Cancer of the Colon, Rectum, and Anus

Editors

ALFRED M. COHEN, M.D.

Professor of Surgery
Cornell University Medical College
Chief, Colorectal Service
Department of Surgery
Memorial Sloan-Kettering Cancer Center
New York, New York

SIDNEY J. WINAWER, M.D.

Professor of Medicine
Cornell University Medical College
Attending Physician and Chief
Gastroenterology and Nutrition Service
Head, Laboratory of Gastrointestinal Cancer Research
Department of Medicine
Memorial Sloan-Kettering Cancer Center
New York, New York

Associate Editors

Michael A. Friedman, M.D.

Associate Director
Cancer Therapy Evaluation Program—
Division of Cancer Treatment
National Cancer Institute—NIH
Bethesda, Maryland

Leonard L. Gunderson, M.D., M.S.

Professor of Oncology
Mayo Medical School
Chairman, Radiation Oncology
Mayo Clinic
Rochester, Minnesota

McGRAW-HILL, INC.

HEALTH PROFESSIONS DIVISION

New York St. Louis San Francisco Auckland Bogotá Caracas Lisbon
London Madrid Mexico City Milan Montreal New Delhi
Paris San Juan Singapore Sydney Tokyo Toronto

Cancer of the Colon, Rectum, and Anus

1234567890 KGPKGP 987654

ISBN 0-07-011601-6

This book was set in Times Roman by Compset, Inc.
The editors were Michael J. Houston and Muza Navrozov.
The production supervisor was Clare B. Stanley.
The cover was designed by N.S.G. Design.
The index was prepared by Irving Conde Tullar.
Arcata Graphics/Kingsport was printer and binder.

Library of Congress Cataloging-in-Publication Data

Cancer of the colon, rectum, and anus / editors, Alfred M. Cohen, Sidney J. Winawer ; associate editors, Michael A. Friedman, Leonard L. Gunderson.
p. cm.
Includes bibliographical references and index.
ISBN 0-07-011601-6 :
1. Colon (Anatomy)—Cancer. 2. Rectum—Cancer.
3. Anus—Cancer.
I. Cohen, Alfred M. II. Winawer, Sidney J.
[DNLM: 1. Colonic Neoplasms. 2. Rectal Neoplasms. WI 520 C216 1995]
RC280.C6C35 1995
616.99'4347—dc20
DNLM/DLC
for Library of Congress 94-7449

To Dr. Claude E. Welch, A Master Twentieth-Century Surgeon,
who taught me and two generations of surgeons
the art and science of caring for patients with cancer

Alfred M. Cohen

To Dr. Stephen E. Hedberg and Dr. Paul Sherlock,
colleagues and friends, whose spirits still encourages us

Alfred M. Cohen
Sidney J. Winawer

To our wives Constance, Andrea, Elizabeth, and Katheryn
for their love, patience, and support

We also dedicate this book to the patients
who have participated in the many research programs delineated in this text

Alfred M. Cohen
Sidney J. Winawer
Michael A. Friedman
Leonard L. Gunderson

NOTICE

Medicine is an ever-changing science. As new research and clinical experience broaden our knowledge, changes in treatment and drug therapy are required. The editors and the publisher of this work have checked with sources believed to be reliable in their efforts to provide information that is complete and generally in accord with the standards accepted at the time of publication. However, in view of the possibility of human error or changes in medical sciences, neither the editors nor the publisher nor any other party who has been involved in the preparation or publication of this work warrants that the information contained herein is in every respect accurate or complete, and they are not responsible for any errors or omissions or for the results obtained from use of such information. Readers are encouraged to confirm the information contained herein with other sources. For example and in particular, readers are advised to check the product information sheet included in the package of each drug they plan to administer to be certain that the information contained in this book is accurate and that changes have not been made in the recommended dose or in the contraindications for administration. This recommendation is of particular importance in connection with new or infrequently used drugs.

Contents

PART 3
Pathology and Biology of Colorectal Cancer

PART 4
Staging and Prognostic Determinants

PART 5
Surveillance and Diagnosis

PART 6
Management of Precancerous Disease

PART 7
Treatment of Colorectal Cancer

PART 8
Surgical Treatment of Potentially Curable Cancer

PART 9
Treatment of Potentially Curable Colonic Cancer

PART 10
Surgical Treatment of Potentially Curable Rectal Cancer

PART 19
Other Anal Cancers

PART 20
Pain Management

Contributors*

Dr. Karl R. Aigner [*89*]
Asklepios Paulinen Klinik
Department of Surgical Oncology
Wiesbaden, Germany

Susan G. Arbuck, M.D. [*92*]
Clinical Research Scientist
Cancer Therapy Evaluation Program
Division of Cancer Treatment
National Cancer Institute
Bethesda, Maryland

Mark W. Arnold, M.D. [*81*]
Assistant Professor
Department of Surgery
The Arthur G. James Cancer Hospital and Research Institute
The Ohio State University Hospitals
Columbus, Ohio

Fadi F. Attiyeh, M.D. [*75*]
Associate Clinical Professor of Surgery
Columbia Presbyterian Hospital
Associate Attending Surgeon
St. Luke's-Roosevelt Hospital Center
New York, New York

Andrew M. Averbach, M.D. [*76*]
Gastrointestinal Oncology Fellow
Washington Cancer Institute
Washington, D.C.

Joseph P. Bannon, M.D. [*62*]
Instructor of Surgery
Jefferson Medical College
Thomas Jefferson University Hospital
Philadelphia, Pennsylvania

*The numbers in brackets following the contributor name refer to chapter(s) authored or co-authored by the contributor.

Robert W. Beart, Jr., M.D. [*52*]
Professor of Surgery
Department of Surgery
University of Southern California
Los Angeles, California

Barbara G. Beatty, Ph.D. [*77*]
Assistant Professor
Department of Pathology
University of Toronto
Toronto, Canada

J. David Beatty, M.D. [*77*]
Executive Director
National Cancer Institute of Canada
Professor
Department of Surgery
Faculty of Medicine
University of Toronto
Toronto, Canada

Colin B. Begg, Ph.D. [*41*]
Chairman
Department of Epidemiology and Biostatistics
Memorial Sloan-Kettering Cancer Center
Professor of Biostatistics and Public Health
Cornell University Medical School
New York, New York

Mansoor H. Beg, M.D. [*89*]
Fellow Surgical Oncology
Tulane University School of Medicine
New Orleans, Louisiana

Lucio Berario, M.D. [*37*]
Director, Italian National
Polyposis Registry
Surgical Division
Istituto Nazionale per lo Studio
e la Cura dei Tumori
Milan, Italy

Jerry G. Blaivas, M.D., F.A.C.S. [*80*]
Clinical Professor of Surgery
Cornell University Medical College
Attending Urologist
The New York Hospital
New York, New York

Kirby I. Bland, M.D. [*60*]
Professor of Surgery
Brown University School of Medicine
Surgeon-in-Chief
Rhode Island Hospital
Executive Surgeon-in-Chief
Brown University School of Medicine Affiliated Hospitals
Providence, Rhode Island

John H. Bond, M.D. [*28*]
Professor of Medicine
University of Minnesota
Chief, Gastroenterology Section
Minneapolis VA Medical Center
Minneapolis, Minnesota

Nicole J. Brittis [*11*]
Research Technician
Memorial Sloan-Kettering Cancer Center
New York, New York

W. Donald Buie, M.D. [*54*]
Clinical Fellow
Division of Colon and Rectal Surgery
Department of Surgery
University of Minnesota
Minneapolis, Minnesota

Randall W. Burt, M.D. [*7, 33*]
Professor of Medicine
University of Utah
Chief, Medical Service
Veterans Administration Medical Center
Salt Lake City, Utah

Nathan I. Cherny, M.B.B.S., F.R.A.C.P. [*109*]
Department of Internal Medicine
Shaave Zedek Medical Center
Jerusalem, Israel

Michaele C. Christian, M.D. [*92*]
Head, Developmental Chemotherapy Section
Investigational Drug Branch
National Cancer Institute
Bethesda, Maryland

Alfred M. Cohen, M.D. [*1, 2, 40, 71*]
Professor of Surgery
Cornell University Medical College
Chief, Colorectal Service
Department of Surgery
Memorial Sloan-Kettering Cancer Center
New York, New York

Katharine E. Cole, Ph.D. [*92*]
Assistant Professor
University of Maryland School of Medicine
Department of Pathology
Baltimore, Maryland

John A. Coller, M.D. [*56*]
Staff Surgeon
Department of Colon and Rectal Surgery
Lahey Clinic Medical Center
Burlington, Massachusetts

Kevin C. Conlon, M.D., M.Ch., F.R.C.S.I. [*23*]
Director, Endosurgical Program
Department of Surgery
Memorial Sloan-Kettering Cancer Center
New York, New York

William R. Connell, M.B., B.S., F.R.A.C.P. [*34*]
Consultant Gastroenterologist
St. Vincent's Hospital
Melbourne, Australia

John A. Conti, M.D. [*78*]
Clinical Assistant Attending Oncologist
Division of Solid Tumor Oncology
Memorial Sloan-Kettering Cancer Center
New York, New York

Bernard J. Cummings, M.B., Ch.B., F.R.C.P.C., F.R.C.R., F.R.A.C.R. [*104*]
Professor and Chairman
Department of Radiation Oncology
University of Toronto
Chief, Department of Radiation Oncology
Princess Margaret Hospital
Toronto, Ontario, Canada

Alan J. Davison, M.D., F.R.C.S.C. [*48*]
Active Staff
Division of General Surgery
Peel Memorial Hospital
Brampton, Ontario, Canada

Dennis F. Devereux, M.D., F.A.C.S. [*68*]
Clinical Professor of Surgery
Robert Wood Johnson School of Medicine
Director of Surgical Services
Helene Fuld Medical Center
Trenton, New Jersey

Chaitanya R. Divgi, M.D., M.S. [*95*]
Assistant Professor
Cornell University Medical College
Assistant Attending Physician
Department of Nuclear Medicine
Memorial Sloan-Kettering Cancer Center
New York, New York

Ralph J. Doerr, M.D. [*77*]
Associate Professor of Surgery
Department of Surgery
University of New York at Buffalo
Buffalo General Hospital
Buffalo, New York

John H. Donohue, M.D. [*82*]
Associate Professor of Surgery
Mayo Medical School
Mayo Clinic
Staff Consultant in General Surgery
Rochester Methodist Hospital
Rochester, Minnesota

Howard D. J. Edington, M.D. *[94]*
Assistant Professor of Plastic Surgery and Surgical Oncology
University of Pittsburgh School of Medicine
Pittsburgh, Pennsylvania

Warren E. Enker, M.D. *[23, 59]*
Professor, Department of Surgery
Cornell University Medical College
Attending Surgeon, Colorectal Service
Department of Surgery
Memorial Sloan-Kettering Cancer Center
New York, New York

Victor W. Fazio, M.B., B.S., F.R.A.C.S., F.A.C.S *[101]*
Professor of Surgery
The Cleveland Clinic Foundation
Chairman, Department of Colorectal Surgery
The Cleveland Clinic
Cleveland, Ohio

L. Peter Fielding, M.B., F.R.C.S., F.A.C.S. *[20]*
Chairman, Department of Surgery
The Genesee Hospital
Rochester, New York

Isaiah J. Fidler, D.V.M., Ph.D. *[17]*
Professor and Chairman
Department of Cell Biology
M.D. Anderson Cancer Center
The University of Texas
Houston, Texas

Marshall S. Flam, M.D., F.A.C.P. *[106]*
Associate Clinical Professor of Medicine
University of California—San Francisco School of Medicine
Hematology-Oncology Medical Group of Fresno
Fresno, California

Betty J. Flehinger, Ph.D. *[27]*
Adjunct Professor of Biostatistics in Public Health
Cornell University Medical College
Manager, Statistics
IBM Research Center
IBM TJ Watson Research Center
Yorktown Heights, New York

Kathleen M. Foley, M.D. *[109]*
Professor of Neurology, Neuroscience, and Clinical Pharmacology
Department of Neurology
Cornell University Medical College
Chief, Pain Service
Memorial Sloan-Kettering Cancer Center
New York, New York

Kenneth A. Forde, M.D. *[45]*
Professor of Clinical Surgery
College of Physicians and Surgeons
Columbia University
Attending Surgeon
Columbia-Presbyterian Medical Center
New York, New York

Eileen A. Friedman, M.D. *[15]*
Associate Laboratory Member
Department of Medicine
Memorial Sloan-Kettering Cancer Center
New York, New York

Michael A. Friedman, M.D. *[50]*
Associate Director
Cancer Therapy Evaluation Program—Division of Cancer Treatment
National Cancer Institute—NIH
Bethesda, Maryland

Cesar Garcia, M.D. *[105]*
Surgical Oncology Fellow
Department of Surgery
The Medical Center of Delaware
Wilmington, Delaware

Hans Gerdes, M.D. *[13]*
Assistant Professor
Cornell University Medical College
Assistant Attending Physician
Memorial Sloan-Kettering Cancer Center
New York, New York

Stanley M. Goldberg, M.D. *[36]*
Clinical Professor of Surgery
Division of Colon and Rectal Surgery
Department of Surgery
University of Minnesota Medical School
Minneapolis, Minnesota

Philip H. Gordon, M.D., F.R.C.S.(C), F.A.C.S. *[61]*
Professor of Surgery
Director of Colon and Rectal Surgery
Sir Mortimer B. Davis—Jewish General Hospital
Professor of Oncology
McGill University
Montreal, Quebec, Canada

Richard L. Grotz, M.D. *[64]*
Clinical Professor
Tufts Medical School
Good Samaritan Medical Center
Stoughton, Massachusetts

José G. Guillem, M.D., M.P.H. *[11, 14]*
Assistant Professor of Surgery
Cornell University Medical College
Assistant Attending Surgeon
Colorectal Service
Department of Surgery
Memorial Sloan-Kettering Cancer Center
New York, New York

Leonard L. Gunderson, M.D., M.S. *[64, 67]*
Professor of Oncology
Mayo Medical School
Chairman, Radiation Oncology
Mayo Clinic
Rochester, Minnesota

Stanley R. Hamilton, M.D. *[18]*
Professor of Pathology and Oncology
Department of Pathology
The Johns Hopkins University School of Medicine
Baltimore, Maryland

Lemuel Herrera, M.D. *[9, 37, 105]*
Professor of Surgery
Director, Surgical Oncology
Department of Surgery
State University of New York Health Science Center at Brooklyn
Brooklyn, New York

Michael J. Hill, D.Sc., F.R.C.(Path.), F.R.S.C. *[4]*
Chairman, European Cancer Prevention Organization
Consultant, Lady Sobell G-1 Unit
Consultant to Research Department
St. Mark's Hospital
Wexham Park Hospital
Slough, Berks, United Kingdom

James Wm. C. Holmes, M.D. *[44]*
Associate Professor of Clinical Surgery
Department of Colorectal Surgery
Attending Surgeon
Tulane University
New Orleans, Louisiana

Herbert C. Hoover, Jr., M.D. *[49]*
Associate Professor of Surgery
Harvard Medical School
Chief, Surgical Oncology
Massachusetts General Hospital
Boston, Massachusetts

Lynn Hornsby-Lewis, M.D. *[6]*
Instructor, Department of Medicine
Cornell University Medical College
Clinical Assistant Physician
GI Nutriton Department of Medicine
Memorial Sloan-Kettering Cancer Center
New York, New York

J. Milburn Jessup, M.D. *[21]*
Associate Professor
Department of Surgery
New England Deaconess Hospital
Harvard Medical School
Boston, Massachusetts

Suresh C. Jhanwar, Ph.D. *[13]*
Associate Professor of Genetics
Cornell University Medical College
Associate Attending Geneticist and Cytogeneticist
Laboratory of Solid Tumor Genetics
Memorial Sloan-Kettering Cancer Center
New York, New York

Garner P. Johnson, M.D. *[52]*
Assistant Professor of Surgery
Albany Medical College
Attending Physician
Albany Medical Center Hospital
Albany, New York

Richard S. Kaplan, M.D., F.A.C.P. *[65]*
Associate Professor of Oncology
University of Maryland Cancer Center
Senior Investigator
Clinical Investigations Branch
National Cancer Institute
Bethesda, Maryland

Donald S. Kaufman, M.D. *[53]*
Associate Clinical Professor of Medicine
Harvard Medical School
Physician, MGH Cancer Center
Massachusetts General Hospital
Boston, Massachusetts

David Kelsen, M.D. *[91]*
Professor of Medicine
Cornell University Medical College
Chief, Gastrointestinal Oncology Service
Memorial Sloan-Kettering Cancer Center
New York, New York

Nancy E. Kemeny, M.D. *[78, 84]*
Professor of Medicine
Cornell University Medical College
Attending Physician, Division of Solid Tumor Oncology
Memorial Sloan-Kettering Cancer Center
New York, New York

Robert C. Kurtz, M.D. *[35, 38]*
Professor of Clinical Medicine
Cornell University Medical College
Director, Gastrointestinal Endoscopy Unit
Attending Physician
Gastroenterology and Nutrition Service
Memorial Sloan-Kettering Cancer Center
New York, New York

Steven M. Larson, M.D. *[95]*
Professor of Radiology
Cornell University Medical College
Chief, Nuclear Medicine Service
Department of Radiology
Memorial Sloan-Kettering Cancer Center
New York, New York

Ian C. Lavery, M.B.B.S., F.R.A.C.S., F.A.C.S. *[42]*
Staff Surgeon
Department of Colorectal Surgery
Cleveland Clinic
Cleveland, Ohio

Henry H. Lee, M.D. *[52]*
Department of Surgery
Cathay General Hospital
Taipei, Taiwan

John E. Lennard-Jones, M.D., F.R.C.P., F.R.C.S. *[34]*
Professor Emeritus of Gastroenterology
University of London
Consulting Gastroenterologist at St. Mark's Hospital and The Royal London Hospital
Hampstead, London, England

Steven K. Libutti, M.D. *[45]*
Senior Resident in Surgery
Department of Surgery
Columbia-Presbyterian Medical Center
New York, New York

Philip O. Livingston, M.D. [*96*]
Associate Professor
Cornell University Medical College
Associate Attending Physician
Department of Medicine
Clinical Immunology Service
Memorial Sloan-Kettering Cancer Center
New York, New York

Kenneth O. Lloyd, Ph.D. [*16*]
Member and Chairman
Immunology Program
Memorial Sloan-Kettering Cancer Center
New York, New York

Michael Lotze, M.D., F.A.C.S. [*94*]
Professor of Surgery
Molecular Genetics and Biochemistry
University of Pittsburgh Medical Center
Chief, Surgical Oncology
Montefiore University Hospital
Pittsburgh, Pennsylvania

Pedro Luna, M.D. [*105*]
Chief, Colorectal Service
Hospital de Oncologia National Medical Center
Mexico City, Mexico

Henry T. Lynch, M.D. [*8*]
Professor and Chairman
Department of Preventive Medicine
and Public Health
Professor of Medicine
Creighton University School of Medicine
Omaha, Nebraska

Jane F. Lynch, B.S.N. [*8*]
Instructor
Department of Preventive Medicine
and Public Health
Creighton University School
of Medicine
Omaha, Nebraska

Robert D. Madoff, M.D., F.A.C.S. [*36*]
Clinical Assistant Professor of Surgery
Director of Research
Department of Surgery
University of Minnesota Medical School
Minneapolis, Minnesota

Gerald J. Marks, M.D. [*62*]
Professor of Surgery
Thomas Jefferson University Hospital
Philadelphia, Pennsylvania

James A. Martenson, Jr., M.D. [*73, 88*]
Associate Professor of Oncology
Mayo Graduate School of Medicine
Mayo Clinic
Rochester, Minnesota

Edward W. Martin, Jr., M.D. [*81*]
Associate Professor
Department of Surgery
Director of Gastrointestinal Cancer Service
The Arthur G. James Cancer Hospital
and Research Institute
The Ohio State University Hospitals
Columbus, Ohio

Patricia McCormack, M.D., F.A.C.S. [*86*]
Associate Professor
Department of Surgery
Cornell University Medical College
Attending Surgeon, Thoracic Service
Department of Surgery
Memorial Sloan-Kettering Cancer Center
New York, New York

Fabrizio Michelassi, M.D., F.A.C.S. [*24*]
Associate Professor of Surgery
Department of Surgery
University of Chicago Medical Center
Chicago, Illinois

Bruce D. Minsky, M.D. [*22, 55, 70*]
Associate Professor of Radiation Oncology
Cornell University Medical College
Associate Attending Physician
Department of Radiation Oncology
Memorial Sloan-Kettering Cancer Center
New York, New York

Carl J. Minnitti, M.D. [*93*]
Fellow, Medical Oncology
Fox Chase Cancer Center
Philadelphia, Pennsylvania

Mohammed Mohiuddin, M.D., F.R.C.R., F.A.C.R. [*69*]
Professor and Chairman
Department of Radiation Medicine
University of Kentucky
Lexington, Kentucky

Timothy D. Moore, M.D. [*92*]
Senior Investigator
National Cancer Institute
National Naval Medical Center
Bethesda, Maryland

James H. Muchmore, M.D., F.A.C.S. [*89*]
Associate Professor
Department of Surgery
Surgical Oncology Program
Tulane University Medical School
New Orleans, Louisiana

David M. Nagorney, M.D. [*82*]
Associate Professor of Surgery
Department of Surgery
Mayo Medical School
Mayo Clinic
Staff Consultant
Rochester Methodist Hospital
Rochester, Minnesota

Heidi Nelson, M.D., F.A.C.S. [*88*]
Assistant Professor of Surgery
Division of Colon and Rectal Surgery
Mayo Medical School
Mayo Clinic
Colorectal and General Surgeon Consultant
Rochester Methodist Hospital
and Saint Mary's Hospital
Rochester, Minnesota

Richard L. Nelson, M.D. [*107*]
Associate Professor of Surgery
Department of Surgery
Assistant Professor, Epidemiology and Biostatistics Program
University of Illinois at Chicago
Attending Colorectal Surgeon
University of Illinois Hospital
Chicago, Illinois

Ronald Lee Nichols, M.D., F.A.C.S. [*44*]
Professor of Microbiology and Immunology
Tulane University School of Medicine
Attending Surgeon
Tulane Medical Center Hospital and Clinic
New Orleans, Louisiana

Santhat Nivatvongs, M.D., F.A.C.S. [*39*]
Professor of Surgery
Mayo Medical School
Consultant in Colon and Rectal Surgery
Mayo Clinic
Rochester, Minnesota

Antonio Obrador, M.D. [*9*]
Attending Surgeon
Service Digestivo
Son Dureta Hospital
Palma de Mallorca, Spain

Michael J. O'Brien, M.D., M.P.H. [*12, 47*]
Professor of Pathology and Laboratory Medicine
Boston University School of Medicine
Chief of Anatomical Pathology
Boston City Hospital and Boston University
Medical Center Hospital
Boston, Massachusetts

Michael J. O'Connell, M.D. [*51, 67*]
Professor of Oncology
Mayo Medical School
Mayo Clinic
Rochester, Minnesota

Peter J. O'Dwyer, M.D. [*93*]
Professor of Medicine
Temple University
Senior Member
Director, Developmental Chemotherapy
Department of Medical Oncology
Fox Chase Cancer Center
Philadelphia, Pennsylvania

David M. Ota, M.D., F.A.C.S. [*43, 46*]
Professor of Surgery
University of Missouri School of Medicine
Medical Director and Chief of Surgery
University of Missouri Ellis Fischel Cancer Center
Columbia, Missouri

Sandip R. Parikh, M.D. [*75*]
Assistant Professor of Surgery
Long Island Jewish Medical Center
Long Island Campus for the Albert Einstein
College of Medicine
New Hyde Park, New York

Philip B. Paty, M.D. [*14, 97, 98, 99*]
Assistant Professor of Surgery
Cornell University Medical College
Assistant Attending Surgeon
Colorectal Service
Department of Surgery
Memorial Sloan-Kettering Cancer Center
New York, New York

Nathan W. Pearlman, M.D. [*87*]
Professor of Surgery
University of Colorado
Health Sciences Center
Department of Surgery
University Hospital
Denver, Colorado

John H. Pemberton, M.D. [*64*]
Associate Professor of Surgery
Mayo Medical School
Consultant, Colon and Rectal Surgery
Mayo Clinic
Rochester, Minnesota

Stuart H. Q. Quan, M.D., F.A.C.S. [*79, 108*]
Clinical Professor of Surgery
Cornell University Medical College
Attending Surgeon, Colorectal Service
Department of Surgery
Memorial Sloan-Kettering Cancer Center
New York, New York

T. S. Ravikumar, M.D. [*83*]
Professor of Surgery and Molecular Biology
Robert Wood Johnson Medical School
Chief of Surgical Oncology and Associate Director
The Cancer Institute of New Jersey
New Brunswick, New Jersey

Tyvin A. Rich, M.D. [*58*]
Professor of Radiotherapy
Department of Radiotherapy
The University of Texas
M. D. Anderson Cancer Center
Houston, Texas

Robert H. Riddell, M.D., F.R.C. (Path.), F.R.C.P.(C) [*10*]
Professor of Pathology
Chief of Service, Anatomical Pathology
McMaster University Medical Centre
Hamilton, Ontario, Canada

Miguel A. Rodriguez-Bigas, M.D. *[37]*
Assistant Professor of Surgery
State University of New York at Buffalo
Associate Chief, Colorectal Service
Director, Familial Polyposis Registry
Department of Surgical Oncology and Endoscopy
Roswell Park Cancer Institute
Buffalo, New York

Charles B. Rosen, M.D. *[82]*
Assistant Professor of Surgery
Mayo Medical School
Senior Associate Consultant
Division of Transplantation Surgery
Mayo Clinic and Mayo Foundation
Rochester, Minnesota

Neal Rosen, M.D., Ph.D. *[14]*
Associate Member
Program in Cell Biology and Genetics
Memorial Sloan-Kettering Cancer Center
New York, New York

David A. Rothenberger, M.D. *[54]*
Clinical Professor of Surgery
Chief, Division of Colon and Rectal Surgery
Department of Surgery
University of Minnesota
Minneapolis, Minnesota

Eugene P. Salvati, M.D. *[57]*
Clinical Professor of Surgery
University of Medicine and Dentistry
Robert Wood Johnson Medical School
Senior Attending Surgeon
Muhlenberg Regional Medical Center
Plainfield, New Jersey

Paul E. Savoca, M.D. *[102]*
Clinical Fellow
Division of Colon and Rectal Surgery
Department of Surgery
University of Minnesota
Minneapolis, Minnesota

Steven E. Schild, M.D. *[73]*
Assistant Professor in Oncology
Mayo Medical School
Rochester, Minnesota
Consultant, Department of Radiation Oncology
Mayo Clinic
Scottsdale, Arizona

Richard L. Schilsky, M.D. *[90]*
Professor of Medicine
and Clinical Pharmacology
Director, Cancer Research Center
University of Chicago
Attending Physician
University of Chicago Hospitals
Chicago, Illinois

Schlomo Schneebaum, M.D. *[81]*
Assistant Professor
Division of Surgical Oncology
Department of Surgery
The Arthur G. James Cancer Hospital
and Research Institute
The Ohio State University Hospitals
Columbus, Ohio

David Schottenfeld, M.D. *[3]*
Professor of Epidemiology and Internal Medicine
Department of Epidemiology
The University of Michigan School of Public Health
Director, Epidemiology, Causation and Prevention Program
The University of Michigan Comprehensive Cancer Center
Ann Arbor, Michigan

Theodore Schrock, M.D. *[63]*
Professor of Surgery
Department of Surgery
Interim Chairman
University of California, San Francisco
San Francisco, California

Karen Seiter, M.D. *[84]*
Assistant Professor of Medicine
New York Medical College
Attending Physician
West County Medical Center
Valhalla, New York

Joe V. Selby, M.D., M.P.H. *[29]*
Assistant Director for Health Services Research
Division of Research
Kaiser Permanente Medical Care Program
Lecturer, Department of Epidemiology
and Biostatistics School of Medicine
University of California, San Francisco
Oakland, California

Ridwan Shabsigh, M.D. *[80]*
Assistant Professor of Urology
Director, Male Reproduction Center
Columbia-Presbyterian Hospital
New York, New York

Brenda Shank, M.D., Ph.D. *[100]*
Professor of Radiation Oncology
Mount Sinai School of Medicine
Director and Attending Physician
Radiation Oncology Department
Mount Sinai Hospital
New York, New York

Paul C. Shellito, M.D. *[53]*
Assistant Professor of Surgery
Harvard Medical School
Associate Visiting Surgeon
Massachusetts General Hospital
Boston, Massachusetts

Moshe Shike, M.D. [*5*]
Associate Professor of Clinical Medicine
Cornell University Medical College
Director, Clinical Nutrition
Attending Physician, Gastroenterology and Nutrition Service
Department of Medicine
Memorial Sloan-Kettering Cancer Center
New York, New York

Elin R. Sigurdson, M.D., Ph.D. [*97, 98, 99*]
Associate Professor of Surgery
Temple University
Member, Fox Chase Cancer Center
Philadelphia, Pennsylvania

Raymond J. Staniunas, M.D. [*56*]
Assistant Professor of Surgery
Case Western Reserve
General Surgeon
Cleveland VA Medical Center
Cleveland, Ohio

Hartley S. Stern, M.D., F.R.C.S.(C), F.A.C.S. [*48*]
Professor and Chairman
Department of Surgery
University of Ottawa
Surgeon in Chief
Ottawa Civic Hospital
Ottawa, Ontario, Canada

Edward T. Stewart, M.D. [*31*]
Professor of Radiology
Medical College of Wisconsin
Chief, GI Radiology
Department of Radiology
Froedtert Memorial Lutheran Hospital
Milwaukee, Wisconsin

Paul H. Sugarbaker, M.D. [*76, 85*]
Director, Surgical Oncology
The Washington Cancer Institute
Washington Hospital Center
Washington, D.C.

Paul Ian Tartter, M.D., F.A.C.S. [*25*]
Associate Professor of Surgery
Mount Sinai School of Medicine
Chief, Breast Service
Department of Surgery
Mount Sinai Medical Center
New York, New York

Joel E. Tepper, M.D. [*66, 74*]
Professor and Chairman
Department of Radiation Oncology
University of North Carolina
at Chapel Hill Medical School
Chapel Hill, North Carolina

Joe J. Tjandra, M.D., F.R.A.C.S., F.R.C.S., F.R.C.P.S. [*101*]
Senior Lecturer in Colorectal Surgery
Consultant Colorectal Surgery
University of Melbourne
Consultant, Colorectal Service
Department of Surgery
Royal Melbourne Hospital
Parkville, Victoria, Australia

Malcolm C. Veidenheimer, M.D., C.M., F.A.C.S., F.R.C.S.C. [*103*]
Vice-Chairman, Department of Surgery
Chief, Division of General Surgery
Health Care International (Scotland) Ltd.
Clydebank, Scotland

Michael P. Vezeridis, M.D. [*72*]
Professor of Surgery and Associate Director
Division of Surgical Oncology
Brown University School of Medicine
Chief, Surgical Oncology Section
Veterans Administration Medical Center
Department of Surgery
Roger Williams Medical Center
Providence, Rhode Island

Marina L. Wasylyshyn, M.D. [*24*]
Clinical Instructor in Surgery
State University of New York
Health Science Center
Syracuse, New York
Surgical Oncologist
United Medical Associates, P.C.
Johnson City, New York

Harold J. Wanebo, M.D. [*72*]
Professor of Surgery
Director, Division of Surgical Oncology
Brown University
Chief of Surgery
Department of Surgery
Roger Williams Medical Center
Providence, Rhode Island

Jerome D. Waye, M.D. [*30, 47*]
Clinical Professor of Medicine
Mount Sinai School of Medicine
Chief, Gastrointestinal Endoscopy
Mount Sinai Hospital and
Lenox Hill Hospital
New York, New York

Leonard Weiss, M.D., Ph.D. [*19*]
Professor Emeritus in Experimental Pathology
Roswell Park Division
Center for Biosurfaces
SUNY at Buffalo
Buffalo, New York

Christopher G. Willett, M.D. [*49, 53*]
Assistant Professor in Radiation Oncology
Harvard Medical School
Associate Radiation Oncologist
Department of Radiation Medicine
Massachusetts General Hospital
Boston, Massachusetts

Sidney J. Winawer, M.D. [*1, 2, 26, 28, 32*]
Professor of Medicine
Cornell University Medical College
Attending Physician and Chief, Gastroenterology
and Nutrition Service
Head, Laboratory for Gastrointestinal Cancer Research
Department of Medicine
Memorial Sloan-Kettering Cancer Center
New York, New York

W. Douglas Wong, M.D., F.A.C.S. *[102]*
Clinical Assistant Professor of Surgery
Director, Residency Training Program
Division of Colon and Rectal Surgery
Department of Surgery
University of Minnesota
Minneapolis, Minnesota

Timothy J. Yeatman, M.D. *[60]*
Assistant Professor of Surgery
H. Lee Moffitt Cancer Center and Research Institute at the University of South Florida
Tampa, Florida

Jian-Nong Zhou, M.D. *[62]*
International Fellow
Division of Colorectal Surgery
Department of Surgery
Thomas Jefferson University
Philadelphia, Pennsylvania
Attending Surgeon
Jiangsu Cancer Institute and Hospital
Nanjing, People's Republic of China

Preface

The purpose of this book is to provide the reader with a timely critical analysis of our knowledge concerning the biology, diagnosis and therapy of cancer of the colon, rectum, and anus. We believe general and colorectal surgeons, internists, gastroenterologists, and all oncologic specialists will find this volume a useful resource. Clinicians will encounter tabulation of the latest treatment strategies within a book that defines the rationale and biologic basis of our knowledge concerning these issues. In addition, laboratory investigators will find insights into the clinical relevancy of their endeavors.

The editors have enlisted the talents of over one hundred authors, each expert in his or her field. The chapters do not represent "library reviews"—they are thoughtful analyses by experienced clinicians and laboratory scientists. Summary abstracts have not been used, but when appropriate, the authors have defined highlights, controversies, and future direction sections. This will help the reader to separate generally accepted facts from opinions when subsequently discussed in the chapter.

The book is divided into twenty major divisions. We begin with chapters on etiology and risk factors, followed by chapters dealing with cell biology, immunology, invasion and metastases, and pathology. These sections are followed by chapters concerning staging and other prognostic determinants. Part 5—Surveillance and Diagnosis—is a collation of ten chapters.

The therapy portion of the book initially discusses management of patients with precancerous disease, followed by chapters addressing general surgical considerations. Surgical and adjuvant therapy of colorectal cancer patients is separated into colonic and rectal sections, since the biology of recurrence and treatment strategies are quite different. Following discussion of surgical considerations, adjuvant therapy with chemotherapy, irradiation or both is discussed in detail. Multimodality management of the complex patients with locally advanced rectal cancer is addressed in a separate section.

The book has nineteen chapters analyzing the management of patients with locally recurrent and metastatic cancer. For locally recurrent lesions, potentially curative approaches are discussed using aggressive multimodality treatment (external irradiation plus concomitant chemotherapy, maximal resection, intraoperative irradiation, additional chemotherapy). In addition to detailed discussions of chemotherapy options, drug resistance and clinical trial design, this section provides information on many areas of future promise. Included are discussions of hepatic artery, pelvic arterial and intraperitoneal regional chemotherapy, monoclonal antibodies for diagnosis and therapy, the potential for generic cancer vaccines, and an update on cellular immunotherapy.

A separate section of this book is devoted to the biology and therapy of cancer of the anal canal. These cancers are much less common than adenocarcinoma of the rectum and present an exciting paradigm for sphincter-saving multidisciplinary therapy. The biology of these lesions and the management of precursor lesions are discussed.

Interspersed throughout the book are discussions concerning palliative and supportive care. We conclude this tome with a detailed consideration of the pathophysiology, differential diagnosis, and treatment of the various pain syndromes in these patients.

The editors and authors are enthusiastic about this new volume which integrates the background, state of our knowledge, and future areas of study in a lucid book useful for clinicians and scientists involved in these disease processes.

ACKNOWLEDGMENT

The preparation of a major textbook involves the teamwork, dedication and contribution of many people, and we would like to acknowledge the assistance of several individuals. First and foremost, the editors would like to thank all the contributors for working with enthusiasm toward the goals set forth for this textbook.

We are also grateful to our secretarial staff for their help in completing this project. Evelyn Otero-Santiago, with her immense organizational skills and diligence, was primarily responsible for our success.

We also acknowledge and wish to thank the entire staff of McGraw-Hill Health Professions Division. Their dedication, skill, imagination, and innovation have helped in guiding this material from concept to bound book. A special thanks to Michael Houston, Muza Navrozov, and Mariapaz Ramos-Englis.

CHAPTER 1

Introduction

Alfred M. Cohen
Sidney J. Winawer

Deaths from cancer of the colon and rectum are the second leading cause of cancer deaths in the United States next to lung cancer. The most common cancer sites in patients in the United States and most western countries are the breast, lung, colon, rectum, and prostate. The number of new colorectal cancer cases has been increasing approximately 5 percent each year until 1993, corresponding to the aging of the population. There is no peak incidence of colorectal cancer; increasing risk is associated with increasing age. In males, the incidence of colonic versus rectal cancer is approximately 2 to 1. However, it is of interest that the ratio in women is approximately 3 to 1. Despite the high incidence of cancer of the colon and rectum, there has been a slow decline in the colorectal cancer mortality, with just over half of all patients being cured. This improvement is attributable partly to improved therapy and to a major extent to earlier diagnosis. This progress in outcome is based on impressive advances in our knowledge of the biology of this cancer as well as advances in diagnostic and therapeutic technology. The editors believe that the magnitude and array of this progress warrants a comprehensive review of colorectal cancer in a single treatise.

This book is organized according to the etiology, biology, diagnosis, and treatment of adenocarcinoma of the colon and rectum and sets forth the current state of knowledge in these areas. Less common malignancies of the large bowel are also discussed. Patterns-of-failure studies indicate that local regional recurrence is a much more common problem in patients with rectal cancer than in those with colonic cancer. This leads to different management algorithms for these two groups of patients, and such considerations are reviewed in separate sections. Last, we will focus on cancers of the anal canal. The large majority of patients with such cancers have squamous cell carcinoma and are curable with chemoradiation therapy without colostomy.

Colorectal cancer was one of the first neoplasms for which a pathologic staging system to predict prognosis was developed. Cuthbert Dukes, in a series of publications over 50 years, described important prognostic determinants in rectal cancer. Such staging approaches—related to the growth of the primary tumor, lymph node metastases, and distant spread—have since been enhanced by the analysis of multiple additional pathologic prognostic factors, cell cycle kinetics, and, more recently, the types of genetic mutations and deletions.

Clinical or preoperative staging and prognosis has been expanded by clinical criteria such as tumor configuration and histologic grade and by new technology such as intrarectal ultrasound, computed tomography (CT), and magnetic resonance imaging (MRI). Enhanced MRI and positron emission tomography (PET) scanning will be areas of investigation over the next few years. In the current climate stressing cost-effectiveness, new, expensive technologies, in order to win acceptance, will have to demonstrate utility by obviating other tests, clearly changing treatment strategies, or—most importantly—improving treatment outcome.

The majority of patients with colorectal cancer will be cured, with surgical resection the mainstay of therapy. However, 15 to 20 percent of patients present with synchronous hematogenous metastases, and such patients are cured only rarely. Earlier diagnosis to minimize the number of patients in this subset will be necessary in order to improve these results. Most of the reduction in the mortality from this disease is related to early diagnosis. This is a highly complex public health issue with considerable financial implications, but there is promise that the mortality from this disease can be considerably reduced. We now have evidence of mortality reduction from fecal occult blood testing and sigmoidoscopy and incidence reduction from polypectomy. Yet to be addressed are the issues of widespread acceptance, cost-effectiveness, and education. Our understanding of heritable factors and the preceding adenoma provides further basis for effective secondary preventive strategies coupled with primary dietary approaches.

The development of flexible endoscopes made a dramatic impact on the evaluation of symptomatic patients as well as the treatment of patients with polyps. Prior to such endoscopes, only patients with large adenomas were diagnosed, and tens of thousands of patients each year underwent surgery involving colotomy and polypectomy for benign disease. As many as half of these patients developed metachronous polyps, and many of them underwent several operations over decades to remove such polyps. It has now become a routine office procedure to examine the entire colon with flexible endoscopy, and the large majority of benign polyps can be removed by snare cautery at the time of the diagnostic evaluation. In addition, color images of these procedures document the extent of disease. Patients cured of colorectal cancer can be kept "adenoma-free" and their likelihood of developing a second colorectal cancer can be markedly reduced.

The prognosis following colectomy for node-negative colon cancer is excellent, with 5-year survival approaching 80 percent. The role of laparoscope-assisted colectomy remains to be defined. We cure approximately half of the patients with nodal metastases by surgical resection alone, but current adjuvant chemotherapy appears to reduce cancer-related deaths by one-third.

The history of the treatment of rectal cancer has primarily involved surgical approaches. Much of the heritage of general surgery involved the evolution of techniques to excise rectal cancer. Attempts in the nineteenth century to deal with rectal cancer primarily involved a perineal or posterior excision of the rectum. J. P. Lockhart-Mummery developed considerable expertise in this approach while working at St. Marks Hospital in London. Patients underwent an initial abdominal operation with a loop colostomy in the left lower abdomen. It was at this point that the patients could be staged in regard to whether their lesions were operable or not. Several weeks later, the rectum was removed from a posterior perineal approach. This was a relatively successful operation for low rectal cancers. Of interest, although this is perceived as an inadequate operation today, 370 patients underwent a perineal proctectomy at St. Marks Hospital in the period from 1910 to 1930, with an 11.6 percent mortality and a 40 percent 5-year survival. This occurred prior to the introduction of antibiotics and blood transfusions and must be considered an impressive result.

Another posterior approach was initially described by Kraske in 1885. In this procedure, a posterior incision was made in the coccyx and a portion of the sacrum removed. The pelvis and ultimately the peritoneum was then entered from the posterolateral approach and the rectum resected. This approach allowed a direct reanastomosis to the lower rectum.

Studies by Ernest Miles and later by Cuthbert Dukes demonstrated the upward spread of cancer of the rectum. This led to combining the abdominal and perineal phases for resection of the rectum. This was initially reported by Czerny in 1883 but ultimately popularized in England and America by Ernest Miles, following his initial report in 1908. Subsequent technical advances by Coffey, McKittrich, Rankind, Lahey, Graye, Turner, and Gabriel established this approach as the definitive operation for mid- and low rectal cancer. It took many decades for this to occur, since in Miles's first 61 cases there was a mortality of 36 percent. Because of this extremely high mortality, Hartmann in 1923 described a technique for the treatment of mid- and upper rectal cancer that involved resecting the rectum and rectosigmoid but leaving the anus and perineum in place.

Technical advances combined with better studies of the local/regional spread of rectal cancer from the 1940s until the present time have improved overall cure and function. Abdominoperineal resection is rarely required for mid- and upper rectal cancer. Surgical "staplers" permit sphincter-saving surgery for most patient with rectal cancer. Experience with distal rectal mucosectomy for patients with ulcerative colitis has led to even fewer abdominoperineal resections by the use of the coloanal reconstruction for midrectal cancer. Internal colon pouches and sexual nerve–preserving surgery improves the functional outcome further.

Through a series of randomized clinical trials carried out over the two decades beginning in the early 1970s, the benefit of adjuvant therapy for patients with rectal cancer has been demonstrated. At present, patients with node-positive and/or transmural rectal cancer receiving adjuvant chemotherapy based on 5-fluorouracil (5-FU) as well as pelvic radiation therapy can expect a one-third reduction in cancer-related mortality and a pelvic recurrence rate of only 10 percent. There is ongoing interest in evaluating the various surgical/radiation therapy sequencing options in regard to both efficacy and toxicity. Current studies will define which type of 5-FU–based chemotherapy appears the most efficacious and whether preoperative or postoperative radiation therapy sequencing has the greatest benefit.

As with early breast cancer, many patients with early rectal cancer can be cured with various local treatment options combined with chemoradiation therapy. Local treatment options include local surgical excision, fulguration, cautery, cryosurgery, and localized radiation therapy. It is likely that with a better understanding of the molecular basis of invasion and metastases, patients will be more appropriately selected for these more conservative approaches to the management of rectal cancer. However, since these represent our most curable subset of patients, it is important not to compromise on cure in order to minimize potential functional deficits.

Despite efforts at early detection, there is still a subset of patients who present with locally advanced rectal cancer. There have been considerable advances in surgical techniques as well as the use of high-dose preoperative radiation therapy combined chemoradiation therapy and extended radical operations that cure many of these patients. By boosting the radiation dose (combining external beam radiation therapy with resection and intraoperative radiation therapy), one can improve local control and survival in these patients as well. This strategy is complex, expensive, and logistically cumbersome. Its exact role is yet to be defined.

Although the rationale for follow-up strategy in patients who had potentially curative operations is fairly straightforward, the benefit of such programs in the early detection, treatment, and possible cure of patients with recurrent disease is unclear. There remains considerable disagreement as to the usefulness of carcinoembryonic antigen (CEA) and other tumor markers in such patients. However, since 25 to 35 percent of patients with limited hepatic metastases can be cured by hepatic resection and since serial CEA assays appear to be a fairly straightforward method to detect such metastases, the use of tumor markers in follow-up will likely continue.

Unfortunately, the ubiquitous presence of the multidrug resistance gene in colorectal cancer cells has limited the efficacy of many chemotherapy agents. However, through laboratory research and clinical trials, there has been incremental improvement in response rates to systemic chemotherapy. There are exciting opportunities for cellular immunotherapy, generic vaccines, and monoclonal antibodies in the treatment of colorectal cancer.

The majority of patients with anal cancer have a variant of squamous cell or epidermoid carcinoma. There is considerable interest in anal cancers because of the presence of precursor lesions, such as Bowen's disease. There appears to be a considerable increase in the incidence of this disease in the HIV-positive patient population; the human papilloma virus may play a role in this. Based on the pioneering work by Nigro and colleagues in the 1970s, the use of chemoradiation therapy has improved survival and avoided colostomies in two-thirds of such patients. All of the initial studies were empiric, and there have been multiple reports of various radiation strategies and different chemoradiation combinations in the management of these patients. Ongoing and future clinical trials will define the most appropriate agents, dose, and sequence of therapies.

This book presents a comprehensive review of the present status of the biology and treatment of colorectal cancer. Enormous progress has been made in treatment, and further incremental advances are expected over the next few years. However, major innovative opportunities for intervention are likely to become clinically available over the next decade. These include the development of a selective screening and prevention strategy based on family history and molecular genetic analysis of individual patients. We may also be able to use our understanding of the molecular biology of colorectal cancer—its initiation and progression—to prevent its clinical development. Finally, for those of our patients who already have such cancer, we may, as well, be able to offer more specifically tailored treatments.

PART 1

Adenocarcinoma of the Colon and Rectum

CHAPTER 2

Overview of Adenocarcinoma of the Colon and Rectum

Sidney J. Winawer
Alfred M. Cohen

Remarkable progress has been made in our understanding of the biology, natural history, prevention, and management of adenocarcinoma of the colon and rectum.[1] This progress is already having an effect in lowering the national mortality from this disease.[2] Although there are certain epidemiologic and biological differences between colonic and rectal cancer, the two conditions are often combined, as they will be in this brief overview for the purpose of discussion and because many of the leading researchers have not clearly separated their findings in terms of the two anatomic sites. In addition, the distinction becomes somewhat blurred as one considers observations over time, since there has been a temporal shift in the proportion of cancers localized to the rectum as opposed to more proximal anatomic sites.[3]

In considering advances in our understanding and treatment of colorectal cancer, we can place these subjects in a biological perspective along with what we now understand of its natural history.[1] This can be viewed in reverse progression, from outcome back to the diagnosis of cancer, to the antecedent benign lesion, the adenomatous polyp, then to the field defect which precedes all colorectal neoplasia, and finally to the hereditable and environmental factors that are responsible for the interaction and progression of the process. This sequence, also termed the *colorectal cancer tumorigenesis model,* has been shown to be associated with a number of genetic alterations that accumulate as the multistep process moves from normal mucosa through the stages of adenoma and on to cancer.[4]

In examining the progression along this natural history sequence, we should first call attention to the improved outcome in patients with diagnosed colorectal cancer who are candidates for adjuvant treatment. This has now been shown to effectively improve survival in patients with stages B_2 and C rectal cancer and stage C colonic cancer, with either combined radiation and chemotherapy in the former or chemotherapy in the latter.[5] However, it is desirable to make the diagnosis at an early stage so that adjuvant treatment is not necessary and the probability of cure is high. There have now been 309,000 people entered into controlled trials of stool blood testing to evaluate this approach to the screening and early diagnosis of colorectal cancer.[1] All of the early outcome variables have been positive, demonstrating that this approach is feasible for average-risk asymptomatic individuals. More recently, evidence has been presented demonstrating the effectiveness of this approach in reducing mortality from colorectal cancer.[6,7] In addition, case-control studies have also shown that screening sigmoidoscopy reduces the mortality from colorectal cancer.[8,9] These data support current guidelines for screening average-risk asymptomatic men and women for colorectal cancer. Major public education programs and a better understanding of the basis for noncompliance will be needed for these approaches to have their maximal impact on national mortality from colorectal cancer.[10]

It is now well established that the adenomatous polyp precedes colorectal cancer. A cross-sectional study has indicated that the average time span from normal mucosa to colorectal cancer is about 10 years, with a 5-year span between the adenomatous polyp and cancer.[11] Adenomatous polyps are quite prevalent in western countries and are strongly age-related. They are the most common neoplastic lesions found in symptomatic people and in those with a positive screening test. It is now known that about two-thirds of the polyps found in the colon are adenomatous, the remainder being mostly normal mucosal tags and hyperplastic polyps. There is a high synchronous rate (50 percent) of additional adenomas at the time of diagnosis of an index adenoma, and there is a high metachronous rate (30 percent) of adenomas at subsequent examinations after the colon has been cleared of all polyps. Recent evidence has demonstrated that longer intervals can be used for follow-up surveillance in individuals after polyps have been removed by colonoscopy.[12] This is consistent with the known long natural history of new growths. We have learned quite a bit about predictive factors for new adenomas found at follow-up and also for high-grade dysplasia in adenomas, the premalignant bridge between benign and invasive cancer. It has recently been shown that removal of adenomas results in a lowering of the incidence of colorectal cancer and therefore, presumably, of its mortality.[13]

It has been demonstrated that the adenomatous polyp arises in a background of abnormal mucosal cell proliferation and maturational arrest that occurs in anatomic patches throughout the colon, the so-called field defect.[1] This field defect has many other associated abnormalities in proliferation, antigen expression, and cytoskeletal structure. The appearance of an adenoma follows the development of this field defect and microscopic adenomatous changes with individual crypts. Although adenomas are removed, the field defects remain, resulting in additional adenomas (both synchronous and metachronous). We now have a better understanding of the heritable factors associated with this sequence of events. Well-delineated inherited syndromes have been described, including familial adenomatous polyposis and hereditary nonpolyposis colorectal cancer. These account for approximately 1 and 5 percent of the new cases each year respectively.[14] However, a large proportion of the remainder of the new cases each year also have associated inherited factors. It has been shown that colorectal cancer and adenomas cluster in families and that the risk in first-degree relatives is increased in the presence in a proband with either an adenomatous polyp or a colorectal cancer. The lifetime probability of colorectal cancer in affected families is about 18 percent, as compared to 6 percent in unaffected families. Mathematical modeling has predicted that the mortality from colorectal cancer can be substantially reduced by surveillance with colonoscopy in affected families. Based on these calculations, new guidelines that include colonoscopy have been recommended for family members when there is a proband with colorectal neoplasia.[15]

With knowledge of the colorectal cancer tumorigenesis model and the available clinical skills, environmental factors can now be studied more effectively. In the past, epidemiologic studies of large populations were needed to obtain clues of environmental factors. However, observations of adenoma recurrence or changes in the field defect on biopsy of the mucosa can lead to an assessment of dietary effects in a much shorter period of time and with fewer cases studied. We have moved observational studies to active intervention trials, which will provide definitive data on the relationship of nutrition to the progression of normal mucosa to adenomas and cancer.[16]

Genetic alterations, growth factor abnormalities, and other biological events have been described in terms of the progression of tumorigenesis.[4] It is now known that several suppressor genes are altered in tumor tissue, permitting cell proliferation to escape from normal control and allowing the neoplastic process to progress. We still do not know much about the early events—that is, what abnormalities produce the field defect that precedes neoplasia. We also do not know much about the genetic-environmental interaction. To what extent are the observed genetic alterations due to inherited susceptibility and/or to environmental effects? In addition, we need to learn more about genetic susceptibility to carcinogens. There is evidence, for example, that people vary in their P450 enzyme and glutathione transferase genotypes and their acetylator status, all of which could affect their ability to handle carcinogens.[17] We do not know much about the relationship of this to familial factors either. However, the dramatic progress in our understanding of the biology of colorectal cancer has already led to new prognostic markers and to possible new approaches to screening as, for example, identifying mutated *ras* oncogenes in the stool as a means of screening for adenomas and for cancer. We also now have clearer insight into the spectrum of the risk in patients with adenomatous polyps, in individuals with a family history of varying strength and age of onset, and in patients with other premalignant conditions such as inflammatory bowel disease.[14,18–20]

In this text, the subject of adenocarcinoma of the colon and rectum has been organized first into a series of sections that deal with pathology, epidemiology, inherited risk, and various aspects of its biology. This is followed by a comprehensive presentation of all aspects of preventive intervention, including screening and diagnosis. The topic of surgical treatment of colonic and rectal cancer is preceded by a full discussion of pathology and staging. It is followed by a presentation of adjuvant treatment and treatment of advanced cancer and its management problems, especially as they relate specifically to the colon and the rectum. Throughout the book, there is a balance between biology and management. The subject matter has been divided into very specific subsections and categories to permit a detailed approach to each area by people with extensive experience and a definite point of view.

This particular aspect of the book's organization makes it unique; every contributor has written from a position of strength, conviction, and personal commitment to the issues presented.

REFERENCES

1. Winawer SJ, Zauber AG, Stewart ET, O'Brien MJ: The natural history of colorectal cancer: Opportunities for intervention. *Cancer* 67:1143–1149, 1991.
2. Chu KC, Kramer BS, Smart CR: Analysis of the role of cancer prevention and control measures in reducing cancer mortality. *J Natl Cancer Inst* 83:1636–1643, 1991.
3. Schottenfeld D, Winawer SJ: Large intestine, in Schottenfeld D, Fraumeni JF Jr (eds): *Cancer: Epidemiology and Prevention*. Philadelphia, Saunders, 1982, pp 703–727.
4. Vogelstein B, Fearon ER, Hamilton SR, et al: Genetic alterations during colorectal tumor development. *N Engl J Med* 319:525–532, 1988.
5. Winawer SJ: Colorectal cancer screening and early diagnosis, in Brodie DR (ed): *Screening and Early Diagnosis of Colorectal Cancer*. Consensus Development Conference Proceedings. Washington, DC, NIH Publication No. 80-2075, 1979, pp 193–210.
6. Winawer SJ, Flehinger BJ, Schottenfeld D, Miller DG: Screening for colorectal cancer with fecal occult blood testing and sigmoidoscopy. *JNCI* 85(16):1311–1318, 1993.
7. Mandel JS, Bond JH, Church TR, et al: Reducing mortality from colorectal cancer by screening for fecal occult blood. *N Engl J Med* 328(19):1365–1371, 1993.
8. Selby JV, Friedman GD, Quesenberry CP Jr, Weiss NS: A case-control study of screening sigmoidoscopy and mortality from colorectal cancer. *N Engl J Med* 326:653–657, 1992.
9. Simon BD, Morrison AS, Lev R, Verhoek-Oftedahl W: Relationship of polyps to cancer of the large intestine. *J Natl Cancer Inst* 84:962–966, 1992.
10. Winawer SJ, Shike M: Dietary factors in colorectal cancer and their possible effects on earlier stages of hyperproliferation and adenoma formation. *J Natl Cancer Inst* 84:74–75, 1992.
11. Winawer SJ, Zauber AG, Diaz B: The National Polyp Study: Temporal sequence of evolving colorectal cancer from the normal colon. *Gastrointest Endosc* 33:A167, 1987.
12. Winawer SJ, Zauber AG, O'Brien MJ, et al: Randomized comparison of surveillance intervals after colonoscopic removal of newly diagnosed adenomatous polyps. *N Engl J Med* 328:901–906, 1993.
13. Winawer SJ, Zauber AG, Ho MN, et al: Prevention of colorectal cancer by colonoscopic polypectomy. *N Engl J Med* 329:1977–1981, 1993.
14. Burt RW, Bishop DT, Lynch HT, et al: Risk and surveillance of individuals with heritable factors for colorectal cancer. *Bull WHO* 68:655–665, 1990.
15. American Cancer Society: *Cancer Facts and Figures*. New York, American Cancer Society, 1993.
16. Shike M, Winawer SJ, Greenwald PH, et al: Primary prevention of colorectal cancer. *Bull WHO* 68:377–385, 1990.
17. Dale Smith CA, Moss JE, Gough AC, et al: Molecular genetic analysis of the cytochrome P450 debrisoquine hydroxylase locus and association with cancer susceptibility. *Environ Health Perspect* 98:107–112, 1992.
18. Levin B, Lennard-Jones J, Riddell RH, et al: Surveillance of patients with chronic ulcerative colitis. *Bull WHO* 69(1):121–126, 1991.
19. Winawer SJ, Zauber AG, Gerdes H, et al: Genetic epidemiology of colorectal cancer: Relationship of familial colorectal cancer risk to adenoma proband age and adenoma characteristics. *Gastroenterology* 102(4)[2]:A409, 1992.
20. Winawer SJ, Zauber AG, Bishop DT, et al: Family history of colorectal cancer as a predictor of adenomas at follow-up colonoscopy: A study based on segregation analysis. *Gastroenterology* 104(4)[2]:A462, 1993.

CHAPTER 3

Epidemiology

David Schottenfeld

HIGHLIGHTS

In the United States, colorectal cancer is the second most common cancer in women (after breast cancer) and the third most frequently occurring cancer in men (after cancer of the prostate and lung). The age-adjusted colorectal cancer mortality (per 100,000) in the United States for 1985–1989 was highest in black males (27.6), exceeding by 33 percent the mortality in black females (20.8); the corresponding rate in white males (24.2) exceeded by 48 percent the mortality in white females (16.4). The incidence rates for colorectal cancer were similar for white (61.0) and black males (60.5). The male:female age-adjusted colorectal cancer incidence ratios exceeded 1.0 by 30 percent in blacks and 45 percent in whites. During the period 1973–1989, colorectal cancer mortality decreased significantly by 20 percent in white females and 8.5 percent in white males; in contrast, mortality increased significantly by 22.5 percent in black males and 2.6 percent in black females.

The highest incidence rates of colonic cancer are reported in North America, Australia, and New Zealand. The rates in western European countries are uniformly lower than those in North America but are consistently higher than the rates in the eastern European countries. The lowest rates are reported in Africa, Asia, and Latin America. In general, colonic cancer is relatively more common in economically advantaged populations exhibiting westernized lifestyle practices.

Dietary hypotheses concerning causative mechanisms for colorectal cancer have been generated from the striking differences in international incidence rates and studies of migrants. The demonstration of a complete transition in risk for colorectal cancer in one generation of migrants, or after a period of 20 to 30 years of residence in a high-risk country, unlike the intermediate pattern exhibited for gastric cancer, has underscored the potential importance of altering dietary practices in adult life. The risk of colorectal cancer can also decline after migration from a high-risk to a low-risk country.

Food preferences are culturally interconnected and biochemically interactive. Dietary preference patterns characterized by the increased consumption of red meat and other sources of saturated fat; decreased consumption of fruits, vegetables and grains which provide insoluble fiber, micronutrient antioxidants and phytochemicals with anticarcinogenic properties; and decreased calcium intake are predictive of increased risk of cancer of the colon and rectum.

Studies of physical activity in men and women have shown that a sedentary lifestyle is associated with an increased risk of colonic cancer. Accurate methods of recording physical activity, both as to amount and type, are required to separate the potentially confounding effects of energy expenditure from energy consumption, correlated dietary practices, concurrent obesity, and body fat composition.

Increased susceptibility to colorectal cancer may be expressed in the first-degree relatives of families with one of the autosomal dominant syndromes: colorectal carcinoma of early onset and right-sided predominance (Lynch syndrome I) or with colonic and/or extracolonic carcinomas of the endometrium, ovary, small bowel, stomach, pancreas, bile ducts, renal pelvis and/or ureter (Lynch syndrome II). Genetically defined syndromes probably represent less than 10 percent of incident cases of colorectal cancer each year in the United States.

Individuals with inflammatory bowel disease are at significant risk of colorectal carcinoma of multicentric origin. The degree of relative risk may be predicted by the extent and duration of mucosal disease accompanied by dysplastic epithelium and by age at diagnosis. The absolute risk or cumulative incidence increases with the length of follow-up, since carcinoma will often appear after a 5- to 15-year latency interval. Inflammatory bowel-associated colorectal carcinoma constitutes 1 percent of new cases of colorectal cancer each year in the United States.

Women with an index primary cancer of the endometrium, breast, or ovary require medical surveillance because of an increased risk of colorectal carcinoma. The determinants of these established mutual risk patterns are uncertain but may reflect common dietary, metabolic, and endocrine mechanisms or in some instances, genetic pleiotropy.

FUTURE DIRECTIONS

Although the international incidence patterns for colonic cancer generally parallel those for rectal cancer, there are perplexing differences in the comparisons of tumors located in the proximal and distal segments of the colon and in the rectum, which have been noted in epidemiologic, genetic, and molecular studies. The marked variations in international incidence patterns that have been reported pertain mainly to colonic cancer and in particular to differences in the incidence of cancer of the sigmoid colon. The male predominance in the incidence of rectal cancer in many countries exceeds that for colonic cancer, and epidemiologic, embryologic, genetic, and molecular studies suggest that there may be mechanistic differences in the development of neoplasms in the proximal as opposed to the distal segments of the large intestine. Future research should be concerned with the biochemistry of the fecal stream in conjunction with molecular studies of biopsied tissues; these observations should be correlated with the distribution of epidemiologic risk factors in association with the anatomic location of dysplastic and invasive neoplastic lesions. In the surveillance studies of high-risk groups, sensitive and specific biomarkers of aberrant mucosal cell proliferation should be employed as intermediate phenotypic end points that may predict future neoplasia.

Cancer of the large intestine accounted for 13 percent of all incident cancers in the United States, or approximately 152,000 cases, in 1993. Colorectal cancer is the second most common cancer in women (after breast cancer) and the third most frequently occurring cancer in men (after cancer of the prostate and lung). After the vital statistics for women and men are combined, it is second only to lung cancer as the leading cause of cancer mortality. The average annual age-adjusted colon cancer incidence per 100,000 individuals in the United States for 1985–1989 was 34 percent higher in males (41.9) when compared, as a ratio of rates, with that in females (31.3); the male predominance was more evident for rectal cancer incidence (73 percent; Table 3-1). In the late 1980s, the lifetime probability of developing colorectal cancer was estimated to be 6.0 percent for women and 6.2 percent for men. The estimation of lifetime probability is based upon life table projections of current annual age-, sex-, and site-specific incidence rates as well as consideration of competing causes of death that serve to remove individuals from subsequent risks of developing cancer. By way of comparison, the cumulative lifetime risk of developing invasive cancer anywhere in the body was estimated to be 39.2 percent for women and 42.5 percent for men. Between 1973 and 1985, the age-adjusted incidence of colorectal cancer in the United States increased relatively by about 19 percent in males (Fig. 3-1); during the subsequent 5-year interval (1985–1989), it declined by 6 percent. For females, the incidence of colorectal cancer increased by 9 percent during 1973–1985; then, during 1985–1989, it declined by almost 10 percent.

Table 3-1
Age-Adjusted[a] Incidence Rates per 100,000 Population and Male-to-Female Rate Ratio for Colorectal Cancer—All Races, United States, 1985–1989

	Incidence[b]		
	Males	*Females*	*Male/female rate ratio*
Colon and rectum	60.8	42.3	1.44
Colon	41.9	31.3	1.34
Rectum	19.0	11.0	1.73

[a]Age-adjusted to 1970 U.S. standard population.

[b]SEER, National Cancer Institute, *Cancer Statistics Review*.

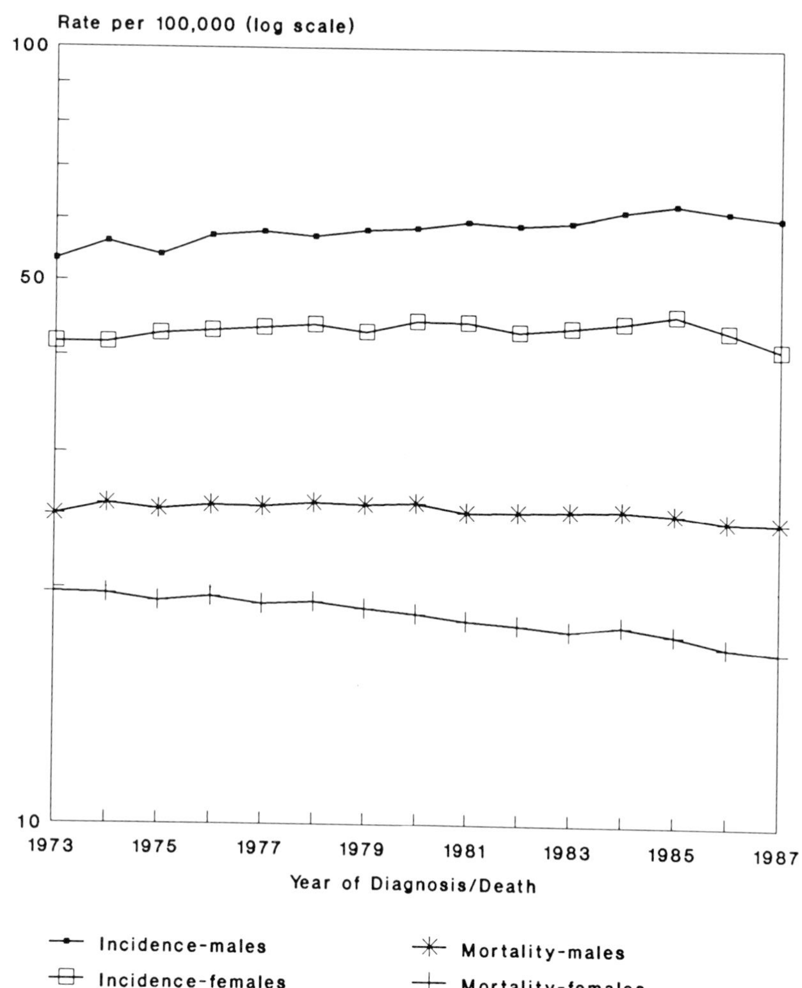

FIG. 3-1. Cancer of the colon and rectum. Age-adjusted (1970 standard) SEER incidence and U.S. mortality rates per 100,000 by sex, 1973–1987.

ANATOMIC DISTRIBUTION

More than half of all colonic cancers occur either in the sigmoid (35 percent) or the cecum (22 percent). The distribution throughout the remaining colon is as follows: ascending colon (12 percent), transverse colon (10 percent), and descending colon (7 percent). The incidence of colonic cancer (36.2 per 100,000) in the United States is about 2½ times that reported for rectal cancer (14.6 per 100,000). Within the large intestine, 69 percent of cancers are in the colon and 31 percent are in the rectum and at the rectosigmoid junction.

Internationally, there is a high positive correlation between the age-adjusted incidence of colonic and rectal cancer (the correlation coefficient exceeds 0.85 for males and females). Countries in which colonic cancer incidence is high demonstrate a relatively higher proportion of sigmoid cancers, whereas in countries with a lower incidence, cancers of the cecum and ascending colon predominate. In countries with low incidence rates of colorectal cancer, the incidence of colonic cancer is lower than that of rectal cancer because of a deficit in the incidence of sigmoid cancer.[1]

The distribution of neoplasms in the large intestine may also be viewed epidemiologically as either right-sided (i.e., including the cecum, ascending colon, hepatic flexure, and transverse colon) or left-sided (i.e., including the splenic flexure, descending colon, sigmoid, rectosigmoid, and rectum). DeJong et al.,[2] in their examination of the subsite distribution of cancers of the large intestine in various populations, described the male preponderance at ages above 65 years for neoplasms in the left side, including the rectum, and the female preponderance at ages below 65 years for all subsites in the colon but excluding the rectum. In a similar analysis based upon the population-based Danish Cancer Registry, Jensen[3] reported that the male:female ratio of age-standardized incidence rates increased in relationship to the more distal location of left-sided lesions.

In an analysis of the anatomic distribution of carcinomas diagnosed throughout the large intestine, based upon information from the Connecticut Tumor Registry, Snyder et al.[4] reported that the proportion of colorectal cancers occurring in the right colon increased gradually over the period 1940–1973. During the period 1940–1944, 26 percent of tumors were located in the cecum, ascending colon, and transverse colon and 74 percent in the descending colon, sigmoid colon, and rectum. During the period 1970–1973, left-sided lesions decreased proportionally to 66 percent.[4] The analysis of the Connecticut experience has been updated by Vukasin et al.,[5] who have questioned the appropriateness in various studies of interpreting the true magnitude of a left-to-right shift based upon the proportional distribution of lesions without the concomitant measurements of temporal trends in site-specific incidence rates.

During the period 1935–1985 in Connecticut, the age-adjusted yearly incidence of cancers of the cecum and ascending colon increased from 3.6 to 16.7 per 100,000 in men and from 4.9 to 14.2 per 100,000 in women; during the same period, the yearly incidence of cancer of the sigmoid colon increased from 8.8 to 18.7 per 100,000 in men and from 7.7 to 12.8 per 100,000 in women. While the age-adjusted incidence of colonic cancer in Connecticut increased proportionally for right-sided and sigmoid lesions, the rates for cancers of the descending colon and rectum did not change significantly over a 50-year period.

INCIDENCE AND MORTALITY IN THE UNITED STATES

The impact of colorectal cancer in the United States may be measured in relation to the available information on temporal trends for mortality, incidence, and survival. Population-based cancer mortality data have been available since 1900, whereas cancer incidence data prior to 1973 were obtainable from periodic surveys conducted in selected geographic areas of the United States during the periods 1937–1939, 1947–1948, and 1969–1971. Before 1973, cancer survival statistics were summarized from hospital-based rather than population-based data under the auspices of the End Results Program of the National Cancer Institute. The evolution of the End Results Program and the periodic incidence surveys resulted in the implementation by the National Cancer Institute of the Surveillance, Epidemiology and End Results (SEER) Program, which has collected data since 1973 on approximately 10 percent of the U.S. population. The SEER program currently coordinates the collection of incidence and follow-up survival information from the states of Connecticut, Iowa, Utah, New Mexico, and Hawaii as well as the metropolitan areas of Atlanta, Detroit, Seattle (Puget Sound), and San Francisco–Oakland.[6]

In the United States in 1990, about 1,040,000 cases of cancer were diagnosed for the first time (incidence); 510,000 deaths were attributable to cancer in all sites and tissues (mortality). Incidence and mortality rates are summarized as the number of events per 100,000 persons at risk per year (person-years) and are age-adjusted by the direct method to the age distribution of the 1970 standard million population of the United States. Since 1973, overall cancer mortality rates have remained relatively stable, while incidence rates have increased 18 and 11 percent among males and females, respectively. Overall cancer incidence in the late 1980s was highest among black males (523.2), followed by white males (427.2), white females (334.5), and black females (322.5). Patterns of incidence and mortality for a specific cancer site may vary in relation to age, gender, and race because of the influence of lifestyle and environmental factors, genetic factors, interactions of exogenous and susceptibility factors, and access to and utilization of optimal screening, diagnostic, and medical care services.

The age-adjusted colorectal cancer mortality (per 100,000) in the United States for 1985–1989 was highest in black males (27.6) and exceeded by 33 percent the mortality in black females (20.8); the corresponding rate in white males (24.2) exceeded by 48 percent the mortality in white females (16.4). The incidence rates for colorectal cancer were similar for white (61.0) and black males (60.5). The male:female age-adjusted incidence ratios for colorectal cancer exceeded 1.0 by 30 percent in blacks and by 45 percent in whites (Table 3-2).

During the period 1973–1989, colorectal cancer mortality among whites decreased significantly—by 20 percent in females and 8.5 percent in males; in contrast, mortality among blacks increased significantly—by 22.5 percent in males and 2.6 percent in females. For whites, the decreases in mortality occurred in all

Table 3-2
Age-Adjusted[a] Mortality and Incidence Rates per 100,000 Population for Colorectal Cancer, Whites and Blacks, Males and Females, United States, 1985–1989

	Whites		*Blacks*	
Colon and rectum	*Males*	*Females*	*Males*	*Females*
Mortality	24.2	16.4	27.6	20.8
Incidence	61.0	42.1	60.5	46.4

[a]Age-adjusted to 1970 U.S. standard population.

age groups except in those aged 85 and above. For blacks, only females under 65 years of age showed a decrease in mortality, which was most evident over the period 1985–1989. The mortality rate for cancer of the rectum, including the rectosigmoid junction, decreased among each of the four race-gender subgroups and particularly in those aged 70 and above. One cautionary caveat in reporting rectal cancer mortality trends in the United States is that there is substantial misclassification of sigmoid colon versus rectum (including rectosigmoid) on the death certificate. An analysis by Percy et al.[7] indicated that as a result of inaccuracies in certification, the mortality rate for colonic cancer is generally overestimated and that for cancer of the rectum and rectosigmoid is generally underestimated by approximately 30 percent. In evaluating the accuracy of death certificates in the United States, Chow and Devesa[8] compared each death certificate with the codified information of the SEER registry. The authors estimated that during 1980–1986, deaths from colonic cancer were overreported by 26 percent and those from rectal cancer were underreported by 53 percent. As a result, the reported decline in rectal cancer mortality between 1950 and 1988 (−65 percent) was, after correcting for underreporting, reduced by about half (−31 percent). In contrast to the *mortality* trends just described for cancer of the rectum, the age-standardized *incidence* rates for cancer of the rectum have been quite stable in the four race-gender subgroups since 1973, which does underscore the cogency of reporting mortality trends for the colon and rectum combined. However, as emphasized by Funkhouser and Cole,[9] even after assuming significant misclassification bias, there has been a residual real decline in the mortality rate for cancer of the rectum, which may have resulted in part from improved survival. From the early 1960s through the 1980s, the relative 5-year survival rate combining all stages has increased from 38 to 55 percent for white patients and from 27 to 44 percent for black patients.

INTERNATIONAL INCIDENCE

Colorectal cancer is the third-ranking cancer in the world, accounting for about 9 percent of the estimated 6.35 million invasive cancers occurring each year. The substantial international variation in incidence rates and the observation that patterns change dramatically after migration indicate the importance of environmental factors, particularly those related to lifestyle. For example, the age-standardized incidence of colonic cancer in Connecticut among white males and females is almost 10 times greater than that reported in Bombay, India; the rate for rectal cancer is more than four times higher in Connecticut than in Bombay.[10]

Colon

The highest incidence rates for colonic cancer are reported in North America, Australia, and New Zealand. The rates in western European countries are uniformly lower than those in North America but are consistently higher than those in eastern European countries. The lowest rates are generally reported in Africa, Asia, and Latin America. Incidence rates in Asia vary considerably in that the rates in the Chinese of Singapore and Hong Kong are approximately twice those in the Shanghai Chinese but are comparable to the rates in western Europeans, Hawaiian Chinese, and Israeli Jews. The age-standardized rates in India and among Israeli non-Jews are among the lowest in the world (Fig. 3-2). In general, colonic cancer is relatively more common in economically advantaged populations exhibiting westernized lifestyle practices.

Rectum

The incidence of colonic cancer varies internationally to a greater extent than that of rectal cancer. In contrast to colonic cancer, rectal cancer is usually more common in males, with an age-standardized male: female incidence rate ratio of 1.5 to 2.0. In areas with low incidence rates for colorectal cancer—such as India, Senegal, and eastern Europe—the rates for rectal cancer may exceed those for colonic cancer (Fig. 3-3).

Race/Ethnicity

The comparison of incidence rates among racial and ethnic groups in the United States reveals the influence of cultural and socioeconomic differences such as lifestyle practices (e.g., dietary habits, use of tobacco and/or alcohol, reproductive patterns, physical activity, high-risk occupations) or possibly the interaction of genetic and environmental factors. Incidence, mortality, and survival patterns in racial and ethnic minorities may be influenced by access to and availability and utilization of quality health care and preventive medical services. In Table 3-3, the distribution of incidence rates by racial/ethnic groups suggests three levels of risk for colorectal cancer in males and females. The highest risk levels are seen in Japanese Americans and in U.S. whites and blacks; the intermediate levels affect Chinese and Filipino Americans; and the lowest levels are seen in Mexican and Native Americans.

Migrants

In migrant studies, the age-standardized mortality (or incidence) from a given disease in a specific racial or ethnic group in the country of origin or birth is com-

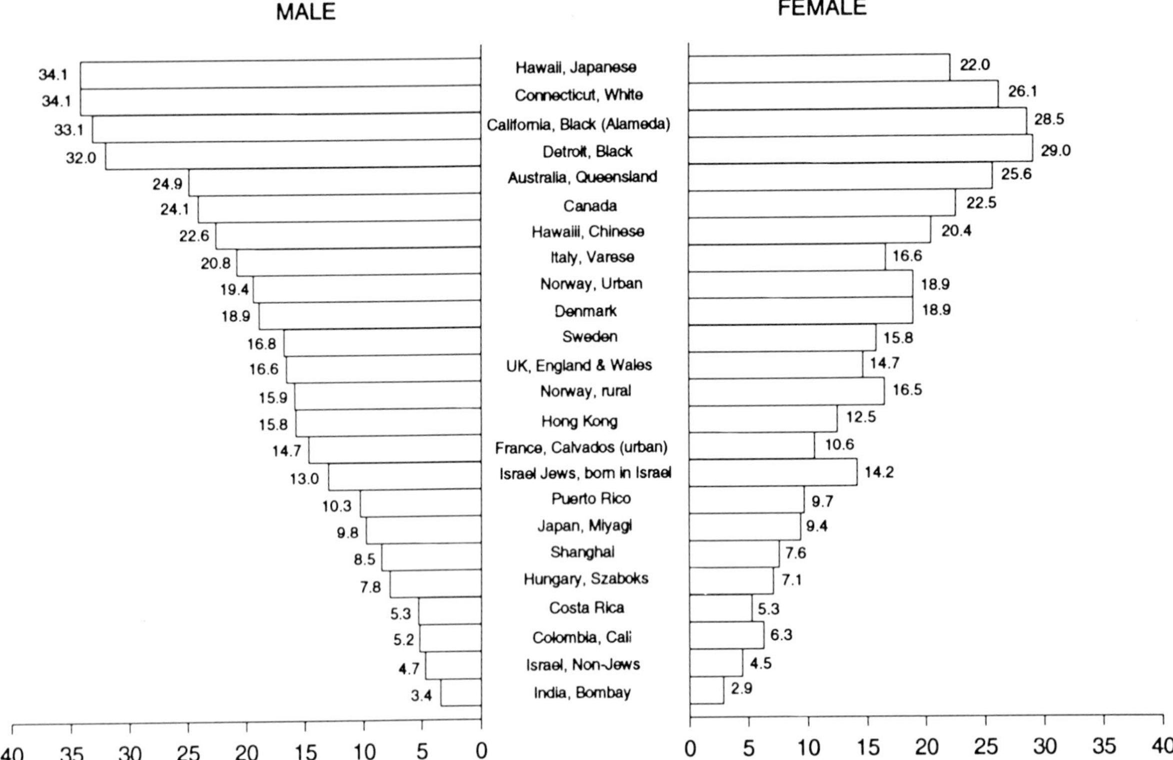

FIG. 3-2. Age-standardized incidence rates per 100,000 (world population) for colonic cancer in 24 selected countries, 1978–1982. (Data from Muir et al.[10] With permission.)

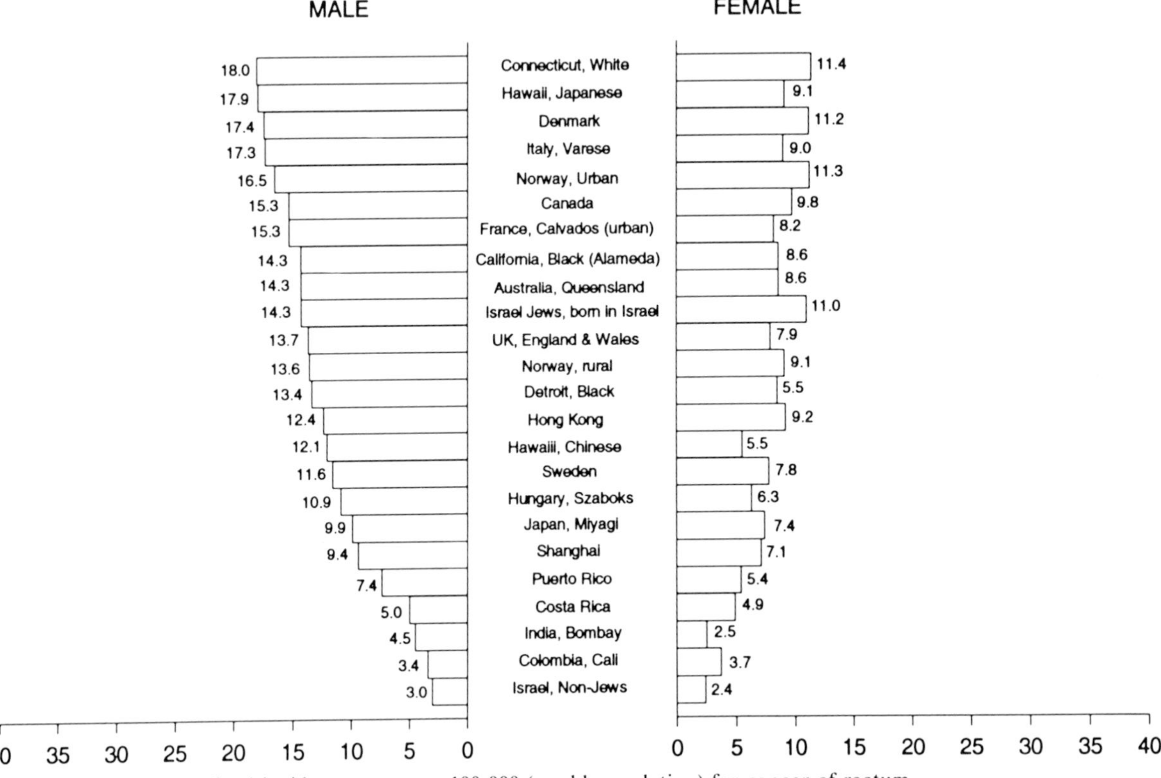

FIG. 3-3. Age-standardized incidence rates per 100,000 (world population) for cancer of rectum (including rectosigmoid junction) in 24 selected countries, 1978–1982. (From Muir et al.[10] With permission.)

Table 3-3
Average Annual Age-Adjusted[a] Incidence Rates per 100,000 Population for Colorectal Cancer by Race, United States, 1977–1983[b]

Race	*Males*	*Females*
Japanese	62.3	37.5
White	59.6	41.9
Black	56.5	46.0
Chinese	48.8	33.0
Filipino	36.7	18.3
Mexican American	28.9	23.9
Native American (New Mexico)	10.4	9.1

[a]Age-adjusted to 1970 U.S. standard population.
[b]SEER, National Cancer Institute.

pared with that in the country of adoption, or the host country. Migrants may be described as *first-generation* (e.g., Issei Japanese) or—with respect to their offspring who reside in the country of adoption—as *second-generation* (e.g., Nisei Japanese). Then there are third and future generations. Those who are of uncertain generation are referred to collectively as *descendants of migrants*. Migrant studies are of particular interest in estimating latency periods and assessing the association with environmental factors. Migrants make up a subset of the country-of-origin population who seek residence in the country of adoption for the sake of economic opportunity or freedom from oppression or for reasons associated with aging and familial dependency. These selective forces may bear on future health risks. With respect to the patterns of displacement of cancer rates, the migrant population is characterized by specific geographic location in the country of origin, age at migration, duration of residence in the country of adoption, and extent of cultural assimilation. Migrant studies are experiments of nature where the populations to be studied are characterized by marked differences in rates at baseline (or prior to migration) and where subsequently, in the current and future generations of migrants, we are able to observe the long-term health effects of transition from one culture to another.

A mortality survey of generations of Japanese Americans during 1949–1952 revealed that although mortality from colorectal cancer was lower among them; it was approaching that among U.S. whites and significantly higher than that seen among the Japanese in Japan. The upward trend was more apparent in males. These trends continued, so that by the early 1970s, the incidence of colorectal cancer and mortality from it in Japanese men and women in Hawaii were similar to those seen in U.S. whites up to age 70. However, these rates remained lower for the group over age 70. It should be noted that over a 25-year period, 1960–1985, mortality from colorectal cancer increased 2.5-fold in Japan. The transitional pattern in the Japanese migrants was associated with a right-to-left shift in anatomic distribution, with a proportionally greater concentration of carcinomas and adenomatous polyps in the sigmoid colon.[11]

The majority of Chinese migrating to the United States have come from Guangzhou province and are identified by their Cantonese dialect. The age-adjusted rates of mortality from colorectal cancer in 1970 among first-generation Chinese American men and women, respectively, were 5.6 and 2.7 times those seen in Guangzhou province.[12]

In 1978–1982, among Israeli Jews who were born in Europe or North America, the incidence of colonic cancer in the men was more than twice that in Israeli Jews born in Africa or Asia and more than four times that in Israeli non-Jews. The rates in Israeli-born Jews, men and women, were intermediate between those in the European/American and African/Asian Jews (Table 3-4). Similar patterns were evident for the incidence of rectal cancer.

Cancer mortality rates in migrants to Australia from southern and eastern Europe and from the United Kingdom have been reviewed for the period 1962–1982. The migrant groups from Poland, Yugoslavia, Greece, and Italy had premigration risks of dying of colonic cancer that were from 0.3 to 0.7 times those in Australia. After living in Australia for 16 years or more, the Polish migrants' relative risk of dying of colonic cancer reached that of the Australian-born; however, the migrating populations from Yugoslavia, Greece, and Italy exhibited risks that were 0.7 times that of the Australian-born. Polish migrants to Australia—by contrast to their fellow immigrants to the United States—were in general of a higher socioeconomic status and drawn from urban areas. This would have affected the baseline premigration level of colorectal cancer mortality.[13]

Table 3-4
Age-Adjusted (World Population) Incidence per 100,000 of Colonic and Rectal Cancer in Israel, 1978–1982, by Religion and Place of Birth

	Males		*Females*	
Israeli population	*Colon*	*Rectum*	*Colon*	*Rectum*
All Jews	16.2	16.6	15.0	13.4
Jews born in Europe or America	21.1	22.6	17.7	15.9
Jews born in Africa or Asia	9.3	10.3	13.3	8.7
Jews born in Israel	13.0	14.3	14.2	11.0
Non-Jews	4.7	3.0	4.5	2.4

SOURCE: From Muir et al.[10] (Reproduced by permission.)

The vast majority of Puerto Rican migrants to the United States arrived after 1945. Unlike the Japanese, Chinese, and Europeans, the Puerto Rican migrants traveled back and forth between the mainland and Puerto Rico, so that environmental and lifestyle exposures accompanied by changing cultural practices were intermittent and of variable duration. Reverse migration was so common that in the 1970s there was a net migration from the United States to Puerto Rico. Warshauer et al.[14] examined the age-adjusted incidence and mortality rates for colorectal cancer during 1975–1979 among Puerto Rican–born residents of New York City. Incidence and mortality for Puerto Rican men and women living in New York City were about twice the rates reported in Puerto Rico and half to two-thirds the rates of white men and women in New York City.

The studies of migrant populations in the United States have demonstrated that, for many racial and ethnic groups throughout the world, the risks of colonic and rectal cancer approach those of the U.S.-born whites in the first generation or after 20 or more years of residence in the country of adoption. The transition for some groups, such as those originating in Mexico or Puerto Rico, may not be complete in the first generation. However, the risk of rectal and colonic cancer appears to change more rapidly and extensively in the first migrating generation than it does for gastric, breast, or prostatic cancers. These differences may reflect the relative importance of earlier versus later exposures to putative carcinogens, genetic factors that influence metabolic processes, and/or the rapidity and degree of change in acculturation that is correlated with determinants of the multistage carcinogenic process. Beyond the ecologic, descriptive studies are case-control and cohort analytic studies that are seeking to identify the major differences in dietary practices and their implications with respect to anatomic displacement in the colon, shifts in incidence and mortality, the occurrence of precursor lesions, or biomarker indicators of aberrant epithelial stem cell proliferation.

Urbanization and Socioeconomic Status

In countries throughout the world, rates of colorectal cancer incidence are consistently higher among urban residents. The urban excess is more apparent for men than for women and for colonic more than for rectal cancer. Current residence in an urban area is a stronger determinant or predictor of colorectal cancer risk than is place of birth. That is, whereas the risk for persons born in rural areas and migrating to large cities resembles that for persons born and currently residing in large cities, the risk for persons born and currently residing in rural areas is about 30 percent less than that for urban residents.

Mortality from colorectal cancer by county in the United States during 1950–1969 was positively correlated with indices of socioeconomic status; that is, the highest risk occurred in the areas of highest income and highest median years of education. Socioeconomic factors, as they are related to access to and quality of medical care, are an important independent predictor of survival in patients with colorectal cancer. In an analysis of colorectal cancer incidence in the United States based upon the Third National Cancer Survey (1969–1971), the correlation of socioeconomic factors was demonstrable only in white males with colonic cancer; the age-adjusted relative risks were increased by 30 to 40 percent in the subgroups with the highest income and median number of years of education. In an analysis of the SEER cancer incidence figures in three U.S. metropolitan areas between 1978 and 1982, Baquet et al.[15] reported a positive association for cancer of the colon, rectum, and rectosigmoid with population density, which is a measure of urbanization. The incidence of colonic cancer in either blacks or whites was not correlated with educational level or median family income based upon data from the 1980 census. The incidence rates for cancer of the rectum were significantly higher for whites than for blacks at every educational level. In summary, in contrast to the international incidence patterns of upper digestive tract squamous cell carcinomas, which are significantly inversely correlated with socioeconomic factors, the current relative risks of colorectal adenocarcinomas in the United States and in other developed countries are neither significantly nor uniformly associated with indices of social and economic advancement.

OCCUPATION: CHEMICAL EXPOSURE OR A SURROGATE MEASURE OF PHYSICAL ACTIVITY?

Colorectal cancer is generally not viewed as an occupational disease. A statistically significant relationship with a particular occupational group may be confounded by social class and lifestyle risk factors or may be due to a specific exposure in the work setting. A causal association has been suggested in the studies of pattern and model makers in the automobile manufacturing industry. Twofold to threefold increases in risk of colorectal cancer incidence and mortality have been described among these skilled workers who were exposed to woods, metals, plastics, fiberglass, and a variety of fumes and solvents.[16,17] Epidemiologic studies have suggested that there is a weak association between asbestos exposure, in particular chrysotile and amosite fibers, and colonic cancer.[18] Asbestos fibers and the formation of asbestos bodies have been demonstrated by light and electron microscopy in tumor tissue in the colons of patients with occupational asbestos exposure.[19] In a population-based case-control study of incident colonic cancer in Los Angeles County, Garabrant et al.[20] reported that there was no association with the intensity, duration, or latency of reported asbestos exposure.

Persky et al.[21] reported that baseline heart rate, which is inversely associated with level of physical activity, was a predictor of mortality from colonic cancer.[21] In a population-based case-control study of risk factors for colorectal cancer in males aged 20 to 64, Garabrant et al.[22] observed that men with sedentary jobs (i.e., less than 20 percent of work time requiring physical activity) experienced a risk of colonic cancer (excluding rectum and rectosigmoid) at least 1.6 times that of men whose jobs required a high level (i.e., more than 80 percent of work time) of activity. The risk ratios—particularly for cancers located in the transverse, descending, and sigmoid colon—increased significantly in a stepwise manner as occupational physical activity level decreased. The protective effect of physical activity was not evident for cancers located in the proximal colon or rectum. The role of occupational physical activity as a risk factor was evident after controlling for race, ethnicity, and socioeconomic status; it did not appear to reflect common environmental chemical exposures. The observed negative association between the risk of colonic cancer and physical activity has been corroborated by numerous epidemiologic studies in various countries.[23-28] Several studies have demonstrated a protective effect of avocational physical activity for distal colonic cancer in men and women. Dietary factors, in particular the average daily consumption of total calories and total fat (saturated and unsaturated), did not confound or obscure the independent association of physical inactivity as a risk factor for colorectal cancer. In the comparative study of colorectal cancer among Chinese in North America and China, Whittemore et al.[29] inferred that saturated fat intakes exceeding 10 g/day in combination with physical inactivity accounted for 60 percent of colorectal cancer incidence among Chinese American men and 40 percent among Chinese American women.[29]

A plausible physiologic explanation has been advanced to reconcile the differential effects of physical activity on the distribution of neoplasms in the proximal and distal colon. Increased physical activity, perhaps through the release of prostaglandins accompanied by neural reflex mechanisms, enhances propagative peristalsis in the colon.[30,31] The accelerated transit time reduces the likelihood of contact at the interface of the fecal stream, which may contain putative mutagens, and the colonic mucosa. This physiologic effect of physical activity would be strongest in the descending and sigmoid colon, where the stool is semisolid and the transit time responsive to extrinsic factors.

WHO IS AT RISK?

The assessment of individual risk factors associated with the incidence of colorectal cancer may be expressed in terms of relative or absolute risk. Relative risk or the risk ratio is the ratio of the incidence rate for a specific disease among individuals with the specific risk factors to the incidence rate among individuals without the specific risk factors. In a case-control study, an analogous ratio measure is derived by dividing the odds of exposure to the specific risk factors among those with the disease by the odds of exposure to the same risk factors among those without disease. When compared with the baseline or null value of 1.0, each independent risk factor is perceived as having a multiplicative effect on the expression of relative risk.

A complementary approach in the assessment of risk is the derivation of absolute risk, which describes the probability that an individual with given risk factors will develop a specific disease over a defined period of time. The magnitude of absolute risk, usually expressed as a percentage, will depend on the distribution of baseline risk factors, including age, gender, and race; competing causes of mortality that tend to reduce expression of absolute risk; and the period of time over which the projection of risk is to be determined. As an example, the lifetime probability of developing colorectal cancer for U.S. men and women is projected to be 6 percent.

Age

The age-specific incidence of colorectal cancer in the United States rises sharply after age 40, with 90 percent of cancers occurring in persons 50 years of age and older (Fig. 3-4). The incidence trends from 1973 to 1989 indicated a relative decline under age 65 of 13.5 percent in white females in contrast to an increase of 15.6 percent in black females; the decrease in white males was minimal, 1.0 percent, in contrast to the increase in black males of 32.4 percent. At 65 years and older, from 1973 to 1989, there were relative increases of 38.4 percent in black males, 16.5 percent in black females, 8.8 percent in white males, and 1.8 percent in white females. Blacks had higher rates than whites for the age groups below 70, and whites exhibited higher rates than blacks for the age groups 70 and above.

Adenomatous Polyp without Familial History

The precursor lesion of colorectal carcinoma may be either an adenoma or nonpolypoid flat mucosa exhibiting epithelial dysplasia of various grades of severity. Neoplastic polyps are associated with perturbations in

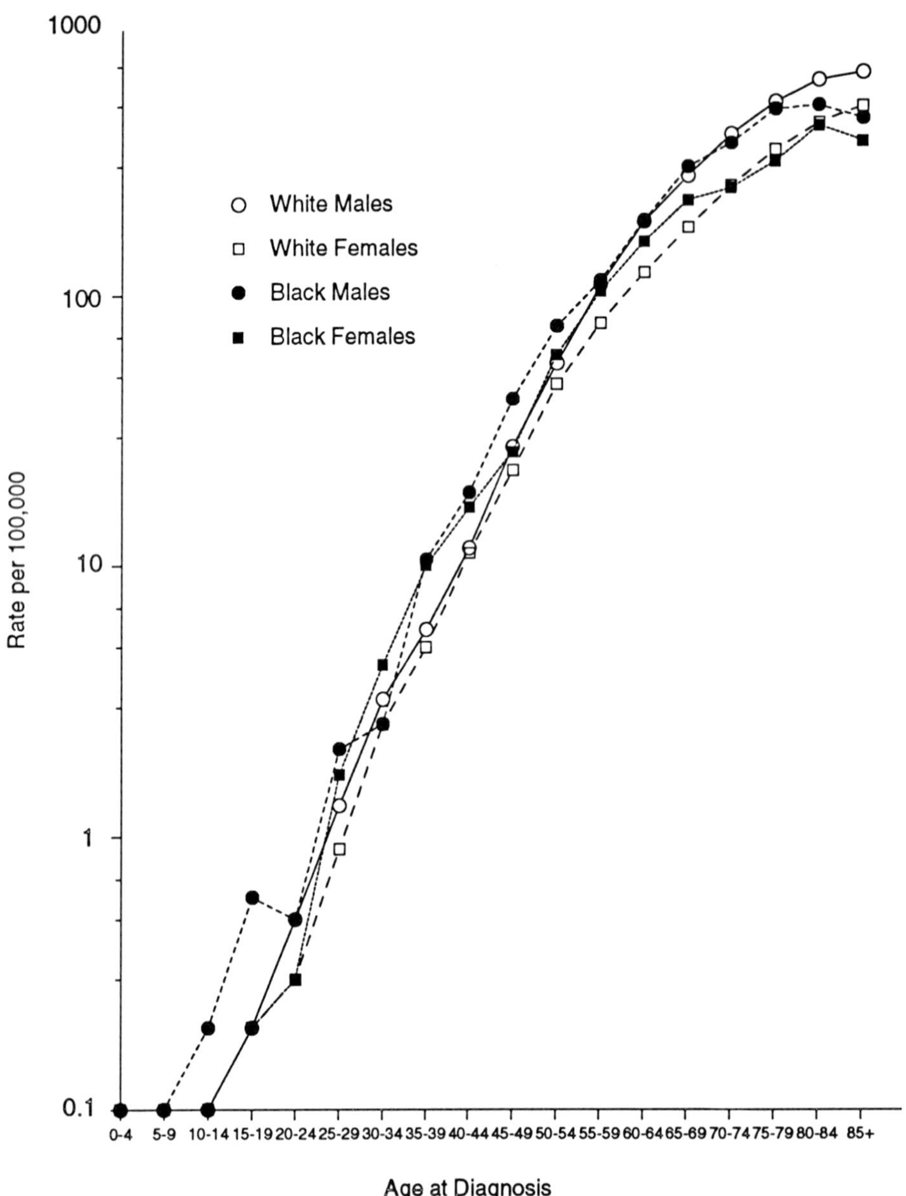

FIG. 3-4. Age-specific incidence rates (per 100,000) for colorectal cancer, by race and sex, United States, 1985–1989.

the mucosal epithelium of the regulation of stem cell proliferation and differentiation.

Thymidine-labeling studies have shown aberrant patterns of DNA synthesis along the crypts of the surface epithelium in patients with dysplastic lesions and adenomas.[32] The malignant potential of an adenoma may be predicted by (1) its size—namely, whether it is 1.0 cm or larger in surface diameter; (2) the presence of high-grade dysplasia; and (3) the predominance of villous features.[33–35] Morson[36] reported that in patients with an adenoma 1.0 cm or larger, the cumulative incidence of colorectal cancer was 10 percent over 15 years of follow-up. The relative risk of colorectal cancer developing in patients with a single adenoma of 1.0 cm or larger may be increased from 1.5 to 3.6 times that expected in a control population. This level of estimated relative risk is multiplied by a factor of approximately 2 in the presence of multiple adenomas and/or a significant component of villous histology.

The frequency of adenomas in various populations varies with the magnitude of colorectal cancer incidence. The positive correlation coefficient worldwide for men and women combined is about 0.7. In cross-sectional studies, the prevalence of colorectal adenomas is reported to be higher in males than in females, and it increases with age in both women and men; larger adenomas are observed more frequently distal to the transverse colon, although an increasing proportion of adenomas have been found on colonoscopy in the cecum and ascending colon in parallel with the shifting anatomic distribution of carcinomas.[37] Giovannucci et al.,[38] in a prospective study of male health professionals, provided evidence in support of the hypothesis that a diet high in saturated fat or in the ratio of red meat to chicken and fish combined was positively associated with the risk of colorectal adenoma after adjusting for total energy intake or amount of kilocalories. Conversely, a high-fiber diet, provided by the regular intake of vegetables, fruits, and grains, was associated with a decreased risk of adenoma. The apparent protective relationship with fiber persisted after adjustment for saturated fat, total calories, and micronutrients commonly found in fruits and vegetables (i.e., vitamins C and E and beta-carotene).[38]

Familial and Hereditary Factors

In addition to the rare autosomal dominant syndrome of familial adenomatous polyposis (FAP) and of Gardner syndrome and the hereditary nonpolyposis colorectal cancer syndromes (Lynch I and II), it is well established that first-degree relatives of patients with cancer of the large bowel or with adenomatous polyps—in the absence of a well-defined monogenic syndrome—have a two- to threefold increased relative risk of colorectal cancer. In the latter, more common instances of familial large bowel cancer where specific inheritance patterns are not apparent, other mechanisms have been suggested such as polygenic inheritance, shared environmental factors, the interactions of genetic and environmental factors, and/or the partial penetrance of an autosomal dominant susceptibility gene.[39]

Inherited conditions as currently defined account for less than 10 percent of incident colorectal carcinomas in the general population. Familial adenomatous polyposis is prototypic of the polyposis-related colorectal cancer syndromes occurring with a frequency of 1/7,000 to 1/24,000 live births. Penetrance has been variously estimated at 80 to 100 percent. About one-third of cases do not present with a family history and are assumed to represent new germline mutants of the FAP gene locus, mapped at 5q21. The cumulative incidence of colorectal carcinoma approaches 100 percent by age 55.

Another category of inherited colorectal cancer manifests itself in the absence of familial polyposis and includes hereditary site-specific colon cancer (Lynch syndrome I) and the cancer family syndrome (Lynch syndrome II). In families with the Lynch syndrome I, the increased risk of colorectal cancer is expressed 15 to 20 years earlier than in the general population. Two-thirds of the malignant neoplasms, often as synchronous and metachronous multiple primaries, occur in the proximal or right half of the colon. Family members of pedigrees with the Lynch syndrome II are distinguished by concomitant or alternative occurrences of extracolonic cancers, most commonly of the endometrium and ovary, but possibly also at other sites in the gastrointestinal, urinary, and biliary tracts.[40,41]

Examination of familial clustering of colorectal cancers in population-based studies indicated that they were not limited to cases characterized by either proximal colonic distribution or early age at onset. However, tumor location proximal to the splenic flexure in the probands identified by population-based tumor registries appeared to be correlated with a higher risk of extracolonic multiple primary cancers in the relatives when compared with the pedigrees of probands with more distal or left-sided cancers.[42] Bulfill[43] has suggested that the neoplasms occurring in the right colon, whether sporadically or in an inherited segregation pattern, appear to be genetically more stable than neoplasms occurring in the distal colon and rectum.[43] Preliminary cytogenetic, flow cytometric, and molecular genetic studies have begun to explore mechanistic differences by distinguishing proximal and distal tumors with respect to polyploidy, aneuploidy, chromosomal abnormalities, c-myc oncogene expression, and allelic deletions.[44]

Inflammatory Bowel Disease

Inflammatory bowel disease (IBD) includes two related but clinically and histologically separate entities: ulcerative colitis and Crohn's disease. Worldwide, the annual incidence of IBD varies from 0.5 to 20 per 100,000, with high-risk areas including northern Europe, the United States, the United Kingdom, Canada, and Israel; intermediate risk exists in central Europe and Australia; and low risk in South America, Asia, and Africa. In most countries, ulcerative colitis is diagnosed more frequently than Crohn's disease, particularly between the ages of 15 and 30. The incidence of IBD has increased significantly in northern Europe and the United Kingdom during the period 1960–1985.

Patients with IBD are at increased risk of colorectal carcinoma; the magnitude of relative and absolute risk increases in relation to the extent of mucosal involvement and the demonstration by biopsy of multicentric foci of dysplasia or, less commonly, adenomatous polyps. In a review of the results of colonoscopic surveillance of patients with IBD, the predictive value for colorectal cancer of a positive biopsy of dysplasia ranged from 15 to 20 percent; severe, or high-grade, dysplasia was associated with a higher predictive value than low-grade, or mild, dysplasia. The overall increase in relative risk for cancer of the large intestine in patients with IBD has been estimated between 4- and 20-fold. In general, the mean age at diagnosis of colorectal cancer in patients with IBD is about 20 to 30 years younger than the mean age at diagnosis in the general population at risk of colorectal cancer. The cumulative incidence of colorectal cancer in patients with ulcerative colitis, after a minimal latency period of 5 to 10 years, increases on average from 0.5 to 1.0 percent per year; thus, after a follow-up period of 30 years, the cumulative incidence of colorectal cancer has been determined to be about 30 to 35 percent.[45,46] Crohn's disease involves the colon in 65 to 70 percent of patients; although the relative risk of colorectal cancer is substantially increased in relation to the extent of inflammatory disease and severity of dysplasia, the cumulative incidence and inference of absolute risk of cancer of the large intestine during a specified interval of surveillance approximates but does not appear to equal the magnitude of risk described in patients with ulcerative colitis.[47,48]

Second Primary Cancers

In the analysis of incidence patterns of multiple primary cancers in a total of 26,804 persons with an index primary cancer of the colon reported by the Connecticut Tumor Registry, the relative risk of a metachronous primary cancer in the remaining large intestine (colon and rectum) was 2.1 (95 percent confidence interval, 1.6 to 2.2), or more than double the incidence expected in the general population. The risk of a second primary varied with age at the time of diagnosis of the index primary: 8.7 when the age was below 45; 3.7 at ages 45 to 54; and 1.8 at age 55 and above. The cumulative incidence of a metachronous primary cancer in the colon and rectum after 10 years of follow-up from the diagnosis of the index primary cancer of the colon was 1.9 percent. Significant increases in relative risk of metachronous primary cancers of the ovary, corpus uteri, and breast have been observed in women with colorectal cancer; the observed increases in relative risk (i.e., at least 50 to 100 percent) were mutual in that women with cancer of the endometrium, ovary, or breast were at increased risk of developing colorectal cancer.[49]

Epidemiologic Patterns and Intestinal Microecology

Variations in the incidence rates of colorectal cancer over a period of years by age, gender, race, ethnicity, country of birth, migration with alteration in cultural practices, and socioeconomic status have generated hypotheses about the causal mechanisms affected by dietary factors and physical activity. The migrant population studies have indicated that low-risk ethnic groups, after establishing residence in a high-risk country for a period of at least 20 to 30 years, assume an elevated risk of colorectal cancer and of the precursor adenomatous polyp equal to or approximately that of the indigenous population.

The incidence of colorectal cancer increases exponentially in the general population with age raised to a power of 4 or 5. Undoubtedly multiple genetic events are required for somatic stem cell initiation, transformation, and clonal progression in carcinogenesis. In their multistage theoretical model, Moolgavkar and Leubeck[50] concluded that there were at least three essential rate-limiting or mutational steps in the genesis of colorectal cancer. They noted that the genetic alterations most consistently demonstrated were two deletions or structural alterations in the colon cancer (DCC) tumor suppressor gene locus on the long arm of chromosome 18 and at the p53 locus, a loss of function of the allele on the short arm of chromosome 17. The mutations described at the FAP gene locus and of the c-*ras* oncogene are interpreted as promoter mutations stimulating clonal expansion but were not viewed by the authors as essential rate-limiting events. Whether or not the proposed theoretical construct adequately explains the cascade of molecular genetic and epigenetic events, it is clear that colorectal cancer exhibits clonal expansion, that it evolves by extensive alteration throughout the genome, and that environmental factors play an essential role in a multistage process.[51]

The dietary patterns of western nations have been correlated with significant international differences in the incidence of colorectal cancer. Most but not all studies have been consistent with the "fat and/or fiber" hypothesis, which, as suggested by Potter,[52] may be alternatively described as the "meat and vegetables" hypothesis. A proposed biochemical mechanism would be that high intake of fat, particularly from animal sources, results in the increased excretion of fatty acids and of bile acids and salts, which are metabolized to secondary bile acids—deoxycholic and lithocholic acids. These metabolic by-products of intestinal fermentation by anaerobic bacteria have been demonstrated experimentally to promote tumor growth. In addition, the cooking of meat protein creates heterocyclic amines which have independent mutagenic and carcinogenic properties.[53] Sources of dietary fiber—namely fruits, vegetables, and grains—may have an anticarcinogenic effect by binding bile acids, increasing stool bulk, reducing intestinal transit time, and lowering the pH.[54–56] Vegetables and fruits are a source of antioxidant micronutrients and of indoles, flavonoids, isothiocyanates, and phenols, which may have potent anticarcinogenic properties. The studies suggesting a protective role of ionized calcium emphasize its potential for binding with fatty acids and bile acids with the formation of insoluble calcium soaps.[57,58]

REFERENCES

1. Ziegler RG, Devesa SS, Fraumeni JF, et al: Epidemiologic patterns of colorectal cancer, in Devita VT, Hellman S, Rosenberg SA (eds): *Important Advances in Oncology*. Philadelphia, Lippincott, 1986, pp 209–232.
2. DeJong UW, Day NE, Muir CS, et al: The distribution of cancer within the large bowel. *Int J Cancer* 10:463–477, 1972.
3. Jensen OM: Different age and sex relationship for cancer of subsites of the large bowel. *Br J Cancer* 50:825–829, 1984.
4. Snyder DN, Heston JF, Meigs JW, et al: Changes in site distribution of colorectal carcinoma in Connecticut, 1940–1973. *Dig Dis* 22:791–797, 1977.
5. Vukasin AP, Ballantyne GH, Flannery JT, et al: Increasing

incidence of cecal and sigmoid carcinoma: Data from the Connecticut tumor registry. *Cancer* 66:2442–2449, 1990.
6. National Cancer Institute: Cancer Statistics Review, 1973–1989. DHHS Publ. No. (NIH) 92-2789. Bethesda, Maryland, 1992.
7. Percy C, Stanek E III, Gloeckler L: Accuracy of cancer death certificates and its effect on cancer mortality statistics. *Am J Public Health* 71:242–250, 1981.
8. Chow WH, Devesa SS: Death certificate reporting of colon and rectal cancers. *JAMA* 267:3028, 1992.
9. Funkhouser E, Cole P: Declining mortality rates for cancer of the rectum in the United States: 1940–1985. *Cancer* 70: 2597–2601, 1992.
10. Muir C, Waterhouse J, Mack T, et al: *Cancer Incidence in Five Continents,* vol 5. IARC Scientific Publ. No. 88. Lyon, France, International Agency for Research on Cancer, 1987.
11. Wynder EL, Fujita Y, Harris RE, et al: Comparative epidemiology of cancer between the United States and Japan. *Cancer* 67:746–763, 1991.
12. King H, Li JY, Locke FB, et al: Patterns of site-specific displacement in cancer mortality among migrants: The Chinese in the United States. *Am J Public Health* 75:237–242, 1985.
13. McMichael AJ, McCall MG, Hartshorne JM, et al: Patterns of gastrointestinal cancer in European migrants to Australia: The role of dietary change. *Int J Cancer Supp* 25:431–437, 1980.
14. Warshauer ME, Silverman DT, Schottenfeld D, et al: Stomach and colorectal cancer incidence and mortality in Puerto Rican-born residents in New York City. *J Natl Cancer Inst* 76:591–595, 1986.
15. Baquet CR, Horm JW, Gibbs T, et al: Socioeconomic factors and cancer incidence among blacks and whites. *J Natl Cancer Inst* 83:551–557, 1991.
16. Schottenfeld D, Warshauer ME, Zauber AG, et al: Study of cancer mortality and incidence in wood shop workers of the General Motors Corporation: Report prepared for the Occupational Health Advisory Board of United Auto Workers. 1980.
17. Swanson GM, Belle SH, Burrows RW: Colon cancer incidence among model makers and pattern makers in the automobile manufacturing industry: A continuing dilemma. *J Occup Med* 27:567–569, 1985.
18. Morgan RW, Foliart DE, Wong O: Asbestos and gastrointestinal cancer. *West J Med* 143:60–65, 1985.
19. Ehrlich A, Gordon RE, Dikman SH: Carcinoma of the colon in asbestos-exposed workers: Analysis of asbestos content in colon tissue. *Am J Indust Med* 19:629–636, 1991.
20. Garabrant DH, Peters RK, Homa DM: Asbestos and colon cancer: Lack of association in a large case-control study. *Am J Epidemiol* 135:843–853, 1992.
21. Persky V, Dyer AR, Leonas J, et al: Heart rate: A risk factor for cancer? *Am J Epidemiol* 114:477–487, 1981.
22. Garabrant DH, Peters JM, Mack TM, et al: Job activity and colon cancer risk. *Am J Epidemiol* 119:1005–1014, 1984.
23. Vena JE, Graham S, Zielezny M, et al: Lifetime occupational exercise and colon cancer. *Am J Epidemiol* 122:357–365, 1985.
24. Wu AH, Paganini-Hill A, Ross RK, et al: Alcohol, physical activity and other risk factors for colorectal cancer: A prospective study. *Br J Cancer* 55:687–694, 1987.
25. Fredriksson M, Bengtsson NO, Hardell L, et al: Colon cancer, physical activity and occupational exposures: A case-control study. *Cancer* 63:1838–1842, 1989.
26. Ballard-Barbasch R, Schatzkin A, Albanes D, et al: Physical activity and risk of large bowel cancer in the Framingham study. *Cancer Res* 50:3610–3613, 1990.
27. Gerhardsson M, Norell SE, Kiviranta H, et al: Sedentary jobs and colon cancer. *Am J Epidemiol* 123:775–780, 1986.
28. Chow W-H, Dosemeci M, Zheng W, et al: Physical activity and occupational risk of colon cancer in Shanghai, China. *Int J Epidemiol* 22:23–29, 1993.
29. Whittemore AS, Wu-Williams AH, Lee M, et al: Diet, physical activity, and colorectal cancer among Chinese in North America and China. *J Natl Cancer Inst* 82:915–926, 1990.
30. Holdstock DJ, Misiewicz JJ, Smith T, et al: Propulsion (mass movements) in the human colon and its relationship to meals and somatic activity. *Gut* 11:91–99, 1970.
31. Demers LM, Harrison TS, Halbert DR, et al: Effect of prolonged exercise on plasma prostaglandin levels. *Prostaglandins Med* 6:413–418, 1981.
32. Lipkin M: Biomarkers of increased susceptibility to gastrointestinal cancer: New application to studies of cancer prevention in human subjects. *Cancer Res* 48:235–245, 1988.
33. O'Brien MJ, O'Keane JC, Zauber AG, et al: Precursors of colorectal carcinoma: Biopsy and biologic markers. *Cancer* 70:1317–1327, 1992.
34. Simons BD, Morrison AS, Lev R, et al: Relationship of polyps to cancer of the large intestine. *J Natl Cancer Inst* 84: 962–966, 1992.
35. Winawer SJ, Zauber AG, O'Brien MJ, et al: Randomized comparison of surveillance intervals after colonoscopic removal of newly diagnosed adenomatous polyps. *N Engl J Med* 328:901–906, 1993.
36. Morson BC: The evolution of colorectal carcinoma. *Clin Radiol* 35:425–431, 1984.
37. Neugut AI, Jacobson JS, DeVivo I: Epidemiology of colorectal adenomatous polyps. *Cancer Epidemiol Biom Prev* 2: 159–176, 1993.
38. Giovannucci E, Stampfer MJ, Colditz G, et al: Relationship of diet to risk of colorectal adenoma in men. *J Natl Cancer Inst* 84:91–98, 1992.
39. Lev R: *Adenomatous Polyps of the Colon.* New York: Springer-Verlag, 1990, pp 45–52.
40. Lynch HT, Watson P, Kriegler M, et al: Differential diagnosis of hereditary nonpolyposis colorectal cancer (Lynch syndrome I and Lynch syndrome II). *Dis Colon Rectum* 31:372–377, 1988.
41. Lynch HT, Richardson JD, Amin M, et al: Variable gastrointestinal and urologic cancers in a Lynch syndrome II kindred. *Dis Colon Rectum* 34:891–895, 1991.
42. Cannon-Albright LA, Thomas TC, Bishop T, et al: Characteristics of familial colon cancer in a large population data base. *Cancer* 64:1971–1975, 1989.
43. Bulfill JA: Colorectal cancer: Evidence for distinct genetic categories based on proximal or distal tumor location. *Ann Intern Med* 113:779–788, 1990.
44. Delattre O, Law DJ, Schwang S, et al: Multiple genetic alterations in distal and proximal colorectal cancer. *Lancet* 2:353–356, 1989.
45. Ekbom A, Helmick C, Zack M, et al: Ulcerative colitis and colorectal cancer—A population based study. *N Engl J Med* 323:1228–1233, 1990.
46. Lennard-Jones JE, Melville DM, Morson BC, et al: Precancer and cancer in extensive ulcerative colitis. Findings among 401 patients over 22 years. *Gut* 31:800–806, 1990.
47. Hamilton SR: Colorectal carcinoma in patients with Crohn's disease. *Gastroenterology* 89:398–407, 1989.
48. Ekbom A, Helmick C, Zack M, et al: Increased risk of large-bowel cancer in Crohn's disease with colonic involvement. *Lancet* 336:357–359, 1990.
49. Schottenfeld D, Winawer SJ: Large intestine, in Schottenfeld D, Fraumeni JF Jr (eds): *Cancer Epidemiology and Prevention.* New York, Oxford University Press (in press).
50. Moolgavkar SH, Laubeck EG: Multistage carcinogenesis: Population-based model for colon cancer. *J Natl Cancer Inst* 84:610–618, 1992.

51. Vogelstein B, Fearon ER, Hamilton SR, et al: Genetic alterations during colorectal tumor development. *N Engl J Med* 319:525–532, 1988.
52. Potter JD: Reconciling the epidemiology, physiology and molecular biology of colon cancer. *JAMA* 268:1573–1577, 1992.
53. Weisburger JH, Wynder EL: Etiology of colorectal cancer with emphasis on mechanism of action and prevention, in DeVita VT, Hellman S, Rosenberg SA (eds): *Important Advances in Oncology*. Philadelphia, Lippincott, 1987, pp 197–220.
54. McKeown-Essen GE: Fiber intake in different populations and colon cancer risk. *Prev Med* 16:532–539, 1987.
55. Heilbrun LK, Nomura A, Hankin JH, et al: Diet and colorectal cancer with special reference to fiber intake. *Int J Cancer* 44:1–6, 1989.
56. Reddy BS, Engle A, Katsifis S, et al: Biochemical epidemiology of colon cancer: Effects of types of dietary fiber on fecal mutagens, acid and neutral sterols in healthy subjects. *Cancer Res* 49:4629–4635, 1989.
57. Buset M, Lipkin M, Winawer SJ, et al: Inhibition of human colonic cell proliferation in vivo and in vitro by calcium. *Cancer Res* 46:5426–5430, 1986.
58. Sorenson AW, Slattery ML, Ford MH: Calcium and colon cancer: A review. *Nutr Cancer* 11:135–145, 1988.

PART 2

Etiology and Risk Factors

CHAPTER 4

Dietary Factors—The Intestinal Milieu

Michael J. Hill

HIGHLIGHTS

The highlights of recent work have been the general acceptance of the importance of the intestinal milieu in colorectal carcinogenesis, the shift toward discussing the role of specific agents in the adenoma-carcinoma sequence, and the translation of the results on etiology into dietary intervention studies.

The importance of the intestinal milieu has become increasingly apparent as the regression of polyps in humans after diversion of the fecal stream has been better documented. This is now supported by a mass of information from animal studies (e.g., comparison of germ-free and conventional animals, the effect of suppression of the gut flora with antibiotics, and the effect of surgical procedures to divert the fecal stream).

In most animal studies, the amount of initiator used is such that it also acts as a powerful promoter, and the adenoma-carcinoma sequence is too fast to permit study of the individual stages. However, this is not so in the human and, increasingly, epidemiologists are studying the etiology of adenomas as precancerous lesions. This awareness has now been translated through to the intervention studies, where adenoma formation and adenoma growth are accepted as suitable targets for inhibition.

With respect to the detailed analysis of the intestinal milieu, tremendous progress has been made in identifying the members of the family of fecapentaenes, the products of pyrolysis of the nitrogenous components of food during cooking, the range of 3-keto steroids present in feces, and the possible importance of the aqueous phase of the feces in mucosal toxicity.

CONTROVERSIES

As with much of science, there is controversy about the interpretation of some of the results of research. The fecapentaenes were initially put forward as possible causative agents of colorectal cancer on the basis of mutagen assay techniques that later proved to be unreliable. They have since been rejected as important participants on the basis of the same unreliable tests. Clearly there is a need to reexamine the epidemiology of fecapentaenes in relation to colon carcinogenesis using tests accepted as reliable. The possible importance of conjugated 4-en-3-one steroids has been rejected, because such compounds are not present in feces in amounts that might be significant. However, if they were formed in the colon, had an opportunity to participate in carcinogenesis, and were later hydrogenated, the products would be indistinguishable from bile acids that had never been unsaturated.

The importance of pyrolysis products is dependent on their ability to reach the colon. The factors controlling this have still to be determined; if they prove to be those that are associated with increased risk of colorectal cancer, this will increase interest in the pyrolysis products.

The controversy in the bile acid field surrounds the importance of the water phase. This has been demonstrated pragmatically but to many is by no means self-evident, since bile acid entry into the colonic mucosa is by passive diffusion in the lipid phase.

NEW DIRECTIONS

All of the most exciting current work is in the area of dietary intervention and its effect on the intestinal milieu and the rate of formation and growth of colorectal adenomas. The most common interventions are justifiable in terms of the bile acid hypothesis: low fat and high fiber cause decreased fecal bile acid concentration; fiber metabolism leads to colonic acidification and the precipitation (and hence detoxification) of fecal bile acids; calcium again precipitates the bile acids and so inactivates them with respect to their capacity to damage the colonic mucosa.

The new directions with respect to pyrolysis products concern their pharmacology and the factor determining their ability to reach the colon.

GENERAL BACKGROUND

The importance of the colonic milieu in colorectal carcinogenesis was initially hypothesized because, although there is obviously an association between diet and colorectal cancer,[1–5] no dietary carcinogens had been reported which could plausibly explain the relationship. It was therefore hypothesized that the diet was a source of benign substrates which could be metabolized in situ in the colon to mutagenic/carcinogenic/promoting agents by bacterial action.[6,7]

That colorectal cancer is caused by a luminal factor is not self-evident, but there is a body of evidence to support it. The fecal stream is important in colorectal carcinogenesis, and its diversion causes regression of tumors in the excluded section of colon or rectum.[8–10] In animal models, the use of germ-free rodents or suppression of the gut bacterial flora results in a considerably decreased number of tumors compared with the conventional animals.[11,12] The distribution of cancer along the human large bowel is consistent with a luminal factor formed in the cecum and concentrated during colonic transit. Further, the human colon contains a rich mixture of carcinogens/promoters formed by gut bacterial action and concentrated during colonic transit. These include the fecapentaenes, the pyrolysis products formed during cooking, the 3-ketosteroids, the bile acids, and a wide range of other metabolites that have received less attention.[13–15] The major factors determining their rate of formation by bacterial action is the luminal pH, particularly in the cecum, and the composition of the gut bacterial flora (also particularly in the cecum).

FECAPENTAENES

Background and Occurrence

In 1977, Bruce et al.[16] described a mutagen present in the feces of a proportion of normal healthy persons. They and others studied the factors affecting its concentration in feces[17–20] and showed that mutagen activity was decreased by dietary fiber and ascorbic acid and increased by fat and meat (in accordance with the epidemiology of colorectal cancer). In consequence, numerous groups studied its concentration in the feces of populations at high and at low risk of colorectal cancer.[21–26] Most of the early reports (Table 4-1) showed a positive association, but their conclusions were criticized by Venitt;[27,28] using the classic methods,[29] the

Table 4-1
Some Representative Studies of Fecal Mutagenicity in Relation to Colorectal Carcinogenesis

Ehrich et al. (1979)	Comparison of urban white, urban black, and rural black populations showed fecal mutagen correlated to cancer risk.
Bruce and Dion (1980)	Compared colon cancer cases and hemorrhoid cases; similar proportion had fecal mutagen.
Reddy et al. (1980)	0/11 Seventh Day Adventists, 2/13 Finns, and 4/13 New Yorkers had fecal mutagen; correlated with cancer risk.
Mower et al. (1982)	Japanese in Hawaii (high risk) have more fecal mutagen than Japanese in Japan (low risk).
Askew et al. (1982)	4/16 colon cancer cases and 7/35 control persons had fecal mutagen. No significant difference.
Reddy et al. (1985)	6/55 from a low-risk area of Finland had fecal mutagen compared with 18/50 from a higher-risk area.
Ferguson et al. (1985)	No significant difference between prevalence of fecal mutagen carriage in Caucasians (with or without colon cancer) and healthy Polynesians.
Venitt et al. (1986)	Auxotrophic growth enhancement limits the usefulness of the Ames test and the fluctuation test.

SOURCE: Summarized from Venitt.[28]

between-sample and within-sample variations in fecal mutagen activity of an individual were so great that epidemiologic results using fecal samples had no validity. Later studies using the same unreliable methods have tended to show no association, and interest has waned in recent years. This is despite the fact that new, more reliable assay systems have been developed which could be applied to epidemiologic studies.[28,30]

Structure

The structure of the mutagens proved to be difficult to determine, but eventually they were demonstrated to be a family of glycerol ethers of conjugated polyenols, the latter containing chain lengths of 8, 10, 12, 14, and 16 carbons;[31] the resultant mutagens are referred to respectively as fecapentaene-8, -10, -12, etc. By far the most important quantitatively is eicosapentenylglycerol ether (fecapentaene-12), the mutagenicity of which has been tested and confirmed in a wide range of bacterial and mammalian cell assay systems.[30]

In Vivo Production

Production of the fecapentaenes has been shown to be the result of the action of the anaerobic bacterial flora. Incubation of freshly voided feces anaerobically at 37°C for 96 h results in a very large increase in mutagen activity; treatment with antibiotics, in contrast, results in decreased fecal activity.[28] The substrates from which the fecapentaenes are released are not known but are presumably glycerides acted on by bacterial lipases. Among a range of gut bacterial anaerobes (159 strains representing 40 species) tested for the ability to produce fecal mutagen from a fecal extract (presumably containing substrate), only strains belonging to five species of the genus *Bacteroides* were strongly positive,[32] although single strains of some minor species were able to release weak mutagenic activity. Fecal samples contained strains able to release mutagen regardless of whether they came from the 20 percent of persons who were fecapentaene-positive or from the 80 percent who were mutagen-negative. Thus the presence of fecal mutagen depends on the presence of substrate rather than of the relevant bacteria. The genus *Bacteroides* are the commonest gut bacteria, usually accounting for 50 percent of fecal organisms.

Controversies and Future Directions

Most of the controversies concerning the fecapentaenes are in the past, but the nature of the substrate, the circumstances in which it is produced in large amounts, its function to the host, and so on have still to be determined.

3-KETOSTEROIDS

Background

There is a large body of evidence suggesting that, under certain circumstances, cholesterol can be carcinogenic;[33,34] in his review of the evidence, Bischoff[34] concluded that it was acting as a solid-state carcinogen. However, Fieser[35] concluded that the phenomenon was, in fact, chemical carcinogenesis and that, since it was inconceivable that such a major endogenous product with such crucial properties for membrane function and so on could also be carcinogenic, the tumors must be due to some contaminant, such as an autoxidation product.[36] He tested a wide range of such oxidation products and showed that, indeed, many of these *were* carcinogens; some could be drawn in the keto or enol form and, when the former, could be conjugated to ring double bonds. During studies of bay ring epoxides, a range of enones and dienones were shown to be carcinogenic, and this led to the suggestion that the tumorigenic action of the bile acids could be due to a 3-keto bile acid with conjugated ring desaturation, with chola-4,6-dien-3-one being the most commonly cited.[37] Its attraction was that it could be formed in vitro using only three enzymes, two of which are widely distributed in intestinal bacteria (the 3-hydroxy-steroid oxidoreductase[6,7] and the 7-dehydroxylase[6,7]) and the third of which has repeatedly been observed to be present in a relatively high proportion of persons with colorectal cancer.[7,37,38] It was shown to be carcinogenic by Rosenkrantz (personal communication).

The epidemiologic results remain an interesting enigma, but interest in these compounds waned when, despite an intensive search in feces, no evidence of the 4,6-dien-3-one could be found.[39] In the absence of convincing evidence of in vivo formation (and of a suitable marker of their formation), it has been impossible to devise plausible epidemiologic studies to investigate their relevance. The presence of allo bile acids in feces[39] is consistent with in vivo formation of 4-en-3-one, but elaborate multiple labeling studies would be needed to demonstrate 4,6-dien-3-one formation as an intermediate (rather than as an end product).

PYROLYSIS PRODUCTS

Background

Mutagens in cooked food were first demonstrated, using the Ames test, by Sugimura et al.[40,41] and by Commoner et al.[42] in grilled fish and ground beef respectively. Table 4-2 lists some of the major groups of mutagens formed by the pyrolysis of protein or amino acids during cooking. The pyridoimidazole and pyridoindole mutagens were amongst the first pyrolysis mutagens to be isolated and identified. The quinoxalines are major mutagens found in fried beef, although almost 90 percent of the mutagens by weight is accounted for by the pyridine mutagen Ph 1P.

Mutagenic activity resulting from pyrolysis is present in most protein sources in the western diet that have been cooked to a "well done" but noncharred state. Cooked fish tends to contain lower mutagen levels than cooked "red meat." Higher levels of mutagen are produced by frying, grilling, or roasting meat than by baking, stewing, or microwave cooking. Overvik et al.,[43–47] in a series of papers, reported that when meat was fried, mutagens were formed in the meat and were present in equal amounts in the pan residues; they were also present in the smoke formed during cooking. Thus use of the pan residues to prepare gravy greatly increased the exposure to mutagen. The amount of mutagen formed was highly dependent on cooking temperature, but so was its distribution between the meat, smoke, and pan residues. At high temperatures, for example, a higher proportion of the mutagen was found in the cooking smoke.

Formation and Activation

Yoshida and Fukahara[48] originally proposed that the mutagens were products of pyrolysis of mixtures of amino acids and creatinine; this is true of many (but not all) of the major ones. Taylor et al.[49] showed that all of the precursors of mutagen formation in meat were water-soluble and had low molecular weights (less than 500). A requirement for water and sugar in some model systems suggested a role for Maillard-type reactions; however, the mutagens can be produced in the absence of either sugar or water.

All of the heterocyclic amine mutagens are, in fact, promutagens and need to be activated by mucosal microsomal enzymes. They tend to be most active in Ames test strains TA 98 and TA 1538, suggesting that they are frame-shift mutagens. The arylamines are activated mainly through *N*-hydroxylation.[50] Detoxification is primarily via ring hydroxylation and then conjugation to glucuronic acid, sulfate, or glutathione. Overvik et al.[47] studied the pharmacology of pyrolysis mutagens in germ-free and conventional rats. The low level of the pyrolysis mutagens recovered from the feces of the germ-free rats suggested a role for the intestinal bacterial flora in their activation. This conclusion was supported by the observation of induction of intestinal cytochrome P-450 enzymes in the conventional but not in the germ-free rats.[47]

Mutagenic and Carcinogenic Activity

Table 4-3 compares the mutagenic activity of various pyrolysis mutagens in the Ames test. They are also active in nonmicrobial systems such as Chinese hamster ovary cells, mouse fibroblasts, V79 cells, *Drosophila*, etc.; they cause unscheduled DNA synthesis in rodent hepatocytes. Further, a number of pyrolysis mutagens have been shown to be carcinogens in rodents (Table 4-4).

Although many studies have reported a correlation between meat intake and colorectal cancer risk,[1,3] few have included data on the method of cooking. Gerhardson et al.[51] carried out such a study of 559 cases and 505 controls. They confirmed the association with meat consumption and further noted that the association was strongest when the meat surface was heavily browned during frying and weakest when the meat was only lightly browned. The relative risks were higher for rectal than for colon cancer (6.0 and 2.8, respectively, for heavily browned meat).

Controversies and Future Work

The main need is for much more epidemiologic work to establish the relevance of these pyrolysis products to human cancer; mutagen levels must be assayed both in the cooked meat and in feces and urine in these studies. Until their relevance is established, they will remain as intellectual curiosities.

Table 4-2
Some of the Mutagens Present in Cooked Meat Products and Produced by Pyrolysis of Amino Acids or Proteins

Mutagen group	*Examples*	*Source*
1. Pyridoimidazole and pyridoindole mutagens	Trp-P-1; Trp-P-2	Pyrolysis of tryptophan
	Glu-P-1; Glu-P-2	Pyrolysis of glutamic acid
	AAC, MeAAC	Pyrolysis of fish
2. Quinolines	IQ; MeIQ	Cooked meat and fish amino acid pyrolysates
3. Quinoxalines	MeIQx; IQx 4,8-diMeIQx	Pyrolysis of amino acids and creatinine; grilled beef
4. Pyridines	PhIP	Phenylalanine and creatinine pyrolysis; fried beef
	DMIP; TMIP	Cooked meat products
5. Benzoxazines	Heterocyclic amines	Cooked meat

Table 4-3
Mutagenic Activity of Various Pyrolysis Mutagens in the Ames Test

Mutagen group	*Mutagen*	*Activity*
Pyridoimidazole	Trp-P-1	39,000
	Trp-P-2	100,000
	Glu-P-1	49,000
	Glu-P-2	1,900
	AAC	300
	MeAAC	200
Quinolines	IQ	433,000
	MeIQ	661,000
Quinoxalines	IQx	100,000
	MeIQx	145,000
	4,8 diMeIQx	206,000
Pyridines	PhIP	2,000

BILE ACIDS

Background

A major role for bile acids in colorectal cancer was originally proposed in order to rationalize the observed association between colorectal cancer and dietary fat (positive) and fiber (inverse). Table 4-5 summarizes the data supporting such a role, and the evidence has been reviewed by Hill.[13,14] There is a mass of evidence from animal and in vitro studies that bile acids are tumor promoters or comutagens (Table 4-6); comparisons of populations have almost all shown higher fecal bile acid concentrations in those at higher risk of colorectal cancer. Case-control studies have given mainly negative results, with only two studies implicating bile acids; but this may be explicable in terms of the choice of cases and of controls.[13] Bile acid receptor sites have been found in colorectal cancers but not in control tissues.[52] Bile acids cause increased cell proliferation[53–56] and mucosal toxicity.[55,56] The bile acid concentration has been correlated to two aspects of progression from colorectal adenoma to carcinoma, namely adenoma size[13,57] and severity of mucosal dysplasia.[13,14,58]

Table 4-5
The Evidence Implicating Bile Acids in Colorectal Carcinogensis

Study type	*Observation*
Comparison of fecal bile acids (FBAs) in feces of populations	In ten studies of populations, the FBA concentration in a population correlated with the risk of colorectal cancer (CRC).
Diet studies	Dietary items (e.g., fat) which increase the FBA concentration are correlated with CRC risk. Those items which are inversely related (e.g., cereal fiber) decrease the FBA concentration.
Animal studies manipulating diets	Dietary changes which increase the number of colorectal tumors increase the FBA concentration, and vice versa.
Patient groups	Surgical treatment by partial gastrectomy or cholecystectomy, which increases FBA concentration, increases the risk of CRC.
Bile acid binding sites	Binding sites for deoxycholic acid were detected in 31% of CRC patients and only 2% of controls.
Mutagenicity/tumor promotion	Deoxycholic and lithocholic acids are tumor promoters in the rodent colon and are comutagenic in bacterial mutagenesis assays.
Mucosal toxicity	Deoxycholic and lithocholic acids cause dysplastic changes in the rodent colon.

Recent Studies

During recent years, interest in the role of bile acids in colorectal cancer has focused on three main areas, namely (1) bile acids in the aqueous phase, (2) the bile

Table 4-4
Carcinogenicity of Various Pyrolysis Mutagens When Fed to Rodents

		Tumor site	
Group	*Compound*	*Mice*	*Rats*
Pyridoimidazoles	Trp-P-1	Liver (F>M)	Liver, intestine
	Trp-P-2	Liver (F>M)	Liver
	Glu-P-1	Liver (F>>M)	Liver, intestine
	Glu-P-2	Liver (F>M)	Liver, intestine
	AAC	Liver (F>M)	—
	MeAAC	Liver (F>M)	—
Quinolines	IQ	Lung, liver, forestomach	Liver, colon
	MeIQ	Liver, forestomach	Oral cavity, colon, breast
Quinoxalines	MeIQx	Lung, liver, intestine	Liver, zymbal gland

Table 4-6
Evidence That Bile Acids Are Carcinogenic, Cocarcinogenic, Mutagenic, or Comutagenic

Test system	*Bile acids found to be active*	*Activity demonstrated*	*Reference*
MNNG-treated rats	Lithocholic acid, deoxycholic acid	Colon cocarcinogens	Narisawa et al., 1974
Skin painting on rats	Deoxycholic acid	Skin cocarcinogen	Cook et al., 1940
Skin painting on mice	Apocholic acid, bisnor-5-cholenic acid	Skin carcinogen	Lacassagne et al., 1961, 1966
Salmonella mutagenesis assay	Deoxycholic acid, lithocholic acid	Comutagenic	Silverman and Andrews, 1977; Wilpart et al., 1983
Hamster embryo cell transformation test	Lithocholic acid	Mutagenic	Kelsey and Pienta, 1979
Bacterial mutagenicity assay	Deoxycholic acid	Mutagenic	Jensen et al., 1951
Drosophila	Deoxycholic acid	Mutagenic	Demerec, 1948

SOURCE: Summarized from Hill.[13]

acid profile, and (3) bile acids in relation to the use of calcium in chemoprevention studies.

The group of Bruce in Toronto was the first to investigate seriously the concentration of bile acids in the aqueous phase compared to the total fecal bile acids;[54,55] work in this area has recently been reviewed by Rafter and Branting,[59] who noted that the tissue damage caused by bile acids is more closely related to the water-soluble bile acids than to the total bile acids. Similarly, the protective effect of calcium in ameliorating the toxic effects of bile acids is more closely related to the precipitation of soluble bile acids than of bile acids per se. The logic of studying the bile acids in the water phase can be justified pragmatically in the above way but is not self-evident. Bile acids are transported across the colon wall in the lipid phase by passive diffusion, so it could be argued that water-soluble bile acids are the *least* important. Further, only a tiny fraction of the total fecal bile acid pool is in the aqueous phase, and these small amounts can present analytic problems. Much work is in progress, and the relative importance of the soluble fraction will become clear in the next few years.

Interest in the fecal bile acid profile has stemmed from attempts by Owen et al.[60] to determine whether lithocholic acid (LA), deoxycholic acid (DC), or the sum of LA and DC was the best marker of colorectal cancer risk; this was done because, in animal studies, both LA and DC had been shown to be potent promoters of colorectal carcinogenesis. In fact, by far the best risk marker was the ratio of LA/DC, and this became explicable following the work of Wilpart et al.[61] They showed in comutagenesis assays, that while DC and LA are both potent comutagens in mixtures, they antagonize each other; thus there is little residual activity in equal mixtures. The human and in vitro data have been put together in a combined paper,[62] and further work on the bile acid ratio as a marker of colorectal cancer risk in individuals is currently in progress. In support of the value of the ratio as a marker, Biasco et al.[63] showed a correlation between the ratio and cell proliferation indices in rectal biopsies. Further, studies of duodenal bile acids showed that the ratio of chenodeoxycholic acid to cholic acid correlated well with colorectal adenoma size and with the presence of carcinoma.[64,65] The ability of LA and DC to ameliorate each other's toxicity could partly explain why the total fecal bile acids have proved a good risk marker in populations but not in individuals; for the latter, a marker which takes into account both the total amount of bile acid and the ratio LA/DC is worth exploring further. McMichael and Potter[66] reported the relation between the fecal bile acid profile in general and the risk of cancer of the proximal colon.

The third area of recent activity has been in the development of the background theories for calcium supplementation in the prevention of colorectal cancer. In their original hypothesis, Wargovich et al.[55] and Newmark et al.[56] suggested that the calcium would precipitate the toxic bile acids and so ameliorate their toxicity. Van der Meer et al.[67] showed that this binding of bile acids could be amplified in the presence of phosphate, and that calcium phosphate was particularly effective in removing the toxic agents from fecal water. There is a considerable amount of work in progress[59,67] which should greatly increase our understanding of the antitumor action of dietary calcium supplements.

CONCLUSIONS

Although the evidence that the intestinal milieu has an important influence on the risk of colorectal carcinogenesis, the mechanism by which this occurs is unclear. Since the best epidemiologic and animal model evidence suggests a role for luminal factors in tumor promotion—the progression from adenoma to carcinoma—it is possible that the factors initiating tumorigenesis have still to be identified. The even distribution of adenomas along the colorectum is most consistent with a systemically delivered "adenogen." However, it could also be a luminal factor that is absorbed or inactivated at a rate which counteracts the concentrating effect of luminal dehydration; this is necessary in order to have a constant luminal concentration of adenogen consistent with the even distribution of adenomas.

There is much to be gained from studying the various stages of the dysplasia-carcinoma sequence separately. Such studies (e.g., of adenoma formation, adenoma growth, severity of dysplasia) are still a relatively new concept, particularly to epidemiologists, but they are likely to yield valuable information in the next few years.

REFERENCES

1. Armstrong B, Doll R: Environmental factors and cancer incidence and mortality in different countries with special reference to dietary practices. *Int J Cancer* 15:617–631, 1975.
2. Wynder EL, Shigematsu T: Environmental factors of cancer of the colon and rectum. *Cancer* 20:1520–1560, 1967.
3. Willett WC, Stampfer MJ, Colditz GA, et al: Relation of meat, fat and fiber intake to the risk of colon cancer in a prospective study among women. *Int J Rad Oncol Biol Phys* 323:1664–1672, 1990.
4. Willett NC, MacMahon B: Diet and cancer—An overview. *N Engl J Med* 310:697–703, 1984.
5. Trock B, Lanza E, Greenwald P: Dietary fiber, vegetables, and colon cancer: Critical review and metaanalysis of the epidemiologic evidence. *J Natl Cancer Inst* 82:650–661, 1990.
6. Aries VC, Crowther JS, Drasar BS, et al: Degradation of bile salts by human intestinal bacteria. *Gut* 10:575–577, 1969.
7. Hill MJ, Drasar BS, Wiliams RED: Faecal bile-acid and clostridia in patients with cancer of the large bowel. *Lancet* 1:535–539, 1975.
8. Rainey JB, Davies PW, Bristol JB, et al: Adaptation and carcinogenesis in defunctioned rat colon: Divergent effects of faeces and bile acids. *Br J Cancer* 48:477–484, 1983.
9. Lewin MR, Ferulano GP, Cruse JP, et al: Experimental factors in the intestinal contents. *Carcinogenesis* 2:1363–1366, 1981.
10. Cole J, Holden WD: Post-colectomy regression of adenomatous polyps in the human colon. *Arch Surg* 79:385–392, 1959.
11. Reddy BS, Narisawa T, Maronpot R, et al: Animal models for the study of dietary factors and cancer of the large bowel. *Cancer Res* 35:3421–3426, 1975.
12. Goldin BR, Gorbach SL: Effects of antibiotics on incidence of rat intestinal tumours induced by 1,2- dimethylhydrazine dichloride. *J Natl Cancer Inst* 67:877–880, 1981.
13. Hill MJ: *Microbes and Human Carcinogenesis*. London, Edward Arnold, 1986.
14. Hill MJ: Colorectal bacteria in colorectal carcinogenesis, in Seitz HK, Simanowski UA, Wright NA (eds): *Colorectal Cancer.* Heidelberg, Springer-Verlag, 1989, pp 160–176.
15. Bruce WR: Recent hypotheses for the origin of colon cancer. *Cancer Res* 47:4237–4242, 1987.
16. Bruce WR, Varghese AJ, Furrer F, et al: A mutagen in human feces, in Hiatt H, Watson J, Winsten J (eds): *Origins of Human Cancer.* New York, Cold Spring Harbor Laboratory, 1977, pp 1641–1646.
17. Bruce WR, Dion PW: Studies relating to a fecal mutagen. *Am J Clin Nutr* 33:2511–2512, 1980.
18. Dion PW, Bright-See EB, Smith CC: The effect of dietary ascorbic acid and α-tocopherol on fecal mutagenicity. *Mutat Res* 102:27–37, 1982.
19. Reddy BS, Sharma C, Simi B: Metabolic epidemiology of colon cancer: Effect of dietary fiber on fecal mutagens and bile acids in healthy subjects. *Cancer Res* 47:644–648, 1987.
20. Reddy B, Engle A, Katsifis S, et al: Biochemical epidemiology of colon cancer: Effects of types of dietary fiber on fecal mutagens, acid, and neutral sterols in healthy subjects. *Cancer Res* 49:4629–4635, 1989.
21. Ehrich M, Aswell JE, Van Tassell RL: Mutagens in the feces of three South African populations at different levels of risk for colon cancer. *Mutat Res* 64:231–240, 1979.
22. Correa P, Paschal J, Pizzolato P: Fecal mutagens and colorectal polyps: Preliminary report of an autopsy study, in Bruce WR, Correa P, Lipkin M, et al (eds): *Gastrointestinal Cancer: Endogenous Factors*. New York, Cold Spring Harbor Laboratory, 1981, pp 119–128.
23. Schiffman MH, Andrews AW, Van Tassell RL, et al: Case-control study of colorectal cancer and fecal mutagenicity. *Cancer Res* 49:3420–3424, 1989.
24. Ehrich M, Aswell J, Van Tassell R, et al: Mutagens in the feces of 3 South African populations at different levels of risk for colon cancer. *Mutat Res* 64:231–240, 1979.
25. Ferguson LR, Alley P, Gribben BM: DNA-damaging activity of feces from New Zealand groups at varying risks of colorectal cancer. *Nutr Cancer* 7:93–103, 1985.
26. Reddy BS, Sharma C, Darby L, et al: Metabolic epidemiology of large bowel cancer: Fecal mutagens in high and low risk populations for colon cancer. *Mutat Res* 72:511–522, 1980.
27. Venitt S: Mutagens in human faeces: Are they relevant to cancer of the large bowel? *Mutat Res* 98:265–286, 1982.
28. Venitt S: Mutagens in human faeces and cancer of the large bowel, in Rowland IR (ed): *Role of the Gut Flora in Toxicity and Cancer.* London, Academic Press, 1988, pp 399–460.
29. Ames BN, McCann J, Yamasaki E: Methods for detecting carcinogens and mutagens with the *Salmonella* mammalian microsome test. *Mutat Res* 31:347–364, 1975.
30. Curren RD, Putman DL, Yang LL: Genotoxicity of fecapentaene-12 in bacterial and mammalian cell assay systems. *Carcinogenesis* 8:349–353, 1987.
31. Gupta I, Baptista J, Bruce WR, et al: Structures of fecapentaenes, the mutagens of bacterial origin isolated from human feces. *Biochemistry* 22:241–245, 1983.
32. Van Tassel RL, MacDonald DK, Wilkins TD: Production of a fecal mutagen by *Bacteroides* spp. *Infect Immun* 37:975–980, 1982.
33. Hieger I: Cholesterol carcinogenesis. *Br Med Bull* 14:159–160, 1958.
34. Bischoff F: Carcinogenic effects of steroids. *Adv Lipid Res* 7:165–244, 1969.
35. Fieser LF: Some aspects of the chemistry and biochemistry of cholesterol. *Science* 119:710–716, 1954.
36. Smith LL: Carcinogenic cholesterol products, in *Cholesterol Autoxidation*. New York, Plenum, 1981, pp 432–446.
37. Hill MJ: The role of colon anaerobes in the metabolism of bile acids and steroids and its relation to colon cancer. *Cancer* 36:2387–2400, 1975.
38. Goddard P, Fernandez F, West B: The nuclear dehydrogena-

tion of steroids by intestinal bacteria. *J Med Microbiol* 8:429–435, 1975.

39. Wait R, Thompson MH, Hill MJ: Faecal steroids and colorectal cancer: Allo bile acids. *Br J Cancer* 52:445–446, 1985.
40. Sugimura T, Nagao M, Kawachi T, et al: Mutagen-carcinogens in food, with special reference to highly mutagenic pyrolysis products in broiled foods, in Hiatt H, Watson J, Winsten J (eds): *Origins of Human Cancer*. New York, Cold Spring Harbor Laboratory, 1977, pp 1561–1576.
41. Sugimura T: Carcinogenicity of mutagenic heterocyclic amines formed during the cooking process. *Mutat Res* 150:33–42, 1985.
42. Commoner B, Vithayathil A, Delora P, et al: Formation of mutagens in beef and beef extract during cooking. *Science* 201:913–916, 1978.
43. Overvik E, Nilsson L, Fredholm L, et al: High mutagenic activity formed in pan-broiled pork. *Mutat Res* 135:149–157, 1984.
44. Nilsson L, Overvik E, Fredholm L, et al: Influence of frying fat on mutagenic activity in lean pork meat. *Mutat Res* 171:115–121, 1986.
45. Overvik E, Nilsson L, Fredholm L, et al: Mutagenicity of gravy and pan residues from fried meat. *Mutat Res* 187:47–55, 1987.
46. Berg I, Overvik E, Nord C-E, et al: Mutagenic activity in smoke formed during broiling of lean pork at 200, 250 and 300°C. *Mutat Res* 207:199–204, 1988.
47. Overvik E: Formation and biological effects of cooked food mutagens. PhD thesis. Stockholm, Karolinska Institute, 1989.
48. Yoshida D, Fukahara Y: Formation of mutagens by heating creatine with amino acids. *Agric Biol Chem* 46:1069–1070, 1982.
49. Taylor RT, Fultz E, Knize MG: Mutagen formation in a model beef supernatant fraction: IV. Properties of the system. *Environ Health Perspect* 67:59–74, 1986.
50. Kato R: Metabolic activation of mutagenic heterocyclic amines from protein pyrolysates. *CRC Crit Rev Toxicol* 16: 307–348, 1986.
51. Gerhardson M, Hagman U, Peters RK, et al: Meat, cooking methods and colorectal cancer: A case-referent study in Stockholm. *Int J Cancer* 49:520–525, 1991.
52. Summerton J, Flynn M, Cooke T, et al: Bile acid receptors in colorectal cancer. *Br J Surg* 70:549–551, 1984.
53. Tempero M: Bile acids, ornithine decarboxylase, and cell proliferation in colon cancer: A review. *Dig Dis* 4:49–56, 1986.
54. Rafter JJ, Eng VW, Furrer R, et al: Effect of dietary calcium and pH on the mucosal damage produced by deoxycholic acid on the rat colon. *Gut* 27:1320–1329, 1986.
55. Wargovich M, Eng VW, Newmark HL, et al: Calcium ameliorates the toxic effect of deoxycholic acid on colonic epithelium. *Carcinogenesis* 4:125–127, 1983.
56. Newmark HL, Wargovich MJ, Bruce WR: Colon cancer and dietary fat, phosphate and calcium: A hypothesis. *J Natl Cancer Inst* 72:1323–1325, 1984.
57. Hill MJ: Biochemical approaches to the intervention of large bowel cancer. *Prog Clin Biol Res* 186:263–276, 1985.
58. Hill MJ, Melville D, Lennard-Jones J, et al: Faecal bile acids, dysplasia and carcinoma in ulcerative colitis. *Lancet* 1:185–186, 1987.
59. Rafter JJ, Branting C: Bile acids—Interaction with intestinal mucosa. *Eur J Cancer Prev* 1(suppl 2):49–54, 1991.
60. Owen RW, Dodo M, Thompson MH, et al: The faecal ratio of lithocholic to deoxycholic acid may be an important aetiological factor in colorectal cancer. *Eur J Cancer Clin Oncol* 19:1307, 1992.
61. Wilpart M, Mainguet P, Maskens A, et al: Mutagenicity of 1,2-dimethylhydrazine towards *Salmonella typhimurium:* Comutagenic effects of secondary bile acids. *Carcinogenesis* 4:45–48, 1983.
62. Owen RW, Thompson MH, Hill MJ, et al: The importance of the ratio of lithocholic to deoxycholic acid in large bowel carcinogenesis. *Nutr Cancer* 9:67–71, 1987.
63. Biasco G, Paganelli GM, Owen RW, et al: Faecal bile acids and colorectal cell proliferation. *Eur J Cancer Prev* 1(suppl 2):63–68, 1991.
64. Moorehead RJ, Campbell GR, Donaldson JD, et al: Relationship between duodenal bile acids and colorectal cancer. *Gut* 28:1454–1459, 1987.
65. Mullan FJ, Wilson HK, Majury CW, et al: Bile acids and the increased risk of colorectal tumours after truncal vagotomy. *Br J Surg* 77:1085–1090, 1990.
66. McMichael AJ, Potter JD: Host factors in carcinogenesis: Certain bile-acid metabolic profiles that selectively increase the risk of proximal colon cancer. *J Natl Cancer Inst* 75:185–191, 1985.
67. Van der Meer R, Kleibeuker J, Lapre J: Calcium phosphate, bile acids and colorectal cancer. *Eur J Cancer Prev* 1(suppl 2):55–62, 1991.

CHAPTER 5

Dietary Factors—Fat, Fiber, and Calories

Moshe Shike

HIGHLIGHTS

It is clear that dietary factors play an essential role in colonic carcinogenesis. Perhaps the strongest evidence for the role of the environment in causing colonic cancer comes from migrant studies, which demonstrate clearly an increase in the incidence of this cancer in populations which move from countries with low incidence to those with high incidence. Excess fat consumption and lack of adequate intake of fruits, vegetables, and cereals are the most important dietary factors in this process. It appears that the diet exerts its effects throughout the various stages of the carcinogenic process.

CONTROVERSIES

The precise mechanisms by which nutrients enhance colonic carcinogenesis have not been elucidated as yet, nor has it been determined how nutrients interact with inherited genetic changes which predispose to colonic cancer.

FUTURE DIRECTIONS

The multicenter polyp prevention trial sponsored by the National Cancer Institute (NCI), currently in progress, is examining the hypothesis that a diet low in fat and high in fruits, vegetables, and grains will result in reduction in risk for colonic cancer by reducing the recurrence rate of adenomas. Another randomized study which is about to begin is the Women's Health Initiative, which—among other issues—will examine the effect of a low-fat diet on the mortality from cancers of the colon and breast. The study will randomize sufficient numbers of women across the United States to allow for a detection of a decrease in mortality from colonic cancer by modification of fat in the diet.

In addition to these large studies, there are now numerous tightly controlled studies in humans which are examining in depth the effect of various nutrients on various stages of colonic carcinogenesis.[1,2] The success of these studies depends on the ability to closely control the diet and on the use of new markers of carcinogenesis in the colon, such as growth factors, gene expression, and cell differentiation.

Worldwide, colorectal cancer is the third most frequent malignant neoplasm, with an estimated incidence of 570,000 annually. In western developed countries, it ranks as the second most common cancer; in underdeveloped countries, it is the eighth ranking cancer.[3] Epidemiologic observations and experimental studies in animals suggest that the diet plays a crucial role in the genesis of colonic cancer and may explain the difference in incidence among various countries and societies.

Emerging concepts on the causes of colonic cancer attribute its development to both inheritance and environment. As pointed out elsewhere in this book, inheritance is important, not only in the well-defined familial colonic cancer syndromes (such as familial polyposis) but also in the much more common sporadic colonic cancer. The development of colonic cancer is a multistage process during which patchy areas of normal mucosa undergo hyperproliferation, and the hyperproliferating crypts give rise to small adenomas. Some of these adenomas enlarge, become dysplastic, and undergo a malignant transformation. Recent studies have demonstrated that this process is associated with an accumulation of genetic abnormalities. As yet, it has not been well established at what stages nutrition- and diet-related metabolic factors exert their carcinogenic effects or how they interact with inherited or acquired changes in the genetic makeup which predispose to colonic cancer.[2] Information from epidemiologic and experimental studies indicates that nutritional factors operate at various stages. Thus, it has been shown from biopsies of normal colonic mucosa that variations in the amounts[3] and types[4] of ingested fat can modulate the rate of cell proliferation. Calcium supplementation reduces cell proliferation of flat mucosa in patients at high risk for colonic cancer.[5] In addition to modulation of the proliferative rate of the mucosa, nutritional factors such as high fat and low fiber are associated with an increased incidence of adenomas[6] and cancers.[7] It is still not clear whether dietary factors exert their effects at earlier stages (by genotoxic effects, modulation, of growth factors, etc.) or later stages (by facilitating the enlargement of adenomas and inducing dysplastic changes and malignant transformation). It is also conceivable that nutritional effects are operative throughout the neoplastic transformation from normal mucosa to cancer and that their influence is not limited to one stage in this process.

The link between dietary components and colorectal cancer has been supported by epidemiologic correlations,[8–13] case control studies,[8,14–19] and experimental studies in animals.[20–23] Recent experimental studies in humans also support this concept. Dietary factors that have been implicated include fat and excess calories, reduced dietary fiber, alcohol, inadequate intake of vitamins (retinoids, ascorbic acid, alpha tocopherol), minerals (calcium), and trace elements (selenium). In the United States, the National Research Council Committee on Diet, Nutrition and Cancer, after performing an exhaustive evaluation of the literature on the association between diet and cancer,[8] concluded that current evidence indicates a strong link between the two. The Council Committee suggested human intervention studies to clearly demonstrate that changes in diet can reduce the risk of cancer.[24]

FAT

Epidemiologic data indicate that increased fat consumption is associated with increased rates of colonic cancer. There is a linear correlation between total dietary fat availability and mortality from colonic cancer in different countries around the world.[25] Although not all the countries fit readily into the graph, the overall positive direct correlation is striking. Direct estimates of dietary fat intake show that populations with a high fat consumption have higher death rates from colorectal cancer.[12,26] Studies in migrants from areas with diets low in animal fat and protein to areas with a "western" type of diet (with high fat) found an increase in the incidence of colonic cancer in the migrants compared to the incidence in their country of origin. Thus, migrants from Japan to Hawaii[27] had a substantial increase in the mortality rate from colonic cancer, and a similar increase was seen in migrants from Poland to Australia. Numerous case control studies have also supported the association between fat intake and colorectal cancer.[19,27] However, other epidemiologic data did not confirm this association, particularly when different regions of the same country were studied. Thus, in the United States, the per capita fat consumption in individual states showed no direct association with mortality from colonic cancer:[28] the incidence of colonic cancer in Utah was found to be significantly lower than the average U.S. incidence, in spite of a similar per capita fat consumption.[29] A prospective cohort study which assessed the dietary intake for 28 days found no difference in fat intake (as a percentage of calories) between those who subsequently developed colonic cancer and those who did not.[30] A recent critical review on the link between dietary fat and colonic cancer concluded that the evidence linking the two was inconclusive.[31] This inconsistency in the epidemiologic data may be due to the fact that in most epidemiologic studies, the dietary factors which may exert a protective effect against colonic cancer, such as fiber, have not been adequately considered. Thus, in a study from Scandinavia,[32] the rate of colonic cancer was found to be markedly higher in a Danish population compared to the rate among Finns, in spite of similar fat intake; the Finns, however, had a substantially higher fiber intake than the Danes, suggesting that fiber may have modified the carcinogenic effect of fat. It is therefore crucial both in epidemiologic and experimental studies to control for all dietary components when assessing the risk from a single nutrient. In a prospective study involving 88,751 women between the ages of 34 and 59, a dietary questionnaire was obtained and the women were then followed for 6 years. Consumption of animal fat was found to be positively associated with a risk for colonic cancer.[33] A recent analysis of the epidemiologic studies on the relationship between fat intake and various cancers concluded that there is considerable consistency in the information regarding the relationship of dietary fat and six cancers, including colorectal cancer.[34]

Most epidemiologic studies did not correlate colonic cancer with a specific dietary fat but rather with the total fat consumed. Another source of inconsistency in the results of epidemiologic studies may be the type of fat used to elucidate the correlation between fat intake and colonic cancer; while some studies incriminate animal fat consumption, other data suggest that vegetable fat[35] shows the strongest positive correlation. When colonic cancer is induced in laboratory animals by dimethylhydrazine, diets with a high concentration of vegetable oil and polyunsaturated fat are associated with a higher incidence of colonic cancer.[23] In contrast, highly polyunsaturated fish oil and monounsaturated olive oil do not seem to exert an enhancing effect on chemically induced colonic cancer in animals.

A recent study demonstrated that in rats with azoxymethane-induced colonic cancer, the type and the amount of fat and, in addition, the time at which it is consumed in relation to the stage of carcinogenesis can all have effects on the development of colonic cancer. A diet high in corn oil (which has high content of polyunsaturated fat) consumed during the postinitiation stage significantly increased tumor incidence but had no effect during the initiation phase. A diet high in omega-3-fatty acids (menhaden oil) reduced colonic cancer incidence both at the initiation and postinitiation stages. A diet high in animal fat increased the incidence of colonic cancer both at the initiation and postinitiation stages.[36] Two recent European case-control studies suggest that monounsaturated fats exert a protective effect against colonic cancer.[37,38] A double-blind placebo-controlled study using thymidine autoradiography examined colonic biopsies from patients with colonic adenomas who had been given fish oil over a 12-week period. Within 2 weeks of fish oil supplementation, there was a decrease in proliferation rate in the upper compartments of the colonic crypts. Such a decrease is thought to suppress adenoma formation.[4]

Almost all the epidemiologic studies examined the relationship between fat consumption and colonic cancer. These studies do not point to the stages of carcinogenesis at which fat exerts its effects. A recent prospective epidemiologic study examined the relationship between fat intake and subsequent finding of colonic adenomas. The study demonstrated a positive association between consumption of saturated fat and incidence of colonic adenomas. There was no such association with consumption of monosaturated or polysaturated fat. Intake of dietary fiber was protective against adenomas independently of saturated fat consumption.[6]

The biochemical mechanisms of the cancer-promoting action of dietary fat in the colon have not been established. Several mechanisms have been proposed: (1) dietary fat induces an increase in biliary sterols, and these compounds damage the colonic epithelium and induce hyperproliferation;[39,40] (2) carcinogenesis is enhanced by free radicals generated during lipid peroxidation;[41] (3) certain fatty acids promote carcinogenesis by incorporating into cell membranes and by inducing changes in the membrane fluidity and in the response to carcinogenic compounds (dietary fat has been shown to determine membrane structure and cell function);[42] (4) overabundance of linoleic acid increases the synthesis of certain prostaglandins, which can act as cancer promoters by stimulating cell proliferation; (5) dietary fat determines the characteristics of the gut bacterial flora, which play an important role in the metabolism of carcinogens; and (6) the cancer-promoting effect of fat is not specific to its chemical composition but is related to its caloric density. Since fat is the most calorically dense among the macronutrients, it is the most carcinogenic.

It has not been determined to what level dietary fat should be restricted in order to achieve significant attenuation of the carcinogenic process in the colon. The average fat content of the American diet and some western European diets is about 40 percent of total calories.[43,44] This is in contrast to third world diets, in which only 10 to 25 percent of total calories are in the form of fat. Animal studies show a dose response of carcinogen-induced colonic tumors when dietary fat is increased from 10 to 40 percent of total calories.[24]

In spite of the inconsistencies in the evidence relating colorectal cancer to fat intake, the data considered as a whole support the hypothesis that increased dietary fat plays a role in enhancing colonic carcinogenesis. However, randomized intervention studies in humans are required to establish this relationship firmly. Recently, a multicenter study was initiated by the NCI to examine whether a low-fat diet (20 percent of calories) that is high in fruits and vegetables can reduce the recurrence rate of colonic adenomas.[45]

FIBER

The hypothesis that a diet high in fiber may protect against colonic cancer was first proposed by Burkitt and Trowell,[46] who observed that African blacks who consumed high-fiber diets had lower death rates from large bowel cancer than whites, whose fiber intake was low. Seventeen epidemiologic studies, of which only two were case control studies, support this hypothesis,[15,47–50] but four other studies, including three case control studies, are inconsistent[51,53] with it. A recent metaanalysis of epidemiologic studies found a significant correlation between fiber intake and the incidence of colonic cancer.[54] The inconsistency of the data has been pointed out in the report of the U.S. National Research Council,[24] and in a more recent report by a committee of the Federation of American Societies for Experimental Biology.[55] This inconsistency may be due to the fact that dietary fiber is not a specific chemical entity but rather a diverse group of complex compounds whose only common features are that they originate in plants and are resistant to the action of human digestive enzymes. Different fibers have different physiochemical properties and can affect the colonic milieu and colonic mucosa in various ways. Some dietary fibers, such as bran, pass through the colon with little change, while others, such as pectins, are almost completely broken down by colonic bacteria, mostly to short-chain fatty acids. These fatty acids modulate the colonic pH and are used by colonocytes as a primary energy source.

Most epidemiologic studies on the correlations between fiber and colonic cancer examined fiber-containing foods in general rather than specific fibers. In some studies, the risk for colorectal cancer was related to specific fibers or specific fiber-containing foods. Thus, consumption of cruciferous vegetables (broccoli, cauliflower, cabbage, brussels sprouts) was found to be protective against colonic cancer.[48] However, it is impossible to tell whether this protective effect is due to the fiber in these vegetables or to chemopreventive agents such as sulforaphans, which stimulate enzymes that neutralize free radicals. Animal models have shown that specific dietary fibers—bran[56] and cellulose[57] but not pectin[58]—protect against carcinogen-induced colonic cancer. Consumption of some fibers has been shown to induce changes in the colonic mucosa suggestive of enhancement of the carcinogenic process. Thus, in experimentally induced colonic cancer in animals, increased DNA synthesis, mucosal mass, and cell migration were associated with consumption of wheat bran, guar, and pectin but not oat bran.[59] It must be emphasized that this response may not be universal and may depend on species, sex, or other factors. Considering the diverse physiochemical makeup of dietary fiber, it is likely that if, indeed, there is a protective effect, it may be specific to certain fibers.

The mechanisms by which fiber can exert a protective effect against colonic carcinogenesis have not been elucidated. Possibilities include (1) reduction of transit time in the colon, thus reducing the exposure of the colonic mucosa to intraluminal carcinogens; (2) binding and dilution of carcinogens in the colonic mucosa to intraluminal carcinogens (such as bile acids) in the colonic lumen, thus neutralizing their harmful effects; (3) changes in the colonic bacterial flora which metabolize bile acids; and (4) decrease of pH in the colon by certain dietary fibers (such as pectins) which are metabolized in the colon to short-chain fatty acids. A decrease in pH can cause deionization of potentially harmful free fatty acids and bile acids.

A recent epidemiologic study provides more insight into the possible mechanisms of the anti-carcinogenic effect of fiber. Analysis of the correlation between stool weight and incidence of colonic cancer from 20 different populations in 12 countries revealed a strong negative correlation between the two.[60] The authors suggest that consumption of 18 grams or more of fiber per day would result in a stool weight exceeding 150 g/day, and such amount of stool would be preventive against colonic cancer.

The protective effect of dietary fiber against colonic cancer could be additive to that of a reduction in dietary fat. Usually, diets low in fat tend to have a high fiber content. In experimental conditions in normal humans, the reduction of fat in the diet resulted in increased fiber consumption (Shike et al., unpublished data), since fats were replaced by complex carbohydrates and other foods.

CALORIES

Animal studies and a few epidemiologic data suggest that excessive caloric intake and obesity increase cancer risk in various organs. Tennenbaum's[61,62] early work in animals and more recent data[63,64] demonstrated that caloric restriction and decreased body weight inhibit chemically induced tumors, including colonic cancer. International epidemiologic correlation studies[12] and case control studies[13,16] suggest that increased caloric consumption and increased body weight enhance the risk for colorectal cancer. A study by the American Cancer Society[65] found that the body weight index (which is presumably related to caloric intake) correlated positively with colonic cancer incidence. A similar finding was noted in Japanese men living in Hawaii.[66] However, other epidemiologic studies did not find a correlation between body weight and colonic cancer.[67]

In a recent symposium on calories and energy expenditure in carcinogenesis,[68] it was concluded that "overnutrition is directly related to high risk of cancer." It must be noted, however, that there is a complex relationship between caloric intake, energy expenditure, body weight, and the hormonal milieu. The studies cited above lend support to the hypothesis that excess calories and increased body weight can enhance carcinogenesis, but additional data are required to separate the effects of calories from the specific effects of fat and to determine whether the effect of calories is independent of the metabolic rate and body weight. This is particularly important, since it has recently been shown that an inherently low metabolic rate can result in decreased caloric expenditure and a tendency toward obesity,[69] underscoring the complex relationship between caloric intake, metabolic rate, and obesity. If, indeed, increased caloric intake enhances carcinogenesis, it remains to be determined whether the primary factor is the direct effect of the calories, the metabolic rate, or the body weight and composition.

DIETARY RECOMMENDATIONS

Although the role of dietary factors in carcinogenesis has not as yet been completely elucidated, there is sufficient evidence to justify the formulation of dietary recommendations for cancer prevention. In the United States as well as in other countries, such recommendations have been presented to the public. In the United States, numerous organizations have issued dietary recommendations over the last few years. These include the American Cancer Society, the NCI, and the Surgeon General. Although the recommendations vary in details from organization to organization, they all include a call for reducing fat and increasing fruits, vegetables, and fiber in the diet.

These are the NCI recommendations:

- Reduce fat intake to less than 30 percent of calories.
- Increase fiber intake to 20 to 30 g daily, with an upper limit of 35 g.
- Include a variety of vegetables and fruits.
- Avoid obesity.
- Consume alcoholic beverages in moderation if at all.
- Minimize consumption of salt-cured, salt-pickled, and smoked food.

The fat reduction (to 30 percent of total calories) in the NCI dietary recommendations is probably too mild. Further reduction to 25 or 20 percent of total calories may be more appropriate.

REFERENCES

1. Shike M, Al-Sabbagh MR, Friedman E, et al: The effect of dietary fat on human colonic cell proliferation. *Gastroenterology* 100:A401, 1991.
2. Winawer SJ, Shike M: Dietary factors in colorectal cancer and their possible effects in earlier stages on hyperproliferation and adenoma formation. *J Natl Cancer Inst* 84:74–75, 1992.
3. Granoth A et al: Time trends in mortality from cancer. WHO document 1988; WHO/CAN 88.5.
4. Anti M, Marra G, Armelo D et al: Effect of omega-fatty acids on rectal mucosal cell proliferation in subjects at risk for colon cancer. *Gastroenterology* 103:883–891, 1992.
5. Lipkin M, Newmark H: Effect of added dietary calcium on colonic epithelial-cell proliferation in subjects at high risk for familial colonic cancer. *N Engl J Med* 313:1381–1384, 1985.
6. Giovannucci E, Stampfer MJ, Colditz G, et al: Relationship of diet to risk of colorectal adenoma in men. *J Natl Cancer Inst* 84:91–98, 1992.
7. Shike M, Winawer SJ, Greenwald PH, et al: *Bull WHO* 68:377–385, 1986.
8. National Research Council, Committee on Diet, Nutrition and Cancer: Washington, DC, National Academy Press, 1982.
9. Berg JW, Howel MA: The geographic pathology of bowel cancer. *Cancer* 34:807–814, 1974.
10. MacLennan R, et al: Diet, transit time, stool weight and colon cancer in two Scandinavian populations. *Am J Nutr* 31:S239, 1978.
11. Martinez IR, Jenson OM, Mosbech J: Factors associated with adenocarcinomas of the large bowel in Puerto Rico, in Birch JM (ed): *Advances in Medical Oncology, Research and Education,* vol 3. New York, Pergamon Press, 1979, pp 45–52.
12. Armstrong B, Doll R: Evironmental factors and cancer incidence and mortality in different countries, with special reference to dietary practices. *Int J Cancer* 617–631, 1975.
13. Reddy BS, Sharmer C, Darby K et al: Metabolic epidemiology of large bowel cancer: Fecal mutagens in high- and low-risk populations for colon cancer: A preliminary report. *Mutat Res* 72:511–522, 1980.
14. Haenszel W, Berg JW, Segi M: Large-bowel cancer in Hawaiian Japanese. *J Natl Cancer Inst* 51:1765–1779, 1973.
15. Modan B, Barrell V, Lubin F et al: Low-fiber intake as an etiologic factor in cancer of the colon. *J Natl Cancer Inst* 55:15–18, 1975.
16. Lyon JL: Energy intake: Its relationship to colon cancer risk. *J Natl Cancer Inst* 78:853–861, 1987.
17. Potter JB, McMichael AJ: Diet and cancer of the colon and rectum: A case control study. *J Natl Cancer Inst* 76:569, 1986.
18. Graham S, Dayal H, Swanson M: Diet in the epidemiology of cancer of the colon and rectum. *J Natl Cancer Inst* 61:709–714, 1978.
19. Jain M, Cook GM, Davis FG: A case-control study of diet and colonrectal cancer. *Int J Cancer* 26:757–768, 1980.
20. Carroll KK: Experimental studies on dietary fat and cancer in relation to epidemiological data, in Ip C, et al (eds): *Dietary Fat and Cancer.* New York, Liss, 1986.
21. Reddy B, et al: Effect of type and amount of dietary fat and 1,2-dimethylhydrazine on biliary bile acids, deval bile acids, and neutral sterols in rats. *Cancer Res* 37:2132, 1977.
22. Nauss KM, et al: Dietary fat and fiber: Relationship to caloric intake, body growth and colon tumorigenesis. *Am J Clin Nutr* 1987.
23. Broitman S, et al: Polyunsaturated fat, cholesterol and large bowel tumorigenesis. *Cancer* 40:2455, 1977.
24. National Research Council: Diet, nutrition and cancer: Directions for research. Washington, DC, National Academy Press, 1983.
25. Carroll KK, Khor HT: Dietary fat in relation to tumorigenesis. *Prog Biochem Pharm* 10:308–353, 1975.
26. Rose DP, et al: International comparison of mortality rates of cancer of the breast, ovary, prostate and colon and per capita food consumption. *Cancer* 58:2364–2371, 1988.
27. Thomas DB, Karagas MR: Cancer in first and second generation Americans. *Cancer Res* 47:5771–5776, 1987.
28. Enstrom JE: Colorectal cancer and consumption of beef and fat. *Br J Cancer* 32:432–439, 1975.
29. Lyon JL, Sorenson AW: Colon cancer in low-risk populations. *Am J Clin Nutr* 31:S227–223, 1978.
30. Garland C, et al: Dietary vitamin D and calcium and risk of colorectal cancer: A 19 year prospective study in men. *Lancet* 1:307–309, 1985:
31. Kolonel LN: Fat and colon cancer: How firm is the evidence? *Am J Clin Nutr* 45:336–341, 1987.
32. Jensen OM, et al: Diet, bowel function, fecal characteristics, and large bowel cancer in Denmark and Finland. *Nutr Cancer* 4:5–19, 1982.
33. Willett WC, Stampfer MJ, Colditz GA, et al: Relation of meat, fat and fiber intake to the risk of colon cancer in a pro-

spective study among women. *N Engl J Med* 323:1664–1672, 1990.

34. Prentice RL, Sheppard L: Dietary fat and cancer consistency of the epidemiologic data, and disease prevention that may follow from a practical reduction in fat consumption. *Cancer Causes Control* 1:81–97, 1990.
35. Enig NG, et al: Dietary fat and cancer trends: A critique. *Fed Proc* 37:2215–2220, 1978.
36. Reddy BS, Burill C, Rigotly J: Effects of diets high in omega-3 and omega-6 fatty acids on initiation and post initiation stages of colon carcinogenesis. *Cancer Res* 51:487–491, 1991.
37. Macquart-Moulin G, et al: Case-control study on colorectal cancer and diet in Marseilles. *Int J Cancer* 183–191, 1986.
38. Tuyns AJ, et al: Colorectal cancer and the intake of nutrients: Oligosaccharides are a risk factor, fats are not: A case-control study in Belgium. *Nutr Cancer* 10:181–196, 1987.
39. Reddy BS: Role of bile metabolites in colon carcinogenesis. *Cancer* 36:2401–2406, 1976.
40. Reddy BS, et al: Metabolic epidemiology of colon cancer: Dietary patterns and fecal sterol concentration of three populations. *Nutr Cancer* 5:34–39, 1983.
41. Welsch CW: Enhancement of mammary tumorigenesis by dietary fat: Review of potential mechanisms. *Am J Clin Nutr* 45:192–202, 1987.
42. Clandinin MT, Cheema S, Field JC, et al: *FASEB J* 5:2761–2789, 1991.
43. US Department of Agriculture/US Department of Health and Human Services: *Nutrition and Your Health: Dietary Guidelines for Americans,* 2d ed, no. 232. Washington DC, US Government Printing Office, 1985.
44. *Household Food Consumption and Expenditure, 1983: Annual Report of the Food Survey Committee.* London, Her Majesty's Stationery Office, 1983.
45. Schatzkin A, Lanza E, Ballard-Barbash R: The case for a dietary intervention study of large bowel polyps. *Cancer Prev* 1:84–90, 1991.
46. Burkitt DP, Trowell HC (eds): *Refined Carbohydrate Foods and Disease.* London, Academic Press, 1975, pp 333–345.
47. US Department of Health and Human Services. *The Surgeon General's Report on Nutrition and Health* DHHS (PHS) publication no. 88-50201. Washington DC, 1988.
48. Kunes S, et al: Case control study of dietary etiological factors: The Melbourne Colorectal Cancer Study. *Nutr Cancer* 9:21–42, 1987.
49. Hill MJ: Metabolic epidemiology of dietary factors in large bowel cancer. *Cancer Res* 35:3398–3402, 1975.
50. LARC Intestinal Microecology Group: Dietary fibre, transit-time, faecal bacteria, steroids and colon cancer in two Scandinavian populations. *Lancet* 2:207–221, 1977.
51. Pickle LW, et al. Colorectal cancer in rural Nebraska. *Cancer Res* 44:363–369, 1984.
52. Miller AB, et al: Food items and food groups as risk factors in a case-control study of diet and colorectal cancer. *Int J Cancer* 32:155–161, 1983.
53. Walker ARP et al: Fecal pH, dietary fibre intake and proneness to colon cancer in four South African populations. *Br J Cancer* 53:489–495, 1986.
54. Trock B, Unza E, Greenwald P: Dietary fiber, vegetables, and colon cancer: Critical review and meta-analysis of epidemiologic evidence. *J Natl Cancer Inst* 82:650–661, 1990.
55. *Physiological Effect and Health Consequences of Dietary Fiber.* Bethesda, Md, Life Science Research Office, Federation of American Societies for Experimental Biology, 1987.
56. Barbolt TA, Abraham R: The effect of bran on dimethylhydrazine-induced colon carcinogenesis in the rat. *Proc Soc Exp Biol Med* 157:656–659, 1978.
57. Freeman HJ, et al: A double-blind study on the effect of purified cellulose dietary fiber on 1,2-dimethylhydrazine-induced rat colonic neoplasia. *Cancer Res* 38:2912–2917, 1978.
58. Freeman HJ, et al: A double-blind study on the effects of differing purified cellulose and pectin fiber diets on 1,2-dimethylhydrazine-induced rat colonic neoplasia. *Cancer Res* 40: 2661–2665, 1980.
59. Jacobs, LR, Lupton JR: Effect of dietary fibers on rat large bowel mucosal growth and differentiation. *Am J Physiol* 246:378–385, 1984.
60. Cummings JH, Bingham SA, Heaton KU, et al: Fecal weight, colon cancer risk, and dietary intake of nonstarch polysaccharides (dietary fat). *Gastroenterology* 103:1783–1789, 1992.
61. Tennenbaum A: The initiation and growth of tumors. *Am J Cancer* 38:335–350, 1940.
62. Tennenbaum A: Relation of body weight to cancer incidence. *Arch Pathol* 30:509–519, 1940.
63. Reddy BS, et al. Effect of restricted caloric intake on azoxymethan-induced colon tumor incidence in male F344 rats. *Cancer Res* 47:1226–1228, 1987.
64. Klurfed DM, et al: Inhibition of chemically induced mammary and colon tumor promotion by caloric restriction in rats fed increased dietary fat. *Cancer Res* 47:2759–2762, 1966.
65. Law EA, Garfinkel L: Variations in mortality by weight among 750,000 men and women. *J Chronic Dis* 32:563–576, 1979.
66. Nomura A, et al: Body mass index as a predictor of cancer in men. *J Natl Cancer Inst* 74:319–323, 1985.
67. Higginson J: Etiological factors in gastrointestinal cancer in men. *J Natl Cancer Inst* 37:527–545, 1988.
68. Calories and energy expenditure in carcinogenesis: Proceedings of a symposium. *Am J Clin Nutr* 45(suppl):149–372, 1987.
69. Ravussin E, et al: Reduced rate of energy expenditure as a risk factor for body-weight gain. *N Engl J Med* 318:467–472, 1988.

CHAPTER 6

Dietary Factors—Vitamins and Minerals

Lynn Hornsby-Lewis

HIGHLIGHTS

Environment influences the incidence of colonic cancer. Rates are low in Asia and Africa and high in the United States, western Europe, and Great Britain. In considering environmental factors, epidemiologic studies have focused on eating habits and food choices which could help explain this difference. There are many variables present whenever diet is considered, since people eat wide varieties of foods and most food products contain multiple nutrients.

This can make it difficult to decipher exactly which nutrient or group of nutrients is playing an important role. Not only have studies looked at such things as fats, fiber, and calories but researchers have also begun to evaluate the effect of micronutrients with antioxidant properties as well as minerals such as calcium.

The antioxidants function to remove or neutralize the damaging effects of certain oxygen metabolites, called free radicals and singlet oxygen. These metabolites are formed during routine biochemical processes throughout the body. They are potentially dangerous because they can damage DNA, lipid membranes, and proteins. It is felt that this type of molecular-level damage to cells helps promote cancer formation if left unchecked.

Several vitamins, minerals, and trace elements have antioxidant properties. Researchers have focused on these substances to see if there is any association between low levels of micronutrients such as vitamins A, C, and E and increased colonic cancer. Exactly which of their functions may have anticancer properties is unclear.

Vitamin A and the provitamin A substances such as beta carotene have been extensively studied in association with cancer. Certain retinoids have been found effective in helping to prevent skin, lung, and bladder cancer.[1–6] They also are used to treat leukoplakia, myelodysplastic syndrome, and promyelocytic leukemia.[7–9] Animal studies have suggested a role for vitamin A in the prevention of colonic cancer.[10–13] Human studies have been less persuasive.[14–17] Therefore the degree of influence vitamin A substances may have on colonic cancer in humans is still unknown.

Vitamin C animal studies have had conflicting results. Some studies showed increased tumors in C-deficient animals, while others showed the opposite.[18,19] There have been epidemiologic studies in humans which have suggested an increased risk, particularly for rectal cancer, in people taking low amounts of vitamin C.[16] Other studies have not shown that effect.[20,21]

Low vitamin E serum levels in some studies have been associated with an increased risk of colonic cancer.[22] Longitudinal studies of serum vitamin E levels have also shown a trend toward lower levels in some cancer patients.[23] Whether vitamin E actually plays a role in colonic cancer is still unknown.

Calcium is a mineral that acts to decrease hyperproliferation in colonic layers of epithelial mucosa. It has been postulated that this local effect may help decrease the risk of colonic cancer, particularly in high-risk groups.[24–26] Epidemiologic studies have also suggested a protective effect with increased intake of calcium.[27] Intervention studies are under way looking for a decrease in polyps or cancer development with supplemental calcium.

Last, some studies have correlated geographic areas that have low selenium levels with an increased cancer mortality.[28–31] Human studies of colonic cancer and selenium blood levels have not shown this correlation for colon cancer.[32,33] Any potential role for selenium in colonic cancer is still unknown.

CONTROVERSIES

There are two major areas of controversy regarding the potential role of vitamins, minerals, and trace elements in the development and prevention of colonic cancer. The first is the complexity of designing the studies themselves. Since people eat so many different foods individually throughout the world, it can be very difficult to know which set of nutrients is actually having an effect on cancer rates. It is also difficult to decide on a tool which can adequately measure that effect. Dietary histories must rely on patient memory, accuracy in proportion estimates, and degree of cooperation in completing the forms. They also measure vitamins only for defined periods of time. These time periods range from a day, using 24-h recall, to a year, as in the food frequency questionnaires. Once the intake is recorded, the program used to quantitate values for nutrients must also be accurate. If a significant source of a certain vitamin is ignored in the calculations, inaccurate assumptions about levels can be made.

Ecological studies and case-cohort studies can be used to help define potential areas of interest for further research. Randomized control studies are then needed to prove whether interventions such as vitamin supplementation can be beneficial. These studies are complex, since many benefits can take years to occur. Therefore, the time in a person's life in which the intervention is made and the length of time studied can have a tremendous impact on the outcome. It is also difficult to know what dose and what form of nutrient should be used. For example, a vitamin supplement may not have the same effect as a vitamin within a complex fruit or vegetable.

Many intervention studies are being performed. They are looking for proof for an effect from specific nutrients and micronutrients on both cancer rates and other systemic diseases. It will be some time before the answers about these potential effects are known. This leads to the second area of controversy.

Because of the recent explosion of interest in antioxidants among researchers and lay people, the most controversial problem is whether to recommend antioxidant supplements to patients now rather than wait for further studies. Many epidemiologic studies suggest protection from the development or progression of certain diseases, varying from heart disease to cancers, when people have a high level of intake of antioxidants.

It is beyond the scope of this chapter to analyze the data from studies in so many different disease systems. The relation between specific nutrients and the development of colonic cancer is still being evaluated. Most studies do consistently show decreased rates for people who eat diets high in fruits and vegetables. As for supplementing with specific micronutrients, there are no positive intervention trials that would support such a recommendation at this time.

Many people argue that toxicity from these substances is minimal, so they are probably not going to cause harm. Others argue that the best dose for supplementation is unknown and that the potential for long-term toxicity from micronutrients given at increased levels is also unknown.

FUTURE DIRECTIONS

Further research will be directed toward both the molecular activities of micronutrients and their clinical applications. A great deal of study has been done looking at the antioxidant factors of micronutrients. Other potential functions can also be addressed. Some researchers are focusing on the molecular genetics of colonic cancer. Chemopreventive agents that interfere with those genetic changes are of importance.

Many complex issues are involved. It is assumed that these chemopreventive agents would act early on to prevent the development of cancer, whereas many of the genetic alterations that occur happen late.[34,35] Therefore, an effect from a chemopreventive agent would need some marker that typically occurs early enough to measure. Also, the processes of gene transformation are extremely complex, involving many pathways and substances. There will be no universal biomarker to measure the effectiveness of all chemopreventive agents.[36,37]

Studies that evaluate the effect of chemopreventive agents may focus on gene products or on the presence or absence of oncogenes themselves. The formation of an oncogene occurs when some normal cellular gene (protooncogene) becomes altered so that its expression is abnormal or a functionally altered protein is produced. Since oncogenes and protooncogenes are often closely related structurally, a drug which would block oncogene function might also block protooncogenes.[38] This could lead to severe toxicity. In the future, studies which attempt to identify genetic alterations occurring due to supplementation or deficiency of various nutrients will be quite complex. They are important, however, to help point researchers toward potentially beneficial substances which can be tested in humans on a prospective basis.

Prospective randomized intervention trials are important. The Polyp Prevention Trial sponsored by the National Cancer Institute is currently following patients on low-fat, high-fiber diets that are high in fruits and vegetables. These patients have a history of adenomas in the colon. They will be colonoscoped over the years to see if the recurrence rate for polyp formation decreases. This study will specifically evaluate whether fruits and vegetables have an antipolyp effect. Other similar trials involving specific micronutrients are under way. It is hoped that these intervention trials will help to answer the questions about micronutrient supplementation and cancer prevention.

Epidemiologic studies suggest that environment plays an important role in the development of colonic cancer. Incidence rates for colorectal cancer vary widely throughout the world. For example, Asia and Africa have very low rates of colonic cancer. Developed western countries such as the United States, Great Britain, and western Europe have much higher rates. Of interest, when people move from a low-risk to a high-risk area, their incidence changes also. Migration studies have shown that first- and second-generation Japanese who moved to the United States increase their colonic cancer mortality to a rate which more closely resembles that of Americans.[39] The Polish population who move to the United States also get colonic cancer near the American rate.[40] People who live in the northeastern United States have a 50 percent higher rate of colonic cancer than people who live in the South. When retirees move to the South, their colonic cancer incidence declines to resemble the rate of southerners.[41]

Since diet is an important part of our environment, many studies have considered its potential effect. Other chapters deal with such factors as fat, calories, and fiber (see Chap. 5). This chapter focuses on the potential role of vitamins, minerals, and trace elements in the development or prevention of colonic cancer.

ANTIOXIDANTS

An exciting field of research which has grown over the past 25 years is that of oxidative injury and the role of antioxidants. Routine biochemical processes, such as the reduction of molecular oxygen to water, result in the production of reactive oxygen molecules called *free radicals*. These molecules are reactive because they have an unpaired electron and can pull electrons from other organic molecules near them. Another oxygen metabolite (singlet oxygen) has an electron which is excited to a different orbital from its usual position. These metabolites can cause damage to multiple structures including nucleic acids, proteins, and lipid membranes.[42] It is felt that these insults help promote the transformation of normal cells to cancer cells. Factors which defend against these oxidative insults are called *antioxidants*. There are many vitamins, minerals, and trace elements which act through various mechanisms to prevent oxidative damage.[43] For example, vitamin A, beta carotene, and related compounds can absorb the energy from a singlet oxygen so that it reverts back to its usual state. Superoxide dismutase and glutathione peroxidase are two enzymes that can neutralize free radicals. Each of these enzymes requires trace elements to function. Depending on its location, superoxide dismutase requires manganese or zinc and copper. Glutathione peroxidase contains selenium. Antioxidant functions on a molecular level can be easily demonstrated; however, translating that function to a clinical effect such as cancer prevention is difficult.

STUDY METHODS

Epidemiologic research may suggest certain associations between specific environmental agents and cancer incidence. Animal and human studies are then needed to clarify those associations and provide information as to possible intervention. Human studies to evaluate the effects of antioxidants fall into several basic groups. Epidemiologic studies often begin with diet histories. Surveys of large population groups or smaller case control cohort studies can be performed. For example, using a dietary history, Freudenheim et al.[44] found a relative risk of 2.9 for rectal but not colonic cancer in patients reporting a low intake of beta carotene and vitamin C. Other studies have shown a trend toward a risk for stomach and colonic cancer in patients on diets low in fruits and vegetables.[45–47] These patients tend to eat more fats; so it is difficult to decipher which nutrient or combination of nutrients is actually associated with the increase. These studies are important because they can point out potential areas of interest for more focused research. There are, however, many problems with the performance of these studies. Depending on the type of study, the choice of dietary history obtained can vary from 24-h recall to multiple-day food diaries to food frequency questionnaires which estimate average intake of nutrients over a year's time. Problems can occur if patients' memories are inaccurate, if they over or underestimate certain foods, or if the period tested for is not representative of their average food intake. The analysis of nutrient values from specific foods must also be correct to avoid misinterpretation of vitamin or mineral levels.

Studies which examine blood levels of certain nutrients have also been used. For example, Comstock et al.[48] did not show an association between low blood levels of beta carotene or vitamin E with rectal cancer. Studies using nutrient blood levels have their own difficulties. Some researchers in the past used stored blood, which would undergo breakdown of certain nutrients, thereby giving a falsely low estimation of patients' serum levels. Also, one vitamin level determination in a person's lifetime may not be a good indicator of his or her typical vitamin status. Last, a low serum vitamin or mineral level may be due to a patient's illness and not necessarily the cause of it.

After a nutrient with possible anticancer effects is identified, the best tests to prove its efficacy are randomized, controlled trials. These trials also are problematic. Decisions must be made about dose and form of nutrients given. Does a supplement have the same effect as nutrients within actual complex foods? Other problems include the length of time the nutrient is given, the size of the group being tested, the expected time frame before a lesion would be expected to develop, and at what time in a person's life the intervention is made. Therefore, a negative test may be truly negative or it may be due to a brief testing time, inappropriate dose, or other problems with the test method itself.

Information gained from animal studies and various types of human studies is examined below for specific nutrients, beginning with vitamins.

VITAMINS

Vitamin A

There are multiple substances that fall into the general category of vitamin A. The common characteristic of these substances is that they have retinol activity. A retinoid can be either a natural vitamin A compound or its synthetic analogue. These substances may or may not have the biological activity of retinols. Carotenoids, such as beta carotene, are compounds found in fruits and vegetables which can be converted to vitamin A activity. These substances are considered provitamin A compounds. The retinol found in dairy products, meat, eggs, and cereals provide most dietary vitamin A in the United States. If excess vitamin A is absorbed, it can be stored in the liver. Only around 25 percent of dietary vitamin A comes from carotenoids in fruits and vegetables.[49] This is because these carotenoids are less well absorbed and their conversion to vitamin A is inefficient. The activities of retinoids and carotenoids against cancer development may differ at the molecular level; therefore studies should distinguish between the two substance groups.

Retinoids can act as antipromoters and immunostimulants. They can cause an increase in natural killer cells and in cell-mediated toxicity. They also are felt to promote cellular differentiation. Multiple studies have shown activity for retinoids against various cancers. A great deal of work has evaluated the role of retinoids in preventing skin cancer.[1–3] Other studies have found a use for certain retinoids in preventing head and neck, lung, and bladder tumors.[4–6] Retinoids are also used to treat such diseases as leukoplakia, acute promyelocytic leukemia, and myelodysplastic syndrome.[7–9]

Animal Studies. There have been animal data that suggest a role for vitamin A deficiency in the development of colonic cancer. Newberne et al.[10] fed diets of differing fat and vitamin A levels to rats. They found that rats fed the high-fat, low vitamin A diet developed the most colonic tumors. Rats receiving a high-fat, normal vitamin A diet got fewer tumors. Studies in which rats were given 13-*cis*-retinoic acid have shown decreases in colonic tumor incidence or delayed development of colonic tumors.[11,12] Another test that involved giving retinol acetate to rats showed a decrease in the numbers of tumors, but several other retinoids in that same study showed no results.[13] Therefore, not all animal studies consistently show preventive effects with retinoids.

Human Studies. Human studies have shown little evidence of any association between retinoids and colonic cancer. Shekelle et al.[14] performed a study on Western Electric employees and evaluated the amount of carotenoids in their diets according to the fruits and vegetables they ate. He found no relation between amount of carotenoids eaten and incidence of colonic cancer. Case control studies in Australia and France failed to demonstrate any relation between retinol or beta carotene to colonic cancer risk.[15,16]

Several studies have been negative for any relation between plasma levels of carotenoids and colonic or rectal cancer.[17,51–54]

Summary. There are very good data to support the use of certain retinoids in the prevention or treatment of many types of cancers. Thus far, the data for any association between vitamin A foods and colonic cancer is more convincing in animal studies than in humans. Further studies will be performed in the future examining possible links between the two.

Vitamin C

Vitamin C is a water-soluble vitamin with many activities. It is capable of promoting the immune system and acting as an antioxidant. It can also block the conversion of nitrites and nitrates to nitrosamines. The exact role that vitamin C might play in the body's attempts to prevent cancer is unknown.

Animal Studies. Researchers trying to establish a tie between vitamin C deficiency and colonic cancer have had mixed results. For example, a study examining methylcholanthrene carcinogenesis in guinea pigs demonstrated increased tumor growth in vitamin C–deficient guinea pigs.[18] However, another study showed that tumor growth was retarded in ascorbate-deficient animals.[19]

Human Studies. Case control studies have been done in humans in an effort to show an association between vitamin C and colorectal cancer. Of note, results for colonic and rectal cancer can differ. A case control study by Potter et al.[15] found a decrease in incidence of rectal cancers, particularly in women who had high intake of vitamin C. A case control study in Australia found similar protective effects from high intakes of vitamin C for rectal cancer.[54] On the other hand, Heilbrun et al.[55] found no such effect in evaluating rectal cancer in Hawaii. As for colonic cancer, some studies have shown a trend toward protection from vitamin C.[56] Other researchers have demonstrated protection with increased intake of vitamin C. The study of Kune et al.[54] in Australia showed a three fold increased risk of developing colon cancer if consumption of vitamin C was in the lowest quintile. Other studies have not shown that association.[21]

Summary. Epidemiologic studies suggest a role for vitamin C in the prevention of colorectal, particularly rectal, cancer. Not all studies are in agreement with that hypothesis, however, and no intervention studies have been done which demonstrate a beneficial effect from supplemental vitamin C in the prevention of colonic cancer.

Vitamin E

Vitamin E is a fat-soluble vitamin that acts as a free radical scavenger and is a lipid antioxidant. It has been postulated that these types of activities may be associated with anticancer effects.

Animal Studies. Animal studies have been contradictory as to the effect of vitamin E in colorectal carcinogenesis.[22,57,58] Results have ranged from showing inhibition of tumor growth to exacerbation of carcinogenesis in various studies.

Human Studies. Longitudinal studies in humans evaluating serum levels of vitamin E and the potential for colorectal cancer did show a lower blood level of vitamin E in colonic cancer patients than in controls. This lower level was not statistically significant.[59] A large case control study in Finland showed a relative risk of 2.1 for colorectal cancer in women in the lowest group of serum vitamin E levels compared to those in the highest. This association was not seen in men, whose relative risk was 1.0.[60]

Other organ systems are also being studied, from lung to skin to pancreas. At this point, it is unknown whether low vitamin E levels actually play a role in the development of colorectal cancer. What mechanism it would act through is also unknown.

Summary. There is some epidemiological evidence for a role of low serum values of vitamin E and cancer development in various organ systems. No studies have adequately evaluated the potential effect of vitamin E supplementation and colon cancer.

MINERALS

Calcium

There has been a great deal of interest in the potential role of calcium as an inhibitor of colonic cancer development. Irritating substances such as bile acids and fatty acids cause damage to the epithelial cell layer and loss of these cells in the gastrointestinal tract. This forces the intestine to make new cells more rapidly than usually necessary. It has been postulated that this increased rate of cell replacement can lead to an increased potential for the development of colonic cancer. Calcium within the gastrointestinal tract lumen can bind with irritating substances such as the bile acids to make insoluble soaps.[24] These soaps should be less irritating to the epithelial cell layer and therefore help prevent colonic cancer development. This hypothesis requires that excess calcium be within the gut lumen to be effective. Other hypotheses examine potential systemic activities of calcium.

Epidemiologic studies have shown an association between latitude and colon cancer. There is decreased colonic cancer incidence in areas that receive more sun. Since vitamin D levels increase with sun exposure, vitamin D is thought to play a role. Some studies have shown a synergistic effect between vitamin D and calcium.[61] Other studies have suggested that increased vitamin D levels can cause an increase in calcium absorption, thereby leaving less calcium to bind with the bile salts.[62]

Animal Studies. Animal studies have shown a decrease in the number of colorectal tumors in rats fed an increased calcium intake.[63–66] Other studies looking at dimethylhydrazine-induced carcinogenesis did not show any protective effect with calcium.[67,68]

Human Studies. Human studies have used cell cultures from intestinal biopsies to look for evidence of hyperproliferation. Studies have indicated that supplemental calcium in patients at increased risk for colorectal cancer can lead to a decrease in hyperproliferation.[24,26,69,70] Studies of patients who already have a low risk of colonic cancer did not show any further benefits from supplemental calcium.[71–73]

Epidemiologic studies of calcium intake and its association with colorectal cancer have also been performed. A 19-year prospective study in Chicago evaluated calcium intake according to diet history. It was found that men with the highest level of calcium and vitamin D intake had a much lower rate of colonic cancer than men with low intakes.[74] A Utah study also showed a decreased colonic cancer rate in men and women who had increased levels of calcium intake.[27] Other studies have shown less evidence for an association between calcium and colorectal cancer. Case control studies in France and Melbourne have shown only a slight protection against colorectal cancer.[16,54] The slight protective effect in the Australian study was seen only in women.

Summary. The idea of calcium as a potential preventer of colorectal cancer is exciting, particularly for those at increased risk. Studies demonstrate a decrease in hyperproliferation when patients are treated with calcium. This normalization of the rate of cell turnover would, one hopes, lead to a decrease in colorectal cancer production. Epidemiologic studies, however, have been mixed when looking for an association between colonic cancer and calcium intake. This may be because only those patients at high risk for the disease would actually demonstrate a benefit. New intervention trials will help determine its role as an anticancer substance.

TRACE ELEMENTS

Trace elements are minerals which occur in small quantity in the body but are needed for biological activity. They are often necessary for specific enzyme reactions. Some examples of trace elements include zinc, manganese, copper, and selenium.

Selenium

Selenium is an essential trace element found in the glutathione peroxidase system, an important tool in antioxidant activity. Soil levels of selenium vary according to geographic differences. Areas in China and New Zealand contain very low levels. The amount of selenium found in plants will vary depending on where they were grown. Selenium has attracted a great deal of interest as a potential agent of anticancer activity. As mentioned previously, it is essential for glutathione peroxidase activity and is an antioxidant. It has also been shown to have cytoxicity toward cells in rapid division and to alter carcinogen metabolism in various animal tumor models.[75,76]

Animal Studies. Animal research has been mixed. Some research suggests a decreased rate of colon cancer in animals receiving supplemental selenium.[77–81] One study, however, suggested a decrease in colonic cancer rates with selenium deficiency.[82] The exact potential mechanism for selenium as an anticancer agent is unknown, but researchers feel that it is not associated with its glutathione peroxidase activity.[83]

Human Studies. Epidemiologic studies have tried to correlate the level of selenium in forage crops with geographic cancer mortality rates. Several correlation studies have shown an increased incidence of human cancers in areas of low selenium.[28–31] Cancers looked at included those of the esophagus, colon, rectum, lung, breast, ovary, cervix, bladder, and pancreas. Case control studies have shown little or no association between blood levels of selenium and cancer. Since selenium levels can vary so widely in foods, dietary analysis is not an adequate approach to estimate selenium intake and status. Therefore, most case controls studies have used blood levels to measure selenium status in patients. Most studies have shown no statistical difference in blood levels between cancer cases and their controls.[29] A prospective study by Peleg et al.[84] also showed no relationship between colonic cancer and intake of selenium.

Summary. Both animal studies and epidemiologic studies of plant levels for selenium suggest a protective role for selenium against colorectal cancer. This has not been borne out by the case control studies or small prospective studies performed on humans. Further studies will be required to delineate any of selenium's potential benefits.

Of note, researchers have also begun to examine other substances such as copper, folate, vitamin B_{12}, and magnesium.[85–88] At present there is no definitive evidence for effects on human carcinogenesis with any of these substances.

RECOMMENDATIONS

This chapter points out the early stage of knowledge about any of these micronutrients in terms of their potential benefits in prevention of colorectal cancer. At this point, studies do indicate a protective effect from fruits and vegetables, but it is unclear whether this effect is due to fiber, vitamins and minerals, or a decrease in fat intake. In general, increasing the amount of vegetables and fruits in one's diet should be beneficial. Specific recommendations about micronutrients seem premature at this point. Many intervention studies with various vitamins and minerals are ongoing in colonic cancer, other cancers, and systemic diseases such as coronary artery disease. It is hoped that more information about potential benefits, doses, and toxicities will become available.

REFERENCES

1. Kraemer KH, Di Giovanna JJ, Mosball AN, et al: Prevention of skin cancer in xeroderma pigmentosum with the use of oral isotretinoin. *N Engl J Med* 318:1633–1637, 1988.
2. Lippman SM, Kessler JF, Al-Sarra FM, et al: Treatment of advanced squamous cell carcinoma of the head and neck with isotretinoin: A phase II randomized trial. *Invest New Drugs* 6:51–56, 1988.
3. Pecks GL, Di Giovanna JJ, Sarnoff DS, et al: Treatment and prevention of basal cell carcinoma with oral isotretinoin. *Am J Dermatol* 19:176–185, 1988.
4. Hong WK, Lippman SM, Itri L, et al: Prevention of second primary tumors with isotretinoins in squamous cell carcinoma of the head and neck. *N Engl J Med* 323:775–780, 1990.
5. Pastorino U, Soresi E, Clevici M, et al: Lung cancer chemoprevention with retinol palmitate: Preliminary data from a randomized trial of stage Ia non small cell lung cancer. *Acta Oncol* 27:773–782, 1988.
6. Studer UE, Biedermann C, Chollet D, et al: Prevention of recurrent superficial bladder tumors by oral etretinate: Preliminary results of a randomized, double blind multicenter trial. Switzerland. *J Urol* 131:47–49, 1984.
7. Hong WK, Endicott J, Itri LM, et al: 13 cis-Retinoic acid in the treatment of oral leukoplakia. *N Engl J Med* 315:1501–1505, 1986.
8. Hwang M, Ye Y, Chen S, et al: Use of all-trans-retinoic acid in the treatment of acute promyelocytic leukemia. *Blood* 72:567–572, 1988.
9. Besa EC, Abraham JL, Bartholomew MJ, et al: Treatment with 13-cisretinoic acid in transfusion dependent patients with myelodysplastic syndrome and decreased toxicity with addition of α-tocopherol *Am J Med* 89:739–747, 1990.
10. Newberne P, Bueche D, Riengropitah S, et al: The influence of dietary levels of vitamin A and fat on colon cancer. *Nutr Cancer* 13:235–242, 1990.
11. Newberne PM, Suphakarn V: Preventive role of vitamin A in colon carcinogenesis in rats. *Cancer* 40:2553–2556, 1977.
12. O'Dwyer PJ, Ravikunas TS, McCabe DP, et al: Effect of 13-cis-retinoic acid on tumor prevention, tumor growth, and metastasis in experimental colon cancer. *J Surg Res* 43:550–557, 1987.
13. Silverman J, Katazana S, Zelenakos K, et al: Effect of retinoids on the induction of colon cancer in F344 rats by *N*-methyl-*N* nitrosourea or by 1,2 dimethylhydrazine. *Carcinogenesis* 2:167–172, 1981.
14. Shekelle RB, Lepper M, Liu S, et al: Dietary vitamin A and risk of cancer in the Western Electric Study. *Lancet* 2:1185–1190, 1981.
15. Potter JD, McMichael AJ: Diet and cancer of the colon and rectum: A case-control study. *J Natl Cancer Inst* 76:557–569, 1986.
16. Macquart-Moulin G, Riboli E, Cornie J, et al: Case-control study on colorectal cancer and diet in Marseilles. *Int J Cancer* 38:183–191, 1986.
17. Connett JE, Kuller LH, Kjelsberg MO, et al: Relationship between carotenoids and cancer: The Multiple Risk Factor Intervention Trial (MRFIT) Study. *Cancer* 64:126–134, 1989.
18. Russel WD, Ortega LR, Wynne EC: Studies on methylcholanthrene induction of tumors in guinea pigs. *Cancer Res* 12:216–218, 1952.
19. Migliozzi JA: Effect of ascorbic acid on tumor growth. *Br J Cancer* 35:448–453, 1977.
20. Bjelke E. Case-control study of cancer of the stomach, colon and rectum, in Clark RL, Cunley RW, McJay JE (eds): *Oncology 1970: Proceedings of the Tenth International Cancer Congress*, vol V. Chicago, Yearbook, 1971, pp 320–334.
21. Tuyas AJ, Hoelterman M, Kaaks R: Colorectal cancer and the intake of nutrients: Oligosaccharides are a role factor, fats are not: A case-control study in Belgium. *Nutr Cancer* 10:181–196, 1987.
22. Knekt P: *Serum Alpha-Tocopherol and the Risk of Cancer*, vol 83. Helsinki, Publications of the Social Insurance Institution, 1988; 1–148.
23. Stahelin HB, Rosel F, Buess E, et al: Cancer, vitamins and plasma lipids: Prospective Basel Study. *J Natl Cancer Inst* 73:1463–1468, 1984.
24. Lipkin M, Newmark H: Effect of added dietary calcium on colonic epithelial cell proliferation in subjects at high risk for familial colonic cancer. *N Engl J Med* 313:1381–1384, 1985.
25. Boffa LC, Mariani MR, Newmark H, et al: Calcium as modulator of nucleosomal histone acetylation in cultured cells. *Proc Am Assoc Cancer Res* 30:8, 1989.
26. Berger D, Weissman G, Bronzo R, et al: Effect of calcium citrate (CC) on colonic epithelial cell proliferation and DNA content in patients with ulcerative colitis (UC). *Gastroenterology* 100:A349, 1991.
27. Slattery ML, Sorenson AW, Ford MH: Dietary calcium intake as a mitigating factor in colon cancer. *Am J Epidemiol* 128:504, 1988.
28. Shamberger RJ, Willis CE: Selenium distribution and human cancer mortality. *Crit Rev Clin Lab Sci* 2:211–221, 1971.
29. Clark LC: The epidemiology of selenium and cancer. *Fed Proc* 44:2584–2589, 1985.
30. Shamberger RJ, Fros DV: Possible protective effect of selenium against human cancer. *Can Med Assoc J*10:682, 1969.
31. Shamberger RJ, Tyko SA, Willis CE: Antioxidants and cancer: Part VI. Selenium and age-adjusted cancer mortality. *Arch Environ Health* 31:231–235, 1976.
32. Coates RJ, Weiss NS, Daling JR, et al: Serum levels of selenium and retinol and the subsequent risk of cancer. *Am J Epidemiol* 128:515–523, 1988.
33. Robinson MF, Godfrey PJ, Thompson C, et al: Blood selenium and glutathione peroxidase activity in normal subjects

and in surgical patients with and without cancer in New Zealand. *Am J Clin Nutr* 32:1477–1485, 1979.

34. Fearon ER, Vogelstein B: A genetic model for colorectal tumorigenesis. *Cell* 61:759, 1990.
35. Vogelstein B, Fearon ER, Hamilton SR, et al: Genetic alterations during colorectal-tumor development. *N Engl J Med* 319:525, 1988.
36. Augenlicht LH, Wahrman MZ, Halsey H, et al: Expression of cloned sequences in biopsies of human colonic tissue and in colonic carcinoma cells induced to differentiate in vitro. *Cancer Res* 47:6017, 1987.
37. Augenlicht LH, Taylor J, Anderson L, et al: Patterns of gene expression that characterize the colonic mucosa in patients at genetic risk for colonic cancer. *Proc Natl Acad Sci USA* 88:3286, 1991.
38. Cooper GM: *Oncogenes*. Boston, Jones and Bartlett, 1990.
39. Haenszel W, Berg JW, Segi M, et al: Large bowel cancer among Japanese in Hawaii. *J Natl Cancer Inst* 51:1765–1779, 1973.
40. Staszewski J, McCall MG, Stenhouse NS: Cancer mortality in 1962–66 among Polish migrants to Australia. *Br J Cancer* 25:599–618, 1971.
41. Ziegler RG, Blot WJ, Hoover R, et al: Protocol for a study of nutritional factors and the low risk of colon cancer in Southern retirement areas. *Cancer Res* 41:3724–3726, 1981.
42. Sun Y: Free radicals, antioxidant enzymes and carcinogenesis. *Free Rad Biol Med* 8:583–599, 1990.
43. Di Mascio P, Marply ME, Sies H: Antioxidant defense systems: The role of carotenoids, tocopherols, and thiols. *Am J Clin Nutr* 53:194S–200S, 1991.
44. Freudenheim JL, Graham S, Marshall JR, et al: Folate intake and carcinogenesis of the colon and rectum. *Int J Epidemiol* 20:368–374, 1991.
45. Chyoi PH, Nomura AMU, Hanlei JH, et al: A case-cohort study of diet and stomach cancer. *Cancer Res* 50:7501–7504, 1990.
46. Negi E, La Vecchia C, Franceschi S, et al: Vegetables and fruit consumption and cancer risk. *Int J Cancer* 48:350–354, 1991.
47. Whittemore AS, Wu-Williams AH, Lee M, et al: Diet, physical activity and colorectal cancer among Chinese in North America and China. *J Natl Cancer Inst* 82:915–926, 1990.
48. Comstock GW, Helzlsouer KJ, Buoh TL: Prediagnostic serum levels of carotenoids and vitamin E as related to subsequent cancer in Washington County, Maryland. *Am J Clin Nutr* 53:2605–2645, 1991.
49. National Research Council: *Recommended Dietary Allowances*. 9th ed. Washington, DC: National Academy Press, 1980.
50. Stahelin HG, Gey KF, Eichholzer M, et al: B-carotene and cancer prevention: The Basel Study. *Am J Clin Nutr* 53(suppl): 2655–2695, 1991.
51. Schober SE, Comstock GW, Morris JS. Serologic precursors of cancer: Prediagnostic serum nutrients and colon cancer risk. *Am J Epidemiol* 126:1033–1041, 1987.
52. Nomura AMY, Stemmerman GN, Heilbrun LK, et al: Serum vitamin levels and the risk of cancer of specific sites in men of Japanese ancestry in Hawaii. *Cancer Res* 45:2369–2372, 1985.
53. Wald NJ, Thompson SG, Densem JW, et al: Serum B-carotene and subsequent risk of cancer results from the BUPA study. *Br J Cancer* 57:428–433, 1988.
54. Kune S, Kune GG, Watson LF: Case-control study of dietary etiological factors: The Melbourne Colorectal Cancer Study, *Nutr Cancer* 9:21–42, 1987.
55. Heilbrun LK, Nomura A, Hankin JH, et al: Diet and colorectal cancer with special reference to fiber intake. *Int J Cancer* 44:1–6, 1989.
56. La Vecchia C, Negri E, Decarlia, et al: A case-control study of diet and colorectal cancer in Northern Italy. *Int J Cancer* 41:492–498, 1988.
57. Chen LH, Boissonneault GA, Glauert HP: Vitamin C, vitamin E and cancer. *Anticancer Res* 8:739–748, 1988.
58. Birt DF: Update on the effects of vitamins A, C, and E and selenium on carcinogenesis. *Proc Soc Exp Biol Med* 183:311–320, 1986.
59. Wald NJ, Thompson SG, Densem JW, et al: Serum vitamin E and subsequent risk of cancer. *Br J Cancer* 56:69–72, 1987.
60. Krekt PK, Aroman A, Mantela J, et al: Vitamin E and cancer prevention. *Am J Clin Nutr* 1:2835–2865, 1991.
61. Sitrin M, Halline A, Brasitus T: Effect of dietary calcium and vitamin D on colonocyte proliferation and dimethylhydrazine-induced colon cancer in rats. *Gastroenterology* 98:A311, 1990.
62. Pence BC, Buddingh F: Inhibition of dietary fat-promoted colon carcinogenesis in rats by supplemental calcium or vitamin D_3. *Carcinogenesis* 9:187, 1988.
63. Appleton GVN, Davies PW, Bristol JB, et al: Inhibition of intestinal carcinogenesis by dietary supplementation with calcium. *Br J Surg* 74:523, 1987.
64. Skyrpec DJ, Bursey RG: Effect of dietary calcium on azoxymethane-induced intestinal carcinogenesis in male F344 rats fed high fat diets. *FASEB J* 3:A469, 1989.
65. Wargovich MJ, Allnutt D, Palmer C, et al: Inhibition of the promotional phase of azoxymethane-induced colon carcinogenesis in the F344 rat by calcium lactate: Effect of simulating 2 human nutrient density levels. *Cancer Lett* 53:17, 1990.
66. Reshef R, Rozen P, Fireman Z, et al: Effect of a calcium-enriched diet on the colonic epithelial hyperproliferation induced by *N*-methyl-*N'*-nitro-nitrosoguanidine in rats on a low calcium and fat diet. *Cancer Res* 50:1764, 1990.
67. Karkara M, Patrick PC, Glauert HP: Effect of dietary calcium and vitamin D on colon tumors induced by 1,2-dimethylhydrazine in Fischer 344 rats. *FASEB J* 3:472, 1989.
68. Kaup SM, Behling AR, Choquette LL, et al: Colon tumor development in DMH-initiated rats fed varying levels of calcium and butterfat, *FAESB J* 3:A469, 1989.
69. Rozen P, Fireman Z, Fine N, et al: Oral calcium suppresses increased rectal epithelial proliferation of persons at risk of colorectal cancer. *Gut* 30:650, 1989.
70. Lynch PM, Wargovich MJ, Howard L: Calcium modulation of colonic mucosal proliferation in high risk subjects: A randomized prospective crossover study. *Gastroenterology* 100: A382, 1991.
71. Lipkin M, Friedman E, Winawar S, et al: Colonic epithelial cell proliferation in responders and nonresponders to supplemental dietary calcium. *Cancer Research* 49:248, 1989.
72. Gregoire RC, Stern HS, Yeung KS, et al: Effect of calcium supplementation on mucosal cell proliferation in high risk patients for colon cancer. *Gut* 30:376, 1989.
73. Cats A, De Vries EGE, Welberg JWM, et al: Increase of epithelial cell proliferation in the sigmoid during dietary calcium supplementation. *Gastroenterology* 100:A353, 1991.
74. Garland C, Shekelle R, Barrett-Connor E, et al: Dietary vitamin D and calcium and risk of colorectal cancer: A 19-year prospective study in men. *Lancet* 2:307–309, 1985.
75. Combs GF, Clark LC: Can dietary selenium modify cancer risk? *Nutr Rev* 43:325–331, 1985.
76. Nelson RL: Dietary minerals and colon carcinogenesis (review). *Anticancer Res* 7:259–270, 1987.

77. Jacobs MM, Jansson B, Griffin AC: Inhibitory effects of selenium on 1,2 dimethylhydrazine and methylazoxymethanol acetate induction of colon tumors. *Cancer Lett* 2:133–138, 1977.
78. Soullier BK, Wilson PS, Nigro NO: Effect of selenium on azoxymethane induced intestinal cancer in rats fed high fat diet. *Cancer Lett* 12:343–348, 1981.
79. Hodzilon D, Graeva D: Effect of combined tigason and selenium treatment on colon carcinogenesis. *J Cancer Res Clin Oncol* 112:285–286, 1986.
80. Reddy BS, Sugie S, Maruyama H, et al: Chemoprevention of colon carcinogenesis of dietary organoselenium, benzylselenocyanate in Fischer 344 rats. *Cancer Res* 47:5901–5904, 1987.
81. Reddy BS, Tanaka T, El-Bayoumy K: Inhibitory effect of dietary *p*-methoxybenzeneselenol in azoxymethane induced colon and kidney carcinogenesis in female F344 rats. *J Natl Cancer Inst* 74:1325–1328, 1985.
82. Reddy BS, Tanaka T: Interactions of selenium deficiency, vitamin E, polyunsaturated fat, and saturated fat on azoxymethane-induced colon carcinogenesis in male F344 rats. *J Natl Cancer Inst* 76:1157–1162, 1986.
83. Medina D: Mechanisms of selenium inhibitors of tumorigenesis: *J Am Coll Toxicol* 5:21–27, 1986.
84. Peleg I, Morris S, Haines CG: Is serum selenium a risk factor for cancer? *Med Oncol Tumor Pharmacol* 2:157–163, 1985.
85. Greene FL, Lamb LS, Barwich M, et al: Effect of dietary copper on colonic tumor production and ascorbic integrity in the rat. *J Surg Res* 42:503–512, 1987.
86. Lashner BA, Heidenreich PA, Su GL, et al: The effect of folate supplementation on the incidence of dysplasia and cancer in chronic ulcerative colitis: A case-control study. *Gastroenterology* 97:255–259, 1989.
87. Yamamoto R: Effect of vitamin B-12 deficiency in colon carcinogenesis. *Proc Soc Exp Biol Med* 163:350–353, 1980.
88. Tanaka T, Tokuro S, Naoki Y, et al: Inhibitory effect of magnesium hydroxide on methylazoxymethane acetate-induced large bowel carcinogenesis in male F344 rats. *Carcinogenesis* 10:613–616, 1989.

CHAPTER 7

Inheritance—General Issues

Randall W. Burt

HIGHLIGHTS

Inheritance is an important factor in the etiology of colonic adenomatous polyps and colorectal cancer. There are rare inherited syndromes as well as frequent familial clustering of common cases. The rare syndromes include familial adenomatous polyposis coli (FAP) and hereditary nonpolyposis colorectal cancer (HNPCC). The latter includes site-specific colorectal cancer and cancer family syndrome. Persons with these syndromes exhibit an extremely high risk of colorectal cancer. The syndromes are described in detail in Chaps. 8 and 9. All together, the rare inherited syndromes account for a small percentage of colonic cancer and adenoma cases, probably less than 5 percent.

The remainder of colonic neoplasms have been referred to as sporadic. It is now well known, however, that increased familial risk is commonly observed among these so-called sporadic cases. First-degree relatives of persons with colonic cancer, for example, exhibit a two- to threefold increased risk of this malignancy. Relatives of persons with adenomas have a similar risk of large bowel cancer. Colonoscopy studies also have shown that first-degree relatives of patients with colonic cancer have a twofold risk of adenomatous polyps. Risk of colonic cancer in families is increased even further if multiple relatives are diagnosed with colonic cancer, if the index case has colonic cancer diagnosed at an age below 55 years, or if the index case exhibits multiple neoplastic lesions.

Kindred studies have shown that the increased familial risk is likely due to inherited susceptibility of a mild to moderate degree. This type of inherited susceptibility appears to be present in a large proportion and possibly the majority of cases of colorectal cancer and adenomatous polyps. Present evidence would suggest that inherited factors determine individual susceptibility to colonic cancer while environmental factors modulate this susceptibility.

CONTROVERSIES

The fundamental question regarding inheritance of colonic neoplasms is whether the commonly observed increased familial risk indeed comes from inherited susceptibility. The weight of evidence favors this hypothesis. The evidence includes consistently observed increased risk in first-degree relatives, risk in more distant relatives, and segregation patterns in families that indicate partially penetrant dominant inheritance. It should be pointed out, however, that environmental factors common to family members could mimic genetic patterns in some cases. Ultimately, genetic marker studies will be required to prove inheritance. It is quite possible that both inherited and environmental factors contribute to the familial clustering and expression of colonic neoplasms. Regardless of the cause, however, familial risk of colonic neoplasms is well established and is important to issues such as screening.

Another controversy is the prevalence of HNPCC. Estimates vary from less than 1 percent to more than 5 or 6 percent. The prevalence in various studies usually reflects the definition used. Application of a very strict definition results in a lower prevalence figure, while a broader definition gives a higher figure. Only identification of the underlying mutant gene or genes will resolve the issue.

The greater issue reflected in both of these controversies is how common inherited susceptibility to colonic neoplasms is and how many different genes and alleles of these genes give rise to susceptibility.

FUTURE DIRECTIONS

Continued assessment of familial risk should be undertaken in family and population studies to determine the risk of neoplasm in relatives more distant than first degree. Other characteristics of the colonic neoplasms, including age of diagnosis, colonic location, multiplicity of lesions, and histology require further study as to their association with familial risk.

The most important research pertinent to inherited susceptibility of colorectal cancers and adenomas is to identify the pertinent genes and mutations within those genes. Characterization of the genes and their mechanisms of action will follow. Clinically accurate markers of risk will emerge and basic and clinical preventive strategies will be suggested. Inherited risk can then be specified genetically and the interaction of inherited susceptibility and environmental factors can be examined.

OVERVIEW OF INHERITANCE

Inheritance plays a much more important role in the pathogenesis of colorectal cancer and adenomatous polyps than previously believed. Present evidence indicates that inherited susceptibility is a factor in a large proportion and possibly the majority of colorectal cancers. The most current hypothesis is that environmental factors, particularly dietary, interact with inherited susceptibility to determine which persons develop small adenomas, larger adenomas, and finally colonic cancer. If inherited susceptibility factors are severe, very little if any adverse environmental exposure is needed. If susceptibility factors are less severe, more environmental exposure is necessary for colonic neoplasms to occur. Finally, in the case of no inherited susceptibility, environmental exposure must be substantial to initiate the growth of adenomas and stimulate their progression to colorectal cancer.

Inherited susceptibility can be divided into the well-characterized syndromes of colonic adenomas and colorectal cancer and the remainder of cases that have traditionally been referred to as "sporadic." The well-characterized inherited syndromes are further divided into those diseases that exhibit intestinal polyposis and those in which only a few polyps are present, referred to as "nonpolyposis" syndromes.

Inherited Polyposis Syndromes

The inherited polyposis syndromes include familial adenomatous polyposis (FAP) and Gardner syndrome (GS) and the hamartomatous polyposis conditions of Peutz-Jeghers disease and familial juvenile polyposis.[1] Each of these diseases is inherited in an autosomal dominant fashion with essentially complete penetrance. Persons with FAP or GS exhibit hundreds to thousands of colonic adenomatous polyps and the inevitable early-age development of colorectal cancer if the colon is not removed. Both conditions are also now known to arise from mutations in the adenomatous polyposis coli (APC) gene that resides on the long arm of chromosome 5.[2]

The hamartomatous polyposis conditions traditionally have been thought to be benign diseases because neither Peutz-Jeghers polyps nor juvenile polyps are histologically neoplastic. Recent surveys, however, have revealed that both disorders exhibit significant risk of gastrointestinal cancer.[3–5] Frequent extraintestinal malignancies also develop in individuals with Peutz-Jeghers syndrome. There are several additional extremely rare polyposis conditions that exhibit colonic cancer risk. Each of the inherited polyposis diseases is reviewed in detail in Chap. 9.

Together, FAP and GS have an occurrence of approximately 1 in 10,000 births. Peutz-Jeghers disease and familial juvenile polyposis are probably about one-tenth as common. Altogether, the polyposis conditions account for less than 1 percent of cases of colonic cancer (Table 7-1). They are nonetheless very important because of the severe cancer risk present, especially in the adenomatous polyposis diseases. Furthermore, our understanding of these diseases has led to very successful cancer prevention in affected families. Finally, these rare diseases have provided important clues to understanding the inherited susceptibility and pathogenesis of the more common forms of colonic cancer.

Hereditary Nonpolyposis Colorectal Cancer

The inherited colonic cancer syndromes that do not exhibit intestinal polyposis are referred to as heredi-

Table 7-1
Source of Colonic Cancer by Inheritance Category

Category	*Percent of cases*
Familial polyposis and Gardner's syndromes	<1
Peutz-Jeghers and juvenile polyposis syndromes	<<1
Hereditary nonpolyposis colorectal cancer	1–5
Sporadic colorectal cancer	>95
with first-degree relatives with colonic cancer	10–20
with possible inherited predisposition	50–100
with no inherited predisposition	0–50

tary nonpolyposis colorectal cancer (HNPCC). These include "site-specific colorectal cancer," also called Lynch syndrome I, and cancer family syndrome, also referred to as Lynch syndrome II.[6,7] In both of these syndromes, colonic cancer is inherited in an autosomal dominant pattern with high penetrance and young age of onset. Synchronous colorectal cancers are frequently observed and the colonic distribution of cancer is shifted proximally. Cancer family syndrome differs from site-specific colorectal cancer in that extracolonic malignancies also occur. Classically these have included uterine and ovarian cancers, but breast, gastric, pancreatic, and other cancers also have been described in some families.

Colonic adenomas frequently occur in persons affected with HNPCC, but there are usually only a few polyps. These polyps are endoscopically and histologically indistinguishable from adenomas that occur in the general population. Studies of polyp histology and clinical characteristics, however, suggest that adenomas in HNPCC on average exhibit more severe pathologic features than do adenomatous polyps in the general population.[8,9] These features include larger size and more villous histology, which may account for the greater cancer risk observed in this condition. It is hoped that molecular genetic markers will soon be available to distinguish persons with HNPCC from those with more common colonic neoplasms. One such marker has recently been found. Two large HNPCC families showed linkage to an area on the short arm of chromosome 2.[10] Other HNPCC families did not. Work is continuing to find the gene at this site and determine what proportion of HNPCC families arise from mutations of this gene. It may be that HNPCC represents several diseases at the DNA level.

A purported variant of HNPCC has been referred to as "the flat adenoma syndrome."[11] Affected individuals exhibit a greater number of adenomas than are usually observed in HNPCC. There are often dozens or even scores of polyps. A number of families with this condition have now been reported in the medical literature. Genetic linkage studies have demonstrated that the disease arises from mutations of the APC gene.[12] This variant is thus more appropriately classified as an attenuated form of FAP. This condition will be further discussed later in this chapter.

Hereditary nonpolyposis colorectal cancer accounts for between 1 and 5 percent of cases of colonic cancer[13] (Table 7-1). The exact prevalence of this disease has been difficult to determine because of definition and ascertainment problems. The prevalence is lower under strict definitions and when population-based estimates are used.[14] Ultimately genetic markers will provide exact frequencies, because the phenotype is often variable and difficult to distinguish from common colonic polyps and cancers. The HNPCC syndromes are reviewed in detail in Chap. 8.

Sporadic Colonic Neoplasms

The remaining 95 percent or more of colonic adenoma and cancer cases have been referred to as "sporadic" (Table 7-1). This term may be misleading, however, as colonic neoplasms are observed in families much more often than expected by chance. In fact, first-degree relatives (parents, siblings, children) of persons with colonic cancer have a two- to threefold increased risk of colonic malignancy.[15] Authors of studies that have found this risk suggest that either incompletely penetrant mendelian genes or shared environmental factors account for it. Large family studies have indicated that inherited suseptibility is the most likely explanation for the increased risk. This chapter reviews familial risk of colonic neoplasms and the family studies suggesting that this risk is inherited. Applicable molecular genetic investigations are also summarized. Finally, the risk data that apply to screening recommendations are reviewed.

RELATIONSHIP OF "SPORADIC" CANCER AND ADENOMAS TO INHERITANCE

Except for the rare inherited syndromes, colonic neoplasms traditionally have been thought to be "sporadic" and to arise because of exposure to certain environmental factors. Diets high in fat and/or low in fiber have been associated with increased risk of colonic cancer in both population and case control studies. Preventive factors have also been identified, including fresh fruits and vegetables, calcium, and vitamins A and C. Migrational studies have demonstrated that persons moving from areas of low to high colonic cancer risk acquire the higher risk within the same generation and possibly within 10 years. These observations leave little doubt as to the importance of environmental factors in the pathogenesis of colorectal cancer.

Numerous investigations, however, have also shown an excess familial occurrence of colonic neoplasms among the so-called sporadic cases. Large family studies would suggest that this familial occurrence results from inherited susceptibility. This section first reviews studies that have determined the risk of colorectal neoplasms in relatives of persons with colonic cancer or adenomas. Population, family, and pertinent molecular genetic studies are then summarized.

Mortality Studies of Colorectal Cancer

The first family risk studies examined the mortality from colorectal cancer in relatives of persons with that malignancy. Woolf,[16] in Utah, investigated the mortality from colonic cancer in all parents and siblings of persons who had died of colon cancer in that state between 1931 and 1951. Any cases of FAP were excluded. A total of 763 relatives of 242 colorectal cancer patients were identified. Review of death certificates revealed 26 deaths from colonic cancer in the relatives. This compared to 8 deaths from colorectal cancer in 763 controls matched for age, gender, and county of birth—a 3.2-fold excess. The number of deaths from other cancers was almost identical in the relative and control groups, 81 compared to 83, indicating no excess overall cancer risk in relatives.

Macklin,[17] in Ohio, compared the number of deaths from colorectal cancer in first- and second-degree relatives of colonic cancer patients to the number expected for that state. A statewide examination of death certificates was undertaken. There were 31 deaths from colorectal cancer in 392 relatives while only 9.7 were expected, also a 3.2-fold excess. A similar excess was observed in fathers, mothers, sisters, and brothers. Second-degree relatives also exhibited an excess of colonic cancer deaths, which was seen in grandfathers, grandmothers, uncles, and aunts. Gastric cancer deaths were not found in excess in colonic cancer relatives. Familial adenomatous polyposis coli was excluded and patterns of single gene inheritance were not observed in the families studied.

Lovett,[18] in London, examined death certificates of parents and siblings of colorectal cancer patients admitted to the St. Marks Hospital over a 4-year period. There were 41 deaths from colorectal cancer in 352 relatives compared to an expected number of 11.7, a 3.5-fold excess. An equivalent excess was found in fathers, mothers, sisters, and brothers. The colonic cancer risk in relatives was further increased if the index case had multiple adenomas in addition to colonic cancer, previous colonic cancer, or a diagnosis of colonic cancer before the age of 40 years. There was no evidence of single gene inheritance in the families examined.

Lovett attempted to determine if an excess number of colorectal cancer cases were also present in spouses of those with colonic cancer. However, the number of cases available was too small for conclusions. A subsequent Swedish study examined this question and failed to show any excess cases in spouses.[19] Twelve cases of colonic cancer were observed in 1094 spouses of persons with colonic cancer. There were 13.4 expected. These results would suggest that environmental factors, at least those encountered in the adult years, are unlikely to account for the excess of colonic cancer cases in relatives.

Incidence Studies of Colorectal Cancer and Adenomas

A number of investigations subsequent to the mortality studies have examined the incident cases of colorectal cancer in relatives of persons with this malignancy. These studies are summarized in Table 7-2. Three of the studies have also investigated colorectal cancer in relatives of persons with adenomatous polyps. In each study, the frequency of a positive family history for persons with colonic neoplasm has been compared to the frequency of positive family history for controls. A positive family history has been defined as one or more first-degree relatives affected with colorectal cancer. This type of study is weakened by differences in family size and age of index cases. Some of the differences between studies are likely due to these factors. Despite these weaknesses, the investigations have consistently demonstrated that cases have a positive family history two to three times more often than controls. The results appeared to be true whether the index case had a colorectal cancer or an adenomatous polyp. These results are very consistent with the mortality studies.

Additional incidence studies have examined colorectal cancer in parents, so as to minimize the problems with family size and age. A study from Italy found a greater than twofold risk of colorectal cancer in parents (as well as siblings) compared to controls, while the risk of other cancers was no different.[20] A Danish study found the risk ratio of colorectal cancer in mothers and fathers compared to controls to be 1.62 and 1.87 respectively.[21] The National Polyp Study in the United States examined the occurrence of colonic cancer in parents of persons with adenomatous polyps and compared its findings to the expected occurrence based on the National Cancer Institute's Surveillance, Epidemiology, and End Results Program (SEER) data.[22] There was a 1.8-fold increased risk of colonic cancer in parents. The risk in parents was then stratified by age. If the index adenoma case was less than 60 years of age, the risk for colorectal cancer in parents was 2.7 times greater than expected. For index cases 60 to 69 years of age, the risk in parents was 1.8-

Table 7-2
Frequency of Positive Family History[a]

Study location	Frequency of positive family history in controls, %	Frequency of positive family history when index case has colonic cancer		Frequency of positive family history when index case has an adenomatous polyp		Reference
		Frequency, %	Risk compared to controls	Frequency, %	Risk compared to controls	
Scotland	2.0	16	8.0			40
France	3.5	19	5.3	15	4.2	41
Italy	5.4	21	3.9	18	3.4	42
Australia	10.0	18	1.8			43
Italy	5.1	11	2.4	14	3.2	44
Australia	7.5	16	2.2			45
United Kingdom	5.0	23	4.6			46

[a]Positive family history defined as one or more relatives with colonic cancer.
SOURCE: Adapted from Ref. 47, with permission.

fold increased; and for cases 70 years of age and older, the risk in parents was 1.4. Only the last category was not statistically significant. Each of these studies in parents again confirms the excess familial risk of colorectal cancer.

Prevalence of Adenomatous Polyps in Relatives

A number of endoscopic studies have assessed the prevalence of adenomatous polyps in first-degree relatives of colonic cancer patients.[23–32] This prevalence has varied from 8 to 63 percent. Only three of the studies, however, had control groups. In each of these three, the prevalence of adenomas in relatives was significantly greater than in controls. These studies further showed that the age-specific prevalence of adenomas was significantly greater in relatives than in controls and that relatives of those with only adenomas also had an increased risk of adenomas. The results of these endoscopic studies are reviewed in greater detail in Chap. 33, where screening of relatives is discussed.

Stratification of Familial Risk

Familial risk varies from mild to severe, with the severe extreme including FAP and HNPCC. Except for HNPCC and FAP, however, there are no obvious syndromes of adenomas and cancer (Table 7-1). Nonetheless, a number of characteristics of common colonic neoplasms appear to predict greater familial risk (Table 7-3). They include age at diagnosis, colonic location of adenomas and cancer, multiplicity of lesions, and number of relatives affected with colonic cancer or adenomas. These characteristics are presented in detail in Chap. 33 but will be summarized here.

Age at Diagnosis. Population studies have demonstrated that familial clustering of colonic cancer cases is common in all age groups. Referral center investigations additionally have suggested that the risk of colonic neoplasms may be even greater if the index case had a diagnosis of colorectal cancer at an age below 50 or 55 years.

Colonic Location of Neoplasms. The presence of proximal colonic tumors has been suspected as a predictor of familial risk because it is a feature of HNPCC. Population studies have demonstrated, however, that both proximal and distal colonic cancers predict familial risk, and to approximately the same degree. The only exception may be rectal cancer, which appears to be somewhat less familial than cancer of other colonic segments.

Multiplicity of Lesions. There are studies indicating that multiple adenomas predict increased familial risk, although this feature requires better definition.

Number of Affected Relatives. Finally, several studies that demonstrated increased risk of neoplasm in first-degree relatives of those with colorectal cancer found that the risk was further increased if two first-degree relatives had colonic cancer. Intermediate lev-

Table 7-3
Characteristics That Predict Increased Familial Risk of Colorectal Cancer

Characteristic	Strength as predictor of familial risk
Age at colonic cancer diagnosis	Good
Colonic location of tumor	Poor[a]
Multiplicity of lesions	Fair
Number of affected relatives	Good
Histology of neoplasm	Possibly

[a]Associated with hereditary nonpolyposis colorectal cancer but not with more common familial clustering.

els of risk were present if a first- and a second-degree relative were diagnosed with colonic cancer.

Thus, age of diagnosis, number of lesions, and number of affected relatives associate with colonic cancer risk in the setting of common colonic neoplasms. It is not known if these features are additive in predicting colonic cancer risk.

FAMILY AND GENETIC STUDIES

Authors of the mortality and to some extent the incidence studies were careful to exclude FAP. Families with obvious monogenetic inheritance of colonic cancer, as would be expected with HNPCC, were rarely found. Postulates to explain the excess familial cases of colonic cancer therefore included (1) partially penetrant mendelian genes, (2) multifactorial or polygenic inheritance, and (3) shared environmental factors. Genealogic data base, kindred, and molecular genetic studies have recently been undertaken to determine which of these mechanisms is causing the observed excess of familial cases.

Genealogic Data-Base Study

A genealogic data-base study examined the relatedness of individuals with colonic cancer in a large population. The data base consisted of genealogies from the Utah Genealogical Society (over 1.5 million entries) that are linked to the Utah Cancer Registry and the Utah Death Registry.[33] The relationship of each individual with a given cancer to all other individuals in the registry with that same cancer was determined.[33–35] This result was compared to the relatedness of a number of equally large age-, sex-, and county-of-birth-matched control groups. The method has the advantage of complete ascertainment and determination of all levels of relatedness (i.e., not just first-degree relatives).

The analysis found persons with colonic cancer to be significantly more related than persons in the control groups. Excess relatedness was observed at all levels of relationship examined, up to fifth degree. Similar comparisons were done for individuals with proximal and distal colorectal cancer considered separately.[34] Excess familial clustering was observed to approximately the same degree in both groups. This investigation further suggested that inherited susceptibility is important to the genesis of colonic cancer because it would be unlikely for environmental factors alone to affect cancer risk in very distant relations.

Kindred Studies

A kindred study was next undertaken to determine the exact mechanism of excess familial cases. The kindred examined was a large family which extended over seven generations and included approximately 10,000 members. Four branches of the kindred were studied. There were multiple cases of colonic cancer in the kindred but no apparent patterns of inheritance when cancer cases alone were considered.[36] Other features of HNPCC, such as proximal colonic cancers and early-age onset of tumors, were likewise absent. Flexible proctosigmoidoscopy was used to screen relatives and spouses for the presence of adenomatous polyps, because these lesions are the precursors of colonic cancer and are also more common than cancer. Adenomas were found significantly more often in relatives compared to spouse-controls [41 of 191 (21 percent) versus 12 of 132 (9 percent), $p<.005$]. Pedigree analysis that considered both adenomas and cancer showed that the familial excess of neoplasms most likely occurred from dominantly inherited susceptibility rather than recessive susceptibility or random occurrence.

Numerous additional kindreds were next systematically selected for study to determine if inheritance of susceptibility to adenomas and colonic cancer was common.[25] A total of 670 subjects (407 relatives and 263 spouses from 34 pedigrees) were examined, including the original large pedigree. Adenomas in first-degree relatives were significantly more prevalent than in controls. Analysis again found the pattern of occurrence of adenomas and cancer in the pedigrees to be consistent with partially penetrant autosomal dominant susceptibility. It also suggested that most of the adenomas clinically detected arose, at least in part, from inherited susceptibility (95 percent confidence limits, 53 to 100 percent). The computed gene frequency in the population examined was 19 percent (95 percent confidence limits, 14 to 28 percent). Gene penetrance was 63 percent by age 80. These findings suggested that most adenomatous polyps identified in the population studied arose from a common, partially penetrant susceptibility gene or genes.

Referral Center Studies

Another approach was taken in Australia, where detailed family histories were collected on all 525 cases of colonic cancer from a single referral practice.[14,37] Of the total, 2 cases were found to arise from HNPCC families; 16 cases had two first-degree relatives with colonic cancer; 69 had one affected first-degree relative, and 438 had no relatives with colonic cancer. Segregation analysis of this data base suggested that a rare gene (gene frequency 0.004) was the most likely explanation for the familial clustering of cases. The gene gave a lifetime risk of 0.5 for developing colonic cancer.

Thus analysis of colonic cancer cases alone suggested a rare gene with high penetrance to account for familial cases of colonic cancer. This finding is somewhat at variance with the results from the kindred studies where adenomas were analyzed. Some of the difference might be because colonic cancers are much less common than adenomas, and the analysis would reflect this. The different results nonetheless define an important question: Does inherited susceptibility for colonic cancer cause more adenomas to form or does it cause the adenoma-to-cancer sequence to progress more rapidly? A combination or the presence of both models is also possible. Further segregation and gene-marker studies will be required to resolve this issue.

Attenuated Adenomatous Polyposis Coli

A phenotype of inherited colonic cancer and multiple adenomatous polyps in a large kindred was recently found linked to the gene for adenomatous polyposis coli (APC).[12] Affected persons in this family did not have FAP. Instead, they exhibited a variable number of adenomatous polyps (usually less than the 100 polyps observed in fully developed APC) and a high risk of colorectal cancer. Many persons with the mutant gene exhibited only one or a few adenomas. The findings in this family demonstrated that more subtle forms of inherited adenomas and colonic cancer could arise from mutations of the APC gene. Several similar families subsequently have been studied and each has shown linkage to the APC gene. These families are referred to as having attenuated adenomatous polyposis coli (AAPC).

Genetics

Specific genetic markers or mutant genes must be identified to prove that common familial clustering of colonic neoplasms arises from inherited susceptibility. Except for FAP and the few families with AAPC, such mutant genes are yet to be identified. A current hypothesis is that "less severe" mutations of the APC gene result in inherited susceptibility to common adenomas and colon cancer.[25]

This premise seems plausible in view of the nature of mutations that give rise to FAP.[2] The APC gene is a large gene with approximately 8500 base pairs. A number of different mutations that cause the syndrome of FAP have been found in the gene. Although the large majority of mutations identified are unique, they are similar in that almost all appear to be gene-inactivating; that is, they give rise to incomplete or absent protein products. They are also either point mutations or small deletions. The point mutations observed inevitably change a DNA triplet from one coding for an amino acid to one coding for a "stop." A stop codon is a triplet that signals termination of the translation of mRNA to protein. An accidental stop thus causes an incomplete protein product. The small deletion mutations found in the APC gene result in a "frame shift" in the reading of DNA and eventually mRNA triplets. In the case of frame shifts, an unexpected stop codon inevitably occurs from the "nonsense" triplet codes that occur downstream from the deletion. An incomplete protein again results.

On a statistical basis, many more mutations should occur that result in simple amino acid changes than those that result in incomplete proteins. Nonetheless, such mutations are not observed in FAP. They apparently are not sufficient to cause the syndrome. Could the inheritance of such less severe mutations of the APC gene give rise to common adenomas and cancer? Such inheritance has not yet been identified. Germline mutations of the APC gene that result in amino acid changes, however, have been found in 13 percent of both normal persons and persons with colonic adenomas and cancer.[38]

Another hypothesis is that inherited mutations of genes other than the APC gene could give rise to susceptibility to colonic neoplasm. There are many proteins involved in cell growth control which could conceivably be involved in cancer predisposition. Furthermore, immune system determinants, bile acid regulation, and many other physiologic systems might relate to cancer susceptibility when they are pathologically altered. A system of recent interest is the metabolic activation of aromatic amine colonic carcinogens. Rapid aromatic amine acetylation ("rapid acetylation") and rapid *N*-oxidation have both been associated with colonic cancer in some studies.[39] A genetically determined higher concentration of colonic carcinogens might well explain an excess of colonic neoplasms in some families. Each of these hypotheses awaits further testing.

Current Hypothesis

The population, family, and genetic studies reviewed demonstrate that familial factors play an important role in the pathogenesis of a significant proportion and possibly the majority of cases of colorectal adenomas and cancer. Current evidence suggests that these familial factors represent inherited susceptibility that varies from mild to severe. The exact nature of this susceptibility is unclear except in the relatively rare syndromes of FAP and HNPCC. Ultimately, genetic markers will be required to confirm and clarify inherited susceptibility and to determine if it arises from a single or multiple genes and/or different mutations within those genes.

Environmental factors, particularly dietary, likely modulate susceptibility and may account for some of the familial cases. The overall model most consistent with current observations is that inheritance defines individual susceptibility to colonic neoplasms while environmental factors modulate this susceptibility to determine which persons develop adenomas and finally colonic cancer.

REFERENCES

1. Haggitt RC, Reid BJ: Hereditary gastrointestinal polyposis syndromes. *Am J Surg Pathol* 10:871–887, 1986.
2. Burt RW, Groden J: The genetic and molecular diagnosis of adenomatous polyposis coli. *Gastroenterology* 104:1211–1214, 1993.
3. Giardiello FM, Welsh SB, Hamilton SR, et al: Increased risk of cancer in the Peutz-Jeghers syndrome. *N Engl J Med* 316:1511–1514, 1987.
4. Foley R, McGarrity TJ, Abt A: Peutz-Jeghers syndrome: A clinicopathologic survey of the "Harrisburg family" with a 49-year follow-up. *Gastroenterology* 95:1535–1540, 1988.
5. Jarvinen H, Franssila KO: Familial juvenile polyposis coli; increased risk of colorectal cancer. *Gut* 25:792–800, 1984.
6. Lynch HT, Watson P, Kriegler M, et al: Differential diagnosis of hereditary nonpolyposis colorectal cancer (Lynch syndrome I and Lynch syndrome II). *Dis Colon Rectum* 31:372–377, 1988.
7. Lynch HT, Smyrk TC, Watson P, et al: Genetics, natural history, tumor spectrum, and pathology of hereditary nonpolyposis colorectal cancer: An updated review. *Gastroenterology* 104:1535–1549, 1993.
8. Jass JR, Stewart SM: Evolution of hereditary non-polyposis colorectal cancer. *Gut* 33:783–786, 1992.
9. Mecklin J-P, Jarvinen HJ: Clinical features of colorectal carcinoma in cancer family syndrome. *Dis Colon Rectum* 23: 160–164, 1986.
10. Paltomaki P, Galtonen LA, Sistonen P, et al: Genetic mapping of a locus predisposing to human colorectal cancer. *Science* 260:810–812, 1993.
11. Lynch HT, Smyrk T, Lanspa SJ, et al: Flat adenomas in a colon cancer-prone kindred. *J Natl Cancer Inst* 80:278–282, 1988.
12. Leppert M, Burt RW, Hughes JP, et al: Genetic analysis of an inherited predisposition to colon cancer in a family with a variable number of adenomatous Polyps. *N Engl J Med* 322:904–908, 1990.
13. Mecklin J-P: Frequency of hereditary colorectal carcinoma. *Gastroenterology* 93:1021–1025, 1987.
14. St John DJB, Bishop DT, Crockford GP: HNPCC or common colorectal cancer? Criteria for diagnosis. *Gastroenterology* 102:A402, 1992.
15. Burt RW, Bishop DT, Lynch HT, et al: Risk and surveillance of individuals with heritable factors for colorectal cancer. *Bull WHO* 68:655, 1993.
16. Woolf CM: A genetic study of carcinoma of the large intestine. *Am J Hum Genet* 10:42–47, 1958.
17. Macklin MT: Inheritance of cancer of the stomach and large intestine in man. *J Natl Cancer Inst* 24L:551–557, 1960.
18. Lovett E: Family studies in cancer of the colon and rectum. *Br J Surg* 63:13–189, 1976.
19. Jensen OM, Sigtryggsson P, Nguyen-Dinh X, et al: Large-bowel cancer in married couples in Sweden: A follow-up study. *Lancet* 2:1161–1163, 1980.
20. Ponz de Leon M, Sassatelli R, Sacchetti C, et al: Familial aggregation of tumors in the three-year experience of a population-based colorectal cancer registry. *Cancer Res* 49:4344–4348, 1989.
21. Sondergaard JO, Bulow S, Lynge E: Cancer incidence among parents of patients with colorectal cancer. *Int J Cancer* 47:202–206, 1991.
22. Winawer SJ, Sauber AG, Gerdes H, et al: Genetic epidemiology of colorectal cancer: Relationship of familial colorectal cancer risk to adenoma proband age and adenoma characteristics. *Gastroenterology* 102:A409, 1992.
23. Gryska PV, Cohen AM: Screening asymptomatic patients at high risk for colon cancer with full colonoscopy. *Dis Colon Rectum* 30:18–20, 1987.
24. Rozen P, Fireman E, Fine N, et al: Oral calcium suppresses increased rectal epithelial proliferation of persons at risk of colorectal cancer. *Gut* 30:650–655, 1989.
25. Cannon-Albright LA, Skolnick MH, Bishop DT, et al: Common inheritance of susceptibility to colonic adenomatous polyps and associated colorectal cancers. *N Engl J Med* 319:533–537, 1988.
26. Grossman S, Milos ML: Colonoscopic screening of persons with suspected risk factors for colon cancer: I. Family history. *Gastroenterology* 39:395–400, 1988.
27. McConnell JC, Nizin JS, Slade MS: Colonoscopy in patients with a primary family history of colon cancer. *Dis Colon Rectum* 33:105–107, 1990.
28. Orrom WJ, Brezezinski WS, Wiens EW: Heredity and colorectal cancer: A prospective, community-based endoscopic study. *Dis Colon Rectum* 33:722, 1990.
29. Baker JW, Gathright JB, Timmicke AE, et al: Colonoscopic screening of asymptomatic patients with a family history of colon cancer. *Dis Colon Rectum* 33:926–930, 1990.
30. Herrera L, Hanna S, Petrelli N, et al: Screening endoscopy in patients with family history positive (FH+) for colorectal neoplasia (CRN) (abstract). *Gastrointest Endosc* 36:211, 1990.
31. Sauar J, Hausken T, Hoff G, et al: Colonoscopic screening examination of relatives of patients with colorectal cancer: I. A comparison with an endoscopically screened normal population. *Scand J Gastroenterol* 27:661–666, 1992.
32. Guillem JG, Forde KA, Treat MR, et al: Colonoscopic screening for neoplasms in asymptomatic first-degree relatives of colon cancer patients. *Dis Colon Rectum* 35:523–529, 1992.
33. Skolnick M: Banbury Report 4: Cancer incidence in defined populations. Cold Spring Harbor, NY, Cold Spring Harbor Laboratory, 1980, pp 285–297.
34. Bishop DT, Skolnick MH: Genetic epidemiology of cancer in Utah genealogies: A prelude to the molecular genetics of common cancers. *J Cell Physiol* (suppl) 3:63–77, 1984.
35. Cannon L, Bishop DT, Skolnick M, et al: Genetic epidemiology of prostate cancer in the Utah Mormon genealogy. *Cancer Surveys* 1:47–69, 1982.
36. Burt RW, Bishop DT, Cannon LA, et al: Dominant inheritance of adenomatous colonic polyps and colorectal cancer. *N Engl J Med* 12:1540–1544, 1985.
37. Bishop DT, St John DJB, Hughes ESR, et al: Genetic susceptibility to common colorectal cancer: How common is it? *Gastroenterology* 102:A346, 1992.
38. Powell SM, Zilz N, Beazer-Barclay Y, et al: APC mutations occur early during colorectal tumorigenesis. *Nature* 359:235–237, 1992.
39. Lang NP, Chu DZJ, Hunter CF, et al: Role of aromatic amine acetyltransferase in human colorectal cancer. *Arch Surg* 121:1259–1261, 1986.
40. Duncan JL, Kyle J: Family incidence of carcinoma of the colon and rectum in northeast Scotland. *Gut* 23:169–171, 1982.
41. Maire P, Morichau-Beauchant M, Drucker J, et al: Familiar prevalence of colorectal cancer: A 3 year case-control study. *Gastroenterol Clin Biol* 8:22–27, 1984.
42. Ponz de Leon M, Antonioli A, Ascari A, et al: Incidence and familial occurrence of colorectal cancer and polyps in a health-care district of northern Italy. *Cancer* 60:2848–2859, 1987.
43. Kune GA, Kune S, Watson LF: The Melbourne colorectal cancer study: Characterization of patients with a family his-

tory of colorectal cancer. *Dis Colon Rectum* 30:600–606, 1987.
44. Bonelli L, Martines H, Conio M, et al: Family history of colorectal cancer as a risk factor for benign and malignant tumours of the large bowel: A case-control study. *Int J Cancer* 41:513–517, 1988.
45. St John DJB, McDermott FT, Datrivessis H, et al: Cancer risk for relatives of patients with sporadic colorectal cancer. Abstract presented at the 2d International Conference on Gastrointestinal Cancer, Jerusalem, Israel, 1989.
46. Stephenson BM, Finan PJ, Gascoyne J, et al: Frequency of familial colorectal cancer. *Br J Surg* 78:1162–1166, 1991.
47. Bishop DT, Thomas HJW: The genetics of colorectal cancer. *Cancer Surveys* 9:585–604, 1990.

CHAPTER 8

Inheritance—Lynch Syndromes I and II

Henry T. Lynch
Jane F. Lynch

HIGHLIGHTS

The Lynch syndromes account for 4 to 6 percent of the total colorectal cancer (CRC) burden. Physicians need to be better informed about their natural history since, in the absence of premonitory physical stigmata and/or biomarkers, the family history is the primary basis for their diagnosis. Paramedical personnel, particularly the registered nurse, can compile the family history data, thereby allowing the physician to devote his or her time more efficiently to the interpretation of the pedigree.

Because of the early age of cancer onset and proximal predilection, surveillance must include colonoscopy, which we initiate at age 25, repeating it every other year through age 35 and annually thereafter. Endometrial aspiration biopsy should be initiated at age 25 and performed annually. Because of the excess of synchronous and metachronous CRC in Lynch syndrome families, prophylactic surgery for CRC should be no less than a subtotal colectomy. And if the patient is a woman in a Lynch syndrome II family, prophylactic total abdominal hysterectomy and bilateral salpingo-oophorectomy should be considered.

CONTROVERSIES

There are no well-developed guidelines for colonoscopic surveillance and surgical management. For example, some physicians believe that repeating colonoscopy every 3 years is sufficient, while others believe that this should be performed every 1 to 2 years.

Insurance companies frequently fail to defray the costs of screening and often give as their reason the opinion that a high genetic risk for cancer is not a "disease."

Physicians are trained to treat a disease once it exists but, unfortunately, they rarely probe the family history and take a hands-on view for encouraging high-risk relatives to participate in surveillance in the interest of prevention. They often believe that this would be a form of solicitation. But physicians may face malpractice litigation for failure to obtain and/or act upon the cancer family history.

FUTURE DIRECTIONS

The International Collaborative Group on Hereditary Nonpolyposis Colorectal Cancer (ICG-HNPCC) has an International Information Service at Creighton University (Henry T. Lynch, M.D., professor and chairman, Department of Preventive Medicine, 2500 California Plaza, Omaha, Nebraska 68178; phone: 402-280-2942; fax: 402-280-1734), which is devoted to improving patient and physician education about the Lynch syndromes, in addition to advancing knowledge about their etiology, heterogeneity, pathogenesis, surveillance, and management. In addition, this group is concerned with development of international collaborations in the interest of achieving these important goals. Sharing of DNA from well-pedigreed Lynch syndrome kindreds in the search for biomarkers of genotypic susceptibility to cancer in the Lynch syndromes has become a high priority for this group.

Cost-benefit research showing the value of screening, with its potential for reducing morbidity and mortality in the Lynch syndromes, must be given a high priority.

For many decades, the only disorder that was known to predispose to colorectal cancer (CRC) was familial adenomatous polyposis (FAP).[1,2] Clearly, FAP is and remains the time-honored paradigm for hereditary CRC. Although it is relatively rare, accounting for <1 percent of the total CRC burden, physicians have learned an enormous amount about the diagnosis, surveillance, and management of hereditary CRC through the study of this disorder.[3–5]

The importance of FAP notwithstanding, hereditary CRC does occur in the absence of multiple colonic polyps. This phenomenon was first described by Warthin[6] when he published his study on family G in 1913. The way in which the study of this family germinated is of particular interest. Warthin's seamstress told him that she would one day die of cancer of the colon or the female organs because "most of my family members die of these cancers." Just as predicted, she died at an early age from endometrial carcinoma. Her family was updated extensively by Warthin[7,8] and later by his colleagues Hauser and Weller.[9] However, the pertinence of Warthin's observation of the aggregation of cancers of the colon (in the absence of multiple colonic polyps), stomach, and endometrium in family G was not appreciated until many years later, when an autosomal dominantly inherited CRC-prone syndrome, originally termed the *cancer family syndrome* (CFS), was described in two extended kindreds.[10] Following this report, all of the original records compiled by Warthin and subsequently by his colleagues were given to Lynch and Krush and used in a study to update "family G."[11] The study represented more than 75 years of follow-up on this family, which was found to fit the same criteria as the CFS.

The cancer family syndrome was subsequently termed *hereditary nonpolyposis colorectal cancer* (HNPCC) and, more recently, *Lynch syndromes I and II*.[12] A key feature of the Lynch syndromes has been the lack of multiple colonic polyps.[13] Segregation analysis disclosed that the mode of genetic transmission of cancer in the Lynch syndromes was most consistent with an autosomal dominant inheritance pattern.[14]

GENETICS

Hereditary Cancer (All Sites)—Considerations Inclusive of FAP

Recognition of primary genetic factors in the etiology of any form of cancer is exceedingly important to patients who are at risk. For example, a first-degree relative of a patient who has CRC or cancer of an anatomic site that is integral to a hereditary CRC syndrome has a cancer risk which exceeds that for any known epidemiologic risk factor.[15] When a cancer-prone family is encountered, it may then be possible to identify family members who could benefit from highly targeted surveillance and/or appropriate preventive surgical management, such as prophylactic colectomy in FAP. This statement notwithstanding, a majority of patients who fit a genetic risk category are not identified soon enough to enable them to benefit from targeted surveillance and management strategies. The main reason these opportunities for cancer prevention and control are missed is due to the fact that the cancer family history remains a neglected portion of the patient's medical workup.[16,17] This problem is seen in high relief in FAP. It has been estimated that 59 percent of individuals with this disease will die of CRC.[18] This is a tragedy, since the phenotype of FAP can be readily recognized by age 15 in 82 percent of high-risk patients, and in virtually 98 percent by age 30.[5]

Diagnosis of the Lynch Syndromes: Family History

An adequate history can provide one of the most powerful bases for recognizing hereditary cancer syndromes and identifying individual family members at risk. This knowledge could lead to effective measures for cancer control by targeting surveillance and management strategies that are wholly responsive to the natural history of the specific hereditary cancer syndrome. Unlike FAP, the Lynch syndromes, which account for approximately 6 percent of the total CRC burden, do not have any premonitory phenotypic signs or biomarkers that can aid the clinician in case/family recognition. Because of this, the family history remains the only key to Lynch syndrome diagnosis.

Family history information regarding cancer can, in most circumstances, be readily gathered by the physician or a trained paramedic. The modified nuclear pedigree (Fig. 8-1) often provides sufficient information for Lynch syndrome diagnosis. This pedigree includes the patient's first-degree relatives (siblings, parents, progeny) as well as selected second-degree relatives (both sets of grandparents, aunts, uncles). These latter second-degree relatives are often highly informative genetically in that they will be older and thereby will have passed through the cancer risk age.

Cancer history should be documented whenever possible. Attention should be focused on the presence

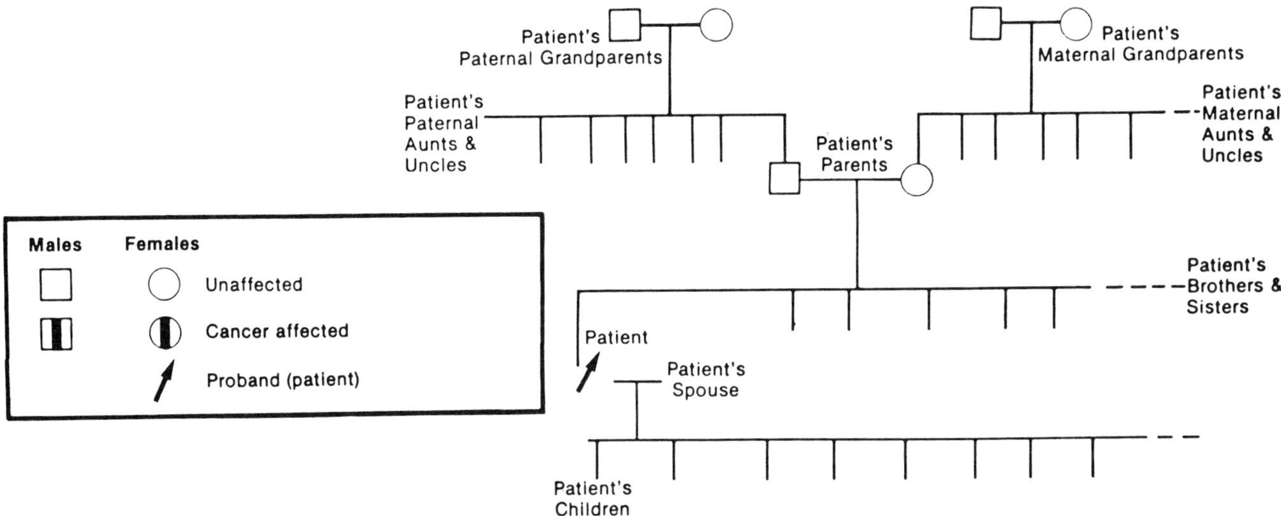

FIG. 8-1. Diagram representing a simple, modified nuclear pedigree for clinical use. [From Lynch HT, Rozen P, Schuelke GS, Lynch JF: Hereditary colorectal cancer review: Colonic polyposis and nonpolyposis colonic cancer (Lynch syndromes I and II), *Surv Dig Dis* 2:244–260, 1984. Reproduced by permission of S. Karger AG, Basel, Switzerland.]

or absence of colonic polyps, their number, age of onset, and location. Particular emphasis must be given to CRC and its location in the colon (proximal versus distal), as well as evidence of synchronous or metachronous CRC. Cancers of all types should be recorded, with special attention given to carcinoma of the endometrium, ovary, and other integrally associated anatomic sites. Possible barriers to interpretation of potential cancer genetic risk include inadequate genealogic, medical, and cancer pathology documentation; small families; early death of key relatives prior to cancer occurrence; missed paternity; or adoptees who are unable to obtain the cancer family history of their natural parents.

Cancer Family Registries

In addition to helping define a hereditary cancer syndrome, the pedigree will aid in identifying high-risk family members. Ideally, the pedigree must be considered a dynamic tool and should be updated continuously so that its informational content can be utilized by those physicians caring for the high-risk family members. However, developing and maintaining such a pedigree may not be a practical task in the usual private practice setting. Hence, it would be prudent to have a publicly supported network of computerized family registries with the capability of disseminating genetic risk information about the physician's patients and recommending surveillance and management considerations for any particular individual. Due attention must be given to maintaining patient confidentiality. A Lynch syndrome registry has been established at Creighton University's Hereditary Cancer Institute.

NATURAL HISTORY OF LYNCH SYNDROMES

Cardinal Features of Hereditary Cancer, Including HNPCC

The following "cardinal features" of the cancer phenotype and its natural history when present in a patient and/or family will characterize virtually all hereditary forms of cancer, inclusive of the Lynch syndromes: (1) early age of cancer onset; (2) multiple primary cancers showing specific combinations within the patients and families; (3) premonitory physical stigmata and/or biomarkers of genotypic susceptibility in certain syndromes; (4) distinctive pathologic features; (5) differences in survival when compared to their sporadic counterparts; and (6) Mendelian patterns of tumor occurrence. Not all of these features will apply in every circumstance, due to variable expressivity of the phenotype and reduced gene penetrance. Nevertheless, they are pervasive enough to effectively assist the clinician in identifying the Lynch syndromes in most instances. These phenotypic characteristics are presented as guidelines so that they can be given careful consideration when assessing familial aggregations of cancer of any anatomic site, including, of course, CRC. In the case of the Lynch syndromes, the reader will see immediately how slight modifications of these cardinal criteria will apply to these disorders.

Extracolonic Cancer in HNPCC

We have compared the observed frequency of cancer at specific anatomic sites in more than 1300 high-risk members of 23 HNPCC kindreds, with expectations based on incidence in the general population [the National Cancer Institute's Surveillance, Epidemiology, and End Results Program (SEER) data], and evaluated the hypothesis that there was heterogeneity in cancer frequency among families.[19]

We observed significantly increased numbers of cancers of the stomach, small intestine, upper urologic tract (transitional cell carcinoma of the renal pelvic and ureter), and ovary. No excess was seen in other types which have been previously associated with HNPCC, including cancer of the breast,[20] pancreas,[21] and urinary bladder.[22] Thus, we hypothesize that significant heterogeneity exists among HNPCC families in the frequencies of endometrial, ovarian, and upper urologic system cancer. With respect to anecdotal family studies showing excesses of cancers of the breast, pancreas, urinary bladder, and potentially other anatomic sites, it is clear that more research will be required in order to ascertain the potential importance of multiple organ sites which may be predisposed to cancer in HNPCC. Efforts are ongoing among our International Collaborative Group on HNPCC (ICG-HNPCC) to determine the significance of extracolonic cancer in HNPCC.[19]

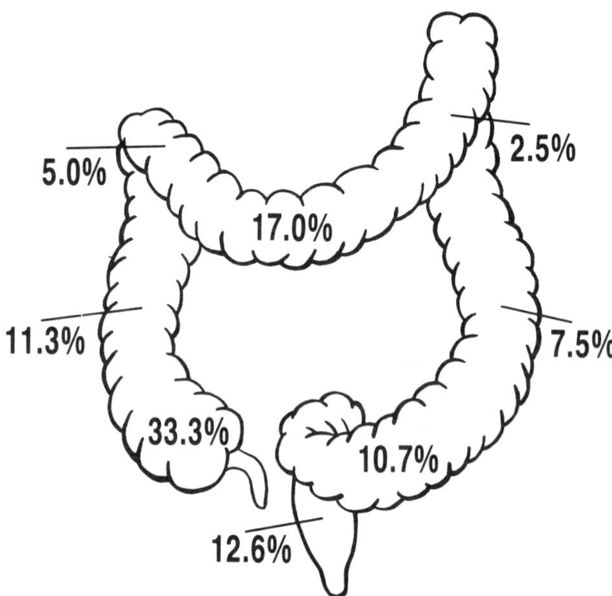

FIG. 8-2. Location of the first colonic cancer. Diagram showing the predominance of right-sided colonic cancer in a series of Lynch syndrome II patients. [From Fitzgibbons RJ, Lynch HT, Stanislau GU, et al: Recognition and treatment of patients with hereditary colon cancer (Lynch syndromes I and II), *Ann Surg* 206:289–295, 1987. Reproduced by permission of S. Karger AG, Basel, Switzerland.]

DIAGNOSIS

Lynch Syndrome Diagnostic Criteria

HNPCC has been subdivided into Lynch syndrome I and Lynch syndrome II. Lynch syndrome I is characterized by an autosomal dominantly inherited susceptibility of site-specific CRC with early (~44 years) age of onset, a proclivity to the proximal colon (70 percent; Fig. 8-2), and an excess of synchronous and metachronous (Fig. 8-3) colonic cancers. Family 4 (Fig. 8-4) is a prime example of an extended Lynch syndrome I family that we have studied since 1976 and which demonstrates the above features for this HNPCC variant. Colorectal cancer has been substantiated in over 30 family members through four generations. The female progenitor (I-2) may also have been affected.[23]

Families have been termed Lynch syndrome II when, in addition to the aforementioned Lynch syndrome I findings, carcinomas of the endometrium and ovary are demonstrated frequently (Figs. 8-5 and 8-6).[12,20,24–26] Other malignancies that have been noted in certain Lynch syndrome II families include transitional cell carcinoma of the ureter and renal pelvis[22] (Figs. 8-6 and 8-7), cancers of the stomach[27] (Figs. 8-8 and 8-9), small bowel[28] [Figs. 8-6 (family 2070), 8-7, and 8-10], and pancreas[21] [Figs. 8-5, 8-6 (family 2070), and 8-11].

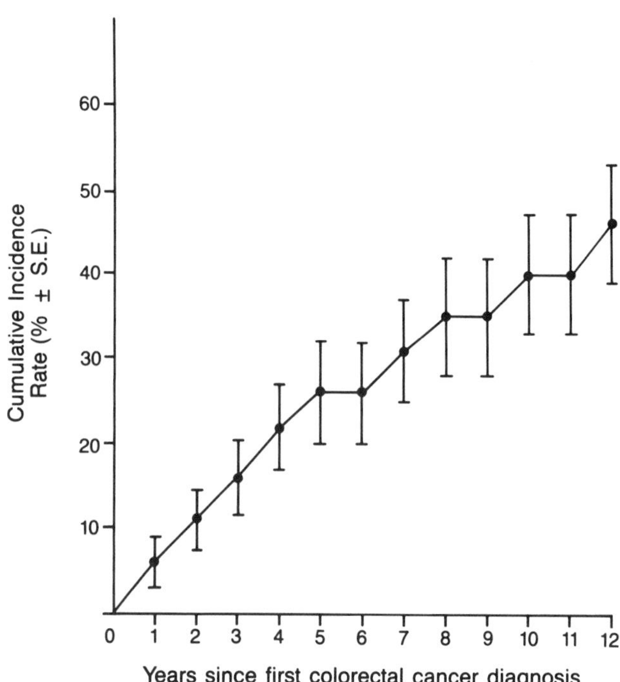

FIG. 8-3. Lifetime analysis showing cumulative incidence of metachronous colorectal cancer among ten HNPCC kindreds. [From Lynch HT, Watson P, Lanspa SJ, et al: Natural history of colorectal cancer in hereditary non-polyposis colorectal cancer (Lynch syndromes I and II), *Dis Colon Rectum* 31:439–444, 1988. Reproduced by permission.]

Probabilities of Early-Onset Colonic and Endometrial Cancer

In order to appreciate the probability of early-onset colonic and endometrial carcinoma—that is, prior to

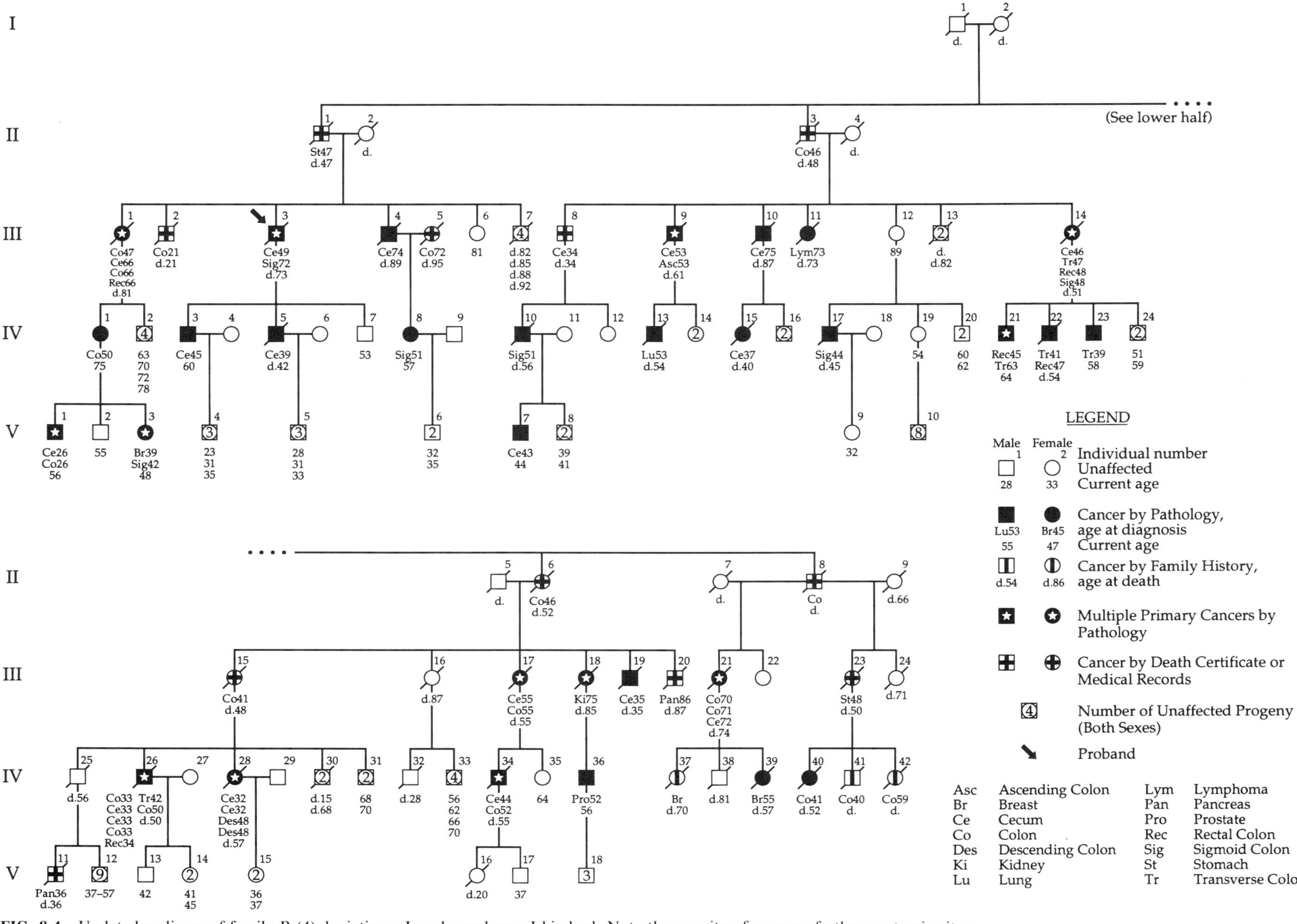

FIG. 8-4. Updated pedigree of family R (4) depicting a Lynch syndrome I kindred. Note the paucity of cancer of other anatomic sites. (From Lynch HT, Harris RE, Bardawil WA, et al: Management of hereditary site-specific colon cancer, *Arch Surg* 112:170–174, 1977. Reproduced by permission.)

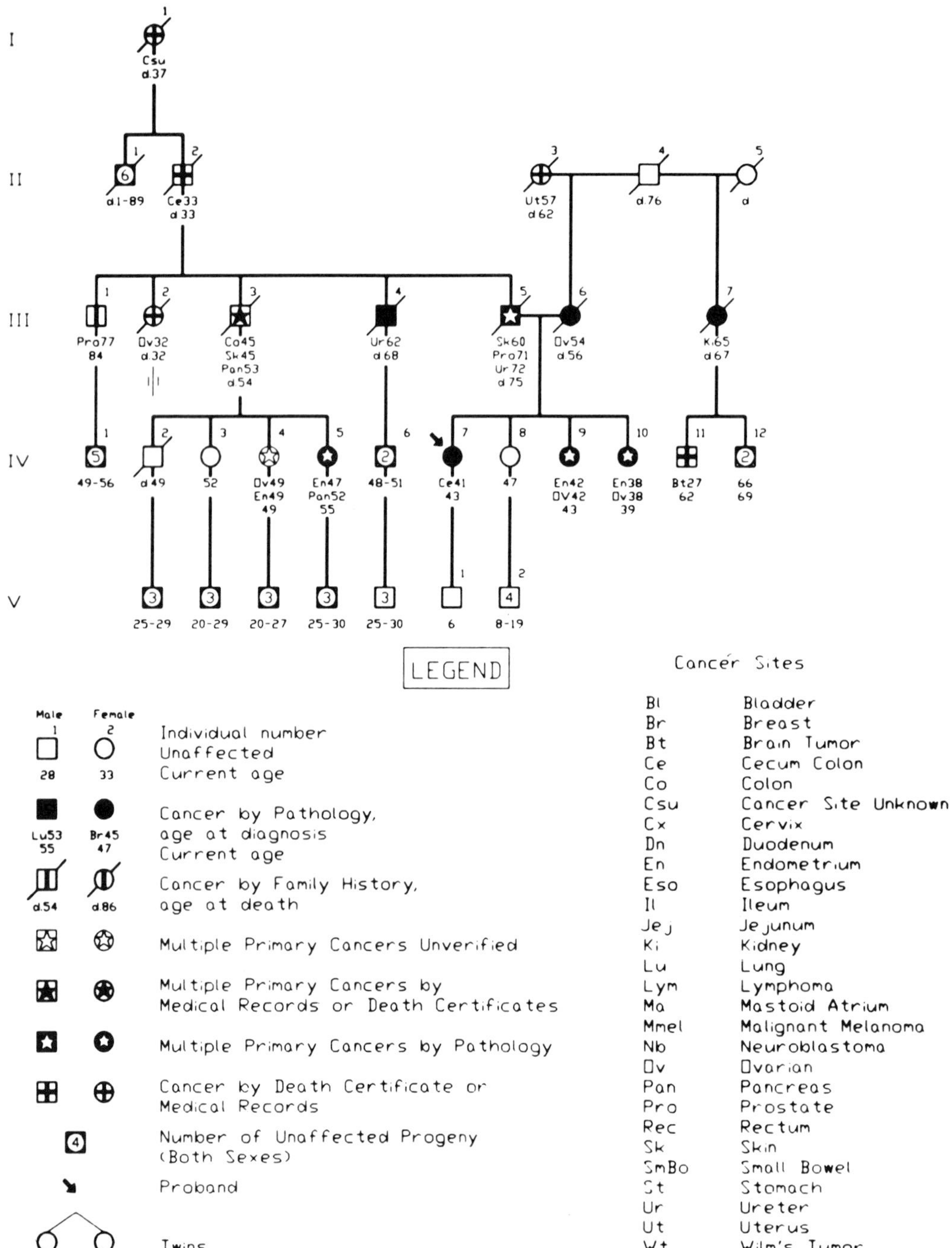

FIG. 8-5. Updated pedigree of family 3208 showing early-onset synchronous carcinoma of the endometrium and ovary in two sisters and a first cousin, early-onset carcinoma of the cecum in the proband, and a pattern of cancer distribution in the paternal lineage consonant with Lynch syndrome II. (From Lynch HT, Cavalieri RJ, Lynch JF, Casey MJ: Gynecologic cancer clues to Lynch syndrome II diagnosis: a family report, *Gynecol Oncol* 44:198–203, 1992. Reproduced by permission.) The legend for symbols and cancer sites is applicable for all subsequent pedigrees.

age 40—we compiled their likelihoods based on age-specific colonic and endometrial cancer incidence from the SEER data. These studies indicated that the probability of manifesting colonic cancer by age 40 was 7×10^{-4} and of endometrial carcinoma 4.4×10^{-4}. The probability of a female having onset of both colonic and endometrial cancer prior to age 40, if these diseases are unrelated, was (.00044)(.0007), or 3 in 10 million. This same probabilistic approach was used to assess proximal colonic cancer, which occurs in about

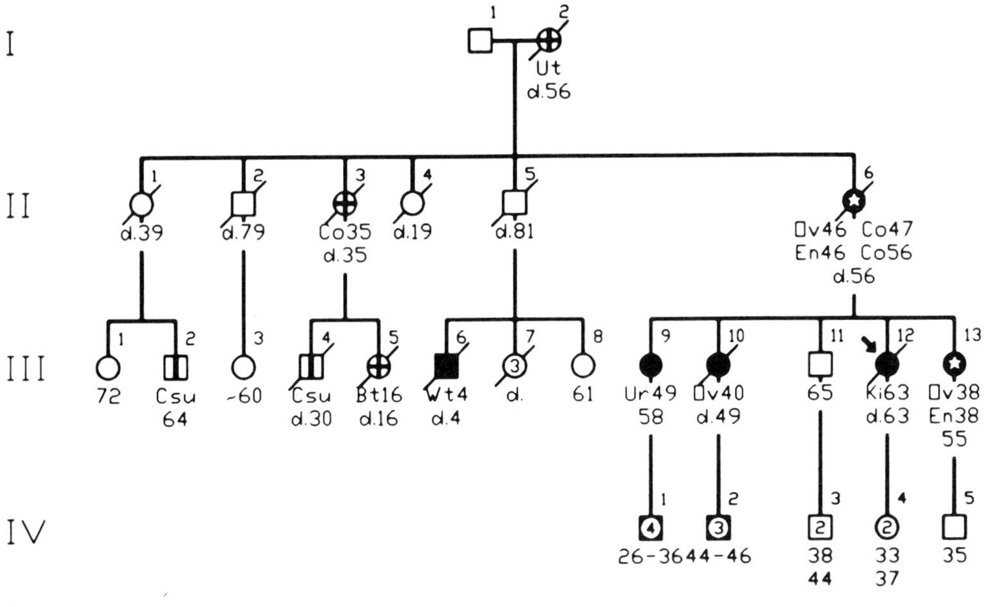

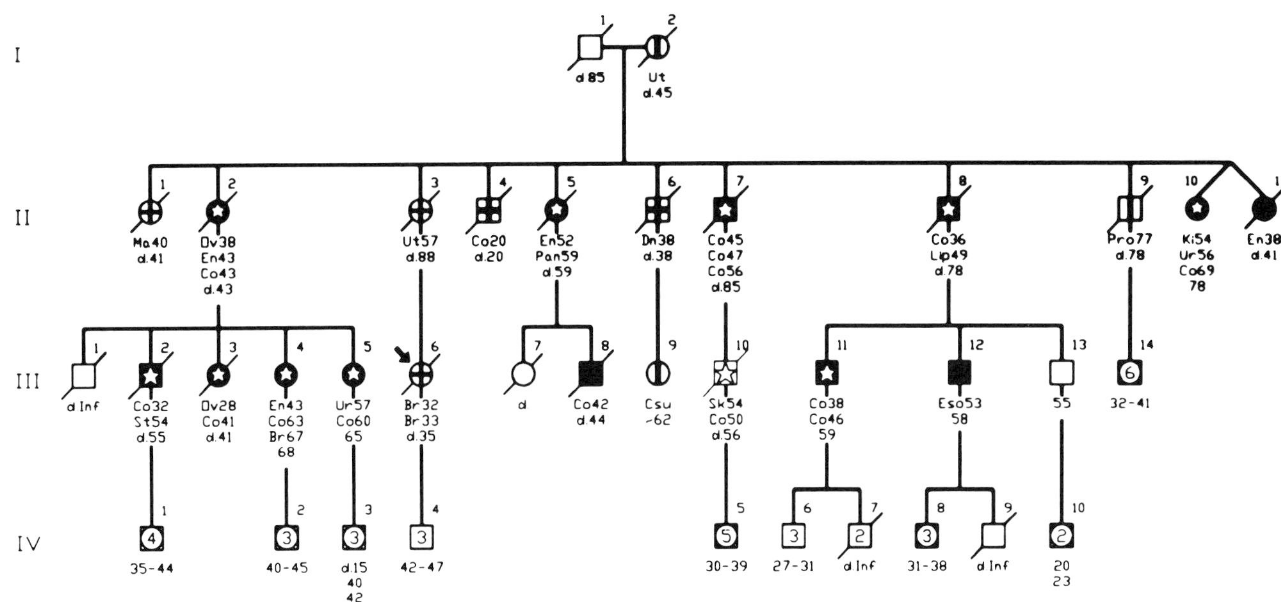

FIG. 8-6. *A.* Pedigree of family 2068 shows a Lynch syndrome II kindred with synchronous carcinomas of the endometrium and ovary in a mother and daughter, and urologic malignancies in two additional daughters. *B.* Pedigree of family 2070 shows an excess of carcinomas of the endometrium, ovary, and urologic system. Cancer of the small bowel and pancreas is also seen in this pedigree. (From Lynch HT, Ens JA, Lynch JF: Lynch syndrome II and urologic manifestations, *J Urol* 143:24–28, 1990. © 1990 Williams & Wilkins. Reproduced by permission.)

35 percent of all patients with colonic cancer. Herein, the probability of proximal colonic cancer in a patient below age 40 was (.35)(.0007), or 2.5×10^{-4}.

Another scenario would be a nuclear family of 8, comprising both parents with a sibship of 6. If all cancer diagnoses in this family were considered as independent, the probability of two cases of proximal colonic cancer at less than age 40 would be equal to 1.7×10^{-6} or 2 in a million. The probability of three cases of proximal colonic cancer at less than age 40 would equal 8.7×10^{-10}, or 1 in a billion.

While these age-specific cancer computations do

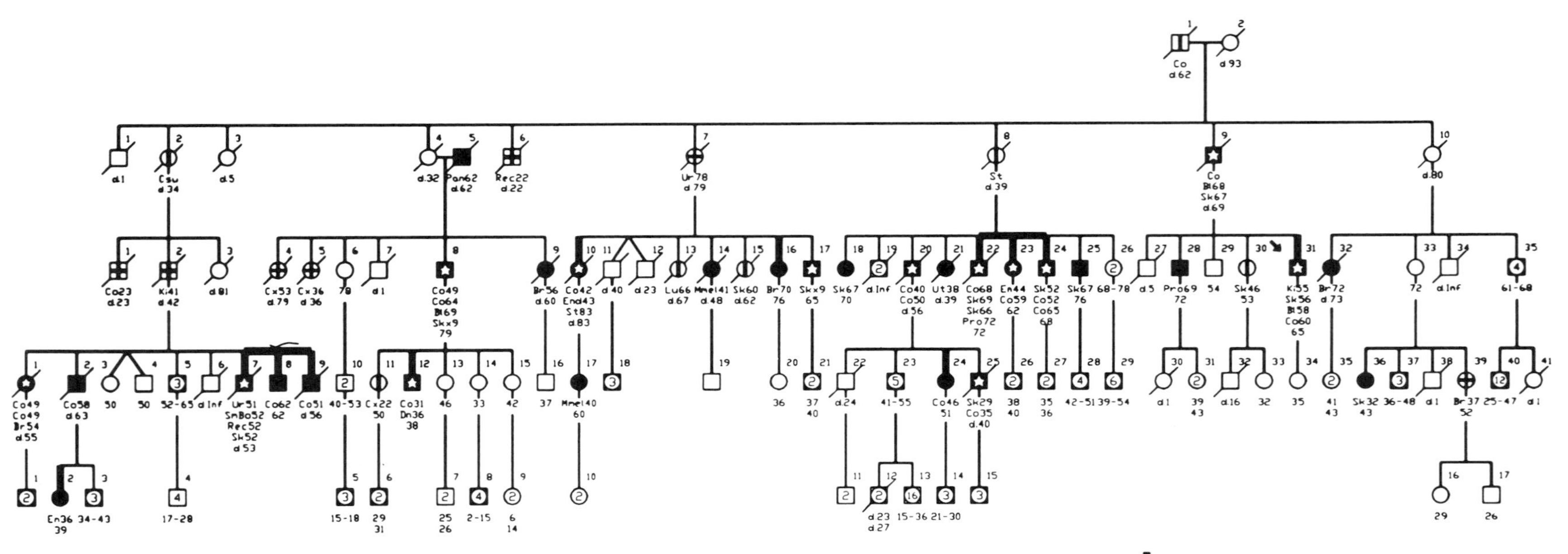

FIG. 8-7. Updated pedigree of family 621 with tumor spectrum consonant with Muir-Torre cutaneous phenotype (III-8, III-22, III-31, and IV-11) in association with Lynch syndrome II (including small bowel and urological malignancies). (From Lynch HT, Fusaro RM, Roberts L, et al: Muir-Torre syndrome in several members of a family with a variant of the Cancer Family Syndrome. *Br J Dermatol* 113:295–301, 1985. Reproduced by permission.)

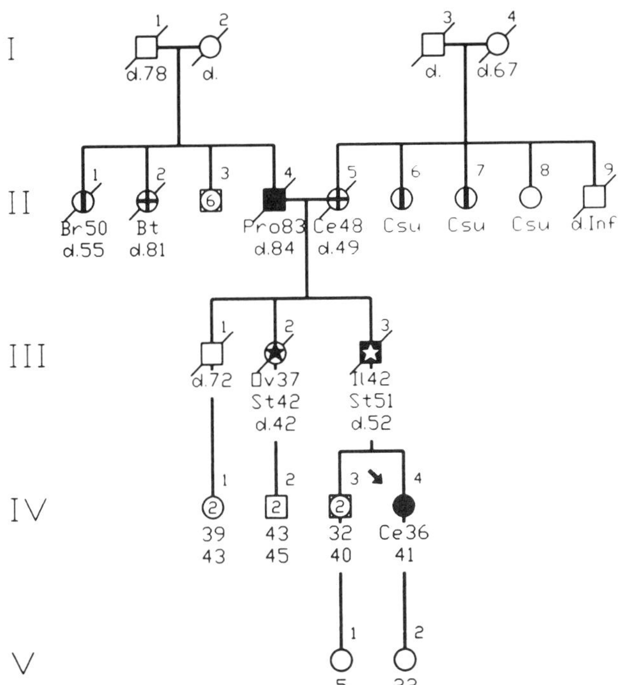

FIG. 8-8. Pedigree of family 2735, a Lynch syndrome II kindred, in which two siblings had multiple primary cancers, including gastric carcinomas.

not portend etiologic significance, they do, nevertheless, provide a basis for comprehending their relative frequencies. Therefore, assessing the clinical significance for early-onset colorectal and endometrial cancer, including both cancers in a single patient, provides an appreciation for their chance expectations in the general population.

Representative Lynch Syndrome Kindreds

The kindreds that follow below will give the reader an overview of the common clinical kindred patterns.

Family 3208 (Fig. 8-5). Initially, the occurrence of ovarian carcinoma in their mother (III-6) at age 54 was given etiologic risk factor consideration when one of her daughters (IV-10) developed midcycle bleeding and was diagnosed with a grade II well-differentiated endometrial carcinoma and a mixed serous and clear cell carcinoma of the ovary at age 38. Subsequently, a second daughter (IV-9) received similar diagnoses. Astute consultants, believing that this might represent a hereditary cancer syndrome, had recommended that the proband (IV-7) and her sisters (IV-8, 9, 10) should undergo colonoscopies. A Dukes A adenocarcinoma of the cecum was diagnosed in the proband (IV-7). She also had a prophylactic total abdominal hysterectomy-bilateral salpingo-oophorectomy (TAH-BSO), as did her sister (IV-8), and the findings were within normal limits. Lynch syndrome II was diagnosed in this family only after the pedigree was extended to include the paternal lineage. Specifically, the proband's father (III-5), her aunt and uncles (III-2, 3, 4), her grandfather (II-2), and a first cousin (IV-5) all had manifested cancers of the type that have been observed in this syndrome. Of interest is the occurrence of pancreatic cancer and colonic cancer in the aunt (III-3). One of her daughters (IV-5) had carcinoma of the ovary at age 47 and at age 52 developed an islet cell carcinoma of the pancreas. Since our initial report of this family,[29] another daughter (IV-4) has, by family report, developed cancer of the ovary and endometrium at age 49.

Family 2068 (Fig. 8-6). This family also has had several members with gynecologic as well as urologic cancers. For example, patient II-6 had four separate primary lesions: cancer of the ovary, cancer of the endometrium, and two cancers in the colon. Four of her five children were affected with cancer. Her daughters had cancers of the ureter (III-9), kidney (III-12), and ovary (III-10), and patient III-13 had separate primary lesions of the ovary and endometrium at age 38.

Family 2070 (Fig. 8-6). Gynecologic cancers and other malignancies that have been reported in association with colonic cancer are represented in this Lynch II pedigree. The progenitor (I-2) had a cancer of the uterus by family history. She had 11 children, all of whom had cancer. A daughter (II-5) had endometrial cancer at age 52 and carcinoma of the pancreas at age 59. A son (II-6) had cancer of the duodenum at age 38, and one twin daughter (II-10) had cancers of the kidney (age 54), ureter (age 56), and colon (age 69). The other twin had endometrial carcinoma at age 38. Another daughter (II-2) had ovarian carcinoma at age 38 and cancers of the colon and endometrium at age 43. Of this last woman's five children, the four who survived to adulthood (III-2, 3, 4, and 5) had multiple primary syndrome cancers that included colon, stomach, ovary, endometrium, and ureter.

Family 621 (Fig. 8-7). This family has been followed by us since 1983, when they were referred by a dermatologist who recognized the classic Muir-Torre syndrome cutaneous phenotype (sebaceous adenomas, sebaceous carcinomas, and multiple keratoacanthomas) in several family members (III-8, III-22, III-31, and IV-11). The proband (III-31) was also treated for urologic malignancies. His mother (II-9), grandfather (I-1), and other family members had an excess of urologic as well as colon cancers. Two field visits were made by us to separate geographic areas of the state where the majority of the family members reside. Educational sessions were held to explain the cardinal features of HNPCC, including risk status and surveillance recommendations. The skin of all family members who attended both sessions was examined; at the

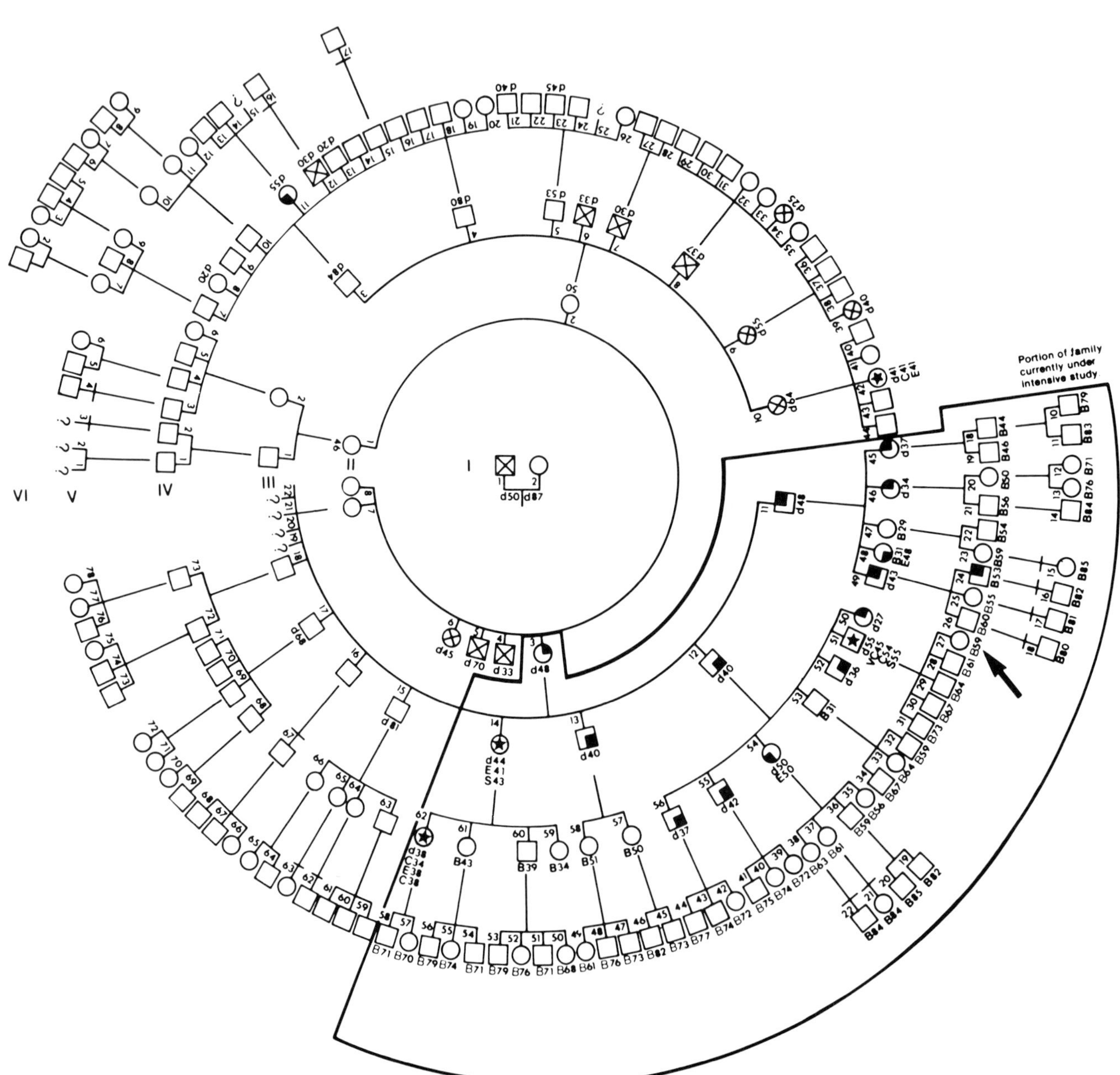

FIG. 8-9. Pedigree of a large Lynch syndrome II family from Italy. Note the excess of gastric carcinoma. (From Cristofaro G, Lynch HT, Caruso ML, et al: New phenotypic aspects in a family with Lynch syndrome II. *Cancer* 60:51–58, 1987. Reproduced by permission.)

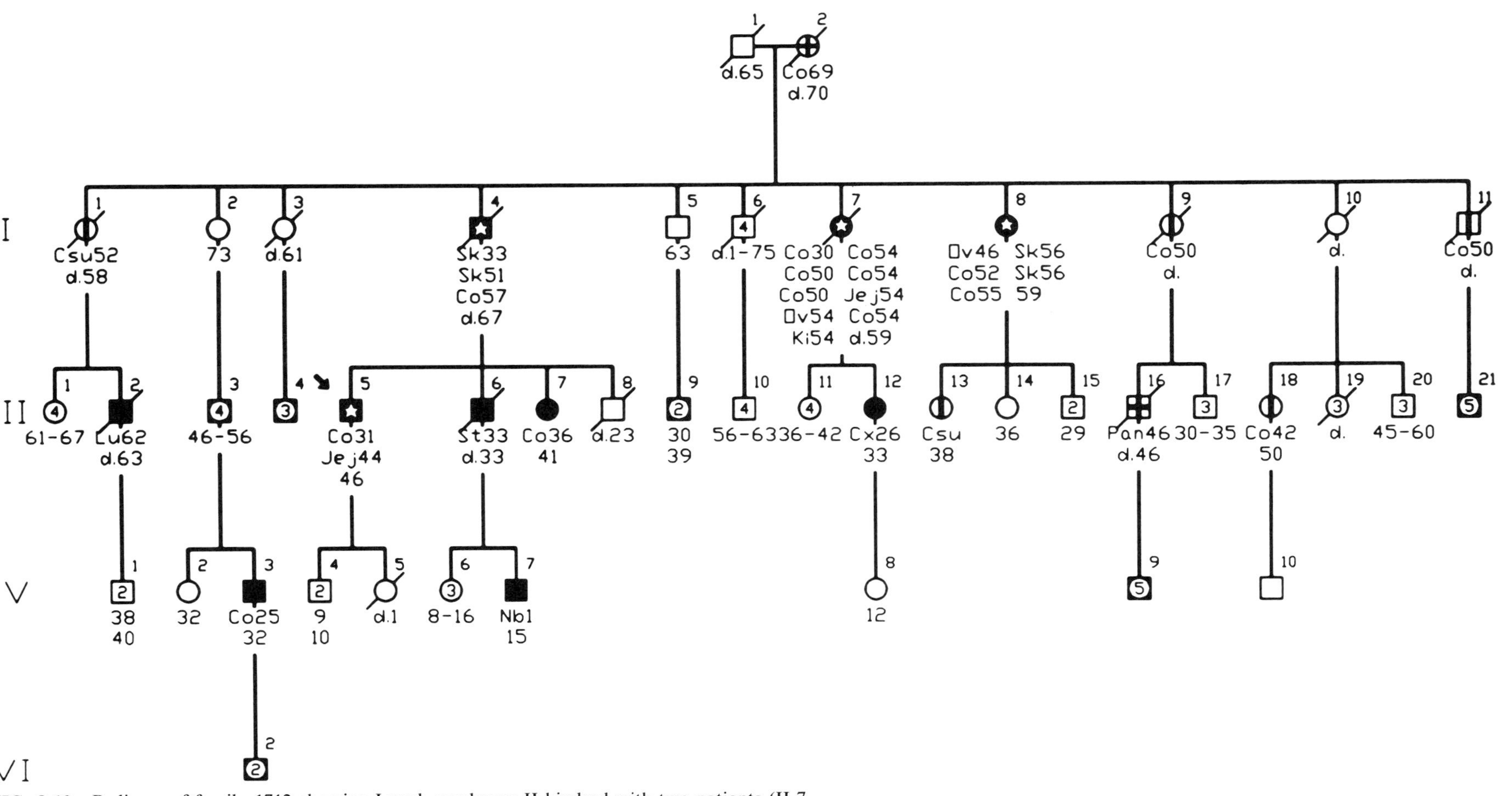

FIG. 8-10. Pedigree of family 1712 showing Lynch syndrome II kindred with two patients (II-7, III-5) with adenocarcinoma of the small bowel. (From Lynch HT, Smyrk TC, Lynch PM, et al: Adenocarcinoma of the small bowel in Lynch syndrome II, *Cancer* 64:2178–2183, 1989. Reproduced by permission.)

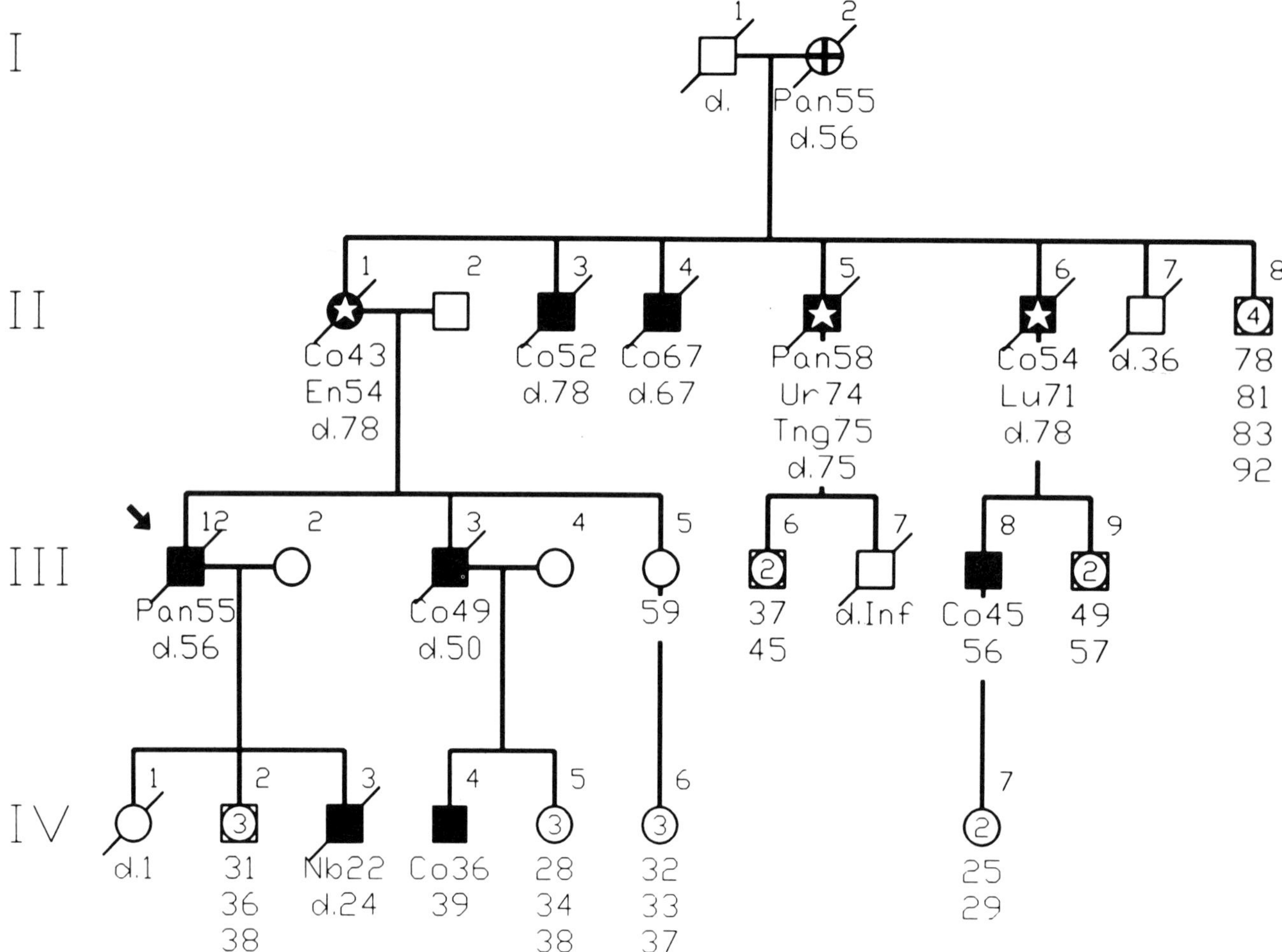

FIG. 8-11. Updated pedigree of family 673 showing pancreatic cancer through three generations in a Lynch syndrome II family. (From Lynch HT, Fitzsimmons ML, Smyrk TC, et al: Familial pancreatic cancer: clinicopathologic study of 18 nuclear families, *Am J Gastroenterol* 85:54–60, 1990. Reproduced by permission.)

second location, colonoscopic screening was performed on selected high-risk members.

Since our initial report of the family in 1985,[30] many new syndrome cancers have been diagnosed, including colonic cancer in the proband at age 60. Patient III-23, who is alive and well at age 62, had endometrial carcinoma at age 44. She had repeatedly told her physician that many of her relatives had had colonic cancer and that she was concerned about developing this disorder. However, she had never had an examination of her colon until she developed symptoms at age 59, at which time a poorly differentiated Dukes C adenocarcinoma of the right colon and distal ileum was diagnosed. Also of interest is patient IV-8. He attended our second field visit in 1990 and was offered the opportunity to undergo a colonoscopy. He did not want his health insurance carrier notified and therefore refused the procedure. Less than 2 years later, in March 1992, he developed shortness of breath and was found to have a hemoglobin of 7g/100 mL. At colonoscopy, an ulcerating lesion was seen in the cecum. A right colectomy was performed. The diagnosis was a grade II moderately differentiated adenocarcinoma, Dukes C, with 3 of 15 lymph nodes involved.

Family 2735 (Fig. 8-8). Although it has been difficult to confirm the cancer history of some of the relatives in generation II, the proband's (IV-4) branch of the family is of interest. She had carcinoma of the cecum at age 36, as did her paternal grandmother (II-5) at age 48. Her father (III-3) had carcinoma of the ileum at age 42 and gastric cancer at age 51. His sister (III-2) also had gastric cancer at age 42 and died of this disease. By family history, she previously had an ovarian carcinoma at age 37. The findings are consistent with a Lynch syndrome II diagnosis.

Family X (Fig. 8-9). This large pedigree provides findings on a Lynch syndrome II family from southern Italy that shows an excess of gastric carcinoma. Warthin's original description of Family G also showed this excess. As might be expected because of the frequent occurrences of gastric cancer in Japan, many of the Lynch II families from that country also express this condition.

Family 1712 (Fig. 8-10). This family is of interest because of the rarely occurring cancer of the jejunum that can be noted in patients II-7 and III-5. Both of these persons had colon cancer many years prior to their lesions in the small bowel. This family shows findings compatible with Lynch syndrome II.

Family 673 (Fig. 8-11). On examination of the pedigree, one can determine that this is a Lynch syndrome II kindred. However, the family was brought to our attention by the proband (III-1), who had developed pancreatic cancer at age 55. He also had a maternal uncle (II-5) and grandmother (I-2) with this condition. The proband's mother (II-1) developed colonic cancer at age 43 and endometrial carcinoma at age 54. She had another son (III-3) who had colonic cancer at age 49, and three of her brothers (II-3, 4, and 6) had carcinoma of the colon, as did the son (III-8) of II-6.

SURVEILLANCE/MANAGEMENT

Surveillance and Management Strategies for Hereditary and Familial CRC

In the case of HNPCC, in the Lynch syndrome I variant, we recommend initiation of colonoscopy at age 25. If the colon is free of polyps or other abnormalities, this procedure should be repeated every 2 years through age 35 and every 1 to 2 years thereafter. Surgical treatment for CRC is subtotal colectomy because of the high risk of subsequent colonic cancer.

In the case of the Lynch syndrome II variant, in addition to the surveillance and management strategies for Lynch syndrome I, we recommend endometrial vacuum curettage beginning at age 25. We are experimenting with pelvic probe ultrasound and CA-125 in certain HNPCC families with a family history of ovarian cancer. In both variants, we recommend that education and genetic counseling be initiated in the late teens. Should a woman in a Lynch syndrome II family who has completed her own family develop CRC, we recommend prophylactic total abdominal hysterectomy–bilateral salpingo-oophorectomy (TAH-BSO) at the time of her subtotal colectomy.

Jass and Stewart[31] call attention to the need for strict diagnostic criteria for the Lynch syndromes when reporting data about colonoscopic screening. To date, only four reports[13,32–34] have employed colonoscopic screening aimed specifically at HNPCC. This is important, since the natural history of HNPCC is distinctive, particularly in terms of its age of onset and proximal predilection for CRC as compared with the natural history of FAP and HFAS. This screening must be responsive to the natural history of hereditary CRC.[35–40]

Jass and Stewart[31] studied 72 volunteers from 8 kindreds wherein criteria for HNPCC were fulfilled (group A) and compared these individuals with 28 patients from 8 families wherein these same criteria were not as rigorously enforced (group B). This included 51 men and 49 women with a mean age of 34 years. Each individual was a first-degree relative of family members who manifested CRC. Findings disclosed 25 adenomas and 2 adenocarcinomas in these two groups. The adenocarcinomas occurred in a 29-year-old male and a 36-year-old female from HNPCC patients in group A. Both of these individuals were asymptomatic. One of these lesions arose within a tubulovillous adenoma in the upper rectum, wherein the spread was limited to the submucosa with no lymph node metastasis and was considered a Dukes A lesion. The tumor was found to be a moderately differentiated mucinous adenocarcinoma. This 29-year-old male underwent a total colectomy and ileorectal anastomosis. The second CRC-affected patient, the 36-year-old female, had a lesion arising in the splenic flexure. It was a well-differentiated adenocarcinoma which had spread beyond the bowel wall, but no lymph node metastases were observed. This was classified as a Dukes B lesion. The patient was treated by colectomy and ileorectal anastomosis.

Adenomas in HNPCC

From a historical viewpoint, the study by Wolfe et al.[41] was possibly the first to show the involvement of the adenomas in the evolution of putative HNPCC based on sigmoidoscopic evaluation. Families which show the typical criteria for HNPCC do not show any evidence of an excess of adenomas.[13] Love,[42] however, in a review of HNPCC families, has demonstrated the presence of malignant change within adenomas. These adenomas developed at an earlier age than that typical of nonhereditary cases. Mecklin et al.[43] have shown a high incidence of adenomas with moderate or severe dysplasia and villous features in HNPCC.

In a pathologic study of adenomas, Jass and Stewart[31] noted the relative infrequency of adenomas in HNPCC but stressed the tendency for these adenomas to occur at an early age and to be relatively large in size. They also demonstrated the origin of carcinoma within adenomas.

Jass et al.[44] believe that villous change and high-grade dysplasia are particularly evident in HNPCC adenomas, a finding also recognized in other studies.[44,45] The Jass et al.[44] study supports the view that adenomas in HNPCC patients are more aggressive than their sporadic counterparts,[44] a finding supported by the rapid growth of adenomas in two of the patients involved in the Jass et al.[44] study. Furthermore, they suggest that "the most likely explanation lies in the HNPCC gene mutation being a critical and rate limiting step for neoplastic evolution, so that its constitutional presence serves to accelerate the evolution of adenoma."

As mentioned, one of the major difficulties in screening for CRC in HNPCC revolves around the definition of HNPCC. For example, an internationally agreed upon definition of HNPCC by the ICG-HNPCC includes four criteria: (1) three family members with CRC; (2) one of whom is a first-degree relative; (3) involvement of at least two successive generations; and (4) one family member who has developed bowel cancer by age 50.[46] Jass et al.,[44] however, believe that this definition is too strict for the purposes of selection for screening. They note that "the children of a parent who developed right-sided bowel cancer at the age of 35 years, but with no additional family history, would be at increased risk of bowel cancer through inheriting the HNPCC gene formed by a new mutation in the parent. It is unlikely, however, that rigid guidelines could be applied, given the complex variables involved. This emphasizes the urgent need for genetic markers. Short interval (annual) follow-up for individuals from definite HNPCC families or families in which most of the HNPCC criteria are met is recommended because of the apparent instability of HNPCC adenomas." We strongly support this view for screening the Lynch syndromes and emphasize the need for giving priority to the identification of genetic markers.

Jass[47] has pioneered concerns about CRC control in New Zealand, where he emphasizes the importance of screening high-risk groups, including those at risk for FAP and the more common HNPCC. He has stressed the need for funding a national (for New Zealand) hereditary bowel cancer registry that would serve the needs of families with FAP and HNPCC. This is particularly appropriate, since New Zealand has the highest rates of bowel cancer in the world,[48] and the incidence there is increasing,[49] in contrast with the declining rates in other western nations.[48] We have stressed the importance of such a family CRC registry in the United States.

Barriers to Screening

While genetic screening has proven to be valuable for diagnosis, there are emotional, financial, insurance, and sociolegal problems that pose barriers to compliance with cancer control programs. For example, one of the more vexing problems is the denial of insurance coverage for screening and management of patients who are genetically at risk. In addition, there is the risk that the insurance companies will cancel policies of genetically cancer-prone patients. Furthermore, the patients' privacy and confidentiality may be violated.[50] Geneticists have recognized these issues, and in the Human Genome Privacy Act (HGPA), attention is given to limiting access of insurers to the patient's genetic information.[51] Clearly, these issues must receive priority research attention in the interest of ameliorating the strife and emotional conflict among patients who suffer the onus of being members of Lynch syndrome families.

Hypothetical Nuclear Pedigrees: Minimal Diagnostic Genetic Clues

In the absence of premonitory physical stigmata and/or biomarkers of genotypic susceptibility, questions arise constantly about putative HNPCC diagnoses when these are based on findings of cancer in the nuclear pedigree. Occasionally, the available information may be too limited to make a definitive diagnosis of HNPCC. Nevertheless, the information may be sufficient to recommend specific surveillance measures for patients who are presumed to be at increased cancer risk. Several hypothetical family history scenarios which, in fact, pose genetic diagnostic problems of the type that are frequently addressed by clinicians are presented in Figs. 8-12 and 8-13, discussed below. In each of the examples, we assume that FAP has been excluded.

Figure 8-12*A*

This problem concerns the potentially increased HNPCC risk to the 25-year-old proband and her 33-year-old brother. Note that their unaffected mother was cancer-free when she died at age 32. However, early-onset endometrial and colon cancers have occurred in three of the mother's first-degree relatives. If this was an HNPCC pedigree, the proband's mother would have been at 50 percent risk; in accord with Mendelian dominant inheritance, the proband and her brother would have a 25 percent risk for the syndrome. *Recommendation:* We would initiate Lynch syndrome II surveillance for the proband and her brother, preferring to err on the side of caution.

Figure 8-12*B*

The proband had phenotypic findings consistent with Lynch syndrome II. However, there was an absence of any additional cancers in the family. Given this information, we would consider the possibility that the proband's cancers resulted from a new germline mutation for Lynch syndrome II. *Recommendation:* We would have the proband's two children under surveillance for Lynch syndrome II at the appropriate age.

Figure 8-12*C*-1

The proband, with relatively late (age 67) onset of carcinoma of the sigmoid colon, has a family history consonant with Lynch syndrome II. However, we can-

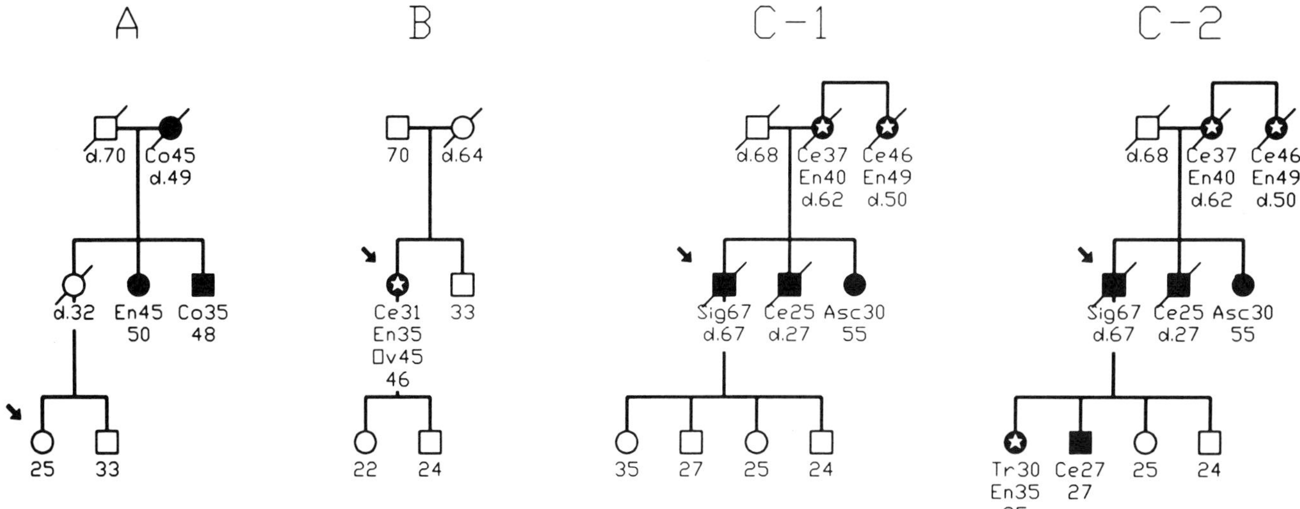

FIG. 8-12. Hypothetical putative Lynch syndrome pedigrees.

not determine whether he represents a late age of onset of the Lynch syndrome II or whether he in fact had "sporadic cancer." *Recommendation:* We would assume that he is genotypically "affected" and would therefore have his four progeny under surveillance for Lynch syndrome II.

Figure 8-12*C*-2

In this scenario, we see that the proband's progeny, as seen originally in Fig. 8-12*C*-1, have now manifested cancers consonant with Lynch syndrome II. Therefore, we would consider the proband to be an obligate gene carrier. *Recommendation:* As in Fig. 8-12C-1, but with added confidence in the Lynch syndrome II diagnosis.

Figure 8-13*D*-1

This is an example of a nuclear pedigree where the proband, her sister, and their mother show gynecologic features of Lynch syndrome II. However, they lack CRC occurrences. *Recommendation:* These patients need colonoscopic surveillance.

Figure 8-13*D*-2

When the pedigree in D-1 is extended, we find evidence of early-onset proximal colon cancers and gynecologic cancer, all consistent with Lynch syndrome II. *Recommendation:* As in D-1, but with added confidence in its Lynch syndrome II diagnosis.

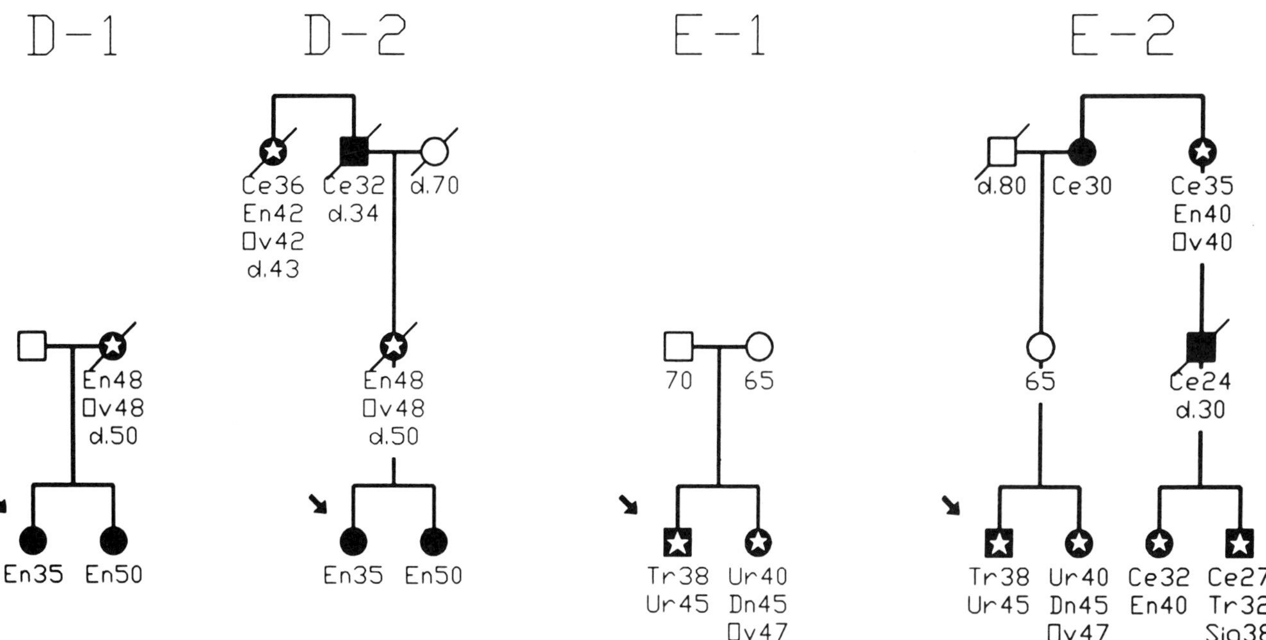

FIG. 8-13. Hypothetical putative Lynch syndrome pedigrees.

Figure 8-13*E*-1

This is an example of urologic cancer in the proband and in his sister. Their mother, at age 65, has not manifested cancer. *Recommendation:* This information is not sufficient to diagnose HNPCC.

Figure 8-13*E*-2

In this depiction of the extended E-1 pedigree, we see that the proband's maternal grandmother died of carcinoma of the cecum at age 30; the grandmother's sister and that sister's son and her grandchildren all had cancers consonant with Lynch syndrome II. *Recommendation:* The proband's mother would be considered an obligate gene carrier. She would warrant intensive surveillance for Lynch syndrome II cancers, including full colonoscopy. The proband and his sister would also warrant an intensive colonoscopic regimen.

DIFFERENTIAL DIAGNOSIS OF HNPCC

In addition to the compilation of a detailed family history, diagnosis of HNPCC requires a physical examination that should focus on the presence or absence of polyps in the colon. For example, the presence of multiple colonic adenomatous polyps in the patient and/or in one or more of his or her immediate relatives would indicate the likelihood that the CRC in the family is secondary to FAP.

Occasionally, patients may present with an unusual history indicating cancer in a single first-degree relative where cancer occurred in the proximal colon before age 30 in the absence of multiple colonic polyps (see "Hypothetical Nuclear Pedigrees," above). This may even be associated with early-onset endometrial and/or ovarian carcinoma, all in the absence of any other positive family history. In this setting, one cannot include or exclude the possibility of HNPCC. It could represent either a new mutation or any of the previously mentioned barriers to family history interpretation. This matter and other complex diagnostic problems are discussed subsequently.

Penetrance of the HNPCC gene is not 100 percent: Therefore, while the cancer phenotype manifested itself in the paternal or maternal lineage, the patient's parent (or other key relative), due to reduced penetrance of the gene, may not have developed a syndrome cancer.[14] Age of onset of cancer may be variable. Thus, late age of cancer onset in key relatives could be consistent with an HNPCC phenotype. Collectively, all of these matters must be reconciled in developing the differential diagnosis for HNPCC.

Until a marker of genotypic susceptibility is identified, the diagnosis of HNPCC will rest on clinical observation in concert with the aforementioned descriptive criteria. The physician who is considering a diagnosis of HNPCC must differentiate the syndrome from disorders with florid adenomatous polyposis of the colon,[4,25] Peutz-Jeghers polyposis,[52–59] and juvenile polyposis.[60–66] Less well defined but also demanding consideration is the recently described hereditary flat adenoma syndrome (HFAS).[67–69]

For example, an extended family with a marked excess of CRCs has been found in which two of the members have FAP-like polyposis but their first degree relatives, including those who developed colonic cancer, did not. Many members of the family developed adenomas at an early age; however, the mean age at diagnosis of CRC was 54 years. Occurrence of multiple adenomas and/or CRC in this family was linked to the locus for FAP on chromosome 5q.[70] This family is similar to other HFAS families described by us,[69] where linkage analysis to 5q markers has also been observed.[71] The first HFAS family we studied was initially believed to represent Lynch syndrome II[67] but subsequently has been linked to the FAP gene at the chromosome 5q locus.[71]

Patients with the Lynch syndromes may have several colonic adenomas.[13] However, the same phenotype may occur in FAP cases having limited phenotypic expression of this trait.[25] In overlap situations such as these, the phenotype of other family members may provide clues to diagnosis; i.e., the FAP patient is more likely to have relatives with florid polyposis than the Lynch syndrome patient. On the other hand, if a putative Lynch syndrome patient with occasional adenomas has a phenotype of flat adenomas with a proximal colonic predilection and the family history shows later age of onset of CRC, HFAS should be considered.[67–69]

Common, isolated adenomatous polyps of the colon may provide clues to hereditary CRC diagnosis. Specifically, Burt et al.[72] described the occurrence of an autosomal dominant inheritance pattern for discrete colorectal polyps and colorectal cancer in a large Utah pedigree. This kindred lacked the natural history characteristics of the "typical" FAP presentation—namely, early age of onset of multiple colonic polyps, an excess of synchronous and metachronous colonic cancer, cancer of extracolonic sites, and variable extracolonic phenotypic stigmata. The findings of colonic cancer in association with discrete polyps in the colorectum were more in accord with those expected in the general population. A reasonable question is whether the heritage of colorectal polyps in families with discrete colorectal polyps represents one end of the colonic mucosal polyp expression with respect to a host-factor susceptibility to the several hereditary CRC syndromes as well as in common CRC.[3]

Cannon-Albright et al.[73] studied 34 kindreds with discrete colorectal adenomas and carcinomas by likelihood analysis. This study provided further evidence for a dominantly inherited susceptibility to adenomatous polyps and subsequent CRC. This phenomenon is believed by those authors to be present in a sizable segment of the general population. Specifically, Cannon-Albright et al.[73] suggested that the frequency of the deleterious gene was about 20 percent, with penetrance of 60 percent by age 60.

Familial CRC, on the other hand, pertains to an individual who may have only a single first-degree relative with CRC. Such a person will have an empirical risk for CRC that is increased about two- to threefold over that for individuals in the general population who do not have a first-degree relative affected with CRC.[25,74] The familial concept, however, is crude, since it does not take into consideration age of onset, location of CRC within the colon, or the presence or absence of synchronous or metachronous CRC—nor does it consider cancers of other anatomic sites in the patient and/or within his or her family.

The assessment of so-called familial CRC[25,74] presents a difficult problem. Given the frequency of CRC in the general population, it is not unlikely that one will encounter familial aggregations of this disease that are due to chance alone. The differentiation of familial clusters of CRC from hereditary CRC will require meticulous attention to the natural history and distribution of cancer within the family, particularly the presence of synchronous and metachronous CRC, age of onset, location within the colon, and association with colonic polyps and extracolonic forms of cancer. It is in these settings that biomarkers of genotypic susceptibility, once identified, will aid the physician in diagnosis and management.

Phenotypic features (including extracolonic manifestations) must be given careful consideration in the assessment of each patient and family. Extracolonic phenotypic stigmata such as congenital hypertrophy of the retinal pigment epithelium (CHRPE) in FAP and osteomas and epidermoid cysts in the Gardner's variant of FAP will be useful discriminants in the differential diagnosis. The cutaneous stigmata of Muir-Torre's syndrome may also be helpful in elucidating hereditary CRC syndrome diagnoses, since these phenotypic features have been observed in a subset of Lynch syndrome II families, such as the one discussed previously (Fig. 8-7).[28,75]

Frequency of the Lynch Syndromes

The first published estimate of the proportion of CRCs due to the Lynch syndromes based on national (Finnish) comprehensive cancer registration was 0.4 percent.[76] This involved the identification of all CRC cases in persons under the age of 40 in a province of Finland. In addition, the criteria were strict and included only CRC. Families affected by extracolonic cancers, such as cancer of the endometrium, and relatively small families had a reduced chance of being identified.

Using a more comprehensive method of identifying Lynch syndrome kindreds and focusing on a single county in Finland, Mecklin[32] showed that from 3.8 to 5.5 percent of CRC cases occurred in Lynch syndrome families. Most of the Lynch syndrome family probands were young; 30 percent of all CRC cases under the age of 50 evidenced a family history consistent with the Lynch syndromes.

Ponz de Leon and colleagues[77] studied familial aggregations of CRC in a population-based registry in a district in northern Italy; they reported that in approximately 5 percent of cases studied, the presence of two relatives (degree unspecified) with CRC, in addition to the proband, suggested the Lynch syndrome. The same report indicates that, when considering only first-degree relatives, "a stronger genetic component" was evidenced in 3.9 percent of the families studied.

Kee and Collins[78] studied all CRC patients in Northern Ireland diagnosed before the age of 55 and thoroughly investigated the medical history of all first-degree relatives of these individuals. They found that 6 percent of the probands had at least two colon cancer–affected relatives, thus meeting their criterion for a Lynch syndrome case. If none of the CRC cases aged 55 and older at diagnosis were Lynch syndrome cases, this means that Lynch syndrome cases accounted for 1 percent of all CRC cases. The authors estimated that the true proportion was from 1 to 2 percent and suggested that the proportion of cases attributable to the syndrome might be lower in Northern Ireland, where overall CRC incidence was high, in contrast to Finland, where CRC is less common.

Stephenson and colleagues[79] studied 100 patients under treatment for CRC by one surgeon in the United Kingdom. Pedigrees of all first-degree relatives were obtained and causes of death were documented. Four percent of the patients were found to have a family history suggestive of the Lynch syndromes in that at least two first-degree relatives of the proband died of CRC or other carcinomas associated with the syndrome.

Family histories of 390 patients under age 50 diagnosed with CRC in southern Alberta, Canada, were investigated, with pathology verification sought for all reported diagnoses of CRC.[80] Twelve cases (3.1 percent) were identified as Lynch syndrome families in that three first-degree relatives with CRC were identified. If "less strict" criteria (unspecified) were used, additional families would be identified, boosting this proportion to 9.5 percent. This study contrasts sharply with Mecklin's[32] estimate that 30 percent of cases in this age group were Lynch syndrome candidates.

It is difficult to reconcile the quantitative differences in these estimates. All investigators used apparently similar criteria for identifying Lynch syndrome families, but subtle differences are present (e.g., use of morbidity versus mortality data; degree of verification of diagnoses; potential for families to qualify based on a cluster of related cases not including the proband). All of these studies have a greater or lesser potential for including non–Lynch syndrome families (including families which happen by chance to have three cases of CRC and unrecognized FAP families); such classification errors would lead to overestimation of the frequency of the Lynch syndromes. Likewise, all of these studies will miss true Lynch syndrome cases, including cases showing endometrial and/or ovarian cancer excess in primary relatives of CRC probands, with CRC in second-degree relatives, including all solitary cases caused by new mutations or incomplete gene penetrance. They would also miss cases where family history was misspecified; such classification errors would lead to underestimation of the frequency. It is not possible to rule out errors in any of these studies until a specific genetic marker can be identified.

Pathology of Colonic Neoplasms in HNPCC

The colonic cancers of Lynch syndrome patients are not accompanied by multiple adenomas. No distinctive precursor lesion has been identified.

Mucinous carcinoma has been considered a feature of CRC and Lynch syndrome. For example, Mecklin[43] found an increased prevalence of mucinous carcinoma in his study of HNPCC in Finland (39 percent versus 20 percent in controls). In our material, there were 27 tumors (25 percent) with more than 50 percent extracellular mucin. There was impressive variability from family to family, with one family accounting for eight mucinous carcinomas and another for six more, suggesting heterogeneity within the Lynch syndromes. Our data set included an unusually large number of signet-ring cell carcinomas (eight), a finding also reported by Mecklin.[43]

Our data support the generally held belief that the Lynch syndrome is not a polyposis-prone disorder. Only 20 percent of colons resected for CRC contained adenomas. This may underestimate the true adenoma prevalence, since our study is partly retrospective and many of the pathology reports did not describe the appearance of the colonic mucosa. Still, there is no evidence that adenomas are more prevalent in patients with Lynch syndrome than in the general population. Mecklin et al.,[43] for example, found adenomas in 39 percent of colons affected by hereditary CRC, compared with 23 percent of colons with sporadic CRC (difference not statistically significant).

In our review, the number of adenomas in affected colons ranged from 1 to 5. Of 37 adenomas available for review, 7 (16 percent) contained areas of high-grade dysplasia. Mecklin et al[43] found high-grade dysplasia in 23 percent of adenomas from hereditary cancer patients versus 13 percent in controls, as did the mentioned study of Jass et al.[30] Still, if one accepts an adenoma-carcinoma sequence, it seems to follow that the adenomatous/dysplastic foci that develop in Lynch syndrome patients are more likely to undergo malignant change than are sporadic adenomas. There may be some inherent defect in the adenomas, the colonic mucosa, or the colonic milieu that encourages the malignant degeneration of dysplastic foci.

Gene Linkage and HNPCC

Gene linkage studies, using blood group and other traditional markers suggested linkage of the JK (Kidd) blood group (lod score 3.19) on chromosome 18 to HNPCC.[20] This linkage was found only in the Lynch syndrome II subset of these families—namely, those in which endometrial cancer occurred. No studies published subsequently have reported linkage between chromosome 18 markers and any hereditary CRC syndrome. Linkage analysis has specifically excluded the DCC gene on chromosome 18q as the locus for susceptibility to HNPCC in five kindreds from Finland.[81] There is no evidence to date that the p53 gene, APC gene, or DCC genes are the site of the germline lesion for HNPCC.

Recently, we have begun linkage studies on 7 HNPCC families selected from a resource of CRC-prone families identified at Creighton University's Hereditary Cancer Institute since the 1960s. Patients were considered affected who had either CRC or endometrial cancer or both specifically mentioned in a pathology report, a medical record, or a death certificate. Patients with a diagnosis of cancer of some other type or of an uncertain primary site were scored as unknown, and those who were believed to have no cancer diagnosis were scored as unaffected. The frequency of the disease gene in the general population was set at 0.001. The penetrance of the gene (i.e., the probability of being affected given a particular genotype at the disease locus) was set according to age-based liability classes. Markers were studied on chromosome 5, very near the APC and MCC genes; on chromosome 13, at the retinoblastoma locus; on chromosome 17, at the site of the p53 gene; and on chromosome 18, at the site of the DCC gene. No evidence of linkage heterogeneity among families was observed with these markers, and the results are generally strongly negative. However, specification of a chromosomal region in which linkage can be said to be excluded awaits further multilocus analyses. (See "Addendum" for recent evidence of gene linkage, below.)

COMMENTARY

We have reviewed the genetics and salient natural history phenotypic features of the Lynch syndromes. Clearly, a detailed family history will be mandatory in attempting to establish the genetic diagnosis for the Lynch syndromes, given the absence of any premorbid physical signs or biomarkers of genotypic risk. Nevertheless, progress is being made and this will likely increase, given the fact that at least 6 percent of the total CRC burden will reside in Lynch syndrome kindreds.

The mentioned absence of distinguishing pathophysiologic characteristics of individuals with the Lynch syndromes has stimulated researchers throughout the world to search for pathologic and molecular genetic clues to its diagnosis. Unfortunately, to date, no such clues to its genotypic status have been identified that can be used at the clinical level.[82,83] This biomarker research has focused on many fronts. It has involved studies attempting to determine whether or not there is a shift in the distribution of proliferating cells at the luminal surface of the crypt in the hereditary CRC setting as compared with controls.[84] Herein, it has been found that the total labeling index among families may or may not demonstrate an abnormality in epithelial proliferation.[19,85–87]

Fluorescent lectin histochemistry has also been studied. The labeling of one of these lectins (*Dolichos biflorus* agglutinin, or DBA) was significantly reduced in normal-appearing HNPCC tissues compared with controls,[82] thereby suggesting an abnormality in normal epithelial maturation in HNPCC. The lectin *Amaranthus caudatus* agglutinin (ACA) in patients with FAP showed significant increase in labeling in the superficial portion of the colonic crypts. In the case of HNPCC, a subset of patients showed an abnormality in ACA that was essentially identical to that seen in FAP.[83] These potential clues to host-factor susceptibility to CRC will require more intensive research.

Relatively few cancer-predisposing genes have been identified to date; of these, an even smaller number have been cloned. The retinoblastoma gene is the paradigm for a cloned tumor suppressor gene.[88] It is clear that cancer-prone families can be used advantageously for DNA-based precancer diagnosis, a concept which has now become a reality in the case of FAP.[89] This is clearly an objective for HNPCC.

The subject of screening and management of FAP has been recently reviewed by Rhodes and Bradburn[90] and may provide a paradigm for HNPCC. Activated oncogenes and tumor suppressor genes, when present in altered form in hereditary cancer syndromes, may also show alteration in sporadically occurring cancers. Such cancer genes may then be identified through the study of patients with what are considered to be generally rare hereditary cancers; this may ultimately prove to be of immense value for the diagnosis and therapy of individuals with commonly occurring cancers in the absence of positive family histories. Knowledge at the molecular level in HNPCC could add significantly to cancer control, comparable to the mentioned experience with FAP.

These studies have significantly advanced molecular genetic research which, in the case of CRC, was heralded by the landmark identification of an interstitial deletion on chromosome 5q in a patient with mental retardation and multiple colonic polyps.[91] This observation enabled investigators to employ gene linkage studies of FAP families to focus immediately on the 5q locus.[92,93] This research culminated in the discovery of the precise location and cloning of the deleterious FAP (APC) gene on chromosome 5q.[94,95]

Hopefully, the strategies which led to the identification and cloning of the APC gene in FAP may one day be successfully employed in the Lynch syndromes and thereby lead to the identification and ultimate cloning of the gene or genes for this more commonly occurring CRC syndrome. This will be extremely important because, as mentioned, there are no premonitory physical stigmata and/or biomarkers of genotypic susceptibility to assist in the diagnosis of the Lynch syndromes.[20,81,96,97]

Clearly, primary attention must be given to the search for biomarkers of genotypic susceptibility in the Lynch syndromes. Expenditure of funds in this quest has the potential for an enormous benefit through the targeting of surveillance on those identified as harboring the deleterious genotype and the ultimate saving of lives.

A problem of major concern pertains to the absence of well-established guidelines for the surveillance of the Lynch syndromes. All physicians agree on the need for full colonoscopic examination, given the proclivity to cancer of the proximal colon. However, there is a substantial lack of agreement on the age for initiation of colonoscopy as well as on its frequency. Nevertheless, insight into this problem may be emerging. Specifically, the work of Jass et al.[31]—showing an increase in villous change and high-grade dysplasia in adenomas from HNPCC patients, a finding confirmed by others[31,45]—provides support for the view that the adenomas of HNPCC patients are more aggressive than adenomas arising sporadically.[31] These findings suggest that adenomas in HNPCC patients undergo rapid growth,[44] thereby indicating that screening may be required more frequently. Clearly, more research is needed. These considerations are very important, given the time and expense of colonoscopy and the limitations of available expertise, particularly when the procedure must be performed with greater frequency. Finally, the recommendation of annual colonoscopy may pose problems in patient compliance.

ADDENDUM

Proof of the genetic basis for HNPCC (Lynch syndrome) has been confirmed recently by genetic linkage analysis. This research has shown the HNPCC locus to be closely linked to the anonymous microsatellite marker D2S123 on chromosome 2p wherein tentative assignment has been designated to 2p 15–16.[98,99] Of keen interest was the finding that most of the familial tumors[100] and to a lesser degree sporadic colorectal carcinoma[99,101,102] showed the unusual feature of microsatellite instability, which was manifest by alterations in the electrophoretic mobility of $(CA)_a$ dinucleotide repeat fragment. These findings of instability are consonant with the hypothesis of a DNA replication error which may result from the chromosome 2p gene defect. Further study of this phenomenon is clearly indicated. The ultimate cloning and characterization of the HNPCC gene should aid in its elucidation.

More recently, Risinger et al.[98] studied endometrial carcinomas from Lynch syndrome II patients and patients with sporadic occurrences of endometrial carcinoma, and herein they pursued the hypothesis that the dinucleotide repeat replication error phenotype would be evident in some fraction of the sporadic cases and those with Lynch syndrome II. The study design included 37 cases of sporadic endometrial carcinoma and endometrial carcinomas from 4 unrelated Lynch syndrome II families in the search for microsatellite instability. Interestingly, microsatellite instability was found in 17 percent of sporadic endometrial carcinomas and in 75 percent of endometrial carcinomas from the Lynch syndrome II kindreds. It was concluded that the HNPCC gene " . . . is also involved in heritable and somatic forms of endometrial carcinoma."

REFERENCES

1. Lynch HT, Smyrk T, Watson P, et al: Hereditary colorectal cancer. *Semin Oncol* 18:337–366, 1991.
2. Lynch HT, Lanspa SJ, Boman BM, et al: Hereditary nonpolyposis colorectal cancer—Lynch syndromes I and II. *Gastrointest Clin North Am* 17:679–712, 1988.
3. Lynch HT, Boman BM, Lanspa SJ, et al: Heritage of colonic polyps, in Herrera L (ed): *Familial Adenomatous Polyposis*. New York, Liss, 1990.
4. Herrera L: *Familial Adenomatous Polyposis*. New York, Liss, 1990.
5. Petersen GM, Slack J, Nakamura Y: Screening guidelines and premorbid diagnosis of familial adenomatous polyposis (FAP) using linkage. *Gastroenterology* 100:1658–1664, 1991.
6. Warthin AS: Heredity with reference to carcinoma as shown by the study of the cases examined in the pathological laboratory of the University of Michigan, 1895–1913. *Arch Intern Med* 12:546–555, 1913.
7. Warthin AS: The further study of a cancer family. *J Cancer Res* 9:279–286, 1925.
8. Warthin AS: Heredity of carcinoma in man. *Ann Intern Med* 4:681–696, 1931.
9. Hauser IJ, Weller CV: A further report on the cancer family of Warthin. *Am J Cancer* 27:434–449, 1936.
10. Lynch HT, Shaw MW, Magnuson CW, et al: Hereditary factors in two large midwestern kindreds. *Arch Intern Med* 117:206–212, 1966.
11. Lynch HT, Krush AJ: Cancer family G revisited: 1895–1970. *Cancer* 27:1505–1511, 1971.
12. Boland CR, Troncale FJ: Familial colonic cancer in the absence of antecedent polyposis. *Ann Intern Med* 100:700–701, 1984.
13. Lanspa SJ, Lynch HT, Smyrk TC, et al: Colorectal adenomas in the Lynch syndromes—Results of a colonoscopy screening program. *Gastroenterology* 98:1117–1122, 1990.
14. Bailey-Wilson JE, Elston RC, Schuelke GS, et al: Segregation analysis of hereditary nonpolyposis colorectal cancer. *Genet Epidemiol* 3:27–38, 1986.
15. Lynch HT: *Cancer Genetics*. Springfield, Ill, Thomas, 1976.
16. David KL, Steiner-Grossman P: The potential use of tumor registry data in the recognition and prevention of hereditary and familial cancer. *NY State J Med* 91:150–152, 1991.
17. Lynch HT: Cancer and the family history trail. *NY State J Med* 91:145–147, 1991.
18. Arvanitis ML, Jagelman DG, Fazio VW, et al: Mortality in patients with familial adenomatous polyposis. *Dis Colon Rectum* 33:639–642, 1990.
19. Watson P, Lynch HT: Extracolonic cancer in hereditary nonpolyposis colorectal cancer. *Cancer* 71:677–685, 1993.
20. Lynch HT, Kimberling WJ, Albano WA, et al: Hereditary nonpolyposis colorectal cancer, parts I and II. *Cancer* 56: 939–951, 1985.
21. Lynch HT, Voorhees GJ, Lanspa SJ, et al: Pancreatic carcinoma and hereditary nonpolyposis colorectal cancer: a family study. *Br J Cancer* 52:271–273, 1985.
22. Lynch HT, Ens JA, Lynch JF: Lynch syndrome II and urologic manifestations. *J Urol* 143:24–28, 1990.
23. Lynch HT, Harris RE, Bardawil WA, et al: Management of hereditary site-specific colon cancer. *Arch Surg* 112:170–174, 1977.
24. Lynch HT, Lynch PM: Tumor variation in the cancer family syndrome: Ovarian cancer. *Am J Surg* 138:439–442, 1979.
25. Lynch PM, Lynch HT: *Colon Cancer Genetics*. New York, Reinhold, 1985.
26. Utsunomiya J, Lynch HT: *Hereditary Colon Cancer*. Tokyo, Springer-Verlag, 1990.
27. Cristofaro G, Lynch HT, Caruso ML, et al: New phenotypic aspects in a family with Lynch syndrome II. *Cancer* 60:51–58, 1987.
28. Lynch HT, Smyrk TC, Lynch PM, et al: Adenocarcinoma of the small bowel in Lynch syndrome II. *Cancer* 64:2178–2183, 1989.
29. Lynch HT, Cavalieri RJ, Lynch JF, et al: Gynecologic cancer clues to Lynch syndrome II diagnosis: A family report. *Gynecol Oncol* 44:198–203, 1992.
30. Lynch HT, Fusaro RM, Roberts L, et al: Muir-Torre syndrome in several members of a family with a variant of the cancer family syndrome. *Br J Dermatol* 113:295–301, 1985.
31. Jass JR, Stewart SM: Evolution of hereditary non-polyposis colorectal cancer. *Gut* 33:783–786, 1992.

32. Mecklin J-P: Frequency of hereditary colorectal carcinoma. *Gastroenterology* 93:1021–1025, 1987.
33. Vasen HFA, den Hartog-Jager FC, Menko FH: Screening for hereditary non-polyposis colorectal cancer: A study of 22 kindreds in The Netherlands. *Am J Med* 86:278–281, 1989.
34. Cameron BH, Fitzgerald GWN, Cox J: Hereditary site-specific colon cancer in a Canadian kindred. *Can Med Assoc J* 140:41–45, 1989.
35. Rozen P, Fireman Z, Figer A, et al: Family history of colorectal cancer as a marker of potential malignancy within a screening program. *Cancer* 60:248–254, 1987.
36. Baker SJ, Preisinger AC, Jessup JM, et al: p53 mutations occur in combination with 17p allelic deletions as late events in colorectal tumorigenesis. *Cancer Res* 50:7717–7722, 1990.
37. Fisher G, Armstrong B: Familial colorectal cancer and the screening of family members. *Med J Aust* 150:22–25, 1989.
38. McConnell JC, Nizin JS, Slade MS: Colonoscopy in patients with a primary family history of colon cancer. *Dis Colon Rectum* 33:105–107, 1990.
39. Houlston RS, Murday V, Harocopos C, et al: Screening and genetic counselling for relatives of patients with colorectal cancer in a family cancer clinic. *Br Med J* 301:366–368, 1990.
40. Luchtfeld MA, Syverson D, Solfelt M, et al: Is colonoscopic screening appropriate in asymptomatic patients with family history of colon cancer? *Dis Colon Rectum* 34:763–768, 1991.
41. Wolfe CM, Richards RC, Gardner EJ: Occasional discrete polyps of the colon and rectum showing an inherited tendency in a kindred. *Cancer* 8:403–408, 1955.
42. Love RR: Adenomas are precursor lesions for malignant growth in non-polyposis hereditary carcinoma of the colon and rectum. *Surg Gynecol Obstet* 162:8–12, 1986.
43. Mecklin JP, Sipponen P, Jarvinen HJ: Histopathology of colorectal carcinomas and adenomas in cancer family syndrome. *Dis Colon Rectum* 29:849, 1986.
44. Jass JR, Stewart SM, Schroeder D, et al: Screening for hereditary non-polyposis colorectal cancer in New Zealand. *Eur J Gastroenterol Hepatol* 4:523–527, 1992.
45. Muto T, Bussey HJR, Morson BC: The evolution of cancer of the colon and rectum. *Cancer* 36:2251–2270, 1975.
46. Vasen HFA, Mecklin J-P, Meera Khan P, et al: Hereditary non-polyposis colorectal cancer. *Lancet* 2:877, 1991.
47. Jass JR: Colorectal cancer—Time to reduce the mortality. *NZ Med J* 105:65–166, 1992.
48. Boyle P, Zaridze DG, Smans M: Descriptive epidemiology of colorectal cancer. *Int J Cancer* 36:9–18, 1985.
49. Jass JR: Subsite distribution and incidence of colorectal cancer in New Zealand, 1974–1983. *Dis Colon Rectum* 34:56–59, 1991.
50. Berg K, Fletcher J: Ethical and legal aspects of predictive testing. *Lancet* 1:1043, 1986.
51. Davies K, Gershon D: Law to keep labels off genes. *Nature* 347:221, 1990.
52. Reid JD: Intestinal carcinoma in the Peutz-Jeghers syndrome. *JAMA* 229:833–834, 1974.
53. DaCruz GMG: Generalized gastrointestinal polyposis: An unusual syndrome of adenomatous polyposis, alopecia, onychorotropia. *Am J Gastroenterol* 47:504–510, 1967.
54. Haggitt RC, Reid BJ: Hereditary gastrointestinal polyposis syndromes. *Am J Surg Pathol* 10:871–887, 1986.
55. Iwama T, Ishida H, Imajo M, et al: The Peutz-Jeghers syndrome and malignant tumor, in Utsunomiya J, Lynch HT (eds): *Hereditary Colorectal Cancer.* Tokyo, Springer-Verlag, 1990, pp 331–336.
56. Lynch HT, Lynch PM, Follett K, et al: Familial polyposis coli: Heterogeneous polyp expression in two kindreds. *J Med Genet* 16:1–7, 1979.
57. Salem OS, Steck WD: Cowden's disease (multiple hamartoma and neoplasia syndrome). *J Am Acad Dermatol* 8:686–696, 1983.
58. Scully RE: Sex cord tumor with annular tubules: A distinctive ovarian tumor of the Peutz-Jeghers syndrome. *Cancer* 25: 1107–1121, 1970.
59. Watanabe H, Ajioka Y, Iwafuchi M, et al: Histogenesis of gastrointestinal carcinoma in Peutz-Jeghers polyp, in Utsunomiya J, Lynch HT (eds): *Hereditary Colon Cancer.* Tokyo, Springer-Verlag, 1990, pp 337–342.
60. Burke AP, Sobin LH: The pathology of Cronkhite-Canada polyps: A comparison to juvenile polyposis. *Am J Surg Pathol* 13:940–946, 1989.
61. Daniel ES, Ludwig SL, Lewin KS, et al: The Cronkhite-Canada syndrome: an analysis of clinical and pathologic features and therapy in 55 patients. *Medicine* 61:293–308, 1974.
62. Jass JR, Williams CB, Bussey HJR, et al: Juvenile polyposis—A precancerous condition. *Histopathology* 13:619–630, 1988.
63. Jass JR: Pathology of polyposis syndromes with special reference to juvenile polyposis, in Utsunomiya J, Lynch HT (eds): *Hereditary Colorectal Cancer.* Tokyo, Springer-Verlag, 1990, p 575.
64. Liu IOL, Kung IJM, Lee JMH, et al: Primary colorectal signet-ring carcinoma in young patients: Report of 3 cases. *Pathology* 17:35, 1985.
65. Rappaport LB, Sperling HV, Stavrides A: Colon cancer in the Cronkhite-Canada syndrome. *J Clin Gastroenterol* 8:199–202, 1986.
66. Walpole IR, Cullity G: Juvenile polyposis: A case with early presentation and death attributable to adenocarcinoma of the pancreas. *Am J Med Genet* 32:1–8, 1989.
67. Lynch HT, Smyrk T, Lanspa SJ, et al: Flat adenomas in a colon cancer-prone kindred. *J Natl Cancer Inst* 80:278–282, 1988.
68. Lynch HT, Smyrk TC, Lanspa SJ, et al: Phenotypic variation in colorectal adenoma/cancer expression in two families: Hereditary flat adenoma syndrome. *Cancer* 66:909–915, 1990.
69. Lynch HT, Smyrk TC, Watson P, et al: Hereditary flat adenoma syndrome: A variant of familial adenomatous polyposis? *Dis Colon Rectum* 35:411–421, 1992.
70. Leppert M, Burt R, Hughes JP, et al: Genetic analysis of an inherited predisposition to colon cancer in a family with a variable number of adenomatous polyps. *N Engl J Med* 322: 904–908, 1990.
71. Spirio L, Otterud B, Stauffer D, et al: Linkage of a variant or attenuated form of adenomatous polyposis coli to the adenomatous polyposis coli (APC) locus. *Am J Hum Genet* 51: 92–100, 1992.
72. Burt RW, Bishop DT, Cannon LA, et al: Dominant inheritance of adenomatous colonic polyps and colorectal cancer. *N Engl J Med* 12:1540–1544, 1985.
73. Cannon-Albright LA, Skolnick MH, Bishop DT, et al: Common inheritance of susceptibility to colonic adenomatous polyps and associated colorectal cancers. *N Engl J Med* 319:533–537, 1988.
74. Lovett E: Family studies in cancer of the colon and rectum. *Br J Surg* 63:13–189, 1976.
75. Lynch HT, Fusaro RM, Pester J, et al: The cancer family syndrome: Rare cutaneous phenotypic linkage of Torre's syndrome. *Arch Intern Med* 141:607–611, 1980.
76. Mecklin J-P, Jarvinen HJ, Peltokallio P: Cancer family syndrome: Genetic analysis of 22 Finnish kindreds. *Gastroenterology* 90:328–333, 1986.
77. Ponz de Leon M, Sassatelli R, Sacchetti C, et al: Familial aggregation of tumors in the three-year experience of a pop-

ulation-based colorectal cancer registry. *Cancer Res* 49:4344–4348, 1989.
78. Kee F, Collins BJ: How prevalent is cancer family syndrome? *Gut* 32:309–312, 1991.
79. Stephenson BM, Finan PJ, Gascoyne J, et al: Frequency of familial colorectal cancer. *Br J Surg* 78:1162–1166, 1991.
80. Westlake PJ, Bryant HE, Huchcroft SA, et al: Frequency of hereditary nonpolyposis colorectal cancer in southern Alberta. *Dig Dis Sci* 36:1441–1447, 1991.
81. Peltomaki P, Sistonen P, Mecklin J-P, et al: Evidence supporting exclusion of the DCC gene and a portion of chromosome 18q as the locus for susceptibility to hereditary nonpolyposis colorectal carcinoma in five kindreds. *Cancer Res* 51:4135–4140, 1991.
82. Sams JS, Lynch HT, Burt RW, et al: Abnormalities of lectin histochemistry in familial polyposis coli and hereditary nonpolyposis colorectal cancer. *Cancer* 66:502–508, 1990.
83. Boland CR: Abnormalities of colonic glycoconjugates in groups at increased risk for colorectal cancer, in Rossini FP, Lynch HT, Winawer SJ (eds): *Recent Progress in Colorectal Cancer: Biology and Management of High Risk Patients*. Amsterdam, Elsevier Science, 1992.
84. Lipkin M, Blattner WA, Gardner EJ, et al: Classification and risk assessment of individuals with familial polyposis, Gardner's syndrome, and familial nonpolyposis colon cancer from [3H] thymidine labeling patterns in colonic epithelial cells. *Cancer Res* 44:4201–4207, 1984.
85. Cats A: Proliferation rate in hereditary nonpolyposis colon cancer. *J Natl Cancer Inst* 83:1687–1689, 1991.
86. Cats A, deVries EGE, Zwart N, et al: Epithelial proliferation in different segments of the colon in hereditary nonpolyposis colon cancer. *Gastroenterology* 102:A348, 1992.
87. Love RR, Surawicz TS, Morrissey JF, et al: Levels of colorectal ornithine decarboxylase activity in patients with colon cancer, a family history of nonpolyposis hereditary colorectal cancer, and adenomas. *Cancer Epidemiol Biomed Prev* 1:195–198, 1992.
88. Lee WH, Bookstein R, Hong F, et al: Human retinoblastoma susceptibility gene: Cloning, identification, and sequence. *Science* 235:1394–1399, 1987.
89. Koorey DJ, McCaughan GW, Trent RJ, et al: Risk estimation in familial adenomatous polyposis using DNA probes linked to the familial adenomatous polyposis gene. *Gut* 33:530–534, 1992.
90. Rhodes M, Bradburn DM: Overview of screening and management of familial adenomatous polyposis. *Gut* 33:125–131, 1992.
91. Herrera L, Kakati S, Gibas L, et al: Gardner syndrome in a man with an interstitial deletion of 5q. *Am J Med Genet* 25:473–476, 1986.
92. Bodmer WF, Bailey CJ, Bodmer J, et al: Localization of the gene for familial adenomatous polyposis on chromosome 5. *Nature* 328:2–4, 1987.
93. Solomon E, Voss R, Hall V, et al: Chromosome 5 allele loss in human colorectal carcinomas. *Nature* 328:616–620, 1987.
94. Groden J, Thliveris A, Samowitz W, et al: Identification and characterization of the familial adenomatous polyposis coli gene. *Cell* 66:589–600, 1991.
95. Kinzler KW, Nilbert MC, Su LK, et al: Identification of FAP locus genes from chromosome 5q21. *Science* 253:661–664, 1991.
96. Mecklin JP, Jarvinen HJ: Clinical features of colorectal carcinoma in the cancer family syndrome. *Dis Colon Rectum* 29:160, 1986.
97. Peltomaki P, Sistonen P, Mecklin J-P, et al: Evidence that the MCC-APC gene region in 5q21 is not the site for susceptibility to hereditary nonpolyposis colorectal carcinoma. *Cancer Res* 52:4530–4533, 1992.
98. Risinger JI, Berchuck A, Kohler MF, et al: Genetic instability of microsatellites in endometrial carcinoma. *Cancer Res* 53:5100–5103, 1993.
99. Peltomaki P, Aaltonen LA, Sistonen P, et al: Genetic mapping of a locus predisposing to human colorectal cancer. *Science* 260:810–812, 1993.
100. Aaltonen LA, Peltomaki P, Leach FS, et al: Clues to the pathogenesis of familial colorectal cancer. *Science* 260:812–816, 1993.
101. Thibodeau SN, Bren G, Schaid D: Microsatellite instability in cancer of the proximal colon. *Science* 260:816–819, 1993.
102. Ionov Y, Peinado MA, Malkhosyan S, et al: Ubiquitous somatic mutations in simple repeated sequences reveal a new mechanism or colonic carcinogenesis. *Nature (Lond)* 363:558–561, 1993.

CHAPTER 9

Hereditary Polyposis Syndromes

Lemuel Herrera
Antonio Obrador

HIGHLIGHTS

Although the study of hereditary polyposis syndromes can be established only by pedigree analysis, initial attention to these syndromes came from the recognition of an increased risk for malignancies following the diagnosis of neoplastic polyps of the large bowel. The study of one of these conditions, familial adenomatous polyposis (FAP), has led the way for the understanding of colorectal cancer in terms of molecular biology, allowing for significant new options in several clinical aspects of the management of that disease.

CONTROVERSIES

The contribution of these syndromes to a premalignant state continues to be established. Their spectrum of phenotypical manifestations continues to be described, while specific biomarkers have yet to be validated.

FUTURE DIRECTIONS

Phenotypical manifestations need to be matched to specific mutations of the FAP gene and their cancer risk. Quality control for DNA testing needs to be established. Effective interventions decreasing morbidity and mortality need to be developed. Issues related to genetic counseling, informed consent, and possible discrimination based on genetic risk need to be clarified.

The study of hereditary polyposis syndromes can best be approached by grouping them histologically into those that express phenotypically as neoplasias, adenomatous (tubular, mixed, or villous) polyps, and nonneoplastic and hamartomatous polyps, because each histologic type has distinct clinical features and outcomes. The analysis can also be approached by the study of specific syndromes, their spectrum of phenotypical manifestations, and their propensity to develop into malignancy.

The diagnosis of a colorectal polyp, particularly in a young individual, should always be considered a potential manifestation of a hereditary polyposis syndrome; therefore, the patient's history should be considered incomplete if the incidence of polyps or gastrointestinal cancer in first-degree relatives is not ascertained. Individuals with a history of a colorectal growth should then be carefully identified and subsequently stratified according to the mode of transmission of these neoplasias. While a pattern of vertical transmission (hereditary) can easily be distinguished in some families, in other families there will be a clustering or aggregation of these pathologic entities without a defined mode of transmission (familial), distinguishable only by inquiring about neoplasias in all relatives, not just first-degree ones. However, in both types of conditions, hereditary and familial, patients and families are at higher risk for the development of colorectal polyps or cancer when compared with a general population without a positive history of colorectal neoplasias. The study of these individuals and families has been prompted by practical clinical issues, which include the recognition that more effective screening policies for relatives at risk for colorectal cancer can be formulated on the basis of the inheritance pattern; the understanding that the elements operative in the adenoma-to-carcinoma histologic sequence are the same in the hereditary, familial, and "sporadic" types of colorectal neoplasias; and the fact that the cellular and biochemical events associated with abnormalities of proliferation and transformation seem to be common to all colonic neoplasias.

In this chapter, FAP is addressed first, followed by Peutz-Jeghers syndrome, juvenile polyposis, Cowden's disease, intestinal ganglioneuromatosis and multiple endocrine neoplasia type IIB, Muir-Torre syndrome, Ruvalcaba-Myhre-Smith syndrome, and Devon family syndrome. Allocations of individuals and families to these syndromes by their phenotypical manifestations have been useful to frame and orient basic research, specifically in the area of genetics. This is especially true with regard to FAP, which has been the model par excellence for furthering the understanding of the adenoma-to-carcinoma sequence, initially at the histologic level and subsequently at the molecular biology level. Because these findings can now be correlated with clinical and epidemiologic data, early diagnosis, genetically directed screening, and early and effective therapeutic interventions for FAP have become clinically relevant. The hope is that this knowledge may be applicable to the understanding and management of "hereditary nonpolypoid" and "sporadic" colorectal cancer, the latter being the most common malignancy affecting both men and women in the United States.

FAMILIAL ADENOMATOUS POLYPOSIS

Familial adenomatous polyposis is inherited in an autosomal dominant fashion, with a high penetrance rate (95 percent).[1] It is characterized by the development of many (usually more than 100) adenomatous polyps in the colon and the rectum. It is associated with the highest risk for the development of colorectal carcinoma; virtually all affected individuals will develop colorectal cancer in the third or fourth decade if a colectomy is not performed.[2]

Familial adenomatous polyposis has been described in all races. It is of interest that in Japan and Africa, where the incidence of colorectal cancer is very low, once individuals are affected with FAP, the possibility of their developing a colorectal malignancy at a young age is 100 percent, the same as in affected individuals living in Western countries, where there is a higher incidence of colorectal cancer. This observation seems to indicate that environmental variations may not be a major contributing factor in inducing the transforming somatic mutations of this disease.

Because FAP is inherited in a dominant mendelian fashion, it affects both sexes. Bulow[3] calculated that the mean annual incidence of FAP in Denmark from 1970 to 1991 was 1.8 per million inhabitants, corresponding to 1 in 6670 live births. This figure is comparable to that of the Swedish estimate of 1 in 7647 births, which was based on national registry data, as was the Danish calculation.[4] Komatsu[5] placed the incidence in Japan at 1 in 9467 births, and Watne[6] estimated 322 new patients per year based on 3,612,000 births in the United States. It is estimated that in about 20 percent of these cases, there is no previous family history; these cases are referred to as *new mutations*. However, these affected individuals will transmit the genetic abnormality to their descendants. Based on polyposis patients born to apparently normal parents from 1931 to 1950, Gedde-Dahl et al.[7] estimated that the rate for new mutations of the adenomatous polyposis coli (APC/FAP) gene was between 1 in 35,333 and 1 in 36,868 births in Norway.

Historically, lesions of the large bowel consistent with polyposis were first described by Menzelio[8] in 1721 in a soldier who ultimately died of chronic dysentery. In 1824, Cooper[9] described a case of rectal polyps in a young man; in 1859, Chargelaigue[10] described a 16-year-old girl and a 21-year-old man with polyadenomatosis; and in 1861, Luschka[11] described a 30-year-old woman with myriad colonic polyps. In 1863, Virchow[12] described many colonic polyps in a 15-year-old boy and coined the term *colitis polyposis*, implying an inflammatory element in the polyps.

In 1882, Cripps[13] presented a paper before the Pathological Society of London reporting familial polyposis coli in two brothers. In 1890, Bickersteth[14] reported polyps in two generations of a family, mother and son, and in that same year, Handford[15] noted the association of the disease with cancer of the large intestine. In 1927, Cockayne[16] was the first to state that colonic polyposis was inherited in a mendelian dominant fashion; this was subsequently validated by a detailed analysis by Veale[17] in 1965.

Little was known, however, about the number and distribution of the adenomas or the age range of onset of the disease. Cuthbert Dukes, a pathologist at St. Mark's Hospital in London, began to interview affected individuals and to inquire about their families in order to construct pedigrees and identify the spectrum of clinical manifestations. Family members were then called and invited to undergo sigmoidoscopic examination. If polyps were found, histologic confirmation was necessary for diagnosis. This led to the publication in 1930 of a comprehensive review of the hereditary factors in multiple intestinal adenomas.[18] A subsequent report coauthored with Lockhart-Mummery, a surgeon at St. Mark's Hospital, demonstrated a vertical pattern of inheritance of the disease and detailed the occurrence in 10 families over three or four successive generations.[19]

In 1939, Descum McKenney[20] from Buffalo, New York, described 21 patients in three families living in North America, all in the third generation of the disease. One of these families was seminal in the development of the Roswell Park Polyposis Registry. McKenney also proposed subtotal colectomy with ileoproctoanastomosis as the operation to be performed.

Among the reports of patients with polyposis, there was the occasional mention of extracolonic manifestations. The first report of such extracolonic manifestations is credited to Devic and Bussey,[21] who in 1912 described a woman with polyposis and osteomas of the mandible, sebaceous cysts of the skull, and subcutaneous lipomas. In 1935, Cabot[22] presented a case of a 36-year-old man with multiple polyposis of the small and large bowels, multiple bony exostoses, a history of fibrosarcoma, sebaceous cysts, and carcinoma of the ampulla of Vater. Miller and Sweet[23] described a 21-year-old woman with polyposis coli and a desmoid tumor in the abdominal wall in 1937, and in 1943 Fitzgerald[24] described a 36-year-old woman with recurrent desmoid tumors of the abdominal wall, bony exostoses, multiple compound odontomas, torus palatinus, and multiple polyps of the bowel. In 1953, Gardner and Richards[25] described the manifestations in a family (kindred 109) in their Utah Registry. Affected members inherited adenomatous polyps of the colon, osteomas of the maxilla and mandible, and exostoses in the skull and facial bones. After a series of subsequent publications, "Gardner's syndrome" became known to encompass soft-tissue tumors (sebaceous cysts and fibromas), bony tumors, osteomas, and adenomatous polyps of the colon. It was also emphasized that colonic polyps in this syndrome had the same growth pattern and malignant potential as the adenomatous polyps in patients with familial polyposis who lacked extracolonic manifestations. In 1967, MacDonald et al.[26] reviewed 118 cases of periampullary carcinomas and Gardner's syndrome reported in the literature. Blair and Trempe,[27] in 1980, described the presence of hyperpigmented lesions of the retina in patients diagnosed with Gardner's syndrome. This finding is currently considered a phenotypical marker for individuals affected with FAP.[28–30] It is now clear that many young patients with FAP have the characteristic lesions of the retina, bilateral and multiple, without other extracolonic manifestations; rarely, nonaffected members of the general population will have them. These lesions can be found in early childhood, preceding the appearance of gastrointestinal polyps.

In 1956, Richards and Woolf[31] published a report on a discrete colonic polyp-cancer syndrome that also seemed to have a mendelian dominant mode of inheritance. Although affected patients had only a few adenomatous polyps of the colon, they had an increased tendency to develop colorectal cancer. They had no extracolonic manifestations. These hereditary and familial aggregation (clustering) elements of the so-called sporadic adenomatous polyps have been reviewed extensively by Burt.[32] Pedigree analysis using likelihood methods and comparing the probability of autosomal dominant, autosomal recessive, and random models suggests that there is a common, underlying, dominantly inherited susceptibility to adenomatous polyps. A problem marring the interpretation of these studies is the selection of controls. By choosing individuals without a positive family history as controls rather than age-specific incidence in the unaffected members of an affected family, it is possible to select as controls individuals from a group with an unknown mutation or individuals with a complete selection against a dominant susceptibility.[33] This clinical entity of heredofamilial polyp-cancer syndrome should be recognized, as it implies an increased risk for colorectal neoplasia but without the connotation of FAP.

Although Gardner's earlier reports suggested a single defective gene for FAP, McKusick,[34] using phenotypical evidence, showed that each of the syndromes resulted from a different genetic abnormality rather than a single one responsible for familial polyposis alone. Bussey[2] had speculated that all polyposis syndromes represented different degrees of manifestations of Gardner's syndrome; in 1983, Gardner[35] suggested that the disease was systemic and called it an *overgrowth syndrome*.

Early cytogenetic studies demonstrated the presence of tetraploidy in "normal" fibroblasts from many of these patients.[36, 37] Others have reported on the presence of an excess of structural and numerical aberrations in in vitro cultures,[38, 39] and it was thought that these findings could be helpful to differentiate relatives at risk without the genetic abnormality and to develop a genetically directed screening program. This was never tested clinically, however. Efforts to localize the genetic defect determining FAP followed a random investigational approach. In 1986, we reported on a patient with colonic polyps and cancer, mental retardation, a large desmoid tumor, and multiple congenital abnormalities.[40] Cytogenetic studies of blood lymphocytes revealed a deletion in the long arm of chromosome 5 (5q15-22) (Fig. 9-1). Based on that report, in the following year, Bodmer et al.[41] and Leppert et al.,[41a] using techniques of restriction fragment length polymorphisms (RFLPs) and the chromosome 5–specific DNA probe c11p11, showed that the gene for FAP was closely linked to the 5q21-22 locus. Using an additional probe (P227), Meera Khan et al.[42] presented data to indicate that the gene was in band 5q22, but closer to 5q21. In 1988, Nakamura et al.[43] demonstrated that both FAP and Gardner's syndrome arose from a genetic defect at basically the same chromo-

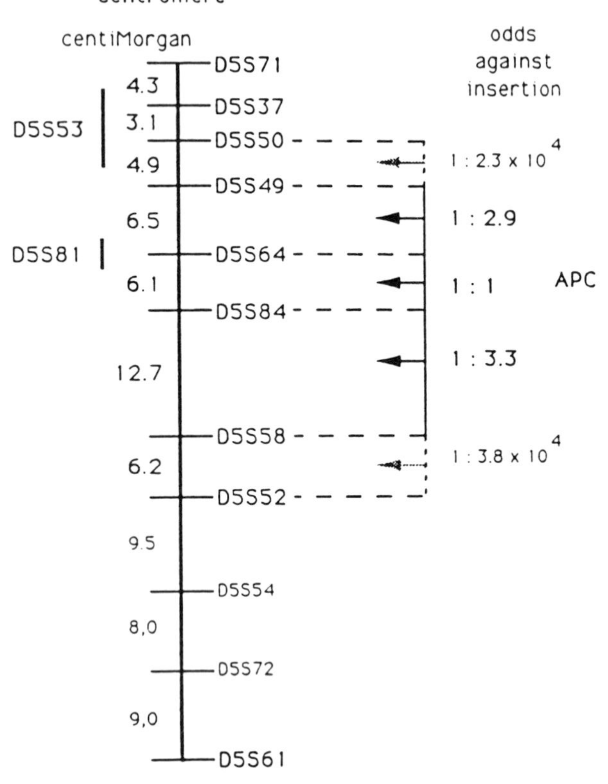

FIG. 9-1. Sex-average map of markers near the adenomatous polyposis coli (APC) locus on chromosome 5. Genetic distances are shown in Kosambi centimorgans. Markers that could be placed (with odds > 1000:1) are shown associated with the *long vertical line*. Only markers in the vicinity of the APC locus are shown. The most likely position for APC was in the D5S49/D5S58 interval. (From Ref. 53, with permission.)

somal location using techniques of genetic markers that flanked the diseased gene.

Genetic modifications of the FAP gene (also called the *APC gene* by geneticists) are germline mutations that can be produced by point mutations, deletions (detectable by cytogenetic analysis), or insertions in the nucleotide sequence. In turn, these alterations may result in termination signals during transcription and possibly faulty or different protein products.[44, 45] The resulting truncated protein may be produced by frameshift, nonsense, or splicing mutations. A recent interesting observation indicates that different mutations of the FAP gene in affected individuals from different families will produce similar phenotypical manifestations.[44–56]

Identification of the FAP/APC gene mutations in affected kindreds (families) and individuals facilitates the presymptomatic diagnosis of relatives at risk with a high degree of confidence. Two types of molecular biologic analysis are currently available for the presymptomatic diagnosis of FAP: (1) The first method is direct mutation analysis of the FAP/APC gene, which is able to detect up to 40 to 70 percent of the affected individuals. Once the specific mutation is identified, highly accurate genetic testing by direct analysis can be performed rapidly by widely available techniques such as protein and allele-specific expression assay and screens for nonsense and frameshift mutations.[56a, 56b] (2) The second method is genetic linkage pedigree analysis and the study of DNA by a set of 12 markers closely associated with and/or flanking the genetic defect and using RFLP techniques (Table 9-1). These techniques use enzymes that cut DNA at specific, well-defined amino acid sequences. This is a highly specific inherited characteristic that is easily traced to progenitors and ancestors and that becomes useful and informative when it is in close proximity to or even flanking the genetic defect. Because of a nonallelic heterogeneity, this linked marker approach for risk estimation is reliable only in those families large enough to prove linkage beyond reasonable doubt (informative kindred). Although limitations to this approach include uninformative pedigree structures or linkage markers and unavailability of key family members or tissues for testing,[57] it was the first strategic approach for identification of affected individuals.[53] The use of these two methods to study well-stratified kindreds provides a powerful research tool and allows for genetic diagnosis in many of the affected individuals with FAP.

Clinical experience from various registries and reports of screening of offspring of patients with FAP have provided an age-at-onset (diagnosis) curve for FAP.[58] More recently, Petersen et al.[59] have suggested the use of this curve in combination with molecular biological analysis as the basis for a screening program. This genetically directed screening program would identify those individuals who have inherited the genetic defect and those who have not. The screening schedule would then be tailored to their risk. In those relatives at risk carrying the FAP mutation characteristic of the kindred, there would be no change in the current screening recommendations. However, in relatives at risk older than 22 years of age with negative molecular biology analysis, it is likely that the lifetime risk for colonic cancer is the same as that of the general population (approximately 3 percent). For them, colonic cancer screening should resume at 50 years of age, with evaluations of the bowel before that only for specific symptoms. A current limitation to adopting this approach as a blanket policy is that each FAP kindred may have a unique FAP/APC gene mutation. At the same time, a prevalent mutation has not been identified in the registered FAP population. This makes it difficult at present to implement a wide genetically directed screening program; however, as experience grows and more kindreds and their mutations are identified, this approach may become clinically useful, al-

Table 9-1
APC Mutations Found by Single-Strand Conformation Polymorphism (SSCP) Analysis in Genomic DNA from 74 Italian Polyposis Patients

Patient	*Exon*	*Position (bp)*	*Mutation type*	*Consequence*
1598	5	541	−CAAA	Frame shift
1506	5	623	CAG → CGG	Glu → Arg[a]
1219	9A	Intron 9	G → T	Exon skipping
1717	11	1485	−T	Frame shift
1669	15B	2504	−CTTCATCAAGAGG	Frame shift
1505	15C	2527	−AGTT	Frame shift
1641	8	904	C → T	Stop
1653	15H	4393	−GAGA	Frame shift
1799	3	419	−AGAG	Frame shift
1871	15G	3926	−AAAAG	Frame shift
1633	15G	3926	−AAAAG	Frame shift
1637	15G	3926	−AAAAG	Frame shift
1381	15G	3926	−AAAAG	Frame shift
1602	15G	3926	−AAAAG	Frame shift
1599	15E	3183	−ACAAA	Frame shift
2182	15E	3183	−ACAAA	Frame shift
1666	15E	3183	−ACAAA	Frame shift
2021	15E	3183	−ACAAA	Frame shift
2104	15E	3183	−ACAAA	Frame shift

[a]No other affected members were available to confirm segregation of this sequence variant with the disease in the family.

SOURCE: Courtesy of L. Bertario, M.D., and L. Varesco, Ph.D., Italian Polyposis Registry.

though the observations of heterogeneity among families, and gene mutations, make a quick screening method doubtful.

Furthermore, there may be psychosocial implications and morbidity associated with presymptomatic DNA testing for FAP. Differences in age of onset and maturity are major factors influencing preparedness for presymptomatic testing and attitude toward a chronic disease. Because these implications may have a major impact on the management of the disease, they should be the object of a carefully designed, executed, and interpreted analysis following an informed consent designed with genetic counselors. The disclosure of test results should be followed by the use of an illness effects questionnaire designed to assess perceived personal family disruptions and emotional upheaval and other manifestations of psychological distress, again with the contribution of appropriate experts.

DNA testing may be useful in individuals with FAP who want testing for completion of a prenatal counseling option, individuals at risk who are planning families, affected individuals with young children at risk who want to establish indications and timing for screening interventions, and affected individuals who want to have supporting proof that their phenotypical manifestations are the result of FAP and wish to know the mutation(s) involved.

If the individual at risk has inherited the affected parent's normal allele, the clinician or genetic counselor can then emphasize the positive aspects of screening management, as this patient has the same risk for colonic cancer as an individual with general risk factors. The genetic defect will not be transmitted to his or her children. We should continue to stress that the key to understanding the results of molecular biological testing remains a well-constructed pedigree based on a reliably obtained family history and a detailed account of the type and onset of benign and malignant phenotypical manifestations.

Although no specific biomarker has been reported to be definitively associated with this disease, we have followed with interest the investigation of ornithine decarboxylase by Luk and Baylin.[60] Ornithine decarboxylase, the gateway enzyme for polyamine biosynthesis, was identified in the "normal" colonic mucosa of individuals who would later express the FAP clinical phenotype.[60] This report was of great interest because of its predictive potential, since stepwise increases in ornithine decarboxylase activity have been reported to be associated with progression from flat mucosa to polyps, dysplasia, and cancer in those with the sporadic type of cancer.[61]

Changes in the type, structure, glucoconjugates, and synthesis of mucin detected by lectin binding may also herald premalignant changes not readily evident in routine histopathologic examination.[62, 63] While Kuroki et al.[64] have reported a decrease in sialic acid content using UEA-1, Muto[65] has reported that the staining for sialomucins in the flat (nonpolypoid) colon biopsies of families of patients with FAP appeared to be associated with the carrier state for the genetic defect, and Boland et al.[65a] have reported on the lectin Griffonia simplicifolia I-A4. Guillem and Weinstein[66] have presented data demonstrating a consistent down-regulation of protein kinase C in colorectal neoplasias. An expanded proliferative compartment of epithelial cells has also been reported in individuals with FAP before the development of gastrointestinal tumors. Baba et al.[67] reported on the differential labeling indices using methods of specimen irrigation with oxygenated artificial blood supplemented with ^{3}H-thymidine and bromodeoxyuridine to label S-phase cells. We have reported on sucrase-isomaltase[68] and crypt-cell antigens,[68a] while others continue to study carbohydrate determinants on the cell surface such as sialyl Le^x and sialyl Le^a and others recognized by monoclonal antibodies.[68b] All of these are potential biomarkers for possible investigation in screening, diagnosis, monitoring, or intervention efforts.

Large Bowel Manifestations

Because the rectum is usually involved in FAP, most clinicians have traditionally begun examining individuals at risk with rectosigmoidoscopy. If polyps are found, a biopsy is always performed to confirm the histologic type of polyp. The need to biopsy these polyps must be emphasized, particularly in children, because they can be inflammatory, not adenomatous. The number of polyps per square centimeter must be counted and their distribution and anatomic location carefully noted, for in a few patients, the disease may be regional, with the rectum spared. The remainder of the large bowel can be evaluated by an air-contrast barium enema, which provides vastly superior information compared with that from a standard barium enema; however, the widespread use of colonoscopy has now supplanted both of these radiographic studies in most institutions. The hallmark of the FAP phenotype is the presence of numerous (usually over 100) mainly adenomatous polyps (Fig. 9-2). Curiously, in some patients, up to several thousand polyps can be present. Histologically, these polyps may exhibit a single pattern or a combination of patterns, which may include tubular, mixed, tubulohyperplastic, mixed tubulovillous, villous adenomas, and occasionally juvenile polyps.[68c] Foci of carcinoma in situ and invasive carcinoma can be found, particularly in the larger polyps. The polyps usually appear during the second or third decade of life, although we have seen them in children as young as 9 years of age and others have noted them to occur as early as 4 months and 7 years

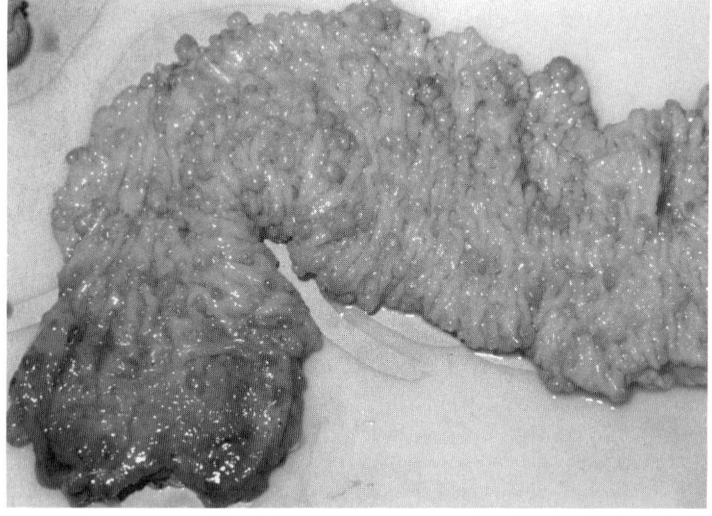

A

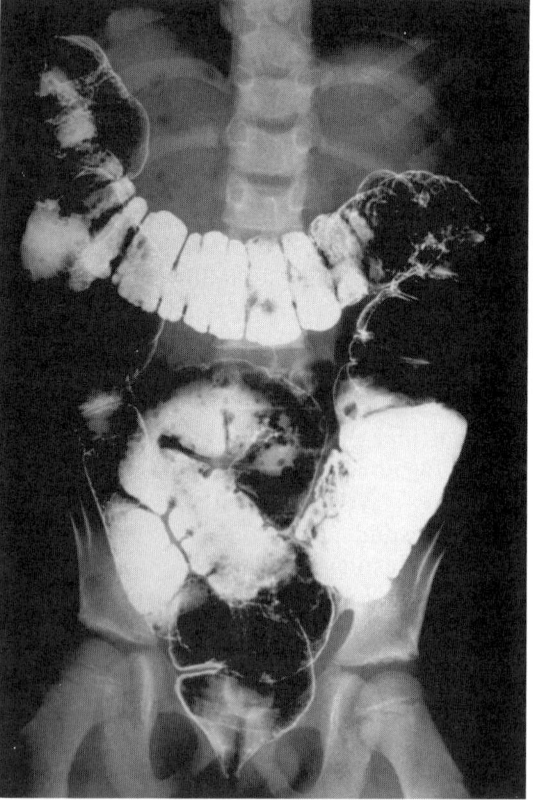

B

FIG. 9-2. *A*. Multiple rectocolonic polyps in a dense pattern in a 9-year-old boy. *B*. Radiograph after barium enema in the same patient. (From Ref. 56, with permission.)

of age.[69, 70] Microscopic adenomatous changes of the epithelium have been seen in even younger children.[71] Individuals at risk in a screening program are usually diagnosed at an average age of 22 years, whereas the average age at diagnosis in patients presenting with symptoms is 36 years. Endoscopically and histologically, polyps occurring in individuals affected with FAP cannot be distinguished from sporadic adenomas occurring in the general population. There are also reports of late-onset FAP, with polyps developing after 40 years of age[70]; however, this is extremely unusual. In affected individuals, polyps may be distributed evenly throughout the colon, with a slight distal colonic excess; occasionally, only segments of colon are affected. The size of the diagnosed polyps depends on the timing and type of the first examination. They can be very large when found in patients who are symptomatic; however, when the polyps are discovered during the implementation of a screening program, they can be minute—that is, microadenomas. Microadenomas (dysplasia or adenomatous changes in a single crypt or even portions of a single crypt, as in Fig. 9-3) are a histologic feature characteristic of patients with FAP but are not observed in the general population. Minute polyps are best recognized by flexible sigmoidoscopy in a well-prepared bowel (Fig. 9-4). They may also be seen in the biopsy specimens of normal-appearing flat mucosa of patients with FAP. It is for this reason that we recommend flexible sigmoidoscopy to 64 cm as the screening procedure, as it affords good magnification and allows for multiple observers. Colonoscopy may be the only way to recognize small flat polyps of regional distribution in certain kindreds. It is of interest that even when there are myriad polyps, most measure less than 5 to 10 mm. The finding of one or more polyps measuring over 1 cm is associated with a 47 percent risk of having a cancer somewhere in the colon.[6] Polyps larger than 2 or 3 cm usually contain a focus of carcinoma. Furthermore, because cancers seem to occur more often when there are many polyps, there is probably some use for stratifying patients into types by their expression of polyps per square centimeter, designated as profuse and sparse, with profuse being >6 to 9 polyps/cm^2 in adults and >3 to 6 polyps/cm^2 in children.

Adenocarcinoma of the colon will invariably develop in all patients with FAP unless the colon is removed. Many reported series have indicated that most

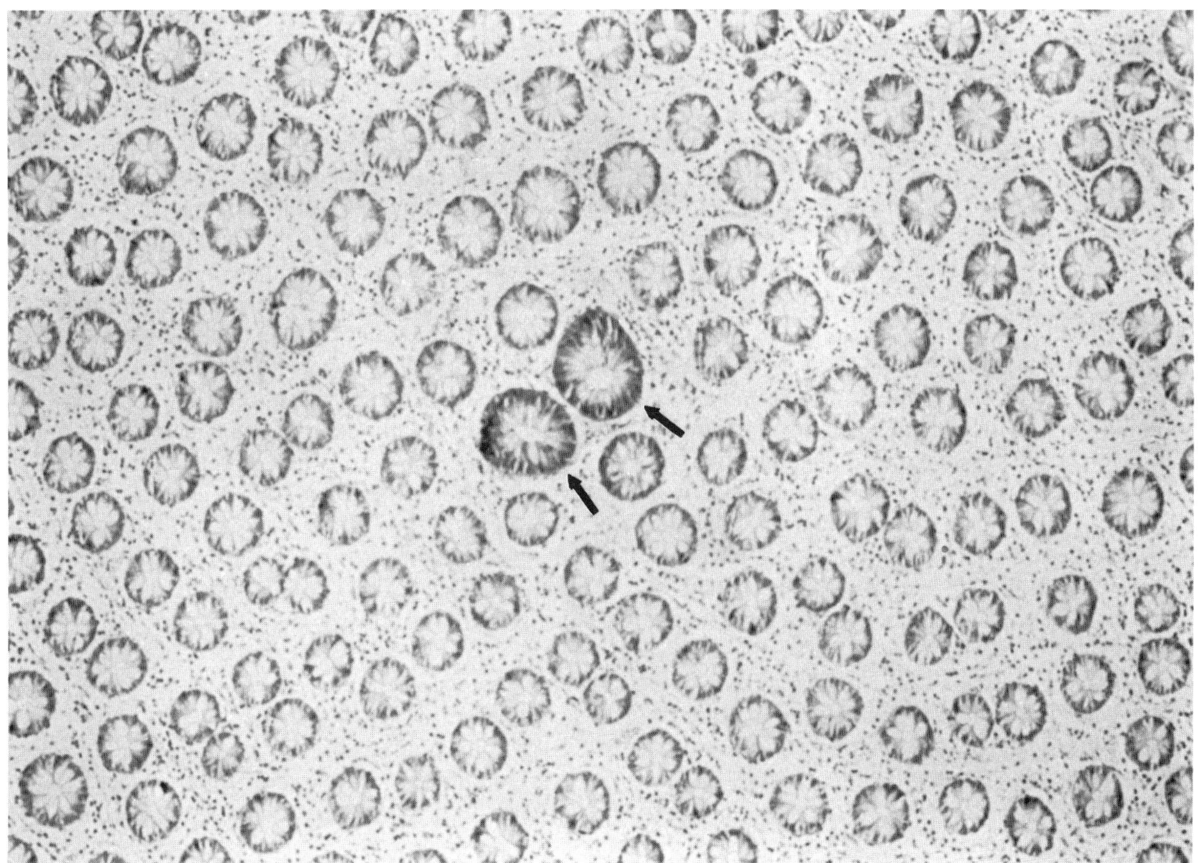

FIG. 9-3. Microadenomas (arrows) detectable only by microscopic examination of grossly "normal" colonic mucosa. (From Ref. 56, with permission.)

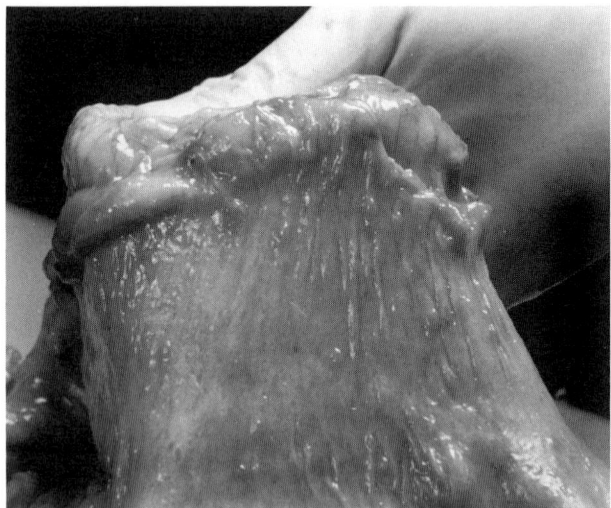

FIG. 9-4. Minute polyps best recognized in a well-prepared bowel.

carcinomas develop approximately 6 years after the appearance of large bowel symptoms. Patients developing these cancers by the middle or late thirties have a crude 5-year survival rate of only 27 percent.[6] Patients diagnosed with FAP because of symptoms are usually found to have cancer at age 39 and are usually dead by age 42.[72] Presciuttini et al.[72a] have observed bimodality at the age of death from colorectal cancer in patients with FAP and have suggested that these variations may be due in part to specific mutations in the FAP/APC gene. However, with the emphasis on screening policies, the greater the number of individuals of younger generations who are examined, the more likely that polyps and cancers will be discovered earlier, in an asymptomatic state, for each successive generation and have a greater possibility of cure.

Extracolonic Manifestations

It is now well accepted that FAP is a generalized growth disorder that may present with protean manifestations in various organs and systems. These extracolonic lesions may be benign or malignant; they may significantly affect management and alter the ultimate prognosis. They may even cause the death of these patients. Lesions with a benign course include most of the tumors of the skin, fibromatosis, osteomas of the jaw or skull, thyroiditis,[73] and congenital pigmentation of the retina.

Previously, these extracolonic manifestations in association with colonic polyposis were denoted as Gardner's syndrome, and for a number of years it was thought that this was a distinct clinical entity. Because recent evidence provided by molecular biology indicates that the spectrum of clinical manifestations described by Gardner is just a protean phenotypical expression of the same basic genetic abnormality and because there are no differences in colorectal pathology with regard to the number, nature, or outcome of the neoplastic lesions that may require a change in management or a radical change in the prognosis, we discourage, in general, use of the eponym *Gardner's syndrome* and favor use of the broader term *familial adenomatous polyposis*.

Many extracolonic cancers have been reported in patients with FAP, including thyroid, adrenal gland, pancreatic, gallbladder and bile duct, urinary bladder, testicular, and embryonal cancer; however, the most common extracolonic lesions can be found in the stomach and duodenum. Those preceded by a premalignant lesion may be very relevant to the management of this disease, because they may lend themselves to preemptive therapeutic intervention. This seems to be the case with neoplastic polyps of the stomach, duodenum, and small bowel, which may also evolve into adenocarcinomas. Comparisons between the Japanese and Western experiences seem to indicate that in these phenotypical expressions, environmental factors could influence the development of these tumors—an observation that does not seem to apply to colorectal cancers.

Gastric Polyps

Although polyps of the stomach were believed to occur infrequently in FAP, it is now clear, with the introduction of routine baseline esophagogastroduodenoscopy, that up to at least one-third of patients with FAP will have gastric polyps.[73a] In 1962, Murphy et al.[74] reported concurrent carcinomas of the colon and stomach in a 16-year-old patient with FAP. Japanese reports indicate a higher incidence of gastric polyps (63.1 percent) and duodenal polyps (80.3 percent) than the Western literature (50.8 percent and 64.1 percent, respectively), possibly because of a higher propensity for intestinal metaplasia. It is important to emphasize that most polypoid lesions in the stomach are the result of a fundic gland hyperplasia (Fig. 9-5*A*), 44 percent in the Japanese series and 33 percent in the Western series, with only a small number found to be adenomatous. This is not a premalignant state. These polyps are common in the body and fundus of the stomach. Hyperplastic polyps are often a conglomerate of irregular prominent folds and polyps (Fig. 9-5*B*), and because of their nonneoplastic nature, they do not represent any threat for malignancy. However, we have seen the occasional patient who has developed the sequence of an adenomatous polyp progressing to carcinoma in situ and invasive carcinoma. Most adenomatous gastric polyps can be found in the antrum, are round or hemispheric, and may differ in size, shape, and consistency from hyperplastic polyps. They may not be amenable to endoscopic removal. Our policy is to biopsy a representative gastric polyp so as to document the diagnosis and to biopsy polyps that are irregular, large (>.2 cm), and ulcerated. Pa-

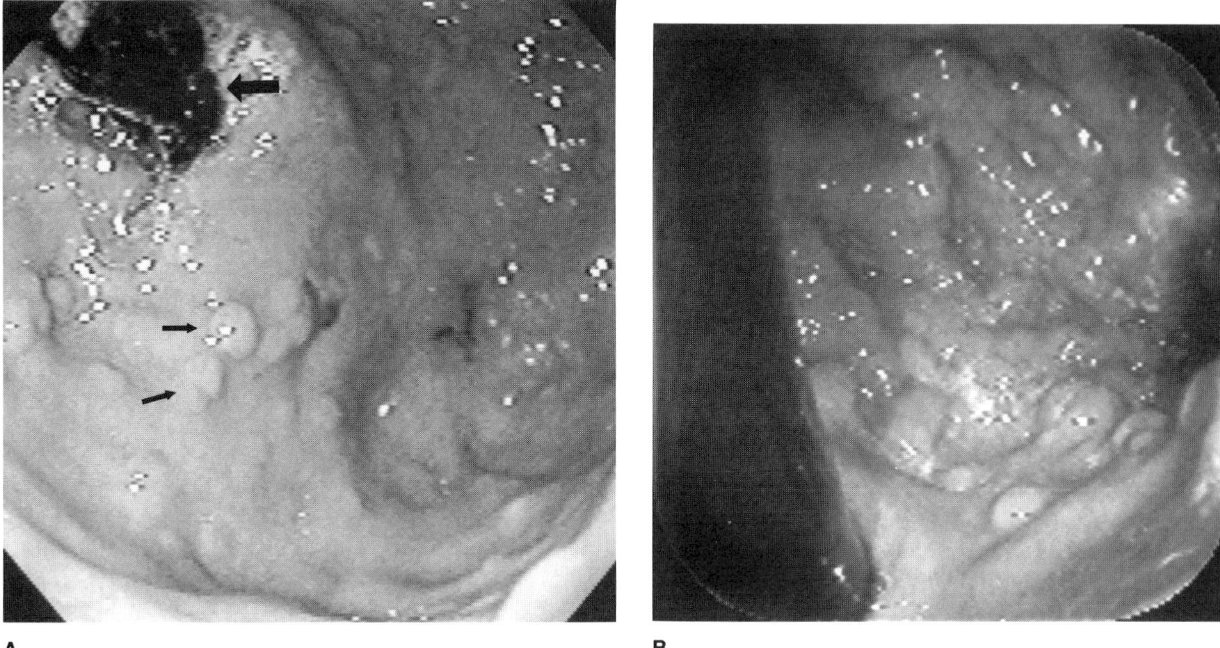
A B

FIG. 9-5. *A*. Fundic gland gastric polyps (small arrows). (Large arrow = retroverted esophagoscope.) *B*. Reversed view of fundus at esophagogastroduodenoscopy revealing multiple polyps. (*B* courtesy of Miguel Rodriguez-Bigas, M.D., Department of Surgery, Roswell Park Cancer Institute, Buffalo, New York.)

tients found to have adenomatous gastric polyps require methodic follow-up and serial endoscopy. Resection is indicated only when polyps are symptomatic or enlarging or when dysplastic progression is documented. In the Japanese experience, the incidence of carcinoma of the stomach was 2.1 percent, which is 3.5-fold higher than that reported in Western series (0.6 percent). Interestingly, the incidence of duodenal cancer in Japanese patients with FAP was 0.6 percent, one-fourth the 2.5 percent incidence in Western patients with FAP.[75]

Duodenal Polyps

In 1904, Funkenstein[76] described duodenal polyps in patients with familial polyposis. Since then, it has been established that duodenal polyps are a common finding in patients with FAP (Fig. 9-6), with a prevalence ranging from 40 to 100 percent. Those in the first portion

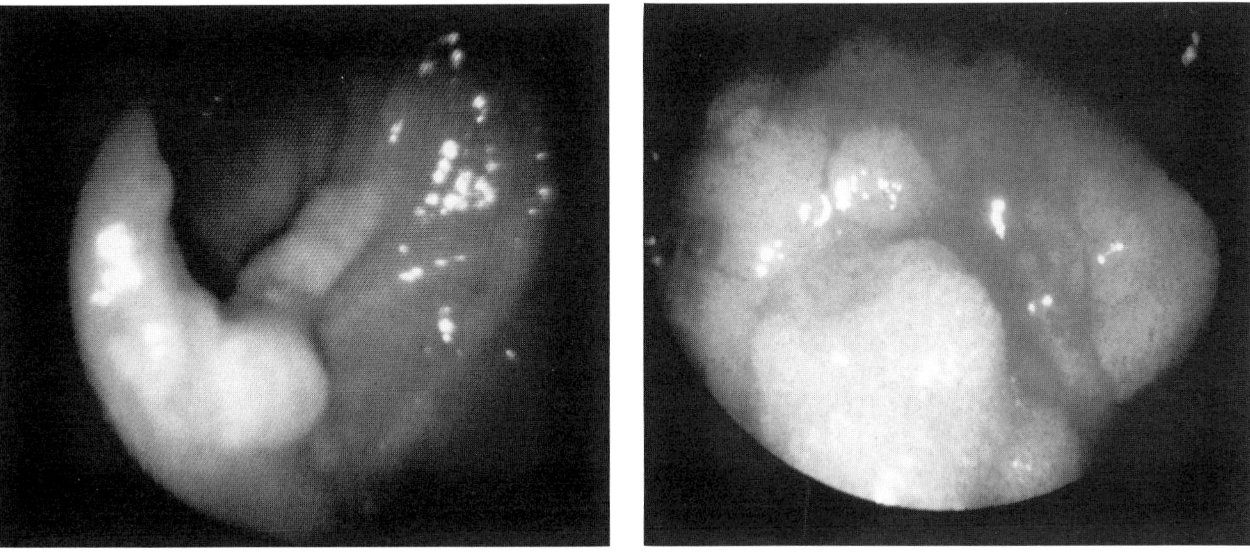
A B

FIG. 9-6. *A*. Adenomatous polyps of the duodenum. *B*. Villous adenoma of the duodenum.

of the duodenum usually do not attain a large size, seldom exceeding 10 mm, but those clustering around the ampulla of Vater may be large. Most duodenal polyps exhibit no symptoms unless they grow to a larger size, then they usually bleed. However, as opposed to those in the stomach, most of these polyps contain adenomatous and dysplastic features; thus, they can be associated with transformation from dysplasia to invasive adenocarcinoma. It is reported that there is a definite risk of malignant change in these polyps in view of a 4 to 12 percent lifetime incidence of duodenal cancer in patients with FAP.[77] Thirty-six of 1255 patients with FAP from the Leeds Castle Polyposis Group Registry developed ampullary cancer at a median of 22 years after colectomy, but it has also been found in younger patients. In addition, patients with FAP possess a risk up to 160 times that of the general population of developing carcinoma of the ampulla of Vater, which may occur from a preceding adenomatous lesion.

The management of these lesions still remains to be settled. Periodic, ongoing endoscopic examinations and biopsies of large polyps, with resection of those lesions undergoing malignant transformation, seem to constitute a prudent approach.[77a]

Small Bowel Polyps

Small bowel polyps have been reported in patients who have undergone surgery for FAP.[78–81] In 1981, Phillips[82] described a man who died as a consequence of a primary adenocarcinoma of the midjejunum and who had multiple benign adenomatous polyps of the small bowel. Ross and Mara[83] described two patients with polyps and adenocarcinoma of the small intestine many years after colectomy for familial polyposis.

Polypoid growths may be seen in the distal ileum at endoscopy or in surgical specimens. They are usually small, sessile, and whitish or translucent. Lymphoid hyperplasia is found on histologic examination. We and others performing small bowel enteroscopy have been able to find a significant number of FAP patients with adenomatous polyps of the small bowel[84, 84a] (Fig. 9-7). These polyps can be pedunculated or sessile. It is likely that some of these polyps occurring in the small bowel may transform to malignancy and may account for a number of the patients with FAP who have died with liver metastases from carcinomas of unknown origin.

Adenomas and carcinomas arising in the extrahepatic bile ducts, gallbladder (Fig. 9-8), and pancreas have been described.[85–89] Other extraintestinal adenomas have been described in patients with FAP, including those in the adrenal glands[6, 90] and thyroid,[73, 91] hepatoblastoma,[92] and islet cell tumors.[93, 94]

Osteomas

Osteomas and bony prominences are usually palpable in the skull and the shins of patients with FAP. In fact, in these locations, they are best detected by palpation; radiologic confirmation is not necessary. Osteomas are almost always benign and do not degenerate into malignancy, although there has been the report of an osteogenic sarcoma. Osteomas, odontomas, and dental abnormalities—including supernumerary, impacted,

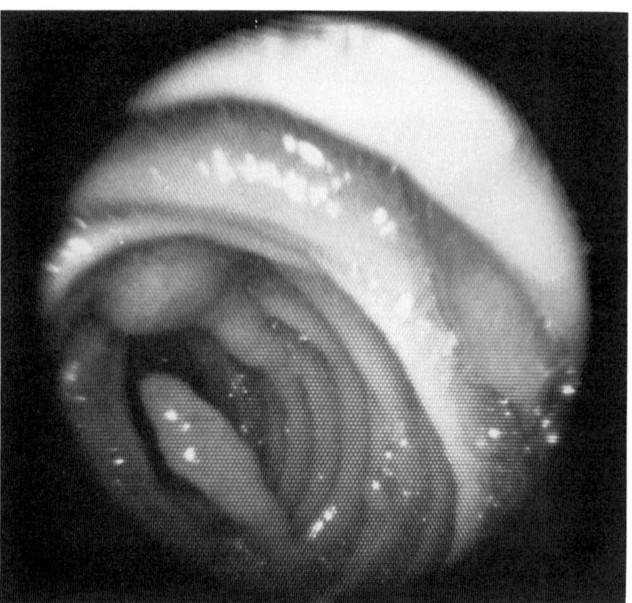

A

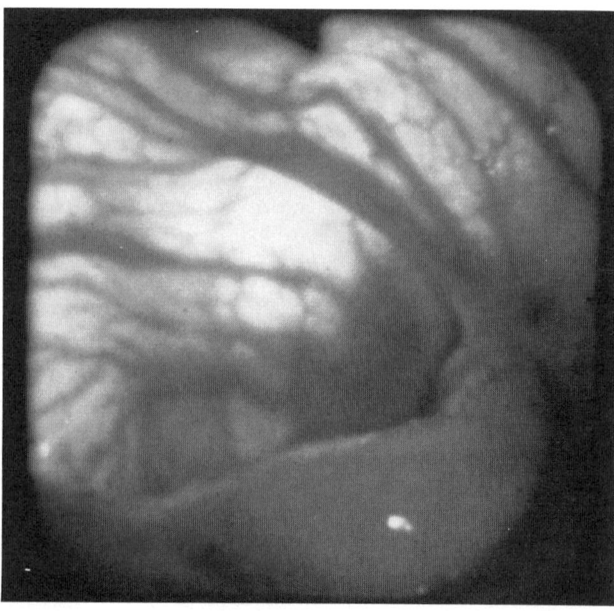

B

FIG. 9-7. *A* and *B*. Intraoperative enteroscopy with a colonoscope introduced through the rectum in a patient with adenomatous polyps in the small bowel.

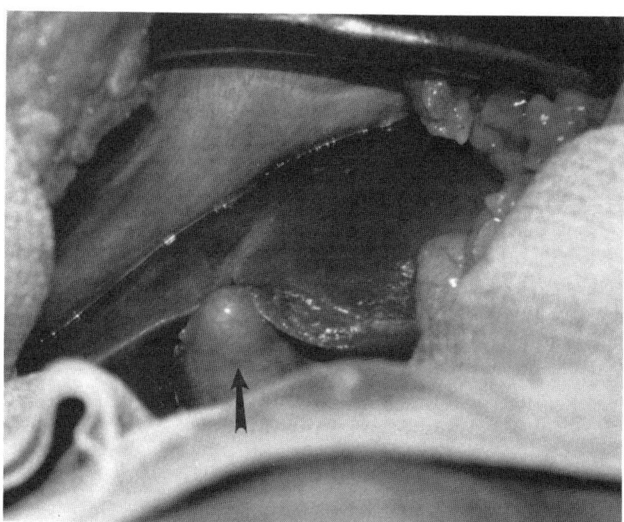

FIG. 9-8. Fundic adenoma of the gallbladder (arrow).

and congenitally absent teeth—can be detected by a panoramic radiograph (Panorex) of the jaw.[95] There is a possible value in using the Panorex of the jaw as the initial screening examination in individuals at risk for FAP, as findings may precede intestinal manifestations in some families (Fig. 9-9). The presence of osteomas does not seem to indicate a higher risk for development of problems in any other parts of the body. The association with multiple cartilaginous exostoses was reported by Zanca in 1956 (Fig. 9-10).[68c]

Soft-Tissue Tumors

In 1953, Gardner and Richards[25] reported that in a family from Utah with many members who had had cancer, cutaneous tumors that were epidermal inclusion

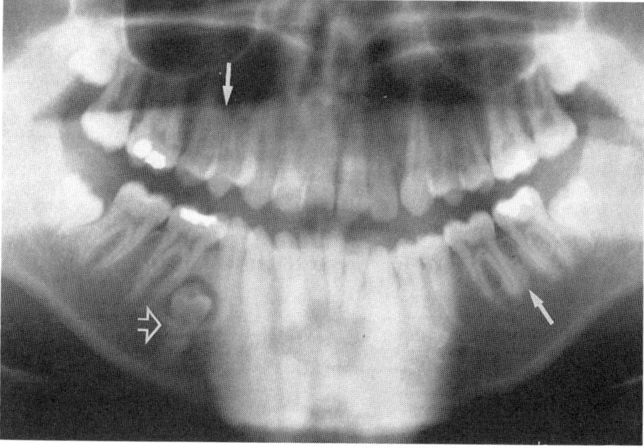

FIG. 9-9. Panoramic radiograph (Panorex) of the maxilla and mandible in a 15-year-old male with a family history of familial adenomatous polyposis (FAP). An impacted mandibular right bicuspid is evident (open arrow). More subtle findings in the right maxilla and left mandible are osseous densities (arrows), a common extracolonic manifestation in patients with FAP. (From Ref. 56, with permission.)

cysts were also common in the family. Although these cutaneous lesions had no malignant potential, they were a phenotypical manifestation of the disease. In 1958, Smith[96] introduced the designation of *Gardner's syndrome* for individuals with colonic polyposis who also had osteomas, sebaceous cysts, and desmoid tumors. Subsequently, other lesions such as fibromas, acrochordons, lipomas, and many more have been described as part of the syndrome. Oldfield[97] noted the association of sebaceous (epidermoid) cysts with polyposis but did not emphasize it as a specific syndrome. Lipomas have been recognized by family members as a family trait, have been observed in a 14-day-old infant, and have preceded the recognition of gastrointestinal polyps.

The association of FAP with fibromatosis has also been well established. The association of FAP and desmoid tumors—locally invasive, nonmetastasizing fibrous tumors—was first reported by Miller and Sweet[23] in 1937. In 1945, Pugh and Nesselrod[98] described a 33-year-old patient with polyposis who had a 5- × 10-cm area in the region of the splenic flexure composed of dense fibrous tissue. Weiner and Cooper[99] described four brothers, three of whom had a typical triad of Gardner's syndrome, whereas Gumpel and Carballo[100] described a patient with a 9 1/2-lb retroperitoneal fibrosarcoma. The development of any fibromatosis in a patient with FAP is usually an ominous sign. Most desmoids associated with FAP arise in the retroperitoneum; involvement of the abdominal wall is usually a secondary manifestation.[100a] Retroperitoneal tumors may cause ureteral obstruction, whereas mesenteric lesions may cause intestinal obstruction, fistulas, and abscesses (Fig. 9-11). Desmoids do not metastasize, but they kill by cachexia owing to their sheer size and metabolic needs. Their temporal history, however, remains unpredictable. The benefits of resection remain controversial, as surgery seems to exacerbate their growth and is associated with significant complications. Complete resections are not often possible, and recurrences are frequent. Furthermore, patients may live with desmoid tumors for many years. Spontaneous remission, although rare, has been reported. In general, surgery should be used only for the treatment of complications, with the exception of those small mesenteric desmoids that are easily resectable. Medical approaches remain investigational; many are based on nonsteroidal anti-inflammatory agents, tamoxifen, doxorubicin, and other agents.[100b] The use of contraceptives is always indicated in patients receiving treatments with potentially teratogenic effects. Other stages of fibroplastic proliferation can be seen, including fibrosarcomas and retroperitoneal fibrosis. Enterline et al.[101] reported a liposarcoma in a patient with polyposis, and Fader et al.[102] described a fibromyosarcoma.

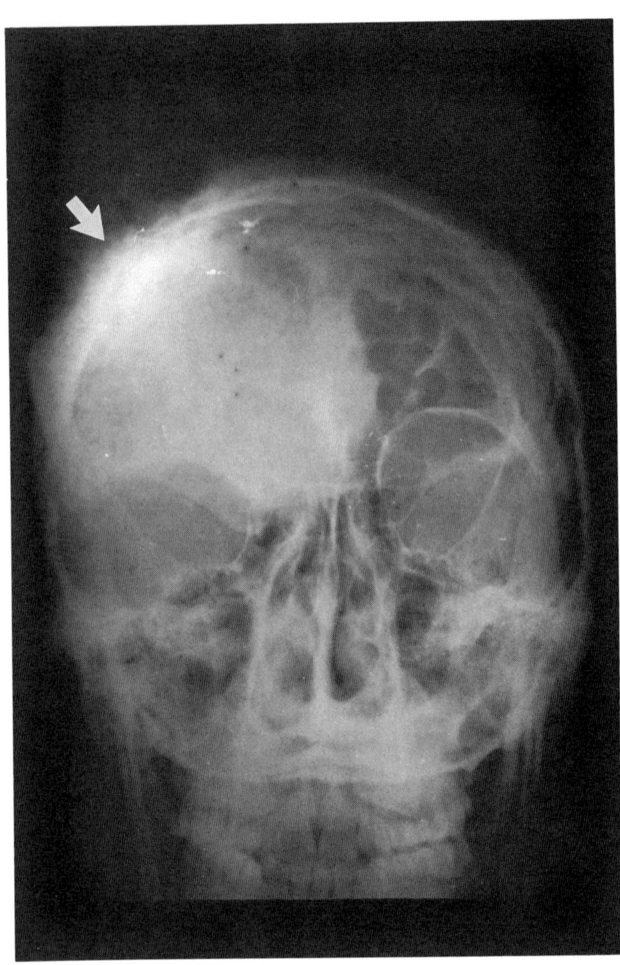

A B

FIG. 9-10. *A*. A 34-year-old Hispanic man with familial adenomatous polyposis and colon cancer, osteophytes, and osteomas (arrows) (Zanca syndrome). *B*. Skull radiograph of the same patient (arrow = osteoma). (Courtesy of Mr. Bravo, Hospital de Oncologia CMN, Mexico City, Mexico.)

Brain Tumors

Brain tumors have been described in patients with FAP. Many of these patients were children near the age of puberty. The association of polyposis with brain tumors has been known as Turcot syndrome, following the description in 1959 by Turcot et al.[103] of two siblings with FAP, one with a medulloblastoma of the spinal cord and the other with a glioblastoma of the frontal lobe. Subsequent reports have been associated with glioblastoma multiforme. Only brain tumors associated with the hereditary form of polyposis should be considered a phenotypical variant of the overall spectrum of FAP, rather than the more common association of brain tumors with sporadic colonic polyps.

Retinal Lesions

Congenital hypertrophy of the retinal pigment epithelium (CHRPE) (Fig. 9-12) is a condition of asymptomatic, multiple, bilateral pigmented spots on the retina detected by indirect funduscopy in 70 to 80 percent of individuals affected with FAP. It is seen only rarely in the general population.[104]

In summary, FAP is not just a colonic disease but can be designated as a genetically determined growth disorder with a wide spectrum of phenotypical manifestations with either benign or malignant behavior. While epidermal inclusion cysts, osteomas, and CHRPE are common and benign, desmoids and carcinomas of the duodenum and thyroid are serious, life-threatening extracolonic manifestations. We emphasize the need for a detailed family history, thorough ascertainment of all pathologic data, construction of a family pedigree, enrollment of families in a registry, and participation in diagnostic and therapeutic protocols (Fig. 9-13) [e.g., sulindac (Fig. 9–14)].

PEUTZ-JEGHERS SYNDROME

This syndrome was originally described by Peutz[105] in 1921 and subsequently clarified by Jeghers et al.[106] in

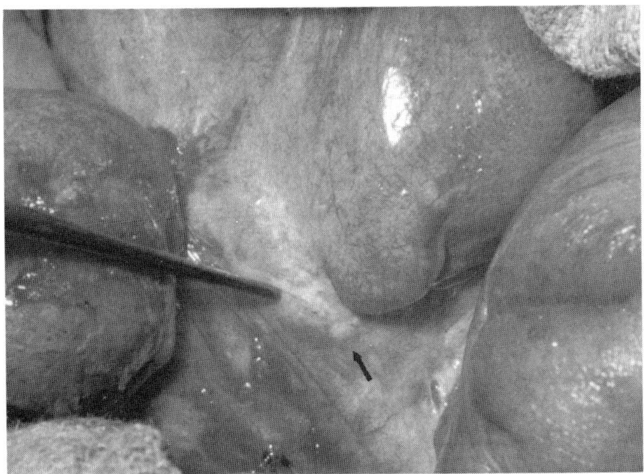
A

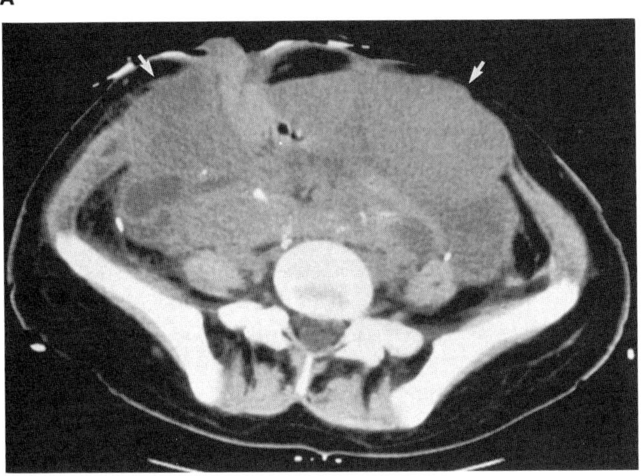
B

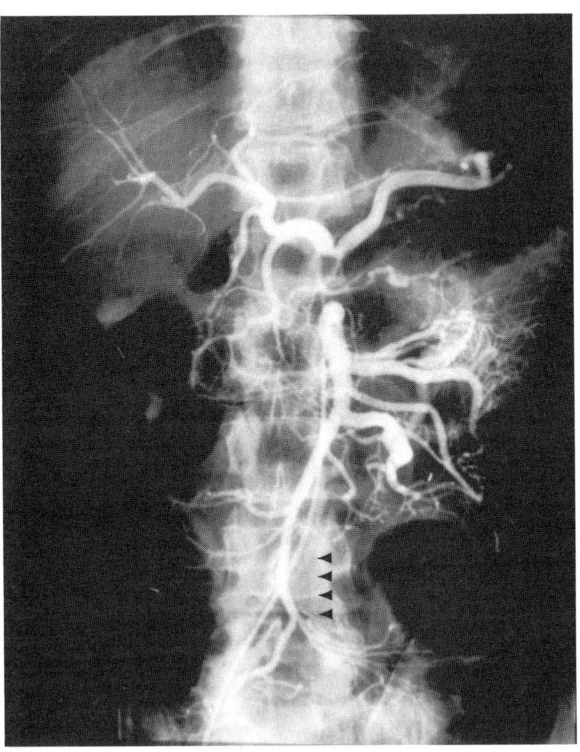
C

FIG. 9-11. *A*. A "sheathlike" desmoid tumor (arrow) involving the mesentery of the small bowel (arrow). *B*. CT scan of abdomen demonstrating the desmoid tumor (arrows). *C*. Arteriogram showing a desmoid tumor (arrowheads) supplied by the distal branches of the superior mesenteric artery. (*B* and *C* from Ref. 56, with permission.)

1949. It is inherited in a mendelian dominant pattern and is characterized by the presence of many hamartomatous polyps in the bowel as well as mucocutaneous pigmented spots.

The pigmented skin lesions are usually found in the perioral region, mainly in the lower lip (Fig. 9-15*A*) and soft palate; however, they can also be found on the hands (Fig. 9-15*B*) and in the perianal region. Histologically, they have a lentiginous appearance and a malformation of muscularis mucosa that appears "treelike."[107] These spots may appear after development of the polyps, and they may actually fade with age, especially those outside the buccal mucosa.[108]

Polyps in the small bowel are most commonly found in the jejunum. They are generally small, usually measuring between 0.1 and 10 mm in diameter, but may grow larger. Histologically, there are muscular fibers in the mucosa and branching of the smooth muscle, often associated with dilated glands full of amorphous acellular material (Fig. 9-16). These polyps begin their growth in the first decade of life and become symptomatic in the second or third decade. The symptoms are usually related to the size of the polyp, and patients most commonly present with severe recurrent abdominal pain secondary to intussusception and intestinal obstruction or with gastrointestinal bleeding. A limited resection of the portion of the bowel involved with polyps should be performed. The role of intraoperative endoscopy remains to be established,[109, 110] but it is a sound recommendation.

Although the polyps are found most often in the small bowel, they can also be found in the stomach and the colon. Colorectal polyps, although they occur infrequently, may be distributed anywhere along the entire large bowel; therefore they may be missed at proctoscopy. Thus it would seem appropriate to recommend screening of children of affected parents with at least a 64-cm flexible rectosigmoidoscope. Certainly if they are symptomatic, they require full colonoscopy.

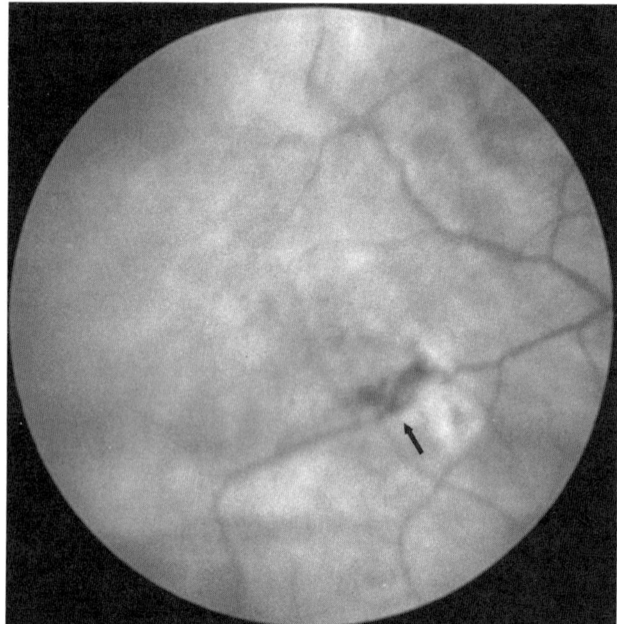

FIG. 9-12. Indirect funduscopy demonstrating congenital hypertrophy of the retinal pigment epithelium (CHRPE) (arrow) in a patient with familial adenomatous polyposis. (From Ref. 56, with permission.)

There is controversy about an increased risk of malignancy in Peutz-Jeghers syndrome.[111] Konishi et al.[112] and Hizawa et al.[113] have documented an increased risk for colonic cancer in young patients with Peutz-Jeghers syndrome. Patients have also been reported with adenomas (in decreasing frequency) in the colon, duodenum, jejunum and stomach, pancreas, bile duct, and liver.[114] Although an actual hamartoma-adenoma-carcinoma sequence in this syndrome has yet to be established, there seems to be little doubt that patients with Peutz-Jeghers syndrome are a risk of 2 to 3 percent for the development of gastrointestinal carcinomas.

Associated breast cancer in these patients can be bilateral.[115] It has also been estimated that 5 percent of female patients with Peutz-Jeghers syndrome develop ovarian tumors[116]; Konishi et al.[112] were able to find only 28 cases. They are sex cord tumors, mostly benign, but with a high percentage being hormonally active. Thus, a thorough gynecologic examination should be part of the initial evaluation.[117] A case of a man with a testicular Sertoli cell tumor has also been reported.[118] A young female patient included in the registry at the Roswell Park Cancer Institute was diagnosed with a periampullar carcinoma, supporting the observations of Konishi et al.[112] and Hizawa et al.[113] of an increased risk for adenocarcinoma of the pancreas and cervix. Interestingly, many of these tumors have also occurred in the early decades of life and in the areas of anatomic involvement, supporting the observation that these tumors are related to the syndrome and not to isolated independent events.[68c]

Screening of relatives at risk must be done by upper gastrointestinal tract endoscopy and colonoscopy as well as enteroclysis or enteroscopy if available. In the asymptomatic patient, enteroclysis may be preferable to small bowel follow-through. The role of preemptive surgical resection is for tumors larger than 10 mm (1 cm), because those are the ones likely to produce complications, and, certainly, for those polyps producing symptoms.

JUVENILE POLYPOSIS (FAMILIAL)

In 1957, Horrilleno et al.[119] introduced the term *juvenile polyp* to describe polyps of the rectum and colon in children. These polyps were hamartomatous (retention) polyps with dilated glands and fibroinflammatory exudate, a smooth surface, and a slender stalk.[120] This rare familial syndrome is characterized by the presence of multiple hamartomatous polyps, usually more than 5 to 10; it is, however, much more common (>70 percent) to find it as a single polyp in the rectum of a child. The inheritance pattern is probably autosomal dominant, but many cases seem to be of the sporadic type. These polyps are usually localized in the large bowel, although they are occasionally found in the stomach and the small bowel. The most common manifestation is rectal bleeding and anemia; however, because a common location is the rectum[121] and because these polyps have a long stalk, they may prolapse through the anus and even autoamputate. The documentation of this type of polyp in young individuals may be an indication for colonoscopy because these polyps may have coexisting adenomas,[121a] and it may be reasonable to evaluate the upper gastrointestinal tract and small bowel in such patients because involvement of the stomach and small bowel is not uncommon. While colonoscopic polypectomy may be appropriate for patients with a single polyp or few polyps, a subtotal colectomy with ileorectal anastomosis may have to be considered when there are multiple polyps in patients who are otherwise good surgical risks. Although seemingly transmitted in an autosomal dominant fashion, cases have been reported in familial aggregation patterns as well as nonfamilial instances. Sachatello and Griffen[122] found that patients with juvenile polyposis may exhibit one of three syndromes: (1) juvenile polyposis of infancy, a non-sex-linked recessive trait associated with early death, (2) juvenile polyposis coli, or (3) generalized juvenile and intestinal polyposis.

It is currently believed that the relative risk of gastrointestinal cancer is 13 percent (confidence interval, 2.7 to 38.1) and that the relative risk for all malignancies is 9 percent (confidence interval, 4.2 to 17.3).[6, 77]

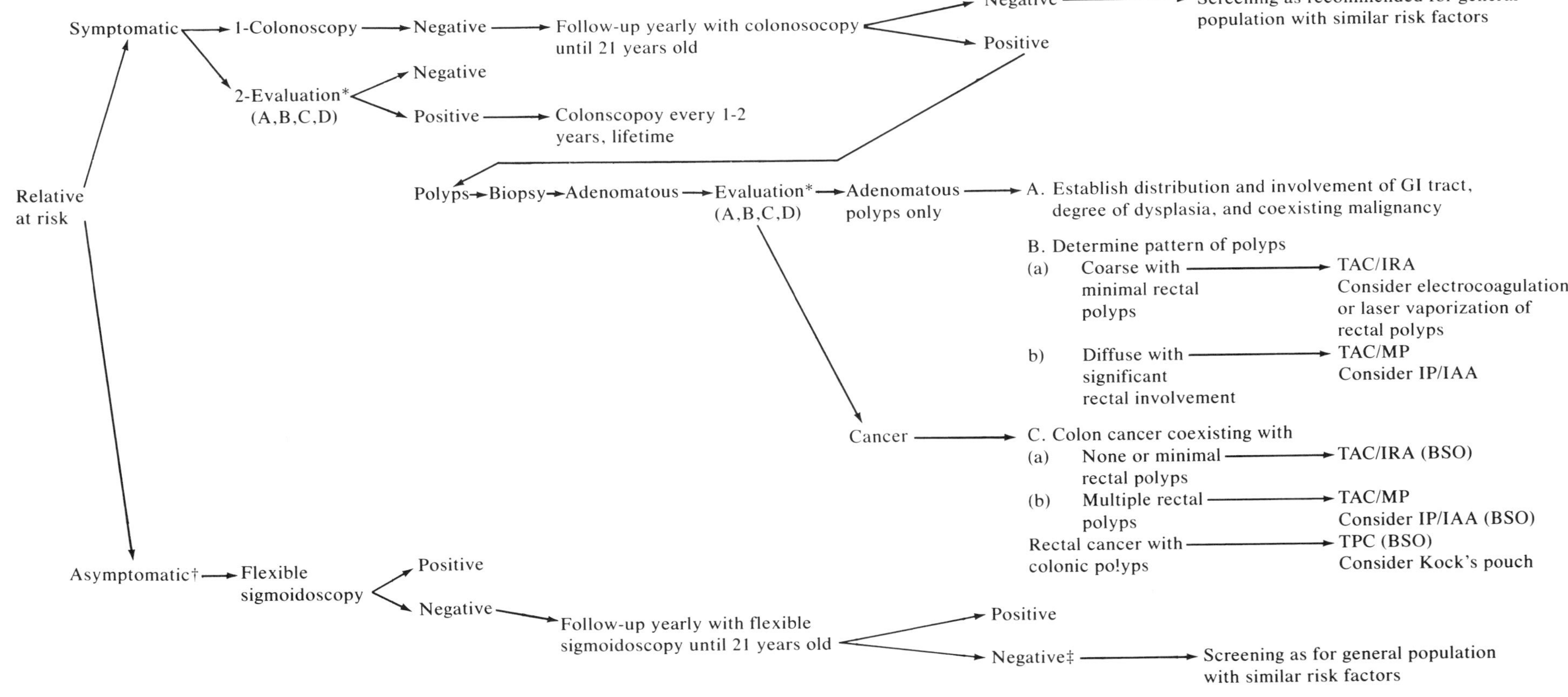

*EVALUATION

A. Phenotypical markers:

Cutaneous:	Epidermal cysts and soft-tissue tumors
Dental:	Malformations of teeth
Ophthalmic:	Congenital hypertrophy of retinal pigment epithelium
Bone:	Osteomas
B. Baseline blood tests:	Complete blood count (CBC), chemistry profile (CP), establishment of lymphoblastoid line for DNA analsysis
C. Baseline x-rays:	Bone survey to include all long bones, skull, Panorex of jaw, intravenous pyelogram, enteroclysis (?)
D. Baseline endoscopy:	Esophagogastroduodenoscopy (fore and side views), colonoscopy, total enteroscopy

BSO = bilateral salpingo-oophorectomy (may be considered complementary to cancer operation)
IAA = ileoanal anastomosis
IP = ileal pouch
IRA = ileorectal anastomosis
MP = mucosal proctectomy
TAC = total abdominal colectomy
TPC = total proctocolectomy

†May consider A and B under Evaluation, above.
‡May consider A, B, C under Evaluation, above; if negative, this will strengthen the decision.

FIG. 9-13. Algorithm for screening and treatment of relatives at risk in familial adenomatous polyposis kindreds.

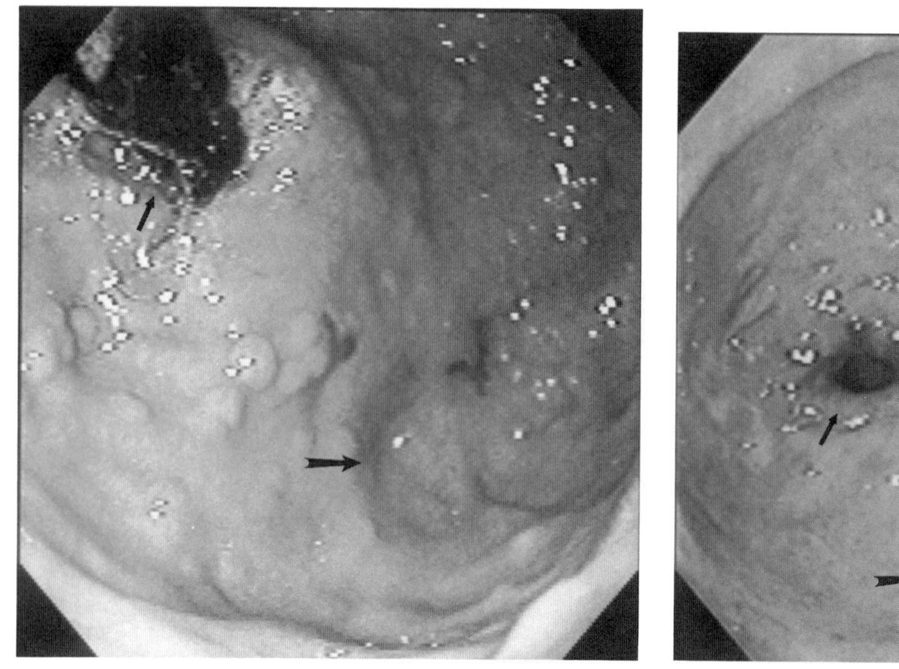
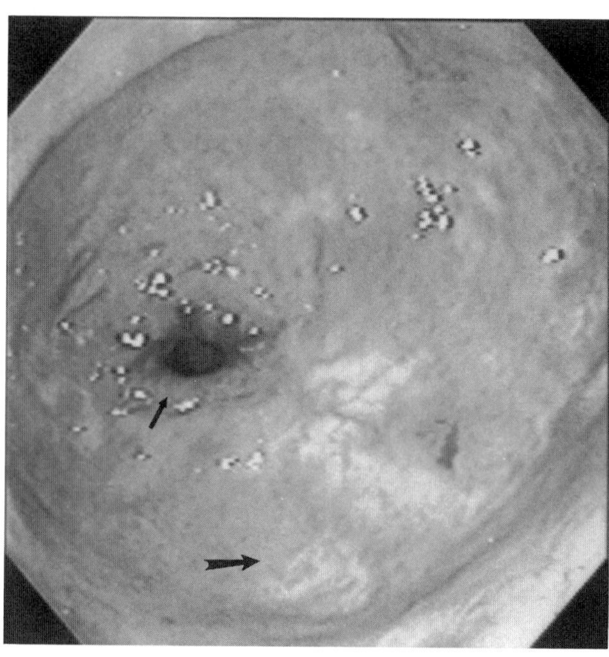

A B

FIG. 9-14. *A*. Rectal remnant carpeted with adenomatous polyps (large arrow) in a 38-year-old man (small arrow = ileoproctostomy). *B*. After 6 weeks of treatment with sulindac (150 mg PO bid), the polyps have disappeared (large arrow) (small arrow = ileoproctostomy).

It appears that these patients are also at increased risk for the development of colorectal cancers; however, it is important to emphasize that cancers do not seem to arise from these polyps.

More recently, there have been increasing reports of patients with these syndromes and colorectal cancer. This association may occur despite the absence of family history. Of interest is the proposition of Sassatelli et al.[123] that these polyps may be precursors of an adenomatous transformation. Congenital abnormalities have been reported in the nonfamilial cases, including hydrocephalus, cardiac lesions, malrotation of the bowel, and mesenteric lymphangiomas,[1] but these lesions are not good as biomarkers in affected families.

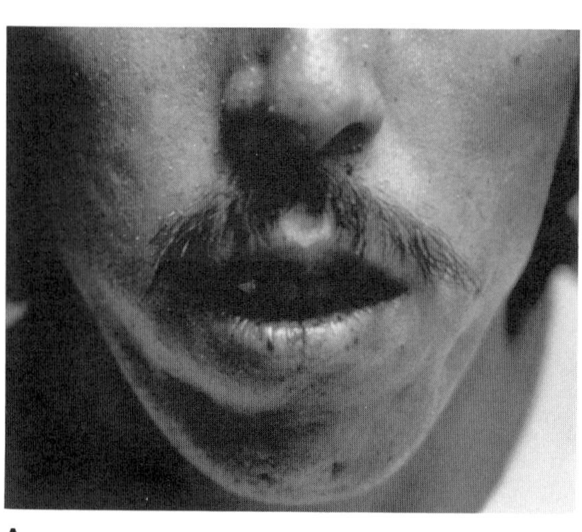
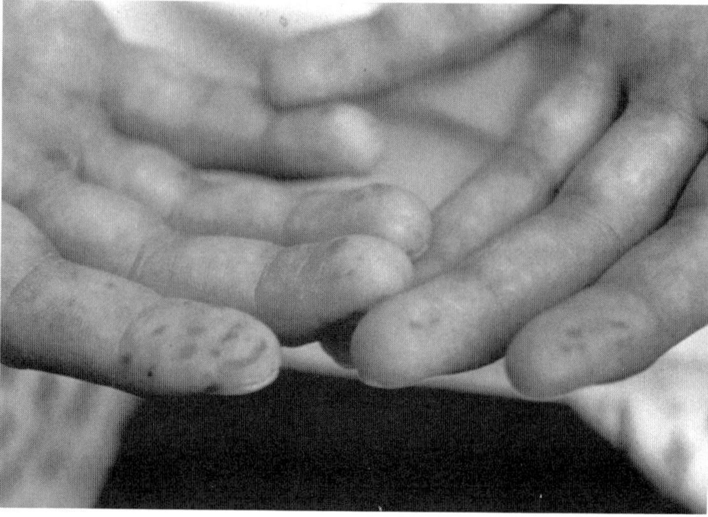

A B

FIG. 9-15. Pigmented skin lesions of the lips (*A*) and hands (*B*) in Peutz-Jeghers syndrome. (*B* from Ref. 84a, with permission.)

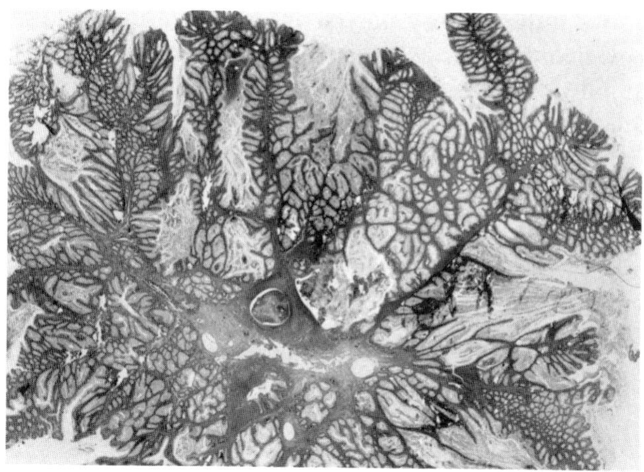

FIG. 9-16. Histologic photograph showing dilated glands filled with amorphous acellular material in polyps in Peutz-Jeghers syndrome. (From Ref. 84a, with permission.)

COWDEN'S DISEASE

This syndrome was initially described in 1963 and named after the affected patient.[124] It is an autosomal dominantly inherited condition characterized by the development of multiple "cobblestone" orocutaneous hamartomas and papillomas as well as other hamartomas on the face and hands. Lesions characteristic of this genodermatosis usually measure between 1 and 5 mm, have a verrucal or hyperkeratotic aspect, and are associated with other cutaneous lesions such as lipomas, hemangiomas, and neuromas.[125] About 35 percent of the patients will have intestinal polyps, which are usually asymptomatic.[126] These hamartomatous polyps can be located in any portion of the gastrointestinal tract; however, the most frequent site is the colon, followed by the stomach, small bowel, and esophagus.[127, 128] Although the widespread phenotypical manifestations would support a disorder of regulation as the basis for this disease, documentation of amplification or rearrangement of HER-s/*neu* and *ras* oncogenes and the estrogen-inducible pS-2 gene could not be established in a recent analysis.[129] The most important clinical aspect of the syndrome is its association with a high incidence for development of internal malignancies in affected individuals; thus, its diagnosis may be helpful for the early detection of various cancers, and screening of the families should be done for breast, thyroid, and gastrointestinal neoplasias. Endoscopy to rule out polyps should be recommended. Malignant tumors described in association with Cowden's disease include carcinomas of the breast (26 cases), thyroid (8 cases), uterus (5 cases), bladder (1 case), lung, and colon as well as liposarcoma, malignant melanoma (3 cases), and squamous cell carcinoma of the skin.[130] Other associated neoplasias include thyroid adenomas, uterine leiomyomas, meningiomas, ganglioneuromas, and developmental anomalies such as a hypoplastic mandible, prominent forehead, high, arched palate, and Down's syndrome.[131–133] Because bilateral carcinoma of the breast (ductal adenocarcinoma) may often occur in middle-aged patients in this setting, this is one of the possible recommendations for a prophylactic total mastectomy.[134]

INTESTINAL GANGLIONEUROMATOSIS

This condition is characterized by a massive proliferation of both ganglionic cells and nerves in the intestinal tract. They differ from neurofibromas in that the cell of origin is the sympathetic nerve cell rather than the supporting Schwann cell. They are commonly found in the retroperitoneum. The transmural type involves all layers of the bowel wall, with predominant involvement of the mesenteric plexus, whereas the limited form involves only the mucosa. It is the latter type that is associated with von Recklinghausen's disease.[135] Mendelsohn and Diamond[136] reported both a child with sporadic polypoid ganglioneurofibromatosis involving the large bowel and a 38-year-old man and 3 children, all of whom had juvenile polyps and ganglioneuromatous polyposis of the colon. Snover et al.[137] have reported on one patient with diffuse mucosal ganglioneuromatosis and adenocarcinoma of the colon.

Familial ganglioneuromatosis of the gastrointestinal tract has also been seen in multiple endocrine neoplasia (MEN) syndrome type IIB. MEN IIB occurs sporadically or as an autosomal dominant trait and is characterized by medullary carcinoma of the thyroid and pheochromocytomas. These neuromas usually consist of a cluster of separate nerve bundles, but without ganglionic cells.[138] Symptoms related to the gastrointestinal tract include severe constipation, chronic blood loss, appendicitis, hormone-secreting states, and intestinal obstruction. In the limited forms, surgical resection of the involved segment may be curative.[139]

MUIR-TORRE SYNDROME

Muir et al.[140] in 1967 and Torre[141] in 1968 described patients with multiple cutaneous sebaceous tumors (Fig. 9-17) and a history of internal malignancies. These cutaneous lesions may be difficult to classify. They seem to involve the hair follicle and resemble a keratoacanthoma.[142] They are asymptomatic, yellow, waxy, papular or nodular lesions of the face, trunk, or scalp. This syndrome can be diagnosed with the minimal criterion of at least one internal malignancy found in combination with a sebaceous gland neoplasia. This genodermatosis seems to be transmitted in a dominant mendelian pattern. The cutaneous sebaceous lesions seem to be a reliable phenotypical biomarker. Colonic

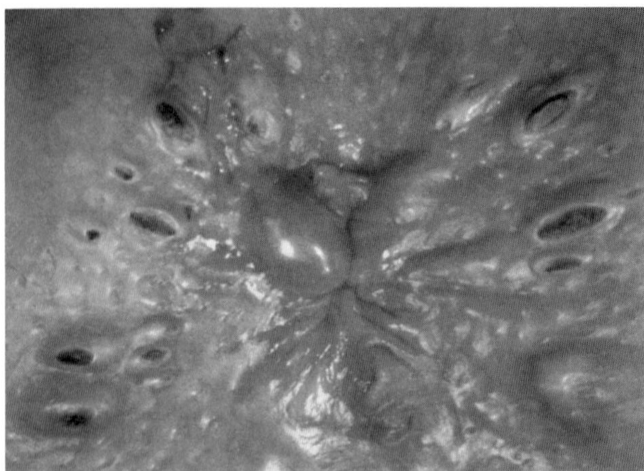

FIG. 9-17. Multiple perianal sebaceous lesions in a patient with Muir-Torre syndrome.

cancer is the tumor most frequently reported in association with this condition (51 percent),[143] followed by tumors of the genitourinary tract (25 percent) and hematologic disorders, although tumors in multiple sites, suggestive of Lynch II syndrome, may occur, denoting a genomic instability in these susceptible patients.[144] Most colorectal cancers are located on the right side and are diagnosed around the age of 50.[145] When this is the only tumor, it is the Lynch I syndrome. They may be preceded by adenomatous polyps.[143] Cancers in this setting seem to be of low biological aggressiveness and are associated with a long survival following surgical therapy.[145a]

RUVALCABA-MYRHE-SMITH SYNDROME

In 1980, Ruvalcaba et al.[146] described two unrelated men with macrocephaly, mental retardation, hyperpigmentation of the skin of the penis, and hamartomatous polyps of the colon, ileum, and tongue but not the stomach. Further reports of this disease, named Ruvalcaba-Myhre-Smith syndrome, indicate that it is transmitted in an autosomal dominant fashion.[147, 148] Other features are ocular abnormalities, lipid storage myopathy, and delayed psychomotor development. Although there seems to be no association of this syndrome with malignant neoplasias,[149] the spectrum of phenotypical manifestations of the syndrome is still being investigated.[150] The clinical presentation and management are similar to those of juvenile polyposis.

DEVON FAMILY SYNDROME

In each one of the three generations of a Devon family, a female member has developed multiple fibroinflammatory polyps of the ileum that have led to persistent and recurrent abdominal pain and intussusception. These inflammatory polyps are localized in the small bowel and gastric antrum. This family remains unique, as no other has been reported. That their pattern of inheritance fits an autosomal dominant mode through X-linked inheritance cannot be excluded.[151] There has been no association with any neoplasia, benign or malignant.[152]

REFERENCES

1. Haggitt RC, Reid BJ: Hereditary gastrointestinal polyposis syndromes. *Am J Surg Pathol* 10:871–877, 1986.
2. Bussey HJR: Historical developments in familial adenomatous polyposis, in Herrera L (ed): *Familial Adenomatous Polyposis*. New York, Liss, 1990, pp 1–7.
3. Bulow S: Diagnosis of familial polyposis. *World J Surg* 15:41–46, 1991.
4. Alm T, Licznerski G: Hereditary colonic polyps in Sweden. *Nord Med* 85:942, 1971.
5. Komatsu I: A clinical genetic study on multiple intestinal polyposis and allied conditions. *Jinrui Idengaku Zasshi* 12:246–297, 1968.
6. Watne AL: The syndromes of intestinal polyposis. *Curr Probl Surg* 24:269–340, 1987.
7. Gedde-Dahl T, Heim S, Lothe R, et al: The polyposis project. *Nord Med* 104:12–15, 1989.
8. Menzelio D: De excrescentals verrucosa cristosis in intestinis crassis dysenteriam passi observatis. *Ast Med Berolinensium* 4:68–71, 1721.
9. Cooper A: Lectures on surgery at Guy's Hospital, London, 1824, cited in Dukes C: The hereditary factor in polyposis intestini or multiple adenomata. *Cancer Rev* 5:241–256, 1930.
10. Chargelaigue A: Des polypes de rectum (thesis). Paris, 1859.
11. Luschka H: Ueber polypose Vegetationen der gesammten Dickdarmschleimhaut. *Arch Pathol Anat Phys Klin Med* 20:133–142, 1861.
12. Virchow RL: *Die Krankhaften Geschwuelste*. Berlin, Hieswald, 1863, p 243.
13. Cripps WH: Two cases of disseminated polyps of the rectum. *Trans Pathol Soc Lond* 33:165–168, 1882.
14. Bickersteth RA: Multiple polypi of the rectum occurring in a mother and child. *St. Bartholomew's Hosp Rep* 26:299–301, 1890.
15. Handford H: Disseminated polypi of the large intestines becoming malignant with stricture (malignant adenoma) of the rectum and of the splenic flexure of the colon: Secondary growths in the liver. *Trans Pathol Soc Lond* 41:133–137, 1890.
16. Cockayne EA: Heredity in relation to cancer. *Cancer Rev* 2:337–347, 1927.
17. Veale AMO: *Intestinal Polyposis*. Cambridge, England, Cambridge University Press, 1965.
18. Dukes C: The hereditary factor in polyposis intestini or multiple adenomata. *Cancer Rev* 5:241–256, 1930.
19. Lockhart-Mummery JP, Dukes CE: Familial adenomatosis of the colon and rectum: Its relationship to cancer. *Lancet* 2:586–589, 1939.
20. McKenney DC: Multiple polyposis: Congenital, heredofamilial, malignant. *Am J Surg* 46:204–216, 1939.
21. Devic A, Bussey HR: Un cas de polypose adenomateuse generalisee a tout de l'intestin. *Arch Mal App Digest* 6:278–289, 1912.
22. Cabot RC: Case records of the Massachusetts General Hospital: Case no. 21061. *N Engl J Med* 212:263–267, 1935.

23. Miller RH, Sweet RH: Multiple polyposis of colon: Familial disease. *Ann Surg* 105:511–515, 1937.
24. Fitzgerald GM: Multiple composite odontomes coincidental with other tumorous conditions: Report of a case. *J Am Dent Assoc* 30:1408–1417, 1943.
25. Gardner EJ, Richards RC: Multiple cutaneous and subcutaneous lesions occurring simultaneously with hereditary polyposis and osteomatosis. *Am J Hum Genet* 5:139–147, 1953.
26. MacDonald JM, Davis WC, Crago HR, Berk AD: Gardner's syndrome and periampullary malignancy. *Am J Surg* 113: 425–430, 1967.
27. Blair NP, Trempe CL: Hypertrophy of the retinal pigment epithelium associated with Gardner's syndrome. *Am J Ophthalmol* 90:661–667, 1980.
28. Lewis RA, Crowder WE, Eierman LA, et al: The Gardner syndrome: Significance of ocular features. *Ophthalmology* 91:916–925, 1984.
29. Traboulsi EI, Krush AJ, Gardner EJ, et al: Prevalence and importance of pigmented ocular fundus lesions in Gardner's syndrome. *N Engl J Med* 316:661–667, 1987.
30. Bertario L, Bandello F, Rosetti C, et al: Congenital hypertrophy of retinal pigment epithelium (CHRPE) as a marker for familial adenomatous polyposis (FAP). *Eur J Cancer Prev* 2:69–75, 1993.
31. Richards RC, Woolf C: Solitary polyps of colon and rectum: Study of inherited tendency. *Am Surg* 22:287–294, 1956.
32. Burt RW: Mode of inheritance of "sporadic" adenomatous polyps, in Herrera L (ed): *Familial Adenomatous Polyposis*. New York, Liss, 1990, pp 17–22.
33. Herrera L, Petrelli NJ: What are the appropriate controls for a colonoscopic screening program? (letter). *Dis Colon Rectum* 36:99–100, 1993.
34. McKusick VA: Genetic factors in intestinal polyposis. *JAMA* 182:271–277, 1962.
35. Gardner EJ: Familial polyposis coli and Gardner syndrome—Is there a difference? *Prog Clin Biol Res* 115:39–60, 1983.
36. Delhanty JD, Pritchard MB, Bussey HJ, Morson BC: Tetraploid fibroblasts and familial polyposis coli (letter). *Lancet* 1:1365, 1980.
37. Danes BS: Occurrence of in vitro tetraploidy in the heritable colon cancer syndromes. *Cancer* 48:1596–1601, 1981.
38. Gardner EJ, Rogers SW, Woodward S: Numerical and structural chromosome aberrations in cultured lymphocytes and cutaneous fibroblasts of patients with multiple adenomas of the colorectum. *Cancer* 49:1413–1419, 1982.
39. Kakati S, Herrera L, Drury RE, Sandberg AA: Comparison of radiation-induced chromosomal damage between normal individuals and patients with familial polyposis coli. *J Cancer Res Clin Oncol* 114:297–300, 1988.
40. Herrera L, Kakati S, Gibas L, et al: Gardner syndrome in a man with an interstitial deletion of 5q. *Am J Med Genet* 25:473–476, 1986.
41. Bodmer WF, Bailey CJ, Bodmer J, et al: Localization of the gene for familial adenomatous polyposis on chromosome 5. *Nature* 328:614–616, 1987.
41a. Leppert M, Dobbs M, Scambler P, et al: The gene for familial polyposis coli maps to the long arm of chromosome 5. *Science* 238:1411–1413, 1987.
42. Meera Khan P, Tops CMJ, vd Broek M, et al: Close linkage of a highly polymorphic marker (D5S37) to familial adenomatous polyposis (FAP) and confirmation of FAP localization on chromosome 5q21-q22. *Hum Genet* 79:183–185, 1988.
43. Nakamura Y, Lathrop M, Leppert M, et al: Localization of the genetic defect in familial adenomatous polyposis within a small region of chromosome 5. *Am J Hum Genet* 43:638–644, 1988.
44. Nishisho I, Nakamura Y, Miyoshi Y, et al: Mutations of chromosome 5q21 genes in FAP and colorectal cancer patients. *Science* 253:665–669, 1991.
45. Joslyn G, Carlson M, Thliveris A, et al: Identification of deletion mutations and three new genes at the familial polyposis locus. *Cell* 66:601–613, 1991.
46. Cottrell S, Bicknell D, Kaklamanis L, Bodmer WF: Molecular analysis of APC mutations in familial adenomatous polyposis and sporadic colon carcinomas. *Lancet* 340:626–630, 1992.
47. Fodde R, van der Luijt R, Wijnen J, et al: Eight novel inactivating germ line mutations at the APC gene identified by denaturing gradient gel electrophoresis. *Genomics* 13:1162–1168, 1992.
48. Groden J, Gelbert L, Thliveris A, et al: Mutational analysis of patients with adenomatous polyposis: Identical inactivating mutations in unrelated individuals. *Am J Hum Genet* 52:263–272, 1993.
49. Miyoshi Y, Ando H, Nagase H, et al: Germ-line mutations of the APC gene in 53 familial adenomatous polyposis patients. *Proc Natl Acad Sci USA* 89:4452–4456, 1992.
50. Miyoshi Y, Nagase H, Ando H, et al: Somatic mutations of the APC gene in colorectal tumors: Mutation cluster region in the APC gene. *Hum Molec Genet* 1:229–233, 1992.
51. Nagase H, Miyoshi Y, Horii A, et al: Screening for germ-line mutations in familial adenomatous polyposis patients: 61 new patients and a summary of 150 unrelated patients. *Hum Mutat* 1:467–473, 1992.
52. Olschwang S, Laurent-Puig P, Groden J, et al: Germ-line mutations in the first 14 exons of the adenomatous polyposis coli (APC) gene. *Am J Hum Genet* 52:273–279, 1993.
53. Olschwang S, Weiffenbach B, Laurent-Puig P, et al: Genetic characterization of the APC locus involved in familial adenomatous polyposis. *Gastroenterology* 101:154–160, 1991.
54. Stella A, Lonoce A, Resta N, et al: Familial adenomatous polyposis: Identification of a new frameshift mutation of the APC gene in an Italian family. *Biochem Biophys Res Commun* 184:1357–1363, 1992.
55. Varesco L, Gismondi V, James R, et al: Identification of APC gene mutations in Italian adenomatous polyposis coli patients by PCR-SSCP analysis. *Am J Hum Genet* 52:280–285, 1993.
56. Aquino A, Garcia C, Dosluoglu H, et al: Familial adenomatous polyposis in Delaware. *Del Med J* 65:627–644, 1993.
56a. Powell SM, Petersen GM, Krush AJ, et al: Molecular diagnosis of familial adenomatous polyposis. *N Engl J Med* 329:1982–1987, 1993.
56b. Varesco L, Groden J, Spirio L, et al: A rapid screening method to detect nonsense and frameshift mutations: Identification of disease-causing APC alleles. *Cancer Res* 53: 5581–5584, 1993.
57. MacDonald F, Morton DG, Rindl PM, et al: Predictive diagnosis of familial adenomatous polyposis with linked DNA markers: Population based study. *Br Med J* 304:869–872, 1992.
58. Neale K, Ritchie S, Thomson JPS: Screening of offspring of patients with familial adenomatous polyposis: The St. Mark's Hospital Polyposis Register experience, in Herrera L (ed): *Familial Adenomatous Polyposis*. New York, Liss, 1990, pp 61–66.
59. Petersen GM, Slack J, Nakamura Y: Screening guidelines and premorbid diagnosis of familial adenomatous polyposis using linkage. *Gastroenterology* 100:1658–1664, 1991.
60. Luk GD, Baylin SB: Ornithine decarboxylase as a biologic marker in familial colonic polyposis. *N Engl J Med* 311:80–83, 1984.
61. Herrera-Ornelas L, Porter C, Pera P, et al: A comparison of ornithine decarboxylase and S-adenosylmethionine decar-

boxylase activity in human large bowel mucosa, polyps, and colorectal adenocarcinoma. *J Surg Res* 42:56–60, 1987.

62. Boland CR, Deshmukh GD: The carbohydrate composition of mucin in colonic cancer. *Gastroenterology* 98(5 pt 1): 1170–1177, 1990.
63. Boland CR, Clapp NK: Glycoconjugates in the colons of New World monkeys with spontaneous colitis: Association between inflammation and neoplasia. *Gastroenterology* 92: 625–634, 1987.
64. Kuroki T, Kubota A, Miki Y, et al: Lectin staining of neoplastic and normal background colorectal mucosa in nonpolyposis and polyposis patients. *Dis Colon Rectum* 34:679–684, 1991.
65. Muto T: Mucin abnormality in colonic mucosa in patients with familial adenomatous polyposis (abstract). *Int J Colorect Dis* 5:60, 1990.

65a. Boland CR, Chen YF, Rinderle SF, et al: Use of the lectin from Amaranthus caudatus as a histochemical probe of proliferating colonic epithelial cells. *Cancer Res* 51:657–665, 1991.

66. Guillem JG, Weinstein IB: The role of protein kinase C in colon neoplasia, in Herrera L (ed): *Familial Adenomatous Polyposis*. New York, Liss, 1990, pp 325–332.
67. Baba S, Morioka S, Ogawa I, Nakamura S: Studies on histogenesis of microadenoma in familial adenomatous polyposis (abstract). *Int J Colorect Dis* 5:55, 1990.
68. Beaulieu JF, Weiser MM, Herrera L, Quaroni A: Detection and characterization of sucrase-isomaltase in adult human colon and in colonic polyps. *Gastroenterology* 98:1467–1477, 1990.

68a. Quaroni A, Weiser MM, Herrera L, Fay D: Crypt cell antigens (CCA): New carbohydrate markers for human colon cancer cells. *Immunol Invest* 18:391–404, 1989.

68b. Dohi T, Hashiguchi M, Yamamoto S, et al: Fucosyltransferase-producing sialyl Le^a and sialyl Le^x carbohydrate antigen in benign and malignant gastrointestinal mucosa. *Cancer* 73:1552–1561, 1994.

68c. Fenoglio-Preiser CM, Hutter RV: Colorectal polyps: Pathologic diagnosis and clinical significance. *CA Cancer J Clin* 35:322–344, 1985.

69. Pierce ER: Some genetic aspects of familial multiple polyposis of the colon in a kindred of 1,422 members. *Dis Colon Rectum* 11:321–329, 1968.
70. Bussey HJR: *Familial Polyposis Coli: Family Studies, Histopathology, Differential Diagnosis, and Results of Treatment*. Baltimore, Johns Hopkins University Press, 1975.
71. Naylor EW, Lebenthal E: Gardner's syndrome: Recent developments in research and management. *Dig Dis Sci* 25:945–959, 1980.
72. Bulow S: Familial polyposis coli. *Dan Med Bull* 34:1–15, 1987.

72a. Presciuttini S, Bertario L, Sala P, et al: Correlation between relatives for colorectal cancer mortality in familial adenomatous polyposis. *Ann Hum Genet* 57(Pt 2):105–115, 1993.

73. Herrera L, Carrel A, Rao U, et al: Familial adenomatous polyposis in association with thyroiditis: Report of two cases. *Dis Colon Rectum* 32:893–896, 1989.

73a. Domizio P, Talbot IC, Spigelman AD, et al: Upper gastrointestinal pathology in familial adenomatous polyposis: Results from a prospective study of 102 patients. *J Clin Pathol* 43:738–743, 1990.

74. Murphy ES, Mireles M, Beltran A: Familial polyposis of the colon and gastric carcinoma: Concurrent conditions in a 16-year-old boy. *JAMA* 179:1026–1028, 1962.
75. Utsunomiya J, Miki Y, Kuroki T, Iwama T: Phenotypic expressions of Japanese patients with familial adenomatous polyposis, in Herrera L (ed): *Familial Adenomatous Polyposis*. New York, Liss, 1990, pp 101–107.
76. Funkenstein O: Uber Polyposis intestinalis. *Z Klin Med Berl* 55:526–548, 1904.
77. Burt RW: Polyposis syndromes, in Yamada T (ed): *Textbook of Gastroenterology*. Philadelphia, Lippincott, 1991, pp 1674–1696.

77a. Jagelman DG: Duodenal and small-intestinal polyps in familial adenomatous polyposis. *Probl Gen Surg* 10:742–748, 1993.

78. Pollack JL, Swinton NW: Congenital polyposis of the colon with extension to the small intestine and stomach. *Lahey Clin Bull* 9:174–179, 1955.
79. Watne AL, Johnson JG, Chang CH: The challenge of Gardner's syndrome. *CA Cancer J Clin* 19:266–275, 1969.
80. Heald RL, Desmond AM: Gardner's syndrome in association with two tumors in the ileum. *Proc R Soc Med* 60:914–915, 1967.
81. Yonemoto RH, Slayback JB, Byron RL Jr, Rosen RB: Familial polyposis of the entire gastrointestinal tract. *Arch Surg* 99:427–434, 1969.
82. Phillips LG Jr: Polyposis and carcinoma of the small bowel and familial colonic polyposis. *Dis Colon Rectum* 24:478–481, 1981.
83. Ross JE, Mara JE: Small bowel polyps and carcinoma in multiple intestinal polyposis. *Arch Surg* 108:736–738, 1974.
84. Ohsato K, Yao T, Watanabe H, et al: Small-intestinal involvement in familial polyposis diagnosed by operative intestinal fiberscopy: Report of four cases. *Dis Colon Rectum* 20:414–420, 1977.

84a. Herrera L, Iwama T, Davidson B, Goedde TA: Endoscopic diagnosis and treatment of gastric, duodenal, and small-intestinal polyps. *Probl Gen Surg* 10:731–741, 1993.

85. Lees CD, Hermann RE: Familial polyposis coli associated with bile duct cancer. *Am J Surg* 141:378–380, 1981.
86. Jarvinen H, Nyberg M, Peltokallio P: Upper gastrointestinal tract polyps in familial adenomatosis coli. *Gut* 24:333–339, 1983.
87. Komorowski RA, Tresp MG, Wilson SD: Pancreaticobiliary involvement in familial polyposis coli/Gardner's syndrome. *Dis Colon Rectum* 29:55–58, 1986.
88. Bombi JA, Rives A, Astudillo E, et al: Polyposis coli associated with adenocarcinoma of the gallbladder. *Cancer* 53: 2561–2563, 1984.
89. Spigelman AD, Williams CB, Talbot IC, et al: Upper gastrointestinal cancer in patients with familial adenomatous polyposis. *Lancet* 2:783–785, 1989.
90. Herrera-Ornelas L, Elsiah S, Petrelli N, Mittelman A: Causes of death in patients with familial polyposis coli (FPC). *Semin Surg Oncol* 3:109–117, 1987.
91. Plail RO, Bussey HJ, Glazer G, Thomson JP: Adenomatous polyposis: An association with carcinoma of the thyroid. *Br J Surg* 74:377–380, 1987.
92. Li FP, Thurber WA, Seddon J, Holmes GE: Hepatoblastoma in families with polyposis coli. *JAMA* 257:2475–2477, 1987.
93. Naylor EW, Gardner EJ: Adrenal adenomas in a patient with Gardner's syndrome. *Clin Genet* 20:67–73, 1981.
94. Painter TA, Jagelman DG: Adrenal adenomas and adrenal carcinomas in association with hereditary adenomatosis of the colon and rectum. *Cancer* 55:2001–2004, 1985.
95. Carl W, Sullivan MA, Herrera L: Dental abnormalities and bone lesions in patients with familial adenomatous polyposis, in Herrera L (ed): *Familial Adenomatous Polyposis*. New York, Liss, 1990, pp 115–120.
96. Smith WG: Multiple polyposis, Gardner's syndrome and desmoid tumors. *Dis Colon Rectum* 1:323–332, 1958.

97. Oldfield MC: Association of familial polyposis of colon with multiple sebaceous cysts. *Br J Surg* 41:534–541, 1954.
98. Pugh HL, Nesselrod JP: Multiple polypoid disease of colon and rectum. *Ann Surg* 121:88–99, 1945.
99. Weiner RS, Cooper P: Multiple polyposis of colon, osteomatosis and soft-tissue tumors: Report of familial syndrome. *N Engl J Med* 253:795–799, 1955.
100. Gumpel RC, Carballo JD: A new concept of familial adenomatosis. *Ann Intern Med* 45:1045–1058, 1956.
100a. Ramos R, Carrel A, Herrera L: Current treatment of desmoids in familial adenomatous polyposis patients, in Herrera L (ed): *Familial Adenomatous Polyposis*. New York, Liss, 1990, pp 133–146.
100b. Lynch HT, Fitzgibbons R Jr, Chong S, et al: Use of doxorubicin and dacarbazine for the management of unresectable intra-abdominal desmoid tumors in Gardner's syndrome. *Dis Colon Rectum* 37:260–267, 1994.
101. Enterline HT, Culberson JO, Rochlin DB, Brady LW: Liposarcoma: A clinical and pathological study of 53 cases. *Cancer* 13:932–950, 1960.
102. Fader M, Kline SN, Spatz SS, Zubrow HJ: Gardner's syndrome (intestinal polyposis, osteomas, sebaceous cysts) and a new dental discovery. *Oral Surg* 15:153–172, 1962.
103. Turcot J, Despres JP, St. Pierre F: Malignant tumors of the central nervous system associated with familial polyposis of the colon: Report of two cases. *Dis Colon Rectum* 2:465–468, 1959.
104. Baba S, Tsuchiya M, Watanabe I, Machida H: Importance of retinal pigmentation as a subclinical marker in familial adenomatous polyposis. *Dis Colon Rectum* 33:660–665, 1990.
105. Peutz J: Very remarkable case of familial polyposis of mucous membranes of intestinal tract and nasopharynx accompanied by peculiar pigmentation of the skin and mucous membranes. *Ned Maandschr Geneeskd* 10:134–146, 1921.
106. Jeghers H, McKusick VA, Katz KH: Generalized intestinal polyposis and melanin spots of the oral mucosa, lips and digits: Syndrome of diagnostic significance. *N Engl J Med* 241:1031–1036, 1949.
107. Hood AB, Krush AJ: Clinical and dermatologic aspects of the hereditary intestinal polyposes. *Dis Colon Rectum* 26: 546–548, 1983.
108. Perzin KH, Bridge MF: Adenomatous and carcinomatous changes in hamartomatous polyps of the small intestine (Peutz-Jeghers syndrome): Report of a case and review of the literature. *Cancer* 49:971–983, 1982.
109. Foutch PG, Sanowski RA, Kelly S: Enteroscopy: A method for detection of small bowel tumors. *Am J Gastroenterol* 80:887–890, 1985.
110. Spigelman AD, Thomson JPS, Phillips RKS: Towards decreasing the relaparotomy rate in Peutz-Jeghers syndrome: The role of preoperative small bowel endoscopy. *Br J Surg* 77:301–302, 1990.
111. Linos DA, Dozois RR, Dahlin DC, Bartholomew LG: Does Peutz-Jeghers syndrome predispose to gastrointestinal malignancy? A later look. *Arch Surg* 116:1182–1184, 1981.
112. Konishi F, Wyse NE, Muto T, et al: Peutz-Jeghers polyposis associated with carcinoma of the digestive organs. *Dis Colon Rectum* 30:790–799, 1987.
113. Hizawa K, Iida M, Matsumoto T, et al: Neoplastic transformation arising in Peutz-Jeghers polyposis. *Dis Colon Rectum* 36:953–957, 1993.
114. Watne AL: Syndromes of polyposis coli and cancer. *Curr Probl Cancer* 7:1–31, 1982.
115. Riley E, Swift M: A family with Peutz-Jeghers syndrome and bilateral breast cancer. *Cancer* 46:815–817, 1980.
116. Scully RE: Sex cord tumor with annular tubules: A distinctive ovarian tumor of the Peutz-Jeghers syndrome. *Cancer* 25:1107–1121, 1970.
117. Burt RW: Colorectal neoplasia: Familial screening. *J Gastroenterol Hepatol* 6:548–551, 1991.
118. Cantu JM, Rivera H, Ocampo-Campos R, et al: Peutz-Jeghers syndrome with feminizing Sertoli cell tumor. *Cancer* 46:223-228, 1980.
119. Horrilleno EG, Eckert C, Ackerman LV: Polyps of rectum and colon in children. *Cancer* 10:1210–1220, 1957.
120. Giardiello FM, Hamilton SR, Kern SE, et al: Colorectal neoplasia in juvenile polyposis or juvenile polyps. *Arch Dis Child* 66:971–975, 1991.
121. Berg HK, Herrera L, Petrelli NJ, et al: Mixed juvenile-adenomatous polyp of the rectum in an elderly patient. *J Surg Oncol* 29:40–42, 1985.
121a. Radi MJ, Fenoglio-Preiser CM: Polyps of the colon, in Kirsner JB, Shorter RG (eds): *Diseases of the Colon, Rectum, and Anal Canal*. Baltimore, Williams & Wilkins, 1988, p 413.
122. Sachatello CR, Griffen WO Jr: Hereditary polypoid diseases of the gastrointestinal tract: A working classification. *Am J Surg* 129:198–203, 1975.
123. Sassatelli R, Bertoni G, Serra L, et al: Generalized juvenile polyposis with mixed pattern and gastric cancer. *Gastroenterology* 104:910–915, 1993.
124. Lloyd KM II, Dennis M: Cowden's disease: A possible new symptom complex with multiple system involvement. *Ann Intern Med* 58:136–142, 1963.
125. Brownstein MH, Mehregan AH, Bikowski J, et al: The dermatopathology of Cowden's syndrome. *Br J Dermatol* 100:667–673, 1979.
126. Chilovi F, Zancanella L, Perino F, et al: Cowden's disease with gastrointestinal polyposis. *Gastrointest Endosc* 36:323–324, 1990.
127. Chen YM, Ott DJ, Wu WC, Gelfand DW: Cowden's disease: A case report and literature review. *Gastrointest Radiol* 12:325–329, 1987.
128. Carlson GJ, Nivatvongs S, Snover DC: Colorectal polyps in Cowden's disease (multiple hamartoma syndrome). *Am J Surg Pathol* 8:763–770, 1984.
129. Williard W, Borgen P, Bol R, et al: Cowden's disease: A case report with analyses at the molecular level. *Cancer* 69:2969–2974, 1992.
130. Haibach H, Burns TW, Carlson HE, et al: Multiple hamartoma syndrome (Cowden's disease) associated with renal cell carcinoma and primary neuroendocrine carcinoma of the skin (Merkel cell carcinoma). *Am J Clin Pathol* 97:705–712, 1992.
131. de la Torre C, Cruces MJ: Cowden's disease and Down syndrome: An exceptional association. *J Am Acad Dermatol* 25(5 pt 2):909–911, 1991.
132. Bagan JV, Penarrocha M, Vera-Sempere F: Cowden syndrome: Clinical and pathological considerations in two new cases. *J Oral Maxillofac Surg* 47:291–294, 1989.
133. Case records of the Massachusetts General Hospital: Weekly clinicopathological exercises, Case 24-1987: A 56-year-old man with a substernal goiter, multiple cutaneous and mucosal lesions, and a positive stool test for occult blood. *N Engl J Med* 316:1531–1540, 1987.
134. Walton BJ, Morain WD, Baughman RD, et al: Cowden's disease: A further indication for prophylactic mastectomy. *Surgery* 99:82–86, 1986.
135. D'Amore ES, Manivel JC, Pettinato G, et al: Intestinal ganglioneuromatosis: Mucosal and transmural types. A clinicopathologic and immunohistochemical study of six cases. *Hum Pathol* 22:276–286, 1991.
136. Mendelsohn G, Diamond MP: Familial ganglioneuromatous

polyposis of the large bowel: Report of a family with associated juvenile polyposis. *Am J Surg Pathol* 8:515–520, 1984.
137. Snover DC, Weigent CE, Sumner HW: Diffuse mucosal ganglioneuromatosis of the colon associated with adenocarcinoma. *Am J Clin Pathol* 75:225–229, 1981.
138. Woodruff JM: The pathology and treatment of peripheral nerve tumors and tumor-like conditions. *CA* 43:290–308, 1993.
139. Chokhavatia S, Anuras S: Neuromuscular disease of the gastrointestinal tract. *Am J Med Sci* 301:201–214, 1991.
140. Muir EG, Bell AJ, Barlow KA: Multiple primary carcinomata of the colon, duodenum, and larynx associated with kerato-acanthomata of the face. *Br J Surg* 54:191–195, 1967.
141. Torre D: Multiple sebaceous tumors. *Arch Dermatol* 98:549–551, 1968.
142. Burgdorf WHC, Pitha H, Fahmy A: Muir-Torre syndrome: Histologic spectrum of sebaceous proliferations. *Am J Dermatopathol* 8:202–208, 1986.
143. Maipang T, Herrera-Ornelas L, Sanford C, et al: Torre's syndrome in association with premalignant and malignant tumors and suspected familial polyposis. *J Surg Oncol* 35:104–106, 1987.
144. Cruz Vigo F, Pardo R, Saenz D, et al: Muir-Torre syndrome with multiple neoplasia. *Br J Surg* 79:1161, 1992.
145. Cohen PR, Kohn SR, Kurzrock R: Association of sebaceous gland tumors and internal malignancy: The Muir-Torre syndrome. *Am J Med* 90:606–613, 1991.
145a. Lynch HT, Fusaro RM: Muir-Torre syndrome: Heterogeneity, natural history, diagnosis, and management. *Probl Gen Surg* 10:765–778, 1993.
146. Ruvalcaba RHA, Myhre S, Smith DW, Sotos syndrome with intestinal polyposis and pigmentary changes of the genitalia. *Clin Genet* 18:413–416, 1980.
147. DiLiberti JH, Weleber RG, Budden S: Ruvalcaba-Myhre-Smith syndrome: A case with probable dominant inheritance and additional manifestations. *Am J Med Genet* 15:491–495, 1983.
148. Dvir M, Beer S, Aladjem M: Heredofamilial syndrome of mesodermal hamartomas, macrocephaly, and pseudopapilledema. *Pediatrics* 81:287–290, 1988.
149. Foster MA, Kilkoyne RF: Ruvalcaba-Myhre-Smith syndrome: A new consideration in the differential diagnosis of intestinal polyposis. *Gastrointest Radiol* 11:349–350, 1986.
150. Gorlin RJ, Cohen MM Jr, Condon LM, Burke BA: Bannayan-Riley-Ruvalcaba syndrome. *Am J Med Genet* 44:307–314, 1992.
151. Allibone RO, Nanson JK, Anthony PP: Multiple and recurrent inflammatory fibroid polyps in a Devon family ("Devon polyposis syndrome"): An update. *Gut* 33:1004–1005, 1992.
152. Anthony PP, Morris DS, Vowles KDJ: Multiple and recurrent fibroid polyps in three generations of a Devon family: A new syndrome. *Gut* 25:854–862, 1984.

CHAPTER 10

Inflammatory Bowel Disease and Colorectal Cancer

Robert H. Riddell

CARCINOMA IN ULCERATIVE COLITIS

Carcinoma complicating ulcerative colitis is uncommon and accounts for only about 1 percent of all large bowel cancers. It occurs primarily in patients with extensive ulcerative colitis or pancolitis at a far greater rate than that observed in the general population, the risk starting after about 10 years of disease. Patients with disease limited to the left colon are probably also at increased risk, but this has the same age spectrum as colorectal carcinoma in the noncolitic population. Patients with ulcerative proctitis and ulcerative proctosigmoiditis are also probably at increased risk, but this risk is likely not sufficiently high to justify surveillance. It is currently estimated that about 3 to 5 percent of the population in North America will develop colorectal carcinoma, so that the increased risk of total ulcerative colitis is probably on the order of 10 to 25 times that of the noncolitic population and even greater in young patients, partly because colorectal carcinoma is rare at this age. There is, however, wide geographic variation of this risk. Some countries, such as Israel, have a low prevalence of dysplasia and carcinoma.[1–4] In Scandinavia, where surgery for severe disease is performed relatively frequently, the population at risk is small and these complications are correspondingly uncommon.[1] One large study suggests a cumulative 25-year probability of only 9 percent.[5]

Age of Presentation and Prognosis

The age at presentation of carcinoma is markedly lower than that seen in the noncolitic population, the mean age of symptomatic presentation being between ages 40 and 45. Because, by definition, the age of half the patients is lower than this, it is not uncommon to see patients in the third and fourth decades of life present with carcinomas.

When patients are compared stage for stage with age-matched controls, the prognosis of cancer in ulcerative colitis is no worse than in the controls, primarily because a large proportion of young patients present and die with advanced disease and aggressive tumors irrespective of the underlying predisposing cause. Most series including a reasonable proportion of young patients have high mortality rates. However, other series have a high proportion of Dukes A carcinomas and a correspondingly good overall prognosis.[6–9]

Risk Factors

The risk factors for colorectal carcinoma complicating ulcerative colitis are reasonably well documented; practically, the only two that really matter are the extent of disease and the length of disease history. However, it is also becoming apparent that an early age of onset may also increase the risk to a degree that exceeds the simple length of history.[10] Although activity of disease is generally considered not to be a significant factor, in one recent study there was a correlation between risk and active disease.[11] The possibility that this might be the result of chronic sulfasalazine administration is intriguing.

Geographic variation may be important. Persons living in countries with a low indigenous rate of colorectal carcinoma are probably also at low risk for developing carcinoma on the background of other diseases that predispose to its development, while some countries with western incidences of colorectal cancer appear to have much less dysplasia and cancer in colitis for reasons that are completely unclear. The corollary of this is whether a family history of colorectal carcinoma is a predisposing risk factor; that is, whether patients at risk for carcinoma in ulcerative colitis are at increased risk if they have a strong family history of colorectal (or other) carcinomas. These factors become important in deciding whether screening programs should be started and may well lead to the reconsideration of decisions regarding whether screening programs should be initiated in some parts of the world or in specific patients.

Extent of Disease

This is the single most important factor predisposing patients with ulcerative colitis to carcinoma. While it is well known that total colitis is a predisposing factor and that idiopathic ulcerative proctitis carries little greater risk than exists in the residual population, considerable uncertainty has arisen about patients falling between these extremes. Patients with disease extending into the right side of the colon can be considered at high risk.[5] Many physicians now include patients in surveillance programs once disease has been demonstrated to extend proximal to the splenic flexure. Extent of disease probably varies depending on how it is assessed. Radiologic assessment even with air-contrast barium enema is less sensitive than endoscopy, while the addition of biopsy in assessing the extent of the disease is likely the most sensitive. However, this creates a further problem by assuming that microscopic disease has the same premalignant potential as gross disease, whether determined radiologically or endoscopically. While this is likely to be the case, evidence to support it is still required. Fortunately this issue concerns a relatively small proportion of the colitic population.

Left-Sided Colitis

Some studies indicate that patients with left-sided colitis may be at slightly increased risk of developing large bowel carcinoma when the disease has been present for at least 20 years.[5] It is not easy to assess this risk without knowing precisely how the diagnosis was made. If the method was endoscopy and biopsy, one would be much more inclined to believe the evidence than if the relatively insensitive single-contrast barium enema was used or the method of diagnosis was not stated. Further about 5 percent of the population at large develops carcinoma in the left colon. For the increased risk in patients with left-sided colitis to be credible, a significant increase over this figure must be demonstrated in patients with no evidence of disease proximal to the splenic flexure.

Histologic Criteria for Involvement

A confounding fact is that the precise criteria for histologic involvement are surprisingly vague. Active (acute) inflammation and/or architectural distortion are clear indicators of current or prior disease. Problems arise in patients with a possible increase in chronic inflammatory cells in the lamina propria. Because lymphoid aggregates are normal in the bowel, these should be ignored. Because a slight increase in plasma cells can be very subjective, we use the criterion of plasma cells regularly extending to the muscularis mucosa, which is a feature limited to chronic inflammatory bowel disease (personal observation). A further confusing factor is that some patients with left-sided disease or even proctosigmoiditis have an inflamed mucosa in the vicinity of the ileocecal valve. The significance of this finding with regard to the patient's cancer risk in the absence of other indicators of extensive disease is unknown. We ignore it in assessing the extent of disease, as there are no data to suggest that it is of clinical significance.

Duration of Disease and Age of Onset

Few patients develop clinically apparent carcinoma before 10 years' duration of disease. However, in most studies, the curve starts to rise at this point.[2] Those who believe that a screening program is required usually start at this time. Others are less comfortable with the fact that cancers may present clinically after 10 years of disease. Assuming that there is a lead time for the dysplasia-carcinoma sequence to be effected, they start screening after 7 years of disease. The actual risk is on the order of 0.5 to 2 percent per year after the first 10 years of disease.[2,8,12] Age of onset of disease is thought to be important, the risk being increased in those developing ulcerative colitis early in life.[10] Other careful analysis of the data suggests that the risk after a given period of time is similar in all age groups.[2]

Activity of Disease

There have also been many attempts to correlate disease activity with the likelihood of developing colorectal carcinoma, but the general conclusion is that lack of activity seems not to be protective. Many patients presenting with colitic cancers have colitis that has been asymptomatic, or easily managed with proprietary preparations, for long periods of time, often decades. Patients under regular medical supervision seem much less likely to present in this manner. Conversely, patients with persistent active disease are much more likely to have a colectomy and will therefore be removed from the group at risk. However, active disease alone seems not to increase the risk of long-term colorectal cancer. Nevertheless, a recent communication raised the issue of whether long-term sulfasalazine-associated induction of remission might be protective.[11]

Site of Tumors

In contrast to noncolitic carcinomas, three-quarters of which are rectosigmoid, colitic cancers have a more diffuse distribution. This has been repeatedly confirmed. Indeed, we have been impressed by how many occur in the ascending colon. Nevertheless, some longterm studies will show a marked prevalence of distal tumors.[5,13] The possibility that some of these might reflect the more distal distribution of colorectal cancer seen in the general population two or three decades ago remains. The clinical implication of this finding is that surveillance colonoscopy must be full colonoscopy. Unless the patient has an ileorectal anastomosis, little sense of security can be gained from a sigmoidoscopy reaching only 60 cm from the anal verge.

Multiple Tumors

The multiplicity of tumors in patients with one colitic cancer is well established, and it has been determined that about 25 percent of patients with one carcinoma will have a second.[14–16] Nevertheless, these figures were obtained in patients presenting with symptoms of carcinoma. The incidence of multiple tumors seems to be much less in patients in whom carcinomas are detected incidentally during surveillance.

CHARACTERISTICS OF COLORECTAL CANCER IN ULCERATIVE COLITIS

Gross and Endoscopic Appearance

Some colitic carcinomas still present with clinical symptoms. These carcinomas are frequently circumferential, stenosing, and may obstruct, with dilatation of the proximal bowel; they may also be multiple (Fig. 10-1). Occasionally a linitis plastica appearance is seen, with long, tubular neoplastic strictures. Some abnormalities seen endoscopically are dysplastic (high- or low-grade) when biopsied, but on subsequent resection some are found to contain invasive adenocarcinoma, so-called dysplasia-associated lesion or masses (DALMs) (Fig. 10-2).[14,15] Smaller lesions, and particularly incidental lesions detected on surveillance colonoscopy, are much more likely to be benign nodules, but the smallest carcinomas are often only plaques, which may be slightly raised, at the same level of the adjacent mucosa, or a slight mucosal irregularity (Fig. 10-2). These small, asymptomatic carcinomas are much more likely to be discovered incidentally in colectomy specimens or at colonoscopy. Rarely, nothing is seen endoscopically, and the diagnosis of carcinoma is made on random biopsy or histologic section. Conversely, a proportion of carcinomas present as large polypoid masses resembling giant inflammatory polyps; surprisingly, infiltration in many of these polyps remains limited to the submucosa or internal muscularis propria. This may be because they were originally giant inflammatory polyps in which dysplasia and cancer have supervened.

The endoscopist carrying out colonoscopy and biopsy for dysplasia and carcinoma in ulcerative colitis and the pathologist taking sections from resected specimens must be acutely aware of the more atypical and subtle appearances of the carcinomas that may be encountered. Histologic detection of these tumors can also be extremely difficult. In resected specimens, their detection is aided if specimens are received fresh, are opened and cleaned, and are then pinned out and fixed overnight. The following day the mucosa is examined carefully, any irregularity is incised through the full thickness of the bowel, and the cut surface is

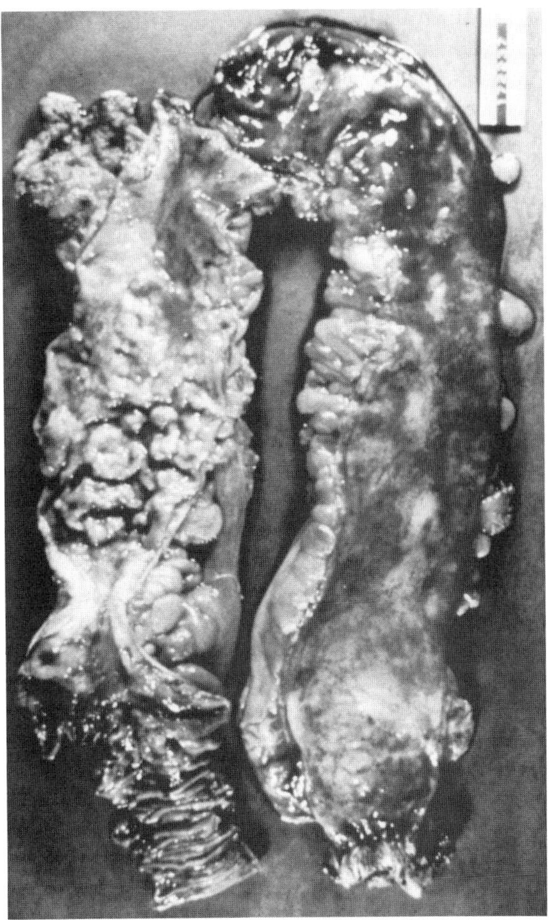

FIG. 10-1. Colectomy from a patient presenting with a right-lower-quadrant mass. Note the annular tumor in the ascending colon and the numerous smaller tumors immediately distal.

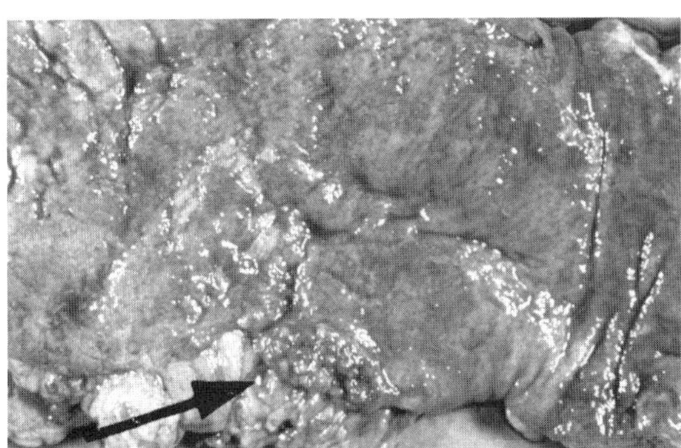

FIG. 10-2. Small incidental carcinoma that had penetrated just through the muscularis propria.

examined for tongues of yellow-white tumor going into the submucosa or beyond or for pools of mucin. Sections are also taken wherever the demarcation of mucosa and submucosa is apparent.

Microscopic Appearance

The microscopic appearance of colitic cancers embraces the same range as that seen in the noncolitic population, but two major differences are apparent. First, many of the tumors are colloid and arise in a villous-like mucosa; these are notoriously difficult to diagnose on biopsy, because even in those patients in whom biopsy is deep enough to detect invasion (rather than the overlying dysplastic mucosa), only mucin or very well differentiated epithelium, often without desmoplasia, is present on biopsy. Hence, the concept of endoscopic DALMs,[14,15] which may prove to be invasive carcinomas endoscopically (see below).

The second difference is that an increased proportion of carcinomas of unusual morphologic subtypes are encountered. Some of these may not be immediately recognized as carcinoma because of the bland appearance of the nuclei; however, these can be seen to infiltrate into the lamina propria or submucosa on biopsy, or beyond in resected specimens. We think of these as "minimal deviation carcinomas." Further, it is apparent that some of the very poorly differentiated carcinomas occurring in ulcerative colitis have dense core granules and represent endocrine carcinomas (see subsequent discussion). Other unusual variants such as squamous cell carcinoma,[17] which can arise in areas of squamous metaplasia within the large bowel[18] or as part of an adenosquamous carcinoma,[19] can occur, as can some of the more unusual variants of adenocarcinoma, including choriocarcinoma and spindle cell variants.

Carcinoid Tumors of the Large Intestine in Ulcerative Colitis

A small proportion of apparent carcinomas occurring in ulcerative colitis (and Crohn's disease) prove to contain numerous dense-core granules on electron microscopy, strongly suggesting that they are poorly differentiated carcinoid tumors (endocrine carcinomas) rather than pure adenocarcinomas.[20–24] However, they tend to behave relatively aggressively. Their presence can be suspected histologically by their infiltrative growth pattern, with little or no gland formation and a high nuclear cytoplasmic ratio. The nuclei often show the typical speckled chromatin pattern so characteristic of these tumors. They tend not to be accompanied by overt dysplasia of the overlying mucosa but rather by hyperplasia of endocrine cells, particularly argentaffin cells,[20–25] and may also include microcarcinoids.[20] However, such endocrine cell hyperplasia may also give rise to mucus-producing tumors in which argentaffin cell granules are readily identified within the intracellular mucus (personal observation).

OTHER CANCERS

Carcinoma at Other Sites in the Gastrointestinal Tract

Rarely, carcinomas occur at colostomy or ileostomy sites.[26] Some are associated with long-standing ostomy dysfunction but seem associated with preexisting disease. Some of these appear to have a large associated villous adenoma and/or area of dysplasia, depending on the interpretation of the morphologic lesion. Particularly in patients with ulcerative colitis, there is a definite although uncommon association with cholangiocarcinoma, primarily of the extrahepatic biliary tree and in association with sclerosing cholangitis. However, there is also a potentially increased risk of carcinoma of the gallbladder.[27]

Tumors outside the Gastrointestinal Tract

The best association in patients with both ulcerative colitis and Crohn's disease are lymphomas and leukemia. Indeed, a small proportion of large bowel tumors arising in patients with ulcerative colitis prove to be lymphomas, usually of B-cell lineage and/or large-cell type. They also tend to arise in patients with long-standing, extensive disease. The anal region may be extensively involved if the underlying disease is Crohn's.[28] Lymphomas are multiple in about one-third as compared to 10 percent of sporadic cases, tend to be left-sided rather than ileocecal, are generally high-grade, and are often advanced at presentation, with a correspondingly poor prognosis. While there are only a handful of reported cases of large bowel lymphoma complicating Crohn's disease, there are many more lymphomas reported in the small bowel.[29,30]

There may be morphologic similarities to lymphomas complicating inflammatory bowel disease and other mucosa-associated tumors, which some have termed *polymorphic*.[31,32] The prognosis tends to be most dependent on the degree of local spread, and patients with disease confined to the mucosa or submucosa and without lymphatic, bone marrow, or other metastasis do best. Most tumors require resection and tend not to completely resolve locally with chemotherapy or radiotherapy.[33]

Leukemia, primarily the acute nonlymphocytic variety, is also well described in both ulcerative colitis and Crohn's disease. In one study, the relative risk was calculated to be increased by about a factor of 5, but, interestingly, none of these patients had been on immunosuppressives.[34]

One population-based study suggested that mesenchymal tumors were encountered with an increased risk of 1.3, a 2.4-fold increase in brain tumors, but a

0.4 risk of breast cancer in females. The same study found that squamous carcinomas of the skin occurred 5.5 times more frequently than expected in patients with Crohn's disease.[35]

CARCINOMA IN CROHN'S DISEASE

The first case of adenocarcinoma in Crohn's disease was reported by Ginzburg et al. in 1956.[36] Since then, the risk of carcinoma of the small and large bowel in these patients has been estimated at 4 to 20 times greater than that of the general population.[33,37–40] The average age at the time of diagnosis of carcinoma is approximately 48 years for cancer of the small bowel and 50 years for that of the large bowel, which is about a decade less than that for carcinoma of these sites in patients without Crohn's disease.[41,42] The incidence is thought to escalate with the increasing duration of Crohn's disease.[33,42,43]

The distribution of gastrointestinal cancers in Crohn's disease is approximately 25 percent in the small bowel (30 percent in the jejunum and 70 percent in the ileum), 70 percent in the large bowel, and 5 percent in the remaining sites.[37,39,42–45] Although the proportion of gastrointestinal cancers that arise in macroscopically normal bowels is greater in Crohn's disease than in ulcerative colitis (33 versus 4 percent),[37] most cancers occur in inflamed segments of bowel, particularly in strictures and long-standing fistulas.[41–44] Bypassed loops of small bowel and excluded colorectum are also vulnerable to cancer.[40,41,45–47] These tumors are now rare as this operation is now not utilized; however, excluded rectal stumps are still sometimes left for long periods of time and are at risk.

Multifocal carcinomas are commonly observed in Crohn's disease.[41–45,48] The preoperative diagnosis of invasive carcinoma in Crohn's disease is even more difficult than in ulcerative colitis due to the difficulty of examining the small bowel and of distinguishing neoplastic from inflammatory stricture. Some carcinomas may be undetectable early, especially if they occur in fistulas or are also of the flat, plaquelike type found in ulcerative colitis. Sometimes, without careful scrutiny, even biopsies of very well differentiated tumors can pass unrecognized morphologically. Patients with Crohn's carcinoma therefore tend to have a very poor prognosis, which may be worse than that of patients with the usual carcinomas or carcinoma in ulcerative colitis.[37,45,49] Mortality is about 80 percent in Crohn's carcinoma.[37,43,44] Grossly and histologically, these carcinomas resemble other advanced small and large bowel and colitic cancers except for the additional presence of Crohn's disease. Also, enteritis or colitis cystica profunda sometimes occurs, which in the presence of dysplasia raises the question of whether this might represent well-differentiated invasive carcinoma. Fortunately, provided that these lesions are well differentiated and remain confined to the submucosa, the limited experience we have suggests that they rarely metastasize. The discussion is therefore largely of academic interest.

Carcinoma in Fistula Tracts

Occasionally, carcinomas in Crohn's disease occur in what appears to be a fistula tract. Most of them are found incidentally in resection specimens. Surprisingly, this is the only group of patients with a good prognosis, presumably because tumor is an incidental finding, has presented asymptomatically, and is largely confined to the bowel wall.

PATHOLOGY OF DYSPLASIA AND ITS IMPLICATIONS

Definition of Dysplasia—Its Uses and Classification

A variety of terms for epithelial abnormalities often reflect not only neoplastic but also reparative (regenerative) changes without distinguishing between them. One reason for this is that regenerative changes are relatively poorly described. The situation is clearly simplified if the definition of dysplasia is restricted to an unequivocally neoplastic proliferation and if all changes that are not unequivocally dysplastic, such as uncertain or reparative lesions, are excluded. Dysplasia can therefore be defined as *an unequivocally neoplastic proliferation essentially equivalent to an adenoma*.[50] A very good analogy can be made with villous adenomas, in which the dysplastic mucosa of the adenoma gives rise directly to an invasive carcinoma that may be occult and found only on resection, sometimes with only low-grade dysplasia being present in the overlying adenoma. Therefore, the most important implication of this definition is that *dysplastic epithelium may not only be a marker or precursor of carcinoma but may itself by malignant and be associated with direct invasion into the underlying tissue*.

Use of Dysplasia in Surveillance of Ulcerative Colitis

The concept of dysplasia in ulcerative colitis is based on the precept that carcinoma arises from a precarcinomatous lesion (dysplasia) and that the identification of dysplasia and excision of the large bowel in these patients prevents subsequent death from disseminated carcinoma. Conversely, patients with quiescent disease and no dysplasia could be followed and not subjected to unnecessary colectomy. This has three major implications. First, prophylactic proctocolectomy in all patients in the high-risk clinical group is unacceptable. Second, a laissez-faire attitude is similarly rejected. Third, there is no good method of anticipating easily which patients in the clinical high-risk group will develop carcinoma. Dysplasia is therefore best regarded as an aid to predicting which patients are at greater risk of developing carcinoma, so that prophylactic surgery would be offered only to this subgroup.

Surveillance in ulcerative colitis depends on several assumptions. The first is that it reduces the mortality from colorectal cancer, although the evidence for this is very limited.[8,51] Ideally, a study proving this would require a control arm with patients not in a surveillance program, but that would obviously be difficult to carry out ethically. In the absence of a controlled study, data are required showing that surveillance prevents the development of lethal cancers. One study used as controls patients who had been lost to follow-up. In the patients under surveillance, 2 cancers were found in 1168 patient-years but with no mortality, compared with 5 cancers, 3 of which were lethal, in 315 patient-years in the patients lost to follow-up.[51] Theoretically, then, cancers which are resected in patients who survive are acceptable. Unfortunately, many surveillance studies include patients who have both developed[52–55] and occasionally even died from carcinoma.[56,57] The second assumption of surveillance is that cancers can either be detected before they become lethal or that a marker, such as the presence of dysplasia, precedes all carcinomas for a long enough period to be detectable, analogous to the adenoma-carcinoma sequence in the noncolitic bowel. It is also assumed that if dysplasia is present, it will be both endoscopically detectable and morphologically identifiable. Many questions have been raised regarding all of these issues.[58]

Classification and Grading of Dysplasia

Practically, when biopsies are being examined, major divisions within the spectrum from negative to high-grade dysplasia need to be made because they are important clinically[51] (Table 10-1). Thus, biopsies can be divided into those that are unequivocally neoplastic (positive for dysplasia) and those that are unequivocally negative for dysplasia; the latter group comprises typical quiescent, active, or resolving colitis, including typical reparative changes. Biopsies representing the midpart of the spectrum—namely, those not falling into either of the previous two categories—are indefinite for dysplasia. Included in this category are samples of epithelium that may be progressing through the spectrum and that may ultimately become dysplastic; samples with exuberant reparative processes which are not considered normal; and biopsies showing other types of epithelial proliferation that is not readily classifiable. Dysplastic epithelium is essentially similar to other benign but neoplastic epithelia such as that seen in adenomas; dysplasia may be subcategorized into high-grade and low-grade on nuclear and architectural grounds.

Table 10-1
Simplified Classification of Dysplasia in Ulcerative Colitis with Clinical Implications for Management

Histologic classification	*Suggested management*
Negative for dysplasia	Regular follow-up
Indefinite for dysplasia	Early rebiopsy
Positive for dysplasia	Consider colectomy, particularly if
Low-grade	(1) found at first colonoscopy
High-grade	(2) associated with an endoscopic lesion
	(3) dysplasia is high-grade
	(4) dysplasia is multifocal

Some prefer three grades of dysplasia (mild, moderate, and severe), but this rapidly turns into five with the addition of mild-moderate (effectively low-grade) and moderate-severe (effectively high-grade). Even a two-grade system has some cases that fall on the boundary, where an argument can be made for either grade. Theoretically both grades merit consideration for colectomy. In practice, this is often not the case (see subsequent discussion of management).

Macroscopic Appearance of Dysplasia

Areas of dysplasia may be raised above the adjacent mucosa, may form obvious nodules or polyps, but may also occur as plaques or irregular areas of nodularity which may be minimally or obviously raised (Fig. 10–3). Sometimes an entire segment of mucosa is affected. The mucosa may also appear finely villous (Fig. 10-4) and brushlike, resembling the pile of a carpet; but, importantly, it may be completely indistinguishable from adjacent nondysplastic mucosa. It may vary in size from a patch that is several millimeters or centimeters in maximum diameter, or it may

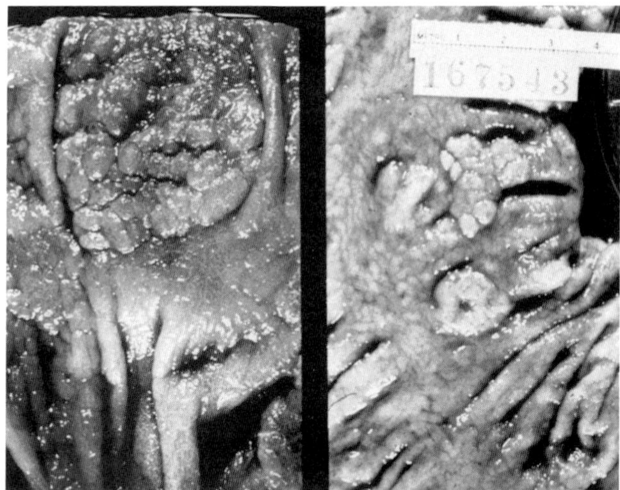

FIG. 10-3. Mucosal plaques and nodules which were dysplastic on biopsy but which were not associated with underlying infiltration on histologic examination.

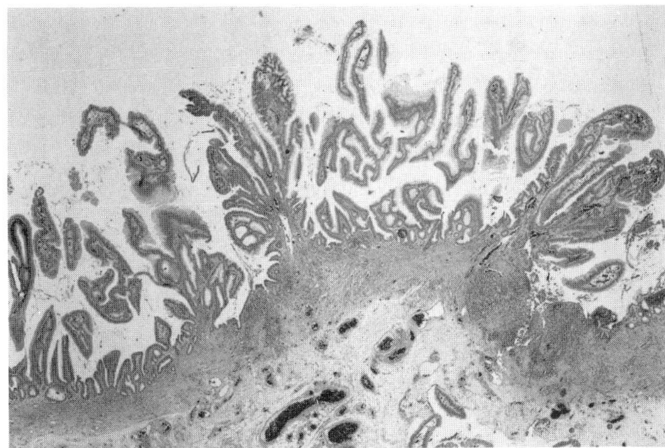

FIG. 10-4. Histologic equivalent of a fine villous pattern identified macroscopically.

involve extensive areas of mucosa. Areas of dysplasia are often poorly circumscribed, in marked contrast to adenomas, which are invariably well circumscribed and penduncULATED, broad-based, or sessile.[16,25] The endoscopic appearances of dysplasia are poorly documented, although some areas of mucin depletion (which appear red) or mucosal irregularity can be recognized. The frequency with which dysplasia is associated with grossly visible abnormalities is similarly difficult to assess.

Histologic Appearances of Dysplasia

Epithelium negative for dysplasia includes normal crypts (Fig. 10-5) and typical regenerative changes (Fig. 10-6). In this, some pathologists would be sufficiently concerned about the size of the nuclei, despite the acute inflammation, to feel uncomfortable about calling it unequivocally negative, preferring to interpret them as indefinite for dysplasia and requesting further biopsies.

By far the most frequent type of dysplasia is that resembling typical adenomas (Fig. 10-7). A much less common type consists of large, hyperchromatic nuclei, each of which occupies as much as one-half of each cell (Fig. 10-8), usually the basal half. If grading is required, it is easiest to restrict it to two grades, high and low, depending on whether the nuclei are confined to the basal halves of the cells (low-grade) or reach the luminal halves (high-grade)[50] (Fig. 10-7). Loss of polarity of nuclei (which some include with in situ carcinoma) is part of high-grade dysplasia, as is the architectural abnormality of a back-to-back (gland-within-gland) appearance which, when associated with dysplasia, is generally recognized as in situ carcinoma. Dysplasia is graded where it is greatest but is usually similar throughout a biopsy.

There are other variants of dysplasia in which the nuclear characteristics are those described previously

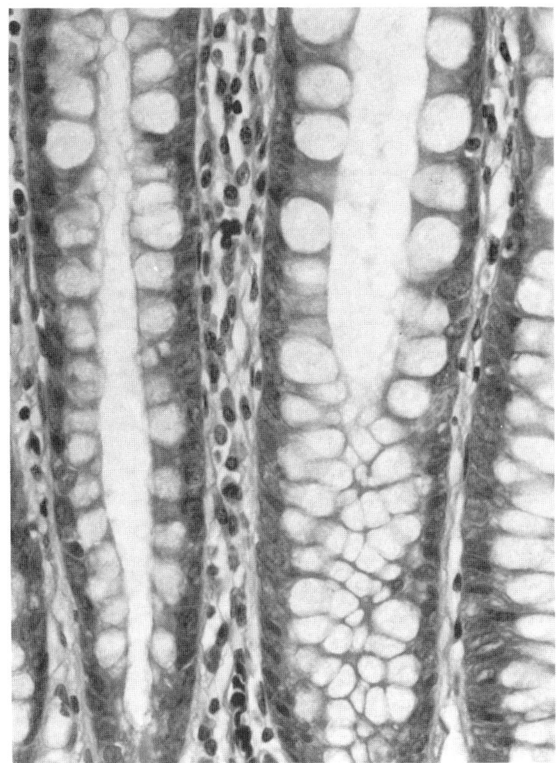

FIG. 10-5. Normal nuclei in crypts containing goblet cells and intervening absorptive cells.

but the cytoplasm may assume other features, such as a nonmucin clear-cell change, dystrophic (upside-down) goblet cells, or the superficial sawtooth appearance similar to that seen in hyperplastic polyps.[50] Although not discussed here, these cells may be found in virtually all phases of colitis.

The classification "epithelium indefinite for dysplasia" encompasses the group of changes in the normal to dysplasia spectrum which are not readily categorized as unequivocally negative or positive (Fig. 10-9). Practically, if one asks whether these changes are unequivocally negative or positive for dysplasia, and the answer to both questions is no, then by definition one is dealing with indefinite changes. Epithelium from biopsies indefinite for dysplasia is often aneuploid when DNA is measured. The importance of this category is that it is not just a hedge for genuine ignorance but usually requires further biopsies within a relatively short period (usually months), so that the behavior of these lesions can be followed closely and their progress to dysplasia or regression documented.

The subcategorization "probably positive" implies that the changes observed are most likely neoplastic but either fail to display sufficient nuclear changes to justify inclusions in that category or contain an overriding factor, usually active inflammation and regeneration, that calls for caution on the grounds that they are unlikely to regress completely and may progress

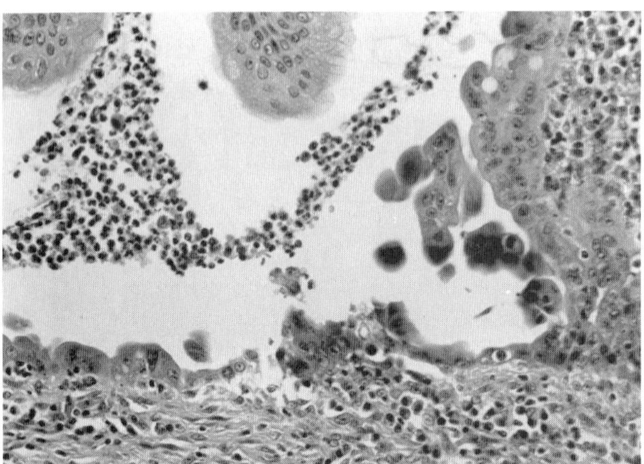
A

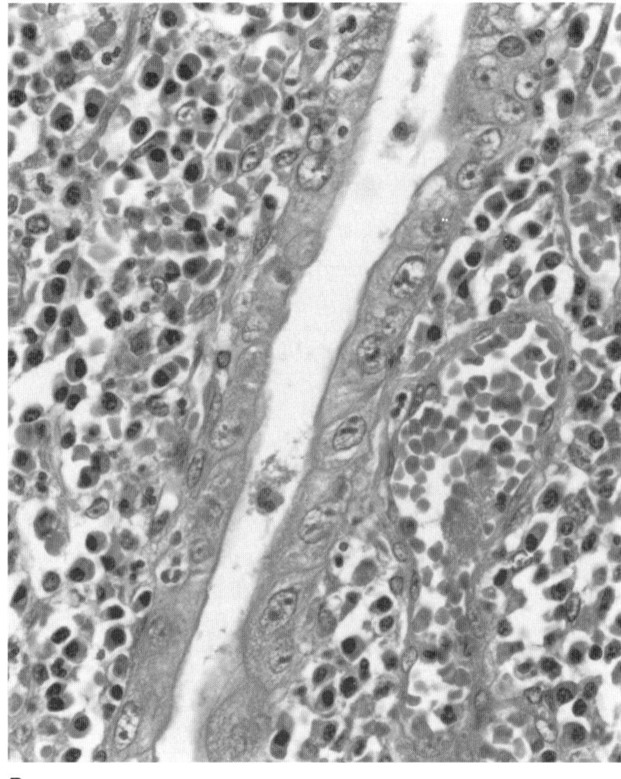
B

FIG. 10-6. Active regeneration (restitution): *A*. Syncitial epithelial cells with hobnail nuclei—a very early regenerative feature. *B*. Restitution with far fewer nuclei than normal, which are in cuboidal cells with indistinct intercellular borders. Note the size of the nuclei but the open chromatin and typical active nucleoli. This change still occasionally causes diagnostic problems.

to unequivocal dysplasia. Also, as detection of aneuploidy becomes more frequent, there may be a trend to subdivide those patients in the "indefinite for dysplasia" group on this basis rather than on the grounds of a subjective morphologic interpretation.

Modification to the Original Classification of Dysplasia

The category "indefinite for dysplasia" was originally subdivided into "probably negative," "unknown," and "probably positive" subgroups. Increasingly, the regenerative and reparative changes originally classified here are being recognized, so that, for experienced observers, the number of biopsies in the "probably negative" category has diminished and its use is now relatively infrequent. Typical reparative changes are included with "negative for dysplasia" rather than with "indefinite for dysplasia—probably negative." If doubt remains they belong in the "indefinite—unknown" category. Early follow-up biopsy is usually requested to ensure that these changes regress with therapy. This leaves only the other two categories ("unknown" and "probably positive") in the "indefinite for dysplasia" category. In practice, it is hardly worthwhile to vacillate between the two, as both have the same clinical implication: a need to gather more data by repeating the endoscopy and biopsies. This results in the simpler classification and suggested management of biopsy specimen, as shown in Table 10-1.

Dysplasia in the Presence of Active Inflammation

Surprisingly, dysplastic epithelium is only occasionally involved with acute inflammation; when the latter is present in dysplastic mucosa, involvement is at best only very focal (Fig. 10-10), with only an occasional crypt abscess. The corollary is that in the presence of active inflammation affecting most of the crypts present and/or in the presence of mucosa actively regenerating epithelium, it is most unwise to classify a biopsy as being dysplastic because it will invariably improve and resolve with therapy, thereby disproving the diagnosis.

Aids in the Diagnosis of Dysplasia

Numerous techniques have been utilized to assist with (or even potentially replace) the histologic diagnosis of dysplasia. These have included carcinoembryonic antigen,[59] mucins,[60–62] and lectin binding.[63,64] A variety of monoclonal and polyclonal antibodies, including those to a variety of growth factors and abnormal gene products, have been unrewarding, showing only

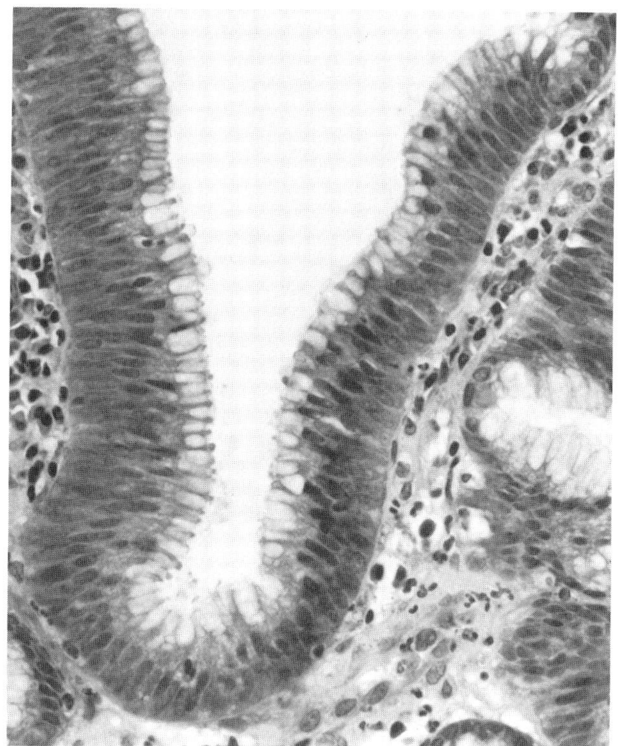

A

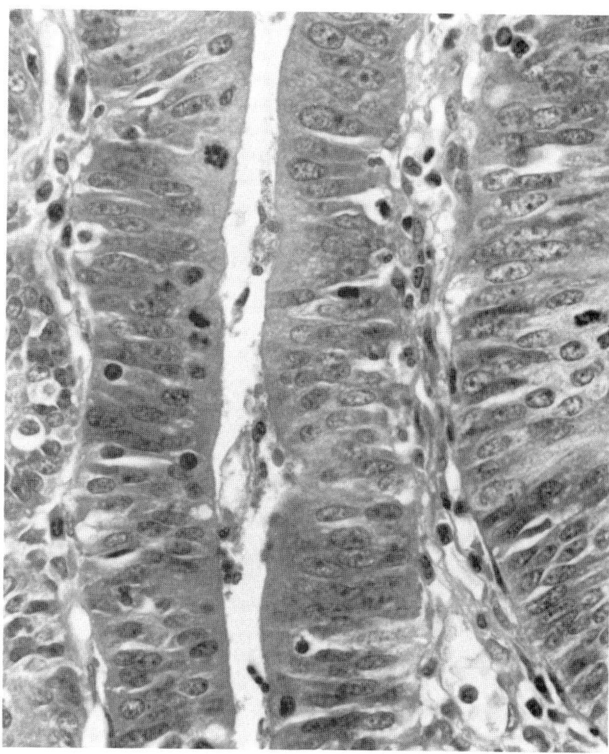

B

FIG. 10-7. Adenomatous-type dysplasia. *A*. Low-grade dysplasia. Compared to Fig. 10-5, nuclei are larger, more hyperchromatic, and stratified. However, they are confined largely to the basal part of the cell. Note also that rather than goblet cells being present as in Fig. 10-5, each cell contains an apical mucous vacuole very similar to gastric foveolar epithelium. *B*. High-grade dysplasia. Nuclei regularly reach the luminal surface of the cells. Compared to low-grade dysplasia, the nuclei tend to be more open and vesicular, and small but prominent nucleoli are present. These are precisely the adjectives used to describe the regenerative features illustrated in Fig. 10-6*B*. Note the size of the cells and the density of nuclei, by which the two are readily distinguished.

trends.[59,65–68] Assay of tissue enzymes such as lactic dehydrogenase or, more hopefully, glucose-6-phosphate dehydrogenase, has been suggested to have potential value,[69] as may scanning electron microscopy.[70]

However, the measurement of DNA content of epithelial nuclei using flow cytometry or image analysis has shown most promise, particularly in predicting which patients with ulcerative colitis have or will develop dysplasia or carcinoma, even if the latter is not aneuploid.[71–75] However, aneuploidy seems unlikely to replace or even be a serious adjunct to conventional microscopy in making the diagnosis of dysplasia or in the management algorithm potentially terminating in colectomy. It may be of value in stratifying patients under surveillance into high- and low-risk groups which could be followed at different intervals.

Work has been carried out on oncogenes and their products (normal and abnormal) and suppressor genes that might be expressed preferentially in adenomas and carcinomas in ulcerative colitis. To date, the little work done suggests that colitic carcinomas may express different mutations to noncolitic carcinomas. c-Ki-*ras* seems less involved in dysplasia and cancer in ulcerative colitis than in noncolitic neoplasia.[76–78] There may be a correlation between high c-*myc* expression and dysplasia.[79] Allelic deletions of tumor suppressor genes are frequently observed in a variety of human tumors. One study of colitic dysplastic and cancerous lesions examined loss of heterozygosity affecting p53, which was found in 47 percent.[80] The retinoblastoma (Rb) gene had been deleted in one-third, while the adenomatous polyposis coli (APC) and adjacent mutated in colon cancer (MCC) genes were also deleted in one-third. In those heterozygous at two or more loci, loss of heterozygosity of p53, Rb, and/or the APC/MCC locus was found in one-half.[81] There have been several studies on p53, the results of which depend to a large extent on the method used for its detection. These abnormalities have been detected in all stages of the dysplasia spectrum from negative for dysplasia to invasive carcinoma, although tending to be

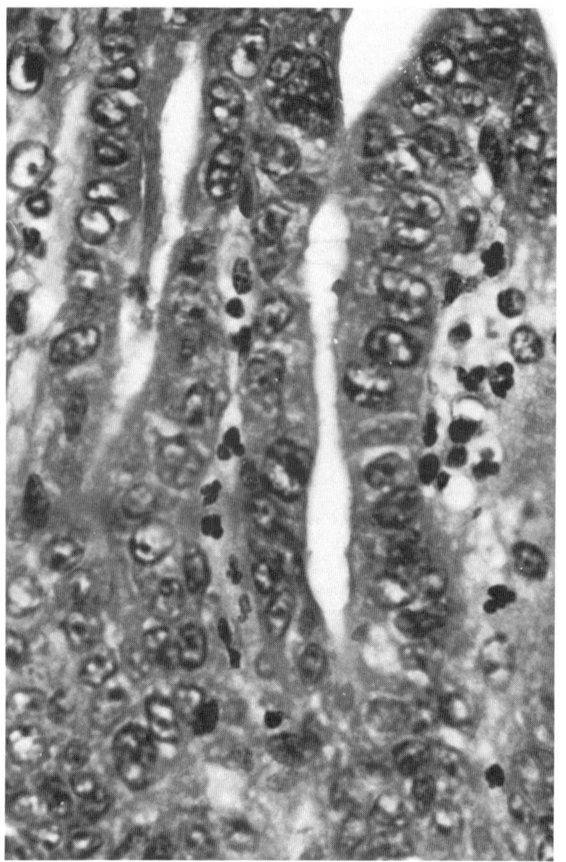

FIG. 10-8. Alternative form of dysplasia characterized by individual large hyperchromatic nuclei occupying most of the cell.

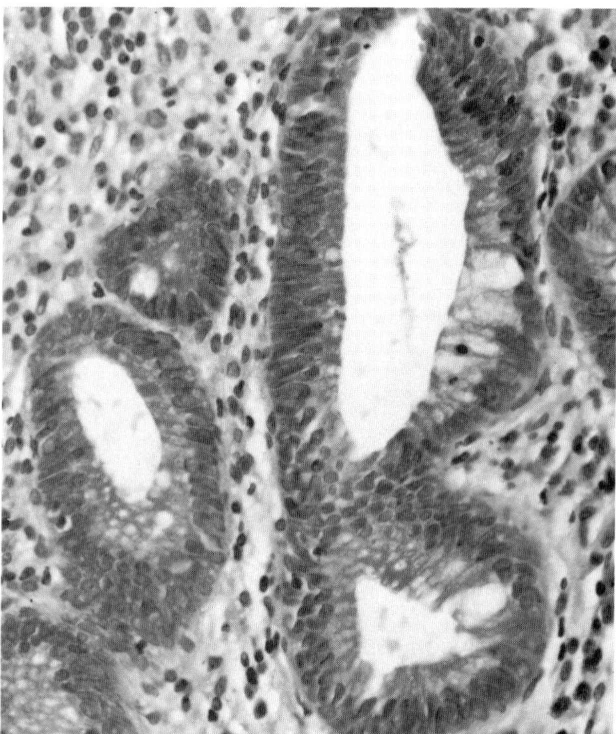

FIG. 10-9. Epithelium indefinite for dysplasia, being neither unequivocally negative as seen in Fig. 10-5 nor unequivocally dysplastic as seen in Fig. 10-7*A*.

increasingly found with increasing degrees of dysplasia.[73,80] While all of these changes presumably play a role in the pathogenesis of dysplasia and cancers in colitis, their potential as markers in dysplasia remains uncertain.

Differences between Adenomas, Dysplasia, and Dysplasia-Associated Lesions and Masses (DALMs)

Adenomas

In ulcerative colitis, pedunculated adenomas are uncommon but do occur. The questions of whether these lesions occur in excess or whether their growth is potentiated by the underlying disease is unclear. However, endoscopic excision of these lesions as if they were simple adenomas appears safe and is not apparently associated with an excess of carcinoma. It must be shown that the lesion has been completely excised locally by demonstrating nondysplastic mucosa in the stalk or lateral margin and by taking multiple biopsy specimens of the adjacent mucosa to ensure that the "adenoma" is not part of a more widespread area of nodular dysplasia. If it is, local excision is not curative and colectomy needs to be considered.

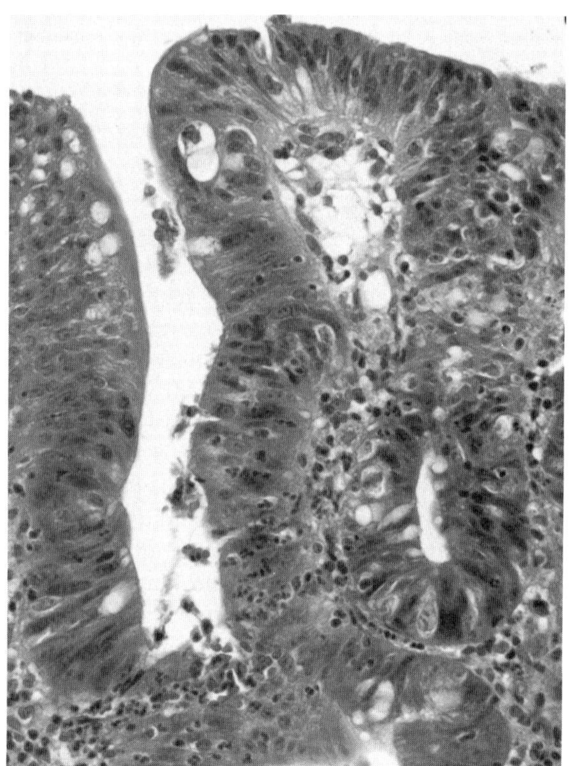

FIG. 10-10. Dysplastic inflamed epithelium. In this biopsy, only a small part contained neutrophils infiltrating the epithelium. However, the nuclei are clearly dysplastic (compare with Fig. 10-7). Nevertheless, this is quite uncommon.

Dysplasia-Associated Lesions and Masses (DALMs)

If dysplastic biopsies are obtained from an endoscopic abnormality such as a plaque, nodule, or polyploid mass (Figs. 10–2 and 10–3), then an underlying carcinoma cannot be excluded unless that lesion is resected and examined histologically. This is because the underlying carcinoma may not be accessible to biopsy forceps, so that without resection, the diagnosis of carcinoma cannot be made. The implication is that simple inflammatory polyps do not need to be biopsied if they are endoscopically classic. However, when this is not the case, the lesion should be excised if on a stalk; it is often wise to biopsy the base of the polyp in addition, to ensure that the attempted local excision is complete. Sometimes there is a focally nodular area of dysplasia and the polypectomy removes only part of the dysplastic area. It is therefore imperative that endoscopists be aware of these lesions and their potential significance in patient management.[15]

The Significance of Dysplasia on a First Endoscopy

This distinction is important; the first colonoscopy is considered *diagnostic* and subsequent colonoscopies are for *surveillance*.[82] If an endoscopic abnormality is found at the first colonoscopy, it is more likely that the changes have been present for a longer period and therefore to have undergone malignant transformation; this may be associated with invasion in about two-thirds of patients.[14] Consequently, if a patient with ulcerative colitis has undergone several surveillance colonoscopies, all of which have yielded biopsy specimens negative for dysplasia, the finding of dysplasia suggests that it has most likely developed more recently and therefore has had less time in which to develop an invasive component. Invasion is therefore less likely to be present but still cannot be excluded other than following histological examination of the resected specimen.

Recommendation for Biopsies at Colonoscopy for the Detection of Dysplasia and Carcinoma

Colonoscopy is directed toward the detection of dysplasia to prevent carcinoma, but practically it may also serve to detect invasive carcinoma that may not have been visualized or been present at a prior endoscopy. Thus endoscopy should be directed primarily at target lesions that cannot be confidently accepted as inflammatory polyps. Alternatively, if numerous inflammatory polyps are present and are not typical in any way, it is reasonable to sample them, together with a biopsy from the stalk if possible, in case it is part of a larger area of dysplasia.

Whether target lesions are visualized or not, some form of sampling is required from the remaining mucosa. There is no ideal number of biopsies, for the obvious reason that if dysplasia is not present, no number of biopsies will detect it; by contrast, if dysplasia involves the entire mucosa, then one biopsy will detect it. Unfortunately, we have no real knowledge of the area of dysplasia when it is first detected by surveillance; it may only be a few square centimeters. It is therefore suggested that two biopsy specimens be taken at the cecal pole, and, possibly using fluoroscopic control, two each in the ascending colon, hepatic flexure, proximal and distal transverse colons, and splenic flexure; then two biopsy specimens may be taken every 10 cm on withdrawal of the scope, finishing with two each in the upper and lower rectum. Each pair of biopsies should be placed in a separate prelabeled container following orientation. Biopsies deemed inadequate in size or consisting of fecal material only should be repeated, but the endoscopy nurse/assistant is in the best position to judge whether adequate tissue is present in a biopsy. The frequency with which surveillance colonoscopy should be carried out is slowly being established as annual. Several studies, including the large study from St. Mark's Hospital in London, have demonstrated that biennial colonoscopy is probably inadequate to prevent patients from developing and dying of carcinoma despite being in a surveillance program.[5,74,83,84] Annual colonoscopy is therefore recommended for surveillance.

Management of Dysplasia

The management of dysplasia involves balancing the risks and benefits of one particular form of therapy, such as colectomy, and any ensuing problems against the risks and benefits of continued follow-up in any particular patient. The real problem is the relative lack of objective data on which to base these judgments.

Controversy continues regarding the management of patients with dysplastic biopsies. The notion that all patients must be managed "individually" continues to guarantee that data will remain difficult to obtain. Numerous factors affect the decision for colectomy, including the extent of disability from the disease, the attitude of both the patient and the physician toward colectomy, the age and life expectancy of the patient, the operative risk, the type of procedure, and the availability of and confidence in both the pathologist and surgeon, the latter particularly if a pouch procedure is contemplated, as this has further problems of its own. The problem is potentiated because many physicians are unclear about whether they are practicing cancer prevention (prophylaxis), its early detection, or a fortuitous combination of both. The management of dysplasia is governed by which of these objectives is being utilized. The presence of dysplasia does not mean that the patient will inevitably have or develop carcinoma; indeed, some never do so. However, a small proportion may already have an invasive carcinoma. This creates further tension in trying to prevent the patient from developing a potentially lethal carcinoma on the one hand (an early curable cancer may be acceptable) and carrying out an unnecessary colectomy on the other.

However, there are circumstances in which there is relatively uniform agreement regarding a recommendation for colectomy. These include the presence of a dysplasia-associated lesion or mass detected endoscopically, irrespective of the grade of dysplasia, which probably has a greater than 50 percent risk of being an invasive cancer on resection, particularly if found on the first (diagnostic) rather than subsequent (surveillance) colonoscopy. Dysplasia found on the first endoscopy seems to carry an increased risk of synchronous invasive carcinoma, and the risk undoubtedly increases with the grade and extent of dysplasia. In many institutions, a single or an occasional biopsy with low-grade dysplasia may not be acted upon. Some find that colectomy—if multiple biopsies have low-grade dysplasia or any have high-grade dysplasia—may be effective in maintaining a population that does not die of colitic cancers. At the time of writing, the data are mainly anecdotal, and good data are required to confirm this approach.

Confirmation of Dysplasia

Confirmation of dysplasia was recommended to ensure that colectomy is not carried out unnecessarily for a false-positive diagnosis of dysplasia.[50] Dysplasia can be confirmed by letting a second pathologist examine the slides interpreted as being dysplastic, or repeating the endoscopy and biopsies, or both. Confirmation by a second pathologist clearly depends on the competence of both pathologists and the gastroenterologist's confidence in that pathologist. Most of the time the diagnosis of dysplasia is straightforward, so that confirmation by a second pathologist is usually necessary only if either party is insecure.

In contrast to patients presenting clinically with invasive carcinoma, in whom dysplasia may be relatively widespread and cancers multiple,[60,61] both of these are uncommon in patients under surveillance. Dysplasia is frequently confined to small areas of the mucosa, which causes major sampling problems for the endoscopist. Unless dysplasia is widespread or an area of dysplasia can be visualized endoscopically, confirmation of dysplasia by repeated endoscopy and biopsy is usually doomed to failure because it has repeatedly been shown that dysplasia is patchy.[8,14–16] Current sampling methods of taking one or two biopsy specimens every 10 cm of bowel assume that perhaps 5 mm^2 of mucosa—that is, at best, 1/2000th of the mucosa—is being sampled. Given this serious sampling problem, if one is fortunate enough to detect dysplasia on biopsy, it makes little sense to ignore it if the criterion for colectomy is the development of dysplasia. To emphasize the sampling problem further, a 2- by 2-cm patch of dysplasia would require about 20 to 25 evenly spaced biopsy specimens in a 10-cm length of bowel to reasonably guarantee its detection. In asking an endoscopist to confirm the presence of dysplasia by repeating the endoscopy and the biopsies, we are being incredibly optimistic and unrealistic and should not be surprised if such missions fail. The end result is that failure to resample an area of dysplasia may be interpreted as regression of the dysplasia, particularly if medical therapy has been increased between endoscopies to reduce inflammatory changes, and implies an original overinterpretation of biopsies.

Options for Patient Management

These are very limited, consisting only of regular surveillance, increased surveillance, or resection.[85] If resection is not recommended for dysplasia, then the option is to repeat the endoscopy and biopsies; the only issue is when and how the results will affect the management algorithm. Some physicians have criteria for consideration of colectomy, which include the repeated demonstration of dysplasia on endoscopic biopsy, the development of high-grade dysplasia, the repeated demonstration of low-grade dysplasia, or the development of a DALM. All of these options are designed to delay colectomy. The assumption is that the risk of a potentially lethal cancer at this time is extremely low. These options deliberately choose to disregard the part of the definition of dysplasia stating that it may give rise directly to invasive carcinoma, irrespective of the grade, and may also be the superficial part of an invasive carcinoma. Or they may regard the likelihood as being too low to justify colectomy. They also ignore the fact that carcinomas may escape endoscopic detection, that it is impossible to time colectomy to the point of minimal invasion, or that these strategies are generally having little impact on the mortality from colorectal cancer in surveillance programs. Nevertheless, if the objective of surveillance is to prevent patients from dying of colitic cancer, the deliberate delay of colectomy for dysplasia should be utilized with caution until it has been shown that these end points achieve their aim.

Dysplasia in Crohn's Disease

Dysplasia adjacent to small bowel carcinomas, as well as those in the large bowel, is well described and similar to that seen in ulcerative colitis. There is therefore no reason why surveillance should not be carried out in Crohn's colitis. However, because of the technical difficulty, cost, and low yield, there is currently little interest in doing so. Dysplastic changes in Crohn's disease are in many ways similar to those seen in ulcerative colitis. However, they may be found adjacent to and/or distant from an infiltrating carcinoma and may extend variably, ranging from widespread to multifocal and focal dysplasia[50,41,47,86,87] Several authors support a dysplasia-carcinoma sequence, especially when high-grade dysplasia is recognized as a precursor of cancer in Crohn's disease,[86–89] but the sensitivity and positive predictive accuracy of dysplasia for adjacent or remote carcinoma are unknown. This raises the question of how dysplasia should be managed whether found incidentally in a biopsy or if an endoscopic lesion is biopsied; there are no data on which to base a decision. If an area of dysplasia is found and endoscopically recognized, endoscopic ablation by a method such as diathermy or laser therapy is an option. However, this does not exclude the possibility of an underlying carcinoma, so that local resection is not unreasonable. This does not answer the question of whether dysplasia is a marker for carcinoma elsewhere in the large bowel. However, extensive resection is probably unjustifiable unless dysplasia is multifocal or widespread. Adenomas arising in patients with Crohn's disease can likely be treated as in ulcerative colitis, namely, by local excision and biopsy of the vicinity of the stalk to ensure that it is not part of a wider area of dysplasia.

REFERENCES

1. Langholz E, Munkholm P, Binder V: Colorectal cancer risk and mortality in patients with ulcerative colitis. *Gastroenterology* 103:1444–1451, 1992.
2. Devroede G: Risk of cancer in inflammatory bowel disease, in Winawer SJ, Schottenfield D, Sherlock P, et al (eds): *Colorectal Cancer: Prevention, Epidemiology and Screening.* New York, Raven Press, 1980, pp 325–326.
3. Gilat T, Fireman Z, Grossman A, et al: Colorectal cancer in patients with ulcerative colitis: A population study in central Israel. *Gastroenterology* 94:870–877, 1988.
4. Maratka Z, Nedbal J, Kocianova J, et al: Incidence of colorectal cancer in proctocolitis: A prospective study of 959 cases over 40 years. *Gut* 26:43–49, 1985.
5. Lennard-Jones JE, Melville DM, Morson BC, et al: Precancer and cancer in extensive ulcerative colitis: Findings among 401 patients over 22 years. *Gut* 31:800–806, 1990.
6. Riddell RH: Why the variation in colitic cancer rates from different centers? in Tytgat GNJ, van Blankenstein M (eds): *Current Topics in Gastroenterology and Hepatology.* Stuttgart, Georg Thieme Verlag, 1990, pp 494–499.
7. Hughes RG, Hall TJ, Block GE, et al: The prognosis of carcinoma of the colon complicating ulcerative colitis. *Surg Gynecol Obstet* 146:46–48, 1978.
8. Lennard-Jones JE, Melville DM, Morson BC, et al: Precancer and cancer in extensive ulcerative colitis: Findings among 401 patients over 22 years. *Gut* 31:800–806, 1990.
9. Lennard-Jones OR, Ritchie JK, Hawley PR, Lennard-Jones JE: Prognosis of carcinoma in ulcerative colitis. *Gut* 22:752–755, 1981.
10. Ekbom A, Helmick C, Zack M, Adami H-O: Ulcerative colitis and colorectal cancer: A population based study. *N Engl J Med* 323:1228–1233, 1990.
11. Ekbom A: Communication, European Conference of Gastroenterology, Madrid, Spain, 1993.
12. Greenstein AJ, Sachar DB, Smith H, et al: Cancer in universal and left-sides colitis: Factors determining risk. *Gastroenterology* 77:290–294, 1979.
13. Woolrich AJ, DaSilva M, Korelitz BI: Surveillance in the routine management of ulcerative colitis: The predictive value of low-grade dysplasia. *Gastroenterology* 103:431–438, 1992.
14. Blackstone MO, Riddell RH, Rogers BHG, Levin B: Dysplasia-associated lesion or mass (DALM) detected by colonoscopy in longstanding ulcerative colitis: An indication for colectomy. *Gastroenterology* 80:366–374, 1981.
15. Rosenstock E, Farmer RG, Petras R, et al: Surveillance for colonic carcinoma in ulcerative colitis. *Gastroenterology* 89:1342–1346, 1985.
16. Butt JH, Konoshi F, Morsom BC, et al: Macroscopic lesions in dysplasia and carcinoma complicating ulcerative colitis. *Dig Dis Sci* 28:18–26, 1983.
17. Mir-Madjlessi SH, Farmer RS: Squamous cell carcinoma of the rectal stump in a patient with ulcerative colitis. *Cleve Clin Q* 52:257–261, 1985.
18. Adamsen S, Ostberg G, Norryd C: Squamous-cell metacarcinoma with severe dysplasia of the colonic mucosa in ulcerative colitis. *Dis Colon Rectum* 31:558–562, 1988.
19. Patterson FK: Adenocanthoma and ulcerative colitis: Case report and review of the literature. *South Med J* 66:681–690, 1973.
20. McNeely B, Owen DA, Pezim M: Multiple microcarcinoids arising in chronic ulcerative colitis. *Am J Clin Pathol* 98:112–116, 1992.
21. Dood SM: Chronic ulcerative colitis complicated by atypical carcinoid tumor. *J Clin Pathol* 39:913–916, 1986.
22. Owen DA, Hwang WS, Thorlakson RH, Wallie JE: Malignant carcinoid tumor complicating chronic ulcerative colitis. *Am J Clin Pathol* 76:333–338, 1981.
23. Miller RR, Sumner HW: Argyrophilic cell hyperplasia and an atypical carcinoid tumor in chronic ulcerative colitis. *Cancer* 50:2920–2925, 1982.
24. Gledhill A, Hall PA, Cruse JP, Pollock DJ: Enteroendocrine cell hyperplasia, carcinoid tumours and adenocarcinoma in long-standing ulcerative colitis. *Histopathology* 10:501–508, 1986.
25. Riddell RH: The precancerous lesion of ulcerative colitis, in Yardley JH, Morson BC, (eds): *The Gastrointestinal Tract.* Baltimore, Williams & Wilkins, 1977, pp 109–123.
26. Gadacz TR, McFadden DW, Gabrielson EW, et al: Adenocarcinoma of the ileostomy: The latent risk of cancer after colectomy for ulcerative colitis and familial polyposis. *Surgery* 107:698–703, 1990.
27. Dorudi S, Chapman RW, Kettlewell MG: Carcinoma of the gallbladder in ulcerative colitis and primary sclerosing cholangitis: Report of two cases. *Dis Colon Rectum* 34:827–828, 1991.
28. Shepherd NA, Hall PA, Williams GT, et al: Primary malignant lymphoma of the large intestine complicating chronic inflammatory bowel disease. *Histopathology* 15:325–337, 1989.
29. Glick SN, Teplick SK, Goodman LR, et al: Development of lymphoma in patients with Crohn's disease. *Radiology* 153: 337–339, 1984.
30. Robertson EJ, Al-Kais WK, Vareska GJ, Ponsky JL: Plasmacytoma of the ileum complicating Crohn's disease: Report of a case and review of the literature. *Surgery* 100:916–923, 1986.
31. Hall PA, Jass JR, Levison DA, et al: Classification of primary gut lymphomas. *Lancet* 2:958, 1988.
32. Shepherd NA, Blackshaw AJ, Coates PJ, Levison DA: Primary malignant lymphoma of the colon: A histopathological

and immunocytochemical study of 45 cases with clinicopathological correlation. *Histopathology* 12:235–252, 1988.
33. Greenstein AJ, Sachar DB, Smith H, et al: A comparison of cancer risk in Crohn's disease and ulcerative colitis. *Cancer* 48:2742–2745, 1981.
34. Mir-Madjlessi SH, Farmer RG, Weich JK: Inflammatory bowel disease and leukemia: Report of seven cases of leukemia in ulcerative colitis and Crohn's disease and review of the literature. *Dig Dis Sci* 31:1025–1031, 1986.
35. Ekbom A, Helmick C, Zack M, Adami HO: Extracolonic malignancies in inflammatory bowel disease. *Cancer* 67:2015–2019, 1991.
36. Ginzburg L, Schneider KM, Dreizin DH, Levinson C: Carcinoma of the jejunum occurring in a case of regional enteritis. *Surgery* 39:347–356, 1956.
37. Greenstein AJ, Sachar DB, Smith H, et al: Patterns of neoplasia in Crohn's disease and ulcerative colitis. *Cancer* 46:403–407, 1980.
38. Weedon DD, Shorter RG, Ilstrup DM, et al: Crohn's disease and cancer. *N Engl J Med* 289:1099–1103, 1973.
39. Gyde SN, Prior P, McCartney JC, et al: Malignancy in Crohn's disease. *Gut* 21:1024–1029, 1980.
40. Shorter RG: Risks of intestinal cancer in Crohn's disease. *Dis Colon Rectum* 26:686–689, 1982.
41. Hamilton SR: Colorectal carcinoma in patients with Crohn's disease. *Gastroenterology* 83:398–407, 1985.
42. Fresko D, Lazarus SS, Dolan J, Reingold M: Early presentation of carcinoma of the small bowel in Crohn's disease ("Crohn's carcinoma"). *Gastroenterology* 82:783–789, 1982.
43. Greenstein AJ, Meyers S, Szporn A, et al: Colorectal cancer in regional ileitis. *Q J Med* 62:33–40, 1987.
44. Korelitz BI: Carcinoma of the intestinal tract in Crohn's disease: Results of a survey conducted by the national foundation for ileitis and colitis. *Am J Gastroenterol* 78:44–46, 1983.
45. Petras RE, Mir-Madjlessi SH, Farmer RG: Crohn's disease and intestinal carcinoma: A report of 11 cases with emphasis on associated epithelial dysplasia. *Gastroenterology* 93:1307–1314, 1987.
46. Glotzer DJ: The risk of cancer in Crohn's disease. *Gastroenterology* 89:438–441, 1985.
47. Traube J, Simpson S, Riddell RH, et al: Crohn's disease and adenocarcinoma of the bowel. *Dig Dis Sci* 25:939–944, 1980.
48. Greenstein AJ, Sachar DB, Pucillo A, et al: Cancer in universal and left-sided ulcerative colitis: Clinical and pathologic features. *Mount Sinai J Med* 46:25–32, 1979.
49. Prior P, Gyde S, Cooke WT, et al: Mortality in Crohn's disease. *Gastroenterology* 80:307–312, 1981.
50. Riddell RH, Goldman H, Ransohoff DF, et al: Dysplasia in inflammatory bowel disease: Standardized classification with provisional clinical implications. *Hum Pathol* 14:931–968, 1983.
51. Jones HW, Grogogno J, Hoare AM: Surveillance in ulcerative colitis: Burdens and benefits. *Gut* 29:325–331, 1988.
52. Kewenter J, Ahlman H, Hulten L: Cancer risk in extensive ulcerative colitis. *Ann Surg* 188:824–828, 1978.
53. Nugent FW, Haggitt R, Colcher H, Kutteruf GC: Malignant potential of chronic ulcerative colitis: Preliminary report. *Gastroenterology* 76:1–5, 1979.
54. Brostrom O, Lofberg R, Ost A, Reichard H: Cancer surveillance of patients with longstanding ulcerative colitis: A clinical endoscopical and histological study. *Gut* 27:1408–1413, 1986.
55. Manning AP, Bulgim OR, Dixon MF, Axon ATR: Screening by colonoscopy for colonic epithelial dysplasia in inflammatory bowel disease. *Gut* 28:1489–1494, 1987.
56. Hulten L, Kewenter J, Ahren C: Precancer and cancer in chronic ulcerative colitis. *Scand J Gastroenterol* 7:6653–6657, 1972.
57. Brasco G, Miglioli M, Di Febo G, et al: Cancer and dysplasia in ulcerative colitis: Preliminary report of a prospective study. *Ital J Gastroenterol* 6:212, 1984.
58. Collins RH, Feldman M, Fordtran JS: Colon cancer, dysplasia and surveillance in patients with ulcerative colitis. *N Engl J Med* 316:1654–1658, 1987.
59. Allen DC, Biggart JD, Orchin JC, Foster H: An immunoperoxidase study of epithelial marker antigens in ulcerative colitis with dysplasia and carcinoma. *J Clin Pathol* 38:18–29, 1985.
60. Ehsanullah M, Naunton Morgan M, Filipe MI, Gazzard B: Sialomucins in the assessment of dysplasia and cancer-risk patients with ulcerative colitis treated with colectomy and ileo-rectal anastomosis. *Histopathology* 9:223–235, 1985.
61. Jass ER, England J, Miller K. Value of mucin histochemistry in follow-up surveillance of patients with longstanding ulcerative colitis. *J Clin Pathol* 39:393–398, 1986.
62. Allen DC, Connolly NS, Biggart JD: Mucin profiles in ulcerative colitis with dysplasia and carcinoma. *Histopathology* 13:413–424, 1988.
63. Boland CR, Lane P, Levin B, et al: Abnormal goblet cell glycoconjugates in rectal biopsies associated with an increased risk of neoplasia in patients with ulcerative colitis: Early results of a prospective study. *Gut* 25:1364–1371, 1984.
64. Ahnen DJ, Warren GH, Greene LJ, et al: Search for specific marker of mucosal dysplasia in chronic ulcerative colitis. *Gastroenterology* 93:1346–1355, 1987.
65. Olding LB, Ahren C, Thurin J, et al: Gastrointestinal carcinoma-associated antigen detected by a monoclonal antibody in dysplasia and adenocarcinoma associated with chronic ulcerative colitis. *Int J Cancer* 36:131–136, 1985.
66. Cooper HS, Steplewski Z: Immunohistologic study with monoclonal antibodies against tumor-associated and/or differentiation antibodies. *Gastroenterology* 95:686–693, 1988.
67. Filipe MI, Sandey A, Ma J: Intestinal mucin antigens in ulcerative colitis and their relationship with malignancy. *Hum Pathol* 19:671–681, 1988.
68. Thor A, Itzhowitz SH, Schlom J, et al: Tumor-association glycoprotein (Tag-72) expression in ulcerative colitis. *Int J Cancer* 43:810–815, 1989.
69. Vatn MH, Elgjo K, Norheim A, Bergan A: Measurement of enzyme activity in colonic biopsies: A test for premalignancy in ulcerative colitis? *Scand J Gastroenterol* 19:889–892, 1984.
70. Shields HM, Bates ML, Goldman H, et al: Scanning electron microscopic appearance of chronic ulcerative colitis with and without dysplasia. *Gastroenterology* 89:62–72, 1985.
71. Rutegard J, Ahgren L, Sterling R, Roos G: DNA content and mucosal dysplasia in ulcerative colitis: Flow cytometric analysis in patients with dysplastic or indefinite morphologic changes in the colorectal mucosa. *Dis Colon Rectum* 32:1055–1059, 1989.
72. Rubin CE, Haggitt RC, Burmer GC, et al: DNA aneuploidy in colonic biopsies predicts future development of dysplasia in ulcerative colitis. *Gastroenterology* 103:1611–1620, 1992.
73. Burmer GC, Rabinovitch PS, Haggitt RC, et al: Neoplastic progression in patients with chronic ulcerative colitis: Histology, DNA content, and loss of the p53 allele. *Gastroenterology* 103:1602–1610, 1992.
74. Porschen R, Robin U, Schumacher A, et al: DNA aneuploidy in Crohn's disease and ulcerative colitis: Results of a comparative flow cytometric study. *Gut* 33:663–667, 1992.
75. Lofberg R, Brostrom O, Karlen P, et al: DNA aneuploidy in ulcerative colitis: Reproducibility, topographic distribution and relation to dysplasia. *Gastroenterology* 102:1149–1154, 1992.
76. Burmer GC, Levine DS, Kulander BG, et al: *C-Ki-Ras* mutations in chronic ulcerative colitis and sporadic colon carcinoma. *Gastroenterology* 99:416–420, 1990.

77. Bell SM, Kelly SA, Hoyle JA, et al: *c-Ki-ras* gene mutations in dysplasia and carcinoma complicating ulcerative colitis. *Br J Cancer* 64:174–178, 1991.
78. Chen J, Compton C, Cheng E, et al: *c-Ki-ras* mutations in dysplastic fields and cancers in ulcerative colitis. *Gastroenterology* 102:1983–1987, 1992.
79. Pavelic ZP, Pavelic L, Kuvelkar R, Gapany SR: High c-myc protein expression in benign colorectal lesions correlates with the degree of dysplasia. *Anticancer Res* 12:171–175, 1992.
80. Greenwald BD, Harpaz N, Yin J, et al: Loss of heterozygosity affecting the p53, Rb, and MCC/APC tumor suppressor gene loci in dysplastic and cancerous ulcerative colitis. *Cancer Res* 52:741–745, 1992.
81. Yin J, Harpaz N, Tong Y, et al: p53 point mutations in dysplastic and cancerous ulcerative colitis lesions. *Gastroenterology* 104:1633–1639, 1993.
82. Fusion JA, Farmer RG, Hawk WA, Sullivan BH: Endoscopic surveillance for cancer in chronic ulcerative colitis. *Am J Gastroenterol* 73:120–126, 1980.
83. Leidenius M, Kellokumpu I, Husa A, et al: Dysplasia and carcinoma in longstanding ulcerative colitis: An endoscopic and histologic surveillance program. *Gut* 32:1521–1525, 1991.
84. Nugent FW, Haggitt RC, Gilpin PA: Cancer surveillance in ulcerative colitis. *Gastroenterology* 101:1241–1248, 1991.
85. Levin B, Lennard-Jones J, Riddell RH, et al: Surveillance of patients with chronic ulcerative colitis: WHO Collaborating Centre for the Prevention of Colorectal Cancer. *Bull WHO* 69:121–126, 1991.
86. Simpson S, Traube J, Riddell RH: The histologic appearance of dysplasia (precarcinomatous change) in Crohn's disease of the small and large intestine. *Gastroenterology* 81:492–501, 1981.
87. Craft CF, Mendelsohn G, Cooper HS, Yardley JH: Colonic "precancer" in Crohn's disease. *Gastroenterology* 80:578–584, 1981.
88. Warren R, Barwick KW: Crohn's colitis with carcinoma and dysplasia: Report of a case review of 100 small and large bowel resections for Crohn's disease to detect incidence of dysplasia. *Am J Surg Pathol* 7:151–159, 1983.
89. Cuvelier C, Behaert E, De Potter C, et al: Crohn's disease with adenocarcinoma and dysplasia: Macroscopical, histological and immunohistochemical aspects of two cases. *Am J Surg Pathol* 13:187–196, 1989.

CHAPTER 11

Additional Personal Risk Factors

José G. Guillem
Nicole J. Brittis

HIGHLIGHTS

While age, inflammatory bowel disease, a family history of familial adenomatous polyposis, nonhereditary polyposis colonic cancer syndromes, or first-degree relatives with colorectal cancer (CRC) have been shown to increase the risk of CRC, a personal history of prior CRC or of breast, ovarian, or uterine cancer as well as prior pelvic irradiation have also been implicated as risk factors for the development of CRC.

CONTROVERSIES

Because of differences in study design and in particular onset, frequency, and duration of surveillance, varying degrees of CRC risk are reported. In patients with a prior history of CRC, the designation of synchronous versus metachronous CRC varies greatly, depending on whether a baseline colonic evaluation had been performed at the time of initial CRC resection. In patients with a prior history of breast, ovarian, or uterine cancer, the increase in observed CRC cases may be due partly to increased surveillance/examination of cancer patients relative to a healthy control population.

FUTURE DIRECTIONS

Further prospective screening studies with long-term follow-up and rigorous cost-benefit analysis are needed not only to further define the subset of "cured" colorectal, breast, ovarian, and uterine cancer patients who may be at significant increased risk for CRC development but also to determine what impact, if any, screening for CRC would have on the overall survival of this cancer population.

Histories of prior pelvic irradiation or prior colorectal, breast, ovarian, or uterine cancer are believed to be risk factors for the development of subsequent CRC. Possible explanations offered for the occurrence of multiple primary cancers include shared risk factors, such as reproductive hormones and dietary factors. In the case of prior pelvic irradiation and prior CRC, the subsequent increased risk of CRC is thought to be due, in part, to "promoted colorectal mucosa." Because of these associations and putative increased risk, the screening of these high-risk populations for colorectal neoplasms has been recommended. However, the data used to generate these calculated risks and recommendations are often not clearly defined. In this chapter, we review the literature and critically analyze available data in an attempt to better define the exact risk of subsequent CRC following a history of prior CRC, pelvic irradiation, or breast, ovarian, or uterine cancer.

BREAST CANCER

The first cases of multiple malignancy were reported by Billroth[1] in 1869. However, one of the earliest descriptions of an association between a history of breast cancer and subsequent CRC was given by Kesteven[2] in 1876. Since then, numerous studies have made use of tumor registry or case-control data and have ex-

Table 11-1
History of Breast Cancer and CRC Risk

Authors	*Colonic cancer*	*Rectal cancer*	*CRC*	*CR adenoma*
Schottenfeld and Berg,[5] 1969	0.9	1.2	1.0	—
Bremond et al.,[10] 1984	—	—	—	2.48
Ewertz,[45] 1985	1.1	1.0	1.1	—
Harvey and Brinton,[6] 1985	1.2[a]	1.1	1.2	—
Teppo et al.,[7] 1985	1.4[a]	1.0	1.2	—
Rozen et al.,[13] 1986	—	—	—	2.7
Agarwal,[46] 1986	2.0	—	—	—
Toma et al.,[11] 1987	—	—	2.0	1.05
Schatzkin et al.,[9] 1988	—	—	1.3	—
Neugut et al.,[8] 1991	—	—	1.1	—
Murray et al.[12] 1992	—	—	—	1.02

[a]$p<.05$.

amined this relationship. The results, as noted in Table 11-1, are quite variable.

The Connecticut Tumor Registry data were analyzed in 1969, to determine the risk of a second primary cancer following a diagnosis of breast cancer.[3] An observed to expected relative risk (RR) of 1.5 and 0.9 for colonic and rectal cancer, respectively, was reported. In contrast, an analysis from the Memorial Sloan Kettering Cancer Center Tumor registry demonstrated an observed to expected ratio of colon and rectal cancer of 0.9 and 1.2.[4,5] In 1985, an updated reevaluation of the Connecticut Tumor Registry noted a relative risk of developing colon and rectal cancer of 1.2 and 1.1, respectively.[6] However, it appeared that the risk of subsequent CRC was dependent on the age of breast cancer diagnosis, with women under the age of 45 having a higher relative risk than older women (1.6 and 1.9 versus 1.1 and 1.0, for colonic and rectal cancer, respectively). A Finnish study demonstrated a similar association between age of breast cancer diagnosis and the relative risk of CRC development.[7] In addition, the length of follow-up after initial breast surgery also appeared to increase the risk of developing rectal (not colonic) cancer. The relative risk for rectal cancer development was 1.66 and 2.05 after 10 and 15 years of follow-up, respectively.

Other studies have, however, yielded conflicting results. Utilizing the National Cancer Institute's Surveillance, Epidemiology, and End Results Program (SEER) data, two studies[8,9] noted a relative risk of 1.3 for developing overall CRC in women with a prior diagnosis of breast cancer. A case control flexible sigmoidoscopy study[10] reported an odds ratio of 2.48 for detecting adenomas in cases relative to controls. Two case control colonoscopy studies[11,12] did not, however, detect an increased risk of adenomatous polyp development in women with a prior history of breast cancer. In contrast, a prospective study of 60-year-old women with a history of breast cancer demonstrated a 2.7 relative risk for having a colonic neoplasm detected via Haemoccult, flexible sigmoidoscopy, or colonoscopy "when indicated."[13]

In summary, it appears that women with a diagnosis of breast cancer at a young age may be at increased risk for the development of CRC, particularly rectal cancer. However, this risk may not become significant until after the first decade of follow-up. Although no firm recommendations have been established, it would appear reasonable to screen the large bowel in long-term survivors of early-age-of-onset breast cancer.

OVARIAN CANCER AND CRC

Surveys by Schottenfeld et al.[4] and Schoenberg et al.[3] of women with a diagnosis of ovarian cancer indicated an increased risk of subsequent primary cancers of the colon, endometrium, and breast. Utilizing follow-up data from the National Cancer Institute End Results Program, the relative risk of CRC in women with a diagnosis of ovarian cancer was further addressed[14] (Table 11-2). Although the relative risk (RR) of colonic

Table 11-2
History of Ovarian Cancer and CRC Risk

	Relative risk	
Authors	*Colonic cancer*	*Rectal cancer*
Schottenfeld and Berg,[5] 1969	3.2	—
Schoenberg et al.,[3] 1969	2.4[a]	1.22
Reimer et al.,[14] 1978	1.3[b]	1.1
	1.9[a,c]	0.3
Curtis et al.,[15] 1985	2.0[a]	1.6[a]
Storm and Ewertz,[21] 1985	1.7[a]	1.2
Teppo et al.,[7] 1985	0.9	2.06

[a]$p<.05$.
[b]non-RT.
[c]RT = radiotherapy.

and rectal cancer in nonirradiated ovarian cancer patients (RR= 1.3 and 1.1, respectively) was not significant, the RR for colonic (not rectal) cancer was significantly increased in ovarian cancer patients receiving radiation therapy (RR=2.8), particularly patients followed for more than 5 years after radiation therapy. Others report a similar increase in both colonic and rectal cancer, with a maximal risk after the first 10 years following radiation therapy.[15]

In contrast, among nonirradiated ovarian cancer patients, the risk for subsequent CRC is limited solely to colonic (not rectal) cancer, with the relative risk ranging from 1.3[14] to 3.2.[5] Among the nonirradiated group, the risk of subsequent colonic cancer was limited to the first 2 years, with a loss of significant risk after the first 5 years.[16]

In summary, it therefore appears that women with a diagnosis of ovarian cancer may be at increased risk for harboring CRC or preneoplastic lesions, particularly in the colon. Furthermore, women with ovarian cancer receiving radiation therapy experience an increased relative risk for both colonic and rectal cancer after the first 5 years of follow-up. These data would therefore suggest that women with ovarian cancer should probably have a baseline evaluation of their colon (air contrast barium enema/sigmoidoscopy or colonoscopy) at the time of diagnosis and a subsequent study 5 years thereafter, particularly those receiving radiation therapy.

UTERINE CANCER AND CRC

Based on parallel variation in distinct geographic locations[17] as well as in migrant populations,[18] it appears that cancers of the uterine corpus, breast, colon, and rectum may share common etiologic factors.[19] Although the specific risks linking uterine cancer to CRC remain unknown, several studies have confirmed Bailar's[20] original 1963 observation.

The relative risk of developing colonic cancer following a diagnosis of corpus uterine cancer ranges from 1.4 to 1.9,[3,5,7,15,21] while the risk for the development of rectal cancer ranges from 0.9 to 2.4.[4,5,7,15,16,21] Of note is the similarity of CRC risk among ovarian and corpus uterine cancer patients. In both cancers, it appears that the risk is greater for colonic as opposed to rectal cancer and that this risk increases with time, especially for patients receiving radiation therapy. Furthermore, in nonirradiated corpus uterine cancer patients, the risk (RR = 1.4) is only significant for colonic and not rectal cancer.[15]

These data would suggest that a baseline colorectal evaluation be performed at the time of diagnosis and subsequent surveillance be performed beginning 5 years later, particularly in those receiving radiation therapy.

PELVIC IRRADIATION AND CRC

A causal relationship between ionizing radiation and carcinogenesis was initially inferred from epidemiological studies on atomic bomb survivors in Japan. Although early results[22] did not show any relationship, long-term follow-up demonstrated a significantly increased risk of CRC mortality.[23]

In 1957, Slaughter[24] reported on the first series of patients to develop mucosal carcinomas, including two in the colon and one in the anus, following radiation therapy.

Evidence, supportive but not conclusive, for a causal relationship between ionizing radiation and CRC comes predominantly from case reports (Table 11-3) and animal studies.[25,26] Case studies suggest that women irradiated for cervical cancer have an increased risk for the subsequent development of CRC cancer.[15,21] The actual radiation-induced risk is difficult to ascertain, since women with gynecologic malignancies are thought to be at increased risk for second cancers, including CRC.[3,4,7,15] However, irradiated ovarian cancer patients followed for more than 5 years have an increased risk of CRC compared to patients that do not receive radiotherapy.[7,15] Similarly, patients

Table 11-3
Pelvic Irradiation and CRC Development

Authors	*No. of cases*	*Interval, years*
Palmer and Spratt,[47] 1956	9	10
Slaughter,[24] 1957	3	11
Rubin,[48] 1961	5	4–12
Smith,[49] 1962	3	19–22
Quan,[50] 1968	2	18–21
DeCosse,[51] 1969	1	31
MacMahon and Rowe,[28] 1971	6	1–25
Castro,[29] 1973	26	5–30
O'Connor,[52] 1979	2	16–31
Jao et al.,[27] 1987	75	0–45
Levitt et al.,[31] 1990	5	16–40

receiving radiation therapy for benign conditions also appear to have an increased risk for CRC.[27]

The following high-risk factors for irradiation-induced CRC development have been established: (1) early radiation proctitis and (2) subsequent secondary proctitis and stenosis or induration of the rectovaginal septum.[28] Although one study[29] demonstrated that 92 percent of radiation-associated mucinous CRC had clinical or histologic evidence of radiation proctitis, the largest published series to date[27] detected clinical manifestations of radiation proctitis in only 17 percent of their cases. This finding runs counter to the view that irradiation-induced CRC develops in areas of chronic/active proctitis. However, cell kinetic studies[30] demonstrating a progressive shift of the major zone of DNA synthesis to the upper third of the crypt in irradiated rectal mucosa with or without the histologic picture of chronic postirradiation proctitis support the notion that even grossly normal-appearing irradiated colorectal mucosa may be at increased risk for CRC development.

Since dosimetry data are lacking from most studies, it is difficult to draw conclusions regarding dosage and risk. Although extensive radiation damage, indicative of moderate to high doses of radiotherapy, has been identified in more than 70 percent of postirradiation cancers, evidence suggest that lower doses may actually produce a greater risk.[31] Doses of 4500 rad have been shown[25] to cause the highest incidence of colonic cancer in rats, compared to 2500, 3500, 5500, or 6500 rads.

In summary, it appears that clinical doses of pelvic irradiation increase the risk for subsequent CRC despite the lack of clinical radiation-induced proctitis. Therefore, careful colorectal surveillance, beginning 5 years after therapy, is recommended.

PRIOR COLORECTAL CANCER

Reports of multiple colorectal carcinomas can be found in the literature as early as the nineteenth century.[32,33] In 1944, Slaughter[24] collected data on 116 published cases and noted that with the exception of the skin, the colon was the most common site of multiple neoplasms confined to the same organ.

A study from St. Mark's Hospital on over 3381 patients who had undergone a resection of a colonic or rectal cancer demonstrated a 1.5 percent incidence of metachronous CRC formation. The incidence rose to 5 percent in patients followed for 25 years and was as high as 10 percent for patients with concomitant polyps at the time of resection.[34] Although the majority of metachronous lesions are discovered within 10 years of the initial CRC resection,[35–39] one study of 700 patients demonstrated a metachronous frequency rate of 3.4 percent, with 67 percent occurring 11 years or more after the original cancer.[40] This would suggest a lifelong risk for metachronous CRC development and a need for indefinite follow-up.[34,41]

Since colonoscopy is regarded as superior to barium enema in detecting colonic neoplasms,[42,43] it is recommended as the surveillance instrument of choice. However, the intervals and long-term yields of surveillance colonoscopy following CRC resection have not been fully determined. As noted in Table 11-4, several studies have attempted to quantitate the colonoscopic yield of metachronous CRC. Although varying in onset and duration of study, metachronous CRCs were detected in 1.7 to 4.6 percent of cases.

The National Polyp Study has shown that, following removal of an adenoma, the yield of "important lesions" at a 3-year follow-up colonoscopy is similar to that at the 1-year study.[44] Therefore, having the first follow-up colonoscopy at 3 years after polypectomy is more cost-effective. An extrapolation of these data would therefore suggest a similar approach for CRC patients with an otherwise normal baseline colonoscopy at the time of initial CRC resection. Surveillance recommendations would, of course, have to be tailored to the individual's risk. Individuals with synchronous neoplasms, first-degree relatives of CRC patients, or multiple neoplasms at the first follow-up colonoscopy may require yearly colonoscopy. In contrast, individuals with limited life expectancy, either from advanced cancer or comorbid disease, may not need any colonoscopic follow-up.

Table 11-4
Detection of Metachronous CRC with Annual Colonoscopy[a]

Author	No. of patients	Duration of study, years	Metachronous CRC, %	Median interval, months
Nava[b],[53] 1982	240	4	11 (4.6)	40
Kronborg,[54] 1983	239	3	4 (1.7)	17
Weber,[55] 1986	75	8	3 (4.0)	18
Juhl,[56] 1990	174	6	4 (2.3)	30

[a]Note that depending on the study, varying percentages of patients had only one colonoscopy.

[b]Figures may be factitiously high, since 25 percent of patients did not have a perioperative baseline colonoscopy.

REFERENCES

1. Billroth T: *Chirurgische K. Wien 1871-6; Nebst einem Gesammt-Bericht über die chirurgischen Klinken in Zurich und Wien wahrend der Jahre 1870-76: Erfahrungen auf dem Gabiete der praktischen Chirurgie*. Berlin, Hirschwald, 1879, p 258.
2. Kesteven WB: *Tr Clin Soc London* 9:77, 1876.
3. Schoenberg BS, Greenberg RA, Eisenberg H: Occurrence of certain multiple primary cancers in females. *J Natl Cancer Inst* 43:15–32, 1969.
4. Schottenfeld D, Berg JW, Vitsky B: Incidence of multiple primary cancers: Index cancers arising in the stomach and lower digestive system. *J Natl Cancer Inst* 43:77–86, 1969.
5. Schottenfeld D, Berg J: Incidence of multiple primary cancers: IV. Cancers of the female breast and genital organs. *J Natl Cancer Inst* 46:161–170, 1971.
6. Harvey EB, Brinton LA: Second cancer following cancer of the breast in Connecticut, 1935–82. *Natl Cancer Inst Monogr* 68:99–112, 1985.
7. Teppo L, Pukkala E, Saxen E: Multiple cancer: An epidemiologic exercise in Finland. *J Natl Cancer Inst* 75:207–217, 1985.
8. Neugut AI, Murray TI, Lee WC, Robinson E: The association of breast cancer and colorectal cancer in men: An analysis of surveillance, epidemiology, and end results program data. *Cancer* 68:2069–2073, 1991.
9. Schatzkin A, Baranovsky AN, Kessler LG: Diet and cancer: Evidence from associations of multiple primary cancers in the SEER program. *Cancer* 62:1451–1457, 1988.
10. Bremond A, Collet P, Lambert R, Martin J-L: Breast cancer and polyps of the colon: A case-control study. *Cancer* 54:2568–2570, 1984.
11. Toma S, Giacchero A, Bonelli L, et al: Association between breast and colorectal cancer in a sample of surgical patients. *Eur J Surg Oncol* 13:429–432, 1987.
12. Murray TI, Neugut AI, Garbowski GC, et al: Relationship between breast cancer and colorectal adenomatous polyps. *Cancer* 69:2232–2234, 1992.
13. Rozen P, Fireman Z, Figer A, Ron E: Colorectal tumor screening in women with a past history of breast, uterine or ovarian malignancies. *Cancer* 57:1235–1239, 1986.
14. Reimer RR, Hoover R, Fraumeni JF, Young RC: Second primary neoplasms following ovarian cancer. *J Natl Cancer Inst* 61:1195–1197, 1978.
15. Curtis RE, Hoover RN, Kleinerman RA, Harvey EB: Second cancer following cancer of the female genital system in Connecticut, 1935–82. *Natl Cancer Inst Monogr* 68:113–117, 1985.
16. Schoenberg BS, Weed-Christine B: The association of neoplasms of the colon and rectum with primary malignancies of other sites. *Am J Proctol* 25:41–60, 1974.
17. Winkelstein W Jr, Sacks ST, Ernster VL, et al: Correlation of incidence rates for selected cancers in the nine areas of the Third National Cancer Survey. *Am J Epidemol* 105:407–419, 1977.
18. Haenzel W: Migrant studies, in Schottenfeld D, Fraumeni JF Jr (eds): *Cancer Epidemiology and Prevention*. Philadelphia, Saunders, pp 194–207, 1982.
19. Kelsey JL, Hildreth NG: *Breast and Gynecologic Cancer Epidemiology*. Boca Raton, Fla, CRC Press, 1983.
20. Bailar JC III: The incidence of independent tumors among uterine cancer patients. *Cancer* 16:842–853, 1963.
21. Storm HH, Ewertz M: Second cancer following cancer of the female genital system in Denmark, 1943–1980. *Natl Cancer Inst Monogr* 68:331–340, 1985.
22. Beebe GW, Kato H, Land CE: Studies of the mortality of A-bomb survivors: VI. Mortality and radiation dose, 1950–1974. *Radiat Res* 75:138–201, 1978.
23. Kato H, Schull WJ: Studies of the mortality of A-bomb survivors: VII. Mortality, 1950–1978: Part I: Cancer mortality. *Radiat Res* 90:395–432, 1982.
24. Slaughter DP, Southwick HW: Mucosal carcinomas as a result of irradiation. *AMA Arch Surg* 74(3):420–429, 1957.
25. Denman DL, Kirchner FR, Osborne JW: Induction of colonic adenocarcinoma in the rat by X-irradiation. *Cancer Res* 38:1899–1905, 1978.
26. Lisco H, Brues AM, Finkel MP, Gundhauser W: Carcinoma of the colon in rats following the feeding of radioactive yttrium. *Cancer Res* 7:721, 1947.
27. Jao S-W, Beart RW, Reiman HM, et al: Colon and anorectal cancer after pelvic irradiation. *Dis Colon Rectum* 30:953–958, 1987.
28. MacMahon CE, Rowe JW: Rectal reaction following radiation therapy of cervical carcinoma: Particular reference to subsequent occurrence of rectal carcinoma. *Ann Surg* 173: 264–269, 1971.
29. Castro EB, Rosen PP, Quan HQ: Carcinoma of large intestine in patients irradiated for carcinoma of cervix and uterus. *Cancer* 31:45–52, 1973.
30. Risio M, Coverlizza S, Candelaresi GL, et al: Late cytokinetic abnormalities in irradiated rectal mucosa. *Int J Colorect Dis* 5:98–102, 1990.
31. Levitt MD, Millar DM, Stewart JO: Rectal cancer after pelvic irradiation. *J Roy Soc Med* 83:152–154, 1990.
32. Czerny II: Aus der Heidelberger chirurgischen Klinik: Nachtrag zur Darmresection. *Berl Klin Wchnschr* 17:683, 1880.
33. Fenger C: Double carcinoma of the colon. *JAMA* 11:606, 1888.
34. Bussey HJR, Wallace MH, Morson BC: Metachronous carcinoma of the large intestine and intestinal polyps. *Proc R Soc Med* 60:208–210, 1967.
35. Ginzburg L, Dreiling DA: Successive independent (metachronous) carcinomas of the colon. *Ann Surg* 143:117–122, 1956.
36. Moertel CG, Bargen JA, Dockerty MB: Multiple carcinomas of the large intestine: A review of the literature and a study of 261 cases. *Gastroenterology* 34:85–98, 1958.
37. Heald RJ, Lockhart-Mummery HE: The lesion of the second cancer of the large bowel. *Br J Surg* 59:16–19, 1972.
38. Agrez MV, Ready R, Ilstrup D, Beart RW: Metachronous colorectal malignancies. *Dis Colon Rectum* 25:569–574, 1982.
39. Welch JP: Multiple colorectal tumors: An appraisal of natural history and therapeutic options. *Am J Surg* 142:274–280, 1981.
40. Lutchefeld MA, Ross DS, Zander JD, Folse JR: Late development of metachronous colorectal cancer. *Dis Colon Rectum* 30:180–184, 1987.
41. Ekelund GR, Phil B: Multiple carcinomas of the colon and rectum. *Cancer* 33:1630–1634, 1974.
42. Durdey P, Westib PMT, Williams NS: Colonoscopy or barium enema as initial investigation of colon disease. *Lancet* 2:549–551, 1987.
43. Reilly JC, Rusin LC, Theuerkauf FJ: Colonoscopy: Its role in cancer of the colon and rectum. *Dis Colon Rectum* 25:532–538, 1982.
44. Winawer SJ, Zauber AG, O'Brien MJ, et al: Randomized comparison of surveillance intervals after colonoscopic removal of newly diagnosed adenomatous polyps. *N Engl J Med* 328:901–906, 1993.
45. Ewertz M, Mouriden HT: Second cancer following cancer of the female breast in Denmark, 1943–1980. *Natl Cancer Inst Monogr* 68:325–329, 1985.
46. Agarwal N, Ulahannan MJ, Mandile MA, et al: Increased risk

of colorectal cancer following breast cancer. *Ann Surg* 203:307–310, 1986.

47. Palmer JP, Spratt DW: Pelvic carcinoma following irradiation for benign gynecological diseases. *Am J Obstet Gynecol* 72:497–505, 1956.
48. Rubin P, Ryplansky A, Dutton A: Incidence of pelvic malignancies following irradiation for benign gynecologic conditions. *AJR* 85:503–514, 1961.
49. Smith JC: Carcinoma of the rectum following irradiation of carcinoma of the cervix. *Proc R Soc Med* 55:701–702, 1962.
50. Quan SH: Fractitial proctitis due to irradiation for cancer of the cervix uteri. *Surg Gynecol Obstet* 126:70–74, 1968.
51. DeCosse JJ, Rhodes RS, Wentz WB, et al: The natural history and management of radiation induced injury of the gastrointestinal tract. *Ann Surg* 170:369–384, 1969.
52. O'Connor TW, Rombeau JL, Levine HS, Turnbull RB Jr: Late development of colorectal cancer subsequent to pelvic irradiation. *Dis Colon Rectum* 22:123–128, 1979.
53. Nava HR, Pagana TJ: Postoperative surveillance of colorectal carcinoma. *Cancer* 49:1043–1047, 1982.
54. Kronborg O, Hage E, Deichgraeber E: The remaining colon after radical surgery for colorectal cancer: The first three years of a prospective study. *Dis Colon Rectum* 26:172–176, 1983.
55. Weber CA, Deveney KE: Routine colonoscopy in the management of colorectal carcinoma. *Am J Surg* 152:87–92, 1986.
56. Juhl G, Larson GM, Mullins R, et al. Six-year results of annual colonoscopy after resection of colorectal cancer. *World J Surg* 14:255–261, 1990.

CHAPTER 12

Colorectal Polyps

Michael J. O'Brien

HIGHLIGHTS

Approximately two-thirds of polyps encountered in a clinical setting are *adenomas*. These are classified histologically as tubular, tubulovillous, and villous and according to whether high-grade dysplasia is present. The most prevalent histologic growth pattern of adenomas is tubular; a purely villous growth pattern is uncommon (<5 percent of all adenomas). Larger adenomas and adenomas with a villous pattern are more likely to show high-grade dysplasia. *Malignant polyps* are defined by the presence of carcinoma invading the submucosa of the polyp head or stalk or, in the case of sessile adenomas, the submucosa of the underlying bowel wall. Other colorectal polyps include *hyperplastic polyps, mucosal polyps* (mucosal tags), *inflammatory polyps, juvenile polyps, hamartomas,* and a variety of nonmucosal lesions. Adenomas are unique among polyps in that only they are known to be direct precursors of carcinoma. Among small polyps (<5 mm), hyperplastic polyps of the distal colon and rectum are as common as adenomas. They have a distinctive histology and seldom grow beyond the 5 mm range in size.

Adenomas represent a monoclonal proliferation of crypt stem cell progeny. The acquired mutation that underlies sporadic adenoma formation is not known, but it is speculated that it may be related to the familial adenomatous polyposis coli (FAP) gene locus. The earliest morphologically identifiable lesion is unicryptal; this progressively expands by mechanisms that result in spread of adenomatous cells along the basement membrane, irregular crypt branching, and crypt elongation. Not all adenomas are polypoid—some show minimal elevation above the mucosal surface and a surface growth pattern; they are called *flat adenomas*.

The concept of the adenoma as the precursor of adenocarcinoma of the colon is strongly supported by epidemiologic and pathologic studies. Recent clinical studies have provided evidence that polypectomy reduces colorectal cancer risk.

CONTROVERSIES

The extent to which clinically inconspicuous nonpolypoid or flat adenomas contribute to the overall incidence of colonic cancer remains to be clarified. There are conflicting data on whether such adenomas have a greater propensity to develop high-grade dysplasia (and cancer). It is agreed, however, that adenomas of this type are more likely to be overlooked at sigmoidoscopy or colonoscopy. There is disagreement in the literature on the interpretation of the observed ecological association between hyperplastic polyp and adenoma prevalence in various populations. Some controversy surrounds whether hyperplastic polyps encountered in the distal colon and rectum of individuals screened by flexible sigmoidoscopy are associated with adenomas located more proximally in the large bowel. A preliminary analysis of data from the National Polyp Study (NPS) provided no evidence to support such an association.

FUTURE DIRECTIONS

Future research is likely to investigate the relationship of growth-factor interactions and cell proliferation to histologic growth patterns. While several specific acquired genetic changes associated with malignant transformation in adenomas have recently been described, these discoveries are applicable mainly to advanced stages of adenoma progression; little is known of factors (environmental or genetic) that are directly related to earlier stages of adenoma evolution and growth. Phenotypic and genotypic characteristics of resected adenomas that are predictive, in a clinically useful context, of an individual's risk for metachronous colorectal neoplasms is also an area worthy of further study.

Polyps of the colon and rectum can be classified as adenomas (67 percent), hyperplastic polyps (11 percent), and a miscellaneous group (22 percent) that includes mucosal polyps (normal mucosa) inflammatory polyps, juvenile polyps, hamartomas, and a variety of nonmucosal lesions[1] (Table 12-1).

COLORECTAL ADENOMAS

Colorectal adenomas represent a family of mucosal neoplasms which show some diversity in their appearance but share certain essential acquired genetic and phenotypic characteristics. They may be encountered at endoscopy in sizes that range from minute 1- to 2-mm protrusions to polyps 10 to 100 times larger. Adenomas may be pedunculated, sessile, or flat; they may be single or multiple; they may show a lobulated or shaggy (Figs. 12-1 and 12-2) type of surface or both; and while they are usually biologically benign when resected, all are considered to have some potential for malignant transformation.

Adenomas represent a disordered noninvasive proliferation of mucosal epithelial cells with an adenomatous phenotype. This phenotype, in addition to a distinctive histologic appearance, can also be described with increasing but still limited insight in terms of the expression of diverse antigens that differ quantitatively and, in some rare instances, qualitatively from those of normal or nonneoplastic mucosa.

MORPHOLOGIC CLASSIFICATION

A typical *tubular adenoma* has a lobulated berrylike external surface that corresponds microscopically to a fissured mucosal surface from which branching tubules or crypts extend into a lamina propria of normal appearance (Fig. 12-1*A* and *B*). The less frequently encountered *villous adenoma* has a shaggy appearance due to thin plates or folia of lamina propria enveloped by adenomatous epithelium (Fig. 12-2*A* and *B*). The *tubulovillous adenoma* is a morphologically intermediate entity with characteristics of both tubular and villous architecture. Adenomas are classified according to the percentage of the villous component: 0 to 25 percent villous are classified as tubular; 25 to 75 percent villous as tubulovillous; and 75 to 100 percent villous as villous.[2]

The component cells of the colorectal adenoma have a distinctive phenotype that is described as *adenomatous*. This phenotype has no exact normal counterpart and most resembles reparative mucosa. The main feature is a tall columnar cell with a large, basally located, oval or cigar-shaped nucleus. It is typically a mucus-depleted cell, but rarely some or all component cells of the adenoma may show abundant mucin. It represents a dysplastic cell type, intermediate between normal and carcinomatous. It is classified according to the severity of cytologic and architectural abnormality as low- or high-grade dysplasia (Fig. 12-3). In low-grade dysplasia, there is an adenomatous phenotype with mild to moderate architectural abnormality. High-

Table 12-1
Characteristics of Polyps at Initial Colonoscopy

		Relative frequency, %
Classification		
Adenomas		67
Hyperplastic polyps		11
Other		22
Mucosal tags		
Inflammatory		
Juvenile		
Hamartomatous		
Lymphoid		
Mesenchymal		
Histologic type of adenomas		
Tubular (0 to 25 percent villous component)		87
Tubulovillous (25 to 75 percent villous component)		8
Villous (75 to 100 percent villous component)		5
Size of adenomas at initial colonoscopy		
Small	(≤0.5 cm)	38
Medium	(0.5 to 1.0 cm)	36
Large	(>1.0 cm)	26
Advanced pathology in adenomas at initial colonoscopy		
High-grade dysplasia		6
Invasive carcinoma		1.5
Classification of polyps <0.5 cm		
Adenomas		50
Hyperplastic polyps		20
Other		
Mucosal tags		25
Indeterminate		1–3
Inflammatory		1–2
Miscellaneous		1–2

SOURCE: Data from National Polyp Study and Ref. 1.

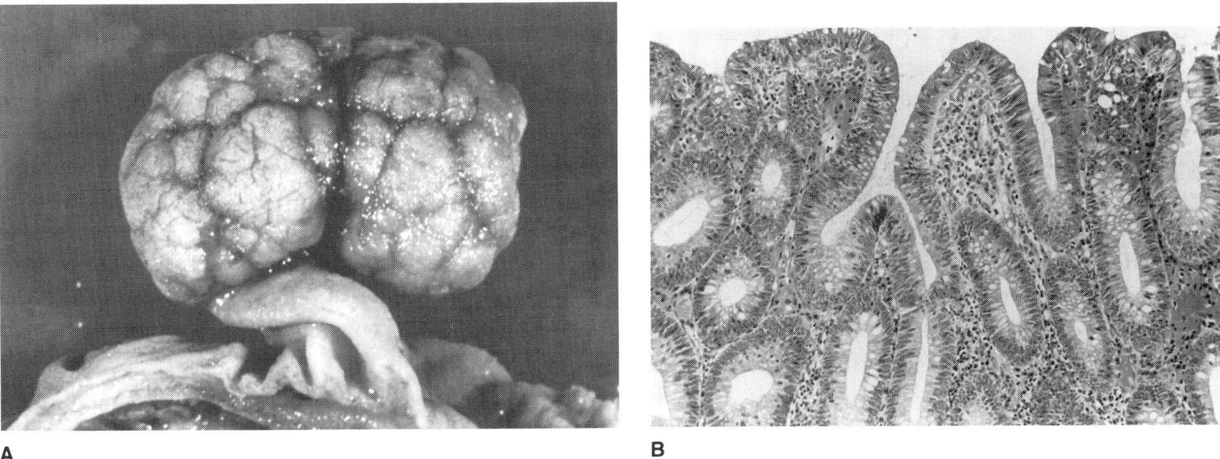

A B

FIG. 12-1. *A*. Pedunculated tubular adenoma. The adenoma surface has a lobulated berrylike appearance. (From O'Brien MJ, Winawer SJ, Waye JD: Colorectal polyps, in Winawer SJ (ed): *Management of Gastrointestinal Diseases*. Gower, New York, 1992. With permission.) *B*. The histology shows branching tubules embedded in the lamina propria.

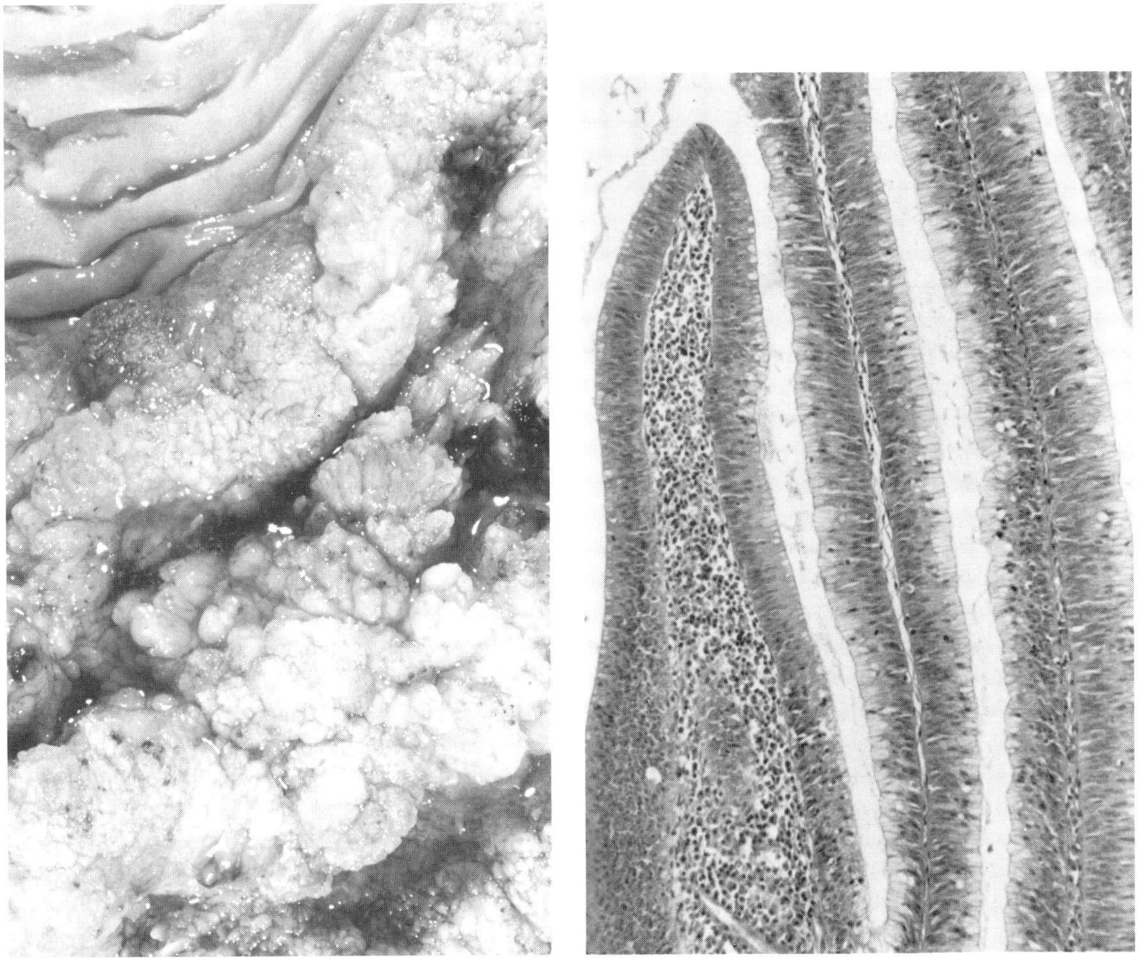

A B

FIG. 12-2. *A*. Sessile villous adenoma. The adenoma surface has a shaggy or villous appearance. *B*. The corresponding histology shows thin plates of lamina propria enveloped in adenomatous epithelium.

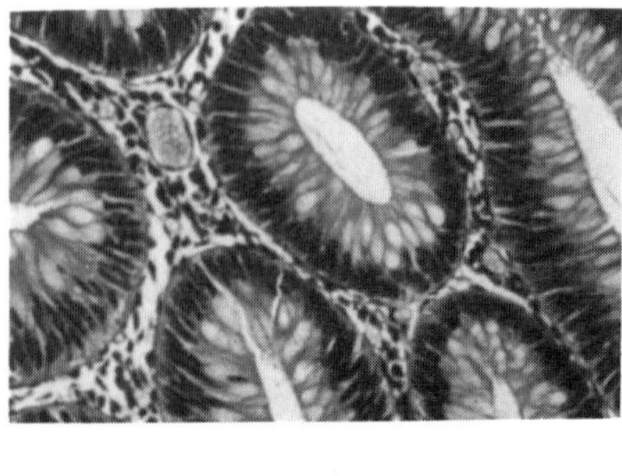
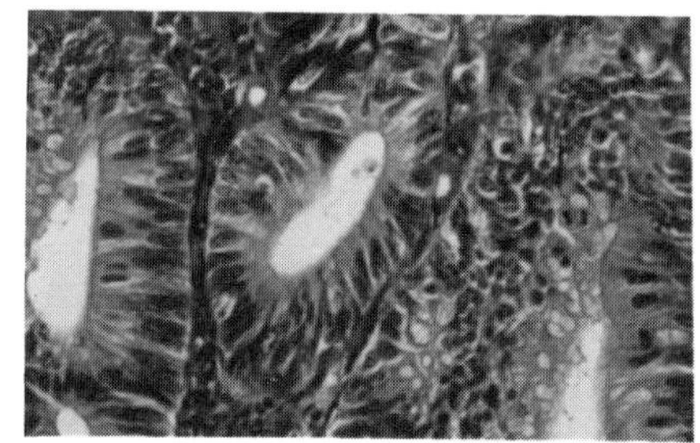
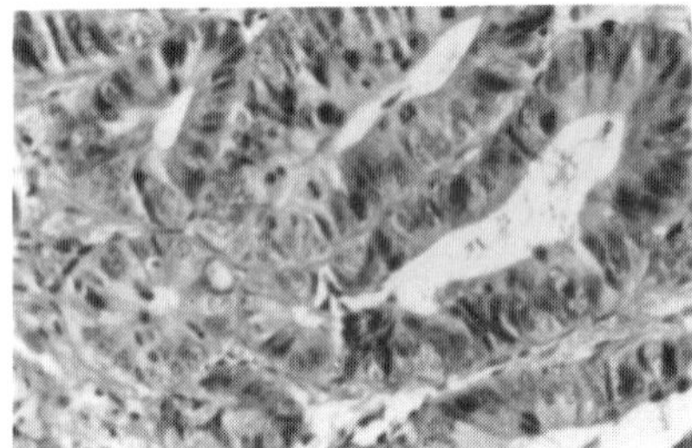
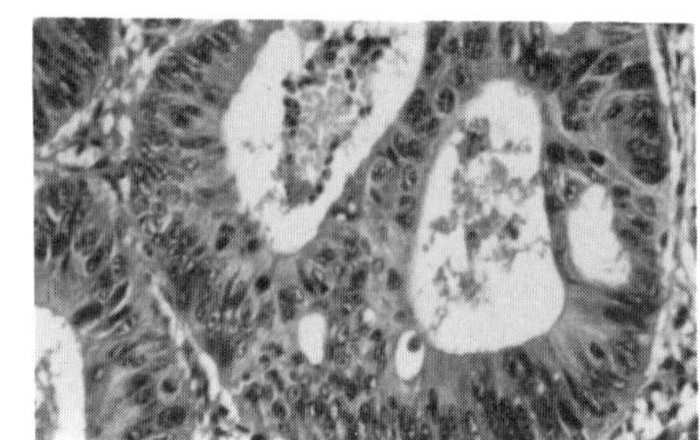

FIG. 12-3. The top frames show adenomatous glands that reveal low-grade dysplasia. The lower two frames are examples of high-grade dysplasia in adenomas. (From O'Brien MJ, Winawer SJ, Waye JD: Colorectal polyps, in Winawer SJ (ed): *Management of Gastrointestinal Diseases*. Gower, New York, 1992. With permission.)

grade dysplasia exists when there are severe alterations of gland patterns, such as papillary infolding, cribriform and back-to-back arrangements with diminution of intervening lamina propria, and/or severe cytologic abnormality. These latter features include high nuclear-to-cytoplasm ratios; loss of basal polarization of nuclei; irregular nuclear membranes; vesicular, clumped, or hyperchromatic chromatin; and large and irregular nucleoli. High-grade dysplasia, according to National Polyp Study data, is found in 6.6 percent of all adenomas removed at initial colonoscopy.[1] The term *severe dysplasia* may be used as the equivalent of *high-grade dysplasia;* a consensus appears to be emerging, however, which rejects the use of the terms *carcinoma in situ* or *intra-mucosal carcinoma* on the grounds that they imply a biological potential for distant spread, which is unwarranted. Approximately 1.5 percent of adenomas that are removed at initial colonoscopy are classified as malignant polyps.[2] A *malignant polyp* is an adenoma in which carcinoma extends from the mucosal portion beyond the muscularis mucosa into the submucosa of the head or stalk in a pedunculated polyp—or, in the case of a sessile polyp, the submucosa of the bowel wall. A malignant polyp is an early carcinoma with the potential for local spread and distant metastases.

EVOLUTION AND GROWTH OF ADENOMAS

Adenomas are monoclonal[3] and thus derived from a single stem cell.[4] The molecular event at the root of sporadic adenoma formation is an acquired genetic mutation, possibly in the FAP locus on the long arm of chromosome 5. The earliest identifiable morphologic change is adenomatous epithelium replacing part or all of a single crypt. Between this microscopic unicryptal lesion and the 1- to 2-mm lesion that is just visible to the endoscopist, there exist intermediate-sized lesions comprising one or more adenomatous crypts and measuring 0.5 to 1.0 mm (microadenomas)[5] (Fig. 12-4). The size of adenomas most frequently encountered at screening colonoscopy is a mere 2 to 5 mm. The manner of continued growth of adenomas is not known for certain, but in the early stages spread along the surface basement membrane (snowplow effect)[6] and irregular branching of crypts close to the mucosal surface are thought to occur. Surface invagination has also been suggested as a mechanism of early growth.[7] Crypt elongation is an important part of the growth process but is thought to contribute mainly in the later stages. It has been suggested that such elongation with compression of intervening stroma is the mechanism of villus formation in *villous adenomas*.[1] Surface growth without crypt elongation may account for the appearance of so-called *flat adenomas*.[8] These latter are adenomas that show minimal elevation above the adjacent mucosa and are thus easily overlooked at endoscopy.[9] They are usually less than 1 cm in diameter, but larger examples may be seen. Microscopic sections show the adenomatous mucosa to be only one to two times the thickness of the adjacent mucosa. Extension of adenomatous epithelium over underlying normal glands is a characteristic feature.

ADENOMA-CARCINOMA SEQUENCE

The concept of the adenoma-carcinoma sequence accounts for the epidemiologic finding that a population's risk for colonic carcinoma is related to the prev-

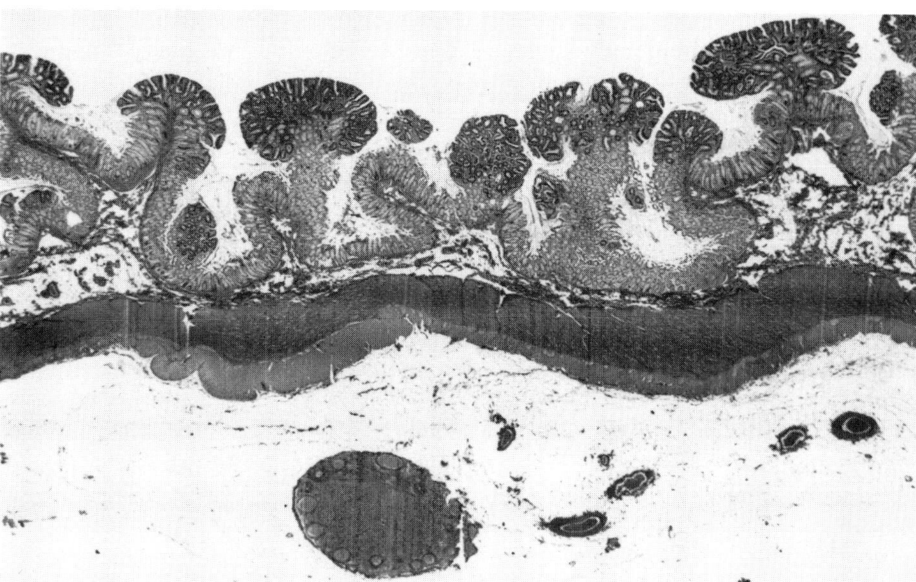

FIG. 12-4. Multiple adenomas in various stages of evolution, from one or two adenomatous crypts to small tubular adenomas, are demonstrated in this section of colon from an individual with familial adenomatous polyposis coli.

alence of colorectal adenomas.[10] It is bolstered by the reported frequency of advanced pathology, such as high-grade dysplasia and focal invasive carcinoma, in large polypectomy series.[11,12] It explains the high concurrence rate of carcinoma and adenomas and the frequent finding of contiguous benign adenoma in resected carcinomas.[13,14] It is manifest also in the natural history of inherited predispositions to colonic cancer, both FAP and related syndromes and hereditary nonpolyposis coli cancer (HNPCC) syndrome. (The latter was originally thought to offer support to the de novo school, but several studies have since demonstrated coexisting and contiguous adenomas associated with HNPCC cancers with a frequency similiar to that observed with sporadic cancers.[15,16])

Proof of the clinical and biological significance of the adenoma-carcinoma sequence should be evident in the extent to which polypectomy affects the incidence and mortality of colorectal cancer. A retrospective cohort study, performed by Gilbertsen[17] in Minnesota in the early 1970s, claimed a large reduction in the incidence of cancer of the sigmoid and rectum in a cohort which had been subjected to screening by rigid sigmoidoscopy. Recently, Selby et al.[18] showed that there was a threefold reduction in the odds for distal carcinoma in individuals who had screening sigmoidoscopy performed at any point in the previous 10 years. A preliminary analysis of NPS data, which showed that patients enrolled in the colonoscopic surveillance program had a greater than 75 percent reduction in the incidence of colonic cancer over the age-matched general population,[19] also provides evidence of prevention of colonic cancer by the interdiction of adenoma growth.

Much of the argument that has been advanced to challenge the adenoma-carcinoma sequence model has been instigated by reports of small or minute nonpolypoid invasive adenocarcinomas without contiguous adenoma.[20–23] Such cases would be of greater consequence if the concept precluded carcinoma or high-grade dysplasia developing in very small adenomas or required that all adenomas be polypoid. While pathologic studies have repeatedly shown a direct correlation between the likelihood of malignant transformation and increasing adenoma size[1,11] (Fig. 12-5), malignant transformation can be found in even the most diminutive adenomas, but proportionately, accounting for their actual rarity and also perhaps for their undue weight in the literature. Recent molecular

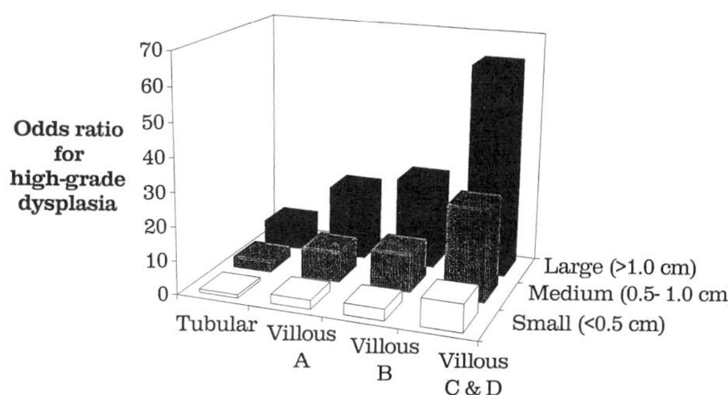

FIG. 12-5. This histogram illustrates the odds ratio for high-grade dysplasia in adenomas (with small tubular adenoma as referent), stratified according to three size categories. Increasing villous component and increasing size make independent and multiplicative contributions to odds for a finding of high-grade dysplasia in an adenoma. (*Data from Ref. 1; figure from Ref. 55. Reproduced by permission.*)

genetic discoveries are also seen to provide support for the adenoma-carcinoma sequence. The ultimate proof and measure of this concept may be the identification of the genetic clonal marker (or markers) of sporadic adenomas in advanced colonic cancer.

EPIDEMIOLOGY OF COLORECTAL POLYPS

There is great variation in the incidence of colonic cancer worldwide. The populations with the highest incidence inhabit the urban centers of western Europe, North America, Australia, and New Zealand. Geographic variation of colorectal cancer mortality shows a strong correlation with adenoma prevalence.[24–30] Adenomas are common in populations with high colorectal cancer incidence, and when populations migrate from a low-risk to a high-risk environment, an increase in the frequency of both adenomas and cancer is seen.[31]

Data on the prevalence of hyperplastic polyps of the colon and rectum in our population are limited. Based on autopsy studies, Hawaiian Japanese appear to have the highest reported prevalence of hyperplastic polyps: 73 percent of males and 51 percent of females.[24] These can be compared with figures of 15 and 14 percent for white and black males respectively from New Orleans.[27] An autopsy study from Liverpool, England, showed a hyperplastic polyp prevalence rate of 34 percent.[25] Clark et al.[32] compared three European centers—Aberdeen in Scotland, Trömso in Norway, and Kuopio in Finland—with respect to colonic cancer incidence and polyp prevalence. They found that variation in the prevalence of both hyperplastic polyps and adenomas paralleled the regional incidence of colonic carcinoma; Aberdeen had the highest prevalence, with rates of 52 and 39 percent for hyperplastic polyps and adenomas, respectively. However, this pattern is not invariably maintained in other studies, and an intermediate colonic cancer incidence area, Barcelona, Spain,[33] for example, has among the lowest reported prevalence rates of hyperplastic polyps—1.6 percent. Cali, Colombia, on the other hand, which has a very low colonic cancer incidence rate, has a prevalence rate of hyperplastic polyps of 11 percent among males and 7 percent among females.[27] Correa et al.[27] have addressed the issue of polyp prevalence as an epidemiologic indicator of colonic cancer risk and concluded that, while adenoma prevalence is a consistently good marker of such risk, this does not appear to be the case for hyperplastic polyps. Their significance as clinical markers of colorectal adenomas is controversial, but the preponderance of the current evidence indicates that they are not useful in identifying patients at risk for adenomas and carcinoma, and there is no pathologic evidence that hyperplastic polyps are precursors of adenomas.

HYPERPLASTIC POLYPS

Hyperplastic polyps are common among small polyps of the distal colon and distal rectum, in particular (Fig. 12-6). The hyperplastic polyp is typically a broad-based, flat, pale nodule, often with a papillary surface, which blends with the normal mucosa at its periphery. It is formed by elongated, funnel-shaped, nonbranching mucosal crypts. The cells in the basal portion of the crypts are cuboidal, of intermediate type, lacking in mucin, and may show mitoses. The upper portion of the crypts shows micropapillary infolding of tall columnar cells or goblet cells, usually the former. Larger hyperplastic polyps may show crypt bifurcation, which is usually basal. Invagination of crypts deep to the muscularis mucosa may also be seen, giving an inverted appearance, as described by Sobin.[34]

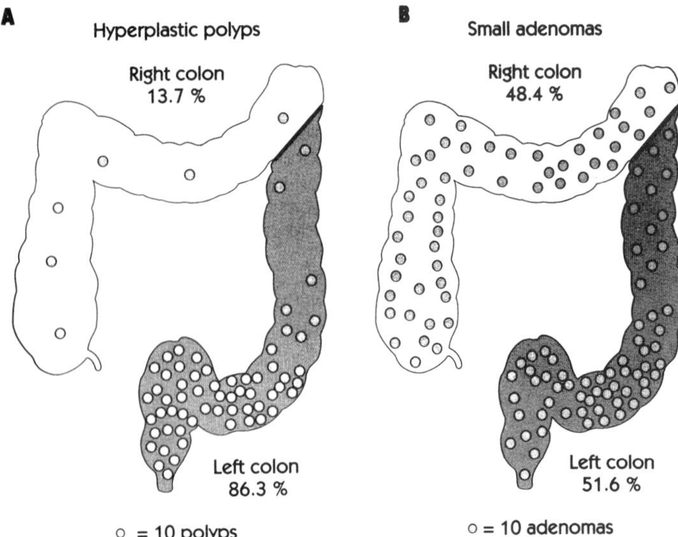

FIG. 12-6. Comparison of distribution of hyperplastic polyps and small adenomas.

Adenomatous change may rarely be encountered in an otherwise typical hyperplastic polyp[35–39] and, conversely, areas resembling hyperplastic polyp may be seen in adenomas. In view of the high prevalence of both lesions in the rectum and sigmoid, occasional juxtapositioning of both entities might be expected. Longacre and Fenoglio-Preiser[39] have drawn attention to a variant of adenoma that resembles the architecture of a hyperplastic polyp, for which they suggested the term *serrated adenoma*.

MUCOSAL POLYPS

Approximately 20 percent of biopsies taken from small mucosal excrescences will be found to represent normal mucosa only. In some cases they represent a miss on biopsy of a small adenoma or hyperplastic polyp. They are small mucosal tags which have no clinical significance; if they could be recognized as such, removal would not be necessary. However, there are no distinguishing endoscopic characteristics that differentiate these from adenomas or hyperplastic polyps.

JUVENILE POLYPS

Juvenile polyps are also referred to as *retention polyps,* a name that relates to the theory that the cystic dilation of mucus-filled glands, typical of these lesions, is due to inflammatory occlusion of the crypt necks. While a majority of patients with juvenile polyps are children under 20 years of age and have solitary lesions located in the distal rectum, these polyps are also encountered in adults.[40] Numerous polyps of this type widely distributed in the colon and rectum suggest the familial juvenile polyposis syndrome.[41]

A juvenile polyp is usually a pedunculated bright-red spheroid 1 to 3 cm in diameter with a granular surface which may bleed on contact. When the specimen is sectioned, it reveals multiple mucus-filled cysts. Microscopically, the surface is a monolayer of columnar cells interrupted by erosions and associated inflammation. The stroma is abundant and separates tubules that range in caliber from that of normal crypts to the macroscopically visible dilated cysts.

INFLAMMATORY POLYPS

Inflammatory polyps are caused by mucosal ulceration and repair. There are three categories that can be defined. One, which is accurately described as a *pseudopolyp,* is produced by confluent ulceration isolating ragged islands of residual inflamed mucosa. A second type, which also occurs in the context of acute colitis, is due to undermining ulceration giving rise to polypoid inflamed mucosal tags. The third type, referred to by Kelly and Gabos[42] as a "mature" inflammatory polyp, is derived from repair and regeneration of these mucosal tags.

Inflammatory polyps usually occur in idiopathic chronic inflammatory bowel disease, most frequently in ulcerative colitis but also in Crohn's disease. Such polyps are seen in 12.5 to 19 percent of patients with ulcerative colitis overall;[43–45] however, in surgical resection specimens, inflammatory polyps are found in over 50 percent.[42,46] Inflammatory polyps are also found in several other inflammatory disorders, including bacillary dysentery, amebic colitis, and schistosomiasis. They have also been reported in ischemic colitis,[47] with stercoral ulcers, and in the vicinity of ureterosigmoidostomies. Inflammatory polyps may be single, multiple, occasionally myriad, and segmental or diffuse in distribution.

Inflammatory polyps are typically of uniform width from base to head and have an "appendagelike" appearance on endoscopy. Variations of this appearance include bulbous enlargement of the polyp head, bifid and arborescent forms, and tubular bridges between polyps and mucosa.

The histology is that of inflamed and regenerative mucosa. Mature inflammatory polyps are covered by mucosa, which encloses a core of muscularis mucosa and submucosa. The mucosal component may be entirely normal or show regenerative or inflammatory changes. Pure granulation tissue polyps and polyps devoid of a submucosal core may also be seen.[46]

Giant Inflammatory Polyps

Inflammatory polyps exceeding 1.5 cm in length are said to be *giant inflammatory polyps*.[48,49] These are often multiple and usually involve a short segment of colon, 15 cm or less.[49] They have the same histologic appearance as smaller "mature" inflammatory polyps. They are encountered most frequently in the transverse colon and, like their smaller counterparts, are least common in the rectum.

Inflammatory Cloacogenic Polyps

A distinctive-appearing polyp which is inflammatory in nature and occurs in the distal rectum has been labeled by Lobert and Appleman[50] as an *inflammatory cloacogenic polyp*. The surface consists of columnar epithelium and variable proportions of squamous or transitional epithelium. Crypts are hyperplastic, and the lesion may be mistaken for a tubular or tubulovillous adenoma. The stroma has a distinctive fibromuscular character.

PEUTZ-JEGHERS POLYPS

A polyp which is characterized by normal mucosal elements draped on a treelike scaffolding of muscularis mucosa is a Peutz-Jeghers polyp.[51] Such mucosal hamartomas are characteristic of the inherited syndrome. They are usually most numerous in the small intestine but are also found in the stomach and colon and usually number less than 100. The mucosa of the colonic polyp is represented by normal mucous goblet and absorptive cells with argentaffin cells and less commonly Paneth cells in slightly irregular crypts.

LYMPHOID POLYPS

A localized hyperplasia of mucosal and submucosal lymphoid tissue may present as a single polyp or, less commonly, multiple polyps and is most frequently encountered in the lower rectum.[52] Physiologic reactive changes distinguish this entity from lymphomatous involvement.

SUBMUCOSAL LESIONS

Carcinoid tumors involving the mucosa and submucosa may present as small polypoid nodules. These lesions are essentially limited to the sigmoid and rectum. They are composed of columnar or cuboidal cells arranged in trabeculae or lobules with a fibromuscular stroma. They show neuroendocrine properties on histochemical and immunochemical staining.

The majority of *lipomas* in the intestinal tract occur in the colon, mostly around the ileocecal valve. These submucosal tumors, 0.5 to 15.0 cm in diameter, are composed of mature adipose tissue. Although they are usually single, multiple lipomatosis of the large bowel has been reported.

Leiomyomas may sometimes present as incidental yellowish white polyps which usually measure less than 1.5 cm in diameter and are benign. Other mesenchymal lesions include neural tumors, *polypoid ganglioneuromas,* and submucosal *neurofibromas* or *schwannomas*. Multiple gastrointestinal neurofibromas may be encountered in von Recklinghausen's disease, but in most reported cases, the location of these tumors has been extraluminal (serosal).[53] Multiple ganglioneuromas as a manifestation of an inherited disorder may be seen in von Recklinghausen's disease in association with multiple endocrine neoplasia type 2 or as an isolated abnormality.[54]

REFERENCES

1. O'Brien MJ, Winawer SJ, Zauber AG, et al: The National Polyp Study: Determinants of high grade dysplasia in colorectal adenomas. *Gastroenterology* 98:371–379, 1990.
2. Winawer SJ, O'Brien MJ, Waye JD, et al: Risk and surveillance of individuals with colorectal polyps. *Bull WHO* 68:789–795, 1990.
3. Fearon ER, Hamilton SR, Vogelstein B: Clonal analysis of human colorectal tumors. *Science* 238:193–196, 1987.
4. Wright NA: The control of cell proliferation in colonic epithelium, in Seitz HK, Simanowski UA, Wright NA (eds): *Colorectal Cancer from Pathogenesis to Prevention.* London, Springer-Verlag, 1989, pp 237–244.
5. Roncucci L, Stamp D, Medline A, et al: Identification and quantification of aberrant crypt foci and microadenomas in the human colon. *Hum Pathol* 22:287–298, 1991.
6. Lane N, Lev R: Observations on the origin of adenomatous epithelium of the colon. *Cancer* 16:751–764, 1963.
7. Maskens AP: Histogenesis of adenomatous polyps in the human large intestine. *Gastroenterology* 77:1245–1251, 1979.
8. Adachi M, Muto T, Morioka Y, et al: Flat adenoma and flat mucosal carcinoma—A new precursor of colorectal carcinoma? *Dis Colon Rectum* 31:236–243, 1988.
9. Muto T, Kamiya J, Sawada T, et al: Small "flat adenoma" of the large bowel with special reference to its clinicopathologic features. *Dis Colon Rectum* 28:847–851, 1985.
10. Correa P: Epidemiology of polyps and cancer, in Morson BC (ed): *The Pathogenesis of Colorectal Cancer,* vol 11. Philadelphia, Saunders, 1978, pp 126–152.
11. Muto T, Bussey HJR, Morson BC: The evolution of cancer of the colon and rectum. *Cancer* 36:2251–2270, 1975.
12. Shinya Y, Wolff WI: Morphology, anatomic distribution and cancer potential of colonic polyps. *Ann Surg* 190:679–683, 1979.
13. Morson BC: The polyp-cancer sequence in the large bowel. *Proc R Soc Med* 67:451–457, 1974.
14. Heald RJ, Bussey HJR: Clinical experience at St. Mark's Hospital with multiple synchronous cancers of the colon and rectum. *Dis Colon Rectum* 18:6–10, 1975.
15. Mecklin JP, Järvinen HJ, Peltokallio P: Cancer family syndrome: Genetic analysis of 22 Finnish kindreds. *Gastroenterology* 90:328–333, 1986.
16. Mecklin JP, Sipponen P, Järvinen HJ: Histopathology of colorectal carcinomas and adenomas in cancer family syndrome. *Dis Colon Rectum* 29:849–853, 1986.
17. Gilbertsen VA: Proctosigmoidoscopy and polypectomy in reducing the incidence of rectal cancer. *Cancer* 34:936–939, 1973.
18. Selby JV, Friedman GD, Quesenberry CP Jr, et al: A case-control study of screening sigmoidoscopy and mortality from colorectal cancer. *N Engl J Med* 326:653–657, 1992.
19. Winawer SJ, Zauber AG, Ho MN, et al: Prevention of colorectal cancer by colonoscopic polypectomy. *N Engl J Med* 329:1977–1981, 1983.
20. Spjut HJ, Frankel NB, Appel MF: The small carcinoma of the large bowel. *Am J Surg Pathol* 3:39–46, 1979.
21. Spratt JS, Ackerman LV: Small primary adenocarcinomas of the colon and rectum. *JAMA* 179:337–346, 1962.
22. Shamusuddin AM, Kato Y, Kunishima N, et al: Carcinoma in situ in nonpolypoid mucosa of the large intestine: Report of a case with significance in strategies for early detection. *Cancer* 56:2849–2854, 1985.
23. Shimoda T, Ikegami M, Fujisaki J, et al: Early colorectal carcinoma with special reference to its development de novo. *Cancer* 64:1136–1146, 1989.
24. Stemmermann GN, Yataui R: Diverticulosis and polyps of the large intestine. *Cancer* 31:1260–1270, 1973.
25. Williams AR, Balasooriya BAW, Day DW: Polyps and cancer of the large bowel: A necropsy study in Liverpool. *Gut* 23: 835–842, 1982.
26. Morten H, Vatn MH, Stalsberg H: The prevalence of polyps of the large intestine in Oslo: An autopsy study. *Cancer* 49:819–825, 1982.
27. Correa P, Sting JP, Reiff A, et al: The epidemiology of colorectal polyps: Prevalence in New Orleans and international comparisons. *Cancer* 39:2258–2264, 1977.
28. Eide TJ, Stalsberg H: Polyps of the large intestine in northern Norway. *Cancer* 42:2839–2848, 1978.

29. Bombi JA: Polyps of the colon in Barcelona, Spain: An autopsy study. *Cancer* 61:1472–1476, 1988.
30. Haghighi P, Nasr K, Mohallatee EA, et al: Colorectal polyps and carcinoma in Southern Iran. *Cancer* 39:274–278, 1977.
31. Correa P: Epidemiology of polyps and cancer, in Morson BC (ed): *The Pathogenesis of Colorectal Cancer,* vol 11. Philadelphia, Saunders, 1978, pp 126–152.
32. Clark JC, Collan Y, Eide TJ, et al: Prevalence of polyps in an autopsy series from areas with varying incidence of large bowel cancer. *Int J Cancer* 36:179–186, 1985.
33. Bombi JA: Polyps of the colon in Barcelona, Spain. An autopsy study. *Cancer* 61:1472–1476, 1988.
34. Sobin LH: Inverted hyperplastic polyps of the colon. *Am J Surg Pathol* 9:265–272, 1985.
35. Urbanski SJ, Kossakowska AE, Marcon N, et al: Mixed hyperplastic adenomatous polyps—An underdiagnosed entity: Report of a case of adenocarcinoma arising within a mixed hyperplastic adenomatous polyp. *Am J Surg Pathol* 8:551–556, 1984.
36. Cooper HS, Patchefsky AS, Marks G: Adenomatous and carcinomatous changes within hyperplastic colonic epithelium. *Dis Colon Rectum* 22:152–156, 1979.
37. Franzin G, Novelli P: Adenocarcinoma occurring in a hyperplastic (metaplastic) polyp of the colon. *Endoscopy* 14:28–30, 1982.
38. Williams GT, Arthur JF, Bussey HJR, et al: Metaplastic polyps and polyposis of the colorectum. *Histopathology* 4:155–170, 1980.
39. Longacre Teri A, Fenoglio-Preiser CM: Mixed hyperplasia adenomatous polyps/serrated adenomas. *Am J Surg Pathol* 14:524–537, 1990.
40. Mazier WP, Bowman HE, Sun KH, et al: Juvenile polyps of the colon and rectum. *Dis Colon Rectum* 17:523–527, 1974.
41. McColl I, Bussey HJR, Veale AMD, et al: Juvenile polyposis coli. *Proc R Soc Med* 57:896–897, 1964.
42. Kelly JK, Gabos S: The pathogenesis of inflammatory polyps. *Dis Colon Rectum* 30:251–254, 1987.
43. De Dombal FT, Watts JMcK, Watkinson G, et al: Local complications of ulcerative colitis: Stricture, pseudopolyposis and carcinoma of the colon and rectum. *Br Med J* 1:1442–1477, 1966.
44. Jalan KN, Sircus W, Walker RJ, et al: Pseudopolyposis in ulcerative colitis. *Lancet* 2:555–559, 1969.
45. Teague RH, Read AE: Polyposis in ulcerative colitis. *Gut* 16:792–795, 1975.
46. Goldgraber M: Pseudopolyps in ulcerative colitis. *Dis Colon Rectum* 8:335–363, 1965.
47. Levine DS, Surawiz CM, Spencer GD, et al: Inflammatory polyposis two years after ischemic colon injury. *Dig Dis Sci* 10:1159–1167, 1986.
48. Hinrichs HR, Goldman H: Localised giant pseudopolyps of the colon. *JAMA* 205:108–109, 1968.
49. Kelly JK, Langevin JM, Price LM, et al: Giant and symptomatic inflammatory polyps of the colon in idiopathic inflammatory bowel disease. *Am J Surg Pathol* 10:420–425, 1986.
50. Lobert PF, Appleman HD: Inflammatory cloacogenic polyp: A clinical inflammatory lesion of the anal transition zone. *Am J Surg Pathol* 5:761, 1981.
51. Morson BC: Histopathology of the small intestine. *Proc R Soc Med* 52:6–10, 1959.
52. Price AB: Benign lymphoid polyps and inflammatory polyps, in Morson BC (ed): *The Pathogenesis of Colorectal Cancer.* Philadelphia, Saunders, 1978, pp 33–42.
53. Hochberg FH, DaSilva AB, Galdabini J, et al: Gastrointestinal involvement in von Recklinghausen's neurofibromatosis. *Neurology* 24:1144–1151, 1974.
54. Haggitt RC, Reid BJ: Hereditary gastrointestinal polyposis syndromes. *Am J Surg Pathol* 10:871–887, 1986.
55. O'Brien MJ, O'Keane JC, Gottlieb LS, et al: Adenoma progression to carcinoma: Classification of phenotypic changes, in Rossini FR, et al (eds): *Recent Progress in Colorectal Cancer: Biology and Management of High-Risk Groups.* Amsterdam, Elsevier, 1992.

CHAPTER 13

Molecular Biology of Familial Cancer and Polyps

Suresh C. Jhanwar
Hans Gerdes

Colorectal cancer is the second most prevalent malignancy in the United States. Well-described inherited syndromes have been reported in families with a high frequency of colorectal cancer. The hereditary or familial colorectal cancer groups include Gardner's syndrome, adenomatous polyposis coli (APC) or familial adenomatous polyposis (FAP), and hereditary nonpolyposis colorectal cancer (HNPCC), including Lynch syndromes I and II.[1]

In 1986, a case report of an interstitial deletion of chromosome 5 in an individual with Gardner's syndrome and colonic adenocarcinoma suggested that this region of the long arm of chromosome 5q may harbor the gene for FAP.[2] Following this observation, Bodmer et al.[3] performed linkage analysis in families with FAP and showed that the gene was closely linked to a chromosome 5 specific probe, c11p11, which is localized to 5q21-22. This observation was concurrently confirmed by other investigators.[4] In addition, the site of the FAP gene also correlated well with the cytogenetic deletion seen in colorectal cancers (Fig. 13-1*A* and *B*). Simultaneously[5] it was also shown that approximately 20 percent of colorectal adenocarcinoma exhibited loss of heterozygosity (LOH) for highly polymorphic probes localized to 5q (Fig. 13-1*C*). These observations suggested that becoming recessive for a gene around 5q21-22 was one of the major steps in the development of many colorectal carcinomas, both sporadic and familial. Since these initial observations, there has been considerable progress in the identification of genetic events associated with colorectal tumorigenesis. Based on such studies, a multistep model of colorectal carcinogenesis has been proposed[6] according to which *ras* mutations, DNA hypomethylation, p53 mutation, and 5q alterations appear to occur early, while allelic deletions of chromosome arms 17p and 18q usually occur at a later stage of tumorigenesis. Furthermore, it has also been suggested that the sequence of events associated with colorectal tumorigenesis in both inherited and sporadic disease is basically similar.[7,8] Following observation by Vogelstein's group that loss of alleles from chromosomes 5, 17, and 18 was important in colorectal carcinogenesis, several reports on cytogenetics and molecular genetic changes have been published which identified allelic losses from several chromosomes in the multistep process of colorectal carcinogenesis. From these reports it also became clear that progression of normal colonic epithelial cells to carcinoma involved at least eight mutational events. Although these events need not be the same or occur in a particular sequence, the gradual accumulation of these alterations is necessary for the progression of benign polyps to frank carcinoma and eventually metastasis. The sequence of genetic events associated with initiation, transformation, and progression of colorectal cancer, therefore, could be divided into three major categories: (1) a predisposing or tissue-specific genetic change, (2) alterations in genes associated with transformation, and (3) alterations associated with progression and metastasis. The colorectal cancer system provides an excellent model for the study of such a sequence of genetic events associated with multistep carcinogenesis. The purpose of this chapter is to summarize the events associated with colorectal tumorigenesis and to develop a unifying model for colorectal tumorigenesis as it relates to familial cancer. An additional elucidation of these events is covered in Chap. 14.

Hypomethylation of DNA

It is well known that a decrease in methylation is associated with gene activation,[9] and alterations in methylation patterns have been observed in several tumor types and transformed cells.[10] Based on methylation

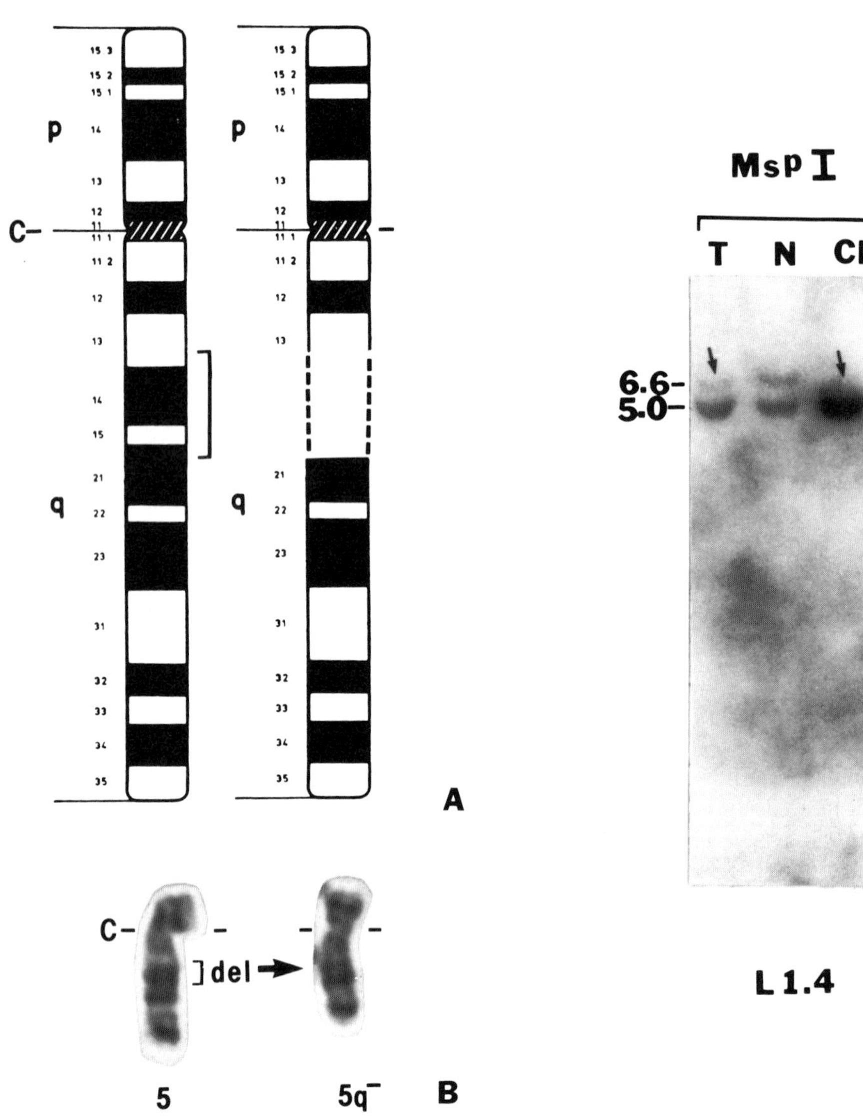

FIG. 13-1. Illustration of the smallest cytogenetic deletion of chromosome 5q(q13q21), including the region to which APC gene has been localized. The extent of deletion is shown by brackets on an idiogram (*A*) and partial karyotype (*B*) of chromosome 5. Also included in the figure is a Southern blot (*C*) to demonstrate allelic deletion on chromosome 5q; note a partial allelic loss in tumor (T) due to normal contamination of cells, whereas complete loss is seen in the cell line (CL) as compared to corresponding normal (N) tissue from the same patient.

pattern studies, Goelz et al.[10] showed that methylation changes occur in the neoplastic process, which in turn may induce selective expression of certain genes and areas of chromosome condensation, leading to aneuploidy.[11] In fact, numerical abnormalities of several chromosomes have been seen in several benign tumors, including polyps.

MCC and APC Gene Mutations and Allelic Losses on Chromosome 5q

Several studies suggested that gene(s) on chromosome band 5q21 are important in colorectal tumorigenesis. By using DNA probes from this region, Kinzler et al.[12] identified a gene called MCC (mutated in colorectal cancer), which encodes for a protein consisting of 829 amino acids. The sequence of amino acids in one short segment showed homology to the G protein–coupled m3 muscarinic acetylcholine receptors, which are important intermediaries for transmitting signals in cells. It was, therefore, suggested that the normal product of this gene may suppress cell growth by interacting with G protein, and that its disruption or mutation may result in uncontrolled proliferation. Although initially, of the 150 colorectal tumors analyzed, only a single tumor showed rearrangement in the coding region of the MCC gene and two additional tumors were found with somatically acquired point mutation, more recent studies by other investigators[13–15] have demonstrated that approximately 15 to 41.5 percent of colorectal tumors may contain gross structural alterations or point mutations of MCC. The precise role of this gene in colorectal tumorigenesis awaits further investigations.

Recently, the APC gene has been cloned and found to be mutated in most if not all cases of APC and sporadic cancer.[13, 15–17] The APC gene consists of 15 exons which code for 2843 amino acids, showing some sequence similarities with myosins and keratins. Two forms of mature transcripts, which differ by an alternative splicing of 303 nucleotides in the 5′ region of the ninth exon, have been identified. The 15th exon of APC is by far the largest (6578 nucleotides) of all known exons in which most known germline mutations associated with FAP have been identified; mutations in exons 4–14, are not frequent. The entire coding region of the APC gene was examined for germline mutations in a total of 555 FAP patients by several investigators.[18–26] Results of these studies, along with the methods of analysis, type, and site of mutations, are summarized in Table 13-1. As shown in the table, of the 186 germline mutations of APC seen in the patients studies, most (98 percent) were alterations causing truncation of the gene product. The APC proteins in 113 patients were disrupted due to frame-shift mutation by 1–5 base-pair insertions or deletions. In 65 patients, single nucleotide changes were detected. Of these, 59 were nonsense mutations, whereas 7 were due to missense mutations. Among point mutations, nucleotide C to A, T, or G_1 was more frequent. Although in general no hot spots were seen, a recent study on identification of APC gene mutations in an Italian population of FAP patients noted a relatively higher number of mutations at positions 3183–3187 and 3926–3939.[26] Similarly, approximately 60 percent of the somatic mutations in the APC gene were clustered within a small region of exon 15, designated as MCR (mutation cluster region), which accounted for less than 10 percent of the coding region.[21] In order to determine the precise role of the APC gene in the early development of colorectal tumorigenesis, Miyoshi et al.[21] examined mutations of the APC gene in 63 colorectal tumors (16 adenomas and 47 carcinomas) derived from FAP and non-FAP patients. Of these tumors, 43 showed at least one mutation in the APC gene; among them, more than 60 percent (9 adenomas and 23 carcinomas) had two mutations. In addition, more than 60 percent of sporadic adenomas and carcinomas—including adenomas as small as 0.5 cm in diameter—were also found to contain APC mutations.[27] Furthermore, *ras* gene mutations specifically detected during the early stages of tumorigenesis were absent in adenomas with APC mutations. These data strongly suggest that mutations of the APC gene play

Table 13-1
Summary of APC Mutations in Familial Adenomatous Polyposis (FAP) Patients

				Nature of mutation			
Study	*No. of patients*	*Method*	*Exon*	*Frame shift*	*Missense*	*Non-sense*	*Total mutation*[a]
Fodde et al.,[18] 1992	33	PCR-DGGE	4–15	4	—	4	1/8
Cottrell et al.,[19] 1992	40	PCR-SSCP	15	5	—	—	5/5
Miyoshi et al.,[20] 1992	79	PCR-RNase protection assay	15	30	4	19	29/53
Miyoshi et al.,[21] 1992	63	PCR-RNase protection assay	15	22	2	16	34/43[b]
Nagase et al.,[22] 1992	10	PCR-RNase protection assay	15	7	1	2	9/10
Groden et al.,[23] 1993	60	PCR-SSCP	15	10	—	2	12/12
Olschwang et al.,[24] 1993	160	PCR-DGGE	1–14	6	—	16	0/26[b]
Paul et al.,[25] 1993	68	PCR-SSCP	15	17	—	—	17/17
Varesco et al.,[26] 1993	42	PCR-SSCP	15	12	—	—	12/12

[a]Number of mutations in exon 15 versus total number of mutations.

[b]Includes three[21] and four[24] mutations which occurred in consensus site of splicing.

a major role in the early development of colorectal cancer and, therefore, can be considered as a tissue-specific predisposing event. Furthermore, these studies also indicate that the molecular defect in FAP and sporadic cancer is similar—inherited in the former and somatically acquired in the latter. The cellular and biochemical pathways involved in the process of inducing clonal expansion of colonic cells, however, are currently unclear. According to a hypothesis proposed,[15] the protein encoded by the APC gene may operate through the same biochemical pathways as the MCC. This is not unexpected, as gene products of both of these share common sequences, particularly those involved in the formation of coiled coils necessary for stable homo- or heteromeric protein complexes with totally absent or greatly reduced suppressor activity. Such complexes in turn might produce a dominant-negative effect if such a truncated protein were able to sequester wild-type APC or MCC. Further biochemical and cellular studies, however, are needed to support the hypothesis. Nevertheless, variability with regard to phenotype, age of cancer onset, and the site of mutation in the APC gene, seen in two families with FAP,[25] lends some support to the above speculation; APC mutations seen near the 5′ end of the gene in two families were associated with fewer polyps and delayed age of cancer onset. On the contrary, there appears to be a correlation between the severity of colonic disease in FAP patients and sporadic colorectal cancers with a more aggressive disease course; 60 to 70 percent of APC mutations were detected between codons 1250 and 1550.[20–22, 27] These data, therefore, are consistent with the hypothesis that functional domains of the APC protein may lie between the above regions of exon 15. Alternatively, this cluster region of exon 15 may be more prone to mutations due to the presence of sequences containing repeat elements.[23, 25, 26]

Last, expression of MCC and APC genes in a variety of tissue types, including normal colon, implies that the product of these two genes is important in maintaining regulated proliferation and a normal state of differentiation.

Recent molecular studies on hereditary cancer syndromes such as retinoblastoma, Wilms' tumor, and others have demonstrated that a minimum of two genetic events are necessary for the development of cancer.[28] One of these events must be a mutation in the tissue-specific cancer predisposing gene, whereas a second event could be either functional loss of the corresponding normal allele or another tumor suppressor gene by mutation or allelic loss. Several studies to identify allelic deletions associated with progression of adenoma to carcinoma in FAP patients have been performed,[29–34] the summary of which is presented in Table 13-2.[29–34] The data from these studies clearly demonstrate that the allelic deletions, although frequently seen in carcinomas, are either absent or rarely seen in adenomas. In addition, allelic deletions of chromosome 5 are always seen in combination with allelic deletions of other chromosomes, such as 17 and 18.

Mutation of the APC gene in one of the alleles is sufficient to cause hyperproliferation and chromosome instability, thus providing a mechanism for further genetic alterations by means of deletion or somatic crossing over, leading to homozygosity or functional hemizygosity for tumor suppressor genes on chromo-

Table 13-2
Summary of Allelic Deletions on Chromosome 5 in Adenomas and Carcinomas in APC Patients[a]

	Histopathologic classification			
Study	*Moderate adenomas*	*Advanced adenomas*	*Intermucosal carcinomas*	*Invasive carcinomas*
Law et al.,[29] 1988	42 (0)	—	—	2 (0)
Okamoto et al.,[30] 1988	22 (0)	—	—	15 (13)
Vogelstein et al.,[31] 1988	40 (0)	—	—	1 (?)
Rees et al.,[32] 1989	48 (4)	—	—	3 (0)
Sasaki et al.,[33] 1989	49 (<2)	—	—	21 (20)
Miyaki et al.,[34] 1990	54 (<2)	33 (20)	24 (26)	26 (56)

[a]Number of tumors analyzed (percent of tumors with LOH).

some 5 and others. In this connection, a study on allelic deletions on chromosome 5 in multiple adenomas and a carcinoma from a single patient with APC[35] is of special interest. According to this study, the same allele was lost in five independent adenomas and one carcinoma, indicating that such deletion of genetic material was caused by a common mechanism during mitosis, which in turn may be related to underlying specific mutation in the APC gene.

Cytogenetics of Polyps and Carcinomas

While cytogenetics suffers from being a tedious method, requiring sufficient cells in culture for analysis of clonal chromosome abnormalities, it provides an indication of which chromosomes are likely to be altered in particular cancers, including leads for the location of genetic susceptibility loci and tumor suppressor genes. Attempts to define chromosomal alterations in polyps, adenomas, and carcinomas from FAP patients have been limited, most probably due to the technical difficulties and possibly due to limited availability of sufficient tissue required for culture. Cytogenetic studies on colonic carcinomas and adenomas from FAP patients revealed recurrent structural abnormalities of chromosomes 1p, 5q, 10q, and 17p and losses of chromosome 18.[36–39] These abnormalities were similar to those reported in sporadic cancers.[40]

In a series of 47 tumors from patients seen at Memorial Sloan-Kettering Cancer Center, the recurrent abnormalities most often involved chromosomes 1, 5, 17, and 18 in a significant proportion of tumors (Fig. 13-2). It was interesting to note that regardless of the extent of deletions on chromosome 5q, the band 5q21 was invariably deleted in 17 of 18 tumors (Figs. 13-1*A* and *B*), which showed abnormalities of chromosome 5. The smallest region involved in deletions included the band to which the gene for FAP (APC) has been localized,[13, 15, 16, 27] thus allowing the localization of the APC gene to this critical region independently of molecular studies. This finding is consistent with the fact that inactivation of the APC gene, either by mutation or deletion, is one of the important initiating events in colorectal carcinogenesis.[19, 21, 27]

The smallest region involved in rearrangement on chromosome 17 was localized to band 17p13, which is consistent with other studies.[41, 42] In addition to these chromosomes, we have also found that chromosome 1 was altered quite frequently in the tumors studied. Of the 47 tumors, 54 percent showed rearrangement of this chromosome. In addition, the rearrangement in-

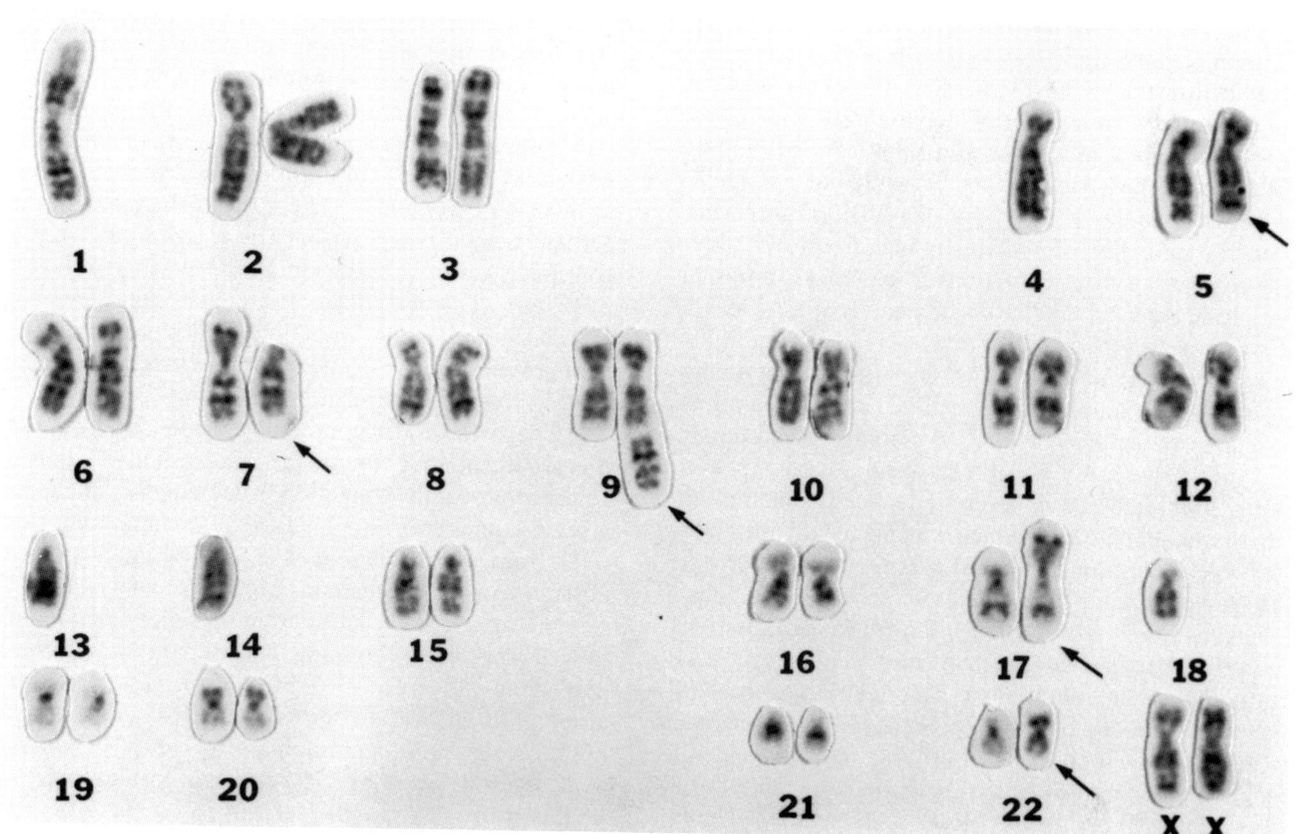

FIG. 13-2. A representative G-banded karyotype from a colorectal carcinoma to show recurrent abnormalities of chromosomes 1, 5, 17, and 18. The chromosome constitution of this cell is 41,XX, −1, −4,del(5)(q13q21),t(7;17)(p11;p11),der(9)t(1;9)(q21;q34), −13, −14, −18,add(22)(p13).

volved loss of 1p, which has previously been shown to be involved in several other tumor types, including colorectal cancer. In this connection, it should be emphasized that with the exception of three tumors, no tumor showed abnormalities of 1p without the alterations of chromosomes 5, 17, or 18. These observations are consistent with the hypothesisthat the genes regulating the normal proliferation and differentiation of colonic mucosa are present on chromosome 5, whereas chromosomes 17 and 18 carry genes required for the neoplastic transformation. Losses of genes from these chromosomes, therefore, are associated with the initiation and neoplastic transformation of colonic cells, whereas the allelic loss of chromosome 1 may be associated with progression. In fact, rearrangements and subsequent deletions of chromosome 1p have been implicated in tumor progression in other tumor types.[43–45]

ras Gene Mutations

The identification of specific point mutations at the amino acids 12, 13, and 61 in the family of *ras* genes in human tumor cells has been one of the most exciting developments in cancer research. The role of such activating mutations in tumorigenesis has been well studied in animal tumors induced by carcinogens. Furthermore, mutated *ras* genes, in cooperation with other oncogenes, have also been implicated in the transformation of normal primary cell cultures into immortalized cell lines.[46, 47] Several earlier studies on the identification and frequency of *ras* mutations in human cancer detected mutations in a significant percentage of tumors. These studies, however, did not provide direct evidence that *ras* oncogene activation causes cancer.[46, 47] Detection of a relatively high frequency (40 to 58 percent) of k-*ras* mutations at codon 12 in human colorectal cancer and premalignant tissues was the first clear evidence that the activation of *ras* mutations may be associated with the development of malignancy.[31, 46, 47] In order to determine if similar mutations occur in patients with FAP, two studies were undertaken.[34, 48] According to these, k-*ras* mutations were very often detected in severe (advanced) adenomas—that is, in 36 percent—which was higher than the percentage seen in intramucosal carcinomas (26 percent) but lower than in invasive carcinomas (44 percent).[34] These studies indicate that although k-*ras* mutations contribute to the development of malignancy in FAP carcinomas, the mutations had no relation to the conversion of adenomas to carcinomas. Based on their studies on the identification of k-*ras* mutations in 135 adenomatous polyps from FAP patients, Ando et al.[49] drew similar conclusions. Regardless of these, however, it was found that the allelic losses of chromosomes most often seen in carcinomas and adenomas from FAP patients showed very low frequencies of LOH.[31, 34] These results are consistent with the concept that k-*ras* mutations occur at an early stage of colorectal tumorigenesis.

Mutations and Loss of Heterozygosity in the p53 Gene in Colorectal Tomorigenesis

Mutations of the p53 tumor suppressor gene are the most common genetic alterations associated with human cancers. Mutations of the p53 gene have been shown to occur in a variety of tumors, including colorectal cancer.[50–54] The p53 mutations are largely dominant negatives, with different mutations having different functional effects and different selective advantages during the process of tumorigenesis.[19] It is therefore suggested that a mutated p53 gene can provide a selective growth advantage promoting tumor progression, even in the presence of a normal p53 allele.[42] Although several investigators have reported p53 mutations in sporadic colorectal cancer, studies on p53 in adenomas and carcinomas in FAP patients are limited. One recent report[55] studied the status of p53 mutations and LOH in 160 tumors from 40 FAP patients. Of these 160 tumors, 58 adenomas with moderate dysplasia showed no p53 mutations; on the other hand, 8 percent (3/37) of advanced adenomas, 15 percent 96/40) of intramucosal carcinomas, and 40 percent (10/25) of invasive carcinomas showed p53 mutation. It was interesting to note that only 3 percent (1/33) of advanced adenomas, 25 percent (6/24) of intramucosal carcinomas, and 40 percent (10/25) of invasive carcinomas showed both mutation and LOH for the p53 gene. Similar results were obtained for nonfamilial APC patients; no adenomas showed both mutation and LOH, but both these alterations were frequently seen in invasive carcinomas. Thus, these studies taken together strongly suggest that the rate-limiting step in p53 inactivation is point mutation, which is followed by loss of wild-type alleles. Both these alterations normally occur near the transition from benign to malignant growth. The p53 gene, therefore, may play an important role in this transition.

Perhaps the most compelling evidence to support the argument that functional inactivation of the p53 genes occurs at the transition from benign to malignant growth comes from the analysis of a single tumor derived from an FAP patient. The tumor contained a carcinoma within an adenoma. Molecular analysis of the regions of adenoma and carcinoma individually, following cryostat sectioning and separation of these two tissues, revealed the APC and *ras* gene mutations along with allelic deletions of the DCC gene in adenoma, whereas the carcinoma also had p53 mutation and allelic deletion of 17p markers. In addition, the mutation of the p53 gene seen in carcinoma at codon 135 was not detected in either allele of the adenoma.[54]

A majority of p53 mutations were due to point mutations and distributed along four hot spots, particularly those seen in intramucosal carcinomas. The co-

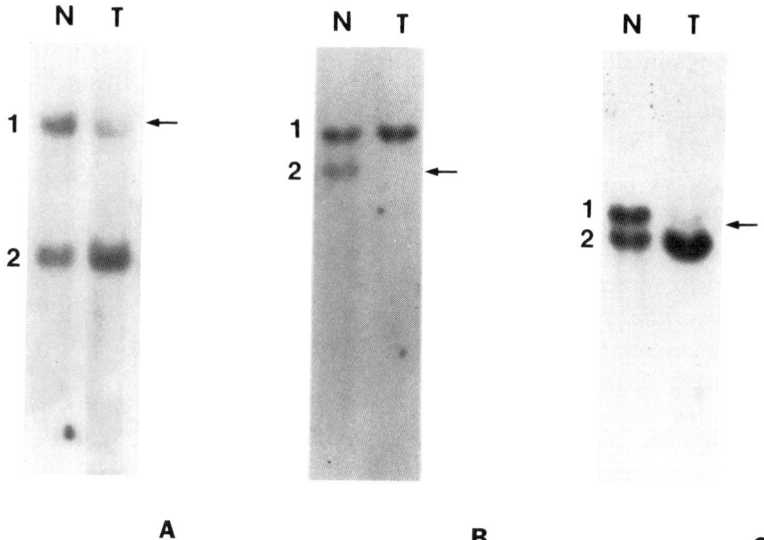

FIG. 13-3. Recurrent allelic deletions of chromosome 17p (*A* and *B*) and 18q (*C*) seen in colorectal cancer. Loss of heterozygosity in tumor (T) as compared to corresponding normal (N) tissue is indicated by arrows.

dons frequently affected were 175, 238, 245, 273, and 282; a great majority (72 percent) of all the mutations were GC-AT transition. In general these results were consistent with other reports on colorectal tumors.[53]

Furthermore, as expected, a close correlation was seen between mutations and protein levels; no mutant protein was detected by immunostaining of p53 protein in adenomas, whereas 86 percent of invasive carcinomas were found to exhibit high levels of mutant p53 protein.

Thus, there is sufficient evidence to suggest that the most common pathway for the functional inactivation of p53 gene is mutation followed by a deletion through LOH (Fig. 13-3*A* and *B*). However, other alternative mechanisms such as mutations in both alleles[56] and loss of message and/or gene product have also been reported.[57] The clinical and biological implications of these various mechanisms, however, are currently unknown. Similarly, the molecular and cellular pathways involved and the interaction of the p53 gene with other genes such as MDM2, APC, DCC, and MCC in the process of colorectal carcinogenesis remain to be elucidated.

Allelic Deletions on Chromosome 18q and the DCC Gene

Vogelstein and associates,[31] who based on their studies on 172 colorectal tumors, showed that a specific region of chromosome 18q was frequently deleted in colorectal carcinomas (73 percent) and in advanced-stage adenomas (47 percent) but was occasionally deleted in moderate adenomas (11 to 13 percent). These studies also identified a carcinoma with a homozygous deletion and yet another one with "gain" of heterozygosity. As a follow-up of this novel observation, Fearon et al.,[58] based on the expression assays using the polymerase chain reaction in an exon-connection strategy, isolated a partial cDNA clone mapping to 18q21. The gene is expressed in several normal tissues including normal colonic mucosa but either absent or drastically reduced in colorectal carcinoma.

The DCC (deleted in colorectal carcinomas) gene is very large, with an mRNA transcript size of 10 to 12 kb. Somatic mutations within the gene have been observed in a number of colorectal cancers; these include a homozygous deletion at the 5′ end of the gene, a point mutation within one of the introns, and 10 examples of DNA insertions within a fragment immediately downstream of one of the exons. The significance of these alterations is not known.

Interestingly, the DCC gene shows significant homology to neural cell adhesion molecules (CAMs) and other related cell surface glycoproteins. The DCC gene contains four immunoglobulin-like domains of the C2 class and a fibronectin type III–related domain similar to the domains present in N-CAM, LI, and other members of the CAM family.

The fact that DCC is related to genes involved in cell-surface interactions is of great significance. There is sufficient evidence that disruption of cell adhesion and cell communications are critical events in neoplastic transformation. Disruption of normal cell-cell contacts is noted in the process of metastasis, and intercellular adhesion mediated by CAMs directly influences differentiation, a process often disrupted in malignancy. Although losses of DCC have been seen in the great majority of patients with sporadic carcinoma (Fig. 13-3*C*), such deletions are invariably absent in adenomas. Furthermore, limited studies performed on intramucosal carcinoma and invasive carcinoma in patients with FAP have identified such deletions only in 40 to 46 percent of tumors studied. Thus, deletions of 18q or DCC are believed to be involved in the progression of intramucosal carcinoma to invasive carcinoma. To the best of our knowledge, mutations of DCC in patients with deleted DCC have not been reported in FAP patients.

Allelic Deletions of Chromosomes other than 5q, 17p, and 18q

In order to determine the extent and variation of allelic losses in colorectal tumors from patients with FAP, Okamoto et al.[30] and Sasaki et al.[33] performed RFLP analysis on a large number of tumors using up to 53 polymorphic probes on all autosomes. According to these studies, in addition to losses of 5q, 17p and 18q, allelic losses of 6, 12, 14, 15, and 22 were noted in a significant proportion of tumors studied. However, the losses were less frequent and involved fewer chromosomes in colorectal adenomas, indicating that the loss of tumor suppressor genes located at these sites of deletions may be involved in the progression of colorectal tumors from adenoma to carcinoma. In an independent study, Miyaki et al.[34] showed that allelic losses of 22q along with 18q were more frequent in invasive carcinoma and therefore suggested that the losses from these two chromosomes may be associated with the progression of intramucosal to invasive carcinoma. In addition, recent studies from our laboratory have demonstrated a high frequency of allelic deletions of 1p and nm-23 (Figs. 13-4*A* and *B*) in high-stage colorectal carcinomas.[40, 57] Furthermore, in a prospective study on nm-23-H1 allelic deletions in colorectal carcinoma in 21 patients, Cohn et al.[59] showed that 73 percent of the patients with nm-23 deletions developed distant metastases, as compared to 20 percent without such deletions. Thus, taken together, these data suggest that losses of genes on these chromosomes—particularly 1p and 22q—along with the loss of nm-23 on 17q may be associated with progression and therefore may confer metastatic potential to tumors carrying such deletions (Fig. 13-5).

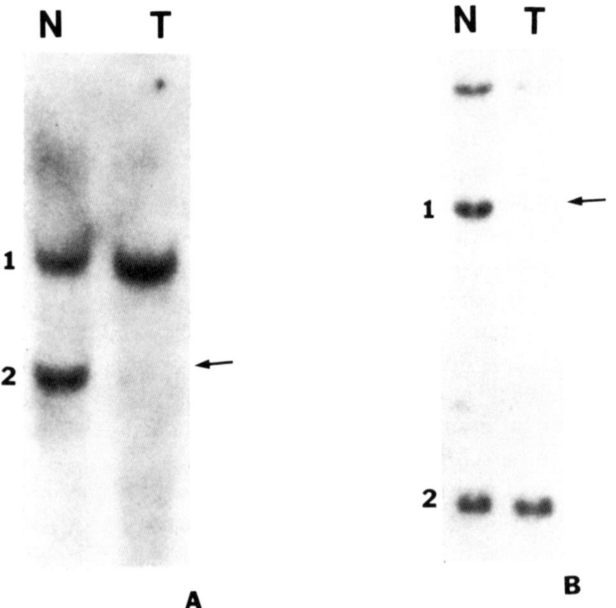

FIG. 13-4. Allelic deletion of chromosome 1p (*A*) and nm23 (*B*) in a metastatic colorectal carcinoma. Loss of heterozygosity in tumor (T) as compared to corresponding normal (N) tissue is indicated by arrows.

Molecular Genetic Alterations in Hereditary Nonpolyposis Colorectal Carcinoma

Although FAP is rare, accounting for only about 1 percent of colorectal cancer patients, HNPCC contributes to approximately 15 percent of patients with colorectal cancers. Although members of HNPCC families do not have multiple polyps or other signs associated with predisposition, they are prone to develop other cancers as well, including cancer of the uterine lining, ovary, kidney, and pancreas, indicating that the genetic component plays an important role here. Linkage analysis in 7 families with HNPCC using polymorphisms from MCC and APC genes provided no evidence for the linkage of HNPCC susceptibility locus to 5q21 region of the chromosome.[60] Similarly, in 5 of the 7 families, data were provided that supported the exclusion of DCC (18q region) linkage to HNPCC.[61] These exclusion studies of HNPCC linkage to any of the genes already known to contribute to colonic cancer prompted researchers to focus on other sites. For such studies, Peltomaki et al.[62] performed linkage analyses in two large families from North America and New Zealand using 345 microsatellite markers. These studies clearly demonstrated a cosegregation between the disease locus and a marker D2S123, which has been mapped to 2p15-16. Thus, the most likely physical location of the HNPCC gene is 2p15-16.

Because recent studies of colorectal cancers in FAP and "sporadic" cases (summarized above) documented the fact that the process of tumorigenesis proceeds through a series of genetic alterations involving both oncogenes and tumor suppressor genes (Fig. 13-5), it was not unreasonable to assume that a similar sequence of events may be associated with the development of cancer in HNPCC patients.

Accordingly, 18 tumors derived from 18 patients from 15 different HNPCC kindreds were studied for k-*ras*, APC, and p53 mutations. Mutations of p53 and at codon 12 or 13 of k-*ras* were identified in approximately 60 to 64 percent of tumors, whereas APC mutations were seen in about 57 percent of tumors in HNPCC patients. The number of mutations of k-*ras* and APC was slightly higher than in sporadic cancers. Some of the hallmarks of classic tumor suppressor genes is the loss of at least one of the two copies in tumor cells. Aaltonen et al.[63] also searched for LOH at the D2S123 locus. Contrary to expectation, however, no such deletions were seen in any of the 14

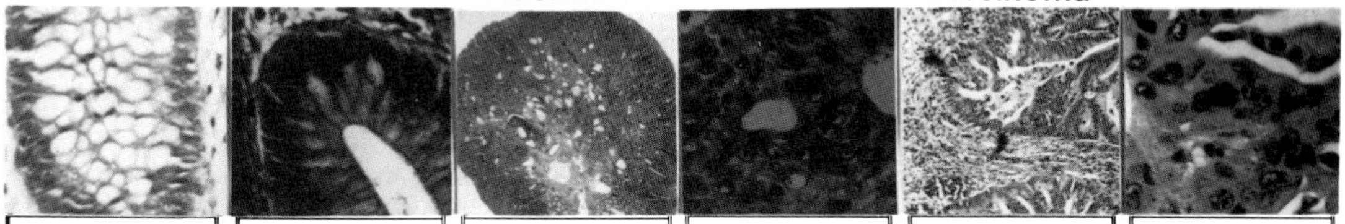

Genetic Alteration		Normal Mucosa	Moderate Adenoma	Severe Adenoma	Intramucosal Carcinoma	Invasive Carcinoma	Metastatic Carcinoma
APC:	Allele 1	**Mutant**	Mutant	Mutant	Mutant	Mutant	Mutant
	Allele 2	Wild-Type	Wild-Type	**Loss**	Loss	Loss	Loss
K-ras:	Allele 1	Wild-Type	**Mutant**	Mutant	Mutant	Mutant	Mutant
	Allele 2	Wild-Type	Wild-Type	Wild-Type	Wild-Type	Wild-Type	Wild-Type
P^{53}:	Allele 1	Wild-Type	Wild-Type	Wild-Type	**Mutant**	Mutant	Mutant
	Allele 2	Wild-Type	Wild-Type	Wild-Type	Wild-Type	**Loss**	Loss
DCC:	Allele 1	Wild-Type	Wild-Type	Wild-Type	Wild-Type	**Loss**	Loss
	Allele 2	Wild-Type	Wild-Type	Wild-Type	Wild-Type	Wild-Type	Wild-Type
NM23:	Allele 1	Wild-Type	Wild-Type	Wild-Type	Wild-Type	Wild-Type	**Loss**
	Allele 2	Wild-Type	Wild-Type	Wild-Type	Wild-Type	Wild-Type	?
Allelic Deletions of 1p,22q		None	None	None	None	**Loss**	Loss

FIG. 13-5. A unifying model of colorectal tumorigenesis in FAP patients. The model is based on data reviewed in this chapter as well as some unpublished observations made in authors' laboratory. The methylation state of DNA at various histologic stages is not specified, as hypomethylation is believed to be a consistent feature of both benign polyps and malignant carcinomas. Similarly, no distinction was made between MCC and APC, due to their physical proximity and the fact that the role of MCC in FAP is not very well defined.

To illustrate the sequence of genetic events associated with the process of tumorigenesis through well-defined histologic stages (moderate adenomas, severe or advanced adenomas, intermucosal carcinomas, and invasive carcinomas) in colonic cells, the status of both the alleles of a given gene is shown for each individual histologic stage. Genetic alterations known to occur for the first time in the history of colorectal tumorigenesis are identified in bold letters. In addition, for simplicity, only those genetic alterations invariably seen in a given histologic stage are included for that particular stage. The model presented here is based on several studies reviewed in this chapter.[6,20,32,33,34,40,57]

HNPCC or the 46 sporadic tumors examined. Instead, remarkable and hitherto unreported shifts in the electrophoretic mobility of (CA)n dinucleotide repeat fragments were seen in the majority of HNPCC-derived tumors and some sporadic cancers. Similar shifts were identified in approximately 43 to 71 percent of the tumors with microsatellite markers from other chromosomes (10, 11, 12, and 13). These observations, therefore, suggested that replication errors (RER) had occurred in these sequences during tumor development. These authors also noted that, overall, the electrophoretic shifts were distributed nonrandomly among the tumors analyzed: 11 of the 14 tumors analyzed had shifts in at least 2 of the 7 markers, whereas the remaining 3 tumors showed no shifts. Based on this, the tumors were classified as RER^+ and RER^- respectively. It was also interesting to note that the RER^+ tumors derived from HNPCC patients as well as RER^+ sporadic tumors were similar with regard to location (both occurred on the right side of the colon) and allelic losses. The data summarized above are consistent with the idea that the genetic instability of the genome can be inherited and may be directly related to a defective gene on chromosome 2 in HNPCC patients. Such a generalized genetic instability, in turn, might contribute to qualitative and quantitative alterations in gene products and thus malignancy of various organs, as seen in HNPCC patients.

Diagnostic and Prognostic Implications of Genetic Alterations in FAP and HNPCC Patients

The results of several studies summarized above provide a basis for presymptomatic diagnosis. Since mutations at several positions (see discussion above) have been shown in approximately 40 percent of the patients studied, it is not unreasonable to begin screening for mutations at these sites using a mutation assay. Only when these sites are negative, half of exon 15 at the 5′ site, which contains 2/3 mutations, should be examined. Furthermore, since 92 percent of the APC mutations in FAP patients result in truncated protein, deletion of such protein products using specific antibodies against the APC protein may be the most appropriate screening test for diagnosis. Alternatively, in individuals known to be at risk because of family history, linkage analysis using multi-allelic CA repeat polymorphism closely linked to the APC gene may help to identify individuals with such mutations. In fact, such an approach has recently been utilized by Spirio et al.[64] to identify 20 of the 31 at risk individuals as either carriers or noncarriers of an APC-predisposing allele. More recently, Varesco et al.[65] have used an elegant and quick assay based on the level of expression of a β-galactosidase coding sequence present at the 3′ end of a PCR-amplified and cloned DNA segment in the expression vector system. They employed this to screen for chain-terminating mutations caused by stop and frameshift mutations in the APC gene.

Although it is important to identify the genetic alterations involved in the development of colorectal cancer so as to find answers to biological questions regarding carcinogenesis, the clinical significance of these findings is not always obvious. The pathologic stage, in general, correlates well with outcome; the course in individual patients cannot be precisely predicted. Since adjuvant therapy has been shown to improve survival, characterization of the genetic alterations in primary cancers may better predict the clinical behavior of the cancer in individual patients and thus enable adjuvant therapy to be used more appropriately. Although no serious attempts have been made to identify prognostic indicators in FAP patients, several studies on the prognostic implications of genetic alterations seen in sporadic colorectal carcinomas have been published.[29, 66, 67] Considering the similarities in genetic alterations between sporadic and tumors derived from FAP patients, it is not unreasonable to assume that similar correlations may exist in FAP patients as well.

In our series of 63 sporadic cancers analyzed, 47 were primary colorectal cancers. Analysis of factors predicting clinical outcome by the Kaplan-Meier method has demonstrated that, in addition to pathologic stage, the finding of genetic alterations involving chromosome 1 or 17 in the cancer predicted poor survival. This finding was in full agreement with two prior reports suggesting that allelic deletions of chromosome 17 are associated with poorer prognosis and one study describing similar predictiveness of chromosome 1 deletions.[67, 68] These findings further strengthen the belief that loss of a normal p53 gene in a tumor harboring a mutated homologue translates into a more aggressive phenotype. In addition, our findings of the importance of chromosome 1 deletions, particularly 1p36, suggest that there is a tumor suppressor gene at this site which is not tissue-specific, as for the case of p53, and confers on the cancer cells a more aggressive character. This finding had been demonstrated earlier in melanoma[43] and was also recently suggested in colonic cancer by Lauren-Puig et al.[68, 69] Our confirmation of this finding further raises the need to focus on this area as the location of another important tumor suppressor gene. The permanent cell lines established from tumors with the abnormalities of chromosome 1p are currently being used to identify a putative tumor suppressor gene.

In an attempt to identify LOH for chromosomes 5, 17, 15, and 18 in 1p and also correlate this with microsatellite alterations in 90 colorectal tumors, Thibodeau et al.[70] performed LOH as well as microsatellite alteration studies. Data from such studies enabled them to conclude that, while microsatellite instability was significantly correlated with the tumor's location in the proximal colon ($p = .003$) and increased patient survival ($p = .02$), the inverse correlation between LOH and microsatellite shifts was clearly seen.

SUMMARY

Tumorigenesis has long been considered to be a multistep process. However, it has only recently become possible to identify the molecular genetic events associated with the initiation and progression of human tumors. Colorectal tumors provide an excellent system to study these underlying genetic events, as sufficient clinical and pathologic data suggest that most, if not all, malignant colorectal cancers arise from preexisting benign tumors (adenomas) through several histopathologically well-defined stages. In addition, both genetic and environmental factors equally contribute to the process of tumorigenesis. Furthermore, loss of tumor suppressor genes appears to be involved in the pathogenesis of these tumors, and—according to recent studies—a net accumulation of genetic events without any well-defined sequence has been proposed.

In the process of colorectal tumorigenesis, however, according to the existing literature (reviewed above), and in the presence of underlying APC mutation, *ras*-gene mutations, DNA hypomethylation, p53 mutation, and 5q alterations appear to occur early, while allelic deletions of chromosome arms 17 p and 18q usually occur at a later stage and therefore may be related to progression. Loss of tumor suppressor genes from other chromosomes such as 1p and 22q and allelic losses of nm23 may be involved in further evolution of the tumor. Thus, based on these studies, a unifying model of colorectal tumorigenesis can be proposed as shown in Fig. 13-5. Furthermore, allelic deletions of certain chromosomes may also help in predicting overall outcome.

The gene for non-FAP patients (HNPCC), however, is located on the chromosome 2. Although the nature of this gene is currently unknown, it is believed to cause genetic instability of the genome as a whole, which, in turn, may initiate the neoplastic process in HNPCC patients.

REFERENCES

1. Gardner, EJ: Familial polyposis coli and Gardner syndrome, in *Prevention of Hereditary Large Bowel Cancer.* New York, Liss, 1983, pp 39–60.
2. Herrara L, Kakati S, Gibas L, et al: Brief clinical report: Gardner syndrome in a man with an interstitial deletion of 5q. *Am J Med Genet* 25:473–476, 1986.
3. Bodmer WF, Bailey CJ, Bodmer J, et al: Localization of the gene for familial adenomatous polyposis on chromosome 5. *Nature (London)* 328:614–616, 1987.
4. Leppert M, Dobbs M, Scambler P, et al: The gene for familial polyposis coli maps to the long arm of chromosome 5. *Science* 238:1411–1413, 1987.
5. Solomon E, Voss R, Hall V, et al: Chromosome 5 allele loss in human colorectal carcinomas. *Nature (London)* 328:616–619, 1987.
6. Fearon ER, Vogelstein B: A genetic model for colorectal tumorigenesis. *Cell* 61:759–767, 1990.
7. Solomon E: Colorectal cancer genes. *Nature (London)*, 343:412–414, 1990.
8. Marshall CJ: Tumor suppressor genes. *Cell* 54:313–325, 1991.
9. Razin, A, Riggs AD: DNA methylation and gene function. *Science* 210:604, 1980.
10. Goelz SE, Vogelstein B, Hamilton SR, et al: Hypomethylation of DNA from benign and malignant human colon neoplasm. *Science* 228:187–190, 1985.
11. Fearon ER, Hamilton SR, Vogelstein B: Clonal analysis of human colorectal tumors. *Science* 238:193–197, 1987.
12. Kinzler KW, Nilbert MC, Vogelstein B, et al: Identification of a gene located at chromosome 5q21 that is mutated in colorectal cancers. *Science* 251:1366–1369, 1991.
13. Kinzler KW, Nilbert MC, Su LK, et al: Identification of FAP locus genes from chromosome 5q21. *Science* 253:661–665, 1991.
14. Ashton-Rickardt PG, Wyllie AH, Bird CC, et al: MCC, a candidate familial polyposis gene in 5q21, shows frequent allele loss in colorectal and lung cancer. *Oncogene* 6:1861–1886, 1991.
15. Nishisho I, Nakamura Y, Miyoshi Y, et al: Mutations of chromosome 5q21 genes in FAP and colorectal patients. *Science* 253:665–669, 1991.
16. Groden J, Thliveris A, Samowitz W, et al: Identification and characterization of the familial adenomatous polyposis coli gene. *Cell* 66:589–600, 1991.
17. Joslyn G, Carlson M, Thliveris A, et al: Identification of deletion mutations and three new genes at familial polyposis locus. *Cell* 66:601–613, 1991.
18. Fodde R, Van der Luijt R, Wijnen J, et al: Eight novel inactivation germ line mutations at the APC gene identified by denaturing gradient gel electrophoresis. *Genomics* 13:1162–1168, 1992.
19. Cottrell S, Bicknell D, Kaklamanis L, et al: Molecular analysis of APC mutations in familial adenomatous polyposis and sporadic colon carcinomas. *Lancet* 340:626–630, 1992.
20. Miyoshi Y, Ando H, Nagase H, et al: Germ-line mutations of the APC gene in 53 familial adenomatous polyposis patients. *Proc Natl Acad Sci USA* 89:4452–4456, 1992.
21. Miyoshi Y, Nagase H, Ando H, et al: Somatic mutations of the APC gene in colorectal tumors: Mutation cluster region in APC gene. *Hum Molec Genet* 1:229–233, 1992.
22. Nagase H, Miyoshi Y, Horii A, et al: Correlation between the location of germ-line mutations in the APC gene and the number of colorectal polyps in familial adenomatous polyposis patients. *Cancer Res* 52:4055–4057, 1992.
23. Groden J, Gelbert L, Thliveris A, et al: Mutational analysis of patients with adenomatous polyposis: Identical inactivating mutations in unrelated individuals. *Am J Hum Genet* 53:263–272, 1993.
24. Olschwang S, Laurent-Puig P, Groden J, et al: Germ-line mutations in the first 14 exons of the adenomatous polyposis coli (APC) gene. *Am J Hum Genet* 52:273–279, 1993.
25. Paul P, Letteboer T, Gelbert L, et al: Identical APC exon 15 mutations result in a variable phenotype in familial adenomatous polyposis. *Hum Mol Genet* 2:925–931, 1993.
26. Varesco L, Gismondi V, James R, et al: Identification of APC gene mutations in Italian adenomatous polyposis coli patients by PCR-SSCP analysis *Am J Hum Genet* 52:280–285, 1993.
27. Powell SM, Zilz N, Beazer-Barclay Y, et al: APC mutations occur early during colorectal tumorigenesis. *Nature (London)*, 359:235–237, 1992.
28. Knudson AG: Hereditary cancer, oncogenes, and antioncogenes. *Cancer Res* 45:1653–1656, 1985.
29. Law DJ, Olschwang S, Monpezat JP, et al: Concerted nonsyntenic allelic loss in human colorectal carcinoma. *Science* 241:961–965, 1988.
30. Okamoto M, Sasaki M, Sugio K, et al: Loss of constitutional heterozygosity in colon carcinoma from patients with familial polyposis coli. *Nature (London)* 331:273–277, 1988.
31. Vogelstein B, Fearon ER, Hamilton SR, et al: Genetic alterations during colorectal tumor development. *N Engl J Med* 319:525–532, 1988.
32. Rees M, Leigh SEA, Delhanty JDA, et al: Chromosome 5 allele loss in familial and sporadic colorectal adenomas. *Br J Cancer* 59:361–365, 1989.
33. Sasaki M, Okamoto M, Sato C, et al: Loss of constitutional heterozygosity in colorectal tumors from patients with familial polyposis coli and those with nonpolyposis colorectal carcinoma. *Cancer Res* 49:4402–4406, 1989.
34. Miyaki M, Seki M, Okamoto M, et al: Genetic changes and histopathological types in colorectal tumors from patients with familial adenomatous polyposis. *Cancer Res* 50:7166–7173, 1990.
35. Miki Y, Nishisho I, Miyoshi Y, et al: Interstitial loss of the same region of 5q in multiple adenomas and a carcinoma derived from an adenomatous polyposis coli (APC) patient. *Genes Chromosomes Cancer 4:81–83, 1992.*
36. Muleris M, Nordlinger B, Dutrillaux B: Cytogenetic characterization of a colon adenocarcinoma from a familial polyposis coli patient. *Cancer Genet Cytogenet* 38:249–253, 1989.
37. Pathak S, Kakati S: Cytogenetics of colorectal cancer, in Augenlicht LH (ed): *Cell and Molecular Biology of Colon Cancer.* Orlando, Fla, CRC Press, 1989, pp 139–163.
38. Ikeuchi T, Yoshida MA, Iwama I, et al: Cytogenetic studies on colon carcinomas and adenomas from patients with familial polyposis coli. in Utsunomiya J, Lynch, HJ (eds): *Hereditary Colorectal Cancer,* Tokyo, Springer-Verlag, 1990, pp 533–540.
39. Paraskeva C, Finerty S, Harper S, et al: Cellular and molecular events involved in tumor progression in colorectal carcin-

ogenesis: A study of the adenoma carcinoma sequence *in vitro,* in Utsunomiya J, Lynch HJ (eds): *Hereditary Colorectal Cancer.* Tokyo, Springer-Verlag, 1990, pp 497–507.

40. Gerdes H, Chen Q, Elahi AH, et al: Recurrent deletions involving chromosomes 1, 5, 17, and 18 in colorectal carcinoma: Possible role in biological and clinical behavior of tumors. *Genes Chromosomes Cancer* (submitted).
41. Baker SJ, Fearon ER, Nigro JM, et al: Chromosome 17 deletions and p53 gene mutations in colorectal carcinomas. *Science,* 244:217–221, 1989.
42. Cho KR, Vogelstein B: genetic alterations in colorectal tumors, in Utsunomiya J, Lynch HT (eds): *Hereditary Colorectal Cancer,* Tokyo, Springer-Verlag, 1990, pp 477–482.
43. Dracopoli NC, Harnett P, Bale SJ, et al: Loss of alleles from the distal short arm of chromosome 1 occurs late in melanoma tumor progression. *Proc Natl Acad Sci USA* 86:4614–4618, 1989.
44. Ladanyi M, Heinemann FS, Huvos AG, et al: Neural differentiation in small round cell tumors of bone and soft tissue with the translocation t(11;22) (q24;q12): An immunohistochemical study of 11 cases. *Hum Pathol* 21:1245–1251, 1990.
45. Offit K, Chaganti RSK: Chromosomal aberrations in non-Hodgkin's lymphoma: Biological and clinical correlations, in Armitage JO (ed): *Hematology/Oncology Clinics of North America,* Philadelphia, WB Saunders, 1991, vol 5, pp 853–869.
46. Bos JL, Fearon ER, Hamilton SR, et al: Prevalence of *ras* gene mutations in human colorectal cancers. *Nature (London)* 327:293–297, 1987.
47. Forrester K, Almoguera C, Han K, et al: Detection of high incidence of K-*ras* oncogenes during human colon tumorigenesis. *Nature (London)* 327:298–303, 1987.
48. Farr CJ, Marshall CJ, Easty DJ, et al: A study of *ras* gene mutations in colonic adenomas from familial polyposis coli patients. *Oncogene* 3:673–678, 1988.
49. Ando M, Takemura K, Maruyama M, et al: Mutations in c-k-*ras* 2 gene codon 12 during colorectal tumorigenesis in familial adenomatous polyposis. *Gastroenterology* 103:1725–1731, 1992.
50. Nigro JM, Baker SJ, Preisinger AC, et al: Mutations in the p53 gene occur in diverse human tumor types. *Nature (London)* 342:705–708, 1989.
51. Rodrigues WR, Rowan A, Smith MEF, et al: p53 mutations in colorectal cancer. *Proc Natl Acad Sci USA* 87:7555–7559, 1990.
52. Caron De Fromentel C, Soussi T: TP53 tumor suppressor gene: A model for investigating human mutagenesis. *Genes Chromosomes Cancer* 4:1–15, 1992.
53. Harris CC, Hollstein M: Clinical implications of the p53 tumor suppressor gene. *N Engl J Med* 329:1318–1327, 1993.
54. Baker SJ, Preisinger CA, Jessup JM, et al: p53 gene mutations occur in combination with 17p allelic deletions as late events in colorectal tumorigenesis. *Cancer Res* 50:7717–7722, 1990.
55. Yanoshita RK, Konishi M, Ito S, et al: Genetic changes of both p53 alleles associated with the conversion from colorectal adenoma to early carcinoma in familial adenamatous polyposis and non-familial adenomatous polyposis patients. *Cancer Res* 52:3965–3971, 1992.
56. Van der Broek MH, Jhanwar SC, Fodde R, et al: p53 mutations in colorectal cancers in the patients of metropolitan New York. *Anticancer Res* 13:1769–1772, 1993.
57. Elahi A, Gerdes H, Chen Qu, et al: Biological and clinical implications of allelic deletions of chromosome 17 in colorectal cancer cell lines. *Proc AACR* 35:601, 1994.
58. Fearon ER, Cho KR, Nigro JM, et al: Identification of a chromosome 18q gene that is altered in colorectal cancer. *Science* 247:49–56, 1990.
59. Cohn KH, Wang F, DeSoto-Lapaix F, et al: Association of nm23-H1 allelic deletions with distant metastases in colorectal carcinoma. *Lancet* 338:722–724, 1991.
60. Peltomaki P, Sistonen P, Mecklin JP, et al: Evidence that the MCC-APC gene region in 5q21 is not the site for susceptibility to hereditary nonpolyposis colorectal carcinoma. *Cancer Res* 52:4530–4533, 1992.
61. Peltomaki P, Sistonen P, Mecklin JP, et al: Evidence supporting exclusion of the DCC gene and a portion of chromosome 18q as a locus for susceptibility to heredity nonpolyposis colorectal carcinoma in five kindreds. *Cancer Res* 51:4135–4140, 1991.
62. Peltomaki P, Aaltonen, LA, Sistonen P, et al: Genetic mapping of a locus predisposing to human colorectal cancer. *Science* 260:810–815, 1993.
63. Aaltonen LA, Peltomaki P, Leach FS, et al: Clues to the pathogenesis of familial colorectal cancer. *Science* 260:812–816, 1993.
64. Spirio L, Nelson L, Ward K, et al: A CA-repeat polymorphism close to the adenomatous polyposis coli (APC) gene offers improved diagnostic testing for familial APC. *Am J Hum Genet* 52:286–296, 1993.
65. Varesco L, Groden J, Spirio L, et al: A rapid screening method to detect nonsense and frameshift mutations: Identification of disease causing APC alleles. *Cancer Res* 53:5581–5584, 1993.
66. Vogelstein B, Fearon ER, Kern SE, et al: Allelotype of colorectal carcinomas. *Science* 244:207–211, 1989.
67. Kern SE, Fearon ER, Tersmette KWF, et al: Allelic loss in colorectal carcinoma. *JAMA* 261:3099–3103, 1989.
68. Laurent-Puig P, Olschwang S, Delattre O, et al: Survival and acquired genetic alterations in colorectal cancer. *Gastroenterology* 102:1136–1141, 1992.
69. Leister I, Weith A, Bruderlein S, et al: Human colorectal cancer: High frequency of deletions at chromosome 1p35. *Cancer Res* 50:7232–7235, 1990.
70. Thibodeau SN, Bren G, Schaid D: Microsatellite instability in cancer of the proximal colon. *Science* 260:816–819, 1993.

CHAPTER 14

Molecular Biology of Colorectal Cancer

José G. Guillem
Philip B. Paty
Neal Rosen

HIGHLIGHTS

Although a genetic basis for cancer has been proposed for over a century, it is only during the past decade that techniques of recombinant DNA analysis have provided direct evidence that cancer is indeed a genetic disease. In this chapter we review the currently known genetic alterations in colorectal cancer, including oncogenes, tumor suppressor genes, and genomic instability.

CONTROVERSIES

The prevalent view of colorectal carcinogenesis is the progressive accumulation of multiple genetic alterations in the alleles of both oncogenes and tumor suppressor genes. However, although several lines of evidence support a functional role for certain genetic alterations, it is likely that many others are a result of genetic instability but do not contribute to the malignant phenotype. Determining how genetic alterations perturb cellular functions and contribute to human tumor progression will require detailed mechanistic testing.

FUTURE DIRECTIONS

Because of the redundancy and feedback control of normal signal transduction and growth regulation, it is likely that tumor development requires alterations in multiple components of normal growth regulation. Future studies aimed at understanding the interactive roles of oncogenes and tumor suppressor genes in normal growth and differentiation may shed light on the mechanisms by which deregulation of these genes and their signaling pathways contribute to colorectal carcinogenesis.

Colorectal carcinogenesis is a complex, multifactorial process resulting from numerous environmental and genetic interactions and leading to both inherited and somatic mutations. Colorectal cancer (CRC) results, in part, from mutations in two classes of genes: (1) oncogenes, positive regulators of cell growth that are activated by somatic mutation of a single allele, and (2) tumor suppressor genes, recessive genes that require loss or inactivation of both alleles to produce a phenotype.

Although the normal colonic mucosa arises from numerous stem cells and is therefore polyclonal, CRCs have a monoclonal composition.[1,2,3] Even the smallest adenomas and earliest cancers are monoclonal, suggesting that polyps and cancers arise from the clonal expansion of a single stem cell.[4] Subsequent genetic alterations involving activation of oncogenes or inactivation of tumor suppressor genes in these initiated cell populations lead to CRC with clonal mutations; i.e., most or all of the neoplastic cells harbor the same mutation. It is possible that such mutations provide a growth advantage, allowing for complete replacement with cells harboring the mutation. An alternative hypothesis is that the mutation may have arisen concomitantly with another, as yet undetected genetic alteration that actually provided the growth advantage.

In addition to specific mutations in oncogenes and loss of tumor suppressor genes, consistent increases in the expression or activity of certain cellular oncogenes (c-*myc* and c-*src*), without a demonstrable structural change in the gene, suggest that deregulation of gene expression of posttranslational changes in protein function may contribute to malignant transformation. Such hypotheses require careful mechanistic testing, since certain cell cycle–related genes may be overexpressed simply because of increased cellular proliferation.[5]

In this chapter, we initially review the molecular alterations most frequently noted in sporadic colorectal cancer: mutations in *ras;* overexpression in c-*myc* and c-*src;* loss of heterozygosity in chromosome 17p (p53 gene), 18q (DCC gene), and 5q (MCC and APC genes); and alterations in chromosome 2p. We then review alterations in protein kinase C (PKC) which suggest a deregulation of PKC in colonic carcinogenesis.

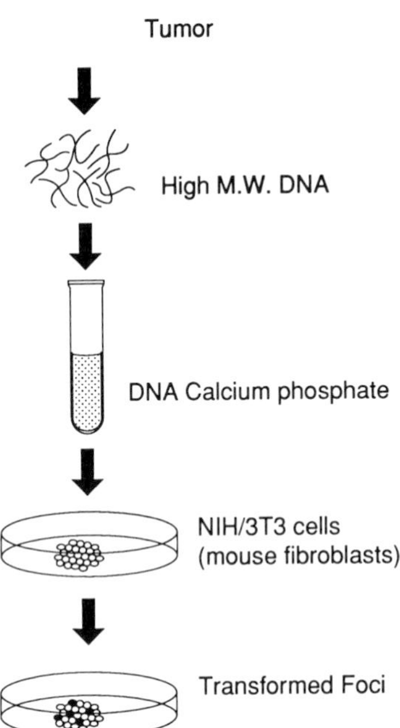

FIG. 14-1. DNA transfection. High-molecular-weight DNA is isolated from tumor cells and introduced into recipient NIH/3T3 fibroblast cells. The monolayer is examined for foci of cells which have been morphologically transformed by the expression of an introduced oncogene.

SOMATIC ALTERATIONS IN ONCOGENES

Ras

The first human oncogene, *ras,* was isolated from a human bladder carcinoma in 1982.[6] Subsequently, all three members (H-*ras,* K-*ras,* and N-*ras*)[7] of this gene family have been found to be mutated in human tumors. All three wild-type genes share strong sequence homology and code for a 21,000-Da protein with the ability to bind guanine nucleotides. Antibodies that block the p21 *ras* product inhibit cellular DNA synthesis.[8]

In 1987, transfection studies (Fig. 14-1) demonstrated that specific *ras* mutations detected in colorectal tumors conferred neoplastic properties in recipient cells.[9] Shortly thereafter, studies using allele-specific oligonucleotides detected mutated *ras* alleles in about 50 percent of colorectal carcinomas[10,11] and in a similar proportion of adenomas over 1 cm in size.[12]

In CRC, 90 percent of *ras* mutations are found in the K-*ras* gene and only 10 percent in the N-*ras* gene. The mutations occur at particular codon "hot spots": codons 12, 13, and 61.[10,11,13] The mutant p21 *ras* proteins are intrinsically active because they bind guanine triphosphate (GTP) and resist its hydrolysis to guanine diphosphate (GDP), thereby remaining in the active GTP-bound state.[14] Therefore, mutated *ras* genes lead to transformation via activation of *ras*-dependent mitogenic signaling pathways. Similarly, overexpression of wild-type p21 *ras* can also lead to transformation. Clinically, this is supported by the frequent elevation of *ras* proteins in CRC and adenomas.[9,15,16]

In adenomatous polyps, the presence of *ras* mutations correlates with the extent of villous histology and of high-grade dysplasia.[16] In well-differentiated CRC with a mucinous and adenomatous component, the prevalence of K-*ras* mutations is 83 percent.[17] In 7 out of 7 CRCs, a diffuse distribution of K-*ras* mutations was demonstrated, whereas in 4 out of 7 adenomas examined, K-*ras* mutations were restricted to discrete areas.[18] These data suggest that (1) *ras* mutations rarely if ever initiate CRC but rather are acquired by discrete tumor cells within small and intermediate adenomas and (2) a *ras*-mutant lineage, once established, expands to populate the entire adenoma and strongly influences subsequent growth pattern and CRC progression.

Ras mutations are found with equal frequency in sporadic and familial adenomatous polyposis (FAP)-associated adenomas and carcinomas.[19,20] In addition, the presence or absence of 5q deletion has no influence on the prevalence of *ras* mutations.[21] This lack of concordance suggests that these are probably independent events. Furthermore, since over 50 percent of sporadic CRCs do not contain K-*ras* mutations, alterations in the K-*ras* locus do not appear to be obligatory events for all CRC formation. This is supported by the low (4 percent) prevalence rate of K-*ras* mutations in ulcerative colitis patients who develop sporadic CRC. It is therefore evident that alternative molecular pathways for CRC progression must exist.

In patients who harbor a CRC with a *ras* mutation (approximately 50 percent of cases), it has been shown that *ras* oncogene mutations can be detected in their stool.[22] This raises the exciting possibility of a noninvasive method of detecting CRC.

C-*myc*

The *myc* oncogene was originally identified as the cellular homologue of the transforming gene of the avian retrovirus MC29, which causes malignancies in infected chickens. Because c-*myc* expression is cell cycle–dependent and rises with mitogen stimulation, it is believed that the c-*myc* protein product is essential for cell proliferation.[23] The c-*myc* gene product, p62cmyc, is a nuclear phosphoprotein involved in transcriptional regulation. It is induced by peptide growth factors and, when overexpressed, can transform cells in culture and induce tumors in animals.[24] A recent study has shown that a peptide, PuF, which binds to a distinctive element of the human c-*myc* promoter has a nucleotide sequence which is virtually identical to the human nm23-H2 nucleoside diphosphate kinase gene, a potential negative regulator of cancer metastasis. This suggest that, at least in vitro, the nm23 protein can regulate the transcriptional expression of c-*myc*.[25]

The *myc* gene family contains numerous members, including N-*myc*, L-*myc*, and c-*myc*. Relative to normal colonic mucosa, elevated levels of c-*myc* RNA are noted in as many as three-quarters of CRC and adenomas.[26–32] In affected tumors, c-*myc* RNA levels are 3- to 40-fold higher than adjacent normal mucosa.[26,28,32] Although, within adenomas, c-*myc* RNA levels increase linearly with increasing polyp size,[30] there is no correlation with villous histology, dysplasia, or Dukes stage of CRC.[30,32]

In normal human colon, immunohistochemical localization of the *myc* protein is noted in the basal-proliferative zone.[31,33] However, in adenomas, positive staining is noted throughout all levels of the crypts.[31] In an azoxymethane-induced rat CRC model, the same pattern is noted,[34] suggesting that elevated c-*myc* expression in adenomas is linked to cell replication and expansion of the proliferative zone. However, in some carcinomas, c-*myc* expression may be uncoupled from proliferation.[34] N-*myc* and L-*myc* overexpression has also been noted in many CRCs.[30,31]

Although isolated reports of c-*myc* amplification exist, there are no data to support the hypothesis that point mutations, rearrangement, or amplification of c-*myc* oncogenes play a role in colonic carcinogenesis. Rather, the proposed theory states that overloading of a cell with an otherwise normal c-*myc* cellular product leads to transformation. In vivo, an abnormal accumulation of c-*myc* product is thought to be secondary to increased synthesis rather than decreased degradation of the c-*myc* RNA. However, there are no data demonstrating a cause-and-effect relationship between increased c-*myc* RNA production and the development of colonic carcinomas.

C-*src*

The c-*src* gene is the cellular homologue of the transforming gene of the Rous sarcoma virus, v-*src*. The c-*src* gene product, pp60-*src*, is a membrane-associated protein tyrosine kinase that functions in mitogenic signal transduction. pp60-*src* is highly activated (five- to tenfold) in 70 percent of CRCs, including large adenomas, primary carcinomas, metastatic tumors, and most CRC cell lines.[35–39] This finding has been corroborated by several investigators and may be important in neoplastic progression. Among adenomas, pp60-*src* activation is greatest in polyps greater than 2 cm in diameter, where the degree of enzyme activation is correlated with villous histology and dysplasia.[38]

The mechanism of pp60-*src* activation is unknown. No primary genetic changes have been observed, and activation appears to involve posttranslational interactions.[35] Other members of the *src* family of tyrosine kinases are expressed at high levels in subsets of CRC cell lines.[40]

LOSS OF TUMOR SUPPRESSOR GENES

Loss of specific chromosomal regions coding for specific genes is detected frequently in many human malignancies, including CRC. These losses, which usually involve only one of the parental chromosome sets, can be detected cytogenetically or with molecular techniques, such as restriction fragment length polymorphisms (RFLP). Through the use of RFLPs, allelic losses or loss of heterozygosity (LOH) can be identified in tumor tissues relative to corresponding normal tissue. Since the remaining allele is sometimes duplicated yet the phenotypic change is nevertheless noted, it appears that the allele lost differs from the one that remains.[1]

The general scheme for LOH leading to an unmasking of a recessive mutation in tumor suppressor genes is based on Knudson's two-hit theory (Fig. 14-2). Individuals who are heterozygous for a defective gene carry a dominantly inherited predisposition to the cancer, which becomes phenotypically evident only after a somatic change results in the loss of the intact allele. In sporadic cases, the same phenotypic change requires two successive events to knock out both alleles.

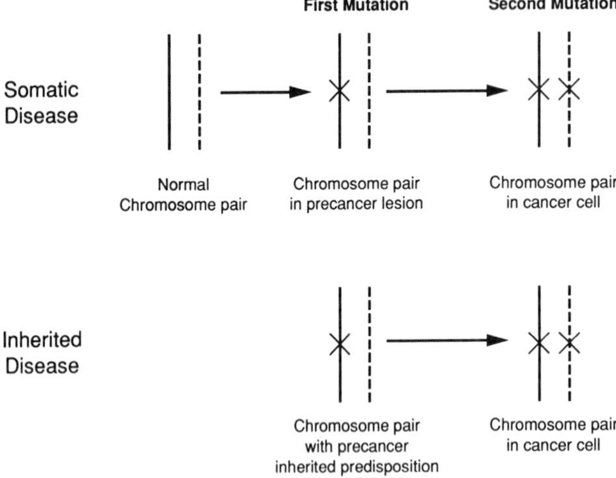

FIG. 14-2. Knudson's two-hit model. This general scheme fits the data on the development of tumors where recessive genetic defects have been detected. The somatic, or sporadic, form of the disease involves two successive somatic genetic events knocking out function of a gene. Individuals who inherit the disease carry a dominantly inherited heterozygous gene which, following a single somatic alteration, becomes defective.

Similarly, tumor suppressor genes, which act recessively, require loss of both the paternal and maternal copies of the gene for the suppressor function to be eliminated. Since chromosomal losses in retinoblastoma and Wilms' tumors have been associated with unmasking of tumor suppressor mutations, it was postulated by Fearon and Volgestein[12,16] that the frequently noted loss of chromosomes 17p and 18q in CRC was probably selected for during CRC development in order to unmask mutations in tumor suppressor genes. In this section, we review the p53, DCC, MCC, and APC genes.

p-53

In over 75 percent of CRC, LOH of chromosome 17p is noted.[1,21] The common region of allelic loss includes the p53 gene.[41] As the name implies, the p53 gene product is a 53-kDa nuclear phosphoprotein.[42] The wild-type protein forms homodimers, binds DNA, is involved in transcription of multiple genes, and appears to regulate cell-cycle progression through late G_1 and entry into S phase.

Acquiring a point mutation in one allele is believed to be the initial and rate-limiting step of p53 inactivation. The majority of mutations reported in CRC show a G:C to A:T transition occurring at the CpG dinucleotide.[43] It is believed that a point mutation in p53 could provide a selective growth advantage, leading to clonal expansion. It has been proposed that mutated p53 alleles and their corresponding proteins, which accumulate at high levels in carcinoma cells,[42,44] might function in a dominant negative manner by binding the wild-type allele, leading to a conformational change and probable alteration of normal cellular function.[45,46] However, the observation that overexpression of exogenous wild-type p53 in CRC cells with mutated p53 alleles suppresses growth[47] suggest that, somewhere during the transition from adenoma to carcinoma, a fine balance between mutated and wild-type protein must be tipped in favor of transformation. Deletion of the other allele follows in the majority of cases as a secondary event.[47]

In general, inactivation of p53 is infrequently detected before the carcinoma stage, with less than 10 percent of adenomas revealing this alteration.[47] Since p53 mutations are rare in adenomas and since CRCs are rare in both animals and humans with germline p53 mutations such as the Li-Fraumeni syndrome,[48] it is unlikely that p53 mutations play a significant role in adenoma formation. However, it is likely that they do play a significant role in the later stages of CRC progression. Several studies have shown that LOH of 17p[49] or increased p53 nuclear protein[44] correlates with poor patient survival.

DCC

In a manner analogous to 17p, LOH of 18q is rarely seen in early-stage adenomas. However, this is noted in nearly 50 percent of advanced adenomas and in over 70 percent of CRCs.[12] A candidate tumor suppressor gene from a common region of allelic loss has been cloned and termed DCC (deleted in colorectal carcinoma).[16] This is a complex gene containing 28 exons that encode a large transmembrane protein.[16,50] The extracellular domain (1100 amino acids) has significant homology with the neural cell adhesion molecule (NCAM) family, which are thought to be involved in cell-cell or cell-matrix interactions. Although the normal function of the DCC gene remains unknown, it is inferred that because of its similarity to NCAM genes, inactivation of this gene may account for alterations in adhesion and invasion noted in advanced CRC. The function of the intracellular domain (324 amino acids) remains unknown. Gene expression may involve complex RNA processing that produces tissue-specific transcripts.

Several lines of evidence, including allelic loss of 18q in 70 percent of CRC, support the hypothesis that DCC is a tumor suppressor gene in CRC. Although the gene is expressed in normal colonic mucosa, it is greatly reduced or absent from most CRC cell lines studied.[16] Furthermore, somatic mutations have been observed in about 15 percent of CRC. In addition, introduction of chromosome 18 into CRC cell lines suppresses their ability to grow in soft agar and form tumors in nude mice.[51] However, tumor suppression via direct transfer of the DCC gene into cells with deficient DCC alleles has yet to be demonstrated. It is conceivable that allelic losses of 18q in CRC result in the unmasking of other tumor suppressor loci, yet to be identified, in addition to DCC.

MCC and APC

A constitutional deletion of chromosomal band 5q21 in a familial adenomatous polyposis (FAP) patient[52] provided the first clue for the cloning of both the APC and MCC (mutated in colon cancer) genes. Utilizing a DNA probe which had been assigned to a region of the long arm of chromosome 5 (5q21-22), linkage studies revealed a polymorphism which was closely linked to the APC phenotype.[53] Subsequent studies demonstrated linkage between 5q21-22 and adenoma development in both FAP and Gardner syndrome.[54] However, the clinical significance of 5q21-22 genes in sporadic, nonfamilial CRC—which constitute the majority of CRC—was demonstrated when 20 to 40 percent of sporadic CRC showed loss of heterozygosity for the 5q21-22 gene.[12,55,56]

In order to identify the tumor suppressor gene or genes possibly located within 5q21-22, large portions of this chromosome were cloned using yeast artificial chromosome (YAC) vectors and chromosome walking techniques.[57,58] The first tumor suppressor gene identified was MCC. It was examined for germline mutations in DNA from lymphocytes of FAP patients and for somatic mutations in DNA from sporadic CRC. Although somatic mutations were noted in sporadic CRC, no germline mutations were detected.[59,60] Subsequent studies in FAP patients identified germline point mutations in a gene (APC) which did not include MCC sequences.

The APC gene is large, producing an RNA message of 8.9 kb, which is divided into 15 exons, the last of which contains more than three-quarters of the coding sequence. Genetic alterations of the APC gene that cause FAP include point mutations, deletions, or insertions in the nucleoside sequence, which then result in termination signals during transcription leading to truncated proteins that lack the carboxyl terminus.[57,60] All APC mutations studied are nonsense or inactivating mutations. This is distinctly different from p53 mutations that are dominant negative, such that different mutations have different functional effects.[61]

The APC mutations occur as an early event in CRC development, since colorectal adenomas (63 percent) are just as likely as CRCs (60 percent) to harbor an APC mutation.[62] These figures probably underestimate the actual mutation rate, since changes in the promoter region, alterations of introns, and large deletions were not evaluated.[62,63] The APC mutations appear to precede *ras* mutations and have been detected in adenomas as small as 5 mm.[62] In contrast to inactivations of the p53 tumor suppressor gene, which increase in frequency in advancing tumors, the frequency of APC mutations remains constant as colorectal tumors progress from benign to malignant stages.

Although the predicted APC gene product has sequence homology with cytoskeletal structural proteins,[58] the functional characterization of the wild and mutant proteins has yet to be determined. However, immunohistochemical localization of the wild-type APC protein to the basolateral aspect of colonocytes with the greatest intensity noted on the luminal surface of the crypts suggests a possible role for the APC protein in colonocyte maturation.[64]

Thus far, 126 germline mutations have been identified in unrelated patients.[65] Certain regions, such as codon 1309, appear to be hot spots, since the mutation rate is approximately 85 times the average for the rest of the gene. Most FAP kindreds appear to possess unique APC alterations. In addition, similar APC mutations appear to lead to both the FAP syndrome and Gardner syndrome.[58]

In sporadic CRC, the functional significance of somatic APC mutations remains to be determined. As previously mentioned, these mutations can become clonal by providing a growth advantage or simply by being concomitantly altered with another genetic alteration for which selection occurs. However, the observation that APC mutations are noted in the earliest adenomas and that the frequency of such mutations remains constant throughout all stages of CRC progression suggest that the APC gene plays an important role in both FAP and sporadic CRC development.

MICROSATELLITE INSTABILITY ON CHROMOSOME 2

Although the data reviewed above would suggest that a large subset of CRC arises as a result of a cellular accumulation of activated oncogenes and the loss of tumor suppressor genes, a recent discovery has provided exciting evidence for the presence of a "mutator" phenotype in approximately 1 percent of CRC.[66] This mutator phenotype is characterized by genomic instability at simple repeated sequences in DNA.[20,66–68] The mechanism appears to involve slippage of DNA strands during replication[69] and is currently thought to be a consequence of a mutation in a gene or genes involved in DNA replication and/or repair. Cells which present the mutator phenotype accumulate insertions and deletions at simple repeated sequences, including long runs of single residues, dinucleotide microsatellites, and triple repeats.[20,66–68] This dynamic process generates millions of mutations in tumor cells.

Although the clinical characteristics of individuals with CRC harboring a mutator phenotype appear to be similar to those of persons with the Lynch syndrome,[70] sporadic cases of CRC with this mutator phenotype are often found in the proximal colon of young individuals.[20,66,67] In Lynch syndrome patients demonstrating a mutator phenotype, inheritance was found to be linked to chromosome 2p15-16. Cloning of the Lynch syndrome mutator gene may provide the basis for a genetic Lynch syndrome test as well as insight into the mechanism by which mutations in this gene lead to sporadic CRC at large.

PROTEIN KINASE C

Protein kinase C (PKC) is a multigene family of serine/threonine kinases central to signal transduction pathways.[71] The endogenous activator of PKC is 1,2-diacylglycerol (DAG), an intracellular second messenger which is generated through receptor-mediated inositol phospholipid turnover. Depending on the cell type, PKC activation leads to a variety of changes, including modulation of gene expression, morphologic changes, and stimulation or suppression of cell proliferation.[72] Because tumor-promoting phorbol esters, such as 12-O-tetradecanoylphorbol 13-acetate (TPA), can activate PKC in a manner similar to DAG,[73] PKC has been implicated in tumor promotion.

Several studies have established a possible role for PKC in colorectal carcinogenesis. Secondary bile acids, elevated in feces of populations consuming high-fat diets, are known to promote CRC in rodents[74,75] and alter PKC activity both in vitro[76] and in vivo.[77] Furthermore, in intact cells, secondary bile acids induce PKC translocation from the cytosol to the membrane as well as the expression of PKC-responsive genes in a manner analogous to DAG stimulation.[78] In human CRC[79] and adenomas[80,81] as well as in carcinogen-induced rat CRC,[82] PKC activity is decreased. Since both preneoplastic colonic mucosa and CRC from 1,2-dimethylhydrazine treated rats have decreased PKC activity, it appears that this is an early event in colonic carcinogenesis. In addition, since intracellular levels of DAG, which are also produced by intestinal microflora,[83] are also decreased in adenomas and CRC,[84,85] it appears that numerous stages in the PKC signal transduction pathway are diminished in CRC.

Recent studies on PKC RNA expression have demonstrated a unique decrease in isoform PKC-beta, suggesting that the noted decrease in overall PKC activity is not simply due to post-translational downregulation but rather to decreases in specific PKC isoform RNA expression.[86] Transfection studies have shown that overexpression of PKC-beta isozyme in established human CRC cell lines inhibits rather than stimulates their in vitro growth and tumorigenicity.[87] These data would suggest that in established CRC, PKC exerts a negative growth influence, while in normal mucosa, it may facilitate CRC promotion through the action of bile acids.[86] This paradoxical observation suggests striking differences in the regulation of PKC signal transduction between normal colonic mucosa and established CRC.[88]

SUMMARY

It is clear that the development of CRC is associated with an acquisition of numerous genetic alterations including oncogenes, tumor suppressor genes, microsatellite instability, and deregulation of signal transduction pathways such as PKC. As heterogenous as the phenotype of CRC appears to be, it is likely that numerous other, yet to be defined genotypic alterations may be required in CRC development. Although the normal physiologic roles of oncogenes and tumor suppressor genes are beginning to be elucidated, the relative impact of each of these alterations on different stages of colorectal carcinogenesis remains to be determined.

The major clinical challenge over the next decade will be the application of our understanding of the molecular biology of colorectal cancer to "translational research," leading to enhanced prevention, diagnosis, therapy, and prognosis.

REFERENCES

1. Fearon ER, Hamilton SR, Vogelstein B: Clonal analysis of human colorectal tumors. *Science* 238:193–197, 1987.
2. Foulds L: The natural history of cancer. *J Chronic Dis* 8:2–37, 1958.
3. Nowell P: The clonal evolution of tumor cell populations. *Science* 194:23–28,1976.
4. Ponder BAJ, Wilkinson MM: Direct examination of the clonality of carcinogen-induced colonic epithelial dysplasia in chimeric mice. *J Natl Cancer Inst* 77:967–976, 1986.
5. Calabretta B, Kaczmarek L, Ming PL, et al: Expression of c-*myc* and other cell cycle-dependent genes in human colon neoplasia. *Cancer Res* 45:6000–6004, 1985.
6. Bos JL: The ras family and human carcinogenesis. *Mutat Res* 196:255–271, 1988.
7. Valencia A, Chardin P, Wittinghofer A, et al: The ras protein family: Evolutionary tree and role of conserved amino acids. *Biochemistry* 30:4637–4648, 1991.
8. Stacey DW, Tasi MH, Yu CL, et al: Critical role of ras proteins in proliferative signal transduction. *Cold Spring Harbor Symp Quant Mol Biol* 53:871–881, 1988.
9. Barbacid M: *Ras* genes. *Annu Rev Biochem* 56:779–827, 1987.
10. Bos JL, Fearon ER, Hamilton SR, et al: Prevalence of *ras* gene mutations in human colorectal cancer. *Nature* 327:239–297, 1987.
11. Forrester K, Almoguera C, Han K, et al: Detection of high incidence of K-*ras* oncogenes during human colon tumorigenesis. *Nature* 327:298–303, 1987.
12. Vogelstein B, Fearon ER, Hamilton SR, et al: Genetic alterations during colorectal-tumor development. *N Engl J Med* 319:525–532, 1988.
13. Perucho M, Forrester K, Almoguera C, et al: Expression and mutational activation of the c-Ki-*ras* gene in human carcino-

mas, in Furth M, Greaves M (eds): *Cancer Cells 7: Molecular Diagnostics of Human Cancer.* Cold Spring Harbor, NY, Cold Spring Harbor Laboratory Press, 1989, pp 141–237.
14. Haubruck H, McCormick F: *Ras* p 21: Effects and regulation. *Biochem Biophys Acta* 1072:215–229, 1991.
15. Salhab N, Jones DJ, Bos JL, et al: Detection of ras gene alterations and ras proteins in colorectal cancer. *Dis Colon Rectum* 32:559–664, 1989.
16. Fearon ER, Vogelstein B: A genetic model for colorectal tumorigenesis. *Cell* 61:759–767, 1990.
17. Laurent-Puig P, Olschwang S, Delattre O, et al: Association of K-*ras* mutation with differentiation and tumor-formation pathways in colorectal carcinoma. *Int J Cancer* 49:220–223, 1991.
18. Shibata D, Schaeffer J, Liz H, et al: Genetic heterogeneity of the c-k-*ras* locus in colorectal adenomas but not in adenocarcinomas. *J Natl Cancer Inst* 85:1058–1063, 1993.
19. Nishiso I, Nakamura Y, Miyoshi Y, et al: Mutations of chromosome 5q21 genes in FAP and colorectal cancer patients. *Science* 253:665–669, 1991.
20. Aaltonen L, Peltomaki P, Leach F, et al: Clues to the pathogenesis of familial colorectal cancer. *Science* 260:812–816, 1993.
21. Vogelstein B, Fearon ER, Kern SE, et al: Allelotype of colorectal carcinomas. *Science* 244:207–211, 1989.
22. Sidransky D, Tokino T, Hamilton SR, et al: Identification of ras oncogene mutations in the stool of patients with curable colorectal tumors. *Science* 256:102–105, 1992.
23. Erisman MD, Scott JK, Astrin SM: Evidence that the familial adenomatous polyposis gene is involved in a subset of colon cancers with a complementable defect in c-*myc* regulation. *Proc Natl Acad Sci USA* 86:4262–4268, 1989.
24. Dang CV: C-myc oncoprotein function. *Biochim Biophys Acta* 1072:103–113, 1991.
25. Postel EH, Berberich SJ, Flint SJ, Ferrone CA: Human c-*myc* transcription factor PuF identified as nm23-H2 nucleoside diphosphate kinase, a candidate suppressor of tumor metastasis. *Science* 261:478–480, 1993.
26. Erisman MD, Rothberg PG, Diegl RD, et al: Deregulation of c-*myc* gene expression in human colon carcinoma is not accompanied by amplification or rearrangement of the gene. *Mol Cell Biol* 5:1969–1976, 1985.
27. Erisman MD, Scott JK, Watt RA, et al: The c-*myc* protein is constitutively expressed at elevated levels in colorectal carcinoma lines. *Oncogene* 2:367–378, 1988.
28. Stewart J, Evan G, Watson J, et al: Detection of the c-*myc* oncogene product in colonic polyps and carcinomas. *Br J Cancer* 53:1–6, 1986.
29. Imaseki H, Hayashi H, Taira M, et al: Expression of c-*myc* oncogene in colorectal polyps as a biological marker for monitoring malignant potential. *Cancer* 64:704–709, 1989.
30. Finley GG, Schultz NT, Hill SA, et al: Expression of the *myc* gene family in different stages of human colorectal cancer. *Oncogene* 4:963–971, 1989.
31. Melham MF, Neisler AI, Finley GG: Distribution of cells expressing *myc* proteins in human colorectal epithelium, polyps, and malignant tumors. *Cancer Res* 52:5853–5864, 1992.
32. Guillem JG, Levy MF, Hsieh LL, et al: Increased levels of phorbin, c-*myc* and ornithine decarboxylase RNAs in human colon cancer. *Mol Carcinogen* 3:68–74, 1990.
33. Tulchin N, Ornstein L, Harpaz N, et al: C-myc protein distribution: I. Neoplastic tissues of the human colon. *Am J Pathol* 140:719–730, 1992.
34. Tulchin N, Ornstein L, Guillem JG, Weinstein IB: Distribution of the c-*myc* oncoprotein in normal and neoplastic tissues of the rat colon. *Oncogene* 3:697–701, 1988.
35. Bolen JB, Veillette A, Schwartz AM, et al: Activation of pp60[c-src] protein kinase activity in human colon carcinoma. *Proc Natl Acad Sci USA* 84:2251–2255, 1987.
36. Rosen N, Bolen JB, Schwartz AM, et al: Analysis of pp60 c-src protein kinase activity in human tumor cell lines and tissues. *J Biol Chem* 261:13754–13759, 1986.
37. Cartwright CA, Kamps MP, Meisler AI, et al: pp60c-*src* activation in human colon carcinoma. *J Clin Invest* 83:2025–2033, 1989.
38. Cartwright CA, Meisler AI, Eckhart W: Activation of the pp60c-*src* protein kinase is an early event in colon carcinogenesis. *Proc Natl Acad Sci USA* 87:558–562, 1990.
39. Talaminti MS, Roh MS, Curley SA, Gallick GE: Increase in activity and level of human colorectal cancer. *J Clin Invest* 91:53–60, 1993.
40. Rosen N, Sartor O, Foss FM, et al: Altered expression of src-related tyrosine kinases in human colon cancer. *Cancer Cells* 7:161–166, 1989.
41. Baker SJ, Fearon ER, Nigro JM, et al: Chromosome 17 deletions and p53 gene mutations in colorectal carcinomas. *Science* 244:217–221, 1989.
42. Levine A, Momand J, Finaly C: The p53 tumour suppressor gene. *Nature* 354:1453–1456, 1991.
43. Lothe RA, Fossli T, Danielsen HE, et al: Molecular genetic studies of tumor supressor gene regions on chromosome 13 and 17 in colorectal tumors. *J Natl Cancer Inst* 84:1100–1108, 1992.
44. Rodrigues N, Rowan, Smith M, et al: p53 mutations in colorectal cancer. *Proc Natl Acad Sci USA* 87:7555–7559, 1990.
45. Herkowitz I: Functional inactivation of genes by dominant negative mutations. *Nature* 329:219–222, 1987.
46. Lane DP, Benchimal S: p53: oncogene or anti-oncogene? *Genes Devel* 4:1–8, 1990.
47. Baker SJ, Preisinger AC, Jessup JM, et al: p53 gene mutations occur in combination with 17p allelic deletions as late events in colorectal tumorigenesis. *Cancer Res* 50:7717–7722, 1990.
48. Malkin D, Li F, Strong LC, et al: Germ line p53 mutations in a familial syndrome of breast cancer, sarcomas, and other neoplasms. *Science* 250:1233–1238, 1990.
49. Kern SE, Fearon ER, Tersmette KW, et al: Clinical and pathological associations with allelic loss in colorectal carcinoma. *JAMA* 261:3099–3103, 1989.
50. Cho K, Vogelstein B: Genetic alterations in the adenoma-carcinoma sequence. *Cancer* 70:1727–1731, 1992.
51. Tanaka K, Oshimuru M, Kikuchi R, et al: Suppression of tumorigeneity in human colon carcinoma cells by introduction of chromosome 5 or 18. *Nature* 349:340–342, 1991.
52. Herrera L, Kakati S, Gibas L, et al: Brief clinical report: Gardner syndrome in a man with an interstitial deletion of 5q. *Am J Med Genet* 25:473–476, 1986.
53. Bodmer WF, Bailey C, Bodmer J, et al: Localization of the gene for familial polyposis on chromosome 5. *Nature* 328: 614–616, 1987.
54. Leppert M, Dobbs M, Scambler P, et al: The gene for familial polyposis coli maps to the long arm of chromosome 5. *Science* 238:1411–1413, 1987.
55. Solomon E, Voss R, Hall V, et al: Chromosome 5 allele loss in human colorectal carcinomas. *Nature* 328:616–619, 1987.
56. Ashton-Rickardt PG, Dunlop MG, Nakamura Y, et al: High frequency of APC loss in sporadic colorectal carcinoma due to breaks clustered in 5q21-22. *Oncogene* 4:1169–1174, 1989.
57. Joslyn G, Carlson M, Thliveris A, et al: Identification of deletion mutations and three new genes at the familial polyposis locus. *Cell* 66:601–613, 1991.
58. Kinsler KW, Nilbert MC, Vogelstein B, et al: Identification

of a gene located at chromosome 5q21 that is mutated in colorectal cancers. *Science* 251:1366–1370, 1991.

59. Groden J, Thliveris A, Samowitz W, et al: Identification and characterization of the familial adenomatous polyposis coli gene. *Cell* 66:589–600, 1991.
60. Nishisho I, Nakamura Y, Miyoshi Y, et al: Mutations of chromosome 5121 genes in FAP and colorectal cancer patients. *Science* 253:665–669, 1991.
61. DeFromentel CC, Soussi T: TP53 tumour suppressor gene: A model for thymine in single-base-pair mismatches with hydroxylamine and osmium tetroxide and its application to the study of mutations. *Proc Natl Acad Sci USA* 85:4397–4401, 1988.
62. Powell S, Zilz N, Barclay Y, et al: APC mutations occur early during colorectal tumorigenesis. *Nature* 359:235–237, 1992.
63. Miyoshi Y, Ando H, Nagase H, et al: Germ-line mutations of the *APC* gene in 53 familial adenomatous polyposis patients. *Proc Natl Acad Sci USA* 89:4452–4456, 1992.
64. Smith K, Johnson K, Bryan T, et al: The *APC* gene product in normal and tumor cells. *Proc Natl Acad Sci USA* 90:2846–2850, 1993.
65. Burt R, Groden J: The genetic and molecular diagnosis of adenomatous polyposis coli. *Gastroenterology* 104:1211–1214, 1993.
66. Ionov J, Peinado MA, Malkhosyan S, et al: Ubiquitous somatic mutations in simple repeated sequences reveal a new mechanism for colonic carcinogenesis. *Nature* 363:558–561, 1993.
67. Peltomaki P, Aaltonen LA, Sistonen P, et al: Genetic mapping of a locus predisposing to human colorectal cancer. *Science* 260:810–812, 1993.
68. Thibodeau S, Bren G, Schaid D: Microsatellite instability in cancer of the proximal colon. *Science* 260:816–819, 1993.
69. Streisinger G, Okada Y, Emrich J, et al: Frameshift mutations and the genetic code. *Cold Spring Harbor Symp Quant Biol* 31:77–84, 1986.
70. Lynch HT, Conway T, Lynch J: Hereditary nonpolyposis colorectal cancer. *Cancer Genet Cytogenet* 143:160–170, 1991.
71. Nishizuka Y: Intracellular signaling by hydrolysis of phospholipids and activation of protein kinase C. *Science* 258:607–614, 1992.
72. Hug H, Sarre TF: Protein kinase C isoenzymes: Divergence in signal transduction? *Biochem J* 291:329–343, 1993.
73. Castagna M, Takai Y, Kaibuchi K, et al: Direct activation of calcium-activated phospholipid-dependent protein kinase by tumor-promoting phorbol esters. *J Biol Chem* 257:7847–7851, 1982.
74. Reddy BS, Weisburger JH, Wynder EL: Effect of dietary fat level and dimethylhydrazine on fecal acid and neutral sterol excretion and colon carcinogenesis in rats. *J Natl Cancer Inst* 52:507–511, 1974.
75. Bull AW, Soullier BK, Wilson PS, et al: Promotion of azoxymethane-induced intestinal cancer by high-fat diets in rats. *Cancer Res* 39:4956–4959, 1979.
76. Fitzer CJ, O'Brian CA, Guillem JG, Weinstein IB: The regulation of protein kinase C by chenodeoxycholate, deoxycholate and several structurally related bile acids. *Carcinogenesis* 8:217–220, 1987.
77. Craven PA, DeRubertis FR: Alterations in protein kinase C system of colonic epithelium during fasting-refeeding. *Dig Dis Sci* 37:1162–1169, 1992.
78. Guillem JG, O'Brian CA, Fitzer CJ, et al: Studies on protein kinase C and colon carcinogenesis. *Arch Surg* 122:1475–1478, 1987.
79. Guillem JG, O'Brian CA, Fitzer CJ, et al: Altered levels of protein kinase C and Ca^{2+}-dependent protein kinases in human colon carcinomas. *Cancer Res* 47:2036–2039, 1987.
80. Kopp R, Noelke B, Sauter G, et al: Altered protein kinase C activity in biopsies of human colon adenomas and carcinomas. *Cancer Res* 51:205–210, 1991.
81. Kusunoki M, Sakanoue Y, Hatada T, et al: Protein kinase C activity in human colon adenoma and colorectal carcinoma. *Cancer* 69:24–30, 1992.
82. Baum CL, Wali RK, Sitrin MD, et al: 1,2-Dimethylhydrazine-induced alterations in protein kinase C activity in the rat preneoplastic colon. *Cancer Res* 50:3915–3920, 1990.
83. Morotomi M, Guillem JG, LoGerfo P, Weinstein IB: Production of diacylglycerol, an activator of protein kinase C, by human intestinal microflora. *Cancer Res* 50:3595–3599, 1990.
84. Phan SC, Morotomi M, Guillem JG, et al: Decreased levels of 1,2-sn-diacylglycerol in human colon tumors. *Cancer Res* 51:1571–1573, 1991.
85. Sauter G, Nerlich A, Spengler U, et al: Low diacylglycerol values in colonic adenomas and colorectal cancer. *Gut* 31:1041–1045, 1990.
86. Levy MF, Pocsidio J, Guillem JG, et al: Decreased levels of protein kinase C (PKC) enzyme activity and PKC mRNA in primary human colon tumors. *Dis Colon Rectum* 36:913–921, 1993.
87. Choi P, Tchou-Wong K-M, Weinstein IB: Overexpression of protein kinase C in HT29 colon cancer cells causes growth inhibition and tumor suppression. *Mol Cell Biol* 10:4650–4657, 1990.
88. Weinstein IB, Borner CM, Krauss RS, et al: Pleiotropic effects of protein kinase C and the concept of carcinogenesis as a progressive disorder in signal transduction, in Brugge J, Curran T, Harlow, McCormick F (eds): *Origins of Human Cancer: A Comprehensive Review.* Plainview, NY, Cold Spring Harbor Laboratory Press, 1991, pp 113–124.

PART 3

Pathology and Biology of Colorectal Cancer

CHAPTER 15

Cell Biology

Eileen A. Friedman

HIGHLIGHTS

Transforming growth factor (TGF)-β_1 acts both as an inducer of differentiation and a growth inhibitor of differentiated colonic tumor cells and as a stimulator of growth and invasiveness of poorly differentiated or metastatic colonic tumor cells. The specific mediators of TGF-β1 signal transduction in controlling cell-cycle progression have yet to be identified, although some evidence points to members of the cyclin-directed kinase family. Fecal diglycerides, which are found in high concentration in vivo, act as growth stimulators of undifferentiated colonic carcinoma cells because these cells have elevated protein kinase c(PKC)-β levels. Activation of PKC-β directly by diglycerides activates the cells' basic FGF signal transduction system downstream of the fibroblast growth factor (FGF) receptor. Normal colonocytes have downregulated PKC-β and therefore are unresponsive to fecal diglycerides. To verify the clinical significance of these observations, the levels of PKC-β in differentiated and undifferentiated resected colonic cancers should be measured. Several members of the epidermal growth factor (EGF) gene superfamily are expressed in colonic cancer cells, but understanding their respective roles is complicated by their overlapping binding affinities for the three EGF receptor family members.

Colonic epithelial cells fall into two major morphologic and functional types, fluid-transporting colonocytes and mucin granule–producing goblet cells, comprising roughly 80 and 20 percent of the cell numbers, respectively. A small fraction of cells per crypt fall into other categories, which have been defined primarily by histochemical means and have not been studied using model systems. These will not be discussed. An exception are the enteroendocrine cell populations which have been studied by Gordon and coworkers[1] in a series of elegant experiments using transgenic mice, which express a transgene composed of the 5′ transcribed region of the mouse liver fatty acid–binding protein gene coupled to the human growth hormone gene as an easily assayable reporter gene. These experiments have revealed several classes of enteroendocrine cells within the usual subclasses of these cells, based on their neuroendocrine products, and indicate the complexity of this lineage.

TRANSFORMING GROWTH FACTOR-β1

The advent of tissue culture methodology several decades ago led to the identification of growth stimulatory and growth inhibitory factors in both sera and tissue extracts. In the last decade, the techniques of molecular biology have been used to define, purify, clone, and sequence many of these growth factors. One such factor which affects many cell types is called, for historical reasons, transforming growth factor β or TGFβ. This is not one molecule but a family of structurally related 25-kDa disulfide-bonded dimeric molecules synthesized and secreted as inactive higher-molecular-weight forms complexed with binding proteins. Three members of this family that are roughly 80 percent homologous in their mature forms are TGF-β1, TGF-β2, and TGF-β3.[2]

Isoform-specific antibodies to TGF-β1, TGF-β2, and TGF-β3 were generated and used to examine expression of these factors in the developing mouse embryo.[3] TGF-β1 was strongly expressed at the tips of villi in the embryonic gut, while the expression was lowest in the crypt, implying a role for TGF-β1 in intestinal cell development. TGF-β2, in contrast, was localized to the basement membrane of the submucosa, and TGF-β3 was present in low abundance. It is well known that cell proliferation ceases as colonic epithelial cells ascend the crypt,[4] and it is likely that TGF-β1 modulates this growth inhibition, with the greatest inhibition occurring at the site of greatest concentration of TGF-β1—the top of the crypt.

TGF-β1 has the necessary biological properties for this role, as it has been shown to be inhibitory to epithelial cell growth in vivo. TGF-β1 in slow-release pellets implanted at mammary end buds inhibited the growth of mammary epithelial cells at these buds,[5] while intravenous TGF-β1 inhibited the early phase of liver regeneration following partial hepatectomy.[6] TGF-β1 inhibits mouse keratinocyte,[7] mink lung epithelial cell,[8] and human colonic enterocytic cell growth,[9] by inhibiting the phosphorylation of the retinoblastoma gene product pRB. The colonic enterocytic cells were reversibly blocked at a point within early G1, so they did not enter S phase and could not proliferate.

A bank of cell lines were cloned from the HT29 colonic carcinoma cell line in the presence of the TGF-β1-inducing and differentiation-inducing compound hexamethylene bisacetamide (HMBA). These lines included two which expressed high levels of TGF-β1 mRNA, secreted the active peptide, and differentiated into colonic enterocytic–like cells when placed in postconfluent growth.[10] These lines were growth-inhibited by TGF-β1 because of the block in retinoblastoma protein phosphorylation, as discussed above. Two other lines were derived by this cloning, which differentiated into goblet cells under appropriate culture conditions. Neither cell line responded to TGF-β1[9,10] because the goblet cells had lost receptors to TGF-β1. Thus response to TGF-β1 distinguishes between the two major lineages in the intestine: enterocytic cells and goblet cells (Table 15-1).

TGF-β1 plays a second role in colonic enterocytic cell differentiation, in addition to its ability to block cell cycle progression. TGF-β1 induces expression of differentiation-related proteins, among them collagen I binding proteins. Both enterocytic cell lines bound more tightly to collagen I films than undifferentiated lines, indicating that collagen I binding proteins were elaborated during enterocytic differentiation. A second bank of HT29 sublines were used for these studies, but the cloning was not done in HMBA, so that lines could be obtained with constitutive low levels of TGF-β1 expression, which could then be modulated. One of these sublines, U4, could be differentiated into an enterocytic cell line by HMBA treatment. The HMBA-treated U4 cells, called U4H cells, were stably altered, like the lines studied earlier which had been generated by cloning in HMBA. A second subline U9 remained undifferentiated and multilayered when treated with HMBA, to yield the U9H cell line. Both HMBA-generated lines, U4H and U9H, synthesized higher levels of TGF-β1 mRNA compared to their precursor lines, and both U4H and U9H lines secreted roughly equal levels of TGF-β1 in mature active form. However, the response of the U4H and U9H cells to their endogenously produced TGF-β1 differed greatly. The enterocytic differentiated U4H cells exhibited four times as much cell surface expression of the collagen I binding protein alpha-2 integrin, twice as much of the accessory collagen binding protein CEA, and almost twice as much binding to collagen I films as undifferentiated U9H cells.[11] TGF-β1 treatment doubled U4 cell collagen I binding, increased expression of alpha-2 integrin fourfold but increased CEA expression only marginally. Thus TGF-β1 treatment of the precursor U4 line was able to reproduce the phenotype of the enterocytic differentiated U4H cells. In addition, U4H cells also responded to TGF-β1 by growth arrest in G1, like the two other enterocytic lines studied earlier by Yan et al.[9] The reasons for the aberrant response of the U9 cells to TGF-β1 is unknown but under investigation. Therefore, TGF-β1 has two roles in colonic enterocytic differentiation: to increase levels of collagen I adhesion proteins and to block enterocytic cells in G1 so they can differentiate.

TGF-β1 plays an opposite role in invasion and metastasis to its role in differentiation. The undifferentiated U9 cell line is a model for a group of resected colonic carcinomas that were either poorly differentiated histologically or metastatic to the liver, which responded to TGF-β1 or the TGF-β1-inducer HMBA by increased growth in primary culture.[12,13] The undifferentiated U9 line also responds to TGF-β1 by growth stimulation.[10] Recent studies have also shown that the in vitro invasive potential of U9 cells can be increased three- to fourfold by TGF-β1.[14] Therefore, TGF-β1 can be bifunctional during the evolution of colonic carcinoma acting as a growth inhibitor and differentiation inducer in the more differentiated carcinomas and then acquiring the opposite facility, the ability to stimulate

Table 15-1
Comparison of Cell Lines

Line	*Differentiation capacity*	*Response to TGF-β1*
U9	Undifferentiated	Increased growth Increased invasiveness Increased phosphorylation of retinoblastoma protein
U4	Preenterocytic	Inhibited growth Increased synthesis of collagen I binding proteins
U4H HD3, HD4	Enterocytic	Growth inhibition Arrest in G1 Decreased phosphorylation of retinoblastoma protein
HD6, HD8	Goblet cell	None, no receptors

growth and invasion, when the carcinoma progresses and becomes less differentiated and more aggressive.

This opposite altered response of colonic cells to TGF-β1 during carcinogenesis is not limited to the colonic system. The experimental metastatic potential of a mammary adenocarcinoma cell line was increased by TGF-β1, which increased the number of surface lung metastases two- to threefold.[15] In the same study, these investigators showed that the in vitro invasive potential of this line was potentiated two- to fourfold by TGF-β1 treatment. The increase in invasive potential was due at least in part to severalfold increases in collagenase and heparanase activity. In an experimental in vivo metastasis system, TGF-β1 released by low metastatic cells stimulated in a paracrine fashion the metastatic potential of more metastatic mammary adenocarcinoma variants.[16] In this way TGF-β1 could enhance the clonal selection of TGF-β1 growth-stimulated metastatic variants in vivo. The local source of TGF-β1 in liver metastasis could be the damaged liver cells themselves or stromal fibroblasts. TGF-β1 is known to inhibit the growth of normal breast epithelial cells in in vivo experiments[17] and to inhibit the growth of some mammary adenocarcinoma cell lines. Thus TGF-β1 acts to inhibit the growth of normal mammary epithelial cells and of the more differentiated, less aggressive mammary tumors while increasing the aggressiveness of the less differentiated, more invasive tumors, parallel to the action of this cytokine in colonic carcinogenesis.

The mechanism for this switch in response to TGF-β1 is unknown but currently under investigation. Yan[9] has shown that TGF-β1 treatment increased the phosphorylation of the product of the cell cycle control retinoblastoma gene in the undifferentiated colon carcinoma cells, consistent with an increased rate of cell cycling. Under the same experimental conditions, TGF-β1 decreased the phosphorylation of the retinoblastoma protein in differentiated colonic carcinoma cells, blocking cell progression in G1. The search for the specific kinases that modulate these different responses to TGF-β1 is under investigation and may be a fruitful direction for future research.

The TGF-β1-sensitive retinoblastoma protein kinases are very likely to be cyclin-directed kinases. These are heterodimeric kinases, the actual kinase subunit of which is 32 to 36 kDa bound to a cyclin subunit, which can be 36 to 60 kDa. Both the kinase and the cyclin belong to multigene families. Ten members of the cyclin-directed or cdc2-related kinase family have been identified by PCR cloning.[18] Cyclins direct the activity of the kinase subunit. Cyclins were originally defined as proteins that are synthesized in each cell cycle and then destroyed at mitosis. As the number of cyclins has increased, it has become apparent that they control progression through other phases of the cell cycle in addition to mitosis. There are at least four G1 cyclins (C's and D's): cyclin A, which appears to have a role in mediating passage through S phase; cyclin B, which mediates cell movement through mitosis; and at least two cyclins, E and F, which may play some role at the G1/S boundary.[19] The cyclins which control entry into S phase could have great significance in the modulation of tumor cell growth. Recent studies have implicated a cyclin E/cdk2 complex as mediating this transition in human cells,[20] but it is likely that the cyclin-directed kinase story will become more complex, because of the large numbers of cyclins active in G1. Purified cdk2 protein can phosphorylate purified retinoblastoma protein,[21] but more studies will need to be done to determine whether cdk2/cyclin E is modulated by TGF-β1 in both the growth-inhibited differentiated colonic carcinoma cells and the growth-stimulated poorly differentiated colonic carcinoma cells.

PROTEIN KINASE C AND FIBROBLAST GROWTH FACTOR

Protein kinase C (PKC) is a central player in eukaryotic signal transduction, mediating many signals from the cell surface. There are at least nine isoforms of PKC, all of which have considerable sequence homology in three of their four constant domains.[22] The presence of this large family of closely related PKCs suggests that the many different cellular responses to external signals may be mediated by different PKC isozymes. The β isoform of PKC is in low abundance in colonic enterocytic cells compared with either undifferentiated colonic cells or goblet cells.[23] Calcium- and phospholipid-dependent protein kinase C activity was reduced about 70 percent in cytosolic fractions. Immunoblotting with isotype-specific antisera demonstrated that the isozyme that was in low abundance was β. In contrast, each of two goblet cell lines exhibited high levels of PKC-β activity and abundance. When PKC-β activity was downregulated in goblet cell lines, they lost their ability to differentiate. These experiments indicate that the relative abundance of PKC-β determines whether the enterocytic or the goblet cell maturation pathway is utilized by colonic epithelial cells.

The undifferentiated cells with elevated PKC-β levels can respond to the mitogen basic fibroblast growth factor (bFGF) by growth, while the differentiated enterocytic cells with low PKC-β levels cannot. The FGF family includes proteins encoded by at least seven separate genes which have a core homology region indicating that they were all derived from a common ancestor.[24] Several of the FGF family members are themselves heterogenous, as they are derived from different splice variants at the mRNA level. This heterogeneity indicates that the number of possible FGF family members that could potentially play a role in colonic tumorigenesis is at least 20. To simplify this pattern in colonic carcinogenesis, studies of the internal mediators of bFGF receptor activation were performed. PKC-β is activated within the cell by long-chain diacylglycerols (DAGs). Both basic and acidic FGF increase the intracellular concentration of long-chain DAGs.[23] Exogeneous long-chain DAGs had the same effect as bFGF, stimulating the growth of undifferentiated colonic carcinoma cells with high PKC-β levels but not differentiated those with low PKC-β levels.[23]

Model cell lines repeated the pattern of DAG response we had noted in an earlier study with primary cultured biopsies from normal colon, adenomas, and carcinomas. Diacylglycerols induced proliferation of epithelial cells from each of 13 adenomas of all histologic classes, 2 of 4 carcinomas[25] and both of the undifferentiated cell lines tested. In contrast, exogeneous DAGs had no effect on the proliferation of normal colonic epithelial cells from 7 patients.[25] The enterocytic differentiated lines with low PKC-β levels modeled the normal colonic epithelial cells, since neither exhibited proliferative response to DAGs. Presumably the two DAG-insensitive resected carcinomas were too differentiated to retain high levels of PKC-β. In the same study,[25] DAGs had been found within fecal extracts at high concentrations of hundreds of millimolars. This observation of high levels of fecal DAGs was confirmed by Weinstein's group.[26] These authors hypothesized that the fecal DAGs were caused by lipolysis of phospholipids by the fecal microflora, while we considered that partial lipolysis of dietary triglycerides was the source. Both hypotheses could be correct, with the high fat content of western diets contributing more triglyerides to the small intestine than can be fully digested and additional DAGs being produced by phospholipid breakdown. Therefore, we hypothesize that fecal DAGs increase the level of intracellular DAGs (Fig. 15-1), which, in turn, stimulate the growth of undifferentiated adenoma cells and undifferentiated colon carcinomas cells by activating their bFGF signal transduction pathways. If this is true, reduction of fat intake among patients who have already grown an adenoma should decrease the size of adenomatous polyps that subsequently arise, perhaps to the point where they will be undetectable by endoscopic examination. A trial to test the role of dietary fat in adenoma recurrence is now underway at our center as part of a multicenter dietary intervention trial.

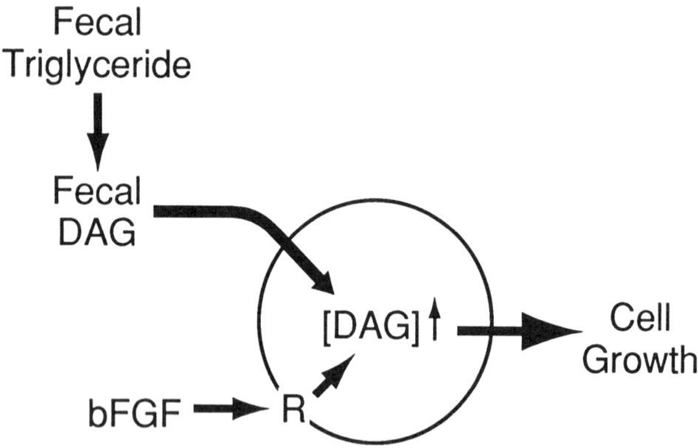

FIG. 15-1. Diglyceride signal transduction.

OTHER GROWTH FACTORS

Other growth-factor systems implicated in the development of colon cancer include the epidermal growth factor/transforming growth factor alpha (EGF/TGF-α) system. Both growth factors bind to the EGF receptor (*erb*B1) and activate its tyrosine kinase activity, leading to signal transduction. Overexpression of TGF-α in transgenic mice led to marked hyperplasia of the colonic epithelium.[27] Expression of TGF-α and the EGF receptor have been observed in colonic carcinoma cell lines,[28] leading to the hypothesis that colonic carcinoma cell growth is often mediated by this growth factor in an autocrine fashion. This simple, attractive hypothesis has been made more complex by the recent identification of homologues to the EGF receptor, *erb*B2 and *erb*B3 which are overexpressed in many malignancies, as well as the identification of ligands for these receptors. The *erb*B2 ligand has been called heregulin by some investigators and Neu differentiation factor by others.[29] Additional members of the EGF supergene family called cripto and amphiregulin have been cloned and may be ligands for *erb*B3. Transcripts for these genes have also been observed in many colonic carcinoma cell lines.[30] Further complexity arises because the ligands can activate more than one of the EGF receptor family members. In addition, the receptors are required to dimerize to transduce growth-factor signals, and different EGF receptor family members can dimerize to form heterodimers. The functional consequences in signal transduction for this multiplicity of ligands and receptor dimers will be a focus of study for some time to come.

Two other growth factors—scatter factor (also called hepatocyte growth factor) and insulinlike growth factor—have been implicated in colonic carcinoma cell growth and differentiation. Scatter factor was initially described as an activity secreted by cells that caused epithelial cell colonies to dissociate or scatter,[31] while more recent studies have shown that binding of scatter factor to its receptor, the oncogene *met,* led to lumenlike differentiation in colon carcinoma cells.[32] Insulinlike growth factors I and II bind to separate receptors, and both have been implicated in colonic carcinoma cell growth modulation. Some colonic carcinoma cell lines also secrete binding proteins for ILGFs which can inhibit tumor cell growth by sequestering the factors.[33] These extracellular modulators of growth-factor action have been identified for other growth factors and again point to the complexity of growth-factor modulation of colonic cell growth. The growth of a colon carcinoma cell will reflect its responses to the growth factors it secretes (autocrine) and those secreted by nearby fibroblasts, inflammatory cells, and other tumor cells (paracrine response). The list described here includes only the best-characterized factors at this writing and does not include interferons and interleukins. From the number of ligands and receptors already described, it is clear that it will take the work of many investigators to obtain a more thorough picture of the responses of normal colonocytes and their transformed derivatives to the various cytokines found in vivo.

REFERENCES

1. Roth KA, Hertz JM, Gordon JI: Mapping enteroendocrine cell populations in transgenic mice reveals an unexpected degree of complexity in cellular differentiation within the gastrointestinal tract. *J Cell Biol* 110:1791–1801, 1990.
2. Moses HL, Yang EY, Pietenpol JA: TGF-β stimulation and inhibition of cell proliferation: New mechanistic insights. *Cell* 63:245–247, 1990.
3. Pelton RW, Saxena B, Jones M, et al: Immunohistochemical localization of TGFβ1, TGFβ2, and TGFβ3 in the mouse embryo: Expression patterns suggest multiple roles during embryonic development. *J Cell Biol* 115:1091–1105, 1991.
4. Deschner E, Lipkin M: Study of human rectal epithelial cells in vitro: III. RNA, protein, and DNA synthesis in polyps and adjacent mucosa. *J Natl Cancer Inst* 44:175–185, 1975.
5. Silberstein GB, Daniel CW: Reversible inhibition of mammary gland growth by transforming growth factor-β. *Science* 233:291–293, 1987.
6. Russell WE, Coffey RJ, Quellette AJ, et al: Type β transforming growth factor reversibly inhibits the early proliferative response to partial hepatectomy in the rat. *Proc Natl Acad Sci USA* 85:5126–5130, 1988.
7. Pietenpol JA, Stein RW, Moran E, et al: TGF-β1 inhibition of c-*myc* transcription and growth in keratinocytes is abrogated by viral transforming proteins with pRB binding domains. *Cell* 61:777–785, 1990.
8. Laiho M, DeCaprio JA, Ludlow JW, et al: Growth inhibition by TGF-β linked to suppression of retinoblastoma protein phosphorylation. *Cell* 62:175–185, 1990.
9. Yan Z, Hsu S, Winawer S, et al: Transforming growth factor B1 (TGF-β1) inhibits retinoblastoma gene expression but not pRB phosphorylation in TGF-B1-growth stimulated colon carcinoma cells. *Oncogene* 7:801–805, 1992.
10. Hafez MM, Infante D, Winawer S, et al: Transforming growth factor β1 acts as an autocrine-negative growth regulator in colon enterocytic differentiation but not in goblet cell maturation. *Cell Growth Diff* 1:616–626, 1990.
11. Hafez MM, Hsu S, Yan Z, et al: Two roles for transforming growth factor β_1 in colon enterocytic cell differentiation. *Cell Growth Diff* 3:753–763, 1992.
12. Schroy PC, III, Carnright K, Winawer SJ, et al: Heterogeneous responses of human colon carcinomas to hexamethylene bisacetamide. *Cancer Res* 48:5487–5494, 1988.
13. Schroy P, Rifkin J, Coffey RJ, et al: Role of transforming growth factor β_1 in induction of colon carcinoma differentiation by hexamethylene bisacetamide. *Cancer Res* 50:261–265, 1990.
14. Hsu S, Huang F, Hafez M, et al: Colon carcinoma cells switch their response to TGF-β1 with tumor progression. *Cell Growth Diff* 5:267–275, 1994.
15. Welch DR, Fabra A, Nakajima M: Transforming growth factor β stimulates mammary adenocarcinoma cell invasion and metastatic potential. *Proc Natl Acad Sci USA* 87:7678–7682, 1990.
16. Theodorescu D, Caltabiano M, Greig R, et al: Reduction of TGF-beta activity abrogates growth promoting tumor cell-cell interactions in vivo. *J Cell Physiol* 148:380–390, 1991.
17. Silberstein GB, Daniel CW: Reversible inhibition of mammary gland growth by transforming growth factor-β. *Science* 237:291–295, 1987.
18. Meyerson M, Enders GH, Wu C-L, et al: A family of human cdc2-related protein kinases. *EMBO J* 11:2909–2917, 1992.
19. Pines J: Cyclins: Wheels within wheels. *Cell Growth Diff* 2:305–310, 1991.
20. Koff A, Giardano A, Desai D, et al: Formation and activation of a cyclin E-cdk2 complex during the G_1 phase of the human cell cycle. *Science* 257:1689–1694, 1992.
21. Akiyama T, Ohuchi T, Sumida S, et al: Phosphorylation of the retinoblastoma protein by cdk2. *Proc Natl Acad Sci USA* 89:7900–7904, 1992.
22. Bell RM, Burns DJ: Lipid activation of protein kinase C. *J Biol Chem* 266:4661–4664, 1991.
23. Lee H, Ghose-Dastidar J, Winawer S, Friedman E: Signal transduction through ERK-like pp57 blocked in differentiated cells having low PKCβ activity. *J Biol Chem* 268:5255–5263, 1993.
24. Goldfarb M: The fibroblast growth factor family. *Cell Growth Diff* 1:439–445, 1990.
25. Friedman E, Isaksson P, Rafter J, et al: Fecal diglycerides as selective endogenous mitogens for premalignant and malignant human colonic epithelial cells. *Cancer Res* 49:544–548, 1989.
26. Morotomi M, Guillem JG, LoGerfo P, et al: Production of diacylglycerol, an activator of protein kinase C, by human intestinal microflora. *Cancer Res* 50:3595–3599, 1990.
27. Sandgren EP, Luetteke NC, Palmiter RD, et al: Overexpression of TGFα in transgenic mice: Induction of epithelial hyperplasia, pancreatic metaplasia, and carcinoma of the breast. *Cell* 61:1121–1135, 1990.
28. Coffey RJ, Goustin AS, Soderquist AM, et al: Transforming growth factor α and β expression in human colon cancer lines: Implications for an autocrine model. *Cancer Res* 47:4590–4594, 1987.
29. Peles E, Bacus SS, Koski RA, et al: Isolation of the Neu/HER-2 stimulatory ligand: A 44 kd glycoprotein that induces differentiation of mammary tumor cells. *Cell* 69:205–216, 1992.

30. Ciardiello F, Kim N, Saeki T, et al: Differential expression of epidermal growth factor-related proteins in human colorectal tumors. *Proc Natl Acad Sci USA* 88:7792–7796, 1991.
31. Stoker M, Perryman M: An epithelial scatter factor released by embryo fibroblasts. *J Cell Sci* 77:209–213, 1985.
32. Tsarfaty I, Resau JH, Vande Woude GF: The *met* proto-oncogene receptor and lumen formation. *Science* 257:1258–1261, 1992.
33. Culouscou J-M, Shoyab M: Purification of a colon cancer cell growth inhibitor and its identification as an insulin-like growth factor binding protein. *Cancer Res* 51:2813–2819, 1991.

CHAPTER 16

Immunology

Kenneth O. Lloyd

Important advances have recently been made in the immunology of colorectal cancer. Although the possibility of the immune surveillance of cancer by the immune system remains controversial, considerable progress has been made in analyzing the antigenicity of tumors, including colorectal cancer, and in utilizing their altered antigenic makeup as targets for antibody-directed diagnosis and therapy and for active immunization. Carcinoembryonic antigen (CEA), which, along with alphafetoprotein, was one of the first cancer-associated antigens to be recognized,[1] remains as a focus for some of these studies. The development of hybridoma technology for the production of monoclonal antibodies (mAbs) led to the development of more suitable anti-CEA antibodies and to the demonstration of a large number of other carcinoma-associated antigens. In colorectal cancer, this approach led to the recognition of the role played by blood group–related antigens as tumor markers and the discovery of a number of novel epithelium-specific and mucin antigens. Although none of these mAbs are completely tumor-specific, many of them have characteristics that make them suitable for use in clinical studies (Table 16-1). Their properties and uses are summarized in this chapter.

BLOOD GROUP ANTIGENS

Two major blood group systems show alterations in colorectal cancer and other carcinomas that result in changes in antigenicity. These are the A, B, O, and Lewis and the T, Tn, and sialylTn families. Both these systems are based on carbohydrate epitopes. The A, B, O, and Lewis determinants are carried on glycoproteins, mucins, and glycolipids, whereas the T, Tn, and sialylTn epitopes are carried exclusively by mucins. The former specificities consist of 3 to 6 sugar residues at the nonreducing end of sugar chains, which in turn are linked as a variety of core structures. The latter specificities are short sugar chains linked directly to the serine or threonine residues in the peptide backbone of mucins.

The A, B, O, and Lewis determinants are a group of interrelated specificities that are biosynthesized from common precursors. These determinants are formed mainly on basic structures termed type 1 and type 2 sugar chains; the former have Galβ1→3GlcNAc sequences and the latter Galβ1→4GlcNAc sequences. More recently, repetitive (type 3) and globo (type 4) structures have been described. The addition of other sugar residues (L-fucose and *N*-acetylneuraminic acid) by specific glycosyltransferases produces the final blood group structure. The blood group type of an individual is genetically determined and is controlled by the array of glycosyltransferases expressed in that person. Blood group antigens are therefore polymorphic alloantigens. The specific structures representing this family are shown in Table 16-2, and their genetic and biosynthetic interrelationships are shown in Fig. 16-1.

Although A, B, O, and Lewis antigens were originally discovered as erythrocyte antigens, it is their occurrence on epithelial tissues and their secretions that make them of interest as carcinoma antigens. The expression of these antigens in epithelial tissues is tissue-specific. Moreover, the pattern of expression in tissues is further complicated by another regulatory mechanism involving the secretor gene. The activity of this gene determines whether or not blood group expression in secretions and some epithelial tissues is the same as or different from the expression on red cells. In brief, most individuals (secretors) have the same blood group expression in both locations, whereas Le^a-positive individuals (nonsecretors) have tissues and secretions that lack the A, B, or O (H) expression of their red cells and synthesize Le^a and Le^x antigens instead.

The pattern of expression of A, B, O, and Lewis antigens in tissues is therefore determined by a complex interaction of genetic and tissue-specific factors. In malignancy, these interactions become disrupted, leading to aberrant expression of these antigens in car-

Table 16-1
Possible Uses of Monoclonal Antibodies in Colorectal Cancer

Immunohistology	Differentiation of tumor from normal or benign tissues
	Differentiation of carcinomas from nonepithelial tumors
	Classification of tumors
Serum assays	Sensitive assays for the diagnosis and monitoring of cancer
Tumor localization	Radiolabeled antibody in the immunoscintigraphic detection of tumors
Therapy	Unconjugated antibodies with suitable effector functions
	Drug-antibody conjugates
	Toxin-antibody conjugates
	Bifunctional antibodies to activate and target cytotoxic antibodies to tumors

cinomas. These changes can serve as targets for antibody-directed diagnosis and therapy and may even serve as targets for active immunotherapy. The range of altered blood group expression that can occur in carcinomas is summarized in Table 16-3. Many of these factors were recognized by the development of mouse monoclonal antibodies to human cancer cells. This is particularly true of the sialyl-Le^a, sialyl-Le^x, and $Lewis^y$ determinants, which had previously been detected by chemical isolation but whose significance as tumor antigens had not been appreciated. Sialyl-Le^a was demonstrated to be the antigen detected by a mouse monoclonal antibody (1116-NS-19-9) raised against a colon cancer cell line.[2] It was found to be present in cells either as a glycolipid or a glycoprotein[3] and in serum as a mucin.[4] A double-determinant assay based on this mAb detects elevated levels of sialyl-Le^a in the serum of colorectal cancer patients.[5,6] Sialyl-Le^x was also detected by a mouse mAb (CSLEX) and was found to have enhanced expression in certain carcinomas and elevated serum levels in these patients.[7]

Numerous mouse mAbs raised to tumors have been shown to detect Le^y antigen, and this antigen remains a subject of many ongoing studies. The normal tissue expression of Le^y antigen in the gastrointestinal tract ranges from strong expression in the stomach[8] to minimal expression in the distal colon.[9] Since the majority of colorectal cancers express high levels of Le^y, this antigen is highly tumor-restricted when only this location is considered. The expression of Le^y in normal tissues is dependent on secretor status, and the expression of Le^y in the tumors of nonsecretor individuals is even more tumor-specific.[9,10] Another factor that contributes to the usefulness of Le^y and other blood group antigens as targets for mAb-directed diagnosis and therapy is the difference in cellular localization of the antigens in normal and malignant tissues. In normal tissues, blood group antigens occur mainly in secretions or on the apical side of epithelial tissues, whereas in tumors the distribution is more inter- and intracellular within the tumor tissue, thus providing better access to mAb. Another factor to be considered in using anticarbohydrate mAb in clinical studies, which is exemplified by the Le^y systems, is their tendency to cross-react with closely related antigens. Thus, many anti-Le^y mAbs cross-react with Le^x or H type 2 structures,[11] and careful screening is necessary to select a suitable mAb. This factor is particularly important in the use of anti-Le^y mAbs, as erythrocytes express H antigen and granulocytes express Le^x antigen, thus precluding the use of such cross-reacting mAbs in patients. Among anti-Le^y mAbs that have been extensively studied are F-3,[11] C14,[12] AH6,[13] B1 and B3,[14] BR55-2,[15] and BR64 and BR96.[16] mAb F-3 was found to react with the majority of colorectal carcinomas,[11] whereas mAbs B1 and B3 react mainly with mucinous tumors.[16] mAb BR96 has been shown to internalize after reacting with tumor cells, thus making it an attractive candidate for targeting drugs and other agents to tumors.[17] Although anti-Le^y mAbs are not entirely specific for tumors, the characteristics of this antigen system make it one of the most attractive blood group antigen targets for further studies. Furthermore, it has been claimed that extended Le^y determinants with internal fucosylation (trifucosyl Le^y) have an even more tumor-restricted distribution.[13]

The second blood group antigen system that has achieved prominence in colorectal cancer is the mucin-borne family consisting of T, Tn, and sialyl-Tn. As shown in Fig. 16-2 these carbohydrate structures are shorter forms of the normal tetrasaccharide structure. Although the exact mechanism has not been elucidated, it appears that the synthesis of these structures is incomplete in malignant epithelia (leading to T and Tn expression) or is prematurely terminated by sialylation on the GalNAc residue (leading to sialyl-Tn expression). The most widely studied mAb detecting these antigens is B72-3 (and a related "second-generation" mAb CC49) generated by Schlom and coworkers.[18] These mAbs had been available for some time before their anti-sialyl-Tn specificity was demonstrated.[19] The significance of T and Tn as carcinoma antigens was first pointed out by Springer and coworkers[20] in the 1970s. MAbs and lectins detecting T and Tn antigens are also available, but they have not been as extensively studied. This family of antigens appears to be minimally expressed in normal colonic mucosa, moderately or highly expressed (often in a heterogeneous distribution) in colorectal cancer, and, interestingly, highly expressed in transitional mucosa.[21] Sialyl-Tn expression has been shown to be inversely correlated with survival in colon cancer pa-

Table 16-2
Structures of Blood Group Determinants and Their Sialosylated Derivatives

	Structure	*Specificity*
Type 1		
	Galβ1 → 3GlcNAcβ1 → 3 Gal-	Precursor (LNT)
	Galβ1 → 3GlcNAcβ1 → 3Gal- 3 ↑ NeuAcα2	Sialyl-LNT
	Galβ1 → 3GlcNAcβ1 → 3Gal- 2 ↑ Fucα1	H-type 1
	Galβ1 → 3GlcNAcβ1 → 3Gal- 4 ↑ Fucα1	Le^{a}
	Galβ1 → 3GlcNAcβ1 → 3Gal- 3 4 ↑ ↑ NeuAcα2 Fucα1	Sialyl-Le^{a}
	Galβ1 → 3GlcNAcβ1 → 3Gal- 2 4 ↑ ↑ Fucα1 Fucα1	Le^{b}
	GalNAcα1 → 3Galβ1 → 3GlcNAcβ1 → 3Gal- 2 ↑ Fucα1	A monofucosyl type 1
	GalNAcαa1 → 3Galβ1 → 3GlcNAcβ1 → 3Gal- 2 4 ↑ ↑ Fucα1 Fucα1	ALe^{b}
	Galα1 → 3Galβ1 → 3GlcNAcβ1 → 3Gal- 2 ↑ Fucα1	B monofucosyl type 1
	Galα1 → 3Galβ1 → 3GlcNAcβ1 → 3Gal- 2 4 ↑ ↑ Fucα1 Fucα1	BLe^{b}
Type 2		
	Galβ1 → 4GlcNAcβ1 → 3 Gal-	Precursor (LNneoT)
	Galβ1 → 4GlcNAcβ1 → 3 Gal- 3 ↑ NeuAcα2	Sialyl-LNneoT
	Galβ1 → 4GlcNAcβ1 → 3Gal- 2 ↑ Fucα1	H-type 2
	Galβ1 → 4GlcNAcβ1 → 3Gal- 3 ↑ Fucα1	X(Le^{x})
	Galβ1 → 4GlcNAcβ1 → 3Gal- 3 3 ↑ ↑ NeuAcα2 Fucα1	Sialyl-Le^{x}
	Galβ1 → 4GlcNAcβ1 → 3Gal- 2 3 ↑ ↑ Fucαa1 Fucα1	Y(Le^{y})

(*Continued on page 168*)

Table 16-2 (*Continued*) Structures of Blood Group Determinants and Their Sialosylated Derivatives

Structure	*Specificity*
GalNAcα1 → 3Galβ1 → 4GlcNAcβ1 → 3Gal- 2 ↑ Fucα1	A monofucosyl type 2
GalNAcα1 → 3Galβ1 → 4GlcNAcβ1 → 3Gal- 2 3 ↑ ↑ Fucα1 Fucα1	ALe^y
Galα1 → 3Galβ1 → 4GlcNAcβ1 → 3Gal- 2 ↑ Fucα1	B monofucosyl type 2
Galα1 → 3Galβ1 → 4GlcNAcβ1 → 3Gal- 2 3 ↑ ↑ Fucα1 Fucα1	BLe^y
Galβ1 → 4GlcNAcβ1 → 3Galβ1 → 4GlcNAc- 3 3 ↑ ↑ Fucα1 Fucα1	Polyfucosyl-Le^x
Galβ1 → 4GlcNAcβ1 → 3Galβ1 → 4GlcNAc- 3/6 3 ↑ ↑ NeuAcα2 Fucα1	Sialy-Le^x isomer
Galβ1 → 4GlcNAcβ1 → 3Galβ1 → 4GlcNAc- 3 3 3 ↑ ↑ ↑ NeuAcα2 Fucα1 Fucα1	Sialyl-polyfucosyl-Le^x
Type 3	
Galβ1 → 3GalNAcα1 → 3Galβ1 → 4GlcNAcβ1 → 3Gal- 2 2 ↑ ↑ Fucα1 Fucα1	H-type 3
GalNAcα1 → 3Galβ1 → 3GalNAcα1 → 3Galβ1 → 4GlcNAcβ1 → 3 Gal- 2 2 ↑ ↑ Fucα1 Fucα1	A-type 3
Type 4	
Galβ1 → 3GalNAcβ1 → 3Galα1 → 4Gal- 2 ↑ Fucα1	Globo-H
GalNAcα1 → 3Galβ1 → 3GalNAcβ1 → 3Galα1 → 4Gal- 2 ↑ Fucα1	Globo-A

tients.[22] This study concluded that tumor ploidy and sialyl-Tn expression were the two variables of most importance for predicting both disease-free and overall survival in these patients.

Anti-sialylTn mAbs have been entered into clinical trials in colorectal and other cancers.[23,24] In one such study, ^{131}I-labeled B72-3 was shown to selectively localize to primary and metastatic colorectal lesions. Ratios of mAb uptake in tumor/normal tissue ranged from 3:1 to 40:1 in 70 percent of the patients.[25] Recent research efforts on this antibody include the generation of mouse/human chimeric forms[26] and the construction of a single-chain (Fv) form of mAb CC49.[27] The rationale for the use of chimeric mAbs is that they will induce a lower and less frequent human anti-mouse Ig (HAMA) response in patients, thus extending the time period over which they can be used. Fv single-chain antibodies are designed for greater tumor penetration by virtue of their smaller size and for better tumor/normal tissue ratios because of their more rapid clearance from the circulation.

Another line of investigation on T, Tn, and sialyl-Tn antigens is in their potential use as tumor vaccines. The rationale for the use of these antigens in active therapy lies in their restricted distribution in normal tissues and, more importantly, their known immunogenicity in humans. Experimental evidence for the efficacy of this approach has been generated in mouse-

TYPE 1 STRUCTURES

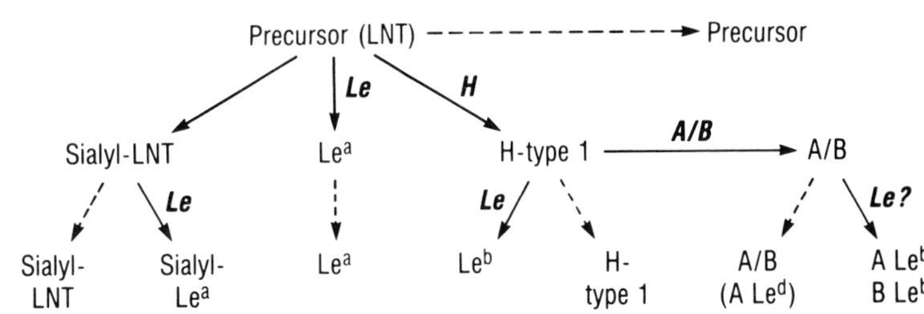

TYPE 2 STRUCTURES

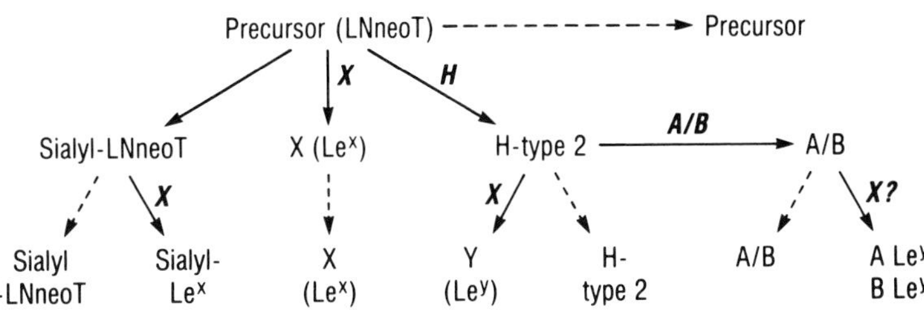

FIG. 16-1. Biosynthetic pathways and genetic interrelationships of A, B, H, Lewis, and related blood group specificities. The genes coding for the glycosyltransferases responsible for the various structures are shown in italics. Dashed arrows indicate absence of a gene, resulting in the expression of the simpler structure as the final specificity.

model systems. Thus, Longnecker and coworkers[28] and Singhal and coworkers[29] have shown that T- and Tn-containing vaccines, respectively, can protect mice against the TA3-Ha murine mammary adenocarcinoma. Human trials have also been initiated. In a study using a synthetic sialyl-Tn protein conjugate, MacLean et al.[30] showed the development of both IgM and IgG anti-sialyl Tn antibodies in breast cancer patients. In a related trial, Livingston and coworkers[31] immunized colon cancer patients with the same conjugate and found antibodies capable of reacting with the immunizing antigen but not with natural mucins. The same group also immunized colorectal cancer patients with partially desialylated ovine submaxillary mucin, or OSM (a rich source of sTn and epitopes). The modified OSM was not immunogenic when given without adjuvant, whereas 5 of 6 patients immunized

Table 16-3
Alterations in Blood Group Antigens Found in Carcinomas

Neosynthesis
Incompatible expression of A antigen in tumors of O or B individuals
Increased sialylation on type 1 and type 2 chains—sialyl Le^a, sialyl Le^x, and polymeric Le^x
Increased fucosylation on type 1 and type 2 chains—Le^b, Le^y, and extended Le^y
Elongation of type 2 chains—i antigen
Inappropriate expression of Le^b and Le^y in tumors of nonsecretor individuals
Expression of sialyl-Tn antigen
Incomplete synthesis
Deletion of A or B antigen in tumors of A or B individuals
Expression of T and Tn antigens
Other factors
Antigen density on cell surface
Antigen accessibility on cell surface
Distribution of antigen within cells and tissues

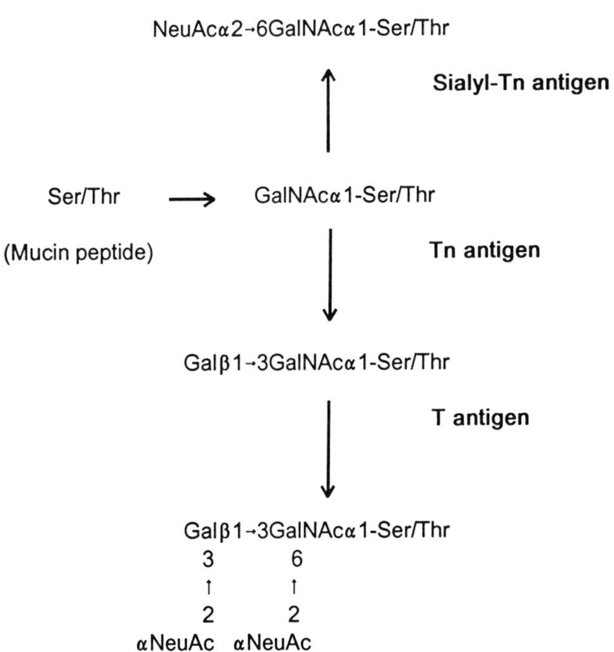

FIG. 16-2. Biosynthetic pathways leading to T, Tn, and sialyl-Tn antigens. In tumors, the conversion of the T-antigen structure to the mature disialylated tetrasaccharide is completely or partially blocked.

with the antigen and BCG responded with increased antibody titers.[32] The antibody response was mainly of the IgM class, but low-level IgG titers were observed in some patients. Future studies in this area will emphasize the use of carbohydrate-protein conjugates (to induce T-cell help and better IgG responses) and improved adjuvants suitable for use in humans.

MUCIN (PEPTIDE) ANTIGENS

Mucins are very high molecular weight glycoproteins of high viscosity and gel-forming properties. They are characterized by the high serine and threonine content of their peptide moiety and the linkage of sugar chains of varying lengths and structures to these amino acids through α-*N*-acetylgalactosaminyl linkages (O-linked chains). The carbohydrate content of mucins is typically greater than 50 percent; in intestinal mucins, the sugar chains may be sialylated or sulfated.

Although the importance of carbohydrate determinants on mucins as tumor-associated antigens has been recognized for some time, the possibility that the peptide moiety of mucins could serve a similar role has only been realized more recently. A key event in this field was the molecular cloning of the cDNA coding for the peptide sequence of a mucin known as polymorphic epithelial mucin (PEM), episialin, and other names.[33] This approach showed that the peptide backbone of this mucin consisted of multiple repeats of a unit coding for 20 amino acids, termed the MUC-1 sequence. Moreover, it was shown that many anti-PEM antibodies were capable of reacting with unglycosylated peptides derived from this sequence. Further studies localized the epitope to a short peptide sequence centered around PDTR (proline-aspartic acid-threonine-arginine).[34] The selective reactivity of some anti-PEM antibodies with epithelial cancers has been postulated to be due to differences in the degree or nature of glycosylation in tumor mucins, resulting in increased exposure of the peptide moiety.

Following this seminal finding, peptide sequences for other mucins have now been elucidated—specifically, pertinent to this chapter, on the two sequences (MUC-2 and -3) identified in intestinal mucins by Kim and coworkers.[35,36] As shown in Table 16-4, these are also tandemly repeated peptide sequences with 23 and 17 amino acids, respectively. These peptide cores are significantly richer in threonine and serine than MUC-1. These residues represent the possibility for a high level of glycosylation in the native mucins. Both these genes are expressed in the normal intestine and colon and in colorectal cancer. It is not known whether the peptide sequences are relatively exposed in tumor mucin, as appears to be the case with PEM; however, antibodies to the MUC-2 tandem repeat react strongly with colonic tumors, indicating that this may be the case.[37,38] The tandem repeat section of MUC-2 was found to be linked to a C-terminal stretch of about 157 amino acids not containing repeat units. The *N*-terminal region was also found to contain a nonrepetitive sequence. Recently the sequence of the region's C-terminal to the tandem repeat unit has been completely elucidated.[39] This region contains some potential *N*-glycosylation sites and, more significantly, numerous cysteine residues. This latter finding is important in terms of the total secondary and tertiary structure of mucins. Of the various models suggested for the structure of mucins, the one suggested by Carlstedt et al.[40] is usually accepted. In this model, the basic structure of a mucin consists of one long peptide chain which has several highly glycosylated tandem repeat regions with intervening, less-glycosylated "naked" sequences. These long chains are postulated to be linked through disulfide bonds to form long, coiled, thread-like structures capable of forming gels. The demonstration of a cysteine-rich region in MUC-2 provides support for this model, although the total structure still needs to be determined.

Despite these recent advances in the field, numerous questions remain concerning the structure, synthesis, and tissue distribution of mucins and their possible alterations in malignancy. Specifically in intestinal tissues, the number of different mucins synthesized remains to be determined, although present data indicate at least four different species (i.e., MUC-1, -2, -3, and 4). Expression of these gene products is differentially regulated in different parts of the gastrointestinal tract.[13] Various alterations in expression, including aberrant or increased synthesis, occur in malignancy. These data were derived from gene cloning

Table 16-4
Tandem Repeat Units Found in Peptide Core of Mucins and mAbs Detecting These Sequences

Designation	*Sequence*	*mAbs*
MUC-1	PDTRPAPGSTAPPAHGVTSA[a]	HMFG-1 and -2, SM3, and others[57]
MUC-2	PTTTPITTTTVTPTPTPTGTQT	LDQ10[37] and CP-31, -37, and -58[38]
MUC-3	HSTPSFTSSITTTETTS	None known

[a]Single-letter code for amino acids: P, proline; D, aspartic acid; T, threonine; R, arginine; A, alanine; G, glycine; S, serine; H, histidine; V, valine; I, isoleucine; Q, glutamine; E, glutamic acid.

approaches and need to be tied in with earlier biochemical data demonstrating two major classes of intestinal mucins—a neutral mucin (rich in fucose) and an acidic mucin (sialylated or sulfated). Another important point remaining to be elucidated is the nature of the glycan substituent on the different mucins. The picture seems to be quite complex, with the possibility that the same carbohydrate structure may be borne by different mucins. For example, Baeckström et al.[41] showed that although the Le^a determinant is carried on two different mucins in COLO205 cells (termed H-CanAg and L-CanAg), sialylLe^a is found only on H-CanAg.

In addition to serving their normal functions (presumably as protective agents and biological lubricants and possibly in cell-cell interactions) and as targets for tumor-directed monoclonal antibodies, it has been postulated that mucins play important roles in determining the metastatic behavior of tumor cells. Evidence has been presented for the role of sialylLe^a and sialylLe^x in the adhesion of tumor cells to activated endothelium.[42] Moreover, it has been claimed that the expression of sialyl dimeric Le^x (as detected by mAb FH6) is inversely correlated with survival in patients with colonic carcinoma.[43]

The peptide portion of mucins may also be involved in immune responses to carcinomas. Both humoral and cellular responses to MUC-1 mucin peptide epitopes have been detected. Finn and coworkers[44] derived cytotoxic T-cell cultures from pancreatic cancer patients—cultures that were capable of lysing many carcinoma cell lines in a non-HLA restricted manner. The susceptible cell lines were shown to be mucin-expressing, and antibodies to mucin peptide epitopes could block the cytotoxicity.[45] Other workers showed that mucin peptide epitopes can also induce antibody responses, as indicated by the isolation of EBV-transformed B-cell lines derived from an ovarian cancer patient that recognized the MUC-1 peptide sequence.[46] These findings suggest the possible use of synthetic peptides for the active immunization of cancer patients.

CARCINOEMBRYONIC ANTIGEN (CEA)

Since its initial discovery by Gold and Freedman,[1] using rabbit antisera, in 1965, CEA has received wide attention as a tumor antigen and marker, particularly in colorectal cancer. This oncofetal antigen is a highly glycosylated protein of 180,000 Da with a protein core of 702 amino acids (72,800 Da). Its carbohydrate component is characteristic of a typical *N*-linked glycoprotein rather than a mucin. CEA is anchored in the plasma membrane by glycosylphosphatidylinositol linkages,[47] and it belongs to the immunoglobulin superfamily of molecules having seven highly conserved Ig loop domains.[48,49] It has been proposed that CEA serves as an intercellular adhesion molecule and may have a role to play in normal epithelial tissue architecture in malignant tissues.[50] A number of CEA-related antigens have been detected, and it is now clear that CEA is but one of a family of related molecules. Nonspecific cross-reacting antigen (NCA) was identified as a normal tissue component that interfered with the determination of CEA in serum and normal tissues. Different forms of NCA have been identified and even CEA may exist in tissue-specific variants.

Following the development of commercial assays for serum levels of CEA, this antigen has become a widely used marker for colonic cancer. Its most important clinical use is in the surveillance of patients in the postoperative phase.[51] CEA Is also an important target in antibody-directed diagnosis and therapy using mouse mAbs.[52] Despite the presence of high levels of CEA in the serum of colonic cancer patients, anti-CEA antibodies localize well to tumors. A number of mouse mAbs to CEA have been developed that show preferential tumor localization. Bivalent [$F(ab')_2$] and monovalent (Fab′ and Fab) fragments are preferred in these studies because they target to tumor and clear blood and other tissues more rapidly, thus reducing background activity. In a recent study, Sharkey et al.[53] evaluated the use of an intact anti-CEA mouse antibody (MN-14) which had a tenfold higher affinity than most previously tested mAbs. They concluded that the antibody targeted tumors very effectively, even in the presence of elevated circulating CEA.

Radioimmunotherapy with anti-CEA antibodies has, as yet, met with only limited success. The limiting factor seems to be the difficulty of delivering adequate doses of radioactivity to the tumor for a sufficient duration of time. With anti-CEA, tumor doses achieved have usually been less than 2000 cGy, whereas more than 5000 cGy may be required for clinical responses.[54] Despite these limitations, a number of trials have demonstrated promising results and further progress can be anticipated in the future. Other approaches that are being pursued for the therapeutic uses of these mAbs include the use of unconjugated antibodies with biological effector functions or the ability to induce inflammation in tumors and the use of drug or toxin conjugates.[55] The limitation of the use of mouse mAb in patients due to a HAMA response is being overcome by the development of less immunogenic "chimeric" or "humanized" antibody using molecular engineering techniques.[56]

OTHER COLORECTAL CANCER ANTIGENS

Epithelial Surface Antigen (ESA)

The immunization of mice with a number of different epithelial cancers has resulted in the production of a large number of mAbs detecting the same adenocarcinoma-associated antigen.[57] This antigen is a cell-surface glycoprotein of about 38,000 Da which is uniformly expressed in the majority of adenocarcinomas and in many normal epithelial tissues also. Biochemical studies have shown that the 38-kDa form of ESA is proteolytically cleaved to 32- and 6-kDa species, which remain linked by disulfide bonds in some cell types.[58] Recently full-length cDNA clones coding for this antigen have been isolated by a number of investigators.[59,60] A second related gene (GA733-1), showing 49 percent homology, to the first gene (GA733-2 or KS 1/4) has also been identified.[61] Both gene products are typical type 1 membrane glycoproteins with three or four *N*-glycosylation sites. Although its biological function has not been firmly established, ESA has been postulated to be involved in adhesion.

Despite the expression of ESA in many normal epithelial tissues, anti-ESA antibodies have been used extensively in clinical trials. Two mAbs have received considerable attention: 17-1A and KS 1/4. Clinical studies with mAb 17-1A have emphasized the use of unconjugated antibody. Overall response rates were 19 percent in one study in advanced colon cancer, although only 2 percent complete responses were noted.[62] The mechanism of tumor destruction in these trials is unclear, although direct tumor cell killing and antibody-dependent cellular cytotoxic (ADCC) effects are possible. The induction of an anti-idiotype response may be an alternate mechanism. On the assumption that ADCC is important, Mellstedt and coworkers[63] have recently carried out a clinical trial in colorectal cancer patients using a combination of mAb 17-1A and granulocyte-macrophage colony-stimulating factor (GM-CSF). Of the 20 patients studied, 2 achieved complete remissions and 3 other patients had stable disease. This result encourages further studies with this approach. Clinical studies with mAb KS1/4 have used drug-antibody conjugates.[64] A phase I study on a methotrexate conjugate tested the antibody in a small number of lung cancer patients.

ESA has also been the target in an alternate approach to cancer therapy—the use of anti-idiotype antibodies as vaccines. The rationale for this method is that anti-idiotype antibodies bear the internal image of the antigen, thus mimicking antigen. In a clinical trial using goat anti-CO17-1A, 6 of 30 patients had a partial remission and 7 patients showed regression of metastases.[65]

A33 Antigen

Monoclonal antibody A33 was developed following immunization of mice with a colorectal cancer cell line.[66] It detects an antigen that is restricted in its expression to normal colon epithelium and colonic carcinoma. Although the antigen has not been precisely characterized, the epitope recognized is heat-stable, protease- and neuraminidase-resistant, and periodate-sensitive and is carried on a high-molecular-weight glycoprotein. It appears to be unrelated to blood group antigens or other antigens known to be expressed on colon cancer. A phase I study has evaluated the biodistribution and imaging characteristics of ^{131}I-labeled mAb A33 in a series of 20 patients with metastatic colon cancer. The antibody demonstrated outstanding localization properties. One week after antibody administration, tumor-to-liver ratios ranged from 6.9:1 to 100:1 and tumor serum ratios from 4.1:1 to 25.2:1. Successful imaging in whole-body scans was observed in most of the patients. In general, the clarity of the images correlated with tumor-to-serum ratios and to a lesser degree with tumor-to-liver ratios. Therapeutic trials using ^{125}I-conjugated mAb A33 are under way.

Table 16-5
Additional Mouse Monoclonal Antibodies Detecting Colorectal Carcinoma Antigens

MAb	*Antigen*	*Reference*
F4/2E10	No data	67
3NM and 17NM	Mucin ?	68
CO-029	32-kDa glycoprotein	69
GA 22-2	180-kDa glycoprotein	69
91.9H	Sulfomucin	70
D612	48-kDa glycoprotein	71
M43	Mucin	72
ND4	160-kDa glycoprotein	73

Other Antigens

A large number of other mouse mAbs detecting colon cancer–associated antigens have been developed over the last 18 years. Apart from the ones discussed earlier in this chapter, none of them have, as yet, reached clinical trials. In recent studies, the motive for generating new mAbs has been to generate mAbs detecting novel antigens, i.e., unrelated to blood group antigens, CEA, ESA, and other well-known carcinoma antigens and to develop mAbs to antigens carried by poorly differentiated non-CEA-producing colorectal tumors. Some of these mAbs are summarized in Table 16-5. After further study, a number of these antibodies may take their place alongside the well-recognized, clinically useful reagents discussed above.

REFERENCES

1. Gold P, Freedman SO: Demonstration of tumor specific antigens in human colonic carcinomata by immunological tolerance and absorption techniques. *J Exp Med* 121:439–462, 1965.
2. Koprowski H, Steplewski Z, Mitchell K, et al: Colorectal carcinoma antigens detected by hybridoma antibodies. *Somatic Cell Mol Genet* 5:957–972, 1979.

3. Magnani JL, Nilsson B, Brockhaus M, et al: A monoclonal antibody-defined antigen associated with gastrointestinal cancer is a ganglioside containing sialylated lacto-*N*-fucopentose. *J Biol Chem* 257:14365–14369, 1982.
4. Magnani JL, Steplewski Z, Koprowski H, et al: The gastrointestinal and pancreatic cancer-associated antigen detected by monoclonal antibody 19-9 in the sera of patients is a mucin. *Cancer Res* 43:5489–5492, 1983.
5. Ritts RE, Del Villano BC, Go VLW, et al: Initial clinical evaluation of an immunoradiometric assay for CA 19-9 using the NCl serum bank. *Int J Cancer* 33:339–345, 1984.
6. Koprowski H, Herlyn D, Steplewski Z, et al: Specific antigen in serum of patients with colon carcinoma. *Science* 212:53–55, 1981.
7. Fukushima K, Hirota M, Terasaki PI, et al: Characterization of sialosylated Lewis^x as a new tumor-associated antigen. *Cancer Res* 44:5279–5285, 1984.
8. Sakamoto J, Watanabe T, Tokumaru T, et al: Expression of Lewis^a, Lewis^b, Lewis^x, Lewis^y, sialyl-Lewis^a, and sialyl-Lewis^x blood group antigens in human gastric carcinoma and in normal gastric tissue. *Cancer Res* 49:745–752, 1989.
9. Sakamoto J, Furukawa K, Cordon-Cardo C, et al: Expression of Lewis A, Lewis B, X, Y blood group antigens in human colonic tumors and normal tissue in human tumor-derived cell lines. *Cancer Res* 46:1553–1561, 1986.
10. Lloyd KO: Philip Levine award lecture: Blood group antigens as markers for normal differentiation and malignant change in human tissues. *Am J Clin Pathol* 87:129–139, 1987.
11. Furukawa K, Welt S, Yin BWT, et al: Analysis of the fine specificities of 11 mouse monoclonal antibodies reactive with type 2 blood group determinants. *Mol Immunol* 27:723–732, 1990.
12. Brown A, Ellis LO, Embleton MJ, et al: Immunohistochemical localization of Y hapten and the structurally related H type-2 blood-group antigen on large-bowel tumours and normal adult tissues. *Int J Cancer* 33:727–736, 1984.
13. Kim YS, Yuan M, Itzkowitz SH, et al: Expression of LeY and extended LeY blood group-related antigens in human malignant, premalignant, and nonmalignant colonic tissues. *Cancer Res* 46:5985–5992, 1986.
14. Pastan I, Lovelace ET, Gallo MG, et al: Characterization of monoclonal antibodies B1 and B3 that react with mucinous adenocarcinomas. *Cancer Res* 51:3781–3787, 1991.
15. Blaszczyk-Thurin M, Thurin J, Hindsgaul O, et al: Blood group B type 2 glycolipid antigens accumulate in a human gastric carcinoma cell line as detected by monoclonal antibody. *J Biol Chem* 262:372–379, 1987.
16. Hellstrom I, Garrigues HJ, Garrigues U, et al: Highly tumor-reactive, internalizing, mouse monoclonal antibodies to Lewis y-related case surface antigens. *Cancer Res* 50:2183–2190, 1990.
17. Garrigues J, Garrigues U, Hellström I, et al: Le^y specific antibody with potent anti-tumor activity is internalized and degraded in lysosomes. *Am J Pathol* 142:607–622, 1993.
18. Nuti M, Teramoto YA, Mariani-Constantini R, et al: A monoclonal antibody (B72.3) defines patterns of distribution of a novel tumor-associated antigen in human mammary carcinoma cell populations. *Int J Cancer* 29:539–545, 1982.
19. Gold DM, Mattes MJ: Monoclonal antibody B72.3 reacts with a core region structure of O-linked carbohydrates. *Tumour Biol* 9:137–144, 1988.
20. Springer GF: T and Tn, general carcinoma autoantigens. *Science* 224:1198–1206, 1984.
21. Xu M, Real FX, Welt S, et al: Expression of TAG-72 in normal colon, transitional mucosa, and colon cancer. *Int J Cancer* 44:985–989, 1989.
22. Itzkowitz SH, Bloom EJ, Kokal WA, et al: A novel mucin antigen associated with prognosis in colorectal cancer patients. *Cancer* 66:1960–1966, 1990.
23. Schlom J: Basic principles and applications of monoclonal antibodies in the management of carcinomas: The Richard and Hinda Rosenthal Foundation Award Lecture. *Cancer Res* 46:3225–3238, 1986.
24. Cohen AM, Martin EW, Lavery I, et al: Radioimmunoguided surgery using iodine 125 B72.3 in patients with colorectal cancer. *Arch Surg* 126:349–352, 1991.
25. Colcher D, Esteban JM, Carrasquillo JA, et al: Quantitative analysis of selective radiolabeled monoclonal antibody localization in metastatic lesions of colorectal cancer patients. *Cancer Res* 47:1185–1189, 1987.
26. Hutzell P, Kashmiri S, Colcher D, et al: Generation and characterization of a recombinant/chimeric B72.3 (human lambda 1). *Cancer Res* 51:181–189, 1991.
27. Milenic DE, Yokota T, Filpula DR, et al: Construction, binding properties, metabolism, and tumor targeting of a single-chain Fv derived from the pancarcinoma monoclonal antibody CC49. *Cancer Res* 51:6363–6371, 1991.
28. Fung PYS, Madej M, Koganty RR, et al: Active specific immunotherapy of a murine mammary adenocarcinoma using a synthetic tumor-associated glycoconjugate. *Cancer Res* 50: 4308–4314, 1990.
29. Singhal A, Fohn M, Hakomori S: Induction of alpha-*N*-acetylgalactosamine-O-serine/threonine (Tn) antigen-mediated cellular immune response for active immunotherapy in mice. *Cancer Res* 51:1406–1411, 1991.
30. MacLean GD, Reddish M, Koganty RR, et al: Immunization of breast cancer patients using a synthetic sialyl-Tn glycoconjugate plus Detox adjuvant. *Cancer Immunol Immunother* 36:215–222, 1993.
31. Adluri M, Calves AD, Livingston PO: Immunogenicity of TF and sTn-KLH conjugates in colorectal carcinoma patients, in *Specific Immunotherapy of Cancer with Vaccines*. New York Academy Science Conference, Washington, DC, January 21–24, 1993, PII-20, abstracts.
32. O'Boyle KP, Zamore R, Adluri S, et al: Immunization of colorectal cancer patients with modified ovine submaxillary gland mucin and adjuvants induces IgM and IgG antibodies to sialylated Tn. *Cancer Res* 52:5663–5667, 1992.
33. Gendler S, Taylor-Papadimitriou J, Duhig T, et al: A highly immunogenic region of a human polymorphic epithelial mucin expressed by carcinomas is made up of tandem repeats. *J Biol Chem* 263:12820–12823, 1988.
34. Burchell J, Taylor-Papadimitriou J, Boshell M, et al: A short sequence, within the amino acid tandem repeat of a cancer-associated mucin, contains immunodominant epitopes. *Int J Cancer* 44:691–696, 1989.
35. Gum JR, Byrd JC, Hicks JW, et al: Molecular cloning of human intestinal mucin cDNAs: Sequence analysis and evidence for genetic polymorphism. *J Biol Chem* 264:6480–6487, 1989.
36. Gum JR, Hicks JW, Swallow DM, et al: Molecular cloning of cDNAs derived from a novel human intestinal mucin gene. *Biochem Biophys Res Commun* 171:407–415, 1990.
37. Gambús G, Bolós C, Andrew D, et al: Detection of the MUC2 apomucin tandem repeat with a mouse monoclonal antibody. *Gastroenterology* 104:93–102, 1993.
38. Xing P-X, Prenzoska J, Layton GT, et al: Second-generation monoclonal antibodies to intestinal MUC2 peptide reactive with colon cancer. *J Natl Cancer Inst* 84:699–703, 1992.
39. Gum JR Jr, Hicks JW, Toribara NW, et al: The human *MUC2* intestinal mucin has cysteine-rich subdomains located both upstream and downstream of its central repetitive region. *J Biol Chem* 267:21375–21383, 1992.

40. Carlstedt I, Sheenan J, Cornfeld AP, et al: Mucus glycoproteins: A gel of a problem. *Essays Biochem* 20:40–76, 1985.
41. Baeckström D, Hansson GC, Nilsson O, et al: Purification and characterization of a membrane-bound and a secreted mucin-type glycoprotein carrying the carcinoma associated sialyl-Le^a epitope on distinct core proteins. *J Biol Chem* 266:21537–21547, 1991.
42. Takada A, Ohmori K, Yoneda T, et al: Contribution of carbohydrate antigens sialyl Lewis A and sialyl Lewis X to adhesion of human cancer cells to vascular endothelium. *Cancer Res* 53:354–361, 1993.
43. Irimura T, Matsushita Y, Hoff SD, et al: Ectopic expression of mucins in colorectal cancer metastasis. *Cancer Biol* 2:129–139, 1991.
44. Barnd DL, Lan MS, Metzgar RS, et al: Specific, major histocompatibility complex-unrestricted recognition of tumor-associated mucins by human cytotoxic T cells. *Proc Natl Acad Sci USA* 86:7159–7163, 1989.
45. Jerome KR, Barnd DL, Bendt KM, et al: Cytotoxic T-lymphocytes derived from patients with breast adenocarcinoma recognize an epitope present on the protein core of a mucin molecule preferentially expressed by malignant cells. *Cancer Res* 51:2908–2916, 1991.
46. Rughetti A, Turchi V, Ghetti CA, et al: Human B-cell immune response to the polymorphic epithelial mucin. *Cancer Res* 53:2457–2459, 1993.
47. Hefta SA, Hefta LJF, Lee TD, et al: Carcinoembryonic antigen is anchored to membranes by covalent attachment to a glycosylphosphatidylinositol moiety: Identification of the ethanolamine linkage site. *Proc Natl Acad Sci USA* 85:4648–4652, 1988.
48. Thompson JA, Pande H, Paxton RJ, et al: Molecular cloning of a gene belonging to the carcinoembryonic antigen gene family and discussion of a domain model. *Proc Natl Acad Sci USA* 84:2965–2969, 1987.
49. Zimmermann W, Ortlieb B, Friedrich R, et al: Isolation and characterization of cDNA clones encoding the human carcinoembryonic antigen reveal a highly conserved repeating structure. *Proc Natl Acad Sci USA* 84:2960–2964, 1987.
50. Benchimol S, Fuks A, Jothy S, et al: Carcinoembryonic antigen, a human tumor marker, functions as an intercellular adhesion molecule. *Cell* 57:327–334, 1989.
51. Bates SE: Clinical applications of serum tumor markers. *Ann Intern Med* 115:623–638, 1991.
52. Goldenberg DM, Blumenthal RD, Sharkey RM: Biological and clinical perspectives of cancer imaging and therapy with radiolabeled antibodies. *Semin Cancer Biol* 1:217–225, 1990.
53. Sharkey RM, Goldenberg DM, Murthy S, et al: Clinical evaluation of tumor targeting with a high-affinity, anticarcinoembryonic-antigen-specific, murine monoclonal antibody, MN-14. *Cancer* 71:2082–2096, 1993.
54. Siegel JA, Pawlyk DA, Lee RE, et al: Tumor, red marrow, and organ dosimetry for 131I-labeled anti-carcinoembryonic antigen monoclonal antibody. *Cancer Res* 50:1039–1042, 1990.
55. Goldenberg DM: Monoclonal antibodies in cancer detection and therapy. *Am J Med* 94:297–312, 1993.
56. Waldmann TA: Monoclonal antibodies in diagnosis and therapy. *Science* 252:1657–1662, 1991.
57. Lloyd KO: Molecular characteristics of tumor antigens. *Immunol Allergy Clin North Am* 10:765–779, 1990.
58. Thampoe IJ, Ng JSC, Lloyd KO: Biochemical analysis of a human epithelial surface antigen: Differential cell expression and processing. *Arch Biochem Biophys* 267:342–352, 1988.
59. Szala S, Froehlich M, Scollon M, et al: Molecular cloning of cDNA for the carcinoma-associated antigen GA733-2. *Proc Natl Acad Sci USA* 87:3542–3546, 1990.
60. Strnad J, Hamilton AE, Beavers LS, et al: Molecular cloning and characterization of a human adenocarcinoma/epithelial cell surface antigen complementary DNA. *Cancer Res* 49: 314–317, 1989.
61. Linnenbach AJ, Seng BA, Wu S, et al: Retroposition in a family of carcinoma-associated antigen genes. *Mol Cell Biol* 13: 1507–1515, 1993.
62. Mellstedt H, Frödin J-E, Masucci G, et al: The therapeutic use of monoclonal antibodies in colorectal carcinoma. *Semin Oncol* 18:462–477, 1991.
63. Raghnhammar P, Fagerberg J, Frödin J-E, et al: Effects of monoclonal antibody 17-1A and GM-CSF in patients with advanced colorectal carcinoma—Long-lasting, complete remissions can be induced. *Int J Cancer* 53:751–758, 1993.
64. Elias DJ, Hirschowitz L, Kline LE, et al: Phase I clinical comparative study of monoclonal antibody KS1/4 and KS1/4-methotrexate immunoconjugate in patients with non-small cell lung carcinoma. *Cancer Res* 50:4154–4159, 1990.
65. Herlyn D, Wettendorff M, Schmoll E, et al: Anti-idiotype immunization of cancer patients: Modulation of the immune response. *Proc Natl Acad Sci USA* 84:8055–8059, 1987.
66. Welt S, Divgi CR, Real FX, et al: Quantitative analysis of antibody localization in human metastatic colon cancer: A phase I study of monoclonal antibody A33. *J Clin Oncol* 8:1894–1906, 1990.
67. Drewinki B, Yang LY, Chan J, et al: New monoclonal antibodies against colon cancer-associated antigens. *Cancer Res* 46:5137–5143, 1986.
68. Hughes NR, Walls RS, Newland RC, et al: Antigen expression in normal and neoplastic colonic mucosa: Three tissue-specific antigens using monoclonal antibodies to isolated colonic glands. *Cancer Res* 46:2164–2171, 1986.
69. Sela B-A, Steplewski Z, Koprowski H: Colon carcinoma-associated glycoproteins recognized by monoclonal antibodies CO-029 and GA22-2. *Hybridoma* 8:481–491, 1989.
70. Irimura T, Wynn DM, Hager LG, et al: Human colonic sulfomucin identified by a specific monoclonal antibody. *Cancer Res* 51:5728–5735, 1991.
71. Fernsten PD, Primus FJ, Greiner JW, et al: Characterization of the colorectal carcinoma-associated antigen defined by monoclonal antibody D612. *Cancer Res* 51:926–934, 1991.
72. Goodgame R, Kiefe C, Rose E, et al: Clinical evaluation of M43: A novel cancer-associated mucin epitope. *Cancer Res* 53:2803–2809, 1993.
73. Salem RR, Wolf BC, Sears HF, et al: A cell surface glycoprotein expressed by colorectal carcinomas including poorly differentiated, noncarcinoembryonic antigen-producing colorectal tumors. *Cancer Res* 48:7257–7263, 1988.

CHAPTER 17

Biological Determinants of Invasion and Metastasis

Isaiah J. Fidler

HIGHLIGHTS

The major cause of death from colonic and rectal carcinomas is metastasis that is resistant to conventional therapies. By the time of diagnosis, and certainly in clinically advanced lesions, malignant neoplasms contain multiple cell populations exhibiting a wide range of biological characteristics, such as cell surface structures, growth rate, sensitivity to various cytotoxic drugs, and the ability to further invade and metastasize. Metastasis is a highly selective process that is regulated by a large number of interdependent mechanisms. Metastatic cells can usurp host homeostatic mechanisms so as to survive and grow preferentially in particular organ environments. The view that cancer metastasis is a selective process stimulates efforts to elucidate its regulatory mechanisms. From the knowledge gained, better approaches to the therapy of human colorectal cancer should emerge.

CONTROVERSIES

Is the metastatic phenotype under the regulation of a single gene or multiple genes? If multiple, are they independent or interrelated? Which tumor cell property or event in the metastatic process is amenable to therapeutic intervention? What mechanisms are responsible for the generation of biological diversity in neoplasms? What does the host contribute to the pathogenesis of metastasis? Are the models used now relevant to the clinical situation? How important is the evidence that malignant human tumors implanted into nude mice produce metastases only from orthotopic sites and not from ectopic sites? What is the contribution of the specific organ microenvironment to the growth and spread of cancer cells?

The cure of metastasis requires the destruction of all tumor cells. Anything short of that can produce only long-term remission. For example, after the eradication of 99.9 percent of a 1-cm^3 tumor, 10^6 cells remain to undergo rapid proliferation and diversification. Moreover, if a particular systemic therapy killed most but not all cells in a heterogeneous tumor cell population, the formation of new tumor cell variants might be enhanced.

FUTURE DIRECTIONS

Understanding the mechanisms responsible for the process of cancer metastasis, for the origin of metastases, and for the development of biological heterogeneity in metastases must be a primary goal of cancer research. Only from this new understanding will come improvements in the design (and thus in the effectiveness) of therapy for malignant disease and in the way physicians deal with cancer metastasis.

The major cause of death from colonic and rectal carcinoma is metastasis that is resistant to conventional therapies. In a large number of patients with colonic and rectal cancers, metastasis has occurred by the time of diagnosis. The metastases can be located in more than one organ and in different discrete anatomic regions of the same organs, thus complicating their treatment. Furthermore, the specific organ environment can modify the response of tumor cells to systemic therapy and hence alter the effects of anticancer drugs.[1]

Before diagnosis, tumors in internal organs may grow to 1 cm^3 (1 g) and consist of approximately 10^9 cells. Assuming that a colonic carcinoma has developed from the proliferation of a single transformed cell,[2,3] it must have doubled about 30 times to attain this size. When a neoplasm weighs 1 kg (believed to be the maximum tumor burden compatible with life), it contains 10^{12} cells. Although impressive, the increase from 1 g to 1 kg takes only 10 doublings. Therefore, at diagnosis, malignant cancers are relatively far advanced in their natural history. The period over which this growth occurs depends on the doubling time of the cancer; but on average, human neoplasms are thought to double every 2 months. Rapidly growing lesions such as testicular cancer may double every month, while more slowly growing tumors such as prostate cancer may take a year or longer to double in size.[1]

The major barrier to the treatment of metastases is the biological heterogeneity of cancer cells in primary and secondary neoplasms. This heterogeneity is exhibited in a wide range of genetic, biochemical, immunologic, and biologic characteristics, such as cell-surface receptors, enzymes, karyotypes, cell morphologies, growth properties, sensitivities to various therapeutic agents, and ability to invade and produce metastasis.[2,3] Exacerbating the problems of treating metastatic disease is the fact that tumor cells in different metastases (intralesional heterogeneity) and in some instances even different zones within an individual metastatic tumor (interlesional heterogeneity) may respond differently to treatment. Although numerous promising anticancer drugs and biological agents have been developed, their effectiveness is still hindered by the presence and accumulation of resistant cells within tumors. The emergence of treatment-resistant tumor cells is due to the heterogeneous nature of malignant neoplasms, and tumor cell resistance to current therapeutic modalities is the single most important reason for the lack of success in treating many types of solid neoplasms.[3]

THE PATHOGENESIS OF METASTASIS

The process of cancer metastasis consists of a series of sequential steps, each of which can be rate-limiting (Fig. 17-1). After the initial transforming event, either unicellular or multicellular, growth of neoplastic cells must be progressive. Extensive vascularization must occur if a tumor mass is to exceed 2 mm in diameter.[4] Local invasion of the host stroma by some tumor cells can occur by several mechanisms that are not mutually exclusive.[5] For example, lymphatic channels or thin-walled venules offer little resistance to penetration by tumor cells and provide the most common pathways for tumor cell entry into the circulation. Although early clinical observations have suggested that carcinomas frequently metastasize via the lymphatic system whereas malignant tumors of mesenchymal origin

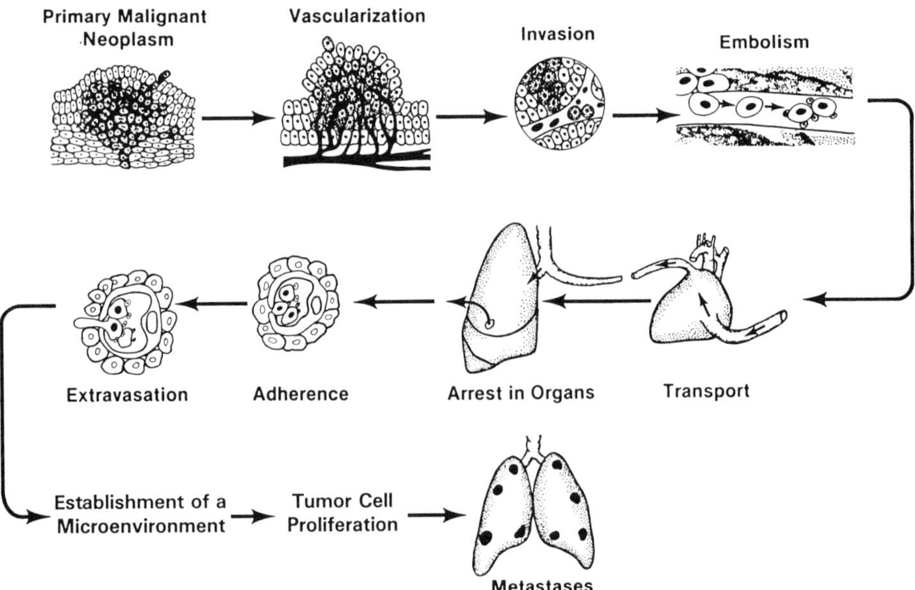

FIG. 17-1. The pathogenesis of cancer metastasis. The process of cancer metastasis consists of sequential, interlinked, and selective steps. The outcome of each step is influenced by the interaction of metastatic cells with homeostatic mechanisms. If a cell fails to complete any of the steps, it is eliminated; hence, the formation of clinically relevant metastases represents the survival and growth of unique subpopulations of cells that preexist in primary neoplasms.

more often spread by the hematogenous route, the presence of numerous venolymphatic anastomoses argues against this belief.[6] Detachment and embolization of small tumor cell aggregates occurs next, and the few tumor cells that survive the circulation must arrest in the capillary beds of organs, using various adhesion molecules.[7] Extravasation occurs next, probably by the same mechanisms that influence initial invasion, and proliferation within the organ parenchyma completes the metastatic process. To produce clinically detectable lesions, the metastases must develop a vascular network, evade the host immune system, and respond to organ-specific factors that influence their growth.[8] Once they do so, the cells can invade host stroma, penetrate blood vessels, and enter the circulation to produce further metastasis, the so-called metastasis of metastases.[1,2]

Only a few cells in a primary tumor can give rise to a metastasis. This is due in part to the elimination of tumor cells that fail to complete any one step in the pathogenesis of secondary tumors. For example, the presence of tumor cells in the circulation does not predict that metastasis will occur, because most tumor cells that enter the bloodstream die rapidly.[9] Using radiolabeled B16 melanoma cells, I observed that by 24 h after entry into the circulation, <1 percent of the cells were still viable, and that <0.01 percent of circulating tumor cells survived to produce metastases. These original observations raised the question of whether the development of metastases represents the chance survival and growth of very few tumor cells or the selective growth of unique subpopulations of malignant cells endowed with special properties. Stated differently, can all cells growing in a primary neoplasm produce metastases, or do only specific and unique cells possess metastatic properties that enable them to metastasize? Most recent data show that neoplasms are biologically heterogeneous and that the process of metastasis is selective.

METASTATIC HETEROGENEITY

Populations of cells that differ from the parent neoplasm in metastatic capacity can be isolated, thus supporting the hypothesis that not all the cells in a primary tumor can successfully disseminate. Two general approaches have been used. In the first, metastatic cells are selected in vivo: tumor cells are implanted into mice and metastatic lesions are harvested. The cells that are recovered can be expanded in culture or used immediately to repeat the process. The cycle is repeated several times, and the behavior of the cycled cells is compared with that of the cells of the parent tumor. This procedure was originally used in my laboratory to isolate the B16-F10 line from the B16 melanoma syngeneic to the C57BL/6 mouse.[10] It has also been successfully used to produce tumor cell lines with increased metastatic capacity from many other experimental tumors. In the second approach, cells are selected for the enhanced expression of a phenotype believed to be important in one or another step of the metastatic sequence, and then they are tested in the appropriate host to determine whether concomitant metastatic potential has been increased or decreased.

The first experimental proof for metastatic heterogeneity in neoplasms was provided by Margaret Kripke and me in 1977 in work with the mouse B16 melanoma.[11] Using the modified fluctuation assay of Luria and Delbruck,[12] we showed that different tumor cell clones, each derived from individual cells isolated from the parent tumor, varied dramatically in their ability to form pulmonary nodules following intravenous inoculation into syngeneic mice. Control subcloning procedures demonstrated that the observed diversity was not a consequence of the cloning procedure.[11] To exclude the possibility that the metastatic heterogeneity found in the B16 melanoma might have been introduced as a result of lengthy cultivation, we studied the biologic and metastatic heterogeneity in a mouse melanoma induced in C_3H mice by chronic exposure to ultraviolet B radiation and painting with croton oil. One mouse thus treated developed a melanoma designated K-1735. The original K-1735 melanoma was established in culture and immediately cloned.[13] The clones differed greatly from each other and from the parent tumor in their ability to produce lung metastases. Moreover, the metastases demonstrated significant variability in their size and pigmentation. Metastases to the lymph nodes, brain, heart, liver, and skin were found in addition to lung metastases; those growing in the brain were uniformly melanotic, whereas those growing in other organs generally were not.

THE SEED-AND-SOIL HYPOTHESIS

Clinical observations of cancer patients have led to the conclusion that certain tumors produce metastasis to specific organs independent of vascular anatomy, rate of blood flow, and number of tumor cells delivered to each organ. The distribution and fate of hematogenously disseminated, radiolabeled melanoma cells in experimental rodent systems amply demonstrate that tumor cells reach the microvasculature of many organs. Extravasation into the organ parenchyma and proliferation of tumor cells occur only in some organs. Therefore, the mere presence of viable tumor cells in a particular organ does not always predict that the cells will proliferate to produce metastases.[9]

The search for the mechanisms that regulate the pattern of metastasis began more than a century ago when, in 1889, Stephen Paget[14] questioned whether the distribution of metastases was due to chance. Paget therefore analyzed 735 autopsy records of women as well as hundreds of records of patients with breast cancer. The nonrandom pattern of visceral metastases suggested to Paget that the process was not due to chance but, rather, that certain tumor cells (the "seed") had a specific affinity for the milieu of certain organs (the "soil"). Metastases resulted only when the seed and soil were matched.

In 1929, Ewing[15] challenged Paget's seed-and-soil theory and hypothesized that metastatic dissemination occurs by purely mechanical factors that are a result of the anatomical structure of the vascular system. These explanations have been evoked separately or together to explain the secondary-site preference of certain types of neoplasms. In a review of clinical studies on secondary-site preferences of malignant neoplasms, Sugarbaker[16] concluded that common *regional* metastatic involvements could be attributed to anatomical or mechanical considerations, such as efferent venous circulation or lymphatic drainage to regional lymph nodes, but that *distant* organ colonization by metastatic cells from numerous types of cancers established their own patterns of site specificity.

Experimental data supporting the seed-and-soil hypothesis were derived from studies on the preferential invasion and growth of B16 melanoma metastases in specific organs.[17] The B16 melanoma cells were injected into the circulation of syngeneic mice. Tumor growths developed in the lungs and in fragments of pulmonary or ovarian tissue implanted intramuscularly. In contrast, metastatic lesions did not develop in renal tissue implanted as a control or at the site of surgical trauma. This study confirmed that sites of metastasis are determined not solely by the characteristics of the neoplastic cells but also by the microenvironment of the host tissue. In vitro experiments demonstrating organ-selective adhesion, invasion, and growth also support Paget's hypothesis. With the B16 melanoma system, cells with increased capacity for organ adhesion, invasion, and growth have been isolated. Moreover, experiments with organ tissue–derived soluble growth factors indicate that soil factors can have profound effects on certain tumor cell subpopulations.[1]

There is no question that the circulatory anatomy influences the dissemination of many malignant cells; however, it cannot, as Ewing proposed,[15] fully explain the patterns of distribution of numerous tumors. Ethical considerations rule out the experimental analysis of cancer metastasis in patients as studied in laboratory animals. The introduction of peritoneovenous shunts for palliation of malignant ascites has, however, provided an opportunity to study some of the factors affecting metastatic spread in humans. The autopsy findings in 15 patients substantiated the clinical observations that the shunts do not significantly increase the risk of visceral organ metastasis. In fact, despite continuous entry of hundreds of millions of tumor cells into the circulation, metastases in the lung (the first capillary bed encountered) were rare.[18] These results provide compelling verification of the seed-and-soil hypothesis.

MODELS FOR HUMAN COLONIC CANCER METASTASIS

The concept that neoplasms are heterogeneous and contain subpopulations of cells with different biological behavior patterns, including metastatic potentials, is no longer controversial. Studies in most rodent tumor systems have also demonstrated that metastasis is a selective process,[10,19,20] that metastases can have a clonal origin,[21] that metastases can develop from the expansion of a single cell,[22] and that the host organ microenvironment can profoundly influence the growth of metastatic tumor cells. Although most data on the metastatic heterogeneity of neoplasms and on host-tumor cell interactions during the metastatic process have been derived from studies in nonhuman systems, data are now accumulating about the biology of metastasis by cells isolated from surgical specimens of human cancers. In large measure, this has been due to improvements in the use of in vivo models for the isolation of metastatic subpopulations of human cancer cells and for testing of their metastatic potential. The discovery of the athymic nude mouse and its adaptation for the study of human cancer growth and metastasis[23] has facilitated the study of many aspects of the biology of human cancer. Reports on the metastatic ability of human tumors subsequent to implantation into nude mice have concluded that it is influenced by variations in experimental techniques.[24] Data from my laboratory show that the capacity to produce metastasis from human tumor cell lines of long duration[25] or recent origin[26,27] depends on both the injection site and on the intrinsic properties of the cells.

A correct model for studies of human cancer metastasis must meet two rigid demands: it must use metastatic cells (seed) growing in the relevant organ environment (soil). To study the properties of metastatic subpopulations from surgical specimens of human cancers, methods for their isolation, propagation, and testing had to be developed. Here, I shall summarize our experience with the isolation and propagation of human colorectal carcinoma (HCC) and discuss the evidence that orthotopic implantation (implantation into anatomically relevant organs of nude mice) is mandatory for accurate assessment of metastatic potential of HCC cells.

HUMAN COLONIC CARCINOMA XENOGRAFTED INTO NUDE MICE

Since the first successful transplantation of a human tumor into a nude mouse,[28] transplantation of colorectal tumors into these animals has been reported by many investigators. Xenografts of colonic tumors in nude mice have been produced either directly from surgical specimens or from cell lines established in culture.[29–33] Before the nude mouse can be used as a relevant model for studies of the biology and therapy of human tumors, it is necessary to ascertain that the tumors maintain their biological characteristics. The histologic parameters of HCCs propagated in nude mice have been reported to resemble those of the tumors of origin.[29–31] We analyzed 30 HCCs subsequent to their growth in nude mice and found a high degree of identity with the human tumor of origin, although occasionally a higher or lower degree of differentiation was found. Morphologic characteristics were maintained after several passages in the nude mouse at different sites of tumor growth and in the metastatic lesions.[29,30] Moreover, the degree of tumor necrosis and the capacity to produce cell products such as mucin were maintained in the transplanted tumors.

The use of polymorphic enzymes allows for the determination of the human origin of tumors proliferating in nude mice.[34] Isoenzyme mobility patterns, which have been considered the most reliable identification of individual tumors, have been shown to be stable even after several passages of tumor cells in nude mice. For instance, tissue-specific isoenzymes maintained stable expression within an individual colonic carcinoma line, although their pattern of expression in some cases differed between lines of different origin. We analyzed six polymorphic enzymes in HCC cells recovered from a total of 30 primary tumors and metastases growing in nude mice; without exception, all the tumors were of human origin.[29,30]

TUMORIGENICITY OF HUMAN COLONIC CANCER CELLS ISOLATED FROM SURGICAL SPECIMENS

In initial studies, we determined whether the growth pattern in nude mouse could distinguish between HCC with low malignant potential (Dukes stage B) and HCC with high malignant potential (Dukes stage D). We transplanted 15 primary HCC and 11 hepatic metastases into the subcutaneous space of nude mice (Fig. 17-1). Continuously growing tumors developed in 53 percent of the mice injected with primary-derived HCCs and 75 percent of the mice injected with cells isolated from hepatic metastases. We did not find significant correlations between the Dukes stage classification of the original neoplasms and tumorigenicity in nude mice. However, even from the first passage, tumor lines derived from metastases grew faster than those derived from primary tumors. In the second serial passage, an increased rate of tumor take (in subcutaneous space) and a decrease in latency time were observed, changes that have been described before[35,36] and could well have been due to host-selection pressures.[23] Nonetheless, the differences in doubling time observed between primary HCC (median doubling time, 7.5 days; range, 5.0 to 8.0 days) and hepatic metastases (median doubling time, 4.0 days; range, 3.5 to 5.0 days) were maintained even on further passages.

Serum levels of carcinoembryonic antigen (CEA) that exceeds 5 ng/mL are associated with a poor prognosis in patients with adenocarcinoma of the colon or rectum and often indicate the presence of visceral metastases. Moreover, in patients with disease limited to the bowel wall or regional lymph nodes, the prognosis is worse when the CEA level is elevated.[37] We examined whether HCC from patients with a preoperative serum CEA level that exceeded 5 ng/mL would be more tumorigenic in nude mice than HCC of patients who had <5 ng/mL CEA. The tumorigenicity of cells from metastases was not significantly greater than that of cells from primary neoplasms. When primary HCC and metastases were considered together, tumors from patients whose preoperative serum CEA exceeded 5 ng/mL were significantly more tumorigenic in nude mice than tumors isolated from patients with normal levels of CEA ($p<.005$; 8.24 by the chi-square test). Furthermore, tumorigenicity did not correlate with standard prognostic factors such as histologic parameters or stage of disease, nor did serum concentration of CEA correlate with the size of the primary tumor in nude mice.[38]

ORTHOTOPIC VERSUS ECTOPIC IMPLANTATION OF HUMAN COLONIC CANCER AND METASTATIC BEHAVIOR IN NUDE MICE

For many years it had been accepted that human tumors did not metastasize in the nude mouse regardless of their malignant potential in patients, thus casting doubt on the validity of this model for studies of the biology of human tumors. More recent reports clearly establish that the production of metastasis depends both on the intrinsic tumor cell properties and on the host response, the experimental technique, and the origin, health, and maintenance of the nude mouse.[23] The importance of the health of the recipient mouse for the success of such studies cannot be overemphasized. Nude mice infected by a pathogenic virus (e.g., mouse hepatitis virus) can resist xenografted tumors and hence metastasis formation. Nude mice must be housed under specific pathogen-free conditions and the injected tumor cells free of pathogenic murine viruses and *Mycoplasma* infections.[23]

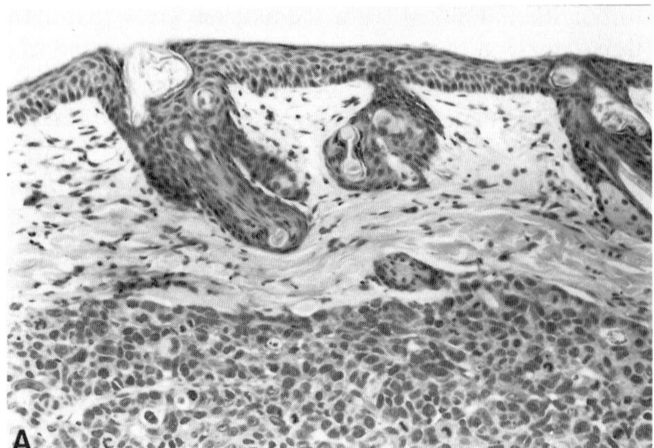

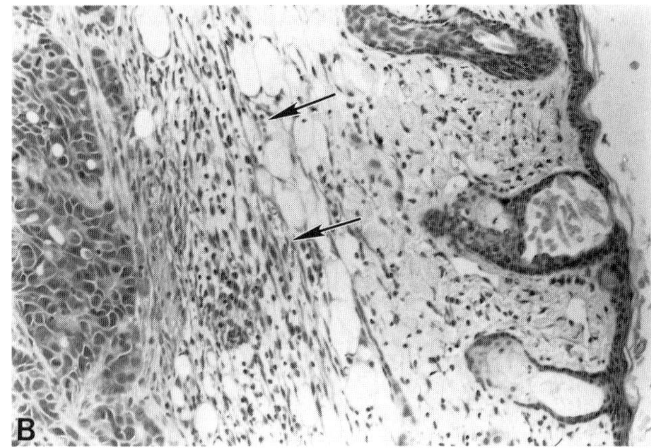

FIG. 17-2. Implantation of HCC into the subcutis of nude mice (ectopic environment). HCC cells produce progressively growing tumors in the subcutaneous space of nude mice (*A*). The tumors can be surrounded by a pseudocapsule (arrows, *B*). The subcutaneous tumors do not produce lymph node or visceral organ metastasis.

Most HCCs studied in nude mice have been implanted into the subcutis, a site that is readily accessible to experimental manipulation but does not correspond with the anatomic origin of the tumor. To determine whether the site of implantation into nude mice influenced the ability of HCC cells to metastasize, we studied eight different HCCs. Four tumor lines were derived from primary HCCs, three from hepatic metastases, and one from a mesenteric lymph node metastasis. All the inoculi consisted of single-cell suspensions obtained by enzymatic dissociation of solid tumors. Tumor cells were injected into multiple sites: the subcutis (Fig. 17-2), the muscle, the venous system, and the spleen (Fig. 17-3).[29,30] In the course of these experiments, we examined by autopsy approximately 600 mice in which HCC had been growing at different sites. Subcutaneous injection, although successful in initiating local tumor growth, yielded metastases to the lung in only one mouse. Histological examination revealed tumor growth in lymph nodes draining the injection site in only 10 mice.[29,30]

In some reports of experimental tumor systems in rodents, multiple metastases developed subsequent to surgical removal of a local tumor. Similarly, the incidence of lung metastases was shown to increase with the prolonged survival of nude mice that had locally recurrent HCC at the site of injection-resection.[39] To examine this possibility, we injected HCC cells into the quadricep femoris of 40 nude mice and amputated the leg when the tumor reached 2 cm. Although most of the mice developed recurrent tumors at the surgical site, metastases were found in the lungs of only two mice, even though all mice survived for 6 months after the initial tumor cell injection. Here again, neither cells from primary HCC nor cells from metastases produced metastasis in nude mice subsequent to subcu-

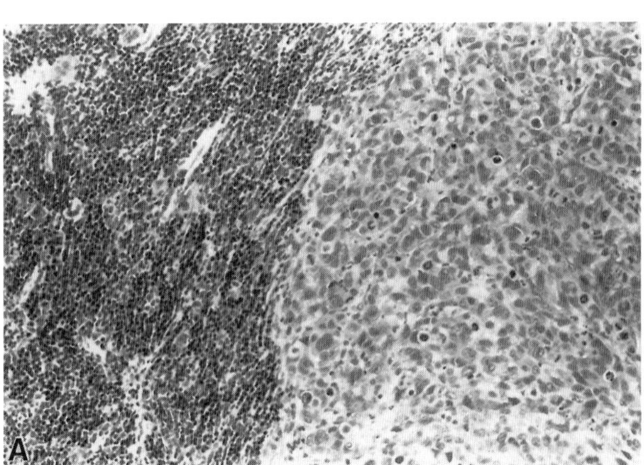

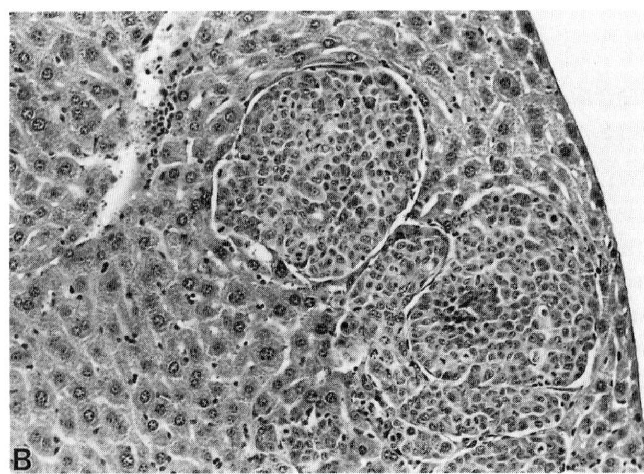

FIG. 17-3. Implantation of HCC cells into the spleen of nude mice and production of hepatic lesions. HCC cells produce large tumors in the spleen of nude mice regardless of their Dukes stage classification (*A*). HCC cells isolated from tumors with high metastatic potential produce liver lesions (*B*) subsequent to intrasplenic administration.

taneous or intramuscular implantation. When the HCC cells were administered intravenously, no correlation was found between the experimental lung metastases and the Dukes stage classification of the original neoplasms.[29]

A NUDE MOUSE MODEL FOR HEPATIC METASTASIS

Hepatic metastases account for many of the deaths from colorectal carcinoma. To develop a reproducible model of hepatic metastasis, we implanted tumor cells into the spleens of nude mice (Fig. 17-3).[29,30] From this site of injection, tumor cells gain access to the bloodstream and then reach the liver to proliferate into experimental hepatic metastases (Fig. 17-3).[40] We investigated the metastatic behavior of 11 human cell lines of different histologic origin and the production of lung and liver metastases in the nude mouse. The extent of metastasis depended on the nature of the tumor cells, with the most dramatic expression of malignancy found for two variants of the HT-29 HCC cell line subsequent to intrasplenic injection.[25] Merely implanting human tumor cells into the spleens of nude mice does not guarantee that metastasis to the liver will occur. I base this conclusion on the results showing that variant lines established from a surgical specimen of a human renal-cell carcinoma produced extensive lung metastasis if the cells were implanted into the kidneys of nude mice, whereas intrasplenic implantation of these cells produced only splenic tumors.[26]

The intrasplenic injection of HCC cells followed by the formation of hepatic lesions allowed us to distinguish HCC with different malignant potentials. Thirty days after the injection of tumor cells derived from two human liver metastases, the mice became moribund. At autopsy, their livers had been completely replaced by tumors. Mice injected with cells from primary HCC classified as Dukes stage B developed few visible tumor foci in the liver by 90 days after intrasplenic injection. Cells of one primary tumor classified as Dukes stage C produced visible liver tumors after 90 days in all the injected mice. The cells recovered from the liver tumors in the nude mice were of human origin (karyotype and isoenzyme analyses).

To further delineate the malignancy of tumors of different origin, we compared the behavior of HCC cells enzymatically dissociated from surgical specimens of one primary HCC (Dukes stage B2), one hepatic metastasis, and one mesenteric lymph node metastasis.[41,42] Intrasplenically injected cells isolated from a patient's liver metastasis produced a rapid growth of tumor cells in the livers of all the injected mice, whereas those derived from a primary colorectal carcinoma (Dukes stage B2) produced but a few liver tumor foci, and these after a longer period of time. The cells from a patient's lymph node metastasis failed to colonize in the liver. All cells produced spleen tumors. All three cell lines were serially passaged in nude mice, and we repeated the experiment at different passages. The three lines maintained their characteristic malignant behavior. The histologic parameters of the original tumors were maintained in the livers of the nude mice; human origin was ascertained by karyotype and isoenzyme analyses. The method of karyotype analysis of the original tumor cells directly established in culture and of the same tumor first grown in the nude mouse and then established in culture is discussed in detail below.[41,42]

CORRELATION BETWEEN HUMAN COLONIC CANCER BIOLOGICAL BEHAVIOR IN NUDE MICE AND CLINICAL OUTCOME

We began to study the ability of HCC to grow and produce metastasis in nude mice in 1984, long enough ago to be able to determine whether the production of experimental hepatic metastases in athymic nude mice by HCC correlated with the clinical outcome in patients. HCC cells from 82 patients were injected into groups of nude mice, either in the flank to assess tumorigenicity or into the spleen to produce experimental metastasis in the liver. Growth of HCC was recorded and compared with clinicopathologic factors and clinical outcome. Growth in either the flanks or the livers of nude mice was associated with the time to recurrence of the disease (postsurgery) in a Wilcoxon analysis. Analysis of the outcome data in a Cox proportional hazards model suggested that there was an interaction between tumorigenicity and metastatic potential of HCC in nude mice and serum CEA concentration in the patient and the stage of disease. A univariate analysis indicated that both tumorigenicity and metastatic potential of HCC in nude mice were significantly associated with the serum CEA concentration in the patient, but not with the other variables such as stage of disease, mucin production, local tissue invasion, or state of differentiation. A subset of 57 patients was surgically treated for cure and followed prospectively for up to 61 months. Tumorigenicity in nude mice and experimental metastatic potential were associated with disease recurrence in 23 of these patients, while 44 developed liver metastasis. Collectively, the ability of HCC cells isolated from surgical specimens to grow in athymic nude mice correlated with the development of advanced disease in patients.[38,43]

ISOLATION OF METASTATIC SUBPOPULATIONS OF CELL FROM PRIMARY NEOPLASMS

The isolation of populations of cells that differ from the parent neoplasm in metastatic capacity has supported the hypothesis that not all the cells in a primary tumor can successfully disseminate.[1] In this procedure, metastatic cells are selected in vivo: tumor cells are implanted into mice and metastatic lesions are harvested. The cells that are recovered can be expanded in culture or used immediately to repeat the process. The cycle is repeated several times and the behavior of the cycled cells is compared with that of the cells of the parent tumor. This procedure was originally used to isolate the B16-F10 line from the wild-type B16 melanoma.[10] It has also been successfully used to produce tumor cell lines with increased metastatic capacity from tumors growing in nude mice.[23]

We undertook a series of orthotopic implantation experiments to select and isolate cells with increased liver-metastasizing potential from heterogeneous primary HCCs. Cells derived from a surgical specimen of a primary HCC, classified as Dukes stage B2, were directly established in culture or were injected into the subcutis, spleen (for liver metastasis), or cecal wall of nude mice. Progressively growing tumors were excised, enzymatically dissociated, and established in culture. Subsequent to implantation into the cecal wall (Fig. 17-4) or spleen (Fig. 17-3) of nude mice, cells from all four lines produced only a few hepatic metastases. Then HCC cells from these rare liver metastases were recovered, expanded in culture, and injected into the spleen of nude mice, thus allowing further cycles of selection. With each successive in vivo selection cycle, the metastatic ability of the isolated-propagated cells increased. After four cycles of selection, we obtained cell lines with very high liver-colonizing efficiency in nude mice.[41,42] In parallel studies using another surgical specimen of a primary HCC classified as a Dukes stage D, we isolated cell lines that were highly metastatic in nude mice. However, successive selection cycles for growth in the liver only slightly increased metastatic properties.

The metastatic potential of the HCC cells in nude mice was determined by both experimental and spontaneous metastasis assays. The first involved the implantation of cells into the spleen for production of liver tumor colonies. The second assay measured the ability of HCC cells to produce lymph node and liver metastases subsequent to implantation into the wall of the cecum. In general, there was agreement on the results of the two assays; a cell line highly metastatic to the liver from intrasplenic implantation was also highly metastatic to the mesenteric lymph nodes and liver after intracecal injection.[41,42]

The classification of a HCC as a Dukes stage B tumor denotes that the lesion is confined to the wall of the colon without any evidence of metastasis. In contrast, a HCC classified as Dukes stage D tumor has

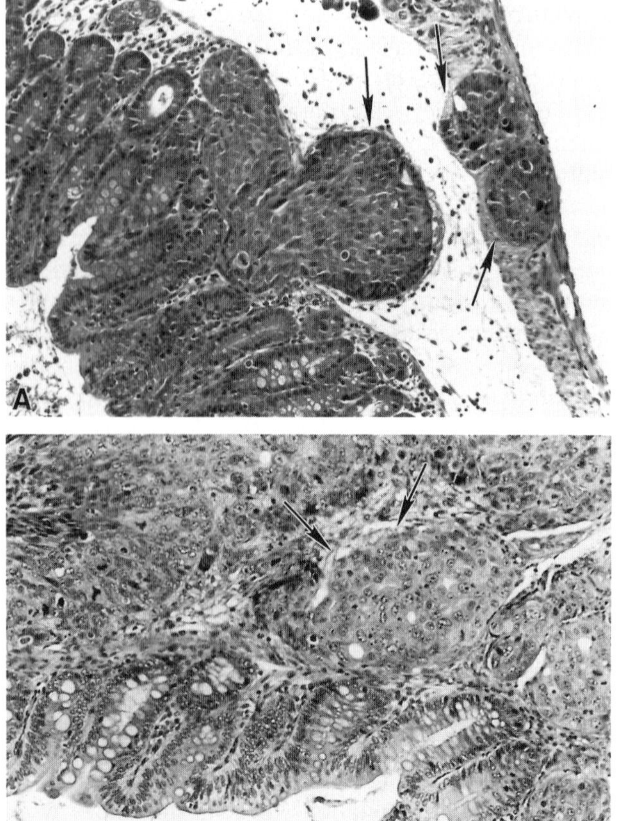

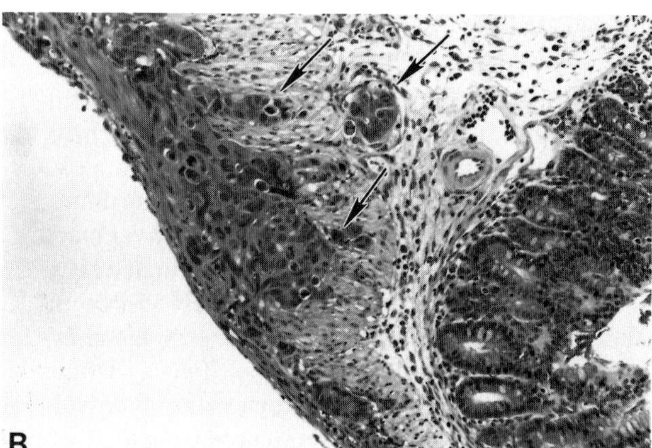

FIG. 17-4. Implantation of HCC cells into the wall of the cecum of the nude mice (orthotopic environment). HCC cells produce progressively growing tumors (arrows) in the cecal wall of nude mice. Note tumor cells invading lymphatics (*A*) or blood vessels (*B*). The HCC can destroy most normal tissue (*C*) and produce fatal obstructions.

produced obvious metastases in the lymph nodes and liver. In general, Dukes stage B tumors are likely to be an earlier manifestation of HCC than Dukes stage D tumors. In fact, clinical observations of various neoplasms have suggested that tumors tend to evolve with the passage of time. Furthermore, neoplasms that are first diagnosed as noninvasive-nonmetastatic can progress to become metastatic.[1] In the case of HCCs, it is entirely possible that, with time, an early Dukes stage B neoplasm can progress to become a Dukes stage D neoplasm. If such were the case, Dukes stage D tumors should contain a large number of metastatic cells, and our data support this assumption.

THE BIOLOGY OF LOCAL-REGIONAL RECURRENT COLONIC CARCINOMAS

Of all patients presenting with colorectal cancer, 70 percent will undergo a potentially curative resection of the localized tumor with no clinical evidence of remaining disease after the operation. Yet 30 to 50 percent of these patients will develop recurrent or metastatic disease, and in 40 percent of the patients the recurrence is limited to a single site. Local or regional recurrent disease may be due to tumor cells dislodged from the primary neoplasm, to cell aggregates in lymphatic vessels, or to micrometastases in the regional lymph nodes.[37] Appropriate animal models are mandatory to advance our understanding of the biological behavior and therapeutic aspects of recurrent and metastatic colorectal cancers. The models should fulfill two requirements. First, the tumor must grow in the colon and produce metastasis in the mesenteric and regional lymph nodes. Second, resection of the primary tumor must be followed by local and/or regional recurrence of the disease.[44]

We injected HCCs directly into the apical follicle of the cecum, which is closely connected to the lymphatic vessels draining into the regional lymph nodes. A high incidence of recurrent disease and lymph node metastasis in the experimental mice was found even when the cecum was resected as early as 10 min after cell injection. This was probably due to the direct and immediate introduction of cells into the lymphatic vessels, as evidenced by injection of latex beads and India ink particles.[44]

Several mechanisms may contribute to the development of recurrent colorectal cancer growth. Although inadequate resection of the primary tumor is an obvious cause, in our study the cecum was removed en bloc and no primary tumor could be found at the margins. Another possibility, the shedding of cells during surgery and subsequent implantation on the cut surface of the cecum, is also unlikely to be the case in our study, since the primary neoplasm (local tumor) was small and distant from the site of surgical resection. Moreover, recurrent disease was not found at any other location in the peritoneum except the surgical site. The last possibility, inadequate removal of tumor cells in lymph vessels, is supported by our data. Therefore, as it does in the clinical situation, recurrent disease originated from a new undetected tumor cells in the lymph system of the large bowel.

THE CONSEQUENCE OF TISSUE DAMAGE/REPAIR ON CANCER GROWTH AND METASTASIS

As discussed above, the outcome of metastasis is influenced by both the intrinsic properties of tumor cells and by host factors likely to be related to homeostasis. For example, factors that control the processes of organ repair, regeneration, or both are known to be organ-specific. For example, subsequent to a partial hepatectomy, the liver undergoes a rapid cell division termed *regeneration*. In a hepatectomized mouse, however, no similar cell division can be found in the kidneys. Similarly, the mouse kidney compensates for unilateral nephrectomy by hypertrophy and hyperplasia, but there is no change in liver growth.

We have recently completed transplantation experiments on HCCs and human renal cell carcinomas in nude mice that have subsequently been subjected to either hepatectomy, nephrectomy, or abdominal surgery (as a trauma control).[1] The results were most interesting. HCC cells implanted subcutaneously demonstrated accelerated growth in partially hepatectomized mice but not in nephrectomized mice. Human renal carcinoma cells established as micrometastases in the lungs of nude mice underwent a significant growth acceleration subsequent to unilateral nephrectomy but not hepatectomy. In other words, liver hyperplasia in nude mice stimulated growth of HCC cells, whereas hypertrophy-hyperplasia of the kidney stimulated the growth of human renal cancer cells. In both studies, the human cancer cells were recent isolates from surgical specimens of human cancers. These results indicate that metastatic cells can respond to physiological signals produced when homeostasis is disturbed. Tumor cells that either originate from or have an affinity for growth in this particular organ can also respond to these signals.

ORGAN-SPECIFIC GROWTH FACTORS

One possible mechanism to explain the accelerated growth of HCC in hepatectomized mice is the production of organ-specific growth factors (GFs). Evidence supporting organ-specific GFs for metastatic cells has been obtained, in part, from experiments on the effects of organ-conditioned medium on the growth of particular neoplastic cells. The presence of stimulatory or inhibitory tissue factors correlates with the site-specific pattern of metastasis.[45] To date, however, only a few of these organ-derived growth factors have been isolated and purified to homogeneity. Liver regeneration that follows major hepatectomy involves quantitative changes in hepatocyte gene expression.[46,47] Recently, transforming growth factor alpha (TGF-α) mRNA was shown to increase approximately twofold in rat hepatocytes during the first 8 to 24 h following partial hepatectomy, coinciding with an increase in epidermal growth factor receptor (EGF-R) mRNA and a downregulation of these receptor proteins as well as a loss of EGF-R protein kinase activity.[48,49] These results suggest that TGF-α is a physiologic regulator of liver regeneration by means of an autocrine mechanism.[50] Moreover, TGF-α production by hepatocytes might also have a paracrine role, stimulating proliferation of adjacent nonparenchymal cells[50] or tumor cells.

Hepatocyte growth factor (HGF), another live mitogen, is synthesized and secreted from nonparenchymal liver cells (endothelial and Kupffer cells). Subsequent to liver damage, a rapid increase is observed in the HGF mRNA of Kupffer cells,[51] paralleling the downregulation of its receptor, the c-*met* protooncogene, in hepatocytes. Like EGF-R, the receptor for HGF (c-*met*) belongs to the tyrosine kinase family of receptors.[52]

Furthermore, TGF-β mRNAs increased in normal nonparenchymal cells, coinciding with hepatocyte DNA replication and mitosis, and TGF-β protein inhibited EGF-stimulated DNA synthesis, implying that it may be a component of a paracrine regulatory loop controlling hepatocyte replication at the late stages of liver regeneration.[53] Therefore, when the liver is damaged (possibly by tumor cells), growth factors are likely to be released and stimulate the proliferation of receptive malignant tumor cells, i.e., those that possess the appropriate receptors.

We assessed the genes encoding for GF receptors of low- and high-metastatic HCC variants.[41,42] Analyses of HCC cells from surgical specimens that differed in malignant potential showed no amplification or rearrangements in the genes encoding the tyrosine kinase receptors EGF-R and c-*erb* B2. Similar results were observed for genes encoding specific GFs or proteins involved in intracellular signal transduction pathways. In contrast, Northern blot analyses demonstrated that high metastatic HCC variants (either Dukes stage D or variant cells selected in nude mice from a Dukes stage B2 tumor) expressed significantly increased EGF-R mRNA transcripts as compared to low-metastatic HCC cell types.[54] The in vitro growth stimulation of cells with high or low metastatic potential to TGF-α demonstrated the functional significance of increased EGF-R numbers on specific cell types. Overexpression or altered expression of EGF-R has been reported for a variety of human carcinomas including breast, liver, pancreas, melanoma, glioblastomas, and metastatic HCC.[55] Although the exact role of the EGF-R in tumorigenesis and/or metastasis remains unclear, the more malignant the tumor, the more cell surface EGF-Rs.[56] EGF-R levels also correlate with advanced-stage disease in a number of human malignancies, including non-small cell lung, bladder, and gastric cancers, as well as with metastatic potential and hence poor prognosis in breast cancer.[57]

Related to, but distinct from the EGF-R, is the c-*met* protooncogene. The protein encoded by the c-*met* protooncogene is the receptor for HGF.[58] In human tissues, the highest levels of c-*met* mRNA expression are found in the liver, kidney, stomach, and thyroid. Similar studies with anti–c-*met* receptor antibodies have shown that receptor protein levels are high in hepatocytes and in gastric and intestinal epithelium (including colon and rectum) among other epithelial cell types. These studies indicate a role for HGF and c-*met* in the growth and turnover of epithelial tissues. Preliminary studies from our laboratory indicate high levels of c-*met* expression in in vitro adapted HCC cell types of either Dukes stage B2, D, or liver metastases.[54] Although preliminary, expression analyses of mRNA isolated directly from HCC tumor specimens versus normal colon mucosa suggest increased c-*met* transcripts in the tumor tissues.

THE INFLUENCE OF THE ORGAN ENVIRONMENT ON THE INVASIVE PHENOTYPE OF HCC

As mentioned above, the first steps in metastasis involve the detachment of tumor cells from the primary tumor, the invasion of host stroma, and entrance into the circulation. For this reason, the implantation site of tumor cells in nude mice influences not only the growth of the local tumor but also the production of metastases. When HCCs are implanted into the subcutis of nude mice, they grow locally but show limited invasiveness. This lack of invasion, as well as the consequent lack of metastasis, has often been associated with the development of a dense fibrous capsule around the tumor.[59]

One tumor cell property that is a prerequisite for metastasis is the ability to degrade connective-tissue extracellular matrix and basement membrane components that constitute barriers against invading tumor cells.[60] Metastatic tumor cells possess various proteases and glycosidases capable of degrading extracellular matrix components.[60] In studying the production of extracellular matrix-degrading enzymes such as type IV collagenase (gelatinase, matrix metalloproteinase 2) and heparinase (heparan sulfate–specific endo-β-D-glucoronidase) in metastatic tumor cells, we found a strong correlation between the type IV collagenase activity of HCC cells and their metastasizing action to the liver after the cells were inoculated into the spleen of nude mice. Type IV collagenolytic metalloproteinases with apparent molecular masses of 98, 92, 80, 68 and 64 kDa were detected in serum-free conditioned media of the highly metastatic KM12 variant cultures. Poorly metastatic parental cells, on the other hand, secreted very low amounts of only 92-kDa metalloproteinase.[42]

The production and secretion of type IV collagenase are modulated by serum factors, growth factors, and tumor cell-extracellular matrix interactions. Plasminogen activators, which are involved in tumor growth and metastatic invasion, are also known to be induced by a variety of growth factors.[61] The plasminogen activator activity in HCC xenografts in nude mice can be modulated by the tissue environment. Gut-implanted xenografts with invasive growth expressed higher plasminogen activator activity than did subcutaneous xenografts growing as noninvasive tumor masses.[62]

We examined the influence of organ environment on the metastasis of HCC cells and on their extracellular matrix-degrading activities using four HCC cell lines with different metastatic potentials. When any of the HCC cells were injected subcutaneously, they did not produce visceral metastases. In contrast, metastatic HCC cells metastasized from the cecum to regional mesenteric lymph nodes and the liver.[41,42,63]

A degradation assay using ^{3}H-labeled type IV collagen and zymography of tumor-conditioned medium clearly demonstrated significant differences in the level of secreted type IV collagenases between HCCs growing subcutaneously or in the cecum. In the medium conditioned by HCCs growing subcutaneously, we detected only a latent form (98-kDa) of the 92-kDa type IV collagenase. In contrast, both latent and active forms of the 92-kDa type IV collagenase were found in culture medium conditioned by HCCs growing in the cecum. Moreover, HCCs growing in the cecum secreted more than twice as much enzymes as the subcutaneous tumors.[63] Significant activities of latent and active forms of the 64-kDa type IV collagenase were found only in the medium conditioned by HCCs growing in the cecum. These results suggest that a factor or factors in the cecum's environment may stimulate the production of both 92-kDa and 64-kDa type IV collagenases in HCC cells. In the subcutis, another factor may suppress production of the 64-kDa enzyme by the HCC cells.

Since the interaction of stromal fibroblasts can influence the tumorigenicity and biological behavior of tumor cells, we determined whether organ-specific fibroblasts could directly influence the invasive ability of HCC cells.[64] Primary cultures of nude mouse fibroblasts, lung, and colon were established. Invasive and metastatic HCC cells were cultured alone or with the fibroblasts. Growth and invasive properties of the HCC cells were evaluated as well as their production of gelatinase activity. HCC cells grew on monolayers of all three fibroblast cultures but did not invade through skin fibroblasts. Those HCC cells that were growing on plastic and on colon or lung fibroblasts produced significant levels of latent and active forms of type IV collagenase, whereas HCC cells cocultivated with nude mouse skin fibroblasts did not. Incubation of HCC cells in serum-free medium containing recombinant human interferon-beta (fibroblast interferon) significantly reduced gelatinase activity. Since the production of type IV collagenase by HCC was specifically inhibited by mouse skin fibroblasts but not by colon or lung fibroblasts, the data support the in vivo data that organ-specific factors can influence the invasive and metastatic properties of HCC cells.[64]

CONCLUSIONS

Human colonic carcinomas are heterogeneous for a variety of biologic properties that include invasion and metastasis. The presence of a small subpopulation of cells with a highly metastatic phenotype has important clinical implications for diagnosis and therapy of cancer. For this reason, it is important to develop animal models for the selection and isolation of metastatic variants from human neoplasms and for testing the metastatic potential of human tumor cells.

We have implanted HCC cells (obtained from a surgical specimen) into different organs of nude mice and then recovered the tumors and established each in culture. The HCCs did not metastasize unless they were implanted orthotopically. These findings indicate that the appropriate nude mouse model for studying the biology and therapy of HCC must be based on the orthotopic implantation of tumor cells. The growth and spread of HCC depends on the interaction of specific tumor cells with homeostatic mechanisms. Cells populating metastases respond to organ-specific growth factors that can also modify the response of tumor cells to therapy.

Our data show that metastasis is a highly selective process that is regulated by a number of different mechanisms. This belief is contrary to the once widely accepted notion that metastasis represents the ultimate expression of cellular anarchy. The view that cancer metastasis is a selective process implies that understanding these regulatory mechanisms will lead to better therapeutic interventions.

REFERENCES

1. Fidler IJ: Critical factors in the biology of human cancer metastasis: Twenty-eighth GHA Clowes Memorial Award Lecture. *Cancer Res* 50:6130–6138, 1990.

2. Poste G, Fidler IJ: The pathogenesis of cancer metastasis. *Nature* 283:139–146, 1979.
3. Fidler IJ, Poste G: The cellular heterogeneity of malignant neoplasms: Implications for adjuvant chemotherapy. *Semin Oncol* 12:207–221, 1985.
4. Folkman J, Klagsburn M: Angiogenic factors. *Science* 235: 444–447, 1987.
5. Liotta LA: Tumor invasion and metastasis—Role of the extracellular matrix: Rhoads Memorial Award Lecture. *Cancer Res* 46:1–7, 1986.
6. Fisher B, Fisher ER: The interrelationship of hematogenous and lymphatic tumor cell dissemination. *Surg Gynecol Obstet* 122:791–797, 1966.
7. Nicolson GL: Cancer metastasis: Tumor cell and host organ properties important in metastasis to specific secondary sites. *Biochem Biophys Acta* 948:175–224, 1988.
8. Fidler IJ, Radinsky R: Genetic control of cancer metastasis (editorial). *J Natl Cancer Inst* 82:166–168, 1990.
9. Fidler IJ: Metastasis: Quantitative analysis of distribution and fate of tumor cell emboli labelled with ^{125}I-5-iododeoxyuridine. *J Natl Cancer Inst* 45:773–782, 1970.
10. Fidler IJ: Selection of successive tumor lines for metastasis. *Nature* 242:148–149, 1973.
11. Fidler IJ, Kripke ML: Metastasis results from pre-existing variant cells within a malignant tumor. *Science* 197:893–895, 1977.
12. Luria SE, Delbruck M: Mutations of bacteria from virus sensitive to virus resistance. *Genetics* 28:491–511, 1943.
13. Fidler IJ, Gruys E, Cifone MA: Demonstration of multiple phenotype diversity in a murine melanoma of recent origin. *J Natl Cancer Inst* 67:947–956, 1981.
14. Paget S: The distribution of secondary growths in cancer of the breast. *Lancet* 1:571–573, 1889.
15. Ewing J: *Neoplastic Diseases,* 6th ed. Philadelphia, Saunders, 1928.
16. Sugarbaker EV: Patterns of metastasis in human malignancies. *Cancer Biol Rev* 2:235–278, 1981.
17. Hart IR, Fidler IJ: Role of organ selectivity in the determination of metastatic patterns of B16 melanoma. *Cancer Res* 41:1281–1287, 1981.
18. Tarin D, Price JE, Kettlewell MGW: Mechanisms of human tumor metastasis studied in patients with peritoneovenous shunts. *Cancer Res* 44:3584–3592, 1984.
19. Talmadge JE, Fidler IJ: Cancer metastasis is selective or random depending on the parent tumor population. Nature 27:593–594, 1982.
20. Price JE, Aukerman SL, Fidler IJ: Evidence that the process of murine melanoma metastasis is sequential and selective and contains stochastic elements. *Cancer Res* 46:5172–5178, 1986.
21. Talmadge JE, Wolman SR, Fidler IJ: Evidence for the clonal origin of spontaneous metastasis. *Science* 217:361–363, 1982.
22. Fidler IJ, Talmage JE: Evidence that intravenously derived murine pulmonary metastases can originate from the expansion of a single tumor cell. *Cancer Res* 46:5167–5171, 1986.
23. Fidler IJ: Rationale and methods for the use of nude mice to study the biology and therapy of human cancer metastasis. *Cancer Metastasis Rev* 5:29–49, 1986.
24. Sharkey FE, Fogh J: Considerations in the use of nude mice for cancer research. *Cancer Metastasis Rev* 3:341–360, 1984.
25. Kozlowski JM, Hart IR, Fidler IJ: A human melanoma line heterogeneous with respect to metastatic capacity in athymic nude mice. *J Natl Cancer Inst* 72:913–917, 1984.
26. Fidler IJ, Naito S, Pathak S: Orthotopic implantation is essential for the selection, growth and metastasis of human renal cell cancer in nude mice. *Cancer Metastasis Rev* 9:149–165, 1990.
27. Fidler IJ: Orthotopic implantation of human colon carcinomas into nude mice provides a valuable model for the biology and therapy of cancer metastasis. *Cancer Metastasis Rev* 10:229–243, 1991.
28. Rygaard J, Povlsen CO: Heterotransplantation of a human malignant tumor to "nude" mice. *Acta Pathol Microbiol Scand* [*A*] 77:758–760, 1969.
29. Giavazzi R, Campbell DE, Jessup JM: Metastatic behavior of tumor cells isolated from primary and metastatic human colorectal carcinomas implanted into different sites in nude mice. *Cancer Res* 46:1928–1933, 1986.
30. Giavazzi R, Jessup JM, Campbell DE: Experimental nude mouse model in human colorectal cancer liver metastases. *J Natl Cancer Inst* 77:1303–1308, 1986.
31. Giovanella BC, Fogh J: Present and future trends in investigations with nude mouse as a recipient of human tumor transplants, in Fogh J, Giovanella BC (eds): *The Nude Mouse in Experimental and Clinical Research,* vol 1. New York, Academic Press, 1978, pp 282–312.
32. Carrel S, Sordat B, Merenola C: Establishment of a cell line (Co-115) from a human colon carcinoma transplanted into nude mice. *Cancer Res* 36:3978–3984, 1976.
33. Bhargava DK, Lipkin M: Transplantation of adenomatous polyps, normal colonic mucosa and adenocarcinoma of colon into athymic mice. *Digestion* 21:225–231, 1981.
34. Wright WC, Daniels WP, Fogh J: Distinction of seventy-one cultured human tumor cell lines by polymorphic enzyme analysis. *J Natl Cancer Inst* 66:239–247, 1981.
35. Caveriviere P, Delsol G: Metastatic behavior of tumor cells isolated from primary and metastatic human colorectal carcinomas implanted into different sites in nude mice. *Cancer Res* 46:1928–1933, 1986.
36. Fogh J, Tiso J, Orfeo T: Thirty-four lines of human tumor categories established in nude mice. *J Natl Cancer Inst* 64:745–751, 1980.
37. August DA, Ottow RT, Sugarbaker PH: Clinical perspective of human colorectal cancer metastasis. *Cancer Metastasis Rev* 3:303–324, 1984.
38. Jessup JM, Giavazzi R, Campbell DE: Growth potential of human colorectal carcinomas in nude mice: Association with preoperative serum concentration of carcinoembryonic antigen. *Cancer Res* 48:1689–1692, 1988.
39. Sordat B, Wang WR: Human colorectal tumor xenografts in nude mice: Expression of malignancy. *Behring Inst Mitt* 74:291–300, 1984.
40. Leduc EH: Metastasis of transplantable hepatomas from the spleen to the liver in mice. *Cancer Res* 19:1091–1095, 1959.
41. Morikawa K, Walker SM, Jessup JM, et al: In vivo selection of highly metastatic cells from surgical specimens of different human colon carcinomas implanted into nude mice. *Cancer Res* 48:1943–1948, 1988.
42. Morikawa K, Walker SM, Nakajima M: Influence of organ environment on the growth, selection, and metastasis of human colon carcinoma cells in nude mice. *Cancer Res* 48:6863–6871, 1988.
43. Jessup JM, Giavazzi R, Campbell DE: Metastatic potential of human colorectal carcinomas implanted into nude mice: Prediction of clinical outcome in patients operated upon for cure. *Cancer Res* 49:6906–6910, 1989.
44. Schackert H, Fidler IJ: Development of an animal model to study the biology of recurrent colorectal cancer originating from mesenteric lymph system metastasis. *Int J Cancer* 44:177–181, 1989.
45. Radinsky R: Growth factors and their receptors in metastasis. *Semin Cancer Biol* 2:169–177, 1991.
46. Michalopoulos GK: Liver regeneration: Molecular mechanisms of growth control. *FASEB J* 4:176–187, 1990.

47. van Dale P, Galand P: Effect of partial hepatectomy on experimental liver invasion by intraportally injected colon carcinoma cells in rats. *Inv Metastasis* 8:217–227, 1988.
48. Fausto N, Mead JE, Braun L: Proto-oncogene expression and growth factors during liver regeneration, in Becker FF, Slaga TF (eds): *Critical Molecular Determinants of Carcinogenesis*. Austin, Texas, University of Texas Press, 1987, pp 69–86.
49. Rubin RA, O'Keefe EJ, Earp HS: Alteration of epidermal growth factor-dependent phosphorylation during rat liver regeneration. *Proc Natl Acad Sci USA* 79:776–780, 1982.
50. Mead JE, Fausto N: Transforming growth factor α may be a physiological regulator of liver regeneration by means of an autocrine mechanism. *Proc Natl Acad Sci USA* 86:1558–1562, 1989.
51. Gherardi E, Stoker M: Hepatocyte growth factor-scatter factor: Mitogen, motogen, and met. *Cancer Cells* 3:227–232, 1991.
52. Ullrich A, Schlessinger J: Signal transduction by receptors with tyrosine kinase activity. *Cell* 61:203–212, 1990.
53. Grupposo PA, Mead JE, Fausto N: Transforming growth factor receptors in liver regeneration following partial hepatectomy in the rat. *Cancer Res* 50:1464–1469, 1990.
54. Radinsky R, Fidler IJ: Regulation of tumor cell growth at organ-specific metastases. *In Vivo* 6:325–332, 1992.
55. Bradley SJ, Garfinkle G, Walker E: Increased expression of the epidermal growth factor receptor on human colon carcinoma cells. *Arch Surg* 121:1242–1247, 1986.
56. Herlyn M, Kath R, Williams N: Growth regulatory factors for normal, premalignant, and malignant human cells in vitro. *Adv Cancer Res* 54:213–234, 1990.
57. Sainsbury JRC, Needham GK, Farndon JR: Epidermal-growth-factor receptor status as predictor of early recurrence and death from breast cancer. *Lancet* 1:1398–1402, 1987.
58. Bottaro DP, Rubin JS, Faletto DL: Identification of the hepatocyte growth factor receptor as the c-met proto-oncogene product. *Science* 215:802–804, 1991.
59. DeVore DP, Houchens DP, Ovejera AA: Collagenase inhibitors retarding invasion of a human tumor in nude mice. *Exp Cell Biol* 48:367–373, 1980.
60. Nakajima M, Irimura T, Nicolson GL: Heparanases and tumor metastasis. *J Cell Biochem* 36:157–167, 1988.
61. Nakajima M, Chop AM: Tumor invasion and extracellular matrix degradative enzymes: Regulation of activity by organ factors. *Semin Cancer Biol* 2:115–127, 1991.
62. Cajot JF, Sordat B, Bachmann F: Human primary colon carcinomas xenografted into nude mice: II. Modulation of tumor plasminogen activator activity by the host tissue environment. *J Natl Cancer Inst* 77:1099–1107, 1986.
63. Nakajima M, Morikawa K, Fabra A: Influence of organ environment on extracellular matrix degradative activity and metastasis of human colon carcinoma cells. *J Natl Cancer Inst* 82:1890–1898, 1990.
64. Fabra A, Nakajima M, Bucana CD, et al: Modulation of the invasive phenotype of human colon carcinoma cells by fibroblasts from orthotopic or ectopic organs of nude mice. *Differentiation* 52:101–110, 1992.

CHAPTER 18

Pathologic Features of Colorectal Cancer

Stanley R. Hamilton

The pathology of large bowel carcinoma is important for its clinical associations, including characteristics affecting screening, surveillance, diagnosis, and management. Assessment of prognosis after resection in relation to therapeutic options is an especially important application of pathology.[1–4]

Nearly every pathologic feature has a range or spectrum of appearances, and dichotomous features are distinctly uncommon. Therefore, classification of almost any pathologic feature typically employs arbitrary distinctions within a continuous spectrum of findings. As a consequence, observer variation has dramatic impact upon the classification of many features,[5] a fact which is often underappreciated in clinical decision making based on pathologic findings. Furthermore, many pathologic features are interrelated rather than distinct from each other. Due to variable topography, assessment of some histopathologic features is highly dependent upon sampling. Thus, even the method of specimen processing by the pathologist influences the findings.[6]

From the "splitters'" perspective as contrasted with that of the "lumpers," each colorectal carcinoma is entirely unique in its combination of particular pathologic features. The challenge is to identify and apply those pathologic features which are reliable and useful in the management of patients. The frequently contradictory and even conflicting data in the literature for nearly any pathologic finding in relation to one or another clinical association often limit meaningful application. This review will address the applications and limitations of the pathology of colorectal carcinoma as it affects the management of patients.

GROSS PATHOLOGY

The pathologic features (Table 18-1) evaluated on visual examination of colorectal neoplasms account for the findings of the radiologist, colonoscopist, and surgeon. Tumors of the large bowel can be located anywhere, from the pouch of the cecum and vermiform appendix to the anorectal junction. Of note in this regard, distinction of rectal from colonic carcinoma often poses a problem, as different landmarks are used by colonoscopists, surgeons, radiologists, and pathologists. The majority of colorectal carcinomas are located distal to the splenic flexure, but the proportion in the proximal colon have been increasing in recent years for reasons that are not clear.[7] Colorectal carcinomas can be tiny to massive, depending upon their status at the time of their discovery. Of note, size is not especially predictive of outcome, because the metastatic phenotype (the properties of cancer cells which permit successful metastasis) can be manifested in some small "early" colorectal cancers and not in some large "late" ones. This discordance between size and metastatic capability is explained by the biologically late phase of all clinically detectable neoplasms: a 1-cm cancer theoretically represents about 30 or more successive generations of malignant cells.[8]

The extent of circumferential involvement of the large bowel is related to size, but occasionally small cancers can be nearly circumferential by contracting the bowel wall as they infiltrate. Obstruction with dilatation of the proximal large bowel occurs with carcinomas which involve much of the circumference and/or physically occlude the lumen (Fig. 18-1).[9–17] Perforation of the obstructed colon or rupture through necrotic areas in the tumor itself occur in occasional patients.[9,12,15,18,19] This finding often signals adverse outcome for the patient, because of peritonitis and sepsis as well as the potential late complication of spread of tumor within the peritoneal cavity. Fistulization into other organs, such as nearby segments of bowel and the genitourinary tract, occurs occasionally.[20,21]

The configuration of colorectal carcinoma is heterogeneous. The tumors can be exophytic and polypoid

Table 18-1
Gross Pathologic Features of Colorectal Carcinoma

Tumor characteristics
Size
Configuration
Extent of circumferential involvement
Depth of invasion
Extensiveness of invasion
Evidence of obstruction
Perforation
Residual adenoma
Consequences of surgery
Length of longitudinal margins of resection
Depth of deep margin of resection
Synchronous lesions
Carcinoma
Polyps (adenomas, hyperplastic polyps, inflammatory polyps, hamartomatous polyps)
Other (e.g., idiopathic inflammatory bowel disease)

with variable extension into the lumen or endophytic with little luminal involvement (Fig. 18-1). Exophytic tumors can be broad-based and sessile or pedunculated on a stalk due to the mechanical effects of the fecal stream. Occasional endophytic tumors have a linitis plastica-like appearance, with diffuse infiltration of the wall of the large bowel but little distortion of the luminal surface, similar to gastric carcinoma of this type.[22,23] The luminal surface of colorectal cancers can be intact or ulcerated (Fig. 18-1). Residual adenoma, representing the precursor lesion, can be seen at the periphery of some tumors. The configuration of colorectal cancers as well as their size affect the detectability of the tumors by various modalities, including radiography, ultrasonography, colonoscopy, and visualization at surgery.

The direct extension and local metastatic spread of colorectal cancers can be evaluated on gross pathology (Fig. 18-1), and these characteristics affect attempts at clinical staging by palpation, computer-assisted tomography, magnetic resonance imaging, and ultrasonography. Longitudinal intramural spread of colorectal cancers is usually limited, and satellite lesions within the bowel wall are rarely seen.[24–27] Deep extension can involve mural structures, soft tissues in the mesentery or perirectal region (Fig. 18-1), serosal surface of the peritoneal cavity, and other organs. The nature of the deep involvement depends upon both the depth and anatomic location of the primary tumor.[14,28,29] This pathologic feature has profound influences on the feasibility of local excision of rectal cancers, laporoscopic excision, and curative extended radical resection.

The gross pathology of lymph node metastases and even distant metastases is notoriously unreliable. Large, apparently involved nodes often show on histopathology only lymphoid hyperplasia as part of the host response to the tumor, rather than metastatic cancer.[30] Conversely, small lymph nodes may harbor mi-

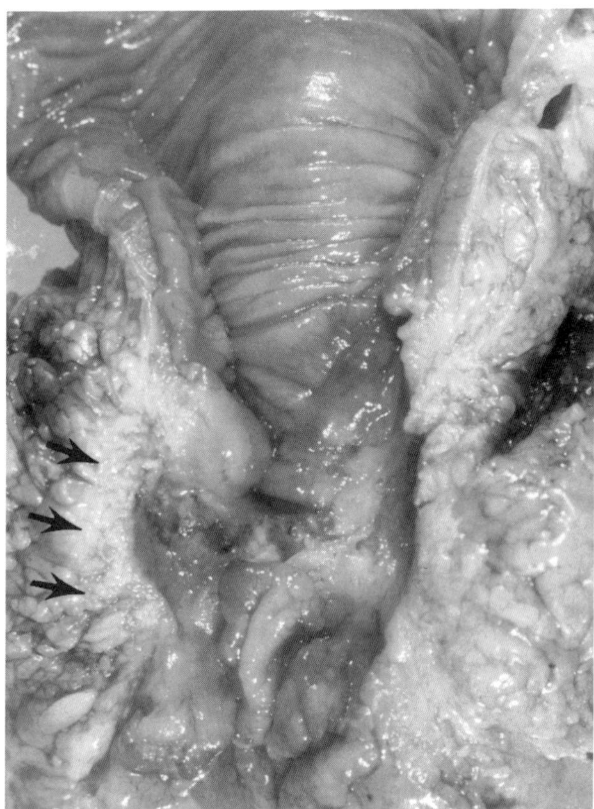

FIG. 18-1. Adenocarcinoma of the proximal rectum in low anterior resection specimen. The tumor is endophytic, with little luminal extension, and ulcerated. The cancer involves the entire circumference of the rectum, producing obstruction evidenced by dilatation of the sigmoid colon above the tumor. The cancer extends through the rectal wall into the perirectal fat (arrow). The distal surgical margin is near the cancer.

crometastases detectable only by histopathology.[31–33] The lack of relationship to gross pathology is reflected in the inaccuracies of the clinical staging and imaging techniques which typically depend on lymph node size.

The margins of excision of colorectal cancers are important in the gross examination of resection specimens. Determination of the length of margins is made difficult by contraction of the specimen once it is removed from the patient, and the length of margin estimated by the surgeon and the pathologist is often dramatically different. The length of margin has a clear-cut relationship to local recurrence, as studies show higher rates of recurrence with closer margins.[27,34–40]

Synchronous lesions are often present in resection specimens with colorectal cancers. These can include synchronous primary carcinomas, which occur in about 3 to 5 percent of patients, adenomas, and hyperplastic polyps.[41] The numbers and types of the synchronous lesions can be important in identifying the association of colorectal cancer with inherited syndromes such as adenomatous polyposis syndrome, juvenile polyposis syndrome, and Peutz-Jeghers syndrome or other predisposing conditions such as idiopathic inflammatory bowel disease.[42]

The gross pathology of suture-line recurrence of colorectal cancer is typically characterized by the predominance of the tumor mass within the wall of the large bowel anastomotic site rather than at the mucosal surface. In occasional cases, metachronous primaries can occur at suture lines.[43]

HISTOPATHOLOGY

The histopathologic features (Table 18-2) of colorectal carcinoma include those related to host response as well as the tumor itself. The tumor type is relatively homogeneous in that the vast majority of colorectal cancers are moderately differentiated, gland-forming adenocarcinomas with relatively characteristic histopathologic features (Fig. 18-2). Pathologists are often able to suggest the large bowel as the primary site of a metastasis of unknown origin based on the characteristic histopathologic appearances of colorectal adenocarcinomas. There is a spectrum of histopathologic findings in typical cancers, however, as the glands may range from large and dilated to small and compact. Occasional papillary carcinomas are seen. At the other extreme of differentiation, glandular architecture may be absent and the carcinoma may form sheets or infiltrate as individual cells, resulting in classification as poorly differentiated carcinoma (Fig. 18-3). Epithelial morphology and cytology also influence classification,[44–49] as highly cellular gland-forming tumors with bizarre cytology can be classified as poorly differentiated. By contrast, cytopathologically bland signet-ring cells with abundant mucin in the cytoplasm which displaces the small nucleus (Fig. 18-4) are usually aggressive tumors.[50] Mixtures of morphology in the same tumor are frequent.

Table 18-2
Histopathologic Features of Colorectal Carcinoma

Tumor characteristics
Type of carcinoma (see Table 18-3)
Grade of differentiation
Depth of direct extension
Extensiveness of invasion
Anatomic site of invasion
Pattern of infiltration
Invasion with potential for metastasis
Lymphatic channels
Venules and veins
Perineural spaces
Regional metastasis
Lymph nodes
Soft tissue
Host response
Angiogenesis
Intratumoral inflammation
Peritumoral lymphoid response
Desmoplasia
Reactive regional lymph nodes
Consequences of surgery
Longitudinal margins of resection
Deep margin of resection

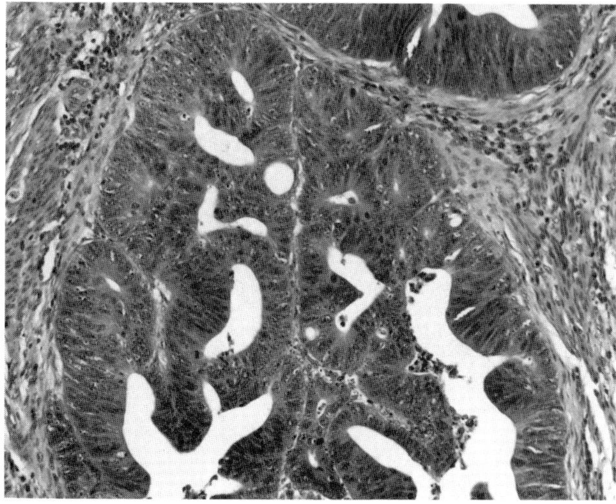

FIG. 18-2. Histopathology of typical moderately differentiated gland-forming adenocarcinoma of the large bowel. The cancer is invading the muscularis propria.

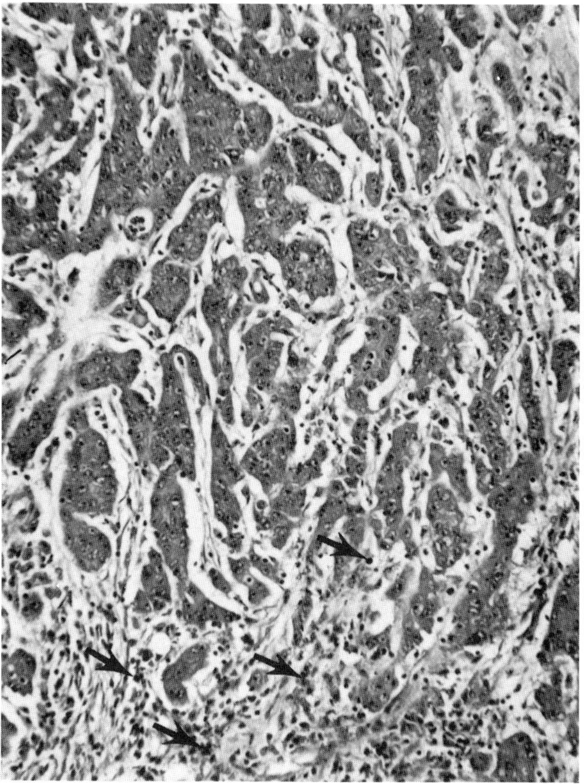

FIG. 18-3. Histopathology of poorly differentiated adenocarcinoma of the large bowel with trabeculae of bizarre tumor cells and no gland formation. Numerous lymphocytes (arrows) are present in the stroma around the aggregates of tumor cells.

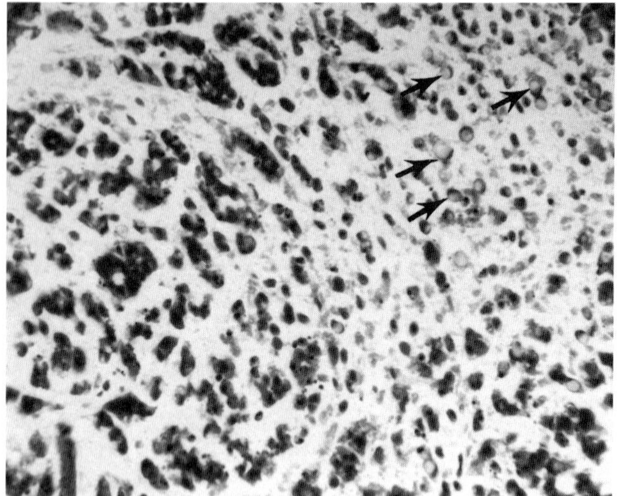

FIG. 18-4. Histopathology of signet-ring cell adenocarcinoma of the large bowel. The cytoplasm of some cells contains a droplet of mucin which displaces the nucleus (arrows).

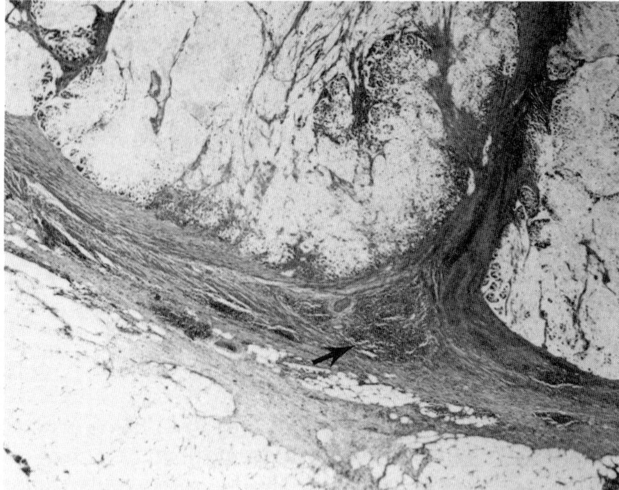

FIG. 18-5. Mucinous adenocarcinoma of the large bowel. The vast majority of the tumor mass consists of extracellular mucin in pools, which contain scattered tumor cells. The carcinoma is invading pericolic fibroadipose tissue in an expansile fashion. A lymphoid aggregate (arrow) is present in the desmoplastic connective tissue at the invasive edge of the carcinoma.

The uncommon variants of colorectal carcinoma are classified on the basis of predominance of one of the unusual patterns (Table 18-3). These include mucinous or colloid carcinomas,[51–58] in which the majority of the tumor consists of mucin pools, which are often of low cellularity (Fig. 18-5). Signet-ring cell carcinomas are occasionally seen.[50] Poorly differentiated colorectal carcinomas can have a variety of features, including neuroendocrine differentiation, when studied with immunohistochemical techniques for chromogranin and other antigens; they are termed poorly differentiated carcinomas with neuroendocrine features. Medullary carcinomas with inflammatory response and small-cell carcinomas[59,60] also occur (Fig. 18-6).

Stromal and inflammatory cells are a variable component of colorectal carcinomas. In some tumors there is marked desmoplasia, whereas in others fibrous connective tissue proliferation may be relatively minor.[61] Angiogenesis is typical at the periphery and in the central portion of infiltrating carcinomas. The host inflammatory response can include lymphocytes[62,63] (Fig. 18-3), eosinophils,[64] mast cells, and macrophages as well as polymorphonuclear leukocytes, which are especially associated with areas of necrosis. In some cases, lymphoid nodules, including germinal centers, are seen at the periphery of infiltrating carcinomas, termed *Crohn's-like lymphoid reaction* (Fig. 18-5).

Residual adenoma is sometimes seen histopathologically at the periphery of infiltrating adenocarcinomas. In some cases, distinction of residual adenoma from lateral spread of carcinoma can be difficult.

The histopathologic characteristics of colorectal carcinomas have been studied extensively as prognostic features. Nearly every histopathologic characteristic has been found to be prognostic in one or another study.[1–3,65–69] It is clear that poorly differentiated car-

Table 18-3
Histopathologic Variants of Colorectal Carcinoma

Mucinous (colloid) adenocarcinoma
Signet-ring cell adenocarcinoma
Adenosquamous carcinoma
Basosquamous carcinoma
Squamous carcinoma
Small-cell carcinoma
Choriocarcinoma
Medullary carcinoma

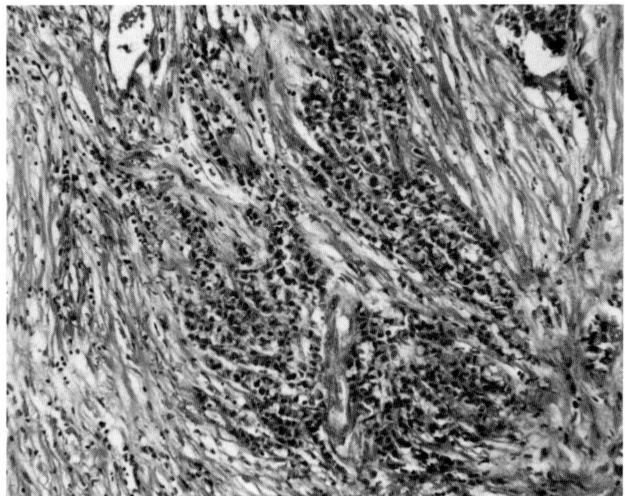

FIG. 18-6. Small cell carcinoma of the large bowel. The tumor cells are infiltrating the desmoplastic stroma in a single-cell pattern.

cinomas have a worse prognosis stage for stage, but there is controversy about the prognostic importance of mucinous carcinoma, with some studies showing poorer outcome but others not.[51–58] Likewise, host response has been associated with better prognosis, including various components such as desmoplasia, inflammatory cell infiltration, and lymphoid response. Intraobserver and interobserver variation in classification of these features in the continuous spectrum seen in colorectal cancers poses a problem for clinical utility, as do interpreting and applying the plethora of histopathologic prognostic indicators, which may conflict among themselves in an individual cancer.

Local invasion by colorectal carcinoma is best assessed by histopathology. The implications differ for colonic as compared to rectal carcinoma because of the anatomic relationships to adjoining structures. In colonic carcinoma, the mesentery and serosal surface are at risk, whereas in rectal carcinoma, the perirectal soft tissue and structures in the pelvis are involved by direct invasion. The pattern of infiltration can vary from pushing or expansile (Fig. 18-5) to infiltrative, with individual cells or small glands leading the invading front (Fig. 18-6). These features have been reported to be of prognostic value.[70] Histopathology also allows assessment of the margins of excision, including the deep areas of the tumor[71–73] as well as the longitudinal margins.

Invasion is clearly important in the metastatic process. Infiltration through the muscularis mucosae is virtually required for risk of metastasis in colorectal carcinoma, as contrasted with gastric carcinoma. As a consequence, "in situ" and "intramucosal" adenocarcinomas of the large bowel are recognized histopathologically but do not represent biological carcinomas, as they pose virtually no threat to the patient.[74] The explanation of failure of intramucosally invasive adenocarcinoma of the large bowel to metastasize is uncertain; it is not explained by the absence of lymphatic channels or venules available for invasion.

The mural structures involved by infiltrating carcinomas serve as the basis for staging classifications. The important landmarks are reflected in the TNM classification and are the muscularis mucosae, the submucosa (T_1), the two-layered muscularis propria (T_2), the subserosal connective tissue (T_3), the perirectal and mesneteric fibroadipose tissue (T_3), the serosal surface (T_4), and other organs (T_4). Involvement of deeper layers obviously increases the likelihood of metastasis or of intraabdominal spread in the case of serosal surface involvement.

Histopathology is essential in the assessment of lymphatic spread. The number and location of lymph nodes involved by metastasis are important prognostic indicators.[75] In particular, involvement of the highest node in resection specimens is of concern, due to the likelihood of more proximal spread which was not removed from the patient. Retrograde lymphatic spread can be recognized in some cases.[76] Assessment of an adequate number of lymph nodes is important for staging, and some authors recommend clearing of adipose tissue for more complete assessment of the number of lymph nodes.[77,78]

Vascular invasion is also detected by histopathology.[79–92] Involvement of capillaries and venules as opposed to lymphatics is often difficult to distinguish histopathologically. The site of venous invasion appears to be important in prognosis because extramural vein involvement is clearly an indicator of worse prognosis, whereas intramural invasion is less concerning. Evidence of hematogenous spread to bone marrow has recently been reported as a prognostic indicator, despite the low frequency of clinically evident osseous metastases.[93,94] Invasion of perineural spaces can also be identified by histopathology.[79,80,84,87,89,95]

Local recurrence of colorectal carcinoma is sometimes seen in anastomotic sites. The tumors in this circumstance generally involve the submucosa, muscularis propria, or extramural soft tissue to a greater extent than the mucosa. The mechanism of suture-line recurrence is the topic of debate.[37,43,96–110] Some authors indicate that exfoliated viable cells implant in the anastomotic site, whereas others suggest that circulating tumor cells[111] have a propensity to become entrapped in the anastomotic site. In occasional cases, a second primary tumor develops in an anastomotic site, probably due to local factors stimulating the neoplastic process, as supported by findings in experimental models of colonic carcinogenesis.

Lymph node metastasis is a hallmark of staging for colorectal carcinomas. Differentiation of lymph node metastasis from venous and lymphatic spread in the mesentery is sometimes difficult because the pathologist cannot differentiate an obliterated lymph node from nodules of tumor initially in lymphatic channels or veins in the soft tissue. For purposes of staging, the nodular metastases in the mesentery are generally included as lymph nodes. Reactive changes in lymph nodes, including follicular hyperplasia and sinus histiocytosis, are sometimes seen.[32] These have been reported to be histopathologic features associated with better prognosis, attributed to host response to the tumor.

CLOSING REMARKS

The pathology of colorectal cancers is remarkably heterogeneous, often making classification of features subjective. Nonetheless, until better markers of metastatic phenotype are found,[112–117] gross pathology and histopathology will continue as mainstays of staging and resultant decisions about patient management.

ACKNOWLEDGMENTS

The manuscript was typed by Mrs. Nancy Folker and Mrs. Connie Knapik. The photomicrographs were taken by Dr. Hoguen Kim and Mr. Raymond E. Lund, RBP.

REFERENCES

1. Qizilbash AH: Pathologic studies in colorectal cancer: A guide to the surgical pathology examination of colorectal specimens and review of features of prognostic significance. *Pathol Annu* 117:1–46, 1982.
2. Cooper HS, Slemmer JR: Surgical pathology of carcinoma of the colon and rectum. *Semin Oncol* 18:367–380, 1991.
3. Shepherd NA, Saraga EP, Love SB, et al: Prognostic factors in colonic cancer. *Histopathology* 14:613–620, 1989.
4. Deans GT, Parks TG, Rowlands BJ, et al: Prognostic factors in colorectal cancer. *Br J Surg* 79:608–613, 1992.
5. Thomas GDH, Dixon MF, Smeeton NC, et al: Observer variation in the histological grading of rectal carcinoma. *J Clin Pathol (Suppl)* 36:385–391, 1983.
6. Sheffield JP, Talbot IC: Gross examination of the large intestine. *J Clin Pathol* 45:751–755, 1992.
7. Bufil JA: Colorectal cancer: Evidence for distinct genetic categories based on proximal or distal tumor location. *Ann Intern Med* 113:779–788, 1990.
8. Tannock IF: Tumor growth and cell kinetics, in Tannock IF, Hill RP (eds): *The Basic Science of Oncology*. New York, Pergamon Press, 1987.
9. Willett C, Tepper JE, Cohen A, et al: Obstructive and perforative colonic carcinoma: Patterns of failure. *J Clin Oncol* 3:379–384, 1985.
10. Chang WYM, Burnett WE: Complete colonic obstruction due to adenocarcinoma. *Surg Gynecol Obstet* 114:353–356, 1962.
11. Floyd CE, Cohn I: Obstruction in cancer of the colon. *Ann Surg* 165:721–731, 1967.
12. Glenn F, McSherry CK: Obstruction and perforation in colorectal cancer. *Ann Surg* 173:983–992, 1971.
13. Welch JP, Donaldson GA: Management of severe obstruction of the large bowel due to malignant disease. *Am J Surg* 127:492–499, 1974.
14. Wolmark N, Wieand HS, Rockette HE, et al: The prognostic significance of tumor and location and bowel obstruction in Dukes B and C colorectal cancer: Findings from the NSABP clinical trials. *Ann Surg* 198:743–752, 1983.
15. Kelley WE Jr, Brown PW, Lawrence W Jr, et al: Penetrating, obstructing, and perforating carcinomas of the colon and rectum. *Arch Surg* 116:381–384, 1981.
16. Konishi F, Muto T, Kanazawa K, et al: Intraoperative irrigation and primary resection for obstructing lesions of the left colon. *Int J Colorect Dis* 3:204–206, 1988.
17. Garcia-Valdecasas JC, Lovera JM, deLacy AM, et al: Obstructing colorectal carcinomas: Prospective study. *Dis Colon Rectum* 34:759–762, 1991.
18. Crowder VH, Cohn I: Perforation in cancer of the colon and rectum. *Dis Colon Rectum* 10:415–420, 1967.
19. Welch JP, Donaldson GA: Perforative carcinoma of colon and rectum. *Ann Surg* 180:734–740, 1974.
20. Hunter JA, Ryan JA Jr, Schultz P: En bloc resection of colon cancer adherent to other organs. *Am J Surg* 154:67–71, 1987.
21. Kroneman H, Castelein A, Jeekel J: En bloc resection of colon carcinoma adherent to other organs: An efficacious treatment? *Dis Colon Rectum* 34:780–783, 1991.
22. Mayo WJ: Grafting and traumatic dissemination of carcinoma in the course of operations for malignant disease. *JAMA* 60:512–513, 1913.
23. Nakahara H, Ishikawa T, Itabashi M, et al: Diffusely infiltrating primary colorectal carcinoma of linitis plastica and lymphangiosis types. *Cancer* 69:901–906, 1992.
24. Black WA, Waugh JM: The intramural extension of carcinoma of the descending colon, sigmoid and rectosigmoid: A pathologic study. *Surg Gynecol Obstet* 87:457–464, 1948.
25. Madsen PM, Christiansen J: Distal intramural spread of rectal carcinomas. *Dis Colon Rectum* 29:279–282, 1986.
26. Lazorthes F, Voight JJ, Roques J, et al: Distal intramural spread of carcinoma of the rectum correlated with lymph nodal involvement. *Surg Gynecol Obstet* 170:45–48, 1990.
27. Sidoni A, Bufalari A, Alberti PF: Distal intramural spread in colorectal cancer—A reappraisal of the extent of distal clearance in fifty cases. *Tumori* 77:514–517, 1991.
28. Russell AH, Tong D, Dawson LE, et al: Adenocarcinoma of the proximal colon: Sites of initial dissemination and patterns of recurrence following surgery alone. *Cancer* 53:360–367, 1984.
29. Russell AH, Tong D, Dawson LE, et al: Adenocarcinoma of the retroperitoneal ascending and descending colon: Sites of initial dissemination and clinical patterns of recurrence following surgery alone. *Int J Rad Oncol Biol Phys* 9:361–365, 1983.
30. Tsakraklides V, Wanebo JH, Sternberg SS, et al: Prognostic evaluation of regional lymph node morphology in colorectal cancer. *Am J Surg* 129:174–180, 1975.
31. Herrera-Ornelas L, Justiniano J, Castillo N, et al: Metastases in small lymph nodes from colon cancer. *Arch Surg* 122:1253–1256, 1987.
32. Davidson BR, Sams VR, Styles J, et al: Detection of occult nodal metastases in patients with colorectal carcinoma. *Cancer* 65:967–970, 1991.
33. Grace R, Scott KEM: The importance of combining xylene clearance and immunohistochemistry in the accurate staging of colorectal carcinoma. *J R Soc Med* 85:713, 1992.
34. Williams NS, Dixon MF, Johnston D: Reappraisal of the 5 centimetre rule of distal excision for carcinoma of the rectum: A study of distal intramural spread and of patient's survival. *Br J Surg* 70:150–154, 1983.
35. Pollett WG, Nicholls RJ: The relationship between the extent of distal clearance and survival and local recurrence rates after curative anterior resection for carcinoma of the rectum. *Ann Surg* 198:159–163, 1984.
36. Kirwan WO, Drumm J, Hogan JM, et al: Determining safe margin of resection in low anterior resection for rectal cancer. *Br J Surg* 75:720, 1988.
37. Manson PN, Corman ML, Coller JA, et al: Anastomotic recurrence after anterior resection for carcinoma: Lahey Clinic experience. *Dis Colon Rectum* 19:219–224, 1976.
38. Karanjia ND, Schache DJ, North WRS, et al: "Close shave" in anterior resection. *Br J Surg* 77:510–512, 1990.
39. Sondenaa K, Kjellevold KH: A prospective study of the length of the distal margin after low anterior resection for rectal cancer. *Int J Colorect Dis* 5:103–105, 1990.
40. Vernava AM, Moran M, Rothenberger DA, et al: A prospective evaluation of distal margins in carcinoma of the rectum. *Surg Gynecol Obstet* 175:333, 1992.
41. Slater G, Aufses AH Jr, Szoporn A: Synchronous carcinoma of the colon and rectum. *Surg Gynecol Obstet* 171: 283–287, 1990.
42. Hamilton SR: "High-risk" and "premalignant" lesions of the colon. *Am J Surg Pathol* 9(suppl 3):21–29, 1985.
43. Wang Q, Gao H, Chen Y-L, et al: Transitional mucosa at anastomosis: A cause of local tumour recurrence in patients with rectal cancer after anterior resection. *Int Surg* 77:37–40, 1992.

44. Jass JR, Atkin WS, Cuzick I, et al: The grading of rectal cancer: Histological persepectives and a multivariate analysis of 447 cases. *Histopathology* 10:437–459, 1986.
45. Grinnell RS: The grading and prognosis of carcinoma of the colon and rectum. *Ann Surg* 109:500–503, 1939.
46. Riboli EB, Secco GB, Lapertosa G, et al: Colorectal cancer: Relationship of histologic grading to disease prognosis. *Tumori* 69:581–584, 1983.
47. Qualheim RE, Gall EA: Is histopathologic grading of colon carcinoma a valid procedure? *Arch Pathol* 56:466–472, 1953.
48. Mitmaker B, Begin LR, Gordon PH: Nuclear shape as a prognostic discriminant in colorectal carcinoma. *Dis Colon Rectum* 34:249–259, 1991.
49. Goldman S, Auer G, Erhardt K, et al: Prognostic significance of clinical stage, histologic grade, and nuclear DNA content in squamous-cell carcinoma of the anus. *Dis Colon Rectum* 30:444–448, 1987.
50. Bonello JC, Sternberg SS, Quan SHQ: The significance of the signet-cell variety of adenocarcinoma of the rectum. *Dis Colon Rectum* 23:180–183, 1980.
51. Minsky BD, Mies C, Rich TA, et al: Colloid carcinoma of the colon and rectum. *Cancer* 60:3103–3112, 1987.
52. Symonds DA, Vickery AL Jr: Mucinous carcinoma of the colon and rectum. *Cancer* 37:1891–1900, 1976.
53. Umpleby HC, Ranson DL, Williamson HC: Peculiarities of mucinous colorectal carcinoma. *Br J Surg* 72:715–718, 1985.
54. Sadhiro S, Ohmura T, Saito T, et al: An assessment of the mucous component in carcinoma of the colon and rectum. *Cancer* 64:1113–1116, 1989.
55. Minsky BD: Clinicopathologic impact of colloid in colorectal carcinoma. *Dis Colon Rectum* 33:714–719, 1990.
56. Sasaki O, Atkin WS, Jass JR: Mucinous carcinoma of the rectum. *Histopathology* 11:259–272, 1987.
57. Green JB, Timmcke AE, Mitchell WT, et al: Mucinous carcinoma—Just another colon cancer? *Dis Colon Rectum* 36:49–54, 1993.
58. Connelly JH, Robey-Cafferty SS, Cleary KR: Mucinous carcinomas of the colon and rectum—An analysis of 62 stage-B and stage-C lesions. *Arch Pathol Lab Med* 115:1022–1025, 1991.
59. Gibbs NM: Undifferentiated carcinoma of the large intestine. *Histopathology* 1:77–84, 1977.
60. Burke AB, Shekitka KM, Sobin LH: Small cell carcinomas of the large intestine. *Am J Clin Pathol* 95:315–321, 1991.
61. Wobbes T, Hendriks T, De Bower HHM: Collagen in colorectal cancer in relation to clinicopathologic stage and histologic grade. *Dis Colon Rectum* 31:778–780, 1988.
62. Svennevig JL, Lunde OC, Holter J, et al: Lymphoid infiltration and prognosis in colorectal carcinoma. *Br J Cancer* 49:375–377, 1984.
63. Pihl E, Malahy MA, Khankhanian N, et al: Immunomorphological features of prognostic significance in Dukes' class B colorectal carcinoma. *Cancer Res* 37:4145–4149, 1977.
64. Fisher ER, Pail SM, Rockette H, et al: Prognostic significance of eosinophils and mast cells in rectal cancer: Findings from the National Surgical Adjuvant Breast and Bowel Project (Protocol R-01). *Hum Pathol* 20:159–163, 1989.
65. Nathanson SD, Schultz L, Tilley B, et al: Carcinoma of the colon and rectum: A comparison of staging classifications. *Am Surg* 52:428–433, 1986.
66. Murray D, Hreno A, Dutton J, et al: Prognosis in colon cancer: A pathologic reassessment. *Arch Surg* 110:908–913, 1975.
67. Hermanek P, Guggenmoos-Holzmann I, Gall FP: Prognostic factors in rectal carcinoma: A contribution to the further development of tumor classification. *Dis Colon Rectum* 32: 593–599, 1989.
68. Payne JE: International colorectal carcinoma staging and grading. *Dis Colon Rectum* 32:282–285, 1989.
69. Michelassi F, Ayala JJ, Balestracci T, et al: Verification of a new clinicopathologic staging system for colorectal adenocarcinoma. *Ann Surg* 214:11–18, 1991.
70. Jass JR, Love SB, Northover JM: A new prognostic classification of rectal cancer. *Lancet* 1:1303–1306, 1987.
71. Quirke P, Durdey P, Dixon MF, et al: Local recurrence of rectal adenocarcinoma due to inadequate surgical resection: Histopathological study of lateral tumor spread and surgical excision. *Lancet* 1:996–999, 1986.
72. Heald RJ: The "Holy Plane" of rectal surgery. *JR Soc Med* 81:503, 1988.
73. Cawthorne SJ, Parmus DV, Gibbs NM, et al: Extent of mesorectal spread and involvement of lateral resection margin as prognostic factors after surgery for rectal cancer. *Lancet* 335:1055–1059, 1990.
74. Haggitt RC, Glotzbach RE, Soffer EE, et al: Prognostic factors in colorectal carcinomas arising in adenomas: Implications for lesions removed by endoscopic polypectomy. *Gastroenterology* 89:328–336, 1985.
75. Shida H, Ban K, Matsumoto M, et al: Prognostic significance of location of lymph node metastases in colorectal cancer. *Dis Colon Rectum* 35:1046–1050, 1992.
76. Grinnell RS: Lymphatic block with atypical and retrograde lymphatic metastasis and spread in carcinoma of the colon and rectum. *Ann Surg* 163:272–280, 1966.
77. Scott KWM, Grace RH: Detection of lymph node metastases in colorectal carcinoma before and after fat clearance. *Br J Surg* 76:1165–1167, 1989.
78. Hyder JW, Talbott TM, Maycroft TC: A critical review of chemical lymph node clearance and staging of colon and rectal cancer at Ferguson Hospital, 1977 to 1982. *Dis Colon Rectum* 33:923–925, 1990.
79. Seefeld P, Bargen JA: The spread of carcinoma of the rectum: Invasion of lymphatics, veins and nerves. *Ann Surg* 118:76–90, 1943.
80. Knudsen JB, Nilsson T, Sprechler M, et al: Venous and nerve invasion as prognostic factors in postoperative survival of patients with resectable cancer of the rectum. *Dis Colon Rectum* 26:613–617, 1983.
81. Sunderalnd DA: The significance of vein invasion by cancer of the rectum and sigmoid: A microscopic study of 210 cases. *Cancer* 2:429–437, 1949.
82. Burns FJ, Pfaff J Jr: Vascular invasion in carcinoma of the colon and rectum. *Am J Surg* 92:704–709, 1956.
83. Talbot IC, Ritchie S, Leighton MH, et al: Spread of rectal cancer within veins: Histologic features and clinical significance. *Am J Surg* 141:15–17, 1981.
84. Horn A, Dahl O, Morild I: The role of venous and neural invasion on survival in rectal adenocarcinoma. *Dis Colon Rectum* 33:598–601, 1990.
85. Minsky BD, Mies C, Recht A, et al: Resectable adenocarcinoma of the rectosigmoid and rectum: II. The influence of blood vessel invasion. *Cancer* 61:1417–1424, 1988.
86. Minsky BD, Mies C, Recht A, et al: Resectable adenocarcinoma of the rectosigmoid and rectum: II. The influence of blood vessel invasion. *Cancer* 61:1408–1416, 1988.
87. Horn A, Dahl O, Morild I: Venous and neural invasion as predictors of recurrence in rectal adenocarcinoma. *Dis Colon Rectum* 34:798–804, 1991.
88. Minsky BD, Mies C, Rich TA, et al: Potentially curative surgery of colon cancer: The influence of blood vessel invasion. *J Clin Oncol* 6:119–127, 1988.
89. Krasna MJ, Flancbaum L, Cody RP, et al: Vascular and neural invasion in colorectal carcinoma: Incidence and prognostic significance. *Cancer* 61:1018–1023, 1988.
90. Khankhanian N, Maulight GM, Russel WO, et al: Prognostic significance of vascular invasion in colorectal cancer of Dukes' B. class. *Cancer* 39:1195–1200, 1977.

91. Minsky BD, Mies C: The clinical significance of vascular invasion in colorectal cancer. *Dis Colon Rectum* 32:794–803, 1989.
92. Shirouzu K, Isomoto H, Kakegawa T, et al: A prospective clinicopathologic study of venous invasion in colorectal cancer. *Am J Surg* 162:216–222, 1991.
93. Schlimok G, Funke I, Bock B, et al: Epithelial tumor cells in bone marrow of patients with colorectal cancer: Immunocytochemical detection, phenotypic characterization, and prognostic significance. *J Clin Oncol* 8:831–837, 1991.
94. Lindemann F, Schlimok G, Dirschedl P, et al: Prognostic significance of micrometastatic tumour cells in bone marrow of colorectal cancer patients. *Lancet* 340:685–689, 1992.
95. Shirouzu K, Isomoto H, Kakegawa T: Prognostic evaluation of perineural invasion in rectal cancer. *Am J Surg* 165:233, 1993.
96. Umpleby HC, Williamson RCN: Anastomotic recurrence in large bowel cancer. *Br J Surg* 74:873–878, 1987.
97. Beahrs OH, Phillips JW, Dockerty MB: Implantation of tumor cells as a factor in recurrence of carcinoma of the rectosigmoid: Report of four cases with implantation at dentate line. *Cancer* 8:831–838, 1955.
98. LeQuesne LP, Thompson AD: Implantation recurrence of carcinoma of rectum and colon. *N Engl J Med* 258:578–582, 1958.
99. McGrew EA, Laws JF, Cole WH: Free malignant cells in relation to recurrence of carcinoma of the colon. *JAMA* 154:1251–1254, 1954.
100. Waltz BJ, Green MR, Lindstron BJ, et al: Anatomical prognostic factors after abdominoperineal resection. *Int J Radiat Oncol Biol Phys* 7:477–484, 1981.
101. Cohn I Jr, Gonzalez EA Jr, Atik M: Spillage and recurrence of colonic carcinoma. *Surg Forum* 12:153–155, 1961.
102. Cohn I Jr, Floyd CE, Atik M: Control of tumor implantation during operations on the colon. *Ann Surg* 157:825–838, 1963.
103. Cohn I Jr, Corley RG, Floyd CE: Iodized suture for control of tumor implantation in a colon anastomosis. *Surg Gynecol Obstet* 116:366–370, 1963.
104. Douglass HO Jr, LeVeen HH: Tumor recurrence in colon anastomoses: Prevention by coagulation and fixation with formalin. *Ann Surg* 173:201–205, 1971.
105. Long RTL, Edwards RH: Implantation metastasis as a cause of local recurrence of colorectal carcinoma. *Am J Surg* 157:194–201, 1989.
106. Pihl E, Hughes ESR, McDermott FT, et al: Recurrence of carcinoma of the colon and rectum at the anastomotic suture line. *Surg Gynecol Obstet* 153:495–496, 1981.
107. Stulc JP, Petrelei NJ: Anastomotic recurrence of adenocarcinoma of the colon. *Arch Surg* 121:1077–1080, 1986.
108. Keynes WM: Implantation from bowel lumen in cancer of the large intestine. *Ann Surg* 153:357–364, 1961.
109. Southwick HW, Harridge WH, et al: Recurrence at the suture line following resection for carcinoma of the colon: Incidence following preventive measures. *Am J Surg* 103:86–89, 1962.
110. McGregor JR, Galloway DJ, McCulloch P, et al: Anastomotic suture materials and implantation metastasis: An experimental study. *Br J Surg* 76:331–334, 1989.
111. Fisher ER, Turnbull RB Jr: The cytologic demonstration and significance of tumor cells in the mesenteric venous blood in patients with colorectal carcinoma. *Surg Gynecol Obstet* 100:102–108, 1955.
112. Delattre O, Law DJ, Remvikos Y, et al: Multiple genetic alterations in distal and proximal colorectal cancer. *Lancet* 2:353–356, 1989.
113. Hamilton SR: Molecular genetic alterations as potential prognostic indicators in colorectal carcinoma. *Cancer* 69: 1589–1591, 1992.
114. Ahlquist DA, Thibodeau SN: Will molecular genetic markers help predict the clinical behavior of colorectal neoplasia? *Gastroenterology* 102:1419–1421, 1992.
115. Laurent-Puig P, Olschwang S, Delattre O, et al: Survival and acquired genetic alterations in colorectal cancer. *Gastroenterology* 102:1136–1141, 1992.
116. Offerhaus GJA, deFeyter EP, Cornelisse CJ, et al: The relationship of DNA aneuploidy to molecular genetic alterations in colorectal carcinoma. *Gastroenterology* 102:1612–1619, 1992.
117. Aznavoorian S, Murphy AN, Stetler-Stevenson WG, et al: Molecular aspects of tumor cell invasion and metastasis. *Cancer* 71:1368–1384, 1993.

CHAPTER 19

Dynamics of Hematogenous Metastatic Patterns

Leonard Weiss

HIGHLIGHTS

Dynamic aspects of the metastatic patterns of colorectal carcinoma are analyzed mainly on the basis of autopsy and clinical data.

A distinction is drawn between the absence of metastatic involvement of target organs and nondetectable involvement, which is a major cause of treatment failure.

Metastatic inefficiency is a major driving force in the development of metastatic patterns. It appears that most cancer cells delivered via the portal vein are arrested and killed in the liver, and only a very small fraction survive and are released to seed the lungs. Of these few cells, most are arrested and killed in the lungs, and very, very few of the viable cancer cells originally entering the portal vein are delivered to other organs by the arterial route. Of these, the majority are again arrested and killed. Therefore, the probability of *synchronous seeding*—from primary colorectal carcinomas—of hematogenous metastases in the liver, lungs, and other organs is less than *metachronous seeding,* in which only liver metastases are predominantly seeded directly from the primary cancer. Pulmonary metastases are predominantly seeded from the hepatic metastases, and arterial metastases are predominantly seeded from the pulmonary lesions.

This sequential development of metastatic pattern creates windows of potential therapeutic opportunity during which disease is localized to the primary cancer alone and metastatic disease is confined to the liver alone or to the liver and lungs, where it should be susceptible to local treatment.

Finally, by use of the novel parameter of the *metastatic efficiency index,* numerical evidence shows that the incidence of arterial metastases in different target organs (excluding liver and lungs) is not accounted for by the amount of cancer cell delivery alone but also depends on differential interactions of the delivered cancer cells with the target organs.

CONTROVERSIES AND FUTURE DIRECTIONS

Controversy over the dynamics of hematogenous metastasis, particularly with respect to synchronous and metachronous seeding, turns on the validity of negative reports of organ involvement in the presence of micrometastases. Noninvasive techniques usually cannot detect metastases less than several millimeters in diameter; invasive techniques are subject to random sampling errors; and composite procedures—such as guided biopsy—require an identifiable suspicious region.

However, the very fact that patients with early primary cancers can be cured by resection alone indicates that diagnosis can be made before metastasis occurs. In addition, in spite of the risk of false-negative reports, autopsy data show that in many cases, metastasis can be limited for some time to the liver or liver and lungs, without involvement of other organs, providing a potential window of opportunity for regional chemotherapy, hopefully with improved drugs and delivery systems.

At present, in spite of the many advances in molecular biology and molecular immunology, there are no metastasis-specific probes which can be used to reliably assess the risk or presence of metastasis in individual patients by examination of a resected primary lesion. Currently much research is directed toward the development of suitable probes to predict the biologic behavior of cancer cells which, when combined with classic morphologic descriptions of the type pioneered by Dukes, would permit an accurate assessment of micrometastatic status with respect to (regional) adjuvant therapy.

Before any attempt is made to analyze the dynamics of hematogenous metastasis from colorectal carcinoma, limitations in available data will be critically assessed.

Noninvasive Procedures

A major problem is the validity of reports of noninvolvement of target organs, the so-called false negative. These cases are of clinical importance because they may well include micrometastases, a well-recognized source of treatment failure.

Current noninvasive diagnostic procedures, including standard X-radiography, computed tomography (CT), magnetic resonance imaging (MRI), scintiscans, and ultrasound do not usually permit the unequivocal detection of metastases less than 0.5 cm in diameter. There may be pathologic enhancement of detection by distortion of adjacent tissues, pathologic fracture of bone, cyst formation, and so on, but this is not invariable. Up to the present, attempts to enhance detection in scintigraphy by the use of radiolabeled probes has not been successful in detecting metastatic lesions less than 0.5 cm in diameter, and enhancement of MRI is still in a preliminary phase of investigation.

Invasive Procedures

Invasive procedures are also subject to sampling errors of the "needle in the haystack" variety when metastatic bulk is low. In the bone marrow for example, the size of the sample has been increased by replacing needle aspiration with long-cylinder core biopsy, with a corresponding increase in sensitivity, and the ability to detect small numbers of cancer cells in these samples has been enhanced by immunocytochemical techniques, particularly in combination with flow cytometry.

Other things being equal, which they seldom are, the chances of detecting metastases increase with increasing size. At any one time, therefore, the recording of metastatic involvement is linked to the relative growth rates of lesions in specific sites, up to the critical detection size of approximately 0.5 cm in diameter. The possibility of site-specific differential growth of metastases is discussed later.

Autopsy Data

An autopsy, all of the results of the prior diagnostic procedures should be available to the pathologist and are supplemented by direct observations, with histologic and possibly immunohistochemical examinations.

For large-scale studies, archival data must often be used, because autopsy rates have fallen sharply. In the United States, for example, they have decreased from 50 percent in the 1940s to 14 percent in 1965; for a variety of reasons, they continue to decline. Selection of cases for autopsy is often made on a scientifically arbitrary basis, and the data therefore cannot be used for demographic studies.

In using archival data, allowance must be made for the trend toward earlier diagnosis of primary cancers, before the development of overt metastases. Together with improved treatment and supportive technologies, this has resulted in overall increased survival and changed patterns of metastasis because the patients tend to live longer with their cancers, potentially permitting the development of more advanced patterns. An extreme example of pattern changes is provided by comparison of those described in patients with a history of breast cancer by Paget in 1889[1] in his classic "seed-and-soil" paper and by Pickren over the period 1958 to 1979;[2] the percentages of involved organs are higher in Pickren's series.

Analyses of metastatic patterns with respect to metastatic cascades (i.e., metastasis from metastases) require details of associations of organ involvement in individual cases;[3] thus, in "cascade" analysis of hematogenous metastasis in colorectal cancer, sufficient data are needed to test the dependence of lung involvement on liver involvement and that of "other" site involvement by arterial dissemination on lung involvement.[4] Analyses of the necessarily large numbers of individual autopsy reports mandate the use of computerized files. Unfortunately, at present, the autopsy has yet to be realistically classified as an "endangered species," and funds are seldom available for the transfer of old autopsy records to computer files, even when they are still available. However, efforts could at least be made to enter current autopsy data in an agreed format for retrieval via computer networks.

Sampling Errors

The presence of microscopic foci cannot be definitively excluded by autopsy because of sampling errors and detection failure. However, the significance of failure in these cases is minimal because they had not developed into clinically significant, overt lesions by the time of death.

Although at present false-negative autopsy reports of target organs have little direct clinical significance, they nonetheless constitute a major problem in the determination of macroscopic mechanisms of metastasis; their validity therefore warrants careful examination. For example, given similar, small metastatic burdens in different target sites, the chances of detecting them in individual organs are expected to decrease with increasing organ bulk. This is related to sampling techniques. At the macroscopic level, the thicker the sections into which organs are cut during autopsy, the greater the chances of missing small metastases. In the absence of relatively easily detectable surface lesions, when the liver is cut into 2-cm thick sections, at the 5 percent probability level, there is the potential of failing to detect as many as ten 0.5-cm nodules if they are present.[5] In contrast, in the adrenal, a single section in the anteroposterior plane, in which the organ is only 0.3 to 0.8 cm thick, will permit the detection of all metastases from 0.15 to 0.4 cm in diameter.

In order to assess the effects of target organ bulk on the differential reported incidence of metastasis, regression analyses were made between average target organ weights and their reported incidence of involvement; no significant correlations were obtained in groups of eight different target organs with respect to putative arterial metastases, and differences were evident in the incidence of involvement in three pairs of different organs of similar weight. Therefore, organ bulk is not a demonstrable, single dominant factor influencing the reported incidence of target organ involvement. The previous calculations clearly indicated a target organ, bulk-dependent potential for failure to detect metastatic lesions. However, in the standard +/− assessments of involvement to be used here, this potential was not realized.

METASTATIC INEFFICIENCY

Numerical analysis of hematogenous metastasis reveals that large numbers of cancer cells are lost at every step of the metastatic process, starting from their release from the primary cancer to the formation of detectable metastatic lesions.[6] Some examples of this inefficiency will be documented both in humans and in the more precise experimental systems utilizing laboratory animals.

Inefficiency in Primary Cancers

The volume doubling times (VDTs) of primary cancers represent the summation of growth and loss processes. In the case of primary colorectal carcinomas, repeated assessment of the volumes of small, actively growing tumors over prolonged periods of time is not usually possible for ethical reasons. Available measurements show a median VDT of 632 days (range, 426 to 938 days.[7] Comparison with VDTs for other carcinomas—including breast (mean, 159 days),[8] large cell bronchial carcinoma (median, 148 days),[7] squamous cell carcinoma of the head and neck (median, 9.5 days)[9] and other carcinomas listed by Steel[7] and others—strongly suggests that the relatively long VDTs of colorectal carcinomas are due mainly to the shedding of cancer cells into the feces and a much smaller loss via intra- or extramural vessels into the metastatic process, as distinct from slow cell multiplication per se. Thus, metastatic inefficiency is expressed at the initial stage of the process, at the level of cancer cell entry.

Inefficiency in the Onset of Invasion

Inefficiency in the progression from noninvasive to invasive cancers may be manifest in terms of temporal delay. Delays of as long as 20 years have been reported for the progression of at least some in situ carcinomas to microinvasive lesions.[6] While this indicates a high degree of metastatic inefficiency, the underlying mechanisms are by no means clear. Are the delays due to a genetic change in the cells in the in situ lesions, resulting in the emergence of subpopulations expressing a more invasive phenotype or genotype? Or do they simply indicate that invasion is a lengthy process punctuated by cancer cell loss and containment and basement membrane repair or a combination of these and other factors?

Inefficiency in Relation to Stage

Hematogenous metastatic disease of the colorectum is almost invariably fatal. Therefore some index of metastatic inefficiency can be obtained from the survival of patients as shown in Table 19-1, which is based on thousands of cases.[10]

Of those patients diagnosed as suffering from localized colonic or rectal cancer, this assessment must have been correct in the 60 and 56 percent, respectively, of cases surviving 20 years (after surgery). This

Table 19-1
Survival Rate (%), Years

	1	*5*	*10*	*15*	*20*
Colon					
Localized	86	68	64	61	60
Regional	76	39	33	33	33
Distant	36	9	7	6	5
Rectum					
Localized	86	66	60	59	56
Regional	77	31	23	23	21
Distant	36	6	4	4	4

SOURCE: Data from Axtell et al.[10]

group includes those with primary carcinomas from T_{is} to T_4 (N_0M_0). However, relatively few tumors are diagnosed in the in situ stage, and few patients diagnosed with tumors at the T_4 stage are expected to survive for 20 years. The survivors in the localized groups are therefore expected to be mainly distributed among T_1 to T_3, which are all invasive carcinomas. The fact that so many of these patients survived so long after surgical removal of their primary lesions indicates a high degree of inefficiency in the postinvasive phases of metastasis. The sharp decline in survival between 1 and 5 years in those patients with regional or distant disease indicates cohorts in which undetected metastases were present prior to resection. The median volume doubling times of colorectal metastases in the liver and lungs are 112[11] and 100[7] days respectively, but these values, which came from measurements of visualized, larger, and relatively slowly growing tumors are longer than expected for undetected lesions less than 0.5 cm in diameter. Assuming exponential increase in volume, which appears warranted for small metastatic lesions, growth of a single cancer cell (diameter 14 μm) to a detectable metastasis measuring 0.5 cm in diameter requires 25 volume doublings, taking somewhat less than 6 years. This would account for the development of diagnosable metastatic disease in 20 percent of patients misdiagnosed as having localized cancer at the time of operation 5 years previously. The subsequent development of lethal metastatic disease is therefore a comparatively efficient (i.e., rapid) process.

Inefficiency after Intravasation

It has been known for many years that there is an apparent gross disparity between the large numbers of circulating cancer cells detected in the blood and the relatively small numbers of metastases that are subsequently detected.[6]

An attempt to quantitate the degree of metastatic inefficiency was based on the observation that samples of blood collected from the ipsilateral renal veins of patients just before nephrectomy for renal cell carcinomas sometimes contained cancer cells in numbers corresponding to prorated release rates in excess of 10^7 cells per 24 h. In spite of this, and in the presence of primary cancers measuring between 8 to 10 cm in diameter, from which cancer cells must have been released for some time before nephrectomy, two of these patients were clinically free of metastasis 6 years after operation.[12] Calculations based on a volume doubling time of 60 days for renal cell carcinomas metastatic to the lungs[7] and the assumption of exponential increase in volume indicate that a single surviving cancer cell is expected to grow into a detectable 0.5-cm metastasis in approximately 4 years; in this situation, the chances of an intravasated cancer cell forming a pulmonary metastasis were 1 in 10^{10}!

More precise estimates of metastatic inefficiency can be made using transplantable tumors in laboratory animals. However, it must not be overlooked that these are adapted to growth following injection and that the degree of inefficiency may be considerably underestimated. In many of these model systems, pulmonary colony counts made at appropriate times after tail vein injection of cancer cells indicate that more than 99.9 percent of the cells perish in the lungs; analogous results are obtained in the liver following portal vein injections. Bioassays have shown that 85 percent or more of the injected cells are lethally damaged within several minutes of arrival in the microvasculature[6] and that the majority of the survivors are killed by slower processes associated with host-defense systems.[13] Intravital videomicroscopy has confirmed that an important cause of rapid, lethal damage to cancer cells is associated with their deformation from spheres to cylinders on entry into capillaries, which results in increases in their surface membrane tension above the level required for rupture.[14]

CANCER CELL TRAFFIC

The significance of metastatic inefficiency is illustrated by studies of cancer cell traffic in laboratory animals. Following tail-vein injection of radiolabeled cancer cells, gamma counts made on the lungs, liver, and blood removed from various circulation access points indicated that the majority of cancer cells arriving in the lungs were arrested and killed in the pulmonary microcirculation. In addition, the majority of injected cells later released from the lungs and delivered to the liver via the hepatic artery were lethally damaged before arrest in the liver.[15]

Analogous studies of liver-to-lung traffic following injection of cancer cells into the portal vein showed that a majority of cells were arrested and killed in the liver and that the majority of the small proportion of cells later released from the liver were incapable of forming colonies after arrival in the lungs.[16]

These results, and many others, in general indicate that each time a blood-borne bolus of cancer cells from a "generalizing" site enters the microvasculature of the first in-line target organ, most of the cells are permanently arrested and killed; very few of the originally injected cells are released into the bloodstream in a viable, tumorigenic state, where they proceed to the target site that is next in line. On the cells' arrival in these sites, the processes of arrest, killing, and release are repeated. This occurs in metastatic "cascades,"[3] or metastasis from metastases.

METASTATIC CASCADES

More than 99.9 percent of the cancer cells arriving in the liver from a primary colorectal carcinoma are arrested and destroyed in the sinusoids. Even if all of the 0.1 percent or less of the surviving cancer cells were released into the hepatic vein and reached the lungs, less than 0.1 percent of these would be expected to survive in the pulmonary microcirculation. If all of these survivors were released from the lungs to gain access to the arterial circulation, due to dilution and distribution factors, less than 0.01 percent of these cells would be expected to have the capacity to form arterial metastases in these other target organs. Therefore, cancer cells released directly from their parent colorectal tumor and following the predominant vascular route from the liver to the lungs, and thence to other organs, would have a 1 : 1000 chance of generating a liver metastasis; a 1 : 1 million chance of generating a lung metastasis, and a 1 : 10 billion chance of generating an arterial metastasis in a target organ receiving 10 percent of the cardiac output. If the calculated value of 10^{10} for the metastatic inefficiency of renal carcinoma cells in the lungs is applicable to cells from colorectal carcinomas, then each of the above calculated odds would have to be reduced by an additional seven orders of magnitude!

Therefore, from statistical considerations, it is improbable that the lungs and other organs are seeded *synchronously* with the liver by the same original bolus of cancer cells leaving the primary cancer. In contrast, if metastatic seeding were to take place *metachronously* in a stepwise manner, by metastasis from metastases, then the chances of a cancer cell released from an hepatic metastasis successfully seeding a pulmonary metastasis would be 1 : 1000 (cf., 1 : 10^6), and the chances of a cancer cell released from a pulmonary metastasis successfully seeding an arterial metastasis would be 1 : 10,000 (cf., 1 : 10^{10}). Synchronous and metachronous seeding are illustrated in Fig. 19-1.

Metachronous seeding would result in pulmonary metastases occurring only in the presence of hepatic metastases, and arterial metastases would require the presence of pulmonary metastases. Analysis of autopsy data on patients dying with a history of colorectal carcinoma have revealed that, in the absence of detectable liver metastasis, 85 percent of cases had no metastases elsewhere; 73 percent of cases with lung metastases had detectable liver metastases; and 50 percent of cases with arterial metastases had detectable lung metastases. After allowing for false-negative reports on the presence of liver and lung metastases and alternative dissemination routes (e.g., Batson's paravertebral plexus), the fit with the concept of metachronous seeding is impressive.[4]

The clinical significance of stepwise, metachronous, hematogenous metastasis is that in its early stages, in the majority of cases, metastatic disease is confined to the liver or liver and lungs, where therapy could be selectively directed at these sites.[17]

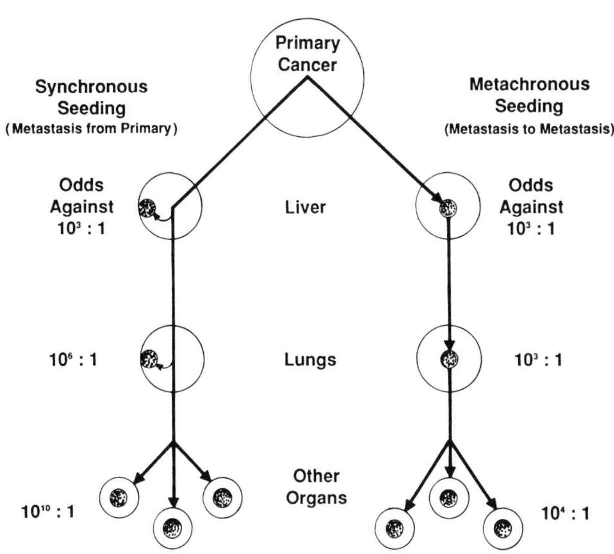

FIG. 19-1. Probabilities of single cancer cells from primary colorectal carcinomas or their metastases generating hepatic, pulmonary, and arterial metastases by synchronous and metachronous seeding mechanisms.

HEMATOGENOUS METASTATIC PATTERNS

The liver and lungs are the two most common sites for metastasis from primary colorectal carcinomas. This is explicable in terms of the anatomy of portal and systemic venous drainage. The pattern of arterial metastasis is accounted for by two nonexclusive hypotheses. The first is the "mechanical" hypothesis,[18] which considers that the major determinant is differential delivery of cancer cells; while this successfully accounts for some features of pattern, it clearly does not account for many, and the data shown in Table 19-2 fail to demonstrate a statistically significant correlation between the incidence of putative arterial metastases in nine different target organs and the blood flow to them ($r = 0.11$). The second, the "seed-and-soil" hypothesis,[1] considers that the major pattern determinants are the favorable or unfavorable interactions occurring in the different target organs after delivery of the cancer cells; these largely undefined interactions account for many of the features of metastatic patterns, as reviewed elsewhere.[19] It should be noted that the liver and lungs are not included in Table 19-2 (because discrimination cannot be made between venous and arterial dissemination to these organs) and that the high incidence of metastasis to the (axial) bone marrow probably reflects dissemination via Batson's plexus.

Some insight into the separate contributions of the delivery and subsequent interactions of cancer cells and their target organ environment may be obtained from *metastatic efficiency indices* (MEIs),[20] which relate the incidence of metastatic involvement to normalized "units" of cancer cells delivered. It is known

Table 19-2
Incidence and Metastatic Efficiency Index in Different Target Organs in Cases of Metastatic Colorectal Carcinoma

Target organs	*Kidneys*	*Brain*	*Bone marrow*	*SkMM*[a]	*Skin*	*Heart*	*Thyroid*	*Adrenals*	*Eye*[b]
Blood flow[c] (mL/min)	1000	750	600	560	400	240	100	90	0.63
Percent incidence[c]	13.0	11.0	27.0	3.0	5.0	2.0	4.0	31.0	4.2
Metastatic efficiency index (MEI)	0.013	0.015	0.045	0.005	0.013	0.008	0.040	0.344	6.7

[a]Skeletal muscle.
[b]Data from Weiss[26] and Nelson et al.[27]
[c]Data from Weiss.[20]

from experiments on animals that when cancer cells are injected into the left ventricular cavity, delivery to different organs correlates closely with the proportions of cardiac output going to each organ ($r = 0.99$). The MEI is therefore calculated by dividing the percentage incidence of target organ involvement by organ blood flow (milliliters per minute) as shown in Table 19-2, and the results indicate the importance of differential organ-environmental effects over and above delivery. For cells from colonic cancers, the most favored environment is the eye, although the incidence of ocular metastases is low on account of low delivery. The next most favored environment is the adrenal gland, where, in spite of relatively low delivery of cancer cells, both the incidence of metastases and the MEI values are high. Although the incidence of bone-marrow metastases is almost as high as in the adrenals and arterial delivery to bone is less than one-sixth of that to the adrenals, the lower MEI value for bone marrow indicates that it is a far more hostile environment. The least favored environments for colonic cancer metastases are skeletal muscle and myocardium, in accord with experiments relating muscle contractility to cancer cell killing.[21,22]

Different target organ environments induce a variety of changes in cancer cells growing in them, which may be reflected in differential metastatic behavior.[23,24] This may contribute to the different arterial metastatic patterns observed at autopsy on cases with histories of carcinomas of the upper and lower thirds of the rectum, in which portal and systemic venous drainage are respectively dominant.[25] The major difference in prearterial metastatic behavior is that tumor cells from the upper third of the rectum progress sequentially from liver to lung to arterial metastasis, whereas those from the lower thirds progress from lung to arterial metastasis. Therefore it is possible that growth of the cancer cells in the liver induces changes in their metastatic behavior, which persist after growth in the lungs.

The existence of site-associated differences between cancer cells in primary lesions and those in secondary (liver), tertiary (lungs), and quarternary (arterial) metastases raises the possibilities of differential growth and differential response to therapy.[17]

REFERENCES

1. Paget S: The distribution of secondary growths in cancer of the breast. *Lancet* 1:571–573, 1898.
2. Pickren JW: *Principles of Metastasis*. Orlando, Fla, Academic Press, 1985, p 232.
3. Viadana E, Bross IDJ, Pickren JW: The metastatic spread of cancers of the digestive system in man. *Oncology* 35:114–126, 1978.
4. Weiss L, Grundmann E, Torhorst J, et al: Haematogenous metastatic patterns in colonic carcinoma: An analysis of 1541 necropsies. *J Pathol* 150:195–203, 1986.
5. Weiss L, Harlos JP: The validity of negative necropsy reports for metastases in solid organs. *J Pathol* 148:203–206, 1986.
6. Weiss L: Metastatic inefficiency. *Adv Cancer Res* 54:159–211, 1990.
7. Steel GG: *Growth kinetics of Tumours*. Oxford, England, Clarendon Press, 1977, p 48.
8. Weiss L: Unpublished collated data, 1990.
9. Galante E, Gallus G, Chiesa F, et al: Growth rate of head and neck tumors. *Eur J Cancer Clin Oncol* 18:707–771, 1982.
10. Axtell LM, Asire AJ: *Cancer Patient Survival*. Report no 5, DHEW (NIH). Washington, DC, US Government Printing Office, 1976, pp 77–992.
11. Finlay IG, Meek DR, Gray HW, et al: Incidence and detection of occult hepatic metastases in colorectal carcinoma. *Br Med J* 284:803–805, 1982.
12. Glaves D, Huben RP, Weiss L: Haematogenous dissemination of cells from human renal carcinomas. *Br J Cancer* 57:32–35, 1988.
13. Orr FW, Buchanan MR, Weiss L: *Microcirculation in Cancer Metastasis*. Boca Raton, Fla, CRC Press, 1991.
14. Weiss L, Nannmark U, Johansson BR, et al: Lethal deformation of cancer cells in the microcirculation: A potential rate regulator of hematogenous metastasis. *Int J Cancer* 50:103–107, 1992.
15. Weiss L: Cancer cell traffic from the lungs to the liver: An example of metastatic inefficiency. *Int J Cancer* 25:385–392, 1980.

16. Weiss L, Ward PM, Holmes JC: Liver-to-lung traffic of cancer cells. *Int J Cancer* 32:79–83, 1983.
17. Weiss L: Metastatic inefficiency and regional therapy for liver metastases from colorectal carcinoma. *Reg Cancer Treat* 2:77–81, 1989.
18. Ewing J: Metastasis, in *Neoplastic Diseases: A Treatise on Tumours*, 3rd ed. Philadelphia, Saunders, 1928, chap 4.
19. Weiss L: *Principles of Metastasis*. Orlando, Fla, Academic Press, pp 160–256, 1985.
20. Weiss L: Comments on hematogenous metastatic patterns in humans as revealed by autopsy. *Clin Exp Metastasis* 10:191–199, 1992.
21. Weiss L: Biomechanical destruction of cancer cells in skeletal muscle: A rate-regulator for hematogenous metastasis. *Clin Exp Metastasis* 7:483–491, 1989.
22. Weiss L: Biomechanical destruction of cancer cells in the heart: A rate-regulator for hematogenous metastasis. *Invasion Metastasis* 8:228–237, 1988.
23. Weiss L: Site-associated differences in cancer cell populations. *Clin Exp Metastasis* 9:193–203, 1991.
24. Grinnell RS: Lymphatic block with atypical and retrograde lymphatic metastasis and spread in carcinoma of the colon and rectum. *Ann Surg* 163:272–280, 1966.
25. Weiss L, Voit A, Lane WW: Metastatic patterns in patients with carcinomas of the lower esophagus and upper rectum. *Invasion Metastasis* 4:47–60, 1984.
26. Weiss L: Analysis of the incidence of intraocular metastasis, *Br J Ophthalmol* 71:149–151, 1993.
27. Nelson CC, Hertzberg BS, Klintworth GK: A histopathologic study of 716 unselected eyes in patients with cancer at the time of death. *Am J Ophthalmol* 95:788–793, 1983.

PART 4

Staging and Prognostic Determinants

CHAPTER 20

Staging Systems

L. Peter Fielding

HIGHLIGHTS

After nearly 100 years of sporadic and somewhat disorganized development of staging for colorectal cancer, certain conclusions can be drawn. At present, the most powerful prognostic information comes from a detailed description of the extent of anatomic tumor spread. This can be identified by using the International Comprehensive Anatomic Terminology (ICAT) checklist (Table 20-1), from which almost all staging systems currently in use worldwide can be derived.

There is an increasing acceptance of the TNM system of the American Joint Committee on Cancer/Union Internationale Contre le Cancer (AJCC/UICC)[1,2] for the staging of colorectal cancer, but this approach has certain problems that will need to be addressed.

CONTROVERSIES

The problems associated with the TNM system are as follows: the amalgamation of distinguishable tumor types in the pT_4 subgroups, the implication that the pN_3 tumors might be incurable, and the poor description of metastatic disease by a single M_1 category.

As investigative methods improve, the problem of "stage migration" must be considered more effectively. These controversial areas are discussed in some detail.

FUTURE DIRECTIONS

Additional clinical and pathologic information of prognostic significance will be integrated into new systems of prognosis. The currently used items are listed in the International Documentation System (IDS) for colorectal cancer (Table 20-2). Furthermore, increasingly sophisticated laboratory techniques will be established, which will achieve two goals: (1) a more accurate description of the anatomic spread of tumor and (2) additional information concerning the degree of tumor aggressiveness, which has prognostic implications.

It is to be hoped that these developments will allow us to more accurately "stage" patients into cohorts with very similar prognosis, and this will contribute to the overall aims of tumor staging in patient management.

PURPOSES OF STAGING

There are several purposes for tumor staging: to help define clinical management, to facilitate communication between physicians, to provide a basis for stratification and analysis of treatment results in prospective studies, and to provide some prognostic information for patients and their families. Currently the most informative staging systems to describe colorectal cancer comprise classification methods that describe the extent of anatomic tumor spread. However, it is also known that certain features of clinical presentation strongly influence outcome. In addition, the histologic grade and other assessments of tumor "aggressiveness"—defined as the rapidity with which tumor metastasizes and grows—have prognostic power, but their relative impact when compared with extent of anatomic tumor spread or clinical features is, at present, small.

Table 20-1
International Comprehensive Anatomic Terminology (ICAT) for Colorectal Cancer

Microscopic description of tumor depth
1. Primary tumor cannot be assessed (pT_X)
2. No evidence of primary tumor (pT_0)
3. Severe dysplasia; carcinoma in situ (pT_{is})
4. Tumor invades submucosa (pT_1)
5. Tumor invades muscularis propria (pT_2)
6. Tumor invades through muscularis propria into the subserosal connective tissue or nonperitonealized pericolic or perirectal tissue (pT_3)
7. Tumor directly invades other organs or structures (pT_4)
8. Tumor to and invading free (serosal) surface of the specimen (pT_4)

Regional lymph node status
9. Cannot be assessed (N_X)
10. Number of lymph nodes examined
11. Number of nodes positive for tumor
12. Line 11 = 0 (pN_0)
13. Line 11 = 1–3 positive nodes (pN_1)
14. Line 11 = >3 positive nodes (pN_2)

Status of nodes on vascular trunk
15. Not recorded
16. Negative for tumor
17. Positive for tumor (pN_3)

Apical node status
18. Not recorded
19. Negative for tumor
20. Positive for tumor (pN_3)

Distant metastasis: Status after definitive treatment
21. Cannot be assessed (M_X)
22. None (M_0)
23. Present (M_1)

Residual tumor: Status after definitive treatment
24. Cannot be assessed (R_X)
25. None (R_0)
26. Locally in line of bowel resection only (shown histologically) (R_1)
27. Distant only (histologically or clinically) (R_2)
28. Both local and distant ($R_1 + R_2$)

Although there have been increasing levels of agreement concerning methods to describe extent of anatomic tumor spread and clinical features of prognostic significance, the description of tumor aggressiveness by the assessment of histology and other biological markers is less well defined and is considered in Chaps. 21–25.

HISTORICAL BACKGROUND

The first cohesive attempt to carry out staging for rectal cancer was made by J. P. Lockhart-Mummery,[3] a surgeon at St. Mark's Hospital in London in 1927, who reported on 200 patients with rectal cancer treated by perineal excision. This system proposed to divide rectal tumors into three categories (A, B, and C), based on depth of invasion of the tumor into the rectal wall. The 5-year cure rate for the patients with A lesions was 74 percent; with B lesions, 44 percent; and with C lesions, 44 percent. Thus the system appeared to successfully identify a patient subgroup with good survival rates following operation, and it set the pattern for this type of tumor classification for the next 50 years.

After the introduction of Lockhart-Mummery's system, St. Mark's Hospital became a major source of new systems for the classification of colorectal cancers. C. E. Dukes became the primary spokesman on this topic, and in 1930 he offered his first modification of the Lockhart-Mummery system.[4] In this article he reported his results on 100 *rectal* cancers and modified the earlier system to include a description of lymph node status. Subsequently, as ideas evolved, Dukes

Table 20-2
International Documentation System (IDS) for Colorectal Cancer

Information type	*Clinical features*	*Pathologic features*
Basic information	Country Hospital (name/code) Patient identification (name/code) Patient race Past tumor history	Number of primary tumors Tumor measurements Appearance of serosal surface Associated pathology Tumor type
Variables of proven prognostic significance	Surgeon (name/code) Patient gender and age Presentation Anatomic extent of tumor Residual tumor	Extent of direct spread Regional nodal status Local residual tumor Distant metastasis status Venous involvement Histology of infiltrating margin Tumor grade
Information of probable prognostic significance	Preoperative treatment Anatomic site of primary Tumor mobility Technique of tumor mobilization Tumor perforation Surgical procedure Resection of distant metastases Postoperative treatments	Tumor perforation Inflammatory cell infiltrate Lymphoid aggregates

continued to modify his staging system. In 1932 he published a system of classification which is generally referred to as the *Dukes classification*.[5] In that article, Dukes modified the 1930 system to reflect the apparent rarity of lymph node involvement until the tumor had penetrated through the full thickness of the rectal wall (Fig. 20-1). According to this new classification, cancers were graded as follows:

"A" cases: Carcinoma limited to the wall of the rectum, there being no extension into the extrarectal tissues and no metastases in lymph nodes.
"B" cases: Spread by direct continuity to the extrarectal tissues but no invasion of the regional lymph nodes.
"C" cases: Metastases within the regional lymph nodes.

Dukes proposed one further modification of his system in 1936:[6] he continued the three divisions of A, B, and C unchanged as described in the 1932 article, but, in addition, the C category was subdivided as follows:

"C_1" cases: Regional lymph nodes are involved, or those in which the upward spread has not yet reached the glands at the point of ligature of the blood vessels.
"C_2" cases: Nodal spread has reached up to the level of the point of ligature of the blood vessels.

The purpose of subdividing the "C" category was to better define the usual sequence of lymph-node involvement in rectal cancer. In the same way that the cancer spreads in a generally orderly manner from the mucosa to the submucosa and then to the muscle wall, it usually spreads first to the pericolic lymph nodes and then upward along the chain of nodes following the superior rectal artery. The implication was that curative surgical treatment was more likely as long as resection was accomplished before the "apical" lymph node became involved with tumor. Although there are exceptions to the postulate, the general statement remains true for both rectal and colonic cancer (Fig. 20-1).

Several other authors have investigated specific areas of these classifications (Simpson and Mayo in 1939;[7] Kirklin, Dockerty, and Waugh in 1949;[8] and Astler and Coller in 1954[9]). However, the purpose of these articles was not to introduce new systems of staging but to specifically address certain detailed ideas within the Dukes system, namely the prognostic implications of involvement of the peritoneal surface with tumor, its association with lymph node positivity, and the significance of the peritoneal reflection in rectal cancer.

These modifications were designed to help judge which surgical approach to lesions of the rectosigmoid and rectum offered the best outcome. Today the very frequent use of low anterior resection of the rectum has subsumed this discussion. However, the controversy lives on in the debate concerning the need for total mesorectal excision during anterior resection of rectal tumors.[10]

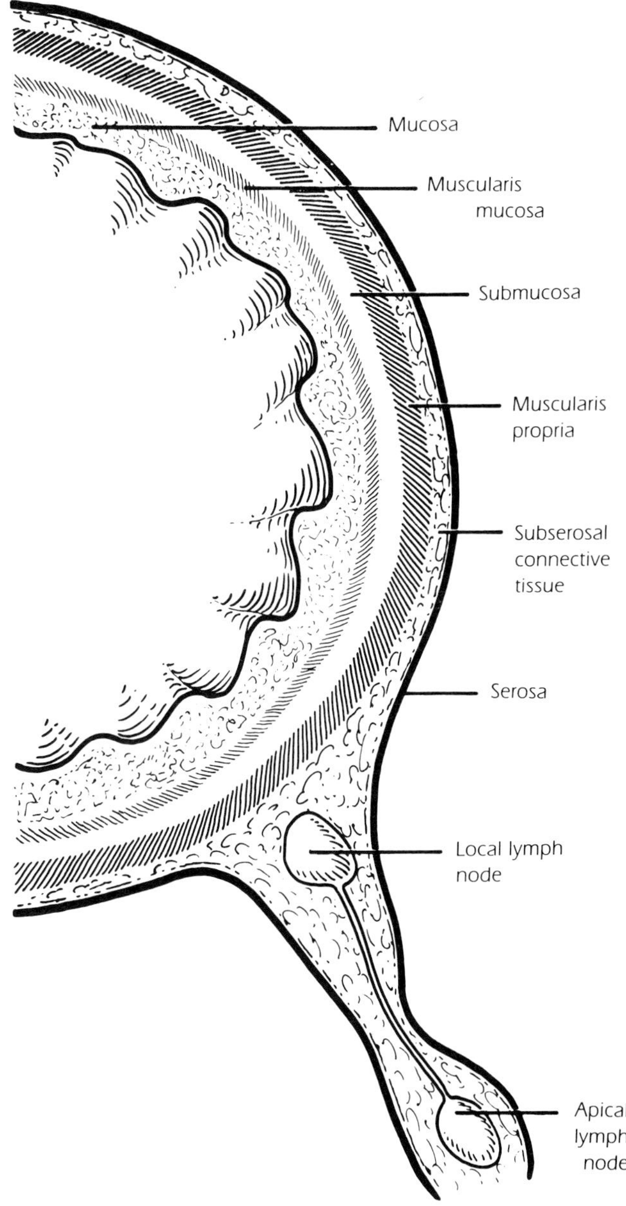

FIG. 20-1. Schematic of bowel wall and nodal location.

An important step forward in these classification systems occurred with the introduction of a "D" category by Turnbull in 1967, which indicated incurability because of metastasis.[11] The most recent of the alphabetized methods was described by Davis and Newland in 1982 (the Australian system); this, in addition to A, B, C, and D, included a category for carcinoma confined to the mucosa (category 0) and an accommodation for local excision or other local procedure done without lymphadenectomy (category X).[12] Although this system is somewhat more complex, once "curative" resections are isolated, the Australian A, B, C,

Table 20-3
American Joint Committee on Cancer/Union Internationale Contre le Cancer—TNM Classification

T_X	Minimum requirements to assess the primary tumor cannot be met.
pT_0	No evidence of primary tumor.
pT_{is}	In situ carcinoma.
pT_1	Tumor extends into the submucosa.
pT_2	Tumor extends into the muscularis propria.
pT_3	Tumor extends through the muscularis propria into the subserosa or into nonperitonealized pericolic or perirectal tissues.
pT_4	Tumor extends directly into other organs or tissues, or tumor perforates the visceral peritoneum of the specimen.
N_X	Minimum requirements to assess the regional lymph nodes cannot be met.
pN_0	No lymph node metastasis.
pN_1	Metastatic tumor in one to three pericolic or perirectal lymph nodes.
pN_2	Metastatic tumor in four or more pericolic or perirectal lymph nodes.
pN_3	Metastatic to any lymph node along the course of a major named vascular trunk.
M_X	Minimum requirements to assess distant metastasis cannot be met.
M_0	No distant metastasis.
M_1	Distant metastasis present.

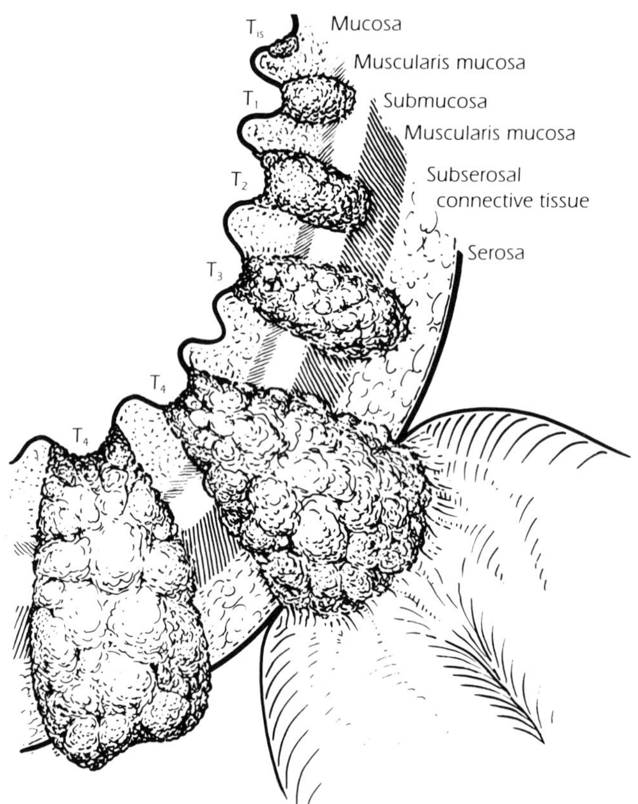

FIG. 20-2. Examples of "T" stages of mural penetration.

D system was found to have greater predictive power than either the TNM or the Astler-Coller systems.[13]

Parallel to these developments, Denoix first presented the TNM (tumor, node, metastasis) system for staging cancers in 1954. It classifies tumors based on the extent of disease utilizing both clinical and pathologic information.[14] The principal advantage of this method is that each column in the classification (T, N, and M) makes no assumption about the status in another part of the system. In other words, it allows for the exceptions to the general rule of "orderly" progression of tumor spread (Table 20-3, Fig. 20-2). However, when the TNM system is grouped into stages (0 to IV), the similarities with the Dukes classification is very substantial (Table 20-4 and Fig. 20-3).

Furthermore, in the TNM method, because nodal involvement is listed as a separate category, there is no assumption that the full thickness of the intestinal wall is penetrated before lymph node involvement occurs. Thus, the TNM system has two major advantages: first, clinical observations are introduced by the inclusion of the metastatic category; and, second, be-

Table 20-4
Stage Group, TNM Features, and Dukes Classification

Stage groupings	*Code*	*Five-year survival rate, %*	*Dukes class*
Stage 0	pT_{is}, pN_0, M_0	100	
Stage I	pT_1, pN_0, M_0	100	A
	pT_2, pN_0, M_0	85	
Stage II	pT_3, pN_0, M_0	70	B
	pT_4, pN_0, M_0	30	
Stage III	Any pT, pN_1, M_0	60	
	Any pT, pN_2, M_0		C
	Any pT, pN_3, M_0	30	
Stage IV	Any pT, any pN, M_1	3	"D"[a]

[a]Indicates common usage of a disseminated tumor category.

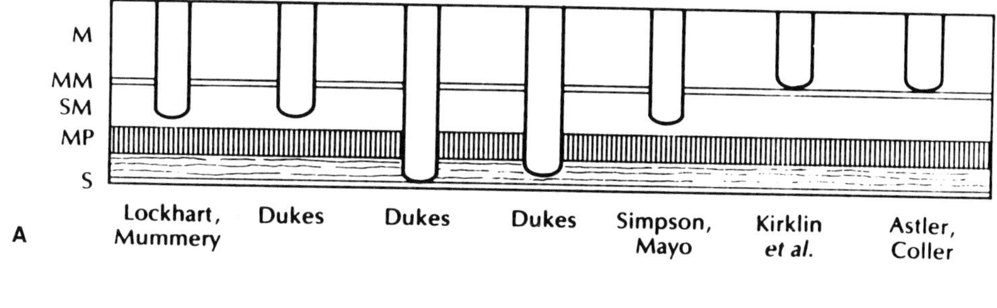

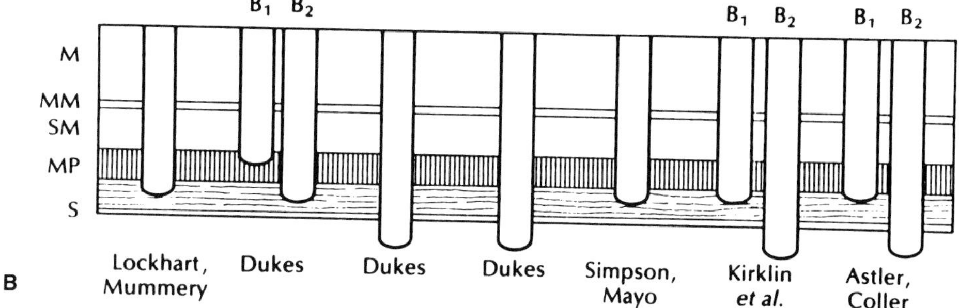

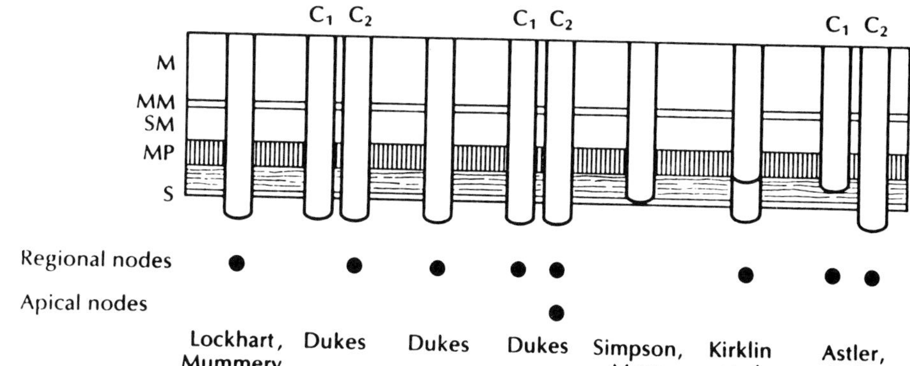

FIG. 20-3. Critical views (panels *A*, *B*, and *C*) of the classification and staging of colorectal cancer. (Adapted with permission from Zinkin LD: A critical review of the classification and staging of colorectal cancer. *Dis Colon Rectum* 26:37–43, 1983 © American Society of Colon & Rectal Surgeons.)

cause a new (nonalphabetized) nomenclature is used, confusion caused by repeated alteration of alphabet definitions is avoided.[14]

PROBLEMS WITH THE TNM SYSTEM

Although the TNM method has been the subject of an extraordinary amount of international work and is a useful contribution, some problems will need additional clarification:

1. Currently, the pT_4 category includes two types of locally advanced tumor: (a) those which have become attached to a contiguous organ but without tumor on the surface (free mesothelial surface) of the specimen and (b) tumor which is apparent on the surface of the specimen. This dichotomy is associated with an identifiable discriminate difference in prognosis in which the presence of tumor on the surface of the specimen, open to the coelomic cavity, is associated with the worse outcome.[15,16] It would be reasonable, therefore, particularly for detailed research protocols, to subdivide the pT_4 classification into (a) and (b) subgroups.
2. The pN_3 category for most tumors suggests incurability because of the unresectability of the nodal involvement beyond the immediate regional lymph nodes, but this is not a universal rule.
3. The M category does not distinguish between locoregional persistence of disease from more widespread tumor dissemination. In addition, it does not take into account the occasional patient who undergoes resection of a distant metastasis for "cure." To solve these problems the M category should be subdivided depending on "residual" tumor status as suggested by Hermanek:[15] R_0 (no residual tumor); R_1 (local/residual tumor in the line of bowel resection only [shown histologically]); R_2 (distant residual tumor only [shown histologically or clinically]); R_1 plus R_2 (both local and distant residual tumor; see Table 20-1).

Despite these problems, the TNM system has been adopted as the surgical staging system of choice in many parts of the world and permits a better understanding of the results from one center to another.

DATA GATHERING FOR STAGING

In an attempt to identify the specific line items of information required for an appropriate description of anatomic extent of tumor, a working party was brought together under the auspices of the World Congresses of Gastroenterology.[17] This group suggested the adoption of an "International Comprehensive Anatomical Terminology" (ICAT) system for colorectal cancer, which consists of a 28-line checklist from which virtually all the currently recognized staging systems for colorectal cancer can be derived (Table 20-1).

REFINEMENTS IN ANATOMIC STAGING METHODS[18]

One of the current dilemmas concerning the determination of outcome in patients with cancer is that tumors with apparently similar anatomic extent of neoplastic spread (stage) may have substantially different clinical outcomes.[19] Such prognostic heterogeneity has prompted attempts to refine our methods to define anatomic stage, not only through enhanced radiologic techniques and improvement in the routine task of tumor sampling but also by the use of the newer methods that more accurately detect the presence of metastasis (especially micrometastasis), such as immunohistochemistry, flow cytometry, and other molecular markers.

These issues are becoming increasingly important for patients with colorectal cancer because adjuvant therapies are being identified, and thus there is an increased need to determine whether there is any evidence of local residual and/or systemic tumor,[20] so that only appropriate subgroups will receive adjuvant treatment.

Before the newer techniques to define the extent of tumor spread are discussed, it is necessary to emphasize that the traditional methods of histopathologic examination be implemented to a high standard. There is some observer variation between pathologists concerning an accurate description of depth of spread of the primary tumor in the organ of origin.[21] The primary tumor must be cut through the maximum depth of tumor penetration in the organ to obtain an accurate pT category. There must also be a vigorous attempt to harvest lymph nodes that drain the tumor by careful dissection of the specimen; this can be helped by using acid-alcohol-containing fixative solutions to increase the visibility and palpability of the nodes during dissection.[22] Xylene clearance of the mesenteric fat[23] has been described, but it is time-consuming, messy, and impractical for routine use.

When regional lymph nodes are involved with tumor, the prognosis for most patients worsens rapidly. When the tumor has disrupted the normal histologic pattern of the node, detection of metastasis is easy to identify using the traditional hematoxylin and eosin staining method. However, recognizing the presence of small foci of metastatic disease (micrometastases) can be more difficult. However, there are tools that can now allow us to recognize micrometastases reliably, even at the single-cell level. These improved techniques have given rise to a redefinition of the term *micrometastasis,* which formerly was defined as foci of tumor cells less than 2 mm in diameter.[24,25] However, with the use of immunologic and molecular markers, we can detect single cells or small cell clusters.[18,26]

Because we are able to identify an increased yield of lymph node specimens that contain tumor, it is necessary to question the biologic meaning of this finding. If it is postulated that the survival of patients with these newly defined micrometastatic "positive lymph nodes" lies somewhere between the outcome of the traditional groups "with" and "without" lymph node involvement, it may take several thousand such cases to determine a clinically significant (e.g., 15 percent) difference for the newly defined group when compared to the other two traditional groups. Furthermore, we should have good statistical and clinical reasons for routinely submitting negative lymph nodes to a wide "battery" of tests in the quest to identify such micrometastasis. Only future research will guide us in this regard. However, it is a reasonable biological premise to suggest that patients in whom micrometastatic disease to the lymph nodes has occurred will fare worse than those patients in whom there are none. Furthermore, we might postulate that it is in these patients that adjuvant chemotherapy might play its greatest role because of minimal tumor bulk.

THE PROBLEM OF "STAGE MIGRATION"

In the previous section, improvements in our diagnostic power to determine anatomic extent of tumor spread more accurately have been discussed. Although such progress is to be applauded, there are some important implications for reporting and comparing the results of treatment because of "stage migration." The most recent lucid explanation of "stage migration" was reported by Feinstein and coworkers.[27] In essence, researchers can be misled by apparent "therapeutic advances" that may be little more than a reflection of changes in patient classification.

Consider a population of cancer patients in which new methods make it possible to identify a group of patients who were formerly classified as having stage II disease but who have, in fact, some degree of metastatic disease. With this new information, these patients would be classified as having stage IV disease. The effect on survival figures comparing the old patient cohort with the new cohort is that the survival figures for the "new stage II" and the "new stage IV" groups *both* would rise, although the prognosis for the patient population as a whole would not change. The reason for the apparent "improvement" in the outcome for the patient subsets can be understood quite readily: the new test identified a number of patients who originally had stage II disease but who, in fact, had disseminated disease. Therefore, they would have a reduced survival potential compared with others with stage II tumors. When these patients are removed from the stage II group and transferred to the stage IV group, the remaining patients have a better overall outlook because the heterogeneity of the group has been reduced by removing patients with a poorer prognosis. Furthermore, those patients who were transferred to the stage IV category are likely to be at an "earlier phase" of tumor dissemination than the others in the stage IV group. Consequently, the effect on prognosis of the new stage IV cohort would be to increase their apparent survival because of "lead-time" bias.

As we progress and refine the accuracy of classifying patients in each of the anatomic tumor prognostic stages, we must be careful to recognize that comparisons of apparently similar stage groups that have been classified by different methods are likely to give different outcomes.

Thus, recognizing the phenomenon of "stage migration," we can draw a number of conclusions:

1. Simplistic interpretations of differences in results from one study to another must be avoided.
2. Randomized studies should be conducted with similar investigational methods to determine tumor anatomic stage throughout the study period.
3. It may be helpful for the interpretation of study results to document "ineligible" and "eligible" patients in a clinical trial so as to examine whether stage migration has occurred.

ADDITIONAL PROGNOSTIC FACTORS

We have considered anatomic tumor spread and its more accurate determination. However, there are several other determinants of prognosis that can be classified arbitrarily into clinical, histopathologic, and several types of molecular prognostic factors. These features must be discussed because they influence patient outcome, although they do not influence a description of anatomic tumor stage per se. However, the identification of anatomic stage is not a goal in and of itself. The purpose of staging is to group patients into a cohort with a similar outcome. If the presence or absence of additional prognostic factors has an effect on outcome in a given anatomic stage, then this factor is relevant to clinical decision making and research protocols.

CLINICOPATHOLOGIC STAGING SYSTEMS

Several types of "clinical" prognostic factors which influence long-term outcome have been identified. Lead-time bias is probably the most important single issue when one is considering the outcome of tumors found by screening programs (i.e., to detect asymptomatic patients with cancer in the population at large) and surveillance programs (i.e., to detect high-risk patient groups) when compared with tumors recognized because of patients' symptoms.[28,29] Furthermore, some patients with tumors may present as emergency admissions to the hospital (e.g., bowel obstruction or perforation), and these patients have substantially reduced survival rates compared with otherwise similar patients who seek elective treatment for symptomatic disease.[19,30]

A controversial but important item is surgeon-related variability, which has been reported as a prognostic variable even when the case mix is similar.[31] Gender and age also may influence outcome.[30]

The overall general health of the patient clearly influences survival, and this factor becomes more relevant with increasing patient age, particularly in patients with distant metastases and those for whom treatment has been unable to achieve removal of all macroscopic tumor. Thus, the presence of comorbid disease (e.g., diabetes or cardiac or pulmonary disease), substantial recent weight loss, corticosteroid or other immunosuppressant administration, and differences in functional status will influence outcome. The Eastern Cooperative Oncology Group and Karnofsky performance scales[32–34] can be used to assess these functions, but an independent effect of these scales on prognosis has not yet been demonstrated in multivariate analyses.

The integration of clinical and pathologic information to produce a more accurate estimate of 5-year patient survival for individual patients has been reported.[19] In this study, prospectively collected information on 2524 patients who had undergone "curative" resection for colorectal cancer was analyzed to establish the rank-order of importance of both clinical and pathologic factors affecting outcome. The patients were divided into two groups. In the first, a statistical weighting was established for each prognostic factor; those that influenced long-term survival were, in order of importance, lymph node status, tumor mobility, number of lymph nodes positive for tumor, presence of bowel obstruction, and depth of primary tumor penetration. Factors that influenced in-hospital mortality were cardiopulmonary complications, intraabdominal sepsis (without anastomotic leak), presence of bowel obstruction, and age. In the second group of patients, these mathematical weightings were applied, and the predicted and observed outcomes were in close agreement. Thus, statistical techniques of this kind will be of value in prognosis and in the analysis of the results of new treatment regimens.

As an extension of the work of the World Congresses of Gastroenterology Working Party on Colorectal Staging, an International Documentation System (IDS) for these tumors was described. This IDS lists the clinical and pathologic features, divided into three subsections: (1) items of general importance; (2) variables of proven prognostic significance; and (3) information of probable prognostic significance (Table 20-2). For those interested in a minimal data set for colorectal cancer documentation, the IDS listing is recommended. This approach of combining both clinical and pathologic prognostic information has been developed into a software program and data management package (Medical Analysis Software Systems, Ridgewood, NJ 07450).

ADDITIONAL MOLECULAR PROGNOSTIC FACTORS

Several other types of determinants of prognosis are described in Chaps. 21–25. However, if the presence or absence of additional prognostic factors has an effect on outcome in a given anatomic stage, then this factor or factors might be relevant to clinical decision making and research protocols. However, to establish that a new putative prognostic factor adds accuracy to estimates of outcome is difficult to establish. McGuire and colleagues[35] have described a set of necessary guidelines for the evaluation of these markers as follows: (1) the factor to be studied should possess clear biologic significance; (2) the study phase from which data have been derived must be defined ("pilot," "definitive," or "confirmatory" types of investigations); (3) the sample size of a study must be sufficient to avoid premature judgments derived from statistical type I or type II errors; (4) every effort must be made to ensure that the study population is representative of the whole population at risk and that the pitfalls of patient selection bias are avoided; (5) laboratory methods must be validated by quality assurance programs of machine-generated data; and (6) appropriate statistical methods must be used, including the concept that for a putative new factor to have "independent" significance, it must be compared, using multivariate and other analytic methods, with other established factors to determine whether the new item adds additional prognostic power.

Although these evaluation guidelines may seem rigorous, the potential consequences of identifying a new prognostic factor inappropriately and integrating it into a highly developed prognostic system are so great that we must insist on the highest possible standards.[18] As with any new technology, there is always the possibility that clinical evaluation may be incomplete, that premature data may be applied in practice, or that erroneous conclusions may be drawn on the basis of incomplete data. Our purpose, therefore, is to prevent these negative possibilities so that treatment selection might be tailored to a patient's individual problems and outlook.

REFERENCES

1. Beahrs OH, Henson DE, Hutter RVP, et al: Philadelphia, Lippincott, 1992, pp 75–82.
2. *UICC TNM Classification of Malignant Tumours*. Berlin, Springer-Verlag, 1987.
3. Lockhart-Mummery JP: Two hundred cases of cancer of the rectum treated by perineal excision. *Br J Surg* 14:110–124, 1927.
4. Dukes C, Simpson WC, Mayo CW: On the spread of cancer in the rectum: The mural penetration of the carcinoma cell in the colon: Anatomic and clinical study. *Br J Surg Gynecol Obstet* 68:872–877, 1939.
5. Dukes CE: The classification of cancer of the rectum. *J Pathol* 35:323–332, 1932.
6. Gabriel WB, Dukes C, Bussey HJR: Lymphatic spread in cancer of the rectum. *Br J Surg* 23:395–413, 1935.
7. Simpson WC, Mayo CW: The mural penetration of the carcinoma cell in the colon: Anatomic and clinical study. *Surg Gynecol Obstet* 68:872–877, 1939.
8. Kirklin JW, Dockerty MB, Waugh JM: The role of the peritoneal reflection in the prognosis of carcinoma of the rectum and sigmoid colon. *Surg Gynecol Obstet* 88:326–331, 1949.
9. Astler VB, Coller FA: The prognostic significance of direct extension of carcinoma of the colon and rectum. *Ann Surg* 139:846–851, 1954.
10. MacFarlane JK, Ryall RD, Heald RJ: Mesorectal excision for rectal cancer. *Lancet* 341:457–460, 1993.
11. Turnbull RB Jr, Kyle K, Watson FR, et al: Cancer of the colon: The influence of the no-touch isolation technique on survival rates. *Ann Surg* 166:420–427, 1967.
12. Davis NC, Newland RC: The reporting of colorectal cancer: The Australian clinico-pathological staging system. *Aust NZ J Surg* 52:395–397, 1982.
13. Chapuis PH, Fisher R, Dent OF, et al: The relationship between staging methods and survival in colorectal carcinoma. *Dis Colon Rectum* 28:158–161, 1985.
14. Zinkin LD: A critical review of the classification and staging of colorectal cancer. *Dis Colon Rectum* 26:37–43, 1983.
15. Hermanek P: Colorectal carcinoma: Histopathological diagnosis and staging. *Baillieres Clin Gastroenterol* 3:511–529, 1989.
16. Newland RC, Dent OF, Chapuis PH, et al: Clinicopathologically diagnosed residual tumor after resection for colorectal cancer: A 20 year prospective study. *Cancer* 72:1536–1542, 1993.
17. Fielding LP, Arsenault PA, Chapuis PHA: Working Party Report to the World Congresses of Gastroenterology, Sydney, 1990: Clinicopathological staging for colorectal cancer: An International Documentation System (IDS) and an International Comprehensive Anatomical Terminology (ICAT). *J Gastroenterol Hepatol* 6:325–344, 1991.
18. Fielding LP, Fenoglio-Preiser CM, Freedman LS: The future of prognostic factors in outcome prediction for patients with cancer. *Cancer* 70:2367–2377, 1992.
19. Fielding LP, Phillips RKS, Fry JS, et al: Prediction of outcome after curative resection for large bowel cancer. *Lancet* 2:904–907, 1986.

20. Fenoglio-Preiser CM: Selection of appropriate cellular and molecular biologic diagnostic tests in the evaluation of cancer. *Cancer* 69:1607–1632, 1992.
21. Blenkinsopp WK, Stewart-Brown S, Blesovsky L, et al: Histopathology reporting in large bowel cancer. *Clin Pathol* 34:509–513, 1981.
22. Sheehan DC, Hrapchak BB: *The Theory and Practice of Histotechnology,* 2d ed. St. Louis, Mosby, 1980.
23. Scott KWM, Grace RH: Detection of lymph node metastases in colorectal carcinoma before and after fat clearance. *Br J Surg* 76:1165–1167, 1989.
24. Huvos AG, Hutter RVP, Berg JW: Significance of axillary macrometastases and micrometastases in mammary cancer. *Ann Surg* 173:44–46, 1971.
25. Pickren JW: Significance of occult metastases: A study of breast cancer. *Cancer* 14:1266–1271, 1961.
26. Davis M, Miller D, Bisson B, et al: Monoclonal antibodies to detect lymph node metastases in colorectal cancer: An expanded study (abstract). Boston, American Society of Colon and Rectal Surgeons. May 1991.
27. Feinstein AR, Sosin DM, Wells CK: The Will Rogers phenomenon: Stage migration and new diagnostic techniques as a source of misleading statistics for survival in cancer. *N Engl J Med* 312:1604–1608, 1985.
28. Hardcastle JD, Chamberland J, Sheffield J, et al: Randomized, controlled trial of faecal occult blood screening for colorectal cancer. *Lancet* 2:1160–1164, 1989.
29. Kronborg O, Fenger C, Olsen J: Interim report on a randomized trial of screening for colorectal cancer with Hemoccult-II, in Millar AB, Chamberlain J, Day NE, et al (eds): *Screening for Cancer.* Cambridge, England, Cambridge University Press, 1991.
30. Chapuis PH, Dent OF, Fisher R, et al: A multivariate analysis of clinical and pathological variables in prognosis after resection of large bowel cancer. *Br J Surg* 72:698–702, 1985.
31. Fielding LP, Stewart-Brown S, Dudley HA: Surgeon-related variables and the clinical trial. *Lancet* 2:778–779, 1978.
32. Beahrs OH, Henson DE, Hutter RVP: *AJCC Manual for Staging of Cancer,* 3d ed. Philadelphia, Lippincott, 1993, pp 8–9.
33. Karnofsky DA, Burchenal JH: The clinical evaluation of chemotherapeutic agents in cancer, in MacLeod CM (ed): *Chemotherapy of Cancer.* New York, Columbia University Press, 1949, pp 191–205.
34. Davies RJ: Staging in cancer, in Moossa AR, Robson MC, Schimpf SC (eds): *Comprehensive Textbook of Oncology.* Baltimore, Williams & Wilkins, 1986, p 67.
35. McGuire WL, Tandon AK, Alfred DC, et al: How to use prognostic factors in axillary node-negative breast cancer patients. *J Natl Cancer Inst* 82:1006–1015, 1990.

CHAPTER 21

Clinical Prognostic Factors in Resectable Colonic and Rectal Cancer Patients

J. Milburn Jessup

HIGHLIGHTS

The most important criterion for assessing a patient's prognosis is the stage of disease. This is determined by how deeply the tumor invades the bowel wall and whether regional nodes or distant sites contain metastatic malignant cells. All other clinical or pathologic factors are usually of secondary importance to staging information.

CONTROVERSIES

It is not clear whether the clinical factors of obstruction or perforation are independent covariates in multivariate analyses of outcome or whether their impact on prognosis is due to their association with an advanced stage of disease. Although a short (1 week or less) duration of symptoms may indicate a poor prognosis, possibly because such a short duration of symptoms is associated with obstruction or perforation, controversy exists as to whether a longer duration of symptoms is associated with a worse outcome. Patients whose cancers cause symptoms for longer than 6 months may not have a worse prognosis in general than patients whose symptoms are present for less than 6 months before definitive therapy. This point is controversial because it suggests that a 1- to 2-month delay in diagnosis and treatment does not adversely affect outcome.

FUTURE DIRECTIONS

The greatest challenge for the future is to reconcile the basic biology of the genotypic and phenotypic alterations that cause colorectal carcinoma with the different clinical factors that are manifestations of the disease. One place to start is to analyze those patients who develop colon or rectal cancer before age 40 in the absence of a familial syndrome. These patients may have a sporadic form of adenocarcinoma produced by an accelerated accumulation of genetic defects that cause colorectal carcinoma and may be paradigms for the analysis of the etiology of cancer of the large bowel.

The most important clinicopathologic determinants of outcome in adenocarcinoma of the large bowel are those that define the stage of disease—i.e., the depth of penetration of the bowel wall by carcinoma, the presence of malignant cells in regional nodes, or the involvement of distant sites by metastases. Other clinical parameters such as age, sex, site of primary lesion, bleeding, duration and type of symptoms are of secondary importance to the factors that constitute stage of disease. Jass et al.[1] demonstrated this in their analysis of a large set of patients with adenocarcinoma of the rectum. Although several pathologic factors in their study were significantly associated with outcome in univariate analysis, none was significant in a multivariate analysis when the stage information was included. Further, many of the variables that appear important in univariate analysis reflect the underlying biology of the disease and may be associated with stage of disease. The study by Jass et al.[1] serves as an example of the importance of both multivariate analysis in identifying important covariates in clinical disease and the dominant effect of stage upon outcome.

In this chapter, clinical factors will be analyzed for their effect upon the prognosis of patients with adenocarcinoma of the colon or rectum. The data are contradictory as to the significance of many of these factors in their effect upon outcome. Where possible, an attempt is made to determine how the clinical factors relate to the underlying stage of disease. Certainly, the presence of obstruction and/or perforation and certain symptoms are associated with stage of disease. The impact of these clinical symptoms on survival may reflect the association with stage more than the effect of the symptom as an independent covariate.

AGE

The effect of age in the outcome of patients with colorectal carcinoma is somewhat controversial. Various authors have felt that the onset of colorectal carcinoma in patients who are less than 40 years of age is an especially poor prognostic sign. Similarly, the diagnosis of carcinoma of the colon and rectum in elderly patients over 75 or 80 years of age has also been thought to portend a poor prognosis. The data now suggest that the outcome for older patients is not nearly as bleak as was once thought, but that the outcome for younger patients still appears to be poor.

The effect of a young age at diagnosis was first noted by Bacon.[2] Early onset of colorectal carcinoma occurs in between 2 to 6 percent of all colorectal carcinoma patients below age 40. There is some question as to whether the delay of symptoms contributes to the purported worse outcome.[3,4] However, the effects of both stage and histologic differentiation may be more important than age itself. Several series have suggested that there is a worse outlook for patients who develop colorectal carcinoma when they are below age 40.[5-10] However, there are two series that suggest that younger patients have the same survival as older patients. Adloff et al.[11] found that the outcome in younger patients was similar to that in older patients. However, in this particular series, the distribution of patients with stage III and IV disease was no different from that of the older patients, albeit with a slight increase in the mucinous and/or poorly differentiated carcinomas. Since the stage distribution was similar in the Adloff series, it is interesting that there was a similar outcome for the series. Heimann et al.[12] reported that the outcome in young patients was not worse than in older patients in a series of rectal carcinoma patients. Interestingly, although there was a slight increase in the proportion of patients with either nodal or visceral metastases, these patients as a whole did not do worse than older patients. The other interesting finding of Heimann et al.[12] is that many of their patients developed carcinomas outside of the colon and rectum even though the investigators specifically excluded patients with known ulcerative colitis or polyposis coli from their cohort. Thus, Heimann et al.[12] raise the possibility that patients with earlier onset of colorectal carcinoma may have disease that is more likely to be genetically induced, possibly related to the Lynch II syndrome. Certainly, current evidence by Fearon and Vogelstein[13] suggests that the accumulation of activated protooncogenes and loss of inhibitory tumor suppressor genes is associated with the induction of colonic or rectal cancer (reviewed elsewhere in this volume). Thus, patients who develop colonic or rectal cancer before age 40 in the absence of a genetic syndrome, such as familial polyposis or hereditary nonpolyposis colonic cancer, may have an accelerated rate of mutation in oncogenes or tumor suppressor genes. These patients may be especially useful for an analysis of the genetic mechanisms that cause colorectal carcinoma.

Other data suggest that the outcome of younger patients is worse because these patients present with more advanced disease and/or disease with a poorer histologic grade of differentiation. Several authors[3,5-9] have shown that younger patients present with more nodal or visceral metastases than older patients. Since stage of disease is the pivotal factor, it is often thought that the more advanced presentation may contribute to the poorer survival. However, the data of Behbehani et al.[7] suggest that, stage for stage, the outcome of younger patients is worse than that of older patients. This is not corroborated by the data of Adkins et al.[9] who demonstrated that well-differentiated carcinomas arising in younger patients have as good an outcome as carcinomas arising in an older cohort. Wong et al.[6] also found that young patients with node-positive cancers had a worse outcome than older patients with the same stage of disease. Taylor et al.[14] also found that patients below age 40 had a poorer survival than older patients who were similarly staged. Smith and Butler[10] found that only 3 percent of their stage III/IV patients were alive at 5 years compared with their historical controls. Thus, it seems that younger patients may present with more advanced disease. However, the disease may also be more aggressive in younger patients.

The frequency of more advanced disease in younger patients may result from later diagnosis than in older patients. This could be because younger patients may neglect their symptoms for a longer period of time than older patients. However, several series suggest that the common presenting signs and symptoms of rectal bleeding or abdominal pain in these young patients are present in a frequency that is similar to that in older patients. Further, in the study of Adkins et al.,[9] 8 of the 45 patients were found incidentally in the course of workups for other causes, suggesting that there could not have been a potential delay in diagnosis. In the series by Smith and Butler,[10] the majority of young patients had a symptom duration of less than 3 months. Similarly, in the study by Taylor et al.,[14] there was no significant difference in the duration of symptoms in comparison to an older concurrent cohort. Adloff et al.[11] also demonstrated a symptom duration that was not significantly different from that of an older cohort of patients. The distribution of the primary carcinomas is not significantly different from that of older patients through these various series. In summary, while there are some data to suggest that the disease may be more aggressive in younger patients, there is general consensus that the disease presents at a more advanced state in younger patients and that this is usually not due to a delay in diagnosis.

Older patients with colorectal cancer are variously defined as being above either age 75 or age 80 at the time of diagnosis. The frequency of older patients may be quite high, since D'Onofrio and Tan[5] demonstrated that approximately 40 percent of patients in their series from western Australia were above 79 years of age at diagnosis. The concern that elderly patients may have a worse outcome appears to be due to comorbid disease as well as to the type of presentation. The series of Payne et al.,[15] Wise et al.,[16] and Hobler[17] suggest that sepsis and complications of surgery may occur more frequently in the elderly population. However, Arnaud et al.[18] demonstrated that the 5-year survival rate of older patients who survive the operation was similar to that of younger patients. In addition, the cancer-specific survival of patients over the age of 75 was the same as that of younger patients in the series by Payne et al.,[15] as was the 3-year survival for the patients reported by Hobler.[17] Thus, an older age at diagnosis does not preclude long-term survival. Further, the biological behavior of these cancers that arise in older patients is not likely to be more aggressive than it is in slightly younger patients. Interestingly, several authors[11,15] suggested that more right-sided cancers arise in the elderly than in the slightly younger population. Whether this leads to an increase in obstruction or perforation is not clear. The elderly seem to have a slightly increased frequency of emergency operations, since 7.4 percent of older patients required emergency surgery, compared to 4 percent for patients below 75 years of age.[15] Thus older age alone does not appear to be a determinant of survival and suggests that older age at diagnosis does not select for cancers that have any different biological behavior than cancers that arise in patients between the ages of 40 and 70. The only effect of age appears to be to increase the risk of operative mortality and morbidity due to comorbid disease.

GENDER

Recently the NSABP[19] reported that, in a prospective randomized trial of adjuvant chemotherapy or radiation therapy in patients with rectal carcinoma, males had a worse outcome than females after surgical resection only. Perhaps as a consequence, these males demonstrated a greater response to adjuvant chemotherapy. The reason for the poorer performance of the male subjects is still not clear but may be related to the practical difficulty of resecting rectal cancers in the narrow male pelvis as compared to the slightly wider female pelvis. This anatomic difference may permit surgeons to resect cancers below the peritoneal reflection with better margins in women compared to men. How likely this explanation is to be correct is not clear, because other large retrospective[20–22] or prospective[23] series have not shown a similar gender bias. Nonetheless, Spratt and Spjut[24] demonstrated that females had a better survival than males. Further, Chapuis et al.[25] found that sex was an independent covariate in a multivariate regression analysis of 709 patients with colorectal carcinoma who underwent a potentially curative operation. Godwin and Brown[26] have shown that even when data were corrected for site, females had better survival than males. Isbister and Fraser[27] have also reported that females had a better outcome than males in a large national study in New Zealand. In a population-based study, Griffin et al.[28] observed that males had a worse survival than females. Since these studies are retrospective analyses of both colon and rectum cancers, it is not clear how or whether anatomic factors play a role. Nor is it clear whether other factors interact with gender to produce a poor prognosis.

RACE

It also appears that there is a difference in outcome associated with race. A recent report by Thomas et al.[29] indicates that inner-city blacks tend to be diagnosed with colorectal carcinoma at an earlier age than white patients, and that trend is significantly greater in black males than in white males. Boring et al.[30] have reported that there has been a significant increase in cancer-specific death rates in both black men and women for colorectal cancer compared to white men and women over the last 30 years. In fact, the cancer-specific death rate declined in white men and women, while it increased in black men and women by 47 and

16 percent, respectively.[30] Interestingly, when incidence rates are stratified by educational level and socioeconomic status, the incidence of cancer of the colon and rectum is higher for whites than for blacks for each stratification.[30] Also, the frequency that cancer is localized at diagnosis tends to be lower in blacks (30 percent) than in whites (36 percent), but it is not significantly lower. Thus, the poorer outcome may be attributable to more limited access to care. Weaver et al.[31] reported their experience over a 10-year period at Meharry Medical College and found that their patients tended to present with more advanced disease than those observed by Boring et al.[30] Their experience may also reflect limited access to health care systems.

PRESENTING SYMPTOMS AND SIGNS

The symptoms and signs of carcinoma of the colon and rectum are rectal bleeding (either gross blood in the stool or a guaiac-positive reaction on digital rectal examination), abdominal pain, change in bowel habits, nausea, vomiting, abdominal distension, weight loss, fatigue, and anemia. Rectal bleeding may be associated with an improved outcome, possibly because it prompts earlier diagnosis. Various authors[23,25,32,33] have observed that rectal bleeding as a presenting symptom was associated with a better overall survival in univariate analyses, but when rectal bleeding was analyzed in multivariate analysis where it was corrected for stage and site, it either had no effect[25,33] or became less important as an independent prognostic variable.[23] However, Garcia-Peche et al.[34] observed in a multivariate analysis of 191 conservative colonic and rectal carcinomas that rectal bleeding was a good prognostic indicator, especially since the lesions that bled were the smaller and more differentiated carcinomas than lesions that did not bleed. In contrast, in a retrospective study of 310 patients with stage I to III disease, Wiggers et al.[35] found that rectal bleeding was not a significant prognostic variable. They suggested that the impact of rectal bleeding on clinical outcome was decreased because their patients had earlier-stage disease than most series, since they did not include patients with visceral metastases and the earlier-stage patients had a better prognosis that decreased the impact of rectal bleeding. This is supported by Cappell and Goldberg,[36] who compared the association of symptoms and signs with patients who had either early (stage I) or late (stage IV) disease. Cappell and Goldberg[36] observed that rectal bleeding was more prevalent at the time of diagnosis in early stage I lesions than in stage IV cancers. Also, Graffner and Olsson[37] reported that rectal bleeding was more frequently associated with rectal (50 percent) than colon (14 percent) cancer. Thus, rectal bleeding may be associated with early-stage lesions and, as a result, may carry a better prognosis.

Abdominal pain is another symptom that may have independent prognostic value. There are two types of abdominal pain that are caused by cancer of the colon or rectum. The first is cramping or colicky pain associated with bowel obstruction. While uncommon in rectal cancer, it may be a presenting symptom in colonic cancer. This symptom may then be best considered as representing the clinical syndromes of obstruction and/or perforation that are discussed under *Obstruction and Perforation* below. Wiggers et al.[35] identified abdominal pain and change in bowel habits as significant covariates in their multivariate analysis of patients with colorectal carcinomas. They felt that both the abdominal pain and change in bowel habits were associated with underlying partial or complete bowel obstruction. Similarly, Cappell and Goldberg[36] observed that abdominal pain was associated with the presence of visceral metastases.

Local pain and/or tenesmus is usually a symptom of a locally advanced rectal cancer and is often associated with involvement of peripheral nerves.[38] Such a locally advanced rectal cancer may be successfully treated, often with a multimodality approach, but it is also more likely to be associated with a stage III rectal cancer than a stage I lesion and, as a result, may have a worse prognosis.

Other complaints such as nausea, vomiting, anorexia, and weight loss of more than 5 kg are uncommon at presentation but are clearly associated with stage IV cancers rather than stage I cancers.[36]

Finally, hemorrhoids as either presenting signs or symptoms are often thought not to have any impact on survival. Anecdotal evidence abounds about delayed diagnosis of rectal cancers that are present in patients with bleeding hemorrhoids. However, in at least one study,[36] hemorrhoids were associated with early-stage cancers of the colon. This is probably because the patients had a benign cause for bleeding (hemorrhoids) and underwent a colonoscopy to rule out a coincident proximal colonic cancer. These data reinforce the need to evaluate the entire colon when a patient presents with rectal bleeding and hemorrhoids.

Anemia secondary to microscopic bleeding—especially from a right-sided colonic cancer—may be a bad prognostic factor especially when it is associated with fatigue and weight loss.[36]

In summary, rectal bleeding may be associated with early-stage disease and better survival. However, when rectal bleeding is corrected for stage and site, the effect of rectal bleeding as a prognostic factor is often lost. Symptoms associated with complete or partial bowel obstruction often adversely affect outcome because of their association with the underlying obstruction or perforation. Constitutional signs and symptoms—such as general malaise, weight loss, and profound anemia—are often associated with advanced disease and reflect the poor outcome of patients who present with visceral metastases.

DURATION OF SYMPTOMS

Although rectal bleeding may be associated with a better outcome, most other symptoms or signs are associated with a worse outcome. Therefore, it is not surprising that patients who are asymptomatic at presentation may enjoy a better chance of surviving colonic or rectal cancer. These are patients whose cancers are found incidentally before they cause bleeding or other problems. Cappell and Goldberg[36] observed that asymptomatic patients were significantly more likely to have a stage I than a stage IV colonic or rectal cancer.

Once the symptoms appear, the duration of symptoms may be an important prognostic factor. Several authors[39–41] have observed that a history of a very short duration of symptoms (usually less than a week) is associated with a poor outcome. This may be because patients with acute onset of pain or other symptoms are presenting with bowel obstruction or perforation. Nonetheless, at least two series[3,42] indicate that such a short duration of symptoms does not have a significant impact on survival. The short duration of symptoms in these last series may have been associated with an earlier stage of disease.[25]

Once symptoms have been present for a week or more, prolongation of the interval before definitive therapy, amazingly, may not be associated with a worsening in prognosis. In early studies, both Irvin and Greaney[43] and McDermott et al.[39] found that patients who had symptoms for longer than 3 months before treatment did not have a worse survival than patients whose symptoms persisted for a shorter period. This was confirmed by Wright and Higgings[44] in a study of right-sided colon cancer. Interestingly, Stubbs and Long[41] reported, in their British study of 211 consecutive patients with colonic or rectal cancer, that patients with stage IV disease have a shorter period of symptoms (the mean was 3.8 months) than patients with $T_1N_0M_0$ disease (whose mean period of symptoms was 11.9 months). Once the bowel wall was breached (stage II) or the regional lymph nodes were involved (stage III), the duration of symptoms was similar to that of the stage IV patients. In fact, several studies that have analyzed the duration of symptoms indicate that 22 to 56 percent of patients have had symptoms for 6 months or more.[3,40,41,45] The median time between the onset of symptoms and diagnosis appears to be similar for colonic and rectal cancer and may be between 17 and 32 weeks.[8,14,46–48]

These results support the concept that the future behavior of carcinomas of the colon and rectum is biologically predetermined at the time of diagnosis. Symptoms are caused by local invasion of malignant cells. The more malignant a cancer is, the greater the probability that it will cause symptoms that require either emergent or urgent care. Thus, the less aggressive early-stage cancers may not cause symptoms and may not necessarily progress to form distant metastases. As a result, all patients whose symptoms are present for more than a week may enjoy the same outcome, whether their symptoms are present for a month or a year. In contrast, patients whose cancers are discovered while asymptomatic may do better because they are likely to have earlier-stage disease. Patients who develop symptoms that require emergency interventions will have a worse outcome because they are more likely to have advanced disease.

OBSTRUCTION AND PERFORATION

The effect of obstruction and/or perforation on the outcome of colonic or rectal carcinoma is not clear because the definitions of both obstruction and perforation are either imprecise or not stated. Much of the literature assumes that the reader knows what an obstruction is, and it does not indicate whether obstruction is complete (i.e., total absence of flatus or bowel movements for at least a day) or partial. Similarly, the type of perforation (e.g., free into the peritoneal cavity or contained, occurring through the cancer or proximal to a complete obstruction) is often not well described. Given this confusion about the entities of obstruction and perforation in bowel cancer, it is not surprising that the impact of either on outcome is not as clear as many clinicians suppose.

The incidence of complete obstruction (as defined above) appears to range between 2 and 16 percent.[13,30,49] The highest incidence occurred in a series which includes as part of the definition how quickly patients were operated upon. Thus, the higher incidence in the series of Serpell et al.[49] may reflect the clinician's desire to operate when he or she has objective clinicopathologic evidence of mechanical blockage to the flow of intestinal contents.

The location of the primary cancer affects the probability of developing a complete obstruction. Levien et al.[50] found that carcinomas of the splenic flexure were more likely to obstruct than carcinomas at other sites. In contrast, obstruction from rectal cancers appears to be uncommon.[51] Fielding et al.[52] suggest that the proportion of patients with obstruction follows the incidence of cancer at each site, while other reports suggest that the left colon[49] or the ascending colon[51] are the most frequent sites of obstruction.

Bowel obstruction may be an independent covariate in a multivariate analysis of outcome, even with stage included in the analysis. Crucitti et al.[22] studied 361 patients with colonic or rectal cancer and found that the presence of obstruction was a significant indicator of death from cancer even when stage was included in the analysis. Similar findings were reported by Wolmark et al.,[53] Serpell et al.,[49] Chapuis et al.,[25] and Griffin et al.[28] Wolmark et al.[53] suggested that the development of obstruction added to the poorer prognosis of right-sided colonic cancer. Right-sided Dukes C colon cancer had a worse prognosis in the NSABP trials than left-sided colonic cancer,[53] and obstruction in a right-sided colonic cancer worsened the prognosis even more. Steinberg et al.[23] did not identify any difference in outcome between right- and left-sided colonic cancers in the Gastrointestinal Tumor Study Group colonic adjuvant therapy trials but did observe that the presence of obstruction had a significant negative impact on outcome.

Several studies suggest that the effect of obstruction may be related to stage of disease rather than to the additional effect of mechanical obstruction worsening prognosis. Garcia-Valdecasas et al.[54] found that the incidence of stage IV disease in patients with obstruction was greater than the incidence of stage IV disease in nonobstructed patients. Further, when patients were compared by stage of disease, the patients with obstruction had the same outcome as did patients without obstruction. Similar findings were reported in a careful pathologic study performed by Ueyama et al.,[51] who found that patients' outcome was dependent upon stage of disease. Korenaga et al.[55] confirmed that obstruction was associated with stage of disease and that stage was a more important prognostic indicator. Willett et al.[56] demonstrated that obstruction was associated with local recurrence and that local recurrence was increased not only with advancing stage of disease but also with the presence of obstruction or, more importantly, perforation.

While controversy exists about the impact of obstruction upon outcome, it is clear that two related clinical situations adversely affect outcome. Both the need for emergency surgery and the presence of free perforation associated with bowel cancer are poor prognostic factors. Fielding et al.[52] studied the effect of obstruction and perforation on outcome in older patients with colonic cancer and found that patients who required emergent operations had a higher operative mortality and morbidity than did patients who were operated upon electively. This may reflect the dehydration and potential sepsis that attend emergent operations. However, Fielding et al.[52] also observed a poorer outcome in those patients who survived the operation. Runkel et al.[57] observed that approximately three-quarters of patients operated upon emergently were obstructed, while one-quarter were perforated. Only one-quarter of the patients who perforated did so either in the prestenotic bowel or the dilated cecum; most patients perforated through the tumor. Of the perforations, half were free perforations into the abdominal cavity while the remainder perforated either into an abscess cavity or a phlegmon. Interestingly, 5 percent of patients perforated on more than one occasion. The presence of visceral metastases also appeared to increase the morbidity and mortality of emergent operations. Perforation appears to be associated with local recurrence of disease, most likely because malignant cells are dispersed throughout the area of infection.[23,28]

In summary, obstruction and perforation appear to affect survival adversely. Perforation—with its immediate risk of both infection and spread of cancer cells in the tissues surrounding the primary cancer—leads to increased mortality and morbidity following an operation often performed under emergent conditions. In addition, there is an increased risk of local recurrence following a perforation. As Ueyama et al.[51] demonstrated, many obstructing cancers penetrate the muscularis propria in such a way that the cancer disrupts the outer muscle layer, replacing it with scar tissue. If this scar necroses, a perforation occurs through a tumor that otherwise might obstruct. The effects of obstructing cancers on postoperative morbidity and mortality are less dramatic than the effects of perforation and, depending upon whether completely or partially obstructing cancers are involved, obstruction may not necessarily significantly decrease the overall survival of patients with colon cancer.

EFFECT OF LOCATION OF PRIMARY CANCER ON PROGNOSIS

Ever since the early report of Spratt and Spjut,[24] most series have suggested that the outcome of rectal cancer is worse than that of colonic cancer. This may be because the pelvis presents certain anatomical boundaries that make complete resection difficult to achieve. Thus, recent reports continue to indicate that cancers arising in the bowel below the peritoneal reflection have a significantly worse outcome than do tumors arising in the colon proximal to the peritoneal reflection.[21,26,58–60] However, other investigators have not found any significant effect on the site of the primary tumor on patients' outcome.[20,28,35,61] With the exception of Fielding's study, most of the studies that do not detect a worsened survival in patients with rectal cancer have a relatively small sample size (around 300 patients or less) and may not be large enough to detect a difference. However, it is not clear why the Large Bowel Cancer Project series fails to display a difference in outcome between rectal and colon cancers. While the anatomy of the pelvis makes it difficult to obtain a negative resection margin in rectal cancer patients, this effect should lead to early recurrence and an early plateau in the incidence of recurrence. However, the data of Eisenberg et al.[58] suggest that the biology of rectal cancer may be quite different from that of colonic cancer. In their series of 704 patients, late recurrences—i.e., recurrences more than 5 years after treatment of the primary—were significantly greater in patients with rectal (11 percent) and left-sided colonic (10 percent) cancer than in patients with right-sided colonic cancer (3 percent). This suggests that cancers of the distal bowel have a greater tendency to recur over time than proximal bowel cancers. Enblad et al.[59] may have noticed a similar effect in their population-based study in Sweden, since the hazard rates for recurrence were not linear with time after surgery and there was a slow, continued decrease in the survival of the rectal cancer patients compared to patients with colonic cancer. These reports suggest that rectal cancer may have a greater proclivity for recurrence than colonic cancer and may be biologically more aggressive than rectal cancer.

Within the colon itself there is a suggestion that right-sided colonic cancers may have a better prognosis than left-sided colonic cancers. Eisenberg et al.[58] found that the 10-year survival of right-sided colonic cancer was 39 percent, versus 28 percent for rectal cancer. This difference in survival for each site was maintained on a stage-for-stage basis and did not just represent the inclusion of more advanced disease in the left-sided colonic cancer. Interestingly, Wolmark et al.[53] suggested that left-sided colonic cancers had a better outcome than right-sided colonic cancers in the NSABP prospective trials. Steinberg et al.[23] did not find a similar difference in outcome between right-sided and left-sided colonic cancers in the prospective trials of the Gastrointestinal Tumor Study Group.

The differences in outcome within the different parts of the colon may depend upon the definition of the part of the colon. Spratt and Spjut[24] demonstrated that the outcome of cecal and rectal cancers was similar and worse than that of the cancers in the sigmoid, ascending, and transverse colon. Further, many reports of the outcome of cancers in different parts of the colon are retrospective studies with relatively small numbers of patients, sometimes stratified by stage.[61,62]

Finally, as the molecular alterations associated with the development of colorectal carcinoma are identified, there should be an association between clinical prognostic factors and the expression of molecular alterations. Halvorsen and Johanessen[60] found that cancers of the rectum had a worse outcome than cancers of the colon, but that ploidy and DNA content were not significantly different between the two sites. They also did not find that DNA ploidy or content were independent covariates of outcome. The sample size (178 patients) was small and may not have been sufficient to detect a significant association. More studies are necessary to define how clinical prognostic factors are associated with alterations in molecular and genetic expression.

REFERENCES

1. Jass JR, Atkin WS, Cuzick I, et al: The grading of rectal cancer: Histological perspectives and a multivariate analysis of 447 cases. *Histopathology* 10:437–459, 1986.
2. Bacon HE: *Anus, Rectum, Sigmoid Colon: Diagnosis and Treatment,* 3d ed. Philadelphia, Lippincott, 1949, pp 603–608.
3. Polissar L, Sim O, Phil M, et al: Survival of colorectal cancer patients in relation to duration of symptoms and other prognostic factors. *Dis Colon Rectum* 24:364–369, 1981.
4. Walton WW, Hagihara PF, Griffen WO: Colorectal adenocarcinoma in patients less than 40 years old. *Dis Colon Rectum* 19:529–534, 1976.
5. D'Onofrio GMD, Tan EGC: Is colorectal carcinoma in the young a more deadly disease? *Aust NZ J Surg* 55:537–540, 1985.
6. Wong SKC, Cheung PSY, Boey J, et al: Colorectal carcinoma in the young. *Aust NZ J Surg* 55:149–152, 1985.
7. Behbehani A, Sakwa M, Ehrlichman R, et al: Colorectal carcinoma in patients under age 40. *Am J Surg* 142:767–769, 1985.
8. Rowe-Jones DC, Azlett DO: Delay in treatment in carcinoma of colon and rectum. *Lancet* 2:972–976, 1965.
9. Adkins RB, DeLozier JB, McKnight WG, et al: Carcinoma of the colon in patients 35 years of age and younger. *Am Surg* 53:141–145, 1987.
10. Smith C, Butler JA: Colorectal cancer in patients younger than 40 years of age. *Dis Colon Rectum* 32:843–846, 1989.
11. Adloff M, Arnaud JP, Schloegel M, et al: Colorectal cancer in patients under 40 years of age. *Dis Colon Rectum* 29:322–325, 1986.
12. Heimann TM, Oh C, Aufses AH: Clinical significance of rectal cancer in young patients. *Dis Colon Rectum* 32:473–476, 1989.
13. Fearon ER, Vogelstein B: A genetic model for colorectal tumorigenesis. *Cell* 61:759–767, 1990.
14. Taylor MC, Pounder D, Ali Ridha NH, et al: Prognostic factors in colorectal carcinoma of young adults. *Can J Surg* 31:150–153, 1988.
15. Payne JE, Chapuis PH, Pheils MT: Surgery for large bowel cancer in people aged 75 years and older. *Dis Colon Rectum* 29:733–737, 1986.
16. Wise WE, Padmanabhan A, Meesig DM, et al: Abdominal colon and rectal operations in the elderly. *Dis Colon Rectum* 34:959–963, 1991.
17. Hobler KE: Colon surgery for cancer in the very elderly: Cost and 3-year survival. *Ann Surg* 203:129–131, 1986.
18. Arnaud JP, Schloegel M, Ollier JC, et al: Colorectal cancer in patients over 80 years of age. *Dis Colon Rectum 34:896–898, 1991.*
19. Fisher B, Wolmark N, Rockette H, et al: Postoperative adjuvant chemotherapy or radiation therapy for rectal cancer:

Results from NSABP protocol R-01. *J Natl Cancer Inst* 80: 21–29, 1988.

20. Fielding LP, Phillips RKS, Fry JS, et al: Prediction of outcome after curative resection for large bowel cancer. *Lancet* 2:904–907, 1986.
21. Kune GA, Kune S, Field B, et al: Survival in patients with large-bowel cancer. *Dis Colon Rectum* 33:938–946, 1990.
22. Crucitti F, Sofo L, Doglietto GB, et al: Prognostic factors in colorectal cancer: Current status and new trends. *J Surg Oncol Suppl* 2:76–82, 1991.
23. Steinberg SM, Barkin JS, Kaplan RS, et al: Prognostic indicators of colon tumors: The Gastrointestinal Tumor Group experience. *Cancer* 57:1866–1870, 1986.
24. Spratt JS Jr, Spjut HJ: Prevalence and prognosis of individual clinical and pathologic variables associated with colorectal carcinoma. *Cancer* 20:1976–1985, 1967.
25. Chapuis PH, Dent OF, Fisher R, et al: A multivariate analysis of clinical and pathological variables in prognosis after resection of large bowel cancer. *Br J Surg* 72:698–702, 1985.
26. Godwin JD, Brown CC: Some prognostic factors in survival of patients with cancer of the colon and rectum. *J Chronic Dis* 28:441–454, 1975.
27. Isbister WH, Fraser J: Survival following resection for colorectal cancer: A New Zealand national study. *Dis Colon Rectum* 28:725–727, 1985.
28. Griffin MR, Bergstralh EJ, Coffey RJ, et al: Predictors of survival after curative resection of carcinoma of the colon and rectum. *Cancer* 60:2318–2324, 1987.
29. Thomas CR Jr, Gale M, Evans N: Racial differences in the incidence of colon and rectal cancer in patients under the age of forty. *Proceedings of the Third International Conference on Anticancer Research*. 1990, abstract 345.
30. Boring CC, Squires TS, Heath CW Jr: Cancer statistics for African Americans. *CA* 42:7–17, 1992.
31. Weaver P, Harrison B, Eskander G, et al: Colon cancer in blacks: A disease with worsening prognosis. *J Natl Med Assoc* 83:133–136, 1991.
32. Mzabi R, Himal HS, Demers R, et al: A multiparametric computer analysis of carcinoma of the colon. *Surg Gynecol Obstet* 143:959–964, 1976.
33. Kim V, Papatestas AE, Aufses AH: Factors influencing survival of colorectal cancer. *Mt Sinai J Med* 45:210–214, 1978.
34. Garcia-Peche P, Vazquez Prado A, Fabra Ramis R, et al: Factors of prognostic value in long-term survival of colorectal cancer patients. *Hepatogastroenterology* 38:438–443, 1991.
35. Wiggers T, Arends JW, Volovics A: Regression analysis of prognostic factors in colorectal cancer after curative resections. *Dis Colon Rectum* 31:33–41, 1988.
36. Cappell MS, Goldberg ES: The relationship between the clinical presentation and spread of colon cancer in 315 consecutive patients: A significant trend of earlier cancer detection from 1982 through 1988 at a university hospital. *J Clin Gastroenterol* 14:227–235, 1992.
37. Graffner MS, Olsson SA: Patient's and doctor's delay in carcinoma of the colon and rectum. *J Surg Oncol* 31:188–190, 1986.
38. Shirouzu K, Isomoto H, Morodomi T, et al: Clinicopathologic study of perineural invasion in rectal cancer. *Kuruma Med J* 39:41–49, 1992.
39. McDermott FT, Hughes ESR, Pihl E, et al: Prognosis in relation to symptom duration in colon cancer. *Br J Surg* 13:846–849, 1981.
40. Pescatori M, Maria G, Beltrani B, et al: Site, emergency, and duration of symptoms in the prognosis of colorectal cancer. *Dis Colon Rectum* 25:33–40, 1982.
41. Stubbs RS, Long MG: Symptom duration and pathologic staging of colorectal cancer. *Eur J Surg Oncol* 12:127–130, 1986.
42. Khubchandani M: Relationship of symptom, duration and survival in patients with carcinoma of the colon and rectum. *Dis Colon Rectum* 28:585–587, 1985.
43. Irvin TT, Greany MG: Duration of symptoms and prognosis of carcinoma of the colon and rectum. *Surg Gynecol Obstet* 144:883–886, 1977.
44. Wright HK, Higgings EF: Natural history of occult right colon cancer. *Am J Surg* 143:169–170, 1982.
45. Dukes CE: Cancer of the rectum: An analysis of 1000 cases. *J Pathol Bacteriol* 50:527–539, 1940.
46. Holliday HW, Hardcastle JD: Delay in diagnosis and treatment of symptomatic colorectal cancer. *Lancet* 1:309–311, 1979.
47. Ratcliffe R, Kiff RD, Walsh SH, et al: Early diagnosis in colorectal cancer: Still no benefit? *J R Coll Surg Edinb* 34:152–155, 1989.
48. MacAdam DB: A study in general practice of the symptoms and delay patterns in the diagnosis of gastrointestinal cancer. *J R Coll Gen Proct* 29:723–729, 1979.
49. Serpell JW, McDermott FT, Katrivessis H, et al: Obstructing carcinomas of the colon. *Br J Surg* 76:965–969, 1989.
50. Levien DH, Gibbons S, Begos D, et al: Survival after resection of carcinoma of the splenic flexure. *Dis Colon Rectum* 34:401–403, 1991.
51. Ueyama T, Yao T, Nakamura K, et al: Obstructing carcinomas of the colon and rectum: Clinicopathologic analysis of 40 cases. *Jpn J Clin Oncol* 21:100–109, 1991.
52. Fielding LP, Phillips RKS, Hittinger R: Factors influencing mortality after curative resection for large bowel cancer in elderly patients. *Lancet* 1:595–597, 1989.
53. Wolmark N, Wieand HS, Rockette HE, et al: The prognostic significance of tumor and location and bowel obstruction in Dukes B and C colorectal cancer: Findings from the NSABP clinical trials. *Ann Surg* 198:743–752, 1983.
54. Garcia-Valdescasas JC, Lovera JM, deLacy AM, et al: Obstructing colorectal carcinomas: Prospective study. *Dis Colon Rectum* 34:759–762, 1991.
55. Korenaga D, Ueo H, Mochida K, et al: Prognostic factors in Japanese patients with colorectal cancer: The significance of large bowel obstruction—univariate and multivariate analyses. *J Surg Oncol* 47:188–192, 1991.
56. Willett C, Tepper JE, Cohen A, et al: Obstructive and perforative colonic carcinoma: Patterns of failure. *J Clin Oncol* 3: 379–384, 1985.
57. Runkel NS, Schlag P, Schwartz V, et al: Outcome after emergency surgery for cancer of the large intestine. *Br J Surg* 78:183–188, 1991.
58. Eisenberg B, DeCosse JJ, Harford F, et al: Carcinoma of the colon and rectum: The natural history reviewed in 1704 patients. *Cancer* 49:1131–1134, 1982.
59. Enblad P, Adami HO, Bergstrom R, et al: Improved survival of patients with cancers of the colon and rectum? *J Natl Cancer Inst* 80:589–591, 1988.
60. Halvorsen TB, Johannesen E: DNA ploidy, tumor site, and prognosis in colorectal cancer. *Scand J Gastroenterol* 25:141–148, 1990.
61. Goh HS, Goh CR, Rauff A, et al: Clinico-pathological prognostic factors of large bowel cancer in Singapore: A multivariate analysis. *Ann Acad Med Singapore* 16:437–440, 1987.
62. Fegiz G, Barillari P, Ramacciato G, et al: Right colon cancer: Long-term results after curative surgery and prognostic significance of duration of symptoms. *J Surg Oncol* 41:250–255, 1989.

CHAPTER 22

Additional Pathologic Prognostic Factors

Bruce D. Minsky

HIGHLIGHTS

Although operative findings and pathologic TNM stage are the major determinants of prognosis in colorectal cancer, other pathologic features may influence the patterns of failure and survival. This chapter will focus on tumor size, configuration, adjacent organ involvement, and differentiation (grade) as well as blood vessel invasion, lymphatic vessel invasion, perineural invasion, and immune response.

CONTROVERSIES

Some of these factors have been reported to be of prognostic importance by univariate analysis. However, many are interrelated and may reflect the same overall characteristic of the cancer. There is a limited number of series which present data analyzed in a multivariate fashion, thereby resulting in contradictory results.

FUTURE DIRECTIONS

The majority of investigators agree that the most important independent pathologic factor for recurrence and/or survival is stage. However, other factors which are independent for survival have been identified. These factors should be used as stratification variables in future clinical trials of adjuvant therapy in colorectal cancer.

A majority of investigators agree that the most important independent pathologic factor for recurrence and/or survival is stage (depth of penetration through the bowel wall and the presence and number of positive lymph nodes).[1-3] Other independent factors for survival have included gross tumor appearance,[4] blood vessel invasion (BVI),[5] lymphatic vessel invasion (LVI),[6] the character of the invasive margin and tumor type,[7] nucleolar organizer regions,[8] number of mast cells,[9] nuclear shape,[10] sedimentation rate and leukocytosis,[11] lymphocytic infiltration,[12] obstruction, perforation, and rectal bleeding,[13] character of the invasive margin and peritumoral lymphocytic infiltration,[14] infiltrating border (lateral margins),[15] age, grade, LVI, gender, and obstruction,[5] ploidy,[16-20] preoperative CEA in $T_{1-4}N_2M_0$ colorectal cancer,[21] and the combination of preoperative CEA, tissue polypeptide antigen, and CA-50. This chapter will focus on tumor size, configuration, adjacent organ involvement, and differentiation (grade) as well as BVI, LVI, perineural invasion, and immune response. The prognostic significance of these factors is summarized in Table 22-1.

PRIMARY TUMOR SIZE

The majority of studies find no significant adverse relationship of tumor size to survival.[1,5,22-28] A limited number have shown improved survival with smaller tumors.[29] In one series, colonic tumors between 6 to 10 cm in size were associated with an improved survival as compared with lesions larger than 11 cm.[2] This relationship of size to survival was not seen in rectal

Table 22-1
Selected Prognostic Factors in Colorectal Cancer

Factor	*Univariate analysis*	*Multivariate analysis*
Tumor size	1+	None
Primary tumor configuration	2+	None
Adjacent organ invasion	3+	1+
Grade	3+	3+
Stromal fibrosis	1+	None
Colloid (any)	1+	None
BVI	3+	2+
LVI	3+	3+
Perineural invasion	3+	2+
Immune response	2+	1+

Key: 1+ = 1–25 percent of published series are positive; 2+ = 26–75 percent of published series are positive; 3+ = >75 percent of published series are positive.

tumors.[1] Some studies have shown an increased depth of tumor penetration through the bowel wall with larger cancers.[24,30] However, size was not associated with an increased incidence of positive nodes.[24] The Gastrointestinal Tumor Study Group (GITSG) analysis of 572 patients in a randomized chemoimmunotherapy trial for colonic cancer found that tumor size was not significant when analyzed as a single factor.[13] However, when the effects of other factors were adjusted for, increasing size had a negative impact on disease-free and overall survival.

PRIMARY TUMOR CONFIGURATION

In an initial report by Grinnell[31] in 1939, survival was higher in patients with tumors projecting into the lumen (83 percent) compared with patients whose tumors were either intermediate (45 percent) or infiltrating (38 percent). Other authors have reported that the possible reasons for such differences in survival include the lower frequency of bowel wall penetration, (24 versus 39 percent),[30] less frequent nodal metastases,[30,32,33] and fewer hematogenous metastases (23 versus 31 percent)[34] by exophytic tumors compared with ulcerating tumors. Overall, exophytic tumors are more frequently limited to the bowel wall (46 percent) than are ulcerating tumors (24 percent).[30] In the GITSG colon cancer adjuvant therapy trial, the presence of an exophytic lesion was associated with a significantly improved survival.[13]

ADJACENT ORGAN INVOLVEMENT

Involvement of adjacent organs or structures (T_4) is seen in approximately 10 percent of colorectal cancers. Spratt and Spjut[25] found that removal of a contiguous pathologically invaded organ had no influence on 5- or 10-year survival. To address the issue of adjacent organ involvement, Gunderson and Sosin devised a modification of the Astler-Coller staging system. This modification added B_3 ($T_4N_0M_0$) and C_3 ($T_4N_{1-2}M_0$), denoting adjacent organ or structure involvement for node-negative or node-positive disease respectively.[35] Several studies have analyzed both local failure and survival using this modified Astler-Coller staging system.[36–40] The additional B_3 and C_3 staging predicted an increase in local failure as well as decreased 5-year survival. In a multivariate analysis of prognostic factors, Nathanson et al.[41] reported that the second most important factor for survival was involvement of adjacent organs, which increased the relative risk of dying of colorectal cancer to 2.6.

A limited number of series have examined the prognostic significance of pathologic confirmation of tumor invasion into an adjacent organ or structure (as opposed to adherence alone) in stages B_3 and C_3 colorectal cancer.[2,42–44] Eldar et al.[44] found a significant decrease in survival in patients with stage B_3 disease in whom tumor invasion was verified microscopically, but not in stage C_3. Minsky and colleagues[1,2] analyzed patients with colonic or rectal cancer according to whether they had stage B_3 or C_3 disease clinically or verified microscopically. Patients with stage B_3 colonic cancer verified pathologically had a 27 percent 5-year actuarial survival rate, which was significantly lower than the 88 percent survival in patients with B_3 disease who were found to have only clinical adjacent organ involvement.[2] This difference was not seen in patients with rectal cancer.[1]

DEGREE OF DIFFERENTIATION (GRADE)

Broders[45] pioneered classifying the adenocarcinomas by their degree of differentiation. He designated four grades, based on the percentage of differentiated tumor cells. Of note, colloid (mucinous) carcinomas were included with well-differentiated cancers. In contrast, Dukes considered colloid carcinomas separately from adenocarcinomas.[46] Because of their relatively poor prognosis, colloid carcinoma and signet-ring cell carcinoma have been considered separately from pure adenocarcinomas by most investigators.

Dukes' grading system considered the arrangement of the cells rather than the percentage of differentiated cells. His initial approach evolved into a three-grade system, now the most widely used. Grade 1 (low-grade) is the most differentiated, with well-formed tubules and the least nuclear polymorphism and mitoses. Grade 3 (high-grade) is the least differentiated, with only occasional glandular structures, pleomorphic cells, and a high incidence of mitoses. Grade 2 (intermediate-grade) is intermediate between grades 1 and 3 (moderately differentiated).[22,47]

Dukes and others reported a correlation of grade with both lymph nodes and distant metastases found at the time of operation.[48–50] Grade has also been correlated with the presence of venous spread,[49,51] risk of lymphatic penetration,[51] extent of local spread,[49] number of lymph node metastases,[30,52] and increasing bowel wall penetration by tumor.[30] In another study, grade was not associated with the extent of local invasion.[53]

Univariate analyses have shown a clear relationship between survival and histologic grade in both colon and rectal cancer. In several series, multivariate analyses revealed that grade was an independent prognostic factor for survival.[5,13,54–57]

The question of how accurately a biopsy reflects the pathologic features of the tumor has been examined.[31,58,59] Overall, agreement between the grade of a resected rectal cancer specimen and the grade of the original biopsy specimen obtained at proctoscopy varied from 56 to 78 percent. It was the least accurate for poorly differentiated tumors (38 to 52 percent) and somewhat better for moderately well differentiated tumors (64 percent).[58,59] In general, the proctoscopy biopsy specimen was usually assigned a lower grade than the surgical specimen.[31] Complete agreement among three pathologists with respect to multiple biopsy specimens and the resected specimen was only 44 percent.[58]

Jass and colleagues[12] use seven parameters in their grading criteria: histologic type, overall differentiation, nuclear polarity, tubule configuration, pattern of growth, lymphocytic infiltration, and amount of fibrosis. This system attempts to broaden the criteria by which to assign a grade. However, it has not yet gained wide acceptance.

In summary, there is no uniform agreement on the grading criteria. Most investigators agree on the use of a three-grade system similar to that described initially by Dukes. A majority of the data suggest that grade should be considered an independent prognostic factor. However, several problems are associated with its use. These include the nonuniformity of grading systems, the designation of the majority of tumors as grade 2 or moderately differentiated, variability of grade in different parts of the tumor,[60] and individual variation among pathologists on grading the same tumor.

STROMAL FIBROSIS

Willett et al.[61] examined the impact of stromal fibrosis in 64 patients who underwent an abdominoperineal resection for stage I ($T_{1-2}N_0M_0$) rectal cancer. Patients with tumors with extensive stromal fibrosis had a significant decrease in freedom from distant metastasis compared with patients with tumors with none, minimal, or moderate stromal fibrosis (77 versus 100 percent, $p<.01$). In the report from Jass et al.[12] from St. Mark's Hospital, the presence of stromal fibrosis was associated with a poorer prognosis by univariate analysis but not by a multivariate analysis.

COLLOID (MUCINOUS) CANCER

Colloid or mucinous adenocarcinoma represents approximately 17 percent (11 to 30 percent) of large bowel cancers.[62] Synonyms include gelatinous carcinoma, myxomatous carcinoma, mucoid carcinoma, mucinous carcinoma, mucous degenerative carcinoma, carcinoma colloides, and degenerative carcinoma.[63] In the broad sense, colloid carcinoma is an adenocarcinoma with an associated clear, gelatinous fluid, which may be either intracellular or extracellular. The intracellular variety, most commonly known as signet cell or signet-ring cell carcinoma, accounts for approximately 4 percent of colloid cancers and 1 to 2 percent of all colorectal cancers. Some signet-ring cell cancers form a linitis plastica appearance by spreading intramurally, usually not involving the mucosa.[49] In most series, signet-ring cell cancer is associated with a very poor prognosis.[64]

The most common variety of colloid is extracellular, and it is this type which is commonly referred to as colloid or mucinous cancer. Although there is a fairly uniform histologic definition of mucin, there is no consensus as to the location or percentage of the colloid pattern in adenocarcinoma which must be present to be defined as colloid carcinoma. Umpelby and associates[65] defined moderate colloid adenocarcinoma as containing 60 to 80 percent of a colloid pattern and high colloid as an adenocarcinoma containing greater than 80 percent of a colloid pattern. Symonds and Vickery[64] defined colloid carcinoma as those tumors containing greater than 60 percent colloid. Minsky et al.[66] defined colloid cancer as an adenocarcinoma growing largely (more than two-thirds) in a colloid pattern. Adenocarcinoma with colloid features was defined as an adenocarcinoma with an intermediate morphology (both ordinary gland-forming and colloid growth patterns, the former predominating). Colloid cancer was a prognostic factor for survival by univariate analysis but not by multivariate analysis. In a prospective study of colorectal cancer using independent pathologic review, there was poor agreement in the grading of mucin secretion among three pathologists.[64]

There is an increased incidence of colloid cancer in the colon compared with the rectum.[64,66–69] In the series from Minsky et al.,[66] as the amount of colloid in the tumor increased, there was a corresponding increased distribution of that histologic type in the colon and decreased distribution in the rectum. There was no clear relationship between stage and the incidence or distribution of colloid cancer.

In most series, there is an increased incidence of colloid cancer in younger patients.[64,68,70–75] In those series which examine age, the average incidence of colloid cancer is 13 percent (8 to 17 percent) in patients with an average or median age greater than 45 years compared with 30 percent (19 to 88 percent) when the average or median age is less than 45 years.

Other pathologic factors are associated with colloid cancer. Compared with pure adenocarcinomas, there is an increased association with villous adenomas[64] and preexisting adenomas.[69] One series reported that patients with colorectal cancer associated with Crohn's disease had a significantly higher incidence of colloid cancer compared with patients with colorectal cancer not associated with Crohn's disease.[76] There is a lower incidence of blood vessel invasion[66,69] and lymphatic vessel invasion[66] with colloid cancers compared with pure adenocarcinomas. Recent data from colon cancer cell lines suggest that mucin production correlates with metastatic potential and affects their ability to colonize in the liver.[77]

VASCULAR INVASION

In 1938, Brown and Warren[78] demonstrated an increase in visceral metastasis in patients with rectal cancer whose tumors had vascular invasion. Since that initial report, a number of investigators have examined the influence of vascular invasion by tumor in colon, rectal, and colorectal cancer. One might predict intuitively that the presence of vascular invasion would be associated with an increased incidence of lymph node and/or distant metastasis and a corresponding decrease in survival. However, this association is not a consistent finding in the literature. Vascular invasion has two distinct components: blood vessel invasion (BVI) and lymphatic vessel invasion (LVI). In many series, *vascular invasion* is a general term which has been used to define BVI and/or LVI. The use of elastic tissue stains is important to help identify BVI. If elastic tissue stains are not used, BVI will be correctly identified in only 16 percent of patients.[79,80] In the series reported by Minsky et al.,[79,80] Krasna and associates,[81] and Inoue et al.[82] elastic tissue stains were used and BVI was clearly identified and scored separately from LVI. Unfortunately, most of the other series examining vascular invasion did not employ elastic tissue or other special stains, thereby introducing uncertainty both in the identification of BVI and in the differentiation of BVI from LVI.

Blood Vessel Invasion

There are two types of BVI. Invasion of blood vessels within the bowel wall is defined as intramural BVI and invasion of blood vessels outside the bowel wall (pericolonic fat or adventitia) as extramural BVI. In general, BVI refers to vein invasion rather than arterial invasion. The overall incidence of arterial invasion is <1 percent.

Rectal Cancer

In rectal cancer, the incidence of BVI varies from 17 to 61 percent and increases with stage and grade.[78,83–87] The first series to carefully examine both the intramural and extramural types of BVI was reported by Talbot et al.[88] In those tumors with BVI, 31 percent was intramural and 69 percent was extramural, compared with 61 and 23 percent, respectively, in the series from Minsky and colleagues.[80] The incidence of liver metastasis was significantly increased in patients with BVI+ tumors compared with BVI− tumors (35 versus 14 percent, $p = .001$). The extramural component of BVI was associated with the most unfavorable results. The incidence of liver metastasis was increased compared with thin-walled extramural BVI+ tumors (57 versus 30 percent; $p = .001$), and survival decreased compared with intramural BVI (33 versus 73 percent; $p = .001$) and thin-walled extramural BVI+ tumors (19 versus 41 percent; $p = .005$).

Minsky and colleagues[80] also found that the extramural component of BVI was responsible for the adverse impact on survival. For the total patient group, actuarial 5-year survival was significantly decreased in patients who had tumors containing extramural BVI compared with patients who had tumors that were BVI− or contained intramural BVI. However, by proportional hazards analysis, BVI was not an independent prognostic factor for survival.

Using a modification of Talbot's definition of BVI, Horn and colleagues[89] found by univariate analysis a significant decrease in 5-year survival in patients with BVI (30 versus 69 percent; $p < .01$). In an update of their results, BVI was found to be an independent prognostic factor for distant metastasis; however, it was less significant than stage.[90]

In the series by Rich et al.,[24] patients with BVI+ tumors experienced a significant increase in local failure at 5 years compared with BVI− tumors [node-negative: (59 versus 33 percent; $p = .013$), node-positive: (100 versus 41 percent; $p = .0001$)]. By proportional hazards analysis, BVI was found to be an independent prognostic factor predicting for increased local failure and distant failure in patients with positive nodes.

In summary, most series suggest that patients with BVI+ tumors have a decreased survival compared with those patients with BVI− tumors. In both the Talbot[88] and Minsky[80] series, the extramural component of BVI may be responsible. Whether BVI is an independent prognostic factor is controversial. By proportional hazards analysis, Minsky et al.[80] showed that BVI was not an independent prognostic factor for survival. However, other series have reported that BVI was an independent factor for local[24] and distant[24,90] failure.

Colonic Cancer

The only series which specifically examines the influence of BVI in colonic cancer is from Minsky et al.[80] The overall incidence of BVI was 42 percent, and the incidence of BVI increased with grade and stage. For the total group, patients whose tumors were BVI+ had a significant decrease in survival (BVI+: 74 percent versus BVI−: 85 percent; $p = .04$). When examined by the type of BVI, those patients whose tumors contained simultaneous extramural and intramural BVI had a significantly lower survival compared to patients with BVI− tumors (32 versus 85 percent; $p = .05$). There was a significant increase in local failure stage in patients with stage $T_3N_{1-2}M_0$ (BVI+: 29 percent versus BVI−: 10 percent; $p = .04$). By proportional hazards analysis, BVI was not an independent prognostic factor for survival.

Colorectal Cancer

In eight series, tumors of the colon and rectum are not analyzed separately. In general, the incidence of BVI varies from 25 to 81 percent and increases with stage and grade.[5,31,81,82,91-94] By multivariate analysis, Chapuis et al.[5] found BVI to be an independent prognostic factor for survival; however, this was not confirmed by Wiggers et al.[91] Shirouzu[94] reported a significant increase in local/regional recurrence, liver metastasis, and survival in patients with BVI+ tumors. Usually the increase was associated with extramural BVI. Only two series used elastic tissue stains and scored BVI separately from LVI.[81,82] Krasna and colleagues[81] reported a significant decrease in 3-year survival in patients with BVI+ compared with those having BVI− tumors (30 versus 62 percent) $p < .003$). The incidence of extranodal metastasis was also higher in patients with BVI+ compared with those having BVI− tumors (60 versus 17 percent; $p < .0001$). The type of BVI did not influence the incidence of failure or survival. In the series from Inoue et al.,[82] patients dead with hematogenous metastasis had a significant increase in BVI+ tumors compared with those dead without hematogenous metastasis (BVI+: 81 versus BVI−: 24 percent; $p < .01$).

Lymphatic Vessel Invasion

There are few data in the literature which examine the impact of LVI in colorectal cancer. Only five series have examined tumors for LVI and analyzed its impact on survival rates.[6,25,86,95,96] The incidence of LVI varies from 8 to 73 percent and increases with stage and grade. All series report a lower survival for patients with LVI+ tumors compared with LVI− tumors.

Three of the series did not define the criteria used for diagnosing LVI, use elastic tissue stains to help differentiate BVI from LVI, or examine the impact of LVI on the patterns of failure. Furthermore, in the series reported by Spratt and Spjut[25] and De Leon et al.,[95] not all tumors were examined for LVI. In the series from Khankhanian et al.,[86] LVI was not reported separately from BVI.

Michelassi and colleagues[96] examined rectal cancer from 110 patients and found vascular or lymphatic microinvasion in 73 percent. There was an increase in local failure in those with LVI+ tumors (23 versus 0 percent) and, by multivariate analysis, LVI was an independent prognostic factor for survival.

In an analysis of 462 patients with colorectal cancer by Minsky et al.,[6] a greater incidence of LVI was found in colonic cancer compared with rectal cancer (15 versus 10 percent). Tumors with both intramural and extramural BVI had the highest incidence of LVI compared with BVI− tumors (52 versus 5 percent; $p = .05$). There was a significantly increased incidence and number of positive lymph nodes in LVI+ tumors compared with LVI− tumors (59 versus 25 percent; $p = .0004$). The average number of positive nodes in patients with LVI+ tumors was 4.8, compared with 2.2 in patients with LVI− tumors ($p = .0003$). There was a significant decrease in 5-year survival in patients with LVI+ tumors compared to those with LVI− tumors in both the colon (57 versus 84 percent; $p = .0001$) and rectum (38 versus 71 percent; $p = .004$). By proportional hazards analysis, LVI was found to be an independent prognostic factor for survival. Therefore, both the Michelassi[96] and Minsky[6] series confirm that LVI is an independent prognostic factor for survival.

Willett et al.[61] examined the impact of LVI in 64 patients who underwent an abdominoperineal resection for stage I ($T_{1-2}N_0M_0$) rectal cancer. The incidence of LVI was 11 percent. By univariate analysis, patients with LVI+ tumors had a significant decrease in 6-year actuarial disease-free survival (48 versus 89 percent; $p < .01$) and local control (56 versus 91 percent; $p = .05$) compared with those who had LVI− tumors.

In summary, it is difficult to draw firm conclusions from the data, and treatment recommendations based solely on the presence of BVI or LVI should be made with caution. However, if LVI is clearly identified and differentiated from elastic tissue stain–confirmed BVI, then BVI and LVI should be used as stratification variables in clinical trials.

PERINEURAL INVASION

The incidence of perineural invasion varies from 14 to 32 percent. The classic study of perineural invasion was reported by Seefeld and Bargen,[84] who noted that malignant spread by growth along perineural spaces occurred as far as 10 cm from the primary tumor. Perineural invasion increases with the degree of local tumor extension. In one study, no patient with Dukes A tumors had perineural invasion, whereas 24 percent of those with Dukes B and 69 percent with Dukes C tumors had perineural invasion, as did 23 percent of patients with Broders grade 2 lesions and 58 percent with grade 3 lesions.[97] Too few patients had Broders grade 1 or 4 lesions to be evaluated.

In general, the incidence of perineural invasion increases with grade and stage. In one series, patients whose tumors had perineural invasion had a higher incidence of local failure in the perineal scar or anastomotic site (81 versus 30 percent) and a lower 5-year survival rate (7 versus 35 percent). Spratt and Spjut[25] also reported a lower survival. In another study of 77 patients with colorectal cancer, there was a significant decrease in survival in those patients whose tumors had neural invasion (30 versus 58 percent; $p<.003$).[98] Feil et al.[99] reported an increase in local failure in patients with rectal cancers with perineural invasion (52 versus 17 percent; $p\leq.001$). Similar results were reported in patients with rectal cancer by Horn and colleagues.[90] There was a significant decrease in 5-year local recurrence–free survival in patients with perineural invasion (64 versus 8 percent; $p=.03$). By multivariate analysis, perineural invasion was an independent prognostic factor for local failure. No independent effect was demonstrated for the development of distant metastasis. Knudson and associates[97] reported that, by multivariate analysis, perineal invasion was an independent prognostic variable.

IMMUNE RESPONSE TO THE PRIMARY TUMOR

There is considerable interest in the prognostic value of local inflammatory reactions at the primary tumor site. Local inflammation has been found in approximately 50 to 75 percent of tumors.[22,100] Spratt and Spjut[25] noted a decrease in survival with a lack of an inflammatory response around the tumor periphery. Murray et al.[100] reported an increased 5-year survival rate for patients with Dukes B and C colonic cancer when local inflammation was present (89 versus 46 percent).

Jass and associates[14] have offered a new prognostic classification of rectal cancer which incorporates the presence of a lymphocytic infiltrate. Using Cox regression analysis, they found that the number of positive nodes, whether the invasive border was pushing or infiltrative, the presence of a conspicuous lymphocytic infiltrate, and the absence or presence of transmural penetration were independent prognostic factors. Each factor was assigned a weighted score and the score range was divided to provide four prognostic stages. Each stage had a significant difference in 5-year survival. By univariate analysis, lymphatic stroma reaction was a prognostic factor for local failure in rectal cancer[99] and lymphocytic infiltration was a prognostic factor for survival in colon cancer.[7] The authors concluded that this prognostic classification was simple to use and superior to the Dukes system.

In contrast, Cawthorne et al.[101] examined 167 patients with rectal cancer and, by multivariate analysis, found that peritumoral inflammatory infiltrate was not an independent prognostic factor for survival. The National Surgical Adjuvant Breast and Bowel Projects (NSABP) performed a comparison of the Dukes (and its modifications) and Jass staging systems using clinical information from the R-01 protocol.[102,103] Survival was significantly decreased with increasing numbers of eosinophils and mast cells present at the tumor border. By multivariate analysis, the number of mast cells was an independent prognostic factor for survival. Jass and associates[12] demonstrated that lymphocytic infiltration was the most important factor in their grading model (Cox regression analysis) and was also important in their "best" model with grade- and stage-related parameters. Carlon et al.[104] similarly noted that lymphocytic infiltrate around the primary and pattern of growth were the most significant prognostic features. Svennevig and colleagues[105] reported a higher number of mononuclear cells in both the peritumoral stroma and within the tumor parenchyma of those patients cured by surgery.

A number of investigators have shown that an apparent immunologic response in regional lymph nodes correlates with improved survival.[100,106–108] In sigmoid colon cancer, Patt et al.[106] noted that sinus histiocytosis and paracortical immunoblastic activity each correlated with an increased survival. When both features were present, survival further increased. There was no survival benefit with increased germinal center activity. Murray et al.[100] also reported an increased survival with sinus histiocytosis of the draining lymph nodes and an even greater increase in survival when this feature was present with a local inflammatory reaction to the primary. Pihl and colleagues[108] observed that paracortical lymph node hyperplasia occupying more than 15 percent of the lymph node section was associated with an improvement in survival.

REFERENCES

1. Minsky BD, Mies C, Recht A, et al: Resectable adenocarcinoma of the rectosigmoid and rectum: I. Patterns of failure and survival. *Cancer* 61:1408–1416, 1988.
2. Minsky BD, Mies C, Rich TA, et al: Potentially curative surgery of colon cancer: I. Patterns of failure and survival. *J Clin Oncol* 6:106–118, 1988.
3. Krook JE, Moertel CG, Gunderson LL, et al: Effective surgical adjuvant therapy for high-risk rectal carcinoma. *N Engl J Med* 324:709–715, 1991.
4. Stahle E, Glimelius B, Bergstrom R, et al: Preoperative prediction of outcome in patients with rectal and rectosigmoid cancer. *Cancer* 63:1831–1837, 1989.
5. Chapuis PH, Dent OF, Fisher R, et al: A multivariate analysis of clinical and pathological variables in prognosis after resection of large bowel cancer. *Br J Surg* 72:698–702, 1985.
6. Minsky BD, Mies C, Rich TA, et al: Lymphatic vessel invasion is an independent prognostic factor for survival in colorectal cancer. *Int J Radiat Oncol Biol Phys* 17:311–318, 1989.
7. Shepherd NA, Saraga EP, Love SB, et al: Prognostic factors in colonic cancer. *Histopathology* 14:613–620, 1989.
8. Moran K, Cooke T, Forster G, et al: Prognostic value of nucleolar organizer regions and ploidy values in advanced colorectal cancer. *Br J Surg* 76:1152–1155, 1989.
9. Fisher ER, Pail SM, Rockette H, et al: Prognostic significance of eosinophils and mast cells in rectal cancer: Findings from the National Surgical Adjuvant Breast and Bowel Project (Protocol R-01). *Hum Pathol* 20:159–163, 1989.
10. Mitmaker B, Begin LR, Gordon PH: Nuclear shape as a prognostic discriminant in colorectal carcinoma. *Dis Colon Rectum* 34:249–259, 1991.
11. Hannisdal E, Thorsen G: Regression analysis of prognostic factors in colorectal cancer. *J Surg Oncol* 37:109–112, 1988.
12. Jass JR, Atkin WS, Cuzick I, et al: The grading of rectal cancer: Histological perspectives and a multivariate analysis of 447 cases. *Histopathology* 10:437–459, 1986.
13. Steinberg SM, Barkin JS, Kaplan RS, et al: Prognostic indicators of colon tumors: The Gastrointestinal Tumor Group experience. *Cancer* 57:1866–1870, 1986.
14. Jass JR, Love SB, Northover JM: A new prognostic classification of rectal cancer. *Lancet* 1:1303–1306, 1987.
15. Quirke P, Durdey P, Dixon MF, et al: Local recurrence of rectal adenocarcinoma due to inadequate surgical resection: Histopathological study of lateral tumor spread and surgical excision. *Lancet* 1:996–999, 1986.
16. Kokal WA, Gardine RL, Sheibani K, et al: Tumor DNA content in resectable, primary colorectal carcinoma. *Ann Surg* 209:188–193, 1989.
17. Heimann TM, Miller F, Martinelli G, et al: Significance of DNA content abnormalities in small rectal cancer. *Am J Surg* 159:525–528, 1989.
18. Jones DJ, Zaloudik J, James RD, et al: Predicting local recurrence of carcinoma of the rectum after preoperative radiotherapy and surgery. *Br J Surg* 76:1172–1175, 1989.
19. Scivetti P, Riccardi A, Marsano B, et al: Flow cytometric DNA index in the prognosis of colorectal cancer. *Cancer* 67:1921–1927, 1991.
20. Armitage NC, Ballantyne KC, Evans DF, et al: The influence of tumor cell DNA content of survival in colorectal cancer. *Br J Cancer* 62:852–856, 1990.
21. Moertel CG, O'Fallon JR, Go VL, et al: The preoperative carcinoembryonic antigen test in the diagnosis, staging, and prognosis of colorectal cancer. *Cancer* 58:603–610, 1986.
22. Qizilbash AH: Pathologic studies in colorectal cancer: A guide to the surgical pathology examination of colorectal specimens and review of features of prognostic significance. *Pathol Annu* 17:1–46, 1982.
23. Rao AR, Kagan AR, Chan PM, et al: Patterns of recurrence following curative resection alone for adenocarcinoma of the rectum and sigmoid colon. *Cancer* 48:1492–1495, 1981.
24. Rich T, Gunderson LL, Lew R, et al: Patterns of recurrence of rectal cancer after potentially curative surgery. *Cancer* 52:1317–1329, 1983.
25. Spratt JS Jr, Spjut HJ: Prevalence and prognosis of individual clinical and pathologic variables associated with colorectal carcinoma. *Cancer* 20:1976–1985, 1967.
26. Godwin JD, Brown CC: Some prognostic factors in survival of patients with cancer of the colon and rectum. *J Chronic Dis* 28:441–454, 1975.
27. Osnes S: Carcinoma of the colon and rectum: A study of 353 cases with special reference to prognosis. *Acta Chir Scand* 110:378–388, 1956.
28. McSherry CK, Cornell GN, Glenn F: Carcinoma of the colon and rectum. *Ann Surg* 169:502–512, 1969.
29. Olson RM, Perencevich NP, Malcolm AW, et al: Patterns of recurrence following curative resection of adenocarcinoma of the colon and rectum. *Cancer* 45:2969–2974, 1980.
30. Cohen AM, Wood WC, Gunderson LL, et al: Pathological studies in rectal cancer. *Cancer* 45:2965–2968, 1980.
31. Grinnell RS: The grading and prognosis of carcinoma of the colon and rectum. *Ann Surg* 109:500–503, 1939.
32. Wolmark N, Fisher ER, Wieand HS, et al: The relationship of depth of penetration and tumor size to the number of positive nodes in Dukes C colorectal cancer. *Cancer* 53:2707–2712, 1984.
33. Coller FA, Kay EB, MacIntyre RS: Regional lymphatic metastasis in carcinoma of the colon. *Ann Surg* 114:56–63, 1941.
34. Sontag SJ, Durczak C, Aranha GV, et al: Fecal occult blood screening for colorectal cancer in a Veteran's Administration hospital. *Am J Surg* 145:89–94, 1983.
35. Gunderson LL, Sosin H: Areas of failure found at reoperation (second or symptomatic look) following "curative surgery" for adenocarcinoma of the rectum: Clinicopathologic correlation and implications for adjuvant therapy. *Cancer* 34:1278–1292, 1974.
36. Wood WQ, Wilkie DPD: Carcinoma of the rectum: An anatomico-pathologic study. *Edinburgh Med J* 40:321–331, 1933.
37. Weiss L, Grundmann E, Torhorst J, et al: Haematogenous metastatic patterns in colonic carcinoma: An analysis of 1541 necropsies. *J Pathol* 150:195–203, 1986.
38. Batson OV: The function of the vertebral veins and their role in the spread of metastases. *Ann Surg* 112:138–149. 1940.
39. Willett CG, Tepper JE, Cohen AM, et al: Failure patterns following curative resection of colonic carcinoma. *Ann Surg* 200:685–690, 1984.
40. Willett C, Tepper JE, Cohen AM, et al: Local failure following curative resection of colonic adenocarcinoma. *Int J Radiat Oncol Biol Phys* 10:645–651, 1984.
41. Nathanson SD, Tilley BC, Schultz L, et al: Perioperative allogeneic blood transfusions: Survival in patients with resected carcinomas of the colon and rectum. *Arch Surg* 120: 734–738, 1985.
42. Eldar S, Kemeny MM, Terz JJ: Extended resections for carcinoma of the colon and rectum. *Surg Gynecol Obstet* 161:319–322, 1985.
43. Astler VB, Coller FA: The prognostic significance of direct extension of carcinoma of the colon and rectum. *Ann Surg* 139:846–851, 1954.
44. Kelley WE Jr, Brown PW, Lawrence W Jr, et al: Penetrating, obstructing, and perforating carcinomas of the colon and rectum. *Arch Surg* 116:381–384, 1981.

45. Broders AC: The grading of carcinoma. *Minn Med* 8:726–730, 1925.
46. Dukes CE: The classification of cancer of the rectum. *J Pathol* 35:323–332, 1932.
47. Hermanek P: Evolution and pathology of rectal cancer. *World J Surg* 6:502–509, 1982.
48. Miles WE: Discussion on the surgical treatment of cancer of the rectum. *Br Med J* 2:730–742, 1920.
49. Dukes CE, Bussey HJR: The spread of rectal cancer and its effect on prognosis. *Br J Cancer* 12:309–320, 1958.
50. Gilbert SG: Symptomatic local tumor failure following abdomino-perineal resection. *Int J Radiat Oncol Biol Phys* 4:801–807, 1978.
51. Winchester DP, Shull JH, Scanlon EF, et al: A mass screening program for colorectal cancer using chemical testing for occult blood in the stool. *Cancer* 45:2955–2958, 1980.
52. Minsky BD, Rich T, Recth A, et al: Selection criteria for local excision with or without adjuvant radiation therapy for rectal cancer. *Cancer* 63:1421–1429, 1989.
53. Riboli EB, Secco GB, Lapertosa G, et al: Colorectal cancer: Relationship of histologic grading to disease prognosis. *Tumori* 69:581–584, 1983.
54. Phillips RKS, Hittinger R, Blesovsky L, et al: Large bowel cancer: Surgical pathology and its relationship to survival. *Br J Surg* 71:604–610, 1984.
55. Davis NC, Newland RC: The reporting of colorectal cancer: The Australian clinico-pathological staging system. *Aust NZ J Surg* 52:395–397, 1982.
56. deMello J, Struthers L, Turner R, et al: Multivariate analysis as aides to diagnosis and assessment of prognosis in gastrointestinal cancer. *Br J Cancer* 48:341–348, 1983.
57. Godwin JD II: Carcinoid tumors: An analysis of 2837 cases. *Cancer* 36:560–569, 1975.
58. Williams NS, Durdey P, Quirke P, et al: Pre-operative staging of rectal neoplasm and its impact on clinical management. *Br J Surg* 72:868–874, 1985.
59. Thomas GDH, Dixon MF, Smeeton NC, et al: Observer variation in the histological grading of rectal carcinoma. *J Clin Pathol (Suppl)* 36:385–391, 1983.
60. Qualheim RE, Gall EA: Is histopathologic grading of colon carcinoma a valid procedure? *Arch Pathol* 56:466–472, 1953.
61. Willett CG, Lewandrowski K, Donnelly S, et al: Are there patients with stage I rectal carcinoma at risk for failure after abdominoperineal resection? *Cancer* 69:1651–1655, 1992.
62. Minsky BD: Clinicopathologic impact of colloid in colorectal carcinoma. *Dis Colon Rectum* 33:714–719, 1990.
63. Trimpi HD, Bacon HE: Mucoid carcinoma of the rectum. *Cancer* 4:597–609, 1951.
64. Symonds DA, Vickery AL Jr: Mucinous carcinoma of the colon and rectum. *Cancer* 37:1891–1900, 1976.
65. Umpleby HC, Ranson DL, Williamson HC: Peculiarities of mucinous colorectal carcinoma. *Br J Surg* 72:715–718, 1985.
66. Minsky BD, Mies C, Rich TA, et al: Colloid carcinoma of the colon and rectum. *Cancer* 60:3103–3112, 1987.
67. Parham D: Colloid carcinoma. *Ann Surg* 77:94–105, 1923.
68. Dajani YF, Zayed I, Malatjabian DA, et al: Colorectal cancer in Jordan and Nova Scotia: A comparative epidemiologic and histopathologic study. *Cancer* 46:420–426, 1978.
69. Sundbald AS, Paz RA: Mucinous carcinomas of the colon and the rectum and their relation to polyps. *Cancer* 50:2504–2509, 1982.
70. Recalde M, Holyoke ED, Elias EG: Carcinoma of the colon, rectum and anal canal in young patients. *Surg Gynecol Obstet* 139:909–913, 1974.
71. Kenda JFN: Cancer of the large bowel in the African: A 15-year survey at Kinshasa University Hospital, Zaire. *Br J Surg* 63:966–968, 1976.
72. Odone V, Chang L, Caces J, et al: The natural history of colorectal carcinoma in adolescents. *Cancer* 49:1716–1720, 1982.
73. Umpleby HC, Williamson RCN: Carcinoma of the large bowel in the first four decades. *Br J Surg* 71:272–277, 1984.
74. Walton WW, Hagihara PF, Griffen WO: Colorectal adenocarcinoma in patients less than 40 years old. *Dis Colon Rectum* 19:529–534, 1976.
75. Russell AH, Pelton J, Reheis CE, et al: Adenocarcinoma of the colon: An autopsy study with implications for new therapeutic strategies. *Cancer* 56:1446–1451, 1985.
76. Hamilton SR: Colorectal carcinoma in patients with Crohn's disease. *Gastroenterology* 89:398–407, 1989.
77. Bresalier RS, Niv Y, Byrd JC, et al: Mucin production by human colonic carcinoma cells correlates with their metastatic potential in animal models of colon cancer metastasis. *J Clin Invest* 87:1037–1045, 1991.
78. Brown CE, Warren S: Visceral metastases from rectal carcinoma. *Surg Gynecol Obstet* 66:611–621, 1938.
79. Minsky BD, Mies C, Rich TA, et al: Potentially curative surgery of colon cancer: The influence of blood vessel invasion. *J Clin Oncol* 6:119–127, 1988.
80. Minsky BD, Mies C, Recht A, et al: Resectable adenocarcinoma of the rectosigmoid and rectum: II. The influence of blood vessel invasion. *Cancer* 61:1417–1424, 1988.
81. Krasna MJ, Flanobaum L, Cody RP, et al: Vascular and neural invasion in colorectal cancer. *Cancer* 61:1018–1023, 1988.
82. Inoue T, Mori M, Shimono R, et al: Vascular invasion of colorectal carcinoma readily visible with certain stains. *Dis Colon Rectum* 35:34–39, 1992.
83. Dukes CE, Bussey HJR: Venous spread in rectal cancer. *Proc R Soc Med* 34:571–581, 1941.
84. Seefeld P, Bargen JA: The spread of carcinoma of the rectum: Invasion of lymphatics, veins and nerves. *Ann Surg* 118:76–90, 1943.
85. Madison MS, Dockerty MB, Waugh JM: Venous invasion in carcinoma of the rectum as evidenced by venous radiography. *Surg Gynecol Obstet* 99:170–178, 1954.
86. Khankhanian N, Maulight GM, Russel WO, et al: Prognostic significance of vascular invasion in colorectal cancer of Dukes' B class. *Cancer* 39:1195–1200, 1977.
87. Heald RJ, Ryall RDH: Recurrence and survival after total meso-rectal excision for rectal cancer. *Lancet* 328:1479–1482, 1986.
88. Talbot IC, Ritchie S, Leighton MH, et al: The clinical significance of invasion of veins by rectal cancer. *Br J Surg* 67:439–442, 1980.
89. Horn A, Dahl O, Morild I: The role of venous and neural invasion on survival in rectal adenocarcinoma. *Dis Colon Rectum* 33:598–601, 1990.
90. Horn A, Dahl O, Morild I: Venous and neural invasion as predictors of recurrence in rectal adenocarcinoma. *Dis Colon Rectum* 34:798–804, 1991.
91. Wiggers T, Arends JW, Volovics A: Regression analysis of prognostic factors in colorectal cancer after curative resections. *Dis Colon Rectum* 31:33–41, 1988.
92. Sunderland DA: The significance of vein invasion by cancer of the rectum and sigmoid: A microscopic study of 210 cases. *Cancer* 2:429–437, 1949.
93. Swinton NW: Cancer of the colon and rectum: A statistical study of 608 patients. *Surg Clin North Am* 39:745–753, 1959.
94. Shirouzu K, Isomoto H, Morimatsu M: A prospective clinicopathologic study of venous invasion in colorectal cancer. *Am J Surg* 162:216–220, 1991.
95. DeLeon ML, Schoetz DJ, Coller JA, et al: Colorectal cancer: Lahey Clinic experience, 1972–1976: An analysis of prognostic indicators. *Dis Colon Rectum* 30:237–242, 1987.
96. Michelassi F, Vannucci L, Ayala JJ, et al: Local recurrence

after curative resection of colorectal adenocarcinoma. *Surgery* 108:787–793, 1990.

97. Knudsen JB, Nilsson T, Sprechler M, et al: Venous and nerve invasion as prognostic factors in postoperative survival of patients with resectable cancer of the rectum. *Dis Colon Rectum* 26:613–617, 1983.
98. Krasna MJ, Flancbaum L, Cody RP, et al: Vascular and neural invasion in colorectal carcinoma: Incidence and prognostic significance. *Cancer* 61:1018–1023, 1988.
99. Feil W, Wunderlich M, Neuhild N, et al: Rectal cancer: Factors influencing the development of local recurrence after radical anterior resection. *Int J Colorect Dis* 3:195–200, 1988.
100. Murray D, Hreno A, Dutton J, et al: Prognosis in colon cancer: A pathologic reassessment. *Arch Surg* 110:908–913, 1975.
101. Cawthorne SJ, Parmus DV, Gibbs NM, et al: Extent of mesorectal spread and involvement of lateral resection margin as prognostic factors after surgery for rectal cancer. *Lancet* 335:1055–1059, 1990.
102. Fisher ER, Sass R, Palekar A, et al: Dukes's classification revisited—Findings from the National Surgical Adjuvant Breast and Bowel Projects (protocol R-01). *Cancer* 64:2354–2360, 1989.
103. Fisher B, Wolmark N, Rockette H, et al: Postoperative adjuvant chemotherapy or radiation therapy for rectal cancer: Results from NSABP protocol R-01. *J Natl Cancer Inst* 80:21–29, 1988.
104. Carlon CA, Fabris G, Arslan-Pagnini C, et al: Prognostic correlations of operable carcinoma of the rectum. *Dis Colon Rectum* 28:47–50, 1985.
105. Svennevig JL, Lunde OC, Holter J, et al: Lymphoid infiltration and prognosis in colorectal carcinoma. *Br J Cancer* 49:375–377, 1984.
106. Patt DJ, Brynes RK, Vardiman JW, et al: Mesocolic lymph node histology is an important prognostic indicator for patients with carcinoma of the sigmoid colon: An immunomorphologic study. *Cancer* 35:1388–1397, 1975.
107. Tsakraklides V, Wanebo HJ, Sternberg SS, et al: Prognostic evaluation of regional lymph node morphology in colorectal cancer. *Am J Surg* 129:174–180, 1975.
108. Pihl E, Malahy MA, Khankhanian N, et al: Immunomorphological features of prognostic significance in Dukes' class B colorectal carcinoma. *Cancer Res* 37:4145–4149, 1977.

CHAPTER 23

DNA Content and Proliferative Index: Prognostic Variables in Colorectal Disease

Kevin C. Conlon
Warren E. Enker

HIGHLIGHTS

DNA ploidy abnormalities are frequently present in human tumors. In many solid tumors (i.e., bladder, breast, lung, ovarian), determination of ploidy and proliferative activity has provided useful prognostic information.[1-3] This chapter will describe the methodology involved in the measurement of DNA/RNA ploidy and its potential for application as a prognostic variable in colorectal cancer. The often conflicting results which have been obtained will be examined.

CONTROVERSIES

Current staging of colorectal cancer is based on morphologic criteria, i.e., the depth of tumor mural penetration, extension to lymphatics, and/or metastatic disease.[4,5] This system accurately predicts the likelihood of disease-free and long-term survival for patients with either early or advanced disease. However, there is a sizable intermediate group of patients in whom the outcome is less certain. The development of methodology such as flow cytometry, an objective and reproducible method for quantitative cytologic analysis, has enabled investigators to study tumor nucleic acid content and cell cycle kinetics, thereby defining a group of molecular variables not included in the standard staging system that may be of independent prognostic significance.

FUTURE DIRECTIONS

Despite the often conflicting reports in the literature, it would appear that the determination of tumor DNA content and proliferative index (PI) in certain subgroups of patients (i.e., with Dukes B lesions) can accurately predict prognosis, thus allowing for the selection of patients who may benefit from adjuvant therapies.

METHODOLOGY

Using radiolabeled precursors of DNA synthesis (i.e., ^{32}P, ^{3}H-thymidine) a model of cellular proliferation has been developed (Fig. 23-1). DNA synthesis appears not to be a continuous process; rather, it occurs during a specific portion of the cell cycle (S phase). Mitosis, during which chromosomal content is doubled, takes place after DNA synthesis has been completed. The

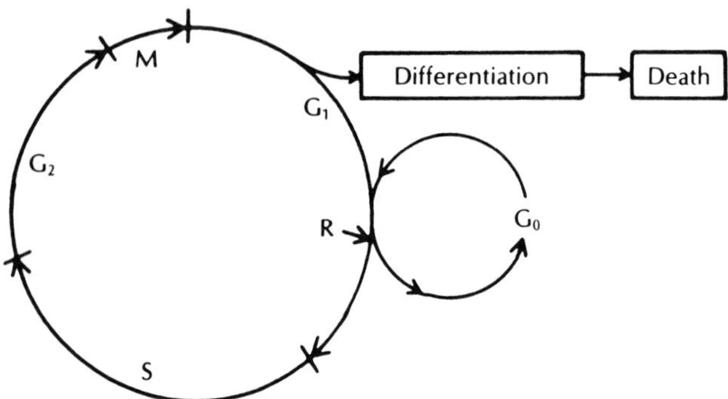

FIG. 23-1. The normal cell cycle. G_0/G_1 is the resting or quiescent phase, in which the majority of normal and neoplastic cells are found. DNA synthesis occurs during the S phase. The portion of the cell cycle during which the chromosomal content is doubled (mitosis) is represented by the M phase. $S + G_{2M}$ phases are often combined to give the proliferative fraction of the cell cycle. (From Enker et al.[53] Reproduced by permission.)

G_1 and G_2 phases are the time periods in which the cell is not actively synthesizing DNA or dividing. Nonproliferating cells arrested between the M and S phases are referred to as G_0 cells. From a proliferative standpoint, cells within the G_0/G_1 phases are resting or quiescent. Thus, the cell cycle can be divided into separate phases: G_0, G_1, S, G_2, and M, the duration of which vary between cells of a population.

Flow cytometry can be utilized to determine the DNA content of tumor cells. A detailed review of flow cytometry methodology is beyond the scope of this chapter. In brief, the technique requires the preparation of an aqueous single-cell suspension. This can be obtained from either fresh, frozen, or formalin-fixed, paraffin-embedded tissue, although each source of cells has potential pitfalls. The cells are stained with one of several fluorescent stains that bind specifically and stoichiometrically to DNA or RNA. Our laboratory uses mainly acridine dyes, such as acridine orange (AO). This is a useful stain, because AO can intercalate with double-stranded DNA to form a monomeric complex (which fluoresces green) and then bind with single-stranded RNA (exhibiting red fluorescence), thus providing information regarding both DNA and RNA content simultaneously. The reader is referred to the reviews by Traganos[6,7] and Shapiro[8] for further information regarding the choice of fluorescent stains. The stained cells suspended in single file pass at high speed through a light source (typically an argon laser) to excite the fluorescent stain. A portion of the emitted fluorescence is captured by one or more photosensors, generating an electrical signal which can be measured, amplified, and recorded by computer (Fig. 23-2). The amount of fluorescence is proportional to the DNA content; thus the technique allows for the measurement of cells containing differing amounts of DNA. Cell separation can be achieved by applying an electrical charge to cells with different fluorescence intensities.

A DNA histogram can be obtained from the fluorescent distribution, as shown in Fig. 23-3. Nonproliferating and quiescent cells (G_0/G_1) contain a normal diploid chromosomal content (2C), whereas those in the

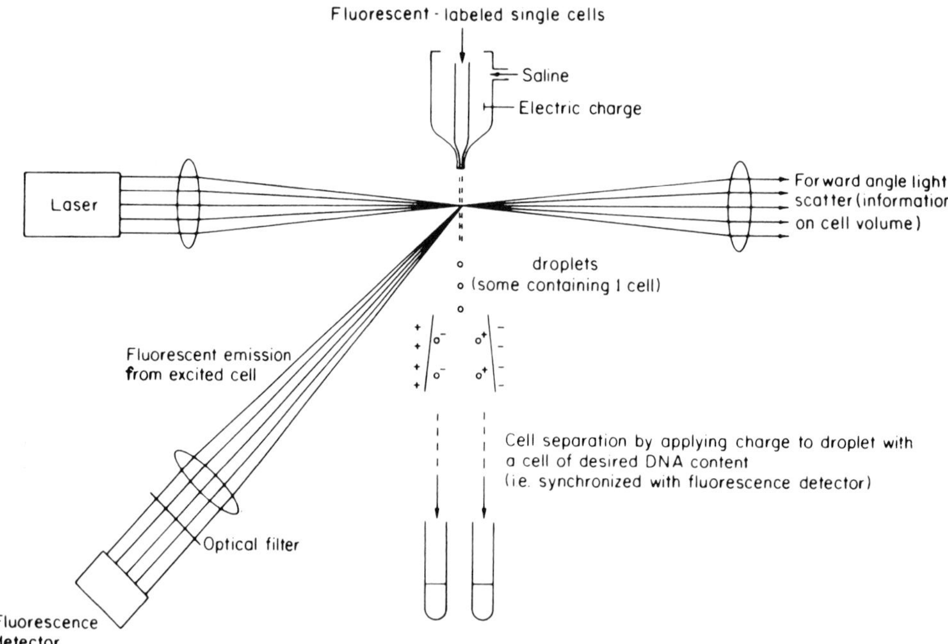

FIG. 23-2. A simplified line diagram of flow cytometry. See text for details. (From DeVita V, Hellman S, Rosenberg S: *Cancer: Principles and Practice in Oncology*. Philadelphia, Lippincott, 1989, p. 7. Reproduced by permission.)

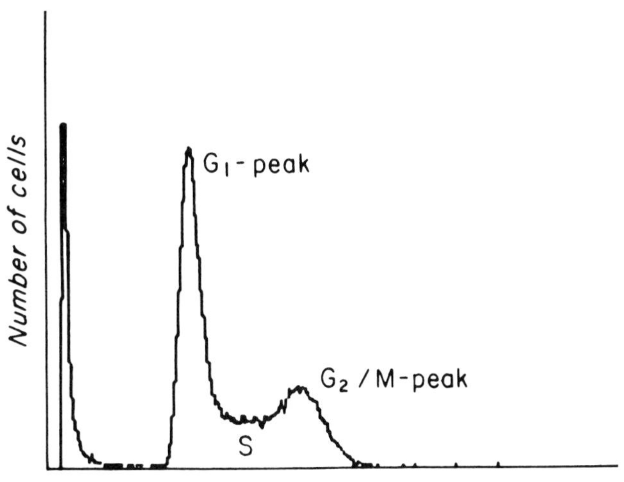

FIG. 23-3. Line diagram of a DNA histogram produced by flow cytometry. (From Enker WE: Perspect Colon Rectal Surg 3(1):1–33, 1990. Reproduced by permission.)

G_2/M phase are tetraploid (4C). Cells in the S phase have an intermediate amount of DNA content. The DNA index (DI) is the ratio of the mean of the relative DNA content of the G_1/G_0 peak to the mean of the G_1/G_0 peak of the reference cells.[9] Cells with a normal diploid karotype have an index of 1.0. DNA aneuploidy is defined by convention as DNA content more or less than 10 percent above the standard chromosomal content. Aneuploidy can be referred to as hypoploidy (DI $<$1.0), hyperploidy (DI $>$1.0), or tetraploidy (DI $>$2.0).

Hedley et al.,[10] in 1983, described a method for the analysis of cellular DNA content in formalin-fixed tissue, allowing archival tissue to be used for flow cytometry. Analysis of either fresh or archival tissue produced comparable results. Similar findings were made by Emdin et al.,[11] who noted a 94 percent concordance between the results obtained from fresh or from paraffin-embedded tumor blocks from the same tumor. Armitage et al.,[12] noted less agreement (75 percent) between fresh and archival tissue, concluding that inadequate sampling from the tumor was responsible. Comparable findings were made by Jones et al.[13] This may in part be due to the cellular heterogeneity within each tumor. Thirty-one percent of colorectal tumors were found by Petersen et al.[14] to be heterogeneous with regard to DNA content. Koha et al.[15] took four fine-needle-aspiration samples from each of 50 patients with colorectal tumors; a heterogenic DNA pattern was identified in 60 percent of these tumors. None of the tumors was homogeneously diploid. Rognum et al.[16] noted that multiple sampling (five samples from each tumor) increases the possibility of detecting an aneuploid peak and achieves concordance rates between fresh and archival tissue exceeding 80 percent.

Kim et al.[17] compared the DNA ploidy of superficial and deep biopsies from the same tumor. They examined tumor specimens from 88 patients with advanced colorectal carcinoma (Dukes stages C2 and D) and found that 78 percent had nondiploid stemlines. There was a 19 percent disagreement between superficial and deep biopsies. Additionally, it was found that the superficial specimens had a similar ploidy to the lymph node metastases, whereas the deeper biopsies reflected the hepatic metastases. Therefore, not only the number of specimens but the nature (i.e., superficial or deep) of the specimen may be of importance in determining an accurate DNA histogram. The lack of consistent methodology between studies and institutions in terms of (1) fresh vs. archival tissue, (2) single versus multiple biopsies, and (3) superficial versus deep biopsies makes the interpretation of results difficult.

CLINICAL STUDIES

Primary Colorectal Carcinoma

The prognostic significance of cellular DNA content has been explored in many retrospective studies.[18] The incidence of aneuploidy varies between 35 to 78 percent in published series.[12,17,19–30] Aneuploid lesions appear to be equally prevalent between the colon and rectum. Most studies have not demonstrated a correlation between DNA index and histologic grade.[20,28,31–33] However, some reports have demonstrated increased aneuploidy in less differentiated lesions.[20,34] Increased expression of carcinoembryonic antigen has been noted with nondiploid tumors and tumors with a high PI.[34] Many reports have demonstrated a correlation between advancing clinical stage and ploidy abnormalities. Kokal et al.,[20] reviewing 147 cases, noted that aneuploid tumors were more likely to be rather poorly differentiated and to have full-thickness mural penetration and/or lymphatic invasion. In a series of young patients ($<$40 years) with rectal cancer, all nondiploid tumors were deeply infiltrating, with 80 percent being associated with nodal or distant metastases.[35] It of interest that in this series there was a lack of correlation between histologic grading, colloid production, and cellular DNA abnormalities.

The potential importance of DNA ploidy abnormalities as an important prognostic variable has been suggested by many of the retrospective studies. Aneuploidy and increased PI have been associated with decreased disease-free survival,[20,28] increased local recurrence,[20,36] and reduced overall survival.[19,20,23,28,35,37,38] Publications seem to be divided between those which have demonstrated that aneuploidy is an important independent prognostic variable[19–23] and those which have demonstrated that the overall contribution of ploidy to prognosis is small[24,25,32,39] and that following multivariate analysis is not statistically significant.[24,40] In specific instances, ploidy may have more significance. Kokal et al.[28] noted that ploidy was a particularly important variable in Dukes B lesions. Similarly, Armitage et al.,[21] reviewing 416 patients with colorectal cancer, noted that DNA content only exerted an influence on Dukes B lesions, moderately differentiated tumors, rectal tumors, and mobile tumors. They found that the influence of pathologic stage was greater than that of ploidy. Chang et al.,[41] reporting the Memorial Sloan-Kettering Cancer Center experience with local excision of early rectal cancer, noted that ploidy was an independent predictor of tumor aggressiveness, with aneuploid patients having an increased incidence of local failure.

A differing pattern of DNA ploidy was noted by Kouri et al.[42] in 59 patients with the cancer family syndrome. Unlike "normal" colorectal carcinomas, these tumors exhibited a predominance of diploid or near-diploid DNA values. Forty tumors were diploid, and only 19 were aneuploid or near-diploid (defined as DNA index 1.1 to 1.3). The DNA index was less than 1.27 in 90 percent of cases. The authors propose that the ploidy characteristics in these patients may in part explain their better prognosis.

Retrospective studies, while posing intriguing questions, have failed to define the value of cellular DNA analysis in the assessment of prognosis. Recent prospective studies have attempted to do so (Fig. 23-4).

Author	Year	N	Result
Hemming et al.[52]	1992	62	Aneuploidy associated with worse Dukes stage
Armitage et al.[12]	1991	236	Significant for recurrence only in Dukes B patients
Rognum et al.[16]	1991	100	Significant for survival
Witzig et al.[49]	1991	694	Significant for recurrence and survival
Albe et al.[46]	1990	171	Significant for survival in subgroup undergoing "curative" surgery
Kouri et al.[42,50]	1990	157	Significant for local recurrence
Jones et al.[13]	1988	123	Not significant

FIG. 23-4. Recent studies analyzing the independent significance of DNA ploidy as a prognostic variable in patients undergoing resection.

The earliest prospective study was published by Wolley et al.[43] in 1982. They measured cellular DNA content in 33 patients with colorectal adenocarcinoma. Of these, 20 patients (61 percent) had a diploid distribution, and the remaining 13 patients (39 percent) were classed as nondiploid. At a median follow-up of 43 months, 70 percent of the patients with diploid tumors were alive and free from disease, whereas, only one patient with a nondiploid tumor was alive with disease. The average survival for patients with non-diploid tumors was 17.7 months. Aneuploidy appeared to correlate with advanced stage and increased tumor aggressiveness.

Banner et al.[33] compared established morphologic prognostic parameters with DNA ploidy in 56 patients studied prospectively between 1983 and 1984. A majority (75 percent) of tumors were non-diploid. Objective parameters of staging (i.e., mural penetration and lymphatic invasion) were strongly related to ploidy. Diploid tumors tended to be Astler-Coller stage A or B, whereas nondiploid lesions were stage C or D. Subjective histologic criteria (i.e., grade) correlated poorly with ploidy. The authors suggested that ploidy could provide useful information regarding tumor invasiveness. In contrast, Hood et al.[44] did not find a correlation with tumor stage or with lymphatic or vascular invasion. However, high-grade carcinomas were more likely to demonstrate aneuploidy—a trend that did not reach statistical significance. Similar results were reported by Jones et al.,[45] who studied 123 patients with colorectal cancer. DNA aneuploidy was seen in 67 percent of cases. There was a trend toward a poorer prognosis in the aneuploid lesions, but this only reached significance in the Dukes stage B patients, and then only in a univariate analysis. A Cox-model regression analysis found that even in these patients ploidy was not of independent significance. The surgeon's assessment of "curability," Dukes stage, and the patient's age were the strongest predictors of survival.

Albe et al.[46] measured DNA histograms in 211 patients with colonic and rectal cancers followed for a maximum of 54 months after surgery. Of these cancers, 88 (42 percent) were diploid and 123 (58 percent) aneuploid. More aneuploid tumors were found in the distal bowel. There was no correlation between ploidy and histologic grade or tumor stage. In patients undergoing "curative" surgery (i.e., Dukes A, B, and C), the tumor stage, differentiation, and ploidy status were independent predictors of survival. Dukes stage and DNA ploidy were also indicators for recurrence. The relationship of ploidy to recurrence was further investigated by Armitage et al.,[12] who reviewed 236 patients following curative surgery and noted a significantly increased rate of recurrence in the patients with nondiploid tumors (52 of 142, or 37 percent) compared to those with diploid tumors (23 of 94, or 24 percent). However, only in the Dukes B lesions was ploidy found to be an independent prognostic factor. The authors stress that ploidy can potentially identify a group of patients who are at high risk for recurrence and are thus candidates for adjuvant therapies.

The importance of the proliferative index (PI) (i.e., proportion of cells in the S + G_2/M phase of the cell cycle) or S-phase values has been investigated in recent reports. Emdin et al.[11] demonstrated at a median follow-up of 30.4 months a significant survival advantage for patients with diploid tumors.

The majority of tumors in this study (23 of 37) were aneuploid, with significantly higher S-phase values compared to diploid tumors. It was suggested by the authors that the PI was an important variable; however, no correlation with ploidy was made. The relationship between ploidy and the PI was also examined by Bauer et al.,[47] who reported a significant correlation between aneuploidy and a high PI.[47] A high PI (defined as >20 percent of cells in S phase) was noted in this study to be a stronger prognostic variable than aneuploidy. A relationship between ploidy and malignant transformation was suggested by Page et al.,[48] who analyzed ploidy and PI in 120 patients. An increase in the percentage of cells in S + G_2/M was noted between adenomas (17 percent), diploid tumors (22 percent), and aneuploid tumors (29 percent). Bauer et al.[47] also noted a significant correlation between aneuploidy and an increased PI index. Witzig et al.[49] studied DNA ploidy and cell kinetic measurements in 694 patients with either Aster-Coller stage B_2 or C colorectal tumors. Ploidy and proliferation index were independent prognostic factors. When these two variables were combined, patients in a favorable grouping (i.e., diploidy and low PI) had a significantly improved survival compared to those in an unfavorable grouping (i.e., aneuploidy with a high proliferative index). The 5-year survival was 74 versus 54 percent, respectively.

In contrast, other studies have failed to demonstrate a correlation between PI and prognosis. Kouri et al.[50] examined ploidy and cell kinetics in 157 patients. Univariate analysis revealed DNA aneuploidy to be associated with a reduced disease-free and overall survival. However, the S-phase measurements did not correlate with prognosis. This study also demonstrated a considerable heterogeneity in S-phase values within the tumors, especially with diploid tumors.

Scott et al.[51] reviewed four mathematical methods for measuring cellular proliferation from the DNA histogram. The mathematically defined distribution of the data fitted to the S phase differed in each case (Fig. 23-5). All were accurate in measuring cell cycle distribution; however, there were obvious differences in the level of cell proliferation indices (S + G_2/M) recorded. This appeared to be due primarily to an underestimation of the S-phase component. The authors suggested that the variability of published clinical series regarding the proliferative index could be a result of this intermethod variation.

Hemming et al.[52] failed to demonstrate, in 61 tumor specimens, any correlation between cellular proliferation as measured by monoclonal antibody (Ki-67) labeling and tumor stage or ploidy. Similar results have been reported by others.[44]

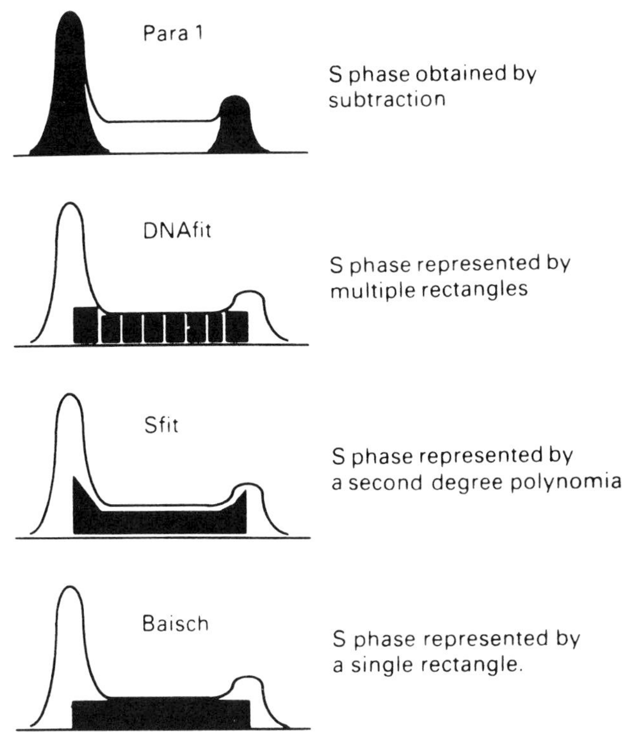

FIG. 23-5. Methodology for S-phase determination. (From Moran et al.[55] Reproduced by permission.)

Experience at Memorial Sloan-Kettering Cancer Center supports the contention that ploidy or the calculation of S phase/PI from the DNA histogram alone will not be useful independent prognostic factors. In a prospective study of 176 patients, Enker et al.[53] found no correlation between aneuploidy and Dukes stage, tumor grade, site, size, or location. The PI was related to increasing tumor stage, but there was no correlation with survival. Similarly, no difference in survival rates was seen between patients with aneuploid or diploid tumors (Fig. 23-6). Currently we are evaluating survival and recurrence patterns in 105 patients whose PI was prospectively determined by the intravenous infusion of 5-bromo-deoxyuridine (BUDR). Incorporation of this S-phase precursor is evaluated both by flow cytometry and by immunohistochemistry. Median follow-up is approaching 33 months.

In view of the often conflicting results, Giaretti et al.[54] proposed the hypothesis that the degree of aneuploidy was important as a prognostic factor. They defined a DNA index (DI) as the ratio of the tumor cells' DNA content to that of non-malignant cells. Diploid tumors had a better prognosis. Among the aneuploid tumors, those with a DI > 1.2 were worse (23 percent greater relative risk of death) than those with a DI < 1.2 and DI = 2.

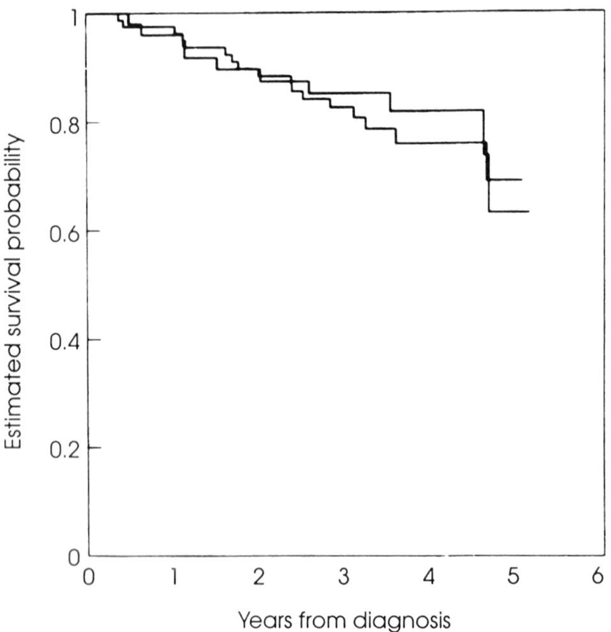

FIG. 23-6. Comparison of survival for patients with colonic and rectal cancers, aneuploid versus diploid (p = not significant). (From Enker et al.[53] Reproduced by permission.)

The actual definition of aneuploidy is another factor that may account for some of the variability seen in published results. Jones et al.[13] considered three alternate definitions of aneuploidy, depending on the proportion of nuclei considered to constitute a separate peak on the DNA histogram: i.e., 5, 10, and 10 percent if the DI is 1.1 to 1.8, but 15 percent if the DI is 1.9 to 2.1. An inverse relationship between the aneuploid peak size and prognosis was noted, implying that thresholds utilized to define aneuploidy influence the prognostic significance of DNA ploidy.

Metastatic Disease

A number of recent studies have addressed the importance of DNA ploidy in colorectal hepatic metastases.[17,32,55–57] Salmon et al.[58] noted that DNA patterns between the primary tumor and hepatic metastatic disease were similar. Analogous results were reported by Kokal et al.,[28] who demonstrated concordance in 78 percent of cases between the primary tumor and the metastases.

Yamaguchi et al.[58] found that ploidy estimation of the metastatic lesion correlated with the recurrence rates in liver. Cady et al.,[56] in a retrospective review of 51 cases, noted an improved disease-free survival for patients with a diploid metastasis. In contrast, Lind et al.[57] performed flow cytometry on 37 archival specimens. Of these, 60 percent were noted to be aneuploid. All metastases from Dukes A primary tumors were noted to be diploid. No difference in either disease-free or overall survival was noted on the basis of ploidy. Similar results were reported by Kokal et al.,[28] who found that there was no significant correlation between DNA ploidy and response to treatment or overall survival. Although the available data are weak, existing evidence questions the importance of ploidy as an additional prognostic variable in this select group of patients.

A possible explanation for the conflicting results is the heterogeneity noted in the DNA content of colorectal hepatic metastases. Graham et al.[59] observed a 21 percent rate of intratumoral heterogeneity in 25 hepatic lesions. Among 24 patients who underwent resection, 8 tumors were diploid while 16 had an aneuploid pattern. All patients with aneuploid tumors have died of their disease—while at the time of the report—3 patients with diploid tumors were disease-free.

Other Tumors

Two recent studies have investigated the prognostic significance of ploidy in squamous cell carcinoma of the anus.[60,61] Scott et al.[60] obtained DNA histograms from 117 patients. Of these tumors, 70 percent had a diploid pattern, 17 percent tetraploid, and 13 percent aneuploid. Ploidy appeared related to the histologic grade of the tumor. However, in a multivariate analysis, only tumor histology and stage were independent prognostic factors, with ploidy manifesting only a marginal influence. In contrast, Shepherd et al.[61] measured ploidy from the archival specimens of 184 patients, 42 of which were non-diploid. Ploidy—along with tumor thickness, anatomic spread, and the status of the inguinal nodes—was noted as an independent prognostic factor.

DNA ploidy has been shown by Tsioulias et al.[62] to be a significant prognostic factor in carcinoid tumors of the rectum. A diploid DNA pattern was demonstrated in 19 of 22 patients, all of whom had localized disease. In contrast, 3 patients with metastatic disease had aneuploid tumors. A further case of metastatic aneuploid rectal carcinoid was reported by Cohn et al.[63]

Benign/Premalignant Conditions

DNA ploidy pattern has been analyzed as a possible marker of malignant potential in certain high-risk patient populations. Premalignant lesions have been shown to have an altered DNA content compared with normal tissue or benign tumors.[64–68] Chronic ulcerative colitis (CUC), a condition in which the definition of patients at risk for colorectal cancer is often difficult, has been extensively studied. Cuvelier et al.[69] noted that patients with "quiescent" colitis had a diploid DNA pattern, whereas 62.5 percent of those with high-grade dysplasia had an aneuploid pattern. Lofberg et al.[70] prospectively followed 53 patients with long-standing ulcerative colitis. Colonoscopy and biopsies were performed at regular intervals. Of the 5 patients who had an aneuploid DNA pattern, 4 also had some degree of dysplasia. In 1 patient, the finding of an abnormal DNA pattern appeared prior to dysplasia, and in another prior to the detection of a Dukes A adenocarcinoma. Four additional patients had reactive, inflammatory changes on their rectal biopsies, none of which were dysplastic or manifested an aneuploid DNA pattern. The authors concluded that flow cytometry may aid existing methods in screening these high-risk patients. In contrast, others[71] have suggested that while ploidy estimation confirms dysplasia and cancer, it does not as yet appear to be an independent predictor of malignant transformation. The adenoma-carcinoma sequence has also been evaluated.[64] Polyp size and histologic subtype are related to the degree of aneuploidy. Goh et al.[65] demonstrated a significant correlation between the degree of dysplasia and aneuploidy.

Association with Cytogenetic Changes

Recent studies have demonstrated multiple, complex genetic alterations in colorectal tumors.[72–74] Genetic changes generally involve the mutation or deletion of tumor suppressor genes or oncogenes.[74–76] Amplification of particular gene loci has also been described.[73] The association of these genetic alterations with DNA ploidy has recently been studied. Meling et al.[75] demonstrated a significant association between amplification of the retinoblastoma gene, a tumor suppressor gene associated with tumorigenesis and DNA aneuploidy. A similar correlation between the expression of epidermal growth factor (another cellular protein implicated in carcinogenesis), aneuploidy, and tumor stage has been reported.[52] These findings suggest that the increased amount of DNA present in tumor cells may reflect specific gene amplifications of importance in tumorigenesis.

Offerhaus et al.[74] compared DNA ploidy with clonal molecular genetic abnormalities in 50 colorectal cancers. Increased DI was correlated with a greater mean fractional allelic loss. Deletion of chromosome 17p was more frequent in aneuploid tumors, whereas *ras* gene mutations were less frequent, compared to diploid tumors. Aneuploid tumors were less well differentiated, however, no correlation between DNA ploidy and lymphatic or distant metastases was noted. Other studies have demonstrated similar associations between aneuploidy, 17p deletion, 18q deletion, and overexpression of the tumor suppressor gene p53. Shackney et al.[77] hypothesized that chromosomal alterations which result in cellular proliferation (i.e. deletion of 17p or increased expression of p53) may be a prerequisite for the establishment of an aneuploid peak on the DNA histogram. All of these observations require further research and future clinical observations before their significance will become evident.

SUMMARY

Recent work has demonstrated that while DNA ploidy estimation overall may not be in itself a strong independent predictor of survival, it may be a significant variable in certain subgroups (i.e., Duke B tumors). The combination of ploidy and PI can accurately predict prognosis. Patients with diploid tumors and a low PI appear to have the best prognosis, whereas those with aneuploid lesions and an increased PI have the worst. Thus, the assessment of DNA content has potential as a means of selecting patients with poor prognosis who would benefit from adjuvant therapies.

REFERENCES

1. Williams NN, Daly JM: Flow cytometry and prognostic implications in patients with solid tumors. *Surg Obstet Gynecol* 171:257–266, 1990.
2. Barlogie B, Raber MN, Schumann J, et al: Flow cytometry in clinical cancer research. *Cancer Res* 43:3982–3997, 1983.
3. Seckinger D, Sugarbaker E, Frankfurt O: DNA content in human cancer: Application and pathology and clinical. *Arch Pathol Lab Med* 113:619–626, 1989.
4. Beahrs OH, Henson DE, Hutter RV, et al (eds): *Manual for Staging of Cancer*, 3d ed. Philadelphia, Lippincott, 1988.
5. American Joint Committee on Cancer: Colon and rectum, in Beahrs OH, Henson DE, Hutter RV, et al (eds): *Manual for Staging of Cancer*, 3d ed. Philadelphia, Lippincott, 1988, pp 75–80.
6. Traganos F: Fly cytometry: Principles and applications, I. *Cancer Invest* 2:149–163, 1984.
7. Traganos F: Flow cytometry: Principles and applications, II. *Cancer Invest* 2:239–258, 1984.
8. Shapiro HM: Flow cytometry of DNA content and other indicators of proliferative activity. *Arch Pathol Lab Med* 113:591–597, 1989.
9. Hiddemann W, Schumann J, Andreff M, et al: Convention on nomenclature for DNA cytometry. *Cytometry* 5:445–446, 1984.
10. Hedley DW, Friedlander ML, Taylor IW, et al: Method for analysis of cellular DNA content of paraffin-embedded pathological material using flow cytometry. *J Histochem Cytochem* 31:1333–1335, 1983.
11. Emdin SO, Stenling R, Roos G: Prognostic value of DNA content in colorectal carcinoma: A flow cytometric study with some methodological aspects. *Cancer* 60:1282–1287, 1987.
12. Armitage NC, Ballantyne KC, Sheffield JP, et al: A prospective evaluation of the effect of tumor cell DNA content on recurrence in colorectal cancer. *Cancer* 67:2599–2604, 1991.
13. Jones DJ, Moore M, Schofield PF: Refining the prognostic significance of DNA ploidy status in colorectal cancer: A prospective flow cytometric study. *Int J Cancer* 41:206–210, 1988.
14. Petersen SE, Lorentsen H, Bichel P: A mosaic subpopulation structure of human colorectal carcinomas demonstrated by flow cytometry. *Acta Pathol Microbiol Scand (A)* 274:412–416, 1981.
15. Koha M, Caspersson TO, Wikstrom B, et al: Heterogeneity

of DNA distribution pattern in colorectal carcinoma: A microspectrophotometric study of fine needle aspirates. *Anal Quant Cytol Histol* 12:348–351, 1990.

16. Rognum TO, Lund E, Meling GI, et al: Near diploid large bowel carcinomas have better five-year survival than aneuploid ones. *Cancer* 68:1077–1081, 1991.
17. Kim YJ, Ngoi SS, Godwin TA, et al: Ploidy in invasive colorectal cancer: Implications for metastatic disease. *Cancer* 68:638–641, 1991.
18. Mileski WJ, Joehl RJ, Rege RV, et al: Treatment of anastomotic leakage following low anterior colon resection. *Arch Surg* 123:968–971, 1988.
19. Armitage NC, Robins RA, Evans DF, et al: Tumour cell DNA content in colorectal cancer and its relationship to survival. *Br J Surg* 72:828–830, 1985.
20. Kokal WA, Gardine RL, Sheibani K, et al: Tumor DNA content in resectable, primary colorectal carcinoma. *Ann Surg* 209:188–193, 1989.
21. Armitage NC, Ballantyne KC, Evans DF, et al: The influence of tumor cell DNA content of survival in colorectal cancer. *Br J Cancer* 62:852–856, 1990.
22. Heimann TM, Miller F, Martinelli G, et al: Significance of DNA content abnormalities in small rectal cancer. *Am J Surg* 159:525–528, 1989.
23. Quirke P, Dixon MF, Clayden AD, et al: Prognostic significance of DNA aneuploidy and cell proliferation in rectal c adenocarcinomas. *J Pathol* 151:285–291, 1987.
24. Jass JR, Mukawa K, Goh HS, et al: Clinical importance of DNA content in rectal cancer measured by flow cytometry. *J Clin Pathol* 42:254–259, 1989.
25. Fisher ER, Siderits RH, Sass R, et al: Value of assessment of ploidy in rectal cancers. *Arch Pathol Lab Med* 113:525–528, 1991.
26. Durrant L, Robins RA, Armitage N, et al: Association of antigen expression and DNA ploidy in human colorectal tumors. *Cancer Res* 46:3543–3549, 1986.
27. Remvikos Y, Laurent-Purg P, Salmon RJ, et al: Simultaneous monitoring of p53 protein and DNA content of colorectal adenocarcinomas by flow cytometry. *Int J Cancer* 45:450–456, 1990.
28. Kokal WA, Duda RB, Azumi N, et al: Tumor DNA content in primary and metastatic colorectal carcinoma. *Arch Surg* 121:1434–1439, 1986.
29. Bird RP: Effect of dietary components on the pathobiology of colonic epithelium: Possible relationship with colon tumorigenesis. *Lipids* 21:289–291, 1986.
30. Rhodes JB, Holmes FF, Clark GM: Changing distribution of primary cancer in the large bowel. *JAMA* 235:1641–1643, 1977.
31. Tribukait B, Hammarberg C, Rubio C: Ploidy and proliferation patterns in colorectal adenocarcinomas related to Dukes' classification and to histopathological differentiation. *Acta Pathol Microbiol Immunol Scand (A)* 91:89–95, 1983.
32. Finan PJ, Quirke P, Dixon MF, et al: Is DNA aneuploidy a good prognostic indicator in patients with advanced colorectal cancer? *Br J Cancer* 54:327–330, 1986.
33. Banner BF, Tomas de la Vega JE, Roseman DL: Should flow cytometric DNA analysis precede definitive surgery for colon carcinoma? *Ann Surg* 202:740–744, 1985.
34. Flijham GH, Schutte B, Reynders MM, et al: Flow cytometric (FCM) determination of ploidy level and life cycle analysis on 297 paraffin-embedded colorectal carcinoma specimens. *Proc Am Soc Clin Oncol* 4:22, 1985.
35. Heimann TM, Martinelli G, Szporn A, et al: Prognostic significance of DNA content abnormalities in young patients with colorectal cancer. *Ann Surg* 210:792–795, 1989.
36. Kimura O, Kijima T, Moriwaki S, et al: DNA index as a significant indicator of lymph node metastasis and local recurrence of rectal cancer. *Dis Colon Rectum* 35:1130–1134, 1992.
37. Schutte B, Reynders MMJ, Wiggers T, et al: Retrospective analysis of the prognostic significance of DNA content and proliferative activity in large bowel carcinoma. *Cancer Res* 47:5494–5496, 1987.
38. Bawani M, Tibrewala S, Copur S, et al: DNA flow cytometry of colorectal carcinoma: Correlation of DNA stemlines with other prognostic indices. *Am J Gastroenterol* 86:191–195, 1991.
39. Goh HS, Jass JR, Atkin WS, et al: Value of flow cytometric determination of ploidy as a guide to prognosis inoperable rectal cancer: A multivariate analysis. *Int J Colorect Dis* 2:17–21, 1987.
40. Bottger TC, Gabbert HE, Stockle M, et al: DNA image cytometry: A prognostic tool in rectal cancer? *Dis Colon Rectum* 35:436–443, 1992.
41. Chang KJ, Enker WE, Melamed M: Influence of tumor cell DNA ploidy on the natural history of rectal cancer. *Am J Surg* 153:184–188, 1987.
42. Kouri M, Laasonen A, Mecklin J-P, et al: Diploid predominance in hereditary nonpolyposis colorectal carcinoma evaluated by flow cytometry. *Cancer* 65:1825–1829, 1990.
43. Wolley RC, Schreiber K, Koss LG, et al: DNA distribution in human colon carcinomas and its relationship to clinical behavior. *J Natl Cancer Inst* 69:15–22, 1982.
44. Hood DL, Petras RE, Edinger M, et al: Deoxyribonucleic acid ploidy and cell cycle analysis of colorectal carcinoma by flow cytometry. *Am J Clin Path* 93:615–620, 1990.
45. Jones DJ, Moore M, Schofield PF: Prognostic significance of DNA ploidy in colorectal cancer: A prospective flow cytometric study. *Br J Surg* 75:28–33, 1988.
46. Albe X, Vassilakos P, Helfer-Guarnori K, et al: Independent prognostic value of ploidy in colorectal cancer. *Cancer* 66:1168–1175, 1990.
47. Bauer KD, Lincon ST, Vera-Roman JM, et al: Prognostic implications of proliferative activity and DNA aneuploidy in colonic adenocarcinomas. *Lab Invest* 57:329–335, 1987.
48. Page M, Bocquillon PG, Daver A: Flow cytometric analysis of ploidy and proliferative index of 120 human colon adenocarcinomas: A comparison with clinical parameters. *Proc Am Assoc Cancer Res* 27:32, 1986.
49. Witzig TE, Loprinzi CL, Gonchoroff NJ, et al: DNA ploidy and cell kinetic measurements as predictors of recurrence and survival in stages B2 and colorectal adenocarcinoma. *Cancer* 68:879–888, 1991.
50. Kouri M, Pyrhonen S, Mecklin J-P, et al: The prognostic value of DNA ploidy in colorectal carcinoma: A prospective study. *Br J Cancer* 62:976–981, 1990.
51. Scott N, Cross D, Plumb MI, et al: An investigation of different methods of cell cycle analysis by flow cytometry in rectal cancer. *Br J Cancer* 65:8–10, 1992.
52. Hemming AW, Davis NL, Kluftinger A, et al: Prognostic markers of colorectal cancer: An evaluation of DNA content, epidermal growth factor receptor, and Ki-67. *J Surg Oncol* 51:147–152, 1992.
53. Enker WE, Kimmel M, Cibas ES, et al: DNA/RNA content and proliferative fractions of colorectal cancers: A five-year prospective study relating flow cytometry to survival. *J Natl Cancer Inst* 83:701–707, 1991.
54. Giaretti W, Danova M, Geido E, et al: Flow cytometric DNA index in the prognosis of colorectal cancer. *Cancer* 67:1921–1927, 1991.
55. Moran MR, Rothenberger DA, Gallo RA, et al: A predictive model for distant metastases in rectal cancer using DNA ploidy studies. *Am J Surg* 163:599–601, 1992.

56. Cady B, Stone MD, McDermott WV Jr, et al: Technical and biological factors in disease-free survival after hepatic resection for colorectal cancer metastases. *Arch Surg* 127:561–569, 1992.
57. Lind DS, Parker GA, Horsley JS, et al: Formal hepatic resection of colorectal liver metastases: Ploidy and prognosis. *Ann Surg* 215:677–684, 1992.
58. Salmon RJ, Remvikos Y, Sano T, et al: Flow cytometric analysis of colorectal cancers and their liver metastases. *Proc Am Assoc Cancer Res* 29:A804, 1988.
59. Graham RA, Teague K, Mclemore D, et al: Regional DNA content heterogeneity in colonic adenocarcinoma: Prognostic significance in patients with liver metastases. *J Surg Oncol* 50:228–232, 1992.
60. Scott NA, Beart RW Jr, Weiland LH, et al: Carcinoma of the anal canal and flow cytometric DNA analysis. *Br J Cancer* 60:56–58, 1989.
61. Shepherd NA, Scholefield JH, Love SB, et al: Prognostic factors in anal squamous carcinoma: A multivariate analysis of clinical, pathological, and flow cytometric parameters in 235 cases. *Histopathology* 16:545–555, 1990.
62. Tsioulias G, Muto T, Kubota Y, et al: DNA ploidy pattern in rectal carcinoid tumors. *Dis Colon Rectum* 34:31–36, 1991.
63. Cohn G, Erhardt K, Cedemark B, et al: DNA distribution pattern in intestinal carcinoid tumors. *World J Surg* 10:548–554, 1986.
64. Van der Ingh HF, Griffioen G, Cornelisse CJ: Flow cytometric detection of aneuploidy in colorectal adenomas. *Cancer Res* 45:3392–3397, 1985.
65. Goh HS, Jass JR: DNA content and the adenoma-carcinoma sequence in the colorectum. *J Clin Pathol* 39:387–392, 1986.
66. Banner BF, Chaco MS, Rosemann DL, et al: Multiparameter flow cytometric analysis of colon polyps. *Am J Clin Pathol* 87:313–318, 1987.
67. Quirke P, Fozard JB, Dixon MF, et al: DNA aneuploidy in rectal adenomas. *Br J Cancer* 53:477–481, 1986.
68. Giaretti W, Sciarello S, Bruno S, et al: DNA flow cytometry of endoscopically examined colorectal adenomas and adenocarcinomas. *Cytometry* 9:238–244, 1988.
69. Cuvelier CA, Morson BC, Roels HJ: The DNA in cancer and dysplasia in chronic ulcerative colitis. *Histopathology* 11: 927–939, 1987.
70. Lofberg R, Tribukait B, Ost A, et al: Flow cytometric DNA analysis in longstanding ulcerative colitis: A method of prediction of dysplasia and carcinoma development? *Gut* 28: 1100–1106, 1987.
71. Allen DC, Hamilton PW, Watt PC, et al: Morphometrical analysis in ulcerative colitis with dysplasia and carcinoma. *Histopathology* 11:913–926, 1987.
72. Fearon ER, Cho KR, Nigro JM, et al: Identification of a chromosome 18q gene that is altered in colorectal cancers. *Science* 247:49–56, 1990.
73. Fearon ER: Genetic alterations underlying colorectal tumorigenesis. *Cancer Surv* 12:119–136, 1992.
74. Offerhaus GJA, De Feyter EP, Cornelisse CJ, et al: The relationship of DNA aneuploidy to molecular genetic alterations in colorectal carcinoma. *Gastroenterology* 102:1612–1619, 1992.
75. Meling GI, Lothe RA, Borresen AL, et al: Genetic alterations within the retinoblastoma locus in colorectal carcinomas: Relation to DNA ploidy pattern studied by flow cytometric analysis. *Br J Cancer* 64:474–480, 1991.
76. Sidransky D, Tokino T, Hamilton SR, et al: Identification of ras oncogene mutations in the stool of patients with curable colorectal tumors. *Science* 256:102–105, 1992.
77. Shackney SE, Smith CA, Miller BW, et al: Model for the genetic evolution of human solid tumors. *Cancer Res* 49:3344–3354, 1989.

CHAPTER 24

Molecular Prognostic Factors

Marina L. Wasylyshyn
Fabrizio Michelassi

HIGHLIGHTS

Preliminary data suggest that the presence of multiple chromosomal mutations in a colorectal cancer is an independent risk factor in the development of metastatic disease. Data also suggest that chromosome 17 deletions and chromosome 18 deletions are each significantly associated with the development of metastatic disease.

CONTROVERSIES

The role this information will play in treatment strategies awaits further studies.

FUTURE DIRECTIONS

Bearing in mind tumor heterogeneity and differences between the primary tumors and their lymph node and distant metastases, the determination of molecular changes in the individual patient may provide unique information as to the likelihood of local failure and metastatic disease. Selected patients with a favorable molecular pattern may undergo limited surgical procedures, and others with a more aggressive pattern may receive aggressive preoperative adjuvant therapy.

The molecular biology of colorectal cancer has been reviewed in previous chapters. This section will delineate the prognostic correlates of some of these molecular alterations.

THE *ras* FAMILY OF ONCOGENES

The *ras* gene mutations are found in various frequencies in different tumor types. In a study by Vogelstein et al.,[1] 47 percent of colorectal carcinomas exhibited *ras* mutations. Adenomas were also examined in this work in an attempt to identify the mutations which occur as a lesion progresses from benign to malignant. The adenomas were divided into three classes. Class I adenomas were small, tubular adenomas with low-grade dysplasia from patients with familial adenomatous polyposis (FAP). Class II adenomas were from patients without FAP. Class III adenomas were those with an associated focus of malignancy. The areas of malignancy were carefully dissected away from the surrounding adenomatous portion of the tumor prior to analysis. The results showed that 12 percent of class I adenomas, 42 percent of class II adenomas, and 57 percent of class III adenomas harbored a *ras* gene mutation. It should be noted that benign adenomas from non-FAP patients had essentially the same rate of *ras* mutation as carcinomas. This suggests that the presence of *ras* mutations does not correlate with the aggressiveness of the tumor.

The question of the role of the *ras* oncogene in determining the aggressiveness of the malignancy was also addressed by Vogelstein's group.[2] In an analysis of 87 cases, they found that the presence of *ras* mutations was not related to the development of metastatic disease during follow-up, nor was it related to survival.

TUMOR SUPPRESSOR GENES

Tumor suppressor genes normally function to control cell growth. Loss or mutation of both copies of a tumor suppressor gene leads to an inactive or absent gene product, which allows the development or progression of malignancy.

Loss of an allele on a particular chromosome suggests the presence of a tumor suppressor gene. Attention is especially drawn to a particular region of a chromosome if allele loss is seen there frequently in a given tumor type. Vogelstein et al.[3] studied every autosomal chromosome in 56 colorectal carcinomas and found that every chromosome revealed allele losses in a certain percentage of tumors. It is not yet known how many of these chromosomes harbor tumor suppressor genes which, upon mutation, play a role in the development of colorectal cancer. To date, tumor suppressor genes have been identified in colorectal cancer on chromosomes 5,[4–7] 17,[8] and 18[9] and others are being actively sought.[10]

Two tumor suppressor genes have been identified on chromosome 5. Attention first focused on this chromosome in 1986, when Herrera reported a deletion on chromosome 5 in a man with Gardner syndrome. Genetic linkage analysis of kindreds followed and localized the FAP gene to the short arm of chromosome 5, 5q.[11,12]

Studies have shown that 23 to 36 percent[1,13,14] of sporadic colorectal carcinomas lose an allele on chromosome 5. Similarly, 24 percent of colorectal carcinomas from FAP patients lose an allele on chromosome 5. Rates of allele loss among benign polyps from FAP patients are very low: 0[1,13] to 2 percent.[14] In contrast, polyps from non-FAP patients reveal allele loss on chromosome 5 in 29 percent of cases,[1] equal to that found in frank carcinomas.

These findings indicate that somatic loss of an allele on chromosome 5 is not required for polyp formation or for the development of carcinoma in FAP patients. Two hypotheses have been proposed to elucidate the role of the FAP gene. Bodmer et al.[15] suggest that fluctuation below some critical level of FAP gene product in patients with an inherited mutation of the FAP gene leads to polyp formation. Vogelstein et al.[1] hypothesize that mutation of one allele of the FAP gene leads to epithelial hyperplasia, and that polyp formation develops following mutations at other loci.

The FAP gene has recently been identified by two groups.[4–7] Germline mutations of this gene are found in individuals with FAP. Mutations of this gene are also found in sporadic colorectal carcinomas, although the prevalence of this mutation in sporadic colorectal malignancies is not yet known.

In the search for the FAP gene, both of these groups identified a second gene, located very close to the FAP gene on chromosome 5. This has been called the *MCC* (mutated in colorectal cancer) gene. The MCC gene is mutated in 15 percent of sporadic colorectal cancers but not in FAP.

Now that the FAP gene has been identified, diagnostic tests for the FAP phenotype are feasible. Further work on the FAP and MCC genes and their products may lead to methods of prevention and treatment of colon cancer.

From 40[16] to 75 percent[1] of colorectal carcinomas lose an allele on chromosome 17. The involved tumor suppressor gene is believed to be the p53 gene,[17] as the p53 gene had been previously localized to this area of deletion.[18] Confirmation of the role of p53 in colorectal neoplasms comes with experiments in which wild-type p53 is inserted into human colorectal carcinoma cell lines and suppresses their growth.[19] The protein product of the p53 gene has an inhibitory effect on the growth of cells.[20] Most p53 mutations produce a protein which lacks adequate growth suppressor function. Different p53 mutations produce proteins which have different abilities to change cell growth.[21] This finding suggests that different p53 mutations may have different biological activities. This suggests a potential role for evaluation of p53 mutations in determining prognosis in colorectal malignancies.

Allele loss occurs on the long arm of chromosome 18 in 75 percent[1] of colorectal carcinomas. Fearon et al.[9] localized and cloned part of what they believe represents the tumor suppressor gene on chromosome 18q, the DCC (deleted in colorectal carcinomas) gene. This gene encodes a protein which resembles neural cell adhesion molecules, suggesting that mutation of this gene might alter cell interactions that normally control growth. This could then enhance tumor development. Expression of this gene is found in most normal tissues examined, including colonic mucosa, but is absent in most colon cancer cell lines. This is evidence that the DCC gene is a tumor suppressor gene.

Tumors with more mutations appear to have a more aggressive clinical behavior. This was studied by Kern et al.[2] in an analysis of 87 carcinomas from 83 patients. They looked at fractional allelic loss (FAL), which they defined as the *number of chromosomal arms with allele loss divided by the number of chromosomal arms for which the patient was informative* (heterozygous for at least one probe). The median FAL was 0.20; that is, 20 percent of chromosomal arms studied had undergone allelic deletion in colorectal carcinoma. In all, 39 chromosomal arms were studied in these tumors.

As shown in Table 24-1, patients with less than the average number of allele losses in their tumors had a better disease-free survival and a better overall survival than patients with a greater than average number of mutations. Of those with a FAL <0.20, 28 percent

Table 24-1
Molecular Correlates of Prognosis

	Number of deaths from metastatic disease	*p value (Wilcoxon-Gehan test, NS, p > .30)*
FAL < 0.2	7/25 (28%)	0.005
> 0.2	14/23 (61%)	
17p—no deletion	2/12 (17%)	0.059
deletion	19/39 (49%)	
18q—no deletion	2/13 (15%)	0.109
deletion	18/35 (51%)	
5 q—no deletion	13/30 (43%)	NS
deletion	8/20 (40%)	
ras genes—no mutation	16/42 (38%)	NS
mutation	16/37 (43%)	
Dukes A	0/12 (0%)	0.011
B	13/28 (46%)	
C	19/39 (49%)	

SOURCE: Adapted from Kern et al.[2] With permission.

died of metastatic disease, compared with 61 percent who had a FAL >0.20. These investigators then specifically looked at *ras* oncogene mutations and at deletions on chromosomes 5, 17, and 18 to determine if they were related to clinical outcome. The results are shown in Tables 24-1 and 24-2.

Chromosome 5 deletions and *ras* oncogene mutations did not correlate with the development of metastatic disease or with death from metastases. Chromosome 17 deletions were significantly associated with the development of metastases in Dukes B and C patients and were significantly associated with death from metastatic disease. Chromosome 18 deletions were also significantly associated with the development of metastases and with death from metastases. There was no association found between FAL, 17p deletion, 18q deletions, 5q deletion, *ras* oncogene mutation, and Dukes classification. Of the 24 patients who had clinically obvious metastatic disease at the time of resection, 71 percent had a high FAL, 94 percent had 18q deletions, and 88 percent had 17p deletions. Of the Dukes B and C patients without evidence of metastases at the time of resection, 6 of the 18 who had 17p deletions eventually developed metastatic disease, while 0 of 10 patients without 17p deletions developed metastatic disease ($p = .049$). There were only two cases of death from local recurrence without metastatic disease, and this was insufficient for separate analysis.

Patients with a family history of colorectal cancer in a first-degree relative had a mean FAL that was twice that of patients without such a family history (0.296 versus 0.150, $p = .0002$). Twice as many chromosomal arms lost alleles in tumors of patients with a family history of colorectal cancer as in patients without. Such a family history was also found to be associated with 17p deletion ($p = .010$).

When tumor location was considered, it was found that 93 percent of left-sided tumors had 18p loss, compared with 60 percent of right-sided tumors ($p = .004$). Mucin-producing tumors accounted for 24 percent of the tumors studied. They had 17p deletions in 44 percent of cases, compared with 88 percent of non–mucin-producing tumors ($p = .001$). Similarly, 18q deletions were found in only 47 percent of mucin-producing tumors, while they were found in 85 percent of non–mucin-producing tumors ($p = .007$). This is an interesting finding, as mucin-producing tumors are more aggressive;[22] it suggests that deletions on other chromosomes will be found to be important in mucin-producing tumors. In this study, 36 percent of the right-sided tumors were mucin-producing, compared with 13 percent of left-sided tumors. After the exclusion of mucin-producing tumors, 96 percent of left-sided tumors had 17p deletions, compared with 78 percent of right-sided tumors.

Table 24-2
Molecular Correlates of Metastases[a]

	Number of patients (Dukes B and C) who developed metastasis during follow-up	*p value, Fisher exact test*
FAL < 0.2	8/21 (38%)	0.031
> 0.2	15/21 (71%)	
17p—no deletion	2/12 (17%)	0.006
deletion	21/33 (64%)	
18q—no deletion	2/11 (18%)	0.010
deletion	20/31 (65%)	

[a]See text for details.

SOURCE: Adapted from Kern et al.[2] With permission.

CONCLUSIONS

In summary, many chromosomal mutations may combine to lead to the development of colorectal malignancy. None of these mutations has yet been found to be necessary or sufficient for the development of carcinoma. It is apparent, however, that the greater the number of mutations in a given tumor, the greater the likelihood of development of metastatic disease and the greater the chance of death from malignancy.

REFERENCES

1. Vogelstein B, Fearon ER, Hamilton SR, et al: Genetic alterations during colorectal-tumor development. *N Engl J Med* 319:525–532, 1988.
2. Kern SE, Fearon ER, Tersmette KWF, et al: Allelic loss in colorectal carcinoma. *JAMA* 261:3099–3103, 1989.
3. Vogelstein B, Fearon ER, Kern SE, et al: Allelotype of colorectal carcinomas. *Science* 244:207–211, 1989.

4. Kinzler KW, Nilbert MC, Su LK, et al: Identification of FAP locus genes from chromosome 5q21. *Science* 253:661–665, 1991.
5. Nishisho I, Nakamura Y, Mitoshi Y: Mutations of chromosome 5q21 genes in FAP and colorectal cancer patients. *Science* 253:665–669, 1991.
6. Groden I, Thilveris A, Samowitz W, et al: Identification and characterization of the familial adenomatous polyposis coli gene. *Cell* 66:589–600, 1991.
7. Joslyn G, Carlson M, Thliveris A, et al: Identification of deletion mutations and three new genes at the familial polyposis locus. *Cell* 66:601–613, 1991.
8. Baker SJ, Fearon ER, Nigro JM, et al: Chromosome 17 deletions and p53 gene mutations in colorectal carcinomas. *Science* 244:217–221, 1989.
9. Fearon ER, Cho KR, Nigro JM, et al: Identification of a chromosome 18q gene that is altered in colorectal cancers. *Science* 247:49–56, 1990.
10. Wasylyshyn ML, Neuman WL, Angriman I, et al: Evidence for a new tumor-suppressor gene involved in gastrointestinal malignancies. *Surgery* 110:265–268, 1991.
11. Bodmer WF, Bailey CJ, Bodmer J, et al: Localization of the gene for familial adenomatous polyposis on chromosome 5. *Nature* 328:614–616, 1987.
12. Leppert M, Dobbs M, Scambler P, et al: The gene for familial polyposis coli maps to the long arm of chromosome 5. *Science* 238:1411–1413, 1987.
13. Solomon E, Voss R, Hall V, et al: Chromosome 5 allele loss in human colorectal carcinomas. *Nature* 328:616–620, 1987.
14. Sasaki M, Okamoto M, Sato C, et al: Loss of constitutional heterozygosity in colorectal tumors from patients with familial polyposis coli and those with nonpolyposis colorectal carcinoma. *Cancer Res* 49:4402–4406, 1989.
15. Bodmer WF, Bailey CJ, Bodmer J, et al: Localization of the gene for familial adenomatous polyposis on chromosome 5. *Nature* 328:2–4, 1987.
16. Lothe RA, Nakamura Y, Woodward S: VNTR (variable number of tandem repeats) markers show loss of chromosome 17p sequences in human colorectal carcinomas. *Cytogenet Cell Genet* 48:167–169, 1988.
17. Baker SJ, Fearon ER, Nigro JM, et al: Chromosome 17 deletions and p53 gene mutations in colorectal carcinomas. *Science* 244:217–221, 1989.
18. Van Tuinen P, Rich DC, Summers KM, et al: Regional mapping panel for human chromosome 17; Application to neurofibromatosis type I. *Genomics* 1:374–381, 1987.
19. Baker SJ, Markowitz S, Fearon ER, et al: Suppression of human colorectal carcinoma cell growth by wild-type p53. *Science* 249:912–915, 1990.
20. Levine AJ, Momand J, Finlay CA: The p53 tumor suppressor gene. *Nature* 351:453–456, 1991.
21. Halevy O, Michalovitz D, Orem M: Different tumor-derived p53 mutants exhibit distinct biological activities. *Science* 250: 113–116, 1990.
22. Cohen AM, Shank B, Friedman MA: Colorectal cancer, in DeVita VT, Jr, Hellman S, Rosenberg, SA (eds): *Cancer Principles and Practice of Oncology,* 3d ed. Philadelphia, JB Lippincott Company 1989, pp 895–964.

CHAPTER 25

Prognostic Factors: Transfusion and Splenectomy

Paul Ian Tartter

HIGHLIGHTS

Considerable clinical and experimental evidence supports the hypothesis that factors which suppress or enhance immune function cause measurable differences in the outcome of cancer surgery. Blood transfusion causes a broad perturbation of immune function, resulting in generalized immune suppression and consequent early recurrence and poor survival following surgery for colon cancer. Splenectomy, on the other hand, removes a source of suppressor cells in experimental animals, thereby enhancing immune function, at least transiently, and inhibiting tumor growth. The single clinical study of colon cancer prognosis following splenectomy in humans suggests that splenectomy is detrimental to the host, not beneficial, in contrast to the experimental studies.

CONTROVERSIES

The prognostic power of blood transfusion for patients with colon cancer may merely reflect transfusion's association with other known prognostic factors. Transfusion may have no inherent prognostic value of its own. Clinical studies of transfusion and colorectal cancer prognosis, even prospective studies, cannot separate transfusion from the other prognostic variables with which it is associated. Only prospective randomized studies comparing autologous to homologous blood recipients will resolve the true prognostic value of transfusion. Splenectomy, too, is associated with other prognostic factors, and its inherent value cannot be judged without randomization, although the likelihood of this is low.

NEW DIRECTIONS

Two randomized prospective trials of autologous and homologous blood for colorectal cancer are under way in Europe. Early results of the Munich study indicate that recurrence rates following receipt of homologous blood are significantly higher than following receipt of autologous blood. The Dutch study has accrued 500 patients with preliminary results indicating no difference. The use of homologous blood for colorectal cancer surgery has declined due primarily to fears of contracting viral diseases.

Since the appearance and growth of neoplasms is dependent to some degree on the immune function of the host, factors which inhibit or depress immunity should increase colon cancer incidence and facilitate growth and regrowth following excision. Two factors which have been found to affect immune function in patients without malignancies are blood transfusion and splenectomy, and both have been evaluated for prognostic value in patients with malignancies. The evidence linking blood transfusion to immune suppression is overwhelming and, not surprisingly, the studies linking perioperative blood transfusion to colorectal cancer recurrence are also convincing. In addition, since prognostic factors often function as risk factors, there are some data indicating that individuals who receive transfusions are at increased risk of developing colorectal cancers. In contrast, the data relating splenectomy to immune suppression is not uniform; experimental studies indicate that splenectomy removes a source of suppressor activity resulting in enhancement of immune function. Splenectomy is not a risk factor for colorectal cancer in clinical studies, and the data linking splenectomy to prognosis are subject to criticism.

TRANSFUSION AND IMMUNE FUNCTION

Immune function following blood transfusion has been thoroughly studied in dialysis patients because renal allografts survive longer in transplant patients who have received multiple pretransplant blood transfusions. Since renal allograft rejection is mediated by lymphocytes, these studies have documented inhibition of lymphocyte responses to antigens, mitogens, and homologous lymphocytes[1] (Table 25-1).

Anti-idiotype antibodies appear in the serum following blood transfusion and may contribute to immune suppression through suppressor cells or by direct contact with lymphocyte surface antibodies.[2] Natural killer cytotoxicity is also significantly inhibited.[3] These immunologic alterations are also observed in patients with functioning kidneys transfused for hemophilia and inherited hemolytic anemias.[4]

Surgery alone, without blood transfusion, is accompanied by a transient rise in serum cortisol, contributing to a decline in circulating levels of all lymphocyte subsets, which return to normal within 24 h.[5] In vitro assays of lymphocyte function may be inhibited by blood transfusions during surgery, but this has not been a universal finding.[6] However, these changes are transient, and if immune inhibition is to influence the outcome following cancer surgery, it must be prolonged.

Evidence of prolonged immune dysfunction following homologous blood transfusion has been noted in several studies. Women tested at ages 25 to 30 who had received neonatal transfusion for Rh incompatibility have significantly depressed levels of lymphocyte reactivity compared to untransfused age-matched controls.[7] Depression of lymphocyte function was also found in women transfused 5-years earlier. In a second study, colorectal cancer patients who had received transfusion more than 7 years previously had significantly lower numbers of lymphocytes and natural killer cytotoxicity than colorectal cancer patients who had never been transfused.[8] In a study of patients undergoing surgery for inflammatory bowel disease, T cells and total lymphocytes were significantly lower 18 months following surgery accompanied by blood transfusion.[9] Finally, among women suffering from habitual abortion, transfusion with spouse leukocytes causes the appearance of antibodies which block lymphocyte responses and successful pregnancy often follows.[10]

These studies certainly indicate that immune dysfunction follows homologous blood transfusion in humans, and these changes are potentially capable of influencing the outcome of cancer surgery. Although the mechanism of immune perturbation by blood is not clear, red cells and their components in culture with lymphocytes and macrophages inhibit phagocytosis[11] and may contribute to improved renal allograft survival through nonspecific immune suppression.[12]

Table 25-1
Immune Dysfunction Associated with Blood Transfusion

Inhibition of lymphocyte responses to mitogens, antigens, and homologous lymphocytes
Increased suppressor activity
Appearance of anti-idiotype antibodies
Decreased natural killer cytotoxicity
Decreased helper T-cell numbers

CLINICAL EVIDENCE LINKING TRANSFUSION TO COLONIC CANCER RECURRENCE

The association of blood transfusion with colorectal cancer recurrence was first noted at Mount Sinai Medical Center, New York, in a group of patients participating in the Gastrointestinal Tumor Study Group's (GITSG) prospective study of adjuvant radiotherapy, chemotherapy, and immunotherapy for colorectal cancer.[13] The patients were accrued for the study prospectively and follow-up was 100 percent, but the data on blood products received were collected in a retrospective manner. There were 122 patients with tumors through the bowel wall with or without lymph node metastases (Dukes B2 and C) and 48 percent were transfused. The 5-year cumulative disease-free survival of the transfused group was 51 percent, compared to 84 percent for untransfused patients ($p <$ .005). This study was expanded to include all patients undergoing potentially curative surgery at the same institution for the same stage of disease from 1976 to 1979.[14] Sixty percent of the 295 patients were transfused, and disease-free survival at 5 years was 51 percent, compared to 65 percent for untransfused patients ($p < .001$). Subgroup analysis indicated that the association of transfusion with recurrence was not due to stage, location, or postoperative therapy. Transfused patients fared worse, whether transfused before, during, or after surgery.

Several additional retrospective studies have been published supporting our original observation (Table 25-2).

Table 25-2
Univariate Studies Relating Transfusion to Colorectal Cancer Recurrence

Studies in which transfusion was a significant prognostic factor

Authors	*Number of patients*	*Percent transfused*	*Percent difference in survival or DFS between transfused and untransfused patients*
Burrows et al.[14]	295	60	14
Waymack et al.[15]	155	65	40
Parrott et al.[16]	517	72	23
Mecklin et al.[17]	520	68	15
Francis & Judson[18]	87	61	10

Studies in which transfusion was not a significant prognostic factor

Authors	*Number of patients*	*Percent transfused*	*Percent difference in survival or DFS between transfused and untransfused patients*
Ross[19]	159	60	13
Vente et al.[20]	212	75	0
Ota et al.[21]	207	78	5

Waymack et al.[15] studied 155 colonic cancer surgery patients (67 percent transfused) and observed a cancer-specific mortality of 64 percent in the transfused group and 28 percent in the untransfused patients ($p < .0001$). Parrott et al.[16] noted that transfused patients had a 20 percent greater probability of recurrence ($p < .005$) and 16 percent more cancer-related deaths ($p < .01$) in their study of 517 patients (72 percent transfused). Differences between transfused and untransfused patients were noted in preoperative hemoglobin, duration of surgery, and operative blood loss; to control for these confounders, the authors matched 203 patients for these variables, and the significance of transfusion for prognosis remained. Mecklin et al.[17] observed a significant transfusion effect in 520 patients undergoing surgery for colonic or rectal cancer in Finland. After elimination of 64 of the 192 colonic cancer patients with emergency surgery, adjacent organ resection, or extended surgery, the transfusion effect in the remaining 128 colonic cancers was no longer statistically significant. The same exclusion criteria did not reduce the statistical significance of the association of transfusion with outcome for rectal cancers in their study ($p < .01$).

Some authors support the hypothesis that blood transfusion is associated with colorectal cancer recurrence, although for their own studies the difference in outcome between the transfused and untransfused groups was not statistically significant. Ross[19] studied 159 patients (60 percent transfused) undergoing transabdominal colorectal cancer resection and observed a transfusion difference which was not statistically significant (47 percent versus 34 percent disease-free). Transfused patients underwent significantly more staged operations for obstructing lesions requiring colostomy than untransfused patients, but otherwise the groups were comparable. Cheslyn-Curtis et al.[22] observed no effect of blood transfusion on the outcome of 961 Large Bowel Cancer Project patients (61 percent transfused). Transfused patients had more advanced tumors and more tumors in the rectosigmoid, but log-rank multivariate analysis correcting for these variables did not reveal differences in recurrence or survival. Transfused patients were significantly more likely to develop lung metastases and less likely to develop liver metastases than untransfused patients ($p < .001$). The investigators concluded that "blood given in the perioperative period may change the biology of the metastatic process." Francis and Judson[18] observed a significant adverse effect of blood given during surgery in comparison to no transfusion ($p < .05$) or blood given before or after surgery ($p < .01$). Preoperative and postoperative transfusions were not significantly related to outcome. They concluded that factors influencing the need for blood during surgery were more important than the receipt of blood per se (see Table 25-3).

There are a few published studies which have found no relationship between transfusion and outcome. Vente et al.[20] studied 212 patients with transfusion data out of 350 entered in a prospective trial comparing usual resection techniques to the no-touch technique and found no relationship between blood transfusion and outcome. The relationship of blood loss and transfusion to operative technique, a subject of seemingly obvious interest, was not alluded to. Ota et al.[21] stud-

Table 25-3
Multivariate Studies Relating Transfusion to Colorectal Cancer Recurrence

Studies in which transfusion was not a significant prognostic factor

Authors	*Number of patients*	*Percent transfused*	*Percent difference in survival or DFS between transfused and untransfused patients*
Cheslyn-Curtis et al.[22]	961	61	4
Weiden et al.[23]	171	60	−13

Studies in which the prognostic value of transfusion was not a significant factor after consideration for other prognostic factors

Authors	*Number of patients*	*Percent transfused*	*Percent difference in survival or DFS between transfused and untransfused patients*
Nathanson et al.[24]	366	54	14
Bentzen et al.[25]	468	67	Not given
Hermanek et al.[26]	598	87	38
Marsh et al.[27]	224	47	Not given

Studies in which transfusion retained significant value after consideration for other prognostic factors

Authors	*Number of patients*	*Percent transfused*	*Survival or DFS between transfused and untransfused patients*
Tartter[28]	339	32	20
Blumberg et al.[29]	197	65	32
Foster et al.[30]	146	45	17
Arnoux et al.[31]	198	94	50
Corman et al.[32]	281	84	21
Liewald et al.[38]	439	69	16
Voogt et al.[33]	113	76	16
Wobbes et al.[34]	270	68	20
Beynon et al.[35]	519	55	20
Creasy et al.[36]	68	49	25

ied 207 patients (78 percent transfused) who underwent transabdominal colonic resection; no relationship between transfusion and prognosis was found, but the number of untransfused patients may have been too small to detect a transfusion effect.

Weiden et al.[23] noted a beneficial effect of transfusion among 171 patients who underwent resection of colorectal cancer in Seattle from 1977 to 1979. This is an important study because the likelihood of detecting a difference between transfused and untransfused patients of 18 percent was 80 percent (power), with a significance level of $p = .05$. They used the Cox proportional hazards model[37] to control for other prognostic factors. Multivariate analysis is necessary in these studies because transfusion is associated with other factors which are known to have prognostic value for colorectal cancer and transfusion's association with outcome may merely reflect transfusion's association with these other prognostic factors.

Transfusion is associated with advanced disease stage and with extensive operative trauma. Preoperative anemia often leads to blood transfusion. Anemia may be due to bleeding from an ulcerating carcinoma or to marrow replacement by tumor. Preoperative anemia is a sign of advanced disease in cancer patients and transfusion would be expected to be associated with early disease recurrence, since it is associated with anemia. Advanced malignancies necessitate extensive surgery, requiring more time and causing greater blood loss. Procedure, duration of surgery, and blood loss are all associated with transfusion and may account for transfusion's association with recurrence. These prognostic factors may not have been adequately controlled in the published reports linking transfusion to cancer recurrence. Preoperative anemia was generally associated with blood transfusion, but few studies examined the relationship between hemoglobin or hematocrit and prognosis. Prolonged procedures were associated with transfusion, but duration of surgery was rarely of significant prognostic importance. Extensive procedures were generally associated with more advanced stage, and advanced stage was often associated with more blood transfusions. Despite this relationship, in many reports there was no correlation between the stage of malignancy and the number of units of blood given. Operative blood loss was universally a significant prognostic factor and correlated directly with the number of blood transfusions.

Despite the accepted prognostic influences of these variables reflecting operative trauma and stage of disease and their relationship to blood transfusion, the majority of the studies evaluated only one or two prognostic variables. These variables are associated with transfusion as well as with recurrence. The contribution of transfusion to the risk of recurrence independent of the risk from variables reflecting advanced disease stage and operative trauma can be calculated statistically using the Cox proportional hazards model. Briefly, the significance of the association between each variable and disease-free survival is calculated using chi-square, and an equation is constructed with disease-free survival as the dependent variable. The most significant "independent" variable is incorporated into the equation and the potential contribution of the remaining variables is recalculated. Additional significant variables are added one at a time, recalculating the significance of each variable after each step.

Complete data for all variables must be obtained for every patient for this method of analysis. A theoretical limitation is that many of the potential independent variables are not truly independent. For example, admission and discharge hematocrit, Dukes stage, blood loss, and transfusion are related to one another and all were significantly associated with disease recurrence using the Cox analysis in our study of colorectal cancer patients.[28] Dukes stage was the most significant variable associated with disease recurrence, and the first step of the analysis was to create an equation relating these two. After consideration for Dukes stage, blood transfusion was the next most significant variable related to disease-free survival, and it was added to the equation. After Dukes stage and transfusion were taken into consideration, the remaining variables were no longer significantly related to disease recurrence. Transfusion's association with disease recurrence may reflect a combination of weak, not statistically significant relationships between several prognostic variables and outcome. We tested for this by forcing all potential variables except transfusion into an equation relating to disease recurrence. After consideration for age, sex, blood loss, tumor differentiation, stage, admission hematocrit, duration of surgery, length of specimen, and tumor size, the association of blood transfusion with recurrence was still significant ($p = .0196$).

Thirteen additional studies used the Cox model to control for potential prognostic factors after finding a statistically significant relationship between blood transfusion and crude recurrence and/or survival. In four of these studies, transfusion was not a statistically significant prognostic variable in the Cox model. Five-year disease-free survival of transfused patients was significantly worse for transfused patients in the study by Nathanson et al.[24] (43 versus 57 percent disease-free, $p = .0049$); but using the Cox model after controlling for stage, age and sex, blood transfusion was not useful in predicting survival ($p > .16$). This study had 199 transfused and 167 untransfused patients, sufficient numbers to detect a significant difference in outcome if it existed. This excellent study attributed the observed transfusion difference to other prognostic factors associated with transfusion. Bentzen et al.[25] observed an adverse effect of blood transfusion on the survival of 468 patients with Dukes B and C tumors of the rectum and rectosigmoid. The Cox proportional hazards model was applied separately to the 260 Dukes B tumors and the 208 Dukes C tumors but did not identify transfusion as a significant prognostic factor. Stage should have been included as a variable in the Cox model for all 468 patients, and transfusion would have been statistically significant.

Hermanek et al.[26] studied 598 patients with colorectal cancer and observed an adverse effect of transfusion with blood or fresh frozen plasma on survival. Blood alone was not a significant prognostic factor in the Cox model, but fresh frozen plasma was statistically significant. In this study, only 14 percent of the patients underwent surgery without blood transfusion. This may be too few untransfused patients to detect significant differences due to transfusion. In contrast, the patients with and without fresh frozen plasma were more evenly distributed (31 versus 69 percent), and the adverse association was significant in the Cox model. In support of Hermanek is the work by Marsh et al.[27] In their study of 224 patients, transfusion with plasma or whole blood doubled the risk of developing recurrence ($p < .05$), although an independent harmful effect of transfusion with red cells was not found.

Nine studies observed a statistically significant prognostic value for transfusion, which remained significant in the Cox model. For Blumberg et al.,[29] data from 197 colorectal cancer patients indicated that blood transfusion was a more significant prognostic factor than stage and remained significant after controlling for age, stage, location, duration of surgery, and year of diagnosis using the Cox model. A second early study confirming our observation that transfusion has significant prognostic value was published by Foster et al.[30] The relative risk of death due to cancer in 146 patients (45 percent transfused) was 2.3 (p = .05) after controlling for age, stage, differentiation, location, and hemoglobin using the Cox model. The disease-free survivals for the two groups were 68 and 51 percent respectively (p = .03).

Arnoux et al.[31] observed prognostic significance for transfusion in 198 patients undergoing surgery for rectal carcinoma; 85 percent of the patients received abdominoperineal resections. Transfusion was significant when given during surgery, but pre- and postoperative transfusions were not associated with a poor prognosis. This group also published a study of 281 nonoverlapping patients who underwent surgery for colorectal cancer.[32] The prognostic value of transfusion in the 74 rectal cancers lost significance in the Cox model, whereas for the 171 patients with colonic cancers, the number of units of blood transfused was highly significant ($p < .001$). Since only 16 percent of rectal cancer patients in this study underwent surgery without transfusion, the number of patients studied is not sufficient to reject the transfusion hypothesis. Liewald et al.[38] published a study of 439 colorectal cancer patients (69 percent transfused) undergoing surgery in Munich, and transfusion was a significant prognostic factor in the Cox model.

The prognostic value of transfusion was also noted in a study from the Netherlands by Voogt et al.[33] The disease-free survivals were 48 percent for the 86 transfused patients and 74 percent for the 27 untransfused patients (p = .007). After adjustment for age, sex, stage, location, procedure, and hemoglobin in the Cox model, transfusion was associated with a relative risk of death due to cancer of 4.25 (p = .03). In a second Dutch study,[34] disease-free survival of the 184 transfused patients was 58 percent, compared to 78 percent for the 86 patients receiving no blood. A difference in survival between patients who received whole blood and packed cells was also noted (51 percent versus 63 percent, p = .08).

In a study by Creasy et al.[36] limited to 68 patients with sigmoid carcinomas, a significant relationship between blood transfusion and prognosis was noted with the Cox model. Stage of disease was more significant than transfusion. Stage ($p < .0001$) and blood transfusion ($p < .003$) were also significant variables determining outcome in the Cox model, using 519 patients collected by Beynon et al.[35] Intraoperative transfusion contributed significantly to adverse outcome ($p < .001$), and increasing numbers of units transfused were associated with increasing risk of recurrence.

A prospective study at Mount Sinai of all patients undergoing potentially curative surgery with a preoperative diagnosis of colorectal cancer[28] accrued and followed 339 patients between 1983 and 1986. In 1991, the 5-year disease-free survival of the 40 percent of the patients who were transfused was 57 percent, with 40 percent suffering from recurrence, compared to 77 percent for untransfused patients with 22 percent developing recurrence ($p < .001$) (see Fig. 25-1).

Clinical evidence that blood transfusion influences the growth of colorectal cancer has been presented by Stephenson et al.,[39] who studied patients undergoing resection of liver metastases. Each unit of blood transfused increased the risk of recurrence by 5 percent (p = .0015); the amount of blood transfused was also a significant prognostic factor using the Cox model.

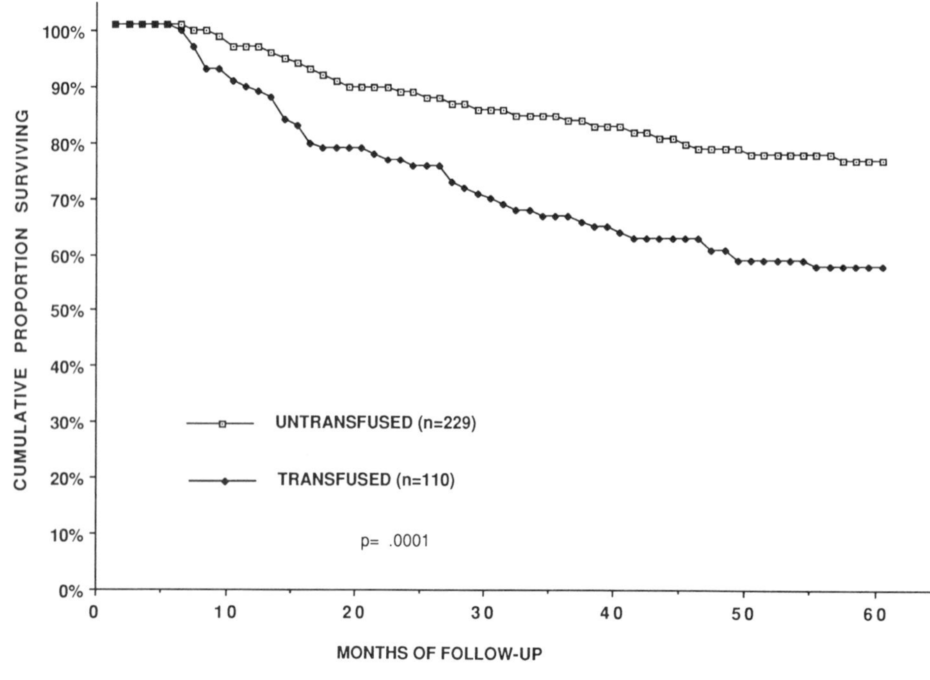

FIG. 25-1. Disease-free survival of transfused and untransfused colorectal cancer patients in a prospective study at the Mount Sinai Medical Center, New York. (From Tartter.[28] Reproduced by permission.)

THE SIGNIFICANCE OF TIMING

If the association of blood transfusion with early recurrence is due to transfusion's relationship to advanced stage rather than to operative trauma, one would expect preoperative transfusions to have more prognostic influence than intraoperative or postoperative transfusions. This is not the case. In the studies by Francis and Judson,[18] Arnoux et al.,[31] and Beynon et al.,[40] only intraoperative transfusions were significantly related to outcome; preoperative and postoperative transfusions were not of significant prognostic value. These studies indicate that the prognostic value of transfusion is not solely related to subtle correlation with stage of disease.

PLASMA VERSUS RED CELLS

In order to reconcile differences in outcome among retrospective studies, Blumberg et al.[29] have suggested that plasma is responsible for the transfusion effect. They base this hypothesis on their studies in colorectal, prostate, and cervical cancers. In all three cancers, a single unit of whole blood was associated with adverse outcome, whereas up to two units of packed red cells did not worsen prognosis. The investigators pooled the data for all three cancers and were able to demonstrate a significant independent prognostic influence of whole blood transfusion. Additional units of whole blood did not worsen the prognosis. On the other hand, with packed red cells, a clear dose-response relationship was observed beginning with four units. These differences in outcome Blumberg et al. attribute to the large volume of plasma given with a transfusion of whole blood versus the small volume of plasma in a unit of packed red cells.

Additional evidence for the importance of plasma comes from studies by Hermanek et al.[26] and Marsh et al.[27] In both studies, plasma alone was a significant independent prognostic factor in the Cox model and transfusion of red cells alone was not associated with adverse outcome.

I have not been able to replicate the findings of Blumberg et al. In prospective[28] and retrospective[13,14] studies of colorectal cancer patients at Mount Sinai, a single unit of packed red cells was significantly associated with recurrence, and additional units did not increase the risk of recurrence. Future prospective studies of randomized patients may resolve this issue.

SUMMARY OF STUDIES

The association of transfusion with immune suppression has been investigated in patients undergoing surgery for a variety of malignancies. The hypothesis is that transfused patients would develop earlier recurrence. Despite the publication of over five dozen studies, the significance of blood transfusion–induced immune suppression for cancer patients is unresolved. Eighty percent of the published studies observed a statistically significant association of blood transfusion with cancer recurrence. Half of the studies found that, using multivariate analysis to control for other potential prognostic factors, blood transfusion continued to have significant prognostic value. A variety of malignancies have been studied, with no consistent relationship between the tissue of origin and the significance of the observation.

If the transfusion effect is real, why have almost 20 percent of studies not observed it? Blumberg has suggested that studies which have not found a transfusion effect suffer from insufficient numbers of patients. In order to identify a true difference in survival of 15 percent (e.g., 80 versus 65 percent) with 80 percent certainty (power = 1 − beta) and accepting 5 percent as the level of significance (p = alpha = .05), one needs 226 transfused patients.[41] Since more patients would be needed to compensate for noncancer deaths and patients lost to follow-up, and assuming equal numbers of transfused and untransfused patients, the minimum study size would have to be over 500 patients. However, an analysis of studies' observation of a transfusion effect in relation to the number of patients does not reveal a consistent relationship: 3 of 10 studies with less than 100 patients and 2 of 11 with more than 400 observed no transfusion effect.

EXPERIMENTAL STUDIES OF TRANSFUSION AND TUMOR GROWTH

In the absence of clinical studies able to prove a cause-effect relationship with certainty, studies in experimental animals become very important. Experimental studies control for tumor burden (disease stage) and extent of the procedure, including duration and blood loss. These studies indicate that allogeneic blood transfusion produces profound changes in the immune systems of experimental animals which are analogous to those observed in humans.

Experimental models of blood transfusion and tumor growth capable of controlling surgical trauma, tumor load, and transfusion[26] could contribute significantly to this area. In fact, several experimental studies have observed promotion or inhibition of tumor growth following allogeneic blood transfusions.[42,43] The effect of transfusion on tumor growth is route-, tumor-, species-, and strain-specific. For example, in mice, tail vein inoculation of basal cell carcinoma produces pulmonary nodules which are inhibited by prior allogeneic transfusion, while no effect is seen if the tumor is given subcutaneously.[44] On the other hand, growth of subcutaneous adenocarcinoma is inhibited by transfusion, while pulmonary nodules are unaffected. Timing of transfusion relative to tumor inoculation may also determine subsequent tumor growth. Various strains of animals inoculated with various tumors have been used in these experiments, in some cases by the same investigator with different results. The variety of animal and tumor models suggests that a good reproducible experimental model for the study of blood transfusion and tumor growth has not been found.

Another problem with many of these studies of tumor growth in experimental animals is the lack of analogy to the situation in the cancer patient. The tumor has been present for some interval, usually years, in patients with malignancies, and some immunologic interaction between the host and the tumor has preceded the effects of surgery and blood transfusion. In the experimental studies, tumor inoculation generally followed allogeneic transfusion.

It is currently impossible to prove that the observed clinical phenomena in humans are not due to viral contamination of transfused blood. Human cytomegalovirus infections are associated with immune suppression,[45,46] and posttransplantation infection is common.[41] The facility with which the clinical studies can be reproduced in animal models makes it unlikelythat viral infections are the cause of these phenomena.

DISCUSSION

An association of blood transfusion with infections has been reproducibly demonstrated in numerous clinical and experimental studies. The relationship of blood transfusion to cancer recurrence is unsettled and to experimental tumor growth highly variable. This probably reflects a fundamental difference between the surface antigens of bacteria and cancer cells. Cancer cells may be antigenically heterogeneous and diverse, but they possess poorly defined tumor-associated antigens of variable immunogenicity. There is evidence of specific anticancer cell-mediated and humoral immune responses in some patients and animals. However, the majority of cancer patients do not mount an effective immune response. It is unreasonable to expect cancer cells to be influenced by the same effectors of immune response as bacteria, because neoplastic cells do not have appropriate surface determinants with which to stimulate the afferent arm. This fundamental difference in antigenicity between bacteria and neoplastic cells leads to an important conclusion. Factors such as blood transfusion, which quite clearly alter the outcome of infections, may have little or no influence on the outcome of tumors—not because they do not affect the immune system, but because in many cases the immune response may have little bearing on tumor behavior.

These problems indicate that a cause-effect relationship between blood transfusion and cancer recurrence cannot be proven with prospective studies in humans limited to homologous blood. Autologous blood may solve many of the problems inherent in these studies provided that patients can be randomly assigned to receive autologous or homologous blood in the event that transfusion is required. It is clear from studies of patients undergoing elective surgery that patients who participate in autologous blood programs and receive autologous blood are significantly healthier than age-matched patients undergoing the same procedures with the same diagnoses receiving homologous blood. This renders randomization between homologous and autologous blood essential for resolving the outstanding issues in this field.

Two randomized prospective trials of colorectal cancer patients are under way in Europe comparing the outcome for recipients of autologous and homologous blood. The Munich Study presented early results at the American Society of Clinical Oncology in March of 1992. The recurrence rate in autologous recipients was 17 percent, compared to 29 percent for homologous recipients. Multivariate regression found that homologous blood transfusion is an independent prognostic parameter ($p = .008$) despite a median follow-up of 21 months. This study and a Dutch study with 500 patients randomized between autologous and homologous blood are being followed with considerable interest.

Autologous blood cannot eliminate immune suppression in patients who are so anemic that autologous donation becomes dangerous. These patients will continue to require exogenous sources of blood or possibly blood substitutes. In addition, trauma patients are not candidates for autologous transfusion programs. Pure preparations of red cells—free of all leukocytes, platelets, and plasma—have been prepared for clinical studies, but the process is extremely expensive. In transplant studies, erythrocytes prepared in this manner are not associated with prolonged allograft survival, but their effect on the outcome of cancer surgery is unknown. Commercially available methods of purifying red cells include freezing blood (glycerolized red cells, frozen, thawed, and deglycerolized) and filtering washed cells. These methods leave a few viable leukocytes as well as leukocyte fragments, both of which affect the outcome of renal transplantation. It is not unlikely that an immunologically inert oxygen-carrying molecule will be developed in the foreseeable future. If and when this happens, a revolution in blood banking is likely to follow, with tremendous simplification or elimination of cross-matching to the benefit of recipients.

SPLENECTOMY

Several experimental studies support the hypothesis that the spleen is a reservoir of nonspecific suppressor activity which suppresses cell-mediated immunity following tumor implantation in the intact animal, allowing the implanted tumor to grow rapidly.[46–48] Removing the spleen removes this source of nonspecific suppressor activity, cell-mediated immunity is not suppressed, and tumor growth is inhibited—at least for a few weeks. Eventually, suppressor activity returns to the splenectomized animal, lymphocytes are inhibited, and tumor growth proceeds. Numerous variables affect the outcome, analogous to the variables which affect tumor growth following allogeneic blood transfusion in experimental animals. These variables include (1) immunogenicity of the tumor cells (spontaneous versus chemically induced tumors), (2) tissue origin, (3) timing of splenectomy relative to tumor inoculation, and (4) dose of tumor cells used.[49] Generally, the growth of inoculated tumors is inhibited by splenectomy, but this finding has not been universal.[50,51] Akamatsu[52] studied the induction of tumors in mice by the carcinogen DMBA relation to splenectomy. The appearance of some tumors was enhanced by removal of the spleen in a given strain while, in other strains, splenectomy inhibited tumors and had no effect in some strains. Splenectomy inhibited the development of mylogenous leukemia in all strains. In male Sprague Dawley rats, splenectomy enhanced the appearance of malignant colon tumors following treatment with DMBA.[53] This suggests that splenectomy should increase the risk of malignancy in humans.[54] However, long-term follow-up of veterans splenectomized for trauma has revealed no increased risk of malignancy of the colorectum or any other site.[55] These studies have led several groups of investigators to study the effect of splenectomy on the outcome of cancer surgery. Several studies of patients undergoing surgery for gastric cancer have observed lower survival rates when gastrectomy was performed at the same time. However, in those studies, splenectomized patients had more advanced disease. In a study of gastric cancer carefully matched for clinical stage, no difference in cumulative survival was seen in relation to splenectomy.[56]

CLINICAL STUDIES SUGGESTING A PROGNOSTIC INFLUENCE OF SPLENECTOMY FOR COLORECTAL CANCER

Davis et al.[57] matched 57 patients with colorectal cancer who had undergone splenectomy for incidental operative trauma, proximity of tumor, or hematologic disease to 57 patients with colorectal cancer with intact spleens by age, sex, tumor grade, stage, and operation. Long-term survival rates of splenectomized patients were significantly lower than for patients with intact spleens. This difference was entirely due to differences in survival among 22 patients with stage C disease. The authors state that there was no difference in the frequency of transfusion between stage C splenectomized patients and controls ($p = .07$), although 73 percent of the splenectomized patients received blood compared to 45 percent of the controls. Five-year survival of transfused patients was 58 percent, compared to 66 percent for untransfused patients ($p = .59$). In the published discussion which follows the paper, it was suggested that the observed survival differences due to splenectomy were not necessarily due to disease recurrence, since this was not measured, or that the splenectomized patients had a higher recurrence rate because splenic injury resulted in less than adequate cancer operations. I might add that although no statistically significant difference in transfusion existed among stage C patients, 73 percent of splenectomized patients received blood compared to 45 percent of the controls. Differences in outcome may have been related to receiving blood.

ACKNOWLEDGMENT

This chapter would not have been possible without the expertise and dedication of Ms. Joan Bratton.

REFERENCES

1. Fisher E, Lenhard V, Seifert P, et al: Blood transfusion-induced suppression of cellular immunity in man. *Hum Immunol* 3:187, 1980.
2. Singal DP, Faguilli L, Joseph S: Blood transfusions induce antiidiotypic antibodies in renal transplant patients. *Trans Proc* 15:1005, 1983.
3. Kaplan J, Sarnaik S, Gitlin J, et al: Diminished helper/suppressor ratios and natural killer activity in recipients of repeated blood transfusions. *Blood* 64:308, 1984.
4. Gascon P, Zoumbos NC, Young NS: Immunologic abnormalities in patients receiving multiple blood transfusions. *Ann Intern Med* 100:173, 1984.
5. Jubert AV, Lee ET, Hersh EM, et al: Effects of surgery, anesthesia and intraoperative blood loss on immunocompetence. *J Surg Res* 15:399, 1973.
6. Tarpley JL, Twomey PL, Catalona WJ, et al: Suppression of cellular immunity by anesthesia and operation. *J Surg Res* 22:195, 1977.
7. Beck I, Scott JS, Pepper M, et al: The effect of neonatal exchange and later blood transfusion on lymphocyte cultures. *Am J Reprod Immunol* 1:224, 1981.
8. Tartter PI: Transfusion history, T cell subsets and natural killer cyotoxicity in colorectal cancer patients. *Vox Sang* 56:80, 1989.
9. Tartter PI, Heimann TM, Aufses AH Jr: Blood transfusion, skin test reactivity, and lymphocytes in inflammatory bowel disease. *Am J Surg* 151:358, 1986.

10. McIntyre JA, Faulk WP, Nichols-Johnson VR, et al: Immunologic testing and immunotherapy in recurrent spontaneous abortion. *Obstet Gynecol* 169, 1986.
11. Keown PA, Descamp B: Suppression of the mixed lymphocyte reaction by autologous red cells and their constituents. *C R Acad Sci (III)* 749:287, 1978.
12. Keoun PA, Descamp B: Improved renal allograft survival after blood transfusions, a nonspecific anthrocyte-mediated immunoregulatory process. *Lancet* 1:20–22, 1979.
13. Burrows L, Tartter P: Effect of blood transfusions on colonic malignancy recurrence rate. *Lancet* 2:662, 1982.
14. Burrows L, Tartter P, Aufses AHJ: Increased recurrence rates in perioperatively transfused colorectal malignancy patients. *Cancer Detect Prev* 10:361, 1987.
15. Waymack JP, Moomaw, Popp MB: The effect of perioperative blood transfusions on long-term survival of colon cancer patients. *Milit Med* 154:515, 1989.
16. Parrot NR, Lennard TWJ, Taylor RMR, et al: Effect of perioperative blood transfusion on recurrence of colorectal cancer. *Br J Surg* 73:970, 1986.
17. Mecklin JP, Jarvinen HJ, Ovaska JT: Blood transfusion and prognosis in colorectal carcinoma. *Scand J Gastroenterol* 24:33, 1989.
18. Francis D, Judson R: Relation between recurrence of cancer of the colon and blood transfusion. *Br Med J* 291:544, 1985.
19. Ross WB: Blood transfusion and colorectal cancer. *J R Col Surg Edin* 32:197, 1987.
20. Vente JP, Wiggers TH, Weidema WF, et al: Peri-operative blood transfusions in colorectal cancer. *Eur J Surg Oncol* 15:371, 1989.
21. Ota D, Alvarez L, Lichtiger B, et al: Perioperative blood transfusions in patients with colon carcinoma. *Transfusion* 25:392, 1985.
22. Cheslyn-Curtis S, Fielding LP, Hittinger R, et al: Large bowel cancer: The effect of perioperative blood transfusion on outcome. *Ann R Col Surg Eng* 172:53, 1990.
23. Weiden PL, Bean MA, Schultz P: Perioperative blood transfusion does not increase the risk of colorectal cancer recurrence. *Cancer* 60:870, 1987.
24. Nathanson SD, Tilley BC, Schultz L, et al: Perioperative allogeneic blood transfusions: Survival in patients with resected carcinomas of the colon and rectum. *Arch Surg* 120:734–738, 1985.
25. Bentzen SM, Balslev I, Pedersen M, et al: Blood transfusion and prognosis in Dukes B and C colorectal cancer. *Eur J Cancer* 26:457, 1990.
26. Hermanek P, Guggenmoos-Holzmann I, Schricker KTH: [Influence of blood and hemoderivatives on the prognosis of colorectal carcinomas.] *Arch Chir* 374:118, 1989 (in German).
27. Marsh J, Donnan PT, Hamer-Hodges DW: Association between transfusion with plasma and the recurrence of colorectal carcinoma. *Br J Surg* 77:623–626, 1990.
28. Tartter PI: The association of perioperative blood transfusion with colorectal cancer recurrence. *Ann Surg* 216:633–638, 1992.
29. Blumberg N, Agarwal MM, Chuang C: Relation between recurrence of cancer of the colon and blood transfusion. *Br Med J* 390:1037, 1985.
30. Foster RS Jr, Costanza MC, Foster JC: Adverse relationship between blood transfusions and survival after colectomy for colon cancer. *Cancer* 55:1195–1201, 1985.
31. Arnoux R, Corman J, Peloquin A, et al: Adverse effect of blood transfusions on patient survival after resection of rectal cancer. *Can J Surg* 131:121, 1988.
32. Corman J, Arnoux R, Peloquin A, et al: Blood transfusions and survival after colectomy for colorectal cancer. *Can J Surg* 29:325–329, 1986.
33. Voogt PJ, van de Velde CJH, Brand A, et al: Perioperative blood transfusion and cancer prognosis: Different effects of blood transfusion on prognosis of colon and breast cancer patients. *Cancer* 59:836, 1987.
34. Wobbes T, Hendriks T, DE Bower HHM: Collagen in colorectal cancer in relation to clinicopathologic stage and histologic grade. *Dis Colon Rectum* 31:778–780, 1988.
35. Beynon J, Davies PW, Billings PJ, et al: Perioperative blood transfusion increases the risk of recurrence in colorectal cancer. *Dis Colon Rectum* 32:975–979, 1989.
36. Creasy TS, Veitch PS, Bell PR: A relationship between perioperative transfusion and recurrence of carcinoma of the sigmoid colon following potentially curative surgery. *Ann R Soc Surg Eng* 69:100, 1987.
37. Cox DR: Regression models and life tables. *J R Statist Soc* 34(series B):187, 1972.
38. Liewald F, Wirshing RP, Zulke C, et al: Influence of blood transfusions on tumor recurrence and survival rate in colorectal carcinoma. *Eur J Cancer* 26:327, 1990.
39. Stephenson KR, Steinberg SM, Hughes KS, et al: Perioperative blood transfusions are associated with decreased time to recurrence and decreased survival after resection of colorectal liver metastasis. *Ann Surg* 208:679–687, 1988.
40. Labayle D, Fischer D, Vielh P, et al: Sulindac causes regression of rectal polyps in familial adenomatous polyposis. *Gastroenterology* 101:635–639, 1991.
41. Tartter PI, Francis DMA: Blood transfusion and tumor growth. *Transplant Proc* 20:1108, 1988.
42. Francis DMA, Shenton BK, Proud G, et al: Tumor growth and blood transfusion. *J Exp Clin Cancer Res* 1:121, 1982.
43. Singh SK, Marquet RL, de Brun RWF, et al: Modulation of tumor growth by allogeneic blood transfusion. *J Cancer Res Clin Oncol* 111:50, 1986.
44. Fiala M, Payne JE, Berne TV, et al: Epidemiology of cytomegalovirus infection after transplantation and immunosuppression. *J Infect Dis* 132:421, 1975.
45. Rand KH, Pollard RB, Merigan TC: Increased pulmonary superinfections in cardiac-transplant patients undergoing primary cytomegalovirus infection. *N Engl J Med* 298:951, 1978.
46. Glenn J: Cytomegalovirus infections following renal transplantation. *Rev Infect Dis* 3:1151, 1981.
47. Meyer JD, Argyris BF, Meyer A: Splenectomy, suppressor cell activity, and survival in tumor bearing rats. *J Surg Res* 29:527–532, 1980.
48. Fujimoto S, Greene MI, Sehon AH: Regulation of the immune response to tumor antigens. *J Immunol* 116:791–799, 1976.
49. Singh SK, Marquet RL, Westbroek DL, et al: Enhanced growth of artifical tumor metastases following blood transfusion: The effect of erythrocytes, leukocytes and plasma transfusion. *Eur J Cancer Clin Oncol* 23:1537, 1987.
50. Yamagishi H, Pellis NR, Kahan BD: Effect of splenectomy upon tumor growth: Characterization of splenic tumor-enhancing cells in vivo. *Surgery* 87:655–661, 1980.
51. Sato N, Michaelides MC, Wallack M: Effect of splenectomy on the growth of murine colon tumors. *J Surg Oncol* 22:73–76, 1983.
52. Akamatsu Y: Neoplasms in strains of splenectomized mice after a single, 7, 12-dimethylbenz[a] anthracene treatment. *J Natl Cancer Inst* 55:893–897, 1975.
53. Hull CC, Galloway P, Gordon N, et al: Splenectomy and the induction of murine colon cancer. *Arch Surg* 123:462–464, 1988.
54. Ziegler RG, Devesa SS, Fraumeni JF, et al: Epidemiology

pattern of colorectal cancer, in Devita VT, Hellman S, Rosenberg SA (eds): *Important Advances in Oncology*. Philadelphia, Lippincott, 1986, pp 209–232.

55. Robinette CD: Splenectomy and subsequent mortality in veterans of the 1939–45 war. *Lancet* 2:127–129, 1977.
56. Suehiro S, Nagasue N, Ogawa Y, et al: The negative effect of splenectomy on the prognosis of gastric cancer. *Am J Surg* 148:645–648, 1984.
57. Davis CJ, Illstrup DM, Pemberton JH: Influence of splenectomy on survival rate of patients with colorectal cancer. *Am J Surg* 155:173–179, 1988.

PART 5

Surveillance and Diagnosis

CHAPTER 26

Surveillance Overview

Sidney J. Winawer

Screening for colorectal cancer has been a concept that has been intensely debated since introduction of the new generation impregnated guaiac cards by Greegor[1] in the late 1960s (see definitions in Table 26-1). Until then, patients had been asked to bring in stool specimens in containers, which were highly unesthetic for both patients and laboratory personnel. These stool specimens were tested by guaiac bench reagents, which were shown to be highly unreliable. The earlier reports by Greegor demonstrated that early cancers could be detected in asymptomatic individuals in the setting of a private office practice by asking patients to prepare slides at home from multiple stool specimens while on a high-fiber meat-free diet. This provided a stimulus to the early detection approach for colorectal cancer. Shortly thereafter, in the early 1970s, the introduction of colonoscopy and colonoscopic polypectomy provided an opportunity for accurately identifying small cancers.[2] In addition, polyps could be identified and removed without the need for major abdominal surgery. At the same time, surgical advances provided a basis for more consistently offering curative surgery to patients and reduced the need for permanent colostomy. The desirability of finding and removing adenomatous polyps by colonoscopy was further justified by a large volume of indirect evidence linking the adenomatous polyp to the development of colorectal cancer.[3] These developments together provided the basis for serious consideration of an early detection approach for colorectal cancer. Considering the high incidence of this cancer and the high mortality rate, the approach appeared to be attractive to physicians and to other health care personnel who were discouraged by the frequent presentation of patients on a day-to-day basis with advanced and fatal colorectal cancer. Early detection with a potential for improved survival, reduced mortality and morbidity, and a better quality of life seemed to be a desirable alternative.

SCREENING TESTS

Stool Blood Testing

Early trials demonstrated that a high proportion of cancers were detected by the guaiac slide test in an early stage (Dukes A and B). Controlled trials were initiated beginning in 1975[2,4] (Table 26-2). These large-scale trials—incorporating individuals coming for comprehensive medical examinations, volunteers, and population studies—put the guaiac slide test through a rigorous evaluation which is still ongoing and which is reviewed in Chap. 28. The guaiac slide, however, is not a test of neoplastic disease or for occult blood but rather for peroxidase activity. The pseudoperoxidase activity of hemoglobin provides a positive test. However, a positive test can result from foods containing peroxidase activity or from benign gastrointestinal sources of bleeding, such as hemorrhoids or diverticulosis (Table 26-3). In addition, neoplastic lesions may not always yield a positive test of subthreshold levels of bleeding generally not exceeding the upper limit of physiologic blood loss or because of an intermittent pattern of bleeding. Because only a random sample of stool is tested, there is also a potential for sampling error.[5] With these problems, and with concern for inadequate sensitivity for neoplastic lesions, attempts were made to modify the test or introduce entirely new methods for stool blood testing. Rehydration of the slides with water before addition of the reagent increased the sensitivity from 50 to 70 percent to more than 90 percent for neoplastic lesions, but at a great loss of specificity that resulted in an increased frequency of false positives from 1 to 2 percent to 6 to 10 percent.[6] A quantitative stool test for blood (HemoQuant) has the same limitation of decreased specificity in relation to enhanced sensitivity.[7,8] More recently, immunochemical tests have been reported that may have a greater sensitivity without loss of specificity.[9] These new immunochemical tests have not yet been

Table 26-1
Glossary of Screening

Acceptability:	The extent to which the members of the target population are willing to undergo the screening procedure.
Compliance:	The extent to which patients follow therapeutic instructions concerning the taking of medications, adherence to recommendations concerning diet, rest, exercise and so forth.
Cost-effectiveness:	An approach to program evaluation that compares dollar costs to results, the latter expressed in a natural unit (such as life years gained) other than dollars.
False negatives:	Individuals who have the disease of interest, yet have a negative result for the screening test under consideration.
False positives:	Individuals who are free of the disease of interest, yet have a positive result for the screening test under consideration.
Mass screening:	The performance of screening upon a substantial portion of the population at large.
Natural history:	The interrelations between man, causal factors for disease, and the remainder of the environment, beginning with their initial interaction and ending with the recovery, death, or permanent disability of the affected individual.
Predictive value:	The proportion of individuals with a positive result for the screening test under consideration who have the disease of interest; "true positives" expressed as a proportion of the sum of "true positives" and "false positives."
Screening:	The separation of individuals into groups with high and low probabilities for a given disease, achieved through the examination of physical characteristics, physiologic functions, blood, and/or excreta. Typically, screening is performed upon lanthanic and apparently well individuals, and the tests are performed rapidly and at minimum cost.
Sensitivity:	The proportion of individuals with the disease of interest who have a positive result of the screening test under consideration; "true positives" expressed as a proportion of the sum of "true positives" and "false negatives."
Specificity:	The proportion of individuals free of the disease of interest who will have a negative result for the screening test under consideration; "true negatives" expressed as a proportion of the sum of "true negatives" and "false positives."

SOURCE: From Sackett D: Periodic examinations of patients at risk, in Schottenfeld D: *Cancer, Epidemiology and Prevention: Current Concepts*. Springfield, Ill, Thomas, 1975, pp 451–452. Reproduced by permission.

Table 26-2
Controlled Trials of Stool Blood Testing in Screening for Colorectal Cancer

				Dukes A and B cancers, %	
	Cohort size	*Positivity rate, %*	*Predictive value, %, adenomas and cancers*	*Screened group*	*Control group*
Goteborg, Sweden	27,000	1.9	22	65	33
Nottingham, England	150,000	2.1	53	90	40
New York, USA	22,000	1.7	30	65	33
Minnesota, USA	48,000	2.4	31	78	35
Fuhnen, Denmark	62,000	1.0	58	81	55

SOURCE: This table is derived from multiple sources and summarizes mainly nonhydrated slide data, although hydrated slides have also been used in a phase of some programs. The data are primarily from initial screening. The Dukes A cancers in the screened groups were 34 to 65% as compared to 8 to 24% in the control groups. (Winawer SJ: Screening for colorectal cancer. *Cancer: Principles and Practice of Oncology Updates* 2(6), 1981. With permission.)

Table 26-3
Peroxidase Levels in 65 Foods[a]

Category	*Mass of food with peroxidase activity equivalent to 1.0 mL blood*	*Food[a]*
1	<5	Broccoli, turnip[b]
2	5 to 10	Rare red meat (roast beef), cantaloupe,[b] cauliflower, red radish,[b] parsnip[b]
3	10 to 20	Jerusalem artichoke, bean shoots,[b] cucumber, french beans, lemon rind, mushroom, parsley,[b] zucchini[b]
4	20 to 50	Grapefruit, carrot,[b] cabbage, potato, pumpkin, fig[b]
5	50 to 100	Peach, celery, lettuce, pepper (pickled), silver beet (spinach)
6	100 to 500	Blackberries, pineapple, watermelon, walnuts, mint, peppers (red, green,[b] dark green)
7	500 to 1000	Bananas, black grapes, pears, plums
8	>1000	Well-cooked red meat (roast beef), apples (Golden Delicious and Gravenstein), apricots, olives, raspberries
9	Peroxidase undetectable	Roast chicken and turkey, boiled fish (tuna); boiled liver, kidney, and brains; boiled pork, ham, and bacon; boiled rabbit; boiled silverside (salted) beef; dates, white grapes, lemon, nectarine, orange, passion fruit, raisins, strawberries, sultanas, and tomato

[a]All foods are raw unless stated otherwise.

[b]No peroxidase detectable when reassayed after 20 min at 100°C.

SOURCE: Adapted from Calisiore P, Macrae FA, St John DJB, et al: Peroxidase levels in food: Relevance to colorectal cancer screening. *Am J Clin Nutr* 35:1487–1489, 1982. Copyright 1982 by the American Cancer Society for Clinical Nutrition. Reproduced by permission.

subjected to large clinical trials. To date, screening and case finding efforts in clinical practice and controlled clinical trials have mostly used the standard guaiac slide test without rehydration.

Digital Examination and Sigmoidoscopy

Approximately 10 percent of colorectal cancers may be detected within reach of 7 to 10 cm from the anus by digital rectal examination, and an additional 25 to 35 percent are potentially within view of a 25-cm rigid sigmoidoscope.[10] However, in clinical practice, the rigid sigmoidoscope may be passed beyond 20 cm only in 50 percent of patients, and the discomfort of the procedure is a deterrent to repeated examinations. The risk of perforation has been reported variously as 1 in 1000 to 1 in 10,000 examinations.[11] Thus, the previously used 25-cm rigid sigmoidoscope has been replaced for the most part by flexible scopes ranging in length from 35 to 60 cm. Compared to the rigid sigmoidoscope, the flexible instrument has been shown consistently to detect approximately a two- to threefold greater number of cancers and polyps and is better tolerated.[11,12] Although the longer 60-cm sigmoidoscope has the potential for reaching the splenic flexure and detecting 50 to 60 percent of colorectal cancers, the average depth of insertion in most patients is usually 40 and 50 cm in the upper sigmoid or distal descending colon. Theoretically, the longer the scope, the greater the yield in a screening setting of asymptomatic average-risk people; however, there has been no significant difference in yield between 35- and 60-cm scopes, although less time and training and lower risk is associated with the shorter scopes. With either instrument, the entire rectum and sigmoid colon can be examined completely and easily with relatively high patient compliance (see Chap. 29). The digital rectal examination is usually performed before sigmoidoscopy.

The effectiveness of sigmoidoscopy in screening for colorectal cancer has not been adequately studied. Many of the previously published studies were cross-sectional or lacked a concurrent control group. In one study, conducted by Hertz et al.[13] in 1960, more than 26,000 primarily asymptomatic patients underwent 47,091 rigid sigmoidoscopic examinations; 58 cancers were detected (0.22 percent). Of these, 81 percent were Dukes A and B, and the 15-year survival rate was 90 percent. This was an uncontrolled study with follow-up limited to the patients with detected cancers. No randomized controlled trials have been conducted specifically to assess the role of rigid or flexible endoscopy in screening. Randomized clinical trials conducted among Kaiser Foundation Health Plan members, 35 through 54 years of age at entry, compared the urging of annual rigid sigmoidoscopy as part of a multiphasic health checkup with the usual pattern of care pursued by the members. Initially, it was concluded that sigmoidoscopy was associated with a decrease in colorectal cancer mortality. Subsequent reanalysis questioned this correlation.

However, a recent case-controlled study from the same institution using data on 261 patients who died of rectosigmoid cancer has provided the best evidence to date that sigmoidoscopy can significantly lower the mortality from rectosigmoid cancer.[14–16] The 60 percent mortality reduction in rectosigmoid cancer was impressive. The absence of any mortality reduction for cancer above the rectosigmoid strengthened this observation. A second study confirmed this mortality reduction.[17] This is reviewed in Chap. 29.

Consideration of Risk Factors in Screening Strategies

In considering screening, individuals can be considered along the spectrum of risk, with the lowest end of the spectrum comprising those at average risk by virtue of age alone who have no other associated high-risk factors (Table 26-4). Individuals at increased risk along this spectrum are those who have had a prior history of colorectal cancer or adenomatous polyps and those who have inflammatory bowel disease or a family history of colorectal cancer.

Colorectal Neoplasia

Patients with one colorectal cancer have a 1.5 to 5 percent risk that an additional colorectal cancer is present at the same time and a 5 to 10 percent risk for a subsequent colorectal cancer.[17] The prevalence of adenomas in western countries is as high as 40 to 50 percent older age groups,[18] and there is considerable evidence that most colorectal cancers arise from an adenoma or neoplastic polyp.[18] Only a proportion of colonic polyps that are detected are true adenomas. In the U.S. National Polyp Study (NPS), adenomas accounted for 68 percent of the polyps removed by colonoscopy in the initial examination. Individuals presenting with one adenoma have a 50 percent likelihood of additional adenomas at that time and a 30 percent likelihood of future additional adenomas after their colons have been cleared of all adenomas.[19]

The overall risk of colorectal cancer in patients with a history of adenomas is increased above that of the general population if their colons have not been cleared of all polyps. This risk appears to be related to size and multiplicity. Size greater than 1 cm confers a threefold increase in risk, while multiplicity increases the risk of sixfold.[20] A population-based study indicated that there was no increased risk for patients with adenomas less than 1 cm in size.[21] Another study from the Mayo Clinic supported the correlation of large size with increased risk.[22] These studies were reported in patients in whom the colon was not cleared by colonoscopy. On the other hand, a recent report from the NPS demonstrated a decrease in colorectal cancer risk when the entire colon was cleared of all polyps.[23]

The time sequence from a normal-appearing colon through the stage of adenoma and then to cancer has been studied using mathematical models and clinical observations. These studies suggest that the process develops slowly over many years, with an average 5-year interval from a clean colon to adenomas and another 5-year interval from adenoma to carcinoma.[19]

Genetic Predisposition

Genetic syndromes include familial adenomatous polyposis; Gardner, Turcot, and Peutz-Jeghers syndromes; juvenile polyposis; and hereditary nonpolyposis colorectal cancer syndrome.[24] These account for approximately 5 percent of the colorectal cancer cases each year, and all follow an autosomal dominant mode of inheritance (Fig.26-1). Until recently, genetic factors were considered to be important only in these syndromes, the majority of colorectal cancer cases being "sporadic." However, several studies have reported a threefold excess of cancer and a high frequency of adenomas among first-degree relatives of patients with colorectal cancer.[24] A sizable proportion of sporadic adenomas and colorectal cancers may be genetically determined by an autosomal dominant mode with low penetrance.[25] This is discussed in more detail in Chaps. 7 to 9.

Table 26-4
Risk Factors for Colorectal Cancer

Risk factors
Average risk
Age 50 years and older, asymptomatic
High risk
Inflammatory bowel disease
Chronic ulcerative colitis
Chronic granulomatous colitis
Familial adenomatous polyposis
Familial polyposis
Gardner's syndrome
Turcot's syndrome
Oldfield's syndrome
Juvenile polyposis
Hereditary nonpolyposis colorectal cancer
Family cancer syndrome
Site-specific inherited colorectal cancer
Family history
Colorectal adenomas
Colorectal cancer
Past history
Colorectal adenomas
Colorectal cancer
Breast, ovarian, and uterine cancer

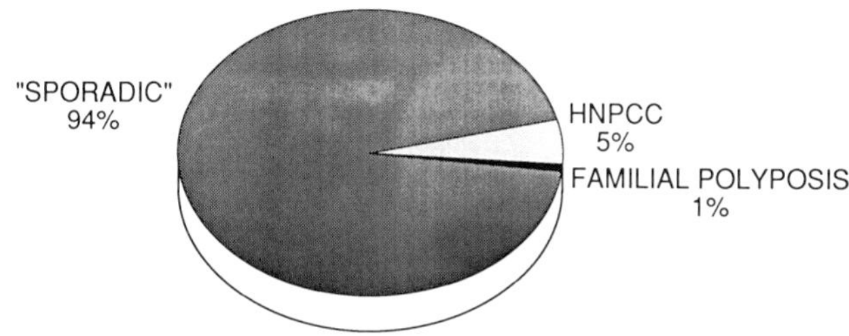

FIG. 26-1. Diagnostic representation of annual percentage of new cancer cases contributed by the characterized familial syndromes of familial adenomatous polyposis and hereditary nonpolyposis colorectal cancer (HNPCC) and by sporadic cases not identifiable as familial.

Inflammatory Bowel Disease

Ulcerative colitis is a risk factor for colorectal cancer[26–28] but accounts for only a small number of new cases each year. Duration of the disease and its anatomic extent are two factors in the cancer risk, which begins to rise after 7 years of disease in patients with involvement of the entire colon and after 15 years when there has been only left-sided colitis. Proctitis alone appears to carry no increased risk[28] (see Chap. 34).

Diagnostic Evaluation of Patients with Positive Screening Tests

Complete diagnostic evaluation of patients with positive screening tests is essential for effectiveness of the screening program. Sensitive techniques are now available for accurate clinical diagnosis of colonic lesions, but there is debate on whether colonoscopy or barium enema should be the initial test of choice.[2] There are no unbiased controlled studies comparing the independent performance of barium enema with colonoscopy except for the NPS currently in progress.[19] The double-contrast barium enema is superior to the single-column type in most hands for the diagnosis of small adenomas and small cancers. The entire colon, including the cecum, can be examined well by experienced endoscopists in more than 90 percent of patients, usually in 15 to 20 min. Colonoscopy has been shown in many studies to have a higher sensitivity than the barium enema for neoplastic lesions of the colon, especially those under 1 cm in size; in addition, biopsies and cytology can be performed and polyps can be removed. The decision to use either of these diagnostic tests is an individual matter based on the above factors as well as on available resources, but colonoscopy is now the preferred diagnostic test in all of the major trials (see Chaps. 30 and 31).

Patient Acceptance of Screening

Patients' acceptance of stool blood testing has been good in controlled trials but was as low as 15 percent in community programs.[29] Sustained interest in rescreening has been difficult to maintain for some programs. In the New York trial, for example, while acceptance was high for the first screen, the patients were reluctant to return personally or to send slides in for rescreening despite intensive efforts.[30] In an English trial,[31] special measures to encourage compliance were found to be very helpful in raising acceptance from 38 percent to over 50 percent. Patients with positive screening tests complied with diagnostic studies to a fairly high degree in all of the trials. Factors influencing patients' acceptance of screening have been studied.[32–35] Acceptors are more likely to have had positive attitudes toward preventive health practices, to have had more recent contacts with medical services, to be better informed about serious illness, and to be more optimistic and less frightened about cancer. An American Cancer Society survey showed that there were often disturbing public misconceptions regarding colorectal cancer.[35] Patients have been shown to have a high acceptance of sigmoidoscopy when they present for a general examination (over 90 percent in the New York program). However, patients in general have not demonstrated a willingness to return for repeat rigid sigmoidoscopy. This attitude may change with greater use of flexible sigmoidoscopes. Although the American Cancer Society surveys indicate an increasing emphasis on early cancer detection and increased use of stool blood testing, there is a variable approach by physicians to the diagnostic investigation of patients with a positive screening test.[36]

Cost-Effectiveness of Screening

One cost-benefit analysis suggested a financial savings and a projected increase in life expectancy as a result of stool blood testing.[37] Mathematical models have given us some insights into the range of cost-benefit and cost-effectiveness expectations.[38] Although these models do not provide definitive answers, they summarize available data and can provide future research directions. The models suggest that screening is cost-effective and is in the same range in this regard as screening for breast cancer with mammography.

Treatment of Detected Cancers and Polyps

Many reviews of colorectal cancer surgery are available, with extensive discussion of surgical oncologic principles and survival statistics[39,40] (see chapters on treatment). Although survival relates clearly to the stage of cancer at the time of resection, aggressive anatomic surgery has been shown to provide the highest chance of cure for each stage. In addition, colorectal cancer provides a unique opportunity for control of the disease because of an identifiable premalignant adenomatous stage. In the past, removal of adenomas above the reach of the rigid sigmoidoscope required laparotomy and colotomy, with the attendant morbidity and mortality. These risks have been markedly decreased with the introduction of colonoscopic polypectomy.

Expected Benefit of Screening

Screening can be considered to be the specific approach within the generic framework of early detection in individuals at average risk. Those individuals who have had neoplastic lesions identified or who are at increased risk, such as those with inflammatory bowel disease or a family history, can be considered to be individuals who should be under surveillance. There is a difference between screening and surveillance as compared to case finding, although the terms are often used synonymously. *Screening* implies a population approach, whereas *surveillance* and *case finding* are approaches that are performed within the framework of medical care with multiple encounters with health care personnel. Case finding provides opportunities for identifying symptoms, changes in risk factors, and the highest level of informed performance of testing by patients. In considering the guidelines by major medical organizations for screening, it must be understood that these are not for population screening outside the framework of medical care but are really for case finding within that framework. *Surveillance* refers to the ongoing monitoring of patients who have been identified as having had a neoplastic lesion that was treated[2] or who are at increased risk, such as patients with a family history of colon cancer or a personal history of ulcerative colitis.

To the extent that we can expand the pool of patients who are candidates for curative surgery, the introduction of a widely applicable, cost-effective screening intervention should have an impact on colorectal cancer survival and mortality.[41] Patients whose cancers are detected in earlier stages (Dukes A and B) have an 85 percent 5-year relative survival rate, compared with 38 percent for patients with later-stage cancers (Dukes C and D). The onset of symptoms is generally associated with the distribution of detected cancers of more advanced stages. The high case fatality rate from colorectal cancer in this country—about one-half of all colorectal cancer patients have died within 5 years of the detection of the disease—is a reflection of the preponderance of cancers detected at later stages.[42] Although environmental factors, particularly a complex of dietary factors and level of physical activity, appear to play a role in the development of colorectal cancer, we have not established how to prevent colorectal cancer through dietary or other lifestyle interventions.[43,44] New adjuvant therapies are promising, but they are likely to have only modest effects on mortality rates.[45] Thus, the most promising opportunity at present to reduce the burden of illness and death associated with colorectal cancer is to detect more cancers in early stages, when they are still curable and before they progress to more advanced stages.

If early detection of colorectal cancer can interrupt or delay the natural course of the disease, detection and removal of the suspected precursors to cancer—colorectal adenomatous polyps—might actually prevent the onset of cancer itself and lower its incidence.[23] For this reason, the concept of colorectal cancer screening has come to encompass a search not only for early cancers but also for adenomas, from which most colorectal cancers are suspected to arise. Not all colorectal polyps are adenomas. It is believed that only a small proportion of these adenomas—probably less than 5 percent—will progress to cancer, but clinicians and investigators agree that the majority of colorectal cancers begin as benign adenomas.[46,47] Thus, detection and removal of adenomas is a second objective of colorectal cancer screening.

At issue is whether a screening test must be shown to reduce the incidence of invasive cancer or mortality to be considered effective, or whether demonstrating a shift in the distribution of detected cancers to earlier stages and the enhancement of survival are sufficient to consider a screening regimen effective. Critics point out that screening and diagnostic follow-up incur medical risk and high costs. Others focus on the heavy burden of illness and death brought about by colorectal cancer and have concluded that the evidence cannot be ignored.[2,4,41,48–52]

EVALUATION OF EVIDENCE

There are varying levels of evidence that support working guidelines. The strongest evidence would be that obtained from a well-designed and well-conducted randomized controlled trial. It is, however, not always practical to conduct such a trial to address every question surrounding the field of screening. As in all other aspects of medicine, guidelines for practice must be based upon information that falls short of a randomized trial. For each guideline, the levels of evidence that support it are listed. In order of strength of evidence, the five levels may be seen in Table 26-5. Case-control and cohort studies provide indirect evidence for the effectiveness of screening.[2] Such studies do not prove a mortality reduction effect, but they can suggest a mortality reduction. Such evidence is particularly compelling for the effectiveness of screening for cervical cancer. There are also recent case-control data related to rectosigmoid cancer.[16] However, the potential for bias in case-control and cohort studies must be recognized. For colorectal cancer, there is level 1 and level 2 evidence from several trials dem-

Table 26-5
Levels of Evidence Supporting Screening for Colorectal Cancer

1. At least one properly randomized, well-designed, and well-conducted controlled trial
2. Well-designed and well-conducted controlled trials without randomization
3. Well-designed cohort or case-control analytic studies, preferably from more than one center or research group
4. Multiple time series with or without the intervention
5. Opinions of respected authorities based upon clinical experience, descriptive studies, or reports of expert committees

Table 26-6
Historical Development of Colorectal Cancer Screening Tests

Phase	*Tests*
1.	Bench guaiac and rigid sigmoidoscopy
2.	Guaiac FOBT[a] slides and rigid sigmoidoscopy
3.	Guaiac FOBT slides and flexible sigmoidoscopy
4.	Immunologic FOBT slides and flexible sigmoidoscopy
5.	Genetic screening and colonoscopy

[a]FOBT = fecal occult blood test.

onstrating a stage shift, improved survival, and significant mortality reduction from the fecal occult blood test (FOBT) screening,[30,53–55] level 3 evidence of a mortality reduction from sigmoidoscopy screening,[16,17] and levels 4 and 5 evidence of expected mortality reduction from mathematical models and opinions.[56]

FUTURE PROSPECTS

Prevention offers promise of benefits for many people at risk for developing colorectal adenomas and cancer. Primary prevention targeted to the general population may possibly reduce the incidence of adenomas and thereby reduce future colorectal cancer incidence and mortality.[43] Secondary prevention strategies may be targeted to the general population over age 50, with the result of detecting earlier-stage cancers or removing adenomas.[4] At present, only a small proportion of those destined to develop colorectal cancer can be identified as having an inherited genetic predisposition. These individuals can be placed under surveillance, as with other high-risk groups. It is expected that, in the future, the majority of those at risk for colorectal cancer will be identified by genetic markers. Periodic colonoscopy could be performed in these individuals to keep their colons free of adenomas, thereby bringing about a dramatic reduction in the incidence of colorectal cancer.[57]

We now have a considerable understanding of the natural history of colorectal cancer as it evolves in the tumorigenesis model from normal mucosa through the successive stages of hyperproliferation, to successively larger adenomas with more advanced and premalignant histology, and finally to early- and late-stage colorectal cancer.[57–59] We have opportunities to apply primary and secondary preventive strategies to intervene in this natural history for the ultimate benefit of the patient.[60] We have learned quite a bit, but we have yet quite a lot more to learn, and data are incomplete on many of these issues. Over the next few years, we will undoubtedly see a refinement of our knowledge of primary prevention and how this interacts with molecular genetic changes and other changes in the cell biology of colonic mucosal cells that are susceptible to the carcinogenic process. It is also certain that over the next few years, we will see improved stool blood tests which will have a better sensitivity and specificity. The early stool blood tests will ultimately be replaced by more specific immunologic occult blood tests and by more sophisticated screening techniques[9] (Table 26-6). It is very likely that these techniques will be related to the molecular genetic abnormalities that are now being uncovered rapidly within tumors and in the genetic high-risk groups as germline changes[58] (Fig.26-2). These research developments will undoubtedly lead to markers that can be used for genetic screening, either in the stool—as, for example, mutated *ras* oncogene or p53 in desquamated cells.[61] A

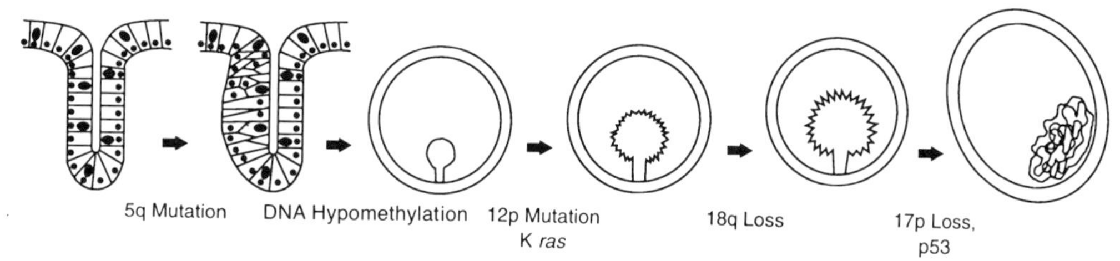

FIG. 26-2. A model of colon carcinogenesis indicating where observed genetic alterations may be influencing progression of normal epithelium to cancer through hyperproliferation and advancing adenoma stages. See references for details.

more attractive approach is one that would be based on circulating markers or abnormalities in cells that are more easily accessible, such as lymphocytes. In addition, we will have to address key issues such as cost-effectiveness, patient compliance, and physician performance of the tests required for preventive strategies.[62] Sophisticated research producing improved interventional strategies will be to no avail without the ability to marshal resources and to influence patient-physician orientation toward preventive approaches. Simple, highly effective, sensitive, and specific screening techniques can do a lot to surmount these obstacles, and easily implemented nutritional interventions such as food supplements will go far to overcome the difficulties in the behavioral modification of large populations. It is clear, however, that even now we have the concepts and techniques to alter the natural history of colorectal cancer in a large proportion of average-risk and high-risk individuals. This can be accomplished today, and the approaches can be modified as new data and improved techniques become available. Eventually, we will undoubtedly see the eradication of colorectal cancer as a major disease by the identification of the majority of individuals and their families at risk. This risk assessment will provide the basis for identifying those individuals destined to develop the premalignant adenomatous polyps and, by periodic examination, will enable us to identify and remove such premalignant adenomas and prevent and reduce the incidence of colorectal cancer, thereby reducing its mortality.

The importance of prevention was appreciated by Thomas Huxley, who at Johns Hopkins University in 1876 said, "The objective of medical education is to train physicians to *prevent diseases* and, where disease is already established, to alleviate or to cure it."

We are finally arriving at that point in our education and clinical perspective where we are beginning to develop a more balanced view of cancer control today that includes prevention as well as treatment.

REFERENCES

1. Greegor DH: Diagnosis of large bowel cancer in the asymptomatic patient. *JAMA* 201:943–945, 1967.
2. Winawer SJ, Schottenfeld D, Flehinger BJ: Colorectal cancer screening (review). *J Natl Cancer Inst* 83:243–253, 1991.
3. Winawer SJ, O'Brien MJ, Waye JD, et al: Risk and surveillance of individuals with colorectal polyps. *Bull WHO* 68:789–795, 1990.
4. Winawer SJ, St. John J, Bond J, et al: Screening of average-risk individuals for colorectal cancer. *Bull WHO* 68:505–513, 1990.
5. Gnauck R, Macrae FA, Fleisher M. How to perform the fecal occult blood test. *CA* 34:134–147, 1984.
6. Fleisher M, Schwartz MK, Winawer SJ: Laboratory studies on the Hemoccult slide for fecal occult blood testing in colorectal cancer, in Winawer SJ, Schottenfeld D, Sherlock P (eds): *Colorectal Cancer: Prevention, Epidemiology, and Screening*. New York, Raven Press, 1980, pp 181–187.
7. St John DJB, Young GP, Cuthbertson AM, et al: Detection of colorectal neoplasia: Comparison of guaiac porphyrin and immunochemical tests for occult blood. *Gastroenterology* 96:A492, 1989.
8. Ahlquist DA, McGill DB, Schwartz S, et al: Fecal blood levels in health and disease: A study using HemoQuant. *N Engl J Med* 312:1422–1428, 1985.
9. St. John DJB, Young GP, Alexeyeff M, et al: Most large and medium colorectal adenomas can be detected by immunochemical occult blood tests. *Gastroenterology* 98:A312, 1990.
10. Schottenfeld D, Winawer SJ: Large intestine, in Schottenfeld D, Fraumeni JF Jr (eds): *Cancer, Epidemiology and Prevention*. Philadelphia, Saunders, 703–727, 1982.
11. Crespi M, Weissman GS, Gilbertsen VA, et al: The role of proctosigmoidoscopy in screening for colorectal neoplasia. *CA* 34:158–166, 1984.
12. Bohlman TW, Katon RM, Lipshutz GR, et al: Fiberoptic pansigmoidoscopy: An evaluation and comparison with rigid sigmoidoscopy. *Gastroenterology* 72:644–649, 1977.
13. Hertz RE, Deddish MR, Day E: Value of periodic examinations in detecting cancer of the rectum and colon. *Postgrad Med* 27:290–294, 1960.
14. Dales LG, Friedman GD, Ramcharan S, et al: Multiphasic check-up evaluation study: III. Outpatient clinic utilization, hospitalization and mortality experience after seven years. *Prev Med* 2:221–235, 1973.
15. Friedman GD, Collen MF, Fireman BH. Multiphasic health check-up evaluation: A 16 year follow-up. *J Chronic Dis* 39:453–463, 1986.
16. Selby JV, Friedman GD, Quesenberry CP Jr, Weiss NS: A case-control study of screening sigmoidoscopy and mortality from colorectal cancer. *N Engl J Med* 326:653–657, 1992.
17. Newcomb PA, Norfleet RG, Storer BE, et al: Screening sigmoidoscopy and colorectal cancer mortality. *JNCI* 84:1572–1575, 1992.
18. Williams AR, Balasooriya BAW, Day DW: Polyps and cancer of the large bowel: A necropsy study in Liverpool. *Gut* 23:835–842, 1982.
19. Winawer SJ, Zauber AG, O'Brien MJ, et al: Randomized comparison of surveillance intervals after colonoscopic removal of newly diagnosed adenomatous polyps. *N Engl J Med* 328:901–906, 1993.
20. Atkin WS, Morson BC, Cuzick J: Long-term risk of colorectal cancer after excision of rectosigmoid adenomas. *N Engl J Med* 326:658–662, 1992.
21. Spencer RJ, Melton LJ, Ready RL, Ilstrup DM: Treatment of small colorectal polyps: A population-based study of the risk of subsequent carcinoma. *Mayo Clin Proc* 59:305–310, 1984.
22. Lotfi AM, Spencer RJ, Ilstrup DM, Melton J: Colorectal polyps and the risk of subsequent carcinoma. *Mayo Clin Proc* 61:337–343, 1986.
23. Winawer SJ, Zauber AG, Ho MN, et al: Prevention of colorectal cancer by colonoscopic polypectomy. *N Engl J Med* 329:1977–1981, 1993.
24. Kussin SZ, Lipkin M, Winawer SJ: Inherited colon cancer: Clinical implications. *Am J Gastroenterol* 72:448–457, 1979.
25. Burt RW, Bishop DT, Cannon LA, et al: Dominant inheritance of adenomatous colonic polyps and colorectal cancer. *N Engl J Med* 312:1540–1544, 1985.
26. Devroede G, Taylor WF: On calculating cancer risk and survival of ulcerative colitis patients with the life table method. *Gastroenterology* 71:505–509, 1976.
27. Kewenter J, Bjork S, Haglind E, et al: Cancer risk in extensive ulcerative colitis. *Ann Surg* 188:824–827, 1978.
28. Greenstein AJ, Sachar D, Smith H, et al: Cancer in universal

and left-sided ulcerative colitis: Factors determining risk. *Gastroenterology* 77:290–294, 1979.

29. Bralow SP, Kopel J. Hemoccult screening for colorectal cancer: An impact study on Sarasota, Florida. *J Fla Med Assoc* 66:915–919, 1979.
30. Flehinger BJ, Herbert E, Winawer SJ, et al: Screening for colorectal cancer with fecal occult blood test and sigmoidoscopy: Preliminary report of the colon project of Memorial Sloan-Kettering Cancer Center and PMI-Strang Clinic, in Chamberlain J, Miller AB (eds): *Screening for Gastrointestinal Cancer.* Toronto, Huber, 1988, pp 9–16.
31. Hardcastle JD, Thomas WM, Chamberlain J, et al: Randomized controlled trial of fecal occult blood screening for colorectal cancer: The results of the first 107,349 subjects. *Lancet* 1:1160–1164, 1989.
32. Farrands PA, Hardcastle JD: Factors affecting compliance with screening for colorectal cancer. *Community Med* 6:12–19, 1984.
33. Dent OF, Bartrop R, Goulston KJ, et al: Participation in fecal occult blood screening for colorectal cancer. *Soc Sci Med* 17:17–23, 1983.
34. Halper MS, Winawer SJ, Brody BS, et al: Issues of patient compliance, in Winawer SJ, Schottenfeld D, Sherlock P (eds): *Colorectal Cancer: Prevention, Epidemiology, and Screening.* New York, Raven Press, 1980, pp 299–310.
35. American Cancer Society: Cancer of the colon and rectum: A summary of a public attitude survey. *CA* 33:31–37, 1983.
36. American Cancer Society: Survey of physicians' attitudes and practices in early cancer detection. *CA* 35:197–213, 1985.
37. Allison JE, Felman R: Cost benefits of Hemoccult screening for colorectal carcinoma. *Dig Dis Sci* 9:860–865, 1985.
38. Eddy DM: Screening for colorectal cancer. *Ann Intern Med* 113:373–384, 1990.
39. Cohen AM, Shank B, Friedman MA: Colorectal cancer, in DeVita VT Jr, Hellman S, Rosenberg SA (eds): *Cancer: Principles and Practices of Oncology,* 3d ed. Philadelphia, Lippincott, 1989, pp 895–964.
40. Enker WE: Extent of operations for large bowel cancer, in DeCosse JJ (ed): *Large Bowel Cancer.* New York, Churchill Livingstone, 1981, pp 78–93.
41. Winawer SJ, Prorok P, Macrae F, et al: Surveillance and early diagnosis of colorectal cancer. *Cancer Detect Prev* 8:373–392, 1985.
42. American Cancer Society: *Cancer Facts and Figures.* New York, American Cancer Society, 1992.
43. Shike M, Greenwald P, Bloch A, et al: Primary prevention of colorectal cancer. *Bull WHO* 68:377–385, 1990.
44. Winawer SJ, Shike M: Dietary factors in colorectal cancer and their possible effects on earlier stages of hyperproliferation and adenoma formation (editorial). *J Natl Cancer Inst* 84:74–75, 1992.
45. Moertel CG, Fleming TR, MacDonald JS, et al: Levamisole and fluorouracil for adjuvant therapy of resected colon carcinoma. *N Engl J Med* 322:352–358, 1990.
46. Winawer SJ, Enker WE, Levin B: Colorectal cancer, in Winawer SJ (ed): *Management of Gastrointestinal Diseases.* New York, Gower, 1992, pp 27.1–27.40.
47. O'Brien MJ, Winawer SJ, Zauber AG, et al: The national polyp study: Patient and polyp characteristics associated with high-grade dysplasia in colorectal adenomas. *Gastroenterology* 98:371–379, 1990.
48. Simon JB: Occult blood screening for colorectal carcinoma: A clinical review. *Gastroenterology* 88:820–837, 1985.
49. Knight KK, Fielding JE, Battista RN: Occult blood screening for colorectal cancer. *JAMA* 261:587–593, 1989.
50. Fleischer DE, Goldberg SB, Browning TH, et al: Detection and surveillance of colorectal cancer. *JAMA* 261:580–585, 1989.
51. American Cancer Society: Guidelines for the cancer-related checkup: Recommendations and rationale. *CA* 30:194–240, 1980.
52. Office of Technology Assessment, US Congress: costs and effectiveness of colorectal cancer screening in the elderly. Publ No OTA-BH-H-74. Washington, DC, US Government Printing Office, 1990.
53. Kronborg O, Fenger C, Sondergaard O, et al: Initial mass screening for colorectal cancer with fecal occult blood test. *Scand J Gastroenterol* 22:677–686, 1987.
54. Mandel JS, Bond JH, Church TR, et al: Reducing mortality from colorectal cancer by screening for fecal occult blood. *N Engl J Med* 328:1365–1371, 1993.
55. Kewenter J, Bjork S, Haglind E, et al: Screening and rescreening for colorectal cancer: A controlled trial of fecal occult blood testing in 27,700 subjects. *CA* 62:645–651, 1988.
56. Eddy DM, Nugent W, Eddy JF, et al: Screening for colorectal cancer in a high-risk population: Results of a mathematical model. *Gastroenterology* 92:682–692, 1987.
57. Burt RW, Bishop DT, Lynch HT, et al: Risk and surveillance of individuals with heritable factors for colorectal cancer. *Bull WHO* 68:655–665, 1990.
58. Vogelstein B, Fearon ER, Hamilton SR, et al: Genetic alterations during colorectal tumor development. *N Engl J Med* 319:525–532, 1988.
59. Solomon E, Voss R, Hall V, et al: Chromosome 5 allele loss in human colorectal carcinoma. *Nature* 328:616–619, 1987.
60. Winawer SJ: The natural history of colorectal cancer: Opportunities for intervention, in Levin B (ed): *Gastrointestinal Cancer: Current Approaches to Diagnosis and Treatment.* Austin, Texas, University of Texas Press, 1988, pp 21–30.
61. Sidransky D, Tokino T, Hamilton SR, et al: Identification of *ras* oncogene mutations in the stool of patients with curable colorectal tumors. *Science* 256:102–105, 1992.
62. Ransohoff DF, Lang CA: Screening for colorectal cancer (review article). *N Engl J Med* 325:37–41, 1991.

CHAPTER 27

Statistical Considerations in Screening

Betty J. Flehinger

HIGHLIGHTS

Cancers detected by screening while patients are still asymptomatic are almost invariably associated with better survival than cancers that come to medical attention because they have caused symptoms. This does not prove that the early detection of disease through screening changes the prognosis for the patient. The survival difference might be attributable to lead-time bias, length-biased sampling, and overdiagnosis bias. The major criterion of efficacy of a screening program is the disease-specific mortality in a population invited to participate in the program.

The preferred method of investigating mortality reduction from screening is the randomly controlled clinical trial in which members of a study group are offered periodic screening tests while members of a control group receive none. The numbers of cancer deaths in the two groups are compared to determine whether screening provides significant mortality benefit.

Careful planning is required so that the sample size and duration of a clinical trial may be adequate to ensure appropriate significance and power. Moreover, special care is required to avoid bias from unequal criteria for assigning patients to study and control groups, from unequal follow-up, or from misdiagnosis of causes of death.

CONTROVERSIES

It is most important that the characteristics of a screening trial, significance and power, be established *in advance*. The significance level guarantees that a worthless screen is unlikely to be accepted because of random differences between study and control groups. Most investigators are well aware of the need to attach significance levels to their findings. Power guarantees that a real opportunity to reduce mortality substantially will not be overlooked. Too often power is neglected; clinical trials are terminated without any proof of significant benefit and the results are interpreted as proving that no benefit exists when in fact sample size or duration were inadequate.

FUTURE DIRECTIONS

A simple mathematical model of the natural history of cancer in the presence of a screening program is described. It is demonstrated that computer simulation based on the model can be used to relate the long-term benefit from screening to the detectability and curability of early-stage disease. An example of a clinical trial carefully designed through simulation for appropriate significance and power is presented.

In this chapter, screening is defined as the routine administration of a medical test with the objective of detecting a specific chronic disease in a presymptomatic, treatable stage and thereby preventing mortality from the disease. The currently available screening tests for colorectal cancer, for example, are sigmoidoscopy and the fecal occult blood test.

Before a test procedure can be considered as a screening tool, it must meet certain basic requirements. It must be inexpensive, acceptable to patients, simple to administer, and free of dangerous side effects. Furthermore, the test should detect the disease in its presymptomatic stage with high probability. The detected disease should be treatable with high probability of long survival and with small probability of adverse side effects. Finally, the test itself should be specific for the disease in question or it should be linked to inexpensive, safe, acceptable diagnostic procedures.

COMMONLY USED STATISTICS

The quantities most often associated with screening tests are sensitivity, specificity, and predictive value.[1] *Sensitivity* (Se) is defined as the probability that a screenee who has the disease in question will exhibit a positive result from the test. *Specificity* (Sp) is defined as the probability that a screenee who does not have the disease will exhibit a negative result from the test. *Predictive value* (PV) is defined as the probability that a patient who exhibits a positive result actually has the disease. The predictive value of a test depends on both sensitivity and specificity, as well as the prevalence (P) of the disease in the population undergoing screening:

$$PV = \frac{SeP}{SeP + (1 - Sp)(1 - P)}$$

In words, the predictive value is equal to the probability of correct detection of the disease divided by the probability of correct detection plus the probability of incorrect detection in a patient free of the disease. These are useful concepts for thinking about planned screening programs, but their applicability is limited because of the following problems.

Sensitivity is usually defined without regard to stage at detection. A screening test with high sensitivity only for advanced symptomatic disease is not valuable. On the other hand, it is impossible to estimate the probability of detecting early, asymptomatic disease directly, since there is no way of counting the undetected cases. Assumptions about the speed with which undetected early cancer will become symptomatic or other assumptions about the progression dynamics of the disease are required before early-stage detectability can be estimated.

Predictive value is the quantity that the clinician would most like to know when faced with a positive result from a screening test. That should tell him or her how likely it is that the patient actually has the disease and should be helpful in deciding on the extent of subsequent workup. However, it is clear from the above equation that predictive value depends not only on the basic characteristics of the test but also on the prevalence of the disease in the population being screened.

SURVIVAL AND MORTALITY

The survival of groups of patients with chronic fatal disease such as colorectal cancer is generally characterized by Kaplan-Meier product limit estimates.[2–4] This estimate is used conveniently when the length of follow-up is variable from patient to patient—i.e., when some patients are followed to death from the disease while others are followed to censorship because of death from other causes or loss of contact. It requires no assumptions about the structure of the survival function, only that censorship be independent of death from the disease.

To perform the calculation, one first enumerates the times $t_1, t_2, \ldots, t_n$ at which deaths occurred. Suppose that at each point t_i, r_i patients were at risk and d_i patients died. The survival function $R(t)$ is then estimated by taking the product over all i for which t_i is less than t of $(1 - d_i/r_i)$. Figure 27-1 displays a typical set of survival estimates for patients treated for colorectal cancer[5–7] after detection in a screening program or after being brought to medical attention because of symptoms. On this graph, the drops in the curves represent deaths and the tick marks represent patients still alive. These curves are quite typical, since it happens almost invariably that a group of patients whose

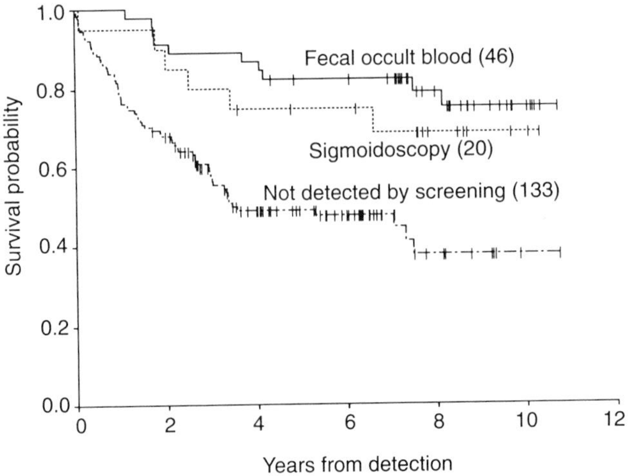

FIG. 27-1. Kaplan-Meier product limit estimate of survival from colorectal cancer by method of detection. Tick marks represent patients who are still alive.

diseases are found while they remain asymptomatic have better survival than a corresponding symptomatic group.

It is important to recognize that this survival difference does *not* prove that the early detection of disease through screening changes the prognosis for the patient. The survival difference might be attributable to several sources of bias. First, lead-time bias results from the delay between the detectability of disease by the screening test and the onset of symptoms. The length of this delay is not measured, since ethical considerations require that detected disease be treated promptly. Second, there is length-biased sampling which arises because chronic diseases like cancer grow at different rates in different patients. The slowest cancers are most likely to be detected in a screening program, since the faster cancers progress to advanced symptomatic stages between screens. These slow cancers are associated with long survival. Often, if the patients with slow cancers were not screened, they might die of other causes before their cancers were even detected. This phenomenon is called overdiagnosis bias. For these reasons the benefit of a screening program cannot be determined by measuring survival difference between screening detections and symptomatic patients. The benefit depends on the change in prognosis induced by screening detection with prompt treatment, and this change is virtually impossible to measure.

The major criterion of efficacy of a screening program is the *mortality* from the disease in question in a population invited to participate in the program—i.e., the number of deaths attributable to the disease per unit of population per year. When this mortality is decreased substantially, the program is a success. Necessary conditions for this success start with the selection of a high-risk population in which, in the absence of screening, mortality from the disease is high. Next comes acceptability of the screening test to members of the population. This is based on willingness to enroll in the program and compliance with test requirements after enrollment. The screening test must be sensitive to presymptomatic disease for which there is an effective treatment. Survival probability must be improved by the treatment. Since these conditions are not directly observable, it is desirable to provide direct proof of mortality reduction before widespread screening programs are initiated.

CLINICAL TRIALS

The preferred method of investigating mortality reduction is the randomly controlled clinical trial. A high-risk population is defined on the basis of age, sex, and other known demographic considerations. Members of this population are invited to participate; volunteers are interviewed and asked to complete questionnaires and consent forms. *After* their eligibility is determined, they are randomized into two or more groups. In the simplest design, members of the *study group* are offered periodic screening tests; they are reminded and urged to comply with these tests promptly. Every positive test is followed by an appropriate diagnostic workup and treatment. Members of the *control group* receive no screening tests. All participants are urged to seek medical attention promptly when symptoms occur. Study and control patients are treated with equal care upon presentation with symptoms. Every participant should be contacted at regular intervals from enrollment to death or the termination of the study. Every death should be carefully reviewed by an unbiased panel to determine whether or not it was caused by the disease under investigation. When the trial is terminated, after a prespecified duration or based on sequential decision criteria, comparison of the numbers of deaths in the study and control groups determines whether the screening program conveys a significant mortality benefit.

Careful planning is required so that the sample size and duration of a clinical trial to investigate the benefits of screening may be adequate to ensure appropriate significance and power. Significance is defined as the probability that the trial will be interpreted as demonstrating a mortality benefit to screening when none in fact is present. A significance level of 0.05 is usually considered appropriate in trials to establish the benefits of screening. Power is the probability that a mortality improvement of a specified magnitude demonstrates a significant benefit in the trial. Power requirements of 0.80 or 0.90 are often used in the design of trials. It is most important that the characteristics of the trial be established *in advance*. The significance level guarantees that a worthless screen is unlikely to be accepted because of random differences between study and control groups. The power guarantees that a real opportunity to reduce mortality substantially will not be overlooked. Too often clinical trials are terminated without any proof of significant benefit, and they are then interpreted as proving that no benefit exists when in fact their power was inadequate.[8] In those cases, important effects may have been overlooked. Methods of calculating approximate significance and power for fixed-length and sequential clinical trials are well known.[9,10] Simulation studies based on mathematical models discussed below are also recommended.

An important caveat in the design of trials relates to imperfect compliance in the study group and contamination of the control group. Members of the study group are always free to omit prescribed screening examinations or even to drop out of the program altogether. Control participants, on the other hand, are likely to seek out screening examinations from private practitioners outside the experimental program. This problem is particularly difficult in societies like the United States, where medical care is primarily private. Calculations of significance and power should take this caveat into account.

There are several sources of bias in screening trials that should be avoided. The first relates to unequal criteria for assigning participants to study and control groups. It is imperative that randomization take place after the participant has agreed to all the rules of the study and after it is completely determined that he or she is eligible to be included. Once randomized, the participant must remain a member of the assigned group even if the protocol of the other group appears preferable. Intense effort is required to provide equal follow-up for study and control groups, since the study group is receiving service and the control group is receiving none. In a free society, the process of keeping track of a large number of people for many years is both expensive and time-consuming. It is important to obtain equally accurate statistics on numbers of deaths and causes of death in the study and control groups. Death certificate information may well be inadequate. A patient who was once treated for colon cancer, for example, is very likely to have colon cancer as an underlying cause of death on the death certificate even though the cancer was completely cured and the patient died of coronary infarction. This problem can only be obviated by impartial review of all deaths.

MODELING THE NATURAL HISTORY OF DISEASE

The effectiveness of a screening program depends strongly on the characteristics of the disease in addition to the characteristics of the screening test. That dependence has been clarified by extensive analysis of a mathematical model based on the following simplified assumptions[11]:

1. In the population to be screened, a subgroup, proportion ρ, is susceptible to the disease in question.
2. In the absence of treatment, the disease, after its onset, passes through two distinct stages followed by death. When the disease enters the advanced stage, it becomes symptomatic immediately.
3. The age of onset and the durations of the early and advanced stages are random variables with means T_0, μ_1, and μ_2.
4. A screening program consists of periodic tests intended to detect the disease in its early stage. Given the presence of early-stage disease, the test gives a positive result with probability p.
5. When early-stage disease is detected, the patient is treated with cure probability c. If the patient is cured, the subsequent survival is the same as if the patient had never had the disease; if not cured, survival is the same as if there had been no treatment.

In this analysis, death is taken as the important end point, so that reduction in mortality from the disease is the measure of benefit from the screening program. The major parameters that determine that benefit are the susceptibility ρ, the mean time in early stage μ_1, the early-stage detectability p, and the early-stage cure probability c. For any specified set of these parameters, computer simulation can be used to calculate the expected disease mortality in a population screened periodically for many years compared to the mortality in the same population without any screening. Table 27-1 displays a typical result of such a simulation. For any given natural history, the mortality benefit increases with early-stage detectability p and early-stage curability c as expected. Thus, the better the methods of detection and treatment, the more lives are saved.

A similar simulation technique can be used to plan a clinical trial. It is assumed that the natural history of the disease is the same as in the prior example, and that both the detectability p and curability c are unknown. Suppose 20,000 participants are randomized into study and control groups. The study participants are screened annually and the controls are not screened at all. All cancers are treated promptly. The trial is terminated after a fixed period T, and the ratio of the number of cancer deaths D_1 in the control group to the number of cancer deaths D_2 in the study group is calculated. If and only if the ratio D_1/D_2 exceeds a critical value R, the conclusion is reached that a significant benefit results from screening. The appropriate value of R depends on the trial duration T. If the trial is to have a significance of 0.05, this means that, if there were no value to the screen (i.e., $p = 0$ or $c = 0$), then 5 percent of all possible experiments would end with D_1/D_2 greater than R—i.e., with a decision that there is indeed a significant mortality benefit. Through simulation, the value of R that is exceeded by D_1/D_2 in 5 percent of all possible trials with $p = 0$ has been estimated and is plotted in Fig. 27-2. For short trials, the number of cancer deaths in the

Table 27-1
Results of Simulation of 35 Years of Colorectal Cancer Mortality in 10,000 Participants with Annual Screening Compared to No Screening

ρ	μ_1	p	c	*Cancers found*	*Cancer deaths*	*Mortality reduction, %*
.2	4	0	0	1047	908	
		0.5	0.5	1240	599	34
		0.5	1	1240	297	67
		1	0.5	1280	509	44
		1	1	1280	129	86

Abbreviations: ρ, proportion susceptible to the disease; μ_1, mean duration of early stage cancers in years; p, probability of a positive test; c, probability of cure.

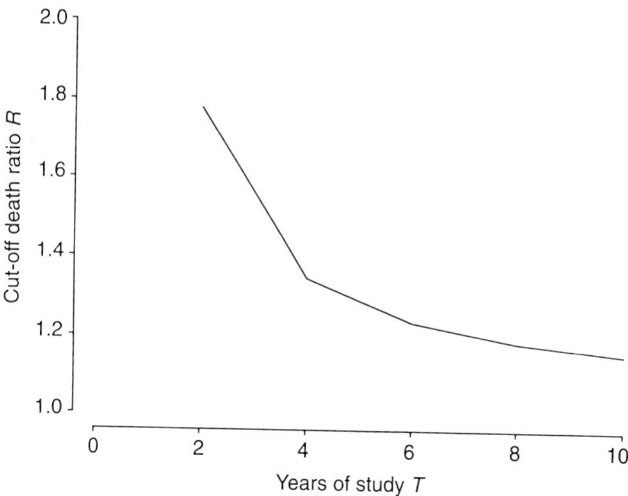

FIG. 27-2. Cutoff value R of D_1/D_2 corresponding to significance 0.05 as a function of trial duration T (10,000 study, 10,000 control participants, susceptibility $\rho = 0.2$, mean duration of early stage $\mu_1 = 4$).

control group must be considerably larger than the number in the study group before a significant benefit is proven. For longer trials in which both D_1 and D_2 are large, values of D_1/D_2 not much larger than 1 are sufficient to prove a significant effect.

Power calculations are also based on simulation. For specified values of p and c, both greater than zero in the study group, and values of R taken from Fig. 27-2, the probability that D_1/D_2 exceeds R represents the power of a trial of duration T. Figure 27-3 exhibits this power as a function of T. To use these curves, the

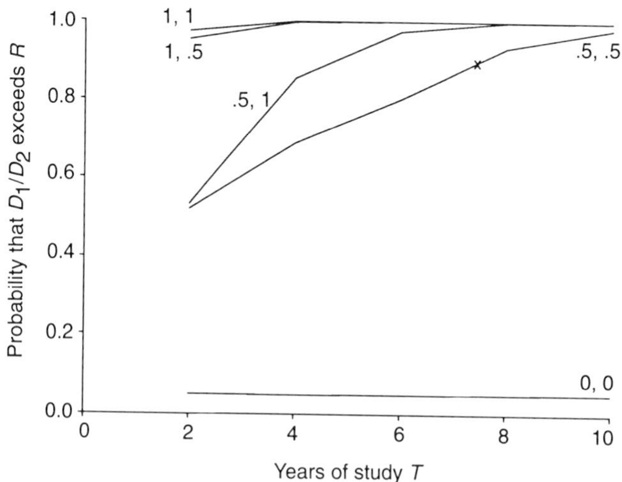

FIG. 27-3. Power of clinical trial as a function of trial duration T for specified values of early-stage detectability p and early-stage curability c (10,000 study, 10,000 control participants, significance = 0.05, susceptibility $\rho = 0.2$, mean duration of early stage $\mu_1 = 4$).

planner first consults Table 27-1 to estimate the true benefit that would be achieved through screening for various values of p and c. For example, suppose the 34 percent mortality reduction associated with $p = 0.5$, $c = 0.5$ is considered good enough that it would be a major mistake to fail to recognize it in the trial. Then a power of 0.9 would be required and, as indicated in Fig. 27-3, the trial should be planned for at least 7.4 years.

This procedure has been described to illustrate the detailed planning that can be carried out through computer simulation. In an actual case, medical information would be used to characterize the natural history of the disease and extensive computer experiments would include varying sample sizes, imperfect compliance, and contamination of the control group in addition to the duration of the trial. Furthermore, various sequential stopping rules would also be investigated. Screening trials require the recruitment and follow-up of very large numbers of participants for long periods of time and are therefore very expensive. Inconclusive results constitute major disappointments that can usually be prevented by adequate planning using statistical analysis and computer simulation.

REFERENCES

1. Winawer SJ, Fleisher M: Sensitivity and specificity of the fecal occult blood test for colorectal neoplasia. *Gastroenterology* 82:986–991, 1982.
2. Kaplan EL, Meier P: Nonparametric estimation for incomplete observation. *J Am Stat Assoc* 53:457–481, 1958.
3. Elandt-Johnson RC, Johnson NL: *Survival Models and Data Analysis*. New York, Wiley, 1980, pp 150–180.
4. Cox DR, Oakes D: *Analysis of Survival Data*. London, Chapman and Hall, 1984, pp 48–61.
5. Winawer SJ, Andrews M, Flehinger B, et al: Progress report on controlled trial of fecal occult blood testing for the detection of colorectal neoplasia. *Cancer* 45:2959–2964, 1980.
6. Winawer SJ, Schottenfeld D, Flehinger BJ: Colorectal cancer screening. *J Natl Cancer Inst* 83:243–253, 1991.
7. Flehinger BJ, Herbert E, Winawer SJ, et al: Screening for colorectal cancer with fecal occult blood test and sigmoidoscopy, in Chamberlain J, Miller AB (eds): *Screening for Gastrointestinal Cancer*. Toronto, Huber, 1988, pp 9–15.
8. Freiman JA, Chalmers JC, Smith H, et al: The importance of beta, the type II error, and sample size in the design and interpretation of the randomized controlled trial, in Bailar JC III, Mosteller F (eds): *Medical Uses of Statistics*. Boston, New England Journal of Medicine Books, 1992, pp 357–373.
9. Peto R, Pike MC, Armitage P, et al: Design and analysis of randomized clinical trials requiring prolonged observation of each patient. *Br J Cancer* 34:585–612, 1976; 35:1–39, 1977.
10. Shapiro SM: *Clinical Trials Issues and Approaches*. New York, Dekker, 1983.
11. Flehinger BJ, Kimmel M: The natural history of lung cancer in a periodically screened population. *Biometrics* 43:127–144, 1987.

CHAPTER 28

Fecal Occult Blood Test Screening Trials

Sidney J. Winawer
John H. Bond

HIGHLIGHTS

Considering the present high incidence rate of 160,000 new cases per year in the United States, a critical question is whether we can produce a shift to an earlier stage in more patients and reduce mortality from colorectal cancer by application of screening tests in asymptomatic people. In this chapter, evidence of the effectiveness of screening with the fecal occult blood test (FOBT) is reviewed. Initial data were reported from community trials and studies of individual physicians, while later studies were designed as prospective controlled trials. Five such trials were initiated and two have been completed and reported. There are now two studies that have demonstrated the effectiveness of screening for colorectal cancer with stool blood testing. The Minnesota randomized trial clearly has shown a reduced mortality in the annually screened group. The New York study demonstrated a reduced mortality significant at the .053 level when stool blood testing was added to sigmoidoscopy as compared to sigmoidoscopy alone. The ongoing European studies and all prior noncontrolled trials have shown a stage shift consistent with the improved survival and mortality reduction of the completed American trials. We now have effective screening methods, the ability to find and remove polyps, and the ability to detect and treat early cancers with effective surgery. Polyp detection makes the screening approach more attractive, since it is the more common neoplastic finding in positive patients, and removal of polyps reduces the incidence of future cancer.

CONTROVERSIES

Many questions remain, however. An important issue is what slide to use. The Minnesota trial used previously rehydrated slides which increased the false-positive rate, while all the other trials used nonhydrated slides with a lower false-positive rate but also with a lower sensitivity. The Swedish trial has nicely demonstrated the sensitivity and specificity of the two approaches. Rehydration of the slides can produce variability of the test performance, so it is not ideal. Newer tests such as the Hemesensa are said to produce a high sensitivity similar to that of the rehydrated slide without loss of specificity. This may be a good choice for the next slide test. There is a critical need to provide this entire screening-diagnostic-treatment approach to people in a cost-effective manner, and there is a tremendous need to educate the public about the importance of colorectal cancer, the availability of these approaches, and the need to have symptoms and risk factors addressed.

FUTURE DIRECTIONS

While we have effective techniques now to reduce the mortality of colorectal cancer, we will, in the future, have better approaches. These undoubtedly will encompass genetic screening followed by colonoscopic polypectomy in individuals with demonstrated susceptibility. To this approach, we can add new concepts of primary prevention when evidence provides a basis for this broad application.

Although techniques are now available for the early detection of colorectal cancer, this disease continues to kill within 5 years almost 50 percent of the people in whom it occurs. This high mortality rate is related directly to the stage at which the diagnosis is usually made; today, only about 40 percent of colorectal cancers are detected at a localized stage without lymph node involvement. The 10-year relative survival rate for patients with localized disease approaches 70 percent, and the majority of patients in whom colorectal cancer is detected at an asymptomatic stage have localized disease and are therefore potentially curable at surgery. Recent evidence has demonstrated that the natural history of colorectal cancer as it evolves from the normal mucosa through the adenoma stage is a long one, with approximately 10 to 15 years of time for the neoplastic process to develop into clinical cancer with symptoms. Considering the present high incidence rate of 150,000 new cases per year in the United States, a critical question is whether we can produce a shift to an earlier stage in more patients and reduce mortality from colorectal cancer by the application of screening tests in asymptomatic people.[1,2]

Early detection encompasses screening and case finding; *screening* being a population approach while *case finding* is an approach that is applied by physicians and other health care personnel within the framework of comprehensive medical care. The two terms have been used interchangeably. Tests for early detection include digital rectal examination, stool blood testing, sigmoidoscopy, and colonoscopy. The first three tests are generally applied to average-risk individuals, while colonoscopy is reserved for high-risk individuals such as those with inflammatory bowel disease, a prior history of polyps or colonic cancer, and those with a family history of colonic cancer.[1] In this chapter, evidence of the effectiveness of screening with the fecal occult blood test is reviewed. Initial data were reported from community trials and studies of individual physicians, while later studies were designed as prospective controlled trials. Five such trials were initiated and two have been completed and reported. The effectiveness of screening, however, rests not only on the introduction of the FOBT and sigmoidoscopy but also on the availability of colonoscopy with the demonstration that polyps removed by colonoscopy result in a reduction in the incidence of colorectal cancer.[3] The effectiveness of screening is also enhanced by surgical progress which now permits excellent anatomic resection of the disease.[4]

Introduction of the impregnated guaiac slide test for the first time permitted testing of stools with a reliable screening test for stool blood. Greegor[5] utilized the new impregnated guaiac slide test in a series of patients in his office with a goal of demonstrating that this test could detect early colonic cancers in asymptomatic patients. In Greegor's initial series, 5 percent of patients had positive tests, 1 had colonic cancer, 2 had diverticulosis, 1 had a polyp, and in only 1 could no disease be found. In Greegor's later experience, the frequency of positive reactions decreased to 2.8 percent, but the findings remained approximately the same. In a collaborative study organized by Greegor, in which 103 physicians reported on the use of this approach, 139 cancers were detected.[6] Of 47 cases that were considered to be silent, 85 percent were reported to be pathologically localized to the bowel wall—that is, Dukes A or B. This compared favorably with the overall national average of about 40 percent localization of detected colonic cancers. Only 20 of the 139 cases were within reach of the rigid sigmoidoscope. In these studies, the impregnated guaiac slide test was prepared by giving patients 6 slides to test over 3 days on a high-roughage meat-free diet. The tests were brought in and tested promptly. Studies initiated in the United States, Israel, West Germany, the United Kingdom, and Italy supported these early observations that screening with stool blood testing in asymptomatic individuals uncovered early-stage cancers and was of potential value.[1,2]

Many questions were asked about the feasibility and effectiveness of this test. Feasibility related to patient compliance with the test, the rate of positives, the false-positive and false-negative rates, sensitivity and specificity, and the type of diagnostic workup required to make the test effective. Effectiveness of the test relates to the stage of cancers detected, the survival of patients with cancers detected, and—the most important issue—whether this test would result in a reduction in mortality in colorectal cancer in a screened group as compared with a control group. It was necessary to design, organize, and implement large-scale long-term trials in order to address the major issue of mortality reduction in addition to demonstrating a stage shift and improved survival. Although a stage shift and improved survival would not completely validate the approach, since these could be related to screening bias, positive findings of these parameters would be necessary to be consistent with a mortality reduction. Demonstration of a mortality reduction from screening would validate the stage shift and survival benefit demonstrated in the early studies and would indicate that these observations were valid and not due to screening bias.

CONTROLLED TRIALS

Prospective controlled trials were initiated by Memorial Sloan-Kettering Cancer Center in collaboration with the Strang Clinic—Preventive Medicine Institute in New York, the University of Minnesota, and later in the United Kingdom (in Nottingham), Sweden, and Denmark.[1] By 1975, it became clear that it was appropriate to evaluate a screening program intended for the early detection of colorectal cancer and for the identification of premalignant adenomas. To be successful, the screening program had to combine the following elements: (1) a simple and inexpensive screening test, (2) accurate and acceptable diagnostic procedures for individuals with positive screening tests, (3) effective methods of nonsurgical adenoma removal, and (4) anatomic cancer surgery without frequent need for colostomy.[7]

Memorial Sloan-Kettering and Preventive Medicine Institute—Strang Clinic Trial

A clinical trial was conducted by Memorial Sloan-Kettering Cancer Center in collaboration with the Preventive Medicine Institute—Strang Clinic in New York from 1975 to 1984.[7] The objective was the evaluation of the FOBT as a supplement to rigid sigmoidoscopy for the detection of colorectal cancer. This study was conducted in the setting of comprehensive preventive medical examination. Since initiation of this trial, other controlled trials evaluating screening of colorectal cancer with the FOBT have been conducted.[8–12]

The clinical trial was initiated with the objectives of answering the several questions: Given a health-conscious, asymptomatic group of people over 40 years of age who attend a preventive medicine clinic, is it feasible to add a routine FOBT to a comprehensive examination? The test would require a restricted diet for 4 days and would be administered in addition to the rigid sigmoidoscopy performed during routine examinations. In the population described above, what is the rate of positivity for the FOBT, and what is its predictive value for colorectal cancer and for adenomas? When members of this population have positive FOBT results, will they comply with recommendations for colonoscopy and barium enema, and will these procedures successfully detect the lesions causing the bleeding? Will screening with the FOBT and sigmoidoscopy result in detection of precancerous adenomas and cancers at an earlier stage than screening by sigmoidoscopy alone? And will detection of colorectal cancer at an earlier stage result in improved long-term survival for patients after correction for lead time? Will a group of patients offered annual screening with the FOBT and sigmoidoscopy have reduced colorectal cancer mortality compared with a similar group offered annual sigmoidoscopy only?

At enrollment, all participants underwent the standard comprehensive examination at the Preventive Medicine Institute—Strang Clinic. This examination included, in addition to a general physical examination, a health history questionnaire and 25-cm rigid sigmoidoscopy. The questionnaire covered the patients' personal and family health history, lifestyle, and symptoms. The only difference for the study and control patients was that patients assigned to either of the study groups (regular or first-time patients) by calendar period were also offered the FOBT, while control patients were not offered this test. Each study patient also received three FOBT slides (Hemoccult) with two windows each and instructions for their use. Patients were instructed to adhere to a meat-free, high-bulk diet for 1 day prior to preparation of the slides and for the 3 days during which stool smears were to be obtained and prepared. The slides were tested without rehydration except for a brief period of 6 months. Slides were brought in at the time of the clinic visit. Whenever a positive result was detected, the patient was referred for a double-contrast barium enema and a full colonoscopy. All patients, study and control, were examined by sigmoidoscopy. Survival probabilities after cancer detection were estimated by the Kaplan-Meier product limit method.[13] Comparisons of survival probability between study and control groups were based on logrank and modified Wilcoxon statistics. Colonic cancer mortality rates were estimated by dividing the number of colonic cancer deaths by the total years at risk in each group. One-sided hypothesis tests were used to compare mortality rates between study and control groups, since it was clear that systematic use of the FOBT screening could not conceivably increase cancer mortality. Given the person-years at risk, a hypothesis test with $\alpha = 0.05$ would provide power $\beta = 0.80$ of detecting a 50 percent reduction in mortality.

Of the 9277 regular patients in trial I, 77 percent were assigned to the study group. This trial was designed primarily to test the feasibility of adding the FOBT to the regular examination of the Preventive Medicine Institute—Strang Clinic. In trial II, 47 percent (5806) of the 12,479 first-time patients were in the study group, so that a comparison of mortality between study and control groups was reasonable. In trial II, the study and control groups were satisfactorily comparable in sample size, age, sex, and other risk factors reported at enrollment. Thus, although allocation to groups was not random, we believe that a comparison of colorectal cancer mortality between study and control groups in trial II was appropriate. Trial I, in which the study and control groups were not balanced in total number of patients, was done primarily to determine whether regular patients at the Preventive Medicine Institute—Strang Clinic would comply with the addition of the FOBT to the extensive annual examinations. However, in both trials, equal attention was given to ensuring adequate follow-up after active follow-up was initiated, and the results of both trials are reported here.

The FOBT was well accepted at the first examination in both study groups. Eighty percent of the first-time patients in trial II complied, while 70 percent of those in trial I complied. However, compliance in trial II decreased rapidly, with only 20 percent compliance at 1 year and 16 percent at 2 years, primarily because these first-time patients failed to return to the clinic. Correspondingly, compliance with sigmoidoscopy started at close to 100 percent for all groups and then rapidly declined, particularly in trial II. There was no difference in frequency of sigmoidoscopy between study and control groups.

A great majority of the FOBTs administered to the study groups in both trials did not involve rehydration of the slides. Rehydration increases the sensitivity but decreases the specificity and positive predictive value of the test.[14] The rate of positivity was higher in trial II (2.6 percent) than in trial I (1.4 percent) and was higher on the first examination than on subsequent examinations conducted 1 or more years after enrollment. Almost 4 percent of the trial II group had positive test results at enrollment. Of the 609 patients with positive test results, 467 (77 percent) received adequate workup within 1 year, including colonoscopy in most cases. Thirty percent (142 patients) of the 467 patients were diagnosed with some neoplasm, either polyp or cancer, with 11 percent (50 patients) being cancerous. In trial II, the predictive value of a positive FOBT on the first examination of 131 patients was 36 percent (47 patients) for all neoplasms and 17 percent (22 patients) for cancer; on subsequent examinations of 74 patients, these figures dropped to 24 percent (18 patients) and 5 percent (4 patients). Corresponding predictive values in trial I were not substantially different.

A total of 199 cases of colorectal cancer were reported and confirmed in participants in the project. Colorectal cancer was detected in 55 patients at the time of study enrollment (prevalence cases): 43 of these patients were participants in trial II. The proportion of patients with cancers detected at study entry was substantially higher in trial II than in trial I. This observation may be ascribed to the fact that the regular patients (trial I) had been screened by sigmoidoscopy in previous years. The study groups had higher prevalence rates than the control groups because a substantial number of cases were detected through FOBTs. A total of 144 cases of colorectal cancer were

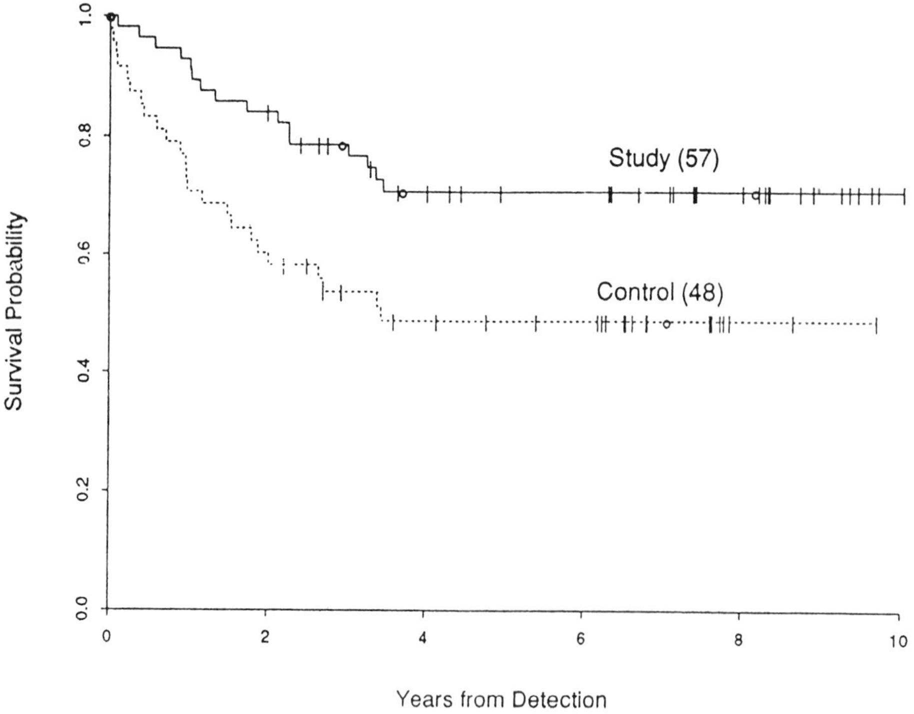

FIG. 28-1. Kaplan-Meier estimates of survival probability in trial II (first-time clinic patients). Tick marks represent patients still alive and circles represent those who died of other causes; these are treated as withdrawals. Mortality difference is highly significant ($p < .001$, logrank and modified Wilcoxon tests). See text and references for details. (From Winawer et al.[7] Reproduced by permission.)

diagnosed after the patients had entered the study (incidence cases), including those found through screening and those diagnosed outside the screening program. Incidence rates in all groups were approximately 1 per 1000 per year. A marked difference in distribution of stages was noted in the trial II prevalence cases; 18 of 26 (69 percent) study cases had Dukes A or B disease compared with 6 of 17 (35 percent) control cases. In the incidence cases, on the other hand, no stage shift was apparent, consistent with the fact that very few of them were detected through screening. There was no difference between study and control subjects in trial I. In trial II, the difference was highly significant ($p < .001$), and with long-term survival of 70 versus 48 percent (Fig. 28-1). Overall mortality was approximately the same in all four groups. As for colorectal cancer mortality, a comparison reveals a rate of 0.63 per thousand per year for the control group versus 0.36 for the study group. This difference is statistically significant at the .053 level (one-tailed test) (Table 28-1). The difference was observed in every age group (Fig. 28-2).

It is now appropriate to consider answers to the questions posed at the beginning of this trial. We found that incorporation of the FOBT into a routine comprehensive clinic examination was feasible and that approximately three-quarters of asymptomatic patients over age 40 were willing to prepare their slides at the time of enrollment in the program. Participation dropped to 16 percent at year 2 and then gradually increased, because of intensive follow-up efforts, to a maximum of 28 percent at year 6. Compliance with slide preparation for screening with the FOBT has varied in other trials from 50 percent or better in large controlled trials to as low as 15 percent in community screening programs.[8–12,15–17] Factors influencing acceptance of the screening concept and compliance with the tests have been studied and reported.[18–22]

Positivity of the FOBT was strongly age-dependent, with few positive test results in patients below the age of 50 years, and the proportion of positive tests demonstrated in the first examination was highest in the group without prior screening experience (3.9 percent). The predictive value of the test for polyps and cancer was age-dependent and was greatest on the first screen. Thus, it was clear that the greatest yield of neoplasms from the FOBT results from screening people aged 50 and older who have not been examined for

Table 28-1
Mortality Rates

	Trial I		*Trial II*	
	Study group	*Control group*	*Study group*	*Control group*
Person-years	51,545	14,640	33,543	34,675
Total deaths	365	94	259	270
Mortality rate[a]	7.1	6.4	7.7	7.8
Colorectal cancer deaths	24	6	12	22
Mortality rate[a]	0.47	0.41	0.36	0.63

[a]Mortality rate = no. of deaths per 1000 per year in the study and control groups. See text and references for details.

SOURCE: From Winawer et al.[7] Reproduced by permission.

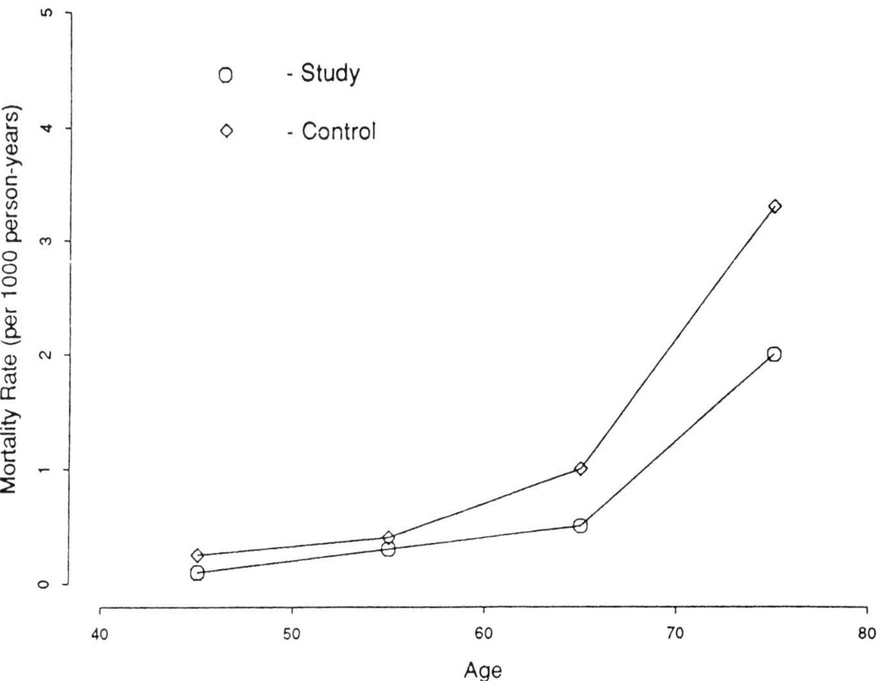

FIG. 28-2. Colorectal cancer mortality rates in Trial II, calculated for age groups 40–49, 50–59, 60–69, and 70+. See text and references for details. (From Winawer et al.[7] Reproduced by permission.)

several years. Our findings agree with those of other controlled trials in several ways: (1) the higher predictive value for neoplasia for the first screen, (2) the strong age-dependency, and (3) the higher yield of adenomas detected compared with cancers detected.[8–12] In one trial, two-thirds of the adenomas detected at screening were greater than 1 cm in size.[12]

Three quarters of patients with positive FOBTs underwent adequate diagnostic procedures after their tests. It was clear that colonoscopy was an essential part of the workup, since the barium enema missed 25 percent of the neoplastic lesions found through colonoscopy. Other large screening trials also depend on colonoscopy for diagnosis.[8–12]

It has not been possible to evaluate directly the effect of detecting and removing precancerous adenomas. Identification and removal of adenomas has been reported in another trial to reduce the incidence of subsequent colorectal cancer.[22] In trial II, a statistically significant difference in the distribution of Dukes staging between study and control groups was observed with respect to those cancers found on the first screen. Furthermore, there was a statistically significant difference in survival probability for all trial II patients, with an estimated long-term survival of 70 percent for the study group compared with 48 percent for the control group. The shift to earlier-stage cancers in the screened group compared with the control group was also observed in other trials.[8–12] Survival has been shown to be improved by the FOBT in one other trial.[23]

Trial II reveals a difference in colorectal cancer mortality of borderline statistical significance. Another trial recently reported has demonstrated a significant reduction in mortality from colorectal cancer in subjects screened annually with rehydrated FOBTs.[23] This will be described in detail below.

University of Minnesota (U.S.) Trial

The Minnesota Colon Cancer Control Study, begun in 1975, reported end-point results of long-term fecal occult blood screening.[23] The study is a randomized controlled trial of the value of fecal occult blood screening in reducing mortality from colorectal cancer. Funded by the U.S. National Cancer Institute, the study enrolled 46,551 participants 50 to 80 years of age from 1975 through 1977. Exclusion criteria included a history of large bowel cancer, familial polyposis, chronic ulcerative colitis, or significant comorbidity. After stratification for age, gender, and place of residence (urban versus rural), participants were randomized to three equal groups. One group was screened annually, one group was screened every other year (biennially), and the third group served as controls.

Participants in the two screening groups were asked to submit six Hemoccult slides containing two fecal smears from each of three consecutive stools after a 24-h meat-free diet and abstinence from vitamin C and aspirin. Because the mailing of slides to the study center delayed their processing for up to 8 days, the process of rehydrating the slides before developing was instituted in 1977.

Participants with a positive screening test (at least one of the six slides positive) were asked to undergo an evaluation, including colonoscopy, at the University of Minnesota Hospital. If colonoscopy was suboptimal or incomplete, a double-contrast barium enema was performed. All visible polypoid lesions were biopsied or resected. Patients with cancers were referred for surgery and patients with neoplasia were subsequently followed by their primary physicians. The participants in all three groups were followed with a mailed annual health questionnaire to ascertain their vital status, the occurrence of colorectal cancer and polyps in the control group participants, and the detection of any colorectal lesions by other means in the screening group. All deaths in the study cohort were reviewed by an independent Deaths Review Committee in order to determine whether colorectal cancer had been the underlying cause of death. Difference in mortality from colorectal cancer between each of the two screening groups and the control group were monitored in a group sequential analysis by means of the sequential logrank statistic as computed from life tables through year 13, the last complete year of follow-up.

The cumulative mortality from colorectal cancer in the annually screened group was reduced by 33 percent compared with that of the control group. This statistically significant reduction appears largely to result from a 50 percent decrease in the number of incurable cancers (stage D) in the screened group compared with the control group. The detection of cancers before they develop to stage D had a profound effect on mortality, since the 5-year survival for patients with stage D cancers was only 2.4 percent. A statistically nonsignificant 6 percent reduction in colorectal cancer mortality was observed in the biennially screened group. Additional follow-up is necessary to evaluate the efficacy of screening every 2 years. The survival data were consistent with the mortality and stage-shift data. Survival was best in the annually screened group, intermediate in the biennially screened group, and poorest in the controls.

The sensitivity of the Hemoccult screening test was determined employing the assumptions that cases of colorectal cancer detected within 1 year after a positive screening test were true positives and that those detected within 1 year after a negative screening were false negatives. Overall, 82.5 percent of the slides were rehydrated. As the result of rehydration, the rate of positive results increased fourfold, from 2.8 to 9.8 percent; sensitivity for colorectal cancer increased from 80.8 to 92.2 percent; and specificity decreased from 97.7 to 90.4 percent. With the loss of specificity, the positive predictive value for cancers decreased from 5.6 to 2.2 percent.

The 33 percent reduction in mortality observed in the annually screened group strongly supports current recommendations for annual fecal occult blood screening by the American Cancer Society, the U.S. National Cancer Institute, and the World Health Organization—U.S. Collaborating Center for the Prevention of Colorectal Cancer. This proven reduction is considered a minimum figure by the Minnesota trial investigators, because 10 percent of the participants assigned to the annual screening group did not participate in any screens, and only 46 percent of this group completed all screens. Furthermore, some screening occurred among the control group participants outside the study, there was a 3-year period during the study in which no screening was done, and only 83 percent of the screening tests were rehydrated.

By the 13th year of this long-term study, an appreciable fraction of the screening group participants had undergone at least one colonoscopy. However, a number of study findings support the independent contribution of the screening test to mortality reduction rather than being the result of "random" colonoscopy. This conclusion is supported by the high sensitivity of the screening test, the increase in the positive predictive value for cancer as the number of positive screening tests out of the set of six increased, a similar association of predictive value for large polyps likely to bleed but not for small polyps, and a much greater cumulative incidence of colorectal cancer among participants with a positive first screen compared with that of participants with a negative first screen or those not screened.

Nottingham (U.K.) Trial

A large population-based, randomized, controlled clinical trial was started more recently in England,[12] where asymptomatic individuals were identified from family physician registries. Recruitment of 156,000 persons aged 50 through 74 was completed in 1989, and rescreening is planned every other year. In the test group (52,258 subjects), 53 percent completed the FOBT, which resulted in 2.3 percent positive tests for nonhydrated slides. The initial yield of cancer was 2.3 per 1000 persons screened, and the predictive value of a positive test for colorectal cancers and adenomas was 53 percent. Fifty-three percent of cancers detected were Dukes A, compared with 10 percent in the control group; overall, 90 percent of cancers detected in the screened group were Dukes A and B, compared with 40 percent in the control group. As a result of the initial examination cycle, sensitivity was estimated at 72 percent and specificity at 98 percent (Table 28-2).

Goteborg (Sweden) Trial

Another randomized, controlled clinical trial of screening is in progress in Sweden[10] and involves 27,700 inhabitants of Goteborg, aged 60 through 64. The rate of positivity in the screened group was 1.9 percent with use of nonhydrated slides and 5.8 percent with rehydrated slides. In the initial screen, 65 percent of the cancers were Dukes A or B, compared with 33 percent in the control group. The estimated sensitivity for cancer was 52 percent with the nonhydrated slides but more than 90 percent with rehydrated slides (Table 28-2).

Table 28-2
Controlled Trials of Stool Blood Testing in Screening for Colorectal Cancer[a]

	Cohort size	*Positivity rate*	*Predictive value, %, adenomas and cancers*	*Dukes A and B cancers, %[b]*	
				Screened group	*Control group*
Goteborg, Sweden	27,000	1.9	22	65	33
Nottingham, England	150,000	2.1	53	90	40
New York, USA	22,000	1.7	30	65	33
Minnesota, USA	48,000	2.4	31	78	35
Fuhnen, Denmark	62,000	1.0	58	81	55

[a]This table, derived from multiple sources, summarizes mainly data from non-hydrated slides, although hydrated slides have also been used in a phase of some programs. The data are primarily from initial screening.

[b]The Dukes A cancers in the screened groups were 34 to 65 percent, compared with 8 percent in the control groups. See text and reference for details.

SOURCE: From Winawer et al.[1] Reproduced by permission.

Odense (Denmark) Trial

A large population-based, randomized, controlled clinical trial has recently been initiated in Denmark.[9] In this study, 62,000 participants aged 50 through 74 were randomly allocated to one of two groups: those who were offered the FOBT every other year and a control group. The first test was completed in 66 percent of those participants offered slides, with a rate of positivity of 1.0 percent, which was the lowest reported on a first screen. A reduction in mortality from colorectal cancer of 27 percent was noted in the screened group, but this did not achieve statistical significance over the relatively short follow-up period (Table 28-2).

Burgundy (France) Trial

This was a study involving 94,000 people aged 45 to 74, half of whom were offered a FOBT, the other half being controls.[24] The number of subjects was calculated as the minimal number necessary to demonstrate a 20 percent decrease in mortality from colorectal cancer after 5 years with a significance of 0.05 and 80 percent power. The screening test was offered to all residents of select towns and administrative districts of the department of Saone et Loire. Controls were residents of areas of similar size in the neighboring region of the Cote d'Or; they had a similar risk of colorectal cancer. The screening program was implemented in two phases: 27,000 subjects were included in 1988 and 22,000 in 1989. The screening campaign was organized with the collaboration of the general practitioners. Documents for public awareness were prepared with an advertising agency and general practitioners. The screening program was advertised in the local papers, municipal brochures, local radio programs, and regional television. Posters with the theme "Don't hide your head in the sand like an ostrich" were hung in the doctors' waiting rooms and offices and in the town halls.

Among the 47,150 people included in the test group 24,562 (i.e., 52.1 percent) performed the screening test. Participation was higher among women (54.7 percent) than among men (49.2 percent; $p < .001$) in all age groups. The test was more often done by people between ages 55 and 69 than those in the youngest or oldest age groups. A total of 56.9 percent of all the tests were performed after a medical consultation, 26.6 percent after mailing the test, and 16.6 percent after a subsequent recall letter. Age and sex had little influence on that distribution. The way of offering the test had an influence on the participation rate: in the areas where it was given away free by the general practitioners, the test was better accepted than in areas where it was prescribed (acceptance rate of 54.0 versus 40.0 percent $p < .001$). The colonic examination was a colonoscopy in 282 cases (98 percent). Twenty-three cancers were discovered (i.e., 1.6 per thousand rate within the population who did the test). Five cancers were located in the rectum, 17 in the left colon, and 1 in the right colon. Carcinomas were Dukes A in 12 cases, Dukes B in 6 cases, and Dukes C in 4 cases; 1 patient had distant metastases. A total of 225 polyps were discovered in 104 subjects. Among those, 194 were recovered for histological examination; there were 160 adenomas (83 percent). One or more adenomas were found in 83 subjects, and in 54 (44 percent) subjects the adenomas were larger than 1 cm. The positive predictive value of the test was 44 percent for a colorectal tumor in general, 8 percent for a cancer, and 19 percent for an adenoma more than 10 mm in diameter.

Federal Republic of Germany Trial

It was decided to conduct a feasibility study in a well-defined geographic region of the Federal Republic of Germany (FRG). The Saarland is one of the ten essential administrative areas (Länder) of the FRG. It covers a population of about 1.0 million and is of particular interest since the only yet functioning population-based cancer registry in the FRG is operating in that area. In addition, the situation in the Saarland was found to be particularly suitable, since its size would give rise to an appropriate number of colorectal deaths and the administrative requirements were deemed to be sufficiently manageable in a population of 1.0 million. In the second half of 1988, the main study was started. From the files of the pathological institutes, 2809 biopsy cases of colorectal cancer were identified which had been diagnosed between 1979 and 1985 in the age range of 45 to 74 years. A follow-up for vital status of these cases through residential registries led to the identification of 676 individuals who died between 1983 and 1986 in the age range of 55 to 74 years. The latter age and time window was defined to be most important for the evaluation of the effect on colorectal cancer mortality of colorectal cancer screening by occult blood test, which started in 1977. For all 676 deaths, contacts to a referring general practitioner were established in order to get information about cause of death and the screening history of the cases. A comparison will be made of colorectal cancer mortality in those screened and not screened. Preliminary evaluation of the data indicates a protective effect of screening.[25]

IMMUNOCHEMICAL/HEMEPORPHYRIN TESTS AND OTHER GUAIAC TESTS

A wide variety of commercial immunochemical tests are available, including the enzyme-linked immunosorbent assay (ELISA), the radial immunodiffusion test, the latex agglutination tests, and the hemagglutination test. These are predominantly qualitative tests, utilizing antibodies directed against the intact globin moiety of human hemoglobin and possibly also against large fragments of globin. As judged by in vitro studies, these tests have differing performance characteristics. As yet, no information is available about the relative merits of the tests based on direct comparisons in patients with colorectal neoplasia, in healthy subjects, or in screening populations. In general, the tests have a higher level of sensitivity for colorectal bleeding than guaiac tests, an even lower level of sensitivity for upper gastrointestinal tract bleeding, and simpler requirements for participants (test results not affected by diet or medication). Their major disadvantage is that at present, these are all laboratory tests, costing substantially more than the guaiac tests. There is little information on which to base recommendations about the various immunochemical tests. Studies on patients with symptomatic colorectal cancer indicate that the ELISA, hemagglutination, and radial immunodiffusion tests have high sensitivity.[26–28] However, in screening programs, the ELISA and radial immunodiffusion tests had disturbingly high positivity rates,[29–32] raising concern about their specificity and the likely impact that this would have on cost-effectiveness of screening. Although preliminary data were based on just 1- and 2-day testing, a lower positivity rate was reported with the hemagglutination test.[33]

The HemoQuant assay[34] is a biochemical method for the measurement of hemoglobin and its degradation products in stools. The method involves conversion of any hemoglobin and free heme to heme-derived porphyrins, followed by solvent extraction of interfering chlorophyll, coproporphyrins, and uroporphyrins with quantitation of heme-derived porphyrins by fluorimetry. On theoretical grounds, the HemoQuant test should detect upper and lower gastrointestinal tract bleeding with equal sensitivity. Moreover, test results are affected by ingestion of animal hemoglobin and myoglobin and by aspirin-induced gastroduodenal bleeding.[35,36] If HemoQuant were to be used as primary screening test, it would be essential for participants to follow a low-heme diet and to exclude aspirin and other NSAIDs. A separation between HemoQuant levels in normal subjects and patients with colorectal cancer was reported,[37] suggesting that HemoQuant could be an effective screening test. Unfortunately, the 106 healthy subjects were all on an appropriate diet free of red meat and had been advised to avoid aspirin, whereas the patients with colorectal cancer did not have any special dietary or drug restriction. These differences between the two groups could have contributed to the separation of results. The high cost of the test and the need for special dietary and drug restrictions are considerable disadvantages for a screening test. A study compared performance of the standard Hemoccult test with (1) Hemoccult SENSA, a new and more sensitive guaiac test; (2) HemeSelect, the hemagglutination test; and (3) HemoQuant in 40 patients with symptomatic colorectal cancer and in 29 patients with colorectal adenomas.[38] All subjects were on appropriate diet and drug restriction and tests were performed in parallel. The new guaiac and hemagglutination tests had higher sensitivity than the standard Hemoccult test and HemoQuant, the hemagglutination test giving particularly encouraging results in patients with adenomas. Importantly, sensitivity for colorectal cancer and adenomas was lowest with HemoQuant (Table 28-3).

STOOL BLOOD TEST COMPLIANCE AND COST EFFECTIVENESS

Patient compliance with stool blood testing has exceeded 50 percent in most controlled trials but has

Table 28-3
Comparison of Sensitivities of Various Fecal Occult Blood Tests for Large Bowel Cancer

		Fecal occult blood test							
		Hemoccult		*Hemoccult SENSA*		*HemeSelect*		*HemoQuant*[a]	
Lesion	*No.*	*n*	*%*	*n*	*%*	*n*	*%*	*n*	*%*
Cancer	49	42	86	44	90	47	96	35	71
Adenoma(s)									
All	28	7	25	12	43	19	68	8	29
≥1 cm	14	6	43	8	57	14	100	5	36
Cancer or adenoma[b]	63	48	76	52	83	61	97	40	63

[a]Positive if HemoQuant value is greater than 2 mg/g.

[b]Adenomas ≥1 cm.

n = number of positive patients. Patients were considered positive if any one of the three samples tested was positive. See text and reference for details.

SOURCE: From Young and St. John.[38] Reproduced by permission.

been as slow as 15 percent in community programs;[17] however, sustained adherence in rescreening has been difficult to achieve for some programs. In the New York trial,[7] patient compliance was high for the first screen, but patients were reluctant to return for examinations or to submit additional slides in spite of intensive efforts. Special letters were found in the English trial[8] to be very helpful in raising compliance from 38 percent to more than 50 percent. Compliance with diagnostic workup in patients with positive screening tests has been shown to be fairly high in all of the trials. Patients have shown a high acceptance of sigmoidoscopy when they present for a general examination; however, patients in general have not demonstrated a willingness to return for repeat rigid sigmoidoscopy.[7] This attitude may change with greater use of flexible sigmoidoscopes. Factors influencing patient compliance in screening have been studied.[19–21] Compliers are more likely to have had positive attitudes toward preventive health practices, to have had more recent contacts with medical services, to be better informed about cancer, and to be more optimistic and less frightened about cancer. An American Cancer Society survey[39] showed frequent disturbing public misconceptions regarding colorectal cancer. Although the American Cancer Society surveys indicate an increasing emphasis on early cancer detection and increasing use of stool blood testing, the approach by physicians to the diagnostic workup of patients with a positive screening test has not been consistent or uniformly systematic.[40]

One cost-benefit analysis suggested a financial savings and a projected increase in life expectancy as a result of stool testing.[41] Mathematical models have provided some insights into the range of cost-benefit and cost-effectiveness expectations.[42,43] The Office of Technology Assessment (OTA) in the United States estimated that screening people over age 65 with stool blood testing annually and flexible sigmoidoscopy every 3 to 5 years would result in a cost of approximately $25,000 per person-year of life saved. This is comparable to the cost-effectiveness of screening mammography in women over age 50. Cost-effectiveness calculations based on the University of Minnesota trial indicated a similar cost per person-year of life saved from annual stool blood testing with rehydrated slides.

CONCLUSION

There are now two studies that have demonstrated the effectiveness of screening for colorectal cancer with stool blood testing. The Minnesota randomized trial clearly has shown a reduced mortality in the annually screened group. Although the group screened every other year has not as yet shown a reduced mortality, they have had a shift to earlier-stage cancers and an improved survival. The New York study demonstrated a reduced mortality significant at the .053 level when stool blood testing was added to sigmoidoscopy as compared with sigmoidoscopy alone. The latter study was controlled and patients were enrolled by calendar period in a busy clinic setting rather than randomized. The ongoing European studies and all prior noncontrolled trials have shown a stage shift consistent with the improved survival and mortality reduction of the completed American trials. It would be difficult to consider that all the positive worldwide data are due to screening bias. Many questions remain, however. An important issue is what slide to use. The Minnesota trial used previously rehydrated slides which increased the false-positive rate,[23] while all the other trials used nonhydrated slides with a lower false-positive rate but also lower sensitivity.[1] The Swedish trial has nicely demonstrated the sensitivity and specificity of the two approaches. Rehydration of the slides can produce variability of the test performance, so it is not ideal. Newer tests such as the Hemesensa are said to produce a high sensitivity similar to that of the rehydrated slide without loss of specificity.[40] This may be a good choice for the next slide test.

We now have effective screening methods, the ability to find and remove polyps, and the ability to detect and treat early cancers with effective surgery. Polyp detection makes the screening approach more attractive, since it is the more common neoplastic finding in positive patients, and removal of polyps reduces the incidence of future cancer.[3] There is a critical need to provide this entire screening-diagnostic-treatment approach to people in a cost-effective manner, and there is a tremendous need to educate the public about the importance of colorectal cancer, the availability of these approaches, and the need to have symptoms and high-risk factors addressed. While we now have effective techniques to reduce the mortality of colorectal cancer, we will in the future have even better approaches. These undoubtedly will encompass genetic screening followed by colonoscopic polypectomy in individuals with demonstrated susceptibility.[45] To this approach, we can add new concepts of primary prevention when evidence provides a basis for this broad application.[46]

REFERENCES

1. Winawer SJ, Schottenfeld D, Flehinger BJ: Colorectal cancer screening. *J Natl Cancer Inst* 84:243, 1991.
2. Winawer SJ, St. John J, Bond J, et al: Screening of average-risk individuals for colorectal cancer. *Bull WHO* 68:505, 1990.

3. Winawer SJ, Zauber AG, Ho MN, et al: Prevention of colorectal cancer by colonoscopic polypectomy. *N Engl J Med* 329:1977, 1993.
4. Enker WE: Extent of operations for large bowel cancer, in DeCosse JJ (ed): *Large Bowel Cancer.* New York, Churchill-Livingston, 1981, pp 78–93.
5. Greegor DH: Diagnosis of large bowel cancer in the asymptomatic patient. *JAMA* 201:943, 1967.
6. Greegor DH: Occult blood testing for detection of asymptomatic colon cancer. *Cancer* 28:131, 1971.
7. Winawer SJ, Flehinger BJ, Schottenfeld D, Miller DG: Screening for colorectal cancer with fecal occult blood testing and sigmoidoscopy. *J Natl Cancer Inst* 85:1311, 1993.
8. Gilbertsen VA, McHugh R, Schuman L, et al: The early detection of colorectal cancer: A preliminary report of the results of the occult blood supply. *Cancer* 45:2899, 1980.
9. Kronborg O, Fenger C, Worm J, et al: Causes of death during the first 5 years of a randomized trial of mass screening for colorectal cancer with fecal occult blood test. *Scand J Gastroenterol* 27:47, 1992.
10. Kewenter J, Bjork S, Haglind E, et al: Screening and rescreening for colorectal cancer: A controlled trial of fecal occult blood testing in 27,700 subjects. *Cancer* 62:645–651, 1988.
11. Kewenter J, Asztely M, Engaras B, et al: A randomized trial of fecal occult blood testing for early detection of colorectal cancer: Results of screening and rescreening of 51,325 subjects, in Miller AB, Chamberlain J, Day NE, et al (eds): Cancer *Screening.* Cambridge, England, Cambridge University Press, 1991, pp 117–125.
12. Hardcastle JD, Thomas WM, Chamberlain J, et al: Randomized, controlled trial of fecal occult blood screening for colorectal cancer: Results of the first 107,349 subjects. *Lancet* 1:1160, 1989.
13. Kaplan EL, Meier P: Non-parametric estimation from incomplete observations. *J Am Stat Assoc* 53:457, 1958.
14. Fleisher M, Schwartz M, Winawer SJ: The false negative Hemoccult test: Rapid communication. *Gastroenterology* 72:782, 1977.
15. Selby JV, Friedman GD, Quesenberry CP Jr, et al: Effect of occult blood testing on mortality from colorectal cancer: A case control study. *Ann Intern Med* 118:1, 1993.
16. Winchester DP, Sylvester J, Maher MI: Risks and benefits of mass screening for colorectal neoplasia with stool guaiac test, in *Detecting Colon and Rectum Cancer.* New York: American Cancer Society, 1983, pp 5–15.
17. Bralow SP, Kopel J: Hemoccult screening for colorectal cancer: An impact study on Sarasota, Florida. *J Fla Med Assoc* 66:915, 1979.
18. Elwood TW, Erickson A, Lieberman S: Comparative educational approaches to screening for colorectal cancer. *Am J Public Health* 68:135, 1978.
19. Farrands PA, Hardcastle JD, Chamberlain J, et al: Factors affecting compliance with screening for colorectal cancer. *Community Med* 6:12, 1984.
20. Dent OF, Bartrop R, Goulston KJ, et al: Participation in fecal occult blood screening for colorectal cancer. *Soc Sci Med* 17:17, 1983.
21. Halper M, Winawer SJ, Brody RS, et al: Issues of patient compliance, in Winawer SJ, Schottenfeld D, Sherlock P (eds): *Colorectal Cancer: Prevention, Epidemiology and Screening.* New York, Raven Press, 1980, pp 299–310.
22. Simon JB: Occult blood screening for colorectal carcinoma: A critical review. *Gastroenterology* 88:820, 1985.
23. Mandel JS, Bond JH, Church TR, et al: Reducing mortality from colorectal cancer by screening for fecal occult blood. *N Engl J Med* 328:1365, 1993.
24. Faivre J, Arveux P, Milan C, et al: Participation in mass screening for colorectal cancer: Results of screening and rescreening from the Burgundy study. *Eur J Cancer Prev* 1:49, 1991.
25. Robra BP, Wahrendorf J: Fecal occult blood screening in the Federal Republic of Germany, in Hardcastle JD (ed): *Screening for Colorectal Cancer.* (Proceedings of an international meeting held at the Royal College of Physicians on May 24, 1989; organized by the United Kingdom Coordinating Committee on Cancer Research.) Bad Homburg, Madrid, Englewood, NJ, Normed Verlag, 1990, pp 70–77.
26. Turunen MJ, Liewendahl K, Partanen P, et al: Immunological detection of fecal occult blood in colorectal cancer. *Br J Cancer* 49:141, 1984.
27. Satio H, et al: An immunological occult blood test for mass screening of colorectal cancer by reverse passive hemagglutination (RPHA). *Jpn J Gastroenterol* 81:2831, 1984.
28. McDonald C, Burford Y, Walls R, et al: Immunochemical testing for fecal occult blood in patients with colorectal cancer. *Med J Aust* 143:141, 1985.
29. Armitage N, Hardcastle JD, Amar SS, et al: A comparison of an immunological fecal occult blood test Fecatwin sensitive/FECA EIA with Haemoccult in population screening for colorectal cancer. *Br J Cancer* 51:799, 1985.
30. Kakkinen I, Paasivuo R, Partanen P: Screening for colorectal tumors using an improved fecal occult blood test: Quantitative aspects. *Gut* 29:1194, 1988.
31. Williams JAR, Hunter R, Thomas DW, et al: Evaluation of immunochemical test for fecal occult blood in screening for colorectal neoplasia in a high risk group. *Aust NZ J Surg* 57:951, 1987.
32. Frommer DJ, Kapparis A, Brown MK: Improved screening for colorectal cancer by immunological detection of occult blood. *Br Med J* 296:1092, 1988.
33. Aisawa T, Saito H, Kawaguchi H, et al: Mass screening for colon cancer using an immunologic fecal occult blood test by reversed passive hemagglutination (RPHA): Comparison of single RPHA with 2 day testing. Proc 8th Asian-Pacific Congress of Gastroenterology 1988; FP23-5.
34. Schwartz S, Dahl J, Ellefson M, et al: The "HemoQuant" test: A specific and quantitative determination of heme (hemoglobulin) in feces and other materials. *Clin Chem* 29:2061, 1983.
35. Rose IS, Young GP, St John DJB, et al: Effect of ingestion of hemoproteins on fecal excretion of hemes and poryphyrins. *Clin Chem* 35:2290, 1989.
36. Fleming JL, Ahlquist DA, McGill DG, et al: Influence of aspirin and ethanol on fecal blood levels as determined by using the HemoQuant assay. *Mayo Clin Proc* 62:159, 1987.
37. Ahlquist DA, McGill DB, Schwartz S, et al: Fecal blood level in health and disease: A study using HemoQuant. *N Engl J Med* 312:1422, 1985.
38. Young GP, St John DJB: Selecting an occult blood test for use as a screening tool for large bowel cancer, in Rozen P, Reich CB, Winawer SJ (eds): *Large Bowel Cancer: Policy, Prevention, Research and Treatment,* vol 18. *Frontiers in Gastroinestinal Research.* Basel, Karger, 1991, pp 135–156.
39. American Cancer Society: Cancer of the colon and rectum: A summary of a public attitude survey. *CA* 333:31, 1983.
40. American Cancer Society: Survey of physicians' attitudes and practices in early cancer detection. *CA* 35:197, 1985.
41. Allison JE, Feldman R: Cost benefits of Hemoccult screening for colorectal carcinoma. *Dig Dis Sci* 9:860, 1985.
42. Eddy DM: Screening for colorectal cancer. *Ann Intern Med* 113:373, 1990.
43. Crespi M, Caperle M, Dellamano R, et al. (edited by V.

Ghetti): Cost-benefit analysis of colorectal cancer screening: A mathematical model. Milan, Italy, Franco Angeli Libri, 1990.

44. St John DJB. Fecal occult blood tests: A critical review, in Hardcastle JD (ed): *Screening for Colorectal Cancer.* (Proceedings of an international meeting held at the Royal College of Physicians on May 24, 1989; organized by the United Kingdom Coordinating Committee on Cancer Research.) Bad Homburg, Madrid, Englewood NJ, Normed Verlag, 1990, pp 54–68.

45. Liu ET: From the molecule to public health (editorial). *N Engl J Med* 329:2028, 1993.

46. Shike M, Winawer SJ, Greenwald PH, et al: Primary prevention of colorectal cancer. *Bull WHO* 68:377, 1990.

CHAPTER 29

Clinical Trials of Screening Sigmoidoscopy

Joe V. Selby

HIGHLIGHTS

Two recently published case-control studies of sigmoidoscopy screening have provided the first evidence from controlled studies that sigmoidoscopy can lead to a reduction in mortality from colorectal cancer. The studies are consistent in suggesting an approximate 60 to 70 percent reduction in mortality from cancers within reach of the sigmoidoscope. Because 50 to 60 percent of all colorectal cancers are detectable by the 60-cm sigmoidoscope, these studies suggest that periodic sigmoidoscopy screening could lower total colorectal cancer mortality by 30 to 40 percent.

One of the studies also provided evidence that the interval between screening examinations could be lengthened to 5 or even 10 years after a negative examination. This finding has important implications for the costs of screening. It also suggests that much of the benefit of screening derives from the removal of premalignant lesions, or adenomatous polyps.

Flexible sigmoidoscopy is an extremely safe procedure in the asymptomatic patient. Screening 60-cm sigmoidoscopy will detect adenomatous polyps in approximately 8 to 10 percent of persons of average colorectal cancer risk who are age 50 years and above. More than 50 percent of these individuals will have only a single small adenoma (less than 1 cm in diameter). Several recent studies have suggested that this group is not at increased risk for colorectal cancer. Thus, it may be possible to forego the currently recommended initial colonoscopy or the subsequent surveillance colonoscopies recommended for this group. If so, the costs of a screening program would be lowered dramatically.

The recent case-control studies provide a new degree of certainty regarding the efficacy of the examination. On the basis of these studies, screening sigmoidoscopy can be recommended for average-risk persons beginning at age 50. Persons at substantially increased risk of colorectal cancer should have full colonoscopy rather than sigmoidoscopy. Such persons include those with inflammatory bowel disease, hereditary adenomatous polyposis syndromes, a family history of hereditary nonpolyposis colorectal cancer, a family history of two or more first-degree relatives with colorectal cancer, or a single first-degree relative who developed the disease before age 55. Persons with a single first-degree relative who develops colorectal cancer after age 55 may have a slight increase in risk, but this relatively large group should be screened with flexible sigmoidoscopy beginning at age 40. Persons found to have an adenomatous polyp either at screening or because of symptoms should also be followed with periodic colonoscopy, particularly if the adenoma is larger than 1 cm in diameter.

CONTROVERSIES

It will be argued that the case-control studies are insufficient evidence on which to base the initiation of large-scale sigmoidoscopy screening, and that only a randomized trial could justify this step. However, the magnitude of the protective effect seen in the two case-control studies is so great that it would be nearly impossible for confounding to explain the bulk of this effect. A randomized trial will take at least 15 years to be completed and runs the risk of failing to show a true effect because of noncompliance in the study group or crossover screening in the control group. Thus, the prudent course would be to initiate screening and to monitor incidence and mortality rates in screened populations.

Disagreement prevails regarding the workup and surveillance of the large numbers of persons who will be found to have only a single small adenoma at screening sigmoidoscopy. Current recommendations are that each of these persons needs full colonoscopy both initially and periodically thereafter. Several authors have recently pointed out that these individuals are not at increased risk for developing colorectal cancer. If they are not, there is little rationale for the intensive workup and surveillance.

There is a lack of consensus on appropriate screening of individuals with a single first-degree relative who has colorectal cancer. Some authorities recommend full colonoscopy for screening; others suggest flexible sigmoidoscopy with or without fecal occult blood testing. A compromise suggestion is to perform colonoscopy if the relative was diagnosed before reaching age 55, in which case genetic risk may be greater, but to perform sigmoidoscopy for the vast majority of individuals with a relative who was diagnosed after reaching age 55.

FUTURE DIRECTIONS

A randomized trial of sigmoidoscopy was initiated in 1992 by the National Cancer Institute. This study will require 15 years to provide mortality data. However, some information may be obtained earlier on incidence, which sigmoidoscopy should also reduce.

Additional data are needed on the findings at initial and surveillance colonoscopies in persons with various sizes and numbers of adenomas at screening sigmoidoscopy. These data should help to clarify the need for colonoscopic workup and surveillance in these individuals. More data are also needed to quantify the degree of risk associated with single first-degree relatives with colorectal cancer, with particular attention to the relative's age at diagnosis.

Periodic endoscopic examination of the rectum and sigmoid colon in asymptomatic persons has been recommended for at least 40 years as a means of reducing mortality from colorectal cancer.[1-3] Colorectal cancer's position as the third leading cause of cancer mortality in both men and women in the United States[4] justifies consideration of large-scale screening for this cancer if a safe, affordable, and effective test can be identified. Sigmoidoscopy offers the potential for both earlier detection of cancers and a reduction in cancer incidence by the discovery and removal of premalignant adenomatous polyps. Nevertheless, most recent reviews[5-7] have not recommended periodic screening sigmoidoscopy for average-risk persons. A lack of controlled study evidence of mortality reduction with screening was cited in two of these reviews,[5,6] while the costs and discomfort associated with sigmoidoscopy explained exclusion of sigmoidoscopy in the third report.[7]

In this chapter we evaluate the available evidence regarding the efficacy of periodic screening sigmoidoscopy for reducing mortality from colorectal cancer in average-risk persons. In particular, we review two recent case-control reports that provide the first controlled study evidence of a reduction in colorectal cancer mortality with sigmoidoscopy screening. The 60-cm flexible sigmoidoscope has become the overwhelming choice for colorectal screening. The performance characteristics of this instrument for screening tests—including its sensitivity, specificity, diagnostic yield, patient and physician acceptability, and safety—are considered. Finally, we discuss the age at which to begin screening and the appropriate interval between screening examinations. Brief mention is made of the workup of patients with a positive screening sigmoidoscopy, because decisions regarding this workup bear heavily on the ultimate costs of a screening program.

EVIDENCE REGARDING THE EFFICACY OF SCREENING SIGMOIDOSCOPY IN ASYMPTOMATIC PERSONS

Randomized Controlled Trials

Ideally, the efficacy of a screening test should be evaluated in an experimental study in which mortality from the disease in question is contrasted between screened and nonscreened groups, with comparability assured by random assignment of participants to the two groups. When mortality is used as the outcome, the analysis tests both the ability of the screening test to detect disease earlier and the superiority of early treatment over treatment delayed until the onset of symptoms.

Although screening sigmoidoscopy has been recommended and practiced for more than 40 years in this country, not a single randomized trial of sigmoidoscopy has yet been conducted. Hesitation in initiating such a trial can probably be attributed to the very large sample size and long follow-up (and therefore high costs) that would be necessary to detect a mortality reduction and to concerns that noncompliance with screening in the intervention group could obscure a true benefit of screening. Despite these concerns, the National Cancer Institute is currently beginning a cancer screening trial that will include periodic sigmoidoscopy along with screening for lung, prostate, and ovarian cancer.[8] This study, which aims to enroll and follow 148,000 persons age 50 and above for at least 16 years, will have sufficient power to detect a 20 percent reduction in colorectal cancer mortality in the intervention group.

In the past, results of the Kaiser Permanente Multiphasic Evaluation Study[9–11] have been cited as randomized trial evidence of the efficacy of sigmoidoscopy. Screening sigmoidoscopy was not, however, the randomized intervention in this study. Rather, 10,713 members of the Kaiser Permanente Medical Care Program between the ages of 35 and 54 years were randomly assigned to a study group which received an annual urging to schedule a multiphasic health checkup or to a control group which received no such urging but was free to attend a checkup whenever desired. At the multiphasic, members of either group who were 40 years of age or older were encouraged to schedule an examination by rigid sigmoidoscope. The study began in 1965. By 7 years of follow-up, study group members had taken nearly three times as many multiphasics as the controls, and a significant difference was already apparent in mortality from colorectal cancer favoring the study group (2 versus 10 deaths in these approximately equally sized groups). This difference persisted after 16 years of follow-up (Table 29-1).

However, reexamination of these data[11] has shown that sigmoidoscopy probably did not lead to this mortality reduction. Review of medical records for the first 10 years of the study (1965–1974) showed that only 31 percent of study group members ever had a sigmoidoscopy, despite the repeated urging, while 26 percent of control group members also had at least one sigmoidoscopy (Table 29-1). This small excess of sigmoidoscopies in the study group would not be expected to lead to discovery of more than one or at most two asymptomatic early cancers.[11]

Mortality was reduced most strikingly for cancers arising within reach of the sigmoidoscope. Approximately two-thirds of this mortality reduction was due to lower cancer incidence in the study group. Yet the polypectomy rate at or after sigmoidoscopy did not differ between groups, suggesting again that screening sigmoidoscopy does not appear to explain this lowered incidence. Most colorectal cancers in each group were detected after the onset of symptoms rather than by screening. The improvement in stage distribution noted for study group tumors was nearly as great for tumors diagnosed because of symptoms as for the patients without symptoms.

In view of the numerous mortality categories examined in this study, the most likely explanation for the striking reduction in colorectal cancer mortality in the study group is chance. It is plausible, however, that exposure to other aspects of the multiphasic ex-

Table 29-1
Colorectal Cancer Incidence, Mortality, and Screening History in the Kaiser Permanente Multiphasic Evaluation Study

	Study group, n=5156	*Control group, n=5557*
Cumulative cancer incidence, 1965–1982 (per 1000 members/18 years)		
Within reach of sigmoidoscope	4.3	6.7[a]
Above reach of sigmoidoscope	4.1	4.9
Cancer mortality, 1965–1982 (per 1000 members/18 years)		
Within reach of sigmoidoscope	1.4	2.7[a]
Above reach of sigmoidoscope	1.7	2.3
Case fatality rate		
Within reach of sigmoidoscope	7/22 (0.32)	15/37 (0.41)
Above reach of sigmoidoscope	9/21 (0.43)	13/27 (0.48)
Number (and %) of persons having at least one sigmoidoscopy, 1965–1974	1585 (30.7)	1434 (25.8)
Total number of colorectal polyps removed, 1965–1974	103	110

[a]$p < .10$ for study-control differences.

amination could have led study group participants to report symptoms from colorectal cancer earlier in the course of their disease or to alter their lifestyles so as to reduce the incidence or aggressiveness of these cancers. It must be emphasized that the Kaiser Permanente Multiphasic Evaluation Study does not provide evidence against the efficacy of screening sigmoidoscopy. It simply was not designed to study sigmoidoscopy. Given its small size and the relatively young age of study participants, it would have been unreasonable to expect a detectable mortality reduction from colorectal cancer due to sigmoidoscopy over the period of follow-up, even if the entire study group had been screened appropriately.

To summarize, there are no randomized trial data regarding the utility of screening sigmoidoscopy, and it is a virtual certainty that there will be none before the year 2008. With this in mind, the need to critically review data from observational studies becomes clear.

Observational Analytic Studies

Nonrandomized comparisons of screened and unscreened groups, designed either as cohort or case-control studies, can also provide information on the efficacy of a screening test.[12,13] However, lack of randomization to screening can introduce bias in these studies. It is possible, for example, that health-conscious, compliant patients will be more likely to undergo sigmoidoscopy screening and less likely to develop or die from colorectal cancer even if sigmoidoscopy has no benefit. Such self-selection factors could create or exaggerate the appearance of a protective effect of screening. It is also possible that higher-risk subjects, such as those with a family history of colorectal cancer, may be more apt to undergo screening. This bias would tend to reduce or obscure a true benefit of screening. Thus, observational studies require careful scrutiny for the possibility of confounding by self-selection factors.

Two case-control studies of sigmoidoscopy screening comprise the entire literature of observational analytic studies of screening sigmoidoscopy.[14,15] The two studies are consistent in suggesting a substantial reduction in mortality from rectal and rectosigmoid cancer in the persons who have been screened. Case-control methods have not yet been used extensively for evaluating screening tests and may be unfamiliar to many clinicians and policymakers. As with case-control studies generally, "cases" are defined as an adverse outcome which screening is intended to prevent. For sigmoidoscopy, this adverse outcome is death from rectal or distal colonic cancer. Controls must be drawn from the same population as the cases. Controls reflect the level of screening that has occurred in that population. A deficit of screening among cases in the period before diagnosis, demonstrated by an odds ratio estimate significantly below 1, suggests a protective effect of the screening test.

Case-control methods are frequently criticized for their susceptibility to several biases, most notably to selection bias associated with choice of either the cases, the controls, or both, and to recall bias, which can occur when exposures are determined after case or control status has been established. These two studies avoided both these biases. Each was conducted in a health maintenance organization (HMO) population, where full ascertainment of fatal cases was possible. Controls could be sampled from the same HMO cohort from which cases were derived. Exposure to screening tests before case diagnosis was recorded from medical records of the HMO. This type of study can be considered a "nested" case-control study because the case-control comparisons are nested within the cohort of HMO members. Nested case-control studies are essentially equivalent to cohort studies, in which a sample of noncases rather than all noncases are selected for detailed ascertainment of exposure history.

The first of these studies[14] was quite small and included only 21 cases of rectal or rectosigmoid cancer. Among these 21 cases and their matched controls, the odds ratio (OR) for ever having had a screening sigmoidoscopy before case diagnosis was 0.23, suggesting a 77 percent reduction in rectal cancer mortality associated with being screened. Curiously, a strong "protective" effect of sigmoidoscopy was also suggested in this study for cancers above reach of the sigmoidoscope (OR = 0.35). Because most colon cancers could not have been reached with sigmoidoscopy, this suggests that some of the apparent benefit of sigmoidoscopy might have been due to confounding self-selection factors.

In a much larger case-control study conducted within the Kaiser Permanente Medical Care Program,[15] exposure to screening during the 10-year period before case diagnosis was compared for 261 cases of fatal colorectal cancer within reach of the rigid sigmoidoscope and 868 matched controls (Table 29-2). A number of possible confounding factors—including number of health checkups taken during the interval, number of other cancer screening tests, personal and family history of colorectal cancer, and a personal history of colorectal adenomas—were determined from medical record review. Each of these factors was related to the likelihood of being screened with sigmoidoscopy. The unadjusted OR for having had at least one screening sigmoidoscopy was 0.30. After adjusting for the entire list of confounders mentioned above, the OR rose to 0.41, which was still highly significant. This adjusted OR is probably a somewhat conservative estimate of effect, because the "confounder" that raised the OR to 0.41 (number of health checkups taken) was a prerequisite for getting screen-

Table 29-2
Results of Case-Control Study of Screening Sigmoidoscopy for Cancers within *and* above Reach of the Sigmoidoscope

Within reach of sigmoidoscope				
Adjustments	*Cases (n = 261)*	*Controls (n = 868)*	*Odds ratio*[a]	*95% confidence interval*
Unadjusted	23 (9%)	210 (24%)	0.30	(0.19–0.48)
History of colorectal cancer, polyp, or family history of colorectal cancer and number of periodic health checkups			0.41	(0.25–0.69)
Above reach of sigmoidoscope				
Adjustments	*Cases (n = 268)*	*Controls (n = 268)*	*Odds ratio*[a]	*95% confidence interval*
Unadjusted	56 (21%)	67 (25%)	0.80	(0.54–1.19)
History of colorectal cancer, polyp, or family history of colorectal cancer and number of periodic health checkups			0.96	(0.61–1.50)

[a]Odds ratios obtained from matched conditional logistic regression models.

ing sigmoidoscopy in some centers. Thus, inclusion of this variable may have "overadjusted" the estimate. The best estimate of the effect of screening sigmoidoscopy from this study is a mortality reduction of 59 to 75 percent for cancers that are within reach of the sigmoidoscope.

To further test for possible confounding by self-selection factors, 268 cases arising above the reach of the sigmoidoscope were compared with 268 matched controls in separate analyses (Table 29-2). For these cancers, sigmoidoscopy should provide little if any true benefit, but confounders could create a spurious protective effect. Suggestion of a small reduction in risk was seen before adjustment (OR = 0.80), but after adjusting for number of health checkups taken, there was no remaining evidence of efficacy (adjusted OR = 0.96). Thus, the adjustments made appeared to account for most confounding factors, suggesting further that the low OR estimate for cancers within reach of the sigmoidoscope reflects true efficacy rather than confounding.

This study also examined the question of the appropriate interval between screening sigmoidoscopies. In analyses that considered the efficacy of an individual's most recent screening examination (Table 29-3), no diminution of efficacy was seen if that sigmoidoscopy occurred as long as 9 to 10 years before diagnosis. This finding suggests that, for persons who have had a negative screening sigmoidoscopy, risk for subsequent mortality will remain reduced for at least 10 years thereafter. Intervals longer than 10 years could not be assessed in this study. However, the finding of persistent risk reduction for 10 years is consistent with what is currently known of the development and progression of colorectal adenomas toward cancer.[16–20] Taken together, these two studies provide the strongest evidence to date that endoscopic visualization of the lower bowel can lead to a reduction in mortality from colorectal cancer in that area. The persistence of the mortality reduction for at least 9 to 10 years indicates that removal of premalignant adenomas, as well as the early detection of cancers, must contribute to the mortality reduction and implies that the majority of colorectal cancers do indeed arise from polyps.

Descriptive Studies

Many descriptive studies have reported the results of series of screening examinations, presenting the stage distribution and mortality experience of the cancers discovered at screening with no reference to unscreened comparison groups. Descriptive studies are often cited as evidence for the effectiveness of screening, because the cancers detected by screening consistently have an earlier stage distribution and carry a better survival rate than cancers detected after the onset of symptoms. However, these differences may not reflect a true benefit of screening.[21,22] Colorectal cancers appear to grow at widely varying rates.[23] At any point in time, slower-growing tumors are more likely to be present but still undetected than more aggressive

Table 29-3
Timing of Most Recent Screening Sigmoidoscopy—253 Cases and 762 Controls Who Had at Most One Screening Examination in 10 Years[a]

Most recent sigmoidoscopy, years	*Cases having sigmoidoscopy in interval*	*Controls having sigmoidoscopy in interval*	*Matched odds ratio[b]*	*95% confidence interval*
	n (%)[c]	*n* (%)[c]		
1–2	4 (1.6)	27 (3.5)	0.41	(0.14–1.22)
3–4	5 (2.0)	20 (2.7)	0.74	(0.27–2.01)
5–6	5 (2.0)	30 (4.2)	0.44	(0.17–1.15)
7–8	1 (0.4)	22 (3.2)	0.11	(0.01–0.83)
9–10	1 (0.4)	21 (3.2)	0.12	(0.02–0.93)

[a]Eight cases and 106 controls with screens in more than one interval were excluded to remove possibility of "healthy screenee" bias.

[b]Estimates obtained from a single conditional logistic regression model. Referent category is persons with no sigmoidoscopy during 10-year interval.

[c]% refers to those still at risk for most recent sigmoidoscopy (i.e., those who had a more recent sigmoidoscopy are excluded from the denominator).

tumors, and they are therefore more likely to be noted at a screening examination. The inclusion of a greater proportion of these less aggressive tumors in series of screen-detected cases than in series of tumors detected because of symptoms has been called *length bias*. *Lead-time bias* refers to the appearance of improved survival in screen-detected cases that results from moving the diagnosis forward by screening, lengthening the interval from diagnosis to death rather than lengthening life. This bias is most notable when short follow-up periods, such as 5-year survival rates, are used. *Prognostic selection bias* can occur if patients undergoing screening, by virtue of having better health habits than the general population, have lower mortality or longer survival because they are more resistant to the tumor or more compliant with therapy. These three biases invalidate comparisons of stage distribution or survival between series of screen-detected cancers and series of cancers detected because of symptoms.

One frequently cited descriptive study covered 47,091 rigid sigmoidoscopic examinations performed in 26,196 patients at the Strang Cancer Prevention Clinic at the Memorial Sloan-Kettering Hospital between 1946 and 1954.[24] A small portion (11.5 percent) of the group presented for symptoms; the remainder were asymptomatic. Eighty-one percent of the cases discovered by sigmoidoscopy were localized (stage B or better) at diagnosis, and the 15-year survival rate was 88 percent. This stage distribution and survival rate are much better than those for series of cancers detected because of symptoms.

Another widely cited descriptive study of rigid sigmoidoscopy is that of Gilbertsen et al.[25,26] In this study, 21,150 persons of age 45 and over underwent initial screening sigmoidoscopy and a variable number of annual follow-up examinations. Participants were dropped from the study if they missed an annual examination. At the initial examination, 27 malignancies were removed, along with an unspecified number of polyps. At 92,650 follow-up annual examinations, 13 new rectal cancers were detected. Of these, 12 were confined to the mucosal or submucosal area (stage A) and 1 showed minimal invasion of the muscularis propria. Mortality among these 13 patients was limited to one perioperative death and one death from cancer of the pancreas 4 years later.

The remarkably early stage distribution and low mortality for these cancers detected at repeat screening examinations are much better than reports from the same study for tumors found at initial screenings.[25] However, it is not entirely clear from the published reports of this study that all incident cancers were detected. According to the authors' description of the follow-up method,[26] a person contributed a year of follow-up only if he or she returned for the annual screening sigmoidoscopy. Follow-up was terminated at the date of the last such examination. One reason for not returning to the next annual screening examination could be discovery of a colorectal cancer because of symptoms in the interim. Nevertheless, the absence of a single advanced cancer in nearly 100,000 follow-up sigmoidoscopies is impressive and is consistent with the low risk for mortality following a single sigmoidoscopy in the case-control studies.

Published studies of screening flexible sigmoidoscopy are much smaller than those of rigid sigmoidoscopy, and only a few cancers have been detected in those studies. Nevertheless, pooling 14 studies[27–40] (Table 29-4) totaling approximately 11,000 screening flexible sigmoidoscopies, 30 cancers were detected, at least 24 of which were still localized at diagnosis.

Table 29-4
Results of 60-cm Flexible Sigmoidoscopy Screening in Asymptomatic Adults

Authors	*Study population*	*Sample size (N)*	*Cancers detected, localized/ total*	*Percent with at least one polyp*	*Percent of hyperplastic polyps*	*Percent of polyps less than 1 cm*	*Complications (perforation)*
Goldsmith et al.,[27] 1977	Adults, age not specified	1000	0	5.3	NA	NA	NA
Lipshutz et al.,[28] 1979	Males, age 40 and above	200	0	19.0	NA	80	None
Marks et al.,[29] 1979	Adults, age not specified	203	0	12.8	NA	NA	One[a]
Meyer et al.,[30] 1980	Males, age 40 and above	122	?/1	12.3	NA	59	None
Wherry et al.,[31] 1981	Adults, age 50 and above	417	0	12.5	NA	68	None
Rosevelt and Frankl,[32] 1984	Adults, age 40 and above	825	3/3	10.6	20	67	None
Johnson et al.,[33] 1984	Adults, age not specified	140	0	2.8	NA	NA	None
Yarborough and Waisbren,[34] 1985	Adults, age 50 and above	483	1/1	19.4	0[b]	48	None
Ujszaszy et al.,[35] 1985	Adults, age 40 and above	3963	8/11	8.5	57	5.7	NA
Dubow et al.,[36] 1985	Adults, age 45 and above	258	0/1	15.0	24	80	None
Rumans et al.,[37] 1986	Adults, age 50 and above, hemoccult neg.	252	0	10.0	0[b]	NA	None
Shida et al.,[38] 1989	Adults, any age	2243	9/9	6	0[b]	89	None
Gupta et al.,[39] 1989	Males, age 40 and above, hemoccult neg.	412	3/4	22.3	26	74	None
Cauffman et al.,[40] 1992	Adults, age 45	1000	0	3.6	0[b]	NA	None

[a]One colonic perforation, not clearly a screening examination.
[b]These studies reported only on adenomatous polyps.
Abbreviations: NA = not available.

Thus, as with rigid sigmoidoscopy, flexible sigmoidoscopy screening also leads predominantly to detection of very early stage cancers.

SENSITIVITY, SPECIFICITY, AND DIAGNOSTIC YIELD OF SIGMOIDOSCOPY

Flexible endoscopic examination is often considered the standard against which other colorectal cancer screening methods, such as fecal occult blood testing or radiography, are evaluated for sensitivity.[41,42] The sensitivity of sigmoidoscopy obviously falls well below 100 percent if the entire colon is considered. In the only published study to compare 60-cm flexible sigmoidoscopy and total colonoscopy in the same asymptomatic patients,[43] sigmoidoscopy detected 64 percent of all patients with adenomas. Three studies of full colonoscopy in a total of 433 asymptomatic patients[44–46] found that 44 to 67 percent of all patients with adenomas had at least one adenoma in the distal 60-cm of insertion. Similarly for colorectal cancer, incidence data[4] indicate that approximately 55 percent of all incident colorectal cancers should be detectable by 60-cm sigmoidoscopy because they arise in the sigmoid colon, the rectosigmoid, or the rectum.

Strictly speaking, a lack of specificity, or the occurrence of false-positive tests, is not an issue with sigmoidoscopy because all potential lesions are directly visualized and can be biopsied or removed. However, the clinical significance of diminutive adenomatous polyps (less than 5 to 6 mm in diameter) is still in question.[47–49] Most current guidelines[50–52] call for initial and surveillance colonoscopies upon discovery of such polyps. If these tiny adenomas do not truly indicate an increased risk for cancer, their discovery could be considered a false-positive test requiring a needless workup.

The diagnostic yield of flexible sigmoidoscopy (i.e., the percentage of asymptomatic patients who will have either an adenomatous polyp or cancer discovered at screening sigmoidoscopy) is difficult to discern from published reports. Table 29-4 summarizes 14 descriptive studies of findings at screening sigmoidoscopy. Many of these studies report the yield of "polyps," including hyperplastic as well as neoplastic (adenomatous) lesions. Polyp prevalence varies widely, depending on the age and gender of study samples and on whether previous screening has occurred.

Across these 14 studies, 60-cm flexible sigmoidoscopy detects approximately 2.5 colorectal adenocarcinomas per 1000 examinations in persons 50 years of age and over (see also Ref. 42). Polyps are detected in 2.8 to 22.3 percent of examinations. However, in the seven studies that include both men and women and report on adenomas separately (Refs. 32–35,37,38, and 40), the prevalence of adenomatous polyps ranged from 3.6 to 19.4 percent, with an average prevalence below 10 percent.

The prevalence of adenomas increases fairly dramatically (to 10 percent or higher) after the age of 50.[32,38] Men have consistently been found to have a prevalence of adenomas nearly twice that of women of the same age with sigmoidoscopy[31,38,40] or colonoscopy screening.[46] Hyperplastic polyps may constitute from 10 to 35 percent of polyps less than 1 cm in diameter.[32,36,39] Once identified histologically, they do not require further workup or expense.[53]

Few studies have reported specifically on the size distribution of the adenomatous polyps found at screening examinations. As with stage distribution for cancer, the average size of polyps detected by screening is apt to be much smaller than that of polyps found in patients with symptoms. In the largest study, Shida and Yamamoto[38] found that 89 percent of 170 adenomas detected at screening sigmoidoscopy were less than 1 cm in diameter.

The importance of size has been emphasized recently by three studies which suggest that single tubular adenomas below 1 cm in diameter, once removed, are not associated with an increased incidence of future cancer[54,55] or with colonoscopy findings more severe than those of the general population.[48] Current recommendations for the workup of patients found to have one or more adenomatous polyps are discussed in detail in Chap. 32. These recommendations, which call for both initial colonoscopy to check for synchronous lesions above the reach of the sigmoidoscope and subsequent surveillance colonoscopies at intervals of every 1 to 5 years, are based on the premise that all adenomas are markers of increased risk for development of colorectal cancer. However, if cancer risk is not truly increased for patients whose only lesion is a single tubular adenoma less than 1 cm in diameter, the colonoscopic workup and/or subsequent surveillance colonoscopies may be unnecessary. Because this group represents 50 percent or more of all patients with adenomas, eliminating some or all of their currently recommended colonoscopies would dramatically lower the total costs of a sigmoidoscopy screening program.[56] Modifications of workup and surveillance guidelines are now beginning to appear,[57] although further data are needed to clarify these recommendations.

PATIENT AND PHYSICIAN ACCEPTANCE OF SIGMOIDOSCOPY SCREENING

Sigmoidoscopy has been dismissed as a screening tool because it was judged to be too uncomfortable and too costly to be widely acceptable,[7] but recent reports suggest that this speculation may be unfounded. Several studies comparing patient tolerance or degree of discomfort indicate that the introduction of flexible sigmoidoscopes has increased acceptability of sigmoidoscopy for patients.[58–60]

McCarthy and Moskowitz[61] found that 79 of 105 subjects (75 percent) scheduled for screening sigmoidoscopy kept their appointment. Although as many as 42 percent of those examined reported pain or discomfort, patients were significantly less embarrassed and felt less discomfort and pain than they had expected, and fully 89 percent stated that they definitely or probably would be willing to have the test again. In a family practice residency setting, 97 percent of more than 2000 patients who had just undergone screening sigmoidoscopy stated that they would agree to have the procedure again in 1 year.[62]

Patients undergoing screening sigmoidoscopy indicate that their physician's recommendation was the most significant factor leading them to schedule and have an examination.[63] This powerful effect of physician recommendation is consistent with data on participant motivation for other cancer screening tests.[64] Thus, any substantial increase in sigmoidoscopy screening is likely to require that physicians be convinced of its benefits. Yet surveys of primary care physicians[65,66] find that as many as 37 percent are unconvinced of the utility of screening sigmoidoscopy. Dissemination of the results of the recent case-control studies of sigmoidoscopy screening may alter this proportion.

Additional barriers mentioned by physicians are the inconvenience and costs of performing sigmoidoscopy in the office setting.[67] Organization of sigmoidoscopy screening in efficient, centralized, high-volume settings with nonphysicians as the primary examiners is an alternative to office screening; it could lower costs per examination and remove the burden of screening from busy physicians without sacrificing the quality of the examination.[32,68]

SAFETY OF SCREENING SIGMOIDOSCOPY

The major potential injury from sigmoidoscopy is colonic perforation. Three large series of rigid sigmoidoscopies (both screening and diagnostic), totaling more than 175,000 examinations, have established that perforation occurs at a rate of approximately 1 per 10,000 examinations.[2,69,70] Studies of flexible sigmoidoscopy are much smaller. Twelve studies (Table 29-4) totaling approximately 6500 examinations reported one perforation. However, the authors noted that the patient had fibrostenotic diverticulitis and did not clearly state that this was a screening examination.[29] One nonfatal perforation was reported in 6481 flexible sigmoidoscopies (mostly 60 cm) in a survey of recently trained primary care physicians.[71] Again, the report did not specify whether the perforation occurred in an asymptomatic patient undergoing screening. Thus, the incidence of perforation with flexible sigmoidoscopy appears to be less than 1 per 5000 examinations and perhaps much lower for screening examinations. To our knowledge, no deaths have been reported as a consequence of flexible sigmoidoscopy screening.

Infectious endocarditis is considered to be an additional rare complication of lower intestinal endoscopy[72] in persons with prosthetic heart valves or congenital or rheumatic valvular heart disease. However, the risk is judged to be lower than the risk of adverse reactions to antibiotic prophylaxis, so that the American Heart Association does not recommend antibiotic prophylaxis for these patients.[73]

SCREENING OF HIGH-RISK GROUPS

Flexible sigmoidoscopy screening is recommended only for average-risk persons. Persons determined to be at substantially increased risk for developing colorectal cancer should have total colonoscopy rather than sigmoidoscopy, because cancer risk is increased throughout the entire colon. Persons with ulcerative colitis, adenomatous polyposis syndromes, or a family history of hereditary nonpolyposis colorectal cancer (HNPCC) are clearly at increased risk[74,75] and should be followed with total colonoscopy.

There is less clarity when the family history is that of one or two first-degree relatives with colorectal cancer. A number of studies have demonstrated that a positive family history is associated with a two- to threefold increased risk of colorectal cancer.[76] However, these studies did not consistently exclude families with multiple cancers (i.e., possible HNPCC families). Three recent studies have compared sigmoidoscopy[75] or colonoscopy findings[77,78] in individuals with a positive family history to control groups of persons with no affected relatives. A slight increase in prevalence of adenomas was found in each study for those with one affected first-degree relative, and findings were increased if two or more first-degree relatives had colorectal cancer.

Colorectal cancer occurs at earlier ages in hereditary syndromes.[76] There is some evidence that age at diagnosis may also be important for common colorectal cancer.[79,80] Recognizing this, the American Cancer Society and others[76] have recently proposed that screening for persons having one first-degree relative with colorectal cancer should consist of sigmoidoscopy and fecal occult blood testing beginning at age 40 if the relative was diagnosed after the age of 55, but periodic colonoscopy should be employed if the affected family member was 55 or less at diagnosis or when two or more first-degree relatives had colorectal cancer. Additional data are needed to further define the risk associated with number and age of affected relatives.

APPROPRIATE AGES AND FREQUENCY FOR SCREENING SIGMOIDOSCOPY

Colorectal cancer incidence rates begin to increase sharply after age 50, reaching 1 case per 1000 persons per year by age 60.[4] The prevalence of adenomatous polyps, arguably the primary target of sigmoidoscopy screening, also rises sharply at about age 50.[32,38] For these reasons, most current guidelines recommend that screening begin at age 50 in average-risk persons.

There are few data on the ideal interval between screening examinations. Here the relevant question is: How long may persons with average colorectal cancer risk wait after a negative sigmoidoscopy before repeating the test? In the case-control study of sigmoidoscopy, risk for developing fatal colorectal cancer remained reduced for at least 9 to 10 years after a single negative examination (Table 29-3). This finding is consistent with data suggesting that the sequence from a "clean" bowel through development of adenomatous polyps and progression to carcinoma requires at least 10 years on average.

Because risk was not reduced to zero even in the first 2 years after a negative test, repeat testing at frequencies as often as yearly could theoretically lower risk further. However, the low residual risk throughout the 10-year period (10 to 30 percent of expected mortality) suggests that screening again during this period would have, at most, a small added benefit. Based on these data, it appears reasonable to lengthen the recommended interval between examinations to at least 5 years. Additional data from other populations are needed to determine if an even longer interval may be appropriate.

CONCLUSIONS

A screening test must be shown to benefit those screened, and, in addition, must be safe, affordable, and acceptable to screenees and physicians. Sigmoidoscopy has been criticized because of the lack of controlled study evidence of efficacy and because of the costs and discomfort associated with the examination. Two recent case-control studies have now provided strong evidence that periodic sigmoidoscopic screening could reduce total colorectal cancer mortality by 30 percent or more. In addition, one study suggests that the screening interval could reasonably be lengthened beyond 5 years. In contrast to many cancer screening tests, sigmoidoscopy offers the opportunity to lower cancer mortality risk through the relatively simple procedure of removing premalignant adenomas.

Introduction of flexible sigmoidoscopes has reduced patient discomfort and increased acceptability. Screening costs could safely be reduced by the employment of nonphysician examiners; by lengthening the interval between screening examinations to 5 years or longer, and by reducing the number of colonoscopies in the workup and subsequent surveillance of screenees who have single small adenomatous polyps (less than 1 cm in diameter).

The available data are now sufficient to support an expansion of sigmoidoscopy screening in average-risk patients beginning at age 50. Randomized controlled trial data will not be available for at least 15 years. Delaying the implementation of screening until these data become available cannot be justified. As populations undergo screening, the incidence and mortality from colorectal cancer should be closely monitored. If the efficacy of sigmoidoscopy is as great as suggested by the case-control studies, a reduction in mortality should be detectable when comparison is made with earlier mortality rates in the same populations or with current rates in populations that have not been offered screening.

REFERENCES

1. Christiansen HW, Tenner RJ: Results of sigmoidoscopic examinations at a cancer detection center. *Am J Surg* 81:14–17, 1951.
2. Portes C, Majarakis JD: Proctosigmoidoscopy—Incidence of polyps in 50,000 examinations. *JAMA* 163:411–413, 1957.
3. Molofsky LC, Hayashi SJ: Proctosigmoidoscopy as a routine part of a multiphasic program. *Am J Med Sci* 235:628–631, 1958.
4. National Cancer Institute: Surveillance, epidemiology and end-results: Incidence and mortality data, 1973–77, monograph no. 57. Bethesda, Md, National Cancer Institute, 1981.
5. Selby JV, Friedman GD: Sigmoidoscopy in the periodic health examination of asymptomatic adults. *JAMA* 261:595–601, 1989.
6. Canadian Task Force on the Periodic Health Examination: Periodic health examination, 1989 update 2. *Can Med Assoc J* 14:209–216, 1989.
7. Frame PS: A critical review of adult health maintenance: Part 3. Prevention of cancer. *J Fam Pract* 22:511–520, 1986.
8. Concept approval granted to trial of prostate, lung, colorectal screens. *Cancer Lett* 15:1–3, 1989.
9. Dales LG, Friedman GD, Collen MF: Evaluating periodic multiphase health checkups: A controlled trial. *J Chronic Dis* 32:385–404, 1979.
10. Friedman GD, Collen MF, Fireman BH: Multiphasic health checkup evaluation: A 16-year follow-up. *J Chronic Dis* 39:453–463, 1986.
11. Selby JV, Friedman GD: Sigmoidoscopy and mortality from colorectal cancer: The Kaiser-Permanente Multiphasic Evaluation Study. *J Clin Epidemiol* 41:427–434, 1988.
12. Morrison AS: Case definition in case-control studies of the efficacy of screening. *Am J Epidemiol* 115:6–8, 1982.
13. Weiss NS: Control definition in case-control studies of the efficacy of screening and diagnostic testing. *Am J Epidemiol* 118:457–460, 1983.
14. Newcomb PA, Norfleet RG, Surawicz TS, et al: Screening sigmoidoscopy and colorectal cancer mortality. *J Natl Cancer Inst* 84:1572–1575, 1992.
15. Selby JV, Friedman GD, Quesenberry CP Jr, et al: A case-control study of screening sigmoidoscopy and mortality from colorectal cancer. *N Engl J Med* 326:653–657, 1992.
16. Morson B: The polyp-cancer sequence in the large bowel. *Proc Soc Med* 67:451–457, 1974.
17. Kozuka S, Nogaki M, Ozeki T, et al: Premalignancy of the mucosal polyp in the large intestine: II. Estimation of the periods required for malignant transformation of mucosal polyps. *Dis Colon Rectum* 18:494–500, 1975.
18. Winawer SJ, Zauber A, Diaz B: The National Polyp Study: Temporal sequence of evolving colorectal cancer from the normal colon. *Gastrointest Endosc* 33:167, 1987.
19. Glick SN, Teplick SK, Balfe DM: Large colonic neoplasms missed by endoscopy. *Am J Roentgenol* 152:513–517, 1989.
20. Hoff G, Foerster A, Vatn MH, et al: Epidemiology of polyps in the rectum and colon—Recovery and evaluations of unresected polyps two years after detection. *Scand J Gastroenterol* 21:853–862, 1986.
21. Eddy DE: Guidelines for the cancer related checkup: Recommendations and rationale. *CA* 30:194–240, 1980.
22. Morrison AS: The effects of early treatment, lead time and length bias on the mortality experienced by cases detected by screening. *Int J Epidemiol* 11:261–267, 1982.
23. Spratt JS: Epidemiology of screening for cancer. *Curr Probl Cancer* 6:1–58, 1982.
24. Hertz RE, Deddish MR, Day E: Value of periodic examination in detecting cancer of the rectum and colon. *Postgrad Med* 27:290, 1960.
25. Gilbertsen VA: Proctosigmoidoscopy and polypectomy in reducing the incidence of rectal cancer. *Cancer* 34:936–939, 1974.
26. Gilbertsen VA, Nelms JM: The prevention of invasive cancer of the rectum. *Cancer* 41:1137–1139, 1977.
27. Goldsmith O, Frankl H, Gerety D: Fiberoptic sigmoidoscopy in an asymptomatic population (abstract). *Gastrointest Endosc* 23:228, 1977.
28. Lipshutz GR, Katon RM, McCool MF, et al: Flexible sigmoidoscopy as a screening procedure for neoplasia of the colon. *Surg Gynecol Obstet* 148:19–22, 1979.
29. Marks G, Boggs HW, Castro AF, et al: Sigmoidoscopic examinations with rigid and flexible fiberoptic sigmoidoscopes in the surgeon's office: A comparative prospective study of effectiveness in 1,012 cases. *Dis Colon Rectum* 22:162–168, 1979.
30. Meyer CT, McBride W, Goldblatt RS: Clinical experience with flexible sigmoidoscopy in asymptomatic and symptomatic patients. *Yale J Biol Med* 53:345–352, 1980.
31. Wherry DC: Screening for colorectal neoplasia in asymptomatic patients using flexible fiberoptic sigmoidoscopy. *Dis Colon Rectum* 24:521–522, 1981.
32. Rosevelt J, Frankl H: Colorectal cancer screening by nurse practitioners using 60-cm flexible fiberoptic sigmoidoscope. *Dig Dis Sci* 29:161–163, 1984.
33. Johnson RA, Quan MA, Rodney WM: Continued assessment of flexible sigmoidoscopy in a family practice residency. *J Fam Pract* 18:723–727, 1984.
34. Yarborough GW, Waisbren BA: The benefits of systematic fi-

beroptic flexible sigmoidoscopy. *Arch Intern Med* 145:95–96, 1985.

35. Ujszaszy L, Pronay G, Nagy GY: Screening for colorectal cancer in a Hungarian county. *Endoscopy* 17:109–112, 1985.
36. Dubow RA, Katon RM, Benner KG, et al: Short (35 cm) versus long (60 cm) flexible sigmoidoscopy: A comparison of findings and tolerance in asymptomatic patients screened for colorectal neoplasia. *Gastrointest Endosc* 31:305–308, 1985.
37. Rumans MC, Benner KG, Keeffe EB: Screening flexible sigmoidoscopy by primary care physicians. *West J Med* 144:756–758, 1986.
38. Shida H, Yamamoto T: Fiberoptic sigmoidoscopy as the first screening procedure for colorectal cancer. *Dis Colon Rectum* 32:404–408, 1989.
39. Gupta TP, Jaszewski R, Luk GD: Efficacy of screening flexible sigmoidoscopy for colorectal neoplasia in asymptomatic subjects. *Am J Med* 86:547–549, 1989.
40. Cauffman JG, Hara JH, Rasgon IM, et al: Flexible sigmoidoscopy in asymptomatic patients with negative fecal occult blood tests. *J Fam Pract* 34:281–286, 1992.
41. Williams CB, Macrae FA, Bartram CI: A prospective study of diagnostic methods in adenoma follow-up. *Endoscopy* 14:74–78, 1982.
42. Neugut AI, Pita S: Role of sigmoidoscopy in screening for colorectal cancer: A critical review. *Gastroenterology* 95: 492–499, 1988.
43. Foutch PG, Mai H, Pardy K: Flexible sigmoidoscopy may be ineffective for secondary prevention of colorectal cancer in asymptomatic, average-risk men. *Dig Dis Sci* 36:924–928, 1991.
44. DiSario JA, Foutch PG, Mai HD, et al: Prevalence of malignant potential of colorectal polyps in asymptomatic, average-risk men. *Am J Gastroenterol* 86:941–945, 1991.
45. Lieberman DA, Smith FW: Screening for colon malignancy with colonoscopy. *Am J Gastroenterol* 86:946–951, 1991.
46. Rex DK, Lehman GA, Hawes RH, et al: Screening colonoscopy in asymptomatic average-risk persons with negative fecal occult blood tests. *Gastroenterology* 100:64–67, 1991.
47. Achkar E, Carey W: Small polyps found during fiberoptic sigmoidoscopy in asymptomatic patients. *Ann Intern Med* 109: 880, 1988.
48. Grossman S, Milos ML, Tekawa IS, et al: Colonoscopic screening of persons with suspected risk factors for colon cancer: II. Past history of colorectal neoplasms. *Gastroenterology* 96:299–306, 1989.
49. Opelka FG, Timmcke AE, Gathright JB Jr, et al: Diminutive colonic polyps: An indication for colonoscopy. *Dis Colon Rectum* 35:178–181, 1992.
50. American Society for Gastrointestinal Endoscopy: The role of colonoscopy in the management of patients with colonic polyps. *Gastrointest Endosc* 34:6S–7S, 1988.
51. Spiro HM: Surveillance for colonic polyps. *Mt Sinai J Med* 55:251–256, 1988.
52. Fleischer DE, Goldberg SB, Browning TH, et al: Detection and surveillance of colorectal cancer. *JAMA* 261:580–585, 1989.
53. Provenzale D, Garrett JW, Condon SE, et al: Risk for colon adenomas in patients with rectosigmoid hyperplastic polyps. *Ann Intern Med* 113:760–763, 1990.
54. Spencer RJ, Melton LJ III, Ready RL, et al: Treatment of small colorectal polyps: A population-based study of the risk of subsequent carcinoma. *Mayo Clin Proc* 59:305–310, 1984.
55. Atkin WS, Morson BC, Cuzick J: Risk of colorectal cancer up to 30 years after adenoma removal. *N Engl J Med* 326:658–662, 1992.
56. Ransohoff DF, Lang CA, Kuo HS: Colonoscopic surveillance after polypectomy: Considerations of cost effectiveness. *Ann Intern Med* 114:177–182, 1991.
57. Levin B, Murphy GP: Revisions in American Cancer Society recommendations for the early detection of colorectal cancer. *CA Cancer J Clin* 42:296–299, 1992.
58. Bohlman TW, Katon RM, Lipshutz GR: Fiberoptic pansigmoidoscopy: An evaluation and comparison with rigid sigmoidoscopy. *Gastroenterology* 72:644–649, 1977.
59. Winnon G, Beri G, Parnish J: Superiority of the flexible to the rigid sigmoidoscope in routine proctosigmoidoscopy. *N Engl J Med* 302:1011–1012, 1980.
60. Rodney WM, Felmar E: Why flexible sigmoidoscopy instead of rigid sigmoidoscopy? *J Fam Pract* 19:471–476, 1984.
61. McCarthy BD, Moskowitz MA: Screening flexible sigmoidoscopy: Patient attitudes and compliance. *J Gen Intern Med* 1992 (in press).
62. Rodney WM, Frame PS: Screening flexible sigmoidoscopy: Is it worthwhile? *J Fam Pract* 25:601–607, 1987.
63. Holt WS Jr: Factors affecting compliance with screening sigmoidoscopy. *J Fam Pract* 32:564–566, 1991.
64. Fox SA, Stein JA: The effect of physician-patient communication on mammography utilization by different ethnic groups. *Med Care* 29:1065–1082, 1991.
65. McPhee SJ, Richard RJ, Solkowitz SN: Performance of cancer screening in a university general internal medicine practice: Comparison with the 1980 American Cancer Society screening guidelines. *J Gen Intern Med* 1:257–281, 1986.
66. Schwartz JS, Lewis CE, Clancy C: Internists' practices in health promotion and disease prevention. A survey. *Ann Intern Med* 114:46–53, 1991.
67. Montano DE, Manders DB, Phillips WR: Family physician beliefs about cancer screening: Development of a survey instrument. *J Fam Pract* 30:313–319, 1990.
68. Shapiro M: Colorectal cancer screening by paramedical personnel. *Dig Dis Sci* 29:159–160, 1984.
69. Bolt RJ: Sigmoidoscopy in detection and diagnosis in the asymptomatic individual. *Cancer* 28:121–122, 1971.
70. Nelson RL, Abcarian H, Prasad ML: Iatrogenic perforation of the colon and rectum. *Dis Colon Rectum* 25:305–308, 1982.
71. Rodney WM, Albers G: Flexible sigmoidoscopy: Primary care outcomes after two types of continuing medical education. *Am J Gastroenterol* 81:133–137, 1986.
72. Norfleet RG: Infectious endocarditis after fiberoptic sigmoidoscopy: With a literature review. *J Clin Gastroenterol* 13:448–451, 1991.
73. Dajani AS, Bisno AL, Chung KJ: Prevention of bacterial endocarditis: Recommendations by the American Heart Association. *JAMA* 264:2919–2922, 1990.
74. Winawer SJD: Detection and diagnosis of colorectal cancer. *Cancer* 51:2519–2524, 1983.
75. Rozen P, Fireman Z, Figer A, et al: Family history of colorectal cancer as a marker of potential malignancy within a screening program. *Cancer* 60:248–254, 1987.
76. Burt RW, Bishop DT, Cannon-Albright L: Population genetics of colonic cancer. *Cancer* 70:1719–1722, 1992.
77. Luchtefeld MA, Syverson D, Solfelt M: Is colonoscopic screening appropriate in asymptomatic patients with family history of colon cancer. *Dis Colon Rectum* 34:763–768, 1991.
78. Guillem JG, Forde KA, Treat MR: Colonoscopic screening for neoplasms in asymptomatic first-degree relatives of colon cancer patients: A controlled prospective study. *Dis Colon Rectum* 35:523–529, 1992.
79. Winawer SJ, Zauber AG, Gerdes H: Genetic epidemiology of colorectal cancer: Relationship of familial colorectal cancer risk to adenoma proband age and adenoma characteristics (abstract). *Gastroenterology* 102:A409, 1992.
80. Bishop DT, St John DBJ, Hughes ESR: Genetic susceptibility to common colorectal cancer: How common is it? (Abstract) *Gastroenterology* 102:A346, 1992.

CHAPTER 30

Colonoscopy and Polypectomy

Jerome D. Waye

The first colonoscopes were short instruments with one-plane tip deflection whose flexibility was developed on the basis of the natural tortuosity of the sigmoid colon. This was determined by inspecting casts of the rectosigmoid area which were obtained by using specially prepared enemas with a silastic foam base. Since the initial introduction of these instruments, colonoscopy has become an accepted and valuable method of examining the colon because of its ability to intubate the entire large bowel with full mucosal inspection. A trained endoscopist should be able to perform total colonoscopy to the cecum in over 90 percent of patients[1,2] within 30 to 45 min. During the initial colonoscopic examination, biopsies can be taken of any area, colonic polyps can be removed, and abnormalities that have been demonstrated on a barium enema x-ray examination can be evaluated. Colonoscopy, usually performed with intravenous sedation, is well tolerated by most patients.

During the introductory phases of colonoscopy, all patients were hospitalized for the procedure. Because of its safety and overall acceptance by patients and physicians, many examinations are now performed in a freestanding office or in a hospital ambulatory endoscopy unit.

Visual inspection with the flexible colonoscope provides an evaluation of the intact colon that is not possible by any other method (Figs. 30-1 through 30-6). In order to interpret the endoscopic findings correctly, the examiner must recognize the gross pathology of the large bowel, since all diseases which affect the mucosal lining of the colon can be directly evaluated with the colonoscope. The excellent intraluminal visualization led to therapeutic applications of this procedure, the most important of which is the removal of colonic polyps. Since a vast majority of colonic carcinomas arise from a preexisting benign colonic polyp,[3] the ability to intervene and remove these at a premalignant phase in their development is expected to markedly alter the incidence of colonic cancer over the next generation.

INSTRUMENTATION

Colonoscopes, which vary from 10 to 13 mm in outside diameter, are available in two standard lengths, 135 cm and 165 cm. The distal tip can be deflected more than 180° by control wheels on the head portion. The "ideal" instrument is stiff enough to permit tip advancement when the shaft is pushed into the rectum and flexible enough to conform to the colonic contours; however, it is not so flexible that it will coil up instead of progressing. Air insufflation, a necessity for visualization, is controlled by a trumpet valve on the instrument head, as is a water jet directed at the distal lens to spray away debris, mucus, and so on. Suction of air or fluid is activated by another fingertip control. Various devices may be passed through the suction/accessory channel of the instrument. These include biopsy forceps, polypectomy snares, foreign-body baskets, grasping forceps, laser fibers, needle injectors, and balloon dilators. Most colonoscopes have one large channel (about 3.8 mm in diameter) which permits aspiration of fluid even though a biopsy forceps occupies the multipurpose conduit. Operative colonoscopes are available with two channels (one for suction, the other for accessories), but these are stiffer than the standard, smaller-diameter, single-channel instruments; they are more likely to cause greater discomfort for the patient.

The displacement of fiberoptic bundles by video technology was a major breakthrough in the imaging capability of flexible endoscopy. A small charge-coupled device (CCD)—actually a sort of television camera—is built into the endoscope tip.[4] This device transmits coded data to a processor, which converts the electronic signal to a color picture on a television monitor. The video colonoscope provides bright images with superb resolution capability and is destined to replace fiberoptic systems while retaining the flexibility and ease in handling developed over the past 25 years.

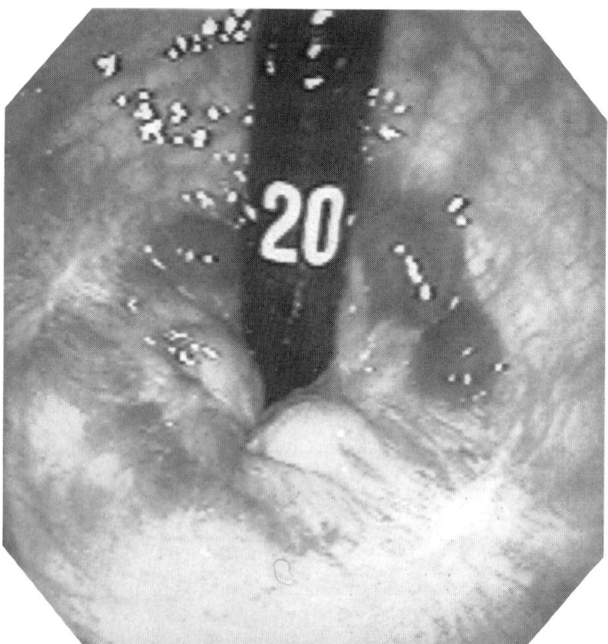

FIG. 30-1. The colonoscope in a U-turn position at the anal canal. Blue hemorrhoidal veins are seen, and scars from previous hemorrhoidectomy are present. (See color Plate 1.)

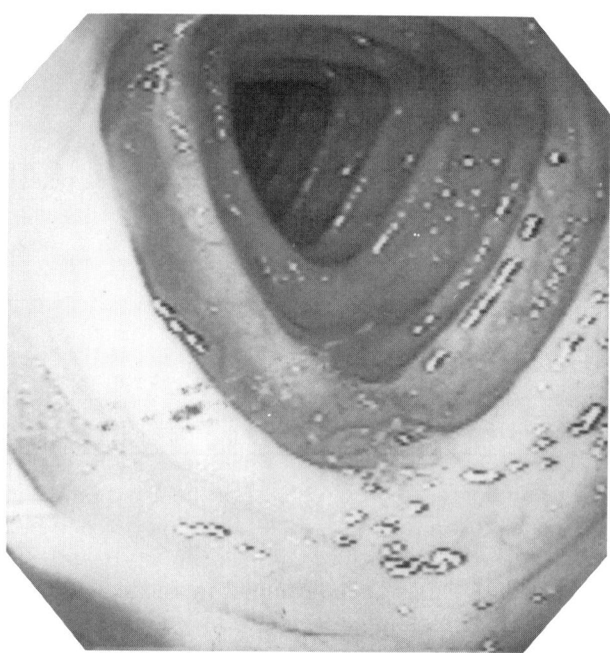

FIG. 30-2. Triangular appearance of the transverse colon. (See color Plate 2.)

Training in Colonoscopy

During the introduction of colonoscopy, no one had any experience, so that anyone who attempted the procedure relied on skills previously acquired during use of the flexible gastroscope, adapting those principles to the convoluted, long, and tortuous colon. Over the years, a body of information has been developed concerning the technique for guiding a 6-ft-long flexible tube from the rectum around to the cecum. Fluoroscopy, thought to be absolutely necessary for the safe performance of colonoscopy in the early years, is still used by a few endoscopists,[5,6] but not by most who perform colonoscopy.[7–9] There are only a limited number of maneuvers available to the endoscopist.

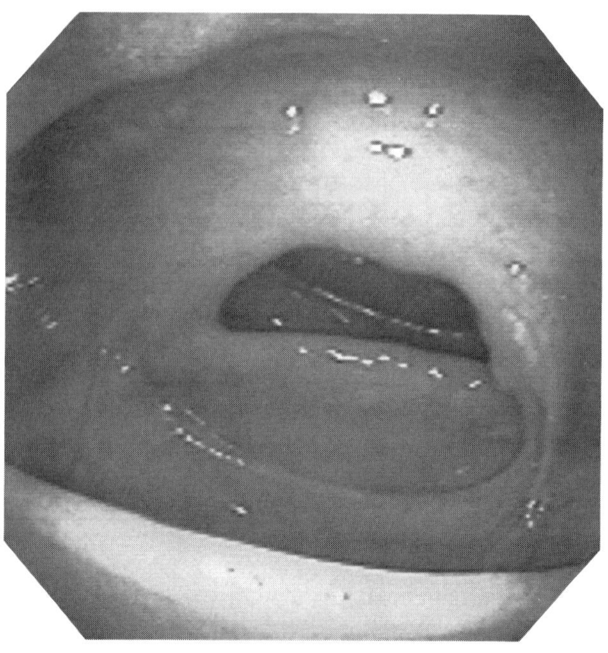

FIG. 30-3. The irregular configuration of a colonic fold, characteristic of the superior lip of the ileocecal valve. (See color Plate 3.)

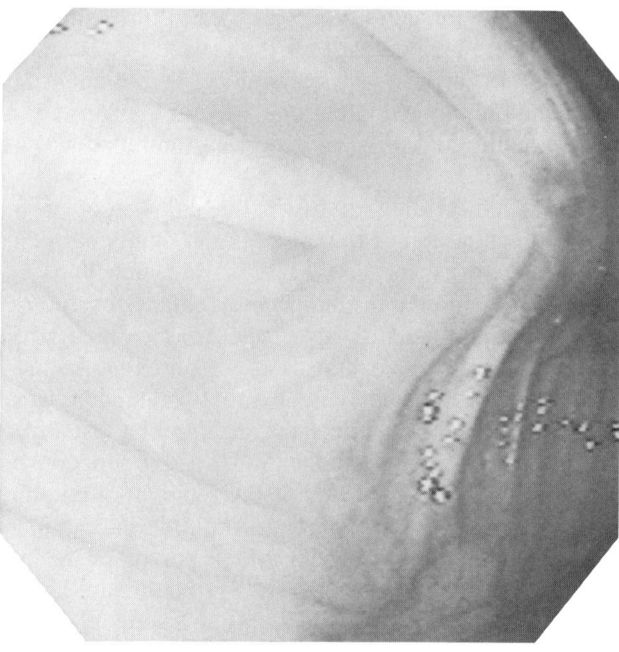

FIG. 30-4. The appendiceal orifice just under a "sling fold" of the cecum. (See color Plate 4.)

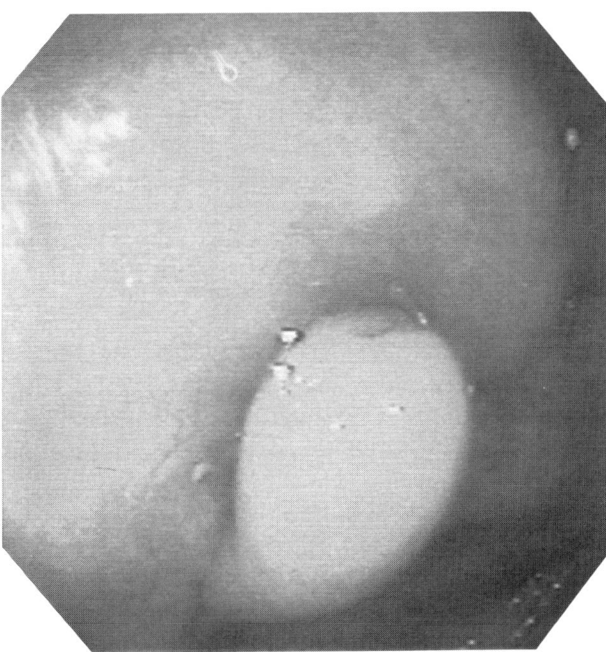

FIG. 30-5. An inverted appendiceal stump. Note the indentation at the apex. (See color Plate 5.)

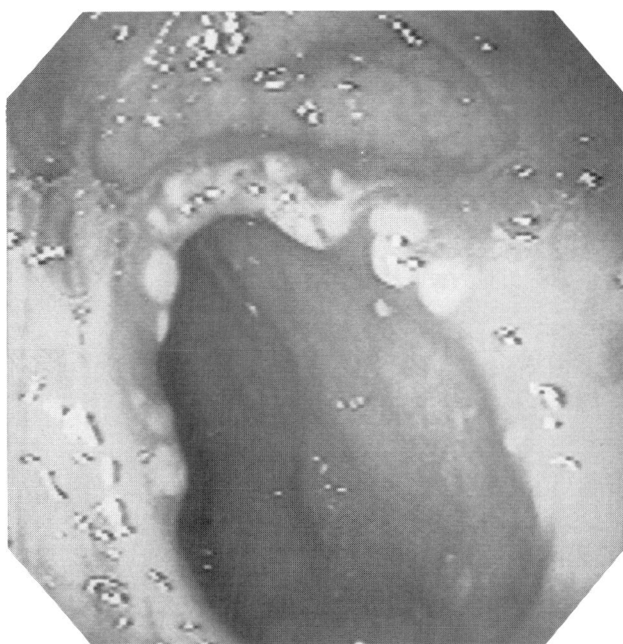

FIG. 30-6. Ileocolic anastomosis with granulation tissue at the edge, on the suture line. (See color Plate 6.)

These include pushing the instrument in or pulling it out, twisting the shaft to the right or left, insufflation or aspiration of air, using dial controls to move the tip up/down or right/left, repositioning the patient, or placing pressure on the abdomen so as to prevent loop formation. The difference between a slow operator who reaches the cecum 70 percent of the time with a prolonged examination and the person who intubates the total colon in 95 percent of patients within an average time of 15 min is the ability to move through the various options quickly and sequentially while using the correct combinations without repeating nonproductive maneuvers. Because of the requirement of performing several functions simultaneously, operator technique is an important factor for successful colonoscopy. The various maneuvers and the decision as to which combinations to use at various stages during the examination can be taught by experts during an apprentice-type training period. Some basic skills may be learned from passing the colonoscope in a variety of plastic or latex models, but the ability to pass the colonoscope in a patient can only be achieved by a one-to-one teacher-to-student learning experience in a clinical setting. A number of groups are developing simulators for endoscopy with interactive computer technology.[10,11] In the future, basic techniques may be learned in a simulation laboratory, thus sparing the patient the initial thrusts of the neophyte colonoscopist. The best way to be trained in colonoscopy is to receive hands-on instruction during a fellowship in gastroenterology or a residency in surgery,[12] where teaching expertise is available. There are very few programs available for physicians who have finished their formal training and want to learn colonoscopy. One method for obtaining skills in a posttraining situation is to locate a proficient colonoscopist and form a teaching relationship with that person as preceptor for 50 to 100 colonoscopic examinations.[13]

The Roles of Colonoscopy and the Barium Enema

The colonoscope presents many imaging features not available through the radiographic examination of the colon. Among these is the ability to see the mucosal vascular pattern and ascertain whether it is normal or abnormal. Other possibilities unique to colonoscopy include the recognition of surface detail (such as blood or mucus in the lumen) and the direct visualization of aphthous ulcerations, erythema, or surface edema. Small, flat lesions such as arteriovenous malformations may be readily seen through the colonoscope (Fig. 30-7), which has such fine resolution that a single human hair is easily discernible. In addition to making use of this visual capability, other diagnostic and therapeutic maneuvers can be performed, such as mucosal biopsy, biopsy of lesions, or removal of polyps and foreign bodies. The extent of diverticulosis is better appreciated by means of the barium enema than by endoscopy, and a fistulous communication from the colon to another loop of bowel or to an adjacent organ is more readily identified roentgenographically than endoscopically, as is displacement of the colon by a mass lesion.

The barium enema has certain advantages over colonoscopy, among which is the fact that barium can

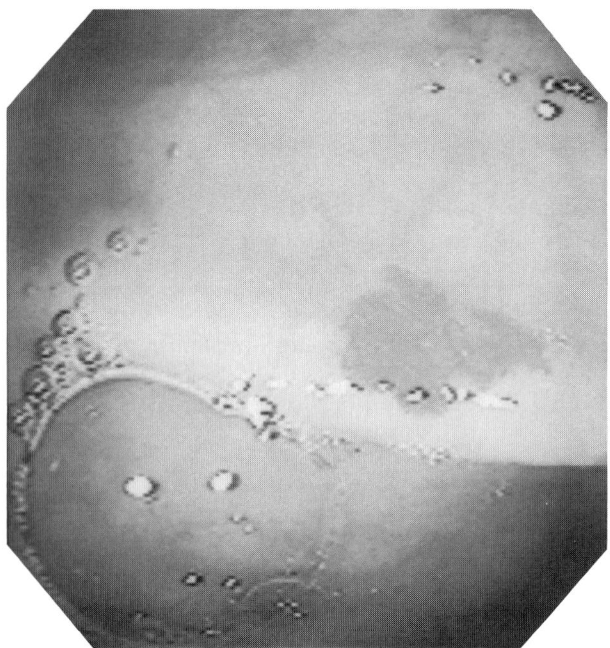

FIG. 30-7. Racemose collection of blood vessels in the cecum. This is a characteristic appearance of a colonic arteriovenous malformation. (See color Plate 7.)

almost always reach the cecum during the x-ray examination, but the colonoscope cannot always be passed through the entire colon. Other positive aspects of the barium enema include its widespread availability, quick completion, low cost, and low morbidity.

Although there are technical skills required for both examinations, colonoscopy demands a considerably greater amount of operator time and direct involvement than even the most rigorous barium enema/air contrast examination. Following the examination, the barium enema provides a standard set of images, which can be reproduced and filed for later review as often as necessary. This capability is not possible with the colonoscope unless the entire examination is videotaped. Video recording of a complete colonoscopy is possible, but it is an onerous task to pick out a defined segment of pathology to compare from one examination to the next, since the reviewer must search through an entire recording to locate an area of interest. In addition, the video cassettes are cumbersome and difficult to store on a long-term basis. Instantly printed photographic hard copy or 35-mm slides may easily be taken during colonoscopy but do not provide a "universal" picture of the entire colon, as is depicted on films taken during the barium enema x-ray examination. During the colonoscopy, pictures are usually taken of specific areas of pathology, as interpreted by the endoscopist, rather than making a photographic map of the entire large bowel.

In comparing the accuracy of each modality, we find that the colonoscope will invariably locate more

Table 30-1
Indications for Colonoscopy after Barium Enema X-Ray

Investigate x-ray abnormality
Mass
Stricture
Filling defect
Unexplained diarrhea
Inability to tolerate barium enema

mass lesions (polyps or cancer),[14,15] and smaller lesions than can be demonstrated by the x-ray examination. However, it is not the final arbiter for determining the presence of lesions in the colon, since some tumors will be missed during colonoscopy.[16] Nevertheless, colonoscopy can achieve a detection rate of over 95 percent for lesions larger than 1 cm.[17] A barium enema is not a prerequisite for colonoscopy, since there is little information from the x-ray that will affect the actual performance of colonoscopy. The radiographic appearance of colonic tortuosity usually cannot be correlated with the degree of difficulty in passing the colonoscope through that area, although excessive redundancy may predict some difficulty. A barium enema may be helpful in identifying a segment of colon requiring close scrutiny, since some segments between intrahaustral septae and around acute flexures may be relatively "blind" areas for the colonoscopist unless attention has been specifically directed to those areas by a previous barium enema.

Evaluation of an Abnormal Barium Enema X-Ray

Concerns over an abnormality on the x-ray can usually be resolved by colonoscopy (Table 30-1). These include unexplained defects found on a barium enema performed for nonspecific lower gastrointestinal symptoms (abdominal cramps, change in bowel habits, or abdominal pain). When an indefinite radiographic interpretation is rendered, colonoscopy rather than a repeat x-ray should be the next modality of investigation, since endoscopy provides the possibility of several ancillary procedures in addition to direct visualization and evaluation by probe palpation. Brush cytology, biopsy, or even polypectomy can be performed at the time of colonoscopy.

INDICATIONS FOR COLONOSCOPY

Primary Colonoscopy

Primary colonoscopy without a preceding barium enema is indicated in specific clinical situations (Table 30-2), as in patients with rectal bleeding, either overt or occult. In many of these cases, patients will have both examinations, although the x-ray is frequently redundant because colonoscopy is often requested when a radiographic lesion has been identified. Endoscopy

Table 30-2
Indications for Primary Colonoscopy[a]

Rectal bleeding
Overt
Occult
Adenoma on flexible sigmoidoscopy
Previous colonic neoplasia
Surveillance based on family history
Surveillance in chronic ulcerative colitis

[a]Colonoscopy without preceding barium enema x-ray.

may be required to biopsy or obtain brush cytology of a mass, remove a polyp, or better evaluate a lesion shown on the x-ray examination. On the other hand, if the barium enema fails to demonstrate a probable cause of occult bleeding, colonoscopy is mandatory, since in these cases about 10 percent of patients will have undetected colonic cancer and 15 percent will have undetected polyps.[18] Another subgroup of patients in whom primary colonoscopy is indicated includes those with an index adenoma discovered on either rigid or flexible sigmoidoscopy, since there is a high incidence of proximal lesions[19,20] and the polyp can be removed during the same examination performed for evaluation of the remainder of the colon. Other patients in high-risk categories for colonic and/or rectal neoplasia are also candidates for primary colonoscopy. These include surveillance for reasons of a strong family history of colonic cancer, since even small adenomas can be discovered and removed at the time of the primary examination. After removal of a polyp or tumor from the colon, there is a high risk for development of subsequent (metachronous) neoplasms; these patients should have interval primary colonoscopy. Patients with long-standing inflammatory bowel disease have a higher incidence of colonic carcinoma than does the general population, and periodic multiple mucosal biopsies are required for histopathologic identification of dysplasia, a premalignant cytologic change.[21,22]

In the absence of rectal bleeding (occult or overt), colonoscopy has a relatively low yield in patients with chronic abdominal pain or a change in bowel habits.[23] Inability to hold barium may be an age-related problem, and it has been suggested by radiologists that colonoscopy in the elderly patient may be a more effective modality than the barium enema.[14]

Unexplained Colonic Bleeding

Rectal bleeding is always abnormal, therefore efforts must be made to explain recurrent bleeding. The ability to visualize the colon in full color provides the endoscopist with a dimension not possible radiographically. Arteriovenous malformations, rarely identified by barium x-ray, can easily be seen through the colonoscope, and streaks of blood on the mucosal surface are readily visible to the endoscopist. Total colonoscopy is the most accurate method of investigating occult gastrointestinal bleeding, while also providing a therapeutic capability.[24,25] During ongoing bleeding, an oral electrolyte purge may clean the lower gastrointestinal tract adequately for subsequent total colonoscopic visualization,[26] but angiography may be necessary for torrential bleeding episodes. Intraoperative colonoscopy along with a large-volume lavage given through a cecostomy has been advocated when the site of massive bleeding cannot be located in the operating theater.[27] Diverticulosis is one of the most common causes for massive lower gastrointestinal bleeding. Colonoscopy can be an important therapeutic tool, since approximately half of patients with acute bleeding will have polyps or arteriovenous malformations.[26]

Inflammatory Bowel Disease

The majority of patients with inflammatory bowel disease can be managed by the clinician without ever requiring colonoscopic intervention.[28] There are specific circumstances when colonoscopy may provide information to supplement the data from the history, physical examination, and sigmoidoscopy. Colonoscopy may aid in making the differential diagnosis between various types of inflammatory bowel disease. The ability to see the areas of mucosal involvement and to directly visualize the type of ulcers along with the biopsy capability enhances the differentiation between ulcerative colitis and Crohn's disease of the colon[29] (Fig. 30-8). Mass lesions seen on a colonic x-ray can be evaluated and, if there is doubt as to their histology, tissue sampling will assist in the correct diagnosis, whether it be an adenoma, pseudopolyp (Fig. 30-9), or carcinoma. Strictures in inflammatory bowel disease should be endoscopically characterized to assess whether they harbor carcinoma (Fig. 30-10). Surveillance for colonic carcinoma is an important use for colonoscopy in inflammatory bowel disease, where the carcinoma risk is considerably higher than in the general population[30] when the patient has universal disease for over eight years' duration. An especially high-risk group of patients with inflammatory bowel disease can be identified by the histopathologic finding of dysplasia on endoscopic biopsies. Repeat biopsies which confirm the presence of high-grade dysplasia in inflammatory bowel disease strongly suggest proctocolectomy to remove the colon and prevent the development of carcinoma. The current recommendation is that, regardless of activity, patients with universal ulcerative colitis who have had their disease for over 8 years should have surveillance colonoscopy and biopsies seeking dysplasia every 1 or 2 years. If it is feasible, patients with Crohn's disease should probably be followed in a similar manner.[31]

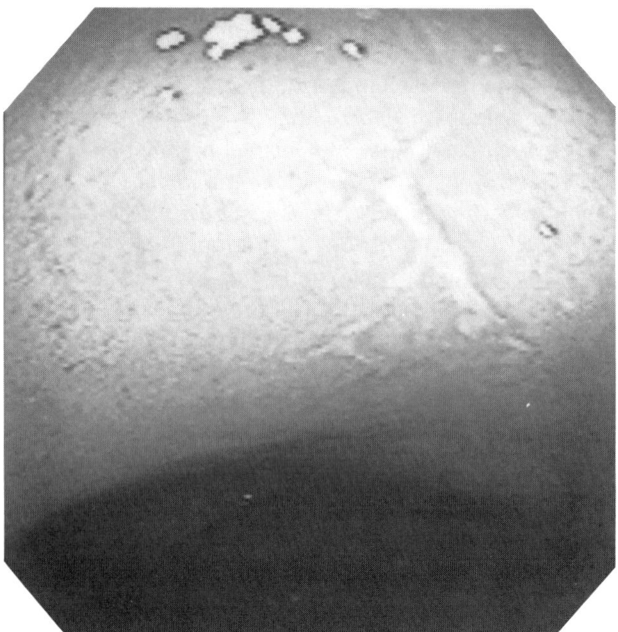

FIG. 30-8. A characteristic appearance of inflammatory bowel disease, with loss of the normal vascular pattern, and a linear ulceration in an area of inflamed mucosa. This patient has ulcerative colitis. (See color Plate 8.)

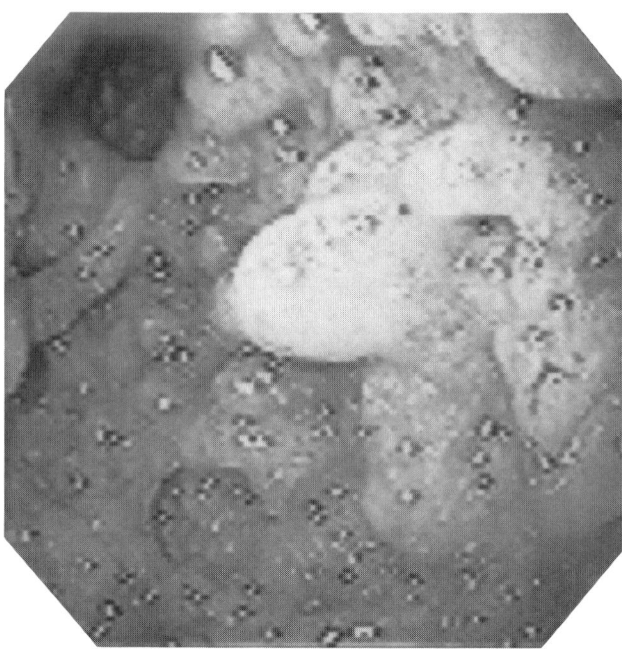

FIG. 30-9. A collection of inflammatory polyps covering the wall of the transverse colon in a patient with chronic ulcerative colitis. (See color Plate 9.)

In ulcerative colitis there is often a disparity between the patient's clinical course and the endoscopic appearance of the mucosa. This lack of correlation argues against the practice of interval colonoscopy to assess the result of therapy or to provide an evaluation of the activity of disease.[29–34]

Infectious Colitis

Most patients with infectious colitis have a self-limited illness and do not require colonoscopy. A detailed history of pertinent events leading to the onset of illness is important, including travel, diet, antibiotic use, and sexual preferences. Differentiating an infectious colitis from idiopathic inflammatory bowel disease may be difficult because of the many features in common. Damage to the mucosal lining of the rectum and colon in either infectious or idiopathic colitis may appear to be similar. This is because some infectious agents cause surface damage which resembles that seen in ulcerative colitis, while others may cause lesions similar to Crohn's disease. Tests should include stool cultures for viral and bacterial agents. If endoscopy is performed, biopsies may help to differentiate an acute infection from chronic inflammatory bowel disease.[35]

Colitis due to previous antibiotic use causes multiple patches of creamy plaquelike "pseudomembrane" on the bowel wall. Biopsies may be diagnostic in revealing "pseudomembranous antibiotic colitis."[36] Ischemia is usually associated with either discrete or diffuse ulcerations which can occur at any area of the colon, the most common being at the splenic flexure.

Perioperative Endoscopy

Total colonoscopy should be considered whenever a carcinoma of the colon is to be resected, since the patient with a carcinoma is at high risk for additional or synchronous neoplasms, especially adenomas; 4 percent will have a synchronous carcinoma.[37] Intraoper-

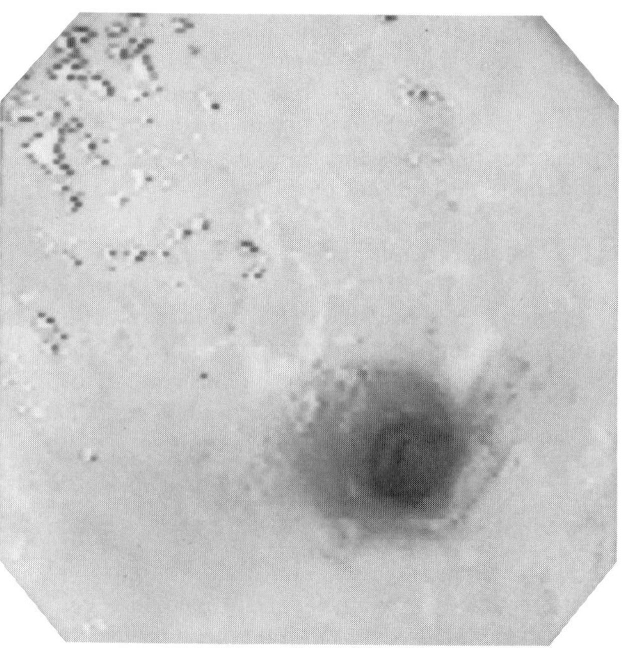

FIG. 30-10. A stricture in Crohn's disease. Note the marked inflammation and ulcerations at the edge of the stricture. This stricture was due to severe inflammation. (See color Plate 10.)

ative colonoscopy can be performed at the time of exploratory laparotomy and is used by some physicians for localization of a polypectomy site where follow-up surgery is performed for removal of a segment from which a malignant polyp was endoscopically removed.[38] At the operating table, the surgeon may not be able to identify the polypectomy site by either palpation or observation of the serosal surface. The need for intraoperative endoscopy is diminished now that it is possible to mark the site of polypectomy with India ink injection (Fig. 30-11), enabling the surgeon to locate the permanent tattoo in the operating theater. India ink localization is becoming an important tool, since precise site identification during primary colonoscopy (without a preceding barium enema x-ray examination) may be unreliable.[39]

Surveillance

Following removal of polyps or surgical resection of colonic cancers, the colon has a propensity to develop metachronous tumors.[40] Colonoscopy is better than a barium enema x-ray examination[41] in the location and treatment of these lesions at an early stage. Endoscopy will result in the highest yield of neoplasia in these high-risk individuals and provides the additional possibility for polyp removal at the same time. The ideal follow-up intervals for endoscopic surveillance following removal of an adenoma are currently being investigated by the National Polyp Study in the United States.[42,43] A 3-year interval is probably sufficient if a single benign adenoma was removed, with more frequent surveillance when multiple polyps have been resected.

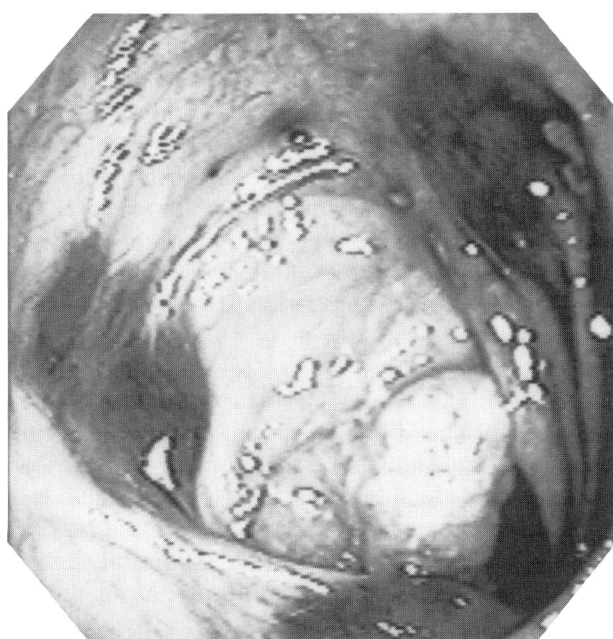

FIG. 30-11. A small carcinoma of the descending colon with circumferential India ink injections for subsequent surgical localization. (See color Plate 11.)

The patient in a high-risk group for the development of colonic cancer requires close surveillance.[41] Relatives of patients with familial polyposis should be examined with colonoscopy or sigmoidoscopy to rule out the presence of colonic polyps, because even tiny adenomas can readily be seen and biopsied. As more information accumulates concerning the role of inheritance in the transmission of colonic cancer and adenomas,[44,45] it appears that colonoscopy is indicated at approximately age 40 in any person who has a first-degree relative with colonic cancer.[46]

Unexplained Chronic Diarrhea

The etiology of diarrhea may be diverse and obscure. Many of the various causes will neither be radiographically identifiable, nor will they produce a positive stool culture. Endoscopy in these patients may demonstrate patchy involvement of the colon with Crohn's disease, while random biopsies may permit the diagnosis of microscopic colitis or collagenous colitis[47] where no grossly visible abnormalities exist.

Endoscopic Therapy

The most important aspect of colonoscopic therapy is the removal of colonic polyps, a major accomplishment in the field of gastroenterology. Removal of adenomas has been reported to markedly diminish the incidence of colonic cancer.[48,49] Polyps, both pedunculated and sessile, can be removed through the colonoscope from any portion of the colon. Most polyps are adenomas, as are the majority of diminutive (less than 5 mm) colonic polyps. Because most polyps are adenomas,[50] any polyp seen during the course of a colonoscopic examination should be removed at that time. Every endoscopist should be able to perform polypectomy at the time of diagnosis, since polyps are frequently encountered.[51] It is unnecessary to require a patient in whom a polyp is found to reprep and return for a subsequent polypectomy. There is no role for strictly diagnostic colonoscopy.

Contraindications to Colonoscopy

There are only a few contraindications to colonoscopy (Table 30-3). In the absence of unusual circumstances, colonoscopy should not be attempted if a patient can-

Table 30-3
Contraindications for Colonoscopy

Recent myocardial infarction
Recent pulmonary embolus
Suspicion of colonic perforation
Acute diverticulitis
Inability to prepare the colon

not be adequately prepared for the examination. Among specific contraindications are recent myocardial infarction or pulmonary embolism. Neither arrhythmias nor chronic cardiorespiratory illness are contraindications to colonoscopy provided that care is taken to assess the patient's status before and during the procedure. The suspicion of a colonic perforation or peritonitis is an absolute contraindication to colonoscopy, where the insufflation of air may "blow out" a confined perforation to communicate freely with the peritoneal cavity. An acute attack of active colitis usually does not require colonoscopy, since the diagnosis may be made by other modalities such as proctosigmoidoscopy, although there has been a report[52] on the effectiveness of colonoscopy in evaluating the intraluminal activity during acute colitis episodes. Relative contraindications are acute or recent diverticulitis and neutropenia. Special attention is necessary in the presence of a coagulation disorder or when the patient is taking anticoagulant medications.

There are several instances in which colonoscopy is rarely of benefit; these include the evaluation of chronic lower abdominal pain, a change in bowel movements without rectal bleeding, or evaluation of weight loss and/or anorexia.

COLONOSCOPY AND POLYPECTOMY

Medication for Colonoscopy

In the United States, general anesthesia is not usually employed for colonoscopy, except under unusual circumstances,[53] even when infants and children are being examined. Most patients will be able to undergo total colonoscopy with conscious sedation; general anesthesia is avoided, since the general opinion is that the endoscopist loses feedback from the patient about pain or discomfort caused by loop formation. However, in a patient who must have colonoscopy and in whom the procedure cannot be accomplished with conscious sedation, general anesthesia may be necessary. The most frequently used drugs for colonoscopy sedation are a combination of meperidine and a benzodiazepine, with dosage adjusted for age and weight. Muscle relaxant medications are used by many during colonoscopy but are of little benefit.

Prophylaxis against Infection

Bacteremia occurs during colonoscopy and may result in endocarditis. The American Heart Association has recommended that prophylactic antibiotics be given to patients who are at high risk for endocarditis, such as those with prosthetic cardiac valves or previous endocarditis and those with damaged valve leaflets. Other patients who may benefit from precolonoscopy antibiotics are those with significant leukocytosis or who are immunocompromised.[54] The antibiotics recommended are ampicillin and gentamicin.[55,56] Oral antibiotic prophylaxis appears to be sufficient for patients with prolapse of the mitral valve and a cardiac murmur.

Techniques of Colonoscopy

There are many different techniques for colonoscopy.[57–60] All call for a clean bowel, which requires the use of a vigorous cathartic with or without enemas or a large volume of orally ingested lavage solution.[61] The scope is passed through the colon by a series of simultaneous and sequential movements utilizing the dials for control of deflection and rotatory torque on the shaft as it is being introduced or withdrawn. Because of the multiple convolutions of the colon, which induce the instrument to assume a loop configuration, continued attempts at straightening of the instrument during the examination are important and result in "accordian pleating" of the colon onto the colonoscope's shaft. Loops may be removed by combinations of withdrawal and torque, rendering fluoroscopy of little benefit for a successful colonoscopy. The current reliance on fluoroscopy is much a matter of habit, since it was thought to be extremely useful in the beginning phases of colonoscopy some 25 years ago. Early in the days of colonoscopy, the use of "slide-by" was fashionable, whereby the colonoscope was pushed into the colon and the mucosa was seen to "slide by" as the tip advanced, with neither visualization of the lumen nor knowledge of its whereabouts. Although this method was frequently successful, there was also a greater risk of perforation; current teaching requires that the direction of the lumen be known at all times. Air is used to distend the bowel for full visualization, but CO_2 has been advocated to diminish postendoscopy discomfort from distension.[62] There is no one "correct" way to perform colonoscopy. The technique has been developed in several centers simultaneously, with the result being a multitude of approaches. The desirable end point must be a safe and thorough examination which is performed by a competent person trained in both the diagnostic and therapeutic aspects of the procedure.

The Endoscopy Assistant

A well-trained gastrointestinal assistant is valuable for the smooth and proper performance of colonoscopy and for the safety of the patient.[63] Among the duties of the gastrointestinal assistant are looking after the comfort and safety of the patient, providing abdominal pressure as needed,[64] preparing the room for the examination, providing the necessary accessory equipment as required (snares, biopsy forceps, etc.), setting up the electrocoagulation apparatus, labeling and identification of biopsy specimens, and recording various aspects of the procedure. After the endoscopic examination has been completed, the work of the endoscopy assistant continues in the postendoscopic observation of the patient, instrument maintenance, cleaning and disinfection, setting up the room for the following procedure, and ordering supplies, drugs, and accessories.

Some endoscopists prefer a two-person colonoscopy technique, where the assistant advances the instrument as the endoscopist steers the dial controls. This technique is cumbersome and somewhat tedious, causing most endoscopists to rely on a "one person—two hand" technique, whereby the left hand manipulates the dial control mechanisms and the air/water/suction controls while the right hand steers the shaft around various colonic turns and twists, withdrawing or advancing the instrument as necessary.

Prepolypectomy Preparation

The colon should be adequately cleansed for purposes of visualization and to reduce potentially explosive concentrations of gases to noncombustible levels.[65] This usually means avoiding the use of fermentable sugars (Mannitol) and cleansing the colon of bacteria and fecal matter. Any method of cleansing the colon—including castor oil and enemas, citrate of magnesia and enemas, phosphosoda or an electrolyte preparation—is adequate to prepare the colon for electrosurgery.[66,67] Carbon dioxide colonic insufflation, once thought necessary for avoidance of spark-induced explosion, is now considered optional, with most endoscopists not using CO_2.[68]

Routine testing for bleeding disorders prior to colonoscopic polypectomy is not necessary.[69] Most patients need not be screened with a platelet count, prothrombin time, bleeding time, or clotting time. A history of a bleeding disorder is important to obtain, including any tendency to bleed excessively following lacerations, a surgical procedure, or dental extraction. Aspirin, having specific antiplatelet properties, should be discontinued for 1 week prior to the endoscopic examination. This includes any aspirin-containing over-the-counter drugs, including Bufferin and Alka-Seltzer. Patients on anticoagulants may be colonoscoped safely, but polypectomy should be avoided because of the risk of bleeding. When polyps are to be removed in the anticoagulated patient at high risk for thrombotic episodes (such as a patient with prosthetic cardiac valves), a period of hospitalization is required, with anticoagulation maintained using heparin, with its short duration of action. Warfarin should be discontinued; when prothrombin levels return to the normal range, polypectomy may be performed within 4 h after discontinuation of heparin therapy. If there is no bleeding during polypectomy, heparin may be given within 4 h and warfarin may be resumed. The patient should remain in the hospital on heparin until prothrombin times return to therapeutic levels.

Equipment for Polypectomy

Any solid-state electrosurgical unit can be used. These units are capable of producing continuous power output (cutting current) or an interrupted waveform (coagulation current). Some may combine the two waveforms with a setting called *blended current*.

Once the electrosurgical unit is adjusted to the optimal range, the setting need not be incrementally raised during polyp removal (whether the size is large or small) or when switching between the polypectomy snare and the hot biopsy forceps.

Several types of snares are available for polypectomy. The large snare is approximately 6 cm in length and 2 cm in width; the small snare is 3 cm long and 1 cm wide. Only a few endoscopists are using the original "homemade" snare technique, preferring to use the commercially manufactured snare wires. Essentially, it makes little difference whether the snare is oval, crescent-shaped, or hexagonal, as the technique is the same in all instances. Thin snare wires will cut through a polyp faster than a thick wire,[70] and this factor must be kept in mind when switching from one type of snare to another.

The hot biopsy forceps is an electrically insulated forceps which permits current to flow through its entire length without current leakage into the colonoscope.[71] This forceps directs electrical energy around the tissue held within the jaws, enabling simultaneous cautery of the polyp base and a biopsy specimen.

In cases of bleeding, it is useful to have equipment available that will assist in hemostasis. A variceal type injector needle is useful, through which a 1:10,000 solution of epinephrine can be injected. A heater probe or a Bicap electrode may be a helpful adjunct to the hemostatic armamentarium when bleeding occurs.

Mechanical Aspects of Polypectomy

Two forces are employed whenever a polyp is transected with the wire snare. Both must be used simultaneously to achieve a clean, bloodless polypectomy without an excessive amount of thermal injury to the colonic wall. These two forces are heat, which results in cauterization, and the guillotine shearing force exerted by tightening the wire loop. Heat alone will not sever a polyp, while guillotine force alone may cut through a polyp but may result in immediate bleeding, as there is no capability for heat-sealing of blood vessels. Either cutting or coagulation current (or a blend of the two) can achieve tissue heating, but transecting a polyp while cells are being exploded by pure cutting current may result in subsequent bleeding from the polypectomy site without adequate hemostasis. It has been demonstrated[72] that use of blended current involved a greater incidence of immediate bleeding, while use of pure coagulation current was associated with a higher rate of delayed postpolypectomy bleeding.

Much of the capability for polyp transection is achieved by the guillotine force generated as the wire snare is withdrawn into its sheath. Proper use of the electrosurgical unit will provide heat sealing of the squeezed coapted blood vessels within the polyp base. Tissue will then be severed by the mechanical force of snare closure.

Polyp Size

Most polyps are less than 1 cm in diameter; only about 20 percent of polyps are larger than this. All large polyps (greater than 35 mm) are adenomas and are usually located in the right colon. In the rectum and distal sigmoid colon, a majority of small (less than 5 mm) polyps are nonneoplastic. Throughout the remainder of the colon, however, approximately 60 to 70 percent of these ≤5-mm polyps are adenomas.[73] Small polyps may be made more visible by chromoscopy,[74] using vital staining during the examination or in the preparation phase. It is not possible to determine the histology of diminutive polyps visually, therefore biopsy should be performed to permit differentiation between adenomas and polyps that are hyperplastic.

Polyp Configuration

There are two basic polyp configurations: pedunculated polyps, attached to the intestinal wall by a stalk, and sessile polyps, which have a broad base and arise directly from the wall. Pedunculated polyps may be attached by a short, thick or long, thin pedicle (Figs. 30-12 and 30-13). Sessile polyps are attached to the mucosal surface in a variety of ways. Those that are less than 8 mm in diameter almost invariably have the shape of a split pea, but larger polyps can assume any of several configurations.[75] The *marble-type* polyp (Fig. 30-14) has a narrow base and resembles a round marble. These polyps are attached to the colonic wall by a small connection, considerably narrower than the polyp's widest diameter. The *mountain-type* is well defined, with attachment by a broad base which is the widest part of the polyp. These are often multilobulated, with the edges distinctly discernible. The *clamshell* polyp is wrapped around a colonic fold (Fig. 30-15). The portion away from the instrument may be difficult to visualize completely because a portion of the mucosal attachment is on the opposite side of the fold. The *carpet* polyp is flat and may extend laterally over a wide area. The limits of this type are often difficult to delineate because its edges blend into the surrounding mucosa. *Extended* polyps have a combination of attachments, with the major component usually being a mountain or clamshell type. The edges of this type of polyp usually extend diffusely into the mucosa.

Some 50 percent of patients with one adenoma will have another, and it is important to perform total colonoscopy to seek synchronous adenomas. No attempt should be made to remove large or difficult polyps during intubation, since larger unresectable polyps or a malignancy may be encountered proximally, which will require surgery. However, there is no contraindi-

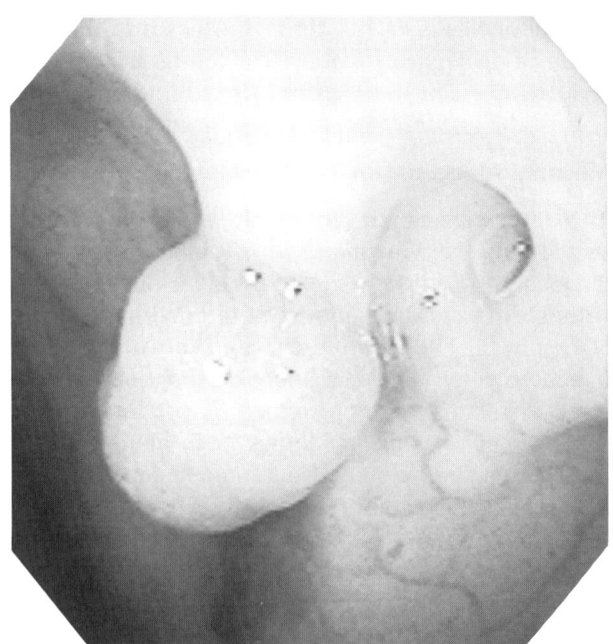

FIG. 30-12. A tubular adenoma attached by a short, thick pedicle. A single diverticulum is adjacent to the base of the pedicle. (See color Plate 12.)

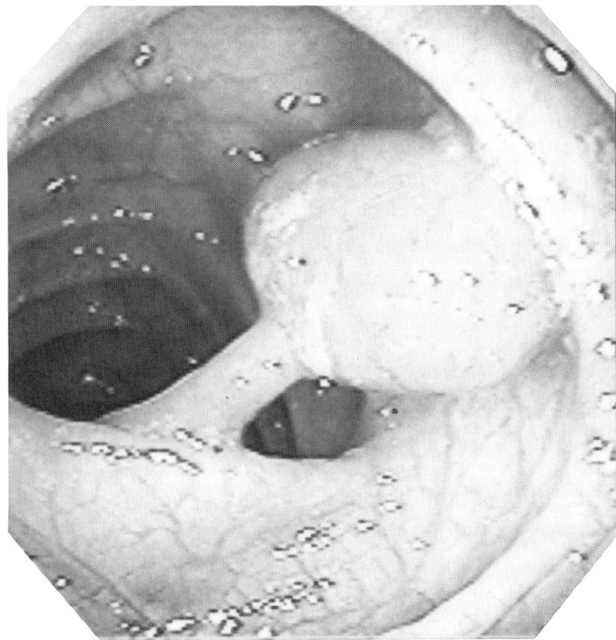

FIG. 30-13. A tubulovillous adenoma on a long, thin pedicle in the transverse colon. (See color Plate 13.)

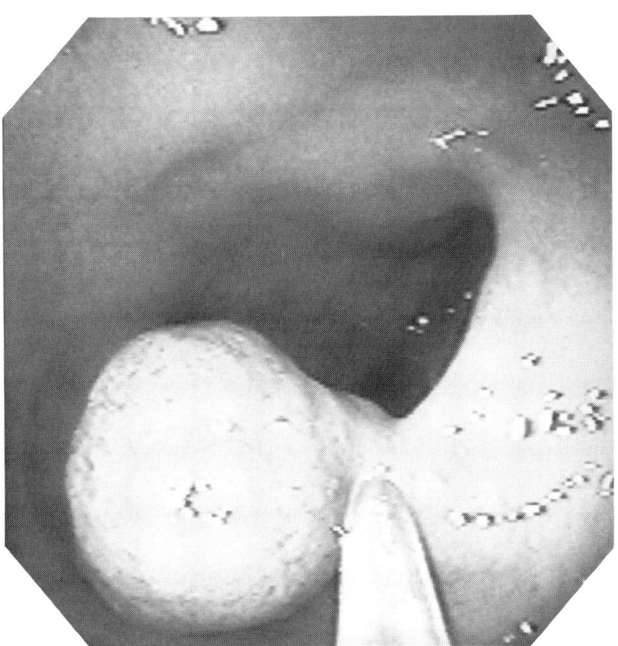

FIG. 30-14. A "marble-type" polyp with a small attachment to the colonic wall. The snare sheath is extended, and the wire loop has been closed around its narrow attachment to the colonic wall. (See color Plate 14.)

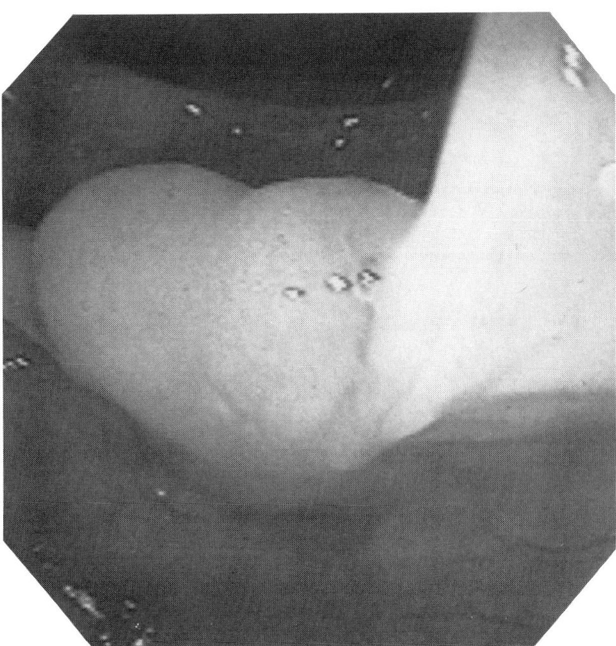

FIG. 30-15. A "clamshell" type of polyp wrapped around a fold in the sigmoid colon. (See color Plate 15.)

cation to removing a polyp during intubation and then continuing the examination to the cecum.

Technique of Polypectomy

The hot biopsy forceps is frequently used for removal of small polyps. A histologically identifiable tissue specimen is provided while electrocoagulation current ablates the polyp base in most instances.[76] When a cold biopsy forceps is used to remove small polyps, fragments will remain and subsequently proliferate.[77] In order to prevent deep thermal injury to the colonic wall, the polyp head, once grasped wholly or in part, should be tented away from the wall toward the colonic lumen. As current is applied, a zone of white thermal injury will become visible on the tented normal mucosa surrounding the polyp base. When this injury zone is 1 to 2 mm in size, current should be discontinued and the specimen retrieved as a normal biopsy. There is a high rate of residual adenoma when incomplete fulguration occurs.[78]

Small polyps may alternatively be removed with a wire snare. The minisnare is suitable, for it can easily be manipulated around the head of the polyp. Small polyps have small nutrient blood vessels and can safely be removed by "cheese-wiring" with the snare in the absence of electric current. This technique is safe and results in minimal bleeding.[79]

Pedunculated polyps are relatively easy to remove by placing the wire loop completely over the polyp head and closing the loop on the stalk. Full and direct vision of both snare and polyp must be maintained during capture and transection. The most important step in polyp capture is to place the catheter tip at the precise site where transection is desired.[70] If the polyp is pedunculated, the tip of the sheath should be advanced to the midportion of the stalk. If it is sessile, the sheath should be advanced to the line of demarcation between adenoma and colonic wall. Closure of the loop will result in seating the snare on the opposite site of the polyp. The wire loop always closes concentrically toward the tip of the snare sheath, which is the fixed point in the polypectomy system.

The mountain-type sessile polyp may require piecemeal resection, with one wire placed along a margin of the polyp base and the opposite wire positioned over a portion of the protruding polyp. Snare closure will result in capture of a portion of the polyp, which is then transected. Several applications may be required, removing fragments until satisfactory polypectomy is achieved.[67,80,81] The decision as to whether large polyps should be removed piecemeal or with one transection is not necessarily related to the size of the polyp but rather to the volume of tissue within the closed snare. A new technique has been developed for the removal of sessile colonic polyps. This involves injection of saline under the polyp and raising it away from the serosal surface on the cushion of saline. This may render polypectomy safer and more complete (Figs. 30-16, 30-17, and 30-18).[82,83]

After piecemeal transection of a wide-based sessile polyp, ragged fragments of tissue are seen at the base. A repeat examination after 4 to 12 weeks may reveal

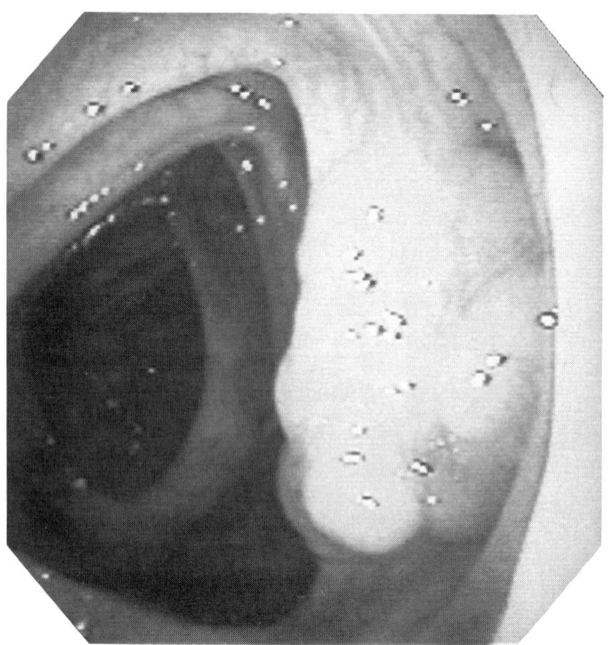

FIG. 30-16. A sessile polyp attached to the wall of the right colon. (See color Plate 16.)

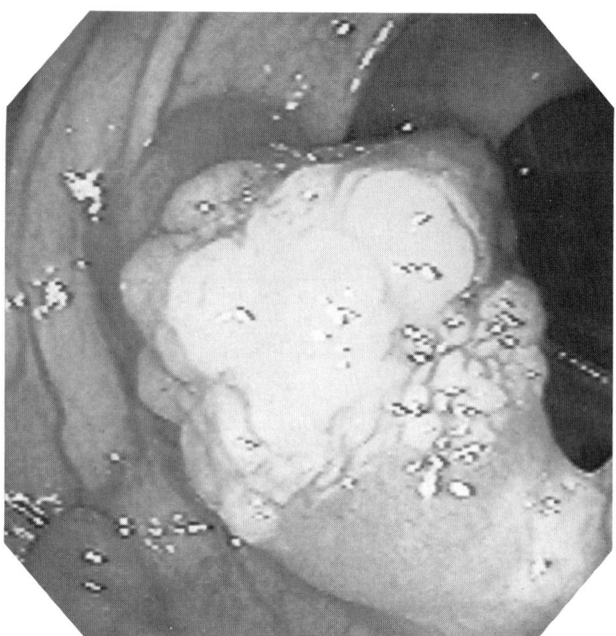

FIG. 30-17. The same polyp as in Fig. 30-16 after submucosal injection of saline. The saline increases the distance between the polyp base and the muscularis propria, rendering colonoscopic polypectomy safer. (See color Plate 17.)

that the polyp has completely disappeared, since thermal energy delivered during polypectomy may slough the residual adenoma. If adenoma is present at the repeat examination, it may be removed with further snare applications,[84] or an assessment as to the need for surgical resection will be necessary.

When precise site identification is desirable after polypectomy, an India ink tattoo[39] may be placed into the submucosa through a long flexible needle to permit subsequent localization either by endoscopy or at the time of surgery.

Laser therapy for enlarging the aperture of a tumor stenosis is usually applicable only in the rectum and lower sigmoid (extraperitoneal portion of the large bowel) where tumor vaporization can be performed with relative safety, a condition not met above the peritoneal reflection.[85] Laser vaporization of polyps may be possible, but it is not a viable alternative in most instances, since tissue cannot be retrieved for histopathologic identification.

Other forms of operative endoscopy include removal of foreign bodies; treatment of arteriovenous malformations[86] (angiodysplasia) with electrofulguration techniques, injection sclerotherapy, or a laser beam; balloon dilation of postoperative strictures or stenoses in Crohn's disease[87]; deflation of acute pseudoobstruction on the basis of ileus or Ogilvie's syndrome[88]; and decompression of volvulus.

Complications of Colonoscopy

Drugs used for conscious sedation may induce cardiorespiratory abnormalities, such as respiratory depression, as well as aberrations in cardiac rhythm (premature contractions). Elderly patients may be particularly susceptible to drug effects, requiring that dosages be adjusted accordingly. All patients must be monitored during colonoscopy by a gastrointestinal assistant. Mechanical external monitoring with electro-

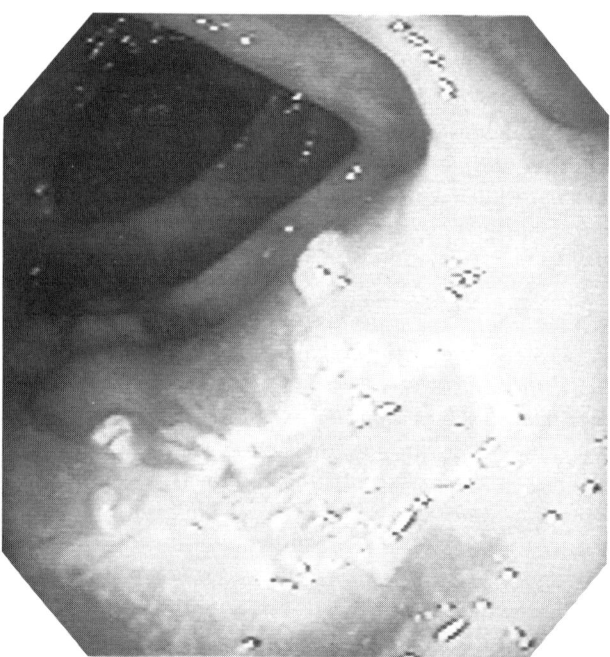

FIG. 30-18. The same polyp as Fig. 30-16. This defect in the wall was the result of total polypectomy of the sessile polyp.

cardiography and/or a pulse oximeter has not been proven to be beneficial during colonoscopy,[89] but it does provide additional information in certain high-risk patients.[90]

The most significant complication of diagnostic colonoscopy is perforation of the colon, which is reported to occur in 0.17 percent of procedures.[91,92] Perforation may be caused by either mechanical or pneumatic pressures or a combination of both.[93] Mechanical perforation may be associated with the use of splinting devices or biopsy forceps, but it is more frequently the result of a large loop formed by the colonoscope shaft which overstretches and splits the bowel. The rectosigmoid junction and sigmoid colon are the most common sites of perforation,[94] as they are the most difficult segments to intubate. The danger of perforation may be increased with oversedation or general anesthesia. Age does not appear to be a factor in colonoscopy complications.[95]

An x-ray of the abdomen is usually indicated for the patient with persistent severe postcolonoscopy distension and abdominal pain. Immediate surgical intervention is the treatment of choice for frank perforation; primary closure may be accomplished if there is no gross fecal contamination of the peritoneal cavity. In the presence of marked fecal soilage, a temporary diverting colostomy may be required. In asymptomatic patients, with minimal pneumoperitoneum or retroperitoneal emphysema, conservative treatment may be considered,[96] with one-third of perforations seen in a large series[97,98] being successfully treated without an operation. Splenic rupture is a rare complication.[99,100]

In addition to the risk of sedative medications, the three major complications of colonic polypectomy are hemorrhage, perforation, and the postpolypectomy coagulation syndrome. Hemorrhage and perforation are reported to occur in 1.7 percent[92,101] of polypectomies. Hemorrhage may occur at the time of polyp separation or up to 10 days following the procedure. Most immediate postpolypectomy hemorrhages can be managed conservatively and controlled at the time of the procedure. Delayed bleeding several days after polypectomy is due to ongoing necrosis from thermal injury, which erodes the wall of a blood vessel. If persistent postpolypectomy bleeding occurs, repeat colonoscopy may be needed with attempt at coagulation of the bleeding site.[102] Only rarely is selective intraarterial vasoconstrictor infusion required, but laparotomy is indicated if bleeding cannot be controlled. Because of the risk of bleeding following polypectomy, all patients undergoing colonoscopy should be instructed to discontinue salicylates for 1 week prior to the examination. Perforation related to polypectomy occurs in 0.04 to 2.1 percent[92] of patients. The causes of perforation are mechanical, such as cutting through the bowel wall or thermal injury from the use of cautery current. The effect of thermal damage and necrosis may be noticed immediately during the procedure or may occur hours or even days following polypectomy. Use of the hot biopsy forceps has been associated with a higher incidence of hemorrhage and perforation than when polyps are removed via a snare technique.[103,104]

Thermal injury to tissue is caused by the heat from electrocoagulation current. The burn effect may extend across the full thickness of the bowel wall to the serosa and cause symptoms of peritoneal irritation, similar to that of a localized peritonitis. The postpolypectomy syndrome[105] is often accompanied by fever, leukocytosis, and localized as well as rebound tenderness over the polypectomy site. This generally does not progress to a free perforation and can usually be treated conservatively.

Cleaning and Disinfection of Instrument

The colonic lumen is laden with bacteria and pathogenic organisms, of which two cause the most concern: hepatitis-B virus and the virus causing acquired immunodeficiency syndrome (AIDS).[106]

There have been only a few reported cases of transmission of bacterial infection and none of viral transmission via contaminated colonoscopes. It has been determined that proper cleaning and disinfection of instruments is sufficient to render them noninfectious. The steps in cleaning a flexible fiberoptic instrument, which cannot be heat-autoclaved, include mechanically cleansing the biopsy/instrument channel with a brush and scrubbing the shaft and outer portions of the endoscope. The instrument should then be placed in a disinfecting solution such as glutaraldehyde for up to 10 min.[107,108] Totally immersible endoscopes are currently being manufactured to allow soaking of the instrument head for more adequate disinfection. Some institutions require that colonoscopes used on patients known to be infected by AIDS should have gas sterilization. However, it has been demonstrated that the human immunodeficiency virus is inactivated by all of the standard disinfecting solutions currently in use. Biopsy forceps, snares, and water bottles must all be disinfected after use.

FUTURE DIRECTIONS

Digital processing of video images is a new field where applications lag behind the technological capabilities of the available instrumentation. The capability exists to measure spectrophotometric bands of color and depth, but there are no clinical correlates at this time. Digitally stored images may be computer-modeled for reconstruction in a three-dimensional format, permitting a polyp to be viewed from multiple directions in several positions. Various types of illumination can potentially be added, so that phosphor dye, which binds to tumors, can be photo-activated during a procedure to assume one color if benign and another when cancer has developed.

Sonographic imaging of the colon wall and surrounding tissue permits accurate assessment of the presence or depth of penetration of a cancer and will identify whether local lymph node involvement has occurred. This is rapidly developing into a valuable diagnostic adjunct.[109] Optical scanning laser fibers can provide instantaneous computer analysis of autofluorescence[110,111] to differentiate normal from neoplastic tissue.

REFERENCES

1. Fleischer DE, Goldberg SB, Browning TH, et al: Detection and surveillance of colorectal cancer. *JAMA* 261:580–585, 1989.
2. Waye JD, Bashkoff E: Total colonoscopy: Is it always possible? *Gastrointest Endosc* 37:152–154, 1991.
3. Muto T, Bussey HJR, Morson BC: The evolution of cancer of the colon and rectum. *Cancer* 36:2251–2270, 1975.
4. Sivak MV, Fleischer DE: Colonoscopy with a videoendoscope: Preliminary experience. *Gastrointest Endosc* 30:1–5, 1984.
5. Rogers BH: Colonoscopy with fluoroscopy (editorial). *Gastroint Endosc* 37:71–72, 1990.
6. Cirocco WC, Rusin LC: Documenting the use of fluoroscopy during colonoscopic examination: A prospective study. *Surg Endosc* 5:200–203, 1991.
7. Waye JD: Colonoscopy intubation techniques without fluoroscopy, in Hunt RH, Waye JD (eds): *Colonoscopy: Techniques, Clinical Practice and Colour Atlas*. London, Chapman & Hall, 1981.
8. Waye JD: Colonoscopy without fluoroscopy (editorial). *Gastroint Endosc* 36:72–73, 1990.
9. Anderson ML, Heigh RI, McCoy GA, et al: Accuracy of assessment of the extent of examination by experienced colonoscopists. *Gastrointest Endosc* 38:560–563, 1992.
10. Baillie J, Jowell P, Evangelou H, et al: Use of computer graphics simulation for teaching of flexible sigmoidoscopy. *Endoscopy* 23:126–129, 1991.
11. Noar MD: Endoscopy simulation—A brave new world (editorial). *Endoscopy* 23:147–149, 1991.
12. Cullado MJ, Porter JA, Slezak FA: The evolution of surgical endoscopic training—Meeting the American Board of Surgery requirements. *Am Surg* 57:4:250–253, 1991.
13. Waye, JD: How to become trained in an endoscopic procedure after the fellowship program (editorial). *Am J Gastroenterol* 81:611–612, 1986.
14. Irvine EJ, O'Connor J, Frost RA, et al: Prospective comparison of double contrast barium enema plus flexible sigmoidoscopy v colonoscopy in rectal bleeding: Barium enema v colonoscopy in rectal bleeding. *Gut* 29:1188–1193, 1988.
15. Williams CB, Macrae FA, Bartram CI: A prospective study of diagnostic methods in adenoma follow-up. *Endoscopy* 41:74–78, 1982.
16. Glick SN, Teplick SK, Balfe DM, et al: Large colonic neoplasms missed by endoscopy. *AJR* 152:513–517, 1989.
17. Hixson LJ, Fennerty MB, Sampliner RE, Garewal HS: Prospective blinded trial of the colonoscopic miss-rate of large colorectal polyps. *Gastrointest Endosc* 37:125–127, 1991.
18. Hunt RH, Swarbrick ET, Teague RH, et al: Colonoscopy for unexplained rectal bleeding. *Gastroenterology* 76:1158, 1979.
19. Lambert R, Sobin LH, Waye JD, Stadler GA: The management of patients with colorectal adenomas. *CA* 34:167–176, 1984.
20. Norfleet RG, Ryan ME, Wyman JB, et al: Barium enema versus colonoscopy for patients with polyps found during flexible sigmoidoscopy. *Gastrointest Endosc* 37:531–534, 1991.
21. Dobbins W: Dysplasia and malignancy in inflammatory bowel disease. *Rev Med* 35:33–48, 1984.
22. Nugent FW, Haggit RC, Gilpin PA: Cancer surveillance in ulcerative colitis. *Gastroenterology* 100:1241–1248, 1991.
23. Brenna E, Skreden K, Waldum HL, et al: The benefit of colonoscopy. *Scand J Gastroenterol* 25:81–88, 1990.
24. Waye JD: A diagnostic approach to colon bleeding. *Mt Sinai J Med* 51:491–501, 1984.
25. Lichtiger S, Kornbluth A, Salomon P, Waye JD: Lower gastrointestinal bleeding, in Taylor MB, Gollan JL, Peppercorn MA, et al (eds): *Gastrointestinal Emergencies*. Baltimore, Williams & Wilkins, 1992.
26. Jensen DM, Machicado GA: Diagnosis and treatment of severe hematocheszia: The role of urgent colonoscopy after purge. *Gastroenterology* 95:1569–1574, 1988.
27. Cussons PD, Berry AR: Comparison of the use of emergency mesenteric angiography and intraoperative colonoscopy with antegrade colonic irrigation in massive rectal hemorrhage. *J R Coll Surg Edinb* 34:91–93, 1989.
28. Waye JD: Endoscopy in idiopathic inflammatory bowel disease, in Kirsner J, Shorter R (Eds): *Inflammatory Bowel Disease*. Philadelphia, Lea & Febiger, 1988.
29. Waye JD, Hunt RH: Colonoscopic diagnosis of inflammatory bowel disease. *Surg Clin North Am* 62:905–913, 1982.
30. Riddell R, Goldman H, Ransohoff D, et al: Dysplasia in inflammatory bowel disease: Standardized classification with provisional clinical applications. *Hum Pathol* 14:931–968, 1983.
31. Sacher DB: New concepts of cancer. *Mt Sinai J Med* 50:133–137, 1983.
32. Modigliani R, Mary JY, Simon JF, et al: Clinical, biological, and endoscopic picture of attacks of Crohn's disease: Evolution on prednisone. Groupe d'Etude Therapeutique des Affections Inflammatoires Digestives. *Gastroenterology* 98: 811–818, 1990.
33. Holmquist I, Ahren C, Fallstrom SP: Clinical disease activity and inflammatory activity in the rectum in relation to mucosal inflammation assessed by colonoscopy: A study of children and adolescents with chronic inflammatory bowel disease. *Acta Paediatr Scand* 79:527–534, 1990.
34. Olaison G, Sjodahl R, Tagesson C: Glucocorticoid treatment in ileal Crohn's disease: Relief of symptoms but not of endoscopically viewed information. *Gut* 31:325–328, 1990.
35. Surawicz CM: Diagnosing colitis: Biopsy is best. *Gastroenterology* 92:538–540, 1987.
36. Waye JD: The differential diagnosis of inflammatory and infectious colitis, in Sivak MV Jr (ed): *Gastroenterologic Endoscopy*. Philadelphia, Saunders, 1987.
37. Chu DZJ, Giacco G, Martin RG, et al: The significance of synchronous carcinoma and polyps in the colon and rectum. *Cancer* 57:445–450, 1986.
38. Cohen JL, Forde KA: Intraoperative colonoscopy. *Ann Surg* 207:231–233, 1988.
39. Hyman N, Waye JD: Endoscopic four quadrant tattoo for the identification of colonic lesions at surgery. *Gastrointest Endosc* 37:56–58, 1991.

40. Matek W, Guggenmoos-Hozman I, Demling L: Follow-up of patients with colorectal adenomas. *Endoscopy* 17:175–181, 1985.
41. Selby JV, Friedman GD: Sigmoidoscopy in the periodic health examination of asymptomatic adults. *JAMA* 261: 4:595–601, 1989.
42. National Polyp Study Work Group: The National Polyp Study: Temporal sequence of evaluating colorectal cancer from the normal colon (abstract). *Gastrointest Endosc* 33: 167, 1987.
43. Winawer SJ, Zauber A, Diaz B, et al and the National Polyp Study Work Group: The National Polyp Study: Overview of Program and Preliminary Report of Patient and Polyp Characteristics, in Steele G Jr, Burt RW, Winawer SJ, Karp JP (eds): *Basic and Clinical Perspectives of Colorectal Polyps and Cancer: Progress in Clinical and Biological Research*, vol. 279. New York, Liss, 1988.
44. Eddy DM: Screening for colon cancer in a high risk population. *Gastroenterology* 92:682–692, 1987.
45. Vogelstein B, Fearon ER, Hamilton SR, et al: Genetic alterations during colorectal-tumor development. *N Engl J Med* 319:525–532, 1988.
46. Guillem JG, Neugut AI, Forde KA, et al: Colonic neoplasms in asymptomatic first-degree relatives of colon cancer patients. *Am J Gastroenterol* 83:271–273, 1988.
47. Lazenby AJ, Yardley JH, Giardiello FM: Lymphocytic ("microscopic") colitis: A comparative histopathologic study with particular reference to collangeous colitis. *Hum Pathol* 20:18–28, 1989.
48. Gilbertsen VA, Nelms JM: The prevention of invasive cancer of the rectum. *Cancer* 41:1137–1139, 1978.
49. Winawer SJ, Zauber AG, Gerdes H, et al: Reduction in colorectal cancer incidence following colonoscopic polypectomy: Report from the National Polyp Study (NPS) (abstract). *Gastroenterology* 100:A410, 1991.
50. Waye JD, Lewis BS, Frankel A, Geller SA: Small colon polyps. *Am J Gastroenterol* 83:120–122, 1988.
51. ASGE Guidelines: The role of colonoscopy in the management of patients with colonic polyps—Guidelines for clinical application. ASGE publication no. 1014. *Gastrointest Endosc* 34(suppl):6–7, 1988.
52. Alemayehu G, Jarnerot G: Colonoscopy during an attack of severe ulcerative colitis is a safe procedure and of great value in clinical decision making. *Am J Gastroenterol* 86: 187–190, 1991.
53. ASGE Guidelines: Preparation of patients for gastrointestinal endoscopy—Guidelines for clinical application. ASGE publication no. 1015. *Gastrointest Endosc* 34(suppl):32–34, 1988.
54. Fleischer D: Recommendations for antibiotic prophylaxis before endoscopy. *Am J Gastroenterol* 84:1489–1491,1989.
55. Neu HC: Recommendations for antibiotic prophylaxis before endoscopy. *Am J Gastroenterol* 84:1488–1489, 1989.
56. Meyer GW: Endocarditis prophylaxis and gastrointestinal procedures (editorial). *Am J Gastroenterol* 84:1492–1493, 1989.
57. Hunt RH, Waye JD (eds): *Colonoscopy Techniques: Clinical Practice and Color Atlas*. Chapman & Hall, London, 1981.
58. Sugawa C, Schuman BM: *Primer of Gastrointestinal Fiberoptic Endoscopy*. Boston, Little, Brown, 1981.
59. Cotton PB, Williams CB: *Practical Gastrointestinal Endoscopy*. London, Blackwell Scientific Publications, 1982.
60. Shinya H: *Colonoscopy: Diagnosis and Treatment of Colonic Diseases*. New York, Tokyo, Igaku-Shoin, 1982.
61. Brouillette DE, Leventhal R, Kuman S, et al: Midazolam versus diazepam for combined esophagogastroduodenoscopy and colonoscopy. *Dig Dis Sci* 34:1265–1271, 1989.
62. Stevenson GW, Wilson JA, Wilkinson J, et al: Pain following colonoscopy: Elimination with carbon dioxide. *Gastrointest Endosc* 38:564–567, 1992.
63. Keeffe EB, O'Connor KW: 1989 ASGE survey of endoscopic sedation and monitoring practices. *Gastrointest Endosc* 36:513–518, 1990.
64. Waye JD, Yessayan SA, Lewis BS, Fabry TL: The technique of abdominal pressure in total colonoscopy. *Gastrointest Endosc* 37:147–151, 1991.
65. Monahan DW, Peluso FE, Goldner F: Combustible colonic gas levels during flexible sigmoidoscopy and colonoscopy. *Gastrointest Endosc* 38:40–43, 1992.
66. Ernstoff JJ, Howard DA, Marshall JB, et al: A randomized blinded clinical trial of a rapid colonic lavage solution (Golytely) compared with standard preparation for colonoscopy and barium enema. *Gastroenterology* 84:1512–1516, 1983.
67. Beck DE, Fazio VW, Jagelman JG: Comparison of oral lavage methods for preoperative colonic cleansing. *Dis Colon Rectum* 29:699–703, 1986.
68. Bond JH, Levitt MD: Colonic gas explosion—Is a fire extinguisher necessary? *Gastroenterology* 77:1349, 1979.
69. Waye JD: Endoscopic treatment of adenomas. *World J Surg* 15:14–19, 1991.
70. Cohen LB, Waye JD: Treatment of colonic polyps—Practical considerations. *Clin Gastroenterol* 15:359, 1986.
71. Williams CB: Diathermy-biopsy: A technique for the endoscopic management of small polyps. *Endoscopy* 5:215, 1973.
72. Van Gossum A, Cozzoli A, Adler M, et al: Colonoscopic snare polypectomy: Analysis of 1485 resections comparing two types of current. *Gastrointest Endosc* 38:472–475, 1992.
73. Waye JD, Lewis BS, Frankel A, Geller SA: Small colon polyps. *Am J Gastroenterol* 83:120, 1988.
74. Mitooka H, Fujimori T, Ohno S, et al: New methods—new materials: Chromoscopy of the colon using indigo carmine dye with electrolyte lavage solution. *Gastrointest Endosc* 38:373–374, 1992.
75. Geenen JE, Fleischer D, Waye JD: *Techniques of Therapeutic Endoscopy*. New York, Saunders and Gower, 1991.
76. Peluso F, Goldner F: Follow-up of hot biopsy forceps treatment of diminutive colonic polyps. *Gastrointest Endosc* 37:604–606, 1991.
77. Woods A, Sanowski RA, Wadas DD, et al: Eradication of diminutive polyps: A prospective evaluation of bipolar coagulation versus conventional biopsy removal. *Gastrointest Endosc* 35:536, 1989.
78. Vanagunas A, Jacob P, Vakil N: Adequacy of "hot biopsy" for the treatment of diminutive polyps: A prospective randomized trial. *Am J Gastroenterol* 84:383, 1989.
79. Tappero G, Gaia E, DeFiuli P, et al: Cold snare excision of small colorectal polyps. *Gastrointest Endosc* 38:310–313, 1992.
80. Nivatvongs S, Snover DC, Fang DT: Piecemeal snare excision of large sessile colon and rectal polyps: Is it adequate? *Gastrointest Endosc* 30:18, 1984.
81. Christie JP: Colonoscopic removal of sessile colonic lesions. *Dis Colon Rectum* 21:11, 1978.
82. Karita M, Tada M, Okita K, Kodama T: Endoscopic therapy for early colon cancer: The strip biopsy resection technique. *Gastrointest Endosc* 37:128–132, 1991.
83. Karita M, Tada M, Okita K: The successive strip biopsy partial resection technique for large early gastric and colon cancers. *Gastrointest Endosc* 38:174–178, 1992.
84. Walsh RM, Ackroyd FW, Shelito PC: Endoscopic resection

of large sessile colorectal polyps. *Gastrointest Endosc* 38: 303–309, 1992.

85. Brunetaud JM, Maunoury V, Cochelard D, et al: Endoscopic laser treatment for rectosigmoid villous adenoma: Factors affecting the results. *Gastroenterology* 97:272–277, 1989.
86. Harford WV: Gastrointestinal angiodysplasia: Clinical features. *Endoscopy* 20:144–148, 1988.
87. Barroso AO, Azizi E, Jordan G, Alpert E: Repeated balloon dilation of a severe colonic stricture. *Gastrointest Endosc* 33:320–322, 1987.
88. Harig JM, Fumo DE, Loo FD, et al: Treatment of acute nontoxic megacolon during colonoscopy: Tube placement versus simple decompression. *Gastrointest Endosc* 34:23–27, 1988.
89. Waye JD: Colonoscopy and sigmoidoscopy, in Cotton PB, Tytgat GNJ, Williams CB (eds): *Annual of Gastrointestinal Endoscopy*. London, Current Science, 1991.
90. Fleischer D: Monitoring the patient receiving conscious sedation for gastrointestinal endoscopy: Issues and guidelines. *Gastrointest Endosc*. 35:262–266, 1989.
91. Reiertsen O, Skjoto J, Jacobsen CD, Rosseland AR: Complications of fiberoptic gastrointestinal endoscopy—Five years' experience in a central hospital. *Endoscopy* 19:1–6, 1987.
92. Habr-Gama A, Waye JD: Complications and hazards of gastrointestinal endoscopy. *World J Surg* 13:193–201, 1989.
93. Rogers BHG: Complications and hazards of colonoscopy, in Hunt RH, Waye JD (eds): *Colonoscopy: Techniques, Clinical Practice and Colon Atlas*. London, Chapman and Hall, 1981, pp 237–264.
94. Soon JC, Shang NS, Coh PM, Rauff A: Perforation of the large bowel during colonoscopy in Singapore. *Am Surg* 56:285–288, 1990.
95. Bat L, Pines A, Shemesh E, et al: Colonoscopy in patients aged 80 years or older and its contribution to the evaluation of rectal bleeding. *Postgrad Med J* 68:355–358, 1992.
96. Kavin H, Sinicrope F, Esker AH: Management of perforation of the colon at colonoscopy. *Am J Gastroenterol* 87:161–167, 1992.
97. Smith LE, Nivatvongs S: Complications in colonoscopy. *Dis Colon Rectum* 18:214, 1975.
98. Taylor R, Weakley FL, Sullivan HB: Non-operative management of colonoscopic perforation with pneumoperitoneum. *Gastrointest Endosc* 24:124, 1978.
99. Rockey DC, Weber JR, Wright TL, Wall SD: Splenic injury following colonoscopy. *Gastrointest Endosc* 36:306–309, 1990.
100. Ong E, Bohmler U, Wurbs D: Splenic injury as a complication of endoscopy: Two case reports and a literature review. *Endoscopy* 23:302–304, 1991.
101. Nivatvongs S: Complications in colonoscopic polypectomy: Lessons to learn from an experience with 1576 polyps. *Am Surg* 54:51–53, 1988.
102. Rex DK, Lewis BS, Waye JD: Colonoscopy and endoscopic therapy for delayed post-polypectomy hemorrhage. *Gastrointest Endosc* 38:127–129, 1992.
103. Wadas DD, Sanowski RA: Complications of the hot biopsy forceps technique. *Gastrointest Endosc* 33:32–37, 1987.
104. Dyer WS, Quigley EM, Noel SM, et al: Major colonic hemorrhage following electrocoagulating (hot) biopsy of diminutive colonic polyps: Relationship to colonic location and low-dose aspirin therapy. *Gastrointest Endosc* 37:361–364, 1991.
105. Waye JD: The postpolypectomy coagulation syndrome. *Gastrointest Endosc* 27:184, 1981.
106. ASGE Guidelines: Infection control during gastrointestinal endoscopy—Guidelines for clinical application. ASGE publication no. 1018. *Gastrointest Endosc* 34(suppl):37–40, 1988.
107. Axon ATR: Disinfection and endoscopy—Summary and recommendations. *J Gastroenterol Hepatol* 6:1:23–24, 1991.
108. Tandon RK: Endoscopic disinfection—Practices and recommendations. *J Gastroenterol Hepatol* 6:1:37–39, 1991.
109. Wiersema MJ, Hawes RH, Tao L-C, et al: Endoscopic ultrasonography as an adjunct to fine needle aspiration cytology of the upper and lower gastrointestinal tract. *Gastrointest Endosc* 38:35–39, 1992.
110. Kapadia CR, Cutruzzola FW, O'Brien KM, et al: Laser-induced fluorescence spectroscopy of human colonic mucosa: Detection of adenomatous transformation. *Gastroenterology* 99:150–157, 1990.
111. Cothren RM, Richards Kortum R, et al: Gastrointestinal tissue diagnosis by laser-induced fluorescence spectroscopy at endoscopy. *Gastrointest Endosc* 36:105–111, 1990.

CHAPTER 31

Air-Contrast Barium Enema Technique

Edward T. Stewart

HIGHLIGHTS

For a number of decades, single-contrast examination of the colon was the best technique available to evaluate those portions of the colon not readily examined digitally or by rigid proctosigmoidoscopy. During those years, the development of improved barium suspensions with better coating characteristics paralleled ever-improving fluoroscopic equipment. The introduction of image intensification with markedly enhanced resolution led to the development of the single-contrast barium enema as the major diagnostic tool in the search for colorectal carcinoma. The single-contrast examination became the "workhorse" of the clinician and especially for the gastroenterologist. Twenty-five years ago, Welin[1] (Sweden) reported the results of a new technique for polyp detection now called the *air-contrast enema,* or *pneumocolon.* Since the introduction of the air-contrast examination (as opposed to the single-contrast examination), its proper role in the examination of the colon has been debated by radiologists.[2] Following the introduction of colonoscopy with fiberoptic equipment in the late 1960s, a new yardstick became available for evaluating the accuracy of these examinations.[3–6] Colonoscopy also came into wide use among gastroenterologists as a primary diagnostic tool for evaluation of the colon. In addition to serving as a diagnostic instrument, the colonoscope also allowed such therapeutic options as biopsy and polypectomy. As a result, the traditional roles of the diagnostic radiologist and gastroenterologist merged as the competing technologies began to interface.

CONTROVERSIES

There is an ongoing debate as to the role of the radiologic and endoscopic examination of the colon. Each discipline has marshaled its results and defended the utilization of "its" technique. From the data available, we now know that as colonic lesions increase in size, the accuracies of the radiologic and endoscopic examinations begin to approach one another in terms of detection.[7,8] Conversely, with diminishing size, polypoid lesions become more difficult to define by both techniques but especially by the radiologic examination. Among endoscopists, the emphasis on the detection of adenoma in an effort to prevent the development of adenocarcinoma has fueled enthusiasm for the detection of diminutive polyps. For this reason, the interest in air-contrast examination has heightened; from available data, it would appear to be a far more sensitive examination for the detection of diminutive colonic polyps than the single-contrast examination. Most comparisons between single- and double-contrast examinations are derived from retrospective studies which compare the results with colonoscopic findings.[9–11] Inferences drawn from these types of studies are subject to a number of variables which may or may not be controlled. Variables such as patient selection, colonic cleansing, examiner expertise, estimation of polyp size, and pathologic documentation are among the problems encountered in comparing these studies. However, based on the available data, it would appear that the air-contrast examination—because of its superiority in the detection of smaller polyps—is the examination of choice in searching for polypoid lesions of the colon. In addition, the rectum is no longer given over to the proctosigmoidoscopist, since the rectum is clearly within the domain of the air-contrast examination for the detection of significant pathology. Radiologists correctly point to the fact that their examinations are *safer, are less time-consuming for the patient, examine the entire colon, and are far less expensive than endoscopic studies*. Since the radiologic examination can detect polypoid lesions equal or greater than 1 cm in size—those that are likely to be malignant—in 90 to 95 percent of individuals, it is deemed to be very satisfactory for screening polypoid lesions in the colon. Endoscopists point to the fact that lesions less than 5 mm in size may be detected only 20 to 30 percent of the time by radiologic examinations, but they *can* be seen endoscopically. Additionally, endoscopists point to the fact that when polyps are found, they can be destroyed or removed and examined histologically.

FUTURE DIRECTIONS

Clearly, the most important new issue facing the diagnosis of carcinoma of the colon and premalignant lesions is cost-effectiveness. In the next few years, the debate over the value in detecting diminutive ($\leq$ 5 mm) polyps during screening will continue. Due to the great cost of screening for such tiny, invariably benign lesions, new recommendations will very likely emerge.[12] Future resource utilization must be looked at very carefully, especially in terms of its financial impact. It may well be that procedures used in detection and screening will be different from those used in follow-up surveillance. The safer, much less expensive radiologic examination may be more important in screening the larger population than in the surveillance of patients who are expected to have diminutive metachronous polyps. Also, the most cost-effective interval for reexamination must be established. If the radiologic examination is perceived as being competitive with endoscopic examinations, the patient is ill served. Properly used, these highly sophisticated procedures should and can be complementary. The combination of flexible sigmoidoscopy and air-contrast enema may ultimately prove to be the most cost-effective approach for the detection and surveillance of colonic neoplasms.[13]

Evaluation of patients on a day-to-day basis by air-contrast examination has many champions and is increasingly being utilized. The detection of early inflammatory disease as well as neoplasms is well suited to this study. When dealing with neoplastic lesions, the role of the exam is to detect primary lesions and any synchronous lesions during the initial screen. During surveillance, positive-contrast exam is directed at the identification of metachronous lesions or recurrent disease. Surveillance studies often deal with postoperative alterations in the colon, such as end-to-end anastamosis or diverting colostomies.

Despite the current emphasis on performing double-contrast studies, the single-contrast study may be preferable in some instances. For example, when the colon is severely deformed by diverticulosis, the single-contrast examination may be preferable for the detection of polypoid masses and strictures. When the objective of the positive-contrast enema is simply to define the level of obstruction, single-contrast examination is generally sufficient (Fig. 31-1). When fistulas—bowel-to-bowel or bowel-to-skin—are suspected, the single-contrast barium study is also preferred. Since endoscopy often follows positive-contrast studies in obstructed patients, water-soluble contrast agents may be useful. For instance, in the presence of high-grade colonic obstruction, water-soluble agents may be used in the examination to confirm the level of obstruction. This step can then be followed immediately by endoscopy without cleansing the colon of residual barium. The proper selection of the contrast study should be the responsibility of the examining radiologist, who is aware of the clinical setting and the goals of the examination.

The following text deals with the technique of air-contrast examination. As with any radiologic study, many variables affect the final results.

INITIAL CONSIDERATIONS IN PATIENT SELECTION

The clinical status of the patient will occasionally determine whether air-contrast examination will be successful. In the performance of air-contrast examination, multiple patient positions are necessary, including prone, supine, lateral, and erect. Patients whose clinical status will not allow proper positioning are not good candidates for air-contrast examination. Orthopedic or monitoring devices which impede the movement of the patient make air-contrast examination extremely difficult if not impossible. Severe musculoskeletal disease, deformity, and contracture may make positioning impossible. Any patient with a se-

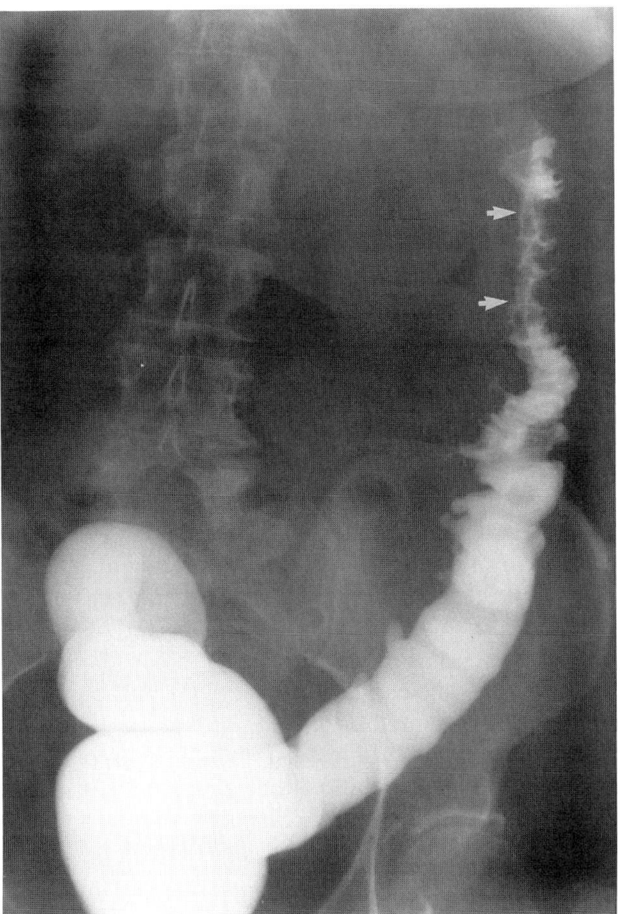

FIG. 31-1. High-grade obstruction due to infiltrating carcinoma of the left colon. A single-contrast examination in this patient is sufficient to show a scirrhous, nodular, infiltrating malignancy in the left colon (arrowheads). The lesion is narrowing the lumen of the colon sufficiently to cause high-grade obstruction to retrograde flow of contrast. A number of diverticula are also demonstrated. The features of this infiltrating process are shown with the single-contrast technique. Endoscopic biopsy proved this to be an infiltrating adenocarcinoma. There is no evidence of high-grade obstruction of the proximal colon in this patient. The appearance of high-grade obstruction during instillation of positive contrast from below is probably due to mucosal prolapse into the lumen of the narrowed colon. This phenomenon is often encountered in barium enema examinations of high-grade strictures despite the absence of clinical obstruction or other radiographic evidence of obstruction.

vere cognitive disorder or other neurologic diseases may not be a candidate for this type of examination.

INDICATIONS

Indications for air-contrast enema cover the gamut of suspected colonic diseases. This includes evaluation of *suspected colonic neoplasm, inflammatory bowel disease, diagnosis of and search for complications of diverticulitis, evaluation of occult gastrointestinal bleeding, ruling out of colonic obstruction, and searching for the cause of abdominal pain.* Since air-contrast enemas examine the entire colon, one of the frequent indications is *incomplete colonoscopy.*[8]

CONTRAINDICATIONS

As with any type of enema, there are situations which may delay or preclude the air-contrast examination. Clinical signs of peritonitis—such as fever, rebound tenderness, and elevated white count—may indicate *perforation or impending perforation* and should be evaluated by the radiologist. Whenever perforation is suspected, the examination is contraindicated. *Suspected toxic megacolon is a contraindication;* when in doubt, delay or cancellation may be necessary.

A far more common issue is the status of *previous colonic biopsy.* Two types of biopsy are generally utilized: *surgical forceps biopsy* or *endoscopic biopsy.* Due to depth of penetration into the muscularis propria, surgical forceps biopsy weakens the colonic wall, so that any type of enema examination before healing takes place is contraindicated.[15,26a] It is customary to allow at least 2 weeks for healing of the mucosal wall and mucosa prior to any positive-contrast study. One exception to this is surgical biopsy on the surface of a large intraluminal tumor mass. In this instance, surgical forceps biopsy does not extend into the bowel wall and there is little danger of perforation. *Endoscopic biopsy,* on the other hand, appears to be a safe procedure and should not preclude subsequent positive-contrast examination. This is due to the superficial nature of the biopsy (no deeper than muscularis mucosa), which does not weaken the colon wall or increase the risk of perforation.

Experimental studies have shown that intraluminal colon pressures generated by air-contrast studies are not sufficient to perforate the colon after endoscopic biopsy but are potentially in a range to do so after surgical forceps biopsy.[16]

Endoscopic polypectomy, which injuries the bowel wall, is a contraindication for positive-contrast studies until the colon has healed. Again, healing of the colonic mucosa and wall generally takes a minimum of 2 to 3 weeks. *It is the responsibility of the ordering physician to relay information concerning biopsy or polypectomy to the radiologist to assist in making the proper decision.* Patients cannot be expected to know what type of biopsy has been performed and often are unaware that a biopsy of any nature has taken place. When there is doubt as to the safety of the examination, communication with the referring physician directly is most useful. It is better to delay and reschedule the examination than to proceed if there are any questions concerning the status of biopsy or polypectomy.

Obviously, pregnancy is a contraindication for positive-contrast studies.

PREPARATION

It should be the radiologist's responsibility to provide the patient with adequate instruction for colonic cleansing and to work with the patient until the colon is satisfactorily cleansed.

The presence of particulate fecal debris presents the same problems for the radiologist as it does for the endoscopist. The confidence level for polyp detection plummets when stool is present. Over the years, a number of regimens have been employed to cleanse the colon and, to some degree, the clinical status of the patient may dictate the type of preparation that is advisable. Various combinations of enemas, saline cathartics, stimulant cathartics, and bulk cathartics have been employed.[17,18] These have been augmented recently by the introduction of the polyethylene glycol (PEG) preparation now favored by most colonoscopists.[14,19,20]

Unfortunately, the presence of water in the colon substantially degrades the quality of air-contrast examinations due to interference with mucosal coating. Therefore, colonic preparations which feature the introduction of large quantities of liquid that may be retained in the colon can cause problems. For this reason, the use of PEG is not favored by most radiologists. This particular 1-day preparation lavages the colon very effectively but leaves it very wet. In order for the colon to be properly "dried out," barium studies must be delayed for at least 12 to 24 h. Often, this delay is unacceptable. In some clinical situations, however, the delay is acceptable, and the PEG preparation is preferred. Among the best examples are patients with inflammatory bowel disease. They respond very nicely to the PEG prep, which lets them avoid the use of stimulant cathartics that may exacerbate their symptoms. The use of tap water or saline enemas to cleanse the colon introduces a time factor and logistics problem for most radiology departments. Also, following the use of cleansing enemas, a time delay is necessary for reabsorption of the water that is invariably retained in the right colon. When cleansing is inadequate, there is a tendency for excess fluid and feces to remain in the right colon. It is not unusual to have a very high confidence exam of the left colon and a poor exam of the right colon.

Most radiologists currently employ a combination of saline and stimulant cathartics combined with hydration and dietary restrictions. We have for sometime employed a preparation featuring clear liquids for 24 h prior to examination, 10 oz of magnesium citrate and 20 mg of bisacodyl (Dulcolax) the evening before the examination, followed by a bisacodyl suppository in the morning prior to the study. Individuals who are not adequately cleansed using the above regimen may require longer and repeated efforts at cleansing the colon, and this is generally done at the discretion of the radiologist.

There is increasing interest in performing double-contrast examinations following flexible sigmoidoscopy.[21] The rationale for this is supported by minimizing the number of colon cleansing regimens for the patient as well as expediting the examinations on a single day. Air-contrast barium enema can sometimes be performed satisfactorily following flexible sigmoidoscopy and the introduction of gas. Although this situation is not optimal for the radiologist, the patient should probably not be refused access to the barium examination simply on the basis of retained gas in the colon. However, in this situation, redundancy of the colon may cause problems in moving the barium because of "air locks" in the gas-filled colon. Also, preparing the left colon for flexible sigmoidoscopy may not adequately clean the right colon. Although the air-contrast examination can be attempted following sigmoidoscopy, the radiologist should be prepared to terminate the examination and reschedule it if the technical quality is for any reason thought to be compromised. Most radiologists would prefer a clean, empty, dry colon for this examination.

COMPLICATIONS

Complications are uncommon but occasionally are encountered. These include *perforation, barium sensitivity, barium impaction, transient bacteremia, patient dehydration, and misplacement of the enema tip into the vaginal vault,* especially in female patients with prior rectovaginal injuries.[21,22] Perforation and mortality are 10 to 20 times less than colonoscopy.[23] Perforation is estimated to occur in 1/10,000 examinations and mortality in 1/50,000 examinations. Perforation of the colon proximal to the rectum is unusual unless the colon is severely diseased and necrotic or subjected to transmural injuries such as polypectomy or surgical biopsy, as previously discussed. Most perforations occur around the rectum and are generally related in some way to the enema tip or balloon device.[24] Balloon devices that are overdistended can disrupt the rectal mucosa and cause transmural tears.[25,26] As the balloon device is inflated to the point that it touches the bowel wall, pressures within the balloon are directly transmitted to the bowel wall. When compliance of the rectal wall is exceeded by the pressure of the balloon, mucosal injury may occur. Perforation of the rectum may be seen immediately or may not be recognized until the balloon is deflated and the barium extravasates through the rectal tear into the perirectal soft tissues. Hard or firm barium enema tips may be driven into the wall of the colon as the balloon device is inflated or the tip is inserted inappropriately. This may occasionally result in significant mucosal and occasional transmural injury. In general practice, the overinflated rectal balloon is usually the culprit. To avoid this potential complication, rectal balloons should be inflated only by the examiner under direct fluoroscopic control.[26] The capacity of the rectum is demonstrated by the instillation of positive contrast prior to balloon distention. The distended balloon should not touch the lateral rectal wall; following satisfactory inflation, the entire assembly is generally pulled down against the internal anal sphincter.

Retention balloon devices are most safely used when they are reserved for patients who demonstrate incontinence. In most cases, the inflatable balloon, although attached to the enema tip, does not need to be inflated, since most patients examined will remain continent. We routinely perform rectal examination and assessment of rectal tone as well as the capacity of the rectal vault. Patients with good sphincter tone are rarely incontinent.[27,28] Patients with very poor sphincter tone are virtually always incontinent. However, the balloon is only inflated after incontinence occurs. Also, during the examination, a continent patient may have the enema tip removed for comfort at the election of the examiner. One of the major advantages of avoiding balloon inflation and removing the enema tip is demonstration of low rectal lesions, which might otherwise be obscured by the enema tip apparatus (Figs. 31-2*A*, 31-2*B*, and 31-3).

Hypersensitivity reactions to the components of barium occasionally occur.[29,30] The recent discovery of severe analphylactic reactions to latex rectal balloons has led to the discontinuation of these retention devices in favor of nonallergenic materials, usually silicone rubber.[31] It is highly likely that some hypersensitivity reactions previously attributed to barium components were, in fact, due to latex sensitivity. Latex sensitivity appears to be related to proteins in latex rubber which are rapidly absorbed by the rectal mucosa. The new silicone rubber inflatable devices are free of this problem and are now in widespread use.

Because of transient bacteremia from enteric pathogens, patients with prosthetic or abnormal cardiac valves might be considered for prophylactic antibiotics during the barium enema exam; at this time, however, there are no formal recommendations concerning this.[32] Improper vaginal placement of the enema tip should be quickly recognized by the radiologist. Although overfilling of the vaginal vault can potentially result in intraperitoneal spillage of contrast via the fallopian tubes, this is very rare. Digital rectal examination should minimize the potential for this error, since rectovaginal tears are easily diagnosed on digital and visual examination.

PHARMACOLOGIC AGENTS

Air-contrast studies require no sedation, which is a major advantage over endoscopy. Routine sedation for colonoscopy procedures leaves the patient heavily sedated for several hours and unable to drive or resume daily activities. Following barium enema, the patient is able to resume normal daily activities immediately. The only pharmacologic aid often employed is the use of a smooth-muscle relaxant. In patients with colonic irritability, pulse doses of glucagon (0.5 and 1.0 mg IV) can be given.[33] Routine use of glucagon is unnecessary. However, in order to diminish colonic irritability and decrease the abdominal cramping experienced by some patients, glucagon should be employed liberally.

TECHNIQUE OF THE RADIOGRAPHIC EXAMINATION

Standard fluoroscopic equipment (either stand-at-the-side or remote control) is satisfactory for air-contrast examination. High kilovoltage (120 kV) technique is preferred for this type of examination, since the higher kilovoltage shortens the exposure and diminishes the effect of motion. Although the examination emphasizes the analysis of the final film, fluoroscopy and compression remain very important parts of the study; therefore, image intensification should be of high quality, allowing for high resolution. Since the patient must be placed in the erect position, the table must be able to elevate to 90° in one direction. Standard spot films and overhead films are employed during the study. The size of spot films is determined by the equipment but varies from 9.5 × 9.5 to 14 × 14 in. Digital radiography is now being utilized in some institutions, where the size of the images is limited to the field of view of the image intensifier.

Prior to the performance of positive-contrast examination of the colon, a plain film of the abdomen is recommended. The value of the plain film is not only to assess the colon for adequate cleansing but also to record artifacts, calcifications, and skeletal abnormalities that may subsequently be obscured or cause confusion in the interpretation of the barium enema examination. The postoperative abdomen often contains metallic clips and sutures, which should be duly recorded. As previously discussed, if the patient has had a previous flexible examination, there may be a considerable amount of gas present in the colon. This is also recorded on the preliminary film.

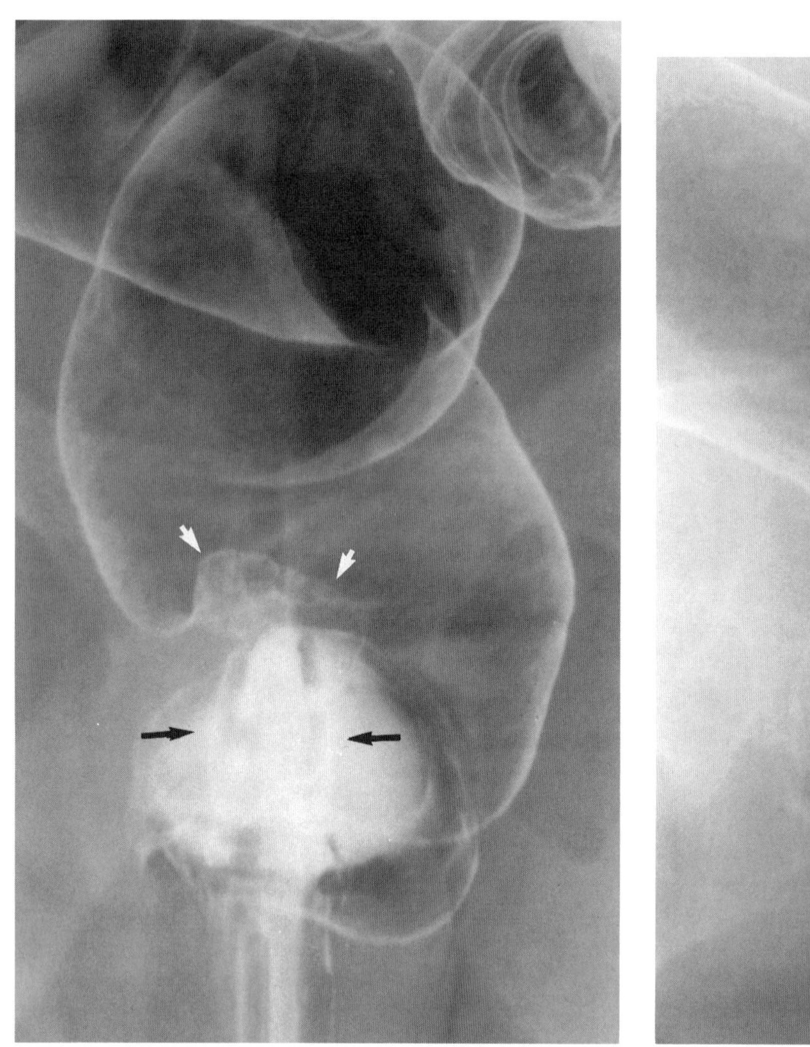

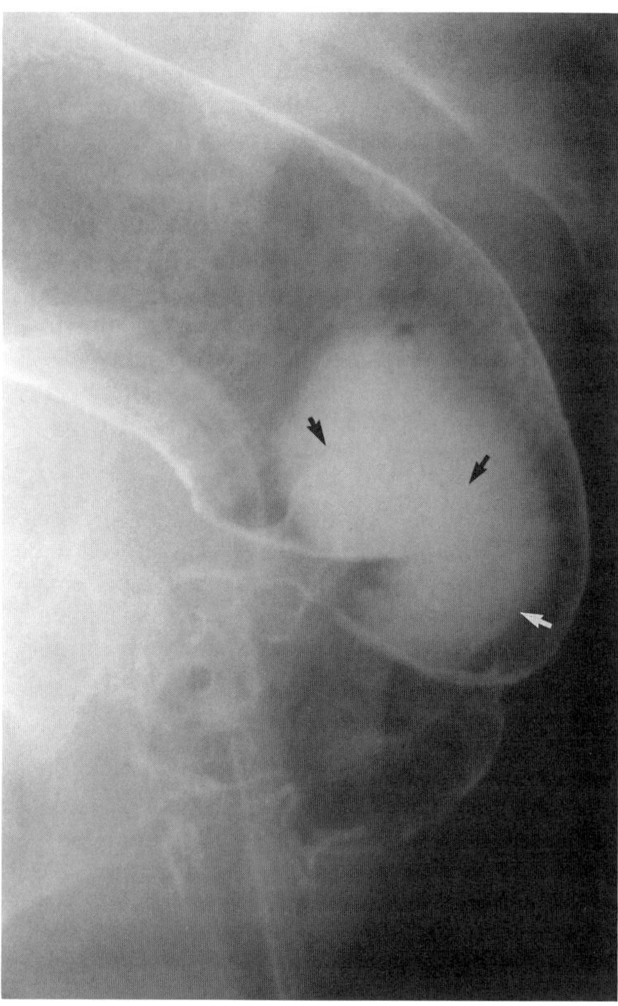

A B

FIG. 31-2. Low-lying rectal carcinoma. *A*. Lobular 3- to 4-cm rectal carcinoma (white arrowheads) extends into the lumen of the rectum from the lateral rectal wall. The enema tip (black arrows) has partially obscured the lumen. The barium in the dependent portions of the colon also partially obscures the lesion. *B*. This is the lateral view of the rectum with the patient in the recumbent position. The tumor mass (arrowheads) is partially obscured by a puddle of barium in the dependent portion of the rectum. Again, notice how close the enema tip is to the tumor mass itself. A balloon-tip catheter with the balloon distended would dobscure much if not all of this low-lying lesion. *C*. The rectum viewed on the lateral decubitus film shows the tumor to much better advantage (arrowheads). Notice that the tumor sits astride the first valve of Houston.

The objective of the air-contrast examination is to visualize the entire colon with the air-contrast technique. In this type of exam, the information gained is generally limited to those areas of the colon which are thinly coated with barium and distended with air. Puddles of barium in the dependent portions of the colon are so dense that they generally obscure pathology. The proper technique for this examination therefore involves the use of optimum amounts of barium and gas. Although CO_2, which is rapidly absorbed, has been employed by some in an effort to reduce colonic cramping and distention which may persist following the examination, most examiners use room air.[34] The type of barium selected for these studies varies from 80% to 100% wt/vol (E-Z EM Company: Liquid Polibar, 100% wt/vol; E-Z-AC, 100% wt/vol; Liquid Polibar Plus, 105% wt/vol; Lafayette Pharmaceutical: HD-85, 85% wt/vol). High-density barium currently available has excellent coating characteristics and contains dispersing agents and simethicone. It is of high viscosity and therefore requires large-bore tubing (½ in. internal lumen) for flow to be satisfactory. The quantity employed generally varies from 500 to 600 mL, but larger volumes may be necessary.

Air-contrast studies are generally begun with the patient in the prone position following the satisfactory

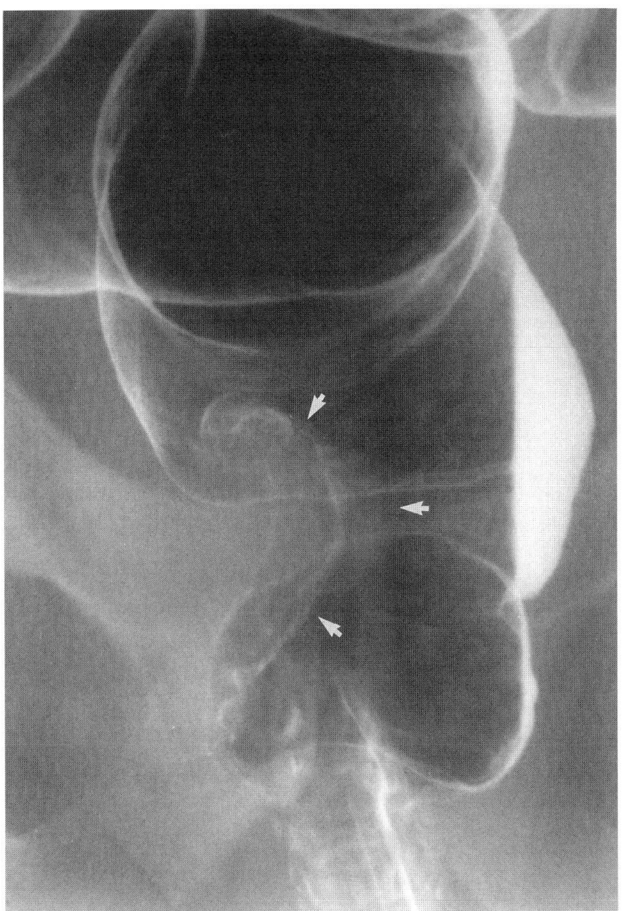

C
FIG. 31-2 (*Continued*)

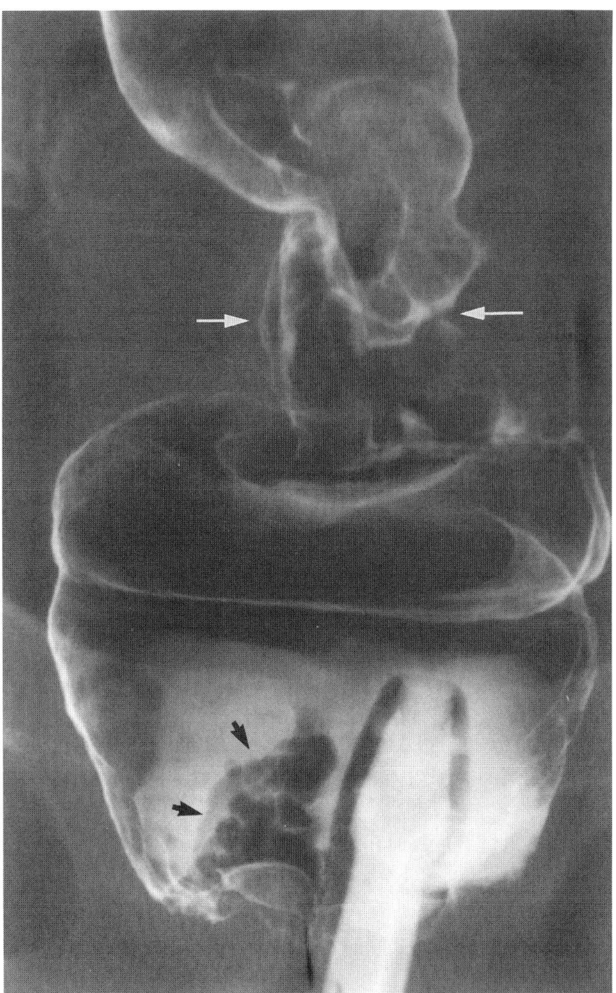

FIG. 31-3. Two rectal carcinomas. The air-contrast examination demonstrates two independent carcinomas. A polypoid tumor is shown just inside the anal canal (black arrowheads). A second annular carcinoma is present in the rectosigmoid (white arrows). Both lesions and their morphologic characteristics are beautifully displayed on this air-contrast examination. Note that the enema tip could be withdrawn in this patient, which would eliminate the artifact produced by the enema tip in the rectum.

placement of the enema tip, which is secured to the skin with tape. This is done because the large-bore tubing required for this exam becomes heavy enough to dislodge the enema tip by gravity when the patient is placed erect. In the prone position, contrast is introduced into the colon and the head of the barium column is followed to the distal transverse colon. At this point, the barium in the rectum is siphoned back into the bag. Air is then insufflated into the rectum, distending the rectum with air and pushing the barium column forward; as more gas is introduced, the barium column is pushed further into the colon and, generally around the hepatic flexure, into the ascending colon. It is important to not let the air column get ahead of the barium. When this happens, it may be impossible to advance the barium column any farther. Initial spot films of the sigmoid colon are taken with the patient in the prone position.

The patient is then placed in the lateral position, facing the examiner, with the right side down. Air is then added in amounts sufficient to push enough barium around the hepatic flexure to allow for a complete examination of the right colon (Fig. 31-4*A* to *H*). Generally, a lateral radiograph of the distended rectum is taken in this lateral position. The patient is then placed supine and films of the sigmoid colon, including oblique views, are obtained. Compression may be employed to displace redundant sigmoid loops for better visualization as well as improved resolution in obese patients. We employ compression in almost all patients. Once the sigmoid colon is satisfactorily imaged, air is insufflated to distend the remainder of the colon satisfactorily. Once the cecum and/or terminal ileum is reached, insufflation of air is stopped. Initial examination of the sigmoid should be performed before reflux into the terminal ileum occurs, avoiding the overlap of small bowel on the sigmoid colon. The patient is then rotated 360° to coat the colon and placed in the erect position; in this position, films are taken of the

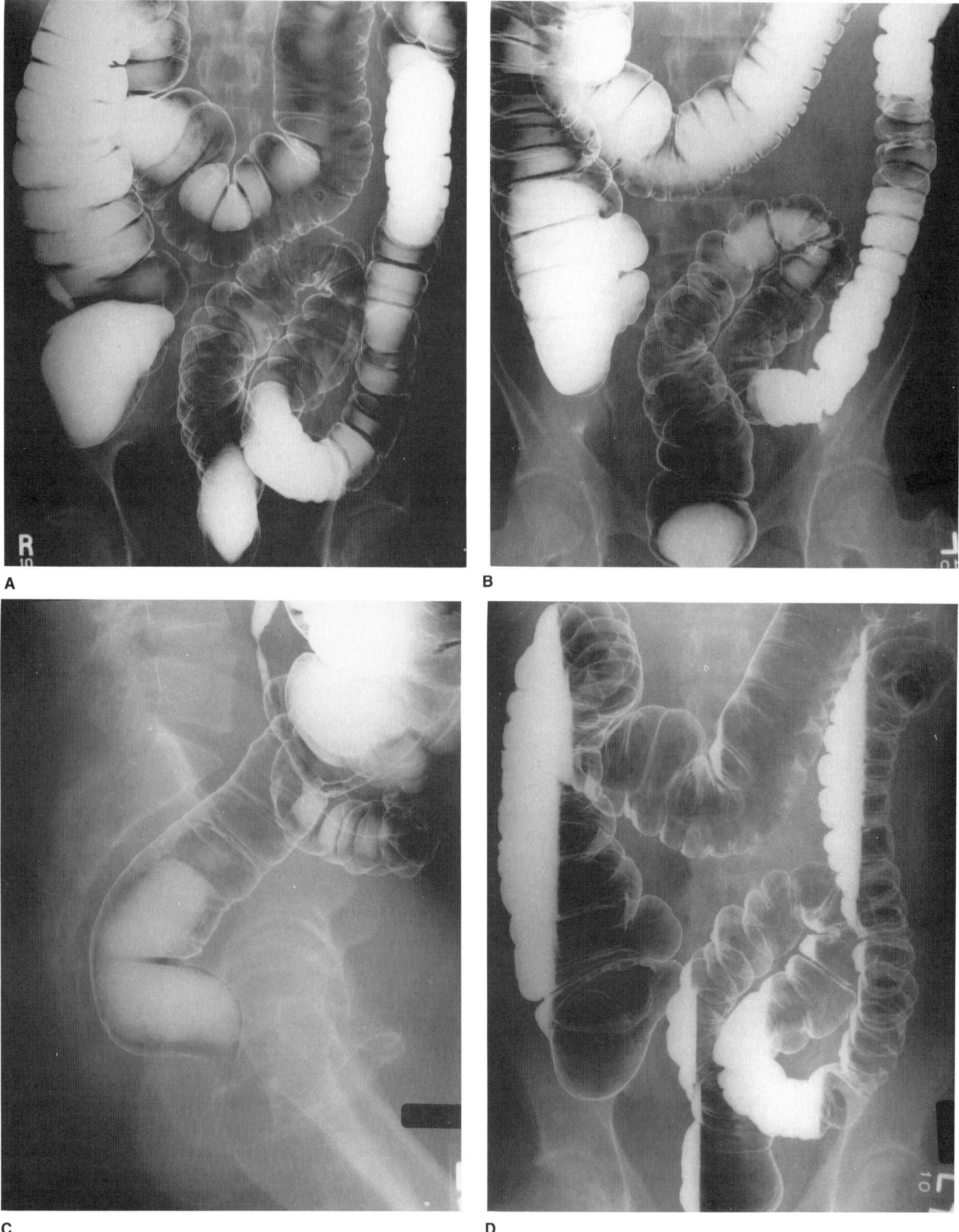

FIG. 31-4. Representative films from a normal pneumocolon. *A*. Supine overhead anterior-posterior 14- × 17-in. film. *B*. Prone overhead posteroanterior 14- × 17-in. film. *C*. Left lateral overhead 10- × 12-in. film. *D*. Right decubitus 14- × 17-in. film (horizontal beam with compensation filtration). *E*. Left decubitus 14- × 17-in. film (horizontal beam with compensation filtration). *F*. Erect spot film (14 × 14 in.). *G*. Erect spot film (14 × 14 in.), left posterior oblique position with compression. *H*. Erect spot film (14 × 14 in.), right posterior oblique position.

As noted in Table 31-1, numerous films are obtained. Each projection requires different positions, so that all of the colon is seen when it is distended and well coated with barium. Because of

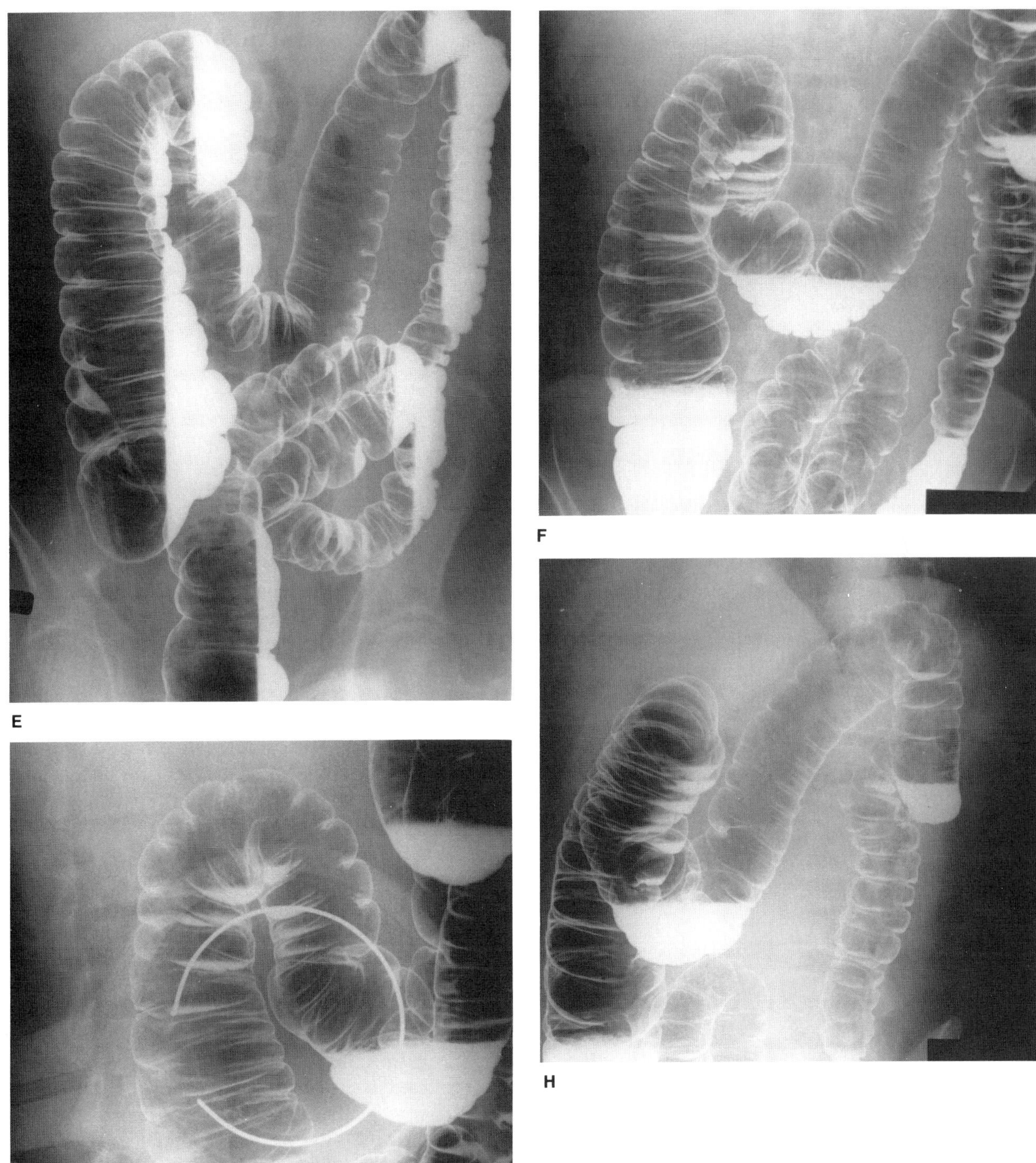

FIG. 31-4 (*Continued*) the very high density of the barium (85 to 100% wt/vol), pools of barium obscure intraluminal pathology, although the contour of the colon is preserved. Note how the erect oblique views of the hepatic (*G*) and splenic flexures (*H*) display them to better advantage. Each redundant overlapping segment can be positioned so that spot films can record abnormalities or normal structures. In addition to these films, it is customary to record the sigmoid on four to six additional spot films. A well-coated mucosal surface is fluoroscopically interrogated by the radiologist. Static films, as displayed here, represent only a portion of the examination, and fluoroscopy remains a very important part of the procedure. Also notice that the enema tip has been removed in this patient, thereby eliminating the artifact of that device.

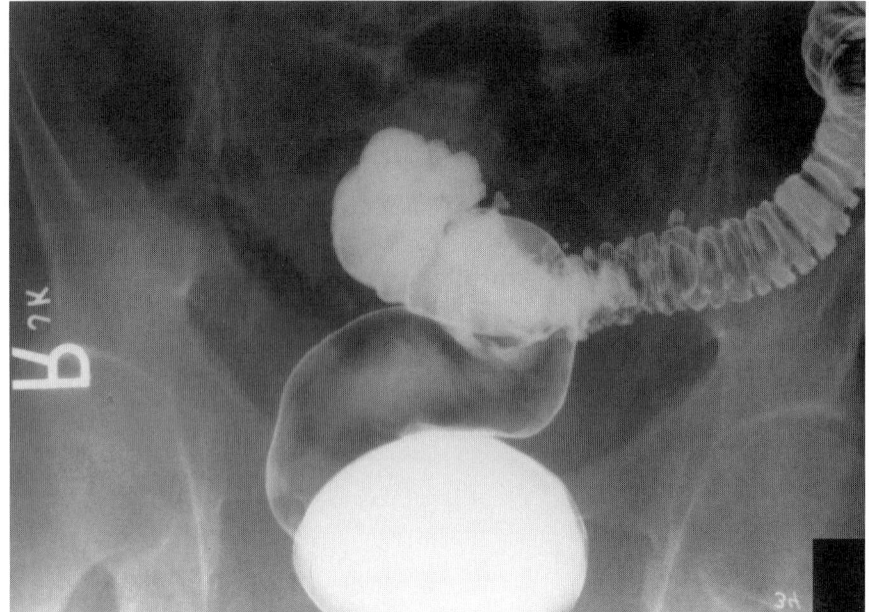

A

FIG. 31-5. Carcinoma of the rectosigmoid. *A*. The anteroposterior supine view of the rectum fails to demonstrate the tumor due to redundant, overlapping barium-filled loops of rectosigmoid. There is considerable smooth muscle hypertrophy as well as sigmoid diverticulosis of the sigmoid colon. *B*. Prone angle view of the rectum. The overhead tube has been angled 15°. The redundancy in the sigmoid colon has been reduced and now the polypoid rectosigmoid tumor (arrowheads) is easily demonstrated. During air-contrast examinations, films should be taken following reduction of redundancy as well as in different positions. All segments of the colon must be adequately examined, preferably in more than one projection to exclude disease with confidence.

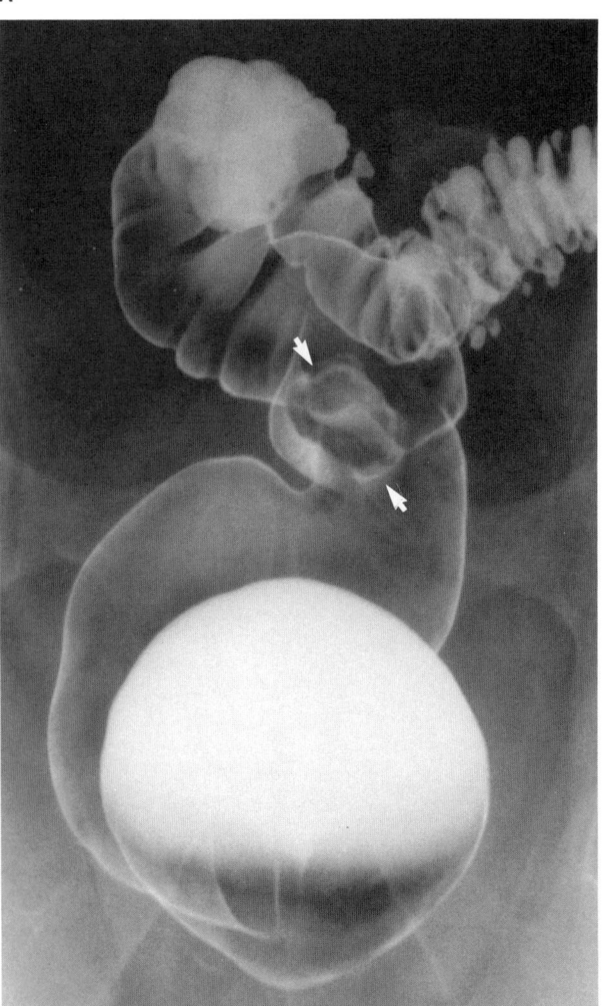

B

descending colon, splenic flexure, transverse colon, hepatic flexure, and lateral rectum. Compression is easily performed with the patient in the erect position. Generally, a film of the cecum is taken after the patient has been returned to the supine position and barium which was in the cecal tip has flowed more proximally. The number of films required is determined by the redundancy of the colon and the size of the spot films as determined by the equipment. If the ileocecal valve has remained competent during the examination and the patient is continent, the enema tip may be electively removed from the rectum prior to placing the patient in the erect position. This makes the patient much more comfortable. An incompetent ileocecal valve, however, may require further instillation of air throughout the examination to maintain proper inflation of the colon, requiring the enema tip to remain in place. If the patient is incontinent of air and/or barium, the enema tip should be left in place and the rectal balloon inflated as necessary.

The value of the numerous spot films is to record the appearance of the colon as redundancy is reduced by fluoroscopically positioning the patient in optimal positions. Remote control equipment, used in some departments, allows for angulation of the fluoroscopy tube, assisting in filming redundant overlapping loops of colon.

After obtaining spot films, overhead views of the colon are taken with the patient prone, supine, and lateral (Fig. 31-5*A* and *B*). Angulation of the overhead tube allows better definition of the redundant rectosigmoid and is a routine part of the examination. A film of the rectum is generally obtained with the patient lying on the right or left side. Some examiners employ a cross-table lateral of the rectum with the patient lying prone. Cross-table horizontal-beam films are taken in both the right and left decubitus positions to include the rectum. Most radiology departments now employ some type of added filtration for the decubitus films. This evens out the density of the films, which is a problem for decubitus horizontal-beam films.

The final result of this type of examination is a combination of overhead films as well as spot films. Generally, six or seven overhead films as well as eight to ten spot films are obtained during a complete examination. Obviously, pathologic abnormalities are often recorded with additional spot films (see Table 31-1).

It is prudent to review all of the films that have been obtained prior to allowing the patient to evacuate, since areas in question will be readily available for reexamination.

Interpretation of these examinations may be easy or can occasionally be extremely difficult, and both technical and perceptual errors may occur. The most common technical problems are too much barium, too little air, excessive unreduced redundancy, fecal contamination, air-bubble contamination, and spasm.

Patients with very redundant colons often require a large amount of barium to completely fill the colon. This large amount of barium is occasionally inadequately drained, so that more barium than is desired remains in the colon. In this situation, the instillation of as much air as possible will significantly decrease the problem of excess barium. Barium preparations contain simethicone. Despite this, some individuals persistently demonstrate small or large air bubbles. Although these may move in a characteristic fashion, some can occasionally be confused with small polyps in the colon. By rotating the patient and recoating the colonic walls, the air bubbles can generally be moved from one position to another. Particulate fecal debris can also markedly lower the confidence level for polyps, especially diminutive polyps. Stool may be adherent and not move about, even though the patient is placed in different positions (Fig. 31-6). Although the horizontal-beam films taken in the decubitus and erect positions can usually discriminate air bubbles and stool, problems can occasionally persist. Spasm is usually controlled with intravenous glucagon but may, on occasion, be unresponsive to pulse doses of glucagon (1 mg IV). In this situation, spot films obtained during periods of relaxation may be the only adequate way to examine the irritable region of the colon. Although the majority of double-contrast exams are satisfactory, reexaminations or alternate approaches may be considered when examinations have proved technically unsatisfactory. A feces-contaminated colon should be reprepped and reexamined at the discretion of the radiologist. A repeat single-contrast examina-

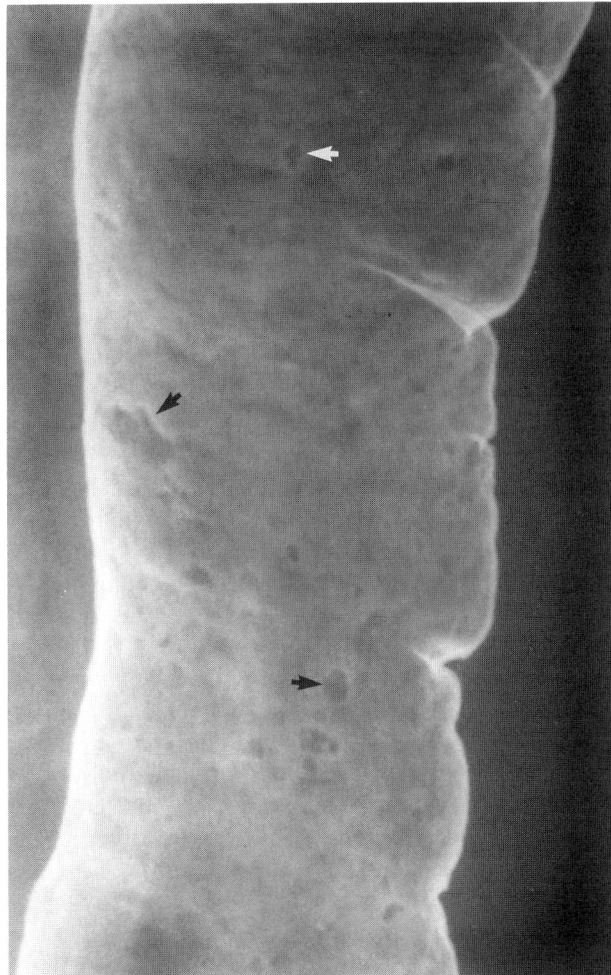

FIG. 31-6. Fecal debris. The air-contrast examination with the patient recumbent shows the appearance of multiple small fecal particles remaining within the colon (arrowheads). Particulate fecal debris is a major problem for the examiner. Horizontal-beam films minimize the influence of particulate fecal debris; however, some debris remains adherent to the colonic wall on occasion. This can cause significant lowering of the confidence level in the interpretation of these studies. For this reason, the colon needs to be cleaned satisfactorily for adequate examination.

Table 31-1
Standard Films Obtained during Air-Contrast Studies

Preliminary KUB
Recumbent films
Four to six spot films of sigmoid colon (prone and supine)
Supine KUB, prone KUB, angle rectum, and lateral rectum
Horizontal-beam films
Right left decubitus abdomen
Erect spot films of the
descending colon
splenic flexure
hepatic flexure
transverse colon
rectum

Abbreviation: KUB = kidney, ureter, and bladder.

tion of the deformed sigmoid with diverticulosis is often more reliable for polyp and stricture evaluation.

The total time of the procedure varies, but it should take an experienced examiner and technologist about 30 min to perform. As with endoscopy, some examinations take much longer, even up to an hour of total room time.

COLOSTOMY EXAMINATIONS

The use of inflatable balloons through colostomies should be avoided due to the danger of perforation. The safest examination of a colostomy is performed by using some type of external colostomy occlusive device.[35] There are commercially available cones which occlude the colostomy snugly with external pressure. An alternative is an inflatable balloon catheter which can be inflated outside the patient and held against the colostomy, sealing the stoma with the tip just inside the colostomy.

Once the occlusive device is secured, examination proceeds in a somewhat limited fashion. The study is done with the patient supine and barium is advanced to the proximal colon. Contrast is drained, followed by insufflation of air into the colon. It is important to be sure that there is enough barium beyond the hepatic flexure to allow complete examination of the ascending colon. Spot films of the colon can generally be obtained with the patient recumbent or semierect; it is possible that a cooperative patient can be placed in the erect position as well. Adequate distention of the colon is achieved by insufflating enough air to maintain distention during the study. Positioning of the patient is limited in this type of examination; generally, however, horizontal-beam films can be obtained with the patient in the erect position and occasionally in one decubitus position as well. It is necessary to maintain occlusion with the enema tip at the ostomy site; this is often achieved by having the patient hold the occlusive device in place with one hand. The number of films obtained in this type of examination is determined by the technical aspects of the examination, with most of the exam being recorded on spot films and with limited use of overhead films.

Following right hemicolectomy and end-to-end small bowel and colonic anastomoses, decompression of air from the colon into the small bowel occurs. Therefore, it may be difficult to maintain adequate distention of the colon. In this situation, spot films during periods of distention may be the best way to record the examination. Adding air just before each overhead film can markedly improve the study. Left hemicolectomy and primary anastomosis should present no significant problems.

RADIOGRAPHIC APPEARANCE OF NEOPLASTIC COLONIC LESIONS

Benign neoplastic polyps are either tubular adenomas, tubulovillous adenomas, or villous adenomas, and they are usually indistinguishable radiologically from nonneoplastic epithelial polyps, such as hyperplastic and inflammatory polyps (Table 31-2).[36]

Adenomatous polyps tend to occur in multiples (Fig. 31-7*A* and *B*). At least 50 percent of patients, when first identified as harboring an adenomatous polyp, will have more than one polypoid lesion occurring synchronously somewhere else in the colon. Therefore, it is imperative to scrutinize the remaining colon closely once a polypoid lesion has been identified (Fig. 31-8). Clustering of adenomatous polyps in the rectosigmoid and distal descending colon accounts for 50 to 60 percent of lesions being detected in this

Table 31-2
Classification of Polypoid Colonic Lesions

- Polypoid colonic lesions of epithelial origin
  - Neoplastic
    - Benign lesions
      - Tubular adenoma
      - Tubulovillous adenoma
      - Villous adenoma
    - Malignant lesions
      - Carcinoma
      - Carcinoid tumor
  - Nonneoplastic
    - Hyperplastic metaplasia
    - Inflammatory pseudopolyp
    - Hamartomas
      - Cystic (juvenile polyp)
      - Cellular (Peutz-Jeghers)
    - Lymphoid tissue
    - Barium granuloma
    - Heterotopic (for example, gastric)
    - Ameboma, tuberculoma
    - Malakoplakia
- Polypoid colonic lesions of subepithelial origin
  - Neoplastic
    - Benign lesions
      - Lipoma
      - Leiomyoma
      - Neurofibroma
      - Hemangioma
      - Lymphangioma
      - Endothelioma
      - Myeloblastoma
  - Malignant lesions
      - Lymphoma
      - Sarcoma
      - Metastases
  - Nonneoplastic
    - Endometriosis
    - Enteric cyst
    - Duplication
    - Pneumatosis
    - Hematoma
    - Varix

SOURCE: From Stewart and Dodds.[36] Reproduced by permission.

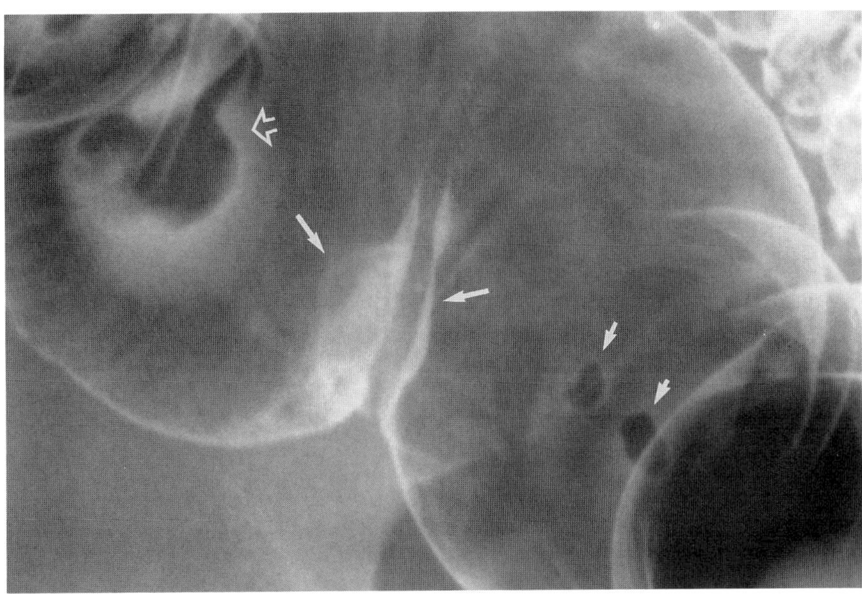

A

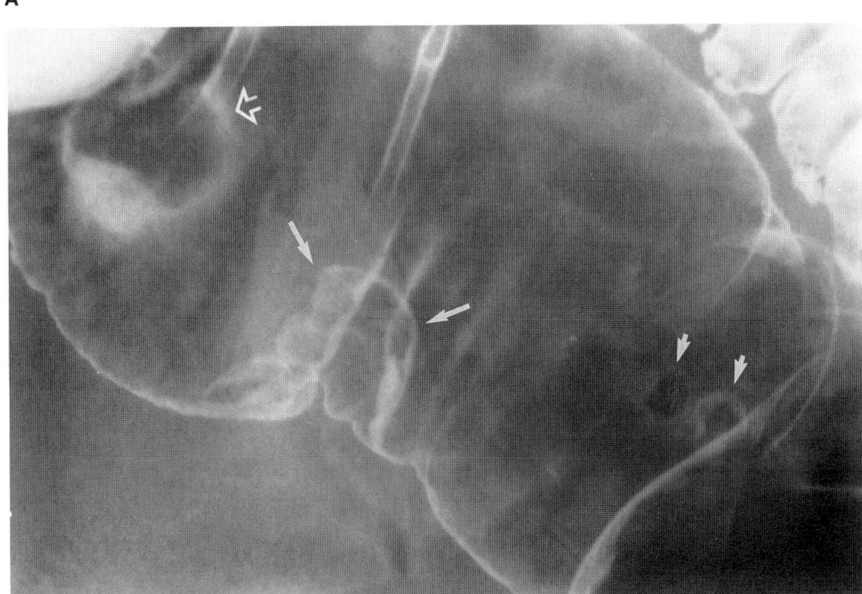

B

FIG. 31-7. Four separate lesions in a segment of sigmoid colon. *A* and *B*. Radiographs taken moments apart during the examination. Note that two small polyps (arrowheads), a large sessile polyp straddling a haustral fold (arrows), and pedunculated polyp (open arrow) are all seen somewhat differently from moment to moment. The two small polyps are seen with and without a small amount of barium surrounding their base. The pedunculated polyp is seen lying in a dependent pool of barium. The true size of the sessile lesion is best seen in Fig. 31-7*B*. Mucosal lesions have morphologic characteristics that may vary from film to film. Additionally, the size of lesions may be better seen on one film than another.

portion of the colon (Fig. 31-9*A*, *B*, and *C*). Unfortunately, this is the region where most redundancy and diverticular deformity occurs. Because of the concentration of neoplastic lesions in this area, meticulous examination and filming of the sigmoid colon is performed during the positive-contrast examination (Fig. 31-10). The other 40 to 50 percent of lesions are scattered throughout the remaining colon. It should be emphasized that during surveillance following polypectomy, the likelihood of diminutive polyps greatly increases, so that metachronous lesions are more likely to be very small. Since diminutive polyps less than 5 mm in diameter are frequent in these patients, the challenge for the air-contrast examination is significant (Fig. 31-11*A* and *B*).

Although the final histologic examination allows for discrimination of neoplastic versus nonneoplastic polyps, their morphologic appearance and size may increase suspicion of neoplasia (Fig. 31-12). Although most polypoid lesions of 5 mm or less were initially thought to be unimportant and due to hyperplastic polyps, we now know that at least half of these polyps are adenomatous polyps; therefore, when detected, they should be reported.

On single-contrast studies, polyps and masses are perceived as filling defects surrounded by barium;

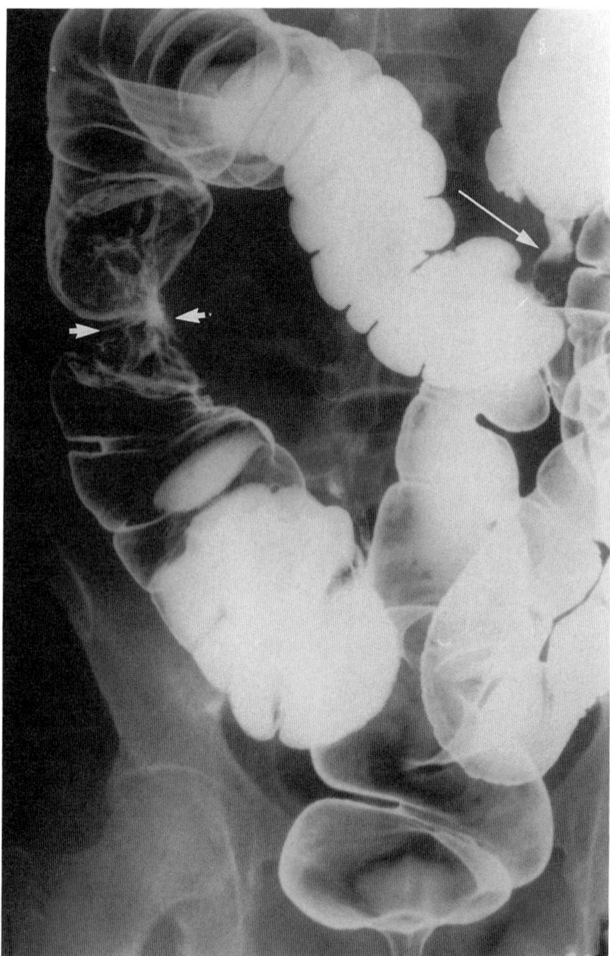

FIG. 31-8. Synchronous carcinomas. Five percent of patients may be expected to have synchronous carcinomas. In this case, there are two annular carcinomas. One is located in the ascending colon (arrowheads). The second lesion is in the distal transverse colon (arrow). Note that the luminal dimensions of the lesion in the transverse colon may be so tight that a colonoscope cannot be advanced through this area. Except in cases of very high grade obstruction, the entire colon is usually available for radiographic examination.

however, on air-contrast exams, they are coated with barium and have a linear appearance (Fig. 31-13*A* and *B*). Perceptually, the reader has to adjust to examining the entire colon for linear abnormalities. Large masses can be misinterpreted as haustral folds. On occasion, a shallow puddle of barium will outline a mass as a filling defect. The value of multiple projections is to confirm abnormalities which might be poorly seen on another view. Subtle changes in position or barium distribution can alter the appearance of the lesion radiographically, sometimes very dramatically (Fig. 31-14*A*, *B*, and *C*). Pedunculated polyps can move about for long distances, depending on the length of the stalk, and decubitus films frequently show them "dangling" on their stalks.

As polypoid lesions increase in size, they take on morphologic characteristics that can be described as *sessile, pedunculated, infiltrating,* and, occasionally, *ulcerated* (Fig. 31-15*A* and *B*). The potential for malignant degeneration accelerates as the adenomatous polyp's size increases. As lesions approach sizes between 1 to 2 cm, the probability of villous architecture increases as well as the probability of carcinoma in situ and invasive carcinoma; therefore *size is very important and should be described.* The sessile appearance or pedunculation are radiographic features which should be described, since pedunculated polyps are less likely to contain invasive carcinoma (Fig. 31-16*A* and *B*). With the exception of ulceration, the surface characteristics of a polyp are poor predictors of malig-

(Text continues on page 337)

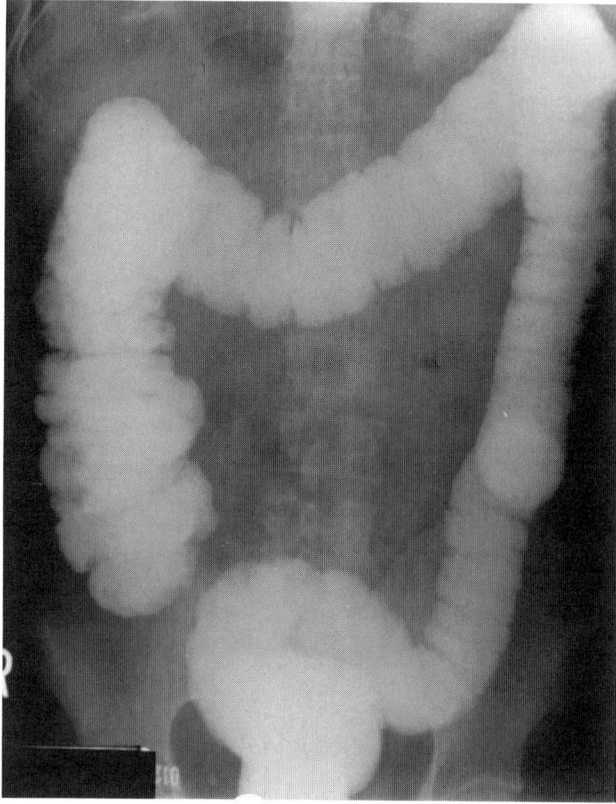

A

FIG. 31-9. Familial polyposis. *A*. Single-contrast examination of the colon. The numerous tiny colonic polyps give the colon a somewhat feathery appearance as seen tangentially. Small polyps are seen through the barium column in this examination. *B*. An air-contrast examination of the same patient demonstrates the multiplicity of tiny colonic polyps to better advantage. This dramatic example of familial polyposis illustrates the utility of the double-contrast examination in the depiction of small polyps. (From Stewart and Dodds.[36] Reproduced by permission.) *C*. A magnified view of the sigmoid colon demonstrates the characteristics of mucosal polyps which, in this patient, are too numerous to count.

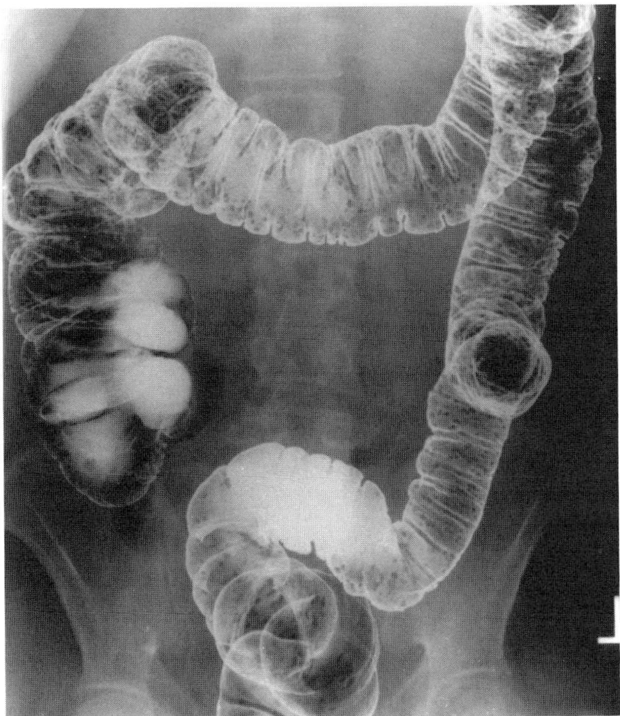

B

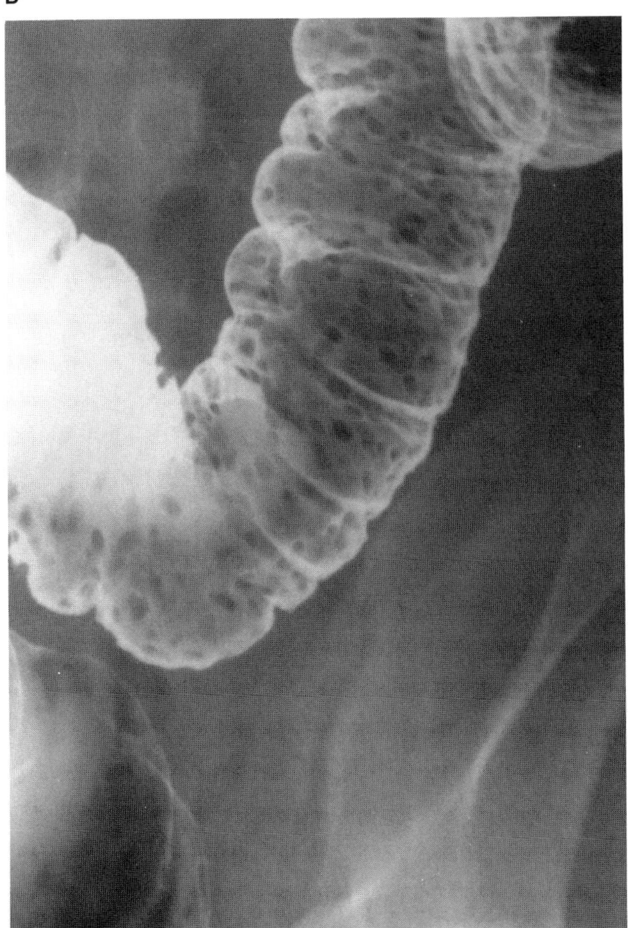

C

FIG. 31-9 (*Continued*)

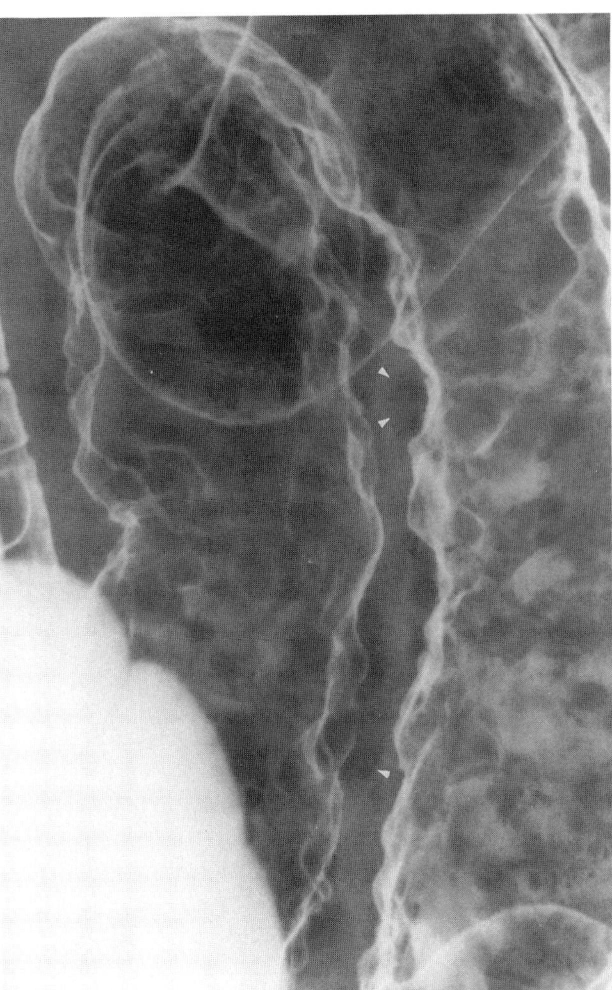

FIG. 31-10. Pneumatosis cystoides intestinalis. An air-contrast examination in a patient with benign asymptomatic pneumatosis cystoides intestinalis might initially be confused with multiple polyposis. The encysted gas presents as polypoid protrusions into the colonic lumen. A tangential view of the colon, however, confirms the presence of intramural gas (arrowheads). The proper diagnosis is readily established once the observation has been made. The same features should be demonstrable during a single-contrast examination.

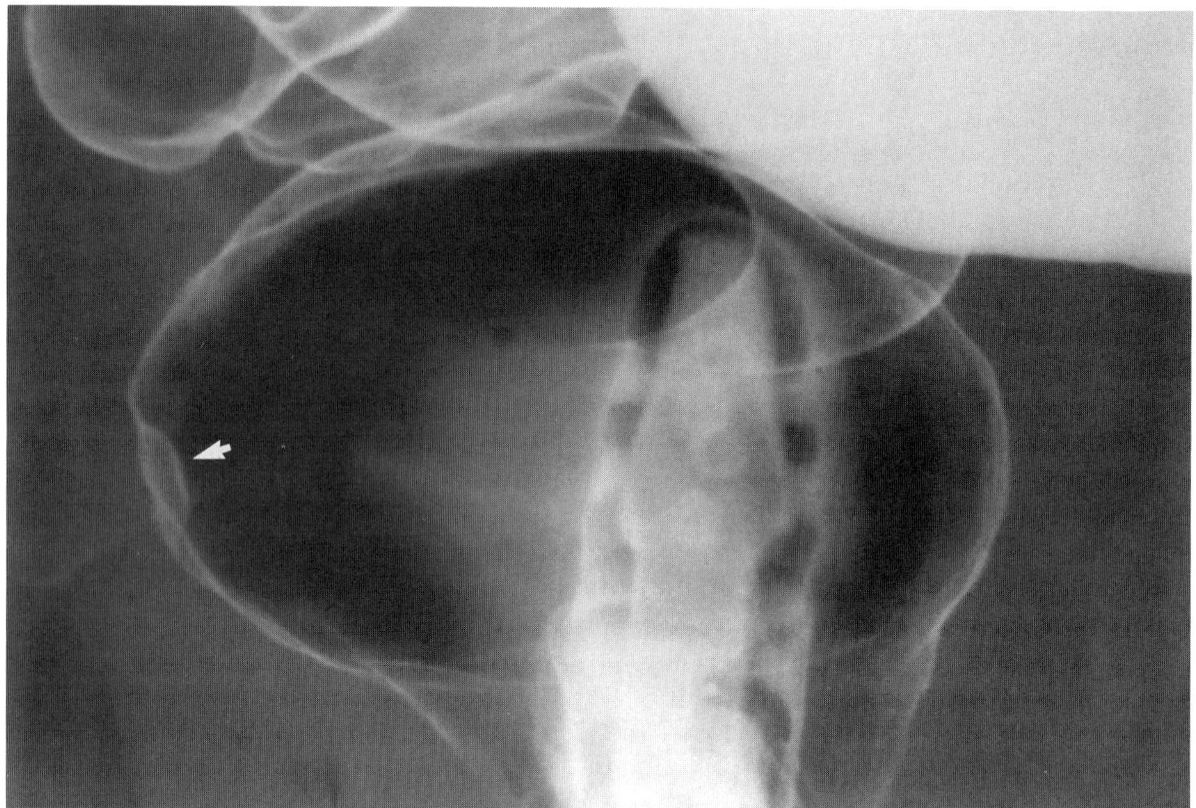

A

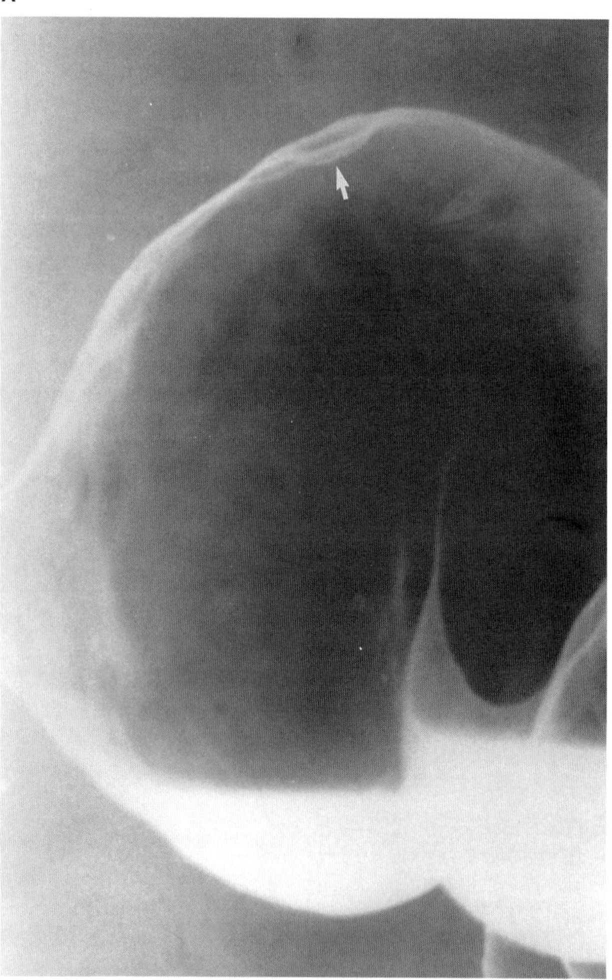

B

FIG. 31-11. Rectal carcinoid tumor. *A*. This recumbent view with the enema tip in place demonstrates a 5- to 7-mm sessile polyp (arrowhead) protruding from the lateral rectal wall. *B*. In the left decubitus position, the enema tip has been removed. The polypoid lesion is confirmed (arrowhead). In this case, the lesion was a rectal carcinoid. High-quality double-contrast examination should be able to demonstrate lesions of this dimension with a high degree of accuracy. The rectum is well examined with the air-contrast technique.

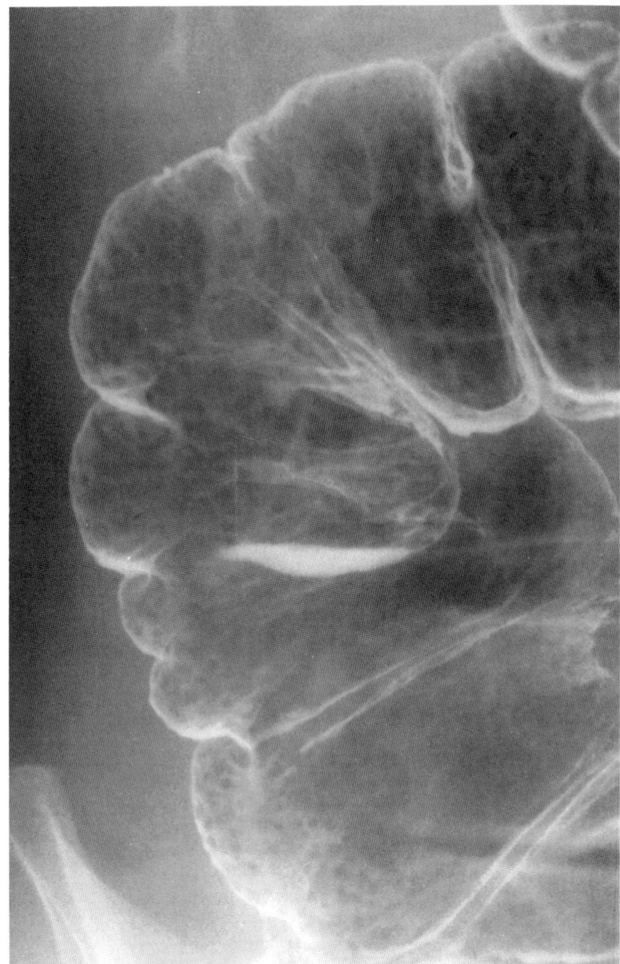

FIG. 31-12. Lymphoid hyperplasia. With the patient in the erect position, lymphoid hyperplasia in the hepatic flexure is very nicely demonstrated. The multiple small lymphoid follicles measuring 1 to 3 mm in diameter are depicted on this high-quality examination. It should be stressed that the air-contrast examination is capable of detecting very tiny colonic lesions.

FIG. 31-13. Carcinoma of the colon. *A*. Recumbent film of the proximal descending colon shows an irregular mass which is not particularly well demonstrated in this projection (arrowheads). Poor definition of this lesion is due to the fact that it is on the anterior wall of the colon in this projection. *B*. The patient is now in the erect position and is turned obliquely. The sessile nodular lesion is seen more tangentially and is much more obvious (arrowheads). The subtleties of lesions are often appreciated only with different projections and repositioning of the patient. Masses appear as lines due to barium coating of the mucosal surface. The tangential surface is seen on the x-ray film as a linear density. Note that a second tiny polyp is seen in Fig. 31-13*A* (arrow). It is partially surrounded by barium and is on the posterior wall of the colon.

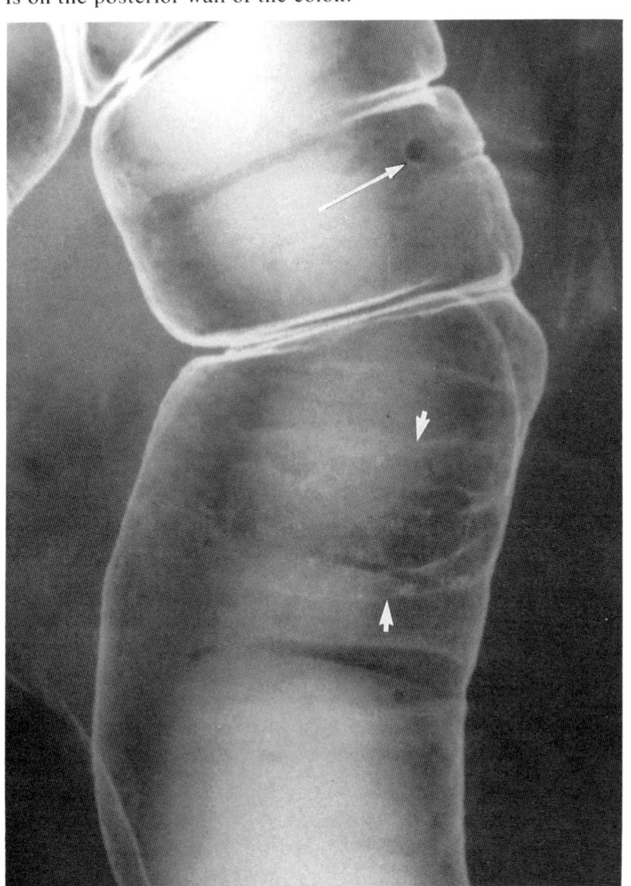

A

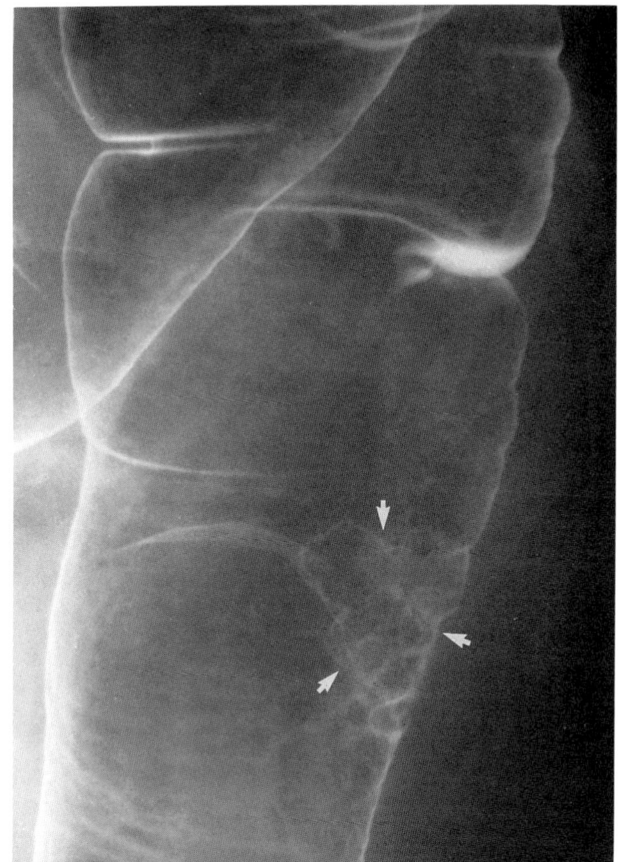

B

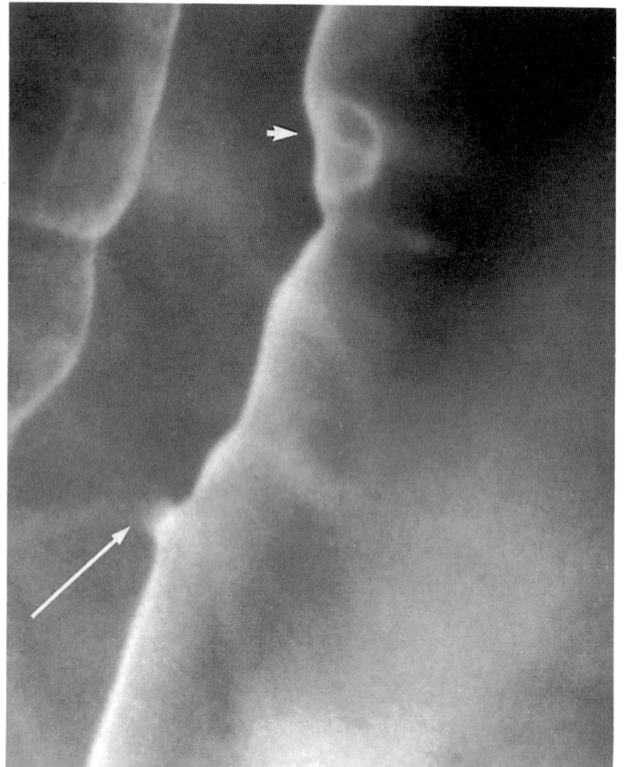

A

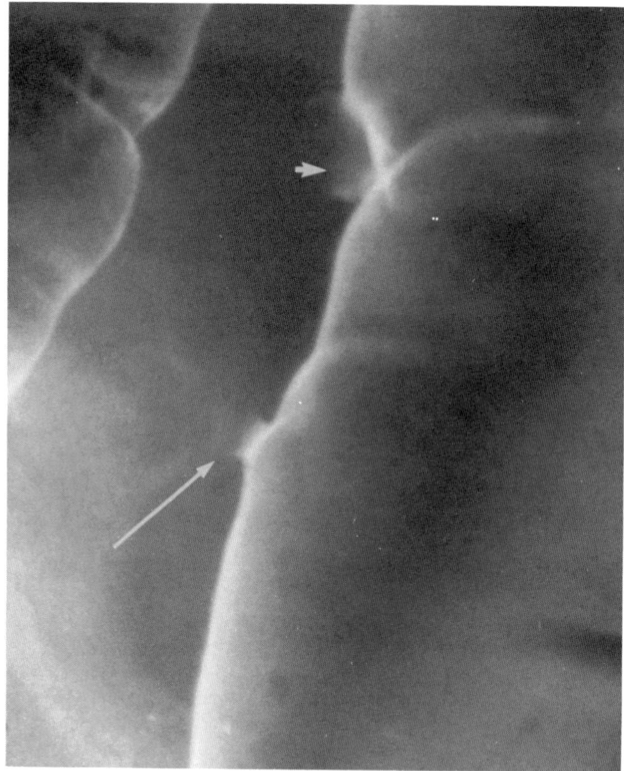

B

C

FIG. 31-14. Diverticulum simulating a polyp. *A*, *B*, and *C*. Two diverticula are present (arrows and arrowheads); both are seen with three different degrees of obliquity. Note that the cephalad, larger of the diverticula (arrowheads) is slowly filling with barium as the examination proceeds. The tangential view and the filling of the diverticulum with barium easily distinguish this as a diverticulum rather than a polyp. Interpretative errors occur in patients with diverticulosis. Multiple views may be necessary to distinguish polyps from diverticula.

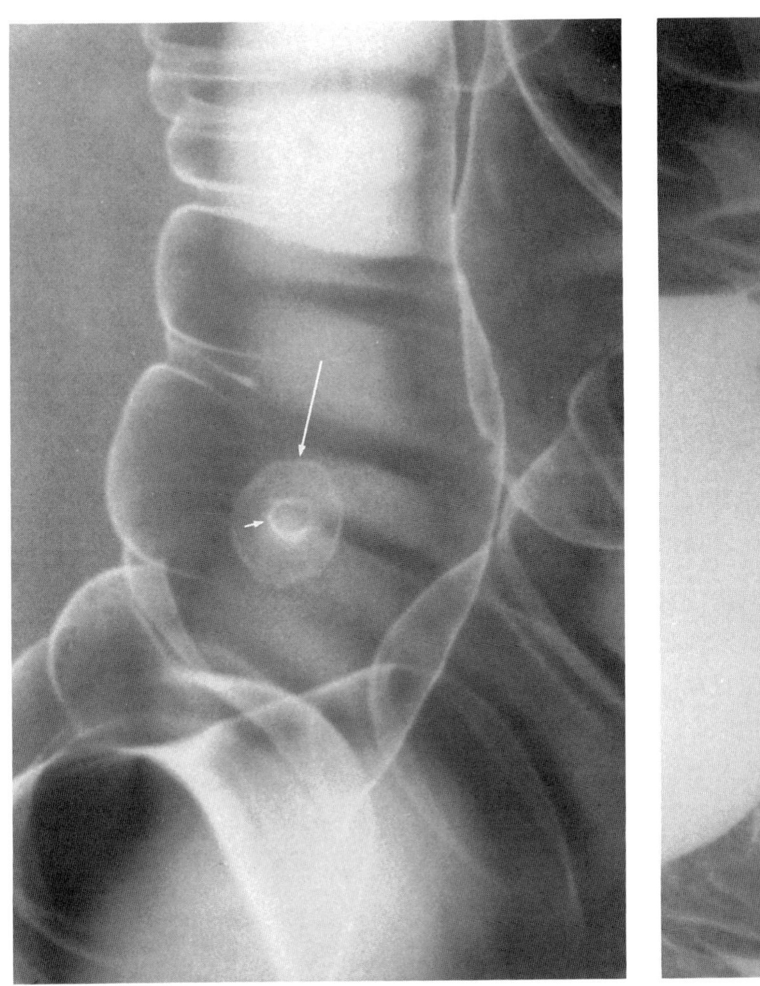

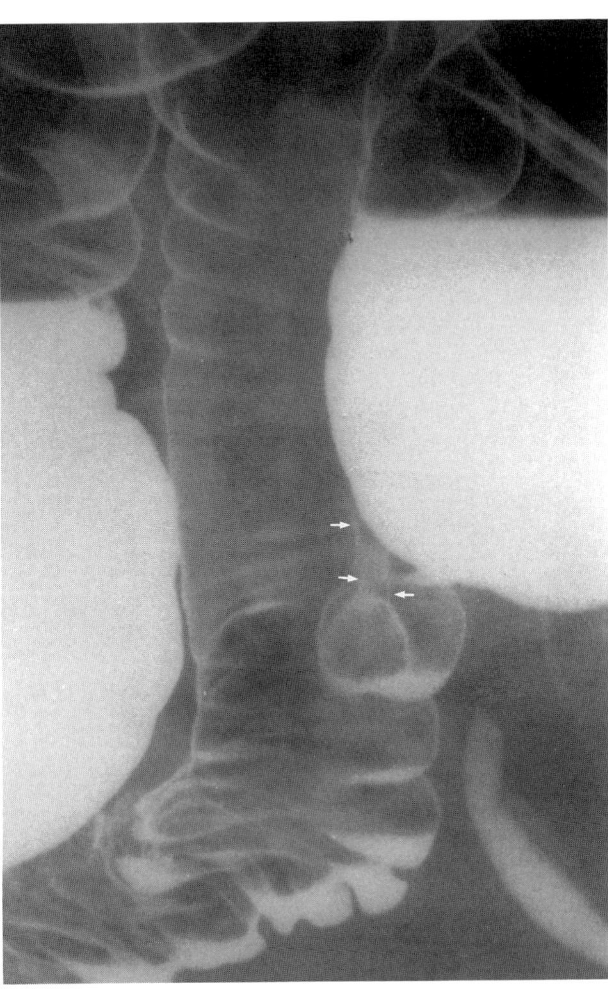

A B

FIG. 31-15. Pedunculated polyp. *A*. A pedunculated polyp hanging off the anterior wall of the colon. The pedicle appears as a ring (arrowhead). The larger head of the polyp is seen as a larger, ringlike density (arrow). *B*. With the patient in the decubitus position, the pedunculated polyp is hanging on its pedicle (arrowheads). Pedunculated polyps on long stalks may move considerable distances within the colon from film to film.

nancy. Ulcerations on a mass should be considered to be a malignant process until proven otherwise. Neoplastic polyps in excess of several centimeters in size often present as large polypoid masses protruding into the colonic lumen. As malignant degeneration and invasion occur, annular or circumferential invasion may result in an "apple core" or "napkin ring" appearance, which is often described (Fig. 31-17*A* and *B*). Long, infiltrating, scirrhous tumors are occasionally seen in the colon and may be confused with a long segment of inflammatory bowel disease (as shown in Fig. 31-1). Carcinoma superimposed on long-standing idiopathic ulcerative colitis can present as a scirrhous infiltrating tumor and have benign radiographic characteristics. Because of this, any benign-appearing stricture demonstrated in a patient with chronic ulcerative colitis should be evaluated with biopsy to exclude the possibility of carcinoma regardless of its other morphologic features seen on air-contrast examination (Figs. 31-18 and 31-19).

The false-positive rate for well-done air-contrast examinations of the colon is low. Because of this, any radiologically detected polypoid lesion which is not found endoscopically should be verified by repeat air-contrast examination of the colon. Failure to detect a lesion by endoscopy by no means confirms the absence of such a lesion. One of the inherent problems in comparing endoscopic findings with double-contrast examination is the location of lesions. Due to telescoping of the colon over the endoscope as well as compliance of colon, the perceived location of the tip of the endoscope may be at variance with the location

(Text continues on page 341)

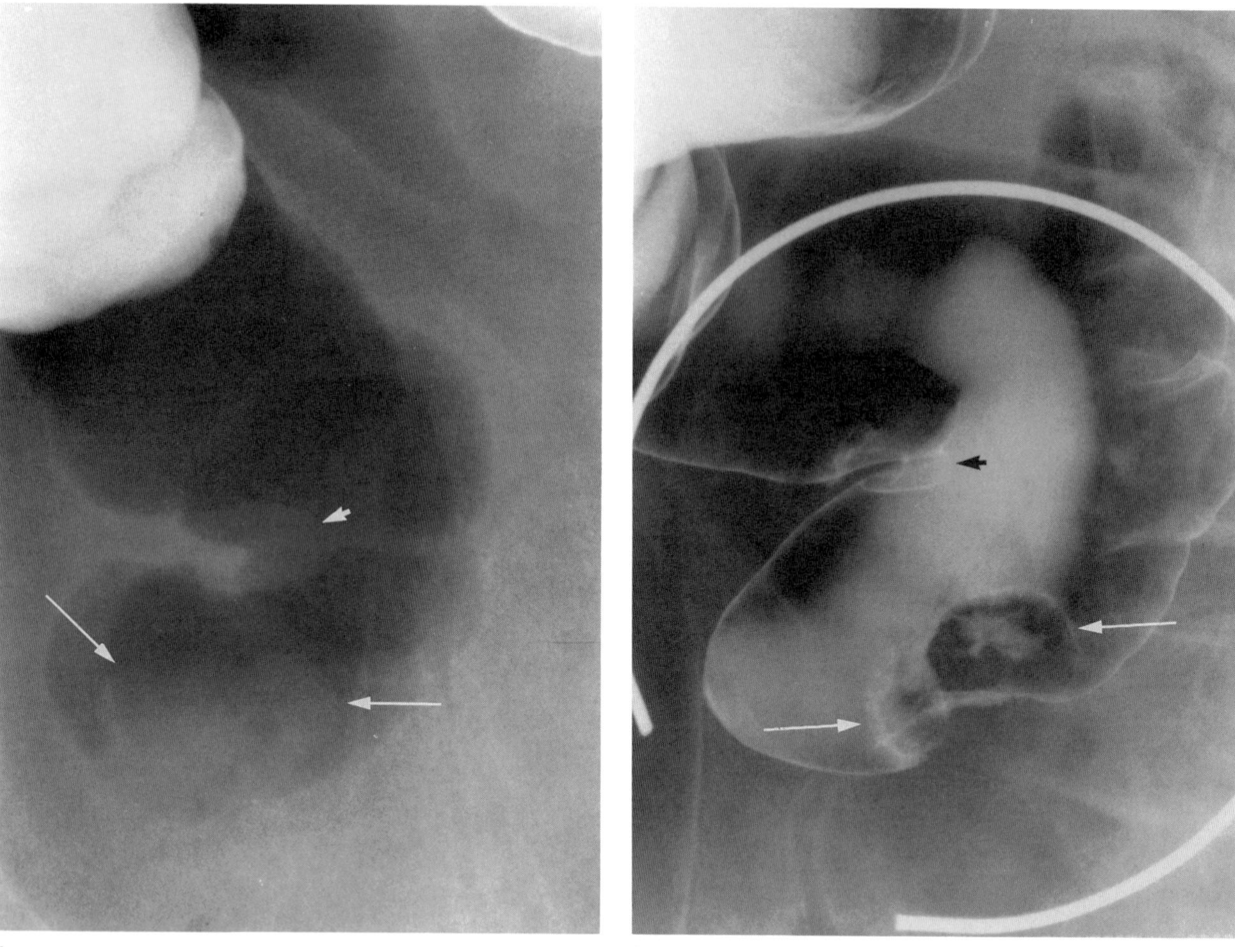

FIG. 31-16. Adenocarcinoma of the cecum. *A*. During the early filling phase of the air-contrast examination, gas in the cecum outlines the ileocecal valve (arrowhead) as well as the soft-tissue mass in the cecum (arrows). *B*. Once air and barium have coated the cecum, the ileocecal valve (arrowhead) and the tumor (arrows) are very nicely seen and confirmed. Soft tissue masses protruding into the air-filled lumen of the colon are often obvious on plain films. Air in the colon has been referred to as "negative contrast"; it often demonstrates pathology without the performance of positive-contrast studies. Figure 31-16*A* is a nice example of this.

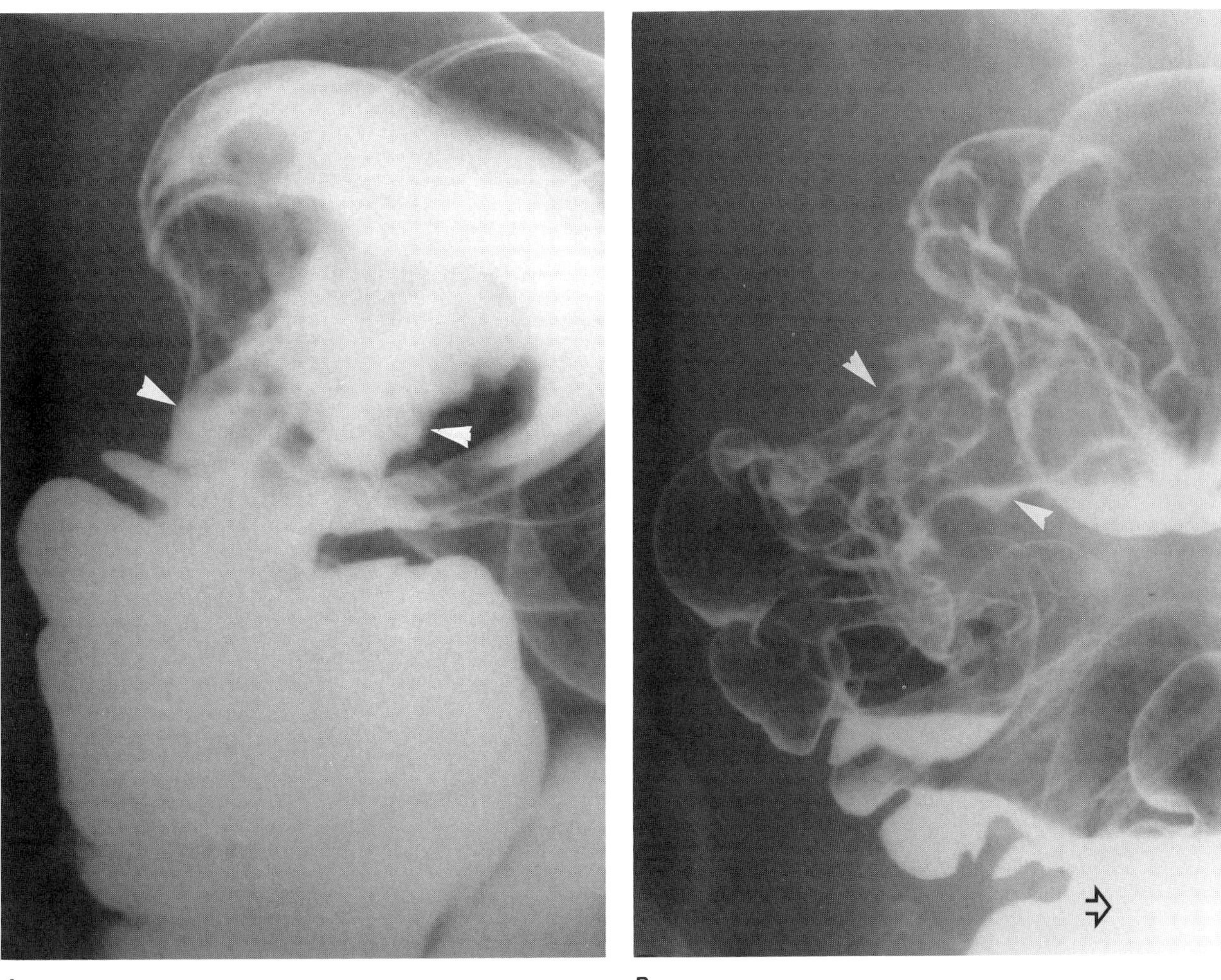

FIG. 31-17. Annular carcinoma of the hepatic flexure. *A*. The single-contrast phase of the examination demonstrates an annular tumor involving the right colon. The tumor encompasses the colon circumferentially, producing the "apple core" or "napkin ring" appearance (arrowheads). *B*. With the patient in the erect position, barium has now accumulated in the dependent portion of the colon near the cecum (open arrow). The tumor (arrowheads) is once again nicely demonstrated. The nodular surface characteristics are better illustrated, since the dense contrast has now been removed from this portion of the colon, leaving the coated surface of the tumor more readily visible.

FIG. 31-19. Stricture of the descending colon in patient with chronic ulcerative colitis. *A* and *B*. The single (*A*) and air-contrast (*B*) phases demonstrate the same stricture. The mucosal nodularity and irregularity due to the chronic ulcerations and small pseudopolyp formation is seen in the strictured segment and on both sides. Any stricture such as this is presumed malignant until proved otherwise, and biopsy through this area is indicated. Also note that the dimensions of this stricture may preclude the advancement of a colonoscope through it. Therefore, an examination of the remainder of the colon is best provided by the positive contrast examination.

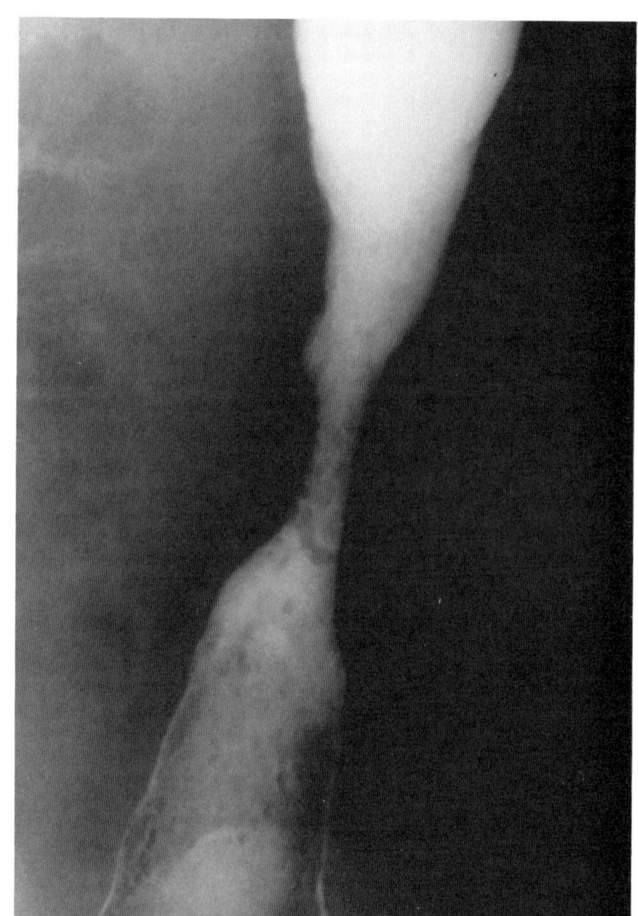

A

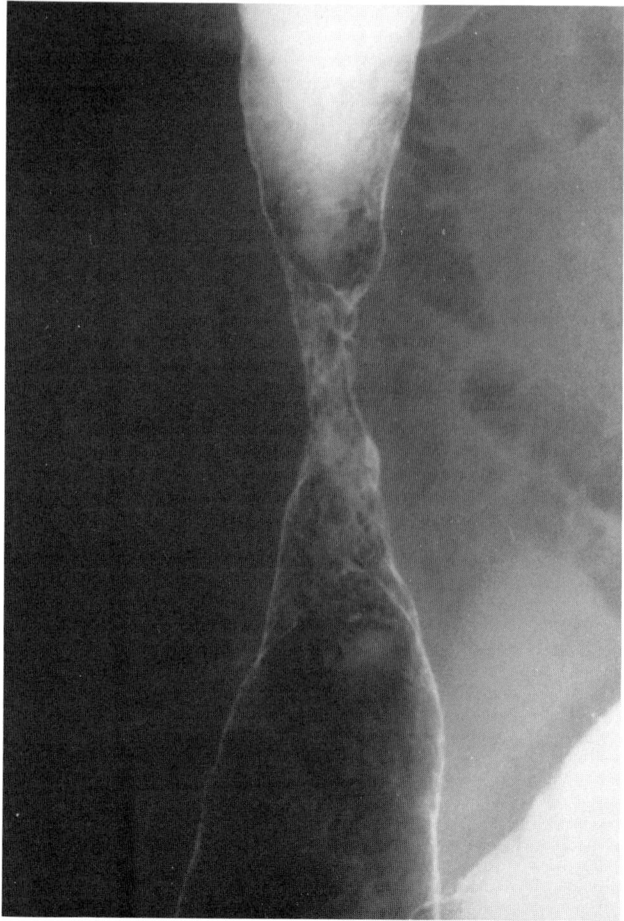

B

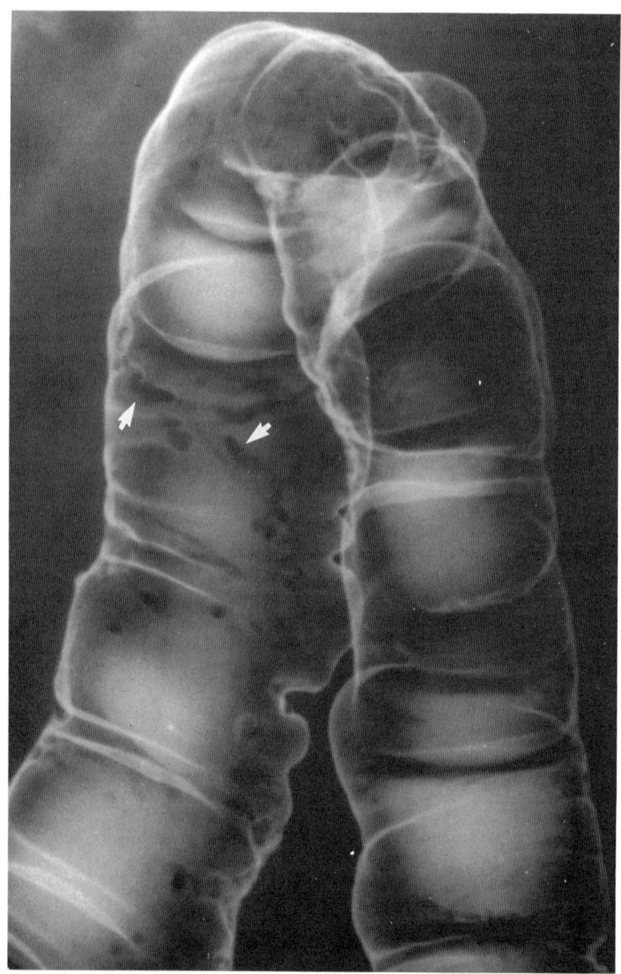

FIG. 31-18. Filiform inflammatory pseudopolyps in patient with chronic ulcerative colitis. The wormlike, or filiform, nature of the pseudopolyps in this patient (arrowheads) with chronic ulcerative colitis are very nicely shown. At times, these may be confused with familial polyposis. As in many of these cases, the appearance of the colon causes confusion because the haustral pattern is preserved and there is no shortening; the morphologic characteristics of the colon may be otherwise normal. The inflammatory nature of these polyps is established quite easily with biopsy. The air-contrast examination in these patients beautifully demonstrates the morphology of these inflammatory pseudopolyps. (From Stewart and Dodds.[36] Reproduced by permission.)

Table 31-3
Studies Comparing the Detection of Polypoid Colonic Lesions

				Percent Detected		
Authors	*Number of patients*	*Number of polyps*	*Polyp size, cm*	*Single contrast*	*Double contrast*	*Colonoscopy*
Thoeni and Menuck[4]	112	219	—	55	88	97
Leinicke et al.[8]	72	133		**Both**		
			<0.5	46		100
			0.5–0.9	46		100
			1.0–1.9	77		87
			>1.9	93		97
Wolff et al.[6]	500	284		**Both**		
			0.5–0.9	27		100
			1.0–1.9	80		100
			2.0–2.9	90		100
			3.0	100		100
Hogan et al.[7]	50	126	<0.5		67	91
			0.5–0.9		52	90
			>1.0		82	97
Williams et al.[5]	64	108	≤0.5	11		100
			0.6–1.0	60		100
			1.1–2.0	75		100
			>2.0	78		100
	118	292	≤0.5		75	100
			0.6–1.0		88	100
			1.1–2.0		99	100
			>2.0		95	100
Ott et al.[11]	54	85	0.5–0.9	72		100
			1.0–1.9	89		100
			≥2.0	100		100
	85	149	0.5–0.9		88	100
			1.0–1.9		97	100
			≥2.0		95	100
Ott et al.[37]	140	190	>0.5		93	100

of the lesions seen on the radiographs. Because of this, errors may be made in estimating the location of lesions removed relative to the findings on the radiograph. This affects the true false-negative and false-positive rates reported for air-contrast studies. Endoscopic misses may simply be due to incorrect estimates of the location of the endoscope. It is wise for the radiologist to identify by location and size each polypoid lesion identified so that, during colonoscopy, mapping of the colon and designation of polyp location and size are correlated with radiographic findings. In this way, there should be minimal discrepancy between the two examinations.

Table 31-3 lists some of the studies comparing the detection rate of polypoid lesions in the colon. In virtually all cases, endoscopy is used as the gold standard. Some studies were not well controlled and compared varying levels of expertise as well as various colonic preparations; they were based on inadequate information as to polyp size; and, often, they compared studies performed at different institutions. However, all the available data support the fact that double-contrast examinations are more sensitive for the detection of diminutive polyps than single-contrast studies. As polypoid lesions increase in size, the ability to detect these lesions endoscopically increases, as it also does with both types of barium exams. Lesions greater than 1 cm in size are more likely to contain dysplasia or malignant degeneration; polypoid lesions of this dimension are detected in the majority of these patients. It is well to remember that the multiplicity of polyps (two or more polyps in 50 percent of patients) tends to protect the patient from a missed diagnosis in the screening examination. Many studies stress that the barium enema exam is universally a complete examination whereas colonoscopy may be incomplete, depending on the skill of the examiner. Although colonoscopy detects 100 percent of lesions in most studies, this merely indicates that colonoscopy is the gold standard. The true false-negative rate for colonoscopy may be as high as 10 to 15 percent. Nevertheless, these data indicate that both barium enema and colonoscopy are effective screening and surveillance examinations for the detection of colonic polyps both benign and malignant.

SUMMARY

The technique of examination of the colon using the air-contrast method requires meticulous attention to a number of factors, beginning with patient selection, colon preparation for the examination, technical factors during the performance of the examination, as well as interpretation of the final record. A well-done air-contrast examination should be very sensitive for the detection of small and large neoplastic lesions. Differentiation of neoplastic disease from benign disease requires definitive visualization and biopsy. The role of the radiologist is to produce high confidence examinations that can reliably be used for screening and surveillance studies in those patients who are at high risk for neoplasms of the colon. Since the entire colon is invariably examined, including the rectum, this examination is uniquely suited for detection of lesions at any location. Too often, endoscopists have elected to simply bypass the positive-contrast examination in favor of direct visualization of the colon. *In my opinion, failure to utilize the air-contrast examination properly places the patient at a disadvantage and substantially increases the cost of patient care. The role of positive-contrast examination in screening for colorectal malignancy is extremely important, since this exam remains the most available, cost-effective, and safe procedure. However, in order to justify the procedure, high-quality studies are necessary and are the responsibility of the consulting radiologist.*

REFERENCES

1. Welin S: Results of the Malmo technique of colon examination. *JAMA* 199:369, 1967.
2. Rice RP: Single- or double-contrast barium enemas: Another opinion. *AJR* 140:1271–1272, 1983.
3. Sugarbaker PH, Vineyard GC, Lewicki AM, et al: Colonoscopy in the management of diseases of the colon and rectum. *Surg Gynecol Obstet* 139:341–349, 1974.
4. Thoeni RF, Menuck L: Comparison of barium enema and colonoscopy in the detection of small colonic polyps. *Radiology* 124:631–635, 1977.
5. Williams WB, Hunt RH, Loose H, et al: Colonoscopy in management of colon polyps. *Br J Surg* 61:673–682, 1974.
6. Wolff WI, Shinya H, Ozoktay S, et al: Comparison of colonoscopy and the contrast enema in five hundred patients with colorectal disease. *Am J Surg* 129:181–186, 1975.
7. Hogan WJ, Stewart ET, Geenen JE, et al: A prospective comparison of the accuracy of colonoscopy vs. air-barium contrast exam for detection of colonic polypoid lesions (abstract). *Gastrointest Endosc* 23:230, 1977.
8. Leinicke JL, Dodds WJ, Hogan WJ, et al: A comparison of colonoscopy and roentgenography for detecting polypoid lesions of the colon. *Gastrointest Radiol* 2:125–128, 1977.
9. Thoeni RF, Petras A: Double contrast barium enema and endoscopy in the detection of polypoid lesions in the cecum and ascending colon. *Radiology* 144:257–260, 1982.
10. Johnson CD, Carlson HC, Taylor WF, et al: Barium enemas of carcinoma of the colon: Sensitivity of double- and single-contrast studies. *AJR* 140:1143–1149, 1983.
11. Ott DJ, Gelfand DW, Chen YM, et al: Single-contrast vs. double-contrast barium enema in the detection of colonic polyps. *AJR* 146:993–996, 1986.
12. Eddy DM, Nugent FW, Eddy JF, et al: Screening for colorectal cancer in a high-risk population: Results of a mathematical model. *Gastroenterology* 92:682–692, 1987.
13. Lehman GA, Buchner DM, Lappas JC: Anatomical extent of fiberoptic sigmoidoscopy. *Gastroenterology* 84:803–808, 1983.
14. Girard CM, Rugh KS, DiPalma JA, et al: Comparison of Golytely lavage with standard diet/cathartic preparation for double-contrast barium enema. *AJR* 142:1147–1149, 1984.
15. Maglinte DD, Strong RC, Strate RW, et al: Barium enema after colorectal biopsies: Experimental data. *AJR* 139:693–697, 1982.
16. Diner WC, Patel G, Texter EC Jr, et al: Intraluminal pressure measurements during barium enema: Full column vs. air contrast. *AJR* 137:217–221, 1981.
17. Present AJ, Jansonn B, Burhenne JH, et al: Evaluation of 12 colon-cleansing regimens with single-contrast barium enema. *AJR* 139:855–860, 1982.
18. Fork F-T, Ekberg O, Nilsson G, et al: Colon cleansing regimens: A clinical study in 1200 patients. *Gastrointest Radiol* 7:383–389, 1982.
19. Chan CH, Diner WC, Fontenot E, et al: Randomized single-blind clinical trial of a rapid colonic lavage solution (Golytely) vs. standard preparation for barium enema and colonoscopy. *Gastrointest Radiol* 10:378–382, 1985.
20. Davis GR, Smith HJ: Double-contrast examination of the colon after preparation with Golytely (a balanced lavage solution). *Gastrointest Radiol* 8:173–176, 1983.
21. Gelfand DW: Complications of gastrointestinal radiologic procedures: I. Complications of routine fluoroscopic studies. *Gastrointest Radiol* 5:293–315, 1980.
22. Masel H, Masel JP, Casey KV: A survey of colon examination technique in Australia and New Zealand with a review of complications. *Australas Radiol* 15:140–147, 1971.
23. Rankin GB: Indications, contraindications, and complications of colonoscopy, in Sivak MC Jr (ed): *Gastroenterologic Endoscopy*. Philadelphia, Saunders, 1987, pp 868–880.
24. Zheutlin N, Lasser EC, Rigler LG: Clinical studies on effect of barium in the peritoneal cavity following rupture of the colon. *Surgery* 32:967–979, 1952.
25. Nelson JA, Daniels AU, Dodds WJ: Rectal balloons: Complications, causes, and recommendations. *Invest Radiol* 14: 48–59, 1979.
26. Dodds WJ, Stewart ET, Nelson JA: Rectal balloon catheters and the barium enema examination. *Gastrointest Radiol* 5:277, 1980.

26a. Harned RK, Williams SM, Maglinte DD, et al: Clinical application of in vitro studies for barium-enema examination following colorectal biopsy. *Radiology* 154:319–321, 1985.

27. Stewart ET, Dodds WJ: Predictability of rectal incontinence on barium enema examination. *AJR* 132:197, 1979.
28. Stewart ET, Dodds WJ: The value of digital rectal examination before barium enema. *Radiology* 137:567, 1980.
29. Schwartz EE, Glick SN, Foggs MB, et al: Hypersensitivity reactions after barium enema examination. *AJR* 143:103–104, 1984.
30. Gelfand DW, Sowers JC, De Ponte KA, et al: Anaphylactic and allergic reactions during double-contrast studies: Is glu-

cagon or barium suspension the allergen? *AJR* 144:405–406, 1985.

31. Gelfand DW: Barium enemas, latex balloons and anaphylactic reactions. *AJR* 156:1–2, 1991.
32. Butt J, Hentges D, Pelican G, et al: Bacteremia during barium enema study. *AJR* 130:715–718, 1978.
33. Thoeni RF, Vandeman F, Wall SD: Effect of glucagon on the diagnostic accuracy of double-contrast barium enema examinations. *AJR* 142:111–114, 1984.
34. Coblentz MCL, Frost RA, Molinaro V, et al: Pain after barium enema: Effect of CO_2 and air on double-contrast study. *Radiology* 157:35–36, 1985.
35. Pochaczevsky R: A colostomy device for barium enema examinations. *Radiology* 143:565, 1982.
36. Stewart ET, Dodds WJ: Polyps, in Margulis AR, Burhenne HJ (eds): *Alimentary Tract Radiology*, 4th ed, vol 1. St. Louis, Mosby, 1989, pp 1017–1049.
37. OH DJ, Gelfand DW, Wu WC, Kerr RM: Sensitivity of double-contrast barium enema: Emphasis on polyp detection. *AJR* 135:327–330, 1980.

CHAPTER 32

Surveillance of Patients with Polyps

Sidney J. Winawer

HIGHLIGHTS

The goal of surveillance is to reduce the future incidence of colorectal cancer. The National Polyp Study (NPS) reported a reduced incidence of colorectal cancer in patients with adenomas in whom all synchronous polyps had been removed by colonoscopy. The presence of an adenoma is associated with a proliferative abnormality of the entire colon, resulting in the high rate of additional (50%) or synchronous adenomas. Several studies have shown that after an adenoma is removed, metachronous adenomas develop. It is not clear what proportion of adenomas found at follow-up are true metachronous adenomas and what proportion are missed synchronous adenomas. It has been estimated that about half of the adenomas found on follow-up examinations were missed initially (about 15 percent). In the NPS, these were mostly small to medium size adenomas with mostly unimportant pathology. Colonoscopy is the preferred method of follow-up examination after removal of an initial adenoma. Current information suggests that after establishing a clean colon, there can usually be an interval of 3 years before the first follow-up examination. Evolving data appear to suggest that much longer intervals between follow-up examinations may be appropriate for the management of some patients after polypectomy, particularly if the first follow-up exam is negative. More frequent examinations are needed after incomplete or piecemeal removal of some large sessile lesions, for patients with malignant polyps or numerous polyps, or after a technically unsatisfactory examination.

CONTROVERSIES

Do all patients with adenomatous polyps regardless of size and pathology require complete colonoscopy? Do patients with small or hyperplastic polyps detected on sigmoidoscopy need full colonoscopy? Can patients be divided into subsets of those requiring more frequent and those requiring less frequent follow-up examinations? Do all patients, including those with small adenomas, require follow-up examinations? What is the cost-effectiveness of follow-up surveillance?

FUTURE DIRECTIONS

The approach to patients with adenomas will change dramatically over the next few years as we begin to understand the biology of the adenoma better. Progress in molecular genetics may provide a basis for identifying those individuals who harbor adenomas with significant pathology and whose adenomas are likely to progress and recur. A logical and cost-effective program could then be developed that would target genetically susceptible individuals for periodic colonoscopy and polypectomy. This would dramatically reduce the future incidence of colorectal cancer.

Surveillance can be defined as the *ongoing periodic reexamination of individuals who have had neoplastic disease identified and treated.* Because of the high frequency of subsequent or metachronous adenomas detected at follow-up examinations, this concept is applied to individuals who had adenomatous polyps removed. The goal of surveillance in such individuals is to reduce their future incidence of colorectal cancer by keeping their colons free of clinically significant adenomas. Within this conceptual framework, several issues need to be addressed. Among these issues are the following: (1) How often and by what method should surveillance be done? (2) Can patients be divided into subsets of those requiring more frequent and those requiring less frequent follow-up examinations? (3) Do all patients, including those with small adenomas, require follow-up examinations? (4) Will this approach reduce the incidence and hence mortality from colorectal cancer by interrupting the adenoma-adenocarcinoma sequence? and (5) Can molecular genetic, pathologic, and familial determinants aid in the follow-up strategies? In addition to follow-up management, certain questions regarding initial management also need to be answered, such as (1) Do all patients with adenomatous polyps require complete colonoscopy? (2) Do patients with small or hyperplastic polyps detected on sigmoidoscopy need full colonoscopy? and (3) What is the approach to surgical considerations in patients having malignant polyps removed? The last of these questions is addressed in Chap. 47.

Initial Management

It is now generally accepted that the entire colon must be examined if a histologically proven adenoma has been removed from the colon or is the pathologic interpretation of a sigmoidoscopic biopsy.[1] This is understandable considering the observations that have been reported of the field defect accompanying adenomas of the colon (Fig. 32-1). In the normal colon, proliferation of cells occurs deep in the crypts, with maturation and differentiation of cells occurring as they migrate toward the luminal surface, losing their proliferative potential. When neoplasia appears in the colon in the form of either an adenoma or cancer, the flat mucosa of the colon demonstrates an abnormality of proliferation, with an extension to the surface of the zone of cell proliferation from deep in the crypt accompanied by delayed maturation of cells on the luminal surface with retention of their capacity to proliferate. This abnormality or field defect is seen throughout the entire colon but is distributed in a patchy manner.[2,3] In addition to expansion of the zone of proliferation to the surface, there is an increase in the number of cells undergoing proliferation, resulting in a high proliferation index. This increase in the number of proliferating cells per colonic crypt is greatest

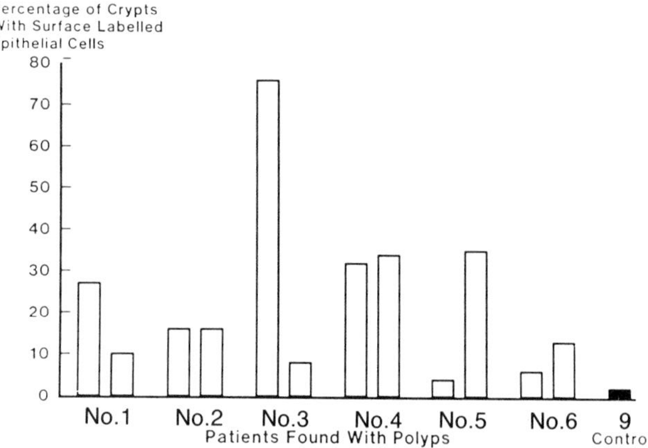

FIG. 32-1. TdR³H (tritiated thymidine) findings in patients with adenoma and in controls.

in the presence of a cancer, intermediate in the presence of large adenomas over 1 cm in size, and increased the least in the presence of adenomas less than 1 cm in size. It is now well established that colonic neoplasia occurs only on the background of a field defect. We can, therefore, understand that the presence of a single adenoma indicates the association of a widespread proliferative abnormality of the entire colon, resulting in the high rate of additional or synchronous adenomas.

When polyps are detected on a screening flexible sigmoidoscopy they can be divided into two broad endoscopic categories: those that are over 0.5 cm in size and those that are under 0.5 cm. The former have a high probability of being adenomas; therefore a full colonoscopy with polypectomy should be done. There will be approximately a 50 percent likelihood of finding additional adenomas more proximally in the presence of an adenoma in the rectosigmoid.[1] Some authors have questioned this concept, citing evidence that patients with small adenomas found on flexible sigmoidoscopy will have unimportant pathology in the additional synchronous adenomas in the proximal colon. In a study reported by Tripp and colleagues,[4] the distribution of synchronous neoplasia was retrospectively analyzed in 220 patients undergoing colonoscopy. In 32 patients with the finding of small ($\leq$ 0.5 cm) adenomas in the rectosigmoid, no cancers were found proximally, and the adenomas found proximally were of unimportant histology. Grossman et al.[5] reported that in 133 patients whose worst index lesion in the rectosigmoid was a single tubular adenoma less than 1 cm in size, there was only a 3 percent prevalence of advanced colonic neoplasia more proximally (adenomas that were $>$ 1 cm in size or with villous features, severe dysplasia, or invasive cancer). In addition, studies have suggested that these patients do not have an increased risk of colorectal cancer over the general population; hence they do not need a clearing colonoscopy to search for synchronous adenomas at the time of initial diagnosis, nor do they require follow-up surveillance. A study from the Mayo Clinic showed no increased future risk of colorectal cancer in patients who had a polyp under 1 cm removed from the rectosigmoid.[6] Another study from this institution demonstrated an increased future risk of colorectal cancer only in patients with polyps over 1 cm in size when initially detected.[7] A recent British study also showed no increase in future risk of colorectal cancer over the general population in patients in whom rectosigmoid adenomas less than 1 cm in size were initially removed.[8] Several of the above studies[6–8] preceded the colonoscopy era; hence patients did not have their colons cleared of polyps. It is now well known that there is a 50 percent synchronous rate of additional adenomas in patients in whom an index adenoma has been identified. Clearly, the increased future risk was related in the above studies[6–8] to the synchronous adenomas that were not removed. More recently, the National Polyp Study (NPS) reported a reduced incidence of future colorectal cancer in patients with index adenomas in whom all synchronous polyps had been removed by colonoscopy.[9] All of these observations agree with our present concepts of the relationship of adenomas to carcinoma. The counterargument to the position of dismissing patients with small adenomas is that once an individual has been identified as having an adenomatous polyp, that individual should have the entire colon cleared of synchronous adenomas and be entered into a follow-up program for metachronous adenomas in order to reduce the risk *below* that of the general population. Should clinicians be satisfied with offering patients a risk of colorectal cancer *equal* to the general population, considering the high risk of colorectal cancer in this country? In patients with identified adenomas, it seems reasonable to offer complete initial colonoscopy and follow-up surveillance in order to achieve the major goal of reducing the incidence and mortality of colorectal cancer regardless of size of the adenoma initially found.

Another controversy in the literature has regarded the approach to patients having small polyps detected on sigmoidoscopy. One suggestive concept is to offer full colonoscopy to all of these individuals. Some studies have suggested that hyperplastic polyps share the same high predictive value for proximal adenomas as do adenomas found on sigmoidoscopy. Achkar and Carey[10] reported that a finding of adenomas or hyperplastic polyps on flexible sigmoidoscopy was of equal predictiveness as proximal adenomas when total colonoscopy was undertaken. Furthermore, this association was significantly greater than that in a control group consisting of patients with a mucosal tag found on initial flexible sigmoidoscopy. In another retrospective study, Ansher et al.[11] found that the percentage of patients harboring a proximal adenoma in the absence of a distal hyperplastic polyp was 13 percent, compared with 48 percent when a distal hyperplastic polyp was also present. The likelihood of finding an isolated right-sided adenoma was increased by a factor of 10 when a left-sided hyperplastic polyp was present. A report by Provenzale et al.,[12] however, did not support this relationship. That study was prospective, involving 274 patients with adenomas and 108 with hyperplastic polyps. The main difficulty in interpreting the significance of the study by Achkar and Carey[10] is the absence of a true control group of patients with completely normal findings in the sigmoid and rectum. The NPS data analysis permitted the comparison of a large cohort of 3067 patients with no lesion on the left side of the colon (distal to splenic flexure) to a group of 1139 with adenomas only on the left and 162 with hyperplastic polyps only on the left. Adenomas on the left, particularly when multiple, were shown to be predictive of adenomas on the right proximal to the splenic flexure. However, the frequency of right-sided adenomas was similar when hyperplastic polyps only or no lesions were found on the left. This study, therefore, strongly supports the view that a hyperplastic polyp in the rectum and sigmoid is not an indication per se for a total colonoscopy.[13]

Once a patient has been identified as having an adenomatous polyp and after the polyp has been completely excised, the specimen should be examined to adequately classify the lesion and delineate any focus of cancer. A total colonoscopy should be done to detect and remove additional synchronous polyps.

In the precolonoscopy era, it was concluded that 90 percent of colonic polyps were hyperplastic. These observations resulted primarily from sigmoidoscopy studies. Based on colonoscopy data, it has been shown that the majority of colorectal polyps are adenomas. The remaining polyps are overgrowths of normal mucosa as well as hyperplastic and other miscellaneous lesions.[14] Adenomas detected in clinical trials are larger than those reported from autopsy studies, since the majority of the former are detected as a result either of symptoms or abnormal x-ray studies. All adenomas show at least mild dysplasia and a lesser proportion show either low-grade or high-grade dysplasia (see Chap. 12).[14] The most common type of adenoma is tubular, and two-thirds are distal to the splenic flexure in clinical studies. In autopsy studies, adenomas tend to be small and uniformly distributed anatomically; they have very little high-grade dysplasia or invasive cancer.[15]

Follow-up Management

Several studies have shown that after an adenoma is removed, metachronous adenomas develop at an increased rate.[16–20] The frequency with which adenomas were detected after polypectomy had been reported to be in the range of 20 to 60 percent prior to the colonoscopy era. Since introduction of colonoscopy, observations of adenoma detection at follow-up have been reported by a number of investigators. In a study by Macrae and Williams[18] of 330 patients, a 37 percent detection rate was observed during an average follow-up period of 3.6 years. Waye and Braunfeld[19] observed a 56 percent detection rate in 227 patients, while Fowler and Hedberg[20] reported a 60 percent detection rate in 383 patients over a 4-year period of follow-up. Matek and colleagues[17] reported a similar rate. The large cooperative multicenter randomized trial in the United States (NPS) also demonstrated a significant detection rate of 29 to 35 percent at follow-up, depending on the number of interventions and the time interval from last colonoscopy.[16] It is clear from all of these studies that a significant number of adenomas are detected after the colon has been thoroughly cleared of all synchronous adenomas.

An important question is what the characteristics of adenomas found at follow-up are. A review of the studies reported above, including the NPS, indicates that adenomas detected at follow-up are generally small, mostly tubular without high-grade dysplasia, and more uniformly distributed than on initial presentation.[16–20] Analysis of the factors associated with detection at follow-up indicate that the independent risk factors are an initial large size of the adenoma, multiplicity, and older age of the patient. It is not at all clear how these observations can be used clinically as yet, since adenomas found at follow-up have been mostly unimportant pathologically.[16–20]

Further management and follow-up surveillance depends on the characteristics of the adenomas removed initially, the quality of the examination, and, of course, the clinical status of the patient (Fig. 32-2). Follow-up management of adenomas containing in situ carcinoma or high-grade (severe) dysplasia is the same as for benign adenomas. Further management of patients with adenomas containing invasive cancer is discussed elsewhere in this book (see Chap. 47). Patients can be separated into two groups in terms of their follow-up requirements.[21] While most patients can have routine follow-up, a small proportion will need individualized follow-up approaches because of special factors. Individuals not having their colon cleared of all polyps with a high degree of confidence—because of redundancy, suboptimal preparation, persistent spasm, or other factors preventing complete examination—will require an additional examination earlier than is usually planned routinely. In addition, in the presence of invasive cancer or a large sessile adenoma, earlier examinations may be needed to be certain that there is no residual adenoma or cancer at the polypectomy site. Individuals having numerous adenomas usually need to be reexamined to see whether there were missed synchronous adenomas.

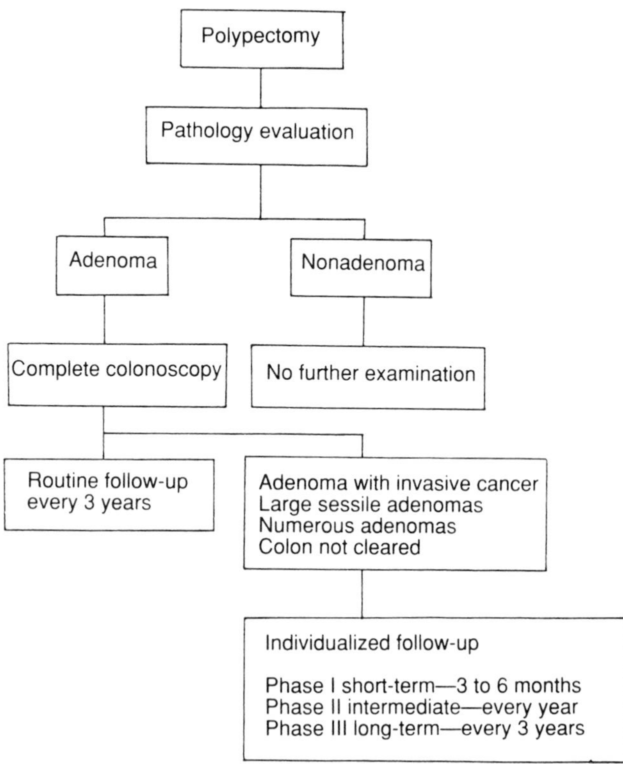

FIG. 32-2. Follow-up management of patients with polyps.

Individuals having no special risk factors (as indicated above) can have routine follow-up surveillance.[21] This can be done either with double-contrast barium enema or with colonoscopy. Colonoscopy is more sensitive for all polyps but especially for polyps less than 1 cm in size, and although it is more costly and more invasive, it has the added advantage of biopsy of suspicious lesions and polypectomy. Considering these factors, colonoscopy is the method of follow-up preferred by most investigators and clinicians. An annual fecal occult blood test has been used as an interval examination, but this is of questionable value in this setting, since periodic colonoscopy is being done anyway. The objective of a follow-up program is to prevent the development of colorectal cancer. The detection rate of adenomas in patients after initial polypectomy is high enough to justify periodic follow-up. In addition, missed synchronous adenomas can be identified during the follow-up examination. However, the follow-up program should be designed so as to protect the patient from the risk and cost of unnecessary examinations and an overwhelming usage of medical resources. The endoscopist should be fairly confident that he or she has established a clean colon free of adenomas before a long-term follow-up program is instituted. This may require more than one examination in some patients, as discussed above. Routine follow-up intervals have not as yet been established. Current data suggest that after establishing a clean colon, and in the absence of the special risk factors discussed above, there can usually be an interval of 3 years before repeat examination. Individual patient considerations, such as associated medical conditions, will affect the decision regarding continued follow-up.

It is not clear what proportion of adenomas found at follow-up are true metachronous adenomas and what proportion are missed synchronous polyps. Several reports have indicated that the 10 to 15 percent of adenomas that are missed on a single colonoscopy are mostly small, with unimportant pathology and very little high-grade dysplasia. In a study reported by Hixson et al.,[22] 90 patients were examined by tandem colonoscopy performed by two alternate examiners. Of 58 lesions detected in 31 patients, no neoplastic lesion greater than or equal to 1 cm in size was missed. It was calculated that 16 percent of small (<0.5 cm) and 12 percent of medium-size (0.6 to 0.9 cm) polyps were missed by the first examiner. The investigators concluded that an experienced endoscopist will miss about 15 percent of polyps less than 1 cm in size. Large (> 1 cm) polyps, however, were rarely missed. The NPS has also estimated that about half of the adenomas found on follow-up examinations were missed initially (about 15 percent). In the NPS, there were mostly small to medium size adenomas with mostly unimportant pathology. It can be estimated that about half of the adenomas detected at the first follow-up colonoscopy are true metachronous adenomas and half are adenomas that were missed on the initial examination.

The justification for removing adenomatous polyps is based on our knowledge of the adenoma-adenocarcinoma progression. The thesis is that removal of adenomas will interrupt this sequence, resulting in a decreased incidence of colorectal cancer and presumably a decreased mortality. This outcome was suggested in a study based on rigid sigmoidoscopy conducted at the University of Minnesota.[23] Details of the pathology of removed polyps and completeness of follow-up were not reported. More recently, a colonoscopic study reported from the NPS demonstrated a reduction in the incidence of colorectal cancer in a cohort in which all adenomas had been removed.[9] The NPS conclusions were based on a comparison of expected versus observed colorectal cancer found at follow-up examinations in a cohort that had all polyps removed initially, that had at least one adenomatous polyp removed initially, that had the entire colon cleared by colonoscopy, and that had approximately a 97 percent follow-up in 8000 person-years of risk. These data provided good evidence for the adenoma-adenocarcinoma progression and the possibility of interrupting it by colonoscopic polypectomy.

The approach to patients with adenomas will change considerably in the next decade, as our understanding of the biology of the adenomas and their relationship to colorectal cancer increases. It is likely that progress in the genetics of heredity will provide a basis for identifying people with adenomas who have a propensity for growth of these adenomas and their transformation into cancer. At present, individuals with adenomas can be viewed as indicators of increased risk among the first-degree relatives of their families. In the past, several studies have demonstrated the increase in familial risk for colorectal cancer and adenomas as a result of colorectal cancer in a first-degree relative.[24] More recently, it has been shown that this increased familial risk is also present when the index individual has an adenomatous polyp.[25] The NPS provided a framework within which to evaluate risk of cancer in the first-degree relatives of probands with adenomas, to further examine the adenoma-carcinoma relationship in families, and to clarify the inheritance of "sporadic" adenomas. To achieve these goals, the Genetic Epidemiology Study was organized utilizing the NPS cohort of more than 9000 patients accrued over a 10-year period from seven participating centers.[25] This database included patients with (1) single and multiple newly diagnosed adenomas having a wide range of histologic features and size, (2) with clean colons, (3) with hyperplastic polyps, and (4) with colon cancer. Colonoscopy was performed only by study investigators and all polyps were prospectively reviewed by a pathology committee. Family history data were obtained from a sample of this cohort by trained telephone interviewers. Confirmatory data were obtained directly from family members when permission was given. Data are currently based on 865 adenoma probands, 150 colorectal cancer probands, 213 probands with nonadenomatous polyps, 224 probands with clean colons, 8725 family members, and 974 spouse controls. The preliminary conclusions reached include the following:

- Families of probands with newly diagnosed adenomas have an increased risk of colorectal cancer; this overall increased risk is the same for probands with single or multiple adenomas.
- With single adenomas, the younger the proband, the greater the familial risk of colorectal cancer.
- For probands with multiple adenomas, the increased familial risk of colorectal cancer did not vary with proband age.

These data provide further evidence for the adenoma-adenocarcinoma relationship and for inheritance as a factor in the formation of adenomas. Younger age of adenoma onset identifies a higher familial risk for colorectal cancer. Further understanding of the risk for growth and recurrence based on initial pathology of adenomas and their phenotypic characteristics will also help classify individuals according to risk and thereby permit more rational follow-up surveillance.[1,26–30] In the interim, the following guidelines can serve for patients who have undergone polypectomy.

Summary Guidelines

Colonoscopy is the preferred method of follow-up examination after removal of an initial adenoma.[1] However, sigmoidoscopy with a high-quality double-contrast barium enema is a possible acceptable alternative in the absence of good colonoscopy. Annual fecal occult blood tests have been used in the follow-up period when the surveillance intervals were longer than 1 year, but they are of questionable value in this setting. The endoscopist must be confident that a "clean colon," free of adenomas, has been established before instituting long-term follow-up. Following apparently complete removal of a pedunculated malignant polyp as judged on combined endoscopic and histologic grounds, most endoscopists perform repeat examination at 3 to 6 months and 1 year before reverting to general follow-up. Individual considerations such as ill health or pathologic predictive factors will affect the age at which follow-up is discontinued.

REFERENCES

1. Winawer SJ, O'Brien MJ, Waye JD, et al: Risk and surveillance of individuals with colorectal polyps. *Bull WHO* 68:789–795, 1990.
2. Deschner EE, Winawer SJ, Long FC, Boyle BS: Early detection of colonic neoplasia in patients at high risk. *Cancer* 40:2625–2631, 1977.
3. Terpstra OT, van Blankenstein M, Dees J, Eilers GAM: Abnormal pattern of cell proliferation in the entire colonic mucosa of patients with colon adenoma or cancer. *Gastroenterology* 92:704–708, 1987.
4. Tripp MR, Morgan TR, Sampliner RE, et al: Synchronous neoplasms in patients with diminutive colorectal adenomas. *Cancer* 60:1599–1603, 1987.
5. Grossman S, Milos ML, Tekawa IS, Jewel NP: Colonoscopic screening of persons with suspected risk factors for colon cancer: II. Past history of colorectal neoplasms. *Gastroenterology* 96:299–306, 1989.
6. Spencer JR, Melton LJ, Ready RL, Ilstrup DM. Treatment of small colorectal polyps: A population based study of the risk of subsequent carcinoma. *Mayo Clin Proc* 59:305–310, 1984.
7. Lotfi AM, Spencer RJ, Ilstrup DM, Melton LJ: Colorectal polyps and the risk of subsequent carcinoma. *Mayo Clin Proc* 61:337–343, 1986.
8. Atkin WS, Morson BC, Cuzick J: Long-term risk of colorectal cancer after excision of rectosigmoid adenomas. *N Engl J Med* 326:658–662, 1992.
9. Winawer SJ, Zauber AG, Gerdes H, et al: Reduction in colorectal cancer incidence following colonoscopic polypectomy: Report from the national polyp study. *Gastroenterology* 100 (5 suppl 2):A410, 1991.
10. Achkar E, Carey W: Small polyps found during fiberoptic sigmoidoscopy in asymptomatic patients. *Ann Intern Med* 109:880–883, 1988.
11. Ansher AF, Lewis JH, O'Kieffe DA, et al: Hyperplastic colonic polyps (HP) as a marker for adenomatous colonic polyps (AP) (abstract). *Gastroenterology* 90:A1328, 1986.
12. Provenzale D, Garrett JW, Condon SE, Sandler RS: Risk for colon adenomas in patients with rectosigmoid hyperplastic polyps. *Ann Intern Med* 113:760–763, 1990.
13. Winawer SJ, Diaz B, Zauber AG, et al: The national polyp study: Colorectal adenomas and hyperplastic polyps (abstract). *Gastroenterology* 94:A499, 1988.
14. O'Brien MJ, Winawer SJ, Zauber AG, et al: The national polyp study: Patient and polyp characteristics associated with high grade dysplasia in colorectal adenomas. *Gastroenterology* 98:371–379, 1990.
15. Eide TJ: Risk of colorectal cancer in adenoma-bearing individuals within a defined population. *Int J Cancer* 38:173–176, 1986.
16. Winawer SJ, Zauber AG, Diaz B, et al: The national polyp study: Overview of program and preliminary report of patient and polyp characteristics, in Steele G Jr, Burt RW, Winawer SJ, Karr JP (eds): *Basic and Clinical Perspectives of Colorectal Polyps and Cancer.* New York, Liss, 1988, pp 35–49.
17. Matek W, Guggenmoos-Holzman I, Demling L: Follow-up of patients with colorectal adenomas. *Endoscopy* 17:175–181, 1985.
18. Macrae FA, Willliams CB: A prospective colonoscopic follow-up study of 500 adenoma patients with multivariate analysis to predict risk of subsequent colorectal tumors. *Gastroenterology* 5:A1122, 1982.
19. Waye JD, Braunfeld SF: Surveillance intervals after colonoscopic polypectomy. *Endoscopy* 14:79–81, 1982.
20. Fowler DL, Hedberg SE: Follow-up colonoscopy after polypectomy. *Gastrointest Endosc* 26:A67, 1980.
21. Lambert R, Sobin LH, Waye JD, Stalder GA: The management of patients with colorectal adenomas, in *Third International Symposium on Colorectal Cancer, 1983.* New York, American Cancer Society, 1984, pp 43–52.
22. Hixson LJ, Fennerty MB, Sampliner RE, et al: Prospective study of the frequency and size distribution of polyps missed by colonoscopy. *J Natl Cancer Inst* 82:1769–1772, 1990.
23. Gilbertsen VA, McHugh R, Schuman L, et al: The early detection of colorectal cancers: A preliminary report of the results of the occult blood study. *Cancer* 45:2899–2901, 1980.
24. Burt RW, Bishop DT, Lynch HT, et al: Risk and surveillance of individuals with heritable factors for colorectal cancer. *Bull WHO* 68:655–665, 1990.
25. Winawer SJ, Zauber AG, Gerdes H, et al: Genetic epidemiology of colorectal cancer: Relationship of familial colorectal cancer risk to adenoma proband age and adenoma characteristics (abstract). *Gastroenterology* 102(suppl 2):A409, 1992.
26. Vogelstein B, Fearon ER, Hamilton SR, et al: Genetic alterations during colorectal tumor development. *N Engl J Med* 319:525–532, 1988.
27. Solomon E, Voss R, Hall V, et al: Chromosome 5 allele loss in human colorectal carcinomas. *Nature* 328:616–619, 1967.
28. Burt RW, Bishop DT, Cannon-Albright LA, et al: Dominant inheritance of adenomatous colonic polyps and colorectal cancer. *N Engl J Med* 312:1540–1544, 1985.
29. Cannon-Albright LA, Skolnick MH, Bishop DT, et al: Common inheritance of susceptibility of colonic adenomatous polyps and associated colorectal cancers. *N Engl J Med* 319:533–537, 1988.
30. Shike M, Greenwald P, Bloch A, et al: Primary prevention of colorectal cancer. *Bull WHO* 68:377–385, 1990.
31. Winawer SJ, Schottenfeld D, Flehinger BJ: Colorectal cancer screening (review). *J Natl Cancer Inst* 83:243–253, 1991.

CHAPTER 33

Surveillance—Family History and Lynch Syndrome Patients

Randall W. Burt

HIGHLIGHTS

Epidemiologic, endoscopic, kindred, and genetic studies have consistently demonstrated an increased familial risk associated with colorectal cancer and adenomas. Current data favor partially penetrant inherited susceptibility as the explanation for the majority of familial cases. Rare inherited syndromes of colonic cancer are well known and account for a small fraction of the familial cases. Hereditary nonpolyposis colorectal cancer (HNPCC) is one of these and may be difficult to distinguish from more common colonic cancers without a defining family history.

Certain characteristics of colorectal cancer and adenomas associate with familial risk. These characteristics can be used in the clinical setting to stratify risk. The most helpful clinical features in this regard include age at diagnosis and number of first-degree relatives affected with colonic cancer. Multiplicity of lesions, colonic location of tumors, and histology may also be helpful but require further study. These characteristics also help to define the disease in the extreme setting of HNPCC. The risk information presented is used to suggest screening strategies for relatives of persons with colorectal cancers and adenomas.

CONTROVERSIES

There is general agreement that screening is indicated in relatives of persons with colonic cancer. Disagreement arises as to what strategy would be optimal in specific situations. Some believe that having a single first-degree relative affected with colorectal cancer is sufficient to warrant complete colonoscopy screening every 5 years. Others maintain that average-risk screening is more appropriate, possibly beginning at a younger age. The degree to which relatives with adenomas and second-degree relatives with colonic cancer should affect screening guidelines is debated. The frequency at which colonoscopy should be done for persons at risk of HNPCC is not known. Intervals from 1 to 3 years have been suggested.

FUTURE DIRECTIONS

Better genetic definition of familial risk is needed. Studies should soon identify genetic markers for HNPCC. A more accurate diagnosis of that disease as well as an understanding of its etiology will then be possible. Genetic markers for the more common familial cases of colonic cancer are also important but are probably a number of years in the future.

Clinical trials and case control studies examining screening strategies in the familial risk setting should be planned. Such studies are needed to validate the suggested screening of persons with familial risk. More attention to specific features of colorectal cancer and adenomas is needed in epidemiologic and endoscopic studies. Such information should help to stratify familial risk more precisely and allow for the development of more effective screening guidelines.

Colonic cancer is known to occur in families more often than expected by chance. First-degree relatives of individuals with colonic cancer, in fact, exhibit a two- to threefold increased risk of this malignancy. A small number of familial cases come from the rare but well-characterized syndromes of familial adenomatous polyposis (FAP) and hereditary nonpolyposis colorectal cancer (HNPCC). The great majority of familial cases, however, do not fit into any syndrome. Current evidence suggests nonetheless that inherited susceptibility plays a role in these cases.[1] This chapter summarizes the evidence for inherited or familial risk (presented in detail in Chap. 7) and reviews data that allow familial risk to be stratified by clinical characteristics. Screening guidelines that consider familial risk are then outlined.

The screening guidelines address both family history in general and HNPCC. These two categories are best considered together because HNPCC is often difficult to distinguish from other familial cases until an extensive family history is obtained. Screening strategies that consider familial risk therefore should include the possibility of HNPCC and be able to identify it when present. Because of its characteristic phenotype, FAP is more easily distinguished.

FAMILIAL RISK

Population and Hospital Studies

The first studies that addressed familial risk of colonic cancer examined the mortality from colorectal cancer in relatives of individuals with that malignancy.[2–4] Subsequent investigations examined incident cases of colonic cancer in relatives.[5–12] Both types of studies consistently demonstrated a two- to threefold increased risk of colonic cancer in first-degree relatives. Studies that included relatives of individuals with colonic adenomas found the same result.[6,7,9] Most of these studies excluded FAP and found little evidence of monogenic inheritance that would be expected with HNPCC.

Endoscopic Studies

Recent studies have used endoscopy to determine the prevalence of adenomatous polyps in relatives of persons with colorectal cancer. Such studies have particular pertinence to screening relatives of colonic cancer patients. Table 33-1 summarizes the endoscopic studies that have been performed to date. Given the wide variation of adenoma prevalence in these investigations, it is difficult to assess excess familial risk without control groups. Only three of the studies had controls. In each of these, the incidence of adenomas was significantly greater in relatives than in controls. The incidence of adenomas also increased with age and was greater in relatives than in controls for each age group in the studies where age was given.[12,13] A flexible sigmoidoscopy study further found that relatives of subjects with only adenomas likewise exhibited a twofold greater risk of adenomas than controls.

Kindred Studies and Inherited Susceptibility

Excess familial clustering of cases could arise either from inherited susceptibility or from common exposure to environmental factors. Kindred investigations were undertaken to determine which of these causes

Table 33-1
Frequency of Adenomas in First-Degree Relatives of Index Cases with Colorectal Cancer

Authors	*Relatives, %*	*Controls, %*	*Study method*
Gryska and Cohen,[40] 1987	63	—	Colonoscopy
Rosen et al.,[22] 1989	8	4	FOBT/FS
Cannon-Albright et al.,[41] 1988	19	12	FS
Grossman and Milos,[42] 1988	18	—	Colonoscopy
McConnell et al.,[43] 1990	12	—	Colonoscopy
Orrom et al.,[44] 1990	20	—	Colonoscopy
Baker et al.,[30] 1990	27	—	Colonoscopy
Herrera et al.,[45] 1990	12	—	FOBT/FS
Sauar et al.,[46] 1992	37	—	Colonoscopy
Guillem et al.,[13] 1992	14	8	Colonoscopy

Abbreviations: FOBT, fecal occult blood test; FS, flexible sigmoidoscopy.

accounted for the excess familial risk observed in the epidemiologic and endoscopic studies. The first kindred study examined members of multiple kindreds for both adenomas and colonic cancer.[14] The analysis indicated that familial clustering probably arose because of commonly occurring genes that conferred susceptibility for adenomatous polyps and colonic cancer. Another study assessed kindred members for the presence of colonic cancers only.[15,16] Results from this investigation suggested an uncommon but more penetrant susceptibility gene or genes for colonic cancer.

Exposure to common environmental factors may also play a role in the familial occurrence of colonic cancer. Genetic marker studies are under way to further clarify inherited susceptibility and, it is hoped, to resolve the issues of gene frequency, gene function, and genetic-environmental interactions. A consistent hypothesis from the present data is that inheritance defines individual susceptibility to colonic adenomas and cancer while environmental factors determine which persons actually form polyps and finally develop cancer.

Stratification of Familial Risk

Despite the ill-defined nature of inherited susceptibility in most familial cases of colonic cancer, present studies leave little doubt that familial factors, probably inherited, play an important role in the pathogenesis of a large proportion and possibly a majority of cases of colorectal adenoma and cancer. The exact nature of this familial clustering or inheritance is unclear except in the relatively rare syndromes of FAP and HNPCC. It is apparent, however, that inheritance varies from mild to severe, with the syndromes representing the most severe end of the spectrum.

Ultimately genetic markers will be required to confirm that inherited susceptibility is common and to determine its severity in each family or case. Until such markers are available, however, certain clinical characteristics appear to be useful in stratifying familial risk. These characteristics include age of diagnosis, colonic location of neoplasms, multiplicity of lesions, and number of affected relatives. Each of these characteristics exhibits extreme features in HNPCC and FAP. Interestingly, they are often also present to some degree in families with the more common but milder forms of inherited susceptibility.

Age at Diagnosis

Excess familial risk of colonic neoplasms appears to be common in all age groups. Many referral-based studies have shown an even higher risk in relatives when the index case was diagnosed at a younger age. Two recent studies should be mentioned. The National Polyp Study found parents of persons with adenomas to have a 1.8-fold increased risk of colonic cancer compared to expected rates.[17] When groups were separated by age of adenoma diagnosis of the index case, parents had a 2.7-, 1.8-, and 1.4-fold increased risk for the age groups of <60, 60 to 69, and >69 years of age, respectively. The excess risk was significant for the first two groups but not for the >69 age group.

A study from Australia found the risk of colonic cancer in first-degree relatives of persons with colonic cancer to be double that of the general population if the index case was diagnosed at age 55 or above.[16] If the index case was diagnosed at age 45 to 54, the risk in relatives was triple that of the general population. The risk was approximately four times that of the general population if the index case was diagnosed at an age below 45.

There are, however, several population and referral center studies that have failed to associate a younger age at diagnosis with increased cancer risk.[11,18–20] These studies have taken a somewhat different approach. They have examined the age at colonic cancer diagnosis in persons with affected relatives and compared this to the age at diagnosis of those who have no affected relatives. In such studies, the age at colonic cancer diagnosis in those with affected relatives has not differed from the age at diagnosis in the general population.

Considering all the data, however, it seems likely that the age at diagnosis probably does correlate with familial risk to some degree. The differing results probably relate to the different methodologies used to examine the problem. For screening purposes, one should remember that familial risk is significant regardless of the age of the index case. But considering the studies reviewed, the risk appears to be even greater if the index case was diagnosed at an age below 55 years. Diagnosis of colonic cancer at a very young age (<30 years) should raise one's suspicion for HNPCC or FAP.

Colonic Location of Adenomas and Cancer

An excess of proximal colonic tumors generally has not been found to be a feature of familial risk outside the syndrome of HNPCC. It has been suggested in some studies[8,13,21] but has not been found in most.[11,18–20,22] Furthermore, proximal and distal colonic cancers both appear to be predictive of familial risk and to approximately the same degree.[19,20] Rectal cancer considered separately, however, may not be associated with familial risk to the same degree as cancer at other locations.[8] Further examination of population-based data should resolve the issues of colonic cancer location and familial risk. Until then, it would seem prudent to regard familial risk as an important consideration for colonic cancer regardless of colonic segment. An excess of proximal colonic tumors *is* a feature of

HNPCC, making full colonoscopy the only acceptable screening tool in that setting.

Multiplicity of Lesions

An increased number of adenomas has been associated with familial risk.[14,23] In the analysis by Morson et al.[24] of Lovett's data, there was a mean number of 1.2 adenomas in colonic cancer patients from families with a single case of colonic cancer. There were 2.2 adenomas in colonic cancer patients from two case families and 4.3 in three case families. It is important that more data be collected on the number of polyps as it relates to family history, as colonoscopists frequently identify persons with multiple adenomas.

Histology

Histology may also correlate with familial risk. Two studies have suggested an association of family history with more severe histology, while other studies have failed to find this association.[13,24,25] A molecular genetic investigation found that the proportion of chromosomal locations exhibiting loss of genetic material (fractional allelic loss) in colorectal cancer tissues correlated with a family history of the disease.[26] There are also suggestions of familial risk related to the presence of hyperplastic polyps in relatives.[27] Further study is required in these areas.

Number of Affected First-Degree Relatives

It appears well established that the number of first-degree relatives with colonic cancer relates to colonic cancer and colonic adenoma risk. The mortality, incidence, and colonoscopy studies all have found that first-degree relatives of persons with colorectal cancer or adenomas have a two- to fourfold increased risk of harboring colonic neoplasm. Many of these studies have also found the risk to be further increased if two first-degree relatives had colonic cancer.[13,28–30] In the colonoscopy study of first-degree relatives by Guillem et al.,[13] 25.0 percent of persons with two affected first-degree relatives were found to have adenomas, compared to 13.1 percent of those with a single affected relative and 8.4 percent of controls. The colonoscopy study of Baker et al.[30] found adenomas in 23.5 percent of persons who had one first-degree relative with colorectal cancer. If two first-degree relatives had colonic cancer, adenomas were found in 32.0 percent. Adenomas were found in 100 percent of those with three or four affected relatives, but there were only 4 and 2 persons, respectively, in these last two groups.

Investigators at St. Mark's Hospital in London calculated the risk for colonic cancer based on previously studied families in order to formulate screening guidelines.[31] These risk are given in Table 33-2. It is again notable that the risk of colonic cancer was more than double if two first-degree relatives were affected with the disease compared to the risk with a single affected relative. The risk of an individual with an affected first- *and* second-degree relative was intermediate. The authors specified that full colonoscopy be the screening tool for any person with risk ≥1 in 10. It should be pointed out that the population risk of colonic cancer in the United States is much higher than the population risk in the United Kingdom. The U.S. lifetime risk of the general population approaches 6 percent, or nearly 1 in 18. Thus, having a single affected first-degree relative would result in a personal risk greater than 1 in 10.

Table 33-2
Lifetime Risks of Colorectal Cancer in First-Degree Relatives of Patients with Colonic Cancer

Category	*Risk*
Population risk	1 in 50
One first-degree relative affected	1 in 17
One first- and one second-degree relative affected	1 in 12
One relative under age 45 affected	1 in 10
Two first-degree relatives affected	1 in 6
Dominant pedigree	1 in 2

SOURCE: From Ref. 31, by permission.

Adenomas in First-Degree Relatives

Previously cited studies[6,7,9] show that first-degree relatives of persons with adenomatous polyps exhibit approximately the same degree of cancer risk as first-degree relatives of persons with colorectal cancer. These studies should be viewed with caution, however, when determining risk and screening strategies. The epidemiologic studies that included adenomas probably ascertained persons with large or symptomatic polyps. It is not clear if the risk would be similar for small adenomas that are so often found with modern endoscopy. Studies need to be done that stratify risk in relatives by size of adenoma. Until such data are available, large adenomas (>1 cm) in relatives should probably be considered near equivalent to colonic cancer as a risk factor. Small adenomas, on the other hand, should be considered a risk factor, but of lesser importance.

FAMILIAL RISK IN HEREDITARY NONPOLYPOSIS COLORECTAL CANCER

There are two categories of HNPCC, site-specific hereditary colonic cancer and cancer family syndrome. These also are referred to as Lynch syndromes I and II, respectively.[32] As discussed in detail in Chap. 8, both Lynch syndromes exhibit a very high risk of colonic cancer that occurs at a relatively young age. Cancers are prone to occur in the proximal colon, and synchronous and metachronous primary malignancies are found more often than expected. Adenomatous polyps occur, but usually only one or several are present.[33] Cancer family syndrome differs from site-specific hereditary colonic cancer only in that extracolonic cancers also occur in affected families. These cancers primarily include ovarian and uterine types, although families have also been studied that exhibit breast, gastric, prostate, pancreatic, and other malignancies.

It is often impossible to determine if Lynch syndrome is present in an isolated individual. The clinician must rely on the family history. Multiple cases of colonic cancer extending over two or three generations is considered the hallmark of the syndrome. A high suspicion for the disease must also be present when colonic cancer occurs at a young age (<30 years) or when three first-degree relatives are affected with colonic cancer.

Genetic studies have now found a chromosomal locus associated with some HNPCC families, although genetic diagnosis is not yet possible.[34] Clinical characteristics must be used to diagnose the disease and determine the most appropriate screening approaches in individuals at risk. Clinical features of HNPCC have also provided clues as to how the underlying genetic mutation affects the pathogenesis of colonic cancer development. It appears that adenomas in HNPCC occur at a younger age, are on average larger, and have a greater villous component than adenomas in the general population.[35,36] There is not an excessive number of adenomas in HNPCC. Instead, the adenoma-to-carcinoma sequence appears to be accelerated.

SCREENING RECOMMENDATIONS

The screening recommendations that consider familial risk are empiric.[1,37,38] They are based on the effectiveness and limitations of available screening and diagnostic tools. They also consider the characteristics of the inherited syndromes and the risks of colonic cancer in families, as outlined above. Modeling studies have addressed screening in individuals with familial risk of colonic cancer,[39] but neither case control studies nor clinical trials have yet been completed. Nonetheless, the known increased risk of colonic cancer in relatives of persons with this malignancy has led to a general consensus that screening in relatives is necessary and appropriate.

All organizations that have formulated screening guidelines for colonic cancer have suggested that screening is necessary for relatives of persons with colonic cancer. The increased predictive value of any screening test in a higher-risk setting is the basis of this opinion. Discussion remains as to the most appropriate screening approaches. The guidelines presented must therefore be considered interim but represent a logical approach to the problem of familial risk in view of present knowledge (Table 33-3).

Relatives of Persons with Colorectal Cancer

1. *One affected first-degree relative:* Average-risk screening should be advised but should begin by age 35 to 40. Average-risk screening should include annual fecal occult blood testing (FOBT) and sigmoidoscopy every 3 to 5 years. Full colonoscopy, starting at age 50 and continuing

Table 33-3
Screening according to Familial Risk

Category	*Test*	*Beginning age, years*	*Frequency*
One 1° rel with CRC	Flex procto,	35–40	Every 3–5 years
	FOBT	35–40	Annually
One 1° rel with CRC <55 years	Colonoscopy,[a]	50	Every 5 years
	FOBT	35–40	Annually
Two 1° rels with CRC	Colonoscopy,	35–40[b]	Every 5 years
	FOBT	35–40[b]	Annually
Three or more 1° rels with CRC	Colonoscopy	35–40[b]	See note[c]
One or more 2° rels with CRC	Flex procto,	50[d]	Every 3–5 years
	FOBT	50	Annually
One 1° and one 2° rel with CRC	Colonoscopy,	50	Every 5 years
	FOBT	50	Annually
1° or 2° rels with adenomas	Flex procto,	50	Every 3–5 years
	FOBT	50	Annually
HNPCC	Colonoscopy	25[b]	Every 2 to 3 years

[a]Flex procto should be done every 3 to 5 years between age 35 and 50.

[b]Or 5 years younger than the earliest case in the family.

[c]Frequency should be determined after initial family screening.

[d]Three or more second-degree relatives may indicate substantial risk, so that colonoscopy might be considered.

Abbreviations: 1° rel, first-degree relative; CRC, colorectal cancer; FOBT, fecal occult blood test; flex procto, flexible proctosigmoidoscopy; HNPCC, hereditary nonpolyposis colorectal cancer.

every 3 to 5 years, can be considered an alternative approach, especially if cancer in the relative was diagnosed at an age below 55.

2. *Two affected first-degree relatives:* Annual FOBT and colonoscopy every 3 to 5 years should begin by age 35 to 40 or at an age 5 years below the age of the earliest colonic cancer in relatives, whichever comes first.
3. *Three or more affected first-degree relatives or a relative with colonic cancer diagnosed below age 30:* Inherited colonic cancer syndrome should be suspected unless colonoscopy screening proves otherwise.
4. *Affected second-degree relatives:* Average-risk screening should be advised. If a first-degree relative is also affected, colonoscopy should be considered.
5. *Relatives affected with adenomas:* Average-risk screening should be advised.

Hereditary Nonpolyposis Colorectal Cancer

Individuals in families with HNPCC should have full colonoscopy every 2 to 3 years beginning at age 25 or beginning at an age 5 years below the age of the earliest colonic cancer diagnosis in the family. More frequent colonoscopy should be considered after age 35 (Table 33-3).

REFERENCES

1. Burt RW, Bishop DT, Lynch HT, et al: Risk and surveillance of individuals with heritable factors for colorectal cancer. *Bull WHO* 68:655–665, 1992.
2. Woolf CM: A genetic study of carcinoma of the large intestine. *Am J Hum Genet* 10:42–47, 1958.
3. Macklin MT: Inheritance of cancer of the stomach and large intestine in man. *J Natl Cancer Inst* 24L:551–557, 1960.
4. Lovett E: Family studies in cancer of the colon and rectum. *Br J Surg* 63:13–189, 1976.
5. Duncan JL, Kyle J: Family incidence of carcinoma of the colon and rectum in northeast Scotland. *Gut* 23:169–171, 1982.
6. Maire P, Morichau-Beauchant M, Drucker J, et al: Familiar prevalence of colorectal cancer: A 3 year case-control study. *Gastroenterol Clin Biol* 8:22–27, 1984.
7. Ponz de Leon M, Antonioli A, Ascari A, et al: Incidence and familial occurrence of colorectal cancer and polyps in a health-care district of northern Italy. *Cancer* 60:2848–2859, 1987.
8. Kune GA, Kune S, Watson LF: The Melbourne colorectal cancer study: Characterization of patients with a family history of colorectal cancer. *Dis Colon Rectum* 30:600–606, 1987.
9. Bonelli L, Martines H, Conio M, et al: Family history of colorectal cancer as a risk factor for benign and malignant tumours of the large bowel: A case-control study. *Int J Cancer* 41:513–517, 1988.
10. St John DJB, McDermott FT, Datrivessis H, et al: Cancer risk for relatives of patients with sporadic colorectal cancer. Abstract presented at the 2d International Conference on Gastrointestinal Cancer, Jerusalem, Israel, 1989.
11. Stephenson BM, Finan PJ, Gascoyne J, et al: Frequency of familial colorectal cancer. *Br J Surg* 78:1162–1166, 1991.
12. Bishop DT, Thomas HJW: The genetics of colorectal cancer. *Cancer Surv* 9:585–604, 1990.
13. Guillem JG, Forde KA, Treat MR, et al: Colonoscopic screening for neoplasms in asymptomatic first-degree relatives of colon cancer patients. *Dis Colon Rectum* 35:523–529, 1992.
14. Burt RW, Bishop DT, Cannon LA, et al: Dominant inheritance of adenomatous colonic polyps and colorectal cancer. *N Engl J Med* 12:1540–1544, 1985.
15. St John DJB, Bishop DT, Crockford GP: HNPCC or common colorectal cancer? Criteria for diagnosis. *Gastroenterology* 102:A402, 1992.
16. Bishop DT, St John DJB, Hughes ESR, et al: Genetic susceptibility to common colorectal cancer: How common is it? *Gastroenterology* 102:A346, 1992.
17. Winawer SJ, Zauber AG, Gerdes H, et al: Genetic epidemiology of colorectal cancer: Relationship of familial colorectal cancer risk to adenoma proband age and adenoma characteristics. *Gastroenterology* 102:A409, 1992.
18. Kee F, Collins BJ: Families at risk of colorectal cancer: Who are they? *Gut* 33:787–790, 1992.
19. Cannon-Albright LA, Thomas TC, Bishop T, et al: Characteristics of familial colon cancer in a large population data base. *Cancer* 64:1971–1975, 1989.
20. Søndergaard JO, Būlow S, Lynge E: Cancer incidence among parents of patients with colorectal cancer. *Int J Cancer* 47:202–206, 1991.
21. Ponz de Leon M, Sassatelli R, Sacchetti C, et al: Familial aggregation of tumors in the three-year experience of a population-based colorectal cancer registry. *Cancer Res* 49:4344–4348, 1989.
22. Rozen P, Fireman E, Fine N, et al: Oral calcium suppresses increased rectal epithelial proliferation of persons at risk of colorectal cancer. *Gut* 30:650–655, 1989.
23. Dunlog MG: Screening for large bowel neoplasms in individuals with a family history of colorectal cancer. *Br J Surg* 79:488–494, 1992.
24. Morson BC, Bussey JHR, Day DW, et al: Adenomas of large bowel. *Cancer Surv* 2:451–477, 1983.
25. Sauar J, Hoff G, Hausken T, et al: Colonoscopic screening examination of relatives of patients with colorectal cancer: II. Relations between tumour characteristics and the presence of polyps. *Scand J Gastroenterol* 27:667–672, 1992.
26. Kern SE, Fearon ER, Tersmette KWF, et al: Allelic loss in colorectal carcinoma. *JAMA* 261:3099–3103, 1989.
27. DiSario JA, Cannon-Albright LA, Samowitz WS, et al: Hyperplastic colorectal polyps in relatives of persons with colorectal neoplasms. *Gastroenterology* 102:A353, 1992.
28. Rozen P, Ron E: A cost-effective analysis of using colonoscopy for screening family members of colon cancer patients. *Gastrointest Endosc* 34:219, 1988.
29. Gillin JS, Winawer SJ, Lipkin M: Prevalence of adenomas detected by colonoscopy in asymptomatic individuals in cancer-prone families. *Gastroenterology* 86:1088, 1984.
30. Baker JW, Gathright JB, Timmicke AE, et al: Colonoscopic screening of asymptomatic patients with a family history of colon cancer. *Dis Colon Rectum* 33:926–930, 1990.
31. Houlston RS, Murday V, Harocopos C, et al: Screening and genetic counselling for relatives of patients with colorectal cancer in a family cancer clinic. *Br Med J* 301:366–368, 1990.
32. Lynch HT, Watson P, Kriegler M, et al: Differential diagnosis of hereditary nonpolyposis colorectal cancer (Lynch syndrome I and Lynch syndrome II). *Dis Colon Rectum* 31:372–377, 1988.
33. Lanspa SJ, Lynch HT, Smyrk TC, et al: Colorectal adenomas in the Lynch syndrome—results of a colonoscopy screening program. *Gastroenterology* 98:1117–1122, 1990.
34. Paltomaki P, Galtonen LA, Sistonen P, et al: Genetic mapping of a locus predisposing to human colorectal cancer. *Science* 260:810–812, 1993.

35. Jass JR, Stewart SM: Evolution of hereditary non-polyposis colorectal cancer. *Gut* 33:783–786, 1992.
36. Mecklin J-P, Jarvinen HJ: Clinical features of colorectal carcinoma in cancer family syndrome. *Dis Colon Rectum* 23: 160–164, 1986.
37. Levin B, Murphy GP: Revision in American Cancer Society recommendations for the early detection of colorectal cancer. *CA* 42:296–299, 1992.
38. Rozen P, Ron E: A cost analysis of screening methodology for family members of colorectal cancer patients. *Am J Gastroenterol* 84:1548–1551, 1989.
39. Eddy DM, Nugent FW, Eddy JF, et al: Screening for colorectal cancer in a high-risk population: Results of a mathematical model. *Gastroenterology* 92:682–692, 1987.
40. Gryska PV, Cohen AM: Screening asymptomatic patients at high risk for colon cancer with full colonoscopy. *Dis Colon Rectum* 30:18–20, 1987.
41. Cannon-Albright LA, Skolnick MH, Bishop DT, et al: Common inheritance of susceptibility to colonic adenomatous polyps and associated colorectal cancers. *N Engl J Med* 319:533–537, 1988.
42. Grossman S, Milos ML: Colonoscopic screening of persons with suspected risk factors for colon cancer: I. Family history. *Gastroenterology* 39:395–400, 1988.
43. McConnell JC, Nizin JS, Slade MS: Colonoscopy in patients with a primary family history of colon cancer. *Dis Colon Rectum* 33:105–107, 1990.
44. Orrom WJ, Brezezinski WS, Wiens EW: Heredity and colorectal cancer: A prospective, community-based endoscopic study. *Dis Colon Rectum* 33:722, 1990.
45. Herrera L, Hanna S, Petrelli N, et al: Screening endoscopy in patients with family history positive (FH+) for colorectal neoplasia (CRN) (abstract). *Gastrointest Endosc* 36:211, 1990.
46. Sauar J, Hausken T, Hoff G, et al: Colonoscopic screening examination of relatives of patients with colorectal cancer: I. A comparison with an endoscopically screened normal population. *Scand J Gastroenterol* 27:661–666, 1992.

CHAPTER 34

Surveillance—Inflammatory Bowel Disease

John E. Lennard-Jones
William R. Connell

HIGHLIGHTS

Cancer in ulcerative colitis is associated with evidence of widespread genetic instability of the epithelium. If ulcerative colitis is treated surgically, the cancer risk can be avoided. Now that treatment increasingly avoids the need for a permanent ileostomy, it is more acceptable to patients. If the proportion of patients treated by surgery rises, the incidence of complicating colorectal cancer is likely to decrease.

A distinction is drawn between cancer screening (an episodic investigation), clinical supervision (which involves investigation of new symptoms), and cancer surveillance (a regular program of investigation).

During the last two decades, exploratory pilot surveillance programs using dysplasia as a marker of precancerous change or carcinoma have given disappointing results. Results are difficult to compare because patients with differing extent and duration of disease have been included. Standardized definitions are recommended for the future. At four referral centers, three in America and one in England, the subsequent diagnosis of carcinoma during surveillance has depended greatly on the findings at the first colonoscopy. When no dysplasia was found at the first examination, the incidence of carcinoma has tended to be lower than among those in whom dysplasia was present.

No series has demonstrated a reduction in cancer mortality compared with a control group. The results of pilot studies are confusing and can be interpreted in two ways. Either the yield of carcinoma was too low to justify the resources involved, or, conversely, the development of carcinoma was unacceptably high. In the present state of uncertainty, cancer surveillance programs for patients with ulcerative colitis should not be regarded as mandatory. Investigation with new markers is needed to show whether these programs are effective and represent a good use of resources.

CONTROVERSIES

The major controversy concerns the clinical value of cancer surveillance in colitis. It is now apparent that dysplasia is an imperfect marker of neoplastic potential. About one-quarter of carcinomas in colitis are not associated with dysplasia at a distance from the tumor. High-grade dysplasia or dysplasia on the surface of an elevated lesion tends to be associated with a carcinoma at the same site or elsewhere in the colon. Clinicians therefore regard these changes as an indication for operation. The clinical significance of low-grade dysplasia is highly controversial; some regard a single biopsy showing this change as an indication for operation, others advise surgery when the change is widespread in the colon or found on repeated examination, and yet others regard it as a clinically insignificant finding. The importance of indefinite dysplasia is likewise controversial.

If it is accepted that cancer surveillance should be undertaken, there is doubt as to whether it should be restricted to patients with inflammation involving the proximal half of the colon or whether patients with left-sided colitis should be included.

FUTURE DIRECTIONS

Genetic abnormalities associated with neoplastic potential are the subject of intense research. Chromosomal abnormalities, recognized as aneuploidy by flow cytometry, tend to suggest a multiclonal abnormality which begins at different sites in the colon. Gene deletions and mutations, such as deletion of one p53 allele, can be detected. Future research will be devoted to assessing the possible role of these genetic abnormalities as markers of precancerous change. A reliable controlled study of the effect of surveillance using these or any other markers is unlikely to be feasible.

Cancer surveillance in ulcerative colitis as practiced in many centers is of unproven benefit. The outcome of surveillance programs during the last two decades can be criticized for two opposing reasons. On the one hand, it can be said of some programs that the incidence of dysplasia or carcinoma has been too low to justify the trouble and expense involved. Conversely, in other series the incidence of carcinoma has been disconcertingly high.

Surgical treatment of ulcerative colitis within the first 10 years of disease removes the cancer risk. A recent population study from Denmark has shown that the incidence of colorectal carcinoma among patients with colitis followed for up to 25 years and treated using a vigorous medical and surgical protocol was the same as in the general population. The colectomy rate was 35 percent within the first 5 years of disease among patients with extensive colitis.[1] In past years, patients often wished to avoid colectomy with a permanent abdominal stoma. Modern surgical treatment increasingly avoids the need for a stoma and is therefore likely to be more acceptable to patients.

Doubts about the efficacy of cancer surveillance in colitis, arising from the results of exploratory programs during the last two decades, remove an ethical obligation to offer patients regular investigation designed to reduce the cancer risk. Surveillance as described in this chapter can be offered to patients who desire it, recognizing that it may reduce but does not eliminate the cancer risk. The cancer risk in Crohn's disease appears to be less than in ulcerative colitis, and the consensus view at present is that surveillance is not indicated. This review will therefore concentrate on cancer surveillance in ulcerative colitis.

It is now recognized that widespread genetic instability in the colitic mucosa usually precedes the development of carcinoma. Current research is devoted to recognition and analysis of these changes at a chromosomal and molecular level, with the aim of detecting them clinically before cancer occurs.

DEFINITION OF CANCER SURVEILLANCE

The word *surveillance* means "to watch over." It is best reserved for the regular investigation of patients initially shown to be free of carcinoma or known markers of incipient or actual neoplastic change (at present, dysplasia) in the colon, with the aim of detecting symptomless precancer or cancer at a stage when surgical prevention or cure is possible.

Surveillance is thus to be distinguished from cancer *screening,* or *detection,* when patients are investigated on a single occasion for the possible finding of symptomless neoplastic change. This is the situation when a patient with a long history of colitis is investigated after a long interval to assess the present state of disease.

Cancer surveillance should not be equated with regular *colonoscopic examination.* Surveillance by regular (flexible) sigmoidoscopy would still be surveillance, though not likely to give as good results as complete examination of the colon.

Surveillance, with its program of regular investigation, is also to be distinguished from clinical *supervision,* when patients are seen regularly but investigations are ordered irregularly as indicated by a change of symptoms or at the suggestion of the patient and/or clinician.

DEFINITION OF EXTENT OF COLITIS

The proportion of the total colonic area affected by colitis lacks proper definition. Sources of confusion are different modes of diagnosis and anatomic descriptions related to differing landmarks.

Before the introduction of colonoscopy in the early 1970s, extent of colitis was assessed by barium enema. The original single-contrast technique is less sensitive than the air-contrast method introduced widely in the 1960s. Disease affecting the ascending or transverse colon recognized by single-contrast x-ray is likely to include a higher proportion of cases with severe structural damage to the colon than when inflammation is recognized by the double-contrast barium enema. When the most sensitive x-ray is normal, direct inspection of the mucosa by endoscopy may show evidence of past or present inflammation. Biopsies may show evidence of inflammation when both the endoscopic and radiologic appearances are normal. There is thus a gradient of severity from microscopic mucosal changes with no visible abnormality on endoscopy to distortion of the outline of the colon on single-contrast barium enema.

The technique of examination of the colon has changed and is changing with time. Single-contrast x-ray studies were superseded by double-contrast barium enema, which is now being replaced by colonoscopy and biopsy.

Thus, it is important to define the technique by which the extent of inflammation is measured. Even a patient with endoscopic changes confined to the rectum may show minimal inflammation of the mucosa throughout the colon on biopsy.

Recommendation: Extent of disease should at present be defined by abnormalities visible on endoscopic examination.

"Total" colitis is generally accepted to mean involvement of the whole colon to the cecum. The terms *extensive, substantial,* and *left-sided* colitis are used differently by different authors. Many authors describe inflammation proximal to the splenic flexure as *extensive*.[2–5] Others limit the term *extensive colitis* to disease up to and including the hepatic flexure[6,7] or involvement of the whole colon.[8,9] In some studies the term *extensive colitis* is used without definition.[10]

Recommendation: The term extensive colitis *should refer to a condition involving endoscopic or radiographic evidence of inflammation of the colon proximal to the splenic flexure; this is a widely used definition and uses a clearly identifiable reference point.*

Proctitis should be defined as inflammation limited on endoscopy to 15 cm from the anal verge on withdrawal of the instrument. All intermediate extents of inflammation between proctitis and the splenic flexure should be described as left-sided colitis.

DEFINITION OF DURATION OF DISEASE

Many authors date the onset of disease to the first symptom or symptoms likely to be due to colitis, often recurrent rectal bleeding. In some studies, the date of clinical diagnosis is used. This may differ from the first symptoms by an interval of only months, but it may also do so by years.

Recommendation: Duration of colitis should date from the first symptoms of the disease.

ARE THE CONDITIONS FOR A POTENTIALLY SUCCESSFUL SURVEILLANCE PROGRAM FULFILLED IN COLITIS?

Is the Cancer Risk Great Enough?

The best estimates of cancer risk in colitis are derived from retrospective population studies of defined geographical areas or, better still, from the prospective study of a cohort of patients. A representative population study was based on two areas in England and one in Sweden and involved 823 patients followed for 17 to 38 years with 97 percent completeness of follow-up. In this population, 35 patients (4.2 percent) developed carcinoma, eight times the expected frequency.[10] When the patients were divided into those with extensive colitis (undefined) and those with left-sided disease or proctitis, the excess risk among the former was almost 20-fold and among the latter about 4-fold more than expected.

Conclusion: A 20-fold relative risk is sufficient to justify prophylactic measures.

Is the Excess Cancer Risk Spread over a Reasonable Time Span?

Life tables calculate the likelihood of developing carcinoma among patients who survive with an intact colon. Calculations refer only to this relatively small group of patients and not to the original cohort among whom the incidence of carcinoma is reduced by colectomy and death from causes other than carcinoma, including colitis. In the study described, the cumulative likelihood of carcinoma among patients with extensive colitis was 0.7 percent [confidence interval (CI) 0 to 1.1] at 10 years, 3.4 percent (CI 1 to 5.8) at 15 years, 7.2 percent (CI 3.6 to 10.8) at 20 years, and 11.6 percent (CI 6.4 to 16.8) at 25 years after onset. This figure at 25 years is similar to that of 13 percent derived in another population study from Sweden for patients with a diagnosis of ulcerative colitis before age 40.[11] These estimates agree with a study in an American private practice, where the cumulative risk was 11.7 percent at 26 years.[12]

It is difficult to assess the cancer risk more than 25 years from onset because the population at risk is small and confidence limits are therefore wide.

Conclusion: About 1 in 8 patients (12 percent) with extensive colitis develops carcinoma during the 15-year period between 10 and 25 years from onset. This is about 1 in 125 per year—a figure just great enough to make surveillance meaningful.

Is a Carcinoma Which Presents Clinically outside a Surveillance Program Surgically Curable?

If all or most carcinomas complicating colitis were surgically curable, there would be no need to develop an expensive program designed to diagnose a precancerous phase or early carcinoma. In fact, analysis of 5 surgical series shows that the 5-year survival after surgical treatment for colorectal cancer complicating colitis diagnosed outside a surveillance program varied between 31 and 42 percent.[13–17] The expected mortality is therefore at most about 1 in 12 (8 percent) among patients with extensive colitis during the period 10 to 25 years from onset of the disease, assuming that the surgical cure rate is 33 percent and that the cumulative cancer incidence is 12 percent at the end of this time.

Can Mortality from Cancer Be Reduced by Earlier Surgical Treatment?

Proctocolectomy removes the risk of colorectal carcinoma. It therefore has been argued that all patients with long-standing, extensive colitis should be advised to accept this operation during the first 10 years of disease. Patients who are well do not usually wish to accept this advice on grounds of the cancer risk alone. Universal surgical treatment cannot therefore be adopted to remove the cancer risk, though all patients with disabling colitis, especially young patients, should be encouraged to accept modern surgical treatment both for improved health and, as a secondary advantage, removal of the cancer risk. *One object of a regular program of clinical supervision or of surveillance is to encourage appropriate patients to accept surgery before there is any evidence of precancerous change or cancer.*

In some patients, recognition of dysplasia leads to operation, with removal of a previously unidentified carcinoma. It seems probable that operation when a carcinoma is symptomless, rather than when it is clinically apparent, improves survival. The removal of a colon with dysplastic change but no carcinoma has not been shown to reduce cancer mortality, though this is a reasonable expectation.

If carcinoma develops, three surgical series[13,15,17] have shown that the 5-year survival after colectomy for a Dukes A carcinoma complicating colitis is greater than 95 percent, as compared with 60 to 70 percent for a Dukes B and only 20 to 56 percent for Dukes C tumors. There is thus good evidence that surgical treatment of carcinoma at Dukes stages A or B is likely to prolong survival.

Are Diagnostic Methods of Sufficient Sensitivity and Specificity Available to Diagnose a Precancerous Phase or Curable Carcinoma?

After 20 years of experience, it is now apparent that the effectiveness of surveillance in colitis is limited by the diagnostic methods available.

Endoscopy

In the normal colon, a polyp or tumor is clearly distinguishable from the surrounding pale flat mucosa. In colitis, the mucosa tends to be pink or red, exudate or spontaneous bleeding may limit vision, and the background may not be flat but distorted by scarring or inflammatory polypoid change. It can thus be difficult for the endoscopist to recognize a slightly raised plaque; a low, broad-based polyp; or the indistinct elevation of villous change—which are the proliferative lesions of dysplasia or early carcinoma. Similarly, a small carcinomatous ulcer with raised edges or a malignant area in a smooth stricture can be missed.

Double-Contrast Barium Enema

Radiology remains a good method for diagnosing carcinoma, often at a clinically late stage,[7] but is of limited value in detecting dysplasia or small flat tumors. Slight abnormalities on barium enema can draw attention to lesions which might otherwise be missed on endoscopy. The need to obtain biopsies and the radiation exposure make barium enema unsuitable for frequent examinations.

Biopsy or Brushings

Endoscopic biopsies with the largest available colonoscopic forceps average 4 to 6 mm in the largest dimension; a technique has been described for taking a larger mucosal biopsy, which is about 50 percent longer, without complication.[18] Even multiple biopsies of this larger type sample only a small proportion of the total mucosal area. It has been estimated that at least 18 of these biopsies are needed to give a 95 percent chance of detecting dysplasia or cancer when both are present.[19] The likelihood of detecting dysplasia is increased if the biopsy is taken from an elevated lesion or stricture.

Brushing samples a wider area than biopsy. The exfoliated cells are mainly epithelial and their cytologic appearance may allow a presumptive diagnosis of neoplastic change, either dysplasia or carcinoma.[20] The technique deserves further study.

Dysplasia

Definition of the presence or absence of dysplasia or its severity have been improved by an international classification of nomenclature.[21] However, interpretation is qualitative and thus subject to interobserver variation.[21-25] Dysplasia consists of cytologic changes sometimes combined with a proliferative component which forms an elevated mucosal plaque, broad-based polyp, or villous change. A distinction can therefore be drawn between dysplastic cytologic changes in flat mucosa or on the surface of an elevated lesion. The latter are always clinically significant because they are often associated with the presence of a carcinoma at the same site or elsewhere in the colon; they are thus markers of cancer rather than precancer.[26,27]

A careful study in which colonoscopy was stimulated by taking 32 specimens with endoscopic biopsy forceps from 50 colectomy specimens with colorectal carcinoma complicating ulcerative colitis and 50 matched specimens without carcinoma has shown that dysplasia was not found in about one-quarter of the colons when carcinoma was present.[28] In about one-third of the colons high-grade dysplasia (HGD) and in just under an additional half indefinite or low-grade dysplasia (LGD) was found at a distance from the tumor. Thus dysplasia is an imperfect marker, though the presence of any dysplasia, especially if it is the high-grade type, means that a coexistent carcinoma may be present. The significance of indefinite or LGD as a marker of carcinoma may be greater than originally supposed.

Indefinite or LGD was also present in about a quarter of the 50 specimens without carcinoma, and one then needs to know if it represents a precancerous change. Evidence is conflicting. In some clinical series, LGD has been found frequently and transitorily without obvious prognostic significance;[3] in other series, a proportion of patients with LGD later developed HGD dysplasia or carcinoma.[7,29]

The fact that carcinoma can occur in the absence of dysplasia and the lack of a specific precancerous phase in the development of dysplasia both imply that dysplasia is an imperfect marker for use in a surveillance program. However, it is not useless, and, if its strengths and deficiencies are appreciated, it remains a clinically useful finding.

Abnormal Chromatin Content of Nuclei as a Measure of Aneuploidy

There is good evidence that widespread genetic instability precedes the development of carcinoma complicating ulcerative colitis. This instability may be manifested by altered chromatin structure, by altered gene expression, or by gene deletion or mutation.

An abnormal chromatin content in the epithelial cell nuclei, or aneuploidy, can be detected by flow cytometry[19,24,30-32] or by the laborious technique of microspectrophotometry,[31] both of which give equivalent results. The techniques compare the amount of chromatin in the epithelial cell nucleus with a standard diploid (or tetraploid) quantity judged by comparison with a standard population of normal cells. Genetic alterations which involve slight changes in chromatin content are not detected. In ulcerative colitis, different areas of the colon may manifest varying numerical values for chromatin content, suggesting that several abnormal clones of cells have developed and expanded over the surface.[32] Aneuploidy can be found in the absence of dysplasia, but it is found with increasing frequency in areas of dysplasia of progressively higher grade and is most commonly present in carcinoma.[19,24,32] However, carcinoma or dysplasia itself can be diploid and can occur without aneuploidy elsewhere in the colon, so, like dysplasia, it is an imperfect marker. In elegant prospective studies, it has been shown not only that the area of aneuploidy expands with time[30] but also that aneuploidy may precede the development of dysplasia.[19,30]

For the clinician, the most interesting and potentially important findings are that aneuploidy may occur in the absence of dysplasia or in areas of indefinite dysplasia. It is too early to know whether aneuploidy in these situations is a reliable marker of precancer. The data do suggest that it is sufficiently reliable to warrant frequent investigation of such patients, at intervals of 6 months or a year, as dysplasia may develop. The special equipment needed does not permit the routine assessment of aneuploidy at present. When it can be detected, dysplasia and aneuploidy combined are likely to give more information than either alone.

Abnormal Gene Expression as Possible Markers of Neoplastic Potential

Much work has been done assessing changes in the structure of mucus, carcinoembryonic antigen,[33] oncoprotein secretion, and enzyme activity without finding a reliable marker of neoplastic potential. In general, the colonic mucosa seems to respond similarly to the proliferative responses of inflammation and neoplasia.

Gene Deletions and Mutations

Loss of heterozygosity for the p53 gene occurs in a proportion of patients with dysplasia and carcinoma.[32] Mutations of the p53 gene occur in dysplasia, but the frequency has not yet been reported. Mutations of the c-Ki-*Ras* protooncogene occur in about 10 to 15 percent of carcinomas complicating colitis, a lower frequency than in sporadic carcinoma. It is therefore not likely that this mutation will be a frequent marker of precancerous genetic change.

It is likely that in the future, gene alterations, found by examining several genes in the same tissue specimen, will be important markers, but at present their use is neither practicable nor established.

Do Patients Comply with a Surveillance Program?

A surveillance program is likely to succeed only if patients accept the protocol. Acceptance depends on understanding the reason for regular observation and willingness, because of this reason, to give the necessary time to investigation which may be inconvenient and incur some discomfort. Continuity of care by one or a few clinicians maintains confidence and collaboration. Inevitably, some patients leave the follow-up because they move from the area, become frail with advancing age, or develop a coincidental illness. In our series, 6 percent of patients have failed to attend because of unwillingness or indifference, though not all other patients follow the protocol exactly for many personal reasons. In other series, about one-quarter of patients have left the program.[3,6] A system is needed to remind patients of missed appointments.

Conclusion

Many of the accepted criteria for a possible successful cancer surveillance program are fulfilled in ulcerative colitis, but currently available markers for precancer and cancer have a lower specificity and sensitivity than is desirable. It is likely that the advantages and limitations of dysplasia have been almost fully explored. Attention is now being given to other markers, but none is yet validated or available for routine clinical use.

EXPERIENCE GAINED FROM SURVEILLANCE PROGRAMS

Five centers in Europe[3,5–7,9] and three in America[2,4,8] have followed cohorts of patients with ulcerative colitis prospectively in planned programs of cancer surveillance (see Table 34-1). During this exploratory period, the selection of patients, the protocols used, and the methods of reporting results have varied, so that it is difficult to generalize from the results. For example, some centers include only patients with total colitis;[8,9] others include those with disease proximal to the hepatic flexure,[6,7] the splenic flexure,[3,5] or the sigmoid colon.[2] In one series, a quarter of the patients gave a history of colitis of less than 8 years at entry.[8] In other series, the minimum duration at entry was 7, 8, and 10 years. Many studies have shown that the cancer risk in ulcerative colitis depends on the extent[10,11,35] and duration of disease, so these variations in practice are likely to affect the results. Series also differ in the geographic origin of the patients, either from a specified local population[6,9] or from an unknown population from a referral center.

Our own experience of surveillance began in 1966 with sigmoidoscopy;[7] colonoscopy was introduced later. The results reported here exclude the first 5 years with sigmoidoscopy only and cover the 20-year period from the first colonoscopies in 1971 until 1991. They include 332 patients, all of whom had disease extending at least up to the hepatic flexure of the colon as judged by double-contrast barium enema or visible changes on colonoscopy and all of whom had a minimum history of 10 years since first symptoms of disease. These patients were followed at regular out-patient visits, when examination by rigid sigmoidoscopy and biopsy was performed. They underwent colonoscopy every 2 years, or more frequently if dysplasia was found. The lessons to be learned from this relatively large series and other published studies allow some conclusions to be drawn about future policy.

Importance of the First Colonoscopy

The ideal surveillance program begins after an initial colonoscopy which shows no evidence of dysplasia or carcinoma. This criterion is particularly important at referral centers, where patients with chronic active disease tend to be seen for the first time after a rela-

Table 34-1
Summary of Results of Eight Endoscopic Surveillance Programs

	Nugent et al.[2]	*Rutegard et al.*[9]	*Lynch et al.*[3]	*Rosenstock et al.*[8]	*Lofberg et al.*[6]	*Lashner et al.*[4]	*Ledenius et al.*[5]	*Lennard-Jones et al.*[a]
Location	Lahey Clinic	Sweden	Leeds	Cleveland	Stockholm	Chicago	Helsinki	London
Patients	213	57	160	248	72	99	66	332
Series duration	13 years	8 years	12 years	11 years	15 years	8 years	13 years	21 years
Complete FU	100%	100%	89%	100%	94%	91%	95%	98.2%
Extent	151 > SF	pancolitis	>SF	pancolitis	>HF	>SF	45%>SF	>HF
Disease duration	> 8 years	67% > 10 years	> 8 years	76% > 8 years	> 8 years	> 8 years	> 7 years	> 10 years
Frequency C	0.5–3 yearly	1–2 yearly	1 yearly	19 monthly	1–2 yearly	1 yearly	1–2 yearly	2 yearly
Colonoscopies	NS	256	739	370	291	416	182	1316
Biopsies per C	19	12	7.8	12	>20	NS	20	9
Cancers	10	1	1	7	2	8	nil	20

[a]Current data.

Abbreviations: FU, follow-up; C, colonoscopies; SF, splenic flexure; NS, not specified; HF, hepatic flexure.

tively long history of disease. In the St. Mark's series, 288 of 332 patients had no evidence of dysplasia at the first colonoscopy; of those who continued in the program, 8 later developed a carcinoma, compared with 7 of 38 patients whose first colonoscopy revealed indefinite or definite dysplasia ($p < .01$).

At the Cleveland Clinic,[8] 13 of 248 patients were found to have HGD at the first colonoscopy; 6 of these had or later developed carcinoma. Likewise, 8 of 213 patients referred to the Lahey Clinic[2] had HGD at the first colonoscopy. Three of them had carcinomas, of which two died. Among 30 patients with indefinite or LGD, 5 subsequently developed carcinoma. In contrast, among the 175 patients without dysplasia, 6 subsequently developed dysplastic changes on biopsy and only 2 developed carcinoma after defaulting from the program for about 3 years after the first colonoscopy. In the Chicago series,[4] 6 patients appear to have had HGD at the first colonoscopy. All were operated upon and 5 cancers were diagnosed, 3 of which proved fatal.

Carcinoma among Patients during Surveillance

Among the St. Mark's series of 332 patients, 20 (6 percent) developed carcinoma: 2 at the outset, 15 while being followed, and 3 after leaving follow-up. At the initial colonoscopy, 2 patients were found to have HGD; at operation, a symptomless Dukes A carcinoma was found in both. Of the 282 patients who continued in the follow-up, 9 symptomless carcinomas (6A, 1B, 2C) and 6 symptomatic carcinomas were treated surgically. Of the symptomless carcinomas, 4 were diagnosed at endoscopy and 5 at surgery, which was advised because HGD (3), LGD and a mass (1), or repeated LGD (1) was found on biopsy. Of the 6 symptomatic tumors, 2 were diagnosed at endoscopy, 2 by barium enema, and 2 at operation. Among 48 patients who left the follow-up, carcinoma presented clinically in 3 (6 percent) 4, 7, and 9 years later (Dukes B, B and disseminated).

In other series, there is a striking contrast between three American studies and four others from northern Europe. At the Cleveland Clinic,[8] 7 of 248 patients developed carcinoma; 1 was found to have carcinoma after the first colonoscopy and 6 were diagnosed later (1A, 2B, 2C). At the Lahey Clinic,[2] 2 fatal cancers developed later among 175 patients with no dysplasia at the first colonoscopy and 8 (1A, 3B, 4C) among 38 patients whose initial biopsies showed indefinite or definite dysplasia. In Chicago,[4] among 99 patients, 5 carcinomas were apparently diagnosed among 6 patients found to have HGD at the first colonoscopy and 3 (1C, 2 disseminated) were diagnosed later in patients found initially to have LGD. The four European series reported 1 carcinoma (B) in 57 patients,[9] 2 (both A) in 72,[6] none in 66,[5] and one (A) in 160 patients.[3]

The difference between the American experience, that at St. Mark's Hospital in England, and the other four European series may be partly explained by differences in definitions of duration and extent of disease, as already discussed, and partly by different referral patterns. It is noteworthy that all the four centers with a relatively high cancer incidence are referral centers. The duration of observation is unlikely to explain the differences, because programs in the four centers with a low incidence of cancer had been undertaken over 8, 12, 15, and 13 years respectively, though the St. Mark's series is the largest and longest experience. It is possible that there is a geographical factor, as colorectal carcinoma in the general population is more common in America than in Europe.

Cancer Incidence and Mortality

Patients in the St. Mark's series were followed for a total 2496 patient-years, and the mean duration of colitis at an end point for the series was 23 ± 9 years. If, from population surveys,[10,11] cumulative incidence of cancer between 10 and 25 years is estimated as 12 percent, the yearly incidence is 0.8 percent. The expected number of cancers in this series would then be 21; the observed number was 20. It is characteristic of all surveillance programs that more tumors are found during early than during later examinations. If dysplasia is a precancerous lesion, it would be expected that some carcinomas would develop after the last date of follow-up. The benefit of earlier operation would not be apparent in the present results.

Of these 20 patients, 5 have died of carcinoma. From surgical results quoted earlier and a population survey,[11] a 5-year mortality of around 50 percent might be expected.

These results suggest that the cancer incidence was not reduced by surveillance, even though 12 patients (see below) were operated upon for dysplasia confirmed in the operation specimen. It does seem possible that the cancer mortality rate was reduced. In our surveillance program with a mean follow-up of 7.9 years, the mortality rate was 1.5 percent among patients judged to be at greatest risk.

High-Grade Dysplasia

In our series, 18 patients had HGD on biopsy, and all of them underwent surgery. In 8 patients carcinomas were present; they were recognized by endoscopy in 3 and detected in the colectomy specimen in 5. The presence of dysplasia (HGD7, LGD1) was confirmed in the colectomy specimen in 8 of the remaining 10 patients. In the three American series, a carcinoma was present in association with HGD in 6 of 15 patients,[8] 6 of 18 patients,[2] and 8 of 12 patients.[4] In the remaining series, the association was 1 in 3,[9] 1 in 4,[34] none in 1 (inconstant finding),[5] and 1 of 1.[3] In total, among 71 patients with HGD, a carcinoma was present in 30 (42 percent), confirming the advice that the finding of HGD is an indication for colectomy.

Indefinite and Low-Grade Dysplasia

Action to be taken on finding indefinite (ID) or LGD remains controversial. The association between LGD and carcinoma in operation specimens has led the Mayo Clinic group to recommend a biopsy showing LGD as an indication for colectomy.[28] Conversely, 40 of 160 patients were found to have LGD in at least one biopsy in the Leeds series.[3] These patients were followed for a total of 223 patient-years with 201 colonoscopies over a mean follow-up of 4.7 to 6.9 years. Half of these patients had no further evidence of dysplasia, 19 showed LGD in at least one subsequent biopsy, and 1 developed HGD associated with two Dukes A carcinomas. Our recent experience has been that about one-half of such patients develop HGD or carcinoma during the next 5 years, rather more than the experience in New York.[29]

Some of the variability in clinical experience may reflect different pathologic interpretation of biopsies,[25] and a blinded review of biopsies in our series suggests that this is the case. It seems likely that widespread LGD in one examination or a consistent finding of LGD on subsequent examinations is more significant than a single biopsy showing LGD without similar changes elsewhere in the colon and no LGD in subsequent biopsies. It is clear that a finding of LGD should be taken seriously and another colonoscopy arranged within 6 months. In the authors' opinion, widespread LGD, especially if confirmed on another examination or repeated single biopsies showing LGD, is an indication for colectomy. A more aggressive policy of investigation and operation on finding LGD might have altered the results in our series, because 13 of 17 patients showed evidence of dysplasia before a carcinoma was found. Of the 4 patients without evidence of dysplasia, 3 presented clinically at a late stage (Dukes 1B, 2C, disseminated). Most clinicians would find it difficult to recommend colectomy for a single biopsy showing LGD unless it was an added indication to a recommendation based on disability.

Action to Be Taken on Finding an Adenoma

An adenoma in a normal colon is by definition dysplastic and can develop malignant change. One or more colonic adenomas are common in the normal population in older age groups.

When an adenoma is encountered in ulcerative colitis, the problem is to know whether it is a sporadic adenoma, such as those found in the normal colon, or whether it is a manifestation of widespread dysplasia or genetic instability.

If the adenoma is situated in normal mucosa proximal to the area of inflammation, particularly if it is pedunculated and the patient is middle-aged or older, it can be treated endoscopically as if it were an adenoma in the normal colon and the prognosis is good.[2]

In contrast, if the adenoma is situated in an area of past or present inflammation, if it is broad-based or villous, and particularly if there is more than one adenoma or it is part of an irregular, widespread lesion, or there is dysplasia elsewhere in the colon, it should be regarded as an elevated dysplastic lesion and operation should be advised.

Great caution is advisable when a single broad-based adenoma is encountered in an area of ulcerative colitis. It should be regarded as a manifestation of dysplasia until proved otherwise. Frequent and repeated endoscopic examination is indicated.

Interval between Negative Colonoscopy and Subsequent Development of Carcinoma

In the St. Mark's series, 7 interval carcinomas were diagnosed 10, 15, 15, 22, 23, 27, and 28 months after a colonoscopy without dysplasia. It is apparent that a 2-year interval between colonoscopies is too long and yearly colonoscopy should be recommended. It has been suggested that the interval between colonoscopies should vary with the length of history—for example, every 2 years in the period 14 to 18 years after onset and then yearly during the period 19 to 33 years.[36] Three of the patients described above had a disease duration of 13, 13, and 15 years respectively, which does not support this recommendation. The premise for more frequent colonoscopies with increasing disease duration was based on the increasing slope of a survival curve but did not take into account the fact that the shape of the curve is due to the fact that, as years pass, each carcinoma that occurs accounts for a larger and larger proportion of the decreasing number of patients remaining in follow-up.

The Complementary Role of Colonoscopy and Sigmoidoscopy

The St. Mark's protocol included regular outpatient visits, at each of which sigmoidoscopy and biopsy were performed, mostly with a rigid but latterly with a flexible instrument. Among 4 symptomless cancers detected endoscopically, 1 was diagnosed by colonoscopy, 1 by sigmoidoscopy, and 2 by colonoscopy after a lesion had been seen at sigmoidoscopy. Detection of dysplasia which led to diagnosis of a symptomless carcinoma at operation occurred in 7 patients, once by colonoscopy, once by sigmoidoscopy, and on five occasions by both. Diagnosis of carcinoma and dysplasia in ulcerative colitis on rectal biopsy taken at sigmoidoscopy has also been reported in a retrospective American series.[37]

Examinations of the rectosigmoid without bowel preparation or the rectum and left colon after minimal preparation (such as a laxative taken on the previous evening or a phosphate enema) during outpatient consultations thus yield useful diagnostic information. They can be performed in the middle of the period between colonoscopies.

Compliance

Of the 48 patients (12 percent) who left the St. Mark's program, 24 moved elsewhere, 6 elected to continue under clinical supervision without colonoscopy, and 18 discontinued attendance (among these, 3 developed carcinomas). It is our practice to send patients another appointment if they do not keep an appointment and then for the doctor in charge to write a personal letter if this appointment is missed.

Failure of compliance in another British series was 26 percent;[3] in three American series, it was not recorded; and in a Scandinavian series, it was 25 percent.[6]

Possible Benefit of the St. Mark's Program and Cost per Patient

During the 21 years of the program, 9 patients were operated upon for a symptomless Dukes A (8) or B (1) carcinoma; all survive. Surgery was also performed in 12 patients because of endoscopic finding of HGD, LGD with a mass, or persistent LGD; in all these patients, dysplasia was found in the operation specimen. If it is assumed that the 9 carcinomas were at a symptomless curable stage and that 12 precancerous colons were removed, benefit accrued to 21 patients.

Over the same period, 1316 colonoscopies were performed as part of the surveillance program, and the protocol required an equivalent number of outpatient consultations with sigmoidoscopy and biopsy. In practice, many patients attended the outpatient clinic more frequently for treatment of their colitis.

The cost of colonoscopy and the laboratory costs of biopsy processing and interpretation was estimated at £150 in 1991.[38] If the additional cost of an outpatient visit with sigmoidoscopy and biopsy is estimated at £50, then the total cost of the program was approximately £267,000 at 1991 prices. The cost for each patient benefited was therefore about £12,700. In 1988, an estimate for each cancer detected in ulcerative colitis—based on colonoscopy (at £125 per patient) for every patient at 8 years of disease and thereafter twice yearly for those with extensive disease—was £6015; this estimate takes no account of the presumed benefit of also diagnosing precancerous lesions.[39]

A theoretical calculation in America based on yearly colonoscopy at a cost of $1000 for each examination estimated the cost of diagnosing each severe dysplastic lesion or curable cancer at $200,000.[40]

Carcinoma among Patients Not Included in the Surveillance Program

Among the 332 patients enrolled in the St. Mark's program, 20 carcinomas occurred over 21 years. During the same period, 16 patients attending the outpatient clinic who had not been included in the program because they were thought to have distal or left-sided colitis developed carcinoma. In fact, 12 of these patients had total colitis at the time of surgery; only 2 had left-sided colitis and 2 were unknown. Furthermore, 11 carcinomas occurred among patients known to have extensive colitis who, for various reasons, did not fulfill the entry conditions for the program (these reasons included their own wish, difficulty in attendance at the clinic due to distance, and supervision elsewhere).

A similar analysis in Leeds[3] has shown that eligible patients were not included in a surveillance program in many instances because their colitis was diagnosed before the program began and they were not seen again until they presented with carcinoma.

Thus, despite considerable effort, a surveillance program did not make a major impact on the incidence of carcinoma among patients attending these two hospitals. It has always been evident that surveillance would be possible for only a small proportion of the total population of patients with colitis. It is apparent that more active measures than hitherto will be necessary to select and recruit appropriate patients if surveillance is to be adopted as a cost-effective program.

CROHN'S DISEASE

Epidemiologic studies show that there is a greater than expected incidence of colorectal carcinoma in Crohn's ileocolitis and colitis. In a large population study, there was about a fourfold excess among such patients.[41] The relative risk among patients diagnosed before age 30 was similar to corresponding figures for ulcerative colitis.[11,41] Dysplasia can be found on biopsy at a distance from the tumor, as in ulcerative colitis. Case reports describe cancer in long-standing small bowel disease, especially bypassed loops, and in association with chronic anal and perianal lesions.[42]

The evidence suggests that patients with long-standing colonic disease, especially those with onset during the first three decades of life, should be offered clinical supervision. Clinicians should be alert for the possible complication of cancer, but regular surveillance investigations are not indicated. New symptoms or signs, particularly obstruction, unusual induration of a chronic anal lesion or of the pelvic-rectal tissues, a mucosal biopsy showing dysplasia, or a newly developed short colorectal stricture[43] should be regarded with suspicion and investigated.

CONCLUSIONS

Cancer Surveillance in Ulcerative Colitis Is Not Mandatory

The cost-effectiveness of cancer surveillance for ulcerative colitis has been questioned by reviewers.[40,44,45] Practical experience, collected with considerable effort over the last two decades, supports their conclusion, but for different reasons in different series. One group[3] has questioned the value of performing 728 colonoscopies in 159 patients during 629 patient-years of follow-up when the yield was one carcinoma (Dukes A). Conversely, the effectiveness of our own program and that of the three American series can be questioned when a relatively large number of carcinomas still occurred, with some cancer deaths. There are thus two conflicting arguments against undertaking a surveillance program: either it is not cost-effective because too few carcinomas are found or it is ineffective because fatal carcinoma is not prevented.

As a consequence of the present uncertainty, it is not mandatory to undertake a surveillance program for patients with ulcerative colitis.

Cancer Surveillance Seeks Precancer, Not Cancer

There is confusion in some people's minds about the aim of a surveillance program. Ideally, a marker of neoplastic potential would be available that had such sensitivity and specificity that colectomy could confidently be advised, before malignant invasion occurred, because the patient was at high risk of incipient carcinoma. The prime aim of a surveillance program is to detect precancer and, failing that, curable carcinoma. When carcinoma develops, there is always the risk that the tumor has spread beyond the colon by the time operation is performed.

The uses and limitations of dysplasia as a marker are now apparent. No marker has yet been validated that replaces or complements dysplasia. With further research, aneuploidy or abnormalities of gene structure or expression may prove to be reliable indicators of malignant potential that allow clinical action to be taken before carcinoma develops. At present, LGD is the nearest approximation to such a marker. It will always be difficult to assess the usefulness of potential markers, as validation entails observing patients until carcinoma develops. This ethical problem has prevented the full validation of dysplasia. The suggested action to be taken when dysplasia is found is illustrated as a flowchart (Fig. 34-1).

Difficulties of Controlled Comparisons of Cancer Mortality

A surveillance program can be judged effective only if it is shown to reduce cancer mortality in comparison with a control group. The logistics of such a comparison are formidable. To show a reduction in colorectal cancer mortality from 8 to 4 percent with 95 percent confidence in 9 out of 10 trials would require about 1000 patients in each group. The trial would have to be carried out over many years to accumulate sufficient numbers and to avoid lead-time and duration bias. The creation of a control group would be ethically difficult, because many patients would decline to be randomized when all the facts were known. Strict criteria for operation would have to be defined, but patients often do not accept such advice. A case-control study between centers, some undertaking surveillance and others not, would be possible, but it would be difficult to define the degree of supervision and investigation at the control centers. The situation is made more difficult because an increased colectomy rate for any reason is bound to reduce the incidence of carcinoma. For these reasons, a formal controlled trial or case-control study is unlikely to be done or, if it is, the results will not be available for many years.

Assessment and Advice for All Patients with Colitis after 8 to 10 Years of Disease

The way forward at present is to recognize that the carcinoma risk in ulcerative colitis is greatest among patients with colitis involving most or all of the colon

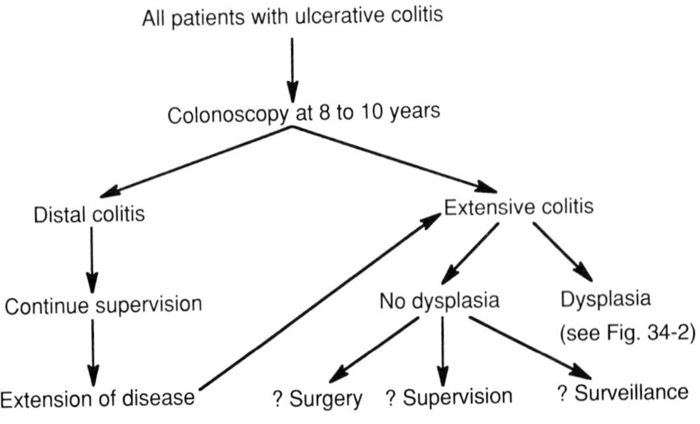

FIG. 34-1. Algorithm for managing cancer risk in patients with ulcerative colitis.

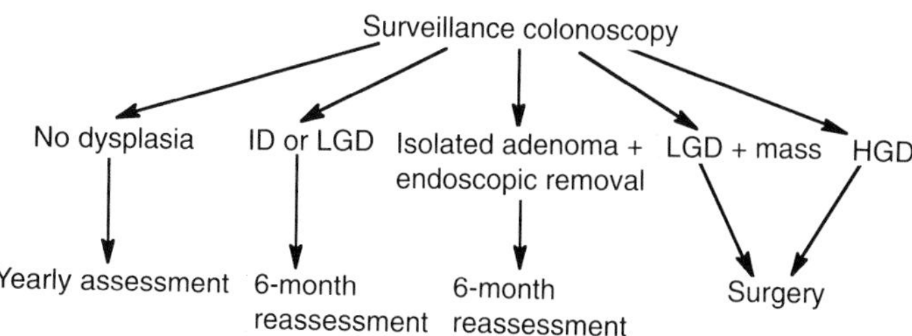

FIG. 34-2. Suggested endoscopic surveillance protocol in patients with ulcerative colitis.

at any time with a disease duration of more than 10 years. Colonoscopy should be offered to every patient with colitis 8 to 10 years after onset, or later if follow-up has been lost, with the aim of defining the visual extent and activity of disease (Fig. 34-2). At the same time, a detailed assessment of symptomatic disability and physical health should be made. If there is evidence of inflammation proximal to the splenic flexure with considerable disability or chronic ill health due to the disease, surgical treatment should be recommended, the cancer risk being one factor in the decision.

If healed or mild inflammation proximal to the splenic flexure is found and the patient is well, the general facts of the carcinoma risk should be discussed without inducing fear. It should be explained that no screening program eliminates the risk of cancer. Regular clinical supervision is advisable because there is still danger from acute attacks of colitis as well as from carcinoma. Supervision may do more to reduce the death rate from acute colitis than from cancer.[46] The patient should be aware of the cancer risk and report any new symptoms. If desired by the patient and if possible with the available medical resources, yearly colonoscopy with multiple (about 20 to 30) biopsies looking for dysplasia or cancer is at present the best available option for cancer surveillance, though its efficacy is unproven. Some patients do not wish to undergo regular colonoscopy, with its associated inconvenience and discomfort. The possible psychological effects of long-continued cancer surveillance must also be recognized.[47] As an alternative to colonoscopy, regular consultation and flexible sigmoidoscopy with biopsies can be considered.

Patients with left-sided colitis or proctitis have a lower risk of acute colitis and cancer than those with extensive colitis. The need for regular follow-up depends on the activity of inflammation. They should be advised to seek medical advice for any recurrence of inflammation, when the possibility of extension of the inflammation should be considered, or for any new symptom when the disease is inactive.

FUTURE RESEARCH

At certain centers equipped for endoscopic and laboratory procedures, a research program should be undertaken to assess new markers of genetic instability and to test the possible benefit of intensive investigation. Patients with the highest risk of carcinoma should be selected to improve the diagnostic yield. Each patient should have suffered from colitis for at least 10 years and colonoscopy should demonstrate visual inflammation proximal to the splenic flexure with no evidence of dysplasia on biopsy. The program should include annual (and occasionally more frequent) colonoscopy alternating every 6 months with clinical consultation to assess disability and treatment, digital examination of the rectum, and flexible sigmoidoscopy. At colonoscopy, observation of the ileocecal valve should be recorded, when possible, as evidence that the whole colon has been examined; an ileal biopsy can confirm the fact. Biopsies should be taken from any suspicious lesion and about 20 from around the circumference of the colon and rectum as the instrument is withdrawn. Multiple biopsies should be taken at flexible sigmoidoscopy. Each biopsy should be examined for dysplasia and genetic markers. Cytologic preparations obtained by brushing should also be examined. Stools should be collected for study of bile acids.[48] Other possible factors associated with an increased risk of colorectal cancer such as family history, folate deficiency, and drug metabolism should be investigated. Indication for operation in such patients would be those currently advised—namely, a severe attack or chronic disability, widespread or repeated finding of LGD, dysplasia associated with villous change or a broad-based elevated lesion, HGD, or carcinoma.

The distribution, progression, or regression of epithelial markers—as well as chemical measurements—would give valuable information about the biology of neoplastic change in colitis and would test the effectiveness of an idealized surveillance program.

REFERENCES

1. Langholz E, Munkholm P, Davidsen M, et al: Colorectal cancer risk and mortality in patients with ulcerative colitis. *Gastroenterology* 103:1444–1451, 1992.
2. Nugent FW, Haggitt RC, Gilpin PA: Cancer surveillance in ulcerative colitis. *Gastroenterology* 100:1241–1248, 1991.
3. Lynch DAF, Lobo AJ, Sobala GM, et al: Failure of colonoscopic surveillance in ulcerative colitis. *Gut* 34:1075–1080, 1992.

4. Lashner BA, Silverstein MD, Hanauer SB: Hazard rates for dysplasia and cancer in ulcerative colitis. *Dig Dis Sci* 34:1536–1541, 1989.
5. Leidenius M, Kellokumpu I, Husa A, et al: Dysplasia and carcinoma in longstanding ulcerative colitis: An endoscopic and histological surveillance programme. *Gut* 32:1521–1525, 1991.
6. Löfberg R, Broström O, Karlén P, et al: Colonoscopic surveillance in long-standing total ulcerative colitis—A 15-year follow-up study. *Gastroenterology* 99:1021–1031, 1990.
7. Lennard-Jones JE, Melville DM, Morson BC, et al: Precancer and cancer in extensive ulcerative colitis: Findings among 401 patients over 22 years. *Gut* 31:800–806, 1990.
8. Rosenstock E, Farmer RG, Petras R, et al: Surveillance for colonic carcinoma in ulcerative colitis. *Gastroenterology* 89:1342–1346, 1985.
9. Rutegård J, Åhsgren L, Stenling R, et al: Ulcerative colitis: Cancer in an unselected population. *Scand J Gastroenterol* 23:139–145, 1988.
10. Gyde SN, Prior P, Allan RN, et al: Colorectal cancer in ulcerative colitis: A cohort study of primary referrals from three centres. *Gut* 29:206–217, 1988.
11. Ekbom A, Helmick C, Zack M, et al: Ulcerative colitis and colorectal cancer—A population based study. *N Engl J Med* 323:1228–1233, 1990.
12. Katzka I, Brody RS, Morris E, et al: Assessment of colorectal cancer risk in patients with ulcerative colitis: Experience from a private practice. *Gastroenterology* 85:22–29, 1983.
13. Öhman U: Colorectal carcinoma in patients with ulcerative colitis. *Am J Surg* 144:344–349, 1982.
14. Johnson WR, McDermott FT, Hughes ESR, et al: Carcinoma of the colon and rectum in inflammatory disease of the intestine. *Surg Gynecol Obstet* 156:193–197, 1983.
15. van Heerden JA, Beart RW Jr.: Carcinoma of the colon and rectum complicating chronic ulcerative colitis. *Dis Colon Rectum* 23:155–159, 1980.
16. Gyde SN, Prior P, Thompson H, et al: Survival of patients with colorectal carcinoma complicating ulcerative colitis. *Gut* 25:228–231, 1984.
17. Lavery IC, Chiulli RA, Jagelman DJ, et al: Survival with carcinoma arising in mucosal ulcerative colitis. *Ann Surg* 195:508–512, 1982.
18. Levine DS, Reid BJ: Endoscopic biopsy technique for acquiring larger mucosal samples. *Gastrointest Endosc* 37:332–337, 1991.
19. Rubin CE, Haggitt RC, Burmer GC, et al: DNA aneuploidy in colonic biopsies predicts future development of dysplasia in ulcerative colitis. *Gastroenterology* 103:1611–1620, 1992.
20. Melville DM, Richman PI, Shepherd NA, et al: Brush cytology of the colon and rectum in ulcerative colitis: An aid to cancer diagnosis. *J Clin Pathol* 41:1180–1186, 1988.
21. Riddell RH, Goldman RH, Ransohoff DF, et al: Dysplasia in inflammatory bowel disease: Standardized classification with provisional clinical applications. *Hum Pathol* 14:931–966, 1983.
22. Dixon MF, Brown LJR, Gilmour HM, et al: Observer variation in the assessment of dysplasia in ulcerative colitis. *Histopathology* 13:385–397, 1988.
23. Dundas SAC, Kay R, Beck S, et al: Can histopathologists reliably assess dysplasia in chronic inflammatory bowel disease. *J Clin Pathol* 40:1282–1286, 1987.
24. Melville DM, Jass JR, Shepherd NA, et al: Dysplasia and deoxyribonucleic acid aneuploidy in the assessment of precancerous changes in chronic ulcerative colitis: Observer variation and correlations. *Gastroenterology* 95:668–675, 1988.
25. Melville DM, Jass JR, Morson BC, et al: Observer study of the grading of dysplasia in ulcerative colitis: Comparison with clinical outcome. *Hum Pathol* 20:1008–1014, 1989.
26. Blackstone MO, Riddell RH, Rogers BHG, et al: Dysplasia-associated lesion or mass (DALM) detected by colonoscopy in long-standing ulcerative colitis: An indication for colectomy. *Gastroenterology* 80:366–374, 1981.
27. Butt JH, Konishi F, Morson BC, et al: Macroscopic lesions in dysplasia and carcinoma complicating ulcerative colitis. *Dig Dis Sci* 28:18–26, 1983.
28. Taylor BA, Pemberton JH, Carpenter HA, et al: Dysplasia in chronic ulcerative colitis: Implications for colonoscopic surveillance. *Dis Colon Rectum* 35:950–956, 1992.
29. Woolrich AJ, DaSilva MD, Korelitz BI: Surveillance in the routine management of ulcerative colitis: The predictive value of low-grade dysplasia. *Gastroenterology* 103:431–438, 1992.
30. Löfberg R, Broström O, Karlén P, et al: DNA aneuploidy in ulcerative colitis: Reproducibility, topographic distribution and relation to dysplasia. *Gastroenterology* 102:1149–1154, 1992.
31. Löfberg R, Caspersson T, Tribukait B, et al: Comparative DNA analyses in long standing ulcerative colitis with aneuploidy. *Gut* 30:1731–1736, 1989.
32. Burmer GC, Rabinovitch PS, Haggitt RC, et al: Neoplastic progression in ulcerative colitis: Histology, DNA content, and loss of a p53 allele. *Gastroenterology* 103:1602–1610, 1992.
33. Ahnen DJ, Warren GH, Greene LJ, et al: Search for a specific marker of mucosal dysplasia in chronic ulcerative colitis. *Gastroenterology* 93:1346–1355, 1987.
34. Grinnell RS: The grading and prognosis of carcinoma of the colon and rectum. *Ann Surg* 109:500–503, 1939.
35. Greenstein AJ, Sachar DB, Smith H, et al: Cancer in universal and left-sided ulcerative colitis: Factors determining risk. *Gastroenterology* 77:290–294, 1979.
36. Lashner BA, Hanauer SB, Silverstein MD: Optimal timing of colonoscopy to screen for cancer in ulcerative colitis. *Ann Intern Med* 108:274–278, 1988.
37. Fochois SE, Sommers SC, Korelitz BI: Sigmoidoscopy and biopsy in surveillance for cancer in ulcerative colitis. *J Clin Gastroenterol* 8:249–254, 1986.
38. British Society of Gastroenterology Working Party: *Provision of Gastro-intestinal Endoscopy and Related Services for a District General Hospital*. London, England, 1991, pp 95–105.
39. Jones HW, Grogono J, Hoare AM: Surveillance in ulcerative colitis: Burdens and benefit. *Gut* 29:325–331, 1988.
40. Collins RH, Geldman M, Fordtran JS: Colon cancer, dysplasia, and surveillance in patients with ulcerative colitis. *N Engl J Med* 316:1654–1658, 1987.
41. Ekbom A, Helmick C, Zack M, et al: Increased risk of large-bowel cancer in Crohn's disease with colonic involvement. *Lancet* 2:357–359, 1990.
42. Connell W, Kamm MA, Ritchie JK, et al: 1992, in press.
43. Yamazaki Y, Ribeiro MB, Sachar DB, et al: Malignant colorectal strictures in Crohn's disease. *Am J Gastroenterol* 86:882–885, 1991.
44. Fozard JBJ, Dixon MF: Colonoscopic surveillance in ulcerative colitis: Dysplasia through the looking glass. *Gut* 30:285–292, 1989.
45. Gyde S: Screening for colorectal cancer in ulcerative colitis: Dubious benefits and high costs. *Gut* 31:1089–1092, 1990.
46. Lashner BA, Kane SV, Hanauer SB: Colon cancer surveillance in chronic ulcerative colitis: Historical cohort study. *Am J Gastroenterol* 85:1083–1087, 1990.
47. Marteau TM: Psychological cost of screening. *Br Med J* 299:527, 1989.
48. Hill MJ, Lennard-Jones JE, Melville DM, et al: Faecal bile acids, dysplasia and carcinoma in ulcerative colitis. *Lancet* 2:185–186, 1987.

CHAPTER 35

Diagnostic Approach to the Symptomatic Patient

Robert C. Kurtz

HIGHLIGHTS

This chapter reviews those symptoms that may be attributable to colorectal neoplasia and details the appropriate evaluation of these symptoms. The evaluation of the symptomatic patient starts with a careful history and physical examination, the development of a list of differential diagnoses, and the ordering of the proper laboratory and diagnostic tests in the correct sequence. The benefits and risks of the various diagnostic tests are described and their expected diagnostic yields are reviewed. Guidelines are presented to aid the reader.

CONTROVERSIES

The major controversy in this chapter deals with whether to use a barium enema examination or colonoscopy to evaluate the symptomatic patient when the entire colon needs to be studied. The merits of each test are detailed, as are the problems of each. The reader should understand why these two procedures are frequently complementary and when to use each.

FUTURE DIRECTIONS

In the future, the evaluation of the symptomatic patient will commonly include more accurate preoperative staging. The use of higher-resolution computed tomography (CT) and endoluminal and extraluminal ultrasound will enable the clinician not only to detect small liver metastases but also to determine, preoperatively, regional lymph node involvement with greater accuracy.

SYMPTOM EVALUATION

Symptomatic colorectal cancer is highly variable due to different growth patterns and their location in the large bowel. Symptoms which may be attributable to colorectal cancer include rectal bleeding, fatigue and other symptoms associated with anemia, recent change in bowel habits, new onset of constipation or diarrhea, decrease in stool caliber, and abdominal pain, which may be chronic or acute due to large bowel obstruction or even perforation.

Rectal bleeding defined as bright red blood, with or without clots, usually at the time of defecation, occurs most often when cancer originates in the rectum or left colon. The bleeding is rarely massive, and if iron deficiency anemia is present, it will be mild. Significant hypochromic, microcytic anemia, often associated with symptoms of progressive fatigue or new congestive heart failure, is more commonly due to a cancer of the right colon. In this part of the colon, the cancer frequently grows to a large size without the development of symptoms of bowel obstruction and may bleed in an occult fashion for a long time before discovery.

Change in bowel habits may also be due to colorectal cancer. Typically, constipation occurs with rectal or left colon tumors. This is new and more severe than previously described by the patient. Often narrow, "pencil-thin" stools may be noted. Abdominal pain of a crampy nature represents the increase in peristaltic activity needed to force the solid fecal stream past the cancer-narrowed left colon lumen. Laxatives used to relieve the worsening constipation may increase this crampy pain and occasionally lead to bowel perforation. Diarrhea may develop paradoxically as the fecal stream is forced past a partially obstructing colon cancer. Acute abdominal pain due to complete bowel obstruction or perforation represents a surgical emergency. While obstruction is most common in the left colon, it may occur anywhere in the large bowel. Welch and Donaldson[1] reported that 8 percent of symptomatic patients with colon cancer at the Massachusetts General Hospital presented with bowel obstruction. Kelly and colleagues[2] found that 3.7 percent of their colorectal cancer patients at the Medical College of Virginia presented with bowel perforation.

Rectal cancers may cause fecal urgency and tenesmus, the passage of mucus and blood, and the sense of incomplete evacuation. Symptoms of rectal cancers also include perineal pain, urinary tract symptoms, and vaginal fistulas.

Symptoms of advanced colorectal cancer include fatigue, anorexia, and weight loss in addition to those that are related to the location of metastases. Jaundice and right-upper-quadrant abdominal pain may represent liver involvement. Abdominal distention may be due to ascites or a large right colon mass. Back pain can follow spread of the cancer to bone or may stem from periaortic nodal metastases. Cough and a pleural effusion may occur with pulmonary metastases.

Young patients with symptoms of colorectal cancer may be incorrectly reassured that their symptoms are related to a benign process and not undergo a proper evaluation. In a series of 481 consecutive patients with colorectal cancer, Galloway and colleagues[3] found that 7.5 percent were under age 50. Half of the older patients in this group presented to the hospital for treatment within 3 months of the development of symptoms, compared with only 17.5 percent of the younger patients ($p < .02$). There was a higher proportion of younger patients with metastatic disease at the time of presentation.

DIFFERENTIAL DIAGNOSIS

It is important that the primary physician aggressively evaluate symptoms that might be attributable to colorectal cancer. Bright red rectal bleeding can be due to a variety of benign causes, including hemorrhoids, colitis, and diverticulosis as well as colonic polyps. It is impossible to differentiate colorectal cancer from these benign conditions solely on the basis of the character of the bleeding. Furthermore, many patients who have colorectal cancer will also have hemorrhoids. Therefore, while a digital rectal examination is important, the finding of hemorrhoids should not end the diagnostic evaluation.

Colonic diverticulosis is the most common cause of massive colonic bleeding, accounting for approximately 70 percent of these episodes.[4] Diverticulosis is a common finding in asymptomatic older patients, and its frequency of diagnosis increases with age. The incidence of bleeding from diverticulosis ranges from 10 to 30 percent, with massive hemorrhage occurring in about 5 percent.[5] Angiodysplasia is being diagnosed more frequently in patients with lower gastrointestinal bleeding. The bleeding may be intermittent and of a chronic nature, with iron-deficiency anemia as the major problem. Baum and colleagues[6] found that one-half of their patients with angiodysplasia presented with massive hemorrhage.

Many of the nonspecific symptoms of colorectal cancer are seen as part of functional bowel disease or the irritable bowel syndrome, which is very common. Drossman[7] estimated that at least 40 percent of gastroenterologists' practice was made up of patients with an irritable bowel. Often patients will complain of lifelong constipation. They may develop gastrointestinal symptoms—such as diarrhea or abdominal bloating and pain—after spicy or fatty foods. Lactose intolerance with crampy abdominal pain, bloating, and diarrhea, associated with the irritable bowel syndrome, is a common problem in adults. The physician must be alert to an abrupt change in the pattern of all of these chronic symptoms and must evaluate the patient thoroughly if chronic symptoms change.

Diverticulitis may present with left-lower-quadrant abdominal pain, fever, and signs of localized perforation. Symptoms and signs of bowel obstruction may also be attributable to colonic diverticula. It is not possible to differentiate these signs and symptoms from those of colonic cancer without appropriate diagnostic studies.

LABORATORY STUDIES

Laboratory evaluation should include a complete blood count and tests of renal and hepatic function. Profound anemia will require preoperative correction. Elevation of serum bilirubin of alkaline phosphatase will increase suspicion of possible liver metastases, so that a preoperative abdominal computed tomography (CT) scan or liver sonogram should be performed. While carcinoembryonic antigen (CEA) levels are often obtained prior to surgical treatment, initial diagnosis and management should not be dependent on plasma CEA levels.

PROCTOSIGMOIDOSCOPY/ FLEXIBLE SIGMOIDOSCOPY

Rigid and flexible sigmoidoscopy are important endoscopic techniques that help the clinician to evaluate the distal colon and rectum. Rigid sigmoidoscopes are usually 25 cm long, whereas flexible instruments are either 35 or 60 cm long. While rigid sigmoidoscopes are less expensive to purchase and maintain and somewhat easier to use than their flexible counterparts, the flexible instruments offer greater depth of insertion, patient comfort, and acceptance.

In symptomatic patients, proctosigmoidoscopy is often the first diagnostic procedure performed. Because of the length of the instrument, however, sigmoidoscopy will miss proximal colon cancers and polyps. This is a significant shortcoming, as colorectal cancer is now less commonly left-sided than it was in past decades. A retrospective review of 1694 consecutive cases of colorectal cancer seen at the University of Chicago Medical Center demonstrated a 10.2 percent increase in the frequency of cancers of the cecum and ascending colon during the 25-year period of the study. During the same period, rectal and rectosigmoid cancers declined by 15.8 percent. The classic teaching that 50 percent of colorectal cancers can be detected by digital rectal examination and proctosigmoidoscopy is no longer valid.[8]

In the symptomatic patient, sigmoidoscopy may be used to complement air-contrast barium enema studies done to evaluate rectal bleeding, anemia, and abdominal pain. In a study comparing flexible sigmoidoscopy with other diagnostic techniques, the combination of sigmoidoscopy and air-contrast barium enema was almost as effective in identifying colonic cancer as was colonoscopy. The identification of small and medium-sized polyps was better with colonoscopy.[9]

Sigmoidoscopy is also useful to assess therapy in the follow-up of patients with inflammatory bowel disease; it may be therapeutic in patients with abdominal pain and radiographic evidence suggesting bowel obstruction due to sigmoid volvulus; it is used to follow patients with familial adenomatous polyposis (FAP) after colectomy and ileorectal reconstruction; and it is helpful in evaluating family members for phenotypic expression of FAP.

Sigmoidoscopy is a very safe procedure. Complications such as perforation of the colon during rigid or flexible sigmoidoscopy, while possible, are very unusual. In one large series of 5000 flexible sigmoidoscopies, no perforations occurred.[10]

BARIUM ENEMA

The barium enema examination is one of the most common ways to evaluate symptoms believed to originate in the colon. In 1987 alone, almost 1 1/2 million barium enema examinations were performed on Medicare patients in the United States.[11] In a southern California multispecialty group, Zarchy and Ershoff[12] reviewed the use of barium enemas.[12] Over 50 percent of the barium enemas were ordered to evaluate symptoms. Abdominal pain represented the most frequent symptom (40 percent), followed by rectal bleeding and change in bowel habits (29 percent). There were 148 (18.6 percent) abnormal barium enemas. Colonic cancer was detected in 23 (2.9 percent) of the 794 patients undergoing barium enema examinations. Colorectal polyps accounted for the most frequent abnormality (70 cases). Four variables that were shown to be significant predictors of colorectal cancer included an abnormal sigmoidoscopy, iron-deficiency anemia, positive stool occult blood, and relevant history.

The type of barium enema examination performed affects the detection of neoplastic lesions. If a single-column barium enema study is performed, the majority of adenomatous polyps and about half of the cancers will be missed, as determined by subsequent colonoscopy. Double- or air-contrast barium enema examinations will identify most lesions over 2 cm in size, but smaller lesions are often missed. In a study from New Zealand,[13] the radiographs and clinical records of 26 patients with colorectal cancers missed on barium enema and then identified by colonoscopy were reviewed. Over three-quarters of the patients were women, and 24 of the 26 patients presented with rectal bleeding. Eight-six percent of the radiographs were air-contrast studies. The most consistent error was missing the lesion in the barium pool. Errors were made by both experienced and inexperienced radiologists. The authors suggest double reading and reporting of barium enema studies to avoid these errors.

Perhaps one of the most difficult areas in the interpretation of barium enema studies is the differentiation of diverticular disease from colonic cancer. Barium enema studies may underestimate the degree and intensity of diverticular inflammation. Strictures due to diverticular disease cannot easily be distinguished from malignant strictures. Colonoscopy, with associated biopsy and cytology, is the most important tool to use in making this distinction.[14] In 44 patients with diverticular disease, Hunt[15] found 6 (13 percent) with unexpected cancer; he was unable to examine the colon adequately in a similar number of patients.

COLONOSCOPY

Colonoscopic examination has become the established method of evaluating and treating diseases of the large bowel. Modern colonoscopes are easier and safer to use, and complete evaluation by direct observation of the rectum and colon as far as the cecum is possible in most patients. Abnormalities seen may be photographed, biopsied, and—in the case of polypoid lesions—often entirely removed. With the currently available lavage preparations, patients can be readied for colonoscopy in 24 h. Patients with acute hematochezia can safely use lavage preparations. In a study of such patients, Caos and colleagues[16] noted excellent mucosal visualization. They were able to identify the colonic cause of the hematochezia in 24 of their 35 patients.

Hematochezia and melena thought not to be from an upper gastrointestinal source should be evaluated by colonoscopy. Brand and colleagues[17] studied over 300 patients with recent rectal bleeding by colonoscopy. They found that the bleeding was due to cancer in about 8 percent of their patients, while it was due to benign colon polyps in over 20 percent. Angiodysplasia was also an important cause of large bowel hemorrhage in this patient population. Tedesco and colleagues[18] performed colonoscopy in 258 patients with rectal bleeding and whose proctosigmoidoscopy and barium enemas studies were either negative or showed only diverticula. In 29 of these patients (11.2 percent), cancer was found by the colonoscopic examination.

There is still debate over whether colonoscopy or air-contrast barium enema should be performed on the symptomatic patient. Radiologists tend to recommend the barium enema, while gastroenterologists prefer colonoscopy. In fact, both tests are complementary and both are often obtained. Colonoscopy is frequently utilized to confirm abnormalities seen on barium enema, to determine the precise nature of the lesion, to remove it if it proves to be a benign-appearing polyp, to biopsy it if it cannot be removed, and to confirm that there are no synchronous lesions elsewhere in the colon.

When a polyp is identified, colonoscopic polypectomy is performed. Wherever possible, the polyp is totally removed and submitted for pathologic assessment. Complete colonoscopy should always be performed at the time of polypectomy to identify and remove any synchronous polyps. Synchronous adenomas occur in about 50 percent of patients with colonic cancer, and separate synchronous colon cancers occur in from 1.5 to 5 percent of patients.[19,20]

Small polyps (7 mm or less in diameter), are often removed by the "hot biopsy" technique, whereby electric current is passed through a special biopsy forceps to cauterize the base of the polyp. The tissue in the forceps is then sent to pathology. Larger polyps are removed by the "snare cautery" technique. A wire loop is passed around the polyp base and an electric current both transects and cauterizes the polyp base. The entire polyp is retrieved and submitted to pathology for analysis. The vast majority of colonic polyps can be managed in this fashion. Large, sessile polyps may need to be removed in a piecemeal approach. A small number of large sessile polyps (greater than 2 cm in diameter), particularly in the cecum, may not be safely removable during colonoscopy; surgical resection will then be necessary. Since it may be important to find the polypectomy site at a future time, the polypectomy site can be marked with an injection of dilute sterile India ink. This has been recommended as an accurate and permanent method of future endoscopic or surgical identification.[21]

The major complications of colonoscopy are bowel perforation and hemorrhage. While this is true for both diagnostic and therapeutic colonoscopy, the rates of occurrence are different. In 4713 diagnostic colonoscopies reported on by the American Society for Gastrointestinal Endoscopy (ASGE), perforation occurred in 0.17 percent.[22] These perforations are usually the result of the mechanical impact of the colonoscope shaft on the sigmoid colon, especially a sigmoid colon affected by diverticular disease or adhesions. In 1901 polypectomy patients reported by the ASGE, the perforation rate was 0.11 percent. In this group, perforation—usually related to the removal of a sessile polyp—almost always occurred at the polypectomy site. Also in the ASGE study, hemorrhage occurred more commonly following polypectomy than diagnostic colonoscopy (2.16 versus 0.01 percent). The syndrome of pain, leukocytosis, and fever after polypectomy does not always represent bowel perforation and may be due to a colonic transmural electrocautery burn. Conservative management in this setting is appropriate.[23]

ULTRASONOGRAPHY

While transabdominal ultrasonography has little or no role in the diagnosis and staging of primary colorectal cancer, a new modality, hydrocolonic sonography, has recently been described. Limberg[24] reported on 300 patients who had conventional transabdominal ultrasonography and hydrocolonic ultrasonography, with the diagnosis confirmed by subsequent colonoscopy. The examinations were performed to evaluate abdominal pain, weight loss, diarrhea, or fecal occult blood. Complete examination from the rectosigmoid to the cecum was obtained in 97 percent of patients with hydrocolonic ultrasound. Conventional ultrasonography only detected 9 of 29 cancers, while the hydrocolonic study correctly found 28 (97 percent). Similar results were noted with colonic polyps. Hydrocolonic ultrasonography found 91 percent of colonic polyps larger than 7 mm and 25 percent of polyps smaller than 7 mm. Because of its ability to evaluate the structure of the bowel wall, hydrocolonic ultrasonography was useful in the staging of the colonic cancers. Seventy-five percent of the T2 tumors, 85 percent of the T3 tumors, and 75 percent of the T4 tumors were correctly staged preoperatively by this method.

GUIDELINES

Evaluation of the symptomatic patient should always start with a history, during which attention should be paid to new and changed symptoms. A thorough family history must be included to explore the possibility of relatives with bowel cancer or polyps. Physical examination should follow, with subsequent hematologic and biochemical laboratory evaluation. It is important to emphasize that the finding of external hemorrhoids on digital rectal examination should never end the diagnostic evaluation, no matter what the age of the patient. The sequence of endoscopic and/or radiologic tests to follow is dependent on available resources and the patient's symptoms. While some would recommend going directly to colonoscopy to evaluate change in bowel habits or rectal bleeding, flexible sigmoidoscopy would be perfectly appropriate in a young patient with occasional bright red rectal bleeding and no family history of bowel cancer or adenomatous polyps. Where colonoscopy is not available or is unsuccessful, the combination of flexible sigmoidoscopy followed by a high-quality double-contrast barium enema is reasonable. In this way, well over 95 percent of colorectal cancers will be correctly identified, and synchronous lesions will be found or excluded.

REFERENCES

1. Welch JP, Donaldson GA: Management of severe obstruction of the large bowel due to malignant disease. *Am J Surg* 127:492–499, 1974.
2. Kelly WE Jr, Brown PW, Lawrence W, et al: Penetrating, obstructing, and perforating carcinomas of the colon and rectum. *Arch Surg* 116:381–384, 1985.
3. Galloway DJ, Burns HJ, Bear H, et al: Colorectal cancer in young adults. *Clin Oncol* 10:205–211, 1984.
4. Cathcart PM, Cathcart RS, Rambo WM: Management of massive lower GI bleeding. *Am J Surg* 43:217–219, 1977.
5. Rigg BM, Ewing MR: Current attitudes on diverticulitis with particular reference to colonic bleeding. *Arch Surg* 92:321–328, 1966.
6. Baum S, Athanasoulis CA, Waltman AC, et al: Angiodysplasia of the right colon: A cause of gastrointestinal bleeding. *Am J Roentgenol* 129:789–794, 1977.
7. Drossman DA: Irritable bowel syndrome: A multifactorial disorder. *Hosp Pract* 23:95–108, 1988.
8. Ghahremani GG, Dowlatshahi K: Colorectal carcinomas: Diagnostic implications of their changing frequency and anatomic distribution. *World J Surg* 13:321–325, 1989.
9. Winawer SJ, Leidner SD, Boyle C, et al: Comparison of flexible sigmoidoscopy with other diagnostic techniques in the diagnosis of rectocolon neoplasia. *Dig Dis Sci* 6:277–281, 1979.
10. Traul DG, Davis CB, Pollock JC, et al: Flexible fiberoptic sigmoidoscopy—The Monroe Clinic experience: A prospective study of 5000 examinations. *Dis Colon Rectum* 26:161–166, 1983.
11. Medical annual data, part B, in *Medicare Barium Enemas*. Washington, DC, Health Care Finance Administration, 1987.
12. Zarchy TM, Ershoff D: Which clinical variables predict an abnormal double-contrast barium enema result? *Ann Intern Med* 114:137–141, 1991.
13. Anderson N, Cook HB, Coates R: Colonoscopically detected colorectal cancer missed on barium enema. *Gastrointest Radiol* 16:123–127, 1991.
14. Marks G, Moses ML: The clinical application of flexible fiberoptic colonoscopy. *Surg Clin North Am* 53:735–756, 1973.
15. Hunt RH: The role of colonoscopy in complicated diverticular disease. *Acta Chir Belg* 78:349–353, 1979.
16. Caos A, Benner KG, Manier J, et al: Colonoscopy after Golytely preparation in acute rectal bleeding. *J Clin Gastroenterol* 8:46–49, 1986.
17. Brand EJ, Sullivan BH, Sivak MV Jr, et al: Colonoscopy in the diagnosis of unexplained rectal bleeding. *Ann Surg* 192:111–113, 1980.
18. Tedesco FJ, Waye JD, Raskin JB, et al: Colonoscopic evaluation of rectal bleeding. *Ann Intern Med* 89:907–1002, 1978.
19. Fowler DL, Hedberg SE: Follow-up colonoscopy after polypectomy (abstract). *Gastrointest Endosc* 26:67, 1980.
20. Winawer SJ, Zauber A, Diaz B, et al: The National Polyp Study: Overview of program and preliminary report of patient and polyp characteristics, in Steele G, Burt R, Winawer SJ, et al (eds): *Basic and Clinical Perspectives of Colorectal Polyps and Cancer*. New York, Alan R. Liss, 1988.
21. Lightdale CJ: India ink colonic tattoo: Blots on the record. *Gastrointest Endosc* 37:99–100, 1991.
22. Gilbert GA, Hallsrom AP, Shaneyfelt SL: The national ASGE colonoscopy survey: Complications of colonoscopy (abstract). *Gastrointest Endosc* 30:156, 1984.
23. Waye JD: The post-polypectomy coagulation syndrome. *Gastrointest Endosc* 27:184, 1981.
24. Limberg B: Diagnosis and staging of colonic tumors by conventional abdominal sonography as compared with hydrocolonic sonography. *N Engl J Med* 327:65–69, 1992.

PART 6

Management of Precancerous Disease

CHAPTER 36

Operative Approaches to Patients with Inflammatory Bowel Disease

Robert D. Madoff
Stanley M. Goldberg

It is widely agreed that patients with chronic ulcerative colitis harbor an increased risk of developing colorectal carcinoma. Long-term estimates of this risk vary considerably and depend in part upon geographic location, the population being studied (e.g., tertiary referral center versus private practice), and the nature of the study itself (e.g., institutional versus population-based). Technical factors in calculating risk such as inclusion of colitis patients presenting with carcinoma at the time of initial referral can markedly skew risk assessment.[1] Current estimates of cancer risk for patients with pancolitis are 1.3 percent at 18 years in Copenhagen,[2] 7.2 percent at 11 years in New York,[3] 13.5 percent at 30 years in Tel Aviv,[4] 20 percent at 30 years in Birmingham, England,[5] and 24.2 percent at 20 years in Goteborg.[6] This risk is not altered by disease activity.

Because colitis-associated carcinoma can be difficult to diagnose and frequently presents at an advanced stage, removal of the colon prior to the development of malignancy is a universal goal. However, several factors balance this tendency toward surgical aggressiveness, particularly in the patient with long-standing quiescent or well-controlled colitis: the need for a major operation with its possible attendant morbidity, the possible need for a permanent ileostomy, and the distinct possibility that quality of life will be diminished rather than enhanced postoperatively. These issues do not pertain to the acute indications for colectomy in chronic ulcerative colitis: hemorrhage, perforation, fulminant colitis, toxic megacolon, or failure to respond to medical therapy. Discussion of these indications lies beyond the scope of this chapter.

There is no perfect way to determine when prophylactic colectomy for chronic ulcerative colitis should be performed. The classic approach to this problem is based upon duration of disease. However, while the risk of carcinoma development clearly increases with time, there is no clear cutoff at which an "acceptable" risk becomes unacceptable, and any fixed rule as to the timing of colectomy is thus at least to some extent arbitrary. Nonetheless, many surgeons consider elective prophylactic colectomy after approximately 15 to 20 years of pancolonic disease.

A more recent approach to the timing of colectomy is based on dysplasia screening of the colon. This technique stems from the observation of Morson and Pang[7] in 1987 that development of cancer in colitic patients is associated with recognizable dysplastic changes either locally or elsewhere in the colon. Dysplasia screening has gained increasing popularity and is utilized by a number of major centers to determine the timing of prophylactic colectomy. Still, the efficacy and cost-effectiveness of this approach remain to be proven, and there are significant caveats regarding its use.[1] First, the technique requires lifelong (until colectomy) colonoscopy screening, which is costly, associated with a small but significant risk of complications, and prone to poor patient compliance, particularly in those with quiescent disease. Dysplasia itself can be difficult to diagnose correctly, especially in the presence of acute inflammation and in particular for the nonspecialist pathologist. Despite frequent dysplasia screening, some cancers are missed and up to 20 percent of cancers are diagnosed only at advanced stages. Finally, it is impossible to say how many "severely dysplastic" colons would not have gone on to develop carcinoma in the near term had they been left in situ (false-positive examinations). The issues surrounding dysplasia screening are discussed in greater detail in Chap. 34.

Once the decision has been made to proceed with surgery, the next question becomes which operation to perform. The four options include total proctocolectomy with permanent Brooke ileostomy, total proctocolectomy with Kock continent ileostomy, total abdominal colectomy with ileorectal anastomosis, and proctocolectomy with ileoanal reservoir (restorative proctocolectomy, Parks pouch). The advantages and disadvantages of the various surgical options for ulcerative colitis are outlined in Table 36-1. Total proctocolectomy with Brooke ileostomy remains the time-proven procedure and should be considered the standard by which all other operations are measured. The procedure's advantages are simple: it cures ulcerative colitis and eliminates the risk of colorectal cancer in a single familiar operation. Disadvantages of this approach include possible pelvic morbidity (impaired sexual and bladder function, unhealed perineal wound) and the need for a permanent ileostomy with an external appliance. These problems are all obviated by abdominal colectomy with ileorectal anastomosis, but the operation is not curative and the retained diseased rectum can lead to persisting symptoms or development of carcinoma. Another approach to avoidance of an external appliance is total proctocolectomy with Kock continent ileostomy. This technique permits creation of a flush ileostomy that is emptied several times a day by means of a catheter. The operation is technically complex and prone to late complications, particularly slippage of the nipple valve. Proctocolectomy with ileoanal reservoir has more recently gained increasing popularity as the procedure of choice for

Table 36-1
Surgical Options for Chronic Ulcerative Colitis (CUC)

Procedure	*Features*	*Advantages*	*Disadvantages*
Total proctocolectomy with permanent Brooke ileostomy	Removal of entire colon, rectum, and anus Permanent Brooke ileostomy	Eliminates risk of colorectal cancer Curative for CUC Routine procedure for the surgeon Usually one operation Known complications Known long-term results	Permanent ileostomy Requires pouching system Possible sexual and bladder dysfunction Perineal wound Further restorative surgery unlikely
Total colectomy with ileorectal anastomosis	Removal of entire colon Ileum joined to rectum	No ileostomy No external pouching system Best approximates normal bowel function Routine procedure for surgeon Usually one operation Further restorative surgery feasible	Not curative Risk of cancer in retained rectum Frequent stools (3–8/day) Requires regular follow-up with proctoscopy Further surgery often necessary
Kock pouch (continent ileostomy)	Removal of entire colon, rectum, and anus Permanent ileostomy with nipple valve Internal abdominal ileal reservoir	Eliminates risk of colorectal cancer Curative for CUC No external pouching system Continence good when procedure works well Usually one operation Ileostomy may be located lower on the abdomen	Permanent ileostomy Patient must intubate and carry supplies to empty pouch Continence variable Requires specialized surgical expertise Operative revision may be needed Possible sexual and bladder dysfunction Perineal wound Pouchitis Further restorative surgery unlikely
Restorative ileoanal reservoir	Removal of entire colon and upper rectum Lining of lower rectum may be removed (rectal mucosectomy) Internal pelvic ileal reservoir Ileal reservoir joined to the anus Temporary ileostomy usually performed	With complete mucosectomy, risk of colorectal cancer is slight and disease usually cured No permanent ileostomy No external pouching system Continence usually good	Temporary ileostomy usually necessary Bowel function variable Requires specialized surgical expertise More than one operation usually necessary Increased surgical complications Pouchitis Long-term results unknown (nutritional effects, cancer risk)

SOURCE: Pena JP, Gemlo BT, Rothenberger DA: Ileal pouch-anal anastomosis: State of the art. *Baillière's Clinical Gastroenterology* 6:113–128, 1992. Reproduced by permission.

chronic ulcerative colitis. The operation was designed to both eradicate all diseased tissue and to eliminate the need for permanent ileostomy. Disadvantages include technical complexity, a relatively high complication rate, the need for a temporary stoma, and variable functional results.

TOTAL PROCTOCOLECTOMY WITH BROOKE ILEOSTOMY

For many years, total proctocolectomy with Brooke ileostomy was the only available surgical procedure for chronic ulcerative colitis. While newer alternative procedures have gained increasing prominence in the surgical literature, proctocolectomy remains a straightforward one-stage operation that cures the underlying disease and eliminates the future risk of large bowel carcinoma. Its fundamental drawback is the need for permanent ileostomy with external appliance.

Patient Selection

Total proctocolectomy is an option for all patients requiring surgery for ulcerative colitis. It is suitable for elderly patients, patients with possible Crohn's disease, patients with impaired anal sphincter function, and patients in whom ileal pouch-anal anastomosis is technically impossible (e.g., due to marked obesity). Furthermore, some patients simply prefer a single-stage definitive procedure with a predictable functional outcome to alternative, more complex reconstructions with their numerous possible complications.

Results

It should be emphasized at the outset that most large series of total proctocolectomy for ulcerative colitis include patients who underwent surgery 20 to 40 years ago. Thus, direct comparison of morbidity and mortality between total proctocolectomy and the more recently described operations is likely to be misleading. Because the pelvic dissection for all procedures requiring proctectomy is similar, some types of morbidity (e.g., pelvic nerve injury) should be comparable. In contrast, there are specific complications related to total proctocolectomy alone that include unhealed perineal wounds and problems related to permanent ileostomy.

Ritchie[8] reviewed the St. Mark's experience with colectomy and ileostomy for ulcerative colitis in 246 patients operated upon between 1955 and 1969. Both morbidity and mortality were directly related to the operative status of the patient. Morbidity was 18.8, 31.3, and 40.0 percent in elective, urgent, and emergent cases respectively; mortality was 1.6, 10.7, and 23.3 percent in these same groups. Readmission for complications decreased over the study period, consistent with both increasing experience and advances in intraoperative and perioperative management. A more modern series of 70 patients who underwent one-stage elective proctocolectomy for ulcerative colitis between 1976 and 1986 demonstrated that the operation still causes significant morbidity (17 percent major and 21 percent minor complications).[9] Readmission was necessary for 25 patients (36 percent) and reoperation for 15 (21 percent); surgical indications included ileostomy dysfunction (11 patients), small bowel obstruction (2 patients), and perineal wound problems (5 patients).

Sexual dysfunction following proctectomy is related to damage of the pelvic sympathetic and parasympathetic nerves; the former mediate ejaculatory function and the latter erectile and urinary function. Perimuscular rectal dissection (anterior to the superior mesenteric vessels) and intersphincteric proctectomy (dissection between the internal and external anal sphincters) are operative techniques designed to keep dissection away from these nerves and thus minimize postoperative sexual dysfunction. While we advocate both of these techniques, some surgeons prefer anatomic mesorectal excision in the plane between the superior rectal vessels and the pelvic autonomic nerves and report comparably low rates of sexual dysfunction.[10,11]

Early series of proctocolectomy for ulcerative colitis in which pelvic nerve sparing was not emphasized demonstrated distressingly high rates of sexual dysfunction. For example, in the series of Goligher et al.,[12] of 41 male colitic patients treated with proctocolectomy and ileostomy, 11 had impaired sexual function, including ejaculatory failure in 2, temporary impotence in 2, and permanent impotence in 7. The same series documents the effect of age on the incidence of sexual dysfunction: 0 of 8 patients below 30 years of age suffered sexual dysfunction postoperatively, versus 5 of 25 (20 percent) patients 30 to 50 years of age and 6 of 8 (75 percent) patients above 50 years of age.

More recent series of proctectomy demonstrate less postoperative sexual dysfunction. Leicester et al.[13] reviewed 98 patients who, at St. Mark's Hospital, underwent intersphincteric proctectomy for inflammatory bowel disease between 1972 and 1978. Of these, 48 were available for follow-up interview. Transient sexual dysfunction was reported by 11 of 23 men (47 percent) and permanent sexual dysfunction by 4 (17 percent). In the latter group, all had difficulties with arousal and maintenance of erection and one had loss of ejaculation. Sexual morbidity was related in part to the presence of a stoma, and no patient under the age of 40 had diminished sexual activity. Of the 113 patients operated upon between 1972 and 1984 and reported by Berry et al.,[14] none had permanent sexual or urinary problems following intersphincteric proctectomy.[14] Similarly, Corman et al.[15] reported one case of temporary and no cases of permanent impotence in a series of 76 men who underwent proctocolectomy for inflammatory bowel disease at the Lahey Clinic.

Sexual function in women is also affected by proctocolectomy. In the series of Leicester et al.,[13] 5 of 25 women (20 percent) complained of dyspareunia and diminished sexual satisfaction following surgery, though all but one could achieve normal orgasm. Metcalf et al.[16] reported improved sexual function in 100 women who underwent proctocolectomy for benign disease at the Mayo Clinic. However, persistent dyspareunia was present in 19 of 50 women (38 percent) with Kock pouch and 9 of 50 women (18 percent) with ileal pouch–anal anastomosis. Diminished orgasm was seen in one patient in each group.

Unhealed perineal wounds represent a significant source of morbidity following proctocolectomy, particularly for inflammatory bowel disease. For example, Ritchie[8] reported that 49 percent of perineal wounds were unhealed at 6 months and 23 percent at 1 year following proctocolectomy for ulcerative colitis.

ABDOMINAL COLECTOMY WITH ILEORECTAL ANASTOMOSIS

Abdominal colectomy with ileorectal anastomosis was championed by Aylett[17] in the 1950s and 1960s as a "sphincter saving" alternative to total proctocolectomy with ileostomy. The operation has a number of attractive attributes: it is relatively simple, pelvic dissection is entirely avoided, and the need for permanent ileostomy is either delayed or avoided entirely. Unfortunately, the operation necessarily leaves behind diseased rectum which can continue to cause symptoms and eventually permit development of rectal cancer. Poor functional results can also lead to operative failure requiring completion proctectomy and permanent ileostomy.

Patient Selection

Because of the late failure rate and persisting risk of rectal carcinoma, ileorectal anastomosis has now largely been supplanted by the ileal pouch-anal anastomosis. Parc et al.,[18] once leading proponents of ileorectal anastomosis, now advocate the procedure only when the diagnosis of ulcerative colitis is in doubt, in patients above 60 years of age, and in circumstances where technical problems prevent completion of restorative proctocolectomy.

Contraindications to ileorectal anastomosis include a fibrotic or strictured rectum, poor anal sphincter function, and preexisting large bowel cancer or dysplasia. While several series fail to document any difference in failure rates between patients with mild and advanced proctitis,[19,20] we do not find the data conclusive and have avoided ileorectal anastomosis in patients with severe distal disease. Grundfest et al.[21] emphasized the need to remove the entire rectum in patients with preexisting cancer or underlying moderate to severe dysplasia. Of 7 such surviving patients in their series, 5 (71 percent) subsequently developed rectal carcinoma or dysplasia. Similarly, Johnson et al.[22] found a 42 percent risk of developing rectal cancer in patients with moderate or severe dysplasia at 9 years after diagnosis.

Functional Results

The functional results of ileorectal anastomosis for ulcerative colitis are depicted in Table 36-2. Jagelman et al.[23] reviewed the functional results of ileorectal anastomosis in 174 patients from Aylett's series. Of these, 94 percent had 6 or fewer bowel movements per day and 40 percent had 3 or fewer. Newton and Baker[24] reported a mean stool frequency of 4.5 bowel movements per day for colitic patients at St. Mark's Hospital; Oakley et al.,[19] 4.3 bowel movements per day at the Cleveland Clinic; and Parc et al.,[25] 4.5 bowel movements per day at the Hospital St. Antoine in Paris.

Table 36-2
Functional Results of Ileorectal Anastomosis for Ulcerative Colitis: Selected Series

Author/Year	*Mean no. BMs/24h*	*Excessive stool frequency*	*Nocturnal evacuation*	*Incontinence*
Oakley et al.,[19] 1985	4.3	N/A	5.4%	0
Newton and Baker,[24] 1975	4.5	18% > 6 BMs/day	70% sometimes 4% always	17%[a]
Parc et al.,[25] 1985	4.5	17% > 6 BMs/day	35%	1% nocturnal seepage 0.5% incontinent
Khubchandani et al.,[26] 1989	1.4	1% > 8 BMs/day	N/A	0

[a]At least one episode of major incontinence in 12 months.

More recently, Khubchandani et al.[26] reported an average stool frequency of 1.4 bowel movements per day following ileorectal anastomosis. Continence following ileorectal anastomosis is generally well preserved.

Beckwith et al.[27] assessed the functional results of older patients (≥ 60 years) who underwent ileorectal anastomosis for various indications at the Mayo Clinic. Patients initially experienced a relatively pronounced increase in stool frequency; however, after 5 years, patients averaged only 1.5 bowel movements per day more than their baseline level. Seven percent of patients were incontinent following ileorectal anastomosis. These data suggest that age alone is not a contraindication to ileorectal anastomosis.

Rectal Carcinoma Risk

The incidence of rectal carcinoma following ileorectal anastomosis as reported in various series is depicted in Table 36-3. More informative than these raw data, however, are calculated cumulative cancer risks defined as a function of time. In reviewing Aylett's series, Baker et al.[28] found that rectal cancer risk was 6 percent at 20 years of disease and 15 percent at 30 years of disease. Grundfest et al.,[21] utilizing similar methodology, calculated the cancer risk in their series to be 0 percent at 10 years, 2.1 percent at 15 years, 5.0 percent at 20 years, and 12.9 percent at 25 years of disease. These figures are surprisingly similar to the modern estimates of long-term large bowel cancer risk in unoperated patients with ulcerative colitis. Thus, while the risk of developing rectal cancer remains relatively small following ileorectal anastomosis, particularly in the first 10 to 15 years of disease, the risk is by no means negligible or obviated.

Unfortunately, cancers arising after ileorectal anastomosis tend to be advanced. Twenty-two patients developed rectal cancer in Aylett's series.[28] Of these, 4 were unoperable and 12 presented with Dukes C lesions. Of 18 patients who underwent resection, 9 were dead within 3 years of surgery. In the Cleveland Clinic series, 5 cancers occurred, 3 of which were Dukes A. However, the remaining 2 lesions were advanced at presentation and both patients died of their disease within 14 months of surgery.[19]

It remains to be seen whether dysplasia screening of the rectal remnant will decrease the incidence of cancer or lead to excision of tumors that do develop at an acceptably early stage. In any case, close and continued follow-up of the retained rectum (with proctoscopy every 6 to 12 months) is indicated for all patients who undergo ileorectal anastomosis for chronic ulcerative colitis.

TOTAL PROCTOCOLECTOMY WITH KOCK POUCH

The continent ileal reservoir was described by Kock[29] in 1969 to provide a continent alternative to conventional ileostomy. The operation creates an internal ileal reservoir to permit storage of ileal effluent and a one-way nipple valve that prevents spontaneous emptying. The patient empties the pouch two to four times daily with a catheter. The advantage of this technique lies in its elimination of the need for an external appliance and any associated psychological and social stigma. In addition, the Kock ileostomy itself is relatively inconspicuous: there is no need for eversion to optimize pouching and the stoma can be located low in the abdominal wall.

Patient Selection

The Kock pouch has seen limited use for two reasons. First, the operation is technically demanding and subject to both complications and failure. In addition, the procedure has largely been supplanted by the pelvic ileal pouch with anal anastomosis, an operation whose reservoir design was inspired by the Kock pouch.

Table 36-3
Ileorectal Anastomosis Failures

Author	*Year*	*N*	*Follow-up, years*	*Rectal cancer*	*Ileostomy/ proctectomy*
Baker[20]	1970	41	2–17	0	18 (44%)
Hughes et al.[94]	1975	37	minimum 15	2	12 (32%)
Baker et al.[28a]	1978	374	2–23	22	47 (13%)
Farnell et al.[95]	1980	63[b]	5–17	0	15 (24%)
Oakley et al.[19]	1985	136	3–25	5	37 (27%)
Johnson et al.[96]	1986	147	5–36	11[c]	22 (15%)
Khubchandani et al.[26]	1989	53	1–28	2	6 (11%)
Lejionmark et al.[97]	1990	51	6–35	0	29 (37%)
Löfberg et al.[98]	1991	46	12–36	0	25 (54%)

[a]Aylett's series.

[b]Ulcerative colitis patients.

[c]Of 286 subtotal colectomies (147 with ileorectal anastomosis).

Nonetheless, there remain a number of significant indications for the Kock pouch in ulcerative colitis. First, a number of patients simply prefer the notion of a predictable number of self-catheterizations to the possibility of an erratic or poor functional result following restorative proctocolectomy. A second indication occurs in patients requiring surgery who have underlying sphincter dysfunction or in whom technical difficulties preclude pouch-anal anastomosis. Similarly, there are a number of patients who have previously undergone proctocolectomy with conventional ileostomy who desire a continent alternative. Finally, a number of patients whose ileal pouch has failed can be converted to continent ileostomy.[30] Kock pouch is contraindicated in patients with known or suspected Crohn's disease. Poorly motivated patients and patients with neuropsychiatric disorders are poor candidates for this operation.

Results

A detailed description of the Kock pouch operation has been published elsewhere.[31] Slippage of the one-way nipple valve is the most bothersome complication following pouch creation. While this complication occurred in up to 50 percent of patients in early series, its incidence has more recently decreased to approximately 10 percent.[31]

Pouch ileitis, analogous to pouchitis following ileal pouch-anal anastomosis, is an inflammatory condition that occurs in 15 to 30 percent of Kock pouch patients.[32] The condition manifests itself by abdominal cramps and excessive ileostomy output with associated electrolyte disturbances and dehydration. Pouchitis is best initially treated with continuous catheter drainage of the pouch and oral metronidazole. Refractory cases may require treatment with steroids or 5-aminosalicylic acid (5-ASA), either orally or by enema.

RESTORATIVE PROCTOCOLECTOMY

Total proctocolectomy with ileal pouch-anal anastomosis, also known as "restorative proctocolectomy," was designed to cure ulcerative colitis without the need for a permanent stoma. While the prototype operation was described by Ravitch and Sabiston[33] in 1947, the early clinical experience of excessive stool frequency and urgency and secondary perineal excoriation led to abandonment of the procedure. However, renewed interest was stimulated in the 1960s with the success of the Soave colonic pull-through procedure for Hirschsprung's disease and the development of the Kock continent ileal reservoir. In 1978, Ferrari and Fonkalsrud[34] combined these concepts to create an ileal pouch pull-through in dogs, and Parks and Nicholls[35] that same year used a similar technique to perform "proctocolectomy without ileostomy" in eight patients.

Since the operation's initial description, several technical modifications have been introduced, and there remain a number of areas of controversy. These include, among others, the ideal pouch configuration, the need for mucosectomy, and the need for temporary ileostomy.

Patient Selection

Appropriate patient selection is of critical importance when restorative proctocolectomy is being considered. While the procedure generally offers good functional results, patients must be made aware that these results still do not approximate "normal" bowel function. Multiple daily bowel movements can be expected, and continence, while generally good, is usually not perfect. These considerations are often less daunting to patients suffering from chronic ulcerative colitis, as many such patients are used to excessive stool frequency; but patients with chronic quiescent colitis undergoing surgery for dysplasia or chronicity must have a clear sense of what to expect postoperatively before choosing this option. Poorly motivated patients and patients with significant emotional and psychiatric disorders are poor candidates for restorative proctocolectomy.

A preoperative or intraoperative diagnosis of Crohn's disease is an absolute contraindication to restorative proctocolectomy. These patients have an unacceptably high complication rate and frequently go on to require pouch excision.[36,37] Hyman et al.[36] reviewed the Cleveland Clinic experience with 25 patients whose postoperative diagnosis was Crohn's disease. While patients with preoperative features suggestive of Crohn's disease did extremely poorly (1 of 9 with a functional pouch at the time of follow-up), patients without preoperative features of Crohn's disease enjoyed results similar to those of patients with typical ulcerative colitis. Patients with "indeterminate" colitis can also expect to do well following restorative proctocolectomy.[36,38]

Compromised anal sphincter function is another absolute contraindication to restorative proctocolectomy. Patients with poor continence preoperatively can be expected to have worse function postoperatively, due to the additional stress of an ileoanal anastomosis. Patients whose sphincter function is suspect (e.g., women who have had traumatic vaginal deliveries) should undergo preoperative anorectal physiologic assessment.

There are a number of relative contraindications to restorative proctocolectomy. Sphincter function deteriorates with age, and functional results are generally worse in patients above age 50.[39] Marked obesity makes the operation technically difficult and occasionally impossible, as a short mesentery may prevent the pouch from reaching the anus. Severe acute (e.g., fulminant colitis, toxic megacolon, shock) or chronic (malnutrition, especially in conjunction with high-dose immunosuppression) illness is not a contraindication to eventual ileal pouch-anal anastomosis, but these patients are best served by initial subtotal colectomy and Brooke ileostomy.

Pouch Physiology

Impaired continence following restorative proctocolectomy is most commonly related to diminished resting anal pressure caused by injury to the internal anal sphincter.[40] Keighley[41] showed that both soiling and impaired internal anal sphincter function were due to the anal retraction required for perineal mucosectomy; patients who underwent transabdominal mucosectomy had a low incidence of soiling, as well as intact resting anal pressures indicative of normal internal anal sphincter function. Preservation of resting anal tone and low rates of soiling are also demonstrable in patients who undergo stapled ileoanal anastomosis without mucosectomy versus those who have mucosectomy with sutured anastomosis.[42,43] Nocturnal leakage is related both to decreased resting anal pressure and to the lack of external sphincter contraction during rapid eye movement sleep.[44]

Anal and pouch sensation may also play a role in determining continence. The pouch's ability to sense filling does not differ from that of the normal rectum.[45] It is not surprising that sensation of the upper anal canal decreases following mucosectomy,[46] but while preservation of the anal transition zone maintains normal sensation, this does not result in a superior clinical result in terms of improved continence.[41] Ambulatory studies demonstrate decreased anal sampling following restorative proctocolectomy,[47] but this function may return with time, and some have correlated its return with improved function.

Stool frequency has been related to pouch capacity, compliance, and emptying efficiency.[48–51] However, increased compliance may simply be a reflection of pouch size,[52,53] and a large pouch that empties poorly is physiologically analogous to a smaller pouch that empties completely. Pouch activity is low until filling occurs, when strong contractile waves lead to evacuation.[47,54] The "threshold volume" for inducing these contractions correlates closely with stool frequency.[54] Twenty-four-hour stool output is also an important determinant of stool frequency,[50] and while small bowel motility is generally slowed following restorative proctocolectomy, abnormally rapid transit may be associated with excessive evacuation frequency.[55]

Technical Controversies in Pouch Construction

Pouch Design

The J pouch, initially described by Utsunomiya et al.,[56] has the advantage of technical simplicity and ease of construction with the linear cutting stapler. Catheterization is rarely if ever required for emptying. Potential disadvantages include its relatively small volume, occasional difficulty reaching the anus, and the need to fashion a side-to-end anastomosis.

S pouches are intermediate in size and do not lend themselves to stapling techniques. While obtaining adequate length can be a problem in any pouch procedure, the S pouch has an easier reach to the anus because its creation requires division of the ileocolic artery to allow the terminal ileum to swing downward into the pelvis.[57,58] Sutured anal end-to-end anastomosis is somewhat easier than the side-to-end anastomosis of the J or W pouch. As noted above, spontaneous evacuation of S pouches can be problematic if a long efferent limb (> 2 to 3 cm) is utilized.

The W pouch, first described by Nicholls and Lubowski,[59] was designed to increase the capacity of the J pouch without the need for an efferent spout. The technique requires construction of two adjacent J pouches, frequently offset to permit a better fit into the pelvic outlet. Most authors suture the pouch,[48,59,60] and the ability to reach the pelvis is similar to that of the J pouch.

Nicholls and Lubowski[59] found improved function in W versus J pouches in sequential series, and Sagar et al.[51] reported improved emptying efficiency and decreased evacuation frequency in W versus S pouches. In contrast, Keighley et al.[61] performed a randomized prospective trial of J versus W pouches and found similar functional results in both groups. However, operating time was almost 1 h longer in the W versus the J group. de Silva[62] compared patients with J, S, and W pouches in a nonrandomized series and found similar functional results in all groups (with the exception of impaired evacuation in the S-pouch group). These conflicting data demonstrate that, at present, no single pouch design has been proven superior to the others.

Rectal Mucosectomy

With the development of the double-staple technique for extended low coloproctostomy, several groups have advocated application of this method to ileal pouch construction.[10,42,63,64] Advocates of this approach argue that it is technically simpler than mucosectomy with handsewn anastomosis, that it leads to a more expeditious operation, and that functional results are improved because damaging anal retraction is avoided. Opponents of this view argue that leaving behind diseased mucosa at risk for symptomatic strip proctitis or late development of carcinoma is unacceptable in an operation initially conceived as "curative."

Several groups have demonstrated improved resting anal pressures following nonmucosectomy restorative proctocolectomy and have correlated these results with superior outcomes.[42,43,65] Upper anal sensation and the ability to discriminate flatus from stool are also better following nonmucosectomy anastomosis.[66] Wexner et al.[64] reported preserved resting and squeeze anal pressures 1 year following double-stapled ileal pouch-anal anastomosis, though the high-pressure zone was shortened due to transection of the proximal internal anal sphincter with stapled anastomosis. Diminished continence was seen only in patients who required transanal repair of anastomotic defects, though this maneuver was required in 3 of 11 patients reported. In contrast, Williams et al.[67] reported significant diminution of resting anal pressures following double-stapled ileal pouch anastomosis.

The extent of cancer risk by retaining a short cuff of anal mucosa remains a contentious issue. Rectal columnar mucosa can extend distally to the dentate line;[68] inflammation is frequently seen in mucosectomy specimens[69] and in the distal anastomotic rings of stapled pouch-anal anastomosis.[70] However, follow-up biopsies frequently show that resolution of colitis and symptomatic strip proctitis is rare following double-stapled anastomosis.[70] Dysplasia is variably reported in the distal anorectum, occurring in from 0[70,71] to 25 percent[69] of cases; one patient in the series of King et al.[69] had an occult adenocarcinoma of the anal canal. However, rectal mucosectomy is no panacea for this problem. Viable rectal mucosa can persist despite grossly complete mucosectomy,[72,73] and rare rectal carcinomas have been reported following restorative proctocolectomy with mucosectomy.[74,75] Indeed, rare carcinomas have even arisen in ileostomies in colitis patients following total proctocolectomy.[76–78]

Functional Results

Functional results of restorative proctocolectomy are depicted in Table 36-4. In most series, patients average four to six bowel movements during the daytime in addition to one or two evacuations at night. Continence is generally good to excellent but frequently imperfect: variable numbers of patients complain of minor soiling, difficulty controlling flatus, or the need to wear a pad. Despite generally favorable results, it must be emphasized that individual results can vary widely between patients, and virtually all large series include patients who are functional failures due to excessive stool frequency and/or poor stool control. While some bad results can be attributed to septic complications,[45] it has generally proved difficult to predict postoperative function based upon preoperative status.

Wexner et al.[79] reviewed the functional results of restorative proctocolectomy at the University of Minnesota in 1989, where 114 patients were available for follow-up with a minimum follow-up of 16 months and a mean follow-up of 5 years. Almost all patients in the series had undergone mucosectomy with sutured S pouch anastomosis. Nine patients (8 percent) required catheterization to empty their reservoirs. All of these patients were operated upon before 1983; since that time, the efferent spout length has been decreased to 2 to 3 cm and the incidence of catheterization has dropped to zero. Inability to evacuate J pouches is, as noted, rare. For example, Pemberton reported a 0 percent catheterization rate in 390 patients who underwent ileoanal J pouch anastomosis at the Mayo Clinic.[39]

Mean evacuation frequencies for various series of restorative proctocolectomy are depicted in Table 36-4. In our series, mean stool frequency is 5.4 ± 2.5 during the day and 1.5 ± 1.0 at night.[79] Evacuation frequency decreases modestly with time.[48,79–83] Most improvement occurs within the first 2 years following

Table 36-4
Functional Results of Ileal Pouch-Anal Anastomosis

Author/Year	*N*	*Type*	*Day evacuation*	*Nocturnal evacuation*	*24-h evacuation*
de Silva et al.,[62] 1991	88	J/S/W	4.4	0	4.4
Becker et al.,[82] 1985	40	J	5.9	0.5	6.4
Chausade et al.,[99] 1989	18	J	4.2	1.1	5.3
Everett,[60] 1989	60	W			3.8
Nicholls and Lubowski,[59] 1987	64	W			3.3
Harms et al.,[48] 1992	89[a]	W	4.6	0.3	4.9
Pemberton et al.,[39] 1987	390	J	6	1	7.0
Morgan et al.,[100] 1987	72	straight			8.3
Wexner et al.,[79] 1989	114	S	5.4	1.5	6.9

[a]Ulcerative colitis patients, results at 1 year.

ileostomy closure, after which evacuation frequency is relatively stable.[39,79]

There is unfortunately little uniformity in assessment of continence following restorative proctocolectomy. Eight-one percent of patients in the University of Minnesota series had good control of flatus, though most had difficulty differentiating gas from liquid and thus preferred to expel flatus on the toilet.[79] Continence was perfect or near perfect in 81 percent of patients during the day; this figure decreased to 76 percent at night. Minor spotting occurred in 39 percent of patients during the day and 57 percent of patients at night. Forty-five percent of patients usually or always wore a pad during the day and 68 percent did so at night. In the Mayo Clinic series, occasional nocturnal spotting occurred in 51 percent of patients and gross nocturnal incontinence occurred in 4 percent of patients 6 months following ileostomy closure; these figures decreased to 20 and 0 percent respectively after 4 years. Daytime continence remained stable over the same time period, with spotting occurring in 20 to 25 percent of patients. Level of continence was inversely correlated to stool frequency, and women were significantly more prone to spotting than were men.[39] Öresland et al.[81] also noted clear improvements in soiling and the need for a protective pad over the first 2 postoperative years.

Complications

Because restorative proctocolectomy is a technically challenging operation, its complication rate is relatively high. Common surgical complications include small bowel obstruction, pelvic sepsis, development of pouchitis, and pouch failure. Not surprisingly, morbidity rates tend to decrease with progressive experience with the operation.

Pouchitis is a clinical syndrome characterized by increased stool frequency, occasionally associated with bleeding, and endoscopic inflammatory changes of the pouch mucosa.[84] The etiology of pouchitis remains uncertain. One intriguing observation is the relative rarity of pouchitis in patients whose indication for surgery was familial adenomatous polyposis.[85] A second important observation is the frequent clinical response of patients to metronidazole therapy. While this finding suggests an anaerobic bacterial etiology, comparative microbiology studies have failed to demonstrate abnormal bacterial ecology in pouches affected with pouchitis versus controls.[86] However, it has been proposed that pouchitis could be mediated by bacterial deconjugation of bile acids, a mechanism that would explain the clinical response to antibiotics.[85] Pouchitis occurs in 7 to 42 percent of patients who undergo restorative proctocolectomy,[87] and its incidence increases with duration of follow-up.[79] The incidence of pouchitis in the University of Minnesota series is 31 percent.[37]

Initial treatment of pouchitis is oral metronidazole. Approximately one-half of patients in our series responded to this therapy. Antidiarrheals may be used for symptomatic relief. Second-line therapy of refractory pouchitis includes steroid or 5-ASA enemas, pouch irrigation, and occasionally oral steroids, sulfasalizine, or 5-ASA. Refractory pouchitis can eventually necessitate pouch excision. Rauh was able to divide pouchitis patients into two groups—those with relatively few episodes, who tended to respond to metronidazole therapy, and those with more frequent episodes, who required more aggressive medical treatment.[84] Strikingly, 50 percent of patients with refractory pouchitis had an underlying diagnosis of indeterminate colitis. It is likely that a number of these patients will eventually prove to have had Crohn's disease.

Pouch failure (requiring pouch excision or permanent diversion) has been reported in 0 to 10 percent of patients in large series.[37,39,48,80] Gemlo et al.[37] recently reviewed the University of Minnesota experience with pouch failure. Of 253 patients, 25 (10 percent) had pouch failure; causes include poor functional results (7), Crohn's disease (6), pelvic sepsis (5), and refractory pouchitis (4). Forty-six percent of patients with unsuspected Crohn's disease and 80 percent of patients who required abdominal exploration for pelvic sepsis experienced pouch failure. Median time to pouch failure was 15 months, with 44 percent of failures occurring within 1 year.

CHOICE OF OPERATION

Numerous quality-of-life studies have been performed to assess the outcomes of each of the operations discussed in this chapter. While some studies do document improved quality of life following Kock ileostomy versus Brooke ileostomy[88,89] and following restorative proctocolectomy versus Kock or Brooke ileostomies,[90] patient satisfaction tends to be high following any of these procedures.[91] McLeod et al.[91] found no difference in quality of life between patients undergoing different operations for ulcerative colitis and made three important observations: patients self-select the procedure they prefer, physical well-being is a major determinant of quality of life, and most patients are able to adapt well to their postoperative status regardless of operation. On the other hand, poor functional results—be it following Brooke ileostomy,[92] Kock pouch, or restorative proctocolectomy[93]—unquestionably affect quality of life in an adverse fashion. Regardless of the operation selected, a well-conceived and well-performed operation will optimize patient well-being and satisfaction.

No operation is ideal for all ulcerative colitis patients. The surgeon must therefore involve the patient in the selection of the procedure and individualize his or her recommendation for the patient's particular situation and lifestyle. While restorative proctocolectomy remains the first choice for most ulcerative colitis patients today, it is not universally applicable, and patients must understand the wide range of functional outcomes that may result following this operation. Restorative proctocolectomy in most instances requires two stages, its technical complexity leads to a relatively high complication rate, and it has unique late complications such as pouchitis. In addition, patients retain an as yet unknown cancer risk when the operation is performed without mucosectomy and thus require long-term proctoscopic surveillance. Accordingly, restorative proctocolectomy is a poor choice for patients who prefer to undergo a single definitive operation.

Despite its drawbacks, ileorectal anastomosis remains a good option for young patients with relative rectal sparing, as they can rapidly resume a normal lifestyle after a single operation and without risk to sexual function or the need for a stoma. It is our clinical impression that functional results, particularly nocturnal continence, are better following ileorectal anastomosis than ileal pouch-anal anastomosis. Patients who undergo this operation must understand that lifelong follow-up of the rectal remnant is mandatory and that conversion either to ileostomy or ileal pouch is often necessary later on. Despite dysplasia screening, development of rectal carcinoma remains a small but significant risk over the long term.

Because of the popularity of the ileal pouch, the Kock pouch has been relegated to a secondary role in ulcerative colitis surgery. Nonetheless, specific indications continue to exist that call for its occasional use. The procedure offers a continent alternative to patients who have poorly functioning or previously excised anal sphincters and for those in whom an ileal pouch-anal anastomosis is technically impossible. Rare patients prefer the predictable self-catheterization of the Kock pouch to the less predictable spontaneous evacuation of the ileoanal pouch.

Development of newer, continence-preserving procedures has not in the least relegated total proctocolectomy with Brooke ileostomy to a minor role in ulcerative colitis surgery. This operation remains the time-proven standard, applicable to any patient, that is simple, curative, and offers a predictable functional outcome. It remains an excellent first choice for elderly patients, patients with impaired sphincter function, and patients who desire a single operation with a low likelihood of late related problems.

REFERENCES

1. Collins RH, Geldman M, Fordtran JS: Colon cancer, dysplasia, and surveillance in patients with ulcerative colitis. *N Engl J Med* 316:1654–1658, 1987.
2. Hendriksen C, Kreiner S, Binder V: Long-term prognosis in ulcerative colitis—based on results from a regional patient group in the county of Copenhagen. *Gut* 26:158–163, 1985.
3. Katzka I, Brody RS, Morris E, et al: Assessment of colorectal cancer risk in patients with ulcerative colitis: Experience from a private practice. *Gastroenterology* 85:22–29, 1983.
4. Gilat T, Fireman Z, Grossman A: Colorectal cancer in patients with ulcerative colitis: A population study in Central Israel. *Gastroenterology* 84:870–877, 1988.
5. Prior P, Gyde SN, Macartney JC, et al: Cancer morbidity in ulcerative colitis. *Gut* 23:490–497, 1982.
6. Kewenter J, Ahlman H, Hulten L: Cancer risk in extensive ulcerative colitis. *Ann Surg* 188:824–828, 1978.
7. Morson BC, Pang LSC: Rectal biopsy as an aid to cancer control and ulcerative colitis. *Gut* 8:423–434, 1987.
8. Ritchie JK: Ulcerative colitis treated by ileostomy and excisional surgery. *Br J Surg* 59:345–351, 1972.
9. Phillips RKS, Ritchie JK, Hawley PR: Proctocolectomy and ileostomy for ulcerative colitis: The longer term story. *J R Soc Med* 82:386–387, 1989.
10. Heald RJ, Allen DR: Stapled ileo-anal anastomosis: A technique to avoid mucosal proctectomy in the ileal pouch operation. *Br J Surg* 73:571–572, 1986.
11. Keighley MRB, Kmiot W: Surgical options in ulcerative colitis: Role of ileo-anal anastomosis. *Aust NZ J Surg* 60:835–848, 1990.
12. Watts JMK, de Dombal FT, Goligher JC: Long-term complications and prognosis following major surgery for ulcerative colitis. *Br J Surg* 53:1014–1023, 1993.
13. Leicester RJ, Ritchie JK, Wadsworth J, et al: Sexual function and perineal wound healing after intersphincteric excision of the rectum for inflammatory bowel disease. *Dis Colon Rectum* 27:244–248, 1984.
14. Berry AR, Campos RD, Lee ECG: Perineal and pelvic morbidity following perimuscular excision of the rectum for inflammatory bowel disease. *Br J Surg* 73:675–677, 1986.
15. Corman ML, Veidenheimer MC, Coller JA: Impotence after proctectomy for inflammatory disease of the bowel. *Dis Colon Rectum* 21:418–419, 1978.
16. Metcalf AM, Dozois RR, Kelly KA: Sexual function in women after proctocolectomy. *Ann Surg* 204:624–627, 1986.
17. Aylett S: Three hundred cases of diffuse ulcerative colitis treated by total colectomy and ileo-rectal anastomosis. *Br Med J* 5494:1001–1005, 1966.
18. Parc R, Legrand M, Frileaux P, et al: Comparative clinical results of ileal-pouch anal anastomosis and ileorectal anastomosis in ulcerative colitis. *Hepatogastroenterology* 36:235–239, 1989.
19. Oakley JR, Jagelman DG, Fazio VW, et al: Complications and quality of life after ileorectal anastomosis for ulcerative colitis. *Am J Surg* 149:23–30, 1985.
20. Baker WNNW: The results of ileorectal anastomosis at St. Mark's Hospital from 1953 to 1968. *Gut* 11:235–239, 1970.
21. Grundfest SF, Fazio V, Weiss RA, et al: The risk of cancer following colectomy and ileorectal anastomosis for extensive mucosal ulcerative colitis. *Ann Surg* 193:9–14, 1981.
22. Johnson WR, McDermott FT, Pihl E, et al: Mucosal dysplasia: A major predictor of cancer following ileorectal anastomosis. *Dis Colon Rectum* 26:697–700, 1983.
23. Jagelman DG, Lewis CB, Rowe-Jones DC: Ileorectal anas-

tomosis: Appreciation by patients. *Br Med J* 1:756–757, 1969.

24. Newton CR, Baker WNW: Comparison of bowel function after ileorectal anastomosis for ulcerative colitis and colonic polyposis. *Gut* 16:785–791, 1975.
25. Parc R, Levy E, Frileux P, et al: Current results: Ileorectal anastomosis after total abdominal colectomy for ulcerative colitis, in Dozois RR (ed): *Alternatives to Conventional Ileostomy*. Chicago, Year Book Medical Publishers, 1985, pp 81–99.
26. Khubchandani IT, Sandfort MR, Rosen L, et al: Current status of ileorectal anastomosis for inflammatory bowel disease. *Dis Colon Rectum* 32:400–403, 1989.
27. Beckwith PS, Wolff BG, Frazee RC: Ileorectostomy in the older patient. *Dis Colon Rectum* 35:301–304, 1992.
28. Baker WNW, Glass RE, Ritchie JK, et al: Cancer of the rectum following colectomy and ileorectal anastomosis for ulcerative colitis. *Br J Surg* 65:862–868, 1978.
29. Kock NG: Intra-abdominal "reservoir" in patients with permanent ileostomy: Preliminary observations on a procedure resulting in fecal continence in five ileostomy patients. *Arch Surg* 99:223–231, 1969.
30. Hulton L: The continent ileostomy (Kock's pouch) versus the restorative proctocolectomy (pelvic pouch). *World J Surg* 9:952–959, 1985.
31. Kock NG, Brevinge H, Ojerskog B: Continent ileostomy. *Perspect Colon Rectal Surg* 2:71–84, 1989.
32. Vernava AM III, Goldberg SM: Is the Kock pouch still a viable option? *Int J Colorect Dis* 3:135–138, 1988.
33. Ravitch MM, Sabiston DC Jr: Anal ileostomy with preservation in patients requiring total colectomy for benign conditions. *Surg Gynecol Obstet* 84:1095–1099, 1947.
34. Ferrari BT, Fonkalsrud EW: Endorectal ileal pullthrough operation with ileal reservoir after total colectomy. *Am J Surg* 136:113–120, 1978.
35. Parks AG, Nicholls RJ: Proctocolectomy without ileostomy for ulcerative colitis. *Br Med J* 2(6130):85–88, 1978.
36. Hyman NH, Fazio VW, Tuckson WB, et al: Consequences of ileal pouch-anal anastomosis for Crohn's colitis. *Dis Colon Rectum* 34:653–657, 1991.
37. Gemlo BT, Wong WD, Rothenberger DA, et al: Ileal pouch-anal anastomosis: Patterns of failure. *Arch Surg* 127:784–787, 1992.
38. Pezim ME, Pemberton JH, Beart RW Jr, et al: Outcome of "indeterminant" colitis following ileal pouch–anal anastomosis. *Dis Colon Rectum* 32:653–658, 1989.
39. Pemberton JH, Kelly KA, Beart RW Jr, et al: Ileal pouch-anal anastomosis for chronic ulcerative colitis. *Ann Surg* 206:504–513, 1987.
40. Nasmyth DG, Johnston D, Godwin PGR, et al: Factors influencing bowel function after ileal pouch-anal anastomosis. *Br J Surg* 73:469–473, 1986.
41. Keighley MRB: Abdominal mucosectomy reduces the incidence of soiling and sphincter damage after restorative proctocolectomy and J-pouch. *Dis Colon Rectum* 30:386–390, 1987.
42. Johnston D, Holdsworth PJ, Nasmyth DG, et al: Preservation of the entire anal canal in conservative proctocolectomy for ulcerative colitis: A pilot study comparing end-to-end ileo-anal anastomosis without mucosal resection with mucosal proctectomy and endo-anal anastomosis. *Br J Surg* 74:940–944, 1987.
43. Lavery IC, Tuckson WB, Easley KA: Internal anal sphincter function after total abdominal colectomy and stapled ileal pouch-anal anastomosis without mucosal proctectomy. *Dis Colon Rectum* 32:950–953, 1989.
44. Smith LE, Orkin BA: Physiology of the ileoanal anastomosis. *Semin Colon Rectal Surg* 1:118–127, 1990.
45. Keighley MRB, Yoshioka K, Kmiot W, et al: Physiological parameters influencing function in restorative proctocolectomy and ileo-pouch-anal anastomosis. *Br J Surg* 75:997–1002, 1988.
46. Nilsson LO, Lock NG, Kylberg F, et al: Sexual adjustment in ileostomy patients before and after conversion to continent ileostomy. *Dis Colon Rectum* 24:287–290, 1981.
47. Miller R, Orrom WJ, Duthie G, et al: Ambulatory anorectal physiology in patients following restorative proctocolectomy for ulcerative colitis: Comparison with normal controls. *Br J Surg* 77:895–897, 1990.
48. Harms BA, Andersen AB, Starling JR: The W ileal reservoir: Long-term assessment after proctocolectomy for ulcerative colitis and familial polyposis. *Surgery* 112:638–648, 1992.
49. Nasmyth DG, Williams NS, Johnston D: Comparison of the function of triplicated and duplicated pelvic ileal reservoirs after mucosal proctectomy and ileo-anal anastomosis for ulcerative colitis and adenomatous polyposis. *Br J Surg* 73:361–366, 1986.
50. O'Connell PR, Pemberton JH, Brown ML, et al: Determinants of stool frequency after ileal pouch-anal anastomosis. *Am J Surg* 153:157–164, 1987.
51. Sagar PM, Holdsworth PJ, Johnston D: Correlation between laboratory findings and clinical outcome after restorative proctocolectomy: Serial studies in 20 patients with end-to-end pouch-anal anastomosis. *Br J Surg* 78:67–70, 1991.
52. Madoff RD, Orrom WJ, Rothenberger DA, et al: Rectal compliance: A critical reappraisal. *Int J Colorect Dis* 5:37–40, 1990.
53. Thayer ML, Madoff RD, Jacobs DM, et al: Comparative intrinsic and extrinsic compliance characteristics of S, J, and W ileoanal pouches. *Dis Colon Rectum* 34:404–408, 1991.
54. O'Connell PR, Stryker SJ, Metcalf AM, et al: Anal canal pressure and motility after ileoanal anastomosis. *Surg Gynecol Obstet* 166:47–54, 1988.
55. Soper NJ, Orkin BA, Kelly KA, et al: Gastrointestinal transit after proctocolectomy with ileal pouch-anal anastomosis or ileostomy. *J Surg Res* 46:300–305, 1989.
56. Utsunomiya J, Iwama T, Imajo M, et al: Total colectomy, mucosal proctectomy, and ileoanal anastomosis. *Dis Colon Rectum* 23:459–466, 1980.
57. Smith L, Friend WC, Medwell SJ: The superior mesenteric artery: The critical factor in the pouch pull-through procedure. *Dis Colon Rectum* 27:741–744, 1984.
58. Cherqui D, Valleur P, Perniceni T, et al: Inferior reach of ileal reservoir in ileoanal anastomosis: Experimental anatomic and angiographic study. *Dis Colon Rectum* 30:365–371, 1987.
59. Nicholls RJ, Lubowski DZ: Restorative proctocolectomy: The four loop (W) reservoir. *Br J Surg* 74:564–566, 1987.
60. Everett WG: Experience of restorative proctocolectomy with ileal reservoir. *Br J Surg* 76:77–81, 1989.
61. Keighley MRB, Yoshioka K, Kmiot W: Prospective randomized trial to compare the stapled double lumen pouch and the sutured quadruple pouch for restorative proctocolectomy. *Br J Surg* 75:1008–1011, 1988.
62. de Silva HJ, de Angelis CP, Soper N, et al: Clinical and functional outcome after restorative proctocolectomy. *Br J Surg* 78:1039–1044, 1991.
63. Kmiot WA, Keighley MRB: Totally stapled abdominal restorative proctocolectomy. *Br J Surg* 76:961–964, 1989.
64. Wexner SD, James K, Jagelman DG: The double-stapled ileal reservoir and ileoanal anastomosis: A prospective re-

view of sphincter function and clinical outcome. *Dis Colon Rectum* 34:487–494, 1991.

65. Tuckson W, Lavery I, Fazio V, et al: Manometric and functional comparison of ileal pouch anal anastomosis with and without anal manipulation. *Am J Surg* 161:90–96, 1991.
66. Holdsworth PJ, Johnston D: Anal sensation after restorative proctocolectomy for ulcerative colitis. *Br J Surg* 75:993–996, 1988.
67. Williams NS, Marzouk DEMM, Hallan RI, et al: Function after ileal pouch and stapled pouch-anal anastomosis for ulcerative colitis. *Br J Surg* 76:1168–1171, 1989.
68. Morson BC, Dawson MP: Normal anal region, in *Gastrointestinal Pathology*. Oxford, Blackwell Scientific Publications, 1979, pp 715–718.
69. King DW, Lubowski DZ, Cook TA: Anal canal mucosa in restorative proctocolectomy for ulcerative colitis. *Br J Surg* 76:970–972, 1989.
70. Schmitt SL, Wexner SD, Lucas FV, et al: Retained mucosa after double-stapled ileal reservoir and ileoanal anastomosis. *Dis Colon Rectum* 35:1051–1056, 1992.
71. Tsunoda A, Talbot IC, Nicholls RJ: Incidence of dysplasia in the anorectal mucosa in patients having restorative proctocolectomy. *Br J Surg* 77:506–508, 1990.
72. Heppell J, Weiland LH, Perrault J, et al: Fate of the rectal mucosa after rectal mucosectomy and ileoanal anastomosis. *Dis Colon Rectum* 26:768–771, 1983.
73. O'Connell PR, Pemberton JH, Weiland LH, et al: Does rectal mucosa regenerate after ileoanal anastomosis? *Dis Colon Rectum* 30:1–5, 1987.
74. Stern H, Walfisch S, Mullen B, et al: Cancer in an ileoanal reservoir: A new late complication? *Gut* 31:473–475, 1990.
75. Puthu D, Rajan N, Rao R, et al: Carcinoma of the rectal pouch following restorative proctocolectomy: Report of a case. *Dis Colon Rectum* 35:257–260, 1992.
76. Berman JJ, Ullah A: Colonic metaplasia of ileostomies: Biological significance for ulcerative colitis patients following total colectomy. *Am J Surg Pathol* 13:955–960, 1989.
77. Gadacz TR, McFadden DW, Gabrielson EW, et al: Adenocarcinoma of the ileostomy: The latent risk of cancer after colectomy for ulcerative colitis and familial polyposis. *Surgery* 107:698–703, 1990.
78. Vasilevsky C-A, Gordon PH: Adenocarcinoma arising at the ileocutaneous junction occurring after proctocolectomy for ulcerative colitis. *Br J Surg* 73:378, 1986.
79. Wexner SD, Jensen L, Rothenberger DA, et al: Long-term functional analysis of the ileoanal reservoir. *Dis Colon Rectum* 32:275–281, 1989.
80. Schoetz DJ Jr, Coller JA, Veidenheimer MC: Ileoanal reservoir for ulcerative colitis and familial polyposis. *Arch Surg* 121:404–409, 1986.
81. Öresland T, Fasth S, Nordgren S, et al: The clinical and functional outcome after restorative proctocolectomy: A prospective study in 100 patients. *Int J Colorect Dis* 4:50–56, 1989.
82. Becker JM, Hillard AE, Mann FA, et al: Functional assessment after colectomy, mucosal proctectomy, and endorectal ileoanal pull-through. *World J Surg* 9:598–605, 1985.
83. Cohen Z, McLeod RS, Stern H, et al: The pelvic pouch and ileoanal anastomosis procedure: Surgical technique and initial results. *Am J Surg* 150:601–607, 1985.
84. Rauh SM, Schoetz JRD, Roberts PL, et al: Pouchitis—Is it a wastebasket diagnosis? *Dis Colon Rectum* 34:685–689, 1991.
85. Madden MV, Farthing MJG, Nicholls RJ: Inflammation in ileal reservoirs: "Pouchitis." *Gut* 31:247–249, 1990.
86. Luukonen P, Valtonen V, Sivonen A, et al: Fecal bacteriology and reservoir ileitis in patients operated on for ulcerative colitis. *Dis Colon Rectum* 31:864–867, 1988.
87. Tytgat GN, van Deventer SJ: Pouchitis. *Int J Colorect Dis* 3:226–228, 1988.
88. Kock NG, Darle N, Kewenter J, et al: The quality of life after proctocolectomy and ileostomy: A study of patients with conventional ileostomies converted to continent ileostomies. *Dis Colon Rectum* 17:287–292, 1974.
89. McLeod RS, Fazio VW: Quality of life with the continent ileostomy. *World J Surg* 8:90–95, 1984.
90. Köhler LW, Pemberton JH, Zinsmeister AR, et al: Quality of life after proctocolectomy. A comparison of Brooke ileostomy, Kock pouch, and ileal pouch-anal anastomosis. *Gastroenterology* 101:679–684, 1991.
91. McLeod RS, Churchill DN, Lock AM, et al: Quality of life of patients with ulcerative colitis preoperatively and postoperatively. *Gastroenterology* 101:1307–1313, 1991.
92. McLeod RS, Lavery IC, Leatherman JR, et al: Factors affecting quality of life with a conventional ileostomy. *World J Surg* 10:474–480, 1986.
93. Fujita S, Kusunoki M, Shoji Y, et al: Quality of life after total proctocolectomy and ileal J-pouch–anal anastomosis. *Dis Colon Rectum* 35:1030–1039, 1992.
94. Hughes ESR, McDermott FT, Masterton JP: Ileorectal anastomosis for inflammatory bowel disease: 15-year follow-up. *Dis Colon Rectum* 22:399–400, 1979.
95. Farnell MB, van Heerden JA, Beart RW, et al: Rectal preservation in non-specific inflammatory disease of the colon. *Ann Surg* 192:249–253, 1980.
96. Johnson WR, Hughes ESR, McDermott FT, et al: The outcome of patients with ulcerative colitis managed by subtotal colectomy. *Surg Gynecol Obstet* 162:421–425, 1986.
97. Leijonmarck C-E, Löfberg R, Ost A, Hellers G: Long-term results of ileorectal anastomosis in ulcerative colitis in Stockholm County. *Dis Colon Rectum* 33:195–200, 1990.
98. Löfberg R, Leijonmarck C-E, Hellers G, et al: Mucosal dysplasia and DNA content in ulcerative colitis patients with ileorectal anastomosis: Follow-up study in a defined patient group. *Dis Colon Rectum* 34:566–571, 1991.
99. Chaussade S, Verduron A, Hautefeuille M, et al: Proctocolectomy and ileoanal pouch anastomosis without conservation of a rectal muscular cuff. *Br J Surg* 76(3): 273–275, 1989.
100. Morgan RA, Manning PB, Coran AG: Experience with straight endorectal pull-through for the management of ulcerative colitis and familial polyposis in children and adults. *Ann Surg* 206:595–599, 1987.

CHAPTER 37

Management and Follow-up of Patients with Familial Adenomatous Polyposis

Miguel A. Rodriguez-Bigas
Lucio Bertario
Lemuel Herrera

HIGHLIGHTS

The management of patients with familial adenomatous polyposis (FAP) relies mainly on prophylatic colorectal surgical resections. There is no "ideal" operation that abolishes the risk of cancer while preserving normal physiology with minimal morbidity and mortality. Surgical procedures can be significantly affected by the extent of associated phenotypical manifestations. Nonsurgical approaches rely on medications that diminish gastrointestinal mucosal proliferation; however, they are still in an experimental clinical phase.

CONTROVERSIES

Discussion exists as to what procedure to perform, at what age, by whom, and in whom.

FUTURE DIRECTIONS

Although the removal of the colon and rectum has significantly decreased the risk for colorectal cancer in patients with FAP, the procedure has not had a decisive effect on the overall mortality due to cancer; that is, many patients die from metastatic gastrointestinal adenocarcinomas or desmoids, indicating a failure to control a disseminated disorder with surgery alone. Research is being directed toward identification of the individuals who will develop carcinomas, the understanding of the biology of desmoid tumors, and the development of drugs that consistently and predictably diminish proliferation of the gastrointestinal mucosa.

Management of the patient with familial adenomatous polyposis (FAP) relies significantly on prophylactic surgery, because the risk of developing colorectal carcinoma is 100 percent in the patient with an intact colon or rectum that contains adenomatous polyps, and resection is the only therapeutic intervention known to alter the evolution of this disease. A number of surgical procedures have been described for this condition. They include segmental resections,[1] total proctocolectomy and ileostomy,[2] subtotal or total abdominal colectomy with ileorectal anastomosis,[3,4] and total colectomy, mucosal proctectomy, and ileoanal anastomosis.[5–8] These procedures can be performed alone or in combination with an array of limited ablative procedures aimed at preservation of continence and other physiologic functions. There is a debate over which of these procedures should be undertaken in the patient with FAP, for each has advantages and disadvantages. It is the goal of this chapter to underscore the factors that must be considered before one of these procedures is recommended, including the extent and distribution of polyps in the gastrointestinal tract, extracolonic manifestations of the disease, presence of carcinoma, social and psychological factors such as ability to handle a stoma, willingness of the patient to comply with lifelong follow-up, expected success of the procedure, and associated morbidity.

SEGMENTAL RESECTIONS

Segmental resections are seldom recommended, although they may play a role in patients with a form of FAP that involves multiple discontinuous segments of bowel, patients in whom there is an advanced metastatic tumor associated with a primary tumor causing obstruction or bleeding, or patients who represent a significant surgical risk.

TOTAL PROCTOCOLECTOMY AND ILEOSTOMY

In 1952, Brooke[9] reported the technique of immediate maturation of the ileal mucosa to the surrounding skin following total proctocolectomy. This procedure is still used in the management of selected patients with FAP, particularly those with a rectum carpeted with polyps. Other patients who may be candidates for this operation are those whose ileoanal reservoir has failed, patients older than age 50,[10] elderly patients with poor sphincter tone, and patients who will not comply with lifelong periodic proctoscopy. The advantages of this procedure include the elimination of all diseased mucosa and the fact that it need not be performed at a specialized center. Disadvantages include the presence of a permanent stoma, associated morbidity (up to 14 percent of patients require reoperation and up to 26 percent develop peristomal skin problems), potential for interference with bladder and sexual function, and the psychological effect that the procedure may have on the patient because of adjustment and acceptance of family members and society at large.[11–13]

Kock[14] described a "continent" ileostomy whereby a reservoir with reversed ileal segments was constructed. It evolved into the construction of a valve mechanism with an intussuscepted portion of small bowel. However, leakages between pouch intubations, problems with stoma nipples and the intussuscepted bowel that functions as a check valve, and the complexity of the procedure have deterred many surgeons from performing it.[15] Nevertheless, a small but definite number of patients do well for several years with this procedure. These patients are usually young, highly motivated, and interested in their care. Long-term observations have shown that in addition to other complications, there is the development of a syndrome characterized by lack of appetite, weight loss, and loose stools. This form of "pouchitis" may be managed by the use of a temporary proximal ileostomy.

SUBTOTAL OR TOTAL ABDOMINAL COLECTOMY AND ILEORECTAL ANASTOMOSIS

Originally described by Mayo and Wakefield[3] in 1936, this procedure involves the removal of the entire abdominal colon, with the anastomosis performed in the true rectum.[16] Abdominal colectomy with ileorectal anastomosis is still the most common procedure performed for FAP. A review of more than 960 patients by the Leeds Castle Polyposis Group and others revealed that it is still performed in approximately 55 percent of patients with FAP, with a mortality rate of 1.1 percent and a morbidity rate of 7.8 percent.[17] The ideal candidate for total colectomy and ileorectal anastomosis is the patient with FAP who has a few polyps or scattered polyps in the rectum amenable to local ablation and who will comply with lifelong periodic endoscopy. The advantages of this procedure include the avoidance of a stoma, relatively normal bowel movements, preservation of bladder and sexual function, and ease of examination of the remainder of the rectal mucosa. The main disadvantage of the procedure is the subsequent risk of developing a carcinoma in the rectal stump. A fourfold increase in the incidence of malignancy in the rectal stump has been reported if a malignancy was noted in the original colectomy specimen.[4] Bess et al.[18] reported an association between the number of rectal polyps present preoperatively and the development of rectal carcinoma as well as a correlation between the presence of cancer in the resected colon and subsequent development of rectal carcinoma.

The risk of carcinoma in the rectal stump has been reported to be as high as 59 percent at 23 years following colectomy and ileorectal anastomosis.[19] Bussey et al.,[20] at St. Mark's Hospital in London, reported a cumulative risk of rectal carcinoma of 13 percent at 25 years after colectomy and ileorectal anastomosis. Most recently, in a retrospective review of patients in 11 member registries who underwent colectomy and ileorectal anastomosis, the Leeds Castle Polyposis Group noted that 50 patients (3.7 percent) had developed an invasive carcinoma in the retained rectum on follow-up.[21] However, the cumulative incidence of rectal cancer was 13 percent at 25 years.[21] In contrast, Iwama et al.[22] reported a cumulative risk of developing carcinoma in the rectal stump of 13 and 37 percent at 10 and 20 years, respectively, in 320 patients undergoing total abdominal colectomy and ileorectal anastomosis (Table 37-1). Although the current policy at St. Mark's Hospital in London for flexible videoendoscopy at fixed 4-month intervals in all patients at risk

Table 37-1
Risk of Rectal Carcinoma after Total Abdominal Colectomy and Ileorectal Anastomosis

				Cumulative risk			
Authors	*Cancer/ patients*	*Follow-up, years*	*Anastomosis length, cm*	*10 years, percent*	*20 years, percent*	*25 years, percent*	*30 years, percent*
Bess et al.[18]	46/123	19.1[a]	19.5	13	26		55
Sarre et al.[23]	10/133	5.4[b]	NS	4	12		
Bussey et al.[20]	11/173	14.3[b]	15.2			13	
Iwama et al.[22]	105/320	NS[c]	10.3[d]	13	37		
Leeds Castle Polyposis Group[21]	50/1363	NS	14.3[e]				
Scandinavian study[21]	14/294	NS	NS	4.5	9.4	13.1	

[a]Median.

[b]Mean.

[c]Not stated.

[d]230 of 320 patients.

[e]40 of 50 patients with cancer.

over 45 years of age is a sound and conservative approach,[10] we recommend mandatory examination of the remainder of the rectum at least every 6 months and more frequently if dysplastic polyps are noted. Any polyps discovered in the rectal stump should be biopsied. A decision should be made to enter a patient in a protocol for dietary and/or nutritional supplementation with the aim of decreasing proliferation of the gastrointestinal mucosa; otherwise, the polyps should be removed and/or destroyed with either electrofulguration or laser therapy. We prefer the latter, as it elicits less cicatricial response and interference with a possible proctectomy. The use of laser contact tips offers distinct advantages over free fiber techniques in terms of possible morbidity and a better control of the energy delivered.

There have been reports of regression of rectal polyps after ileorectal anastomosis. Such "spontaneous" regression occurred in approximately 33 percent of the patients in the Cleveland Clinic experience.[23] The mechanism for this regression has not been elucidated, although some authors have implicated a decrease in secondary bile acid excretion in feces as a possible mechanism.[24,25] However, the polyps may recur, suggesting that other factors—such as genetic alterations or a decrease in short-chain fatty acids—influence redevelopment of polyps in the rectal stump.[25,26]

TOTAL ABDOMINAL COLECTOMY, MUCOSAL PROCTECTOMY, AND ILEOANAL ANASTOMOSIS

Despite several reports of this procedure after it was originally described in the 1940s, it was not until the late 1970s that it was added to the armamentarium of the surgeon managing patients with FAP.

Total abdominal colectomy and mucosal proctectomy with ileoanal anastomosis should be reserved for patients who have a large number of rectal polyps with no evidence of invasive carcinoma, those who develop a large number of polyps after ileorectal anastomosis, and those who desire to minimize the risk of rectal carcinoma.[11] Advantages of this procedure include the virtual elimination of colorectal mucosa, thus decreasing the risk of developing carcinoma in the rectum; avoidance of a permanent stoma; relatively good sphincter control, thus maintaining continence; and usually preservation of sexual function.[12] Ileal reservoirs of several shapes—including the J, S, and W pouches—have been described. The differences among them include the type of anastomosis performed between the pouch and the anal mucosa (end-to-end versus side-to-end) and the amount of small bowel used to create the double, triple, or quadruple reservoir.[6,7,27] These aspects have been discussed in a preceding chapter.

Complications associated with this procedure include wound problems, anastomotic breakdown, pelvic abscess, and early and late small bowel obstruction; the last may be triggered or compounded by the development of desmoid tumors. Functional problems such as fecal incontinence, sexual dysfunction, pouchitis, perianal skin excoriation, and stricturing of the ileoanal anastomosis can occur. Although some authors have reported performing ileoanal anastomosis without a temporary ileostomy,[6,28] the majority of surgeons undertaking this procedure will perform a temporary completely diverting (loop) ileostomy, which will be closed at a later time.

The morbidity of ileoanal anastomosis in patients with FAP is considerable. In a series of 37 patients with FAP who underwent ileoanal anastomosis at St. Mark's Hospital in London, the combined postoperative stay after total abdominal colectomy, mucosal proctectomy, and ileoanal anastomosis and ileostomy closure was 24 days, compared with 11 days after colectomy and ileorectal anastomosis.[29] The morbidity rate after ileoanal anastomosis, including closure of the ileostomy, was 60 percent, versus 21 percent after ileorectal anastomosis, with a risk of reoperation of 29 percent for the former and 3 percent for the latter.[29] One-third of the complications and reoperations after ileoanal anastomosis in that series were related to closure of the temporary ileostomy.[29] In contrast, in a series from the Mayo Clinic in which 94 patients with FAP underwent total colectomy, mucosal proctectomy, and ileoanal anastomosis, the morbidity rate was 28 percent, compared with 17 percent after total colectomy and ileorectal anastomosis.[30] This difference was not statistically significant. The rate of small bowel obstruction requiring reoperation was not different between the two procedures, being 5 percent for ileoanal anastomosis and 6 percent for ileorectal anastomosis.[30] Dayton et al.[31] reported a 16 percent complication rate with no major morbidity after total colectomy, mucosal proctectomy, and ileoanal anastomosis in 38 patients with FAP (Table 37-2).

Several factors can affect the quality of life after ileoanal anastomosis. Foremost is the frequency of daily stools. Nicholls and Pezim[34] postulated that the frequency of evacuation was inversely related to the capacity of the reservoir. In their series, they reported a mean capacity of 172 mL for a J pouch versus 325 mL for a W pouch, with a frequency of evacuation of 5.5 and 4.1 per 24 h, respectively. In a retrospective study of J pouch versus S pouch reservoirs, Tuckson and Fazio[35] reported a mean tolerated volume of 250 mL in the J pouch compared with 275 mL in the S pouch, with a significantly different compliance of 7.6 mL/mmHg in the J pouch compared with 14.1 mL/mmHg in the S pouch. Patients with the J pouch had a median of 6 bowel movements per 24 h, whereas those with the S pouch had 5 bowel movements per 24 h. Compliance was significantly different in patients with the W pouch, but this did not translate into a decrease in stool frequency.[36] Age has also been found to influence daytime stool frequency. Pemberton et al.[37] reported that older patients had more bowel movements than younger patients after ileoanal anastomosis. In patients with FAP who have undergone ileoanal anastomosis, the average daily stool frequency has varied from 3.4 ± 0.4 to 6.7, with nocturnal frequency varying from 0.2 to 1.2.[30,31,38]

Fecal spotting and incontinence after ileoanal anastomosis are other factors affecting quality of life. In 94 patients with FAP at 36 months follow-up, Dozois et al.[38] reported a daytime incidence of spotting and incontinence of 4 and 9 percent, respectively, while nighttime spotting was 26 percent and incontinence was 4 percent. Fecal incontinence after ileoanal anastomosis has been reported to improve with time.[31,33] Diet may affect bowel function after ileoanal anastomosis. Excessive fluid intake, fatty foods, and green vegetables have been associated with increased soiling and defecation.[39] In some patients, it may be necessary to utilize antidiarrheal and/or bulk-forming agents.

Sexual dysfunction (i.e., impotence, retrograde ejaculation, and dyspareunia) has been reported after ileoanal anastomosis. In the series of Dozois et al.,[38] the incidence was 4 percent. The incidence of pouchitis in FAP patients after ileoanal anastomosis has been noted to be 0 to 7 percent.[30–32,40] Although most investigators have questioned the existence of pouchitis in patients with FAP, expressing the view that this entity occurs only in patients with inflammatory bowel disease,[41] a form of pouchitis does seem to develop years after the procedure, as mentioned earlier.

Subjective satisfaction of patients with FAP after ileoanal anastomosis varies depending on the complications that affect their quality of life. It has been reported that 76 to 95 percent of patients are satisfied with the results after ileoanal anastomosis.[42,43]

Performing a total abdominal colectomy, mucosal proctectomy, and ileoanal anastomosis is complex and tedious. Several technical points in the construction and anastomosis of the reservoir need special atten-

Table 37-2
Complications after Total Colectomy, Mucosal Protectomy, and Ileoanal Anastomosis

Authors	*Patients*	*Type of pouch*	*Overall complication rate, percent*
Ambroze et al.[30]	94	J	28
Dayton et al.[31]	38	J	16
McMullen et al.[32]	25	S, J	28
Harms et al.[33]	19	W	10
Madden et al.[29]	69	NS	60[a]

[a]Combined complications with closure of temporary ileostomy.

tion. The reader is referred to the previous chapter for details.

Because of the complexity of the procedure as well as the multiple extracolonic manifestations of FAP, which may complicate its performance, we recommend that ileoanal anastomosis in patients with FAP be performed in specialized centers with special teams with interest in the care of this unique group of patients.

It can be appreciated that there is no simple answer as to which surgical procedure is better in the management of patients with FAP. Each patient should be approached individually, and factors such as age, extent of polyposis, extracolonic manifestations of the disease, presence or absence of carcinoma, morbidity associated with each procedure, and social factors as well as compliance should be carefully considered in the decision-making process. Compliance is of utmost importance, because these patients have a risk of developing not only carcinoma in the rectal stump after ileorectal anastomosis but also primary carcinoma in the ileostomy and in the ileoanal reservoir as well as in the remaining gastrointestinal tract, thyroid, brain, and adrenals; they are also at risk of developing desmoid tumors.[44–47]

The medical therapies comprise interesting approaches to the treatment of patients with FAP. Lipkin and Newmark[48] have reported on tests that permit the analysis of proliferative activity of gastrointestinal epithelial cells, such as the use of (^{3}H) d-thymidine-labeled epithelial cells to obtain morphometric measurements and indices per crypt and crypt compartments. Administration of oral calcium supplements produces a decrement in epithelial cell proliferation and induces the gastrointestinal mucosa into a quiescent state.[49] Sulindac, a nonsteroidal anti-inflammatory drug that produces significant gastritis, has been associated with the regression of polyps.[50] In a randomized, double-blind, placebo-controlled study of 22 patients with FAP, including 18 who had not undergone colectomy, Giardello et al.[51] demonstrated a statistically significant decrease in the mean number of polyps and their mean diameter in patients treated with sulindac. No patient had complete resolution of polyps; however, although both the number and size of the polyps increased when treatment was stopped, they remained at values lower than baseline.

Desmoid tumors are among the most challenging manifestations associated with FAP. They are slow-growing, locally invasive, benign fibrous tissue tumors with no metastasizing potential that originate in the musculoaponeurotic structures throughout the body.[52] Desmoid tumors occur in 3.5 to 38 percent of patients with FAP,[47,52–57] mainly in areas of previous surgery.[52,58] At the Roswell Park Cancer Institute, 20 of 24 patients with FAP developed desmoid tumors at a median of 38 months (range, 12 to 164 months) after abdominal surgery (19 colectomies, 1 hysterectomy).[57] In the majority of reports, desmoid tumors are more common in women than in men. Although estrogen has also been implicated in their growth rate,[58,59] as estrogen receptors can be found in these tumors, studies have not distinguished between desmoid tumors associated with FAP and those not associated with it. Although desmoid tumors may occur in the abdominal wall in patients with FAP, they will most frequently occur in the mesentery of the small bowel and extend into the retroperitoneum.[60] It must be stressed that desmoid tumors in patients with FAP behave differently than "sporadic" desmoid tumors, which are not associated with FAP, as the latter are seldom mesenteric or retroperitoneal and are amenable to surgical control if resected with 1- to 2-cm healthy margins. In FAP, these mesenteric desmoid tumors are often unresectable because of encroachment on the superior mesenteric vessels. Even if they are resected, the recurrence rate for mesenteric desmoid tumors is as high as 77 percent, and the major surgical morbidity rate is as high as 60 percent.[57,61,62] At the Roswell Park Cancer Institute, 6 patients who had exploratory surgery alone for mesenteric desmoid tumors are alive at a median of 118 months (range, 14 to 155 months) after their diagnosis;[57] 5 patients are alive with no evidence of disease after curative resections (3 patients had recurrent disease and underwent reresection) at a median follow-up of 198 months (range, 40 to 256 months); and 6 patients died with disease at a median of 26 months after their diagnosis (range, 3 to 129 months).

Multiple medical treatments have been used in an attempt to arrest the growth of these slow-growing tumors. These include nonsteroidal anti-inflammatory agents such as sulindac and indomethacin; hormonal manipulation with tamoxifen and toremifene, testolactone, megestrol, and corticosteroids; as well as chemotherapy and radiation therapy. Mixed results have been obtained with the medical treatment of desmoid tumors,[60] most of them disappointing. At present, our policy of management of intraabdominal desmoid tumors in patients with FAP is one of restraint with regard to surgical intervention except for small mesenteric desmoid tumors that can easily be resected. Surgical management is reserved for patients with desmoid tumors causing significant symptoms or complications. Surgical therapeutic interventions aim to relieve specific symptoms. In at least one patient, small bowel transplant has been tried as a possible alternative, but the patient did not survive long enough to be evaluated.

In summary, the management and follow-up of patients with FAP depend greatly on the type of procedure performed. Several options exist, but none fulfills the criteria for an "ideal" operation—one that would abolish the risk of cancer with minimal interference with physiologic functions and minimal morbidity and mortality. Because each procedure has advantages and disadvantages, there is a need for a highly individualized recommendation, which can be made only with the help of a team of individuals with an in-depth knowledge of the natural evolution of this fascinating disorder.

REFERENCES

1. Handford H: Disseminated polypi of the large intestine. *Trans Pathol Soc Lond* 41:133–137, 1890.
2. Hoxworth PI, Slaughter DP: Polyposis (adenomatosis) of the colon. *Surgery* 24:188–211, 1948.
3. Mayo CW, Wakefield EG: Disseminated polyposis of the colon: New surgical treatment in selected cases. *JAMA* 107:342–348, 1936.
4. Thomson JPS: Editorial comments, in Herrera L (ed): *Familial Adenomatous Polyposis*. New York, Liss, 1990, pp 207–208.
5. Ravitch MM, Sabiston DC Jr: Anal ileostomy with preservation of the sphincter: Proposed operation in patients requiring total colectomy for benign lesions. *Surg Gynecol Obstet* 84:1095–1099, 1947.
6. Parks AG, Nicholls RJ: Proctocolectomy without ileostomy for ulcerative colitis. *Br Med J* 2:85–88, 1978.
7. Utsunomiya J, Iwama T, Imajo M, et al: Total colectomy, mucosal proctectomy and ileoanal anastomosis. *Dis Colon Rectum* 23:459–466, 1980.
8. Ferrari BT, Fonkalsrud EW: Endorectal ileal pullthrough operation with ileal reservoir after total colectomy. *Am J Surg* 136:113–120, 1978.
9. Brooke BN: Management of ileostomy including its complications. *Lancet* 2:102–104, 1952.
10. Nugent KP, Phillips RKS: Rectal cancer risk in older patients with familial adenomatous polyposis and an ileorectal anastomosis: A cause for concern. *Br J Surg* 79:1204–1206, 1992.
11. Jagelman DG: Choice of operation in familial adenomatous polyposis. *World J Surg* 15:47–49, 1991.
12. Beart RW Jr, Welling DR: Surgical alternatives in the treatment of familial adenomatous polyposis, in Herrera L (ed): *Familial Adenomatous Polyposis*. New York, Liss, 1990, pp 199–208.
13. Roy PH, Sauer WG, Beahrs OH, Farrow GM: Experience with ileostomies: Evaluation of long-term rehabilitation in 497 patients. *Am J Surg* 119:77–86, 1970.
14. Kock NG: Intra-abdominal "reservoir" in patients with permanent ileostomy: Preliminary observations on a procedure resulting in fecal "continence" in five ileostomy patients. *Arch Surg* 99:223–231, 1969.
15. Sackier JM, Wood CB: Ulcerative colitis and polyposis coli: Surgical options. *Surg Clin North Am* 68:1319–1338, 1988.
16. Jagelman DG: Familial polyposis coli. *Surg Clin North Am* 63:117–128, 1983.
17. Herrera L: The article reviewed: Jagelman DG: Extra-colonic manifestations of familial adenomatous polyposis. *Oncology* 5:31–33, 1991.
18. Bess MA, Adson MA, Elveback LR, Moertel CG: Rectal cancer following colectomy for polyposis. *Arch Surg* 115:460–467, 1980.
19. Moertel CG, Hill JR, Adson MA: Surgical management of multiple polyposis: The problem of cancer in the retained bowel segment. *Arch Surg* 100:521–526, 1970.
20. Bussey HJR, Eyers AA, Ritchie SM, Thomson JPS: The rectum in adenomatous polyposis: The St. Mark's policy. *Br J Surg* 72(suppl):S29–S31, 1985.
21. DeCosse JJ, Bulow S, Neale K, et al: Rectal cancer risk in patients treated for familial adenomatous polyposis: The Leeds Castle Polyposis Group. *Br J Surg* 79:1372–1375, 1992.
22. Iwama T, Mishima Y, Utsunomiya J: The impact of familial adenomatous polyposis on the tumorigenesis and mortality at the several organs: Its rational treatment. *Ann Surg* 217:101–108, 1993.
23. Sarre RG, Jagelman DG, Beck GJ, et al: Colectomy with ileorectal anastomosis for familial adenomatous polyposis: The risk of rectal cancer. *Surgery* 101:20–26, 1987.
24. DeCosse JJ, Miller HH, Lesser ML: Effect of wheat fiber and vitamins C and E on rectal polyps in patients with familial adenomatous polyposis. *J Natl Cancer Inst* 81:1290–1297, 1989.
25. Cats A, Kleibeuker JH, Kuipers F, et al: Changes in rectal epithelial cell proliferation and intestinal bile acids after subtotal colectomy in familial adenomatous polyposis. *Cancer Res* 52:3552–3557, 1992.
26. Farmer KCR, Phillips RKS: Colectomy with ileorectal anastomosis lowers rectal mucosal cell proliferation in familial adenomatous polyposis. *Dis Colon Rectum* 36:167–171, 1993.
27. Harms BA, Hamilton JW, Yamamoto DT, Starling JR: Quadruple-loop (W) ileal pouch reconstruction after proctocolectomy: Analysis and functional results. *Surgery* 102:561–567, 1987.
28. Sugerman HJ, Newsome HH, DeCosta G, Zfass AM: Stapled ileoanal anastomosis for ulcerative colitis and familial polyposis without a temporary diverting ileostomy. *Ann Surg* 213:606–619, 1991.
29. Madden MV, Neale KF, Nicholls RJ, et al: Comparison of morbidity and function after colectomy with ileorectal anastomosis or restorative proctocolectomy for familial adenomatous polyposis. *Br J Surg* 78:789–792, 1991.
30. Ambroze WL Jr, Dozois RR, Pemberton JH, et al. Familial adenomatous polyposis: Results following ileal pouch-anal anastomosis and ileorectostomy. *Dis Colon Rectum* 35:12–15, 1992.
31. Dayton MT, Faught WE, Becker JM, Burt R: Superior results of ileoanal pull through (IAPT) in polyposis coli vs ulcerative colitis patients. *J Surg Res* 52:131–134, 1992.
32. McMullen K, Hicks TC, Ray JE, et al: Complications associated with ileal pouch-anal anastomosis. *World J Surg* 15:763–767, 1991.
33. Harms BA, Andersen AB, Starling JR: The W ileal reservoir: Long-term assessment after proctocolectomy for ulcerative colitis and familial polyposis. *Surgery* 112:638–648, 1992.
34. Nicholls RJ, Pezim ME: Restorative proctocolectomy with ileal reservoir for ulcerative colitis and familial polyposis: A comparison of three reservoir designs. *Br J Surg* 72:470–474, 1985.
35. Tuckson WB, Fazio VW: Functional comparison between double and triple ileal loop pouches. *Dis Colon Rectum* 34:17–21, 1991.
36. Harms BA, Pahl AC, Starling JR: Comparison of clinical and compliance characteristics between S and W ileal reservoirs. *Am J Surg* 159:34–40, 1990.
37. Pemberton JH, Kelly KA, Beart RW Jr, et al: Ileal pouch-anal anastomosis for chronic ulcerative colitis: Long-term results. *Ann Surg* 206:504–513, 1987.
38. Dozois RR, Kelly KA, Welling DR, et al: Ileal pouch-anal anastomosis: Comparison of results in familial adenomatous polyposis and chronic ulcerative colitis. *Ann Surg* 210:268–273, 1989.

39. Fujita S, Kusunoki M, Shoji Y, et al: Quality of life after total proctocolectomy and ileal J-pouch-anal anastomosis. *Dis Colon Rectum* 35:1030–1039, 1992.
40. Lohmuller JL, Pemberton JH, Dozois RR, et al: Pouchitis and extraintestinal manifestations of inflammatory bowel disease after ileal pouch-anal anastomosis. *Ann Surg* 211:622–629, 1990.
41. Shepherd NA, Jass JR, Duval I, et al: Restorative proctocolectomy with ileal reservoir: Pathological and histochemical study of mucosal biopsy specimens. *J Clin Pathol* 40:601–607, 1987.
42. Salemans JM, Nagengast FM, Lubbers EJ, Kuijpers JH: Postoperative and long-term results of ileal pouch-anal anastomosis for ulcerative colitis and familial polyposis coli. *Dig Dis Sci* 37:1882–1889, 1992.
43. Everett WG: Experience of restorative proctocolectomy with ileal reservoir. *Br J Surg* 76:77–81, 1989.
44. Gadacz TR, McFadden DW, Gabrielson EW, et al: Adenocarcinoma of the ileostomy: The latent risk of cancer after colectomy for ulcerative colitis and familial polyposis. *Surgery* 107:698–703, 1990.
45. Wiltz O, Hashmi HF, Schoetz DJ Jr, et al: Carcinoma and the ileal pouch-anal anastomosis. *Dis Colon Rectum* 34:805–809, 1991.
46. Starke J, Rodriguez-Bigas M, Marshall W, et al: Primary adenocarcinoma arising in an ileostomy. *Surgery,* 114:125–128, 1993.
47. Jagelman DG: Extra-colonic manifestations of familial adenomatous polyposis. *Oncology* 5:23–27, 1991.
48. Lipkin M, Newmark H: Application of intermediate biomarkers and the prevention of cancer of the large intestine. *Prog Clin Biol Res* 279:135–150, 1988.
49. Lipkin M, Friedman E, Winawer SJ, Newmark H: Colonic epithelial cell proliferation in responders and nonresponders to supplemental dietary calcium. *Cancer Res* 49:248–254, 1989.
50. Waddell WR, Ganser GF, Cerise EJ, Loughry RW: Sulindac for polyposis of the colon. *Am J Surg* 157:175–179, 1989.
51. Giardello FM, Hamilton SR, Krush AJ, et al: Treatment of colonic and rectal adenomas with sulindac in familial adenomatous polyposis. *N Engl J Med* 328:1313–1316, 1993.
52. Naylor EW, Gardner EJ, Richards RC: Desmoid tumors and mesenteric fibromatosis in Gardner's syndrome: Report of kindred 109. *Arch Surg* 114:1181–1185, 1979.
53. Smith WG: Desmoid tumors in familial multiple polyposis. *Proc Mayo Clin* 34:31–38, 1959.
54. Jones EL, Cornell WP: Gardner's syndrome: A review of the literature and report on a family. *Arch Surg* 92:287–300, 1966.
55. Shiffman MA. Familial multiple polyposis associated with soft-tissue and hard-tissue tumors. *JAMA* 179:514–522, 1962.
56. Sener SF, Miller HH, DeCosse JJ: The spectrum of polyposis. *Surg Gynecol Obstet* 159:525–532, 1984.
57. Rodriguez-Bigas MA, Mahoney MC, Karakousis CP, Petrelli NJ: Desmoid tumors in familial adenomatous polyposis (abstract), in *Proceedings of the Society of Surgical Oncology: 46th Annual Cancer Symposium*. Los Angeles, California, 1993, p 210.
58. Hayry P, Reitamo JJ, Totterman S, et al: The desmoid tumor: II. Analysis of factors possibly contributing to the etiology and growth behavior. *Am J Clin Pathol* 77:674–680, 1982.
59. Dahn I, Jonsson N, Lundh G: Desmoid tumours: A series of 33 cases. *Acta Chir Scand* 126:305–314, 1963.
60. Ramos R, Carrel A, Herrera L: Current treatment of desmoids in familial adenomatous polyposis patients, in Herrera L (ed): *Familial Adenomatous Polyposis*. New York, Liss, 1990, pp 133–146.
61. Easter DW, Halasz NA: Recent trends in the management of desmoid tumors: Summary of 19 cases and review of the literature. *Ann Surg* 210:765–769, 1989.
62. Jones IT, Jagelman DG, Fazio VW, et al: Desmoid tumors in familial polyposis coli. *Ann Surg* 204:94–97, 1986.

CHAPTER 38

Upper Gastrointestinal and Biliary Neoplasms in Patients with Familial Adenomatous Polyposis

Robert C. Kurtz

HIGHLIGHTS

Cancers of the upper gastrointestinal tract and abdominal desmoid tumors have replaced colorectal cancers as the life-threatening illnesses that patients with familial adenomatous polyposis (FAP) are now facing. This chapter reviews the prevalence of upper gastrointestinal polyps and cancer in FAP patients, the locations most affected, and present management and follow-up.

CONTROVERSIES

The whole topic of surveillance for the development of adenomatous upper gastrointestinal polyps and cancers is controversial. While it would seem prudent to recommend periodic endoscopic evaluation in these patients, there has never been a prospective study that demonstrates the effectiveness of endoscopic surveillance. As we continue to follow these patients, this issue should become clearer.

Another area of controversy is the management of patients with duodenal adenomatous polyps and severe dysplasia. What type of treatment, if any, should be used? Is there a role for non-steroidal drugs in these patients?

FUTURE DIRECTIONS

Prospective trials of nonsteroidal anti-inflammatory drugs will be done in an attempt to control not only rectal polyps but also those in the upper gastrointestinal tract. Better data allowing rational surveillance programs will become available and, it is hoped, controlled studies of the various modalities for management will be performed.

Upper gastrointestinal polyps and cancers have, for many years, been known to occur in FAP patients. Since prophylactic colectomy is now routinely performed when the diagnosis of polyposis is made, other phenotypic expressions of polyposis, including desmoid tumors and upper gastrointestinal neoplasia, have become the major management problems in these patients (Table 38-1).

In 1935, Cabot[1] first reported the occurrence of periampullary cancer in a polyposis patient. At a meeting of the Southern Surgical Association in 1947, Dr. Charles W. Mayo noted: "There is one point in the examination of multiple polyposis . . . that is too often neglected . . . in about 5% of the cases . . . there are also polyps in the stomach or small intestine . . . roentgenographic studies of these portions of the digestive tract should be included for complete examination in each case."[2] In 1953, when Gardner and Richards[3] first defined the syndrome of familial polyposis with extracolonic expressions of epidermoid

Table 38-1
Location of Neoplastic Upper GI Polyps and Cancers in FAP

Location	*Probability*
Duodenum	+ + + +
Ampulla	+ + +
Jejunum and ileum	+ +
Stomach	+ +
Bile duct	+
Pancreas	+
Esophagus	+/−

cysts, osteomas, and fibromas and later dental abnormalities and desmoid tumors,[4] they did not include upper gastrointestinal neoplasia.

Subsequently, other investigators have described the association of benign upper gastrointestinal polyps and cancer in polyposis patients. Polyps and cancers have been described in the duodenum and more distally in the jejunum and ileum as well as the bile duct and gallbladder.[5–7] In 1974, Utsunomiya[8] described multiple gastric polyps in polyposis patients. Endoscopic surveys of the prevalence of gastric and duodenal polyposis, stimulated by Japanese investigators, have only recently been reported. Populations with FAP in Japan,[8–10] Europe, and the United States[11–15] have been studied. Investigators report gastric polyp prevalence rates ranging from 39 to 100 percent and duodenal polyp prevalence rates ranging from 46 to 93 percent. Adenomatous changes have frequently been identified in pathologic evaluations of endoscopic biopsies of the ampulla of Vater. When they are looked for, polyps are often found in other small bowel sites. Utilizing the technique of push enteroscopy, Iida and colleagues[16] described their findings in 10 polyposis patients, of whom 8 had both duodenal and jejunal polyps, 1 had no polyps, and 1 had only jejunal polyps.

A prevalence study of upper gastrointestinal (UGI) neoplasia in this patient population was performed at Memorial Sloan-Kettering Cancer Center.[17] A total of 41 asymptomatic American FAP patients—representing 68 percent of a group of 62 patients in a chemoprevention trial—underwent upper gastrointestinal endoscopy. Of these 42 patients, 18 were found to have UGI polyps on endoscopy. Of the 10 patients who had duodenal polyps, 9 had biopsies performed, and 8 of these 9 had adenomatous duodenal polyps on histopathology. Gastric fundal polyps were seen in an additional 8 patients. These fundal polyps showed only hyperplastic changes on histopathology. No gastric adenomatous polyps were noted.

Other extracolonic expressions of polyposis were found in 11 of the 18 patients with UGI polyps (61 percent) and in 9 of 23 patients without UGI polyps (39 percent). These findings were suggestive of an association between UGI polyps and other extracolonic manifestations, but they were not statistically significant ($p = .14$).

Gastric polyps were concentrated in the fundus and body of the stomach. These polyps appeared as sessile nodules or mucosal excrescences and were very small, usually 2 to 3 mm in diameter. They were diffuse or in clusters and were always multiple. Duodenal polyps tended to be larger than the gastric polyps, were generally sessile, and were often extensively involved the second portion of the duodenum. In several patients, an enlarged ampulla was noted. The mucosa of the duodenal polyps was different from the surrounding mucosa, in contrast to the gastric polyps, where the mucosa was similar to that of the surrounding gastric mucosa (Figs. 38-1 and 38-2).

Gastric adenomatous polyps have been described in polyposis. When they occur, they are almost exclusively in the distal stomach and antrum. Gastric cancers have been described, mainly by the Japanese, to occur in the gastric antrum of polyposis patients.[18]

In one longitudinal study of individuals with polyposis, 18 of 20 Japanese patients found to have duodenal polyps were followed for a mean time of 7.1 years.[19] During this follow-up period, duodenal polyp number increased and decreased in only 4 patients, with no change in 13 patients. A 49-year-old patient was noted to have an advanced duodenal cancer, but on reviewing the previous studies, this was felt to have been overlooked earlier and not to have developed during the follow-up period.

Most investigators believe that, over time, some duodenal and ampullary adenomatous polyps become invasive cancers in a fashion similar to the polyp-cancer sequence in the colon. In those patients with polyposis who have undergone colectomy at St. Mark's Hospital over the last 40 or so years, periampullary cancer now represents the most common cause of death and exceeds colorectal cancer by almost a 2:1 ratio.[20] To further define the occurrence of UGI cancers in polyposis patients, the Leeds Castle polyposis group retrospectively reviewed 1255 FAP patients, representing 10 polyposis registries.[21] Invasive UGI cancers were noted in 57 patients (4.5 percent). The patients with cancer included 38 men and 19 women, with a mean age of 52 years. The majority of the cancers (37) were detected after identification and treatment of the colonic polyposis. Of the total, 39 cancers were in the second portion of the duodenum or in the periampullary region while 19 cancers were disseminated. Gastric cancer was seen in 7 patients. Bile duct obstruction occurred in 7 patients with ampullary cancer and 3 with duodenal cancer. In addition to stomach and duodenum, other cancer sites included jejunum, ileum, bile duct, and pancreas.

The Leeds Castle group emphasized that their data supported the adenoma-carcinoma sequence in the

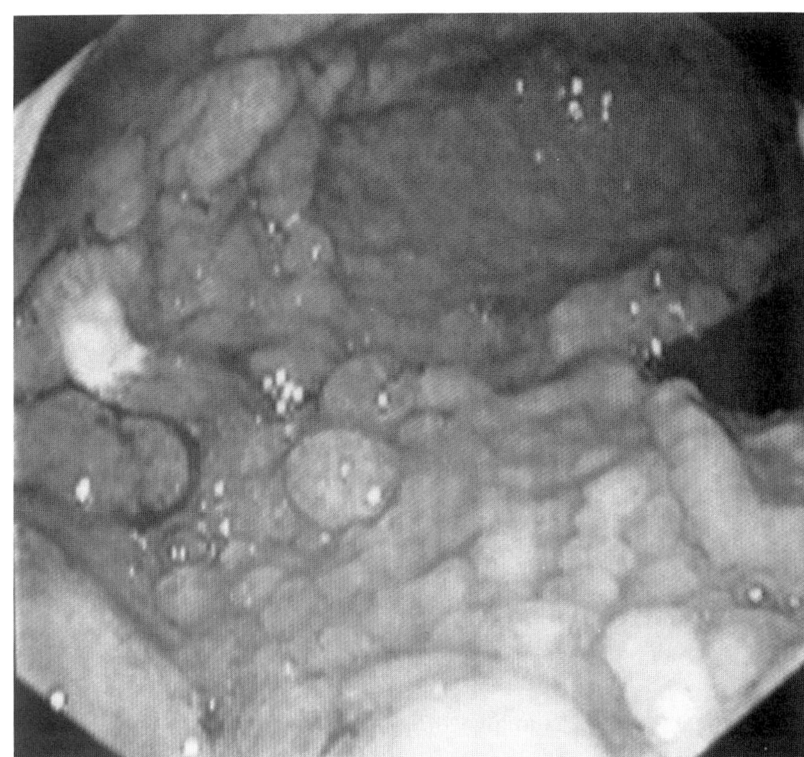

FIG. 38-1. An endoscopic photograph of gastric polyps in familial adenomatous polyposis. The endoscope is retroflexed looking back at the cardioesophageal junction. The cardia and fundus of the stomach are carpeted with small, sessile polyps which are hyperplastic on biopsy.

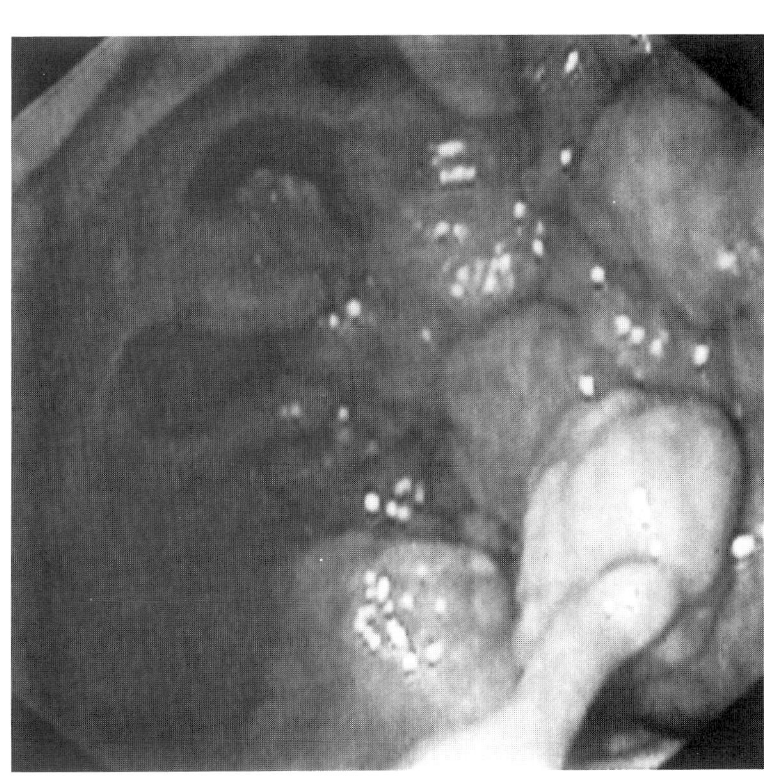

FIG. 38-2. An endoscopic photograph of the second portion of the duodenum in a patient with familial adenomatous polyposis. Multiple sessile polyps line the duodenum. In addition, large, pedunculated polyps can also be noted. Biopsy of the polyps revealed true adenomas. Endoscopic treatment of these polyps would be difficult if not impossible.

UGI tract in this patient population. Of note, since many of their patients had only recently been entered into their registries, they believed that the UGI cancer risk had been potentially underestimated.

Several groups have attempted to study factors that may be associated with the development or progression of UGI polyps in polyposis patients. The fact that the UGI cancers seem to be centered around the ampulla has led to speculation that bile may have a promoting effect. This has encouraged studies of bile and its content. Spigelman and associates[22] tested duodenal bile from post-colectomy polyposis patients for mutagenicity, using techniques that detect point mutations in bacteria. While the polyposis bile appeared to be more mutagenic than control bile, this result was believed to be due to a feeding effect. Another study by the same group looked at bile acid profiles in 29 polyposis patients before and after colectomy.[23] They found that the bile of polyposis patients had a higher bile acid concentration and a greater proportion of chenodeoxycholic acid than the bile of patients without polyposis.

A Danish group[24] examined the plasma concentration of epidermal growth factor (EGF), insulin, glucagon, adrenocorticotropic hormone (ACTH), gastrin, somatostatin, parathyroid hormone, prolactin, pancreatic polypeptide, neurotensin, vasoactive intestinal polypeptide (VIP), calcitonin, and secretin in polyposis patients with UGI polyps. All of the plasma concentrations for these regulatory peptides were normal. They then looked at the duodenal and polyp mucosa and found increased immunoreactivity to EGF in adenomatous tissue in 3 of 7 polyposis patients. The significance of this finding remains to be worked out.

MANAGEMENT AND FOLLOW-UP

While it seems clear that FAP patients with UGI polyps carry an increased risk for the development of invasive periampullary and duodenal cancer, the best methods of treatment remain to be established. Certainly, when invasive cancer is diagnosed endoscopically and there is no evidence for metastatic disease, surgery is indicated. Waiting for symptoms to develop may be waiting too long. A retrospective review of 14 polyposis patients was performed by Beckwith and associates[25] at the Mayo Clinic. Of 8 patients with symptoms, 6 had invasive UGI cancer; surgical procedures performed included local excision, pancreaticoduodenectomy, and palliative bypass. Of these 6 patients, 4 died, with a mean survival of 13 months after diagnosis. Of 6 asymptomatic patients found to have duodenal polyps on surveillance endoscopy, 4 were treated by endoscopic means. Another patient had a local surgical excision, and the sixth was found to have carcinoma in situ and had a pancreaticoduodenectomy. Of these asymptomatic patients, 5 were alive at a mean follow-up interval of 20 years.

Endoscopic management of the duodenal polyps with either laser therapy or snare-cautery is a potential alternative to surgery, but there is risk of perforation, and in many patients it may be impossible to safely destroy all of the polyps when the duodenum is carpeted, as it is in the most seriously affected patients.

In a French study reviewing endoscopic management of ampullary cancer and adenomas in nonpolyposis patients, 11 patients (9 with adenomas and 2 with adenomas and cancer) had endoscopic tumor destruction.[26] Snare resection in 3 patients was felt, by histologic examination, to be curative and remained so on follow-up examinations. Three patients who had a snare resection but were deemed not cured received follow-up photodynamic laser therapy (PDT). Of these 3 patients, 1 was found to have a recurrence of a villous adenoma at 24 months and required additional PDT. Five patients were treated with Nd:YAG laser coagulation after snare removal and were believed to be cured on follow-up examination. Argon laser was used alone in 3 patients but produced complete destruction of the tumor in only 1. Eight patients who were not surgical candidates received only laser therapy for their adenocarcinomas. Tumor destruction was incomplete in all of these patients.

Complications of endoscopic therapy occurred infrequently. One patient with an adenoma developed arterial hemorrhage after snare resection and required surgery. Laser therapy complications included mild pancreatitis and ulcerative duodenitis that healed with medical treatment. These data suggest that endoscopic treatment is feasible.

Sulindac, a nonsteroidal anti-inflammatory drug, has been shown to cause a reduction in size and number of polyps in the rectum and colon of polyposis patients.[27] It has also been shown to reduce the size and number of colonic polyps in polyposis and nonpolyposis patients.[28] Because of these reports, there has been a significant interest in trying this or a similar drug in patients with UGI polyps. Anecdotal results have, so far, been mixed, and a randomized, blinded, controlled trial needs to be done.

At present, endoscopic surveillance is the most important option available. Guidelines for surveillance and follow-up based on our current knowledge can be established. All patients diagnosed as having colonic involvement with polyposis should have an initial UGI endoscopy performed, with both forward and side-viewing endoscopes, prior to colectomy. If no UGI polyps are identified, follow-up endoscopic examinations should be performed at 3- to 5-year intervals. If duodenal polyps are identified and confirmed to be adenomas histopathologically, annual UGI endoscopy and biopsies, looking for dysplasia, should be performed. If severe or high-grade dysplasia is identified, the patient should be referred for surgical treatment with local excision. If the ampulla is involved or the duodenum is carpeted with polyps, the patient may have to undergo a pancreaticoduodenectomy. If there is evidence of invasive cancer, the more extensive surgical procedure should be considered. Endoscopic ablation techniques may also be considered, in skilled hands, for severe dysplasia if the polyps are not too numerous, if they are localized, and if the ampulla appears normal. Here again, there are no controlled, prospective studies that define the approach to the management of these patients. As such, these recommendations should be individualized based on the resources available and the skills of the physicians and surgeons involved.

REFERENCES

1. Cabot RC: Case records of the Massachusetts General Hospital. *N Engl J Med* 212:263–267, 1935.
2. Mayo CW: Discussion of a paper by Estes WL. *Ann Surg* 127:1055–1056, 1949.
3. Gardner EJ, Richards RC: Multiple cutaneous and subcutaneous lesions occurring simultaneously with hereditary polyposis and osteomatosis. *Am J Hum Genet* 5:139–147, 1953.
4. Gardner EJ: Follow-up study of a family group exhibiting dominant inheritance for a syndrome including intestinal polyps, osteomas, fibromas and epidermal cysts. *Am J Hum Genet* 14:376–390, 1962.
5. Hoffman DC, Gologher JC: Polyposis of the stomach and small intestine in association with familial polyposis coli. *Br J Surg* 58:126–128, 1971.
6. Ungar H: Familial carcinoma of the duodenum in adolescence. *Br J Cancer* 3:321–330, 1949.
7. Scully RE, Mark EJ, McNeely BU: Case records of the Massachusetts General Hospital. *N Engl J Med* 307:1566–1573, 1982.
8. Utsunomiya J, Maki T, Iwama T: Gastric lesions of familial polyposis coli. *Cancer* 34:745–754, 1974.
9. Ushio K, Sasagawa M, Doi H: Lesions associated with familial polyposis coli: Studies of lesions of the stomach, duodenum, bones and teeth. *Gastrointest Radiol* 1:67–80, 1976.
10. Watanabe H, Enjoji M, Yoo T: Gastric lesions in familial adenomatosis coli: Their incidence and histologic analysis. *Hum Pathol* 9:269–283, 1978.
11. Bulow S, Laurifsen KB, Johansen A: Gastroduodenal polyps in familial polyposis coli. *Dis Colon Rectum* 28:90–93, 1985.
12. Jarvinen H, Nyberg M, Peltoralleo P: Upper gastrointestinal tract polyps in familial adenomatosis coli. *Gut* 24:333–339, 1983.
13. Sivak MV, Jagelman DG: Upper gastrointestinal endoscopy in polyposis syndromes: Familial polyposis coli and Gardner's syndrome. *Gastrointest Endosc* 30:102–104, 1984.
14. Burt RW, Berenson MM, Lee RG: Upper gastrointestinal polyps in Gardner's syndrome. *Gastroenterology* 86:295–301, 1984.
15. Ranzi T, Castagnone D, Velio P: Gastric and duodenal polyps in familial polyposis coli. *Gut* 22:363–367, 1981.
16. Iida M, Matsui T, Itoh H, et al: The value of push-type jejunal endoscopy in familial adenomatosis coli/Gardner's syndrome: Upper gastrointestinal neoplasia in familial polyposis. *Am J Gastroenterol Dig Dis Sci* 32:459–465, 1987.
17. Kurtz RC, Sternberg SS, Miller HH, et al: Upper gastrointestinal neoplasia in familial polyposis. *Dig Dis Sci* 32:605–611, 1987.
18. Iida M, Yao T, Itoh H: Natural history of gastric adenomas in patients with familial adenomatosis coli/Gardner's syndrome. *Cancer* 61:605–611, 1988.
19. Iida M, Yao T, Itoh H: Natural history of duodenal lesions in Japanese patients with familial adenomatosis coli (Gardner's syndrome). *Gastroenterology* 96:1301–1306, 1989.
20. Spigelman AD, Phillips RKS: Polyposis follow-up and management of the rectum. *Ann R Coll Surg Engl* 71:269–277, 1989.
21. Jagelman DG, DeCosse JJ, Bussey HRJ: Upper gastrointestinal cancer in familial adenomatous polyposis. *Lancet* 1:1149–1151, 1988.
22. Spigelman AD, Crofton-Sleigh C, Venitt: Mutagenicity of bile and duodenal adenomas in familial adenomatous polyposis. *Br J Surg* 77:878–881, 1990.
23. Spigelman AD, Owen RW, Hill MJ: Biliary bile acid profiles in familial adenomatous polyposis. *Br J Surg* 78:321–325, 1991.
24. Olsen PS, Bulow S, Jorgensen PN: Gastrointestinal regulatory peptides in familial adenomatous polyposis. *Digestion* 46:228–232, 1990.
25. Beckwith PS, van Heerden JA, Dozois RR: Prognosis of symptomatic duodenal adenomas in familial adenomatous polyposis. *Arch Surg* 126:825–828, 1991.
26. Ponchon T, Berger F, Chavaillon A: Contribution of endoscopy to diagnosis and treatment of tumors of the ampulla of Vater. *Cancer* l64:161–167, 1989.
27. Giardiello F, Hamilton SR, Krush AJ, et al: Treatment of colonic and rectal adenomas with sulindac in familial adenomatous polyposis *N Engl J Med* 328:1313–1316, 1993.
28. Rigau J, Pique JM, Rubio E: Effects of long-term sulindac therapy on colonic polyposis. *Ann Intern Med* 115:952–954, 1991.

CHAPTER 39

Management of Villous Adenoma

Santhat Nivatvongs

HIGHLIGHTS

Villous adenoma is a premalignant neoplasm. A patient who is found to have a villous adenoma is categorized as belonging to a high-risk group and should have the index polyp removed as well as a complete colonic workup, especially colonoscopy. Villous adenoma is unique in that the size may vary from a few millimeters to so large that it occupies the entire circumferential surface of the colon or rectum. Soft rectal adenomas should not be biopsied prior to excision. Particularly in the rectum, a variety of techniques are available to remove the lesion. Surgeons must be adept and efficient in various surgical techniques in order to remove the lesion successfully while saving the rectum.

CONTROVERSIES

A villous adenoma should be removed regardless of size. How to remove it is a matter of the surgeon's familiarity with the techniques. Questions as to what to do often arise when the villous adenoma removed subsequently shows a focal area of invasive adenocarcinoma. Some authors believe that carcinoma arising from villous adenoma is more aggressive than usual and therefore calls for radical surgery. Others contend that the risk of lymph node metastasis in these lesions is not high so long as the invasion is limited to the submucosa and that a wide local excision should be adequate. The role of local excision followed by chemoradiation is not yet known.

FUTURE DIRECTIONS

Villous adenomas, particularly flat ones, can easily be missed on colonoscopy. It is possible to enhance their detection by using a dye spray which makes the lesion stand out with blue color. A large villous adenoma that cannot be removed transanally or via the colonoscope may be ideal for a laparoscopic colon and rectal resection. With the rapid improvement of techniques and equipment, laparoscopic surgery will undoubtedly be widely used—if not becoming a standard treatment for these lesions—in the near future. The advance in endoscopic ultrasonography to differentiate between benign and malignant lesions or staging of the malignant lesions will enhance case selection for local excision and laparoscopic procedures.

GENERAL CONSIDERATIONS

Adenomas are the most common neoplasms of the large bowel. They are classified into three types according to their histologic appearance—tubular, tubulovillous, and villous adenomas. Tubular adenomas account for 75 percent, villous adenomas, 10 percent, and tubulovillous adenomas 15 percent of all neoplastic polyps.[1]

Adenoma-carcinoma sequence has been well accepted as the process in the development of carcinoma of the colon and rectum. This hypothesis is based on the evidence that showed gradation from the adenoma with a microscopic focus of invasive adenocarcinoma to the obvious cancer with some residual benign tumor at the adjacent area. In the St. Mark's series, the malignancy rate of tubular adenomas is 5 percent, but it rises to 40 percent in villous adenomas. The rate of intermediate or tubulovillous type, 22 percent, suggests that the tumors behave more like villous than tubular adenomas.[2] As adenomas grow, there is an increasing tendency for them to adopt a villous type of structure. The malignant potential of adenomas has been calculated on the basis of their size and histologic type. Tubular adenomas smaller than 1 cm in diameter have a very low malignant potential, whereas small villous tumors, which are rare, have a 10 percent malignant rate. The intermediate histologic type, also rarely this size, has a malignant potential of about 4 percent.

At over 2 cm in diameter, the malignant potential is significantly greater for tumors with a villous component than for adenomatous polyps. One reason why villous tumors have a much greater cancer rate than the adenomatous type could be just that they are usually much larger. A study of the cytologic appearance of three histologic types of polyps emphasizes the importance of the degree of epithelial atypia and explains why even small villous tumors have a ten times greater malignant potential than adenomatous polyps of the same size.[3] It, thus, can be said that villous adenoma is a premalignant lesion.

MORPHOLOGY

Villous adenomas are most commonly found in the rectum, followed by the cecum. Most of them are flat and sessile, and they may occupy the entire circumference of the bowel, particularly in the rectum (Fig. 39-1). Pedunculated villous adenomas are much less common and are usually found in the sigmoid colon. Villous adenomas can be distinguished from tubular adenomas in that they are tan in color instead of reddish or purplish. They can also be recognized by their frondlike appearance. Flat villous adenomas can easily be missed on proctoscopy, flexible sigmoidoscopy, or colonoscopy because they usually are of the same color as the large bowel mucosa. By its nature, a villous adenoma is soft and difficult to palpate on abdominal exploration. Histologically, their long, frondlike appearance can be easily distinguished from that of the tubular adenoma (Fig. 39-2).

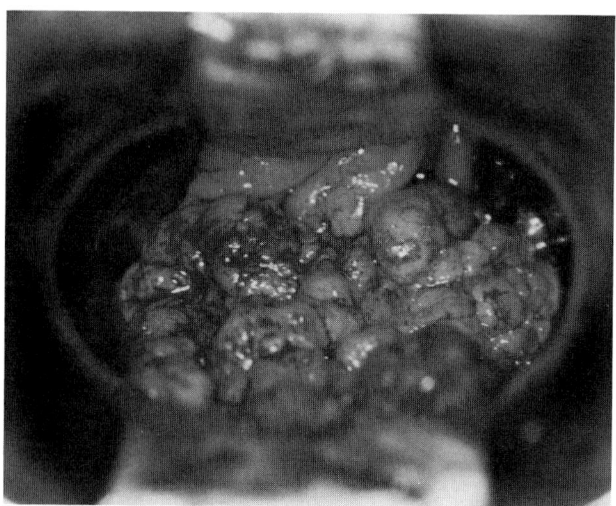

FIG. 39-1. A circumferential villous adenoma of the rectum.

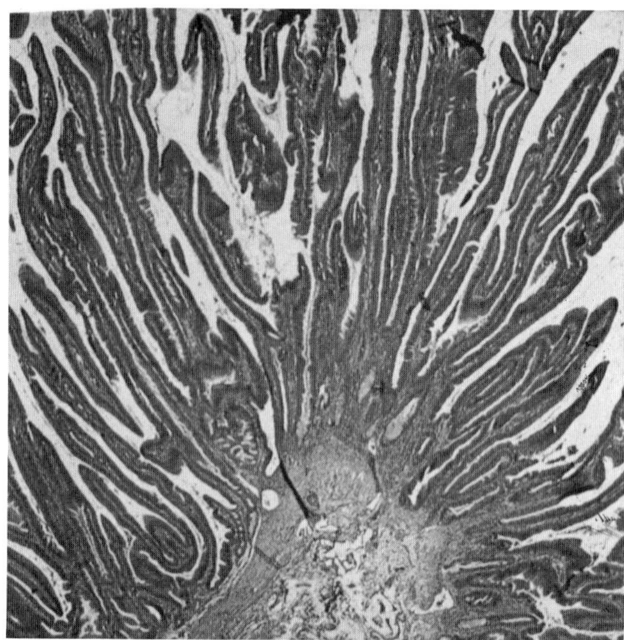

FIG. 39-2. Frondlike glands of villous adenoma on microscopy.

DIAGNOSIS

Like tubular adenomas, villous adenomas are usually found or detected on a routine large bowel workup with proctoscopy, flexible sigmoidoscopy, colonoscopy, or barium enema. Unless they are malignant, they do not cause bowel obstruction even if they are large except in circumstances when they cause intussusception. A large villous adenoma of the low or middle rectum is well known to cause water diarrhea—from its large amount of secretion—or the passage of mucus and blood. Hypokalemia from excessive loss of potassium is uncommon but has been reported. Occasionally, a large and bulky villous adenoma of the low and middle rectum prolapses through the anus; this must not be confused with a rectal prolapse.

WORKUP OF PATIENTS WITH VILLOUS ADENOMA OF THE LARGE BOWEL

A patient with villous adenoma found in the rectum requires a complete colonic examination to rule out a synchronous lesion. Ideally, a total colonoscopy should be done. An alternative is a proctoscopy or flexible sigmoidoscopy followed by a barium enema.

MANAGEMENT

It is important that the management of villous adenoma of the large bowel be individualized. This depends on the site, size, and shape of the lesion.

Induration is the single most important sign of malignancy. If the lesion is soft, regardless of size, it has a 90 percent chance of being benign.[4,5] The entire lesion should be excised in one piece or at least piecemeal for an adequate histopathologic examination. Preoperative biopsies are unreliable and have produced high false-positive and false-negative reports with regard to invasive carcinoma.[6,7] Biopsy also makes a subsequent per anal or snare excision more difficult. One-half to two-thirds of villous adenomas with cancer show only in situ changes, curable by local excision. A biopsy should be taken only if the lesion is indurated or ulcerated.

The bowel should be prepared with mechanical bowel preparation as for colon resection, including prophylactic antibiotics. However, antibiotics are usually not given for the lesions that are to be removed via the colonoscope.

Villous Adenoma of the Cecum and Other Parts of the Colon

A pedunculated villous adenoma with a stalk smaller than 1.5 cm can be snared in one piece (Fig. 39-3). Sessile villous adenomas 2 to 3 cm in size can be snared piecemeal. Villous adenomas larger than 1 cm in diameter that cannot be reached by colonoscopy and snaring should be removed via an exploratory celiotomy if there are no contraindications. A colotomy, polypectomy, or a colonic resection may be performed. Large sessile polyps (larger than 3 cm) in the cecum and right colon should be considered for colonic resection, since the risk of recurrence and complications from colonoscopic polypectomy, especially perforation and bleeding, are significant. However, a large sessile polyp (larger than 3 cm) in the rectum or sigmoid colon can usually be safely snared piecemeal.[8]

Villous Adenoma of the Upper Rectum (11 to 15 cm from the Anal Verge)

Most polyps up to 4 cm in diameter in the upper rectum can be snared piecemeal via a proctoscope or a colonoscope. A very large polyp calls for resection of the rectosigmoid colon.

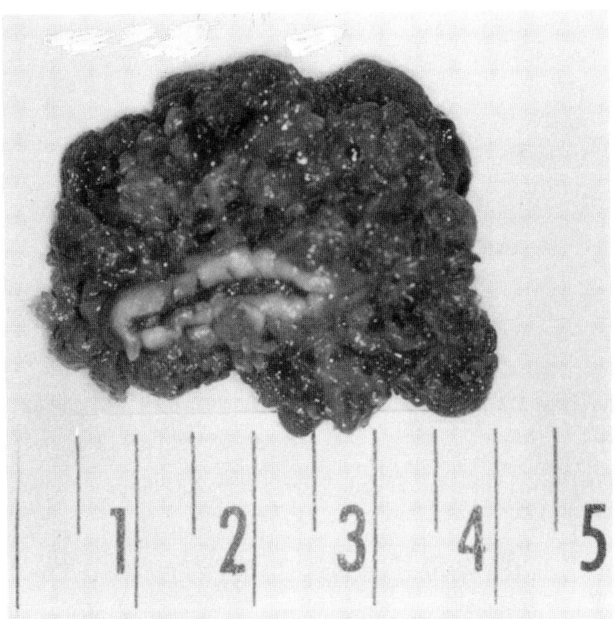

FIG. 39-3. A pedunculated villous adenoma.

Villous Adenoma of the Midrectum (7 to 11 cm from the Anal Verge)

Lesions at this level can usually be snared in one piece or piecemeal, depending on the size, via a proctoscope or a colonoscope. The mucosa around the base should be thoroughly electrocoagulated to minimize the risk of recurrence. Other methods are also available and should be carefully applied according to the site and size of the lesion.

Submucosal Pedicle Technique

Villous adenoma of the mid rectum in which the upper margin is at the 8- to 9-cm level can be excised through the anus, using a submucosal pedicle technique, if the lesion does not involve more than one-fourth of the circumference. This technique was originally described by Faivre.[9]

Technique. The anorectal mucosa and the anal canal are infiltrated with saline containing 1:200,000 epinephrine. A Fansler or a Pratt anal speculum is used to expose the anorectum. An elliptical excision is made with a scissors or an electrocautery blade starting at the dentate line. The mucosa and submucosa are dissected from their underlying muscle, creating a tongue of pedicle about 1 cm in width (Fig. 39-4). As the dissection is carried proximally, it is made to encompass the lesion with a normal margin of 7 to 10 mm until the upper margin has been reached and tran-

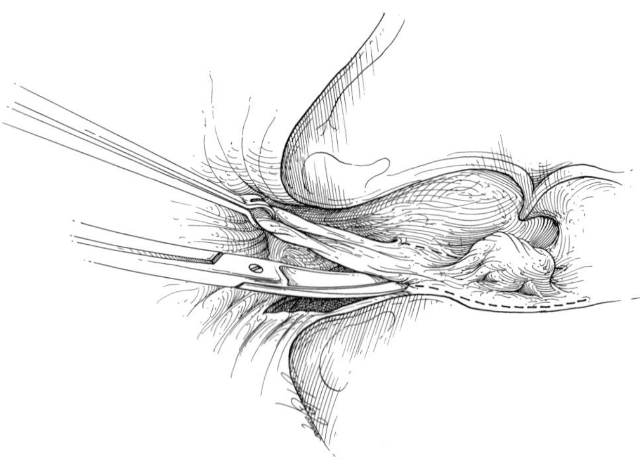

FIG. 39-4. Submucosal pedicle technique: An elliptical excision starts at the dentate line.

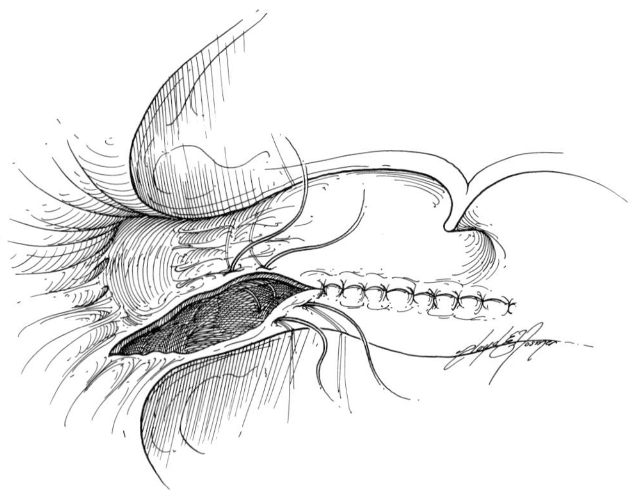

FIG. 39-6. Submucosal pedicle technique (continued): Closure of wound with running absorbable suture.

sected (Fig. 39-5). If the anorectal wall does not prolapse when the submucosal pedicle is pulled, a Sawyer or Hill Ferguson retractor should be used instead. The wound is closed with running 3-0 absorbable suture (Fig. 39-6), marsupialized, or left open. A diverting colostomy is not indicated.

Posterior Proctotomy Approach (Kraske's Approach)

A large villous adenoma of the midrectum may be impossible to excise via the anus unless the rectum can be prolapsed through the anus. This higher lesion, however, can be reached by opening the rectum posteriorly. Because of the potential for serious complications, the posterior approach to the rectum should be reserved for cases in which other alternatives are not suitable.

Technique. With Kraske's approach, the patient is placed in prone jackknife position. A midline incision is made from the sacrococcygeal joint to a point just proximal to the anus (Fig. 39-7*A*). The anococcygeal ligament is separated along the midline or detached from the coccyx, with removal of the coccyx to gain exposure. The incision is deepened to expose the levator ani muscle, which is incised in the midline to expose the posterior rectal wall (Fig. 39-7*B*). The rectum is opened through the posterior wall (Fig. 39-7*C*) and the polyp is excised submucosally (Fig. 39-7*D*). The defect is approximated using 4-0 absorbable suture. The posterior proctotomy wound is closed vertically or transversely with one layer absorbable 4-0 suture, depending on which method is easier to accomplish without compromising the lumen. The entire wound is irrigated with normal saline solution and a closed suction drain is placed. The muscles are closed in layers using 3-0 absorbable suture (Fig. 39-7*E*). The skin is closed with subcuticular 4-0 absorbable suture.

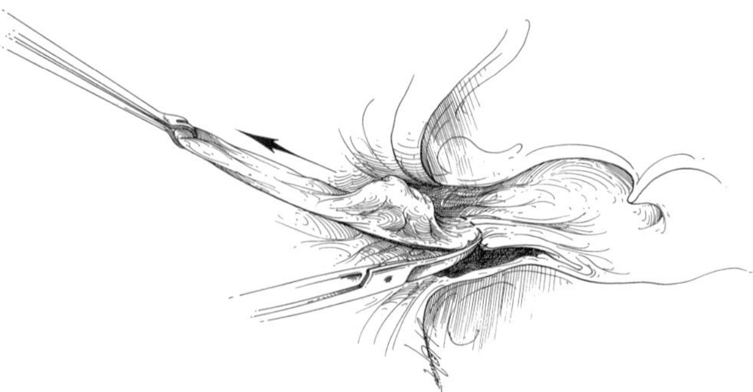

FIG. 39-5. Submucosal pedicle technique (continued): With traction to prolapse the submucosal pedicle, the lesion is completely excised.

Posterior Transsphincteric Approach (York-Mason's Approach)

The sphincter muscles, the pelvic floor muscles, and the anorectal wall are laid open posteriorly in order to provide better exposure of the interior of the rectum.

Technique. The patient is placed in prone jackknife position. A left parasacral incision is made from the middle sacrum, passing obliquely downward to the anal verge in the midline (Fig. 39-8*A*). The exposure can be widened by incising the lower part of the gluteus muscle. The incision is deepened to expose the external sphincteric complex and the levator ani muscles. They are divided along the lines of incision and the divided edges are tagged step by step. It is important to mark each layer and component of the muscles accurately with stay sutures to allow correct identification when reapproximating them (Fig. 39-8*B*). The nerve supply to these muscles lies lateral to the incision and is, therefore, safe from injury.

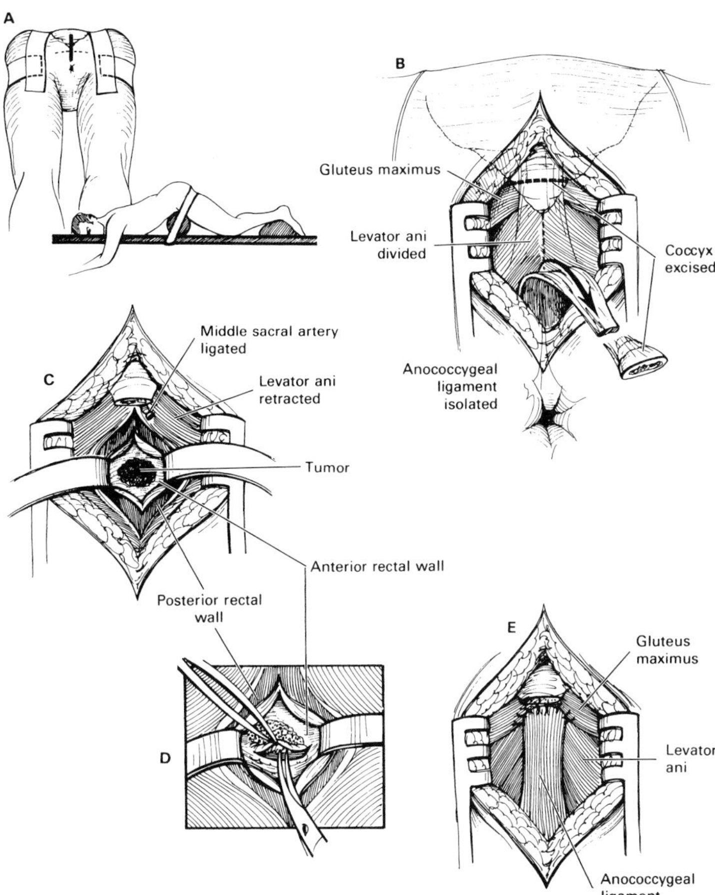

FIG. 39-7. Kraske's approach. *A*. Prone jackknife position and line of incision. *B*. Incision through external sphincter and levator ani muscle in midline or coccyx can be removed with detachment of the anococcygeal ligament. *C*. Incision of posterior rectal wall to expose interior of rectum. *D*. The lesion is excised submucosally. *E*. The wound is closed in layers. [From Goldberg SM, Gordon PH, Nivatvongs S (eds): *Essentials of Anorectal Surgery*. Philadelphia, Lippincott, 1980, p 242. Reproduced by permission.]

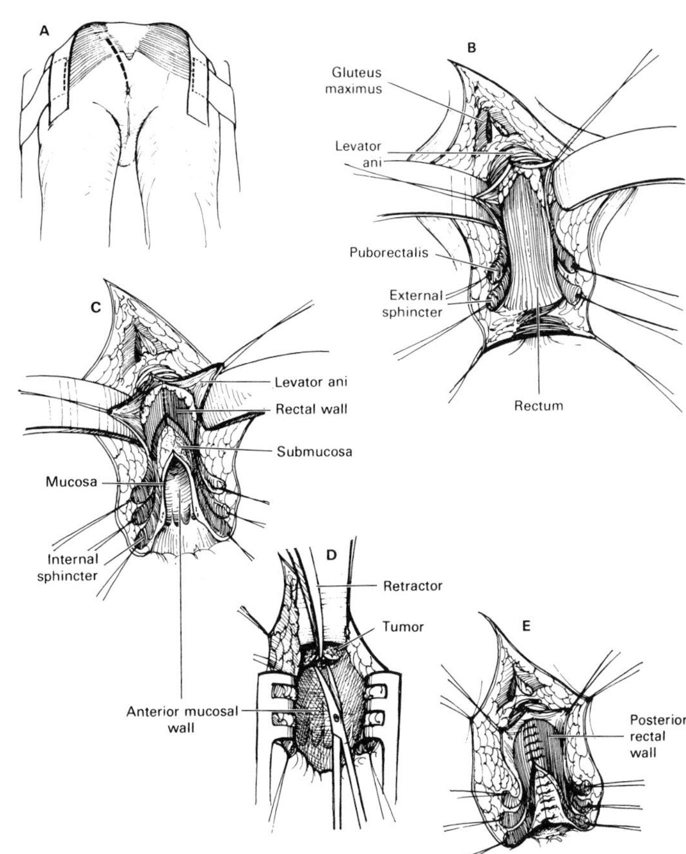

FIG. 39-8. York-Mason's approach. *A*. Prone jackknife position and line of incision. *B*. The incised sphincter muscles and levator ani muscles are individually marked with sutures for later accurate closure. *C*. Posterior rectal wall is incised to expose the interior anorectum. *D*. The lesion is excised submucosally. *E*. The wound is closed in layers. [From Goldberg SM, Gordon PH, Nivatvongs S (eds): *Essentials of Anorectal Surgery*. Philadelphia, Lippincott, 1980, p 243. Reproduced by permission.]

Next, the internal sphincter is divided with proximal extension to the thinner muscle wall of the rectum. The submucosa and the mucosa are incised to expose the interior of the rectum and the anal canal (Fig. 39-8*C*). The lesion is excised (Fig. 39-8*D*). The bowel is closed in layers. The mucosa and submucosa are closed with running or interrupted 4-0 absorbable suture; the internal sphincter is closed with interrupted or running 3-0 absorbable suture (Fig. 39-8*E*). The external sphincter and the puborectalis and levator ani muscles are closed with 3-0 absorbable suture. A suction drain is placed in the subcutaneous space and the skin is closed with subcuticular suture of 4-0 absorbable suture. York-Mason's approach is used more widely than Kraske's approach because of its superior exposure. Although the sphincteric muscle is cut during the procedure, anal incontinence has not been a problem.

Circumferential Villous Adenoma of the Rectum

A circumferential villous adenoma with the lower margin in the lower rectum can be removed even if the proximal margin extends to the upper rectum. Although Parks and Stuart[10] removed it in three to four longitudinal strips, this type of lesion can be removed in one piece as a submucosal tube. A smaller villous adenoma at this level can be excised in one piece using electrocautery.

Technique. Using the Pratt anal speculum or Parks's retractor to expose the anorectum, a circumferential incision is made around the dentate line in the submucosal plane with an electrocautery blade. Diluted epinephrine may be injected to raise the submucosal plane. The anal speculum or Parks's retractor is then replaced by Gelpi retractors positioned at a right angle to each other at the dentate line; better yet is a Lone Star self-retaining retractor. The submucosal dissection is carried as far proximally as needed. The circumferential dissection of the submucosa apparently allows the rectum to prolapse during traction.

After the entire adenoma has been dissected from the underlying anorectal wall, the proximal cut end of the mucosa and submucosa can be brought down along with the denuded muscle wall to approximate circumferentially with the lower cut end at the dentate line (Fig. 39-9*A*). At completion, the anorectal wall will be imbricated in the longitudinal plane (Fig. 39-9*B*). Incontinence of gas and liquid stool may last for a few weeks.

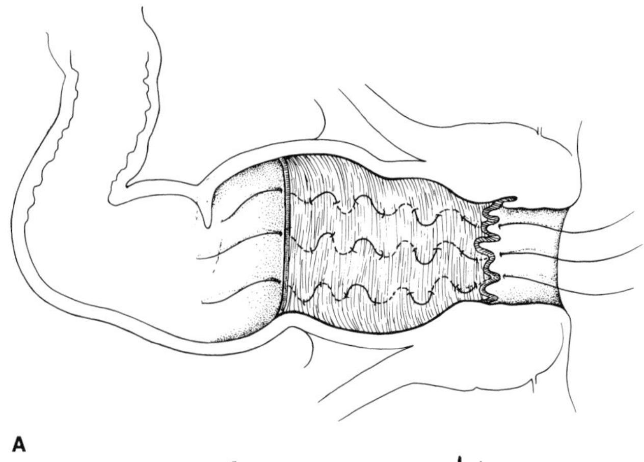

A

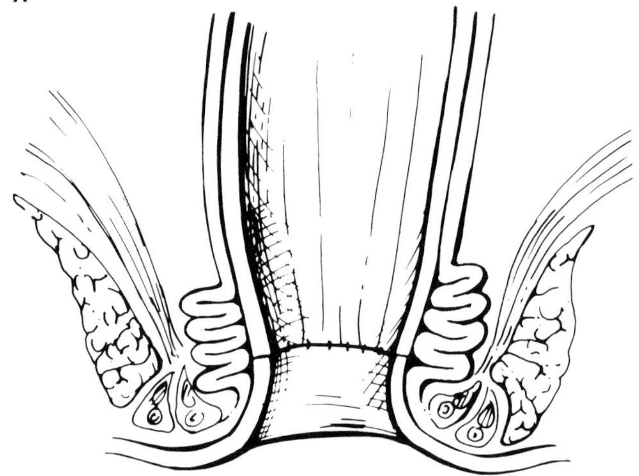

B

FIG. 39-9. Excision of circumferential villous adenoma. *A*. A circumferential submucosal sleeve dissection starts from the dentate line to above the proximal margin. The proximal cut end is brought down along with the denuded muscular wall to approximate with the dentate line, using absorbable sutures. *B*. At completion, the anorectal wall is pleated.

REFERENCES

1. Morson BC: The polyp-cancer sequence in the large bowel. *Proc R Soc Med* 67:451–457, 1974.
2. Muto T, Bussey HJR, Morson BC: The evolution of cancer of the colon and rectum. *Cancer* 36:2251–2270, 1975.
3. Morson BC: Polyps and cancer of the large bowel, in Yardley JH, Morson BC, Abell MR (eds): *The Gastrointestinal Tract*. Baltimore, Williams & Wilkins, 1977, pp 101–108.
4. Nivatvongs S, Nicholson JD, Rothenberger DA, et al: Villous adenomas of the rectum: The accuracy of clinical assessment. *Surgery* 87:549–551, 1980.
5. Galandiuk S, Fazio VW, Jagelman DG, et al: Villous and tubulovillous adenomas of the colon and rectum: A retrospective review, 1964–1985. *Am J Surg* 153:41–47, 1987.
6. Taylor EW, Thompson H, Oates GD, et al: Limitations of biopsy in reoperative assessment of villous papilloma. *Dis Colon Rectum* 24:259–262, 1981.
7. Roge MMP: Surgical management of villous tumors of the colon and rectum. *Dig Surg* 1:168–171, 1984.
8. Nivatvongs S, Snover DC, Fang DT: Piecemeal snare excision of large sessile colon and rectal polyps: Is it adequate? *Gastrointest Endosc* 30:18–20, 1984.
9. Faivre J: Transanal electroresection of rectal tumor by means of tractable mucocutaneous anal flap. *Coloproctology* 2:77–80, 1980.
10. Parks AG, Stuart AE: The management of villous tumors of the large bowel. *Br J Surg* 9:688–695, 1973.

PART 7

Treatment of Colorectal Cancer

CHAPTER 40

Overview of Colorectal Cancer Treatment

Alfred M. Cohen

Treatment of patients with colorectal cancer varies from a simple endoscopic polypectomy alone or fairly straightforward surgical procedures to complex, expensive multidisciplinary strategies accompanied by high morbidity. The next sections will focus on the management of patients with potentially curable colorectal cancer. We will start with a discourse on clinical trials, focusing on the many caveats in the interpretation of such studies. This is followed by a series of chapters devoted to surgical considerations. These chapters provide more than just technical detail. An analysis of preoperative evaluation practice parameters is provided. After three chapters on surgical technique, we provide the reader with important information relevant to managing patients with cancer within adenomatous polyps as well as patients with Lynch syndromes and synchronous large bowel cancers. Last, we address the issue of the potential value of prophylactic oophorectomy in women with primary colorectal cancer.

Although many of the same biological and therapeutic considerations apply to all cancers of the large bowel, several important management distinctions warrant dividing our discussion of treatment into separate sections on colonic and rectal cancer. The rectum is generally considered to be 15 cm in length. In their reports, some groups have limited their experience in the treatment of rectal cancer to patients with tumors below the level of 11 cm; others have included tumors up to 18 cm of the rectosigmoid. The distinction is not related to distance or the presence of the tumor involving the bowel in the pelvis. The major issue involves differences in surgical technique and the subsequent risks of pelvic recurrence. Under these circumstances, rectal cancer is defined as that in which *the lower edge of the tumor is at or below the peritoneal reflection*. When *tumors involve the pelvic colon or rectosigmoid,* patients should be considered to have colonic cancer.

Clinical trials of adjuvant chemotherapy initially included patients with both colonic and rectal cancer. Only a single trial of adjuvant single-agent 5-fluorouracil (5-FU) reported the rectal cancer patients separately. Hence, it was many years later that the benefit of adjuvant chemotherapy was demonstrated in rectal cancer patients.

Systemic adjuvant chemotherapy for patients with node-positive colonic cancer improves disease-free and likely overall survival. Ongoing trials are assessing the most effective modulator of 5-FU. However, there has not been a large enough trial of 5-FU alone to rule out significant benefit of high-dose therapy with just this single agent.

Because of several negative trials indicating no reduction in subsequent hepatic metastases, there is little interest in the United States in portal vein chemotherapy programs, although such is not the case in the United Kingdom and Europe. However, there has not been a trial utilizing intensive multicycle portal vein chemotherapy. All such reported programs utilized treatment durations of only 1 week to 2 months. Last, there have not been any trials combining systemic and portal vein chemotherapy. The identification of relevant biological-pathologic determinants of high-risk node-negative patients who may benefit from adjuvant chemotherapy remains a challenge.

The influence of surgical technique on the management of patients with rectal cancer has not been addressed in randomized clinical trials. Control groups in adjuvant chemoradiation trials and historical controls indicate local failure rates of 20 to 45 percent in node-positive rectal cancer and 15 to 30 percent in transmural node-negative patients. However, a few nonrandomized reports from centers focusing on surgical technique to maximize the lateral (peripheral or tangential) margins report local failure rates of 10 percent or less with surgical resection alone.

Although clinical trials confirm the efficacy of preoperative radiation or postoperative chemoradiation in reducing local recurrence, there remains a possibility that a more effective technical operation could replace adjuvant radiation in selected patients. More adept technical procedures can minimize the need for permanent colostomy, which is often accompanied by sexual and urinary dysfunction.

There is a concern that adjuvant radiation or more radical pelvic surgery for patients with rectal cancer may not be a useful strategy because *overall* survival may not be increased. This concern does not adequately consider the catastrophic symptomatic consequences of pelvic recurrence. One-quarter of patients who die from rectal cancer have isolated pelvic recurrence at autopsy, and three-quarters of all rectal cancer deaths have pelvic recurrence. Since such recurrences frequently lead to severe pain, any strategy that minimizes this consequence, as long as it does not *reduce* overall survival, is to be encouraged. Long-term adverse effects of sophisticated contemporary adjuvant pelvic radiation are small.

A current Intergroup trial comparing preoperative versus postoperative radiation-surgery sequencing is addressing not only local control and survival issues but also early and late toxicity related to the entire multidisciplinary program. The impact of adjuvant radiation on bowel function in patients undergoing sphincter-saving surgery is as yet undefined.

There are a large number of surgical options in the management of patients with rectal cancer. A small subset of patients with "early" cancer can be cured with "localregional" or conservative approaches. These strategies include local excision, fulguration, laser therapy, cryosurgery, transanal microsurgery, and several radiation therapy treatments. Such approaches had been developed for use in patients in poor medical condition, where radical en bloc resection of the rectum was precluded. Currently such approaches are also recommended in younger, healthier, *highly selected* patients. Clinicopathologic criteria allow a rational selection process, but biological determinants of a nonmetastatizing phenotype will allow more appropriate utilization of these approaches.

CHAPTER 41

Statistical Considerations in the Interpretation of Clinical Trials

Colin B. Begg

HIGHLIGHTS

Medical journals are dominated by scientific reports of clinical research studies. Specialists should have the ability to critically evaluate articles on an individual basis, and this requires some familiarity with important methodologic concepts. Prominent among these are the distinction between experimental and observational studies, the need for control groups to serve as a benchmark for evaluating new treatments, and the importance of randomization for unbiased evaluation of new treatments. The credibility of the evidence in an article is determined by the nature of the design and conduct of the study in addition to the quantitative statistical evidence from the analysis.

CONTROVERSIES

Few experts would contest the methodologic principles described in this article. However, there is some controversy surrounding the use of randomization. Some prominent commentators believe it is unethical, and some believe it is unnecessary. These points of view are very much in the minority.

FUTURE DIRECTIONS

Metaanalysis is being used increasingly to summarize findings from the global experience on a topic of interest. This has focused attention on the methodologic attributes of individual studies. The technique of metaanalysis has methodologic problems of its own, and further research on how to conduct a metaanalysis will be a focus of attention in the next few years.

In academic medicine, much current knowledge regarding the appropriate management of patients is disseminated via journal articles reporting the results of individual clinical trials. Since the clinical trial involves the application of the scientific method to clinical research, the reporting necessarily involves a good deal of technical material. Therefore, for specialists who wish to keep up to date with developments in the field, it is necessary to absorb the results of the many trials published in their specialty. To do this effectively, one needs the ability to critically appraise the merits of individual published trials from a methodologic as well as a clinical standpoint. The purpose of this chapter is to explain the essential attributes of a high-quality clinical trial, with an emphasis on the randomized clinical trial, to provide a framework for a critical evaluation of the literature.

A central feature of any published clinical trial is the analysis of the data. Consequently, statistical methods play a prominent role. Therefore, in order to interpret the results, it is necessary to have some familiarity with the purposes and jargon of the commonly used statistical techniques in addition to a grasp of their limitations. While the field of statistics is huge and literally thousands of individual tests and methods are available, there are a few standard methods that are commonly used in cancer trials. In this article we will mention briefly these key methods and some related basic concepts.

The appropriateness and credibility of any statistical analysis is, however, largely determined by the design and conduct of the trial. Therefore, in evaluating a study, critical appraisal of these aspects is of paramount importance. Later in this chapter we will describe and justify the key methodologic attributes of a high-quality study and describe some of the important links between the design and the statistical analysis.

The chapter is divided into three sections. In the first we describe a variety of different types of study design and clarify their relative strengths and limitations, emphasizing the role of the randomized clinical trial as the "gold standard" for evaluating medical inoerventions. In the second section we discuss the identifiable attributes of a high-quality clinical trial to help readers evaluate and understand individual trials. In the final section we focus on statistical terminology and discuss some basic statistical concepts and methods.

RATIONALE FOR CONTROLLED CLINICAL TRIALS

Before evaluating the relative merits of different clinical trial designs, we must clarify what a clinical trial is. The clinical trial represents the embodiment of the *experimental* approach to medical research, in which a scientific hypothesis is evaluated prospectively. (For an illuminating historical perspective, see Silverman.[1]) A loose definition of a clinical trial is "a prospective evaluation of a prescribed therapy in a sample of patients from a defined population, using measures of effectiveness which are defined and reproducible." The converse of an experimental study is an *observational* study, that is, "an analysis of a therapy using data derived from patients treated in accordance with regular medical practice, uninfluenced by any research protocol." In other words, the major distinguishing feature of a clinical trial is that it involves a planned intervention that is repeated on a series of patients. This distinction is very important methodologically, since in general the degree of aggressiveness of treatment (in the unplanned setting) is related to the severity of the condition. Therefore, observational studies of different treatment approaches are very susceptible to systematic biases, which make it difficult to distinguish the impact of different treatments from factors representing the natural course of the disease.

Often, when one is reading a journal article, it will not be immediately obvious which type of study is being presented, since the style of presentation of the results, the analysis of the data, and the claimed conclusiveness of the findings may be very similar. Nonetheless, the distinction between a clinical trial and an observational study is the single most crucial methodologic issue in determining the credibility of the findings.

There are some other, less obvious reasons why prospective clinical trials typically produce more reliable findings. The clinical trial will involve the use of a research protocol, which must necessarily be developed to obtain approval from the institutional review board. In cancer trials, where patient care is complex and dynamic, the protocol will usually contain detailed instructions regarding treatment modifications and supportive care. Consequently, the need for medical judgments is reduced and the treatment experience is more prescriptive and therefore more reproducible. In addition, the nature of the patient population is more clearly defined in a protocol-based study. Finally, in a well-conducted trial, the precise definition of the end points, the schedule for data collection, and other aspects of data management will have been considered in advance, in contrast to the typical retrospective observational study, in which data must be abstracted post hoc from the medical record—an approach that can easily result in incomplete and biased data.

Of course, the term *clinical trial* covers a range of types of study with different purposes. Drug trials are usually classified as phase I, phase II, or phase III. Phase I trials are "dose-finding" trials, and these involve a relatively small number of patients treated at various dosages. Phase II trials are noncomparative "efficacy" trials, in which a relatively small number of patients, typically 20 to 50, are treated at a common dose to evaluate potential efficacy. Phase II trials are by nature exploratory, and it is not uncommon for the results of such studies to be given undue prominence. A striking illustration of the potential pitfalls has been provided by Moertel,[2] who assembled the results of 21 seemingly identical phase II trials of fluorouracil in advanced colon cancer. These trials produced tumor response rates ranging from 8 to 85 percent, a variation far larger than could be explained by statistical fluctuation. There are probably many factors which contributed to the variation, including differences in the patient populations with regard to extent of pretreatment, differences in the methods for evaluating response, and selective inclusion of patients in the report.

The important lesson to be learned from these phase II studies is the fact that you cannot evaluate treatment efficacy in a definitive way without a benchmark against which to compare the results of the experimental treatment. In short, one needs a *control* group, comprising patients treated according to a standard therapy—or no therapy depending on the circumstances—evaluated for the end points of interest in a manner comparable to the experimental treatment.

There are various methods for selecting controls, each of which is used quite commonly in the literature. We shall discuss the strengths and limitations of each of these in turn. These are, in ascending order of scientific validity: literature controls, historical controls, concurrent (nonrandomized) controls, and randomized controls.

There are many methodologic problems with using literature controls—that is, using data from a published study as the benchmark. Most of the problems associated with historical controls, which are described just below, are applicable to literature control also. However, a specially prominent concern is publication bias, which is caused when studies with unusual or positive results are preferentially selected for publication, either due to the increased motivation on the part of the investigator or editorial preference for studies with striking results.[3] This phenomenon is, of course, not just restricted to the use of literature comparisons but can affect the reliability of results from published studies using more valid control groups, although there is evidence that publication bias has much less impact on randomized trials than on trials with nonrandomized controls.[4]

The use of a historical control group is common in evaluating new treatments. As the name suggests, historical controls comprise patients treated in an earlier time period, often in the same hospital as the experimental group. While such groups may provide a useful benchmark, there are several ways in which comparisons might be biased. First there is no guarantee that the groups will be prognostically comparable. That is, the doctors may, either consciously or subconsciously, preferentially select, say, good-risk patients for the experimental treatment, thus leading to bias. There is no guarantee that the end points will be comparably evaluated. In fact, for end points that involve measuring time to an event, such as death, the length of follow-up is necessarily different for a historical cohort. Finally, time trends due to changing referral patterns or supportive care can plausibly skew the results. Indeed, cancer is a disease with a continually evolving epidemiology, and the mortality rates for selected cancers have changed markedly in recent years, although colorectal cancer has been relatively stable.[5]

The temporal bias can clearly be eliminated by using concurrent controls. However, the use of controls which are merely contemporaneous does not guarantee that the treatment groups are prognostically comparable, since the treating physicians may still subconsciously select patients for the experimental treatment in a preferential way. The only way to resolve this problem definitively is to deny the physician any influence on the treatment selection. To accomplish this, one must use *randomization* to allocate treatments. In a randomized trial, the patient gives consent to participate with full knowledge of the alternative possible treatments and the fact that the actual treatment to be administered will be selected by a chance mechanism. Recognizing that the prognosis of patients is heterogeneous, randomization ensures that, in the long run, a similar mix of good- and poor-risk patients are assigned to each treatment. In practice, one can further refine the allocation process to avoid chance prognostic imbalances by *stratifying* patients on the basis of known prognostic factors. For further technical details of randomization and stratification, see the paper by Zelen.[6]

EVALUATION OF RANDOMIZED TRIALS

In considering how to evaluate published clinical trials, we will focus on important methodologic issues pertinent to randomized trials. Most of the issues are of similar concern in evaluating nonrandomized trials. Throughout this section we will use as an example the Intergroup randomized trial of levamisole and fluorouracil for adjuvant therapy of node-positive colon carcinoma, a pivotal study in demonstrating a statistically significant survival advantage for adjuvant therapy. Most of the important methodologic aspects of cancer clinical trials are clearly detailed in the article reporting the results of this study.[7]

Briefly, the trial involved a randomized comparison of three treatment strategies in patients with node-positive disease: levamisole plus fluorouracil; levamisole alone; observation (control). The primary end point was patient survival, with time to recurrence a major secondary end point. Between 1984 and 1987, 971 patients were enrolled in the study. The trial was terminated prematurely due to the accumulating evidence in favor of treatment with levamisole plus fluorouracil.

We will discuss in turn a number of important methodologic and analytic issues relevant to the evaluation of the trial.

Randomization Procedures

The randomization procedure was stratified on the basis of the major prognostic factors: invasion by the primary lesion, interval since surgery, and number of involved lymph nodes. The authors were consequently able to display in tabular form the close balance of the treatment groups with regard to these and other prognostic factors, thereby adding credibility to the conclusion that observed differences in survival were indeed due to the treatments.

Sample Size

The number of patients in the trial is a very important issue. Because individual patients are invariably heterogeneous with regard to prognosis, their outcomes are unpredictable to a greater or lesser extent, and this introduces statistical "noise" or uncertainty into the estimates of treatment efficacy, such as the percent survival at 5 years, etc. However, the law of averages ensures that as the sample size increases, such estimates inevitably stabilize around the correct or "true" estimate. Consequently, the larger a study, the more definitive are its conclusions, all other things being equal. It is good practice in the design of trials to determine in advance the sample size that is necessary to achieve a required level of precision. In the levamisole-fluorouracil study, this projection was complicated by the fact that a sequential monitoring scheme was used (see below). Nonetheless, the achieved sample size of 971 patients is large by any standards and therefore provides strong evidence regarding the hypothesis under study.

Comparable Evaluation of End Points

Merely by using randomization one does not guarantee an unbiased study. It is also important to ensure that the end points are evaluated in a comparable manner for each of the treatment groups. This is of special concern in studies with subjective end points, where both patients and physicians may subconsciously influence the evaluation of the end points differently for each treatment due to their knowledge of which treatment was administered. Subjective end points are increasingly common in cancer trials—for example, trials with quality-of-life end points, such as pain control. The use of a double-blind placebo-controlled trial disguises the treatment from the patient (by using a placebo) and from the physician (via blinding). Such trials are uncommon in cancer, since the modes of administration and the side effects of therapy typically render the blinding a pointless exercise. In the levamisole-fluorouracil trial, the primary end points were death and tumor recurrence, seemingly objective outcomes. In fact, the investigators took care to minimize the possibility of biased reporting by using similar evaluation schedules for the control patients and the treated patients.

The "Intent-to-Treat" Principle

Assuming that the end points are evaluated comparably, randomization guarantees an unbiased comparison of the groups of patients assigned to each treatment. However, in most trials, circumstances arise which encourage the investigators to withdraw patients from the analysis. This may occur because some patients do not actually receive the treatments to which they were assigned, in which case the investigators may elect to compare the patient groups "as treated" rather than "as randomized." This approach has a clear potential for bias if the refusers comprise an especially good- or poor-risk selection of the patients. Another common reason for exclusion is ineligibility for the protocol, although the potential for bias is lower in this case, especially if the rates of exclusion are similar in the treatment groups. From a strictly technical standpoint, the correct, unbiased way to analyze the data is to compare the groups "as randomized." That is, each comparison group is characterized by the "intention to treat" with the assigned therapy.[8] In the levamisole-fluorouracil trial, the investigators chose to exclude 42 ineligible patients (4.3 percent) but retained in the analysis the 14 patients (1.4 percent) who refused their assigned therapies.

Adjustments for Prognostic Factors

In comparative studies in general, one must be concerned that apparent differences (or similarities) in the effects of the treatments may be caused or skewed by differences in the case mix of the patients. If there are factors known to independently affect the end points, e.g., prognostic factors, then imbalances in these factors may have an impact on the apparent treatment effects. In order to offset this problem, one can perform analyses to "adjust" for the effects of the prognostic factors. If there are several factors, it is common practice to use statistical "regression" techniques to make these adjustments. In a well-designed, large randomized trial, adjustments are unlikely to have a substantial effect, since the purpose of randomization in the first place is to offset this problem by making the treatment groups comparable with regard to the prognostic factors, rendering the adjustments unnecessary. However it is good practice to perform adjusted comparisons, in addition to straightforward unadjusted comparisons, to check that there are no serious discrepancies. In the levamisole-fluorouracil study, the investigators performed an analysis using the "Cox model" to make the adjustments. This is a commonly used statistical method which involves applying a regression model to the analysis of lengths of survival.[9] The statistical significance of the treatment effects was unaffected by the adjustments, as one would expect.

Interim Analyses

Every clinical trial takes place over a period of time, and there is always concern that evidence might be mounting in favor of one of the treatments under study to the extent that it is inappropriate to continue the trial. Consequently, investigators will typically analyze the results repeatedly as the trial progresses. Unfortunately, a mathematical consequence is that the chance of observing a statistically significant difference where no real difference exists, i.e., a false-positive result, increases markedly as more interim analyses are performed. To circumvent this problem, statistical researchers have found ways of adjusting conventional statistical tests to standardize the chance of a false-positive result over the entire trial. However, this requires deciding in advance a precise schedule for performing the interim analyses. Such methods are called "group sequential methods." To stop the trial early, one must invariably achieve a significant result at a more pronounced level of significance than the conventional 5 percent level. In the levamisole-fluorouracil trial, a formal group sequential plan was followed. This resulted in the trial being terminated at the second planned interim analysis, when the *p* value of the survival analysis was less than the required 0.0098.

Metaanalysis

Techniques for evaluating published clinical trials have become much more formalized in the last few years due to the prominence of metaanalysis, the name given to the formal statistical aggregation of data from all available trials on a given topic. The impetus for metaanalysis derives from the fact that so many similar trials are being conducted, often with seemingly contradictory conclusions, and from the promise of greatly increased statistical power when you combine the information from several trials. However, the use of this technique is controversial and poses clear methodologic problems. Prominent among these are the possibility of combining studies which are too dissimilar for meaningful aggregation and the risk of biased selection of studies for inclusion, especially due to publication bias.[3] In any well-conducted metaanalysis, the authors will necessarily be concerned with the issues discussed previously, namely the use of randomization, the sample sizes of the component studies, the use of comparable end points, the inappropriate exclusion of patients from reported results of the component studies, adjustments for prognostic factors, and the influence of interim analyses on the results. A good example of the use of this technique is the metaanalysis of adjuvant studies of colorectal cancer, conducted by Buyse et al.[10]

STATISTICAL METHODS AND TERMINOLOGY

This section is not intended as an introduction to biostatistics, as such a topic would require a much more elaborate document. The purpose is simply to discuss briefly some very basic concepts that are relevant to the interpretation of published trials and to explain some commonly used terminology.

Probably the most important issue is one that has been mentioned previously, concerning the fact that virtually all statistical tests and related methods are generic in the sense that they are applied regardless of the manner in which the data were collected. That is, they are computed without reference to the study design. As an example, suppose you have two clinical trials, each designed to compare response rates on two treatments, but one trial is randomized and the other uses historical controls. Suppose also that these trials produce identical data. Then the same chi-square test can be applied to each trial and the same *p* value will be calculated, yet we know that the results from the randomized trial are more credible. However, this difference in credibility is not reflected in the *p* value, even though the *p* value is usually interpreted as a quantitative reflection of the strength of evidence in a study (against the null hypothesis). In other words, in interpreting strength of evidence from a study, it is necessary to pay careful attention to the features of the design and conduct of the study which bear upon the credibility of the trial as outlined in the previous section, in addition to the reported statistical summaries and *p* values.

Tests and Confidence Intervals

The most commonly reported statistical summary is the *p* value. This is reported in the context of testing a hypothesis, such as the hypothesis that two treatments are identical with regard to their efficacy. In interpreting the meaning of the *p* value, you must first assume that the hypothesis is true. The *p* value is then the probability of observing the data in the trial or a less likely configuration. If this probability is small, say less than 5 percent, this provides strong evidence against the (null) hypothesis on the grounds that if the hypothesis (e.g., equivalence of treatment effects) were true, it is unlikely that such a data configuration would have been observed. The use of $p < .05$ (i.e., probability less than 5 percent) is a widely used though arbitrary convention. It is important to be aware that tests are used to refute hypotheses, but they cannot provide strong evidence in favor of a (null) hypothesis. If one wishes to establish the equivalence of two treatments, say, it is necessary to use confidence intervals (see below) to show that there is a low probability that the treatments differ by more than, say, a clinically relevant difference. For more details of the distinction between conventional trials and "equivalence" trials, see Durrleman and Simon.[11]

Confidence intervals are used generally to provide a range of values within which a quantity of interest must lie with high probability. For example, if one obtains an estimated response rate of 30 percent in a phase II trial, such an estimate is influenced by random factors and as such is inaccurate due to statistical variation. By calculating a confidence interval, one can provide a range of values within which the true response rate lies with high probability (say 95 percent). In general, one wants such ranges to be narrow, and this is directly related to the sample size in the study.

Commonly Used Statistical Methods

Literally thousands of statistical tests and techniques have been developed as the field has developed during this century. In this section we mention briefly those key methods that are used repeatedly in reports of cancer clinical trials. We restrict attention to three basic types of methods: descriptive methods, tests, and methods for adjusting analyses for prognostic factors. Another important distinction concerns the nature of the end point. Two very common end points are the time to an adverse event, such as death or tumor recurrence, and the presence or absence of a response to treatment.

Descriptive statistics of response rates are straightforward. However, description of the survival experience of a sample of patients requires special techniques. The *Kaplan-Meier survival curve* is an especially widely used method, illustrated in Fig. 41-1, where the recurrence-free survival is reproduced for the three treatment groups in the levamisole-fluorouracil study. The curve provides the probability that a patient will remain in remission at any given time period subsequent to treatment. For example, at 3 ½ years this probability is 63 percent for patients receiving levamisole plus fluorouracil, or 5-FU (thin line), obtained by observing the height of the curve at 42 months. By contrast, this probability is 47 percent for the control patients (solid line). The median survival is defined to be the time at which 50 percent of the patients are expected to fail, i.e., the time at which the curve has dropped to 50 percent. This is in the region of 2 ½ to 3 years for the two lower curves. However, the upper curve has not yet dropped to 50 percent. In this case, further follow-up is required to estimate the median. Notice however, that fewer than half the patients have actually relapsed (failed) for any of the treatments. Estimation of the median is still possible, since these failures are spread over the entire curve due to the fact that accrual to the study took place over a period of several years; therefore the length to follow-up is highly variable among patients. In fact, the median follow-up time is often quoted as a measure of the maturity of the data for meaningful analysis. In general, the power of the statistical analysis is directly related to the number of failures rather than the total sample size (denoted as "at risk" in Fig. 41-1).

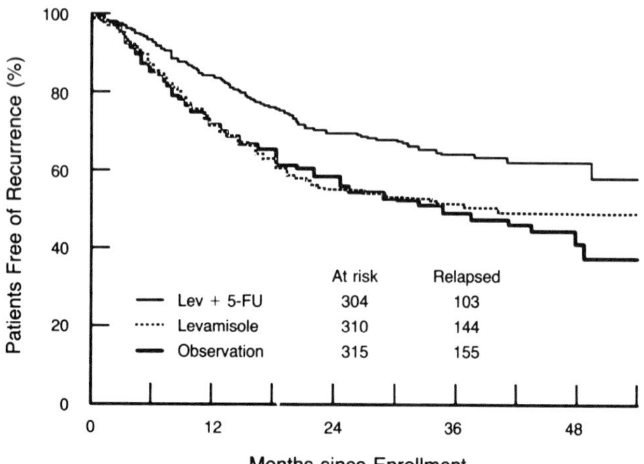

FIG. 41-1. Randomized adjuvant trial in node-positive colon cancer. (Reprinted by permission of *The New England Journal of Medicine* 322:352–358, 1990.)

There are a variety of statistical tests for comparing treatments. For a comparison of proportions, the *chi-square test* is commonly used, although a technique known as the *exact test* is more appropriate if the sample sizes are small. Survival curves can be compared using various techniques, of which the *logrank test* is the most commonly used.

The most direct way to accommodate the influence of prognostic factors is to partition the patients into mutually exclusive subgroups and compare the treatments directly within each subgroup. In practice, this becomes unmanageable if there are several factors, in which case one uses statistical "regression" models to effect the adjustments. For survival data, the model used is the *Cox model,* sometimes referred to as the *proportional hazards model*. The analogous model for analyzing proportions is called *logistic regression*.

For a useful textbook on biostatistical techniques which describes the commonly used methods in detail, see Altman.[12]

Interpretive Pitfalls

As mentioned earlier, the real strength of evidence supporting a conclusion as embodied in, say, a p value depends as much on the sequence of steps leading up to the analysis as on the magnitude of the p value itself. This was mentioned earlier in the context of the relative credibility of randomized versus nonrandomized studies and in relation to the number of times a formal analysis is performed during the course of a study. However, the strategy employed in the statistical analysis is also extremely important. To be specific, the chance of obtaining a statistically significant result increases steadily as more analyses are performed. This is true regardless of whether the experimental treatment has any merit. For instance, one could perform tests in different subgroups individually, such as men and women, early stage and late stage, and so on; the more subgroups, the greater the chances of spurious false-positive tests. The false-positive rate is also increased if you perform the analysis in different ways, by leaving out ineligible patients or, alternatively, by including them, by trying out different statistical tests to see which ones give the most significant results, and so forth. It is for these reasons that many statisticians encourage the use of formal rules for analyzing data from trials, such as specifying in advance the definition of the major end point, the stopping rule, and the precise analytic strategy that will be emphasized, e.g., use of the "intent-to-treat" principle. In any event, evidence of these details in the published article lends credibility to the reported conclusions of the study.

SUMMARY

In absorbing information from the medical literature in colorectal cancer, readers cannot in general accept the conclusions presented at face value without a critical appraisal of the methodology employed in the study. Uncontrolled evaluations of new therapeutic approaches must always be regarded as exploratory and therefore nondefinitive. In comparative trials, the use of randomization is a crucial methodologic device. However, even in randomized trials, one must be concerned to evaluate whether other important methodologic principles were observed. Specifically, the end points should be defined in advance and evaluated in a comparable manner for each of the treatment groups, the study should be planned with a sufficient sample size to give reliable conclusions, all data should be reported and exclusions of patients from the analysis should be justified and preferably minimized, and the statistical analytic strategy should be explained in sufficient detail to give readers confidence that the data have not been manipulated to give prominence to the most striking results. A readership educated in these methodologic principles will further the cause of science by encouraging prominence for those trials which are observant of these standards.

REFERENCES

1. Silverman WA: *Human Experimentation: A Guided Step into the Unknown*. New York, Oxford University Press, 1985.
2. Moertel CG: Improving the efficiency of clinical trials: A medical perspective. *Stat Med* 3:455–465, 1984.
3. Begg CB: Publication bias and dissemination of clinical research. *J Natl Cancer Inst* 81:107–115, 1989.
4. Dickersin K, Min YI, Meinert CL: Factors in influencing publication of research results: Follow-up of applications submitted to two institutional review boards. *JAMA* 267:374–378, 1992.
5. American Cancer Society: *Cancer Facts and Figures*. Atlanta, Georgia, American Cancer Society, 1992.
6. Zelen M: The randomization and stratification of patients to clinical trials. *J Chron Dis* 27:365–375, 1974.
7. Moertel CG, Fleming TR, MacDonald JS, et al: Levamisole and fluorouracil for adjuvant therapy of resected colon carcinoma. *N Engl J Med* 322:352–358, 1990.
8. Peto R, Pike MC, Armitage P, et al: Design and analysis of randomized clinical trials requiring prolonged observation of each patient: I. Introduction and design. *Br J Cancer* 34:585–612, 1976.
9. Cox DR: Regression models and life tables. *J R Stat Soc B* 34:187–220, 1972.
10. Buyse M, Zeleniuch-Jacquotte A, Chalmers TC: Adjuvant therapy of colorectal cancer: Why we still don't know. *JAMA* 259:3571–3578, 1988.
11. Durrleman S, Simon R: Planning and monitoring of equivalence studies. *Biometrics* 46:329–336, 1990.
12. Altman DG: *Practical Statistics for Medical Research*. London, Chapman and Hall, 1991.

PART 8

Surgical Treatment of Potentially Curable Cancer

CHAPTER 42

Preoperative Evaluation

Ian C. Lavery

After the diagnosis of a large bowel cancer has been made, it is necessary to make a judgment on the most appropriate form of treatment for the person involved. Most cancers are treated by surgical excision, hopefully in order to achieve a cure. The excision may be a wide one executed at laparotomy, or it may be a local excision done transanally. If the tumor is considered to be incurable, palliation either by resection or bypass may still require a laparotomy. Only with far advanced metastatic disease is laparotomy or some form of surgery not performed. Most patients are in generally good condition. Even in the presence of obstruction, electrolyte imbalance is a late phenomenon. Elderly patients commonly have associated cardiovascular and respiratory problems or some other comorbid condition that may influence a decision on their suitability for surgery. Considering the dire consequences of no surgery, given the nature of the disease, it is uncommon not to operate. Table 42-1 provides an outline of the general medical assessment of these patients.

A well-conducted clinical examination is the most important initial step in evaluating patients in general, with reference to their suitability for an anesthetic and, in particular, for the extent of disease. In extensive disease, abdominal distension may be due to ascites or to feces or flatus from an obstructed colon. Even in a normally protuberant abdomen, a careful clinical examination will provide a reliable assessment.

A mass may be palpated, which may be from a tumor. If it is on the left side, the palpable mass may be feces proximal to a stenotic tumor. An extensively involved liver is usually unmistakably involved, as it has a characteristic irregular feel. Tumors in the lower third of the rectum or anal canal may have caused secondary involvement of the inguinal lymph nodes.

Apart from specific features related to the tumor to be looked for and other potential findings that may influence the course of events, two areas of note should be examined. In females, a breast examination and a complete pelvic examination should not be omitted. Breast cancer is becoming increasingly more common, and there is an association between cancer of the colon and rectum and uterine cancer. In male patients, while the digital examination of the rectum is being performed, note is made of the prostate—its size and shape and any suspicious nodules.

As well as being integral parts of the procedure to diagnose a cancer of the large bowel, digital examination of the rectum, sigmoidoscopy, contrast studies, and/or colonoscopy are also measures taken to assess the tumor preoperatively. These studies should all be done in sequence and are complementary to each other.

Digital Examination

A digital examination of the rectum for a rectal tumor enables assessment of the location of the tumor with respect to its location and its distance from the anal margin as well as the extent of involvement of the circumference of the rectal wall. Mobility or fixation of the tumor is assessed, providing information necessary to determine suitability of local treatment in small early lesions. At the other end of the spectrum, it must be ascertained whether the lesion is resectable at all. Extrarectal spread, submucosal spread, and occasionally discrete nodes are palpable. These signs do not portend well for cure and may prompt preoperative adjunctive therapy in an attempt to improve the outcome.

In colonic tumors, a digital examination will enable palpation of peritoneal metastases in the rectovesicle or rectouterine pouch, if they are present.

Sigmoidoscopy

If the tumor is visible with a sigmoidoscope, the degree of obstruction or involvement of the circumference is assessed. The mobility of a tumor can also be assessed with the tip of the instrument. During assessment of rectal cancers, a rigid sigmoidoscopic examination will provide a more accurate measurement from

Table 42-1
Preoperative Evaluation of Patients with Cancer of the Large Bowel

Clinical	
Age	
Comorbid conditions	
Suitability for anesthesia	
Suitability for surgery	
Suitability for adjunctive therapy	
Digital examination of rectum	
Proctosigmoidoscopy	
Colonoscopy	
Breast examination	
Prostate examination	
Extent of disease	
Synchronous lesions	
Local extent	
Size	
Regional spread	
Local spread	
Distant disease	
Intraabdominal	
	Local
Peritoneal	Diffuse
	Pelvic
Hepatic	
Extraabdominal	
Pulmonary	
Osseous	Rare
Cerebral	Rare
Laboratory	
Essential	
Complete blood count	
Liver function tests	
Renal function	
Coagulation profile	
Electrocardiogram	
Recommended	
Carcinoembryonic antigen	
Radiology/Endoscopy	
Essential	
Chest x-ray	
Air-contrast barium enema, sigmoidoscopy or colonoscopy	
Recommended	
Computed tomography, abdomen and pelvis	
Doubtful value as routine	
Magnetic resonance imaging	
Ultrasound of the liver	
Endolumenal ultrasound, possibly helpful for cancers in the lower two-thirds of the rectum	
Monoclonal antibodies	
Prostate-specific antigen	

the anal margin, or the top of the sphincter mechanism, to the lower border of the tumor than a measurement taken with a flexible instrument. It is important to determine the distance to the lower border of the tumor when a decision is to be made between a sphincter-saving procedure and an abdominoperineal resection with a permanent end colostomy.

Air Contrast Barium Enema/Colonoscopy

If the diagnosis of a colonic cancer is made on the basis of a barium enema exam, the question arises as to the reliability of detecting synchronous polyps or cancers. It is difficult to make a case for the routine use of a full-column barium enema. These studies will demonstrate only the most gross lesions. In my opinion, there is no place for this study in the preoperative evaluation of large bowel cancers. The reliability of an *air-contrast barium enema* approaches that of a colonoscopy.[1-4] The accuracy is dependent on the radiologist and the technique used. "Significant" lesions are detected with the same accuracy as with colonoscopy. Smaller lesions, such as polyps 2 to 3 mm in size, are detected more accurately on colonoscopy. The benefit of a colonoscopic examination is that it allows biopsies to be taken from a tumor and/or polyps and makes it possible to treat many benign lesions detected.

Colonoscopy

If colonoscopy is not used to make the diagnosis (but rather an air-contrast barium enema), its value as part of the preoperative evaluation becomes debatable. The rationale of preoperative colonoscopy is to detect synchronous colonic cancers, which are reported to be present in 1.5 to 7.6 percent of these cases, and synchronous colonic polyps, at 25 to 40 percent.[5-9] Sollenberger et al.[5] avoid preoperative endoscopy on the basis that manipulation of the tumor may cause hematogenous or lymphatic seeding of neoplastic cells. Howard and Greene[10] examined a group of patients with colonic or rectal cancer and concluded—on the basis of comparison of rates of recurrence, distant metastases, and survival of matched patients—that there was no disadvantage to those patients undergoing preoperative endoscopy.

Preoperative colonoscopy has been reported to change the planned procedures in patients: from 10.8 to 13.3 percent.[9,11,12] At the Cleveland Clinic, from 1989 to 1992, 96 preoperative colonoscopies were performed (65 males, 31 females). In 44 patients, no other pathology was found; 20 had one polyp; 26 had multiple polyps; and 6 had additional cancers.

The results of the preoperative colonoscopy influenced a change in the planned surgical procedures in 9 of the 96 patients. In a further 51 patients (31 males, 20 females), intraoperative colonoscopy was performed and found to be helpful (see Table 42-2).

In 8 cases, the findings on colonoscopy changed the planned surgery. (Personal communication: Dr. James Church.)

Arguments are made as to the value of special investigations and to what extent these should be performed in the preoperative evaluation of patients with large bowel cancer.

A *chest x-ray* is usually required by the anesthesiologist. If extensive metastases are found, this may be a deterrent to proceeding with an operation. However, if one or two metastases are found, this will not influence the decision to proceed. In some circumstances pulmonary lesions may be suitable for resec-

Table 42-2
Intraoperative Colonoscopy at the Cleveland Clinic

Indication	*Changes in plan*
Examine for polyps or synchronous cancers (31)	Extra resection (4)
Locate a polyp (11)	Colotomy and polypectomy (4)
Locate a small cancer (5)	
Locate a polypectomy site (4)	

Note: numbers in parentheses indicate number of patients.

tion, if there is no other evidence of metastatic disease after the primary tumor has been resected.

Computed Tomography

This procedure is used to determine the presence or absence of clinically undetectable distant metastases, and the extent of local spread. Even in the presence of clinically undetectable metastases, with lesions seen on a computed tomography (CT) scan, a surgeon will, in the vast majority of cases, proceed with a laparotomy. At this time, clinical assessment and possible evaluation with intraoperative ultrasound of the liver is made. In some circumstances, the presence of extramural spread, paraaortic adenopathy, or extensive hepatic metastases may influence a change in therapy to a less radical procedure with less morbidity. If a solitary hepatic metastasis is found preoperatively, theoretically the surgeon may prepare for a synchronous resection of the liver metastasis. A CT scan of the pelvis is accurate in the assessment of local disease in 70 to 80 percent of cases, but it is not as accurate for early lesions.[13–15] The ability of CT scans to detect involved lymph nodes is poor. In one study, the accuracy of CT scans in pararectal lymph node evaluation was only 57 percent.[16]

Liver metastases are present at the time of surgery in 15 to 20 percent of patients with large bowel cancers.[17–20] After surgery, occult metastases not found at laparotomy will develop within 2 years of surgery in about 30 percent of patients. Longo et al.[21] performed a retrospective analysis of 119 consecutive patients undergoing excision of rectal cancer who had a preoperative CT scans at the Cleveland Clinic. Of these patients, 102 underwent laparotomy; 89 (88 percent) preoperatively were thought to have a normal CT scan. This was confirmed in 86 patients at laparotomy. However, 3 patients with negative scans had liver metastases and 5 with positive scans had no metastases at operation. A positive scan helped in decision making in 5.9 percent of the total number of patients or 7.5 percent of the patients with Dukes B ($T_3N_0M_0$) or Dukes C ($T_3N_1M_0$) lesions. Almost all the liver metastases occurred in patients with Dukes C cancers; only one occurred in a patient with a Dukes B cancer. The yield from performing a CT scan in Dukes A or B cancers is very low, making routine CT scans difficult to justify on this basis. In patients with Dukes C lesions (which are larger), the yield is higher and may influence the operative approach. However, in practice, many patients with colorectal cancer do have postoperative adjunctive therapy and most protocols require a baseline CT scan. There is a high incidence of cysts and hemangiomas in the liver, and having baseline studies to eliminate doubt is beneficial. The same argument can be made for patients with a rectal cancer in whom preoperative adjunctive radiotherapy is planned to include extrapelvic disease. The CT scan assists in assessing response (or lack of it) to the radiotherapy.

Endolumenal ultrasound is a relatively more recent tool to be made available to clinicians to help in preoperative staging of rectal cancers. This is to be covered in another chapter.

RADIOIMMUNODETECTION WITH MONOCLONAL ANTIBODIES

The use of monoclonal antibodies (MoAbs) to deliver diagnostic radioisotopes to sites of disease is a new technique. The utility of this technique for imaging colorectal cancers results from the ability to detect lesions not detected by conventional techniques. The targeting is directly related to antigen expression and thus provides a higher degree of specificity than other techniques which rely on nonspecific physical properties of tumors. In patients who have occult disease with elevated serum markers, detection rates of up to 95 percent have been reported.[22] This rate of detection surpasses the rate of detection by CT of extrahepatic tumor.[23] Computed tomography scans are more sensitive than immunoscintigraphy in the assessment of liver involvement. In the diagnosis of hepatic metastases, the sensitivity of CT is 86 percent and scintigraphy 54 percent. Immunoscintigraphy allows scanning of the entire body using a gamma camera or multiple sequential images. Single photon emission computed tomography (SPECT) allows three-dimensional images to be made of the tumor, which allows better localization of metastases. Immunoscintigraphy is able to detect tumors in regional and distant lymph nodes that are less than 2 cm in size and appear normal on CT scans. The information provided by the labeling of tumor with a radiolabeled monoclonal antibody can augment information obtained by other diagnostic tests. Previously unidentified disease may be detected in the retroperitoneum or mesentery, enabling a change in treatment if indicated.

Localization of the monoclonal antibody when other studies are equivocal enhances diagnostic accuracy. When used intraoperatively utilizing the RIGS system and antibody CC49 labeled with 1 to 2 mCi iodine 125, Arnold et al.[24] reported 83 percent positive antibody localization at surgery in 36 patients. Of the patients in whom localization occurred, staging changes were made in 34 percent (11 patients). Operative changes were made in 9 patients (25 percent). When more specific MoAbs become readily available, the technique promises to have a significant impact on the management of patients with colorectal cancer.

RECOMMENDED GUIDELINES

Initially, a good *general clinical examination* should be performed. The tumor should be assessed by *digital examination, sigmoidoscopy,* and *colonoscopy.*

Endolumenal ultrasound will give accurate information on the depth of invasion of the tumor in the lower two-thirds of the rectum. The reliability of the detection of involved lymph nodes is not yet convincing, though if an ultrasound-guided biopsy is positive, it is clearly valuable information.

Computed tomography is not as accurate as ultrasound in defining local involvement either in depth of spread or local invasion or in the detection of lymph nodes. However, CT scans are indicated for preoperative assessment of the liver and extraperitoneal sites of metastases. They are indicated in patients who will have preoperative radiotherapy or postoperative adjunctive therapy.

Unless the patient is unable to have a laparotomy because of severe associated medical problems or clear evidence of extensive disease likely to cause an early demise, virtually all patients will have a laparotomy for a resection or bypass and should have a preoperative CT scan.

The developing technology of radiolabeled *monoclonal antibodies* with immunoscintigraphy and radioimmunoguided surgery is showing promise in improving our preoperative and intraoperative assessment of the extent of the tumor, but it is not yet available or recommended for routine use.

Laparoscopic bowel surgery is in its infancy. Questions still exist regarding the desirability of performing curative cancer surgery by this technique. Intuitively, we would expect palliative surgery performed laparoscopically to be beneficial, though there are no data to support this. If laparoscopic resection is possible, CT or hepatic ultrasound should be performed to evaluate for distant spread. Deep metastases in the liver cannot be detected laparoscopically, since there is no tactile sensibility.

REFERENCES

1. Thoeni RF, Petras A: Double-contrast barium-enema examination and endoscopy in the detection of polypoid lesions in the cecum and ascending colon. *Radiology* 144:257, 1982.
2. Rex DK, Lehman GA, Lappas JC, et al: Sensitivity of double-contrast barium study for left-colon polyps. *Radiology* 158: 69, 1986.
3. Leinicke JL, Dodds WJ, Hogan WJ, et al: A comparison of colonoscopy and roentegenography for detecting polypoid lesions of the colon. *Gastrointest Radiol* 2:125, 1977.
4. Fork FT: Double contrast enema and colonoscopy in polyp detection. *Gut* 22:971, 1981.
5. Sollenberger LL, Eisenstat TE, Rubin RJ, et al: Is preoperative colonoscopy necessary in carcinoma of the colon and rectum? *Am Surg* 54:113–115, 1988.
6. Eklund GR, Pihl E: Multiple carcinoma of the colon and rectum. *Cancer* 33:1630–1634, 1974.
7. Hancock RJ: Synchronous carcinoma of the colon and rectum. *Am Surg* 41:560–563, 1975.
8. Heald RJ, Bussey HJR: Clinical experience at St. Mark's Hospital with multiple synchronous cancers of the colon and rectum. *Dis Colon Rectum* 18:6–10, 1975.
9. Pagana TJ, Ledesma EJ, Mittelman A, et al: The use of colonoscopy in the study of synchronous colorectal neoplasms. *Cancer* 53:356–359, 1984.
10. Howard ML, Greene FL: The effect of preoperative endoscopy on recurrence and survival following surgery for colorectal carcinoma. *Am Surg* 56:124–127, 1990.
11. Askew A, Ward M, Cowen A: The influence of colonoscopy on the operative management of colorectal cancer. *Med J Aust* 145:254–255, 1986.
12. Isler JT, Brown PC, Billingham RF: The role of preoperative colonoscopy in colorectal cancer. *Dis Colon Rectum* 30:435–439, 1987.
13. Adalsteinsson B, Glimeliss B, Fraffman S, et al: Computed tomography in staging rectal carcinoma. *Acta Radiol Diagn* 26:45–55, 1985.
14. Van Waes PF, Koehler PR, Feldberg MAM: Management of rectal carcinoma: Impact of computed tomography *AJR* 140:1137–1142, 1983.
15. Thoeni RF, Moss AA, Schnyder P, Margulis AR: Detection and staging of primary rectal and rectosigmoid cancer by computed tomography. *Radiology* 141:135–138, 1981.
16. Beynon J, Mortensen NJM, Foy DMA, et al: Preoperative assessment of mesorectal lymph node involvement in rectal cancer. *Br J Surg* 76:276, 1989.
17. Lundstedt C, Elcberg H, Hedefstrom E, et al: Radiologic diagnosis of liver metastases in colorectal carcinoma: Prospective evaluation of angiography, ultrasonography, computed tomography and computed tomographic angiography. *Acta Radiol* 28:431–438, 1987.
18. Reed WP, Haney PJ, Elias EG, et al: Ethiodized oil emulsion enhanced computerized tomography in the preoperative assessment of metastases to the liver from the colon and rectum. *Surg Gynecol Obstet* 162:131–138, 1986.

19. Temple DF, Parthasarthy KL, Bakshi SP, et al: A comparison of isotopic and computerized tomographic scanning in the diagnosis of metastasis to the liver in patients with adenocarcinoma of the colon and rectum. *Surg Gynecol Obstet* 156:205–208, 1983.
20. Matsui O, Takashima T, Kadoya M, et al: Liver metastases from colorectal cancers: Detection With CT during arterial portography. *Radiology* 165:65–69, 1987.
21. Longo WE, Church JC, Lavery IC, et al: What is the role of preoperative CAT scan in patients with rectal cancers? (In press.)
22. Patt YZ, Lamki LM, Shanken J, et al: Imaging with indium III labeled anti-carcinoembryonic antigen monoclonal antibody ZCE-025 of recurrent colorectal or carcinoembryonic antigen-producing cancer in patients with rising serum carcinoembryonic antigen levels and occult metastases. *J Clin Oncol* 8:1246–1254, 1990.
23. Siccardi AG, Buraggi GL, Callegro L, et al: Immunoscintigraphy of adrenocarcinomas by means of radiolabeled F(ab')2 fragments of an anticarcinoembryonic antigen monoclonal antibody: A multicenter study. *Cancer Res* 49:3095–3103, 1989.
24. Arnold MW, Schnecbaum S, Bueno A, et al: Radioimmune guided surgery challenges traditional decision making in patients with primary colorectal cancer. *Surgery* 112:624–630, 1992.

CHAPTER 43

Surgical Considerations

David M. Ota

HIGHLIGHTS

The standard treatment for resectable colon carcinoma is a hemicolectomy and a regional lymphadenectomy. The regional node dissection is based on the regional arterial supply. Because effective adjuvant chemotherapy is available for Dukes C colon carcinoma, the nodal dissection is important for staging and local control of disease. A randomized trial showed there was no difference in survival with the "no-touch" technique.

CONTROVERSIES

The definition of a regional lymphadenectomy for left-sided colon cancers is unclear. Ligation of the inferior mesenteric artery at its origin is advocated by some, while others argue that a regional arterial ligation at either the left colic or superior rectal artery is adequate. The management of obstructing colon cancers seems to be changing. While multistage procedures have been advocated in the past, the success of single-stage procedures using intraoperative lavage or involving a subtotal colectomy may reduce the need for follow-up procedures.

FUTURE DIRECTIONS

Adjuvant therapies are improving the outlook for locally advanced colon cancers. These postoperative systemic and regional therapies must be considered during operative therapy.

The primary treatment of localized colonic adenocarcinoma is surgical resection, and the object of operative procedures is to maximize the chance of cure. Theoretically, wide excision and regional lymphadenectomy should result in the highest cure rate from the locally invasive and regional metastatic aspects of colonic carcinoma. Hence, the operative techniques have developed around the regional arterial blood supply of the colon. Taking the regional artery at its origin has defined the boundaries of the mesenteric, lymphatic, and colonic resection. Operative considerations that may influence survival include the no-touch technique and intraluminal spread of exfoliated tumor cells. In addition to these, other management problems such as acute obstruction and perforation from colon carcinomas require special attention. Last, treatment of adjacent organ involvement requires an understanding of the pathology and of postoperative adjuvant therapy.

PATHOLOGIC CONSIDERATIONS

While the invasive and metastatic properties of colonic carcinoma are reviewed in other chapters, these pathologic events figure prominently in the operative management of potentially curable colonic carcinomas. The American Joint Committee on Cancer has defined local invasion according to the depth of penetration into the bowel wall.[1] In addition to bowel invasion, colonic carcinoma also spreads to regional lymphatic vessels and lymph nodes. Exfoliation of tumor cells into the peritoneal cavity and subsequent implantation can result in carcinomatosis. Blood vessel invasion is a crucial event that leads to metastatic disease. These pathologic features are important because they form the theoretical basis of surgical management of this disease.

NO-TOUCH TECHNIQUE

The theory of the no-touch technique was that intraoperative manipulation of the primary tumor during dissection of the colon and mesentery could dislodge tumor cells into regional venules and veins, potentially disseminating disease to distant organs. For these reasons the initial step in the no-touch technique was ligation of the regional arterial and venous blood supply before the colon and mesentery were mobilized. Turnbull et al.[2] popularized the no-touch technique as a means of reducing the risk of systemic and intraperitoneal dissemination, thus improving survival. Other investigators have argued that their results could be attributed to patient selection and that similar results could be obtained with extended resection and lymphadenectomy.[3,4]

One of the major limitations of Turnbull's theory was the absence of prospective randomized data. In 1988, Wiggers et al.[5] reported the results of a prospective randomized trial of the no-touch isolation technique versus a conventional resection technique. Patients were registered and randomized preoperatively. Eligibility and exclusion criteria were defined and were judged reasonable. There were 117 patients in the no-touch group and 119 in the control arm. All evaluable patients had resectable disease. Complications were equal in both treatment groups but survival was not significantly different among them. While the authors saw a trend toward improved survival with the no-touch technique, there was no statistical improvement in survival. In general, the no-touch technique is not widely practiced and does not offer a survival advantage.

INTRALUMINAL SPREAD

Another potential problem is intraluminal exfoliation of tumor cells and implantation on the anastomotic site, giving rise to so-called suture line recurrence. The incidence of suture line recurrence for rectal carcinomas has ranged from 10 to 35 percent, while that for colonic carcinomas is below 1 percent. Possible explanations for recurrences include (1) implantation of exfoliated tumor cells at the suture line, (2) proximity of the tumor to the anastomosis, and (3) extraluminal residual disease growing into the suture line. Precautionary methods include (1) isolation of the colon with constricting tapes, (2) painting the anastomotic site with alcohol solutions, and (3) chemical lavage of the colonic lumen. However, it should be pointed out that there have been no randomized trials comparing these precautionary techniques. Because the incidence of suture line recurrence is so low, it is unlikely that these maneuvers will reduce this problem further. Adequate distal and proximal luminal resection (5 to 10 cm) should be obtained to prevent suture line recurrence.

EXTENT OF COLONIC RESECTION

The extent of colonic resection and lymphadenectomy has been controversial since Miles[6] published his paper on the rationale for the abdominoperineal resection. The theory behind extended lymphadenectomy is that a wider dissection removes more lymph nodes with potential metastatic deposits and thereby increases the chance for cure. Although the early studies by Gabriel et al.[7] showed that lymphatic metastases advanced in an orderly fashion from proximal to more distant nodes, the concept of "skip" lymph node metastases was proposed to explain nodal metastases far from the primary tumor without involvement of adjacent lymph nodes. This phenomenon was attributed to unusual lymphatic drainage or clogging of lymphatic vessels, resulting in retrograde lymphatic flow and development of lymph node metastases far from the primary tumor.[8]

In 1982 Sugarbaker and Corlew[9] analyzed the results of lymphadenectomy from several studies that retrospectively compared extended regional hemicolectomy with a regional colectomy. An extended regional hemicolectomy included the regional arterial blood supply and perioaortic node dissection. The definition of a regional hemicolectomy is a colonic resection with removal of the regional arterial blood supply. The investigators concluded that the extended regional hemicolectomy resulted in a theoretical 5 percent survival advantage over regional hemicolectomy, and no statistical significance was found in the studies that were reviewed. Admittedly, there are no randomized trials that have attempted to resolve the controversy over whether "wider is better." The current recommendation is that a colectomy should be performed with at least 5 to 10 cm of proximal and distal luminal margins and that the regional arterial blood supply should be taken at its origin, thus assuring an adequate mesenteric resection. A lesion in the right colon requires a colonic resection with the ileocolic, right colic, and right branch of the middle colic artery (Fig. 43-1). Figure 43-1 also shows the extent of resection for carcinomas of the hepatic flexure, transverse colon, and splenic flexure. For a splenic flexure lesion, taking the left and middle colic vessels but leaving the ileocolic vessels is also acceptable.

Figure 43-2 shows the extent of mesenteric dissection for left and sigmoid colon carcinomas. The interior mesenteric artery (IMA) is taken at its origin, but it is unclear whether a high ligation and removal of

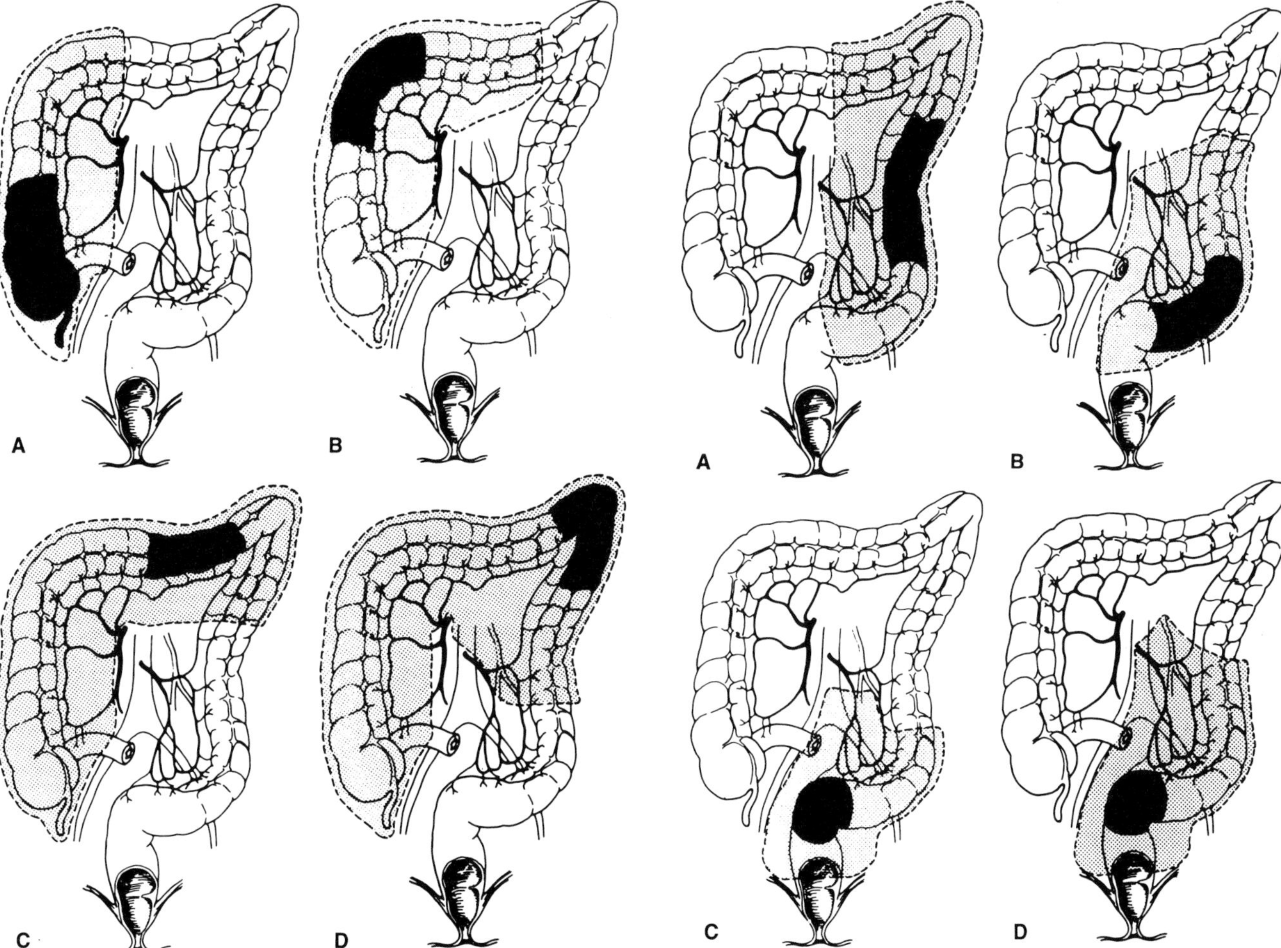

FIG. 43-1. Surgical resection for right and transverse colon cancers. (From DeVita VT, Jr, Hellman S, Rosenberg SA (eds): *Cancer: Principles and Practice of Oncology,* 4th ed. Philadelphia, Lippincott, reproduced by permission.)

FIG. 43-2. Surgical resection for left and sigmoid colon cancer. (From DeVita VT, Jr, Hellman S, Rosenberg SA (eds): *Cancer: Principles and Practice of Oncology,* 4th ed. Philadelphia, Lippincott, reproduced by permission.)

central lymph nodes around the IMA has therapeutic value. Enker et al.[4] reported excellent survival data in their colonic carcinoma series, and they attributed this to extensive lymphadenectomy. However, when Grinnell[10] reviewed his 17 patients with positive nodes at the IMA, he found that all patients had died of recurrent disease. Hence, it is not clear whether high ligation at the IMA leads to a survival advantage. It can be argued that left colonic tumors can be resected at the left colic artery and sigmoid colonic tumors require a mesenteric resection taking the superior rectal artery at its origin. Only a randomized trial comparing high ligation at the IMA with regional arterial ligation will resolve this issue.

Although the extent of lymphadenectomy may not necessarily influence survival, important prognostic information is available in the regional lymph nodes of the resected mesentery. Cady[11] has put forth the evolving concept that regional lymph nodes are not "governors" but rather "indicators" of survival. For solid tumors such as those of the breast, prostate, bladder, and cervix removal of regional lymph nodes provides important staging information and may not add to survival. The surgical treatment of colonic adenocarcinomas may evolve in a similar direction when more data become available.

There is another reason to perform an adequate regional node dissection for colonic cancer. Postoperative adjuvant systemic chemotherapy improves survival in patients with node-positive tumors ($T_{any}N_1M_0$ stage; stage III; Dukes C tumors) while no benefit was seen with node negative tumors ($T_{1-3}N_0M_0$; stage II, Dukes B tumors).[12] Therefore, an adequate lymph node sampling during a curative colonic resection is necessary in order to stage the disease and to select those patients who will benefit from postoperative adjuvant chemotherapy. Resecting colon and mesentery according to the regional arterial blood supply will provide sufficient node sampling for determining postoperative adjuvant chemotherapy.

OBSTRUCTING COLONIC CARCINOMAS

Obstructing colonic carcinomas are most frequently found in the sigmoid and left colon and less frequently in the right colon.[13] This clinical problem had traditionally been managed by a three-stage operative approach involving (1) a proximal colostomy, (2) a second-stage tumor resection about 14 days later, and (3) a colostomy closure at an even later date. If the patient can tolerate an open laparotomy and resection, a two-stage procedure can be done. In this situation the obstructed left or sigmoid colon and tumor are resected, the proximal end is brought out as a colostomy, and the distal end is stapled. Some 4 to 6 weeks later a second operation is performed with a prepared bowel to establish intestinal continuity. The rationale for these staged procedures is that it is unsafe to perform an intestinal anastomosis with an unprepared and obstructed colon.

There are alternatives to these staged procedures. An obstructing cecal lesion involving the ileocecal valve can be treated with a single-stage right colonic resection and primary anastomosis. For left-sided obstructing tumors, a colonic resection and intraoperative colonic lavage with a primary anastomosis has been described. The rationale is that the intraluminal lavage can decompress the bowel and reduce the fecal load. The anastomosis can then be performed in a clean, unladen intestine. This step adds at least 60 min to the procedure.

Another alternative is a subtotal colectomy with an ileo–descending colon or ileo–sigmoid colon anastomosis. This procedure removes the entire obstructed proximal colon with its fecal load, after which an anastomosis from the distal ileum to the distal colon can often be performed safety. The drawback to a subtotal colectomy is increased stool frequency, which can be exacerbated if systemic adjuvant chemotherapy is given.

While single-stage procedures for obstructing colonic cancer can be done safely, caution should be exercised in performing them. In seriously ill patients with significant comorbid diseases in whom a longer operation is precluded, a two-stage procedure should be considered. If patients are healthy and hemodynamically stable, a single-stage procedure may be preferable. Because obstructing lesions carry a worse prognosis,[15] these patients must complete surgical therapy in a timely fashion in order to start their systemic adjuvant chemotherapy. For this reason a single-stage procedure is more appealing.

PERFORATING CANCERS

Free perforation of the colon requires prompt surgical intervention with resection of the involved segment of colon, peritoneal lavage, and antibiotics. If fecal contamination of the peritoneal cavity is significant, a two-stage procedure with colonic resection of the perforation and tumor and a proximal colostomy is the safest approach. A localized perforation with abscess formation can be related to either diverticulitis, appendicitis, or malignancy. Resection of the colon and abscess is preferred.

CONTIGUOUS ORGAN INVOLVEMENT

Adjacent organ involvement is uncommon but poses major management problems. The goal of an operative resection for colonic carcinoma that has invaded an adjacent structure is to obtain a tumor-free margin. Although its attachment may be either inflammatory or direct tumor penetration, the adjacent organ should be resected en bloc with the colon. This may include either the small bowel, the dome of bladder, or the gallbladder. The area of invasion should be marked with metal clips and postoperative radiotherapy should be considered. An active Intergroup trial is evaluating the benefits of postoperative radiotherapy in such patients.

REFERENCES

1. American Joint Committee on Cancer: *Manual for Staging Cancer*, 3d ed. Philadelphia, JB Lippincott, 1988.
2. Turnbull RB Jr, Kyle K, Watson FR, et al: Cancer of the colon: The influence of the no-touch isolation technic on survival rates. *Ann Surg* 166:420–427, 1967.
3. Stearns MW, Schottenfeld D: Techniques for the surgical management of colon cancer. *Cancer* 28:165–169, 1971.
4. Enker WE, Laffer UT, Block GE: Enhanced survival of patients with colon and rectal cancer is based upon wide anatomic resection. *Ann Surg* 190:350–360, 1979.
5. Wiggers T, Jeekel J, Arends JW, et al: No-touch isolation technique in colon cancer: A controlled prospective trial. *Br J Surg* 75:409–415, 1988.
6. Miles EE: A method of performing abdomino-perineal excision for carcinoma of the rectum and of the terminal portion of the pelvic colon. *Lancet* 2:1812–1813, 1908.
7. Gabriel WB, Dukes C, Bussy HJ: Lymphatic spread in cancer of the rectum. *Br J Surg* 23:395–413, 1935.
8. Grinnell RS: Lymphatic block with atypical and retrograde lymphatic metastasis and spread in carcinoma of the colon and rectum. *Ann Surg* 163:272–280, 1966.
9. Sugarbaker PH, Corlew S: Influence of surgical techniques on survival in patients with colorectal cancer: A review. *Dis Colon Rectum* 25:545–557, 1982.
10. Grinnell RS: Results of ligation of inferior mesenteric artery at the aorta in resections of carcinoma of the descending and

sigmoid colon and rectum. *Surg Gynecol Obstet* 120:1031–1036, 1965.

11. Cady B: Lymph node metastasis: Indicators but not governors of survival. *Arch Surg* 119:1067–1072, 1984.
12. Steele G: Adjuvant therapy for patients with colon and rectal cancer: Clinical indications for multimodality therapy in high-risk groups and specific surgical questions for future multimodality trials. *Surgery* 112:847–849, 1992.
13. Ohman U: Prognosis in patients with obstructing colorectal carcinoma. *Am J Surg* 143:742–747, 1982.
14. MacKenzie S, Thomson SR, Baker LW: Management options in malignant obstruction of the left colon. *Surg Gynecol Obstet* 174:337–345, 1992.
15. Wolmark N, Wieand HS, Rockette HE, et al: The prognostic significance of tumor location and bowel obstruction in Dukes B and C colorectal cancer. *Ann Surg* 198:743–752, 1983.

CHAPTER 44

Intestinal Preparation before Colorectal Surgery

Ronald Lee Nichols
James Wm. C. Holmes

HIGHLIGHTS

Preoperative preparation of the intestine is a prerequisite for modern elective colorectal surgery. This consists of a mechanical cleansing of the large bowel followed by preoperative oral antibiotic prophylaxis and perioperative parenteral antibiotic therapy using antimicrobial agents with coverage of the aerobic and anaerobic colonic microflora. Such a protocol markedly reduces the infectious complication of colorectal operations.

CONTROVERSIES

The importance of mechanical bowel preparation prior to elective large bowel surgery has been universally accepted, while preoperative oral antibiotic prophylaxis followed by perioperative parenteral antibiotic administration has become the standard of care. Controversy exists as to which agents should be utilized for large bowel prophylaxis preoperatively and for antimicrobial therapy in the perioperative and postoperative periods. The drugs used must have appropriate coverage for the aerobic and anaerobic organisms found in the large bowel. Other important factors in the choice of antibiotics are the cost of the drugs as well as their frequency of administration.

FUTURE DIRECTIONS

Development and testing of antibiotic preparations with both aerobic and anaerobic antimicrobial activities continues.

Elective outpatient preoperative preparation of the large bowel increases patient comfort and decreases hospitalization costs. Patient compliance is good but requires preoperative instruction as to administration of purgatives and antibiotics.

Intraoperative colonic lavage allows resection of the bowel with primary anastomosis in selected cases.

The human colon and distal small intestine contain an enormous reservoir of aerobic and anaerobic bacteria that are excluded from the rest of the body by a mucous membrane.[1] If this membrane barrier is disturbed by disease or trauma or if the colon is opened to the peritoneal cavity during operation, bacteria may escape into adjacent tissues and cause serious infection. Most of these infections are limited to the operative wound, resulting in patient discomfort and anxiety in addition to a lengthened hospital stay and increased expense. Other complications—such as intraabdominal sepsis, septicemia, or anastomotic leakage—pose grave therapeutic challenges that result in a high degree of morbidity and mortality. One technique used to minimize this risk is mechanical cleansing of the colon; however, mechanical cleansing does not kill bacteria but merely removes some bacteria-laden waste material from the colon. To prevent infection, the colonic microflora must be suppressed. A reliable method of sterilization has been a goal of surgeons throughout this century. In the past 20 years, results of clinical trials have clearly shown that to reduce septic complications significantly after elective colonic surgery, it is necessary to employ antibiotics that act against both colonic aerobes such as *Escherichia coli* and colonic anaerobes such as *Bacteroides fragilis*. There is still some controversy over what the best antibiotic regimen is and how it should be administered.[2]

BACTERIOLOGY OF THE GASTROINTESTINAL TRACT

The human gastrointestinal tract in utero is sterile.[1] Within a few hours of birth, the oral and anal orifices are colonized and organisms can be cultured from the rectum. The intestinal flora at this time is variable and is derived from the environment of the infant. A few days after birth, a more stable gastrointestinal flora begins to establish itself. The types of bacteria that colonize the colon at this time depend on whether the newborn infant is formula- or breast-fed. The stool of the breast-fed infant is characterized by large concentrations of gram-positive organisms, predominantly *Lactobacillus bifidus*. The stool flora of formula-fed infants is more complex, with a predominance of gram-negative aerobic and anaerobic organisms, and resembles the stool of older children eating a mixed diet.

Smith and Crabb[3] studied the stool flora of a variety of newborn animals and human infants. During the early weeks of life, the flora was similar in all species. As the animals grew older, however, differences developed. *Bacteroides* and *Lactobacillus* were the most common organisms found in the stool of human infants, and clostridia, coliforms, and streptococci predominated in the feces of lower animals. *Staphylococcus aureus* was never isolated from animals and appeared only in human stool. Because of such species differences in fecal flora, study results of antibiotic preparation of the colon in lower animals must be applied with considerable caution to humans.

During the last 20 years, many thoughtfully designed and scientifically accurate studies have outlined the gastrointestinal flora in both healthy and diseased colons.[4] These reports have demonstrated that anaerobic, nonsporulating, gram-negative rods, predominately *Bacteroides*, are the most prevalent bacteria in the colon. These anaerobic microorganisms are 1000 to 100,000 times more numerous than aerobic coliforms. Stool specimens usually contain 10^{10} to 10^{11} anaerobic bacteroides per gram, and aerobic coliforms number 10^6 to 10^8 organisms per gram. Other major fecal organisms are microaerophilic lactobacilli, anaerobic lactobacilli or bifidobacteria, and streptococci. The minor bacterial constituents of human stool include *Proteus, Pseudomonas, Clostridium,* and *Staphylococcus*.

Most recently, emphasis has been placed on studying both the luminal and mucosal-associated colonic flora.[5,6] These qualitatively and quantitatively different populations of colonic bacteria may have varying degrees of influence on bacterial translocation, anastomotic healing, and wound or intraabdominal infections.

RISK FOR INFECTION IN COLONIC SURGERY

Many clinical studies of risk factors for infection in specific operative procedures have been published during the 1980s. Knowledge of the presence or absence of these risk factors in the perioperative period may allow for the modification of infection control techniques in studies conducted during the 1990s.[7]

Kaiser et al.,[8] studying elective colonic resection and different approaches to preoperative antibiotic prophylaxis, have shown a direct correlation between the duration of the operation and the postoperative infection rate. In operations lasting less than 3 h, no infections were identified when the antibiotic prophylaxis was with a parenteral agent alone or a combination of oral and parenteral agents. However, in operations lasting more than 4 h, a significant reduction of infection was observed in those patients receiving the combination prophylactic regimen. Coppa and Eng,[9] in a similar study of elective colonic resection, have stressed that postoperative wound infections are associated with the length of operation and location of the colonic resection (intraperitoneal colonic resection versus rectal resection). These authors showed that the wound infection rate in high-risk patients with long operations (>215 min) and rectal resection could significantly benefit from the use of a combination of oral and parenteral prophylactic antibiotics.

GENERAL RULES OF ANTIBIOTIC PROPHYLAXIS IN SURGERY

Reviews of a large number of clinical studies dealing with surgical prophylaxis have classified those patients who may be expected to benefit from perioperative antibiotics.[10,11] Prophylactic antibiotics are indicated in patients undergoing clean-contaminated procedures, such as colonic or rectal.

Choice of Antibiotics

No single antibiotic agent or combination should be relied upon for effective prophylaxis in all operations. The agent or agents should be chosen primarily on the basis of their efficacy against the exogenous and endogenous microorganisms usually known to cause infectious complications in each clinical setting as well as the agents' safety profile and cost. Where multiple individual drug choices have been proven equally efficacious and safe, local hospital cost analyses and utilization studies may lead to choosing the agent that will result in the greatest savings. Worldwide, the cephalosporins are the most widely used antibiotics for surgical prophylaxis.[12] It has been stressed that antibiotic coverage for all the potential pathogens is not a desired feature of a prophylactic regimen. However, it is important to maintain a local up-to-date hospital analysis of the antimicrobial susceptibilities of wound isolates so as to detect important shifts in patterns of resistance.

Timing of Antibiotic Prophylaxis

The effective use of prophylactic antibiotics depends to a great extent on the appropriate timing of their administration. Historically, the most common errors observed, which dulled the luster of this technique, were faulty timing of the initial administration and the common practice of continuing the antibiotic beyond 72 h.[13]

Current recommendations indicate that the parenteral antibiotics used in prophylaxis should be given in sufficient dosage within 30 min preceding incision.[10,11] This can be facilitated by having the anesthesiologist administer the antibiotic in the operating room, when the intravenous lines are started, shortly before operative incision. This timing replaces the former approach of giving the antibiotic "on call" to the operating room, a technique that frequently resulted in delays of 3 or 4 h before operative incision and subsequently low or absent serum and tissue levels of antibiotic at the actual time of operation. A recent large clinical study of the timing of prophylactic antibiotic administration in almost 2900 patients has shown that administration of the antibiotic within 2 h of incision reduces the risk of subsequent wound infections.[14] Starting the antibiotic agent within 30 min of incision results in therapeutic drug levels in the wound and surrounding tissues during the operation. Evidence from clinical trials is mounting that a single preoperative dose of antibiotic results in the same efficacy as multiple doses given during the perioperative course. Those that advocate single-dose prophylaxis generally recommend that another dose be given in operations lasting over 2 to 3 h.

In oral preoperative antibiotic preparation—commonly utilized before elective colonic resection—the chosen agents should be given during the 24 h before surgery in order to attain significant intraluminal (local) and serum (systemic) levels.[11] In utilizing oral neomycin and erythromycin base, it is necessary to give only three doses of each agent during the 19 h prior to operative incision in order to accomplish appropriate levels. Longer periods of preoperative preparation are not necessary and have been associated with the isolation of resistant organisms within the colonic lumen at the time of resection.

Route of Administration of Prophylactic Antibiotics

Intravenous administration of the prophylactic antibiotic is preferred in most patients undergoing an operative procedure. When this is accomplished in a relatively small volume over a short period of time (20 to 30 min), one can expect high serum and tissue levels. The pharmacokinetics of each individual antibiotic agent largely determine the period of time efficacious serum levels are maintained. Agents with short half-lives (<1 h) should be redosed for every 2 to 3 h of operative time. There are a number of agents with different half-lives that are used in surgical prophylaxis for prolonged operations, but as yet no study comparing them has been done. Oral administration of antibiotics currently plays a major role only in the preparation of patients for elective colonic operations.[11]

PREPARATION BEFORE COLONIC RESECTION

Prior to the 1970s, the majority of surgeons utilized primarily mechanical cleansing before elective colonic surgery.[1] The oral antibiotics (neomycin, kanamycin, streptomycin, and sulfonamides) that had been utilized most often at that time were found later only to suppress the facultative aerobic colonic flora and were associated with high percentages of clinical failures. In addition, the use of these oral antibiotics for 3- to 5-day periods before elective colonic resection was frequently associated with the overgrowth of staphylococci and yeast within the colonic lumen.[11]

Mechanical Preparation

Mechanical cleansing of the colonic lumen before elective colonic resection is a time-tested procedure that, when done appropriately, reduces total fecal mass, thus facilitating operative manipulation of the colon and enhancing the action of oral antibiotics. Vigorous mechanical cleansing alone, however—whether it includes lavage or follows the classic approach (dietary restriction, enemas, and cathartics)—does not significantly reduce the number of microorganisms in residual colonic material.[15,16] This microbiologic failure of mechanical cleansing alone also translates to clinical failure. More than 40 percent of patients undergoing elective colonic resection developed septic complications following mechanical cleansing alone in two large prospective randomized, double-blind clinical trials investigating the efficacy of oral antibiotic prophylaxis.[17,18]

Approaches to mechanical cleansing vary considerably. For many good reasons, the time-honored 5-day preoperative preparation has long been abandoned. Among the most important of these reasons are the severe iatrogenically induced metabolic abnormalities that were reported more than 20 years ago. Modern approaches fall into two general categories: (1) whole-gut lavage with either an electrolyte solution, 10% mannitol, or polyethylene glycol on the day before operation and (2) standard mechanical cleansing, which utilizes dietary restriction, cathartics, and enemas for a 2-day period.[19–22] It is possible, as well as advisable in these cost-conscious days, to perform the preoperative bowel preparation when possible on an outpatient basis, thereby saving hundreds of dollars per admission.[23]

In patients presenting with partially obstructing lesions of the large bowel, surgery is more often urgent than elective. Although these individuals will often not tolerate a rapid mechanical preoperative bowel preparation, they will, fortunately, generally tolerate decelerated mechanical bowel preparation. Such a partially obstructed patient who is stable and in good clinical condition is admitted to the hospital while undergoing preoperative bowel preparation. Resuscitation with parenteral fluids and their continuation at a maintenance rate is usually necessary, although many patients will tolerate clear liquids by mouth. Fleet Phospho-Soda (a buffered oral saline laxative) is also given orally in 10-mL aliquots at hourly intervals for 6 doses on day 2 preoperatively and is repeated starting at 6 A.M. on preoperative day 1. If the patient develops worsening abdominal distension or signs of complete obstruction, the oral mechanical bowel preparation is stopped and the patient is prepared for urgent surgery using an appropriate perioperative parenteral antimicrobial agent or agents. In the patient who tolerates the decelerated mechanical bowel preparation, oral preoperative antibiotic prophylaxis is given and surgery is done the following morning, utilizing a parenteral perioperative antibiotic coverage.

Emergency situations often require immediate surgical intervention, which precludes preoperative mechanical and oral antibiotic bowel preparation. In selected patients with limited intraabdominal disease and without peritonitis or free pus, resection of the diseased segment of large bowel with primary anastomosis is possible. This is routinely done without the benefit of preoperative mechanical bowel preparation in patients with lesions of the right colon. Under identical clinical settings, emergency surgery for distal colonic lesions presents a greater challenge. Intraoperative antegrade colonic lavage following resection of the diseased distal segment of colon or rectum will facilitate primary anastomosis in many such cases. This technique has a place in the surgeon's armamentarium. However, it is not recommended for the surgeon operating alone and is most useful when adequate assistance is available to allow a group effort, so as to prevent loss of control of either the proximal or distal ends of the lavage circuit. Such a loss of control can cause gross fecal contamination of the abdominal cavity, which leads to disastrous results in the patient's postoperative course.[24,25] Perioperative coverage with parenteral antibiotic agents with aerobic and anaerobic activity are indicated in these emergency procedures.

Antibiotic Preoperative Preparation

The vast majority of surgeons today employ antibiotics and mechanical cleansing for preoperative preparation before elective colonic resection.[2,26] The antibiotics chosen should be effective in suppressing both the colonic aerobes and anaerobes (Table 44-1). There continues to be some interest concerning which agents are ideal and which route of administration is preferred. Those investigators who advocate oral antibiotic usage generally stress the importance of the reduction of microorganisms within the colonic lumen prior to opening the colon, while those who rely on parenteral agents stress the importance of adequate tissue levels of antibiotics.

Oral Antibiotic Agents

In a recently reported survey of 500 board-certified colorectal surgeons, 92 percent of the 370 respondents said that they utilized oral antibiotics in their preoperative preparation.[26] At the present time, three regimens of oral agents are utilized, combining neomycin

Table 44-1
Selected Single and Combination Parenterally Administered Antibiotic Agents That Cover Facultative/Anaerobic Colonic Microflora

Facultative coverage—to be combined with a drug having anaerobic activity
Amikacin
Aztreonam
Cefotaxime
Ceftriaxone
Ciprofloxacin
Gentamicin
Tobramycin
Anaerobic coverage—to be combined with a drug having facultative activity
Chloramphenicol
Clindamycin
Metronidazole
Facultative-anaerobic coverage—single agents
Ampicillin-sulbactam
Cefotetan
Cefoxitin
Ceftizoxime
Imipenem-cilastatin
Piperacillin-tazobactam
Ticarcillin-clavulanic acid

with either erythromycin base, metronidazole, or tetracycline.[2,11] The greatest experience in the United States has been with the neomycin–erythromycin base preparation, which was introduced in 1972,[27,28] while the use of metronidazole plus either kanamycin or neomycin is popular in Great Britain.[2] Reviews of antibiotic prophylaxis for colonic surgery continue to support the value of oral neomycin–erythromycin base bowel preparation in preventing infections following elective colonic resection.[2,10,11,29] The pharmacokinetics of this preparation have been studied in healthy volunteers and in patients undergoing elective colonic resection.[30,31] These studies suggest that when adequate mechanical preparation is used, a significant intraluminal (local) level of both antibiotics is achieved, as well as a serum (systemic) level of erythromycin, and that both mechanisms may play a role in the prevention of infection after colonic surgery. The timing of administration of these oral agents appears to be critical. It is recommended that only 1 g of each agent, neomycin and erythromycin base, be given at 1 P.M., 2 P.M., and 11 P.M. on the day prior to surgery (6 g total). Surgery should be scheduled to be at about 8 A.M. when this approach is utilized. If the operation is scheduled for later in the day, the time sequence of administration should be appropriately changed to preserve the 19-h schema.

Parenteral Antibiotic Agents

The first prospective randomized, double-blind study of parenteral antibiotic prophylaxis usage in elective colonic resection was published in 1969, utilizing perioperative cephaloridine administered intramuscularly.[31] This study revealed a significant reduction in postoperative infections (7 versus 30 percent) in the group of patients receiving antibiotics and mechanical preparation as compared to the use of mechanical preparation alone. However, other clinical studies utilizing the same or similar first-generation cephalosporin prophylaxis failed to show the efficacy of this approach when compared with placebo (mechanical preparation alone) or with oral neomycin and erythromycin base.[2] Clinical studies comparing parenteral cephalosporin alone in this setting showed a lack of efficacy unless the antibiotic possessed facultative and anaerobic activity.[2] Most investigators recommend the perioperative use of one to five doses of parenteral agent during the 24-h period starting shortly before operation.

Combination of Parenteral and Oral Antibiotic Agents

Most surgeons presently utilize both oral and parenteral antibiotic agents and mechanical cleansing as preoperative preparation before elective colonic resection in the hope of reducing the postoperative infection rate.[2] According to the previously mentioned 1990 survey of 350 board-certified colorectal surgeons, all utilized antibiotics in addition to mechanical cleansing.[26] Three percent utilized only oral agents, 8 percent utilized only systemic agents, and the remaining 89 percent utilized a combination of both oral and parenteral agents. Studies utilizing single parenteral antibiotics with both facultative and anaerobic coverage (e.g., cefotetan, cefoxitin, or ceftizoxime) in addition to oral neomycin and erythromycin base have been shown to be associated with a low incidence of infection.[2] It appears at this time that the addition of one dose of parenteral antibiotic such as mentioned above, given within 30 min of incision to the oral and mechanical bowel preparation, may be beneficial. A complete review of all agents utilized and recommended for preoperative antibiotic preparation throughout the world has recently been updated.[2]

CONCLUSIONS

The use of preoperative mechanical bowel preparation and preoperative oral antibiotic prophylaxis in conjunction with perioperative parenteral antibiotics has revolutionized colorectal surgery. Morbidity and mortality have been drastically reduced and surgical control of a disease process can now often be achieved at one time rather than in two or three staged operations, thereby further reducing the incidence of cumulative postoperative complications.

The morbidity of the preoperative preparatory process can be greatly lessened by performing it in an accelerated manner over 1 to 2 days prior to surgery rather than the time-honored 3 to 5 days. Patient comfort is enhanced by allowing the use of no-residue liquid dietary supplements as well as a clear liquid diet. Both the cost of each hospitalization and the risk of postoperative wound infection are reduced when the mechanical and oral antibiotic bowel preparations are administered on an outpatient basis. Certainly all patients undergoing elective colorectal surgery should undergo preoperative preparation consisting of mechanical cleansing of the bowel followed by preoperative antibiotic prophylaxis. We recommend oral erythromycin base and neomycin preoperatively in conjunction with a single dose of preoperative parenteral antibiotic which has both aerobic and anaerobic antimicrobial action against the endogenous flora of the large bowel.

REFERENCES

1. Nichols RL, Condon RE: Preoperative preparation of the colon—Collective review. *Surg Gynecol Obstet* 132:323–337, 1971.
2. Nichols RL: Bowel preparations, in Wilmore DW, Brennan MF, Harken AH, et al (eds): *Care of the Surgical Patient*, 2nd

ed, vol VI, *Preoperative Care*. New York, Scientific American, 1990, chap 4, pp 1–10.
3. Smith WH, Crabb WE: The fecal bacterial flora of animals and man: Its development in the young. *J Pathol Bacteriol* 82:53–64, 1961.
4. Nichols RL: *Surgery Annual*. East Norwalk, Conn, Appleton & Lange, 1981, pp 205–238.
5. Lindsey JT, Smith JW, McClugage SG, et al: Effects of commonly used bowel preparations on the large bowel mucosal-associated and luminal microflora in the rat model. *Dis Colon Rectum* 33:554–560, 1990.
6. Smith MB, Goradia VK, Holmes JW, et al: Suppression of the human mucosal-related colonic microflora with prophylactic parenteral and/or oral antibiotics. *World J Surg* 14:636–664, 1990.
7. Nichols RL: Surgical wound infection. *Am J Med* 91 (suppl 3B):54s–64s, 1991.
8. Kaiser AB, Herrington JL Jr, Jacobs JK, et al: Cefoxitin versus erythromycin, neomycin, and cefazolin in colorectal operations. *Ann Surg* 198:525–530, 1983.
9. Coppa GF, Eng K: Factors involved in antibiotic selection in elective colon and rectal surgery. *Surgery* 104:853–858, 1988.
10. Antimicrobial prophylaxis in surgery. *Med Lett Drug Ther* 35:91–94, 1993.
11. Nichols RL: Prophylaxis for surgical infections, in Gorbach SL, Bartlett JG, Blacklow NR (eds): *Infectious Diseases*. Philadelphia, Saunders, 1992, pp 393–403.
12. Gorbach SL: The role of cephalosporins in surgical prophylaxis. *J Antimicrob Chemother* 23(suppl D):61–70, 1989.
13. Shapiro M, Townsend TR, Rosner B, et al: Use of antimicrobial drugs in general hospitals: Patterns of prophylaxis. *N Engl J Med* 301:351–355, 1979.
14. Classen DC, Evans RS, Pestotnik SL, et al: The timing of prophylactic administration of antibiotics and the risk of surgical wound infection. *N Engl J Med* 326:281–286, 1992.
15. Nichols RL, Gorbach SL, Condon RE: Alteration of intestinal microflora following preoperative mechanical preparation of the colon. *Dis Colon Rectum* 14:123–127, 1971.
16. Bartlett JG, Condon RE, Gorbach SL, et al: Veterans Administration cooperative study on bowel preparation of elective colorectal operations: Impact of oral antibiotic regimen on colonic flora, wound irrigation cultures and bacteriology of septic complications. *Ann Surg* 188:249–254, 1978.
17. Clarke JS, Condon RE, Bartlett JG, et al: Preoperative oral antibiotics reduce septic complications of colon operations. *Ann Surg* 186:251–259, 1977.
18. Washington JA, Dearing WH, Judd ES, et al: Effect of preoperative antibiotic regimen on development of infection after intestinal surgery: Prospective randomized double-blind study. *Ann Surg* 180:567–572, 1974.
19. Beck DE, Harford FJ, DiPalma JA: Comparison of cleansing methods in preparation for colonic surgery. *Dis Colon Rectum* 28:491–496, 1985.
20. Bowden TA Jr, DiPiro JT, Michael KA: Polyethylene glycol electrolyte lavage solution (PEG-ELS): A rapid, safe mechanical bowel preparation for colorectal surgery. *Am Surg* 53:34–39, 1987.
21. Jagelman DG, Fazio VW, Lavery IC, et al: A prospective, randomized, double-blind study of 10% mannitol mechanical bowel preparation combined with oral neomycin and short-term, perioperative, intravenous Flagyl as prophylaxis in elective colorectal resections. *Surgery* 98:861–870, 1985.
22. Keighley MRB: A clinical and physiological evaluation of bowel preparation for elective colorectal surgery. *World J Surg* 6:464–468, 1982.
23. Frazee RC, Roberts J, Symmonds R, et al: Prospective randomized trial of inpatient vs. outpatient bowel preparation for elective colorectal surgery. *Dis Colon Rectum* 35:223–226, 1992.
24. Muir EG: Safety in colonic resection. *Proc R Soc Med* 61:401–408, 1968.
25. Murray JJ, Schoetz DJ Jr, Coller JA, et al: Intraoperative colonic lavage and primary anastomosis in nonelective colon resection. *Dis Colon Rectum* 34:527–531, 1991.
26. Solla JA, Rothenberger DA: Preoperative bowel preparation—A survey of colon and rectal surgeons. *Dis Colon Rectum* 33:154–159, 1990.
27. Nichols RL, Condon RE, Gorbach SL, et al: Efficacy of preoperative antimicrobial preparation of the bowel. *Ann Surg* 176:227–232, 1972.
28. Nichols RL, Broido P, Condon RE, et al: The effect of preoperative neomycin-erythromycin intestinal preparation on the incidence of infectious complications following colon surgery. *Ann Surg* 178:453–462, 1973.
29. Gorbach SL, Condon RE, Conte JE, et al: General guidelines for the evaluation of new anti-infective drugs for prophylaxis of surgical infections: Evaluation of new anti-infective drugs for surgical prophylaxis. *Clin Infect Dis* 15(suppl 1):S313–S338, 1992.
30. Nichols RL, Condon RE, DiSanto AR: Preoperative bowel preparation—Erythromycin base serum and fecal levels following oral administration. *Arch Surg* 112:1493–1496, 1977.
31. Polk HC Jr, Lopez-Mayor JF: Postoperative wound infections: A prospective study of determinant factors and prevention. *Surgery* 66:97–103, 1969.

CHAPTER 45

Surgical Considerations—Bowel Anastomosis

Steven K. Libutti
Kenneth A. Forde

In the performance of a bowel resection for colon cancer, the restoration of bowel continuity is as important to the patient's outcome as the resection itself. A poorly constructed anastomosis can result in complications such as stricture formation, breakdown, and leakage. Morbidity and mortality are increased secondary to obstruction, abscess formation, and sepsis; therefore careful anastomotic technique is of critical importance.

The term *anastomosis* is defined as a union of two hollow or tubular structures created by surgery, trauma, or disease and is derived from the Greek *anastomoun:* to furnish with an outlet. The earliest anastomoses were performed in order to repair the traumatic disruption of bowel continuity resulting from injuries sustained in battle. References to anastomotic techniques can be found as far back as 460 B.C. in the writings of Hippocrates and, later, in those of Celsus (30 B.C. to A.D. 30), a celebrated Roman authority on medicine.[1,2]

The fear of creating a stricture, which would most certainly lead to death, led some of the earliest practitioners of the art of surgery to avoid performing anastomoses of the bowel in any form. Galen (A.D. 130–200) wrote of the evils of suturing either the large or small bowel, and Celsus was opposed to the suturing of the small bowel, although he felt that the large bowel could be successfully repaired.[1] In an effort to avoid these complications, certain basic principles for constructing anastomoses emerged. These can be found in the writings of such nineteenth-century surgeons as Travers, Lembert, Czerny, Senn, and Halsted.[2,3] It was during the nineteenth century that many of the techniques still in use today were developed. In order to evaluate and critically analyze various anastomotic techniques, it is first essential that one understand the scientific evidence supporting these basic principles.

PRINCIPLES OF ANASTOMOTIC TECHNIQUE

The following are critical to the success of any colonic anastomosis: (1) adequate blood supply, (2) absence of tension (both external and internal), (3) absence of inflammation, and (4) absence of infection. We will examine the importance of each of these "four A's" of anastomotic technique in the setting of the normally healing wound. Several authors have stressed understanding the phases of wound healing in order to examine the traditional doctrines of intestinal suturing and the experimental foundations on which they are based.[3,4] The events following the apposition of two cut edges of tissue, which will ultimately lead to a restoration of tissue integrity, can be divided into three phases.[3,5,6]

Immediately following tissue injury, there is a brisk inflammatory response. This phase is marked by changes in vascular permeability, cellular infiltration by polymorphonuclear leukocytes, and the release of cytokines. During this period, which lasts approximately 4 to 5 days, debris is cleared from the wound edges and the early strength of the wound is provided by a fibrin mesh. Throughout the lag phase of wound healing, the immature wound is at its weakest and is almost entirely reliant upon the strength of the suture material to avoid complete disruption.

The second phase of wound healing is referred to as the period of fibroplasia.[3,5,6] Fibroplasia begins during the inflammatory phase, usually on day 3, and will last approximately 21 days. Fibroblasts and macrophages predominate and immature collagen is deposited. Tensile strength begins to increase exponentially between days 5 and 14. It is after day 5 that the suture material holding the wound together begins to take on less significance.

Finally, beginning on or about day 10, the phase of maturation begins. Collagen accumulation continues until day 21, after which further collagen deposition ceases. However, tensile strength continues to increase exponentially as the collagen undergoes remodeling and cross linking.[7] The period of wound maturation may last as long as 1 year.

Many of the studies on which our understanding of these events is based were conducted using skin models. However, this sequence of events was confirmed in healing intestinal anastomoses as well.[8,9] Factors which tend to prolong the lag phase of wound healing and therefore delay the onset of fibroplasia will result in a weaker anastomosis, which will be more prone to leakage and disruption. With the phases of wound healing as a framework, we can begin to understand the importance of the four A's of anastomotic technique.

Adequate blood supply to the tissue edges of the anastomosis is critical for healing to occur. If the blood supply is compromised, necrosis will ensue, resulting in an increased inflammatory response. In addition, oxygen is necessary for the proper synthesis of collagen. Blood flow is needed for the removal of toxic metabolites and for successful clearing of cellular debris. In the absence of an adequate blood supply, the lag phase of wound healing is prolonged and the anastomosis is doomed to failure, regardless of the technique used for its creation.

Tension on the anastomosis will lead to suture line ischemia. The absence of tension is therefore important for an anastomosis to be successful. Adequate mobilization of the two bowel segments to be joined is critical and care should be taken to eliminate this source of external tension. Internal tension is also detrimental to adequate healing. An adequate mechanical bowel preparation is important to reduce the bulk of material present in the lumen and therefore the internal tension (distension) on the anastomosis.

The presence of inflammation at and near the lines of resection will delay the healing of intestinal anastomoses.[10–12] Inflammation may be secondary to necrotic debris, suture material, or trauma to the tissues during the creation of the anastomosis.[12] Halsted, and later Whipple, emphasized the importance of minimizing inflammation by minimizing the presence of foreign body and damaged tissue in the wound.[12] In various studies comparing different suturing techniques, the techniques which produced the least inflammation resulted in the highest tensile strength and the most rapid rate of healing.[12–14]

The presence of infection has often been cited as an etiologic factor contributing to the development of anastomotic leaks.[12] This phenomenon occurs secondary to an inflammatory response to bacteria and by stimulation of collagenase activity. Several studies addressing the mechanism by which the presence of infection contributes to anastomotic dehiscence have demonstrated that bacterial contamination increases collagenolytic activity, resulting in lower bursting strengths secondary to decreased collagen content.[12,15–17] The use of oral antibiotics, such as erythromycin and kanamycin, in attempts to minimize the presence of bacteria in the colon prior to anastomosis has been shown to result in significantly increased tensile strength when compared to controls.[12,18] Therefore, the presence of infection adversely affects the strength and integrity of intestinal anastomoses by at least two mechanisms: promoting inflammation as well as increasing collagenase activity and therefore delaying wound healing.

The ideal anastomotic technique would obviously maximize blood supply and minimize tension, inflammation, and infection. With this in mind, we can critically analyze the various techniques for reestablishing bowel continuity that have evolved since antiquity.

SUTURED ANASTOMOSES

As mentioned above, the earliest recorded examples of successful suturing of the intestine date back as far as ancient Greece,[1,2] and the Roman Celsus wrote of having closed intestinal injuries using a "glover's stitch," a continuous running suture commonly used at that time by glove makers.[1,2] During the next several centuries, various variations on this theme were proposed, making use of both interrupted and continuous single-layer closures. As early as the eleventh century, the importance of aseptic technique was recognized, and both transverse and longitudinal wounds were closed using stents when necessary to prevent stricture formation.[1,2] However, it was not until the nineteenth century, with the introduction of anesthetics, that elective bowel resection became a reality.[1] It was this achievement that led to an explosion in the development of anastomotic techniques and to many of the principles to which we still rigorously adhere.

Hand-sewn colonic anastomoses are commonly performed in a two-layer fashion. A continuous inner layer of absorbable suture material (gut, Vicryl, Dexons, etc.) is used to approximate the mucosa, and an interrupted outer layer of nonabsorbable suture (silk, silver, stainless steel) is used to create an inverted serosa-to-serosa apposition incorporating submucosa for strength. This method is based on the Czerny modification of the Lembert anastomosis.[1,12] The importance of including the subumucosa with each stitch in order to provide strength to the anastomoses is a concept first proposed by Halsted and since supported by multiple experimental studies demonstrating that the submucosal layer provides all of the strength.[3]

The use of an inverting suture as opposed to an everting suture was made popular by Lembert. Prior to this, Travers had been a proponent of a single-layer everting anastomosis. While studies have not definitively proven the superiority of one over the other, there is experimental evidence to suggest that while everting anastomoses may result in a lower rate of stricture formation, they are by and large weaker than inverting anastomoses and produce more adhesions.[3]

All suture material, whether absorbable or nonabsorbable, produces inflammation at the suture lines.[3,12] The passage of a needle through tissue similarly produces inflammation. The presence of multiple sutures results in suture line ischemia. We have already established that a successful anastomosis is dependent on the minimization of inflammation and ischemia. Therefore, if one is going to employ sutures to create an anastomosis, it is important to choose the material and the technique that will minimize these factors.

Several studies have been performed comparing different types of suture material.[4,12,19–21] Comparisons have been based on measurements of tensile or bursting strength, amount of inflammation evoked, and rates of infection. While no single suture material can be termed ideal, the collective conclusions of many studies suggest that sutures with smooth surfaces that evoke minimal tissue reaction—such as those produced from polyglycolic acid, polypropylene, monofilament nylon, and Teflon-coated Dacron—are among the best.

The earliest hand-sewn anastomoses were created using a single layer of suture material. The first two-layer anastomosis is credited to Larry[1] who added a second layer for "added strength." Czerny popularized the two-layer closure with his modification of Lembert's technique. There is still considerable debate among surgeons as to whether one should perform a one-layer or two-layer closure. However, there is an increasing body of experimental evidence which would tend to favor a single-layer closure based on the principles of anastomotic technique we have already outlined.

Direct comparisons of double-layer Czerney-Lembert and single-layer Lembert anastomoses have been performed in a canine model.[12,22] Results suggested that the two-layer technique resulted in a significant reduction in the anastomotic lumen as well as increased inflammation. Others have shown that a two-layer technique decreases tensile strength and increases anastomotic leakage by reducing the arterial supply and obstructing venous and lymphatic return.[12,23] This leads to increased tissue necrosis and a prolongation of the inflammatory phase. Single-layer anastomoses have been shown to result in increased tensile strength as well as collagen content during the lag phase of wound healing as well as advanced rates of healing during the period of fibroplasia.[24,25]

In spite of this large body of experimental data, there still exists debate regarding single- versus double-layer anastomoses. This is due in part to a paucity of large clinical studies comparing the two techniques. While there are no large series which directly compare one- versus two-layer closures in a prospective randomized fashion, reports are now emerging which describe large experiences with methods of single-layer closure. One such method makes use of a continuous single-layer polypropylene suture to construct colocolic, colorectal, ileocolic, and ileorectal anastomoses. The largest of these studies was reported by Max et al.,[26] who described their experience with 1000 consecutive single-layer continuous polypropylene anastomoses performed over a 9-year period. Their results demonstrated a leakage rate of 1 percent for intraperitoneal anastomoses, a rate of obstruction of 2 percent, a wound complication rate of 2 percent, and a mortality rate of 1 percent. These rates are comparable to and in most instances better than those reported for two-layer and stapled techniques (Table 45-1). These data are supported by other, smaller series at different institutions.[27,28]

Therefore—based on the four A's of anastomotic technique, a large body of experimental data and multiple clinical trials now emerging—we can draw the following conclusions regarding hand-sewn anastomoses. The type of suture material used is important only with regard to minimizing tissue reaction and inflammation. There are many materials available currently which will meet these criteria. Care must be taken in the handling of the tissue edges and in the passage of the needle to minimize tissue trauma. And finally, single-layer closure, whether interrupted or continuous,[28] appears to be superior to a two-layer closure with respect to minimizing inflammation and ischemia, although the definitive prospective randomized clinical trial has yet to be performed.

STAPLED ANASTOMOSES

Stapling devices have gained widespread popularity since their introduction in the United State by Ravitch et al.[29] in 1959. They are commonly used for anastomoses of both the intra- and extraperitoneal colon as well as other gastrointestinal viscera. Perhaps the first anastomotic "stapler" was a device used by Henroz in 1850, which consisted of two self-securing intraluminal disks. Prongs were attached to one disk which pierced the bowel and fit into small openings in the other disk. The prongs were then crimped, thus securing the bowel edges together.[1]

Table 45-1
Review of Several Series Assessing Clinical Leakage Rate, Rate of Obstruction, and Mortality Resulting from Various Anastomotic Techniques

Study	*No. patients*	*Type of anastomosis*	*Clinical leak, %*	*Clinical obstruction, %*	*Mortality, %*
Corman et al. *Dis Colon Rectum* 32:183, 1989	162	Sutures (DL)	2	2	2
	54	Staples	2	4	4
	222	VALTRAC	3	4	2
Debas et al. *Surg Gynecol Obstet* 135:747, 1972	838	Interrupted sutures (DL)	8	2	5
Harder et al. *Am J Surg* 155:611, 1988	143	Continuous sutures (SL)	0	Not stated	0
Lazorthes et al. *Int J Colorect Dis* 12:96, 1986	82	EEA stapler	4	Not stated	1
Friend et al. *Surg Gynecol Obstet* 171:373, 1990	114	EEA stapler	4	Not stated	3
	125	Interrupted sutures (SL)	9	Not stated	1
Griffen et al. *Ann Surg* 211:745, 1990	75	EEA + TA-55 Double staple technique	3	3	0
Max et al. *Am J Surg* 162:461, 1991	1000	Continuous sutures (SL)	1	2	1
Kennedy et al. *Dis Colon Rectum* 26:145, 1983	265	Circular stapler	5	1	1
Trollope *Am J Surg* 152:11, 1986	205	EEA stapler	2	3	1
Antonsen et al. *Dis Colon Rectum* 30:579, 1987	178	EEA stapler[a]	15	Not stated	3

[a]These anastomoses were all extraperitoneal.
Abbreviations: SL = single layer; DL = double layer.

The forerunner of the modern stapler was first presented by Hültl in 1908 at the second congress of the Hungarian Surgical Society.[12] This device weighed approximately 5 kg and was difficult to assemble, precluding widespread use.[12,30] In 1924, Von Petz introduced a stapling instrument that provided a leakproof and hemostatic seal of the stomach, duodenum, or colon.[12,30] The staples formed the correct B formation but the tissue distal to the staple line was crushed and therefore ischemic. There was only a single line of staples, and in order to provide a secure closure, the practice of the day was to place a row of inverting sutures distal to the staple line.[30] These drawbacks, along with the large size of the instrument, led to further modifications. H. Friedrich of Ulm, in 1934, introduced the first stapler with a replaceable preloaded cartridge and a two-handle firing design.[30] This instrument never gained widespread use but provided a preview of future devices.

Credit for the development of the technology which forms the basis for our present-day staplers must be given to the researchers at the Institute for Experimental Surgical Apparatus and Instruments in Moscow. Using their basic design but incorporating disposable cartridges which contained the stapling mechanism, American companies have modified and improved these devices. Presently, there are three stapling formats which are widely used for colon transection and anastomosis.

The gastrointestinal anastomosis (GIA) device, the thoracoabdominal (TA) series of staplers, and the end-to-end anastomosis (EEA) stapler (Autosuture, United States Surgical Corporation) are shown in Fig. 45-1. The GIA and TA units are direct descendants of the Russian design. The EEA stapler was introduced in 1977 and was the first commercially available instrument that permitted the construction of an end-to-end inverted anastomosis. There have been modifications and refinements of the basic design in the form of the intraluminal stapler (ILS, Ethicon Inc.[3]), and the circular EEA (CEEA);[32] however, the advantages of the original EEA have been obvious from its introduction. The EEA made the construction of very low colonic anastomoses much easier than hand-sewn counterparts. It also allowed for more generous distal margins on resection specimens. All of the devices shortened the time required to reestablish intestinal continuity and were relatively easy to operate. The critical ques-

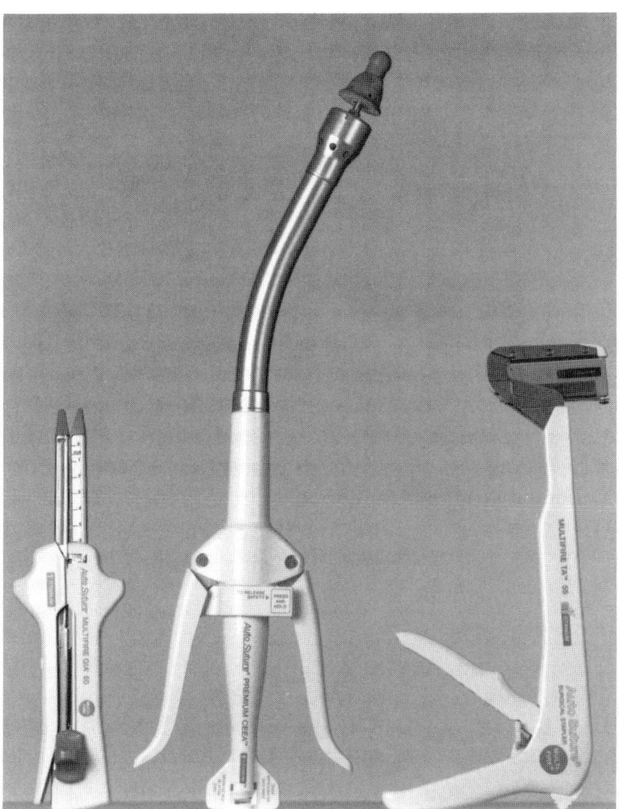

FIG. 45-1. Three common stapler formats. From left to right: gastrointestinal anastomosis (GIA), circular end-enteric anastomosis (CEEA), and thoracoabdominal (TA) staplers. (Autosuture Division, United States Surgical Corp.)

tion that had to be answered was whether there was any difference between anastomoses constructed with staplers and conventional hand-sewn anastomoses in terms of rates of leakage and stenosis.

Several studies over the last two decades have attempted to directly compare stapled and hand-sewn anastomoses. Proponents of stapled techniques assert that staples result in less inflammatory response and decreased anastomotic edema. Supporters of hand-sewn techniques claim that stapled anastomoses are more prone to stricture formation secondary to increased ischemia at the staple line and long-term foreign body reaction to the staples.

Most of the early experimental data directly comparing stapled to hand-sewn closures came from studies of canine bronchial stumps. Stumps closed by staples showed less inflammation as well as significantly higher bursting pressures.[33] These results were later supported by studies comparing single-layer continuous Dacron suture to the EEA device for end-to-end colorectal anastomoses.[12,34] The stapled closures demonstrated a significantly increased bursting strength and were consistently stronger than the sewn anastomoses during the lag phase of healing.

However, clinical data have failed to universally support the advantages of stapled over hand-sewn anastomoses in terms of significantly reducing leakage rates. Friend et al.[35] examined 250 patients undergoing anastomosis of the left side of the colon and rectum. Patients were randomized to one of two groups. Group 1 had their anastomoses performed with an EEA stapling device, while group 2 received single-layer anastomoses hand-sewn with monofilament nylon. The results failed to demonstrate any difference in roentgenologic or clinical leakage rate. The only significant difference found was that the leakage rate for surgeons in training was higher in the hand-sewn group; it was therefore concluded that the benefits of experience are more marked in hand-sewn anastomoses but that, in experienced hands, there is no difference.

With respect to anastomotic edema, Kozol et al.,[36] using radiolabeled albumin, compared EEA to two-layer hand-sewn anastomoses in dogs and found no difference in edema formation. Both techniques resulted in a significant amount of edema in the first 28 h following anastomosis. Polglase and colleagues,[37] questioning earlier results by others, compared end-to-end stapled to sutured anastomoses in dogs, measuring bursting strengths, and found no significant difference. Although there have been some studies suggesting an increased rate of stenosis in stapled anastomoses,[38] there have not been enough prospective randomized long-term studies directly comparing sutures to staples to allow for any definitive conclusions.

The relative speed and ease with which one can perform a stapled anastomosis compared to a sutured anastomosis become even more evident during laparoscopic procedures. While suturing through the laparoscope is possible, it can be very tedious and time-consuming. The use of the laparoscope for colon resections is becoming increasingly popular, and authors have described techniques for both laparoscope-assisted as well as full laparoscopic colectomies.[39] In the assisted procedure, the colon resection is performed laparoscopically while the anastomosis is created extracorporeally through a small incision, either hand-sewn or completed with a variety of stapled techniques. For the full laparoscopic colectomy, both the resection and the anastomosis are performed intracorporeally. Bowel continuity is restored in a side-to-side fashion using a laparoscopic GIA stapler. As the benefits of minimally invasive surgery become more evident, there is no doubt that novel stapling techniques and devices will be created.

INTRALUMINAL ANASTOMIC DEVICES

In 1826, Felix-Nicholas Denans described a device he used to perform an end-to-end ileoileostomy in a dog and exhibited the animal at a meeting of the Société

Royale de Médecine de Marsailles. The apparatus consisted of two outer rings and an inner cylinder which, when properly assembled, created a "sutureless" inverted serosa-to-serosa anastomosis. As healing of the serosal surfaces occurred, the inner margins were sloughed and the device passed in the stool.[40] This was the first intraluminal compression device and was designed to combine the advantages of serosa-to-serosa apposition as described by Lembert with a stent to ensure luminal patency. Theoretically, the use of a device capable of joining the intestine in an end-to-end fashion without suture material, which would be passed in the stool following adequate healing, could have several advantages over suture techniques. Such a device could minimize inflammation and ischemia as well as the long-term presence of a foreign body. While Denans's instrument failed to gain widespread use and acceptance, it sparked a surge of interest and research into the use of sutureless mechanical devices for creating bowel anastomoses.[40]

The most popular prototype anastomotic device was the Murphy button[41] described in 1892 and quickly adopted worldwide as a safe and effective means of constructing quick anastomoses.[40] Consisting of two metal mushrooms with hollow stems, Murphy's button was secured in the bowel by a purse-string suture around the hollow stems. The stems were telescoped, thus compressing the mushroom caps together and forming a serosa-to-serosa apposition.[40] An internal spring helped to maintain the compression and an internal opening allowed for a patent channel through the intestine. As healing progressed, the button was passed in the stool. Limitations of the Murphy button were that (1) it caused pressure necrosis at the site of the anastomosis; (2) it was a metallic foreign body that remained in the lumen of the bowel until intestinal slough occurred at the anastomosis and the device was passed in the stool; and (3) the lumen for passage of intestinal contents was small.

Recently, there has been renewed interest in sutureless anastomoses. Advances in the production of synthetic materials as well as engineering technologies have given rise to a new generation of intraluminal anastomotic devices. While several designs are currently available, there are two which have gained popular attention. Both are based on the concepts advanced by Denans and Murphy over 100 years ago.

Rosati and colleagues,[42] in 1988, introduced a new mechanical device which they developed for performing end-to-end anastomoses. Their anastomotic compression button (ACB) consists of three molded polypropylene rings (an outer, an intermediate, and an inner button) carried by a gun much like an EEA stapling device that introduces them via the rectum into the bowel. The rings are available 30 mm and 25 mm in diameter. Purse-string sutures are place around each of the transected colonic ends. The device is introduced and the distal bowel end is secured around the intermediate button and shaft of the gun. The outer button is inserted into the proximal stump and the purse-string suture secured. By rotating the instrument's handle, the outer button and the intermediate button are approximated at a fixed distance of 1.2 mm. When the device is fired, by closing the handles, the inner button enters and expands, thus locking the intermediate to the outer button. A circular knife then cuts through the colonic edges and the outer button, leaving an inverted serosa-to-seroa anastomosis. The gun is withdrawn and the three interlocking buttons are left in place. When the trapped tissue becomes necrotic and sloughs, the buttons are passed in the stool. After the device is fired, the two tissue doughnuts that result must be inspected to ensure a complete circumferential anastomosis.

Rosati et al.[42] performed 58 colonic anastomoses in dogs using the ACB and compared them to 23 stapled colonic anastomoses. They reported no leakages in either the ACB or the stapled anastomoses. Bursting pressures were also similar. These results led them to evaluate the ACB in humans. They performed 13 anastomoses and found a subclinical leakage rate of 7.7 percent without any observed stenoses.[42] This device was independently evaluated by Malthioner et al.[43] in a canine model. They compared the ACB to the ILS stapler and assayed for mucosal blood flow, bursting pressure, and anastomotic indices. They concluded that the ACB was easier to use and displayed better healing than stapled anastomoses on histologic examination. They did, however, point out that the tissue doughnuts must be carefully inspected, and they recorded one subclinical leak and two postoperative deaths due to anastomotic disruption. All occurred in dogs with incomplete doughnuts. This led them to recommend that in the presence of an incomplete doughnut, the anastomosis should be taken down and reconstructed. The ACB system is at present limited by the fact that it is not completely disposable, and since the rings are not absorbable, the system can be used only in colonic and colorectal anastomoses. Further modifications are currently being performed and a refined instrument is expected from Deknatel Inc.

In 1985, Hardy et al.[44] first reported an experimental study of a completely biofragmentable anastomosis ring (BAR) which included some of the basic features of the Murphy button. The Valtrac BAR (Davis & Geck, Medical Device Division), is a fragmentable device designed to facilitate anastomosis of the inverted ends of the bowel and then to fragment and pass out of the body. It is composed of polyglycolic acid with barium sulfate 12 percent added for x-ray visualiza-

FIG. 45-2. The Valtrac biofragmentable anastomotic ring. (Davis and Geck Inc.)

tion. The device is made up of two identical segments which, when locked into place, hold the serosal surfaces of the bowel in close approximation (Fig. 45-2). The BAR is available in diameters of 25, 28, 31, and 34 mm. The closed gap sizes (distance between the approximated rings) range from 1.5 to 2.5 mm. In his experimental studies, Hardy et al.[44] compared the BAR to both sutured and stapled anastomoses. He concluded that while healing appeared equivalent with all three techniques, burst pressure was highest at time zero and overall necrosis was least with the BAR. Since its introduction there have been many experimental and clinical studies to support the efficacy of the BAR system.[45–51]

SUTURELESS LASER AND LASER-ASSISTED ANASTOMOSES

The ideal technique for creating a bowel anastomosis would minimize ischemia, eliminate tension, and avoid the use of foreign bodies. Eliminating foreign body reaction would result in reduced inflammation. While the use of intraluminal anastomotic devices approaches this ideal, these devices still rely on the introduction of foreign bodies and the use of sutures for a limited amount of time. A truly "sutureless" anastomosis would eliminate the use of any foreign bodies and "fuse" the ends of the bowel together, thus restoring intestinal continuity. Laser tissue welding is a technique whereby laser energy is applied to two apposed ends of tissue, resulting in tissue fusion.

While the exact mechanism for laser tissue fusion is debated, it is generally accepted that a photothermal mechanism is involved.[52] Incident laser light is absorbed by water or pigment in the target tissue and converted to heat. The rise in surrounding tissue temperature results in tissue changes, which are responsible for welding of the tissue edges. A large body of experimental and clinical data has been accumulated over the last 10 to 12 years demonstrating advantages of laser tissue welding over conventional suture and stapling techniques.[52] These advantages have included shorter operative time, absence of foreign body reaction, absence of scar formation, and a more natural healing profile whereby the laser-created anastomosis "grows" with the surrounding tissue. This phenomenon has been postulated as having the potential to reduce late stricture formation.

Most of the early data on laser tissue welding come from experiments on vascular tissue. The earliest clinical reports described the creation of arteriovenous fistulas for hemodialysis patients as well as the formation of femoropopliteal and distal popliteal bypasses using saphenous vein.[53] These early techniques employed CO_2 lasers, whch are absorbed by water in the substrate tissue. These lasers were cumbersome to use (requiring articulating arms and mirrors) and, due to the nonselective nature of water absorption, the amount of collateral thermal injury was often high. In 1990, White and Kopchok[54] reported on a series of 10 patients who underwent creation of forearm Brescia-Cimino arteriovenous fistulas using the argon laser. This device emits energy at a wavelength of 480 to 532 nm, which is strongly absorbed by hemoglobin, allowing for more selective targeting of laser energy to bloodstained surfaces and therefore the use of lower power outputs. This translates directly to less collateral thermal injury. Furthermore, the argon laser energy can be delivered via a fiberoptic cable, making the system far less cumbersome than its CO_2 counterpart. After 4.5 years of follow-up, 7 of the 10 patients in the White-Kopchok[54] study continue to have functioning fistulas without evidence of hematomas, false aneurysms, or stenosis. These techniques have been improved and applied to the creation of end-to-end bowel anastomoses.

The techniques described above relied on hand-held delivery of laser energy and a subjective determination by the surgeon of appropriate end points. In an effort to make the welding process more reproducible and to allow for more accurate dosing of laser energy, certain novel devices have been created. The ExoScope (LaserSurge Inc.) is a circumferential clamping device with a circular array of laser fibers. An absorbable stent is placed into the lumen of the colon and the cut edges of tissues are brought into apposition by the ExoScope. The ExoScope is then coupled to a computer-controlled laser that provides reproducible, uniform dosing of the energy delivered to the anastomosis. Anastomoses made in this way are more reliable than those made with hand-held units and the use of subjective judgments as to welding end points. Using this device, Sauer and colleagues[52,55] have created end-to-end bowel anastomoses in a canine model with bursting pressures and indices of healing superior to both sutured and stapled counterparts. In addition to devices such as the ExoScope, there have been other advances in laser tissue welding that have allowed for broader application of this technology.

One of the principal drawbacks to laser systems has been their expense. There are now available new solid-state laser systems, such as the diode laser, which are relatively inexpensive, low-power, air-cooled devices that until recently had limited applications in surgery. Their power outputs are an order of magnitude lower than argon, CO_2, KTP, Nd:YAG, or THC:YAG units. These low-power diode units emit at wavelengths from 800 to 900 nm, which are poorly absorbed by native tissues and water. These units alone have not been useful for tissue welding because their power outputs were not high enough. However, through the use of exogenous dyes which absorb at 800 to 900 nm, successful laser welding can be performed at very low output powers. Use of a laser-energy absorbing dye enhances the selective localization of heat with less collateral injury and allows use of less energy for the weld.[56]

Laser energy can be even further localized to the site of the anastomosis through the use of laser-activated "glues" or "solders." These protein-based substances can be used for the creation of native welds or for the reinforcement of either sutured or stapled anastomoses (Fig. 45-3). The use of solders makes the welding process more flexible. Whereas otherwise one would have to rely on the tissues to absorb the laser energy, here the majority of the heat generated by the laser is absorbed by the protein solder. The solder joins the tissues together and thus reduces the amount of thermal injury to them. In our laboratory, we have evaluated the use of a multicomponent solder for laser tissue welding both in experimental animals and clinically. Multicomponent solders consisting of a naturally occurring protein such as albumin or fibrinogen, a tissue matrix or ground substance component such as hyaluronic acid, and a laser-absorbing dye such as indocyanine green allow the tailoring of the physical and optical properties of the solder by varying the proportions of the individual components. In this way, the ideal glue can be formulated for each tissue system being welded. We have used laser-solder techniques for the creation of arteriovenous fistulas in dialysis patients,[57] the reinforcement of colon anastomoses,[58,59] and the reinforcement of "high-risk" anastomoses in the esophagus, pancreas, and biliary system.[60]

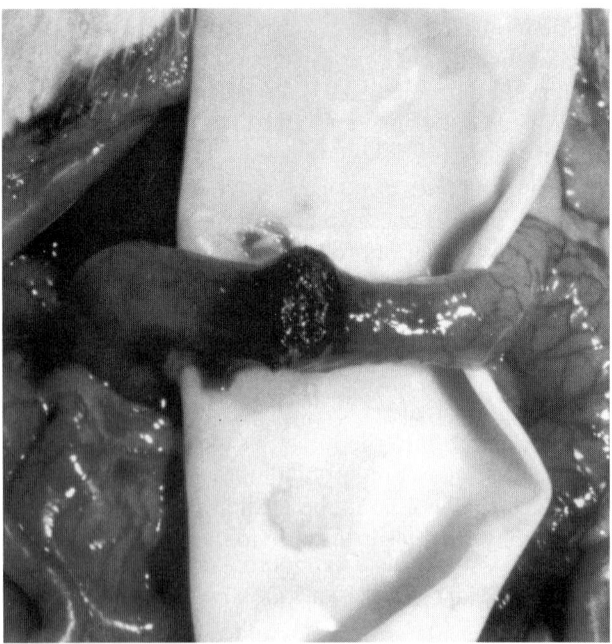

FIG. 45-3. An end-to-end transverse colonic anastomosis created with a laser-activated protein solder composed of fibrinogen, albumin, sodium hyaluronate, and indocyanine green dye. The solder was activated using an 810-nm diode laser in a continuous wave (CW) mode with an output power of 1.5 W. Stay sutures were used during the welding process and were removed at the completion of the anastomosis.

The future acceptance of tissue welding for the creation of anastomoses may rely on the widespread use of laparoscopic techniques. Laser tissue welding is ideally suited to laparoscopic surgery as it is relatively easy to deliver laser fibers and laser solders via laparoscopic ports. The engineering difficulties of building reliable stapling devices which can fit down reasonably sized laparoscopic ports is considerable. We have described several methods for performing laparoscopic anastomoses using laser-activated protein solders.[61] As laser technology becomes more affordable, these techniques may replace suturing and stapling for the creation of laparoscopic anastomoses.

ANASTOMOTIC COMPLICATIONS AND THEIR MANAGEMENT

The major complications of colonic anastomoses include leakage, dehiscence, and stricture formation. While strict adherence to the principles of good anastomotic technique will reduce the incidence of complications, it is important for the surgeon to recognize when they occur and to know the appropriate ways to manage them in order to reduce morbidity and mortality.

Anastomic dehiscence is probably the most serious complication, with an incidence of 4 to 18 percent, depending on the series and on the location of the anastomosis.[62] Mortality resulting from sepsis can be as high as 30 percent, depending to some degree on coexisting illness. Subclinical leaks may occur in as many as 35 percent of anastomoses.[62] While small leaks can often be treated expectantly, leaks which result in large collections and which are symptomatic should be addressed. There are a variety of techniques both surgical and nonsurgical which can be used to manage an anastomotic leak and the resulting abscess collection.

The options available to the surgeon include closure of the leak with or without drainage; proximal decompression of the colon by a loop colostomy with or without drainage; resection of the anastomosis with proximal colostomy and closure or exteriorization of the distal stump; or drainage alone.[63] Drainage can be accomplished either open or with CT guided percutaneous techniques. Each of the above alternatives was evaluated by Mileski and coworkers,[63] who studied the treatment of anastomotic leaks following anterior colon resection.

By studying 405 consecutive cases of anterior colon resection, Mileski et al.[63] discovered a clinical leakage rate of 4 percent. Of their patients with leaks, they noted that 94 percent demonstrated fever, leukocytosis, and pelvic pain. Proximal decompression and drainage was employed for 69 percent of these patients with a resultant mortality of 36 percent. Improved outcomes were noted in the 19 percent of patients receiving resection of the anastomosis, end colostomy, and distal closure or exteriorization (no deaths recorded). Similarly, the 13 percent who underwent drainage alone did not suffer any mortal outcomes. The investigators concluded, based on their data, that the management of anastomotic dehiscence should include a procedure involving a takedown of the anastomosis, end colostomy, and closure of the rectum. Each case must be evaluated individually. While a frank anastomotic dehiscence with ongoing fecal soilage requires an aggressive approach such as this, a small, self-contained leak may be readily managed by percutaneous drainage alone.

Anastomotic stricture is often a late complication of colon surgery, occurring in as many as 2 to 5 percent of patients[64] and attributed by some to a wider use of stapling techniques.[65] Patients often present with symptoms attributable to bowel obstruction after unsuccessful attempts colonoscopy or after evaluation of the colon by barium enema. We recently reviewed our 10-year experience with endoscopic alternatives for the management of colonic strictures.[66] Of the 61 patients evaluated, 14 underwent endoscopic management. Half of these patients had developed a stricture as the result of an anastomosis. A variety of endoscopic techniques have been developed which are essential to the successful management of strictures.

These techniques can be divided into those involving divulsion and those involving ablation. Divulsion techniques include the use of bougies, balloons, and endoscopes. All of these devices work by tearing at the tissues in the weakest section of the anastomosis, thus enlarging the lumen. While these techniques are not demanding technically, they are not precise and can result in perforation. Ablation techniques involve the use of electrocautery and lasers. Tissue is ablated in order to enlarge the diameter of the anastomosis. Ablation is often better suited to the management of obstructing masses such as suture line recurrences rather than benign colonic strictures following anastomosis. Of the seven patients with anastomotic strictures that we managed endoscopically, 86 percent achieved successful resolution. A dilating endoscope was employed in 71 percent of cases, balloons in 57 percent, bouginage in 43 percent, and electrocautery in 14 percent. An average of 2.6 sessions were required for each patient (range 1 to 5). In the patient who failed endoscopic dilatation, a diverting colostomy was performed.

While operative management of strictures, including resection and reanastomosis, is possible, repeated operation is technically difficult and carries an increased morbidity and mortality in high-risk patients. It is our belief that with caution and appropriate selection, colonic strictures can be ablated or dilated with reasonable results and avoidance of repeated operation. Endoscopic failures, however, should be managed surgically.

SUMMARY

There are many options available to the surgeon for the restoration of bowel continuity following colonic resection. These include hand-sewn techniques, stapled closures, the use of intraluminal anastomotic devices, and new technologies such as laser tissue welding. Despite this variety, the most important factors for a successful anastomosis continue to be adequate blood supply, absence of tension, absence of inflammation, and absence of infection. While careful attention to the four A's of anastomotic technique will minimize morbidity and mortality, prompt recognition and management of anastomotic complications is critical. As advances in minimally invasive surgery continue, there will no doubt be new techniques developed. Careful attention to basic principles and an understanding of the healing process will always be of paramount importance.

REFERENCES

1. Getzen LC: Intestinal suturing: Part I. The development of intestinal sutures. *Curr Probl Surg* Aug:3–48, Aug 1969.
2. Senn W: Enterorrhaphy: Its history, technic, and present status. *JAMA* 21:215, 1893.
3. Ballantyne GH: Intestinal suturing: Review of the experimental foundations for traditional doctrines. *Dis Colon Rectum* 26:836–843, 1983.
4. Lord MG, Broughton AC, Williams HTG: A morphometric study on the effect of suturing the submucosa of the large intestine. *Surg Gynecol Obstet* 146:211–216, 1978.

5. Mathes SJ, Abouljoud M: Wound healing, in Davis JH (ed): *Clinical Surgery*. St. Louis, Mosby, 1987, p 475.
6. Peacock EE Jr: Wound healing and wound care, in Schwartz SI, Shires GT, Spencer FC (eds): *Principles of Surgery,* 5th ed. New York, McGraw Hill, pp 318–320, 1989.
7. Madden JW, Peacock EE Jr: Biology of collagen during wound healing. *Ann Surg* 174:511, 517, 1971.
8. Herrmann JB, Woodward MD, Pulaski J: Healing of colonic anastomoses in the rat. *Surg Gynecol Obstet* 119:269–275, 1964.
9. Jiborn H, Ahonen J, Zederfeldt B: Healing of experimental colonic anastomoses: II. Breaking strength of the colon after left colon resection and anastomosis. *Am J Surg* 136:595–599, 1978.
10. Houck JC: The effect of local necrosis upon collagen content in uninjured distal skin. *Surgery* 51:770–773, 1962.
11. De Haan BS, Ellis H, Wilks M: The role of infection on wound healing. *Surg Gynecol Obstet* 138:695–700, 1974.
12. Ballantyne GH: The experimental basis of intestinal suturing effect of surgical technique, inflammation, and infection on enteric wound healing. *Dis Colon Rectum* 27:61–71, 1984.
13. Hamilton JE: Reappraisal of open intestinal anastomosis. *Ann Surg* 165:917–924, 1967.
14. Getzen LC, Roe RD, Holloway CK: Comparative study of intestinal anastomotic healing in inverted and everted closures. *Surg Gynecol Obstet* 123:1219–1227, 1966.
15. Irvin TT, Hunt JK: Pathogenesis and prevention of disruption of colonic anastomoses in traumatized rats. *Br J Surg* 61:437–439, 1974.
16. Yamakawa T, Patin CS, Sobel S, et al: Healing of colonic anastomoses following resection for experimental "diverticulitis." *Arch Surg* 103:17–20, 1971.
17. Hawley PR, Faulk P, Hunt JK, et al: Collagenase activity in gastro-intestinal tract. *Br J Surg* 57:896–900, 1970.
18. Leveen HH, Wapnicks S, Falk D, et al: Effects of prophylactic antibiotics of colonic healing. *Am J Surg* 131:47–53, 1976.
19. Forrester JC, Zederfeldt BH, Hayes JL, et al: Tape-closed and sutured wounds: A comparison by tensiometry and scanning electron microscopy. *Br J Surg* 57:729–737, 1970.
20. Shambaugh P, Dunphy JE: Postoperative wound infections and the use of silk: An experimental study. *Surgery* 1:379–385, 1937.
21. Van Winkle W Jr, Hastings JC: Considerations in the choice of suture material for various tissues. *Surg Gynecol Obstet* 135:113–126, 1972.
22. Sako Y, Wagensteen OH: Experimental studies on gastrointestinal anastomoses. *Surg Forum* 2:117–123, 1951.
23. Hamilton JE: Reappraisal of open intestinal anastomoses. *Ann Surg* 165:917–924, 1967.
24. Letwin E, Williams HTG: Healing of intestinal anastomosis. *Can J Surg* 10:109–116, 1967.
25. McAdams HJ, Meikle AG, Taylor JO: One or two layer colonic anastomoses. *Am J Surg* 120:546–550, 1970.
26. Max E, Sweeny WB, Bailey HR, et al: Results of 1,000 single-layer continuous polypropylene intestinal anastomoses. *Am J Surg* 162:461–467, 1991.
27. Harder F, Vogelbauch P: Single-layer end-on continuous suture of colonic anastomoses. *Am J Surg* 155:611–614, 1988.
28. Sarin S, Lightwood RG: Continuous single-layer gastrointestinal anastomosis: A prospective audit. *Br J Surg* 76:493–495, 1989.
29. Ravitch MM, Brown IW, Daviglus GF, et al: Experimental and clinical use of the Soviet bronchus stapling instruments. *Surgery* 46:1, 1959.
30. Ravitch MM: Staples in abdominal and thoracic surgery. *Contemp Surg* 4:58–65, 1974.
31. Nance FC: Gastrointestinal anastomosis with a disposable intraluminal stapler. *Contemp Surg* 19:11–18, 1981.
32. Dziki AJ, Duncan MD, Harmon JW, et al: Advantages of hand-sewn over stapled bowel anastomosis. *Dis Colon Rectum* 34:442–448, 1991.
33. Scott RN, Farac RP, Goodman DG, et al: The role of inflammation in bronchial stump healing. *Ann Surg* 181:381–385, 1975.
34. Greenstein A, Rogers P, Moss G: Doubled fourth-day colorectal anastomotic strength with complete retention of intestinal mature wound collagen and accelerated deposition following full enteral nutrition. *Surg Forum* 29:78–81, 1978.
35. Friend PJ, Scott R, Everett WG, et al: Stapling or suturing for anastomoses of the left side of the large intestine. *Surg Gynecol Obstet* 171:373–376, 1990.
36. Kozol RA, Mulligan M, Downes RJ, et al: Early colonic anastomotic edema, evaluation of stapled vs. hand-sewn anastomoses. *Dis Colon Rectum* 31:503–506, 1988.
37. Polglase AL, Hughes ES, McDermott FT, et al: A comparison of end-to-end staple and suture colorectal anastomosis in the dog. *Surg Gynecol Obstet* 152:792–796, 1981.
38. Luchtefeld MA, Milsom JW, Senecgore A, et al: Colorectal anastomotic stenosis: Results of a survey of the ASCRS membership. *Dis Colon Rectum* 32:733–736, 1989.
39. Quilici PJ: *New Developments in Laparoscopy*. United States Surgical Corporation: Auto Suture Co., Norwalk, CT, 1992.
40. Steichen FM, Ravitch MM: History of mechanical devices and instruments for suturing. *Curr Probl Surg* 19:1–52, 1982.
41. Murphy JB: Cholecysto-intestinal, gastrointestinal, enterointestinal anastomosis and approximation without sutures. *Med Rec* 42:665–676, 1892.
42. Rosati R, Rebuffat C, Pezzuoli G: A new mechanical device for circular compression anastomosis. *Ann Surg* 207:245–252, 1988.
43. Malthoiner RA, Hakki FZ, Saini N, et al: Anastomotic compression button: A new mechanical device for sutureless bowel anastomosis. *Dis Colon Rectum* 33:291–297, 1990.
44. Hardy TG, Pace WG, Maney JW, et al: A biofragmentable ring for sutureless bowel anastomosis: An experimental study. *Dis Colon Rectum* 28:484–490, 1985.
45. Maney JW, Katz AR, Lehmann K, et al: Biofragmentable bowel anastomosis ring: Comparative efficacy studies in dogs. *Surgery* 103:56–62, 1988.
46. Hardy TG, Aquilar PS, Stewart WRC: Initial clinical experience with a biofragmentable ring for sutureless bowel anastomosis. *Dis Colon Rectum* 30:55–60, 1987.
47. Corman ML, Prager ED, Hardy TG: Comparison of the Valtrac BAR with conventional suture and stapled anastomosis in colon surgery. *Dis Colon Rectum* 32:183–187, 1989.
48. Dyess DL, Curreri PW, Ferrara JJ: A new technique for sutureless intestinal anastomosis. *Am Surg* 56:71–75, 1990.
49. Bubrick MP, Corman ML, Cahill CJ, et al: Prospective randomized trial of the BAR. *Am J Surg* 161:136–143, 1991.
50. Cahill CJ, Betzler M, Grunez JA, et al: Sutureless large bowel anastomosis: European experience with the biofragmentable anastomosis ring. *Br J Surg* 76:344–347, 1989.
51. Forde KA, McClarty AJ, Tsai J, et al: Murphy's button revisited: Clinical experience with the biofragmentable anastomotic ring. *Ann Surg* 217:78–81, 1993.
52. Treat MR, Oz MC, Bass LS: New technologies and future applications of surgical lasers: The right tool for the right job. *Surg Clin North Am* 72:705–742, 1992.
53. Okadu M, Shimizu K, Ikuta H: An alternative method of vascular anastomosis by laser: Experimental and clinical study. *Lasers Surg Med* 7:240–248, 1987.
54. White RA, Kopchok GF: Laser vascular tissue fusion: De-

velopment, current status and future perspectives. *J Clin Laser Med Surg* 8:47–54, 1990.
55. Sauer JS, Hinshaw JR, McGuire KP: The first sutureless, laser-welded, end-to-end bowel anastomosis. *Lasers Surg Med* 9:70–73, 1989.
56. Chuck RS, Oz MC, Delohery TM, et al: Dye-enhanced laser tissue welding. *Lasers Surg Med* 9:471–477, 1989.
57. Oz MC, Bass LS, Williams MR, et al: Clinical experience with laser enhanced tissue soldering of vascular anastomoses. *Lasers Surg Med* 77(suppl 3):74, 1991.
58. Libutti SK, Oz MC, Forde KA, et al: Canine colonic anastomoses reinforced with dye-enhanced fibrinogen and a diode laser. *Surg Endosc* 4:97–99, 1990.
59. Moazami N, Oz MC, Bass LS, et al: Reinforcement of colonic anastomoses with a laser and dye-enhanced fibrinogen. *Arch Surg* 125:1452–1454, 1990.
60. Libutti SK, Bessler M, Chabot J, et al: Reinforcement of high risk anastomoses using laser activated protein solders: A clinical study, in White JV, White RA, Bass LS (eds): *Lasers in Otolaryngology, Dermatology and Tissue Welding Proc SPIE* 1876:164–167, 1993.
61. Bass LS, Oz MC, Auteri JS, et al: Laparoscopic applications of laser-activated tissue glues. *Proc SPIE* 1421:164–168, 1991.
62. Daly JM, DeCosse JS: Complications in surgery of the colon and rectum. *Surg Clin North Am* 63:1215–1231, 1983.
63. Mileski WJ, Joehl RJ, Rege RV, et al: Treatment of anastomotic leakage following low anterior colon resection. *Arch Surg* 123:968–971, 1988.
64. Thies E, Lange V, Miersch WD: Peranal dilatation of postsurgical colonic stenosis by means of flexible endoscope. *Endoscopy* 15:327–328, 1983.
65. Gordon PH, Vasilevsky CA: Experience with stapling in rectal surgery. *Surg Clin North Am* 64:555–568, 1984.
66. Oz MC, Forde KA: Endoscopic alternatives in the management of colonic strictures. *Surgery* 108:515–519, 1990.

CHAPTER 46

Laparoscopic Colectomy for Colonic Carcinoma

David M. Ota

HIGHLIGHTS

The accepted treatment for resectable colonic carcinoma is exploratory laparotomy and hemicolectomy. The technique of a colonic resection is well known, but there are reports that this procedure can be done using advanced laparoscopic techniques. This chapter describes the technique of laparoscopic-assisted colectomy for colonic carcinoma.

CONTROVERSIES

A potential advance in the operative management of colonic carcinoma is the laparoscopic colectomy. Surgeons can mobilize the right, left, or sigmoid colon and perform a regional lymphadenectomy using laparoscopic instruments and advanced video imaging equipment. The advantages of the laparoscopic colectomy are that the abdominal incisions are relatively smaller and postoperative stress and pain are thereby reduced. Currently, this procedure is undergoing evaluation to determine whether laparoscopic colectomy is similar to open laparotomy and colectomy for controlling malignant disease without increasing health care costs. A randomized trial comparing open laparotomy versus laparoscopic resection is necessary to establish that laparoscopic colectomy is equivalent to the open laparotomy technique.

FUTURE DIRECTIONS

Significant advances in surgical technology are forthcoming. Video imaging and surgical instruments are constantly improving. Laparoscopic ultrasound as well as radioactive and Doppler probes may soon be available to assist in detecting occult metastases and finding the regional arterial blood supply. Robotic arms that attach to the bedside may become available, and within a few years robotic instruments controlled by a surgeon sitting at a console may be available to perform hemicolectomies without a surgical assistant. However, as this technology develops, the surgeon must keep in mind (a) the principles of cancer surgery in order to maximize local control of disease and (b) the need to reduce health care costs.

The primary treatment of localized colon adenocarcinoma is surgical resection, and the objective of operative procedures is to obtain sufficient distal and proximal luminal margins and a regional lymphadenectomy. Recently, there has been tremendous interest in developing minimally invasive surgical techniques to treat inflammatory and neoplastic diseases of the gastrointestinal tract. The laparoscopic cholecystectomy procedure rapidly became the standard treatment for cholelithiasis and laparoscopic appendectomy and Nissen fundoplication may also replace the open laparotomy technique. Laparoscopic surgery is being developed for gastrointestinal cancer surgery, and there are several reports describing a series of patients who have had laparoscopic-assisted colectomy for resectable malignant disease.[1–7] While the procedure is feasible, it is not clear whether laparoscopic colectomy is equivalent to open colectomy. Issues such as compromised cancer control, complications, quality of life, and health care costs must be considered. In order to clarify the potential benefits and limitations of laparoscopic colectomy, this chapter reviews the technique and controversies of this procedure.

COLECTOMY BY OPEN LAPAROTOMY

The standard colorectal resection for curative adenocarcinoma is based on adequate resection of proximal and distal margins with a regional lymphadenectomy. For intraabdominal carcinomas, at least 10 cm of proximal and distal colon are sufficient. The regional lymphadenectomy is based on the arterial blood supply to that particular portion of the intraabdominal colon. A lesion in the right colon requires removal of mesentery with the ileocolic and right colic arteries with the right branch of the middle colic artery. Transverse colonic lesions require resection of the mesentery with the middle colic artery. Lesions in the descending colon require removal of the left colic artery and its associated mesentery. Sigmoid colonic lesions require removal of the superior rectal artery and sigmoid branches with an anterior anastomosis.

LAPAROSCOPIC COLECTOMY

Laparoscopic surgery is rapidly evolving. A number of procedures have been developed for benign diseases, and cholecystectomy, appendectomy, and hysterectomy are becoming routine. Advances in laparoscopic instrumentation have resulted in new procedures such as colonic resections for polyps or malignant disease. T_1, T_2, and T_3 tumors are amenable to laparoscopic resection, while T_4 tumors (invasion of adjacent organs) require open laparotomy. Lesions located in the ascending, descending, and sigmoid colons are amenable to laparoscopic colectomy. At the present time the transverse colon is difficult to resect because of the greater omentum. Another indication for laparoscopic colectomy is a near obstructing colonic lesion with unresectable metastatic disease. Significant palliation can be achieved with a laparoscopic segmental colectomy, resulting in faster recovery and better quality of life. Ondrula et al.[8] have described the significant comorbid disease processes that increase the morbidity of colorectal resections. Those patients with significant congestive heart failure, history of myocardial infarction, and severe chronic obstructive pulmonary disease can benefit from minimal-access surgery that reduces postoperative stress and pain.

Experience with laparoscopic colectomy for colonic neoplasms is increasing, but there are few data detailing the benefits and risks of these procedures. Prospective trials are under way, and they will determine (1) learning time, (2) factors that contribute to open laparotomy, (3) operative time, (4) complications, (5) hospital stay, and (6) pathologic assessment of the resected specimen. Preliminary reports indicate that laparoscopic colectomy results in less postoperative pain, shorter hospital stay, and earlier return to work.[1–7] There are numerous questions that remain to be answered regarding this technique.

Presently, laparoscopic colectomy for resectable colonic carcinomas is investigational. As with all new treatment modalities, comparison with traditional open colectomy is necessary and a multi-institutional randomized trial is needed. Such a trial should compare extent of node sampling, proximal and distal luminal margins, conversion rates, hospitalization/operating room costs, and patterns of recurrence and survival. Until these issues are resolved, laparoscopic colectomy should be done under a protocol approved by an institutional review board in order to monitor complications, extent of resection, conversion rates, and hospitalization time.

The objective of laparoscopic colonic resections is to obtain at least 10 cm of proximal and distal colon with a regional lymphadenectomy. The lymphadenectomy requires that the major arterial blood supply be taken with the resected specimen. The steps to this procedure include (1) port placement, (2) inspection of the abdominal cavity, (3) mobilization of the colon and mesentery, (4) dissection of the mesentery and securing of the regional arterial and venous blood vessels, (5) transection of the bowel and specimen removal, and (6) anastomosis. At all times the surgeon should be aware of reasons for converting a laparoscopic procedure to an open laparotomy. These include (1) poor exposure because of adhesions, extensive tumor or obesity, (2) bleeding, (3) injury to other organs, and (4) lack of progress after 1 h.

For the laparoscopic right hemicolectomy, the patient is placed in a supine position with the left arm tucked to the side. The ports are placed as shown in Fig. 46-1. The TV monitor is placed on the right side of the patient and the surgeon stands on the left side. The first assistant is the camera operator, who stands on the left side as well. The same 10-mm ports are used at all sites. The port in the left upper quadrant is placed through the rectus abdominis muscle, using a cutdown technique and inserting a Hasson cannula. Grasping instruments such as modified Babcock clamps are placed through the left and right ports and used to grasp and retract the bowel. The spatula cautery instrument is placed through the lower port. The surgeon controls the spatula cautery and left grasper while the first assistant holds the camera and the right grasper. The patient is then placed in a Trendelenburg position with the table rotated to the left. This is done

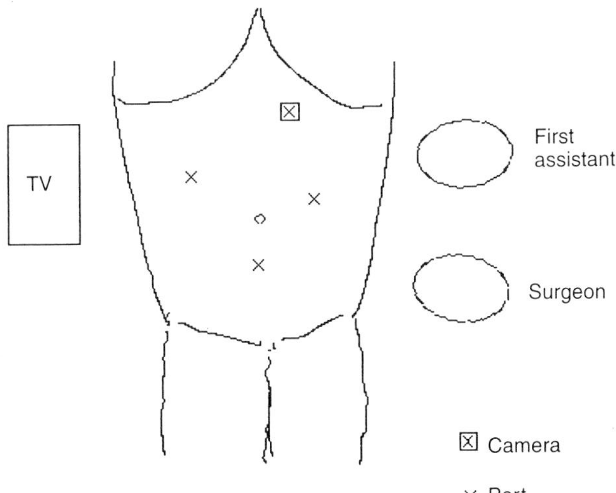

FIG. 46-1. Port placement for laparoscopic right hemicolectomy. The patient is placed in a supine Trendelenburg position. A 10-mm Hasson port is placed in the left upper quadrant for the laparoscope. Left and lower-midline 10-mm ports are placed as shown. The right 10-mm port is placed over the transverse colon. The surgeon and assistant stand on the left side, facing the monitor on the right side. The ileum and colon are exteriorized through a 5-cm transverse incision around the right port.

to keep the small bowel out of the pelvis (see Fig. 46-2). The grasping instruments are used to retract the terminal ileum and cecum to the left upper quadrant. The spatula-cautery is then used to immobilize the terminal ileum and cecum from the retroperitoneum. The cautery is initially used to break the peritoneum on the inferior side of the ileum. The spatula is then used to bluntly dissect the ileum and cecum from the retroperitoneum. By staying in the appropriate plane, bleeding is minimized and the cecum and right colon are easily mobilized with identification of the right ureter (see Fig. 46-3). Mobilization of the terminal ileum is important, because this leads to the correct plane of dissection. Attempts to dissect the right colon along the paracolic gutter can increase the risk of entering the plane which is deep to the colonic mesentery and can lead to bleeding and ureteral injury. All dissection is performed with constant gentle tension on the bowel. After the ileum and cecum are mobilized, the white line of Toldt is cauterized and the right colonic mesentery is mobilized off the retroperitoneum, using blunt dissection. The greater omentum is retracted over the transverse colon toward the stomach. This then exposes the hepatic flexure, which is taken down with careful cautery dissection. As the hepatic flexure is taken down, using electrocautery and blunt dissection, the duodenum and right kidney come into view. After the terminal ileum, cecum, right colon, and mesentery have been mobilized, attention is directed to the right colonic mesentery. The cecum and terminal ileum are placed back into the right lower quadrant and held up with the graspers or Babcocks, putting tension on the ileocecal mesentery (see Figs. 46-4 and 46-5). This has the effect of bow-stringing the ileocolic artery, and the cautery is then placed in the left port. The mesentery along the ileocolic artery is cauterized and a window is created in the mesentery along the ileocolic artery. Once the window is created, the grasper and the spatula are inserted into the window and are spread to increase its size. This opening is extended to the ileocolic vessels. The artery and vein are identified with blunt dissection (see Fig. 46-6). The artery is then doubly clipped and transected. A laparoscopic loop suture is then placed around the proximal

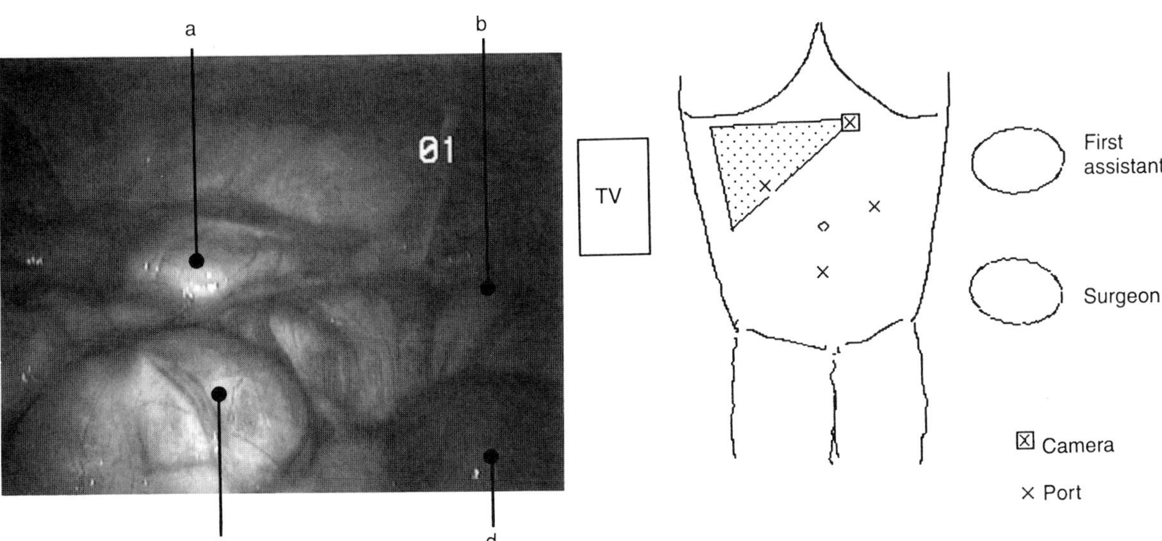

FIG. 46-2. This is the view of the right abdominal cavity from the camera in the left-upper-quadrant port. The gallbladder (d), transverse colon (c), hepatic flexure (b), and right colon (a) are easily seen. (See color Plate 18.)

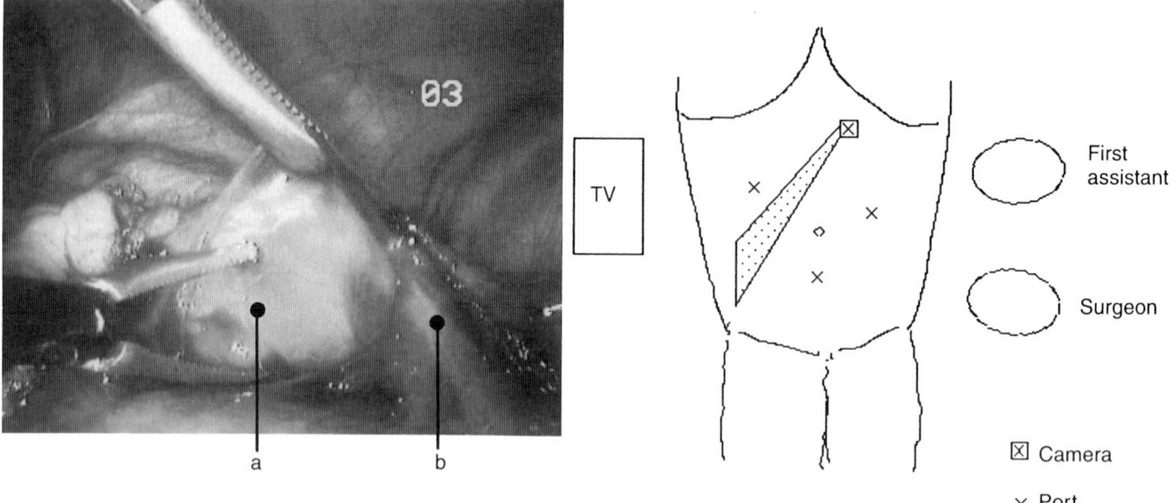

FIG. 46-3. This is a view from the camera in the left-upper-quadrant port looking into the right lower quadrant. The terminal ileum, cecum, and right colon have been mobilized off the retroperitoneum and retracted to the left upper quadrant with a laparoscopic Babcock instrument (not seen) in the right port. The two instruments shown in this picture are in the left and lower-midline ports and are gently dissecting the retroperitoneum (b) to identify the right ureter (a). (See color Plate 19.)

arterial stump and secured. The vein is treated in a similar manner. The dissection is then continued superiorly along the base of the right colonic mesentery toward the transverse colon, using the cautery to cut the peritoneum and adipose tissue (Fig. 46-7). The right colic artery is doubly clipped on both sides and transected; a laparoscopic loop suture is then placed around the proximal stump (Fig. 46-8). The mesentery is then further dissected toward the transverse colon until the right branch of the middle colic artery is seen. At this point the terminal ileum and right colon are fully mobilized. The cecum is grasped with the Babcock clamp in the right-sided port, and this port is enlarged to approximately 5 to 7 cm. The incision is extended through the fascia into the abdominal cavity. The port is then removed with the Babcock clamp and the specimen. The terminal ileum is readily identified and transected using a standard stapler. The proximal terminal ileum is then grasped with a standard Babcock clamp and held at skin level. The remaining mes-

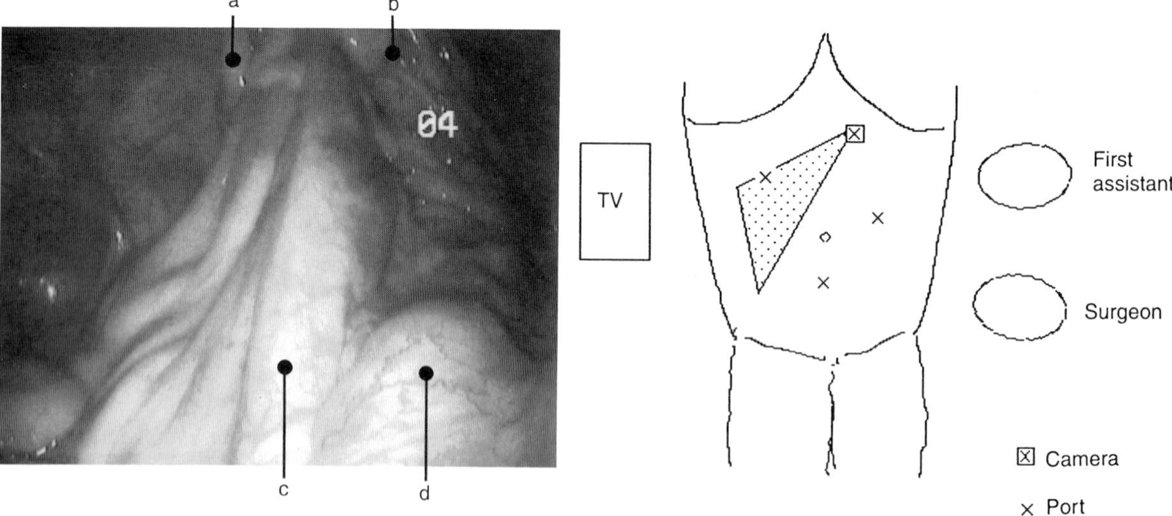

FIG. 46-4. After the ileum (a), right colon, and hepatic flexure are mobilized, they are placed back in the right lower quadrant. A laparoscopic Babcock clamp in the right port is used to grasp the ileocecal junction (b). This picture is a view from the left upper quadrant looking into the right lower quadrant. The ileocecal junction is grasped and lifted up. This puts the mesentery on stretch and creates a bowstring effect (c), thus identifying the ileocolic artery. The transverse colon (d) is seen in the right lower corner. (See color Plate 20.)

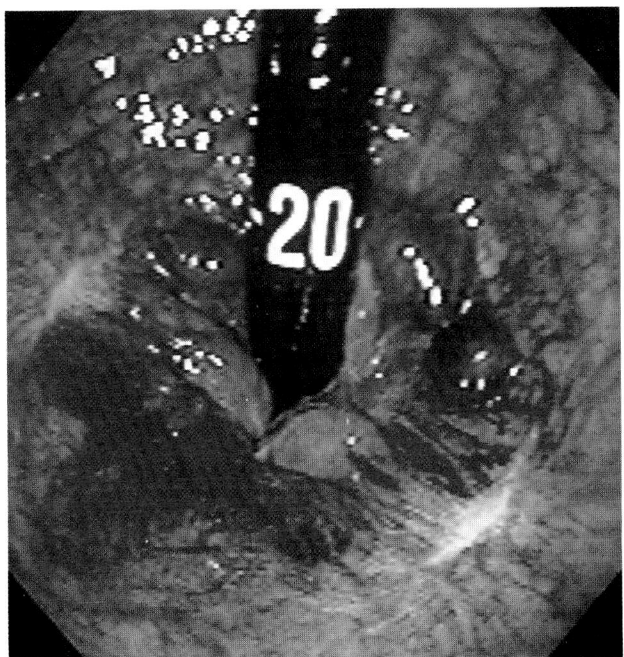

Plate 1. The colonoscope in a U-turn position at the anal canal. Blue hemorrhoidal veins are seen, and scars from previous hemorrhoidectomy are present. The plate is cited in Chap. 30.

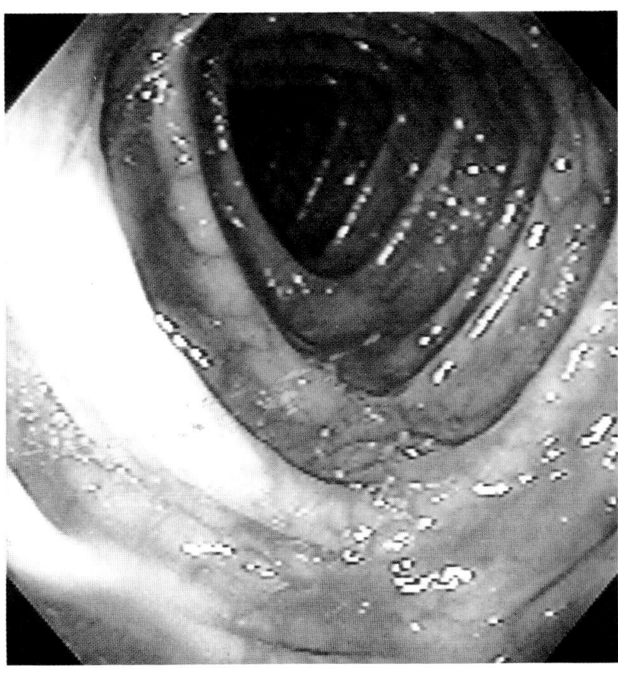

Plate 2. Triangular appearance of the transverse colon. The plate is cited in Chap. 30.

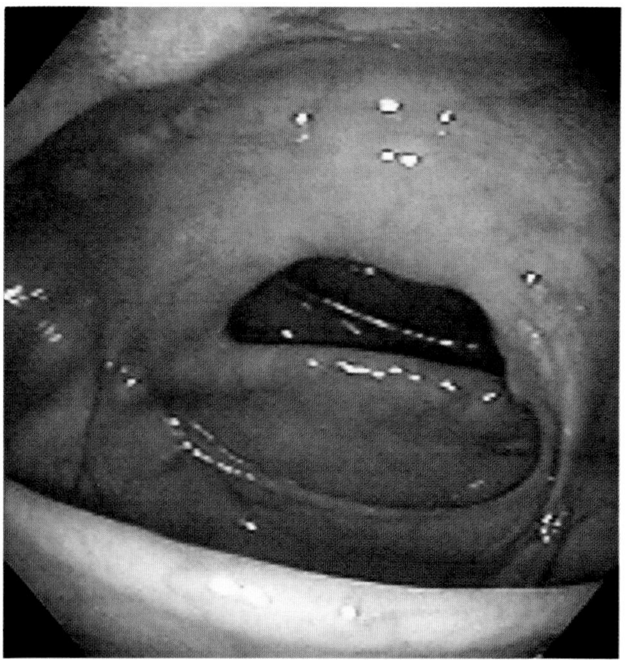

Plate 3. The irregular configuration of a colonic fold, characteristic of the superior lip of the ileocecal valve. The plate is cited in Chap. 30.

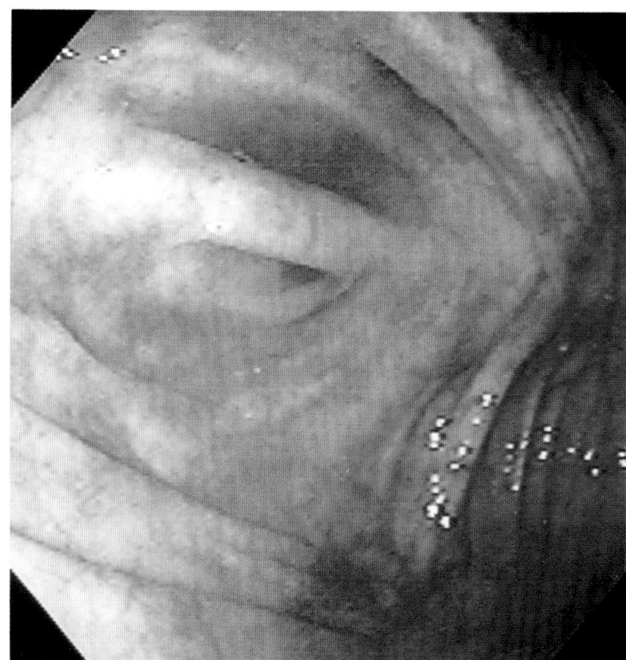

Plate 4. The appendiceal orifice just under a "sling fold" of the cecum. The plate is cited in Chap. 30.

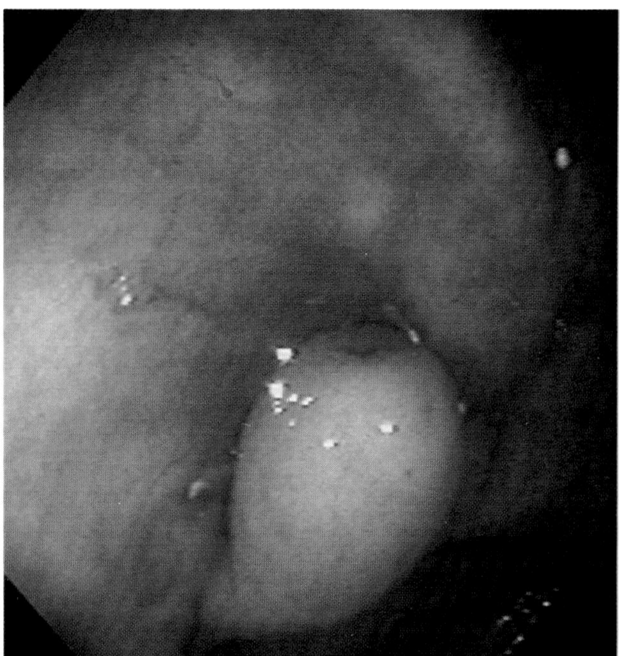

Plate 5. An inverted appendiceal stump. Note the indentation at the apex. The plate is cited in Chap. 30.

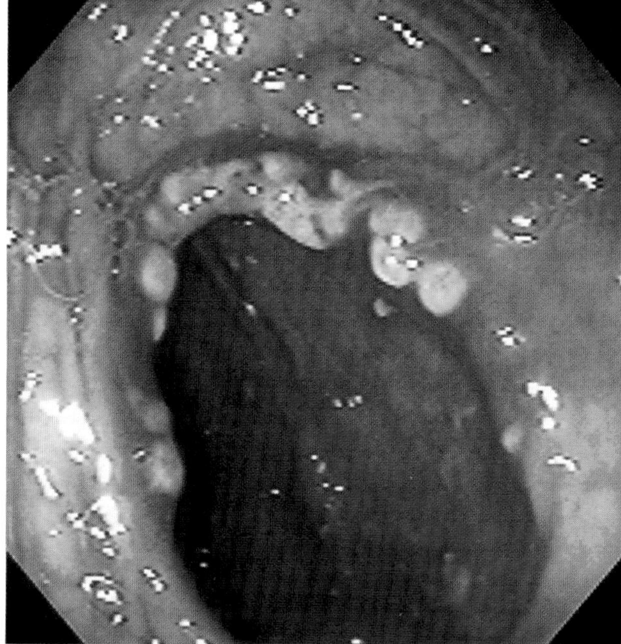

Plate 6. Ileocolic anastomosis with granulation tissue at the edge, on the suture line. The plate is cited in Chap. 30.

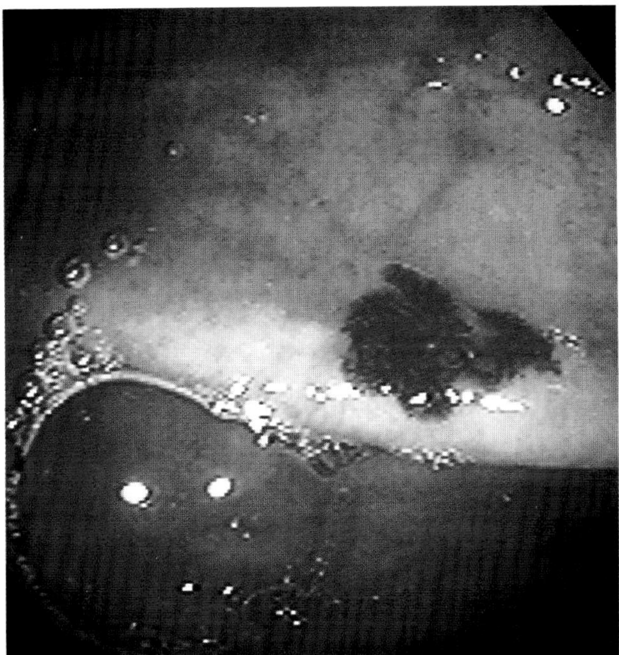

Plate 7. Racemose collection of blood vessels in the cecum. This is a characteristic appearance of a colonic arteriovenous malformation. The plate is cited in Chap. 30.

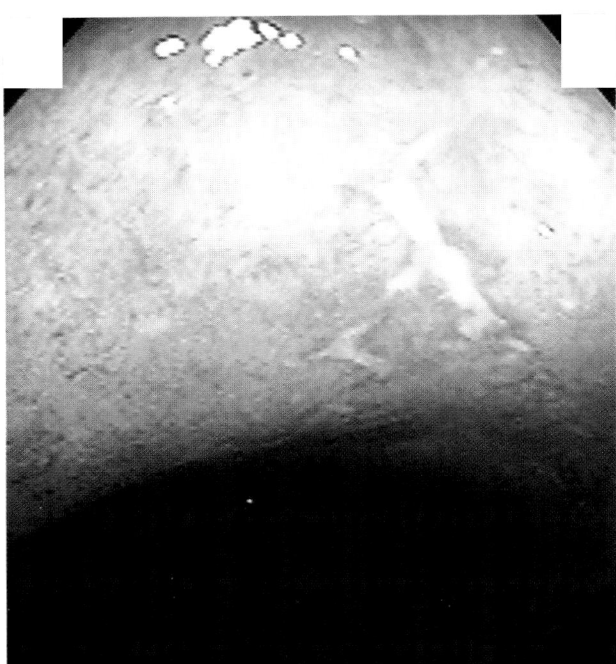

Plate 8. A characteristic appearance of inflammatory bowel disease, with loss of the normal vascular pattern, and a linear ulceration in an area of inflamed mucosa. This patient has ulcerative colitis. The plate is cited in Chap. 30.

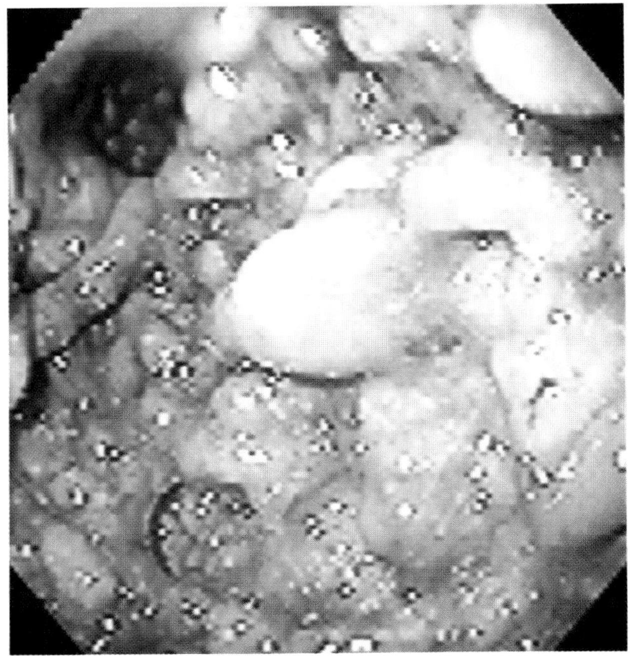

Plate 9. A collection of inflammatory polyps covering the wall of the transverse colon in a patient with chronic ulcerative colitis. The plate is cited in Chap. 30.

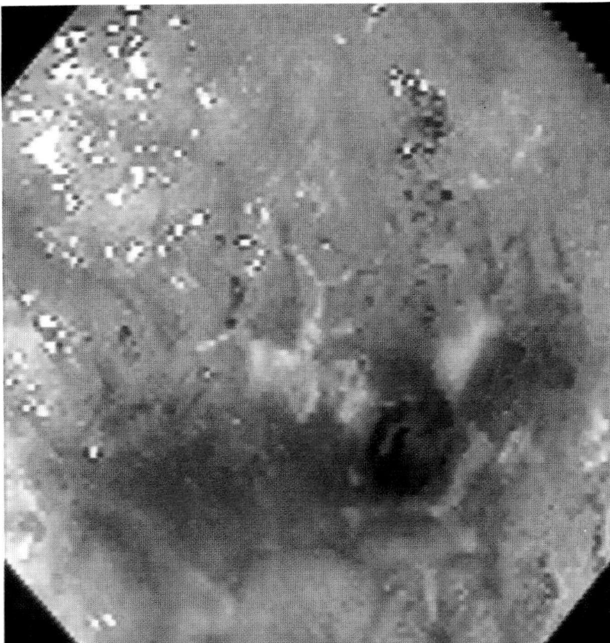

Plate 10. A stricture in Crohn's disease. Note the marked inflammation and ulcerations at the edge of the stricture. This stricture was due to severe inflammation. The plate is cited in Chap. 30.

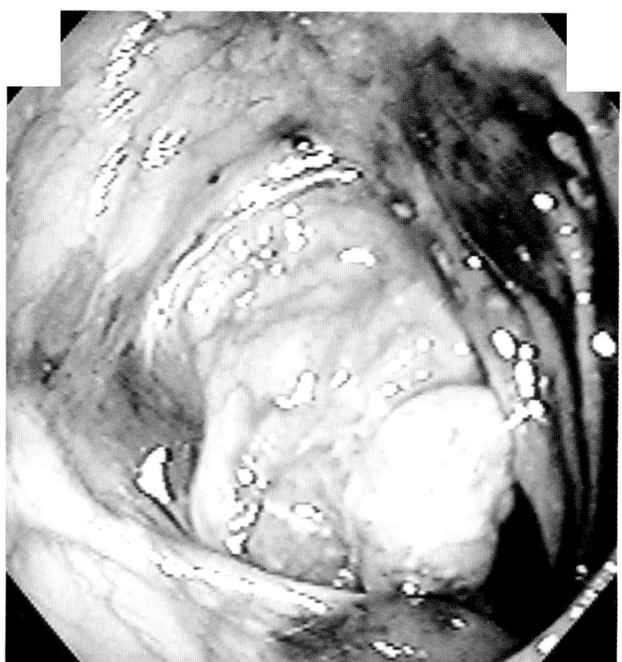

Plate 11. A small carcinoma of the descending colon with circumferential India ink injections for subsequent surgical localization. The plate is cited in Chap. 30.

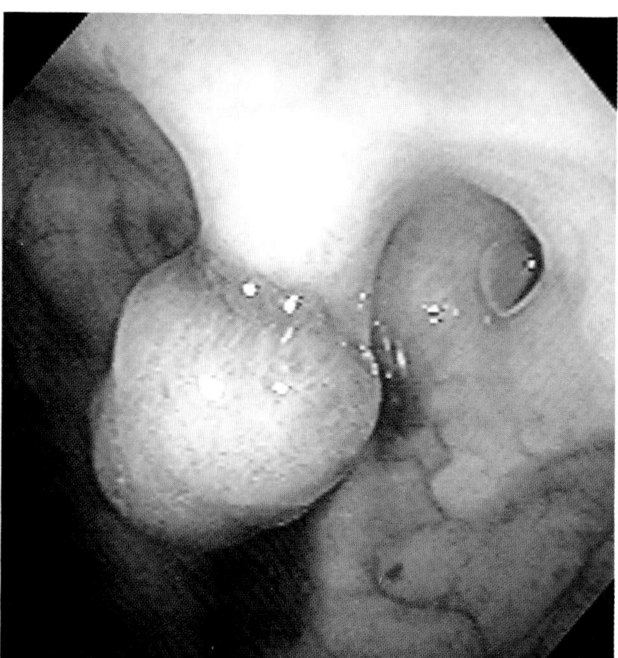

Plate 12. A tubular adenoma attached by a short, thick pedicle. A single diverticulum is adjacent to the base of the pedicle. The plate is cited in Chap. 30.

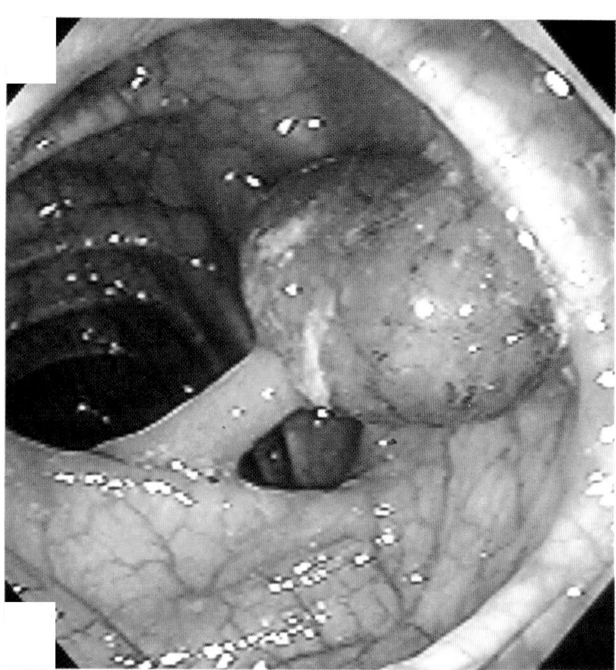

Plate 13. A tubulovillous adenoma on a long, thin pedicle in the transverse colon. The plate is cited in Chap. 30.

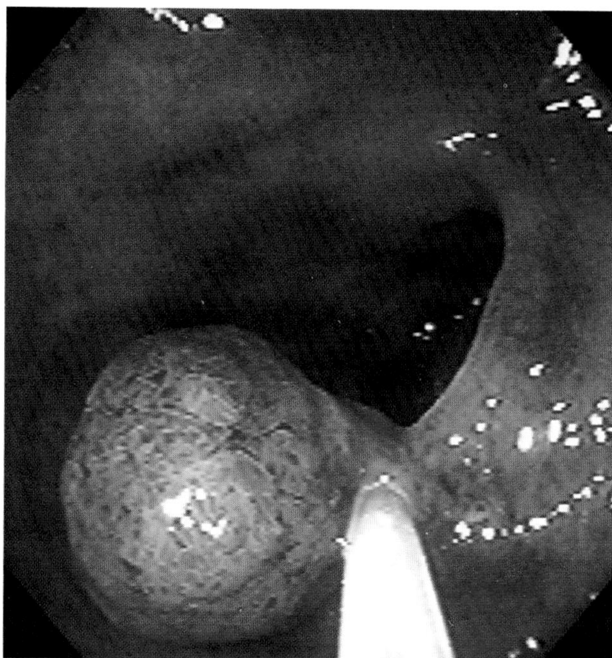

Plate 14. A "marble-type" polyp with a small attachment to the colonic wall. The snare sheath is extended, and the wire loop has been closed around its narrow attachment to the colonic wall. The plate is cited in Chap. 30.

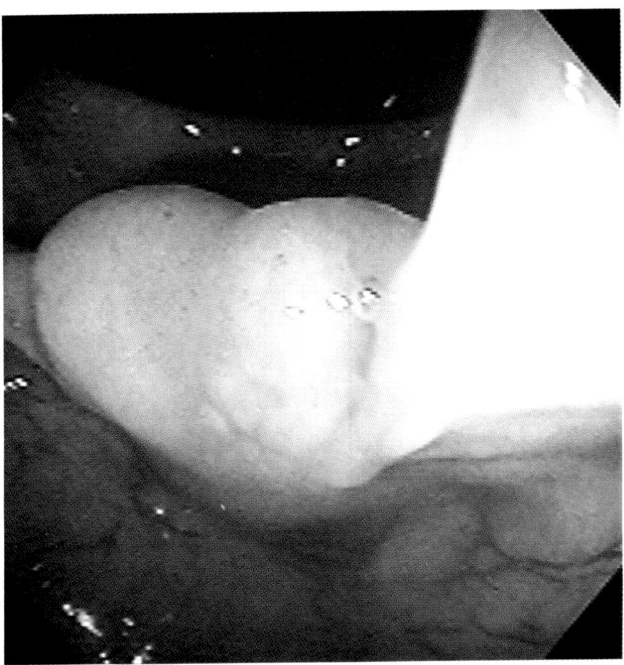

Plate 15. A "clamshell" type of polyp wrapped around a fold in the sigmoid colon. The plate is cited in Chap. 30.

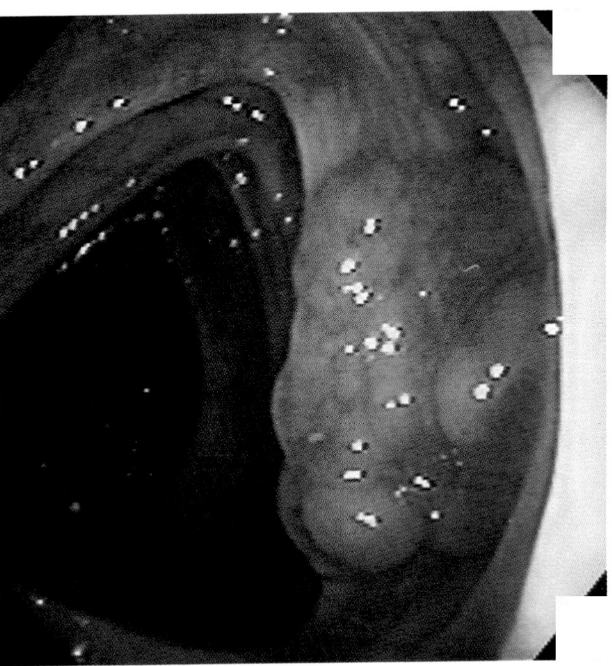

Plate 16. A sessile polyp attached to the wall of the right colon. The plate is cited in Chap. 30.

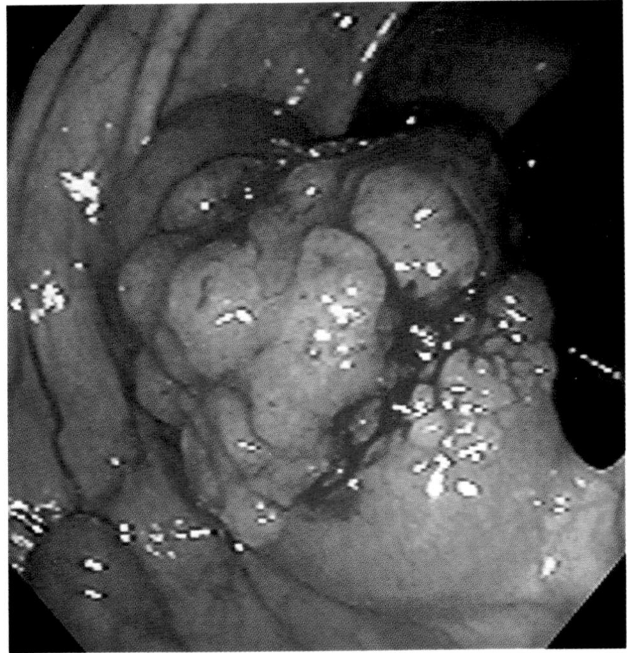

Plate 17. The same polyp as in Plate 17 after submucosal injection of saline. The saline increases the distance between the polyp base and the muscularis propria, rendering colonoscopic polypectomy safer. The plate is cited in Chap. 30.

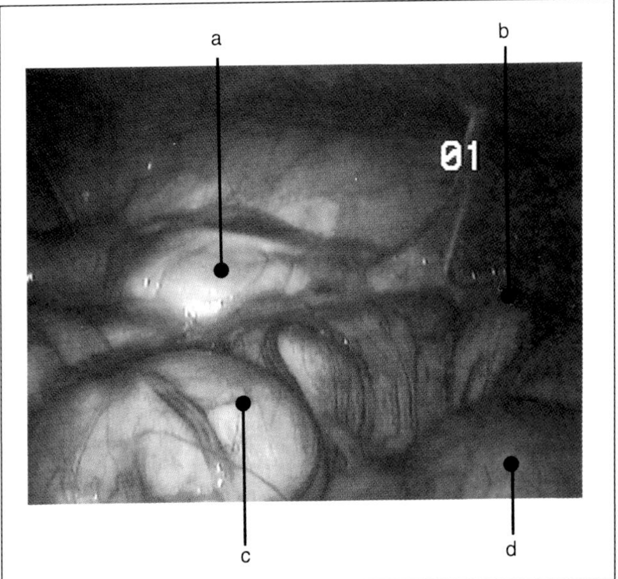

Plate 18. This is the view of the right abdominal cavity from the camera in the left upper-quadrant port. The gallbladder (d), transverse colon (c), hepatic flexure (b), and right colon (a) are easily seen. The plate is cited in Chap. 46.

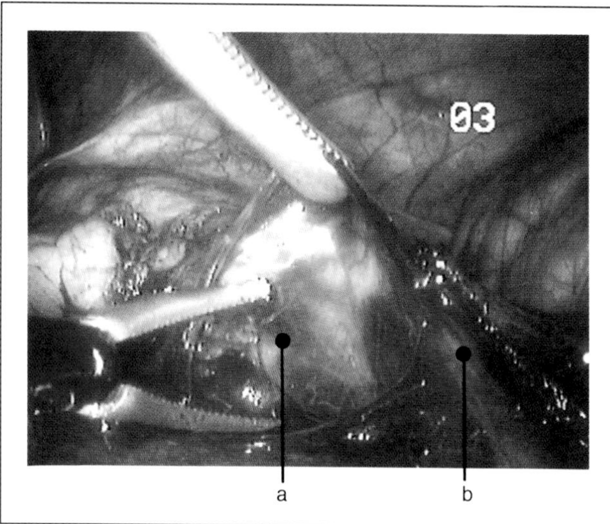

Plate 19. This is a view from the camera in the left upper-quadrant port looking into the right lower quadrant. The terminal ileum, cecum, and right colon have been mobilized off the retroperitoneum and retracted to the left upper quadrant with a laparoscopic Babcock instrument (not seen) in the right port. The two instruments shown in this picture are in the left and lower-midline ports and are gently dissecting the retroperitoneum (b) to identify the right ureter (a). The plate is cited in Chap. 46.

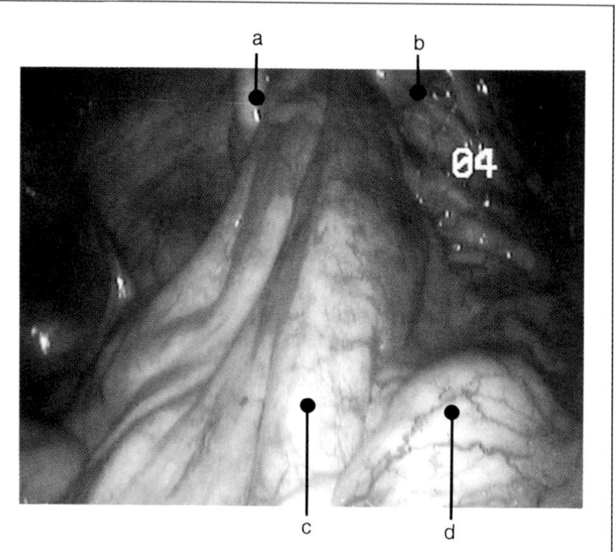

Plate 20. After the ileum (a), right colon, and hepatic flexure are mobilized, they are placed back in the right lower quadrant. A laparoscopic Babcock clamp in the right port is used to grasp the ileocecal junction (b). This picture is a view from the left upper quadrant looking into the right lower quadrant. The ileocecal junction is grasped and lifted up. This puts the mesentery on stretch and creates a bowstring effect (c), thus identifying the ileocolic artery. The transverse colon (d) is seen in the right lower corner. The plate is cited in Chap. 46.

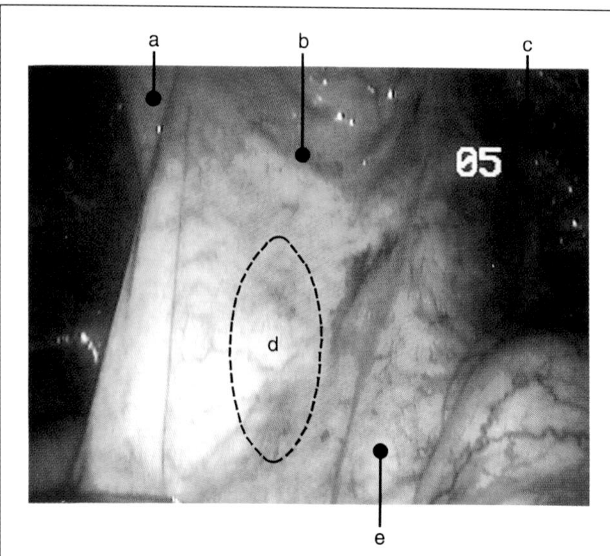

Plate 21. A grasper is placed in the lower midline port and the terminal ileum (a) is gently lifted. An ileal artery (b) is an arcade vessel from the superior mesenteric artery to the ileocolic artery. The cecum (c) is gently grasped with a Babcock clamp. The avascular mesentary adjacent to the ileocolic artery is seen. A cautery spatula in the left port is used to create an opening in the mesentery (d) parallel to the ileocolic artery (e). This opening is carried down to the base of the mesentery and up to the bowel wall. The plate is cited in Chap. 46.

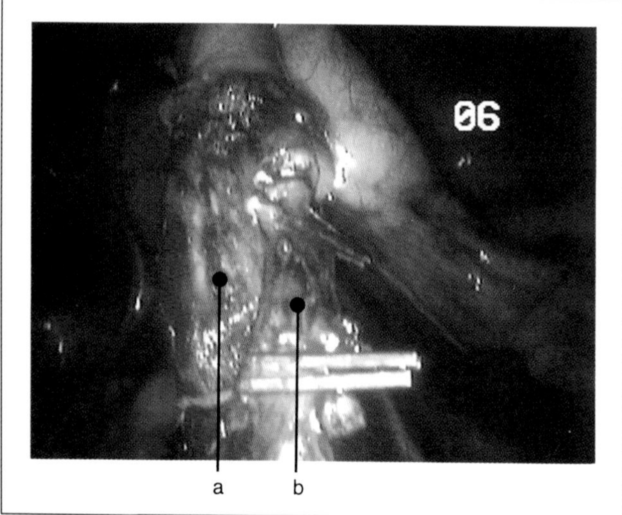

Plate 22. The ileocolic artery (a) and vein (b) have been separated, and double clips have been placed proximally and distally on the vein. The vein is then transected. The artery is behind and will also be doubly clipped. A loop suture will then be placed on the proximal stump. The plate is cited in Chap. 46.

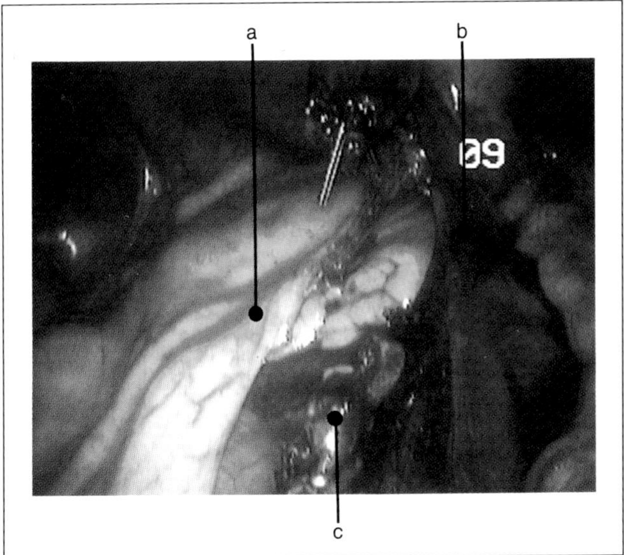

Plate 23. This is a view from the camera in the lower midline port looking cephalad. The proximal (c) and distal (a) ends of the ileocolic vessel are seen. The mesentery (b) is taken toward the transverse colon. The plate is cited in Chap. 46.

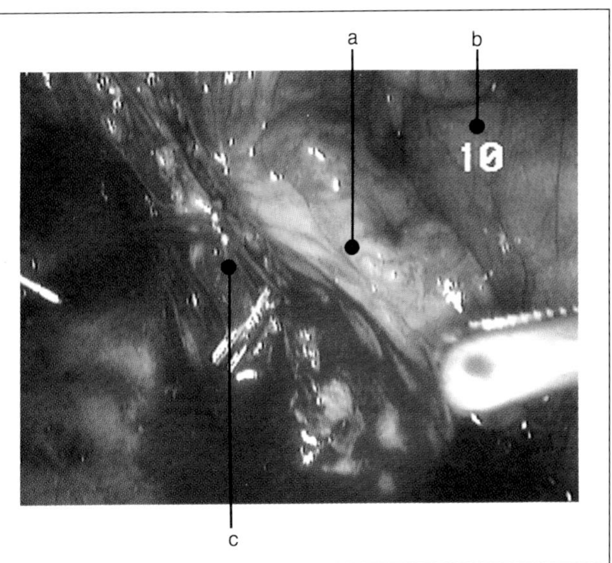

Plate 24. The right colic artery (a) and vein (c) are found in the mesentery and are doubly clipped and transected. At this point the terminal ileum, cecum, right colon, hepatic flexure, and mesentery from ileum to transverse colon (b) have been mobilized and the incision in the right upper quadrant is enlarged 5 to 7 cm to remove the specimen, transect the bowel, and perform a side-to-side anastomosis. The plate is cited in Chap. 46.

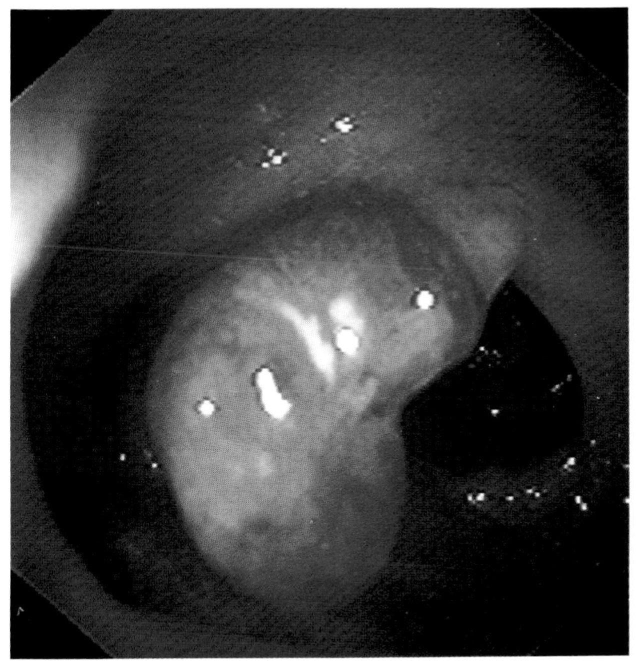

A

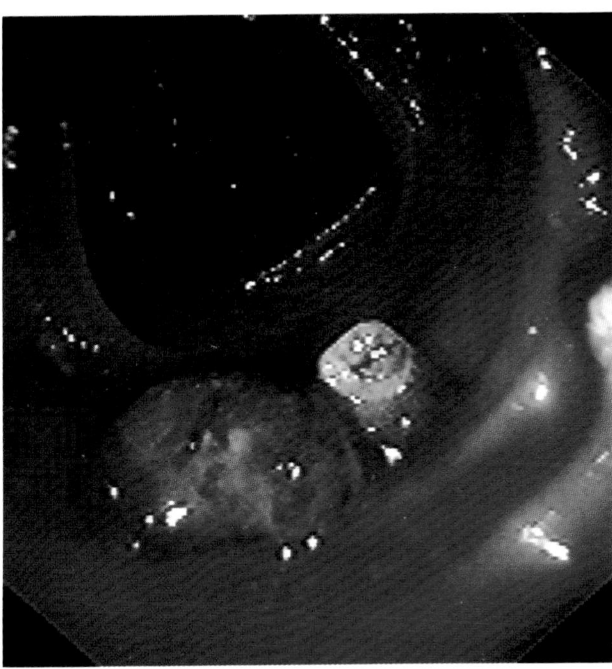

B

Plate 25. Malignant polyp with favorable histologic features. *A* and *B*. Bean-shaped pedunculated polyp before and after endoscopic resection. The histologic features are favorable. The plate is cited in Chap. 47.

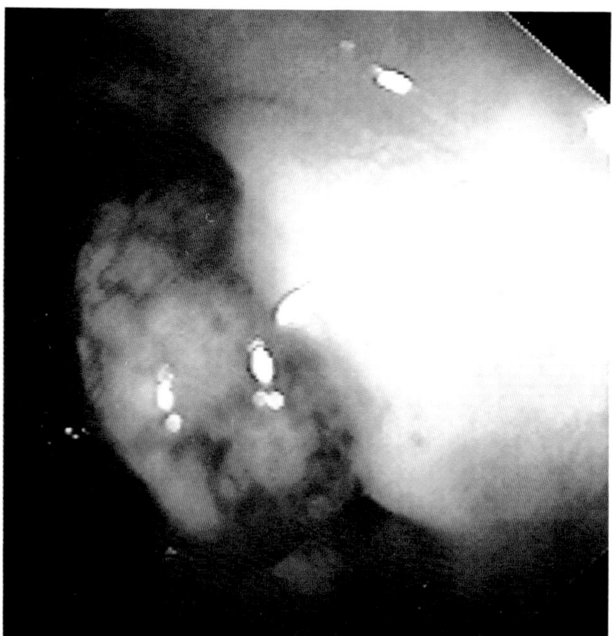

Plate 26. Malignant polyp with unfavorable histologic features. Broad-based sessile malignant polyp with smooth head. Lymphatic invasion was present on histologic examination. Subsequent surgery showed no residual or nodal cancer. The plate is cited in Chap. 47.

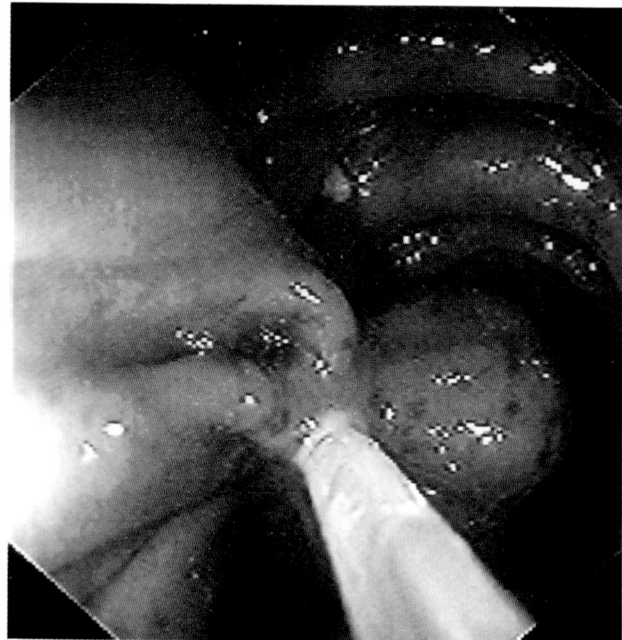

Plate 27. Malignant polyp with favorable histologic features. Snare encircling the upper portion of a broad-based polyp. Although benign-appearing, this polyp had invasive cancer. There was a 3-mm margin of noninvolved adenoma at the resection margin. Surgery was not recommended. The plate is cited in Chap. 47.

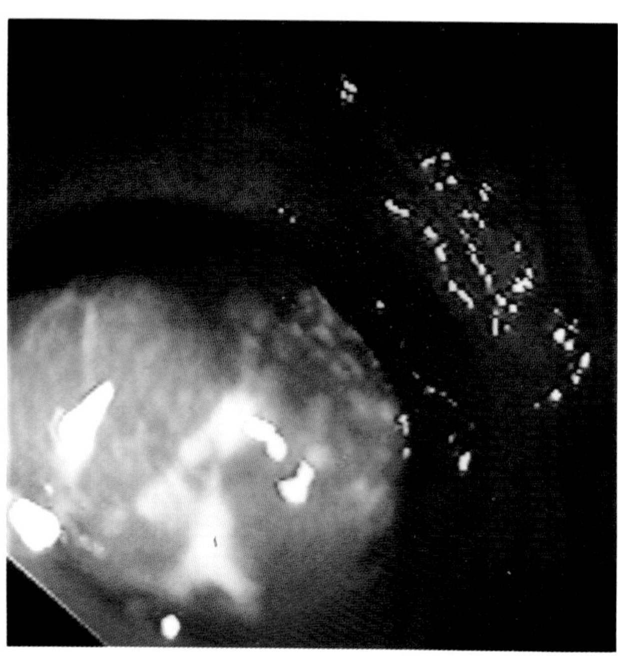

Plate 28. Malignant polyp with unfavorable histologic features. Smooth polyp with broad base that had carcinoma at the margin of endoscopic resection. The plate is cited in Chap. 47.

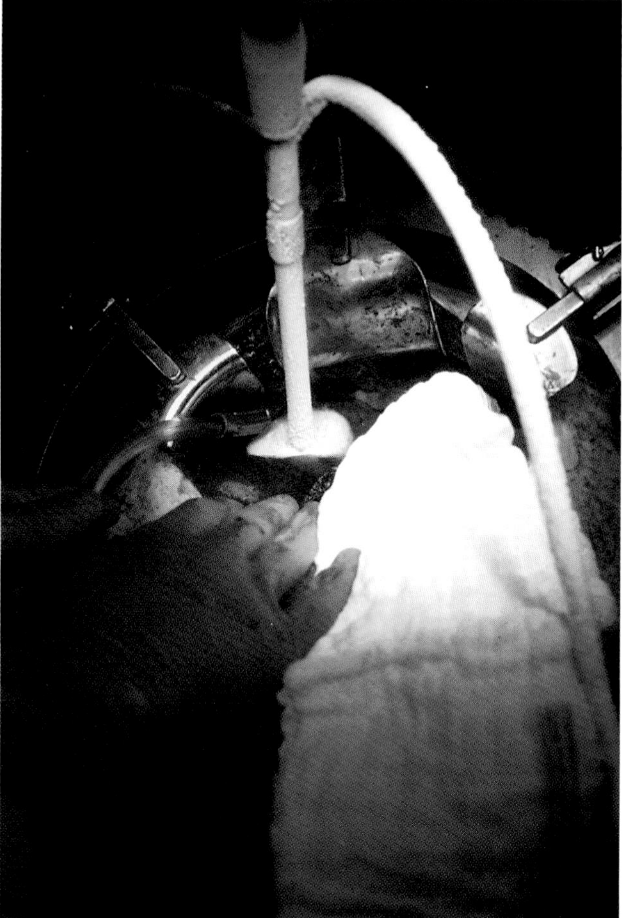

Plate 29. Cryosurgery in progress. Demonstration of liver exposure, probe placement, and freezing. The plate is cited in Chap. 83.

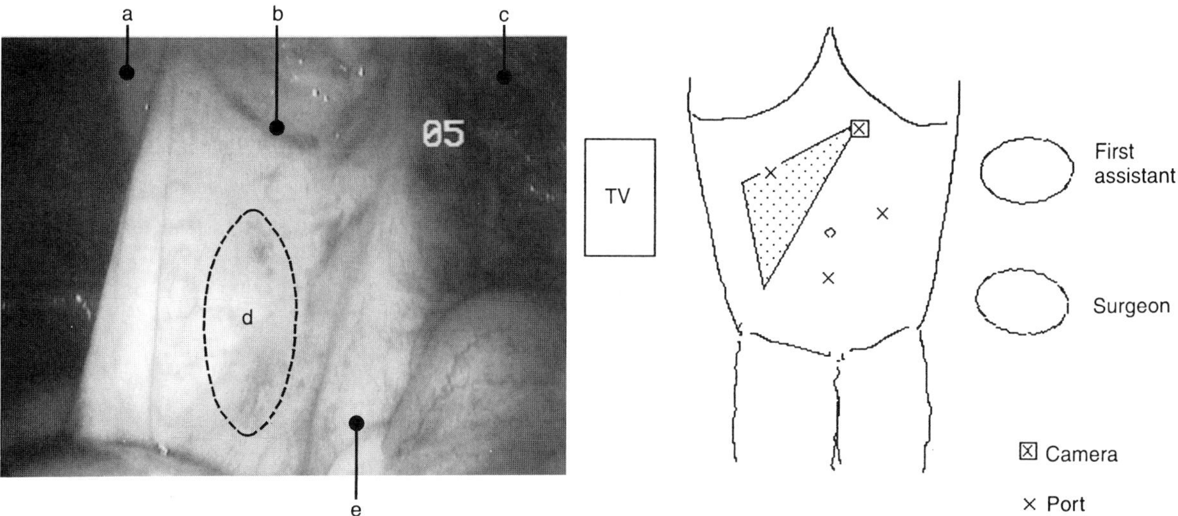

FIG. 46-5. A grasper is placed in the lower midline port and the terminal ileum (a) is gently lifted. An ileal artery (b) is an arcade vessel from the superior mesenteric artery to the ileocolic artery. The cecum (c) is gently grasped with a Babcock clamp. The avascular mesentary adjacent to the ileocolic artery is seen. A cautery spatula in the left port is used to create an opening in the mesentery (d) parallel to the ileocolic artery (e). This opening is carried down to the base of the mesentery and up to the bowel wall. (See color Plate 21.)

entery of the transverse colon is then taken down and the right branch of the middle colic artery is identified, secured, and transected. The transverse colon is transected using a standard intestinal stapler. A side-to-side extracorporeal anastomosis is performed using the stapler. The ends of the bowel are lined up together and two adjacent enterotomies are made for the forks of the stapler. The stapler is introduced and fired. The common opening is closed with another reload of the stapler. The anastomosis can be reinforced using 3-0 Lembert silk sutures. The anastomosis is dropped back into the abdominal cavity. The defect in the mesentery is left open. The incision in the right side of the abdomen isclosed in a two-layer fashion using absorbable monofilament suture. The laparoscope is then reintroduced into the abdominal cavity and the anastomosis is observed to check for any significant bleeding. The abdominal cavity can be irrigated with warm saline at this time. The other remaining ports are removed and closed appropriately. The fascia for the Hasson cannula is closed using absorbable braided suture material.

The ports to the left colectomy are shown in Fig. 46-9, while the ports for the sigmoid resection in Fig.

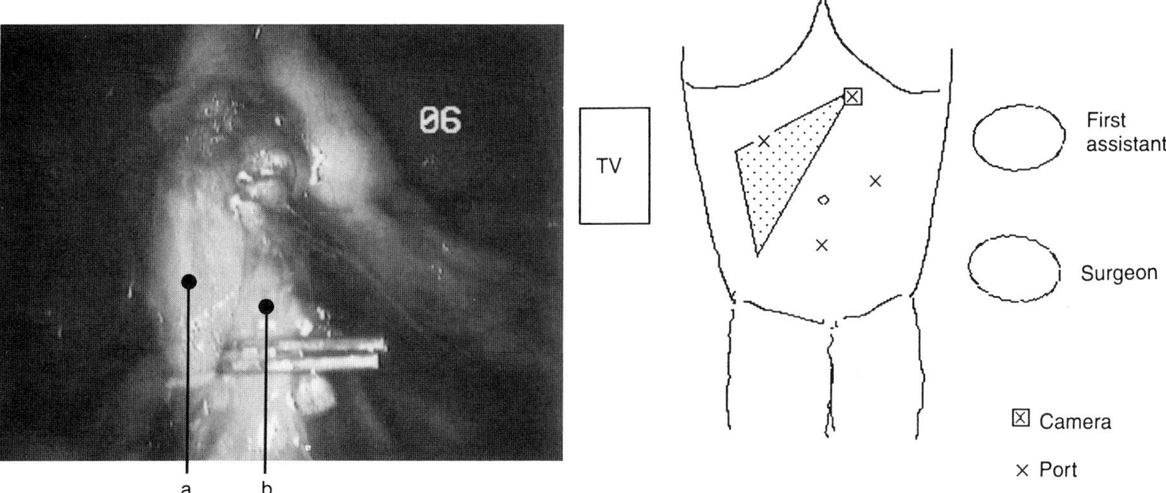

FIG. 46-6. The ileocolic artery (a) and vein (b) have been separated and double clips have been placed proximally and distally on the vein. The vein is then transected. The artery is behind and will also be doubly clipped. A loop suture will then be placed on the proximal stump. (See color Plate 22.)

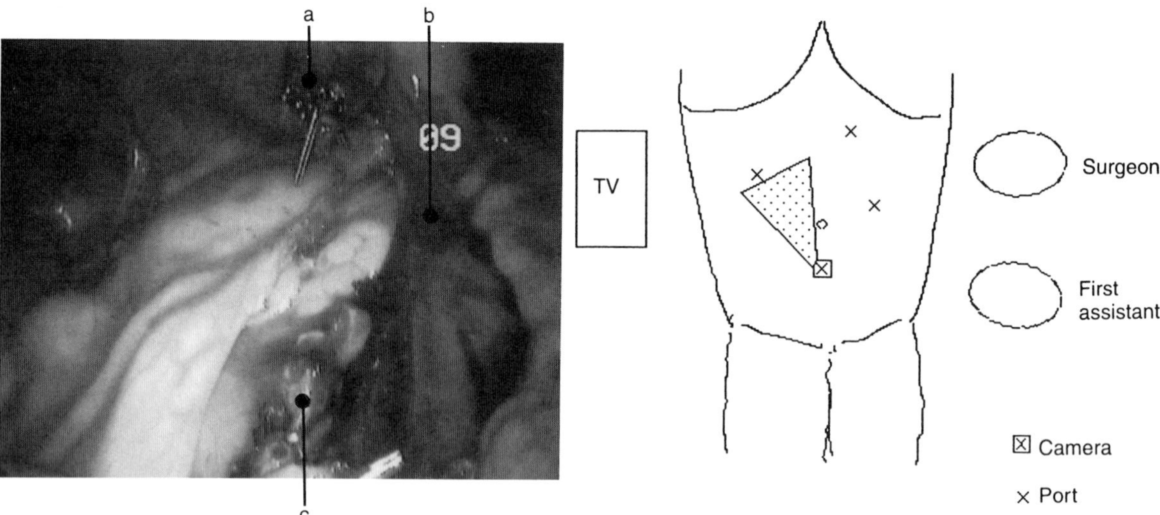

FIG. 46-7. This is a view from the camera in the lower-midline port looking cephalad. The proximal (c) and distal (a) ends of the ileocolic vessel are seen. The mesentery (b) is taken toward the transverse colon. (See color Plate 23.)

46-10. The patient is placed in a lithotomy position. This position is necessary in the event that (1) flexible sigmoidoscopy is needed to localize the lesion and (2) the anastomosis requires an end-to-end stapler that is introduced from below. Villous adenomas and T_1–T_3 lesions in the left and sigmoid colon may not be visible via the laparoscope, and intraoperative endoscopic localization can identify the area that must be resected. Once the ports have been inserted, the patient is placed in a Trendelenburg position in order to retract the small bowel out of the pelvis. The sigmoid colon is gently retracted and dissected off the left lateral abdominal and pelvic walls with electrocoagulation and blunt dissection using the spatula. The white line of Toldt along the left paracolic gutter is taken down using the spatula cautery. Once the peritoneum is broken, the spatula is used to bluntly dissect the left and sigmoid colon off the retroperitoneum. The left colonic mobilization continues to the splenic flexure by gently retracting the left colon toward the right lower quadrant. The Trendelenburg position keeps the spleen and greater omentum in the upper abdomen. With careful retraction, the splenic flexure is taken down; this is an important step to bring the left colon out of the abdo-

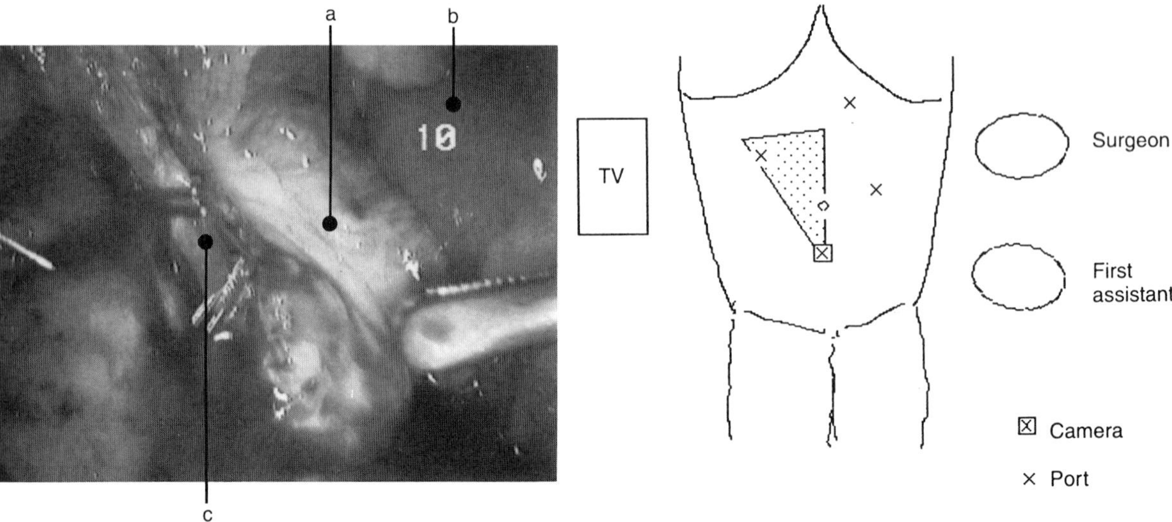

FIG. 46-8. The right colic artery (a) and vein (c) are found in the mesentery and are doubly clipped and transected. At this point the terminal ileum, cecum, right colon, hepatic flexure, and mesentery from ileum to transverse colon (b) have been mobilized and the incision in the right upper quadrant is enlarged 5 to 7 cm to remove the specimen, transect the bowel, and perform a side-to-side anastomosis. (See color Plate 24.)

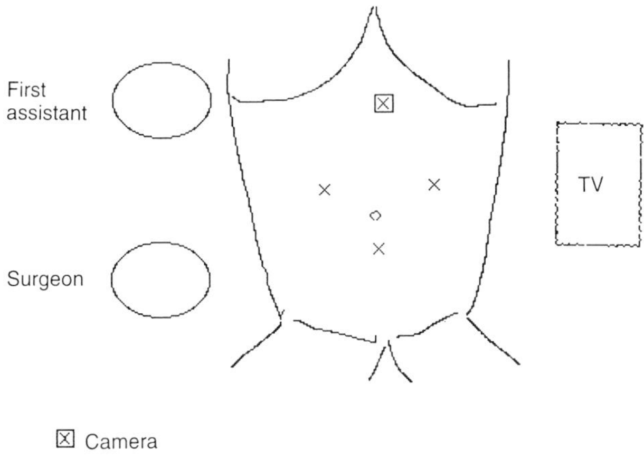

FIG. 46-9. Port placement for laparoscopic left hemicolectomy. The patient is placed in a lithotomy position. A 10-mm Hasson port is placed in the left upper quadrant. The surgeon stands on the patient's right side and the assistant stands between the legs. Additional ports (10-mm) are placed in the infraumbilical, left, and right sides of the abdomen. The laparoscope is placed in the infraumbilical port. The TV monitor is placed on the patient's left side. The patient is placed in a lithotomy position because this permits a flexible sigmoidoscopy procedure in order to localize the lesion and provides a better position for the assistant to control the laparoscope and the left port grasping instrument. After the sigmoid colon, left colon, and splenic flexure are mobilized, a transverse incision is made around the left port and the colon is exteriorized.

men through a small left abdominal incision. At this point it may be necessary to localize the lesion if the tumor is superficial. In order to perform the endoscopic localization, a laparoscopic bowel clamp must be placed across the proximal colon. This will prevent insufflation of air into the proximal colon. If excessive air is introduced into the proximal colon and small bowel, exposure is limited and conversion to open laparotomy is more likely.

A flexible sigmoidoscope is inserted into the rectum and passed into the sigmoid and left colon. When the lesion is seen through the flexible sigmoidoscope, it is then localized with the laparoscope by identifying the transilluminated light from the flexible sigmoidoscope. This portion of the bowel is marked with the laparoscopic metal clips. The flexible sigmoidoscope is then withdrawn, removing the insufflated air. Once the lesion is identified, the goal is to obtain at least a 10-cm proximal and distal luminal margin with removal of the regional artery and mesentery. Lesions in the left colon can be resected in a fashion similar to that described for the right colon. The left colon is placed back in the left side of the abdomen and held up with a full visualization of the colonic mesentery from the right side. At the base of the left colonic mesentery, the inferior mesenteric artery is dissected from its surrounding tissues. The inferior mesenteric artery is then doubly clipped on each side and transected; the stump of the left inferior mesenteric artery is secured with a laparoscopic loop suture. The mesentery is scored to allow at least a 10-cm proximal and distal luminal margin from the primary tumor. The sigmoid mesentery is bluntly dissected. This dissection is continued all the way to the lumen of the sigmoid colon. The proximal mesentery of the left colon is taken down with blunt dissection as well. Major vessels such as the inferior mesenteric vein can be doubly clipped on each side, transected, and secured with an endoscopic loop suture. If the tumor is in the proximal portion of the descending colon, the colon can be exteriorized through a 5- to 7-cm incision on the left side of the abdomen at the left port site. A transverse incision is made and the bowel is exteriorized, transected proximally and distally, and a side-to-side anastomosis is performed using stapling instruments or an end-to-end anastomosis can be done with hand suturing techniques. If the lesion is in the distal descending colon

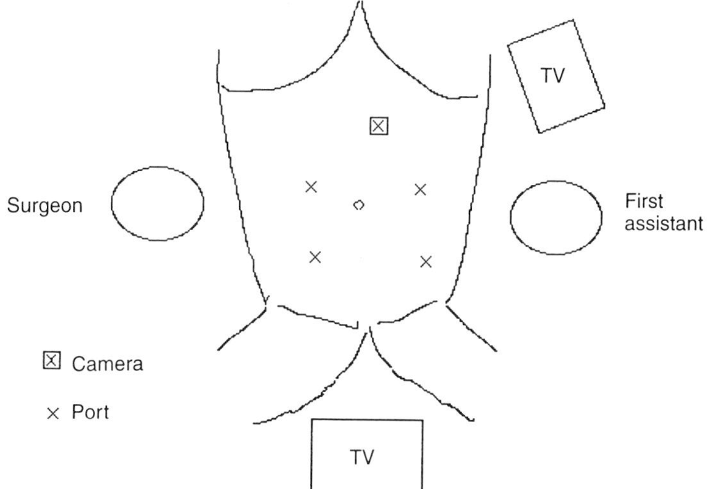

FIG. 46-10. Port placement for laparoscopic sigmoid colectomy and anterior anastomosis. The patient is placed in a lithotomy position. A 10-mm Hasson port is placed in the left upper quadrant. Three additional 10-mm ports are placed as shown. The endoscopic intestinal stapler is placed through the right lower port to transect the sigmoid colon at least 10 cm distal to the tumor. The colon and tumor are exteriorized through a 5-cm transverse incision around the left port. The proximal end of the colon is transected and the head of the circular stapler is inserted into the proximal end. The colon is dropped into the abdominal cavity and the incision is closed at fascia. Under laparoscopic viewing, the stapler is brought up through the rectum and mated to the head in the proximal end. The stapler is approximated and fixed to complete the anastomosis.

or sigmoid colon, the anastomosis may have to be performed intracorporeally, using an approximating circular stapler from the rectum. In this situation the distal sigmoid colon is transected using a laparoscopic intestinal stapler. The resected bowel is then brought up through a 7-cm transverse incision that is located at the left abdominal port site. The bowel is exteriorized, the proximal colon is transected, and the specimen is removed. The anvil and head are then inserted into the proximal lumen and dropped back into the abdominal cavity. The transverse incision is then closed in a two-layer fashion. Under laparoscopic visualization, the head is joined to the shaft of the stapler. The stapler is approximated and fired. The stapler is then withdrawn from the rectum and checked for two complete doughnuts. If incomplete doughnuts are obtained, the abdomen will have to be opened to reinforce the incomplete stapled suture line. The defect in the colonic mesentery is left open.

The postoperative management of laparoscopic colonic resection is similar to that for open colectomies. Nasogastric decompression is not routinely used. The patients are kept NPO until bowel sounds are heard; then they are started on clear liquids. A patient-controlled analgesia (PCA) pump is used for 24 to 48 h and then discontinued. By the third or fourth postoperative day, the patients are advanced to oral pain medication. The amount of postoperative pain is similar to that due to appendectomy incisions. Patients are usually discharged by the fourth or fifth day after surgery.

Both operative technique and instrumentation for laparoscopic surgery will undergo significant changes in the next few years. The technology of Doppler and ultrasonography have been or will soon be incorporated into laparoscopic instruments, and these will enhance a surgeon's ability to dissect the colonic mesentery and identify blood vessels. Video technology will continue to improve and progress to three-dimensional imaging, virtual reality imaging, and split-screen technology. Computers will also be incorporated into our imaging instruments, and robotic instruments controlled by the surgeon sitting at a control console may be available within the next decade. This technology will undoubtedly transform the operating room environment. The surgeon's goal is to obtain adequate luminal margins and adequate lymph node sampling. If new surgical technology can be applied cost-effectively while maintaining optimal standards of anatomic resection, then minimally invasive surgery will be a welcome advance.

CANCER CONTROL

There are important cancer control issues regarding laparoscopic colectomy. These include the extent of lymph node dissection, tumor implantation at port sites, and adequacy of intraperitoneal staging. The role of lymphadenectomy in colorectal resections has been controversial for many years. Miles'[9] theory was that a wider lymph node dissection removed more nodes that contained metastatic disease and thereby increased the chance for cure. Sugarbaker et al.[10] analyzed the results of lymphadenectomy from several studies that compared an extended regional lymph node dissection with a regional dissection and found no evidence for improved survival. Thus, the concept of "wider is better" has been questioned in recent years.

Laparoscopic colectomy has resurrected the issue of lymphadenectomy. The number of nodes found in a resected specimen has been equated with adequacy of node sampling. When 20 nodes are reported in the final surgical pathology assessment, the surgeon feels satisfied with his or her technique. When only six nodes are reported, the surgeon typically cites the pathologist for not spending more time dissecting out nodes. A normal variation in node number of a resected colon is also another explanation. We recently reviewed the number of nodes in resected specimens from Dukes B and C colonic tumors (Table 46-1). Only those tumors in the right, left, and sigmoid colons were examined. The node count varied significantly according to site, with the right colon having the highest count. The count then progressively decreased in the left and sigmoid colon. In comparing laparoscopic-assisted colectomy with open colectomy, these differences in nodal count according to large bowel location should be considered.

It is possible that a laparoscopic colectomy results in a lesser lymphadenectomy. Several reports suggest that lymph node counts in laparoscopic-assisted colectomy specimens are similar to those in open colectomy specimens.[1-7] However, these studies had a considerable mix of proximal and distal colorectal carcinomas and—because there is considerable variabil-

Table 46-1
Number of Lymph Nodes in Resected Specimens for Astler-Coller Dukes B and C Colon Carcinomas

Location[a]	*n*[b]	*Mean nodes ± SD*[c]
Right	101	18.8 ± 11.2(±1.1)
Left	60	15.8 ± 16.2(±2.1)[d]
Sigmoid	43	11.0 ± 8.6(±1.3)[e]

[a]Lesions were located in the right, left, and sigmoid colon. Dukes A and D tumors were excluded. Carcinomas of the hepatic flexure, transverse colon, and splenic flexure were excluded. B_1 = 39 patients, B_2 = 104 patients, C_1 = 7 patients, and C_2 = 54 patients.

[b]Number of patients who underwent colectomy.

[c]Number of lymph nodes found in resected specimens. (±) = ± SE.

[d]$p < .002$ compared with right colon (Mann-Whitney test).

[e]$p < .00001$ compared with right colon (Mann-Whitney test).

ity in node counts from proximal to distal colon—analyses of node counts that do not consider this variation may be misleading. A recent study of 14 laparoscopic-assisted right hemicolectomies found that the mean node count was 8.8 ± 5.4 (± SD), and this was significantly less than what was observed in the historic right colon resections shown in Table 46-1 ($p < .05$). Vayer et al.[11] had a similar finding. They also compared laparoscopic right colectomies with open laparotomy right colonic resections during a similar time period. The mean node count for the laparoscopic group was 6.6; this was significantly less than the 9.6 nodes found in the open colectomy group.

It is unclear whether significant differences in node counts between laparoscopic-assisted and open colectomy are clinically meaningful. There is significant prognostic information in resected lymph nodes.[12] Systemic adjuvant chemotherapy has been shown to be effective in increasing the survival of colonic cancer patients who are node-positive.[13] If laparoscopic colectomy results in fewer lymph nodes than it does with open colectomy, then there is a potential for understaging this disease. This could lead to withholding postoperative systemic adjuvant chemotherapy from patients who might otherwise benefit from it, resulting in lower survival. Another important consideration is whether a lesser lymphadenectomy will affect local/regional control of disease. We continue to live under the specter of Miles, and only a randomized trial comparing laparoscopic with open colectomy will resolve all these issues.

Tumor implantation at either a port site or the specimen wound is another cancer-control issue. There are several reports that have described tumor implantation at port sites for a variety of abdominal malignancies originating in the gallbladder, stomach, pancreas, and ovary.[14–18] Similar reports regarding tumor implantation at wound or port sites after laparoscopic colectomy have now appeared in the literature.[19–21] Such reports point out that new operative technology, while having short-term benefits such as shorter hospitalization, can have long-term consequences for cancer control. Wound recurrence is uncommon with open colectomy, but the true incidence of port-site recurrence with laparoscopic colectomy will never be known until a large prospective study is done. The potential mechanism of port-site recurrence is the shedding of malignant cells during the procedure. From a technical standpoint, the laparoscopic surgeon should avoid grasping the colonic wall near the tumor. Laparoscopic Babcock clamps are now available and should be used carefully.

Intraoperative staging is another limitation of laparoscopic colectomy. The surgeon is no longer able to palpate the liver for metastases, although the surface of the liver can be seen. Preoperative staging with either ultrasound or computed tomography may be necessary. Intraperitoneal metastases to the ovaries, pelvic cul-de-sac, or paracolic gutters can be missed. The incidence of such understaging is unknown and, one hopes, is low enough to rule out the need for systemic adjuvant chemotherapy such as that in trials now under way.

COMPLICATIONS

During the early development of laparoscopic cholecystectomy, unusual complications such as common bile duct injury, cystic duct leakage, and stones scattered throughout the peritoneal cavity were reported. The laparoscopic approach to colonic resection has also resulted in unusual complications. Ureteral injury is rare with open laparotomy, but such injuries have been observed with the laparoscopic technique. Some surgeons routinely place lighted ureteral stents prior to the procedure in order to visualize the structure, but this obviously increases the cost. Inadvertent and undetected small bowel perforation is another significant injury. This presumably occurs because the grasping instruments can traumatize the bowel wall or cauterizing instruments can injure the bowel outside the range of laparoscope view. Other injuries include uncontrolled hemorrhage, bladder injury, and hypercapnia-induced cardiac arrhythmias or decompensation.

COST ANALYSIS AND QUALITY OF LIFE

Advocates of laparoscopic surgery point out that this new technology results in faster patient recovery, lower health care costs, and better quality of life compared with open laparotomy.[22,23] Shorter hospitalization time and fewer postoperative complications should reduce costs. Less postoperative pain and faster return to normal activity may result in improved quality of life. While many surgeons would agree with these impressions, attempts to quantify these parameters often resemble the search for the Holy Grail. Under the pressure of growing concern over spiraling medical costs, economic analysts have developed new tools that make it possible to conduct rational analyses of the economic and quality-of-life effects of new medical interventions.[24] These studies have been applied to controversial cancer therapy, with intriguing results and conclusions.[25]

The goal of a randomized trial of laparoscopic colectomy for resectable disease is to determine whether it is equivalent to open colectomy in terms of disease-free and overall survival. If laparoscopic colectomy does not meet that test, then the issues of cost and quality of life are irrelevant. If this procedure does not compromise survival, then the choice between laparoscopic and open procedures should be guided by costs and quality of life. Because laparoscopic technology is new and seemingly less traumatic, one should not assume that it is better. Tate et al.[26] recently reported their randomized trial of laparoscopic versus open appendectomy. They found that hospitalization time and return to work were similar, while operating room time was greater with the laparoscopic approach. Their conclusion is that the procedures are equivalent. Therefore they question whether the laparoscopic approach is better. A prospective study comparing open versus laparoscopic colectomy is necessary in order to resolve the issues of outcome, cost, and quality of life before the new procedure is accepted as standard of therapy.

CONCLUSIONS

Laparoscopic surgery has the potential to have a significant impact on abdominal surgery. Minimally invasive techniques may have an important role in palliating the symptoms of advanced disease, but the application of this type of surgery to the treatment of potentially curable colonic carcinoma is controversial. The surgeon's goal is to obtain adequate luminal margins and adequate lymph node sampling. If new surgical technology can be applied cost-effectively while maintaining optimal standards of anatomic resection, then minimally invasive surgery will be a welcome advance.

Before laparoscopic colectomy can replace open colectomy, a prospective randomized clinical trial comparing disease control, complications, costs, and quality of life must be done.

REFERENCES

1. Jacobs M, Verdeja JC, Goldstein HS: Minimally invasive colon resection (laparoscopic colectomy). *Surg Laparosc Endoscopy*, 1:144–150, 1991.
2. Fowler DL, White SA: Laparoscopy-assisted sigmoid resection. *Surg Laparosc Endosc* 1:183–188, 1991.
3. Schlinkert RT: Laparoscopic-assisted right hemicolectomy. *Dis Colon Rectum* 34:1030–1031, 1991.
4. Phillips EH, Franklin M, Carroll BJ, et al: Laparoscopic colectomy. *Ann Surg* 216:703–707, 1992.
5. Falk PM, Beart RW, Wexner SD, et al: Laparoscopic colectomy: A critical appraisal. *Dis Colon Rectum* 36:28–34, 1993.
6. Scoggin SD, Frazee RC, Snyder SK, et al: Laparoscopic-assisted bowel surgery. *Dis Colon Rectum* 36:747–750, 1993.
7. Peters WR, Bartels TL: Minimally invasive colectomy—Are the potential benefits realized? *Dis Colon Rectum* 36:751–756, 1993.
8. Ondrula DP, Nelson RL, Prasad ML, et al: Multifactorial index of preoperative risk factors in colon resections. *Dis Colon Rectum* 35:117–122, 1992.
9. Miles EE: A method of performing abdomino-perineal excision for carcinoma of the rectum and of the terminal portion of the pelvic colon. *Lancet* 2:1812–1813, 1908.
10. Sugarbaker PH, Corlew S: Influence of surgical techniques on survival in patients with colorectal cancer: A review. *Dis Colon Rectum* 25:545–557, 1982.
11. Vayer AJ, Larach SW, Williamson PR, et al: Cost effectiveness of laparoscopic assisted colectomy. *Proceedings of the American Society of Colon/Rectal Surgeons, 92nd Annual Meeting*, 1993. p 37.
12. Cady B: Lymph node metastasis: Indicators but not governors of survival. *Arch Surg* 119:1067–1072, 1984.
13. Steele G: Adjuvant therapy for patients with colon and rectal cancer: Clinical indications for multimodality therapy in high-risk groups and specific surgical questions for future multimodality trials. *Surgery* 112:847–849, 1992.
14. Cava A, Ronian J, Gonzalez Quintala A, et al: Subcutaneous metastasis following laparoscopy in gastric adenocarcinoma. *Eur J Surg Oncol* 16:63–67, 1990.
15. Clair DG, Lautz DB, Brooks DC: Rapid development of umbilical metastases after laparoscopic cholecystectomy for unsuspected gallbladder carcinoma. *Surgery* 113:355–358, 1993.
16. Fong Y, Brennan MF, Turnbull A, et al: Gallbladder cancer discovered during laparoscopic surgery: Potential for iatrogenic tumor dissemination. *Arch Surg* 128:1028–1032, 1993.
17. Gleeson NC, Nicosia SV, Mark JE, et al: Abdominal wall metastases from ovarian cancer after laparoscopy. *Am J Obstet Gynecol* 169:522–523, 1993.
18. Delcastillo CF, Warshaw L: Peritoneal metastases in pancreatic carcinoma. *Hepatogastroenterology* 40:430–432, 1993.
19. Walsh DCA, Wattchow DA, Wilson TG: Subcutaneous metastases after laparoscopic resection of malignancy. *Aust NZJ Surg* 63:563–565, 1993.
20. O'Rourke N, Price PM, Kelly S, Sikora K: Tumor inoculation during laparoscopy. *Lancet* 342:368, 1993.
21. Fusco MA, Paluzzi MW. Abdominal wall recurrence after laparoscopic-assisted colectomy for adenocarcinoma of the colon. *Dis Colon Rectum* 36:858–861, 1993.
22. Fritts LL, Orlando R, Thompson WR, et al: Laparoscopic appendectomy—A safety and cost analysis. *Arch Surg* 128:521–525, 1993.
23. Bass EB, Pitt HA, Lillemoe KD: Cost-effectiveness of laparoscopic cholecystectomy versus open cholecystectomy. *Am J Surg* 165:466–471, 1993.
24. Detsky AS, Naglie I: A clinician's guide to cost-effective analysis. *Ann Int Med* 113:147–154, 1990.
25. Smith TJ, Hillner BE, Desch CE: Efficacy and cost-effectiveness of cancer treatment: Rational allocation of resources based on decision analysis. *J Natl Cancer Inst* 85:1460–1474, 1993.
26. Tate JJT, Dawson JW, Chung SCS, et al: Laparoscopic versus open appendicectomy—Prospective randomized trial. *Lancet* 342:633–637, 1993.

CHAPTER 47

Cancer in Polyps

Jerome D. Waye
Michael J. O'Brien

HIGHLIGHTS

A malignant polyp is an adenoma in which an invasive carcinoma involves the submucosa of the polyp's head or stalk, or, in the case of a sessile polyp, the submucosa of the underlying bowel wall. A segmental resection of the bowel is not considered a necessary intervention if the polyp meets the following favorable criteria: (1) the resection margin is not involved, (2) the histology is well or moderately differentiated, (3) there is no evidence of lymphatic or vascular space invasion, (4) the endoscopist considers the lesion totally removed. To achieve the best outcome for the patient, the decision to operate after endoscopic resection of a malignant polyp involves balancing the risk of residual cancer at the excision site and regional lymph node metastases against that of mortality from abdominal surgery. In general, the risk of death from elective colonic surgery varies from 0.2 to 2 percent, with the patient younger than age 50 being at lowest risk. A summary analysis of the recent literature yields an estimate of the risk of residual tumor or nodal cancer in colonoscopically resected pedunculated malignant polyps with favorable criteria as 0.3 percent and that for sessile malignant polyps as 1.5 percent.

Patients of any age with favorable endoscopic resection criteria who have pedunculated malignant polyps resected endoscopically should not have a subsequent surgical resection. Among healthy patients under age 50 with sessile malignant polyps with favorable criteria, the risk of residual tumor or nodal disease is similiar to or slightly higher than the risk of death from surgery, and the argument can be made that this subgroup of patients should have surgical resection of that segment of bowel. Subsequent cancer surgery with bowel resection and node dissection will result in a cure of residual cancer in only about 50 percent of the patients with nodal metastases. Malignant polyps in the distal rectum require special consideration because a permanent colostomy is an issue. Malignant polyps in this location are also unique in that they are amenable to proctologic surgical techniques that permit deep excisions, which are not applicable in the colon.

In the event that a decision for follow-up colonoscopy only is made, a full repeat colonoscopic examination need not be undertaken immediately after the index colonoscopy if the initial examination was completed to the cecum. Endoscopy for evaluation of the polypectomy site may be performed in 4 to 12 weeks in order to assess completeness of resection, and again in 3 to 6 months. If no recurrent tumor is present, annual examinations should be performed for 2 years, after which routine polyp follow-up is recommended. If recurrent tumor is seen at the polypectomy site, surgical bowel resection should be carried out.

CONTROVERSY

While some feel that sessile malignant polyps always warrant bowel resection, a consensus is emerging for a conservative approach if free endoscopic resection margins can be demonstrated. This conservative approach is most compelling when the patient is older or is a poor surgical risk. Polypoid carcinoma (a malignant polyp without residual adenoma) has also, in the past, been considered an a priori indication for bowel resection, but there is considerable evidence that criteria similar to those pertaining to malignant polyps should determine the need for surgery in these cases also.

FUTURE DIRECTIONS

Staging by endoscopic ultrasound will be increasingly used in early colorectal cancer. Multi-institutional studies will permit prospective comparisons of conservative with surgical management strategies for malignant polyps. Multivariate analysis of pathologic and clinical characteristics that relate to adverse outcomes are needed.

DEFINITIONS

The expression *cancer in a polyp* has been used to refer to a broad spectrum of polypoid neoplasms ranging from an adenoma manifesting the biologically benign entity *carcinoma in situ* or *high-grade dysplasia* to an advanced adenocarcinoma in which residual adenoma has persisted. The term *malignant polyp* refers to an adenoma in which invasive carcinoma extends from the mucosal portion beyond the muscularis mucosa into the submucosa of the polyp; in a pedunculated polyp, the submucosa is found in the head or stalk, whereas in a sessile polyp it is contiguous with the submucosa of the underlying bowel wall. A malignant polyp represents an early carcinoma. A distinction is often made between *malignant polyp* and *polypoid carcinoma* which differs from the former in that the totality of the mucosal part of the polyp head is replaced by malignant tumor and it lacks a component of residual adenoma; but it also represents an early carcinoma, and its management is the same as that of the malignant polyp.

Published studies are unanimous that when cells that have the morphologic characteristics of cancer are present in the mucosal layer of an adenoma only and have not penetrated through the muscularis mucosae, there is no potential for recurrence or for metastasis once the adenoma is resected, and such an adenoma is therefore not a "malignant polyp."[1] This is true whether the adenoma is sessile or pedunculated. Terms used synonymously for carcinoma confined to the mucosal layer of a polyp include *severe dysplasia, high-grade dysplasia,* and *carcinoma in situ*. Use of the latter term is discouraged by many authors, including those of the WHO Classification, because of a concern that it may be misinterpreted and lead to overtreatment. For the same reason most authors discourage use of the term *intramucosal carcinoma,* used by some to describe extension of carcinoma into the lamina propria of the mucosa; they recommend that the terms *high-grade dysplasia* and *severe dysplasia* be used to encompass all variations of carcinoma confined to the mucosal layer of an adenoma.

THE MALIGNANT POLYP

When the "malignant polyp" is defined as above, the primary treatment is usually polypectomy and a second decision must be made as to whether the polypectomy has provided adequate therapy and prospect of cure. This contrasts with the situation where the primary treatment has been a surgical resection for a polypoid mass presumed to be an advanced cancer or an adenoma too large to be resected endoscopically. In such cases there is the advantage of accurate tumor staging and prognostication based on the histologic examination of the resected bowel and lymph nodes. When the primary treatment is polypectomy, however, the stage and prognosis must of necessity be inferred indirectly. The future course can be predicted with considerable accuracy from pathologic and endoscopic criteria because of the known propensity for colonic cancer to follow an orderly anatomic pattern in its progression.

The literature concerning malignant polyps is somewhat confusing. Some authors devise their own independent classification system of the depth of cancer invasion, while others mix results from polyps with severe dysplasia (carcinoma in situ) with those from invasive cancer, while some do not differentiate between polyps resected endoscopically or surgically. Occasionally, there is no mention of whether the polyp was sessile or pedunculated.

Frequency of Malignant Polyps

It is currently accepted that both size of the adenoma and degree of villous component are positively correlated with the probability of cancer developing within a polyp.[2] For a polyp less than 0.6 cm in diameter, the cancer risk is extremely low,[3] on the order of 0.1 percent. About 1 percent of polyps 1 cm diameter will contain carcinoma, while the rate has been reported to be as high as 40 percent in polyps larger than 3 cm.[4] (This latter figure is based on a series that included polyps resected surgically.[5]) While the relative risk for a finding of malignancy is greatest in very large polyps, these are much less prevalent than small or medium-sized polyps, so that they account for only a fraction of malignant polyps. The median size of malignant polyps removed endoscopically is 1 to 2 cm. The frequency of a finding of invasive cancer in polyps resected endoscopically is in the range of 2.0 to 9.3 percent [4,6–18] (Table 47-1). The figure reported by the National Polyp study in patients with polyps undergoing polypectomy for the first time was 1.5 percent.[6]

Endoscopic Assessment of the Malignant Polyp

The endoscopic appearance of a polyp may suggest carcinomatous invasion, although most malignant polyps have a benign appearance at endoscopy.[1,11,19] Gross features of malignancy include[15,20] an irregular surface contour, ulceration, firm (or hard) consistency when the head is pushed with a snare or forceps, and broadening of the stalk.

Although polyps with these features are not invariably malignant, the endoscopist should pay special attention to any lesion with malignant characteristics, since it may be advantageously managed somewhat differently from the routine adenoma. If cancer is suspected by any of the above criteria, the snare should be placed more toward the wall when resecting a pedunculated polyp than toward the head, as is the usual practice. Special care must be directed toward recovering all of the fragments for histopathologic evaluation and to localize the polyp's position in the colon precisely should subsequent surgery be needed.

The initial evaluation by the endoscopist may be of great significance, since the morphology of the lesion is frequently incompletely assessed once resection occurs. Following resection, it may not be possible to ascertain whether a polyp was sessile or pedunculated, because a short pedicle may retract completely into the polyp head. Polyps tend to curl up in formalin and the site of attachment of sessile polyps may not be recognizable in the pathology laboratory.[20,21] The resection site of each endoscopically removed polyp suspected of harboring a malignancy should be identified by marking it with India ink or impaling the polyp on a fine hypodermic needle through the cut margin before placing it in fixative.

Table 47-1
Frequency of Invasive Cancer in Adenomas

Authors	*No. of polyps*	*No. with invasive cancer*	*Percent*
Wolff and Shinya,[33] 1975	892	46	5.2
Coutsoftides et al.,[68] 1978	477	18	3.8
Colacchio et al.,[18] 1981	729	39	5.3
Bartnik et al.,[69] 1985	178	9	5.0
Cranley et al.,[1] 1987	1523	41	2.7
Rossini et al.,[11] 1988	2095	60	2.8
Eckardt et al.,[16] 1988	1769	61	3.4
Sugihara et al.,[19] 1989	1213	25	2.0
Muller et al.,[70] 1989	367	34	9.3

The endoscopist can tell, with some confidence, whether a complete polypectomy has been effected when the polyp is pedunculated, since the naked stalk is readily identified and the absence of residual adenoma is easily discerned. The determination is more difficult when a *sessile* polyp is resected, although the clean base without adjacent, elevated, reddened tissue usually attests to the completeness of resection. This assurance may be difficult to achieve when a polyp has been removed in piecemeal fashion, because fragments at the base could equally prove to be nonviable coagulum or residual adenomatous tissue.

The Pedunculated Malignant Polyp

Criteria to determine the adequacy of endoscopic polypectomy are well defined for the pedunculated malignant polyp. They are that the carcinoma is well or moderately differentiated, that there is no invasion of the lymphatic or vascular spaces in the head or stalk of the polyp, that the carcinoma does not involve the excision margin on microscopic examination, and that the endoscopist's assessment is that the entire lesion has been removed. When these favorable criteria are encountered in an endoscopically resected pedunculated malignant polyp, there is small or negligible risk of recurrent disease, lymph node metastases, or distant spread[22–27] (Fig. 47-1).

The Sessile Malignant Polyp

The sessile malignant polyp has, in the past, received separate consideration, and many experts have considered surgery appropriate in all such cases, because invasive carcinoma in sessile polyps by definition invades the submucosa of the underlying bowel wall.[28,29] Haggitt et al.[17] reported that invasion of the submucosa of the bowel wall accounted for 7 of 8 adverse outcomes in their series of 64 malignant polyps. However, as they pointed out, this criterion yielded a false-positive result in 75 percent of instances when applied to their cases. A more precise measure to predict an adverse outcome would clearly be of value, especially for patients who are poor operative risks or for those with polyps located in the distal rectum. According to Christie,[20] evidence of complete local excision was justification for a conservative approach to sessile lesions with favorable histology in high-risk patients. Cranley et al.[1] found that among five sessile lesions which were operated on, in no case was the sessile nature of the polyp alone associated with an adverse outcome. They suggested that the *positive predictive value* for an adverse outcome of carcinoma at the resection margin

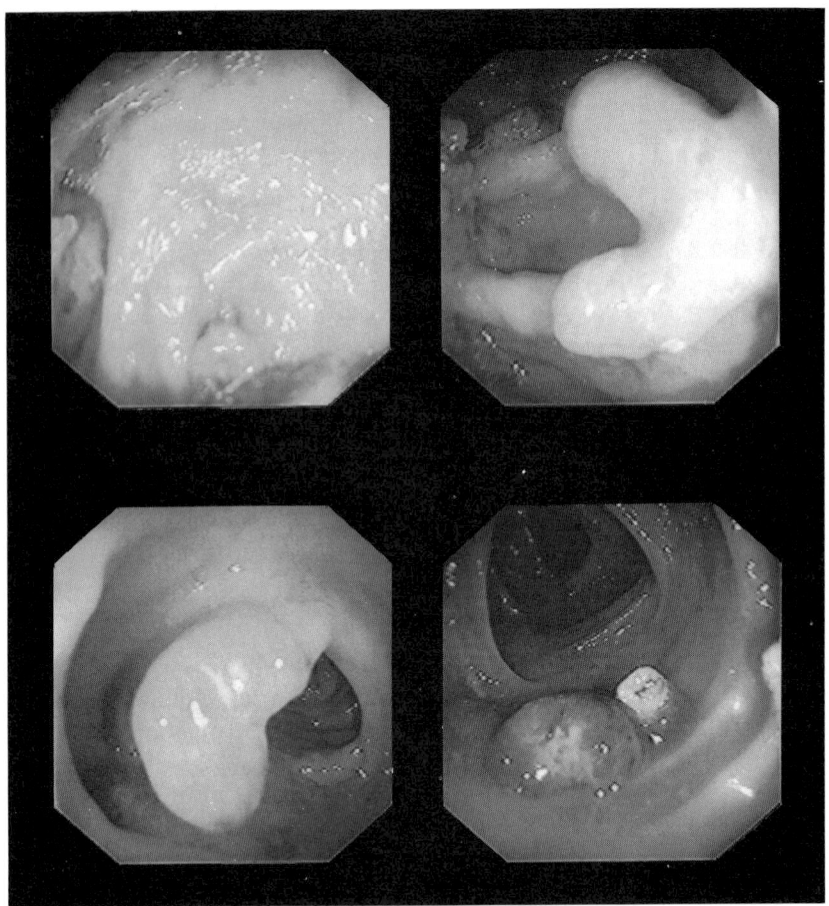

A B

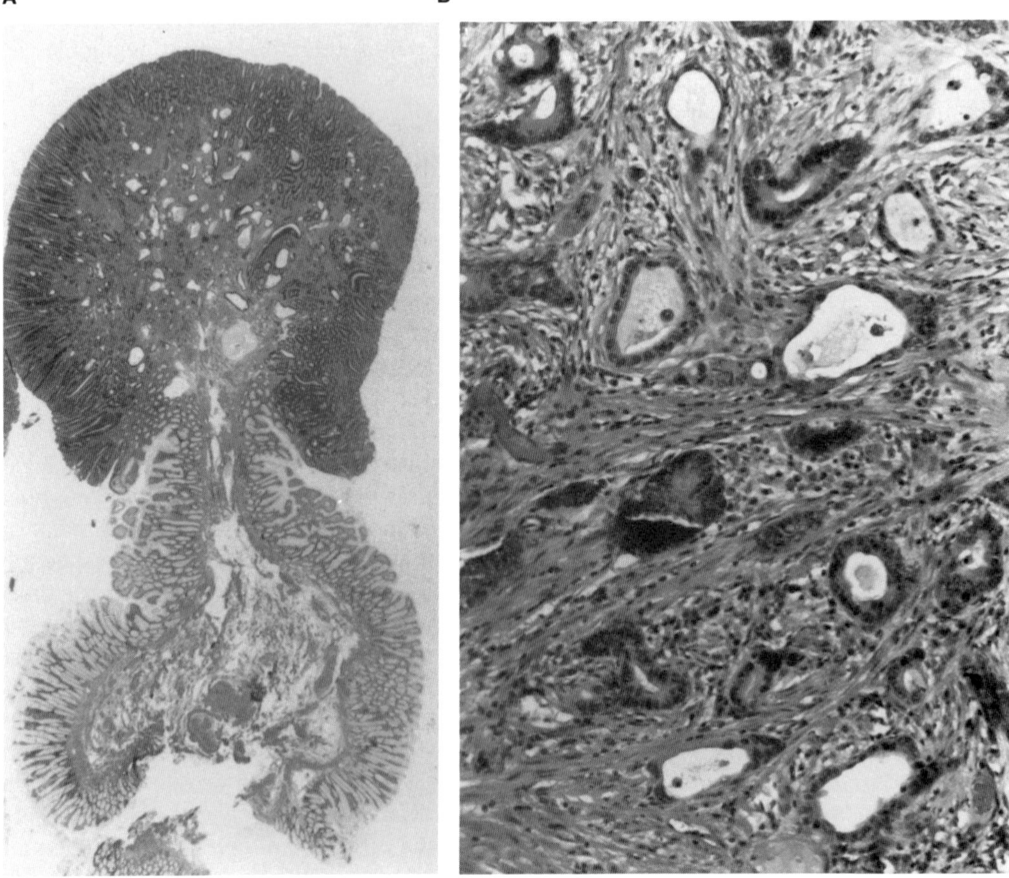

C

FIG. 47-1. Malignant polyp with favorable histologic features. *A* and *B*. Bean-shaped pedunculated polyp before and after endoscopic resection (see color Plate 25). The histologic features are favorable. *C*. This pedunculated adenoma shows a moderately differentiated adenocarcinoma infiltrating the submucosa of the head of the polyp (*detail on right*) to the level of the neck. There is no invasion of the stalk and the resection margin is clear.

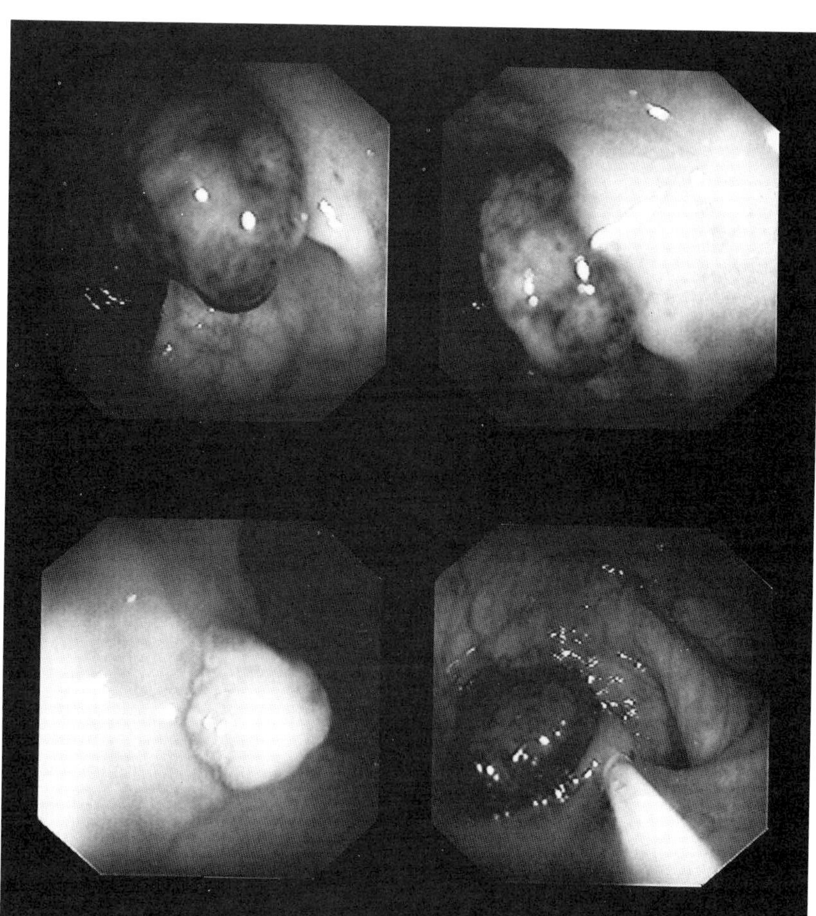

FIG. 47-2. Malignant polyp with unfavorable histologic features. Broad-based sessile malignant polyp with smooth head. Lymphatic invasion was present on histologic examination. Subsequent surgery showed no residual or nodal cancer (see color Plate 26).

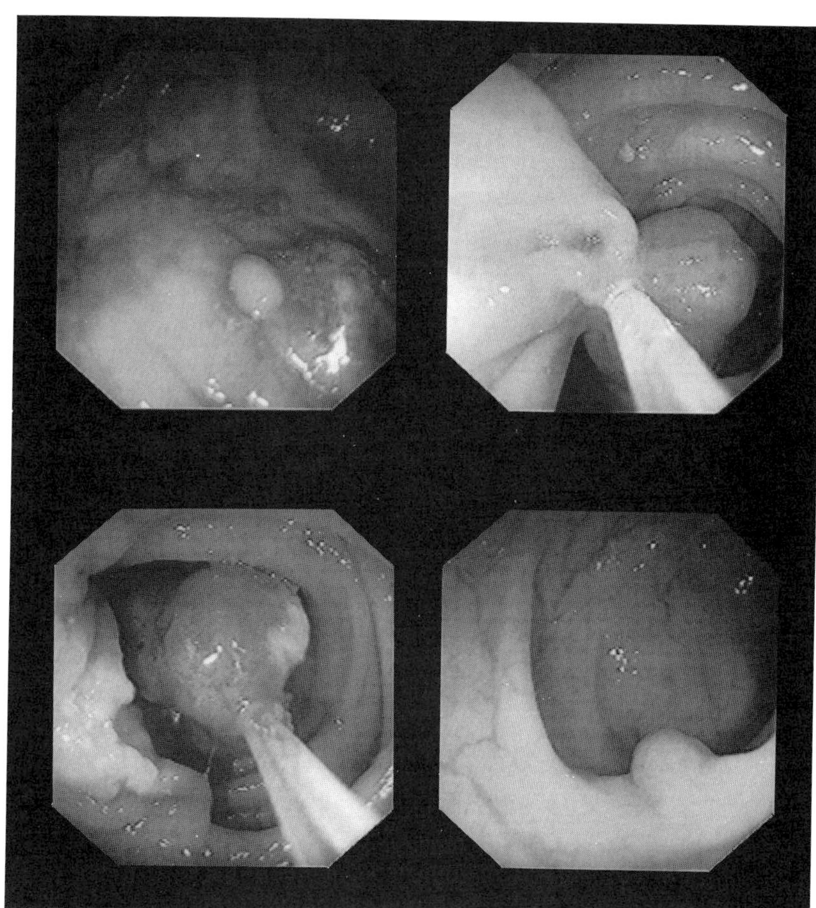

FIG. 47-3. Malignant polyp with favorable histologic features. Snare encircling the upper portion of a broad-based polyp. Although benign-appearing, this polyp had invasive cancer. There was a 3-mm margin of noninvolved adenoma at the resection margin. Surgery was not recommended (see color Plate 27).

would be considerably higher. A 1987[30] decision analysis report based on a literature review, however, concluded that all sessile malignant polyps should have an operative resection if the patient was a good surgical candidate (Fig. 47-2). A 1988 literature review,[31] on the other hand, concluded that neither sessile nor pedunculated malignant polyps differed in their risk for residual and/or metastatic disease if the resection criteria were favorable. An experience with 249 "early" colonic cancers which were resected surgically[22] demonstrated lymph node metastases in only 3 percent of 130 patients, independently of whether the original cancer was found in a pedunculated or sessile adenoma (Fig. 47-3). The authors' definition of "early colonic cancer" included infiltration of the submucosa without involvement of the muscle coat, the muscularis propria. There was 100 percent 10-year survival, and the authors concluded that if rigid selection criteria are met, the survival rate for early colonic cancer is the same whether treatment is endoscopic polypectomy, local surgical excision, segmental resection, or radical surgery.

POLYPOID CARCINOMA

There is some uncertainty as to whether the criteria for determining adequacy of polypectomy for malignant polyps apply equally in those cases where no residual adenoma is evident in the polyp, so-called *polypoid carcinomas*. Such cases were excluded from consideration in some reports; in others, such as that of Shinya et al.[2] a recommendation for bowel resection in these cases was made even though the study cases had no adverse outcomes. No large single series of these cases has been reported, but if the small numbers from the reports of Haggitt et al.,[17] Christie et al.,[20] Cooper,[32] Cranley et al.,[1] and Shinya et al.[33] are combined, an adverse outcome is observed in only 2 of a total of 33 cases, and in both of these cases the resection margins of the polyps were positive for carcinoma. Many experts now share the view of Williams et al.[15] that polypoid carcinoma patients are not automatically candidates for surgery, but that the decision should be based on the presence or absence of criteria identical to those for malignant polyps, namely, positive resection margins, or the presence of adverse histologic features, such as poorly differentiated carcinoma and invasion of the vascular space.

FLAT ADENOMAS AND CANCER

The adenoma-carcinoma sequence may not always evolve[34] within a polypoid lesion.[3] Recent contributions to the literature describe small, flat, invasive cancers, which, if they did not arise de novo, are thought likely to have developed within a preceding flat adenoma (Fig. 47-4). Flat adenomas, originally described by Muto et al.,[35] have been reported to have greater propensity to develop into cancer, and they invade the submucosa more readily than polypoid adenomas.[36–38] An association between small, flat adenomas and cancer has been reported in the Lynch syndrome[39] of hereditary nonpolyposis colorectal cancer (HNPCC). While these associations are controversial, it is accepted that cancer may develop in flat nonpolypoid adenomas and present particular problems for diagnosis and resection. These tumors may be difficult to identify endoscopically.[40] Dye spraying—with either topical spray of 0.2% indigo carmine on the colonic surface or by oral ingestion of dye during the preparation phase prior to colonoscopy—may aid in their endoscopic visualization.[41] Small, flat adenomas,

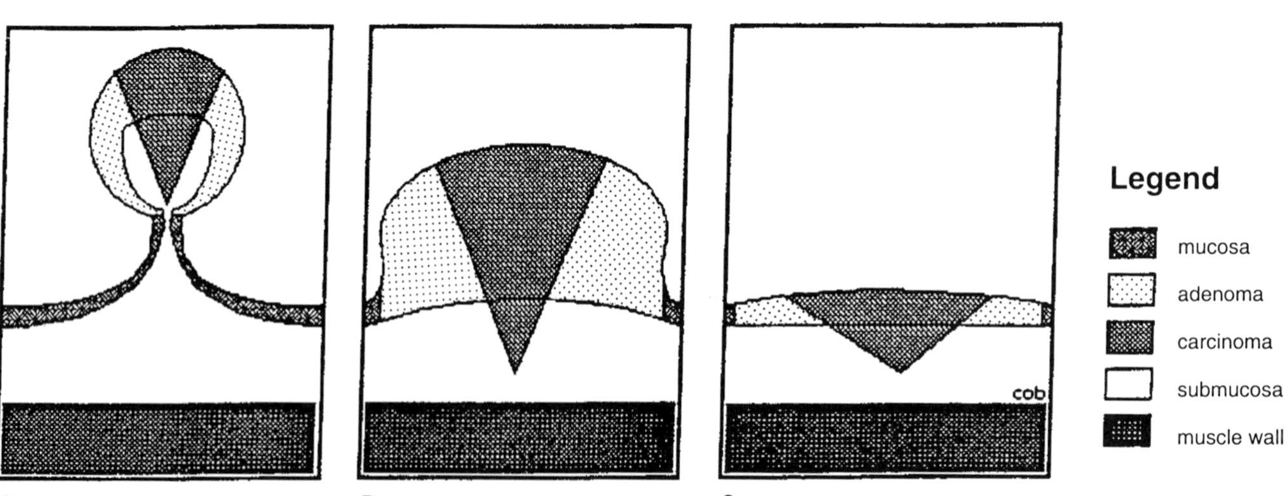

FIG. 47-4. Invasive carcinoma in colorectal adenomas—a schematic representation of malignant polyps. *A*. pedunculated, *B*. sessile, and *C*. invasive carcinoma in a flat adenoma.

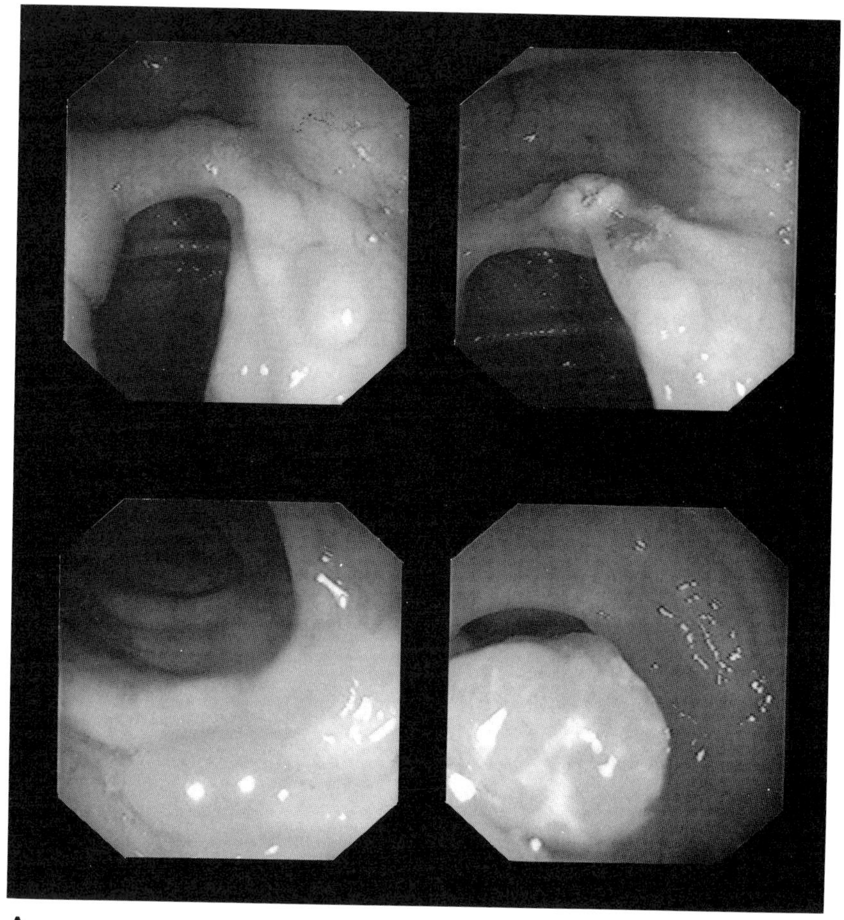

A

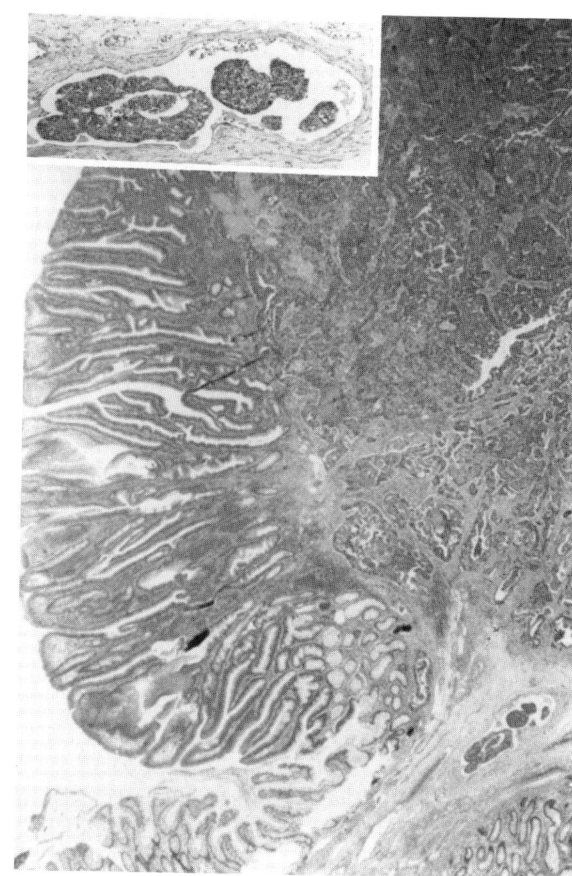

B

FIG. 47-5. Malignant polyp with unfavorable histologic features. *A*. Smooth polyp with broad base that had carcinoma at the margin of endoscopic resection (see color Plate 28). *B*. This pedunculated adenoma shows extensive replacement of the head by poorly differentiated adenocarcinoma. A dilated lymphatic in the stalk of the polyp shows invasion by carcinoma. This is detailed in the inset at top left.

some of which contain invasive carcinoma, have been resected and cured by the submucosal injection of saline followed by removal with an endoscopic snare.[40]

There are only a few reports of flat adenomas in the English literature,[42,43] leading to speculation[44] that they are not recognized and, therefore, "missed" during colonoscopy. The relative paucity of English-language reports may reflect either a difference in prevalence or the fact that they are seen and removed but not separately categorized by western endoscopists. Either of these two possibilities is more plausible than the theory that these small lesions are being repeatedly and systematically overlooked,[44] since rigorous follow-up of patients by the National Polyp Study (NPS) has demonstrated an extremely low incidence of subsequent cancer in colons from which all adenomas were removed by the NPS endoscopists.[45,46] The latter of these two explanations would appear to be the "best fit" to available data, since, when specifically sought, flat adenomas *are* found in North Americans.[43]

RESECTION MARGIN

There appears to be substantial support in the recent literature for the view that the single most useful criterion to guide the management of patients with malignant polyps is the status of the polyp resection margin[27,47] (Fig. 47-5). The definition of a negative margin in a malignant polyp can be open to diverse interpretations, however, with some investigators requiring a 1-,[13] 2-,[1,31] or 3-[15,45] mm cancer-free zone; others[11] are satisfied with a "healthy" margin; while yet others[26] state that the presence of malignant cells at the resection margin is the only criterion which predicts a poor outcome. A long-term follow-up of malignant polyps in which the malignancy appeared to involve the resection line in microscopic sections but the endoscopist considered it to be totally resected was reported from St. Mark's Hospital.[21] It was found that no patients had evidence of malignancy at a mean 5-year follow-up interval. Consultation between pathologist and endoscopist is clearly highly desirable in reaching a final determination of resection margin status. Notwithstanding such cooperation, the piecemeal resection that is often necessary for large, sessile polyps[48] may leave the status of the resection margin indeterminate. Such an indeterminate status may be acceptable if there is no evidence of gross residual tumor on direct inspection or by endoscopic ultrasound in a lesion located in the distal rectum or even in a more proximal location in an elderly patient with serious medical problems, but it would normally be an indication for surgery in an otherwise healthy patient.

The frequency with which further treatment decisions are necessary following endoscopic resection of polyps found to have invasive cancer involves about 5 percent of all polypectomies performed with the colonoscope. These decisions are relatively easy to make when minute focal carcinomatous invasion is present, but they are much more difficult when the tumor is close to or at the resection margin or when the patient is elderly and in good health. One polyp in 20 that are resected via the colonoscope will subsequently be found, at pathologic examination, to harbor cancer that crosses the muscularis mucosa and invades the submucosa of the polyp.

THE DECISION TO OPERATE

In order to achieve the best outcome, the decision to operate on a patient who has had an endoscopically resected malignant polyp involves balancing the risk of residual cancer at the excision site and regional lymph node metastases against that of mortality from abdominal surgery (Tables 47-2 and 47-3). In general, the risk of death from elective colonic surgery varies from 0.2 to 2 percent, with the patient below age 50 being at lowest risk[22,30] (Table 47-4). A summary analysis of the recent literature[1,49] yields an estimate of the risk of residual tumor or nodal cancer in colonoscopically resected pedunculated malignant polyps with favorable criteria as 0.3 percent and that for sessile malignant polyps as 1.5 percent.

Patients of any age with favorable resection criteria who have pedunculated malignant polyps resected endoscopically should not have a subsequent surgical resection, nor normally should patients over 50 years of age with *sessile* malignant polyps with favorable resection criteria.[50] Among healthy patients under age 50 with sessile malignant polyps with favorable criteria, the risk of residual tumor or nodal disease is similar to or slightly higher than the risk of death from surgery, and the argument can be made that this group of patients should have surgical resection of that segment

Table 47-2
Malignant Colorectal Polyps—Factors Relevant to the Decisions to Operate Postpolypectomy

Pathologic evaluation	Status of resection margin Degree of differentiation Vascular or lymphatic invasion
Endoscopic assessment	Completeness of excision
Patient risk and benefit	Distal rectal location Operative risk Life expectancy

Table 47-3
High-Risk Invasive Cancer in Adenomas

Authors	*Polyps with invasive CA*	*No. with high risk*	*R, LN, or MET*	*Percent high risk with R, LN, or MET*
Lipper et al.,[26] 1983	19	6	1	17
Cooper,[32] 1983	56	36	5	14
Langer et al.,[14] 1984	19	6	4	67
Bartnik et al.,[69] 1985	9	2	0	0
Haggitt et al.,[17] 1985	64	31	4	13
Cranley et al.,[1] 1987	41	24	10	42
Conte et al.,[47] 1987	30	4	4	100
Richards et al.,[24] 1987	80	10	10	100
Williams et al.,[15] 1987	90	27	4	15
Christie,[20] 1988	106	30	1	3
Rossini et al.,[11] 1988	60	10	4	40
Sugihara et al.,[19] 1989	25	18	3	17
Muller et al.,[70] 1989	34	15	8	53
Coverlizza et al.,[71] 1989	81	14	5	36
Nivatongs et al.,[29] 1991	151	35	11	31
Kyzer et al.,[27] 1992	44	21	3	14

Abbreviations: CA, cancer; R, residual or recurrent cancer; LN, positive lymph nodes; MET, metastatic disease.

of bowel. Subsequent cancer surgery with bowel resection and node dissection will result in a cure of residual cancer in only about 50 percent of the patients with nodal metastases[51] (Fig. 47-6). Malignant polyps in the distal rectum require special consideration, because a permanent colostomy is an issue. Malignant polyps in this location are also unique in that they are amenable to proctologic surgical techniques that permit deep excisions, which are not applicable in the colon.

Table 47-4
Low-Risk Invasive Cancer in Adenomas—Frequency of Residual Cancer, Lymph Node, or Distant Metastases

Authors	*Polyps with invasive CA*	*No. with low risk*	*R, LN, or MET*	*Percent low risk with R, LN, or MET*
Colacchio et al.,[18] 1981	39	24	2	8
Cooper et al.,[32] 1983	56	32	0	0
Lipper et al.,[26] 1983	19	6	0	0
Langer et al.,[14] 1984	19	13	1	8
Fried et al.,[7] 1984	22	22	0	0
Bartnik et al.,[69] 1985	9	7	0	0
Haggitt et al.,[17] 1985	64	33	0	0
Cranley et al.,[1] 1987	41	14	0	0
Williams et al.,[15] 1987	90	63	0	0
Conte et al.,[47] 1987	30	26	0	0
Richards et al.,[24] 1987	80	70	0	0
Christie,[20] 1988	106	46	1	2
Rossini et al.,[11] 1988	60	49	0	0
Sugihara et al.,[19] 1989	25	7	0	0
Muller et al.,[70] 1989	34	16	1	6
Coverlizza et al.,[71] 1989	81	67	0	0
Nivatongs et al.,[29] 1991	151	38	0	0
Geraghty et al.,[73] 1991	81	62	1	2
Kyzer et al.,[27] 1992	44	23	0	0

Abbreviations: CA, cancer; R, residual or recurrent cancer; LN, positive lymph nodes; MET, metastatic disease.

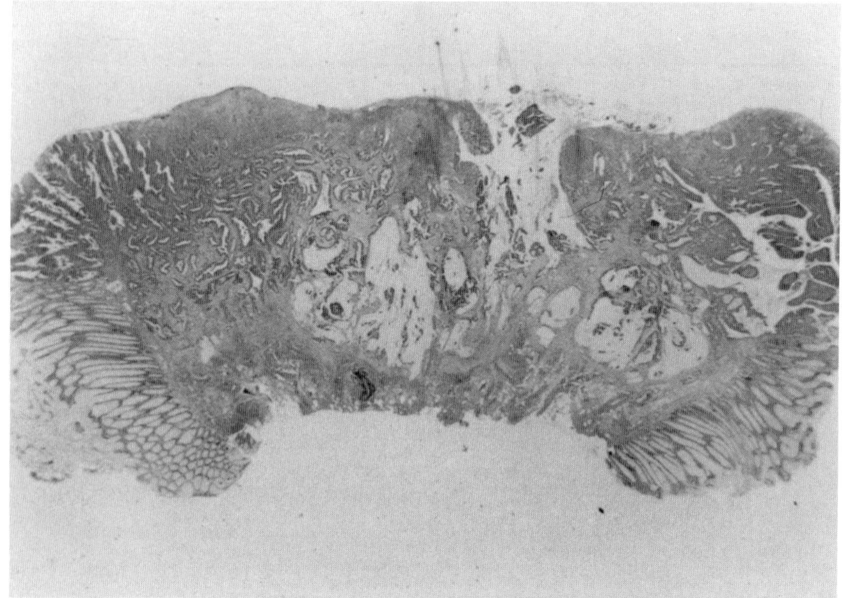

FIG. 47-6. Malignant polyp with unfavorable histologic features. This sessile polypoid carcinoma consisted of a moderately differentiated adenocarcinoma (partly mucinous) which entirely replaced the head of the polyp and invaded to the level of the resection margin. A colectomy was performed which revealed no residual carcinoma in the bowel wall, but 2 of 7 lymph nodes contained metastatic carcinoma.

FOLLOW-UP AFTER RESECTION OF THE MALIGNANT POLYP

If a decision for endoscopic follow-up has been made and the initial examination was completed to the cecum, a full repeat colonoscopic examination need not be undertaken immediately after the index colonoscopy. Endoscopy for evaluation of the polypectomy site may be performed in 4 to 12 weeks, in order to assess completeness of resection, and again in 3 to 6 months. If no recurrent tumor is present, annual examinations should be performed for 2 years, after which routine polyp follow-up is recommended. If recurrent tumor is seen at the polypectomy site, surgical bowel resection should be carried out.

Colonic ultrasound may prove worthwhile in patients who have had malignant polyps removed. The technique of endoscopic ultrasound provides an evaluation of the depth of tumor penetration and also offers an opportunity to assess adjacent lymph nodes.[52,53]

When high-grade dysplasia (carcinoma in situ) is present in an endoscopically resected adenoma, there is no possibility of metastatic disease. These polyps can be regarded as completely benign biologically. There is no need for subsequent surgical resection or for any increased follow-up surveillance over and above that which would be recommended for a polyp of similar size and morphology that did not contain high-grade dysplasia (carcinoma in situ or intramucosal carcinoma).

SITE LOCALIZATION

Following endoscopic resection of a malignant polyp, a small percentage of patients will require surgical resection to ensure that local or nodal disease is eradicated. Site identification becomes necessary when a portion of the large bowel requires resection and the area from which the polyp was removed is not readily apparent by visual or palpatory exploration.[48] Many patients have not had a preceding barium enema, since primary colonoscopy is frequently employed to evaluate patients at high risk for neoplastic disease, such as those who have had a colonic cancer or adenoma previously removed, a positive fecal occult blood test, a long history of ulcerative colitis, or a significant family history of colonic cancer.

Reliance on the endoscopist's estimate of lesion location may be inadequate because of several factors, including the major problem that the actual number of centimeters of instrument inserted may bear no relationship with the actual tip location within the colon.[54] The use of endoscopic landmarks is imprecise for exact localization of areas between the rectum and cecum.[22,55] Even the most experienced colonoscopists may falter in their estimates of tip location.[56,57]

Now that laparoscopy-assisted surgical colonic resection has developed, there is even greater urgency to have precise lesion location, since the laparoscopist cannot palpate the colon manually at exploratory laparotomy. Because clips placed on the mucosa endoscopically tend to fall off at an average of approximately 10 days,[58] the surgeon cannot be assured that a palpable clip has not become detached just prior to surgery and is now located at some distance from the original placement.

Locating the site of an endoscopically resected malignant tumor is the most common indication for intraoperative colonoscopy.[59–62] An indelible marker injected colonoscopically at the polypectomy site will direct the attention of the surgeon or endoscopist.[57] Indocyanine green is visible up to 7 days after injection,[63,64] while India ink is a permanent marker.[49,65,66] Complications have been reported with India ink injection,[67] but they are infrequent.

REFERENCES

1. Cranley JP, Petras RE, Carey WD, et al: When is endoscopic polypectomy adequate therapy for colonic polyps containing invasive carcinoma? *Gastroenterology* 91:419–427, 1987.
2. Ackroyd FW, Hedberg SE: Colonic polyps. *Annu Rev Med* 36:619–625, 1985.
3. Simon JB: Colonic polyps, cancer and fecal occult blood (editorial). *Ann Intern Med* 118:71–72, 1993.
4. Cohen LB, Waye JD: Treatment of colonic polyps—Practical considerations. *Clin Gastroenterol* 15:359–376, 1986.
5. Morson BC: Precancerous conditions of the large bowel. *Proc R Soc Med* 64:959–962, 1971.
6. O'Brien MJ, Winawer SJ, Zauber AG, et al: The National Polyp Study. *Gastroenterology* 98:371–379, 1990.
7. Fried GM, Hreno A, Duguid WP, et al: Rational management of malignant colon polyps based on long-term follow-up. *Surgery* 96:815–821, 1984.
8. Stryker SJ, Wolff BG, Culp CE, et al: Natural history of untreated colonic polyps. *Gastroenterology* 93:1009–1013, 1987.
9. Morson BC: The pathogenesis of colorectal cancer, in *Major Problems in Pathology,* 10th ed. Philadelphia, Saunders, 1978.
10. Fenoglio CM, Kaye GI, Lane N: Distribution of human colonic lymphatics in normal hyperplastic and adnomatous tissue. Its relationship to metastasis from small carcinomas in pedunculated adenomas. *Gastroenterology* 64:51–66, 1973.
11. Rossini FP, Ferrari A, Coverlizza S, et al: Large bowel adenomas containing carcinoma—a diagnostic and therapeutic approach. *Int J Colorect Dis* 3:47–52, 1988.
12. Jaurequi HO, Nadra L, Kessimian N: Colonic polyps and cancer. *RI Med J* 72:317–321, 1939.
13. Fucini C, Wolff BG, Spencere RJ: An appraisal of endoscopic removal of malignant colonic polyps. *Mayo Clin Proc* 61:123–126, 1986.
14. Langer JC, Cohen A, Taylor BR, et al: Management of patients with polyps containing malignancy removed by colonoscopic polypectomy. *Dis Colon Rectum* 27:6–9, 1984.
15. Williams CB, Whiteway JE, Jass JR: Practical aspects of endoscopic management of malignant polyps. *Endoscopy* 19:31–37, 1987.
16. Eckardt VF, Fuchs M, Kanzler G, et al: Follow-up of patients with colonic polyps containing severe atypia and invasive carcinoma. *Cancer* 61:2552–2557, 1988.
17. Haggitt RC, Glotzbach RE, Soffer EE, et al: Prognostic factors in colorectal carcinomas arising in adenomas: Implications for lesions removed by endoscopic polypectomy. *Gastroenterology* 89:328–336, 1985.
18. Colacchio TA, Forde KA, Scantlebury VP: Endoscopic polypectomy: Inadequate treatment for invasive colorectal carcinoma. *Ann Surg* 194:704–707, 1981.
19. Sugihara K, Muto T, Morioka Y: Management of patients with invasive carcinoma removed by colonoscopic polypectomy. *Dis Colon Rectum* 32:829–834, 1989.
20. Christie JP: Polypectomy or colectomy? Management of 106 consecutively encountered colorectal polyps. *Am Surg* 54:93–99, 1988.
21. Morson BC, Whiteway JE, Jones EA, et al: Histopathology and prognosis of malignant colorectal polyps treated by endoscopic polypectomy. *Gut* 25:437–444, 1984.
22. Hermanek P, Gall FP: Early (microinvasive) colorectal carcinoma: Pathology, diagnosis, surgical treatment. *Int J Colorect Dis* 1:79–84, 1986.
23. Rosseland AR, Bakka A, Reiersten O: Endoscopic treatment of colorectal carcinoma. *Scand J Gastroenterol Suppl* 149:102–105, 1988.
24. Richards WO, Webb WA, Morris SJ, et al: Patient management after endoscopic removal of the cancerous colon adenoma. *Ann Surg* 205:665–672, 1987.
25. Russell JB, Chu DZ, Russell MP, et al: When is polypectomy sufficient treatment for colorectal cancer in a polyp? *Am J Surg* 160:665–668, 1990.
26. Lipper S, Kahn LB, Ackerman LV: The significance of microscopic invasive cancer in endoscopically removed polyps of the large bowel: A clinicopathologic study of 51 cases. *Cancer* 52:1691–1699, 1983.
27. Kyzer S, Begin LR, Gordon PH, et al: The care of patients with colorectal polyps that contain invasive adenocarcinoma: Endoscopic polypectomy or colectomy? *Cancer* 70:2044–2050, 1992.
28. Riddell RH: Hands off "cancerous" large bowel polyps. *Gastroenterology* 89:432–435, 1985.
29. Nivatongs S, Rojanasakul A, Reiman HM, et al: The risk of lymph node metastasis in colorectal polyps with invasive adenocarcinoma. *Dis Colon Rectum* 34:323–328, 1991.
30. Wilcox GM, Beck JR: Early invasive cancer in adenomatous colonic polyps: Evaluation of the therapeutic options by decision analysis. *Gastroenterology* 92:1159–1168, 1987.
31. Ehrinpreis MN, Kinzie JL, Jaszewski R, et al: Management of the malignant polyp. *Gastroenterology* 17:837–850, 1988.
32. Cooper HS: Surgical pathology of endoscopically removed malignant polyps of the colon and rectum. *Am J Surg Pathol* 7:613–623, 1983.
33. Wolff WI, Shinya H: Definitive treatment of "malignant" polyps of the colon. *Ann Surg* 182:516–524, 1975.
34. Koretz RL: Malignant polyps: Are they sheep in wolves' clothing? *Ann Intern Med* 118:63–68, 1993.
35. Muto T, Kamiya J, Sawada T, et al: Small "flat adenoma" of the large bowel with special reference to its clinicopathologic features. *Dis Colon Rectum* 28:847–851, 1985.
36. Karita M, Tada M, Okita K, et al: Endoscopic therapy for early colon cancer: The strip biopsy resection technique. *Gastrointest Endosc* 37:128–132, 1991.
37. Inoue H, Takeshita K, Hori H, et al: Endoscopic mucosal resection with a cap-fitted panendoscope for esophagus, stomach, and colon mucosal lesions. *Gastrointest Endosc* 39:58–62, 1993.
38. Shimoda T, Ikegami M, Fujisaki J, et al: Early colorectal carcinoma with special reference to its development de novo. *Cancer* 64:1138–1146, 1989.
39. Lynch HT, Smyrk T, Lanspa SJ: The colonoscopist and the Lynch syndromes. *Gastrointest Endosc* 36:156–158, 1990.
40. Matsumoto T, Lida M, Kuwano Y, et al: Minute non-polypoid

adenoma of the colon detected by colonoscopy: Correlation between endoscopic and histologic findings. *Gastrointest Endosc* 38:645–650, 1992.

41. Mitooka H, Fujimori T, Ohno S, et al: Chromoscopy of the colon using indigo carmine dye with electrolyte lavage solution. *Gastrointestinal Endosc* 38:373–374, 1992.
42. Wolber RA, Owen DA: Flat adenomas of the colon. *Hum Pathol* 21:70–74, 1991.
43. Lanspa SJ, Rouse J, Smyrk T, et al: Epidemiologic characteristics of the flat adenoma of Muto: A prospective study. *Dis Colon Rectum* 35:543–546, 1992.
44. Riddell R: Flat adenomas and carcinomas seeking the visible? (editorial). *Gastrointest Endosc* 38:721–722, 1992.
45. Winawer SJ, Zauber AG, Gerdes H, et al: Reduction in colorectal cancer incidence following colonoscopic polypectomy: Report from the National Polyp Study (NPS) (Abstract). *Gastroenterology* 100:A410, 1991.
46. Winawer SJ, Zauber AG, O'Brien MJ, et al: Randomized comparison of surveillance intervals after colonoscopic removal of newly diagnosed adenomatous polyps. *N Engl J Med* 328:901–906, 1993.
47. Conte CC, Welch JP, Tennant R, et al: Management of endoscopically removed malignant colon polyps. *J Surg Oncol* 36:116–121, 1987.
48. Walsh RM, Ackroyd FW, Shellito PC: Endoscopic resection of large sessiled colorectal polyps (see comments). *Gastrointest Endosc* 38:303–309, 1992.
49. Cohen LB, Waye JD: Colonoscopic polypectomy of polyps with adenocarcinoma: When is it curative? in Barkin JS, Rogers AI (eds): *Difficult Decisions in Digestive Diseases*. Boca Raton, Fla, Year Book, 1989.
50. Bond JH: Polyp Guideline: Diagnosis, treatment, and surveillance for patients with nonfamilial colorectal polyps. *Ann Intern Med* 119:836–846, 1993.
51. Haggitt RC: Controversies, dilemmas, and dialogues: When is colonoscopic resection of an adenomatous polyp containing a "malignancy" sufficient? *Am J Gastroenterol* 85:1564–1568, 1990.
52. Niederhuber JE: Colon and rectum cancer: Patterns of spread and implications for workup. *Cancer* 71:4187–4192, 1993.
53. Roseau G, Palazzo L, Paolaggi JA: Endoscopic ultrasonography in colorectal diseases. *Biomed Pharmacother* 46:133–138, 1992.
54. Frager DH, Frager JD, Wolf EL, et al: Problems in the colonoscopic localization of tumors: Continued value of the barium enema. *Gastrointest Radiol* 12:343–346, 1987.
55. Waye JD, Atchison MAE, Talbott MC, et al: Transillumination of light in the right lower quadrant during total colonoscopy (letter). *Gastrointest Endosc* 34:69, 1988.
56. Waye JD: Colonoscopy without fluoroscopy (editorial). *Gastrointest Endosc* 36:72–73, 1990.
57. Hilliard G, Ramming K, Thompson J Jr, et al: The elusive colonic malignancy: A need for definitive preoperative localization. *Am Surg* 56:742–744, 1990.
58. Tabibian N, Michaletz PA, Schwartz JT, et al: Use of an endoscopically placed clip can avoid diagnostic errors in colonoscopy. *Gastrointest Endosc* 34:262–264, 1988.
59. Forde KA, Cohen JL: Intraoperative colonoscopy. *Ann Surg* 207:231–233, 1988.
60. Richter RM, Littman L, Levowitz BS: Intraoperative fiberoptic colonoscopy: Localization on nonpalpable colonic lesions. *Arch Surg* 106:228, 1973.
61. Sakanoe Y, Nakao K, Shoji Y, et al: Intraoperative colonoscopy. *Surg Endosc* 7:84–87, 1993.
62. Kuramoto S, Thara O, Sakai S, et al: Intraoperative colonoscopy in the detection of nonpalpable colonic lesions—How to identify the affected bowel segment. *Surg Endosc* 2:76–80, 1988.
63. Hammond DC, Lane FR, Welk RA, et al: Endoscopic tattooing of the colon: An experimental study. *Am Surg* 55:457–461, 1989.
64. Hammond DC, Lane FR, MacKeigan JM, et al: Endoscopic tattooing of the colon: Clinical experience. *Am Surg* 59:205–210, 1993.
65. Ponsky JL, King JF: Endoscopic marking of colon lesions. *Gastrointest Endosc* 22:42–43, 1975.
66. Hyman N, Waye JD: Endoscopic four quadrant tattoo for the identification of colonic lesions at surgery. *Gastrointest Endosc* 37:56–58, 1991.
67. Lightdale CJ: India ink colonic tattoo: Blots on the record. *Gastrointest Endosc* 37:99–100, 1991.
68. Coutsoftides T, Sivak MV, Benjamin SP, et al: Colonoscopy and the management of polyps containing invasive carcinoma. *Ann Surg* 188:638–641, 1978.
69. Bartnik W, Burtuk E, Orlowska J: A conservative approach to adenomas containing invasive carcinoma removed colonoscopically. *Dis Colon Rectum* 28:673–675, 1985.
70. Muller S, Chesner IM, Egan MJ, et al: Significance of venous and lymphatic invasion in malignant polyps of the colon and rectum. *Gut* 30:1385–1391, 1989.
71. Coverlizza S, Risio M, Ferrari A, et al: Colorectal adenomas containing invasive carcinoma: Pathologic assessment of lymph node metastatic potential. *Cancer* 64:1937–1947, 1989.
72. Martin ED, Potet F: Pathology of endocrine tumors of the GI tract. *Clin Gastroenterol* 3:511–532, 1974.
73. Geraghty JM, Williams CB, Talbot IC: Malignant colorectal polyps: Venous invasion and successful treatment by endoscopic polypectomy. *Gut* 32:774–778, 1991.

CHAPTER 48

Additional Specific Management Problems

Alan J. Davison
Hartley S. Stern

HIGHLIGHTS

This chapter, at first glance, deals with a potpourri of management issues related to specific subsets of patients with colorectal cancer. However, what is common to patients with synchronous colonic cancers, Lynch syndrome, ovarian metastases, and synchronous hepatic metastases is the high risk of recurrence these patients have. Each is phenotypically unique in terms of how the risk is expressed. In each case we define the problem, describe its recognition, and offer a rational management plan.

CONTROVERSIES

In the Lynch syndrome, concern exists in defining families early in the expression of the problem. Of even greater debate is how to screen and follow these families, because even patients on intensive screening programs are not completely protected from developing advanced colonic cancer.

We are still concerned with the familiar problem of prophylactic oophorectomy, particularly in premenopausal women, and we attempt to address this in this chapter.

Although it now appears that isolated hepatic metastases can clearly be resected for cure, it is necessary to define the subset most optimally suited for such procedures. Additionally, the timing of intervention is an issue that is addressed in this chapter.

FUTURE DIRECTIONS

The trend for most of the issues dealt with in this chapter could be defined as a more aggressive approach. However, it is clear that better methods of recognition of the subsets of patients who will benefit from this approach, particularly with molecular genetic techniques, will play an important role in future and current management.

Table 48-1
Multiple Colorectal Cancers

	Synchronous	*Metachronous*	*Lynch syndrome*
Incidence	6.3%	1–7% (depends on surveillance)	~5%
Synchronous polyps	>50%	>50%	Frequent
Age	60–70	Older	Younger
Site prediction	None	None	Proximal colon
Stage	80% stage 1	Early if colonoscopy used	Variable
Treatment	Subtotal colectomy	Subtotal colectomy	Subtotal colectomy
Prognosis	Depends on stage of index cancer	Depends on stage	Depends on stage

Patients with concomitant or metachronous colorectal tumors represent a heterogeneous group in regard to surgical management. An overview of the major subsets of patients is provided in Table 48-1.

MANAGEMENT OF THE PATIENT WITH SYNCHRONOUS TUMORS

Definition of the Problem

Synchronous colorectal carcinomas may be defined as two or more distinct cancers separated by normal mucosa and bowel wall, with invasion of malignant cells below the muscularis mucosa.[1] Neoplastic polyps with in situ carcinoma are classified as benign. Not included in this discussion are patients with ulcerative colitis, familial polyposis, or histology other than adenocarcinoma. Carcinoma diagnosed within an arbitrary period of 6 months after the initial cancer has been considered synchronous in some reports. However, it has been estimated that a minimum of 5 years is required for an adenomatous polyp to evolve into a cancer.[2,3] In a large series from St. Mark's hospital, Finan et al.[4] reported a 3.4 percent rate of synchronous carcinoma but found that 29 percent of all the *metachronous* (subsequent) cancers appeared within 3 years of the initial diagnosis. Similarly, Kiefer et al.[5] found that 40 percent of metachronous cancers were identified within 2 years of the index cancer. It seems likely that many of these "early metachronous" cancers in fact represent synchronous cancers missed by inadequate perioperative examination. This concept is supported by the consistent finding of more advanced Dukes stages in early metachronous lesions.[4,5,7–10]

Before the advent of colonoscopy, the reported incidence of synchronous carcinoma varied widely, probably because of a lack of uniformity in diagnostic criteria and the use of inadequate methods to detect simultaneous lesions.[11–15] Air-contrast barium enema has been shown to miss the second cancer in a significant proportion of synchronous cancers subsequently discovered at colonoscopy or operation.[7,16–19] Of 59 synchronous carcinomas reviewed by Finan et al.,[4] only 51 percent were palpable at laparotomy. Early series relied on intraoperative palpation and examination of surgical specimens to determine the incidence of second cancers. Perhaps not surprisingly, these reports tended to find most of the synchronous cancers in the same surgical colon segment.[7,20] They were not able, however, to accurately examine unresected bowel.

The true incidence of synchronous carcinoma can be established only by colonoscopic evaluation of the entire mucosal surface prior to surgery or within a 6-month postoperative period. Studies utilizing perioperative colonoscopy have found rates of synchronous carcinoma between 4.4 and 9.3 percent and rates of synchronous neoplastic polyps between 18 and 27 percent.[9,16–18,21–24] Combining all patients in these series yields an incidence of synchronous carcinoma of 6.3 percent. Patients with two or more carcinomas have a remarkably high risk of synchronous adenomas, ranging from 38 to 86 percent, depending on the size of the polyp included. For instance, Evers et al.[17] found that 48 percent of patients with synchronous colonic cancers also had associated adenomas greater than 1 cm in size.

Management of the patient with synchronous carcinomas of the colon demands consideration of many aspects of colorectal cancer. Therapeutic strategies should be individualized but must take into account current knowledge about the natural history of benign and malignant colonic neoplasms and the prognostic significance of synchronous carcinoma. The adenoma-cancer sequence, which is the most widely accepted mechanism of malignant transformation, has implications for the patient with synchronous carcinoma. Colonoscopy influences surgical management through its role in both preoperative evaluation and postoperative surveillance. The extent of colonic resection for synchronous carcinoma is controversial but is based on respect for oncologic principles, the natural history of synchronous cancer, and morbidity.

Characteristics and Behavior of Synchronous Tumors

What is the biologic and clinical significance of the synchronous carcinomas and adenomas commonly discovered in colorectal cancer? The answers may be found by examining characteristics of these lesions such as site distribution, Dukes stage, and risk of metachronous tumors. The timing of detection in relation to surgery also has an important influence on patient management.

It is important to exclude series in which patients with ulcerative colitis and familial polyposis are included. Differences in age of presentation are difficult to determine. Synchronous carcinoma tended to occur in a slightly older age group in three series, including that of Slater et al.,[25] in which 54 patients had an average age of 72.4 years, compared to 68.8 years in overall groups of colorectal cancer patients.[15,26,27] However, one additional review reported a lower average age in synchronous cancer patients. In this study, 2 of the 21 patients were below age 40 and the mean age was 60.[17]

The data regarding site distribution are also difficult to assess because of the discrepancy between early retrospective reviews which reported a majority of synchronous cancers occurring in the same anatomic segment[7,28] and more recent prospective studies with colonoscopy which consistently found the second cancer to be widely distributed in the colon.[16,18,22] Prior to colonoscopy, early cancers were less readily detected by barium enema and intraoperative palpation.[7,26] The majority of studies utilizing colonoscopy support the concept that most synchronous cancers are widely separated in the colon.[18,22,24] Slater et al.,[25] reviewing the distribution of synchronous cancers just prior to the era of colonoscopy, classified lesions as being in the right, transverse, or left colon and found 63 percent of cancers in different segments. Although some series have suggested a predominance of right-sided synchronous tumors,[13,15,25,26] others found a lower incidence involving the right colon,[4,8,17] and the groups using colonoscopy reported no site predilection.[16,18,22,24]

Synchronous cancers tend to be discovered at an earlier pathologic stage than the primary cancer, although this depends to some extent on the means of detection. Lesions diagnosed at colonoscopy, or as an incidental finding in the same surgical specimen, are frequently adenomatous polyps or early invasive adenocarcinoma. In a review of patients operated on before 1975, Chu et al.[28] reported 53 synchronous carcinomas, 80 percent of which were Dukes A. This finding was confirmed by a 75 percent rate of Dukes A lesions in another early study of 59 synchronous cancers.[4] Series utilizing colonoscopy found that most of the second cancers were Dukes A or stage I lesions, including many polypoid tumors with focal invasion.[16–18]

Prognostic Significance of Synchronous Carcinoma

In addition to the very high incidence of synchronous polyps, there is evidence that patients with synchronous lesions have a greater risk of metachronous polyps. In studies of colonoscopic surveillance after surgery for colorectal cancer, there are significantly more patients with synchronous cancer and polyps who develop metachronous polyps (54 to 57 percent) than those without synchronous polyps (11 to 26 percent).[9,29] The incidence of metachronous carcinoma in these series is too low to suggest a similar tendency during the median follow-up period of 28 to 31 months. In fact, the median interval to development of metachronous polyps was 19 months, and most polyps were 10 mm or less in size.[29] Heald and Bussey,[7] in a review of 157 patients with synchronous colorectal cancers before 1970, stated that the accumulated risk of developing a metachronous tumor increases to 8 percent after resection of two cancers, compared to 3.5 percent after a solitary cancer, with an average interval of over 12 years. Despite this assertion, it has not been demonstrated that synchronous colorectal cancer predisposes to subsequent carcinoma. With careful perioperative evaluation and regular endoscopic surveillance with polypectomy, it seems unlikely that many cancers in evolution will be missed. But if one accepts the adenoma-cancer sequence, it may be inferred that the documented higher risk of metachronous polyps also carries a higher risk of carcinoma.

Little information exists concerning the prognosis of patients with multiple colonic carcinomas. Kaibara et al.[8] reviewed over 800 patients prior to 1980 with simultaneous multiple cancers or early in situ carcinomas but excluded patients with obstruction or perforation and those undergoing reoperation for the second lesion within 1 year. Among 535 patients followed, there was no difference in 5-year survival rates between patients with concurrent advanced cancers and those with both advanced and "early" cancers (69 percent). Some of the earlier series have reported decreased 5-year survival rates of 10 to 21 percent for patients with synchronous colorectal carcinoma.[12,27,30] However, Ekelund and Pihl[11] found no survival disadvantage for 44 patients with synchronous tumors. A corrected 5-year survival rate of 66 percent was reported by Heald and Bussey,[7] who felt that the second cancer, even a Dukes B or C lesion, had no effect on the prognosis. Adloff et al.[20] found no significant difference in 5-year survival rates (49 versus 39 percent) between groups with synchronous and single cancers even when analyzed by Dukes stage.

Surgical Strategies

There is no universally accepted surgical management of the patient with synchronous colonic cancers. In an ideal situation, the cancers would be diagnosed preoperatively, resection would be based on oncologic principles with minimal morbidity, and planning of both the surgical procedure and postoperative surveillance would take into consideration the increased risk of subsequent colonic neoplasia. However, in reality, patients sometimes present with obstructing or perforated cancers, or preoperative assessment of the entire colon may otherwise be impossible. Suspected synchronous cancers may be discovered during operation. The lifetime risk of a young patient with synchronous carcinomas may suggest to a surgeon that subtotal colectomy be recommended. The same surgeon might favor separate resections of tumors in an elderly patient to preserve colonic mucosa if there is concern about morbidity.

Preoperative colonoscopy preferably, or air-contrast barium enema, should be routinely performed to assess the presence of second neoplasms.[21,24] In many cases, synchronous cancers/adenomas require an alteration of the planned resection, but if they are not diagnosed until postoperative colonoscopy, a second operation may become necessary. Preoperative colonoscopy obviously has an advantage over barium enema in treating the frequently associated polyps and therefore is the major component in the secondary prevention of subsequent malignancy.

The primary consideration in the surgical management of simultaneous colorectal cancers must be the same as in single tumors, i.e., adequate resection of each carcinoma and its corresponding mesenteric lymphatic drainage area. For lesions in widely separate areas of the colon or rectum, this would entail discontinuous segmental resections and anastomoses. Subtotal colectomy is an option; for many surgeons, it is the procedure of choice for multiple colonic tumors, since it also removes much of the remaining mucosa at risk for synchronous and metachronous disease.[28,30–33] Unsuspected synchronous carcinomas and malignant polyps were discovered in 17 (26 percent) of 72 subtotal colectomy specimens in patients with obstruction, polyps associated with carcinoma, or known synchronous carcinomas.[34] Synchronous neoplasms, most of which were located proximal to the index tumor, were found in 58 percent of patients with occluding colonic cancer.[35] In patients with synchronous cancer or polyps, Carlsson et al.[29] found that 55 percent (21/38) were located proximal to the first cancer. Subtotal resection removes these incidental neoplasms and simplifies endoscopic follow-up.

Subtotal colectomy has been shown to be a safe operation, with acceptable mortality and morbidity, in a number of clinical settings (Table 48-2).[34,36,38] When compared to colocolic anastomosis, the ileocolic anastomosis has a lower rate of technical complications and leakage, and suture line recurrence is rare.[34,39,40] Although disabling diarrhea is a concern, particularly in the elderly, most series report good long-term functional results, even if the anastomosis is to the rectum, as long as an adequate length of terminal ileum is retained.[32,34,36,41–43] However, the authors believe that the best results in their series of 40 subtotal colectomies were obtained when a few centimeters of sigmoid colon were preserved.

One-stage subtotal colectomy has also been advocated as the procedure of choice in obstructing left-sided colonic cancer.[34,36,37,41–44] Morbidity and mortality are lower than the cumulative rates of the staged approach.[34,43] Contraindications to subtotal colectomy in this setting include poor-risk patients who are inadequately resuscitated or have massive proximal bowel distention.[34] Even in patients presenting without obstruction, complete evaluation of the large bowel mucosa may be technically difficult because of redundant colon or narrowing of the lumen by a cicatrizing cancer. This problem does not significantly affect the management of a right-sided tumor, as distal lesions will likely be detected and occult proximal lesions will be included in the right hemicolectomy. For the most commonly seen left-sided carcinomas, however, failure to visualize the proximal colon before surgery requires careful intraoperative assessment. Second cancers or large polyps may be found by palpation, but this cannot be considered reliable.[4,7,22] Indeed, the pa-

Table 48-2
Advantages and Disadvantages of Subtotal Colectomy

Advantages	*Disadvantages*
Reduces colonic mucosa at risk	Frequent bowel movements (temporary)
Treats synchronous neoplasia	Higher morbidity and mortality than with partial colectomy
Facilitates endoscopic follow-up	No effect on survival
Lower rate anastomotic complications	
Decreased incidence suture-line recurrence	
In obstruction, avoids morbidity of colostomy and staged surgery	

tient may subsequently manifest an "early metachronous" malignancy. It is therefore mandatory that these patients have colonoscopy within 3 to 6 months of surgery.[18,45]

Some authors recommend intraoperative colonoscopic evaluation of the large bowel proximal to a constricting cancer, suggesting that complete examination is usually possible and adds 15 to 20 min to operating time.[4,46,47] Many surgeons, including the authors, would find this procedure to be time-consuming and technically difficult while also adding potential risk of complications.[45]

Early invasive carcinoma in a polyp may be adequately treated by colonoscopic polypectomy during preoperative evaluation of a synchronous cancer. In this situation, segmental resection of the initial lesion would seem appropriate. Similarly, simultaneous cancers confined to the same anatomic segment of colon might be suitable for partial colectomy. If however, there are other associated polyps or if lifelong colonoscopic surveillance is problematic, then subtotal colectomy would be preferable because of the high risk of future neoplasms in such a patient.

There is no evidence to suggest that subtotal colectomy for synchronous cancers confers any survival benefit as compared with regional resection. Even if one accepts equal operative mortality rates for the two procedures, the individual patient's prognosis depends solely on the staging of the colonic carcinomas. Metachronous neoplasms occur with somewhat greater frequency in these patients—but, as previously described, most of these are benign polyps or early invasive carcinomas easily dealt with by endoscopic polypectomy or curative resection. However, since these patients do require intensive follow-up, those having subtotal colectomy will need only sigmoidoscopy. This is by far the simplest and safest follow-up method. Moreover, it may be the most cost-effective method, although this has not been clearly addressed. For all of these reasons, it is the authors' preference to perform subtotal colectomy in the majority of patients with synchronous cancers. When one of the tumors is in the upper rectum, we utilize an anastomosis between the cecum and the rectum to preserve the ileocecal valve and improve the functional result following combined subtotal colectomy and anterior resection.

Summary and Recommendations

Patients undergoing preoperative colonoscopy for colorectal carcinoma have an incidence of coexisting colonic cancer of approximately 6.3 percent. Most simultaneous lesions are early invasive cancers curable by endoscopic polypectomy or resection at the time of surgery for the initial cancer. Because there is no site predilection for synchronous tumors, their discovery may dictate more extensive resection. If left undetected, they may subsequently appear as advanced "metachronous" cancers. Early postoperative colonoscopy is mandatory when complete evaluation of the colon is impossible before surgery.

Synchronous colonic cancers carry a greater than 50 percent risk of associated concurrent neoplastic polyps. Available evidence points to a relationship between synchronous carcinoma, the adenoma-cancer pathogenetic sequence, and future likelihood of colorectal malignancy. Indeed, more than 50 percent of patients with synchronous cancers and polyps will develop metachronous polyps in the first 2 to 3 years of follow-up. This tendency toward development of neoplastic disease has led to the emphasis placed on managing this high-risk group of patients by either removal of or close surveillance of the colonic mucosa at risk.

Subtotal colectomy should be considered for many synchronous carcinomas, particularly in young patients without locally advanced or metastatic disease or if there are associated adenomatous polyps. Partial colectomy is appropriate for synchronous lesions that can be resected in a curative manner in patients who are amenable to lifelong colonoscopic surveillance.

MANAGEMENT OF LYNCH SYNDROME PATIENTS

There is increasing interest in the role of genetic factors in the etiology of colorectal cancer. Familial adenomatous polyposis (FAP) is a well-known syndrome that has numerous benign and malignant manifestations and an established genetic linkage.[48] The multiple polyps of FAP serve as a readily identifiable phenotype which is absent in other forms of hereditary colorectal cancer, such as familial colorectal cancer and hereditary nonpolyposis colorectal cancer syndrome (HNPCC or the Lynch syndromes). While HNPCC is not common, it has been estimated to represent 5 to 6 percent of colonic cancer cases—compared with the 1 percent attributed to FAP. (It has been described in hundreds of families of many nationalities and races.[49]) Management strategies for Lynch syndrome patients are different than those for FAP or sporadic colonic cancer. They have evolved from an understanding of the natural history of HNPCC and its genetic implications. Fundamental to the management of HNPCC is its recognition, which is based predominantly on the family history as well as some distinctive clinical features.

Diagnosis

Patients with HNPCC may be distinguished from those with familial or sporadic colonic cancer despite the lack of physical signs or biological markers. Lynch has proposed diagnostic criteria derived from pedigree analysis of affected families.[50] Strictly applied, these criteria describe only rare large-family groups. However, HNPCC may represent a heterogeneous set of syndromes influenced by genetic or environmental factors. The majority of potential HNPCC patients may be sporadic cases or involve a small family, with the result that the diagnosis may be obscured.[51] In these situations, recognition of the clinical characteristics of HNPCC may lead to the identification of affected individuals and families.

The cardinal features of Lynch syndrome I are (1) proximal colon cancer, (2) increased incidence of synchronous and metachronous colonic lesions, (3) early age of onset, and (4) autosomal dominant transmission.[50] Lynch syndrome II has the same features, with the addition of extracolonic malignancies, including cancers of the female genital tract, stomach, small intestine, urinary tract, and others.[52]

The presence of certain components of HNPCC in a patient with colorectal cancer or in the family history may be sufficient for a presumptive diagnosis. This has important implications in the treatment of the patient and in a surveillance program for the patient's primary relatives.[52]

Treatment Recommendations

The Lynch syndrome patient with newly diagnosed colonic cancer should have subtotal colectomy with ileorectal anastomosis.[53] This recommendation is based on the natural history of HNPCC. There was an excess of both synchronous (18 percent) and metachronous (24 percent) colonic cancers in the families reviewed by Fitzgibbons et al.[53] Life table analysis suggested that the risk of metachronous colonic cancer in HNPCC patients is 40 percent by 10 years.[53] Removal of most of the colonic mucosa at risk is justified by the high incidence of multiple tumors. Ileorectal anastomosis is preferred to proctectomy, with its attendant morbidity, because the majority (87 percent) of colonic cancers in Lynch syndromes are proximal to the rectum.[54] Frequent sigmoidoscopic examination of the remaining large bowel is recommended. Follow-up data on patients treated with this approach are not yet available. It is not known whether there is a significant risk of cancer in the retained rectum.[54]

In the Creighton University registry, extracolonic cancers of the Lynch syndrome II patients have occurred primarily in the female genital tract.[53] For female Lynch syndrome II patients presenting with colonic cancer, Fitzgibbons et al.[53] advise prophylactic hysterectomy and bilateral salpingo-oophorectomy at the time of colonic resection. In younger patients—in whom childbearing issues and the long-term effects of estrogen replacement therapy are considerations—a surveillance program is substituted. This consists of pelvic examinations, endometrial aspiration and cytology, and ovarian ultrasound.[54]

Regular surveillance of individuals in an affected family is recommended, since there is a 50 percent risk of transmission of the Lynch syndrome according to its autosomal dominant inheritance. Biannual fecal occult blood testing is advised at age 20, and yearly colonoscopy is initiated at age 25 or 5 years before the earliest onset of colonic cancer in the family.[53] Integrally inherited extracolonic cancers in Lynch syndrome II patients may be screened according to the individual pedigree. Compliance with screening regimens is encouraged by counseling about the natural history of the Lynch syndrome. Invasive carcinoma may develop rapidly without readily apparent precursor lesions, such as the "flat adenoma," making frequent examination necessary.[54,55] Patients at 50 percent risk for the Lynch syndrome have been followed in colonoscopy studies, which demonstrate an increased incidence of both adenomas and carcinoma in certain families, though there appears to be marked genetic and phenotypic heterogeneity.[55,56] Patients need to be aware that surveillance may not necessarily protect completely against the development of carcinoma.

A patient who has had a previous partial colectomy and is subsequently recognized to be a member of a Lynch syndrome family faces a risk of developing a metachronous cancer of approximately 40 percent at 10 years.[53] An aggressive screening program has been recommended, although it is the authors' preference to recommend a complete subtotal colectomy.

SYNCHRONOUS HEPATIC METASTASES

Definition of the Problem

The discovery of metastases in the liver at the time of presentation of colorectal cancer is a common occurrence and almost invariably implies a dismal prognosis. There are, however, occasional patients who tend to have prolonged survival even without treatment.[57–60] Moreover, prognostic factors have been determined which identify those patients who might be cured by resection of hepatic metastases.[60–64] There is some controversy regarding the long-term value of such surgery; indeed, no prospective randomized trial addressing the issue exists.[65–67] Nonetheless, it has been demonstrated that resection of colorectal metastases to the liver can achieve 5-year survival rates of 25 to 40 percent in a selected group of patients.[60,62–64,68–74] Whether metastases present as synchronous lesions with the primary colorectal carcinoma or later as metachronous disease, the critical issue governing surgical management is selection of the small fraction of patients likely to benefit from hepatic resection.

Natural History and Tumor Biology of Synchronous Hepatic Metastases

The prognosis for patients with metastatic liver disease appears to be determined by biological factors such as tumor extent, tumor behavior, and patient characteristics rather than temporal factors such as early diagnosis.[72] To evaluate treatment, information regarding the natural history of untreated hepatic metastases is required. Median survival time in untreated patients is between 4 and 15 months, depending largely on the degree of liver involvement.[57,58,75–77] However, unselected and unstaged historical data should not be compared to current treatment groups, which largely represent patients with less advanced disease.[66,78]

Long-term survival with unresected liver metastases from colorectal cancer is possible but rare.[57,58] Hughes et al.[60] found only 14 patients reported in the literature who lived without resection for 5 years, and all eventually died of cancer. For unselected solitary metastatic nodules, Wagner et al.[58] reported a median survival of 21 months and a 20 percent 3-year survival rate. Despite concerns about using historical series for comparisons, it is generally accepted that the small subset of patients with favorable hepatic metastases achieve improved survival with resection. Clearly the only chance for cure is obtained with surgical treatment.

Synchronous metastases diagnosed at the initial presentation of the colorectal primary occur in 8 to 25 percent of patients.[57,59,65,77,79] In most cases there is diffuse hepatic involvement or extrahepatic disease, but up to 25 percent of metastases confined to the liver are solitary or few in number and thus potentially amenable to resection.[59,62,80–82]

Adverse tumor factors include extensive hepatic involvement, extrahepatic metastases, and an advanced stage of the primary colorectal tumor.[60–64,83] Prolonged survival after hepatic resection is associated with an adequate resection margin, fewer than three liver metastases, and possibly a prolonged disease-free interval.[60–62,69,72,80,84] Patients with liver dysfunction or poor clinical performance status have a limited prognosis.[75] The importance of tumor biology in survival is further suggested by the fact that patients with nodal involvement of the primary tumor have resectable hepatic metastases less frequently than do node-negative patients and tend to have a worse outcome even if resection is possible.[60,72]

Survival is equivalent in synchronous colonic and hepatic resection compared to delayed hepatic resection.[61,62,83,85,86] Conversely, early resection of metastases does not improve survival. In fact, interval delay may allow the biological behavior of metastatic disease to be determined. Many patients will develop diffuse hepatic metastases during this delay, which enables the selection of patients with favorable features for resection.[82,87]

Diagnosis

In the absence of clinical evidence of liver involvement, hepatic metastases are usually suspected preoperatively because of abnormal liver imaging or less sensitively altered liver function tests. At operation, evaluation of palpable liver metastases is fairly accurate without biopsy, but up to 25 percent of patients may have occult metastases.[88–90] In cases of potentially resectable metastases, biopsy is inadvisable.[91] Histologic confirmation is preferred by some authors, particularly if chemotherapy is contemplated for unresectable disease.[79,84] A technique has been described to facilitate needle biopsy through a low abdominal incision.[92] Preoperative imaging of the liver by computed tomography (CT) or ultrasound can affect the conduct of the procedure in several ways. Incurable liver metastases found with ultrasound may dictate a more limited resection. Conversely, solitary lesions detected preoperatively may suggest synchronous hepatic resection.

Intraoperative ultrasound has assumed a greater role in surgery for hepatic metastases.[82,89,90] It is more accurate than the combination of preoperative ultrasound and CT and demonstrates lesions that are neither visible nor palpable at surgery.[90] It should be routinely employed prior to resection to exclude unsuspected metastatic deposits in the liver and to determine the extent of resection required.

Surgical Strategy

With an understanding of the biological behavior of hepatic metastases and their prognostic significance, a strategy for managing synchronous colorectal metastases to the liver has been developed. The rationale for this strategy is based on optimally selecting patients for hepatic resection while avoiding the morbidity of major liver surgery in patients destined to develop widespread metastatic disease.

The most important considerations are the appropriate cancer resection of the primary tumor and accurate staging, including biopsy of liver lesions when indicated. Assessment of the right upper quadrant may prove difficult through a lower abdominal incision, particularly if adhesions are present or there are nodules on the superior dome of the liver. When complete exploration is possible, extrahepatic metastases should be searched for. Bimanual palpation of the liver should be complemented by hepatic mobilization and intraoperative ultrasound—if available—when synchronous resection appears feasible. In addition, the porta hepatis should be examined for lymph node metastasis, which would preclude curative resection.[60]

There are specific circumstances in which synchronous liver resection ought to be contemplated. Issues to be considered include the surgeon's experience, availability of blood, and informed consent. For cure, the primary tumor must be resectable, with no evidence of residual local disease or extrahepatic spread. If the incision can easily be extended to allow complete evaluation of the liver, a minor hepatic resection for an apparently isolated liver metastasis may be reasonable. Wedge resection or left lateral segment resection adds little to the operative morbidity and offers the possibility of cure if the metastasis is truly solitary. However, major hepatic surgery combined with resection of the primary colorectal cancer is probably contraindicated. Some groups advocate simultaneous colorectal and hepatic resections as safe procedures which yield survival rates equal to metachronous resections.[71,86] It is difficult to justify increased operative morbidity and mortality when most patients have either occult metastases or will develop incurable disease. Additionally, these types of operations are probably best performed by experienced hepatic surgeons. Staged hepatic resection does not compromise survival.[61,62,83,85,86] On the contrary, because patients with favorable criteria will be selected, the survival rates for interval resection may be enhanced.[62,93] Additionally, this allows referral to tertiary centers with experienced hepatic surgeons.

An occasional patient is best served by nonoperative management of synchronous colorectal cancer and hepatic metastases (Table 48-3). When extensive hepatic metastases are demonstrated by imaging studies, survival is generally measured in terms of months. If an occult primary tumor is subsequently found, it may, in some circumstances, be judged unlikely to become symptomatic during the expected remaining period of life.

Resection of the primary lesion is indicated in incurable disease when complications such as intestinal obstruction, bleeding, or pain can be palliated. Patients with a relatively small burden of unresectable hepatic metastases may have prolonged survival and in most circumstances would benefit from surgery to avoid future intestinal symptoms. Since the potential for cure has been lost, any procedure to excise a primary colorectal cancer in the presence of unresectable metastases should be planned with the patient's morbidity and quality of life in mind. Colostomy might be avoided in partially obstructing lesions with a low-residue diet and the use of mineral oil.

Laparoscopic colectomy may be utilized in some cases to minimize postoperative discomfort. Any concern about the oncologic appropriateness of the laparoscopic resection is outweighed by the surgical intent to control symptoms. Using a similar rationale, "palliative" abdominal-perineal resection of rectal carcinoma with widespread metastases cannot be justified in most patients. Less aggressive surgery that removes the rectal tumor but preserves the anal sphincter is preferable to a colostomy in the incurable patient. Alternatives to tumor excision include Nd-Yag laser, palliative radiation, or chemotherapy. However, abdominal-perineal resection may be of benefit for symptomatic bulky or recurrent rectal cancer.

OOPHORECTOMY

Background

Metastasis of colonic carcinoma to the ovary may present at the time of initial colonic surgery or as a late recurrence sometimes requiring reoperation. Ovarian involvement is often associated with widespread metastatic disease and implies a poor prognosis. As a result, prophylactic oophorectomy at the original operation for colonic carcinoma has been advocated by some for many years. The indications for this policy and the benefits of the procedure are controversial. To evaluate the problem, we have reviewed the biology of ovarian metastasis and its clinical significance.

Strictly defined, a Krukenberg tumor describes an ovarian metastasis that contains significant numbers of signet-ring cells in a cellular stroma derived from

Table 48-3
Management of Primary Tumor with Unresectable Hepatic Metastases

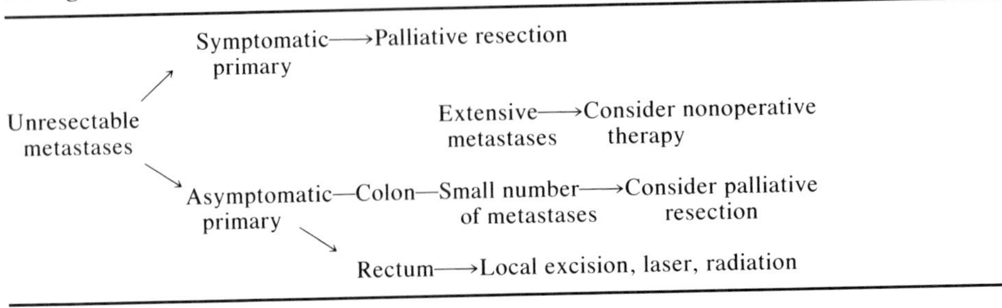

the ovary.[94–96] The eponym refers to metastatic epithelial tumors to the ovary such as gastric carcinoma; histologically, however, very few colorectal primaries can be classified as Krukenberg tumors, since large acini are usually present microscopically.[95,96]

The reported incidence of ovarian metastasis from colonic cancer varies from 1.4 to 10.3 percent.[97–102] In combined series, synchronous ovarian involvement by direct extension or metastasis occurred in 33 of 584 women (5.7 percent) selected to have oophorectomy at the time of colon surgery.[99–103] Many of these patients had only microscopically detectable disease. The actual incidence of gross ovarian metastasis is probably significantly lower. Some cases diagnosed at operation are in fact tumors invading the ovary directly from the primary lesion. No randomized controlled study of prophylactic oophorectomy versus no treatment exists, and selection criteria for oophorectomy were not stated in the largest retrospective series. MacKeigan and Ferguson[100] performed prophylactic oophorectomy in 137 of 484 women with colorectal carcinoma and reported an incidence of ovarian metastasis of 7.4 percent. An autopsy study found a 13.6 percent incidence of ovarian metastasis in colorectal cancer patients, most with widespread disease.[104]

A more relevant figure in the assessment of prophylactic oophorectomy is the proportion of patients requiring surgery for late ovarian metastases. Estimates of this problem range from 0 to 2 percent.[96,98–102,105] In a long-term follow-up study of 882 women after resection of colorectal carcinoma, only 13 (1.5 percent) required operation for ovarian recurrence.[97] Cutait et al.[102] saw no late ovarian recurrence in 134 patients followed for at least 5 years. Rarely does metastatic colonic cancer involve only the ovary; therefore surgery for symptomatic disease is strictly palliative. Morrow and Enker[106] found that of 926 women with metastatic colonic cancer, 63 (6.8 percent) had developed metachronous ovarian metastases at reoperation after a mean interval of 17 months from the time of colonic surgery (Table 48-4). Over half of these patients had diffuse intraabdominal metastases, while only 4 of the 63 patients had disease apparently confined to the ovary.[106]

Table 48-4
Surgery for Late Ovarian Metastases

Reference	*No. female patients*	*No. requiring surgery, %*
4	882	13 (1.5%)
9	134	0
13	926[a]	63 (6.8%)

[a]Metastatic cancer.

Biology of Ovarian Metastasis

The ovary is a frequent site of metastatic spread of breast, endometrial, and gastrointestinal tumors. Ovarian involvement is bilateral in over half of affected colonic cancer patients.[95,107,108] It is not clear whether the ovary is by nature more susceptible to metastatic colonic carcinoma or whether it is merely associated with diffuse intraabdominal carcinomatosis. Steroid hormone receptors in primary colonic cancer have been studied by Alford et al.,[109] who found that 30 percent of tumors had a high estrogen receptor affinity. Seventy percent of tumors had a high affinity for at least one steroid receptor. Subsequent reports have not confirmed this finding.[110,111] Estrogen receptor positivity is also found in breast and stomach carcinoma and may be a causative factor in the predisposition toward implantation and growth in hormone-producing tissue such as the ovary.[96]

The pathogenesis of metastasis to the ovary most likely involves hematogenous spread.[96,108] Theoretically, ovarian implantation could result from the exfoliation of malignant cells into the peritoneal cavity after full-thickness tumor invasion of the bowel wall.[112] This might then be the mechanism behind bilateral ovarian metastases and peritoneal implants. However, the surface epithelium of the ovary bearing metastatic disease is usually intact on histologic examination, so cancer cell "capture" and implantation is unlikely.[96] Moreover, metastatic peritoneal seeding may be absent despite the presence of ovarian metastases. Lymphatic spread is also improbable. Though tumors may rarely be seen in the lymphatics of the ovary, there are no direct lymphatic channels between colon and ovary.[96]

The hematogenous route of metastasis is consistent with the finding of an intact ovarian capsule. Additionally, since no site of primary colonic cancer carries a greater risk of ovarian metastasis, the implantation route seems less plausible. Metastatic ovarian spread is seen most often from tumors in the left colon, but this corresponds to the expected distribution of primary lesions.[97,98,100,101,108,113] It has also been suggested that premenopausal women, who have increased ovarian blood supply and function, have a greater incidence of metastasis.[97,100,113,114] MacKeigan and Ferguson[100] reported that 6 of 24 (25 percent) premenopausal patients with colonic cancer had metastasis to the ovaries either at the time of surgery or subsequently.

Rationale for Prophylactic Oophorectomy

It is known that the ovary is a favored site of metastasis for colonic carcinoma and that patients with spread to the ovaries have a dismal prognosis. Although there are occasional patients with prolonged survival, three series reported a mean survival of 16 months after surgery for ovarian metastases.[97,106,108] Nonetheless, it has not been demonstrated that prophylactic oophorectomy in women with colonic cancer improves survival. An early study by Deddish[103] compared patients undergoing radical lymphadenectomy plus bilateral oophorectomy to patients having only conservative nodal dissection during excision of rectal carcinoma. Although 2 of 5 patients with resected ovarian metastases were free of disease at 5 years, the group treated by radical node dissection plus oophorectomy showed no improvement in 5-year survival. In a retrospective analysis of 201 women who had prophylactic oophorectomy, there was a trend toward slightly decreased survival compared to a non-oophorectomy group.[102] This difference might be explained by the slightly greater number of patients with rectal cancer and node-positive disease in the oophorectomy group. No significant effects of oophorectomy were found when Dukes B or C patients were segregated or when groups were compared by menopausal status. No prolonged survival was seen in the 4 patients with gross or microscopic metastasis that had oophorectomy.[102] Another retrospective study of women with surgically curable colonic cancer found no significant benefit in disease-free interval or survival for patients who had removal of their ovaries at the time of initial surgical therapy for colonic cancer[115] or who had previous bilateral oophorectomy for other reasons. Again, there was no significant difference between groups with and without oophorectomy even when stratified by tumor grade, Dukes stage, tumor location, or menopausal status.

Despite the fact that no study assessing the impact of oophorectomy has shown a survival advantage, there remain advocates for prophylactic oophorectomy.[96,102,105,115] Burt[116] recommended the procedure for all women with colorectal carcinoma to avoid a second operation for metastatic disease. Rendleman and Gilchrist[117] performed oophorectomy in 42 of 102 patients, finding three metastatic lesions. They restricted oophorectomy to patients with gross ovarian involvement, serosal invasion, peritoneal implants, or widespread metastatic disease. Knoepp et al.[118] suggested similar criteria but felt that prophylactic oophorectomy was indicated in all postmenopausal patients.

More recently, several groups have argued for prophylactic oophorectomy regardless of menopausal status.[100,105–107] Morrow and Enker[106] felt that the role of the procedure in premenopausal women would expand with increasing use of adjuvant therapy for colorectal cancer.[106] Cutait et al.[102] found a 2 percent risk to late ovarian cancer, but no patient developed metastases from colonic cancer to the ovary in long-term follow-up. Based on this, adjunctive oophorectomy was recommended for all postmenopausal women to protect against ovarian cancer. Only those premenopausal patients at higher risk for developing ovarian cancer because of previous malignancy or a strong family history were considered candidates for oophorectomy.[102] Blamey et al.[97] held that routine prophylactic oophorectomy was not justified, since a second operation for ovarian recurrence was necessary in only 1.5 percent of 882 patients studied.

A randomized, controlled trial would be required to demonstrate any advantage in disease-free interval or survival for women having prophylactic oophorectomy. Only then could its role be determined within the context of other adjuvant treatments currently employed in colorectal cancer.

Summary and Recommendations

Ovarian metastases from recurrent colorectal carcinoma may necessitate further surgery for palliation of symptoms. It is estimated that less than 2 percent of women followed after the initial resection for colorectal cancer will require such a reoperation. Metastases are rarely confined to the ovary. More commonly, there is widespread disease with an associated poor prognosis.

If there is evident ovarian involvement at the time of resection for colonic carcinoma, bilateral oophorectomy is advisable. However, routine prophylactic oophorectomy appears to confer no survival benefit. It may be justified in postmenopausal patients to prevent subsequent ovarian cancer, either primary or metastatic, since the additional operative morbidity is negligible. It should be recognized that only a small fraction of these patients are likely to benefit. For most premenopausal women, induction of menopause, loss of fertility, and possibly increased morbidity outweigh this potential advantage. A subset of patients with diffuse intraabdominal disease at the initial bowel resection may benefit from bilateral oophorectomy to prevent subsequent symptomatic ovarian disease.

MANAGEMENT OF METACHRONOUS CANCERS

Little meaningful information is available regarding the incidence, characteristics, and prognosis of metachronous cancers. Previous studies addressing this subject were undertaken before colonoscopy was widely utilized. As a result, many asynchronously discovered tumors probably represent simultaneous cancers missed at the time the index tumor was found.

In a report of postoperative colonoscopic surveillance, 24 of 91 patients (26 percent) developed metachronous adenomatous polyps at a median interval of 19 months.[29] In 1 patient (0.8 percent), metachronous cancer in a polyp was detected at 10 years. Evers et al.[17] found that 5 of 320 (2 percent) patients treated for colorectal cancer had metachronous carcinoma. The two patients who survived both had $T_1N_0M_0$ lesions identified by colonoscopy at 2 and 3 years after resection of the primary tumor. Three other patients presented up to 23 years after their initial cancer and died of advanced metachronous carcinoma. In another series, 78 patients had colonoscopy at an average of 3.7 years after treatment of the index cancer; of these, 6 (7.7 percent) had metachronous carcinoma, all of which were Dukes A or focal invasion in a polyp.[18]

Such results, while not definitive, suggest the importance of close endoscopic follow-up in patients with colorectal cancer. As previously described, there is a significant incidence of metachronous polyps in this population, and this presents the possibility of secondary prevention or cure of further malignancy. With postoperative colonoscopic surveillance, benign precursor polyps should be detected and removed. Theoretically, intervention in the adenoma-carcinoma sequence will be possible at a more favorable stage and metachronous cancers will in future be much less frequent.

Management of a metachronous colorectal carcinoma follows the same principles as those used for synchronous cancers. With the recognition that the entire colonic mucosa is at high risk of neoplastic transformation, preoperative examination with colonoscopy, where possible, is recommended. Subtotal colectomy should be considered to treat the high incidence of synchronous polyps and to facilitate endoscopic follow-up. Factors mitigating against subtotal colectomy included advanced age, concurrent medical problems, and incurable disease.

REFERENCES

1. Moertel CG, Bargen JA, Dockerty MB: Multiple carcinomas of the large intestine: A review of the literature and a study of 261 cases. *Gastroenterology* 34:85–88, 1958.
2. Morson BC: The polyp-cancer sequence in the large bowel. *Proc R Soc Med* 67:451–457, 1974.
3. Muto T, Bussey HJ, Morson BC: The evolution of cancer of the colon and rectum. *Cancer* 36:2251–2270, 1975.
4. Finan P, Ritchie JK, Hawley PR: Synchronous and "early" metachronous carcinomas of the colon and rectum. *Br J Surg* 74:945–947, 1987.
5. Kiefer PJ, Thorson AG, Christensen MA: Metachronous colorectal cancer: Time interval to presentation of a metachronous cancer. *Dis Colon Rectum* 29:378–382, 1986.
6. Heald RJ, Lockhart-Mummery HE: The lesion of the second cancer of the large bowel. *Br J Surg* 59:16–19, 1972.
7. Heald RJ, Bussey HJ: Clinical experiences at St. Mark's Hospital with multiple synchronous cancers of the colon and rectum. *Dis Colon Rectum* 18:6–10, 1975.
8. Kaibara N, Koga S, Jinnai D: Synchronous and metachronous malignancies of the colon and rectum in Japan with special reference to a coexisting early cancer. *Cancer* 54:1870–1874, 1984.
9. Dasmahapatra KS, Lopyan K: Rationale for aggressive colonoscopy in patients with colorectal neoplasia. *Arch Surg* 124:63–66, 1989.
10. Agrez MV, Ready R, Ilstrup D, Beart RW: Metachronous colorectal malignancies. *Dis Colon Rectum* 29:378–382, 1986.
11. Ekelund GR, Pihl B: Multiple carcinomas of the colon and rectum. *Cancer* 33:1630–1634, 1974.
12. Travieso CR, Knoepp LF, Hanley PH: Multiple adenocarcinomas of the colon and rectum. *Dis Colon Rectum* 15:1–6, 1972.
13. Lasser A: Synchronous primary adenocarcinomas of the colon and rectum. *Dis Colon Rectum* 21:20–22, 1978.
14. Hancock RJ: Synchronous carcinoma of the colon and rectum. *Am Surg* 41:560–563, 1975.
15. Cunliffe WJ, Hasleton PS, Tweedle DE, Schofield PF: Incidence of synchronous and metachronous colorectal carcinoma. *Br J Surg* 71:941–943, 1984.
16. Langevin JM, Nivatvongs S: The true incidence of synchronous cancer of the large bowel: A prospective study. *Am J Surg* 147:330–333, 1984.
17. Evers BM, Mullins RJ, Matthews TH, et al: Multiple adenocarcinomas of the colon and rectum: An analysis of incidences and current trends. *Dis Colon Rectum* 31:518–522, 1988.
18. Reilly JC, Rusin LC, Theuerkauf FJ: Colonoscopy: Its role in cancer of the colon and rectum. *Dis Colon Rectum* 25:532–538, 1982.
19. Thorson AG, Christensen MA, Davis SJ: The role of colonoscopy in the assessment of patients with colorectal cancer. *Dis Colon Rectum* 29:306–311, 1986.
20. Adloff M, Arnaud J, Bergamaschi R, Schloegel M: Synchronous carcinoma of the colon and rectum: Prognostic and therapeutic implications. *Am J Surg* 157:299–302, 1989.
21. Weber CA, Deveney KE, Pellegrini CA, Way LW: Routine colonoscopy in the management of colorectal carcinoma. *Am J Surg* 152:87–92, 1986.
22. Sugrue M, Black R, Watts J et al: Peri-operative colonoscopy detects synchronous tumours in patients with colorectal cancers. *Aust NZ J Surg* 61:25–28, 1991.
23. Maxfield RG: Colonoscopy at a routine preoperative procedure for carcinoma of the colon. *Am J Surg* 147:477–480, 1984.
24. Pagana TJ, Ledesma EJ, Mittelman A, Nava HR: The use of colonoscopy in the study of synchronous colorectal neoplasms. *Cancer* 53:356–359, 1984.
25. Slater G, Aufses AH, Szporn A: Synchronous carcinoma of the colon and rectum. *Surg Gynecol Obstet* 171:283–287, 1990.
26. Welch JP: Multiple colon and rectum tumours: An appraisal of natural history and therapeutic options. *Am J Surg* 142:274–280, 1981.
27. Devitt JE, Roth-Mayo LA, Brunon FN: The significance of multiple adenocarcinomas of the colon and rectum. *Ann Surg* 169:364–367, 1969.
28. Chu DZ, Giacco G, Martin RG, Guinee VF: The significance of synchronous carcinoma and polyps in the colon. *Cancer* 57:445–450, 1986.
29. Carlsson G, Petrelli NJ, Nava H, et al: The value of colonoscopic surveillance after curative resection for colorectal cancer or synchronous adenomatous polyps. *Arch Surg* 122:1261–1263, 1987.
30. Enker WE, Dragacevic S: Multiple carcinomas of the large bowel: A natural experiment in etiology and pathogenesis. *Ann Surg* 187:8–11, 1978.
31. Brief DK, Brener BJ, Goldenkranz R, et al: An argument for increased use of subtotal colectomy in the management of carcinoma of the colon. *Am Surg* 49:66–72, 1983.

32. Lillehei RC, Wangensteen OH: Bowel function after colectomy for cancer, polyps and diverticulitis. *JAMA* 159:163–170, 1955.
33. Fogler R, Weiner E: Multiple foci of colorectal carcinoma. *NY State J Med* 80:47–51, 1980.
34. Brief DK, Brener BJ, Goldenkranz R, et al: Defining the role of subtotal colectomy in the treatment of carcinoma of the colon. *Ann Surg* 213:248–252, 1991.
35. Bat L, Neumann G, Shemesh E: The association of synchronous neoplasms with occluding colorectal cancer. *Dis Colon Rectum* 28:149–151, 1985.
36. Halevy A, Levi J, Orda R: Emergency subtotal colectomy: A new trend for treatment of obstructing carcinoma of the left colon. *Ann Surg* 210:220–223, 1989.
37. Stephenson BM, Shandall AA, Farouk R, Griffith G: Malignant left-sided large bowel obstruction managed by subtotal/total colectomy. *Br J Surg* 77:1098–1102, 1990.
38. Skinner MA, Yler D, Branum GD, et al: Subtotal colectomy for familial polyposis. *Arch Surg* 125:621–624, 1990.
39. Wright HK, Thomas WH, Cleveland JC: The low recurrence rate of colonic carcinoma in ileocolic anastomosis. *Surg Gynecol Obstet* 129:960, 1969.
40. Fielding L: Anastomotic integrity after operations for large bowel cancer. *Br Med J* 281:411, 1980.
41. Deutsch AA, Zelokovski A, Sternberg A, Reiss R: One-stage subtotal colectomy with anastomosis for obstructing carcinoma of the left colon. *Dis Colon Rectum* 26:227–230, 1983.
42. Morgan WP, Jenkins N, Lewis P, Aubrey DA: Management of obstructing carcinoma of the left colon by extended right hemicolectomy. *Am J Surg* 149:327–329, 1985.
43. Klatt GR, Martin WH, Gillespie JT: Subtotal colectomy with primary anastomosis without diversion in the treatment of obstructing carcinoma of the left colon. *Am J Surg* 141:577–578, 1981.
44. Glass RL, Smith LE, Cochran RC: Subtotal colectomy for obstructing carcinoma of the left colon. *Am J Surg* 145:335–336, 1983.
45. Tate JJ, Rawlinson J, Royle GT, et al: Pre-operative or post-operative colonic examination for synchronous lesions in colorectal cancer. *Br J Surg* 75:1016–1018, 1988.
46. Kaibara N, Kimura O, Nishidoi H, et al: Intraoperative colonoscopy for the diagnosis of multiple cancers of the large intestine. *Japan J Surg* 12:117–121, 1982.
47. Unger SW, Wanebo HJ: Colonoscopy: An essential monitoring technique after resection of colorectal cancer. *Am J Surg* 145:71–75, 1983.
48. Bodmer WF, Bailey CJ, Bodmer J, et al: Localization of the gene for familial adenomatous polyposis on chromosome 5. *Nature* 328:614–616, 1987.
49. Lynch PM, Lynch HT: *Colon Cancer Genetics*. New York, Reinhold, 1985.
50. Lynch HT, Rozen P, Schuelke GS, Lynch JF: Hereditary colorectal cancer review: Colonic polyposis and nonpolyposis colonic cancer (Lynch Syndrome I and II). *Surg Dig Dis* 2:244–260, 1984.
51. Utsunomiya J: The concept of hereditary colorectal cancer and the implications of its study, in *Hereditary Colon Cancer*. Tokyo, Springer-Verlag, 1990, pp 3–16.
52. Lynch HT, Smyrk T, Watson P, et al: Hereditary colorectal cancer. *Semin Oncol* 18:337–366, 1991.
53. Fitzgibbons RJ, Lynch HT, Stanislav GV, et al: Recognition and treatment of patients with hereditary nonpolyposis colon cancer. *Ann Surg* 206:289–295, 1987.
54. Fitzgibbons RJ, Lynch HT, Lanspa SJ, et al: Surgical strategies for management of the Lynch syndromes, in *Hereditary Colon Cancer*. Tokyo, Springer-Verlag, 1990, pp 211–217.
55. Lanspa SJ, Lynch HT, Smyrk C, et al: Colorectal adenomas in the Lynch syndromes: Results of a colonoscopy screening program. *Gastroenterology* 98:1117–1122, 1990.
56. Vasen HF, den Hartog Jager FC, Menko FM, et al: Screening for hereditary nonpolyposis colorectal cancer: A study of 22 kindreds in the Netherlands. *Am J Med* 86:278–281, 1989.
57. Wood CG, Gillis CR, Blumgart LH: A retrospective study of the natural history of patients with liver metastases from colorectal cancer. *J Clin Oncol* 2:285–288, 1976.
58. Wagner JS, Adson MA, Van Heerden JA, et al: The natural history of hepatic metastases from colorectal cancer. *Ann Surg* 199:502–508, 1984.
59. Greenway B: Hepatic metastases from colorectal cancer: Resection or not. *Br J Surg* 75:513–519, 1988.
60. Hughes KS, Simon RM, Songhorabodi S, et al: Resection of the liver for colorectal carcinoma metastases: A multi-institutional study of indications for resection. *Surgery* 103:278–288, 1988.
61. Ekberg H, Tranberg KG, Andersson R, et al: Determinants of survival in liver resection for colorectal secondaries. *Br J Surg* 73:727–731, 1986.
62. Scheele J, Stangl R, Altendorf-Hofmann A, Gall FP: Indicators of prognosis after hepatic resection for colorectal secondaries. *Surgery* 110:13–29, 1991.
63. Fornter JG, Silva JS, Golbey RB, et al: Multivariate analysis of a personal series of 242 consecutive patients with liver metastases from colo-rectal cancer: I. Treatment by hepatic resection. *Ann Surg* 198:306–316, 1984.
64. Doci R, Gennari L, Bignami P, et al: One hundred patients with hepatic metastases from colorectal cancer treated by resection: Analysis of prognostic determinants. *Br J Surg* 78:797–801, 1991.
65. Ridge JA, Daly JM: Treatment of colorectal hepatic metastases. *Surg Gynecol Obstet* 161:597–607, 1985.
66. Silen W: Hepatic resection for metastases from colorectal carcinoma is of dubious value. *Arch Surg* 124:1021–1022, 1989.
67. Adson MA: The resection of hepatic metastases. *Arch Surg* 124:1023–1024, 1989.
68. Wilson ST, Adson MA: Surgical treatment of hepatic metastases from colorectal cancers. *Arch Surg* 111:330–334, 1976.
69. Foster JH, Berman MM: Solid liver tumours. *Major Probl Clin Surg* 22:1–342, 1977.
70. Wanebo HJ, Semoglou C, Attiyeh F, et al: Surgical management of patients with primary operable colorectal cancer and synchronous liver metastases. *Am J Surg* 135:81–85, 1978.
71. Iwatsuki S, Esquivel CO, Gordon RD, et al: Liver resection for metastatic colorectal cancer. *Surgery* 100:804–809, 1986.
72. Cady B, McDermott WV: Major hepatic resection for metachronous metastases from colon cancer. *Ann Surg* 201: 204–209, 1985.
73. Butler J, Attiyeh FF, Daly JM: Hepatic resection for metastases of the colon and rectum. *Surg Gynecol Obstet* 162:109–113, 1986.
74. Cobourn CS, Makowka L, Langer B, et al: Examination of patient selection and outcome for hepatic resection for metastatic disease. *Surg Gynecol Obstet* 165:239–246, 1987.
75. Cady B, Monson DO, Swinton NW: Survival of patients after colonic resection for carcinoma with simultaneous liver metastases. *Surg Gynecol Obstet* 131:697–700, 1970.
76. Goslin R, Steele G, Zamcheck N, et al: Factors influencing survival in patients with hepatic metastases from adenocarcinoma of the colon or rectum. *Dis Colon Rectum* 25:749–753, 1982.

77. Bengtsson G, Carlsson G, Hafstrom L, et al: Natural history of patients with untreated liver metastases from colorectal cancer. *Am J Surg* 141:586–589, 1981.
78. Langer B: Colorectal cancer: Managing distant metastases. *Can J Surg* 28:419–421, 1985.
79. Bengmark S, Hafstrom L: The natural history of primary and secondary malignant tumours of the liver: I. The prognosis for patients with hepatic metastases from colonic and rectal carcinoma verified by laparotomy. *Cancer* 23:198–202, 1969.
80. Taylor B, Langer B, Falk RE, et al: Role of resection in the management of metastases to the liver. *Can J Surg* 26:215–217, 1983.
81. Adson MA: Resection of liver metastases—When is it worthwhile? *World J Surg* 11:511–520, 1987.
82. Saenz NC, Cady B, McDermott WV, et al: Experience with colorectal carcinoma metastatic to the liver. *Surg Clin North Am* 69:361–371, 1989.
83. Adson MA, Van Heerden JA, Adson MH, et al: Resection of hepatic metastases from colo-rectal cancer. *Arch Surg* 119:647–651, 1984.
84. Logan SE, Meier SJ, Ramming KP, et al: Hepatic resection of metastatic colorectal carcinoma. *Arch Surg* 117:25–28, 1982.
85. Morrow CE, Grage TB, Sutherland DE, et al: Hepatic resection for secondary neoplasms. *Surgery* 92:610–614, 1982.
86. Vogt P, Raab R, Ringe B, et al: Resection of synchronous liver metastases from colorectal cancer. *World J Surg* 15:62–67, 1991.
87. Cady B, Stone, MD: The role of surgical resection of liver metastases in colorectal carcinoma. *Semin Oncol* 18:399–406, 1991.
88. Finlay IG, McArdle CS: Occult hepatic metastases in colorectal carcinoma. *Br J Surg* 73:732–735, 1986.
89. Machi J, Isomoto M, Kurohiji T, et al: Detection of unrecognized liver metastases from colorectal cancers by routine use of operative ultrasonography. *Dis Colon Rectum* 29:405–409, 1986.
90. Clarke MP, Kane RA, Steele G, et al: Prospective comparison of preoperative imaging and intra-operative ultrasonography in the detection of liver tumours. *Surgery* 106:849–855, 1989.
91. Cohen AM: Surgical considerations in patients with cancer of the colon and rectum. *Semin Oncol* 18:381–387, 1991.
92. Cohen AM: Technique for needle biopsy to confirm suspected hepatic metastases at laparotomy. *Surg Gynecol Obstet* 166:281–282, 1988.
93. Schlag P, Hohenberger P, Herfarth C: Resection of liver metastases in colorectal cancer—Competitive analysis of treatment results in synchronous versus metachronous metastases. *Eur J Surg Oncol* 16:360–365, 1990.
94. Thomas R, Barnhill D, Worsham F, et al: Krukenberg tumour of the ovary from an occult appendiceal primary: Case report and literature review. *Obstet Gynecol* 65:95s–98s, 1985.
95. Woodruff JD, Novak ER: The Krukenberg tumour: Study of 48 cases from the Ovarian Tumour Registry. *Obstet Gynecol* 15:351–360, 1960.
96. Birnkrant A, Sampson J, Sugarbaker PH: Ovarian metastasis from colorectal cancer. *Dis Colon Rectum* 29:767–771, 1986.
97. Blamey SL, McDermott FT, Pihl E, Hughes ES: Resected ovarian recurrence from colorectal adenocarcinoma: A study of 13 cases. *Dis Colon Rectum* 24:272–275, 1981.
98. Burt CA: Prophylactic oophorectomy with resection of the large bowel for cancer. *Am J Surg* 82:571–577, 1951.
99. Quan SH, Sehdev MK: Pelvic surgery concomitant with bowel resection for carcinoma. *Surg Clin North Am* 54:881–886, 1974.
100. MacKeigan JM, Ferguson JA: Prophylactic oophorectomy and colorectal cancer in premenopausal patients. *Dis Colon Rectum* 22:401–405, 1979.
101. Graffner HO, Alm PO, Oscarson JE: Prophylactic oophorectomy in colorectal carcinoma. *Am J Surg* 146:233–235, 1983.
102. Cutait R, Lesser ML, Enker WE: Prophylactic oophorectomy in surgery for large-bowel cancer. *Dis Colon Rectum* 26:6–11, 1983.
103. Deddish MR: Surgical procedures for carcinoma of the left colon and rectum, with five-year end results following abdominopelvic dissection of lymph nodes. *Am J Surg* 99:188–190, 1960.
104. Abrams HL, Spiro R, Goldstein N: Metastases in carcinoma: Analysis of 1,000 autopsied cases. *Cancer* 3:74–85, 1950.
105. O'Brien PH, Newton BB, Metcalf JS, Rittenbury MS: Oophorectomy in women with carcinoma of the colon and rectum. *Surg Gynecol Obstet* 153:827–830, 1981.
106. Morrow M, Enker WE: Late ovarian metastases in carcinoma of the colon and rectum. *Arch Surg* 119:1385–1388, 1984.
107. Antoniades K, Spector HB, Hecksher RH: Prophylactic oophorectomy in conjunction with large-bowel resection for cancer. Report of two cases. *Dis Colon Rectum* 20:506–510, 1977.
108. Herrera LO, Ledesma EJ, Natarajan N, et al: Metachronous ovarian metastases from adenocarcinoma of the colon and rectum. *Surg Gynecol Obstet* 154:531–533, 1982.
109. Alford TC, Do HM, Geelhoed GW, et al: Steroid hormone receptors in human cancers. *Cancer* 43:980–984, 1979.
110. Wobbes TH, Beex LV, Koenders AM: Estrogen and progestin receptors in colonic cancer? *Dis Colon Rectum* 27:591–592, 1984.
111. Di Leo A, Linsalata M, Cavallini A, et al: Sex steroid hormone receptors, epidermal growth factor receptor, and polyamines in human colorectal cancer. *Dis Colon Rectum* 35:305–309, 1992.
112. Mason M, Kovalcik P: Ovarian metastases from colon carcinoma. *J Surg Oncol* 17:33–38, 1981.
113. Harcourt KF, Dennis DL: Laparotomy for "ovarian tumours" in unsuspected carcinoma of the colon. *Cancer* 21:1244–1246, 1968.
114. Israel SL, Helsel EV, Hausman DH: The challenge of metastatic ovarian carcinoma. *Am J Obstet Gynecol* 93:1094–1101, 1965.
115. Ballantyne GH, Riegel MM, Wolff BG, Ilstrup DM: Oophorectomy and colon cancer. *Ann Surg* 202:209–214, 1985.
116. Burt CA: Carcinoma of the ovaries secondary to cancer of the colon and rectum. *Dis Colon Rectum* 3:352–357, 1960.
117. Rendleman DF, Gilchrist RK: Indications for oophorectomy in carcinoma of the gastrointestinal tract. *Surg Gynecol Obstet* 109:364–366, 1959.
118. Knoepp LF, Ray JE, Overby I: Ovarian metastases from colorectal carcinoma. *Dis Colon Rectum* 16:305–311, 1973.

PART 9

Treatment of Potentially Curable Colonic Cancer

CHAPTER 49

Overall Survival and Patterns of Failure for Surgery of Colonic Cancer

Herbert C. Hoover, Jr.
Christopher G. Willett

HIGHLIGHTS

The extent of spread at the time of resection of colonic cancer best predicts outcome. Extension beyond the bowel wall and into the regional lymph nodes is of paramount importance. The number of positive lymph nodes inversely relates to prognosis, but the outcome is significantly better in patients with three or less than in those with four or more positive lymph nodes.

Analogous to rectal cancer, lesions of "immobile bowel," namely, the ascending and descending colon and the flexures, may have compromised radial or pericolonic operative margins. Local failure following resection increases as a function of anatomic immobility and with progressive extension of disease through the bowel wall. Local failure is especially prevalent when there is gross extension of tumor into the adjacent fat. Thus, anatomic factors as well as stage are important in estimating the risk of local recurrence and the need for a localized adjuvant treatment such as postoperative radiation therapy. This is especially important, since local failure occurs predominantly in the tumor bed and adjoining structures and not in the lymph nodes.

Overall survival in patients with potentially curable colonic cancer is dependent upon a number of clinical, pathologic, cell cycle, molecular, and biological prognostic factors that have been discussed in previous chapters. Since the extent of spread at the time of surgical exploration and resection best predicts outcome, such data are usually used in reporting overall survival in surgically resected patients. Staging systems have been previously described and will be related to overall survival in this chapter.

Cuthbert Dukes[1] in 1932 proposed a classification for rectal cancer based upon the depth of bowel wall penetration of the tumor and the presence of metastasis to regional lymph nodes. The classification was later modified to include patients with colonic cancer. Numerous modifications of the Dukes classification have been used to report survival data as related to the extent of growth through the bowel wall and into the regional lymph nodes. Unfortunately, the modification of Dukes' classification have varied considerably, making comparison of various reported series difficult or impossible.

Astler and Coller[2] in 1954 published a careful analysis of 352 cases of colonic and rectal cancer staged according to a modification of the Dukes classification by Kirklin et al.[3] in 1949. Their criteria were as follows: A = lesions limited to the mucosa; B_1 = lesions extending into the muscularis propria but not penetrating it, with negative nodes; B_2 = penetrating the muscularis propria, with negative nodes; C = lesions of either B_1 or B_2 type but with lymph node metastasis. Astler and Coller modified it further by dividing Dukes C into C_1, representing tumor limited to the wall with positive nodes, and C_2, representing transmural extension with positive nodes. Distribution of lesions and 5-year survival of Astler and Coller's patients are

Table 49-1
Astler-Coller Series (1940–1944)

Modified Dukes Stage	*No. of cases*	*Percent of cases*	*5-Year survival, %*
A	1	0.28	100
B_1	48	13.64	66.6
B_2	164	46.59	53.9
C_1	14	3.98	42.8
C_2	125	35.51	22.4

SOURCE: From Dukes.[2] With permission.

shown in Table 49-1. Their series reflected an obvious delay in diagnosis, with 82 percent of the patients showing transmural growth and 40 percent having regional metastasis. Their data were graphic evidence that survival progressively declined as the depth of colon wall penetration increased, and that lymph node involvement lessens survival even more dramatically.

The Astler-Coller modification of the Dukes classification has been used for staging in the major series reported since its introduction. The Gunderson-Sosin[4] modification of the Astler-Coller classification adds a B_3 stage, representing extension through the entire bowel wall with adherence or invasion of adjacent organs or structures and with negative nodes. Stage C_3 is identical except the nodes are positive. The tumor/node/metastasis (TNM) system has been jointly agreed to by the International Union Against Cancer (UICC) and The American Joint Committee on Cancer (AJCC) and is currently the staging system recommended to most accurately translate other systems into a standard format. However, the literature to date does not reflect its use. The 5-year survival rates following resection of colonic cancer are reviewed by selected series in Table 49-2. These series were chosen because they had clearly separated colonic cancer from rectal cancer and were clearly broken down by the modified Dukes stages. Interestingly, the same trend toward advanced stages of disease as shown in the Astler-Coller series exists with only 6 percent Dukes A cases, while there are 61 percent Dukes B (B_1 = 12 percent, B_2 = 42 percent, B_3 = 7 percent) and 33 percent Dukes C cases (C_1 = 17 percent, C_2 = 12 percent, C_3 = 4 percent). Unfortunately, most major series do not report data according to the number of positive nodes in Dukes C patients, information that is most likely the best determinant of survival. Cohen[5] makes a convincing argument that all clinical trials of adjuvant therapy of colonic cancer should stratify by the number of involved nodes. While the National Surgical Adjuvant

Table 49-2
Five-Year Survival in Colonic Cancer Patients Treated Only by Surgical Resection

Study	*No. of patients*	*Modified Astler-Coller stage*	*Actuarial 5-year survivals, %*	*Actuarial 10-year survivals, %*
Willett et al.[8]	29	A	90	—
Minsky et al.[9]	52	A	100	—
Michelassi et al.[10]	12	A	92	100
Willett et al.[8]	89	B_1	75	—
Minsky et al.[9]	44	B_1	93	—
Michelassi et al.[10]	37	B_1	100	95
Willett et al.[8]	163	B_2	70	—
GITSG[7]	67	B_2	77	—
Minsky et al.[9]	141	B_2	90	—
Michelassi et al.[10]	218	B_2	83	72
Willett et al.[8]	83	B_3	64	—
Minsky et al.[9]	16	B_3	64	—
Willett et al.[8]		C_1	63	—
Minsky et al.[9]	9	C_1	76	—
GITSG[7]	55	C_1(1–4 nodes)	56	—
		C_2(>4 nodes)	26	—
Michelassi et al.[10]	173	$C_1 + C_2$	49	40
Willett et al.[8]	100	C_2	45	—
Minsky et al.[9]	63	C_2	56	—
Willett et al.[8]	49	C_3	38	—
Minsky et al.[9]	9	C_3	33	—

Breast/Bowel Project (NSABP)[6] and the Gastrointestinal Tumor Study Group (GITSG)[7] subcategorized node-positive patients into two groups: (1) 1 to 4 or (2) 5 or >, Cohen's multivariate data analysis confirmed that the number of positive nodes was related inversely to prognosis, but the optimal dichotomization was (1) 3 or < or (2) 4 or >. In 306 node-positive colon cancer patients who underwent potentially curative resection at Memorial Sloan-Kettering Cancer Center in New York, the Kaplan-Meier 5-year survival with 1 to 3 positive nodes was 66 percent and with 4 or greater was 37 percent (Fig. 49-1). Table 49-3 lists the actuarial 5-year survival for each nodal group.

Although survival rates stage for stage for colon cancer have improved significantly in the 50 years since the publication of the Astler-Coller series, there has been little improvement in the past 10 to 20 years in the results achieved by surgical resection alone. It is unlikely that advances in surgical technique will add further improvements. Clearly, adjuvant therapy is needed to improve on the present accomplishments of surgical resection.

Table 49-3
Actuarial 5-Year Survival and Nodal Status for Colonic Cancer Patient Treated with Resection Only

No. of positive nodes	*Number of patients*	*Five-year survival, %*
1	117	69
2	72	61
3	32	63
4	19	56
5	21	42
≥6	45	27

SOURCE: Cohen et al.[5] With permission.

FAILURE PATTERNS

Unlike the rectum, which is a retroperitoneal and immobile structure without serosa or mesentery, the large bowel (above the peritoneal reflection) has varying degrees of serosal covering, mesentery, and mobility. The ascending and descending colon and hepatic and splenic flexures are partially (and variably) retroperitoneal and immobile structures without a true mesentery and a serosal surface often limited to the anterior wall. At the other extreme, the sigmoid and transverse colon are freely mobile and completely intraperitoneal, having a complete mesentery and serosal covering. The cecum and proximal and distal segments of the sigmoid and transverse colon also have a variable mesentery and mobility. Analogous to rectal carcinoma, lesions of "immobile bowel"—ascending and descending colon and flexures invading through the bowel wall, in particular the lateral and posterior wall—may have compromised radial or pericolonic

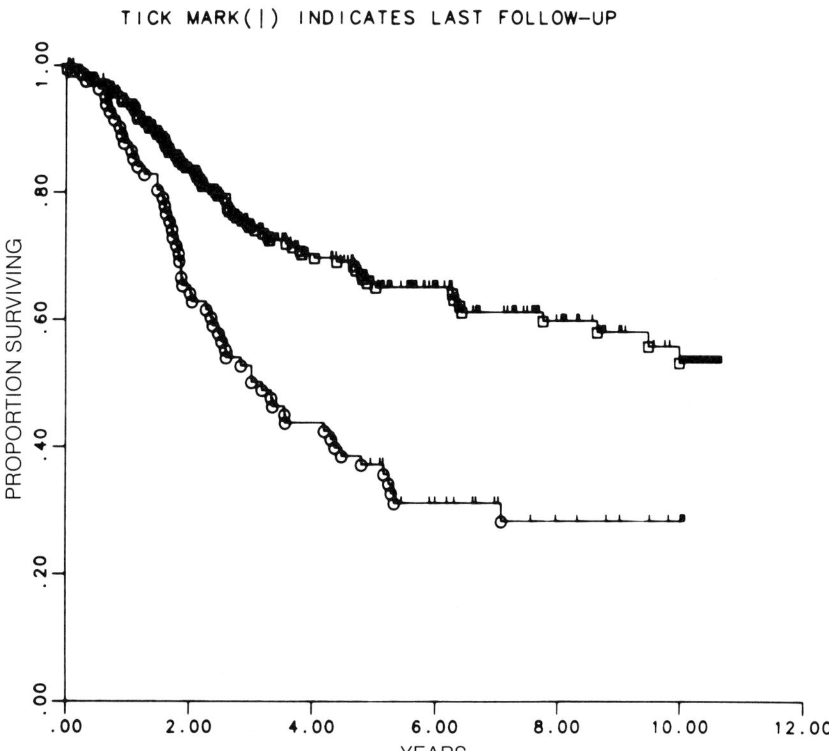

FIG. 49-1. Kaplan-Meier survival for colonic cancer with 1 to 3 and 4 or more positive node dichotomy. □, 1 to 3 positive nodes (out of 221 patients, 143 censored); ○, 4+ positive nodes (out of 85 patients, 29 censored); tick mark(|) indicates last follow-up. (From Cohen et al.[5] Reproduced by permission.)

operative margins, as often only a small surgical margin is possible. Lesions extending anteriorly to the serosal surface may also be at risk for peritoneal spread. For tumors of mobile bowel—sigmoid and transverse colon—the surgeon can usually obtain a wide circumferential margin and the risk of a subtotal resection is usually limited to situations when there is tumor invasion or adherence to adjoining structures. The risk of peritoneal seeding may be increased in advanced lesions arising from this portion of bowel. Because of their variable mesentery and retroperitoneal position, tumors arising in the cecum and proximal and distal portions of the transverse and sigmoid colon (partially mobile bowel) with extracolonic extension may have compromised radial resection margins.

A number of recent studies have examined the failure patterns of colonic carcinoma following resection with curative intent.[8–15] Gunderson et al.[11] reported on 91 patients with predominantly stage C_1–C_3 disease (73 patients) who had reoperation after initial resection and observed a 48 percent incidence of locoregional failure. For patients with stages C_2 and C_3 disease, a further analysis was done stratifying patients according to the anatomic mobility of the primary site: mobile bowel (transverse colon and cecum) and immobile bowel (ascending and descending colon and flexures). Local failure increased as a function of anatomic immobility and with progressive extension of disease through the bowel wall. For patients with stage C_2 disease with microscopic extension into fat, local failure occurred in 13 percent of tumors located in mobile bowel and 29 percent of tumors located in immobile bowel. For patients with stage C_2 disease with gross extension into fat, local failure was seen in 22 percent of tumors located in mobile bowel and 72 percent of those in immobile bowel.

In the Massachusetts General Hospital (MGH) series of 533 patients undergoing resection of colonic cancer, both the 5-year survival and incidence of local failure were closely correlated to stage (Table 49-4).[8,12,13] The determinate incidence of local failure according to stage was as follows: A, 1/29 (3 percent); B_1, 2/89 (2 percent); B_2, 18/163 (11 percent); B_3, 25/83 (30 percent); C_1, 0/20 (0 percent); C_2, 32/100 (32 percent); C_3, 24/49 (49 percent). Local failure occurred predominantly in the tumor bed and adjoining structures (82 percent) and not by nodal failures (18 percent). In this series, stratification according to stage and primary site was also done (Table 49-5). For all stage A, B_1 and C_1 tumors, the risk of local failure was low, whereas a moderately high incidence of local failure was seen for patients with stage C_2 and C_3 disease. Patients with stage B_3 disease at most sites and selected B_2 sites (high and low sigmoid and splenic and hepatic flexures) experienced local failure rates of at least 16 percent. Thus, anatomic location as well as stage may be important in estimating the risk for local recurrence and the need for a localized adjuvant treatment such as postoperative radiation therapy. Adjuvant postoperative radiotherapy to the tumor bed and adjoining structures could be considered for the following subgroups of patients after resection of colonic carcinoma: (1) patients with stage B_3 and C_3 disease at all sites within the bowel and (2) patients with stage C_2 disease at all sites except the midsigmoid and midtransverse colon.

Although local failure is common after resection of colonic carcinoma, distant metastases also occur fre-

Table 49-4
Determine 5-Year Disease-Free Survival and Local Failure after Surgery Alone for Carcinoma of the Colon (Massachusetts General Hospital)

Stage	*Total*	*5-year DFS,[a] %*	*Local failure,%*
A	29	90	3
B_1	89	75	2
B_2	163	70	11
B_3	83	64	30
C_1	20	63	0
C_2	100	45	32
C_3	49	38	49

[a]DFS = disease-free survival.

Table 49-5
Colonic Cancer Incidence of Local Failure according to Location and Stage (Massachusetts General Hospital)

Site	*B_2*	*B_3*	*C_2*	*C_3*	*Total LF*
Group 1[a]	—	15/61 (25)	20/58 (34)	17/35 (49)	52/154 (40)
Group 2[b]	13/61 (21)[c]	10/22 (45)	12/42 (29)	7/14 (50)	42/139 (30)
Total	—	25/83 (30)	32/100 (32)	24/49 (49)	94/293 (32)

[a]Group 1: Cecum, ascending, mid sigmoid, transverse, descending colon.

[b]Group 2: High sigmoid, low sigmoid, hepatic and splenic flexures.

[c]Numbers in parentheses indicate percentage.

Table 49-6
Stage versus Site of Abdominal Failure (Massachusetts General Hospital)

		Liver		*Peritoneal surface*		*Abdominal lymph nodes*	
Stage	*Total*	*Only*	*Total*	*Only*	*Total*	*Only*	*Total*
A	29	0 (0)[a]	0 (0)	1 (3)	1 (3)	0 (0)	0 (0)
B_1	89	2 (2)	6 (7)	0 (0)	0 (0)	0 (0)	0 (0)
B_2	16	36 (4)	20 (12)	2 (1)	6 (4)	0 (0)	0 (0)
B_3	83	9 (11)	15 (18)	2 (2)	3 (4)	1 (1)	5 (6)
C_1	20	1 (5)	3 (15)	0 (0)	0 (0)	0 (0)	1 (5)
C_2	100	7 (7)	29 (29)	2 (2)	16 (16)	0 (0)	5 (5)
C_3	49	6 (12)	15 (31)	2 (4)	7 (14)	2 (4)	7 (14)
Total	533	31 (6)	88 (17)	9 (2)	33 (6)	3 (1)	21 (4)

[a]Numbers in parentheses indicate percentage.

quently in advanced-stage patients. In the MGH series, the incidence of distant metastases was 25 percent (131/533).[8] Only 21 patients had failure limited to extraabdominal sites, while 110 patients failed abdominally (liver, peritoneal surface, or abdominal lymph nodes). Of these 110 patients, 50 failed in association with extraabdominal metastases and 60 failed exclusively in the abdomen. The rate of distant metastases rose from 3 percent for stage A disease to 45 percent for stage C_3 disease. The highest incidence of abdominal failure occurred in stage B_3, C_2, and C_3 patients with rates between 24 and 43 percent, but the rate was only 15 percent for stages B_2 and C_1. Within the abdomen, the liver was the most common site of metastasis (Table 49-6). The highest failure rates occurred in C_2 and C_3 patients with liver failure rates of 29 and 31 percent, respectively. The incidence of failure in peritoneal surface was highest in stage C_2 and C_3 disease—16 and 14 percent respectively—but less than 4 percent for less advanced tumors. Based on these data, adjuvant treatment to the liver or peritoneal surfaces could be considered for patients with stage B_3, C_2, and C_3 disease.

REFERENCES

1. Dukes CE: The classification of cancer of the rectum. *J Pathol Bacteriol* 35:323–332, 1932.
2. Astler VB, Coller FA: The prognostic significance of direct extension of carcinoma of the colon and rectum. *Ann Surg* 139:846–851, 1954.
3. Kirklin JW, Docherty MB, Waugh JW: The role of the peritoneal reflection and the prognosis of carcinoma of the rectum and sigmoid colon. *Surg Gynecol Obstet* 88:326–331, 1949.
4. Gunderson LL, Sosin H: Areas of failure found at reoperation (second or symptomatic look) following "curative surgery" for adenocarcinoma of the rectum: Clinical pathologic correlation and implications for adjuvant therapy. *Cancer* 34:1278–1292, 1974.
5. Cohen AM, Tremiterra S, Candela F, et al: Prognosis of node-positive colon cancer. *Cancer* 67:1859–1861, 1991.
6. Wolmark N, Fisher B, Wienand HS: The prognostic value of the modifications of the Dukes' C class of colorectal cancer: An analysis of the NSABP clinical trials. *Ann Surg* 203:115–122, 1986.
7. Gastrointestinal Tumor Study Group: Adjuvant therapy of colon cancer: Result of a prospectively randomized trial. *N Engl J Med* 310:737–743, 1984.
8. Willett CG, Tepper JE, Cohen AM, et al: Failure patterns following curative resection of colonic carcinoma. *Ann Surg* 200:685–690, 1984.
9. Minsky BD, Mies C, Rich TA, et al: Potentially curative surgery of colon cancer: Patterns of failure in survival. *J Clin Oncol* 6:106–118, 1988.
10. Michelassi F, Ayala JJ, Balestracci T, et al: Verification of a new clinical pathologic staging system for colorectal adenocarcinoma. *Ann Surg* 214:11–18, 1991.
11. Gunderson LL, Sossin H, Levitt S: Extrapelvic colon: Areas of failure in a reoperation series: Implications for adjuvant therapy. *Int J Radiat Oncol Biol Phys* 11:731–742, 1985.
12. Willett CG, Tepper JE, Cohen AM, et al: Local failure following curative resection of colonic adenocarcinoma. *Int J Radiat Oncol Biol Phys* 10:645–651, 1984.
13. Willett CG, Tepper JE, Cohen AM, et al.: Obstructive and perforative colonic carcinoma: Patterns of failure. *J Clin Oncol* 3:379–384, 1985.
14. Olson RM, Perencevich NP, Malcolm AW, et al.: Patterns of recurrence following curative resection of adenocarcinoma of the colon and rectum. *Cancer* 45:2969–2974, 1980.
15. Cass AW, Pfaff FA, Million RR: Patterns of recurrence following surgery alone for adenocarcinoma of the colon and rectum. *Cancer* 37:2861–2869, 1976.

CHAPTER 50

Adjuvant Therapies Overview

Alfred M. Cohen
Michael A. Friedman

The considerable improvements in survival obtained in the treatment of patients with colonic cancer have been accomplished by early detection and better staging as well as by improved therapy. Despite the fact that a majority of patients who present with colonic cancer successfully undergo surgical resection of all gross disease, the cure rate with extirpation alone is approximately one-half for node-positive patients and two-thirds for node-negative patients. Over 100,000 Americans each year are diagnosed with colonic cancer, and adjuvant therapy offers us the opportunity to save a large number of additional lives.

As with all adjuvant treatment strategies, analyses of the patterns of failure are essential in the construction of improved adjuvant programs. These data are presented in detail in the preceding chapter. In summary, suture-line recurrence is rare, with the majority of cancer-related deaths occurring from widespread disease. The major sites of clinical failure are the liver and lungs, with frequent subclinical involvement of the retroperitoneum, the retroperitoneal nodes, and the peritoneal cavity.

Several surgical procedures should be considered as part of the broad strategy of adjuvant therapy. The ovaries are a potential site of failure, and "prophylactic oophorectomy" could be considered an adjuvant procedure, removing potential sites of micrometastasis. The data relevant to this issue are discussed in Chap. 48. Patients with inherited cancer propensity or those with multiple cancers or cancer and multiple polyps may be candidates for subtotal colectomy. This, however, is a form of prophylactic rather than adjuvant therapy.

Since hematogenous or transcoelomic spread are the major mechanisms of dissemination, systemic therapies have been the primary consideration for adjuvant therapy. Isolated local/regional failure or combined systemic/local failure is a relatively more common problem encountered in the management of patients with rectal cancer than it is for those with colonic cancer. Hence, systemic cytotoxic chemotherapy has been the fundamental strategy for colonic adjuvant treatment. In the 1960s, perioperative therapy was first utilized; in the 1970s, various approaches with single-agent fluorouracil were introduced; and in the early 1980s, fluorouracil was combined with other agents. Ironically, despite 30 years of clinical research, there has not been a proper clinical trial of intensive single-agent fluorouracil versus surgery alone with a sample size and adequate power to detect a 10 percent survival benefit. However, as analyzed in detail in the chapter that follows, there is strong evidence that the use of fluorouracil combined with levamisole is effective in increasing the disease-free and overall survival in node-positive colon cancer patients.[1] These benefits can be achieved with minuscule mortality and modest morbidity rates. Recently completed trials comparing fluorouracil/levamisole with several fluorouracil/leucovorin programs are maturing, with pending analyses of morbidity and survival.

Since two-thirds of patients with recurrent colonic cancer have liver metastases and one-third of these patients appear to have isolated hepatic metastases at autopsy, it is not surprising that regional chemotherapy has been utilized as an adjuvant strategy. Based on pharmacokinetics and vascular physiology data, for advanced hepatic metastatic disease regional therapy is most advantageous using the hepatic artery route. However, in order to deal most effectively with microscopic metastatic disease (<1 mm), the portal vein may be more appropriate and logistically more realistic for adjuvant therapy. Chapter 52 delineates the clinical trials associated with this approach, suggesting survival benefit in several randomized trials. However, analysis of patterns of failure suggests that the benefit may be due more to a systemic effect than to a regional one.[2,3] Since portal vein therapy is routinely given not only as subsequent adjuvant treatment but also in the immediate postoperative period, an Intergroup trial of immediate postoperative systemic fluorouracil infusion (combined with subsequent standard systemic therapy) has been initiated to define this important issue.

Although clinically local/regional recurrence as an isolated phenomenon is uncommon, autopsy data suggest that this failure pattern is recognizable. With modern radiation therapy technique, local/regional radiation to moderate therapeutic doses can be safely delivered. An ongoing randomized clinical trial is exploring the potential benefit of adjuvant regional radiation in addition to systemic fluorouracil/levamisole for that subgroup of patients at highest risk of this type of metastatic pattern.

With large numbers of patients with a common malignancy enrolled in national adjuvant trials, it may be possible to demonstrate relatively small incremental survival benefits that achieve "statistical significance." Under these circumstances, it is imperative to analyze the morbidity, mortality, and costs associated with such programs. Sample-size decisions in current studies may allow the detection of a one-fifth reduction in cancer mortality. However, this means that in the treatment of node-positive colonic cancer patients, the overall survival increment is only approximately 10 percent. Such benefits have to be carefully weighed against any harm done to the large number of patients who are not benefited by such treatments. Broader comparative analyses are essential. In addition, assessments of the use of inpatient versus outpatient services, bolus versus infusional strategies, and return to work and other quality-of-life issues will be as important as the actual drug treatment costs.

Cost-effectiveness issues in the use of adjuvant fluorouracil/levamisole have been elegantly addressed by Brown and colleagues.[4] The reader is referred to this article, which uses computer simulation of a patient population cross section to (1) estimate the cost-effectiveness of such treatment, (2) estimate the social return on the research investment made by the National Institutes of Health, and (3) evaluate the impact of quality-of-life adjustment on such estimates.

In addition to the comparative clinical trials under way and planned for the remainder of this decade, an equally important aspect of analysis is the improved selection of patients at high enough risk for micrometastases to justify adjuvant therapy. The fluorouracil/levamisole Intergroup trial in node-negative colonic cancer patients shows a consistent trend toward adjuvant benefit, but the end results with surgery alone are so favorable as to make reaching traditional statistical significance difficult, even with increased maturation of the data.

Ruling out occult (but detectable) metastatic foci by intraoperative ultrasound of the liver[5] or with intraoperative radioimmunodetection using iodine 125–labeled monoclonal antibody and a hand-held gamma-detecting probe[6] may be helpful adjuncts. Multivariate pathologic analyses with computer-assisted prognostic determinants will likely refine or even replace standard TNM staging.[7] Such analyses are able to quantify the adverse prognostic impact of age >75 years, pathologic involvement of the apical node, transmural penetration through the serosa, venous invasion, high grade, and male gender. Serosal cytology appears to offer a quick an inexpensive method of determining serosal penetration.[8] Preoperative measurement of serum carcinoembryonic antigen is useful.[9] In order to better define the risk profile for such patients, ploidy[10,11] and p53[12,13] analyses on fixed tissue can be done if the nodes are pathologically negative. It is likely that additional molecular and biological determinants will be useful in prognostic stratification.

In summary, clinical trials over the past decade have produced adjuvant therapies in colonic cancer capable of saving thousands of lives each year. Issues of patient selection and improvement of such programs with acceptable morbidity and appropriate cost-effectiveness will be the challenge for the next decade.

REFERENCES

1. Moertel CG, Fleming TR, Macdonald JS, et al: Levamisole and fluorouracil for adjuvant therapy of resected colon carcinoma. *N Engl J Med* 322:352–358, 1990.
2. Wolmark N, Rockette H, Wickerham DL, et al: Adjuvant therapy of Dukes' A, B, and C adenocarcinoma of the colon with portal-vein fluorouracil hepatic infusion: Preliminary results of national surgical adjuvant breast and bowel project protocol C-02. *J Clin Oncol* 8:1466–1475, 1990.
3. Fielding LP, Hittinger R, Grace RH, et al: Randomised controlled trial of adjuvant chemotherapy by portal-vein perfusion after curative resection for colorectal adenocarcinoma. *Lancet* 340:502–506, 1992.
4. Brown ML, Nayfield SG, Shibley LM: Adjuvant therapy for stage III colon cancer: Economics returns to research and cost-effectiveness of treatment. *J Natl Cancer Inst* 86:424–430, 1994.
5. Machi J, Isomoto H, Kurohiji T, et al: Accuracy of intraoperative ultrasonography in diagnosing liver metastasis from colorectal cancer: Evaluation with postoperative follow-up results. *World J Surg* 15:551–557, 1991.
6. Arnold MW, Schneebaum S, Berens A, et al: Radioimmunoguided surgery challenges traditional decision making in patients with primary colorectal cancer. *Surgery* 112:624–629, 1992.
7. Newland RC, Dent OF, Lyttle MNB, et al: Pathologic determinants of survival associated with colorectal cancer with lymph node metastases: A multivariate analysis of 579 patients. *Cancer* 73:2076–2082, 1994.
8. Zeng Z, Cohen AM, Hajdu S, et al: Serosal cytologic study to determine free mesothelial penetration of intraperitoneal colon cancer. *Cancer* 70:737–740, 1992.
9. Arnaud JP, Koehl C, Adloff M: Carcinoembryonic antigen (CEA) in diagnosis and prognosis of colorectal carcinoma. *Dis Colon Rectum* 23:141–144, 1980.

10. Witzig TE, Loprinzi CL, Gonchoroff NJ, et al: DNA ploidy and cell kinetic measurements as predictors of recurrence and survival in stages B2 and colorectal adenocarcinoma. *Cancer* 68:879–888, 1991.
11. Moran MR, Rothenberger DA, Gallo RA, et al: A predictive model for distant metastases in rectal cancer using DNA ploidy studies. *Am J Surg* 163:599–601, 1992.
12. Scott N, Sagar P, Stewart J, et al: p53 in colorectal cancer: Clinicopathological correlation and prognostic significance. *Br J Cancer* 63:317–319, 1991.
13. Remvikos Y, Laurent-Purg P, Salmon RJ, et al: Simultaneous monitoring of p53 protein and DNA content of colorectal adenocarcinomas by flow cytometry. *Int J Cancer* 45:450–456, 1990.

CHAPTER 51

Systemic Adjuvant Therapy of Colonic Cancer

Michael J. O'Connell

HIGHLIGHTS

Until recently, there was no convincing evidence that postoperative systemic adjuvant therapy was effective in decreasing the risk of tumor relapse and death in patients undergoing surgery for primary colonic cancer. However, mature data from two prospectively randomized clinical trials has clearly established that 5-fluorouracil (5-FU) combined with levamisole can substantially improve relapse-free and overall survival in patients with node-positive stage III (stage C) colonic cancer. Emerging data suggests that 5-FU combined with leucovorin may also be an effective systemic surgical adjuvant therapy, although follow-up of these clinical trials is not currently sufficient to accurately assess impact on 5-year survival.

CONTROVERSIES

The dosage and administration schedule of 5-FU combined with levamisole in the effective adjuvant therapy regimen was chosen empirically rather than being based on preclinical laboratory observations or hypotheses. Further, the mechanism underlying the cytotoxic interaction between levamisole and 5-FU has not been clearly defined. Thus, the optimal dose and schedule of 5-FU and levamisole given in combination as surgical adjuvant therapy may not have been identified.

Some have questioned the contribution of levamisole to the effectiveness of the regimen comprising 5-FU plus levamisole, since levamisole alone has no apparent antitumor activity in patients with colonic cancer. The role of levamisole is being evaluated in two surgical adjuvant trials which recently completed patient accrual. These studies will directly compare the standard 5-FU plus levamisole regimen with a drug combination that does not include levamisole (5-FU and leucovorin, given in one of two different administration schedules). These studies will also evaluate 5-FU combined with both leucovorin and levamisole to determine whether the use of two 5-FU–modulating agents in combination will provide additional benefit.

The optimal timing of initiation and duration of adjuvant therapy is not known. The studies that established the efficacy of 5-FU and levamisole began treatment 3 to 5 weeks following surgery and continued treatment for 1 year. However, with other solid tumors such as breast cancer, it has been demonstrated that 6 months of chemotherapy is as effective as longer periods of treatment. A controlled surgical adjuvant trial randomizing patients to receive either 12 months or 6 months of postoperative chemotherapy has completed patient accrual and should provide valuable information to address this issue. Other studies will evaluate a 7-day course of 5-FU given in the immediate postoperative period.

Postoperative management of patients with node-negative stage II (modified Astler-Coller stages B_2 and B_3) colonic cancer remains controversial. Although the intergroup trial of the standard regimen of 5-FU and levamisole demonstrated some improvement in time-to-tumor relapse in comparison with surgery alone (84 versus 77 percent tumor-free at 3½ years), these results were of borderline statistical significance ($p = .06$). Likewise, there was no improvement in patient survival. Some studies have suggested that a profile comprising histopathologic characteristics of the primary tumor (i.e., T stage) and DNA flow cytometry pattern (ploidy status and cell proliferative index) may be useful in identifying high- and low-risk node-negative colonic cancer patients. Such a profile might be helpful in clinical decision making with regard to the use of postoperative adjuvant systemic chemotherapy.

FUTURE DIRECTIONS

There is considerable interest in modifying the dose and schedule of levamisole to optimize its antitumor interaction with 5-FU. Cell culture experiments have indicated a dose-dependent enhancement of 5-FU cytotoxicity with increasing concentrations of levamisole against human colonic cancer cells in vitro. A pilot study suggests that the dose of levamisole may be safely increased five- to sixfold above the level given in the standard adjuvant therapy regimen in combination with 5-FU and leucovorin. The hypothesis that this high-dose levamisole regimen will be more effective than a standard-dose levamisole regimen as postoperative adjuvant therapy is now being tested in a controlled trial.

There is increasing interest in testing continuous-infusion methods of 5-FU administration in the surgical adjuvant setting for patients with colonic cancer. This interest is based in part upon preliminary data from a national intergroup trial suggesting that including continuous infusion 5-FU as a component of postoperative adjuvant therapy for patients with high-risk rectal cancer significantly decreases the tumor relapse rate compared to regimens employing 5-FU given exclusively by bolus administration. Such continuous-infusion 5-FU schedules may also be tested in combination with modulating agents such as levamisole and/or leucovorin.

Finally, dramatic insights into the biology of colonic cancer have been afforded by recent advances in molecular biology. With a more precise understanding of the malignant process at the molecular level, new targets for pharmacologic intervention may be elucidated which will lead to entirely new treatment strategies for systemic adjuvant therapy of colonic cancer in the future.

SINGLE-AGENT CHEMOTHERAPY

The use of single-agent postoperative systemic adjuvant chemotherapy for colonic cancer is primarily of historical interest at this point in time. Early studies conducted by a university hospital cooperative group[1] and the Veterans Administration Surgical Oncology Group (VASOG)[2] evaluated the alkylating agent thiotepa. This agent, which was not effective in the treatment of advanced colorectal cancer, was similarly ineffective when used as a postoperative adjuvant.

The fluorinated pyrimidines 5-FU and fluorodeoxyuridine (FUDR) were extensively studied as single agents in a series of randomized trials conducted by VASOG[3–6] and the Central Oncology Group (COG).[7] Disease-free and overall survival in the patient groups receiving chemotherapy were compared with the experience of the groups treated with surgery alone. The chemotherapy regimens consisted of two intravenous courses of FUDR or 5-FU, repeated 5-day courses of 5-FU at 6- to 8-week intervals for 18 months, or 5-FU given in a single intravenous loading course followed by weekly injections over a period of 1 year.

None of these studies indicated a statistically significant improvement in survival among patients receiving postoperative adjuvant chemotherapy compared with randomized controls treated with surgery alone. Some of these trials indicated a slight trend toward improved survival among patients receiving adjuvant therapy, and statistically significant survival advantages were seen within certain patient subsets. These trends and retrospective subset analyses could not be considered to provide adequate scientific evidence of therapeutic benefit. Taken as a group, these studies failed to establish a role for single-agent fluourinated pyrimidine therapy in the management of colorectal cancer.

There is interest among several groups in further evaluating single-agent 5-FU given in the immediate postoperative period by continuous intravenous infusion for 7 days. This interest is based upon the theoretical consideration that chemotherapy given early in the perioperative period might be more successful in eradicating microscopic foci of malignant cells than similar treatment given after tumor implantation and growth has advanced. In addition, some studies of perioperative portal vein infusions of 5-FU have suggested a possible improvement in time to progression and in survival, even though the incidence of hepatic metastases was not reduced compared to randomized control patients.[8] This suggests a possible systemic treatment effect. The value of perioperative systemic infusions of 5-FU is currently being addressed in several randomized clinical trials but has not yet been established.

Preliminary data from a national intergroup trial of postoperative combined-modality therapy for patients with high-risk rectal cancer suggests that the administration of protracted continuous-infusion of 5-FU as a component of therapy improves time to relapse as well as survival by comparison with 5-FU given solely by rapid intravenous injection.[9] This observation, coupled with reports of improved objective tumor response rates with protracted infusions of 5-FU in some studies of patients with advanced colorectal cancer, provides a rationale for the investigation of this method of 5-FU administration with or without the addition of modulating agents such as leucovorin or levamisole as adjuvant therapy for colonic cancer.

COMBINATION CHEMOTHERAPY

5-FU plus Semustine Regimens

The use of several cytotoxic agents with different mechanisms of action and nonoverlapping toxicities given in combination was found to produce major advances in the treatment of malignancies such as Hodgkin's disease. Early studies combining 5-FU with semustine (methyl CCNU) and vincristine based on this strategy suggested improved objective tumor response rates in patients with advanced colorectal cancer.[10] Preclinical studies of murine colonic adenocarcinomas also suggested an enhanced adjuvant effect when semustine was combined with 5-FU. Based on these observations, a series of controlled trials of 5-FU and semustine with or without vincristine was conducted by various cooperative groups including the Gastrointestinal Tumor Study Group (GITSG),[11] VASOG,[12] Southwest Oncology Group (SWOG),[13] Eastern Cooperative Oncology Group (ECOG),[14] and National Surgical Adjuvant Breast and Bowel Project (NSABP).[15] The GITSG, VASOG, and SWOG studies failed to demonstrate a significant treatment benefit for the groups of patients randomly assigned to receive 5-FU plus semustine chemotherapy compared to control patients treated with surgery alone. Likewise, the ECOG study indicated no advantage for 5-FU plus semustine compared to single-agent 5-FU. The NSABP trial indicated a small benefit in disease-free and overall survival at a borderline level of statistical significance for patients receiving 5-FU plus semustine plus vincristine compared to untreated controls. Several cases of leukemia and other blood dyscrasias attributed to delayed semustine toxicity were reported in these trials.

The overall results of this set of clinical trials failed to establish the efficacy of adjuvant therapy for colonic cancer based on 5-FU plus semustine. These studies were valuable, however, in establishing the mechanisms with which to study large groups of patients so as to assure adequate sample size to detect clinically meaningful improvements in survival and to establish appropriate quality-control procedures. The importance of a randomized study design using a group of patients treated with surgery alone was also highlighted by these trials, since control patients participating in these studies who did not receive any adjuvant therapy were found to have substantially superior survival compared to historical series reported in the medical literature.

5-FU plus Levamisole

The combination of 5-FU and levamisole was developed as a systemic adjuvant therapy for colonic cancer by the North Central Cancer Treatment Group (NCCTG) in 1978.[16] Levamisole was chosen for study on the basis of its immunostimulatory effects, antineoplastic activity in some animal model systems, and positive results from a small surgical adjuvant trial conducted by Verhaegen et al.[17] which suggested a survival benefit for patients receiving levamisole postoperatively compared to others treated with surgery alone. The schedule of 5-FU chosen (a single intravenous loading course followed by weekly injections for 1 year) was based on the earlier adjuvant therapy trial conducted by COG[7] which showed a trend (not statistically significant) toward survival improvement in patients treated with this regimen. The specific administration schedule of 5-FU and levamisole in combination was therefore chosen on a purely empiric basis (see Table 51-1).

Table 51-1
Dosage and Administration Schedule of 5-FU and Levamisole Given as Postoperative Adjuvant Therapy[a]

Drug	*Dose*	*Route*	*Schedule*
5-FU	450 mg/m^2	Rapid intravenous injection	Daily for 5 consecutive days, then once weekly beginning on day 28
Levamisole	50 mg tid	Oral	Daily for 3 consecutive days, repeated every 2 weeks

[a]Treatment initiated 3 to 5 weeks following surgery and continued for a total duration of 1 year.

Patients eligible for this trial included those who had undergone complete gross resection of a colorectal cancer which had extended through the muscularis to invade serosa or pericolonic fat (stage B_2 or B_3; $T_{3\text{-}4}N_0M_0$) or had metastasized to regional lymph nodes (stage C; $T_{1-4}N_{1-3}M_0$). Patients were stratified according to depth of tumor invasion, number of positive regional lymph nodes, and anatomic location within the large bowel. Randomization was carried out within 5 weeks following surgery to one of three options: (1) observation; (2) levamisole alone, (3) levamisole plus 5-FU. Levamisole was given in the same dose schedule in treatment arms 2 and 3 as indicated in Table 51-1. Treatment was continued for 1 year.

Of the 408 patients, 401 (98.3 percent) entered on this trial were eligible. Two-thirds of the patients had stage C disease. Median follow-up was over 7 years at the time of publication. Levamisole plus 5-FU, and to a lesser extent levamisole alone, reduced cancer recurrence in comparison with no adjuvant therapy. These differences, after correction for imbalances in prognostic variables, were only suggestive for levamisole alone (p = .05) but were quite significant for levamisole plus 5-FU (p = .003). Furthermore, an improvement in survival was seen in stage C patients treated with levamisole and 5-FU (p = .03).

The NCCTG trial provided suggestive evidence of therapeutic benefit for postoperative adjuvant therapy, particularly for stage C patients treated with levamisole plus 5-FU. The results were not considered definitive, however. Therefore, a confirmatory national intergroup study was initiated by NCCTG, SWOG, and ECOG in 1984 to further evaluate these treatment regimens.[18] Patient selection for this intergroup trial was similar to that for the earlier NCCTG study with the exception that patients with rectal cancer were specifically excluded. The dosage and administration schedules for the levamisole alone and levamisole plus 5-FU regimens were identical to those for the NCCTG study. However, patients with node-negative stage B_2 or B_3 tumors were randomized to one of two treatment options: observation or levamisole plus 5-FU. Patients with stage C tumors were separately randomized to the three arms of the earlier NCCTG study: observation, levamisole alone, or levamisole plus 5-FU.

A total of 1296 patients entered this trial. Of the 325 stage B_2 or B_3 patients, 318 (97.8 percent) were eligible, as were 929 (95.7 percent) of the 971 stage C patients. Median follow-up at the time of publication was 3 years. Among patients with stage C disease, therapy with levamisole and 5-FU produced a highly significant improvement in recurrence-free interval (p = .0002; Fig. 51-1) and patient survival (p = .006; Fig. 51-2). These improvements in time to recurrence and patient survival were even more pronounced in fully mature analyses performed with a median follow-up in

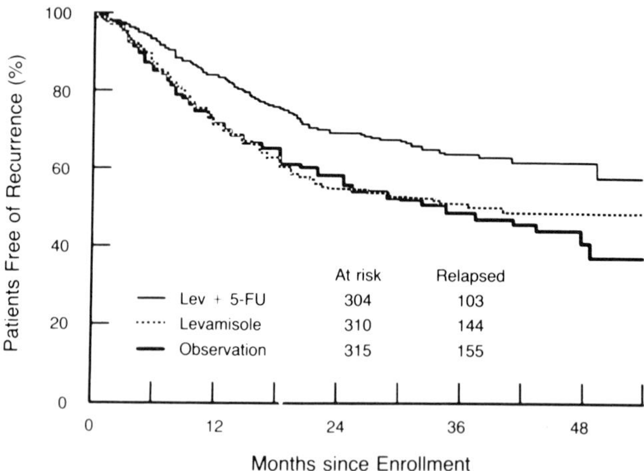

FIG. 51-1. Recurrence-free interval for stage C patients managed with levamisole plus 5-FU, levamisole alone, or observation following surgical resection. (From Moertel et al.[18] Reprinted by permission of *The New England Journal of Medicine* 322:355, 1990.)

excess of 5 years.[19] No benefit was associated with levamisole alone. Toxicity of the levamisole and 5-FU combination consisted of nausea, vomiting, stomatitis, diarrhea, dermatitis, arthralgia, and mood-altering effects. These reactions were usually not severe. One patient among the 304 patients treated with levamisole plus 5-FU in this trial died of chemotherapy-related leukopenia and sepsis.

A National Institutes of Health Consensus Development Panel has endorsed this treatment for stage III (Dukes C) colonic cancer patients,[20] and the Food and Drug Administration has approved levamisole in combination with 5-FU for this indication in the United States.

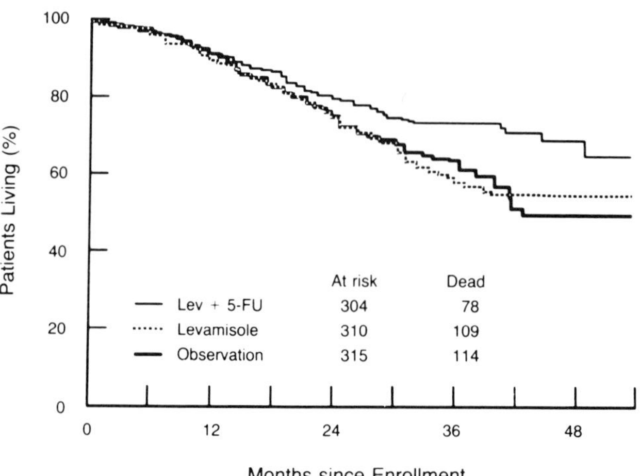

FIG. 51-2. Survival for stage C patients. (From Moertel et al.[18] Reprinted by permission of *The New England Journal of Medicine* 322:357, 1990.)

Among those with stage B_2 or B_3 disease, 84 percent of patients who received levamisole plus 5-FU and 77 percent of patients who underwent observation were free of tumor recurrence at 3½ years. These differences were not statistically significant, however (p = .06). No survival benefit was associated with treatment with levamisole plus 5-FU, perhaps because of a disproportionate number of deaths due to causes not associated with recurrence on this treatment arm. Thus, this study did not clearly establish the efficacy of levamisole plus 5-FU for this relatively good-prognosis cohort of node-negative patients.

The use of flow cytometry to determine DNA content (ploidy) and cell proliferation indices on tumor specimens has been found to be of value as an adjunct to traditional surgical and histopathologic staging in determining prognosis for patients with resectable primary colonic cancer.[21] Aneuploid tumors and those with a high proliferative index (the sum of the percent of cells in S phase plus G2M phase greater than 20 percent) have a worse prognosis independent of Dukes' stage. It has been possible to subdivide patients with stage II colon cancer into high- and low-risk groups based upon ploidy status and T stage.[22] Patients with aneuploid tumors and/or those with T_4 lesions (perforation of the colonic wall or adherence to or invasion into adjacent anatomic structures) had a 39 percent chance of tumor recurrence, contrasted with patients with diploid T_3 tumors (penetration through muscularis but no perforation, adherence, or invasion), who had a 12 percent recurrence rate. Patients with high-risk node-negative colonic cancer may reasonably be considered for postoperative adjuvant therapy, but the efficacy of treatment has not been proven by controlled trial in this specific subset of patients.

5-FU plus Leucovorin

Preclinical studies have clearly indicated that leucovorin (folinic acid) can increase the cytotoxic effect of 5-FU against cultured tumor cells. Multiple clinical trials (reviewed elsewhere) have established a significant increase in objective tumor response rates, and some have indicated extension of median survival time with 5-FU plus leucovorin compared to single-agent 5-FU for patients with advanced colorectal cancer. Three separate controlled trials of different administration schedules of 5-FU and leucovorin given as postoperative adjuvant therapy for patients with colonic cancer are being conducted by NSABP;[23] NCCTG, ECOG, and SWOG;[24] and the National Clinical Trials Group of Canada (NCIC) in collaboration with a consortium of European investigators.[25] The preliminary results from these trials indicate a significant improvement in time to relapse. Although an improvement in long-term survival may reasonably be anticipated, follow-up is not currently sufficient to confirm that these observations will translate into a significant improvement in 5-year survival.

IMMUNOTHERAPY

To date there is no conclusive evidence that immunotherapy of any type is effective as adjuvant therapy for colon cancer. Although levamisole is known to have a variety of immune-modulating effects, this agent is entirely ineffective when given alone as adjuvant therapy for colonic cancer.[18] The combination of levamisole plus 5-FU is an effective adjuvant regimen, as described above. However, there is no evidence that immune stimulation by levamisole is the basis for its mechanism of action. Laboratory studies conducted at the National Cancer Institute[26] and at the Mayo Clinic[27] have indicated a direct dose-dependent enhancement of 5-FU cytotoxicity against a variety of cultured human tumor cell lines with high concentrations of levamisole. It has been suggested[27] that inhibition of tyrosine phosphatase may be responsible for the potentiation by levamisole of the inhibitory activity of 5-FU in vitro, completely independent of any immune modulation. Inhibition of dephosphorylation of regulatory phosphoproteins may therefore be related to the efficacy of levamisole combined with 5-FU in the adjuvant treatment of colonic cancer.

In a study conducted by the GITSG,[11] active nonspecific immunotherapy with the methanol extraction residue of bacillus Calmette-Guérin (BCG) given postoperatively alone or in combination with chemotherapy to patients with colonic cancer was ineffective compared to surgery alone in randomized control patients. Likewise, SWOG found no significant advantage for the addition of BCG to adjuvant chemotherapy compared to surgery alone or surgery followed by chemotherapy.[13]

Active specific immunotherapy with tumor vaccine as adjuvant therapy is also being studied in patients with colonic cancer. A small pilot study to determine the feasibility of administering a mixture of BCG and a vaccine prepared from the patient's own tumor cells has been reported,[28] and ECOG is currently conducting phase III studies to determine if this approach has any value from a therapeutic standpoint.

It is possible that further understanding of tumor immunology at a basic level will lead to new investigational approaches to immunotherapy as systemic adjuvant treatment for colonic cancer in future controlled clinical trials.

REFERENCES

1. Dixon WJ, Longmire WP Jr, Holden WD: Use of triethylenethiophosphomamide as adjuvant to the surgical treatment

of gastric and colorectal cancer: Ten year follow-up. *Ann Surg* 173:26–39, 1971.

2. Dwight RW, Higgins GA, Keehan RJ: Factors influencing survival after resection in cancer of the colon and rectum. *Am J Surg* 117:512–522, 1969.
3. Dwight RW, Humphrey EW, Higgins GA, et al: FUDR as an adjuvant to surgery in cancer of the large bowel. *J Surg Oncol* 5:243–249, 1973.
4. Higgins GA, Dwight RW, Smith JV, et al: Fluorouracil as an adjuvant to surgery in carcinoma of the colon. *Arch Surg* 102:339–343, 1971.
5. Higgins GA, Humphrey E, Juler GL, et al: Adjuvant chemotherapy and the surgical treatment of large bowel cancer. *Cancer* 38:1461–1467, 1976.
6. Higgins GA Jr, Donaldson RC, Humphrey EW, et al: Adjuvant therapy for large bowel cancer: Update of Veterans Administration Surgical Oncology Group Trial. *Surg Clin North Am* 61:1311–1320, 1981.
7. Grage TB, Moss SE: Adjuvant chemotherapy in cancer of the colon and rectum: Demonstration of effectiveness of prolonged 5-FU chemotherapy in a prospectively controlled randomized trial. *Surg Clin North Am* 61:1321–1329, 1981.
8. Wolmark N, Rockette H, Wickerham DL, et al: Adjuvant therapy of Dukes' A, B, and C adenocarcinoma of the colon with portal-vein fluorouracil hepatic infusion: Preliminary results of national surgical adjuvant breast and bowel project protocol C-02. *J Clin Oncol* 8:1466–1475, 1990.
9. O'Connell M, Martenson J, Rich T, et al: Protracted venous infusion (PVI) 5-fluorouracil (5FU) as a component of effective combined modality postoperative surgical adjuvant therapy for high-risk rectal cancer (abstract). *ASCO Proc* 12: 193, 1993.
10. Moertel CG, Schutt AJ, Hahn RG, et al: Therapy of advanced colorectal cancer with a combination of 5-fluorouracil, methyl 3-cis (2-chlorethyl)-1-nitrosourea and vincristine. *J Natl Cancer Inst* 54:69–71, 1975.
11. Gastrointestinal Tumor Study Group: Adjuvant therapy of colon cancer: Results of a prospectively randomized trial. *N Engl J Med* 310:737–743, 1984.
12. Higgins GA, Amadeo JH, McElhinney J, et al: Efficacy of prolonged intermittent therapy with combined 5-fluorouracil and me-CCNU following resection for carcinomas of the large bowel. *Cancer* 53:1–8, 1984.
13. Panettiere FJ, Goodman PJ, Costanzi JJ, et al: Adjuvant therapy in large bowel adenocarcinoma: Long-term results of a Southwest Oncology Group study. *J Clin Oncol* 6:947–954, 1988.
14. Mansour EG, MacIntyre JW, Johnson R, et al: Adjuvant studies in colorectal carcinoma: Experience of the Eastern Cooperative Oncology Group (ECOG)-preliminary report, in Gerard A (ed): *Progress and Perspectives in the Treatment of Gastrointestinal Tumors.* New York, Pergamon Press, 1981, pp 68–75.
15. Wolmark N, Fisher B, Rockette H, et al: Postoperative adjuvant chemotherapy or BCG for colon cancer: Results from NSABP Protocol C-01. *J Natl Cancer Inst* 80:30–36, 1988.
16. Laurie JA, Moertel CG, Fleming TR, et al: Surgical adjuvant therapy of large-bowel carcinoma: An evaluation of levamisole and the combination of levamisole and fluorouracil. *J Clin Oncol* 7:1447–1456, 1989.
17. Verhaegen H, DeCree J, DeCock W, et al: Levamisole therapy in patients with colorectal cancer, in Terry WD, Rosenberg SA (eds): *Immunotherapy of Human Cancer.* New York, Excerpta Medica, 1982, pp 225–230.
18. Moertel CG, Fleming TR, Macdonald JS, et al: Levamisole and fluorouracil for adjuvant therapy of resected colon carcinoma. *N Engl J Med* 322:352–358, 1990.
19. Moertel C, Fleming T, Macdonald J, et al: The intergroup study of fluorouracil (5FU) plus levamisole (LEV) and levamisole alone as adjuvant therapy for stage C colon cancer. *Proc Am Soc Clin Oncol* 11:161, 1992.
20. NIH Consensus Conference: Adjuvant therapy for patients with colon and rectal cancer. *JAMA* 264:1444–1450, 1990.
21. Witzig TE, Loprinzi CL, Gonchoroff NJ, et al: DNA ploidy and cell kinetic measurements as predictors of recurrence and survival in stages B2 and colorectal adenocarcinoma. *Cancer* 68:879–888, 1991.
22. Moertel CG, Loprinzi CL, Witzig TE, et al: The dilemma of stage B2 colon cancer: Is adjuvant therapy justified? A Mayo Clinic/North Central Cancer Treatment Group Study. *Proc Am Soc Clin Oncol* 9:108, 1990.
23. Wolmark N, Rockette H, Fisher B, et al: The benefit of leucovorin-modulated fluorouracil as postoperative adjuvant therapy for primary colon cancer: Results from National Surgical Adjuvant Breast and Bowel Project protocol C-03. *J Clin Oncol* 11:1879–1887, 1993.
24. O'Connell M, Mailliard J, Macdonald J, et al: An intergroup trial of intensive course 5-FU and low dose leucovorin as surgical adjuvant therapy for high risk colon cancer (abstract). *ASCO Proc* 12:190, 1993.
25. Zaniboni A, Erlichman C, Seitz JF, et al: FUFA increases disease-free survival in resected BZC colon cancer: Results of a prospectively pooled analysis of 3 randomized trials (abstract). *ASCO Proc* 12:191, 1993.
26. Grem JL, Allegra CJ: Toxicity of levamisole and 5-fluorouracil in human colon carcinoma cells. *J Natl Cancer Inst* 81:1413–1417, 1989.
27. Kovach JS, Svingen PA, Schaid DJ: Levamisole potentiation of fluorouracil antiproliferative activity mimicked by orthovanadate, an inhibitor of tyrosine phosphatase. *J Natl Cancer Inst* 84:515–519, 1992.
28. Hoover HC Jr, Surdyke M, Dangel RB, et al: Prospectively randomized trial of adjuvant active specific immunotherapy for human colorectal cancer. *Cancer* 55:1236–1243, 1985.

CHAPTER 52

Adjuvant Portal Vein Chemotherapy

Garner P. Johnson
Robert W. Beart, Jr.
Henry H. Lee

HIGHLIGHTS

Seven randomized trials of short-term early-postoperative portal vein chemotherapy have produced variable results, with survival advantage in three studies.

CONTROVERSIES

It is unclear whether demonstrable benefit is related to the systemic chemotherapy activity or the regional infusion strategy.

FUTURE DIRECTIONS

Longer-duration multidrug portal vein chemotherapy as a component of an overall adjuvant program should be considered.

Portal vein chemotherapy (PVC) is a regional adjuvant infusional therapy employed immediately following curative resection of colorectal carcinoma in patients without demonstrable hepatic metastases. The liver is the primary site for recurrence of colorectal carcinoma in 40 to 60 percent of patients following curative resection of the primary lesion. The goal of PVC is to inhibit the growth of viable tumor cells and micrometastases shed via the portal venous system to the hepatic circulation and parenchyma. Several prospective randomized studies were undertaken in the 1980s to evaluate this treatment modality. Recent experimental data derived from animal models may be helpful in designing future studies.

BACKGROUND

The liver is the site of treatment failure in the overwhelming majority of patients who suffer recurrent colorectal carcinoma. Hepatic metastases are present in 10 to 20 percent of patients with colorectal carcinoma at the time of initial diagnosis. About half of the patients without hepatic metastases are cured by local regional therapy. The remaining patients may have clinically occult micrometastases. Tumor cells may spread to the liver via lymphatic and hematogenous routes. Hematogenous routes include both the systemic circulation and the portal venous system.[1]

The metastatic potential of colorectal carcinoma is defined by the heterogeneity of tumor cells, viability of the circulating cells, host defenses, and target cell tropism.[2,3] It is estimated that the portal vein is the primary blood supply for micrometastases less than 1 mm in diameter.[4] As the metastasis grows, the blood supply shifts to the hepatic artery.

Tumor cells, individually and in clumps, are found in the mesenteric veins draining the primary cancer as well as in the systemic circulation. Fisher and Turnbull[5] recovered tumor cells from mesenteric veins in 32 percent of cases of colorectal carcinoma. Their study included patients in whom venous infiltration was not seen histologically and a few patients with stage Dukes A lesions. Similar findings have been reported by others[6–9]—for example, by Moore et al.,[10]

2 years later—but they grouped all gastrointestinal malignancies together. Tumor cells were recovered from the adjacent mesenteric veins in 52 percent of the patients. Furthermore, 44 percent of the same group of patients demonstrated tumor cells in peripheral veins. As a result of their data, Fisher and Turnbull recommended early ligation of mesenteric veins and the "no-touch technique." However, others showed no quantitative differences in the presence or absence of tumor cells in the mesenteric circulation before or after surgical manipulation.[10,11] A direct relationship between histologic grade of colorectal tumors and the presence of circulating tumor cells was shown by Engell.[11] In his series, survival was not influenced by the detection of tumor cells in the blood. It is assumed that metastases are already established at the time of surgery. Although tumor shedding at the time of surgery and tumor manipulation may have an incremental effect, the fundamental problem that needs to be addressed concerns the already established micrometastases.

In an effort to decrease the clinical development of hepatic metastases and improve survival rates for patients with colorectal carcinoma, several centers initiated PVC trials 10 to 15 years ago. In Sweden, preliminary work in animals and humans with various types of hepatic metastases and hepatocellular carcinoma by Almersjö et al.[12] demonstrated the feasibility and safety of PVC with 5-fluorouracil (5-FU).[12] Such infusions of 5-FU achieved high portal vein and low systemic concentrations. Bone marrow depression was seen after 5-FU was administered systemically but did not occur when it was infused via the portal vein. Patients tolerated 5-FU at a dose of 15 mg/kg/24 h; toxicity was seen in one patient at a dose of 30 mg/kg/24 h.

CHEMOTHERAPY TRIALS (TABLE 52-1)

At the University of Liverpool, Taylor et al.[13,14] started a prospective, randomized trial in 1975 to evaluate the efficacy of adjuvant PVC. Preoperatively, patients were randomized by closed envelope technique to surgery alone versus portal vein chemotherapy. A standard metastatic evaluation was performed prior to surgery. Patients with evidence of metastatic disease were excluded. Therefore, only patients with Dukes A, B, or C colonic and rectal carcinoma were studied. The umbilical vein was cannulated following curative en bloc resection of the involved bowel. The position of the portal vein catheter was verified by a contrast study, and the catheter was manipulated to ensure flow to both lobes. Catheters were not placed in the control group. Notably, the patients were not stratified for stage or tumor location.

The treatment group received 1 g of 5-FU in D5W with 5000 U of heparin by continuous infusion over 24 h for 7 days starting in the immediate postoperative period. The chemotherapy was well tolerated. No patients developed significant neutropenia or thrombocytopenia. A mild, transient elevation in the results of liver function tests was noted during infusion of 5-FU. More patients in the treatment group experienced nausea or diarrhea than did controls.

A preliminary report from Taylor et al.[13] in 1977 of the first 50 patients was encouraging. At 15 months mean follow-up, 6 control patients had developed hepatic metastases compared to none in the treatment group. Taylor's group published their 5-year survival data in 1985,[14] comprising 127 evaluable patients in the control arm and 117 in the treatment arm ($n = 244$). A decreased incidence of liver metastases was suggested by the data for patients who received PVC versus controls. The 5-year overall survival for controls versus PVC was 41 and 70 percent, respectively. When analyzed by stage and site of tumor, PVC conferred a survival advantage to patients with Dukes B colon carcinoma only (control 50 percent versus PVC 97 percent; $p < .002$). Improved survival was not demonstrated for patients with rectal cancer or Dukes C colonic cancer. The number of patients in each subgroup ranged

Table 52-1
Results of Various Treatment Protocols

Trial	*Site*	*Control*	*DFS advantage*	*Survival advantage*	*Hepatic metastasis*
Taylor et al.[14]	C/R	Surgery	Yes	Dukes B	Yes
Beart et al.[16]	Colon	Surgery	No	No	No
Ryan et al.[17]	C/R	Surg/Hep	No	No	No
Metzger et al.[18,20]	C/R	Surgery	No	No	No
Wolmark et al.[21]	Colon	Surgery	No	Yes	No
Gray et al. (Austr–NZ)[22]	Colon	Surgery	Yes	Yes	—
Wereldsma et al. (Rotterdam)[23]	C/R	Surgery	Yes	Yes	Yes

Abbreviations: DFS, disease-free survival; C/R, patients with carcinoma of the colon and rectum.

from 19 to 38. The authors recommended further study to verify the role of PVC in the prevention of liver metastases and improved survival. They concluded that PVC reduced hepatic metastases and improved survival.

The preliminary report from the University of Liverpool served as the impetus for eight other study groups to initiate prospective, randomized trials comparing a surgery-only group to one or more treatment groups. The results of two trials in Europe are pending. One is directed by the European Organization for Research and Treatment of Cancer (EORTC/GITCCG protocol 40812), which is limited to colonic carcinoma. The other is from Düsseldorf, Germany (Evangelisches Krankenhaus Düsseldorf Trial), which closed in 1990 and included *both* colon and rectal carcinoma. A third study by Fielding et al.[15] from St. Mary's in London was recently published; it summarizes data from the remaining six studies. These studies were unable to show both a reduction in hepatic metastases *and* a survival advantage in patients receiving PVC as reported by Taylor et al.

NO SURVIVAL ADVANTAGE; NO REDUCTION IN HEPATIC METASTASIS

The North Central Cancer Treatment Group and the Mayo Clinic randomized patients with colonic cancer intraoperatively to surgery only versus PVC.[16] The study accrued 219 eligible patients with a mean follow-up of 5.5 years. Treated patients ($n=110$) received 5-FU at a dosage of 500 mg/m^2/24 h with 5000 U heparin in D5W for 7 days beginning in the immediate post-operative period. The average daily dose of 5-FU was 930 mg. Recurrence-free survival for control versus PVC was 68 and 70 percent, respectively ($p=.57$). Thirteen percent of control patients and 15 percent of treated patients developed hepatic metastases ($p=.58$). Analysis by Dukes stage showed no differences between the two groups.

Ryan et al.[17] reported the results of the trial from Virginia Mason Medical Center. Patients ($n=232$) with colonic (73 percent) and rectal cancer were randomized to surgery only versus heparin only by portal vein versus PVC. Mean follow-up was 22 months. Patients receiving PVC were bolused with mitomycin (12 mg/m^2) and then received 5-FU at a dosage of 1 g/m^2/24 h with heparin 5000 U/m^2/24 h in D5W for 5 days, which began immediately after surgery. The heparin-only group received the same dosage as the chemotherapy group. No recurrence-free survival advantage was found by Kaplan-Meier projections or logrank test for Dukes B or C patients in either treatment group when compared to surgery only.

Metzger et al.[18–20] reported the results of a trial supported by the Swiss Group for Clinical Cancer Research (SAKK 40/81). This multicenter trial randomized 469 patients with colonic ($n=302$) and rectal carcinoma to surgery alone versus PVC. Mitomycin was bolused via the portal vein immediately following surgery at 10 mg/m^2, as in the study by Ryan et al. Then 5-FU at a dose of 500 mg/m^2/24 h with 5000 U heparin in D5W for 7 days was infused. Mean follow up was 48 months. The differences in overall survival did not reach significance ($p=.10$). Actuarial disease-free survival showed a trend favoring PVC (62 percent) versus controls (53 percent; $p=.09$). Of the patients randomized to the treatment group, 41 did not complete the chemotherapy. Subgroup analysis suggested that patients with colonic cancer only ($p=.07$) and node-positive disease ($p=.11$) benefited the most. Liver metastases were found in 14.6 percent of controls and 12.3 percent of patients who received PVC. Eight patients in the PVC arm developed transient leukopenia or thrombocytopenia.

Trial design has made it difficult to evaluate and compare these studies. In particular, different stratification and treatment paradigms, various medications and dosage regimens, and the lack of surgical technique control—particularly in multicenter studies—are confounding details.

SURVIVAL ADVANTAGE; NO REDUCTION IN HEPATIC METASTASIS

A large multicenter randomized trial conducted by the National Surgical Adjuvant Breast and Bowel Project (protocol C-02) compared surgery only versus PVC in patients with colonic carcinoma.[21] A total of 989 eligible patients were followed for an average of 41.8 months. Patients in the PVC group (414) received 5-FU at a dosage of 600 mg/m^2/24 h with 5000 U heparin in D5W for 7 days. Disease-free survival at 4 years was significantly improved in the treatment group (74 percent) as compared to controls (64 percent; $p < .02$). Overall survival nearly reached significance ($p=.07$). Of the control patients, 82 suffered recurrence, and in 27 (33 percent) the liver was the first site of failure. Following PVC, 31 of 46 (67 percent) patients developed hepatic metastases. Subgroup analysis was not performed when the global test for interaction (proportional hazards analysis) did not reach significance. Four patients in the PVC group developed small bowel infarctions from catheter-related thrombosis.

The Australian and New Zealand Bowel Cancer Trial (ANZBCT 8201) randomized patients ($n=232$) with Dukes B and C colonic cancer to three groups.[22] One group received PVC at a dosage of 600 mg/m^2/24 h for 7 days. The second group received the same dosage systemically. Both were compared to a surgery-only group. There was no significant improvement in the overall disease-free interval between treated patients and controls. Subgroup analysis showed that patients with Dukes C colonic cancer treated with PVC had an improved disease-free interval compared to controls ($p = .02$). There was a significant improvement in overall survival for patients receiving PVC ($p = .037$ versus controls). Subgroup analysis showed that this was seen only in Dukes C patients versus controls, where 4-year survival was 77 percent and 21 percent, respectively. The number of patients in each subgroup was less than 40. Mean length of follow-up was not discussed.

NO SURVIVAL ADVANTAGE; IMPROVED RECURRENCE-FREE SURVIVAL

Four hospitals in Rotterdam, Netherlands, participated in a prospective trial reported by Wereldsma et al.[23] Patients ($n = 304$) with colonic (58 percent), rectosigmoid, and rectal carcinoma were randomized to one of three groups with a mean follow up of 44 months. Group I was given 5-FU at a dosage of 1 g/24h with 5000 U heparin in D5W for 7 days via the portal vein. Group II (thrombolytic agent) received a single dose of 10,000 U urokinase in normal saline over 24 h. Group III was treated with surgery only. Catheter problems precluded infusion in 15 to 20 percent of group I and II patients. The overall 5-year survival was 65 percent (group I) versus 59 percent (group II) versus 59 percent (group III). In group I (PVC), 7 percent of patients developed hepatic metastases, compared to 23 percent in the control group, $p < .01$. The relative hazard rate for hepatic metastases in group I was 0.27 ($p < .001$ compared with controls). In this study, therefore, patients treated with PVC had one-third the risk compared with surgery alone.

EXPERIMENTAL ANIMAL MODELS

The timing of the infusion of chemotherapeutic agents in the human studies described above was based on the early work of Fisher and Turnbull,[5] Engell,[11] and Moore,[10] suggesting that viable tumor cells may circulate at the time of surgery and with manipulation of the tumor. Chemotherapy was infused within 6 to 24h of surgery and continued for 5 to 7 days in the hope of killing viable tumor cells in the portal circulation. Experimental evidence from animal models suggests that timing is critical.

Sigurdson et al.[24] developed a rat model with DMH-induced colonic cancer cells introduced to the portal circulation by splenic injection. Portal vein infusion of FUdR was begun on day zero (immediate) and on day three (delayed) and compared to controls (no FUdR). A significant reduction in hepatic metastases occurred only in the immediate-infusion group. Archer et al.[25] injected the portal vein of rats with a colonic carcinoma cell line. On days zero, two, four, and six, 5-FU was infused via the portal vein (group I) and hepatic artery (group II) and the reduction in metastases was compared to controls (no treatment). A 91 percent reduction in tumor metastasis ($p < .01$) was seen following portal vein infusion on day zero. No tumor response was seen after portal vein infusion on days two, four, or six. Tumor nodules averaged 0.33 mm in nonresponders. The infusion of 5-FU via the hepatic artery was associated with a 61 percent reduction in liver metastases on day zero and also on days two, four, and six. The sensitivity of micrometastases in these animal models to PVC is directly proportional to the lead time prior to implantation and growth acceleration. These studies suggest that the prompt infusion of chemotherapeutic agents via the portal vein may effectively reduce the number of circulating tumor cells in the liver.

The actual *uptake* of chemotherapeutic agents by tumor cells following portal or hepatic artery infusions in humans is difficult to quantify. Ridge et al.[26] looked at uptake of radiolabeled doxorubicin (Adriamycin) by hepatic tumors induced in rabbits using the VX-2 cell line. Blood flow to the metastases was assessed using radiolabeled macroaggregated albumin (^{99m}Tc MAA). Labeled and cold doxorubicin and ^{99m}Tc MAA were infused via the hepatic artery (group I), the portal vein (group II), and a peripheral vein (group III). The animals were sacrificed 30 min later. Tumor levels of doxorubicin were compared with normal hepatic parenchyma and found to be highest following hepatic artery infusion (34.3 nmol/g) versus portal vein (6.5 nmol/g) and peripheral vein (11.5 nmol/g). A similar study from Japan by Kuroda et al.[27] (Engish abstract) showed tumor uptake of doxorubicin following sacrifice at 2 and 3h was greatest following portal vein infusion compared with hepatic artery infusion. Another group infused tritiated FUdR and ^{99m}Tc MAA via the portal vein (group I), hepatic artery (group II), and peripheral vein (group III) in rabbits with *established* VX-2 hepatic implants.[28] Uptake of labeled FUdR was significantly increased when administered by hepatic artery. No uptake occurred after portal vein infusion. A significant increase in tumor blood flow from the hepatic artery was also demonstrated. Finally, a provocative animal study comparing portal vein (group II) versus intraperitoneal (group III) instillation of 5-FU in rats was introduced by Archer et al.[29] Treatment (for 5 days) was initiated 2 days after a colonic cell line was inoculated into the portal vein and peritoneal cavity. The results were compared to those from control rabbits who developed advanced intraperitoneal and hepatic metastases. The investigators found that intraperitoneal 5-FU effectively eliminated peritoneal metastases in 57 percent, as well as producing a 50 percent reduction in hepatic metastases. Following portal vein 5-FU, a similar reduction in hepatic metastases was seen, but the peritoneal tumor burden increased compared with controls. Intraperitoneal 5-FU produced a homogeneous reduction in hepatic tumor growth. A qualitative assessment of the heterogeneous pattern of failure in the liver suggested that the delivery of PVC may be influenced by streaming effects of portal venous flow. Alternatively, micrometastases may have been in different stages of implantation, thus reducing contact with portal vein blood flow.

These experimental efforts and recent relevant discoveries shed light on the role of regional therapy. First, as the polymorphic nature of genetic abnormalities becomes clear, the appropriateness of various tumor models used to evaluate regional therapy will be called into question. The pattern of genetic abnormality may prove relevant to the means of therapy.

Second, variables that have proven to be important (e.g., timing and duration of agent administration, route of administration, etc.) will need to be stratified and critically assessed. These factors will be easier to assess when the chemotherapeutic regimen is clearly efficacious. The 5-FU–leucovorin and 5-FU–levamisole combinations may prove more effective when given regionally than when given systemically—particularly when given for prolonged periods of time.

FUTURE CONSIDERATIONS

The results from seven prospective, randomized trials evaluating the efficacy of PVC to reduce the incidence of hepatic metastases are inconclusive. Longer follow-up is necessary in some of the published trials and final results are pending in three others. Animal studies suggest that the timing of PVC is critical with regard to the initial inoculum. In patients with colorectal carcinoma, tumor cells are continuously shed into the portal venous system prior to and during surgical intervention. Implantation of single tumor cells and micrometastases may have occurred before the infusion of PVC in patients who failed and ultimately developed hepatic metastases. Further analysis of the data generated from PVC trials is awaited with interest.

Newly emerging technology and assays may lead to the detection of small liver metastases and improve the selection of patients for PVC. Intraoperative liver ultrasound combined with preoperative monoclonal antibody scans and biliary carcinoembryonic antigen (CEA) determinations are modalities currently available.

If regional chemotherapy is going to be proven effective, several controversial issues will have to be resolved. Studies must be stratified to have homogeneous and anatomically reasonable treatment groups. Stratification parameters must include primary tumor site, stage, grade, and biologic characteristics such as flow cytometric status. Ultimately, genetic features will likely constitute a stratification group.

More effective chemotherapy must be used. 5-FU and leucovorin or FUdR and leucovorin may be more cytotoxic. Hopefully, more effective agents will become available.

Since these agents kill in a logrithmic fashion, perfusion for more prolonged periods will likely be necessary. Modes of administration that will allow weeks rather than days of administration will be necessary.

It remains unclear if any apparent benefit from regional chemotherapy is regionally dependent or merely a systemic effect. In view of the logistic complexity of regional perfusion, it is important to discern the mechanism of action.

REFERENCES

1. Weiss L, Grundmann E, Torhorst J, et al: Haematogenous metastatic patterns in colonic carcinoma: An analysis of 1541 necropsies. *J Pathol* 150:195–203, 1986.
2. Liolla LA, Stetler-Stevenson G: Principles of molecular cell biology of cancer: Cancer metastasis, in DeVito VT Jr, et al (eds): *Cancer Principles and Practices of Oncology*. Philadelphia, Lippincott, 1989, pp 98–115.
3. Kerbel RS: Growth dominance of the metastatic cancer cell: Cellular and molecular aspects. *Adv Cancer Res* 55:87–132, 1990.
4. Talbot IC, Ritchie S, Leighton MH, et al: The clinical significance of invasion of veins by rectal cancer. *Br J Surg* 67:439–442, 1980.
5. Fisher ER, Turnbull RB Jr: The cytologic demonstration and significance of tumor cells in the mesenteric venous blood in patients with colorectal carcinoma. *Surg Gynecol Obstet* 100:102–108, 1955.
6. Ackerman NB: Experimental studies on the role of the portal circulation in hepatic tumor vascularity. *Cancer* 58:1653–1657, 1986.
7. Taylor I, Bennett R: The blood supply of colorectal liver metastases. *Br J Cancer* 39:749–756, 1979.
8. Lin B, Linderquist A, Hagerstrand L, et al: Post mortem examination of the blood supply and vascular patterns of small liver metastases in man. *Surgery* 96:517–526, 1984.
9. Ridge JA, Bading JR, Gelbard AS, et al: Perfusion of colorectal hepatic metastases. *Cancer* 59:1547–1553, 1987.
10. Moore GE, Sandberg A, Schubarg JR: Clinical and experimental observations of the outcome and fate of tumor cells in the blood stream. *Ann Surg* 146:580–587, 1957.
11. Engell HC: Cancer cells in the circulating blood. *Acta Chir Scand Suppl* 201: , 1955.
12. Almersjö O, Brandberg, Gustavsson B: Concentration of biologically active 5-fluorouracil in general circulation during continuous portal infusion in man: A preliminary report. *Cancer Lett* 1:113–118, 1975.
13. Taylor I, Brooman P, Rowling JT: Adjuvant liver perfusion in colorectal cancer: Initial results of a clinical trial. *Br Med J* 2:1320–1322, 1977.

14. Taylor I, Machin D, Mullee M, et al: A randomized controlled trial of adjuvant portal vein cytotoxic perfusion in colorectal cancer. *Br J Surg* 72:359–362, 1985.
15. Fielding LP, Hittinger R, Grace RH, et al: Randomised controlled trial of adjuvant chemotherapy by portal-vein perfusion after curative resection for colorectal adenocarcinoma. *Lancet* 1:502–506, 1992.
16. Beart RW Jr, Moertel CG, Wieand HS, et al: Adjuvant therapy for resectable colorectal carcinoma with fluorouracil administered by portal vein infusion. *Arch Surg* 125:897, 1990.
17. Ryan J, Weiden P, Crowley J, et al: Adjuvant portal vein infusion for colorectal cancer: A 3-arm randomized trial. *Proc Am Soc Clin Oncol* 7:A95, 1988.
18. Metzger U, Mermillod B, Aeberhard P, et al: Intraportal chemotherapy in colorectal carcinoma as an adjuvant modality. *World J Surg* 11:452–458, 1987.
19. Metzger U: Adjuvant portal infusion chemotherapy in colorectal cancer. *Recent Results Cancer Res* 110:95–100, 1988.
20. Metzger U, Laffer U, Castiglione M, et al: Adjuvant intraportal chemotherapy for colorectal cancer—4 year results of the randomized Swiss study. *Proc Am Soc Clin Oncol* 8:105, 1989.
21. Wolmark N, Rockette H, Wickerham DL, et al: Adjuvant therapy of Dukes' A, B, and C adenocarcinoma of the colon with portal-vein fluorouracil hepatic infusion: Preliminary results of national surgical adjuvant breast and bowel project protocol C-02. *J Clin Oncol* 8:1466–1475, 1990.
22. Gray BN, deZwart J, Fisher R, et al: The Australia and New Zealand trial of adjuvant chemotherapy in colon cancer, in Salmon SE (ed): *Adjuvant Therapy of Cancer,* vol 5. New York, Grune & Stratton, 1987, pp 537–546.
23. Wereldsma JCJ, Bruggink ERM, Meijer WS, et al: Adjuvant portal liver infusion in colorectal cancer with 5-fluorouracil/heparin versus urokinase versus control: Results of a prospective randomized clinical trial (colorectal adenocarcinoma trial I). *Cancer* 65:425–432, 1990.
24. Sigurdson ER, Sutanto-Ward E, Lincer R, et al: Adjuvant portal vein (PV) chemotherapy for colorectal liver metastases: Timing of chemotherapy. *Proc Annu Meet Am Assoc Cancer Res* 32:A2552, 1991.
25. Archer SG, McCulloch RK, Gray BN: A comparative study of pharmacokinetics of continuous portal vein infusion versus intraperitoneal infusion of 5-fluorouracil. *Reg Cancer Treat* 2:105–111, 1989.
26. Ridge JA, Collin C, Bading JR, et al: Increased adriamycin levels in hepatic implants of rabbit VX-2 carcinoma from regional infusion. *Cancer Res* 48:7, 1988.
27. Kurodo K, Horita Y, Sakane M, et al: Hepatic artery and portal vein infusion of adriamycin in experimental liver metastasis. *Gan To Kagaku Ryoho* 16:2859–2862, 1989.
28. Butler JA, Trezona TP, Nordestgaard A, et al: Hepatic artery versus portal vein and systemic infusion of fluorodeoxyuridine of rabbit VX-2 hepatic implants. *Am J Surg* 157:126–129, 1989.
29. Archer SG, Gray BN: Intraperitoneal 5-fluorouracil infusion for treatment of both peritoneal and liver micrometastases. *Surgery* 108:502–507, 1990.

CHAPTER 53

Adjuvant Radiation Therapy for Colonic Cancer

Christopher G. Willett
Donald S. Kaufman
Paul C. Shellito

HIGHLIGHTS

Unlike the situation for patients with rectal carcinoma, there has been little systematic examination of the value of postoperative radiation therapy for patients with colonic carcinoma. Postoperative radiation therapy has been applied in three settings: (1) irradiation of the tumor bed of patients with colonic tumors judged to be at risk for local recurrence, (2) elective hepatic irradiation, and (3) elective whole abdominal radiotherapy. Retrospective studies have suggested that failure rates in the operative bed are reduced and survival rates improved in patients receiving tumor-bed irradiation, compared to historical controls. With regards to hepatic irradiation, one randomized trial from the Gastrointestinal Tumor Study Group has demonstrated no benefit of elective hepatic irradiation with 5-fluorouracil (5-FU) compared to a surgical control group alone. Prospective phase I/II studies from the Southwestern Oncology Group suggest improved local, peritoneal, and hepatic control rates with acceptable toxicity for patients receiving combinations of 5-FU and whole abdominal radiation therapy.

CONTROVERSIES

There are no available prospective randomized data supporting the use of postoperative tumor-bed irradiation or whole abdominal radiation therapy versus standard treatment of 5-FU and levamisole for high-risk colonic cancer. The first issue is to determine the merits of each of these treatments compared to standard adjuvant chemotherapy. The second issue would be to address the relative merits of tumor-bed irradiation to approaches irradiating the whole abdomen.

FUTURE DIRECTIONS

A randomized prospective intergroup trial combining postoperative radiation therapy with 5-FU and levamisole versus 5-FU with levamisole but no radiation has recently been started. Efforts are under way to initiate a phase III trial evaluating whole abdominal irradiation versus 5-FU and levamisole.

TUMOR-BED REGIONAL RADIATION THERAPY

Unlike the situation for patients with rectal carcinoma, there has been little systematic examination of the value of postoperative radiation therapy for patients with colonic carcinoma. This is largely due to the perception that colonic carcinoma (as opposed to rectal cancer) is much more likely to recur systemically than locally, so local treatment offers little survival benefit.

Although distant metastases do occur frequently in patients with colonic tumors, there are subsets at risk for local failure. Local failure is an important consideration for patients with colonic tumors arising in locations where a wide radial retroperitoneal margin is difficult to achieve and for patients with tumors invading transmurally to involve fixed adjacent structures. Postoperative radiation therapy may be useful in patients with tumors arising in the ascending and descending colon with a compromised (less than 1 cm) retroperitoneal resection margin and for patients with modified Astler-Coller stage B_3 and C_3 tumors.[1-4] Patterns of failure in such patients are described in Chap. 49. Because of the improved survival seen in patients with node-positive colonic carcinoma who receive 5-FU–based chemotherapy, adjuvant radiation therapy for these patients will have to be combined with systemic chemotherapy.

Reports on the use of adjuvant postoperative radiation therapy for colonic carcinoma suggest that failure rates in the operative bed are reduced in patients receiving radiation therapy compared with *historical* controls. Loeffler described 10 patients with stage B_3 to C_3 cecal carcinoma who received adjuvant regional postoperative radiation therapy to doses of 6500 to 7500 cGy with use of two daily fractions of 70 to 75 cGy and observed no local failure.[5] However, 5 patients developed distant metastases within follow-up periods of 7 to 76 months. Shehata et al.[6] described 19 patients with stage B_2 (14 patients) and stage C_2 (5 patients) cecal carcinoma treated with regional postoperative radiation therapy to 4500 cGy and weekly doses of 5-FU. When matched with a similar group treated with right hemicolectomy, no statistical difference in the median survival or incidence of distant metastases was noted; however, the incidence of local failure was 5 percent in the patients who received radiation therapy versus 19 percent in those who underwent surgery alone. In a study at the Princess Margaret Hospital, 48 patients with stages B_1 to C_2 colon carcinoma received adjuvant postoperative local irradiation. In patients with stage B_1 and B_2 tumors, the local failure rate was 15 percent (3/20 patients); whereas for patients with stage C_1 and C_2 lesions, the rate was 32 percent (9/28 patients).[7]

Since 1976, patients at the Massachusetts General Hospital (MGH) with completely resected but high-risk colonic carcinoma have been considered for postoperative radiation therapy to the tumor bed.[8,9] These high-risk groups included patients with stage B_3 and C_3 disease, patients with stage C_2 disease except middle sigmoid and transverse colon cancer, and selected patients with stage B_2 disease with tight margins. In all, 169 patients (1976–1989) have received postoperative radiation therapy via a high-energy linear accelerator by parallel opposed fields or multifield techniques to treat the tumor bed with approximately a 3- to 5-cm margin to a total dose of 4500 cGy in 180-cGy fractions. This was followed by a shrinking-field technique, sparing the small bowel, to 5040 cGy. Additional treatment above 5040 cGy was attempted in patients with stage B_3 and C_3 disease only if the small bowel could be displaced from the field. These 169 patients receiving postoperative radiation therapy were compared with 395 patients in the MGH series with stage B_2, B_3, C_2, and C_3 tumors who underwent surgery only during the period from 1970 to 1977.[1]

Table 53-1 shows by stage the 5-year actuarial local control and recurrence-free survival rates for patients undergoing postoperative radiation therapy and patients having surgery alone. Local control and recurrence-free survival was statistically improved for patients with stage B_3 and C_3 tumors receiving postoperative radiation therapy compared with similarly matched surgical patients. Local control rates for irradiated patients with stage B_3 and C_3 tumors were 93 and 72 percent, whereas these figures were 69 and 47 percent, respectively, in patients having surgery only. Patients with stage B_3 and C_3 disease receiving postoperative radiotherapy experienced a 14 and 15 percent point increase in disease-free survival, respectively, compared with the group that had surgery only. In contrast, local control and recurrence-free survival was not improved for B_2 and C_2 patients receiving postoperative radiation therapy compared with surgery alone. It should be noted, however, that for irradiated patients with stage B_2 and C_2 lesions, these comparisons may be unfavorably biased against radiation, since most were referred because of concerns about the adequacy of local control with surgery alone. In this context, to have achieved similar local control and recurrence-free survival in the "high-risk" irradiated B_2 and C_2 patients may actually represent a positive gain.

Table 53-1
Five-Year Actuarial Local Control and Recurrence-Free Survival after Surgery and Postoperative Radiotherapy versus Surgery Alone according to Stage

	Surgery plus radiation			*Surgery alone*		
Stage	*No. of patients*	*LC, %*	*RFS, %*	*No. of patients*	*LC, %*	*RFS, %*
B_2	23	91	72	163	90	78
B_3	53	93	78	83	69	64
C_2	54	69	46	100	64	48
C_3	39	72	53	49	47	38

Abbreviations: LC, local control; RFS, recurrence-free survival.

To assess the merits of postoperative radiation therapy for selected patients with colonic cancer, a randomized prospective intergroup trial combining postoperative radiation therapy plus 5-FU and levamisole versus 5-FU and levamisole alone has recently been activated. Eligible patients include those with B_3 and C_3 lesions and select C_2 tumors with gross tumor penetration into the retroperitoneum. This trial will evaluate the impact of treatment on disease-free and overall survival as well as any impact on local-regional control in tumor bed and regional nodes.

HEPATIC AND WHOLE ABDOMINAL IRRADIATION

Because of the high incidence of hepatic metastases and peritoneal failures developing in patients with advanced-stage colonic carcinoma, there have been clinical investigations of the efficacy of adjuvant hepatic irradiation as well as whole abdominal radiation therapy. There has only been one randomized prospective trial. The Gastrointestinal Tumor Study Group reported the results of a phase III trial of adjuvant *hepatic irradiation.*[10] In this study, 300 patients with completely resected transmural or node-positive colon carcinoma were randomized between two treatment arms: (1) observation or (2) 5-FU and 2100 cGy to the liver (150 cGy per fraction for 14 treatments). The 5-FU was given as an intravenous bolus during the first 3 days of radiation therapy as well as maintenance treatment. No statistical differences in survival, recurrence-free survival, or liver recurrence were seen between the control patients and the treated patients.

Several investigators have reported the results and toxicity of *whole abdominal irradiation* as an adjuvant treatment for patients at risk for hepatic and peritoneal failure. None of these studies had concurrent controls. Wang et al.[11] reported the experience at Princess Margaret Hospital of 3000 cGy patients receiving whole abdominal irradiation of 1400 to 2500 cGy over 3 to 5 weeks with or without local tumor boost. The 5-year actuarial survival was 55 percent. For patients without regional nodal involvement, the survival was 72 percent, compared with 41 percent for patients with nodal involvement. After treatment, 4 patients had failure in the peritoneum and 12 had hepatic and extraabdominal failure. Brenner et al.[12] described 21 patients with Dukes C colonic cancer who received whole abdominal radiation therapy to 2000 cGy in eight fractions with a boost dose of 2000 to 3000 cGy in 3 weeks to areas at high risk and concurrent weekly 350-mg/m^2 doses of 5-FU given intravenously. The patients who underwent radiation therapy were compared with a matched control group of patients who underwent surgery alone, and a statistically significant improvement in the disease-free survival was noted (55 versus 12 percent, respectively).

In 1988, the results of a phase I/II Southwestern Oncology Group Study utilizing 3000 cGy of whole abdominal irradiation over 6 weeks with a 1600-cGy tumor boost plus an intravenous bolus of 5-FU given at the beginning and end of treatment were described.[13] The 32-month actuarial disease-free survival for all 38 patients was 62 percent. Liver relapse and local control occurred in 24 and 9 percent, respectively, of all patients. More recently, this group has reported the preliminary results of a phase I/II study of continuous infusion of 5-FU and whole abdominal radiation therapy for 42 patients with stage C_2 colonic cancer.[14] Patients received continuous-infusion 5-FU at 200 mg/m^2 with 3000-cGy whole abdominal irradiation followed by a 1600-cGy boost to the tumor bed. An additional 9 cycles of 5-FU was given after radiation therapy. The 3-year actuarial survival of all 42 patients was 76 percent. For patients with less than five nodes, the disease-free survival was 76 percent; whereas for patients with more than five nodes, this figure was 66 percent. Liver failure occurred in 8 patients, while peritoneal seeding was observed in 2 and 4 patients experienced a local failure. Grade 3 or 4 toxicity occurred in 15 percent of the patients. Based on these results, these investigators propose that this regimen be evaluated against 5-FU and levamisole in a phase III trial.

REFERENCES

1. Willett CG, Tepper JE, Cohen AM, et al: Failure patterns following curative resection of colonic carcinoma. *Ann Surg* 200:685–690, 1984.
2. Willett CG, Tepper JE, Cohen A, et al: Obstructive and perforative colonic carcinoma: Patterns of failure. *J Clin Oncol* 3:379–384, 1984.
3. Gunderson LL, Sosin H, Levitt S: Extrapelvic colon areas of failure in a reoperation series: Implications for adjuvant therapy. *Int J Radiat Oncol Biol Phys* 11:731–741, 1984.
4. Willett CG, Tepper JE, Shellito PC, Wood WC: Indications for adjuvant radiotherapy in extrapelvic colonic carcinoma. *Oncology* 3:25–33, 1989.
5. Loeffler RK: Postoperative radiation therapy for Duke's C adenocarcinoma of the cecum using two fractions per day. *Int J Radiat Oncol Biol Phys* 10:1881–1883, 1984.
6. Shehata WM, Meyer RL, Krause RJ, et al: Postoperative adjuvant irradiation and 5-fluorouracil for adenocarcinoma of the cecum. *Cancer* 54:2850–2853, 1984.
7. Wong CS, Harwood AR, Cummings BJ, et al: Postoperative local abdominal irradiation for cancer of the colon above the peritoneal reflection. *Int J Radiat Oncol Biol Phys* 11:2067–2071, 1985.
8. Duttenhaver JR, Hoskins RB, Gunderson LL, Tepper JE: Adjuvant postoperative radiation therapy in the management of adenocarcinoma of the colon. *Cancer* 57:955–963, 1986.
9. Willett CG, Tepper JE, Skates SJ, et al: Adjuvant postoperative radiation therapy for colonic carcinoma. *Ann Surg* 206:694–698, 1987.

10. The Gastrointestinal Tumor Study Group: Adjuvant therapy with hepatic irradiation plus fluorouracil in colon carcinoma. *Int J Radiat Oncol Biol Phys* 21:1151–1156, 1991.
11. Wang CS, Harwood AR, Cummings BJ, et al: Total abdominal irradiation for cancer of the colon. *Radiother Oncol* 2:209–214, 1984.
12. Brenner HJ, Bibe C, Chaitchik S: Adjuvant therapy for Dukes' C adenocarcinoma of colon. *Int Radiat Oncol Biol Phys* 9:1789–1792, 1983.
13. Fabian CJ, Reddy E, Jewell W, et al: Phase I/II pilot of whole abdominal radiation and concomitant 5-FU as an adjuvant in colon cancer: A Southwest Oncology Group Study. *Int J Radiat Oncol Biol Phys* 15:885–892, 1988.
14. Giri PG, Fabian C, Estes N, et al: Concurrent 5-FU chemotherapy and whole abdominal irradiation in patients with stage C2 extrapelvic colon cancer. *Int Radiat Oncol Biol Phys* 24(suppl):155, 1992.

PART 10

Surgical Treatment of Potentially Curable Rectal Cancer

CHAPTER 54

Local Regional Staging of Rectal Cancer

David A. Rothenberger
W. Donald Buie

HIGHLIGHTS

Endorectal ultrasound (ERUS) is the best method of preoperative staging of rectal cancer available to the surgeon today. It is well tolerated by the patient, is reproducible, and has accuracy rates of 85 to 90 percent for depth of invasion and 85 percent for predicting lymph node metastases. With further experience and technologic advancements, the accuracy rates should improve further. Routine computed tomography (CT) is not recommended for local staging of primary rectal tumors and should be reserved for patients in whom locally extensive or widespread disease is suspected. Added information from CT may influence the decision for preoperative adjuvant radiotherapy and help determine the operative approach. Magnetic resonance imaging (MRI) has no advantage over CT at the present time.

CONTROVERSIES

Preoperative local regional staging presupposes that rectal cancer should be treated on an individual basis. In spite of increasing evidence, not all surgeons treat their patients in this manner. The ultimate value of preoperative staging of rectal cancer will be determined by demonstrating that this procedure not only influences selection of treatment but also increases patient survival and local control. At the present time, no study has demonstrated that the increasingly accurate staging of rectal cancer has altered patient survival. At our own institution, we have reviewed all patients from 1985 to 1991 who were selected for local excision, and as yet we have been unable to demonstrate a survival benefit in patients selected with ERUS versus those selected by traditional clinical methods. Demonstrating cause and effect is difficult because of inaccuracies inherent in the staging process and may be impossible due to the myriad of variables influencing patient outcome.

FUTURE DIRECTIONS

Ultimately, local regional staging will allow complete and accurate preoperative evaluation of local and regional disease. When combined with traditional pathologic data and patient variables into a predictive model, it will provide accurate prognostication and optimization of treatment, whether it be local therapy, radical resection without adjuvant therapy, or adjuvant preoperative chemoradiotherapy followed by radical resection. Enhanced MRI using intrarectal coils and positron emission tomography (PET) will have to be explored.

Patients with selected rectal cancers can be treated by either local excision or endocavitary radiation, thus avoiding the morbidity and mortality of a major resection. At the other extreme, patients with locally advanced tumors may benefit from preoperative adjuvant chemoradiotherapy.

Optimal treatment selection for individual patients requires assessment of patient characteristics, including operative risks and patient desires; disease status (i.e., synchronous lesions and distant metastases); and primary tumor characteristics such as size, location, morphology, histology, DNA ploidy and—most importantly—accurate preoperative local regional staging. This chapter is restricted to a discussion of the various methods of local regional staging of primary rectal cancer. While important, local regional staging is not the only factor determining treatment; the ultimate decision must be modified by an assessment of disease status in conjunction with tumor and patient characteristics. Additional clinical pathologic correlates will be discussed in greater detail in the following chapter.

The goal of local regional staging is the accurate classification of patients by disease stage to allow precise patient selection for individual treatment options. To accomplish this, three questions must be answered: (1) What is the depth of intramural invasion? (2) Is there extramural invasion? and (3) Are lymph node metastases present?

CLINICAL STAGING

Clinical staging includes a thorough abdominal, inguinal, digital rectal, and proctoscopic examination with biopsy of the lesion. A pelvic examination may contribute additional information in female patients. Digital examination remains an important clinical method for local regional staging of rectal cancer and is used to assess distance from the anal verge, mobility, accessibility and size. While it is essential, it is only useful for lesions located in the distal rectum and permits only a gross estimate of local stage. York Mason[1] documented a 75 percent accuracy rate in predicting pathologic stage with digital examination (Table 54-1). This was confirmed in a study by Nicholls et al.[2] in 1982, where rectal examination by an experienced clinician correctly predicted local versus regional disease in 80 percent of patients. While the presence and extent of extrarectal invasion was identified with reasonable accuracy, the precise depth of intramural invasion was difficult to predict. Mesorectal lymph node involvement is very difficult to detect unless the nodes are enlarged and firm. In the Nicholls study, only half of the pathologically proven node-positive patients were identified by clinical examination alone. Thus, accuracy of clinical examination is highest for locally advanced lesions and lowest for early lesions, which limits its ability to select patients for local therapy.

Primary tumor characteristics do not provide staging information in a strict sense; however, they do give additional information as to the tendency of a specific tumor to be more advanced at the time of diagnosis. Macroscopically, tumors that are ulcerated as opposed

Table 54-1
Clinical Staging System for Rectal Cancer

Stage	*Definition*	*Pathologic correlation, percent*
CS_1	Freely movable over muscle, indicating confinement to mucosa and submucosa	70
CS_2	Mobile but not movable separately from rectal wall, indicating absence of transrectal spread	75
CS_3	Mobility of tumor but rectum slightly fixed, indicating infiltration of perirectal fat	90
CS_4	Fixed rectal wall, indicating infiltration of adjacent structures	

SOURCE: From York Mason.[1] Reproduced by permission.

to those that are polypoid or sessile have a poorer prognosis and are more likely to have local regional involvement.[3,4] Multiple directed biopsies of viable tumor should be taken both to confirm the diagnosis of adenocarcinoma and to examine the tumor for histologic grading and DNA content. Histologic grading has some predictive value with respect to prognostic and lymph node metastases (LNM). Cohen et al.[5] and Minsky et al.[6] reported a 63 and 50 percent incidence of LNM respectively for poorly differentiated carcinomas regardless of depth of tumor invasion (T stage). Well-differentiated tumors regardless of T stage had an incidence of LNM of 0 and 38 percent, and moderately differentiated tumors, 30 and 57 percent respectively.[5,6] A recent study by Brodsky et al.[7] of T_1/T_2 tumors demonstrated LNM in 22 percent of those that were moderately differentiated and in none of those that were well differentiated. Generally, tumors that are mucin-producing[6,8,9] or that are accompanied by vascular or lymphatic invasion are more likely to have spread locally and have a poor prognosis.[9–11] Unfortunately, there is a 40 percent error rate between grade based on biopsy versus final tumor grade based on the complete pathology specimen,[12] thus lessening the utility of histologic differentiation based on preoperative biopsies.

The primary use of DNA ploidy analysis thus far has been as a predictor of prognosis in colorectal cancer, with diploid tumors having a better prognosis than aneuploid tumors.[13–18] Standard pathologic tumor characteristics such as degree of differentiation, patterns of tumor invasion, and lymphocytic response do not correlate with DNA ploidy.[13–17] The incidence of DNA aneuploidy does seem to be higher in tumors with vascular invasion.[19,20] There is some evidence that DNA aneuploidy increases with pathologic stage.[16,17,20] Although this relationship is weak, it may have some predictive value for distant metastases and possibly lymph node metastases.[16,21] DNA ploidy based on biopsy has been shown to correlate very closely with DNA ploidy of the complete specimen. Although they do not strictly constitute local regional staging, histology and ploidy analysis contribute to surgical decision making by identifying patients whose tumors point to a poor prognosis and who may benefit from preoperative adjuvant therapy.

CROSS-SECTIONAL IMAGING

Endoscopic and barium enema examinations have sensitivities of over 90 percent in detecting rectal cancer. They do not allow complete staging due to their inability to assess local regional extent and distant spread. This requires some form of cross-sectional tumor imaging. Computed tomography (CT), magnetic resonance imaging (MRI), and endorectal ultrasound (ERUS) have all been used to provide clinicians with additional information concerning the staging of rectal cancer. Their accuracy varies greatly.

Computed Tomography

Computed tomography has been used both for local regional staging and for the detection of distant metastases in both the liver and lungs. Early reports suggested that CT staging of local and regional spread correlated well with surgical and histologic findings, with reported accuracy rates of 77 to 100 percent.[22–26] Later studies reported much lower accuracy rates of 53 to 79 percent (Table 54-2), due to low sensitivity for detecting local tumor extension (53 to 77 percent) and lymph node metastases (22 to 36 percent).[22,25,27–32] The ability of CT to detect local extension depends on the stage of the tumor. It is not possible to determine depth of invasion accurately with CT because it cannot delineate the layers of the intestinal wall; however, it is more accurate in determining extrarectal spread. This explains in part the variability in reported accuracy, since many early series consisted predominantly of more advanced tumors. In a study by Freeny et al.,[29] where CT staging was compared to pathologic staging (Astler-Coller modification of Dukes' staging), only 4 of 18 A and B_1 tumors and 12 of 31 B_2 tumors were staged correctly. The accuracy rate for identifying local tumor extension beyond the serosa was 69 percent, with a sensitivity of 61 percent and a specificity of 81 percent. Overall, however, the correlation with pathologic stage was only 47 percent. The low correlation between CT staging and pathologic stage was also reported by Adalsteinsson et al.,[32] who found a 42 percent correlation with Dukes' staging. Overall, the accuracy of CT for determining transmural invasion is about 70 percent.[27,29,30,32] Computed tomography appears to be reasonably accurate for assessing locally advanced cancers, especially those with adjacent organ involvement.[32]

Computed tomography is also very inaccurate in detecting lymph node metastases, as it relies on the detection of enlarged nodes (Table 54-3). Nodal size does not necessarily correlate with metastatic involvement, as there is a relatively high prevalence of micrometastases in nodes less than 1.5 cm in diameter. Overall, accuracy in detecting lymph node metastases is about 40 to 45 percent,[22,25,27–30,32] with a sensitivity of 22 to 36 percent. Obliquity of the pelvis and the variation in pelvic vasculature makes lymph node metastases difficult to visualize and gives high false-positive and false-negative rates. Most authors feel that all lymph nodes visualized adjacent to the tumor should be regarded as involved nodes; however, each author uses different criteria, making comparisons between series difficult. Decreasing threshold size for diagnosing lymph node metastases increases the sensitivity, with a concomitant loss of specificity. Several different techniques are being tried to increase the accuracy of CT. A recent report by Angelelli et al.,[33] using complete distension of the rectum with water, reports an overall staging accuracy of 83 percent, with an accuracy of detecting local invasion of 98 percent and lymph node metastases of 79 percent.

An additional problem with CT is intra- and interobserver agreement. Shank et al.[34] in 1990 gave the CT

Table 54-2
Computed Tomographic Determination of Level of Invasion in Rectal Carcinoma

Authors	*No.*	*Accuracy, %*	*Sensitivity, %*	*Specificity, %*
Dixon et al.,[22] 1981	47	78	72	89
Grabbe et al.,[25] 1983	154	79	74	92
Adalsteinsson et al.,[32] 1985	94	62	62	61
Freeny et al.,[29] 1986	80	62	61	61
Thompson et al.,[28] 1986	25	70	77	57
Holdsworth et al.,[27] 1988	36	94[a]	100	67
Rifkin et al.,[30] 1990	81	53[a]	53	53

[a]Invasion into fat.

Table 54-3
Computed Tomographic Determination of Lymph Node Metastases in Rectal Carcinoma

Authors	*No.*	*Accuracy, %*	*Sensitivity, %*	*Specificity, %*
Dixon et al.,[22] 1981	47	49	36	96
Grabbe et al.,[25] 1983	54	56	34	92
Freeny et al.,[29] 1986	80	35	26	75
Thompson et al.,[28] 1986	25	35	22	75
Holdsworth et al.,[27] 1988	36	70	25	85
Rifkin et al.,[30] 1990	81	72	27	88

scans of 91 patients with proven rectal cancer to two different radiologists. In addition, one radiologist reread the scans at a later date to determine intraobserver variation. They found that agreement between the two observers with respect to stage occurred in only 37 percent of the cases, while agreement between the two stagings performed by the same observer was only 51 percent. In this study, CT staging was in agreement with the final pathology only 33 percent of the time and most frequently erred on the side of understaging.

At the present time, CT should not be relied upon for definitive local regional staging. Its primary use is to aid in the selection of patients with advanced tumors for adjuvant preoperative treatment by evaluating local invasion and liver metastases. Knowledge of extrarectal extension may assist in planning preoperative radiotherapy. There are no large series demonstrating a survival benefit; however, CT-guided radiotherapy has two major advantages.[35] First, it ensures that all areas of macroscopic involvement are included in the field of radiation. Unfortunately, the inability of CT to identify microscopic disease may allow some tissue to escape treatment. Second, CT can also demonstrate the relationship of the tumor to other uninvolved radiosensitive regions. This allows the planning of radiation fields to maximize tumor dose and minimize dosages to sensitive organs such as the bladder and small bowel. The involvement of pararectal organs identified on CT will also change the surgical approach, preparing the surgeon in advance and perhaps enhancing the safety of the operation. The presence of unresectable liver metastases will change surgical intent from curative to palliative and may influence the decision to perform a local rather than a resective procedure in a poor-risk patient. It would also obviate the need for preoperative adjuvant chemoradiation.

Magnetic Resonance Imaging

Magnetic resonance imaging has the same limitations as CT in staging rectal cancer. It is unable to delineate the layers of the bowel wall and relies on enlargement of nodes to predict LNM. Overall staging accuracy is around 74 to 79 percent, but only small series have been reported.[36–39] Hodgman et al.[36] compared staging by CT and MRI. They found that MRI staged 59 percent of patients accurately with respect to depth of invasion but only 13 percent correctly with respect to LNM, in contrast to CT, where 80 percent were staged correctly for depth of invasion and 40 percent were staged correctly with respect to LNM. Most of the lesions in this study were advanced, and the investigators concluded that, overall, CT was more accurate than MRI. In predicting lymph node metastases, MRI was as specific as, but less sensitive than CT. Butch et al.,[38] in 16 patients, found that CT and MRI were equally effective in staging local tumor extent. Neither CT nor MRI could accurately determine the degree of extension through the rectal wall or spread to normal-sized lymph nodes. De Lange et al.,[39] in 1990, examined 29 patients with rectal cancer, using a surface coil and balloon distension of the rectum. They reported accuracies of 90 percent for depth of invasion. However, all cases of extramural invasion had macroscopic disease, which enhanced the results because of greater sensitivity. Only 4 of 7 patients with nodal disease were identified correctly. A recent report on endorectal coils is very promising, as resolution is greatly enhanced with their use. The preliminary study found that 11 of 12 patients were correctly staged for depth of invasion but, again, only 4 of 7 patients were correctly staged for nodal metastases.[40] At the present time there is no distinct advantage of MRI over CT in local regional staging of rectal cancer, although future technologic developments utilizing endorectal coils may enhance the usefulness of this modality.

Endorectal Ultrasound

Of all the cross-sectional imaging modalities, endorectal ultrasound (ERUS) has emerged as the modality of choice for accurately determining the depth of invasion of rectal cancer. It has also proven accurate for lymph node metastases.[41]

The major advantage of ultrasound is its ability to accurately determine depth of tumor infiltration. Using a 7.0 MHz transducer, the bowel wall is imaged as a five-layer structure. There has been some disagreement as to the interpretation of these layers; however, we have found the five-layer model of Beynon[42] to be the most useful (Fig. 54-1). The layers are alternately echogenic and echo poor. The inner white line represents the interface of the balloon and the mucosal surface. The inner black line represents the mucosa and the muscularis mocusa, while the middle white line represents the submucosa. The outer black line represents the muscularis propria, while the outer white line represents the interface of the muscularis propria and the pararectal fat (Fig. 54-2).

The examination is limited by the technique, skill, and experience of the examiner. The entire length of the tumor must be imaged, as the level of tumor invasion is not uniform. The middle white line, corresponding to the submucosa, is very important, as a break in this layer signifies invasive cancer (Fig. 54-3). Once this has been established, attention is turned to the thickness of the muscularis propria and the integrity of the outer white line. If the outer white line is broken, the tumor is invading the pararectal fat.

A modification of the TNM staging system was proposed by Hildebrandt and Feifel[43] for preoperative ultrasonic staging of rectal tumors. In this system, an ultrasonic T_1 lesion (uT_1) is a malignant lesion confined to the submucosa, a uT_2 lesion is confined to the rectal wall with invasion into but not through the muscularis propria, a uT_3 lesion denotes invasion into the pararectal fat, and a uT_4 lesion invades adjacent organs such as the prostate, vagina, or bladder. N_0 denotes no evidence of regional nodal metastases and N_1 implies involvement of a pararectal node with metastatic disease. An in situ or a benign lesion is designated by uT_0.

Endorectal ultrasound can be highly accurate in assessing the depth of rectal wall invasion. A wide range of accuracy is reported with this method, which emphasizes its dependence on the operator. Overall, pathologic correlation with ultrasonic staging (accuracy) for the determination of depth of invasion is 87 to 94 percent, with approximately 5 to 10 percent overstaged and 1 to 9 percent understaged (Table 54-4).[27,42,44–50] The results of our own experience from 1986 to February 1990 demonstrates the importance of experience in interpreting ERUS.[50] Overall accuracy for depth of invasion in our initial report on 106 pa-

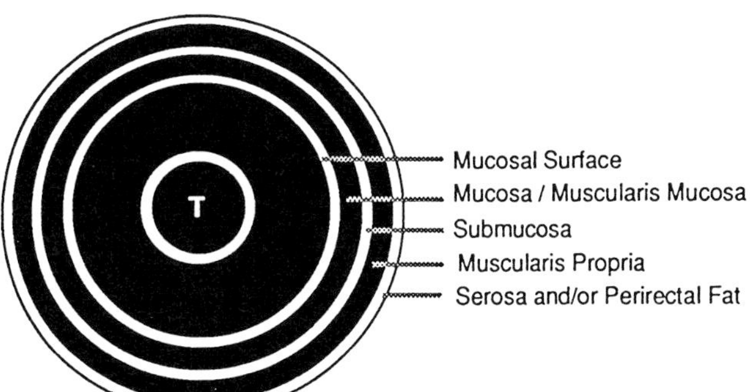

FIG. 54-1. Five-layer anatomic model for interpretation of endorectal ultrasonographic scans. Three echogenic (white lines) and two echo-poor (dark lines) layers are visualized. (From Orrom et al.[50] Reproduced by permission.)

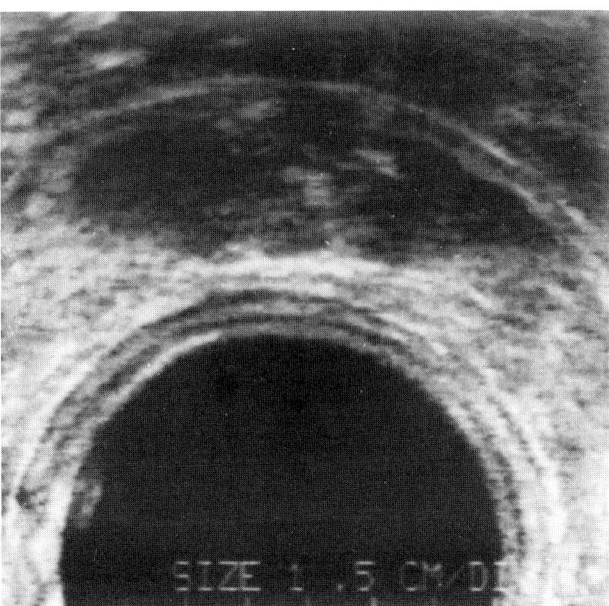

FIG. 54-2. Normal rectal wall. The five layers of the rectal wall are clearly visible.

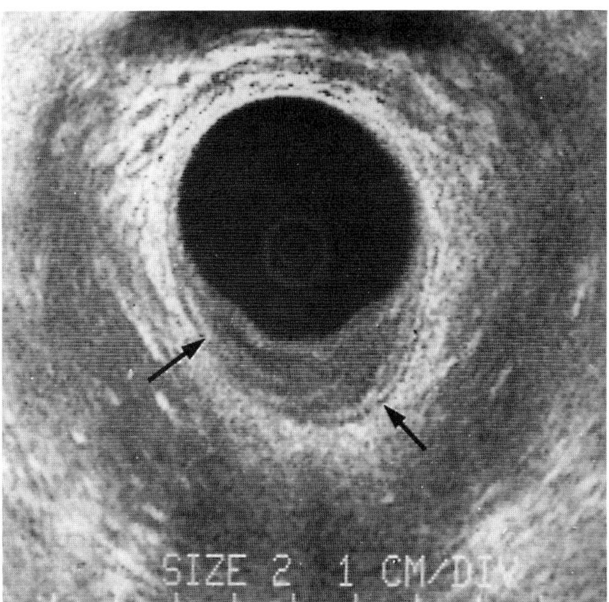

FIG. 54-3. A UT_1 lesion signifying invasion of the submucosa.

Table 54-4
Endorectal Ultrasound Assessment of Recal Wall Invasion

Authors	*No.*	*Accuracy, %*	*Overstage, %*	*Understage, %*
Romano et al.,[48] 1985	23	87	4	9
Boscaini et al.,[44] 1986	11	91	0	9
Hildebrandt et al.,[45] 1986	76	88	11	1
Accarpio et al.,[49] 1987	54	94	4	2
Beynon et al.,[42] 1989	100	93	5	2
Holdsworth et al.,[27] 1988	36	86	11	3
Orrom et al.,[50] 1990	49	88	8	4
Glaser et al.,[46] 1990	110	87	8	5
Katsura et al.,[47] 1992	120	92	4	4

tients was 59 percent, but this figure had increased to 88 percent by the end of the study (Fig. 54-4). These results compare favorably with other series (mean accuracy = 89 percent).

As with all cross-sectional imaging modalities, accuracy improves with advancing tumor stage. Staging of perirectal fat invasion with ERUS approaches an accuracy of 90 percent (Table 54-5). Beynon[42] reported that ultrasound had a 97 percent accuracy rate for invasion beyond the muscularis propria, with a sensitivity of 97 percent and a specificity of 91 percent. In our own series, our sensitivity in determining perirectal fat invasion was 92 percent, with a specificity of 90 percent. The low false-negative rates gives a negative predictive value of 98 percent, meaning that ERUS is very reliable in determining that a tumor is confined to the rectal wall.

As with CT and MRI, lymph node size is not necessarily related to the presence of metastases. Large nodes are often reactive and small nodes may be involved with microscopic tumor. Normal nodes and most reactive nodes are not imaged on an ultrasonic scan. As malignant nodes are usually located at the level of or just proximal to the primary lesion, any hypoechoic lesion regardless of size in the pararectal tissues should be reported as a potential node with metastatic involvement. A recent study by Katsura et al.[47] found that histologically positive nodes tended to be greater than 5 mm in diameter, had sharply defined borders, and an uneven and markedly hypoechoic image pattern similar to that of the primary tumor. Blood vessels are echogenic and can be mistaken for lymph nodes; but by assessing their entire length and identifying branching or extension, one can distinguish vessels from lymph nodes. Ultrasound cannot differentiate involved nodes from islands of tumor outside the rectum, but this distinction is probably of little clinical significance.

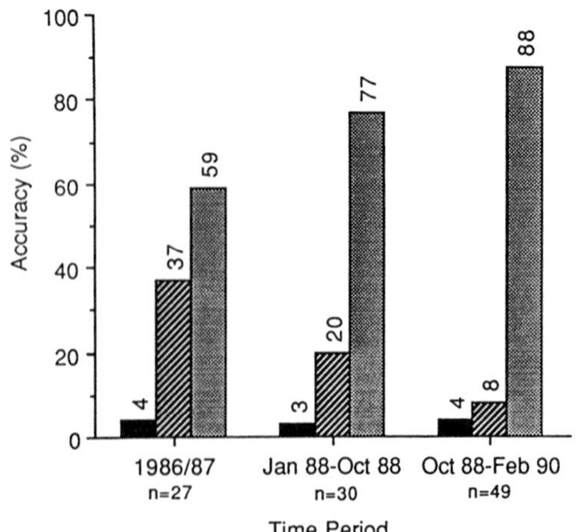

FIG. 54-4. Endorectal ultrasonographic learning curve graphically demonstrated by comparison with our early, middle, and recent experience. ■, Undercall; ▨, overcall; ▩, correct. (From Wong et al.[41] Reproduced by permission.)

Overall the accuracy rates for identifying lymph node metastases range from 61 to 83 percent (Table 54-6).[27,30,42,46,51] Rifkin et al.[30] in 1989 demonstrated a sensitivity of 45 percent and a specificity of 93 percent, implying a relatively high rate of false positives. This was confirmed by Beynon et al.[52] The addition of ultrasound guided fine-needle aspiration and core biopsy promises to increase the accuracy for identifying nodal spread and should decrease the false-positive rate.[53]

In comparative studies, ERUS has proven superior to both CT and clinical staging for detecting local invasion and identifying lymph node metastases from rectal cancer (Table 54-7).[27,30,42,48,54-57] Beynon[42] imaged 100 patients and demonstrated an accuracy for local invasion of 93 percent versus only 74 percent with CT and 58 percent for clinical staging. Rifkin et al.[30] imaged 102 patients with ERUS, 82 of whom also had a CT scan. They found that ERUS was more accurate than CT at all stages. For stage A and B_1 tumors, ERUS had an accuracy of 75 percent versus only 52 percent for CT. The difference in diagnostic accuracy between CT and ERUS, however, decreases in imaging more advanced tumors. In 17 patients with penetration of tumor through the rectal wall, Holdsworth et al.[27] found that the accuracy for CT and ERUS was

Table 54-5
Endorectal Ultrasound Staging of Perirectal Fat Invasion

Authors	*Accuracy, %*	*Sensitivity, %*	*Specificity, %*	*Positive predictive value, %*	*Negative predictive value, %*
Rifkin et al.,[30] 1989	71	67	77	73	72
Holdsworth et al.,[27] 1988	86	96	50	87	80
Beynon,[42] 1989	97	97	91	97	95
Glaser et al.,[46] 1990	92	97	90	98	90
Rothenberger et al. 1992 (current series)		92	90	72	98

86 and 94 percent respectively. Pappalardo et al.[58] reported that ERUS was 100 percent accurate for extramural disease while CT was only 78 percent accurate. Accuracy rates for the detection of lymph node metastases are higher for ERUS than for CT. In Beynon's series, accuracy for mesorectal lymph node metastases was 83 percent for ERUS versus only 57 percent for CT.[42]

Endorectal ultrasound has also been investigated for the staging of rectal cancer after treatment with preoperative radiotherapy. Radiotherapy causes marked tissue edema and disrupts the planes of the intestinal wall, and neither CT nor MRI has been helpful in postradiotherapy staging. Napoleon et al.[59] in 1990 reported on the accuracy of ERUS following preoperative radiotherapy. The rectal wall became markedly thickened and wall invasion was correctly staged in only 47 percent of the irradiated group as compared with 86 percent of the nonirradiated group. The accuracy for lymph node involvement did not change (84 percent following radiotherapy versus 85 percent without radiotherapy). These results were confirmed by Dershaw et al.,[60] who also found that, following preoperative radiation, fibrosis and edema made ERUS staging unreliable. The importance of postradiotherapy staging before surgery depends entirely on whether radiotherapy actually downstages rectal cancer and, more importantly, whether any perceived downstaging would alter surgical management.

Limitations

Endorectal ultrasound is limited by any situation which precludes complete tumor imaging. This includes severe stenosis which will not allow the advancement of the probe and lesions above 15 cm from the anal verge. The entire length of the tumor must be examined, as the level of invasion is not uniform throughout the tumor and lymph node metastases can occur at any level. Imaging, although reproducible, is operator-dependent, and there is a steep learning curve.[50]

ILEOPELVIC LYMPHOSCINTIGRAPHY

Lymphoscintigraphy has been singularly disappointing in the staging of rectal cancer.[61,62] The largest study, by Reasbeck et al.,[61] examined 18 patients with carcinoma of the rectum or sigmoid colon, 4 with inflammatory disease, and 20 controls. The presence or absence of nodal uptake demonstrated by either abdominal scans or in vitro scans of excised specimens was not related to the presence or absence of nodal metastases. They concluded that there was no demonstrable value in lymphoscintigraphy for the staging of rectal cancer.

RADIOLABELED ANTIBODY IMAGING

Radiolabeled antibody imaging is a technique whereby tumor cells are tagged with a radiolabeled monoclonal

Table 54-6
Endorectal Ultrasound Staging of Lymph Node Metastases

Authors	*No.*	*Accuracy, %*	*Sensitivity, %*	*Specificity, %*
Rifkin et al.,[54] 1986	59	83	72	86
Beynon,[42] 1989	95	83	88	79
Holdsworth et al.,[27] 1988	36	61	57	64
Rifkin et al.,[30] 1989	102	81	45	93
Glaser et al.,[46] 1990	97	80	78	78
Hildebrandt et al.,[51] 1990	113	78	72	83
Rothenberger et al. 1992 (current series)	63	86		

Table 54-7
Comparative Studies for Determining Depth of Invasion by Digital Examination, Endorectal Ultrasound, and CT Scanning

		Accuracy to depth of invasion, %		
Authors	*No.*	*Digital*	*Endorectal ultrasound*	*CT scanning*
Romano et al.,[48] 1985	23	—	87	83
Rifkin et al.,[54] 1986	59	—	93	69
Holdsworth et al.,[27] 1988	36	—	86	94[a]
Waizer et al.,[55] 1989	68	83	76	66
Beynon,[42] 1989	100	58	93	74
Rifkin et al.,[30] 1989	102	—	72	—
	82	—	—	53
Milsom and Graffner,[56] 1990	52	48	83	—

[a]Invasion into fat.

antibody (MAb). The MAb is injected intravenously or intraperitoneally and subsequently imaged either preoperatively with an external detector or intraoperatively with a hand-held detector.[63] This form of imaging has been used primarily for the detection of recurrent occult disease. The MAbs which have been most successful are the anti-CEA[64,65] and B72.3.[66,67] They have demonstrated both the location of cancer recurrence and localized additional tumor not identified with conventional imaging techniques. Intraoperatively, they have been used to identify unsuspected microscopic disease and tumor margins demonstrating the need for a more extensive resection.[68–70]

MAbs have also been used to stage primary colorectal carcinomas, although the benefit of this application has not been proven conclusively. In a study of 22 patients imaged preoperatively with monoclonal antibodies to CA19.9 and CEA, 12 of 23 primary tumors were identified with a sensitivity of 52 percent.[71] There was one false positive and 10 false negatives, but the radioimmunolocalization did not add any information to that gained by conventional procedures. Sensitivity was increased if the blood levels of at least one of the tumor markers was increased. In a large multicenter trial examining preoperative external imaging, a single infusion of an immunoconjugate of a monoclonal antibody (B72.3) was administered to 116 patients with primary or recurrent colorectal carcinoma.[69] Of these patients, 103 underwent a surgical procedure for diagnosis and/or treatment. The overall accuracy was 72 percent for detecting disease, with a sensitivity of 70 percent and a specificity of 90 percent. Occult disease (not detected by a standard surgical workup) was detected in 12 percent of patients. The sensitivity for detecting disease in the pelvis was 74 percent, compared with 59 percent with CT scans. Antibody imaging contributed to surgical decision making in 26 percent of patients.

At present there are several problems with MAbs. First, most of the MAbs tested are murine MAbs, and approximately 50 percent of patients develop human antimouse antibodies (HAMA) following a second injection. This may cause an anaphylactic reaction but—more importantly—causes the MAb to be rapidly excreted. Second, tumor cells often express a wide variety of antigens (tumor heterogeneity), which prevents MAbs from completely coating all cells. The most commonly used MAb, B72.3, binds to only 75 to 80 percent of tumor cells. Third, tumor cell populations may undergo antigenic modulation during metastasis, which prevent the coating of those metastatic populations.

This technique is promising but is limited at present by the lack of complete specificity of individual MAbs to tumor cells. In addition, staging for depth of invasion is impossible, as the layers of the intestine cannot be identified. As new MAbs with new radiolabels are developed and tested, however, the accuracy of this method will improve. It is the only modality at present that can image micrometastases.

APPLICATION OF LOCAL REGIONAL STAGING

Local regional staging of rectal cancer is useful only if the information is used to determine or alter management decisions.[72] How does accurate local regional staging accomplish this? First, it allows rational planning of surgical strategy. Accurate staging selects patients in whom local therapy will be curative, selects out those patients who will benefit from preoperative adjuvant therapy, and identifies preoperatively those patients who require extended regional procedures to effect local regional control. Second, it provides prognostic information to surgeons and patients preoperatively. Third, it enables accurate allocation preoperatively in controlled clinical trials for improved comparison.

Preoperative local regional staging centers around the identification of three groups of patients: (1) those who are suitable for local therapy; (2) those who require adjuvant preoperative therapy; and (3) poor-risk patients in whom treatment decisions must be a compromise. All patients diagnosed with rectal cancer must undergo a complete physical examination including digital assessment, a proctoscopy with biopsy, and a complete colonoscopy to rule out synchronous lesions. Depending on the results of the examination, the patient should undergo either an ERUS or a CT. An ERUS is used to determine the depth of invasion and to identify lymph node metastases in patients who appear, on clinical examination, to have local disease. Depth of invasion correlates well with prognosis and the presence of nodal disease.[1] Any hypoechoic nodule which is suspicious for cancer is biopsied transanally with ERUS guidance; if the result is positive, the patient is excluded from curative local therapy. Patients without evidence of nodal metastases who have a small distal cancer confined to the bowel wall are candidates for local therapy if the tumor is well to moderately differentiated, not mucin-producing, not DNA-aneuploid, and has no evidence of blood vessel or lymphatic invasion.[6] The presence of any of these factors increases the probability of extrarectal spread. Endorectal ultrasound is also helpful in low and midrectal tumors if adjacent structures such as the vagina and the prostate are involved.

Patients presenting on initial examination with a very large tumor, a tumor adherent to adjacent structures, or one with palpable lymph nodes are potential candidates for preoperative adjuvant radiotherapy. These patients are imaged by CT primarily to delineate the extent of pelvic disease for planning radiotherapy but also to examine the liver for metastatic disease. Patients who have extensive liver metastases, regardless of the local stage of their disease, should not undergo an extensive course of preoperative chemoradiotherapy, as the benefits do not outweigh the risks.

Patients who are poor risks may not tolerate a formal cancer resection. Endorectal ultrasound will identify a tumor which, although metastatic, may still be amenable to local therapy to gain local control. In patients with a high operative risk, the surgeon must be flexible in the application of tumor characteristics as selection criteria for local therapy.[73]

REFERENCES

1. York Mason A: Rectal cancer: The spectrum of selective surgery. *Proc R Soc Med* 69:237–244, 1976.
2. Nicholls RJ, York Mason A, Morson BC, et al: The clinical staging of rectal cancer. *Br J Surg* 69:404–409, 1982.
3. Bjerkeset T, Morild I, Mork S, et al: Tumor characteristics in colorectal cancer and their relationship to treatment and prognosis. *Dis Colon Rectum* 30:934–938, 1987.
4. Schmitz-Moormann GW, Himmelmann UB, Niles M: Morphological predictors of survival in colorectal carcinoma: Univariate and multivariate analysis. *J Cancer Res Clin Oncol* 113:586–592, 1987.
5. Cohen AM, Wood WC, Gunderson LL, et al: Pathological studies in rectal cancer. *Cancer* 45:2965–2968, 1980.
6. Minsky BD, Rich T, Recth A, et al: Selection criteria for local excision with or without adjuvant radiation therapy for rectal cancer. *Cancer* 63:1421–1429, 1989.
7. Brodsky JT, Richard GK, Cohen AM, et al: Variables correlated with the risk of lymph node metastasis in early rectal cancer. *Cancer* 69:322–326, 1992.
8. Symonds DA, Vickery AL Jr: Mucinous carcinoma of the colon and rectum. *Cancer* 37:1891–1900, 1976.
9. Umpleby HC, Ranson DL, Williamson HC: Peculiarities of mucinous colorectal carcinoma. *Br J Surg* 72:715–718, 1985.
10. Phillips RKS, Hittinger R, Blesovsky L, et al: Large bowel cancer: Surgical pathology and its relationship to survival. *Br J Surg* 71:604–610, 1984.
11. Krasna MJ, Flancbaum L, Cody RP, et al: Vascular and neural invasion in colorectal carcinoma: Incidence and prognostic significance. *Cancer* 61:1018–1023, 1988.
12. Elliott MS, Todd IP, Nicholls RJ: Radical restorative surgery for poorly differentiated carcinoma of the midrectum. *Br J Surg* 69:273–274, 1982.
13. Armitage NC, Robins RA, Evans DF, et al: Tumour cell DNA content in colorectal cancer and its relationship to survival. *Br J Surg* 72:828–830, 1985.
14. Kokal W, Sheibani K, Terz J, et al: Tumor DNA content in the prognosis of colorectal carcinoma. *JAMA* 255:3123–3127, 1986.
15. Scott NA, Wieand HS, Moertel CG, et al: Dukes' stage, tumor site, preoperative plasma CEA level, and patient prognosis related to tumor DNA ploidy pattern. *Arch Surg* 122:1375–1379, 1987.
16. Banner BF, Tomas-de la Vega JE, Roseman DL, et al: Should flow cytometric DNA analysis precede definitive surgery for colon carcinoma? *Ann Surg* 202:740–744, 1985.
17. Suzuki H, Matsumoto K, Masuda T, et al: DNA ploidy of colorectal carcinoma: Correlation with conventional prognostic variables. *J Clin Gastroenterol* 10:176–178, 1988.
18. Quirke P, Dixon MF, Clayden AD, et al: Prognostic significance of DNA aneuploidy and cell proliferation in rectal C adenocarcinoma. *J Path* 151:25–229, 1987.
19. Schutte B, Reynders MMJ, Wiggers T: Retrospective analysis of the prognostic significance of DNA content and proliferative activity in large bowel carcinoma. *Cancer Res* 47:5494–5496, 1987.
20. Scott NA, Rainwater LM, Wieand HS, et al: The relative prognostic value of flow cytometric DNA analysis and conventional clinicopathologic criteria in patients with operable rectal carcinoma. *Dis Colon Rectum* 30:513–520, 1987.
21. Moran MR, Rothenberger DA, Gallo RA, et al: A predictive model for distant metastases in rectal cancer using DNA ploidy studies. *Am J Surg* 163:599–601, 1992.
22. Dixon AK, Fry IK, Morson BC, et al: Pre-operative computed tomography of carcinoma of the rectum. *Br J Radiol* 54:655–659, 1981.
23. Thoeni RF, Moss AA, Schnyder P, et al: Detection and staging of primary rectal and rectosigmoid cancer by computed tomography. *Radiology* 141:135–138, 1981.
24. Zaunbauer W, Haertel M, Fuchs WA: Computed tomography in carcinoma of the rectum. *Gastrointest Radiol* 6:79–84, 1981.

25. Grabbe E, Lierse W, Winkler R: The perirectal fascia: Morphology and use in staging of rectal carcinoma. *Radiology* 149:241–246, 1983.
26. van Waes PFGM, Koehler PR, Feldberg MAM: Management of rectal carcinoma: Impact of computed tomography. *Am J Radiol* 140:1137–1142, 1983.
27. Holdsworth PJ, Johnston D, Chalmers AG, et al: Endoluminal ultrasound and computed tomography in the staging of rectal cancer. *Br J Surg* 75:1019–1022, 1988.
28. Thompson WM, Halvorsen RA, Foster WL Jr, et al: Preoperative and postoperative CT staging of rectosigmoid carcinoma. *Am J Radiol* 146:703–710, 1986.
29. Freeny PC, Marks WM, Ryan JA, et al: Colorectal carcinoma evaluation with CT: Preoperative staging and detection of postoperative recurrence. *Radiology* 158:347–353, 1986.
30. Rifkin MD, Ehrlich SM, Marks G: Staging of rectal carcinoma: Prospective comparison of endorectal US and CT. *Radiology* 170:319–322, 1989.
31. Balthazar EJ, Megibow AJ, Hulnick D, et al: Carcinoma of the colon: Detection and preoperative staging by CT. *AJR* 150:301–306, 1988.
32. Adalsteinsson B, Glimelius B, Graffman S, et al: Computed tomography in staging of rectal carcinoma. *Acta Radiol Diagn* 26:45–55, 1985.
33. Angelelli C, Macarini L, Lupo L, et al: Rectal carcinoma: CT staging with water as contrast medium. *Radiology* 177:511–514, 1990.
34. Shank B, Dershaw DD, Caravelli J, et al: A prospective study of the accuracy of preoperative computed tomographic staging of patients with biopsy-proven rectal carcinoma. *Dis Colon Rectum* 33:285–290, 1990.
35. Williams MP, Husband JE: CT scanning in carcinoma of the rectum: A review. *J Roy Soc Med* 80:701–703, 1987.
36. Hodgman CG, MacCarty RL, Wolff BG, et al: Preoperative staging of rectal carcinoma by computed tomography and 0.15 T magnetic resonance imaging: Preliminary report. *Dis Colon Rectum* 29:446–450, 1986.
37. Guinet C, Buy JN, Ghossain MA, et al: Comparison of magnetic resonance imaging and computed tomography in the preoperative staging of rectal cancer. *Arch Surg* 125:385–388, 1990.
38. Butch RJ, Stark DD, Wittenberg J, et al: Staging rectal cancer by MR and CT. *Am J Radiol* 146:1155–1160, 1986.
39. De Lange EE, Fechner RE, Edge SB, et al: Preoperative staging of rectal carcinoma with MR imaging: Surgical and histopathologic correlation. *Radiology* 176:623–628, 1990.
40. Chan TW, Kressel HY, Milestone B: Rectal carcinoma: Staging at MR imaging with endorectal surface coil. *Radiology* 181:461–467, 1991.
41. Wong WD, Orrom WJ, Jensen LL: Preoperative staging of rectal cancer with endorectal ultrasononography. *Perspect Colon Rectal Surg* 3:315–334, 1990.
42. Beynon J: An evaluation of the role of rectal endosonography in rectal cancer. *Ann Roy College Surg Eng* 71:131–139, 1989.
43. Hildebrandt U, Feifel G: Preoperative staging of rectal cancer by intrarectal ultrasound. *Dis Colon Rectum* 28:42–46, 1985.
44. Boscaini M, Masoni L, Montori A: Transrectal ultrasonography: Three years' experience. *Int J Colorect Dis* 1:208–211, 1986.
45. Hildebrandt U, Feifel G, Schwarz HP, et al: Endorectal ultrasound: Instrumentation and clinical aspects. *Int J Colorect Dis* 1:203–207, 1986.
46. Glaser F, Friedl P, Ditfurth BV, et al: Influence of endorectal ultrasound on surgical treatment of rectal cancer. *Eur J Surg Oncol* 16:304–311, 1990.
47. Katsura Y, Yamada K, Ishizawa T, et al: Endorectal ultrasonography for the assessment of wall invasion and lymph node metastasis in rectal cancer. *Dis Colon Rectum* 35:362–368, 1992.
48. Romano G, deRosa P, Vallone G, et al: Intrarectal ultrasound and computed tomography in the pre- and postoperative assessment of patients with rectal cancer. *Br J Surg* 72:S117–S119, 1985.
49. Accarpio G, Scopinaro G, Claudiani, F, et al: Experience with local rectal excision in light of two recent preoperative diagnostic methods. *Dis Colon Rectum* 30:296–298, 1987.
50. Orrom WJ, Wong WD, Rothenberger DA, et al: Endorectal ultrasound in the preoperative staging of rectal tumors: A learning experience. *Dis Colon Rectum* 33:654–659, 1990.
51. Hildebrandt U, Klein T, Feifel G, et al: Endosonography of pararectal lymph nodes—In vitro and in vivo evaluation. *Dis Colon Rectum* 33:863–868, 1990.
52. Beynon J, Mortenson NJ, Foy DMA, et al: Preoperative assessment of mesorectal lymph node involvement in rectal cancer. *Br J Surg* 76:276–279, 1989.
53. Neilson MB, Pedersen JF, Hald J, et al: Recurrence extraluminal rectal carcinoma: Transrectal biopsy under sonographic guidance. *AJR* 158:1025–1027, 1992.
54. Rifkin MD, McGlynn ET, Marks G: Endorectal sonographic prospective staging of rectal cancer. *Scand J Gastroenterol* 21(suppl 123):99–103, 1986.
55. Waizer Z, Zitron S, Ben-Baruch D, et al: Comparative study for preoperative staging of rectal cancer. *Dis Colon Rectum* 32:53–56, 1989.
56. Milsom JW, Graffner H: Intrarectal ultrasonography in rectal cancer staging and in the evaluation of pelvic disease: Clinical uses of intrarectal ultrasound. *Ann Surg* 212:602–606, 1990.
57. Milsom JW, Graffner H: Intrarectal ultrasonography in rectal cancer staging and in the evaluation of pelvic disease. *Ann Surg* 212:602–606, 1990.
58. Pappalardo G, Reggio D, Frattaroli FM: The value of endoluminal ultrasonography and computed tomography in the staging of rectal cancer: A preliminary study. *J Surg Oncol* 43:219–222, 1990.
59. Napoleon B, Pujol B, Berger F, et al: Accuracy of endosonography in the staging of rectal cancer treated by radiotherapy. *Br J Surg* 78:785–788, 1991.
60. Dershaw DD, Warren EE, Cohen AM, et al: Transrectal ultrasonography of rectal carcinoma. *Cancer* 66:2336–2340, 1990.
61. Reasbeck PG, Manktelow A, McArthur AM, et al: An evaluation of pelvic lymphoscintigraphy in the staging of colorectal carcinoma. *Br J Surg* 71:936–940, 1984.
62. Bucci L, Salfi R, Meraviglia F, et al: Rectal lymphoscintigraphy. *Dis Colon Rectum* 27:370–375, 1984.
63. Lange MK, Martin EW Jr: Monoclonal antibodies in imaging and therapy of colorectal cancer. *World J Surg* 15:617–622, 1991.
64. Serafini AN, Goldenberg DM, Higginbotham-Ford EA: A multicenter trial of cancer imaging with fragments of CEA monoclonal antibodies. *J Nuclear Med* 30:748, 1989.
65. Riva P, Moscatelli G, Paganelli G, et al: Antibody-guided diagnosis: An Italian experience on cea-expressing tumors. *Int J Cancer Suppl* 2:1114–1200, 1988.
66. Renda A, Salvatore M, Sava M, et al: Immunoscintigraphy in the follow-up of patients operated on for carcinoma of the sigmoid and rectum: Preliminary report with a new monoclonal antibody—B72.3 (abstract). *Dis Colon Rectum* 30:683–686, 1987.
67. Carrasquillo JA, Sugarbaker P, Colcher D, et al: Radioimmunoscintigraphy of colon cancer with iodine-131-labeled B72.3 monoclonal antibody. *J Nucl Med* 29:1022–1030, 1988.
68. Beatty JD, Hyams DM, Morton BA, et al: Impact of radiola-

beled antibody imaging on management of colon cancer (abstract). *Am J Surg* 157:13–19, 1989.

69. Doerr RJ, Abdel-Nabi H, Krag D, et al: Radiolabeled antibody imaging in the management of colorectal cancer: Results of a multicenter clinical study. *Ann Surg* 214:118–124, 1991.
70. Nieroda CA, Mojzisik C, Sardi A, et al: The impact of radioimmunoguided surgery (RIGS TM) on surgical decision-making in colorectal cancer. *Dis Colon Rectum* 32:927–932, 1989.
71. Germa-Lluch JR, Alvarez I, Carrio I: Radioimmunolocalization of colorectal carcinoma: A correlation among RIL results, surgical findings, serum tumor marker levels and the presence of CEA and CA 19.9 in tumor tissue: The experience of the Hospital de la Santa Creu i Sant Pau. *Ann Oncol* 2:409–415, 1991.
72. Cohen AM: Preoperative evaluation of patients with primary colorectal cancer. *Cancer* 70:1328–1332, 1992.
73. Rothenberger DA, Wong WD: Preoperative assessment of patients with rectal cancer. *Semin Colon Rectal Surg* 1:2–10, 1990.

CHAPTER 55

Clinical-Pathologic Selection Issues for Local Therapy

Bruce D. Minsky

HIGHLIGHTS

This chapter focuses on the available clinical and pathologic features which can help predict the stage of local-regional rectal cancer. Exophytic mobile rectal cancer without adverse pathologic factors is well treated by conservative local-regional strategies.

CONTROVERSIES

A major limitation of the conservative management of rectal cancer is the absence of complete surgical staging. The overall accuracy of transrectal ultrasound in predicting transmural penetration is 70 to 90 percent; however, it is only 50 to 60 percent accurate in predicting the presence of positive mesorectal/pelvic lymph nodes. Therefore, the stage must be estimated from clinical, radiographic, and biopsy information. There is significant disagreement as to which factor or combination of factors most accurately predicts the true stage.

FUTURE DIRECTIONS

At the present time, intrarectal ultrasound offers the best clinical assessment of T stage, and pathologic analysis of the biopsy provides the most accurate clinical assessment of nodal status. Advances in clinical staging may be possible with improved understanding of pathologic, biological, and genetic features as well as the use of advanced magnetic resonance imaging (MRI) techniques such as a rectal coil and image analysis.

Conservative management (non–en bloc resection) has been used to treat both favorable and unfavorable rectal cancers. Favorable rectal cancers include small, exophytic, mobile tumors without adverse pathologic factors [i.e., high grade, blood vessel invasion (BVI), lymphatic vessel invasion (LVI), colloid histology, or the penetration of tumor into or through the muscularis propria].[1–3] These selected tumors represent 3 to 5 percent of all rectal cancers and are adequately treated with a variety of local therapies such as local excision alone,[4–11] cryosurgery,[12] electrocoagulation,[13] or intracavitary (contact) radiation therapy.[14] Unfavorable rectal cancers include those tumors that are not suitable for one of the local therapies outlined above due to the presence of one or more of the following features: (1) invasion of tumor into or through the muscularis propria, (2) positive pelvic lymph nodes, or (3) the presence of one or more adverse clinical or pathologic factors. In the context of conservative management, these tumors are considered relatively unfavorable, since local therapy alone may not provide adequate treatment.

Current radiologic techniques to assess the local-regional stage of rectal cancer were discussed in the previous chapter. As with most imaging techniques, accuracy is a function of the sensitivity of the instrument as well as the experience of the interpreter. This chapter will focus on clinical-pathologic correlates that may allow patient selection for local therapy options.

CLINICOPATHOLOGIC STAGING SYSTEMS

Since pathologic systems involve postsurgical staging, they cannot be used for the selection of patients for local therapy. Therefore, a number of clinical staging systems for rectal cancer have been developed. These systems attempt to predict the pathologic stage by using a combination of clinical and pathologic information.

Abrams[15] correlated the size of the tumor, the presence or absence of ulceration, and the degree of differentiation with the final Dukes' stage. Ulceration was the primary feature, with 63 percent of nonulcerated cancers being classified as Dukes A, compared with only 28 percent of ulcerated lesions. Another clinical staging system devised by a group from the Princess Margaret Hospital.[16] Since this system included patients with advanced disease, not all stages are applicable to treatment with a local therapy. The staging system was based on several prognostic variables including the degree of circumference, the presence or absence of metastases, mobility, and clinical symptoms of weight loss, anorexia, weakness, and anemia. These variables were grouped into four clinical classes. In class I, none of the variables were present. Class II was characterized by an annular rectal tumor or the presence of systemic symptoms. Class III denoted a fixed rectal tumor; and in class IV metastases were present. Comparing clinical class and Dukes' stage revealed good correlation with survival but not with stage. Univariate and multivariate analyses of prognostic features were performed on 824 rectal cancer patients in the preoperative radiation therapy trial from the British Medical Research Council.[17,18] Mobility of the tumor was the most important feature related to the ability to perform a curative resection.

An Australian clinicopathologic staging system combined features of both a clinical and pathologic staging system on the basis of local tumor characteristics.[19,20] York Mason has also suggested the use of a clinical staging system based on mobility of the primary tumor. In their system, clinical stage (CS) I represented a freely mobile tumor, CS II, a mobile tumor; CS III, tethered mobility; and CS IV, fixed tumor.[21] Nicholls et al.[22] tested the accuracy of the digital examination by comparing it with the final pathologic stage. They assessed the morphology, number of quadrants involved, fixation, and presence of extrarectal involvement. In 70 tumors, there was 67 to 83 percent correlation with the final pathology by the consulting physicians. The association was less accurate (44 to 68 percent) when tumors were assessed by physicians with less experience. In a subsequent publication, Nicholls et al.[23] reported that clinical determination of the local extent and penetration correlated with survival.

The Dijon clinical staging system[24] takes into account the tumor size and depth of penetration of the rectal wall. Briefly, CS T_1A tumors are defined as superficial, exophytic, and <3 cm in size; CS T_1B tumors have a limited infiltrative component and are <3 cm in size; CS T_2A are superficial, exophytic, and are 3 to 5 cm in size; CS T_2B tumors have a limited infiltrative component and are 3 to 5 cm; and CS T_3 tumors are deeply infiltrative or fixed regardless of size. High-grade and colloid tumors are excluded. The rationale for the different T stages is based on the technical parameters of intracavitary radiation. Tumors ≤3 cm are easily covered with the intracavitary cone, whereas tumors >3 cm require overlapping of fields and therefore a higher level of technical expertise.

According to the Dijon guidelines, patients with CS T_1A tumors can be treated adequately with intracavitary radiation alone. Stages CS T_1B and T_2A require the combination of intracavitary radiation and interstitial ^{192}Ir brachytherapy; CS T_2B tumors should receive preoperative external beam followed by either surgery or intracavitary radiation, depending on the tumor response.

In summary, the present clinical staging systems have only moderate predictive capability. Improved clinical staging systems, combined with careful histologic and biological analyses of various markers—such as flow cytometry,[25] monoclonal antibodies,[26] DNA probes,[27] and ^{31}P magnetic resonance spectroscopy[28]—may better enable investigators to define the appropriate subsets of rectal cancer patients for these treatment strategies.

CLINICOPATHOLOGIC STAGING TECHNIQUES

To determine which tumors are likely to have a high enough incidence of local failure or positive pelvic lymph nodes to consider adjuvant radiation therapy following local therapy, it must first be determined which tumors are adequately treated with local therapy alone. The selection of tumors for local therapy is based on both clinical and pathologic factors. Clinical information such as tumor size, mobility, location, and circumference can be obtained at the time of physical examination. Accurate pathologic information is more difficult to obtain from a biopsy. Of the available local therapies, only a full-thickness local excision provides accurate pathologic information.

Depth of Tumor Penetration

Most series in which patients are treated with local excision alone are highly selective and exclude patients whose tumors have adverse clinical and pathologic features. Historically, adverse clinical features have included tumors greater than 3 to 5 cm and those that are circumferential, fixed, or ulcerated. Adverse pathologic features have included high grade, BVI, LVI, colloid histology, signet-ring cells, or penetration of tumor into or through the muscularis propria ($\geq T_2$). Biggers et al.[4] reported the Mayo Clinic experience of 141 patients with T_2 rectal cancers who underwent local excision alone. The 5-year survival was 65 percent and the local failure rate 27 percent. Hager and associates[7] performed a local excision on 20 patients with T_2 rectal cancers which were otherwise "low-risk" (nonmucinous, well to moderately differentiated, no LVI, and negative margins). The incidence of local failure was 17 percent. Other series have reported local failure rates as high as 43 percent in patients with T_2 cancers following either local excision or transanal extirpation.

Willett et al.[30] reported a group of 40 patients who underwent local excision alone. In this series, a separate analysis was performed of those patients whose tumors had unfavorable clinical and pathologic factors. Factors included tumor size >3 cm, high grade, $\geq T_2$, vascular invasion (BVI and/or LVI), moderate or marked stromal fibrosis, a fragmented resection, or positive margins and were associated with a local failure rate of ≥20 percent as well as an increase in distant metastasis.

Lymph Nodes

Another goal in the development of selection criteria for conservative management is the prediction of the incidence of positive lymph nodes. Data are available that allow prediction of the incidence of positive nodes based on various clinical and pathologic factors (Table 55-1).[1,6,9,15,31–33] However, most series use univariate analysis and examine only a few factors, thereby limiting their predictive capability.

Since a lymph node dissection is not performed at the time of a local excision, the only method by which to assess the incidence of positive nodes is to examine surgical specimens from patients who have undergone a low anterior resection or an abdominoperineal resection. To use such data to predict the incidence of positive nodes in patients undergoing local excision, it must be assumed that the pathologic information obtained at the time of local excision is representative of that present during a low anterior resection or an abdominoperineal resection. This may not always be accurate. Since an adequate local excision should include the gross tumor with negative margins, it is reasonable to assume that the pathologic information obtained from the primary tumor is representative of that obtained in a more radical procedure.

Brodsky and colleagues[34] examined 154 patients with T_1 or T_2 tumors who underwent a low anterior resection or abdominoperineal resection. Elastic tissues stains were not used when examining for BVI. The incidence of positive nodes was 12 percent for T_1 tumors and 22 percent for T_2 tumors. Regardless of T stage, none of the 12 patients with well-differentiated tumors had positive nodes, compared with 24 percent for patients with moderately or poorly differentiated tumors ($p = .04$). There was a significant increase in positive nodes in patients with VI+ (LVI and/or BVI+) tumors compared with VI- tumors (31 versus 17 percent). There was a trend toward decreased positive nodes for sessile nonulcerated tumors. Tumor size and colloid histology had no significant impact on the incidence of positive nodes. Based on their data, patients with T_1 well- or moderately differentiated BVI/LVI-cancers or T_2 well-differentiated cancers had a low incidence of positive nodes and were adequately treated with local excision alone.

The only series that performed a multivariate analysis is from the New England Deaconess Hospital.[1] In this study, 168 patients who underwent a low anterior resection or an abdominoperineal resection and various clinical and pathologic factors were correlated with pelvic nodal status. By univariate analysis, the incidence of positive nodes increased with T stage, high grade, and any colloid histology. This was confirmed by logistic regression analysis. Using 2 × 2 contingency tables, the presence of BVI, LVI, colloid histology, and high grade further increased the incidence of positive nodes with increasing T stage. In patients with invasive ($\geq T_2$) rectal cancer—regardless of the tumor size, grade, histology, or presence of BVI or LVI—the incidence of positive nodes was at least 10 percent. Based on these data, patients with invasive rectal cancer, regardless of the presence or absence of associated clinical or pathologic factors, have a high enough incidence of positive nodes to make local therapy alone an inadequate treatment.

RECOMMENDATIONS

A major limitation of the series that examine local excision alone is that most are univariate rather than multivariate. Therefore, clinical and pathologic factors are not examined as independent variables. Further, the series vary in patient selection, the definition of clinical and pathologic features, and the length of follow-up among the series. Variations in patient selection sometimes stems from the individual surgeon's preference. This subjective difference makes it difficult to make firm recommendations for the selection of patients for conservative management based solely on clinical criteria. The most reasonable approach is to consider that if a local excision can be performed adequately (i.e., full thickness, nonfragmented, and

Table 55-1
The Incidence of Positive Lymph Nodes by Clinical and Pathologic Features in Rectal Cancer

Series	Total no.	T stage	No.	Percent LN+	Tumor size, cm	No.	Percent LN+	Grade	No.	Percent LN+	Combined Features	No.	Percent LN+
Nelson	76	T2	N/A	20	<2	7	29	W	21	38	T2:		
et al.[33]		T3	N/A	67	≤4	36	50	M	47	57	≤4 cm	17	24
											W+M	23	22
											≤4 cm, W+M	15	27
Grigg et al.[32]	268	T1	46	6.5	≤3	268	17						
Morson	2084	T1	46	11[a]									
et al.[9]		T2	N/A	12									
		T3	N/A	58									
Greaney	68				2[b]	6	67				≤5 cm:		
and Irvin[6]											Polypoid	9	11
											Ulcerative	43	49
											>5 cm:		
											Polypoid	5	80
											Ulcerative	11	64
Abrams[15]	167				≤3	48	31				≤5 cm:		
					3–5	67	42				Ulcerated	69	39
					≤5	115	38				Nonulcerated	30	23
					>5	37	38						
Cohen	247				≤4	75	33	W	31	29	≤4 cm:		
et al.[31]					>4	129	50	M	106	32	W	15	33
								P	48	63	M	40	30
											P	17	35
											Colloid	3	2/3
											>4 cm:		
											W	16	25
											M	66	33
											P	31	77
											Colloid	18	83
											Exophytic	50	35
											Ulcerative	148	57
Minsky	168	T1	9	0	<5	71	27	W	7	0	T1–4:		
et al.[1]		T2	50	28	≥5	97	37	M	127	30	BVI+	77	37
		T3	92	36				P	12	50	BVI−	91	30
		T4	17	53							LVI+	16	50
											LVI−	152	32
											Adenocarcinoma	145	30
											Total colloid	21	52
Brodsky	154	T1	26	12				W	12	0	VI +	32	31
et al.[34]		T2	128	22				M–P	142	24	VI −	122	17

Abbreviations: N/A, data not available; W, well-differentiated adenocarcinoma; M, moderately differentiated adenocarcinoma; P, poorly differentiated adenocarcinoma; LN+, positive lymph nodes; BVI, blood vessel invasion; LVI, lymphatic vessel invasion.

[a]Three-fifths were poorly differentiated.

[b]Ulcerated only.

with negative margins), the clinical criteria for a local excision have been met.

Pathologic criteria are more objective. Patients with T_1 tumors without adverse pathologic factors have a low enough incidence of local failure and positive nodes that local therapy alone is probably sufficient for the majority. However, once adverse pathologic factors are present (high grade, BVI, LVI, colloid histology, signet-ring cells)[1,30] or the tumor invades into or through the muscularis propria,[4,7,29] the local failure rate with local excision alone is at least 17 percent and the incidence of positive nodes is at least 10 percent.[1] Therefore, local therapy alone is inadequate for the majority of tumors with these adverse pathologic factors. In order to address the issues of patient selection and end results, a phase II intergroup trial of local excision and postoperative radiation and chemotherapy is currently under way.

REFERENCES

1. Minsky BD, Rich T, Recth A, et al: Selection criteria for local excision with or without adjuvant radiation therapy for rectal cancer. *Cancer* 63:1421–1429, 1989.
2. Minsky BD, Cohen AM: Conservative management of invasive rectal cancer: Alternative to abdominoperineal resection. *Oncology* 3:137–147, 1989.
3. Baker AR: Local procedures in the management of rectal cancer. *Semin Oncol* 7:385–391, 1980.
4. Biggers OR, Beart RW Jr, Ilstrup DM: Local excision of rectal cancer. *Dis Colon Rectum* 29:374–377, 1986.
5. Gingold BS, Mitty WF, Jr, Tadros M: Importance of patient selection in local treatment of carcinoma of the rectum. *Am J Surg* 145:293–296, 1983.

6. Greaney MG, Irvin TT: Criteria for the selection of rectal cancer for local treatment: A clinicopathologic study of low rectal tumors. *Dis Colon Rectum* 20:463–466, 1977.
7. Hager T, Gall FP, Hermanek P: Local excision of rectal cancer. *Dis Colon Rectum* 26:149–151, 1983.
8. Locke MR, Cairns DW, Ritchie JK, et al: The treatment of early colorectal cancer by local excision. *Br J Surg* 65:346–349, 1978.
9. Morson BC, Bussey HJR, Samoorian S: Policy of local excision for early cancer of the colorectum. *Gut* 18:1045–1050, 1979.
10. Stearns MW, Sternberg SS, DeCosse JJ: Treatment alternatives. Localized rectal cancer. *Cancer* 54:2691–2694, 1984.
11. Whiteway J, Nicholls RJ, Morson BC: The role of surgical local excision in the treatment of rectal cancer. *Br J Surg* 72:694–697, 1985.
12. Osborne DR, Higgins AF, Hobbs KEF: Cryosurgery in the management of rectal tumors. *Br J Surg* 65:859–861, 1978.
13. Hughes EP, Veidenheimer MC, Corman ML, et al: Electrocoagulation of rectal cancer. *Dis Colon Rectum* 25:215–218, 1982.
14. Papillon J, Montbarbon JF, Gerard JP, et al: Interstitial curietherapy in the conservative treatment of anal and rectal cancers. *Int J Radiat Oncol Biol Phys* 17:1161–1169, 1989.
15. Abrams JS: Clinical staging of colorectal cancer. *Am J Surg* 139:539–543, 1980.
16. Zorzitto M. Germanson T, Cummings B, et al: A method of clinical prognostic staging for patients with rectal cancer. *Dis Colon Rectum* 25:759–765, 1982.
17. Duncan W, Smith AN, Freedman LF, et al: Clinico-pathological features of prognostic significance in operable rectal cancer in 17 centres in the U.K. *Br J Cancer* 50:435–442, 1984.
18. Freedman LS, Macaskill P, Smith AN: Multivariate analysis of prognostic factors for operable rectal cancer. *Lancet* 2:733–736, 1984.
19. Davis NC, Newland RC: The reporting of colorectal cancer: The Australian clinico-pathological staging system. *Aust N Z J Surg* 52:395–397, 1982.
20. Chapuis PH, Dent OF, Newland RC, et al: An evaluation of the American Joint Committee (pTNM) staging method for cancer of the colon and rectum. *Dis Colon Rectum* 29:6–10, 1986.
21. York Mason A: Rectal cancer: The spectrum of selective surgery. *Proc R Soc Med* 69:237–244, 1976.
22. Nicholls RJ, York Mason A, Morson BC, et al: The clinical staging of rectal cancer. *Br J Surg* 69:404–409, 1982.
23. Nicholls RJ, Galloway DJ, Mason AY, et al: Clinical local staging of rectal cancer. *Br J Surg* 72:S51–S52, 1985.
24. Horiot JC, Roth SL, Calais G, et al: The Dijon clinical staging system for early rectal carcinomas amenable to intracavitary treatment techniques. *Radiother Oncol* 18:329–337, 1990.
25. Scott NA, Grande JP, Weiland L: Flow cytometric DNA patterns from colorectal cancers—How reproducible are they? *Mayo Clin Proc* 62:331–337, 1987.
26. Leyden MJ, Thompson CH, Lichtenstein M, et al: Visualization of metastases from colon carcinoma using an iodine 131–radiolabeled monoclonal antibody. *Cancer* 57:1135–1139, 1986.
27. Heerdt BG, Molinas S, Deitch D, et al: Aggressive subtypes of human colorectal tumors frequently exhibit amplification of the c-*myc* gene. *Oncogene* 6:125–129, 1991.
28. Merchant TE, Kasimos JN, deGraaf PW, et al: Phospholipid profiles of human colon cancer using 31P magnetic resonance spectroscopy. *Int J Color Dis* 6:121–126, 1991.
29. Horn A, Halvorsen JF, Morild I: Transanal extirpation for early rectal cancer. *Dis Colon Rectum* 32:769–772, 1989.
30. Willet CG, Tepper JE, Donnely S, et al: Patterns of failure following local excision and local excision and postoperative radiation therapy for invasive rectal adenocarcinoma. *J Clin Oncol* 7:1003–1008, 1989.
31. Cohen AM, Wood WC, Gunderson LL, et al: Pathological studies in rectal cancer. *Cancer* 45:2965–2968, 1980.
32. Grigg M, McDermott FT, Pihl EA, et al: Curative local excision in the treatment of carcinoma of the rectum. *Dis Colon Rectum* 27:81–83, 1984.
33. Nelson JC, Nimr AF, Thomford NR: Criteria for the selection of "early" carcinomas of the rectum. Are they valid? *Arch Surg* 122:533–536, 1987.
34. Brodsky JT, Richard GK, Cohen AM, et al: Variables correlated with the risk of lymph node metastasis in early rectal cancer. *Cancer* 69:322–326, 1992.

CHAPTER 56

Treatment of Rectal Cancer by Local Excision

Raymond J. Staniunas
John A. Coller

HIGHLIGHTS

This chapter on local excision for rectal cancer will discuss the selection criteria for tumors amenable to local therapy. These criteria are based on the degree of tumor fixation, stage, and differentiation. The current techniques of local excision will be illustrated. These include the two major local intraluminal excisional techniques of transanal excision and transanal endoscopic microsurgery and the extraluminal transsacral and transsphinteric approaches. With appropriate selection, results with local excision have generally been good to excellent.

CONTROVERSIES

One of the most disturbing aspects of distal rectal cancer therapy is that we deal with uncertainties after the fact as well as before. Should we have done more? Did we do too much? One has to consider that the performance of an abdominoperineal resection (APR) is standard maximal surgery for a distal rectal cancer. The operation that does not remove the regional lymph node chain will surely be inadequate for those patients who have lymph node metastasis. Even though not all stage C patients will be cured by APR, those that are would not have been had a lesser procedure been performed. By inference, it is also quite likely that some stage A and B lesions that did not appear to require APR may, in fact, not have been cured by something short of radical resection.

FUTURE DIRECTIONS

There are two major challenges for the immediate future. First, we need to develop greater precision in determining just which lesions are most suitable for local excision for cure and which need a more substantial resectional approach. The use of combined diagnostic modalities such as transrectal ultrasonography (TRUS), magnetic resonance imaging (MRI), and immunoscintigraphy using radiolabeled tumor-specific monoclonal antibodies may be helpful in identifying lesions that have extended beyond the limits of local excision. More effective cytologic assessment—as might be obtained with flow cytometry—may help to minimize inappropriate undertreatment.

A second challenge is the determination of appropriate adjuvant therapy. What combination of chemotherapeutic agents and/or radiotherapy might extend the effectiveness of local excision? The use of radiation therapy and local excision of rectal cancers is controversial. Patients who appear to have lesions favorable to local excisional therapy but in fact turn out to be failures may represent that cohort of occult metastasis that are most likely to benefit from adjuvant therapy. Prospective, randomized, controlled studies are needed to clarify these issues.

Standard therapy for low-lying rectal cancer—that is, within approximately 6 cm of the dentate line—is abdominoperineal resection (APR). This approach provides maximal extirpation of both the primary tumor and the regional lymphatic drainage. During the past decade, it has been possible to lower the 6-cm level in a number of patients whose anatomy so permits. Improved instrumentation for low anterior resection and greater experience with coloanal techniques have enabled many patients to benefit from the anatomic completeness of APR without losing sphincter function. However, it is clear that some patients will not receive additional benefit from a procedure that does any more than remove the primary lesion. If, in fact, all of the disease that exists is confined to the bowel wall, then local excision will suffice as treatment. It is, of course, the uncertainty of knowing just which lesions are so confined and thus amenable to local curative treatment and which will be inadequately treated that tempers our wholesale enthusiasm for such therapy.

Most local excisional techniques are performed transanally. However, there are also those that involve a transmural approach to the rectum. These operations, which incorporate transsphincteric and transsacral approaches, may be suitable for the removal of mid- to high rectal lesions otherwise unreachable by luminal techniques. It must be kept in mind that, with the transmural approaches, normal tissue planes beyond what is essential are laid open and may be exposed to viable exfoliated malignant cells. Although this concern does not necessarily translate into therapeutic failure, it is a theoretical risk that can be minimized with the transanal approach.

SELECTION CRITERIA FOR LOCAL EXCISION

The decision to advise local excision may be based upon the surgeon's judgment that a high likelihood of cure exists. On the other hand, a less favorable lesion may be treated by local excision because of the patient's aversion to a more appropriate major abdominal procedure. The selection criteria for local excision to be outlined here are a brief reiteration of those discussed in Chap. 55.

Local excisional therapy with an intent for cure should be applied only to patients whose tumors are not biologically aggressive, that are without obvious evidence of lymph node metastases, and which can be completely excised with a low incidence of local recurrence. The current modalities employed to properly stage patients who fit the criteria for local excision are digital rectal examination, TRUS, computed tomography (CT), and pathologic and histologic grading.

Digital rectal examination is performed to assess the tumor's degree of mobility as well as to detect enlarged regional lymph nodes. Immobile or fixed tumors must be assumed to penetrate all layers of the rectal wall and to extend beyond the perirectal tissue. Consequently, such lesions do not lend themselves to local excision for cure. A tumor that is freely mobile has been shown by Mason[1] to most probably be an "early" lesion and therefore most likely cured by local excision. Mason has also shown that tumors that are not fixed but "tethered" generally invade the pararectal tissue, with associated lymph node metastases as high as 90 percent. Local excision with intent to cure should not be applied to tethered lesions.

The accuracy of digital examination in assessing the depth of invasion is only about 75 percent.[2] Therefore, other modalities are used to stage patients more accurately. Transrectal ultrasonography has been reported to be between 75 and 94 percent accurate in assessing the depth of invasion of rectal cancer.[3] The assessment of lymph nodes by TRUS is less accurate than depth of invasion but is reported to be as high as 80 percent.[4,5] This is certainly higher than the percentage for clinical examination.

Computed tomography has also been utilized to stage patients with rectal cancer preoperatively. However, it has been shown to be less accurate than TRUS. The CT scan detects positive perirectal lymph nodes in only 35 percent of patients and depth of invasion in 70 percent.[6] It is probably no better than digital examination in accurately staging patients with rectal cancer.

Certain morphologic and histologic criteria should be met in selecting tumors amenable to local excision. The tumor should be small—less than 4 cm in diameter. Preoperative biopsy should demonstrate well- or moderate-to-well differentiated histology. Mucin production should not be excessive.[7] An exophytic structure is favorable, whereas deep ulceration is an adverse characteristic. It has been shown by Greaney and Irvin[8] that polypoid tumors less than 5 cm in diameter are associated with an 11 percent incidence of lymph node metastases. Ulcerated or larger tumors are associate with a 50 percent incidence of lymph node metastases and therefore are much less likely to be cured with local excision.

TECHNIQUES OF LOCAL EXCISION

There are currently four surgical approaches to the local removal of rectal cancer. These are transanal, transsacral, transsphincteric, and transanal endomicroscopic. As with all rectal cancer operations whether local or not, patients undergo a full mechanical and oral and parenteral antibiotic bowel preparation.

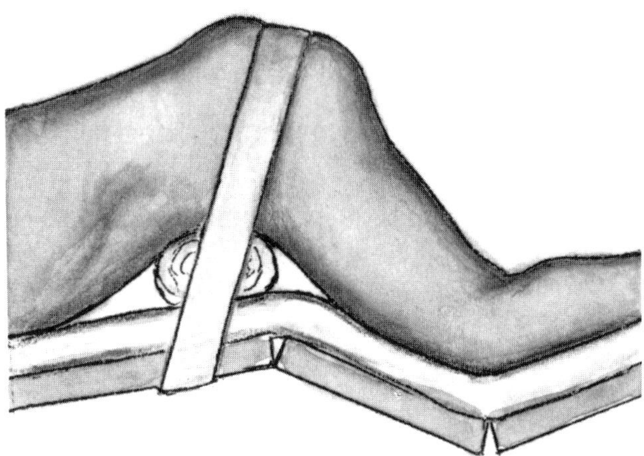

FIG. 56-1. Transanal local excision. Patient positioning.

TRANSANAL EXCISION

Patient Position

The patient should be positioned so that the lesion is in the most accessible location. For lesions that are predominantly anterior, the patient should be placed in the prone Bowie position (Fig. 56-1). Additional hip flexion is obtained by placing a blanket roll at the level of the iliac crest. Fleshy buttock tissue can be retracted to the side with tape. This position, combined with head-down table angulation, provides good access by the surgeon and an assistant from either side of the table. If the tumor is in the posterior quadrant, the patient is placed in the dorsal lithotomy position. Using gynecologic stirrups, the legs are severely flexed. It is essential that both surgeon and assistant have good access to the anus.

After the patient has been positioned, a sponge soaked with povidone-iodine is used to swab out the rectum. If residual stool is encountered during the operation, the operative site is irrigated with povidone-iodine until all fecal debris has been cleared.

Excision of Tumor

The anal sphincter is slowly and progressively dilated. A Ferguson plastic anoscope is the retractor that is most likely to provide adequate exposure throughout the operation (Figs. 56-2*A* and 2*B*). The shortest scope with the largest diameter should be selected. The operative site should be drawn down to the scope rather than advancing a longer scope up to the lesion. Alternatively, it is sometimes helpful to use a pair of long narrow Denver or narrow malleable retractors. If, because of incidental anal stricture, an adequate-diameter retractor cannot be inserted, a submucosal sphincterotomy may have to be performed. To facilitate excision, it is essential that the operator and the assistant use long instruments. Very helpful in this regard is a double-action needle holder. This instrument provides strong grasping power while at the same time being long enough to keep the surgeon's hands from blocking a narrow field of view. Long, narrow-shafted laparoscopic instruments are often helpful. The approach to excision should anticipate the wound closure. Lesions of 1 cm can be removed with surrounding border and the wound closed in either a horizontal or vertical axis. On the other hand, the defect that remains after removing a large lesion should be closed in a transverse axis so as not to narrow the rectal lumen.

A full-thickness incision is made with electrocautery using either a coagulation current or a blended cutting current with maximal coagulation. The proximal and distal margins are developed simultaneously for a distance of about 1.5 cm (Fig. 56-3). Dissection incorporates the full thickness of the muscular wall to the perirectal fat. By sequentially incising with the electrocautery and then placing a few more stitches,

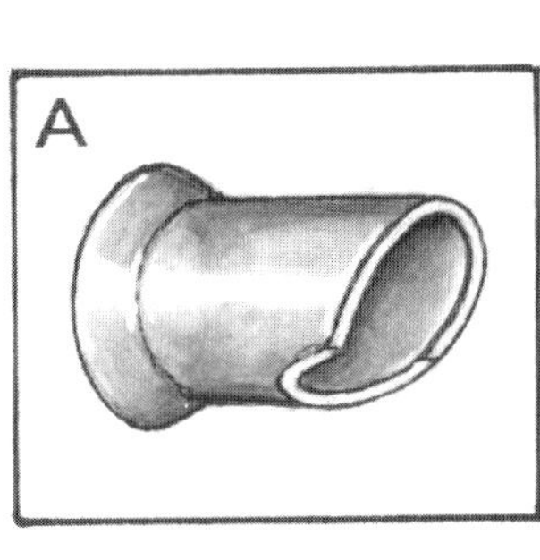

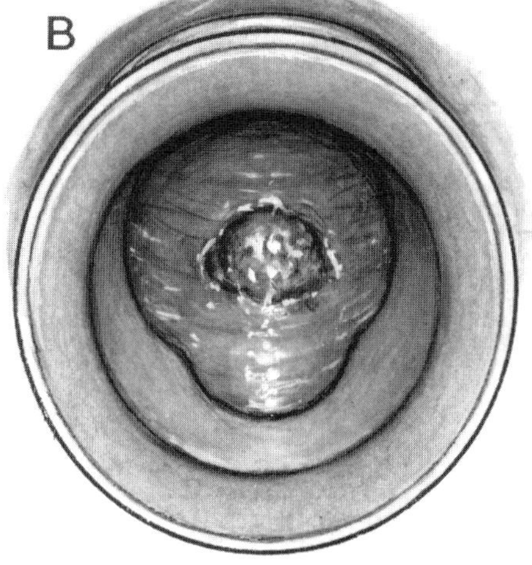

FIG. 56-2. *A* and *B*. Transanal local excision. A Ferguson anoscopic retractor is used for operative exposure.

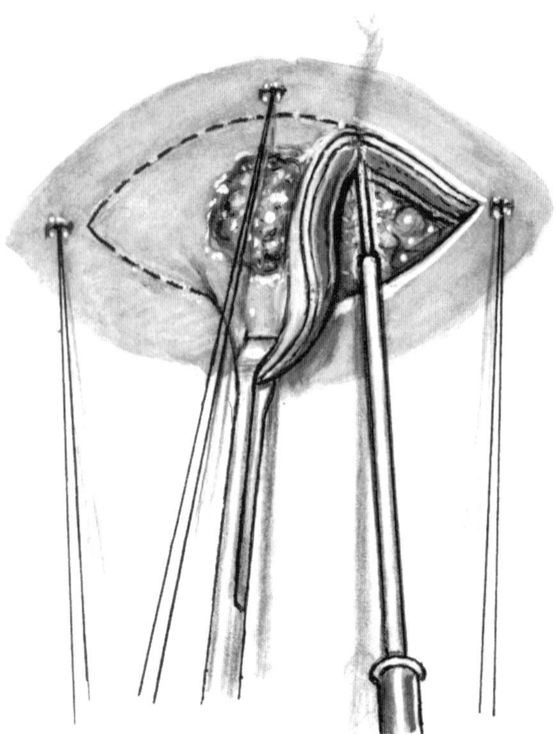

FIG. 56-3. Transanal local excision. The limits of excision are outlined with the needle-tip electrocautery. Stay sutures are placed to assist retraction. (Full-thickness excision is accomplished with the electrocautery.)

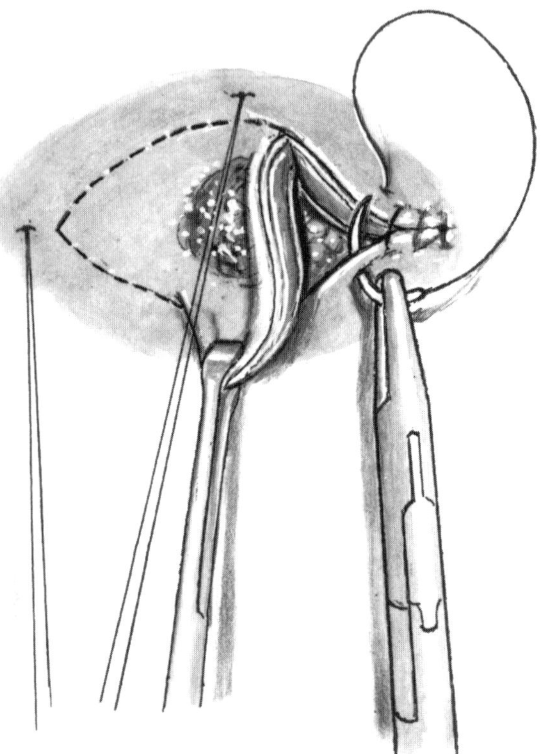

FIG. 56-4. Transanal local excision. A running closure is performed as excision proceeds.

the lesion can be removed without losing control of the wound or the tumor (Fig. 56-4).

POSTERIOR AND TRANSSPHINCTERIC TECHNIQUES

Most local excisional techniques are performed transanally; however, there are those that involve a transmural approach to the rectum. These operations, which incorporate posterior transsphincteric and transsacral approaches, may be suitable for the removal of mid- to high-rectal lesions and for those otherwise unreachable through luminal techniques. It must be kept in mind that with the transmural approaches, normal tissue planes beyond what is essential are laid open and exposed to the malignancy.

Transsacral (Kraske) Excision

The transsacral posterior proctotomy approach to high or midrectal tumors was first described by Kraske in 1885. His technique was reviewed in the English literature by Hargrove in 1979.[9] The patient is positioned in the prone jackknife position with the buttocks taped apart (Fig. 56-5). The utility of this approach can often be predicted by simple examination. Patients who have a substantial distance between the anal verge and the tip of the coccyx will have good exposure during operation. If the coccyx is positioned close to the sphincter and the anococcygeal raphe is short, there will be minimal working room. Under such circumstances, it is quite likely that the coccyx will have to be removed and the midline incision carried cephalad alongside the sacrum in order to facilitate exposure.

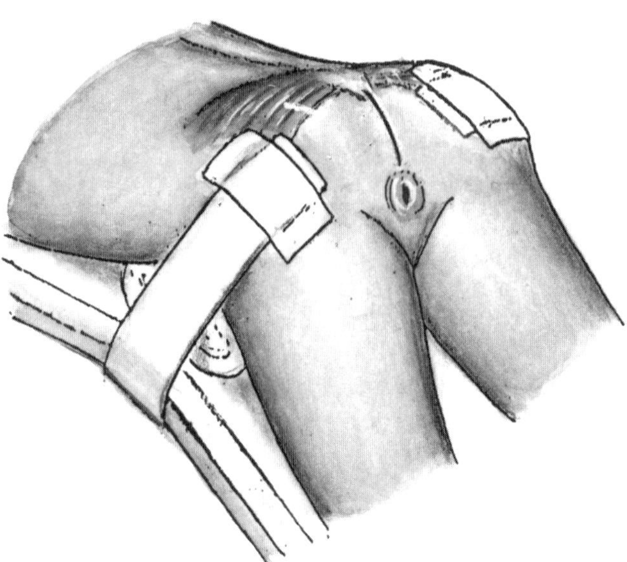

FIG. 56-5. Transsacral excision. Posterior midline incision from sacrum to just above external sphincter.

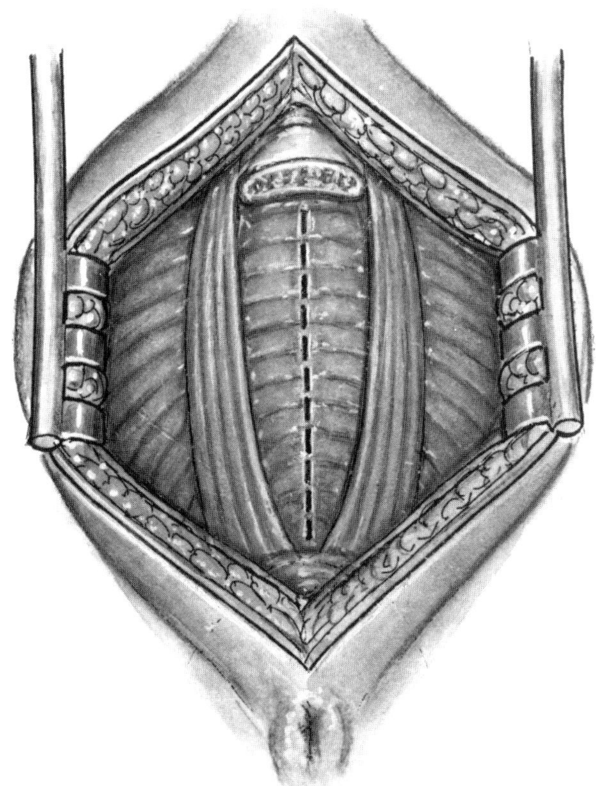

FIG. 56-6. Transsacral excision. The coccyx has been removed. The posterior raphe is separated and the levator ani divided.

For more proximal access, the lower two sacral segments can be removed as Kraske originally described. However, in light of current techniques for treating proximal rectal lesions from above, we believe that there is little to be gained from stretching a Kraske approach to its cephalad limit.

A posterior midline incision is performed from the tip of the coccyx to just proximal to the anus and external sphincter. The incision is carried through the muscular layers of levator ani to the retrorectal fat and the posterior wall of the rectum (Fig. 56-6). After fullthickness excision of the tumor with at least a 1-cm margin, the rectal wall and muscular layers are meticulously reapproximated, usually with absorbable suture material, in a continuous manner. The wound is drained with one or two closed suction drains.

Transsphincteric (Bevan-York Mason) Technique

A posterior transsphincteric approach, first described by Bevan in 1917,[10] was reintroduced and popularized by York Mason[11] in 1970. This technique is most suitable for those lesions that occupy more than a quarter of the circumference in the anterior hemisphere of the distal rectum. A tumor in this location may, on occasion, be difficult to remove cleanly by transanal excision. If the lesion does not encroach upon the requisite posterior incision line, this access considerably eases tissue excision and bowel reapproximation. The two principal concerns with this approach are unnecessary tissue exposure to cancer, as previously noted, and overt damage to the anal sphincter.

Injury to the anal sphincter is a risk of sphincter division and reapproximation. However, the functional outcome of this procedure is generally satisfactory if postoperative infection is avoided. Indeed, there is probably no greater risk to sphincter integrity from planned division and careful reapproximation than there is when excessive dilatation is required for adequate exposure during the transanal approach.

The technique, as depicted in Figs. 56-7 through 56-9, involves a parasacral incision that courses to the posterior midline below the coccyx and is carried to the anal verge. Division through the anal sphincter is undertaken precisely and sequentially. Scalpel dissection or blended electrocautery with low wattage is used in order to minimize distortion of tissue margins. Each muscular layer is carefully tagged so as to facilitate accurate reapproximation. In order to ensure adequate exposure, it is essential that both the levator ani above the level of the puborectalis and the rectal wall be incised to a level cephalad to the lesion.

York Mason reported success with this approach in a series of 50 patients harboring rectal cancer, with few complications noted.[1] In a series by Allgower et al.[12] in 79 patients, 36 had rectal cancer. There was no operative mortality, but there was a notable incidence of wound abscess (22 percent) and a substantial recurrence rate (25 percent).

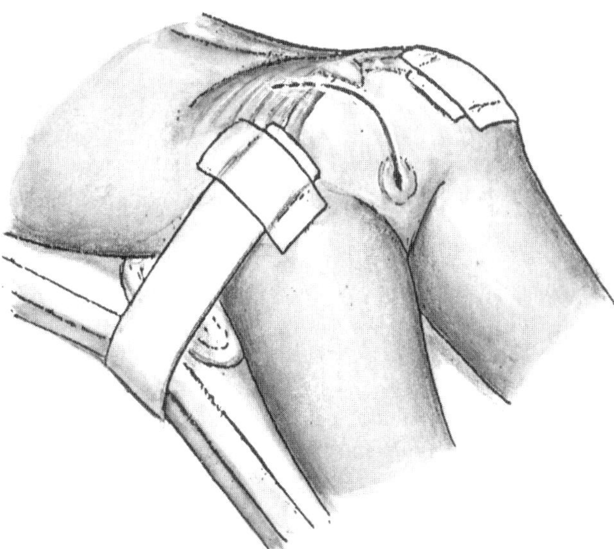

FIG. 56-7. Transsphincteric excision. Posterior incision from alongside sacrum to midline at anal verge.

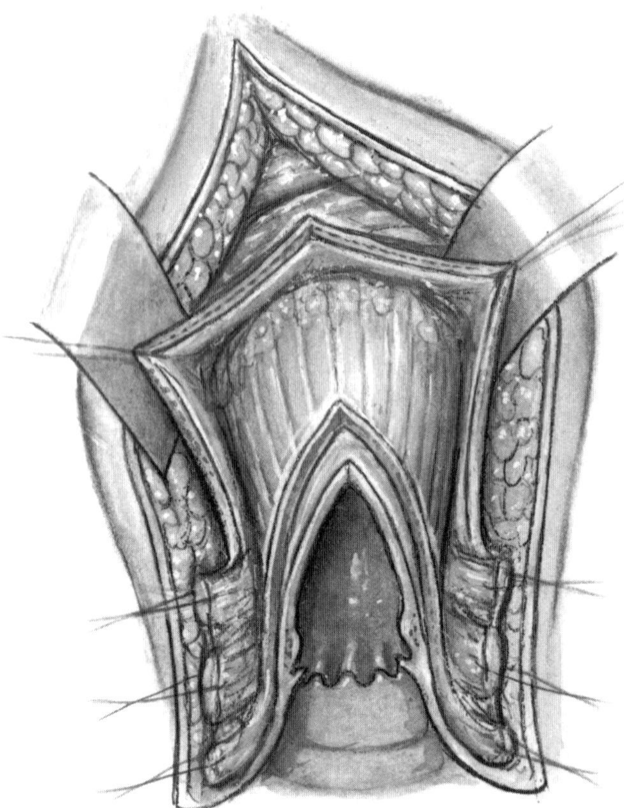

FIG. 56-8. Transsphincter excision. All elements of the external and internal sphincter are tagged for identification as they are divided.

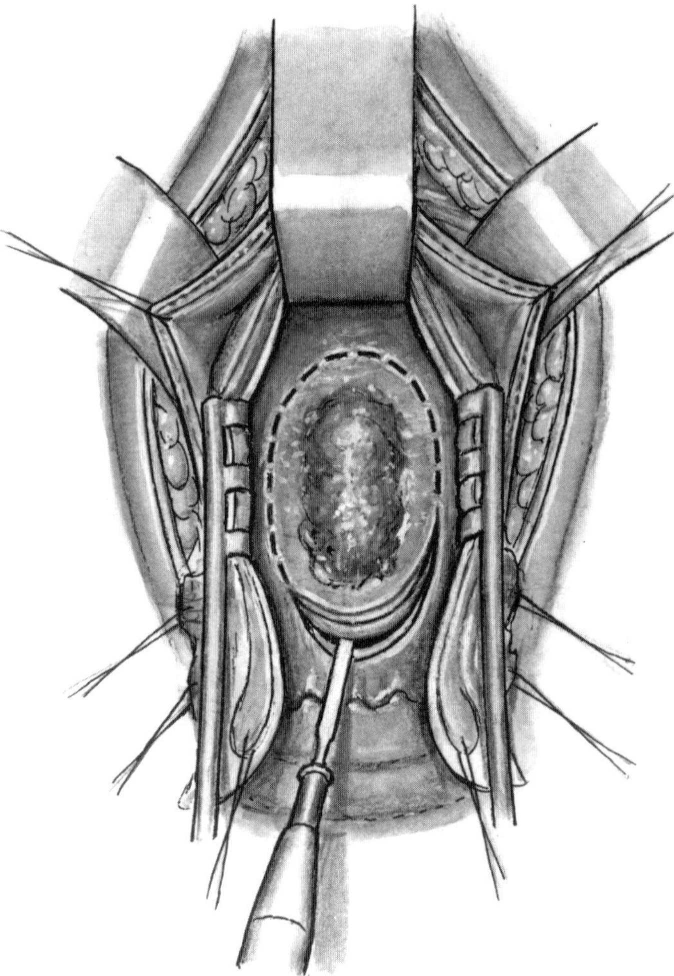

FIG. 56-9. Transsphincteric excision. Anterior lesion close to dentate line is excised with electrocautery.

TRANSANAL ENDOSCOPIC MICROSURGERY (TEM)

Standard transanal excisional techniques may not be applicable to some lesions of the midrectum due to exposure difficulties. An appropriate alternative includes the newly developed transanal endoscopic microsurgery (TEM) method of Buess et al.[13] from Germany. Using a closed system, the rectum is distended with gas, the dissection is performed with endoscopic instruments, and the operating field is viewed with a binocular stereoscope (Richard Wolf Medical Instruments Corporation, Vernon Hills, Ill.). Full-thickness excision of tumors that are located as high as 20 cm from the anal verge may be possible with this approach.[14]

As depicted in Fig. 56-10, the operating proctoscope is 20 cm long and 4 cm in diameter, with four operating ports. Dissecting instruments—including graspers, scissors, needle holders, electrocautery probe, and suction tubes—are inserted through the four operating ports. A binocular stereoscope is used for visualization. Remote imaging to a video monitor can be achieved with an accessory scope. Rectal distention is maintained during the operation by the continuous insufflation of CO_2 at up to 6 L/min. Intrarectal pressure is maintained at between 12 and 15 mmHg.

Buess et al.[13] reported their results of local excision with transanal endoscopic microsurgery on 310 patients. There was a 5 percent morbidity and a 0.3 percent mortality. Only 74 patients had carcinoma, many of whom were not suspected preoperatively. Thus, from a staging standpoint, the reported cases represent a very select group of patients who would be expected to have an exceptionally good outcome when treated by conventional means. For a mean follow-up of 14.2 months, the recurrence rate for patients with low-risk histology (well-differentiated tumors without venous or lymphatic invasion) whose primary was classified as pT1 was 1 in 28, or 3.5 percent. In a smaller series from the United States reported by Smith[15] and utilizing the transendoscopic system in 27 patients, there were no deaths and no cancer recurrence in the 9 patients with malignancy.

Transanal endoscopic microsurgery requires rather expensive specialized equipment. There is a definite learning curve to mastering the surgical technique.

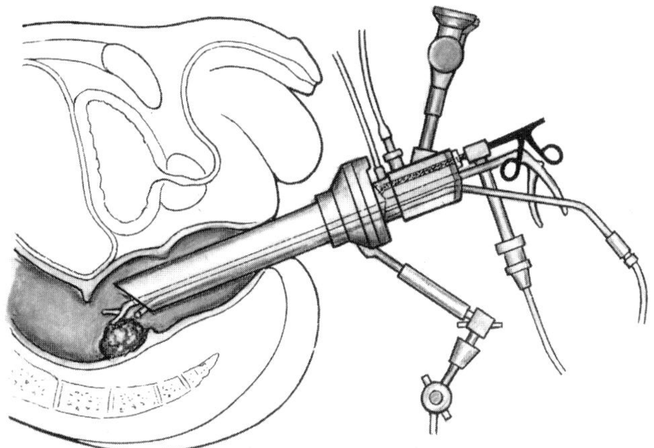

FIG. 56-10. Transanal endoscopic microsurgery instrumentation. (Richard Wolf Medical Systems, Vernon Hills, Illinois.)

Consequently, it cannot be recommended for a practice that infrequently deals with the appropriate tumor. However, this clearly provides a viable option for selected lesions that might be curable by local excision and are above the level of the most distal rectum.

RESULTS OF LOCAL EXCISION

Several series of local excisions of rectal cancer have reported excellent results with regard to morbidity, mortality, and survival. Graham et al.,[16] in 1990, reviewed the results of 10 such series (Table 56-1). There were a total of 404 patients, most of whom had T_1 or T_2 lesions. The collective cancer-specific survival was 94 percent with a 19 percent recurrence rate. Of these recurrences, more than half were salvaged. Even when examining only those cases with 5-year follow-up, the cancer-specific survival was 89 percent. Despite a recurrence rate of 24 percent, nearly half of these (42 percent) were considered cured by further operation. These results compare favorably with those obtained by abdominoperineal resection for similarly staged tumors. Grigg et al.[17] reported an 88 percent 5-year survival for patients undergoing rectal resection for lesions of the same stage as those in most local excision series. The adverse prognostic factors which increased recurrence and decreased survival are outlined in Table 56-2. The most significant were positive surgical margins, poorly differentiated histology, and increasing depth of bowel wall invasion. Interestingly, size greater than 3 cm was not an adverse prognostic variable. These data suggest that, for the properly staged lesion and in the absence of adverse prognostic clinical or histopathologic variables, local excision can be performed on rectal cancer with curative intent.

The results with local excision might be improved by the addition of radiotherapy. This is discussed in greater depth in Chap. 58. The expected benefits of radiation therapy are to control disease, both locally and in surrounding lymph nodes. There are only a few reports which addressed this issue.[15,18–20] However, none of them are prospective, randomized, controlled studies. Two of the studies addressed the issue of combined radiation and local excision for a subset of patients with more aggressive tumors. Marks et al.[20] reported the use of preoperative radiation and local excision in 14 patients who did not fit the standard criteria for local excision alone. The recurrence rate was 21 percent and the 3-year survival 61 percent. Rich et al.[18] reported the results of 17 patients who, after local excision, had pathologic variables which would put them in a high-risk category for local failure. After postoperative radiation, for the most part with doses greater than 4500 cGy, the local failure rate was only 6 percent (1 of 17). These results show that, for patients at increased risk for recurrence, radiation therapy may provide an additional margin of safety. However, if the tumor is properly staged and fits the rigid criteria for local excision, the majority should be "early" lesions at low risk for recurrence; therefore adjuvant radio-

Table 56-1
Results of Local Excision—Collected Results from 10 Series with Total of 404 Patients

	All series, %	*Series with > 5-year follow-up, %*
Absolute survival	69	66
Cancer-specific survival	94	89
Local recurrence	19	24

SOURCE: From Ref. 16. With permission.

Table 56-2
Effect of Pathologic Criteria upon Patient Outcome

	Mortality, %	*Local recurrence, %*
Surgical margins		
Negative	1	6
Postitive	35	52
Histologic differentiation		
Well to moderate	3	11
Poor	26	33
Depth of invasion		
T_1	1	5
T_2	8	18
T_3	20	22
Size of tumor		
≤ 3 cm	4	11
> 3 cm	18	33

SOURCE: From Ref. 16. With permission.

therapy would offer no additional benefits. Also, radiation has substantial adverse effects such as fibrosis, proctitis, and sphincter dysfunction.

CONCLUSION

For the appropriately selected lesion and patient, local excisional therapy for rectal cancer can provide cure rates equal to those obtained with more extensive resection. The conduct of the transanal operations, as outlined in this chapter, should not compromise the standards of cancer surgery. Currently, very few patients with rectal cancer would fit the criteria for local surgical therapy. Until more accurate preoperative staging methods become available, it appears that the recommendation for local therapy will continue to be beset with substantial uncertainty.

REFERENCES

1. Mason AY: Transsphincteric approach to rectal lesions. *Surg Annu* 9:171–194, 1977.
2. Gall FP: Cancer of the rectum—Local excision. *Int J Colorect Dis* 6:84–85, 1991.
3. Beynon J, Mortenson NJ, Channer JL, et al: Rectal ultrasonography accurately predicts depth of penetration in rectal cancer. *Int J Colorect Dis* 7:4–7, 1992.
4. Glaser F, Schlag P, Herfarth C: Endorectal ultrasonography for the assessment of invasion of rectal tumours and lymph node involvement. *Br J Surg* 77:883–887, 1990.
5. Katsura Y, Kamada K, Ishizawa T, et al: Endorectal ultrasonography for the assessment of wall invasion and lymph node metastasis in rectal cancer. *Dis Colon Rectum* 35:362–368, 1992.
6. Thompson WM, Halvorsen RA, Foster WL Jr, et al: Preoperative and postoperative CT staging of rectosigmoid carcinoma. *Am J Radiol* 146:703–710, 1986.
7. Hildebrandt U: Local curative treatment of rectal cancer. *Int J Colorect Dis* 6:74–76, 1991.
8. Greaney MG, Irvin TT: Criteria for the selection of rectal cancer for local treatment: A clinicopathologic study of low rectal tumors. *Dis Colon Rectum* 20:463–466, 1977.
9. Hargrove WC III, Gertner MH, Fitts WT Jr: The Kraske operation for carcinoma of the rectum. *Surg Gynecol Obstet* 148:931–933, 1979.
10. Bevan AD: Carcinoma of the rectum—Treatment by local excision. *Surg Clin Chicago* 1:233–239, 1917.
11. York Mason A: Rectal cancer: The spectrum of selective surgery. *Proc R Soc Med* 69:237–244, 1976.
12. Allgower M, Durig M, Hochstetter AV, et al: The parasacral sphincter-splitting approach to the rectum. *World J Surg* 6:539–548, 1982.
13. Buess G, Theiss R, Gunther M, et al: Endoscopic surgery in the rectum. *Endoscopy* 17:31–35, 1985.
14. Buess G, Mentges G, Manncke K, et al: Minimal invasive surgery in the local treatment of rectal cancer. *Int J Colorect Dis* 6:77–81, 1991.
15. Smith LE: Transanal endoscopic microsurgery. *Semin Colon Rectal Surg* 3:9–12, 1992.
16. Graham RA, Garnsey L, Jessup JM: Local excision of rectal carcinoma. *Am J Surg* 160:306–312, 1990.
17. Grigg M, McDermott FT, Pihl EA, et al: Curative local excision in the treatment of carcinoma of the rectum. *Dis Colon Rectum* 27:81–83, 1984.
18. Rich TA, Weiss DR, Mies C, et al: Sphincter preservation in patients with low rectal cancer treated with radiation therapy with or without local excision or fulguration. *Radiology* 156:527–531, 1985.
19. Willett CG, Tepper JE, Donnely S, et al: Patterns of failure following local excision and postoperative radiation therapy for invasive rectal adenocarcinoma. *J Surg Oncol* 7:1003–1008, 1989.
20. Marks G, Mohiuddin MM, Masoni L, et al: High-dose preoperative radiation and full-thickness local excision—A new option for patients with select cancers of the rectum. *Dis Colon Rectum* 33:735–740, 1990.

CHAPTER 57

Fulguration of Rectal Cancer

Eugene P. Salvati

HIGHLIGHTS

The use of electrocoagulation to destroy distal rectal cancers less than 4 cm in diameter that are movable and moderately or well differentiated results in a 65 percent crude 5-year survival rate. The low mortality and morbidity rates as compared with abdominoperineal resection—with its attendant colostomy and risk to potency—makes electrocoagulation even more appealing. Its advantage over local resection is its relative ease of performance. In case the procedure to control the cancer fails, radical salvage surgery can frequently be performed afterwards.

CONTROVERSIES

The primary argument against the use of electrocoagulation for the treatment of distal rectal cancer is the inability to properly stage the tumor, because only a portion of the specimen is submitted to the pathologist. Rectal ultrasound is not reliable in detecting nodal metastasis, since it can only indicate enlarged nodes which may be inflammatory, and even small nodes can harbor metastatic deposits. If nodal metastases are present, adjuvant chemotherapy would be beneficial.

FUTURE DIRECTIONS

Improved staging and adjuvant chemotherapy should allow for improved local control and cure rates with this modality.

The use of electricity to destroy cancer was first described by Byrne[1] in 1989. The application of this modality to the treatment of cancer of the rectum as well as other cancers was carried out and reported by Strauss et al.[2] in 1935. They believed that antibodies were produced by electrocoagulation of the cancer. This theory, however, could never be proved and to our satisfaction was disproved using the leukocyte migration test.[3]

In 1961, Jackman[4] published a 10-year study of 250 patients with rectal cancer who were treated by fulguration. He observed his patients for 8 to 18 years and stated that the procedure was successful in 96.2 percent of the cases. The next reports to appear in the literature were those of Madden and Kandalaft[5,6] in 1967 and 1971. Since that time, they have published other reports[7] and they have probably had the greatest experience in this modality.

Crile and Turnbull[8] treated 62 cases of cancer of the rectum by electrocoagulation and demonstrated a 68 percent 5-year survival. It was their conclusion that all cancers of the distal rectum should be treated by electrocoagulation first and that this, if necessary, should then be followed by an abdominoperineal resection.

Hughes et al.[9] reported their results with electrocoagulation of rectal cancer in 1982; this was followed by a paper from Gingold et al.[10] in 1983. The present writer has coauthored papers on the topic published in 1972,[11] 1976,[12] 1982,[13] and 1988.[14]

RATIONALE

It is generally accepted that cancer of the rectum located higher than 5 or 6 cm from the anal verge can best be treated by some type of sphincter-saving procedure, whether that be by a low anterior resection, a coloanal anastomosis, or some other technique, while offering the patient the same chance for survival as a more radical procedure such as an abdominoperineal resection.

Deddish and Stearn,[15] in 1961, compared the 5-year survival rate for cancer of the rectum 6 cm from the anal verge treated by anterior resection as opposed to abdominoperineal resection in almost 398 cases. There was no difference statistically in the 5-year survival rate between the two approaches.

More recently, Wolmark et al.[16] found no difference in the 4-year survival rate between abdominoperineal resection and a sphincter-saving procedure in Dukes B and C rectal cancer. Thus, in a good-risk patient, some type of sphincter-saving procedure should be carried out for any rectal cancer 5 to 6 cm proximal to the anal verge. The use of the double-staple technique with the intraluminal stapler or a coloanal anastomosis facilitates this approach. If one agrees with the above, this leaves only distal rectal lesions below 5 to 6 cm from the anal verge to be treated by a radical abdominoperineal resection or by a local approach.

CRITERIA

The indications for the application of electrocoagulation to the treatment of distal rectal cancer resolves themselves into matters of size, fixation, configuration, and differentiation of the tumor. Most surgeons experienced in the treatment of rectal cancer agree that the cancer should be no greater than 3 to 4 cm in diameter to be amenable to any type of local treatment in the good-risk patient. Our statistics indicate that the survival rate dropped from 65 to 30 percent in patients with lesions over 4 cm in diameter. A freely movable tumor is one that has not fully penetrated the muscular wall of the bowel and is amenable to local treatment. Studies have shown that one can accurately stage rectal lesions by digital palpation in 80 percent[17] of patients, and this accuracy can be increased to 95 percent by the use of rectal ultrasound.[18]

A detailed discussion of selection criteria is offered in a previous chapter.

PROCEDURE

The technique of fulguration varies slightly among groups. Our own approach is described below.

The patient is given a general anesthetic and placed in the lithotomy position. This anesthetic is supplemented by the use of a local anesthetic consisting of a combination of 50 mL of a 0.25% solution of bupivacaine and 1:200,000 epinephrine to which two ampules of hyaluronidase [300 turbidity reducing (TR) units] have been added. This local anesthetic is administered peri- and intraanally, subcutaneously, and submucosally, intrarectally. The use of a local anesthetic permits profound relaxation of the sphincter mechanism; thus the general anesthetic can be relatively light. Since these procedures are done primarily in the elderly this, of course, is a distinct advantage. An operating proctoscope (Fig. 57-1) specifically designed for this technique is then inserted into the rectum. The instrument has a diameter of 4 cm and a length of 15 cm. It has a 45° oblique canal and a channel for the insertion of a fiberoptic light source as well as a smoke ejection channel. An obturator is provided for insertion. Occasionally, it is necessary to perform a partial lateral internal sphincterotomy in order to insert the instrument into the rectum without tearing or overstretching the internal sphincter. The tumor should fit inside the diameter of the instrument (Fig. 57-2). If it does not, the tumor should not be treated by electrocoagulation. An electrocoagulating tip 5 mm in diameter attached to a Cameron electrosurgical unit is then applied, utilizing the bipolar current to char the entire surface of the tumor. A right-angle biopsy forceps is then used to remove the necrotic burnt tumor (Fig. 57-3). The process is then repeated until all tumor is destroyed, as demonstrated visually and by palpation (Fig. 57-4). A 1-cm halo of normal bowel is destroyed

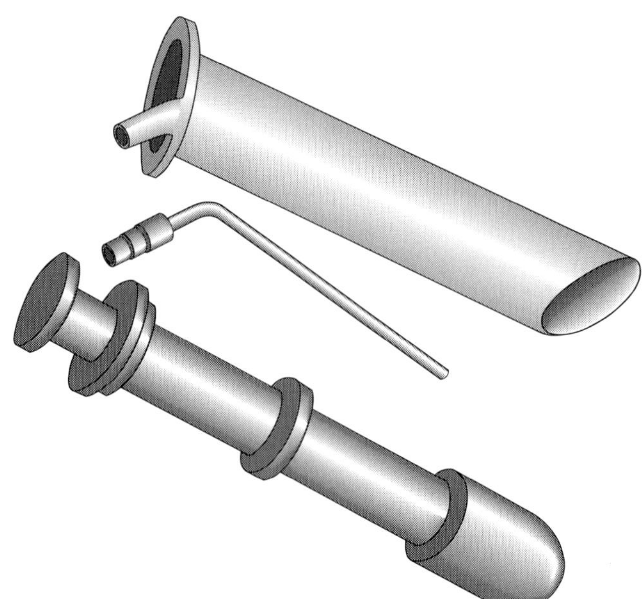

FIG. 57-1. An operating proctoscope. (Manufactured by Electro-Surgical Instruments, Electro-Surgical Instrument Company, 37 Centennial Street, Rochester, New York 14611.)

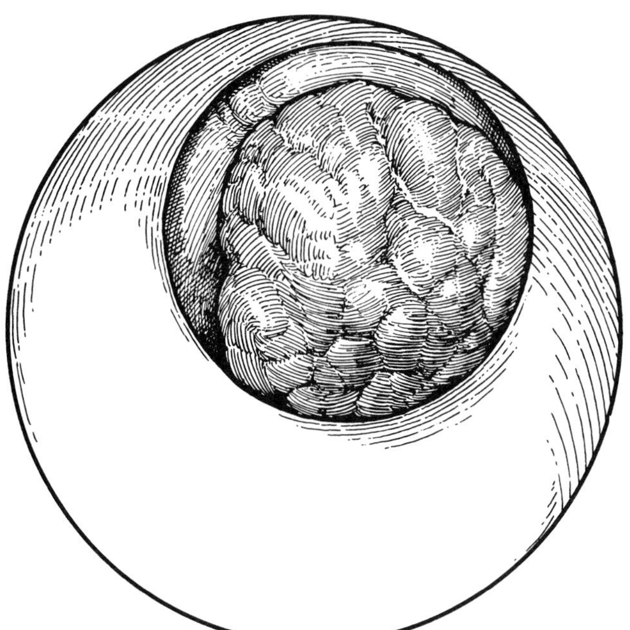

FIG. 57-2. Polypoid rectal cancer.

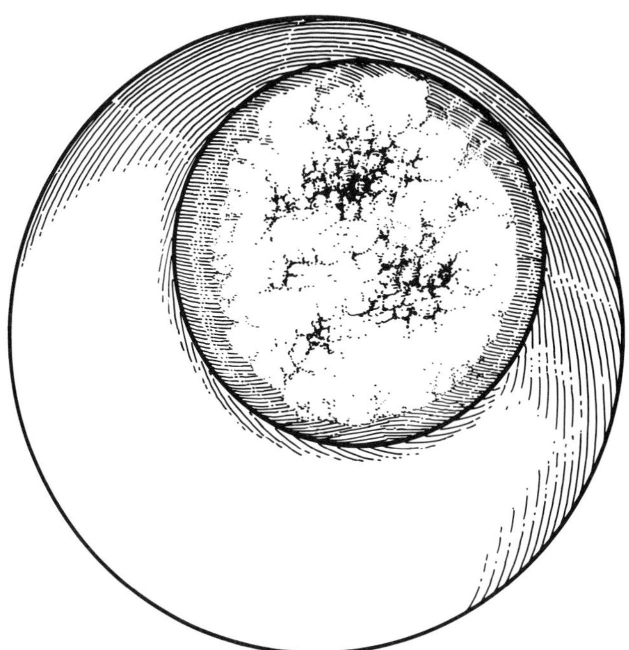

FIG. 57-4. Rectal cancer after electrocoagulation.

circumferentially about the tumor. Posteriorly, one can burn right through the bowel wall into the presacral fascia. Laterally, the tumor can be destroyed to the perirectal fat. Anteriorly, one must, of course, be careful not to burn into the prostate or through the posterior wall of the vagina. Considerable smoke and debris are produced and two suctions must be available. Irrigation utilizing an asepto syringe is carried out frequently. Bleeding can be brisk but is easily controlled. It is necessary to change the electrocoagulating tip frequently, as burning is ineffective once the tip has become covered with carbon. The process is tedious and takes 60 to 90 min to complete. One should note that this technique is different from that carried out by Madden[5] and Crile,[8] in that they insert a needle directly into the tumor and then apply the current. The end achieved, however, is essentially the same.

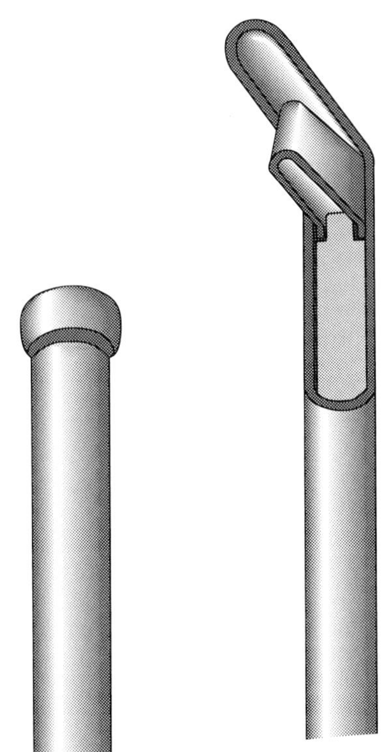

FIG. 57-3. Cameron 5-mm electrocoagulating electrode and right-angled biopsy forceps.

Postoperatively, most of these patients become febrile, frequently up to 104°F. Aspirin or acetaminophen is used; it has not been found necessary to use antibiotics. A regular diet and a stool softener (dioctyl sodium sulfosuccinate) are given and the patient is discharged when afebrile, generally within 2 to 3 days. The wound created heals by secondary intention and is practically closed when the patients are seen in 1 month, at their first visit.

Examination, digital and endoscopic, is then performed at monthly intervals for the first year, every 3 months thereafter for 2 years, at 6-month intervals for 3 years, and yearly after that. Any questionable area of hardness indicating a possible recurrence is biopsied again. Evaluation under general anesthesia is occasionally necessary, and this should be done without hesitation. If a recurrence is proved, then repeat electrocoagulation can be performed, again depending upon whether the bowel wall is penetrated or not. It is obvious that if the tumor is fixed, one should not persist in utilizing electrocoagulation. In such an instance, an abdominoperineal resection should be performed in the good-risk patient. Reasonable salvage can be expected under these circumstances even with a Dukes C lesion.

RESULTS

In the past 30 years, a total of 215 patients with rectal cancer have been treated by electrocoagulation. Of this number, 114 have been followed for more than 5 years. In this latter group, the tumor involved up to 50 percent of the circumference of the rectum. There were 62 males and 52 females, 50 percent over age 70. A total of 33 patients were treated for palliation, and of this group only 1 required a colostomy; thus, 32 patients were carried to their deaths without requiring fecal diversion. Among the 81 patients treated for cure, the overall crude 5-year survival rate was 47 percent (Fig. 57-5). Of this group, 50 patients were treated by electrocoagulation alone, with a survival rate of 58 percent; however, the survival rate for lesions more than 4 cm in diameter was only 30 percent. There were 40 patients with lesions less than 4 cm in diameter, and their survival rate was 65 percent. Among the 31 patients requiring abdominoperineal resection following electrocoagulation, the survival rate was 29 percent. In this group, 10 patients had a Dukes B lesion and 21 had a Dukes C lesion. The overall mortality rate was 2.1 percent and the morbidity rate 21 percent. Complications included bleeding (7.0 percent), stricture (6.0 percent), urinary retention (2.6 percent), electrical burns (2.6 percent), perianal abscess (0.9 percent), and perforation (0.9 percent). Bleeding was controlled in all instances by electrocoagulation on an outpatient basis. All strictures were dilated in the office with the rigid sigmoidoscope. Electrical burns were the result of improper placement of the grounding pad. The perianal abscess did not result in a fistula and the perforation occurred in a patient whose tumor extended above the peritoneal reflection and who was being treated for palliation.

These results can be compared with the major recent series of rectal cancer treated with electrocoagulation (Table 57-1). The largest series is that of Madden and Kandalaft.[7] They report a 55.9 percent crude survival rate in 114 patients, with no mortality. All lesions were within 10 cm of the anal verge. Their complication rate was 23 percent, which compares favorably with ours (21 percent). The survival rate of patients with lesions less than 3 cm in diameter was 10 percent greater than that of those with larger lesions. There was no restriction as to size of lesion treated; the only contraindication was an anterior location in the female with fixation of the rectovaginal septum. This series, however, is somewhat flawed by the inclusion of 32 patients with malignancies arising in villous adenomas.

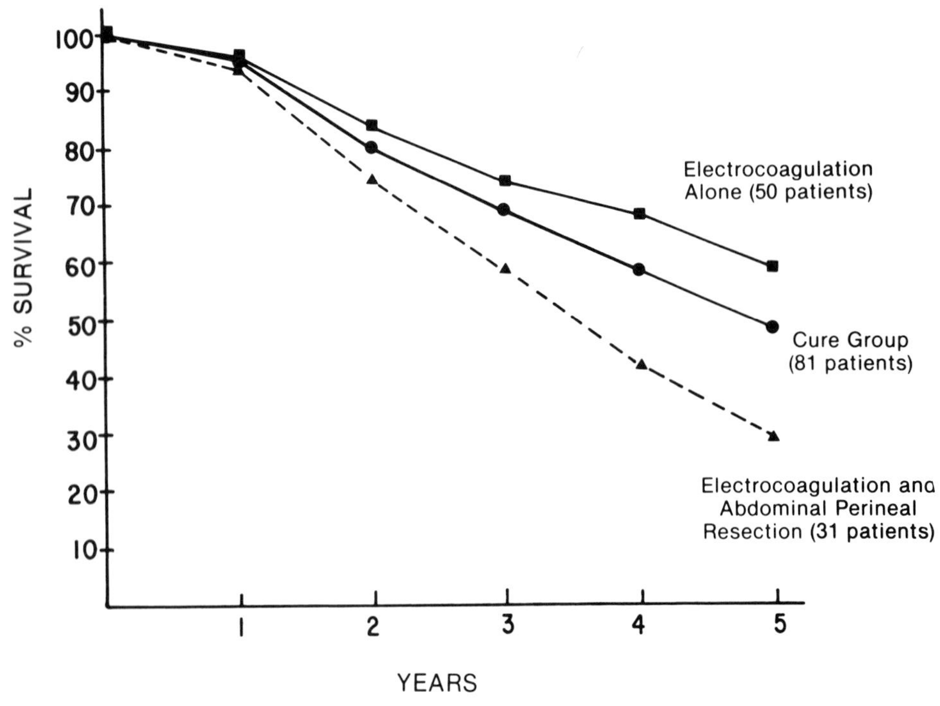

FIG. 57-5. Survival of patients with rectal carcinoma treated for cure with electrocoagulation—five-year crude survival rates. (From Salvati et al.[14] Reproduced by permission of Surgery, Gynecology, and Obstetrics.)

Table 57-1
Five-Year Determinant Survival Rates after Electrocoagulation for Rectal Cancer

Author	*Year*	*No. of patients*	*Percent*
Crile and Turnbull[8]	1972	62	55.9
Hughes et al.[9]	1982	41	67.1
Madden and Kandalaft[7]	1983	114	55.9
Salvati et al.[14]	1988	81	47.0
		Average	56.4

Crile and Turnbull[8] compared their results with electrocoagulation against those with abdominoperineal resection for distal rectal cancer. They treated 226 patients with rectal cancer with abdominoperineal resection, with a survival rate of 61 percent, versus 62 cases treated with electrocoagulation, with a survival rate of 67 percent. However, when this is corrected for patients with no residual tumor, it becomes 55.9 percent. These series are not strictly comparable, since the status of the nodes remains unknown in the electrocoagulated patients. The authors observed that patients lived at least a year longer with their disease when treated with electrocoagulation rather than surgery. Their mortality rate was zero as compared to our 2.7 percent. They calculated that the mortality rate of abdominoperineal resection must be below 3 percent to compensate for any increased survival stemming from the removal of involved lymph nodes. All of their lesions were below 10 cm from the anal verge.

Hughes et al.[9] treated 48 patients with cancer of the distal 10 cm of the rectum by electrocoagulation. They had 2 intraoperative deaths (4.5 percent), and 5 patients required a subsequent abdominoperineal resection. Of these, 4 died of their disease within 2 years and one is still alive at 2 years. Of the 7 patients treated with electrocoagulation, only 1 died of the disease and 6 were alive without disease; however, these patients were followed for less than 5 years. Thus, their crude 5-year survival rate (28 of the 41 patients) was 67.2 percent. The authors found that the success rate with the exophytic lesions was 92 percent, versus 33 percent for ulcerative lesions. The overall survival rate for abdominoperineal resection at the Lahey Clinic for the same period was 61.6 percent.

REFERENCES

1. Byrne J: *Electrocautery in Uterine Surgery.* New York, William Wood, 1889.
2. Strauss AA, Strauss SF, Crawford RA: Surgical diathermy of carcinoma of rectum: Its clinical end results. *JAMA* 104:1480–1484, 1935.
3. Greco RS, Rubin RJ, Salvati EP: A comparison of cellular immunity in the patients undergoing electrocoagulation and resection for adenocarinoma of the rectum. *Surg Gynecol Obstet* 151:471, 1980.
4. Jackman RJ: Conservative management of selected patients with carcinoma of the rectum. *Dis Colon Rectum* 4:429–434, 1961.
5. Madden JL, Kandalaft SI: Electrocoagulation: A primary and preferred method of treatment for cancer of the rectum. *Ann Surg* 166:413–419, 1967.
6. Madden JL, Kandalaft SI: Clinical evaluation of electrocoagulation in the treatment of cancer of the rectum. *Am J Surg* 122:347–352, 1971.
7. Madden JL, Kandalaft SI: Electrocoagulation as a primary curative method in the treatment of carcinoma of the rectum. *Surg Gynecol Obstet* 157:164–179, 1983.
8. Crile G, Turnbull RB: Role of electrocoagulation in the treatment of carcinoma of the rectum. *Surg Gynecol Obstet* 135:391–396, 1972.
9. Hughes EP, Veidenheimer MC, Corman ML, et al: Electrocoagulation of rectal cancer. *Dis Colon Rectum* 25:215–218, 1982.
10. Gingold BS, Mitty WF Jr, Tadros M: Importance of patient selection in local treatment of carcinoma of the rectum. *Am J Surg* 145:293–296, 1983.
11. Swerdlow DB, Salvati EP: Electrocoagulation of cancer of the rectum. *Dis Colon Rectum* 15:228–232, 1972.
12. Salvati EP, Rubin RJ: Electrocoagulation as primary therapy for rectal carcinoma. *Am J Surg* 132:583–586, 1976.
13. Eisenstat TE, Deak ST, Rubin RJ, et al: Five-year survival in patients with carcinoma of the rectum treated by electrocoagulation. *Am J Surg* 143:127–131, 1982.
14. Salvati EP, Rubin RJ, Eisenstat TE, et al: Electrocoagulation of selected carcinoma of the rectum. *Surg Gynecol Obstet* 166:393–396, 1988.
15. Deddish MR, Stearns MW: Anterior resection for carcinoma of the rectum and rectosigmoid area. *Ann Surg* 154:961–966, 1961.
16. Wolmark N, Gordon PH, Fisher B, et al: A comparison of stapled and hand-sewn anastomoses in patients undergoing resection of Dukes B and C colorectal cancer: An analysis of disease-free survival and survival from the NSABP prospective trials. *Dis Colon Rectum* 29:344–350, 1986.
17. Nicholls RJ, York Mason A, Morson BC, et al: The clinical staging of rectal cancer. *Br J Surg* 69:404–409, 1982.
18. Orrom WJ, Wong WD, Rothenberger DA, et al: Endorectal ultrasound in the preoperative staging of rectal tumors: A learning experience. *Dis Colon Rectum* 33:654–659, 1990.

CHAPTER 58

Local Therapy—Radiation Therapy

Tyvin A. Rich

HIGHLIGHTS

Rectal cancer is increasingly managed by surgical techniques aimed at preserving the anal sphincter and the rectal vault. There are also several radiotherapeutic options for sphincter preservation, including endocavitary irradiation with or without implant and external irradiation alone. The most commonly used irradiation option is the logical combination of limited surgery and postoperative radiotherapy (XRT), because this treatment philosophy has been successful in curing locally invasive rectal cancers. Radiotherapy after limited surgery allows for pathologic tumor staging, so that comparisons can be made to the results of more conventional treatment approaches. Radiotherapy parameters such as optimal field size, total dose, and the role for chemotherapy are aspects of treatment requiring further study.

Limited surgery following preoperative XRT and chemotherapy for patients with T_3 tumors is another attractive approach, since the resulting downstaging of tumor preoperatively permits more limited surgery in patients who might otherwise not be good candidates for conservation therapy. Conservation management of rectal cancer will become more widely used as the issues of treatment selection and therapy sequencing are better defined.

CONTROVERSIES

Radial or circumferential resection margins in specimens of low rectal cancer after "radical" surgery are < 10 mm. Many surgeons underestimate the extent of a safe margin, and the standard pathology report does not give enough detail about its adequacy. With limited surgery for tumors with a median diameter < 4 cm, radial margins of only 3 mm have been reported. Obtaining the widest surgical margin possible, especially in the patient with transmural disease, may be a key element to the success of either conservation or more standard surgical procedures. In future trials, data on radial margins should be correlated with treatment outcome.

FUTURE DIRECTIONS

The first area for new research will be to examine "quality of life" objectively based on anal, rectal, and sexual function in patients receiving standard therapy, limited surgery alone (i.e., coloanal anastomosis), or conservation surgery and XRT. A second challenging area will be to refine patient selection using newer clinical and laboratory methods. For example, kinetic and genetic assays of tumor cells designed to predict the recurrence of local and distant disease may allow clinicians to select those patients most likely to have a complete pathologic response. As in squamous cell cancer of the anus, which is now treated with chemoradiation, some patients with rectal cancer may now be curable with no surgery at all. If this notion is to be extended to the treatment of invasive rectal cancer, it must be explored in clinical trials.

In the conservation approach to rectal cancer arising in the lowest third of the rectum, clinicians now strive to obviate the need for colostomy while attempting to ensure the longest possible survival and the best quality of life. Once strongly held opinions regarding the necessity of radical surgery are being challenged successfully by the results of XRT and limited surgery for patients with distal rectal cancers. The success of alternative therapies to radical surgery depends as much on the patient selection process as the surgical and XRT techniques.

PATIENT SELECTION FOR CONSERVATION THERAPY

The lowest rectal segment, measured from the dentate line to the first rectal valve of Houston, is usually no more than 8 cm long and is the target of newer combined-modality therapies. Here, the Miles resection or abdominoperineal resection (APR) has been the standard radical operation used to achieve margins of normal tissue along three directions of tumor spread (upward, downward, and around).[1] However, because of radial tumor infiltration, the surgical margin around the tumor is frequently compromised. For example, the currently accepted margin of distal rectum is > 2 to 3 cm, because recurrence rates increase when margins are smaller[2]; yet the adequacy of the radial margin in surgical series where it has been examined in detail shows that tumor-free resection margins range only from 6 to 9.0 mm in patients undergoing APR and low anterior resection.[3–6] In all studies, the ability to secure tumor-free radial margins is inversely correlated to the extent of tumor penetration through the bowel wall. In a study by Quirke and Scott,[5] 85 percent of patients with positive radial margins later experienced pelvic recurrence. These authors concluded that standard pathologic reporting of radial tumor extent did not adequately describe this margin and that the surgeon frequently underestimated the problem of tumor spread in the lateral zone.[4,5] These data parallel the pathologic staging reports for operable rectal cancer, which demonstrate that the quantitation of extramural (radial) tumor extension, when incorporated into a modification of the Dukes staging, predicts for pelvic recurrence after radical surgery.[2,7,8] In addition to high pathologic stage and positive margin status, other pathologic factors that produce a high risk of local recurrence after surgery are high tumor grade, lymphatic invasion, and colloid tumor histology.[7,9]

One of the main selection criteria for conservation treatment is a tumor diameter < 3 cm. The importance to surgeons of small tumor size is evident from a review of over 750 patients treated conservatively. Of these, 85 percent had tumor diameters < 3 cm.[10] Although tumor size lacks prognostic significance in rectal cancer, conservation procedures are more practical if performed on patients with small tumors. The distance above the anal verge has also been used as a criterion to select favorable patients for surgery that spares the anus/rectum.[11]

A small, accessible, mobile tumor is a prerequisite for conservation therapy, but preoperative tumor staging is also mandatory. Ideally, clinical staging of rectal cancer should determine the degree of muscle penetration and unequivocally identify involved lymph nodes. Staging based on the digital rectal exam (DRE), mainly using an assessment of mobility, has been found to be 90 percent accurate in predicting tumor penetration through the bowel wall.[12] The utility of DRE has been shown on the basis of its ability to distinguish between mobile and fixed/tethered lesions, which have significantly different 5-year survival rates.[13] However, the clinical accuracy of this approach is generally not accepted by clinicians; most do not assess the lesions as carefully as did the authors who published these studies.

Clinical staging by DRE can now be augmented by endoscopic or endorectal ultrasound (EUS), computed tomography (CT), or magnetic resonance imaging (MRI). Endorectal ultrasound is 85 to 93 percent accurate in demonstrating the degree of transmural tumor extension. It describes five layers of the normal rectal wall, and tumor extension within and through the muscle wall can be assessed easily; its determination of lymph node involvement, however, is controversial, since universally accepted criteria for nodal positivity do not exist.[14,15] Nodal size is usually not helpful,[16] while some consider round and echo-poor perirectal structures to be indicative of tumor involvement.[15] Nevertheless, it may be possible to predict lymph node involvement with an 80 percent sensitivity and 89 percent specificity[15]; operator experience and judgment in interpretation of the scan are important. A proposed TNM staging of rectal cancer based on EUS follows the classification of the American Joint Commission on Cancer/Union Internationale Contre le Cancer (AJCC/UICC): a stage uT_1 lesion is a cancer confined to the submucosa; stage uT_2, a lesion that invades into but not through the muscularis propria; stage uT_3, a lesion that invades into the perirectal fat; and stage uT_4, a lesion that invades into an adjacent organ or structure (prostate, bladder, or sacrum).[17,18] For nodal staging, uN_1 implies that there are features consistent with nodal involvement.

Other radiologic staging methods—such as CT and MRI of the abdomen and pelvis—are helpful in assessing the presence of extramural tumor[14] and in revealing high pelvic and paraaortic nodal involvement and liver metastasis. Similarly, MRI with endorectal coils has shown 88 percent accuracy in determining transmural extension, though it was only 57 percent accurate in determining lymph node involvement.[19] The use of paramagnetic scanning materials may improve accuracy further.

SURGICAL AND RADIOTHERAPY TECHNIQUES

The conservation approach currently used at the University of Texas M. D. Anderson Cancer Center in the patient with low rectal cancer is shown in Fig. 58-1. As preservation of fecal reservoir function is one of the main goals of surgical therapy, as much rectal length as possible is spared. Preservation of rectal function must be weighed against the risk of recurrence and the need to provide for adequate wound healing. The types of conservative surgical procedures that have been employed with XRT include transanal resection, abdominosacral resection, abdominotranssphincteric resection, and the Kraske procedure. Many procedures are designed to minimize postoperative disruption of the anastomostis; the frequency of this may be greater when surgery is combined with preoperative XRT. All of these procedures have been used to treat rectal cancer, and some present unique technical challenges.[1]

In our protocols, XRT is given either pre- or postoperatively with external beam irradiation in combination with a low-dose, continuous infusion of 5-fluorouracil (5-FU). Following tumor excision, postoperative XRT should be delayed until wound healing is complete, usually 3 to 5 weeks later. During this interval, the patient can regain anal and rectal function; however, many patients still have frequent, loose bowel movements related to the decreased capacity of the rectal vault. Some patients may need anticholinergics to control symptoms prior to beginning irradiation. In our experience, many of those with coloanal anastomoses will be incontinent even 8 weeks after surgery; they are more difficult to treat during the acute phase of XRT toxicity.

For those receiving postoperative XRT, our treatment policy is to include the anastomotic area as well as a 3- to 5-cm margin around the primary tumor site. We include the pelvic lymphatics up to the sacral promontory. In patients with a visible skin incision, tissue-equivalent bolus material is placed over the scar and is included in all treatment fields. If transsphincteric excision has been performed, the scar will extend down into the anal verge, and it too is treated for its entire length. Scars extending between the gluteal cleft are self-bolusing; the patient will experience a moist reaction in this area with doses of 45 Gy in 25 fractions. The anatomy of some patients will favor taping the buttocks apart and applying bolus over the scar instead of using the self-bolusing technique. After 45 Gy, the treatment fields are reduced off the scar area and the total dose to the tumor bed is taken to 53 Gy. The last four fractions are administered at 2.0 Gy/day; doses are calculated at the 95 percent isodose.

For patients treated preoperatively, dose is limited to 45 Gy and field placement is easier, since there are no scars to treat. The patient is treated prone on an open tabletop device with a three-field plan (Fig. 58-2).[20]

The 5-FU is given as a low-dose protracted infusion at a dosage of 300 mg/m^2/day administered for 5 days/week coinciding with each radiotherapy treatment.[21] Acute toxicity reactions have included diarrhea, stomatitis, nausea, hand-foot syndrome, loss of appetite, and flare of solar keratoses. These side effects are nearly always treated with medications; 5-FU administration rarely requires interruption because of toxicity. Use of the open tabletop is especially helpful in decreasing acute toxicity of combined modality therapy; it or an alternative bowel-exclusion technique should always be employed.

Local excision alone results in local recurrence rates ranging from 0 to 27 percent.[22] Local excision alone may cure the majority of properly selected pa-

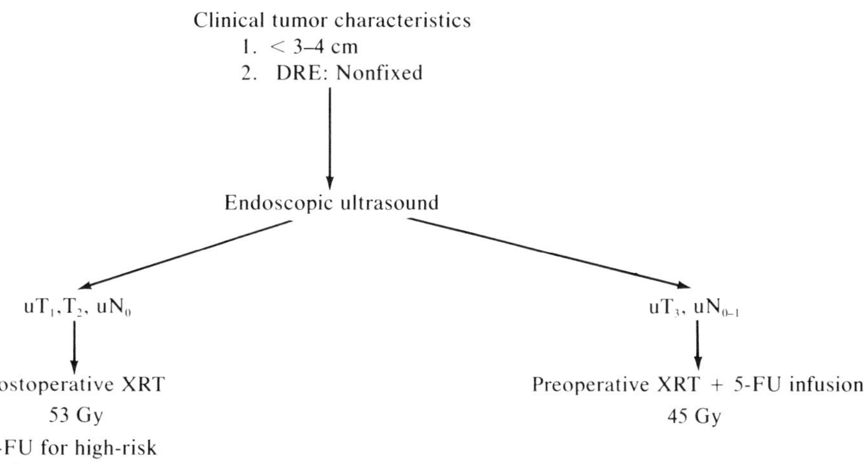

FIG. 58-1. The treatment approach for low rectal cancer at M. D. Anderson Cancer Center. The tumor is examined by ultrasound and staged according to the American Joint Committee on cancer's rectal cancer staging system (see Refs. 17 and 18).

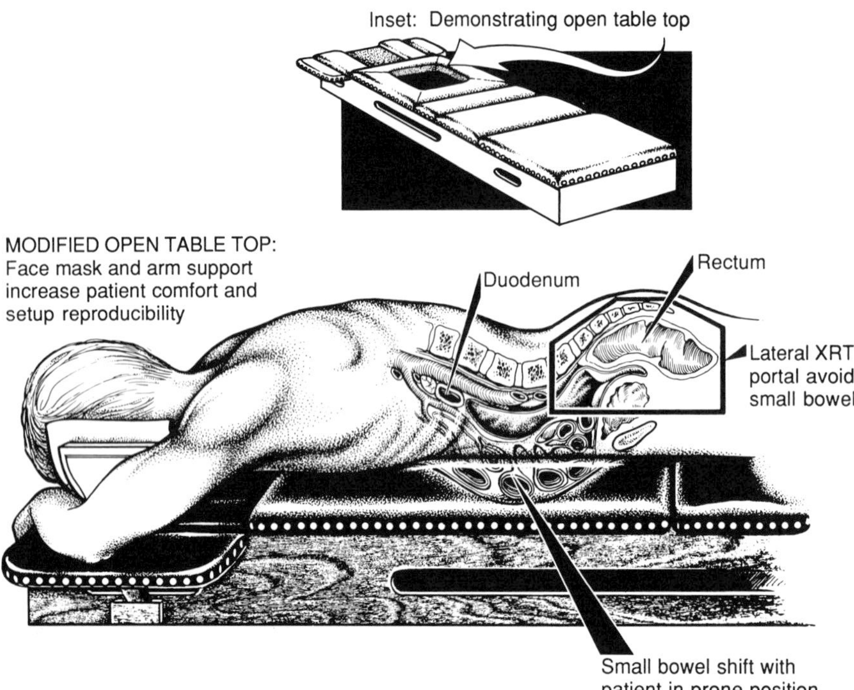

FIG. 58-2. The treatment position used at M. D. Anderson Cancer Center for irradiation of the pelvis, showing the mobilization of the small intestine out of the pelvis to reduce early and late radiation-related morbidity. (From Ref. 20. Reproduced by permission.)

tients. However, for the minority in whom treatment fails locally, one approach has been to perform a more radical operation when disease recurs. This philosophy unfortunately results in permanent colostomy, since a local recurrence can rarely be treated with an operation less radical than an APR. An alternative management philosophy employed at M. D. Anderson is to offer adjuvant treatment to all patients immediately after excision to maximize anal and rectal preservation. This "up-front" treatment approach reduces the overall need for colostomy, but admittedly, at the price of overtreating some.

RESULTS OF VARIOUS COMBINATIONS

Conservation surgery followed by XRT has now been reported in several series (Table 58-1). The results generally show local control rates > 90 percent and high survival rates with variable follow-up between 1 to 5 years. The initial series were similar in that patients were usually referred for XRT because of concern about the adequacy of surgery.[10,23] More recently, prospective phase I–II trials have been done in an effort to understand the toxicity, limitations, efficacy, and functional results of various combinations of limited surgery and XRT.[11,24–27] For example, the largest series is a prospective study from M. D. Anderson for patients with stages T_1, T_2, and T_3 disease who refused radical surgical excision. A total of 46 patients were treated with transanal, Kraske, transsphincteric, or abdominosacral operations and postoperative XRT between 1985 and 1989. There was one local failure in 31 T_1/T_2 patients, with follow-up ranging from 30 to 43 months; these results are consistent with those reported by others (Table 58-1). In contrast, there was 20 percent (3/15) local failure rate in T_3 patients.

Two explanations for local pelvic recurrence in patients treated on this protocol are (1) the presence of microscopic disease in the regional lymph nodes and (2) inadequate margins of resection. In our series, 3 patients had positive margins on final pathologic sections.[28] In an analysis of all locally excised rectal cancer patients referred for XRT at M. D. Anderson, positive margins were an independent prognostic factor associated with local failure. Most patients with positive margins were treated before the inception of the prospective phase I–II protocol. Further analysis of the M. D. Anderson patients undergoing limited surgery and postoperative XRT shows that the average tumor margin was only 3 mm while the average tumor size was 3 cm. The use of limited excision and postoperative XRT appears to be a reasonable alternative to APR for patients with T_1 and T_2 low rectal cancers regardless of margin status. Patients with pathologically staged T_3 disease, those having compromised resection margins, or those with tumors staged uT_3 N_1 are at higher risk for local recurrence. Although it is feasible, we have not yet treated these patients with further excision and/or higher doses of XRT.

As outlined in Fig. 58-1, patients with stage uT_3 tumors are now treated by a protocol of preoperative chemoradiation: 45 Gy in 25 fractions and concomitant

Table 58-1
Results of Local Excision and Postoperative Radiotherapy for Early Rectal Cancer

Authors	No. of patients	Type of surgery	XRT dose, Gy	Pathology tumor stage T_1	T_2	T_3	Local control, %	Salvage	Survival,[a] %
Rich et al.,[23] 1985	17	TA,FUL,EC, IB,CRY	<60	2	11	3	94	—	88
Rich,[10] 1988	15	TA,TS	53[b]	9		4	93	1/1	80
Gryska and Cohen,[34] 1987	26	TA,K,FUL	59[b]	—	—	—	85	2/4	—
Summers et al.,[24] 1992	14	FTLE	50.4	3	7	4	79	2/3	88
Summers et al.,[24] 1992	19	TA,TSC	<55	13	4	—	84	2/3	68
Wood and Willett,[25] 1992	20	TA,TS,K	<65	5	11	1	100	—	100
Jessup et al.,[26] 1992	21	TA,TSC	<54	6	13	2	100	—	100
Ota et al.,[27] 1992	46	TA,TS,TAS,K	<55	16	15	15	91	—	93
Wong et al.,[35] 1993	25	TA,EC	50	13	7	3	76	—	75

[a]Survival < 5 years; varies with series.

[b]Median dose.

Abbreviations: TA, transanal; FUL, fulguration; EC, electrocoagulation; IB, incisional biopsy; CRY, cryotherapy; TS, transsphincteric; K, Kraske; FTLE, full-thickness local excision; TSC, transsacral excision; TAS, transabdominosacral.

low-dose infusion of 5-FU.[29] The chemotherapy is given from Monday morning until Saturday morning by a portable infusion pump. This chemoradiation protocol was first assessed in patients with T_4 disease and found to be well tolerated; it has now been used in patients with less advanced stages of cancer. The rationale here is to achieve a preoperative downstaging of tumor, thereby improving the likelihood of successful conservative surgery. The disadvantages of this preoperative approach are the delay in wound healing and an increase in acute and late complications, including decreased anal, rectal, and sexual function. Early results show that the complications encountered are minimal and that this approach is feasible and safe. We have seen complete pathologic responses in >30 percent of patients and about another 45 percent have only microscopic residual disease; the anus has been preserved in about 80 percent.[29]

ENDOCAVITARY IRRADIATION WITH OR WITHOUT IMPLANT BOOST

Endocavitary XRT is a form of external treatment that does not conform to the basic notions of conventional fractionated external beam XRT because of the use of extremely large fractional doses and the pattern and method of treatment application. The treatment philosophy here is to deliver a cytocidal dose of XRT to the rectal cancer and a small amount of surrounding normal colonic mucosa. The classic selection criteria for this procedure are nearly identical to those chosen for surgical conservation procedures, as is the necessity for adequate follow-up.[30] Based on the pioneering work of Papillon, this approach is now a proven alternative for curative treatment for patients who are medically unfit for an anesthetic or surgical resection.

Selection of patients suitable for endocavitary XRT is constrained by tumor diameter and the depth of tumor invasion in the rectal wall. The largest diameter of the treatment applicator is 3.0 cm, although two overlapping treatment fields can be aligned to treat lesions that are < 3 × 5 cm. The lesion thickness that can be treated with endocavitary irradiation is limited by the beam's energy. The most common treatment machine for endocavitary XRT is a Philips 50 kV rod-anode device that emits irradiation axially with a focus to target distance of 4 cm. The filtration used is 0.5 mm Al, which produces a dose rate at 2 cm from the tip of 20 Gy/min. The penetration of this beam is limited; within 2 cm of the surface of treatment, the beam decays to 10 percent of the applied dose.

Endocavitary treatment can be considered a form of radiocautery. The usual total dose is 100 to 140 Gy given over 6 to 7 weeks in four to five applications. The long treatment intervals are necessary to permit tumor regression, thus allowing the applicator to rest directly on the remaining and deeper layers of tumor at the next treatment session. The rapidity of shrinkage has been used by Papillon as a guideline for the the application of subsequent dose levels and interfraction intervals. For example, exophytic cancer tumors usually display rapid shrinkage after the first or second dose and can be treated with endocavitary XRT alone according to the schedule described. However, for patients with ulceration, induration, and tethering after two treatments, Papillon's recommendation is that surgery should be performed because these clinical findings indicate perirectal involvement not amenable at endocavitary XRT. For selected patients with residual cancer who are not candidates for surgery, an interstitial implant using an afterloading iridium 192 forked needle can be used to deliver an additional 20 Gy to the base of the tumor.[30]

The treatment results from several institutions indicate that endocavitary XRT can obtain local control from 76 to 93 percent, depending on careful patient selection.[30–33] A clinical staging system has been proposed by the Dijon group and is based on size (> or < 3 cm) and deep fixation on DRE.[33] Tumor control with endocavitary XRT alone was better for lesions on the anterior wall versus other wall locations, and it was better for midrectal versus low or high rectal cancers.[33] This proposed staging system may be used to select patients who may be treated with endocavitary irradiation alone or with an implant boost. Because of the specialized nature of this procedure and the lack of wide availability of this equipment, referral to larger centers with experience with this technique is commonly done.

SUMMARY AND FUTURE DIRECTIONS

Limited surgery and postoperative XRT for selected patients can maximize local control and minimize the need for permanent colostomy for patients with early-stage low rectal cancer. Establishing reliable criteria for the selection of patients for newer modalities will improve the clinician's ability to select those with truly minimal disease for limited surgical or radiotherapeutic treatment.

In patients with slightly more extensive disease or in those with identifiable risk factors for local recurrence, the use of preoperative chemoradiation appears to be a very reasonable approach, based on pilot studies. This treatment has been found to be well tolerated and highly effective at downstaging rectal cancer, thus permitting limited surgery.

REFERENCES

1. Curley SA, Roh MS, Rich TA: Surgical therapy and early rectal carcinoma. *Hematol Oncol Clin North Am* 3:87–102, 1989.
2. Wolmark N, Fisher B: An analysis of survival and treatment failure following abdominoperineal and sphincter-saving resection in Dukes' B and C rectal carcinoma. *Ann Surg* 204:480–489, 1986.
3. Chan KW, Boey J, Wong SKC: A method of reporting radial invasion and surgical clearance of rectal carcinoma. *Histopathology* 9:1319–1327, 1985.
4. Quirke P, Durdey P, Dixon MF, et al: Local recurrence of rectal adenocarcinoma due to inadequate surgical resection: Histopathological study of lateral tumor spread and surgical excision. *Lancet* 1:996–999, 1986.
5. Quirke P, Scott N: The pathologist's role in the assessment of local recurrence in rectal carcinoma. *Surg Oncol Clin North Am* 1:1–17, 1992.
6. Rich TA, Terry NHA, Meistrich M, et al: Pathologic, anatomic, and biologic factors correlated with local recurrence of colorectal cancer. *Semin Radiat Oncol* 3:13–19, 1993.
7. Rich T, Gunderson LL, Lew R, et al: Patterns of recurrence of rectal cancer after potentially curative surgery. *Cancer* 52:1317–1329, 1983.
8. Gunderson LL, Sosin H: Areas of failure found at reoperation (second or symptomatic look) following "curative surgery" for adenocarcinoma of the rectum: Clinicopathologic correlation and implications for adjuvant therapy. *Cancer* 34:1278–1292, 1974.
9. Minsky BD, Mies C, Rich TA, et al: Colloid carcinoma of the colon and rectum. *Cancer* 60:3103–3112, 1987.
10. Rich TA: Radiotherapy for early rectal cancer, in Levin B (ed): *Gastrointestinal Cancer.* Austin, Texas, University of Texas Press, 1988, pp 167–175.
11. Enker WE, Paty B, Minsky BD, et al: Restorative or preservative operations in the treatment of rectal cancer. *Surg Oncol Clin North Am* 1:57–69, 1992.
12. Nichols RJ, Mason AY, Morson BC: The clinical staging of rectal cancer. *Br J Surg* 69:404–409, 1982.
13. Duncan W: Adjuvant radiotherapy in rectal cancer: The MRC trials. *Br J Surg* 72:S59–S62, 1985.
14. Grabbe E, Lierse W, Winkler R: The perirectal fascia: Morphology and use in staging of rectal carcinoma. *Radiology* 149:241–246, 1983.
15. Wong WD, Orrom WJ, Jensen LL: Preoperative staging of rectal cancer with endorectal ultrasonography. *Perspect Colon Rect Surg* 3:315–334, 1990.
16. Hinder JM, Chu J, Bokey EL, et al: Use of transrectal ultrasound to evaluate direct tumor spread and lymph node status in patients with rectal cancer. *Aust NZ J Surg* 60:19–23, 1990.
17. Hildebrandt U, Feifel G: Preoperative staging of rectal cancer by intrarectal ultrasound. *Dis Colon Rectum* 28:42–46, 1985.
18. American Joint Committee on Cancer: Colon and rectum, in Beahrs OH, Henson DE, Hutter RV, et al (eds): *Manual for Staging of Cancer,* 3rd ed. Philadelphia, Lippincott, 1988, pp 75–80.
19. Chan TW, Kressel HY, Milestone B, et al: Rectal carcinoma: Staging at MR imaging with endorectal surface coil. *Radiology* 181:461–467, 1991.
20. Rich TA: Treatment planning for tumors of the gastrointestinal tract, in Paliwal BR, Griem ML (eds): *Syllabus: A Categorical Course in Radiation Therapy Treatment Planning.* Oak Brook, Ill, RSNA Division, Editorial and Publishing Services, 1986, pp 47–55.
21. Rich TA: Chemoradiation for gastrointestinal cancer, in Meyer JL, Vaeth J (eds): *Radiotherapy/Chemotherapy Interactions in Cancer Therapy, Front Radiat Ther Oncol.* Basel, Karger, 1992, pp 115–130.
22. Graham RA, Garnsey L, Jessup JM: Local excision of rectal carcinoma. *Am J Surg* 160:306–312, 1990.
23. Rich TA, Weiss DR, Mies C, et al: Sphincter preservation in patients with low rectal cancer treated with radiation therapy with or without local excision or fulguration. *Radiology* 156:527–531, 1985.
24. Summers GE, Mendenhall WM, Copeland EM III: Update on the University of Florida experience with local excision and postoperative radiation therapy for the treatment of early rectal carcinoma. *Surg Oncol Clin North Am* 1:25–130, 1992.
25. Wood WC, Willett CG: Update of the Massachusetts General Hospital experience of combined local excision and radiotherapy for rectal cancer. *Surg Oncol Clin North Am* 1:131–136, 1992.
26. Jessup JM, Bothe A, Stone MD, et al: Preservation of sphincter function in rectal carcinoma by a multimodality treatment approach. *Surg Oncol Clin North Am* 1:137–145, 1992.

27. Ota DM, Skibber J, Rich TA: MD Anderson Cancer Center experience with local exicision and multimodality therapy for rectal cancer. *Surg Oncol Clin North Am* 1:147–152, 1992.
28. Skibber JM, Rich TA, Schumate RC, et al: Local excision and postoperative radiotherapy for low rectal cancer (abstract). *Proceedings of Society of Surgical Oncology.* March 1992.
29. Meterissian S, Skibber J, Rich T, et al: Patterns of residual disease after preoperative chemoradiation in ultrasound T3 rectal carcinoma. *J Surg Oncol,* 1994.
30. Papillon J: Conservative treatment by Irradiation—An alternative to radical surgery. in Papillon J (ed): *Rectal and Anal Cancer.* New York, Springer-Verlag, 1982, pp 66–95.
31. Sischy B, Granery MJ, Hinson EJ: Endocavitary irradiation for adenocarcinoma of the rectum. *CA* 34:333–339, 1984.
32. Lavery IC, Jones IT, Weakley FL, et al: Definitive management of rectal cancer by contact (endocavitary) Irradiation. *Dis Colon Rectum* 30:835–838, 1987.
33. Roth SL, Horiot JC, Calais G, et al: Prognostic factors in limited rectal cancer treated with intracavitary irradiation. *Int J Radiat Oncol Biol Phys* 16:1445–1451, 1989.
34. Gryska PV, Cohen AM: Screening asymptomatic patients at high risk for colon cancer with full colonoscopy. *Dis Colon Rectum* 30:18–20, 1987.
35. Wong CS, Stern H, Cummings BJ: Local excision and postoperative radiation therapy for rectal carcinoma. *Int J Radiat Biol Phys* 25:669–675, 1993.

CHAPTER 59

Operative Considerations in Rectal Cancer—The Pelvic Dissection

Warren E. Enker

HIGHLIGHTS

In the operative treatment of rectal cancer, the extent of resection and its techniques determine cure, local control, the need for adjuvant therapy, sphincter preservation, and the loss of or the preservation of sexual and urinary functions. Planes of dissection, pathophysiology, definitions of margins, and other determinants of successful outcome are discussed. Avoidance of both long-term sexual and urinary dysfunction and loss of sphincter function will be coordinated with extent of resection.

CONTROVERSIES

Modern operative technique may be associated with markedly decreased rates of pelvic recurrence in T_3N_0 and T_3N_1 rectal cancers—i.e., 3 to 12 percent as opposed to 20 to 45 percent local recurrence rates following conventional surgery. This may obviate the need for adjuvant radiation therapy.

FUTURE DIRECTIONS

Pathologic markers of tumor behavior—i.e., nonnodal separate foci of metastatic disease of lymphatic vascular invasion within the mesentery—and molecular markers are under investigation. Such findings may lead to revisions in the way adjuvant therapy is currently selected and administered.

DETERMINANTS OF PELVIC RECURRENCE

The determinants of pelvic recurrence include clinical, pathologic, operative, and other factors.

Clinical Factors

Pelvic Configuration

Rectal cancer is more difficult to cure in the male patient. In the male, the true pelvis may vary from a severely android pelvis, offering no room for the operating surgeon's hand, to the gynecoid pelvis, approaching the dimensions of a small female pelvis. A bulky rectal cancer within the true pelvis in a male patient with an enlarged prostate represents a challenge to a curative resection. While these frustrating circumstances often lead to blunt dissection and frequently hamper sphincter preservation, one must, nevertheless, maintain all efforts at sharp dissection along appropriate planes. If surgery is further hampered by obesity, significant difficulty may be encountered in performing an adequate resection.

Adjacent Organ Involvement

Adjacent organ involvement or adherence is encountered in approximately 10 percent of patients with rectal cancer. While adjacent organ involvement is traditionally staged by Turnbull as stage D (incurable) disease, Memorial Sloan-Kettering Cancer Center data as well as those of other institutions suggest that it is one more manifestation of local/regional disease.

The principles dictating treatment are (1) adequate regional resection with resection of the involved adjacent organ sufficient to provide negative surgical and pathologic margins of resection and (2) primary reconstruction of the adjacent organ wherever possible. To knowingly leave gross or microscopic tumor attached to an adjacent organ, relying on radiation therapy to eliminate such disease, is condemned as a violation of the rules of cancer treatment and a guarantee of persistent/recurrent disease despite all nonoperative modalities.[1,2]

Similarly, perforation with extension toward an anterior organ—such as the uterus—is treated in the same fashion as adjacent organ involvement. Pelvic peritoneal seeding, while treated aggressively for palliation, is rarely cured.

Pathologic Factors

T Stage

The general view following conventional surgery for rectal cancer indicates that 20 to 45 percent of patients with rectal cancer experience local recurrence following curative resection. This risk of local failure will increase proportionately in relation to the extent of transmural penetration by the tumor and/or the presence of lymph node metastases. While multiple factors may contribute to such recurrence, virtually all instances of local failure appear to be related to inadequate resection of regional disease.[3]

Pelvic recurrence has been traditionally associated with T stage. Significant recurrence rates are associated with penetration of the full thickness of the rectal wall into perirectal adipose tissue. In a seminal study reported in 1986, Quirke and coworkers[4] demonstrated the inadequacy of this approach. Analyzing rectal cancers using transverse whole-mount cross sections of resected specimens, they demonstrated unsuspected carcinoma at the lateral margins of resection in 14 of 52 analyzed specimens. Of the 14 patients, 12 developed a local pelvic recurrence. These authors indicated that prior methods of analyzing specimens resulted in a failure to appreciate this mechanism from a pathologic standpoint, and they concluded that pelvic recurrence of rectal cancer is the result of inadequate surgery, i.e., inadequate lateral clearance of regional tumor present in any and all forms of spread. Subsequent studies have confirmed their original data.[3] Some authors[5] would suggest that the risk of local recurrence is as great due to full-thickness penetration of the bowel wall as one would expect with lymph node involvement. Recent work suggests that increasing involvement of lymph nodes in the perirectal fat is associated with the increasing degree of primary tumor penetration and that the majority of such lymph nodes measure less than 5 mm. Such lymph nodes could escape detection in routine pathologic assessment, thus understaging N_1 disease and leaving one with the impression that a patient has $T_3N_0M_0$ disease.[6] In the presence of adequate resection and in the absence of other adverse pathologic features, T_3N_0 rectal cancer seems to represent no special risk and is highly amenable to cure and local control.

N Stage

Lymph node metastases within the mesorectum define several subgroups, each with its own unique surgical outcome. In several published series, patients with T_3N_1 disease with only one involved lymph node have fared as well—in terms of both local control and cure—as patients with T_3N_0 disease.[7,8] While rare, patients with T_2N_1 rectal cancer have been noted to have a significantly higher survival in these same published series.[8]

Where N_1 disease is defined as 1 to 3 positive lymph nodes, the traditional recurrence rates are 20 to 45 or 30 to 50 percent in published series.[9] Such findings prompt the aggressive use of adjuvant therapy in patients with any number of positive lymph nodes. Within the past decade, surgeons who have demonstrated the advantages of complete resection of all regional pelvic disease related to the spread of rectal cancer have published local recurrence ranging from only 3 to 12 percent in patients with N_1 disease.[8,10–14] Significantly, many of the tumors that did recur in the pelvis had more aggressive pathologic features, which are not accounted for in either the traditional Dukes' or the TNM staging systems. When present, such factors—including lymphatic vascular invasion—may play a stronger role in recurrence than lymph node metastases alone.[11,15] Unpublished data in 251 patients who underwent low anterior resection between 1979 and 1989 suggest a 4.5 percent local recurrence rate. Fifty percent of the patients experiencing local pelvic failure had some additional risk factor—e.g., lymphatic vascular or perineural invasion—in addition to their T or N stage.[13] MacFarlane et al.[14] have recently published similar results in which adherence to the principle of total mesorectal excision yielded local recurrence rates of only 5 percent and cancer-free survival figures far better than conventional resections, despite the purported advantages of adjuvant radiation and chemotherapy.

One is drawn to the conclusion that T_3 disease or N_1 disease *alone* may not represent an ominous prognostic factor in the face of complete mesorectal excision. In the setting of conventional surgery as it is routinely practiced (blunt dissection, generally along the visceral planes instead of the parietal fascia, with violations of the mesentery), both T_3 and N_1 disease are considered significant risks for pelvic recurrence, prompting aggressive adjuvant therapy.

N_2 disease (four or more positive lymph nodes) in and of itself is a significant risk factor for local recurrence. Despite the potential risks of postoperative radiation and chemotherapy, patients harboring N_2 disease should receive adjuvant therapy no matter what the extent of operative dissection. With the additional presence of either lymphatic or perineural invasion or poorly differentiated disease, such additional systemic and regional treatment is mandatory.

N_3 disease (metastases to extraregional lymph nodes, e.g., periaortic or obturator) constitutes a high risk for local failure and for the further development of systemic disease. Aggressive combined chemotherapy and radiation should precede surgery where such disease is staged preoperatively. Alternatively, aggressive postoperative combined chemotherapy and radiation should be employed in the hope of a rare cure and significant palliation.

Lymphatic Vascular Invasion

Lymphatic vessel invasion is a significant independent prognostic factor for survival in colorectal cancer.[11,15] Michelassi et al.[11] described an overall local recurrence rate of 12 percent in patients undergoing parietal pelvic dissection at the University of Chicago. No patients experienced local recurrence in the presence of N_1 disease alone. All patients who did experience local recurrence had lymphatic vascular invasion within the resected specimen. In and of itself, T_3N_1 disease may represent surgically curable regional disease; however, lymphatic vascular invasion probably represents more widespread pelvic disease with a higher incidence of pelvic failure and systemic spread. In a similar vein, perineural invasion may represent an ominous prognostic variable. Perineural invasion is often associated with local and systemic failure despite aggressive efforts at adjuvant therapy.

While the mechanism of spread is as yet unclear, the presence of separate foci of metastatic disease within the surrounding mesorectum or mesocolon may be a manifestation of both lymphatic vascular and perineural spread. In contrast to nodal spread, where metastases are visible either in lymph nodes or replacing lymph nodes with an ovoid deposit, separate, nonnodal mesenteric implants represent stellate foci within the mesentery, portions of which demonstrate no evidence of a preexisting node. Special stains suggest that this widespread form of regional disease takes place along neural sheaths and lymphatic vessels. The pathway may not be as important as the fact that such foci represent widespread regional disease with extremely poor survival and a high rate of pelvic failure.[16] Molecular factors controlling tumor behavior may be more important in this setting than the specific pathway of spread adopted by the tumor.[17]

Ploidy

Tumor cell DNA content and proliferative indices have been related to aggressive tumor behavior in both colonic and rectal cancer. In general, retrospective studies find that ploidy is an independent prognostic variable. Prospective studies have found that ploidy *alone* is of little significance in prognosis[18] and that the contribution of ploidy to prognosis is marginal in a multivariate analysis.[19] Aneuploidy may be associated with local recurrence following local excision or ablation of rectal cancer[20] (see Chap. 23).

When combined with proliferative index, ploidy may offer more prognostic value. Patients with diploid tumors of low proliferative index appear to have very benign cancers, while patients whose tumors are both aneuploid and of high proliferative index have extremely aggressive tumors. Tumors that are either aneuploid with low proliferative index or diploid with high proliferative index manifest no unusual behavior.

Operative Factors

Beginning with the work of Dukes,[21,22] it has been evident that cancers of the rectum have a progressively increasing chance of spread to regional lymph nodes based on the degree of mural penetration by the primary cancer. The traditional rates of local recurrence following conventional surgery are 20 to 45 percent for T_3N_0 or T_3N_1 disease, with a 30 to 35 percent 5-year survival for N_1 disease. Following operations that utilize complete mesorectal excision, local recurrence rates average 3 to 12 percent, with 55 to 60 percent 5-year survival in N_1 disease.[10,11,14,23]

The traditional rates of local recurrence—20 to 45 percent—are associated with inadequate surgery and positive *lateral* margins due to inadequate clearance of the entire mesorectum.[4] Along with the effects of complete mesorectal excision, one must appreciate the benefits of sharp pelvic dissection as opposed to the traditional blunt technique. Sharp dissection allows careful, deliberate, and hemostatic dissection along the parietal pelvic fascia, whereas blunt technique results in injury to the mesorectum, violation of tumor close to the margins of resection, and local recurrence rates reflecting complete versus inadequate resection. In addition, blunt dissection in the pelvis, particularly at the level of the third sacral vertebra (i.e., the anterior curve of the sacrum), is associated with bleeding due to gross disruption of the sacral venous complex. By contrast, sharp dissection along the parietal pelvic fascia, which includes the presacral fascia, is virtually bloodless when performed under direct control using cautery and small hemoclips for hemostasis. Together with the avoidance of sexual and urinary morbidity by the identification of the pelvic autonomic nerves, sharp dissection with complete mesorectal excision, and sphincter preservation constitute a synthesis of goals in the operative treatment of rectal cancer.[14,23]

Distal Margin of Resection (the Cancer-Free Mural Margin) as a Factor in Local Recurrence

The traditional 5-cm distal margin in the operative treatment of rectal cancer was introduced by Goligher et al.[24] in 1951. Subsequently, these authors modified their recommendation to a 2.5- to 3-cm distal margin of resection. This recommendation accompanied increasing experience with circular stapling devices and improvement of surgical standards regarding cancer clearance combined with low anterior resection. Attempts to correlate the distance of the distal margin in the fresh unpinned specimen, in the pinned specimen, or in the fixed pathologic specimen have demonstrated how elusive this goal may be. The elasticity of the rectum and difficulty in determining the distal edge of the primary tumor in vivo may make it quite difficult to determine the distal margin of resection intraoperatively. Recently, Vernava and coworkers[25] have studied the influence of the distal margin of resection on the incidence of pelvic recurrence prospectively. Patients were categorized as having a distal margin of resection of 1, 2, or 3 cm beyond the tumor in the fresh, resected, unpinned specimen. In 243 patients, there was no significant difference in the anastomotic, pelvic, or distal recurrence rates or in the rate of survival until the distal margin of resection was less than 0.8 cm.

These data reflect the distal margin measured *after* the surgeon has become committed to division of the rectal wall distal to the tumor. More often than not, the actual or accurate intraoperative determination of the distal margin of resection can prove difficult. Obesity, prior pelvic surgery, or radiation therapy may compound the problem. Be it digital examination, intraoperative sigmoidoscopy, marking the rectum with a suture, or any other maneuver that may be necessary, accurate identification of the distal margin is one of the factors important to a successful outcome. In the completely mobilized rectum, the distal margin of resection is not too significant an issue. As discussed below, the major issue intraoperatively is the distal margin of *dissection* and the adequate clearance of all cancer. The actual distal margin will vary with the circumstances, rarely being as little as 1 cm and generally more like 3 or 4 cm. Surgical experience and identification of the distal margin as well as complete lateral clearance will all influence the selection process.

Cancer Cell Exfoliation

The fragmentation of primary tumors and the exfoliation of tumor cells take place as a consequence of manipulation of the primary tumor during pelvic dissection, be it blunt or sharp. While little proof exists that exfoliation may be responsible for local pelvic recurrence, the presence of numerous tumor cells within the lumen distal to the primary cancer is a certainty. The possibility that exfoliated tumor cells or fragments of tumor can implant within a stapled anastomosis remains a consideration during any form of closed anastomosis.[3] For this reason, all "closed anastomoses" (i.e., created by double-stapling) require that copious irrigation of the distal rectum be performed prior to the application of the transverse staple line. Some surgeons practice universal irrigation of the distal rectal stump. Copious pelvic irrigation is equally helpful in the elimination of exfoliated cells that may be exposed to the true pelvis during the division of the rectum and the execution of any open anastomosis. Nevertheless, exfoliation is mostly a theoretical issue and is unlikely to account for any but the rarest case of recurrence at the anastomosis or at a distal site of injury such as an anal fissure.

FACTORS AFFECTING THE DISTAL MARGINS OF RESECTION AND DISSECTION

Distal intramural spread by a primary rectal cancer via the lymphatics or via direct submucosal spread is rarely observed beyond the lowest visible point of the gross lesion. Even when present, such spread is not likely to extend beyond 2 cm. In the majority of cases in which the distal margin of resection is positive due to intramural spread and not surgical misadventure, other adverse pathologic features are virtually always present—features such as poorly differentiated cancer, signet-ring cells, multiple separate foci of mesenteric implants, and so on—all signs of locally widespread disease.

Williams and coworkers,[26] among others, have evaluated the relationship between distal margin and local pelvic recurrence. In the absence of the above features—i.e., in the conventional, well-circumscribed, well- or moderately well differentiated carcinoma with or without nodal involvement—pathologic distal margins of 2 cm or more are generally not associated with local failure.[26]

The spread of rectal cancer into the mesorectum beyond the lowest edge of the primary tumor is postulated as one cause of pelvic recurrence. Heald and Ryall[10] have suggested that among the key features of an adequate resection is the complete resection of the "distal mesorectum." In examining this postulate, Quirke and Scott[3] discovered that 4 of 20 specimens did contain tumor spread to the mesorectum distal to the lowest edge of the primary but that 2 of these cases also had involvement of lateral surgical margins. In their opinion, distal mesorectal spread was not so much a mechanism of recurrence as a marker of advanced disease in which resection alone would be highly unlikely to address the issue of local control.

In most instances, the issue of the distal margin of *resection* is confused with and mistaken for the issue of the distal margin of *dissection*. For decades, the prevailing guideline has been a distal margin of 5 cm in resections of the rectum. Realistically, this means that without stretching the indications, patients with midrectal cancers 6 to 10 cm from the anal verge can have sphincter-preserving operations with an acceptable distal margin, but not patients with cancers of the distal rectum situated up to 5 cm from the anal verge.

Focusing on the reconstruction rather than on the cancer resection—i.e., "coning down" to the site of the distal transection of the specimen-to-be—represents an operative approach that is most responsible for compromise of the distal margin and of all surgical margins. All are agreed that the potential for spread within the mesorectum is the most important consideration in the planning of any resection. With 65 to 80 percent of curable patients harboring mesorectal disease either by direct extension or by spread, total resection of the mesorectum proximal lateral and distal to the primary tumor is the most important principle of treatment in rectal cancer.

In order to prevent compromise to the resection of the mesentery, the complete rectum must be mobilized, from the point of entry into the true pelvis to the anal hiatus in the levator ani muscles. Once mobilization has been accomplished, a point for transection of the mesorectum and rectum can be selected. A rectal examination to confirm the location of the primary tumor, palpation, placement of a marking stitch, or any other indicator of the distal edge of the primary can be helpful to the operating surgeon. If, after identifying the distal edge of the primary tumor in a completely mobilized rectum, one transects the bowel and the mesentery less than 5 cm from the distal margin, few patients will die as a result of distal compromise. If, however, the *dissection* proceeds for a distance of *only* 5 cm beyond the lowest palpable edge of tumor, with the mesentery transected and the bowel prepared for an anastomosis *without prior complete mobilization*, the placement of a bowel clamp prior to rectal transection will frequently compromise the distal margin.

PLANES OF PELVIC DISSECTION IN RELATION TO CURATIVE RESECTIONS FOR RECTAL CANCER

In the operative treatment of rectal cancer there are five major goals. These include the following:

1. Cure
2. Local control (the avoidance of pelvic recurrence)
3. Restoration of continuity
4. Preservation of anorectal sphincter function
5. Preservation of sexual and urinary function

Cure, local control, and the avoidance of sexual and urinary morbidity are related to the extent and technique of pelvic dissection. The extent of lateral dissection within the pelvis will rarely influence one's ability to accomplish sphincter preservation. The choice between abdominoperineal resection of the rectum or colorectal anastomosis is more often dependent upon the location of the primary tumor (its distance from the anal verge) and of the presence or absence of gross residual pelvic disease.

A working knowledge of the planes of pelvic anatomy is of signal importance to the surgeon operating on rectal cancer. This chapter will compare claims regarding cure, local control, and the avoidance of sexual and urinary morbidity in terms of operations that define the planes of anatomy utilized by experienced surgeons.

General Features of Pelvic Anatomy

The pelvis may be divided into various compartments. In the male patient, there are two pelvic visceral compartments, the anterior one containing the male genitourinary structures and the posterior one the rectum and its related structures. For convenience, in the female, the uterus and vagina may be included within the anterior visceral compartment. Such arbitrary divisions, while educationally useful, do not obviate the need for adjacent organ resection in certain cancers involving either compartment.

A second distinction can be made between the visceral compartments in general and the parietal compartment of the pelvis. Within the visceral compartments are the male and female genitourinary tracts and the rectum, while in the parietal compartment one finds the musculoskeletal boundaries of the pelvic side walls, the major vessels, and the various branches of the pelvic autonomic nervous system (Fig. 59-1). The extent of primary rectal cancer spread is best viewed as the extent of lateral or circumferential spread within the posterior visceral compartment. It is this relationship between the potential extent of spread and the planes of surgical resection that forms the essence of ongoing debate regarding which planes of pelvic dissection provide the best likelihood of cure with the least likelihood of operative morbidity.

Planes of Pelvic Dissection in Relation to Rectal Cancer

The true pelvis is radiographically defined as that portion of the pelvic caudad or distal to a line drawn from the sacral promontory to the symphysis pubis on the lateral x-ray. The rectum is that portion of the large intestine found within the true pelvis. For convenience, the American College of Surgeons defines the rectum as having three portions, the lower rectum, situated up to 5 cm from the anal verge; the midrectum,

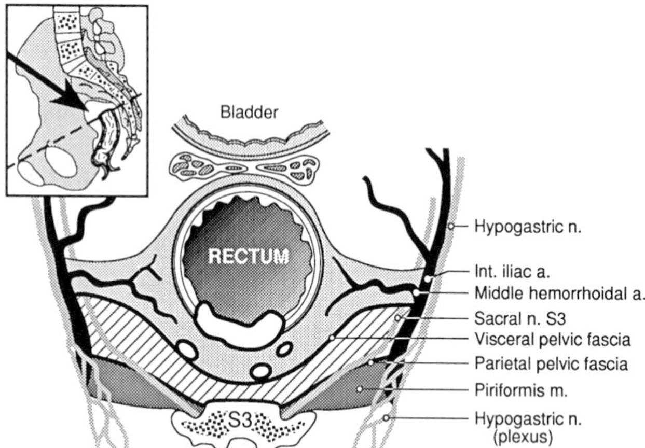

FIG. 59-1. A transverse cross-sectional view of the pelvis at the level of the middle of the true pelvis, i.e., the piriformis muscles. This level corresponds to S3 and to the anterior curvature of the sacrum. Shown here is the posterior visceral compartment with both the visceral and parietal fascia outlined. Potentially involved lymph nodes are situated along the visceral plane of the fascia investing the mesorectum. (Reprinted with permission of Primary Care and Cancer, PRR Inc., Publishers, Huntington, N.Y., 1993.)

lying 6 to 10 cm from the anal verge; and the upper rectum, situated 10 to 15 cm from the anal verge. In reality, the rectum situated within the true pelvis is rarely 15 cm long. A rectum of that length is usually found only in large male patients.

Clinical evidence from patterns of recurrence[27] and from the Gastrointestinal Tumor Study Group of the National Cancer Institute[28] suggests that the rectum is that portion of the distal colon situated up to 12 cm from the anal verge. This distinction is based upon patterns of local failure following operations for rectal cancer, with the traditional high incidence of local failure falling dramatically for tumor situated above 11 or 12 cm when compared to those situated below that level. Surgical series including data on cancers of the rectum defined as higher than 11 or 12 cm project falsely optimistic rates of local recurrence based on a liberal definition of the rectum as opposed to any new benefits of therapy.

A cross section of the pelvis at the midrectum (at approximately the level of the piriformis muscles of the pelvis) will show the following anatomic relationships. The rectum itself will be relatively thick-walled and circular. Laterally, the rectum will be held in place by two structures, the lateral ligaments or stalks. Within the lateral ligaments emanating from the pelvic sidewall and running to the rectum can be found the middle hemorrhoidal arteries, the rectal visceral blood supply from the internal iliac artery. The rectal blood supply derived from the inferior mesenteric artery is situated posterior to the rectum and runs within the generous fat-containing mesorectum. The rectum, the lateral ligaments, and the mesorectum are surrounded by an investing layer of fascia known previously as the fascia propria of the rectum. Recent and more accurate nomenclature refers to this layer as the visceral layer of the endopelvic fascia.

The mesorectum anterior to the rectum is quite thin and borders on a fascial plane separating the anterior visceral compartment from the rectum. This layer is referred to as the fascia of Denonvillier and constitutes the anteriormost boundary of resection for a typical rectal cancer. The parietal pelvic boundaries, also referred to as the pelvic side wall, is composed of the bony skeletal boundaries of the pelvis, comprising the sacrum and the ischial tuberosities, the muscular boundaries (the piriformis and the obturator muscles), the great vessels of the pelvis (the external, internal, and common iliac vessels), and the pelvic nerves (the sympathetic and parasympathetic nerves of the pelvic autonomic nervous system). While the vessels have their own adventitia—which is lateral to any lymphatic or lymph node–containing tissue—all of these structures are invested by a fascial layer which defines the inward surface of the pelvic side walls—the parietal layer of the endopelvic fascia.

Anatomic Planes of Dissection in Relation to Curative Resections

As one moves outward or centrifugally from the center of the rectum, there are four adventitial, relatively avascular planes for dissection in relation to the anatomy of the rectum and the natural history of rectal cancer. These are (1) the visceral layer of the endopelvic fascia, (2) the parietal layer of the endopelvic fascia, (3) the vascular adventitia, and (4) the extrapelvic anatomic spaces (i.e., obturator).

All discussion of dissection along selected planes assumes the use of sharp as opposed to blunt dissection. Blunt dissection frequently violates tissue planes and cannot be relied upon to maintain the integrity of a dissection along a chosen pathway. Sharp dissection is gentler, more controlled and hemostatic, anatomically truer, and less likely, due to the creation of unnatural stresses, to fracture tumor located along the margins of resection. The traditional operation performed in the western world for rectal cancer generally involves blunt dissection along the plane immediately surrounding the mesorectum (i.e., the visceral plane of the endopelvic fascia).

Most regional disease will be found within the structures of the posterior visceral compartment—the area restricted to the wall of the rectum and the mesorectum. As indicated by the work of Quirke et al.,[4] approximately 25 percent of the patients will harbor disease at or near the edge of the mesorectum, the traditional margin of resection. The most efficient plane for the resection of all regional disease, including the potential margins outlined by Quirke and coworkers, is the parietal plane of the pelvic fascia. For the majority of patients undergoing resection, the use of the parietal layer as the plane of dissection achieves negative margins and complete resection in two ways: (1) all structures of the posterior visceral compartment are included in the resection and (2) one can invariably identify a unique layer of areolar-lymphatic tissue between the mesorectum and the plane of dissection, which layer can be separated from the posterior surface of the mesorectum in the pathology laboratory. It is this layer which provides the all-important barrier between the plane of dissection and any potential disease along the margins of the mesorectum (the visceral plane of the pelvic fascia).[13]

Data from surgeons who are known to operate along the parietal plane of the endopelvic fascia using sharp technique and who have reported their results in a literature indicate a dramatic difference in local recurrence rates when compared with reports from surgeons of a more traditional bent. The former surgeons[11,14,23] report recurrent rates of 3 to 12 percent for T_3N_0 or T_3N_1 lesions, as opposed to the traditional 20 to 45 percent of local failure which is associated with conventional surgery. In some cases, recurrence is not associated with either transmural penetration or lymph node involvement until additional risk factors which are not captured by *any* staging system are present. These risk factors include lymphatic or vascular invasion within the mesentery, separate foci of metastatic disease, poor degree of differentiation, signet-ring features, and microscopically positive margins. Enker[23] and Heald et al.[14] have also reported small numbers of patients in whom direct extension of disease required the en bloc resection of named pelvic side-wall blood vessels and in whom local control was successfully achieved.

EXTRAORDINARY EFFORTS IN THE MANAGEMENT OF RECTAL CANCER

Surgical efforts to cure rectal cancer have led to the development of aggressive operations that have widened the scope of operation and have incorporated extensive lateral dissection. To evaluate such efforts, one must weigh reports of cure against established morbidity. The three operations which fall into this category are as follows:

1. Abdominopelvic lymphadenectomy[29]
2. Internal iliac, hypogastric, or pelvic lymphadenectomy[7]
3. Combined pelvic and extrapelvic lymphadenectomy[12,30]

Abdominopelvic Lymphadenectomy

In 1940, Coller and coworkers reported on the lymphatic spread of rectal cancer. They indicated that cancers of the rectum could spread centrally to lymph nodes in the mesorectum, adjacent to the primary tumor, and laterally to lymph nodes situated along the internal iliac arteries and veins, the hypogastric lymph nodes. In addition, "skip disease"—i.e., lymph node metastases located more proximally within the sigmoid mesocolon, having bypassed the immediately adjacent lymph nodes—was also observed. On this basis, Coller suggested that the scope of operation for rectal cancer should include (1) ligation of the inferior mesenteric artery at its origin from the aorta, (2) complete resection of the sigmoid mesentery, (3) complete resection of the mesorectum, (4) en bloc resection of the internal iliac lymph nodes via a hypogastric or internal iliac lymphadenectomy in association with the mesorectum, and (5) complete resection of the ischiorectal fat and the levator muscles out to the lateral pelvic side walls, completing the abdominoperineal resection.

Pelvic Lymphadenectomy

The significance of lateral spread by rectal cancer to the internal iliac lymph nodes has been the focus of decades of debate. To some, lateral internal iliac lymph node spread represents a primary feature of the natural history of rectal cancer in a small number of patients. To others, spread to the internal iliac lymph nodes represents a late feature of disease when lymphatics adjacent to or proximal to the primary tumor within the mesorectum are blocked and alternate patterns of lymphatic flow are initiated by centrally located lymphatic obstruction.

The incidence of lateral or internal iliac lymph node involvement ranges from 1 to 7 percent in meticulous studies on lymph node distribution performed by Japanese investigators.[30] Until recently, the 5-year survival of patients in whom lateral or internal iliac lymph node involvement was detected was reported to be in the range of 10 percent. More recently, an incidence of 14 percent has been reported, with a 5-year survival of 50 percent in patients undergoing en bloc removal of the internal iliac lymph nodes.[12] En bloc resection of the pelvic lymph nodes would potentially increase cure or local control from 0.7 percent of all patients to 7 percent if all efforts at pelvic lymphadenectomy successfully cured or at least provided local control The detection of disease in the hypogastric lymph nodes is difficult. Gross disease observed on computed tomography (CT) or at laparotomy can certainly be resected en bloc. In our experience, finding involvement of the lateral or internal iliac lymph nodes is rarer than reported by Japanese authors. In addition, a significant proportion of patients with lymph node involvement by rectal cancer have systemic disease, primarily to the liver and lung. The majority of such patients die of systemic disease. Using the available figures, the highest imaginable yield would be 3.5 percent 5-year survival attributable to internal lymphadenectomy alone.

At the present time the indications for hypogastric node dissection are limited to the gross presence of disease approaching the lateral pelvic side wall, where such dissection would allow the creation of negative margins or the detection, either by CT or at operation, of gross disease along the internal iliac lymph nodes.

Combined Hypogastric and Obturator Lymphadenectomy

Based on the prior observations of primary, lateral lymph node spread, various investigators have pursued a course of en bloc pelvic lymphadenectomy combined with obturator lymphadenectomy. At the very least, obturator lymph node metastases will be classified as N_3 disease. Hojo and Koyama[30] originally reported a 7 percent incidence of positive lymph nodes with a 10 percent 5-year survival, with the majority of deaths due to systemic disease.[30] Moriya and coworkers[12] recently reported a 14 percent incidence of lateral lymph nodes involved with a 50 percent 5-year survival following hypogastric and obturator lymphadenectomy. It remains difficult to assess the importance of such observations, as the role of radiation therapy and/or combined chemotherapy and radiation is not addressed in their reports.

The long-term morbidity includes a significant incidence of impotence, with 76 percent of patients being impotent and a total of 96 percent experiencing significant sexual dysfunction. Attempts to preserve the sympathetic or hypogastric nerves and the parasympathetic or sacral nerves S3 and S4, while anatomically successful, fail to be functional. Dissection lateral to the nerves generally devascularizes the nerve trunks and, while the nerves do remain anatomically preserved, they scar and fibrose secondary to the ischemic damage.

SEXUAL AND URINARY DYSFUNCTION IN RELATION TO SURGERY FOR RECTAL CANCER

Postoperative impotence and urinary dysfunction have traditionally been associated with radical operations for rectal cancer. To date there has been little clinical application of the anatomic knowledge derived from the elegant dissections of the pelvic autonomic nerves[31] responsible for sexual and urinary function.

Postoperative impotence has been directly related to the lateral extent of pelvic surgery. Most commonly, injury to the hypogastric or sympathetic nerves takes place with initial entry into the true pelvis as part of rectal mobilization. Such injuries result in failure of complete bladder filling and in loss of emission, ejaculation, and vaginal lubrication. The most common forms of injury to the sacral parasympathetic nerves include traction or avulsion injuries attributable to blunt pelvic dissection or to unrecognized division of the nerves during division and ligation of the lateral ligaments. Sacral parasympathetic nerve injuries result in loss of awareness of the urge to urinate and in impotence in the male, defined as the loss of spontaneous erection, and in the loss of recognizable responses to sexual arousal in the female. Combined injuries contribute to the loss of both sympathetic and parasympathetic functions and may also result in the loss of the bulbocavernosus spasm associated with orgasm in both sexes.

In keeping with the relationship of nerve injury to the extent of lateral pelvic dissection, "conservative" proctectomies for inflammatory bowel disease have been associated with low rates of postoperative impotence—that is, 3.4 percent—while "radical" proctectomies for rectal cancer have been associated with significantly higher rates of postoperative impotence, averaging 46.3 percent.[23]

In view of the high rates of local failure associated with conservative resection, and in view of the fact that the hypogastric plexus is not responsible for any major sexual function, we were prompted by the works of Walsh[32] and of Lee et al.[31] to design an autonomic nerve-preserving pelvic parietal dissection that maintains the integrity of the parietal pelvic dissection while also preserving bilaterally the main trunks of the sympathetic and the parasympathetic nerves along with their functions. The operation is described above.[23] The anatomic relationships between the pelvic autonomic nerves and the rectum are based upon the anatomic dissections of Lee et al.[31]

Recently we have reported the initial results of *en bloc* autonomic nerve-preserving pelvic side-wall dissection (ANP-PSWD) in male patients undergoing sphincter-preserving operations for rectal cancer. In 42 male patients who underwent ANP-PSWD for primary rectal cancer, the operations adhered to the following guidelines:

1. *En bloc* resection of the rectum, the mesorectum, and the lymphatic tissues surrounding the mesorectum—that is, within the parietal pelvic fascia
2. Sharp dissection and meticulous hemostasis throughout the dissection from the aortic bifurcation to the anal hiatus of the levator diaphragm
3. Dissection within the parietal pelvic fascia, with identification and preservation of the major trunks of the hypogastric (sympathetic) and sacral parasympathetic nerves within the "posterior visceral compartment" of the pelvis

Forty-two male patients underwent a low anterior resection or low anterior resection with coloanal anastomosis for a rectal cancer situated within 11 cm of the anal verge. All temporary stomas were closed prior to the assessment of sexual function, as some patients had an aversion to resuming sexual activity while temporary stoma endured.

Of the 38 evaluable patients, 33 (86.8 percent) were capable of having a spontaneous erection following recovery from surgery. All 33 were able to sustain their erection for the duration of sexual intercourse. Of these 33 patients, 28 (84.8 percent) experienced a postoperative erection whose capacity was at least 75 percent of their own preoperative norm. Six patients (17.6 percent) experienced a postoperative erection of 50 to 75 percent of their own preoperative norm. Five of these six were among the patients who exhibited a psychological impediment to the resumption of sexual activity. Of the 33 patients, 29 (87.9 percent) experienced a normal ejaculate postoperatively, whereas 5 patients experienced either a diminished or absent ejaculate. Age was a significant factor in the postoperative outcome. The mean age of patients who sustained normal potency was 54.3 years, while the mean age of those who were impotent postoperatively was 68.0 years. Only one patient under the age of 60 years became impotent as a result of pelvic dissection, a patient who had undergone orchiectomy and radiation for a testicular carcinoma 10 years previously. Of 12 patients 60 to 69 years of age, 9 (75 percent) remained potent, while of 2 patients 70 years or older, 1 (50 percent) remained potent. While age was a significant factor affecting potency, it was not related to the extent of the postoperative erection. The mean age of the 6 patients whose postoperative extent of erection was 50 to 75 percent of preoperative capacity was 55.2 years (median, 54 years).

Stage, radiation therapy, chemotherapy, or the incidence of preoperative genitourinary dysfunction had no bearing on the postoperative outcome when compared individually in each patient.

Over the past two decades, operations for rectal cancer have been evolving toward the best likelihood for cure *combined with* the least consequent morbidity. Sphincter-preserving operations (i.e., low anterior resection or low anterior resection with coloanal anastomosis) have significantly reduced one aspect of morbidity by restoring colorectal continuity with both voluntary and involuntary continence and with satisfactory long-term anorectal function. Impotence has persisted as a serious and a frequent consequence of rectal cancer treatment. The operation described above seems to address the avoidance of impotence successfully in the vast majority of cases.

REFERENCES

1. Prohaska JV, Govostis MC, Wasick M: Multiple organ resection for advanced carcinoma of the colon and rectum. *Surg Gynecol Obstet* 97:177–182, 1953.
2. Eisenberg SB, Kraybill WG, Lopez MJ: Long-term results of surgical resection of locally advanced colorectal carcinoma. *Surgery* 108:779–786, 1990.
3. Quirke P, Scott N: The pathologist's role in the assessment of local recurrence in rectal carcinoma. *Surg Oncol Clin North Am* 1:1–17, 1992.
4. Quirke P, Durdey P, Dixon MF, et al: Local recurrence of rectal adenocarcinoma due to inadequate surgical resection: Histopathological study of lateral tumor spread and surgical excision. *Lancet* 1:996–999, 1986.
5. Rao AR, Kagan AR, Chan PM, et al: Patterns of recurrence following curative resection alone for adenocarcinoma of the rectum and sigmoid colon. *Cancer* 48:1492–1495, 1981.
6. Brown MT, Luna-Perez P, Petrelli NJ, et al: Factors associated with nodal involvement of rectal adenocarcinomas. *Surgical Oncol Clin North Am* 1:25–38, 1992.
7. Enker WE, Laffer UT, Block GE: Enhanced survival of patients with colon and rectal cancer is based upon wide anatomic resection. *Ann Surg* 190:350–360, 1979.
8. Enker WE, Heilweil ML, Hertz REL, et al: En bloc pelvic lymphadenopathy and sphincter preservation in the surgical management of rectal cancer. *Ann Surg* 203:426–433, 1986.
9. Twomey P, Burchell M, Strawn D, et al: Local control in rectal cancer: A clinical review and meta-analysis. *Arch Surg* 124:1174, 1989.
10. Heald RJ, Ryall RDH: Recurrence and survival after total meso-rectal excision for rectal cancer. *Lancet* 1:1479–1482, 1986.
11. Michelassi F, Block GE, Vannucci L, et al: A 5- to 21-year follow-up and analysis of 250 patients with rectal adenocarcinoma. *Ann Surg* 208:379–389, 1988.
12. Moriya Y, Hojo K, Sawada T, et al: Significance of lateral node dissection for advanced rectal carcinoma at or below the peritoneal reflection. *Dis Colon Rectum* 32:307–315, 1989.
13. Enker WE: Unpublished data.
14. MacFarlane JK, Ryall RDH, Heald RJ: Mesorectal excision for rectal cancer. *Lancet* 341:457–460, 1993.
15. Minsky BD, Mies C, Rich TA, et al: Lymphatic vessel invasion is an independent prognostic factor for survival in colorectal cancer. *Int J Radiol Oncol Biol Phys* 17:311–318, 1989.
16. Paty PB, Lauwers G, Enker WE, et al: Discrete mesenteric implants of metastatic colorectal cancer. Unpublished.
17. Michelassi F, Erroi F, Roncella M, et al: Ras oncogene and the acquisition of metastasizing properties by rectal adenocarcinoma. *Dis Colon Rectum* 32:665–668, 1989.
18. Enker WE, Kimmel M, Cibas ES, et al: DNA/RNA content and proliferative fractions of colorectal cancers: A five-year prospective study relating flow cytometry to survival. *J Natl Cancer Inst* 83:701–707, 1991.
19. Enker WE: Flow cytometric determination of tumor cell DNA content and proliferative index as prognostic variables in colorectal cancer. *Perspect Colon Rectal Surg* 3:1–32, 1990.
20. Chang KJ, Enker WE, Melamed M: Influence of tumor cell DNA ploidy on the natural history of rectal cancer. *Am J Surg* 153:184–188, 1987.
21. Dukes CE: Cancer of the rectum: An analysis of 1000 cases. *J Pathol Bacteriol* 50:527–539, 1940.
22. Dukes CE, Bussey HJR: The spread of rectal cancer and its effect on prognosis. *Br J Cancer* 12:309–320, 1958.
23. Enker WE: Potency, cure and local control in the operative treatment of rectal cancer. *Arch Surg* 127:1396–1402, 1992.
24. Goligher JC, Dukes CE, Bussey HJR: Local recurrences after sphincter-saving excisions for carcinoma of the rectum and rectosigmoid. *Br J Surg* 39:199–211, 1951.
25. Vernava AM, Moran M, Rothenberger DA, et al: A prospec-

tive evaluation of distal margins in carcinoma of the rectum. *Surg Gynecol Obstet* 175:333–336, 1992.

26. Williams NS, Dixon MF, Johnston D: Reappraisal of the 5 centimetre rule of distal excision for carcinoma of the rectum: A study of distal intramural spread and of patient's survival. *Br J Surg* 70:150–154, 1983.
27. Pilipshen SJ, Heilweil M, Quan SHQ, et al: Patterns of pelvic recurrence following definitive resections of rectal cancer. *Cancer* 53:1354–1362, 1984.
28. Gastrointestinal Tumor Study Group: Prolongation of the disease-free interval in surgically treated rectal carcinoma. *N Engl J Med* 312:1465–1472, 1985.
29. Deddish MR: Surgical procedures for carcinoma of the left colon and rectum with five year end results following abdomino-pelvic dissection of lymph nodes. *Am J Surg* 99:188–191, 1960.
30. Hojo K, Koyama Y: The effectiveness of wide anatomical resection and radical lymphadenectomy for patients with rectal cancer. *Jpn J Surg* 12:111–116, 1982.
31. Lee JF, Maurer VM, Block GE: Anatomic relations of pelvic autonomic nerves to pelvic operations. *Arch Surg* 107:324–328, 1973.
32. Walsh PC: Radical prostatectomy, preservation of sexual function, cancer control: The controversy. *Urol Clin North Am* 14:663–673, 1987.

CHAPTER 60

Sphincter-Saving Procedures for Operable Rectal Cancer

Timothy J. Yeatman
Kirby I. Bland

HIGHLIGHTS

Oncologic and Technical Considerations

The decision to create a permanent colostomy is one of the most difficult decisions that a surgeon must face when caring for the patient with rectal cancer. Although there are many oncologic problems best suited to abdominoperineal resection, it is clear that more and more patients are undergoing sphincter-saving procedures. Whether or not a patient is eligible for a sphincter-preserving procedure is often a decision that must be made at the operating table and is based on both oncologic and technical factors. Preoperative considerations such as the patient's age, sex, and psychological complexion—as well as stage of disease—must also be factored into the decision-making process.

CONTROVERSIES

Local Excision

Local excision of invasive, distal rectal cancers remains controversial because of the associated risk of lymph node metastases, which are not addressed surgically, as they are with anterior approaches and abdominoperineal resection. Appropriate selection of patients eligible for local excision (T_{1-2} N_0 M_0 distal rectal tumors in older patients) combined with the judicious use of adjuvant radiotherapy and chemotherapy may permit results equivalent to those of more radical procedures. Endorectal ultrasound is helpful in staging patients prior to surgery.

Preoperative versus Postoperative Adjuvant Therapy

For rectal cancers, there are adequate data to support the use of a combination of chemotherapy, radiotherapy, and surgical resection over surgery alone for the purposes of improving survival and reducing local (pelvic) recurrences. Whether these modalities should be administered preoperatively or postoperatively remains controversial; but ultimately, this issue is determined by the goals of therapy and the stage and location of disease at presentation.

FUTURE DIRECTIONS

Neoadjuvant Therapy to Increase Sphincter Salvage through Downstaging

Because preoperative therapy may significantly reduce the size and extent of rectal cancers, there are certain circumstances when sphincter preservation might be possible after therapy, when otherwise an abdominoperineal resection would have been indicated. The use of radiosensitizing agents such as 5-fluorouracil may increase the rate of pathologic complete responses in patients undergoing neoadjuvant therapy.

New Technology

Endorectal ultrasound has recently gained favor due to its ability to determine T stage preoperatively with adequate precision. Similarly, laparoscopic technology has become popular because it has permitted the surgeon to perform invasive surgery with less tissue destruction. Laparoscopic techniques for application to bowel surgery are currently under development.

Operable rectal cancer can be treated by one of any number of surgical techniques with or without the addition of adjuvant or neoadjuvant therapy when appropriately indicated. For the surgeon, difficulties arise in two basic circumstances: low-lying rectal lesions approaching the anal sphincter complex and large, deeply invasive, locally advanced lesions at high risk for local recurrence. Small lesions that do not traverse the bowel wall and are not distal in location may generally be treated by low anterior resection with handsewn or stapled anastomoses.

When faced with a lesion that is easily palpable on digital exam (i.e., within 2 to 3 cm of the palpable internal sphincter complex) or one that is clearly deeply penetrating into ischiorectal fat that may or may not be involving adjacent organs (bladder, vagina, prostate, uterus), a decision must be made as to whether or not sphincter preservation is feasible. This decision is a complex one that not only involves extensive preoperative evaluation but also requires extensive consultation with the patient, who must clearly understand the risks and benefits of attempting sphincter preservation.

This chapter will outline the sphincter-saving procedures available to most surgeons and will discuss some of the many operative factors that must be considered in contemplating such a procedure.

BACKGROUND

Although sphincter-saving techniques (SST) were developed more than a century ago, their popularity has recently resurged. We have seen an upsurge in the number of SST procedures used to treat rectal cancers in place of the "gold standard" abdominoperineal resection (APR).[1] Surgeons have come to realize that, in many cases, sphincter preservation is possible without compromising oncologic principles. This change in philosophy has been due largely to a better understanding of the biology of rectal cancer. While lymph node metastases were once thought simply to represent stations along the course of tumor spread from the primary site to distant organs, we now recognize a different concept—that the lymph node metastasis is a marker for the potential of tumor to thrive outside of the primary tumor's environment. That is, if tumor can survive in a lymph node separate from the primary tumor site, it is likely that tumor can survive and thrive elsewhere (and it may do so in the form of occult or detected distant metastases). Thus, Halsted's principle of extending the margins of surgical resection in the attempt to encompass all disease for curative purposes (despite having positive effects on local control) may not be applicable to rectal cancer. A better understanding of the biology of rectal cancer has permitted consideration for SST when APR would have otherwise been indicated. This concept has dramatically altered the management of breast cancer, where lumpectomy and axillary dissection with breast radiotherapy are now routinely substituted for modified radical mastectomy and nearly always substituted for radical mastectomy without any compromise of oncologic end results.[2,3]

The introduction of new stapling technology (such as the EEA stapler), which has permitted the construction of very low anastomoses, has also had a significant impact on the number of sphincter-preserving procedures performed.[4] Similarly, the introduction of neoadjuvant radiotherapy and chemotherapy has led to an increase in the number of patients eligible for SST due to tumor shrinkage.[5,6]

Despite the overall trends toward sphincter preservation and the availability of new technology and adjuvant therapies that make these procedures possible, the decision to use SST must ultimately be based on sound surgical judgment—that is, on numerous preoperative and intraoperative considerations in addition to a thorough understanding of the natural history of the disease and the end results of various treatment regimens.

CONSIDERATIONS PRIOR TO SELECTION OF SST OVER APR

Local Recurrence Is Predictable and Preventable

For the patient with rectal cancer, local (pelvic) recurrence is unfortunately an all too common problem. For the surgeon, local recurrence is a very difficult problem to manage and is often fraught with poor end results. Pelvic recurrences frequently portend an ominous prognosis and often lead to intractable physical disability that includes pelvic pain, tenesmus, and fecal soiling.[7] Because pelvic recurrences are associated with the development of metastatic disease, 5-year survival rates following these recurrences are as low as 5 percent.[8] The determinants of local failure include factors such as the location of the tumor in relation to the anal verge, the distal and radial resection margins, and tumor characteristics including grade, size, and depth of invasion (see Chap. 59). Knowledge of some of the high-risk factors prior to surgical intervention may help prevent devastating local recurrences.

APR Is Not Better than SST in Preventing Local Recurrence or in Prolonging Survival

The question that must be asked is whether or not SSTs in and of themselves lead to increased rates of local recurrence. Multiple studies have attempted to address this issue. Retrospective studies have, for the most part, demonstrated that local recurrences are similar for patients undergoing APR and SST.[9] Cass et al.[10] found recurrence rates of 31 percent and 29 percent for APR and low anterior resection (LAR) respectively. Neville et al.[11] studied APR versus LAR in 373 patients who underwent curative resections and found no significant differences (19 versus 17 percent). Reports of low rates of recurrence by Parks and Percy[12] using an abdominotransanal (coloanal) technique and by Localio et al.[13] using an abdominotranssacral method have been noted. Similarly, Drake et al.[14] and Hautefeuille et al.[15] have reported low rates of recurrence (5 and 17 percent, respectively) with distal resections and coloanal anastomoses.

A prospective study performed by the National Surgical Adjuvant Breast and Bowel Project (NSABP) has also addressed the issue of local recurrence for rectal cancer and found that although treatment failures were less for APR than for LAR (5 versus 13 percent), there was no survival advantage for one procedure over the other in similarly staged patients.[16] This study did identify several risk factors for local recurrence that included advanced Dukes staging, poorly differentiated tumors, and tumors of the low and middle rectum.

In order to prevent local recurrence, the surgeon can carefully select those patients who are good candidates for SST based on the aforementioned factors in addition to performing the technical exercise of resecting the mesorectum whenever possible as well as incorporating adjuvant therapy into the management of the disease.

Adjuvant Therapy Reduces the Risk of Local Recurrence

Adjuvant radiotherapy, whether given preoperatively or postoperatively, has a permanent role in the management of rectal cancer. It has been conclusively shown in multiple randomized trials involving several thousand patients that radiotherapy has a significant influence on local control rates but has not improved survival. In general, local recurrence rates may approach 30 to 50 percent in patients with full-thickness (T_3) lesions treated by surgery alone, whereas the addition of radiotherapy often halves these recurrences.[17,18] In a recent publication by Krook et al.,[19] it was determined by a prospectively randomized study that patients undergoing radiation alone had significantly higher recurrence rates (25 percent) than those undergoing radiation and chemotherapy (13 percent) in the postoperative setting. This study, like its predecessor performed by the Gastrointestinal Tumor Study Group (GITSG),[20] also demonstrated a survival advantage for the patients treated by radiation therapy and chemotherapy versus radiation therapy alone. These studies have collectively led to the conceptual use of 5-fluorouracil as a radiosensitizer to help reduce local recurrence rates as well as to the use of combined therapy to increase survival in patients who have adverse prognostic factors, including regional node metastasis, and invasion of perirectal fat or adjacent organs.

Functional Results of SST

There is no dispute over the fact that the quality of life after excision for low rectal cancer is better following SST than after APR. Williams and Johnston[16] assessed 78 patients following surgical resection of low rectal cancers and found that patients undergoing SST had fewer bowel actions and less flatus, fewer dietary restrictions, and a lower incidence of sexual dysfunction and depression. Perhaps most interesting was the finding that while only 40 percent of patients undergoing APR returned to work within 1 year, 83 percent of patients undergoing SST returned to work.

The distance from the *palpable anorectal ring* determines both the risk of local recurrence and the likelihood of a poor functional result. The closer the cancer is to the sphincter complex, the less likely it is that an adequate oncologic procedure will be performed. Similarly, it is more difficult to obtain satisfactory sphincter function as more and more nerve and muscle fibers are sacrificed by necessity and sphincters are manually dilated for better exposure with distal dissections and coloanal procedures.

In general, the majority of stapled anastomoses (EEA) are well tolerated, with the exception of staple-line-associated strictures that may occur. These may be reduced in frequency through the use of larger-diameter (28- to 31-mm) stapling devices. Hand-sewn coloanal anastomoses tend to result in a greater incidence of continence problems for the patient, presumably due to the greater degree of manipulation of the anal sphincter complex required. The majority of patients, however, despite having frequent bowel movements early (4 to 8 per day), develop normal bowel function by 1 year.[21,22] Hautefeuille et al.,[15] for example, reported that the majority of their patients could differentiate between flatus and stool, although 50 percent of patients had frequent bowel actions through the first year. Only 1 patient (of 31 in the series) had unsatisfactory results. Skibber et al.[23] recently reported that the functional results following local excision procedures (n = 46) (including transanal, transsacral, and Kraske procedures) were quite good, with a fecal incontinence rate of 2 percent and an alteration of sexual function in 11 percent. Sixty-five percent of patients, however, experienced transient diarrhea. Overall, few patients undergoing SST require conversion to permanent colostomy due to incontinence problems.

THE DECISION FOR SST OVER APR

Contraindications

The easiest way to determine whether or not a patient is eligible for sphincter preservation preoperatively is to first determine when such a procedure would be contraindicated (Table 60-1). One absolute contraindication would be the presence of sphincter invasion by tumor. Although radiotherapy and chemotherapy, when delivered in a combined fashion preoperatively, have been shown to produce complete pathologic responses in up to 38 percent of cases,[24] there are currently no data to support or justify a reduction (or elimination) of distal resection margins (<2 cm); thus it is difficult to imagine that any tumor invading the sphincter complex would be resectable with SST. Furthermore, sphincter invasion often causes symptomatic pain and tenesmus, which often do not improve with adjuvant therapy even when a significant downstaging response has been noted. It is reasonable to assume that tumors lying within 2 cm of the *palpable anorectal ring* (or within approximately 4 cm of the anal verge) would likewise be unresectable by SST because adequate distal margins may not be attainable. Likewise, tumors that are locally advanced (large, ulcerated, full-thickness lesions) are not easily treated by SST per primum but often require preoperative therapy (radiotherapy and/or chemotherapy) prior to consideration of surgical resection. Other contraindications include a very narrow pelvis or a very large prostate in the male that preclude a good technical result or the lack of good sphincter function—which may be related to the patient's age, childbirth or other perineal trauma, or to a history of previous anal surgery. Anal function can be assessed preoperatively by anal manometric techniques.

Table 60-1
Unfavorable Clinicopathologic Determinants for Sphincter-Saving Surgery: Qualities That May Contribute to a Poor End Result

Physical characteristics	*Tumor characteristics*
Male sex Narrow pelvis Large prostate	Distal location Sphincter invasion Obstructing lesion Full-thickness penetration Fixation to adjacent organs/ bony pelvis Deep ulceration Palpable perirectal lymph nodes Indurated intramural lymphatics

Indications

The female pelvis is ideally suited for distal pelvic dissections due to its wider pelvic brim. The younger the patient, generally the better the functional result due to better acclimatization to new bowel habits (i.e., increased frequency, occasional incontinence, etc). Otherwise, patients with tumors that are more than 5 cm from the anal verge and are not locally advanced are eligible for SST.

Intraoperative Decisions

Although all attempts are made to stage patients adequately preoperatively (by proctoscopic exams, computed tomography, and endorectal ultrasound) to determine which patients are best suited for SST, these decisions must often be made (or finalized) in the operating room after the initial pelvic dissection has been performed. In certain circumstances, not as much distal margin is cleared as was anticipated and the procedure is converted to an APR for oncologic reasons. In circumstances when it is obvious that adequate tumor margins are unlikely to be achieved, it is inappropriate to cut across tumor in a desperate attempt to avoid a colostomy.

The choice of SST most appropriate for the patient must be based on the size, stage, and location of the

Table 60-2
Sphincter-Saving Options

Anterior resection[a]	*Local excision*[b]	*Local treatment*
Low anterior resection	Transanal	Fulguration
Abdominosacral resection	Transsphincteric	Endocavitary x-ray therapy
Coloanal resection	Kraske (transsacral)	Cryosurgery
	Transanal microsurgery	

[a] ± Preoperative or postoperative x-ray therapy ± chemotherapy.
[b] ± Postoperative x-ray therapy ± chemotherapy.

Table 60-3
Results of Locally Excised Favorable Grade T_1–T_2 Tumors without Radiotherapy

Authors	*Lesion*	*No. of patients*	*Local recurrence, %*	*Cancer-specific death rate, %*
Morson et al.,[33]	T_1	91	3	0
Hager et al.,[34]	T_1–T_2	59	10	3
Grigg et al.,[35] 1984	T_1	16	6	0
Knoch,[36] 1984	T_1	94	2	0
Whiteway et al.,[37]	T_1–T_2	19	0	0
Heberer et al.,[38] 1987	T_1–T_2	36	3	5
De Cosse et al.,[39]	T_1–T_2	27	7	0

tumor. The most common approach is to attempt to perform an LAR using either a stapled or hand-sewn approach. The hand-sewn approach, when very low, is often best performed via the anus as a coloanal procedure. Only in rare circumstances are other procedures—such as the abdominosacral or Kraske procedures—utilized, the latter being generally considered a "local excision" procedure because of its inability to resect significant mesorectum with the tumor.

Matching the Procedure to the Patient

Of the five or six surgical procedures[25] that have been devised and used with some body of experience to preserve sphincter function, only a few have gained widespread use (Table 60-2). The most common SST is the LAR performed with the EEA stapling device in combination with an angulated stapling device (the double staple technique). Occasionally, with suitable pelvic anatomy, an EEA staple line may be placed as low as the palpable anorectal ring by dividing the rectum at the level of the pelvic diaphragm. If this is not possible, a coloanal anastomosis is the next most common solution to the problem of a distal rectal cancer. With this procedure, a hand-sewn anastomosis between the proximal colon and the dentate line (denuded of its mucosa 1 cm proximal to the dentate line, leaving a muscular cuff) is made through the anus. This procedure is more technically demanding than the LAR but may provide acceptable functional results if done properly in patients with good preoperative sphincter function. If neither of these procedures is considered to be ideally suited for the patient, other procedures such as local excision techniques or local treatments may be contemplated.

Local Excision: A Procedure for a Highly Selected Group of Patients

Local excision of distal rectal cancer is perhaps one of the most controversial issues. It has been estimated that approximately 45,000 cases of adenocarcinoma of the rectum will be diagnosed each year in the United States, with less than 10 percent—or 4000 to 5000 patients—involving superficial lesions (T_1 or T_2) and thus eligible for conservative, sphincter-preserving surgery. While T_1 lesions portend a good prognosis, T_2 lesions may be associated with significant rates of recurrence (20 to 27 percent)[26] and thus require adjuvant therapy if a local procedure is contemplated. Locally resected T_3 lesions have an unacceptably high rate of local recurrence (>20 percent). The results of multiple series of locally excised cancers, both without (Table 60-3) and with (Table 60-4) adjuvant radiotherapy, have demonstrated favorable results in highly selected patients.

Local excision is an attractive alternative to standard treatment regimens such as LAR and APR because of the low rates of associated morbidity and mortality. Local procedures are particularly suited to patients with comorbid medical risk factors that might preclude general anesthesia (as opposed to epidural) or an abdominal wall incision. By comparison, the APR has an operative mortality of up to 7 percent, a 5 to 40

Table 60-4
Results of Locally Excised T_1–T_3 Tumors with Adjuvant Radiotherapy

Authors	*Lesion*	*No. of patients*	*Local recurrence, %*	*Cancer-specific death rate, %*
Bailey et al.,[40] 1992	T_1–T_2	53	8	4
Ellis et al.,[41] 1988	T_1	9	0	0
McCready et al.,[42] 1989	T_1–T_3	24	0	0
Coco et al.,[43] 1992	T_1–T_2	36	3	6

percent rate of impotence, and a local failure rate as high as 30 percent.[27]

Ultimately, the decision to perform local excision must be based on the presence of favorable tumor characteristics and comorbid medical risk factors that justify a conservative approach, which generally does not sample the mesorectal lymph nodes.

EVOLVING THERAPIES

Laparoscopy

The role of the laparoscope is currently in evolution. Although there are as yet no randomized prospective trials conclusively demonstrating the benefits of laparoscopic colectomy over an open procedure, it is clear that the technology is improving and that laparoscopic bowel surgery is possible. There is an existent body of literature supporting the use of the laparoscope in the performance of a colonic resection.[28–30] The hope is that this sort of procedure, while perhaps more costly and time-consuming, might ultimately be attractive due to decreased rates of morbidity and shorter associated hospital stays, with earlier returns to work. The further development of endoscopic stapling devices and better means of intracorporeal suturing may lead to improved operative capabilities such that, for example, the majority of abdominal (anterior) dissections could be performed laparoscopically. Currently, however, laparoscopic colectomy remains experimental and should be *protocol-driven,* because there are many unanswered questions—such as the amount of mesentery that must be resected for adequate oncologic results, as well as the actual benefits of the procedure versus the risks.

Preoperative versus Postoperative Adjuvant Therapy

Although there is no question as to whether or not radiotherapy[31] and chemotherapy[32] have a role in the management of rectal cancer, it has not yet been conclusively demonstrated that adjuvant therapy is better prior to surgery rather than following surgery. There are advantages and disadvantages to both regimens. For example, preoperative combined therapy ensures that all patients undergoing definitive surgical treatment also obtain the benefits of adjuvant therapy. Preoperative radiotherapy generally results in less small bowel toxicity because, in the unoperated patient, the small bowel moves randomly throughout the radiation fields. With preoperative radiotherapy, smaller volumes of radiation are generally permitted, as fields do not need to encompass the surgical wounds but rather can be focused on the tumor. There are theoretical advantages to radiating patients without scar tissue, which tends to be hypoxic and reduces the effectiveness of radiation, which depends on the presence of oxygen for effect. Additionally, preoperative therapy may downstage or shrink tumors, such that lesions that were otherwise unresectable become resectable and, in some instances, lesions that would otherwise have required APR may be treated by a sphincter-preserving procedure.

The arguments against preoperative therapy include increased risks of wound complications, fistulization, and risks of overtreating patients who might otherwise not require adjuvant therapy if staged pathologically (postoperatively). Yet to be answered are questions concerning the meaning of a pathologic complete response following neoadjuvant therapy, the prognostic factors that predict which patients will have a significant or complete response, and whether or not less surgery can be done in conjunction with more complete responses. These are issues that can only be addressed using prospective clinical trials.

REFERENCES

1. Lockhart-Mummery HE, Ritchie JK, Hawley PR: The results of surgical treatment for carcinoma of the rectum at St. Marks Hospital from 1948–1972. *Br J Surg* 63:673–677, 1976.
2. Fisher B, Redmond C, Poisson R: Eight-year results of a randomized clinical trial comparing total mastectomy and lumpectomy with or without irradiation in the treatment of breast cancer. *N Engl J Med* 320:822–828, 1989.
3. Fisher B, Redmond C, Fisher ER: Ten-year results of a randomized clinical trial comparing radical mastectomy and total mastectomy with or without radiation. *N Engl J Med* 312:674–681, 1985.
4. Rain SN, Patin S, Morganstern L: Use of mechanical apparatus in low colorectal anastomosis. *Arch Surg* 110:1079–1082, 1975.
5. Enker WE, Paty PB, Minsky BD, et al: Restorative or preservative operations in the treatment of rectal cancer. *Surg Oncol Clin North Am* 1:57–69, 1992.
6. Marks G, Mohiuddin M, Masoni L, et al: High-dose preoperative radiation therapy as the key to extending sphincter-preservation surgery for cancer of the distal rectum. *Surg Oncol Clin North Am* 1:71–86, 1992.
7. Wanebo HJ, Gaker DL, Whitehill R, et al: Pelvic recurrence of rectal cancer. *Ann Surg* 205:482–495, 1987.
8. Carlsson U, Lasson A, Ekelund G: Recurrence rates after curative surgery for rectal carcinoma, with special reference to their accuracy. *Dis Colon Rectum* 30:431–434, 1987.
9. Williams NS: The rationale of preservation of the anal sphincter in patients with low rectal cancer. *Br J Surg* 71:575–581, 1984.
10. Cass AW, Million RR, Pfaff WW: Patterns of recurrence following surgery alone for adenocarcinoma of the colon and rectum. *Cancer* 37:2861–2865, 1976.
11. Neville R, Fielding PL, Amendola C: Local tumor recurrence after curative resection for rectal cancer: A ten hospital review. *Dis Colon Rectum* 30:12–17, 1987.
12. Parks AG, Percy JP: Resection and sutured colo-anal anastomosis for rectal carcinoma. *Br J Surg* 69:301–304, 1982.
13. Localio SA, Eng K, Coppa GF: Abdominosacral resection for mid-rectal cancer. *Ann Surg* 198:320–324, 1983.
14. Drake DB, Penberton JH, Beart RW: Coloanal anastomosis

and the management of benign and malignant rectal disease. *Ann Surg* 206:600–605, 1987.

15. Hautefeuille P, Valleur P, Perniceni T, et al: Functional and oncologic results after coloanal anastomosis for low rectal carcinoma. *Ann Surg* 207:61–64, 1988.
16. Williams NS, Johnston D: The quality of life after rectal excision for low rectal cancer. *Br J Surg* 70:460–462, 1983.
17. Higgins GA: Adjuvant therapy for carcinoma of the colon and rectum. *Int Adv Surg Oncol* 7:77–111, 1984.
18. Quan SHQ, Deddish MR, Stearns MW: The effect of preoperative roentgen therapy upon the 10- and 5-year results of the surgical treatment of cancer of the rectum. *Surg Gynecol Obstet* 111:507–508, 1960.
19. Krook JE, Moertel CG, Gunderson LL, et al: Effective surgical adjuvant therapy for high-risk rectal carcinoma. *N Engl J Med* 324:709–715, 1991.
20. Gastrointestinal Tumor Study Group: Prolongation of the disease-free interval in surgically treated rectal carcinoma. *N Engl J Med* 312:1465–1472, 1985.
21. Lane RHS, Parks AG: Function of the anal sphincters following colo-anal anastomosis. *Br J Surg* 64:596–599, 1977.
22. Pappalardo G, Toccaceli S, Dionisio P, et al: Preoperative and postoperative evaluation by manometric study of the anal sphincter after coloanal anastomosis for carcinoma. *Dis Colon Rectum* 3:119–122, 1988.
23. Skibber JM, Rich TA, Schumate CR, et al: Local excision and adjuvant therapy for rectal adenocarcinoma (Abstract). PS4.9. SSO 144, 1992.
24. Rich TA, Ota DM, Skibber JM, et al: Preoperative radiotherapy and 5-FU concomitant infusion for low rectal adenocarcinoma (Abstract). *Soc Surg Oncol* 241, 1992.
25. Yeatman TJ, Bland KI: Sphincter-saving procedures for distal carcinoma of the rectum. *Ann Surg* 209:1–18, 1989.
26. Steele G Jr, Hamilton JM, Karr JP: A rational next step in a treatment of some rectal adenocarcinomas. *J Clin Oncol* 7:988–990, 1989.
27. Adloff M, Arnaud JP, Schloegel M: Factors influencing recurrence after abdominoperineal resection for cancer of the rectum. *Dis Colon Rectum* 28:413–415, 1985.
28. Schlinkert RT: Laparoscopic-assisted right hemicolectomy. *Dis Colon Rectum* 34:1030–1031, 1991.
29. Cooperman AM, Katz V, Zimmon D, et al: Laparoscopic colon resection: A case report. *J Laparoendosc Surg* 1:221–224, 1991.
30. Beart RW Jr: Quality assurance: The use of endoscopy in cancer care. *Cancer* 64:266–268, 1989.
31. Mendenhall WM, Bland KI, Copeland EM, et al: Does preoperative radiation therapy enhance the probability of local control and survival in high-risk distal rectal cancer? *Ann Surg* 215:696–706, 1992.
32. NIH Consensus Conference: Adjuvant therapy for patients with colon and rectal cancer. *JAMA* 264:1444–1450, 1990.
33. Morson BC, Bussey HJR, Samoorian S: Policy of local excision for early cancer of the colorectum. *Gut* 18:1045–1050, 1977.
34. Hager T, Gall FP, Hermanek P: Local excision of rectal cancer. *Dis Col Rect* 26:149–151, 1983.
35. Grigg M, McDermott FT, Pihl EA, et al: Curative local excision in the treatment of carcinoma of the rectum. *Dis Colon Rectum* 27:81–83, 1984.
36. Knoch HG: Early rectal carcinoma—Treatment and late results. *Colo-Proctology* 6:26–28, 1984.
37. Whiteway J, Nicholls RJ, Morson BC: The role of surgical local excision in the treatment of rectal cancer. *Br J Surg* 72:694–697, 1985.
38. Heberer G, Denecke H, Demmel N, et al: Local procedures in the management of rectal cancer. *World J Surg* 11:499–503, 1987.
39. DeCosse JJ, Wong RJ, Quan SHQ, et al: Conservative treatment of distal rectal cancer by local excision. *Cancer* 63:219–223, 1989.
40. Bailey HR, Huval WV, Max E, et al: Local excision of carcinoma of the rectum for cure. *Surgery* 111:555–561, 1992.
41. Ellis LM, Mendenhall WM, Bland KI, et al: Local excision and radiation therapy for early rectal cancer. *Am Surg* 54:217–220, 1988.
42. McCready DR, Ota DM, Rich TA, et al: Prospective phase I trial of conservative management of low rectal lesions. *Arch Surg* 124:67–70, 1989.
43. Coco C, Magistrelli P, Granone P, et al: Conservative surgery for early cancer of the distal rectum. *Dis Colon Rectum* 35:131–136, 1992.

CHAPTER 61

Radical Surgery—Low Anterior Resection

Philip H. Gordon

HIGHLIGHTS, CONTROVERSIES, AND FUTURE DIRECTIONS

The successful performance of a low anterior resection of the rectum depends upon attention to a series of details. The points the author considers important are outlined in detail. The author's preference for the reestablishment of intestinal continuity has been the circular stapler; consequently the technique, together with potential pitfalls and avoidance of such pitfalls, has been extensively outlined. As with many facets in the disciplines of medicine and surgery, certain controversies prevail. For example, some surgeons prefer the double-staple technique, but this chapter places little emphasis on that method since it has not been adopted by the author. Other surgeons prefer to utilize the traditional hand-sutured anastomosis. Here there is also controversy as to whether a one- or two-layer anastomosis should be employed, what suture material should be used, and whether the selected sutures should be placed in an interrupted or a continuous manner. Other techniques not described but which might play a role in the future include the biofragmentable anastomotic ring used by some surgeons for more proximal anastomoses and the use of biological glue to diminish the risk of anastomotic leaks.

The term *low anterior resection* is applied when the operation necessitates full mobilization of the rectum and transection of both lateral ligaments. The anastomosis is performed below the anterior peritoneal reflection.

Because of the lateral curves of the rectum, it is possible that a carcinoma at the 7-cm level may be at the 12-cm level after full rectal mobilization. This is especially true with a posterior lesion. The feasibility of low anterior resection is decided upon only after the rectum has been completely mobilized posteriorly, anteriorly, and laterally. If low anterior resection is to be done, the distal clearance should be at least 2.0 cm from the lower margin of the carcinoma. The splenic flexure must be taken down if there is any question of tension at the anastomosis. At the completion of the anastomosis, the pelvic peritoneum is left open so that the hollow of the sacrum is freely communicating with the peritoneal cavity to allow drainage of the accumulated fluid. Closed suction drainage may be used in selected cases when the pelvis is not completely dry. Proximal colostomy is rarely performed, but in those circumstances where the surgeon is not entirely satisfied with the integrity of the anastomosis, there should be no hesitation to perform a complementary transverse colostomy. The following description of low anterior resection of the rectum has been taken from a recent publication.[1]

POSITION

The patient is placed in the supine position in slight Trendelenburg for better exposure of pelvic structures and aid in venous return from the lower extremities. The lower extremities are placed in stirrups, with the buttocks slightly elevated and near the edge of the table. With the knees flexed and the hips minimally flexed and abducted simultaneously, access to the abdomen and perineum is obtained (Fig. 61-1). Caution should be exercised to avoid excess abduction; therefore, the lower extremities are best placed in a neutral position with only enough abduction to permit access

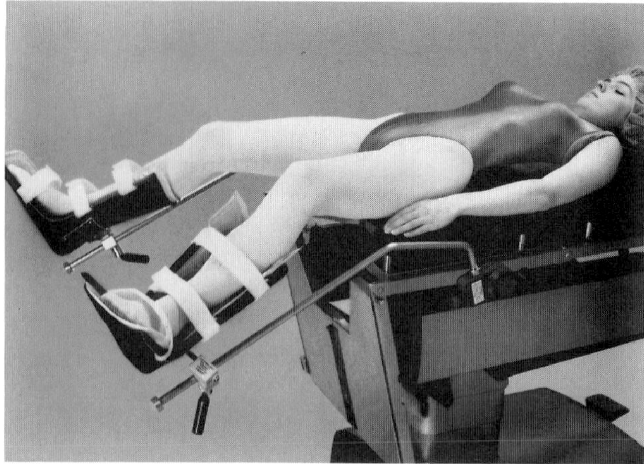

FIG. 61-1. Allen stirrups. With simple padding, the design of these stirrups minimizes the risk of pressure on the calf and eliminates pressure on the peroneal nerve. The thighs are slightly abducted and the hips and knees slightly flexed. (Courtesy Allen Medical Systems, Bedford Heights, Ohio.)

to the perineum. Pressure over the fibular head has the potential for the development of a peroneal nerve palsy, and undue calf pressure may result in a compartment syndrome.[2] Therefore, adequate padding should be employed. The second assistant can be positioned between the legs. A catheter is inserted into the bladder and the urine output is monitored continuously throughout the operation.

INCISION

Depending upon the body habitus, both a transverse incision at a level between the pubis and umbilicus and a lower midline incision provide satisfactory exposure (Fig. 61-2*A*). If the proposed transverse incision interferes with the ideal location of a possible stoma, a midline incision should be used. A self-retaining retractor aids exposure.

MOBILIZATION OF THE SIGMOID COLON

After the small bowel has been packed into the upper abdomen, the sigmoid colon is mobilized by incising the lateral peritoneal reflection (white line of Toldt). The incision is carried cephalad to the distal descending colon and caudad parallel to the rectum up to the cul-de-sac (Fig. 61-2*B*). The extent of proximal mobilization will depend upon the redundancy of the sigmoid colon. If the sigmoid colon is short, the splenic flexure may require mobilization. This can conveniently be accomplished with a cautery or a scissors. The intersigmoid fossa acts as a useful guide to the ureter located just behind it. The retroperitoneal areolar tissue is pushed aside with a stick sponge so that a fan-shaped flap of sigmoid mesentery is created. The left spermatic or left ovarian vein can be identified. At the level of the iliac crest, the ureter is just medial to this vein. Next, the peritoneum on the right side of the sigmoid and rectum is incised, starting near the sigmoid vessels and continuing toward the origin of the inferior mesenteric artery. A T-shaped incision is made in the peritoneum, again parallel to the rectum, and carried down to the pelvis up to the cul-de-sac. Unless there is invasion or inflammation in the pelvis, the right ureter is not routinely identified. The inferior mesenteric artery is identified and it is doubly clamped, divided, and doubly ligated just distal to the takeoff of the left colic artery (Fig. 61-2*C* and *D*). Prior to clamping the inferior mesenteric artery, care should be exercised to ensure that the ureter is out of harm's way. The inferior mesenteric vein is ligated at the corresponding level.

POSTERIOR MOBILIZATION OF THE RECTUM

By drawing the rectum taut, a plane of areolar tissue behind the rectum at the level just above the promontory of the sacrum can be identified. Using sharp dissection, the retrorectal space can usually easily be entered with minimal bleeding. Care must be exercised at this point to develop the plane *anterior* to the presacral nerves. At the level just below the promontory they can be seen bifurcating (Fig. 61-2*E*). The hand is swept laterally on each side, developing the lateral stalks (Fig. 61-2*F*). The plane is developed by a combination of sharp and blunt dissection. At the S3 or S4 level, the rectosacral fascia—which varies from a thin fibrous band to a thick ligament—is encountered. It is cut with a long heavy scissors or electrocautery (Fig. 61-2*G*). Failing to do so risks tearing the presacral venous plexus, which may then bleed profusely and can be difficult to control. Once this fascia is cut, the coccyx is reached.

Bleeding may arise directly from basivertebral veins through the sacral foramina.[3] Bleeding may be controlled by electrocoagulation or direct pressure, or, if it arises from the bone, a titanium thumbtack described by Nivatvongs and Fang[4] may be used. In rare circumstances, prolonged packing, which is removed several days later, can be employed.[5,6]

ANTERIOR MOBILIZATION OF THE RECTUM

In men, the peritoneum at the rectovesical reflection is incised and mobilization is continued in the plane between the seminal vesicles and Denovillier's fascia. Dissection is extended distally until the rectum is separated from the seminal vesicles; it is then continued distal to the prostate (Fig. 61-2*H*). Bleeding can be controlled with electrocoagulation. In women, the rectovaginal reflection is incised and the plane between

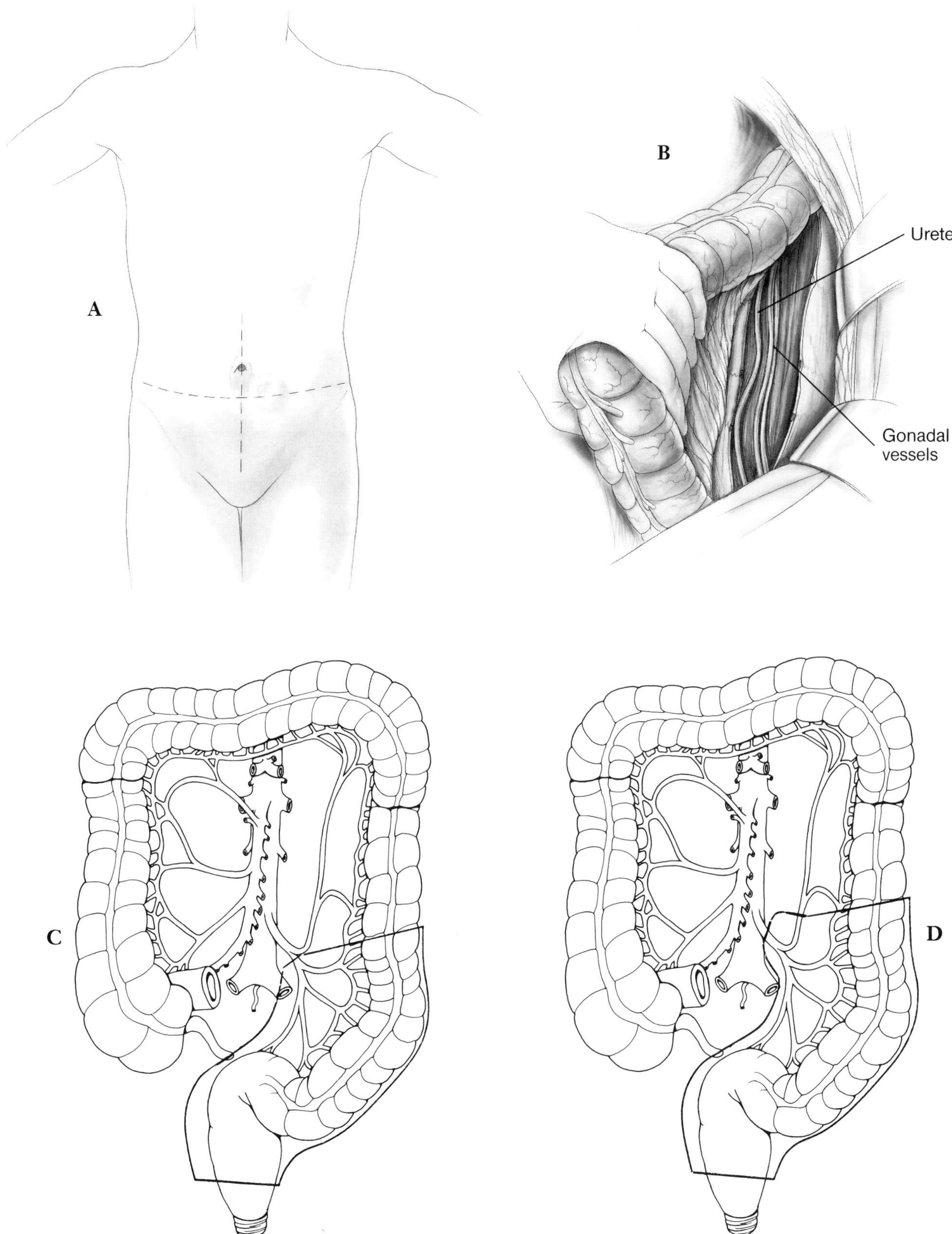

FIG. 61-2. Low anterior resection. *A*. Incision selection. *B*. Mobilization of the sigmoid colon. *C*. Ligation of the superior hemorrhoidal vessels. *D*. Ligation of the inferior mesenteric vessels. *E*. Identification of presacral nerve at the level of sacral promontory. *F*. Hand mobilization of the posterior rectal wall and development of lateral stalks. At the level of the sacral promontory the presacral space is entered and developed. *G*. Division of rectosacral fascia. *H*. Anterior mobilization of the rectum. *I*. Division of lateral stalks. *J*. Right angled bowel clamp placed distal to the carcinoma. (From Gordon PH: Malignant neoplasms of the rectum, in Gordon PH, Nivatvongs S (eds.): *Principles and Practice of Surgery for the Colon, Rectum, and Anus*. St. Louis: Quality Medical Publishing, Inc., 1992, pp. 600–603. Reproduced by permission.)

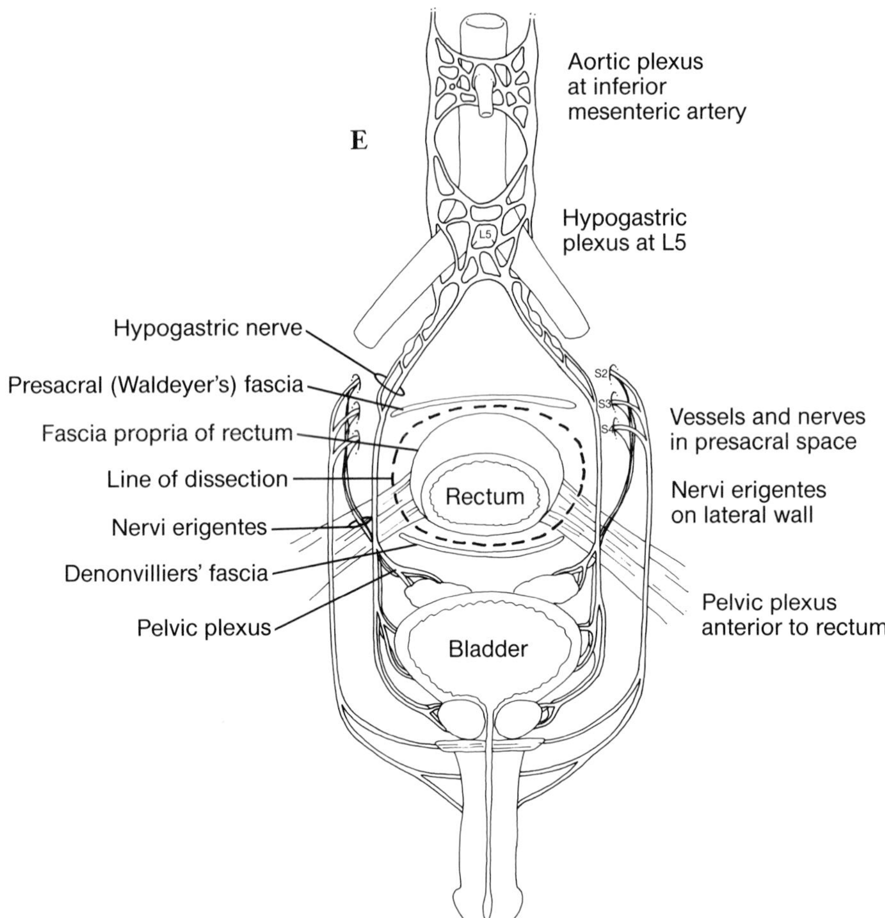

FIG. 61-2 (*Continued*).

the rectum and vagina developed until the pubis can be felt anteriorly. Exposure may be facilitated by passage of a suture around each fallopian tube, with elevation and retraction of the uterus anteriorly, by attaching the sutures to the self-retaining retractor.

DIVIDING THE LATERAL LIGAMENTS (STALKS)

At this stage, the rectum has been mobilized posteriorly to the tip of the coccyx and anteriorly to the level of the pubis. It is still attached laterally on each side by the pelvic fascia, called lateral ligaments (containing the accessory middle rectal vessels). The rectum is pulled taut with the left hand and the right hand is placed behind the rectum and sweeps laterally on each side of the ligament, care being taken to avoid the ureters and the S3 and S4 parasympathetic nerves. The ligaments are then clamped, divided, and ligated (Fig. 61-2*I*). Alternatively, the ligaments can be divided by electrocautery.

On the basis of the recommendation by Heald et al.[7,8] an effort is made to excise the mesorectum rather than follow the tendency to cone down through the mesorectum to the proposed distal line of resection. The latter technique leaves mesorectum in the pelvis, and Heald et al. have cautioned that this is the main reason for local recurrence. For lesions located higher in the rectum, the distal portion of mesorectum may be left undisturbed. But given an adequate distal margin, transection of the mesorectum is performed perpendicular to the rectal wall and not in a cone fashion. When adequate mobilization has been achieved, a right-angle bowel clamp is placed across the rectum distal to the carcinoma (Fig. 61-2*J*). At this point, many surgeons irrigate the rectal stump with water or a cancerocidal agent. Saline is probably adequate.

ANASTOMOSIS WITH THE CIRCULAR STAPLER

The introduction of staplers has markedly facilitated intestinal anastomoses. The advent of the circular stapler has extended the limits of low anterior resection by enabling surgeons to perform highly reliable anastomoses at a lower level than was technically possible with a traditional hand-sewn anastomosis, thus sparing a considerable number of patients from abdomi-

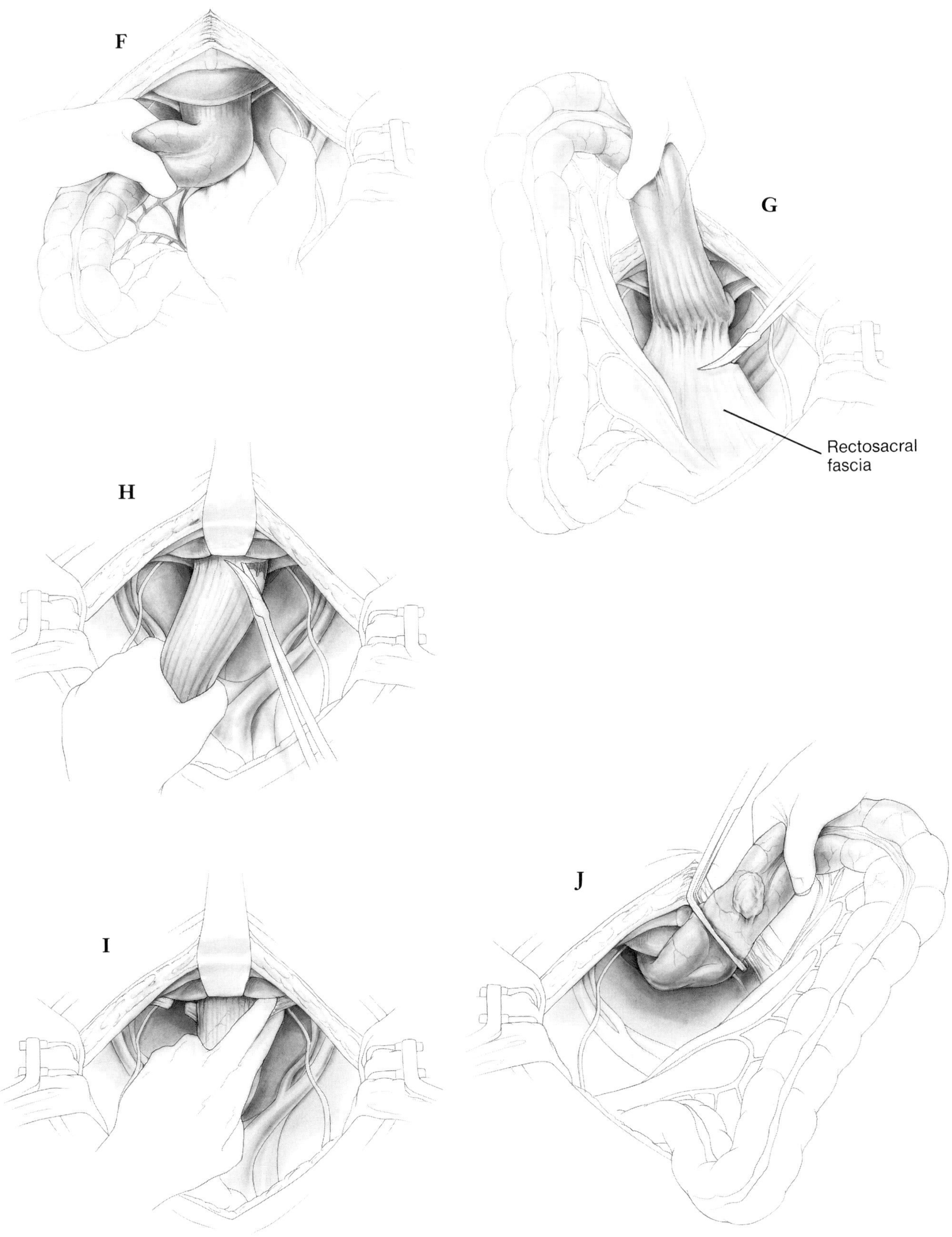

FIG. 61-2 (*Continued*).

noperineal resection and permanent colostomy. It should be pointed out that the general principles of anastomoses must be maintained (i.e., tissues not fit to sew should not be stapled). Unfavorable conditions in which a surgeon would be reluctant to do a handsewn anastomosis are not situations suitable for staples. Staples are only one method, albeit a convenient one, to establish intestinal continuity. Considerations of adequate blood supply, absence of tension, accurate apposition of tissue, and absence of sepsis apply equally to both stapled and hand-sutured anastomoses. A variety of staplers are commercially available.

The technique and pitfalls with the use of the circular stapler have previously been described in detail.[9] Having determined that a low anterior resection with a circular stapler is feasible, the surgeon prepares the proximal bowel by clearing 1.0 to 1.5 cm from the proposed margin of proximal resection. A purse-string suture may conveniently be applied using the specially designed fenestrated clamp (Fig. 61-3*A*). The rectum is prepared in a similar manner except that, for low anastomoses, the width of the pelvis is not adequate to permit application of the instrument and a Keith needle. A right-angle clamp is placed distal to the carcinoma and the bowel transected. A whipstitch of 2-0 Prolene is placed on the rectal stump, taking evenly spaced bites 4 to 5 mm from the cut edge (Fig. 61-3*A*). The purse-string suture may be placed on the outside of the rectum only prior to dividing the rectum.[10] Sizers are used to determine the appropriate diameter of the stapler cartridge.

Before insertion of the EEA stapler, the operator must confirm that the instrument has been properly assembled and must take special care to ensure the presence of the staples, circular knife, and Teflon ring. For the totally disposable stapler, only the cartridge and the head need be checked. The appropriate-size cartridge is selected, lubricated, and inserted in the closed position with the handle up. The instrument is advanced until the tip of the anvil protrudes through the rectal lumen, and the stapler is opened fully by turning the wing nut counterclockwise. The distal purse string is secured around the central shaft (Fig. 61-3*B*). The proximal bowel is advanced over the anvil, and the proximal purse string is secured around the central rod (Fig. 61-3*C*). The stapler is closed by turning the wing nut clockwise, while the abdominal operator ensures that the gap is free of mesentery, bladder, other tissues, and sponges (Fig. 61-3*D*). When the stapler is fully closed, the safety is released and the stapler fired by squeezing the handle firmly. This action places a double staggered circular row of stainless steel staples that join the two ends of the bowel while a circular knife simultaneously cuts two rings of tissue inside the staple line, thus creating an inverted end-to-end anastomosis (Fig. 61-3*E*). When the CEEA is used, the anvil is detached from the instrument and inserted into the proximal bowel after its transection.

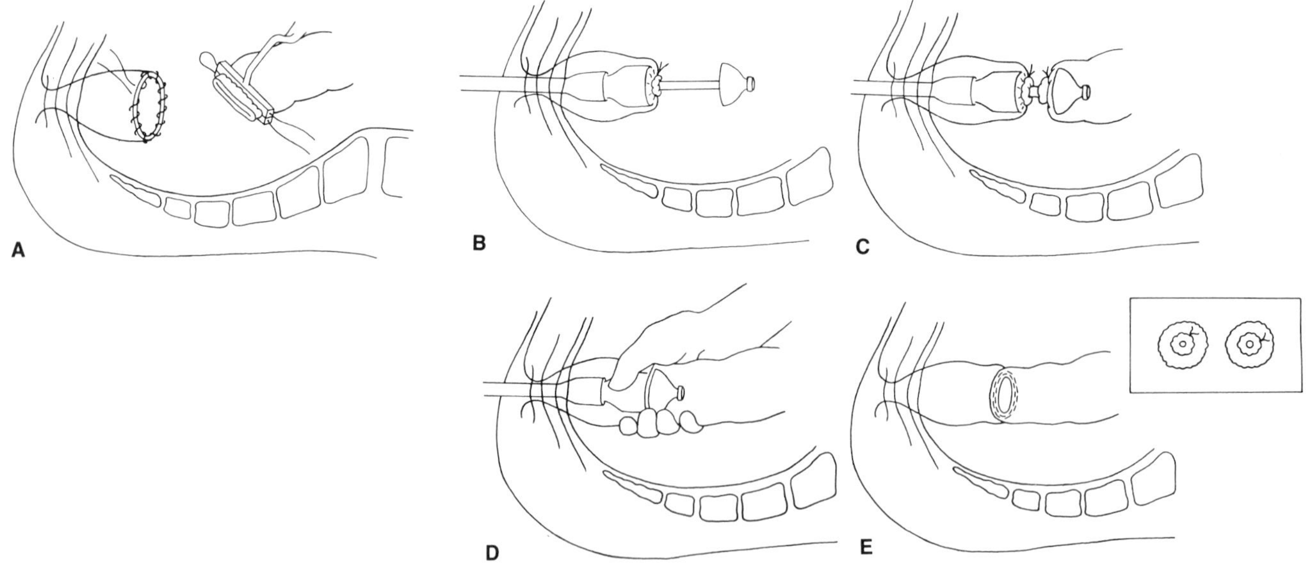

FIG. 61-3. Construction of anastomosis with the use of the circular stapler. *A*. Application of proximal purse-string suture using a specially designed fenestrated clamp and of distal purse-string suture with a whip suture of 2-0 polypropylene. *B*. The distal purse-string suture is secured around the central shaft. *C*. The proximal purse-string suture is secured around the central shaft. *D*. Manual exclusion of extraneous tissue during approximation of the bowel ends. *E*. A completed anastomosis with "rings of confidence." (From Gordon PH, Vasilevsky CA: Experience with stapling in rectal surgery. *Surg Clin North Am* 64:555–566, 1984. Reproduced by permission.)

The proximal purse string is tied, and this avoids any contamination from the proximal bowel. Attention is then directed to the distal stump. The CEEA is inserted through the anus, the central shaft extruded, and the distal purse string tied. The anvil is then engaged into the central shaft and the anastomosis created with the same precautions.

To remove the instrument, the stapler is opened by turning the wing nut counterclockwise three complete turns. The stapler is rotated; it should move independently of the bowel. The instrument is then removed by a simple, gentle, simultaneous withdrawing and back-and-forth rotational motion. When difficulty is encountered in extracting the instrument, guide sutures are placed through the anastomosis to help lift the anastomosis over the anvil (Fig. 61-4). A check is made to ensure that the rings of tissue excised are intact. Anastomoses may be inspected directly with a sigmoidoscope, and the physician should look for bleeding or obvious disruption. The integrity of the anastomosis is further tested by insufflating air into the bowel via the sigmoidoscope, with saline in the pelvis. The abdominal operator checks for bubbles arising from the anastomosis. Should an air leak be present, sutures can be placed to correct the defect.

If there is excess laxity in bowel, the peritoneum on the right side of the pelvis is closed. One side is left open to freely communicate with the generalized peritoneal cavity so that any fluid will be readily absorbed. More recently, the peritoneum has not been closed at all and no adverse effects have appeared, since it is unlikely a loop of small bowel will pass around the colon led to the pelvis.

A technical problem that is not infrequently encountered is the discrepancy in the diameter of the bowel ends to be anastomosed. Probably the simplest way to enlarge the bowel lumen is by insertion of progressively larger sizers (manufactured by the Autosuture Co.). A second option is the use of a sponge forceps

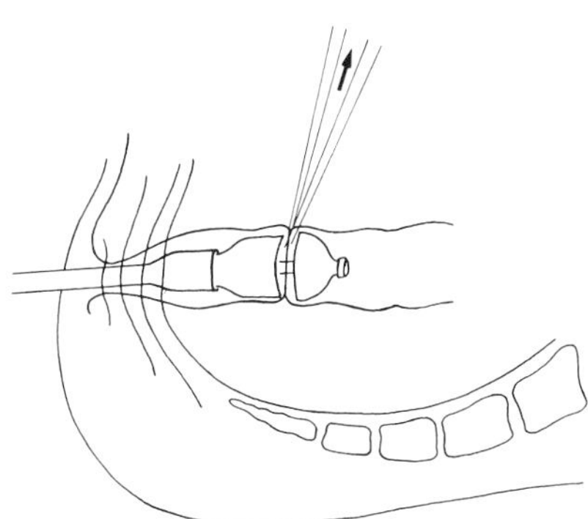

FIG. 61-4. Suture placement through the anastomosis to help lift the anastomosis over the anvil. (From Gordon PH, Vasilevsky CA: Experience with stapling in rectal surgery. *Surg Clin North Am* 64:555–566, 1984. Reproduced by permission.)

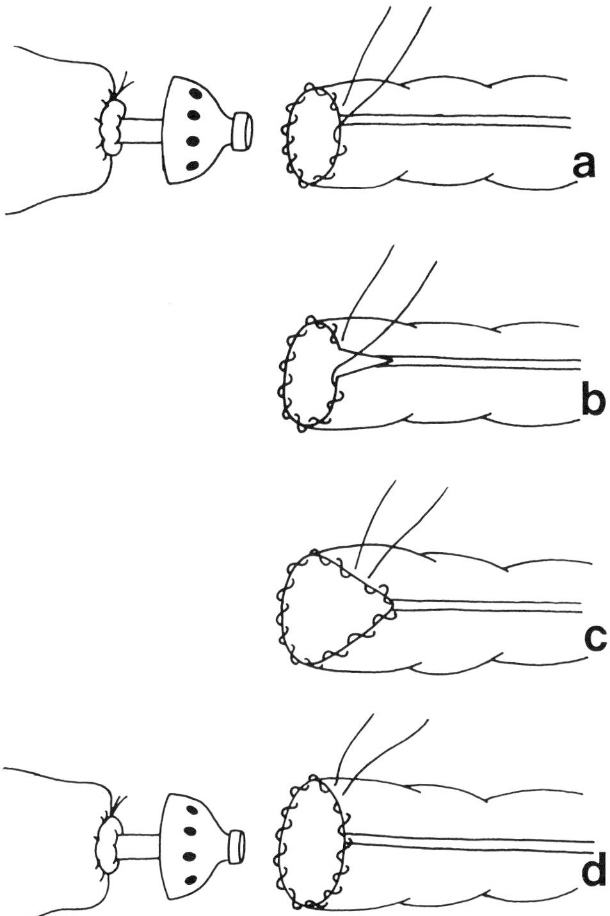

FIG. 61-5. Application of purse-string clamp so that one end is on the antimesenteric border. *B*. Incision of bowel along tenia between sutures. *C*. Continuation of suture along newly created border. *D*. Completed application of purse-string suture. (From Tchervenkov and Gordon.[12] Reproduced by permission.)

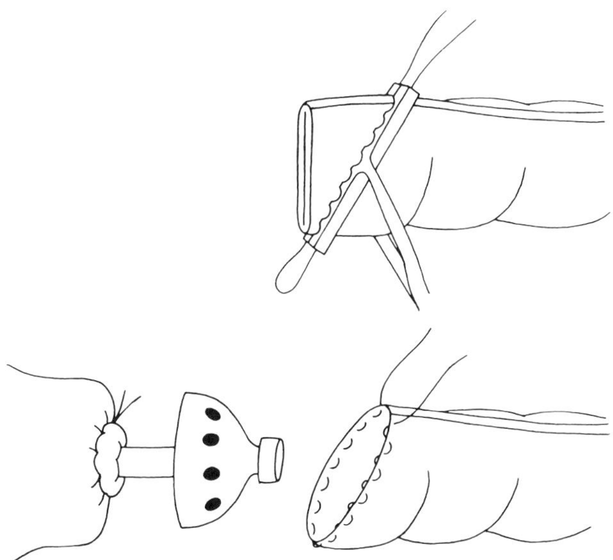

FIG. 61-6. Oblique application of purse-string clamp. (From Tchervenkov and Gordon.[12] Reproduced by permission.)

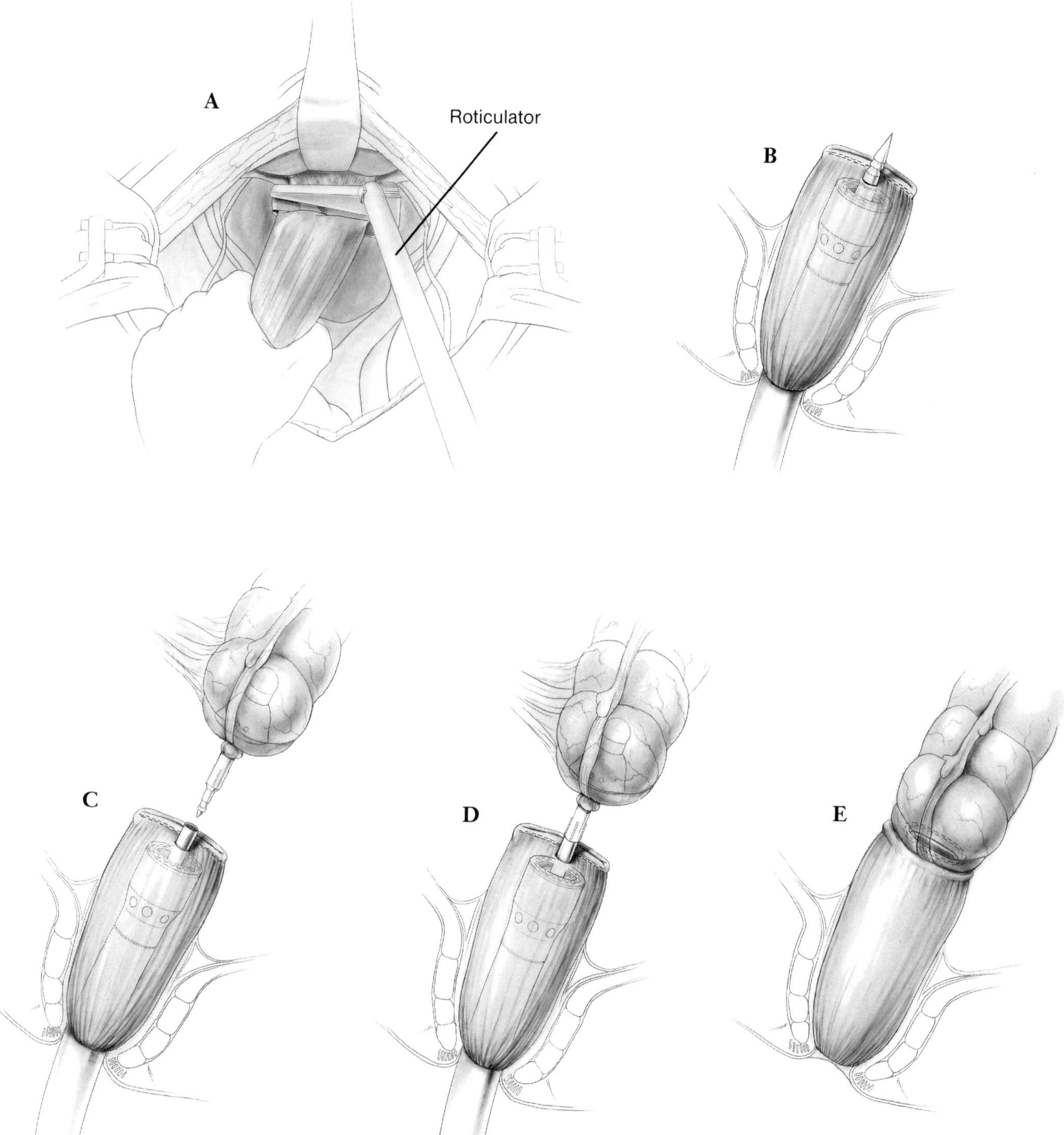

FIG. 61-7. Double staple technique. *A*. Roticulator applied to distal rectum and purse-string clamp applied to proximal colon. *B*. CEEA introduced with trocar piercing at level of anastomosis. *C*. Trocar removed and detachable anvil inserted into proximal bowel. *D*. Anvil engaged in central shaft. *E*. Anastomosis completed. (From Gordon PH: Malignant neoplasms of the rectum, in Gordon PH, Nivatvongs S (eds.): *Principles and Practice of Surgery for the Colon, Rectum, and Anus*. St. Louis: Quality Medical Publishing, Inc., 1992, p. 608. Reproduced by permission.)

to stretch the bowel. Another technique is the very slow expansion of a 30-cc Foley catheter balloon with saline after it is positioned in the bowel lumen.[11] All these methods of dilatation may result in tearing of the bowel wall. Simple techniques of enlarging the diameter of the bowel lumen for performance of end-to-end anastomoses using the EEA stapler were described by Tchervenkov and Gordon.[12] If the transected bowel end cannot be dilated to accept a staple cartridge of appropriate size and the purse-string suture has already been applied, an incision can be made along the antimesenteric border of the colon. Ideally, the purse-string suture will have been placed so that the free ends are at the antimesenteric position of the circumference of the bowel (Fig. 61-5*A*). It is a simple matter to incise the bowel between the two ends of the suture (Fig. 61-5*B*) and then continue the suture along the newly created border past the apex of the incision to meet the other end of the suture (Fig. 61-5*C*). The new configuration of the circumference will be egg-shaped (Fig. 61-5*D*).

If it is apparent from the outset that the bowel caliber is definitely too small and will not be successfully dilated by the previously described methods, the oblique application of the purse-string clamp will result in a larger diameter of the bowel end (Fig. 61-6).

Double-Staple Technique

Knight and Griffin[13] introduced the double-staple technique (Fig. 61-7). The advantage of this technique is the elimination of the need to place the distal purse-string suture, and it avoids the size discrepancy problem. A linear staple line is placed on the rectum distal to the carcinoma. The instrument is fired, a right angle bowel clamp is applied distal to the carcinoma, and the rectum is transected just proximal to the stapler. The CEEA instrument is ideally suited to construct the anastomosis. The detachable anvil is removed, a trochar is placed in the central shaft, and this is then retracted within the cartridge. The instrument is introduced through the anus and advanced to the staple line. The trochar is extruded through the staple line and removed. Then the anvil previously inserted into and secured on the proximal bowel is engaged into the central shaft. The anvil is approximated to the cartridge and the instrument activated. The instrument is withdrawn and the anastomosis inspected, as was done for the regular circular stapler. Care should be exercised to ensure that the trochar penetrates the suture line or immediately adjacent to it. If there is a rim of tissue between the stapled rectum and the ring of tissue excised, it may become ischemic and result in a leak.

For their most recent publication, Griffin et al.[14] reviewed 75 patients and found an anastomotic leak rate of 2.7 percent, with an incidence of stenosis which required treatment of 2.7 percent. There were no deaths.[14] Other surgeons have successfully employed this technique.[15,16]

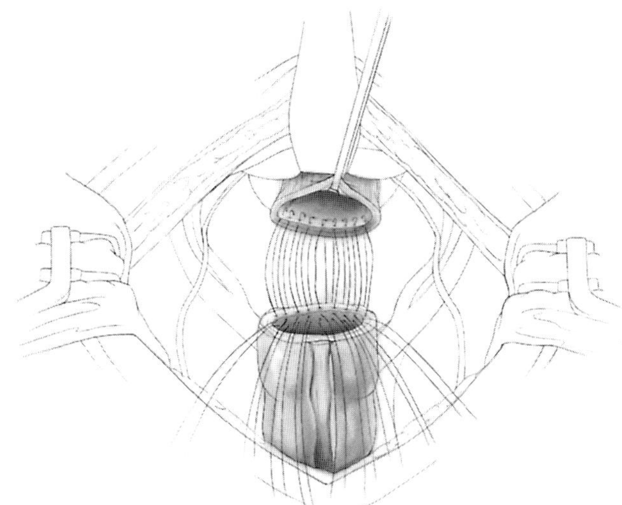

FIG. 61-8. Single-layer hand-sutured anastomosis. Alignment of posterior wall and placement of sutures before tying. (From Gordon PH: Malignant neoplasms of the rectum, in Gordon PH, Nivatvongs S (eds.): *Principles and Practice of Surgery for the Colon, Rectum, and Anus*. St. Louis: Quality Medical Publishing, Inc., 1992, p. 608. Reproduced by permission.)

HAND-SUTURED ANASTOMOSES

Many surgeons still prefer hand-sutured anastomoses. Although two-layered anastomoses were once considered standard technique, there has been a move toward single-layer anastomoses. If adopted, the open technique with no clamps applied on the bowel ends prevents injury to the bowel wall. For approximation of the posterior wall, vertical mattress sutures are used: the first bite is full-thickness on each side, but on the return bite only mucosa and submucosa are included (Fig. 61-8). Widely used sutures are 4-0 polypropylene or 4-0 polyglycolic acid or polyglactin. All knots are tied inside the lumen. An interrupted full thickness with only mucosal inversion as described by Gambee is used for the anterior wall. Many surgeons prefer a two-layer anastomosis: an outer seromuscular layer of 4-0 nonabsorbable suture and a continuous inner layer of 4-0 absorbable suture.

REFERENCES

1. Gordon PH: Malignant neoplasms of the rectum, in Gordon PH, Nivatvongs S (eds): *Principles and Practice of Surgery for the Colon, Rectum, and Anus*. St Louis, Quality Medical Publishing, 1992, pp 598–609.
2. Bergqvist D, Bohe M, Ekelund G: Compartment syndrome after prolonged surgery with leg supports. *Int J Colorect Dis* 5:1–5, 1990.

3. Qinyao W, Weijun S, Youren Z, et al: New concepts in severe hemorrhage during proctectomy. *Arch Surg* 12:1013–1020, 1985.
4. Nivatvongs S, Fang DT: The use of thumbtacks to stop massive presacral hemorrhage. *Dis Colon Rectum* 29:589–590, 1986.
5. Metzger PP: Modified packing technique for control of presacral pelvic bleeding. *Dis Colon Rectum* 31:981–982, 1988.
6. Zama N, Fazio VW, Jagelman DG, et al: Efficacy of pelvic packing in maintaining hemostasis after rectal excision for cancer. *Dis Colon Rectum* 31:923–928, 1988.
7. Heald RJ: Rectal cancer: Anterior resection and local recurrence—A personal view. *Perspect Colon Rectal Surg* 1:1–26, 1988.
8. Heald RJ, Ryall RDA: Recurrence and survival after total meso-rectal excision for rectal cancer. *Lancet* 1:1479–1482, 1986.
9. Gordon PH, Dalrymple S: The use of staples for reconstruction after colonic and rectal surgery, in Ravitch MM, Steichen FM (eds): *Principles and Practice of Surgical Stapling*. Chicago, Year Book, 1987, pp 402–431.
10. Cohen AM: Purse-string placement for transanal intraluminal circular stapling. *Dis Colon Rectum* 29:532–533, 1986.
11. Minichan DP: Enlarging the bowel lumen for the EEA stapler. *Dis Colon Rectum* 25:61, 1982.
12. Tchervenkov CI, Gordon PH: Simple techniques of enlarging the diameter of the bowel lumen for the performance of end-to-end anastomoses using the EEA stapler. *Dis Colon Rectum* 27:630–631, 1984.
13. Knight CD, Griffin FD: Techniques of low rectal reconstruction. *Curr Probl Surg* 20:391–456, 1983.
14. Griffin FD, Knight CD, Whitaker JM, et al: The double stapling technique for low anterior resection—Results, modifications, and observations. *Ann Surg* 211:745–752, 1990.
15. Feinberg SM, Parker F, Cohen Z, et al: The double stapling technique for low anterior resection of rectal carcinoma. *Dis Colon Rectum* 29:885–890, 1986.
16. Julian TB, Ravitch MM: Evaluation of the safety of end-to-end (EEA) stapling anastomosis across linear stapled closures. *Surg Clin North Am* 64:567–577, 1984.

CHAPTER 62

Radical Surgery—Coloanal Reconstruction

Gerald J. Marks
Joseph P. Bannon
Jian-Nong Zhou

HIGHLIGHTS

The traditional 5-cm rule for the distal margin in patients with rectal cancer has been shown to be fallacious. The lateral margin is the major determinant of local recurrence. Distal margins of 2 cm, and perhaps less with the use of radiation therapy, frequently suffice. Such biological findings allow increased use of sphincter-saving strategies and, in particular, the coloanal anastomotic approach.

CONTROVERSIES

Patient selection and technical expertise remain the major problems in the widespread application of this approach. The definition of adequate margins with the use of preoperative radiation therapy remains unclear.

FUTURE DIRECTIONS

Patient selection based on molecular-biological determinants, improved clinical staging with ultrasound (US), and enhanced magnetic resonance imaging (MRI) techniques are important areas of investigation. Data from the Swedish randomized trial of colon J-pouch anal reconstruction should help to define the expected functional outcome of bowel surgery. Integration of these approaches with autonomic nerve preservation will likely improve the functional results further.

The heightened interest in coloanal anastomosis (CAA) performed in conjunction with radical proctosigmoidectomy in the treatment of low-lying rectal cancers can be attributed in major part to Sir Allan Parks,[1] who described an endoanal mucosal stripped-sleeve type anastomosis in 1972. This interest was amplified further by the widespread application of ileoanal anastomoses in managing ulcerative colitis and the realization that, because the proprioceptive arm of the continence reflex originates in the puborectalis and levator muscles, anal sphincteric competence does not require any length of rectal wall or mucosa.[2] Experience with ileoanal anastomoses encouraged a progressive reduction in the length of distal rectum sleeve and gave rise to the use of a direct "cuffless" anastomosis. Direct anastomosis without anal eversion has been accomplished by the transanal,[3] transsacral,[4] and transsphincteric routes.[5] The colonic J-type reservoir has been used in conjunction with these procedures and studied for its effectiveness in reducing bowel frequency.[6–8] Instrumentation which allows circular stapling has produced wider usage of the low-rectal supraanal anastomosis, which is often referred to erroneously as a coloanal anastomosis. With the availability of an increasing number of technical options to create anastomoses at lower levels of the rectum and anorectum, surgeons are more inclined to perform sphincter-preservation surgery for cancer of the distal rectum.

DETERMINANTS OF LOCAL FAILURE IN RECTAL CANCER

One of the traditional areas of surgical attention has focused on obtaining an adequate distal mucosal and mural margin in the treatment of patients with rectal cancer. A need for the "required" distal 5-cm margin cannot be documented. Clinicopathologic studies from many centers indicated that a 2-cm distal mural margin may be adequate.[9–11] Obtaining an adequate lateral margin appears to be far more important in avoiding local recurrence.[12] Clearing the mesorectum above the levators maximizes chances for truly negative pelvic margins.[13,14]

PREOPERATIVE RADIATION THERAPY

Transmural tumor penetration into perirectal fat in the lower third of the rectum may lead to microscopic tumor invasion of the pelvic floor. It is possible that high-dose radiation therapy, particularly preoperatively, can sterilize such peripheral tumors and permit sphincter-saving surgery options. In theory, such operations could replace the abdominoperineal resection except in cases of direct invasion of the anal sphincters or gross penetration into the levators.

There are multiple randomized trials using adjuvant preoperative radiation.[15–19] The data suggest that high-dose radiation is effective in reducing local recurrence. The lowest local failure rates with adjuvant radiation are reported in nonrandomized series from the United States using 4500 to 5000 rads in 180- to 200-rad fractions. With this approach, the leak rates with sphincter-saving surgery have not increased.[20–23]

COLOANAL/ENDOANAL RECONSTRUCTION

During the past 50 years, multiple anal sphincter-saving operations using the endoanal approach or direct coloanal reconstruction have been described. The various surgical considerations are outlined in Table 62-1.

Table 62-1
Options in Coloanal Reconstruction

A. Exposure approaches
   1. Abdominosacral
   2. Eversion of rectal stump
   3. Transsphincteric
   4. Endoanal
      a. Direct
      b. Submucosal
      c. Intersphincteric
B. Level of anastomosis
   1. Distal rectum
   2. Pelvic floor (anorectal ring)
   3. Anal canal (dentate line)
C. Anastomosis
   1. Timing
      a. Primary
      b. Delayed
   2. Type
      a. Handsewn
      b. Stapled
D. Reconstruction
   1. Straight
   2. J pouch

Exposure

Mobilization and exposure of the distal rectum is feasible using the abdominosacral approach described by D'Allaines and reported extensively by Localio and associates.[24] The more direct perineal approach can utilize distal rectal eversion, a transsphincteric approach, or the endoanal route. Eversion has been an essential component of the "pull-through" procedures.[18,25–30] Anal dilatation and possible nerve damage are inherent in this approach, and functional end results appear to be less than ideal. A posterior transsphincteric approach allows direct visualization for low colorectal or coloanal anastomosis. In selected series, this approach is successful.[31,32]

Various endoanal approaches with improved functional results have been reported. The lower rectum may be mobilized by a direct endoanal dissection at the level of the most distal rectum, excluding the anal canal. Incorporating the upper anal canal is feasible usually by a submucosal dissection beginning at the dentate line.[7,33–38] The internal sphincter may be included with the endoanal dissection.[39–41]

Level of Anastomosis

The abdominosacral and various eversion endoanal approaches may be used to anastomose the proximal bowel down to the level of the lower rectum. For more distal rectal cancers, the anastomosis is made at the level of the pelvic floor (levators, anorectal ring)[41,42]; or, combined with a submucosal or intersphincteric dissection, a true coloanal anastomosis at the level of the dentate line is feasible.[7,33–39,41]

Anastomosis

Additional variables include the timing and type of anastomosis. The pull-through procedures may have a primary or a delayed anastomosis. Major complications with the delayed anastomosis are fewer.[27] Anastomosis at the level of the lower rectum or the anorectal ring may be hand-sewn[42] or stapled.[41] The endoanal reconstructions at the level of the dentate line are hand-sewn.[7,33–38,41]

Recognition of the difficulties associated with an anterior transabdominal approach to cancers located less than 2 cm from the anorectal ring for the purpose of creating either an anterior or transsacral anasto-

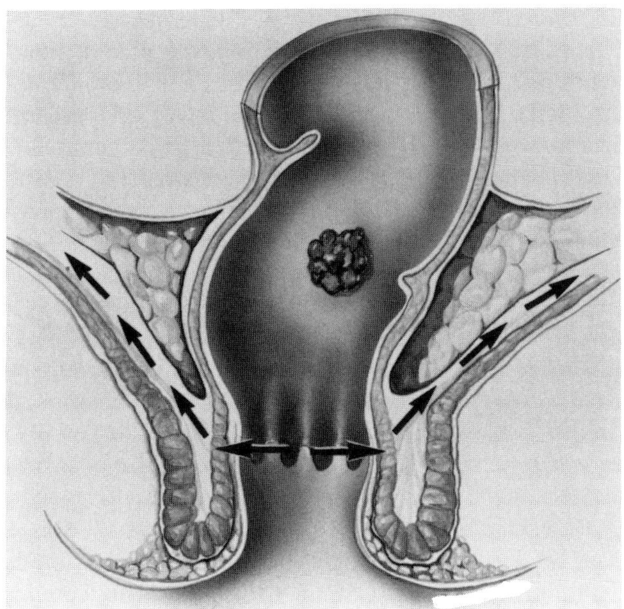

FIG. 62-1. Graphic plane of dissection.

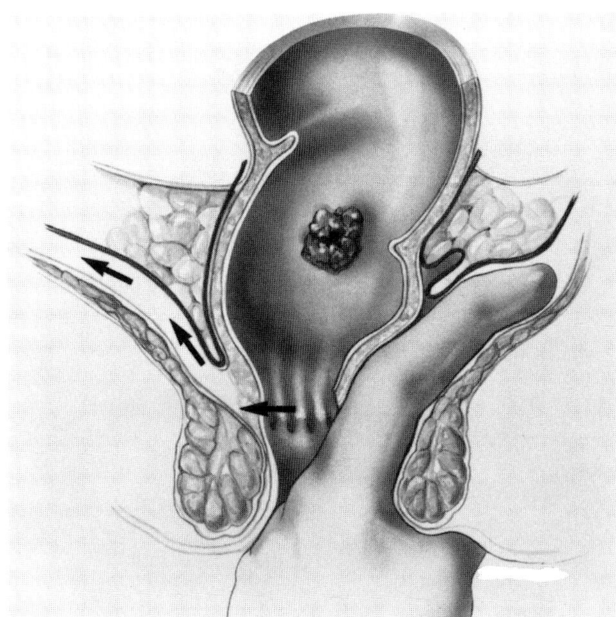

FIG. 62-2. Endopelvic fascia advancing in front of finger.

mosis brought about the development of a procedure in which the initial step is mobilization of the rectum through a full-thickness incision of the rectal wall at or just above the pectinate line (Fig. 62-1). The endopelvic fascia is pushed superiorly and creates an additional layer around the rectum and tumor in a manner unachievable when dissection is begun anteriorly (Fig. 62-2). The splenic flexure is fully mobilized and the descending colon (Fig. 62-3) used for a perianal sutured anastomosis (Fig. 62-4).

Pouches

Although fecal continence is usually obtained, bowel dysfunction from loss of the normal rectal reservoir

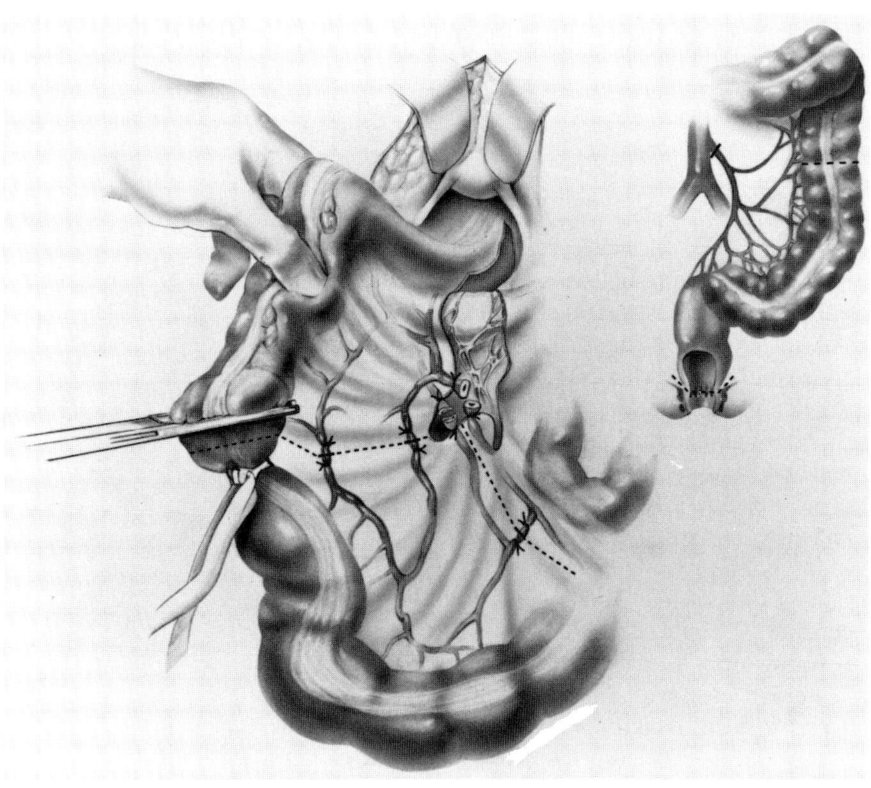

FIG. 62-3. Intraperitoneal dissection.

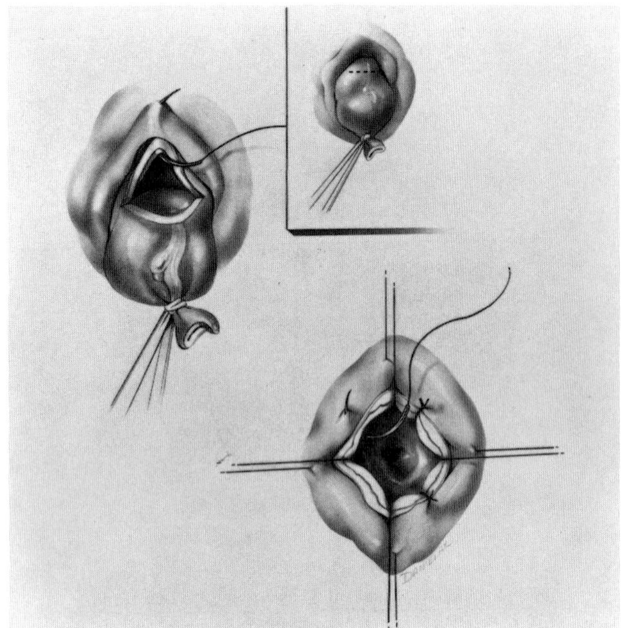

FIG. 62-4. Transanal anastomosis.

may remain problematic, even after a year of adaptation.[43] Use of the descending colon for the anastomosis precludes some of the dysfunction. Stool frequency, urgency, nocturnal movements, and episodic frequent movements during the 6 months following operation are bothersome to the patient.[44] Use of dietary manipulation, bulking agents, antidiarrheal medications, and, more recently, the construction of a small colonic pouch as part of the restorative reconstruction have been utilized.[7,36,38,43,45,46] A randomized trial is under way in Sweden comparing the straight anastomosis with a pouch.

RESULTS

Thomas Jefferson University Experience

Of 289 patients who received primary treatment for rectal cancer with high-dose preoperative radiation and sphincter-preservation surgery, 65 underwent CAA for cancers of the distal 3 cm of the rectum.[47] A 72-year-old man who underwent a CAA and died 6 weeks after sustaining a delayed hemorrhage represents the one death in the entire series. Intraoperative presacral venous hemorrhage occurred in 3 patients, but no perioperative radiation- or procedure-specific morbidity has been identified. All 4 significant pelvic infections responded to percutaneous or surgical drainage, and while 3 major anastomotic disruptions occurred, 2 were reconstituted. No patient was lost to follow-up. Mild strictures were common, and all yielded easily to digital dilatation. Function was surprisingly satisfactory after the customary early diarrhea. It was discovered that 2 patients had unsuspected obstetric sphincter function. No patient operated on was excluded from analysis. The overall Kaplan-Meier 5-year actuarial survival was 85 percent. The overall local recurrence rate was 9 percent. Survival in the postradiated favorable stages T_0, T_1, and T_2 was 95 percent. All local recurrences were in postradiated $T_3 \pm N_1$ cancers.

Memorial Sloan-Kettering Cancer Center Experience

A total of 134 patients with distal rectal cancer underwent CAA reconstruction.[48] Actuarial 5-year survival was 73 percent; T_2N_0, 79 percent; T_3N_0, 70 percent; and node-positive, 58 percent. Local failure occurred in 11%.

Determinants of pelvic recurrence were T_3 stage, positive margins, mesenteric tumor implants, perineural invasion, blood vessel invasion, and high grade. Poor functional results were primarily associated with the use of postoperative radiation therapy.[43]

CONCLUSIONS

In experienced hands, proctectomy and coloanal reconstruction avoids permanent colostomy in almost all patients, yields fair functional results, and provides good local control in selected patients.

REFERENCES

1. Parks A: Transanal technique in low rectal anastomosis. *Proc R Soc Med* 65:975–976, 1972.
2. Scharli AF, Kieswetter WB: Defecation and continence: Some new concepts. *Dis Colon Rectum* 13:81–107, 1970.
3. Paty PB, Enker WE: Coloanal anastomosis following low anterior resection. *Hepatogastroenterology* 39:202–206, 1992.
4. Marks GJ, Mohiuddin M, Borenstein BD: Preoperative radiation therapy and sphincter preservation by the combined abdominotranssacral technique for selected rectal cancers. *Dis Colon Rectum* 28:565–571, 1985.
5. Lazorthes FP, Fages P, Chiotasso P, et al: Synchronous abdomino-trans-sphincteric resection of low rectal cancer: New technique for direct colo-anal anastomosis. *Br J Surg* 73:573–575, 1986.
6. Lazorthes FP, Fages P, Chiotasso P, et al: Resection of the rectum with construction of a colonic reservoir and colo-anal anastomosis for carcinoma of the rectum. *Br J Surg* 73:136–138, 1986.
7. Parc R, Tiret E, Frileux P, et al: Resection and colo-anal anastomosis with colonic reservoir for rectal carcinoma. *Br J Surg* 73:139–141, 1986.
8. Nicholls RJ, Lubowski DZ, Donaldson DR: Comparison of colonic reservoir and straight colo-anal reconstruction after rectal excision. *Br J Surg* 75:318–320, 1988.
9. Williams NS: The rationale of preservation of the anal sphincter in patients with low rectal cancer. *Br J Surg* 71:575–581, 1984.
10. Pollett WG, Nicholls RJ: The relationship between the extent of distal clearance and survival and local recurrence rates af-

ter curative anterior resection for carcinoma of the rectum. *Ann Surg* 198:159–163, 1984.
11. Hojo K: Anastomotic recurrence after sphincter-saving resection for rectal cancer: Length of distal clearance of the bowel. *Dis Colon Rectum* 29:11–14, 1986.
12. Quirke P, Durdey P, Dixon MF, et al: Local recurrence of rectal adenocarcinoma due to inadequate surgical resection: Histopathological study of lateral tumor spread and surgical excision. *Lancet* 1:996–999, 1986.
13. Heald RJ, Ryall RDH: Recurrence and survival after total meso-rectal excision for rectal cancer. *Lancet* 1:1479–1482, 1986.
14. Enker WE, Heilweil ML, Hertz REL, et al: En bloc pelvic lymphadenopathy and sphincter preservation in the surgical management of rectal cancer. *Ann Surg* 203:426–433, 1986.
15. Gerard A, Buyse M, Nordlinger B, et al: Preoperative radiotherapy as adjuvant treatment in rectal cancer: Final results of a randomized study of the European Organization for research and treatment of cancer (EORTC). *Ann Surg* 208:606–614, 1988.
16. Roswit B, Higgins GA Jr, Keehn R: Preoperative irradiation for carcinoma of the rectum and rectosigmoid colon: Report of a national Veterans Administration randomized study. *Cancer* 35:1597–1602, 1975.
17. Bruckner R, Kempf P, Kutzner J, et al: Preliminary results of preoperative radiotherapy in carcinoma of the rectum. *Dtsch Med Wochenschr* 102:195–198, 1977.
18. Turnbull RB Jr., Cuthbertson AM: Abdomino-rectal pull-through resection and Hirschsprung's disease. *Cleve Clin Q* 28:109–115, 1961.
19. Stockholm Rectal Cancer Study Group: Short-term preoperative radiotherapy for adenocarcinoma of the rectum. *Am J Clin Oncol* 10:369–375, 1987.
20. Mohiuddin M, Maarks GJ: High dose preoperative radiation and sphincter preservation in the treatment of rectal cancer. *Int J Radiat Oncol Biol Phys* 13:389–842, 1987.
21. Friedman P, Garb JL, Park WC, et al: Survival following moderate-dose preoperative radiation therapy for carcinoma of the rectum. *Cancer* 55:967–973, 1985.
22. Mendenhall WM, Bland KI, Rout WR, et al: Clinically resectable adenocarcinoma of the rectum treated with preoperative irradiation and surgery. *Dis Colon Rectum* 31:287–290, 1988.
23. Fortier GA, Constable W, Meyers H: Preoperative radiation therapy for rectal cancer. *Arch Surg* 121:1380, 1986.
24. Localio SA, Eng K, Coppa GF: Abdominosacral resection for mid-rectal cancer. *Ann Surg* 198:320–324, 1983.
25. Bacon HE: Evolution of sphincter muscle preservation and re-establishment of continuity in the operative treatment of rectal and sigmoid cancer. *Surg Gynecol Obstet* 2:113–127, 1949.
26. Babcock WW: Experiences with resection of the colon and the elimination of colostomy. *Am J Surg* 46:186–203, 1939.
27. Cutait DE, Cutait R, Ioshimoto M, et al: Abdominoperineal endoanal pull-through resection: A comparative study between immediate and delayed colorectal anastomosis. *Dis Colon Rectum* 28:294–299, 1985.
28. Kennedy JT, Muomish D, Bennett RC, et al: Abdomino-anal pull-through resection of the rectum. *Br J Surg* 57:589–596, 1970.
29. Goligher JC, Duthie HL, Dedombal FT, et al: Abdomino-anal pull-through excision for tumors of the mid third of the rectum—A comparison with low anterior resection. *Br J Surg* 52:323–335, 1975.
30. Khubchandani IT, Karamchandani MC, Sheets JA, et al: The Bacon pull-through procedure. *Dis Colon Rectum* 30:540–544, 1987.
31. York-Mason A: Trans-sphincteric surgery of the rectum. *Prog Surg* 13:66–97, 1974.
32. Lazorthes F, Fages P, Chiotasso P, et al: Synchronous abdominotransphincteric resection of low rectal cancer: New technique for direct colo-anal anastomosis. *Br J Surg* 73:573–575, 1986.
33. Parks AG, Percy JP: Resection and sutured colo-anal anastomosis for rectal carcinoma. *Br J Surg* 69:301–304, 1982.
34. Parks AG: Per-anal anastomosis. *World J Surg* 6:531–538, 1982.
35. Gardner B, Kottmeier P, Harshaw D: A modified one stage pull-through operation for carcinoma or prolapse of the rectum. *Surg Gynecol Obstet* 136:95–99, 1973.
36. Nicholls RJ, Lubowski DZ, Donaldson DR: Comparison of colonic reservoir and straight colo-anal reconstruction after rectal excision. *Br J Surg* 75:318–320, 1988.
37. Hautefeuille P, Valleur P, Perniceni T, et al: Functional and oncologic results after coloanal anastomosis for low rectal carcinoma. *Ann Surg* 207:61–64, 1988.
38. Drake DB, Pemberton JH, Beart RW Jr, et al: Coloanal anastomosis in the management of benign and malignant rectal disease. *Ann Surg* 206:600–605, 1987.
39. Castrini G, Papalardo G, Mobarhan S: A new technique for ileo-anal and coloanal anastomosis. *Surgery* 97:111–116, 1985.
40. Pappalardo G, Toccaceli S, Dionisio P, et al: Preoperative and postoperative evaluation by manometric study of the anal sphincter after coloanal anastomosis for carcinoma. *Dis Colon Rectum* 3:119–122, 1988.
41. Enker WE, Stearns MW Jr, Janov AJ: Peranal coloanal anastomosis following low anterior resection for rectal carcinoma. *Dis Colon Rectum* 28:576–581, 1985.
42. Basso Minervini S, Marcelli M: Modified abdomino-transanal resection for cancer of the lower third of the rectum. *Dis Colon Rectum* 30:641–643, 1987.
43. Paty PB, Cohen AM, Friedlander-Klar H: Long-term functional results of coloanal anastomosis for rectal cancer. *Am J Surg* 167:90–95, 1994.
44. Schoetz DJ Jr: Postcolectomy syndromes. *World J Surg* 15:605–608, 1991.
45. Huguet C, Harb J, Bona S: Coloanal anastomosis after resection of low rectal cancer in the elderly. *World J Surg* 14:619–623, 1990.
46. Lazorthes F, Fages P, Chiotasso P, et al: Resection of the rectum with construction of a colonic reservoir and colo-anal anastomosis for carcinoma of the rectum. *Br J Surg* 73:136–138, 1986.
47. Marks GJ, Mohiuddin M, Masoni L, et al: High dose preoperative radiation therapy as the key to extending sphincter-preservation surgery for cancer of the distal rectum. *Surg Oncol Clin North Am* 1:71–85, 1992.
48. Paty PB, Enker WE, Cohen AM, et al: Treatment of rectal cancer by low anterior resection with coloanal anastomosis. *Ann Surg* 219:365–373, 1994.

CHAPTER 63

Abdominoperineal Resection—Technique and Complications

Theodore R. Schrock

HIGHLIGHTS

Upward spread through lymphatics along the superior hemorrhoidal and inferior mesenteric vessels is an important feature of rectal carcinoma. Control of this route is the foundation of abdominoperineal resection (APR). Whenever possible, a sphincter-preserving operation is performed for rectal cancer, but APR remains the standard curative surgical procedure for carcinoma of the distal rectum.

The abdominal and pelvic phases of the operation involve dissection through anatomic planes. The ureters and major vascular structures are identified and protected. The preaortic and presacral sympathetic nerves are avoided. Dissection posterior to the rectum should be done under direct vision, when possible, rather than bluntly. All of the soft tissue lateral to the rectum should be excised to the pelvic side wall. Anteriorly, the rectum is separated from the urogenital structures. A colostomy is established through the left rectus abdominis muscle.

The perineal phase should incur little blood loss. Management of the perineal wound is controversial, but one of the closed techniques clearly is advantageous over packing the perineal wound open.

The operative mortality rate should be no greater than 3 percent today. Intraoperative, early postoperative, and late postoperative complications are common but usually not serious.

CONTROVERSIES

Surgeons differ in their preference for two-stage or combined synchronous APR, mainly depending on the availability of a second surgeon to do the perineal phase at the same time. If the operation is done synchronously, of course the patient must be in the lithotomy position. Some surgeons who do the procedure in separate abdominal and perineal phases prefer the left lateral decubitus position for the perineal dissection.

The level of ligation of the vessels to the distal colon and rectum is still somewhat controversial. Although involved nodes may remain in the patient if the vessels are not ligated at the origin of the inferior mesenteric artery, these patients prove to be incurable anyway. Ligation just distal to the origin of the left colic artery seems to be a practical compromise.

Sigmoid colostomies are prone to paracolostomy herniation regardless of measures taken to minimize this risk. Bringing the colostomy through an extraperitoneal tunnel avoids the potential for obstruction of small bowel that is trapped in the lateral gutter, but the incidence of subsequent herniation is not altered appreciably.

Management of the pelvic peritoneal floor and the perineal wound is a point of controversy. The trend is toward closure of the perineal wound in layers. It is unnecessary to close the pelvic peritoneum, and a controlled trial showed that the perineum healed with fewer problems if this approach was used. On the other hand, postoperative radiation therapy may injure small bowel that is adherent in the pelvis, a more likely phenomenon in the early postoperative period if the pelvic floor is left open.

Completeness of excision of the levators is debatable. Complete excision of muscle to the bony side wall has the theoretical benefit of more radical extirpation of cancer-bearing tissue, but it makes primary closure of the perineal wound more difficult and is probably unnecessary.

FUTURE DIRECTIONS

Laparoscopic performance of the abdominal phase of APR has become a reality, and the future probably will see more surgeons adopting this approach, at least selectively. Palliative APR in a patient with distant metastases is an ideal indication for the laparoscopic procedure if the primary tumor is not too bulky.

Abdominoperineal resection (APR) was established as the preferred operation for cancer of the distal rectum by the work of Ernest Miles, first published in 1908.[1] Miles was convinced, from study of older perineal approaches, that the zone of upward spread could not be controlled by that route alone. He determined that surgical treatment of rectal cancer requires complete removal of the rectum and anus, part of the sigmoid colon and mesocolon with its contained vessels and nodes, the mesorectum, pelvic peritoneum adjacent to the rectum, and much of the ischiorectal fat and the levators.[1–3] Miles concluded that the only way to excise all of these structures was through a combined abdominal and perineal approach. The rationale of the operation is still valid today, and APR remains the standard of comparison for treatment of cancer of the distal rectum. This chapter describes conventional open APR; laparoscopic APR is a new procedure that is rapidly growing in popularity, and no doubt future discussions will emphasize the role of the laparoscopic approach.

ASSESSMENT AND PREPARATION

Assessment of the Patient

Assessment of operability depends on the characteristics of the tumor and the general condition of the patient.[2] Associated medical conditions are evaluated and treated. With today's anesthetic techniques and preoperative and postoperative care, it is most unusual for a patient to be categorically inoperable because of associated medical conditions. Ascites is a strong contraindication to APR because ascitic leak through the perineal wound may be troublesome or even fatal if it leads to peritonitis.

Assessment of the Tumor

Sphincter-preserving procedures are of course preferred over APR if the cancer is high enough for anastomosis or small enough for local excision. It is anatomically impossible to resect and anastomose a cancer with its distal edge lower than about 5 cm above the anal verge (3 cm above the dentate line). In practice, many midrectal cancers that are large, deeply invasive, or poorly differentiated cannot be dealt with by sphincter preservation; these judgments depend in part on other factors including the patient's habitus and preferences. Sometimes the final decision of APR versus sphincter preservation can be made only during the operation.

Digital rectal examination and rigid proctosigmoidoscopy are fundamental steps in the clinical assessment of rectal cancer.[2,4] Fixity on digital palpation is an unreliable sign on which to decide whether a tumor is unresectable.[2] Many patients are declared inoperable because their lesions are thought to be fixed, but in most of them it is possible to dissect the growth free.[2]

Palliative APR

Excision of the primary tumor is the most effective form of palliation of rectal adenocarcinoma.[5,6] Tenesmus is a distressing symptom, and prevention or relief of tenesmus is a goal worth pursuing even in the patient who has distant metastases or other evidence of incurability. Tenesmus is not relieved by fecal diversion and it is not reliably eliminated by radiation therapy, fulguration, or laser photocoagulation. Other symptoms of advanced rectal cancer include bloody mucoid rectal discharge, sacral and sciatic pain, and fistulas externally or into other organs.[2]

Preparation

Standard bowel preparation using cathartics and oral antibiotics is given. Intravenous antibiotics are used as for other colorectal resections. Intravenous fluids are given.

THE OPERATION

Anesthesia

Regional anesthesia alone is not recommended because patients must be tilted head down for at least part of the procedure, an uncomfortable position for an awake patient.

Positioning

Positioning of the patient depends on plans to perform APR in separate stages with a single operator or synchronously with two teams.[2] The synchronous technique requires a second experienced surgeon who is capable of performing the perineal dissection.[7]

If the two-stage approach is selected, the patient is supine for the abdominal part. The classic Miles procedure calls for a steep (15 to 20°) Trendelenburg position for the abdominal phase, but so steep a tilt requires the use of shoulder rests which carry the risk of brachial plexus injuries, and it is really unnecessary.[2] For the perineal phase, the patient is placed in either the lithotomy or the left lateral decubitus position. Lithotomy is easier in some ways. The surgeon is seated and one or two assistants stand on either side of the perineum. The lateral decubitus position is more cumbersome because the patient must be turned, but exposure of the anterior structures is superb. In a difficult patient with an extensive tumor on the anterior wall, the lateral decubitus position is advantageous.

For the synchronous procedure, the lower extremities are supported on Lloyd-Davies leg rests or Allen universal stirrups.[2,3] The sacrum is protected on a padded rest. The thighs should be separated widely enough for the surgeon and an assistant to gain access.[2]

Preparation

A Foley catheter is placed into the bladder in the operating room after the patient is anesthetized unless there is some need for it earlier. The tumor should be examined once again with the patient anesthetized; occasionally, the findings will differ from the preoperative evaluation and a decision will be made to alter the operative plan to sphincter-preservation or transanal excision. The rectum is irrigated to remove gross feces from the distal bowel; saline is sufficient, although some surgeons use a cancerocidal solution for this purpose. The anus is closed with a purse-string suture of heavy material if APR is a certainty; two sutures, one within the other, are advisable.

Incision

Various incisions have been suggested for performance of APR.[2] Requirements are adequate exposure of the lower abdomen and pelvis and preservation of the left midabdominal wall for placement of a colostomy. A midline wound is preferred for its simplicity, distance from the colostomy, relatively bloodless planes, and flexibility to deal with unexpected findings.

Exploration of the Abdomen

The abdomen is explored with special attention to possible hepatic metastases, periaortic node involvement, and peritoneal and omental implants. The pelvis is palpated to determine resectability. Lesions at the anterior pelvic peritoneal reflection or above may be palpable, and extension into the vagina, uterus, or male urogenital structures may be apparent. The tumor may have invaded through the rectal wall to present on the surface of the rectum or the pelvic peritoneum.

Fixation of the rectal tumor is determined by palpation. If the tumor can be moved at all before the dissection is begun, it can usually be excised. Sometimes it is necessary to begin the dissection before resectability can be assessed.[2] It should be possible to determine whether the anterior structures (uterus especially) must be resected *en bloc* to effect cure. If the tumor is unresectable, the only recourse is usually sigmoid colostomy and postoperative radiation therapy (if maximal irradiation has not been given previously) followed by another attempt to resect the tumor.

Mobilization of the Sigmoid and Mesosigmoid

The sigmoid colon and mesocolon are retracted out of the abdomen to the right as much as possible to expose the lateral attachments for division. This step and most others throughout the operation can be performed with scissors or electrocautery. No part of the procedure so clearly separates the experienced from the neophyte surgeon than the simple maneuver to divide the bloodless congenital attachments of appendices epiploica, the sigmoid colon, and the mesocolon from the lateral and posterior parietal peritoneum. If the proper plane is not followed, the appendices are injured and the small vessels supplying the colon are interrupted, the mesocolon is entered and the sigmoidal vessels are torn, or the posterior parietal peritoneum is incised in the incorrect place. If the retroperitoneum is entered too far laterally, the gonadal vessels are encountered and usually injured. Further, improper dissection in the retroperitoneal plane brings one to the ureter from the lateral direction. It is much better if the colon and mesocolon are mobilized off the intact posterior parietal peritoneum so the ureter can be approached from the medial side.

With the colon and mesocolon retracted up and to the patient's right, the posterior parietal peritoneum is incised at the base of the mesocolon on the left, *medial* to the ureter. The ureter is easily seen in most instances. The peritoneal incision is carried longitudinally, parallel to the course of the ureter, for a distance of 10 cm or so, and the ureter is swept laterally to avoid injury during subsequent vascular ligation.[2] It is unnecessary to mobilize the ureter circumferentially in most patients; therefore the risk of postoperative ureteral ischemia, although very low, can be avoided entirely. The left common iliac artery and the large and impressive left common iliac vein are exposed to view.

The posterior parietal peritoneum at the base of the mesosigmoid on the right is now incised, with the small bowel retracted out of the way and the sigmoid held firmly upward and to the left to place the mesosigmoid on tension. This incision exposes the aorta and the right common iliac artery. The previous dissection plane on the left is joined by dissection posterior to the superior hemorrhoidal or inferior mesenteric vessels. Care should be taken to avoid injury to the preaortic sympathetic nerves; they should be left alone, closely adherent to the aorta.[2,8,9] The incision is carried cephalad toward the duodenum a variable distance, depending on the planned level of ligation of vessels.

Ligation of Vessels

The level at which vessels should be ligated during performance of APR is controversial. Miles ligated at the aortic bifurcation, just below the origin of the left colic or first sigmoid artery.[2] Subsequent authors recommended ligation at the origin of the inferior mesenteric artery to remove the few nodes that remain with ligation more distally.[2,6,8] Data are consistent, however, that the level of ligation does not influence survival rates.[2,7,10,11] Presumably, if cancer has spread to the nodes at the origin of the inferior mesenter artery, surgical cure is unlikely. Most surgeons today ligate the artery and adjacent vein just distal to the origin of the left colic artery.

Division of Mesocolon and Colon

The mesocolon is divided radially to the planned point of transection of the colon. The colon may be transected now or after the pelvic dissection has been completed. The colon is most conveniently divided with the linear stapling device that applies parallel rows of staples and cuts between them.

Pelvic Dissection

Injury to the sympathetic nerves of the superior hypogastric plexus (presacral nerve) should be avoided. The plexus lies at the level of the aortic bufurcation and divides into the left and right hypogastric nerves, which extend into the pelvis.[2,8,9]

The technique of posterior dissection has changed. In the classic method, the presacral connective tissue was incised for a short distance, the right hand was inserted, and the rectum was pulled forward and upward as the mesorectum was separated from the endopelvic fascia by blunt dissection, creating a characteristic suction sound.[2,3] This technique is unnecessarily crude, consisting as it does of tearing the soft tissues in what is hoped will be the proper plane. The uncontrolled trauma sometimes results in bleeding from the presacral veins, and the completeness of posterior excision of node-bearing tissue is unpredictable. In my view, this technique should be abandoned except in the most difficult situation, e.g., an obese male, where the surgeon has limited visibility of the posterior pelvis. Instead, one can pull the rectum forward with a deep pelvic retractor and cut the loose areolar tissue between the intact mesorectum and the intact endopelvic fascia using electrocautery or scissors under direct vision. This dissection is bloodless if electrocautery is used to coagulate the few tiny vessels in the areolar tissue. Posterior dissection is carried down to the surface of the levators.

The pelvic peritoneum is incised bilaterally about 1 cm medial to the ureters. Flaps of peritoneum are created for subsequent closure of the peritoneal floor. The anterior dissection begins by connecting the lateral incisions in the midline. It is important to include a flap of about 2 cm of peritoneum from the surface of the bladder or vagina with the specimen, and then the proper anatomic plane is struck unless the anterior organs are to be removed as well. In men, the seminal vesicles are denuded and the fascia of Denonvilliers is included with the rectum down to the base of the prostate, where it is incised.[2] In women, care must be taken to avoid injury to the vagina.

The lateral dissection aims to remove completely the node-bearing tissue up to the pelvic side wall but not external to the parietal pelvic fascia. Some surgeons prefer sharp dissection to ensure complete excision of potential lymph node–bearing tissue.[2] The lateral ligaments are divided entirely from the abdominal side in most cases, although it is possible to do it from below.[2] The pelvis should be devoid of lateral soft tissue when this dissection is complete. The extent of the pelvic dissection is delineated in Figs. 63-1, 63-2, and 63-3.

Extended Pelvic Lymphadenectomy

Many attempts have been made to improve local eradication of rectal cancer by extended lymphadenectomy in which the internal iliac lymph nodes are excised.[2] These nodes lie external to the parietal pelvic fascia and are not removed during standard APR.[2] Japanese surgeons have reported improved results with extended lateral dissection of lymph nodes, and it is claimed that this goal has been achieved without undue urinary or sexual dysfunction.[12–14] Experience reported from Europe and North America, however, is nearly unanimous in concluding that the additional operating time, blood loss, and potential for postoperative sexual and bladder dysfunction is not worth the minimal potential gain from excision of these

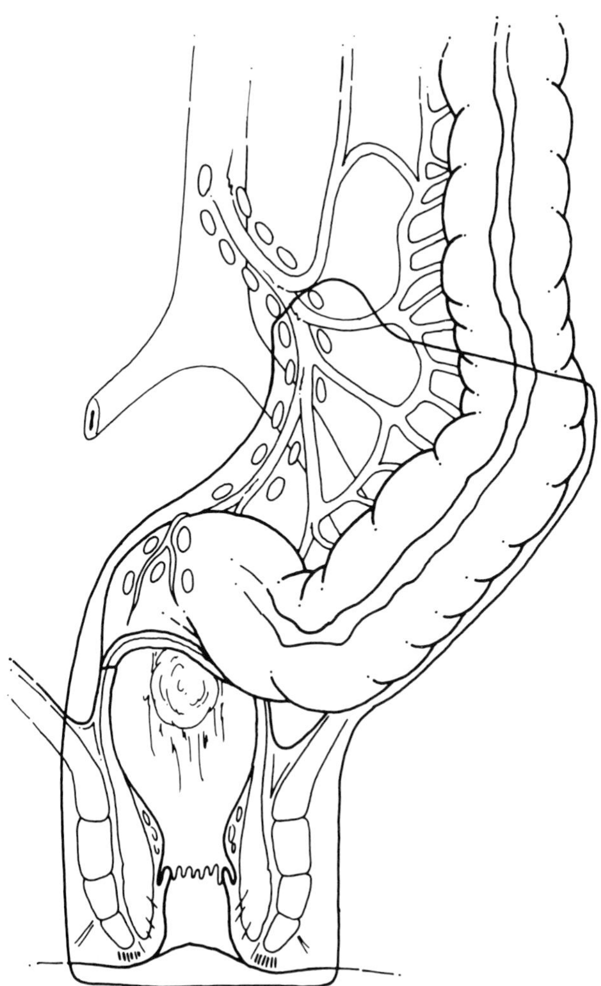

FIG. 63-1. Extent of the resection. (From Gordon PH: "Malignant neoplasms of the rectum," in Gordon PH, Nivatvongs S (eds.): *Principles and Practice of Surgery for the Colon, Rectum, and Anus*. St. Louis, Quality Medical Publishing, 1992, p. 598. Reproduced by permission.)

nodes.[2,15,16] In this view, if the internal iliac nodes are involved, the lesion has progressed too far for cure by surgical means, and adjuvant treatment must be relied upon to complete the task.[2]

Closure of the Pelvic Peritoneal Floor

Some surgeons do not close the pelvic peritoneum routinely.[2] In a few patients, it is impossible to close this layer because of previous pelvic surgery or irradiation. With the pelvic peritoneal floor open, the small bowel falls into the pelvis, but intestinal obstruction is probably no more frequent with this technique.[7] If postoperative radiation therapy is likely, the pelvic peritoneal floor probably should be closed. If there is insufficient peritoneum for this purpose, the omentum can be used to create a floor or polyglycolic acid mesh can be used.[17]

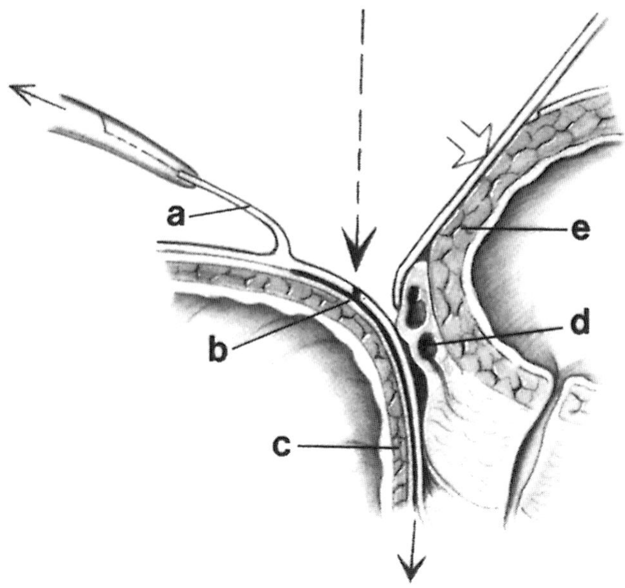

FIG. 63-2. Anterior dissection in the male. (From Goligher J: *Surgery of the Anus, Rectum, and Colon. 5th ed.* London, Bailliere, Tindall, 1984, p. 632. Reproduced by permission.)

Colostomy

The colostomy site should be marked preoperatively by the surgeon or enterostomal therapist. The proposed incision, natural skin folds, bony prominences, and scars should be avoided. The stoma is best placed below the belt line in most patients, although occasionally a higher site is better. The colostomy should pass through the rectus abdominis muscle rather than

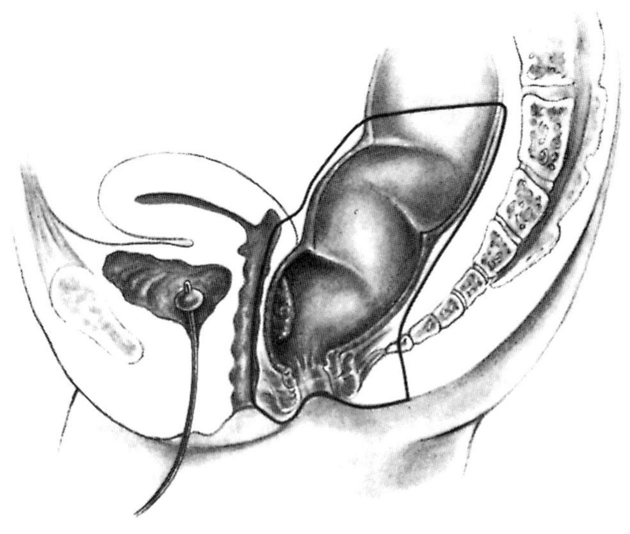

FIG. 63-3. Anterior dissection in women, taking the posterior wall of the vagina and leaving the uterus. (From Corman ML: *Colon and Rectal Surgery, 2d ed.* Philadelphia, Lippincott, 1989, p. 498. Reproduced by permission.)

the oblique muscles; large paracolostomy hernias typically develop when the stoma is placed too far laterally.

It is important to make sure that the layers of the abdominal wall are properly aligned as the aperture is made; in some instances, it is a good plan to make the aperture down to the level of the peritoneum before incising the abdomen. The circular skin opening should be about 2.5 cm in diameter. It is unnecessary to excise subcutaneous fat. The anterior rectus sheath is incised longitudinally for about 3.5 cm, depending on the caliber of the colon and the thickness of the mesocolon. The fascia may be incised laterally for a short distance, but incision medially should be avoided. The rectus muscle is split, and the peritoneum is then incised longitudinally.

The conventional sigmoid colostomy is made by bringing the colon straight through the abdominal wall. That leaves a space lateral to the colon through which small bowel can herniate and obstruct. This space should be closed.[18] Alternatively, the colostomy can be placed extraperitoneally.[2] The main advantage is complete obliteration of the lateral space. Hopes that extraperitoneal colostomy would result in fewer paracolostomy hernias have not been realized.[2] The peritoneum is tightly adherent to the fascia at the lateral border of the rectus, and creation of the extraperitoneal tunnel goes easily until this point is reached. Often the peritoneum is torn at this level and must be repaired with sutures. If the extraperitoneal method is used, the pelvic peritoneum should not be closed until the colon is brought through the tunnel.[2] The advantages of extraperitoneal colostomy do not seem to justify the additional time and effort.

Although protrusion above the skin level is essential for an ileostomy, it is not necessary with a colostomy. The stoma is matured with interrupted sutures of absorbable material after the abdominal incision is closed.

Perineal Phase

An elliptical incision encompassing the anus is made with scalpel or electrocautery. A shield-shaped incision recommended by some surgeons invariably leaves a dog ear anteriorly when the perineal skin is closed.[2,7] The incision is carried through the ischiorectal fat, including much but usually not all of this tissue with the specimen. Large rake retractors are used to expose the levators. A self-retaining perineal retractor of the St. Mark's Hospital pattern is useful.

The anococcygeal raphe is incised just anterior to the coccyx. Amputation of the coccyx is unnecessary in the routine case.[2] With the anus retracted forward, the white Waldeyer's fascia is exposed and incised transversely. The pelvic dissection space is thus entered, and the surgeon can insert one or two fingers to define the levators for division with electrocautery. Vessels in the muscle must be controlled during this step.

When the levators have been divided, the specimen can be delivered through the posterior part of the perineal wound, leaving only the anterior attachments. The transverse perinei muscles are separated from the external anal sphincter, and the puborectalis and pubococcygeus muscles are divided. Anterior dissection is facilitated by placing a finger between the rectum and the anterior structures to help define the plane. The tissue that tethers the rectum to the vagina or to the prostate and membranous urethra is incised carefully to avoid entry into the rectum or injury to the urogenital structures. The specimen is then removed.

The Perineal Wound

There are several methods of handling the perineal wound.[19] If the pelvic peritoneal floor is closed, the perineal wound can be sutured in layers with drainage or the perineal wound can be packed open. Alterna-

Table 63-1
Results of Controlled Trial of Management of Perineal Wound

	Method 1[a]	*Method 2*[b]	*Method 3*[c]	*p value*
No. of patients	34	34	34	—
Primary healing	—	18 (53%)	29 (85%)	<.01
Perineal infection	5 (15%)	16 (47%)	5 (15%)	<.001 method 2 vs. 1 or 3
Mean length of stay (days)	36	24	15	—

[a]Method 1: Close pelvic peritoneal floor, pack perineum open.
[b]Method 2: Close pelvic peritoneal floor, close perineum with drainage.
[c]Method 3: Leave pelvic peritoneal floor open, close perineum with drainage.
SOURCE: Campos et al.[19] With permission.

tively, the pelvic peritoneal floor can be left open and the perineal wound closed. The trend is definitely toward primary closure of the perineal wound whenever possible, because delayed healing is more common when wounds are left open (Table 63-1). If the pelvic peritoneal floor and the perineum are closed, the pelvic space must be drained with one or two suction drains. If bacterial contamination is heavy, the perineal wound is left open or partially closed with drainage.

Resection of Other Viscera

Resection of adherent small intestine adds little to the scope of APR. Anterior distal rectal cancers often call for excision of the posterior vaginal wall so as to obtain an adequate margin. Hysterectomy in continuity with rectal excision is also fairly routine. Adherence to the prostate or seminal vesicles may be dealt with by shaving off a portion of the prostate to be included with the rectal specimen.[2] Involvement of ureters is managed by excision of ureter with repair or replantation as needed. If the tumor invades into the prostate or base of the bladder, total cystoprostatectomy in continuity with the rectal excision may be appropriate if the patient's outlook warrants it.[2] The ureters are implanted into an ileal conduit in most cases. Total pelvic exenteration and combined resections including the sacrum are discussed in other chapters.

POSTOPERATIVE CARE

A few issues are specific for postoperative care following APR. One is the question of ambulation. In the past, patients were kept at bed rest for several days in the belief that herniation of the small bowel through the pelvic floor would be less likely by avoidance of erect posture. This concern seems unjustified, and patients today are allowed to walk a few steps the day after APR if they are hemodynamically stable. If a pelvic floor hernia is going to occur, it will do so in the supine patient as readily as in the ambulatory one. Moreover, it is impossible to keep a patient in bed until the risk of hernia has entirely passed.

The bladder catheter is kept in for at least 5 days postoperatively, mainly because some patients have difficulty voiding after APR (see below). Also, distension of the bladder in a patient who cannot void might have some harmful effect on integrity of the pelvic peritoneal floor if it was closed.

Colostomy care and training of the patient is an essential aspect of postoperative care in these patients. We teach patients how to irrigate the colostomy, and, when at home, patients make their own decisions regarding continuation of the practice.

COMPLICATIONS

This discussion is limited to complications that are rather specific to APR or other forms of radical excision of the rectum. The overall complication rate is 35 percent in this predominantly elderly patient population, but most of the complications (e.g., atelectasis or postoperative urinary retention) are relatively minor.[3,6,18,20]

Intraoperative Complications (Table 63-2)

Hemorrhage

Intraoperative hemorrhage most commonly arises from injury to the presacral veins. In a personal series, this problem developed in 3 percent of patients.[18] Bulky tumors, previous radiation therapy, narrow pelvis, and obesity are patient factors that make this complication more likely. Separation of the rectum from the sacrum under direct vision is always preferable to blunt dissection. If presacral veins are torn, bleeding may stop with pressure. Some of these thin-walled veins can be controlled with cautery or fine suture ligatures. If the vessel is torn where it emerges from the bone, cautery and suture may not be effective. Special metal tacks are available for the purpose of controlling these vessels, but we have never found it necessary to use them. The last resort would be to pack the pelvis and return to the operating room to remove the pack 2 to 3 days later.

Bleeding from hypogastric veins or the left common iliac vein is much less common, but it can be torrential and pose a grave threat to survival of the patient. Direct suture control is the only solution.

Ureteral or Urethral Injury

Injury to the left ureter requires immediate repair. If the ureter has been divided cleanly, end-to-end repair with an indwelling stent is sufficient. If the ureter has been devascularized for a distance or if the injury is distal, special techniques are required.[21] The urethra is vulnerable to injury during the anterior perineal dissection, but fortunately injury occurs very seldom.[18] The injured urethra should be repaired primarily and a

Table 63-2
Intraoperative Complications of Abdominoperineal Resection

Complication	*Incidence, %*	*References*
Hemorrhage	3	18
Ureteral injury	0.5	2,7,18
Urethral injury	<0.5	2,3,7,18
Vaginal injury	2	18
Rectal perforation	3	18

suprapubic cystostomy tube placed. Urethral stricture is a late consequence.[7]

Perforation of the Rectum

The rectum can be torn during the posterior pelvic dissection or during the perineal phase. The greatest concern is contamination of the field by malignant cells; bacterial contamination is also problematic but less serious. In the event of entry into the rectal lumen, the field should be irrigated thoroughly with water and/or a cancerocidal agent such as dilute povidone-iodine.

Injury to the Vagina

The thin vagina is vulnerable to injury during the anterior pelvic dissection and during the anterior portion of the perineal dissection. In either situation, direct repair with absorbable sutures usually results in healing. If the posterior vaginal wall must be excised with the rectum, the vagina is reconstructed, and usually it heals well. Heavily irradiated tissues, of course, heal less well.

Early Postoperative Complications

Small Bowel Obstruction

Reoperation for small bowel obstruction from all mechanisms is required in the early postoperative period in about 5 percent of patients.[18] Abdominoperineal resection carries the risk of intestinal obstruction by two special mechanisms: (1) Herniation of the small bowel through the paracolic gutter lateral to the colostomy causes obstruction in about 7 percent of patients, about equally divided between the immediate postoperative period and the later period,[18] and (2) herniation through the pelvic peritoneal floor. The latter complication is rare, but when it occurs the risk of strangulation is significant.[2] In the usual course of events, postoperative small bowel obstruction is not recognized immediately, and operation is delayed.

Urinary Tract Complications

Bladder dysfunction and/or urinary tract infection (usually cystitis) are the most common complications of APR; they occur in up to 40 percent of patients.[2,7,18,22–24] Some patients, especially elderly men, have bladder outlet obstruction as a preexisting problem, and the operation just brings the prostatic enlargement to light. Posterior displacement of the bladder is another contributory factor.[23] Weakness and recumbency of the elderly postoperative patient and inability to relax the pelvic floor may play a role as well. The most important factor, however, is denervation of the bladder. If the patient cannot void upon initial removal of the catheter, it is reinserted and another attempt made in a day or two. Urologic consultation should be obtained if difficulty persists. Most patients are able to void satisfactorily eventually, although a variable number of days or even weeks may be needed to achieve recovery.

Colostomy Complications

Bleeding from the colostomy seldom poses any serious problem. Troublesome bleeding from the cut edge of bowel can be controlled by suture. Bleeding from the mesocolon from a tear or slipped ligature may require return to the operating room for control.

Necrosis of the colostomy is a consequence of dividing too much mesocolic blood supply or, occasionally, bringing the colon through too tight an abdominal wall aperture. Extensive loss of viability requires reoperation.

Retraction of the colostomy is usually associated with necrosis, but sometimes it results simply from too much tension. If the stoma retracts for most of its circumference, it is best to refashion the colostomy.

Paracolostomy abscess is surprisingly uncommon, given the inevitable bacterial contamination of the soft tissues adjacent to the stoma. Most abscesses can be drained by separating the stoma from the skin with a hemostat, but occasionally a separate incision is needed.

Other Complications

Fistulas from vagina, bladder, or urethra to the perineal wound may result from intraoperative injury to these structures.

Late Postoperative Complications

Perineal Wound Problems

Perineal wound complications occur in about 15 percent of patients who undergo APR for rectal cancer.[18,19] *Perineal sinus* is an unhealed wound. Definitions vary, but certainly a perineal wound that remains unhealed 6 months after APR qualifies as a perineal sinus. The pelvic space after APR is bounded by bone posteriorly and laterally; the only soft tissues available to obliterate the space are the small bowel above and the urogenital structures anteriorly. The pelvic space after APR closes mainly by descent of the pelvic peritoneal floor. Posterior shift of the vagina and uterus are of some help in women, but the urogenital structures do not contribute much in men. The perineal wound does not "granulate in," as surgeons once said, because if the pelvic space fills with granulation tissue, the patient has a perineal sinus.

Once a sinus forms, it cannot heal without intervention. Cautery with silver nitrate sticks may suffice for very superficial sinuses, and curettage to freshen the edges may work for larger ones. Very large or deep sinuses require more radical steps. Coccygectomy may help perineal soft tissues collapse into the space. Alternatively, gracilis or gluteus muscle flaps can be mobilized into the cavity. Induration of the perineal tissues in heavily irradiated patients presents a formidable challenge. Indeed, an irradiated patient with indurated perineal tissues may be better served by placement of muscle flaps into the perineal wound at the time of the APR rather than waiting for a large, infected, painful, odorous wound that will be difficult to treat secondarily.

Perineal hernia is uncommon after APR, perhaps occurring in 1 percent or so. It is more frequent if the levators are excised widely. Patients typically complain of heaviness in the perineum and a sensation of sitting on a mass. Eventually the hernia will be palpable to the patient and the examining surgeon. Small hernias do not require repair. Large ones are repaired from the abdominal side with placement of prosthetic mesh deep in the pelvis. Combined repair from above and below has been described.[2]

Colostomy Complications

Stenosis of a colostomy is unusual today because colostomies are matured primarily. It is unnecessary to digitally dilate a normally functioning colostomy, as had once been the routine. Simple revision of the stoma at the skin level can be done under local anesthesia.

Paracolostomy hernia is very common, possibly inevitable, after APR.[2] Small hernias should be left alone. A large, troublesome hernia may need revision, usually by transplanting the stoma to a new site, but the hernia nearly always recurs in the new site. Repair of a paracolostomy hernia with prosthetic mesh, leaving the stoma in its original location, has been disappointing in our experience.

Prolapse is another uncommon complication of an end sigmoid colostomy. It is revised by amputation of redundant colon through the colostomy site.

Sexual Dysfunction

Sexual dysfunction in men after APR is usually neurogenic, but advanced age and psychological factors may play a role as well.[9] The overall incidence of these complications ranges widely, from 25 to 100 percent of men.[2,7,9] Impotence, inability to achieve or sustain an erection, is the consequence of parasympathetic nerve injury.[9] Total impotence occurs in 15 to 40 percent of men after APR in recent reports.[7] Erection without ejaculation is the result of sympathetic nerve injury; the incidence of this problem varies from 3 to 39 percent.[7] Urologists today have a wide range of investigative and therapeutic options for these men, and many are returned to satisfactory function.[9]

Table 63-3
Mortality Rates of Abdominoperineal Resection since 1980

Author	*Year*	*No. of patients*	*Deaths*	*Mortality, %*
Bokey et al.[20]	1990	189	6	3.1
Cunsolo et al.[27]	1989	167	0	0
Elliott et al.[28]	1984	196	4	2.0
Heberer et al.[29]	1987	317	23	7.3
Rosen et al.[25]	1982	230	4	1.7
Rothenberger and Wong[7]	1992	125	4	2.6
Schrock[18]	1993	125	1	0.8
Tagliacozzo and Accordino[26]	1992	44	3	6.8

Sexual dysfunction in women may result from psychological problems related to altered body image. Dyspareunia, presumably from pelvic fibrosis, is reported by as many as 50 percent of women after APR.[24]

Mortality Rates

The operative mortality of APR in Miles's original report was 42 percent.[1] During the 1940s and 1950s, the mortality rate was brought below 10 percent, and reports from the next two decades consistently had a mortality rate of less than 5 percent.[2,25] Today, the operative mortality rate for APR ranges from 0 percent to 7.3 percent, with the majority of contemporary series reporting mortality rates of 2 to 3 percent[2,7,18,20,25–29] (Table 63-3). Most deaths are from cardiovascular complications and pulmonary embolus. When surgery is done by experienced hands, surgical complications leading to death are increasingly uncommon.

REFERENCES

1. Miles WE: A method of performing abdominoperineal excision for carcinoma of the rectum and of the terminal portion of the pelvic colon. *Lancet* 2:1812–1813, 1908.
2. Goligher JC: *Surgery of the Anus, Rectum and Colon,* 4th ed. London, Bailliere, Tindall and Cassell, 1993, pp 590–779.
3. Corman ML: *Colon and Rectal Surgery,* 2d ed. Philadelphia, Lippincott, 1989, pp 470–578.
4. Durdey P, Williams NS: Pre-operative evaluation of patients with low rectal carcinoma. *World J Surg* 16:430–436, 1992.
5. Modlin J, Walker SJ: Palliative resections in cancer of the colon and rectum. *Cancer* 2:767–776, 1949.
6. Gordon PH, Nivatvongs S: *Principles and Practice of Surgery for the Colon, Rectum, and Anus.* St Louis, Quality Medical Publishing, 1992, pp 596–653.
7. Rothenberger DA, Wong WD: Abdominoperineal resection for adenocarcinoma of the low rectum. *World J Surg* 16:478–485, 1992.
8. Hughes ESR: Treatment of carcinoma of the rectum. *Curr Probl Surg* November 1965. Year Book, pp. 3–32.

9. Aboseif SR, Marzel KE, Lue TF: Sexual dysfunction after rectal surgery. *Persp Colon Rectal Surg* 3:157–172, 1990.
10. Pezim ME, Nicholls RJ: Survival after high or low ligation of the inferior mesenteric artery during curative surgery for rectal cancer. *Ann Surg* 200:729–733, 1984.
11. Bland KI, Polk HC: Therapeutic measures applied for the curative and palliative control of colorectal carcinoma. *Surg Ann* 15:123–161, 1983.
12. Hojo K, Sawada T, Moriya Y: An analysis of survival and voiding, sexual function after wide iliopelvic lymphadenectomy in patients with carcinoma of the rectum, compared with conventional lymphadenectomy. *Dis Colon Rectum* 32:128–133, 1989.
13. Koyama Y, Moriya Y, Hojo K: Effects of extended systemic lymphadenectomy for adenocarcinoma of the rectum: Significant improvement of survival rate and decrease of local recurrence. *Jpn J Clin Oncol* 14:623–632, 1984.
14. Hojo K, Vernava AM III, Sugihara K, et al: Preservation of urine voiding and sexual function after rectal cancer surgery. *Dis Colon Rectum* 34:532–539, 1991.
15. Enker WE, Laffer UT, Block GE: Enhanced survival of patients with colon and rectal cancer is based upon wide anatomic resection. *Ann Surg* 190:350–360, 1979.
16. Wolff BG: Lateral margins of resection in adenocarcinoma of the rectum. *World J Surg* 16:467–469, 1992.
17. Devereux DF: The PGA sling procedure for prevention of radiation damage to the small bowel. *Persp Colon Rectal Surg* 1:68–81, 1988.
18. Schrock TR: Unpublished data.
19. Campos RR, Ayllon JG, Paricio PP: Management of the perineal wound following abdominoperineal resection: Prospective study of three methods. *Br J Surg* 79:29–31, 1992.
20. Bokey EL, Chapuis PH, Hughes WJ: Morbidity, mortality and survival following resection for carcinoma of the rectum at Concord Hospital. *Aust N Z J Surg* 60:253–259, 1990.
21. Presti JC Jr, Carroll PR: Intraoperative management of the injured ureter. *Persp Colon Rectal Surg* 1:98–106, 1988.
22. Cunsolo A, Bragaglia RB, Manara G, et al: Urogenital dysfunction after abdominoperineal resection for carcinoma of the rectum. *Dis Colon Rectum* 33:918–922, 1990.
23. Watson PC, Williams I: The urological complications of excision of the rectum. *Br J Surg* 40:19–28, 1952.
24. Cunsolo A, Bragaglia RB, Manara G: Urogenital dysfunction after abdominoperineal resection for carcinoma of the rectum. *Dis Colon Rectum* 33:918–922, 1990.
25. Rosen L, Veidenheimer MC, Coller JA: Mortality, morbidity, and patterns of recurrence after abdominoperineal resection for cancer of the rectum. *Dis Colon Rectum* 25:202–208, 1982.
26. Tagliacozzo S, Accordino M: Pelvic recurrence after surgical treatment of rectal and sigmoid cancer: A prospective clinical trial on 274 patients. *Int J Colorect Dis* 7:135–140, 1992.
27. Cunsolo A, Bragaglia RB, Petrucci C: Survival and complications after radical surgery for carcinoma of the rectum. *J Surg Oncol* 41:27–32, 1989.
28. Elliott MS, Steven DM, Terblanche J: Abdominoperineal resection of the rectum for carcinoma at Groote Schuur Hospital, Cape Town, 1971–1982. *S Afr Med J* 65:411–413, 1984.
29. Heberer C, Denecke H, Demmel N: Local procedures in the management of rectal cancer. *World J Surg* 11:499–503, 1987.

CHAPTER 64

Treatment Results with Radical Surgery

Richard L. Grotz
John H. Pemberton
Leonard L. Gunderson

HIGHLIGHTS

While surgery is the optimal modality for cure of rectal cancer, randomized trials have demonstrated that the addition of irradiation and chemotherapy improves disease control and survival in high-risk patients. The principal goal of surgery is complete removal of the tumor and adjacent nodes, including perhaps organs to which tumor is adherent and pelvic lymph nodes, with as wide a margin as is technically feasible, is safe, and will result in a satisfactory quality of life. The definitive surgical treatment for rectal cancer has not been established conclusively due to patient variability and, often, unpredictable tumor biology. However, operations for midrectal cancer which spare the anal sphincter appear comparable to abdominoperineal resection (APR) in terms of local control and survival.

CONTROVERSIES

Abdominoperineal resection is still a viable operation for patients with rectal cancer; it has been all but supplanted, however, by sphincter-preserving operations which eradicate the tumor without leaving the patient with a permanent colostomy. Survival and local regional control after sphincter-saving procedures have been compared to the traditional standard of APR with results that are controversial. This chapter will focus on the results of *standard* surgical options for cancer of the rectum.

FUTURE DIRECTIONS

The most important measures of success, 5- and 10-year survivals following curative resection of rectal carcinoma, have not been altered significantly since the introduction of anterior resection in the 1940s by Dixon.[1] Only small gains have been made by minimizing perioperative morbidity and mortality. Hopes for improving patient survival therefore lie mostly in the areas of prevention and earlier diagnosis of rectal cancer and improved perioperative adjuvant therapy.

Perhaps the method of rectal resection which may have the most impact in the future is laparoscopy. Laparoscopy has long been successfully used for gynecologic pelvic disorders and, more recently, has been advocated for appendicitis and pelvic lymph node biopsy for prostatic malignancies. Laparoscopy assisted surgery is certainly possible in patients with benign colorectal disorders. Currently, laparoscopic colon surgery requires a minilaparotomy or placement of large cannulas to remove the specimen and complete the anastomosis. In procedures involving the rectosigmoid, the distal bowel is not easily mobilized to the anterior abdominal wall for the purpose of performing an anastomosis. Alternatively, a transanal stapling device may facilitate restoration of intestinal continuity.

A legitimate and important question is whether a laparoscopic approach to rectal cancer compromises local recurrence and survival by virtue of inadequate margins of resection. In properly selected patients, the technique of perirectal and mesorectal dissection and proximal lymphovascular pedicle ligation is clearly feasible laparoscopically. Preliminary data (J. R. Monson, personal communication) suggest that the en bloc resection achieved during laparoscopic resection is comparable to that achieved by conventional excision. These questions will be resolved only when sufficient experience has been gained with laparoscopic colorectal surgery, so that results can be compared with matched-pair analyses of patients treated by standard resection. Prospective randomized trials comparing laparoscopic and standard resection may be indicated (although clearly difficult to initiate) if pilot studies show acceptable if not improved patient tolerance with laparoscopic methods and acceptable local control.

Relapse of tumor locally or systemically following curative resection of rectal cancer is an ominous event. The diagnostic means and manner of measuring and reporting data affect the rates of relapse. The incidence of relapse of tumor at all sites is underestimated by clinical studies which report only the incidence of initial failure by site (actually initially diagnosed failure), since asymptomatic lesions often escape early detection. Because of the selective nature of reoperating for recurrent cancer, and the inability of the surgeon to detect all sites of disease, exploratory laparotomy will also underestimate the amount and distribution of both locally recurrent and metastatic tumor. The drawback of an autopsy series is that initially localized failures may disseminate, thus reflecting the end stage of tumor relapse rather than the initial site of failure. Generally, autopsy and reexploration studies show higher rates of relapse than do clinical studies with regard to tumor bed and nodal and peritoneal sites. Identification of sites of failure are most accurate if a combination of clinical, radiographic, and surgical or autopsy methods are utilized.

The exact incidence of local tumor recurrence is thus difficult to determine accurately. Between 45 and 74 percent of local recurrences manifest themselves within the first year postoperatively and 67 to 95 percent by the end of the second year.[2–6] In fact, many cases of local recurrence are likely to be residual tumor from the "curative" operation. Moreover, residual tumor deposits may escape detection for long periods of time due to the limited sensitivity of clinical detection of recurrent disease.

Carlsson et al.[7] compared relapse rates in two separate patient groups undergoing curative rectal excision. In the group with 5-year follow-up, total and local failure rates were 39 and 24 percent, respectively. After 18 years, total and local failure rates increased to 54 and 38 percent, respectively. A second study, using primarily autopsies for detection of relapse, found a 13 percent relapse rate at 17 years in patients with no clinical evidence of disease at 10 years.[8] Thus, long-term follow-up will identify additional patients with recurrent rectal cancer previously thought to have been cured.

In general, presence of regional lymph node metastases and the depth of intramural and extramural invasion are the principal risk factors for relapse.[2,4,9–19] The incidence of local failure by Dukes stage of disease following resection of a malignant rectal tumor is quite variable (Table 64-1).

Gunderson et al.[20] noted that local recurrence rates were associated with both the degree of extramural spread and lymph node involvement. For example, local failure in patients with involved nodes but with tumors confined to the rectal wall varies from 20 to 40 percent by series, compared to 20 to 35 percent for those tumors with extension beyond the wall with negative nodes (Table 64-2). Patients with both lymph nodal involvement *and* extension through the bowel wall had a risk of local recurrence between 30 and 65 percent in clinical series and up to 70 percent in a reoperation series. Furthermore, the degree of extraluminal extension (modified Astler-Coller B_3 versus B_2) correlated directly with an increased local recurrence rate.

Mossa et al.,[21] reporting on 152 patients who underwent APR for rectal and rectosigmoid carcinoma, found depth of bowel wall penetration, age below 60 years, and lymph node involvement to be prognostic

Table 64-1
Local Alone or Component of Local Recurrence Rates and Dukes Stage following Low Anterior or Abdominoperineal Resection

		Dukes Stage		
Author	*N*	*A, %*	*B, %*	*C, %*
Patel et al.[96]	435	13	17	37
Rich et al.[97]	142	8	31	50
Pilipshen et al.[37]	412	14	30	40

Table 64-2
Extent of Disease versus Incidence of Pelvic Failure after "Curative Resection" with No Adjuvant Therapy[a]

Astler-Coller Stage[b]	*Ref. 28*		*Ref. 98*		*Ref. 97*		*Ref. 99*		*Ref. 100*		*Ref. 22*		*Modified Astler-Coller Stage*[b]
	No.[c]	*(%)*	*No.*	*(%)*	*No.*	*(%)*	*No.*	*(%)*	*No.*	*(%)*	*No.*	*(%)*	
Within Wall													
A	0/14	—	0/1	—	0/3	—	—	—	2/12	(17)	—	—	A
B_1	5/23	(22)	6/42	(14)	3/36	(8)	149	(3)	0/21	(0)			B_1
C_1	9/24	(38)	1/5	—	2/4	—	12	(32)	2/7	(29)	4/17	(24)	C_1
Beyond Wall													
B_2 $(+B_3)$[b]	10/45	(22)	13/37	(35)	10/44	(23)	198	(15)	6/38	(16)	—	—	B_2
					8/15	(53)	11	(31)	1/5	—	—	—	B_3
C_2 $(+C_3)$[b]	11/29	(38)	24/37	(65)	16/34	(47)	92	(28)	14/38	(37)	28/40	(70)	C_2
					4/6	(67)	34	(62)	1/2	—	—	—	C_3

[a]All percentages are of total group at risk.

[b]Represents number at risk.

[c]Represents number of local failures/number at risk.

SOURCE: From Gunderson LL: Colorectal cancer, in Perez CA, Brady LW (eds): *Principles and Practice of Radiation*. New York, Raven Press, 1987, p 816. Reproduced by permission of the publisher.

factors for local recurrence. Furthermore, low rectal lesions were associated with a 32 percent local recurrence rate, in comparison to 4 percent for tumors located in the intraperitoneal rectum. In contrast, a series of patients undergoing reoperation following APR resection for rectal cancer reported that the pelvic component of failure was approximately 50 percent whether the tumor was located 0 to 5 cm, 6 to 10 cm, or over 10 cm above the dentate line.[22]

PATTERNS OF RECURRENCE

Local recurrence from rectal cancer occurs more commonly than from colonic cancer, presumably because of the anatomic limitations of the pelvis. The extraperitoneal rectum closely approximates the pelvis posteriorly and laterally, and the base of the bladder, vagina, and uterus or prostate anteriorly. In fact, in an analysis by Gilbertsen,[23] these structures were frequent sites of tumor recurrence following *curative* resection.

Contiguous visceral involvement by tumor adherence or invasion certainly contributes to increased local recurrence rates (Table 64-2). Pelvic recurrences are easier to diagnose than peritoneal seeding. The latter risk may be overrepresented as the sole pattern of failure but underestimated with regard to total incidence, especially quoting only initial incidence data.

Gunderson and Sosin[22] evaluated the areas of failure found at reoperation following curative resection of rectal cancer in 74 patients. Local regional metastases in the pelvis or in periaortic nodes was the sole source of failure in 48 percent of the 52 patients who relapsed and, in combination with distant metastatic disease, comprised 92 percent of all failures. Of the 67 patients with an abdominoperineal resection, a pelvic or perineal component of relapse occurred in 37 patients (71 percent of those with failure and 49 percent of those at risk). Distant metastases alone consisted of only 8 percent of all relapses but were found as a component of failure in 70 percent with relapse. Peritoneal seeding as a component of failure occurred in only 3 patients (6 percent of relapses and 4 percent of patients at risk).

Welch and Donaldson[24] reviewed autopsies on 145 patients dying from colorectal cancer. They found that rectal tumors recurred locally in 25 percent, distant metastases alone in 25 percent, and a combination of local and distant dissemination in the remaining 50 percent of patients. Unilateral and bilateral ureteral obstruction was identified in 25 and 21 percent of autopsies, respectively. Recurrent rectal cancer resulted in large or small bowel obstruction in 14 percent of cases. In this series, hepatic metastases were more common than local lymph node involvement and 75 percent of the patients actually died from distant metastases.

Peculiar to sphincter-saving rectal resections is the complication of so-called suture-line recurrence. An autopsy study found that 20 percent of recurrences after anterior resection were *adjacent* to the anastomosis.[3] Suture line recurrences are more likely related to secondary invasion of the adjacent bowel from a pelvic recurrence than to actual growth of tumor cells on the anastomotic line.[25,26] In one study, reexploration for 11 presumed suture line recurrences identified advanced pelvic malignancy in *all* patients; salvage APR yielded only one 5-year survivor.[27] Importantly, fear of a suture-line recurrence should in no way dissuade the surgeon from performing an anastomosis in the pelvis.

Overall, local tumor relapse is responsible for significant morbidity and from 50 to 75 percent of cancer-related deaths.[21,28–31] These reports are in contrast to a report by McDermott et al.,[18] who found that 48 percent of patients died from systemic spread only, compared to 27 percent for local recurrence and 24 percent with combined local and distant spread.

Comparing rectal and colonic carcinomas, Michelassi et al.[32] found that the median time to diagnosis of local recurrence for rectal cancer was 15 months, while it was 21 months for colonic tumors. Furthermore, median survival with distant metastases was 25 months for rectal lesions versus 38 months for colonic tumors. Survival without distant metastases was 44 months and 85 months for rectal and colonic tumors, respectively. Overall, 5-year survival following local recurrence was 22 percent for rectal and 37 percent for colonic cancers. Finally, the authors found that the local recurrence rate increased as the site of the tumor moved distally: 6 percent for cecal tumors, 12 percent for rectal tumors.

Tumors originating in the intraperitoneal rectum have a lower local recurrence rate than do extraperitoneal lesions in most series; specifically, tumors in the lower third of the rectum are especially prone to local recurrence.[33–36] Morson et al.[26] reviewed 1596 APRs and reported an overall rate of clinically evident pelvic recurrence of 10 percent; 80 percent of the failures were identified within 2 years of operation. The rate of pelvic recurrence was 15 percent in tumors of the lower third of the rectum. McDermott et al.[18] reported rates of pelvic failure for upper-, middle-, and lower-third rectal lesions of 14, 21, and 26 percent, respectively. However, Pilipshen et al.[37] found no difference in rates of pelvic failure following resection for tumors in the middle and lower rectum (both 30 percent), yet proximal tumors recurred in only 10 percent of cases. The pelvis is the earliest and most prominent site of recurrence for distal lesions following surgery alone. The reason for the increased relapse rates with distal lesions is incompletely understood but is likely related to inadequate distal and/or radial margins (lateral, anterior, or posterior) and the aggressiveness of the tumor. Low rectal lesions are more difficult to resect due to anatomic limitations, and adequate margins are most difficult to achieve with lateral or anterior extraluminal spread.

CHOICE OF OPERATION

Evolution of treatment of cancer of the rectum has progressed from APR for all lesions at any level to aggressive attempts at sphincter preservation. Initial success with low anterior resection was reported by Dixon[1] in 1948.

He cited an astonishing 64 percent 5-year survival and concomitant 3 percent operative mortality with anterior resection for proximal rectal and distal sigmoid lesions. More than a decade later, a second report from the Mayo Clinic reconfirmed the validity of restorative resection and, furthermore, made the observation that an intraperitoneal anastomotic location was associated with fewer complications than an extraperitoneal anastomosis.[38]

The popularity of restorative resection has increased to such a degree that APR is now performed rarely; Heald and Ryall[39] used APR in only 11 percent of 115 patients with low and middle rectal cancers. This is based not only on the surgeons desire to preserve the anal sphincter but also on the knowledge that distal margins need not be 5 cm or more to minimize local recurrence;[12,13,40,41] distal intramural spread occurs in only 10 percent of tumors and is, moreover, a poor prognostic sign often associated with extensive lymphatic involvement and disseminated disease. Indeed, patients may not be salvaged by wider resection margins. Similarly, high ligation of the inferior mesenteric vessels has not been shown to confer any added survival benefit to distal ligation.[42,43]

Quirke et al.[44] suggested that local recurrence is predominantly a factor of incomplete circumferential clearance when the tumor extends beyond the muscularis propria. Heald and Ryall[39] performed complete mesorectal excision in patients with potentially curable rectal cancers and achieved a 3 percent local recurrence rate. These results are completely uncontrolled and have not been achieved by any other author.

In similar fashion, extended pelvic lymphadenectomy has been advocated to eradicate undetectable tumor deposits residing in the lymphatics left behind after APR or low anterior resection.[10,45] For instance, Hojo et al.[45] combined high ligation of the inferior mesenteric vessels with removal of all lymphatic tissue in the paraaortic area, medial to the ureters, along the iliac vessels, and at the hypogastric plexus. Overall, the local recurrence rate and 5-year survival for stage III disease was 13 and 61 percent, respectively. The average operating time was increased by 10 percent, with a 27 percent greater blood loss, compared to conventional resection. Furthermore, anastomotic dehiscence occurred in 23 percent of patients. With preservation of the pelvic autonomic nerves, postoperative urinary and sexual dysfunction is decreased.[46] To date, no prospective controlled trial comparing extended lymphadenectomy to conventional resection has been performed. Moreover, retrospective analysis has shown that extended lymphadenectomy has not translated into improved survival.[47,48]

Williams et al.[49] reported a reduction in APRs from 59 percent during the 5-year period of 1968 to 1972 to 30 percent by 1986. The introduction of endoluminal stapling has facilitated intestinal reconstitution for lesions which, in many surgeons' hands, would have demanded complete rectal excision. For select early lesions, increased use of local measures for the treatment of rectal cancer—including local excision, endocavitary radiation, and fulguration—has also contributed to fewer abdominoperineal excisions. Indeed, most agree that sphincter preservation is contraindicated with invasion of the sphincter mechanism and bony or visceral pelvic fixation. For lesions less than 3 cm from the dentate line, sphincter preservation is difficult to achieve except for early lesions, in which local treatment may suffice, or the patient in whom a coloanal anastomosis is feasible.

The goal of surgery for rectal cancer is to minimize the risk of tumor recurrence within the context of acceptable morbidity and mortality. Today, there is little argument that upper rectal cancers are nearly always amenable to anterior resection. Abdominoperineal resection is often selected for large, more advanced, or poorly differentiated lesions located in the lower rectum.

The controversial area is middle-third rectal lesions, where the decision is based on the patient's body habitus and availability of adequate margins. The ultimate concern is whether survival or local recurrence rates are compromised by aggressive attempts to preserve the anal sphincter. Comparisons are difficult because of the varied location of the tumors in each series and the addition of adjuvant irradiation and chemotherapy on a fairly routine basis since the mid-1980s. Undoubtedly, the site of the tumor in the rectum influences the selection of the surgical procedure by the surgeon. Furthermore, no randomized prospective trial comparing APR and low anterior resection will be performed because of the strong desire of patients to avoid a permanent colostomy.

With locally advanced lesions (modified Astler-Coller B_2, C_1, and C_2), *higher local recurrence rates* for low anterior resection compared to abdominoperineal resection have been reported.[14,50–55] In one, the report of the Large Bowel Cancer Project, the higher local recurrence rate for anterior resection compared to APR was 12 versus 18 percent, respectively ($p<.02$).[14] This uncontrolled retrospective report pooled data from various institutions and did not stratify tumor location evenly within the rectum. In fact, the same project demonstrated wide variation in the local recurrence rates reported by the surgeons participating in the study.[56] Local recurrence following restorative resection may manifest itself earlier than after complete rectal excision due to the ease of detection from endoluminal protrusion of tumor extrinsic to the bowel wall.[5,14,57] This may bias the results reported in the literature.

Table 64-3
Local Regional Recurrence Rates following Abdominoperineal Resection and Sphincter-Saving Procedure

			Recurrence	
Author	*N*	*Distance AV, cm*	*APR, %*	*SSP, %*
Deddish and Stearns[60]	297	6–10	46	55
	187	11–16	52	23
Slanetz et al.[58]	189	8–18	25[a]	23[a]
	215	8–18	38[b]	33[b]
Patel et al.[96]	435	< 10	16	16
Jones et al.[101c]	186	< 15	9	13
Williams and Johnston[59]	83	7.5–12	8	11
Morson et al.[26]	1238	< 15	10	7
Odou and O'Connell[102]	199	5–10	22	20
Dixon[1]	287	< 20	14	6
Fick et al.[103]	59	< 15	15	13
Heimann et al.[104]	118	< 20	17	16

[a]Dukes B lesions.
[b]Dukes C lesions.
[c]Preoperative pelvic irradiation given to some patients.
Abbreviations: AV, above anal verge; APR, abdominoperineal resection; SSP, sphincter-saving procedure.

Nonetheless, multiple retrospective reviews document that rectal cancers are treated by complete proctectomy or sphincter preservation with comparable (usually equal) local regional recurrence (Table 64-3) and survival rates (Table 64-4). It is apparent, however, that there is a wide range of results. This is due to several variables: distribution of tumor location, tumor stage, histologic grade, and the definition of relapse. Often, a poorly differentiated or locally extensive middle to low rectal cancer is treated with APR without consideration for restorative techniques. Prospective studies have not been done comparing sphincter preservation or extirpation while controlling

Table 64-4
Five-Year Survival following Abdominoperineal Resection and Sphincter-Saving Procedure

Author	*N*	*Distance AV, cm*	*APR, %*	*SSP, %*
Mayo and Cullen[38]	34	5–9	69	72
Deddish and Stearns[60]	223	6–10	62	65
	175	11–16	72	78
Slanetz et al.[58]	333	8–13	47	56
Patel et al.[96]	435	< 10	56	64
Nicholls et al.[61]	199	8–12	57	73
Jones et al.[101]	186	< 15	52	67
McDermott et al.[18]	439	6–11	71	68
Williams and Johnston[59]	83	7.5–12	62	74
Dixon[1]	287	< 20	64	52
Fick et al.[103]	59	< 15	59	72

Abbreviations: AV, above anal verge; APR, abdominoperineal resection; SSP, sphincter-saving procedure.

for tumor location. Yet in the most controversial area, the middle rectum, retrospective studies examining treatment results with APR and anterior resection have demonstrated comparable results.[18,58–61] These results support the tenet that anterior resection contends with the "zone of upward spread" in a fashion similar to APR. Furthermore, since lateral and cephalad spread of carcinoma in the upper rectum is uncommon,[62–65] anterior resection appears suitable for most upper rectal tumors. Hence, local pelvic recurrence and long-term survival have not been adversely affected by the increased use of sphincter-saving operations.

Indeed, there is little question that survival after abdominoperineal or low anterior resection is usually dependent on the biology of the tumor rather than on the actual procedure performed. Tumor extent has the greatest negative impact on survival and relapse rates than any other tumor, patient, or operative variable. Direct extension of tumor beyond the muscularis propria, nodal involvement, or both impact negatively on local recurrence and survival (Tables 64-2 and 64-5). Moreover, survival is dependent upon the location and number of nodes involved: 1 to 4 nodes correlates with a 50 to 55 percent survival; 5 or more nodes, a 22 to 28 percent survival.[66,67] Similarly, poorly differentiated tumors reduce 5-year survival rates to 25 percent, compared to 60 percent for well-differentiated lesions.[68] However, modified Astler-Coller C_1 patients have a prognosis similar to that of patients with B_3 tumors (Table 64-2). Other issues that affect outcome but which are not necessarily controlled by the type of operation performed include DNA ploidy, obstruction and perforation, neural and blood vessel invasion, and tumor size.

Table 64-5
Five-Year Survival following Low Anterior, Abdominoperineal, and Abdominosacral Resection for Rectal Cancer

		Dukes Stage		
Author	*N*	*A, %*	*B, %*	*C, %*
Gilbertsen,[23] 1960	125	80	50	23
Slanetz et al.,[58] 1972	496	81	52	33
Rich et al.,[97] 1983	142	77	44	23
Localio et al.,[105] 1983	360	89	57	36
Williams and Johnston,[59] 1984	83	82	77	56
Pilipshen et al.,[37] 1984	412	84	64	39
Rosen et al.,[73] 1985	119	86	65	33
Malmberg et al.,[75] 1986	96	96	72	45
McDermott et al.,[106] 1986	265	93	71	41
Ohman,[76] 1986	87	84	63	52
Athlin et al.,[107] 1988	99	86	55	29
Kune et al.,[108] 1990	1105	78	55	31
DiMatteo et al.,[109] 1990	131	89	67	46
Dixon et al.,[90] 1991	287	100	70	50

TECHNIQUES OF ANASTOMOSIS

Surgical staplers have had a great impact upon the frequency of restorative resections for rectal carcinoma. Yet some authors continue to question whether rectal cancers are adequately eradicated when a stapling device is used. Studies comparing local recurrence rates between hand-sewn and stapled anastomoses have shown considerable discrepancies. These reports have addressed lesions located in the middle rectum primarily; the data must therefore be extrapolated carefully to tumors in the lower rectum, where clinical trials have not been performed.

Several studies have reported local recurrence rates after stapled restorative resection to vary between 20 and 32 percent.[19,55,69,70] Varying follow-up periods and small sample sizes make comparisons between these retrospective studies difficult. How the stapling device might actually increase local recurrence rates is completely unclear. Explanations proffered include increased intraluminal trauma leading to exfoliated tumor cell implantation,[71] impaired mucosal healing with stapled anastomoses,[72] and transplantation of tumor cells at the anastomosis by way of the stapler.[73]

Favorable experiences with regards to low local recurrence rates using the stapled anastomosis have also been reported.[4,57,59,74–77] Moreover, differences in local recurrence rates are not evident when stapled and hand-sewn techniques are compared directly (Table 64-6); the differences in recurrence rates and overall survival are most likely explained by other technical issues and tumor biology. A multi-institutional trial of 181 patients undergoing sphincter-saving operations and 232 undergoing abdominoperineal excision revealed no difference in survival for either technique at 48 months follow-up; however, many of these patients received postoperative radiation or chemotherapy.[78]

Table 64-6
Local Regional Recurrence Rates of Hand-Sewn versus Stapled Low Anterior Resection

	Recurrence			
Author	*N*	*Stapled, %*	*N*	*Sutured, %*
Bokey et al.[110]	44	14	108	22
Leff et al.[111]	70	11	58	17
Rosen et al.[73]	76	21	43	14
Williams[89]	35	17	31	13
Neville et al.[111]	76	24	105	17
Sauven et al.[80]	7	29	6	16
Amato et al.[79]	40	13	38	11

Table 64-7
Local Regional Recurrence Rates of Stapled Low Anterior Resection and Abdominoperineal Resection (APR)

	Recurrence			
Author	*N*	*Stapled, %*	*N*	*APR, %*
Colombo et al.[112]	61	10	32	14
Christiansen[113]	22	23	11	23
Vlasak et al.[52]	38	26	61	15
Amato et al.[79]	78	13	69	11
Gillen and Peel[114]	55	15	45	25
Graf et al.[115]	51	16	105	17
Ohman[76]	29	9	39	19

Finally, when series have examined local recurrence rates following stapled low anterior resection and APR, results were similar (Table 64-7).

Amato et al.[79] found no increased risk of local recurrence in patients with anastomotic leaks following anterior resection for cancer. However, contrast enemas were not used routinely to identify all dehiscences. A correlation between anastomotic leak and increased pelvic recurrence has been observed by other authors.[80,81] Akyol et al.[82] cited a 47 percent incidence of tumor recurrence in patients with anastomotic leaks, compared to 19 percent without a leak. Furthermore, cancer specific mortality at 2 years was 37 percent in those with leaks and 13 percent in those without leaks. Unfortunately, the level of the anastomotic sites and the frequency of perioperative transfusion were dissimilar in the two groups.

Spillage of viable tumor cells is one presumed etiology responsible for local recurrence in the presence of an anastomotic leak. The effect of intraoperative irrigation of the rectal stump and proximal bowel with tumoricidal agents is inconclusive. Retrospective, uncontrolled studies suggest a benefit with various agents and techniques, yet these have not translated into improved survival.[82–84]

A newer anastomotic technique is the double-staple procedure. Recently, Griffen et al.,[85] reporting upon their own series, found anastomotic leak and stricture rates to be 2.7 percent, with no operative deaths. Feinberg et al.[86] reported a local recurrence rate of 16 percent. Technical problems with the stapling device occurred in 6 percent of patients, and 8 percent developed anastomotic leaks. Stool frequency ranged from 2 to 5 bowel movements per day. An additional study prospectively comparing the single- and double-stapling techniques identified a trend but no statistical difference toward fewer anastomotic leaks with the double-stapling method.[87] The double-stapling technique has become the preferred technique of restoring intestinal continuity in most situations when the resulting anastomosis will be below 5 cm.

OPERATIVE MORTALITY

Because the age at which most patients present with rectal cancer is greater than 60 years, perioperative mortality is usually related to concomitant medical disease. The operative mortality for the first series of anterior resections was reported by Dixon to be only 3 percent.[1] Twenty years later, Deddish and Stearns[60] found an operative mortality rate of 9 percent for midrectal tumors and 4 percent for upper rectal tumors following anterior resection; in contrast, the rate was 2 percent for APR. Goligher[88] had a 7 percent operative mortality rate for anterior resection of tumors at various levels in the rectum, compared to 7 percent for APR. Lockhart-Mummery et al.[68] reported mortality rates of 3 and 2 percent for anterior resection and APR, respectively. More recent results have confirmed that APR and hand-sewn or stapled restorative resection can be performed with similar operative mortalities.[14,89–92] Thus, constructing a large bowel anastomosis in the pelvis regardless of technique does not increase the risk of perioperative mortality. The trend to lower perioperative mortality is no doubt due in large part to improved anesthetic management and general supportive care rather than advancement in surgical techniques.

A note of caution: the operative mortality for abdominoperineal excision has been reported to be as high as 16 percent in patients over age 80.[93,94] More recently, however, operative mortalities for *elective* colorectal operations were similar in patients over age 80 (7.4 percent) compared to younger patients (4.5 percent).[95] However, perioperative deaths, most commonly resulting from coexisting medical illnesses, were significantly higher in older than in younger patients for *emergency* procedures (54 versus 15 percent, respectively). Although 5-year survival was significantly higher for younger than for older patients (46 versus 35 percent, respectively), many deaths in the elderly population were not related to tumor regrowth or metastasis.

CONCLUSION

Cancer recurrence after a "curative" resection is usually dependent on the nature of the tumor rather than the method of excision. The differences in rates of perioperative morbidity and mortality may be explained by differences in surgical technique and patient selection criteria. The proportion of restorative procedures for rectal cancer has increased steadily; most investigators agree that this has not had an adverse effect on survival. Sphincter-saving procedures are well accepted for upper and middle rectal tumors and may be used cautiously for low rectal tumors. Furthermore, most patients who undergo restorative resection achieve satisfactory control of defecation with time. Thus, sphincter-sparing operations are favored for most rectal cancers because (1) they confer no survival or recurrence *dis*advantage, (2) they obviate the need for a perineal wound, (3) a stoma is not needed, (4) most patients are or become continent, and (5) restoring intestinal continuity allows easier detection of local recurrence. For these reasons, restorative and not extirpative surgery is the treatment of choice for most rectal cancers.

REFERENCES

1. Dixon CF: Anterior resection for malignant lesions of upper part of rectum and lower part of sigmoid. *Ann Surg* 128:425–442, 1948.
2. Mendenhall WM, Million RR, Pfaff WW: Patterns of recurrence in adenocarcinoma of the rectum and rectosigmoid treated with surgery alone: Implications in treatment planning with adjuvant radiation therapy. *Int J Radiat Oncol Biol Phys* 9:977–985, 1983.
3. Welch JP, Donaldson GA: Detection and treatment of recurrent cancer of the colon and rectum. *Am J Surg* 135:505–510, 1973.
4. Kennedy HL, Langevin JM, Goldberg SM, et al: Recurrence following stapled coloproctostomy for carcinomas of the mid portion of the rectum. *Surg Gynecol Obstet* 160:513–516, 1985.
5. Tagart REB: Restorative rectal resection: An audit of 220 cases. *Br J Surg* 73:70–71, 1986.
6. Polk HC, Spratt JS Jr: Recurrent colorectal carcinoma: Detection, treatment and other considerations. *Surgery* 69:9–23, 1971.
7. Carlsson U, Lasson A, Ekelund G: Recurrence rates after curative surgery for rectal carcinoma, with special reference to their accuracy. *Dis Colon Rectum* 30:431–434, 1987.
8. Berge T, Ekelund G, Mellner C, et al: Carcinoma of the colon and rectum in a defined population. *Acta Chir Scand [Suppl]* 438:11–86, 1973.
9. Chapuis PH, Dent OF, Fisher R, et al: A multivariate analysis of clinical and pathological variables in prognosis after resection of large bowel cancer. *Br J Surg* 72:698–702, 1985.
10. Enker WE, Heilweil ML, Hertz REL, et al: En bloc pelvic lymphadenopathy and sphincter preservation in the surgical management of rectal cancer. *Ann Surg* 203:426–433, 1986.
11. Wolmark N, Wieand HS, Rockette HE, et al: The prognostic significance of tumor and location and bowel obstruction in Dukes B and C colorectal cancer: Findings from the NSABP clinical trials. *Ann Surg* 198:743–752, 1983.
12. Williams NS, Dixon MF, Johnston D: Reappraisal of the 5 centimetre rule of distal excision for carcinoma of the rectum: A study of distal intramural spread and of patient's survival. *Br J Surg* 70:150–154, 1983.
13. Pollett WG, Nicholls RJ: The relationship between the extent of distal clearance and survival and local recurrence rates after curative anterior resection for carcinoma of the rectum. *Ann Surg* 198:159–163, 1984.
14. Phillips RKS, Hittinger R, Blesovsky L, et al: Local recurrence following curative surgery for large bowel cancer. *Br J Surg* 71:17–20, 1984.
15. Heald RJ, Husband EM, Ryall RDH: The meso-rectum in rectal cancer surgery: The clue to pelvic recurrence. *Br J Surg* 69:613–616, 1982.
16. Feil W, Wunderlich M, Neuhild N, et al: Rectal cancer: Factors influencing the development of local recurrence after radical anterior resection. *Int J Colorect Dis* 3:195–200, 1988.
17. Huguier M, Depoux F, Houry S, et al: Adenocarcinoma of the rectum treated by abdominoperineal excision: Multivariate analysis of prognostic factors. *Int J Colorect Dis* 5:144–147, 1990.
18. McDermott FT, Hughes ESR, Pihl E, et al: Local recurrence after potentially curative resection for rectal cancer in a series of 1,008 patients. *Br J Surg* 72:34–37, 1985.
19. Anderberg B, Enblad P, Sjodahl R, et al: Recurrent rectal carcinoma after anterior resection and rectal stapling. *Br J Surg* 70:1–4, 1983.
20. Gunderson LL, Sosin H, Levitt S: Extrapelvic colon—Areas of failure in a reoperation series: Implications for adjuvant therapy. *Int J Radiat Oncol Biol Phys* 11:731–741, 1985.
21. Moosa AR, Ree PC, Marks JE, et al: Factors influencing local recurrence after abdominoperineal resection for cancer of the rectum and rectosigmoid. *Br J Surg* 62:727–730, 1975.
22. Gunderson LL, Sosin H: Areas of failure found at reoperation (second or symptomatic look) following "curative surgery" for adenocarcinoma of the rectum: Clinicopathologic correlation and implications for adjuvant therapy. *Cancer* 34:1278–1292, 1974.
23. Gilbertsen VA: Adenocarcinoma of the rectum: Incidence and locations of recurrent tumor following present-day operations for cure. *Ann Surg* 151:340–348, 1960.
24. Welch JP, Donaldson GA: The clinical correlation of an autopsy study of recurrent colorectal cancer. *Ann Surg* 189:496–502, 1979.
25. Umpleby HC, Williamson RCN: Anastomotic recurrence in large bowel cancer. *Br J Surg* 74:873–878, 1987.
26. Morson BC, Vaughan EG, Bussey HJR: Pelvic recurrence after excision of rectum for carcinoma. *Br Med J* 2:13–18, 1963.
27. Sannella NA: Abdominoperineal resection following anterior resection. *Cancer* 38:378–381, 1976.
28. Cass AW, Million RR, Pfaff WW: Patterns of recurrence following surgery alone for adenocarcinoma of the colon and rectum. *Cancer* 37:2861–2865, 1976.
29. Rao AR, Kagan AR, Chan PM, et al: Patterns of recurrence following curative resection alone for adenocarcinoma of the rectum and sigmoid colon. *Cancer* 48:1492–1495, 1981.
30. Floyd CE, Corley RG, Cohn I: Local recurrence of carcinoma of the colon and rectum. *Am J Surg* 109:153–159, 1965.
31. Taylor FW: Cancer of the colon and rectum—A study of routes of metastases and death. *Surgery* 52:305–308, 1962.
32. Michelassi F, Vannucci L, Ayala JJ, et al: Local recurrence after curative resection of colorectal adenocarcinoma. *Surgery* 108:787–793, 1990.
33. Enker WE, Pilipshen SJ: Patterns of failure resulting after definitive resections for rectal or colonic cancer. *Cancer Treat Symp* 2:173–180, 1983.
34. Michelassi F, Block GE, Vannucci L, et al: A 5- to 21-year follow-up analysis of 250 patients with rectal adenocarcinoma. *Ann Surg* 208:379–389, 1988.
35. Warneke A, Petrelli NJ, Herrera L: Local recurrence after sphincter-saving resection for rectal adenocarcinoma. *Am J Surg* 158:3–5, 1989.
36. Secco GB, Fardelli R, Campora E, et al: Factors influencing local recurrence after curative surgery for rectal surgery. *Oncology* 46:10–13, 1989.
37. Pilipshen SJ, Heilweil M, Quan SHQ, et al: Patterns of pel-

vic recurrence following definitive resections of rectal cancer. *Cancer* 53:1354–1362, 1984.

38. Mayo CW, Cullen PK Jr: Symposium on surgery of the colon: An evaluation of the one-stage low anterior resection. *Proc Mayo Clin* 36:474–476, 1961.
39. Heald RJ, Ryall RDH: Recurrence and survival after total meso-rectal excision for rectal cancer. *Lancet* 1:1479–1482, 1986.
40. Penfold JB: A comparison of restorative resection of carcinoma of the middle third of the rectum with abdomino-perineal excision. *Aust NZ J Surg* 44:354–356, 1974.
41. Baker JW, Margetts LH, Schutt RP: The distal and proximal margin of resection in carcinoma of the pelvic colon and rectum. *Ann Surg* 141:693–706, 1955.
42. Pezim ME, Nicholls RJ: Survival after high or low ligation of the inferior mesenteric artery during curative surgery for rectal cancer. *Ann Surg* 200:729–733, 1984.
43. Surtees P, Ritchie JK, Phillips RKS: High versus low ligation of the inferior mesenteric artery in rectal cancer. *Br J Surg* 77:618–621, 1990.
44. Quirke P, Durdey P, Dixon MF, et al: Local recurrence of rectal adenocarcinoma due to inadequate surgical resection. Histopathological study of lateral tumor spread and surgical excision. *Lancet* 1:996–999, 1986.
45. Hojo K, Sawada T, Moriya Y: An analysis of survival and voiding, sexual function after wide iliopelvic lymphadenectomy in patients with carcinoma of the rectum, compared with conventional lymphadenectomy. *Dis Colon Rectum* 32:128–133, 1989.
46. Hojo K, Vernava AM III, Sugihara K, et al: Preservation of urine voiding and sexual function after rectal cancer surgery. *Dis Colon Rectum* 34:532–539, 1991.
47. Moriya Y, Hojo K, Sawada T, et al: Significance of lateral node dissection for advanced rectal carcinoma at or below the peritoneal reflection. *Dis Colon Rectum* 32:307–315, 1989.
48. Glass RE, Ritchie JK, Thompson HR, et al: The results of surgical treatment of cancer of the rectum by radical resection and extended abdomino-iliac lymphadenectomy. *Br J Surg* 72:599–601, 1985.
49. Williams NS, Durdey P, Johnston D: The outcome following sphincter-saving resection and abdominoperineal resection for low rectal cancer. *Br J Surg* 72:595–598, 1985.
50. Wolmark N, Gordon PH, Fisher B, et al: A comparison of stapled and hand-sewn anastomoses in patients undergoing resection of Dukes' B and C colorectal cancer: An analysis of disease-free survival and survival from the NSABP prospective trials. *Dis Colon Rectum* 29:344–350, 1986.
51. Ziv BD, Waizer A, Flex D, et al: Local recurrence after low anterior resection using the EEA stapling device. *Dis Colon Rectum* 31:945–947, 1988.
52. Vlasak JW, Wagner D, Passaro E, et al: Local recurrence after curative resection of rectal cancer: A comparison of low anterior resection and abdominoperineal resection. *J Surg Oncol* 41:236–239, 1989.
53. Rubbini M, Vettorello GF, Guerrera C, et al: A prospective study of local recurrence after resection and low stapled anastomosis in 183 patients with rectal cancer. *Dis Colon Rectum* 33:117–121, 1990.
54. Pheils MT, Chapuis PH, Newland RC, et al: Local recurrence following curative resection for carcinoma of the rectum. *Dis Colon Rectum* 26:98–102, 1983.
55. Hurst PA, Prout WG, Kelly JM, et al: Local recurrence after low anterior resection using the staple gun. *Br J Surg* 69:275–276, 1982.
56. Phillips RKS, Hittinger R, Blesovsky L, et al: Local recurrence following "curative" surgery for large bowel cancer: I. The overall picture. *Br J Surg* 71:12–16, 1984.
57. Lasson ALL, Ekelund G, Lindstrom CG: Recurrence risk after stapled anastomosis for rectal carcinoma. *Acta Chir Scand* 150:85–89, 1984.
58. Slanetz CA Jr, Herter FP, Grinnell RS: Anterior resection versus abdominoperineal resection for cancer of the rectum and rectosigmoid. *Am J Surg* 123:110–117, 1972.
59. Williams NS, Johnston D: Survival and recurrence after sphincter saving resection and abdominoperineal resection for carcinoma of the middle third of the rectum. *Br J Surg* 71:278–282, 1984.
60. Deddish MR, Stearns MW: Anterior resection for carcinoma of the rectum and rectosigmoid area. *Ann Surg* 154:961–966, 1961.
61. Nicholls RJ, Ritchie JK, Wadsworth J, et al: Total excision or restorative resection for carcinoma of the middle third of the rectum. *Br J Surg* 66:625–627, 1979.
62. Enquist IF, Block IR: Rectal cancer in females: Selection of proper operation based upon anatomic studies of rectal lymphatics. *Prog Clin Cancer* 2:73–85, 1966.
63. Grinnell RS: Lymphatic block with atypical and retrograde lymphatic metastasis and spread in carcinoma of the colon and rectum. *Ann Surg* 163:272–280, 1966.
64. Gilchrist RK, David VC: A consideration of pathological factors influencing five year survival in radical resection of the large bowel and rectum for carcinoma. *Ann Surg* 126:421–438, 1947.
65. Coller FA, Kay EB, MacIntyre RS: Regional lymphatic metastasis in carcinoma of the colon. *Ann Surg* 114:56–63, 1941.
66. Wolmark N, Fisher B, Wieand HS: The prognostic value of the modifications of the Dukes' C class of colorectal cancer. *Ann Surg* 203:115–122, 1986.
67. Hojo K, Koyama Y, Moriya Y: Lymphatic spread and its prognostic value in patients with rectal cancer. *Am J Surg* 144:350–354, 1982.
68. Lockhart-Mummery HE, Ritchie JK, Hawley PR: The results of surgical treatment for carcinoma of the rectum at St. Marks Hospital from 1948–1972. *Br J Surg* 63:673–677, 1976.
69. Reid JDS, Robins RE, Atkinson KG: Pelvic recurrence after anterior resection and EEA stapling anastomosis for potentially curable carcinoma of the rectum. *Am J Surg* 147:629–632, 1984.
70. Bisgaard C, Suanholm H, Jensen AS: Recurrent carcinoma after low anterior resection of the rectum using the EEA staple gun. *Acta Chir Scand* 152:157–160, 1986.
71. Norgen J, Svensson JO: Anal implantation metastasis from carcinoma of the sigmoid colon and rectum: A risk when performing anterior resection with the EEA stapler? *Br J Surg* 72:602, 1985.
72. Polglase AL, Hughes ESR, McDermott FT, et al: A comparison of end-to-end staple and suture colorectal anastomosis in the dog. *Surg Gynecol Obstet* 152:792–796, 1981.
73. Rosen CB, Beart RW, Ilstrup DM: Local recurrence of rectal carcinoma after hand-sewn and stapled anastomoses. *Dis Colon Rectum* 28:305–309, 1985.
74. Belli L, Beati CA, Frangi M, et al: Outcome of patients with rectal cancer treated by stapled anterior resection. *Br J Surg* 75:422–424, 1988.
75. Malmberg M, Graffner H, Ling L, et al: Recurrence and survival after anterior resection of the rectum using the end to end anastomotic stapler. *Surg Gynecol Obstet* 163:231–234, 1986.
76. Ohman U: Curative potential of EEA stapler in rectal carcinoma. *Acta Chir Scand* 152:59–64, 1986.

77. Waxman BP: Large bowel anastomoses: II. The circular staplers. *Br J Surg* 70:64–67, 1983.
78. Wolmark N, Fisher B: An analysis of survival and treatment failure following abdominoperineal and sphincter-saving resection in Dukes' B and C rectal carcinoma: A report of the NSABP clinical trials. *Ann Surg* 204:480–487, 1986.
79. Amato A, Pescatori M, Butti A: Local recurrence following abdominoperineal excision and anterior resection for rectal carcinoma. *Dis Colon Rectum* 34:317–322, 1991.
80. Sauven P, Playforth MJ, Evans M, et al: Early infective complications and late recurrent cancer in stapled colonic anastomoses. *Dis Colon Rectum* 32:33–35, 1989.
81. Akyol AM, McGregor JR, Galloway DJ, et al: Anastomotic leaks in colorectal cancer surgery: A risk factor for recurrence? *Int J Colorect Dis* 6:179–183, 1991.
82. Akyol AM, McGregor JR, Galloway DJ, et al: Recurrence of colorectal cancer after sutured and stapled large bowel anastomoses. *Br J Surg* 78:1297–1300, 1991.
83. Long RTL, Edwards RH: Implantation metastasis as a cause of local recurrence of colorectal carcinoma. *Am J Surg* 157:194–201, 1989.
84. Labow AB, Salvati EP, Rubin RJ: Suture line recurrence in carcinoma of the colon and rectum. *Dis Colon Rectum* 18:123–125, 1975.
85. Griffen FD, Knight CD, Whitaker JM, et al: The double stapling technique for low anterior resection: Results, modifications, and observations. *Ann Surg* 211:745–75? 1990.
86. Feinberg SM, Parker F, Cohen Z, et al: The double stapling technique for low anterior resection of rectal carcinoma. *Dis Colon Rectum* 29:885–890, 1986.
87. Moritz E, Achleitner D, Holbling N, et al: Single vs. double stapling technique in colorectal surgery: A prospective randomized trial. *Dis Colon Rectum* 34:495–497, 1991.
88. Goligher JC: *Surgery of the Anus, Rectum and Colon,* 3d ed. London, Baillière, 1975, p 815.
89. Williams NS: The rationale of preservation of the anal sphincter in patients with low rectal cancer. *Br J Surg* 71:575–581, 1984.
90. Dixon AR, Maxwell WA, Holmes JT: Carcinoma of the rectum: A 10-year experience. *Br J Surg* 78:308–311, 1991.
91. Beart RW Jr, Kelly KA: Randomized prospective evaluation of the EEA stapler for colorectal anastomoses. *Am J Surg* 141:143–147, 1981.
92. Brennan SS, Pickford IR, Evans M, et al: Staples or sutures for colonic anastomoses—A controlled clinical trial. *Br J Surg* 69:722–724, 1982.
93. Cohen JR, Theile DE, Holt J, et al: Carcinoma of the large bowel in patients aged 70 years and over. *Aust NZ J Surg* 48:405–408, 1978.
94. Hughes ESR, McDermott FT, Masterton JP, et al: Operative mortality following excision of the rectum. *Br J Surg* 67:49–51, 1980.
95. Arnaud JP, Schloegel M, Ollier JC, et al: Colorectal cancer in patients over 80 years of age. *Dis Colon Rectum* 34:896–898, 1991.
96. Patel SC, Tovee EB, Langer B: Twenty-five years of experience with radical surgical treatment of carcinoma of the extraperitoneal rectum. *Surgery* 82:460–465, 1977.
97. Rich T, Gunderson LL, Lew R, et al: Patterns of recurrence of rectal cancer after potentially curative surgery. *Cancer* 52:1317–1329, 1983.
98. Gilbert SG: Symptomatic local tumor failure following abdomino-perineal resection. *Int J Radiat Oncol Biol Phys* 4:801–807, 1978.
99. Withers HR, Causay L, Mason KA, et al: Elective radiation therapy in the curative treatment of cancer of the rectum and rectosigmoid colon, in Stroehlin JR, Romsdahl MM (eds): *Gastrointestinal Cancer.* New York, Raven Press, 1981, pp 351.
100. Walz BJ, Green MR, Linstrom RE, et al: Anatomic prognostic factors after abdominal perineal resection. *Int J Radiat Oncol Biol Phys* 7:477–482, 1981.
101. Jones DJ, Zaloudik J, James RD, et al: Predicting local recurrence of carcinoma of the rectum after preoperative radiotherapy and surgery. *Br J Surg* 76:1172–1175, 1989.
102. Odou MW, O'Connell TX: Changes in the treatment of rectal carcinoma and effects on local recurrence. *Arch Surg* 121:1114–1116, 1986.
103. Fick TE, Baeten CGMI, von Meyenfeldt MF, et al: Recurrence and survival after abdominoperineal and low anterior resection for rectal cancer, without adjunctive therapy. *Eur J Surg Oncol* 16:105–108, 1990.
104. Heimann TM, Szporn A, Bolnick K, et al: Local recurrence following surgical treatment of rectal cancer: Comparison of anterior and abdominoperineal resection. *Dis Colon Rectum* 29:862–864, 1986.
105. Localio SA, Eng K, Coppa GF: Abdominosacral resection for mid-rectal cancer. *Ann Surg* 198:320–324, 1983.
106. McDermott FT, Hughes ESR, Pihl EA, et al: Changing survival prospects in rectal carcinoma: A series of 1,306 patients managed by one surgeon. *Dis Colon Rectum* 29:798–803, 1986.
107. Athlin L, Bengtsson NO, Stenling R: Local recurrence and survival after radical resection of rectal carcinoma. *Acta Chir Scand* 154:225–229, 1988.
108. Kune GA, Kune S, Field B, et al: Survival in patients with large-bowel cancer. *Dis Colon Rectum* 33:938–946, 1990.
109. Di Matteo G, Cancrini A Jr, Boemi L, et al: Techniques of rectal oncologic surgery. *Int Surg* 75:208–214, 1990.
110. Bokey EL, Chapuis PH, Hughes WJ, et al: Local recurrence following anterior resection for carcinoma of the rectum with a stapled anastomosis. *Acta Chir Scand* 150:683–686, 1984.
111. Neville R, Fielding LP, Amendola C: Local tumor recurrence after curative resection for rectal cancer: A ten-hospital review. *Dis Colon Rectum* 30:12–17, 1987.
112. Colombo PL, Scotti, Foglieni CL, et al: Analysis of recurrence following curative low anterior resection and stapled anastomoses for carcinoma of the middle third and lower rectum. *Dis Colon Rectum* 30:457–464, 1987.
113. Christiansen J: Place of abdominoperineal excision in rectal cancer. *J R Soc Med* 81:143–145, 1988.
114. Gillen P, Peel ALG: Comparison of the mortality, morbidity and incidence of local recurrence in patients with rectal cancer treated by either stapled anterior resection or abdominoperineal resection. *Br J Surg* 73:339–341, 1986.
115. Graf W, Pahlman L, Enblad P, et al: Anterior versus abdominoperineal resections in the management of mid-rectal tumours. *Acta Chir Scand* 156:231–235, 1990.

PART 11

Adjuvant Therapy for Rectal Cancer

CHAPTER 65

Adjuvant Chemotherapy

Richard S. Kaplan

HIGHLIGHTS

Patients with primary sites in the rectum were not distinguished from patients with more proximal adenocarcinomas in the late 1960s–early 1970s generation of adjuvant single-agent chemotherapy trials that failed to demonstrate consistent evidence of benefit. Subsequently, however, recognition of the higher risk of local recurrence led to randomized trials specific for rectal cancer patients, usually incorporating a combined-modality approach to address both the characteristic local and distant patterns of failure.[1–5]

By the early 1990s, combined chemoradiation surgical adjuvant therapy for modified Astler-Coller B_2–C ($T_{3-4}N_{0-3}$) rectal cancer had become a community standard in the United States based upon the results of the randomized trials of the Gastrointestinal Tumor Study Group (GITSG) and the Mayo/North Central Cancer Treatment Group (NCCTG) randomized trials[6–8] and the analysis of the 1990 NIH Consensus Conference on Adjuvant Therapy of Large Bowel Cancer.[9]

CONTROVERSIES

Nonetheless, a number of controversies remain, and there are numerous questions about the optimal administration of adjuvant therapy. Chemotherapy without radiation did not demonstrate significant survival benefit in the GITSG study[6] but did so in the National Surgical Adjuvant Breast and Bowel Project (NSABP) R-01 randomized trial,[10] so there remains uncertainty as to the role of chemotherapy based on 5-fluorouracil (5-FU) as a single modality. Conversely, the necessity of the radiation remains a topic of disagreement, because the subsequent NSABP R-02 trial, for which only early data are available, has as yet not shown that radiation plus chemotherapy is superior to chemotherapy alone.

Furthermore, the chemotherapy utilized by the GITSG, Mayo/NCCTG, and NSABP in all these trials incorporated 5-FU and semustine (methyl-CCNU) with or without the addition of vincristine; but a subsequent prospectively randomized Intergroup trial (NCCTG 86-47-51) has proven that methyl-CCNU is not a necessary element of the therapy[11] and was associated with substantial acute and chronic toxicity. Current adjuvant trials, therefore, have adopted various regimens, based upon results of advanced disease trials, which add leucovorin, levamisole, or both to 5-FU. However, adjuvant trials of these regimens are not yet mature and no one regimen has yet been established or can be considered "standard" for rectal cancer.

The same large NCCTG 86-47-51 Intergroup trial that demonstrated the ineffectiveness of methyl-CCNU also randomly allocated patients to either bolus 5-FU or protracted continuous venous infusion (PVI) of 5-FU during the radiation phase of treatment. It was found that PVI was associated with superior overall disease-free survival (DFS) with fewer distant metastases, implying that the effect was not due merely to superior local control[12] (and M. J. O'Connell, personal communication). This finding has led to additional new studies to investigate which of the current chemotherapy regimens may provide optimal benefit.

FUTURE DIRECTIONS

Key questions to be resolved by forthcoming data from completed studies and/or the next generation of prospective randomized trials include:

1. Whether PVI chemotherapy administered throughout the sequence of postoperative adjuvant treatment (rather than just during the radiation) will yield further benefit
2. Whether the addition of levamisole to 5-FU provides the same type of additional benefit as is apparent for colonic cancer adjuvant therapy
3. Whether the addition of leucovorin (as a modulator) to 5-FU is superior to 5-FU alone
4. Whether tumor levels of thymidylate synthase (TS), the primary target enzyme for 5-FU therapy, can be utilized to predict which patients will benefit from 5-FU–based adjuvant therapy
5. Similarly, whether recently identified allelic deletions of the *p53* gene on chromosome 17p, the *dcc* gene on 18q, or other genetic changes will be predictive of prognosis or response to adjuvant therapy
6. Whether preoperative (neoadjuvant) chemoradiation may be superior to the now conventional postoperative adjuvant chemoradiation
7. Whether preoperative chemoradiation can lead to a superior rate of sphincter-preserving surgery for rectal cancer

---

For resected TNM stage II (modified Astler-Colter $B_{2,3}$) and III (modified Astler-Colter C) rectal adenocarcinomas (as distinct from colonic adenocarcinomas), adjuvant postoperative pelvic radiotherapy as a single modality decreased the incidence of pelvic recurrences compared to surgery-only controls in two randomized multi-institutional trials of the first (modern) generation, begun in the 1970s by the GITSG (GITSG 7175)[6,7] and the NSABP (NSABP R-01).[10] However, overall survival was not improved (see Chap. 67).

Adjuvant chemotherapy as a single modality was also compared to a surgery-only control arm in both of these trials. In GITSG 7175, with roughly 50 patients per arm, adjuvant chemotherapy utilizing 5-FU plus methyl-CCNU also failed to improve survival.[6,7] However, combined-modality adjuvant therapy with pelvic radiotherapy, 5-FU, and methyl-CCNU demonstrated statistically superior 5-year DFS (71 percent, versus 47 percent for surgery only) and overall survival (OS) (59 versus 43 percent) as well as improved local control. On the other hand, NSABP R-01 with approximately 180 patients in each arm, and using 5-FU, methyl-CCNU and vincristine ("MOF") showed that chemotherapy *alone* (without radiation) was associated with a DFS advantage (42 versus 30 percent) and a marginal advantage in OS (53 versus 43 percent). An unplanned subgroup analysis suggested that this chemotherapy was beneficial only in male patients.[10] Combined radiation and chemotherapy was not tested in this trial.

These data (and others described below) were evaluated in an NIH Consensus Development Conference on adjuvant therapy for patients with colonic and rectal cancer in 1990[9] and updated in an NCI Clinical Announcement in 1991, following which there have been no further U.S. trials with surgery-only control arms for TNM stage II and III rectal cancer. Thus there are no further data available to resolve directly the role of chemotherapy as a single adjuvant modality for rectal cancer. To a certain extent, however, this topic may be assessed indirectly by examining to what extent chemotherapy and radiation are or are not additive in other trials.

Another of the first-generation randomized trials was a two-arm study conducted by the NCCTG and Mayo Clinic that specifically tested whether chemotherapy improved survivorship by comparing postoperative 5-FU + methyl-CCNU + radiation versus radiation alone. It was felt that, considering the relatively small size of the GITSG 7175 trial, confirmation was required that radiation alone was not sufficient therapy. This NCCTG 79-47-51 study enrolled about 100 patients per arm; DFS was increased from 42 percent for radiation alone to 63 percent with the addition of chemotherapy, and OS increased from 47 to 58 percent.[8] These differences were all statistically significant and confirmed that chemotherapy was a required element for successful adjuvant therapy. No gender differences in outcome or toxicity were evident.

A second-generation NSABP trial reevaluated the alternative question, whether radiation added additional benefit to chemotherapy. This trial, NSABP R-02, compared chemotherapy alone (5-FU + leucovorin in females; MOF versus 5-FU + leucovorin in males) to chemotherapy + radiation. It accrued 741 patients and closed in late 1992. The data therefore are not mature, but thus far they appear only to confirm the expected lower rate of local recurrence for those receiving radiation; no advantage in DFS has yet been seen. This trial clearly requires longer follow-up for any definitive conclusion, but if an advantage does not appear, it would suggest that the chemotherapy is the critical element.

How, then, are we to interpret these perhaps superficial disparities among chemotherapy results in rectal cancer adjuvant trials to date? It is certainly possible that 5-FU + leucovorin, with which the majority of patients on NSABP R-02 were treated, is a superior regimen to 5-FU + methyl-CCNU (± vincristine) used in the previous generation of studies. Indeed, for colonic cancer adjuvant therapy, another NSABP randomized trial appears to demonstrate this conclusively.[13] It seems reasonable to tentatively extrapolate this superiority to rectal cancer trials, in which case the adjuvant effect of 5-FU + leucovorin may be large enough either to obscure any additional benefit from radiation or, perhaps, even to obviate the need for radiation.

Indeed, additional rectal adjuvant trials, and extrapolation of results from large colonic adjuvant studies, support both the central importance of 5-FU–based regimens and the likelihood that there are some meaningful differences among regimens. In several different schedules and doses, 5-FU + leucovorin has been demonstrated to be superior to 5-FU in advanced disease[14–19] and has been widely assumed to have the potential to be a superior adjuvant regimen as well. In colon cancer adjuvant therapy, the NSABP C-03 trial, completed in 1989, was recently reported to demonstrate unequivocally that 5-FU + leucovorin (using the weekly, high-dose leucovorin Roswell Park schedule) is superior to the MOF combination.[13] The NSABP R-02 trial, described above, will yield data on the comparison in rectal cancer.

The combination of 5-FU and levamisole has been the regimen reproducibly demonstrated to improve DFS and OS in TNM II and III colonic cancer[20,21] (see Chap. 51). In rectal cancer, this regimen has been compared to 5-FU alone, 5-FU + leucovorin (by the monthly 5-day, low-dose leucovorin NCCTG schedule), and 5-FU + leucovorin + levamisole, in a large Intergroup study (INT-0114) chaired by CALGB and completed in late 1992. Results from this trial are not likely to be available until 1995.

It has certainly become clear that methyl-CCNU is not an important component of adjuvant therapy for either colon or rectal cancer. For colon cancer, NSABP C-03 demonstrated that 5-FU + leucovorin was better than MOF.[13] In rectal cancer, a GITSG trial failed to show that methyl-CCNU + 5-FU was superior to 5-FU alone, both in combination with radiotherapy.[22] A much larger Intergroup study, NCCTG 86-47-51, yielded an identical conclusion.[11]

The latter trial, however, was particularly interesting because, in addition to the methyl-CCNU question, this study had a second independent randomization as to the method of administering 5-FU during the 5- to 6-week radiation phase of the regimen. The control arm utilized intravenous bolus 5-FU for 3 consecutive days during weeks 1 and 5 of radiation therapy, as has been standard for the other studies. The experimental arm substituted protracted venous infusion of 5-FU (PVI) at 225 mg/m²/day continuously throughout the entire radiation course, using a venous access device and portable infusion pump. This regimen was chosen for study because of experimental evidence that it might provide better radiosensitization and thus improve local/regional disease control. Thus far, the local control has been good in both arms but, surprisingly, early results (median follow-up = 43 months) have demonstrated that PVI produced significant improvements in both DFS (p = .01) and survival (p = .02), indicating that PVI 5-FU had an important *systemic* effect even though PVI was administered for only a brief portion of the overall 6-month chemoradiation regimen.[12]

Possible explanations for this significant difference based only on the schedule of 5-FU administration certainly include biochemical alterations that are associated with the infusion schedule,[23] or suspected superiority of infusion 5-FU as a radiosensitizer.[24,25] However, another important consideration is that the dose intensity of PVI 5-FU is markedly higher with this schedule, which provides 6300 mg/m²/28 days in comparison to the bolus × 3 schedule (3000 mg/m²/31 days at best) or even in comparison to 5-FU when used in other trials on the Roswell Park or NCCTG schedules (2000 to 2400 and 1875 to 2100 mg/m²/28 days, respectively). There have been only a few direct randomized comparisons of continuous infusion regimens to other 5-FU schedules in advanced or recurrent colorectal cancer[23,26,27] and these have each been criticized as having some design flaws, but they have consistently pointed to an advantage for infusion over bolus.

The observation regarding PVI 5-FU from Intergroup/NCCTG 86-47-51 will serve as the basis for the next Intergroup cooperative post-op rectal adjuvant trial, SWOG 9304. The control arm of this study will replicate the NCCTG 86-47-51 regimen of bolus courses of 5-FU during the pre- and post-RT phases plus PVI during the sandwiched pelvic radiation (*arm A*). Both investigational arms will also adopt the PVI 5-FU during the radiation: *arm B:* PVI 5-FU in all three phases; *arm C:* PVI 5-FU + leucovorin in the pre- and post-RT phases. It is hoped that this design will ascertain whether PVI throughout therapy and/or the additional biochemical modulation by leucovorin will lead to another incremental improvement in outcome.

The difference in survival by gender identified in NSABP R-01, which was unexpected and remains unprecedented and unexplained, has been the subject of a good deal of speculation and doubt. One possibility is that such a difference could be related to higher levels of O^6-guanyl methyl transferase, the enzyme responsible for repair of methyl-CCNU damage to DNA, in tumors of females. However, the data supporting this explanation are very scanty and were not derived from analysis of tumors of patients who were actually receiving this therapy.[28] Unless a comparable gender difference is seen in subsequent studies, this question is likely to remain unresolved, since methyl-CCNU is no longer being used.

Perhaps a more promising explanation will emerge from the current evaluation of thymidine synthase (TS) expression in rectal tumors. This key target enzyme for 5-FU–based therapy is being assayed in the primary tumors of patients actually randomized on adjuvant trials, and the results correlated with stage and survival. There are encouraging preliminary data that these correlations may be predictive of potential benefit from adjuvant therapy.

Johnston and colleagues at the NCI–Navy Medical Oncology Branch and NSABP investigators studied rectal tumor specimens from patients on NSABP R-01 and compared the findings to the recurrence and survival results of this mature clinical trial. Their initial findings indicated that patients whose tumors expressed lower levels of TS (measured by an immunohistochemical method[29]) had a better chance of survival, 60 to 65 percent at 5 years, compared to 35 to 40 percent for those with high levels.[29a] Although larger tumors tended to have higher TS levels, the TS level was predictive after correction for size. Even more interestingly, it appeared that only those patients with high levels of TS derived benefit from 5-FU–based adjuvant chemotherapy (MOF in this trial). Whether or not there may be any gender differences, however, is not yet known.

Several cooperative groups are pursuing these observations prospectively in current adjuvant trials. If similar findings are replicated in another cohort, it could lead to a significantly improved capacity to select patients for adjuvant therapy, since patients whose tumors expressed low levels of TS could be predicted to have a lower risk and less chance of benefit, while patients with high-TS tumors would have a higher risk and a greater likelihood of benefit from adjuvant 5-FU–containing chemotherapy regimens.

Indeed, one of the most exciting aspects of the next generation of colorectal cancer adjuvant studies relates to the possibility that it may become feasible to better quantitate the risk of recurrence for individual patients—based on tumor levels of TS, flow cytometry parameters, or molecular genetic alterations. This may be of particular importance for patients with Dukes B tumors who may have a risk of recurrence in the range of 20 percent for colonic primaries and 30 to 40 percent for rectal sites.

There is preliminary evidence that DNA ploidy and proliferation index may be of use as prognostic markers that, in addition to Dukes stage, can classify patients into high- and low-risk groups. Investigators from the NCCTG studied paraffin blocks of both Dukes B_2 and C tumors from several NCCTG colonic and rectal adjuvant therapy trials.[30] They found that the combination of diploid chromosome number and low proliferation index (proportion of cells in S + G2/M phases) was associated with a 74 percent 5-year survival, compared to 54 percent for the unfavorable (opposite) combination. This finding was statistically significant for both colon and rectal primaries and for Dukes B_2 and Dukes C. Whether or not these findings could be related to response to adjuvant therapy was not assessible in these trials, since all patients received 5-FU–based treatment.

Additional potential prognostic indicators for colorectal cancers may be found in their well-characterized and frequent acquired molecular genetic alterations. Several small-scale investigations have shown that allelic deletion of the *p53* gene region on the short arm of chromosome 17 (17p), or deletion of the *dcc* gene region on the long arm of chromosome 18 (18q), or both, may be independently associated with a higher likelihood of disseminated disease and poorer survival.[31–36] Recently, methods have been developed for performing these studies on paraffin blocks[31] so these analyses will be undertaken for both retrospective and prospective evaluation on large series of patients on adjuvant trials in both colon and rectal cancer. There are no data thus far that would bear on any possible relationship to response to therapy.

One further direction for investigation of adjuvant treatment of rectal carcinoma is the exploration of preoperative (neoadjuvant) chemotherapy and radiotherapy, which is the focus of the current NSABP R-03 and intergroup trials. This approach is based on several compelling clinical and experimental rationales. Experimentally, various animal-model tumors have long been known to undergo an increase in growth rate of metastases associated with the removal of the primary.[37–39] This phenomenon conceivably may be prevented by preoperative exposure of micrometastases to effective chemotherapy, though the same data would also support enhanced vulnerability of micrometastases in the immediate postoperative period. However, the administration of chemotherapy immediately after surgery is problematic in terms of possible interference with healing of rectal anastomoses.

Clinically, neoadjuvant chemoradiation has had a major impact on the management of anal carcinoma and localized esophageal cancer, in both of which it has reduced the requirement for surgery; it may have an advantage in several other solid tumors as well.[40]

The possible survival advantage of preoperative radiation (as a single modality) in rectal adenocarcinoma is discussed in Chap. 69. Preoperative combined-modality therapy (chemoradiation) has been used in selected cases of unresectable or marginally resectable tumors, with good patient tolerance, apparent "downstaging," sparing of the rectal sphincter in some cases, and encouraging rates of survival, including in a number of patients with no subsequent resection.[41–44] These results, especially in view of the potential for sphincter sparing, make a strong argument for extension of such a strategy to the more favorable group of rectal cancer patients with less advanced, conventionally resectable tumors (Chap. 70).

The NSABP R-03 trial is randomizing patients between identical regimens of 5-FU + leucovorin + pelvic radiation but with markedly different timing. In the control arm, patients undergo resection and then receive 2 months of chemotherapy, then combined chemoradiation, followed by 2 further months of chemotherapy. In the neoadjuvant arm, the chemotherapy and radiation therapy sequence is the same, but the surgery is not done until after the chemoradiation (about 4 months after initiation of therapy) unless there is clinical evidence that the primary tumor is progressing. Two of the possible outcomes of this trial would be encouraging, either a prolongation of survival or at least an increase in the number of patients without colostomies, as long as survival is not compromised. This general approach will also be evaluated in a separate Intergroup trial, coordinated by RTOG, in which the details of sequencing therapy differ in that chemoradiation (5-FU/leucovorin) is utilized first rather than chemotherapy followed by chemoradiation.

REFERENCES

1. Gunderson LL, Sosin H: Areas of failure found at reoperation (second or symptomatic look) following "curative surgery" for adenocarcinoma of the rectum: Clinicopathologic correlation and implications for adjuvant therapy. *Cancer* 34:1278–1292, 1974.
2. Rich T, Gunderson LL, Lew R, et al: Patterns of recurrence of rectal cancer after potentially curative surgery. *Cancer* 52:1317–1329, 1983.
3. Pilipshen SJ, Heilweil M, Quan SH, et al: Patterns of pelvic recurrence following definitive resections of rectal cancer. *Cancer* 53:1354, 1984.
4. McDermott FT, Hughes ES, Pihl E, et al: Local recurrence after potentially curative resection for rectal cancer in a series of 1008 patients. *Br J Surg* 72:34, 1985.
5. Schild SE, Martenson JA Jr, Gunderson LL, et al: Postoperative radiation therapy of rectal cancer: An analysis of disease control, survival, and prognostic factors. *Int J Radiat Oncol Biol Phys* 17:55–62, 1989.
6. Gastrointestinal Tumor Study Group: Prolongation of the disease-free interval in surgically treated rectal carcinoma. *N Engl J Med* 312:1465, 1985.
7. Gastrointestinal Tumor Study Group: Survival after postoperative combination treatment of rectal cancer. *N Engl J Med* 315:1294–1295, 1986.
8. Krook JE, Moertel CG, Gunderson LL, et al: Effective surgical adjuvant therapy for high-risk rectal carcinoma. *N Engl J Med* 324:709–715, 1991.
9. NIH Consensus Conference: Adjuvant therapy for patients with colon and rectal cancer. *JAMA* 264:1444–1450, 1990.
10. Fisher B, Wolmark N, Rockette H, et al: Postoperative adjuvant chemotherapy or radiation therapy for rectal cancer: Results from NSABP protocol R-01. *J Natl Cancer Inst* 80:21, 1988.
11. O'Connell M, Wieand H, Krook J, et al: Lack of value for methyl-CCNU as a component of effective rectal cancer surgical adjuvant therapy: Interim analysis of intergroup protocol 86-47-51. *Proc ASCO* 10:134, 1991.
12. O'Connell M, Martenson J, Rich T, et al: Protracted venous infusion (PVI) 5 fluorouracil (5FU) as a combined modality postoperative surgical adjuvant therapy for high risk rectal cancer. *Proc ASCO* 12:193, 1993.
13. Wolmark N, Rockette H, Fisher B, et al: The benefit of leucovorin-modulated fluorouracil as postoperative adjuvant therapy for primary colon cancer: Results from National Surgical Adjuvant Breast and Bowel Project protocol C-03. *J Clin Oncol* 11:1879–1887, 1993.
14. Advanced Colorectal Cancer Meta-Analysis Project: Modulation of fluorouracil by leucovorin in patients with advanced colorectal cancer: Evidence in terms of response rate. *J Clin Oncol* 10:896–903, 1992.
15. Erlichman C, Fine S, Wong A, et al: A randomized trial of 5-fluorouracil (5-FU) and folinic acid (FA) in metastatic colorectal carcinoma. *J Clin Oncol* 6:469, 1988.
16. Doroshow JH, Bertrand M, Multhauf P: A prospective randomized trial comparing 5-FU and high-dose folinic acid (HDFA) for treatment of advanced colorectal cancer. *Proc ASCO* 6:96, 1987.
17. Petrelli N, Herrera L, Rustum Y, et al: A prospective randomized trial of 5-fluorouracil versus 5-fluorouracil and high-dose leucovorin versus 5-fluorouracil and methotrexate in previously untreated patients with advanced colorectal carcinoma. *J Clin Oncol* 5:1559, 1987.
18. Poon MA, O'Connell MJ, Moertel CG, et al: Biochemical modulation of fluorouracil: Evidence of significant improvement of survival and quality of life in patients with advanced colorectal carcinoma. *J Clin Oncol* 7:1407, 1989.
19. Valone FH, Friedman MA, Wittlinger PS, et al: Treatment of patients with advanced colorectal carcinomas with 5-FU alone, high-dose leucovorin plus 5-FU or sequential methotrexate, 5-FU, leucovorin: A randomized trial of the Northern California Oncology Group. *J Clin Oncol* 7:1427–1436, 1989.
20. Laurie JA, Moertel CG, Fleming TR, et al: Surgical adjuvant therapy of large-bowel carcinoma: An evaluation of levamisole and the combination of levamisole and 5-fluorouracil. *J Clin Oncol* 7:1447, 1989.
21. Moertel CG, Fleming TR, MacDonald JS, et al: Levamisole and fluorouracil for adjuvant therapy of resected colon carcinoma. *N Engl J Med* 322:352–358, 1990.
22. Gastrointestinal Tumor Study Group: Radiation therapy and fluorouracil with or without semustine for the treatment of patients with surgical adjuvant adenocarcinoma of the rectum. *J Clin Oncol* 10:549–557, 1992.
23. Lokich JJ, Ahlgren JD, Gullo JJ, et al: A prospective randomized comparison of continuous infusion fluorouracil with a

conventional bolus schedule in metastatic colorectal carcinoma: A Mid-Atlantic Oncology Program Study. *J Clin Oncol* 7:425–432, 1989.
24. Byfield J: Theoretical basis and clinical applications of 5-fluorouracil as a radiosensitizer, in Rosenthal CJ, Rotman M (eds): *Clinical Applications of Continuous Infusion Chemotherapy and Concomitant Radiation Therapy*. New York, Plenum Press, 1986, pp 113–126.
25. Smalley SR, Kimler BF, Evans RG: 5-Fluorouracil modulation of radiosensitivity in cultured human carcinoma cells. *Int J Radiat Oncol Biol Phys* 20:207–211, 1990.
26. Seifert P, Baker LH, Reed ML, et al: Comparison of continuously infused 5-fluorouracil with bolus injection in treatment of patients with colorectal adenocarcinoma. *Cancer* 36:123–128, 1975.
27. Weinerman B, Shah A, Fields A, et al: systemic infusion versus bolus chemotherapy with 5-fluorouracil in measurable metastatic colorectal cancer. *Am J Clin Oncol* 15:518–523, 1992.
28. Citron M, White A, Levin L, et al: O6-methylguanine-DNA methyltransferase (MGMT) in human normal and colorectal tumor tissue. *Proc AACR* 33:A3267, 1992.
29. Johnston PG, Drake JC, Steinberg S, Allegra CJ: Quantitation of thymidylate synthase in human tumors using an ultrasensitive enzyme-linked immunoassay. *Proc AACR* 34:A2460, 1993.
29a. Johnston PG, Fisher E, Rockette HE, et al: Thymidylate synthase expression is an independent predictor of survival/disease-free survival in patients with rectal cancer. *Proc ASCO* 12:202, 1993.
30. Witzig TE, Loprinzi CL, Gonchoroff NJ, et al: DNA ploidy and cell kinetic measurements as predictors of recurrence and survival in stages B2 and C colorectal adenocarcinoma. *Cancer* 68:879, 1991.
31. Jen J, Kim H, Piantadosi S, et al: Allelic loss of chromosome 18q and prognosis in colorectal cancer. *N Engl J Med* 331:213–221, 1994.
32. Offerhaus GJA, DeFeyter EP, Cornelisse CJ, et al: The relationship of DNA aneuploidy to molecular genetic alterations in colorectal carcinoma. *Gastroenterology* 102:1612–1619, 1992.
33. Hamilton SR: Molecular genetic alterations as potential prognostic indicators in colorectal carcinoma. *Cancer* 69(suppl): 1589–1591, 1992.
34. Hamilton SR: Molecular genetics of colorectal carcinoma. *Cancer* 70(suppl):1216–1221, 1992.
35. Laurent-Puig P, Olschwang S, Delattre O, et al: Survival and acquired genetic alterations in colorectal cancer. *Gastroenterology* 102:1136–1141, 1992.
36. Ahlquist DA, Thibodeau SN: Will molecular genetic markers help predict the clinical behavior of colorectal neoplasia? *Gastroenterology* 102:1419–1421, 1992.
37. Simpson-Herren L, Sanford AH, Holmquist JP: Effects of surgery on the cell kinetics of residual tumor. *Cancer Treat Rep* 60:1749–1760, 1976.
38. Gunduz N, Fisher B, Saffer EA: Effect of surgical removal on the growth and kinetics of residual tumor. *Cancer Res* 39:1361–1365, 1979.
39. Fisher B, Gunduz N, Saffer EA: Influence of the interval between primary tumor removal and chemotherapy on kinetics and growth of metastases. *Cancer Res* 43:1488–1492, 1983.
40. Trimble EL, Ungerleider RS, Abrams JA, et al: Neoadjuvant therapy in cancer treatment. *Cancer* 72:3515–3524, 1993.
41. Minsky BD, Cohen AM, Kemeny N, et al: Combined modality therapy of rectal cancer: Decreased acute toxicity with the preoperative approach. *J Clin Oncol* 10:1218–1224, 1992.
42. Minsky BD, Cohen AM, Kemeny N, et al: Enhancement of radiation-induced downstaging of rectal cancer by fluorouracil and high-dose leucovorin chemotherapy. *J Clin Oncol* 10:79–84, 1992.
43. Minsky BD, Cohen AM, Kemeny N, et al: Pre-operative combined 5-FU, low dose leucovorin, and sequential radiation therapy for unresectable rectal cancer. *Int J Radiat Oncol Biol Phys* 25:821–827, 1993.
44. Marks GM, Mohiudin M, Rakinic J: New hope and promise for sphincter preservation in the management of cancer of the rectum. *Semin Oncol* 18:388–398, 1991.

CHAPTER 66

Principles of Radiation Therapy for Rectal Cancer

Joel E. Tepper

HIGHLIGHTS

Radiation therapy can be used to treat locally advanced rectal cancer or, in patients who have undergone a potentially curative resection, to decrease the risk of local failure and improve the survival rate. It can also be used in combination with more limited surgical resections to maintain anal function while still producing a low local recurrence rate. A number of general principles have evolved defining the proper radiation dose and fields, as described below. There is also now substantial information showing that the small bowel is the major normal tissue limiting radiation dose and that surgical and radiotherapeutic techniques need to be followed to minimize toxicity. Finally, it has become clear that in most clinical situations where radiation is used in the treatment of rectal cancer, the concurrent use of a chemotherapy regimen based on 5-fluorouracil (5-FU) improves the local control and, in the case of adjuvant treatment, the survival rate. Primarily postoperative irradiation has been used in most of the adjuvant trials in the United States, but there is still a good rationale for testing the use of preoperative irradiation.

CONTROVERSIES

There are two major controversies regarding the use of radiation therapy as an adjuvant in the treatment of rectal cancer. The first is whether radiation should be given preoperatively or postoperatively. There is one randomized trial that demonstrates a lower local recurrence rate in patients who received preoperative therapy, but there was no effect on overall survival rates. There are theoretical and practical reasons to prefer one treatment to another, but it is yet to be established which is better. There are also significant uncertainties about the optimal timing of postoperative radiation and chemotherapy. The second major issue is how radiation should be combined with 5-FU–based chemotherapy. Substantial data show an advantage to the combined modality therapy, but the mechanism of the interaction is unclear. There are reasons to recommend a variety of regimens—including continuous infusion 5-FU, 5-FU plus leucovorin, or 5-FU plus other combinations—in order to increase the combined modality effect, but no one regimen has been demonstrated to be optimal.

FUTURE DIRECTIONS

Further studies are needed to define the optimal timing of radiation therapy with other therapies, including surgery and chemotherapy. At present, randomized studies are beginning to test this point. Perhaps of greater interest is a clearer understanding of the interaction between chemotherapy and radiation and of the manipulation of that interaction to the patient's advantage. This could influence the timing of the delivery of 5-FU and radiation, the mode of delivery (bolus versus short-term infusion versus long-term infusion), and the use of 5-FU modulators such as leucovorin or interferon.

Radiation therapy can be used for a variety of reasons in the treatment of rectal cancer. It is commonly used as an adjuvant to surgical resection in conjunction with chemotherapy in order to prevent local recurrence and the accompanying symptomatology and to improve the long-term survival rate. It can be used for palliation in patients who have symptomatic pelvic disease, either primary or recurrent, and to shrink bulky rectal tumors, allowing a potentially curative surgical resection to be performed. It can also help to destroy small amounts of known gross or microscopic residual disease. Last, it can be combined with a limited surgical resection in patients who have small, relatively localized carcinomas of the rectum in order to preserve sphincter function while still maximizing local control.

Although all of these approaches to radiation therapy are different, there are similarities in how radiation is used. In planning radiation therapy, there are a number of basic principles which must be followed. These include (1) defining the rationale for the therapy, (2) determining the sequence of radiation with the other therapeutic modalities, (3) defining the optimal radiation dose, and (4) defining the optimal radiation fields and techniques. The rationale for therapy in individual clinical situations is defined elsewhere in this book, as are specific issues of timing of radiation, surgery, and chemotherapy. However, some general principles may appropriately be discussed here.

PATIENT SELECTION

A number of studies have evaluated the patterns of failure after potentially curative surgical resection of rectal cancer. These studies have demonstrated a high local failure rate in patients treated with surgery alone when the tumor extends through the bowel wall into extraperitoneal perirectal soft tissue, when there is positive lymph node disease, or both.[1–4] Generally the incidence of local failure increases as the extent of the disease increases. Patients with positive nodal disease plus extension through the bowel wall have a higher incidence of local failure than patients with only one of these characteristics. In addition, there is information to suggest that patients with tumors located low in the rectum have a higher incidence of local failure than patients with disease located high in the rectum.[5]

There has been some disagreement in the literature as to what qualifies a tumor as a rectal cancer as contrasted to a colonic cancer. The distance from the anal verge by itself is of relatively little importance, since there is no anatomic significance to this distance. However, since local failure stems primarily from tumor extension into retroperitoneal soft tissue, a good operational definition of a rectal tumor is one that is located at or below the peritoneal reflection. Tumors located above the reflection are intraperitoneal and are not likely to extend locally into tissues that cannot easily be resected; thus such lesions are less likely to lead to local failure. Therefore, the rationale for a local treatment adjuvant such as radiation therapy applies to tumors with invasion through the bowel wall and/or with positive lymph nodes when the primary tumor lies at or below the peritoneal reflection. Since the anterior peritoneal reflection extends lower than does the posterior reflection, this is also a somewhat ambiguous definition. However, if there is a risk of the tumor extending into bowel at a site where there is no peritoneal covering, the tumor should be treated as a rectal cancer. These are primarily the patients who have been studied in the past and in whom an advantage has been demonstrated from the use of radiation.

TIMING OF RADIATION THERAPY

Radiation in rectal cancer is delivered either alone, preoperatively, or postoperatively and can be combined in all these situations with chemotherapy. For many years there have been discussions regarding the role of adjuvant pre- versus postoperative radiation therapy. There are a number of reasons to consider either the pre- or postoperative approach.

Preoperative

1. Early radiation treatment might decrease the size of the tumor mass and thereby make surgical resection easier.
2. Preoperative radiation, when given in relatively high doses, would destroy many logs of tumor cells, decreasing the risk of tumor cell implantation and dissemination at the time of surgery.
3. The radiation fields, when delivered preoperatively, can be more limited than those given postoperatively. Areas that would be at risk for tumor involvement because of surgical manipulation and possible seeding, such as the perineal scar after abdominoperineal resection, would not need to be treated preoperatively but would need to be treated postoperatively.
4. Tumors might be more sensitive to preoperative radiation, as the amount of tumor hypoxia (which makes the cells relatively radioresistant) would likely be less prior to surgical manipulation.
5. Giving radiation prior to surgery avoids irradiating the small bowel which is fixed within the pelvis; this would increase the treatment-related morbidity. When a patient is irradiated preoperatively, the small bowel is relatively free, and the likelihood of a single bowel loop receiving high doses of radiation is less.
6. Preoperative irradiation might produce tumor shrinkage, allowing for surgery with anal sphincter preservation.

Postoperative

1. A significant number of patients (those with disease limited to the bowel wall) are at low risk of pelvic recurrence after surgery alone and could be spared adjuvant therapy

if the disease were accurately staged surgically prior to any other therapy.

2. Important prognostic information is lost when the tumor is treated prior to surgical resection. Factors such as lymph node status might never be accurately known if the patient is downstaged by radiation, a not uncommon occurrence. As chemotherapy is now used routinely for tumors extending through the bowel wall or with positive lymph nodes, the loss of this prognostic information could cause significant problems in determining which patients require additional chemotherapy.
3. Postoperative radiation does not pose the risk of increasing operative morbidity, as does preoperative irradiation.
4. Certain anatomical areas which are at the highest risk for local recurrence may not be known prior to surgery. These areas could be underdosed (or not receive a maximum boost) when using preoperative therapy, but they could be treated to high dose postoperatively. In addition, if one wants to give a postoperative boost in addition to the preoperative therapy, it might not be possible to deliver the boost till many weeks after the surgical procedure. The time delay between the two portions of the radiation would lessen the effectiveness of the total radiation dose.

Some of the arguments mentioned above are partially hypothetical. It is, however, clear that there could be meaningful differences in outcome based on which approach is chosen. Unfortunately, there is relatively little information that allows these techniques to be compared. A study has been reported by Pahlman and Glimelius[6] from Sweden, where patients received adjuvant treatment for rectal cancer with either a rapid course of preoperative irradiation (25.5 Gy in 5 to 7 days) or high-dose postoperative irradiation (60 Gy in 8 weeks). The local recurrence rate was statistically significantly lower after preoperative irradiation (12 percent) than after postoperative irradiation (21 percent). However, there was no survival difference or difference in the rate of distant metastases between the two arms. Toxicity was also evaluated. Although more patients in the preoperative arm had perineal wound sepsis causing prolongation of the hospital stay, the postoperative irradiation was not tolerated as well overall as the preoperative treatment. There were no complications noted during the preoperative radiation course, while most of the patients who received postoperative radiation therapy had mild to moderate symptoms of diarrhea, fatigue, nausea, skin reactions, and urinary disorders. Only 9 of the postoperative patients had their treatment completed without adverse effects. A major problem with this study is that there was no arm utilizing adjuvant chemotherapy given concurrently with the radiation. Recent trials of postoperative radiation combined with 5-FU–based chemotherapy demonstrate a decreased local recurrence with the addition of chemotherapy, with local control rates very similar to those reported by Pahlman and Glimelius[7] with preoperative irradiation. Thus, these data do not allow one to draw any conclusions regarding the efficacy of these two approaches. At present in the United States, the majority of patients treated with adjuvant radiation therapy are treated postoperatively.

When delivering radiation therapy for locally advanced disease, the situation is different. Most investigators would support the concept of using high-dose preoperative radiation when the primary tumor cannot easily be resected with negative margins. Although no formal randomized studies have been performed, it is generally thought to be preferable to try to shrink a tumor preoperatively and make it potentially resectable rather than attempt to control residual disease after an inadequate operation.

DOSE

There are many arguments regarding the optimal total dose and dose fractionation schedule. A general tenet of radiation biology is that the higher the dose of radiation given in a single fraction, the greater the likelihood of local tumor control. This is supported by multiple in vitro studies, with minimal contradictory data. However, when radiation is delivered clinically, it is not given as a single fraction but rather as multiple daily fractions. In most tumor-normal tissue settings, the overall therapeutic ratio is improved by the use of lower radiation doses per fraction. In other words, the dose delivered in a single fraction which would be needed to control microscopic residual disease would likely produce an unacceptable amount of injury to normal tissue. A higher total dose, given in divided daily fractions, would be able to produce the same level of tumor control with less morbidity to normal tissue. It is for this reason that radiation doses in the range of 180 to 200 cGy/day are normally used in the United States. In Europe and Canada, patients are often treated with higher doses per fraction (225 to 250 cGy/day), but there have been no comparative studies of the two approaches. There is fairly good evidence to suggest that, for many other clinical situations, there is an improvement in the therapeutic ratio with a decrease in the dose per fraction from doses of 200 cGy per fraction, but there is relatively little information to suggest what the optimal dose per fraction is. It is possible that further decreases in daily dose would be beneficial.

However, potential problems are associated with the use of lower daily doses, and these relate to possible tumor cell proliferation during the course of radiation therapy. Although this problem has been best studied in cancer of the head and neck, tumors appear to have the potential to go into an accelerated growth phase once treatment has started. This increased proliferation could negate some of the benefits that might result from a more protracted course of radiation, with the tumor proliferating as rapidly as the cells are being killed by the radiation. Tumor-cell kinetics have not been well studied during radiation therapy of colorectal cancers, but most radiation oncologists are concerned about the possible adverse effects of a treatment course that is too protracted. This has resulted in the desire not to decrease the daily dose below 180 cGy.

One strategy that has been used to avoid these problems is to treat patients with a fraction size of less than 180 cGy (typically in the range of 120 to 160 cGy) but to use multiple radiation fractions per day. As long as there are at least 4 to 6 h between the radiation fractions, the sublethal radiation injury produced from the first dose will have been repaired and the tumor and normal tissues will respond as if the doses were given with a prolonged separation. This approach has been used most commonly in more rapidly proliferating tumors, such as squamous cell carcinomas of the head and neck, but could be applicable to colonic and rectal tumors as well. One must be aware that acute reactions will reflect the total dose given in a certain time, so that even though the twice-daily schedule might decrease the late normal tissue injury (small bowel obstruction, ulceration, etc.), the acute side effects (diarrhea, etc.) could be greater.

Despite the fact that there is no definite information on these questions of radiation dose or dose per fraction, there are some reasonable guidelines which can be used until better information is available. High doses per fraction should probably be avoided at the present time because of the risk of late morbidity, and there is little information for colon and rectal cancer to show a benefit of low doses per treatment. Thus, a fraction size in the range of 180 cGy should be considered standard at present. A dose to the pelvis of 4500 cGy is reasonably well tolerated in most clinical situations and, combined with a boost radiation dose of 540–900 cGy, produces local control in a high percentage of patients. In high-risk situations, such as with tumor adherence or fixation to adjacent structures, doses up to 6000 cGy should be given to the boost field if the small bowel can be completely eliminated from the boost. Under special situations, such as residual pelvic disease, the maximal dose to the boost volume could be up to 7000 cGy, or perhaps higher with sophisticated treatment planning techniques, if all sensitive normal structures are out of the high-dose volume.

RADIATION FIELDS

Whenever radiation therapy is delivered, the radiation oncologist must consider the design of the radiation field in order to minimize the irradiation of normal tissues while maximizing the irradiation of tissues thought to be at high risk of tumor involvement. In the treatment of rectal cancer, the high-risk areas have been defined by earlier analyses of recurrence patterns, such as that performed by Gunderson and Sosin[1] in reviewing the reoperation series from the University of Minnesota.

These studies have demonstrated that the primary site of local failure is in the soft tissues surrounding the rectum, especially in the presacral space, along the pelvic side walls, and anteriorly along the vagina or prostate. These are sites where it is difficult for the surgeon to obtain a wide margin around the tumor, so that a high incidence of local recurrence results. It follows that the radiation oncologist must pay special attention in obtaining adequate coverage of these sites. There must be an adequate margin to allow for dosimetric variation around the edges of the beam, specifically to allow for coverage of the presacral space. It is also important to realize that the regional lymph nodes are a potential tumor-bearing area that must be irradiated. Unless the tumor involves the anus, the risk of involvement of the external iliac nodal chain is very low; therefore this does not have to be encompassed in the radiation field. However, the internal iliac nodal chain, an area that is not dissected in the normal abdominoperineal resection, is at risk for involvement in patients with rectal cancer and should be treated with radiation therapy. The mesenteric lymph nodes are usually dissected adequately by the surgeon, so no specific efforts need be made to treat this site.

In addition, one must be sure to treat other areas at risk for tumor involvement. After an abdominoperineal resection, the perineal incision and soft tissue are at risk for tumor involvement and should be treated, as should any drain sites in the perineum.

Generally, radiation therapy is given to patients with rectal cancer as an adjuvant with a multiple-field approach that includes anteroposterior–posteroanterior (AP-PA) and lateral fields. In order to cover these high-risk areas adequately, the radiation fields should be designed to treat laterally to at least 1 cm lateral to the bony pelvis, to extend inferiorly approximately 5 cm below the lowest extent of the tumor after a low anterior resection or to the perineal incision after an abdominoperineal resection, and to extend to the lower portion of the L-5 vertebral body in order to encompass fully the retroperitoneal soft tissues into which the tumor could have infiltrated. Posteriorly, there must be at least a 1½-cm margin to the anterior border of the sacrum; anteriorly, there must be a margin on the vagina in females or the prostate in males (Fig. 66-1*A* and *B*). Good dose distributions can generally be obtained with the use of all four fields. We generally use either equally weighted fields or fields with a modest decrease in the weighting of the anterior

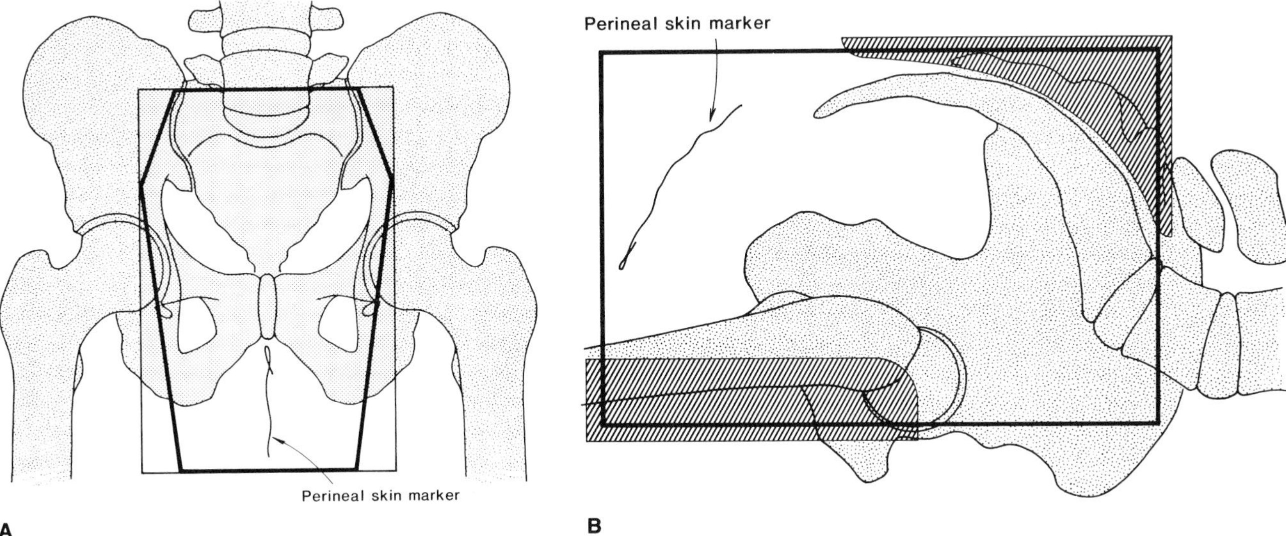

FIG. 66-1. Typical radiation fields for patients treated postoperatively after an abdominoperineal resection for rectal cancer. The fields extend inferiorly to include the perineal incision. In a low anterior resection those fields would typically extend 3 to 5 cm below the anastomosis to the level of the obturator foramen. *A*. The AP-PA fields. *B*. The lateral fields.

field. A sample dose distribution for an equally weighted four-field arrangement is shown in Fig. 66-2. These fields are generally treated to a dose of 4500 cGy using a fraction size of 180 cGy. At this point the fields are reduced so as to eliminate as much small bowel as possible from the radiation field with a boost of an additional 540 to 900 cGy when radiation is given as a postoperative adjuvant.

A critical factor in the delivery of radiation is to be sure that normal tissues do not receive a dose of radiation so high as to produce substantial morbidity. The primary normal tissue of interest for late radiation injury is the small bowel, a structure that can safely tolerate a dose of 4500 to 5000 cGy at 180–200 cGy per fraction. It is, however, possible to treat the pelvis to doses higher than this by being certain that the small bowel is not in the high-dose region. This can be done by visualizing the small bowel with contrast during the radiation simulation and blocking the bowel during the

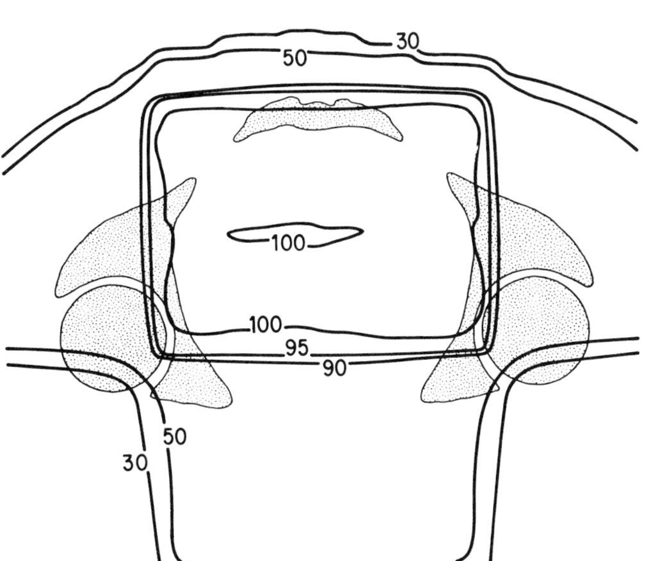

FIG. 66-2. Typical dose distribution for an equally weighted four-field arrangement to the pelvis. There are no significant hot spots and the dose distribution is relatively uniform.

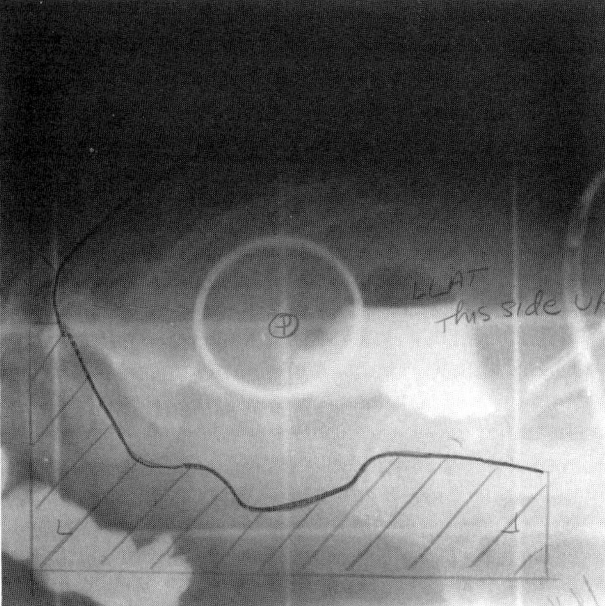

FIG. 66-3. Lateral simulation film of the pelvis with small bowel contrast. The ability to spare the small bowel by the use of the lateral fields is well illustrated.

boost field. In order to accomplish this, it is very helpful to have the surgeon define the areas at highest risk of tumor involvement with surgical clips and to move the small bowel out of the pelvis surgically. This can be done by reperitonealizing the pelvic floor, retroverting the uterus into the pelvis, or constructing a sling of absorbable mesh. Any of these maneuvers will move the bowel out of the high-dose radiation field and will facilitate the safe delivery of radiation. Often the use of lateral fields during the boost dose of radiation is effective in minimizing the amount of small bowel in the radiation field, as much of the small bowel is often located anteriorly in the pelvis (Fig. 66-3).

INTERACTION OF CHEMOTHERAPY AND RADIATION

A number of studies done over the years strongly suggest that, in the adjuvant setting, the combination of radiation and a chemotherapy regimen based on 5-FU improves local control and long-term survival compared to therapies utilizing radiation alone. The work of Moertel et al.[8] from the Mayo Clinic, which was reported in 1969, spurred much of the interest in combined-modality therapy. In this report, patients with locally advanced cancers from a number of sites were treated with either radiation therapy plus a placebo or radiation therapy plus 5-FU chemotherapy, using low doses of chemotherapy (50 mg/kg over 3 days), delivered during the first 3 days of the radiation therapy. Despite the very low dose of 5-FU which was used, this study demonstrated that there was a survival advantage to the combined-modality therapy. More recently, this has been supported by data from the Gastrointestinal Tumor Study Group (GITSG)[9] as well as from the Mayo/North Central Cancer Treatment Group.[7] The GITSG trial randomized patients with stage B_2 and C rectal cancer to receive either (1) no postoperative therapy, (2) postoperative treatment with 5-FU and semustine (methyl CCNU), (3) radiation therapy, or (4) combined-modality chemotherapy and radiation therapy. Patients treated with the combined-modality therapy had improved local control, disease-free survival, and overall survival compared to patients treated with surgery alone. In a more recent trial from the Mayo Clinic/North Central Cancer Treatment Group,[7] patients were randomized to receive either postoperative radiation therapy alone or two cycles of chemotherapy with 5-FU and methyl CCNU followed by concurrent radiation therapy and 5-FU and two more cycles of chemotherapy. The results of this study show a definite advantage in disease-free survival to the combined-modality approach. At present, when radiation is being used either as preoperative or postoperative therapy in rectal cancer, 5-FU–based chemotherapy should be used concomitantly.

The question of the optimal timing of the combination therapy is more difficult. A number of in vitro studies have been performed to try to elucidate the mechanism of the combined-modality effect with radiation and 5-FU. However, the way in which these agents work in combination is not at all certain. Possible modes of action of 5-FU include DNA incorporation of the 5-FU, incorporation of the 5-FU into RNA, inhibition of DNA synthesis, inhibition of repair of sublethal radiation injury, or cell cycle effects. The radiation enhancement of 5-FU could be due to any combination of the above factors. Data suggest that it is probably not primarily related to altered repair of sublethal radiation injury.[10] A better understanding of the reason for the enhancement would make it possible to modify the effect more intelligently. It is known from in vitro data that the amount and duration of exposure of the cells to 5-FU is a very important factor in attaining radiation sensitization. This is important, since it is well known that the half-life of 5-FU after bolus administration is approximately 15 min, which means that the duration of exposure in the typical clinical setting is short.

Since the exact mechanism of action is not known, it is unclear how the drug should be optimally delivered to maximize radiation sensitization. With the very short half-life of 5-FU, drug delivered prior to the radiation would likely not be present at the time radiation is delivered in the standard clinical setting. There are some data to suggest that the maximum combined-modality effect is seen when 5-FU is given shortly after radiation therapy, but these data are not clear.[10]

Because of these issues, a study has recently been completed to evaluate the potential benefit of continuous infusion 5-FU in conjunction with radiation therapy. The aim here was to try to improve the radiation sensitization of the 5-FU by prolonging the exposure of the cells to the radiation. Results of this study are not as yet available.

Other strategies that need to be investigated include the use of other agents to increase radiosensitization. The drug leucovorin acts to increase the binding of 5-FU to thymidilate synthase and to stabilize the ternary complex, thereby producing further inhibition of DNA synthesis. It is reasonable to think that by effectively keeping the drug around longer, the radiation sensitization may be increased by effectively increasing drug exposure. Leucovorin is known to increase cell killing by 5-FU. One in vitro study has been completed which shows increased radiation sensitization when using the deoxyribonucleoside derivative of 5-FU (FUdR) plus leucovorin with radiation compared to the same regimen without FUdR.[11] This concept is being tested in an intergroup trial of the adjuvant therapy of rectal cancer.

REFERENCES

1. Gunderson LL, Sosin H: Areas of failure found at reoperation (second or symptomatic look) following "curative surgery" for adenocarcinoma of the rectum: Clinicopathologic correlation and implications for adjuvant therapy. *Cancer* 34:1278–1292, 1974.
2. Rich T, Gunderson LL, Lew R, et al: Patterns of recurrence of rectal cancer after potentially curative surgery. *Cancer* 52:1317–1329, 1983.
3. Mendenhall WM, Million RR, Pfaff WW: Patterns of recurrence in adenocarcinoma of the rectum and rectosigmoid treated with surgery alone: Implications in treatment planning with adjuvant radiation therapy. *Int J Radiat Oncol Biol Phys* 9:977–985, 1983.
4. Fisher B, Wolmark N, Rockette H, et al: Postoperative adjuvant chemotherapy or radiation therapy for rectal cancer: Results from NSABP protocol R-01. *J Natl Cancer Inst* 80:21–29, 1988.
5. Tepper J: Reflections in rectosigmoid: Retro-peritoneal vs. intra-peritoneal. *Int J Radiat Oncol Biol Phys* 14:1043–1046, 1988.
6. Pahlman L, Glimelius B: Pre- or postoperative radiotherapy in rectal and rectosigmoid carcinoma: Report from a randomized multicenter trial. *Ann Surg* 211:187–195, 1990.
7. Krook JE, Moertel CG, Gunderson LL, et al: Effective surgical adjuvant therapy for high-risk rectal carcinoma. *N Engl J Med* 324:709–715, 1991.
8. Moertel C, Childs D, Reitemeier R, et al: Combined 5-fluorouracil and supervoltage radiation therapy of locally unresectable gastrointestinal cancer. *Lancet* 2:865–867, 1969.
9. Gastrointestinal Tumor Study Group: Prolongation of the disease-free interval in surgically treated rectal carcinoma. *N Engl J Med* 312:1465–1472, 1985.
10. Byfield JE, Calabro-Jones P, Klisak I, et al: Pharmacologic requirements for obtaining sensitization of human tumor cells in vitro to combined 5-fluorouracil of ftorafur and x-rays. *Int J Radiat Oncol Biol Phys* 8:1923–1933, 1982.
11. Lawrence T, Heimburger D, Shewach D: The effects of leucovorin and dipyridamole on fluoropyrimidine-induced radiosensitization. *Int J Radiat Oncol Biol Phys* 20:377–381, 1991.

CHAPTER 67

The Postoperative Chemotherapy/ Irradiation Adjuvant Strategy

Leonard L. Gunderson
Michael J. O'Connell

HIGHLIGHTS

Although complete surgical resection with negative margins remains a vital component of treatment for mobile rectal cancers, a moderate to high risk of local or systemic failure or decreased survival exists in patients with primary tumor extension beyond the rectal wall, involved nodes, or both when treated with surgery alone, and adjuvant treatment is, therefore, indicated. The ideal adjuvant treatment for resected high-risk rectal cancer would preferably decrease both local recurrence and systemic metastases, increase both disease-free and overall survival, and accomplish such with acceptable morbidity. The efficacy of adjuvant treatment for rectal cancer was determined by the outcomes of three primary scientific end points at the 1990 National Institutes of Health (NIH) Consensus Conference on Adjuvant Therapy of Large Bowel Cancer[1]: (1) disease-free survival (time to relapse), (2) overall survival, and (3) incidence of pelvic (local) recurrence. Inclusion of local recurrence as a separate scientific end point is pertinent in view of the significant morbidity of pelvic recurrence[2] and the difficulty of achieving subsequent salvage for cure. While distant metastases result in less patient-months of morbidity than local recurrence after surgery alone,[2] subsequent cure can be achieved only when metastases in the liver or lung can be resected. In future trials, reduction in the incidence of distant metastases with effective systemic adjuvants would be a justifiable separate end point.

Single-Modality Adjuvants

Neither postoperative irradiation nor chemotherapy as a single adjuvant has met all suggested criteria of efficacy with regard to disease control and survival. Although postoperative irradiation diminishes the incidence of local recurrence in both nonrandomized single-institutional as well as randomized multi-institutional trials, this has not translated into an improvement in overall survival in randomized trials.[3,4] Adjuvant chemotherapy produced a significant improvement in disease-free survival and marginal improvement in overall survival in a single trial,[4] but survival benefits from chemotherapy alone have not been demonstrated in other controlled trials.[3,5] No significant improvement in local control has been seen with chemotherapy as a single adjuvant in any randomized study of rectal cancer.

Combined-Modality Adjuvants

Combined-modality adjuvant treatment with postoperative irradiation plus chemotherapy has demonstrated efficacy in all parameters (improved local control of tumor, disease-free survival, and overall survival) in two prospectively randomized trials for resected high-risk rectal cancer.[3,5,6] In both trials, 5-fluorouracil (5-FU) was given during irradiation, and patients received 5-FU methyl-CCNU either after the combined treatment or both before and after. On the basis of these randomized data, the NIH Consensus Conference noted that

"Combined postoperative chemotherapy and radiation therapy improves local control and survival in stages II and III patients [with rectal cancer] and is recommended."[1] (Dukes B or C; Astler-Coller B_2, C_1, or C_2; modified Astler-Coller B_{2-3} or C_{1-3}; TNM $T_{3-4}N_0$, T_{is-4} N_{1-3}). Subsequent randomized trials have demonstrated that methyl-CCNU does not produce an additive benefit to irradiation plus 5-FU.[7,8] Postoperative irradiation plus 5-FU has, therefore, served as the standard of treatment and was the control arm in the recently completed intergroup trial that randomized over 1800 patients to one of four treatment arms. The study was designed to determine the best method of achieving both local control (irradiation plus bolus 5-FU or 5-FU plus low-dose leucovorin) and systemic control (5-Fu ± low-dose) leucovorin + levamisole, or all three drugs combined). Since distant metastasis is the predominant pattern of failure following combined-modality treatment with postoperative irradiation plus chemotherapy, the incidence of such failures will be an important fourth independent end point in this and future studies.

CONTROVERSIES

Five years ago the basic controversies in adjuvant treatment of rectal cancer were markedly different than today, since there was little agreement on a standard recommendation for high-risk patients who had undergone resection. The existing controversies were as follows: (1) Is irradiation a necessary component of treatment, since—as a single adjuvant—it does not improve survival? (2) Does chemotherapy as a single adjuvant add to the local benefits of irradiation? (3) Is adjuvant treatment necessary in all patients with high-risk primary tumors?

Since combined-modality adjuvant treatment with postoperative irradiation plus chemotherapy has demonstrated a statistically significant impact on both local and systemic disease control and survival, *current treatment-related controversies* center around how to combine irradiation and chemotherapy rather than whether to utilize either or both. Issues to be resolved in randomized trials include sequencing of adjuvant modalities when given postoperatively (e.g., Does chemotherapy need to be instituted before irradiation or can both be started concomitantly with equivalent effect?) and sequencing of modalities relative to resection (i.e., Would preoperative irradiation plus chemotherapy be more effective than postoperative irradiation plus chemotherapy in potentially resectable but high risk patients?).

Appropriate patient selection for adjuvant trials has not been a major controversy, but this should potentially be reevaluated. At present all patients with primary tumor extension beyond the muscularis propria, nodal involvement, or both are eligible for current intergroup trials and are usually treated in nonstudy settings. However, the risks of local recurrence or distant metastases can vary markedly within these subsets of patients, and the potential for overtreatment exists. For instance, in patients with uninvolved nodes but extension beyond the muscularis propria, the risk of local recurrence after resection alone varies markedly on the basis of degree of extension beyond the muscularis propria. In a single-institution analysis from Massachusetts General Hospital (MGH), the risk of local recurrence in patients with microscopic extrarectal involvement was 17 percent (2/12) versus 53 percent (8/15) in patients with adherence to or involvement of adjuvant organs or structures.[9] While inclusion of all patients with the latter operative/pathologic extent of disease is justified, 80 percent of the former group may not need either irradiation or chemotherapy. In our institution, selected patients with minimal extrarectal extension of 1 to 2 mm and good radial resection margins ($\geq$ 1 to 1.5 cm) are offered the option of close follow-up.[10] Select node-positive patients with high rectal primaries which are confined to the rectal wall and involve only one or two nodes are also at lower risk for relapse, either locally or systemically, and could possibly be observed closely instead of automatically receiving adjuvant treatment.[11]

Conversely, most patients with the primary tumor confined to the rectal wall and with uninvolved nodes are currently excluded from adjuvant treatment in randomized trials and most single-institution nonstudy treatment approaches. Whereas the risk of local recurrence or distant metastases in this group of patients is $\leq$10 percent in most surgery-alone series, it approaches 20 percent in other series or in subset analyses. Therefore, we may currently be undertreating subsets of patients with T_2N_0 lesions.

FUTURE DIRECTIONS

Future trials need to define optimal combinations of irradiation and chemotherapy (what drugs, route, and timing of delivery, sequencing of radiation and chemotherapy, etc.) and to determine whether some patients can be spared the most aggressive treatment combinations (i.e., limited B_2 and C_1). There is a need to evaluate both which drugs and methods of delivery should be used during irradiation to enhance its effect and which drugs are most effective in altering systemic patterns of failure. It will be important to determine the role of tumor DNA content (ploidy) as determined by flow cytometry, peritoneal cytology, and other parameters in predicting patterns of failure and prognosis and to determine total as well as initial patterns of failure as an aid in the design of future studies.

In view of improvements in local control with single-modality pre- versus postoperative irradiation in a Swedish randomized trial,[12] it would be of interest to randomly compare full-dose preoperative and postoperative radiation plus concomitant chemotherapy in patients with mobile, clinically resectable $T_{3-4}N_{0-2}$ or $T_{1-4}N_0$ rectal cancers. An extensive evaluation should be conducted prior to randomization to assure—to the extent possible—that patients have equivalent stages of disease (i.e., to be certain that any differences in results are due to treatment effect and not imbalances in disease extent). In addition to routine studies (serum chemistries, chest film, colon x-ray plus proctoscopy or colonoscopy), transrectal ultrasound and abdominal/pelvic computed tomography (CT) should be obtained.

PATIENT SELECTION

Patients with rectal cancer who are appropriate candidates for adjuvant treatment after complete surgical resection are those with a moderate to high risk of local or systemic failure if treated with surgery alone. In the Mayo–North Central Cancer Treatment Group (NCCTG) randomized trial (79-47-51),[6] the *required characteristics for patient entry* were as follows: (1) Patients with histologic proof of adenocarcinoma of the rectum in whom a potentially curative resection had been performed with neither gross nor microscopic evidence of residual disease. (2) The resected specimen had an indicator of poor prognosis, i.e., modified Astler-Coller stage B_{2-3} (invasion of perirectal fat or adjacent organs by direct extension) or C_{1-3} (involvement of regional lymph nodes with or without perirectal involvement). See Table 67-1. (3) The inferior edge of the primary lesion was at the sacral promontory or below (i.e., within the sacral hollow) or within 12 cm of the anal verge. (4) Patients must have recovered from the acute effects of surgery and had to be maintaining normal oral nutrition. (5) Patients with abdominoperineal resections whose perineal incisions were not adequately healed by day 56 could enter the study up to day 70 postoperatively. *Contraindications to protocol entry* included the following: (1) A leukocyte count of less than 4000 or a platelet count less than 130,000. (2) Any prior radiation therapy to the pelvis. (3) Any prior chemotherapy. (4) Any malignant disease within the previous 5 years except superficial squamous or basal cell carcinoma of the skin or in situ carcinoma of the cervix. (5) Any evidence of distant metastasis. (6) Regional metastasis that could not be resected en bloc with the primary lesion. (7) Any active and significant coexistent disease which, in the judgment of the investigator, would make the risks of chemotherapy or radiation therapy prohibitive.

With regard to appropriate patient selection for adjuvant treatment in either a controlled protocol setting or in clinical practice in a nonstudy setting, there is

Table 67-1
Comparison of Staging Systems for Colorectal Adenocarcinoma

Dukes	*TNM*		*TNM*[a]		*Modified Astler-Coller (MAC)*
A	I	T_{is}	N_0	M_0	A
		T_1 T_2	N_0	M_0	B_1
B	II	T_3 T_{4a}	N_0	M_0	B_2
		T_{4b}	N_0	M_0	B_3
C	III	T_1 T_2	N_1 N_2 N_3	M_0	C_1
		T_3 T_{4a}	N_2 N_2 N_3	M_0	C_2
		T_{4b}	N_1 N_2 N_3	M_0	C_3
D	IV	Any T	Any N	M_1	D

[a]T_{is}, carcinoma in situ; T_1, tumor invades submucosa; T_2, tumor invades muscularis propria; T_3, tumor invades through the muscularis propria into the subserosa or into nonperitonealized pericolic or perirectal tissues; T_{4a}, tumor perforates the visceral peritoneum; T_{4b}, tumor (is adherent to or directly invades) other organs or structures (surgical or pathologic definition). N_0, no regional lymph node metastasis; N_1, metastasis in 1 to 3 pericolic or perirectal lymph nodes; N_2, metastasis in ≥4 pericolic or perirectal lymph nodes; N_3, metastasis in any lymph node along the course of a named trunk; M_0, no distant metastasis; M_1, distant metastasis.

Note: T_4 is substaged and information in parentheses added to more clearly define patients with differential failure risks.

[b]Lymph nodes beyond those encompassed by standard resection of the primary tumor and regional lymphatics (e.g., retroperitoneal nodes) are considered distant metastases.

SOURCE: Adapted from O'Connell and Gunderson.[14] Reproduced by permission.

little disagreement with regard to required characteristics 1 and 4 noted previously or with contraindication 7. For controlled investigational trials, all contraindications are appropriate; but for purpose of nonprotocol adjuvant treatment, exceptions could be made for items 1 through 6 for selected patients. In patients with reduced WBC or platelet counts, pelvic irradiation would usually be feasible; but the medical oncologist would have to determine whether the reduced counts would allow safe delivery of 5-FU during as well as before or after irradiation. Prior pelvic irradiation may not preclude further irradiation but may only alter irradiation dose levels or field design. If an abdominoperineal resection were performed and the surgeon utilized reconstruction methods to exclude small bowel from the pelvis, it may be possible to safely deliver an additional 4000 to 5000 cGy in 180-cGy fractions even in patients who received a prior dose of ≤4500 cGy (decision dependent on time interval from prior irradiation, patient risk factors, informed consent regarding increased risks, etc.). Prior chemotherapy should not preclude the use of concomitant chemotherapy with irradiation or subsequent maintenance chemotherapy but may affect choice of agents or dose level. If solitary distant or regional metastases have been resected in patients with high risks for local recurrence, aggressive combined-modality treatment to reduce both systemic and local/regional risks would be quite appropriate. If patients have unresected distant metastases, chemotherapy alone would usually be the most appropriate treatment, with irradiation reserved for symptomatic local recurrence. Nonprotocol combined-modality treatment for patients with a successfully treated prior malignancy may again be indicated, depending on the nature of the prior cancer, disease extent of the new lesion, and factors of patient tolerance.

The major current questions in patient selection for adjuvant treatment of rectal cancer center around the definition of high-risk factors, what constitutes a rectal versus sigmoid lesion, and in which patients treatment can be given safely. If therapeutic gains in local tumor control are to be achieved with acceptable normal-tissue tolerance, it helps if initial tumor extent is defined radiographically or with surgical clips to allow the use of shrinking-field irradiation techniques. Knowledge of lymphatic drainage can also aid the design of appropriate radiation fields. Some patients with upper rectal cancers are currently being excluded from protocol or nonprotocol adjuvant combined-modality treatment because of the following: (1) Physicians do not understand the anatomy of the large bowel. (2) Studies have not been obtained to define tumor location. (3) The surgeon's operative note contains insufficient information, and the radiation and medical oncologists see the patient 1 month postoperatively, when the surgeon cannot remember enough anatomic information to reconstruct lesion location. As noted in the preceding discussion of controversies, the definition of the term *high-risk lesions* based on operative pathologic extent is so generalized that some patients with apparent local or distant risks ≤10 percent are being treated and some with risks ≥20 percent are not. In an attempt to clarify these issues or at least highlight potential controversies, summary information on diagnostic evaluation, anatomy, and staging and is presented below.

Diagnostic Evaluation

The radiation oncologist is often consulted only after a patient's malignancy has been resected and must use information obtained from preoperative studies, operative findings, and pathologic review to design appropriate radiation fields. Studies that evaluate the local extent of disease should be performed on every patient prior to exploration and should include digital exam, proctoscopy and/or colonoscopy, and a barium enema study, including cross-table lateral views. While endoscopy procedures are of value in diagnosis, they should not be performed as a substitute for a barium enema study, since the findings are of limited worth to the radiation oncologist in reconstructing tumor volume in three-dimensional fashion for the purpose of sparing normal structures. When endoscopy is performed, the lesion's position on the bowel wall should be described as well as its distance from the anal verge, its size, the degree of circumference involved, and whether the lesion is exophytic or ulcerative. When lesions are palpable, one should note the inferior extent relative to the anal verge, lesion location (anterior, posterior, etc.), degree of circumference involved, and whether the lesion is clinically mobile or is fixed to extrarectal structures. If low or midrectal lesions are immobile or fixed, CT of the pelvis can confirm the presence or absence of free space between the malignancy and a structure that may or may not be surgically resectable.

Anatomical Considerations

The large bowel consists of rectum and colon. The rectum begins in the hollow of the upper to middle presacrum as a continuation of the sigmoid colon. While the sigmoid colon has a complete peritoneal covering (serosa) and mesentery, the upper rectum is covered by peritoneum anteriorly and laterally (Fig. 67-1). The lower half to two-thirds of the rectum is below the peritoneal reflection (infraperitoneal) and is surrounded by fibrous fatty tissue as well as organs and structures that can be involved by direct tumor ex-

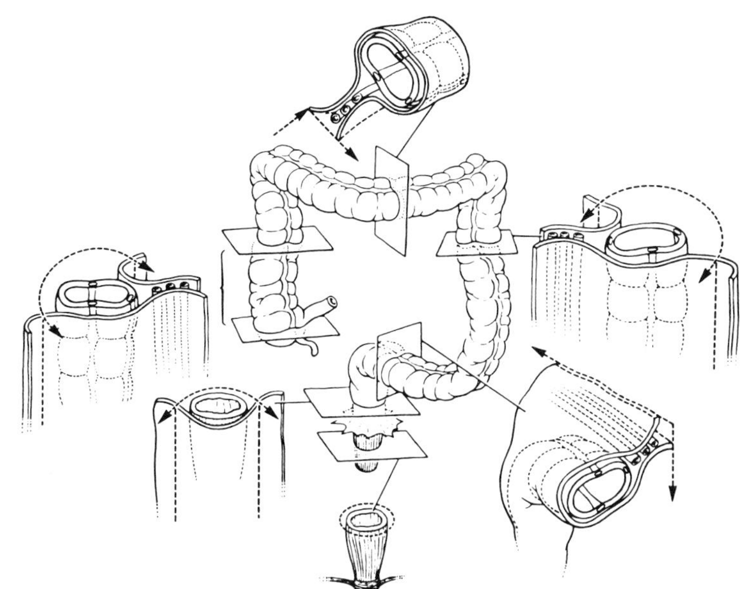

FIG. 67-1. Idealized depiction of peritoneal relationships in the colon and rectum. The transverse and sigmoid colon are intraperitoneal, with a complete peritoneal covering (serosa) and mesentery. The ascending and descending colon are retroperitoneal, lack a true mesentery, and usually do not have a peritoneal covering posteriorly or laterally. The upper rectum begins above the peritoneal reflection and has peritoneum anteriorly and laterally. The lower half to two-thirds of the rectum is below the peritoneal reflection (infraperitoneal).

tension (bladder, prostate, ureters, vagina, sacrum, nerves, and vessels).

The rectum is sometimes incorrectly defined as starting at the level of the peritoneal reflection or at 12 cm above the anal verge. Both definitions have been used in protocol settings in an attempt to standardize for purposes of quality control, but neither is a true anatomic definition. With regard to definition on the basis of 12 cm above the verge, the length of rectum will vary greatly in large versus small patients. The location of the peritoneal reflection can also vary widely. If a preoperative barium enema with a cross-table lateral view has been obtained, the anatomic separation of sigmoid and rectum may be easier. If not, the surgeon can define sigmoid from rectum by the presence of a complete peritoneal covering and mesentery in the former (Fig. 67-1).

Staging

Some of the difficulties encountered in patient selection or attempting to compare treatment results by series are differences in staging systems or incorrect interpretations of such. Details have been covered in previous chapters. While the original Dukes system was useful in predicting general survival outcome after surgical resection, subsets of patients within Dukes stage C were shown to have markedly different outcomes. This resulted in the Astler-Coller modification of Dukes' system (C_1—nodes positive, primary tumor confined to rectal wall; C_2—nodes positive, primary beyond rectal wall). What becomes confusing about the terminology of stages C_1 and C_2 in the literature is the fact that three different systems exist: Dukes (based on location of nodes), Astler-Coller (depth of primary tumor invasion), and the Gastrointestinal Tumor Study Group (GTSG; number of nodes). A subsequent modification of Astler-Coller (MAC) by Gunderson and Sosin subdivided stages B_2 and C_2 on the basis of degree of extrarectal or extracolonic tumor extension: microscopic (m), gross or macroscopic (g), or operative or pathologic adherence to or invasion of surrounding organs or structures (B_3 or C_3).[13] When the MAC system was used to analyze survival and patterns of release after potentially curative resection, significantly different risks were found for both survival and local failure for subsets of patients with either Dukes B or C lesions.[9] In the NIH Consensus Conference statement,[1] it was noted that the MAC staging system was used most commonly within the United States, but a plea was made for more standard use of the TNM system jointly agreed to by the Union Internationale Contre le Cancer (UICC) and American Joint Committee on Cancer (AJCC). The T and N portions of the TNM system have advantages over most other staging systems with regard to a more precise definition of the degree of primary tumor extension in lesions confined to the rectal wall and of node involvement by both number and location. However, there is some confusion with regard to the correct placement of lesions with primary tumor adherence to other organs or structures, since adherence is not defined within the TNM system. Separate authors from our own institution have substaged adherent lesions as either T_{3c}[6] or T_{4b}.[14] While we prefer the latter, the most important factor in future articles by ourselves or others will be a clear definition of lesion extent with regard to both primary lesion and nodes. If stage is defined only by TNM stages I through IV, however, much valuable information will be lost concerning differential survival and local recurrence risks within stages II and III (Dukes B and C), as previously discussed.

ADJUVANT RADIATION THERAPY: NONRANDOMIZED SINGLE-INSTITUTION DATA

The rationale for the use of irradiation as a component of adjuvant treatment is based on the risks of local recurrence after surgery alone and evidence that radiation alone can achieve local control and cure in some patients whose primary lesions are not resected. In 1962, Wang and Schulz[15] reported long-term survival in 12.5 percent (2/16) of irradiated patients who were medically inoperable or had surgically unresectable lesions. Patients received 35 to 50 Gy in 4 to 5 weeks. Cummings et al.[16] presented a series from Princess Margaret Hospital in which primary irradiation was given in 67 patients with tumor fixation and 56 with clinically mobile lesions. The latter patients were either medically inoperable or refused AP resection. Doses of 45 to 50 Gy in 20 fractions over 4 weeks yielded the best results. For patients with tumor fixation, local control and 5-year actual survival were low at 9 percent (6/67) and 2 percent, respectively. However, in those with mobile lesions, local control was achieved in 38 percent (21/56), and 5-year actuarial survival was 40 percent. Although the latter results are not competitive with combined-modality treatment that includes resection, they nonetheless strongly support the curative potential of irradiation as a single modality.

Postoperative Irradiation Plus/Minus Chemotherapy

In prospective but nonrandomized series of resected but high-risk patients, local recurrence has been decreased from an incidence of 35 to 50 percent with surgery alone to 10 to 20 percent with the addition of postoperative irradiation at doses of 45 to 55 Gy in 1.8- to 2.0-Gy fractions.[17–19] In spite of apparent improvements in local control, distant failures still occurred in 25 to 30 percent of patients.

Local recurrence was compared at an interval of 3 years from resection in sequential MGH series of 103 patients with surgery alone versus 95 patients with resection and postoperative irradiation.[17] An apparent reduction in local recurrence was found for most subsets of patients who received irradiation (MAC stages $B_{2[g]}$, B_3, C_1, and C_2). In a subsequent update by Tepper et al.,[18] a group of 165 irradiated patients continued to have a lower incidence of local recurrence by stage; only 15 received 5-FU during irradiation. The incidence of local recurrence in irradiated B_2 and B_3 patients was quite low at 8 percent (5/60); but in node-positive patients, the incidence still exceeded 20 percent.

In the most recent MGH update by Willett et al.,[20] simultaneous 5-FU was given during weeks 1 ± 5 of irradiation in 41 of 261 irradiated patients.[20] A trend for improved local control and disease-free survival was seen in MAC B_2 and C_2 patients who received 5-FU with irradiation (Table 67-2). Patients with C_3 lesions did poorly in spite of adjuvant irradiation or combined-modality treatment because of high rates of both local and systemic failure.

Systemic risks have been found to be higher in irradiated patients whose primary tumors exhibited both high-risk pathologic factors (beyond the rectal wall, nodes positive). In separate analyses from MGH and the Mayo Clinic, the incidence of distant metastases after adjuvant treatment was 40 to 60 percent with MAC C_2 ± C_3 lesions versus 20 percent with MAC B_2, B_3, and C_1.[17,19] The difference in the incidence of systemic failure appeared to translate into a survival difference. A 5-year survival range of 70 to 90 percent was achieved at both institutions with B_2, B_3, and C_1 disease versus 40 percent with C_2 (both) and 17

Table 67-2
Actuarial Local Control (LC) and Disease-Free Survival (DFS) with Irradiation ± 5-FU, at Massachusetts General Hospital

	Irradiation ± 5-FU, 5 years			*Irradiation alone, 3 years*			*Irradiation + 5-FU, 3 years*		
MAC stage	*No.*	*LC, %*	*DFS, %*	*No.*	*LC, %*	*DFS, %*	*No.*	*LC, %*	*DFS, %*
B_2	83	87	74	64	87	75	19	100	93
B_3	12	83	55	11	100	72	1	100	0[a]
C_1	20	76	62	15	79	67	4	100	50
C_2	121	77	41	105	82	49	14	90	71
C_3	21	23	10	18	37	22	3	33	0[b]
Total No.	257			213			41		

[a]At 22 months.
[b]At 15 months.

SOURCE: Adapted from Willett et al.[20] Reproduced by permission.

percent with C_3 lesions (MGH). In the Mayo analysis, 5-year overall survival appeared to be better with combined irradiation plus chemotherapy versus irradiation alone (70 versus 57 percent, $p = .01$).

Low-Dose Preoperative Plus/Minus Postoperative Irradiation

Low-dose preoperative irradiation (5 Gy × 1 or 5 × 2 Gy) has been combined with selective postoperative irradiation (45 to 50 Gy in 25 to 28 fractions) in view of some theoretical advantages over either high-dose preoperative or postoperative irradiation. Analyses of series from MGH[11] and Thomas Jefferson University Hospital (TJUH)[21,22] suggest that one can safely delete patients who do not require the postoperative component of irradiation (MAC stages A and B_1 with or without select early $B_{2[m]}$ and C_1 lesions) and yet achieve excellent local control and good survival.

In a recent update of the TJUH series, 120 patients were at risk for a minimum of 5 years following curative resection.[22] Of the 86 patients with TNM stage II or III lesions, 32 received only low-dose preoperative irradiation (5 Gy × 1), on the basis of surgeon or patient preference, and 54 received an additional 45 Gy in 25 fractions postoperatively. The addition of the postoperative component of treatment appeared to reduce the incidence of local failures in patients with TNM stages II and III lesions when compared with low-dose preoperative irradiation alone at 9 percent (5/54) versus 34 percent (11/32). Distant failure was also lower in the pre- and postoperative group at 19 percent (10/54) versus 28 percent (9/32). This appeared to translate into an improvement in 5-year absolute and 10-year actuarial survival of 72 versus 54 percent (5-year) and 62 versus 38 percent (10-year actuarial).

ADJUVANT IRRADIATION: RANDOMIZED TRIALS

Postoperative Irradiation

Treatment schema and results for four randomized U.S. trials are shown in Table 67-3. The impact of treatment on patterns of failure (local, distant) and survival (disease-free, overall) is summarized. Although irradiation-alone adjuvant arms existed in three of the four studies, the information discussed in this section will be limited to the two trials with surgery-alone control arms. While local control has been improved with adjuvant postoperative irradiation when compared with a surgery-alone control arm, no survival advantage was demonstrated.

In the GTSG trial (7175),[3,5] patients with TNM stages II and III lesions (Dukes B and C) were randomized between a surgery-alone control arm versus adjuvant treatment arms of postoperative irradiation (40 or 48 Gy), postoperative chemotherapy (5-FU plus methyl-CCNU), or a combination thereof (irradiation dose lowered to 40 or 44 Gy). The incidence of local recurrence as the initial site of failure was decreased in irradiated versus nonirradiated patients. The local risk was lowest with combined irradiation plus chemotherapy versus irradiation alone at 11 versus 20 percent.

The National Surgical Adjuvant Breast and Bowel Program (NSABP)[4] conducted a three-arm trial (RO1) comparing surgery alone with postoperative irradiation (46 to 47 Gy in 25 to 27 fractions) and postoperative chemotherapy [5-fluorouracil (5-FU), methyl-CCNU, vincristine]. In patients randomized to receive irradiation, there was a decrease in local recurrence from 25 percent to 16 percent ($p = .06$), which did not translate into improved survival. Of those patients randomized to irradiation, 14 percent did not receive such.

Pre- versus Postoperative Irradiation

A Swedish randomized trial compared high-dose-per-fraction preoperative irradiation to standard-fraction postoperative irradiation as single adjuvants.[12] The preoperative dose was 25.5 Gy in 25 fractions over 5 to 7 days with resection within 1 week—dose considered equivalent to 45 to 47 Gy in 2 Gy fractions by the authors. The postoperative dose was 60 Gy in 30 fractions of 2 Gy over 8 weeks with a 2-week break after 40 Gy; field size was reduced for the last 10 Gy. In those patients who had a curative resection (~90 percent in both groups), local failure was statistically lower in the preoperative group at 12 versus 21 percent ($p = .02$), but this did not translate into differences in either survival or the incidence of distant metastases.

Postoperative Plus/Minus Low-Dose Preoperative Irradiation

A randomized comparison of postoperative plus/minus low-dose preoperative irradiation has been conducted in a combined Radiation Therapy Oncology Group–Eastern Cooperative Group trial (RTOG-ECOG). Patients were randomized to either receive or not receive low-dose preoperative irradiation (5.0 Gy in one fraction) followed by immediate resection.[23] All patients with TNM stages II or III disease were to receive 45 Gy in 25 fractions to the pelvis postoperatively. Preliminary results in 304 analyzable cases demonstrated a trend toward improved 3-year actuarial pelvic (local) control in 148 patients receiving pre- and postoperative irradiation versus 156 patients with postoperative irradiation alone at 79 versus 69 percent. There was no statistical difference in the 3-year actuarial incidence of distant metastases (33 percent for both groups) or survival (75 percent preoperative and postoperative, 68 percent postoperative alone).

Table 67-3
Adjuvant Postoperative Randomized Rectal Trials, United States—Irradiation and Chemotherapy (MAC B_2, B_3, C_1, C_2, C_3)

					Advantage in tumor control		*Survival advantage*	
Group or institution	*Treatment regimen*	*XRT dose (Gy) schedule*	*Chemotherapy*	*No. patients*	*Local*	*Distant*	*Disease-free*	*Overall*
GITSG[3,5] 7175	(1) Op'n alone	None	None	58	—	—	—	—
	(2) XRT	40 or 48/1.8 Gy Fx	None	50	Yes[a]	No	Inc	Inc
	(3) CT	None	5-FU + MeCCNU	48	No	Yes[b]	Inc	Inc
	(4) XRT + CT	40 or 44	5-FU 500 mg/m² 3 d wk 1 ± 5 XRT; 5-FU + MeCCNU	46	Yes[a] $p = .08$	Yes[b]	Yes $p = .009$	Yes $p = .005$
Mayo/NCCTG[6] 79-47-51	(1) XRT	50.4/28 Fx	None	101	—	—	—	—
	(2) XRT + CT	Same	5-FU MeCCNU; 5-FU 500 mg/m² 3 d wk 1 ± 5 XRT; 5-FU MeCCNU	103	Yes $p = .04$	Yes $p = .01$	Yes $p = .002$	Yes $p = .025$
NSABP[4] R01	(1) Op'n alone	None	None	173	—	—	—	—
	(2) XRT	47/26 Fx	None	177	Yes ($p = .06$)	Dec	Equal	Equal
	(3) CT	None	5-FU, MeCCNU, VCR	178	Inc	Equal	Yes $p = .006$	Yes $p = .05$
GTSG[2] 7180	(1) XRT + CT (5FU)	41.4/23 Fx	5-FU 500 mg/m² 3 d wk 1 ± 5 XRT;5FU	104	Equal	Yes $p = .05$	Inc $p = .20$	Inc $p = .58$
	(2) XRT + CT (5-FU + MeCCNU)	Same	5-FU + XRT (as in #1); 5-FU + MeCCNU	95	Equal	—	—	—
NCCTG 864751[25] (intergroup)	(1) XRT + CT (bolus 5FU ± MeCCNU)	50.4 to 54/ 28-30 Fx	Same as arm 2 79-47-51	332	—	—	—	—
	(2) XRT + CT (bolus 5-FU ± MeCCNU) CI5-FU	Same	Bolus 5-FU ± MeCCNU; CI5-FU during XRT; 5-FU ± MeCCNU	328	Inc	Yes $p = .03$	Yes $p = .01$	Yes $p = .005$

[a]Local control advantage to XRT versus no XRT, $p = .08$.

[b]Distant control advantage to CT versus no CT.

Abbreviations: MAC, modified Astler-Coller stage. Op'n, operation; XRT, external irradiation; Fx, fractions; CT, chemotherapy; CI5-FU, continuous-infusion 5-FU; LF, local failure; SR, survival; DFS, disease-free SR; Inc, increased survival or tumor control but not statistically significant; Dec, decreased. Yes, marginal or statistically significant improvement.

SOURCE: Adapted from Gunderson et al.[33] Reproduced by permission.

ADJUVANT CHEMOTHERAPY: RANDOMIZED TRIALS

Chemotherapy as a single modality has not had an impact on all suggested criteria of efficacy as adjuvant therapy for rectal cancer. While a marginal improvement in overall survival was seen in the NSABP trial,[4] no significant improvement in local control has been demonstrated with chemotherapy as a single adjuvant in any randomized rectal study.

The GTSG trial[3,5] failed to demonstrate any significant improvement with the use of postoperative 5-FU plus methyl-CCNU chemotherapy in either disease-free or overall survival compared to surgery alone or surgery followed by postoperative irradiation. No apparent impact on local control was seen with chemotherapy as a single adjuvant with that treatment arm having the highest incidence of local recurrence at 27 percent. An apparent impact on distant failures was noted in those patients who received chemotherapy alone or with irradiation versus those who received no chemotherapy.

The subsequent much larger NSABP trial[4] demonstrated a small overall survival advantage for patients receiving postoperative chemotherapy with 5-FU plus methyl-CCNU plus vincristine compared to surgery alone (53 versus 43 percent 5-year survival) at a borderline level of statistical significance ($p = .05$). Disease-free survival was superior in patients receiving chemotherapy (42 versus 30 percent 5-year disease-free survival; $p = .006$), but there was no improvement in local tumor control. Thus, although it is possible that adjuvant chemotherapy with 5-FU plus methyl-CCNU plus vincristine may have some treatment effect, the magnitude of any benefit is small and has not been confirmed by other studies. Methyl-CCNU is no longer used in any cooperative group trials in the United States because of its marginal efficacy and substantial immediate and delayed toxicities.

It has recently been shown that postoperative adjuvant chemotherapy with 5-FU plus levamisole has significantly increased both disease-free and overall survival in patients with node-positive colonic cancer (TNM stage III or Dukes C).[24] This drug combination has not been tested as surgical adjuvant therapy for rectal cancer but was evaluated in combination with irradiation in the recently completed intergroup trial (INT 0114) in the United States.

ADJUVANT IRRADIATION PLUS CHEMOTHERAPY: RANDOMIZED TRIALS

Two randomized trials[3,5,6] (GTSG and Mayo Clinic/NCCTG), have demonstrated a decrease in local recurrence and an improvement in both disease-free and overall survival with the combination of postoperative irradiation and chemotherapy for patients with resected high-risk rectal cancer. Bolus 5-FU was given for 3 days during weeks 1 ± 5 of irradiation and patients received 5-FU plus methyl-CCNU after (GTSG) or before and after (Mayo Clinic/NCCTG) irradiation plus 5-FU.

In the GTSG trial, although the disease-free survival of all three adjuvant arms was higher than surgery alone, a statistically significant advantage was achieved only in a comparison of the combined irradiation/chemotherapy arm versus the surgery-alone control arm.[3,5] Statistically significant differences in both disease-free and overall survival were demonstrated with combined-modality treatment (p = .009 and .005). A nearly significant difference in disease-free survival was achieved with the combined-modality arm versus irradiation alone (p = .06). There was still uncertainty regarding the preferred postoperative adjuvant therapy, however, since radiation doses were lower than in the major prospective single-institution studies and the incidence of local recurrence was 20 percent in the radiation-only arm.

In the Mayo Clinic/NCCTG randomized trial (79-47-51), the minimum irradiation dose within the boost field in both the irradiation and irradiation-plus-chemotherapy adjuvant arms was 50.4 Gy/28 fractions/5½ weeks.[6] The combined/modality arm achieved statistically significant improvements in both disease control and survival. The incidence of local recurrence was half that seen with irradiation alone, at 13.5 versus 25 percent (p = .04), and distant metastases were reduced from 46 to 29 percent (p = .01). Both disease-free and overall survival were improved in the combined-modality arm (59 versus 37 percent, p = .002; 58 versus 48 percent, p = .025). This is the only randomized trial in which a course of full-dose chemotherapy was given before irradiation in an attempt to decrease the incidence of distant metastases.

Two subsequent randomized postoperative trials, GTSG 7180 and NCCTG coordinated intergroup trial (NCCTG 86-47-51), have demonstrated that methyl-CCNU does not produce an additive benefit to irradiation plus 5-FU. In the GTSG trial, all patients received irradiation plus concomitant 5-FU and were randomized to receive further chemotherapy with escalating doses, as tolerated, of either 5-FU alone or 5-FU plus methyl-CCNU.[7] Both disease-free and overall survival at 3 years were better in the 5-FU arm, and distant metastases were reduced (68 versus 54 percent, p = .20; 75 versus 66 percent, p = .58; 26 versus 40 percent, p = .05). While only preliminary results have been reported in the NCCTG coordinated intergroup trial (NCCTG 86-47-51), enough events have occurred to make it highly unlikely that the arm containing 5-FU and methyl-CCNU could achieve superiority over the arm containing 5-FU alone ($p < .05$).[8] As a result of these two studies, the current standard of treatment and control arm in the most recent intergroup rectal adjuvant study (INT 0114) was postoperative irradiation plus bolus 5-FU. The 5-FU is given as two 5-day courses before and after irradiation and two 3-day courses during weeks 1 and 5 of irradiation.

In spite of the disease-control advantages found with combined-modality postoperative adjuvant treatment, both local and systemic control of disease need to be improved further. In both GTSG 7175[3] and Mayo Clinic/NCCTG 79-47-51,[6] although local failure was decreased by half with the combined modality treatment, the incidence of local failure was still 11 to 13 percent. The Schild et al.[19] analysis from Mayo demonstrated that use of data on the initial failure pattern underestimates the true risk of local failure by 33 percent.[19] Therefore, the true incidence of local failure as a component of failure at any time in follow-up is probably ≥15 percent even with combined irradiation plus chemotherapy. The goal would be to reduce this to ≤5 percent if this could be accomplished with acceptable morbidity. In patients with extension of the primary tumor beyond the rectal wall, local control may be more difficult to achieve when the surgeon's radial margin of resection is narrow. This information has been monitored, when available, in the last two intergroup rectal adjuvant trials, but the impact on local control has not yet been evaluated.

There is a need to determine the most effective combination of irradiation and concomitant chemotherapy with regard to optimization of local control. The completed intergroup trial NCCTG 86-47-51 tested the best method of giving 5-FU with irradiation (bolus versus continuous infusion) with a 2 × 2 randomization design in 664 patients. A planned interim analysis of disease control and time to relapse indicated a significant advantage for patients who received continuous-infusion 5-FU during irradiation[25] (Tables 67-3 to 67-5). Although the analysis also revealed an improvement in overall survival, further follow-up is required for definitive evaluation of a long-term survival benefit. During the recently completed intergroup trial INT 0114, patients received either bolus 5-FU alone or bolus 5-FU plus low-dose leucovorin during irradiation. Data regarding the impact of treatment on local and distant control of disease will be unavailable for several years.

Systemic failures, as an initial pattern of failure, existed in 26 to 29 percent of patients in both GTSG 7175[3] and NCCTG 79-47-51.[6] There is certainly a need to evaluate the delivery of the most effective systemic therapy during the irradiation component of treatment—as well as before and after—in order to avoid delays of 2 ½ to 3 months between sequences of effective systemic therapy. In the latest intergroup adjuvant rectal trial (INT 0014), four different types of chemotherapy were given before and after combined postoperative irradiation plus chemotherapy (5-FU, 5-FU plus levamisole, 5-FU plus low-dose leucovorin, or all three drugs). As we attempt to optimize systemic control of disease, we may need new and more effective drug combinations with C_2 and C_3 lesions ($\pm$ C_1 with $\geq$4 lymph nodes) as opposed to B_2, B_3 and C_1 (all versus <4 lymph nodes).

A replacement intergroup study, to be coordinated by the Southwest Oncology Group (SWOG), has been developed to further pursue optimal combinations of irradiation and chemotherapy. The control arm will be the positive arm of intergroup study 86-47-51, wherein systemic treatment will consist of two cycles of bolus 5-FU before and after irradiation plus continuous-infusion 5-FU. One investigative arm will be taken from the just completed intergroup trial 0114 (systemic treatment with all three drugs and bolus 5-FU plus low-dose leucovorin during irradiation). The third arm will test continuous-infusion 5-FU as both systemic treatment and in combination with irradiation.

PREOPERATIVE VERSUS POSTOPERATIVE IRRADIATION PLUS/MINUS CHEMOTHERAPY

In Tables 67-4 and 67-5 an effort has been made to compare the efficacy of moderate-dose preoperative irradiation (utilizing data generated in two large ran-

Table 67-4
Pre- versus Postoperative Irradiation—Impact on Survival[a]

Sequence XRT/Op'n	*Advantage seen*	*Disease-free, % (p value)*	*Overall, % (p value)*	*Reference no.*
Preop (all stages)				
EORTC				
Curative	Preop XRT vs op'n alone	not given	69 vs 59 (.08)	26
Total	None	56 vs 51 (.54)	52 vs 49 (.69)	
Rotterdam				
T_3, T_4	Preop XRT vs op'n alone	not given	50 vs 18 (.001)	29
T_2	None	not given	62 vs 70 (NS)	
Postop[b] (5-year actuarial data and 2-tail *p* values unless specified)				
GTSG 7175	XRT CT vs op'n	70 vs 46 (.009)	58 vs 45 (.005, 1-tail)	3, 5
	XRT CT vs XRT	70 vs 52 (.06)	58 vs 52 (not given)	
NCCTG/Mayo 794751	XRT CT vs XRT	59 vs 37 (.002)	58 vs 48 (.025)[c]	6
NSABP RO1	CT vs op'n	41 vs 30 (.006)	53 vs 43 (.05)	4
GTSG 7180 (3-year data)	XRT 5-FU $\pm$ MeCCNU	68 vs 54 (.20)	75 vs 66 (.58)	29
NCCTG 864751 (4-year data)	XRTCI5-FU vs XRT bolus 5-FU	63 vs 53 (.01)	70 vs 60 (.005)	25
Preop vs Postop (all stages)				
Swedish	Preop vs Postop	not given for total group	43 vs 37 (.43)	12
Low-Dose Preop $\pm$ *Postop* (TJUH 5-year absolute and RTOG ECOG 5-year actuarial; TNM stages II & III)				
TJUH (nonrandomized)	Pre & post vs preop	not given	72 vs 54 (.006)	22
RTOG ECOG	Pre & post vs postop	not given	75 vs 68 (NS)	23

[a]All data are from controlled multi-institution randomized trials except for the TJUH series.

[b]Postop – MAC stages B_2, B_3, C_1, C_2, C_3 (TNM stage II, III, or $T_{3\text{-}4}$ NO, $T_{is\text{-}4}$ N+).

[c]Mayo 5-year overall SR 70 vs 57% postop XRT CT vs XRT (*p* .01).[19]

Abbreviations: See Table 67-3.

Table 67-5
Pre- versus Postoperative Irradiation—Impact on Disease Control

Sequence XRT/Op'n	*Incidence local recurrence, %*					*Incidence distant metastasis, %*				
	Op'n	*CT*	*XRT*	*XRT/CT*	*p value*	*Op'n*	*CT*	*XRT*	*XRT/CT*	*p value*
Preop (5-year actuarial)										
EORTC										
Total	35	—	20	—	.02	—	—	—	—	—
Curative	30	—	15	—	.003	25	—	25	—	.87
Rotterdam										
T_2	18	—	0	—	NS	26	—	45	—	NS
T_3, T_4	36	—	14	—	.08	45	—	32	—	NS
Postop (initial failure, crude incidence)										
GTSG 7175	24	27	20	11	.08[a]	34	27[b]	30	26[b]	—
NCCTG/Mayo Clinic 79-47-51	—	—	25	13.5	.04	—	—	46	29	.01[c]
NSABP										
Published	25	21	16	—	.06	26	24	31	—	NS
Consensus Conf.	30	—	19	—	.03					
GTSG 7180	—	—	—	17 vs 16	NS	—	—	—	26 vs 40	.05[d]
NCCTG 86-47-51	—	—	—	8 vs 12	NS[e]	—	—	—	31 vs 40	.03[e]
Postop vs Postop (crude incidence, local recurrence; 5-year actuarial distant metastasis)										
Swedish trial	—	—	12 vs 21	—	.02	—	—	28 vs 37	—	.30
Low-Dose Preop ± *Postop* (crude incidence)										
TJUH										
Pre &post vs preop	—	—	9 vs 34	—	not given	—	—	18 vs 28	—	not given
TJUH										
Pre & postop vs postop	—	—	21 vs 31	—	not given	—	—	both 33%	—	not given

[a]XRT vs no XRT.

[b]GTSG advantage to chemotherapy vs no chemotherapy at 20% vs 30% (DM only), 27% vs 32% (any DM).

[c]Mayo 5-year actuarial distant metastases (DM) rate of 33% vs 52%, XRT CT vs XRT.[19]

[d]Advantage XRT 5-FU vs XRT 5-FU Me-CCNU.

[e]Advantage to XRT CI5-FU vs XRT bolus 5-FU.

Abbreviations: See Table 67-3.

domized European trials) with postoperative irradiation plus/minus chemotherapy (data from four randomized U.S. trials), pre- versus postoperative irradiation as single adjuvants (Swedish randomized trial), and postoperative plus/minus low-dose preoperative irradiation (nonrandomized TJUH and randomized RTOG/ECOG data). Neither patient selection factors nor methods of analysis are equivalent from series to series. Therefore, the intent is not to compare actual percentages between series but rather to evaluate the impact of treatment modality and sequence on both disease control (local and systemic) and survival (disease-free and overall) within the respective series.

The only uniform benefit of adjuvant pre- and postoperative irradiation, as single adjuvants, is the ability to decrease the risk of local recurrence for resected high-risk lesions. A survival benefit was achieved only in subset analyses in the preoperative trials. In the Rotterdam study,[26] irradiation of T_3 and T_4 lesions resulted in an overall survival benefit (50 versus 18 percent, $p = .001$) and marginal significance in local control, but no benefit was achieved with irradiation of T_2 lesions concerning either local control or survival. In the European Organization for Research and Treatment of Cancer (EORTC) trial,[27] a statistical improvement in local control was noted in the total group and those with curative resection; this translated into a marginal improvement in overall 5-year survival only in patients with curative resection (69 versus 59 percent, $p = .08$). As noted previously, in the postoperative trials only the combined irradiation/chemotherapy arms had an impact on both local control and survival (Table 67-3).

In a Swedish trial that compared high-dose-per-fraction preoperative irradiation to postoperative irradiation as single adjuvants, the local recurrence risk in patients with curative resection was less in the preoperative group at 12 versus 21 percent ($p = .02$).[12] No significant difference was seen in survival or distant metastasis rates.

At this time it is uncertain whether the combination of low-dose preoperative irradiation with moderate-dose postoperative irradiation should be evaluated further. The nonrandomized single-institution analysis from TJUH certainly suggested an advantage of pre- plus postoperative irradiation over low-dose preoperative irradiation alone for high-risk patients (TNM stages II and III) with regard to both disease control and survival.[22] While the single-institution analysis from TJUH also suggested both disease control and survival advantages for the combined pre- and postoperative irradiation versus the option of postoperative irradiation alone, this has not been demonstrated to date in the randomized RTOG/ECOG trial.[23] While the latter series needs further maturation of data, the current trend toward improvements in local control has not yet translated into a corresponding improvement in survival. Since the incidence of distant metastases is similar in both arms, chemotherapy is probably needed in the combined pre/postoperative approach, as seen with postoperative irradiation alone.

An impact on distant metastases has not been demonstrated with either pre- or postoperative irradiation as a single adjuvant in randomized studies. This would suggest that most distant metastases are not due to cells disseminated at the time of surgical resection of mobile lesions but instead are due to preexistent micrometastases or circulating cells or arise from locally recurrent lesions. The only treatment with a statistically significant impact on distant metastasis is combined-modality postoperative irradiation plus chemotherapy.[6]

TOLERANCE ISSUES

Chemotherapy Tolerance Issues

Several clinical factors and laboratory parameters must be carefully evaluated to determine whether postoperative adjuvant chemotherapy is likely to be well tolerated. Patients should have recovered from surgery and any postoperative complications, be ambulatory, and be able to undergo chemotherapy treatments on an outpatient basis. The surgical incision should be well healed, and there should be no sign of active infection. Patients should be maintaining adequate oral nutrition and should not be experiencing frequent vomiting or watery diarrhea. Hematologic parameters should be satisfactory, in particular a WBC of ≥4000 cells/mm^3 and platelets ≥100,000 cells/mm^3.

Subsequent chemotherapy doses should be reduced to avoid severe toxicity in the event of significant stomatitis, diarrhea, leukopenia, or dermatitis following a cycle of treatment, and further chemotherapy should be delayed until any major side effects have resolved. Chemotherapy should be discontinued entirely if prolonged (>6 weeks) leukopenia or thrombocytopenia occurs following pelvic irradiation.

Toxicity observed from the chemotherapy component of treatment in reported clinical trials can be quantified with regard to acute events, but its contribution to chronic or delayed toxicity is less certain. The primary acute side effects of 5-FU chemotherapy consist of stomatitis, diarrhea, and leukopenia. Nausea, vomiting, and thrombocytopenia were also frequently seen when methyl-CCNU was included in the regimen, but they are uncommon when 5-FU is given as a single agent. In the randomized Mayo Clinic/NCCTG rectal adjuvant trial,[6] the incidence of severe toxicity (≥grade 3) due to chemotherapy given prior to or following 5-FU plus irradiation was as follows (Table 67-6): stomatitis, 1 percent; nausea, 10 percent; vomiting, 6 percent; diarrhea, 21 percent; thrombocytopenia, (<25,000), 4 percent; and leukopenia (<2000), 15 percent. Diarrhea and leukopenia are the predominant acute side effects during combined irradiation and 5-FU. Recent studies evaluating 5-FU and leucovorin combined with irradiation have indicated an increase in severe diarrhea (approximately 25 percent) compared to the use of single-agent 5-FU with irradiation (15 percent).

Radiation Plus/Minus Chemotherapy

A suitable therapeutic ratio between local control and complications is achieved only with close interaction between the surgeon and the radiation oncologist and the use of sophisticated radiation techniques.[28,29] Factors which should be considered surgically include clip placement to indicate areas of tumor adherence and pelvic reconstruction techniques to displace small bowel. Radiation considerations include use of lateral fields for a portion of treatment to decrease the volume of irradiated small bowel, treatment with bladder distention unless the tumor was adherent to bladder, and shrinking-field or boost techniques after a dose of 45 to 50 Gy.

The incidence of small bowel obstruction requiring hospitalization or reoperation when patients have received postoperative irradiation plus/minus chemotherapy appears to vary by treatment technique. When irradiation was given with only parallel opposed anteroposterior-posteroanterior (AP-PA) fields in early trials of M.D. Anderson Hospital, the incidence of severe small bowel problems was 17.5 percent in irradiated patients versus 5 percent with surgery alone.[30] When the superior extent of the treatment field was reduced from the L2-3 region down to L5, the risk decreased to 12 percent. In the postoperative MGH rectal series with shaped-multiple-field techniques, use of bladder distention, etc., the incidence of small bowel obstruction requiring operative intervention was essentially equal in the group receiving postoperative irradiation as compared with surgical resection alone at 6 percent versus 5 percent, respectively.[17,18] The Mayo Clinic/NCCTG rectal trial 79-47-51 was the first group trial to use multiple-field irradiation techniques. The incidence of severe small bowel problems in that study was ≤5 percent with either adjuvant irradiation alone or in combination with chemotherapy (Table 67-6).[6]

Gallagher et al.[31] evaluated the effect of volume of irradiated small bowel on acute and chronic tolerance following pelvic irradiation for a variety of malignancies, including rectal.[31] Patients with an abdominoperineal resection had more small bowel within irradiation fields than did those without prior surgery or with a lesser pelvic procedure. Volumes of irradiated small bowel were also markedly reduced with four-field versus AP-PA techniques, and some volume advantage was found for prone position with external compression and bladder distention. Dose and volume had a relationship to both acute and chronic tolerance. With regard to chronic tolerance, subsequent small bowel obstruction occurred in 0/75 patients with no previous pelvic surgery, 3 of 25 or 12 percent following abdominoperineal resection, and 2 of 50 or 4 percent with other pelvic operations.

A separate analysis from the same institution evaluated the influence of use of small bowel contrast during irradiation simulation on field design and long-term risks in 115 patients irradiated for endometrial or rectal cancer.[32] For patients in whom contrast was used, the overall incidence of side effects as well as chronic complications was reduced from the level seen in those simulated without contrast (overall, 77 percent versus 93 percent, $p = .026$; chronic, 23 percent versus 50 percent, $p = .014$). The superior field extent was commonly in a more inferior location in those simulated with contrast, thereby excluding small bowel from treatment fields.

The impact of sequencing of surgery and irradiation on later complications can be evaluated in the pre- versus postoperative irradiation trial for rectal cancer reported by Pahlman and Glimelius.[12] Perioperative mortality in the pre- versus postoperative groups was 3 and 5 percent, respectively (the latter risk was before

Table 67-6
Acute and Chronic Treatment-Related Side Effects in Postoperative Adjuvant Mayo Clinic/NCCTG Protocol 79-47-51

	Incidence by regimen, %		
	CT[a]	*XRT + CT*	*XRT*
Acute Intolerance	(N = 101)	(N = 96)	(N = 99)
Nausea			
any	73	38	6
severe	10	2	0
Vomiting			
any	54	11	1
severe	6	2	0
Diarrhea			
any	76	59	42
severe	21	20	5
Stomatitis			
any	23	4	0
severe	1	1	0
Leukopenia			
<4000	83	78	21
<2000	15	18	0
Thrombocytopenia			
<100,000	35	9	2
<25,000	4	0	0
Dermatitis			
any	0	28	22
severe	0	5	0
Chronic Intolerance (Severe)			
Small bowel[b]	—	6	4
Rectal perforation	—	0	1
Sigmoid obstruction	—	1	0
Pelvic fibrosis	—	1	1

[a]Alopecia in 16%, severe in 1%.

[b]Total 10 patients: 9 obstruction, 1 hemorrhage (6 XRT + CT, 4 XRT).

Abbreviations: CT, chemotherapy (before or after combined irradiation plus 5-fluorouracil, or 5-FU); XRT, external irradiation; XRT + CT, external irradiation plus concomitant chemotherapy with 5-FU.

irradiation and due solely to patient and surgical factors). For patients with minimum follow-up of 5 years, no differences were found in late effect, including small bowel obstruction, between patients treated with surgery alone versus those with adjuvant preoperative irradiation or adjuvant postoperative irradiation.

When patients receive multimodality therapy combining surgery, irradiation, and chemotherapy, the final result is usually a combined treatment effect with regard to both positive antitumor effects and negative normal-tissue effects. If patients have surgery, irradiation, and chemotherapy, how does one determine which treatment modality caused a subsequent complication? With multimodality treatment approaches, the term *treatment-related morbidity/mortality* should be used. Although both the GTSG and Mayo Clinic/NCCTG trials had a higher incidence of severe acute toxicities with combined irradiation plus chemotherapy than with irradiation as a single adjuvant, it is of interest that, in the initial report of GTSG 7175, all cases of small bowel obstruction were defined as "radiation enteritis."[3] In the GTSG trial, severe or worse nonhematologic toxicity occurred in 35 percent of patients on the combined-modality arm versus 16 percent with irradiation as a single adjuvant. Two patients in the combined arm died of complications of enteritis, free of disease. With regard to severe acute GI or hematologic intolerance, the randomized Mayo Clinic/NCCTG trial 79-47-51 demonstrated a significantly higher level of intolerance with combined irradiation plus chemotherapy versus irradiation alone (severe diarrhea, 20 percent versus 5 percent; WBC $\leq$2000, 18 percent versus 0 percent) (Table 67-6).[6] Chronic tolerance was similar, however, and the imbalance in acute intolerance was offset by the previously discussed advantages in disease control and survival for combinations of postoperative irradiation and chemotherapy versus postoperative irradiation alone.

ACKNOWLEDGMENTS

The authors appreciate the assistance of Julie Chambers and the Mayo Clinic Typing Service for assistance in the preparation of this manuscript.

REFERENCES

1. NIH Consensus Conference: Adjuvant therapy for patients with colon and rectal cancer. *JAMA* 264:1444–1450, 1990.
2. Gilbert SG: Symptomatic local tumor failure following abdomino-perineal resection. *Int J Radiat Oncol Biol Phys* 4:801–807, 1978.
3. Gastrointestinal Tumor Study Group: Prolongation of the disease-free interval in surgically treated rectal carcinoma. *N Engl J Med* 312:1465–1472, 1985.
4. Fisher B, Wolmark N, Rockette H, et al: Postoperative adjuvant chemotherapy or radiation therapy for rectal cancer: Results from NSABP protocol R-01. *J Natl Cancer Inst* 80:21–29, 1988.
5. Gastrointestinal Tumor Study Group: Survival after postoperative combination treatment of rectal cancer. *N Engl J Med* 315:1294–1295, 1986.
6. Krook JE, Moertel CG, Gunderson LL, et al: Effective surgical adjuvant therapy for high-risk rectal carcinoma. *N Engl J Med* 324:709–715, 1991.
7. Gastrointestinal Tumor Study Group: Radiation therapy and fluorouracil with or without semustine for the treatment of patients with surgical adjuvant adenocarcinoma of the rectum. *J Clin Oncol* 10:549–557, 1992.
8. O'Connell M, Wieand H, Krook J, et al: Lack of value for methyl-CCNU (MeCCNU) as a component of effective rectal cancer surgical adjuvant therapy: Interim analysis of Intergroup Protocol 86-47-51 (abstract). *Proc ASCO* 10:134, 1991.
9. Rich T, Gunderson LL, Galdabini J, et al: Patterns of recurrence of rectal cancer after potentially curative surgery. *Cancer* 52:1317–1329, 1983.
10. Chan KW, Boey J, Wong SKC: A method of reporting radial invasion and surgical clearance of rectal carcinoma. *Histopathology* 9:1319–1327, 1985.
11. Gunderson LL, Dosoretz DE, Hedberg SE, et al: Low-dose preoperative irradiation, surgery, and elective postoperative radiation therapy for resectable rectum and rectosigmoid carcinoma. *Cancer* 52:446–451, 1983.
12. Pahlman L, Glimelius B: Pre- or postoperative radiotherapy in rectal and rectosigmoid carcinoma: Report from a randomized multicenter trial. *Ann Surg* 211:187–195, 1990.
13. Gunderson LL, Sosin H: Areas of failure found at reoperation (second or symptomatic look) following "curative surgery" for adenocarcinoma of the rectum: Clinicopathologic correlation and implications for adjuvant therapy. *Cancer* 34:1278–1292, 1974.
14. O'Connell MJ, Gunderson LL: Adjuvant therapy for adenocarcinoma of the rectum. *World J Surg* 16:510–515, 1992.
15. Wang CC, Schulz MD: The role of radiation therapy in the management of carcinoma of the sigmoid, rectrosigmoid and rectum. *Radiology* 79:1–5, 1962.
16. Cummings BJ Jr, Rider WD, Harwood AR, et al: Radical external beam radiation therapy for adenocarcinoma of the rectum. *Dis Colon Rectum* 26:30–36, 1983.
17. Hoskins B, Gunderson LL, Dosoretz D, et al: Adjuvant postoperative radiotherapy in carcinoma of the rectum and rectosigmoid. *Cancer* 55:61–71, 1985.
18. Tepper JE, Cohen AM, Wood WC, et al: Postoperative radiation therapy of rectal cancer. *Int J Radiat Oncol Biol Phys* 13:5–10, 1987.
19. Schild SE, Martenson JA Jr, Gunderson LL, et al: Postoperative adjuvant therapy of rectal cancer: An analysis of disease control, survival, and prognostic factors. *Int J Radiat Oncol Biol Phys* 17:55–62, 1989.
20. Willett CG, Tepper JE, Kaufman DS: Adjuvant postoperative radiation therapy for rectal adenocarcinoma. *Am J Clin Oncol* 15:371–375, 1992.
21. Mohuiddin M, Dobelbower R, Kramer S: A new approach to adjuvant radiotherapy in rectal cancer. *Int J Radiat Oncol Biol Phys* 6:205–207, 1980.
22. Mohuidden M, Lingareddy N, Marks G: Long-term results of "selective sandwich" adjunctive radiotherapy for cancer of the rectum. *Am J Clin Oncol* (in press).
23. Sause WT, Martz KL, Noyes D, et al: RTOG 81-15 ECOG 83-23: Evaluation of preoperative radiation therapy in operable rectal carcinoma. *Int J Radiat Oncol Biol Phys* 19:179, 1990.
24. Moertel CG, Fleming TR, Macdonald JS, et al: Levamisole

and fluorouracil for adjuvant therapy of resected colon carcinoma. *N Engl J Med* 322:352–358, 1990.

25. O'Connell M, Martenson J, Wiland HS, et al: Improved adjuvant therapy for rectal cancer by combining protracted venous infusion fluorouracil and radiation therapy after curative surgery. *N Engl J Med* (in press).
26. Wassif SB, Langenhorst BL, Hop CJ: The contribution of preoperative radiotherapy in the management of borderline operability rectal cancer, in Salmon SE, Jones SE (eds): *Adjuvant Therapy of Cancer,* vol 2. New York, Grune & Stratton, 1974, pp 612–626.
27. Gerard A, Buyse M, Nordlinger B, et al: Preoperative radiotherapy as adjuvant treatment in rectal cancer: Final results of a randomized study of the European Organization for Research and Treatment of Cancer (EORTC). *Ann Surg* 208:606–614, 1988.
28. Gunderson LL, Russell AH, Llewellyn HJ, et al: Treatment planning for colorectal cancer: Radiation and surgical techniques and value of small-bowel films. *Int J Radiat Oncol Biol Phys* 11:1379–1393, 1985.
29. Gunderson LL, Martenson JA: *Technological Basis of Radiation Therapy,* in Levitt S, Khan F, Potish R (eds): Cancers of the colon and rectum. Philadelphia, Lea & Febiger, 1991, pp 342–350.
30. Withers HR, Romsdahl MM, Saxton JP: Elective radiation therapy in the curative treatment of cancer of the rectum and rectosigmoid colon, in Strocklein JR, Romsdahl MM (eds): *Gastrointestinal Cancer.* New York, Raven Press, 1981, pp 351–362.
31. Gallagher MJ, Brereton HD, Rostock RA, et al: A prospective study of treatment techniques to minimize the volume of pelvic small bowel with reduction of acute and late effects associated with pelvic irradiation. *Int J Radiat Oncol Biol Phys* 12:1565–1573, 1986.
32. Herbert SH, Curran WJ, Solin LJ, et al: Decreasing gastrointestinal morbidity with the use of small bowel contrast during treatment planning for pelvic radiation. *Int J Radiat Oncol Biol Phys* 20:835–842, 1991.
33. Gunderson LL, Martenson JA: *Current Therapy in Hematology-Oncology,* in Carbone P (ed): Colorectal cancer: radiation therapy. Philadelphia, BC Decker, 1992, pp 251–261.

CHAPTER 68

Surgical Approaches to Minimize Risk of Radiation-Induced Small Bowel Damage

Dennis F. Devereux

HIGHLIGHTS

The surgeon plays a pivotal rose in excluding the small bowel from the pelvis, thus minimizing the risk of radiation enteritis when radiation therapy follows surgery. Surgical technique utilized for the intestinal sling procedure (ISP) is outlined.

CONTROVERSIES

Prevention of small bowel damage following radiation treatment is no longer an area of controversy. The ISP, which elevates the small bowel out of the radiation beam's path, achieves this without undue harm to the patient. It has not been established, however, whether the small bowel must be excluded from the entire radiation field or merely from the true pelvis by covering the pelvic inlet.

FUTURE DIRECTIONS

Patients are often selected for postoperative radiation therapy based on T_3 or deeper (Astler-Coller B_2 or C) rectal lesion. Mid- or high-rectal carcinomas frequently require intraabdominal colonic mobilization. It is at this time that an absorbable mesh is placed. In patients with low-lying, fixed, and bulky rectal carcinomas, preoperative radiation therapy should be followed by transanal resection in appropriate cases. These patients would not require the ISP, as there is no intraabdominal surgical component; therefore, radiation-associated small bowel injury (RASBI) is unlikely even if postoperative radiation follows.

Future trials in patients undergoing abdominoperineal resection (APR) or low anterior anastomoses should be used to answer the question "Is small bowel exclusion from the true pelvis or from the entire radiation field necessary to prevent RASBI?"

The most common indications for pelvic radiation therapy continue to be for carcinoma of the cervix, endometrium, and ovary followed by carcinoma of the rectum and prostate. As effective as radiation is in the treatment of pelvic malignancies, the down side becomes equally problematic. During a patient's course of radiation treatment, normal tissues unfortunately sustain varying amounts of damage, either directly or by scatter. And although the response to the radiation damage by the normal tissue varies—due to factors such as previous pelvic surgery, diabetes mellitus, endomorphic body habitus, hypertension, and other predisposing phenomena—nonetheless, tumoricidal doses of radiation therapy (greater than 4500 cGy) begin to damage the intestines of even the most normal patients. When truly effective doses of radiation treatment are given in the 5000- to 6000-cGy range, the patient may trade cure from a malignant condition to an increase in morbidity and mortality from radiation-associated small bowel injury (RASBI).[1]

Retrospective data indicate that the true incidence of RASBI in postoperative patients ranges from 10 to 37 percent when doses of 4500 to 5000 cGy are administered.[2] In fact, some observers believe that RASBI may range as high as 71 percent.[3] However, this depends upon the manner in which the abnormality is defined. For example, Newman et al.[4] demonstrated that 16 of 17 women who had undergone pelvic irradiation for malignant gynecologic tumors developed malabsorption of bile salts. Most observers would probably agree, however, that the true incidence of RASBI following effective pelvic radiation therapy will never be known. It is also important to recognize that the type of surgical procedure that precedes radiation treatment affects this incidence. Patients undergoing pelvic exenteration or abdominoperineal resection have demonstrated a higher incidence of RASBI, as the volume of small bowel remaining in the pelvis following surgery is increased.[2]

Early radiation therapists observed the effects of acute radiation damage on their own small bowel, with nausea, vomiting, diarrhea, and cramps.[5] Today, nausea, vomiting, diarrhea, and cramps continue to be the clinical criteria by which the initial diagnosis of acute RASBI is entertained. Late effects of radiation therapy on the small intestine are primarily those of stricture, followed by perforation and fistula formation[1,6] secondary to progression of the underlying vascular problem.

In attempts to minimize the acute and chronic radiation changes associated with tumoricidal doses, fractionation techniques of supervoltage radiation therapy are now employed. However, assurances that fraction techniques protect the small intestine from damage may take many years to become evident, and as Dietel and associates[6] have reported, radiation therapy causing small bowel complications may appear as long as 30 years following effective treatment.

PATHOGENESIS

Radiation therapy disrupts not only the tumor but also normal cellular elements in the following way. The high-energy beam produces increased numbers of free radicals from intracellular water, which then interact with DNA to prevent its replication, transcription, and eventual protein synthesis. Some of these intracellular defects can be repaired; however, most result in lethal injuries to the cells.[7] This produces cell death and ultimately tissue loss from the intestinal villus and crypts; even the high mitotic rate noted in the small intestine of irradiated animals is insufficient to compensate for the mucosal tissue loss from the villi into the lumen. Therefore, ulceration takes place.[8]

The acute response to radiation injury is best explained on a cellular basis. Cells in the DNA synthetic phase (S phase) are the most radioresistant. Cells in the quiescent (nondividing *interphase*) require much larger doses of radiation before cellular damage and death occurs than do replicating cells. Cells in G_1 (the postmitotic phase) are the most vulnerable to radiation damage. Therefore, the cells with the highest turnover rate will be most affected. In the gastrointestinal tract, the cells with the highest turnover are the replicating cells deep within the intestinal crypts. Again, with loss of these rapidly dividing cells, there is no progressive maturation up the intestinal villi; the result is denudation, ulceration, and ultimately bleeding.

The most important clinical aspect of radiation damage to the small intestine, however, lies not in the acute mucosal tissue loss but in the chronic, progressive changes noted in the mucosa. Chronic changes are due to the effects of the ionizing radiation on the endothelial cells of the blood vessels supplying the intestinal mucosa. And although these endothelial cells are apparently more radioresistant than are the crypt cells, their loss is long-lasting, progressive, and the most troublesome. It is this chronic vascular damage, and not the acute mucosal loss, which ultimately results in the stenosis, obstruction, and fistula formation seen in patients so affected.

These endothelial cells swell in their initial response to radiation damage and eventually necrose, leaving behind denuded areas in the vascular lumen. This eventuates in thrombosis and vascular occlusion. Endothelial cell loss leads to an increase in vascular permeability, local tissue edema, damage to other small vessels in the area, and initiation of a fibrotic response in the subendothelial space, which is progressive and eventually, over long periods of time, occludes the vascular lumen. So although there is an obliteration of these small vessels in the submucosa, the damage results from a connective tissue response (fibrosis) to the radiation exposure, which eventually leads to ischemia, necrosis, stenosis, and fistula formation. In the long term, the normal vascular responses to trauma—such as dilatation, hyperemia, and repair of the damaged mucosa—are retarded because of the poor vascular response secondary to this obliterative arteritis. The wall of the affected segments therefore becomes thickened, indurated, and fibrotic, resulting in stenosis of the lumen and presenting frequently with complications of obstruction.

In addition to the problems secondary to fibrosis and obstruction, the affected bowel is compromised in its ability to absorb nutrients. These patients generally have carbohydrate malabsorption; this is best quantified utilizing a labeled CO_2, and the hydrogen breath test is also frequently abnormal in these patients. In one study, following 1 week of pelvic irradiation, 13 percent of patients had abnormal hydrogen breath tests, which ultimately increased to 45 percent of patients by the fifth postirradiation week. The inability to absorb the products of carbohydrate digestion results in bacterial fermentation and release of carbon dioxide, hydrogen, and methane gas.[9] Passive uptake of lipids, unlike active absorption of carbohydrates, is also affected in a negative way by abdominal irradiation.[10] Thus, radiation damage to the small bowel affects both active and passive transport of carbohydrates and lipids into the portal circulation,[11] giving rise to malabsorption and ultimately weight loss.

METHODS OF PREVENTING RADIATION-ASSOCIATED SMALL BOWEL INJURY (RASBI)

It has been reported that up to 70 percent of patients treated for gynecologic tumors demonstrate the chronic effects of successful radiation treatment primarily through an increased frequency of daily bowel movements.[12] However true, chronic diarrhea has been reported to affect only about 15 percent of patients.[13] The acute manifestation of RASBI is a function of the amount of radiation received by the small bowel. Damage is usually seen when 150 cGy/day or greater are targeted to the pelvis. When doses approach 6500 cGy 5 percent of patients so treated will suffer severe intestinal complications within 5 years.[3] Reduced radiation dosages of only 4000 cGy combined with chemotherapy can produce severe complications and even death from small bowel damage.[14]

Chemical Agents

Symptoms of chronic RASBI may be treated if the underlying cause can be postulated or is known. The problem of malabsorption is clinically managed by gluten-free diets, low-carbohydrate and lactose-free diets, as well as fat restriction. Cholestyramine is used if documented bile salt malabsorption occurs. Acetylsalicylic acid has proved successful in treating the symptoms of cramps and diarrhea in some patients.[15] The use of steroids in acute or chronic RASBI has met with limited success and should not be advocated on a routine basis.

Because the medical management of RASBI has continued to be a major problem for the clinician, several investigators have utilized various agents in attempts to prevent damage to the small bowel should it remain in the path of the radiation beam. Borgstrom et al.[16] claim protection from RASBI by administering intraarterial vasopression during fractional abdominal radiation in pigs. Hanson and Thomas[17] claim a radioprotective effect when mouse intestinal cells are pretreated by prostaglandins before radiation therapy. A sulfhydryl thiol, WR-2721, is a well-studied, well-documented radioprotective agent against acute and chronic small bowel damage when administered intracolonically in rats.[18] Whether any of these agents will be useful in protecting humans remains to be proved.

Elemental Diets

The use of elemental diets during the course of radiation treatment has gained recent attention. Mulholland et al.[19] demonstrated in guinea pigs that the intraluminal contents, particularly biliary and pancreatic secretions present during radiation treatment, exacerbate RASBI. It therefore followed that reducing the biliary-pancreatic secretion exposure by using elemental diets may be protective. A recent study in patients with invasive bladder cancer who received an elemental diet for 3 days prior to and 4 days during radiation therapy showed that these patients seemed to be protected from acute RASBI. Although 400 cGy/day was administered, a total dose of only 2000 cGy was received. The addition of glutamine to the diet of rats has been shown to be protective in some instances and may be associated with the reversal of intestinal damage.[20] These dietary formulations need to be studied prospectively in patients following abdominal surgery who are treated with tumoricidal doses of radiation therapy (4500 to 5000 cGy) before any conclusions about effectiveness can be made.

Techniques Employed by Radiation Therapists

Several techniques have been employed to displace the small bowel from the pelvis. If the small intestine is out of the radiation beam's path, it should suffer less direct damage. Again, it has been well documented that both acute and chronic RASBI correlates directly with the degree of exposure to the small intestine.

Investigators have used nitrous oxide gas insufflated into the peritoneal cavity,[21] bladder distention, and abdominal wall compression with the patient in the prone position[22] in attempts to displace the small intestine from the pelvis.

Patients with mid- or low rectal carcinomas who have not been explored previously are often treated with preoperative radiation therapy, particularly if the tumor is fixed. In them, the small bowel is not at risk of damage as (1) it is not fixed in position from previous surgery and (2) the radiation portals receiving tumoricidal doses are below the peritoneal reflection. Therefore, preoperative radiation therapy in this setting is relatively risk-free, as the small intestine receives only "scatter" or nondamaging radiation doses.

Bladder distention with saline or placing the patient in a head-down position is often tried. In patients having anterior pelvic fixation of the small bowel, lateral-field boost techniques can be used. This limits out-of-field radiation exposure of the small intestine to 4500 rads or less. It also allows a boost to the tumor bed (up to 6000 rads) through the lateral field.

The technique of covering the pelvic inlet with Dexon mesh would probably allow the lateral-field boost technique to be employed even though the entire small intestine were not completely out of the radiation field. As noted (Fig. 68-1), the small bowel will be located anteriorly to the boost area.

Unproved Surgical Techniques (Table 68-1)

Silicon skin expanders[23] and breast prosthetic tissue expanders,[24] both aimed at elevating the small bowel out of the pelvis and the radiation beam's path, have been used. Others have reported on the use of the omentum as a sling or a pedicle flap,[25] while De Luca and Ragins[26] used the omentum as an envelope to support the small bowel and prevent its descent into the pelvis. Follow-up data on these reports need to address complication rates and actual prevention of RASBI, which to date they have not. Kavanagh et al.[27] reported that surgical techniques such as reperitonealization of the pelvic floor or the use of the omentum (frequently surgically absent or, more often, too thin to support any intestinal weight) more often fail than succeed. Feldman et al.[28] demonstrated in a prospective, blinded study that use of host tissues does not reliably exclude the small bowel from the radiation portal.

Effective Surgical Techniques (Table 68-1)

With the commercialization of an absorbable polyglycolic acid mesh (Fig. 68-2), studies were initiated in rats to determine if the mesh could effectively keep the small bowel out of the pelvis.[29] The experiments were conducted over a 9-month period documenting, by upper gastrointestinal contrast x-ray studies, that this displacement was easily accomplished. Further work in a baboon model corroborated the effectiveness of this maneuver in an upright, ambulating primate model.[29] A serendipitous finding was that, following complete absorption, use of the PGA mesh resulted in an adhesion-free peritoneal cavity (Fig. 68-3).

However, although the mesh was capable of elevating the small bowel out of the pelvis, it was not known whether it would support the small bowel long enough to actually prevent RASBI. This would require a comparison with non-mesh-treated animals. The use of another primate model, the Cebus monkey, helped us to answer that question. All animals were subjected to a low anterior anastomosis. Half of the animals received the intestinal sling (mesh) while the other one half did not. Animals were then irradiated with 2000 cGy as a single dose in a blinded fashion. The sacral promontory was the superiormost boundary of the radiation portal. Animals were killed at intervals and notation of gross peritoneal appearance as well as histologic assessment of ileum, jejunum, and duodenum plus rectum and bladder was made.

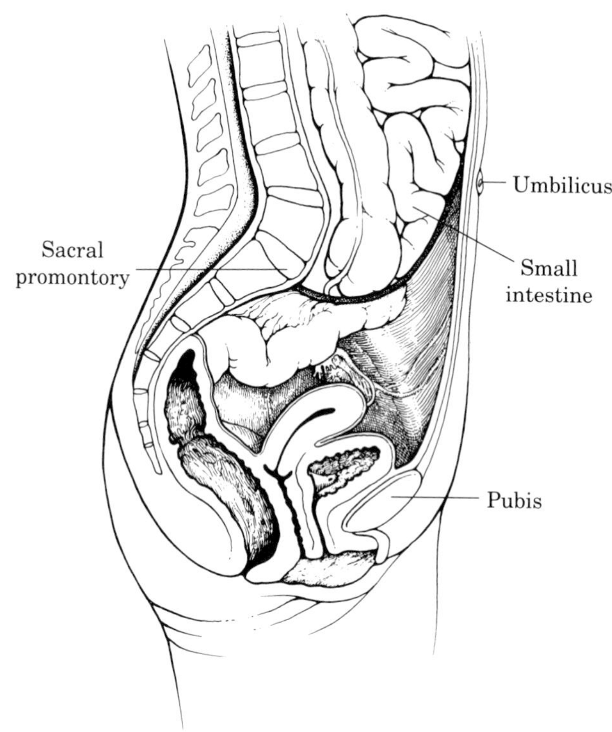

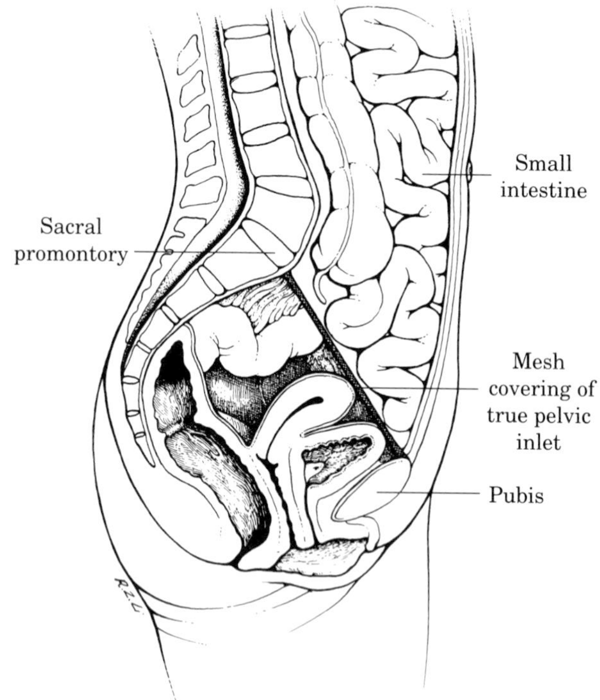

FIG. 68-1. *A*. Intestinal sling procedure in sagittal section. Position of small bowel seen in sagittal views is totally outside the pelvic radiation fields. Mesh is anchored at sacral promontory, around abdominal side walls and above umbilicus. *B*. Mesh covering pelvic inlet in sagittal section. Note that the small bowel is outside of the radiation fields in lateral projection but not in anteroposterior projection. Mesh is anchored to sacral promontory and to pubis. Mesh position defines true conjugate line.

Table 68-1
Operative Techniques to Prevent Small-Bowel Descent into the Pelvis

Surgical technique	*Clinical data on effectiveness*	*Comment*
Autologous tissue		
Uterus (uteropexy to sacral promontory)	Anecdotal—no data reported on effectiveness of RASBI prevention.	• Often surgically absent • Effectiveness depends on size ratio between uterus and pelvic inlet, i.e., small uterus in wide pelvis often allows small bowel to descend laterally into the pelvis. Not a totally reliable method of small bowel exclusion.
Bladder (vesicopexy to sacral promontory)	Anecdotal—no data reported on effectiveness of RASBI prevention.	Effectiveness depends on ability to mobilize the bladder—often troublesome and difficult. Inadvertent cystomies have been reported. Not a totally reliable method of small bowel exclusion.
Omentum (used as sling or envelope)	Anecdotal—published reports limited to post operative radiographs not on confirmations of RASBI prevention.	Often too thin in many patients to support small bowel even when used as a pedicle flap or envelope. No proven efficacy demonstrated.
Reperitonealization (mobilization of "peritoneum")	Anecdotal—often reported but seldom studied. No data on effectiveness of RASBI prevention.	The peritoneum is only several cell layers thick and is not vascularized. Therefore, mobilizing this diaphanous tissue with the expectation of supporting the small bowel is hopeful at best. No proven efficacy demonstrated.
Prosthetic materials		
Nonabsorbable		
Breast prothesis, silicone elastomer skin expanders or pelvic molds. (Fills pelvis with foreign body as method of small bowel exclusion.)	Has been demonstrated to prevent acute RASBI in a few patients. Follow-up too short to determine if it prevents chronic enteritis.	There is a risk of erosion when leaving a foreign body in a radiated field adjacent to host tissues. The pelvic mold requires a surgical procedure for its removal. **Use not recommended.**
Absorbable (mesh)		
Vicryl (90% polyglycolic acid, 10% lactic acid; *chemically different* than Dexon. Used as an intestinal sling or cover to pelvic inlet.)	Has been evaluated commitantly with Dexon in animals and humans. *Vicryl use is associated with dense adhesions and numerous pelvic abscesses,* however, it remains in patients long enough to prevent acute RASBI. Long-term follow-up regarding effectiveness is lacking.	In laboratory studies, Vicryl mesh is proven to suppress peritoneal leukocyte response to bacterial challenge. It is also demonstrably more adhesion provoking. Several investigators have reported serious complications with Vicryl use in the peritoneal cavity.[a,b] Its use in the peritoneal cavity cannot be recommended.
Dexon (Mesh #2) (100% polyglycolic acid used as an intestinal sling or covering for pelvic inlet.)	Has been investigated extensively in the laboratory and clinically. Dexon, when used as an intestinal sling (ISP) to prevent acute and chronic RASBI has been reported in over 250 cases. Its use has not been associated with adhesion formation nor pelvic abscess in uncomplicated cases.	Side effects associated with the ISP are limited to prolonged illness. Dexon mesh #2 can be used as an intestinal sling (1) to keep the small bowel out of the radiation field totally or (2) as a covering to the pelvic inlet which excludes the small bowel from the true pelvis. Dexon mesh has demonstrable peritoneal leukocyte stimulating properties in both animal and human studies, which probably accounts for its low pelvic abscess rate. Once dissolved, few if any adhesions remain and the small bowel descends back into the pelvis.

[a]Rodier JF, Janser JC, Rodier D, et al: Prevention of radiation enteritis by an absorbable polyglycolic acid mesh sling. A 60-case multicentric study. *Cancer* 68: 2549, 1991. With permission.

[b]Dasmahaptra KS, Swaminathan AP: The use of a biodegradable mesh to prevent radiation-associated small bowel injury. *Arch Surg* 126:366–369, 1991. With permission.

Abbreviations: RASBI, radiation associated small bowel injury; TCL (true conjugate), an imaginary line connecting sacral promontory to pubis in sagittal plane below which is true pelvis.

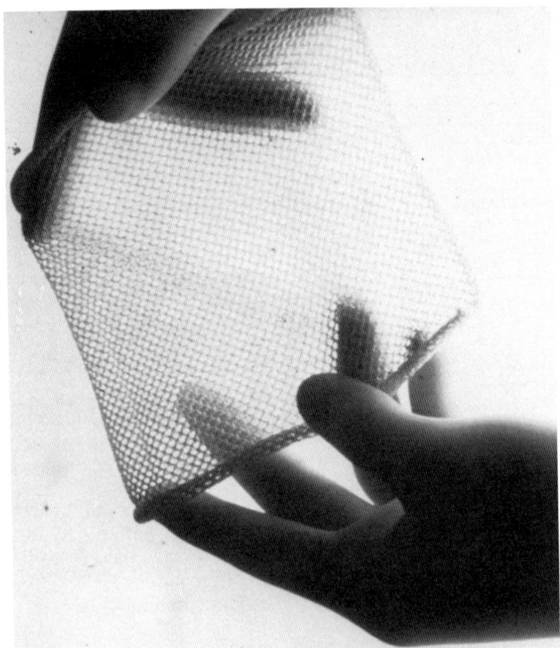

FIG. 68-2. Absorbable 100 percent polyglycolic acid mesh from Davis & Geck (Dexon mesh #2), Danbury, Connecticut.

Biologically, the experiment really ended at 2 months postoperatively, as all non-mesh-treated animals had died of acute RASBI (Fig. 68-4*A* and *B*), while the intestinal-sling-treated animals prospered in weight and biochemical parameters. The small bowel histology in mesh-treated animals remained normal (compared to nonoperated, nonradiated controls; Fig. 68-4*C*). This study confirmed that if the small bowel remains out of the radiation portal, its function and histologic appearance remain completely within normal limits.

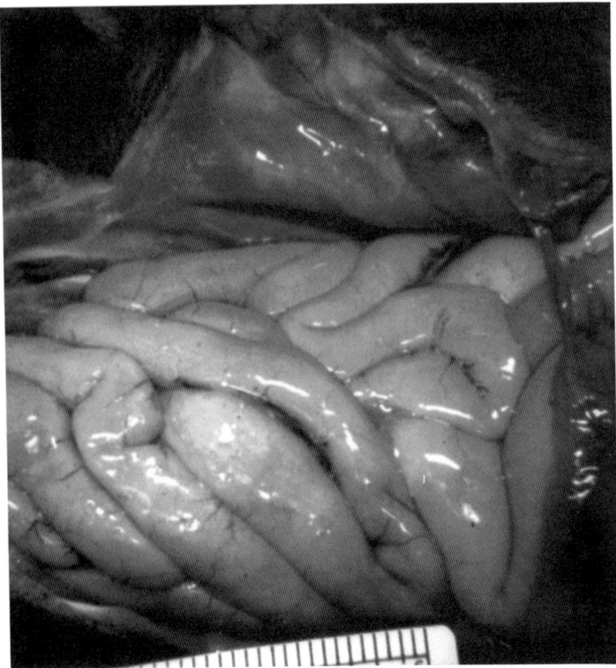

FIG. 68-3. Postmortem examination of a monkey 2 to 4 months postoperatively shows lack of adhesions following complete absorption.

Use of the intestinal sling procedure (ISP) with PGA mesh in humans has been found to have similar results.[30] For this procedure, we use Dexon mesh #2 only, as we have not noted a single septic intraabdominal episode attributable to it in uncomplicated cases. This has also been confirmed by others.[31,32] It appears that pure polyglycolic acid acts as a peritoneal white cell stimulant, increasing phagocytosis, intracellular hydrogen peroxide production, and bacterial killing (O'Connell, Spain, Robertson, Devereux, unpublished observations). Use of the PGA mesh results in elevation of the small bowel out of the pelvis for at least 3 months[29] (Fig. 68-5*A* and *B*); following total absorption, there are no residual adhesions (Fig. 68-6). This is because PGA is removed through hydrolysis, a noninflammatory process.

Elevation of the small bowel out of the pelvis results in a 5- to 7-day ileus, which is best prevented by leaving the nasogastric tube in place until passage of flatus.[33] Of critical importance to this discussion is that not a single case of acute radiation enteritis (nausea, vomiting, cramps, diarrhea, or dietary change) has been noted; this is compared to a high of 82 percent of patients treated with tumoricidal doses of radiation therapy whose small bowel remained in the pelvis.[34] Others have used PGA mesh to partition the small bowel in the right flank so high-dose radiation therapy could be administered to the left flank for colorectal carcinoma[35]—again, without noting acute radiation damage to the small intestine.

TECHNIQUE OF INTESTINAL SLING PLACEMENT

The intestinal sling procedure may be used in any patient with a pelvic malignancy. It is useful in patients undergoing either an abdominoperitoneal resection or a low anterior resection with similar protective results. The techniques are basically the same in both cases save for the handling of the descending colon in the case of anterior anastomoses.

The intestinal sling is initially sutured by two separate 2-0 Dexon sutures, each to be run in opposite directions. The sutures are placed deep into the sacral promontory under the aortic bifurcation (Fig. 68-7). Care is taken when sewing on either side of the great vessels. (Visualization of the ureter is mandatory.) Sutures are placed 1 cm apart with locking bites placed gently but deeply into the psoas and iliacus muscles (Fig. 68-8). On the right side, we recommend mobilization of the cecum and terminal ileum. Suturing is carried out laterally and always upward toward the lat-

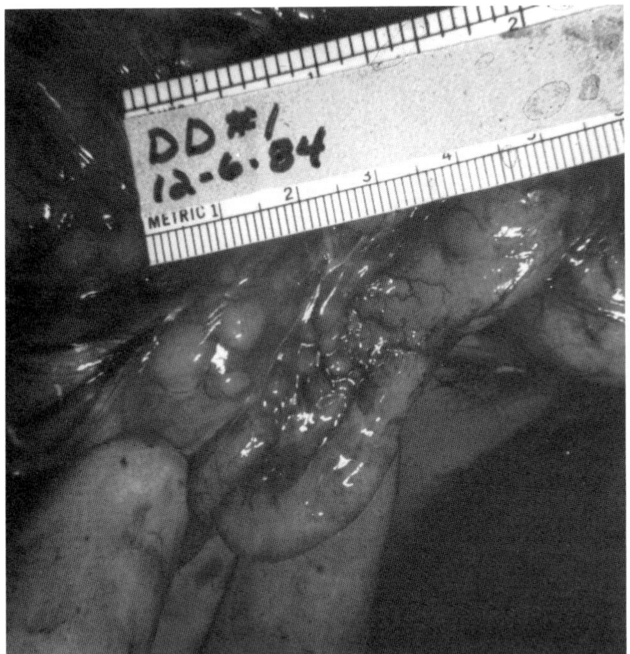

A

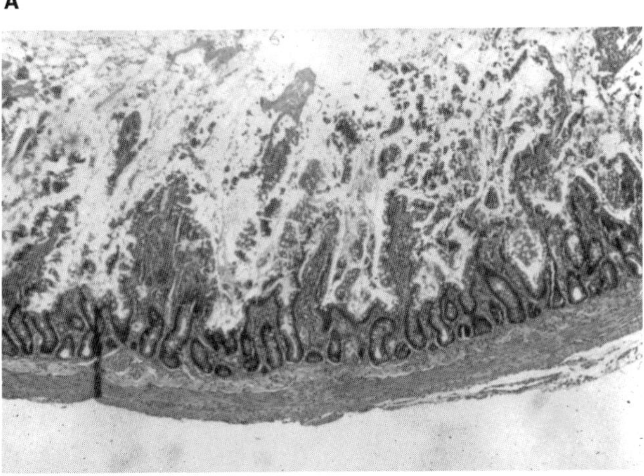

C

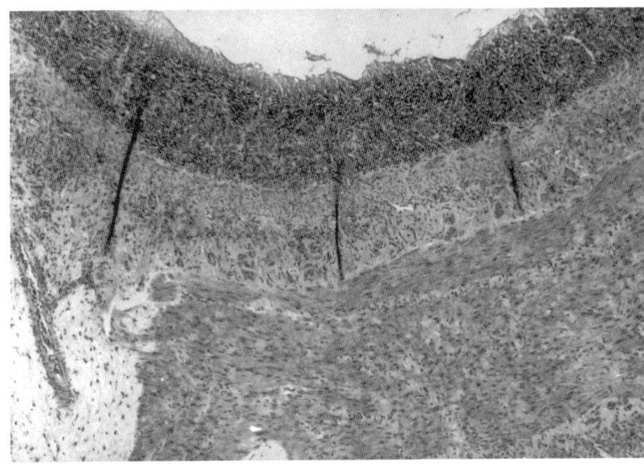

B

FIG. 68-4. *A*. Acute radiation damage to nonmesh Cebus monkey ileum at 1 month following a single dose of 2000 cGy. Note stricture, telangiectasia, and mesenteric adenopathy. *B*. Histology of strictured segment in *A*. Note loss of villi, edematous submucosa, thickened circular and longitudinal muscle, and presence of multinucleated giant cells so characteristic of radiation damage. (Courtesy Dr. Linda Sanhaus, Department of Pathology.) *C*. Cebus monkey whose small bowel was taken out of the radiation beam's path by suspending it with mesh. Note normal ileal villi and thin circular and longitudinal muscle. This photomicrograph is similar to those from nonoperated monkeys. (Courtesy Dr. Linda Sandhaus, Department of Pathology, Robert Wood Johnson Medical School, New Brunswick, New Jersey.)

eral gutter and cephalad toward the umbilicus. Once the lateral gutter is reached, deep bites are taken into the posterior aspect of the anterior abdominal wall. On the patient's left, crossing the vessels and ureter with 1- to 2-cm locking bites, we sew upward on the sigmoid mesentery (if present; if not present, we create a "mesh mesentery," as in Fig. 68-9), and then place seromuscular bites over and around the descending colon until the mesh or sigmoid mesentery is reached. Bites are then taken deep into the lateral gutter and posterior aspect of the anterior abdominal wall, always heading toward the umbilicus.

When right and left sutures reach the midline, we begin to close the midline incision from the top to create, in effect, a roof over the right and left sutures (Fig. 68-10). The right and left sutures gather up excess mesh and are sewn into the undersurface of the newly created roof. The small bowel is now completely contained within the mesh (Fig. 68-11). We place a drain in the pelvis and bring it out through an abdominal-wall stab wound. It is usually removed by the fourth postoperative day. The remainder of the midline is closed and the procedure terminated. Oral antibiotics are used for bowel prep; parenteral antibiotics are rarely used.

We utilize the ISP in all patients with a bulky rectal tumor or one that seems likely to have penetrated the muscularis propria. If, histologically, the lesions prove to be graded Astler-Coller A or B_1, we do not administer postoperative radiation therapy immediately. If the tumor is a grade B_2 or C lesion, we administer at least 5500 cGy to the pelvis, usually in conjunction with a 5-FU–based chemotherapy regimen.

When a tumor is too bulky to resect or is fixed in the pelvis, we employ the ISP, administer high-dose radiation therapy, and then reexplore 3 months later or when indicated. By then, the tumor has usually shrunk enough to allow removal. In all our patients who have received postoperative radiation therapy of the magnitude of 5000 cGy or less, we have not seen a single case of acute or chronic RASBI. And if we believe the literature of pediatric radiation oncology, which reports no observations of chronic RASBI that was not preceded by acute RASBI, then we should not expect to discover a single case of chronic RASBI in ISP-treated patients in the future.[34]

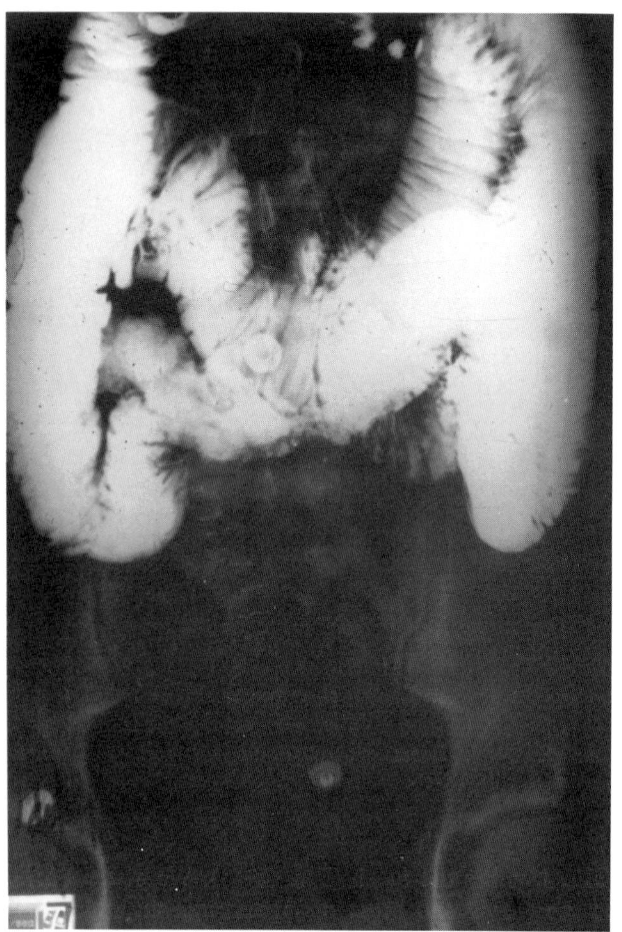

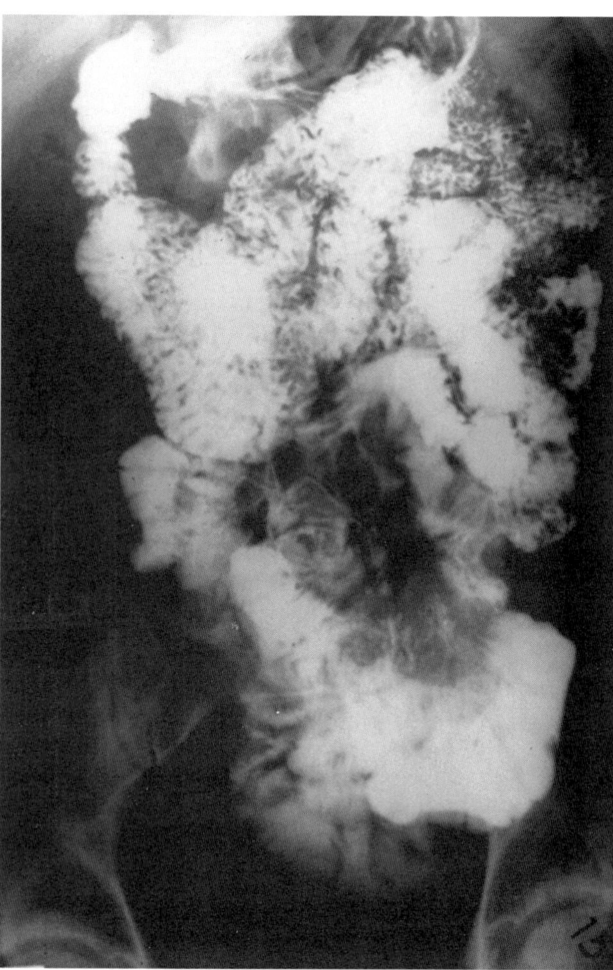

A B

FIG. 68-5. *A*. Contrast study taken of small bowel in the immediate postoperative period in patient with grade C_1 rectal carcinoma. Note displacement of small bowel out of pelvis. *B*. Same patient 3 months postoperatively. Note return of small bowel to pelvis and no evidence of obstruction. Radiation therapy was completed by 2 months and 1 week following placement of the intestinal sling.

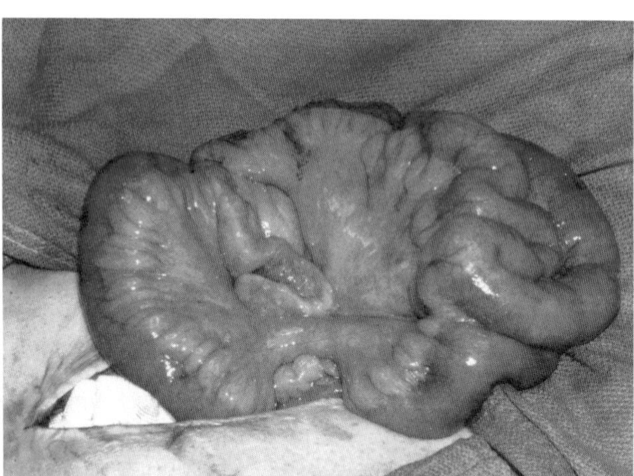

FIG. 68-6. Patient at reoperation, following resorption of mesh for closure of Hartmann colostomy. Note lack of adhesions, as in nonhuman primate study.

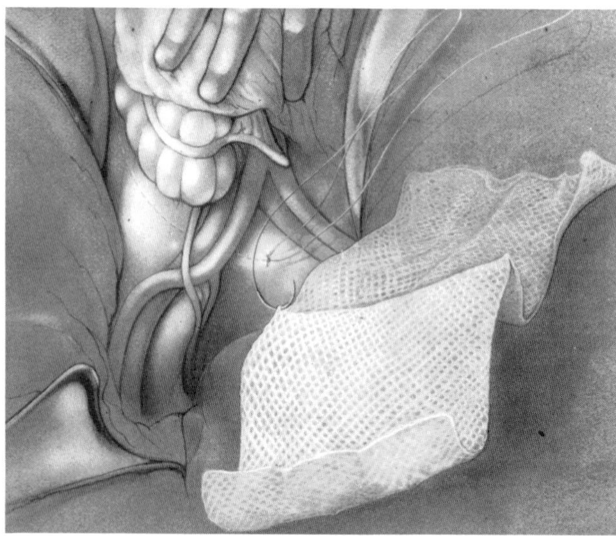

FIG. 68-7. Initiation of the intestinal sling procedure. Two sutures of 2-0 Vicryl or Dexon are placed deep into the sacral promontory to be run in opposite directions.

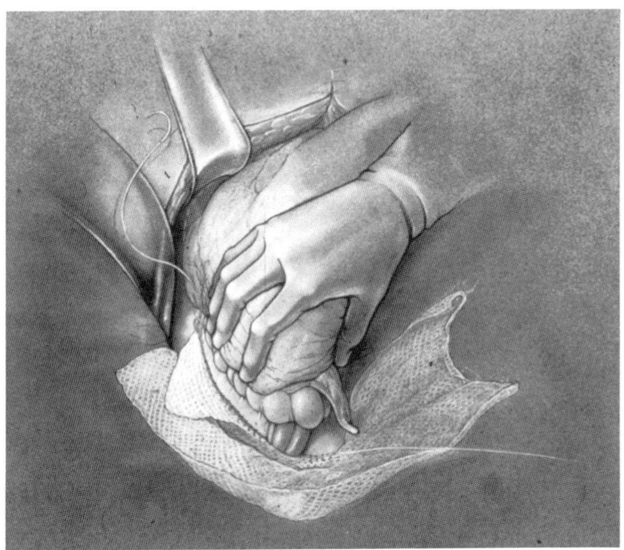

FIG. 68-8. Sutures are placed 1 cm apart with locking bites. Care is taken to sew over the iliac vessels and ureter (which must be seen), always progressing toward the head.

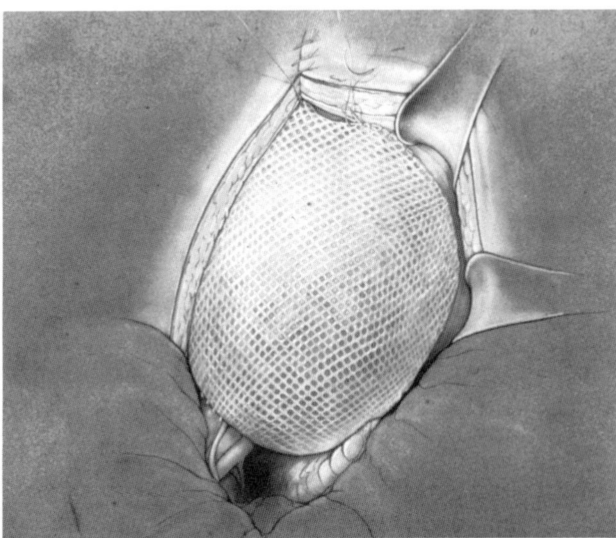

FIG. 68-10. Closure of the upper part of the incision is done first in order to create a roof under which the right and left sutures can be sewn to close the sling and its contents. The remainder of the midline incision is then closed following placement of a Jackson Pratt pelvic drain.

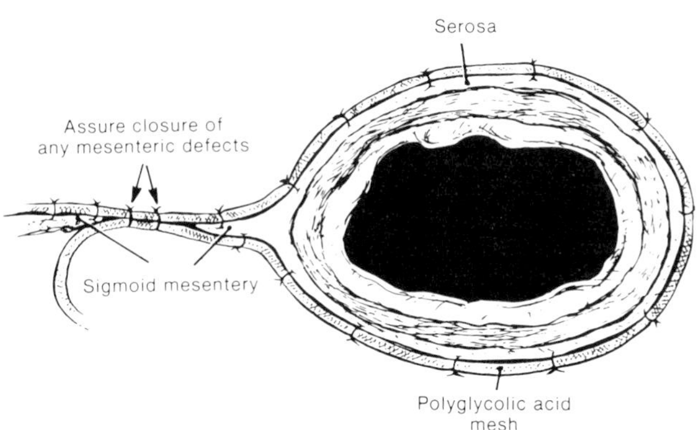

FIG. 68-9. Neosigmoid mesentery is fashioned by opposing mesh to mesh in the area devoid of sigmoid mesentery. This prevents the small bowel from descending into the pelvis from behind the anastomosis.

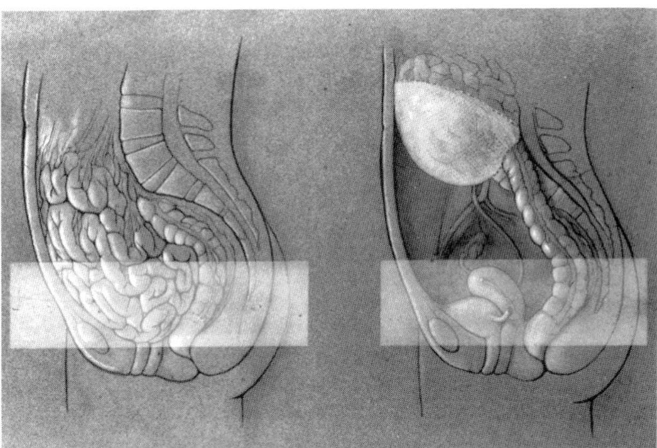

FIG. 68-11. Artist's rendering of completed intestinal sling placement, showing suspension of small bowel out of the radiation beam's (light gray) path. This is compared to a small bowel that is in beam's path and is subject to severe damage.

REFERENCES

1. Devereux DF, Sears HF, Ketcham AS: Intestinal fistula following pelvic exenterative surgery: Predisposing causes and treatment. *J Surg Oncol* 14:227–234, 1980.
2. Mennie AT, Dalley VM, Dinneen LC: Treatment of radiation-induced gastrointestinal distress with acetylsalicylate. *Lancet* 2:942, 1975.
3. Wittich G, Salomonowitz E, Szepesi T, et al: Small bowel double-contrast enema in stage III ovarian cancer. *Am J Roentgenol* 142:299–304, 1984.
4. Newman A, Katsaris J, Blendis LM: Small intestinal injury in women who have had pelvic radiotherapy. *Lancet* 2:1471, 1973.
5. Walsh D: Deep tissue traumatism from roentgen ray exposure. *Br Med J* 2:272, 1897.
6. Deitel M, To TB: Major intestinal complications of radiotherapy: Management and nutrition. *Arch Surg* 122:1421–1424, 1987.
7. Smith DH, DeCosse JJ: Radiation damage to the small intestine. *World J Surg* 10:189, 1986.
8. Dewit L, Oussoren Y: Late effects in the mouse small intestine after a clinically relevant multi-fractionated radiation treatment. *Radiat Res* 110:372–384, 1987.
9. Braslow SP, Marks G: Radiation injury to the gut, in Burk, Bockus (eds): *Gastroenterology,* 4th ed. Philadelphia, Saunders, 1985, pp 2593–2599.
10. Thomson ABR, Cheeseman CI, Walker K: Effect of external abdominal irradiation on the dimensions and characteristics of the barriers to passive transport in the rat intestine. *Lipids* 19:405–418, 1984.
11. Cheeseman CI: The effects of abdominal radiation on intestinal transport in the rate as assessed by isolated epithelial cells. *Radiat Res* 101:131–143, 1985.
12. Yeoh E, Horowitz M: Radiation enteritis. *Br J Hosp Med* 39:498, 1989.
13. DeCosse JJ, Rhodes RS, Wentz WB, et al: The natural history and management of radiation-induced injury of the gastrointestinal tract. *Ann Surg* 170:369, 1969.
14. Krook JE, Moertel CG, Gunderson LL, et al: Effective surgical adjuvant therapy for high-risk rectal carcinoma. *N Engl J Med* 324:709–715, 1991.
15. Miholic J, Schlappack O, Klepetko W, et al: Surgical therapy of radiation-induced small bowel lesions: Report of 34 cases with a high share of patients with combined chemotherapy. *Arch Surg* 122:923–926, 1987.
16. Borgstrom S, Aronsen KF, Augustson NE, et al: The protective effect of intra-arterial vasopressin injections on the small bowel during fractionated abdominal irradiation. *Acta Radiat Oncol* 24:401–405, 1985.
17. Hanson WR, Thomas C: 16,16-dimethyl prostaglandin E2 increases survival of murine intestinal stem cells when given before photon radiation. *Radiat Res* 96:393–398, 1983.
18. France HG Jr, Jirtle RK, Mansbach CM: Intracolonic WR 2721 protection of the rat colon from acute radiation injure. *Gastroenterology* 91:644, 1986.
19. Mulholland MW, Levitt SH, Song CW: The role of luminal contents in radiation enteritis. *Cancer* 54:2396, 1984.
20. Klimberg VS, Souba WW, Dolson DJ, et al: Prophylactic glutamine protects the intestinal mucosa from radiation injury. *Cancer* 66:62–68, 1990.
21. Cole H: Displacement of small bowel from pelvic radiation field. *Lancet* 2:1341, 1988.
22. Gallagher MJ, Brereton HD, Rostock RA, et al: A prospective study of treatment techniques to minimize the volume of pelvic small bowel with reduction of acute and late effects associated with pelvic irradiation. *Int J Radiat Oncol Biol Phys* 12:1565–1573, 1986.
23. Dische S, Dowdell JW: A method to reduce radiation injury to intestine—A preliminary report. *Radiother Oncol* 1:277–279, 1984.
24. Armstrong JG, Harrison LB, Dattoli M, et al: The use of a prosthetic tissue expander to displace bowel from a brachytherapy implant site. *Int J Radiat Oncol Biol Phys* 19:1521–1523, 1990.
25. Russ JE, Smoron GL, Gagnon JD: Omental transposition flap in colorectal carcinoma: Adjunctive use in prevention and treatment of radiation complications. *Int J Radiat Oncol Biol Phys* 10:55–62, 1984.
26. DeLuca FR, Ragins H: Construction of an omental envelope as a method of excluding the small intestine from the field of postoperative irradiation to the pelvis. *Surg Gynecol Obstet* 160:365, 1985.
27. Kavanah MT, Feldman MI, Devereux DF, et al: New surgical approach to minimize radiation-associated small bowel injury in patients with pelvic malignancies requiring surgery and high-dose irradiation: A preliminary report. *Cancer* 56:1300–1304, 1985.
28. Feldman MI, Kavanah MT, Devereux DF, et al: New surgical method to prevent pelvic radiation enteropathy. *Am J Clin Oncol* 11:27, 1988.
29. Devereux DF, Chandler J, Eisenstat T, et al: Efficacy of an absorbable mesh in keeping the small bowel out of the human pelvis following surgery. Presented to the American Society of Colon and Rectal Surgeons, Washington, DC, April 1987. *Dis Colon Rectum* 31:17–21, 1988.
30. Devereux D, Kavanagh M, Feldman MI, et al: New surgical approach to minimize radiation associated small bowel injury in patients with pelvic malignancy: A preliminary report (unpublished). Boston, New England Cancer Society, November 1983.
31. Dasmahapatra KS, Swaminathan AP: The use of a biodegradable mesh to prevent radiation-associated small bowel injury. *Arch Surg* 126:366–369, 1991.
32. Trimbos JB, Snijders-Keilhold T, Peters AA: Feasibility of the application of a resorbable polyglycolic-acid mesh (Dexon mesh) to prevent complications of radiotherapy following gynecological surgery. *Eur J Surg* 157:281–284, 1991.
33. Devereux D: *Perspectives: Colon & Rectal Surgery.* St Louis, Quality Medical Publishing, 1988.
34. Bounous G: Elemental diets in the prophylaxis and therapy for intestinal lesions: An update. *Surgery* 105:571, 1989.
35. Evans D, Shumate CR, Ames FC, et al: Use of a Dexon mesh for abdominal partitioning above the peritoneal reflection. *Dis Colon Rectum* 34:833–835, 1991.

CHAPTER 69

Radiation: The Preoperative Adjuvant Strategy

Mohammed Mohiuddin

HIGHLIGHTS

In spite of recent advances in surgery, results of surgical treatment for cancer of the rectum have shown only modest improvement over the last several decades. Local recurrence of disease (30 to 35 percent) continues to be the dominant pattern of failure.[1-4]

Several adjunctive radiation therapy programs have been used in an effort to improve survival and decrease local recurrence rates. Among these, preoperative radiation has had a long history in the treatment of this disease. The relatively low doses of radiation used at first did not produce any substantial improvement in survival, although this treatment appeared to reduce local recurrence rates. Randomized moderate-dose preoperative radiation trials have shown a statistical increase in local control and suggested improvement in survival in subset analyses.

More recently, high-dose preoperative radiation (>4000 cGy delivered at 180 to 200 cGy per fraction) has been utilized, but many surgeons remain unwilling to operate on patients because of unwarranted fear of radiation effects. High-dose preoperative radiation can sterilize the peripheral margins of a lesion, making surgical resection more complete as long as surgical principles of tumor resection are not compromised. It can also lead to downstaging of marginally resectable tumors, making them surgically curable, and allows safe sphincter-sparing surgical resection with limited longitudinal surgical margins in the distal rectum.

CONTROVERSIES

The major controversies in adjunctive preoperative radiation for rectal cancer are patient selection criteria (clinical staging), dose/time/volume of radiation, the use of systemic chemotherapy, and the role of intraoperative radiation (IORT).

1. Patient selection criteria: The lack of a generally accepted clinical staging system has been a significant impediment to progress in establishing the value of preoperative radiation. Physical examination and imaging studies are not yet precise enough to allow fine definition of disease extent. Histopathologic stage of disease is the strongest prognostic indicator, and tumor downstaging as a result of preoperative radiation leads to uncertainty as to the original stage of tumor; hence this method cannot be used in assessing the effectiveness of therapy. Many early tumors are cured by surgery alone and do not require pre- or postoperative adjunctive therapy. Patients with more advanced disease need to be categorized preoperatively by degree of "unfavorability," so as to allow the use of adjunctive therapy based on well-balanced risk/reward ratios. A clear, easily reproducible clinical staging system is essential for designing and interpreting the results of programs of adjunctive preoperative radiation.
2. Dose/time/volume: Optimal parameters for adjunctive preoperative radiation therapy still need to be established for different clinical stages of disease. Historically, low-dose

radiation was an accommodation to surgeons fearful of operating on the irradiated bowel. Recent large series indicate that surgery can be performed safely following high-dose radiation (≥4000 cGy in 20 fractions over 4 weeks). Higher doses of radiation have proved more effective in reducing local recurrence of disease following surgery but may be associated with a higher risk of small/large bowel complications.

3. Surgical quality control: Success in any adjunctive therapy program depends on good surgical quality control. Poor surgical technique, inappropriate patient selection, or compromised tumor margins are likely to nullify the benefits of preoperative radiation, after which a failure of surgical technique can be interpreted incorrectly as a failure of adjunctive therapy.
4. Integration of systemic chemotherapy with adjunctive radiation: Recent studies indicate that combined chemotherapy and radiation is more effective than either modality alone in the adjunctive treatment of rectal cancer. Among presently available drugs, 5-fluorouracil (5-FU) is the most effective. There is debate about optimal dosage, mode of administration, length of infusion, and the toxicity/benefit ratio of 5-FU/leucovorin combinations with radiation.
5. Use of intraoperative radiation: IORT has proved useful as "boost" radiation in the management of recurrent and locally advanced primary rectal cancers. It appears most suitable for slowly growing tumors with a propensity for local recurrence after surgical resection. Appropriate doses/volume factors for IORT still remain to be established.

FUTURE DIRECTIONS

It is hoped that future developments will include a clinical staging system that is easily reproducible and provides for clearly defined selection criteria for adjunctive therapy treatment options; optimization of radiation dose/time/volume parameters; use of combined systemic chemotherapy in conjunction with preoperative radiation for high-risk patients; and, finally, the integration of IORT. These developments should help bring about the optimal management of rectal cancer.

Adjunctive radiation for cancer of the rectum has been in use for several decades. The clinical and biological basis for the use of preoperative radiation lies in the fact that significant tumor shrinkage can be obtained with relatively modest doses of radiation. Preoperative radiation can reduce the likelihood of local recurrence of disease by reducing the volume of tumor and eliminating tumor cells at the margins of surgical resection. This is especially important in the peripheral region of the surgical field, where microscopic aggregations of tumor cells may be present in lymphatic channels or tissue spaces and may not be appreciated during surgery. Preoperative radiation is also useful in distal rectal cancer, where the tumor is in close proximity to the pelvic side walls and the confines of the rigid, funnel-shaped pelvis limits the circumferential margins of surgical resection.

An additional benefit of preoperative radiation is that tumor sterilization of the pararectal tissues can reduce the probability of disseminating viable tumor cells during surgery. While this has been observed in several animal models even after relatively low doses of radiation,[5,6] it has not been demonstrated so far with human colorectal tumors.

The observation that less than curative doses of radiation can result in dramatic tumor shrinkage of initially resectable lesions has also expanded the use of preoperative radiation in the treatment of marginally resectable and/or unresectable cancers. Regression can make these tumors amenable to radical curative surgery with potential for long-term cure.

Preoperative radiation has the potential advantage of greater therapeutic efficacy than postoperative radiation with equivalent doses, as the blood supply and hence oxygenation of tumor tissues is likely to be better before surgical disruption of blood vessels or the development of postsurgical fibrosis. Radiosensitivity is vitally dependent on the oxygen concentration within tumors, with well-oxygenated cells being three times more sensitive than hypoxic cells.

Another potential advantage of preoperative over postoperative radiation is a lower risk of treatment-related morbidity. Adhesions following surgical exploration of the abdomen may result in loops of small bowel becoming fixed within the pelvis if surgical reconstruction has not been performed. Fixed bowel has a propensity for obstructive changes, edema, and bacterial invasion and is known to be at high risk for radiation complications. Preoperatively, small bowel is less likely to be fixed and is therefore less prone to radiation damage.

There are, however, some disadvantages to the use of preoperative radiation. Surgery is often delayed by it. This delay can be minimized by the use of moderate-dose preoperative radiation (<3000 cGy), as surgery can be performed immediately afterward. With higher doses of radiation, it may be necessary to allow for the recovery of normal tissues from radiation effects (4 to 6 weeks) before surgery is undertaken. In some studies, high-dose preoperative radiation has been associated with delayed wound healing, especially after high doses per fraction and short waiting periods to surgery. Longer waiting periods can be difficult for both patients and surgeons. However, in rectal cancer, it has been demonstrated that tumors undergo shrinkage slowly, over several months following treatment.[7] A delay of several weeks before surgery may actually be desirable, especially with large tumors, to allow maximum regression of disease prior to resection. Studies to date have failed to demonstrate any increased risk of metastatic spread during preoperative radiation or the subsequent waiting period.

A further disadvantage in the use of preoperative radiation is that tumor shrinkage often obscures the initial stage of disease. Historically, histopathologic tumor stage has been considered the most important prognostic indicator and is the yardstick most often used to evaluate outcome of treatment. Downstaging of disease following radiation leads to uncertainty of the initial stage of the tumor and makes it difficult to assess the results of treatment or to make valid comparisons with other treatments. A standardized clinical/pathologic staging system will allow better patient selection and clear definition of criteria for adjuvant therapy and for comparison of results from different studies.

Another disadvantage of preoperative radiation is that in spite of careful clinical assessment of disease, some patients with early cancers (node-negative tumors confined to the bowel wall) who are not likely to benefit from the treatment may receive adjuvant therapy. At the same time, patients with metastatic disease may not be identified until surgical exploration of the abdomen. The advent of newer imaging techniques—computed tomography (CT), transrectal ultrasonography (TRUS), and magnetic resonance imaging (MRI)—can help to stage clinical disease more accurately and to improve our ability to select appropriate patients for preoperative radiation.

LOW-DOSE PREOPERATIVE RADIATION (TABLE 69-1)

Early trials of preoperative radiation in rectal cancer involved the use of relatively low doses (<3000 cGy).[8,9] A retrospective review covering the period 1939–1951 at Memorial Sloan Kettering Cancer Center (MSKCC) indicated that patients with rectal cancer treated preoperatively with 2000 cGy in 1 week had better survival at 5 years than patients treated with surgery alone (43 versus 27 percent).[10] A subsequent randomized study at MSKCC failed to substantiate the benefit for the treated group over surgery alone.[11]

A randomized study of 700 patients by the Veterans Administrative Surgical Adjuvant Group (VASAG) for adenocarcinoma of the rectum and rectosigmoid was designed to assess the results of the first MSKCC study.[12] Patients were treated either by surgery alone or surgery after low-dose preoperative radiation (2000 cGy in 2 weeks). Initial reports showed improved survival for resected patients treated with preoperative radiation (39 versus 31 percent; $p<.05$). This advantage appeared to be most marked for patients undergoing abdominoperineal resection, or APR (41 versus 28 percent; $p=<.01$). A second trial (VASAG II) in 361 male patients suitable for APR, utilizing higher doses of preoperative radiation (3150 cGy delivered in 18 fractions), failed to confirm these results.[13] No significant difference was noted in survival ratio between the two groups. A similar randomized study by the Medical Research Council (MRC),[14] comparing the re-

Table 69-1
Randomized Studies of Low-Dose Preoperative Radiation

		Local recurrence		*5-year survival*	
	Radiation dose, Gy/no. fractions/days	*Radiation plus surgery, percent*	*Surgery alone, percent*	*Radiation plus surgery, percent*	*Surgery alone, percent*
MRC[14]	5/1/1	45	43	42	38
	20/10/14	47	43	40	38
Stearns et al.[11] (MSKCC)	20/10/14	11	17	52	59
Roswit et al.[12] (VASAG I)	20/10/14	29	40	39	31
Higgins et al.[13] (VASAG II)	31.5/18/24	—	—	35	35
Stockholm trial[15a]	25/5/5	8	20	45	45

[a]Moderately high dose.

NOTE: None of the results were statistically significant for survival.

sults of low-dose preoperative radiation (500 cGy in a single fraction or 2000 cGy in 2 weeks) and surgery alone, also failed to show any significant difference in local control or survival.

More recently, a Swedish randomized study[15] comparing surgery alone and moderately high-dose preoperative radiation (2500 cGy in 5 fractions over 5 days) also failed to show any survival benefit for irradiated patients, although the incidence of local recurrence was substantially less in irradiated patients. Postoperative complications, especially wound sepsis, were slightly more common in the irradiated patients due in part to the higher radiation dose (500 cGy) per fraction.

Although slight decreases in local recurrence rates were noted in several of these studies, the lack of improvement in survival rates indicates that low-dose preoperative radiation has little or no role in the routine management of cancer of the rectum.

HIGH-DOSE PREOPERATIVE RADIATION

The systematic use of high-dose preoperative radiation for cancer of the rectum began relatively recently. Surgeons have been reluctant to operate on patients following high doses of radiation for fear of complications. Primary anastomosis of the irradiated rectum is still considered hazardous by many. Recent results indicate that high-dose preoperative radiation can be delivered safely, is an effective mode of adjunctive therapy with improved local control, and may improve survival.

The lack of a clinical staging system has hampered the development of optimized guidelines for high-dose preoperative radiation and the interpretation of results in some of the studies. Tumor mobility,[16,17] location in the rectum,[2–4,12] obstruction,[18] perforation,[19] and so on are recognized as significant prognostic indicators of disease. In most studies, patients were not stratified according to prognostically significant clinical features. Moreover, patient eligibility has been loosely defined, as indicated by the use of phrases like "curative resection,"[11] "tumors of the rectum and rectosigmoid,"[20] "adenocarcinomas proved by sigmoidoscopy,"[21] or "suitable for radical resection."[22] Such loose definition of disease status hampers the assessment of treatment efficacy, so that comparison of results between various studies becomes meaningless.

An additional difficulty in interpreting results of various studies is the failure to standardize surgical techniques. It has been well established that extent and quality of surgical resection often affects the outcome of treatment.[23–26] In spite of these shortcomings, recent results from randomized and nonrandomized studies indicate that preoperative radiation warrants serious consideration in the management of cancer of the rectum.

HIGH-DOSE NONRANDOMIZED RADIATION (TABLE 69-2)

In the 1970s, Stevens and colleagues[27] at the University of Oregon treated 97 rectal cancer patients with preoperative radiation to doses of 5000 to 6000 cGy in 200 cGy fractions over 5 to 8 weeks. Of these patients, 57 were considered clinically operable and 50 underwent surgical resection 4 to 7 weeks following radiation. At that time, 5 patients (10 percent) had no evidence of residual cancer. The 5-year survival rate in these patients was 53 percent, compared to 38 percent for historical controls treated with surgery only. None of the patients receiving preoperative radiation who underwent curative resection suffered a local recurrence. Although 40 additional patients were initially considered inoperable, 22 of these became resectable following radiation and 20 underwent resection. Of these 20 patients, 3 were alive at 5 years and 1 patient, who did not undergo surgery, was also alive at 7 years.

Patients with locally advanced rectal cancer treated with preoperative radiation provide *additional* infor-

Table 69-2
Nonrandomized Studies of High-Dose Preoperative Radiation

			Local recurrence		*5-year survival*	
Study	*No. of patients*	*Dose, fraction size (Gy)*	*Radiation plus surgery, percent*	*Surgery alone, percent*	*Radiation plus surgery, percent*	*Surgery alone, percent*
Stevens et al.[27a]	50	50–60/2	0		53	38
Mendenhall et al.[30]	132	30–45/1.8–3	8	29	66	40 (p = .0001)
Fortier et al.[49]	60	45/1.8–2	16	40	52	48
Reed[32]	149	40–45/1.7–2	9	18	68	52
Kodner et al.[33]	72	45/1.8	2	—	86	—
Kerman et al.[34]	120	45/1.8	4	—	66	—
Mohiuddin and Marks[37]	220	45–70/1.8	15	—	72	—

[a]Only in resected patients.

mation supporting this strategy. Pilepich et al.[28] were able to perform complete resections in 27 of 44 patients with initial unresectable rectal cancer who were treated preoperatively to a dose of 4500 to 5000 cGy in 25 fractions. Of these patients, 22 remained disease-free, with a median follow-up of 27 months. In a similar study, Dosoretz et al.[29] reported a 5-year survival rate of 43 percent in 18 patients with initially unresectable (fixed) rectal cancer following high-dose preoperative radiation. The incidence of local recurrence was 43 percent in resected patients.

Mendenhall et al.[30] reported on 132 patients with "clinically resectable" adenocarcinoma of the rectum who received preoperative radiation in doses ranging from 30 Gy in 3.5 to 4 weeks to 45 Gy in 5 weeks. The incidence of positive pelvic nodes was 17 percent, almost half that of historical controls treated with surgery alone (38 percent).[31] The local recurrence rate was 8 percent (10/132) in patients given preoperative radiation versus 29 percent for historical controls, and the 5-year absolute survival rate was 66 percent for patients given radiation, versus 40 percent for the historical group ($p = .0001$). No increase in acute or late complications was observed with the use of preoperative radiation.

Reed et al.[32] compared 40 patients with "unfavorable" rectal cancer (bulky, >5 cm or circumferential) treated with preoperative radiation (4000 to 4500 cGy in 4 to 4.5 weeks), with 109 patients treated with surgery alone. A 5-year survival rate of 68 percent was observed in patients treated with radiation as compared with 52 percent in patients treated without radiation ($p < .05$). The local recurrence rate was 6 percent in treated patients as compared with 18 percent in patients undergoing surgery alone.

More recently, several nonrandomized studies have reported an even more impressive benefit associated with high-dose preoperative radiation. Kodner et al.[33] treated 90 patients with 4500 cGy preoperative radiation over a 5-week period, followed by surgical resection 6 weeks later. Of their patients, 72 (with Dukes A, B, and C lesions) had a 5-year survival of 86 percent and a local recurrence rate of 1.8 percent. The 5-year survival rate in the 12 patients who presented with fixed, poorly differentiated cancers was 27 percent. In a similar study of 120 patients with "resectable" rectal cancer treated with preoperative radiation, Kerman et al.[34] reported a 5-year survival of 66 percent and a local recurrence rate of 4 percent. Anastomotic leakage was not increased.

The customized approach to preoperative radiation utilized at Thomas Jefferson University Hospital follows similar principles, but in a more systematic fashion. This approach to adjunctive therapy of rectal cancer is based on the clinical staging system shown in Table 69-3.[35] Tumors were classified as favorable or unfavorable on the basis of tumor mobility/fixation, deep ulceration, obstruction and/or perforation, and location of disease in the rectum relative to the anorectal junction (0 level). Proximal tumors above the middle valve of Houston were classified as favorable lesions (>6 cm), whereas those below the middle valve were subdivided into a mid (3 to 6 cm) and lower (0 to 3 cm) group by the position of the inferior valve. Patients were treated according to the treatment schema shown in Fig. 69-1, with escalating doses of preoperative radiation for "unfavorable" stages of cancer.[35] Cases of "favorable" proximal cancer (clinical stage 1A) were treated with combined low-dose preoperative and selective high-dose postoperative radiation (selective sandwich technique).[36] Cases of favorable distal cancers (clinical stage 1B, 1C) were treated with high-dose preoperative radiation to allow sphincter-preserving surgical resection to be performed with smaller-than-recommended distal margin of resection. Unfavorable cancers with extrarectal fixation (clinical stages 2 and 3) were treated with dose escalation, using a shrinking-field technique, to 5500 to 6000 cGy, followed by surgical resection. Patients whose advanced tumors had invaded adjacent organs (clinical stage 4) are now treated with radiation to >7000 cGy, followed by surgical resection. More recently, patients with

Table 69-3
Clinical Classification of Rectal Cancer[a]

Stage I	Mobile	Free movement in all directions
Stage II	Partial fixation Tethered	Movable in at least one direction (cephalocaudad or lateral).
Stage III	Fixed	Immovable in any direction due to fixation (not size) or perforated, obstructed, deep ulceration
Stage IV	Advanced fixation	Invasion of pelvic side walls and/or sacrum; unresectable.

[a]Each clinical stage is divided into four subgroups based on location in the rectum measured from the anorectal junction, or "zero" level. These subgroups are as follows: (a) proximal, >6 cm; (b) mid, 3 to 6 cm; (c) lower, 0 to 3 cm; (d) extending into the anal canal.

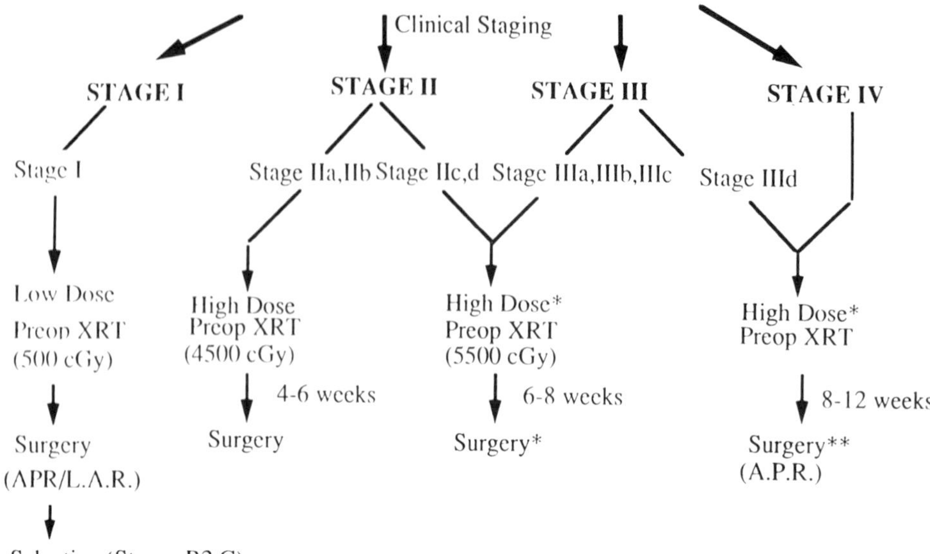

FIG. 69-1. Treatment scheme for selective high-dose preoperative radiation for rectal cancer based on the Jefferson staging system. Radiation given in 1.8-Gy fractions 5 days a week. *+Chemotherapy (stages IIIb, IIc, and IV): 350 mg 5-FU continuous infusion for duration of treatment. **+I.O.R.T. (stages III and IV): microscopic disease, 1500 cGy; gross disease, 2000 cGy.

fixed cancers received concurrent 5-fluorouracil (5-FU) infusional chemotherapy as a radiation sensitizer in order to produce maximum regression of disease and allow more complete surgical resection. The 5-year survival rate in 220 patients treated with this customized adjunctive high-dose preoperative radiation and surgery regimen is 72 percent.[37] Comparative survival in patients with potentially more favorable tumors treated with surgery alone in cooperative group studies is only 45 to 50 percent.[38,39] The rate of local recurrence at Jefferson was 15 percent (32/220), which also appears lower than the 25 to 38 percent rate with surgery alone. The Jefferson series included many fixed rectal cancers 146/220 (66 percent), which are excluded from most surgical series. The Medical Research Council (MRC) study[14] of low-dose preoperative radiation for rectal cancer included patients with fixed cancer and reported a survival rate of 48 percent for mobile tumors, 29 percent for partially fixed cancers, and 15 percent for fixed cancers—considerably lower than the Jefferson series 5-year survival rate of 87 percent for mobile cancers, 65 percent for partially fixed cancers, and 70 percent for fixed cancers.[17]

It is also instructive to look at survival and local recurrence according to the "postresection" Astler-Coller stages of disease. The results at Jefferson are given in Table 69-4, but it is important to remember that these represent postradiation stages, and preoperative radiation—especially at high doses—can result in considerable downstaging of tumor. That can mask the beneficial effects of preoperative radiation.

The Jefferson experience is also unique in that 72 percent (158/220) of the patients underwent sphincter-preserving surgery with primary anastomosis of the irradiated rectum after the high-dose radiation therapy. Many of these patients had tumors below the middle valve of Houston. In the patients undergoing sphincter preservation, Marks et al.[40] reported an actuarial 5-year survival rate of 80 percent and a local recurrence rate of only 13 percent. There was no significant increase in complications due to the preoperative radiation. The key to this successful integration of high-dose preoperative radiation with surgery has been the use of a clinical staging system with clearly defined patient selection criteria and dose escalation for high-risk patients.

Table 69-4
The Jefferson Experience with High-Dose Preoperative Radiation, 45 to 70 Gy

Postradiation stage	*No. of patients*	*Local recurrence, percent*	*5-year survival, percent*
O, A, B_1	72	4 (6)	92
B_2	72	13 (18)	71
C_1	14	3 (21)	75
C_2	46	9 (20)	47
Total	220	29 (13)	69

RANDOMIZED HIGH-DOSE PREOPERATIVE TRIALS (TABLE 69-5)

While these results of high-dose preoperative radiation in nonrandomized single-institution studies are impressive, results in randomized studies also appear favorable.

At Yale, Kligerman et al.[20] randomized 31 patients with resectable rectal cancer to either preoperative radiation (4500 cGy in 5 weeks) or surgery alone. The

Table 69-5
Randomized Studies of High-Dose Preoperative Radiation

Study	No. of patients	Dose, Gy/no. fractions/days	Local recurrence: Radiation plus surgery, percent	Local recurrence: Surgery alone, percent	5-year survival: Radiation plus surgery, percent	5-year survival: Surgery alone, percent
Kligerman et al.[20]	31[a]	45/25/35	—	—	41	25
EORTC[22]						
(all patients)	466	34.5/15/19	20	31 (p = .023)	52	49 (p = .69)
(curative)	341		15	30 (p = .003)	69	59 (p = .08)
Brazil[41]	68	40/20/28	3	24	80	34
Rotterdam[54]						
T_2	42	34.5/15/21	0	18	63	70 (NS)
T_3, T_4	54		14	36	50	18 (p = .001)

[a]Incidence of liver metastases at time of exploration was 6/16 in the surgery group versus 1/13 in the preoperative radiation group. Therefore results may be significantly affected.

5-year survival rate of the treated group was significantly better (41 percent) than that of patients treated with surgery alone (25 percent). However, some of these differences may have been due to patient selection, as the surgery-only group had a higher incidence of liver metastasis. The incidence of positive lymph nodes was also lower than expected in patients treated with radiation (22 versus 43 percent).

A randomized study from Brazil[41] in a small group of 68 patients with rectal cancer reported a 5-year survival rate of 80 percent for patients treated with preoperative radiation (4000 cGy in 20 fractions over 4 weeks) as compared with 34 percent for patients treated with surgery only (actual 5-year survival rate of 73 versus 30 percent). Local recurrence alone was observed in 2.9 percent of patients receiving radiation and 23.5 percent of patients treated with surgery alone. Local recurrence as a component of total overall failure was observed in 14.7 percent of irradiated patients as compared with 47 percent in patients treated without radiation.

In a study conducted by the European Organization for Research and Treatment of Cancer (EORTC), patients were randomized to receive either preoperative radiation (3450 cGy in 15 fractions at 230 cGy per fraction) or surgery alone.[22] The overall 5-year survival rate in those 466 patients was similar in both treatment arms: 51 percent for the preoperative radiation group and 49 percent for the surgery-alone group (p = .69). At the same time, among the 341 patients who underwent "curative" surgical resection, the survival was 69 percent for patients receiving preoperative radiation and 59 percent for patients treated by surgery alone, which approaches statistical significance (p = .08). Subset analysis revealed that the difference was most marked for patients below 55 years of age, with a 5-year survival rate of 80 percent for preoperative radiation versus 48 percent for surgery alone (p = .004). Preoperative radiation also led to a marked improvement in local recurrence rates: 15 percent compared with 30 percent for surgery alone (p = .003). While postoperative morbidity was slightly more frequent and at a higher degree of severity after preoperative radiation, overall the difference was not statistically significant.

A recent Swedish multicenter trial[42] compared the effects of moderately high dose preoperative radiation with postoperative radiation for rectal and rectosigmoid cancers. In this study, 471 patients were randomized to receive either 2550 cGy in 5-Gy fractions over 5 to 7 days preoperatively or 6000 cGy delivered in 2-Gy fractions over an 8-week period (2-week split). With a minimum follow-up of 3 years and a mean follow-up of 6 years, no difference has been observed in survival between the two groups (43 versus 40 percent). However, the local recurrence rate was significantly lower in patients with curative resection who had received preoperative radiation (12 percent) compared to curative resection patients who received postoperative radiation (21 percent; p = .02).

From these studies, it would appear that while the major impact of high-dose preoperative radiation has been in reducing the rate of pelvic recurrence, survival may also be improved. Subset analyses suggest a greater benefit from preoperative radiation in patients with fixed rectal cancer and distal rectal cancer, but subset analyses must be viewed with caution and future, better-designed trials are required to confirm these results.

HIGH-DOSE PREOPERATIVE RADIATION AND SPHINCTER PRESERVATION FOR DISTAL RECTAL CANCER

The advent of endoluminal stapling devices in the late 1970s sparked new interest in extending sphincter preservation techniques to the mid- and distal rectum. However, Steele et al.[43] estimated that no more than

4000 to 5000 of the estimated 18,000 cancers of the distal rectum diagnosed annually undergo sphincter-preserving treatment. Technical problems of impaired visibility and restricted space in the rigid confines of the pelvis make application of clamps and instruments difficult. For many years, surgeons believed that a 5-cm length of the distal rectum was necessary to maintain fecal continence and to minimize recurrence due to intramural spread of rectal cancer. Recent published data indicate that margins of less than 2 cm may be adequate to encompass distal spread of disease.[44,45] High-dose preoperative radiation can sterilize microscopic tumor extension along the rectum and reduce the length of required distal and circumferential margins of resection, thereby extending the scope of sphincter-preservation surgical techniques to all regions of the rectum. The combined abdominotranssacral resection (CATS), the transanal-abdominal-transanal resection (TATA), the pull-through procedures, and other new surgical techniques with coloanal anastomosis have now made it possible to perform sphincter preservation in tumors as low as the anorectal junction. Marks et al.[46] reported on 86 patients with tumors below 6 cm from the anorectal junction with half of these tumors below the inferior valve of Houston (3 cm). Patients received high-dose preoperative radiation, 4500 to 5500 cGy in 180-cGy fractions, followed 4 to 6 weeks later by sphincter-preserving surgical techniques. A local recurrence rate of 16 percent and a 5-year survival rate of 79 percent was observed. Patients with tumors at or below the inferior valve (3 cm) had a 5-year actuarial survival rate of 85 percent. Anal sphincter function was maintained in 91 percent of patients and overall function as determined by clinical assessment was considered satisfactory.

In a smaller study of 22 patients with distal rectal cancer treated at Memorial Sloan Kettering Cancer Center, Minsky et al.[47] reported a 3-year survival rate of 69 percent and a local recurrence rate of 14 percent following high-dose preoperative radiation and sphincter-preserving surgical techniques. There was no significant increase in complications and excellent quality of life was maintained.

From these evolving experiences, it would appear that effective sphincter preservation can be accomplished in the distal rectum by new surgical options following high-dose preoperative radiation of selected rectal cancers. Distal surgical margins as small as 5 mm may be adequate after high-dose radiation. Maintenance of normal anal sphincter function, an important quality-of-life issue to both patients and surgeons, can be achieved without compromising survival.

TOXICITY

The low-dose radiation studies have shown no significant increase in acute or late radiation-related morbidity. High-dose preoperative radiation has not led to any reports of increased technical difficulty with surgical resection.[22,30,33,40] However, several studies have noted a delay in the healing of abdominal and perineal wounds.[22,42] A greater delay in healing, especially of the perineal wound, has been observed in patients who underwent resection immediately after the completion of radiation in comparison to patients whose surgery was delayed 6 to 8 weeks (Table 69-6). High doses per fraction (350 to 500 cGy) and the short interval between completion of radiation and surgery may be key factors in wound-healing difficulties.

High morbidity due to disruption of primary anastomosis of the irradiated rectum was observed in early studies, but this has been reduced significantly by using an unirradiated proximal segment of bowel to anastomose to the irradiated distal rectum. Temporary colostomy may be helpful in reducing anastomotic complications. Gary-Bobo et al.[48] reported two anastomotic leaks in 37 patients who underwent anterior

Table 69-6
Complications following High-Dose Preoperative Radiation

Study	*Radiation dose, Gy/no. of fractions/days*	*Interval to surgery, days*	*Complication rate, percent*	*Comment*
Stockholm[15]	25/5/5	Immediate	24	Wound sepsis
	Controls	—	12 ($p = .005$)	
EORTC[22]	34.5/15/19	11	48	Perineal wound infection
	Controls	—	29 ($p < .001$)	
Mendenhall et al.[30]	30/10/14	—	10	Second intra-abdominal surgery
	45/25/35	31	6	
Kodner et al.[33]	20/5/7	1	14	Perineal wound
	45/25/35	35–49	9	
Kerman et al.[34]	45–50/25/35	—	5	Major surgical

resection after preoperative radiation of 4000 cGy. The Swedish randomized study[42] showed no increase in anastomotic failure after a short intensive course of moderately high radiation. In general, most recent studies of preoperative radiation have not demonstrated any more complications in irradiated patients than in patients treated with surgery only.

DOSE/TIME/VOLUME

As discussed earlier, low-dose preoperative radiation appears to be of limited value in the management of rectal cancer. For high-dose preoperative radiation, a significant dose-response has been observed in several studies.

Fortier et al.[49] found that increasing the dose by 1000 cGy had a substantial effect on the rate of local control of disease (67 percent incidence with 4000 cGy and 91 percent with 5000 cGy). Overgaard et al.[50] reported a dose-response relationship for doses ≥5600 cGy versus less in a series of patients treated with radiation alone. At doses ≥5600 cGy, 40 percent of patients had a 2-year actuarial complete response compared with rates of 7, 4, and 0 percent at doses of 46 to 55 Gy, 36 to 45 Gy, and less than 35 Gy, respectively. A recent analysis of the Jefferson experience[51] with high-dose preoperative radiation showed that 20 percent (31/156) of patients developed a local recurrence at doses ranging from 4000 to 4500 cGy (group 1) compared with 6 percent (7/119) at doses of 5000 to 5500 cGy (group 2). Local recurrence by stage of disease was 11 percent for postirradiation stages O, A, and B_1; 27 percent for stage B_2, and 23 percent for stage C in group 1, compared with 2, 11, and 7 percent respectively for group 2.

High doses of radiation, however, carry the potential for increased complications, and therefore a risk-reward ratio based on clinical staging must be utilized. Mobile tumors, where the intention is to sterilize subclinical disease, may be treated adequately preoperatively at doses equivalent to 4500 cGy in fractions over 5 weeks. On the other hand, fixed rectal cancers require higher doses of radiation, in part because tumor shrinkage is necessary in allowing a satisfactory plane of surgical resection. For unresectable disease, even higher doses may be required, together with concurrent chemotherapy and/or intraoperative radiation.

Radiation dose/time fractionation is also of crucial importance in promoting satisfactory healing, especially when plans call for a primary anastomosis of the bowel. Higher doses per fraction may lead to increased complications, as observed in the EORTC[22] and the Swedish[42] studies. Treatment of large volumes with AP/PA techniques may further contribute to poor healing of tissues. Daily fractionation doses of 180 to 200 cGy are desirable, especially when higher total doses (>4000 cGy) are planned.

Volume of preoperative radiation has varied widely in reported studies. The Oregon study[27] involved small-volume radiation encompassing just the primary rectal tumor (usually a 10 x 10 cm field). Other groups[12,20] have utilized radiation of the pelvis and paraaortics to include the lymph nodes along the inferior mesenteric artery and vein. Most recent studies have confined preoperative radiation fields to the pelvis only. A four-field technique is recommended, utilizing high-energy photons and treating all fields every day. (Field arrangements are shown in Figs. 69-2 and 69-3.) Customized Cereband blocking techniques to exclude as much of the small bowel as possible should be utilized. The Jefferson study[37] utilized a volume where the superior part of the fields extends to the L5, S1 interspace. The lateral border is 1 cm beyond the bony pelvis. The inferior border includes the anal canal for low rectal cancers below the middle valve of Houston and for proximal tumors is at the anorectal junction. The anterior border of the lateral field encompasses the external iliac lymph nodes for low rectal cancers but excludes the external iliac chain for proximal rectal tumors. Posteriorly, the field extends 1 cm posterior to the sacrum to allow for adequate buildup of dose in the presacral tissues, especially when high-energy photons are utilized. Patients should be treated with a full bladder to minimize the volume of small bowel in the pelvis. With this approach, the reported incidence of small bowel complications after high-dose preoperative radiation is less than 5 percent.[22,30,33,40]

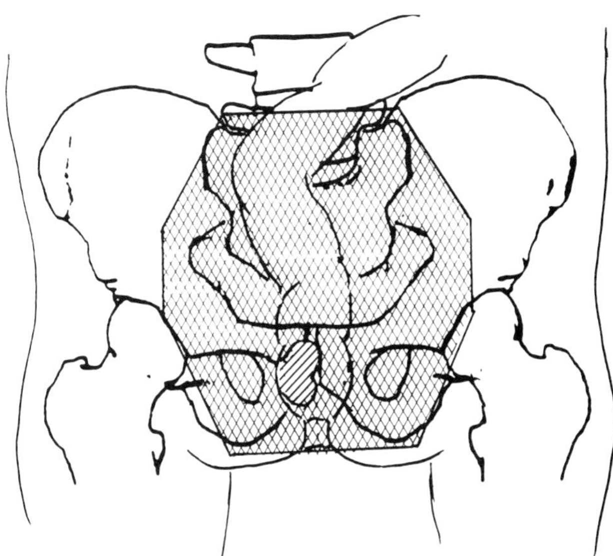

FIG. 69-2. Anteroposterior/posteroanterior treatment fields for low rectal cancers.

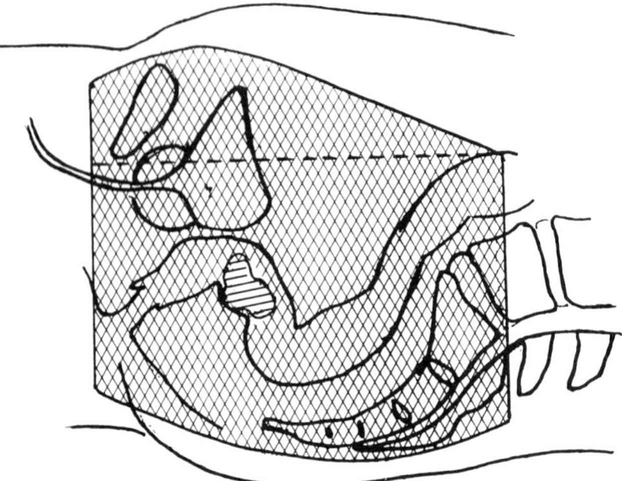

FIG. 69-3. Lateral fields for low rectal cancer (dashed line defines anterior border of field for proximal lesions).

COMBINED CHEMORADIATION

Recent studies of adjuvant therapy in rectal cancer indicate that combined chemotherapy and radiation is more efficacious than adjunctive radiation alone. In laboratory studies, 5-FU has been shown to have a strong synergism with radiation;[52] it is also the most effective cytotoxic agent for this disease. The Gastrointestinal Tumor Study Group (GITSG) found that adjunctive postoperative chemoradiation utilizing 5-FU and methyl-CCNU was significantly better than surgery alone.[39] For stages B_2 and C rectal cancer, the 5-year survival rate in the combined-modality arm was 60 percent, compared with 45 percent for surgery alone ($p = .005$); the incidence of local recurrence was also substantially lower (11 versus 24 percent). The Mayo North Central Cancer Treatment Group (NCCTG) study, comparing adjunctive chemoradiation (5-FU and methyl-CCNU) with postoperative radiation alone (5040 cGy in 28 fractions) also demonstrated a statistically significant improvement of the 5-year survival rate in the combined-modality arm (55 percent) as compared with postoperative radiation alone (45 percent; $p = .025$).[53] Local recurrence was less frequent (14 versus 25 percent; $p = .036$), and the rate of distant metastasis was reduced (29 versus 46 percent; $p = .011$).

Clinicians have had relatively little experience with combined chemotherapy and preoperative radiation. Wassif-Boulis et al.[54] randomized patients to receive adjunctive preoperative radiation and chemotherapy or either preoperative radiation alone or surgery alone for borderline operable rectal cancer. The combined-modality group had a 97 percent resectability rate, compared with 93 percent for the preoperative radiation-alone group and 78 percent for the surgery-alone group. The 62 percent survival rate in the combined-modality group was significantly better than the 49 percent rate in the preoperative radiation group and the 31 percent rate in the surgery-alone group. However, while the results of treatment appeared better with the combined-modality approach, several studies of combined chemotherapy and radiation—especially postoperative radiation—suggest higher potential morbidity with combined treatment.[39,55] Aggressive combined chemoradiation must be used with care and may not be indicated for mobile tumors, but it remains an option for the management of fixed rectal cancers and for unresectable disease. Randomized preoperative radiation trials have not demonstrated a decrease in distant metastases or an increase in survival except in subset analyses. The data from randomized trials of postoperative adjunctive therapy would suggest that chemotherapy may be a necessary part of combined modality treatment if survival is to be improved.

INTRAOPERATIVE RADIATION

Recent interest in the use of intraoperative radiation therapy (IORT) using an electron beam indicates that the most effective use of this modality is as a booster dose in conjunction with high-dose adjunctive radiation therapy. "Unfavorable" rectal cancers with extrarectal fixation in the pelvis (especially to the sacrum) are ideally suited for IORT in conjunction with high-dose preoperative radiation. Studies at Massachusetts General Hospital (MGH)[56] and the Mayo Clinic[57] indicate a substantial improvement in the local control of advanced rectal cancers with IORT in combination with external-beam radiation. In the MGH experience, the technique led to local control of 85 percent of 31 advanced primary cancers and 30 percent of recurrent rectal cancers, with a 3-year survival rate of 52 and 25 percent, respectively. The optimum dose of IORT for suspected or known residual cancer of various stages remains to be established. General guidelines recommend doses of 1000 to 1500 cGy for microscopic residual disease and doses of 1500 to 2000 cGy for macroscopic residual disease.

CONCLUSION

In summary, recent results of high-dose preoperative radiation for rectal cancer show considerable promise in reducing the probability of local recurrence and possibly improving survival. The use of sphincter-preserving surgical techniques can safely be expanded in conjunction with high-dose preoperative radiation. The addition of systemic chemotherapy and/or intraoperative radiation can salvage more patients with fixed rectal cancers or those with initial unresectable disease.

Future directions require the establishment of a clinical staging system and appropriate selection criteria with dose escalation of preoperative radiation, integration of systemic chemotherapy and IORT in the total management of this disease.

REFERENCES

1. Adlof M, Arnaud JP, Schloegel M, et al: Factors influencing local recurrence after abdominoperineal resection for cancer of the rectum. *Dis Colon Rectum* 28:413–415, 1985.
2. Pilipshen SJ, Heilweil M, Quan SHQ, et al: Patterns of pelvic recurrence following definitive resections of rectal cancer. *Cancer* 53:1354–1362, 1984.
3. Rao AR, Kagan AR, Chan PM, et al: Patterns of recurrence following curative resection alone for adenocarcinoma of the rectum and sigmoid colon. *Cancer* 48:1492–1495, 1981.
4. Gunderson LL, Sosin H: Areas of failure found at reoperation (second or symptomatic look) following "curative surgery" for adenocarcinoma of the rectum: Clinocopathologic correlation and implications for adjuvant therapy. *Cancer* 34:1278–1292, 1974.
5. Agostino D, Nickson JJ: Preoperative x-ray therapy in a simulated colon carcinoma in the rat. *Radiology* 74:816–818, 1960.
6. Powers WE, Tolmach LJ: Preoperative radiation therapy: Biological basis and experimental investigation. *Nature* 201:172–204, 1964.
7. Cummings BJ: A critical review of adjuvant preoperative radiation therapy for adenocarcinoma of the rectum. *Br J Surg* 73:332, 1986.
8. Morodomi T, Isomoto H, Shirouzu K, et al: An index for estimating the probability of lymph node metastasis in rectal cancers. *Cancer* 63:539–543, 1989.
9. Enstrom JE: Health and dietary practices and cancer mortality among California Mormons, in Lyon JL, Skolnick M (eds): *Cancer Incidence in Defined Populations*. Cold Spring Harbor, New York, Cold Spring Harbor Laboratory, 1980, pp 69–90.
10. Quan SHQ, Deddish MR, Stearns MW: The effect of preoperative roentgen therapy upon the 10- and 5-year results of the surgical treatment of cancer of the rectum. *Surg Gynecol Obstet* 111:507–508, 1960.
11. Stearns MW, Deddish MR, Quan SH, et al: Preoperative roentgen therapy for cancer of the rectum and rectosigmoid. *Cancer* 37:2866–2874, 1974.
12. Roswit B, Higgins GA Jr, Keehn R: Preoperative irradiation for carcinoma of the rectum and rectosigmoid colon: Report of a national Veterans Administration randomized study. *Cancer* 35:1597–1602, 1975.
13. Higgins GA, Humphrey EW, Dwight RW, et al: Preoperative radiation and surgery for cancer of the rectum: Veterans Administration Surgical Oncology Group trial II. *Cancer* 58:352–359, 1986.
14. Second report of an MRC working party. The evaluation of low dose pre-operative x-ray therapy in the management of operable rectal cancer; results of a randomly controlled trial. *Br J Surg* 71:21–25, 1984.
15. Stockholm Rectal Cancer Study Group: Short-term preoperative radiotherapy for adenocarcinoma of the rectum. *Am J Clin Oncol* 10:369–375, 1987.
16. Habib NA, Peck MA, Sawyer CN, et al: Does fixity affect prognosis in colorectal tumours? *Br J Surg* 70:423–424, 1983.
17. Duncan W, Smith AN, Freedman LF, et al: Clinico-pathological features of prognostic significance in operable rectal cancer in 17 centres in the UK. *Br J Cancer* 50:435–442, 1984.
18. Loefler I, Hafner CD: Survival rate in obstructing carcinoma of the colon. *Arch Surg* 89:716–718, 1964.
19. Sanfelippo PM, Beahrs OH: Factors in the prognosis of adenocarcinoma of the colon and rectum. *Arch Surg* 104:401–406, 1972.
20. Kligerman MM, Urdaneta N, Knowlton A, et al: Preoperative irradiation of rectosigmoid carcinoma including its regional lymph nodes. *Am J Roentgenol Radium Ther Nucl Med* 114:498–503, 1972.
21. Higgins GA Jr, Conn JH, Jordan PH Jr, et al: Preoperative radiotherapy for colorectal cancer. *Ann Surg* 181:624–631, 1975.
22. Gerard A, Buyse M, Nordlinger B, et al: Preoperative radiotherapy as adjuvant treatment in rectal cancer: Final results of a randomized study of the European Organization and Research for Treatment of Cancer (EORTC). *Ann Surg* 208:606–614, 1988.
23. Enker WE, Heilweil ML, Hertz REL, et al: En bloc pelvic lymphadenopathy and sphincter preservation in the surgical management of rectal cancer. *Ann Surg* 203:426–433, 1986.
24. Hojo K, Koyama Y: The effectiveness of wide anatomical resection and radical lymphadenectomy for patients with rectal cancer. *Jpn J Surg* 12:111–116, 1982.
25. Heald RJ, Husband EM, Ryall RDH: The meso-rectum in rectal cancer surgery: The clue to pelvic recurrence. *Br J Surg* 69:613–616, 1982.
26. Nicholls RJ: Surgery: Recent results. *Cancer Res* 83:101–112, 1982.
27. Stevens KR Jr, Allen CV, Fletcher WS: Preoperative radiotherapy for adenocarcinoma of the rectosigmoid. *Cancer* 37:2866–2874, 1976.
28. Pilepich M, Munzenrider J, Tak W, et al: Preoperative irradiation of primarily unresectable colorectal carcinoma. *Cancer* 42:1077–1081, 1978.
29. Dosoretz DE, Gunderson LL, Hedberg S, et al: Preoperative irradiation for unresectable rectal and rectosigmoid carcinomas. *Cancer* 52:814–818, 1983.
30. Mendenhall WM, Bland KI, Copeland EM, et al: Does preoperative radiotherapy enhance the probability of local control and survival in high-risk distal rectal cancer? Presented at the meeting of the Southern Surgical Association, Hot Springs, Virginia, December 1–5, 1991.
31. Mendenhall WM, Million RR, Bland KI, et al: Preoperative radiation therapy for clinically resectable adenocarcinoma of the rectum. *Ann Surg* 202:215–222, 1985.
32. Reed WP, Garb JL, Park WC, et al: Long-term results and complications of preoperative radiation in the treatment of rectal cancer. *Surgery* 103:161–167, 1988.
33. Kodner IJ, Shemesh EI, Fry RD, et al: Preoperative irradiation for rectal cancer: Improved local control and long-term survival. *Ann Surg* 209:194–199, 1989.
34. Kerman H, Roberson S, Bloom T, et al: Long-term experience with moderately high-dose preoperative radiation and low anterior resection. *Cancer* 69:2813–2819, 1992.
35. Mohiuddin M, Marks G: Adjuvant therapy for colon and rectal cancer. *Semin Oncol* 18:411–420, 1991.
36. Mohiuddin M, Derdel J, Marks G, et al: Results of adjuvant radiation therapy in cancer of the rectum: Thomas Jefferson University Hospital experience. *Cancer* 55:350–353, 1985.
37. Mohuiddin M, Marks G: High dose preoperative irradiation for cancer of the rectum, 1976–1988. *Int J Radiat Oncol Biol Phys* 20:37–43, 1991.
38. Fisher B, Wolmark N, Rockette H, et al: Postoperative adjuvant chemotherapy or radiation therapy for rectal cancer:

Results from NSABP protocol R-01. *J Natl Cancer Inst* 80:21–29, 1988.
39. Gastrointestinal Tumor Study Group: Survival after postoperative combination treatment of rectal cancer. *N Engl J Med* 315:1294–1295, 1986.
40. Marks J, Mohiuddin M, Kakinic J: New hope and promise for sphincter preservation in the management of cancer of the rectum. *Semin Oncol* 18:388–398, 1991.
41. Reis Neto JA, Quilici FA, Reis JA Jr: A comparison of nonoperative vs preoperative radiotherapy in rectal carcinoma: A 10-year randomized trial. *Dis Colon Rectum* 32:702–710, 1989.
42. Pahlman L, Glimelius B: Pre- or postoperative radiotherapy in rectal and rectosigmoid carcinoma: Report from a randomized multicenter trial. *Ann Surg* 211:187–195, 1990.
43. Steele G, Hamilton JM, Karr JP: A rational next step in the treatment of some rectal adenocarcinomas. *J Clin Oncol* 7: 988–990, 1989.
44. Weese JL, O'Grady MG, Ohevey FD: How long is the 5 cm margin? *Surg Gynecol Obstet* 163:101–103, 1986.
45. Williams NS, Dixon MF, Johnston D: Reappraisal of the 5 centimetre rule of distal excision for carcinoma of the rectum: A study of distal intramural spread and of patients' survival. *Br J Surg* 70:150–154, 1983.
46. Marks G, Mohiuddin M, Mason L, et al: High-dose preoperative radiation therapy as the key to extending sphincter-preservation surgery for cancer of the distal rectum. *Surg Oncol Clin North Am* 1:71–86, 1992.
47. Minsky BD, Cohen AM, Enker WE, et al: Phase I/II trial of pre-operative radiation therapy and coloanal anastomosis in distal invasive resectable rectal cancer. *Int J Radiat Oncol Biol Phys* 23:387–392, 1992.
48. Gary-Bobo J, Pujol H, Solassol CI, et al: L'irradition preoperatoire du cancer rectal: Resultats a 5 ans de 116 cas. *Bull Cancer (Paris)* 66:491–496, 1979.
49. Fortier GA, Krochak RJ, Kim JA, et al: Dose response to preoperative irradiation in rectal cancer: Implications for local control and complications associated with sphincter sparing surgery and abdominal resection. *Int J Radiat Oncol Biol Phys* 12:1559–1563, 1986.
50. Overgaard M, Overgaard J, Sell A: Dose-response relationship for radiation therapy of recurrent, residual, and primarily inoperable colorectal cancer. *Radiother Oncol* 1:217–225, 1984.
51. Ahmad N, Marks G, Mohiuddin M: High-dose preoperative radiation for cancer of the rectum: Impact of radiation dose on patterns of failure and survival. *Int J Radiat Oncol Biol Phys* 27:773–778, 1993.
52. Byfield JE, Calabro-Jones P, Klisak I, et al: Pharmacologic requirements for obtaining sensitization of human tumor cells in vitro to combined 5-fluorouracil of ftorafur and x-rays. *Int J Radiat Oncol Biol Phys* 8:1923–1933, 1982.
53. Krook JE, Moertel CG, Gunderson LL, et al: Effective surgical adjuvant therapy for high-risk rectal carcinoma. *N Engl J Med* 324:709–715, 1991.
54. Wassif-Boulis S: The role of pre-operative adjuvant therapy in management of borderline operability of rectal cancer. *Clin Radiol* 33:353–358, 1982.
55. Mansour M, Lefkopoulou R, Johnson R, et al: A comparison of post-operative chemotherapy, radiotherapy or combination therapy in potentially curable resectable rectal carcinoma: An ECOG study est 4276. Abstract 484. *Proc ASCO* 10:154, 1991.
56. Tepper JE, Shipley WU, Wood WC, et al: Intraoperative radiation therapy at the Massachusetts General Hospital, in Dobelbower RB, Abe M (eds): *Intraoperative Radiation Therapy*. Boca Raton, Florida, CRC Press, 1989.
57. Gunderson LL, Martin JK Jr, Earle JD, et al: Intraoperative and external beam irradiation with or without resection: Mayo pilot experience. *Mayo Clin Proc* 59:691–699, 1984.

CHAPTER 70

The Preoperative Adjuvant Radiation/ Chemotherapy Strategy

Bruce Minsky

HIGHLIGHTS

The encouraging results seen in patients who received adjuvant postoperative combined-modality therapy has prompted increased interest in preoperative combined-modality therapy. Advantages of preoperative combined-modality therapy include higher chemotherapy doses, enhanced downstaging, and decreased acute toxicity. This chapter will examine the rationale and results of the preoperative combined-modality approach to patients with rectal cancer.

CONTROVERSIES

The successful integration of chemotherapy and radiation therapy requires the use of careful radiation techniques as well as a phase I dose-escalation trial to determine the maximum tolerated dose of chemotherapy. Most studies have not employed these approaches. The optimal chemotherapy agents, doses, and schedule of preoperative combined-modality therapy are still being determined.

FUTURE DIRECTIONS

Based on the ability to deliver higher chemotherapy doses, enhanced downstaging, and decreased acute toxicity in patients with unresectable disease, preoperative combined-modality therapy is an attractive approach. Trials of preoperative versus postoperative radiation therapy and chemotherapy for patients with resectable rectal cancer are in progress.

Preoperative radiation therapy offers a number of potential advantages over postoperative radiation therapy in the treatment of patients with rectal cancer. These include (1) biological advantages—decreased tumor seeding at the time of surgery and increased radiosensitivity due to more oxygenated cells; (2) functional advantages—ability to conserve the rectum by changing the operation from an abdominoperineal resection to a low anterior resection/coloanal anastomosis; (3) surgical advantages—increasing the resectability rate in patients with unresectable disease; and (4) toxicity-related advantages—lower acute side effects due to the absence of postsurgical small bowel fixation in the pelvis.

The major theoretical disadvantage of preoperative radiation therapy is possibly overtreating 10 to 15 percent of patients (i.e., those patients with stages $T_{1-2}N_0M_0$ disease who do not require adjuvant therapy). With the use of computed tomography (CT) and magnetic resonance imaging (MRI),[1,2] which increase the detection of unsuspected liver metastasis, and intrarectal ultrasound,[3,4] which increases the detection of transmural tumor penetration, the true incidence of overtreatment may be less. In addition, there are pathologic features which can help predict the presence of positive pelvic nodes.[5] Preoperative radiation therapy has been delivered at low to intermediate doses (500 to 3450 cGy) and standard doses (≥ 4500 cGy).

Many nonrandomized trials of preoperative radiation therapy alone for patients with clinically resectable rectal cancer have been performed.[6–9] Overall, the retrospective data suggest that standard-dose preoperative radiation therapy downstages pelvic lymph nodes and decreases local failure.

There are eight modern randomized trials of preoperative radiation therapy alone for resectable rectal cancer.[10–17] All used low to intermediate doses of radiation. Some show a decrease in local failure, and in two of the series (Stockholm[11] and the European Organization for Research and Treatment of Cancer, or EORTC[10]) this difference reached statistical significance. The Stockholm trial[11] showed a significant advantage in disease-free survival, and the EORTC combined-modality trial[15] revealed a borderline advantage in survival ($p = .06$). The most impressive improvement in results was reported from São Paulo Catholic University; however, a statistical analysis was not performed.[17]

There are significant flaws in the design of all the randomized trials of preoperative radiation therapy. First, none use standard radiation doses (≥4500 cGy). Second, the interval between the completion of radiation and surgery is inadequate. An interval of 4 to 6 weeks is recommended for maximum tumor downstaging and the recovery of normal tissues. Third, the radiation techniques employed were suboptimal and are known to be associated with an increased incidence of complications. For example, all used AP/PA rather than multiple field techniques and made no attempt to limit the dose to the small bowel. The superior border in most series was extended to L2 (rather than the more standard L5/S1), thereby further increasing the volume of small bowel in the radiation field. Furthermore, the fraction sizes were unconventional and were as high as 510 cGy/day. These inferior radiation techniques contributed to the significant increase in complications, most notably in the EORTC[10] and Stockholm[11] series.

Early trials of leucovorin (LV) with 5-fluorouracil (5-FU) in patients with metastatic colorectal cancer reported responses with cancers refractory to 5-FU alone as well as improved results compared with those expected with 5-FU alone in previously untreated patients.[18,19] Following these initial reports, many institutions have tested various LV/5-FU combinations in patients with advanced colorectal cancer.[20–26] The doses and schedules vary widely; however, the response rates are usually higher (10 to 50 percent) than those reported with 5-FU alone (5 to 25 percent). Although some trials report an advantage of LV/5-FU, it is not yet clear whether the increased response rate to LV/5-FU translates into an improvement in survival compared with high-dose 5-FU alone.

The encouraging results seen in patients with resectable rectal cancer who received adjuvant postoperative combined-modality therapy[27–29] has prompted increased interest in preoperative combined-modality therapy. As discussed above, there are potential advantages to preoperative radiation therapy. Likewise, there are advantages to preoperative combined-modality therapy. First, patients are able to tolerate higher chemotherapy doses and experience lower acute toxicity.[30] Second, in patients with unresectable disease, the addition of chemotherapy to preoperative radiation therapy increases downstaging and the resectability rate.[31] Third, there is no delay in starting systemic therapy. Finally, a theoretical reason for adding systemic chemotherapy at the time of diagnosis is to deliver therapy when the metastatic burden is the smallest.[32]

This chapter will examine the rationale and results of the preoperative combined-modality approach to rectal cancer. Since there is limited experience with this approach in patients with resectable rectal cancer, most of the discussion will present data obtained from patients with unresectable rectal cancer.

DESIGN OF PREOPERATIVE COMBINED-MODALITY TRIALS

The successful integration of chemotherapy and radiation therapy requires the use of careful radiation techniques. A limited number of trials have used preoperative combined-modality therapy in a systematic fashion [Wong et al.,[33] Haghbin et al.,[34] Frykholm et al.,[35] Boulis-Wassif et al. (EORTC),[15] Bosset et al.,[36] and Minsky et al.[30,37,38]] All have used bolus 5-FU–based chemotherapy (Table 70-1). The EORTC trial is a phase III trial and the remainder are single arm, nonrandomized trials. The only trials that use conventional radiation therapy techniques are from Minsky et al.[30,37,38] and Bosset et al.[36]

The toxicity associated with unconventional radiation techniques and failure to use a recommended chemotherapy dose level from a phase I trial is evident in the trial from Wong et al.[33] The investigators reported the results of 22 patients with unresectable recurrent rectal cancer who received concurrent radiation therapy (4500 to 5000 cGy), bolus 5-FU (15 mg/kg/day × 3), and mitomycin-C (10 mg/kg/day × 1). Rather than starting at a lower chemotherapy dose and escalating to determine the maximum tolerated dose (MTD), the investigators chose a dose of chemotherapy that, even after a dose attenuation, was above the MTD. Ten patients (45 percent) were unable to complete the proto-

Table 70-1
Preoperative Combined Modality Therapy for Rectal Cancer

Series	*No. of patients*	*Resectability*	*Radiation dose, cGy*	*Chemotherapy*	*Type of trial*
Wong et al.[33]	22	Unresectable	4000–4500	5-FU/MMC	Phase II
Haghbin et al.[34]	64	Resectable + Unresectable	4000	5-FU/MMC	Phase II
Frykholm et al.[35]	21	Unresectable	4000	5-FU/MTX/LV	Phase II
Boulis-Wassif et al.[15]	121[a]	Resectable	3450	5-FU	Phase III
Bosset et al.[36]	73	Resectable + Unresectable	4500	5-FU/LV	Phase II
Minsky et al.[30]	20	Unresectable	5040	5-FU/LV	Phase I
Minsky et al.[37]	12	Unresectable	5040	5-FU/LV	Phase I
Minsky et al.[38]	17	Resectable + Unresectable	5040	5-FU/LV	Phase I

[a] = Combined modality arm only.
Abbreviations: 5-FU = bolus 5-fluorouracil, MMC = mitomycin-C, MTX = methotrexate, LV = leucovorin.

col due to toxicity. The incidence of grade 3+ toxicity included hematologic, 23 percent; stomatitis, 9 percent; gastrointestinal, 32 percent; and nadir sepsis, 23 percent. There was one neutropenic death. The excessive acute toxicity may have been partly due to the unconventional radiation techniques. For example, patients received large fraction sizes (250 cGy/day), AP/PA techniques were used, and there was no attempt to limit the dose to the small bowel.

The EORTC randomized 247 patients with clinically resectable rectal cancer to preoperative radiation therapy plus 5-FU (375 mg/m^2 bolus days 1–4) versus radiation therapy alone.[15] Like other European preoperative randomized trials in resectable rectal cancer, the total dose (3450 cGy), fraction size (230 cGy/fraction), field size (extended to the superior border of L2), technique (AP/PA), and short radiation–surgery interval (2 weeks) were not conventional. There was no difference in local control; however, patients who received the combined-modality therapy had a decrease in liver metastasis (8 versus 18 percent; $p = .07$). Overall, combined-modality therapy had a negative impact on survival (46 versus 59 percent; $p = .06$). Since 5-FU was not employed as a systemic therapy with monthly cycles and the radiation therapy techniques were unconventional, it is not surprising that this was a negative study.

Based on the possible advantage of continuous-infusion 5-FU compared with bolus 5-FU,[39] Rich[40] from the M. D. Anderson Hospital designed a preoperative combined-modality program. Patients receive 4500 cGy and continuous infusion 5-FU (250 mg/m^2/day) and cisplatin (4 mg/m^2/day) during the entire course of the radiation therapy. In this study, conventional radiation techniques are used. The results are pending at this time.

The only trials that employed a phase I escalation to determine the MTD are from Memorial Sloan-Kettering Cancer Center (MSKCC).[37,38,41] Based on the suggestion of an advantage of 5-FU/LV compared with 5-FU alone in patients with metastatic colorectal cancer[20,23,42–46] and the in vitro[34,47] and in vivo[48] evidence of 5-FU sensitization of radiation therapy, three consecutive trials of preoperative combined-modality therapy have been performed. All three trials employed bolus 5-FU/LV (two cycles) and radiation therapy (5040 cGy) followed by surgery (with or without intraoperative brachytherapy) and 10 cycles of postoperative bolus 5-FU/LV. The 5-FU was escalated while the dose of radiation and LV remained constant. Conventional radiation techniques were used. The treatment scheme for the three trials is seen in Fig. 70-1. Since they were phase I trials, the primary end point of the trials was the determination of the MTD of 5-FU during the preoperative combined-modality segment.

The first MSKCC phase I trial (sequential high-dose LV) was based on the experience of Erlichman et al.[20] and used high-dose LV (200 mg/m^2); 20 patients with primary (13) or recurrent (7) unresectable rectal cancer limited to the pelvis were enrolled. Chemotherapy was started on day 1 and radiation therapy on day 8. The resectability rate (with negative margins) was 89 percent and the pathologic complete response rate was 20 percent. For the 6 patients who received preoperative 5-FU at the recommended dose level (250 mg/m^2), the incidence of any grade 3+ toxicity was as follows: diarrhea, 17 percent, and frequent bowel movements, 17 percent. With a median follow-up of 36 months, the local control rate was 74 percent and the 3-year actuarial survival was 69 percent.[49] However, since optimal doses of 5-FU to treat systemic disease could not

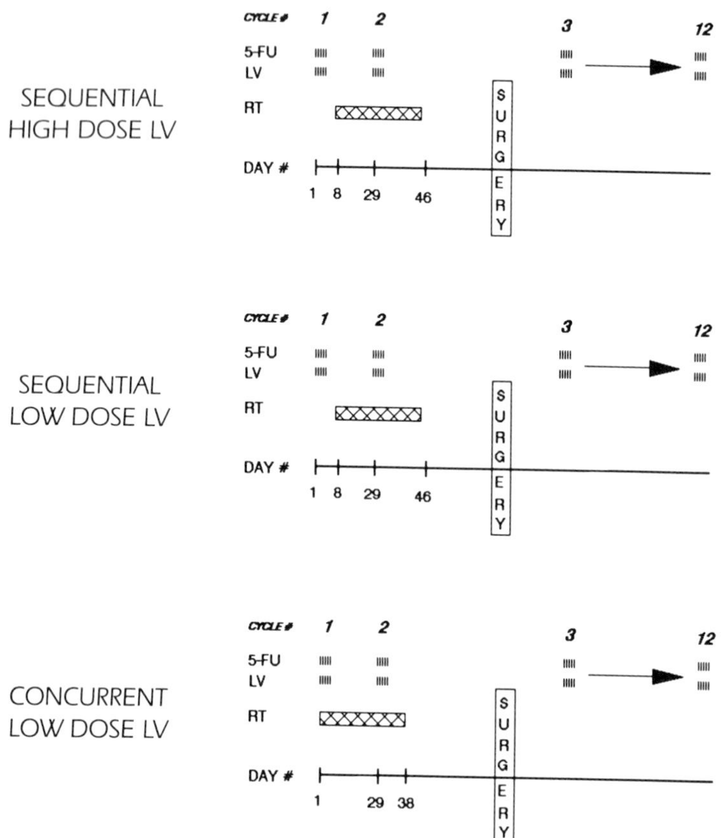

FIG. 70-1. Treatment schema for MSKCC phase I preoperative combined-modality trials.

be delivered until the postoperative chemotherapy segment (cycle 3), the high-dose LV regimen was discontinued and a new trial using low-dose LV (20 mg/m^2) was developed.

Based on the Mayo Clinic/North Central Cancer Treatment Group (NCCTG) experience in patients with metastatic colorectal cancer with 5-FU and low-dose LV,[22,25] two subsequent consecutive phase I trials with 5-FU, radiation therapy, and low-dose LV were performed at MSKCC. In the first trial, 12 patients with unresectable disease received 5-FU/LV on day 1 and radiation on day 8.[37] The MTD of 5-FU during the preoperative combined-modality segment was 325 mg/m^2. The recommended dose was lower. Therefore, since optimal doses of 5-FU to treat systemic disease could not be delivered until the postoperative chemotherapy segment (cycle 3), this sequential low-dose LV regimen was also discontinued.

A second trial was performed in which the schedule rather than the chemotherapy dose was altered.[38] A total of 17 patients with unresectable (1), locally advanced (12), or resectable but bulky disease (4) were entered. In this trial, preoperative radiation therapy, 5-FU, and low-dose LV was delivered concurrently (from day 1) rather than sequentially (chemotherapy on day 1 and radiation on day 8). The MTD of 5-FU during the preoperative combined-modality segment of the trial was 375 mg/m^2; therefore the recommended dose was 325 mg/m^2. The clinical complete response rate was 19 percent (3/16). Two patients (13 percent) had a pathologic complete response and 1 patient had negative nodes and a microscopic focus of tumor in the bowel wall. The resectability rate with negative margins was 100 percent. Limiting the analysis to the 15 patients who received 5-FU at the recommended dose level, the incidence of any grade 3 toxicity during the combined-modality segment was as follows: diarrhea, 7 percent; frequent bowel movements, 7 percent; erythema, 14 percent; the incidence of total grade 3 toxicity was 20 percent (3/15). None had grade 4 toxicity. Two patients (13 percent) had a postoperative perineal wound abscess. At MSKCC, this regimen is recommended as a phase II preoperative adjuvant therapy for patients with clinically staged $T_{3-4}N_{0-2}M_0$ rectal cancer.

A similar trial of concurrent preoperative radiation therapy, bolus 5-FU, and low-dose LV was performed by the EORTC. A total of 73 patients with resectable, residual, locally recurrent, or fixed rectal cancers were entered.[36] Patients received treatment according to a schedule similar to that used in the MSKCC concurrent low-dose LV trial (bolus daily × 5, days 1 and 29 of radiation therapy). However, rather than performing a phase I dose-escalation trial, a phase II trial with a dose-attenuation schedule was performed. The 5-FU dose started at 425 mg/m^2 and was attenuated to 350 mg/m^2. At the recommended dose level (350 mg/m^2), the incidence of WHO grade 2+ toxicity during the preoperative combined-modality segment was 14 percent (1/7).

In summary, both the MSKCC[38] and EORTC[36] preoperative concurrent low-dose LV trials recommend similar dose levels of 5-FU (325 mg/m^2 and 350 mg/m^2, respectively) while also reporting a similar incidence of significant toxicity during the combined-modality segment (20 and 14 percent, respectively).

Chemotherapy Dose Issues

The optimal preoperative combined-modality therapy program must use chemotherapy doses adequate to treat systemic disease. Therefore, the chemotherapy dose levels in any combined-modality programs should be compared with those used in patients with advanced disease.

In the MSKCC high-dose LV trial, the recommended dose of 5-FU during the combined-modality segment was 250 mg/m^2, which is 68 percent of Erlichman's recommended dose of 370 mg/m^2. In the MSKCC concurrent low-dose LV trial, the recommended dose of 5-FU during the combined-modality segment was 325 mg/m^2, which is 76 percent of the Mayo Clinic/NCCTG recommended dose of 425 mg/m^2. The EORTC recommended dose was 350 mg/m^2, which is 82 percent of the Mayo Clinic/NCCTG recommended dose of 425 mg/m^2. The dose of LV remained constant in all trials.

Intergroup adjuvant postoperative rectal trial no. 114 is also based on the Mayo Clinic/NCCTG 5-FU/low-dose LV regimen. Arm no. 2 of the trial uses the same doses and schedules of 5-FU/LV as the MSKCC concurrent low-dose LV and EORTC trials. However, during the combined-modality segment of the intergroup trial (cycles 3 and 4 of chemotherapy), the chemotherapy dose and schedule is attenuated. The LV dose remains at 20 mg/m^2 but is given for only 4 rather than 5 days. Likewise, the 5-FU is decreased to 400 mg/m^2 × 4 days. With this schedule, the total dose per cycle of LV is 80 mg/m^2 and of 5-FU is 1600 mg/m^2. These doses are similar to the 100 mg/m^2 of LV and 1625 mg/m^2 of 5-FU in the MSKCC[38] concurrent low-dose LV trial and the 100 mg/m^2 of LV and 1750 mg/m^2 of 5-FU in the EORTC[36] trial. Therefore, although there was concern that optimal doses of 5-FU to treat systemic disease were not being delivered during the combined-modality segments of the MSKCC concurrent low-dose LV and EORTC trials, it should be recognized that a similar dose reduction is needed when the therapy is delivered postoperatively in the intergroup adjuvant trial. The 5-FU is delivered at 75 percent and LV at 80 percent of the recommended Mayo/NCCTG dose.

POTENTIAL ADVANTAGES OF PREOPERATIVE COMBINED-MODALITY THERAPY

Higher Chemotherapy Doses

Nonrandomized data from MSKCC suggest that higher doses of chemotherapy can be delivered with preoperative compared with postoperative radiation therapy. This difference was noted when comparing two MSKCC Phase I trials of combined 5-FU, high-dose LV, and sequential radiation therapy.[30,41,50] Patients with unresectable disease[41] received preoperative radiation therapy and two cycles of 5-FU/LV (sequential high-dose LV) followed by surgery and postoperative 5-FU/LV. Patients with resectable disease[50] received the same 5-FU/LV and radiation therapy except postoperatively. The MTD of 5-FU was higher with preoperative (300 mg/m^2) than with postoperative combined-modality therapy (250 mg/m^2). However, it should be emphasized that measurement of dose intensity, which accounts for additional dose-related variables, may offer a more accurate assessment.

Enhanced Downstaging

Following full-dose preoperative radiation therapy alone for patients with resectable rectal cancer, 10 to 15 percent had a complete pathologic response (T_0N_0).[9,51–53] The incidence of positive pelvic nodes was 16 to 48 percent.[9,52–55]

In patients with unresectable disease (as opposed to those with resectable disease) who receive preoperative radiation therapy, none had a complete pathologic response[56,57] and the incidence of positive mesorectal/pelvic nodes was 40 to 86 percent.[52,53,56,58,59] Overall, 46 to 64 percent were converted to a resectable status with negative margins.[56,57,60]

Nonrandomized data from MSKCC suggest that 5-FU and high-dose LV enhances radiation-induced downstaging (Table 70-2).[31] For this comparison, three groups of patients who were treated with identical doses and techniques of preoperative pelvic radiation therapy (total dose, 5040 cGy) were examined.

Group 1 included 20 patients with unresectable disease who received radiation therapy, 5-FU, and high-dose LV (sequential high-dose LV). Group 2 included 11 patients with unresectable disease who received preoperative radiation therapy. Group 3 included 21 patients with invasive, resectable, primary disease who received preoperative radiation therapy.

Patients with unresectable disease who received LV/5-FU had a higher rate of pathologic complete response (20 versus 0 percent) and a lower incidence of positive mesorectal/pelvic nodes (30 versus 64 per-

Table 70-2
The Impact of Radiation Therapy and Chemotherapy on Downstaging in Rectal Cancer

	Group I			*Group 2*			*Group 3*	*Groups 2 and 3*
	Primary	*Recurrent*	*Total*	*Primary*	*Recurrent*	*Total*	*All patients*	*All patients*
No. of patients	13	7	20	9	2	11	21	32
Stage[a]								
T_0N_0[b]	15%	29%	20%	0	0	0	10%	6%
$T_2N_{0\text{-}2}$	46%	29%	40%	0	0	0	38%	25%
$T_3N_{0\text{-}2}$	15%	29%	20%	78%	0	64%	52%	56%
$T_4N_{0\text{-}2}$	23%	14%	20%	22%	2/2	36%	0	13%
% Resectable[c]	85%	100%	90%	78%	0/2	64%	N/A[d]	N/A
% Node +	38%	14%	30%	56%	2/2	64%	48%	53%

[a]None had T_1 tumors after treatment.
[b]No identifiable tumor remaining (pathological CR).
[c]Complete resection with negative margins.
[d]Not applicable (all patients in group 3 presented with resectable disease).
SOURCE: Modified from Minsky et al.[31] (Reproduced by permission.)

cent) compared with those who did not receive chemotherapy. Even when the most favorable group of patients (group 3) was included, patients who received 5-FU/LV still had a higher complete response rate (20 versus 6 percent) and a lower incidence of positive mesorectal/pelvic nodes (30 versus 53 percent) compared with those who received radiation therapy without chemotherapy. Among patients with initially unresectable disease, the resectability rate was higher in those who received 5-FU/LV compared with those who did not receive 5-FU/LV (90 versus 64 percent). Patients who received 5-FU/LV experienced slightly more grade 1–2 fatigue, stomatitis, and nausea and grade 3 diarrhea, tenesmus, and dysuria.

Despite the fact that patients who received chemotherapy (group 1) had more advanced disease compared with those with resectable disease (group 3), the addition of 5-FU/LV increased the resectability and downstaging rates. These data should be interpreted with caution, since this was not a prospective randomized trial. The improvement in results may have been due to other factors such as patient selection and differences in other clinicopathologic variables. However, since the doses and techniques of radiation therapy were identical in the three groups of patients, the addition of 5-FU/LV may have been partly responsible for the improvement.

The data suggest that preoperative combined-modality therapy increases the chance of a complete resection. This is of significance, since patients with initially unresectable rectal cancer who have microscopic or gross residual disease remaining after preoperative radiation therapy have higher local failure and lower survival rates compared with those who undergo a complete resection.[61–63] The ultimate impact of a complete response as well as a decrease in the incidence of pelvic nodes on local control and survival remains to be determined.

Decreased Acute Toxicity

Preoperative combined-modality therapy may be associated with lower acute toxicity compared with postoperative combined-modality therapy. Although both the Gastrointestinal Tumor Study Group (GITSG)[28,29] and Mayo/NCCTG[27] postoperative adjuvant trials revealed an advantage in survival for the combined-modality arm, the acute toxicity of therapy was not inconsequential. In the GITSG trial, the total incidence of grade 3+ toxicity in patients who received the combined-modality therapy was hematological, 26 percent (WBC < 2000), and nonhematologic, 35 percent. Due to toxicity, 35 percent of the patients never finished all the planned cycles of chemotherapy.

In a separate randomized trial from the GITSG (GITSG #7182), patients received combined postoperative 5-FU and radiation therapy and then were randomized to either 5-FU/MeCCNU or escalating doses of 5-FU alone.[64] The incidence of grade 3+ toxicity was 50 to 53 percent.

The Mayo/NCCTG trial reported toxicity for the combined-modality segment as well as for the total treatment course.[27] For the total treatment course, the most substantial grade 3+ toxicities included diarrhea (41 percent) and leukopenia (33 percent). Similar to the GITSG trial, 35 percent of the patients never finished all the planned cycles of chemotherapy due to toxicity. Furthermore, in the Mayo/NCCTG trial, an additional 5 percent of patients did not finish all the planned cycles of chemotherapy due to patient refusal. Another technique that could be used to measure acute toxicity is the number of patients requiring a dose reduction. These data were not reported in the manuscript. Limiting the analysis to the combined-modality segment, 19 percent (18/96) of patients in the Mayo/NCCTG trial were unable to receive the second cycle of chemotherapy due to grade 3+ toxicity. The incidence of grade 3+ toxicity was as follows: diarrhea, 20 percent; leukopenia, 18 percent; dermatitis, 5 percent; nausea and vomiting, 2 percent; and stomatitis, 1 percent.

A major disadvantage of delivering radiation therapy in the postoperative setting is the possibility of fixed loops of small bowel in the pelvis. Following pelvic surgery, the small bowel commonly extends into the pelvis. Complications of radiation therapy related to the small bowel are directly proportional to the volume of small bowel in the radiation field.[65] The increased volume of small bowel in the radiation fields may have been partly responsible for the increased toxicity seen in patients receiving postoperative therapy. The use of absorbable mesh to exclude the small bowel from the pelvis may decrease some of the small bowel complications.[66] However, since radiation therapy in the intergroup rectal trial no. 114 begins at least 4 months postoperatively and absorbable mesh is usually completely reabsorbed by 6 months, the use of absorbable mesh may be of limited benefit.

In the Mayo/NCCTG trial, conventional radiation techniques were used and the only grade 3+ toxicity with radiation therapy alone was a 5 percent incidence of diarrhea.[27] Therefore, the increased toxicity of postoperative combined-modality therapy cannot be explained by radiation therapy alone. Other factors that may contribute to the higher incidence of toxicity include radiation-chemotherapy synergy as well as slower recovery of the postoperative patient.

To determine if combined-modality therapy had less acute toxicity when delivered preoperatively as opposed to postoperatively in patients with rectal cancer, the combined-modality therapy segments of two separate parallel phase I trials from MSKCC were compared.[30,41,50] Patients with unresectable disease received preoperative radiation therapy, 5-FU, and high-dose LV (sequential high-dose LV) followed by surgery and postoperative 5-FU/LV.[41] Patients with resectable disease received identical doses, techniques, and schedules of radiation and 5-FU/LV except that all therapy was delivered postoperatively.[50] The National Cancer Institute's (NCI) Common Toxicity Criteria modified for gastrointestinal toxicity were used.[41]

The results are seen in Table 70-3. Although more patients (75 versus 32 percent; $p = .02$) received the higher dose level of 5-FU (250 mg/m^2), significantly fewer experienced acute nonhematologic grade 3+ toxicity with preoperative versus postoperative combined-modality therapy (13 versus 48 percent; $p = .045$). There was no difference in hematologic toxicity. Although the study was not a randomized trial, the data suggest that with the doses and schedule as used in these trials, combined-modality therapy has less acute toxicity when it is delivered preoperatively rather than postoperatively. These differences may be partly due to the volume of small bowel in the radiation therapy field as well as slower recovery of the postoperative patient.

In contrast with short-term (acute) toxicity, it is difficult to compare the long-term toxicity of preoperative compared with postoperative combined-modality therapy. Patients with postoperative grade 3+ complications sometimes are not referred for adjuvant therapy. This introduces a bias against preoperative therapy, since patients with surgical complications may not be included in the overall toxicity of postoperative therapy. Therefore, outside of a phase III trial where patients are randomized prior to surgery, the only fair comparison is one of acute toxicity.

FUTURE APPROACHES TO PREOPERATIVE COMBINED-MODALITY THERAPY

Most randomized trials comparing 5-FU/LV with 5-FU alone in patients with metastatic colorectal can-

Table 70-3
Acute Toxicity of Preoperative Compared with Postoperative Combined-Modality Therapy for Rectal Cancer

	Total grade 3+ acute toxicity,[a] 5-FU dose level						
	200 mg/m²		*250 mg/m²*		*Total*		
	No. of pts.	*No. grade 3+*	*No. of pts.*	*No. grade 3+*	*No. of pts.*	*No. grade 3+*	
Preoperative	4	0 (0%)	12	2 (17%)	16	2 (13%)	($p = .045$)
Postoperative	17	7 (41%)	8	5 (63%)	25	12 (48%)	

[a]Highest toxicity per patient. Multiple toxicities in the same patient are scored as a single event and the results are expressed as a percentage of patients evaluable at each dose level.

SOURCE: Modified from Minsky et al.[30] (Reproduced by permission.)

cer suggest an advantage of 5-FU/LV.[23,24,44–47] Additional controversy exists as to the efficacy of low-dose LV compared with high-dose LV. Most of the randomized trials of 5-FU/LV versus 5-FU have used high-dose LV. Recent nonrandomized data from the Mayo Clinic/NCCTG suggest that 5-FU and low-dose LV is as effective and better tolerated than 5-FU and high-dose LV in patients with metastatic colorectal cancer.[44] In addition, the route of administration of 5-FU (bolus versus infusion) may influence the response rates.[47,67] A recent analysis of the Mayo Clinic/NCCTG four-arm postoperative adjuvant rectal trial (86-47-51) revealed a significant improvement in 3-year survival in patients who received combined modality therapy with continuous-infusion 5-FU compared with bolus 5-FU (with or without MeCCNU).[68] A number of approaches have been used to try to decrease the toxicity of combined-modality therapy. These include changing the schedule or doses of chemotherapy.

Schedule

Other chemotherapy schedules are still associated with toxicity. Using a weekly administration schedule, the GITSG reported an advantage with 5-FU plus even higher doses of LV (500 mg/m^2) compared with low-dose (25 mg/m^2) LV in patients with metastatic colorectal cancer.[23] However, with this schedule of weekly high-dose LV, the incidence of treatment-related mortality was 6.5 percent. Likewise, 27 percent of patients in the Roswell Park study required hospitalization, primarily for management of severe diarrhea.[45] Therefore, the ideal schedule is not yet known.

High-Dose versus Low-Dose Leucovorin

To determine if there was a difference in toxicity between high- and low-dose LV regimens in patients who received chemotherapy alone for metastatic colorectal cancer, the Mayo Clinic/NCCTG compared the incidence of grade 3+ toxicity in their previously reported trials.[22,25] There was no difference in the incidence of severe diarrhea (16 versus 19 percent) and a small decrease in leukopenia (22 versus 15 percent); however, there was a significant increase in the incidence of hospital admissions (15 versus 5.4 percent; $p = .015$) in those patients who received low-dose LV as opposed to high-dose LV. It should be emphasized that the dose of 5-FU is higher in the low-dose than the high-dose LV regimen. Therefore the dose of 5-FU may be partly responsible for the differences in toxicity. The question of toxicity differences between the low- and high-dose LV regimens remains unresolved.

In summary, the optimal chemotherapy agents, doses, and schedule of preoperative combined-modality therapy are still being determined. Based on the potential to deliver higher chemotherapy doses, enhanced downstaging, and decreased acute toxicity in patients with unresectable disease, preoperative combined-modality therapy is an attractive approach. Trials of preoperative versus postoperative radiation therapy and chemotherapy for patients with clinically staged $T_{3-4}N_{0-2}M_0$ rectal cancer are in progress.

REFERENCES

1. Butch RJ, Stark DD, Wittenberg J, et al: Staging rectal cancer by MR and CT. *Am J Radiol* 146:1155–1160, 1986.
2. Koehler PR, Feldberg MAM, van Waes PFGM: Preoperative staging of rectal cancer with computerized tomography: Accuracy, efficacy, and effect on patient management. *Cancer* 54:512–516, 1984.
3. Hildebrandt U, Feifel G: Preoperative staging of rectal cancer by intrarectal ultrasound. *Dis Colon Rectum* 28:42–46, 1985.
4. Rifkin MD, Marks GJ: Transrectal US as an adjunct in the diagnosis of rectal and extrarectal tumors. *Radiology* 157: 499–502, 1985.
5. Minsky BD, Rich T, Recht A, et al: Selection criteria for local excision with or without adjuvant radiation therapy for rectal cancer. *Cancer* 63:1421–1429, 1989.
6. Mendenhall WM, Million RR, Bland KI, et al: Preoperative radiation therapy for clinically resectable adenocarcinoma of the rectum. *Ann Surg* 202:215–222, 1985.
7. Reed WP, Garb JL, Park WC, et al: Long-term results and complications of preoperative radiation in the treatment of rectal cancer. *Surgery* 103:161–167, 1988.
8. Marks J, Mohiuddin M, Kakinic J: New hope and promise for sphincter preservation in the management of cancer of the rectum. *Semin Oncol* 18:388–398, 1991.
9. Minsky BD, Cohen AM, Enker WE, et al: Phase I/II trial of pre-operative radiation therapy and coloanal anastomosis in distal invasive resectable rectal cancer. *Int J Radiat Oncol Biol Phys* 23:387–392, 1992.
10. Gerard A, Buyse M, Nordlinger B, et al: Preoperative radiotherapy as adjuvant treatment in rectal cancer: Final results of a randomized study of the European Organization for Research and Treatment of Cancer (EORTC). *Ann Surg* 208:606–614, 1988.
11. Stockholm Rectal Cancer Study Group: Preoperative short-term preoperative radiation therapy in operable rectal cancer: A randomized trial. *Cancer* 66:49–55, 1990.
12. Higgins GA, Humphrey EW, Dwight RW, et al: Preoperative radiation and surgery for cancer of the rectum: Veterans Administration Surgical Oncology Group trial II. *Cancer* 58:352–359, 1986.
13. Rider WD, Palmer JA, Mahoney LJ, et al: Preoperative irradiation in operable cancer of the rectum: Report of the Toronto Trial. *Can J Surg* 20:335–338, 1977.
14. Roswit B, Higgins GA Jr, Keehn R: Preoperative irradiation for carcinoma of the rectum and rectosigmoid colon: Report of a national Veterans Administration randomized study. *Cancer* 35:1597–1602, 1975.
15. Boulis-Wassif S, Gerard A, Loygue J, et al: Final results of a randomized trial on the treatment of rectal cancer with preoperative radiotherapy alone or in combination with 5-fluorouracil, followed by radical surgery. *Cancer* 53:1811–1818, 1984.
16. Duncan W: Adjuvant radiotherapy in rectal cancer: The MRC trials. *Br J Surg* 72:S59–S62, 1985.
17. Reis Neto JA, Quilici FA, Reis JA Jr: A comparison of non-operative vs preoperative radiotherapy in rectal carcinoma: A 10-year randomized trial. *Dis Colon Rectum* 32:702–710, 1989.

18. Machover D, Schwarzenberg L, Goldschmidt E, et al: Treatment of advanced colorectal and gastric adenocarcinomas with 5-FU combined with high-dose folinic acid: A pilot study. *Cancer Treat Rep* 66:1803–1807, 1982.
19. Bruckner HW, Roboz J, Spigelman M, et al: An efficient leucovorin and 5-FU sequence: Dosage escalation and pharmacological monitoring. *Proc AACR* 24:138, 1983.
20. Erlichman C, Fine S, Wong A, et al: A randomized trial of fluorouracil and folinic acid in patients with metastatic colorectal carcinoma. *J Clin Oncol* 6:469–475, 1988.
21. Doroshaw JH, Multhauf P, Leong L, et al: Prospective randomized comparison of fluorouracil versus fluorouracil and high dose continuous infusion leucovorin calcium for the treatment of advanced measurable colorectal cancer in patients previously unexposed to chemotherapy. *J Clin Oncol* 8:491–501, 1990.
22. Poon MA, O'Connell MJ, Moertel CG, et al: Biochemical modulation of fluorouracil: Evidence of significant improvement of survival and quality of life in patients with advanced colorectal carcinoma. *J Clin Oncol* 7:1407–1418, 1989.
23. Petrelli N, Douglass HO Jr, Herrera L, et al: The modulation of fluorouracil with leucovorin in metastatic colorectal carcinoma: A prospective randomized phase III trial. *J Clin Oncol* 7:1419–1426, 1989.
24. Valone FH, Friedman MA, Wittlinger PS, et al: Treatment of patients with advanced colorectal carcinomas with fluorouracil alone, high-dose leucovorin plus fluorouracil, or sequential methotrexate, fluorouracil and leucovorin: A randomized trial of the Northern California oncology group. *J Clin Oncol* 7:1427–1436, 1989.
25. Poon MA, O'Connell MJ, Wieand HS, et al: Biochemical modulation of fluorouracil with leucovorin: Confirmatory evidence of improved therapeutic efficacy in advanced colorectal cancer. *J Clin Oncol* 9:1967–1972, 1991.
26. O'Dwyer PD, Wittes RE: Development of folates and folinic acid antagonists in cancer therapy. *Natl Cancer Inst Monogr* 5:1–223, 1987.
27. Krook JE, Moertel CG, Gunderson LL, et al: Effective surgical adjuvant therapy for high-risk rectal carcinoma. *N Engl J Med* 324:709–715, 1991.
28. Gastrointestinal Tumor Study Group: Prolongation of the disease-free interval in surgically treated rectal carcinoma. *N Engl J Med* 312:1465–1472, 1985.
29. Douglass HO, Moertel CG, Mayer RJ, et al: Survival after postoperative combination treatment of rectal cancer. *N Engl J Med* 315:1294–1295, 1986.
30. Minsky BD, Cohen AM, Enker WE: Combined modality therapy of rectal cancer: Decreased acute toxicity with the preoperative approach. *J Clin Oncol* 10:1218–1224, 1992.
31. Minsky BD, Cohen AM, Kemeny N, et al: Enhancement of radiation-induced downstaging of rectal cancer by fluorouracil and high-dose leucovorin chemotherapy. *J Clin Oncol* 10:79–84, 1992.
32. Kelsen DP, Hilaris B, Martini N: Neoadjuvant chemotherapy and surgery of cancer of the esophagus. *Semin Surg Oncol* 2:170–176, 1986.
33. Wong CS, Cummings BJ, Keane TJ, et al: Combined radiation therapy, mitomycin C, and 5-fluorouracil for locally recurrent rectal carcinoma: Results of a pilot study. *Int J Radiat Oncol Biol Phys* 21:1291–1296, 1991.
34. Haghbin M, Sischy B, Hinson J: Combined modality therapy in poor prognostic rectal adenocarcinoma. *Radiother Oncol* 13:75–81, 1988.
35. Frykolm G, Glimelius B, Pahlman L: Preoperative irradiation with and without chemotherapy (MFL) in the treatment of primary non-resectable adenocarcinoma of the rectum: Results from two consecutive studies. *Eur J Clin Oncol* 11:1535–1541, 1989.
36. Bosset JF, Pavy JJ, Hamers HP, et al: Low dose 5-FU-leucovorin and concomitant radiotherapy for locally advanced rectal cancer: Determination of an optimal dosage of 5-FU (abstract). A phase III study of the EORTC cooperative group of radiotherapy (73 patients). *Radiother Oncol* 24:S101, 1992.
37. Minsky BD, Cohen AM, Kemeny N, et al: Pre-operative 5-FU, and low dose leucovorin and sequential radiation therapy for unresectable rectal cancer. *Int J Radiat Oncol Biol Phys* 25:821–827, 1993.
38. Minsky B, Cohen A, Enker W, et al: Pre-operative 5-FU, low dose leucovorin, and concurrent radiation therapy for rectal cancer. *Proc ASCO* 12:194, 1993.
39. Byfield JE: Useful interactions between 5-fluorouracil and radiation in man: 5-fluorouracil as a radiosensitizer, in Hill BT, Belamy AS (eds): *Antitumor Drug-Radiation Interactions*. Boca Raton, Florida, CRC Press, 1990, p 87.
40. Rich TA: Chemoradiation for gastrointestinal cancer. *Front Radiat Ther Oncol* 26:115–130, 1992.
41. Minsky BD, Kemeny N, Cohen AM, et al: Preoperative high-dose leucovorin/5-fluorouracil and radiation therapy for unresectable rectal cancer. *Cancer* 67:2859–2866, 1991.
42. Houghton JA, Maroda SJ Jr, Philips JO, et al: Biochemical determinants of responsiveness to 5-fluorouracil and its derivatives in xenografts of human colorectal adenocarcinomas in mice. *Cancer Res* 41:144–149, 1981.
43. Noboile MT, Vidili MG, Sobrero A, et al: 5-fluorouracil (5-FU) alone or combined with high-dose folinic acid (FA) in advanced colorectal cancer patients: A randomized trial (abstract). *Proc ASCO* 7:97, 1988.
44. O'Connell MJ: A Phase III trial of 5-fluorouracil and leucovorin in the treatment of advanced colorectal cancer: A Mayo Clinic/North Central Cancer Treatment Group Study. *Cancer* 63:1026–1030, 1989.
45. Petrelli N, Herrera L, Rustum Y, et al: A prospective randomized trial of 5-fluorouracil versus 5-fluorouracil and high dose leucovorin versus 5-fluorouracil and methotrexate in previously untreated patients with advanced colorectal carcinoma. *J Clin Oncol* 5:1559–1565, 1987.
46. Valone FH, Drakes T, Flam M, et al: Randomized trial of 5-FU vs. leucovorin (lv) plus 5-FU vs. sequential methotrexate (mtx), 5-FU, leucovorin in patients with advanced colorectal carcinoma: A Northern California Oncology Group Trial (abstract). *Proc ASCO* 7:95, 1988.
47. Byfield JE, Frankel SS, Hoenback CL, et al: Phase I and pharmacological study of 72 hour infused and hyperfractionated cyclical radiation. *Int J Radiat Oncol Biol Phys* 11:791–800, 1985.
48. Rotman M, Aziz H: Concomitant continuous infusion chemotherapy and radiation. *Cancer* 65:823–835, 1990.
49. Minsky BD, Cohen AM, Kemeny N, et al: Efficacy of preoperative 5-FU, high dose leucovorin, and sequential radiation therapy for unresectable rectal cancer. *Cancer* 1993 (in press).
50. Minsky BD, Cohen AM, Enker WE: Phase I trial of postoperative 5-FU, radiation therapy and high-dose leucovorin for resectable cancer. *Int J Radiat Oncol Biol Phys* 22:139–145, 1993.
51. Mendenhall WM, Bland KI, Rout WR, et al: Clinically resectable adenocarcinoma of the rectum treated with preoperative irradiation and surgery. *Dis Colon Rectum* 31:287–290, 1988.
52. Stevens KR Jr, Allen CV, Fletcher WS: Preoperative radiotherapy for adenocarcinoma of the rectosigmoid. *Cancer* 37:2866–2874, 1976.
53. Mohiuddin M, Marks G: High dose preoperative irradiation

for cancer of the rectum, 1976–1988. *Int J Radiat Oncol Biol Phys* 20:37–43, 1991.

54. Kligerman MM: Preoperative radiation therapy in rectal cancer. *Cancer* 36:691–695, 1975.
55. Kodner IJ, Shemesh EI, Fry RD, et al: Preoperative irradiation for rectal cancer: Improved local control and long-term survival. *Ann Surg* 209:194–199, 1989.
56. Mendenhall WM, Bland KI, Pfaff WW, et al: Initially unresectable rectal adenocarcinoma treated with preoperative irridiation and surgery. *Ann Surg* 205:41–44, 1986.
57. Minsky BD, Cohen AM, Enker WE, et al: Radiation therapy for unresectable rectal cancer. *Int J Radiat Oncol Biol Phys* 21:1283–1289, 1991.
58. Fortier GA, Constable W, Meyers H: Preoperative radiation therapy for rectal cancer. *Arch Surg* 121:1380, 1986.
59. Muto T, Masaki T, Suzuki K: DNA ploidy pattern of flat adenomas of the large bowel. *Dis Colon Rectum* 34:696–698, 1991.
60. Dosoretz DE, Gunderson LL, Hedberg S, et al: Preoperative irradiation for unresectable rectal and rectosigmoid carcinomas. *Cancer* 52:814–818, 1983.
61. Willett CG, Shellito PC, Tepper JE, et al: Intraoperative electron beam radiation therapy for primary locally advanced rectal and rectosigmoid carcinoma. *J Clin Oncol* 9:843–849, 1991.
62. Willett CG, Shellito PC, Tepper JE, et al: Intraoperative electron beam radiation therapy for recurrent locally advanced rectal or rectosigmoid carcinoma. *Cancer* 67:1504–1508, 1991.
63. Gunderson LL, Martin JK, Beart RW: Intraoperative and external beam irradiation for locally advanced colorectal cancer. *Ann Surg* 207:52–60, 1988.
64. Gastrointestinal Tumor Study Group: Radiation therapy and fluorouracil with or without semustine for the treatment of patients with surgical adjuvant adenocarcinoma of the rectum. *J Clin Oncol* 10:549–557, 1992.
65. Herbert SH, Curran WJ, Solin LJ, et al: Decreasing gastrointestinal morbidity with the use of small bowel contrast during treatment planning for pelvic radiation. *Int J Radiat Oncol Biol Phys* 20:835–842, 1991.
66. Devereux DF, Chandler JJ, Eisenstat T, et al: Efficacy of an absorbable mesh in keeping the small bowel out of the human pelvis following surgery. *Dis Colon Rectum* 31:17–21, 1988.
67. Petrelli N, Stablein D, Bruckner H, et al: A prospective randomized phase III trial of 5-fluorouracil (5FU) versus 5FU + high dose leucovorin (hdfa) versus 5FU + low dose leucovorin (ldcf) in patients (pts) with metastatic colorectal adenocarcinoma: A report of the Gastrointestinal Tumor Study Group (abstract). *Proc ASCO* 7:94, 1988.
68. O'Connell M, Martenson J, Rich T, et al: Protracted venous infusion (PVI) 5-fluorouracil (5FU) as a component of effective adjuvant therapy for high-risk rectal cancer. *Proc ASCO* 12:193, 1993.

PART 12

Treatment of Primary Locally Advanced Rectal Cancer

CHAPTER 71

Overview of the Management of Patients with Locally Advanced Rectal Cancer

Alfred M. Cohen

Despite efforts to encourage early detection among both patients and physicians, a subset of patients continues to present with locally advanced rectal cancer. Many of these patients will have concomitant hepatic or pulmonary metastases. However, presumably related to biological factors, there is a group of patients with bulky locally advanced rectal cancer, frequently node-negative, that can be cured with aggressive local/regional treatment strategies. It is among this subset of patients that maximizing local/regional (pelvic) control will likely have a considerable impact on the overall cure of the cancer.

A complete evaluation—including complete symptom history, pelvic examination (sometimes under anesthesia), and computed tomography of the chest, abdomen, and pelvis—is required to determine the extent of disease. Cystoscopy, magnetic resonance imaging, and intrarectal ultrasound may play a role in management as well.

Anteriorly based distal rectal cancers in women may invade or be adherent to the vagina. Extending abdominoperineal resection to include a hysterectomy and posterior vaginectomy or just posterior vaginectomy alone is common surgical practice for such patients. Transmural anteriorly based proximal rectal cancers in women may invade the cervix or posterior uterus. In such patients rectal resection incontinuity with a radical hysterectomy (posterior exenteration) provides improved margins. In women with a past history of hysterectomy and locally advanced rectal cancer, bladder invasion may occur. Total pelvic exenteration may be appropriate in selected patients.

Patients with tumors adherent or fixed to lateral or posterior pelvic structures (side wall, sacrum) have benefited from multidisciplinary therapy. The most effective strategy routinely utilized is preoperative radiation therapy. Additional approaches to supplement preoperative radiation therapy and resection include combined chemoradiation, hyperthermia, or the use of brachytherapy or other forms of intraoperative radiation therapy. All of these approaches will be discussed in the chapters that follow.

It is important to stress that a considerable subset of patients with locally advanced rectal cancer can be cured by radical surgery or combinations of surgery, radiation, and chemotherapy. The treating clinician should rule out distant disease and then pursue an aggressive treatment strategy.

CHAPTER 72

Radical Operative Approaches in the Treatment of Rectal Cancer

Michael P. Vezeridis
Harold J. Wanebo

HIGHLIGHTS

Despite the advances in early detection, a subset of patients will present with locally advanced rectal cancer. In the absence of distant disease, combined-modality therapy or ultraradical operative procedures offer a chance for cure and considerable palliation by avoiding the development of symptoms associated with uncontrolled growth of pelvic malignancy. Abdominoperineal resection with concomitant hysterectomy, formal posterior exenteration, total pelvic exenteration, and the composite abdominosacral exenteration all play a role in the management of such patients.

CONTROVERSIES

Patient selection for these highly morbid operative procedures remains the most difficult aspect of their management.

FUTURE DIRECTIONS

Improved methods of patient selection by molecular studies of the primary tumor, monoclonal antibody imaging, and improved radiologic imaging are important areas currently under investigation. Technical improvements to avoid urostomies are also a goal, since this has a far greater impact on the quality of life than the colostomy.

Despite the potential for early detection of rectal cancer and public education efforts, some patients still seek medical attention only when their disease is locally advanced and requires treatment by radical surgical procedures. While some locally advanced rectal cancers may be amenable to less radical resections, such as abdominoperineal resection combined with hysterectomy and posterior vaginectomy, others will require resections of great magnitude, such as total exenteration or abdominosacral resection. Although these extensive surgical procedures present a formidable challenge to the surgeon and entail significant short-term risks and long-term sequelae for the patient, they can result in long-term survival of a significant proportion of selected patients with locally advanced rectal cancer. In addition, the surgical removal of the rectal tumor has the potential to improve quality of life by preventing the development of unrelenting symptomatology of uncontrolled pelvic malignancy, particularly intractable pelvic pain and tenesmus. These radical procedures are, therefore, a valuable part of the surgical armamentarium, and physicians treating colorectal cancer should be familiar with their technical aspects as well as their indications and selection criteria.

INDICATIONS, PATIENT SELECTION, AND PREOPERATIVE ASSESSMENT

Radical resections are indicated for locally advanced rectal cancers invading pelvic viscera adjacent to the rectum but without extrapelvic spread or distant metastases. Indications for radical resection in the treatment of advanced rectal cancer are outlined in Table 72-1. Adherence or invasion of the posterior vagina is indication for an abdominoperineal resection with posterior vaginectomy, while adherence or invasion of the uterus and the posterior vagina will require a hysterectomy and posterior vaginectomy. Invasion at the cul-de-sac is indication for posterior exenteration. Invasion of the bladder, with or without involvement of the prostate and seminal vesicles, will necessitate a total pelvic exenteration. Invasion of the sacrum with or without involvement of other pelvic viscera is indication for abdominosacral resection. Nodal involvement should not be considered a contraindication to a radical resection if the nodes can be included in the resection field. Occasionally, radical resections may be performed purely for palliation, but as a rule the intent of such procedures should be curative. Obviously, an abdominoperineal resection and posterior vaginectomy with or without hysterectomy is a procedure of substantially lesser magnitude with less pronounced functional consequences than a total pelvic exenteration or an abdominosacral resection; therefore, it can be used more liberally for palliation.

The main goals of the preoperative workup are to rule out metastatic dissemination, determine resectability of the tumor, and assess the general medical status of the patient. The preoperative metastatic workup should be based on the patterns of dissemination of rectal carcinoma. Computed tomographic (CT) scanning of the abdomen and pelvis will demonstrate the local extent of the primary tumor and may also reveal enlarged periaortic nodes and liver metastases. In the presence of suspicious findings, laparoscopy can provide direct visualization and access to biopsy and histologic confirmation. A plain chest x-ray is usually sufficient, but a normal chest CT may be more reassuring. Magnetic resonance imaging (MRI) may provide supplemental data, particularly in regard to the sacrum. Since metastases to the bones and the brain from rectal cancer are very infrequent, it is not necessary to obtain bone scan and head CT routinely. These tests are indicated only in cases with symptoms or physical findings suggestive of bone or brain metastases. Despite the fact that metastases to peripheral lymph nodes are also very uncommon, they should be evaluated during physical examination and suspicious nodes biopsied, particularly inguinal nodes. Although the final determination of resectability can be made only intraoperatively, the preoperative assessment of the extent of the rectal tumor is of great importance in designing the proper operative procedure and preparing both the surgeon and the patient. Low rectal lesions are easily accessible to digital examination, which can provide valuable information regarding fixation of the tumor to the pelvic side walls. Digital rectal examination, however, has significant limitations in the assessment of involvement of contiguous structures. Similarly, it is extremely difficult to distinguish between sacral fixation due to inflammatory reaction and that caused by true tumor infiltration. A CT scan of the pelvis can be a very helpful diagnostic test in these situations. It can demonstrate tumor invasion into adjacent structures such as bladder, prostate, seminal vesicles, sacrum, and levator muscles. Cystoscopy is useful in evaluating the extent of involvement of the urinary bladder. Limited involvement of the dome of the bladder may allow the performance of partial cystectomy, thus preserving bladder function.

Table 72-1
Radical Resections for Advanced Rectal Cancer: Indications for Operative Procedures

Extent of disease	*Procedure*
Adherence to or invasion of the posterior vagina	Abdominoperineal resection with posterior vaginectomy ± vaginal reconstruction
Adherence to or invasion of the uterus and the posterior vagina	Abdominoperineal resection with hysterectomy and posterior vaginectomy ± vaginal reconstruction
Invasion of the anterior vagina	Posterior exenteration
Invasion of the cul-de-sac	
Invasion of the bladder in women with previous hysterectomy	Total exenteration
Invasion of the bladder, prostate, and seminal vesicles in men	
Invasion of the sacrum and any of the above	Abdominosacral resection

The assessment of the patient's general medical status prior to undertaking radical resections is of paramount importance, since operations of this magnitude constitute a major insult that may cause significant disturbances to the patient's homeostasis and impose a heavy burden on the reserves of the various organ systems. Subsequently, all major organ systems should be carefully assessed preoperatively. Cardiac, respiratory, and renal function should be studied and optimized. Chronic metabolic disorders such as diabetes mellitus, if present, should be properly evaluated and controlled. Assessment of the patient's nutritional status is of great importance. Nutritional deficits may affect healing and predispose the patient to infectious complications. These deficiencies should be corrected preoperatively with enteral or parenteral nutrition. Coagulation status should be evaluated and any abnormalities should be corrected. Hematologic parameters should also be studied and optimized. Evaluation of the colon with barium enema or colonoscopy is important to search for synchronous lesions, which may alter the extent of the resection.

Assessment of the patient's mental status is of no lesser importance than that of the physiologic condition. Radical operations for rectal cancer cause major functional alterations which may have profound psychological effects on the patient, calling for an ability to adjust and the motivation for self-care and rehabilitation. Therefore, severe psychological or mental impairment may be a contraindication to such operations. In patients with adequate mental capacity, preoperative teaching and psychosocial preparation are of paramount importance.

SURGICAL PROCEDURES

Abdominoperineal Resection with Hysterectomy and Posterior Vaginectomy

The abdomen is entered through a long midline incision and a meticulous abdominal exploration is performed to exclude extrapelvic lesions. The lower abdomen and pelvis are exposed, the sigmoid colon is mobilized by incising the lateral parietal peritoneum along the white line of Toldt, and the ureter and the gonadal vessels are separated from the mesocolon. The site of transection of the sigmoid colon is selected for the formation of a permanent colostomy. The peritoneum on the medial and lateral aspects of the mesosigmoid is incised from the level of the inferior mesenteric artery (IMA), and this incision parallels the ureters to the inferior pelvic reflection overlying urogenital structures.

The pelvic peritoneum is incised between the rectum and the bladder from ureter to ureter in the male. In the female, the peritoneum is incised anterior to the uterus if it is to be included. The ureters are identified early and encircled with a vascular loop to facilitate mobilization during the dissection. It is also helpful to have stents placed if a difficult dissection is anticipated. The mesosigmoid is serially clamped, divided and ligated down to the level of the IMA or first branched vessel (left colic or sigmoid). At this point, the sigmoid is transected using the linear gastrointestinal stapler. The rectosigmoid is grasped and pulled forcefully cephalad and anteriorly and the retrorectal plane is dissected sharply down to the distal rectum, producing a clear separation of perirectal tissue and mesentery from Waldeyer's fascia.

After posterior dissection to the level of the tip of the coccyx is completed, the lateral attachments of the proximal rectum are dissected sharply to the peritoneal reflexion. The ureters are protected by sweeping them laterally. The fibro-fatty lateral attachments of the rectum are divided by sharp dissection close to the pelvic side walls. Many branches of the pelvic autonomic nerves are intertwined with the lymph node–bearing tissue that the surgeon is trying to excise in this area. These can be dissected free and protected in some but not all patients. The lateral stalks of the rectum are divided with the electrocautery, and vessels which are visualized are clamped and ligated. After wide lateral mobilization is accomplished, the anterior plane is entered at the level of the previously incised peritoneal reflection and dissection is carried down to the level of the seminal vesicles in men and the uterine cervix in women. If the tumor is adherent to the bladder wall anteriorly, dissection between the bladder and rectum should be avoided even in cases where dissection appears to be technically easy. Although adherence between the rectum and the adjacent structures may be caused by desmoplastic reaction surrounding the tumor, it should be attributed to tumor invasion unless proven otherwise if the catastrophic consequences of dissecting through tumor are to be avoided. Dissection through tumor is almost synonymous with local recurrence, with all its detrimental effects on the patient's quality of life. In such cases, an early transverse cystotomy with adequate visualization of the ureteral orifices and the trigone should be performed. Partial resection of the bladder may then be performed, followed by two-layer closure of the bladder. In males, Devonvilliers' fascia should be included in the resected specimen by resecting close to the prostate capsule and then reentering the plane adjacent to the wall of the rectum, below the growth.

After dissection is complete to the level of the levator ani muscles, the perineal part of the operation is started with the performance of an elliptical incision around the anus. In the female, the perianal incision may have to include the posterior vaginal wall if there is tumor extension to the vagina and/or uterus. The tip of the coccyx is identified, the anococcygeal raphe is divided with the electrocautery, and the presacral space is entered. The levator ani muscles are divided with the electrocautery. Dissection is then performed anteriorly with special care being taken to avoid injury to the urethra in males or entry into the rectum. Identification of the proper plane of dissection by palpating the Foley catheter helps in avoiding injury to the urethra. The rectum is separated from the prostate by a combination of sharp and blunt dissection to the level of the seminal vesicles, completing the dissection anteriorly. If the prostate appears to be involved by tumor, it must be resected in continuity with the rectum, which usually mandates removal of the bladder (total exenteration). In females, dissection between the rectum and vagina is usually carried out easily. However, in cases with limited tumor involvement of the posterior vaginal wall, a posterior vaginectomy with or without hysterectomy (Figs. 72-1 and 72-2) may be performed and the vaginal wall and introitus recon-

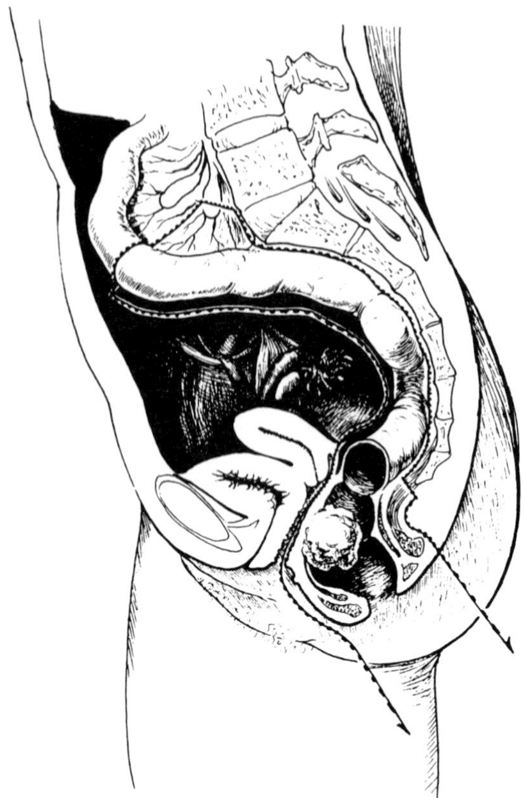

FIG. 72-1. Outline of abdominoperineal resection with posterior vaginectomy for advanced rectal cancer.

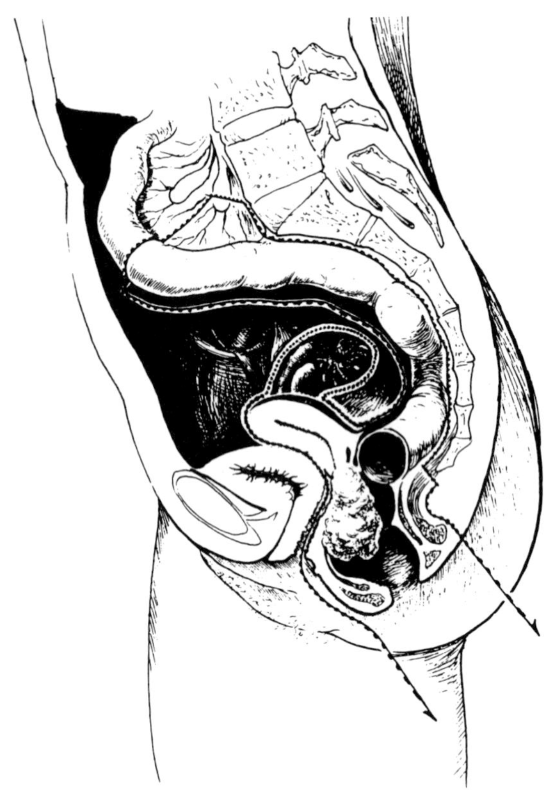

FIG. 72-2. Outline of abdominoperineal resection with hysterectomy and posterior vaginectomy for advanced rectal cancer.

structed. The anterior part of the perianal phase involves an extension of the perianal incision to include the midportion of the introitus and vagina, so that a hemicircle of vagina is included in the resection. In case of tumor extension into the uterus and posterior vagina, a hysterectomy and posterior vaginectomy are commonly performed. The hysterectomy is accomplished in the standard way, with transection of the infundibulopelvic ligament and bisection of the uterine artery and vein overlapping the ureters. The anterior vaginal wall is incised to enter the vagina away from the tumor and the midvaginal wall is incised bilaterally (this incision communicates with the perianal dissection). The posterior vagina can be reconstructed by mobilizing myocutaneous gracilis or rectus abdominis flaps and approximating the skin side to the remaining vaginal wall. After the perineal resection is completed, the specimen is delivered through the perineal incision. The pelvis is copiously irrigated with warm normal saline solution, and two closed suction drains are placed in the pelvis. The subcutaneous tissues are closed with interrupted absorbable sutures and the skin edges approximated with staples (levator ani muscles cannot be approximated in most cases).

If adjuvant radiotherapy has not been used preoperatively, an absorbable polyglycolic acid mesh is placed across the pelvic inlet to suspend the small bowel out of the pelvis (or the pelvic floor is reconstructed by mobilizing the peritoneum and cecum). A colostomy is fashioned in the left lower quadrant, essentially at McBurney's point, and the abdomen is closed.

POSTERIOR EXENTERATION (TOTAL HYSTERECTOMY AND VAGINECTOMY)

Entering of the abdomen and exploration are performed as previously described. After proper exposure of the lower abdomen and pelvis, the parietal peritoneum is incised laterally to the iliac artery below the infundibulopelvic ligament; the retroperitoneal space is entered; and careful blunt dissection is carried down to the level of the ureters, which are identified and protected from injury (may be encircled with vascular loop). The infundibulopelvic ligaments are clamped, divided, and suture-ligated. The peritoneal incision is extended along the external iliac arteries to the round ligaments, which are divided at their point of exit from the pelvic wall. The incision on the peritoneum is then extended upward laterally along the white line of Toldt and medially to the root of the mesocolon at the level of the sacral promontory. The sigmoid colon is mobilized laterally by separating the ureter from the mesocolon. The site of transection of the sigmoid colon is

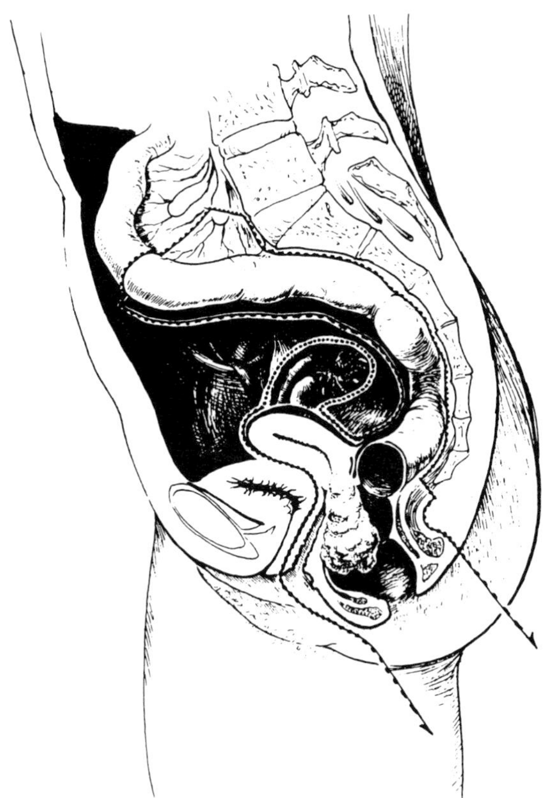

FIG. 72-3. Outline of posterior pelvic exenteration for advanced rectal cancer.

selected, ensuring the adequacy of length and blood supply of the left colon to be used for the creation of the permanent colostomy. The peritoneum of the medial aspect of the mesosigmoid is incised directly over and parallel to the aorta at the level of the inferior mesenteric artery. The mesosigmoid is serially clamped, divided, and ligated down to the level of the sacral promontory and the sigmoid is transected using the linear gastrointestinal stapler. The rectosigmoid is grasped and pulled cephalad anteriorly, the retrorectal space is entered sharply at the sacral promontory, and the retrorectal tissues are dissected to the coccyx, as previously described for abdominoperineal resection. The lateral attachments of the rectum are divided at the pelvic side walls. The uterosacral ligaments and cardinal ligaments are clamped, divided, and ligated. The lateral stalks of the rectum are divided with the electrocautery, and vessels which are visualized are clamped and ligated. Although autonomic nerves to the bladder can be identified and protected in selected patients with early cancer, this is not indicated in patients with advanced rectal cancer. Dissection is thus completed to the level of the levator ani muscles bilaterally.

The uterine artery is clamped, divided, and suture-ligated with 0-silk ligatures bilaterally. Sharp dissection is carried out anteriorly below the uterine cervix along the anterior vaginal wall down to the pelvic floor. The same considerations and concerns regarding invasion of the bladder by large tumors, which were discussed earlier, apply also in cases where posterior exenteration is contemplated.

The perineal part of the procedure is completed as described above. An outline of this procedure is shown in Fig. 72-3.

TOTAL PELVIC EXENTERATION (AND PELVIC NODE DISSECTION)

Preparatory steps are the same as those described for abdominoperineal resection. After a thorough abdominal exploration excludes extrapelvic disease, the posterior peritoneum is incised over the distal aorta and the common iliac vessels bilaterally. The round ligaments are divided and ligated at the pelvic wall and the ureters identified and teased away, safely avoiding injury to them. Pelvic node dissection begins at the level of the aortic bifurcation and continues downward along the iliac arteries and veins. The adipose tissue overlying these vessels is dissected sharply and reflected medially, and the external and internal iliac vessels are skeletonized bilaterally. After identification of the obturator nerve bilaterally, dissection is carried along the nerve into the obturator space. The obturator vessels are divided and ligated, but the nerve is protected. Adipose tissue and nodes are swept away from the nerve medially. The hypogastric artery and vein are clamped, divided, and ligated distal to the bifurcation of the common iliac vessels. The ureters are divided in the pelvis, their distal ends are tied, and #8 feeding tubes are placed in the proximal ends and attached to drainage tubes off the side of the table.

The sigmoid colon is mobilized by incising the lateral parietal peritoneum and separating the ureter from the mesocolon. The incision in the lateral parietal peritoneum is extended down into the pelvis. The site of transection at the sigmoid colon is selected and the peritoneum of the medial aspect of the mesosigmoid is incised from the chosen point of transection to the root of the mesocolon to meet the previously performed peritoneal incision below the terminal ileum and cecum. The sigmoid is transected using the linear gastrointestinal stapler, and the mesosigmoid is serially clamped, divided, and ligated down to the level of the sacral promontory. The retrorectal space is entered and sharp dissection is carried down to the tip of the coccyx, using the same technique described for abdominoperineal resection. The lateral stalks of the rectum are divided with the electrocautery and visualized vessels are clamped and ligated.

The bladder is separated from the pubic symphysis and the pubic rami. The space of Retzius is entered and the bladder is freed by sharply dividing the anterior and lateral peritoneal attachments. Attention to hemostasis is essential in this vascular area. At this point, the urethra is divided at the level of the pelvic floor and the endopelvic fascia is divided bilaterally on the pelvic sidewall. The lateral attachments of the bladder to the pelvic wall contain a plexus of hypogastric vessels and lymph node-bearing tissue, which is included in the specimen. The anterior dissection finishes at the levator ani muscles.

At this point, with the specimen fully mobilized anteriorly, laterally, and posteriorly, the only remaining attachments are the vagina and the rectum. Now the perineal part of the procedure begins. An elliptical incision is made from the tip of the coccyx to a point anterior to the urethral orifice in women and to the bulb of the penis in men. The distance of the skin incision lateral to the anal margin is determined by the proximity of the tumor to the anal canal. For very low lying lesions, a wide excision of perineal skin is needed, removing ischiorectal fat and transecting the levator ani muscles at the pelvic wall. The subcutaneous tissue is divided with electrocoagulation, the tip of the coccyx is identified, the anococcygeal rhaphe is divided, and the presacral space is entered. The levator ani muscles are divided by electrocautery to the ischial tuberosity. The dissection is completed anteriorly at the pubic symphysis and the specimen is removed en bloc through the abdominal incision. After satisfactory hemostasis is ascertained, closed suction drains are placed in the pelvis and brought out anteriorly, and the perineal incision is closed. An ileal conduit is then fashioned for urinary diversion, using terminal ileum approximately 10 cm from the ileocecal valve. Irradiated ileum must be avoided. If the terminal ileum is irradiated, a more proximal segment of ileum or transverse colon should be used.

The proximal end of the ileal sites for the ureteral anastomosis are selected to allow anastomosis without tension. The anastomosis may be performed over the ureteral catheters, already in place, or a number 8 pediatric feeding tube may be inserted into the ileal segment (outside in) and exited through two small stab wounds and passed retrograde up the ureters to the kidney. Mucosa-to-muscosa sutures are placed with 5-0 polyglycolic monofilament thread (usually six sutures are needed). A second row of 5-0 serosal silk sutures are placed to bolster the anastomosis. The ureteral catheters are brought out through the stoma and sutured to the skin so as to permit the stoma appliance to be placed. The closed end of the ileal loop is sutured to the periosteum of the sacral promontory to prevent twisting of the mesentery.

The distal end of the ileal loop and the divided end of the sigmoid are exteriorized through openings at preselected areas of the abdominal wall (Fig. 72-4). An omental J flap can often be moved down into the pelvis

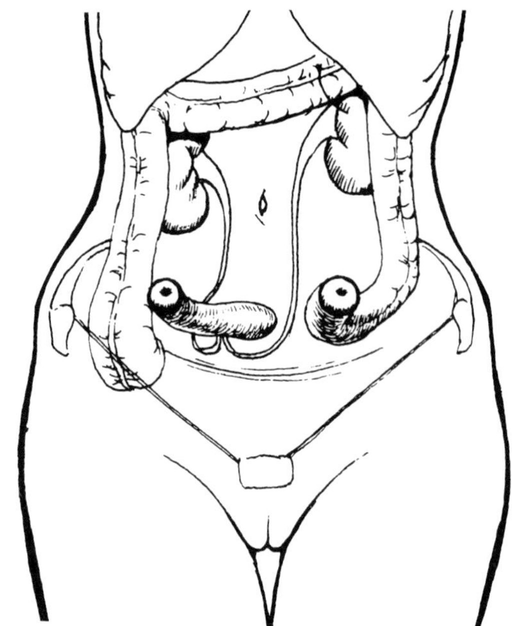

FIG. 72-4. Ileal loop and end sigmoid colostomy after total pelvic exenteration.

and sutured to the pelvic side walls to help keep the small bowel out of the true pelvis and provide additional blood supply to previously irradiated pelvic tissue. After closure of the abdominal incision, the stomas are matured with 4-0 Vicryl sutures. The ureteral stents are transfixed to the skin surrounding the stoma of the ileal loop, left in place for 5 to 7 days, and removed only after anastomotic integrity is confirmed by a retrograde contrast study.

ABDOMINOSACRAL RESECTION

Pelvic devascularization is accomplished by dividing and suture-ligating the internal iliac arteries and veins bilaterally (Fig. 72-5).[1] It is preferable, if possible, to ligate the internal iliac artery beyond the origin of the superior gluteal branch to preserve adequate vascularization of the skin and muscle flaps used for closure. The peritoneal floor is reformed with the use of a Vicryl mesh, an omental pedicle, or a local peritoneal flap, and the abdominal incision is closed. For the sacral stage of the procedure, the patient is placed in the prone position. A posterior sacral incision extending from the spinous process of L5 to the perineum is performed. The lower part of the incision is designed in elliptical fashion to include the anus. Full-thickness flaps are raised at the level of the sacral periosteum to the lateral extent of the sacrum. The gluteus maximus and medius muscles are dissected from their sacral origins, maintaining a fascial cuff on the muscles for the subsequent midline wound closure. The sciatic nerve is located by retracting the gluteus maximus and

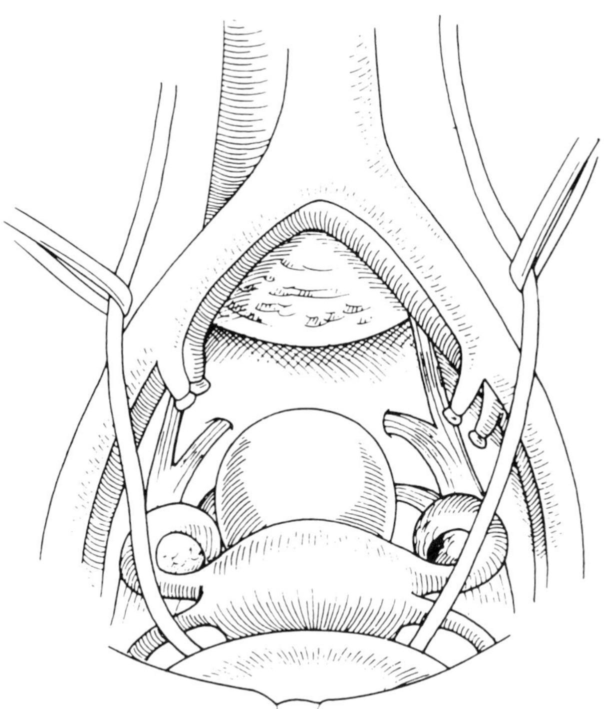

FIG. 72-5. Abdominosacral resection. Pelvic devascularization has been accomplished by dividing and suture ligating the internal iliac artery and vein bilaterally. (From JJ Bauer (ed): *Colorectal Surgery Illustrated.* St Louis, Mosby-Yearbook, 1993, p 243. Reproduced by permission.)

the underlying pyriformis muscles superiorly and at the lateral aspect of the midsacrum. The nerve lies superficially to the obturator internus and gemelli muscles as it courses inferolaterally midway between the ischial tuberosity and the greater trochanter. The sciatic nerve is encircled with a vessel loop for ease of identification during the dissection. The sacrotuberous and sacrospinous ligaments are incised at the level of their attachments to the ischial tuberosity and the ischial spine. A finger is inserted medially to the sciatic nerve and advanced deeply, beneath the pyriformis muscles and through the underlying endopelvic fascia (Fig. 72-6).[1] Using this maneuver, the surgeon "breaks through" the endopelvic fascia to reach the anterior surface of the sacrum and into the area of pelvic dissection performed during the abdominal part of the procedure. This approach will direct the subsequent sacral osteotomy and ensure adequate margin proximal to the tumor. Further dissection is carried out around the sacrum by incising the pyriformis muscles and the soft tissues surrounding the sciatic nerve.

A laminectomy is performed proximal to the planned level of sacral transection, usually between L5 and S1, to ligate the terminal end of the dural sac. The proximal sacral roots are identified and an effort is made to preserve the roots by dissecting them free from the portion of the sacrum to be resected. After determining the resection line on both sides of the sacrum, an osteotome or oscillating saw is used to transect the sacrum. The surgeon's finger is positioned anteriorly to protect the intraabdominal contents. For higher resections, above the level of S3, the line of resection is continued through the sacroiliac joints laterally. Care is taken not to injure the lumbar component of the sciatic nerve. The sacral components of the nerve are dissected as needed. The sacrum, pelvic side walls, and tumor-bearing rectum are removed en bloc. If other pelvic structures—such as uterus, vagina, or bladder—are attached to the tumor, these are also removed in continuity with the rest of the specimen.

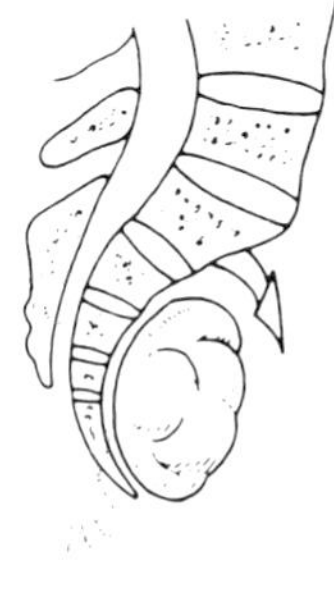

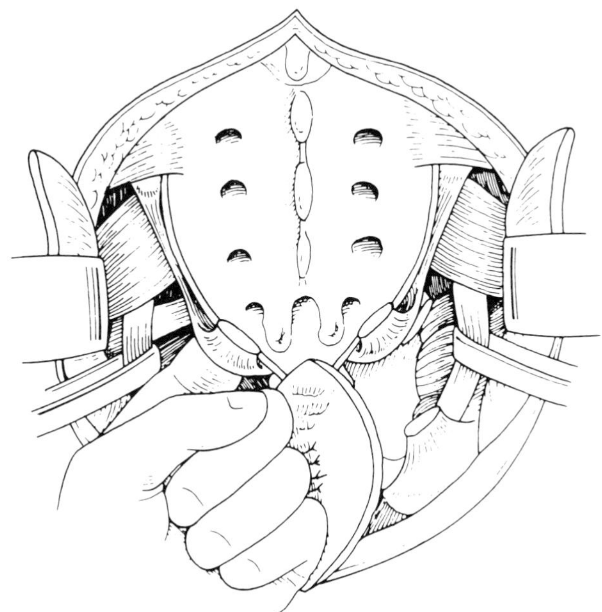

FIG. 72-6. Abdominosacral resection. The surgeon's finger is inserted medially to the sciatic nerve and advanced deeply, beneath the pyriformis muscles and through the underlying endopelvic fascia, to reach the anterior surface of the sacrum into the area of the pelvic dissection performed during the abdominal part of the procedure. (From JJ Bauer (ed): *Colorectal Surgery Illustrated.* St Louis, Mosby-Yearbook, 1993, p 245. Reproduced by permission.)

Closure of the sacral wound follows. If the fascial origin of the gluteus maximus has been preserved and the gluteus maximus is adequately mobile, the muscles are approximated in the midline with a heavy nonabsorbable monofilament suture, thus forming a new pelvic floor. A relaxing incision at the level of the lateral fixation of the gluteus maximus on the greater trochanter may be necessary to allow greater medial advancement of the muscle. The subcutaneous tissue is approximated with interrupted absorbable sutures and the skin with staples.

MORTALITY, MORBIDITY, END RESULTS

The potential complications of radical operative procedures for rectal carcinoma cover the entire spectrum of complications encountered during major abdominal operations. In addition, complications unique to the urinary diversion and the stomas may and do occur. Obviously, postoperative morbidity is more significant following more extensive resections, such as total pelvic exenteration and abdominosacral resection. The prolonged anesthesia and operative time and the associated major blood loss, requiring massive replacement with crystalloids and blood products, may present a formidable challenge to the patient. Therefore, close intraoperative and postoperative hemodynamic monitoring are of paramount importance. Severe postoperative hemorrhage leading to death has been reported.[2–5] Mortality from uncontrolled bleeding should be preventable in most cases by proper handling of the pelvic vasculature during the operation and achievement of satisfactory hemostasis before the end of the procedure. When satisfactory hemostasis cannot be accomplished, as in the case of dilutional coagulopathy, a safe and effective approach is to pack the pelvis and, 48 h later, after the coagulation has been normalized, return the patient to the operating room for removal of the pack.

Cardiopulmonary complications are likely to occur after procedures of this magnitude and have been reported.[2–4,6,7] Massive fluid shifts, rapid administration of large volumes of crystalloids intraoperatively, and significant continuing losses in the immediate postoperative period make these patients particularly vulnerable to cardiac complications. Essential to the prevention of such complications is close hemodynamic monitoring with proper replacement of fluids and correction of electrolyte imbalances. The presence of adequate urine output is a good index of adequate hydration and renal function as well as evidence of integrity and patency of the ureteral anastomosis.

Wound infections have been reported in the literature[4,6–8] and represented a significant cause of morbidity in earlier series.[3] In abdominosacral resections, wound infection and flap separation are markedly more frequent after resections for recurrent disease occurring exclusively in patients who had been heavily irradiated.[8]

Intestinal obstruction is a rather frequent early postoperative complication[3,4,6–8] which may lead to significant morbidity if it is not diagnosed in time and properly treated.[5] The main factors predisposing to this serious complication are the empty, deperitonealized pelvis and the presence and position of the urinary diversion conduit.[3,9–11] The former factor also predisposes to the formation of enteroperineal fistula.[11–14] Delaying the surgical management of early postoperative intestinal obstruction entails the risk of entering the pelvis after the formation of adhesions, substantially increasing the surgical morbidity and mortality.[5] Sound clinical judgment dictates that if the bowel cannot be safely dissected free from the pelvis, the obstruction should be relieved by an intestinal bypass procedure.[3,12,14,15] The incidence of this complication is significantly higher in patients who have had preoperative radiation treatment, particularly in those who did not undergo pelvic reconstruction with omental or myocutaneous flaps or colonic advancement.[9,11] It is therefore advisable to perform a pelvic reconstruction using these techniques in patients who have been irradiated prior to surgery. Obliteration of the pelvic defect with omentum or muscles should also be considered in patients who did not have preoperative radiation but are likely candidates for postoperative radiation, in order to prevent descent of the small intestine into the lower part of the pelvis, which may result in exposure to radiation and its associated complications.[16] Gracilis, rectus abdominis, tensor fascia lata, and inferior gluteal flaps have been used successfully for filling pelvic defects.[17–19]

Dehiscence of intestinal and ureteral anastomoses has been reported[3,6,7] and appears to be more frequent following preoperative radiation. It can be minimized by using nonirradiated ileum or, if necessary, colon for the formation of the ileal conduit.[3] Other reported complications include fecal and urinary fistulas, urinary tract infections, hydronephrosis, retraction or separation of the stomas, thrombophlebitis, pulmonary embolism, evisceration, psychosis, cerebrovascular accident, prolonged ileus, atelectasis, and pneumonia.[3,4,6–9,11,20]

Late complications occur quite frequently, making evident the importance of continued surgical follow-up of these patients. Late intestinal obstruction and enteroperineal fistula formation have been reported, and their surgical management entails a significant surgical risk.[3] The surgical management is the same as that described for the early postoperative complications. Again, if the risk associated with dissection of the small intestine from the pelvis is high, an intestinal bypass procedure should be performed. Although it is very unlikely that an enteroperineal fistula will close after a bypass procedure, leaving a draining fistula in the perineum may be the proper choice if the risk of dissecting the small intestine from the pelvis is prohibitive.[3] Extensive resections of the small bowel should be avoided, as they may lead to short-bowel syndrome, which will compromise the patient's quality of life.

Pyelonephritis occurs as a late complication and is usually easily controlled with the proper antibiotics if there is no mechanical obstruction at the ureteral anastomosis causing stasis. However, if obstruction is present, it should be corrected surgically. Extensive dissection of the ureters in the irradiated patient incurs risk of ischemic damage to the ureter, with hazard of ureteral fibrosis and/or fistula. An acute episode of ureteral obstruction in such a patient may be managed by percutaneous nephrostomies to permit controlled urinary decompression. This will allow time to assess the problem and plan reconstruction at an elective future date. Other late complications include perineal, paracolostomy, and incisional hernia[3,4] which are usually amenable to surgical repair with conventional techniques, the use of synthetic mesh, or the use of myocutaneous flaps.[3,21–23]

The morbidity rates in the literature range from 26 to 80 percent after pelvic exenteration[2,5,9,11,20,24,25] and from 25 to 50 percent after multivisceral resection for colorectal carcinoma,[6,7,26–33] with mortality rates ranging from 5 to 33 percent for the former and from 1.7 to 13 percent for the latter. It is noticeable that the operative mortality rates have declined in patients who underwent radical procedures in more recent years.[2,9,34,35] This decline in operative mortality can be attributed to better patient selection, refinement of surgical techniques, and improvements in perioperative care.[2,9,25,34–36] In the literature, 5-year survival rates following pelvic exenteration range from 20 to 67 percent, with an average of 37 percent. Mortality, morbidity, and 5-year survival data from the literature are summarized in Tables 72-2 and 72-3. Long-term survival is influenced by the presence of unidentified tumor dissemination, pericolorectal invasion, and regional lymph node involvement.[3] Obviously, tumors with favorable biological behavior and associated with a higher probability of long-term survival are those that tend to grow locally but metastasize late in their course.

Abdominosacral resection is a procedure associated with significant blood loss and morbidity. In the most recent series reported by Wanebo et al.,[8] the mean operative time was 18.5 hours, with a mean blood loss of 10,000 mL. The total long-term hospital mortality rate was 7.8 percent (6 of 76 patients). Mortality and morbidity in these series are summarized in Table 72-4.

Survival differed according to the origin and histology of the tumor. Of 18 patients with primary tumors of the posterior pelvis, 9 were alive without evidence of disease from 14 to 136 months after surgery, with an estimated 5-year survival of 52 percent. Of the 47 patients resected for pelvic recurrence of rectal cancer, 41 were resected with curative intent and 6 for palliation. In the patients resected for palliation, the survival ranged from 2 to 12 months, while of the patients resected for cure, 5 patients survived from 67 to 168 months. The overall median survival was 36 months; the median disease free survival was 24 months; and the estimated 5-year survival was 24 percent.

The functional results after resection depend on the extent and level of sacral resection. In patients with sacral resections at or distal to the level of S3, anorectal function was normal. Bilateral resections above the

Table 72-2
Mortality, Morbidity, and Survival of Patients with Pelvic Exenteration for Colorectal Cancer

Authors	*No. of patients*	*Operative morbidity, %*	*Operative mortality, %*	*5-year survival, %*
Appleby,[37] 1950	6	—	17	67
Brintnall and Flock,[38] 1950	9	—	33	—
Brunschwig,[39] 1954	21	—	5	23
Kiselow et al.,[5] 1967	43	44	16	30
Symmonds et al.,[34] 1975	12	—	8	33
Deckers et al.,[24] 1976	5	80	20	20
Rutledge et al.,[35] 1977	15	—	10	41
Eckhauser et al.,[25] 1979	12	75	8	37
Ledesma et al.,[20] 1981	30	26	10	43
Boey et al.,[2] 1982	49	51	27	38
Takagi et al.,[36] 1985	13	—	8	38
Jakowatz et al.,[11] 1985	28	77	8	27
Lopez et al.,[9] 1987	24	26	20	41
Totals	267	54	15	37

Table 72-3
Mortality and Morbidity Rates after Multivisceral Resections for Colorectal Carcinoma

Authors	*No. of patients*	*Mortality, %*	*Morbidity, %*
Kelley et al.,[26] 1981	66	9	—
Bonfanti et al.,[29] 1982	61	8	30
McGlone et al.,[30] 1982	24	8	25
Pittam et al.,[31] 1984	44	13	—
Eldar et al.,[6] 1985	84	5	28
Gall et al.,[27] 1986	121	12	—
Hunter et al.,[28] 1987	28	1.7	—
Heslov and Frost,[32] 1988	58	5	—
Fedorov et al.,[33] 1989	242	5.4	50
Eisenberg et al.,[7] 1990	58	1.7	31

SOURCE: Expanded and modified from Eisenberg et al.[7] By permission.

S3 level compromised the anorectal and urogenital functions. Generally, for anatomic reasons, female patients had problems of urinary retention less frequently. Patients with resections at the S1, S2 level could manage urologic function by practicing Crede at defined intervals. Male patients with high sacral resections, through the S1 level, additionally required periodic catheterizations. In some cases, incontinence was improved by taking ephedrine.

Persistent postoperative pain, typically new phantomlike pain or causalgia and local symptoms related to delayed wound healing, were observed in 12 of 34

Table 72-4
Mortality and Complications after Resection of Tumors of the Musculoskeletal Pelvis

Perioperative mortality	*Rectal adenocarcinoma (n = 47)* *4 (8.5%)*	*Epidermoid carcinoma (n = 11)* *1*	*Primary tumors (n = 18)* *1*
Complications			
Cardiovascular			
Myocardial ischemia, arrhythmia	2	1	0
Pneumonia	2	0	0
Pulmonary insufficiency (prolonged intubation/ ARDS)	8	2	0
Intraoperative coagulopathy	1	0	2
Postoperative hemorrhage	6	0	3
Fistula			
Small bowel/large bowel	5	3	1
Bladder/ureteral	3	0	2
Infection			
Sepsis	14	1	0
Urinary tract	5	0	0
Wound complications			
Wound infection	7	5	1
Posterior wound infection/ flap separation	15	1	1
Bowel/urinary			
Small bowel obstruction	4	0	0
Renal failure	5	0	1
Hydronephrosis, ureteral stricture	0	1	0
Urinary incontinence	0	0	3
Urinary retention	0	0	1
Vascular/nerve			
Perineal nerve palsy	3	1	0
Deep venous thrombosis	2	2	2
Myonecrosis	0	0	1

SOURCE: Wanebo et al.[8] Reproduced by permission.

patients (35 percent). Although long-term neurologic sequelae were unusual, many patients did incur short-term lower-extremity weakness. Patients reported unsteadiness, diminished lower-leg strength, and sensory deficits in the foot. Overall, serious locomotor dysfunction was evident only in patients having resections involving the S1 and S2 roots bilaterally. The rehabilitation outcome was good. Overall, 66 percent of the patients returned to their previous lifestyle and 43 percent returned to work. The duration of impaired function was, in general, about 3 months. All patients were referred for rehabilitation, and they generally required aggressive outpatient therapy.

Although radical pelvic resections and particularly total pelvic exenteration and abdominosacral resection are associated with substantial postoperative morbidity, the hospital mortality rate in properly selected patients treated in experienced centers should not exceed 10 percent, with an anticipated 5-year survival of 40 percent or higher.[3,4,9] The radical operative approaches described in this chapter can provide meaningful long-term survival in a small subset of patients having advanced colorectal cancer with favorable biologic features.

Although, as a general rule, these procedures should be undertaken with curative intent, using them on specific occasions for palliation may improve the patient's quality of life significantly by providing relief from the unrelenting symptoms of advanced pelvic tumors.[9,24] Sound clinical judgment should be exercised in the selection of patients for palliative pelvic exenteration, because the probability of disastrous consequences is significant if the selection is not proper. Incomplete resection or transection through tumor invariably leads to rapid recurrence, which results in severe compromise in the quality of life because of refractory symptomatology.

The need for careful follow-up of these patients should be emphasized. In addition to the fact that a significant percentage of these patients will develop recurrence or metastases, late complications related to the operation may occur and psychological or marital problems may arise. The role of the surgeon in the coordination of follow-up and management of these problems cannot be overestimated. Despite the profound anatomic and functional changes associated with radical pelvic surgery, these patients can, with proper support and rehabilitation, adjust and live meaningful and productive lives.

REFERENCES

1. Wanebo HJ, Turk PS: Abdominal sacral resection for recurrent rectal cancer, in Bauer JJ (ed): *Colorectal Surgery Illustrated*. St Louis, Mosby-Yearbook, 1993, pp 241–250.
2. Boey J, Wong J, Ong GB: Pelvic exenteration for locally advanced colorectal carcinoma. *Ann Surg* 195:513–518, 1982.
3. Bricker EM, Kraybill WG, Lopez MJ, et al: The current role of ultraradical surgery in the treatment of pelvic cancer. *Curr Probl Surg* 23:871–953, 1986.
4. Kraybill WG, Lopez MJ, Bricker EM: Total pelvic exenteration as a therapeutic option in advanced malignant disease of the pelvis. *Surg Gynecol Obstet* 166:259–263, 1988.
5. Kiselow M, Butcher HR Jr, Brocher EM: Results of the radical surgical treatment of advanced pelvic cancer. *Am Surg* 166:428–434, 1967.
6. Eldar S, Kemeny MM, Terz JJ: Extended resections for carcinoma of the colon and rectum. *Surg Gynecol Obstet* 161:319–322, 1985.
7. Eisenberg SB, Kraybill WG, Lopez MJ: Long-term results of surgical resection of locally advanced colorectal carcinoma. *Surgery* 108:779–786, 1990.
8. Wanebo JH, Koness RJ, Turk PS, et al: Composite resection of posterior pelvic malignancy. *Ann Surg* 215:685–695, 1993.
9. Lopez MJ, Kraybill WG, Downey RS, et al: Exenterative surgery for locally advanced rectosigmoid cancers: Is it worthwhile? *Surgery* 102:644–651, 1987.
10. Jaffe BM, Bricker EM, Butcher HR: Surgical complications of ileal segment urinary diversion. *Ann Surg* 167:367–376, 1968.
11. Jakowatz JG, Porudominsky D, Riihimaki DU, et al: Complication of pelvic exenteration. *Am J Obstet Gynecol* 145:325–332, 1983.
12. Lifshitz S, Johnson R, Roberts JA, et al: Intestinal fistula and obstruction following pelvic exenteration. *Am J Obstet Gynecol* 145:3250–3332, 1983.
13. Devereaux DF, Sears HF, Ketcham AS: Intestinal fistula following pelvic exenteration surgery: Predisposing causes and treatment. *J Surg Oncol* 14:227–232, 1980.
14. Polk HC, Butcher HR Jr, Bricker EM: Perineal fecal fistula following pelvic exenteration. *Surg Gynecol Obstet* 123:308–312, 1966.
15. Wheeles CR: Small bowel bypass for complications related to pelvic malignancy. *Obstet Gynecol* 42:661–666, 1973.
16. Devine RM, Dozois RR: Surgical management of locally advanced adenocarcinoma of the rectum. *World J Surg* 16:486–489, 1992.
17. Palmer JA, Vernon CP, Cummings BJ, et al: Gracilis myocutaneous flap for reconstructing perineal defects resulting from radiation and radical surgery. *Can J Surg* 26:510–512, 1983.
18. Temple WJ, Ketcham AS: The closure of large pelvic defects by extended compound tensor fascia lateral and inferior gluteal myocutaneous flaps. *Am J Clin Oncol* 5:573–577, 1982.
19. Miller LB, Steele G, Cady B, et al: Resection of tumors in irradiated fields with subsequent immediate reconstruction. *Arch Surg* 122:461–466, 1987.
20. Ledesma EJ, Bruno S, Mittleman A: Total pelvic exenteration in colorectal disease. *Ann Surg* 194;701–703, 1981.
21. Ego-Aguirne E, Spratt JS, Butcher HR, et al: Repair of perineal hernias developed subsequent to pelvic exenteration. *Ann Surg* 159:66–71, 1964.
22. Leuchter RS, Lagasse LD, Hacker NF, et al: Management of postexenteration perineal hernias by myocutaneous axial flaps. *Gynecol Oncol* 14:15–22, 1982.
23. Powell WJ, Parsons L: Perineal hernia repair with nylon mesh. *Surgery* 43:447–451, 1958.
24. Deckers PJ, Olssom C, Williams LA, et al: Pelvic exenteration as palliation of malignant disease. *Am J Surg* 131:509–515, 1976.
25. Eckhauser FE, Lindenauer SM, Morley GW: Pelvic exenteration for advanced rectal carcinoma. *Am J Surg* 138:411–414, 1979.

26. Kelley WE Jr, Brown PW, Lawrence W Jr, et al: Penetrating, obstructing, and perforating carcinomas of the colon and rectum. *Arch Surg* 116:381–384, 1981.
27. Gall FP, Tonak J, Altendorf A: Multivisceral resections in colorectal cancer. *Dis Colon Rectum* 30:337–341, 1987.
28. Hunter JA, Ryan JA Jr, Schultz P: En bloc resection of colon cancer adherent to other organs. *Am J Surg* 154:67–71, 1987.
29. Bonfanti G, Bozzetti F, Doci R, et al: Results of extended surgery for cancer of the rectum and sigmoid. *Br J Surg* 69:305–307, 1982.
30. McGlone TB, Bernie WA, Elliot DW: Survival following extended operations for extracolonic invasion by colon cancer. *Arch Surg* 117:595–599, 1982.
31. Pittam MR, Thornton H, Ellis H: Survival after extended resection for locally advanced carcinomas of the colon and rectum. *Ann R Coll Surg Engl* 66:81–84, 1984.
32. Heslov SF, Frost DB: Extended resection for primary colorectal carcinoma involving adjacent organs or structures. *Cancer* 62:1637–1640, 1988.
33. Fedorov VD, Odaryuk TS, Shelygin YA: Results of radical surgery for advanced rectal cancer. *Dis Colon Rectum* 32:567–571, 1989.
34. Symmonds RE, Pratt JH, Webb MJ: Exenterative operations: Experience with 198 patients. *Am J Obstet Gynecol* 121:907–918, 1975.
35. Rutledge FN, Smith JP, Wharton JT, et al: Pelvic exenteration: Analysis of 296 patients. *Am J Obstet Gynecol* 129:881–889, 1977.
36. Takagi H, Morimoto T, Yasue M, et al: Total pelvic exenteration for advanced carcinoma of the lower colon. *J Surg Oncol* 28:59–62, 1985.
37. Appleby LH: Proctocystectomy: The management of colostomy with ureteral transplants. *Am J Surg* 79:57–60, 1950.
38. Brintnall ES, Flocks RH: En masse pelvic viscerectomy with ureterointestinal anastomosis. *Arch Surg* 61:851–864, 1950.
39. Brunschwig A: Pelvic exenteration for carcinoma of the lower colon. *Surgery* 40:691–695, 1956.

CHAPTER 73

External Radiation Therapy for Primary Locally Advanced Rectal Cancer

James A. Martenson, Jr.
Steven E. Schild

HIGHLIGHTS

External radiation therapy can result in complete response in a minority of patients with locally advanced rectal cancer. Unfortunately, virtually all patients treated in this way will experience local progression and die of their disease.[1] The use of 5-fluorouracil (5-FU) in combination with external radiation therapy in patients with primary unresectable colorectal cancer was associated with improved survival and better palliation in one randomized prospective trial.[2] Approximately 44 to 65 percent of patients with unresectable lesions will have potentially curative resections subsequent to preoperative radiation therapy.[3-6] Unfortunately, approximately half of the patients whose lesions are converted to resectable status will experience local recurrence, and only a small minority will be cured of their disease. For patients with borderline resectable or tethered lesions, randomized trials suggest an improvement in survival,[7] resectability,[7] and local control.[7,8] In patients initially treated with incomplete resection followed by postoperative radiation therapy, long-term survival rates are poor (approximately 20 percent).

CONTROVERSIES

Despite the randomized trial from the Mayo Clinic[2] suggesting improved outcome with the combination of 5-FU and primary external radiation therapy, some investigators believe that the amount of improvement is too small to adopt 5-FU as a component of standard therapy. Although preoperative radiation therapy in unresectable disease converts some lesions to resectable status, definitive interpretation of the value of this approach is limited by a lack of prospective trials. Randomized trials in patients with tethered or borderline resectable lesions suggest improved local control with this approach. Improved survival has not been consistently demonstrated, however.[7,8] Radiation therapy after subtotal resection results in long-term survival and local control in a minority of patients.[9-15] Most studies of postoperative radiation therapy, however, have analyzed only small numbers of patients with short follow-up; thus, definitive interpretation of the impact of this form of treatment is precluded.

FUTURE DIRECTIONS

The recent finding of more effective systemic treatment (5-FU modulated by levamisole or leucovorin) for colorectal cancer[16-19] indicates that prospective clinical trials of these regimens used in combination with radiation therapy should be undertaken in patients with locally advanced disease. Regardless of the regimen used, local control is still achieved in only a small minority of patients who present with locally advanced rectal cancer. Measures for improving local control—such as intraoperative radiation therapy, hyperthermia, and use of radiation sensitizers—should be studied. The future understanding of the utility of various new approaches for locally advanced disease will be maximized if addressed within the context of prospective clinical trials.

Complete surgical resection is the treatment of choice for patients with rectal cancer. However, at the time of initial presentation, some patients have unresectable disease. In an analysis of 1137 patients with colorectal cancer from Ellis Fischel Hospital, 87 (8 percent) did not have resection because of locally advanced disease, and an additional 69 (6 percent) underwent noncurative resections. Five-year survival rates for these two groups were 1 and 9 percent, respectively.[20] Among 149 patients with rectosigmoid cancer at the University of Oregon who were referred for consideration of preoperative irradiation, 22 (15 percent) were thought to have locally unresectable disease.[3] External radiation therapy assumes an important role when curative primary surgical resection is not possible because of locally advanced disease.

PLANNING RADIATION THERAPY: GENERAL CONSIDERATIONS

Helpful studies for the planning of radiation therapy include preoperative barium enema and computed tomography. These studies document tumor location and spatial relationships to surrounding dose-limiting structures. This information can then be used for the proper design of irradiation fields.

In patients whose lesions are unresectable for cure at initial operation, attention to specific surgical details can help improve subsequent radiotherapy. Metal clips can be placed at the tumor borders, and these can later be viewed at simulation. The presence of clips can help prevent marginal misses and improve the accuracy of smaller boost fields. Pelvic reconstruction techniques can be used to prevent radiation-induced injury to the small bowel by moving the small intestine away from the tumor or tumor bed.[21]

Radiation therapy techniques to decrease injury to the small bowel include use of a multifield technique, a shrinking-field approach, and the prone position during treatment. Bladder distention is appropriate if it does not displace the tumor out of the radiation therapy fields. Small bowel films obtained at simulation can be used to aid in designing boost fields that minimize or exclude exposure of the small intestine.[21]

The target volume for the initial fields includes the tumor bed, sacral canal, and presacral and internal iliac lymph nodes. External iliac nodes are included if the tumor involves structures that drain to these lymph nodes, such as the bladder, prostate, uterus, cervix, or vagina. The superior edge of the radiation therapy fields generally lies at the mid–fifth lumbar vertebral body. The bottom of the fields is usually below the obturator foramina and includes a 3- to 5-cm margin below the tumor in patients treated primarily or after low anterior resection. The fields should cover the perineal scar after combined abdominoperineal resection. The lateral edges of the anteroposterior: posteroanterior fields should include the pelvic inlet with 1.5 to 2.0 cm of margin. The lateral fields should include the sacral canal with 1.5 cm or more of margin, tumor or tumor bed, and the draining lymph nodes mentioned above. The use of lateral portals allows for some sparing of small bowel and bladder. Boost fields should include the tumor or tumor bed with a minimum 2-cm margin, and they should be designed to minimize the volume of small intestine in the radiation field. Complete exclusion of small bowel after approximately 50 Gy is recommended.

Initially, patients are generally treated to 45 to 50 Gy at 1.8 to 2.0 Gy per day to fields designed to treat both the primary tumor and the regional lymph nodes. In preoperatively treated patients, an additional boost of 5 to 9 Gy in 3 to 5 fractions to reduced fields is then given for a total cumulative dose of 50 to 55 Gy. Patients with unresectable disease or residual disease after operation may benefit from higher doses.

PRIMARY EXTERNAL RADIATION THERAPY

At the Princess Margaret Hospital, external radiation, generally 50 Gy in 20 fractions, was used as the primary treatment in a group of 67 patients with "fixed" rectal cancer.[1] Of 8 patients (12 percent) who had a complete response to treatment, 2 subsequently developed local recurrence; thus, the overall local control rate was only 9 percent. Within a subgroup of 43 patients who did not have colostomy at the time of initiation of radiation therapy, 57 percent remained colostomy-free for the remainder of their lives. The limited value of radiation therapy as a single modality is illustrated in Fig. 73-1. Only 1 of the 67 patients treated survived 5 years.

A randomized clinical trial performed at the Mayo Clinic provided evidence that the use of 5-FU as an adjuvant to primary radiation therapy results in improved outcome.[2] A total of 65 patients with unresectable large bowel cancer were randomized to receive conventionally fractionated radiation therapy alone to a total dose of 35 to 40 Gy or radiation therapy in combination with 5-FU. Approximately half of the patients

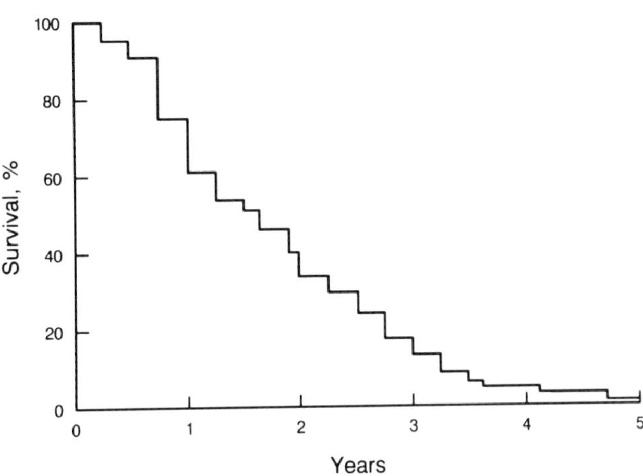

FIG. 73-1. Survival rate in 67 patients with fixed rectal tumors treated with primary radiation at Princess Margaret Hospital. (From Cummings et al.[1] Reproduced by permission of the American Society of Colon and Rectal Surgeons.)

in each group experienced "substantial or complete relief" of symptoms subsequent to treatment. The duration of symptom control was longer in the patients who received 5-FU than in those who did not (17 months versus 11 months). Both the interval to progression and the survival rate were statistically significantly better in patients randomized to 5-FU (Fig. 73-2).

PREOPERATIVE RADIATION THERAPY

Nearly all patients treated with primary radiation therapy without resection will experience local progression with or without distant metastasis and will eventually die of their disease. In an effort to improve these results, preoperative external radiation therapy has been used in combination with surgical resection. In patients with locally advanced rectal cancer, the primary goal of preoperative radiation therapy is conversion of the primary lesion from unresectable to resectable status. In general, approximately 45 to 65 percent of patients who receive preoperative radiation therapy will be able to have a potentially curative resection of their tumor (Table 73-1).[4–6,22] Unfortunately, a significant proportion of patients with apparently curative resections will subsequently experience local recurrence and death from disease. At the University of Florida, for example, 23 patients with unresectable rectal cancer received 30 to 60 Gy (median, 50 Gy) of conventionally fractionated pelvic radiation therapy; 11 patients (48 percent) subsequently underwent "apparently complete resection of their cancer."[4] Among the 11 patients with potentially curative resection of tumor, 6 had local recurrence. The overall 5-year survival rate for the entire group of 23 patients was 9 percent. In a study of 25 patients at Massachusetts General Hospital (MGH), those with unresectable (21 patients) or borderline resectable (4 patients) lesions received preoperative radiation therapy to a dose of 40 to 52 Gy. A total of 16 (64 percent) then had potentially curative resection; of these, 5 subsequently experienced pelvic failure. For the 25 patients who had preoperative radiation therapy, the 6-year survival rate was 17 percent.[6]

The use of systemic chemotherapy in combination with preoperative radiation therapy is one potential way of improving the results of preoperative radiation therapy. In patients with metastatic colonic and rectal cancer, treatment with 5-FU and leucovorin has been shown to result in improved response rates and sur-

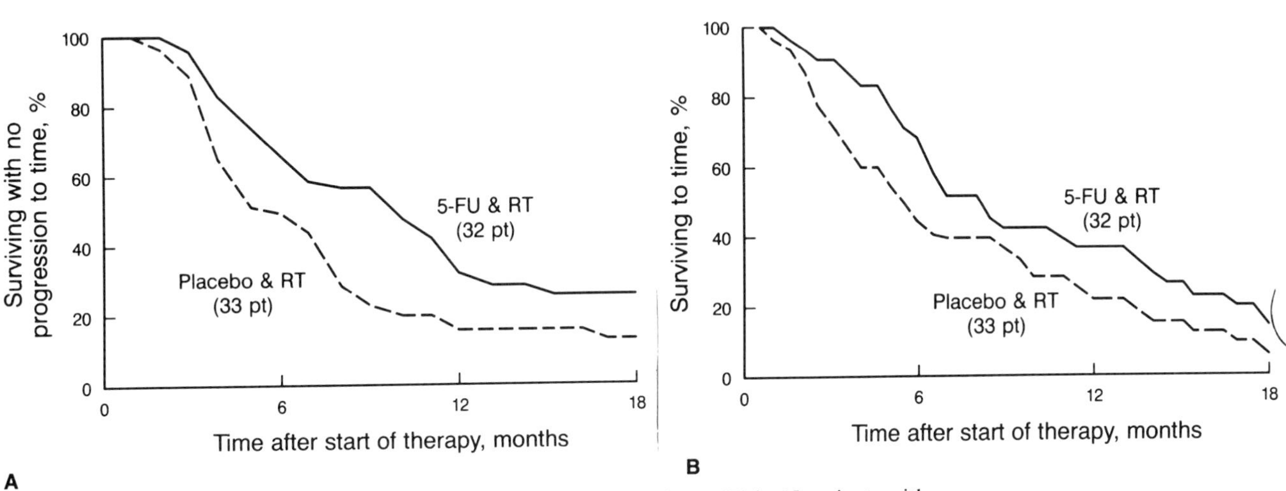

FIG. 73-2. Survival rate without progression (*A*) and overall survival rate (*B*) in 65 patients with unresectable colorectal cancer treated with 35 to 40 Gy radiation and randomized to 5-FU or placebo. A statistically significant improvement for both end points was observed for patients randomized to 5-FU. (From Moertel et al.[2] Reproduced by permission of the journal *Lancet*.)

Table 73-1
Literature Summary: Preoperative Radiation Therapy for Locally Advanced Rectal Cancer

Reference	*Cases included*	*Total dose, Gy*	*No. patients*	*Potentially curative resections*		*Local failure*		*Survival*		*Follow-up*
				No.	*%*[a]	*No.*	*%*[a]	*No.*	*%*[a]	
Allen and Fletcher[3]	Rectum, rectosigmoid	50	22	10	45	Not stated		10	45	Variable[b]
Dosoretz et al.[6]	Rectum, rectosigmoid	40–52	25	16	64	11	50[c]	7	28	5 years
Mendenhall et al.[4]	Rectum	35–60	23	11	48	17	74	2	9	5 years
Emani et al.[5]	Colon, rectum	45–60	44[d]	26	59	25	56	Not stated		Not stated[e]

[a]All percentages are based on the original number of patients receiving radiation therapy unless noted otherwise.

[b]Of 10 patients who became resectable, 3 survived >30 months, and 7 of 12 patients who did not become resectable survived (minimum follow-up not stated).

[c]Three patients who had complete resection and died of postoperative complications were regarded as invaluable for purposes of calculating local failure rate.

[d]Rectum, 28 cases; rectosigmoid, 11 cases; sigmoid colon, 4 cases; transverse colon, 1 case.

[e]Five-year survival, 70% in patients undergoing curative resection; figures for entire group were not provided.

vival in comparison with the use of 5-FU alone.[16] On the basis of this result, Minsky and colleagues[23] treated 20 patients who had unresectable rectal cancer (13 with primary unresectable disease and 7 with locally recurrent disease) with preoperative radiation (50.4 Gy in 28 fractions), 5-FU, and leucovorin in a phase I study. Results were compared with those in 11 patients who had locally advanced rectal cancer (9 with primary unresectable disease and 2 with locally recurrent disease) treated by radiation without chemotherapy. Among patients with primary unresectable disease, 15% of those who received radiation therapy, 5-FU, and leucovorin had no residual tumor at the time of surgical resection, whereas none of the patients with primary unresectable disease who were treated with radiation alone had similar downstaging. Among the entire group of patients, the rates of potentially curative resection for combination therapy and for radiation therapy alone were 90 and 64 percent, respectively (Table 73-2). These results indicate a need for continued prospective studies to investigate the value of radiation therapy and chemotherapy in patients with advanced rectal cancer.

The strongest scientific evidence for a beneficial effect of preoperative radiation therapy is in patients with "borderline resectable"[24] tumors. In one study, for example, 60 patients with rectal cancer who generally had "advanced borderline resectable and inoperable lesions" received preoperative radiation therapy.[24] At the time of operation, 52 of 56 patients

Table 73-2
Memorial Sloan-Kettering Results with Radiation Therapy, 5-Fluorouracil (5-FU), and Leucovorin versus Radiation Therapy Alone

	Radiation therapy, 5-FU, leucovorin			*Radiation therapy*		
	Primary	*Recurrent*	*Total*	*Primary*	*Recurrent*	*Total*
No. of patients	13	7	20	9	2	11
Stage,[a] no. of patients (%)						
T_0N_0[b]	2 (15)	2 (29)	4 (20)	0	0	0
T_2N_{0-2}	6 (46)	2 (29)	8 (40)	0	0	0
T_3N_{0-2}	2 (15)	2 (29)	4 (20)	7 (78)	0	7 (64)
T_4N_{0-2}	3 (23)	1 (14)	4 (20)	2 (22)	2 (100)	4 (36)
% resectable[c]	11 (85)	7 (100)	18 (90)	7 (78)	0	7 (64)
% node-positive[c]	5 (38)	1 (14)	6 (30)	5 (56)	2 (100)	7 (64)

[a]Pathologic stage of tumor after radiation therapy.

[b]T_0N_0, no identifiable tumor remaining (pathologic complete response).

[c]Complete resection with negative margins.

SOURCE: From Minsky et al.[23] Reproduced by permission of the American Society of Clinical Oncology.

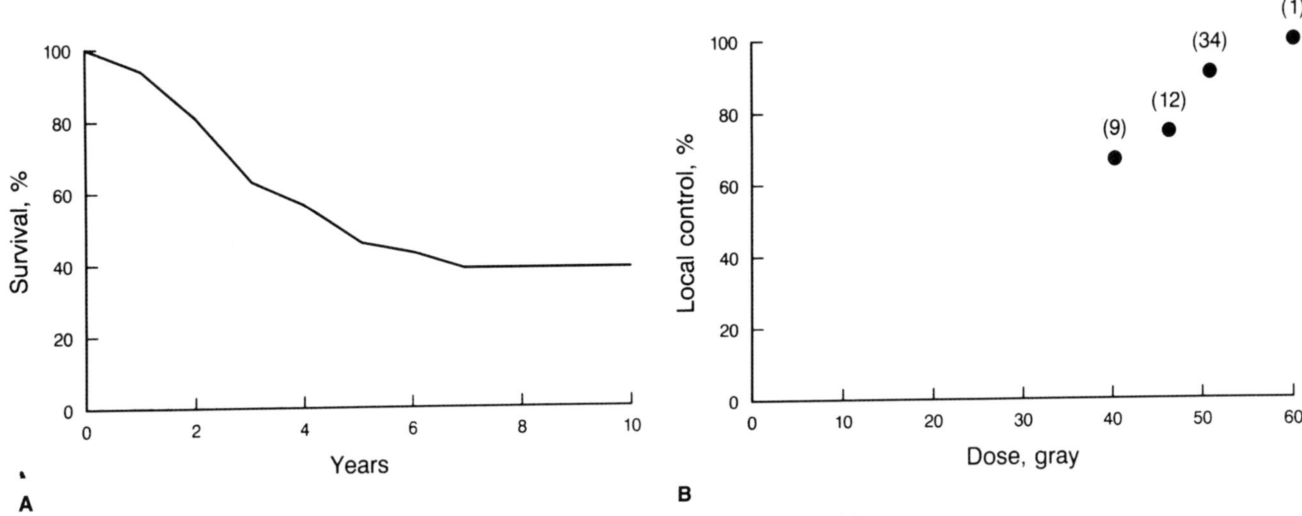

FIG. 73-3. *A*. Survival rate in 56 patients treated with preoperative radiation followed by operation. *B*. Dose versus local control in the 52 patients who had potentially curative operation. The numbers in parentheses are the number of patients at risk at each data point. (From Fortier et al.[24] Reproduced by permission of Pergamon Press.)

without evidence of metastasis had potentially curative resections. The 5-year survival rate was 45 percent (Fig. 73-3*A*). Among the 52 patients resected for cure, there was a suggestion of improved local control with increasing dose (Fig. 73-3*B*).

Two randomized clinical trials suggest that preoperative radiation therapy may result in improved local control in patients with borderline-operable rectal cancer. At the Rottersdamsch Radio-Therapeutisch Instituut, 100 patients with "border operability rectal carcinoma" were randomized either to operation alone or to preoperative radiation therapy (34.5 Gy in 15 fractions over 18 days) followed by operation.[7] No differences in outcome were observed in patients with T_2 disease. Among patients with T_{3-4} disease, potentially curative resections were possible in 97 percent after preoperative radiation therapy and in only 68 percent treated with operation alone. After radical resection, freedom from local recurrence in patients with T_{3-4} disease at 5 years was 88 percent in preoperatively irradiated patients and 65 percent in those treated with operation only (p = .08). The survival rate was better in patients with T_{3-4} disease treated with preoperative radiation (Fig. 73-4). Jones et al.[8] described results in 262 patients with "locally advanced, tethered rectal carcinomas" who were randomized to receive operation only or 20 Gy in four daily fractions followed by operation. The incidence of local recurrence was reduced

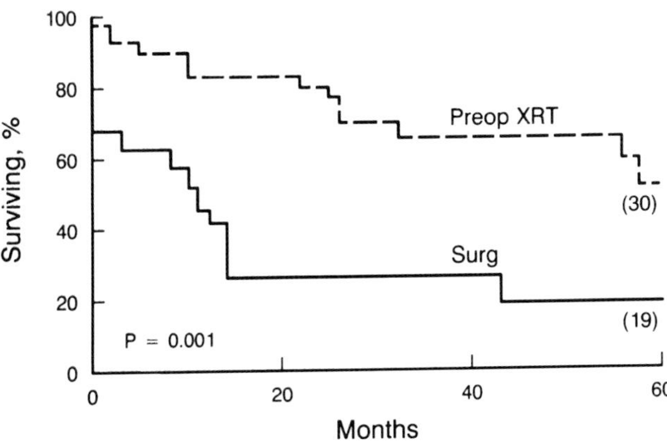

FIG. 73-4. Survival rate in patients with T_{3-4} tumors according to treatment—by surgery (Surg) alone or preoperative radiation therapy (Preop XRT; 34.5 Gy in 15 fractions) followed by operation in the randomized trial from Rotterdam. (From Wassif et al.[7] Reproduced by permission of Grune & Stratton, the publisher.)

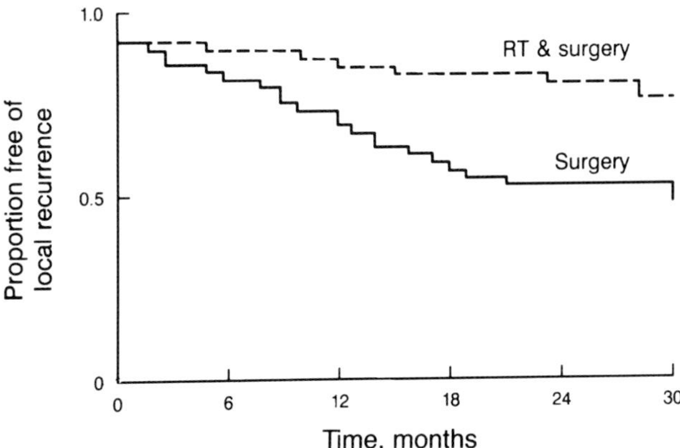

FIG. 73-5. Analysis of local recurrence according to treatment—with or without preoperative radiation therapy (RT; 20 Gy in 4 fractions)—in a randomized trial from Manchester. (From Jones et al.[8] Reproduced by permission of Butterworth-Heinemann Ltd., Publishers.)

Table 73-3
Literature Summary: Subtotally Resected Rectal Cancer Treated with External Beam Radiation

			Results by residual disease			
			Microscopic residual[a]		*Gross residual*	
Reference	*Cases included*	*Dose including boost, Gy*	*LF*	*Survival*	*LF*	*Survival*
Wang and Schulz[10]	Sigmoid, rectum	20–50			Not stated	2/9 (25%) [b]
Ghossein et al.[9]	Colorectal	31–60	2/13 (15%)	10/13 (77%)	9/18 (50%)	7/18 (39%)
Allee et al.[14]	Colorectal	45–70	9/30 (30%)	42% at 5 years	13/23 (57%)	4% at 5 years
Brizel and Tepperman[12]	Sigmoid, rectum	9–64	6/19 (32%)[b]	Not stated	4/14 (29%)[c]	Not stated
Rominger et al. (RTOG)[11]	Sigmoid, rectum	50–70	5/18 (28%)	11/19 (58%) at 2 years	8/16 (50%)	5/18 (28%) at 2 years
Schild et al.[13]	Rectum	40–60	7/10 (70%)	3/10 (30%) at 5 years	6/7 (86%)	1/7 (14%) at 5 years
De Neve et al.[15]	Sigmoid, rectum	30–60	6/21 (28%)	40% at 5 years	8/19 (42%)	12% at 5 years

[a]Number of patients with local failure/number of patients in group.
[b]Authors stated that these patients had "obvious residual."
[c]Only histologically confirmed pelvic recurrences were considered local failures.
Abbreviations: LF, local failure.

in the patients who received radiation therapy (Fig. 73-5). Survival rates were similar for the two groups of patients.

POSTOPERATIVE RADIATION THERAPY

Postoperative external radiation therapy is potentially curative for a minority of patients who have undergone subtotal resection of rectal cancer. Results with external beam radiotherapy for subtotally resected colorectal cancers are summarized in Table 73-3.

Local failure was reported in 15 to 32 percent of patients with microscopic residual disease except in the Mayo series,[13] which reported a 70 percent local failure rate. Local failure was reported in 29 to 57 percent of patients with gross residual disease except in the Mayo series,[13] which reported an 86 percent local failure rate. The higher rate of local failure reported from Mayo may be related to the longer follow-up used in this series and the less restrictive criteria used for judging local failure.[13]

Survival rates are unfavorable. Reported 5-year projected survival rates range from 30 to 42 percent in patients with microscopic residual disease and 4 to 14 percent in those with gross residual disease (Table 74-3). Although the Mayo series reported poorer rates for local control, the survival rates were similar to those reported by other institutions. In the MGH experience,[14] survival was better among patients with microscopic disease (42 percent at 5 years) than those with gross disease (4 percent at 5 years). When patients with microscopic disease subsequent to surgery were further divided into those with pathologically confirmed residual disease and those with presumed residual disease, survival was poorer in the former group (14 versus 50 percent at 5 years) and local failure was higher (43 versus 26 percent).

Systemic failure is also a significant problem. At Mayo, for example, distant metastases developed in 59 percent of the patients.[13] Interestingly, no Mayo patient had distant disease develop in the absence of local failure.

Given the relatively unfavorable survival results with external beam irradiation alone, other additional therapeutic measures should be considered in an attempt to improve survival. The addition of 5-FU to radiation therapy appears to result in better survival when compared with radiation therapy alone.[2] Future clinical trials may show that modulators of 5-FU, such as leucovorin[16,17] and levamisole,[18,19] are of benefit in patients with locally advanced disease, since such combinations appear to provide more effective systemic treatment. Measures for improving local control—such as intraoperative radiation therapy, hyperthermia, and radiation sensitizers—should also be studied.

REFERENCES

1. Cummings BJ Jr, Rider WD, Harwood AR, et al: Radical external beam radiation therapy for adenocarcinoma of the rectum. *Dis Colon Rectum* 26:30–36, 1983.
2. Moertel CG, Childs DS Jr, Reitemeier RJ, et al: Combined 5-fluorouracil and supervoltage radiation therapy of locally unresectable gastrointestinal cancer. *Lancet* 2:865–867, 1969.
3. Allen CV, Fletcher WS: A pilot study of preoperative irradiation of rectosigmoid carcinoma. *Am J Roentgenol* 114:504–508, 1972.

4. Mendenhall WM, Million RR, Bland KI, et al: Initially unresectable rectal adenocarcinoma treated with preoperative irradiation and surgery. *Ann Surg* 205:41–44, 1987.
5. Emami B, Pilepich M, Willett C, et al: Effect of preoperative irradiation on resectability of colorectal carcinomas. *Int J Radiat Oncol Biol Phys* 8:1295–1299, 1982.
6. Dosoretz DE, Gunderson LL, Hedberg S, et al: Preoperative irradiation for unresectable rectal and rectosigmoid carcinomas. *Cancer* 52:814–818, 1983.
7. Wassif SB, Langenhorst BL, Hop WCJ: The contribution of preoperative radiotherapy in the management of borderline operability rectal cancer, in Jones SE, Salmon SE (eds): *Adjuvant Therapy of Cancer II*. New York, Grune & Stratton, 1979, pp 613–620.
8. Jones DJ, Zaloudik J, James RD, et al: Predicting local recurrence of carcinoma of the rectum after preoperative radiotherapy and surgery. *Br J Surg* 76:1172–1175, 1989.
9. Ghossein NA, Samala EC, Alpert S, et al: Elective postoperative radiotherapy after incomplete resection of colorectal cancer. *Dis Colon Rectum* 24:252–256, 1981.
10. Wang CC, Schulz MD: The role of radiation therapy in the management of carcinoma of the sigmoid, rectosigmoid, and rectum. *Radiology* 79:1–5, 1962.
11. Rominger CJ, Gelber RD, Gunderson LL, et al: Radiation therapy alone or in combination with chemotherapy in the treatment of residual or inoperable carcinoma of the rectum and rectosigmoid or pelvic recurrence following colorectal surgery. Radiation Therapy Oncology Group study (76-16). *Am J Clin Oncol* 8:118–127, 1985.
12. Brizel HE, Tepperman BS: Postoperative adjuvant irradiation for adenocarcinoma of the rectum and sigmoid. *Am J Clin Oncol* 7:679–685, 1984.
13. Schild SE, Martenson JA, Gunderson LL, et al: Long-term survival and patterns of failure after postoperative radiation therapy for subtotally resected rectal adenocarcinoma. *Int J Radiat Oncol Biol Phys* 16:459–463, 1989.
14. Allee PE, Tepper JE, Gunderson LL, et al: Postoperative radiation therapy for incompletely resected colorectal carcinoma. *Int J Radiat Oncol Biol Phys* 17:1171–1176, 1989.
15. De Neve W, Martijn H, Lybeert MM, et al: Incompletely resected rectum, recto-sigmoid, or sigmoid carcinoma: Results of postoperative radiotherapy and prognostic factors. *Int J Radiat Oncol Biol Phys* 21:1297–1302, 1991.
16. Poon MA, O'Connell MJ, Moertel CG, et al: Biochemical modulation of fluorouracil: Evidence of significant improvement of survival and quality of life in patients with advanced colorectal carcinoma. *J Clin Oncol* 7:1407–1418, 1989.
17. Petrelli N, Douglass HO Jr, Herrera L, et al: The modulation of fluorouracil with leucovorin in metastatic colorectal carcinoma: A prospective randomized phase III trial. *J Clin Oncol* 7:1419–1426, 1989.
18. Moertel CG, Fleming TR, Macdonald JS, et al: Levamisole and fluorouracil for adjuvant therapy of resected colon carcinoma. *N Engl J Med* 322:352–358, 1990.
19. Laurie JA, Moertel CG, Fleming TR, et al: Surgical adjuvant therapy of large-bowel carcinoma: An evaluation of levamisole and the combination of levamisole and fluorouracil. *J Clin Oncol* 7:1447–1456, 1989.
20. Spratt JS Jr, Spjut HJ: Prevalence and prognosis of individual clinical and pathologic variables associated with colorectal carcinoma. *Cancer* 20:1976–1985, 1967.
21. Gunderson LL, Russell AH, Llewellyn HJ, et al: Treatment planning for colorectal cancer: Radiation and surgical techniques and value of small-bowel films. *Int J Radiat Oncol Biol Phys* 11:1379–1393, 1985.
22. Pilepich MV, Munzenrider JE, Tak WK, et al: Preoperative irradiation of primarily unresectable colorectal carcinoma. *Cancer* 42:1077–1081, 1978.
23. Minsky BD, Cohen AM, Kemeny N, et al: Enhancement of radiation-induced downstaging of rectal cancer by fluorouracil and high-dose leucovorin chemotherapy. *J Clin Oncol* 10:79–84, 1992.
24. Fortier GA, Krochak RJ, Kim JA, et al: Dose response to preoperative irradiation in rectal cancer: Implications for local control and complications associated with sphincter sparing surgery and abdominoperineal resection. *Int J Radiat Oncol Biol Phys* 12:1559–1563, 1986.

CHAPTER 74

Intraoperative Radiation Strategies

Joel E. Tepper

HIGHLIGHTS

The data that have been developed on the use of radiation therapy boost techniques for patients with locally advanced carcinomas of the rectum suggest that increased radiation dose can improve both local control and survival rates. The radiation boost can theoretically be delivered by the use of external beam therapy, intraoperative electron beam radiation therapy (IORT), or intraoperative radioactive implant. At present most of the data are based on patients treated with electron beam techniques. These data suggest that for patients with primary locally advanced cancers, local control can be obtained in over 80 percent and long-term survival in approximately 50 percent. The complication rate in these patients does not appear to be substantially increased over that obtained with more conventional treatment approaches. In patients with locally recurrent tumors, the local control and survival rates are less good and the complication rate is increased, especially complications related to poor wound healing and nerve entrapment, producing significant pain syndromes. Nonetheless, 15 to 20 percent of patients can be salvaged with aggressive radiation and surgical resection. IORT needs to be viewed as part of an overall combined-modality strategy of preoperative external beam irradiation, surgical resection, and IORT boost.

CONTROVERSIES

There are still a number of uncertainties relating to the role of IORT in the treatment of locally advanced rectal cancer. It has not yet been definitively demonstrated that the combined-modality therapy of preoperative external beam irradiation, surgical resection, and IORT is superior to the same therapy without IORT, although the data strongly suggest that the boost is necessary. Issues relating to patient selection could have favorably influenced the IORT results to suggest a greater benefit than in fact exists. It is also unclear that, even if a radiation boost has a beneficial effect on long-term results, equally good results would not be obtained by the use of a boost delivered with external beam or implant techniques. This is important because of the greater access to the other boost techniques and the substantially increased cost of an IORT facility compared to that for an implant. The role of IORT in patients with locally recurrent disease is not defined. Although some patients can be cured with the use of an IORT boost, the complication rate is high and the incremental benefit needs to be established. Despite the increased complication rate with this approach, some physicians are willing to use IORT in patients who have already received some external beam pelvic irradiation, although other investigators do not think the morbidity in this situation is acceptable.

FUTURE DIRECTIONS

It is important that we work to define the answers to some of the questions mentioned above. A randomized trial is in progress to determine the relative benefit of an IORT boost compared to an external beam radiation boost in patients with primary locally advanced tumors. This will not answer the question as to the value of an implant but will nonetheless provide valuable information. A randomization evaluating implant techniques would be of great interest. Further data also need to be developed on the value of IORT in patients with recurrent disease. These patients are very difficult to manage, and a better understanding of their response to therapy would be of value. Because of the difficulty in obtaining a high incidence of local control in patients with gross residual disease, even when using the high doses that can be delivered intraoperatively, it is important to search for strategies to enhance the effectiveness of IORT. Exploration of the use of concurrent hyperthermia or chemical radiation sensitizers with IORT could be of value. Regardless of the improvement in local control with these approaches, it will be essential to continue efforts to find better systemic agents to decrease the incidence of distant metastases.

The treatment of patients with locally advanced rectal cancer is difficult in terms of both patient evaluation and treatment. The literature in this area is often confusing. One of the major problems is defining what is meant by a locally advanced tumor. Some authors refer to any tumor that has invaded through the bowel wall as locally advanced, whereas others limit the definition to tumors that cannot be resected at all. A good working definition of a locally advanced tumor is a tumor that cannot be resected without leaving microscopic or gross residual disease in the local site because of tumor adherence or fixation to that site. A rectal tumor is most commonly locally advanced because of its adherence to the sacrum, pelvic side wall, vagina, or prostate, although the vagina is not as important clinically because it can be resected with relatively little morbidity, whereas the other sites cannot easily be resected.

RESULTS WITH EXTERNAL IRRADIATION

In the past, the management of locally advanced rectal tumors has been variable. Some patients have had incomplete surgical resections alone, while others have had radiation alone or surgery combined with pre- or postoperative irradiation. A commonly used approach has been preoperative irradiation to shrink the tumor mass, followed by an attempt to perform a complete surgical resection. This approach has been tried at a number of institutions, with some beneficial results (Table 74-1).[1–3] In these series, approximately 50 to 75 percent of patients were able to have a potentially curative surgical resection after preoperative irradiation, with 5-year cure rates of approximately 25 percent in the patients who were thought to have a good resection. Although a substantial percentage of patients had local control with this approach, the local failure rate was still in the range of 40 to 75 percent despite the use of aggressive combined-modality therapy.

The fact that a moderate number of patients were cured with this approach and that local failure remained a substantial problem led to the possibility that a more aggressive local therapy could increase the local cure rate as well as long-term survival. As a more aggressive surgical therapy was generally not feasible, much of the emphasis was given to utilizing radiation boost techniques, which would increase the dose to the area at highest risk for residual tumor.

RADIATION BOOST TECHNIQUES

There are three main possibilities for the boost radiation: external beam radiation therapy, intraoperative implant techniques, and IORT. The use of higher doses of external beam has not been fully pursued because of concern about the morbidity to small intestine secondary to higher radiation doses. However, it may be possible to increase the external beam radiation dose if there is surgical displacement of small bowel from the radiation field and if the high-risk area is well defined. Nonetheless, there is relatively little information available on this approach.

Table 74-1
Preoperative Radiation Therapy and Resection of Locally Advanced Rectal Cancer

	Number of patients	*Resectable for cure, percent*	*Local control of those resected, percent*	*Five-year survival of those resected, percent*
University of Oregon	72	39	32	10
Massachusetts General Hospital	25	72	62	43[a]
Tufts University	28	50		41

[a]Six-year survival, 26 percent.

There are sporadic reports of the use of radioactive implants placed at the time of surgery, but there is no organized body of information on the use of this technique. Implants are appealing because the radiation can be delivered at a low dose rate, which might decrease the late normal tissue injury, and because the radiation dose can be well localized. There are some potential problems with the use of implants. One is that small bowel could fall into the radiation field and abut the implant, resulting in a very high radiation dose to a small segment of small bowel. In addition, there are some clinical situations where it is difficult to obtain a good physical implant placement and other situations where the dose distribution is suboptimal. Nonetheless, this is an approach that deserves further investigation.

INTRAOPERATIVE RADIATION BOOST TECHNIQUES

Perhaps the most clinical information is available on the use of IORT given with a conventional external beam radiation therapy machine after the tumor has been resected. Most of the IORT in the United States has utilized intraoperative electrons, but there has been some use of IORT given with x-rays from orthovoltage machines. Electrons are clearly superior dosimetrically to orthovoltage x-ray radiation, since with electrons little dose is delivered beyond a defined depth in tissue, thereby protecting deep normal tissues from the high radiation dose. Orthovoltage radiation has been used primarily because it is less expensive to develop a dedicated IORT setup with orthovoltage than with electrons. The discussion of IORT in the rest of this chapter will be based on the IORT experience with electrons.

The basic concept behind the use of IORT is that a large single dose of radiation can be given during the operative procedure, when the volume at risk for tumor involvement is well defined. In addition, by using electrons (where the depth of penetration of the radiation beam is limited and can be adjusted), the amount of normal tissues irradiated deep to the tumor mass can be minimized. Since the radiation is delivered during the time of surgery, other normal tissues such as small bowel can be moved out of the path of the radiation beam or shielded from the radiation by the use of lead cutouts. Thus, there is the potential to deliver a high, biologically effective dose of radiation while minimizing the damage to normal tissue.

The exact biological efficacy of radiation given as a large single dose is unclear; it probably varies with the normal tissue involved. There are some radiobiological data on the late effects of IORT on normal tissues. These data indicate that, for most soft tissues, the high single doses of IORT used clinically should produce an acceptably low complication rate. However, for tissues such as peripheral nerves which cannot be moved or shielded from the radiation field and for visceral structures, the late effects can be substantial.[4–12] Specific concerns have been raised regarding the likelihood of osteosarcoma formation and late nerve tissue injury; these will need to be addressed in clinical trials. Although there are no firm data, some investigators have estimated that a single high dose of radiation given intraoperatively has approximately 2 1/2 times the biological effectiveness of the same dose of radiation given in a standard fractionated course. Thus, an IORT dose of 2000 cGy could be biologically equivalent to 5000 cGy of conventional fractionated radiation.

The original clinical experience with IORT was that of Abe and Takahashi[13] at Kyoto University, but relatively little work on rectal cancer has been done by the Japanese. Studies have been performed by a few institutions in the United States, but the treatment philosophy at these institutions has been relatively consistent. Most centers have tried to take advantage of the tumor downstaging that usually occurs with high-dose preoperative irradiation, have utilized surgical resection to maximize tumor debulking, and have utilized IORT as a boost dose of radiation to the high-risk areas.

A typical treatment approach has been first to define the patient as having locally advanced disease with the criteria mentioned above, relying on the clinical examination as well as radiographic studies. The patient then receives preoperative external beam irradiation to a dose of approximately 5000 cGy using a multifield approach, treating the pelvis with a field encompassing the primary tumor and the regional lymphatics. Most investigators now use 5-fluorouracil (5-FU) chemotherapy as a radiation sensitizer in conjunction with the external beam irradiation. After a rest of approximately 4 weeks, the patient is taken to surgery. Generally an abdominoperineal resection is performed, but sometimes a low anterior resection is possible. Attempts are made to resect as much disease as possible, even if some gross residual disease remains. The surgical specimen and the tumor bed should be evaluated pathologically to define areas of possible residual disease, microscopic positive margins, or gross residual tumor. It is critical to define all high-risk areas accurately so as to determine the optimal position for the IORT field.

After the abdomen is partially closed, the patient is transferred to the radiation treatment room. A few centers have dedicated IORT suites where the operation is done and where the radiation is delivered, but this is the exception. A series of treatment applicators are available which attach to the machine head and are placed over the site to be irradiated. These applicators allow the geometry of the applicator to fit the specific situation of tumor versus normal tissue. The applicator must abut the site being treated, which can be difficult if the high-risk area is located in an anatomically confined region such as the pelvis. Further, the angle of the edge of the applicator should optimally be placed flat against the body surface so as to maximize dose homogeneity. It is important that the applicator be placed so that the tumor is fully covered, that sensitive normal tissues are not included in the beam, and that there is no fluid buildup in the treatment area. If necessary, lead sheets can be cut out to block sensitive normal tissues that cannot be removed from the path of the beam; retraction and packing are often necessary to move normal tissues. After the applicator is placed, it is attached to the treatment machine. All personnel leave the room during the therapy and the patient is monitored via closed circuit television and electronics placed outside of the room.

At the completion of the treatment, the radiation field should be rechecked to be certain that the intended areas were in fact treated. The surgery is then completed either in the treatment room or after the patient is transported back to the operating room. Typical doses of radiation delivered intraoperatively are in the range of 1000 to 2000 cGy with the lower doses being given for minimal residual disease and the higher doses for gross residual disease after resection.

RESULTS WITH IORT

One of the difficulties in evaluating the results of IORT in locally advanced rectal cancer is that the clinical definition of which tumors are locally advanced is subjective, making the comparison of results between institutions difficult. Nonetheless, the data suggest an advantage to the use of IORT compared to conventional treatment alone. One can compare IORT data to those obtained using high-dose preoperative radiation therapy and surgical resection without IORT as long as one understands the difficulties inherent in such a comparison and the fact that a comparison of this sort is never definitive.

Most of the data on IORT in locally advanced rectal cancer come from two institutions, the Massachusetts General Hospital (MGH)[14–16] and the Mayo Clinic,[17,18] although others have also reported results of interest.[19] These institutions have employed virtually identical treatment approaches, adding IORT to an otherwise conventional preoperative irradiation regimen. There are many factors which could have a major impact on prognosis, including the following:

1. Whether the patients have received prior external beam irradiation. As the complication rates are high when reirradiation is used, many centers are not willing to re-treat patients after prior pelvic radiation therapy.
2. Whether the patients are being treated for their initial rectal tumor or for locally recurrent disease, with the recurrence being locally advanced.
3. Whether, after the surgical resection, the patient has minimal residual disease or gross residual tumor.

Generally, the patients with the best prognosis are those who are treated for the first time for their rectal cancer (that is, those who are not being treated for locally recurrent disease) and in whom there is no known residual disease after the preoperative irradiation and surgery. Data from the MGH demonstrate an 88 percent 5-year actuarial local control and a 5-year disease-free survival of 53 percent in these patients.[16] For patients treated for their primary tumor but in whom a complete surgical resection cannot be accomplished, the results are not as good, with a local control of 69 percent for patients with microscopic residual disease and 50 percent for those with gross residual disease. The 5-year disease-free survival in this cohort is 47 and 17 percent respectively (Table 74-2).

Patients with locally recurrent rectal cancer do less well than those with locally advanced primary lesions. Local control was obtained in only 37 percent of the patients at the MGH, and disease-free survival was 27 percent.[15] These figures are substantially poorer than those for patients treated for their primary tumor. Similar survival data have been reported from the Mayo Clinic, but their local control results are slightly higher (Table 74-3).[17,18] Whether the difference in local con-

Table 74-2
Primary Locally Advaced Rectal Cancer—IORT Regimens

	Number	*Local control*	*Survival, percent*
Massachusetts General Hospital, overall	42	77% (5-year actuarial)	43 (5-year disease-free)
Complete resection	20	88%	53
Microscopic residual	16	69%	47
Macroscopic residual	6	50%	17
Mayo Clinic			
External alone	17	24% (4/17)	24 (3-year)
External plus IORT	20	80% (16/20)	50

Table 74-3
Recurrent Locally Advanced Rectal Cancer

	Number	*Local control*	*Survival, percent*
Massachusetts General Hospital (determinate)	36	36% (13/36)	28 (5-year)
Complete resection	13	62% (8/13)	54
Partial resection	17	18% (3/17)	6
Resection without IORT	6	33% (2/6)	33
Mayo Clinic	59	60% (5-year actuarial)	34 (3-year actuarial)

trol is due to different criteria for defining local failure, higher overall IORT doses in the Mayo series, or other reasons is unclear.

COMPLICATIONS OF IORT

Complications are an important part of the analysis when one is using a new modality and that modality is being used in an aggressive fashion. Complications have been evaluated carefully in an earlier subset of patients from the MGH[19] (Table 74-4). Patients with locally advanced rectal tumors were divided into two groups: those who were treated for their primary tumor and those treated for locally recurrent disease. These patients were then compared to two other (nonconcurrent) cohorts from the MGH: (1) patients treated at an earlier time for locally advanced rectal cancer with high-dose preoperative irradiation and resection without IORT and (2) a cohort with non–locally advanced tumors treated with surgical resection alone. These data demonstrate no evidence of a major increase in toxicity with the use of IORT as compared with surgical resection and irradiation. The one group that appeared to have a clear increase in complications were those who were treated for locally recurrent disease. These patients had a complication rate near 50 percent (Table 74-4) and, as noted previously, results with the aggressive salvage treatment were not as good as for primary lesions.

Table 74-4
Complications of Intraoperative Radiation Therapy for Locally Advanced Rectal Cancer

	Surgery alone	*RT plus surgery*	*IORT, primary*	*IORT, recurrent*
Soft tissue	6	6	3	7
Gastrointestinal	4	1	0	1
Other	3	3	3	1
Total complications	13	10	6	9
Total patients	80	23	24	17
Percent of patients with complications	16%	35%	21%	47%

The types of complications seen in these series have been varied and generally reflect the toxicities seen with aggressive surgery and radiation. They include pelvic abscess, small bowel obstruction, small bowel fistula, and delayed perineal healing. Most of these complications resolved with either medical or surgical management but did not cause long-term patient morbidity. The complications that have been of the greatest concern are those which are not easily managed. Among these, the major complication is neuropathy, which is rarely seen with conventional therapy. However, in the series from the Mayo Clinic,[17] symptomatic or objective neuropathy occurred in 32 percent (12 of 37) of patients followed for <12 months. The neuropathy presented as pain in all 12 (resolved in 5), sensory in 8, and motor in 7 (resolved in 1). Fortunately, the pain syndrome was severe in only 3 of 12 patients with pain (3 of 37 patients at risk), and the motor deficit was severe in only 1 patient. In the MGH series, neuropathy was much less frequent and occurred in only 3 patients. Interestingly, all of these patients were treated for locally recurrent rectal cancer.

The other complication of note is ureteral obstruction. At the Mayo Clinic, of 12 ureters irradiated with IORT, 9 were unobstructed prior to IORT, and hydronephrosis developed in 4. Ureteral obstruction resolved in 2 of the 3 patients in whom there was ureteral obstruction from tumor prior to the IORT. Thus, although there is significant morbidity from this treatment regimen, it has generally been acceptable in patients treated for a primary tumor but less so in patients treated for recurrence.

DISCUSSION

When results in IORT series are compared with the historical data of high-dose preoperative radiation therapy and resection for locally advanced primary rectal cancers, the data with the addition of IORT appear to be superior. As shown in Tables 74-1 and 74-2, the long-term survival appears to improve from approximately 25 to 50 percent with the addition of IORT. One must question the comparability of the patient groups, as there may be significant biases in patient selection. However, the data are even more encouraging when one realizes that the older series generally report survival results only on patients who had a potentially curative surgical resection rather than on the entire patient population. This favorable subset is the group with the best results in the IORT series—those with no gross residual disease after resection.

While the exact role of IORT in the treatment of locally advanced rectal cancer is not clear, these data clearly suggest an advantage to the use of a boost dose of radiation in improving local control and survival. This advantage seems most clear in patients who present with their initial tumor and who have not received any prior therapy. In addition, patients in whom a complete surgical resection can be obtained do better than those in whom gross residual disease remains. However, in all these series, IORT is used as part of the overall treatment regimen and as a boost therapy after high-dose preoperative external beam irradiation and surgical resection. IORT should not be viewed as the primary treatment modality in these patients but as part of the overall treatment plan.

Because of the significant morbidity seen in patients with localized recurrence who have received previous radiation therapy, the value of IORT in this situation is uncertain. Patients who are treated with IORT for a local recurrence after previous treatment with surgery alone do not have as good a prognosis as do patients with primary lesions. However, there is a 15 to 20 percent salvage rate with this approach, so IORT should be considered a reasonable component of aggressive treatment in properly selected patients.

It is well known that, in animal tumors, the presence of hypoxic cells can decrease radiation sensitivity. There are also agents, such as certain nitroimidazoles, that are well known to increase the radiation sensitivity of hypoxic cells to ionizing radiation. Since one would expect hypoxia to have its maximum effect in situations where a single high dose of radiation was delivered, these sensitizers could have a beneficial role in clinical situations where local control with present techniques is suboptimal. It would be worthwhile to conduct clinical trials, to see whether local control and survival could be improved with the addition of such sensitizers in patients who have gross residual disease after preoperative radiation therapy and surgical resection.

In addition, a number of chemotherapeutic agents have been shown to produce radiation sensitization and improvement of local control when combined with radiation therapy. The most notable example of this is 5-FU, which has been shown to decrease the incidence of local failure and distant metastases when combined with radiation therapy alone in the adjuvant treatment of rectal cancer after surgical resection. Other agents, such as certain platinum compounds, are known to produce radiation sensitization in vitro and could also be explored in patients with locally advanced disease in order to improve local control over that obtained with IORT alone.

Since 5-FU has been shown to be effective in the adjuvant setting in decreasing the incidence of distant metastases, its use—either alone or combined with leucovorin or levamisole (agents demonstrated to improve results in colonic and/or rectal cancer in certain clinical situations)—could be of benefit in improving long-term survival. Clearly it would be helpful to have other systemic agents available or other methods of drug delivery to decrease the incidence of distant metastases further, but no other regimens have yet been shown to be of value.

A major question which is yet unanswered is whether IORT is superior to other methods of delivering boost doses of radiation. As mentioned above, it is possible to deliver a radiation boost by the use of external beam therapy (if small bowel can be removed from the field). Of even greater interest is the use of an intraoperative brachytherapy boost using a temporary implant with iridium 192 or a permanent implant with iodine 125. Although this approach has been used at a number of centers, there is no large body of information that would permit a comparison of the results with these approaches to those obtained with IORT. Regardless of which type of radiation boost is used, the suggestion that long-term cure and local control can be improved with high-dose, carefully directed radiation therapy is an exciting development.

REFERENCES

1. Dosoretz DE, Gunderson LL, Hedberg S, et al: Preoperative irradiation for unresectable rectal and rectosigmoid carcinomas. *Cancer* 52:814–818, 1983.
2. Emami B, Pilepich M, Willett C, et al: Effect of preoperative irradiation on resectability of colorectal carcinomas. *Int J Radiat Oncol Biol Phys* 8:1295–1299, 1982.
3. Stevens KR, Fletcher WS: High dose pre-operative irradiation for unresectable adenocarcinoma of the rectum or sigmoid. *Int J Radiat Oncol Biol Phys* 9:148, 1983.
4. Gilette EL, Powers BE, McChesney SL, et al: Response of aorta and branch arteries to experimental intraoperative irradiation. *Int J Radiat Oncol Biol Phys* 17:1247–1255, 1989.
5. Sindelar WF, Morrow BM, Travis EL, et al: Effects of intraoperative electron irradiation in the dog on cell turnover in intact and surgically anastomosed aorta and intestine. *Int J Radiat Oncol Biol Phys* 9:523, 1983.
6. Sindelar WF, Tepper JE, Travis EL, et al: Tolerance of retroperitoneal structures to intraoperative radiation. *Ann Surg* 196:601, 1982.
7. Tepper JE, Sindelar WF, Travis E, et al: Tolerance of canine anastomoses to intraoperative radiation therapy. *Int J Radiat Oncol Biol Phys* 9:987, 1983.
8. Gillette EL, Powers BE, McChesney SL, et al: Aortic wall

injury following intraoperative irradiation. *Int J Radiat Oncol Biol Phys* 15:6:1401–1406, 1988.

9. Gillette EL, Powers BE, McChesney SL, et al: Response of aorta arteries to experimental intraoperative irradiation. *Int J Radiat Oncol Biol Phys* 15(suppl 1):202–203, 1988.
10. LeCouteur RA, Gillette EL, Powers BE, et al: Response of peripheral nerves to experimental intraoperative radiotherapy. *Int J Radiat Oncol Biol Phys* 15(suppl 1):203, 1988.
11. McChesney SL, Gillette EL, Powers BE, et al: Ureteral injury following experimental intraoperative radiation. *Int J Radiat Oncol Biol Phys* 15(suppl 1): 204, 1988.
12. Powers BE, Gillette EL, McChesney SL, et al: Bone necrosis and tumor induction following experimental intraoperative irradiation. *Int J Radiat Oncol Biol Phys* 15(suppl 1):204, 1988.
13. Abe M, Takahashi M: Intraoperative radiotherapy: The Japanese experience. *Int J Radiat Oncol Biol Phys* 7:863, 1981.
14. Tepper JE, Cohen AM, Wood WC, et al: Intraoperative electron beam radiotherapy in the treatment of unresectable rectal cancer. *Arch Surg* 121:421–423, 1986.
15. Willett CG, Shellito PC, Tepper JE, et al: Intraoperative electron beam radiation therapy for recurrent locally advanced rectal or rectosigmoid carcinoma. *Cancer* 67:1504–1508, 1991.
16. Willett CG, Shellito PC, Tepper JE, et al: Intraoperative electron beam irradiation therapy for primary locally advanced rectal and rectosigmoid carcinoma. *J Clin Oncol* 9:843–849, 1991.
17. Gunderson LL, Martin JK, Beart RW: Intraoperative and external beam irradiation for locally advanced colorectal cancer. *Ann Surg* 207:52–60, 1988.
18. Gunder LL, Dozois RR: Intraoperative irradiation for locally advanced colorectal carcinomas. *Perspec Colon Rectal Surg* 5:1–23, 1992.
19. Calvo FA, Algarra SM, Azinovic I, et al: Intraoperative radiotherapy for recurrent and/or residual colorectal cancer. *Radiother Oncol* 15:133–140, 1989.
20. Wooley PV, Ayoob MJ, Smith FP, et al: A controlled trial of the effect of 4-hydroxy-pyrazolopyrimidine (allopurinol) on the toxicity of a single bolus dose of 5-fluorouracil. *J Clin Oncol* 3:103–109, 1985.

PART 13

Follow-up after Potentially Curative Treatment

CHAPTER 75

Rationale for Follow-up Strategies

Sandip R. Parikh
Fadi F. Attiyeh

HIGHLIGHTS

Follow-up strategies are designed for early recognition of local/regional recurrences or metastases that are amenable to cure with a second operation. Approximately 50 percent of the patients who undergo a "curative" operation are found to develop a recurrence. The remainder cured by primary surgery are at increased risk of developing a second colorectal cancer or a second primary cancer in another organ.

Recurrence of colorectal cancer may be local, distant, or both and depends largely on the site and histology of the tumor. It can occur at any time after the primary resection, but the majority of recurrences appear during the first 18 to 24 months after the initial surgery. Follow-up strategies should therefore be more intensive during the initial 2 years and can be less frequent thereafter.

Knowledge of the patterns of recurrence based on tumor characteristics and adverse prognostic indicators will help guide the follow-up evaluation appropriately and result in earlier detection. A number of methods are currently used in surveillance for recurrence of colorectal cancer. These range from simple history and physical examination to sophisticated radiologic studies. Reliance on clinical assessment alone has not proved to be adequate. Certain laboratory and radiologic studies, as well as patient education, should be a part of the follow-up schedule.

Early detection of colorectal cancer recurrence can be a daunting and costly task in this era of budget cuts and cost containment, especially since the rewards are few when looked upon in the context of the vast number of patients treated for colorectal cancer every year. However, the rewards are real, and some patients can be cured as a result of diligent follow-up.

CONTROVERSIES

Intuitively, close follow-up is quite sensible in view of the risk of recurrent cancer, metachronous cancer, and cancer in other organs following surgery for colorectal cancer. The value of long-term clinical follow-up after curative surgery for colorectal carcinoma remains controversial. One can find studies in the literature supporting follow-up and aggressive surgery for recurrent disease because they are found to result in prolonged survival. One can also find studies that fail to demonstrate any benefit of postoperative follow-up. Most studies are retrospective and without controls or only historical controls.

It is not known whether more local recurrences can be resected when detected at planned follow-up examinations. There is no evidence that the rate of curative reoperation of local recurrences discovered during follow-up visits is actually increasing. Whether the morbidity and mortality from colorectal carcinoma are reduced as a result of close follow-up is not known. Reported rates of recurrence after reoperation for recurrent colorectal cancer are as high as 60 percent, and most of these patients die of their disease. Despite aggressive follow-up, 60 to 80 percent of recurrences present with a systemic dissemination of the carcinoma.

Survival with untreated recurrent colorectal cancer is extremely poor. The median survival is about 5 months. If this is compared to the median survival after reoperation for recurrent colorectal cancer, which is reported to be as long as 60 months, the advantages of a follow-up program become evident.

FUTURE DIRECTIONS

Does follow-up after curative resection for colorectal cancer result in an earlier recognition of recurrences? Does it lead to earlier and more effective treatment? The existing studies in the literature have not answered these questions definitively. Prospective investigations of follow-up versus no follow-up are lacking. Controlled, prospective studies that test the effectiveness of follow-up versus no follow-up are desirable and needed.

Until such studies come forth, experience suggests that some degree of follow-up is beneficial in patients with a resected colorectal cancer. The follow-up ought to be meticulous yet practical, cost-effective, and simple. The early detection of recurrent cancer, a second primary colorectal cancer, or a second primary cancer in another organ may offer the only hope of long-term disease-free survival—by way of a second curative operation—that these patients have.

DETECTION OF RECURRENT CANCER

Surgical resection of carcinoma of the colon and rectum does not always result in long-term cure. The biological behavior of the particular carcinoma plays a major role in determining eventual outcome. The cure rates for patients who have undergone resection of carcinoma of the colon and rectum have remained stationary for the past 40 years. In fact, about 50 percent of all patients undergoing a "curative" resection eventually develop recurrent disease.[1] Unfortunately, the majority of these patients are not curable by surgery, which is the only treatment modality at present that can result in a potential cure. However, a certain number of patients with recurrent disease can be offered a curative reresection, especially with early detection of the recurrence. A palliative resection may also be of benefit to some of these patients.

Follow-up strategies are aimed at the early diagnosis of recurrent disease and the selection of those patients who might benefit from reoperation. The value of long-term clinical follow-up of patients after curative colorectal resection remains controversial. There are many studies in the literature crediting follow-up and aggressive surgery for recurrent disease resulting in prolonged survival.[2–6] Other studies[7–10] have failed to demonstrate any great benefit of the "classic" postoperative follow-up schedules. In an international symposium concerning the management of recurrent colorectal cancer,[11] authorities on the subject had differing views on whether earlier diagnosis and treatment of recurrent disease resulted in a sufficiently improved survival rate to justify the cost and the effort.

From personal experience, resection of recurrent disease has resulted in prolonged 5-year survival rates in patients with anastomotic and mesenteric recurrence, abdominal wall implants, ovarian and groin metastases, and also hepatic and pulmonary metastases.[12,13] There is a selected group of individuals for whom a cure can still be achieved or quality of life improved if recurrent tumor is recognized early.

Recurrence of colonic and rectal carcinoma can theoretically develop at any time following the initial curative operation. The risk is directly related to the stage and the presence or absence of adverse pathologic features of the primary tumor. For reasons related to the biological behavior of the tumor, host factors, or largely unknown conditions, tumor cells can remain dormant for varying periods of time until they manifest with obvious recurrent disease. The majority of recurrences, however, occur within the first 24 months after the initial surgery (Table 75-1). The data in Table 75-1 include figures for both colonic and rectal cancers. The risk of recurrence is noted to decrease exponentially as time goes on. The recurrence rates vary from 8 to 50 percent in several series. Numerous factors responsible for the variability have significant implications in follow-up strategies.

Factors that influence the rate of recurrence include stage, histology, gross appearance, lymphatic and stromal reaction, venous invasion, perineural invasion, and margin of clearance of the primary tumor.[14] The site of recurrence may be local in the operative field (anastomotic, perianastomotic, perineal, pelvic wall, and anterior genitourinary, as classified by Pilipshen),[15] distant from the site of the primary tumor (liver, lung, ovary, bone, brain), or a combination of both.

In general, the most common site of colorectal cancer recurrence is the liver, followed by local recurrence at the primary site of resection, including the anastomoses. In Table 75-2, the pattern of recurrence from several studies is presented. More recently, a trend toward decreased incidence of local as compared

Table 75-1
Time to Recurrence after Curative Resection of Colorectal Cancer

Study	*No. of patients*	*No. of recurrences*	*Median time, months*
Polk and Spratt,[24] 1971	386	121 (31%)	18
Makela and Haukipuro,[89] 1982	173	81 (47%)	13
Schiessel et al.,[90] 1985	915	156 (22%)	12
McDermott et al.,[91] 1985	934	191 (20%)	20
Sugarbaker et al.,[2] 1987	66	33 (50%)	17
Ovaska et al.,[6] 1989	402	120 (30%)	7
Hulton and Hargreaves,[8] 1989	114	38 (33%)	19
Michelassi et al.,[21] 1990	627	50 (8%)	18
Camunas et al.,[9] 1991	151	61 (40%)	10
Galandiuk et al.,[18] 1992	818	353 (43%)	17
Safi et al.,[92] 1993	1054	350 (33%)	38

to distant recurrence was demonstrated. This may be a reflection of the effects of adjuvant therapy. Rosen et al.[16] reported that local recurrence appeared much earlier in patients with Dukes C lesions than in those with Dukes B lesions (6 months versus 21.5 months). However, once recurrence appeared, differences in survival time from recurrence to death were not significant.

The first site of recurrence in more recent studies[17,18] was either distant alone or distant combined with a regional location in the majority of patients except those with rectal cancers. The most frequent sites of recurrence were hepatic and pulmonary, 33 and 22 percent, respectively.

Carcinoma of the rectum may exhibit two different patterns of growth: (1) infiltrative, without lymph node involvement, associated with a higher rate of local recurrence because of direct extension, and (2) lesions with lymphatic involvement and a high incidence of distant recurrence due to lymphatic or hematogenous spread.[18] Transmural rectal carcinomas, with or without positive nodes, are associated with significantly more local recurrences than comparable colonic carcinomas. This demonstrates the propensity of rectal cancer to spread laterally to the pelvis and the uncertainty of surgical removal of this disease.

The histology of the primary tumor has a direct bearing on the risks of recurrent disease and perhaps the success in its retreatment. Several studies[17,19–21] revealed higher rates of local recurrence in patients with poorly differentiated cancers as compared with well- or moderately well-differentiated ones (Table 75-3). The incidence of local recurrence increased as the site of the primary tumor progressed more distally (Table 75-4).

Knowledge of the patterns of recurrence—based on the tumor characteristics and adverse prognostic factors (Table 75-5)—permits more specific follow-up evaluation and may allow earlier detection at a time when effective reoperation is feasible.

Early detection of recurrence and a radical approach to reoperative surgery will benefit some patients in the short run by extending good quality of life and may possibly benefit a few patients in the long run by improving survival. When technically feasible, the best chance of cure of a recurrence is reresection. The results of surgical treatment of local recurrence are seen in Table 75-6. Surgical procedures for local recurrences include abdominoperineal resection, sacral resection, pelvic exenteration, and reresection and anastomosis. Some authors[22,23] believe that pelvic recurrence is not curable by operation or any other mo-

Table 75-2
Pattern of Recurrence of Colorectal Cancer

Study	*Percentage of local recurrence*	*Percentage of distant recurrence*
Gunderson and Sosin,[93] 1974	50	50
Welch and Donaldson,[94] 1978	25	75
Olson et al.,[17] 1980	33	67
Rosen et al.,[16] 1982	23	77
Galandiuk et al.,[18] 1992	21	79
Safi et al.,[92] 1993	21	79

Table 75-3
Recurrence by Histology

Well differentiated	110 patients	Recurrences	21 (19.0%)
		Regional	5 (4.5)%
		Distant	11 (10.0%)
		Both	5 (4.5%)
Moderately well differentiated	144 patients	Recurrences	39 (27.1%)
		Regional	14 (9.7%)
		Distant	18 (12.5%)
		Both	7 (4.9%)
Poorly differentiated	27 patients	Recurrences	9 (33.3%)
		Regional	5 (18.5%)
		Distant	3 (11.1%)
		Both	1 (3.7%)

SOURCE: Olson et al.[17] With permission.

dality. Although no long-term cures were seen, significant palliation was achieved.

Survival with untreated recurrent colorectal carcinoma is very poor. Polk and Spratt[24] reported a median survival of about 5 months after initial detection of recurrence for 48 patients who received no treatment directed toward ablation of the residual cancer. Comparing these data with those in Table 75-6, the advantages of follow-up strategies are clearly evident, especially when a curative reresection is feasible.

As mentioned earlier, colonic and rectal carcinoma can recur at any time after the initial operation. Mayo and Schlicke[25] observed that 7 percent of patients dying within 30 days of a curative resection, presumably of operative and postoperative complications, had residual carcinoma discovered at autopsy. Operations that seem to be curative are sometimes not actually so.

The follow-up of patients should begin soon after curative resection of the colorectal cancer and should be carried out indefinitely. The goal of the follow-up strategy is to identify recurrence at the presymptomatic and hopefully treatable stage. A number of methods are currently used in surveillance for recurrent colorectal cancer. To select an optimal regimen of studies, one must know which patients are likely to have recurrence, when they will have the recurrence, and the site at which it will develop.

Evaluations during follow-up visits should be intensive and complete. History and physical examinations should be comprehensive, taking note of new symptomatology and abnormal physical findings. Many physicians feel that physical examination is unrewarding for identifying an early recurrence. By the time palpation of the abdomen reveals a tumor in the liver or recurrent disease in the peritoneal cavity, the cancer is said to be unresectable. However, some prospective studies[2,26] have shown that certain symptoms, physical findings, or both may provide the first indication of recurrent tumor in 21 to 48 percent of cases. Symptoms that should raise suspicion of recurrence include coughing, abdominal or pelvic pain, change in bowel habits, rectal bleeding, bone pain, weight loss, anorexia, and malaise.

Detection of occult blood in the stool is of little value to diagnose recurrent carcinoma because the vast majority of recurrences are extraluminal and do not disrupt the colonic mucosa. Beart and O'Connell[26] reported that only 6 out of 48 patients with recurrent carcinoma had occult blood in the stool. However, fecal occult blood testing is simple and inexpensive, and it should be used routinely to screen for anastomotic

Table 75-4
Percentage of Local Recurrence by Location by Primary Cancer in the Colon and Rectum

Location	*No. of patients*	*Local recurrence*
Cecum	90	4 (4.4%)
Ascending colon	50	3 (6.0%)
Transverse colon	75	5 (6.7%)
Descending colon	80	7 (8.8%)
Sigmoid colon	184	13 (7.1%)
Rectum	148	18 (12.0%)

SOURCE: Michelassi et al.[21] With permission.

Table 75-5
Adverse Prognostic Factors in Colorectal Cancer

Male versus female	$p = .015$
Rectal location versus colon	$p = .0015$
Dukes C versus B	$p = .0001$
Grade 3 to 4 versus 1 to 2	$p = .0329$
Adhesion/invasion versus none	$p = .001$
Perforation versus none	$p = .0006$
Nondiploid versus diploid	$p = .001$

SOURCE: Galandiuk et al.[18] With permission.

Table 75-6
Results of Curative Surgical Therapy of Local Recurrence

Study	*Number of patients*	*Number of patients reresected*	*Median survival, months*
Bacon and Berkley,[95] 1959	79	32 (41%)	36
Schiessel et al.,[90] 1985	126	53 (42%)	17
Wanebo et al.,[96] 1986	28	24 (86%)	36
Ovaska et al.,[5] 1990	112	25 (22%)	60
Camunas et al.,[9] 1991	61	6 (10%)	40
Martin and Carey,[4] 1991	86	40 (47%)	60

recurrences. Its main advantage is in the detection of metachronous colorectal cancers. A 5-year prospective study by Crowson et al.[27] showed that screening for occult blood detected anastomotic recurrence in 7.2 percent of patients, compared with 2.1 percent detected historically. In this study, patients were tested every 3 months for 5 years or until recurrence was noted. Half of the patients with recurrence had a curative resection, with a 5-year survival of 30 percent. In the most recent randomized trial,[28] annual fecal occult blood testing decreased the 13-year cumulative mortality for primary colorectal cancer by 33 percent.

Digital rectal examination, palpation for groin nodes, pelvic examinations in females, and rigid sigmoidoscopy are simple and should be done at each follow-up office visit, particularly if the anastomosis is within reach of the scope (20 to 25 cm). Flexible sigmoidoscopy can be used in lieu of rigid sigmoidoscopy, but its use requires more staffing in the office and better preparation by the patient. This method of follow-up is of considerable importance after such operations as low anterior resection and local excision of rectal cancer.

Colonoscopy and/or barium enema are important in the initial workup of the index carcinoma and in the follow-up of patients after curative resection. Colonoscopy is preferred over barium enema because of its therapeutic capabilities. The probability of finding synchronous lesions with the index cancer is high, and their detection is desirable, as it may lead to a modification of the primary operative procedure. In some situations—such as an obstructing tumor, perforation, or various medical emergencies—colonoscopy may not have been performed preoperatively. If this is the case, it should be employed early on in the follow-up period for detection of the "missed" synchronous lesions. Reilly et al.[29] performed perioperative colonoscopy on 92 patients and found synchronous cancers in 8 percent. An additional 8 percent had metachronous cancers after 3 or more years following treatment of the index cancer.

A true suture-line recurrence is uncommon. In the study by Galandiuk et al.,[18] of 353 patients with recurrent colorectal cancer, only 5.6 percent had recurrent intraluminal disease. Colonoscopy should be a part of postoperative monitoring for detecting "missed" synchronous and metachronous polyps and cancers. Several reports[30–32] have demonstrated that the majority of these cancers detected by surveillance colonoscopy were asymptomatic, mostly localized, and resectable for cure.

Chest x-rays should be performed annually as part of the follow-up schedule to identify patients with pulmonary metastases. The odds are equally divided for a new lesion on chest x-ray to be either a primary lung tumor or a metastatic lesion.[33] Resection of a solitary lung lesion that is metastatic from a primary colorectal carcinoma has a better chance of cure than does a primary lung carcinoma.[33] McCormack and Attiyeh[12] reported a 5-year survival rate of 22 percent following resection of the pulmonary metastases. Other studies[34,35] have also reported 5-year survival rates between 14 and 21 percent.

More sophisticated imaging techniques—such as ultrasound, computed tomography (CT), magnetic resonance imaging (MRI), liver and spleen scintigraphy, and radioimmunoscintigraphy—have been used to detect recurrent or metastatic colorectal cancer. These tests are not cost-effective and not warranted on a routine follow-up basis. A prospective evaluation[2] of several of these imaging methods revealed that they identified tumor recurrence in only 4 of 33 documented cases of recurrent carcinoma. Abdominal CT scan, when used in a routine manner as part of the follow-up schedule, had a high false-positive rate (45 percent). These tests should be reserved for use when there is suspicion of recurrence based on clinical and laboratory evaluation.

Imaging of liver recurrences is important because resection of hepatic metastases is an established and widely accepted modality, with a 5-year survival rate of 35 percent.[13,36,37] The survival rate is not significantly different between patients with a solitary metastasis and those with multiple lesions, and it is not influenced by the size of the metastasis.[13] Whereas CT can detect 50 percent of liver recurrences, radioimmunoguided surgery (RIGS) has a sensitivity of 89 percent in detecting recurrent disease.[38,39] Its major drawback is the 3- to 4-week waiting period. There are ongoing efforts to develop new monoclonal antibodies for more accurate detection of recurrent cancer.

Clinical assessment rarely produces sufficient information to allow timely surgery for recurrence. Wangensteen,[40] in 1948, initiated the concept of planned second-look laparotomy following curative resection of Dukes C carcinoma of the colon and rectum. This was performed on asymptomatic patients 6 to 9 months following the primary surgery and also on symptomatic patients with suspected recurrence. More patients in the asymptomatic group were rendered disease-free, but the overall resectability rate was low.

Since the discovery of carcinoembryonic antigen (CEA) in 1965, it has been used extensively in the follow-up of patients after curative resection of cancer of the large bowel. Although CEA is not useful in screening patients with colorectal cancer, its determination preoperatively may correlate with tumor histology and pathologic stage,[41–43] risk of recurrence,[44] and prognosis.[45–47] CEA levels are raised in 95 percent of patients with well-differentiated tumors, while they are raised in only 30 percent of those with poorly differentiated adenocarcinomas. The percentage of patients with elevated CEA levels increases proportionately with the Dukes stage (A to C) and 80 to 90 percent of patients with liver metastases have elevated levels.[48] Herrera et al.[44] found that only 35 percent of those with normal preoperative CEA values developed clinical evidence of recurrence by 18 months, compared to 83 percent of those with an elevated preoperative CEA level. If preoperative plasma CEA levels are elevated, they will become normal in nearly all patients after complete resection of the carcinoma. If they do not fall into the normal range within 1 to 4 months postoperatively, an incomplete resection should be suspected.

Plasma CEA determination has become the hallmark of follow-up aimed at detecting recurrent disease. Of importance is defining an abnormal CEA level. In addition, CEA levels from different laboratories should not be compared because of differences in the calibration of the assays. It must be emphasized that in up to 12 percent of patients, a transient rise in CEA level may not be due to recurrent disease and can be attributed to some intercurrent disease affecting another system or to a change in smoking or drinking habits.[49] In another study, of 663 patients,[50] 14.2 percent were found to have transient elevations of CEA postoperatively without subsequent recurrence. These transient elevations in CEA can usually be distinguished from the consistent rise produced by recurrent cancer.

Several investigators have documented the usefulness of plasma CEA monitoring as a predictor of recurrent cancer (Table 75-7). These studies reflect the results of second-look laparotomies based on CEA elevations. The sensitivity of elevated CEA levels in predicting recurrent disease is noted to be 62 to 95 percent. In documented cases of recurrence, the CEA levels were elevated in 68 to 83 percent of patients.[2,6,7,51,52] In general, the group with resectable disease had lower preoperative (second-look surgery) CEA elevations, shorter time delays, and slower rate of elevations than the unresectable group.[11] In the group of patients that are reresected, a 5-year survival of at least 26 percent is noted. It is therefore essential that CEA levels be determined frequently following curative resections for colorectal carcinoma and that abnormally elevated values be acted upon promptly. It has been estimated that postoperative CEA monitoring may provide a lead time for the detection of recurrence of up to 4.5 months.[53]

To clarify the issue of whether CEA-prompted second-look surgery decreases mortality and morbidity, Northover and Slack,[54] in the United Kingdom, launched a prospective, randomized, controlled study involving 2000 patients. Patients are monitored clinically and by CEA levels after radical primary surgery; clinicians are blinded to routine CEA results. If a CEA

Table 75-7
Predictive Value of Plasma CEA Level in Recurrent Colorectal Cancer

Study	*Number of patients with elevated CEA*	*Number of recurrences*
Martin et al.,[97] 1980	53	46 (87%)
Attiyeh and Stearns,[3] 1981	53	46 (87%)
Minton,[98] 1985	146	139 (95%)
Wilking et al.,[99] 1986	36	27 (75%)
Schiessel et al.,[90] 1986	16	15 (94%)
Barillari,[55] 1989	34	21 (62%)
Wanebo et al.,[100] 1989	45	42 (93%)

rise is recorded by the Trials Center, randomization into "CEA Aggressive" and "CEA Conventional" arms occurs. Patients in the "Aggressive" arm undergo second-look laparotomy after exclusion of distant incurable metastases. Those in the "Conventional" arm are managed by clinical detection of recurrence alone. Morbidity and mortality were to be compared at 5 years. Until the results of this study are available for review, the CEA level will remain the mainstay in the follow-up scheme. It represents the best chance for improving patient survival in recurrent carcinoma of the colon and rectum.

Because of the limited specificity of CEA as a tumor marker, the search for a specific marker for colonic and rectal cancer continues. Other tumor markers such as CA 19-9, tissue polypeptide antigen,[55] villin,[56] carbohydrate CA-50,[57] and various tumor associated antigens[48] have been shown to be useful in the follow-up of patients with colorectal cancer. As indicators of recurrent disease, their role is not well defined and their use is not as widely accepted as that of CEA.

Patient education, although not proven, should also be a part of the follow-up strategy. Active patient involvement in the detection of recurrence may increase awareness, leading to better recognition of specific signs and symptoms and allowing for earlier detection. Patient compliance will improve as the benefits of early detection of recurrence are realized. The demands of follow-up may exceed institutional resources. In the present state of increased health care cost awareness, a planned patient education program, both preoperatively and as an integral part of the postoperative follow-up, may prove to be beneficial.

DETECTION OF OTHER TUMORS OF THE LARGE BOWEL

The goals of the follow-up of patients after resection of colorectal carcinomas should include detection of metachronous primary colorectal adenomas and cancers. It is reasonable to speculate that if one area of the colonic mucosa develops a tumor, there is an increased chance that other portions of the mucosa, being continuously subjected to the insult of one or more factors that are presently largely unknown and which possibly caused the original tumor, will then develop one or more additional lesions. Synchronous lesions are present in approximately 30 to 40 percent of patients with colorectal cancer. Most of these are benign adenomas and only about 2 to 4 percent are malignant.[1,58,59]

Ideally, synchronous lesions should be identified before operation for the index cancer with the help of colonoscopy and/or barium enema examination. If this is not feasible, as in conditions of surgical emergency, obstruction, or perforation, the remainder of the colon should be examined within 6 months after the surgery.

Even if the colon and rectum are completely cleared of all neoplastic lesions at the time of the initial operation, true metachronous cancers can develop. This occurs in 2 to 6 percent of patients within 3 to 20 years.[60–62] Bulow et al.[63] reported the appearance of metachronous cancers in 9 percent of patients who were under 40 years of age at the time of curative resection and followed for 41 years. The cumulative risk of developing a metachronous colorectal cancer was 30 percent after 41 years of observation. In the same study, of 44 patients with metachronous colorectal cancer, 27 (61%) underwent curative reresection. The 5-year survival rate was 53 percent, comparable to that in other series.[64,65] These results are not different from those associated with the index cancer.[66]

The incidence of metachronous adenomas after polypectomy for adenomas is about 30 to 50 percent, and some of these patients may develop colorectal cancer.[67–69] Lofti et al.[70] reported a threefold increase in the risk of developing a primary colorectal carcinoma in patients who have had an adenoma compared to that in the general population. The adenoma-carcinoma sequence is now well accepted.[71] Gilbertsen and Nelms[72] have shown that regular proctosigmoidoscopy with removal of new adenomas can reduce the expected incidence of rectal carcinoma by 85 percent.

Hyperplastic polyps are considered nonneoplastic and are not regarded as playing a role in the adenoma-carcinoma sequence.[73] Recently,[68] it has been shown that the combination of multiple adenomas and hyperplastic polyps was a good predictor for the development of new adenomas. In patients with multiple adenomas and synchronous hyperplastic polyps, there was a threefold increase in the likelihood of developing new adenomas compared to those patients having adenomas without concomitant hyperplastic polyps. Collectively, clinical, histologic, and immunohistochemical studies[73] suggest that there are similarities between hyperplastic polyps and colorectal carcinomas, but the exact cellular mechanisms remain unknown. Although the relationship of hyperplastic polyps to adenomas and carcinomas is still unresolved, all colorectal polyps should be removed to prevent possible precancerous lesions from being left behind. Patients with hyperplastic polyps should be followed as frequently as those with adenomas.

DETECTION OF OTHER PRIMARY TUMORS IN OTHER ORGANS

A person who has had colorectal cancer is more likely to develop primary cancers in other organs than a person without prior history of cancer. Several studies[74–78] have demonstrated that the overall relative risk

Table 75-8
Relative Risk of Second Primary Cancers following Cancers of the Colon and Rectum

Site of second cancer	*Sex*	*Relative risk*	*(95% confidence)*
Kidney	Male	1.5	(1.2–2.0)
	Female	1.5	(1.1–2.0)
Bladder	Male	1.5	(1.2–1.8)
	Female	2.0	(1.4–2.6)
Breast	Female	1.3	(1.2–1.5)
Endometrium	Female	1.7	(1.3–2.2)
Cervix	Female	1.1	(0.7–1.6)
Ovary	Female	3.0	(2.5–3.5)
Prostate	Male	1.3	(1.1–1.4)

SOURCE: Adapted from Enblad et al.[78]

of developing a second primary cancer is 30 percent greater than that in a population with no cancers. Excluding metachronous colorectal cancers, the most common second primary sites in men are the bladder, kidney, and prostate and in women the ovary, bladder, endometrium, kidney, breast, and cervix (Table 75-8).

Some studies[75,77,78] have also shown that there is an increased risk of developing rectal carcinoma after colonic carcinoma, and vice versa. The subsequent risk of bladder and kidney cancer was increased only after colonic cancer, not rectal cancer, and was increased during the entire 14 years of follow-up after the index cancer. A 30 percent increased risk of breast cancer was noted, supporting the association between colorectal and breast cancer. This is also suggested by a Swedish study[79] on breast cancer reporting a 20 percent increased risk of subsequent colonic cancer. The risk of subsequent cancer of the ovary is also increased mainly after colonic cancer and remains for many years. However, prophylactic oophorectomy during surgery for colorectal cancer is still not widely accepted.[80]

Colorectal carcinoma may present as part of the cancer family syndrome (CFS), also known as hereditary nonpolyposis colorectal cancer (HNPCC) and Lynch syndromes.[81] In addition to early onset of colorectal cancers, HNPCC family members are at increased risk for cancers of the gastrointestinal tract organs and, especially in some families, cancers of the upper urologic and female genital tract. The most common extracolonic tumors associated with CFS are endometrial and gastric carcinomas. Other less common sites include small intestine, renal pelvis and ureter, ovary, and the biliary tract.[82]

Colorectal adenomas may be found in up to 30 percent of patients with the Lynch syndromes.[83] They are more proximally located, corresponding to the site of cancer distribution in the Lynch syndromes. A high rate of synchronous and metachronous lesions is also found. While colonoscopic follow-up of adenomas in patients not selected for the Lynch syndrome yields metachronous lesions in 3 to 18 percent,[84] that in Lynch syndrome patients will yield 86 percent.[83] Because of the early age of onset of colorectal cancer in patients with the Lynch syndrome, yearly colonoscopy beginning at age 25 and aggressive follow-up of even diminutive polyps is recommended.

Multiple primary malignant neoplasia (MPMN) involves the presence of more than one primary malignant tumor in any one patient. In a large study from the Mayo clinic,[85] of 37,500 patients with a malignancy, 1900 had two malignancies, 74 had three, 4 had four, and 1 had five. The highest number of primary cancers in a single patient is seven.[86] In all these patients, colonic cancer is invariably present. In patients with five or more cancers, the natural history is similar in that they are often locally advanced yet rarely metastasize. These patients survive far longer than would be predicted from the stage of their tumors.

The frequency of multiple synchronous primary cancers depends upon the thoroughness of examination and investigation. The number of new lesions detected after initial therapy for colorectal carcinoma is dependent upon the length and accuracy of the follow-up schemes. Polk et al.[87] reported a 33 percent incidence of subsequent primary cancers in patients surviving at least 5 years after diagnosis of their initial colorectal carcinoma. Unless such persons are carefully followed up indefinitely at frequent intervals, most of them will succumb to their new primary cancers.

GUIDELINES FOR FOLLOW-UP

The optimal chance for cure of colonic and rectal cancer is during the primary operation. However, from the above discussion, it is realized that recurrent, synchronous, and metachronous cancers occur in a significant number of patients. Recurrent disease will not be found unless it is looked for. Knowledge of the pat-

Table 75-9
Suggested Frequency of Follow-up Examinations after Curative Resection of Cancer of the Colon and Rectum

	Frequency of examinations per year				
Follow-up method	*Year 1*	*Year 2*	*Year 3*	*Year 4*	*>4 years*
Hx and physical (including groin and pelvic)	3–4	3–4	2	2	1
Occult fecal blood	3–4	3–4	2	2	1
Rigid or flexible sigmoidoscopy[a]	3–4	3–4	2	2	1
Plasma CEA level	3–4	3–4	2	2	1
Colonoscopy or barium enema[b]	1	—	—	1	q 3 years
Chest x-ray	1	1	1	1	1
CT, MRI, US[c]	—	—	—	—	—

[a]For rectal or rectosigmoid cancer patients.

[b]If colon was not cleared preoperatively, then colonoscopy/barium enema should be performed within 6 months postoperatively. If cleared, then every 3 years is sufficient follow-up.

[c]These tests are used only if there is suspicion of recurrence.

terns of recurrence based on tumor characteristics will allow for the most effective follow-up protocol.

The value of different follow-up schemes after radical surgery for colorectal cancer has not been proven. A review from St. Mark's Hospital, London,[60] pointed out the difference in prognosis in patients who developed a second cancer while attending a follow-up clinic regularly as compared with those who did not. The 41 tumors in the follow-up group were diagnosed earlier, and approximately 70 percent were at Dukes stage A or B. Of the 17 patients, 8 in the non-follow-up group had inoperable growths at the time of diagnosis. Polk and Spratt[88] implemented a follow-up program at a metropolitan university hospital and reported that the detection of apparently localized disease increased from 9 to 36 percent of all recurrences. Unfortunately, prospective, randomized, controlled studies to validate follow-up strategies do not exist at the present time.

Based on the currently available information, the recommended guidelines for routine surveillance after curative resection for colorectal carcinoma are shown in Table 75-9. Primary tumors in the colon tend to recur at distant sites and those in the rectum tend to recur locally. Of all recurrences, 50 percent manifest within 24 months and 85 percent do so within 30 months after resection.

There are several benefits from continued follow-up in patients with a resected colorectal cancer. The follow-up must be acceptable to the patient, meticulous yet practical, cost-effective, and simplified. Follow-up allows the health care system to analyze the results of treatment and compare these results with those of other institutions and groups. The early detection of recurrent cancer, a second primary colorectal cancer, or a second primary cancer in another site may be the only hope for these patients of a second curative operation with the potential for long-term disease-free survival.

REFERENCES

1. Attiyeh FF: Guidelines for the follow-up of patients with carcinomas and adenomas of the colon and rectum, in Stearns MW (ed): *Neoplasms of the Colon, Rectum, and Anus*. New York, Wiley, 1980.
2. Sugarbaker PH, Gianola FJ, Dwyer A, et al: A simplified plan for follow-up of patients with colon and rectal cancer supported by prospective studies of laboratory and radiologic test results. *Surgery* 102:79–87, 1987.
3. Attiyeh FF, Stearns MW: Second-look laparotomy based on CEA elevations in colorectal cancer. *Cancer* 47:2119–2125, 1981.
4. Martin EW Jr, Carey LC: Second-look surgery for colorectal cancer: The second time around. *Ann Surg* 214:321–327, 1991.
5. Ovaska JT, Jarvinen HJ, Kujari H, et al: Follow-up of patients operated on for colorectal carcinoma. *Am J Surg* 159:593–596, 1990.
6. Ovaska JT, Jarvinen HJ, Mecklin JP: The value of followup programme after radical surgery for colorectal carcinoma. *Scand J Gastroenterol* 24:416–422, 1989.
7. Beart RW, Metzger PP, O'Connell MJ, et al: Postoperative screening of patients with carcinoma of the colon. *Dis Colon Rectum* 24:585–589, 1981.
8. Hulton NR, Hargreaves AW: Is long-term follow-up of all colorectal cancer necessary? *J R Coll Surg Edinb* 34:21–24, 1989.
9. Camunas J, Enriquez JM, Devesa JM, et al: Value of follow-

up in the management of recurrent colorectal cancer. *Eur J Surg Oncol* 17:530–535, 1991.
10. Kronborg O, Hage E, Deichgraeber E: Follow-up after radical surgery for colorectal cancer. Design of a randomized study. *Dis Colon Rectum* 26:172–176, 1983.
11. Sugarbaker PH, Attiyeh FF, Killingback M, et al: The management of recurrent colorectal cancer (symposium). *Int J Colorect Dis* 1:133–151, 1986.
12. McCormack PM, Attiyeh FF: Resected pulmonary metastases from colorectal cancer. *Dis Colon Rectum* 22:553–556, 1979.
13. Attiyeh FF, Wichern WA: Hepatic resection for primary and metastatic tumors. *Am J Surg* 156:368–372, 1988.
14. Feil W, Wunderlich M, Neuhild N, et al: Rectal cancer: Factors influencing the development of local recurrence after radical anterior resection. *Int J Colorect Dis* 3:195–200, 1988.
15. Pilipshen S: Cancer of the rectum: Local recurrence, in Fazio VW (ed): *Current Therapy in Colon and Rectal Surgery.* Toronoto, Decker, 1990, pp 137–149.
16. Rosen L, Veidenheimer MC, Coller JA: Mortality, morbidity, and patterns of recurrence after abdominoperineal resection for cancer of the rectum. *Dis Colon Rectum* 25:202–208, 1982.
17. Olson RM, Perencevich NP, Malcolm AW, et al: Patterns of recurrence following curative resection of adenocarcinoma of the colon and rectum. *Cancer* 45:2969–2974, 1980.
18. Galandiuk S, Moertel, CG, Fitzgibbons RJJ, et al: Patterns of recurrence after curative resection of carcinoma of the colon and rectum. *Surg Gynecol Obstet* 174:27–32, 1992.
19. Spratt JS Jr, Spjut HJ: Prevalence and prognosis of individual clinical and pathologic variables associated with colorectal carcinoma. *Cancer* 20:1976–1985, 1967.
20. Michelassi F, Block GE, V Annucci L, et al: A 5- to 21-year follow-up and analysis of 250 patients with rectal adenocarcinoma. *Ann Surg* 208:379–389, 1988.
21. Michelassi F, V Annucci L, Ayala JJ, et al: Local recurrence after curative resection of colorectal adenocarcinoma. *Surgery* 108:787–793, 1990.
22. Stearns MW Jr: Diagnosis and management of recurrent pelvic malignancy following combined abdominoperineal resection. *Dis Colon Rectum* 23:359–361, 1980.
23. Segall MM, Goldberg SM, Nivatvongs S: Abdominoperineal resection for recurrent cancer following anterior resection. *Dis Colon Rectum* 24:80–84, 1981.
24. Polk HC, Spratt JS Jr: Recurrent colorectal carcinoma: Detection, treatment and other considerations. *Surgery* 69:9–23, 1971.
25. Mayo CW, Schlicke CP: Carcinoma of the colon and rectum: A study of metastasis and recurrences. *Surg Gynecol Obstet* 74:83, 1942.
26. Beart RW Jr, O'Connell MJ: Postoperative follow-up of patients with carcinoma of the colon. *Mayo Clin Proc* 58:361–363, 1983.
27. Crowson MC, Jewkes AJ, Acheson N, et al: Haemoccult testing as an indicator of recurrent colorectal cancer: A 5-year prospective study. *Eur J Surg Oncol* 17:281–284, 1991.
28. Mandel JS, Bond JH, Church TR, et al: Reducing mortality from colorectal cancer by screening for fecal occult blood. *N Engl J Med* 328:1365–1371, 1993.
29. Reilly JC, Rusin LC, Theuerkauf FJ Jr: Colonoscopy: Its role in cancer of the colon and rectum. *Dis Colon Rectum* 25:532, 1982.
30. Brady PG, Straker RJ, Goldschmid S: Surveillance colonoscopy after resection for colon carcinoma. *South Med J* 83:765–768, 1990.
31. Juhl G, Larson GM, Mullins R, et al: Six-year results of annual colonoscopy after resection of colorectal cancer. *World J Surg* 14:255–261, 1990.
32. Michael Z, Potdar N, Nargun VH, et al: Colonoscopic surveillance after diagnosis of carcinoma of the colon and rectum. *Ann Chir* 43:568–569, 1989.
33. Cahan WG, Castro EB, Hajdu S: The significance of a solitary lung shadow in patients with colon carcinoma. *Cancer* 33:414–421, 1976.
34. Wilking N, Petrelli NJ, Herrera L, et al: Surgical resection of pulmonary metastases from colorectal adenocarcinoma. *Dis Colon Rectum* 28:562, 1985.
35. Brister SJ, de Varennes B, Gordon PH, et al: Contemporary management of pulmonary metastases of colorectal origin. *Dis Colon Rectum* 31:786, 1988.
36. Attiyeh FF, Wanebo HJ, Stearns MW: Hepatic resection for metastasis from colorectal cancer. *Dis Colon Rectum* 21:160–162, 1978.
37. August DA, Sugarbaker PH, Schneider PD: Lymphatic dissemination of hepatic metastases: Implications for the follow-up and treatment of patients with colorectal cancer. *Cancer* 55:1490–1494, 1985.
38. Nieroda CA, Mojzisik C, Sardi A, et al: The impact of radioimmunoguided surgery (RIGS TM) on surgical decision-making in colorectal cancer. *Dis Colon Rectum* 32:927–932, 1989.
39. Sardi A, Agnone CM, Nieroda CA, et al: Radioimmunogical surgery in recurrent colorectal cancer: The role of carcinoembryonic antigen, computerized tomography, and physical examination. *South Med J* 82:1235–1244, 1989.
40. Wangensteen OH: Cancer of the colon and rectum. *Wis Med J* 48:591, 1949.
41. Goslin R, Steele G, MacIntyre J, et al: The use of pre-operative plasma CEA levels for the stratification of patients after curative resection of colorectal cancer. *Ann Surg* 192:747–751, 1980.
42. Zamcheck N: CEA in diagnosis, prognosis, detection of recurrence, and evaluation of therapy of colo-rectal cancer. *Excerpta Medica* 439:64–79, 1978.
43. Armitage NC, Davidson A, Tsikos D, et al: A study of the reliability of carcinoembryonic antigen blood levels in following the course of colorectal cancer. *Clin Oncol* 10:141–147, 1984.
44. Herrera MA, Chu TM, Holyoke ED: Carcinoembryonic antigen (CEA) as a prognostic and monitoring test in clinically complete resection of colorectal carcinoma. *Ann Surg* 183:5–9, 1976.
45. Wanebo JH, Rao B, Pinsky CM, et al: Pre-operative carcinoembryonic antigen level as a prognostic indicator in colorectal cancer. *N Engl J Med* 299:448–451, 1978.
46. Arnaud JP, Koehl C, Adloff M: Carcinoembryonic antigen (CEA) in diagnosis and prognosis of colorectal carcinoma. *Dis Colon Rectum* 23:141–144, 1980.
47. Wolmark N, Fisher B, Wieand HS, et al: The prognostic significance of preoperative carcinoembryonic antigen levels in colorectal cancer: Results from NSABP clinical trials. *Ann Surg* 199:375–382, 1984.
48. Kurtzman SH, Cohen AM: Tumor markers in colorectal cancer. *Res Staff Phys* 38:57–60, 1992.
49. Rittgers RA, Steele G Jr, Zamcheck M, et al: Transient carcinoembryonic (CEA) elevations following resection of colorectal cancer: A limitation in the use of serial CEA levels as an indicator for second-look surgery. *J Natl Cancer Inst* 61:315–318, 1978.
50. Hine KR, Dykes PW: Serum CEA testing in the post-operative surveillance of colorectal carcinoma. *Br J Cancer* 49:689–693, 1984.

51. Filella X, Molina R, Bedini JLA: Clinical usefulness of CEA as tumor marker in patients with colorectal cancer. *J Nucl Med All Sci* 34:107–110, 1990.
52. Northover JMA: Carcinoembryonic antigen and recurrent colorectal cancer. *Br J Surg* 72(suppl):44–45, 1985.
53. Boey J, Cheung HC, Lai CK, et al: A prospective evaluation of serum carcinoembryonic antigen levels in the management of colorectal carcinoma. *World J Surg* 8:279–286, 1984.
54. Northover J, Slack WW: A randomized controlled trial of CEA-prompted second look surgery in recurrent colorectal cancer: A preliminary report. *Dis Colon Rectum* 27:576, 1984.
55. Barillari P, Ramacciato G, de Angelis R, et al: The role of CEA, TPA, and CA 19-9 in the early detection of recurrent colorectal cancer. *Int J Colorect Dis* 4:230–233, 1989.
56. Dudouet B, Jacob L, Beuzeboc H, et al: Presence of villin, a tissue-specific cytoskeletal protein, in sera of patients and an initial clinical evaluation of its value for the diagnosis and follow-up of colorectal cancers. *Cancer Res* 50:438–443, 1990.
57. Holmgren J, Lindholm L, Persson B, et al: Detection by monoclonal antibody of carbohydrate antigen CA-50 in serum of patients with carcinoma. *Br Med J* 288:1479–1482, 1984.
58. Howard ML, Greene FL: The effect of preoperative endoscopy on recurrence and survival following surgery for colorectal carcinoma. *Am Surg* 56:124–127, 1990.
59. Helwig EB: Adenomas and the pathogenesis of cancer of the colon and rectum. *Dis Colon Rectum* 2:5, 1959.
60. Ellis H: Recurrent cancer of the large bowel. *Br Med J* 287:1741–1742, 1983.
61. Tornqvist A, Ekelund G, Leandoer L: Early diagnosis of metachronous colorectal carcinoma. *Aust NZ J Surg* 51:442–445, 1981.
62. Luchtefeld MA, Ross DS, Zander JD, et al: Late development of metachronous colorectal cancer. *Dis Colon Rectum* 30:180–184, 1987.
63. Bulow S, Svendsen LB, Mellemgaard A: Metachronous colorectal carcinoma. *Br J Surg* 77:502–505, 1990.
64. Ekelund GR, Pihl B: Multiple carcinomas of the colon and rectum. *Cancer* 33:1630–1634, 1974.
65. Agrez MV, Ready R, Ilstrup D, et al: Metachronous colorectal malignancies. *Dis Colon Rectum* 25:569–574, 1982.
66. Kronborg O: Controversies in follow-up after colorectal carcinoma. *Theor Surg* 1:40–46, 1986.
67. Kronborg O: World progress in surgery—colorectal polyps—introduction. *World J Surg* 15:1–2, 1991.
68. Kellokumpu I, Kyllonen L: Multiple adenomas and synchronous hyperplastic polyps as predictors of metachronous colorectal adenomas. *Ann Chir Gynaeco* 80:30–35, 1991.
69. Morson BC, Bussey HJR: Magnitude of risk for cancer in patients with colorectal adenoma. *Br J Surg* 72(suppl):23, 1985.
70. Lofti AM, Spencer RJ, Ilstrup DM, et al: Colorectal polyps and the risk of subsequent carcinoma. *Mayo Clin Proc* 61:337–343, 1986.
71. Tierney RP, Ballantyne GH, Modlin IM: The adenoma to carcinoma sequence. *Surg Gynecol Obstet* 171: 81–94, 1990.
72. Gilbertsen VA, Nelms JM: The prevention of invasive cancer of the rectum. *Cancer* 41:1137–1139, 1978.
73. Jass JR: Do all colorectal carcinomas arise in preexisting adenomas? *World J Surg* 13:45–51, 1989.
74. Schoenberg BS, Myers MH: Statistical methods for studying multiple primary malignant neoplasm. *Cancer* 40(suppl): 1892–1898, 1977.
75. Hoar SK, Wilson J, Blot JW, et al: Second cancer following cancer in the digestive system in Connecticut, 1935–82, in Greenwald P (ed): *Multiple Cancers in Connecticut and Denmark*. National Cancer Institute Monograph 68. Washington DC, U.S. Government Printing Office, 1985, pp 49–82.
76. Lynge E, Jensen OM, Carstensen B: Second cancer following cancer in the digestive system in Denmark 1943–80, in Greenwald P (ed): *Multiple Cancers in Connecticut and Denmark*. National Cancer Institute Monograph 68. Washington, DC, U.S. Government Printing Office, 1985, pp 277–308.
77. Teppo L, Pukkala E, Saxen E: Multiple cancer: An epidemiologic exercise in Finland. *J Natl Cancer Inst* 75:207–217, 1985.
78. Enblad P, Adami HO, Glimelius B, et al: The risk of subsequent primary malignant diseases after cancers of the colon and rectum. *Cancer* 65:2091–2100, 1990.
79. Adami HO, Bergkvist L, Krusemo UB, et al: Breast cancer as a risk factor for other primary malignant diseases: A nationwide cohort study. *J Natl Cancer Inst* 43:77–86, 1984.
80. Dwyer WA Jr: The role of the ovary in colon cancer management. *Contemp Surg* 38:15–20, 1991.
81. Watson P, Lynch HT: Extracolonic cancer in hereditary nonpolyposis colorectal cancer. *Cancer* 71:677–685, 1993.
82. Mecklin JP, Jarvinen HJ, Virolainen M: The association between cholangiocarcinoma and hereditary nonpolyposis colorectal carcinoma. *Cancer* 69:1112–1114, 1992.
83. Lanspa SJ, Lynch HT, Smyrk TC, et al: Colorectal adenomas in the Lynch syndromes: Results of a colonoscopy screening program. *Gastroenterology* 98:1117–1122, 1990.
84. Grossman S, Milos ML, Tekawa IS, et al: Colonoscopic screening of persons with suspected risk factors for colon cancer: II. Past history of colorectal neoplasms. *Gastroenterology* 96:299–306, 1989.
85. Moertel CG, Dockerty MB, Baggenstross AH: Multiple primary malignant neoplasms. *Cancer* 14:221–248, 1961.
86. Baigrie RJ: Seven different primary cancers in a single patient: A case report and review of multiple primary malignant neoplasia. *Eur J Surg Oncol* 17:81–83, 1991.
87. Polk HC, Spratt JS, Butcher HR: Frequency of multiple primary malignant neoplasms associated with colorectal carcinoma. *Am J Surg* 109:71–75, 1965.
88. Polk HC Jr, Spratt JS: Recurrent cancer of the colon. *Surg Clin North Am* 63:151–160, 1983.
89. Makela J, Haukipuro K: Surgical treatment of recurrent colorectal cancer. *Arch Surg* 124:1029–1032, 1989.
90. Schiessel R, Wunderlich M, Herbst F: Local recurrence of colorectal cancer: Effect of early detection and aggressive surgery. *Br J Surg* 73:342–344, 1986.
91. McDermott FT, Hughes ESR, Pihl E, et al: Local recurrence after potentially curative resection for rectal cancer in a series of 1008 patients. *Br J Surg* 72:34–37, 1985.
92. Safi F, Link KH, Beger HG: Is followup of colorectal cancer patients worthwhile? *Dis Colon Rectum* 36:636–644, 1993.
93. Gunderson LL, Sosin H: Areas of failure found at reoperation (second or symptomatic look) following "curative surgery" for adenocarcinoma of the rectum: Clinicopathologic correlation and implications for adjuvant therapy. *Cancer* 34:1278–1292, 1974.
94. Welch JP, Donaldson GA: Detection and treatment of recurrent cancer of the colon and rectum. *Am J Surg* 135:505–510, 1973.
95. Bacon HE, Berkley JL: The rationale of re-resection for recurrent cancer of the colon and rectum. *Dis Colon Rectum* 2:549, 1959.
96. Wanebo HJ, Gaker DL, Whitehill R, et al: Pelvic recurrence of rectal cancer. *Ann Surg* 205:482–495, 1987.
97. Martin EW Jr, Cooperman M, Carey LC, et al: Sixty second-

look procedures indicated primarily by rise in serial carcinoembryonic antigen. *J Surg Res* 28:389–394., 1980.

98. Minton JP, Hoehn JL, Gerber DM, et al: Results of a 400 patient carcinoembryonic antigen second-look colorectal cancer study. *Cancer* 55:1284–1290, 1985.
99. Wilking N, Petrelli NJ, Herrera L, et al: Abdominal exploration for suspected recurrent carcinoma of the colon and rectum based upon elevated carcinoembryonic antigen alone or in combination with other methods. *Surg Gynecol Obstet* 162:465–468, 1986.
100. Wanebo HJ, Llaneras M, Martin T, et al: Prospective monitoring trial for carcinoma of colon and rectum after surgical resection. *Surg Gynecol Obstet* 169:479–487, 1989.

CHAPTER 76

Use of Tumor Markers and Radiologic Tests in Follow-up

Andrew M. Averbach
Paul H. Sugarbaker

HIGHLIGHTS

Thorough follow-up of colorectal cancer patients may increase the number of long-term survivors by detecting asymptomatic recurrence and new primary cancers. For that purpose, numerous methods of radiologic evaluation have been recommended, but the accuracies of these methods are quite different, as are their abilities to disclose particular sites of recurrence (local/regional, liver, intraperitoneal, lungs, etc.). Tumor markers remain the most efficacious surveillance method.

Currently, approximately 5 percent of patients subjected to follow-up can be salvaged from recurrent colon or rectal cancer by sophisticated reoperative surgery. For routine follow-up, a relatively simple and sensitive group of tests should be used in order to retain a cost-effective program. For successful use of any tumor marker or radiologic test, it is necessary to obtain the baseline value or image after bowel resection for subsequent evaluation. The goal of follow-up should be to detect a second primary or recurrent cancer by a simple, sensitive, and inexpensive group of tests (symptom review, physical examination, tumor marker assay, colonoscopy, and chest x-ray). Subsequent examinations by comprehensive and more accurate radiologic tests are performed in patients with a detected abnormality.

The intensiveness of follow-up should be adjusted to low- and high-risk recurrence groups as well as patients' suitability for further therapy by virtue of medical conditioning and age.

CONTROVERSIES

The results of tumor marker assay are dependent on the assay system used and the criteria for elevation of the marker. A progressive rise of a titer rather than a single abnormal assay reflects the progression of recurrent disease. Non-tumor elevations of a marker are frequent occurrences. Moreover, not all patients and not all anatomic sites of recurrence demonstrate an increase in tumor marker level.

The numerous radiologic methods frequently used in follow-up present a major controversy. The poor outcome as regards long-term results and the high expense of surveillance create a major cost-benefit dilemma for the whole follow-up program. It is still uncertain what tests or combinations of tests are indicated and when should they be applied to favorably influence treatment results.

FUTURE DIRECTIONS

The ability of follow-up programs to improve the overall survival of colorectal cancer patients remains to be confirmed in prospective randomized trials. In order to be cost-effective, improved patient selection for follow-up programs based on molecular and biological assays of the primary tumor will be required.

Approximately 30 to 40 percent of patients will experience the relapse of the disease after potentially curative resection. Numerous publications support intensive follow-up in order to detect tumor recurrence early enough for successful treatment. Yet the impact of follow-up on increased resectability or treatment of recurrent tumor and increased survival remains controversial. Some studies have shown that thorough follow-up did not result in increased resectability and survival.[1-3] In contrast, others have demonstrated significant improvement in early detection rate and resectability of recurrent tumor as a result of close follow-up.[4-6] Ovaska and coauthors[30] have shown not only a significantly higher resectability rate but also that the timely treatment of relapses tended to improve survival. This difference did not reach statistical significance when compared to patients outside the follow-up program. It was estimated by Sugarbaker and colleagues[8] that follow-up efforts plus aggressive reoperative surgery could result in a cure of 20 percent patients with local or distant recurrence, thus decreasing the *overall* mortality of colorectal cancer patients by 5 percent (Fig. 76-1). The resectability rate of recurrent tumors in follow-up series varied between 13 and 58 percent, being about 40 to 50 percent in most of these studies. Despite the lack of clear-cut evidence of increased overall survival resulting from thorough follow-up, there are numerous publications suggesting the essential nature of this management strategy.

Anatomic Sites for Reoperative Surgery

All the theoretical discussions of cost-benefit of follow-up cannot negate the fact that selected patients are cured of recurrent cancer by reoperative surgery. The 5-year survival after hepatic resection of isolated colorectal metastases in the liver varies from 18 to 52

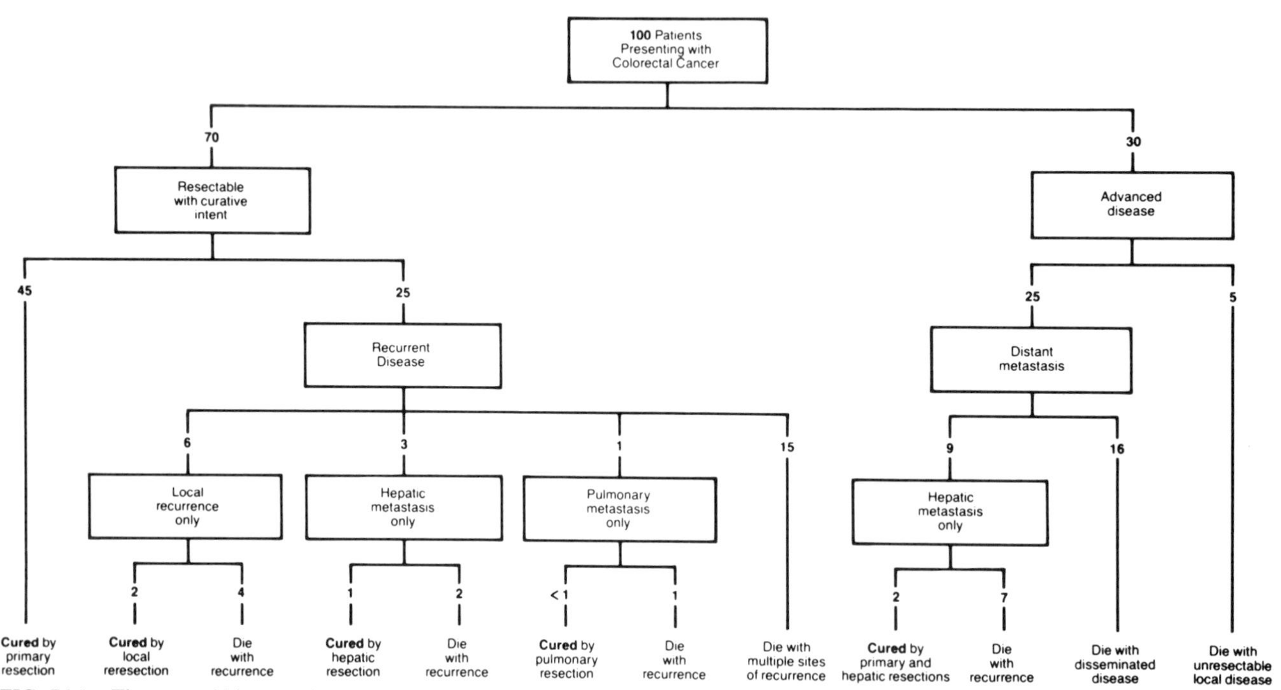

FIG. 76-1. The natural history of surgically treated colonic cancer. Of 100 patients with colorectal cancer, 45 are cured by resection of the primary lesion, and 2 are cured by resection of the primary lesion and synchronous hepatic metastases. Of the 25 patients who develop recurrent disease following "curative" primary resection, 2 are cured by reresection of a local recurrence, 1 by resection of hepatic metastases, and an occasional patient by resection of pulmonary metastases. (From August et al.[33] Reproduced by permission.)

percent.[9–16] Similarly, lung metastases can be resected with a respective 5-year survival of 32 to 67 percent.[17,18] The incidence of solitary metastases to the lungs is not well established. Pihl and coauthors[19] have found the overall incidence of lung metastases to be 11.5 and 3.5 percent after curative resection for rectal and colon cancer, respectively. The resectability rate in this large series of patients was 6.6 percent of the complete population.

Local recurrence at the resection site is a frequent finding. It occurs more commonly in the rectal cancer patient. Surgical removal of the recurrent pelvic tumor results in significant improvement in long-term survival and quality of life for this group of patients.[20] Resection with negative margins remains the only chance for cure.[21] The curative resection rate for local recurrence varies from 2 to 14 percent in most reports. Recently, there was a report of a resection rate of 40 percent in a prospective follow-up study.[5]

Approximately 6 percent of women with cancer of the large bowel develop ovarian metastases at some point during the follow-up period.[22] In half of these cases metastases are unresectable due to diffuse peritoneal seeding. It is important to recognize that patients who were rendered disease-free by surgery lived a mean of 48 months, compared to 9.6 months for patients with unresected disease.[23] This suggests that a complete surgical response may prolong survival even if a surgical cure is not possible.

Symptoms, Signs, and CEA as Indicators of Recurrence

Several prospective studies have demonstrated that patients' symptoms and physical signs had provided the first indication of tumor recurrence in 21 to 48 percent of cases. Cochrane and coauthors[2] have shown that of patients with recurrent tumors who were diagnosed clinically, 11.4 percent were treated surgically. In only 0.71 percent of the entire group was a long-term survival achieved. At the same time, progressively rising CEA level was found to be a first indicator of recurrence in 67 percent of cases.[24] In another study, 89 percent of patients had an elevated plasma CEA level before the recurrence was detected by any other means.[25] Moertel and colleagues[26] and Wedell and coauthors[27] recorded a CEA rise in similar circumstances in only 18 to 25 percent of patients and thought it to be of no value for follow-up and treatment of recurrent disease. This fact can in part be explained by the CEA methodology and interpretation used by this group (the methodologic aspects of CEA assays are discussed further on in this chapter). Most researchers have found that serum CEA rises on average 4 months before there is a clinical evidence of recurrence. But because an elevated serum CEA level is related to a large tumor bulk in a significant proportion of cases the CEA-indicated recurrence is beyond cure.[28,29] Nevertheless, when elevated CEA level in asymptomatic patients has been used as an indication for surgical exploration,[4] 95 percent of patients have been found to have recurrent disease and 58 percent of patients resected were made free of disease. There is strong evidence that follow-up detects resectable recurrent tumor in a significantly higher proportion of patients as compared to patients with no follow-up.[2,30] What one needs to establish is a subsequent increase in overall survival in a followed group of patients as compared to those who are not monitored.

Rationale for Thorough Follow-up

There are several aspects of the natural history of colonic and rectal cancer that support a follow-up program designed to provide improved survival and quality of life for patients. First, one must assume a stepwise progression of primary disease. The colorectal malignancy predictably progresses through a process of local/regional, then regional, and then systemic dissemination. Metastasis occurs by hematogenous routes to the liver and by lymphatic routes to local lymph nodes. Spread occurs through the bowel wall, eventually progressing to peritoneal carcinomatosis. Only if local/regional disease goes unchecked does the recurrence finally progress to incurable disease. This hypothesis suggests that a "window of opportunity" exists during which there are periods of local/regional (intraabdominal) spread of the disease that allow for further curative or life-prolonging therapy to be administered.[31,32]

Second, there are surgical procedures and other treatments that can destroy all of the recurrent malignancy if the treatment occurs in a timely fashion. This treatment is most likely to be reoperative surgery with added effects of radiation and chemotherapy. For some patients, surgery becomes its own "adjuvant therapy" in that repeat cancer resections complement the removal of the primary malignancy.

Third, the earliest possible detection of recurrent disease found in the asymptomatic state will allow more cures with less treatment-related morbidity and mortality. This assumption may be a safe one that can be accepted as a principle of management. Every malignant process has a higher cure rate if diagnosed early as opposed to late in the natural history of the disease. This is a truism associated with all effective treatment regimens. It can be assumed to be operative in the management of recurrent colorectal cancer.

Selection Factors

To select an optimal follow-up plan, one must know which patients are most likely to have recurrences, when these are expected to appear, and which sites of potential recurrence should be monitored. For example, there is little reason to thoroughly follow-up patients with limited life expectancy. Finally, the cost of a follow-up program and its limited benefits must be considered in relation to other treatment offered by the health care industry.

To make accurate predictions on a low or high risk of recurrence and subsequently to select an appropriate follow-up strategy, one must gather pertinent information describing the TNM stage of the primary cancer. Also, treatments employed must be factored in, as well as reliable data on preoperative and postoperative CEA levels and details concerning other prognostic features.

Patterns of Recurrence

Knowledge of the patterns of recurrence following potentially curative resection of primary colorectal cancer is essential to an understanding of the causes of surgical treatment failure. Resection site recurrence was reported in 10 to 40 percent of all patients who had undergone curative resections. Hepatic metastases occurred in 10 to 20 percent and pulmonary metastases in 5 to 10 percent. In 15 percent of the patients, recurrent tumor will be limited to a single site and reoperative surgery for cure is a possibility.[33]

August and colleagues[33] speculated on the condition of 100 patients initially evaluated for colorectal cancer. At presentation, 30 will have advanced disease that is incurable by surgical resection. Of the remaining 70 patients, 45 will be cured by resection of the primary tumor. Twenty-five patients undergoing potentially curative resection will develop recurrent tumor; 10 of these 25 patients will have isolated sites of recurrent disease and will be candidates for reoperative surgery (Fig. 76-1).

In a prospective study, Sugarbaker and colleagues[24] demonstrated that a large proportion of initial recurrences after primary curative surgery appear within the abdominal cavity (Fig. 76-2). Recurrence within the abdominal cavity, including liver metastases, was noted in 84 percent of cases. Distant metastases, thought to be disseminated through hematogenous routes, disseminate predominantly to lungs, adrenal glands, bones, brain, and some other sites. Although intraabdominal recurrence was isolated in approximately one-third of the patients, isolated distant metastases were rare.

Time to Recurrence

The majority of colorectal cancer recurrences take place within 2 years of removal of the primary tumor. In a study of 906 patients, 92 percent of tumor recurrences took place within 4 years of primary surgery.[34] Galandiuk and colleagues[35] have found the median

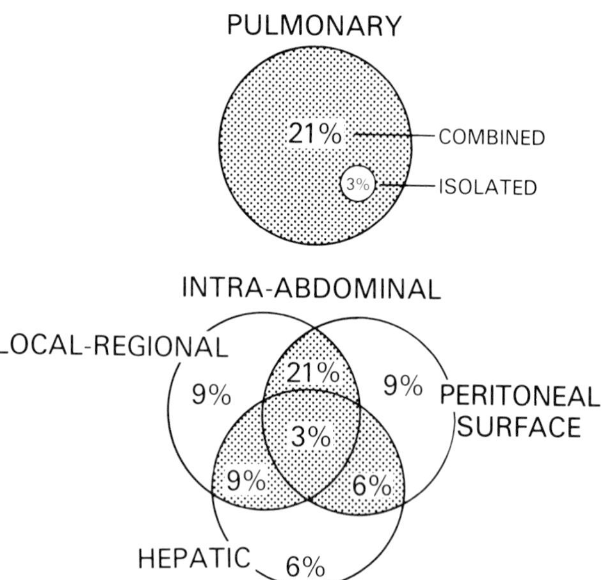

FIG. 76-2. Sites of recurrent colonic or rectal cancer in 33 instances. (From Sugarbaker et al.[24] Reproduced by permission.)

time to recurrence for all patients to be 16.7 months, with a range from 1 month to 7.5 years. Sugarbaker and coworkers[24] attempted, in a prospective trial, to determine when patients are at greatest risk of large bowel cancer recurrence. Figure 76-3*A* shows a modified Kaplan-Meier plot of time of recurrence for all patients. Figure 76-3*B* shows the same patients with the particular anatomic sites of initial recurrence identified. These data show that 85 percent of patients had recurrent disease within 30 months of primary cancer resection and that, at all sites, recurrences developed at approximately the same time. Median time to recurrence in this study was 17 months. In this report, the authors studied a homogeneous group of patients at high risk of recurrence, with the majority of patients having Dukes C cancer. Patients with less advanced stages of the disease at the time of the primary surgery may show clinical evidence of recurrence over a more prolonged period of time.

Quantitation of colorectal cancer progression was better understood as a result of the pioneering work of Collins and coworkers.[36] They developed a hypothesis of "growth rate patterns of human tumors" which supports subsequent clinical use of tumor doubling time. Joseph and colleagues[37] modified the nomogram developed by Collins and associates, thus allowing the calculation of tumor doubling time from direct measurement of the changing diameters of metastases. Their data suggested that aggressive surgical resection for pulmonary metastases was indicated when a tumor doubling time of less than 40 days was calculated. For that group of patients, long-term survival was significantly higher. Havelaar and coworkers[38] used com-

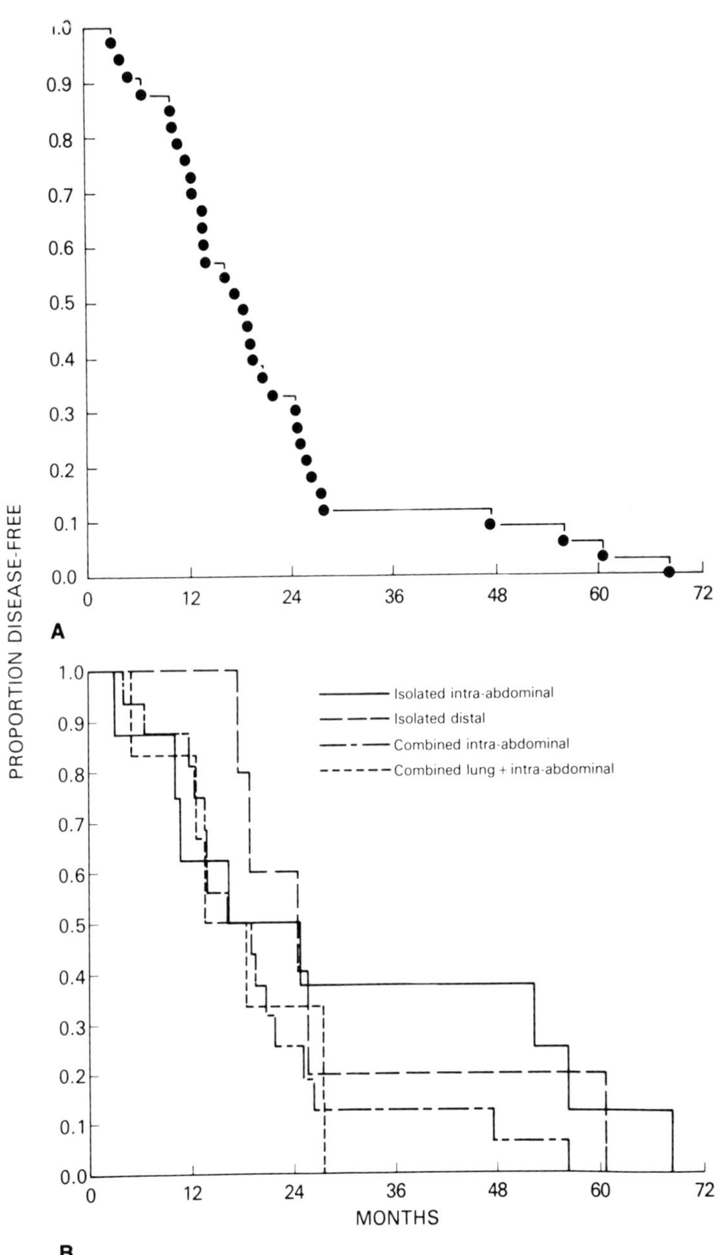

FIG. 76-3. *A*. Modified Kaplan-Meier plot of disease-free survival of all patients. *B*. Modified Kaplan-Meier plot of recurrence at particular anatomic sites. (From Sugarbaker et al.[24] Reproduced by permission.)

puted tomography (CT) in combination with a liver contrast agent to show that intraabdominal metastases in the absence of chemotherapy have a doubling time of 62 to 70 days (Table 76-1). The studies show that in colorectal cancer, metastases grow at a much faster rate than has been reported for primary tumors. Moreover, different tumors within the same liver may show different growth rates. This fact obviously reflects the heterogeneity of metastatic deposits from the primary malignancy (Fig. 76-4*A* and *B*). The data concerning the rate of progression of colorectal cancer metastases is relevant to the design of developing follow-up plans. The follow-up plan of colonic and rectal cancer patients must not only search after recurrent cancer but also detect other primary large bowel malignancies and cancers at other anatomic sites.

Second Primary Colorectal Cancer

Patients with colorectal cancer are at increased risk for synchronous and metachronous second primary tumors, which may develop within the remainder of the colon as well as in other anatomic sites (such as breast, ovary, prostate). The incidence of second primary colon cancer ranged from 2 to 8 percent.[39–41] The time interval may range from 3 months to 29 years (average, 8.5 years).[42] Multiple carcinomas are more likely to develop in patients with associated polyps. The high in-

Table 76-1
Growth Characteristics of Pulmonary and Colorectal Carcinoma

	Mean tumor doubling time, days	*No. of lesions*	*References*
Primary pulmonary adenocarcinoma	269	7	Spratt et al.[170]
Primary colorectal carcinoma	639	1	Spratt and Ackerman[171]
	620	20	Welin et al.[172]
Pulmonary metastases of colorectal carcinoma	116	25	Collins[123]
	109	36	Welin et al.[172]
Hepatic metastases of colorectal carcinoma	70	6	Havelaar[38]
Intraabdominal metastases of colorectal carcinoma	66	1	Havelaar[38]
Lymph node metastases of colorectal carcinoma	62	1	Havelaar[38]

SOURCE: From Havelaar et al.[38] With permission.

cidence of primary tumor recurrence in the first 2 to 3 years suggests that intensive follow-up is valuable during this period. But the relatively high incidence of metachronous disease indicates the need for long-term follow-up as well.

The cost-effectiveness of follow-up of colorectal cancer patients is currently in need of a critical appraisal. This study must evaluate the cost in dollars, the clinical benefits, and the quality-of-life benefits. The goal in follow-up is to create a relatively cost-ef-

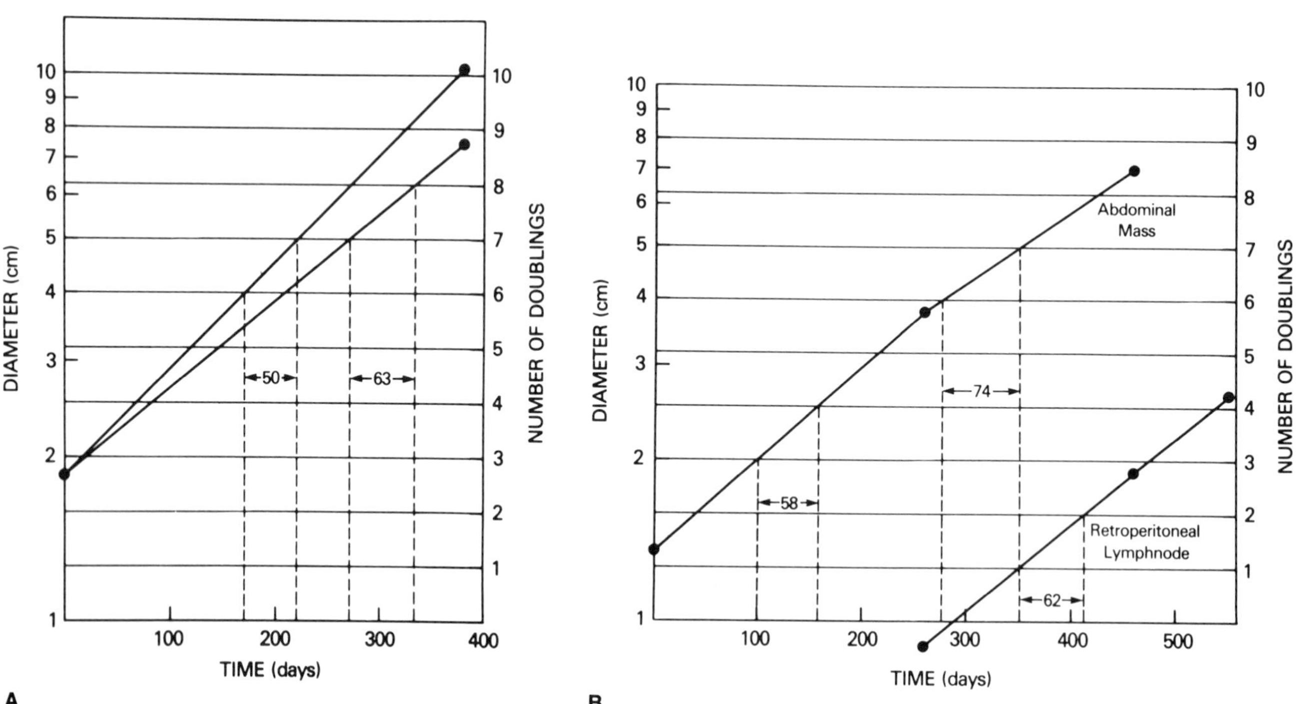

FIG. 76-4. *A*. Tumor-doubling-time curves of patient 2 over approximately a 1-year time interval. The doubling time was calculated according to the method first introduced by Collins, by measuring the lesion through its two largest dimensions and plotting the average diameter against the time in days. The vertical axis on the left side of the graph is the tumor diameter in centimeters on a semilogarithmic scale. On the right side, the number of tumor doublings is shown. In this patient the tumor doubling time was 50 and 63 days for the two lesions. *B*. Tumor-doubling-time curve of patient 3. Plotted are the diameters of the intraperitoneal tumor as well as the progression of lymph node involvement. (From Havelaar et al.[38])

fective, simple plan that will accurately distinguish between high probable absence or presence of recurrent disease. The more definitive and costly radiologic studies should be used only when a surveillance program provides evidence of abnormality.

The following discussion is devoted to a critical assessment of the utility of known tumor markers and radiologic tests in the follow-up of curatively treated colorectal cancer patients. Finally, using knowledge of the natural history of the disease and the effectiveness of follow-up tests, a strategy of follow-up that meets the criteria of simplicity, appropriate sensitivity, timing, and cost-effectiveness is outlined.

TUMOR MARKERS

General Concepts

A large number of "biological markers" have been described for cancer, and these markers are the focus of much ongoing research. Tumor products were originally studied in an attempt to develop a screening test for early detection of the cancer. However, clinical experience with tumor markers makes them more applicable to the surveillance or monitoring of specific patient populations than to screening. Even this use of tumor markers has substantial limitations, which include (1) a general rather than quantitative correlation of circulating marker level and tumor mass; (2) an absence of quantitative criteria for directly establishing cancer recurrence and tumor marker blood level; (3) a less than 100 percent specificity, with many elevations occurring as a result of non-malignant conditions.

Most tumor markers are not cancer-type or site-specific. They can be identified in a wide range of tumors. Nonetheless, they may be of great value in an individual patient as a monitor of therapy. In fact, for many tumors, the heterogeneity of the tumor cell population may dictate the clinical necessity for the use of multiple markers. Lokich[43] summarized the problems of interpreting the level of tumor markers as follows:

- Criteria need to be established for changes in circulating levels as well as for optimal intervals for monitoring.
- The clinical situation may be obfuscated by metabolic alterations in the host.
- The clinical interpretation of the results of tumor marker monitoring relates to the type and time of the assay. In general, the difference between assay runs is in the range of 10 percent.
- Circadian rhythm is a characteristic of many biological functions. Although no data are specifically available for tumor markers, it is not unreasonable to presume that a circadian phenomenon may occur.

Carcinoembryonic Antigen

More than 25 years have passed since Gold and Freedman[44] described the nonspecific tumor marker carcinoembryonic antigen (CEA). They initially suggested that CEA was a uniform molecular structure. Molecular weight was estimated at 200,000 and the structure was that of a complex glycoprotein. Further studies showed that the substances that have CEA immunoreactivity consisted of a family of related glycoprotein molecules.

CEA shows cross-reactivity with closely related molecules. The first substance immunologically cross-reactive with CEA was named nonspecific cross-reacting antigen (NCA).[45] In order of molecular weight NCA-160, NCA-95, NCA-55, low-molecular-weight CEA, normal fetal antigen (NFA-1), and biliary glycoprotein 1 (BGP-1) have been described.[46]

The biological function of the CEA molecule remains unclear, but a protective role in the turnover of the digestive epithelium is suggested and a role in the metastatic process has been proposed.[47] Its inconsistent presence in the host with epithelial tumors plus the fact that its production may cease while the malignant process continues makes its production unlikely as an essential step in the malignant process. The degree to which the neoplastic cell machinery reverts to CEA production over and above that produced by normal tissues may be a random and therefore inconsistent event.

Elevated CEA may result from overproduction by cancer or from non-cancerous inflammation. A prominent pathophysiologic cause for nontumor CEA elevation is decreased metabolism by the liver. There is strong evidence that CEA degradation and excretion take place almost exclusively in the liver.[48–51] Since the antigen is eliminated mainly by the liver, liver insufficiency is a frequent cause of increased plasma CEA.[52]

Practical Problems in CEA Monitoring

In a follow-up treatment protocol, the clinician will monitor serial CEA results. The consistent use of a single assay system is mandatory, since the normal levels and sensitivity of a system may vary according to the assay used.

Nisselbaum and coworkers[53] have published the results of comparative evaluation of different CEA measurement methods. These authors concluded that the precision of all methods compared was acceptable and that concordance among all exceeded 90 percent. Earlier, Davidson and colleagues[54] detected lack of comparability between CEA analyses using three different methods. The same topic has been addressed in several other publications.[55–57] The most reasonable explanation for these occasional discrepancies between assay systems is that CEA comprises a family of related glycoproteins with varying carbohydrate portion of the molecule and a variable primary amino acid composition of the protein portion. Thus, the results obtained with CEA assays that utilize different antibody preparations would be expected to differ to the extent that the antibody preparation was dissimilar to the

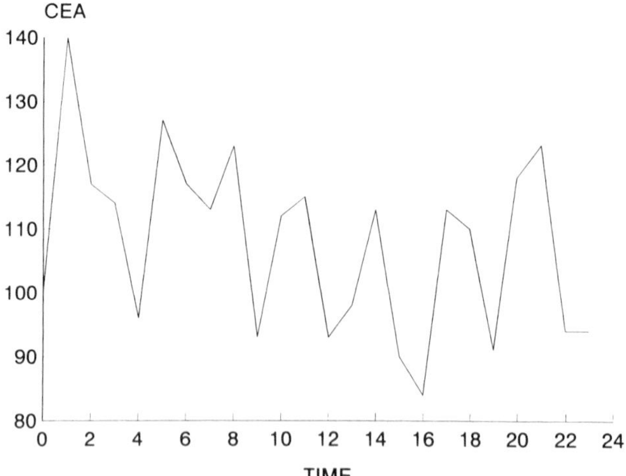

FIG. 76-5. Hourly CEA values (ng/mL) over a 24-h period in an advanced cancer patient. (From Lokick.[43] Reproduced by permission.)

CEA preparations used as a standard. One more interesting fact has been pointed out by Fleisher and collaborators.[58] They have mentioned that discordance of results between two methods tested by them were more common for patients with disseminated cancer than for those with localized disease (35 versus 18 percent, Roche versus Abbott test systems respectively).

Significant discordance in CEA for colonic carcinoma with metastases to the liver may be related to the role of the liver in CEA clearance. Differences in antibody recognition of heterogenic CEA, impaired liver degradation, and abnormal production of CEA may all contribute to the observed discordance of CEA assay results seen in different test systems.

Circulating CEA levels may vary over time, independent of the tumor mass. The observation that levels obtained on an hourly or daily basis may vary by as much as 50 percent suggests that a type of intrinsic secretory rhythm may be common for tumor markers, as is common for the secretion of endogenous hormones. Fig. 76-5 demonstrates the biologic fluctuations in circulating CEA levels over a 24-h period.

Nontumor CEA Elevations

Zamcheck and collaborators established through clinical studies that CEA elevations could result from many nontumor disease processes. Alcoholic patients often had CEA levels greater than 2.5 ng/mL but less than 10 ng/mL.[59,60] Numerous other nontumor causes of CEA elevation have been reported: pancreatitis, recent blood transfusion, ulcerative colitis, heavy cigarette smoking, gastritis following partial gastrectomy, and colonic polyps.

The following suggestions can be made to assist in differentiating tumor from nontumor elevations. First, the magnitude of elevations is important. CEA elevations in the 2.5- to 10-ng/mL range may or may not be from tumor. However, nontumor elevations above 10 ng/mL are very unlikely without jaundice and other obvious signs of biliary tract obstruction. Therefore, only patients with moderate CEA elevations (2.5- to 10-ng/mL range) are likely to pose dilemmas. Second, in patients with moderate CEA elevations, the clinician must make a search for possible nontumor causes. Most commonly, as emphasized by Gardner and coworkers,[61] these conditions are in an active state when associated with plasma CEA elevations. These clinical entities can usually be identified by careful medical history and routine laboratory and radiologic tests. Third, to differentiate tumor from nontumor CEA elevation, several sequential CEA assays as opposed to individual determinations may be required. If the titer is progressively rising, cancer is the most likely cause; if the serial titers are erratic, with both elevated and normal values, nontumor causes are more common. There is one more reason for nontumor elevation of CEA level that was recently emphasized by Moertel and colleagues.[62] As has been discovered by these authors, an adjuvant chemotherapy with fluorouracil and levasomile caused CEA titers increase in some 21 percent of patients. The CEA level rose in association with the liver function tests due to the hepatotoxic effect of the adjuvant treatment.

Serial CEA in Monitoring Cancer Therapy: Assessment of the Adequacy of Surgical Removal of Primary Tumor

After surgical excision of a colorectal cancer, elevated preoperative CEA levels usually fall into the normal range of 2.5 ng/mL or less within 4 to 8 weeks. Several groups have noted that failure of postoperative CEA values to fall into the normal range is associated with poor prognosis.[63–67] In a careful study from the Royal Victoria Hospital, Montreal, colorectal cancer patients were divided into three groups, according to preoperative and postoperative CEA levels.[67] Group 1 had preoperative and postoperative levels below 2.5 ng/mL. In group 2, CEA levels were elevated preoperatively and fell to less than 2.5 ng/mL postoperatively. Group 3 had a preoperative CEA levels above 2.5 ng/mL, but the postoperative values failed to decline below 2.5 ng/mL. In group 1, 14 percent of patients had a recurrence by 19 months postoperatively; in group 2, 18 percent patients had a recurrence; and in group 3, 73 percent of patients had a recurrence (Fig. 76-6).

Gianola and coworkers[68] compared a variety of tests done postoperatively after resection of a colonic or rectal cancer. They studied full-lung tomography, liver-spleen scan, CT of the abdomen, intravenous pyelogram, bone scan, and postoperative CEA assay (Table 76-2). Occult metastases were defined as those

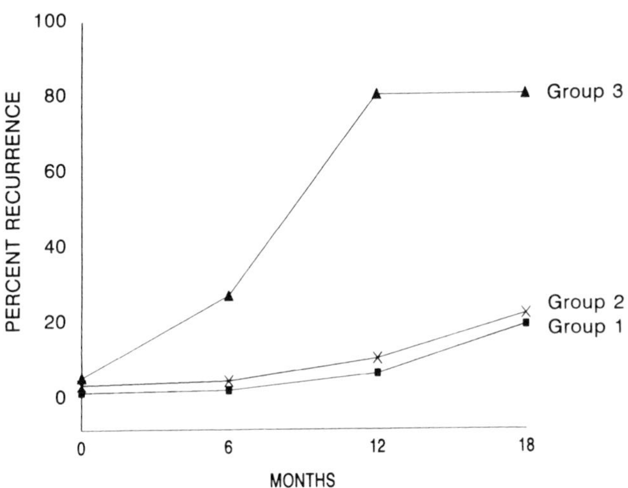

FIG. 76-6. Postoperative baseline CEA level and prognosis of colorectal cancer patients. The 36 patients in group 1 had preoperative and postoperative CEA values of less than 2.5 ng/mL. The 11 patients in group 2 had a preoperative CEA value greater than 2.5 ng/mL, but postoperative values were all less than 2.5 ng/mL. In the 14 patients in group 3, the preoperative and postoperative values were greater than 2.5 ng/mL. Highly significant differences between those with elevated postoperative CEA levels and normal postoperative CEA levels were observed. (From Oh and MacLean.[67] Reproduced by permission.)

that occurred at a particular anatomic site within the first year of follow-up. Patients included in this study were those thought to be at high risk for recurrence because of lymph node positivity, obstruction, or perforation of primary tumor. All site-specific recurrences were confirmed by biopsy or radiologic demonstration of an expanding lesion with continued follow-up.

In 53 patients, CEA assays were obtained within the first postoperative month after "curative resection" of a colonic or rectal cancer. The preoperative CEA was not considered in this analysis. Eleven patients had postoperative elevations from 2.6 to 5.0 ng/mL and 6 had CEA levels above 5.1 ng/mL. In this group of 17 patients with postoperative CEA elevations, 12 had developed recurrent disease. Of the 21 patients with recurrence, 12 had elevated postoperative baseline CEA tests (Table 76-2). If the preoperatively elevated CEA level fails to decrease to normal range postoperatively, this strongly suggests persistent disease. In summary, in this battery of tests, CEA appeared to be the most accurate one by which to identify a group of colorectal cancer patients with persistent cancer following potentially curative surgery.

Table 76-2
Comparison of CEA and Other Diagnostic Tests in the Detection of Occult Colorectal Cancer

		Sensivity		
	Total no. patients	*No. patients w/site-specific disease*	*No. of positive tests*	*True-positive percentage, no. of patients*
Full-lung tomography	52	1	1	(1/1)
Liver/spleen scan	52	9	3	33(3/9)
Computed tomogram, abdomen	60	15	6	40(6/15)
Intravenous pyelogram	25	0	0	—
Bone scan	30	0	0	—
Postoperative baseline CEA>2.5 ng/mL	53	21	12	57(12/21)

	Specificity		
	No. patients without site-specific disease	*No. of positive tests*	*False positive percentage, no. of patients*
Full-lung tomography	51	6	12(6/51)
Liver/spleen scan	43	5	12(5/43)
Computed tomogram, abdomen	45	3	7(3/45)
Intravenous pyelogram	25	2	8(2/25)
Bone scan	30	2	7(2/30)
Postoperative baseline CEA>2.5 ng/mL	32	5	16(5/32)

SOURCE: From Gianola et al.[68] With permission.

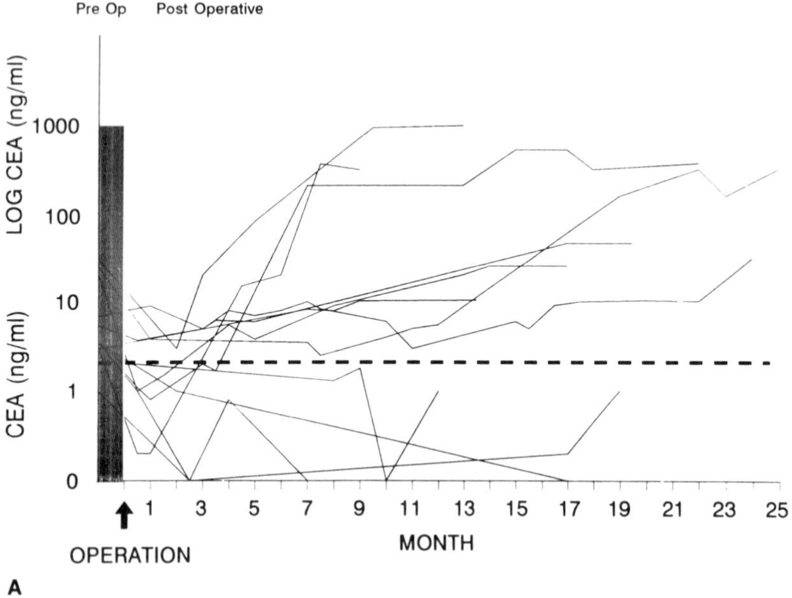

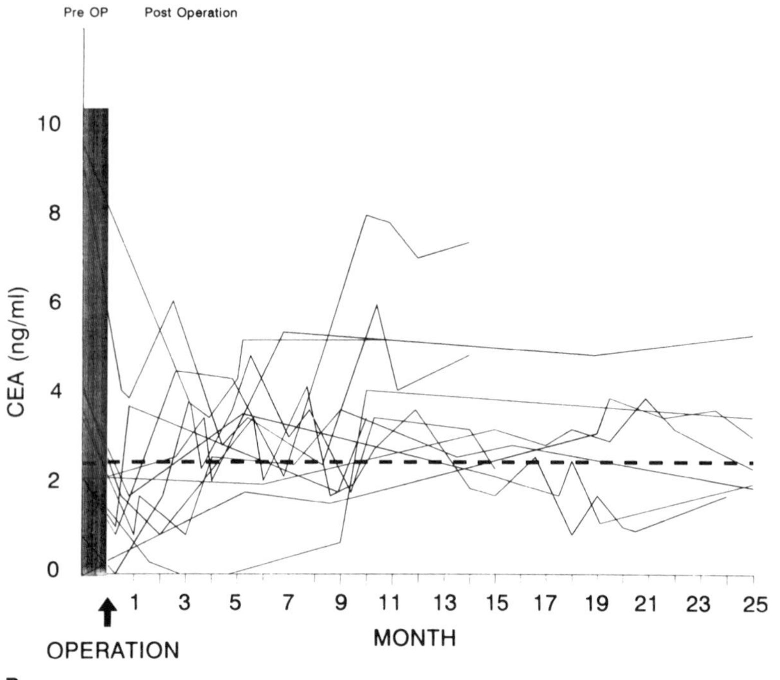

FIG. 76-7. Postoperative CEA profiles of patients in follow-up after resection of colonic and rectal adenocarcinoma. *A*. In 12 patients with recurrence, 8 showed progressively rising CEA titers. Time at which recurrent cancer became clinically evident is shown by arrows. Of the 12 patients, 4 showed no CEA elevation with recurrent disease. However, in 8 of the 12 patients with recurrence, the CEA titers signaled recurrent disease 3 to 18 months prior to other clinical evidence of disease recurrence. *B*. Eleven patients with stable, elevated postoperative CEA titers who did not show recurrent cancer. The CEA titer in patient 13 was associated with hepatitis. *C*. Nine patients, all free of recurrent disease, who had CEA titers consistently below 2.5 ng/mL. (From Sugarbaker et al.[83] Reproduced by permission.)

Serial CEA in the Detection of Recurrent Colorectal Cancer

Perhaps the most important current use of CEA is as an indicator of early recurrent colorectal cancer and a guide to selected second-look surgery. Usually the rise of CEA associated with disease recurrence is gradually progressive. If the CEA profile postoperatively is erratic, with multiple elevations that return to the normal range with repeat determinations, the CEA elevation does not correlate with cancer recurrence. The progressively rising CEA level has great clinical importance.[27,69–79]

The literature has reported various decision rules for predicting tumor recurrence based on postoperative CEA monitoring.[26,80–82] These include CEA levels exceeding cutoff values of 4.0, 5.0, 7.5, 10, or 20 ng/mL and progressively rising CEA levels exceeding a specific rate of change. This multiplicity of rules, each one tested on a different patient sample, has led to dif-

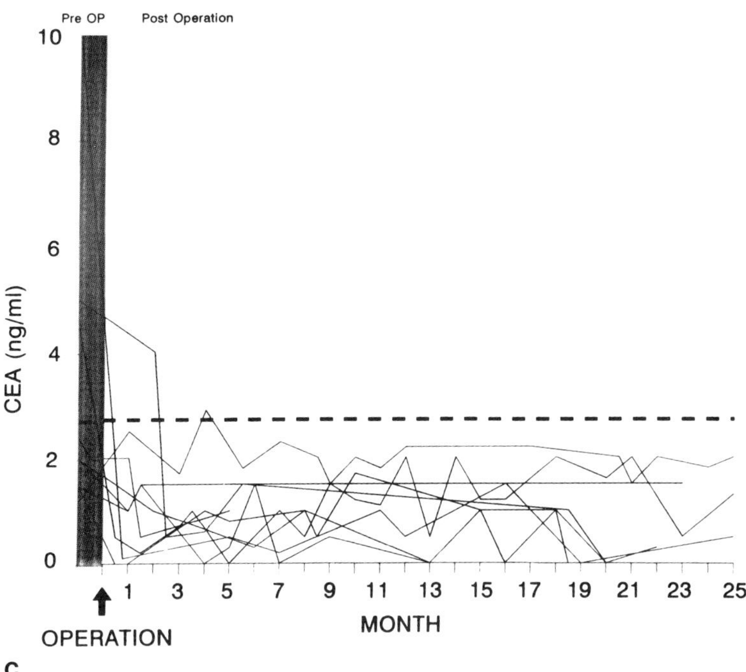

FIG. 76-7. (*Continued*)

ferences of opinion regarding the clinical usefulness of CEA monitoring. This issue has major therapeutic and economic significance.

In an attempt to eliminate certain benign conditions as a source of false-positive results, some authors have developed decision rules that depend on trends in CEA rather than a given cutoff value. This allows each patient to act as his or her own control and might be expected to boost the specificity of CEA-based decision rules. Sugarbaker and coworkers[83] introduced the concept of "progressively rising CEA" level as the postoperative pattern most likely to signal recurrent disease. Steele and colleagues[84] suggested a CEA slope–based rule. According to this rule, recurrence is predicted by a greater than 3 percent monthly increase in the slope of the regression line relating log (1 + CEA) to time. This decision rule gave a sensitivity of 0.69, specificity of 0.66, and false-positive rate of 0.54. Another decision rule by Boey and associates[82] was similar to Steele's method and used a slope exceeding a 5 percent monthly rise in CEA level. Despite impressive estimated sensitivity and specificity results of 0.86 and 0.76, a high false-positive rate of 30 percent was noted. Denstman and coworkers[85] derived another slope-based decision rule by plotting CEA against postoperative time and examining rate of change, expressed as a slope of the regression line. A slope greater than 12.6 percent per month predicted tumor recurrence. When different variables were entered into discriminate analysis together with the 12.6 percent decision rule, only tumor stage contributed significantly to the multivariate criterion.

Denstman et al.[85] have pointed out that the length of patient follow-up is an important variable that can adversely affect the criteria by which diagnostic tests are judged. Their analysis suggested that late recurring tumors are less likely to produce abnormal amounts of CEA than rapidly recurring ones.

In a prospective study, Sugarbaker and coworkers[83] analyzed serial postoperative CEA titers following surgical removal of a colonic and rectal cancer. Three types of postoperative profile were recognized: (1) a progressively rising titer associated with recurrence; (2) stable elevated titers, which may or may not go on to rise; and (3) a titer that remains within the normal range (Fig. 76-7). This study and others suggest that progressively rising serial CEA assays point to recurrent cancer in all patients. These authors also compared CEA with physical examination, barium enema, chest x-ray, and liver scan in the early detection of recurrent cancer. In two-thirds of patients, CEA was the first indication of disease recurrence. The lead time to detection of recurrence by serial CEA over all other diagnostic tests was between 1 and 18 months, with a median of 3 months.

Minton and colleagues[77] performed serial postoperative CEA assays in 400 patients with colorectal cancer. Second-look surgery was performed in 75 of these patients. In 43 patients, reoperation was performed because of rising CEA levels; in 32, because of clinical indications. Recurrent tumor was confirmed in 96 percent of patients. Tumors were resected for cure in 59 percent of CEA-directed reoperations and in 50 percent of clinically directed cases. Patients monitored with serial CEA determinations at 1- to 2-month intervals had a higher 5-year disease-free survival—that is, 33 percent—compared to only 10 percent when CEA levels were determined at any less frequent interval. A 5-year disease-free survival was 37 percent in CEA-directed and 34 percent in clinically directed groups. The authors recommended CEA determinations with a 1- to 2-month interval and reoperation before CEA level exceeds 11 ng/mL, since the highest resectability rate (63 percent) and the best 5-year disease-free survival (68 percent) occurred in this group.

Rittgers and colleagues[76] express concern regarding the transient CEA elevations occasionally seen following resection of colorectal cancer. About 40 percent of their patients showed transient elevations without recurrence upon follow-up and close clinical investigation. It has been stressed that trends in serial CEA titers rather than isolated CEA values must be used along with all other clinical and laboratory data available in making the decision to perform a second-look surgical procedure.

An interesting study was designed in the early 1980s. In a multicenter trial, an attempt was made to quantify the effect on morbidity of CEA-prompted second-look surgery. In each case, a monthly CEA assay and three monthly clinical examinations in the first 2 years and less frequently later were used. In a case of "aggressively" significant CEA rise, the patients were randomly allocated to the "aggressive" and "conventional" arms. In the former case surgeons were notified of the CEA increase; in the latter, surgeons were not informed. Unfortunately, the last brief description of the results was published only in 1985,[86] and at that time the number and length of follow-ups were insufficient to allow more meaningful analysis of data. Mavligit and McMurtey[87] as well as Wanebo and associates[69] supported the usefulness of CEA in detection of liver metastases. Sugarbaker[88] emphasized the high percentage of early CEA elevations in patients with hepatic metastases. Barillari and colleagues[89] also called attention to the benefits of CEA assays in the detection of hepatic metastases compared to other sites of colorectal cancer recurrence. The overall value of serial CEA assays in the follow-up of colorectal cancer patients can be illustrated by the result of a prospective study conducted in Germany.[78] At the time of tumor recurrence, CEA levels were elevated in 50.3 percent of the patients. Increased CEA level were found in 20.8 percent of patients 3 months before tumor recurrence could be localized by other follow-up studies. Some 53.9 percent of patients with distant metastases and 74.1 percent of patients with both distant metastases and local recurrences showed an increased CEA level at the time of recurrence. In 23.3 percent of the patients with local recurrence, there was an increased CEA level. Only in 0.67 percent of cases was there a false-positive increased CEA level. In this particular patient, the CEA level was abnormally high preoperatively and did not decrease postoperatively despite the fact that the patient remained free of recurrence for 6 years.

At the same time, elevations of alkaline phosphatase, aminotransferase, or bilirubin in association with a CEA test increase were mentioned in 21 percent of patients without colonic cancer recurrence due to hepatotoxic side effect of adjuvant chemotherapy.[62] This phenomenon creates a real problem in applying CEA monitoring to this patient population, and in this clinical setting liver function tests may add some valuable clinical information.

CEA Assay Correlated with Other Laboratory Tests

As a single test, CEA lacks 100 percent accuracy. Taken alone, it should not convince a surgeon to reoperate. Repeated assessment and correlation with other laboratory tests is essential to clinical utility.

CEA and Liver Function Tests

As critical studies of liver function tests have accumulated, it becomes clear that there is no single test by which the presence or absence of hepatic metastases can be determined. For many years, alkaline phosphatase has been regarded as the best laboratory test for that purpose.[90] Other reports exploring the role of lactic dehydrogenase (LDH)[91] and gamma glutamyl transpeptidase (GGTP)[92] have been published. Kemeny and coworkers[93] attempted to determine the reliability of laboratory tests that indicated the presence of hepatic metastases. In a prospective study, it was shown that CEA and GGTP were the most sensitive laboratory tests. The accuracy ranged from 53 to 65 percent, with no significant difference between any of the tests. The sensitivity of the CEA as a single test was 86 percent, with a specificity of 60 percent and an accuracy of 79 percent.

An analysis of composite testing showed a pair of tests that complement each other in accuracy. While CEA and LDH had an 87 percent sensitivity, the specificity was 44 percent; the resulting accuracy of 62 percent was less than that for LDH alone (64 percent). Thus, composite testing seemed to be of little value.

Rachlin and colleagues[94] also reported the efficacy of the liver function tests along with that of CEA for early detection of liver metastases. A direct comparison of CEA with each of the individual liver function tests revealed that CEA was statistically significantly more frequently elevated than any of the individual tests. Among the liver function tests, LDH was the best predictor of metastases, though not as good as CEA. Comparing CEA with LDH revealed that CEA was statistically significantly more frequently elevated (87 versus 30 percent, respectively). Suspicion of liver metastases would have been delayed by omission of liver function tests in only 2.2 percent of patients. These authors concluded that liver function tests should be deleted from the follow-up of colorectal cancer patients, decreasing cost without significantly decreasing accuracy. Deveney and Way[95] also stated that there was no benefit to the routine use of liver function tests during follow-up.

Additional data on the CEA value in the follow-up of patients with colonic cancer were recently published by Moertel and colleagues.[62] They described the results of CEA monitoring during an adjuvant chemotherapy trial. The CEA tests were performed in 1017 of 1217 (84 percent) patients. It was a multicenter, nonrandomized assessment of CEA role in the follow-up of curatively treated colonic cancer patients. There was no regimentation as to whether and how the tests should be performed and how the tests should be interpreted. Performance of the test was optional, according to the usual practice of the responsible physician. The number of tests performed varied from 1 to 39, but 80 percent of patients were tested seven times or more. A value greater than 5 ng/mL was considered a positive test result. The sensitivity of the test rose in accordance with the increase in cutoff values from 5 to 15 ng/mL, but the specificity correspondingly decreased. A total of 345 patients (34 percent) of those tested had CEA elevations, and 247 of them had recurrent tumor. The rate of false-negative tests was 41 percent; that of false positives was 16 percent. Sensitivity was reasonably higher for hepatic and retroperitoneal recurrences (78 and 75 percent, respectively) but low for peritoneal and pulmonary metastasis as well as local recurrence. Recurrent tumor was resected for cure in 13.6 percent of patients with elevated CEA levels and in 11.5 percent of clinically detected recurrences (the difference was not statistically significant). The proportion of patients alive and free of disease 1 or more years after reoperation was 2.9 percent in the CEA-elevated group, 1.9 percent in the CEA-non-elevated group, and 2 percent in the clinically monitored group. These authors have concluded that the maximum anticipated gain from CEA monitoring will be a small number of lives saved after resection of hepatic metastases, probably less than 1 percent of the patients monitored. In view of the cost of the test itself and the cost of initiating further examination—as well as the psychological burden for patients—Moertel and coworkers have found it appropriate to consider alternative strategies of follow-up that are not CEA-based.

As it has been mentioned before, this was not a randomized study, and there could have been systemic differences between monitored and unmonitored patients that would account for the observed lack of effect. More careful and aggressive monitoring by CEA test would have gotten better results, but as Moertel and associates have pointed out, their data are probably representative of routine colonic cancer follow-up practice nationwide. This study indicates that 84 percent of patients with resected colonic cancer will have CEA testing postoperatively. In this study, the CEA test identified 59 percent of recurrences; and in 16 percent of patients, test results were falsely positive. Of all CEA-monitored patients with recurrences, 4.6 percent were resected for cure and 2.3 percent were alive and free of disease long-term. Perhaps if progressively rising CEA titers instead of simple cutoff values had been used as diagnostic criteria, these figures would have been higher. It is worthwhile to mention that in this study the median time between the first positive CEA test and diagnosis of recurrence was 4.5 months. In any case, with all these possibilities, the impact of a CEA-based follow-up program on the long-term outcome for colorectal cancer patients with recurrence probably does not exceed 5 percent.

CEA and Acute-Phase Reactant Proteins

Acute-phase reactant proteins (APRPs) were defined by Koj[96] as inflammation-inducible liver-produced glycoproteins. A rise of APRP can be revealed in various disease states, including acute and chronic inflammation, connective tissues disorders, pregnancy, and malignancy. In the latter, increased serum levels may occur in response to an as yet unknown signal from the host-tumor interface; some investigators suggest that the level of increase is related to the degree of tumor invasion.

Ward and coworkers[97] suggested that a combination of APRP and CEA could distinguish metastatic from nonmetastatic malignant tumors preoperatively and may be of use in monitoring the progress of large bowel carcinoma. However, the proteins measured were alpha-1-antitrypsin and haptoglobin, and they show a considerable variation in their response to the reaction produced by a malignant tumor.

A strong correlation has been demonstrated between the level of serum protein hexose and the presence of large bowel malignancy. Walker and Gray[98] showed that hexose closely correlates with the disease status after curative resection of large bowel cancer. Among other APRP associated with malignancy were ceruloplasmin, seromucoid, transferrin, C-reactive protein, and alpha-1-acid glycoprotein.

Table 76-3
Characteristics of CEA, TPA, and CA 19-9

	CEA, %	*TPA, %*	*CA 19-9, %*
Positive predictive value	64.9	66.7	83.3
Negative predictive value	69.0	74.2	69.0
Sensitivity	72.7	78.8	60.1
Specificity	60.6	60.6	87.9
Accuracy	66.7	69.7	74.4

SOURCE: From Barillari et al.[89] With permission.

As no single marker is entirely reliable, several authors have attempted to use combinations of different tumor markers in an effort to enhance the sensitivity for detecting malignancy. Walker and coworkers[99] used six APRP and CEA determinations to monitor 128 patients with large bowel cancer who underwent curative surgery. The results indicated that APRPs have a higher diagnostic rate for the presence of a malignancy than does CEA. Estimation of the serum protein hexose alone is of greater diagnostic value than that of a combination of APRPs. Furthermore, serum protein hexose and CEA are complementary and, when combined, will reflect the presence of cancer in a greater number of patients than either alone. Thus, in 36 patients with recurrences, CEA was elevated in 78 percent, compared to 47 percent for hexose and 31 percent for other three APRPs. However, the combination of CEA and hexose resulted in a detection rate of 92 percent. These investigators concluded that in the monitoring of colorectal cancer patients, the combination of APRP and CEA increases the predictive value for the detection of the recurrence.

A similar conclusion was reached by Verazin and colleagues[100] after studying total sialic acid (TSA; a constituent of glycoproteins and glycolipids), total protein (TP), and CEA in 146 consecutive colorectal cancer patients. CEA was elevated less often than the TSA/TP ratio. This ratio may predict tumor burden less reliably than CEA. The TSA/TP ratio, according to Verazin and colleagues, is useful in monitoring colorectal cancer patients who do not show elevated CEA.

CEA and Other Tumor-Associated Antigens

Putzki and coworkers[101] compared the results of CEA, CA 19-9, and tissue polypeptide antigen (TPA) measurements in 103 patients with colorectal cancer. They found that CEA has the greatest sensitivity for colorectal carcinoma, followed by TPA and CA 19-9. This conflicts with the results of Oehr and colleagues[102] and Luthgens and Schlegel,[103] who reported that TPA was more sensitive. The combination of these antigens provided no greater sensitivity than the single-marker assay. Putzki and coworkers[101] concluded that in colorectal carcinoma, the sensitivity of CEA is not reached by TPA or CA 19-9.

The same group of tumor markers was tested for detection of colorectal cancer recurrence by Barillari and colleagues.[89] In 66 patients, 33 recurrences were detected between 6 and 42 months postoperatively. The effectiveness of CEA, TPA, and CA 19-9 assays is shown in Table 76-3. In 23 out of 33 cases, the rise in the value of CEA, TPA, or CA 19-9 was the first sign of recurrence.

Earlier, Mavligit and McMurtey[87] stressed the usefulness of CEA to detect liver metastases but pointed out that it lacks capability to consistently detect pelvic recurrence. Barillari and coworkers[89] demonstrated a very interesting relationship between localization of recurrent tumors and different tumor marker sensitivities (Table 76-4). Thus, for 16 hepatic metastases CEA showed the greatest sensitivity as compared to TPA and CA 19-9. Among 6 patients with local recurrence the sensitivity of TPA was 100 percent, that of CA 19-9 was 83.3 percent, and that of CEA was only 50 percent. Among 3 patients with peritoneal carcinomatosis, only TPA was of value and reached 100 percent sensitivity. For multiple sites of metastases, there were no significant difference among the three markers.

Yamaguchi and colleagues[104] examined CEA, CA 19-9, and serum NCC-ST 439 in 36 patients with recurrent large bowel cancer. The combination assay of three markers was positive in 88.9 percent of patients, thus improving the sensitivity. For example, NCC-ST 439 was positive in only 66.7 percent of recurrences, while the NCC-ST 439 plus CEA combination was

Table 76-4
Relationship between Marker Sensitivity and Localization of Metastases

	Hepatic, %	*Local, %*	*Polyps, %*	*Peritoneal, %*	*Multiple, %*
CEA	93.7	50.0	19.0	0	75.0
TPA	68.7	100	38.1	100	75.0
CA 19-9	62.5	83.3	23.8	0	62.5

SOURCE: From Barillari at al.[89] With permission.

positive in 88.9 percent of cases. It was concluded that a combination of tumor markers is particularly useful in the diagnosis of recurrences because of improved diagnostic accuracy. Determination of NCC-ST 439 serum levels was as effective as that of CEA for the detection of liver, local, and distant recurrences. At the same time, CEA was, surprisingly, twice (100 percent) as sensitive as NCC-ST 439 in the detection of peritoneal carcinomatosis. The sensitivity of CA 19-9 was below 0.40 for all recurrence sites.

CEA remains the tumor marker most frequently used for monitoring colorectal cancer patients. The National Cancer Institute consensus panel (1989) concluded that CEA is the best presently available noninvasive technique for the postoperative surveillance of patients to detect disseminated recurrence of colorectal cancer. The accuracy of CEA estimations in detecting recurrences may be improved by combination with other tumor-associated and nonspecific tumor markers.

RADIOLOGIC EVALUATION

Detection of Local (Anastomotic) Recurrences and Second Primary Cancers

All clinicians acknowledge the necessity of including some method of examination of the remaining part of colon and rectum in the follow-up of treated patients. Opinions differ only in respect to what particular method should be used. Barium enema has probably been the most often used test in follow-up programs. On the other hand, colonoscopy is frequently advocated for the initial evaluation of the entire colon in order to make a direct visual assessment of the anastomosis.

Local recurrence can be intraluminal or predominantly extraluminal. Barkin and coworkers[105] estimated the rate of intraluminal recurrence to be about one-third of all local recurrences, and these cases constituted 14 percent of all recurrent cases. In a vast majority of cases, local recurrence is associated with other patterns of metastatic disease. Anastomotic recurrences are more likely to occur after resections of the distal colon and rectum, and usually the residual extraanastomotic tumor grows into the suture line. Barkin and coworkers[105] mentioned that only 5.6 percent of all recurrences were initially detected by endoscopy. Clinical symptoms, such as a positive occult blood test, usually appear only with advanced disease.

Chen and colleagues,[106] in an article comparing the results of barium enema and CT in the evaluation of local recurrences, showed that barium enema exams disclosed 97 percent of locally recurrent cancers provided that the double-contrast technique was used. A variety of radiographic appearances ranging from anastomotic narrowing, usually eccentric or irregular, to adjacent-mass effect and obstruction were found. As a relatively rare sign of recurrence, smooth, symmetrical narrowing of the anastomosis was sometimes found to be associated with a mass effect, suggesting local recurrence. Progressive stenosis owing to local recurrence was difficult to distinguish from benign stricture and usually required a colonoscopy with multiple biopsies. When barium enema demonstrated an anastomotic recurrence with a mass effect, CT scans often showed more extensive disease adjacent to an involved anastomosis.

With some limitations, CT scan remains the imaging technique of choice for detecting and evaluating a regional recurrence. Its ability to visualize both the anastomosis, when present, and perirectal or pericolic areas provides a global view of postoperative anatomy.[107] Good distention of the colorectal lumen at the level of anastomosis either by contrast material or insufflating air is an important technical consideration during the CT study.[106] Thin sections (5 mm) through the region of the anastomosis can also be helpful for the display of subtle findings.

Ultrasound Examination in the Follow-up of Colorectal Cancer Patients

There are a variety of ultrasound (US) techniques that could be used for the postoperative follow-up of colorectal cancer patients. Conventional abdominal and pelvic US may be used for the detection of liver metastases, retroperitoneal lymph node involvement, ovarian metastases, and local/regional recurrence, especially in the pelvis. The accuracy of the US exam has increased with technical development (i.e., higher resolution and real-time scanning) and with growing experience among sonographers. The accuracy of US is quite good in comparison with that of other imaging procedures. As US is cheaper than other procedures, generally available, and noninvasive, it could be regarded as one of the primary imaging methods in follow-up programs.

Transrectal US is of specific interest for the detection of local recurrences after sphincter-preserving surgery for rectal and distal sigmoid cancer. Endosonography is also used transvaginally after abdominoperineal resections.

Ultrasound of Liver Metastases

Metastases of 1 to 2 cm can be detected and lesions larger than 2 cm are detected with high accuracy.[108,109] The areas behind the portal vein in the anterior and lateral regions represent some difficulties for the detection of small lesions.[110]

The sonographic appearance of metastatic lesions is variable. It was classified by Rosenbusch and coworkers[110] and Scheible and coworkers[112] as follows:

- Echo-free: rare, due to extensive necrosis of the tumor, especially in colonic carcinoma.
- Hypoechoic: occurs in about one-third of patients.
- Hyperechoic: frequent.
- Hyperechoic with dorsal acoustic shadow: occurs in calcification of necrotic metastases, very characteristic for colorectal cancer metastases.
- Combination of hyperechoic and hypoechoic lesions.
- Hyperechoic with hypoechoic area around; "bull's eye-lesion."
- Hypoechoic with hyperechoic area around; "target lesion."
- Diffuse alteration of architecture.

Transcolorectal Ultrasound

Despite the strong interest in transcolorectal US diagnosis, only a few articles are available concerning the benefits of the method in the follow-up of patients after surgery.[113–116] This is because of the limited usage of the method mainly in rectal cancer patients. Introduction of flexible echoendoscopes may further improve detection of local/regional recurrence in colorectal cancer patients. Some projections regarding follow-up using this method could be made, extrapolating from the results of preoperative transcolorectal US staging.

Digital rectal examination has obvious limitations, including subjectivity, interrelations of accuracy to clinical experience, and distance limitations in that only the distal 8 to 10 cm of the rectum may be evaluated. Endosonography can be performed transrectally after sphincter-preservation surgery or transvaginally in females following abdominoperineal resection. Transrectal US is reported to be twice as accurate as the digital exam[117] in estimating wall penetration and lymph node involvement. Rifkin and coworkers[118] found transrectal US to be more sensitive and specific than CT in the determination of bowel wall penetration and nodal involvement. Rifkin and Marks[113] briefly mentioned that transrectal US is of value for the assessment of extrarectal structures. Romano and coworkers[114] detected 8 local recurrences, confirmed by various means, in their follow-up group of 42 patients. They also had two false-positive cases which proved to be postoperative fibrosis after percutaneous biopsy. Hildebrandt and associates[115] detected 22 recurrences, but only 6 of them were noted with US alone. The study of Beynon and coworkers[116] showed that endosonography gave good information on established recurrence and allowed the detection of recurrent tumor not apparent on routine clinical examination. The authors stressed that after US identification of abnormal areas, histopathologic confirmation is essential. This is of particular importance in irradiated patients or after an anastomotic leak. It was shown in this study that five ultrasonic layers are clearly identified in the neorectum, as described elsewhere,[119] and the presence of staples did not affect interpretation. The US anatomy of the pelvis will be altered after surgery; interpretation will be assisted by a base-line scan performed 3 months after surgery. The established recurrent tumor had the same US pattern as a primary tumor. Also, it was possible to interpret the degree of invasion in the same manner as for primary cancer. Extrarectal tumors were detected at an early stage. They appear as echo-poor defects, but nevertheless it was not possible to judge them as malignant just from the US characteristics. In such cases close observation or immediate transperineal biopsy was advocated. Very similar conclusions were reached by Milsom and Graffner.[117] Charnley et al.[120,121] suggested that transrectal US provided new information in approximately 25 percent of patients with uncertain pelvic disease and that this modality should be considered early in the management of patients with pelvic problems.

Detection of Lung Metastases

A comprehensive guideline for assessing patients for possible lung metastases has been suggested by Davis.[122] The examination should begin with chest x-rays in the anterior-posterior and lateral positions. If multiple tumor nodules are clearly present, there is no need for a subsequent CT. If a solitary nodule or equivocal findings are revealed, a CT scan should be obtained.[111]

An important practical issue is the optimal frequency of serial chest examinations. Surveillance should be of significance (most intense) during the time in which metastases are more likely to occur—1 to 2 years after primary surgery. According to Collins[123] and Welin and coworkers,[172] the mean doubling time of colorectal cancer pulmonary metastases is 109 to 116 days. Hence, if there is no evidence of recurrent disease, the 3- to 6-month interval between examinations is justifiable; if there is some suspicion, then this interval should not exceed 2 to 3 months.

Computed Tomography Imaging of Hepatic Metastases and Peritoneal Carcinomatosis

Since the early 1980s, CT has been the preferred test for the detection of liver metastases. It has been reported to be more accurate than US and scintigraphy in the detection of metastases and a best single test for their detection.[125,126] The sensitivity of CT is approximately 90 percent in detecting hepatic metastases. However, its specificity is lower, especially when a solitary lesion is encountered and the result is highly dependent on size, vascularity of the tumor, and examination technique. When CT findings are nonspecific, complementary imaging studies may help to provide a specific diagnosis. The detection rates of hepatic masses by CT and magnetic resonance imaging (MRI) are currently comparable. The ability of a CT scan to show extrahepatic pathology is superior to that of MRI; therefore CT scanning is currently the most frequently used method for detecting liver metastases.

Peritoneal involvement by colorectal cancer and other malignant neoplasms is a common occurrence for which CT has assumed an increasingly important role in initial diagnosis and follow-up. Theoretically, CT should directly visualize peritoneal tumor implants. A spectrum of characteristic CT findings in peritoneal carcinomatosis has been offered.[127–131] Most studies reported the preoperative imaging of peritoneal carcinomatosis and only a few reported on detection of peritoneal carcinomatosis during the follow-up period. Needless to say, tumor in scars and/or adhesions between the loops may be difficult or impossible to discriminate by CT from postoperative changes. Extrapolation of preoperative CT findings in a defined patient population with peritoneal carcinomatosis to a follow-up setting must be done with caution.

The technique of CT assessment of peritoneal carcinomatosis[132,133] usually comprises slices with a 8- to 10-mm thickness at 10-mm intervals from the dome of the diaphragm to the bottom of the pelvic cavity. Examination is usually accompanied by the oral administration of contrast, barium enema, or air insufflation of the rectum and the use of intravenous contrast material.

Peritoneal carcinomatosis is an advanced stage of cancer; its CT appearance usually reflects multiple abnormalities. That is why the characteristic appearance in particular sites of involvement will be discussed on a lesion-by-lesion basis rather than a patient-to-patient basis.

In the early studies,[128,134] peritoneal implants detected by CT were described as nodules attached to parietal peritoneum. It was clear that the size of the nodule was crucial for identification. The bigger it was, the higher the probability of detection. The major limitation of CT was its inability to detect peritoneal metastases less than 2 or 3 cm in diameter.[135–137] The presence of ascitic fluid lateral to the right liver was correlated with the presence of peritoneal carcinomatosis. The omentum is a common site for peritoneal seeding. Levitt and coworkers[138] originally described the advanced stage of omental metastatic tumor as a thickened, diffusely infiltrated entity commonly referred to as an "omental cake." Cooper and colleagues[129] pointed out that although the omentum is readily visible on CT, smaller omental nodules may be overlooked without a careful search. Megibow and coworkers[130] observed that tumor manifested as reticular, lacelike areas of increased density within fat was often not recognized at CT interpretation. Nelson and colleagues[133] as well as Jacquet and coworkers[139] found the sensitivity of CT detection of omental metastases to be the lowest (50 percent) among other sites and independent of using intraperitoneal (IP) contrast material. Walkey and colleagues[132] have explained this phenomenon by the differing involvement of the omentum in the metastatic process during the course of the disease. Early disease is manifested as irregular soft tissue densities. Later, discrete homogenous nodules are seen. The most advanced stage of infiltration corresponds to the omental cake.

With the advent of higher-resolution scanners, detection of smaller metastases was suggested.[130,131,140] Implants became visible not only as nodules but as a diffuse thickening of the peritoneal surface. This appearance was accentuated in the presence of the intravenous contrast material. Diffuse thickening was correlated with the presence of confluent miliary seeding of the peritoneal surface, documented at surgery. Parietal peritoneal thickening and enhancement, according to Walkey and coworkers,[132] showed some predilection for the right hemidiaphragm, Douglas pouch, and right paracolic gutter, but it could be seen upon occasion in all regions. Occasionally, involvement of the entire peritoneal surface was observed. Subdiaphragmatic thickening was often seen bilaterally, although it is usually more advanced on the right side. All these data correspond to the classic, definite paths of peritoneal fluid movement and collection in certain spaces described by Autio[141] and Meyers.[142]

Facilitation of tumor implant detection in the presence of ascites led to attempts at the intraperitoneal infusion of contrast material. Guinta and coworkers[143] used 3000 mL of contrast material and reported a sensitivity of 67 percent in patients with carcinomatosis that was previously undetected by CT. In a patient analysis, CT with IP contrast material had a sensitivity of 84 percent and a specificity of 79 percent. Nelson and colleagues[133] compared CT and CT with IP contrast administration and received equally low sensitivity, 59 percent and 61 percent, respectively.

Several features of peritoneal carcinomatosis that could be of value in detection of metastatic disease should be mentioned. One manifestation of tumor involvement of small bowel mesentery is disarray of the normal bowel mesentery pattern. This suggests peritoneal tumor spread even when discrete masses cannot be localized. The "stellate mesentery" is another common feature of metastatic involvement of the mesentery. This is caused by straightened blood vessels held rigid in a mesentery coated by cancer. This could be misleading unless measurable thickening of mesenteric surfaces is demonstrated. Involvement of the bowel wall by cancer is rather common. By CT, bowel wall distortion or thickening is observed. Bowel obstruction is readily determined by CT. Mucinous implants tend to have the characteristic CT appearance of discrete, rounded masses with central low density (mucin) and well-defined enhancing rims.[131,144] They tend to be multiple and occur with or without ascites. Finally, ascites is a common feature of CT in patients with peritoneal carcinomatosis. Small amounts of ascitic fluid are easier to detect in the right subphrenic space, lateral gutters, and Douglas pouch. A characteristic feature of malignant ascites is the presence of loculation.[145] Loculated ascites collections were found in 46 percent of patients with malignant ascites.[132] The presence of loculated ascites in the upper pelvis was associated with the absence of fluid in the Douglas pouch. Walkey and coworkers[131] found ascites to be the most common feature of peritoneal carcinomatosis CT (73 percent), while Nelson and colleagues[133] detected ascites only in every fourth case of IP fluid collection.

Nelson and colleagues[133] studied the sensitivity of CT in different abdominal regions. They showed that the right and left subphrenic space and splenic hilum had the highest sensitivity rate (83 to 88 percent) compared, for example, to the greater omentum, mesentery, etc.

In a recent prospective study, Jacquet and associates[139] demonstrated that tumor volume directly influences sensitivity. When tumor nodules were less than 0.5 cm in diameter, the sensitivity was 28 percent (Fig. 76-8); but it increased to 90 percent when nodules were larger than 5 cm. The data from 783 observations in 45 patients clearly demonstrate that sensitivity rises as the tumor volume increases. Similar data were calculated for tumor extent, with nearly identical results.

Nelson and coworkers[133] compared site-specific results of CT and CT with IP contrast in patients with a clinical diagnosis of peritoneal carcinomatosis. They showed that accuracy differs significantly within the abdominal cavity, being highest in subphrenic spaces, the splenic hilum, and the paracolic gutters and lowest in the greater omentum, small bowel, mesentery, and abdominal wall—areas that had the highest frequency of seeding. Both CT techniques demonstrated 100 percent specificity at all sites with exception of the right subphrenic space (86 percent) and pelvis (67 percent) and the left paracolic gutter (86 percent).

Jacquet and coworkers,[139] using CT with oral and intravenous contrast (no IP contrast), published very similar data of greater sensitivity in upper and lateral aspects of the abdominal cavity and extremely low sensitivity and specificity in the pelvic region and retroperitoneum. A large proportion of false-negative scans were recorded for the abdominal wall and greater omentum. The large bowel was divided into anatomic segments and it was determined that the rectosigmoid region was the area where the inaccurate readings were most common.

Hughes and coworkers[146] and Jacquet and associates[139] described phenomena of peritoneal implants impressed into Glisson's capsule and impinging on the external contour of the liver. These findings can be misdiagnosed as an intrahepatic tumor. Computed tomography may give some clues to extrahepatic disease: extrahepatic tumor is frequently depicted as a lens-shaped defect with its greatest diameter tangential to the liver surface.

Tumor implants of minimal or moderate volume (individual focus of tumor <0.5 cm in diameter or con-

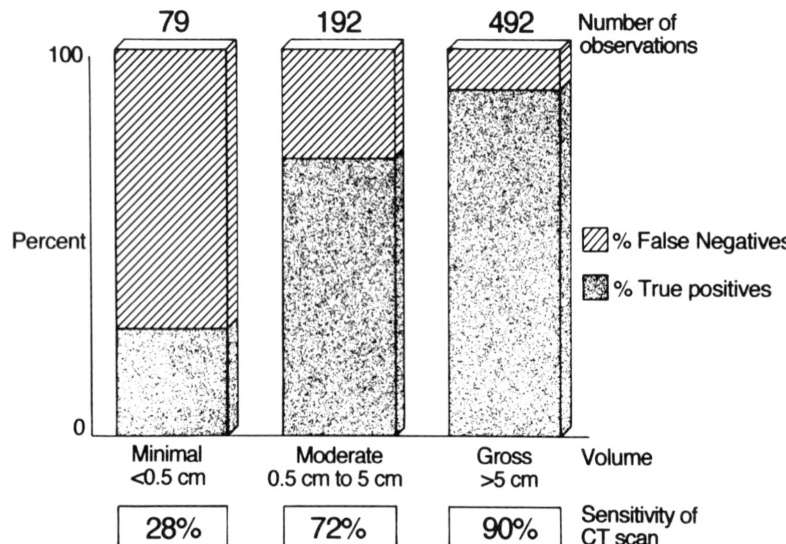

FIG. 76-8. Influence of tumor volume on sensitivity of CT scan. (From Jacquet P et al.[139] Reproduced by permission.)

fluent foci with preserved integrity of a organ, respectively) or location in the rectosigmoid colon, greater omentum, and upper liver surface may cause up to 20 percent of false-negative CT findings.[139] These data are similar to those of Megibow and colleagues,[130] who have found this rate to be 28 percent. It should be kept in mind that both studies were performed with modern equipment and high-resolution scanners.

Nelson and coworkers,[133] having shown that both CT and CT with IP have high specificity but variable sensitivity depending on the site of peritoneal metastases, concluded that CT with IP does not produce sufficient additional information over that gained with conventional CT. Intraoperative correlation and overall patient discomfort during the procedure have resulted in rare requests for CT with IP.

All these data taken together suggest a guarded role of CT in detection of peritoneal carcinomatosis. Greater reliability of CT scan interpretation may come about if the radiologist reads according to specific anatomic sites and uses intravenous and bowel contrast or air to increase visualization in difficult anatomic sites. The study by Jacquet and colleagues[139] suggested the regular use of intrarectal contrast to improve images within the pelvis. Unfortunately, the size-dependent sensitivity makes this method insufficiently reliable for the early detection of peritoneal carcinomatosis when cytoreductive surgery with IP chemotherapy promises improvement in long-term survival to each fourth of patients (see Chap. 89).

Computed Tomography in the Detection of Local/Regional Recurrences

Early studies suggested the usefulness of CT scans in determining the presence of local recurrence and metastases to retroperitoneal lymph nodes.[147,148] Initially, very high sensitivity and accuracy were reported (93 to 95 percent) because patients with advanced disease were studied. More recent investigations have indicated accuracy rates ranging from 69 to 88 percent.[106,149–151] Most errors in interpretation result from CT's inability to differentiate recurrent cancer from postoperative changes or to detect small nodules of metastatic tumor less than 1 to 2 cm in size. Computed tomography is unable to assess the presence or absence of metastatic foci in normal-sized lymph nodes, even if a diameter of 1 cm or less is considered normal. Visualization of early recurrence at the anastomotic site is rarely possible, although good distension of the bowel with contrast material or air plus thin sections (5 mm) through the region of interest are usually helpful for detecting recurrent tumors. Obliteration of adjacent fascial or fat planes and enlargement of regional pelvic nodes may also suggest tumor recurrence. Comparison to a prior baseline examination may be of great help in providing a definite CT interpretation.

Postoperative changes in anatomy may cause difficulties in distinguishing local recurrence from postoperative change (hematoma, abscess, and fibrosis—especially postradiation).[152] For CT to be of optimal value in setting a postoperative follow-up baseline, a CT 2 to 3 months after surgery is required. Kelvin and coworkers[153] reported that 60 percent of presacral masses caused by postoperative fibrosis tended to diminish in size and become better defined over time, while 40 percent of abnormalities showed no change. Masses caused by recurrent tumor enlarged and became less well defined on serial studies.

Butch and colleagues[154] evaluated 28 cases of presacral masses after abdominoperineal resection. They found 78 percent of them to be recurrent tumors verified by percutaneous needle biopsy. At the same time, only 3 of 5 lesions with central areas of low density were recurrent tumors, and none of the 4 gas-containing masses contained tumor. These authors emphasized the necessity of CT-guided biopsy for a suspicious mass. Every attempt to acquire an appropriate contrast image of a cylindrical mass in the pelvis should be made prior to percutaneous needle biopsy. This will minimize the damage to the low loops of small bowel.

Krestin and associates[149] showed that postoperative CTs have a low accuracy when imaging abnormal pelvic changes. In this study, MRI was superior to CT for the assessment of local recurrence. In addition to indirect morphologic criteria, different signal intensities in scar and tumor facilitated differentiation of the two tissues. Evaluation of an anastomosis or the bowel was more accurate with CT. Therefore, it was concluded that in patients who have undergone sphincter-saving resections and in whom previous CT scans were obtained in subsequent follow-up, CT scanning may be considered as accurate as MRI. If there is a discrepancy in clinical or CT findings, an MRI should be obtained.

The value of CT in the detection of local/regional recurrence for colonic cancer is limited. Perianastomotic recurrences are rare after a colonic resection; lymph node metastases in the retroperitoneal space occur much more frequently. The accuracy of CT depends on the size of the tumor. The use of intravenous and oral contrast material for the visualization of bowel loops and ureters that may be displaced or compressed by metastatic tumor must be emphasized.

Magnetic Resonance Imaging of Hepatic Metastases

Magnetic resonance imaging is currently being evaluated as an alternative approach to CT for the optimal detection of liver metastases. Reinig and coworkers[155] demonstrated the slightly better sensitivity of MRI than of EOE-13 CT scanning (95 and 87 percent, respectively). The size threshold for detection of the lesions with both techniques was approximately 1 cm. Most comparative studies have been done with conventional and nonenhanced MRI and only a few[156] compare CT with MRI performed with contrast agent. Despite the fact that comparative studies have produced inconsistent results, with superiority of either MRI or CT, most have found the accuracy of MRI for the detection of liver metastases at least comparable to that of CT.[155–161] Magnetic resonance imaging displays more clearly the internal structure and content of hepatic tumors and their relationship to vessels by its ability to display hepatic venous and portal anatomy without contrast agents. Direct coronal and sagittal MRI can improve the localization of lesions prior to surgery. Surgical clips (excluding titanium ones) do not affect MRI but produce streak artifacts in CT.

Hepatic metastases usually appear as masses with a greater intensity than normal liver on T2-weighted images and with low intensity on T1-weighted images. Metastatic lesions are characterized by prolongation of T_1 and T_2 relaxation times. There is considerable variation in the pattern of the signal intensity that may be observed with metastases. The lesions may be well defined and homogenous. On T2-weighted images, hepatic metastases may show diffuse enhancement, centrally enhanced signal upon necrosis, or a characteristic bright peripheral halo surrounding a low-density or isointense nodule. This peripheral halo is present in approximately one-fourth of the lesions and is never observed in benign lesions. Other signs indicating metastases are as follows: on T1-weighted pulse sequences, a low-signal-intensity mass containing a central lower-signal-intensity area; on T2-weighted pulse sequences, a mass with a central high-intensity region surrounded by a rim of tissue whose signal intensity is less than that of the çentral area (target sign). This variability may be seen even within one patient.[160]

About 10 percent of the adult population possesses either a benign hepatic hemangioma or simple liver cysts. So the problem of differential diagnosis—i.e., specificity—is of great clinical value. On T1-weighted images, all space-occupying lesions (tumor, abscess, hemangioma, cyst) except some hepatomas, lipomas, or hematomas have a similar low-signal, dark appearance with few identifying features. Small tumors and hemangiomas produce similar dark lesions. On T2-weighted images, both tumors and hemangiomas appear bright. Hemangiomas have a contrast-to-noise ratio quantitatively larger than that of tumors. Malignant liver neoplasms tend to have a heterogenous appearance with poorly defined margins and are not as intense as hemangiomas. Metastases secondary to colonic cancer have a less elevated signal than hemangiomas on T2-weighted sequences. For imaging, at 1.5 T the T2-weighted image has the highest sensitivity for hepatic metastases[160] and provides the critical morphologic and signal intensity information to help distinguish benign from malignant lesions.

Outwater and coworkers[162] reviewed the MRI findings and pathologic appearance of 157 metastatic colorectal tumors. Their results support the superiority of T2- to T1-weighted images in demonstrating metastases at 1.5 T. About one-half of the lesions were relatively homogeneous. Some degree of relative central hypointensity was displayed by 49 percent of the nodules. Many of the latter displayed the "halo" sign. However, these patterns form a continuum with hypointense areas, ranging from small central foci to large areas surrounded by a thin, hyperintense rim. The central areas of high signal intensity were usually surrounded by these low-intensity areas. Both of these types of signal change were correlated to the size of the metastases; all of the largest tumors showed some degree of change in signal intensity within the tumor. The authors suggested that these changes represent a spectrum of internal histologic changes related to the tumor's growth.

The halo sign appeared not to be a representation of edema of liver parenchyma around the lesion but the tumor itself. All the histologic specimens reviewed had a predominantly peripheral distribution of carcinoma and few carcinoma cells centrally. Internal desmoplastic reactions were often a dominant feature of these lesions and contributed to the central areas of low signal intensity. The authors concluded that metastases to the liver from colorectal cancer have typical patterns of MRI appearance. Metastatic lesions were usually hyperintense on T2-weighted images. The presence of central low signal intensity within the hyperintense nodule was size-dependent and correlated to areas of desmoplastic stroma, cellular necrosis, and mucin accumulation. Peripheral halos were found to encompass the growing tumor margin and variable degrees of necrosis at the tumor rim. Hypointense peripheral rims corresponded to abnormalities of hepatic parenchyma, hepatocellular atrophy, fibrosis, and congested sinusoids adjacent to the tumor edge.

MRI of Locally Recurrent Tumor

Several investigators found MRI to be superior to CT for the assessment of postoperative local recurrence of rectal cancer.[149,163–165] For an overall abdominal evaluation of nonlocal and liver recurrence, MRI is less valuable than CT or US.

Pelvic presacral masses can readily be detected with MRI. Krestin and coworkers[149] found CT to be more accurate for the evaluation of anastomosis of the bowel wall, since suture material can produce artifacts at high magnetic field strength. Therefore, after abdominoperineal resections, MRI is the preferred method of examination as opposed to CT. If clinical and CT findings are discordant, an MRI can provide additional information.

Initial reports suggested that fibrosis after surgery with or without irradiation could be distinguished from recurrent tumor on the basis of MRI findings. Recurrent tumors were supposed to have a higher signal intensity on T2-weighted images.[149,163,164] But subsequent studies have demonstrated serious doubts about MRI's ability to distinguish between recurrent tumor, fibrosis, and inflammation.[165,166] Using the T2-weighted images, it was shown that it is impossible to differentiate early fibrosis and recurrent tumor (1 to 6 months after surgery), but the low signal intensity of late fibrosis (more than 12 months) could be clearly distinguished from the high signal intensity of recurrent tumor.[149,165,167] A comprehensive investigation of this relationship was conducted by de Lange and colleagues,[168] who compared the results of MRI with those of histologic examination. They found the signal intensities of malignant versus benign lesions to be indistinguishable. All lesions showed areas of high signal intensity that correlated with carcinoma and tumor necrosis or with nonneoplastic inflammation and edema. Areas of low signal intensity corresponded to reactive fibrous tissue (desmoplastic reaction) with small islands of tumor or to nonneoplastic fibrosis. The authors concluded that MRI can be useful in determining the extent of suspected tumors, but signal intensities on T2-weighted images do not permit the establishment of a histologic diagnosis; in particular, they do not allow for a distinction between benign tissue and malignant tissue with a desmoplastic reaction. It is important that, in the latter case, even percutaneous needle biopsy may show only fibrous tissue and no malignant cells.

Chan and coworkers[169] demonstrated that MRI with endorectal coil enhancement correctly established depth of invasion in more than 90 percent of primary cases. This method was much less able to identify positive perirectal nodes (57 percent). Thus, endorectal MRI is a promising technique for the possible detection of local recurrence of rectal cancer after sphincter-saving surgery.

Strategy of Follow-up

The overall recurrence rate is 40 to 45 percent, and only 10 to 15 percent of patients will be secondarily resected for cure, resulting in only a 2 to 5 percent overall survival benefit (Table 76-5). Hence, for routine follow-up to be cost-effective, a relatively simple

Table 76-5
Tests Available for Follow-up and Early Detection of Recurrence—Long-Term Outcome of Follow-up

	Site of recurrence					
Test	*Liver*	*Lungs*	*Local/ regional*	*Intra-abdominal*	*Retro-peritoneal*	*Ovarian*
Symptom review	+ −	+ −	+		+ −	
Physical examination	+ −		+	+ −		+ −
Pelvic examination						+
Stool occult blood test						
CEA blood test	+			+	+ −	
Colonoscopy			+			
Double-contrast barium enema			+			
Chest x-ray		+				
Full-lung tomography		+				
Chest CT scan		+				
CT scan of abdomen and pelvis with contrast	+			+	+	+
MRI	+		+			
US	+		+			+
Transrectal US or MRI			+			
Percutaneous guided biopsy	+		+			
First site recurrence incidence[a]	10%	3%	6%	6%	3%	5%
Curative treatment of recurrent tumor	3%	0.5%	2%	1.2%	0.3%	2%
Long-term survivors	1%	0.1%	0.5%	0.4%	0.1%	1%

[a]Percentage of total group of patients subjected to follow-up.

Table 76-6
Tests Available for Detection of Recurrent Tumor, Second Primary Colorectal Tumor, and Other Primary Cancer

Test	*Recurrent tumor*	*Second primary C/R tumor*	*Other primary cancer*
Symptom review	+	+	+
Physical examination	+	+	+
Pelvic examination	+	−	+
Stool occult blood test	+	+	−
CEA blood test	+	+	−
Colonoscopy	+	+	−
Double-contrast barium enema	+	+	−
Chest x-ray	+	−	+
CT of abdomen, pelvis	+	−	+
US examination	+	−	+
Mammography	−	−	+
Probable rate of detection[a]	33%	5%	5%
Probable rate of curative resections	3–5%	4%	4%
Long-term survivors of those resected for cure	30–40%	65%	60–70%

[a]Percentage of the entire group of patients subjected to follow-up.

Table 76-7
Current Recommendation for Follow-up Plan in Colorectal Cancer: the 2, 4, 6 Plan[a]

	Time interval				
Test	*Preop.*	*Postop.*	*Every 2 months, year 1*	*Every 4 months, years 2–3*	*Every 6 months, years 4–5*
Basic tests					
Symptom review	+	+	+	+	+
Physical examination including rectal[b]	+		+	+	+
CEA blood test (+TPA, CA 19-9 or other)	+	+	+	+	+
Colonoscopy/Double contrast barium enema	+	+[c]		+[d]	+
Chest x-ray (annually)	+		+	+	+
CT of abdomen, pelvis or US examination	+	+[e]			
Site-specific tests	Anytime when indicated				
Full-lung tomography or chest CT					
CT with contrast enhancement, CT-AP, CTA, CT-IP					
MRI of liver, pelvis					
Radioimmunodetection					
Transrectal US or MRI					
Laparoscopy					
Second-look laparotomy					
Tests for other primaries	Once in 2 years				
Mammography					
Pelvic examination with US and cervical cytology					

[a]The 2, 4, 6 plan is not indicated for T_1N_0 cancers, debilitated patients, or patients above age 70.
[b]Visualize suture line with colorectal anastomosis.
[c]If not done preoperatively.
[d]Yearly if positive, every 3 years after two negative exams.
[e]Subsequent abdominal CT for suspect recurrence only.

Table 76-8
Follow-up Schedule for Colonic and Rectal Carcinoma with Low and High Risk of Recurrence (2, 4, 6 Plan versus 1, 2, 6 Plan)

Test	*Primary cancer risk* / *Time interval*[a]	*Colon* *Low* 1	2	3	*Colon* *High* 4	5	6	*Rectum* *Low* 1	2	3	*Rectum* *High* 4	5	6
First line													
Symptoms review		+	+	+	+	+	+	+	+	+	+	+	+
Phys. examination		+	+	+	+	+	+	+	+	+	+	+	+
CEA (TPA + CA19-9)		+	+	+	+	+	+	+	+	+	+	+	+
Procto-sigmoidoscopy		–	–	–	–	–	–	+	+	+	+	+	+
Second line[b]													
Chest x-ray		Annually			Twice a year			Annually			Twice a year		
CT (or MRI, US) of liver and pelvis		If indicated by first-line tests											
Double-contrast barium enema		If indicated by first-line tests											
Colonoscopy[c]		Biannually			Annually			Biannually			Annually		
Transrectal US		If indicated by first-line tests											

[a]Time interval: 1—every 2 months for year 1; 2—every 4 months for years 2 to 3; 3—every 6 months for years 4 to 5; 4—every month for year 1; 5—every 2 months for years 2 to 3; 6—every 6 months for years 4 to 5.
[b]Time intervals may be shorter if indicated by first-line tests.
[c]Yearly if positive, every 3 years after two negative exams.

and sensitive test or group of tests should be used. At the first stage of surveillance, it is appropriate to suspect or detect abnormality. Further investigation with comprehensive and more accurate tests will allow a determination of the precise diagnosis and extent of disease. The set of basic (first-line) tests that should be used for routine follow-up may include one or two reliable tests capable of detecting the presence or recurrence of tumor at all important sites (Table 76-6).

This set of basic tests should be used in accord with the 2,4,6 plan (Table 76-7). That is, the time intervals during the first year of follow-up should be 2 months; during the second and third years, 4 months; and during the fourth and fifth years, 6 months for basic or first-line tests. Any symptoms or findings serve as indications for thorough radiologic evaluation (second-line site-specific tests). This plan includes perioperative evaluation of the entire colon, tumor bed area, liver, and lungs as a baseline for further follow-up. More intensive follow-up plan with 1- to 2-month intervals between first-line tests and shorter intervals between radiologic tests may be applied if there are indicators of a high risk of recurrence (Table 76-8).

REFERENCES

1. Tornquist A, Ekelund G, Leandoer L: The value of intensive follow-up after curative resection for colorectal carcinoma. *Br J Surg* 69:725–728, 1982.
2. Cochrane J, Williams J, Faber R, et al: Value of outpatient follow-up after curative surgery for carcinoma of the large bowel. *Br Med J* 280:593–595, 1980.
3. Ekman C-A, Gustavsson J, Henning A: Value of a follow-up study of recurrent carcinoma of the colon and rectum. *Surg Gynecol Obstet* 145:845–847, 1977.
4. Martin EW Jr, Minton JP, Carey LC: CEA-directed second-look surgery in the asymptomatic patient after primary resection of colorectal cancer. *Ann Surg* 202:310–317, 1985.
5. Schiessel R, Wunderlich M, Herbst F: Local recurrence of colorectal cancer: Effect of early detection and aggressive surgery. *Br J Surg* 73:342–344, 1986.
6. Morson B, Bussey H: Magnitude of risk for cancer in patients with colorectal adenomas. *Br J Surg* 72(suppl):23–25, 1985.
7. Nelson R, Chezmar J, Sugarbaker P, et al: Comparison of CTA-portography, delayed CT and MRI for the preoperative evaluation of hepatic tumors. *Radiology* 174:621–626, 1990.
8. August DA, Ottow RT, Sugarbaker PH: Clinical perspective of human colorectal cancer metastasis. *Cancer Metast* 3:303–324, 1984.
9. Wilson S, Adson M: Surgical treatment of hepatic metastases from colorectal cancer. *Arch Surg* 111:330–334, 1976.
10. Foster J, Berman M: Solid liver tumors, in Ebert P (ed): *Major Problems in Clinical Surgery*. Philadelphia, Saunders, 1977, pp 209–234.
11. Iwatsuki S, Shaw B, Starzl T: Experience with 150 liver resections. *Ann Surg* 197:247–253, 1983.
12. Fortner JG, Silva JS, Cox EB, et al: Multivariate analysis of a personal series of 247 patients with liver metastases from colorectal cancer. *Ann Surg* 199:317–323, 1984.
13. Cady B, McDermott W: Major hepatic resections for metachronous metastases from colon cancer. *Ann Surg* 201: 204–209, 1985.
14. Hughes K, Scheele J, Sugarbaker PH: Surgery for colorectal cancer metastatic to the liver. *Surg Clin North Am* 69:339–359, 1989.
15. Scheele J, Stangl R, Altendorf-Hofmann A: Hepatic metastases from colorectal carcinoma: Impact of surgical resection on the natural history. *Br J Surg* 77:1241–1246, 1990.

16. Petrelli N, Gupta B, Piedmonte M, et al: Morbidity and survival of liver resection for colorectal adenocarcinoma. *Dis Colon Rectum* 34:899–904, 1991.
17. Goya T, Miyazawa N, Kondo H, et al: Surgical resection of pulmonary metastases from colorectal cancer: 10-year follow-up. *Cancer* 64:1418–1421, 1989.
18. Mori M, Tomoda H, Ishida T, et al: Surgical resection of pulmonary metastases from colorectal adenocarcinoma: Special reference to repeated pulmonary resections. *Arch Surg* 126:1297–1302, 1991.
19. Pihl E, Hughes ESR, McDermott FT, et al: Recurrence of carcinoma of the colon and rectum at the anastomotic suture line. *Surg Gynecol Obstet* 153:495–496, 1981.
20. Sugarbaker PH: *Pelvic Surgery and Treatment for Cancer* Mosby Year Book, St. Louis, 1994.
21. Beart R, O'Connel M: Postoperative follow-up of patients with cancer of the colon. *Mayo Clin Proc* 58:361–363, 1983.
22. Birnkraft A, Sampson V, Sugarbaker PH: Ovarian metastasis from colorectal cancer. *Dis Colon Rectum* 29:767–771, 1986.
23. Morrow M, Enker WE: Late ovarian metastases in carcinoma of the colon and rectum. *Arch Surg* 119:1385–1388, 1984.
24. Sugarbaker PH, Gianola FJ, Dwyer A, et al: A simplified plan for follow-up of patients with colon and rectal cancer supported by prospective studies of laboratory and radiologic test results. *Surgery* 102:79–87, 1987.
25. Wanebo HJ, Llaneras M, Martin T, et al: Prospective monitoring trial for carcinoma of colon and rectum after surgical resection. *Surg Gynecol Obstet* 169:479–487, 1989.
26. Moertel CG, Schutt AJ, Go LW: Carcinoembryonic antigen test for recurrent colorectal cancer. *JAMA* 239:1065–1066, 1978.
27. Wedell J, Essen PM, Luu TH, et al: A retrospective study of serial CEA determinations in the early detection of recurrent colorectal cancer. *Dis Colon Rectum* 24:618–621, 1981.
28. Hine KR, Dykes PW: Prospective randomized trial of early cytotoxic therapy for recurrent colorectal carcinoma detected by serum CEA. *Gut* 25:682–688, 1984.
29. Fucini C, Tommasi M, Cardona G, et al: Limitations of CEA monitoring as a guide to second-look surgery in colorectal cancer follow-up. *Tumori* 69:359–364, 1983.
30. Ovaska J, Jarvinen H, Kujari H, et al: Follow-up of patients operated on for colorectal carcinoma. *Am J Surg* 159:593–596, 1990.
31. Weiss L: *Principles of Metastasis*. Orlando, Florida, Academic Press, 1985.
32. Sugarbaker PH: Recurrent colorectal cancer: Tumor biology and therapeutic implications, in Mortensen N (ed): *Baillier's Clinical Gastroenterology*. London, Bailliere, Tindall, Saunders, 1989.
33. August D, Ottow R, Sugarbaker P: Clinical perspective of human colorectal cancer metastasis. *Cancer Metast Rev* 3:303–324, 1984.
34. Berge I, Ekelund C, Meller B: Carcinoma of the colon and rectum in a defined population. *Acta Chir Scand* 438 (suppl):1–86, 1973.
35. Galandiuk S, Wieand H, Moertel C, et al: Patterns of recurrence after curative resection of carcinoma of the colon and rectum. *Surg Gynecol Obstet* 174:27–32, 1992.
36. Collins V, Loeffler R, Tivey H: Observation on growth rates of human tumors. *Am J Roentgenol* 76:988–1000, 1956.
37. Joseph W, Morton D, Adkins P: Prognostic significance of tumor doubling time in evaluating operability in pulmonary disease. *J Thorac Cardiovasc Surg* 61:23–32, 1971.
38. Havelaar IJ, Sugarbaker PH, Vermess M, et al: Rate of growth of intraabdominal metastases from colorectal cancer. *Cancer* 54:163–171, 1991.
39. Cunliffe W, Hasleton P, Tweedle D: Incidence of synchronous and metachronous colorectal carcinoma. *Br J Surg* 71:941–943, 1984.
40. Finan P, Ritchie J, Hawley P: Synchronous and early metachronous colorectal carcinoma. *Br J Surg* 71:941–943, 1984.
41. Langevin JM, Nivatvongs S: The true incidence of synchronous cancer of the large bowel. *Am J Surg* 147:330–333, 1984.
42. Bussey H, Wallace M, Morson B: Metachronous carcinoma of the large intestine and intestinal polyps. *Proc R Soc Med* 60:208–210, 1967.
43. Lokich J: Tumor markers: General concepts, in Schein P (ed): *Decision Making in Oncology*. Toronto, Decker, 1989, pp 2–5.
44. Gold P, Freedman SO: Demonstration of tumor specific antigens in human colonic carcinomata by immunological tolerance and absorption techniques. *J Exp Med* 121:439–462, 1965.
45. van Kleist S, Chavanel G, Burtin P: Identification of an antigen from normal human tissue that crossreacts with the CEA. *Proc Natl Acad Sci USA* 69:2492–2494, 1972.
46. Hammarstrom S: Chemistry and immunology of CEA, CA19-9 and CA50, in Holmgern J (ed): *Tumor Marker Antigens*. Lund, Sweden, Studenten-Litteratur, 1985, pp 34–51.
47. Jessup J, Thomas P: CEA: Function in metastasis by human colorectal carcinoma. *Cancer Metast Rev* 3:263–280, 1989.
48. Schuster J, Silverman M, Gold P: Metabolism of human CEA in xenogeneic animals. *Cancer Res* 33:65–68, 1973.
49. Thomas P, Heims P: The hepatic clearance of circulating CEA antigen by the mouse. *Biochem Soc Trans* 5:312–313, 1977.
50. Holyoke E, Reynoso G, Chu T: CEA in patients with carcinoma of the digestive tract, in *Proceedings of Second Conference on Embryonic and Fetal Antigens in Cancer*. National Technical Information Service, Springfield, VA, US Department of Commerce, 1972, p 215.
51. Dyce B, Haverback B: Free and bound CEA in neoplasms and in normal adult and fetal tissues. *Immunochemistry* 11:423–430, 1975.
52. Begent RHJ: The value of CEA measurement in clinical practice. *Ann Clin Biochem* 21:231–238, 1984.
53. Nisselbaum J, Smith C, Schwartz D, et al: Comparison of Roche RIA, Roche EIA, Hybritech EIA, and Abbott EIA methods for measuring CEA. *Clin Chem* 34:761–764, 1988.
54. Davidson H, Pledger D, Belfield A: Lack of comparability between CEA analyses using three different methods. *Ann Clin Biochem* 22:94–97, 1985.
55. Felder R, MacMillan R, Bruns P: Two monoclonal based assays for CEA. *Clin Chem* 33:700–704, 1987.
56. Klee G, Dodge L, Reguoso G: Discrepancies in CEA measurements: Survey and control vs values for patients. *Clin Chem* 33:563–566, 1987.
57. Special section: A decade of CEA testing. *J Clin Immunoassay* 7:101–132, 1984.
58. Fleisher M, Nisselbaum J, Loftin L, et al: Roche RIA and Abbott EIA carcinoembryonic antigen assays compared. *Clin Chem* 30:200–205, 1984.
59. Khoo S, Warner N, Lie J, et al: CEA activity in tissue extracts: A quantitative study of malignant and benign neoplasms, cirrhotic liver, normal adults and fetal organs. *Int J Cancer* 11:681–687, 1973.
60. Kupchik J, Zamcheck N: CEA(s) in liver disease: I. Clinical and morphological studies. *Gastroenterology* 63:88–94, 1972.
61. Gardner R, Feinerman A, Kantrowitz P, et al: Serial CEA levels in patients with ulcerative colitis. *Am J Dig Dis* 23:129–133, 1978.

62. Moertel ChG, Fleming ThR, Macdonald JS, et al: An evaluation of the CEA test for monitoring patients with resected colon cancer. *JAMA* 270:943–947, 1993.
63. Dhar P, Moore T, Zamcheck N, et al: CEA in colonic cancer: Use in preoperative and postoperative diagnosis and prognosis. *JAMA* 221:31–35, 1972.
64. LoGerfo P, Herter F, Hansen J: Tumor-associated antigen in patients with carcinoma of the colon. *Am J Surg* 123:127–131, 1972.
65. Livingstone A, Hampson L, Schuster J, et al: CEA in the diagnosis and management of colorectal carcinoma. *Arch Surg* 109:259–264, 1974.
66. Sorokin JJ, Sugarbaker PH, Zamcheck N, et al: Serial carcinoembryonic antigen assays: Use in detection of cancer recurrence. *JAMA* 228:49–53, 1974.
67. Oh J, MacLean L: Prognostic use of preoperative and immediate postoperative CEA determinations in colonic cancer. *Can J Surg* 20:64–67, 1977.
68. Gianola F, Sugarbaker P, Dwyer A, et al: Prospective studies of laboratory and radiologic tests in the management of colon and rectal cancer patients. *Dis Colon rectum* 27:811–818, 1985.
69. Wanebo JH, Rao B, Pinsky CM, et al: Pre-operative carcinoembryonic antigen level as a prognostic indicator in colorectal cancer. *N Engl J Med* 299:448–451, 1978.
70. Minton J, Martin E: The use of serial CEA determinations to predict recurrence of colon cancer and when to do a second-look operation. *Cancer* 42:1422–1427, 1993.
71. Cohen A, Wood, W: CEA levels as an indicator for reoperation in patients with carcinoma of the colon and rectum. *Surg Gynecol Obstet* 149:22–26, 1979.
72. Steele G Jr, Zamcheck N, Mayer R, et al: Results of CEA-initiated second-look surgery for recurrent colorectal cancer. *Am J Surg* 139:544–548, 1980.
73. Gray B, Walker C, Barnard R: Value of serial CEA determinations for early detection of recurrent cancer. *Med J Aust* 1:177–178, 1981.
74. Koch M, Washer G, Gaedke H, et al: CEA: Usefulness as a postsurgical method in the detection of recurrence in Dukes stages B2 and C colorectal cancers. *J Natl Cancer Inst* 69:813–815, 1982.
75. Carlsson U, Stewenius J, Ekelund G, et al: Is CEA analysis of value in screening for recurrences after surgery for colorectal carcinoma? *Dis Colon Rectum* 26:369–373, 1983.
76. Rittgers R, Steele G, Zamcheck N, et al: Transient CEA elevations following resection of colorectal cancer: A limitation in the use of serial CEA levels as an indicator for second-look surgery. *J Natl Cancer Inst* 61:315–318, 1978.
77. Minton JP, Hoehn JL, Gerber DM, et al: Results of a 400-patient carcinoembryonic antigen second-look colorectal cancer study. *Cancer* 55:1284–1290, 1985.
78. Bohm B, Schwenk W, Huche H, et al: Does methodic long-term follow-up affect survival after curative resection of colorectal carcinoma? *Dis Colon Rectum* 36:280–286, 1993.
79. Northover J: Carcinoembryonic antigen and recurrent colorectal cancer. *Gut* 27:117–122, 1986.
80. Mach J, Vienny H, Jaeger P, et al: Long-term follow-up of colorectal carcinoma patients by repeated CEA radioimmunoassay. *Cancer* 42:1439–1447, 1978.
81. Beart RW, Metzger PP, O'Connell MJ, et al: Postoperative screening of patients with carcinoma of the colon. *Dis Colon Rectum* 24:585–589, 1981.
82. Boey J, Cheung HC, Lai CK, et al: A prospective evaluation of serum carcinoembryonic antigen levels in the management of colorectal carcinoma. *World J Surg* 8:279–286, 1984.
83. Sugarbaker PH, Zamcheck N, Moore FD: Assessment of serial carcinoembryonic antigen assays in postoperative detection of recurrent colorectal cancer. *Cancer* 38:2310–2315, 1976.
84. Steele G Jr, Ellenberg S, Ramming K, et al: CEA monitoring among patients in multi-institutional adjuvant G.I. therapy protocols. *Ann Surg* 196:162–169, 1982.
85. Denstman F, Rosen L, Khubchandani IT, et al: Comparing predictive decision rules in postoperative CEA monitoring. *Cancer* 58:2089–2095, 1986.
86. Northover JMA: Carcinoembryonic antigen and recurrent colorectal cancer. *Br J Surg* 72(suppl):544–645, 1985.
87. Mavligit G, McMurtey M: Role of CEA—A challenge of a verdict (letter). *JAMA* 240:1714, 1978.
88. Sugarbaker P: Carcinoma of the colon—Prognosis and operative choice. *Curr Probl Surg* 18:755–802, 1981.
89. Barillari P, Bolognese A, Chirletti P, et al: Role of CEA, TPA and CA19-9 in the early detection of localized and diffuse recurrent cancer. *Dis Colon Rectum* 35:471–476, 1992.
90. Costagna J, Benfield J, Yamada H, et al: The reliability of liver scans and function tests in detecting mestastases. *Surg Gynecol Obstet* 134:463–466, 1972.
91. Ranson J, Adams P, Localio S: Preoperative assessment for hepatic metastases in carcinoma of the colon and rectum. *Surg Gynecol Obstet* 137:435, 1973.
92. Baden H, Andersen B, Augustenborg G, et al: Diagnostic value of gamma-glutamyl transpeptidase and alkaline phosphatase in liver metastases. *Surg Gynecol Obstet* 1333:769–1971, 1993.
93. Kemeny NM, Sugarbaker PH, Smith TJ, et al: A prospective analysis of laboratory tests and imaging studies to detect hepatic lesions. *Ann Surg* 195:163–167, 1982.
94. Rachlin M, Senagore A, Talbott T: Role of CEA and liver function tests in the detection of recurrent colorectal carcinoma. *Dis Colon Rectum* 34:794–797, 1991.
95. Deveney KE, Way LW: Follow-up of patients with colorectal cancer. *Am J Surg* 148:717–722, 1984.
96. Koj A: Acute phase reactants, in Allison A (ed): *Structure and Function of Plasma Proteins,* 10th ed. London, Plenum Press, pp 73–131, 1974.
97. Ward AM, Cooper EH, Turner R, et al: Acute-phase reactant protein profiles: An aid to monitoring large bowel cancer by CEA and serum enzymes. *Br J Cancer* 35:170–178, 1977.
98. Walker C, Gray B: Acute-phase reactant proteins and CEA in cancer of the colon and rectum. *Cancer* 52:150–154, 1983.
99. Walker C, Grace BN: Acute-phase reactant proteins and carcinoembryonic antigen in cancer of the colon and rectum. *Cancer* 52:150–154, 1983.
100. Verazin G, Riley WM, Gregory J, et al: Serum sialic acid and carcinoembryonic levels in the detection and monitoring of colorectal cancer. *Dis Colon Rectum* 33:139–142, 1990.
101. Putzki H, Student A, Jablonski M, et al: Comparison of the tumor marker CEA, TPA, and CA 19-9 in colorectal carcinoma. *Cancer* 59:223–226, 1987.
102. Oehr P, Derigs G, Altmann R: Evaluation and characterization of tumor-associated antigens by conversion of inverse distribution function values into specificity-sensitivity diagrams. *Tumor Diagnostik* 2:283–290, 1981.
103. Luthgens M, Schlegel G: Combined use of CEA and TPA in oncologic therapy and surveillance. *Cancer Detect Prev* 6:51–59, 1983.
104. Yamaguchi A, Kurosaka Y, Ishida T, et al: Clinical significance of tumor marker NCC-ST 439 in large bowel cancers. *Dis Colon Rectum* 34:921–924, 1991.
105. Barkin J, Cohen M, Flaxman M, et al: Value of the routine follow-up endoscopy for the detection of recurrent colorectal carcinoma. *Am J Gastroenterol* 88:1355–1360, 1988.
106. Chen YM, Ott D, Wolfman P, et al: Recurrent colorectal car-

cinoma: Evaluation with barium enema examination and CT. *Radiology* 163:307–310, 1987.

107. Taylor AJ, Youker JE: Imaging in colorectal carcinoma. *Semin Oncol* 18:99–110, 1991.
108. Gunven P, Makuchi MM, Takayasu K, et al: Preoperative imaging of liver metastases: Comparison of angiography, CT scan, and ultrasonography. *Ann Surg* 202:573–579, 1985.
109. Suramo I, Paivansalo M, Pamilo M: Unidentified liver metastases at ultrasonography or CT. *Acta Radiol Diagn* 25:385–389, 1984.
110. Rosenbusch G, Smits N, Reeders J: Ultrasonography in hepatobiliary and pancreatic malignancies, in Lygidakis N, Tytgat G (eds): *Hepatobiliary and Pancreatic Malignancies*. Thieme, 1989, 51–65.
111. Friedman G, Bohndorf K, Kruger J: Radiology of pulmonary metastases. *Thorac Cardiovasc Surg* 34:120–124, 1986.
112. Scheible W, Gosink B, Leopold G: Gray-scale echographic patterns of hepatic metastatic disease. *AJR* 129:983–987, 1977.
113. Rifkin MD, Marks GJ: Transrectal US as an adjunct in the diagnosis of rectal and extrarectal tumors. *Radiology* 157: 499–502, 1985.
114. Romano G, deRosa P, Vallone G, et al: Intrarectal ultrasound and computed tomography in the pre- and postoperative assessment of patients with rectal cancer. *Br J Surg* 72(suppl):S117–S119, 1985.
115. Hildebrandt U, Feifel G, Schwarz H, et al: Endorectal ultrasound: Instrumentation and clinical aspects. *Int J Colorect Dis* 1:203–207, 1986.
116. Beynon J, Mortensen M, Foy D, et al: The detection and evaluation of locally recurrent rectal cancer with rectal endosonography. *Dis Colon Rectum* 32:509–517, 1989.
117. Milsom JW, Graffner H: Intrarectal ultrasonography in rectal cancer staging and in the evaluation of pelvic disease: Clinical uses of intrarectal ultrasound. *Ann Surg* 212:602–606, 1990.
118. Rifkin MD, Ehrlich SM, Marks G: Staging of rectal carcinoma: Prospective comparison of endorectal US and CT 1. *Radiology* 170:319–322, 1989.
119. Beynon J, McC Mortensen NJ, Foy DMA, et al: Pre-operative assessment of local invasion in rectal cancer: Digital examination, endoluminal sonography or computed tomography? *Br J Surg* 73:1015–1017, 1986.
120. Charnley RM, Dye G, Awar S, et al: The early detection of recurrent rectal carcinoma by rectal endosonography. *Br J Surg* 75:1232, 1988.
121. Charnley RM: The early detection of recurrent and metastatic colorectal cancer. *Diss Abstr Int (B)* 52:2494, 1991.
122. Davis S: CT evaluation for pulmonary metastases in patients with extrathoracic malignancy. *Radiology* 180:1–12, 1991.
123. Collins VP: Time of occurrence of pulmonary metastasis from carcinoma of colon and rectum. *Cancer* 15:387–395, 1962.
124. Sikora K, Chan S, Evan G, et al: C-myc oncogene expression in colorectal cancer. *Cancer* 59:1289–1295, 1987.
125. Zeman RK, Paushter DM, Schiebler ML, et al: Hepatic imaging: Current status. *Radiol Clin North Am* 23:473–487, 1985.
126. Bernardino M, Ervin B, Steinberg H, et al: Delayed hepatic CT scanning: Increased confidence and improved detection of hepatic metastases. *Radiology* 159:71–74, 1986.
127. Reuter K, Raptopoulos V, Reale F, et al: Diagnosis of peritoneal mesothelioma: CT, sonography and fine-needle aspiration biopsy. *AJR* 140:1189–1194, 1983.
128. Whitley N, Brenner D, Francis A, et al: Use of the CT whole body scanner to stage and follow patients with advanced ovarian carcinoma. *Invest Radiol* 16:479–486, 1981.
129. Cooper C, Jeffrey R, Silverman P, et al: CT of omental pathology. *J Comput Assist Tomogr* 10:62–66, 1986.
130. Megibow A, Bosniak M, Belelr U, et al: Accuracy of CT in detection of persistent or recurrent ovarian carcinoma correlation with second-look laparotomy. *Radiology* 166:341–345, 1988.
131. Walkey M, Friedman A, Sohotra P, et al: CT manifestation of peritoneal carcinomatosis. *Am J Roentgenol* 150:1035–1041, 1988.
132. Walkey M, Friedman A, Radecki P: CT of peritoneal carcinomatosis. *Radiol Rep* 1:152–170, 1989.
133. Nelson R, Chezmar J, Hoel M, et al: CT of peritoneal carcinomatosis prior to cytoreductive surgery: Experience with intraperitoneal contrast material. *Radiology* 182:133–138, 1992.
134. Jeffrey R: CT demonstration of peritoneal implants. *Am J Roentgenol* 135:323–326, 1980.
135. Amendola M, Walsh J, Amendola B, et al: CT in the evaluation of carcinoma of the ovary. *J Comput Assist Tomogr* 5:179–186, 1981.
136. Mamtora H, Isherword I: CT in ovarian carcinoma: Patterns of disease and limitations. *Clin Radiol* 33:165–171, 1982.
137. Levitt R, Koechler R, Sagel S, et al: Metastatic disease of the mesentery and omentum. *Radiol Clin North Am* 20:501–510, 1982.
138. Levitt R, Sogel S, Stanley R: Detection of neoplastic involvement of the mesentery and omentum by CT. *AJR* 131:835–838, 1978.
139. Jacquet P, Jelinek J, Steves M, et al: Evaluation of CT in patients with peritoneal carcinomatosis. *Cancer* 72(5):1631–1636.
140. Whitley N: Mesenteric disease, in Meyers M (ed): *CT of the Gastrointestinal Tract Including the Peritoneal Cavity and Mesentery*. New York, Springer-Verlag, 1986, pp 139–181.
141. Autio V: The spread of intraperitoneal infection: Studies with roentgen contrast medium. *Acta Chir Scand Suppl* 321:1–31, 1964.
142. Meyers M: The spread and localization of acute intraperitoneal effusions. *Radiology* 95:547–554, 1970.
143. Guinta S, Tipaldi L, Diotellevi F, et al: CT demonstration of peritoneal metastases after intraperitoneal injection of contrast media. *Clin Imaging* 14:31–34, 1990.
144. Mayers G, Chuang V, Fisher R: CT of pseudomyxoma peritonei. *AJR* 136:807–808, 1981.
145. Jeffery R: CT of the peritoneal cavity and mesentery, in Moss A, Gamsu G, Genant H (eds): *Computed Tomography of the Body*. Philadelphia, Saunders, 1983, pp 955–986.
146. Hughes KS, Rosenstein RB, Songhorabodi S, et al: Resection of the liver for colorectal carcinoma metastases: A multi-institutional study of long-term survivors. *Dis Colon Rectum* 31:1–4, 1988.
147. Ellert J, Kreel L: The value of CT in malignant colonic tumors. *J Comput Assist Tomogr* 4:225–240, 1980.
148. Husband J, Hadson N, Parsons C: Use of CT in recurrent rectal tumors. *Radiology* 134:677–682, 1980.
149. Krestin G, Steinbrich W, Friedman G: Recurrent rectal cancer: Diagnosis with MRI vs CT. *Radiology* 168:307–311, 1988.
150. Thompson WM, Halvorsen RA, Foster WL Jr, et al: Preoperative and postoperative CT staging of rectosigmoid carcinoma. *Am J Radiol* 146:703–710, 1986.
151. Freeny PC, Marks WM, Ryan JA, et al: Colorectal carcinoma evaluation with CT: Preoperative staging and detection of postoperative recurrence. *Radiology* 158:347–353, 1986.
152. Reznek R, White F, Young J, et al: The appearance on CT

after abdominoperineal resection for carcinoma of the rectum. *Br J Radiol* 56:237–240, 1983.

153. Kelvin F, Gardiner P, Vas W, et al: Colorectal carcinoma missed on double-contrast barium enema study: A problem in perception. *AJR* 137:307–313, 1981.
154. Butch RJ, Stark DD, Wittenberg J, et al: Staging rectal cancer by MR and CT. *Am J Radiol* 146:1155–1160, 1986.
155. Reinig JW, Dwyer AJ, Miller DL, et al: Liver metastasis detection: Comparative sensitivities of MR imaging and CT scanning. *Radiology* 162:43–47, 1987.
156. Nelson R, Chezmar J, Steiberg H, et al: Focal hepatic lesions: Detection by dynamic and delayed CT vs short TE/TR spin echo and fast field echo MRI. *Gastrointest Radiol* 13:115–122, 1988.
157. Vermes M, Leung A, Bydder G, et al: MRI of the liver in primary hepatocellular carcinoma. *J Comput Assist Tomogr* 9:749–754, 1985.
158. Reinig J, Dwyer A, Miller D, et al: Liver metastases: Detection with MRI at 0,5 and 1,5 T. *Radiology* 170:149–153, 1989.
159. Curati W, Halevy A, Gibson R, et al: Ultrasound, CT and MRI comparison in primary and secondary tumors of the liver. *Gastrointest Radiol* 13:123–128, 1988.
160. Wittenberg J, Stark D, Forman B, et al: Differentiation of hepatic metastases from hepatic hemangiomas and cysts by using MRI. *AJR* 151:79–84, 1988.
161. Hahn P, Stark D, Saini s, et al: The differential diagnosis of ringed hepatic lesions in MRI. *AJR* 154:287–290, 1990.
162. Outwater E, Tomaszewski J, Daly J, et al: Hepatic colorectal metastases: Correlation of MRI and pathologic appearance. *Radiology* 180:327–332, 1991.
163. Glazer H, Lee J, Levitt R, et al: Radiation fibrosis: Differentiation from recurrent tumor by MRI. *Radiology* 156:721–726, 1985.
164. Gomberg J, Friedman A, Radecki P: MRI differentiation of recurrent colorectal carcinoma from postoperative fibrosis. *Gastrointest Radiol* 11:361–363, 1986.
165. Ebner F, Kressel H, Mintz M, et al: Tumor recurrence versus fibrosis in female pelvis: Differentiation with MRI. *Radiology* 166:333–340, 1988.
166. Rafto S, Amendola M, Gefter W: MRI of recurrent colorectal carcinoma vs fibrosis. *J Comput Assist Tomogr* 12:521–523, 1988.
167. Dixon AK, Fry IK, Morson BC, et al: Pre-operative computed tomography of carcinoma of the rectum. *Br J Radiol* 54:655–659, 1981.
168. de Lange E, Fechner R, Wanebo H: Suspected recurrent rectosigmoid carcinoma after abdominoperineal resection. *Radiology* 170:323–328, 1989.
169. Chan T, Kressel H, Milestone B, et al: Rectal carcinoma: Staging at MRI with endorectal surface coil. *Radiology* 181:461–467, 1991.
170. Spratt JS, Spjut HJ, Roper CL: The frequency distribution of the rates of growth and the estimated duration of primary pulmonary carcinomas. *Cancer* 16:687–693, 1963.
171. Spratt JS, Ackerman LV: The growth of a colonic adenocarcinoma. *Ann Surg* 27:23–28, 1961.
172. Welin S, Youker J, Spratt JS: The rates and patterns of growth of 375 tumors of the large intestine and rectum observed serially by double contrast enema study. *Am J Roentgenol* 90:673–687, 1963.

CHAPTER 77

Radioimmunoscintigraphy

J. David Beatty
Barbara G. Beatty
Ralph J. Doerr

HIGHLIGHTS

Over the past two decades there has been steady progress in our knowledge and the application of that knowledge for localization of solid tumors using radiolabeled antibodies and gamma camera imaging (radioimmunoscintigraphy). The first decade, early 1970s to early 1980s, was marked by technical advances in monoclonal antibody (MAb) production, radiolabeling, and radionuclide detection. Techniques for affinity purification of polyclonal antibodies were replaced by MAb technology. Large quantities of high-affinity MAbs specific for the antigens associated with colorectal cancer—carcinoembryonic antigen (CEA) and TAG-72—became available for study. Radioiodination of antibodies with iodine 131 and 125 (^{131}I and ^{125}I) was replaced by chelation techniques for radiometals such as indium 111 (^{111}In), which produced radioimmunoconjugates that were more stable and more attractive for scintiscan studies. The planar gamma cameras for radionuclide detection were enhanced by digital subtraction and then by innovative computed tomographic technology—single photon emission, computed tomography (SPECT)—allowing smaller lesions to be detected and localized more accurately.

The second decade, early 1980s to early 1990s, has been marked by clinical advances: presurgical testing of preparations in vitro and in vivo, comparison with other imaging techniques such as computed tomography (CT), utilization of intraoperative gamma detection probes, and identification of the clinical value and limitations of radioimmunoscintigraphy. Anecdotal reports of tumor localization were replaced by prospective presurgical studies which allowed surgical and pathologic verification of scintiscan findings. The resultant evaluation of radioimmunoscintigraphy was significantly more valid and critical than clinical evaluations previously undertaken for new imaging technologies—i.e., CT and magnetic resonance imaging (MRI). The sensitivity of ^{111}In-labeled anti-CEA and anti-Tag-72 MAbs was 70 to 100 percent for primary colorectal cancer, 20 to 40 percent for hepatic metastasis, and 50 to 85 percent for extrahepatic metastasis.

The clinical value of radioimmunoscintigraphy was identified for two categories of colorectal cancer patients: (1) in those found to have a rising level of serum CEA (>5 mg/mL) following a resection of colorectal cancer with curative intent and in whom no site of recurrence was identified by conventional testing, radioimmunoscintigraphy was of value in tumor localization, and (2) in those with known hepatic metastasis of colorectal cancer, radioimmunoscintigraphy was of value in preoperative investigation. In 40 to 50 percent of these high-risk cases, either extraabdominal lesions were identified and confirmed, thereby avoiding major abdominal procedures, or extrahepatic intraabdominal lesions were identified and the abdominal operative procedures significantly altered to incorporate the additional finding. The intraoperative localization of the sites of radionuclide accumulation seen on the scintiscans was greatly enhanced by the use of a hand-held gamma detection probe (C-Trak, Carewise, Morgan Hill, California) appropriately shielded and collimated for ^{111}In. Both ^{111}In-labeled anti-TAG-72 MAb (OncoScint, Cytogen Corporation, Princeton New

Jersey, and Knoll Pharmaceutical Company, Whippany, New Jersey) and a probe for use with ^{111}In are now commercially available.

CONTROVERSIES

Although many labeled MAb preparations have been put forward, few have been prospectively evaluated presurgically in patients, resulting in many claims of efficacy which remain unsubstantiated. The rapid appearance of new MAbs and new labeling techniques and the relative unavailability of most preparations for widespread critical evaluation significantly reduce confidence in radioimmunoscintigraphy as a practical clinical tool. Reliance on anecdotal reports of radioimmunoscintigraphy or large series of cases without surgical and pathologic confirmation for clinical decisions regarding the role and value of this technique has been a concern and is strongly discouraged. Confirmed critical evaluation of new preparations in prospective presurgical trials is strongly encouraged.

Some controversy has resulted from the clinical interpretation of the data obtained using the two well-tested preparations for the detection of colorectal cancer, ^{111}In-labeled MAb directed against CEA or TAG-72. Both effectively localize primary lesions already documented by conventional tests (barium enema, colonoscopy). However, the value of radioimmunoscintigraphy in patients with primary disease without other evidence of hepatic or extrahepatic metastasis is small, and its routine use in these patients is controversial. Concentration of radiolabeled MAb in lymph nodes draining primary and metastatic colorectal cancer has been well documented for both MAbs, but the presence of tumor in these nodes is variable. The routine use of radioimmunoscintigraphy for the staging of primary colorectal cancer and determining the extent of lymph node involvement prior to surgical exploration remains controversial and is not recommended.

Both preparations are relatively ineffective for localizing hepatic metastases and moderately effective for identifying and localizing extrahepatic disease. However, in both regions the radioimmuniscintiscan findings complement and enhance the CT findings. The routine use of these preparations prior to surgical exploration for hepatic metastasis or for a rising serum CEA in colorectal cancer patients is logical but will require careful dissemination of information to radiologists and surgeons regarding scan interpretation and intraoperative probe utilization.

The currently available MAb preparations are derived from the mouse and often result in a host (human) immune response. The immune response in the form of human antimurine antibody (HAMA) can be detected in 5 to 70 percent of patients, depending upon the dose of MAb used and the frequency of administration. While single low-dose regimens are favored, it is possible to give multiple MAb doses and to undertake serial imaging of tumors despite the development of HAMA. However, the presence of HAMA does interfere with the measurement of serum CEA, giving rise to artifactually elevated levels. Thus, multiple-dose regimens of radiolabeled MAb for diagnostic purposes are discouraged except in unusual circumstances, such as a second abdominal reexploration for metastatic disease. The use of serial radioimmunoscintigraphy for the follow-up of colorectal cancer patients after resection with curative intent or for response of recurrent disease to systemic therapy should await humanized MAb preparations that will not elicit the host immune response and artifactual serum CEA elevation. In addition, patients who have received murine MAb and who develop an elevated serum CEA must have the assay carefully repeated under conditions which eliminate the effect of HAMA. This will rule out an artifactual CEA elevation before the CEA value is used in clinical decisions.

FUTURE DIRECTIONS

In the future, recombinant DNA technology will allow the production of designer antibodies and engineered preparations of biological substances. These will be combined in a controlled fashion with radionuclides, which will be utilized for tumor localization and therapy. Radioimmunodiagnosis and radioimmunotherapy will be combined with other biological and pharmacologic manipulations to enhance tumor uptake and limit toxicities. With improvement in the antibody and radionuclide technology will come an enhanced understanding of the biodistribution and metabolism of radiolabeled antibody and peptide preparations in the body and improved efficacy, especially in occult and early disease.

Radioimmune localization of tumors was initially pioneered by Pressman and Korngold[1] in 1953, using osteosarcomas. Since the first detection of human colorectal cancer using radioiodinated antibodies against CEA, published in 1978,[2] numerous antibodies and radiolabels have been studied for their ability to detect known and occult cancers. Goldenberg et al.[2] administered ^{131}I-labeled affinity-purified anti-CEA antibody to 18 patients with advanced neoplastic disease of diverse organs, and total body scans were performed. Ordinary scans proved difficult to interpret, and radiolabeled albumin was used for computer subtraction of blood pool activity. Tumor localization was demonstrated at 48 h in almost all cases. Scans were negative in patients without demonstrable tumors or with tumors devoid of CEA. High plasma levels of CEA did not prevent successful tumor imaging in this study.

Although successful imaging of colorectal tumors utilizing radioiodinated antibodies was reported,[2–8] cumbersome background blood pool subtraction techniques were required and the quality of images from total body scans were poor. However, enthusiasm for the potential of radioimmunolocalization of tumors was maintained by the appearance of exciting new biological and physical technologies. With the advent of MAb technology in the late 1970s,[9] the ability to produce large quantities of highly specific, high-affinity MAbs directed against specific tumor membrane antigens resulted in significant progress in the clinical availability of MAbs as diagnostic agents. In 1982, the use of transaxial tomoscintigraphy, or SPECT, by Mach and coworkers[4] showed an increase in both the sensitivity and specificity of radioimmunodetection of ^{131}I-labeled anti-CEA MAbs in 17 patients with primary, recurrent, and metastatic disease.

The best characterized tumor-associated antigen for human solid tumors is CEA.[10] The cellular, tissue, and organism distribution of CEA has been well documented[11,12] and CEA was found in over 90 percent of colorectal adenocarcinomas. Monoclonal antibodies to CEA have been raised by several groups[13–17] and CEA-producing human tumors have been targeted by anti-CEA MAbs in both animals[18–22] and humans.[2,3,23–25]

The development of labeling techniques for radioisotopes other than radioiodine led several groups to investigate the usefulness of indium-labeled MAbs.[20,24,26–28] Indium 111, a gamma emitter, was an attractive alternative to radioiodine because of its low energy (24 and 171 keV), higher number of photons per disintegration (two) favorable dosimetry (no high-energy beta emissions), and shorter half-life (2.83 days). However, indium requires appropriate bifunctional chelating agents, such as ethylenediamine tetracetic acid (EDTA) and diethylenetriamine pentaacetic acid (DTPA) derivatives, to link the radiometal to the antibody.

In order for a radiolabeled antibody to be an effective clinical tumor imaging agent, it must be easily and reproducibly labeled, stable, and nontoxic. It must demonstrate stability and effective preferential specific targeting to tumor tissue in vivo. Using nude mice xenogafted with CEA-expressing human tumors, it was demonstrated that anti-CEA MAbs labeled with ^{111}In fulfilled these criteria but also resulted in substantial spleen and liver uptake.[20,22] In human studies,[24,25,27,29–32] ^{111}In-labeled anti-CEA MAbs proved to be effective tumor imaging agents but presented two major problems: (1) marked nonspecific uptake in the normal liver parenchyma and (2) long biological half-life, which necessitated the performance of at least two scintiscan sessions over a period of a week following administration of the radioimmunoconjugate.

INDIUM-LABELED ANTI-CEA ANTIBODY

Over 200 patients have been studied at the City of Hope National Medical Center in Duarte, California, using murine MAbs directed against CEA. Most of the patients studied had early or locally recurrent disease and were scheduled for elective surgical procedures for diagnosis or therapy of colorectal cancer. This section focuses upon these patients. Three murine antibodies were evaluated and compared: T84.66, an IgG1 MAb produced and purified at City of Hope; ZCE025, an IgG1 MAb obtained from Hybritech, Inc. (San Diego, California); and C110, an IgG1 MAb obtained from Abbott Laboratories (Abbott Park, Illinois). Imaging accuracy, clinical value, and the human immune response were examined.

The preclinical studies[22,23] indicated that (1) ^{111}In could be firmly attached to anti-CEA MAb with retention of antibody activity; (2) the ^{111}In-DTPA–anti-CEA complex (Indacea) was stable in vitro and in vivo; and (3) Indacea was concentrated in CEA-bearing human tumor xenografts with resulting tumor gamma camera imaging. The focus of the initial clinical trials was presurgical imaging in colorectal cancer patients. This allowed careful evaluation of Indacea's tumor localization efficacy in comparison with the surgical/pathologic findings. Results were tabulated on the basis of clinically significant regions (primary disease, hepatic metastasis, extrahepatic abdominal metastasis, and extraabdominal metastasis), and the clinical significance of Indacea imaging was identified. A lesion-by-lesion analysis was completed in which the accuracy of Indacea and conventional CT imaging were compared. Presurgical imaging also afforded the opportunity to examine tumor and normal tissues directly by immunohistology, gamma well counting for ^{111}In uptake, and high-performance liquid chromatography (HPLC) for metabolism of Indacea. Finally, the host immune response to Indacea was assessed and the impact of Indacea upon the host was examined and characterized.

T84.66 Studies

The initial studies utilized T84.66 anti-CEA MAb-labeled with ^{111}In. The dose of murine protein was very low (200 μg) so as to minimize the human immune response. The amount of radionuclide was similarly low (2 mCi), which limited the imaging to two sessions at 24 and 48 h following the Indacea infusion. It should be noted that the T84.66 MAb has a high affinity for CEA (2.6×10^{10} M^{-1}). Subsequent animal studies have indicated that a low dose of this high-affinity anti-CEA MAb will result in the formation of labeled CEA-Indacea complexes that are rapidly cleared to the liver.[25,34,35]

The first clinical studies[36] provided a steep learning curve, with only 3 of 10 primary colonic cancers recognized and 4 of 10 primary lesions considered equivocally identified. Hepatic metastases were seen only as filling defects in 5 of 13 patients, although a "hot rim" was documented in some hepatic lesions using liver/spleen scans for digital subtraction. The most limiting aspect of the imaging proved to be the uptake of Indacea by the histologically normal liver. Perhaps the most interesting aspect of these early observations related to the tissue biodistribution studies. It was noted that the primary tumor uptake of ^{111}In (4.53 ± 0.44 percent of the injected dose per kilogram of tissue corrected for physical decay of the isotope—% ID/kg) was much greater than that of the adjacent bowel (1.1 ± 0.2 % ID/kg) or mesenteric fat (0.18 ± 0.04 % ID/kg) and that the greatest variation in tissue uptake occurred in histologically normal lymph nodes (24.3 ± 6.7 % ID/kg). Indeed, nodes close to the tumor had uptake of Indacea that was often over tenfold greater than that of the adjacent tumor. As the distance from the tumor increased, the content of ^{111}In decreased dramatically. It was suspected that this was the result of the formation of labeled CEA-MAb complexes in the tumor interstitium and the clearance of these complexes naturally by the lymphatics as part of the process of clearing proteins from the interstitial spaces. These lymph nodes with high uptake of ^{111}In had relatively low CEA content (by enzyme immunoassay, or EIA), which was located intracellularly (by immunohistology). By HPLC analysis, the ^{111}In was in the form of a low-molecular-weight metabolite similar to that observed in the murine liver within 24 h of Indacea administration.[37]

As more patients were studied, it became apparent that approximately 70 percent of primary tumors were visualized.[24,27,38] The tumors that were imaged had a higher uptake of ^{111}In (10.7 ± 3.5 % ID/kg versus 3.6 ± 1.5 % ID/kg), were larger (38.1 ± 17.8 cm^3 versus 6.0 ± 1.7 cm^3), and—after homogenization—had a higher content of CEA as measured by EIA (12.0 ± 3.6 μg/g versus 3.3 ± 1.7 μg/g) than those primary tumors not visualized. Grossly, the tumors that were imaged tended to be fungating rather than ulcerating, perhaps an indication of a better vascularity. Immunohistologically, all tumors demonstrated some CEA positivity, but the intensity of staining or proportion of cells demonstrating CEA positivity was unrelated to imaging efficacy. However, the cellular location of the CEA was important. All tumors with a predominant pattern of staining in apical or tumor intraluminal regions were successfully imaged, whereas only half of the tumors with a predominantly cytoplasmic staining pattern were imaged. Overall, these results suggested that the best imaging results would be seen for tumors that were large, were well vascularized, and had substantial amounts of CEA accessible to MAb in the interstitial spaces. These results confirmed the preclinical animal studies,[22] but a relationship between tumor size and ^{111}In uptake was not established, as it had been in the animal models.[38–40] It was presumed that this was because all the human tumors were over 1 g in size. In the animal xenograft model, a negative power relationship between tumor mass and ^{111}In uptake was seen, but for tumors over 1 g, the difference became very small.

In these initial clinical studies, the hepatic uptake was substantial and dominant. Hepatic metastases were visualized as negative defects in approximately 40 percent of the cases. As with conventional liver/spleen imaging, the hepatic metastases that imaged tended to be large (>4 cm) and multiple. No extrahepatic metastatic sites were visualized, but knowledge of the radionuclide concentration in draining lymph nodes allowed the localization and resection of a solitary pulmonary metastasis.[24] In 74 percent of male patient images, we observed significant uptake in the testes.[41] This led to a careful histologic and biochemical analysis of the adult human testis and the first description of CEA in the germ cell of the normal human testis.

ZCE025 Studies

The next studies utilized a lower-affinity MAb (ZE025) obtained from Hybritech. This antibody was labeled with ^{111}In using technology developed by Meares et al.[42] Higher amounts of MAb were utilized (20 to 40 mg) and increased amounts of radionuclide (5 mCi) allowed for imaging up to a week after Indacea administration. As a result of these changes, the ability to localize primary tumors increased, some hepatic metastases were visualized as areas of increased uptake, and the rate of imaging of extrahepatic metastases increased dramatically.[25,30] As more patients were studied, it became evident that Indacea imaging of patients with early disease (primary tumors only) did not make a substantial contribution to patient management. However, in patients with known hepatic metastasis or suspected recurrence based upon a rising plasma CEA, Indacea imaging prior to abdominal exploration was frequently of benefit to the patient. In 40 percent of these patients, unsuspected extrahepatic disease was identified at exploratory surgery. The antibody scan identified over 50 percent of these previously undocumented recurrences preoperatively, resulting in a change of management or even cancellation of a major surgical procedure in many of these patients. While we continue to consider Indacea imaging an area of clinical investigation, we now also consider it to be part of the appropriate presurgical workup of these high-risk patients with colorectal cancer.

T84.66/ZCE025 Comparison

Upon completion of the ^{111}In-ZCE025 studies, a comparison of the two Indacea preparations was performed.[25,30] In total, 152 colorectal cancer patients were studied and 130 underwent subsequent surgical exploration. Of these (130), 65 were infused with T84.66 Indacea and 65 with ZCE025 Indacea. All sites of increased uptake of ^{111}In, both visualized on the scintiscans and interpreted as indicative of colorectal adenocarcinoma and in which confirmation of disease at the site of ^{111}In accumulation would affect patient management, were evaluated surgically and pathologically. Approximately 80 percent of lesions were surgically assessed and 70 percent were pathologically assessed. At presentation but before the Indacea scan, 57 patients were considered to have primary disease; 53 to have hepatic metastases; and 8 to have a local or anastomotic recurrence. Of these patients, 8 had known disease in more than one region. There were also 20 patients with occult disease who were suspected of colorectal cancer recurrence based upon a rising plasma CEA. The scintiscans for each patient were scored as true or false, positive or negative in each of the clinically relevant regions: primary disease, hepatic metastasis, extrahepatic abdominal metastasis/recurrence, and extraabdominal metastasis.

Overall, ZCE025 Indacea scintiscans were significantly more sensitive (65.7 versus 30.5 percent) and more accurate (83.9 versus 76.9 percent) than T84.66 Indacea scintigraphy (Table 77-1). The improved sensitivity was due to improvement in identification of primary lesions and hepatic metastases and most dramatically to improvement in identification of extrahepatic abdominal metastases (Table 77-2). The ZCE025 Indacea scintigraphy was very sensitive and accurate (over 80 percent) for identifying the presence of primary, extrahepatic abdominal, and extraabdominal disease. However, ^{111}In accumulation in normal liver remained a problem and identification of hepatic metastasis as an area of increased ^{111}In uptake on scintiscan, while improved, remained disappointingly low (20 percent).

Next we asked the question: What is the impact of Indacea imaging of colorectal cancer on patient management? Three groups of patients were selected for analysis: 48 patients who presented with primary disease only, 45 patients who presented with hepatic metastasis only, and 20 patients who presented with occult metastasis. The incidence of metastatic disease was low in the primary disease patients but high in the other two groups of patients (Table 77-3). It would be anticipated that the primary disease ("low-risk") group would have little benefit from the Indacea scanning, whereas the "high-risk" patients with hepatic or occult metastases might have substantial benefit. Of the 48 low-risk primary disease patients, only 3 (6 percent) had an additional biopsy based upon the Indacea scans; in 2 of these, localization of Indacea had identified previously unsuspected extraabdominal metastasis. Thus the scan was of benefit to only 4 percent (2 of 48) of the low-risk patients. Of the 65 hepatic and occult disease (high-risk) patients, 8 (12 percent) had an additional previously unplanned surgical procedure (extraabdominal) based upon Indacea scan findings and 19 (29 percent) had a modification in the abdomi-

Table 77-1
Overall Comparison of Two Murine Monoclonal Antibodies by Combined Disease Region Analysis (^{111}In-Labeled Anti-CEA Monoclonal Antibody Imaging of Colorectal Cancer)

	T84.66 (200 μg, 2 mCi) n = *65*, *percent*	*ZCE025 (20–40 mg, 5 mCi)* n = *65*, *percent*
Sensitivity	30.5[a]	65.7[a]
Specificity	98.3[b]	92.5[b]
Positive predictive value	89.3	81.2
Negative predictive value	74.5[c]	84.4[c]
Accuracy	76.9[d]	83.9[d]

[a–d] $p < .05$.

Table 77-2
Comparison of T84.66 and ZCE025 by Disease Region (^{111}In-Labeled Anti-CEA Monoclonal Antibody Imaging of Colorectal Cancer)

	T84.66 (200 μg, 2 mCi) n = *65, percent*	*ZCE025 (20–40 mg, 5 mCi)* n = *65, percent*
Primary disease		
Sensitivity	67.7 (18/27)[b]	97.8 (30/31)[b]
Accuracy	86.2 (56/65)[c]	98.5 (64/65)[c]
Hepatic metastasis[a]		
Sensitivity	2.6 (1/38)[d]	20.0 (6/30)[d]
Accuracy	43.1 (28/65)[e]	63.1 (41/65)[e]
Extrahepatic abdominal metastasis		
Sensitivity	23.1 (3/13)[f]	83.3 (15/18)[f]
Accuracy	81.5 (54/65)	81.5 (53/65)
Extraabdominal metastasis		
Sensitivity	75.0 (3/4)	83.3 (5/6)
Accuracy	97.9 (63/65)	92.3 (60/65)

[a]Metastasis identified as area of increased uptake on scintiscan.
[b–f]$p < .05$.

nal exploration. The scan proved to be of benefit in identifying disease in 18 of these high-risk patients. This represents a benefit in 28 percent of the high-risk group overall, but a benefit in 67 percent of the patients with an Indacea scan finding suggestive of disease. On the basis of these studies, we currently recommend presurgical Indacea scintiscanning of all patients in these two high-risk groups (hepatic or occult metastasis) prior to abdominal exploration for diagnosis or therapy. On the basis of the combined extrahepatic disease incidence (Table 77-3) and the scan sensitivity for combined extrahepatic metastasis (83.3 percent, Table 77-2), we would anticipate that the presurgical ZCE025 Indacea scan could benefit approximately 24 percent of patients with hepatic metastasis and 50 percent of patients with occult disease.

Lesion Analysis

The Indacea scan (IS) using ZCE025 was compared with conventional CT in patients who had undergone both studies prior to an abdominal exploration.[43] Rather than a regional scoring for each modality, a lesion-by-lesion analysis was performed. A lesion was defined as any area considered to represent colorectal cancer by any one of the following: IS, CT, surgery, or pathology. In 45 patients, 186 lesions were identified, and 147 were examined surgically and pathologically. Overall, CT was more sensitive and more accurate than IS (Table 77-4). This was due to the much better sensitivity and accuracy of CT for hepatic metastases (Table 77-5). However, for extrahepatic abdominal metastases, IS was more sensitive than CT. Both in the liver and outside the liver, the two studies complemented one another. Both IS and CT were sensitive and accurate for the identification of large (>3-cm) lesions, but not for small (≤3-cm) lesions (Table 77-6). However, IS did identify 29.2 percent of these small lesions, while CT localized only 12.5 percent. The addition of SPECT technology increased the localization of hepatic metastases by IS from 17 to 31 percent (Table 77-7) but did not significantly enhance cancer localization in other regions.

On the basis of these observations, high-risk presurgical IS patients are now undergoing routine CT scanning of the chest and abdomen. The CT scan identifies lesions in the liver and lungs more effectively; the IS scan identifies lesions in the peritoneal and retroperitoneal areas and the mediastinum more effec-

Table 77-3
Incidence of Metastatic Disease in Colorectal Cancer Patients at Surgical Exploration

Status at presentation	*Hepatic metastasis*	*Extrahepatic abdominal metastasis*	*Extra-abdominal metastasis*	*Combined extrahepatic metastasis*[a]
Primary disease only	6/48 (12.5%)	4/48 (8.3%)	2/48 (4.2%)	5/48 (10.4%)
Hepatic metastasis only	43/45 (95.6%)	12/45 (26.7%)	1/45 (2.2%)	13/45 (28.9%)
Occult metastases	9/20 (45.0%)	9/20 (45.0%)	5/20 (25.0%)	12/20 (60.0%)

[a]Each patient is counted only once.

Table 77-4
Sensitivity, Positive Predictive Value, and Accuracy of Indacea Scan (ZCE025) and Computed Tomography (CT) on a Lesion-by-Lesion Basis (n = 147)[a]

Image modality	*TP*	*FP*	*FN*	*TN*	*Sensitivity, %*	*Positive predictive value, %*	*Accuracy, %*
IS	49	10	72	16	40.5[b]	83.1	44.2[c,d]
CT	74	10	47	16	61.2[b]	88.1	61.2[c]
IS+CT	88	18	33	8	72.7	83.0	65.3[d]

Abbreviations: TP, true positive; FP, false positive; FN, false negative; TN, true negative.
[a]Sensitivities and accuracies were compared using McNemar's test of symmetry.
[b]p = .0006.
[c]p = .00013 (one-sided).
[d]p = .00001 (one-sided).

tively; the CT and IS scans complement one another in all areas. Examination of the liver by SPECT and of any other area suspected of recurrence is performed based on planar IS or additional clinical information.

Probe

Recently, a gamma detection probe (C-Trak, Carewise Medical Products Corp., Morgan Hill, California) has been used during the operative procedure to aid localization of areas of increased ^{111}In accumulation (Table 77-8). In addition to identifying the sites of ^{111}In accumulation seen on the IS, the probe was also of value in identifying other sites of increased accumulation of ^{111}In and in ensuring that the entire site of increased ^{111}In accumulation had been resected. In 3 of 11 patients studied with the C-Trak gamma detection probe, management was modified by probe findings.[44]

Artifactual Serum CEA Elevation

A potential complication in patient management following the use of radiolabeled MAbs for imaging colorectal cancers is that of falsely elevated serum CEA levels. Retrospective analysis of 108 patients who had undergone presurgical radioimmunoscintigraphy with ^{111}In-labeled anti-CEA MAb showed that 11 patients demonstrated a marked elevation of serum CEA postoperatively without evidence of residual or recurrent disease.[45] The bases for the falsely elevated titers of CEA lie first in the CEA EIA, which is a double-antibody or two-site sandwich immunoassay employing two murine anti-CEA MAbs, and secondly in the production of HAMA in the patient following injection of the murine MAb.[45–48] Normally the capture and detection MAbs specific for the antigen in the immunoassay are bridged by the antigen, such as CEA, being measured in the assay. However, in the presence of HAMA, the two murine MAbs could be bridged by the HAMA, giving the appearance that antigen is being measured. To counteract this, addition of nonspecific murine polyclonal IgG[45] or a mixture of the murine monoclonal antibody isotypes IgG1, IgG2a, and IgG2b[48] to serum prior to assay was carried out. This

Table 77-5
Analysis of Imaging Modality (IS and CT) by Region of Localization[a]

Region	*Image*	*TP*	*FP*	*FN*	*TN*	*Sensitivity, %*	*Positive predictive value, %*	*Accuracy, %*
Primary colorectal tumor (n=26)	IS	23	3	0	0	100.0	88.5	88.5
	CT	20	1	3	2	87.0	95.2	84.6
	IS+CT	23	3	0	0	100.0	88.5	88.5%
Hepatic metastasis (n=71)	IS	11	0	51	9	17.7[b]	100.0	28.2[c,d]
	CT	41	6	20	3	67.7[b]	87.5	63.4[c,e]
	IS+CT	45	6	17	3	72.6	88.2	67.6[d,e]
Extrahepatic abdominal metastases (n=50)	IS	15	7	21	7	41.7	68.2	44.0
	CT	12	3	24	11	33.3	80.0	46.0
	IS+CT	20	9	16	5	55.6	69.0	50.0

[a]Sensitivities and accuracies were compared using McNemar's test of symmetry.
[b]$p < .0001$.
[c]$p < .0001$.
[d]$p < .0001$ (one-sided).
[e]$p = .04$ (one-sided).
Abbreviations: TP, true positive; FP, false positive; FN, false negative; TN, true negative.

Table 77-6
Analysis of Imaging Modality (IS and CT) by Lesion Size ($n = 66$)[a]

Lesion size, cm	*Image*	*TP*	*FP*	*FN*	*TN*	*Sensitivity, %*	*Predictive value, %*	*Accuracy, %*
≤3.0	IS	7	6	17	7	29.2	53.8	37.8
($n = 37$)	CT	3	2	21	11	12.5	60.0	37.8
	IS + CT	8	8	16	5	33.3	50.0	35.1
>3.0	IS	23	0	5	1	82.1	100.0	82.8
($n = 29$)	CT	24	1	4	0	85.7	96.0	82.8[b]
	IS + CT	27	1	1	0	96.4	96.4	93.1

Abbreviations: TP, true positive; FP, false positive; FN, false negative; TN, true negative; IS, immunoscintigraphy; CT, computed tomography.
[a]Sensitivities and accuracies were compared using McNemar's test of symmetry.
[b]$p = .04$ (one-sided).

procedure eliminated the interference of HAMA and corrected the artifactual elevation of the serum marker (CEA).

Positive correlation between the presence of HAMA and an artifactual increase in serum CEA titers has been demonstrated in a group of 30 patients.[49] Of the serum samples taken from these patients, 58 tested positively for CEA (> 5 μg/L). However, only 15 were truly positive, with the remaining samples (21) either falsely positive with CEA values <5 mg/L following addition of murine IgG or (22) artifactually elevated, with CEA values >5 mg/L but significantly lower following addition of murine IgG. Only these last two groups with falsely positive or artifactually elevated serum CEA values showed measurable levels of HAMA above the normal value range.

Since the CEA assay is important in the management of colorectal cancer patients with CEA-positive tumors, detection and removal of this interference is crucial. Any patient who has received murine MAb for diagnosis or treatment has the potential to form HAMA, which, in turn, can interfere with any double antibody immunoassay unless steps have been taken to remove HAMA from the assay. For CEA immunoassays, HAMA can be removed by heat inactivation[48] or the addition of murine IgG.[45,49] It is important that clinicians work closely with the laboratory personnel in determining the significance of CEA-positive assays in patients who have received murine MAbs.

Human Antimurine Antibodies (HAMA)

The production of HAMA in patients who have been given murine MAbs for diagnostic scintiscans or therapeutic treatment was shown to increase as the dose of administered MAb increased (> 20 mg) or as multiple injections were given.[50–53] Measurement of HAMA has not been standardized, as several different assay methods are being used both commercially and in research laboratories. As well, the use of different units for reporting, different positive controls, and different MAbs administered to patients makes it difficult to compare results from one laboratory to another. The type of HAMA (species-, isotype-, or idiotype-

Table 77-7
Analysis of Immunoscintigraphy (IS)–Planar and SPECT ($n = 96$)[a]

Image	*TP*	*FP*	*FN*	*TN*	*Sensitivity, %*	*Positive predictive value, %*	*Accuracy, %*
Planar alone	13	3	65	15	16.7[b]	81.2	29.2[c,d]
SPECT alone	21	2	57	16	26.9[b]	91.3	38.5[c]
IS (planar + SPECT)	24	3	54	15	30.8	88.9	40.6[d]

[a]Sensitivities and accuracies were compared using McNemar's test of symmetry.
[b]$p = .03$.
[c]$p = .01$ (one-sided).
[d]$p = .0005$ (one-sided).
Abbreviations: TP, true positive; FP, false positive; FN, false negative; TN, true negative; SPECT, single photon emission computed tomography.

Table 77-8
Intraabdominal Lesion Comparison ($n = 11$ patients)

Lesion	Total no.	IS	Diagnostic modalities			Pathology		
			Probe	CT	Surgery	CA	Benign	NA
Liver	8	5	5	8	8	7	0	1
Portal LN	4	4	4	0	2	0	3	1
Pelvis	3	3	3	2	2	3	0	0
Retroperitoneal LN	1	1	1	0	0	1	0	0
Colon	3	1	3	0	2	3	0	0
Peritoneal implants	3	0	2	0	3	3	0	0
Total	22	14 (64%)	18 (82%)	10 (45%)	17 (77%)	17	3	2

Abbreviations: IS, immunoscintigraphy; CT, computed tomography; CA, cancer; NA, not available; LN, lymph node.

specific) varies with the detection assay and depends on the assay capture and detection antibody and the relation of the assay antibody to the antibody administered to the patient. Results of an international study in which 17 different sera and two plasma samples were tested in 10 laboratories provided evidence for significant variation in HAMA titers obtained using different assays.[54] An indirect EIA with polyclonal mouse IgG as the capture antibody, which measured species-specific HAMA, gave different quantitative results from the same assay utilizing the murine MAb that was administered to the patient as the capture antibody, which measured species-, isotype-, and idiotype-specific HAMA. Since the quantitative units are based on a positive control, differences in positive controls are also critical and need to be standardized.

Detection and quantitation of HAMA resulting from administration of radioimmunoconjugates remains a critical issue for two reasons. First, HAMA can interfere in double-antibody assays such as the CEA assay and result in artifactual elevations of serum CEA. Thus, measurement of HAMA is crucial in the follow-up management of presurgically imaged high-risk patients in whom serum CEA levels are routinely used for assessment of disease progression and major management decisions such as "second-look" laparotomy. Second, in selected high-risk patients, it may be appropriate to consider administration of a second dose of antibody, either for tumor detection or tumor therapy. The presence of HAMA will result in the formation of HAMA-MAb complexes which are rapidly cleared, thereby compromising the potential tumor localization with its detection or therapeutic value. Knowledge of the presence of HAMA and its concentration will allow the clinician to avoid inappropriate decisions and to learn more rapidly the appropriate roles for murine MAb in the clinic. It has been our policy to recommend that any practitioner administering murine antibodies to patients should follow those patients carefully for the presence and titer of HAMA.

INDIUM-LABELED ANTI-TAG-72 ANTIBODY

B72.3 Studies

Another MAb, B72.3, has been developed by Schlom et al.[55] It recognizes the cell-surface glycoprotein TAG-72. This represents a non-CEA recognition system. The tumor-associated antigen TAG-72 reacts with the MAb B72.3 in up to 94 percent of colonic adenocarcinomas and virtually 100 percent of ovarian carcinomas. Tumor TAG-72 expression is also seen on a significant number of non–small cell lung cancers[56] and a small number of gastric and pancreatic adenocarcinomas. A favorable imaging aspect of the TAG-72 is the paucity of expression of this antigen on normal tissues.

The MAb B72.3 has been extensively investigated as a tumor imaging agent. In one early trial, ^{131}I-labeled B72.3 was administered intravenously to 20 patients with colorectal cancer. Of all tumor lesions, 70 percent demonstrated radiolocalization that was at least three times that of surrounding normal tissues.[57] Again, in a separate series, 30 patients being evaluated for recurrent colorectal cancer were given ^{111}In-labeled B72.3. All 5 instances of local recurrence and 3 out of 5 liver metastases were successfully identified with immunoscintigraphy.[58]

Multicenter trial results with ^{111}In-B72.3 (CYT-103 or OncoScint) were reported in 1991.[59] Of 116 evaluable patients, half presented with primary colorectal cancer (Fig. 77-1*A* and *B*) and half were being evaluated for recurrent disease. Each patient received 1 mg of B72.3 radiolabeled with 4.21 mCi of ^{111}In. A total of 103 patients ultimately underwent biopsy or operation for diagnosis and/or treatment. Colorectal adenocarcinoma was confirmed in 92 patients, of whom had a second primary (small cell lung cancer). The remaining 10 patients were free of disease.

Thus ^{111}In-B72.3 correctly identified at least 1 histopathologically confirmed lesion in 64 of the 92 patients with adenocarcinoma (70 percent sensitivity),

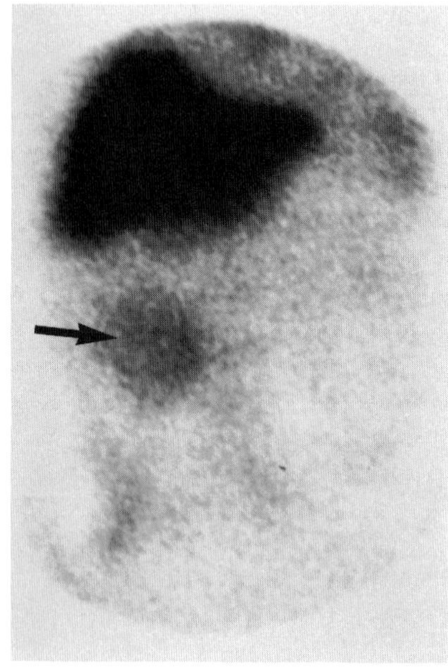

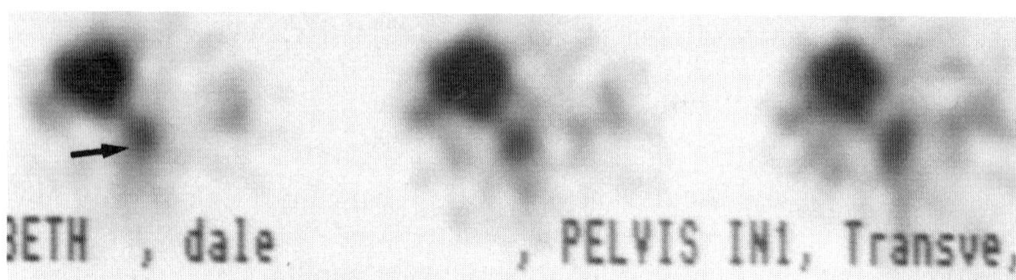

A B

FIG. 77-1. *A*. Planar scan of primary right colon adenocarcinoma (arrow). *B*. SPECT scan of lymph node metastasis (arrow) from primary right colonic cancer.

and the antibody scans were negative for 9 of 10 patients who were free of malignancy (90 percent specificity). The correct diagnosis was rendered for 73 of 102 patients, for an overall accuracy of 72 percent. False-positive findings in this study included three inflammatory lesions, a tubular villous adenoma, and one normal lymph node.

Occult disease tumor lesions not detected by standard preoperative workup were identified by B72.3 immunoscintigraphy in 11 of the 92 patients (12 percent) with confirmed adenocarcinoma (Fig. 77-2). There was no difference in accuracy whether the patient had primary or recurrent disease or had received adjuvant chemotherapy or radiation treatments.

Importantly, in the 18 of 22 patients confirmed to have isolated pelvic or liver recurrences, the B72.3 antibody scans found no other evidence of additional disease (Fig. 77-3). Nine other patients harbored extraabdominal metastatic disease identified by B72.3 immunoscintigraphy. These sites included lymph nodes, lung, bone, and brain.

In the expanded multicenter trial in which 169 patients were evaluated, a vigorous comparison of the imaging efficacy of immunoscintigraphy with CT scanning was performed.[60] Interestingly, the overall imaging results of ^{111}In-B72.3 and CT scan were virtually identical with respect to sensitivity, specificity, and accuracy in positive and negative values. In 70 percent

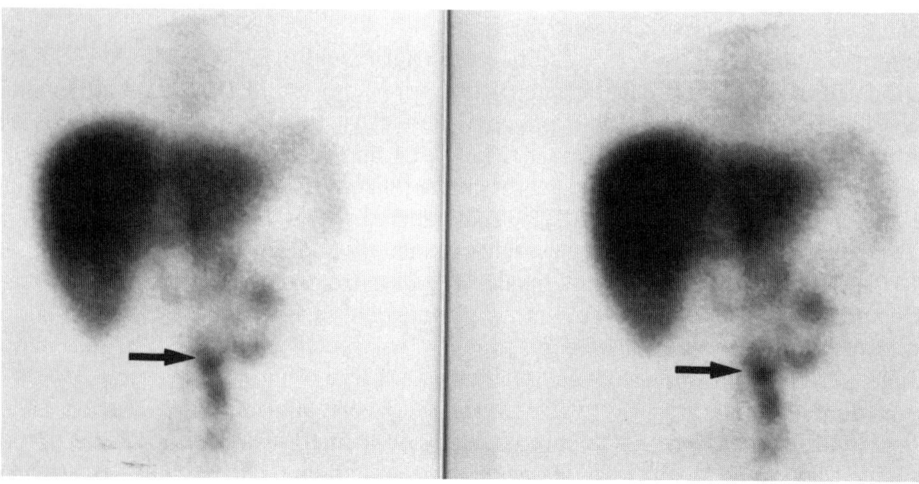

FIG. 77-2. Planar scan of recurrent colonic cancer metastasis to the paraaortic lymph nodes (arrow) in a patient with rising CEA and negative workup.

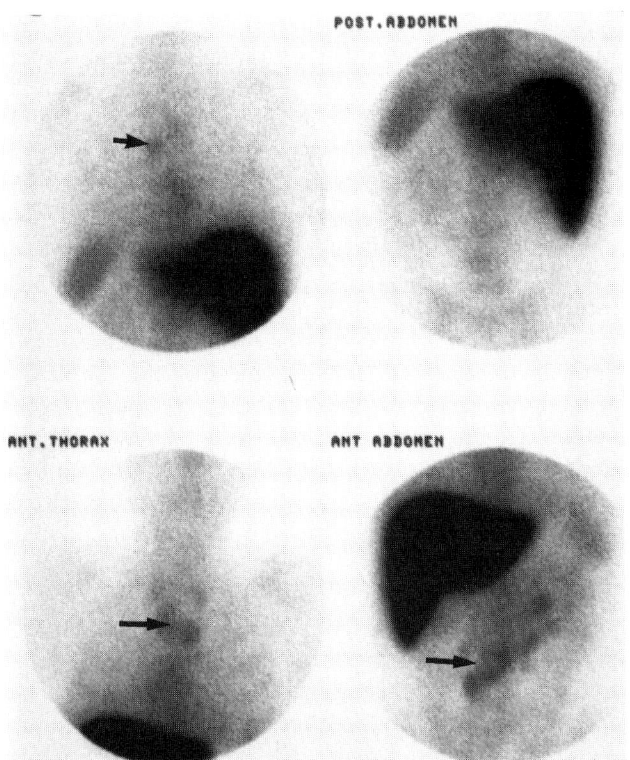

FIG. 77-3. Planar scans of patient with presumed isolated liver metastasis. Arrows indicate mesenteric and mediastinal lymphadenopathy (biopsy positive for adenocarcinoma).

of patients confirmed histologically to have colorectal carcinoma, at least one lesion was identified by immunoscintigraphy or CT scan. Of patients predicted to be negative for tumor, 77 percent had no evidence of malignant disease at surgery. While the overall tumor detection rates for immunoscintigraphy and CT scanning were similar, each modality demonstrated a greater sensitivity for a different subset of tumor lesions, depending on the anatomic location. Scans with B72.3 MAb detected a significantly greater number of tumors in the pelvis (66 versus 34 percent) than CT scanning. Due to the intrinsic ^{111}In activity in the liver, CT scanning identified a greater proportion of hepatic metastases (84 versus 41 percent).

The clearest indication for B72.3 immunoscintigraphy is presented by the patient with a high suspicion of colorectal cancer recurrence based on an elevated serum CEA and a negative conventional workup, including a noncontributory CT scan (Table 77-9). By detecting these occult tumor lesions, immunoscintigraphy provides new diagnostic information that contributes to the medical and/or surgical decision making. In the multicenter trial, patient management was felt to be changed on the basis of the MAb scan in 20 percent of the primary cases and 32 percent of the patients with recurrences.[59]

Table 77-9
Indications for Immunoscintigraphy

Primary disease
Detection of extraabdominal metastases
Road map of local/regional disease for hand-held intraoperative gamma detecting probe
Recurrent disease
Rising CEA with negative conventional workup
Exclusion of extrahepatic disease with isolated liver metastasis
Exclusion of extrapelvic disease with isolated pelvic recurrence

Of all patients with recurrent colorectal cancer who have isolated local, hepatic, or pulmonary lesions, 20 to 30 percent can be cured with reoperation.[61] Unfortunately, in most patients with suspected isolated and resectable recurrences, additional disease is found at the time of surgery. Immunoscintigraphy, with its whole-body imaging and high positive predictive value, can contribute significantly to identifying the patient with truly isolated recurrent or metastatic disease.

FUTURE DIRECTIONS

Although significant progress has been made in the field of radioimmunoscintigraphy over the past decade, there still remains the limitation of suboptimal tumor uptake. It has been demonstrated that factors such as tumor size, tumor vascularity, vascular permeability, level of antigen expression, diffusion characteristics of the antibody, and biological half-life of the radionuclide all play a significant role in determining antibody uptake, penetration, kinetics, and radiation dose distribution within the tumor.[62] As technology improves and our understanding of the mechanisms of antibody processing in vivo increases, it is anticipated that more effective tumor-specific localization of radiolabeled diagnostic agents will be achieved. One current area of investigation is the use of radionuclides with a shorter radiation half-life, such as technetium 99m (^{99m}Tc, with a half-life of 6 h) which has the advantage of permitting earlier scintiscans without the requirement of background subtraction procedures necessary with ^{131}I and ^{123}I-labeled MAbs.[2,3] Technetium 99m is a pure gamma emitter, is inexpensive and easily obtained, and has a high photon flux. However, attachment of ^{99m}Tc to MAbs is not as straightforward and efficient as iodination, due to its more complicated chemistry.[63] In addition, radionuclides with a shorter radiation half-life should be matched to an antibody or antibody fragment with a short biological half-life.

The longer half-life radionuclide ^{111}In (2.8 days) may be better suited to whole-antibody labeling in situations where several imaging sessions would be performed over a period of a week or even longer. The concern of high nonspecific uptake of ^{111}In-labeled MAbs in the liver and spleen stimulated the quest to understand the mechanisms involved.[35,37] The results of these studies suggested the use of high doses of unlabeled MAb to minimize the nonspecific accumulation of radiolabeled MAb in the liver, careful attention to antibody affinity to minimize the formation of antigen-antibody complexes, and the need for new metabolizable chelators, or more sophisticated chelators, which are not retained in liver tissue.[64]

With the new recombinant and gene transfection technologies that have become available, the thrust of many laboratories is in the direction of "designer" antibodies. Chimerized and humanized MAbs are being developed to overcome the antimurine reactions that occur with the present murine MAbs.[65–68] Complementarity-determining region (CDR) grafting of murine CDRs onto a human antibody framework has been used to produce humanized antibodies that retain an active antigen binding site.[69–71] Antibodies can be tailored for increased tumor penetration and attachment by using fragments,[72,73] single-chain antibodies[74,75] with increased antigen binding-site affinities, and hypervariable-region peptides, or molecular recognition units.[63] Finding the minimum size that effectively interacts with tumor cells but is not so small that it is cleared before this interaction can occur is crucial. Single-chain antibodies contain only the variable heavy- and light-chain regions of the antigen combining site linked by a short peptide and no Fc region, thus decreasing antigenicity in vivo. Hypervariable-region peptides are synthesized peptides having the same amino acid sequences as the hypervariable regions of the parent antibody and can be as small as 16 to 31 residues. Size may be critical here in balancing rapid clearance rates with enhanced penetrating ability.

Other approaches include alteration in clearance properties and effector functions by manipulation of the Fc domains[76] and formation of bifunctional antibodies.[77–80] Production of bifunctional antibodies in which one arm (Fab) of the antibody is specific for one tumor antigen and the other arm (Fab) is specific for a different tumor antigen addresses the concern of tumor heterogeneity. This approach may be more appropriate than the "cocktail" approach using mixtures of different antitumor MAbs, as it decreases the potential for the high background radioactivity that is inherent with the antibody cocktails. Bifunctional antibodies which have both tumor binding ability and another effector function,[80] such as binding to radiolabeled low-molecular-weight compounds,[77,79] T-cell receptors,[78] or boron-containing reagents can also be engineered and may play an important role in both radioimaging and therapy.

Combinations of treatments such as external beam radiation, hyperthermia, cytokines (gamma interferon), and chemotherapeutic agents together with radioimmunolocalization reagents may further enhance the diagnostic effectiveness of radiolabeled MAbs.[81] Treatments such as external beam radiation and hyperthermia increase tumor vascularity, allowing better penetration of the radiolabeled MAb, and may also aid in decreasing tumor size.[82,83] Cytokines such as gamma interferon and chemotherapeutic agents such as 5-fluorouracil (5-FU) have been shown to increase tumor antigen expression, thus increasing the antibody-binding capacity of the tumor.[84–86] As well, doses shown to be most effective in enhancing antigen expression were shown to have significant cytotoxic effects on tumor cells.[84] Coordination of these treatment combinations may provide substantial enhancement of radioimmunodiagnostic efficacy and should be investigated further.

As noted in the preceding paragraph, combinations of treatments may prove more effective than either treatment alone. This concept can also be applied to the coordination of radioimmunolocalization of tumors and radioimmunotherapy. For overt colorectal disease, pretreatment planning involving radioimmunolocalization may prove more specific and more helpful for radioimmunotherapy than it has been for surgical therapy of patients with high-risk disease, such as hepatic metastases, or a rising, elevated serum CEA. The subsequent antibody immunotherapy regimen may be customized to the tissue biodistribution of radiolabeled antibody as documented by scintigraphy. The use of radioisotopes such as copper 67 (^{67}Cu), which have both gamma emissions for scintigraphy and beta emissions for therapy, may prove most helpful in this regard.

Animal studies have shown a strong inverse relationship between tumor mass and radiolabeled antibody uptake for small tumors ($<$1 g).[39,40] These small tumors in humans would usually not be visible by current tomographic localization techniques (CT, MRI, SPECT, and positron emission tomography), yet the smaller the tumor, the greater the uptake of antibody conjugate directed against an appropriate tumor marker. This suggests that radioimmunotherapy or immunotherapy with antibody conjugates may be most effective for occult disease in association with or adjuvant to other forms of treatment. Finally, a potential role for radioimmune detection in follow-up of patients with both overt or occult disease after antibody conjugate immunotherapy has yet to be evaluated in an orderly fashion.

CONCLUSIONS

Significant progress has been made over the past decade in the use of radiolabeled antibodies for the detection of colorectal cancer. Radioimmunoscintigraphy remains a rapidly developing area for clinical investigation. A role for radioimmunoscintigraphy with murine antibodies in the presurgical evaluation of patients with hepatic metastasis or occult recurrence identified by a rising CEA has been documented. This is a relatively small subset of colorectal cancer patients who lend themselves well to continued careful study for imaging effectiveness and side effects such as artifactual elevation of serum CEA due to the production of HAMA. As new antibody preparations, new radionuclides, and new conjugates develop, the role for radioimmunoscintigraphy will become more established in the management of colorectal cancer.

REFERENCES

1. Pressman D, Korngold L: The in vivo localization of anti-Wagner osteogenic sarcoma antibodies. *Cancer* 6:619–623, 1953.
2. Goldenberg DM, DeLand F, Kim E, et al: Use of radiolabeled antibodies to carcinoembryonic antigen in the detection and localization of diverse cancers by external photoscanning. *N Engl J Med* 298:1384–1388, 1978.
3. Mach JP, Chatal JF, Lumbroso JD, et al: Tumor localization in patients by radiolabeled monoclonal antibodies against colon carcinoma. *Cancer Res* 43:5593–5600, 1983.
4. Berche C, Mach JP, Lumbroso JD, et al: Tomoscintigraphy for detecting gastrointestinal and medullary thyroid cancers: First clinical results using radiolabelled monoclonal antibodies against carcinoembryonic antigen. *Br J Med* 185:1447–1451, 1982.
5. Armitage NC, Perkins AC, Pimm MV, et al: The localization of an anti-tumour monoclonal antibody (791t/36) in gastrointestinal tumours. *Br J Med* 71:407–412, 1984.
6. Duncan W: Adjuvant radiotherapy in rectal cancer: The MRC trials. *Br J Surg* 72:S59–S62, 1985.
7. Dykes PW, Hine KR, Bradwell AR, et al: Localization of tumour deposits by external scanning after injection of radiolabeled anti-carcinoembryonic antigen *Br Med J* 26:220–222, 1980.
8. Farrad PA, Pinn MV, Embleton MJ, et al: Radioimmune detection of human colorectal cancers by an anti-tumour monoclonal antibody. *Lancet* 2:397–400, 1982.
9. Kohler G, Milstein C: Continuous cultures of fused cells secreting antibody of predefined specificity. *Nature* 256:495–497, 1975.
10. Gold P, Freeman SO: Specific carcinoembryonic antigens of the human digestive system. *J Exp Med* 122:467–481, 1965.
11. Beatty JD, Terz JJ: Value of carcinoembryonic antigen in clinical medicine, in Ariel IM (ed): *Progress in Clinical Cancer,* vol 8. New York, Grune & Stratton, 1982, pp 9–29.
12. Wiggers T, Jeekel J, Arends JW, et al: The no-touch isolation technique in colon cancer: A prospective controlled multicenter trial. *Proc Am Soc Clin Oncol* 5:269, 1986.
13. Primus FJ, Kuhns WJ, Goldenberg DM: Immunological heterogeneity or carcinoembryonic antigen: Immunohistochemical detection of carcinoembryonic determinants in colonic tumors with monoclonal antibodies. *Cancer Res* 43:693–701, 1983.
14. Accolla RS, Carrel S, Mach J-P: Monoclonal antibodies specific for carcinoembryonic antigen and produced by two hybrid cell lines. *Proc Natl Acad Sci USA* 77:563–566, 1980.
15. Hedin A, Hammarstrom S, Larsson A: Specificity and binding properties of eight monoclonal antibodies against carcinoembryonic antigen. *Mol Immunol* 19:1641–1648, 1982.
16. Wagener C, Yang YHJ, Crawford FG, et al: Monoclonal antibodies for carcinoembryonic antigen and related antigens as a model system: A systematic approach for the determination of epitope specificities of monoclonal antibodies. *J Immunol* 130:2308–2315, 1983.
17. Kuroki M, Koga Y, Matsuoka A: Monoclonal antibodies to carcinoembryonic antigen: A systematic analysis of antibody specificities by using related normal antigens and evidence for allotypic determinants on carcinoembryonic antigen. *J Immunol* 133:2090–2097, 1984.
18. Buchegger F, Haskell CM, Schryer M, et al: Radiolabeled fragments of monoclonal antibodies against carcinoembryonic antigen for localization of human colon carcinoma grafted into nude mice. *J Exp Med* 148:413–427, 1983.
19. Pimm MV, Armitage NC, Perkins AC, et al: Localization of an anti-CEA monoclonal antibody in colorectal carcinoma xenografts. *Cancer Immunol Immunother* 19:8–17, 1985.
20. Halpern SE, Hagan PL, Garver PR, et al: Stability, characterization and kinetics of ^{111}In-labeled monoclonal antitumour antibodies in normal animals and nude mouse-human colon tumour models. *Cancer Res* 43:5347–5355, 1983.
21. Hedin A, Wahren B, Hammarstrom S: Tumour localization of CEA-containing human tumours in nude mice by means of monoclonal anti-CEA antibodies. *Int J Cancer* 30:547–552, 1982.
22. Jakowatz JG, Beatty BG, Vlahos WG, et al: High-specific-activity ^{111}In-labeled anticarcinoembryonic antigen monoclonal antibody: Biodistribution and imaging in nude mice bearing human colon cancer xenografts. *Cancer Res* 45:5700–5706, 1985.
23. Goldenberg DM, Kim Ee, Bennett SJ, et al: Carcinoembryonic antigen radioimmunodetection in the evaluation of colorectal cancer and in the detection of occult neoplasms. *Gastroenterology* 84:524–532, 1983.
24. Beatty JD, Duda RB, Williams LE, et al: Preoperative imaging of colorectal carcinoma with indium 111-labelled anticarcinoembryonic antigen monoclonal antibody. *Cancer Res* 46:6494–6502, 1986.
25. Beatty JD, Williams LE, Yamauchi D, et al: Presurgical imaging with indium-labeled anti-carcinoembryonic antigen for colon cancer staging. *Int J Cancer* 50:922s–926s, 1990.
26. Hnatowich DJ, Griffin TW, Kosciuczyk C, et al: Pharmacokinetics of an indium-111 labeled monoclonal antibody in cancer patients. *J Nucl Med* 26:849–858, 1985.
27. Duda RB, Beatty JD, Sheibani K, et al: Imaging of human colorectal adenocarcinoma with indium-labeled anticarcinoembryonic antigen antibodies. *Arch Surg* 121:1315–1319, 1986.
28. Fairweather DS, Bradwell AR, Dykes PW, et al: Improved tumour localization using indium-111 labeled antibodies. *Br Med J* 287:167–170, 1983.
29. Abdel-Nabi HH, Schwartz AN, Higano CS, et al: Colorectal carcinoma: Detection with indium-111 anticarcinoembryonic-antigen monoclonal antibody zce-025 1 (abstract). *Radiology* 164:617–621, 1987.
30. Beatty JD, Hyams DM, Morton BA, et al: Impact of radiolabeled antibody imaging on management of colon cancer (abstract). *Am J Surg* 157:13–19, 1989.
31. Patt YZ, Lamki LM, Haynie TP, et al: Improved tumor localization with increasing dose of indium-111-labeled anti-carcinoembryonic antigen monoclonal antibody zce-025 in metastatic colorectal cancer (abstract). *J Clin Oncol* 6:1220–1230, 1988.
32. Patt YZ, Lamki LM, Shanken J, et al: Imaging with indium-111-labeled anticarcinoembryonic antigen monoclonal antibody zce-025 of recurrent colorectal or carcinoembryonic

antigen-producing cancer in patients with rising serum carcinoembryonic antigen levels and occult metastases. *J Clin Oncol* 8:1246–1254, 1990.

33. Paxton RJ, Jakowatz JG, Beatty JD, et al: High-specific-activity ^{111}In-labeled anticarcinoembryonic antigen monoclonal antibody: Improved method for the synthesis of diethylenetriaminepentaacetic acid conjugates. *Cancer Res* 45:5694–5699, 1985.
34. Beatty BG, Beatty JD, O'Connor-Tressel M, et al: Effect of specific antibody pretreatment on liver uptake of ^{111}In-labeled anti-CEA MAB in nude mice bearing human colon cancer xenografts. *Cancer Res* 49:1587–1594, 1989.
35. Beatty JD, Beatty BG, O'Conner-Tressel M, et al: Mechanism of tissue uptake and metabolism of radiolabeled antibody—Role of antigen:antibody complex formation. *Cancer Res* 50:840s–845s, 1990.
36. Beatty JD, Philben VJ, Beatty BG, et al: Imaging of colon carcinoma with ^{111}Indium labeled anti-CEA MAB. *Arch Surg* 121:1315–1319, 1986.
37. Beatty BG, O'Conner-Tressel M, Do T, et al: Mechanism of decreasing liver uptake of ^{111}In-labeled anti-carcinoembryonic antigen monoclonal antibody by specific antibody pretreatment in tumor bearing mice. *Cancer Res* 50:846s–851s, 1990.
38. Beatty JD, Duda RB, Beatty BG, et al: Imaging of colorectal carcinoma with Indacea, in Pruzanski W, Seligmann M (eds): *Clinical Immunology*. Amsterdam, Elsevier Science Publishers, 1987, pp 287–292.
39. Philben VJ, Jackowatz JG, Beatty BG, et al: The effect of tumour CEA content and tumour size on tissue uptake of indium 111–labeled anti-CEA monoclonal antibody. *Cancer* 57:571–576, 1986.
40. Williams LE, Duda RB, Proffitt RT, et al: Tumour uptake as a function of tumour mass: A mathematic model. *J Nucl Med* 29:103–109, 1988.
41. Beatty BG, Paxton RJ, Sheibani K, et al: Testis imaging with ^{111}In-labeled anti-CEA MAB: Identification of CEA in normal germ cells. *Cancer Res* 46:6503–6508, 1986.
42. Meares CF, McCall MJ, Reardan DT, et al: Conjugation of antibodies with bifunctional chelating agents. *Ann Biochem* 142:68–78, 1984.
43. Corbisiero RM, Yamauchi DM, Williams LE, et al: Comparison of immunoscintigraphy and computerized tomography for identifying colorectal cancer: Individual lesion analysis. *Cancer Res* 51:5704–5711, 1991.
44. Wilson LA, Kuhn JA, Williams LE, et al: A technical analysis of an intraoperative radiation detection probe. *Med Phys* 19:1219–1223, 1992.
45. Morton BA, O'Connor-Tressel M, Beatty BG, et al: Artifactual CEA elevation due to human anti-mouse antibodies. *Arch Surg* 123:1242–1246, 1988.
46. Primus FJ, Kelley EA, Hansen HJ, et al: "Sandwich" type immunoassay of carcinoembryonic antigen in patients receiving murine monoclonal antibodies for diagnosis and therapy. *Clin Chem* 34:261–264, 1988.
47. Kricka LJ, Schmerfeld-Pruss D, Senior M, et al: Interference by human anti-mouse antibody in two-site immunoassays. *Clin Chem* 36:892–894, 1990.
48. Hansen HJ, La Fontain G, Newman ES, et al: Solving the problem of antibody interference in commercial "sandwich" type immunoassays of carcinoembryonic antigen. *Clin Chem* 35:146–151, 1989.
49. Price T, Beatty BG, Beatty JD, et al: Human anti-murine antibody interference in measurement of carcinoembryonic antigen assessed with a double-antibody enzyme immunoassay. *Clin Chem* 37:51–57, 1991.
50. Miller RA, Levey R: Response of cutaneous T-cell lymphoma to therapy with hybridoma monoclonal antibody. *Lancet* ii:226–230, 1981.
51. Courtenay-Luck NS, Epenetos AA, Moore R, et al: Development of primary and secondary immune responses to mouse monoclonal antibodies used in the diagnosis and therapy of malignant neoplasms. *Cancer Res* 46:6489–6493, 1986.
52. Shawler DL, Bartholomew RM, Smith LM, et al: Human immune response to multiple injections of murine monoclonal IgG. *J Immunol* 135:1530–1535, 1985.
53. Schroff RW, Foon KA, Beatty SM, et al: Human anti-murine immunoglobulin responses in patients receiving monoclonal antibody therapy. *Cancer Res* 45:879–885, 1985.
54. Kricka LJ, Schmerfeld-Press D, Kaladas P, et al: Interlaboratory survey of methods for measuring human anti-mouse antibodies. *Clin Chem* 38:172–173, 1992.
55. Thor A, Ohuchi N, Szpak CA, et al: Distribution of onco-fetal antigen tumour-associated glycoprotein-72 defined by monoclonal antibody B72.3. *Cancer Res* 46:3118–3124, 1986.
56. Colcher D, Carrasquillo JA, Esteban JM, et al: Radiolabeled monoclonal antibody B72.3 localization in metastatic lesions of colorectal cancer patients. *Nucl Med Biol* 14:251–262, 1987.
57. Esteban JM, Colcher D, Sugarbaker P, et al: Quantitative and qualitative aspects of radiolocalization in colon cancer patients of intravenously administered Mab B72.3. *Int J Cancer* 39:50–59, 1987.
58. Renda A, Salvatore M, Sava M, et al; Immunoscintigraphy in the follow-up of patients operated for carcinoma of the sigmoid and rectum. *Dis Colon Rectum* 30:683–686, 1987.
59. Doerr RJ, Abdel-Nabi H, Krag D, et al: Radiolabeled antibody imaging in the management of colorectal cancer. *Ann Surg* 214:118–124, 1991.
60. Collier BD, Abdel-Nabi H, Doerr RJ, et al: Immunoscintigraphy performed with IN-111 labeled CYT-111 labeled CTY-103 in the management of colorectal cancer: Comparison with CT. *Radiology* 185:179–186, 1992.
61. August DA, Ottow RT, Sugarbaker PH: Clinical perspective of human colorectal cancer metastasis. *Cancer Metast Rev* 3:303–324, 1984.
62. Jain RK: Physiological barriers to delivery of monoclonal antibodies and other macromolecules in tumours. *Cancer Res* 50 (suppl):814s–819s, 1990.
63. Serafini AN: From monoclonal antibodies to peptides and molecular recognition units: An overview. *J Nucl Med* 34:533–536, 1993.
64. Beatty BG, Paxton RJ, Hawthorne MF, et al: Parmacokinetics of an anti-carcinoembryonic antigen monoclonal antibody conjugated to a bifunctional transition metal carborane complex (Venus flytrap cluster) in tumour bearing mice. *J Nucl Med* 34:1294–1302, 1993.
65. Morrison SL, Oi VT: Genetically engineered antibody molecules. *Adv Immunol* 44:65–93, 1989.
66. Neumaier M, Shively L, Chen FS, et al: Cloning of the genes for T84.66, an antibody that has a high specificity and affinity for carcinoembryonic antigen, and expression of chimeric human/mouse T84.66 genes in myeloma and Chinese hamster ovary cells. *Cancer Res* 50:2128–2134, 1990.
67. Hardman N, Gill LL, De Winter RFJ, et al: Generation of a recombinant mouse-human chimaeric monoclonal antibody directed against human carcinoembryonic antigen. *Int J Cancer* 44:424–433, 1989.
68. Koga H, Kanda H, Nakashima M, et al: Mouse-human chimeric monoclonal antibody to carcinoembryonic antigen (CEA): In vitro and in vivo activities. *Hybridoma* 9:43–56, 1990.
69. Jones PT, Dear PH, Foote J, et al: Replacing the complemen-

tarity-determining regions in a human antibody with those from a mouse. *Nature* 321:522–525, 1986.

70. Queen C, Schneider WP, Selick HE, et al: A humanized antibody that binds to the interleukin 2 receptor. *Proc Natl Acad Sci USA* 86:10029–10033, 1989.
71. Co MS, Deschamps M, Whitley RJ, et al: Humanized antibodies for antiviral therapy. *Proc Natl Acad Sci USA* 88:2869–2873, 1991.
72. Buchegger F, Pelegrin A, Delaloye B, et al: Iodine-131-labeled MAb F(ab')2 fragments are more efficient and less toxic than intact anti-CEA antibodies in radioimmunotherapy of large human colon carcinoma grafted in nude mice. *J Nucl Med* 31:1035–1044, 1990.
73. Larson SM, Carrasquillo JA, Krohn KA, et al; Localization of ^{131}I-labeled p97-specific Fab fragments in human melanoma as a basis for radiotherapy. *Clin Invest* 72:2101–2114, 1983.
74. Bird RE, Hardmann KD, Jacobson JW, et al: Single-chain antigen-binding proteins. *Science* 242:423–426, 1988.
75. Huston JS, Mudgett-Hunter M, Tai MS, et al: Protein engineering of single-chain Fv analogs and fusion proteins. *Methods Enzymol* 203:46–88, 1991.
76. Mueller BM, Reisfeld RA, Gillies SD: Serum half-life and tumour localization of a chimeric antibody deleted of the CH2 domain and directed against the disialoganglioside GD2. *Proc Natl Acad Sci USA* 87:5702–5705, 1990.
77. Frincke JM, Halpern SE, Chang CH, et al: Radioimmunodetection (RID) approach using a ^{111}In hapten (H) Monoclonal antibody (MoAb): Studies in the nude mouse-human colon tumour model. *J Nuc Med* 28:711–712, 1987.
78. Staerz UD, Bevan MJ: Hybrid hybridoma producing a bispecific monoclonal antibody that can focus effector T-cell activity. *Proc Natl Acad Sci USA* 83:1453–1457, 1986.
79. Anderson LD, Meyer DL, Battersby TR, et al: Optimization of ligand structure for imaging with a bifunctional antibody. *J Nuc Med* 29:835–836, 1988.
80. Smith W, Gore VA, Brandon DR, et al: Suppression of well-established tumour xenografts by a hybrid-hybrid monoclonal antibody and vinblastine. *Cancer Immunol Immunother* 31: 157–163, 1990.
81. Wong JYC, Yan X, Buras RR, et al: Strategies to improve the efficacy of radioimmunotherapy: Radiobiologic aspects. Proceedings of the 5th International Radiopharm Dosimetry Symposium, May 1991, pp 8–25, Oak Ridge, TN, 1992.
82. Wong JYC, Williams LE, Paxton RJ, et al: The effects of tumour mass, tumour age and external beam radiation on tumour-specific antibody uptake. *Int J Radiat Oncol Biol Phys* 16:715–720, 1989.
83. Wong JYC, Mivechi N, Paxton RJ, et al: The effects of hyperthermia on tumour antigen expression. *Int J Radiat Oncol Biol Phys* 17:803–808, 1989.
84. Kuhn JA, Beatty BG, Wong JYC, et al: Interferon enhancement of radioimmunotherapy for colon cancer. *Cancer Res* 51:2335–2339, 1991.
85. Kuhn JA, Wong JYC, Beatty BG, et al: Gamma-interferon enhancement of a multiple treatment regimen for radioimmunotherapy. *Antib Immunoconj Radiopharm* 4:837–845, 1991.
86. Kuhn JA, Wong JYC, Beatty BG, et al: Gamma interferon enhancement of carcinoembryonic antigen expression in human colon carcinoma xenografts. *J Immunother* 11:257–266, 1992.

CHAPTER 78

Prognostic Determinants in Metastatic Colorectal Cancer

John A. Conti
Nancy E. Kemeny

HIGHLIGHTS

Many studies have been performed to determine prognostic factors in metastatic colorectal cancer, mostly in patients with liver metastases. Analyses in untreated patients with liver metastases has shown percentage of liver involvement to be the most important prognostic factor and revealed a more variable survival in this group of patients. Surgical series have determined a large number of determinants, but most concur that a positive pathologic margin and the presence of extrahepatic disease predict a poor outcome after hepatic metastasis resection. Data derived from chemotherapy studies again emphasize that the percent of liver involvement along with pretreatment lactic dehydrogenase (LDH) and alkaline phosphatase value are all poor prognostic factors. Staging systems for liver metastases have been proposed based on prognostic data derived from surgical series and usually incorporate some combination of percentage of liver involvement, presence of extrahepatic disease, performance status, and liver function abnormalities.

CONTROVERSIES

Controversy exists regarding the use of adverse prognostic factors in surgical series as contraindications to hepatic metastasis resection. Most sources would not advocate resection in the presence of extrahepatic disease, but there is debate as to the maximum number of metastases which should be resected. The importance of metastasis "size" and whether this is an important prognostic factor independent of percentage of liver involvement and pathologic margin has also been questioned.

FUTURE DIRECTIONS

Interesting observations such as the adverse effect of perioperative transfusion in hepatic metastasis resection, the better prognosis of lung-only versus liver-only metastasis, and the influence of primary tumor stage on prognosis all require closer examination. The application of modern molecular biological techniques to metastatic disease as they have previously been applied to colorectal cancer primaries may provide more accurate prognostic factors. Finally, future prognostic evaluations require prospective studies in larger patient groups, with incorporation into treatment protocols, to improve the utility of prognostic determinants in colorectal cancer hepatic metastases.

Synchronous hepatic metastases are present in 14 to 25 percent[1] of patients with colorectal cancer and occur in 60 to 80 percent[2] of patients with recurrent disease. Studies conducted in the 1960s suggested that all patients with colorectal cancer metastatic to the liver had a uniformly poor prognosis and brief survival duration.[2] Later studies, however, revealed a more diverse natural history. Multiple prognostic determinants have been derived from analyses of surgical and chemotherapy series as well as retrospective accounts of untreated patients. These sources will be reviewed, along with staging systems utilizing these factors. Limited data on other metastatic sites, such as lung, will also be analyzed. The prospect for newer molecular biology techniques to be used for prognosticating hepatic metastases will be described.

UNTREATED HEPATIC METASTASES

The prognostic factors examined in selected series of patients with untreated hepatic metastases are shown in Table 78-1. Most of these reviews were performed in the 1960s and 1970s and hence reflect a difference in technology available at the time, such as less sensitive imaging modalities and less sophisticated statistical methods. The two series which specifically addressed prognostic factors[3,4] were performed without multivariate analysis. Despite these drawbacks, several observations can be drawn from these studies. The natural history of untreated liver metastases from colorectal cancer can be variable, with median survivals as shown in Table 78-1 ranging from 4.5 to 24 months. The most important determinant of survival in this setting is the extent of hepatic involvement by tumor. Finan et al.[5] had a median survival of 16.4 months for patients with liver involvement of <20 percent versus 5.6 months for those with >20 percent ($p<.005$). Palmer et al.[6] noted a 20-month mean survival for patients with ≤ 25 percent liver involvement but only 12 months in those with >25 percent. In a widely quoted study, Wagner et al.[7] demonstrated that the *mean* survival of untreated patients with solitary, multiple unilateral, and widespread metastases were 24, 16, and 11 months, respectively. In this study, however, *widespread* was defined as metastases unresectable by lobectomy or right-sided trisegmentectomy. This category could therefore include patients with varying degrees of percent liver involvement by tumor depending upon the metastasis size. If this study is consistent with other series, we suspect that the pa-

Table 78-1
Prognostic Determinants in Series of Patients with Untreated Hepatic Metastases

Authors	*Median survival, months*	*Significant prognostic factors*
Stearns and Brinkley,[42] 1954	11	Resection of primary tumor
Bacon and Martin,[43] 1964	8	None
Jaffe et al.,[3] 1968	6	Primary tumor site, histologic tumor type, degree of differentiation
Bengmark and Hafstrom,[44] 1969	5.7	Level of serum alkaline phosphatase
Oxley and Ellis,[45] 1969	12	Resection of primary tumor
Cady et al.,[8] 1970	13[a]	Weight loss, intestinal symptoms, ascites, peritoneal seeding, extension of primary tumor to other viscera, histologic involvement of lymph nodes or blood vessels, location within the colon, extent of surgical therapy (of primary tumor)
Abrams and Lerner,[47] 1971	7	Resection of primary tumor
Nielsen et al.,[48] 1973	12	Number of liver metastases, resection of primary tumor
Baden and Anderson,[49] 1974	10	None
Wilson and Adson,[50] 1976	18[b]	None
Wood, 1976[50a]	6.6[a]	Extent of liver metastases
Wanebo et al,[51] 1978	7	Resection of primary tumor
Bengtsson et al.,[52] 1981	4.5–5.0	Percent of liver involvement, level of serum alkaline phosphatase
Goslin et al.,[4] 1982	12.5	Extent of liver metastases, histologic grade of tumor
Wagner et al.,[7] 1984	12–24	Extent of hepatic involvement, presence of extrahepatic disease
Finan et al.,[5] 1985	10.3	See text and Table 78-2
Palmer et al.,[6] 1989	12	Percent of liver involvement

[a]Mean survival.

[b]Extrapolated from survival curve provided.

tients of Wagner et al. with widespread metastases who had a longer survival probably had lesser percent liver involvement, though this is not explicitly stated by the authors. In general, untreated patients with a very small volume (25 percent or less) of metastatic liver disease may occasionally have long-term survival.

Cady et al.[8] stated that certain characteristics—such as depth of invasion of the primary, weight loss, and ascites—were probably not independent prognostic factors but simply reflected bulk of disease. Similar conclusions would be formally determined in the multivariate analysis performed in the 1980s on treated patients. The study by Jaffe et al.[3] combined untreated patients with liver metastases but with different primary tumors. This study had a median survival for untreated colon cancer patients with liver metastases of 5 months, versus 2 months in patients with gastric or pancreatic cancer. Finan et al.[5] conducted a multivariate analysis in 90 patients presenting with synchronous hepatic metastases, determining factors influencing survival and constructing a clinical scoring index and computer survival model. Characteristics found to be significant are listed in Table 78-2. Many of these

Table 78-2
Significant Variables Affecting Survival Following Presentation with Synchronous Liver Metastases

	Median survival, months	*Mantel-Cox p value*
Clinical features		
Appetite loss		
Yes	7–4	
No	12–4	.0–.04
Weight loss (≥3 kg)		
Yes	6–2	
No	13–0	<.001
Clinically enlarged liver		
Yes	4–6	
No	11–0	.002
Biochemical and hematological parameters		
Alkaline phosphatase		
≤13 KAU	13–5	
>13 KAU	4–6	<.001
Serum albumin		
>30 g/L	10–0	
≤30 g/L	4–3	.02
Serum bilirubin		
>20 μmol/L	5–0	
≤20 μmol/L	10–7	.01
White cell count × 10^3		
<7–0	15–8	
7–12.0	7–0	
>12.0	3–5	<.005
Tumor characteristics		
Operative procedure		
Resection	12–5	
Bypass	5–0	
Nil	2–0	<.01
Fixity of primary tumor		
Yes	9–0	
No	11–0	.04
Tumor staging		
Dukes B	16–7	
Dukes C	10–8	<.01
Tumor grading		
Well/moderate	13–0	
Poor	7–0	.005
Percentage liver involvement		
<20%	16–4	
20–80%	5–6	<.005
Distribution of metastases within the liver		
Single in one or both lobes	15–5	
Multiple liver metastases	8–0	<.01

Abbreviations: King–Armstrong units.
SOURCE: From Finan et al.[5] Reproduced by permission.

features are also statistically significant in the series to be described later in this chapter, implying that they are reliable prognosticators regardless of disease treatment.

SURGICAL SERIES

There have been multiple surgical series examining the prognostic factors after resection of hepatic metastases from colorectal cancer. Results of 15 recent studies are summarized in Table 78-3. The principle behind surgical series has been to try to determine the optimal candidates for liver resection and conditions which would contraindicate such surgery. Surgical series have examined patient characteristics and preoperative laboratory values, characteristics of the primary lesion, and characteristics of the metastases (preoperative and postoperative).

Patient Characteristics and Preoperative Laboratory Values

Most studies have not examined the role of age nor gender as prognostic determinants. In some studies, overall survival rates have been lower in patients above age 70,[9,10] but no study has shown age to be a statistically significant factor in disease-free survival. A few smaller studies showed gender to be of borderline significance (some favoring women,[11,12] some favoring men[13]); larger series have discounted gender as a prognostic determinant.

Few surgical series have examined the prognostic value of preoperative laboratory values after hepatic resection. This may reflect the lack of extreme laboratory values in suitable operative patients (i.e., patients with jaundice or profound hypoalbuminemia would not undergo hepatic resections). Similarly, LDH may reflect disease bulk and hence be more commonly elevated in patients with unresectable disease.[14] Of the three studies[15–17] which tested the significance of liver function tests, none found any correlation between abnormal values and survival.

The significance of preoperative serum carcinoembryonic antigen (CEA) level has varied between studies, though the survival curves from Hepatic Metastasis Registry data[18] and the study by Cady et al.[19] present strong support for its significance. In the registry data, there is a threefold difference in 5-year actuarial disease-free survival between patients with a CEA of 0 to 5 ng/mL (42 percent) versus those with a CEA of >30 ng/mL (14 percent; $p = .15$).[20] In the study by Cady et al.[19] none of 17 patients with a CEA of ≥200 ng/mL survived more than 2 years. Though preoperative CEA is an important prognostic factor, Hughes et al.[18] feel that patients should not be denied surgery because their CEA level is elevated. Cady et al.,[19] however, believe that a hepatic resection should

Table 78-3
Prognostic Determinants in Series of Patients with Colorectal Metastases Resection

Author	*Fortner et al.,[15] 1984*	*Wagner et al.,[7] 1984*	*Olak et al.,[23] 1985*	*Butler et al.,[27] 1986*	*Ekberg et al.,[16] 1986*	*Iwatsuki et al.,[9] 1986*	*Nordlinger et al.,[53] 1987*	*Hughes et al.,[18] 1989*	*Wagman et al.,[54] 1990*	*Doci et al.,[11] 1991*	*Scheele et al.,[24] 1991*	*Steele et al.,[17] 1991*	*Younes et al.,[28] 1991*	*Cady et al.,[19] 1992*	*Van Ooijen et al.,[22] 1992*
No. of patients	65	141	25	62	72	60	80	800	35	100	266	87	16	129	118
Patient characteristics															
Gender	NEG	POS	—	NEG	NEG	—	—	NEG	—	POS	—	—	—	—	NEG
Age	NEG	—	—	—	—	—	—	NEG	—	NEG	—	NEG	NEG	—	—
Laboratory values (preop)															
CEA	NEG	—	—	—	—	—	—	POS	—	NEG	—	NEG	POS	POS	—
LDH	NEG	—	—	—	—	—	—	—	—	—	—	—	—	—	—
Alkaline phosphatase	NEG	—	—	—	NEG	—	—	—	—	—	—	NEG	—	—	—
Bilirubin	NEG	—	—	—	NEG	—	—	—	—	—	—	NEG	—	—	—
Characteristics of primary lesion															
Site (colon versus rectum)	NEG	NEG	—	NEG	NEG	—	—	NEG	—	NEG	—	—	POS	—	NEG
Grade	—	NEG	—	—	—	—	—	—	—	—	POS	—	—	—	—
Dukes stage	POS	POS	POS	POS	NEG	POS	NEG	POS	POS	POS	POS	—	NEG	—	NEG
Characteristics of metastases (preop)															
Size	—	—	—	NEG	—	—	NEG	NEG	—	—	NEG	—	POS	NEG	—
Solitary versus multiple	NEG	NEG	NEG	NEG	—	NEG	—	NEG	—	—	—	—	—	—	NEG
Number of metastases	NEG	—	—	NEG	POS	POS	NEG	POS	POS	NEG	NEG	—	POS	—	POS
Metastasis distribution[a]	—	—	—	NEG	NEG	—	—	NEG	—	POS	—	—	NEG	—	NEG
Disease-free interval	NEG	—	POS	NEG	NEG	NEG	NEG	POS	—	NEG	POS	NEG	NEG	—	NEG
Percentage hepatic involvement	—	—	—	—	NEG	—	—	—	—	POS	—	—	—	—	—
Characteristics of metasteses (postop)															
Type of resection	—	—	POS	—	NEG	POS	—	NEG	—	POS	POS	POS	NEG	NEG	NEG
Margin of resection	—	—	—	—	POS	—	—	POS	—	—	POS	—	—	POS	NEG
Presence of extrahepatic disease	POS	POS	—	—	POS	—	—	NEG	—	—	NEG	POS	—	—	—

Key: POS = Significant correlation found with survival; NEG = No significant correlation found with survival; — = Not examined.

[a]Unilobar versus bilobar.

not be attempted in patients with a CEA level >200 mg/mL. The issue remains unresolved and merits further study.

Characteristics of the Primary Lesion

The strongest prognostic factor in patients with localized colorectal cancer is the lymph node status. This relationship, as expressed by the Dukes stage of the tumor, also holds true for patients with hepatic metastases. Though a Dukes stage C lesion has a 50 percent lower 5-year survival than a stage B lesion (20 versus 40 percent in the Hepatic Metastases Registry data[18]), most surgeons do not consider a Dukes stage C primary lesion a contraindication to surgery.

Most series have not demonstrated a difference between colonic and rectal lesions in relation to hepatic metastasis resection. Rectal origin might be assumed to have a worse prognosis due to a greater predisposition to local recurrence and the ability to spread by both the portal and systemic circulation.[21] Rectal cancer patients who are candidates for hepatic metastasis resection, however, are usually selected because their local tumor is controlled and they have no evidence of extrahepatic metastases.[21]

Most series have not examined primary tumor grade as a prognostic determinant. This is surprising, since grade is an important factor in the previously described series of untreated patients. One source hypothesized that undifferentiated lesions are often associated with other conditions that would preclude consideration of hepatic resection.[21] With the recent advances in pathology, this biologic determinant needs to be researched further.

Characteristics of Metastases (Preoperative)

The most important preoperative characteristic of hepatic metastases associated with survival has been the percentage of liver involvement by tumor. Staging systems for liver metastases, as described later in this chapter, all incorporate this parameter because of its prognostic value. Doci et al.,[11] for example, noted 5-year survival rates of 40, 19, and 0 percent in resected patients with percent liver involvement of ≤25, 25 to 50, and >50 percent, respectively ($p<.001$). Though not a significant multivariate variable in the analysis by Ekberg et al.,[16] percent liver involvements of <25, 25 to 49, and 50 to 74 percent again showed differences in 5-year survival: 24, 7, and 0 percent, respectively. The other surgical series did not directly examine this parameter.

After percent liver involvement, the number of metastases is probably the most important factor, though this was positive in only 6 of 11 surgical series in which it was examined. The relevant question is whether a cutoff exists for the maximum number of resectable metastases above which a significant prognostic decline occurs. Hughes et al.[18] noted 5-year survival rates of 37, 34, 9, and 18 percent after resection of one, two, three, and four metastases, respectively. Though Hughes et al. acknowledged that patients with four or more metastases have a poorer prognosis, they did not believe an upper limit on the number of resectable metastases could be derived from the registry data. Cady et al.[19] advocate against surgery in patients with four or more metastases. In the studies by Ekberg et al.[16] and Iwatsuki et al.,[9] none of the patients survived more than 3 years; in the series by van Ooijen et al.,[22] none of the patients with >2 metastases resected survived more than 5 years. Number of metastases is clearly a significant prognostic factor, but because long-term survivors do exist, we concur with Hughes et al. that >4 metastases should not be an *absolute* contraindication to surgery but that such patients should be resected only in the context of a clinical trial.[1]

An important study conducted by Adson et al.[12] from the Mayo Clinic investigated the relationship between lesion number (defined as solitary versus multiple) and size (defined as <4 cm, or "small," and ≤4 cm, or "large"). They found that the overall survival rate of patients with multiple liver lesions resected did not differ from that of patients with solitary lesions resected. Though the sample sizes were too small for statistical analysis, survival after resection of multiple small lesions was similar to that of patients after resection of a solitary large lesion. Though not specifically examined by the authors, this observation, again, is probably a prognostic determinant.

Most other surgical series have found neither the metastasis distribution (unilobar versus bilobar) nor the metastasis size to be significant prognostic factors. One reason for this lack of significance is that these factors are interrelated with metastasis number and percent liver involvement. The "size" of hepatic metastases was most closely examined in the Hepatic Metastases Registry study.[20] Hughes et al.[20] examined size by analyzing survival data in two categories, size of solitary lesion (<8 versus >8 cm) and largest lesion in patients with multiple metastases (<2, 2 to 4, and 4 to 8 cm versus >8 cm). In both cases, no significant relationship was found between size and survival.

Disease-free interval has often been suspected to be an important factor after resection of hepatic metastasis with the hypothesis that a longer disease-free interval reflects a slower tumor doubling time.[1] Though most studies have examined this factor, only the two largest series and a small Canadian study have been able to demonstrate its significance.[18,23,24]

Characteristics of Metastases (Postoperative)

Almost all sources have demonstrated that the margin of uninvolved liver removed beyond a resected metastasis is of prognostic significance. The usual cutoff is 1.0 cm, but as demonstrated in the Hepatic Metastasis Registry data, even tumors which are removed with positive margins can still have a 13 percent five-year actuarial survival.[18]

A frequently asked question is whether the extent of hepatic resection is an independent adverse prognostic factor. It is difficult to analyze the extent of the resection separately from preoperative characteristics of number, distribution, and size of the metastases.[25] For example, as discussed by Adson et al.,[21] survival is better after small operations done for small lesions than after extended resections of large tumors. With smaller lesions, however, the percentage of liver involvement is less and postoperatively the resection margin is usually greater. These factors are more important prognostically than the choice of operation. Hughes et al.[18] observed that anatomic resection of a solitary lesion >4 cm in size yielded a better survival than a wedge resection of a similar-sized solitary metastasis. Again, this may reflect the greater chance of obtaining a >1 cm resection margin with the more extensive operation. Number, size, distribution of metastases and resection margin should therefore be closely examined in studies in which the type of resection is found to be a statistically significant factor.

Most studies have found that the presence of extrahepatic disease is a very poor prognostic factor, and some sources advocate this as a surgical contraindication.[15,16,19] The Hepatic Registry Data demonstrated a trend toward decreased survival in patients with extrahepatic disease and advised hepatic resection only in "good-risk patients" who can be made clinically free of disease with combined hepatic and extrahepatic resection.[18] Most sources, including the registry, hold that hepatic lymph node metastases are an especially poor prognostic feature and advise against hepatic resection in their presence.

Miscellaneous Factors

Factors not listed in Table 78-3 which have been examined in some surgical series include the use of adjuvant chemotherapy,[27] the presence of satellite metastasis,[24] era of resection,[24] preoperative 5′-nucleotidase,[15] presence of symptoms,[19] weight of tumor resected,[19] and ploidy of resected tumor.[16,19] Most of these factors were either not significant, correlated with better-studied features, or have been tested only in a small number of patients. The finding of statistical significance by Younes et al.[28] of number of perioperative hypotensive episodes and the related observation by van Ooijen et al.[22] of perioperative blood loss as prognostic factors is intriguing. Perioperative blood transfusions have also been found to possibly be an adverse prognostic factor in primary colonic resections and should be examined further in future hepatic surgery series.[29]

CHEMOTHERAPY SERIES

The role of prognostic factors in the survival of patients with metastatic colorectal cancer treated with chemotherapy has been systematically examined via combined univariate and multivariate analyses. Nine chemotherapy series are listed in Table 78-4 and commented upon below. Table 78-5 illustrates the univariate survival variables found to be significant in a recent analysis performed by Kemeny et al.[30]

Patient Characteristics and Laboratory Values

As in surgical series, most studies found neither age nor gender to be significantly correlated with survival. In the study by Bedikian et al.,[31] the survival difference for gender was minimal (female = 7 months; male = 5 months; $p = .06$). The data presented by Chang et al.,[32] with a median survival of 19.3 months for men and 10.2 months for women ($p = .02$), have not been confirmed in the other trials in which gender has been examined, and in Chang's study, gender was no longer significant in the multivariate analysis. The correlation with age in the 1983 study by Kemeny and Brown[14] is interesting in that the older patients did better (<40, 4.0 months; >40, 10 months; $p < .001$). This, too, has not been found in other studies, and may reflect the referral of younger patients with more advanced disease to a tertiary cancer center. As with the gender observation of Chang et al., this age difference was not statistically significant in the multivariate analysis.

Performance status is usually strongly correlated with survival. As weight loss and the presence of symptoms are reflected by performance status, it is not surprising that the studies which examined these parameters also found them to be useful prognostic indicators.

Laboratory Characteristics

Table 78-4 lists nine of the more common laboratory factors studied as having possible prognostic value; others studied but not listed include prothrombin time,[32,33] gamma-glutamyl transpeptidase,[34] SGPT,[32,34] leukocyte count,[31] and monocyte count.[31] An analysis of the nine listed parameters is instructive in illustrating the difficulties in comparing studies and deriving conclusions. In the 1983 study by Kemeny et al.,[32] CEA values are strongly correlated with survival as a univariate variable: patients with normal versus ab-

Table 78-4
Prognostic Determinants of Survival in Chemotherapy Series

Author	*Lavin et al.,*[36] *1980*	*Lahr et al.,*[33] *1983*	*Kemeny and Brown,*[14] *1983*	*Bedikian et al.,*[31] *1984*	*Fortner et al.,*[26] *1984*^{a}	*Ekberg et al.,*[34] *1986*	*Chang et al.,*[32] *1989*	*Kemeny et al.,*[30] *1989*	*Graf et al.,*[35] *1991*
No. of patients	1314	175	220	232	117	73	67	112	340
Patient characteristics									
Gender	—	NEG	NEG	POS^{u}	NEG	NEG	POS^{u}	NEG	—
Age	—	NEG	POS^{u}	—	NEG	NEG	NEG	NEG	—
Performance	—	POS^{u}	—	POS^{u}	—	—	—	—	—
status							—		—
Presence of symptoms	—	POS^{u}	—	—	—	—	—	—	—
Presence of weight loss	POS^{m}	—	—	POS^{u}	—	—		POS^{m}	
Laboratory values									
CEA	—	NEG	POS^{u}	—	NEG	—	POS^{u}	NEG	—
Hemoglobin	—	—	—	POS^{u}	—	—	—	—	POS^{m}
WBC	—	—	POS^{m}	—	—	—	—	POS^{u}	—
Albumin	—	POS^{m}	—	POS^{m}	—	—	NEG	POS^{u}	—
Alkaline phosphatase	—	POS^{m}	POS^{u}	POS^{m}	NEG	POS^{m}	POS^{m}	POS^{u}	—
Bilirubin	—	POS^{m}	—	—	NEG	—	NEG	—	—
LDH	—	POS^{u}	POS^{m}	—	NEG	—	POS^{u}	POS^{u}	—
5′-NT	—	—	POS^{u}	—	NEG	—	—	—	—
SGOT	—	—	—	—	POS^{m}	NEG	NEG	—	—
Characteristics of primary lesion									
Site (colon versus	—	NEG	NEG	—	NEG	NEG	NEG	NEG	POS^{u}
rectum)		NEG		—		NEG		—	
Grade	—		—		—		NEG		—
Dukes stage	—	—	—	POS^{u}	NEG	NEG	NEG	—	—
Primary unresected	—	POS^{m}	—	POS^{m}	—	—	—	—	POS^{m}
Characteristics of metastases									
Liver metastases									
Presence or absence	POS^{m}	—	M^{b}	POS^{u}	—	—	—	—	POS^{u}
No. of metastases	—	POS^{u}	—	—	—	NeG	—	—	—
Percentage hepatic involvement	—	—	—	—	POS^{m}	POS^{m}	POS^{m}	POS^{m}	—
Hepatic node status	—	—	—	—	POS^{m}	POS^{m}	NEG	—	—
Extrahepatic metastases									
Presence or absence	—	—	—	—	—	POS^{u}	POS^{u}	—	—
Presence of lung metatases	NEG	—	M^{b}	—	—	NEG	—	—	NEG
Presence of peritoneal metastases	POS^{u}	—	—	—	NEG	—	—	—	POS^{u}
Disease-free interval	—	NEG	NEG	POS^{u}	NEG	NEG	NEG	NEG	POS^{m}

^{a}Multivariate analysis only.

^{b}Analyzed as metastatic site: lung versus liver (see text).

Key: POS^{u} = Significant correlation found with survival in univariate analysis only; POS^{m} = Significant correlation found with survival in both multivariate and univariate analyses; NEG = No correlation found with survival; — = Not examined.

normal CEA levels had median survivals of 23 and 9.2 months, respectively, with a p value of $<.001$ (though no longer significant as a multivariate variable). A normal CEA level probably reflects a better prognosis, though methodologic problems have prevented this from being proved in some studies. White blood cell count was a significant multivariate variable in the 1983 study by Kemeny and Brown.[14] Patients in that study with white blood cell counts of 10,000/mm^3 or less had a median survival of 11 months, while those with white blood cell counts $>$10,000/mm^3 had a median survival of 7.0 months ($p <.002$). In the 1989

Table 78-5
Significant Variables Affecting Survival in Patients with Liver Metastases Treated with Hepatic Arterial Chemotherapy

Prognostic factors	*Subgroup*	*No. of patients*	*Median survival, months*	*Logrank p value*
% Liver involvement	≥30%	49	23.6	.00001
Medical	>30%	62	9.9	
Weight loss at entry	Present	17	6.1	.00001
	Absent	93	16.0	
Albumin	>4	33	26.4	.00025
	≤4	78	10.7	
LDH	≤500	75	18.9	.00006
	>500	37	8.6	
KPS	≥80	85	16.1	.0004
	<80	27	7.2	
% Liver involvement	≤30%	42	24.7	.00006
Surgical	>30%	69	10.7	
WBC	≤10,000	80	16.0	.02
	>10,000	31	10.5	
Response	Response	38	18.9	.02
	No response	71	11.7	
Perfusion status	Good	63	17.7	.03
	Poor	32	9.9	
Sex	Male	73	12.8	.08
	Female	39	18.1	
Site of disease	Rectum	19	10.6	.13
	Other	92	14.8	
CEA	≤5	9	22.0	.10
	>5	103	13.1	
Alkaline phosphatase	≤300	71	17.7	.001
	qr>300	41	10.2	
Age	≤50	16	15.3	.20
	>50	96	13.3	
Diagnosis to metastases	>0	55	14.8	.80
	=0	57	13.1	

Abbreviations: LDH, lactic dehydrogenase; KPS, Karnofsky performance status; WBC, white blood count; CEA, serum carcinoembryonic antigen.

SOURCE: Kemeny et al.[30] (Reproduced by permission.)

study by Kemeny et al.,[30] where only patients with liver metastases were included, white blood cell count was significant in the univariate analysis but not in the multivariate analysis. White blood cell count may reflect prognosis because of a possible relationship to bulk of disease. This was supported in the 1989 analysis by Kemeny et al.[30] by the significant association between percent liver involvement and LDH and white blood cell count. These results merit further examination in future chemotherapy series. Hemoglobin has not been examined sufficiently to comment upon its utility as prognostic factors, but again, it deserves further research.

Of the six liver function tests listed, LDH and alkaline phosphatase appear to be the most useful prognostic markers; LDH probably reflects bulk of disease and is also employed as a prognosticator in other malignancies, such as lymphoma, multiple myeloma, and testicular cancer.[14] Alkaline phosphatase is a sensitive indicator of hepatic metastatic disease and may also reflect the bulk of liver metastases. A greater degree of liver involvement is necessary for hyperbilirubinemia and hypoalbuminemia. Thus, these two factors would also reflect prognosis as a "mirror" of liver involvement, though probably not as accurately as alkaline phosphatase. Serum glutamic-oxaloacetic transaminase has been insufficiently studied for a comment upon its role; 5′-nucleotidase offers little advantage over alkaline phosphatase and is a more costly test.

Characteristics of Primary Lesion

The characteristics of the primary colorectal lesion as it relates to survival in chemotherapy series has not been as thoroughly studied as in surgical series. As in untreated patients, an unresected primary is a poor prognostic factor,[31,33,35] possibly reflecting more advanced local disease. Dukes stage was not prognostically important in three of the studies.[26,32,34] In the study by Bedikian et al., "Dukes D_1/D_2" at diagnosis is worse than "Dukes A–C."[31] This is different from most of the surgical series, which compared Dukes A/B with C primaries in an attempt to gauge the importance of node positivity as a prognostic factor in the setting of liver metastatic disease. The stage and grade of the primary tumor should be more closely examined in future studies. Most studies have assessed the prognostic difference between colonic and rectal primaries; in 6 of 7 studies, no difference was found.

Characteristics of Metastases

The importance of location (i.e., lung, liver, abdomen, etc.) of the metastases as a prognostic factor has not been adequately addressed by most studies. Six of the nine studies[26,30–34] analyzed only patients with liver metastases. In three series, the presence of lung metastases had no adverse effect on prognosis,[34–36] as would be expected. In the 1983 study by Kemeny and Brown,[14] patients with lung-only metastases had a better prognosis than those with liver-only metastases, 12.0 versus 8.0 months, respectively ($p < .002$). The prognostic significance of metastatic site should be addressed in larger studies and in metanalysis. Four of the studies restricted only to patients with liver metastases[26,30,32,34] demonstrated a direct relationship between percent hepatic involvement by tumor and survival. In all four studies, percent liver involvement was a significant variable in both the univariate and multivariate analysis. In the series by Fortner et al.,[26] percent liver involvement emerged as the most significant variable, with a p value $<.000001$. Kemeny et al.[30] noted a median survival of 26.3 months in patients medically assessed as having ≤30 percent liver involvement versus 10.6 months in patients with >30 percent liver involvement ($p = .00001$).

Very few studies examined the relationship between response to intrahepatic chemotherapy and percent liver involvement. In the 1989 study by Kemeny et al.,[30] there was no significant correlation between response and percent liver involvement using a cutoff of ≤30 percent versus 30 percent liver involvement. We recently reviewed response and survival data from our past systemic and intrahepatic chemotherapy protocols to confirm the prognostic significance of percent liver involvement. This analysis found that a 40 percent liver involvement was a significant value for prognosis. For intrahepatic chemotherapy, patients with ≤40 percent involvement had a median survival of 29.3 months, versus 15.6 months for patients with >40 percent ($p < .00001$). Complete plus partial response rate was also statistically significant: 65 percent for patients with ≤40 percent, 38 percent for patients with >40 percent ($p = .009$). For systemic chemotherapy, patients with ≤40 percent had a median survival of 19.4 months, versus 11.9 months for patients with >40 percent ($p = .001$).

Positive hepatic nodes represented a poor prognostic factor in two of the chemotherapy series, as in surgical series.[26,34] Patients with positive hepatic nodes are excluded from most current regional chemotherapy studies because they represent an extrahepatic site of disease. The presence of other extrahepatic metastasis sites may also be a poor prognostic factor in combination with hepatic metastases,[32,34] possibly reflecting a more virulent natural history.

Most chemotherapy studies similar to the surgical series do not find a correlation between disease-free interval and survival. Disease-free interval was defined in three different ways in the chemotherapy studies: synchronous versus metachronous (=0 versus >0),[26,30,33,34] 1 month versus >1 month,[32] and 0 to 12 months versus 12 months.[14,31,35] These differences make comparison of this variable among the chemotherapy studies difficult. Despite this, 7 of 9 studies showed no correlation with survival; in the positive study of Bedikian et al.,[31] the variable was associated only in the univariate analysis with a borderline p value of .03.

STAGING SYSTEMS FOR COLORECTAL CANCER HEPATIC METASTASES

Multiple authors have proposed staging systems for hepatic metastases from colorectal cancer, but no uniform one exists to date. Table 78-6 lists some of the most recent proposals. Most of the staging systems are based on data gathered from retrospective reviews, usually surgical series. None has been extensively validated prospectively. Common to all these systems is inclusion of percent liver involvement by tumor, illustrating its strong correlation with survival. Figure 78-1 illustrates a survival curve from Memorial Hospital demonstrating how medical assessment of liver involvement accurately reflects prognosis.[30] Four staging systems[26,38–40] also incorporate the presence of extrahepatic disease (including portal node metastases) because this factor has a significant correlation with survival. The "presence of symptoms" in some staging systems again shows the importance of performance status as a prognostic factor. The ideal staging system still does not exist and awaits further analyses of larger studies and refinements in imaging techniques.

MOLECULAR BIOLOGICAL FACTORS AS PROGNOSTIC DETERMINANTS

Most of the newer molecular biological techniques have been applied only to the study of colonic primaries. These factors are summarized in Table 78-7 and are discussed in detail elsewhere in this text. As the technology progresses, techniques which have previously been applied to the colorectal cancer primaries will also be extended to hepatic metastases. One recent study, for example, found that the labeling index

Table 78-6
Proposed Staging Systems for Colorectal Cancer Liver Metastases

1. Fortner[26] classification, 1984
   - I PHR: ≤ 50%
   - II PHR: 55 to 80%
   - III PHR: >80%
   - A No extra hepatic involvement or prior chemotherapy.
   - B Either nodal metastases and/or prior chemotherapy.

   PHR = percent hepatic replacement by tumor

2. Gennari[38] classification, 1984
   - H_1 PHR: ≤25%
   - H_2 PHR: 25 to 50%
   - H_3 PHR: >50%
   - s Single metastasis
   - m Multiple metastases to one surgical lobe
   - b Bilateral metastases
   - I Infiltration of adjacent organs or structures
   - F Impairment of liver function

   Stage
   - I H_{1s}
   - II $H_{1m,b}$ H_{2s}
   - III $H_{2m,b}$ $H_{3s,m,b}$
   - IV A "Minimal" intraabdominal extrahepatic disease (detected only at laparotomy)
     B Extrahepatic disease

3. International Staging System,[39] 1986
   - P_1 PHR: 25%
   - P_2 PHR: 25 to 75%
   - P_3 PHR: >75%
   - E Concurrent extrahepatic disease
   - S Symptoms attributable to liver metastases

   Stage
   - O Curatively resected metastases
   - I P_1, no E, no S
   - II P_2, no E, no S
   - III P_3, no E, no S
     Any P, + E, any S
     Any P, any E, + S

4. Lausanne classification,[55] 1984
   Stage
   - I PHR <25% with stratification F, S, FS
   - II PHR: 25 to 75% with stratification F, S, Fs
   - III PHR >75%, all patients with FS

   F, abnormal liver function tests; S, patient with symptoms

5. Petrelli[40] classification, 1984
   - I PHR: ≤25%
   - II PHR: 25 to 50%
   - III PHR: >50%
   - E Extrahepatic intraabdominal disease documented at laparotomy

   Preoperative alkaline phosphatase
   - a <2 × normal level
   - b > 2 × <4 × normal level
   - c >4 × normal level

   Performance status
   - 0 Normal activity
   - 1 Symptoms but ambulatory
   - 2 In bed <50% of the time
   - 3 In bed >50% of the time
   - 4 In bed 100% of the time

   Example: 1_{oa} or III_{3c}

of hepatic metastases correlated well with prognosis: patients with hepatic metastases with a high labeling index (>10 percent) had a much worse prognosis than those with a low labeling index.[41] The future application of modern technology to hepatic metastases should, it is hoped, improve their management by providing more accurate prognostic factors.

SUMMARY

Many studies have been performed to study the prognostic factors in metastatic colorectal cancer; but what can be concluded from this large body of information? For untreated hepatic metastases, percent liver involvement is most likely the most important prognos-

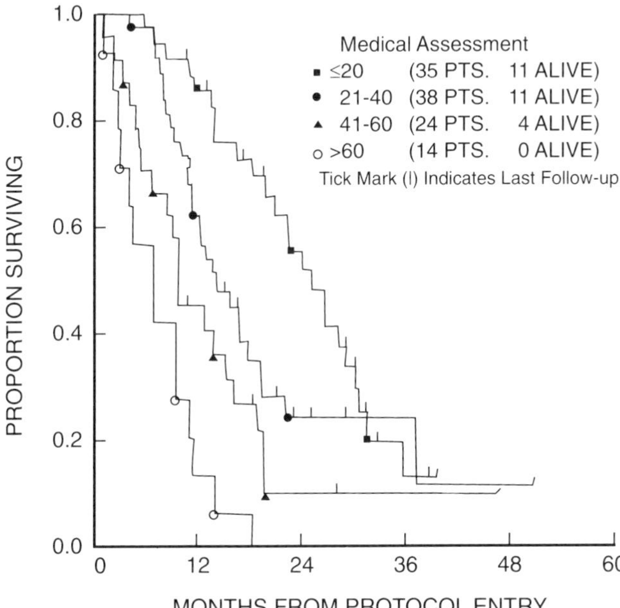

FIG. 78-1. Survival distributions by percent of liver involvement assessed medically, with a median survival of 24.5 months for patients with <20% involvement versus 6.1 months for those with >60% involvement.

tic factor, and recent studies reveal a variable survival in this group of patients. The presence of extrahepatic disease, including portal node metastases and a positive pathologic margin, yields the most important information predicting a poor outcome after hepatic metastasis resection. Pretreatment LDH and alkaline phosphatase are independent prognostic factors which, along with percent liver involvement, are the most useful prognosticators in chemotherapy series. Limited data suggest that lung-only metastases have a better prognosis than liver-only metastases, although more definitive studies are needed. Most staging systems include some combination of percent liver involvement, extrahepatic disease status, performance status, and liver function abnormalities; none has been commonly accepted or validated prospectively in large patient series. Molecular biological factors have not been extensively examined in hepatic metastases but—as in colorectal cancer primaries—will probably provide interesting prognostic information in the future. Future prognostic evaluations require study in larger patient groups, prospective validation, application of newer molecular biological techniques, and incorporation into treatment protocols to improve the utility of prognostic determinants in colorectal cancer hepatic metastases.

REFERENCES

1. Hughes KS, Sugarbaker PH: Resection of the liver for metastatic solid tumors, in Rosenberg S (ed): *Surgical Treatment of Metastatic Cancer.* Philadelphia, Lippincott, 1987, pp 125–164.
2. Levitan N, Hughes KS: Management of non-resectable liver metastases from colorectal cancer. *Oncology* 4:77–84, 1990.
3. Jaffe BM, Donegan WL, Watson F, et al: Factors influencing survival in patients with untreated hepatic metastases. *Surg Gynecol Obstet* 127:1–11, 1968.
4. Goslin R, Steele G, Zamcheck N, et al: Factors influencing survival in patients with hepatic metastases from adenocarcinoma of the colon and rectum. *Dis Colon Rectum* 25:749–754, 1982.
5. Finan PJ, Marshall RJ, Cooper EH, et al: Factors affecting survival in patients presenting with synchronous hepatic metastases from colorectal cancer: A clinical and computer analysis. *Br J Surg* 72:373–377, 1985.
6. Palmer M, Petrelli NJ, Herrera L: No treatment option for liver metastases from colorectal adenocarcinoma. *Dis Colon Rectum* 32:698–701, 1989.
7. Wagner JS, Adson MA, van Heerden JA, et al: The natural history of hepatic metastases from colorectal cancer: A comparison with resective treatment. *Ann Surg* 199:502–508, 1984.
8. Cady B, Monson DO, Swinton NW: Survival of patients after colonic resection for carcinoma with simultaneous liver metastases. *Surg Gynecol Obstet* 131:697–700, 1970.
9. Iwatsuki S, Esquivel CO, Gordon RD, et al: Liver resection for metastatic colorectal cancer. *Surgery* 100:804–810, 1986.
10. Foster JH: Survival after liver resection for secondary tumors. *Am J Surg* 135:389–394, 1978.
11. Doci R, Gennari L, Bignami P, et al: One hundred patients with hepatic metastases from colorectal cancer treated by re-

Table 78-7
Molecular Biological Factors Studied in Colorectal Cancer

Flow cytometric DNA index	Higher DNA index is an independent prognostic factor predictive of survival[56]
Molecular genetic alterations	Specific genetic deletions (e.g., p 53 gene, DCC gene) and allelic loss are associated with a poorer prognosis[57]
p53 protein	Elevated p53 expression in tumor tissue may correlate with a poor prognosis[58]
Ploidy	Aneuploid tumors tend to have a poorer survival than diploid tumors[59]
S-phase fraction or proliferation index (S phase + G_2M phase)	Higher S-phase fractions or proliferation indices are associated with poorer survival[60]

section: Analysis of prognostic determinants. *Br J Surg* 78:797–801, 1991.

12. Adson MA, van Heerden JA, Adson MH, et al: Resection of hepatic metastases from colorectal cancer: Major hepatic resection for metachronous metastases from colon cancer. *Arch Surg Ann Surg* 201:204–209, 1985.
13. Cady B, McDermott WV: Major hepatic resection for metachronous metastases from colon cancer. *Ann Surg* 201:204–209, 1985.
14. Kemeny N, Brown DW: Prognostic factors in advanced colorectal carcinoma: The importance of lactic dehydrogenase, performance status and white blood cell count. *Am J Med* 74:786–794, 1983.
15. Fortner JG, Silva JS, Cox EB, et al: Multivariate analysis of a personal series of 247 patients with liver metastases from colorectal cancer. I. Treatment by hepatic resection. *Ann Surg* 199:306–316, 1984.
16. Ekberg H, Tranberg K-G, Anderson R, et al: Determinants of survival in liver resection for colorectal secondaries. *Br J Surg* 73:727–731, 1986.
17. Steele G Jr, Bleday R, Mayer RJ, et al: A prospective evaluation of hepatic resection for colorectal carcinoma metastases to the liver: Gastrointestinal Tumor Study Group protocol 6584. *J Clin Oncol* 9:1105–1112, 1991.
18. Hughes K, Scheele J, Sugarbaker PH: Surgery for colorectal cancer metastatic to the liver. *Surg Clin North Am* 69:339–359, 1989.
19. Cady B, Stone MD, McDermott WV Jr, et al: Technical and biologic factors in disease-free survival after hepatic resection for colorectal cancer metastases. *Arch Surg* 127:561–569, 1992.
20. Hughes KS, Simon R, Songhorabodi S, et al: Resection of the liver for colorectal metastases: A multi-institutional study of indications for resection. *Surgery* 103:278–288, 1988.
21. Adson MA: Resection of liver metastases: When is it worthwhile? *World J Surg* 11:511520, 1987.
22. van Ooijen B, Wiggers T, Meijer S, et al: Hepatic resection for colorectal metastases in the Netherlands. *Cancer* 70:28–34, 1992.
23. Olak J, Wexler MJ, Rodriguez J, et al: Hepatic resection for metastatic disease. *Can J Surg* 29:435–439, 1986.
24. Scheele J, Stangl R, Altendor-Hofmann A, et al: Indicators of prognosis after hepatic resection for colorectal secondaries. *Surgery* 110:13–29, 1991.
25. Greenway B: Hepatic metastases from colorectal cancer: Resection or not. *Br J Surg* 75:513–519, 1988.
26. Fortner JG, Silva JS, Cox EB, et al: Multivariate analysis of a personal series of 247 patients with liver metastases from colorectal cancer. II. Treatment by intrahepatic chemotherapy. *Ann Surg* 199:317–323, 1984.
27. Butler J, Attiyeh FF, Daly JM: Hepatic resection for metastases of the colon and rectum. *Surg Gynecol Obstet* 162:109–113, 1986.
28. Younes RN, Rogatko A, Brennan MF: The influence of intraoperative hypotension and perioperative blood transfusion on disease-free survival in patients with complete resection of colorectal liver metastases. *Ann Surg* 214:107–113, 1991.
29. Wu H-S, Little AG: Perioperative blood transfusions and cancer recurrence. *J Clin Oncol* 6:1348–1354, 1988.
30. Kemeny N, Niedzwiecki D, Shurgot B, et al: Prognostic variables in patients with hepatic metastases from colorectal cancer: Importance of medical assessment of liver involvement. *Cancer* 63:742–747, 1989.
31. Bedikian AY, Chen TT, Malaky MA, et al: Prognostic factors influencing survival of patients with advanced colorectal cancer: Hepatic artery infusion versus systemic intravenous chemotherapy for liver metastases. *J Clin Oncol* 2:174–180, 1984.
32. Chang AE, Steinberg SM, Culnane M, et al: Determinants of survival in patients with unresectable colorectal liver metastases. *J Surg Oncol* 40:245–251, 1989.
33. Lahr CJ, Soong S-J, Cloud G, et al: A multifactorial analysis of prognostic factors in patients with liver metastases from colorectal carcinoma. *J Clin Oncol* 1:720–726, 1983.
34. Ekberg H, Tranberg KG, Lundstedt C, et al: Determinant of survival after intraarterial infusion of 5-fluorouracil for liver metastases from colorectal cancer: A multivariate analysis. *J Surg Oncol* 31:246–254, 1986.
35. Graf W, Glimelius B, Påhlman L, et al: Determinants of prognosis in advanced colorectal cancer. *Eur J Cancer* 27:1119–1123, 1991.
36. Lavin P, Mittelman A, Douglass H, et al: Survival and response to chemotherapy for advanced colorectal adenocarcinoma: An Eastern Cooperative Oncology Group Report. *Cancer* 46:1536–1543, 1980.
38. Gennari L, Doci R, Bozzetti F, et al: Proposal for staging liver metastases. *Recent Results Cancer Res* 100:80–84, 1986.
39. van de Velde CJH: The staging of hepatic metastases arising from colorectal cancer. *Recent Results Cancer Res* 100:85–90, 1986.
40. Petrelli NJ, Bonnheim DC, Herrera LO, et al: A proposed classification system for liver metastasis from colorectal carcinoma. *Dis Colon Rectum* 27:249–252, 1984.
41. Silvestrini R, Costa A, Gennari L: Cell kinetics of hepatic metastases as a prognostic marker in patients with advanced colorectal carcinoma. *HPB Surgery* 2:135–144, 1990.
42. Stearns MW, Brinkley GJ: Palliative surgery for cancer of the rectum and colon. *Cancer* 7:1016–1019, 1954.
43. Bacon HE, Martin PV: The rationale of palliative resection for primary cancer of the colon complicated by liver and lung metastases. *Dis Colon Rectum* 7:211–217, 1964.
44. Bengmark S, Hafstrom L: The natural history of primary and secondary malignant tumors of the liver: I. the prognosis for patients with hepatic metastases from colonic and rectal carcinoma at laparatomy. *Cancer* 23:198–202, 1969.
45. Oxley EM, Ellis H: Prognosis of carcinoma of the large bowel in the presence of liver metastases. *Br J Surg* 56:149–152, 1969.
47. Abrams MS, Lerner HJ: Survival of patients at Pennsylvania Hospital with hepatic metastases from carcinoma of the colon and rectum. *Dis Colon Rectum* 14:431–434, 1971.
48. Nielsen J, Barlslev I, Jensen HE: Carcinoma of the colon with liver metastases. *Acta Chir Scand* 137:463–465, 1971.
49. Baden H, Anderson B: Survival of patients with untreated liver metastases from colorectal cancer. *Scand J Gastroenterol* 10:221–223, 1975.
50. Wilson SM, Adson MA: Surgical treatment of hepatic metastases from colorectal cancers. *Arch Surg* 111:330–334, 1976.

50a. Wood CB, Gillis CR, Blumgort LH: A retrospective study of the natural history of patients with liver metastases from colorectal cancer. *Clin Oncol* 2:285–288, 1976.

51. Wanebo HJ, Semoglou C, Attiyeh F, et al: Surgical management of patients with primary operable colorectal cancer and synchronous liver metastases. *Am J Surg* 135:81–84, 1978.
52. Bengtsson G, Carlsson G, Hafstrom L, et al: Natural history of patients with untreated liver metastases from colorectal cancer. *Am J Surg* 141:586–589, 1981.
53. Nordlinger B, Parc R, Delva E, et al: Hepatic resection for colorectal liver metastases. *Ann Surg* 205:256–263, 1987.
54. Wagman LD, Kemeney MM, Leong L, et al: A prospective, randomized evaluation of the treatment of colorectal cancer metastatic to the liver. *J Clin Oncol* 8:1885–1893, 1990.
55. Pettavel J, Levoraz S, Douglas P: The necessity for staging liver metastases and standardizig treatment response criteria: The case of secondaries of colorectal origin, in Van de Velde

CJH, Sugarbaker PH (eds): *Liver Metastasis: Basic aspects, Detection and Management*. Boston, Nijhoff, 1984, pp 154–168.

56. Giaretti W, Danova M, Geido E, et al: Flow cytometric DNA index in the prognosis of colorectal cancer. *Cancer* 67:1921–1927, 1991.
57. Hamilton SR: Molecular genetic alterations as potential prognostic indicators in colorectal carcinoma. *Cancer* 69:1589–1591, 1992.
58. Scott N, Sagar P, Stewart J, et al: p53 in colorectal cancer: Clinicopathological correlation and prognostic significance. *Br J Cancer* 63:317–319, 1991.
59. Crissman JD, Zarbo RJ, Ma CK, et al: Histopathologic parameters and DNA analysis in colorectal adenocarcinomas. *Pathol Annu* 24:103–147, 1989.
60. Witzig TE, Loprinzi CL, Gonchoroff NJ, et al: DNA ploidy and cell kinetic measurements as predictors of recurrence and survival in stages B_2 and colorectal adenocarcinoma. *Cancer* 68:879–888, 1991.

CHAPTER 79

Management of Bowel Dysfunction following Surgery

Stuart H. Q. Quan

From the patient's perspective, bowel dysfunction following surgery for colorectal cancer may be defined as any deviation from the preoperative bowel pattern. Preoperative and immediate postoperative discussion between surgeon and patient should always take into consideration the possible changes of subsequent bowel function, which might take place due to the anatomic and functional modifications brought on by the surgical operation as well as by adjuvant therapies. The acute dysfunctional effects of surgery, chemotherapy, and radiation and the appropriate therapy to deal with these are well defined. Acute treatment-related diarrhea responds to antispasmodics and treatment interruption or dose modification. Early postoperative bowel dysfunction is best treated with a low-fiber diet. Highlights of the management of chronic bowel dysfunction will be discussed.

Patients should be reeducated to eat a well-balanced low-fat, high-fiber diet (with the exception of the postileostomy patient). The patient whose colon also revealed diverticuli is asked to avoid seeds, nuts, and skins. Excessively gas-producing foods such as beans, cabbage, onions, milk, and citrus fruits can be warned against. Hyperlaxation can come from overconsumption of fresh fruits, coffee, spices, and so on, whereas constipation can come from overingestion of tea, starchy foods, cheese, and red meats.

ILEOSTOMY

To avoid bowel dysfunction, the patient with an ileostomy should adhere to a modified, *low*-residue diet. The avoidance of seeds, nuts, pulps, skins, and particularly fruits should be strictly enforced. A wide variety of foods included in a well-balanced diet—such as poultry, fish, cooked fruit and vegetables, and cereals, etc.—are tolerated by ileostomy patients. Occasional constipation can be corrected by small doses of mild laxatives, such as mineral oil and/or milk of magnesia.

Recent studies support the beneficial effect of adding calcium to the diet to diminish the frequency of movements, particularly in patients undergoing total proctocolectomy and construction of an ileal pouch anastomosis. A secondary benefit of dietary calcium supplement is the diminished production of crypt cells. Thus, in patients with adenomatous polyposis coli who have retained a rectal stump following total colectomy and ileorectal anastomosis, there is a decrease in the formation of rectal polyps.[1]

COLOSTOMIES

Although the colostomy openings may appear the same, the anatomic location of the stoma is different for the transverse and sigmoid colostomate, and, indeed, reactions to dysfunction will also differ. Because of the shorter existent colon, a transverse colostomy will tend to have looser rather than firmer stools. On the other hand, because of the longer existent colon, a sigmoid colostomy will tend to have more solid movements. Thus, the patient with a transverse colostomy is encouraged to consume bulkier foods in order to solidify the stool and will rarely require a colostomy irrigation. The patient with a sigmoid colostomy, on the other hand, may easily constipate, like any person with a full colon, and may be helped by the use of a laxative or colostomy irrigation as indicated. From a practical point of view in management, most patients prefer sigmoid colostomy irrigations every other day. Between irrigations they usually remain clean and require only a simple cover dressing over the stoma.

The reader is referred to other recent books for detailed discussion of enterostomal therapy.[2]

RIGHT AND LEFT COLECTOMY

There is usually little difference in the cause and effect of bowel dysfunction in patients with either right or left colectomies. If either type of patient ingests the wrong food, the same malfunction will result. The tendency, again, is for the patient with the shorter remaining colon (absent left colon) to have looser bowel action than the patient with the longer remaining colon (absent right colon). Occasionally, severe diarrhea following colectomy may require bile salt binding with cholestyramine.

For proper management, however, anastomotic stricture, whether from recurrent disease or scar tissue formation, must be ruled out. Tumor recurrence at the anastomotic site may require operative intervention and renewed attempts at cure. Anastomotic stricture from scar tissue formation rarely if ever requires operative correction. The judicious use of a stool softener, liquefaction, and an occasional strong cathartic can almost always open up an anastomotic diaphragm, the lumen of which may appear to be only 3 to 4 mm in diameter and through which the endoscopist is afraid to transduce even the smallest endoscopic instrument.

LOW ANTERIOR RESECTION OR COLOANAL ANASTOMOSIS

In recovering from low anterior resection with primary colorectal or coloanal anastomosis, the patient's understanding of bowel dysfunction is highly relevant to his or her post-operative comfort. It is these patients who will have to learn how to adjust to their "new" rectum and their "old" anosphincter. The patient must understand that dysfunction is the norm when most or all of the rectum, its innervation, and some of its immediate adjacent supporting structures have been removed and replaced by a segment of upper colon which has been brought down and attached to the lower remnant of the rectum or to the anosphincter itself. The loss of the normal preoperative anorectal angle and the operative manipulation or actual dilation of the anal sphincter itself at the time of anastomosis all contribute to the disappearance of the normal sensation of a full bowel or rectal urge. Henceforth, and even when this sensation comes back, it may be only a facsimile thereof and not wholly reliable. Patients may be continent of stool but unable to control or even be aware of the passage of flatus. Furthermore, various degrees of anastomotic stricturing usually set in. On the positive side is the fact that the anastomosis is usually within the reach of the surgeon's finger; therefore the assessment and correction of this complication can be more readily accomplished.

From the patient's point of view, the accumulation of stool proximal to the anastomotic scar may produce a "log jam" effect or impaction, so that the patient often suffers from urgent, uncontrollable, episodic, frequent night and/or day movements that are watery, or from tiny movements as the more liquid stool escapes around the impaction (paradoxical diarrhea). The best way to prevent this syndrome is to advise the patient to be sure to have adequate bowel movements at least two or three times a week. This may require continuous modest laxation plus periodic enemas or the use of strong cathartics (castor oil, cascara, etc.) at least twice a week. Again, proper dieting always plays a role. Added bulk (Metamucil, Konsyl) passing through the constricted, scarred lumen might aid in dilating the stricture; yet too much bulk may add to the impaction in some patients. Symptomatic patients may benefit from cautery or balloon dilatation.[3,4] Patients with extreme spasm of the denervated neorectum may benefit from antispasmodic medications such as Lomotil or Imodium. This is particularly helpful prior to leaving home for social functions.

Much of the urgency and frequency encountered following these operations is related to the reduced capacity of the neorectal reservoir.[5] With patience, the functional results generally improve over 6 to 12 months. A number of investigators have implemented construction of a colonic J pouch to facilitate the more rapid development of an adequate neorectal reservoir. Two groups from France were the first to report the use of colonic J pouches as part of the Parks coloanal reconstruction. Parc and colleagues[6] in Paris utilized this approach in 31 patients, with a mean number of 1.1 daily bowel movements. However, 25 percent of the patients were unable to evacuate spontaneously, requiring the use of an enema every other day. Lazorthes and associates[7] in Toulouse have used pouches in 20 patients, all with coloanal anastomoses. Of these patients, 87 percent had 1 to 2 bowel movements per day at 1 year, compared to 33 percent of a group of 33 patients with straight coloanal anastomoses. Bowel frequency correlated with reservoir size. The importance of the pouch in reducing stool frequency has been confirmed by Nicholls and associates[8] from St. Mark's Hospital and by Kusunoki et al.[9] in Japan. The use of an 8-cm colonic J pouch has also been reported by Drake and coworkers[10] from the Mayo Clinic. Data from Memorial Sloan-Kettering Cancer Center also confirm the safety and efficacy of a small colonic J pouch for restorative proctectomy.[11] The group utilized this pouch in 25 patients for both low stapled colorectal reconstruction as well as hand-sewn coloanal anastomosis. Functional results were good to excellent within a few months of the operation. No patient required antispasmodic medications and none was enema-dependent. A randomized clinical trial is under way in Sweden to confirm the utility of the pouch.

REFERENCES

1. Barsoum GH, Winslet M, Youngs D: Influences of dietary calcium supplements on ileoanal pouch function and cytokinetics. *Br J Surg* 79:129–132, 1992.
2. Bubrick MP, Rolstad BS: Intestinal stomas, in Gordon P, Nivatvongs S (eds): *Principles and Practice of Surgery for the Colon, Rectum, and Anus*. St Louis, Missouri, QMP, Inc, 1992, pp 855–904.
3. Oz MC, Forde KA: Endoscopic alternatives in the management of colonic strictures. *Surgery* 108: 513–519, 1990.
4. Venkatesh KS, Ramanujam PS, McGee S: Hydrostatic balloon dilatation of benign colonic anastomotic strictures. *Dis Colon Rectum* 35:789–791, 1992.
5. Schoetz DJ Jr: Postcolectomy syndromes. *World J Surg* 15:605–608, 1991.
6. Parc R, Tiret E, Frileux P, et al: Resection and colo-anal anastomosis with colonic reservoir for rectal carcinoma. *Br J Surg* 73:139–141, 1986.
7. Lazorthes F, Fages P, Chiotasso P, et al: Resection of the rectum with construction of a colonic reservoir and colo-anal anastomosis for carcinoma of the rectum. *Br J Surg* 73:136–138, 1986.
8. Nicholls RJ, Lubowski DZ, Donaldson DR: Comparison of colonic reservoir and straight colo-anal reconstruction after rectal excision. *Br J Surg* 75:318–320, 1988.
9. Kusunoki M, Shoji Y, Yanagi H, et al: Function after anoabdominal rectal resection and colonic J pouch–anal anastomosis. *Br J Surg* 78:1434–1438, 1991.
10. Drake DB, Pemberton JH, Beart RW Jr, et al: Coloanal anastomosis in the management of benign and malignant rectal disease. *Ann Surg* 206:600–605, 1987.
11. Taylor BA, Pemberton JH, Carpenter HA, et al: Dysplasia in chronic ulcerative colitis: Implications for colonoscopic surveillance. *Dis Colon Rectum* 35:950–956, 1992.

CHAPTER 80

Urinary and Sexual Dysfunction

Ridwan Shabsigh
Jerry G. Blaivas

HIGHLIGHTS

Voiding dysfunction is particularly common after abdominoperineal resection of the rectum due to injury to the pelvic plexus. Symptoms may include urinary retention, incontinence, or both. Many patients recover or improve within a year. Urodynamic evaluation is very important for the accurate diagnosis and proper planning of treatment.

Erectile dysfunction is also common after abdominoperineal resection. As in voiding dysfunction, the mechanism is frequently neurogenic, although occasionally a vascular factor may coexist. In recent years, progress has been achieved in the area of treatment of erectile dysfunction. Effective treatment options have become available, including nonsurgical methods—such as the pharmacologic erection program (penile self-injections) and vacuum restriction devices—as well as surgical methods (i.e., penile prostheses).

Individualization of treatment of voiding and sexual dysfunctions—taking into consideration the patient's age, preoperative and postoperative symptoms, cancer status, and other relevant issues—is highly important.

CONTROVERSIES

Patient selection for the various pharmacologic and mechanical interventions in the management of male erectile dysfunction remains problematic.

FUTURE DIRECTIONS

Research continues to result in improvements and progress in all subfields of urology. For the purpose of treating voiding and sexual dysfunctions related to colorectal surgery, expected areas of improvement in the future include intraoperative nerve localization to avoid nerve injury; electrostimulation for induction of bladder function, sphincter control, and/or erection; reinnervation surgery; and more effective pharmacologic agents.

Radical pelvic surgery is well known to be associated with voiding and sexual dysfunctions. The improvements in early detection of colonic malignancy and the consequent improvement in prognosis and postoperative survival have brought increased attention to the sequelae of treatment and the quality of life following recovery from surgery. Modern management of voiding and sexual dysfunction can restore satisfactory functions in the majority of patients.

ANATOMY AND PHYSIOLOGY

The autonomic innervation of the lower urinary tract, including the bladder and the urethral sphincter, originates in the spinal cord. Innervation of the penis follows similar pathways. Parasympathetic innervation is derived from the sacral roots of S2 through S4, forming the pelvic nerves. Sympathetic innervation is derived from thoracolumbar roots of T10 through L1, forming the hypogastric nerves.[1] The pelvic and the hypogastric nerves merge on either side of the pelvic viscera and run from the lateral wall of the pelvis to the base of the bladder. The plexus is in the immediate proximity of the ureter and the visceral pelvic vessels. The posterior portion of the plexus is adjacent to the anterolateral wall of the rectum. The anterior portion of the plexus is adjacent to the prostate and seminal vesicles.[2] It is obvious from this anatomic arrangement that surgery of the rectum may result in injury to the innervation of the bladder, sphincter, and/or penis, resulting in voiding and/or sexual dysfunction. For example, during abdominoperineal resection, the rectum is mobilized, resulting in pulling the pelvic plexuses away from the posterolateral wall of the pelvis. At this point, blunt or sharp dissection on the lateral walls of the rectum may result in damage to the nerves. Figure 80-1 summarizes the neuroanatomy of the bladder, sphincter, and penis.

PATHOPHYSIOLOGY

Iatrogenic nerve injury is the cause of most voiding dysfunction in patients undergoing resection of the rectum. Most of the damage is inflicted upon the pelvic plexus, which includes parasympathetic and sympathetic neurons, resulting in a neurogenic bladder.[3,4] It has been indicated that the extent of denervation is related to the local stage of the malignancy.[5] Denervation is greatest in patients with invasive or highly malignant tumors and in those with posterior or encircling tumors.[5] This information is very important for colorectal surgeons if they are to provide proper preoperative patient counseling. Neurogenic bladder commonly results in an incompetent proximal urethra, decreased detrusor compliance, poor or absent detrusor contractility, and compromised external urethral sphincteric function.[3,6,7] Therefore, with great individual variability, there will usually be some residual ves-

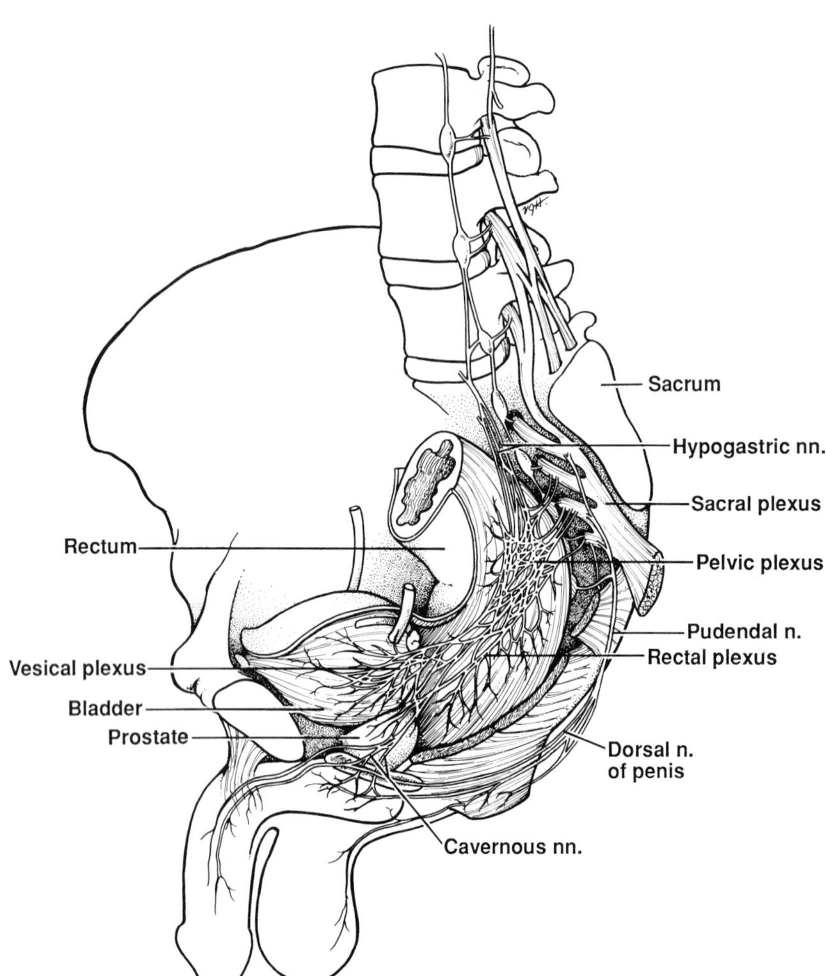

FIG. 80-1. Autonomic innervation of the urinary bladder, urinary sphincter, and penis.

icourethral activity and some responsiveness of the bladder and urethra to pharmacologic agents after pelvic plexus injury. However, the degree of activity and responsiveness to drugs is unpredictable. Detrusor abnormalities are usually due to a lesion in the pelvic parasympathetic nerves, and sphincter abnormalities stem from a lesion in the sympathetic and pudendal nerves.[3] Frequently, the lesions are incomplete and some neural function is maintained. Complete bilateral ablation of the pelvic plexuses causes decentralization of the bladder and urethra from central neural control rather than denervation.[1]

During recovery from pelvic plexus injury, reinnervation occurs to some degree.[8] The extent of reinnervation varies from patient to patient, resulting in various degrees of clinical recovery.[9] The return of continence has been shown to correlate with restoration of somatic sphincter activity in the area of the urogenital diaphragm.[6]

VOIDING DYSFUNCTION

Clinical Presentation

Voiding dysfunction is particularly common after abdominoperineal resection of the rectum, as reported in up to 80 percent of patients undergoing abdominoperineal resection for adenocarcinoma of the rectum or ulcerative colitis.[4] The symptoms may include difficulty in voiding and/or incontinence. The difficulty in voiding is caused by detrusor failure, which is made worse by failure of relaxation of the sphincter mechanism. Sphincter incontinence occurs because of failure of the sphincter to maintain urethral closure pressure and to respond to stress. Incomplete bladder emptying and a large postvoid residual may also aggravate incontinence and, in addition, cause urgency and frequency if sensation is preserved or overflow incontinence if sensation is lost.[1] Incomplete bladder emptying may also cause recurrent urinary tract infections and/or stone formation. The extent of symptoms varies from individual to individual. In some patients, the symptoms may be very minimal, while others may have complete urinary retention or severe incontinence. Preexisting urologic disorders may contribute to the severity of symptoms. Such conditions may include benign prostatic hyperplasia, urethral stricture, previous bladder or urethral surgery, and others. Fortunately, symptoms in most patients subside within the first 3 to 6 months after surgery.[3] After recovery from the initial postoperative symptoms, the secondary development of voiding symptoms in a patient who has had resection of the rectum for a rectal carcinoma may be a sign of local recurrence.

Diagnostic Evaluation

History

The voiding history in addition to the past urologic and general history of the patient prior to colorectal surgery is very important. If the patient had no voiding symptoms prior to colorectal surgery and has developed voiding dysfunction since the operation, the problem clearly relates to a neurogenic injury at the time of the operation. On the other hand, an elderly patient who has had a long history of progressive bladder obstruction prior to the operation represents a more complex problem, especially if such a patient develops urinary retention. Urodynamic evaluation is crucial for the proper diagnosis and management of these patients.

Physical Exam

Physical examination may reveal a distended bladder. Otherwise, little can be gained from the physical exam.

Laboratory Evaluation

Generally, urinalysis, urine culture, complete blood count (CBC), and serum chemistry profile (including creatinine, urea, and electrolytes) are all that is needed in laboratory evaluation.

Urodynamic Evaluation

Multichannel pressure-flow study provides the best information regarding bladder and sphincter abnormalities. In the immediate postoperative period (up to 1 year after surgery), there is usually detrusor areflexia; but with the passage of time, these patients often develop low bladder compliance as well. The end result is an areflexic high-pressure bladder which, without proper treatment, poses a major risk to the upper urinary tract. The sphincter abnormality usually results in stress incontinence. At first, the symptoms seem paradoxical: the patient has urinary incontinence due to the combination of the sphincteric abnormality and the high pressures generated by the low bladder compliance, yet there is incomplete emptying due to the areflexic bladder.

The pressure at which voiding of incontinence occurs (the leak-point pressure) is an important determinant of upper tract damage. Low bladder compliance poses a major risk to the upper urinary tract because, during bladder filling, detrusor pressure rises to very high levels. Untreated patients with low compliance have a very high likelihood of developing hydronephrosis, vesicoureteral reflex, urolithiasis, infection, and renal failure.[10] Thus treatment of low compliance is essential in order to prevent renal deterioration.

Radiologic Evaluation

Imaging of the upper urinary tract with ultrasound or intravenous pyelography may be performed in patients who face the risk of developing renal deterioration, such as those with a long history of unresolved voiding symptoms, abnormal serum creatinine/urea, or high bladder pressures.

Management

In the majority of patients, voiding dysfunction resolves or improves significantly with time, especially in the first year after colorectal injury. Therefore, initial therapy should be nonsurgical, and any potentially irreversible therapy should be withheld until a year after the operation.

In the patient with mild voiding symptoms, conservative, careful follow-up may be all that is needed. The indications for intervention are significant voiding symptoms, urinary retention, and/or urinary incontinence.[1]

Treatment should be directed at the underlying abnormalities. Detrusor areflexia, which is the most common abnormality, is best managed by intermittent self-catheterization. In some patients, this alone is sufficient to prevent incontinence and protect the upper urinary tract provided that it is done often. In other patients, incontinence persists because it is sphincteric in nature. Although alpha-adrenergic agonists may be useful in some patients, many require sphincter-enhancing operations such as the placement of an artificial urinary sphincter (Fig. 80-2) or periurethral injection of bulking agents. In others, low bladder compliance may require that intermittent catheterization be done at such frequent intervals as to make it impractical. These patients may be offered a trial of anticholinergic agents in addition to intermittent self-catheterization designed to lower intravesical pressure and increase bladder capacity. If the drug fails, augmentation cystoplasty is usually effective.

As mentioned above, patients with incomplete voiding who also have coexisting benign prostatic enlargement represent a special case for diagnosis, management, and counseling. Urodynamic evaluation should be performed prior to considering prostatectomy. In patients with sphincteric incompetence, continence depends on the internal sphincteric mechanism (i.e., the bladder neck and prostate may become incontinent after prostatectomy).[11] In such cases, intermittent catheterization will provide complete bladder emptying and in many instances prevent incontinence.

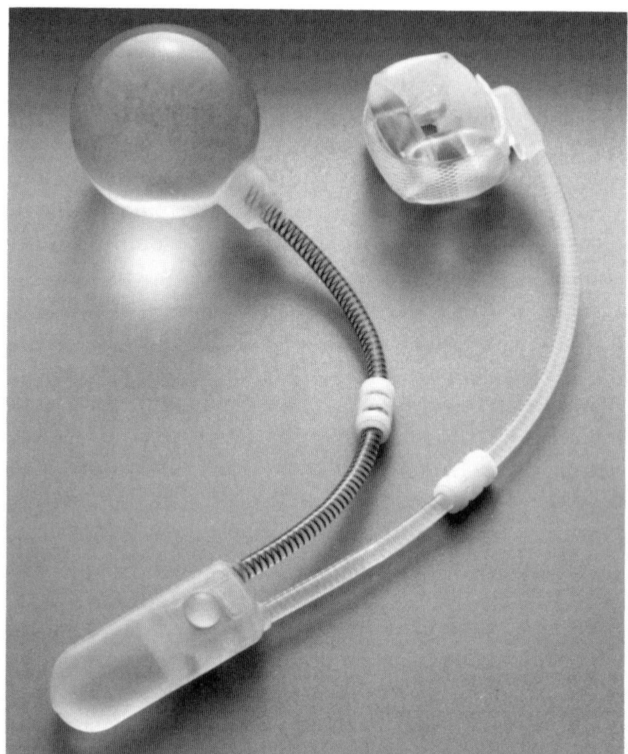

FIG. 80-2. Artificial urinary sphincter AS-800. (Courtesy of American Medical Systems, Minneapolis, Minnesota.)

SEXUAL DYSFUNCTION

Clinical Presentation

One type of sexual dysfunction is erectile dysfunction. During the 1980s, the neural pathways of erectile function were described in detail. As in the classic work of Lue et al.,[12] it is clear that the sacral parasympathetic roots S2–S4 are the origin of the pelvic plexus. The cavernous nerves originate from the pelvic plexus and are truly the "erection nerves" or *nervi erigentes*. The anatomic proximity of the pelvic plexus to the rectum explains the high incidence of erectile dysfunction secondary to resection of the rectum. Indeed, the incidence of erectile dysfunction has been reported to range between 15 and 100 percent following abdominoperineal resection.[13–17]

Another type of sexual dysfunction is ejaculatory dysfunction. Ejaculatory function is dependent upon intact innervation from T10–L1 through the sympathetic hypogastric nerves. These nerve pathways provide innervation to the vas deferens and the seminal vesicles, affecting seminal emission, as well as to the bladder neck, assuring its closure during intercourse. Injury to these sympathetic pathways results in various degrees of ejaculatory dysfunction, ranging from absent emission to retrograde ejaculation. In clinical practice, erectile dysfunction is more significant than ejaculatory dysfunction because, at the age of diagnosis, many colon cancer patients may already have had all the children they desire.

Diagnostic Evaluation

Evaluation of the impotent patient is performed for certain goals: to confirm the diagnosis, to discover possible reversible causes, and to review the medical, surgical, and psychological contributing factors. In some instances, the diagnostic evaluation is performed for research or medicolegal reasons. The history and physical exam are the two indispensable and agreed upon methods. The other diagnostic methods are utilized as indicated in individual patients.[18]

History

This includes sexual history since and prior to colorectal surgery in addition to medical, surgical, psychological, and marital histories.

Physical Exam

In cases of impotence secondary to colorectal surgery, physical examination may not be rewarding because of lack of detectable abnormalities. However, in general, patients with erectile dysfunction should have a complete exam to check their general state of health, secondary sex characteristics, genital and rectal condition, and peripheral vascular and neurologic status.

Laboratory Evaluation

These include the following: serum testosterone and prolactin, CBC, serum chemistry, and glucose tolerance.[19]

Nocturnal Penile Tumescence (NPT) Monitoring

With development of home monitors of penile tumescence and rigidity such as the Rigiscan device, it is now possible to perform reasonably economical studies. Monitoring of NPT can provide evidence of organic erectile dysfunction.[20,21] This becomes very important in medicolegal cases.

Neurologic Evaluation

Initial screening includes neurologic physical exam and bioesthesiometry. Examination of genital sensation to pinprick and temperature is standard, in addition to anal sphincter tone and bulbocavernosus reflex. Bioesthesiometry utilizes a vibrator to test the somatosensory threshold in the penis. More elaborate testing methods are available.[22] However, the diagnostic yield of the screening neurologic evaluation is generally low in patients who have had an abdominoperineal resection.

Vascular Evaluation

A simple office-based test includes penile injection with vasoactive drugs followed by manual stimulation. A rigid erection indicates that the patient is a responder to the pharmacologic erection program (PEP) and may benefit from home injections. Other penile vascular tests include penile duplex Doppler ultrasound, cavernosometry and cavernosography, and pudendal arteriography.[18] These studies are rarely indicated in patients with erectile dysfunction secondary to abdominoperineal resection. The details of these studies are beyond the scope of this chapter.

Treatment

Nonsurgical Treatment

Currently, PEP and vacuum constriction devices are the two standard treatment options. Other medical methods are being developed and investigated, including topical treatments.

Pharmacologic Erection Program. Penile self-injections also known as the pharmacologic erection program (PEP), have become very popular as a nonsurgical treatment of erectile dysfunction.[23–26] The physiologic principle of PEP is the induction of smooth muscle relaxation in the corpora cavernosa, resulting in increased arterial inflow, filling of the sinusoidal spaces, and restriction of venous outflow. Various combinations of medications have been utilized, including papaverine alone, prostaglandin E_1 alone, papaverine + phentolamine, prostaglandin E_1 + phentolamine, and papaverine + phentolamine + prostglandin E_1. The PEP is performed in two phases: the initiation phase and the follow-up phase. In the initiation phase, test injections are given in the office for two purposes: to test the patient's response and to instruct the patient in the self-injection technique. Usually this takes an average of two office visits, with test injections during each visit. Once the patient demonstrates satisfactory self-injection technique, he will be provided with the medication for home use and a prescription for sterile disposable 1-mL insulin syringes with 28G or 29G needles. The dose may be adjusted as required based upon the results of the first few home injections. In the follow-up phase, the patient is seen every 3 months to review the injection technique, results of home injections, patient's and partner's comments and concerns, and possible side effects and complications, as well as to perform a physical exam of the penis. Medication is then resupplied. The overall response rate is approximately 80 percent. Prior to inclusion of the patient in the PEP, it is important to consider his motivation, compliance, manual dexterity, past medical history, and genital anatomy. The absolute contraindications to PEP are sickle cell disease or trait or the use of monoamine oxidase MAO inhibitors. Complications include development of fibrosis at the injection sites in the corpora cavernosa, penile pain, ecchymosis, and priapism. The latter can be prevented by starting patients on low doses of injectable drugs and increasing the dose gradually until a satisfactory response is reached. The dropout rate from PEP ranges from 30 to 50 percent. The reasons for dropping out include loss of partner, dissatisfaction with this method, loss of effective treatment, pain, fibrosis, cost, and loss of interest in sexual activity. Newer, improved injectable drugs are being investigated.

Vacuum Constriction Devices. Such an external device consists of a suction pump operated either manually or electrically to induce an erection-like state.[27–32] An elastic band or ring is applied to the base of the penis in order to maintain the erection (Fig. 80-3). The patient is instructed to remove the restrictive elastive band within 30 min in order to prevent any possible ischemia. A report by a multidisciplinary team has elucidated the beneficial effects of vacuum restriction devices on sexual, psychosocial, and marital functions.[33] The advantages of this method include (1) noninvasiveness—no medications are used and no surgery is performed; (2) noncommitment—this method can be discontinued at any time and another method can be chosen for the treatment of erectile dysfunction; (3) low cost—vacuum devices obviously are less expensive than other treatment methods. While several reports have have reported the efficacy of vacuum devices, only one report has thus far suggested the presence of penile ischemia during vacuum constriction.[34] Other reported minor side effects include petechiae and ecchymosis, painful ejaculation, dusky discoloration, and numbness. Many patients comment that the erection is "hinged," because it exists only distal to the constrictive elastic band. Vacuum devices can be combined with penile self-injections simultaneously or alternately in order to help patients who cannot achieve satisfactory erections with either method.[35]

Surgical Treatment

In the past three decades, significant progress has been made in the field of penile prostheses. Modifications of the original designs have provided a variety of very reliable penile implants made by different manufacturers. Basically, there are two distinct types of penile prosthesis: the semirigid or malleable and the inflatable. The semirigid prostheses consist of paired rods implanted surgically inside the corpora cavernosa (Fig. 80-4). When positioned in a straight position, they provide the penis with the needed rigidity for intercourse. Semirigid prostheses do not change in length or circumference, thus providing continuous erection. In spite of this unphysiologic feature, semirigid prostheses continue to have a role in clinical practice because of their simplicity, reliability, and lack of mechanical failure. The inflatable prostheses have the important advantage of functioning similarly to a natural penis—that is, providing tumescence, or increased length and girth, in addition to satisfactory rigidity when an erection for intercourse is desired. When deflated, such prostheses provide a natural-looking flaccid penis. The ability of the patient to con-

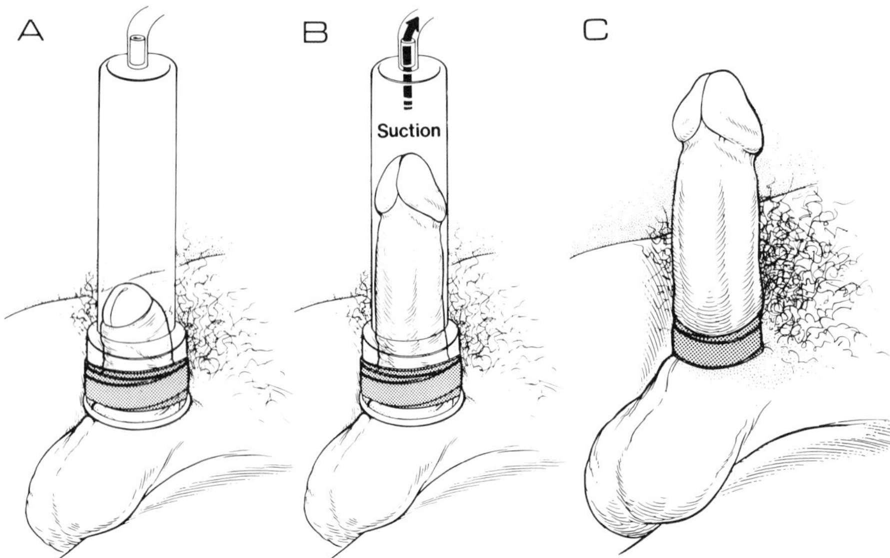

FIG. 80-3. Vacuum constriction device. (From *J Urol Nurs* 6:10, 1987. Reproduced by permission.)

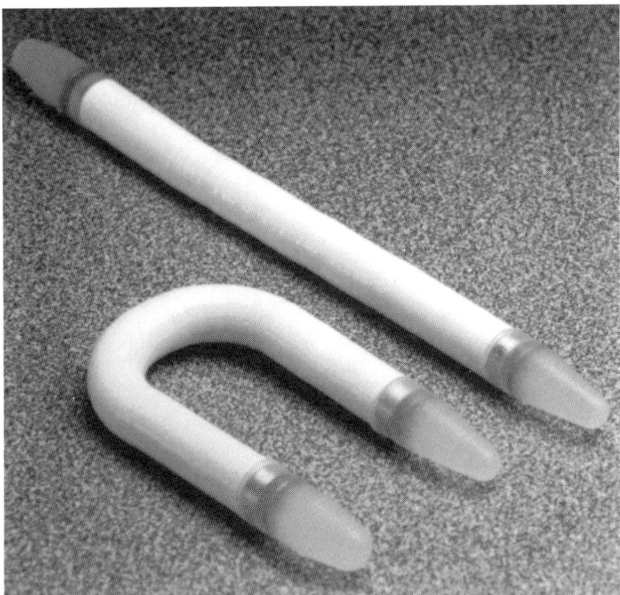

FIG. 80-4. Duraphase penile prosthesis. The design of this malleable prosthesis provides for reliable positioning and excellent concealment. (Courtesy of Dacomed Corp., Minneapolis, Minnesota.)

trol flaccidity and erection is an important and distinct benefit. As a trade-off, inflatable penile prostheses can have mechanical failures, such as fluid leak, that require reoperation, although the newer versions are more durable and reliable.[36–37] There are three types of inflatable penile prosthese. The one-piece penile prostheses consist of paired rods implanted surgically inside the corpora cavernosa. They have a self-contained inflation and deflation mechanism that is operated by the patient as desired. Figure 80-5 shows a

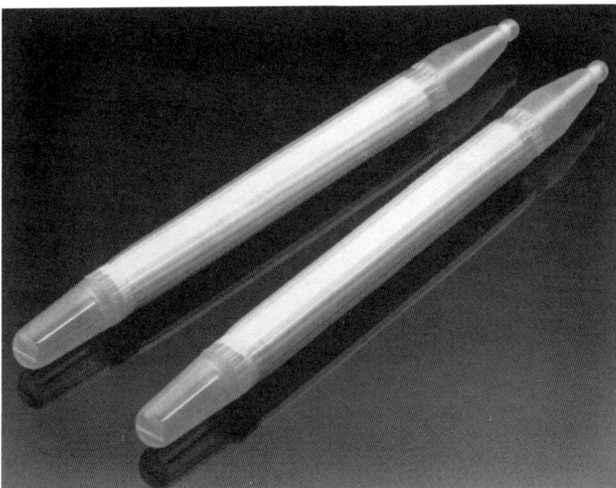

FIG. 80-5. Dynaflex, a one-piece self-contained inflatable penile prosthesis. From distal to proximal end, each rod consists of an inflation pump, a deflation valve, and a fluid reservoir. (Courtesy of American Medical Systems, Minneapolis, Minnesota.)

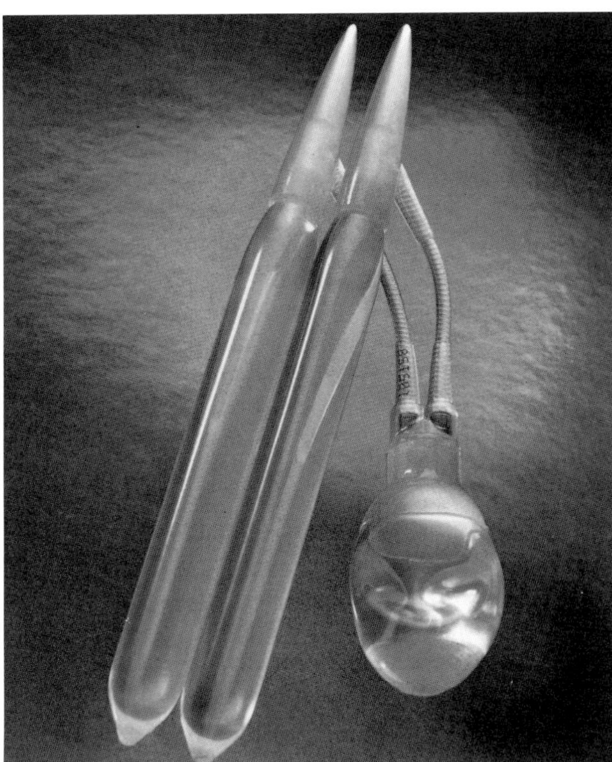

FIG. 80-6. Mentor-Mark II, a two-piece inflatable penile prosthesis. The two cylinders are connected to a "scrotal piece" that contains an inflation pump, a deflation valve, and a fluid reservoir. (Courtesy of Dacomed Corp., Goleta, California.)

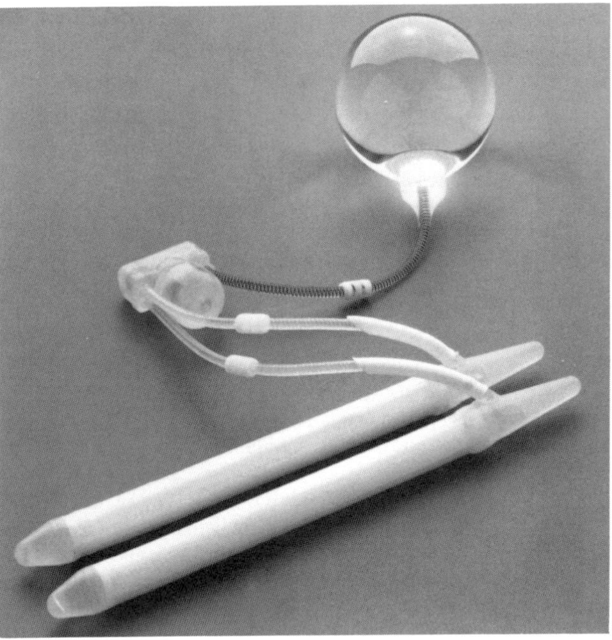

FIG. 80-7. AMS Ultrex, a three-piece inflatable penile prosthesis. The two cylinders are placed inside the corpora cavernosa. The fluid reservoir is placed retropubically or extraperitoneally posterior to the abdominal wall muscles. The pump, which contains an inflation pump and a deflation valve, is placed in the scrotum. (Courtesy of American Medical Systems, Minneapolis, Minnesota.)

one-piece prosthesis, the Dynaflex. The advantages of such prostheses are simple surgical implantation and lack of need for intraoperative fluid filling and tube connections. The two-piece prostheses consist of paired inflatable cylinders implanted inside the corpora cavernosa and connected to a "scrotal piece" that contains an inflatable pump, a deflation valve, and a fluid reservoir. Figure 80-6 shows a two-piece penile prosthesis, the Mentor-Mark II. Three-piece penile prostheses consist of paired inflatable cylinders implanted inside the corpora cavernosa and connected to fluid reservoir implanted retropubically through a scrotal pump. The scrotal pump contains an inflation pump and a deflation valve. Figure 80-7 shows a three-piece penile prosthesis, the AMS Ultrex.

Proper preoperative selection of patients and informed consent are indispensable for the success of penile prosthesis surgery. Postoperative care and patient instruction are crucial, especially for patients receiving inflatable implants. Patient and partner satisfaction has been reported to be in the 95 percent range. In experienced hands, penile prosthesis surgery has very acceptable complication rates. The important possible complications can be divided into mechanical and nonmechanical types. The mechanical complications may include breakage of the core of a semirigid prosthesis, fluid loss from leakage, and tube kinking. Nonmechanical complications may include infection, the most frequent infecting organism being *Staphylococcus epidermidis,* and injury to adjacent organs such as the urethra.

REFERENCES

1. Mundy AR: An anatomical explanation for bladder dysfunction following rectal and uterine surgery. *Br J Urol* 54:501, 1982.
2. Mundy AR: Pelvic plexus injury, in Mundy AR, Stephenson TP, Wein AJ (eds): *Urodynamics, Practice and Principles, and Application.* Churchill Livingstone. Edinburg, New York, 1984, pp 273–277.
3. Blaivas JG, Barbalias GA: Characteristics of neural injury after abdomino perineal resection. *J Urol* 129:84, 1983.
4. Eickenberg HU, Amin M, Klompus W, Lich R Jr: Urologic complications following abdominoperineal resection. *J Urol* 115:180, 1976.
5. Fowler JW, Bremner DN, Moffat LEF: The incidence and consequences of damage to the parasympathetic nerve supply to the bladder after abdominoperineal resection of the rectum for carcinoma. *Br J Urol* 50:95, 1978.
6. Yalla SV, Andriole GL: Vesicourethral dysfunction following pelvic visceral ablative surgery. *J Urol* 132:503, 1984.
7. McGuire EJ: Urodynamic evaluation after abdominoperineal resection and lumbar intervertebral disk herniation. *Urology* 6:63, 1975.
8. Neal DE, Bogue PR, Williams RE: The histology of the innervation of the bladder in patients with denervation after excision of the rectum for carcinoma. *Br J Urol* 54:658, 1982.
9. Norlen L: The autonomous bladder. *Scand J Urol Nephrol* 10 (Suppl 36):5–29, 1976.
10. McGuire EJ, Woodside JR, Borden TA, Weiss RM: The prognostic value of urodynamic testing in myelodysplastic patients. *J Urol* 126:205, 1981.
11. Gillespie L, Barbatic Z, Raz S: Effects of abdominal perineal resection on genitourinary tract. *Urology* 25:259, 1985.
12. Lue TF, Zeineh SJ, Schmidt RA, Tanagho EA: Neuroanatomy of penile erection: Its relevance to iatrogenic impotence. *J Urol* 131:273, 1984.
13. Goligher JC: Sexual function after excision of the rectum. *Proc R Soc Med* 44:824, 1951.
14. Long DM Jr, Bernstein WC: Sexual dysfunction as a complication of abdominoperineal resection of the rectum in the male: An anatomic and physiologic study. *Dis Colon Rectum* 2:540, 1959.
15. Bernstein WC, Bernstein EF: Sexual dysfunction following radical surgery for cancer of the rectum. *Dis Colon Rectum* 9:328, 1966.
16. Weinstein M, Roberts M: Sexual potency following surgery for rectal carcinoma: A follow-up of 44 patients. *Ann Surg* 185:185, 1977.
17. Yeager ES, Van Heerden JA: Sexual dysfunction following prostatectomy and abdominoperineal resection. *Ann Surg* 191:169, 1980.
18. Shabsigh R, Fishman IJ, Scott FB: Evaluation of erectile impotence. *Urology* 32:83, 1988.
19. Deutsch S, Sherman L: Previously unrecognized diabetes mellitus in sexually impotent men. *JAMA* 244:2430, 1980.
20. Morales A, Condra M, Reid K: Role of nocturnal penile tumescence monitoring in diagnosis of impotence: Review. *J Urol* 143:441, 1990.
21. Kaneko S, Bradley WE: Evaluation of erectile dysfunction with continuous monitoring of penile rigidity. *J Urol* 136:1026, 1986.
22. Bradley WE, Lin JTY, Johnson B: Measurement of conduction velocity of dorsal nerve of penis. *J Urol* 131:1127, 1984.
23. Abber JC, Lue TF, Orvis BR, et al: Diagnostic tests for impotence: A comparison of papaverine injection with the penile brachial index and nocturnal penile tumescence monitoring. *J Urol* 135:923, 1986.
24. Zorgniotti AW, Lefleur RS: Auto-injection of the corpus cavernosum with a vasoactive drug combination for vasculogenic impotence. *J Urol* 133:39, 1985.
25. Virag R, Shoukry K, Floresko J, et al: Intracavernous self-injection of vasoactive drugs in the treatment of impotence: 8-year experience with 615 cases. *J Urol* 145:287, 1991.
26. Lakin MM, Montague DK, Medendorp SV: Intracavernous injection therapy: Analysis of results and complications. *J Urol* 143:1138, 1990.
27. Nadig PW, Ware JC, Blumoff R: Noninvasive device to produce and maintain an erection-like state. *Urology* 27:126, 1986.
28. Witherington R: External aids for treatment of impotence. *J Urol Nurs* 6:10, 1987.
29. Marmar JL, DeBenedictis TJ, Praiss DE: The use of vacuum constrictor device to augment partial erection. *J Urol* 140:975, 1988.
30. Witherington R: Vacuum constriction device for the management of erectile impotence. *J Urol* 141:320, 1989.
31. Moul JW, McLeod DG: Negative pressure devices in the explanted penile prosthesis population. *J Urol* 142:729, 1989.
32. Nadig PW: Six-year experience with the vacuum constriction device. *Int J Impotence Res* 1:55, 1989.
33. Turner LA, Althof SB, Tobias TR, et al: Treating erectile dys-

function with external vacuum devices: Impact upon sexual, psychosocial, and marital functioning. *J Urol* 144:79, 1990.
34. Katz PG, Haden HT, Mulligan T, Zasler ND: The effect of vacuum devices on penile hemodynamics. *J Urol* 143:55, 1990.
35. Lue TF: Impotence: A patient's goal-directed approach to treatment. *World J Urol* 8:67, 1990.
36. Fishman IJ, Scott FB, Light JK: Experience with inflatable penile prosthesis. *Urology* 23:86, 1986.
37. Quesada ET, Light JK: The AMS-700 penile prosthesis: Long-term experience with the controlled expansion cylinders. *J Urol* 149:46, 1993.
38. Fishman IJ: Experience with the Hydroflex penile prosthesis. *Semin Urol* 4:239, 1986.

PART 14

Regional Treatment of Recurrent and Metastatic Cancer

CHAPTER 81

Second-Look Operations

Mark W. Arnold
Schlomo Schneebaum
Edward W. Martin, Jr.

Second-look operations in the therapy of metastatic colonic and rectal cancer have been and remain the most underused of treatment options. Unfortunately, in spite of improvements in the surgical treatment of primary colonic and rectal cancer over the past 60 years, since Dukes first developed a classification predictive of survival, there has been no significant improvement in long-term outcome. Less than half of all patients with lymph node metastasis at the initial resection will survive 5 years.[1] When one considers the relatively high success rate of aggressive second-look surgery compared to current chemotherapeutic options, it is unclear why these procedures are not performed more frequently.

Wangensteen et al.[2] are credited with originating the concept of second-look surgery for colonic cancer. Their defining case underwent 5 subsequent reoperations to clear recurrent disease, mostly in the retroperitoneum, at approximately 6-month intervals. On the final exploration, she was disease-free. Wangensteen commented that while preliminary experience with second-look surgery often exposes involvement of the "para vena cava and aorta lymph node," no surgeons in the "initial operation for cancer of the colon and rectum . . . excise regularly this secondary chain of lymph nodes." As the studies progressed, however, their initial enthusiasm was dampened, because only 6 of 103 patients who underwent second-look surgery at 6 to 8 months after the primary operation for cancer of the stomach, colon, and rectum benefited from the procedure. Griffen et al.[3] later reported a similar salvage rate of only 6.2 percent.[3] It was apparent that better selection of patients for second-look surgery was necessary, since over 90 percent of patients failed to benefit.

The identification of carcinoembryonic antigen (CEA) by Gold and Freedman[4] in 1965 established a potential method of discrimination. In 1977, Martin et al.[5] reported on 25 colonic and rectal cancer patients undergoing second-look surgery 8 to 20 months after initial resection because of rising CEA.[5] Of these 25 patients, 6 had locally resectable disease, 16 were found to have unresectable metastatic disease, but only 3 underwent negative laparotomies. It was concluded that any CEA change "greater than two standard deviations from the baseline value strongly suggests recurrence and supports the decision for a second-look procedure."[5] The next year, Wanebo et al.[6] reexplored 16 Dukes B and C patients for a rising CEA, reresecting 7 of these for potential cure. Minton et al.,[7] collecting the results of 400 CEA-directed second-look operations performed by members of the Society of Surgical Oncology, concluded that reoperation was more successful if done before the CEA level had risen above 11 ng/mL.

The use of CEA-directed second-look surgery has resulted in an increased 5-year salvage rate of approximately 30 percent.[8] While that is a significant improvement over the experience of Wangensteen and Griffin, more than 50 percent of all patients still have not benefited by reexploration. In 1984, the Radioimmunoguided Surgery (RIGS) system was introduced, using radiolabeled antitumor monoclonal antibodies (MAbs) and a hand-held, gamma-detecting probe (Fig. 81-1) to identify occult metastatic disease during surgery.[9] Since then, the RIGS system has been used by researchers in over 1000 second-look procedures. This system is potentially an important component of second-look surgery because of its impact on tumor detection and intraoperative decision making.[10]

PATIENT PREPARATION

Two days prior to RIGS radiolabeled antibody injection, patients are started on an oral saturated solution of potassium iodine (SSKI) solution to block radioac-

FIG. 81-1. The Neoprobe 1000 gamma-detecting probe.

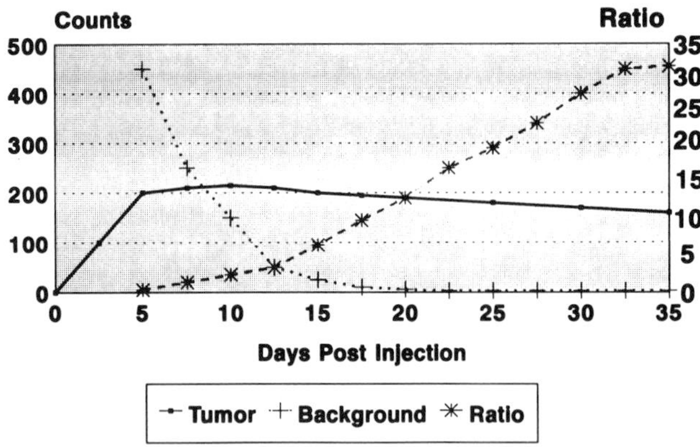

FIG. 81-2. As the blood pool background decreases, the binding of ^{125}I to colonic and rectal cancer cells remains relatively constant.

tive iodine uptake in the thyroid gland. Over 1000 injections have been administered to date without complication in RIGS research conducted worldwide. It generally takes 2 to 3 weeks for the radiolabeled MAbs to clear from the body, allowing blood background count to fall to less than 20 every 2 s (Fig. 81-2).

SECOND-LOOK SURGERY

The first part of any second-look procedure is a traditional surgical exploration. Each area of the abdomen is carefully palpated and inspected for recurrent disease. Particular care is given to the liver; the gastrohepatic ligament; celiac, colonic, and small bowel mesentery nodes; the primary anastomosis if present; the pelvis; and the retroperitoneal, vena cava, and aortic nodes. Intraparenchymal liver lesions are often difficult to palpate, so intraoperative ultrasound of the liver is performed routinely.

If the patient has been injected with a radiolabled MAb for intraoperative detection, a RIGS exploration is performed. The same areas are again surveyed for recurrent tumor, this time with the hand-held gamma detector (Fig. 81-1). The siren sound made by the gamma-detecting probe is first squelched on the aorta (i.e., sound made by the lower-level background radiation is suppressed). The siren sound is then heard only when the probe detects 2-s counts greater than 2 SD above the mean count of the background. Counts are not considered positive unless they are 2.0 times background counts and greater than 20/2 s. When the surgeon surveys an area with the probe, it is in a continuous counting mode while the detector face is slowly moved across the tissue. Direct tissue contact is optimal (Fig. 81-3).

At this point an intraoperative assessment is completed and a decision is made on the therapeutic plan. There are, in general, four possible outcomes of second-look surgery which dictate treatment. First, no tumor is found on either traditional or RIGS exploration. This is an unusual finding, but it does occasionally occur. Under these circumstances there is little to do but

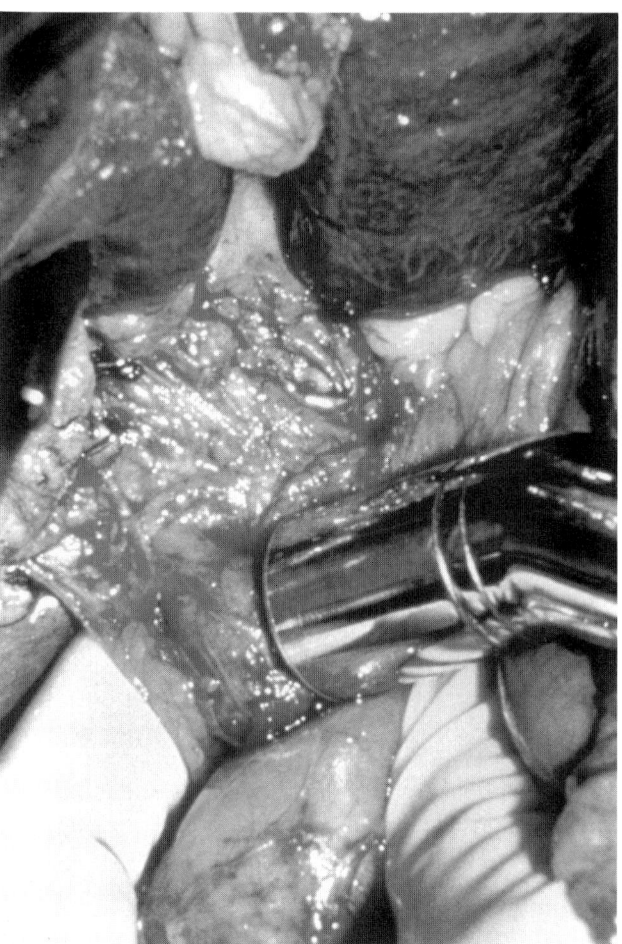

FIG. 81-3. When the surgeon surveys an area with the gamma-detecting probe, direct tissue contact is optimal.

to close the abdomen and terminate the procedure. It must be assumed that preoperative indications of recurrent disease are the result of extraabdominal disease overlooked during first surgery or, perhaps, nonmalignant conditions, as discussed earlier. Second, isolated and limited recurrences that are clearly resectable are found. Our approach is to proceed with resection in every case where removal of tumor is feasible. Multiple locations of resectable tumor are resected. Third, one or more tumor sites are found which are not all resectable but which may be treatable by radiation therapy or other modalities. Resectable lesions are resected if nonresectable lesions can also be treated. Fourth, metastatic disease is clearly unresectable. This could be either carcinomatosis or multiple nonresectable lesions which are also untreatable with alternative approaches.

INTRAOPERATIVE RADIOIMMUNODETECTION

The RIGS technology was developed to find occult metastatic tumor deposits that are not found by traditional methods. These RIGS procedures are used for both primary and recurrent colonic and rectal cancer. In primary cancer, the goal is to find and excise any micrometastatic disease that may already be present. In our initial study with CC49, we found that 34 percent of patients were upstaged from stage I or II to stage III or IV.[10] These patients received therapy more appropriate to the actual status of their disease. The goal of using the RIGS technique in second-look surgery is also to find additional recurrent disease but not to evaluate staging. The additional information RIGS provides often changes the procedure and therapeutic plan for patients with recurrences.[11] Many patients initially thought to be resectable on traditional examination are found to be unresectable because of additional disease found on RIGS examination. These patients are saved the experience of undergoing surgery that may cause significant morbidity and mortality. Other patients undergo a more complete resection with the goal of better prognosis.

The RIGS system has been studied and refined over the past 9 years both through better engineering and better bioengineering. The gamma-detecting probe has been improved to provide better detection of radioactive MAbs with less background noise. The choice of MAb has also improved, providing better lymph node targeting. The RIGS system currently uses second-generation anti-TAG antibodies CC49 and CC83, among others.

The antibody is radiolabeled with iodine 125 (^{125}I) and injected approximately 3 weeks prior to the planned surgical date. Initially the tumor-to-background ratio is extremely low, since most of the radioactivity is in the blood. As the blood-pool background decreases, the tumor-to-background ratio increases (Fig. 81-2). Radiolabeled antibody which preferentially accumulates at tumor sites clears much more slowly than background radiation. Surgery is delayed until the blood-pool background counts are less than 20/2 s, as determined by precordial counts taken at weekly intervals.

The radiolabeled isotope ^{125}I has been chosen for its low energy and long half-life. Low energy allows for tissue shielding and discrimination of relatively discrete and very small areas of radioactivity. Usually, because of the inverse square law, the probe needs to be in contact with suspect tissue to register activity. In most areas of the abdomen, this close contact is an advantage. In the liver, however, it is a disadvantage. The size of the liver makes it unlikely that small lesions in the parenchyma will be picked up with the probe placed on the surface. The lesion may be too distant from the signal. The sensitivity of the RIGS system, however, is far superior to a high energy radionuclide, such as technetium 99m (^{99m}Tc), which would not allow for discrete discrimination of micrometastatic disease.

RESULTS

In 1985, Martin et al.[8] published a series of 146 asymptomatic Ohio State University patients who had elevated CEA and underwent CEA-directed second-look surgery. At surgery, 139 (95 percent) were found to have a recurrence. Of those, 81 (55 percent) were resectable for cure. Of the 45 patients who had surgery from 1976 to 1979, 14 (31 percent) were 5-year survivors. The two most frequent findings were liver disease and carcinomatosis. Less frequent were anastomotic recurrence and mesenteric invasion.

The introduction of RIGS has, to a large extent, changed the approach and subsequent results of second-look surgery. The RIGS system provides the operating surgeon with more intraoperative information, allowing better intraoperative decision making.

Cohen et al.[12] reported the results of a phase II multicenter study using RIGS with ^{125}I-labeled B72.3. A total of 26 primary and 72 recurrent colonic and rectal cancer patients were entered into the protocol. Tumor localization occurred in 78 percent of all patients. Of 32 tumor sites in patients with primary cancers, 24 (75 percent) were localized. In patients with recurrent colorectal cancer, 126 of 199 (63 percent) sites were localized. The overall sensitivity was 77 percent, and the positive predictive value of RIGS localization was 78 percent. All these sites were histologically confirmed for cancer with hematoxylin and eosin (H&E) staining. Of those undergoing reexploration for recurrent cancer in this study, 27 patients were determined by traditional means to be unresectable. An additional 10 patients were found to be unresectable by RIGS exploration. In 8 of 26 resectable patients, the extent of resection was enlarged by RIGS findings. Overall, 30 clinically normal sites in 26 patients were found to have occult cancer by the RIGS technique.

Martin and Carey[13] reviewed the 2, 3, 4, and 5-year survival of 86 patients who underwent RIGS second-look surgery using the anti-TAG antibody B72.3. Of these, 53 patients (62 percent) were considered resectable by traditional examination; however, only 40 (47 percent) were considered resectable by RIGS examination. The other 33 patients were deemed unresectable by traditional examination alone. The survival data were then evaluated on three patient groups: RIGS resectable ($n = 40$), traditional resectable/RIGS unresectable ($n = 13$), and traditional unresectable ($n = 33$). At 3 years' follow-up, survival for the three groups was 83, 7, and 30 percent. The survival rate of the resectable group was significantly higher than that of the two unresectable groups ($p < .001$ and $p = .0008$, respectively). The two unresectable groups behaved similarly, with no 5-year survivor in spite of other therapies. It was concluded that excluding patients with unresectable disease as determined by RIGS will result in better survival rates in those patients found to be resectable. It is hoped, although not yet proven, that performing a more complete operation in those patients being resected will result in increased survival.

We have recently completed a review of our first 60 patients who underwent a RIGS procedure using the second-generation anti-TAG antibody CC49 with the gamma-detecting probe.[14] Of 21 primary tumors, 18 (86 percent) were localized by the CC49 MAb and the gamma-detecting probe. Of 30 recurrent tumors, 29 (97 percent) had localization. Antibody dose did not affect tumor localization.

Specimens located by the RIGS system were divided into four tissue types, depending on whether or not they were identified as neoplasm and by which method. Type I is tissue that is RIGS-negative (i.e., not located by the gamma-detecting probe) and histologically negative (i.e., not identified with H&E staining). Type II tissue is RIGS-negative and histologically (H&E) positive. Type III tissue is RIGS-positive and histologically (H&E) negative. Type IV tissue is both RIGS-positive and histologically (H&E) positive. Next, the specimens were grouped into those tissues found by traditional techniques (i.e., inspection and palpation) and those found only by the RIGS system (i.e., occult neoplasms). There 79 separate specimens were removed from 30 recurrent cancer patients. Of these, 9 specimens were histologically (H&E) confirmed, occult tumor sites found by RIGS (type IV); 16 specimens were RIGS-positive but histologically negative (type III). The mean localization ratios (target tissue to normal tissue) of these groups were 7.7 and 7.4, respectively. There was no significant difference between these groups ($p = .73$) and they behaved similarly. In contrast, 45 specimens found by traditional means were histologically (H&E) confirmed, RIGS-positive tissues. The mean ratio of this group was 23.8, a significantly higher localization ratio than that for either of the other groups ($p < .02$). For the 30 patients undergoing second-look surgery for recurrent disease, RIGS findings changed 17 operative procedures in 14 patients (47 percent of total patients). It is possible that many of the RIGS-positve, H&E negative tissues harbor occult micrometastatic disease which is difficult to detect with traditional pathologic techniques. Use of cytokeratin stains and serial sectioning increases the tumor yield in lymph node analysis. In a limited study done on some of the RIGS-positive, H&E negative blocks removed from CC49-injected patients, 10 of 24 blocks (42 percent) were found, with serial sectioning and special staining, to have micrometastatic disease.[15] In our opinion, all RIGS-positve tissues with the exception of the spleen identified at second-look surgery should be considered cancerous and treated as such.

SUMMARY

Relatively few therapeutic options exist to produce long-term survival in patients with recurrent and metastatic colorectal cancer. Since the large majority of such patients have cancer limited to the abdominal cavity, surgical exploration of selected patients offers the potential for benefit. Radiolabeled MAb with probe-directed second-look surgery appears to help in intraoperative decision making, both avoiding unproductive resections or expanding the scope of such operations in order to encompass additional sites of cancer.

REFERENCES

1. Corman ML: *Colon and Rectal Surgery*, 2d ed. Philadelphia, Lippincott, 1988, pp 469–578.
2. Wagensteen OH, Lewis FJ, Tongen LA: The "second-look" in cancer surgery. *Lancet* 1:303–307, 1951.
3. Griffen WO Jr, Humphrey L, Sosin H: The prognosis and management of recurrent abdominal malignancies. *Curr Probl Surg* 6:2–43, 1969.
4. Gold P, Freedman SO: Demonstration of tumor specific antigens in human colonic carcinoma by immunological tolerance and absorption techniques. *J Exp Med* 121:439–462, 1965.
5. Martin EW, James KK, Hurtubise PE, et al: The use of CEA as an early indicator for gastrointestinal tumor recurrence and second look procedures. *Cancer* 39:440–446, 1977.
6. Wanebo HJ: Are carcinoembryonic antigen levels of value in the curative management of colorectal cancer? *Surgery* 89: 290–295, 1981.
7. Minton JP, Hoehn JL, Gerber DM, et al: Results of a 400-

patient carcinoembryonic antigen second-look colorectal cancer study. *Cancer* 55:1284–1290, 1985.

8. Martin EW Jr, Minton JP, Carey LC: CEA-directed second-look surgery in the asymptomatic patient after primary resection of colorectal cancer. *Ann Surg* 202:310–317, 1985.
9. Aitken DR, Hinkle GH, Thurston MO, et al. A gamma detecting probe for radioimmune detection of CEA-producing tumours: Successful experimental use and clinical case report. *Dis Colon Rectum* 27:279–282, 1984.
10. Arnold MW, Schneebaum S, Berens A, et al: Intraoperative detection of colorectal cancer with radioimmunoguided surgery and CC49, a second-generation monoclonal antibody. *Ann Surg* 216:627–632, 1992.
11. Arnold MW, Schneebaum S, Berens A, et al: Radioimmunoguided surgery challenges traditional decision making in patients with primary colorectal cancer. *Surgery* 112:624–630, 1992.
12. Cohen AM, Martin EW, Lavery I, et al: Radioimmunoguided surgery using iodine 125 B72.3 in patients with colorectal cancer. *Arch Surg* 126:349–352, 1991.
13. Martin EW Jr, Carey LC: Second-look surgery for colorectal cancer—The second time around. *Ann Surg* 214:321–327, 1991.
14. Houchens D, Cote R, Saad A, et al: Presence of occult tumor detected by injected ^{125}I-labeled monoclonal antibody CC49. Proceedings of the eighty-third annual meeting of the American Association for Cancer Research. San Diego, Calif. *Am Assoc Cancer Res* 33:317, 1992.
15. Houchens D, Cote R, Saad A, et al: Radioimmunoguided surgery in colorectal cancer: Histologic and immunohistochemical analysis of lymph nodes from patients injected with ^{125}I labeled monoclonal antibody CC49. Presented at the 7th International Conference on Monoclonal Antibody Immunoconjugates for Cancer, San Diego, Calif, March 5–7, 1992.

CHAPTER 82

Liver Resection for Metastatic Colonic and Rectal Carcinoma

Charles B. Rosen
John H. Donohue
David M. Nagorney

HIGHLIGHTS

Liver resection for metastatic colonic and rectal carcinoma is associated with 25 to 35 percent five-year patient survival. Asymptomatic patients with metastatic disease involving only the liver, limited liver involvement, and a clear margin of resection have the best prognosis. Patients with advanced disease manifested by clinical presentation, extensive liver involvement, multiplicity of lesions, satellite configuration of multiple metastases, and extrahepatic or locally recurrent disease have a poor prognosis.

Despite potentially curative liver resection, over 90 percent of patients eventually succumb to metastatic disease. Reappearance of tumor usually occurs in the liver, lungs, and peritoneal cavity. A few highly selected patients have undergone repeat liver resection, and results have been similar to those achieved by initial liver resection.

CONTROVERSIES

Although surgical extirpation of liver metastases has been practiced since the 1950s,[1] a great deal of controversy persists concerning the actual efficacy of the procedure.[2,3] The rationale for operative intervention is that the natural history of untreated liver metastases is dismal, whereas prolonged survival is clearly possible after liver resection. Indeed, median survival for patients with untreated metastases is less than 2 years, and survival for 5 years is exceedingly rare. Several retrospective studies with historical control groups provide strong but inconclusive evidence that liver resection prolongs patient survival.[4,5] A prospective, randomized trial has never been conducted to unequivocally demonstrate efficacy of liver resection for metastatic disease. At present, such a study seems impractical due to ethical considerations and the high number of patients which would be required to achieve a statistically significant result.

FUTURE DIRECTIONS

It is doubtful that further delineation of prognostic determinants will help with patient selection and afford an improvement in survival. Many factors do have statistically significant associations with survival, but the actual differences in survival are too small to affect clinical decisions.

Improvement in survival may result from advances in tumor imaging, which will afford earlier detection of resectable disease and exclusion of patients with clinically undetectable disease which would be a contraindication for resection.

Adjuvant chemotherapy has not, to date, been shown to improve patient survival after liver resection. Nevertheless, the high likelihood of tumor recurrence after liver resection and the encouraging results with adjuvant therapy for primary disease warrant further study.

Recently, several studies have reported that perioperative blood transfusion may affect tumor behavior and have an adverse effect on patient survival.[6–9] These studies need corroboration, but perioperative blood loss should be minimized to avoid or reduce the need for transfusion.

Clinical experiences are reviewed herein in order to determine the natural history of untreated liver metastases; assess the efficacy of liver resection; identify appropriate criteria for patient selection; develop guidelines for patient evaluation, treatment, and follow-up; and examine the feasibility of conducting a prospective, randomized trial designed to demonstrate the efficacy of liver resection.

Since the major goal of liver resection is to afford prolongation of life for patients with metastatic disease, patient survival data are the best measure of success. Disease-free survival data have inherent inaccuracies due to the difficulty of determining when a recurrence was detected. Moreover, carcinoma does not actually recur; carcinoma persists, progresses, and subsequently reappears to the clinical observer. The time of this reappearance is too dependent on technology and intensity of follow-up to allow meaningful analysis. Thus, this review, whenever possible, is restricted to studies which specifically address patient survival.

NATURAL HISTORY

The development of visceral metastases is an ominous finding, because this occurrence indicates a biologically aggressive malignancy at an advanced stage. Current treatment modalities are of limited value in treating these tumors. However, if all metastases are clinically apparent, surgical excision of gross disease should result in cure. While no prospective, controlled study has demonstrated a positive impact by surgical resection of hepatic metastases from colorectal cancer on patient survival, there are numerous reports of patient outcome with hepatic metastases from colorectal carcinoma with and without treatment for comparison.

If patients with hepatic metastases from large bowel carcinoma do not undergo treatment, the median survival is less than 2 years, and 5-year survivors are rare. These findings are consistent in multiple reports over the last three decades (Table 82-1).[4,5,10–22] Lead-time bias could arise from earlier detection of metastases by improved imaging techniques and serum tumor markers, but current data show no clear-cut trend in more recent studies toward longer median survival. The improved survival seen with 5-fluorouracil plus leucovorin for patients with metastatic colorectal cancer[23,24] will prolong median survivals but will have minimal or no impact on the few patients alive 5 years after the diagnosis of hepatic metastases.

The prognosis for patients with untreated hepatic metastases is most closely related to the extent of liver replacement by tumor.[5,11,13,16,18–21] Not surprisingly, the adequacy of the residual parenchymal function, as de-

Table 82-1
Survival of Patients with Untreated Hepatic Metastases from Colorectal Carcinoma

Study	N	*Median survival, months*	*Five-year survival, percent*
Pestana et al.,[10] 1964	353	9[a]	—
Jaffe et al.,[11] 1968	177	5	0
Oxley and Ellis,[12] 1969	112	NS	1
Bengmark and Hafström,[13] 1969	38	5.7[a]	0
Cady et al.,[14] 1970	269	13[a]	1
Abrams and Lerner,[15] 1971	58	6	2
Wood et al.,[16] 1976	113	6.6[a]	1
Morris et al.,[17] 1977	49	11.4	2
Bengtsson et al.,[18] 1981	155	4.5	0
Goslin et al.,[19] 1982	125	12.5	0
Lahr et al.,[20] 1983	175	6.1	1
Wagner et al.,[4] 1984	252	19	2
Finan et al.,[21] 1985	90	10.3	0
De Brauw et al.,[22] 1987	83	8.4	1
Scheele et al.,[5] 1990	921 unresectable	6.9	0
	62 resectable	14.2	

[a]Mean survival.

termined by serum chemistries, also correlates with patient outcome.[12,13,18–22] Primary tumor characteristics such as grade and stage are inconsistently related to patient survival. However, the overall health of the patient, as measured by performance status, is a significant prognostic variable.[19,21,25] Healthy patients with adequate hepatic reserve and minimal liver involvement by the cancer are most likely to be long-term survivors without treatment. These selective criteria are used by surgeons to select candidates for hepatic resection of metastases. Both proponents[26] and opponents[3,27] of liver surgery for metastatic disease have questioned whether careful patient selection is the reason for improved patient outcome after resection.

Both Adson et al.[4,28] and Scheele et al.[5] have attempted to compare survival in comparable patient populations with either curative hepatic resection or no treatment of their liver metastases. Wilson and Adson[28] compared the survival of 60 patients with resection of metastases to those of 60 patients with a comparable number of lesions and extent of disease who had only biopsy of their metastases. None of the biopsied patients lived 5 years, but 5- and 10-year survivals were 25 and 19 percent, respectively, in the resection group. A subsequent comparison of 116 patients treated by potentially curative liver resection with a group of 70 patients with potentially resectable metastases who did not undergo liver resection at the Mayo Clinic[4] showed a 25 percent 5-year survival after resection but only a 2 percent 5-year survival without resection (Fig. 82-1). More recently, Scheele et al.[5] compared 921 patients deemed unresectable and 62 patients who were judged resectable but did not have curative surgery with 183 patients who had a curative procedure for liver metastases. The patients with limited unresected tumor had a longer median survival than the unresectable patients (14.2 months versus 6.9 months), but no patient in either group survived 5 years after diagnosis. In contrast, the curative surgical group had a median survival of approximately 30 months and a 38 percent actuarial 5-year survival. Although the difference in each study was highly significant, all of these studies are retrospective and uncontrolled. While intriguing, they do not prove benefit from surgical intervention beyond scientific doubt. The apparent improved survival, even when comparing patient outcome for solitary or limited unresected metastases, is strong but inconclusive evidence of an improvement in the natural history of selected patients with colorectal metastases.

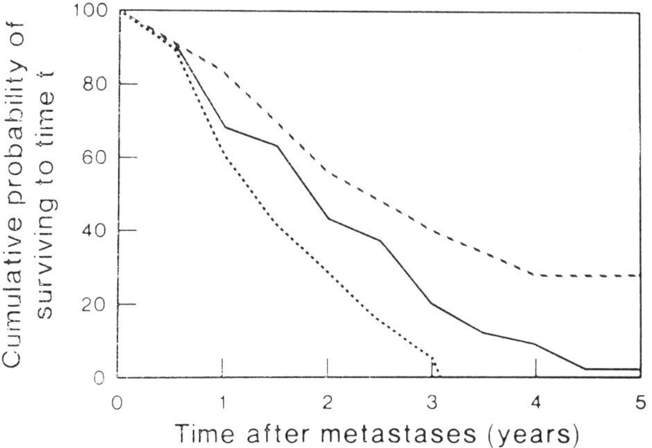

FIG. 82-1. Comparison of the survival of 116 patients who had solitary and multiple hepatic metastases *resected* without evidence of residual primary tumor or extrahepatic metastases to 70 patients who had *unresected* potentially resectable solitary and multiple hepatic metastases.

HEPATIC RESECTION

Hepatic resection has become increasingly important in the multimodal treatment of cancer. Safe resection is predicated upon a clear understanding of hepatic anatomy. Although the regenerative capacity and metabolic reserve of the liver are appreciable, resection based on anatomic consideration reduces operative risk and optimizes postresection liver function. The major anatomic features of the liver relevant to resection have been detailed elsewhere.[29]

Anatomy

Briefly, the liver is divided functionally on the basis of hepatic arterial and portal venous blood supply and biliary and hepatic venous drainage (Fig. 82-2). The two major subdivisions of the liver (right and left) are based on the bifurcation of the portal vein and the corresponding biliary drainage from the right and left hemiliver. The principal plane of the liver divides the two major subdivisions and extends from the gallbladder fossa through the inferior vena cava. The middle hepatic vein lies within the principal plane.

Each major subdivision is further divided into sectors based on the distribution of hepatic veins and portal pedicles. The three major hepatic veins divide the liver into four sectors: right lateral, right paramedian, left paramedian, and left lateral. Each plane dividing the liver along the major hepatic veins is called a scissura. Each sector is supplied by a separate portal pedicle. Each pedicle consists of a bile duct, a hepatic artery, and a portal vein branch. The portal pedicles are best identified as the initial divisions of the portal vein distal to the bifurcation of the main portal vein, with the associated arteries and bile ducts.

The sectors composing each major functional division of the liver can be further subdivided into segments based on the initial bifurcation of each portal pedicle or segmental pedicles. No clear morphologic boundaries exist among the separate liver segments.

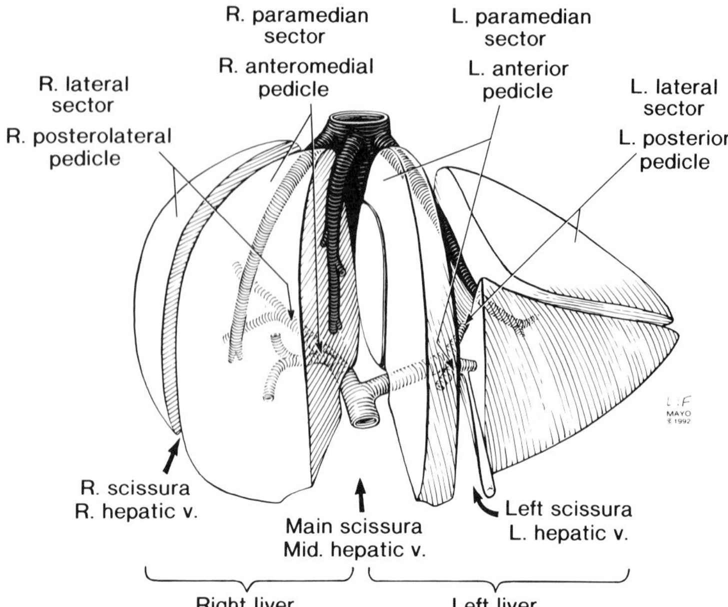

FIG. 82-2. Sectoral anatomy of the liver.

Segments 1 through 4 compose the left hemiliver and segments 5 through 8, the right hemiliver. In practice, liver segments represent the smallest functional subdivisions of the liver from which anatomic resections can be performed reliably.

The vasobiliary sheaths are particularly relevant to hepatic resection (Fig. 82-3). The vasobiliary sheaths represent fusion of the endoabdominal fascia around the bile duct, portal vein, and hepatic artery. These fibrous sheaths invest the components of the pedicles from the portal vein bifurcation to the sinusoids. Because a similar fibrous envelope does not invest the hepatic veins, they are more fragile. The density of the vasculobiliary sheaths increases as the pedicle forms at the base of the liver. At the liver hilus, these sheaths fuse to form plates, which broadly surround the portal pedicles both anteriorly and posteriorly. The divisions of these plates are required to expose and mobilize the portal pedicle during resection. Three primary plates are recognized: the cystic, hilar, and umbilical plates. There are no interplate boundaries. Recognition of the vasobiliary sheaths and the liver plates allows precise access to the hilar structures for either resection or bilioenteric bypass.

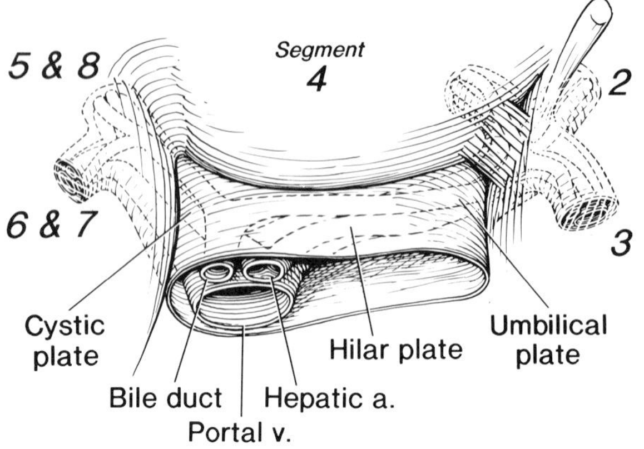

FIG. 82-3. Fibrous plates of the liver: hilar, cystic, and umbilical.

General Principles

Resection should never risk permanent compromise of liver function. The extent of resection depends on size, location, and relation of the major afferent-efferent vasculature and bile ducts to the tumor. Formal anatomic resection should be considered for large or deeply seated lesions or lesions whose margins are indistinct intraoperatively. Metastatic tumors require resection with a margin of normal liver parenchyma. A 1- to 2-cm margin is preferred to reduce risk of marginal recurrence. Margins of resection for malignancies should never risk compromise to the major hepatic vasculature, which may result in hepatic insufficiency. The afferent and efferent vasculature of the anticipated postresection liver remnant must be scrupulously protected. Exclusion of gross bilobar tumor multicentricity and distant metastatic disease is essential for candidacy for resection of malignancies. Intraoperative ultrasonography should be employed to exclude occult intrahepatic metastases.

Preparation

Preparation for hepatic resection is similar to that of any major pancreatobiliary procedure. If jaundice or cholangitis from bile duct obstruction is present, biliary decompression is preferred to control infection and improve hepatic function. In general, major hepatic resection is not undertaken unless total serum bilirubin is less than 5 to 10 g/dL and biliary infection is controlled. Biliary drainage is established for the anticipated postresection liver remnant. If malnutrition or extensive fatty infiltration is present, nutritional indices are corrected preoperatively.

Operation

Safe hepatic resection is dependent upon control of hemorrhage. Circumferential access to the hepatoduodenal ligament should be secured early to permit total hepatic vascular inflow occlusion for control of hemorrhage, especially from the high-pressure afferent vasculature. Hemorrhage from the low-pressure hepatic veins can be controlled temporarily from packing, digital pressure, or parenchymal compression. Exposure of the hepatic veins at the junction of the inferior vena cava requires complete division of liver ligaments. Hepatic veins ideally are approached only after afferent vascular control. If the tumor obscures the hepatic vein at its junction with the inferior vena cava (IVC), total hepatic vascular isolation should be considered. The suprahepatic infradiaphragmatic IVC and infrahepatic IVC should be circumferentially exposed. Ligation of the right adrenal vein combined with infra- and supra-IVC clamping and inflow vascular occlusion results in total hepatic vascular isolation and permits controlled, near bloodless exposure for resection.[30,31]

Bile duct injury is a potential source of major morbidity, and unequivocal identification is required before ligation of any major lobar branches. If ductal anatomy is unclear initially, identification can be obtained by deferring ductal ligation until parenchymal transection exposes the major ducts at the level of the hilar plate or by performing a choledochotomy and cannulation of the proximal ducts with instruments for unequivocal identification.

Types of Resection

Wedge resections are performed without reference to segmental or sectoral anatomy, i.e., nonanatomic resections. Wedge resections are typically subsegmental and frequently cross intersegmental planes. These resections are tolerated well by the liver because they are used for small, peripheral, nonhilar tumors.

The liver parenchyma can be transected by a variety of methods: the compression method (finger fracture or clamp fracture), contact methods ([cavitation ultrasonic aspirator (CUSA), (Valleylab, Inc., Boulder, CO), waterjet]), or thermal methods (electrocautery, laser).[31–33] Each method has advantages and disadvantages. Each disrupts parenchyma to expose vessels and ducts for ligation. Typically, structures greater than 2 mm require ligation. Although some degree of parenchymal necrosis adjacent to the transection plane will occur, depending upon methods used, microscopic zones of devitalized parenchyma are clinically insignificant. Importantly, the surgeon must conceptualize a transection plane during parenchymal transection to eliminate parenchymal devascularization along the interface.

Anatomic Resection

Resections of a single liver segment or multiple contiguous liver segments require identification and ligation of the segmental vasculobiliary pedicles and parenchymal division through anatomic intersegmental planes. This factor is the major difference between nonanatomic wedge resections and anatomic segmental or lobar resections. Ligation of the appropriate segmental pedicle must be obtained for accurate anatomic segmental resection. Both portal and segmental pedicles can be assessed by proximal dissection from the hilar bile ducts and vasculature to the appropriate pedicle or by direct rapid parenchymal transection along an estimated intersegmental plane with ultrasound guidance. Dissection from the hilus is most applicable for the anterior liver segments.[31–34] The latter approach is more appropriate for ligation of the pedicles in segments 7 and 8. Both approaches are facilitated by temporary inflow vascular occlusion to reduce hemorrhage and by use of the CUSA to rapidly expose the pedicle through the intervening parenchyma. Alternatively, methylene blue injection of the segmental or portal pedicle using ultrasound guidance can provide accurate segmental or sectoral anatomic definition. The latter approach is more technically demanding in terms of expertise in operative ultrasonography. Hepatic venous ligation is performed after control of the segmental pedicle has been achieved.

Lobar resections are actually polysegmental resections based on the main right and left vasculobiliary pedicles. Operative risk of blood loss is reduced by ligation of the appropriate lobar hepatic arterial and portal venous branch prior to parenchymal transection. Additionally, ligation of the corresponding hepatic veins before parenchymal transection further reduces blood loss.[34] Major lobar resections may be extended either anatomically or nonanatomically. Anatomic extensions are performed by removing the involved liver segments adjacent to the principal plane. Nonanatomic extensions are self-explanatory. Full liver mobilization is required for extended lobar resections. Inflow vascular occlusion or total liver isolation will reduce hemorrhage.[35] Postoperative suction drainage adjacent to the transected liver surface is optimal.

SURVIVAL AFTER HEPATIC RESECTION OF COLORECTAL MESTASTASES

Two large multicenter experiences of hepatic resection of colorectal metastases have been reported. Nordlinger et al.[36] compiled data from members of the French Association of Surgery. These data comprise 1118 patients who underwent potentially curative liver resection at 85 centers between 1959 and 1991. Operative mortality was 2.4 percent; 3 percent for major resections and 1.2 percent for minor resections. Actuarial survival was 84 percent at 1 year, 40 percent at 3 years, and 25 percent at 5 years (Table 82-2). The Registry of Hepatic Metastases compiled by Hughes et al.[37] includes data from 859 patients treated with potentially curative liver resection at 24 institutions between 1948 and 1985. Patients suffering perioperative death were excluded from the analysis. Actuarial 5-year patient survival was 33 percent (Table 82-2).

Five studies[7,9,38–40] included 100 or more patients and reported 25 to 37 percent actuarial 5-year survival, with 28- to 34-month median survival after liver resection. Operative mortality ranged from 4 to 6 percent. Eight studies[8,41–47] included 50 to 100 patients with 25 to 45 percent 5-year survival, 26- to 59-month median survival, and 0 to 10 percent operative mortality. Nine studies[48–56] included fewer than 50 patients with 20 to 51 percent 5-year survival, 21- to 40-month median survival, and 0 to 14 percent operative mortality.

Only five studies specifically reported the causes of death.[7,38,40,47,48] These combined studies included 707 patients and a total of 445 deaths. Thirty-five (8 percent) were perioperative deaths, 383 (86 percent) were due to clinically recurrent disease, and 27 (6 percent) occurred in the absence of known disease. Excluding perioperative mortality, 93 percent of the deaths were due to clinically recurrent disease and only 7 percent occurred in the absence of known disease.

As discussed earlier, retrospective studies have demonstrated that the natural history of untreated but potentially resectable liver metastases is considerably worse than after liver resection, and survival beyond 5 years is exceedingly rare.[4,5] Despite the apparent efficacy of liver resection for metastatic colorectal carcinoma in these reports, this issue remains controversial. Some investigators have proposed conduction of a randomized, prospective trial designed to demonstrate efficacy. Rosen et al.[7] estimated the number of patients required for such a study with an exponential

Table 82-2
Results of Hepatic Resection for Colorectal Metastases

Study	N	*Years of study*	*Operative mortality*	*Actuarial survival, percent: 1 year*	*3 years*	*5 years*	*Median survival, months*	*Deaths: Operative*	*Cancer*	*Disease-free*	*Comments*
Logan et al.,[56] 1982	19	1971–1980	5	[a]	~50[a,b]	~50[a,b]	27	—	—	—	
Morrow et al.,[49] 1982	29	1961–1978	—	—	—	27	—	—	—	—	
Tomas-de la Vega et al.,[51] 1984	38	1972–1982	8	76	33	—	21	—	—	—	All had synchronous metastases
Coppa et al.,[54] 1985	25	1972–	4	85	58	25	29	—	—	—	
Butler et al.,[45] 1986	62	1950–1981	10	—	50	34	—	—	—	—	29 of 31 operative deaths prior to 1968
Iwatsuki et al.,[46] 1986	60	1975–1985	0	95	53	45	—	—	—	—	
Cobourn et al.,[50] 1987	41	1974–1986	0	—	—	25	—	—	—	—	
Ekberg et al.,[44] 1987	68	1971–1984	6	—	—	~20[a]	22	—	46	—	
Little and Hollands,[53] 1987	26	1970–	0	—	—	51	36	—	—	—	
Nordlinger[42] 1987	80	1970–1985	5	~75[b]	41	25	—	—	—	—	
Attiyeh and Wichern,[55] 1988	20	1978–1986	0	100	-55	35	40	—	—	—	All had negative hepatic lymph nodes and ≤2 lesions
Fortner,[43] 1988	77	1971–1985	6	95[a]	65[a]	49[a]	59	—	—	—	
Hughes et al.,[37] 1988	859	1948–1985	Excluded	—	—	33[a]	—	Excluded	—	—	24 contributing institutions
Stephenson et al.,[8] 1988	55	1976–1985	0	—	—	30	40	—	—	—	
Schlag et al.,[40] 1990	122	1981–1989	4	~85/~80[b]	~40/~25[b]	~30/~10[b]	32/24	5	66	1	Metachronous/ synchronous
Doci et al.,[39] 1991	100	1980–1989	5	—	—	30	28	—	—	—	
Petrelli et al.,[41] 1991	62	1963–1988	8	—	—	27	25	5	—	—	
Scheele et al.,[38] 1991	219	1960–1988	6	—	—	37	—	15	95	12	
Vogt et al.,[48] 1991	36	1977–1987	0	~90[b]	~40[b]	20[b]	28	0	20	0	
Younes et al.,[9] 1991	133	1987–1989	—	91	—	—	N/A	—	—	—	Very short follow-up (13.2 months)
Lind et al.,[47] 1992	50	1980–1991	9	~85[b]	~45[b]	28	~26[b]	5	30	1	Excluded wedge resections
Nakamura et al.,[52] 1992	31	1978–1990	3	—	—	45[a]	28	—	—	—	
Nordlinger et al.,[36] 1992	1818	1959–1991	2.4	84	40	25	—	43	—	—	
Rosen et al.,[7] 1992	280	1960–1987	4	84	47	25	34	10	174	13	

[a]Operative deaths excluded.
[b]Approximation (~) of value from published figure.

survival model. If such a study were to have a 90 percent chance of demonstrating a significant difference in survival at 5 years ($p < .05$ by logrank test), with all patients accrued during the first year and a 5-year survival of 25 percent for the resection group, the necessary number of patients would be 36, 74, 164, or 428 if 5-year survival without resection were to be 1, 5, 10, or 15 percent. Such a study appears impractical at present due to the number of patients required and the ethical concerns about denying patients with a favorable prognosis a chance for curative resection.

DETERMINANTS OF PROGNOSIS

Many surgeons have proposed the possibility of increasing patient survival by refining patient selection for operation. If clinical factors with consistent prognostic value were identifiable, operation could be encouraged for those patients with a high probability of survival. Potential prognostic factors include patient, primary tumor, and metastatic disease characteristics. In addition, the relationship of survival to medical and surgical intervention has been examined. Although associations between potential prognostic factors and survival are best identified by analysis of patient survival data, several studies which are based on disease-free survival data are included.

Patient and Primary Tumor Features

A number of patient and primary tumor features have been subjected to statistical analysis to identify associations with survival (Table 82-3). These features include patient age and gender, primary tumor stage (local/regional stage without regard to distant metastases), histologic grade, location, and size.

Patient Age. Only the multi-institutional study by Hughes et al.[37] reported an association between patient age and survival after liver resection; patients above age 70 fared worse than younger patients. This finding is probably related to the large number of patients in this study. Because most deaths are caused

Table 82-3
Patient and Primary Tumor Features—Association with Survival

		Patient Factors		*Primary tumor characteristics*				
Study	N	*Age*	*Gender*	*Stage*	*Grade*	*Location*	*Size*	*Comments*
Logan et al.,[56] 1982	19	—	—	NS	—	NS	—	
Fortner et al.,[58] 1984	77	NS	NS	Sig	—	NS	—	
Butler et al.,[45] 1986	62	NS	—	Sig	—	NS	—	
Iwatsuki et al.,[46] 1986	60	NS	—	Metachronous lesions only	—	—	—	Only two stage B primary tumors of 13 with synchronous metastases (opposite Rosen's and Scheele's findings).
Cobourn et al.,[50] 1987	41	—	—	NS	—	—	—	
Ekberg et al.,[44] 1987	68	—	—	NS	NS	NS	—	
Nordlinger et al.,[42] 1987	80	—	—	NS	—	—	—	
Attiyeh and Wickern,[55] 1988	20	—	—	Sig	—	—	—	
Hughes et al.,[37] 1988	859	NS >70 fared worse	—	Sig	—	—	—	
Stephensen et al.,[8] 1988	55	—	—	NS	—	—	—	
Doci et al.,[39] 1991	100	NS	Sig	Sig	—	NS	—	
Scheele et al.,[38] 1991	219	NS	NS	Sig	Sig	NS	—	Association between stage and survival entirely due to synchronous metastases group. Stage had no effect for metachronous group.
Vogt et al.,[48] 1991	36	—	NS	NS	NS	—	—	
Younes et al.,[9] 1991	133	NS	—	NS	—	Sig	—	Assessed disease-free survival. Prognosis better for sigmoid and left colon tumors.
Cady et al.,[59] 1992	129	NS	—	NS	—	NS	—	
Nakamura et al.,[52] 1992	31	NS	NS	NS	—	—	—	
Nordlinger et al.,[36] 1992	1818	NS	NS	Sig	—	NS	—	
Rosen et al.,[7] 1992	280	—	NS	Synchronous lesions only	NS	NS	NS	Stage B with synchronous metastases had greater survival than stage C with synchronous metastases.

by disease progression regardless of age, only a large study population would allow detection of significant association between survival and non-tumor-related deaths.

Patient Gender. An early study from the Mayo Clinic[28] reported a better prognosis for women. However, the difference had only borderline[57] or nonprognostic[7] significance in subsequent reports. Doci et al.[39] found a significantly better prognosis for women than men (40 versus 23 percent 5-year survival; $p = .026$), but five other studies[36,38,48,52,58] did not.

Primary Tumor Stage. The multi-institutional studies by Nordlinger et al.[36] and Hughes et al.[37] and seven single institutional studies[7,38,39,45,46,55,58] found an adverse association between advanced primary tumor stage (regional lymph node involvement—American Joint Committee on Cancer—AJCC—stage III) and patient survival. Hughes et al.[37] reported 47 and 23 percent 5-year survival for patients with Dukes B (stage II) and Dukes C (stage III) primary tumors, respectively. The difference in 5-year survival was 13 percent in the French multicenter study (33 versus 20 percent)[36] and ranged from 10 to 20 percent in three other reports.[38,39,48] Rosen et al.[7] could detect a difference in prognosis only by primary tumor stage for patients with a synchronous diagnosis of metastatic disease. The French multicenter study also found a difference in 5-year survival associated with the primary tumor's depth of penetration: 35 percent when it was confined to bowel wall versus 20 percent with involvement of serosa or perirectal fat.[36] Although there is a relationship between primary tumor stage and survival, the actual difference in survival is not sufficient to preclude liver resection.

Primary Tumor Grade. A single study by Scheele et al.[38] reported that high primary tumor grade was as-

Table 82-4
Metastatic Disease Features—Associations with Survival

Study	N	*Presentation*	*Temporal relationship*	*Diagnostic interval*	*Multiplicity, 1 vs. multiple*	*Number, 1–3 vs. 4*	*Size*	*Grade*	*Location*	*Distribution of multiple metastases, uni– vs. bilobar*	*Satellite configuration*	*Extent of liver involvement, % tumor volume*	*Hepatic lymph node involvement*	*Extrahepatic disease*	*CEA level*	*Ploidy*
Fortner et al.,[58] 1984	77	—	—	—	—	—	—	—	—	—	—	—	Sig	Sig	—	—
Coppa et al.,[54] 1985	25	—	NS	—	NS	—	—	—	—	—	—	—	—	—	—	—
Butler et al.,[45] 1986	62	—	NS	NS	NS	—	NS	—	—	—	—	—	—	—	—	—
Iwatsuki et al.,[46] 1986	60	—	—	NS	—	Sig	—	—	—	—	—	—	—	—	—	—
Cobourn et al.,[50] 1987	41	—	NS	—	Sig	—	—	—	—	—	NS	—	—	—	—	—
Ekberg et al.,[44] 1987	68	—	NS	—	NS	Sig	NS	—	—	Sig	—	Sig	Sig	Sig	—	—
Little and Hollands,[53] 1987	26	—	—	—	—	Sig	—	—	—	Sig	—	Sig	—	—	—	—
Nordlinger et al.,[42] 1987	80	NS	NS	NS	NS	NS	NS	—	—	—	—	—	—	—	—	—
Hughes et al.,[37] 1988	859	Sig	—	Sig	NS	Sig	Sig, <8 vs. ≥ 8 cm	—	—	NS	—	—	Sig	—	Sig	—
Stephenson et al.,[8] 1988	55	—	—	NS	—	Sig	Sig	—	—	—	—	—	—	—	—	—
Schlag et al.,[40] 1990	122	—	Sig	Sig	—	—	—	—	—	—	—	—	—	—	—	—
Doci et al.,[39] 1991	100	—	—	NS	NS	NS	—	—	—	Sig	—	Sig	—	—	NS	—
Petrelli et al.,[41] 1991	62	—	—	—	—	NS	NS	—	—	—	—	—	—	—	—	—
Scheele et al.,[38] 1991	219	—	Sig	NS	NS	NS	NS	NS	—	NS	Sig	—	—	NS	—	—
Vogt et al.,[48] 1991	36	—	—	—	NS	NS	—	—	—	—	—	—	—	—	—	—
Younes et al.,[9] 1991	133	—	—	NS	—	Sig	Sig	—	—	—	—	—	—	—	Sig	—
Cady et al.,[59] 1992	129	—	—	NS	—	Sig	NS	—	—	NS	NS	—	Sig	—	Sig	Sig
Lind et al.,[47] 1992	50	—	—	—	—	—	—	—	—	—	—	—	—	—	—	NS
Nakamura et al.,[52] 1992	31	—	—	NS	NS	—	—	NS	NS	—	—	—	NS	—	—	—
Nordlinger et al.,[36] 1992	1818	—	NS	Sig, <2 vs. ≥ 2 years	—	Sig	Sig, <5 vs. ≥ 5 cm	—	—	NS	—	—	Sig	Sig	Sig	—
Rosen et al.,[7] 1992	280	Sig	Sig for stage B primary tumors only	—	NS	Sig by proportional hazards analysis	NS	NS	—	—	Sig	—	Sig	Sig	NS	—

sociated with a worse prognosis, but three other studies did not find such an association.[7,44,48]

Primary Tumor Location. Younes et al.[9] found that patients with primary tumors of the sigmoid and descending colon had a better prognosis after liver resection than patients with primary tumors of rectal or other colonic sites of origin, but the finding has not been corroborated by other studies.[7,36,38,39,44,45,56,58,59]

Features of Metastatic Disease

Many features relating to diagnosis, presentation, and pathology of metastatic disease have been investigated (Table 82-4). These features include the clinical presentation of metastases (symptoms, signs, and test results); the temporal relationship between the diagnoses of primary and metastatic disease (synchronous versus metachronous); the time between diagnoses (diagnostic interval) for patients with metachronous liver metastases; the multiplicity (single versus multiple) or actual number of liver lesions; the size, histologic grade, and location of liver lesions; the distribution of multiple lesions (unilobar versus bilobar); the configuration of multiple lesions (satellite versus scattered); the extent of liver involvement; perihepatic lymph node involvement; the presence of extrahepatic metastases or local recurrence; levels of carcinoembryonic antigen (CEA); and DNA ploidy.

Presentation. Hughes et al.[37] found that patients with symptoms related to metastatic disease fared significantly worse than asymptomatic patients (32 versus 45 percent 5-year survival; $p = 0.05$). Likewise, Rosen et al.[7] reported that patients with metastatic disease initially suspected because of symptoms, signs, or a liver enzyme abnormality fared significantly worse than patients with metastatic disease discovered incidentally at operation, by CEA elevation, or by surveillance imaging (Fig. 82-4). Thus, symptoms and signs of metastatic disease or a liver enzyme abnormality (usually an elevation of serum alkaline phosphatase) often indicate widespread or extensive disease. Even if a potentially curative liver resection can be accomplished, there is a high likelihood of residual disease.

Temporal Relationship and Diagnostic Interval. Whether the temporal relationship between the diagnoses of primary and metastatic disease is associated with survival remains unclear. Nordlinger et al.[36] found no difference in survival between patients with synchronous (within 3 months) and metachronous (after 3 months) liver metastases. However, patients with metachronous metastases fared significantly better if the interval between diagnosis of the primary tumor and metastases was at least 2 years (30 versus 25 percent; $p < 0.001$). Likewise, Hughes et al.[37] did not find a difference in survival between patients with a diagnosis of liver metastases within 1 month versus 2 to 12 months after diagnosis of the primary tumor, but patients with a diagnostic interval of at least 1 year had significantly higher survival at 5 years (42 versus 24 percent; $p \leq 0.01$). Other studies have reported a better prognosis for patients with metachronous diagnoses,[38,40] particularly for patients with Dukes stage B primary tumors (no regional lymph node involvement).[7]

Multiplicity and Number of Metastases. There is little if any difference in survival between patients with solitary and multiple liver metastases after liver resection. However, an association between the number of metastases and survival does become apparent when survival is compared for patients with a few lesions (one to three) and those with many lesions (four or more). Five-year survival in the French multicenter

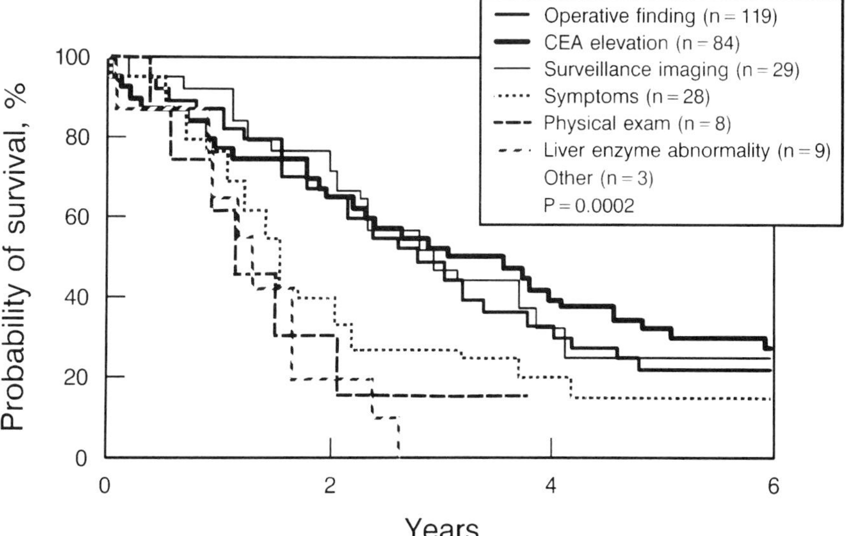

FIG. 82-4. Presentation of metastatic disease and probability of survival after liver resection.

study was 28 percent for patients with less than four metastases and 13 percent for those with four or more lesions, $p < 0.0001$.[36] Hughes et al.[37] found that 5-year survival was less for patients with three or more lesions. Rosen et al.[7] showed a tendency toward poorer survival for patients with two to three lesions and four or more lesions compared to patients with solitary lesions. This trend was proven significant by proportional hazards analysis, which treated the number of lesions as a continuous variable. In contrast, Doci et al.[39] and Scheele et al.[38] did not find an association between the number of metastases and survival, but proportional hazards analysis was not performed. Nevertheless, few patients with four or more liver lesions have disease amenable to potentially curative resection, and the actual differences in survival between those patients with solitary, two, and three lesions are small.

Size of Metastases. Hughes et al.[37] reported that patients with metastases greater than 8 cm fared worse than patients with smaller tumors (27 versus 38 percent 5-year survival). Nordlinger et al.[36] reported a small clinical difference in 5-year survival between patients with metastases less than 5 cm and those with metastases 5 cm or larger (29 versus 24 percent, respectively; $p < 0.0001$). Several studies have identified a similar association,[8,9] but others have not.[7,38,41,42,44,45,59] The clinical differences in survival between patients with large and small tumors should not affect the clinical decision for resection.

Histologic Grade of Metastases. Metastatic tumor histology was not found to be associated with patient survival in two studies.[7,16]

Location and Distribution of Metastases. The location of metastatic lesions in the liver has not been associated with patient survival. Several investigations reported that patients with multiple metastases have a worse prognosis if the distribution of the metastases is bilobar rather than unilobar,[39,44,53] but other studies have not identified a difference in survival.[8,36–38,59]

Satellite Configuration. Liver metastases occasionally occur in a satellite configuration, which is defined as two or more lesions located in close proximity within the liver, suggesting intrahepatic tumor spread. Scheele et al.[38] and Rosen et al.[7] both identified a significant association between satellite configuration and a poor prognosis. Five-year survival was 17 percent with satellite configuration compared to 45 percent without satellite configuration ($p = 0.0003$) in the study by Scheele et al.[38] Rosen et al.[7] showed a 5-year survival of 30 percent for solitary lesions, 18 percent for multiple scattered lesions, and 11 percent for satellite lesions ($p = 0.005$; Fig. 82-5). Thus, satellite configuration of metastases portends a poor prognosis.

Extent of Involvement. The percentage of liver that is involved with metastatic disease has been associated with survival. Doci et al.[39] and Ekberg et al.[44] reported 40 and 22 percent 5-year survival for patients with $\leq$ 25 percent liver involvement, compared to 19 and 9 percent for those with 25 to 50 percent liver involvement. Neither study had any 5-year survivors when liver involvement exceeded 50 percent. Extensive liver involvement is thus a contraindication for liver resection.

Perihepatic Lymph Node Involvement. Perihepatic lymph node involvement has been associated with a poor prognosis. Because the exact site of lymph node involvement is seldom specified (i.e., hilar, choledochal, hepatic, celiac, or portal), the term *perihepatic* has been used to denote regional involvement. Hughes et al.[37] reported results with liver resection for 24 patients with pericholedochal and celiac lymph node involvement; 17 patients had died and none had lived 5

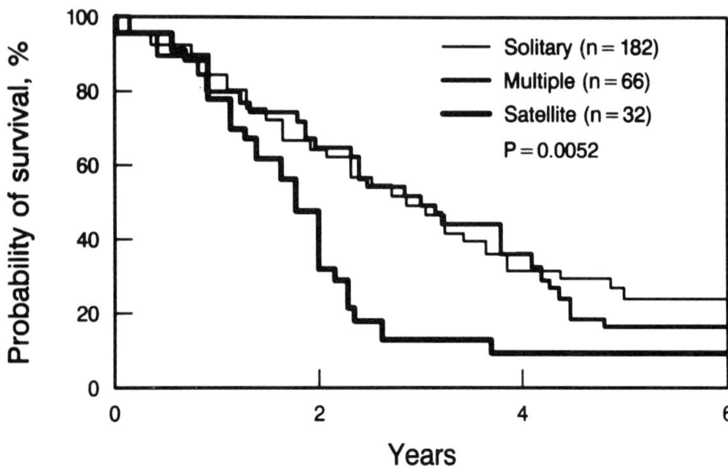

FIG. 82-5. Configuration of metastases and probability of survival after liver resection.

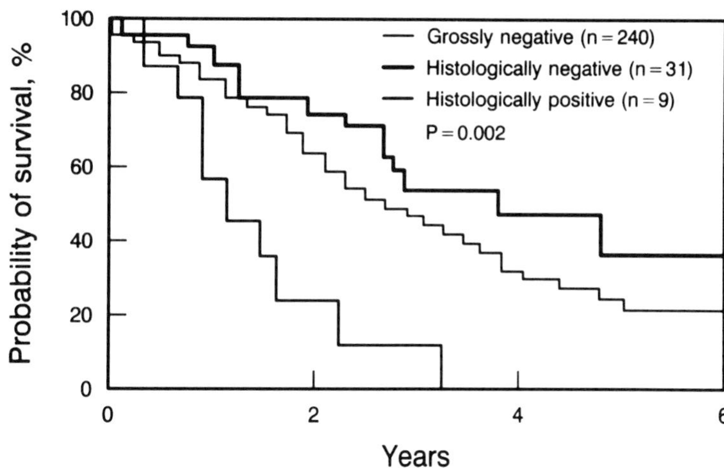

FIG. 82-6. Extrahepatic lymph node involvement and probability of survival after liver resection.

years. Rosen et al.[7] reported results of liver resection for 9 patients with biopsy-proven perihepatic lymph node involvement; none survived beyond 3.5 years. Furthermore, 5-year survival was greater for 31 patients who had histologically negative biopsies of perihepatic lymph nodes than for the 240 patients who were presumed to have uninvolved nodes (37 versus 25 percent 5-year survival, $p < 0.05$; Fig. 82-6).

Although perihepatic lymph node involvement was also associated with a poor prognosis in the French multicenter study (28 versus 12 percent 5-year survival; $p < 0.0001$), long-term survival did occur. Nakamura et al.[52] have performed hepatic hilar lymphadenectomy and reported prolonged survival despite lymph node involvement. Of twenty-two patients who underwent hepatic hilar lymph node dissection, 6 were found to have involvement. For these 6 patients, 4-year survival was 40 percent; 2 patients who underwent repeat hepatic resection were alive at 49 and 66 months.

Perihepatic lymph node involvement generally has been an adverse prognostic factor. Results with resection in such patients have been poor. Unless resection combined with regional lymphadenectomy has demonstrable efficacy through further study, perihepatic lymph node involvement should be considered a contraindication for liver resection.

Extrahepatic Disease. Patients with concurrent hepatic and extrahepatic metastases or locally recurrent disease at the time of liver resection have had poor results from operation, even with complete extirpation of extrahepatic disease. Rosen et al.[7] reported 27 percent 5-year survival for 249 patients without extrahepatic disease, 18 percent for 12 patients with locally recurrent disease, 0 percent for 5 patients with lung metastases, and 8 percent for 14 patients with multiple other sites involved by disease ($p = 0.015$), even though all known extrahepatic and locally recurrent tumor was removed in each case. Likewise, Ekberg et al.[44] reported no 5-year survivors among 12 patients with extrahepatic disease, and median survival was only 6 months. Thus, extrahepatic metastases and locally recurrent disease are relative contraindications for liver resection even if all known tumor can be removed.

CEA Level. Several studies have found an adverse association between high preresection CEA levels and patient survival.[9,36,37,59] In the French multicenter study, 5-year survival was 30, 25, and 18 percent for patients with preoperative CEA levels 0 to 5, 5.1 to 30, and > 30 ng/mL, respectively ($p < 0.0001$).[36] Hughes et al.[37] found that 5-year survival for patients with CEA levels ≤ 4 ng/mL was 47 percent, compared to 30 and 28 percent for patients with CEA levels of 4 to 30 ng/mL and ≥ 30 ng/mL, respectively ($p = 0.08$). Cady et al.[59] demonstrated a statistically significant association between survival and serum CEA levels. None of their 18 patients with CEA levels ≥ 200 ng/mL remained disease-free beyond 2 years after liver resection. Thus, a high CEA level is an indication of widespread or extensive metastatic disease. However, abnormal CEA levels alone should not be used as an absolute contraindication to hepatic resection.

Tumor DNA Ploidy. The relationship between metastatic tumor DNA ploidy and survival remains unclear. Cady et al.[59] found that patients with diploid tumors by flow cytometry fared significantly better than patients with nondiploid tumors. None of the patients with nondiploid tumors remained disease-free beyond 2.5 years. Tsushima et al.[60] found a significant difference in patient survival favoring patients with diploid tumors and a DNA index ≥ 1.5. Although the differences were statistically significant, the actual difference in survival was small—less than 15 percent at 5

Table 82-5
Interventional Factors—Associations with Survival

Study	N	*Year of operation*	*Preresection biopsy*	*Type or extent of resection*		*Margin of resection*	*Operative interval for synchronous diagnoses*	*Perioperative blood transfusion*
				Type	*Extent*			
Coppa et al.,[54] 1985	25	—	—	NS	—	—	—	—
Petrelli et al.,[72] 1985	36	—	—	NS	—	—	—	—
Iwatsuki et al.,[46] 1986	60	—	—	Sig	—	—	—	—
Little and Holland,[53] 1987	26	—	—	—	—	Sig	—	—
Hughes et al.,[37] 1988	859	—	—	NS	Sig for tumors ≥ 4 cm	Sig, <1 vs. ≥1 cm	—	—
Stephenson et al.,[8] 1988	55	—	—	NS	—	Sig	—	Sig
Doci et al.,[39] 1991	100	—	—	—	Sig	—	—	—
Scheele et al.,[38] 1991	219	NS	—	Sig	—	Sig	NS	—
Vogt et al.,[48] 1991	36	—	—	—	—	—	NS	—
Younes et al.,[9] 1991	133	—	—	—	—	—	—	Sig
Cady et al.,[59] 1992	129	—	—	—	Sig	Sig	—	NS
Nakamura et al.,[52] 1992	31	—	—	NS	—	—	—	—
Nordlinger et al.,[36] 1992	1818	—	—	NS	—	Sig, <1 vs. ≥ 1 cm	—	—
Rosen et al.,[7] 1992	280	NS	NS	NS	—	NS	—	Sig

years. In contrast, Lind et al.[47] did not find any difference in patient survival between those with diploid and aneuploid tumors.

Intervention

Interventional factors which have been investigated as possible determinants of prognosis include year of operation, performance of a preresection liver biopsy, type or extent of liver resection, margin of tumor resection, delay between the operations for primary and metastatic disease despite synchronous diagnoses, and perioperative blood transfusion (Table 82-5).

Year of Operation. Butler et al.[45] noted a decrease in operative mortality after 1968; 29 of 31 deaths occurred prior to that year. Otherwise, there has not been a significant association between the year of liver resection and outcome.[7,38] Indeed, survival data have remained remarkably consistent in the studies from the Mayo Clinic—3.1–year mean survival for 8 patients reported in 1963,[1] 28 percent 5-year survival for 60 patients reported in 1976,[28] 41 percent 3-year survival for 34 major resections reported in 1980,[61] 23 percent 5-year survival for 140 patients reported in 1987,[62] and 25 percent 5-year survival for 280 patients reported in 1992.[7]

Preresection Biopsy. Rosen et al.[7] did not find any difference in survival associated with performance of either a percutaneous or operative biopsy of metastatic disease before liver resection. There is no apparent contraindication for biopsy of an indeterminate liver lesion in a patient with a history of colorectal carcinoma, though histologic confirmation of metastases seldom affects management in patients with resectable disease.

Type or Extent of Resection. Although Hughes et al.[37] did not find a difference in survival between patients who underwent limited nonanatomic (wedge) and major anatomic resections, there was a tendency for patients with tumors ≥ 4 cm to fare better after major resection. Scheele et al.[38] found that patients fared significantly better after anatomic resection (45 versus 26 percent 5-year survival; $p = 0.013$). These results suggest that nonanatomic wedge resection may compromise tumor clearance.

In contrast, the French multicenter study,[36] Rosen et al.,[7] and Stephenson et al.[8] did not find any difference in survival after major anatomic versus wedge resection. Iwatsuki et al.[46] also did not find a difference in survival related to the type of resection except that patients requiring trisegmentectomy had poorer survival. These patients had extensive liver involvement, which is clearly associated with decreased patient survival. Importantly, the choice of operation must encompass the extent of disease.

Margin of Resection. Nearly all studies which have addressed margin of resection have found a significant association with patient survival. Nordlinger et al.[36] reported 30 percent 5-year survival for 1112 patients with margins of resection > 1 cm versus 15 percent for 456 patients with margins < 1 cm, $p < 0.0001$. Likewise, Hughes et al.[37] reported a significant difference in 5-year survival between 203 patients with positive margins or margins ≤ 1 cm and 107 patients with margins > 1 cm (23 versus 47 percent). Scheele et al.[38] also identified this relationship; 5-year survival was 46 percent for 81 patients with margins ≥ 10 mm, 35 percent for patients with 5- to 9-mm margins, and 31 percent for 80 patients with margins ≤ 4 mm. Scheele et al.[5] have also reported that survival was nearly identical for a group of 43 patients who underwent liver resection and had positive margins or residual microscopic disease (median survival 14.2 months) and a highly selected group of 62 patients with potentially resectable lesions who did not undergo resection (median survival 13.3 months). In contrast, Rosen et al.[7] did not identify an association between margin of resection and survival, but all patients with positive margins were excluded from the study. Nevertheless, a positive margin of resection portends a poor prognosis. Liver resection should not be undertaken without imaging data substantiating the technical possibility of obtaining a clear margin, preferably greater than 1 cm.

Operative Interval. Neither Scheele et al.[38] nor Vogt et al.[48] found a delay between operations for the primary tumor and metastatic disease to have either an adverse or beneficial effect on survival. Although liver resection can often be performed concurrently with treatment of the primary tumor, hepatic resection should be delayed if conditions are not optimal for a combined operation.

Perioperative Blood Transfusion. Stephenson et al.[8] reported that patients who received more than 11 units of blood had significantly shorter disease-free intervals and worse survival than patients who received 3 to 10 units of blood. Furthermore, they calculated that the transfusion of each additional unit of blood increased the risk of death by 7 percent. Younes et al.[9] also reported that transfusion of whole blood during operation and up to 72 h afterward was associated with a shorter disease-free interval by univariate analysis. However, multivariate analysis indicated that an increasing number of intraoperative hypotensive episodes was more predictive of earlier recurrence.

Rosen et al.[7] reported that 81 patients who did not receive any whole blood or packed red blood cells during the perioperative period (1 week before to 2 weeks after operation) had significantly longer survival than 183 patients who received at least 1 unit of either blood component. Although the exclusion of operative deaths attributes the difference to tumor behavior, more patients in the transfused group had metastases

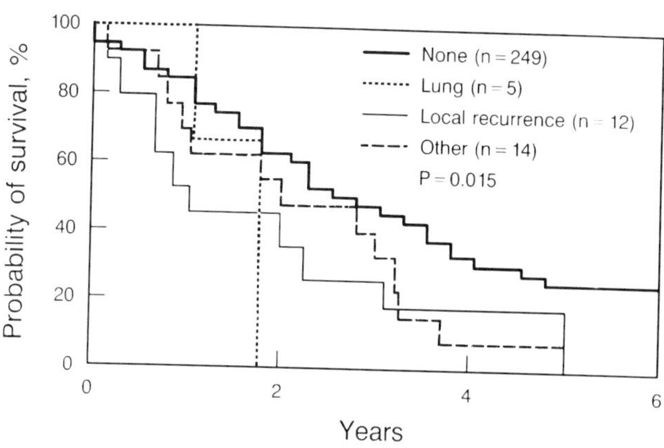

FIG. 82-7. Extrahepatic disease (resected) and probability of survival after liver resection.

initially detected by symptoms, signs, or a liver enzyme abnormality, which are also associated with a poor prognosis. Even though the differences in survival were significant, the actual difference was only 11 percent at 5 years (Fig. 82-7). Although perioperative blood transfusion may have an immunomodulatory effect that encourages growth or spread of residual disease,[6] further research to corroborate these findings is clearly warranted. Regardless of this association, blood loss should be minimized during liver resection to reduce transfusion-associated morbidity and mortality.

Although many putative prognostic factors have been identified, the significance of each varies between studies. Subtle and unrecognized differences in patient and disease characteristics, referral patterns, and changing indications for operation can profoundly affect results of operation and thus explain differences between studies. Moreover, most of the actual differences in patient survival that have been attributed to these prognostic factors are too small to exclude a given patient from operative treatment.

Liver resection clearly does afford selected patients a reasonable chance for long-term survival (25 to 35 percent at 5 years). Long-term survival is possible only if complete extirpation of tumor is accomplished (uninvolved margin of resection). Advanced disease manifested by clinical presentation, extensive liver involvement, multiplicity of lesions, satellite configuration of metastases, and extrahepatic or locally recurrent disease all denote a poor prognosis. Perihepatic lymph node involvement portends a dismal prognosis and is a contraindication for liver resection.

RECURRENCE AND REPEAT HEPATIC RESECTION

Recurrence (or reappearance) of tumor after potentially curative liver resection usually involves the liver, lungs, and peritoneal cavity. In the French multicenter study,[36] 1013 of 1569 patients (65 percent) with available information developed clinically recurrent disease. The liver was involved in 638 patients (63 percent of recurrences), including 480 patients (47 percent of recurrences) with recurrent disease limited to the liver. Hughes et al.[63] reported data on recurrent disease affecting 424 of 607 (70 percent) patients in the Registry of Hepatic Metastases. A total of 316 patients had recurrence in a single organ: 149 (47 percent) in the liver, 73 (23 percent) in the lung, 30 (10 percent) local, and 61 (19 percent) in other sites. Sixty patients initially had multiple sites of recurrence, including 42 liver recurrences, 24 lung recurrences, and 16 other sites. Ekberg et al.[44] studied recurrent disease in 53 patients. The liver was involved in 44 (83 percent) patients and was the only known site of recurrence in 19 (36 percent) patients. A total of 15 (28 percent) patients had lung involvement, and the lungs were the only known site of recurrence in 3 (6 percent) patients. Locally recurrent disease occurred in 8 (15 percent) patients and peritoneal or intraabdominal lymph node involvement was apparent in 12 (23 percent) patients. Other sites of involvement included bone, skin, brain, and extraabdominal lymph nodes.

Selective repeat operative intervention for recurrence limited to one site has been considered.[38,43] Nordlinger et al.[36] reported 78, 30, and 16 percent 1-, 3-, and 5-year survival for 146 patients who underwent repeat liver resection in the French multicenter study. Fourteen patients underwent a third liver resection, and survival was 74 percent at 1 year and 16 percent at 2 years. Several other series of repeat liver resection have been reported,[38,42,47,48,52,64] but the numbers of patients in each study are too small to assess survival statistically. Long-term survival is possible, however. Twenty-one repeat resections were performed at the Mayo Clinic between 1983 and 1991, and survival was similar to results with initial liver resection (median survival 3.4 years, actuarial 5-year survival, 30 percent).[65]

Table 82-6
Adjuvant Chemotherapy following Hepatic Resection of Colorectal Metastases

Study	*Study design*	N	*Drugs*	*Route of delivery*	*Complication rates*	*Median survival, months*
Rajpal et al.,[73] 1982	NR	13	5-FU, 5-FU/ hydrea, methyl-CCNU, semustine, dacarbazine	Systemic	—	30
August et al.,[74] 1985	NR	21	5-FU	Intraportal	27%, type unspecified	—
O-Connell et al.,[75] 1985	NR	26	5-FU, semustine (oral)	Systemic	69% vomiting 58% diarrhea 38% stomatitis 23% bone marrow suppression	34
Iwatsuki et al.,[46] 1986	NR	22	5-FU	Systemic	—	>60
Kemeny et al.,[76] 1986	R	15	5-FUdR	CHAI (pump)	60% chemical hepatitis 33% gastritis 20% sclerosing cholangitis	>33
Lasser et al.,[77] 1986	NR	12	5-FU	Intraportal	25% technical failure 17% pain	—
Elias et al.,[78] 1987	NR	12	5-FU	Intraportal	42% technical failures 33% pain 08% portal vein thrombosis	—
Patt et al.,[79] 1987	NR	20	5-FU mitomycin C	CHAI (percutaneous)	66% chemical hepatitis 25% mucositis 17% bone marrow suppression 17% gastritis	52
Barrone et al.,[80] 1990	NR	17	5-FUdR	CHAI (port)	18% chemical hepatitis 12% sclerosing cholangitis, death	25
Moriya et al.,[81] 1991	NR	16	5-FU, mitomycin C, HCFU (oral)	CHAI (port)	25% bone marrow suppression 19% chemical hepatitis 19% sclerosing chlolangitis	—
Pancera et al.,[82] 1992	NR	49	5-FU	Systemic	—	41

Abbreviations: NR, nonrandomized; R, randomized; CHAI, continuous hepatic artery infusion.

ADJUVANT CHEMOTHERAPY

Adjuvant chemotherapy after hepatic resection of colorectal metastases has been advocated because of the significant risk of tumor recurrence. Data presented herein show unequivocally that the probability of recurrence and tumor-related death exceeds survival. Although the initial site of disease recurrence varies, both intrahepatic and extrahepatic organs are at risk for tumor progression. To reduce the risk of tumor progression after hepatic resection of colorectal metastases, multiple chemotherapy approaches have been designed. Treatment approaches have varied by chemotherapeutic agents, route and schedule of administration, and duration. Studies which have examined the results of adjuvant chemotherapy after resection of hepatic metastases from colorectal carcinoma are shown in Table 82-6. Several investigations which employed adjuvant chemotherapy after hepatic resection of colorectal metastases were not included because of insufficient data on treatment design, drugs administered, or outcome.[37,45,58,66,67] The efficacy of adjuvant chemotherapy after hepatic resection of colorectal metastases cannot be determined by the studies reported to date. Indeed, a significant difference in survival between patients treated by resection alone and resection with adjuvant chemotherapy is not evident from these data. Nevertheless, risk of recurrence after hepatic resection of colorectal metastases clearly warrants further prospective study of adjuvant therapy to improve survival. Future trials of adjuvant therapy after hepatic resection of colorectal metastases must address the patterns of tumor recurrence and account for adjuvant chemotherapy given previously, after resection of the primary colorectal carcinoma.

PREFERRED APPROACH TO LIVER METASTASES

Despite the controversy regarding the efficacy of liver resection, it is our opinion that all patients with colorectal carcinoma metastatic to the liver should be evaluated for liver resection. We recommend evaluation of operative candidates by complete physical examination; blood tests including a complete blood count, chemistry panel, and CEA level; colonoscopy or proctoscopy with barium enema; and chest x-ray or preferably chest CT scan. An abdominal and pelvic computed tomography (CT) scan is obtained to evaluate the liver and rule out extrahepatic and locally recurrent disease. Other studies, such as bone scan and head CT scan, are obtained when signs or symptoms warrant further investigation.

Liver resection can generally be accomplished safely through an abdominal (bilateral subcostal) incision. After assessment of liver involvement and complete abdominal exploration, including careful examination of the bowel and site of the primary tumor, several regional hepatic lymph nodes (a pericholedochal and a hepatic artery lymph node) are excised and examined by frozen section. While awaiting pathology interpretation, the liver is carefully examined by intraoperative ultrasound, which has identified unrecognized metastases in 10 to 15 percent of patients and may determine whether resection is feasible.[68,69] If no contraindications for resection are encountered, liver resection is performed with meticulous technique. We attempt to achieve a free margin of resection (preferably at least 1 cm), to avoid devitalization of unresected parenchyma, and to minimize blood loss and the need for transfusion. We have been able to keep our perioperative transfusion requirement below 3 units (mean 2.6 units, median 2 units)[7] with selected utilization of inflow occlusion. Recently, we have utilized total vascular isolation as described by Huguet et al.[70] for lesions which are large or close to the inferior vena cava. For patients with synchronous diagnoses of primary tumor and liver metastases, liver resection may be performed during the primary tumor operation if the primary procedure is uncomplicated, exposure is satisfactory, and the liver resection can be accomplished safely. Recommendations for follow-up include a complete blood count, chemistry panel, CEA level, chest x-ray, and abdominal CT or ultrasound at 3-month intervals for 2 years, then 6-month intervals until 5 years after operation, and annually thereafter. Annual follow-up for recurrent or metachronous colorectal carcinoma should be performed concurrently.

REFERENCES

1. Woodington GF, Waugh JM: Results of resection of metastatic tumors of the liver. *Am J Surg* 105:24–29, 1963.
2. Adson MA: The resection of hepatic metastases: Another view. *Arch Surg* 124:1023–1024, 1989.
3. Silen W: Hepatic resection for metastases from colorectal carcinoma is of dubious value. *Arch Surg* 124:1021–1024, 1989.
4. Wagner JS, Adson MA, van Heerden JA, et al: The natural history of hepatic metastases from colorectal cancer: A comparison with resective treatment. *Ann Surg* 199:502–508, 1984.
5. Scheele J, Stangl R, Altendorf-Hofmann A: Hepatic metastases from colorectal carcinoma: Impact of surgical resection on the natural history. *Br J Surg* 77:1241–1246, 1990.
6. Francis DMA: Relationship between blood transfusion and tumor behavior. *Br J Surg* 78:1400–1428, 1991.
7. Rosen CB, Nagorney DM, Taswell HF, et al: Perioperative blood transfusion and determinants of survival after liver resection for metastatic colorectal carcinoma. *Ann Surg* 216: 493–505, 1992.
8. Stephenson KR, Steinberg SM, Hughes KS, et al: Perioperative blood transfusions are associated with decreased time to recurrence and decreased survival after resection of colorectal liver metastasis. *Ann Surg* 208:679–687, 1988.
9. Younes RN, Rogatko A, Brennan MF: The influence of intraoperative hypotension and perioperative blood transfusion on disease-free survival in patients with complete resection of colorectal liver metastases. *Ann Surg* 214:107–113, 1991.

10. Pestana C, Reitemeyer RJ, Moertel CG, et al: The natural history of carcinoma of the colon and rectum. *Am J Surg* 108:826–829, 1964.
11. Jaffe BM, Donegan WL, Watson F: Factors influencing survival in patients with untreated hepatic metastases. *Surg Gynecol Obstet* 127:1–11, 1968.
12. Oxley EM, Ellis H: Prognosis of carcinoma of the large bowel in the presence of liver metastases. *Br J Surg* 56:149–152, 1969.
13. Bengmark S, Hafstrom L: The natural history of primary and secondary malignant tumors of the liver: I. The prognosis for patients with hepatic metastases from colonic and rectal carcinoma at laparotomy. *Cancer* 23:198–202, 1969.
14. Cady B, Monson DO, Swinton NW: Survival of patients after colonic resection for carcinoma with simultaneous liver metastases. *Surg Gynecol Obstet* 131:697–700, 1970.
15. Abrams MS, Lerner HJ: Survival of patients at Pennsylvania Hospital with hepatic metastases from carcinoma of the colon and rectum. *Dis Colon Rectum* 14:431–434, 1971.
16. Wood CB, Gillis CR, Blumgart LH: A retrospective study of the natural history of patients with liver metastases from colorectal cancer. *Clin Oncol* 2:285–288, 1976.
17. Morris MJ, Newland RC, Pheils MT: Hepatic metastases from colorectal carcinoma: An analysis of survival rates and histopathology. *Aust NZ J Surg* 47:365–368, 1977.
18. Bengtsson G, Carlsson G, Hafström L: Natural history of patients with untreated liver metastases from colorectal cancer. *Am J Surg* 141:586–589, 1981.
19. Goslin R, Steele G, Zamcheck N: Factors influencing survival in patients with hepatic metastases from adenocarcinoma of the colon and rectum. *Dis Colon Rectum* 25:749–754, 1982.
20. Lahr CJ, Soong S-J, Cloud G, et al: A multifactorial analysis of prognostic factors in patients with liver metastases from colorectal carcinoma. *J Clin Oncol* 1:720–726, 1983.
21. Finan PJ, Marshall RJ, Cooper EH, et al: Factors affecting survival in patients presenting with synchronous hepatic metastases from colorectal cancer: A clinical and computer analysis. *Br J Surg* 72:373–377, 1985.
22. De Brauw LM, De Velde CJH, Bouwhuis-Hoogerwerf ML: Diagnostic evaluation and survival analysis of colorectal cancer patients with liver metastases. *J Surg Oncol* 34:81–86, 1987.
23. Poon MA, O'Connell MJ, Moertel CG, et al: Biochemical modulation of fluorouracil: Evidence of significant improvement of survival and quality of life in patients with advanced colorectal carcinoma. *J Clin Oncol* 7:1407–1418, 1989.
24. Poon MA, O'Connell MJ, Wieand HS, et al: Biochemical modulation of fluorouracil with leucovorin: Confirmatory evidence of improved therapeutic efficacy in advanced colorectal cancer. *J Clin Oncol* 9:1967–1972, 1991.
25. Kemeny N, Niedzwiecki D, Shurgot B, et al: Prognostic variables in patients with hepatic metastases from colorectal cancer: Importance of medical assessment of liver involvement. *Cancer* 63:742–747, 1989.
26. Steele G Jr, Ravikumar TS: Resection of hepatic metastases from colorectal cancer. *Ann Surg* 210:127–138, 1989.
27. Hunt TM, Carty M, Johnson CD: Resection of liver metastases from a colorectal carcinoma does not benefit the patient. *Ann R Coll Surg Engl* 72:199–205, 1990.
28. Wilson SM, Adson MA: Surgical treatment of hepatic metastases from colorectal cancers. *Arch Surg* 111:330–334, 1976.
29. Couinaud C: *Surgical Anatomy of the Liver Revisited*. Paris, Denk, 1989.
30. Delva E, Camus Y, Nordlinger B, et al: Vascular occlusions for liver resections: Operative management and tolerance to hepatic ischemia: 142 cases. *Ann Surg* 209:211–218, 1989.
31. Tranberg K-G, Rigotti P, Brackett KA, et al: Liver resection: A comparison using the Nd-YAG laser, an ultrasonogic surgical aspirator, or blunt dissection. *Am J Surg* 151:368, 1986.
32. Schroder T, Hasselgren PO, Brackett K, et al: Techniques of liver resection: Comparison of suction knife, ultrasonic dissector, and contact neodymium-YAG laser. *Arch Surg* 12: 1166, 1987.
33. Putnam CW: The surgeon at work: Techniques of ultrasonic dissection in resection of the liver. *Surg Gynecol Obstet* 157:475, 1983.
34. McEntee GP, Nagorney DM: Use of vascular staplers in major hepatic resections. *Br J Surg* 78:40–41, 1991.
35. Huguet C, Gavelli A, Chieco PA, et al: Liver ischemia for hepatic resection: Where is the limit? *Surgery* 111:251–259, 1992.
36. Nordlinger B, Jaeck D, Guiget M, et al: Multicentric retrospective study by the French Surgical Association, in Nordlinger B, Jaeck D (eds): *Treatment of Hepatic Metastases of Colorectal Cancer*. Paris, Springer-Verlag, 1992, pp 129–146.
37. Hughes KS, Simon R, Songhorabodi S, et al: Resection of the liver for colorectal metastases: A multi-institutional study of indications for resection. *Surgery* 103:278–288, 1988.
38. Scheele J, Stangl R, Altendor-Hofmann A, et al: Indicators of prognosis after hepatic resection for colorectal secondaries. *Surgery* 110:13–29, 1991.
39. Doci R, Gennari L, Bignami P, et al: One hundred patients with hepatic metastases from colorectal cancer treated by resection: Analysis of prognostic determinants. *Br J Surg* 78:797–801, 1991.
40. Schlag P, Hohenberger P, Herfath C: Resection of liver metastases in colorectal cancer—Competitive analysis of treatment results in synchronous versus metachronous metastases. *Eur J Surg Oncol* 16:360–365, 1990.
41. Petrelli N, Gupta B, Piedmonte M, et al: Morbidity and survival of liver resection for colorectal adenocarcinoma. *Dis Colon Rectum* 34:899–904, 1991.
42. Nordlinger B, Quilichini MA, Parc R, et al: Hepatic resection for colorectal liver metastases: Influence on survival of preoperative factors and surgery for recurrences in 80 patients. *Ann Surg* 205:256–263, 1987.
43. Fortner JG: Recurrence of colorectal cancer after hepatic resection. *Am J Surg* 155:378–382, 1988.
44. Ekberg H, Tranberg KG, Andersson R, et al: Pattern of recurrence in liver resection for colorectal secondaries. *World J Surg* 11:541–547, 1987.
45. Butler J, Attiyeh FF, Daly JM: Hepatic resection for metastases of the colon and rectum. *Surg Gynecol Obstet* 162:109–113, 1986.
46. Iwatsuki S, Esquivel CO, Gordon RD, et al: Liver resection for metastatic colorectal cancer. *Surgery* 100:804–810, 1986.
47. Lind DS, Parker GA, Horsley JS, et al: Formal hepatic resection of colorectal liver metastases. *Ann Surg* 215:677–684, 1992.
48. Vogt P, Raab R, Ringe B, et al: Resection of synchronous liver metastases from colorectal cancer. *World J Surg* 15:62–67, 1991.
49. Morrow CE, Grage TB, Sutherland DER, et al: Hepatic resection for secondary neoplasms. *Surgery* 92:610–614, 1982.
50. Cobourn CS, Makowks L, Langer B, et al: Examination of patient selection and outcome for hepatic resection for metastatic disease. *Surg Gynecol Obstet* 165:239–246, 1987.
51. Tomas-de la Vega JE, Donahue EJ, Doolas A, et al: A ten-year experience with hepatic resection. *Surg Gynecol Obstet* 159:223–228, 1984.
52. Nakamura S, Yokoi Y, Suzuki S, et al: Results of extensive surgery for liver metastases in colorectal carcinoma. *Br J Surg* 79:35–38, 1992.

53. Little JM, Hollands M: Hepatic resection for colorectal metastases—Selection of cases and determinants of success. *Aust NZ J Surg* 57:355–359, 1987.
54. Coppa GF, Eng K, Ranson JCH, et al: Hepatic resection for metastatic colon and rectal cancer: An evaluation of preoperative and postoperative factors. *Ann Surg* 302:203–208, 1985.
55. Attiyeh FF, Wichern WA: Hepatic resection for primary and mestatic tumors. *Am J Surg* 156:368–372, 1988.
56. Logan SE, Meier SJ, Ramming KP, et al: Hepatic resection of metastatic colorectal carcinoma. *Arch Surg* 117:25–28, 1982.
57. Adson MA, van Heerden JA, Adson MH: Resection of hepatic metastases from colorectal cancer. *Arch Surg* 119:647–651, 1984.
58. Fortner JG, Silva JS, Cox EB, et al: Multivariate analysis of a personal series of 247 patients with liver metastases from colorectal cancer. *Ann Surg* 199:317–323, 1984.
59. Cady B, Stone MD, McDermott WV, et al: Technical and biological factors in disease-free survival after hepatic resection for colorectal cancer metastases. *Arch Surg* 127:561–569, 1992.
60. Tsushima K, Nagorney DM, Rainwater LM, et al: Prognostic significance of nuclear deoxyribonucleic acid ploidy patterns in resected hepatic metastases from colorectal carcinoma. *Surgery* 102:635–643, 1987.
61. Adson MA, van Heerden JA: Major hepatic resections for metastatic colorectal cancer. *Ann Surg* 191:576–583, 1980.
62. Adson MA: Resection of liver metastases: When is it worthwhile? *World J Surg* 11:511–520, 1987.
63. Hughes KS, Simon R, Songhorabodi S, et al: Resection of the liver for colorectal carcinoma metastases: A multi-institutional study of patterns of recurrence. *Surgery* 100:278–284, 1986.
64. Griffith DK, Sugarbaker PH, Chang AE: Repeat hepatic resections for colorectal metastases. *Surgery* 107:101–104, 1990.
65. Que FG, Nagorney DM: Resection of "recurrent" colorectal metastases to the liver. *Br J Surg* 81(2):255–258, 1994.
66. Nims TA: Resection of the liver for metastatic cancer. *Surg Gynecol Obstet* 158:46–48, 1984.
67. Bengmark S, Hafstrom L, Jeppsson B, et al: Metastatic disease in the liver from colorectal cancer: An appraisal of liver surgery. *World J Surg* 6:61–65, 1982.
68. Machi J, Isomoto H, Yamashita Y, et al: Intraoperative ultrasonography in screening for liver metastases from colorectal cancer: Comparative accuracy with traditional procedures. *Surgery* 101:678–684, 1987.
69. Parker GA, Lawrence W Jr, Horsley JS III, et al: Intraoperative ultrasound of the liver affects operative decision making. *Ann Surg* 209:569–577, 1989.
70. Huguet C, Addario-Chieco P, Gavelli A, et al: Technique of hepatic vascular exclusion for extensive liver resection. *Am J Surg* 163:602–605, 1992.
71. Morson BC: Factors influencing the prognosis of early cancer of the rectum. *Proc R Soc Med* 59:607–608, 1966.
72. Petrelli NJ, Nambisan RN, Herrera L, et al: Hepatic resection for isolated metastasis from colorectal carcinoma. *Am J Surg* 149:205–209, 1985.
73. Rajpal S, Dasmahapatra KS, Ledesma EJ, et al: Extensive resections of isolated metastasis from carcinoma of the colon and rectum. *Surg Gynecol Obstet* 155:813–816, 1982.
74. August DA, Sugarbaker PH, Ottow RT, et al: Hepatic resection of colorectal metastases: Influence of clinical factors and adjuvant intraperitoneal 5-fluorouracil via Tenckhoff catheter on survival. *Ann Surg* 201:210–218, 1985.
75. O'Connell MJ, Adson MA, Schutt AJ, et al: Clinical trial of adjuvant chemotherapy after surgical resection of colorectal cancer metastatic to the liver. *Mayo Clin Proc* 60:517–520, 1985.
76. Kemeny MM, Goldberg D, Beatty JD, et al: Results of a prospective randomized trial of continuous regional chemotherapy and hepatic resection as treatment of hepatic metastases from colorectal primaries. *Cancer* 57:492–498, 1986.
77. Lasser PH, Elias D, Rougier PH: Chimiothérapie intraportale adjuvante précoce (CIPAP) après hépatectomie pour métastases d'origine colo-rectale. *J Chir (Paris)* 123:318–319, 1986.
78. Elias D, Lasser PH, Rougier PH, et al: Early adjuvant intraportal chemotherapy after curative hepatectomy for colorectal liver metastases—A pilot study. *Eur J Surg Oncol* 13:247–250, 1987.
79. Patt YZ, McBride CM, Ames FC, et al: Adjuvant perioperative hepatic arterial mitomycin C and floxuridine combined with surgical resection of metastatic colorectal cancer in the liver. *Cancer* 59:867–873, 1987.
80. Barone R, Goldfarb P, Saleh F, et al: Liver resection and adjuvant intra-arterial FUDR therapy for the treatment of metastatic colon carcinoma (abstract). *Proc ASCO* 9:1114, 1990.
81. Moriya Y, Sugihara K, Hojo K, et al: Adjuvant hepatic intraarterial chemotherapy after potentially curative hepatectomy for liver metastases from colorectal cancer: A pilot study. *Eur J Surg Oncol* 17:519–525, 1991.
82. Pancera G, Nitti D, Civalleri D, et al: A retrospective analysis of 199 patients (pts) with resected metastases from colorectal cancer (cc): Is there a role for adjuvant chemotherapy (CT) (abstract). *Proc ASCO* 11(March):177, 1992.

CHAPTER 83

Cryosurgery for Hepatic Metastases

T. S. Ravikumar

HIGHLIGHTS

Cryosurgery offers a technically sound and biologically rational approach to the treatment of liver metastasis from colon cancer. Technological advances have made it possible to reproducibly deliver liquid nitrogen to the depths of the liver by insulated probes and to monitor the cryoablation precisely by ultrasound. Rapid freezing of tissues to subzero temperature and slow thawing lead to several physicochemical changes in tissues, resulting in necrosis. The accrued data so far on pathologic evaluation and follow-up by tumor markers and computed tomography (CT) strongly support the usefulness of cryosurgery as a new modality in treating hepatic metastasis. This method is very safe, with minimal morbidity.

CONTROVERSIES

Cryosurgery is nonspecific, based primarily on the chemical and physiologic sequelae of simple physical changes of freeze-thaw. Since characteristics of tissues differ so much from patient to patient, concerns remain as to the uniform effectiveness of cryosurgery. Tumors close to major hepatic vessels may not reach temperatures low enough (due to the thermal sink effect of the warm blood) to achieve 100 percent cell death. Therefore a high likelihood of recurrence exists. Often, cryosurgery is practiced for ablating multiple liver tumors. In such circumstances, the likelihood of additional, as yet undetectable, metastases in the liver is so high that cryosurgery directed at grossly detectable tumors only may not satisfy the biological rationale. Placement of trocar-type cryoprobes into the tumor may result in spillage of tumor cells into the peritoneal cavity upon withdrawal of the probe at the end of freeze-thaw. But this has not been an issue based on the clinical experience, perhaps because the cells close to the probe tract are not viable.

FUTURE DIRECTIONS

Further advances in technology to enable simultaneous multiple-probe applications and to shorten freezing times by more effective cryogens may further refine this approach. Addition of other regional therapies (chemotherapy, biologicals) to cryosurgery may improve long-term outcome in patients with unresectable liver metastases from colorectal cancer. Research may lead to the development of new agents that potentiate cytotoxicity at low temperatures, thus acting synergistically with cryosurgery. Biological and immunological mechanisms involved in the antitumor effects of cryosurgery need further investigation.

It is estimated that among the patients diagnosed with colorectal cancer in the United States each year, about 10,000 to 15,000 will develop focal liver metastases.[1] Surgical resection, while effective, plays a very limited role. A majority of the patients have unresectable tumors due to (1) bilobar disease, (2) multiplicity of tumors, (3) anatomic location of metastases, or (4) severe comorbid conditions precluding safe resection. Several novel regional treatment strategies have been explored. One such approach is interstitial therapy for unresectable hepatic metastases. Such strategies include cryosurgery, interstitial radiotherapy, alcohol injection, hyperthermia, and laser ablation.[2–6] The term *cryosurgery* refers to a method of freezing tissues in situ at subzero temperatures. The following terms are used interchangeably: *cryosurgery, cryotherapy, cryoablation,* and *cryodestruction. Cryotherapy* may have much broader implications, including the use of cold temperatures to alleviate pain and reduce tissue swelling.[7] *Cryosurgery,* as used here, would imply complete destruction of tissues in a defined area by special instrumentation using cryogens at subzero temperatures.

It has been recognized since the mid-nineteenth century that freezing techniques would reduce the size of tumor and palliate cancer-related pain, bleeding, and discharge in patients with carcinoma of the breast and uterine cervix.[7] At the turn of the century, with the advent of liquid air (liquification of permanent gases: oxygen, nitrogen, and hydrogen), extensive experience accrued with regard to the effectiveness of freezing in the treatment of carcinoma of the skin.[8] Although solidified carbon dioxide improved the techniques, it was not until 1950, with the introduction of liquid nitrogen (−196°C) and the experimental studies to define the usefulness of cryosurgery, that additional impetus was provided to develop modern cryosurgery.[9] A variety of surface malignancies and noncancerous conditions were treated by cryosurgery with varying success. However, treatment of deep tissue was not controllable and posed a problem. In the mid-1980s it was demonstrated that ultrasonography can accurately predict the lesion created by cryosurgery.[10] Thus evolution of the mechanical devices to deliver liquid nitrogen to the precise depth required and to monitor this process accurately with intraoperative ultrasonography provided the basis for the current techniques of cryosurgery.

MECHANISMS OF TUMOR LYSIS

The physiologic principles underlying the effectiveness of cryosurgery for the treatment of cancer are rapid freeze, slow thaw, and repetition of the freeze-thaw cycle.[7] To achieve total cell kill, tissue temperatures of −50°C or below are required, the temperature being kept at this low level for a period of 3 min or more.[11] At temperatures below −20°C, most cells undergo internal freezing and will be killed either immediately or during the subsequent slow-thaw phase.[12] Repetitive freeze-thaw cycles increase the probability of complete tissue destruction. Experimental studies have demonstrated that at least two freeze-thaw cycles may be necessary.[13] Therefore, in clinical circumstances, two or three freeze-thaw cycles are commonly used. Thawing should be complete before the next freeze cycle if maximal potential is to be realized. It is also demonstrable that both tumors and normal tissues alike are sensitive to cryosurgery; hence this method is not tumor-specific. Nor is it clear that any specific histologic types of tumor are more sensitive than others. Physicochemical changes bring about the destruction of tumors and the obliteration of small blood vessels following freeze-thaw cycles, with resultant microcirculatory failure and hypoxic cell death.[7,12,14]

Experimental models have been used to define the mechanism of tissue damage from cryosurgery (of the liver) as a function of rate of cooling. There seems to be a U-shaped curve when cell death and rate of cooling are graphed, with the maximum survival occurring at moderate cooling rates.[14,15] At slow cooling rates, ice formation occurs in the vascular structures and spreads through the hepatic sinusoids, dehydrating the hepatocytes and leading to structural damage of the architecture. With faster cooling rates, ice crystals form in the hepatocytes, and the expansion of the sinusoids by ice formation is less impressive. As a net consequence of these effects, cell shrinkage occurs, with ensuing high intracellular ionic concentration culminating in cell death. Rapid freezing produces intracellular ice crystals with mechanical destruction of cell membranes. During a slow thaw, ice crystals continue to grow intracellularly, increasing the mechanical damage. Thus, mechanical, electrochemical, and vascular changes contribute to cryosurgery-mediated tissue necrosis. Neel et al[16] have shown that for maximum cell destruction in hepatic cryosurgery, the critical factors are a large probe-tip surface area, low probe-tip temperature, and rapid and repetitive freezing. To this we may add additional factors such as the type of cryogen used as well as the vascularity of the tumor and liver, which may be partly controlled by inflow occlusion.

In order to establish the mechanical and biological ground rules for hepatic cryosurgery of tumors in vivo, a rat colonic carcinoma liver metastasis model was used.[13] Using subcutaneous isografts as well as established liver metastases, we have shown that at least two freeze-thaw cycles are required to achieve 100 percent cell death. One freeze-thaw cycle resulted in a 10 percent failure rate in this model. Studies by others have also shown that rapid freezing on the order of 30°C/min followed by slow complete thawing (5°C/min) is perhaps the optimal combination for lethality.[11] While immune-mediated tumor destruction has been reported to contribute to the effectiveness of cryosurgery, we and others have not observed this to be a significant phenomenon in the antitumor effectiveness of hepatic cryosurgery.[13,17,18]

INSTRUMENTATION AND TECHNIQUE

Current methods of hepatic cryosurgery require a laparotomy. After careful evaluation of the peritoneal cavity to rule out peritoneal carcinomatosis and extra-

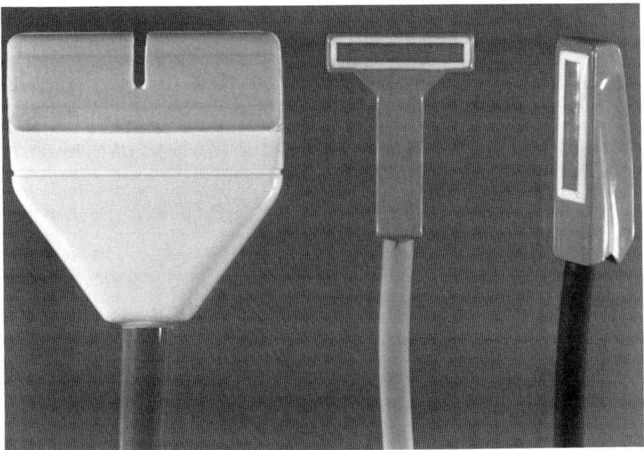

FIG. 83-1. Intraoperative ultrasound transducers. The 5.0-mHz transducer with biopsy channel is shown on the left. The T + 1 configuration 7.5-mHz transducers are on the right.

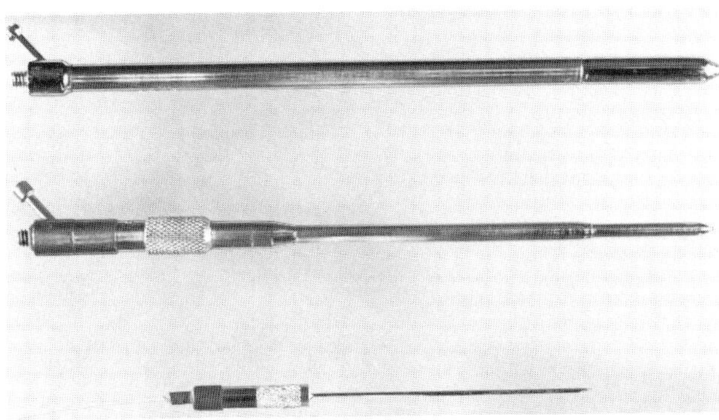

FIG. 83-3. Cryoprobes and thermocouples. Shown are 10-mm and 6-mm trocar-type cryoprobes. The liquid nitrogen inlet and gas exhaust channels are shown on the left. The probe in the bottom is the thermocouple used for temperature measurement at the periphery of the lesion.

hepatic lymph node involvement, a careful bimanual palpation of the liver is performed. Intraoperative bimanual palpation (to detect small lesions on Glisson's capsule missed by preoperative scanning methods) combined with intraoperative ultrasonography (to detect lesions as small as 3 to 5 mm in diameter in the depth of the liver) seems to be most sensitive in detecting hepatic lesions.[19] The 5.0- and 7.5-mHz "linear array" transducers are commonly used (Fig. 83-1). The 5.0-mHz transducer with biopsy channel serves a general purpose as it facilitates ultrasound-guided needle biopsy of any suspicious lesions. Furthermore, ultrasonography helps in the conduct of cryosurgery in several ways.[19] Intraoperative ultrasound is useful in the placement of cryoprobes so as to avoid injury to major vessels and bile ducts. It monitors the freeze-thaw process accurately (Fig. 83-2). The freeze front is demonstrated as a hyperechoic rim with posterior acoustic shadowing. This rim advances as the freeze front progresses during the freezing process and recedes during the thawing process. In general, this freeze front is allowed to encompass the tumor and 1-cm rim of normal tissue around the perimeter of the tumor. After complete thawing, the surrounding normal liver loses its echogenicity while the tumor characteristics remain unchanged ultrasonographically, revealing a halo around the treated tumor and thereby ensuring the completeness of cryoablation.

Liquid nitrogen (−196°C) is the most common cryogen used in the liver. For surface lesions, disk probes

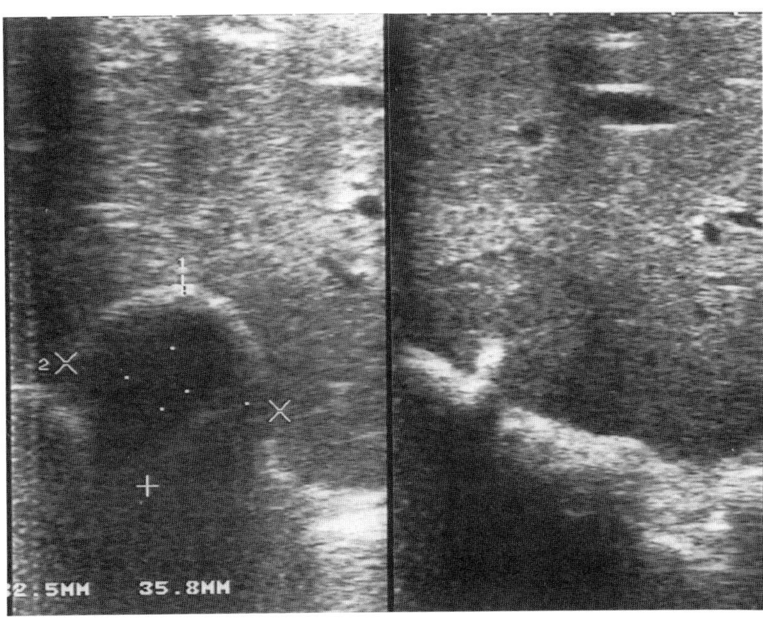

FIG. 83-2. Intraoperative ultrasound monitoring of hepatic cryosurgery. The panel on the left shows hyperechoic rim of freeze front encompassing a liver tumor. The panel on the right represents completion of freeze-thaw process, with the tumor remaining relatively echogenic compared with the surrounding frozen-thawed liver.

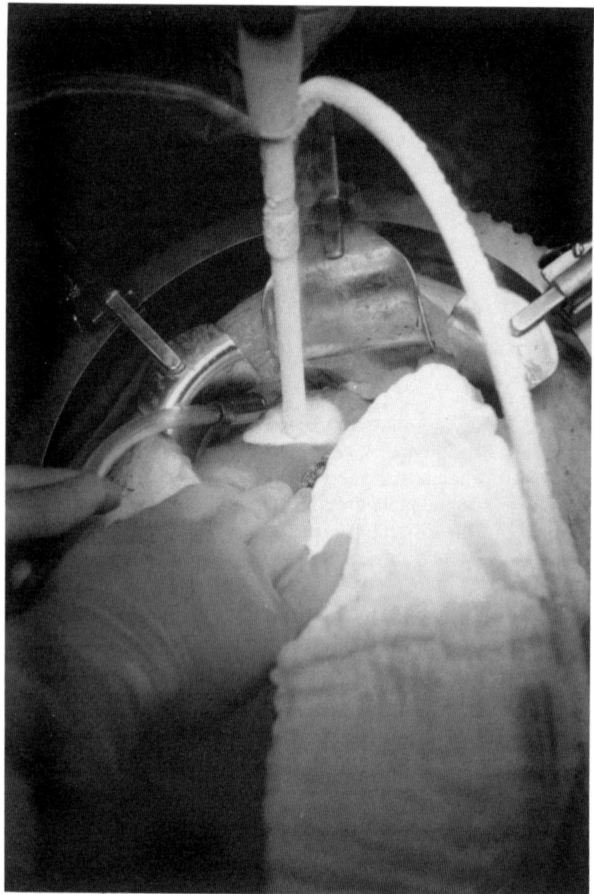

FIG. 83-4. Cryosurgery in progress. Demonstration of liver exposure, probe placement, and freezing. (See color Plate 29.)

are placed under direct vision; for deep-seated lesions trocar probes 6 to 12 mm in diameter are used (Fig. 83-3). The probes we commonly use are 6 to 10 mm in diameter, which produce an iceball of 4 cm and 6 cm respectively (Fig. 83-4). Larger iceballs and more rapid freezing can be accomplished by transient inflow occlusion. For lesions larger than 4 cm, multiple probe placements may be needed. As outlined above, two freeze-thaw cycles are commonly used. After completion of the freeze-thaw cycles, the probe is allowed to rewarm prior to its removal. Brisk transient bleeding from the trocar introduction site is easily controlled by packing with hemostatic material.

COMPLICATIONS

Potential intraoperative complications are accidental freezing of adjacent tissues, cracking of liver parenchyma and bleeding resulting from the introduction of trocar probes, hypothermia and related cardiac arrhythmias, nitrogen embolism, and injury to bile ducts or major vascular structures in the liver.[20]

Despite these potential problems, hepatic cryosurgery has been demonstrated to be a safe procedure with no postoperative mortality to date in the published studies.[2,21–23] It is important to insulate the diaphragm, adjacent bowel, and skin from the liver during surgery to prevent accidental freezing of these normal structures. Bleeding from the probe tract has not been a problem and is easily controlled during the operation by packing with hemostatic material and application of pressure for 10 to 15 min. Experimental and clinical studies have demonstrated that large areas of liver can be frozen without fear of damage to large blood vessels (hepatic veins, portal veins, and hepatic artery).[2,20,24] Large vessels tolerate freezing extremely well, without rupture or occlusion, due to the dissipation of thermal energy by blood flow.[25] Large bile ducts will, however, be susceptible to freezing injury, and caution should be exercised in treating tumors near the hilum.[22] Biochemical abnormalities are not uncommon in the immediate postoperative period.[19] These include transient elevation of liver enzymes (two to three times normal) and mild leucocytosis to about 16,000 cells per milliliter, which normalize within about a week. Temperature elevations to about 102°F for 3 to 4 days is common. Development of right pleural effusion is commonly noted, perhaps resulting from diaphragmatic irritation. We have not noted any abscess formation in the necrotic tissue left in situ after cryoablation. Subphrenic abscess or bile leakage requiring debridement, postoperative wound dehiscence, and hepatorenal syndrome have been reported. This last complication of renal failure has been reported in one study to be the result of myoglobinuria, the etiology of which is unclear.[22]

TUMOR CHARACTERISTICS

A variety of primary and metastatic liver tumors have been treated by cryosurgery. The metastatic tumors include those from colorectal carcinoma, neuroendocrine tumors, and a variety of other tumors, including adenocarcinomas in the liver from unknown primary sites.[2,26] Colorectal liver metastases are the most commonly treated. The number of tumors treated in a single patient varies from 1 to 12.[13,21,22] If cryosurgery alone is used as a therapeutic tool, we feel that the number of tumors treated should be three or fewer, extrapolating from the lessons we have learned from the resection of liver metastases from colorectal carcinoma. Since the statistical chance of occult micrometastasis in the remaining liver is extremely high in patients with four or more tumors, there is a sound rationale for combining cryoablation of gross tumors with regional infusion chemotherapy in this cohort of patients. Larger series of patients and longer follow-up will give us further information with regard to the efficacy of cryosurgery in the treatment of multiple liver metastases. Preliminary reports on the combination of cryosurgery and intrahepatic chemotherapy support the rationale for judicious use of these modalities.[27] A prospective study would have to be conducted to analyze the efficacy of using cryosurgery for the destruction of grossly visible multiple tumors and of combining this modality with regional infusion chemotherapy for micrometastasis. Such a combination approach would then allow the surgical oncologist to expand the opportunities to treat a larger cohort of patients who would otherwise not be curable. Since cryosurgery is not tumor specific, liver tumors of disparate histologies could be treated by this modality.

The effects of cryoablation on the gross morphology of normal and tumor tissue are known.[19] The frozen components of normal liver become distinct, with a darker red-brown color, and softer. No such demarcation between frozen and unfrozen areas was seen within the tumor itself. Microscopically, there seems to be a clear delineation of both the tumor and the normal liver into frozen and unfrozen areas, with the frozen tissue showing coagulative necrosis and loss of tissue architecture, signifying immediate cell necrosis. The margin of destruction is very sharp, corresponding to the intraoperative ultrasound characteristics.

LATE EFFECTS AND LONG-TERM CONTROL OF TUMORS BY CRYOSURGERY

The delayed effects and long-term effectiveness of cryosurgery have been monitored by three methods. The first is histologic proof of long-term control by rebiopsy of the previously frozen lesions during liver surgery at a later stage. Months after cryosurgery, the biopsies reveal focal scarring without any evidence of residual tumors.[13,19] The second method of follow-up is to evaluate the levels of carcinoembryonic antigen (CEA). The kinetics of a decline in CEA levels demonstrates that it can take 2 to 3 months for these levels to normalize in patients who have a complete tumor response.[19] Elevation of the CEA level after the initial decline may signify tumor recurrence, either at the treated site or at other sites, including the liver and extrahepatic tissues.[19,27] The third method of long-term follow-up is radiologic evaluation. This includes computed tomography (CT), ultrasound, or magnetic resonance imaging (MRI). Of these, the most studied modality is CT. The initial studies on cryosurgery included CT scans during the immediate postoperative period and subsequently at intervals of 3 or 6 months. In the immediate postoperative period (5 to 7 days following cryoablation), the CT scans show evidence of necrosis, including the presence of gas bubbles in the cryolesions.[19] The gas bubbles do not signify abscess formation. Later tumor response is manifested by progressive shrinkage of the cryoablated area. Although, on rare occasions, complete disappearance of the lesion can be demonstrated, the residual scar usually persists without significant change after a period of shrinkage of 6 months to 1 year.[2,22]

Since clinical experience with the use of cryosurgery is limited, long-term data with respect to survival and patterns of failure are sparse. Table 83-1 provides a summary of three of the published series that evaluated long-term response and survival.[13,21,22] The patients' ages ranged from 35 to 81 years, and the number of metastases treated in individual patients varied from 1 to 12. A disease-free survival of about 25 percent could be expected at a median follow-up of about 2 to 3 years. Some of the studies have combined cryosurgery with chemotherapy, making any meaningful analysis very difficult. It is not also known whether the number of freeze-thaw cycles correlates with better long-term tumor control. Until a completed 5-year follow-up is available, cryosurgery should be reserved for patients who have either unresectable disease or those with significant comorbid conditions precluding major liver resection. Furthermore, cryosurgery may

Table 83-1
Summary of Published Series of Cryosurgery for Colorectal Liver Metastases

Authors	*No. of patients*	*No. freeze-thaw cycles*	*Additional chemotherapy*	*Follow-up, months—range, median/mean*		*Disease-free survival, %*	
Ravikumar et al.[13]	24	2–3	No	5–60	24	29	62
Onik et al.[22]	18	1–3	Yes	NA	28.8	22	NA
Charnley et al.[21]	11	1	NA	NA	NA	9	NA

Abbreviation: NA, not available.

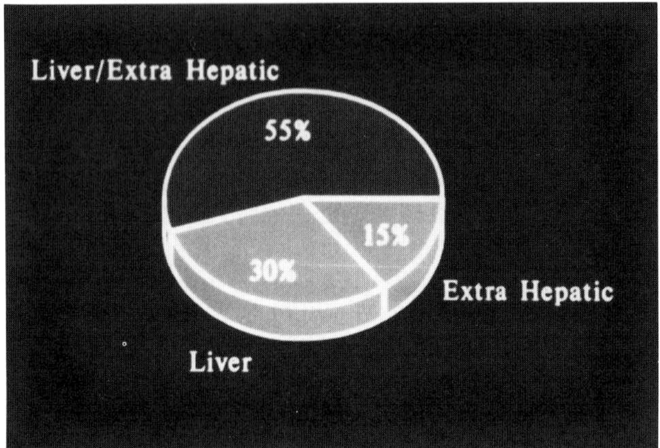

FIG. 83-5. Patterns of failure following cryosurgery of colorectal liver metastases.

extend the indications for liver surgery by allowing the surgeon to combine resection with cryoablation in tumors that are multiple and/or bilateral. Our analysis of patterns of failure (Fig. 83-5) reveals that about 50 percent of the recurrences occur in the remaining section of the liver and at extrahepatic sites such as lung, peritoneum, and bone.[13] The remaining section of the liver was the only site of failure in 35 percent of the patients, while 6 percent of recurrences affected extrahepatic sites only.

CONCLUSIONS AND FUTURE PROSPECTS

The clinical studies so far have established that cryosurgery is a safe and effective modality in the treatment of primary and metastatic liver tumors. Surgical resection should still be the first choice of management, cryoablation being reserved for patients with bilobar tumors and those who are otherwise poor surgical risks. Larger studies with longer periods of follow-up and detailed analysis of patterns of failure are necessary to make an objective evaluation of this modality in comparison with surgery and chemotherapy. Clinical trials addressing the combination of cryosurgery with regional infusion chemotherapy must be conducted. Further research should explore the immunologic effects and potentiation of antitumor cytotoxicity of cryosurgery by chemotherapy and biologicals in experimental systems. While the technology has evolved during the past decade in terms of cryogenic instrumentation and ultrasonography, further progress will undoubtedly be made in the coming years. Laparoscopic approaches to the treatment of liver metastases are bound to become clinical realities, and cryosurgery will be one such method.

REFERENCES

1. Steele GJ, Ravikumar TS: Resection of hepatic metastases from colorectal cancer: Biologic perspectives. *Ann Surg* 210:127–138, 1989.
2. Ravikumar TS, Kane R, Cady B, et al: A 5-year study of cryosurgery in the treatment of liver tumors. *Arch Surg* 126: 1520–1524, 1991.
3. Dritschilo A, Grant EG, Harter KW, et al: Interstitial radiation therapy for hepatic metastases: Sonographic guidance for applicator placement. *AJR* 146:275–278, 1986.
4. Shina S, Yasuda H, Muto H, et al: Percutaneous ethanol injection in the treatment of liver neoplasms. *AJR* 149:949–952, 1987.
5. Masters A, Steger AC, Brown SG: Role of interstitial therapy in the treatment of liver cancer. *Br J Surg* 78:518–523, 1991.
6. Hashimoto D, Takami M, Idezuki Y: In depth radiation therapy by Nd:YAG laser for malignant tumors of the liver under ultrasonic imaging. *Gastroenterology* A1663:88, 1985.
7. Gage AA: Cryosurgery in the treatment of cancer. *Surg Gynecol Obstet* 174:73–92, 1992.
8. White AC: Possibilities of liquid air to the physician. *JAMA* 49:371–375, 1907.
9. Cooper IS: Cryogenic surgery: A new method of destruction or extirpation of benign or malignant tissues. *N Engl J Med* 268:743–749, 1963.
10. Gilbert JC, Onik GM, Hoddick WK, et al: Real-time ultrasonic monitoring of hepatic cryosurgery. *Cryobiology* 22:319–330, 1985.
11. Gage AA, Guest K, Montes M, et al: Effect of varying freezing and thawing rates in experimental cryosurgery. *Cryobiology* 22:175–182, 1985.
12. Farrant J, Walter CA: The cryobiological basis for cryosurgery. *J Dermatol Surg Oncol* 3:403–407, 1977.
13. Ravikumar TS, Steele G Jr, Kane R, et al: Experimental and clinical observations on hepatic cryosurgery for colorectal metastases. *Can Res* 51:6323–6327, 1991.
14. Rubinsky B, Bastacky LC, Onik G: The process of freezing and the mechanism of damage during hepatic cryosurgery. *Cryobiology* 27:85–97, 1990.
15. Gage AA: Workshop report—Progress in cryosurgery. *Cryobiology* 29:300–304, 1992.
16. Neel BH, Ketcham AS, Hammond WG: Requisites for successful cryogenic surgery of cancer. *Arch Surg* 102:45–48, 1971.
17. Wing MG, Goepel JR, Jacob G, et al: Comparison of excision versus cryosurgery of an HSV-2 induced fibrosarcoma: Survival extent of metastatic disease and host immunocompetence following surgery. *Cancer Immunol Immunother* 26: 161–168, 1988.
18. Miya K, Sayi S, Morita T, et al: Immunological response to regional lymph nodes after tumor cryosurgery: Experimental study in rats. *Cryobiology* 23:290–295, 1986.
19. Ravikumar TS, Steele G: Hepatic cryosurgery. *Surg Clin North Am* 69:433–440, 1989.
20. Bayjoo P, Jacob G: Hepatic cryosurgery: Biological and clinical considerations. *J R Coll Surg Edinb* 37:369–372, 1992.
21. Charnley RM, Thomas M, Morris DL: Effects of hepatic cryotherapy on serum CEA concentration in patients with multiple inoperable hepatic metastases from colorectal cancer. *Aust NZ J Surg* 61:55–58, 1991.
22. Onik G, Rubinsky B, Zemel R, et al: Ultrasound-guided hepatic cryosurgery in the treatment of metastatic colon carcinoma—Preliminary results. *Cancer* 67:901–906, 1991.

23. Atkinson D, Zemel R, Weaver ML, et al: Hepatic cryosurgery for metastatic carcinoma. *Proc Am Soc Clin Oncol* 11:A473, 1992.
24. Dutta P, Montes M, Gage AA: Large-volume freezing in experimental hepatic cryosurgery: Avoidance of bleeding in hepatic freezing by an improvement in the technique. *Cryobiology* 16:50–55, 1979.
25. Gage AA, Fazekas G, Riley EE Jr: Freezing injury to large blood vessels in dogs. *Surgery* 61:748–754, 1967.
26. Ravikumar TS, Kane R, Cady B, et al: Hepatic cryosurgery with intraoperative ultrasound monitoring for metastatic colon carcinoma. *Arch Surg* 122:403–409, 1987.
27. Horton MD, Clingan PR, Walters A, et al: Hepatic cryotherapy and regional chemotherapy provide good control of hepatic metastases from colorectal cancer. *Proc Am Soc Clin Oncol* 11:A576, 1992.

CHAPTER 84

Hepatic Arterial Chemotherapy

Nancy E. Kemeny
Karen Seiter

HIGHLIGHTS

Liver metastases are a frequent cause of morbidity and mortality in patients with metastatic colorectal cancer. To date, systemic regimens have yielded low response rates and have had little impact on survival. In contrast to normal hepatocytes, which have a dual blood supply, liver metastases derive their blood supply almost completely from the hepatic artery. Thus, the hepatic infusion of drugs that undergo significant extraction by the liver results in high local concentrations of drug with minimal systemic toxicity. The development of a totally implantable infusion pump has allowed for the safe administration of hepatic arterial chemotherapy in the outpatient setting.

There are now seven large randomized trials comparing hepatic arterial chemotherapy with systemic therapy in metastatic colorectal cancer. All of the studies show an increased response rate for hepatic arterial infusion (HAI) compared with systemic administration. The usual toxicities seen with the systemic administration of fluoropyrimidines were not observed. Instead, ulcers and hepatobiliary toxicity were the predominant side effects. Ulcers result from perfusion of the stomach and duodenum with chemotherapy via collateral vessels from the hepatic artery; they can be minimized by careful dissection of these vessels at the time of pump placement. Hepatic toxicity is due to combined inflammatory and ischemic effect on the bile ducts; it can be minimized by careful monitoring of liver function tests and prompt adjustments of 5-fluorouracil-2-deoxyuridine (5-FUDR) dose.

CONTROVERSIES

Controversy exists as to whether the increase in response rates observed with HAI translates into a survival advantage. Most of the randomized studies do not show a survival advantage; however, there are many problems with these trials:

- Most of the trials are small.
- Trials allowed patients to cross over to HAI after failing systemic therapy.
- In some trials, patients did not receive the treatment to which they were randomized.
- Most trials included patients with positive hepatic lymph nodes.
- Presently a survival benefit has not been shown, which leaves the question as to whether a laparotomy is worth the cost and inconvenience.

It should be noted that 15 percent of patients have liver metastases at presentation and could have a pump placed at the time of primary resection. In addition, once the pump is placed, patients feel well because of the lack of systemic side effects.

FUTURE DIRECTIONS

The current modifications being studied include methods to decrease toxicity, further increase response rates, and decrease extrahepatic metastases. Since biliary toxicity is at least partially related to inflammatory infiltrate around the bile ducts, dexamethasone may decrease such toxicity. Variable infusion of 5-FUDR according to the circadian rhythm decreases toxicity; however, the effect on response rates is not reported. Alternating bolus 5-fluorouracil (5-FU) with infusional 5-FUDR, both via the hepatic artery, yields response rates comparable to 5-FUDR alone, but with less toxicity. Two ways being studied to further increase response rates are the use of combination chemotherapy such as 5-FUDR, mitomycin, and bischloroethylnitrosourea (BCNU) or biochemical modulation of 5-FUDR by leucovorin. The ability of the concurrent administration of systemic fluorouracil to decrease extrahepatic disease is a final area that is being studied.

In summary, HAI yields high response rates in patients with liver metastases from colorectal cancer and offers an effective alternative to systemic chemotherapy. Further improvements to decrease toxicity and increase response rates should widen the general acceptance of this treatment modality.

HEPATIC ARTERIAL CHEMOTHERAPY

Sixty percent of patients with metastatic colorectal cancer develop liver metastases during the course of their illness; in half, the liver is the only or predominant site of disease.[1] To date, systemic chemotherapy regimens have produced responses in only a minority of patients and have made no significant impact on patient survival.

Hepatic arterial chemotherapy has both an anatomic and a pharmacologic rationale. First, in contrast to hepatocytes, which derive their blood supply from both the portal vein and hepatic artery, liver metastases are perfused almost exclusively by the hepatic artery.[2] Following the injection of ^{3}H-5-FUDR into either the hepatic artery or portal vein of patients, mean liver concentrations of drug do not differ depending on the route of injection; however, mean tumor ^{3}H-5-FUDR levels are significantly increased (15-fold) when the drug is injected via the hepatic artery.[3] Second, the use of drugs that are largely extracted by the liver during the first pass results in high local concentrations of drug with minimal systemic toxicity.

Ensminger et al.[4] demonstrated that 94 to 99 percent of 5-FUDR is extracted by the liver in the first pass, compared to 19 to 55 percent of 5-FU. This makes 5-FUDR the ideal drug for hepatic arterial chemotherapy. The pharmacologic advantages of various chemotherapeutic agents for hepatic arterial infusion are summarized in Table 84-1.[5]

In a review of the pharmacologic principles of regional delivery, Collins[6] emphasized the need for drugs with a high total body clearance for hepatic infusion. The area under the concentration-versus-time curve (AUC) is a function not only of drug clearance but also of hepatic arterial flow. Since hepatic arterial blood flow has a high regional exchange rate (100 to 1500 mL/min), drugs with a high clearance rate are needed. Table 84-2 demonstrates the high total body clearance of such drugs as 5-FUDR, 5-FU, and cytosine arabinoside (ARA C).[7] If a drug is not rapidly cleared, recirculation through the systemic circulation mitigates the advantage of intraarterial therapy over systemic therapy.

Another rationale for hepatic arterial chemotherapy, especially for patients with metastatic colorectal cancer, is the concept of a stepwise pattern of meta-

Table 84-1
Drugs for Hepatic Arterial Infusion (HAI)

Drug	*Half-life, min*	*Estimated increase by hepatic arterial exposure*
5-Fluorouracil (5-FU)	10	5 to 10-fold
5-Fluorouracil-2-deoxyuridine (5-FUDR)	<10	100 to 400-fold
Bischlorethylnitrosourea (BCNU)	<5	6 to 7-fold
Mitomycin C	<10	6 to 8-fold
Cisplatin	20–30	4 to 7-fold
Adriamycin (doxorubicin hydrochloride)	60	2-fold
Dichloromethotrexate (DCMTX)	—	6 to 8-fold

Table 84-2
Regional Drug Delivery Advantage for Selected Anticancer Drugs When QHA = 250 mL/min

CLTB, mL/min	*Drug*	R, *mL/min*
25,000	5-FUDR	101
4,000	5-FU	17
3,000	ARA C	13
1,000	BCNU	5
900	Adriamycin	4.6
400	AZQ	2.6
400	cis-DDP	2.6
200	Methotrexate	1.8
40	VP-16	1.2

Abbreviations: ARA C, cytosine arabinoside; AZQ, aziridinylbenzoquinone; cis-DDP, cis-diamminedichloroplatinum; CLTB, total body clearance of drug; R, regional drug delivery advantage, given CLTB and QHA and hepatic extraction of the drug; QHA, blood flow in hepatic artery; VP-16, etoposide.

SOURCE: Adapted from Collins.[7]

Table 84-3
Hepatic Arterial 5-FUDR Infusion with Internal Pump: Responses

Investigators	*No. of patients*	*Percent prior chemo*	*Partial response, percent*	*Percent decrease in CEA*	*Median survival, months*
Niederhuber et al.[12]	70	45	83	91	25
Balch and Urist[13]	50	40	—	83	26
Kemeny et al.[14]	41	43	42	51	12
Shepard et al.[15]	53	42	32	—	17
Cohen et al.[16]	50	36	51	—	—
Weiss et al.[17]	17	85	29	57	13
Schwartz et al.[18]	23	—	15	75	18
Johnson et al.[19]	40	—	47	—	12
Kemeny et al.[20]	31	50	52	—	22

static progression.[8,9] This theory states that hematogenous spread occurs first via the portal vein to the liver, then from the liver to the lungs, and then to other organs. Thus, aggressive treatment of metastases confined to the liver (i.e., either resection or hepatic infusion) may yield prolonged survival for some patients.

Initial trials of HAI utilized external pumps and percutaneously placed catheters, which required hospitalization and patient immobilization for chemotherapy administration. Although response rates of 50 percent were seen, catheter-related complications such as hemorrhage, hepatic arterial thrombosis, and catheter migration occurred frequently.[10] The development of a totally implantable infusion pump allowed for the safe administration of hepatic arterial chemotherapy in the outpatient setting.[11] Early trials using an implantable pump and continuous 5-FUDR therapy produced a median response rate of 45 percent and a median survival of 17 months (Table 84-3).

RANDOMIZED STUDIES

One of the first randomized trials was conducted at Memorial Sloan-Kettering Cancer Center (MSKCC).[21] This prospective randomized trial compared hepatic arterial infusion to systemic infusion using the same chemotherapeutic agent (5-FUDR), the same drug schedule (a 14-day continuous infusion), and the same method of administration (the Infusaid pump) in both groups. The only difference between the two groups was that a lower dose of 5-FUDR was given in the systemic group (0.125 mg/kg/day compared with 0.3 mg/kg/day for the HAI group) in order to avoid severe systemic toxicity. These doses were calculated from the patient's weight and were not readjusted to account for the dead space. All patients underwent exploratory laparotomy not only for pump placement but also to ensure that the two study groups were comparable by accurately defining the extent of liver involvement and assuring that there was no extrahepatic disease. Patients with a resectable hepatic lesion or extrahepatic disease were considered ineligible for the protocol.

Prior to randomization, patients were stratified for extent of liver involvement by tumor and baseline LDH level, two factors that have been shown to be important prognostic indicators of survival (Figs. 84-1 and 84-2).[22,23] Patients randomized to hepatic infusion had the hepatic artery catheter connected to the Infusaid pump. In patients randomized to systemic therapy, the hepatic artery catheter was connected to a subcutaneously implanted access port, and the pump was connected to an additional catheter placed in the cephalic vein. This study design allowed for a cross-

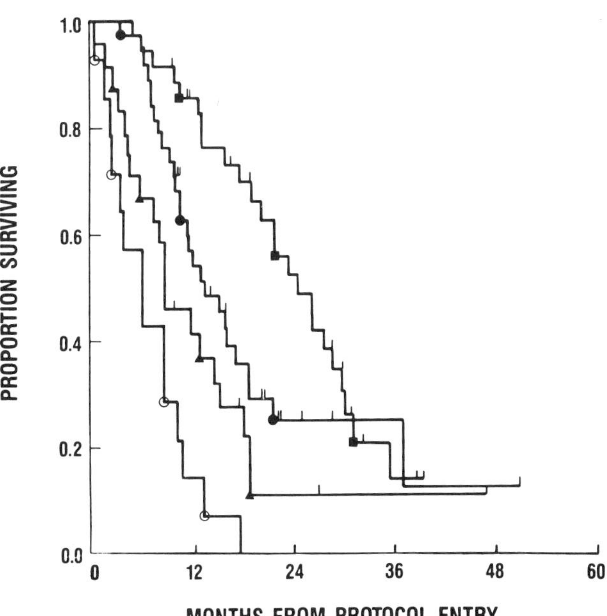

FIG. 84-1. Median survival of 25 months for patients with <20 percent involvement versus 6 months for >60 percent involvement. (From Kemeny et al.[22] Reproduced by permission.)

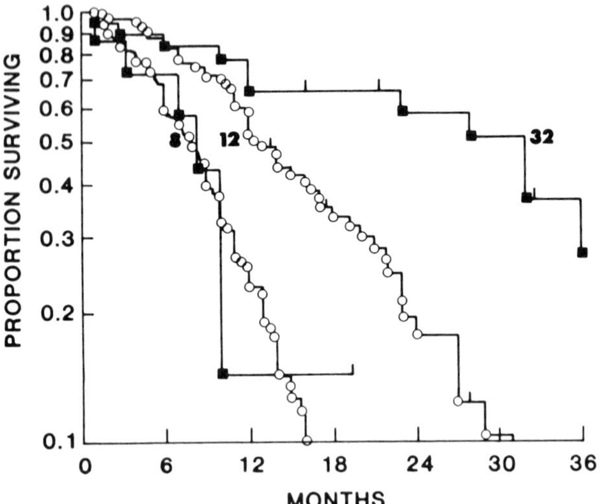

FIG. 84-2. Survival curves according to initial LDH and CEA levels. The median survival of patients with normal LDH and CEA levels at initiation of chemotherapy was 32 months, whereas it was 8 months if both values were abnormal ($p < .001$). (From Kemeny N, Schneider A: Regional treatment of hepatic metastases and hepatocellular carcinoma. *Curr Probl Cancer* 13:197–284, 1989. Reproduced by permission.)

Table 84-4
Intrahepatic versus Systemic 5-FUDR Infusion—Randomized Study, Memorial Sloan-Kettering Cancer Center

	Intrahepatic, n = *48*	*Systemic,* n = *51*	
Complete response	2	0	
Partial response	23 (52%)	10 (20%)	p = .001
>50% decrease in CEA	29	13	
Extrahepatic metastases	27	19	p = .09
Toxicity			
Ulcer	8	3	
Elevated enzymes	20 (42%)	12	
Bilirubin > 3	9	2	
Diarrhea	1	36 (70%)	
Survival (months)			
Total	17	12	p = .424
Crossover		18	
No crossover		8	

over from systemic therapy to hepatic arterial therapy by a minor surgical procedure (ligation of the systemic catheter followed by connection of the pumps to the hepatic catheter) in the event of tumor progression on systemic therapy. Of the 178 patients referred, 12 refused randomization and 4 had an inadequate arterial blood supply; therefore, 162 were randomized. At laparotomy, 63 patients were excluded: 33 had extrahepatic disease, 25 had their tumor resected, 4 had no tumor, and 1 had an abdominal infection.

Of the 99 evaluable patients, there were two complete and 23 partial responses (53 percent) in the group receiving HAI and 10 partial responses (21 percent) in the systemic group, $p = .001$ (Table 84-4). Of the patients randomized to systemic therapy, 31 (60 percent) crossed over to HAI after tumor progression. Of these patients, 25 percent went on to a partial response after the crossover and 60 percent had a decrease in CEA levels.

Toxicity differed between the two groups. In the HAI group, toxicity was predominantly hepatic and gastrointestinal. An increase in aspartate aminotransferase level exceeding two times the baseline occurred in 42 percent of patients and an elevation in serum bilirubin level to higher than 3.0 mg/dL occurred in 19 percent. Biliary sclerosis developed in 4 patients (8 percent); it was reversible in 3. Also 8 patients (17 percent) developed endoscopically confirmed gastrointestinal ulcers and 4 (8 percent) gastritis. In the systemic group, diarrhea occurred in 70 percent of patients, with 9 percent requiring admission for intravenous hydration. Mucositis occurred in 10 percent of patients receiving systemic infusion. Interestingly, 23 patients on the systemic arm developed hepatic enzyme elevations, and 6 percent developed ulcers or gastritis.

The median survival for the HAI and systemic groups was 17 and 12 months, respectively ($p = .424$). The interpretation of survival is difficult in this study because 60 percent of the patients in the systemic group crossed over and received intrahepatic therapy after demonstrating tumor progression on systemic therapy. Patients who were unable to cross over (usually for mechanical reasons such as clotting of the hepatic arterial catheter) had a median survival of only 8 months, compared with 18 months for those patients who crossed over to hepatic infusion ($p = .04$; Fig. 84-3). An analysis of baseline characteristics in the crossover and noncrossover groups revealed no significant differences.

A similar randomized study conducted by the Northern California Oncology Group (NCOG) also used 5-FUDR infusion in both the HAI and systemic groups.[24] Patients were stratified prior to randomization by extent of liver involvement based on computed tomography (CT), baseline bilirubin values, and performance status. The doses of 5-FUDR were 0.2 and 0.075 mg/kg/day for 14 days in the hepatic arterial and systemic groups, respectively. These were the actual doses administered, since recalculation taking into account the residual volume in the pump was preferred. Of 143 entered, only 117 were eligible. A 42 percent complete and partial response rate in the HAI group and 10 percent in the systemic group ($p < .0001$) was reported. The median time to progression was 401 days in the HAI group and 201 days in the systemic group ($p = .009$; Table 84-5).

Toxicity was again different in the two groups, with 16 percent of patients in the HAI group developing bil-

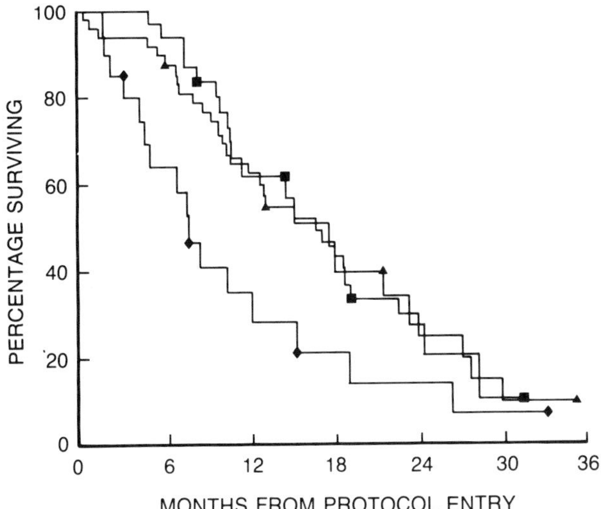

FIG. 84-3. Crossover procedure for patients whose tumor failed to respond to systemic infusion. *Left,* minor surgical procedure required to allow crossover to intrahepatic artery. *Right,* final result. (From Kemeny et al.[21] Reproduced by permission.)

iary tract toxicity, which was reversible in all but 10 percent of patients. Grade 2 or greater diarrhea occurred in 40 percent of patients in the systemic group.

The median survival was 503 days and 484 days for the hepatic and systemic groups, respectively. Although a crossover design was not built into the study, 43 percent of the patients in the systemic group crossed over to intrahepatic therapy after tumor progression on systemic therapy. Of these patients, 19 benefited from the treatment (3 partial responses; 16 had either minor response or stable disease). Thus, the crossover may have again negated any difference in survival.

Table 84-5
Northern California Oncology Group (NCOG) Study—Randomized HAI versus IV 5-FUDR Infusion

	HAI n = 67	*IV* n = 76	p *value*
Complete response	8%	5%	
Major response	34%	5%	.0001
Biliary > grade 3	16%	0	
Irreversible jaundice	10%	0	
Diarrhea ≥ grade 3	0	18%	
Nausea, vomiting	14%	45%	
Mucositis	0	18	
Median time to progression (days)	401	201	.009
Median survival (days)	503	484	
No crossover		362	
Crossover		702[a]	

[a]Patients in systemic group who subsequently received hepatic arterial therapy.

SOURCE: From Hohn et al.[24] With permission.

Another factor that makes an interpretation of survival difficult is that patients with metastases to hepatic lymph nodes were included in both study groups. Since the concept being tested here was whether regional therapy is effective for a certain population of patients, the inclusion of patients with extrahepatic disease interfered with the interpretation of the results. Positive hepatic lymph nodes are considered a contraindication to liver resection. In a large series of patients who underwent liver resections, no patients with positive hepatic lymph nodes were alive at 5 years.[25] These concepts should apply to patients receiving regional hepatic therapy as well. Since the number of patients with extrahepatic disease in the two groups was not reported in the Northern California Oncology Group (NCOG) trial, the possibility of an imbalance in a very important prognostic variable (i.e., portal node involvement) cannot be ruled out.

A National Cancer Institute (NCI) study compared hepatic arterial to systemic infusion of 5-FUDR in 64 patients.[26] Again, there was a significantly improved response rate for hepatic infusion compared with systemic therapy (62 versus 17 percent, respectively; $p<.003$). The authors state that the improved response rate did not translate into a significantly increased survival rate; however, 26 percent of the patients who entered the trial never received chemotherapy: 11 (34 percent) of the HAI group and 3 (9 percent) of the systemic group. Of the patients in the HAI group, 38 percent had positive hepatic lymph nodes. In addition, this was a very small study, so that the power to detect even a moderate difference in survival was very low. Despite these limitations, in the subset of patients without extrahepatic disease, the 2-year survival was 47 percent in the HAI group versus 13 percent in the systemic group ($p=.03$; Table 84-6).

Another small study conducted by the Mayo Clinic (69 patients) compared hepatic arterial 5-FUDR 0.3 mg/kg/day × 14 days to systemic bolus 5-FU 500 mg/m^2 IV × 5 days.[27] Patients were stratified by baseline performance status, extent of hepatic metastases, and the presence of measurable disease. The trial permitted entry of symptomatic patients only and did not allow a crossover to an alternative treatment. Objective tumor response was observed in 48 percent of patients receiving hepatic arterial 5-FUDR and in 21 percent of patients receiving intravenous 5-FU ($p=.02$). Time to hepatic progression was significantly longer in the HAI group (15.7 months versus 6 months, respectively; $p=.0001$). Despite the increase in response rate and time to hepatic progression, survival was similar in the two groups (12.6 months for HAI versus 10.5 months for the systemic group). Again, several factors must be considered regarding the survival data. First, as previously stated, this is a small trial such that the power to detect a survival advantage is very low. Sec-

Table 84-6
National Cancer Institute (NCI) Study—Randomized HAI versus Systemic Chemotherapy

Value	*HAI* n = *32*	*IV* n = *32*	p *value*
Treated	21	29	
Positive hepatic nodes	8	7	
Complete response	1	1	
Partial response	12 (62%)	4 (17%)	.003
Reduction in CEA >50%	12/20	3/26	
Toxicity			
Bilirubin >3	33%	0	
Biliary sclerosis	21%	0	
Ulcer	16%	0	
Diarrhea		59%	
Hospitalization for diarrhea		21%	
Survival median (months)	22	12	.06
Actuarial 2-year survival	34%	17%	.03
Actuarial 2-year survival without positive nodes	47%	13%	

SOURCE: From Chang et al.[26] With permission.

Table 84-7
Mayo Clinical Trial—Randomized HAI versus Systemic Chemotherapy

	HAI[a] n = *36*	*Sys* n = *33*	p *value*
Treated	31	30	
Extrahepatic disease	7	?	
Tumor response	45%	21%	.02
Hepatic progression (months)	15.7	6	.0001
Survival (months)	12.6[b]	10.5	.31
Improved symptoms	61%	45%	.3

[a]Patients treated on HAI reported more subjective satisfaction with pump and less side effects than systemic patients.

[b]Five (15 percent) not treated, 7 had extrahepatic disease, 5 hepatic artery thrombosis or pump malfunction, but all were included in survival analysis.

ond, of the 36 patients in the HAI group, 5 (14 percent) never received treatment, 7 (19 percent) had extrahepatic disease, 3 (9 percent) had hepatic artery thrombosis, and 2 (6 percent) had pump malfunction. The fact that all of these patients were included in the survival analysis, even though 48 percent either were not adequately treated or had extrahepatic disease, may have influenced the survival data. The investigators report that the survival of patients with extrahepatic disease is significantly shorter than that of those without extrahepatic disease ($p = .04$); therefore inclusion of these patients in the HAI group will have a negative impact on survival. There is no comment in the report about the survival in the adequately treated patients (Table 84-7).

In a trial by a multicenter group in France, 163 patients were randomized to either hepatic arterial 5-FUDR for 14 days or systemic bolus 5-FU daily × 5 every 4 weeks.[28] The groups had comparable clinical and laboratory characteristics, including percent of liver involvement and baseline LDH levels. In patients with measurable disease, the response rate was 49 percent in the HAI group and 14 percent in the systemic group. Median time to hepatic progression was 15 months for the HAI group and 6 months for the systemic group. Median survival was 14 months for the HAI group and 10 months for the systemic group. The 2-year survival was 22 percent for the hepatic group and 10 percent for the systemic group ($p < .02$; Table 84-8).

The size of this trial and the lack of crossover in the design allow this study to demonstrate a significant increase in 2-year survival for the HAI group. This increase in survival holds despite excessive biliary toxicity in the HAI group. One criticism of the study was that treatment in the systemic group was not uniform and did not always start immediately following randomization.

A study comparing HAI 5-FUDR therapy with systemic 5-FU treatment in symptomatic patients is being conducted in England.[29] To date, there has been a substantial decrease in liver involvement by tumor in the HAI group and an increase in liver involvement in the systemic group. More definitive response data are pending. This study will address both survival and quality-of-life issues.

In an intergroup study,[30] participants compared three types of treatment: HAI, systemic, and combined intrahepatic and systemic therapy. However, they were only able to accrue 43 patients. The response rates were 58, 38, and 56 percent, respectively,

Table 84-8
French Trial—Randomized HAI versus Systemic Chemotherapy

	HAI n = *81*	*Sys* n = *82*	
Complete response	13%	2%	
Partial response	36%	12%	
Time to progression, months	15	6	
Extrahepatic metastases	44%	39%	
Sclerosing cholangitis	25%	0	
Median survival, months	14	10	
1-year survival	61%	44%	
2-year survival	22%	10%	$p < .02$

SOURCE: From Rougier et al.[28] With permission.

Table 84-9
Randomized Study of Resection ± Hepatic Artery Chemotherapy

Groups	*No. of patients*	*Time to failure*	*Survival*
Solitary metastasis resection	6	9	28
A1 resection only	6	9	28
A2 resection + HAC	5	31	37
Multiple resection			
B1 resection + HAC	10	15	19
B2 resection only	14	9	22
Unresectable			
C1 HAC	31	9	14
C2 systemic then HAC	10	8	12
C3 + portal nodes, HAC	15	6	9

SOURCE: From Wagman et al.[31] With permission.

for the three treatments. The small sample size makes it difficult to discuss response and survival.

Another randomized study conducted at the City of Hope[31] asked a different question: Does HAI added to hepatic tumor resection increase the time to progression and improve overall survival? Ninety-one patients were entered in three different groups. In group A, after solitary metastasis resection, patients were randomized to either no further treatment (A1) or HAI (A2). In group B, after resection of multiple metastases, the patients were randomized to no further treatment (B2) or HAI (B1). In group C, there was no resection and patients were randomized to HAI (C1) or systemic 5-FU followed by HAI (C2). In the group with a solitary liver metastasis, time to failure was 9 months in the resection-alone group (group A1) and 31 months in resection plus HAI (A2), $p<.03$. In the B group, 30 percent of patients who had resection plus HAI were alive at 5 years versus 7 percent of those receiving resection alone. Thus, this study suggests a benefit for HAI in patients who have undergone resection of liver metastases (Table 84-9).

SUMMARY OF RANDOMIZED STUDIES

There are now seven randomized trials demonstrating a significantly higher response rate for hepatic arterial chemotherapy versus systemic therapy in patients with hepatic metastases from colorectal carcinoma (Table 84-10). In every study, the complete and partial response rates were higher for the HAI groups. Whether this increase in response rate translates into increased survival remains controversial. Several factors complicate this issue. First, most of the trials contain relatively few patients, so that the power to observe differences in survival rates is low. An analogous situation is the issue of adjuvant chemotherapy in colorectal carcinoma. For many years, patients with Dukes C colonic cancer did not receive chemotherapy because the many small studies available failed to show a significant increase in survival. When a large study was finally completed, there was a significant increase in survival, suggesting a benefit of adjuvant therapy.[32] Second, because of the early successes with HAI, some of these studies allowed patients in the systemic arm to cross over to intrahepatic therapy after tumor progression on systemic therapy. This crossover may have negated any difference in survival between the two groups. The studies do demonstrate a survival advantage for the groups who received subsequent HAI, with a mean 1-year survival of 69 percent for the patients who had crossed over from systemic therapy to HAI versus 35 percent for the group who did not cross over (Table 84-11). A third factor is that, in several trials, many patients did not receive the therapy that they were randomized to. For example, in the Mayo Clinic trial, 53 percent of the patients randomized to HAI either were not adequately treated or had extrahepatic disease. These three factors demonstrate the need for HAI regimens that maximize response rates (especially complete responses) and impact on survival even more definitively and also for a large, carefully controlled randomized trial.

Table 84-10
Randomized Studies of Intrahepatic versus Systemic Chemotherapy for Hepatic Metastases

Group	*No. of patients*	*HAI drug*	*Response, percent*	*Drug*	*Systemic response, percent*	p *value*
MSKCC[21]	162	5-FUDR	52	5-FUDR	20	.001
NCOG[24]	143	5-FUDR	42	5-FUDR	10	.0001
NCI[26]	64	5-FUDR	62	5-FUDR	17	.003
Consortium[30]	43	5-FUDR	58	5-FU	38	—[a]
City of Hope[20]	41	5-FUDR	56	5-FU	0	—
Mayo Clinic[27]	69	5-FUDR	48	5-FU	21	.02
French[28]	163	5-FUDR	49	5-FU	14	—

[a]— = not stated.

Table 84-11
Randomized Study of Hepatic (HA) versus Systemic (Sys) Chemotherapy

	Survival, percent alive at 1 year		*Survival, percent alive at 2 years*		*Survival, percent alive at 1 year*		*Survival, percent, alive at 2 years*	
Group	*HA*	*Sys*	*HA*	*Sys*	*Cross-over*	*No cross-over*	*Cross-over*	*No cross-over*
MSKCC	60	50	25	20	60	28	25	14
NCOG	60	42	30	20	78	42	40	17
NCI[a]	85	60	44	13				
France	61	44	22	10				
Mean	66	49	30	18	69	35	37	15

[a]Excluding patients with positive hepatic lymph nodes.

TOXICITY OF INTRAHEPATIC THERAPY

A summary of the gastrointestinal toxicities noted by investigators using the implantable pump are listed in Table 84-12. The side effects of systemic chemotherapy are almost never observed with HAI. Myelosuppression does not occur with intrahepatic 5-FUDR.[14,33,34] While intrahepatic mitomycin C or BCNU may depress platelet counts, the absolute depression and frequency of depression occur to a lesser degree than with systemic administration. Nausea, vomiting, and diarrhea do not occur with HAI of 5-FUDR. If diarrhea does occur, shunting to the bowel should be suspected.[35] The most common problems with HAI are ulcer disease and hepatic toxicity.[14,33] Ulcer disease is the result of inadvertent perfusion of the stomach and duodenum with drug via small collateral branches from the hepatic artery and can be prevented via careful dissection of these collaterals at the time of pump placement.[36] This toxicity can also be reduced by careful dose reactions when any gastrointestinal symptoms occur. Hepatobiliary toxicity is the most problematic toxicity seen with hepatic arterial chemotherapy. Although there is some evidence of hepatocellular necrosis and cholestasis on liver biopsies,[37] most studies point to a combined ischemic and inflammatory effect on the bile ducts as the most important etiology of this toxicity. The bile ducts are particularly sensitive to HA chemotherapy because, like hepatic tumors, the bile ducts derive their blood supply almost exclusively from the hepatic artery.[38] Pettavel[39] prospectively studied 21 liver biopsy and 4 autopsy specimens of 13 patients in whom biliary toxicity developed after hepatic arterial treatment with 5-FUDR. The liver biopsies were characterized by portal or diffuse inflammatory changes that were predominantly mononuclear. Other changes included focal atrophy of hepatocytes and increased collagen formation. The autopsy specimens showed gross bile duct damage and intimal fibrous thickening of the small arteries with narrowing or obstruction of the lumens. These changes have been confirmed by other studies.

Clinically, biliary toxicity is manifested as elevations of aspartate aminotransferase (AST), alkaline

Table 84-12
Hepatic Arterial 5-FUDR Infusion with Internal Pump: Toxicity

Investigator	*No. of patients*	*Gastritis, percent*	*Ulcer, percent*	*SGOT percent*	*Bilirubin, percent*	*Diarrhea percent*	*Biliary sclerosis percent*
Niederhuber et al.[12]	70	56	8	32	24	—	—
Balcher and Urist[13]	50	—	6	23	23	0	—
Kemeny et al.[14]	41	29	29	71	22	0	5
Shepard et al.[15]	53	—	20	49	24	—	—
Cohen et al.[16]	50	—	40	10	25	—	—
Weiss et al.[17]	17	50	11	80	23	23	—
Schwartz et al.[18]	23	53	—	77	20	10	—
Johnson et al.[19]	40	—	8	50	13	0	5
Kemeny et al.[20]	31	17	6	47	—	8	19
Hohn et al.[24]	61	35	2	0	78	11	29

phosphatase, and bilirubin. The incidence of these toxicities in the randomized studies is summarized in Table 84-12. Elevation of AST is an early manifestation of toxicity; elevation of alkaline phosphatase or bilirubin is evidence of more severe damage. In the early stages of toxicity, hepatic enzyme elevations will return to normal when the drug is withdrawn and the patient is given a rest period. In more advanced cases, jaundice does not resolve.

In patients with severe toxicity, endoscopic retrograde cholangiopancreatography (ERCP) demonstrates lesions resembling idiopathic sclerosing cholangitis.[40] Since the ducts are sclerotic, sonograms are usually normal. In some patients, the strictures are more centralized, and drainage procedures either by ERCP or by transhepatic cholangiogram may be helpful. Computed tomography (CT) of the liver should be done to exclude metastatic lesions as a cause of strictures.

Close monitoring of liver function tests is necessary to avoid biliary sclerosis. If the serum bilirubin becomes elevated, no further treatment should be given until the bilirubin returns to normal, and then only with a small test dose (0.05 mg/kg/day). In patients who cannot tolerate even a low dose for 2 weeks, it may be possible to continue treatment by giving the 5-FUDR infusion for 1 week rather than the usual 2 weeks.

At MSKCC, it was found that serum AST is a useful laboratory test to monitor hepatic toxicity.[14] A review of the liver function tests obtained every 2 weeks revealed that, in 23 of the original 45 patients, the AST increased at the end of 5-FUDR infusion (2 weeks after treatment began) and then returned to normal or almost normal levels prior to the next dose (4 weeks after treatment began). This pattern occurred in all patients who later developed severe hepatic toxicity (bilirubin >3 mg/mL). In some of the reports with excessive biliary sclerosis, liver function tests were checked only monthly. These investigators may have missed the 2-week elevation and therefore may not have reduced doses appropriately at the time of the next treatment. At MSKCC, we modify treatment as outlined (Table 84-13).

Table 84-13
Dose Modification for Hepatic Toxicity

SGOT	*Bilirubin*	*Alkaline phosphatase*	*FUDR dose*
2× baseline	—	—	80%
3× baseline	1.5 baseline	1.5×	50%
>3× baseline	2 baseline	2×	Hold

In older trials, cholecystitis occurred in up to 33 percent of patients receiving hepatic arterial chemotherapy.[41,42] In more recent series, the gallbladder has been removed at the time of catheter placement to prevent this complication and to avoid the confusion of these symptoms with other hepatic side effects from pump treatment.

NEW APPROACHES TO DECREASE HEPATIC TOXICITY

New approaches to decrease the hepatic toxicity induced by hepatic arterial 5-FUDR are being studied. Since portal triad inflammation may lead to ischemia of the bile ducts, the hepatic arterial administration of dexamethasone (D) may decrease biliary toxicity.[43] In patients with established hepatobiliary toxicity from HAI, dexamethasone promotes resolution of the liver function abnormalities. A prospective double-blind randomized study of intrahepatic 5-FUDR with D versus 5-FUDR alone was conducted at MSKCC in order to determine whether the simultaneous administration of D with 5-FUDR would prevent biliary toxicity and thereby allow for the administration of higher doses of chemotherapy.[44] Prior to randomization, patients were stratified for the percentage of liver involvement by tumor and the perfusion pattern on macroaggregated albumin perfusion scan (MAA). Although a significant increase in tolerable 5-FUDR dose was not documented, the response rate in 49 evaluable patients was 71 percent for the 5-FUDR + D group versus 40 percent for 5-FUDR alone ($p = .03$). Survival also favored the 5-FUDR + D group: 23 months versus 15 months for 5-FUDR alone. In addition, there was a trend toward decreased bilirubin elevation in patients receiving 5-FUDR + D compared to the group receiving 5-FUDR alone (9 versus 30 percent; $p = .07$). (See Table 84-14.)

Table 84-14
Randomized Trial of HAI 5-FUDR in 5-FUDR plus Dexamethasone (D)

	5-FUDR, n = 25	*5-FUDR + D, n = 24*	p *value*
Complete response + partial response	40%	71%	.03
>50% reduction in CEA	64%	84%	
Bilirubin >3	30%	9%	.07
Sclerosing cholangitis	8%	8%	
Time to progression, months	12	19	
Survival, months	15	23	.06

SOURCE: From Kemeny et al.[49] With permission.

The use of circadian modification of hepatic intraarterial 5-FUDR infusion is a second method to decrease hepatic toxicity. In a retrospective, nonrandomized study at the University of Minnesota,[45] a comparison of constant (flat) infusion versus circadian modified (CM) hepatic arterial 5-FUDR infusion was conducted in 50 patients with metastatic colorectal carcinoma. The initial dose was 0.25 to 0.3 mg/kg/day for a 14-day infusion. The group with circadian modification received 68 percent of each daily dose between 3 P.M. and 9 P.M., 2 percent between 3 A.M. and 9 A.M., and 15 percent in each of the adjacent 6-h periods. Over nine courses of treatment, the patients with CM infusion tolerated almost twice the daily dose of 5-FUDR (0.79 mg/kg/day versus 0.46 mg/kg/day). CM infusion resulted in 46 percent of patients having no hepatic toxicity versus 16 percent of patients after flat 5-FUDR infusion. Unfortunately, the authors do not present information on response rates achieved in both groups.

Another approach to decrease toxicity from HAI is to alternate intraarterial (IA) 5-FUDR with IA 5-FU. Weekly IA bolus of 5-FU has similar activity to IA 5-FUDR and does not cause hepatobiliary toxicity; however, it frequently produces treatment-limiting systemic toxicity or arteritis. Stagg et al.[46] used an alternating hepatic arterial 5-FUDR and hepatic arterial 5-FU regimen: HAI 5-FUDR 0.1 mg/kg/day × 7 days followed by hepatic artery bolus 5-FU 15 mg/kg via the pump side port on days 14, 21, 28, repeating this cycle every 35 days. The response rate was 51 percent, and median survival was 22.4 months. In contrast to the experience with single-agent HAI 5-FUDR, no patient had treatment terminated because of drug toxicity.

METHODS TO INCREASE RESPONSE RATE

Based on the fact that systemic combination chemotherapy regimens are more effective than single agents, the potential benefit of multidrug hepatic arterial therapy is being evaluated. In an early study using mitomycin C, BCNU, and 5-FUDR, Cohen et al.[47] produced a 70 percent partial response rate. In a randomized trial at MSKCC comparing this three-drug regimen with 5-FUDR alone, there was a slight increase in response rate and survival with the three-drug regimen.[48] In the 67 patients who entered this trial (all of whom had received prior systemic chemotherapy), the response rates were 45 percent for the three-drug regimen and 32 percent for 5-FUDR alone. The median survivals from the initiation of hepatic arterial therapy were 18.9 and 14.9 months, respectively (Table 84-15). It should be noted that the response rates in both arms were much higher than would be expected with a second systemic regimen. Thus, in addition to its role as front-line treatment, hepatic arterial infusion should also be considered in patients who have failed systemic therapy.

Table 84-15
A Randomized Trial of Hepatic Arterial 5-FUDR (F) + Mitomycin + BCNU (FMB) versus 5-FUDR Alone in Previously Treated Patients with Liver Metastases from Colorectal Cancer

Response	*FMB* (n = *29)*	*F* (n = *34)*
Partial response	45%	32% (p = .31)
Duration of response, months, median	15.0	9.1 (p = .04)
Survival, months, median	18.8	14.9 (p = .05)
Toxicity	*FMB* (n = *29)*	*F* (n = *34)*
Percent of patients with		
Bilirubin >3 mg/dL	28%	21% (p = .52)
Biliary sclerosis	10%	3% (p = .23)
WBC <3000/mm³	14%	9% (p = .41)
Platelets <100K/mm³	28%	6% (p = .02)

In another attempt to improve survival and response rate, a combination of hepatic arterial 5-FUDR and leucovorin (LV) was evaluated.[49] This study was based on success of systemic 5-FU/LV regimens as well as laboratory studies suggesting that LV may actually be a better modifier of 5-FUDR than 5-FU. Twenty-four patients were treated at three dose levels. The overall response rate was 72 percent, but 25 percent of patients developed biliary sclerosis. Nevertheless, 75 percent of the patients were alive after 1 year, 66 percent after 2 years, and 33 percent at 3 years. 5-FUDR plus LV appears to have a high response rate in the treatment of hepatic metastases from colorectal carcinoma, but hepatic toxicity appears greater than previously reported with 5-FUDR alone.

METHODS TO DECREASE EXTRAHEPATIC DISEASE

Extrahepatic disease develops in 40 to 70 percent of patients undergoing hepatic arterial infusion. Such metastases can occur even when the patient is still responding in the liver; in many patients, they can be the cause of death. Safi[50] studied the ability of concomitant systemic chemotherapy to reduce the development of extrahepatic metastases in patients receiving hepatic arterial therapy. Ninety-five patients were randomized to either intraarterial (IA) 5-FUDR (0.2 mg/kg/day for 14 of 28 days), or a combination of IA 5-FUDR (0.21 mg/kg/day) and IV 5-FUDR (0.09 mg/kg/day), given concurrently for 14 of 28 days (IA/IV). The response rates were 60 percent for both arms of the study. However, the incidence of extrahepatic disease was significantly less in patients receiving the IA/IV treatment (56 percent) compared with those receiving IA treatment (79 percent, $p<.01$). No significant difference in survival was found between the two groups ($p = .08$). The results of this trial warrant further study of combined systemic/intraarterial regimens.

CONTROVERSIES REGARDING HEPATIC ARTERIAL INFUSION

Despite the consistently increased response rates seen with HAI, many physicians feel its use is not justified. One reason is that a survival benefit has not been demonstrated. As previously stated, there are many reasons why the studies to date do not adequately address this issue. However, a comparison with survival rates obtained with systemic chemotherapy suggests that HAI may be superior. For example, the use of systemic 5-FU and leucovorin is considered standard treatment for metastatic colorectal carcinoma because several randomized trials have demonstrated increased response rates for 5-FU/LV compared with 5-FU alone.[51–56] In these trials, the mean response rate for 5-FU/LV was 38 percent compared to 12 percent for 5-FU alone. An analysis of the survival data shows that 52 percent of the 5-FU/LV-treated patients were alive at 1 year, compared with 43 percent of the 5-FU-treated patients. At 2 years, 19 percent of the combined-treatment patients and 16 percent of the 5-FU-treated patients were alive. If we compare this information to survival data from the randomized pump studies using intrahepatic 5-FUDR with or without other agents, the percent alive at 1 and 2 years is greater for those receiving HAI: At 1 year, the mean survival of the HAI patients was 73 percent, versus 52 percent for the patients treated with systemic 5-FU and leucovorin (Table 84-16). The mean 2-year survival was 37 percent for the HAI group and 19 percent for the systemic group. One might argue that these studies do not contain comparable patient groups and that the HAI-treated patients had a better survival because of a difference in prognostic variables. In fact, the systemic therapy trials should have had a better survival because they included patients with lung metastases. Patients with lung metastases have a median survival of 12 months, while those with liver metastases only have a median survival of 8 months. Patients with both lung and liver metastases have a median survival of 10.7 months.[23] The 2-year survivals for these three groups of patients (liver alone, lung and liver, and lung alone) were 0, 10, and 30 percent, respectively. Therefore, patients with only liver metastases have the worst prognosis and are often poor candidates for systemic therapy.

Another criticism of pump therapy is that the patient must undergo an additional laparotomy. This is correct; however, 15 percent of patients (roughly 20,000 patients per year) with colorectal carcinoma have hepatic metastases at presentation. In many of these patients, pump placement at the time of initial surgery would decrease cost and avoid another laparotomy. Once the pump is in, patients feel better than systemically treated patients, as they experience none of the irritating side effects of systemic therapy. The pump patients do experience side effects; however, severe symptomatic hepatic toxicity is seen in only 8 percent of patients. This enhanced quality of life may outweigh the negative aspects of laparotomy.

A theoretical disadvantage of hepatic arterial chemotherapy is the development of extrahepatic metas-

Table 84-16
Survival Comparison of Systemic FU + LV Trials to Trial of Hepatic Arterial Infusion of 5-FUDR

	Systemic 5-FU + LV survival, percent			*HAI 5-FUDR survival, percent*	
	1 year	*2 years*		*1 year*	*2years*
Valone et al.[51]	46	18	MSKCC[21]	60	25
Erlichman et al.[52]	55	18	NCOG[24]	60	30
GISTG[53]	58	18	NCI[26]	85	44
NCCTG[54]	51	18	France[28]	61	22
Doroshow et al.[55]	61	20	Mayo[27]	60	18
Petrelli et al.[56]	42	25	MSKCC[49] [a]	90	59
			MSKCC[44] [b]	90	52
			Stagg[46] [c]	70	35
			Safai[50]	80	50
Mean survival, percent	52	19		73	37

[a] + LV.

[b] + Decadron.

[c] + FU.

tases. Actually, randomized studies of HAI versus systemic chemotherapy have not demonstrated a significant increase in extrahepatic metastases in the intrahepatic therapy groups. An argument has been made for early intensive treatment of hepatic metastases by resection and/or intraarterial infusion to prevent the stepwise spread of colorectal carcinoma to other organs.

CONCLUSION

There are several advantages to HAI. From a pharmacologic standpoint, intrahepatic infusional therapy is more effective than systemic therapy since higher drug levels are achieved at the sites of metastatic disease. Utilizing agents with high hepatic extraction virtually eliminates the systemic toxicity observed with "standard" therapy (intravenous 5-FU or 5-FU/LV).

The 50 percent response rate obtained in trials of intrahepatic 5-FUDR therapy has, to date, not been matched by any systemic therapy. The randomized pump studies do not clearly evaluate the issue of survival, because in some a crossover was allowed; in others, patients with positive portal nodes were included in the HAI treated groups.

Severe toxicity may occur with either intrahepatic or systemic therapy. Intrahepatic therapy produces severe gastrointestinal or hepatic toxicity in roughly 10 percent of patients. However, one study of 5-FU/LV reported a mortality rate of 6 percent and severe gastrointestinal toxicity (diarrhea, mucositis, nausea, and vomiting) and/or myelosuppression in roughly 20 percent of patients. The toxicity of intrahepatic therapy may be minimized with better surgical technique, close monitoring of liver function tests and perhaps, circadian dose adjustment, and intrahepatic dexamethasone.

Because the liver is often the initial site of metastatic disease in patients with colorectal carcinoma, early intensive therapy with surgical resection and/or intrahepatic infusion at a time when the tumor burden is small may prevent the progression of metastases to other sites. While intrahepatic therapy is only applicable to a minority of patients with metastatic colorectal carcinoma (those with only hepatic metastases), it may be the best available therapy for these patients.

REFERENCES

1. Coller FA: *Cancer of the Colon and Rectum.* New York: American Cancer Society, 1956.
2. Breedis C, Young C: The blood supply of neoplasms in the liver. *Am J Pathol* 30:969, 1954.
3. Sigurdson ER, Ridge JA, Kemeny N, Daly JM: Tumor and liver drug uptake following hepatic artery and portal vein infusion. *J Clin Oncol* 5:1836–1840, 1987.
4. Ensminger WD, Rosowsky A, Raso V: A clinical pharmacological evaluation of hepatic arterial infusions of 5-fluoro-2-deoxyuridine and 5-fluorouracil. *Cancer Res* 38:3784–3792, 1978.
5. Ensminger WD, Gyves JW: Clinical pharmacology of hepatic arterial chemotherapy. *Semin Oncol* 10:176–182, 1983.
6. Collins JM: Pharmacologic rationale for regional drug delivery. *J Clin Oncol* 2:498–504, 1984.
7. Collins JM: Pharmacologic rationale for hepatic arterial therapy. *Recent Results Cancer Res* 100:140–148, 1986.
8. Weiss L, Grundmann E, Torhorst J, et al: Hematogenous metastatic patterns in colonic carcinoma: An analysis of 1541 necropsies. *J Pathol* 150:195–203, 1986.
9. Weiss L: Metastatic inefficiency and regional therapy for liver metastases from colorectal carcinoma. *Reg Cancer Treat* 2:77–81, 1989.
10. Sugarbaker P, Kemeny N: Treatment of metastatic cancer to liver, in DeVita V, Hellman S, Rosenberg S (eds): *Cancer: Principles and Practice of Oncology,* 3d ed. Philadelphia, Lippincott, 1989, pp 2275–2293.
11. Blackshear PJ, Dorman FD, Blackshear PJ Jr, et al: The design and initial testing of an implantable infusion pump. *Surg Gynecol Obstet* 134:51–56, 1972.
12. Niederhuber JE, Ensminger W, Gyves J, et al: Regional chemotherapy of colorectal cancer metastatic to the liver. *Cancer* 53:1336–1343, 1984.
13. Balch CM, Urist MM: Intraarterial chemotherapy for colorectal liver metastases and hepatomas using a totally implantable drug infusion pump. *Recent Results Cancer Res* 100:123–147, 1986.
14. Kemeny N, Daly J, Oderman P, et al: Hepatic artery pump infusion toxicity and results in patients with metastatic colorectal carcinoma. *J Clin Oncol* 2:595–600, 1984.
15. Shepard KV, Levin B, Karl RC, et al: Therapy for metastatic colorectal cancer with hepatic artery infusion chemotherapy using a subcutaneous implanted pump. *J Clin Oncol* 3:161–169, 1985.
16. Cohen AM, Kaufman SD, Wood WC, et al: Regional hepatic chemotherapy using an implantable drug infusion pump. *Am J Surg* 145:529–533, 1983.
17. Weiss GR, Garnick MB, Osteen RT, et al: Long-term arterial infusion of 5-fluorodeoxyuridine for liver metastases using an implantable infusion pump. *J Clin Oncol* 1:337–344, 1983.
18. Schwartz SI, Jones LS, McCune CS: Assessment of treatment of intrahepatic malignancies using chemotherapy via an implantable pump. *Ann Surg* 201:560–567, 1985.
19. Johnson LP, Wasserman PB, Rivkin SE: FUDR hepatic arterial infusion via an implantable pump for treatment of hepatic tumors. *Proc ASCO* 2:119, 1983.
20. Kemeny MM, Goldberg D, Beatty JD, et al: Results of a prospective randomized trials of continuous regional chemotherapy and hepatic resection as treatment of hepatic metastases from colorectal primaries. *Cancer* 57:492–498, 1986.
21. Kemeny N, Daly J, Reichman B, et al: Intrahepatic or systemic infusion of fluorodeoxyuridine in patients with liver metastases from colorectal carcinoma. *Ann Intern Med* 107: 459–465, 1987.
22. Kemeny N, Daly J, Oderman P, et al: Prognostic variables in patients with hepatic metastases from colorectal cancer: Importance of medical assessment of liver involvement. *Cancer* 63:742–747, 1989.
23. Kemeny N, Braun DW: Prognostic factors in advanced colorectal carcinoma: The importance of lactic dehydrogenase, performance status, and white blood cell count. *Am J Med* 74:786–794, 1983.
24. Hohn D, Stagg R, Friedman M, et al: A randomized trial of

continuous intravenous versus hepatic intraarterial floxuridine in patients with colorectal cancer metastatic to the liver: The Northern California Oncology Group Trial. *J Clin Oncol* 7:1646–1654, 1989.

25. Hughes KS, Hepatic Metastases Registry: Resection of the liver for colorectal metastases: a multi-institutional study of patterns of recurrence. *Surgery* 100:278–284, 1986.
26. Chang AE, Schneider PD, Sugarbaker PH: A prospective randomized trial of regional versus systemic continuous 5-fluorodeoxyuridine chemotherapy in the treatment of colorectal liver metastases. *Ann Surg* 206:685–693, 1987.
27. Martin JK Jr, O'Connell MJ, Wieand HS, et al: Intra-arterial floxuridine vs systemic fluorouracil for hepatic metastases from colorectal cancer. A randomized trial. *Arch Surg* 125:1022–1027, 1990.
28. Rougier P, Laplanche A, Huguier M, et al: Hepatic arterial infusion of floxuridine in patients with liver metastases from colorectal carcinoma: Long-term results of a prospective randomized trial. *J Clin Oncol* 10:1112–1118, 1992.
29. Mersh TG: Personal communication.
30. Niederhuber JE: Arterial chemotherapy for metastatic colorectal cancer in the liver, in *Conference Advances in Regional Cancer Therapy*. Giessen, West Germany, 1985.
31. Wagman LD, Kemeny MM, Leong L, et al: A prospective randomized evaluation of the treatment of colorectal cancer metastatic to the liver. *J Clin Oncol* 8:1885–1893, 1990.
32. Moertel CG, Fleming TR, MacDonald JS, et al: Levamisole and fluorouracil for adjuvant therapy of resected colon carcinoma. *N Engl J Med* 322:352–358, 1990.
33. Kemeny N: Role of chemotherapy in the treatment of colorectal carcinoma. *Semin Surg Oncol* 3:190–214, 1987.
34. Lesser ML, Cento SJ: Tables of power for the F-test for comparing two exponential survival distributions. *J Chronic Dis* 34:533–544, 1981.
35. Gluck WI, Akwari OE, Kelvin FM, et al: A reversible enteropathy complicating continuous hepatic artery infusion chemotherapy with 5-fluoro 2-deoxyuridine. *Cancer* 56:2424–2427, 1985.
36. Hohn DC, Stagg RJ, Price DC, et al: Avoidance of gastroduodenal toxicity in patients receiving hepatic arterial 5-fluoro-2'-deoxyuridine. *J Clin Oncol* 3:1257–1260, 1985.
37. Doria MI Jr, Shepard KV, Levin B, et al: Liver pathology following hepatic arterial infusion chemotherapy. *Cancer* 58:855–861, 1986.
38. Northover JM, Terblanche J: A new look at the arterial supply of the bile duct in man and its surgical implications. *Br J Surg* 66:379–384, 1979.
39. Pettavel J, Gardiol D, Bergier N, et al: Necrosis of main bile ducts caused by hepatic artery infusion of 5-fluoro-2-deoxyuridine. *Reg Cancer Treat* 1:83–92, 1988.
40. Kemeny M, Battifora H, Blayney D, et al: Sclerosing cholangitis after continuous hepatic artery infusion of FUDR. *Ann Surg* 202:176–181, 1985.
41. Buchwald H, Grage TB, Vassilopoulos PP, et al: Intraarterial infusion chemotherapy for hepatic carcinoma using a totally implantable infusion pump. *Cancer* 45:866–869, 1980.
42. Ensminger W, Niederhuber J, Dakhil S, et al: Totally implanted drug delivery system for hepatic arterial chemotherapy. *Cancer Treat Rep* 65:393–400, 1981.
43. Paquette P, Campos LT, Flax I, et al: Prevention and treatment of sclerosing cholangitis related to chemotherapy delivered by Infusaid pump. *Proc ASCO* 6:89, 1987.
44. Kemeny N, Seiter K, Niedzwiecki D, et al: A randomized trial of intrahepatic (IH) infusion of FUDR with dexamethasone (D) vs FUDR alone in the treatment of metastatic colorectal cancer. *Cancer* 69:327–334, 1992.
45. von Roemeling R, Hrushesky WJM: Circadian patterning of continuous floxuridine infusion reduces toxicity and allows higher dose intensity in patients with widespread cancer. *J Clin Oncol* 7:1710–1719, 1989.
46. Stagg RJ, Venook AP, Chase JL, et al: Alternating hepatic intra-arterial floxuridine and fluorouracil: A less toxic regimen for treatment of liver metastases from colorectal cancer. *J Natl Cancer Inst* 83:423–428, 1991.
47. Cohen A, Schaeffer N, Higgins J: Treatment of metastatic colorectal cancer with hepatic artery combination chemotherapy. *Cancer* 57:1115–1117, 1986.
48. Seiter K, Kemeny N, Cohen A, et al: A randomized trial of hepatic arterial FUDR + mitomycin + BCNU versus FUDR alone in the treatment of liver metastases of colorectal cancer. *Proc ASCO*, 1991.
49. Kemeny N, Cohen A, Bertino JR, et al: Continuous intrahepatic infusion of floxuridine and leucovorin through an implantable pump for the treatment of hepatic metastases from colorectal carcinoma. *Cancer* 65:2446–2450, 1990.
50. Safi F: Continuous simultaneous intraarterial and intravenous therapy of liver metastases of colorectal carcinoma: Results of a prospective randomized trial. *Proc ASCO* 11:169, 1992.
51. Valone FH, Friedman MA, Wittinger PS, et al: Treatment of patients with advanced colorectal carcinoma with fluorouracil alone, high-dose leucovorin plus fluorouracil, or sequential methotrexate, fluorouracil, and leucovorin: A randomized trial of the North California Oncology Group. *J Clin Oncol* 7:1427–1436, 1989.
52. Ehrlichman C, Fine S, Wong A, Elhakim T: Randomized trial of fluorouracil and folinic acid in patients with metastatic colorectal carcinoma. *J Clin Oncol* 6:469–475, 1988.
53. Petrelli N, Douglass HO, Herrera L, et al: The modulation of fluorouracil with leucovorin in metastatic colorectal carcinoma: A prospective randomized phase III trial. *J Clin Oncol* 79:1419–1426, 1989.
54. O'Connell MJ: A phase III trial of 5-fluorouracil and leucovorin in the treatment of advanced colorectal cancer. *Cancer* 63:1026–1030, 1989.
55. Doroshow JH, Multhauf P, Leong L, et al: Prospective randomized comparison of fluorouracil versus fluorouracil plus high-dose continuous infusion leucovorin calcium for the treatment of advanced measurable colorectal cancer inpatients previously unexposed to chemotherapy. *J Clin Oncol* 8:491–501, 1990.
56. Petrelli N, Herrera L, Rustum Y, et al: A prospective randomized trial of 5-fluorouracil versus 5-fluorouracil and high-dose leucovorin versus 5-fluorouracil and methotrexate in previously untreated patients with advanced colorectal carcinoma. *J Clin Oncol* 5:1559–1565, 1987.

CHAPTER 85

Intraperitoneal Chemotherapy and Cytoreductive Surgery in Patients with Peritoneal Carcinomatosis from Appendiceal, Colonic, and Rectal Cancer

Paul H. Sugarbaker

HIGHLIGHTS

A frequent cause of death in patients with colorectal malignancy is peritoneal carcinomatosis. Prior to the use of cytoreductive surgery and intraperitoneal chemotherapy, this was a uniformly fatal disease process resulting in intestinal obstruction over the course of months or years. Occasionally, patients with low-grade malignancies would survive long-term, but all end reporting shows a fatal outcome with this clinical situation. This chapter is designed to acquaint the physician with the methods of treatment and prevention developed for peritoneal carcinomatosis from colorectal and appendiceal cancer. The results of therapy in selected patients are favorable. As a result of treatment of large numbers of patients, prognostic groups have been defined and selection factors identified. The grade of the malignancy, the status of lymph nodes, and the completeness of cytoreductive surgery are the determining clinical factors. In patients with peritoneal seeding from colonic cancer, the preoperative volume of cancer on peritoneal surfaces is also an important prognostic feature.

CONTROVERSIES

The major controversy in treating patients with peritoneal carcinomatosis concerns the route and timing of chemotherapy, the timing of the surgical procedure, and the nature of this surgical event. Medical oncologists generally use systemic chemotherapy for patients with this regional disease process. No long-term survivors with this approach have been reported, although definite palliation can occur. Efforts to cure peritoneal carcinomatosis are limited to treatment plans that utilize intraperitoneal chemotherapy during the early postoperative period. Optimally, chemotherapy for peritoneal carcinomatosis from colonic cancer would utilize both an intraperitoneal and a systemic route of drug administration.

The timing of surgery for patients with peritoneal carcinomatosis is also controversial. Some physicians advocate surgery only when palliation is required. However in the treatment of peritoneal carcinomatosis, as in the treatment of other malignancies, the volume of tumor present at the time therapy is initiated is extremely important in determining outcome. The use of cytoreductive surgery and intraperitoneal chemotherapy for high-grade tumor has shown little success in patients with large-volume disease. Considerable success has been achieved with treatment of low-volume disease. Therefore, it seems likely that successful treatments should be instituted just as soon as peritoneal carcinomatosis has been diagnosed.

Finally, there is, as yet, no consensus on the nature of the surgical procedure in patients with peritoneal carcinomatosis. Some surgeons merely bypass obstructing segments of bowel and do the least amount of surgery possible in order to bring temporary relief from intestinal obstruction. Other surgeons have advocated complete resection of all tumor, including stripping of involved abdominal surfaces, undersurfaces of the diaphragm, and surfaces of the pelvis as well as resection of involved organs. These extensive cytoreductive procedures are, of course, associated with additional morbidity and mortality. However, if all visible tumor can be removed or if the cytoreduction reduces tumor to a few millimeters in diameter, then the effects of intraperitoneal chemotherapy should be much more complete. The maximal surgical efforts to remove tumor from the abdomen combined with maximal intraperitoneal chemotherapy has been referred to as the cytoreductive approach for peritoneal carcinomatosis.

FUTURE DIRECTIONS

Controlled clinical trials in patients at high risk for peritoneal carcinomatosis constitute the most important next step in defining the utility of intraperitoneal chemotherapy. Patients at high risk for death from peritoneal carcinomatosis include those with low-volume peritoneal seeding, adjacent organ involvement, tumor spill intraoperatively, positive margins of resection, and extensive lymph node metastases. Only by enrolling large numbers of patients who have the random allocation of regional versus systemic therapy can the application of these new concepts in cancer management be established.

In patients with established high-grade disease, improving the local control becomes the most important next step in improving these therapies. At the present time, patients with grade I cancer are made disease-free long-term by combinations of cytoreductive surgery using the peritonectomy procedures and early postoperative intraperitoneal chemotherapy. A majority of patients with high-grade disease still have recurrences, in most instances, within the abdominal cavity. Experiments with heated chemotherapy, biological response modifiers, and new technologies for cytoreductive surgery are indicated.

PRINCIPLES

Intraperitoneal chemotherapy works because of the "peritoneal plasma barrier."[1] The peritoneal membrane is a metabolically active tissue. The surface area of the parietal and visceral peritoneum is about the same as that of the skin. The visceral peritoneum accounts for a large proportion of the total surface area. The functional area of the peritoneum that participates in the exchange of soluble substances is estimated to be 0.5 percent of the total area. It has been suggested that only the peritoneal surface in immediate juxtaposition to the capillaries participates in solute transfer and only 20 percent of the capillaries are in the perfused state.[2]

The peritoneal plasma barrier is a complex biophysical entity. It consists of the fluid in the dialysate, the mesothelium, the endothelium and basement membrane of the adjacent capillary network, the intervening interstitium, and the blood. The mesothelium is composed of flattened cells lying on a continuous basement membrane. It has been suggested that the structureless areas of the interstitium form channels for the movement of fluids and solutes.[3]

There are large and small pores that selectively allow molecules and cells to leave the peritoneal cavity. Diffusion occurs through the parietal peritoneal surface and through both the visceral and peritoneal surfaces. Direct absorption into lymphatics occurs through the large pores (open lymphatic channels), which are most prominent beneath the hemidiaphragm and in the omentum. The small water-soluble molecules pass through the small pores. Small molecules diffuse from the peritoneal cavity, cross channels of the interstitium, and pass into the vascular system. In humans, the minimal distance separating blood vessels from the peritoneal surface is 5 to 20 μm. The venous drainage of the parietal peritoneal surface is to the systemic circulation; that of the visceral surface, to the portal circulation. A report by Torres and coworkers[4] showed that the net fluid movement from the peritoneal cavity into plasma occurs at a maximal rate of 30 to 35 mL/h.[4] It is estimated that 80 percent of the fluid within the abdominal cavity is absorbed via the portal circulation.

Absorption via lymphatic drainage into the large pores occurs for proteins, macromolecules, red blood cells, and tumor cells.[5] The lymphatic channels are present mainly on the diaphragmatic peritoneum but are also found on the omentum. From the diaphragm, retrosternal lymph channels drain into the mediastinal and internal mammary lymph nodes.

DISTRIBUTION OF PERITONEAL FLUID

If the intraperitoneal instillation of chemotherapeutic agents is to be effective in killing all macroscopic tumor deposits present in the abdominal cavity, the drug-containing fluid must reach all peritoneal surfaces. This intraperitoneal fluid distribution was studied by Rosenshein et al.[6] They showed—by injecting radiolabeled tracer material in monkeys—that a small volume of fluid tended to puddle in the peritoneum near the site of instillation and that subsequent, even drastic, manipulation of the subject failed to ensure wide, uniform distribution. But when a large volume of fluid was instilled, the distribution of the radiopaque fluid was excellent in patients studied by Myers et al.[7] With this "belly bath" technique, they demonstrated that 1.8 to 2.0 L of fluid is sufficient to give satisfactory distribution.

In patients with peritoneal carcinomatosis, the distribution of peritoneal fluid can be assumed to be nonuniform. These patients have usually had one or more surgical procedures. As a result, adhesion formation and closed intraabdominal spaces are common. Second, multiple tumor masses may be present. These tumors adversely affect fluid distribution by causing adherence of intestinal surfaces. Also, tumor masses over a few millimeters in size block access of chemotherapy to cancer in the center of a nodule. However, with the instillation of large volumes of fluid in patients with advanced ovarian cancer, as reported by Howell and coworkers,[8] the fluid distribution was surprisingly uniform in most of the patients studied.

PHARMACOKINETICS OF INTRAPERITONEAL DRUG ADMINISTRATION

The peritoneal cavity, an open space, has boundaries that function as a diffusion barrier, tending to prevent the escape of directly instilled drugs. Absorption occurs through the small intercellular pores and transcellularly. The passage of drug through intercellular pores is governed by the molecular size of the drugs ("Stokes-Einstein" radius). Transcellular movement is through a bilayer lipid membrane and is a function of lipid solubility. Since most commonly used anticancer drugs are hydrophilic, molecular size is the primary determinant of peritoneal absorption.

MODELS OF DRUG DISTRIBUTION

Dedrick and colleagues[9,10] created mathematical models describing the concentration gradients to be expected across body compartments. If a bolus of drug is introduced into a vein, a high concentration is present immediately in the blood. This may be maintained for several minutes but decays over 2 to 4 h. If the same drug is instilled directly into the peritoneal cavity as a bolus in a large volume of fluid, the peak concentration in the abdomen may persist for many hours and the concentration difference is maintained at all times. This pattern may be expected with any hydrophilic agent administered intraperitoneally. The area under the curve (AUC) ratio from concentration-versus-time curves increases as the molecular weight of the drug increases. The larger the drug, the longer the half-life. For example, Sugarbaker and colleagues[11] showed that the AUC ratio in the first few days after a surgical procedure for 5-fluorouracil is 250 and for mitomycin C, 72.

However, this simple model may understate the pharmacokinetic advantages of intraperitoneal delivery. It does not explain the possibility of extensive metabolism of a drug during its first-pass through the liver, which markedly reduces the drug's bioavailability. Moreover, a simple two-compartment model can only predict the concentration of drugs in the peritoneal cavity itself. This concentration is relevant only for the surfaces directly adjacent to the peritoneal surface and free-floating cells. In order to quantitate solute transport and tissue penetration in particular Flessner and colleagues[12,13] developed a distribution model. Although some guidelines for normal tissues are available, the actual penetration distances in pathologic tissues such as tumor nodules is largely unexplored. The ramifications of this distribution theory remain to be fully explored.

DRUG PENETRATION INTO TUMOR TISSUE

The ability of chemotherapeutic agents to penetrate into tumor depends on drug characteristics (concentration, time of exposure, hydrostatic pressure, diffusion coefficient) and tumor characteristics (geometry, surface, diffusivity). A study reported by Collins et al.[14] of 5-fluorouracil after intraperitoneal administration predicted that drug concentration would be 5 percent of that in intraperitoneal fluid at a depth of 600 μm from the peritoneal surface. For cisplatin, the cytotoxic concentration following intraperitoneal delivery was found only at a depth of 1 to 3 mm from the surface.[15,16] These data show that intraperitoneal therapy will be effective only in tumor nodules with a cross-sectional diameter of no more than several millimeters.

Once the drug penetrates into tumor tissue, its half-life depends on the uptake by capillary blood flow. Jain[17] has shown that a significant fraction of these tumor vessels have wide interendothelial junctions and discontinuous or no basal lamina. This suggests that the tumor vessels should have relatively high permeability and that cytotoxic drugs may move into and through tumor tissue faster than through normal cells. Besides the higher vascular permeability, an increased interstitial pressure in tumor has also been demonstrated. This may have severe consequences for tumor tissue exposure to cytostatic drug. Chemotherapeutic agents can be washed out of the tumor tissue rapidly via the vascular system. On the other hand, some cystadenocarcinoma tumors contain an extensive extracellular mucinous matrix. This may function as a simple nonmetabolic reservoir for chemotherapy and thus may increase drug effects. The mucin contains no capillaries or lymphatics to diffuse chemotherapy away from the malignant cells suspended in a gelatinous matrix.

FACTORS THAT MAY ALTER THE PERITONEAL-PLASMA BARRIER

The local-regional nature of drug distribution is modified by prolonged intraperitoneal treatment. Sugarbaker et al.[18] showed that the peritoneal clearance of 5-fluorouracil increased and blood levels rose more rapidly and to higher levels after previous 5-fluorouracil administration. The authors suggested that changes of an inflammatory nature in the peritoneal surface resulting from chemotherapy caused these problems.

Extensive removal of intraabdominal surfaces by peritonectomy procedures does not change the pharmacokinetics of intraperitoneal drug delivery.[19] The effectiveness of the peritoneal plasma barrier does not change significantly if drugs are instilled in the immediate postoperative period (Fig. 85-1). These data suggest that the peritoneal plasma barrier cannot be the mesothelial lining, as postulated in the past. Similarly, Rubin and colleagues[20] studied the effect of evisceration on peritoneal transport. Surprisingly, the peritoneal clearance of glucose, urea, and inulin were unaffected by omentectomy, mesenterectomy, or small bowel resection in dogs.

The physical nature of this peritoneal plasma barrier has not been clearly defined. Further pharmacologic studies need to be performed in order to achieve a better understanding of this interesting metabolic phenomenon. At present one suspects that a diffusion barrier that consists of subserosal tissues exists. The serosa itself participates little or not all in the diffusion process.

CHANGES IN ROUTE AND TIMING OF CHEMOTHERAPY FOR COLORECTAL CANCER

For the chemotherapeutic agents used to treat peritoneal carcinomatosis or peritoneal sarcomatosis, the AUC ratios of intraperitoneal (IP) to intravenous (IV) exposure are favorable. Table 85-1 presents the AUC IP/IV for the drugs commonly used intraperitoneally.[11,19] In our studies, these include 5-fluorouracil, mitomycin C, doxorubicin (Adriamycin), and cisplatin. One unique feature of regional chemotherapy stems from this change in the *route* of chemotherapy administration.

Sugarbaker and colleagues[19] have advanced a theory to explain the high incidence of peritoneal seeding in patients who undergo the surgical treatment of intraabdominal adenocarcinoma. This theory relates the high incidence of tumor implantation to (1) free intraperitoneal tumor emboli present at the time of surgery from serosal penetration by malignant cells, leakage from transected lymphatics, and from trauma to the cancer as a result of dissection; (2) fibrin entrapment of intraabdominal tumor emboli on traumatized peritoneal surfaces; and (3) tumor promotion of these entrapped cells through growth factors involved in the wound-healing process. In order to interrupt the widespread implantation of tumor cells on intraabdominal

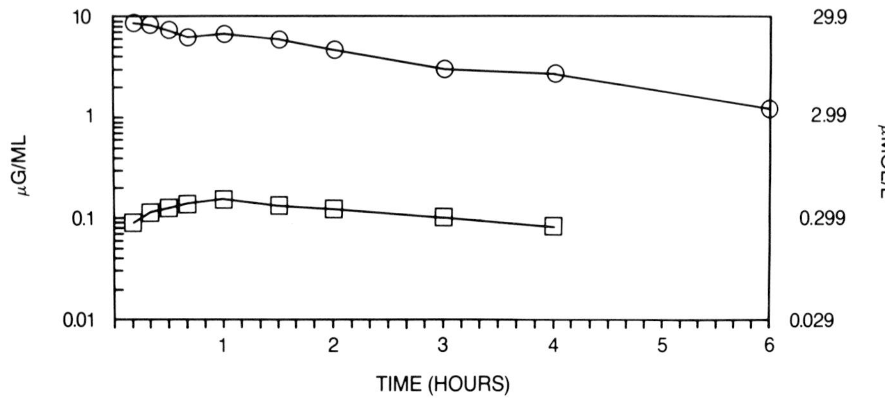

FIG. 85-1. When instilled into the peritoneal cavity, large-molecular-weight compounds are requested at that site for long periods of time. The physiologic barrier to the release of intraperitoneal drugs is called the peritoneal plasma barrier. In this experiment, 15 mg of mitomycin C was infused into the peritoneal cavity as rapidly as possible. Intraperitoneal (◯) and intravenous (□) mitomycin C concentrations were determined by high-pressure liquid chromatography (HPLC) assay.

Table 85-1
Area Under-Curve Ratios for Drugs Used to Treat Gastrointestinal Cancer

Drug	*Molecular weight*	*Area-under curve ratio*
5-Fluorouracil	130	250
Mitomycin C	334	750
Doxorubicin (Adriamycin)	544	500
Cisplatin	300	20

and pelvic surfaces, the abdomen is flooded with chemotherapeutic agents in the early postoperative period. Therefore, the strategy for treatment and prevention of peritoneal carcinomatosis and sarcomatosis involves not only a change in the *route* but also a change in the *timing* of the administration of chemotherapy.

This new approach to intraabdominal malignancy begins in the operating room, with proper placement of tubes and drains for the delivery of intraperitoneal chemotherapy. In the immediate postoperative period, an abdominal lavage removes tissue debris and blood products from the abdominal cavity, so that there is little or no accumulation of fibrin. Any tumor cells that remain behind within the thousands of crevices found in the abdominal cavity can be destroyed by pharmacologic concentrations of intraperitoneal chemotherapy.

The chemotherapy not only destroys tumor cells directly but also eliminates viable platelets, white blood cells, and monocytes from the peritoneal cavity. This diminishes the enhancement of tumor growth associated with the wound-healing process.[21]

PROGNOSTIC GROUPS OF PATIENTS WITH PERITONEAL CARCINOMATOSIS

Predictions of outcome for patients with peritoneal carcinomatosis have become available. Prognostic groups are based on (1) the grade of the malignant tumor, (2) the presence or absence of lymphatic or hematogenous metastases, and (3) the completeness of the surgical removal of cancer from the abdomen and pelvis.[22] Table 85-2 presents the prognostic groups for peritoneal carcinomatosis from colon or rectal cancer now being used clinically to predict outcome.

INDICATIONS

Currently a conservative list of indications exists for the use of intraperitoneal chemotherapy (Table 85-3). Cytoreductive surgery plus intraperitoneal chemotherapy should be considered for patients with malignant pseudomyxoma peritonei. These treatments have demonstrated benefits for grade I cystadenocarcinoma. Cancers of low malignant potential may arise from the colon or appendix and seed the abdominal or pelvic cavity extensively.

Higher-grade adenocarcinomas of colonic or appendiceal origin are selectively treated at this time with induction intraperitoneal chemotherapy followed by cytoreductive surgery. It should be noted that in patients with large-volume cancer, only palliative treatments for peritoneal carcinomatosis should be considered. In those patients with low-volume *peritoneal seeding*, intraperitoneal chemotherapy treatments are routinely employed. The treatments shown in Fig. 85-2 present the options currently in use. We estimate that approximately 10 percent of the total number of patients with colonic cancer and 70 percent of those with appendiceal cancer have peritoneal seeding documented at the time of resection of the primary cancer.

A major role for intraperitoneal chemotherapy is the prevention of subsequent peritoneal carcinomatosis or sarcomatosis. Virtually every patient who has a free intraabdominal *perforation* of colonic cancer through the malignancy itself develops peritoneal carcinomatosis. We recommend intraperitoneal chemotherapy in the early postoperative period for all patients with perforated gastrointestinal cancers.

Not infrequently, patients who are undergoing the resection of a large intraabdominal tumor will have a *tumor spill*. This is extremely common with advanced or recurrent rectal malignancy. With resections of ad-

Table 85-2
Prognostic Groups for Peritoneal Carcinomatosis and Sarcomatosis

Prognostic group	*Grade*	*Metastases*	*Completeness of cytoreduction*	*Number*	*Three-year survival, percent*
I	Grade I	None	Complete	60	96
II	Grade II or III	None	Complete	22	61
III	Any	Present	Complete	20	45
IV	Any	Any	Residual disease	50	22

Table 85-3
Current Indications for Early Postoperative Intraperitoneal Chemotherapy

1. Limited peritoneal seeding.
2. Tumor spill.
3. Perforated gastrointestinal cancer or cancers adherent to adjacent structures.
4. Stage II or greater ovarian cancer.
5. Large-volume grade I peritoneal carcinomatosis or sarcomatosis after definitive cytoreductive surgery.
6. Chemotherapy-resistant recurrent ovarian cancer after definitive cytoreductive surgery.

vanced primary or recurrent colonic cancer, it may occur almost routinely. If there is a tumor spill, then—in order to prevent subsequent development of peritoneal carcinomatosis—we recommend the use of intraperitoneal chemotherapy. Peritoneal seeding, perforation, and tumor spill are considered absolute indications for the use of early postoperative and adjuvant intraperitoneal chemotherapy.

In the current approach, there is a fundamental change in the selection criteria by which patients are treated with intraperitoneal chemotherapy. The treatment of bulk disease in the abdominal cavity is always to be avoided. Only patients with peritoneal surface cancer of very low volume should be treated with intraperitoneal chemotherapy. Small-volume disease widely scattered on peritoneal surfaces should be expected to respond and constitutes an indication for induction (preoperative) chemotherapy. If large-volume disease is present, a complete surgical cytoreduction must preceed the administration of intraperitoneal chemotherapy.[23]

EARLY POSTOPERATIVE INTRAPERITONEAL CHEMOTHERAPY FOR ADENOCARCINOMA

In order to keep the catheters for drug instillation and abdominal drainage clear of blood clots and tissue debris, an abdominal lavage is begun in the operating room. This requires tubes and drains to be positioned prior to closure of the abdomen. We have utilized large volumes of fluid rapidly infused and then drained from the abdomen after a short dwell time. The standardized orders for postoperative lavage are given in Table 85-4.

For early postoperative intraperitoneal chemotherapy following complete cytoreduction in patients with colonic or rectal adenocarcinoma and in those with appendiceal cancer, we have utilized mitomycin C and 5-fluorouracil. In patients who have neurologic toxicities from systemic cisplatin, no more of this drug should be used. These patients are also treated with mitomycin C and 5-fluorouracil. If patients have renal toxicity from systemic cisplatin, then intraperitoneal 5-fluorouracil alone should be used. The standardized orders for administration of intraperitoneal mitomycin C

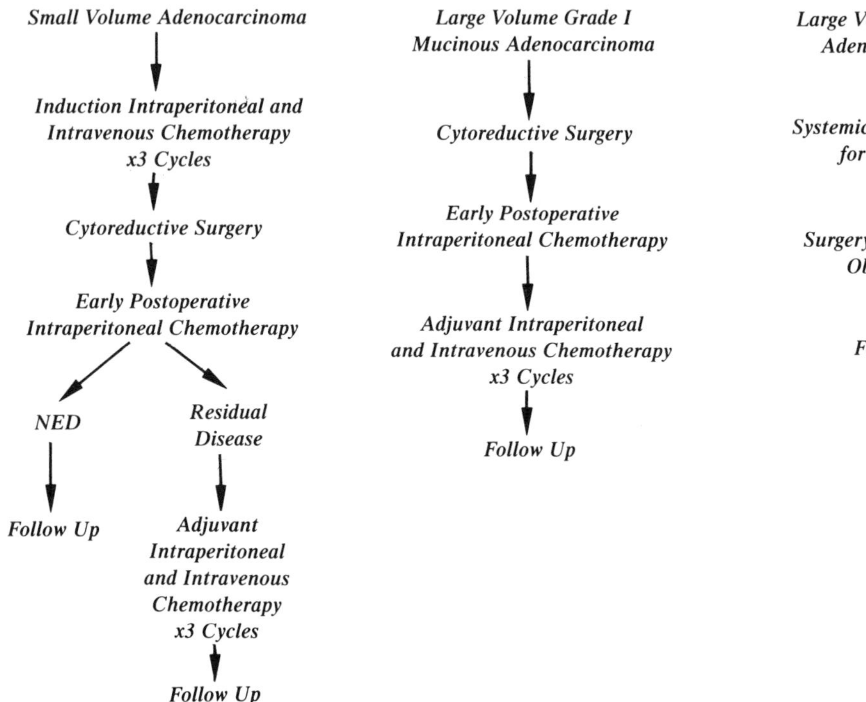

FIG. 85-2. Treatment options for patients with peritoneal carcinomatosis. (From Sugarbaker.[22] Reproduced by permission.)

Table 85-4
Immediate Postoperative Abdominal Lavage

Day of operation:

1. Run in 1000 mL 1.5% dextrose peritoneal dialysis solution as rapidly as possible. Warm to body temperature prior to instillation. Clamp all abdominal drains during infusion.
2. No dwell time.
3. Drain as rapidly as possible through Tenkhoff catheter and abdominal drains.
4. Repeat irrigations q 1 h for 4 h then q 8 h until returns are clear, then each shift until chemotherapy begins.
5. Change dressing at Tenkhoff catheter and abdominal drain skin exit sites using sterile technique once daily and prn.
6. Record intake and output of dialysis fluid by weight.

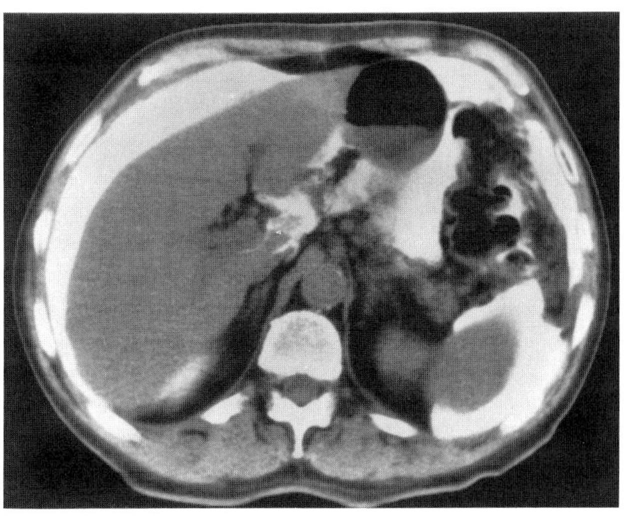

FIG. 85-3. Computed tomography scan of a patient who has received intraperitoneal contrast documents wide distribution of contrast material to peritoneal surfaces.

and 5-fluorouracil are shown in Table 85-5. All intra-abdominal catheters are withdrawn before the patient is discharged from the hospital.

ADJUVANT INTRAPERITONEAL CHEMOTHERAPY

The routine at this point for the delivery of intraperitoneal chemotherapy involves four cycles of treatment. One of these is an early postoperative intraperitoneal treatment. Other cycles follow on a monthly basis. Each cycle comprises 5 consecutive days of treatment.

Access to the peritoneal cavity can be achieved in one of two ways. An intraperitoneal catheter connected to a subcutaneous port is often used. This catheter is positioned surgically in the left upper quadrant, with its tip as close to the ligament of Treitz as possible. The jejunum is a portion of the small bowel that is in the most active peristalsis. Fewer catheter-related failures to infuse occur if the cannula is in the midabdomen and surrounded by loops of small bowel.

A majority of patients treated for peritoneal carcinomatosis have extensive peritoneal adhesions. To maximize distribution, chemotherapy is administered through a temporary catheter, which is placed under radiologic control by paracentesis (8.3 French All Purpose Drain Catheter, Medi-tech, Watertown, MA 02272). These patients have a catheter placed and the adequacy of chemotherapy distribution accessed radiologically for each cycle of treatment. Routinely, computed tomography (CT) with intraperitoneal contrast is employed (Fig. 85-3). The standardized orders for delivery of adjuvant intraperitoneal and intravenous chemotherapy are shown in Table 85-6.

Table 85-5
Early Postoperative Intraperitoneal Chemotherapy with Mitomycin C and 5-Fluorouracil

Postoperative Day 1

1. Add to 100 mL 1.5% dextrose peritoneal dialysis solution _____ mg mitomycin C (10 mg/m^2 × _____ m^2) (maximal dose 20 mg).
2. Drain all fluid from the abdominal cavity prior to instillation and then clamp abdominal drains.
3. Run into abdominal cavity as rapidly as possible the 1 L of chemotherapy solution. Dwell for 23 h with all abdominal drains clamped, then drain for 1 h.

Postoperative Days 2–5

4. Add to 1000 mL 1.5% dextrose peritoneal dialysis solution: (a) _____ mg 5-fluorouracil (15 mg/kg × _____ kg) (maximal dose 1500 mg) and (b) 50 meq sodium bicarbonate.
5. Drain all fluid from the abdominal cavity prior to instillation, then clamp abdominal drains.
6. Run into abdominal cavity as rapidly as possible the 1 L of chemotherapy solution. Dwell for 23 h and drain for 1 h prior to next instillation.
7. Continue to drain abdominal cavity after final 23-h dwell until Tenkhoff catheter is removed.
8. Use 25 percent dose reduction for age greater than 65 or prior radiotherapy.

Table 85-6
Adjuvant Intraperitoneal 5-Fluorouracil and Intravenous Mitomycin C Chemotherapy

Cycle # ____

1. CBC, platelets, profile A, and appropriate tumor marker prior to treatment; and CBC, platelets 10 days after initiation of treatment.
2. 5-Fluorouracil ____ mg (20 mg/kg) (maximum dose 1600 mg) and 50 meq sodium bicarbonate in 1000 mL 1.5% dextrose peritoneal dialysis solution via intraperitoneal catheter q day × 5 days. Last dose ________. Dwell for 23 h, drain for 1 h. Continue with next administration even if no drainage obtained.
3. On day 3 (date ________): 500 mL lactated Ringer's solution intravenously over 2 h prior to mitomycin C infusion.
   Mitomycin C ____ mg (10 mg/m^2 × ____ m^2) (maximum dose 20 mg) in 200 mL 5% dextrose and water intravenously over 2 h.
4. Follow routine procedure for peripheral extravasation of a vesicant if extravasation should occur.
5. Compazine 25 mg per rectum q 4 h prn for nausea.
   OUTPATIENT ONLY: May dose × 4 for use at home.
6. Percocet 1 tablet po q 3 h prn for pain.
   OUTPATIENT ONLY: May dose × 4 for use at home.
7. Routine vital signs.
8. Out of bed ad lib.
9. Diet: Regular as tolerated.
10. Daily dressing change to intraperitoneal catheter skin exit site.
11. Use 25 percent dose reduction for age greater than 65 or prior radiotherapy.

INDUCTION INTRAPERITONEAL AND SYSTEMIC CHEMOTHERAPY

The standardized regimens for induction intraperitoneal and systemic chemotherapy for either colorectal or appendiceal adenocarcinomas are shown in Table 85-6. It should be emphasized that intraperitoneal chemotherapy is given only to patients with low-volume disease which is not confluent in the abdomen. After the three cycles of combined intraperitoneal and systemic chemotherapy have been delivered, all treatments are discontinued for at least 3 months. When the patient has recovered full strength, a complete exploratory laparotomy with meticulous cytoreduction of all residual cancer is performed. A final cycle of early postoperative intraperitoneal chemotherapy is utilized (Table 85-5).

PERITONECTOMY PROCEDURES

Not all of these dissections will be required in all patients. The peritoneal surfaces are stripped of tumor only where there is visible disease. The goal of the surgical cytoreduction is to remove as much tumor as possible. The smaller the volume of cancer that remains for chemotherapy treatments, the better the results will be.

1. *Position and incision.* The patient is placed in a supine modified lithotomy position.
2. *Abdominal exposure, greater omentectomy, and splenectomy.* The abdomen is opened from xiphoid to pubis. The standard tool used to dissect tumor on peritoneal surfaces from the normal tissues is a ball-tipped electrosurgical apparatus. The ball-tipped instrument is placed at the interface of tumor and normal tissues. The focal point for further dissection is placed on strong traction. Electrosurgery is used on pure cut at high voltage. The 2-mm ball-tipped electrode is used for dissecting on visceral surfaces, including stomach, small bowel, and colon.

   Using ball-tip electrosurgery on pure cut creates a large volume of plume because of the carbonization and electroevaporation of tissue. In order to maintain visualization of the operative field and to preserve a smoke-free atmosphere in the operating theater, a smoke filtration unit is utilized.

   In order to free the midabdomen of a large volume of tumor, a complete greater omentectomy is performed. The greater omentum is elevated and then separated from the transverse colon using ball-tip electrosurgery. This dissection continues beneath the peritoneum that covers the transverse mesocolon so as to expose the anterior surface of the pancreas. The gastroepiploic vessels on the greater curvature are clamped, ligated, and divided. A splenectomy is performed at this time.
3. *Peritoneal stripping from beneath the left hemidiaphragm.* The left-upper-quadrant peritonectomy involves the stripping of all tissue from beneath the left hemidiaphragm so as to expose the diaphragmatic muscle, left adrenal gland, superior aspect of pancreas, and cephalad half of Gerota's fascia.
4. *Peritoneal stripping from beneath the right hemidiaphragm.* Peritoneum is stripped away from the right pos-

terior rectus sheath to begin the peritonectomy in the right upper quadrant of the abdomen.

The stripping of tumor from the muscular surface of the right diaphragm continues until the bare area of the liver is encountered. At this point, tumor on the anterior surface of the liver is electroevaporated until the liver surface is visualized. With both blunt and ball-tip electrosurgical dissection, one lifts tumor off the dome of the liver, moving through or beneath Glisson's capsule. Ball-tip electrosurgery is also utilized to extirpate tumor from in and around the falciform ligament, round ligament, and umbilical fissure of the liver.

Tumor from beneath the right hemidiaphragm, from the right subhepatic space, and from the surface of the liver forms an envelope as it is removed en bloc. The dissection is greatly simplified if the tumor specimen can be maintained intact. The dissection continues laterally on the right to encounter Gerota's fascia covering the right kidney. Also, the right adrenal gland is visualized as tumor is stripped out of Morrison's pouch (right subhepatic space). Care is taken not to traumatize the vena cava or to disrupt caudate lobe veins that pass between the vena cava and segment 1 of the liver.

5. *Lesser omentectomy and cholecystectomy.* The gallbladder is removed in a routine fashion. The plate of tissue that is superior to the structures that constitute the porta hepatis is usually heavily infiltrated by tumor. With the help of strong traction, the cancerous tissue that covers these structures is stripped from the base of the gallbladder bed toward the duodenum. The lesser omentum is resected.
6. *Pelvic peritonectomy.* To initiate the pelvic peritonectomy, the peritoneum is stripped from the posterior surface of the lower abdominal incision, exposing the rectus muscle. The muscular surface of the bladder is seen as ball-tip electrosurgery strips tumor bearing peritoneum and preperitoneal fat from this structure. The urachus must be divided and is often the leading point for this dissection. A rectosigmoid resection (and hysterectomy in women) is usually required.

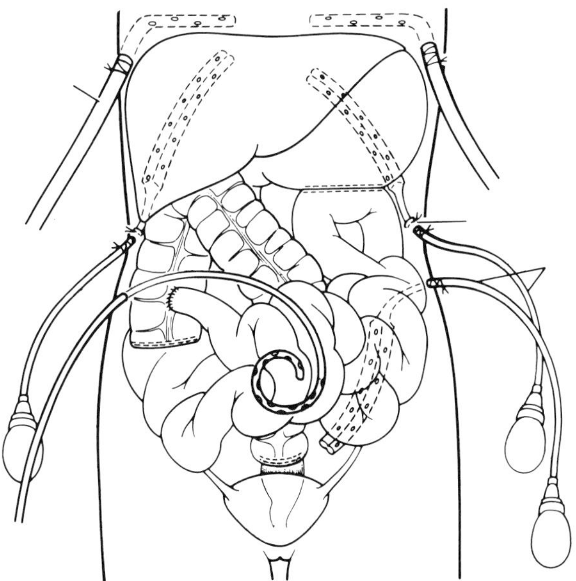

FIG. 85-4. Tubes and drains required for early postoperative intraperitoneal chemotherapy. (From Sugarbaker.[24] Reproduced by permission.)

Table 85-7
Prognostic Features of 155 Patients with Peritoneal Carcinomatosis from Colorectal and Appendiceal Cancer Treated by Cytoreductive Surgery and Intraperitoneal Chemotherapy

Prognostic feature	*Three-year survival, percent*	*p value*
Site		
Appendix	64	
Colon	33	.0001
Histology		
Grade I	85	
Other	29	.0001
Resection		
Complete	71	
Incomplete	20	.0001
Metastases		
Absent	63	
Present	19	.0001
Prior chemotherapy		
Some/None	59	
Heavy	32	.0005
Volume colon		
Moderate	62	
Large	18	.0033

TUBES AND DRAINS REQUIRED FOR EARLY POSTOPERATIVE INTRAPERITONEAL CHEMOTHERAPY (FIG. 85-4)

Closed suction drains are placed in the dependent portions of the abdomen. This includes the right subhepatic space, the left subdiaphragmatic space, and the pelvis. A catheter is placed through the abdominal wall and positioned within the loops of small bowel. All transabdominal drains and tubes are secured with a purse-string suture at the peritoneal level. Thoracostomy tubes are inserted on both the right and left in order to prevent fluid accumulation in the chest as a result of intraperitoneal chemotherapy.[24]

As soon as the abdomen in closed, irrigation of the abdomen with 1.5% dextrose dialysis solution is begun. Standardized orders for early postoperative intraperitoneal lavage and chemotherapy are instituted (Tables 85-4, 85-5, and 85-7).

RESULTS OF TREATMENT

The current disease-free survival of 155 patients with colorectal or appendiceal carcinomatosis is shown in

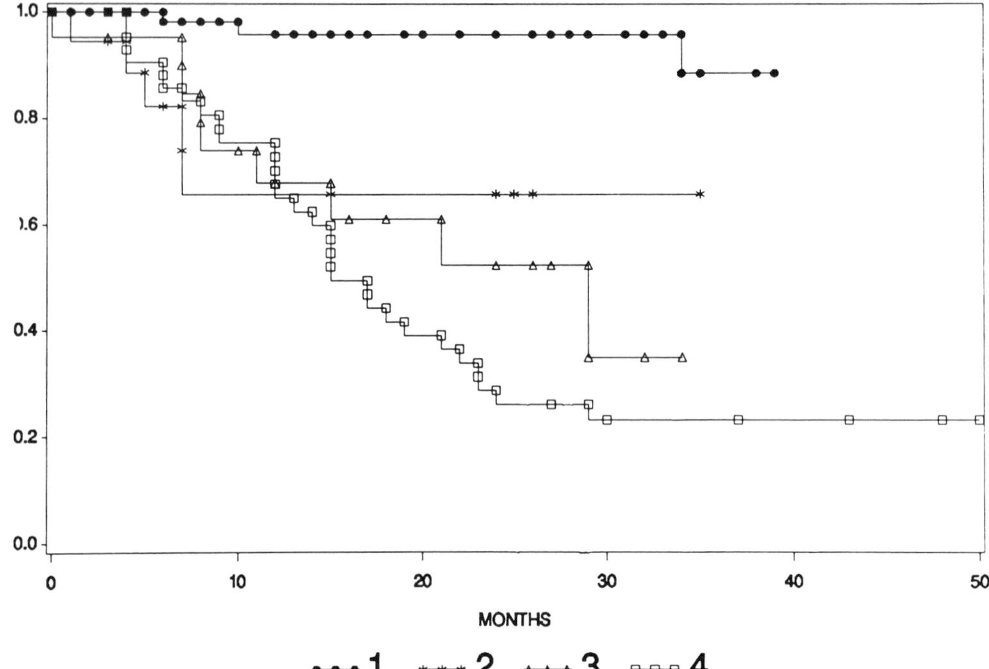

FIG. 85-5. Survival of patients with peritoneal carcinomatosis (minimum 2-year follow-up). Groups 1, 2, 3, and 4 correspond to the groups described in Table 85-2.

Fig. 85-5. This is a minimum 2-year follow-up. High-grade tumor, metastases, and incomplete cytoreduction are the major variables pointing to a poor prognosis (Table 85-7). These survival statistics were accumulated from 155 consecutive patients with peritoneal carcinomatosis of colorectal or appendiceal origin. There were 106 patients with an appendiceal primary cancer and 47 with a colorectal primary. Two had unknown primary cancer but a history and pathology compatible with appendiceal malignancy. The survival of patients with appendiceal cancer was significantly improved over that of patients with colonic cancer, with a p value < .001.

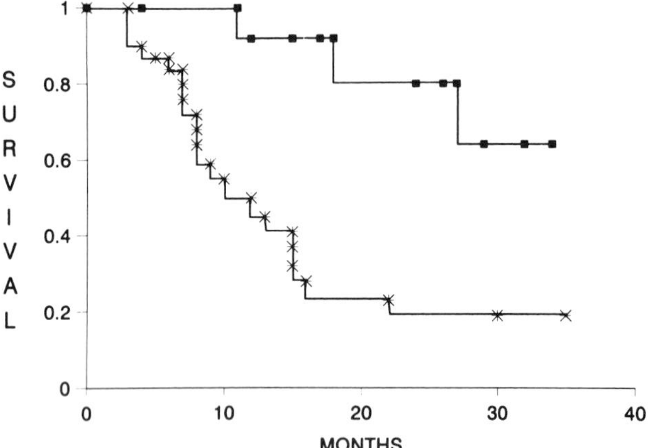

FIG. 85-6. Survival of low- and moderate- (■) versus large-volume (×) peritoneal carcinomatosis in patients with colonic cancer. Volume of cancer preoperatively was not a prognostic factor in appendiceal cancer patients.

The importance of tumor volume in selecting patients for treatment is illustrated in Fig. 85-6. It shows the survival of patients with colon cancer who had small- and moderate- versus large-volume peritoneal carcinomatosis. In this group of patients, volume of malignancy is an important prognostic variable. Patients with large-volume disease from colonic cancer are unlikely to benefit from extensive surgery plus intraperitoneal chemotherapy. Patients with small-volume disease are much better candidates for this treatment strategy. They also have minimal morbidity and mortality.

CONCLUSIONS

Changes in the use of chemotherapy in patients with intraabdominal cancer have been presented, along with early favorable results of treatment. A change in timing has occurred so that chemotherapy begins early postoperatively and is continued for the first 5 postoperative days. Also, a change in the route of drug administration has occurred. Chemotherapy is given intraperitoneally or by combined intraperitoneal and intravenous routes. Finally, there is a change in the tumor treated. Only minimal-volume intraperitoneal tumor is likely to respond. Induction chemotherapy is used for small-volume tumor seeding scattered throughout the abdominal cavity. Treatment of large-volume low-grade tumors following complete cytoreduction is also recommended. Treatment of a large volume of high-grade intraabdominal cancer is unlikely to produce long-term benefits.

REFERENCES

1. Jacquet P, Vidal-Jove J, Zhu BW, Sugarbaker PH: Peritoneal carcinomatosis from intraabdominal malignancy: Natural history and new prospects for management. *Acta Belg Chir* (in press).
2. Wu GG, Oreopoulos DG: Preservation of peritoneal clearance. *Int J Artif Organs* 10:67–71, 1987.
3. Lukas G, Brindle SD, Grengard P: The route of absorption of intraperitoneally administered compounds. *J Pharmacol Exp Ther* 178:562–566, 1971.
4. Torres IG, Litterest CL, Guarino AM: Transport of model compounds across the peritoneal membrane in the rat. *Pharmacology* 17:330–340, 1987.
5. Feldman GB, Knapp RI: Lymphatic drainage of the peritoneal cavity and its significance in ovarian cancer. *Am J Obstet Gynecol* 119:991–994, 1974.
6. Rosenshein N, Blake D, McIntyre P, et al: The effect of volume on the distribution of substances installed into the peritoneal cavity. *Gynecol Oncol* 6:106–110, 1978.
7. Myers CE, Collins JM: Pharmacology of intraperitoneal chemotherapy. *Cancer Invest* 1:395–407, 1983.
8. Howell S, Pleifle C, Wung WE, et al: Intraperitoneal cisplatin with systemic thiosulfate protection. *Ann Intern Med* 97:845–851, 1982.
9. Flessner MF, Dedrick RL, Schultz JS: Exchange of macromolecules between peritoneal cavity and plasma. *Am J Physiol* 248:H15–H25, 1985.
10. Dedrick RL: Theoretical and experimental bases of intraperitoneal chemotherapy. *Semin Oncol* 12:1–6, 1985.
11. Sugarbaker PH, Graves T, DeBruijn EA, et al: Early postoperative intraperitoneal chemotherapy as an adjuvant therapy to surgery for peritoneal carcinomatosis from gastrointestinal cancer: Pharmacological studies. *Cancer Res* 50:5790–5794, 1990.
12. Flessner MF, Dedrick RL, Schultz JS: A distributed model of peritoneal-plasma transport: Theoretical considerations. *Am J Physiol* 246:R597–R607, 1984.
13. Flessner MF, Dedrick RL, Schultz JS: A distributed model of peritoneal-plasma transport: Analysis of experimental data in the rat. *Am J Physiol* 248:F413–F424, 1985.
14. Collins JM, Dedrick RL, Flessner MF, Guarino AM: Concentration-dependent disappearance of fluorouracil from peritoneal fluid in the rat: Experimental observations and distributed modeling. *J Pharm Sci* 71:735–738, 1982.
15. McVie JG, Dikhoff TG, Van der Heide J: Tissue concentration of platinum after intraperitoneal cisplatinum administration in patients. *Proc Am Assoc Cancer Res* 26:162–167, 1982.
16. Los G: *Experimental Basis of Intraperitoneal Chemotherapy.* Amsterdam, Vrije Universiteit te Amsterdam, 1990.
17. Jain RK: Delivery of novel therapeutic agents in tumors: Physiological barriers and strategies. *J Natl Cancer Inst* 81:570–576, 1986.
18. Sugarbaker PH, Klecker BS, Gianola FJ, Speyer JL: Prolonged treatment schedules with intraperitoneal 5-fluorouracil diminish the local-regional nature of drug distribution. *Am J Clin Oncol* 9:1–7, 1986.
19. Sugarbaker PH, Cunliffe WJ, Belliveau J, et al: Rationale of integrating early postoperative intraperitoneal chemotherapy into the surgical treatment of gastrointestinal cancer. *Semin Oncol* 16:83–97, 1989.
20. Rubin J, Jones Q, Planch A, et al: The importance of the abdominal viscera to peritoneal transport during peritoneal dialysis in the dog. *Am J Med Sci* 292:203–208, 1986.
21. Eggermont AMM, Steller EP, Marquet RL, et al: Local promotion of tumor growth after abdominal surgery is dominant over immunotherapy with interleukin-2 and lymphokine activated killer cells. *Cancer Detect Prevent* 12:421–429, 1988.
22. Sugarbaker PH: Peritoneal carcinomatosis treated by cytoreductive surgery and intraperitoneal chemotherapy (submitted).
23. Sugarbaker PH, Steves MA: Treatment of peritoneal carcinomatosis from colon or appendiceal cancer with induction chemotherapy *Ref Cancer Treatment* (in press).
24. Sugarbaker PH: Peritonectomy procedures (submitted).

CHAPTER 86

Surgery for Pulmonary Metastases

Patricia McCormack

HIGHLIGHTS

Two to four percent of colorectal cancer patients will have isolated pulmonary metastases; they are the focus of this chapter. The outlook for untreated lung metastases is poor, with almost all patients dying within 2 years. Candidate selection is based on the number and location of metastases, the absence of disease other than pulmonary, an adequate pulmonary function reserve, and a good medical condition. Resection of pulmonary metastases results in 5-year survival ranging from 20 to 44 percent in recent series.

CONTROVERSIES

Careful selection of candidates who will benefit from this approach is crucial. Criteria have been established to help in the choice. They include disease limited to the lung in a patient whose primary tumor has been controlled or is deemed to be controllable when the primary tumor and the lung metastases present simultaneously; pulmonary function testing proving that lung capacity is sufficient for the needed resection; medical condition not precluding lung surgery; no better means of treatment currently available; computed tomography (CT) indicating that a complete resection of the lung tumor is predictable.

The role of chemotherapy remains controversial. Since there are no 5-year survivors among patients treated for stage IV carcinoma of the colon, the question as to the adjuvant role for chemotherapy arises. Should it be given preoperatively? And if there is a response, should it be continued postoperatively? How long should the preoperative treatment be continued? If there is no response to preoperative chemotherapy, should a different form of immuno- or chemotherapy be given postoperatively when the tumor burden is minimal? What role does the level of carcinoembryonic antigen (CEA) play in documenting the presence of recurrent tumor? Does it have any significance in predicting survival in a given case?

The presence of surgically resectable tumor in more than one site is being approached aggressively by several centers. In properly selected patients, this approach makes a difference in survival and should not be denied to a patient who understands and agrees to it.

FUTURE DIRECTIONS

Thoracoscopy as a method of resecting lung nodules has rapidly accelerated over the past 2 years. Caution must be exercised, however. Palpation of the entire lung parenchyma is a crucial element in the resection of metastases. Frequently, more lesions are felt and removed than are required on either the chest x-ray or CT scan. Often the tumors are seated deeply in lung tissue rather than on the surface. In these cases, a thoracoscopic wedge resection results in incomplete resection of all tumor. The use of intraoperative ultrasound is under investigation. This may help in tumor detection.

PATIENT SELECTION

Since by definition all patients needing resection of pulmonary metastases have stage IV disease, selection criteria are of considerable importance:

1. Disease must be limited to the lungs. At minimum, a CT scan of the abdomen and pelvis is needed to rule out intraabdominal masses, lymphadenopathy, and spread to the liver.[1] Colonoscopy will rule out anastomotic recurrence and intramural spread.[2] Magnetic resonance imaging (MRI) or sonography may also be utilized for further evaluation of suspicious findings on the CT scan.
2. For the patient being evaluated, no better treatment method is available. New chemotherapeutic drugs have been utilized over the years with mixed results.[3–15]
3. Primary tumor has been resected or is deemed resectable. When a primary colonic cancer and pulmonary metastasis present simultaneously, the same criteria are applied to each tumor site. If the primary colorectal tumor meets the criteria for resection and the lung lesion likewise, both are resected. The sequence of operations is determined by the presence of urgency for either site (e.g., bleeding or obstruction). If these elements are absent, the colon should be resected first. At laparotomy, a complete examination of the abdomen is better than any diagnostic study to detect spread.
4. Medical and pulmonary status are adequate. General cardiovascular medical clearance is indicated for the older patient or for any patient with symptoms. Pulmonary status is assessed by pulmonary function tests, including diffusion capacity and arterial blood gases. When results are borderline or if lobectomy or pneumonectomy are contemplated, a ventilation/perfusion lung scan should be added.

   Guidelines for safe metastasectomy include a residual FEV_1 of 1000 mL, a diffusion capacity of over 50 percent, and adequate P_{O_2} and P_{CO_2} postoperatively. Patients with borderline lung function will benefit from a brief preoperative period of intravenous bronchodilators and aggressive respiratory therapy to reduce postoperative complications.
5. The CT scan shows that complete resection of pulmonary metastases is possible. A CT scan with contrast gives clear anatomic details that will enable the surgeon to judge resectability with acceptable accuracy. Incomplete resection does not lead to survival advantage.

SURGICAL APPROACH

Guidelines governing lung resection for metastases are *complete resection and preservation of functional lung parenchyma*.

Wedge resections are usually performed, since most lesions are small and peripherally located. Tumors situated at the hilum of a lobe or lung require complete removal of the lobe or lung. There is no survival difference in type of resection performed so long as the resection is complete (Table 86-1).

In the early decades of lung surgery, the approach used was the standard posterolateral thoracotomy. In instances of bilateral lesions, two operations were staged, approximately 7 to 10 days apart, during one hospitalization. In 1983, Johnson[41] reported using a median sternotomy. When there were bilateral lesions, both lungs were approached through one incision. In cases of unilateral lesions, the opposite lung was explored, looking for lesions missed by the CT scan. This approach was excellent for lesions that were small, few in number, and located peripherally. Larger, centrally placed lesions or those located in the left lower lobe make an anterior-central approach difficult if all tumor is to be resected. A left lower lobectomy is difficult to achieve with safety through a sternotomy. When indicated, this incision is less painful and decreases the time of hospitalization. Most recently a transverse sternotomy with bilateral anterior thoracotomies, as used in bilateral lung transplantation, has been utilized. This accesses all parts of both lung adequately for any resections. Anesthesia is delivered

Table 86-1
Significance of Survival Indicators after Lung Resection

Authors	*No. of patients*	*Disease Free Interval*	*No. of lesions*	*No. of primary lesions*	*Stage of resection*
Cahan,[31] 1974	20	No	—	No	—
McCormack,[32] 1979	35	No	No	Yes	—
Wilking,[33] 1985	27	No	Yes	No	—
Mansel,[34] 1986	66	Yes	Yes	No	No
Brister,[35] 1988	27	Yes	No	No	No
Goya et al.,[18] 1989	62	No	Yes	No	No
Sauter et al.,[16] 1990	18	No	Yes	—	—
Scheele,[36] 1990	45	No	No	No	No
Mori,[37] 1991	35	No	No	No	No
McAfee et al.,[17] 1992	139	No	Yes	No	No
McCormack et al.,[21] 1993	144	No	No	No	No

via a double-lumen tube or using a bronchial blocker. The lung being operated upon is deflated.

SURGICAL TECHNIQUE

Sixty-six percent of metastases can be excised by wedge resection. When the tumor is located subpleurally, the deflated lung is grasped between lung clamps and the tumor removed by using a stapler applied 1 to 2 cm from the palpable edge of the tumor. When the nodule is growing in the center of a lobe, a core excision is carried out to spare normal lung tissue. This can be done with an electrocautery or using a YAG laser. Larger vessels encountered as the dissection progresses are clipped and cut. The edges of the pleura are reapproximated with sutures to prevent air leaks and bleeding. Anatomic segmentectomies, lobectomies, or even pneumonectomies are performed in routine fashion when indicated.

RESULTS

Operative morbidity reported from several series is 10 to 12 percent. Table 86-2 reviews reported results from the last 20 years. Mortality averages 1 percent and the majority report no mortality, making this a safe approach to achieve a good survival in patients with advanced disease.

Five-year survival rates in the 16 reported series varies from 13 to 44 percent. Two-thirds of these authors salvage one out of three patients; for three of the authors, nearly one-half of their patients reach the 5-year mark in survivorship. Indeed, this approach has been proven both safe and effective and deserves to be offered to every proper candidate.

Analysis of 144 patients in the Memorial[29] study found 50 with CEA levels. Results are shown in Table 86-3. More data regarding the relevance of CEA as a valid prognostic indicator are needed. However, an elevated CEA seems to indicate a poorer prognosis. This may be due to disease outside the lung that has remained undetected.

Table 86-2
5-Year Survival and Operative Mortality following Resection of Pulmonary Metastases

Authors	*No. of patients*	*Operative mortality, %*	*5-Year survival*
Cahan et al.,[31] 1974	31	0	30
Vincent et al.,[38] 1978	13	4	31
Wilkins et al.,[39] 1978	34	0	28
Mountain et al.,[40] 1978	28	—	28
McCormack et al.,[32] 1979	35	0	22
Brister et al.,[35] 1988	27	0	21
Goya et al.,[18] 1989	65	4	42
Sauter et al.,[16] 1990	18	4	47
Scheele et al.,[36] 1990	45	2	44
Mori et al.,[37] 1991	35	—	38
McAfee et al.,[17] 1992	139	1.4	30.5
McCormack et al.,[21] 1993	144	0	44

Table 86-3
Relevance of CEA versus Survival in 50 Patients

CEA[a] level	*No. of patients*	*Median survival, months*	*5-Year, %*	*10-Year, %*
0–5	29	35	50	38
6–10	5	34	50	38
11–982	16	17	15	0

[a]Carcinoembryonic antigen.

Resection of metastasis from a colorectal primary carcinoma is now the accepted form of therapy in properly selected patients. Experience has recently demonstrated that dual resection of liver and lung metastases leads to salvage of some patients. Whether these lesions present simultaneously or before or after resection of a metastatic lesion from either the liver or the lung, good results achieved by pursuing these metastases warrant a continuation of this approach.[16]

Of 135 patients reported from the Mayo Clinic, 20 underwent resection of localized extrapulmonary colorectal cancer.[17] Of these patients, 5 had anastomotic recurrence and underwent reresection. The other 15 were found to have a solitary metastasis. There were 7 in the liver, 5 in the brain, 2 in the pelvis, and 1 in the abdominal wall. All were resected and survival was the same as from resected lung metastasis: 30.5 percent at 5 years.

Synchronous or metachronous liver metastasis occurred in 14 of our 144 patients. Resection was done and yielded 32 percent 5-year survival (McCormack; unpublished data). The National Cancer Center Hospital in Tokyo reported 5 of 62 patients undergoing liver and lung resections. Of these, 3 died within 1 year and 2 survived 2 and 5 years respectively.[18]

The application of video-assisted thoracoscopic resection of lung metastases has been advocated.[19,20] This approach is appealing, since it utilizes multiple smaller incisions, leading to a decrease in postoperative discomfort. A cautionary note was raised, however, by McCormack,[21] who reported that a complete resection of all tumor is a prerequisite for a good survival outcome. Our existing imaging studies fail to detect all lesions. A manual examination of the lung is mandatory to detect and resect all tumor deposits.

The CT scan has replaced whole lung tomography for imaging the lung parenchyma.[22] Chest x-rays should be ordered as a part of the routine follow-up for

Table 86-4
Patterns of Failure after Lung Metastasectomy

Authors	*No. of patients*	*Lung only*	*Abdomen and liver*	*Liver only*	*Brain*	*Bone*	*Lung and general*
Mori,[37] 1991	21/35 (60%)	11	7	2	1	0	
Scheele et al.,[36] 1990	19/45 (42%)	15	2	2	0	0	7 + 2 liver
McAfee et al.,[17] 1992	101/139 (74.3%)	38	0	16	7	3	37

resected colorectal carcinoma patients. If a lesion is detected, a CT scan is performed. If it confirms the presence of lesion(s) in the lung, a complete extent-of-disease search is warranted, including colonoscopy and CT scan of abdomen and pelvis.

The reliability of the preoperative CT-scan diagnosis was analyzed in patients with pulmonary metastasis from osteosarcoma and colorectal cancer and was reported by Miura et al.[23] These results were compared with surgical findings and final pathology results. Of 111 surgically proven metastatic nodules, 76 were detected by the CT scan; 32 percent of the metastases were therefore missed. The CT scan was found to fail mostly in the subpleural or apical regions and in nodules of less than 2 to 3 mm in diameter. A similar study was carried out by Peuchot et al.[24] In 84 patients with previously treated malignancies, they examined 100 lungs, excluding 10 patients with radiologic evidence of bronchogenic carcinoma. Of a total 237 resected nodules, 173 (or 73 percent) had been seen on CT scan; 27 percent were not seen preoperatively; 87 percent were metastases, 9 percent were benign; and 4 percent were primary lung cancers. Only 54 percent of the solitary nodules detected by chest x-ray were indeed solitary, yet 80 percent of the solitary nodules detected by CT scan proved to be solitary.

The rate of failure following pulmonary metastasectomy varies from 42 to 78 percent in the four authors who detailed their findings (Table 86-4). Sites varied from the central nervous system and spine only to lung only or liver only. Close surveillance increased the diagnostic accuracy.

When recurrence is limited to the lung alone or liver alone, several authors advocate that a second metastasectomy should be considered. Survival in these patients was found to be identical to that following the first resection.[25–30] Criteria for selecting patients for repeat thoracotomy are the same each time.

REFERENCES

1. Kemeny NM, Sugarbaker PH, Smith TJ, et al: A prospective analysis of laboratory tests and imaging studies to detect hepatic lesions. *Ann Surg* 195:163–167, 1982.
2. Keynes WM: Implantation from bowel lumen in cancer of the large intestine. *Ann Surg* 153:357–364, 1961.
3. Dwight RW, Humphrey EW, Higgins GA, et al: FUDR as an adjuvant to surgery in cancer of the large bowel. *J Surg Oncol* 5:243–249, 1973.
4. Higgins GA, Amadeo JH, McElhinney J, et al: Efficacy of prolonged intermittent therapy with combined 5-fluorouracil and me-CCNU following resection for carcinomas of the large bowel. *Cancer* 53:1–8, 1984.
5. Kligerman MM, Urdaneta N, Knowlton A, et al: Preoperative irradiation of rectosigmoid carcinoma including its regional lymph nodes. *Am J Roentgenol Radium Ther Nucl Med* 114:498–503, 1972.
6. Sischy B: The place of radiotherapy in the management of rectal adenocarcinoma. *Cancer* 50:2631–2637, 1982
7. Kemeny N, Yagoda A, Braun D Jr, et al: Randomized study of 2 different schedules of methyl CCNU, 5-FU, and vincristine for metastatic colorectal carcinoma. *Cancer* 43:78–82, 1979.
8. Kemeny N, Yagoda A, Braun J: Metastatic colorectal carcinoma: A prospective trial of methyl CCNU, 5-fluorouracil (5FU) and vincristine (MOF) versus MOF plus streptozotocin (MOF-Strep). *Cancer* 51:20–25, 1983.
9. Higgins GA, Donaldson R, Rogers L, et al: Efficacy of MER immunotherapy when added to a regimen of 5-fluorouracil and methyl-CCNU following resection for carcinoma of large bowel. *Cancer* 54:193–198, 1984.
10. Duncan W: Adjuvant radiotherapy in rectal cancer: The MRC trials. *Br J Surg* 72:S59–S62, 1985.
11. Hilaris BS, Nori D, Anderson LL: *Atlas of Brachytherapy.* New York, Macmillan, 1988.
12. Kemeny N, Golbey R: A chemotherapeutic approach to colorectal carcinoma, in Stearn MR Jr (ed): *Neoplasm of the Colon, Rectum, and Anus.* New York, Wiley, 1980, pp 155–168.
13. Gastrointestinal Tumor Study Group: Adjuvant therapy of colon cancer: Results of a prospectively randomized trial. *N Engl J Med* 310:737–743, 1984.
14. Duncan W, Arnott SJ, Jack WJL, et al: Results of two randomized trials of neutron therapy in rectal adenocarcinoma. *Radiother Oncol* 8:191–198, 1987.
15. Kemeny N, Israel K, Niedzwiecki D, et al: Randomized study of continuous infusion fluorouracil versus fluorouracil plus cis-platin in patients with metastatic colorectal cancer. *J Clin Oncol* 8:313–318, 1990.
16. Sauter ER, Bolton JS, Willis GQ, et al: Improved survival after pulmonary resection of metastatic colorectal carcinoma. *J Surg Oncol* 23:135,1990.
17. McAfee MK, Allen MS, Trastik VF, et al: Colorectal lung metastases: Results of surgical excision. *Ann Thorac Surg* 53:780, 1992.
18. Goya T, Miyazawa N, Kondo H, et al: Surgical resection of

pulmonary metastases from colorectal cancer. *Cancer* 64: 1418, 1989.

19. Dowling RD, Wachs ME, Ferson PF, et al: Thoracoscopic meodymium: YAG laser resection of a pulmonary metastasis. *Cancer* 70:1873, 1992.
20. Dowling RD, Ferson PF, Landreneau RJ: Thoracoscopic resection of pulmonary metastases. *Chest* 102:1450, 1992.
21. McCormack PM, Ginsberg KB, Bains MS, et al: Accuracy of chest x-ray and CT scan in lung metastases and the implication for the role of thoracoscopy. *Ann Thorac Surg* 56:863–866, 1993.
22. Pass HI, Dwyer A, Maruch R, et al: Detection of pulmonary metastases in patients with osteogenic and soft tissue sarcoma: The superiority of CT scans compared with conventional linear tomograms using dynamic analysis. *J Clin Oncol* 3:1261, 1985.
23. Miura K, Mori K, Equchi K, et al: The usefulness of CT in the pre-operative diagnosis of metastatic lung nodules—A study with resected cases. *Gan No Rinsho Japan J Cancer Clin* 32:41, 1986.
24. Peuchot M, Libshitz HI: Pulmonary metastatic disease: Radiologic surgical correlation. *Radiology* 164:719–722, 1987.
25. Weiss L, Ward PM, Holmes JC: Liver-to-lung traffic of cancer cells. *Int J Cancer* 32:79–83, 1983.
26. Murphy P, Alexander P, Kerkham N, et al: Pattern of spread of bloodborne tumour. *Br J Surg* 73:829, 1986.
27. Viadana E, Bross IDJ, Pickren JW: Cascade spread of bloodborne metastases in solid and non-solid cancers of humans, in Weiss L, Gilbert HA (eds): *Pulmonary Metastasis*. Boston, Hall, 1978, p 142.
28. Nelson WR, Brown RK, Baer S: The repeated surgical attack on solitary metastatic neoplasms. *Ann Surg* 146:790, 1967.
29. McCormack PM, Burt ME, Bains MNS, et al: Lung resection for colorectal metastases: 10-year results. *Arch Surg* 127: 1403, 1992.
30. August DA, Ottow RT, Sugarbaker PA: Clinical perspective of human colorectal cancer metastases. *Cancer Metast Rev* 3:303, 1984.
31. Cahan W, Castro EI, Hajdu S: The significance of a solitary lung shadow in patients with colon carcinoma. *Cancer* 33:414–421, 1974.
32. McCormack PM, Attiyeh FF: Resected pulmonary metastases from colorectal cancer. *Dis Colon Rectum* 22:553–556, 1979.
33. Wilking N, Petrelli NJ, Herrera L, et al: Surgical resection of pulmonary metastases from colorectal adenocarcinoma. *Dis Colon Rectum* 28:562, 1985.
34. Mansel JK, Zinmeister AR, Pairolero PC, et al: Pulmonary resection of metastatic colorectal adenocarcinoma, a 10-year experience. *Chest* 89:109–112, 1986.
35. Brister SJ, de Varennes B, Gordon PH, et al: Contemporary management of pulmonary metastases of colorectal origin. *Dis Colon Rectum* 31:786, 1988.
36. Scheele J, Altendorf-Hofmann A, Stangl R: Pulmonary resection for metastatic colon and upper rectum—is it useful? *Dis Colon Rectum* 33:745–752, 1990.
37. Mori M, Tomoda H, Ishida T, et al: Surgical resection of pulmonary metastases from colorectal adenocarcinoma: Special reference to repeated pulmonary resections. *Arch Surg* 126: 1297–1302, 1991.
38. Vincent RG, Chaski LB, et al: Surgical resection of the solitary pulmonary metastasis, in Weiss L, Gilbert HA (eds): *Pulmonary Metastases*. Boston, Hall, 1978, pp 232–242.
39. Wilkins EW, Jr: The status of pulmonary resection of metastases: Experience at MGH, in Weiss L, Gilbert HA (eds): *Pulmonary Metastases*. Boston, Hall, 1978, pp 271–281.
40. Mountain CF, Ckoli KG, Hermes KE, et al: The contribution of surgery to the management of carcinomatous pulmonary metastases. *Cancer* 42: 83–840, 1978.
41. Johnson MR: Median sternotomy for resection of pulmonary metastases. *J Thor Cardiovasc Surg* 85:516–522, 1983.

. . . END OF CHAPTER . . .

CHAPTER 87

Surgery for Pelvic Recurrences

Nathan W. Pearlman

HIGHLIGHTS

Pelvic recurrence of rectal cancer historically occurs in 14 to 30 percent of patients and is a major cause of overall treatment failure. Management of this problem is difficult. The salvage rate with standard surgery is only 5 to 14 percent. Most patients are considered inoperable and treated with irradiation, colostomy, and/or urinary diversion. Palliation is often less than complete and of short duration; survival averages 12 to 16 months. Thus there is a need for new approaches.

CONTROVERSIES

Recurrence is often attributed to implantation of exfoliated cells at the suture line or inadequate distal resection margins, but a more likely cause is lateral spread of cancer in the mesorectum. The incidence of pelvic recurrence may be as low as 2.6 percent after "total" excision of the mesorectum; however, not all investigators have been equally successful with this approach, and it is unclear whether radical excision of the mesorectum will, in fact, prevent most recurrences.

FUTURE DIRECTIONS

One new approach combines standard external beam irradiation with debulking surgery (anterior or abdominoperineal resection) and intraoperative radiation therapy (IORT). Eligible patients cannot have been irradiated previously, and local control is variable (37 to 83 percent); but treatment-related mortality is nil and the salvage rate may be 27 to 28 percent.

A second approach is extended resection (abdominal sacral resection, sacropelvic exenteration) using dissection planes outside the sacrum and pelvic side wall. This type of surgery can be used after prior irradiation, and the salvage rate is similar to that of IORT (24 to 38 percent). Operative mortality is 5 to 9 percent, however, and the local recurrence rate is 33 to 36 percent. Because of these mixed results, the eventual role of IORT and extended resection remains to be determined.

Pelvic recurrence of rectal cancer historically occurs in 14 to 30 percent of patients undergoing curative resection and is a major source of treatment failure (Table 87-1). The incidence of recurrence is greater in stage B or C disease than in stage A cancer, but it tends to be about the same for both anterior and abdominoperineal resection (Table 87-2). Taking into account differences in patient mix from institution to institution and different reporting methods (some authors report all pelvic relapses, others only those without distant metastases), the frequency of this problem seems relatively unchanged over the past two decades, and recurrence in up to 25 percent of patients might appear the norm. Heald and Ryall,[1] however, reported a local relapse rate of only 2.6 percent after "total mesorectal excision." We have used a similar approach for the past decade and added postoperative irradiation for stage B_2 or stage C disease; at present, we

Table 87-1
Incidence of Local Recurrence Alone, with Distant Metastases, and as a Percentage of All Treatment Failures

Authors	*LR alone, %*	*LR + DM, %*	*Total LR, %*	*LR as percentage of all treatment failures*
Olson et al.,[30] 1980	15	4	19	52
Chung et al.,[54] 1983	14	12	26	81
Rich et al.,[55] 1983	17	13	30	65
Pilipshen et al.,[31] 1984	13	12	25	57
McDermott et al.,[32] 1985	11	9	20	53
Williams et al.,[52] 1985	16	14	30	53
Heimann et al.,[56] 1986	8	9	17	
Neville et al.,[70] 1987		19		49
Colombo et al.,[57] 1987	9			45

Abbreviations: LR, local recurrence; DM, distant metastases.

have a 5 percent incidence of local failure (unpublished data). Steele et al.[2] recently reported no local recurrences in a small series of patients with T_2 or T_3 (American Joint Committee on Cancer classification) tumors when local excision or coloanal resection was combined with postoperative irradiation. All of this suggests recurrence is primarily a technical rather than a biological problem and is preventable in most patients. This is far from a universally held view, however.

The causes of recurrence have been debated for years, often without resolution. One reason for this is that treatment failure can be defined in several ways: relapse at the suture line, recurrence in the resection bed, or tumor anywhere in the pelvis. In addition, recurrence of a stage A or stage B_1 tumor may be due to causes other than recurrence of stage B_2 or stage C disease, but it is often grouped with the latter. Defining cause is important, however, for it will help determine the best course of treatment for a given patient. For that reason, the different types of recurrence will be considered separately in the following discussion.

Table 87-2
Local Recurrence by Stage and Procedure

Authors	*By stage, %* A	B	C	*By procedure, %* LAR	APR
Chung et al.,[54] 1983	0	12	23		
Pheils et al.,[58] 1983	0	8	15	14	5
Rich et al.,[55] 1983	5	19	27		
McDermott et al.,[32] 1985				19	23
Williams et al.,[52] 1985				14	19
Heimann et al.,[56] 1986	0	14	24	16	17
Colombo et al.,[57] 1987	0	9	15	10	14
Terranova et al.,[33] 1988	0	8	15	14	5

Abbreviations: LAR, low anterior resection; APR, abdominoperineal resection.

RECURRENCE AFTER LOCAL THERAPY

Criteria for local excision of rectal cancer are generally as follows: (1) a mobile tumor; (2) size less than 3 to 4 cm or involvement of less than half of the bowel lumen; and (3) low- to intermediate-grade malignancy.[3–5] Similar criteria are used for curative irradiation or electrofulguration,[6–11] and in 80 to 90 percent of cases, for select patients with stage A or stage B_1 disease.[12,13] It is estimated that less than 10 percent of rectal cancers satisfy these criteria.[3,6,14] While the relapse rate after local therapy may be as high as 27 to 31 percent,[5,10] this still represents a small number of patients to analyze for potential causes and/or treatment outcomes. Biggers et al.[5] reported that 73 percent of patients who had recurrences after local excision still had a stage A or stage B tumor. In studies by De Graaf and associates[7] and Papillon,[6] about 50 percent of the relapses after electrofulguration or curative irradiation were local and 50 percent in regional nodes. Such differences aside, these findings suggest that most recurrences after local therapy will be due to persistent lo-

Table 87-3
Surgical Salvage after Failure of Local Excision

Authors	*No. of patients*	*No. salvaged*
Willett et al.,[59] 1989	7	1 (14%)
Killingback,[60] 1985	9	2 (22%)
Whiteway et al.,[3] 1985	4	1 (25%)
Stearns et al.,[a,14] 1984	8	5 (62%)
Hager et al.,[4] 1983	6	4 (67%)

[a]Repeat local excision in three patients.

Table 87-4
Surgical Failure after Electrofulguration or Primary Irradiation

Authors	*Prior therapy*	*No. of patients*	*No. salvaged*
Wanebo and Quan,[61] 1974	EF	14	3 (21%)
Salvati et al.,[10] 1988	EF	31	9 (29%)
DeGraaf et al.,[7] 1985	EF	12	4 (33%)
Papillon,[6] 1984	XRT	25	6 (24%)
Cummings et al.,[62] 1983	XRT	17	5 (29%)
Sischy et al.,[11] 1988	XRT	9	5 (55%)

Abbreviations: EF, electrofulguration; XRT, radiation therapy.

cal regional disease and, as such, eminently curable with a standard salvage procedure, such as abdominoperineal resection. As seen in Tables 87-3 and 87-4, this is rarely the case. Salvage rates range from 14 to 67 percent after such surgery, with most at the low end of the spectrum. The reasons for this are unclear. Perhaps the observations of Biggers et al.,[5] De Graaf et al.,[7] and Papillon[6] were isolated and recurrence in most patients is more extensive than they suggest. Alternatively, standard surgery may be insufficiently radical for this type of recurrence, regardless of its presumed local extent. Whatever the reasons, the results of current approaches to failure of local therapy leave much to be desired.

RECURRENCE AFTER ANTERIOR RESECTION

Pelvic relapse after anterior resection is often discussed as if it were two distinct problems: recurrence at the suture line versus that elsewhere in the pelvis. In the past, suture-line relapse was often attributed to needle implantation of exfoliated cells.[15–18] Rosenberg,[19] however, found no evidence that exfoliated colonic cancer cells were viable in humans or would grow at a suture line in experimental animals. He also noted that essentially all of Goligher's[15] suture-line recurrences were due to extramural disease left behind during palliative resection. Because of this, the degree to which implantation contributes to suture-line relapse remains open to question.

Another explanation for this problem is residual distal intramural disease left behind by inadequate distal resection margins. This concept seems to have arisen in 1954 with Grinnell,[21] who found distal spread of cancer in 9 (12 percent) of 76 patients and concluded that distal margins should be at least 5 cm wide to encompass such disease. Only 3 (4 percent) of these patients had as much as 4 cm of distal spread, however; in the other 6 (8 percent), the extent of spread was just 1 to 1.5 cm. In studies other than Grinnell's,[15,22–25] distal spread of more than 1.5 cm was seen in less than 3 percent of patients with curable disease, and recurrence rates were the same whether distal margins were greater or less than 3 cm. Thus, inadequate distal margins seem an unlikely cause of many anastomostic recurrences.

A more intriguing possibility is mucosal field change. In 1969, Felipe[26] noted that mucosa near an established colorectal cancer had an abnormally high content of sialomucins. Subsequent work by others[20,27] suggested this "transitional" mucosal was premalignant. Roe and associates[28] also found in experimental animals that mucosa near a colonic anastomosis was more susceptible to carcinogenesis than mucosa elsewhere in the bowel. Suture-line recurrence may, therefore, be nothing more than a variant of metachronous disease, but more work is needed before it is clear that this is indeed the case.

Given the attention it has received, one might expect recurrence at the suture line to be a major problem. However, it represents only 4 to 20 percent of all pelvic failures after anterior resection.[30–33] In addition, if the causes of such recurrence were primarily intramural, as suggested by the foregoing discussion, one would expect a high rate of cure when abdominoperineal resection was used for salvage. In fact, only 5 to 14 percent of patients are cured by such surgery.[13,31,34,35] It is difficult to conclude from this that suture-line recurrence is a unique form of relapse. Instead, it would appear to be just part of the overall problem and, in most patients, due to the same causes as those which account for most recurrence.

The traditional view of rectal cancer assumes that lymphatic spread is almost exclusively upward—first to perirectal nodes, then to those higher in the superior hemorrhoidal chain—and these are the nodes, removed by most standard resections. Studies by Hoju et al,[35] Keighley and Hall,[36] and Durdey's group[37] show, however, that 20 to 38 percent of midrectal tumors also spread laterally—either to lymphatics at the periphery of the mesorectum or to nodes at the pelvic side wall. In the latter two studies, 50 to 75 percent of patients with lateral spread had local recurrences. Heald and Ryall[1] contend that incomplete removal of the mesorectum is the main cause of pelvic recurrence and suggest that the reason for incomplete removal is the tendency of most resections to "cone in" toward the rectal wall in the mid- and lower pelvis. Their results with "total" removal of the mesorectum (presumably from pelvic side wall to pelvic side wall and down to the pelvic floor) support this view. It is also supported by Penfold's[38] observation that middle hemorrhoidal nodes were never seen in the 546 specimens from St. Mark's Hospital that he reviewed. Since 1980, we have evaluated 24 patients for recurrence after an anterior resection. Only 1 (4.3 percent) had cancer confined to the suture line and just 2 (8.7 percent) had

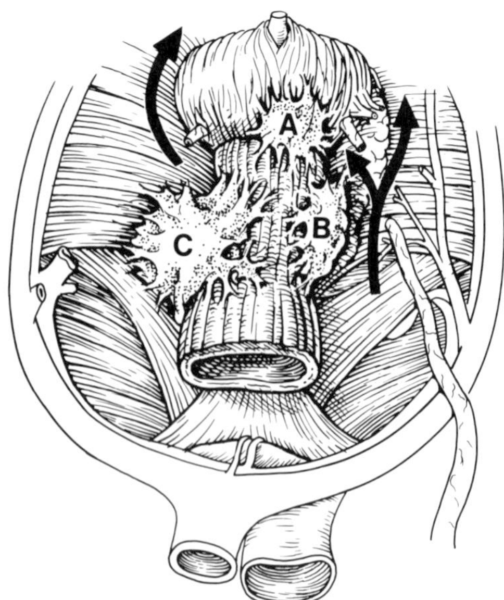

FIG. 87-1. Lateral dissection planes for abdominoperineal resection and standard pelvic exenteration (*arrows*) encompass central (A) or intramural recurrence with limited lateral spread (B) but not tumor fixed to the pelvic side wall (C).

disease which could be encompassed by an abdominoperineal resection. Relapse in the others primarily involved the prostate (5), pelvic side wall (4), or presacral tissues (13).

All of this suggests that recurrence is due to lateral, not cephalad, spread of disease. It also suggests that aggressive removal of the mesorectum might go far toward reducing the extent of this problem. On the other hand, Glass et al.[39] carried out resections that were seemingly as extensive as Heald and Ryall's and had a local relapse rate of 13.6 percent, which was no different than their results with conventional resection. Thus this issue is far from resolved.

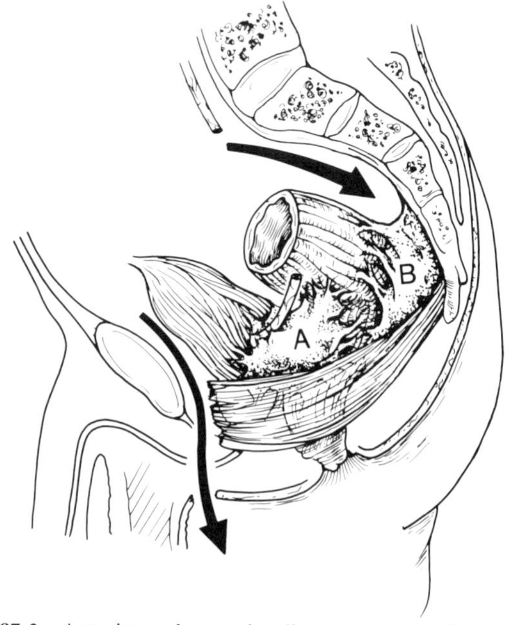

FIG. 87-2. Anterior and posterior dissection planes for standard exenteration (*arrows*). Once again, central disease (A) is encompassed but not tumor fixed to the sacrum (B).

The fact that most recurrence after anterior resection originates outside the bowel perhaps explains why only 5 to 14 percent of patients are salvaged by an abdominoperineal resection or standard pelvic exenteration.[13,31,34,35] These procedures come at the problem from above and are confined by the sacrum posteriorly and by the coccygeus and proximal levator muscles laterally. Because of this, they inevitably cut through tumor which is fixed to these structures (Figs. 87-1 and 87-2). As noted above, such fixation is present in upward of 75 percent of cases. For that reason, standard resection would seem best limited to patients with just central or intramural recurrence.

RECURRENCE AFTER ABDOMINOPERINEAL RESECTION

In contrast to anterior resection, there is little doubt that recurrence after abdominoperineal resection arises from residual extramural disease. It is usually fixed to the prostate, pelvic side walls, and/or sacrum. Since this type of disease does not lend itself to standard resection, most of these patients are considered inoperable and treated, if at all, with irradiation and/or urinary diversion. Although 50 to 85 percent will obtain some palliation with such measures, the duration of relief tends to be 6 months or less and survival averages 9 to 20 months (Table 87-3). In a few instances, the tumor may seem more limited and confined to the perineum. Local excision of such disease yields a median survival of just 12 months, however, and no long-term survivors.[40] Thus, recurrence after abdominoperineal resection, like much of that which follows anterior resection, is a problem of the whole pelvis. This should be kept in mind in considering salvage surgery.

PRIOR PELVIC IRRADIATION

Pre- or postoperative irradiation has become relatively standard for most stage B_2 or stage C tumors. Since these are the most likely to recur, one can assume that most patients with local regional relapse will be radiation failures when seen. If this is not the case, one might consider treatment with external beam therapy, standard surgery, and intraoperative irradiation (IORT). Local control is variable (37 to 83 percent) but treatment-related mortality is nil and upwards of 27 to 28 percent of these patients may be salvaged by such an approach.[42,42]

Most patients will not be candidates for IORT because of prior irradiation. This will add to the risks of subsequent operation and require appropriate measures to minimize risk, but it has not, in our experience, been a contraindication to surgery. One must ensure that the blood supply to any anastomosis is more than adequate and that exposed blood vessels and bone are covered by tissue with its own blood supply. In addition, any potential dead space must be obliterated. If these steps are taken, even heavily irradiated patients can undergo resection with acceptable morbidity and mortality.

EXENTERATIVE SURGERY

As noted earlier, standard approaches to recurrent rectal cancer tend to fail because they come at it from inside the pelvis. In 1981, Wanebo and Marcove[43] described an approach to this problem from outside the pelvis, using dissection planes normally employed for sacral resection. They termed the procedure *abdominal sacral resection,* and their initial report contained 7 patients who had undergone it for cure and 4 who had resections for palliation. Although operative mortality was 9 percent, there was a suggestion that 2-year survival would be 24 percent. The latter figure was supported by subsequent reports from Sugarbaker[44] and Takagi et al.[45] Wanebo et al.[46,47] have periodically updated their experience and have changed the name of the operation to *composite pelvic resection.* Their series now consists of 47 patients with posterior recurrence, 41 of whom were operated on for cure. Operative mortality is about the same (8.5 percent), local recurrence is 33 percent, and actuarial survival remains about 24 percent, this time at 5 years. This is perhaps less than what might be hoped for from such a radical undertaking but still an improvement over standard procedures.

We began using the transsacral approach to fixed rectal cancer (both primary and recurrent) in 1980. We termed the operation *sacropelvic exenteration* to distinguish it from the *abdominosacral resection* of Localio et al.,[48] and we have stayed with this term. Initially, only patients with potentially curable (i.e., intrapelvic) disease were treated. With increasing experience, however, operative mortality dropped and we began to use the procedure for palliation in those with extrapelvic cancer as well. During this time, an attempt was made to tailor the type of resection used to the extent of disease present in hopes of minimizing morbidity. Sacropelvic exenteration was employed for posterior and posterolateral recurrence, but standard exenterations were used when the tumor was centrally located. In addition, a procedure called *extended proctectomy* was undertaken in a few patients who had isolated unilateral recurrence after anterior resection. This consisted of an en bloc resection of the rectum, involving portions of bladder, one distal ureter, and an ipsilateral hypogastric artery, vein, and levator muscle. The transected ureter was reimplanted into a reconstructed bladder.[49]

To date, we have treated 41 patients with recurrent disease, 25 for cure and 16 for palliation. Patient characteristics are shown in Table 87-5, with extent of disease, operations performed, and perioperative outcome portrayed in Table 87-6. Operative mortality was 5 percent (2 patients), and both deaths occurred early in the series (patients 3 and 7). Operative morbidity was initially 44 percent, but it has since become 18 percent with the introduction of continent ileocolonic urinary reservoirs to fill the empty pelvis.[50] Actuarial survival, as shown in Fig. 87-3, is presently 38 percent for patients undergoing curative resection. For comparison purposes, the survival of 13 additional patients who underwent a sacropelvic exenteration for primary postirradiation fixed rectal cancer is also shown. The curve is similar to that of curative resection for recurrent disease, suggesting that the problem is not whether the tumor is primary or recurrent but whether the operation adequately encompasses points of fixation.

Perhaps as important as any survival benefit is the palliation achieved by such surgery. In the series of Wanebo et al.,[47] 96 percent of patients obtained relief

Table 87-5
Results of Irradiation for Relapse after Anterior or Abdominoperineal Resection

Authors	*cGy, rads*	*Relief of symptoms, %*	*Duration of relief, months*[a]	*Survival median, months*	*Three years, %*
Ciatto and Pacini,[63] 1982	3500–5000	55	6		5
Carlsson et al.,[64] 1986	4500	65	6	9	
Rominger et al.,[65] 1985	>4500		6	17	
Dobrowsky et al.,[66] 1985	4500–5400	55		20	12
Overgaard et al.,[67] 1984	4600–5500	50		16	10
Taylor et al.,[68] 1987	4500–5500	60		12	10
Pacini et al.,[69] 1986	>5000	85	4.5	15	

[a]Or time to tumor progression.

Table 87-6
Patient Characteristics

Number of patients	41
Male	31
Female	10
Age range	35–82
Prior therapy	
Abdominoperineal resection	23
Anterior resection	18
Prior radiation therapy	38
Ureteral obstruction	36
Severe pain[a]	31
Bleeding and/or tenesmus	5

[a]Morphine or dihydromorphone required.

[b]Symptoms in patients without severe pain.

of pain, sensation of a mass, or fistulas. Using varied procedures (abdominoperineal resection, exenteration, etc.), Benotti et al.[51] were able to palliate 79 percent of patients with recurrent pelvic cancer. Of our patients, 36 had ureteral obstruction at presentation and all were relieved of this problem. Of the 31 who were taking morphine sulfate or dihydromorphone for relief of pain, 15 (48 percent) became pain-free, and another 9 (29 percent) were able to reduce their analgesic requirement to acetominophen with or without codeine. In total, 77 percent of these patients obtained substantial relief of pain—this after failure of previous irradiation. The operation was not always successful, however, and 15 (37 percent) patients recurred locally: 9 (36 percent) after curative resection and 6 (38 percent) after palliative procedures (Table 87-7). Thus, extended resection represents an improvement on standard measures but cannot, as yet, be considered a definitive answer to the problem of pelvic relapse.

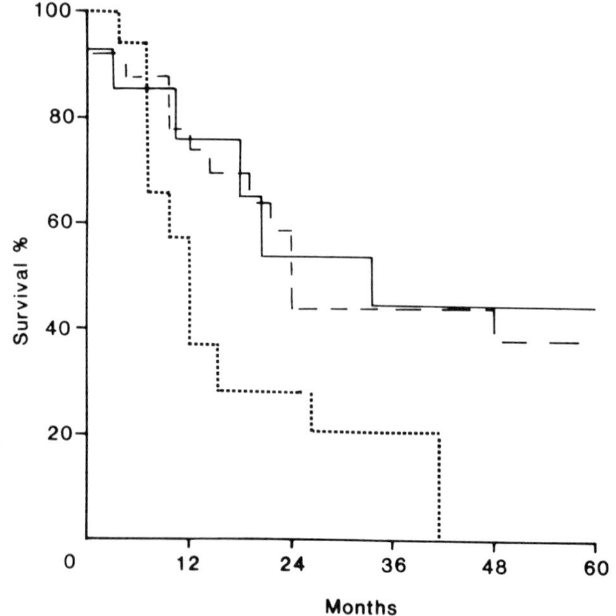

FIG. 87-3. Product-limit survival for curative (—) and palliative (····) resection of recurrent disease; curative resection of primary fixed rectal cancer (---).

SURGICAL TECHNIQUES

Techniques of local excision, anterior or abdominoperineal resection, and standard pelvic exenteration are well described and need not be repeated here. Those of composite pelvic resection and/or sacropelvic exenteration are still evolving, however, and will be reviewed. Wanebo et al.[43,47] describe a staged approach, with the abdominal phase undertaken on day 1 and the perineal phase on day 2 or 3. We have confined the operation to one sitting. To do so, we initially placed patients in a high lithotomy position and stayed with this position throughout the procedure.[53] Exposure to the proximal sacrum was often less than optimal, however. We now use a supine position for the abdominal portions of the procedure and change to a modified lateral position for the posterior dissection.

After entering the abdomen, a search is made for any extrapelvic disease; if this is found, a determination is made as to whether resection for palliation is warranted. We generally proceed if the extrapelvic disease represents less than 10 to 15 percent of the total tumor bulk. Any small bowel in the pelvis is now removed, resecting that which is attached to tumor. The presacral plane is opened to a point just above the tumor; if this point is not beyond S-2, the patient is declared inoperable. Assuming that the presacral plan can be developed past S-2, the ureters are mobilized and divided about 1 cm above their point of obstruction or where they enter the tumor. Each ureter is then cannulated with a plastic catheter connected to a drainage bag. The hypogastric arteries are next isolated at their origins. If possible, the trunk and poste-

Table 87-7
Extent of Disease, Procedures, and Perioperative Outcome

Pelvic disease alone[a]	26
Pelvic + extrapelvic disease[b]	15
Sacropelvic exenteration	32
Standard exenteration	5
Extended proctectomy	4
Postoperative deaths	2
Relief of ureteral obstruction	36
Substantial pain relief[c]	24
Relief of bleeding, tenesmus	5
Local failure/recurrence	15
After curative resection	9
After palliative resection	6

[a]Curative resection.

[b]Palliative resection.

[c]Pain-free (15) or using only acetaminophen with or without codeine (9).

rior branches of one artery are preserved to provide a blood supply for a gluteal muscle flap (to be used later). The other hypogastric artery is ligated with heavy silk but not divided (which increases the chance of postoperative rupture). Nothing is done to the hypogastric veins at this time. The pre- and paravesical spaces are now opened down to the puboprostatic (pubovesical) ligaments anteriorly and to the pelvic floor anterolaterally. This completes the initial abdominal dissection. The incision is temporarily closed with towel clips or a heavy running skin suture and covered with an adherent plastic drape.

The patient is then repositioned in a lateral decubitus position, as for a posterolateral thoracotomy, with the pelvis allowed to roll forward as far as possible. This approximates a prime, jack knife position but is easier to accomplish. An inferiorly based bucket-handle incision is carried out from ischial tuberosity to ischial tuberosity and superiorly to posterior iliac spines. The flap is reflected down to expose sacrum from S-1 to coccyx. Sacral attachments of gluteus maximus are taken down, and the subjacent sacro tuberous and sacrospinous ligaments are divided, taking care to avoid the pudendal vessels. Depending on the level of the tumor, the posterior sacral cortex is taken down with a rongeur between S-2 and S-3 or S-3 and S-4 (Fig. 87-4). The anterior cortex is not formally divided, but fractured forward, leaving the anterior spinal ligament intact.

Puboprostatic (pubovesical) ligaments and the ureter are now divided on the pubis to communicate with the previously opened prevesical dissection plane (Fig. 87-5). The surgeon places a finger in the pelvis to assure that the operative site is beyond tumor anterolaterally; if so, the levators are transected flush with the pelvic side wall. If the site is not beyond the cancer at this point, dissection proceeds upward within the obturator internus to obtain the necessary lateral clearance. The specimen is now pushed farther forward to elevate 2 to 3 cm of anterior spinal ligament off the proximal sacrum. The ligament is divided with cautery (Fig. 87-5), and suture ligatures are used as needed to control the anterior spinal arteries. Remaining attachments now lie posterolaterally and consist of each coccygeus muscle fused, on its ventral surface, to distal hypogastric artery and vein. These are best treated as one large pedicle, to be divided between heavy clamps and then suture-ligated (Fig. 87-6). The specimen is then removed. Frozen sections of margins can be obtained at this point but, in our experience, are unreliable, since the tumor is embedded in scar tissue and easily missed. We now rely on palpation alone to determine the extent of resection.

One is now faced with an enormous perineal defect and the absence of a pelvic floor to prevent herniation. Since most patients have been heavily irradiated, we avoid use of prosthestic mesh to recreate a floor and, instead, rotate the lower half of one gluteus muscle into the field for this purpose (Fig. 87-7). Skin flaps are then closed over suction catheters and the patient is returned to the supine position. After the abdomen is reentered, whatever omentum remains is used to

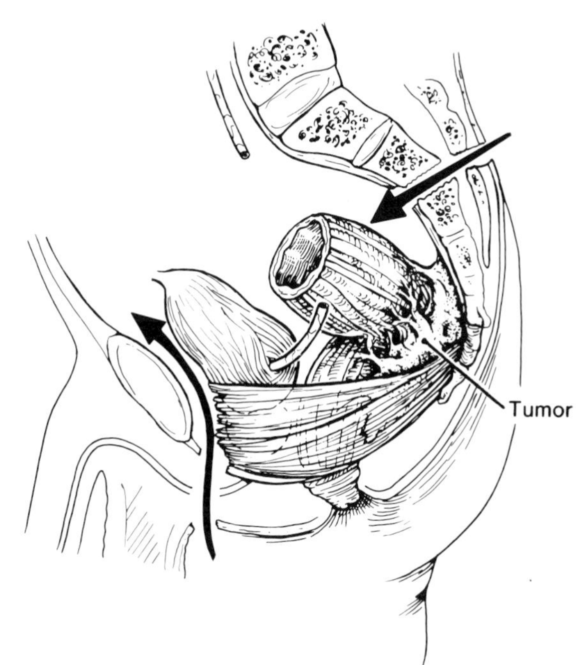

FIG. 87-5. Puboprostatic (pubovesical) ligaments, urethra, and anterior spinal ligaments divided (*arrows*) to mobilize specimen anteriorly and posteriorly.

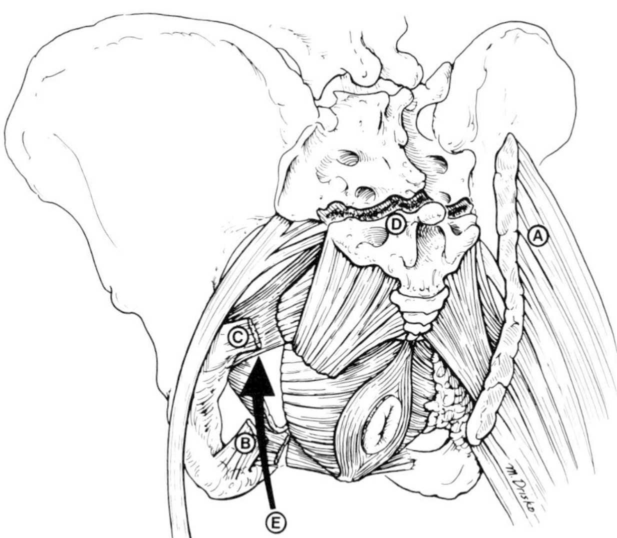

FIG. 87-4. Gluteus maximus (A) is separated from sacrum to expose sacrotuberous (B) and sacrospinous (C) ligaments, which are divided. Each ischiorectal fossa is opened fully (*arrow*) and sacrum transected above tumor (D).

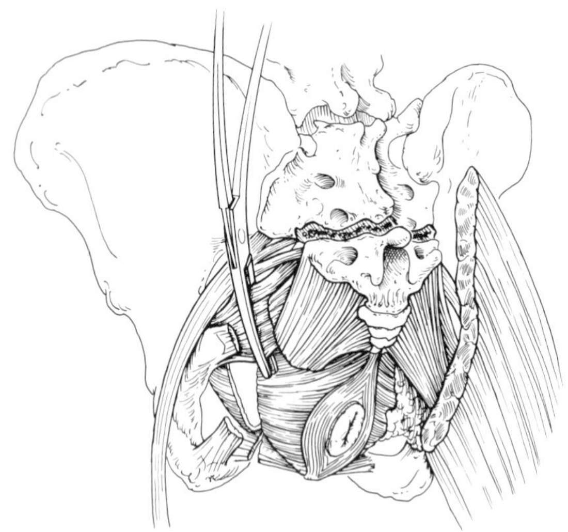

FIG. 87-6. After residual posterior-lateral attachments (coccygeus and distal hypogastric artery and vein) are divided, specimen can be removed.

FIG. 87-7. Lower half of one gluteus maximus muscle is detached from femur and rotated into perineal defect to recreate a pelvic floor and prevent herniation.

cover exposed blood vessels. There is usually not enough omentum to cover other raw surfaces adequately or obliterate dead space; a continent ileocolonic urinary reservoir is rotated into the pelvis to accomplish the latter two aims.[50] Operating time is about 8 to 10 h and blood loss is 1000 to 2000 mL.

REFERENCES

1. Heald RJ, Ryall RDH: Recurrence and survival after total meso-rectal excision for rectal cancer. *Lancet* 1:1479–1482, 1986.
2. Steele G Jr, Busse P, Huberman MS: A pilot study of sphincter-sparing management of adenocarcinoma of the rectum. *Arch Surg* 126:696–702, 1991.
3. Whiteway J, Nicholls RJ, Morson BC: The role of surgical local excision in the treatment of rectal cancer. *Br J Surg* 72:694–697, 1985.
4. Hager T, Gall FP, Hermanek P: Local excision of rectal cancer. *Dis Colon Rectum* 26:149–151, 1983.
5. Biggers OR, Beart RW Jr, Ilstrup DM: Local excision of rectal cancer. *Dis Colon Rectum* 29:374–377, 1986.
6. Papillon J: New prospects in the conservative treatment of rectal cancer. *Dis Colon Rectum* 27:695–700, 1984.
7. De Graaf PW, Roussel JG, Gortzak E: Early-stage rectal cancer: Electrofulguration in comparison to abdominoperineal extirpation or low-anterior resection. *J Surg Oncol* 29:123–128, 1985.
8. Heberer G, Denecke H, Demmel N, et al: Local procedures in the management of rectal cancer. *World J Surg* 11:499–503, 1987.
9. Hoekstra HJ, Verschueren RCJ, Oldhoff JAP: Palliative and curative electrocoagulation for rectal cancer. *Cancer* 55:210–213, 1985.
10. Salvati EP, Rubin RJ, Eisenstat TE: Electrocoagulation of selected carcinoma of the rectum. *Surg Gynecol Obstet* 166:393–396, 1988.
11. Sischy B, Hinson EJ, Wilkinson DR: Definitive radiation therapy for selected cancers of the rectum. *Br J Surg* 75:901–903, 1988.
12. Morson BC: Factors influencing the prognosis of early cancer of the rectum. *Proc R Soc Med* 59:607–608, 1966.
13. Cohen AM, Wood WC, Gunderson LL, et al: Pathological studies in rectal cancer. *Cancer* 45:2965–2968, 1980.
14. Stearns MW, Sternberg SS, DeCosse JJ: Treatment alternatives: Localized rectal cancer. *Cancer* 54:2691–2694, 1984.
15. Goligher JC, Dukes CE, Bussey HJR: Local recurrences after sphincter-saving excisions for carcinoma of the rectum and rectosigmoid. *Br J Surg* 39:199–211, 1951.
16. Southwick HW, Harridge WH, et al: Recurrence at the suture line following resection for carcinoma of the colon: Incidence following preventive measures. *Am J Surg* 103:86–89, 1962.
17. Cohn I Jr, Corley RG, Floyd CE: Iodized suture for control of tumor implantation in a colon anastomosis. *Surg Gynecol Obstet* 116:366–370, 1963.
18. Bacon HE, Mcgregor JK: Prevention of recurrent carcinoma of the colon and rectum. *Dis Colon Rectum* 6:209–214, 1963.
19. Rosenberg IL: The aetiology of colonic suture-line recurrence. *Ann R Coll Surg Engl* 61:251–257, 1979.
20. Deddish MR, Stearns MW: Anterior resection for carcinoma of the rectum and rectosigmoid area. *Ann Surg* 154:961–966, 1961.
21. Grinnell RS. Distal intramural spread of carcinoma of the rectum and rectosigmoid. *Surg Gynecol Obstet* 99:421–430, 1954.
22. Williams NS, Dixon MF, Johnston D: Reappraisal of the 5 centimetre rule of distal excision for carcinoma of the rectum: A study of distal intramural spread and of patient's survival. *Br J Surg* 70:150–154, 1983.
23. Madsen PM, Christiansen J: Distal intramural spread of rectal carcinomas. *Dis Colon Rectum* 29:279–282, 1986.
24. Wilson SM, Beahrs OH: A curative treatment of carcinoma of the sigmoid, recto-sigmoid and rectum. *Ann Surg* 183:556–565, 1976.
25. Quer EA, Dahlin DC, Mayo CW: Retrograde intramural spread of carcinoma of the rectum and rectosigmoid. *Surg Gynecol Obstet* 96:24–30, 1953.
26. Felipe MI: Mucus secretion in rat colonic mucosa during carcinogenesis induced by dimethylhydrazine: A morphological and histochemical study. *Br J Cancer* 32:60–77, 1975.
27. Wood CB, Dawson PM, Habib NA: The sialomucin content of colonic resection margins. *Dis Colon Rectum* 28:260–261, 1985.

28. Roe R, Fermor B, Williamson RCN: Proliferative instability and experimental carcinogenesis at colonic anastomoses. *Gut* 28:808–815, 1987.
29. Olson RM, Perencevich NP, Malcolm AW, et al: Patterns of recurrence following curative resection of adenocarcinoma of the colon and rectum. *Cancer* 45:2969–2974, 1980.
30. Pilipshen SJ, Heilweil M, Quan SHQ, et al: Patterns of pelvic recurrence following definitive resections of rectal cancer. *Cancer* 53:1354–1362, 1984.
31. McDermott FT, Hughes ESR, Pihl E, et al: Local recurrence after potentially curative resection for rectal cancer in a series of 1,008 patients. *Br J Surg* 72:34–37, 1985.
32. Terranova O, Celi D, Martella B, et al: Local recurrence of rectal cancer: Anterior resection versus abdomino-perineal resection. *Int Surg* 73:111–113, 1988.
33. Sannella NA: Abdominoperineal resection following anterior resection. *Cancer* 38:378–381, 1976.
34. Segall MM, Goldberg SM, Nivatvongs S: Abdominoperineal resection for recurrent cancer following anterior resection. *Dis Colon Rectum* 24:80–84, 1981.
35. Hojo K, Koyama Y, Moriya Y: Lymphatic spread and its prognostic value in patients with rectal cancer. *Am J Surg* 144:350–354, 1982.
36. Keighley MRB, Hall C: Anastomotic recurrence of colorectal cancer—A biological phenomenon or an avoidable calamity. *Gut* 28:786–791, 1987.
37. Durdey P, Quirke P, Dixon MF, et al: Lateral spread of rectal cancer, the key to local recurrence (abstract). *Br J Surg* 73:1042, 1986.
38. Penfold JCB: A comparison of restorative resection of carcinoma of the middle third of the rectum with abdominoperineal excision. *Aust NZ J Surg* 44:354–356, 1974.
39. Glass RE, Ritchie JK, Thompson HR, et al: The results of surgical treatment of cancer of the rectum by radical resection and extended abdomino-iliac lymphadenectomy. *Br J Surg* 72:599–601, 1985.
40. Polk HC Jr, Spratt JS Jr: The results of treatment of perineal recurrence of cancer of the rectum. *Cancer* 43:952–955, 1979.
41. Gunderson LL, Martin JK, Beart RW: Intraoperative and external beam irradiation for locally advanced colorectal cancer. *Ann Surg* 207:52–60, 1988.
42. Willett CG, Shellito PC, Tepper JE, et al: Intraoperative electron beam radiation therapy for recurrent locally advanced rectal or rectosigmoid carcinoma. *Cancer* 67:1504–1508, 1991.
43. Wanebo HJ, Marcove RC: Abdominal sacral resection of locally recurrent rectal cancer. *Ann Surg* 194:458–471, 1981.
44. Sugarbaker PH: Partial sacrectomy for en bloc excision of rectal cancer with posterior fixation. *Dis Colon Rectum* 25:708–711, 1982.
45. Takagi H, Morimoto T, Kato T: Diagnosis and operation for locally recurrent rectal cancer. *J Surg Oncol* 28:290–296, 1985.
46. Wanebo HJ, Gaker DL, Whitehill R, et al: Pelvic recurrence of rectal cancer. *Ann Surg* 205:482–495, 1987.
47. Wanebo HJ, Koness RJ, Turk PS, et al: Composite resection of posterior pelvic malignancy. *Ann Surg* 215:685–695, 1992.
48. Localio SA, Eng K, Coppa GF: Abdominosacral resection for mid-rectal cancer. *Ann Surg* 198:320–324, 1983.
49. Pearlman NW, Stiegmann GV, Donohue RE: Extended resection of fixed rectal cancer. *Cancer* 63:2438–2441, 1989.
50. Pearlman NW, Donohue RE, Wettlaufer JN, et al: Continent ileocolonic urinary reservoirs for filling and lining the post-exenteration pelvis. *Am J Surg* 160:634–637, 1990.
51. Benotti PN, Bothe A, Eyre RC, et al: Management of recurrent pelvic tumor. *Arch Surg* 122:457–460, 1987.
52. Williams NS, Durdey P, Johnston D: The outcome following sphincter-saving resection and abdominoperineal resection for low rectal cancer. *Br J Surg* 72:595–598, 1985.
53. Pearlman NW, Donohue RE, Stiegmann GV, et al: Pelvic and sacropelvic exenteration for locally advanced or recurrent anorectal cancer. *Arch Surg* 122:537–541, 1987.
54. Chung CK, Stryker JA, DeMuth WEJ: Patterns of failure following surgery alone for colorectal carcinoma. *J Surg Oncol* 22:65–70, 1983.
55. Rich T, Gunderson LL, Lew R, et al: Patterns of recurrence of rectal cancer after potentially curative surgery. *Cancer* 52:1317–1329, 1983.
56. Heimann TM, Szporn A, Bolnick K, et al: Local recurrence following surgical treatment of rectal cancer: Comparison of anterior and abdominoperineal resection. *Dis Colon Rectum* 29:862–864, 1986.
57. Colombo PL, Scotti, Foglieni CL, et al: Analysis of recurrence following curative low anterior resection and stapled anastomoses for carcinoma of the middle third and lower rectum. *Dis Colon Rectum* 30:457–464, 1987.
58. Pheils MT, Chapuis PH, Newland RC, et al: Local recurrence following curative resection for carcinoma of the rectum. *Dis Colon Rectum* 26:98–102, 1983.
59. Willet CG, Tepper JE, Donnely S, et al: Patterns of failure following local excision and local excision and postoperative radiation therapy for invasive rectal adenocarcinoma. *J Clin Oncol* 7:1003–1008, 1989.
60. Killingback MJ: Indications for local excision of rectal cancer. *Br J Surg* 2S:54–56, 1985.
61. Wanebo HJ, Quan SHQ: Failures of electrocoagulation of primary carcinoma of the rectum. *Surg Gynecol Obstet* 138:174–176, 1974.
62. Cummings BJ Jr, Rider WD, Harwood AR, et al: Radical external beam radiation therapy for adenocarcinoma of the rectum. *Dis Colon Rectum* 26:30–36, 1983.
63. Ciatto S, Pacini P: Radiation therapy of recurrences of carcinoma of the rectum and sigmoid after surgery. *Acta Radiol Oncol* 21:105–109, 1982.
64. Carlsson G, Hafstrom L, Jonsson PE: Unresectable and locally recurrent rectal cancer treated with radiotherapy or bilateral internal iliac artery infusion of 5-fluorouracil. *Cancer* 58:336–340, 1986.
65. Rominger CJ, Gelber RD, Gunderson LL, et al: Radiation therapy alone or in combination with chemotherapy in the treatment of residual or inoperable carcinoma of the rectum and rectosigmoid or pelvic recurrence following colorectal surgery. Radiation Therapy Oncology Group study (76-16). *Am J Clin Oncol* 8:118–127, 1985.
66. Dobrowsky W, Schmid AP: Radiotherapy of presacral recurrence following radical surgery for rectal carcinoma. *Dis Colon Rectum* 28:917–919, 1985.
67. Overgaard M, Overgaard J, Sell A: Dose-response relationship for radiation therapy of recurrent, residual, and primarily inoperable colorectal cancer. *Radiother Oncol* 1:217–225, 1984.
68. Taylor RE, Karr GR, Arnott SJ: External beam radiotherapy for rectal adenocarcinoma. *Br J Surg* 74:455–459, 1987.
69. Pacini P, Cionini L, Pirtoli L, et al: Symptomatic recurrence of carcinoma of the rectum and sigmoid: The influence of radiotherapy on the quality of life. *Dis Colon Rectum* 29:865–868, 1986.
70. Neville R, Fielding LP, Amendola C: Local tumor recurrence after curative resection for rectal cancer. A ten-hospital review. *Dis Colon Rectum* 30:12–17, 1987.

CHAPTER 88

Radiation Therapy for Locally Recurrent Rectal Cancer

James A. Martenson, Jr.
Heidi Nelson

HIGHLIGHTS

External radiation therapy is a very effective palliative treatment modality in patients with locally recurrent rectal cancer. Doses ranging from 5 to 10 Gy in one fraction to 55 to 70 Gy in 30 to 39 fractions provide effective relief of pain in most patients. Unfortunately, relief of pain is often transitory, and most patients have subsequent development of local progression of cancer and die of their disease.

CONTROVERSIES

Definitive prospective randomized trials have not been performed to determine the optimal dose of external radiation therapy. Although one study[1] of the relationships among dose, symptom relief, local control, and survival suggests a benefit for radiation therapy doses of more than 56 Gy, interpretation of this study is complicated by the heterogeneity of the patients analyzed and by the lack of randomization. Retrospective studies suggest a benefit when 5-fluorouracil (5-FU)-based chemotherapy is used in combination with external beam irradiation. Indirect support for a role for 5-FU can also be found in a prospective randomized trial conducted in patients with primary locally advanced disease.

Patients who receive intraoperative radiation therapy (IORT) seem to have better local control and survival results when compared with prior results obtained with external radiation therapy alone. The possibility that these results are due to case selection rather than to treatment can be definitively addressed only by a randomized trial. An initial pilot study suggests that neutron therapy may provide effective palliation. It is unclear, however, whether this form of treatment will have results superior to those obtained with conventional photon therapy.

FUTURE DIRECTIONS

A clear need exists for randomized trials to determine such issues as the optimal dose of external radiation, the role of IORT, and the potential value of neutrons and other heavy particles. Other innovative methods that need further investigation include radiation sensitizers and hyperthermia. Systemic failure remains a serious problem, and the recent finding that levamisole and leucovorin are effective modulators of 5-FU[2,3] suggests that clinical trials of these regimens should be undertaken. Innovative methods of delivering systemic treatment, such as by continuous 5-FU infusion with leucovorin,[4–7] are another potentially fruitful area for clinical research.

Radiation therapy is of clear palliative benefit in patients with locally recurrent rectal cancer and is associated with long-term survival in a minority. In most patients, however, progressive disease will develop and they will die of their cancer. Clearly, improved methods of treatment are needed if better results are to be achieved. Well-designed prospective clinical trials provide the best hope for developing improved therapy.

In patients with previous resection of rectal cancer, development of local recurrence portends an ominous subsequent clinical course. Local recurrence is completely resectable in only a small minority of patients.[8,9] Most patients experience local progression that ultimately leads to death.[10] Moreover, before the disease causes the patient's death, prolonged problems with local pain and other symptoms are common.[11]

Radiation is an important therapeutic method in patients with locally recurrent rectal cancer. This chapter discusses the role of standard external beam radiation therapy for palliation in locally recurrent rectal cancer. Because external radiation therapy has only minimal curative potential in this setting, the role of more aggressive radiotherapeutic approaches is also discussed.

EXTERNAL BEAM RADIATION THERAPY

External beam radiation therapy, either alone or in combination with chemotherapy, has definite palliative value in the treatment of locally recurrent rectal cancer. Approximately 50 to 95 percent of symptomatic patients will experience palliation of pelvic pain subsequent to radiation therapy.[1,12–15] Unfortunately, the median duration of pain relief is generally only a few months,[12,14] and virtually all patients experience local progression and death from disease.[1,14–16] There are only occasional long-term survivors. For example, in one clinical trial of external pelvic radiation therapy (50 Gy in 6 weeks) in patients with locally advanced (14 patients) or locally recurrent (30 patients) rectal cancer, 90 percent had local progression at some time subsequent to radiation therapy, and the projected 5-year survival rate was 0 percent.[14]

Modest doses of radiation can provide effective palliation in patients with locally recurrent rectal cancer. Whiteley and colleagues,[17] for example, found that significant relief of symptoms was obtained in 82 (80 percent) of 103 patients with locally recurrent disease treated with 20 to 25 Gy over 8 to 12 treatment days. In a small series of patients from Queen Elizabeth Hospital in Birmingham, England, Allum and colleagues[12] found that 8 of 12 patients treated palliatively with single doses of 5 to 10 Gy experienced "good or moderate" palliation. This result was similar to that in patients treated with moderate doses of 30 to 45 Gy in 10 to 15 fractions. The median duration of symptomatic relief was 3 months and was similar in both groups. Habeshaw and colleagues[18] used weekly doses of 6 Gy, delivering 3 to 7 total fractions with parallel opposed fields, in combination with 5-FU in 32 patients (28 of whom had pelvic disease) with advanced large bowel cancer. Of 22 evaluable patients, 14 (64 percent) "achieved useful palliation of symptoms" for a median duration of 8 months. Among 20 patients who survived for longer than 6 months, 6 (30 percent) had development of subcutaneous fibrosis, although this did not result in significant symptomatic problems. In one patient, who was treated to a cumulative dose of 42 Gy, severe radiation proctitis developed, which was ultimately thought to contribute to his death.

Single large radiation fractions of 5 to 10 Gy can provide effective palliation and are particularly appropriate for debilitated patients with advanced disease for whom daily transport to a radiation oncology department may pose an excessive burden. For patients who have an expectation of survival beyond a few months, however, single large radiation fractions to the pelvis may pose an excessive risk of complications.[19]

Dose-response relationships in patients treated predominantly with external beam radiation were analyzed by Overgaard and colleagues.[1] Among 113 patients with locally advanced colorectal cancer, 63 percent experienced complete or partial relief of symptoms lasting 6 months or more. Among those who received less than 56 Gy, 47 to 61 percent had symptomatic relief, although no obvious dose-response relationship was observed at this dose level. All patients who received 56 Gy or more experienced significant relief of symptoms (Table 88-1). In addition

Table 88-1
Relationship between Symptom Relief and Total Radiation Dose: Radiumstationen, Denmark Analysis

Dose of radiation, Gy	*No. responses/ No. patients*	*Patients with symptomatic relief,[a] percent*
≤35	9/19	47
36–45	17/28	61
46–55	19/31	61
≥56	11/11	100[b]

[a]Complete or significant alleviation of symptoms lasting 6 months or longer or until death.
[b]$p < .01$ comparing 56 Gy or more with less than 56 Gy.
SOURCE: From Overgaard et al.[1] By permission of Elsevier Science Publishers B.V.

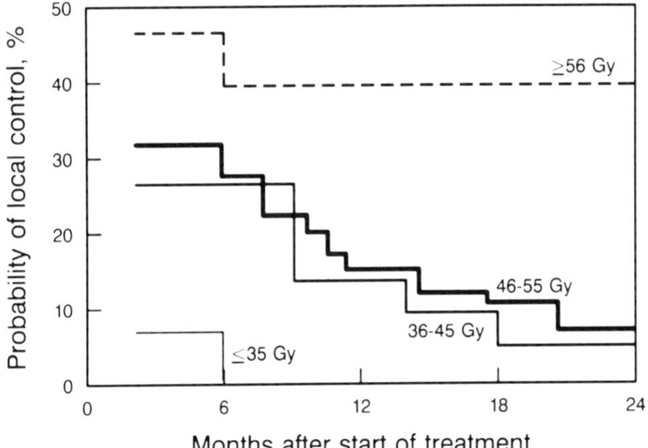

A

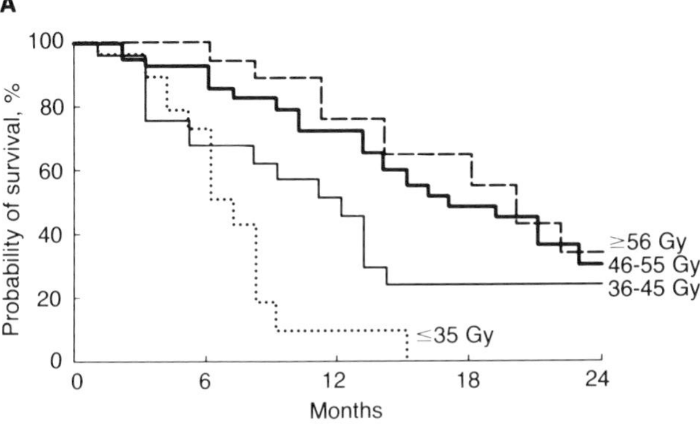

B

FIG. 88-1. Relationship of total radiation dose to local control (*A*) and survival (*B*) in patients with locally advanced colorectal cancer. (*A* from Overgaard et al.[1] Reproduced by permission of Elsevier Science Publishers B.V.)

to improved palliation, there was a trend toward improved local control and survival (Fig. 88-1) in patients treated with higher radiation doses. Although this analysis suggests improved results with higher doses, it must be interpreted with caution because of the retrospective nature of the study and the heterogeneous composition of the study population, which included 28 patients with distant metastasis and 36 with inoperable or incompletely resected disease.

For patients receiving conventionally fractionated moderate-dose radiation therapy, the use of 5-FU may add to the palliative benefit of treatment.[13,15] At West Virginia University Health Sciences Center, for example, 48 patients with locally recurrent rectal cancer were treated with 50 or more Gy external radiation with or without 5-FU. Complete relief of pelvic pain occurred in 87 percent of patients who received 5-FU and in 55 percent who did not. A trend toward improved survival was also noted with 5-FU.[15] Although this was not a randomized clinical trial, the improved result in patients receiving 5-FU is indirectly supported by a randomized study in which patients with primary locally advanced colonic and rectal cancer received radiation therapy and 5-FU. These patients had both better symptom control and better survival than patients treated with radiation alone.[20]

The use of high-dose pelvic external radiation therapy must be undertaken with careful attention to the technical details of treatment. Treatment of patients exclusively with anteroposterior-posteroanterior (AP-PA) fields can result in an excessive risk of morbidity, particularly if doses exceed 55 Gy. In one clinical trial, 3 (27 percent) of 11 patients with locally advanced rectal cancer who received 5-FU and 57 to 63 Gy with AP-PA techniques developed severe small bowel complications.[16] In contrast, only 8 (6 percent) of 129 patients treated in a Radiation Therapy Oncology Group trial[21] had resultant severe small bowel toxicity. The lower rate of small bowel toxicity in that study may have been due to a protocol requirement excluding all small bowel in radiation therapy fields treated to doses of more than 55 Gy. Small bowel exposure and complications can be minimized by the use of multiple fields (AP-PA and lateral), which allows exclusion of anterior bowel from the high-dose region of the radiation therapy field, and by the use of techniques designed to reduce the volume of small bowel in the pelvis, such as the prone position and bladder distention.[22] When a laparotomy is undertaken before external radiation therapy, the volume of small bowel in the pelvis can be reduced by the use of an absorbable mesh sling.[23]

NEUTRON THERAPY

Neutron therapy attempts to improve on the results of conventional photon treatment. Theoretically, neutrons may have a therapeutic advantage over photons because of their decreased dependence on oxygenation in the tumor for cell killing.[24] Engenhart and colleagues[24] treated 21 patients who had unresectable locally recurrent rectal cancer with mixed-beam therapy; 40 Gy was given with photons followed by a boost of 6.6 to 10 Gy with neutrons. All patients had severe pain before treatment. All patients experienced considerable pain relief, and 12 (57 percent) had complete pain relief. Acute toxicity was modest and did not exceed that expected with conventional photon therapy. Because the mean duration of follow-up was only 8.5 months, long-term results of this treatment have yet to be determined.

INTRAOPERATIVE RADIATION THERAPY

Because of poor results in terms of both long-term local control and survival in patients treated with external beam radiation, surgical resection and intraoperative radiation therapy (IORT), either alone or in combination with external radiation, have been used in patients with locally recurrent cancer. Treatment with IORT is potentially advantageous because at operation an electron beam can be used to deliver high-dose radiation to a localized site of tumor with little or no radiation exposure to normal dose-limiting tissues. In some cases, operation can provide complete or near-complete tumor resection, and fields encompassing known or suspected residual disease can be precisely defined for IORT. Radiosensitive normal structures such as bowel, ureter, and bladder can, in many cases, be mobilized out of the radiation field if appropriate (i.e., if uninvolved by tumor).

Theoretically, IORT may offer an advantage by delivering single high-dose treatment fractions. A large single dose of radiation has more biological effect than the same total dose of fractionated treatment. For example, when a large IORT boost of 15 Gy is added to a conventional external beam dose of 45 to 50 Gy, delivered in daily 1.8-Gy fractions, the biological result may be equivalent to 75 to 95 Gy of conventionally fractionated radiation.[25]

The initial assessment to determine whether a patient is eligible for radical operation plus IORT is performed by the radiation oncologist and surgeon. After a review of pertinent oncologic records, examination of the patient, and initial studies, patients are considered appropriate for the combined approach if (1) they are physically able to withstand a major operation, (2) operation alone is not feasible to accomplish complete resection with negative margins, and (3) potentially curative external beam doses would exceed normal tissue tolerance. Once the patient is considered an appropriate candidate, additional studies are obtained to establish that the recurrence is localized and resectable and to plan optimal preoperative and intraoperative treatments.

The extensive nature of the surgical undertaking necessitates a thorough metastatic workup before consideration of radical operation and IORT. The records of prior surgical treatments and related pathology should be reviewed to establish the patient's risk of local, regional, and distant failure. A complete physical examination will establish the general fitness of the patient and help detect focal signs of advanced noncurative malignant disease. Patients with pelvic recurrence should be specifically questioned and examined for signs of sciatic nerve involvement, which contraindicates radical sacrectomy. Similarly, the presence of nonregional nodal involvement contraindicates aggressive surgical therapy. If the patient is a candidate, and extensive resection, such as pelvic exenteration, is anticipated, then it is also useful to examine the patient with an eye to reconstructive options.

Laboratory investigations should include a complete blood cell count, serum chemistries, and a radiograph of the chest. Computed tomography (CT) of the abdomen and pelvis can assess the primary site of recurrence and distant sites in the liver and retroperitoneum. Once distant metastases are excluded, the focus should be on determining the resectability of the site of recurrence, including the presence of distinct tissue planes between the lesion and adjacent organs. Tumor resectability is determined not only by the size and site of the lesion but also, more importantly, by its anatomic approximation to other organs and structures.

Although recurrent lesions are not strictly confined to anatomic locations, it is useful to consider the principal tumor location (anterior, posterior, or lateral) when planning combination therapy with operation and IORT. Anterior lesions most often involve the uterus in the female and the bladder or prostate in the male. When bladder involvement is suspected based on computed tomography scan or clinical symptoms, a urologist can be consulted with the intent of performing cystoscopy and ureteral stent placement at the beginning of the procedure and for the purpose of creating an ileal conduit should cystectomy be required. Females with possible tumor involvement of the uterus or vagina should be prepared for sterilization and for the possibility of vaginal reconstruction should extensive resection be required. Posterior tumors frequently violate the presacral tissue planes and involve the sacrum. More advanced sacral involvement is usually obvious by evidence of bony erosion on CT scan. When sacral involvement extends proximally to involve the sacrum between S-4 and S-2, an orthopedic surgery consultation is obtained. Finally, lateral or pelvic side-wall lesions are generally the most difficult to evaluate preoperatively and to manage intraoperatively. Patients should be counseled about the possibility that the lesion will not be resectable because of the proximity of bony and vascular pelvic structures.

Before the procedure, the large bowel should be inspected for metachronous primary lesions and for evidence of anastomotic lesions. The bowel can be evaluated either with proctosigmoidoscopy and barium enema or with colonoscopy. For patients who have recurrence at the rectal anastomosis, proctoscopy with biopsy will readily provide histologic proof of recurrence. Endorectal ultrasonography, when available, can be used to delineate the extent of disease beyond the bowel wall.

In most cases, patients who are considered for combined radical operation and IORT are given preoperative chemotherapy and external beam radiation therapy. Theoretically, preoperative radiation therapy may provide tumor shrinkage, improve resectability, and provide potentiation of IORT effects. Preoperative radiation therapy, between 45 and 55 Gy in 1.8-Gy fractions over 5 to 6 weeks, is administered in conjunction with 5-FU-based chemotherapy. After completion of external radiation therapy and a 3- to 5-week recovery period, patients are reevaluated for metastatic disease and prepared for operation.

At operation, an initial exploration is performed to detect the presence or absence of metastatic disease. Tumor resection is performed with the intent of complete total resection, including en bloc resections of adherent organs when appropriate. It is generally most difficult to accomplish complete resection when the tumor has recurred along the lateral pelvic side wall or when it has spread as a sheet, covering retroperitoneal structures. Areas of suspected or known residual disease are jointly evaluated by the surgeon and radiation oncologist for the feasibility of IORT. Sites of adherence, or residual disease, are then fitted with a suitably sized translucent cone specifically designed for delivery of the electron beam. The tumor is incorporated into one or more electron fields and normal tissues are shielded from the path of the beam to the maximal possible extent. The doses of IORT are selected according to the amount of disease subsequent to surgical resection: 10 Gy for microscopic disease, 15 Gy for gross disease 2 cm or less in diameter, and 17.5 to 20 Gy for gross disease 2 cm or more in diameter. In most cases, the pelvic defect created by the resection can be filled with mobilized omentum. In rare cases, it is necessary to use a myocutaneous rectus abdominis flap to close large perineal and sacral defects. Finally, if additional postoperative radiation therapy is anticipated, a mesh sling can be fashioned to exclude the small bowel from the pelvis.

Results of therapy with external radiation with or without 5-FU, surgical resection, and IORT at the Mayo Clinic have been reported for 39 patients with recurrent colorectal cancer (rectal, 29 patients; sigmoid, 6 patients; extrapelvic colon, 4).[25] Of the 39 patients, 7 also received 5-FU during the course of their external radiation therapy. The survival rate at 4 years was 23 percent. Recently updated results for both local control and survival in 59 patients are shown in Fig. 88-2. Results of IORT are less satisfactory in patients with a history of pelvic radiation therapy who subsequently present with recurrence or progression in the pelvis. At 2.5 years, the projected survival rate is 60 percent, the disease-free survival rate is 15 percent, and the rate of freedom from local failure is 54 percent. (Fig. 88-3).

At Massachusetts General Hospital, 39 patients with locally recurrent rectal or rectosigmoid cancer entered a program of planned preoperative external beam radiation therapy followed by IORT.[26] Techniques were essentially identical to those used at the Mayo Clinic. For all 39 patients, the 5-year actuarial survival rate was 29 percent; the disease-free survival rate was 21 percent. Nine patients did not receive IORT for the following reasons: (1) findings of unresectable or metastatic cancer (3 patients); (2) IORT not technically feasible because of circumferential adherence of tumor in the pelvis (4 patients); and (3) tumor completely resected with negative margins and no sites of adherence within the pelvis (2 patients). Five-year local control and disease-free survival rates in the 30 patients who received IORT were 26 and 19 percent, respectively. Local control was related to the de-

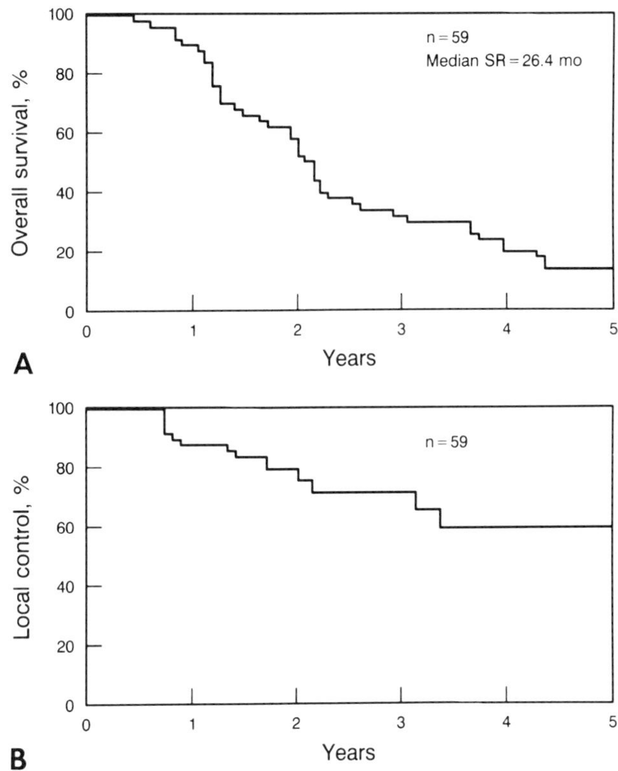

FIG. 88-2. Survival (*A*) and local control (*B*) in patients with locally recurrent colon and rectal cancer after external radiation therapy and IORT at the Mayo Clinic. SR = survival.

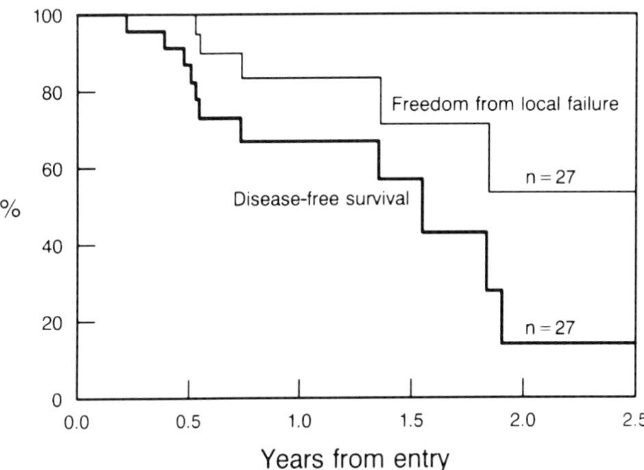

FIG. 88-3. Disease-free survival and rates of freedom from local failure in patients with locally recurrent colon and rectal cancer after prior pelvic radiation therapy.

gree of surgical resection done before IORT. When complete resection was performed (13 patients), the local control rate was 62 percent. When only partial resection was possible (17 patients), the local control rate was only 18 percent. Four patients received no or minimal preoperative radiation because of a history of prior pelvic radiation therapy. Of these 4 patients, 3 had local failure and all 4 died—3 of cancer and 1 of intercurrent disease. Patients with locally recurrent rectal cancer who have a history of pelvic radiation therapy are currently not considered candidates for IORT at Massachusetts General Hospital.[26]

At Rush-Presbyterian Hospital, 26 patients received external radiation therapy and IORT for localized pelvic recurrence of large bowel cancer.[27] Actuarial 3-year relapse-free and overall survival rates were 15 and 25 percent, respectively. Local failure occurred in 11 of 18 patients with gross residual disease and 4 of 8 patients with microscopic residual disease. The local failure rate was higher in patients who received external radiation therapy doses of < 40 Gy (11 of 15, or 73 percent) than in those who received > 40 Gy (4 of 11, or 36 percent). Like the Massachusetts General Hospital group, these investigators have abandoned IORT when a full course of external pelvic radiation therapy is not possible.

Significant complications can result from aggressive therapy in patients with locally recurrent rectal cancer. Table 88-2 describes the complications for the 39 patients in the Massachusetts General Hospital series.[26] At the Mayo Clinic, a detailed analysis of neurologic and ureteral toxicity in patients given IORT has been performed.[28] In 50 evaluable patients, peripheral neuropathy developed subsequent to IORT in 32 percent. The risk of neuropathy was highest in patients who received IORT to the pelvic side wall (47 percent). Among the 16 patients with neuropathy, 100 percent had pain (which was severe in 19 percent), 50 percent experienced weakness, and 69 percent experienced numbness or tingling. Resolution of pain was documented in 6 (42 percent) of 14 evaluable patients. Weakness and sensory problems resolved in 13 and 36 percent of patients with these problems, respectively. When a ureter was included in an IORT field, the risk of subsequent obstruction was 63 percent, a complication that can be mitigated with use of a ureteral stent. An analysis in patients with locally advanced rectal cancer, however, did not find a statistically significant increased risk of severe or worse complications when patients treated with preoperative external radiation and surgical resection were compared with those managed with external radiation, surgical resection, and IORT.[29]

Table 88-2
Complications in 39 Patients[a] Treated with a Program of External Radiation Therapy (RT), Surgery, and Intraoperative Radiation Therapy (IORT)

Complications	*No. of patients*
Postoperative	
Pelvic abscess requiring drainage and small bowel resection	2
Ureterovesical fistula	1
Deep venous thrombosis	1
External beam RT/operation	
Small bowel obstruction requiring operation	2
Radiation enteritis	1
External beam RT/operation/IORT	
Necrotic pelvic/perineal wound requiring debridement	1
Perineal-vesical fistula requiring bladder resection	1
Sacral/soft tissue necrosis requiring sacral resection and flap reconstruction	1
Pelvic neuropathy (sensory or motor)	3

[a]Of the 39 patients, 36 underwent resection and 30 of the 39 received IORT.
SOURCE: From Willett et al.[26] Reproduced by permission of the American Cancer Society.

Although the addition of IORT to external radiation therapy and maximal resection may result in improved local control and possibly improved survival, long-term follow-up demonstrates an overall survival rate of less than 20 percent, even in optimally treated patients (Fig. 88-2). There is a clear need to develop better methods for achieving local control and preventing distant metastasis. Radiation sensitizers and hyperthermia may be useful in improving local control. Modulation of 5-FU activity by levamisole[2] or leucovorin[3] or by specialized delivery methods, such as continuous infusion,[4–7] may provide improved systemic disease control. Investigation of these and other innovative treatment methods within the context of prospective clinical trials provides the best hope for improving outcomes in the future.

REFERENCES

1. Overgaard M, Overgaard J, Sell A: Dose-response relationship for radiation therapy of recurrent, residual, and primarily inoperable colorectal cancer. *Radiother Oncol* 1:217–225, 1984.
2. Moertel CG, Fleming TR, Macdonald JS, et al: Levamisole and fluorouracil for adjuvant therapy of resected colon carcinoma. *N Engl J Med* 322:352–358, 1990.
3. Poon MA, O'Connell MJ, Wieand HS, et al: Biochemical modulation of fluorouracil with leucovorin: Confirmatory evidence of improved therapeutic efficacy in advanced colorectal cancer. *J Clin Oncol* 9:1967–1972, 1991.
4. Leichman CG, Leichman L, Spears CP, et al: Phase II study of prolonged infusion 5-fluorouracil (PIFU) with weekly leucovorin (LV) in disseminated colorectal cancer (CRC). *Proc AMSCO* 10:143, 1991.
5. Isacoff WH, Jacobs AD, Taylor O: Continuous infusion (CI) 5-fluorouracil (5-FU) combined with calcium leucovorin (LV), mitomycin-C (Mito-C), and dipyridamole (D) in ad-

vanced colorectal carcinoma (abstract). *Proc AMSCO* 10:154, 1991.

6. Leichman CG, Leichman L, Spears CP, et al: Biological modification of protracted infusion of 5-fluorouracil with weekly leucovorin: A dose seeking clinical trial for patients with disseminated gastrointestinal cancers. *Cancer Chemother Pharmacol* 26:57–61, 1990.
7. Tempero M, Mitchell M, Higginbotham P: Tolerance of protracted infusion 5-fluorouracil and oral leucovorin (abstract). *Proc AMSCO* 10:160, 1991.
8. Mäkelä J, Haukipuro K, Laitinen S, et al: Surgical treatment of recurrent colorectal cancer: Five-year follow-up. *Arch Surg* 124:1029–1032, 1989.
9. Pheils MT, Chapuis PH, Newland RC, et al: Local recurrence following curative resection for carcinoma of the rectum. *Dis Colon Rectum* 26:98–102, 1983.
10. Rao AR, Kagan AR, Chan PM, et al: Patterns of recurrence following curative resection alone for adenocarcinoma of the rectum and sigmoid colon. *Cancer* 48:1492–1495, 1981.
11. Gilbert SG: Symptomatic local tumor failure following abdomino-perineal resection. *Int J Rad Oncol Biol Phys* 4:801–807, 1978.
12. Allum WH, Mack P, Priestman TJ, et al: Radiotherapy for pain relief in locally recurrent colorectal cancer. *Ann R Coll Surg Engl* 69:220–221, 1987.
13. Arnott SJ: The value of combined 5-fluorouracil and x-ray therapy in the palliation of locally recurrent and inoperable rectal carcinoma. *Clin Radiol* 26:177–182, 1975.
14. O'Connell MJ, Childs DS, Moertel CG, et al: A prospective controlled evaluation of combined pelvic radiotherapy and methanol extraction residue of BCG (MER) for locally unresectable or recurrent rectal carcinoma. *Int J Radiat Oncol Biol Phys* 8:1115–1119, 1982.
15. Sinha PP: In locally recurrent carcinoma of the recto-sigmoid: Radiation therapy with/without simultaneous weekly 5 FU. *West Virginia Med J* 85:137–141, 1989.
16. Danjoux CE, Gelber RD, Catton GE, et al: Combination chemo-radiotherapy for residual, recurrent, or inoperable carcinoma of the rectum: ECOG Study (EST 3276). *Int J Radiat Oncol Biol Phys* 11:765–771, 1985.
17. Whiteley HW Jr, Stearns MW Jr, Leaming RH, et al: Palliative radiation therapy in patients with cancer of the colon and rectum. *Cancer* 25:343–346, 1970.
18. Habeshaw T, Adam JS, Kirk J: Weekly large fraction radiotherapy and 5 fluorouracil as a palliative treatment for large bowel carcinoma: A pilot study. *Int J Radiat Oncol Biol Phys* 8:1127–1130, 1982.
19. Halle JS, Rosenman JG, Varia MA, et al: 1000 cGy single dose palliation for advanced carcinoma of the cervix or endometrium. *Int J Radiat Oncol Biol Phys* 12:1947–1950, 1986.
20. Moertel CG, Childs DS Jr, Reitemeier RJ, et al: Combined 5-fluorouracil and supervoltage radiation therapy of locally unresectable gastrointestinal cancer. *Lancet* 2:865–867, 1969.
21. Rominger CJ, Gelber RD, Gunderson LL, et al: Radiation therapy alone or in combination with chemotherapy in the treatment of residual or inoperable carcinoma of the rectum and rectosigmoid or pelvic recurrence following colorectal surgery: Radiation Therapy Oncology Group study (76-16). *Am J Clin Oncol* 8:118–127, 1985.
22. Martenson JA, Jr., Gunderson LL: Colon and rectum, in CA Perez, LW Brady (eds): *Principles and Practice of Radiation Oncology*. Philadelphia, Lippincott, 1992, pp 1000–1014.
23. Devereux DF, Eisenstat T, Zinkin L: The safe and effective use of postoperative radiation therapy in modified Astler-Coller stage C3 rectal cancer. *Cancer* 63:2393–2396, 1989.
24. Engenhart R, Kimmig B, Marin-Grez M, et al: Combined neutron-photon-therapy of locally recurrent rectosigmoidal tumors. *Strahlenther Onkol* 165:327–329, 1989.
25. Gunderson LL, Martin JK, Beart RW: Intraoperative and external beam irradiation for locally advanced colorectal cancer. *Ann Surg* 207:52–60, 1988.
26. Willett CG, Shellito PC, Tepper JE, et al: Intraoperative electron beam radiation therapy for recurrent locally advanced rectal or rectosigmoid carcinoma. *Cancer* 67:1504–1508, 1991.
27. Kramer T, Share R, Kiel K, et al: Intraoperative radiation therapy of colorectal cancer, in Abe M, Takahashi M (eds): *Intraoperative Radiation Therapy*. New York, Pergamon Press, 1991, pp 308–310.
28. Shaw EG, Gunderson LL, Martin JK, et al: Peripheral nerve and ureteral tolerance to intraoperative radiation therapy: Clinical and dose-response analysis. *Radiother Oncol* 18:247–255, 1990.
29. Tepper JE, Gunderson LL, Orlow E, et al: Complications of intraoperative radiation therapy. *Int J Radiat Oncol Biol Phys* 10:1831–1839, 1984.

CHAPTER 89

Regional Chemotherapy for Advanced Intraabdominal and Pelvic Cancer

James H. Muchmore
Karl R. Aigner
Mansoor H. Beg

Presently, cancer of the colon and rectum is the second most frequent cause of cancer death in the United States. Unfortunately, the overall 5-year survival for this disease has improved only slightly over the last 10 years, from 50 to 58 percent.[1] For approximately 70 percent of patients, the predominant site of treatment failure for colorectal cancer is within the abdominal cavity. Liver metastases together with local recurrence are the most common sites of initial failure following a curative colonic resection (Table 89-1).[2,3]

Local recurrence in the pelvis is the most common site of failure following a curative resection of rectal cancer.

The primary approach to advanced intraabdominal disease in colorectal cancer should be surgical resection. Patients with recurrent or metastatic disease who undergo a complete resection have achieved long-term disease-free survivals. Unfortunately, only 10 percent of patients diagnosed with advanced or recurrent colorectal cancer have resectable neoplasms.[4]

Patients with resectable extrahepatic, intraabdominal metastases have an average 5-year survival of 20 percent.[4] Second-look operations prompted by a rising carcinoembryonic antigen (CEA) level have generated survival rates approaching 31 percent at 5 years following resection of recurrent intraabdominal disease.[5]

Patients with pelvic recurrences of colorectal cancer, besides those with hepatic recurrences, make up another group commonly treated for locally recurrent disease. These patients are primarily treatment failures following surgery for rectal cancer. Several series of selected surgically treated patients with pelvic recurrence of rectal cancer have reported 5-year survivals approaching 25 percent.[6–8]

Most patients with recurrent or intraabdominal disease have multiple sites of involvement within the peritoneal cavity. When isolated regional recurrences are found, the disease is usually extensive, and most of these patients are beyond the purview of the surgeon. Only a very small number of patients with recurrent or advanced disease are effectively treated by surgery alone; therefore, surgical exploration is usually not considered a treatment option.

ADJUVANT THERAPY OF ADVANCED DISEASE

Adjuvant chemotherapy improves the survival of patients with primary colonic cancer with regional lymph node metastases.[9,10] There are no data to support the use of adjuvant chemotherapy following resection of recurrent or colorectal cancer within the abdominal cavity or pelvis. Similarly, the combination of regional chemotherapy and surgical resection for advanced or recurrent large bowel cancer has yielded results that at best are hard to define in terms of a survival benefit.

STAGING OF ADVANCED COLORECTAL CANCER

The difficulty in establishing survival benefit following regional chemotherapy stems in part from the lack of an adequate staging system for patients with advanced intraabdominal disease. The International Staging System of liver metastases from colorectal cancer constitutes the only systematic attempt at staging advanced or recurrent disease.[11] However, there is no adequate staging system for recurrent or advanced colorectal cancer within the abdominal cavity. The best approach to classifying recurrent or advanced colonic cancer

Table 89-1
Patterns of Failure and Recurrence following Curative Surgery for Colorectal Cancer

	Site	*Percent*
Colon		
	Local recurrence	21
	Liver metastases	33
	Intraabdominal recurrence	28
	Distal metastases	26
Rectum		
	Local recurrence	32
	Liver metastases	28
	Intraabdominal recurrence	24
	Distal metastases	36

SOURCE: Adapted from Galandiuk et al.[3]

would be to devise a system that defines both the site and volume of disease. Tentatively, a proposal for a staging system of advance intraabdominal colorectal cancer is presented below. Stage I-R (R = recurrent tumor) would be a single site of recurrence with a particular volume (V_1) of tumor (Table 89-2). Stage II-R would indicate two sites plus V_2 and stage III-R as multiple sites of recurrence in the abdomen plus V_3. Volume of disease would be designated as V_1, less than 5 cm^3; V_2, 5 to 10 cm^3; V_3, 10 to 15 cm^3; and V_4, greater than 15 cm^3. Stage IV-R would indicate multiple sites, or a volume (V_4) of tumor greater than 15 cm^3 and the presence of ascites or jaundice, the rationale being that above a certain tumor volume the patient will essentially have incurable disease and not be salvageable. The presence of jaundice or ascites also makes cure of these patients very unlikely.

RATIONALE FOR REGIONAL INTRAARTERIAL CHEMOTHERAPY

The theoretical basis of regional chemotherapy remains unchanged from the 1950s. It simply states that the amount of drug delivered to a tumor-bearing region can be increased over systemic chemotherapy while limiting systemic toxicity. Most chemotherapeutic agents have a steep dose-response curve, and the resultant systemic toxicity prohibits the use of an effective tumoricidal drug dose. Data from in vitro tissue culture assay shows that most colorectal cancers are resistant to the majority of chemotherapeutic agents at normal systemic dosages.[12] Therefore, regional intraarterial chemotherapy was viewed as a method of achieving regional dose intensification. Theoretically, a complete or significant partial response after regional chemotherapy followed by curative surgery should improve the long-term survival of the patient with an advanced colorectal cancer.

In 1950, the first intraarterial infusion of nitrogen mustard was reported simultaneously by Klopp et al.[13] and Beirman et al.[14] Regional chemotherapy was noted to have enhanced response rates in comparison with systemic chemotherapy. Bierman et al.[15] then applied this technique to patients with hepatic metastases from colorectal cancer. Widespread application of regional chemotherapy was hampered by the lack of a safe delivery system. Common complications included catheter displacement, bleeding, and infection, which were prevalent with temporary arterial catheter systems.[16] Most technical problems and patient reservations were resolved in the 1970s after the development of better arterial catheters and implantable catheter post systems. The Infusaid (Shiley Infusaid Inc., Norwood, MA) implantable pump for hepatic arterial infusion chemotherapy led to a resurgence of interest in regional chemotherapy for metastatic disease from colorectal cancer.[17,18]

Table 89-2
Staging System for Intraabdominal Colorectal Metastases

Stage	*Site*	*Volume of disease*	
Stage I-R	Single site of recurrence—liver, abdominal cavity, or pelvis	V_1	< 5 cm^3
Stage II-R	Two sites of recurrence	V_2	< 10 cm^3
Stage III-R	Multiple sites of recurrence, carcinomatosis	V_3	< 15 cm^3
Stage IV-R	Multiple sites of recurrence, obstructive jaundice, ascites	V_4	< 20 cm^3

PHARMACOKINETIC BASIS FOR REGIONAL CHEMOTHERAPY

In 1974, Eckman et al.[19] formulated a mathematical model describing the pharmacokinetics of regional intraarterial infusions. This model predicted an advantage to regional arterial drug delivery versus systemic therapy as an integral of concentration multiplied by time ($C \times T$). The advantage was dependent on the rate of drug delivery, regional blood flow, and rate of systemic clearance.

During the last several years, most of the emphasis of regional chemotherapy has been directed toward the use of hepatic artery infusion (HAI). Since the liver effectively and rapidly clears several different chemotherapeutic agents, Chen and Gross[20] developed a mathematical model based on the liver as the target organ of regional chemotherapy. The pharmacologic advantage is determined by three factors: (1) regional drug extraction or metabolism, (2) regional blood flow, and (3) total body clearance of the drug. The rapidity of regional drug extraction and clearance in this model primarily determines the regional advantage of drug administration. Total body clearance becomes an important determining factor if the infused drug is cleared more rapidly systemically than regionally. This is particularly true for the use of extrahepatic intraarterial infusions. The model also predicts that the regional advantage would be increased by a low perfusion rate through the target region. However, this advantage may be negated by a high regional blood flow through the target organ containing a hypovascular tumor.

Ensminger et al.[21,22] thoroughly investigated the pharmacokinetics of floxuridine (FUDR) and 5-fluorouracil (5-FU) when delivered through the hepatic artery. A distinct regional advantage was seen for FUDR, because up to 92 percent of the drug is cleared on the first pass through the target organ. There was also a regional advantage for 5-FU, with a 50 percent hepatic extraction rate on the first pass through the liver. The rest of the drugs mitomycin C (MMC), doxorubicin (Adriamycin), carmustine (BCNU), and cisplatin have relatively little regional advantage. However, none of the chemotherapeutic agents are more rapidly cleared regionally than systemically outside of the liver.

Collins[23] has demonstrated an advantage to regional drug therapy over systemic treatment when drug delivery to the tumor-bearing region is evaluated as the area-under-the-concentration-versus-time (AUC_T) curve. A more exacting method to evaluate regional therapy is to determine the uptake or incorporation of a cytotoxic agent into tumor DNA in comparison to normal DNA of the targeted tumor or tumor-bearing region. In studying the treatment of hepatic metastases from colorectal cancer, Chang et al.[24] demonstrated that iododeoxyuridine (IdUrd) has a two- to sevenfold increase in uptake into tumor DNA in comparison to normal liver with regional drug delivery.

Finally, a regionally infused chemotherapeutic agent can be rapidly recovered from the regional venous drainage by extracorporeal hemoperfusion or hemofiltration before the drug reaches the systemic circulation. Total body clearance is artificially enhanced. This technique permits the use of regional intraarterial chemotherapy outside the liver for certain selected chemotherapeutic agents. Dedrick et al.[25] originally described a system of regional chemotherapy plus extracorporeal hemoperfusion for treating patients with primary brain tumors. This technique allows an increase in regional drug dose and thus the regional drug advantage because of rapid total body clearance of the infused chemotherapeutic agent.

RESULTS AND LIMITATIONS

A significant amount of research has focused on the treatment of liver metastases using regional chemotherapy. Response rates following hepatic arterial infusion by either a temporary catheter or implanted pump range from 29 to 88 percent, with an average response rate of 50 percent or approximately twice that with systemic chemotherapy.[26] Unfortunately, regional chemotherapy has been of only limited benefit in treating recurrent colorectal cancer confined to the pelvis.[27]

Patt et al.[27] reported on 21 patients with recurrent pelvic colorectal cancer who had failed radiotherapy or systemic chemotherapy. Only one patient had had no prior treatment. An objective tumor response was noted in only 20 percent of the patients, but 45 percent of them had improvement in pain control. Percivale et al.[28] reported on 9 patients with recurrent colorectal cancer in the pelvis using regional chemotherapy in conjunction with an implantable pump system. The patients in this study had only improvement in pain control, with no significant objective tumor response.

Estes et al.,[29] in studying the combination regional intraarterial chemotherapy plus hyperthermia for patients with recurrent disease in the pelvis, found no better tumor response than that with regional chemotherapy alone. Only 22 percent (2/9) of the patients studied had a partial response, but 88.8 percent achieved good control of their pain.

There are several reasons why the regional chemotherapy of colorectal cancer does not work as well as expected. Most colorectal cancers have considerable resistance to virtually the entire spectrum of chemotherapeutic agents. In tissue culture, 85 percent of the colorectal cancers are found to express high levels of the multidrug resistance (mdr-1) gene or its gene product, the P-170 glycoprotein. These tumors then express mdr-1 without any prior exposure to chemotherapeutic agents.[30] In vitro, the expression of this glycoprotein is associated with induced resistance to multiple structurally unrelated chemotherapeutic agents.

Tissue culture data show that most colorectal cancers are resistant to the majority of chemotherapeutic agents at plasma drug levels obtained with systemic chemotherapy. However, at drug concentrations five to ten times above the normal peak plasma level, colorectal tumor cells become sensitive to almost the entire spectrum of chemotherapeutic agents.[31] Regional intraarterial chemotherapy can at best increase the regional drug dose only two to three times over that of systemic chemotherapy.[32] Therefore, it is not surprising that regional chemotherapy of metastatic colorectal cancer results in only a marginal improvement, at best, in survival.

Another reason that regional chemotherapy for colorectal cancer has lower-than-expected response rates is that it produces only a small pharmacokinetic advantage. Aside from FUDR, regional delivery of most drugs exhibits only a marginal advantage over systemic delivery, and this marginal advantage applies only to the treatment of hepatic metastases.[21] There is no advantage from the pharmacokinetic treatment of recurrent colorectal cancer within the abdomen or pelvis. The regional drug intensification achieved by intraarterial chemotherapy is still far below the 5 to 10 times increased peak drug dose needed to improve tumor response.

A third very important aspect of regional chemotherapy is the variability of regional blood supply and flow to the tumor-bearing area. Patients with intraabdominal and pelvic disease may show significant variability in the blood supply of the treated area. Often, the arterial blood supply to a tumor-bearing region is not identifiable. Additionally, extrahepatic metastatic disease may be hypovascular due to postsurgical scarring or adjuvant radiotherapy.

Tumor vascularity has been reported to determine the responsiveness of hepatic colorectal metastases to chemotherapy.[33] Likewise, Daly et al.[34] have shown that vascularity and the delivery of cytotoxic agents into the nutrient blood supply of metastatic tumor nodules can improve the responsiveness of colorectal cancer to regional chemotherapy. However, again, these data for hepatic metastatic colorectal cancer may not be applicable to intraabdominal or pelvic recurrences. Tseng and Park[35] studied 30 patients with metastatic unresectable pelvic colorectal cancer and, more importantly, evaluated their response to regional chemotherapy in terms of the vascularity of the tumor. Of the total, 8 patients had avascular tumors, 16 had hypovascular tumors, and only 9 had hypervascular or well-vascularized tumors. Interestingly, no differences in tumor response were attributable to the vascularity of the recurrent pelvic disease.

Finally, and probably more important in preventing the delivery of an optimal dose of chemotherapy to the tumor-bearing region, may be the microvascular environment of the tumor. Intratumor vascular shunts, tissue hypertension, and hypoxia are the more likely to be determining factors responsible for the decreased delivery of antineoplastic agents to the tumor DNA.[36] Also, local hypoxia significantly prolongs the chemical reaction time between chemotherapeutic agents and the tumor DNA, making most drugs used in this situation ineffective.

ISOLATED REGIONAL PERFUSION

Isolated regional perfusion can increase the drug dose delivered to the tumor-bearing area 6 to 10 times over that of systemic chemotherapy.[37] The use of isolated regional perfusion for the treatment of advanced cancers, mainly of the limbs, was introduced by Creech et al.[38] in 1957. Ryan et al.[39] published their experience in treating advanced pelvic and recurrent colorectal cancers in 1963 (Fig. 89-1). The drugs (nitrogen mustard, actinomycin D, and 5-FU) used in isolated perfusion had minimal activity against colorectal metastatic disease. Since only a few partial responses were achieved with no improvement in survival, regional perfusion as a treatment modality was discontinued. The pharmacokinetics of 5-FU in this system were not understood. An antimetabolite, 5-FU has little antitumor effect when delivered as a high-dose bolus injection or short-term infusion over 1 h. Because the antitumor effect of 5-FU is time-dependent, it is not well suited for regional perfusion.[40] Alkylating agents and antibiotics are dose-dependent for their antitumor effect (i.e., the higher the delivered dose of drug, the better the response) and therefore are a better choice for isolated regional perfusion.

Despite the lack of encouraging results, hyperthermic regional perfusion remains the most effica-

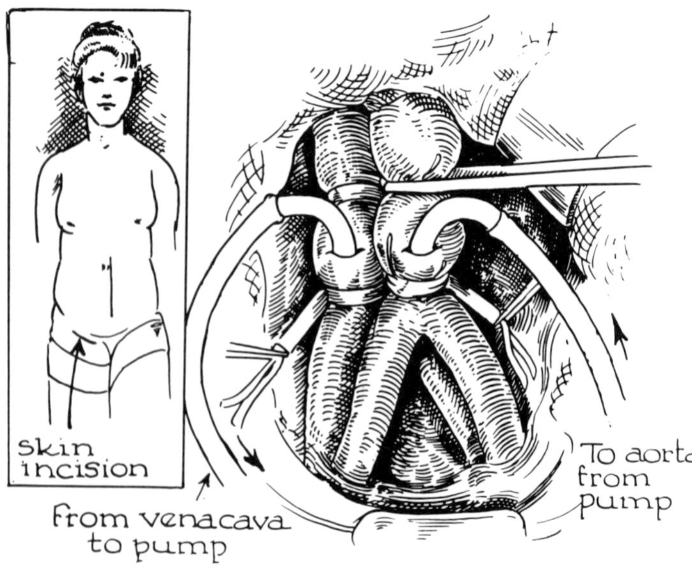

FIG. 89-1. Diagram for pelvic perfusion by a transperitoneal or direct approach to the abdominal aorta and vena cava. Tourniquets are placed around the proximal thighs and inflated during the time of the perfusion to promote the increase in drug levels within the perfused region.

cious method of delivering a tumoricidal concentration of cytotoxic drug to a tumor-bearing region. The combination of 6 to 10 times the systemic drug dose, hyperthermia, and hyperoxygenation can be used to overcome some of the problems of drug resistance and drug delivery related to hypovascular and hypoxic solid tumors.

Recently, there has been a renewed interest in the treatment of colorectal metastatic disease using regional isolated perfusion. In 1987, Wile and Smolin[41] treated 20 patients who had advanced rectal cancer with hyperthermic isolated perfusion. Of the 17 evaluable patients, 1 (5 percent) had a complete response and 7 (35 percent) had partial responses.[41] Up to 3 g of 5-FU was used in the perfusate to treat the patients.

Muller and Aigner[42] have evaluated regional perfusion in the treatment of 29 patients with advanced unresectable rectal carcinomas. Two drug combinations, (1) MMC, 5-FU, and (1-4-amino-2-methyl-5-pyrimidinyl)-methyl-3-(2-chloroethyl)-3-nitrosourea (ACNU) and (2) MMC and mitoxantrone, were evaluated to assess their efficacy within the perfusion system. For these patients with rectal cancer, a 76 percent response rate was noted (10 percent complete response, 66 percent partial response), and there was a resectability rate of 60 percent. This is significantly better than the results reported in earlier studies. The best survival rates were achieved in patients who had a complete or partial response, which was followed by a curative surgical resection.

The response rates and, more importantly, the complete response rates are much better than those obtained with regional intraarterial chemotherapy. Improvement in survival is seen only after a significant number of patients obtain a complete response. Also, the data available suggest that regional chemotherapy techniques are most effective when used in a neoadjuvant setting and then combined with surgical therapy rendering the patient free of disease.

Isolated regional perfusion, as it exists, has a number of drawbacks. The principal problem with this technique is that advanced extrahepatic, intraabdominal malignancies do not have an isolatable blood supply. However, it is possible to treat the entire intraabdominal cavity using a hemicorporeal perfusion, a modification of the pelvic isolated regional perfusion technique. Using intraaortic and intracaval blocking catheters, it is possible to extend the area of perfusion from the pelvis up to the level of the diaphragm.

The second problem is that even though many advanced intraabdominal malignancies appear to be localized, they actually involve the entire abdominal cavity. Local recurrences are often associated with peritoneal seeding or involvement of the retroperitoneal lymphatic drainage system. Therefore, treating pelvic recurrences as limited disease would result in subsequent recurrence within the abdominal cavity and eventual extraabdominal systemic spread.

A third drawback to isolated perfusion is that it can be performed only once or at most twice in the course of treating a patient. Most colorectal cancers appear to be more responsive to repeated treatments as opposed to a single treatment.

REGIONAL CHEMOTHERAPY WITH EXTRACORPOREAL HEMOFILTRATION

Since 1988, a new technique related to isolated regional perfusion has been studied to address the issues of both localized and regional colorectal cancer within the abdominal cavity. Regional intraarterial chemotherapy in combination with extracorporeal hemofiltration has been evaluated as a semiclosed system to deliver high-dose chemotherapy to localized cancer within the liver, peritoneal cavity, or pelvis and simultaneously limit systemic toxicity.[43,44] Also, the technical feasibility of treating various regional areas within the abdominal cavity has been studied and evaluated with respect to response in patients with advanced or recurrent colorectal cancer.

Regional chemotherapy combined with extracorporeal retrieval of the agents was first described by Dedrick et al.[25] for the treatment of primary brain tumors. The advantage, as discussed in an earlier section of this chapter, stems from the rapid total body clearance of the infused drug plus the regional advantage of the infused chemotherapeutic agent.

Aigner et al.[45] then reported on the use of this technique for the treatment of colonic cancers that had metastasized to the liver.[45] Muchmore et al.[46,47] investigated the use of high-dose intraarterial chemotherapy plus extracorporeal hemofiltration as a variant of isolated regional perfusion for advanced hepatic and gastrointestinal tract malignancies. The primary intention of most of these studies was to use regional chemotherapy with hemofiltration as an induction treatment prior to surgical intervention in managing advanced intraabdominal malignancies. This sequencing of therapies has produced a small number of long-term survivors in cases where the disease was considered incurable.

Mitomycin C (MMC), an antibiotic that is concentration-dependent for its tumoricidal effect, has been used in conjunction with 5-FU to treat intraabdominal adenocarcinomas. At higher drug concentrations, MMC has increased tumor cytotoxicity, as supported by tissue culture assay data. The normally obtainable peak plasma level with the systemic administration of MMC is 1 μg/mL. In tissue culture at levels 5 to 10 times over 1 μg/mL, MMC has been shown to be effectively cytotoxic against most colonic adenocarcinomas.[12,48] The duration of tumor cell exposure to

MMC is just as important as drug concentration for producing the optimum cytotoxic drug effect.[48]

Since MMC has a low molecular weight, 334 Da, and is only 15 percent protein-bound in vivo, it can be rapidly recaptured using a modified Gambro hemofiltration system.[47,49] Thus, using high-dose regional chemotherapy plus hemofiltration, the plasma half-life of MMC as well as its systemic toxicity can be significantly reduced.

MATERIALS AND TREATMENT TECHNIQUES

During the past 4 years, 11 patients with advanced or recurrent intraabdominal colorectal cancer were treated by the Department of Surgery, Tulane University Medical Center. Twenty-three courses of high-dose regional chemotherapy with concomitant hemofiltration were used in the treatment of these patients, of whom 5 (45 percent) were men and 6 (55 percent) were women. Their mean age was 56 (range 37 to 70) years. In 5 patients, the disease was limited to the abdominal cavity and the liver; 3 had only peritoneal disease, and 3 patients had recurrences confined to the pelvis.

Patients with combined liver and peritoneal metastases had a hepatic arterial catheter inserted angiographically plus an aortic catheter placed retrograde from the common femoral artery and positioned above the celiac axis at the level of the 10th thoracic vertebra (T-10) just prior to treatment (Fig. 89-2). Patients with primarily pelvic disease had only an aortic arterial catheter inserted by means of a common femoral artery cutdown. The arterial catheters were positioned with fluoroscopy in the lower thoracic aorta at the level of T-10. The correct location was then confirmed with an injection of full-strength radiopaque dye.

Patients with peritoneal and liver disease were simultaneously infused through both aortic and hepatic catheters. Patients with peritoneal and/or pelvic disease were infused only by means of an aortic catheter, and during the infusion (30 to 35 min), tourniquets placed around both upper thighs were inflated to 300 mmHg.

Using the same groin incision employed for the arterial catheter placement, a Plastik fur Medizin (PFM) 16F double-lumen filtration catheter was threaded through a saphenous venotomy and, using fluoroscopic guidance, positioned above the hepatic veins and just below the right atrium. All patients were systemically heparinized with heparin, 150 to 175 U/kg, prior to the placement of their arterial or venous catheters.

The filtration catheter was then connected to a modified Gambro hemofiltration unit with a 1.2-m^2 hollow-tube filter (Fig. 89-3). A balanced hemofiltration was established with a flow rate of 350 to 500 mL/

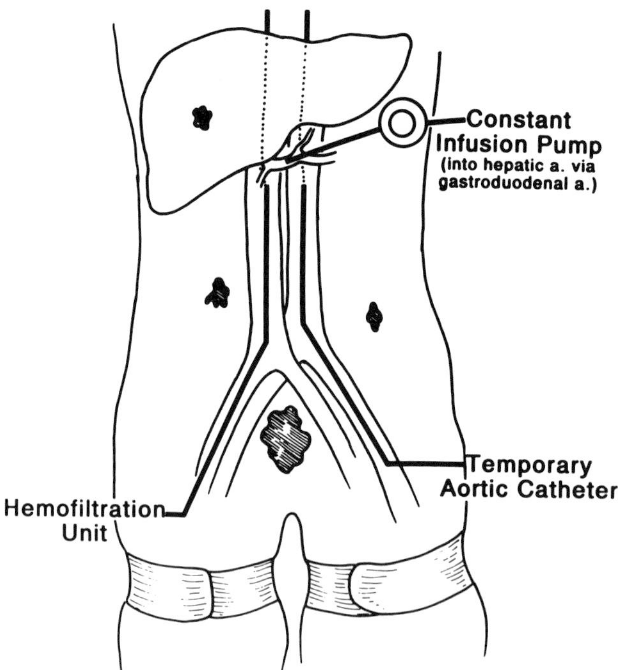

FIG. 89-2. Arterial catheter system used for patients with combined hepatic and intraabdominal colorectal metastases. An implanted catheter and port system is placed in the gastroduodenal artery. A temporary catheter is inserted by means of the common femoral artery and positioned above the celiac axis. For patients with only peritoneal or pelvic disease, only a temporary aortic catheter is inserted. Tourniquets are placed around the thighs and inflated to 300 mmHg during the time of drug infusion.

min and an ultrafiltration rate of 150 mL/min. A modified, bicarbonate-based renal hemofiltration replacement solution (Table 89-3), prewarmed to 38°C (100.4°F), was returned to the patient at essentially the same rate as the efflux of the ultrafiltrate.[49] The balance between the replacement solution and the ultrafiltrate was monitored by a scale maintaining a zero balance between the two. In cases where the patient's systolic blood pressure fell below 100 to 110 mmHg, additional replacement solution was given. Because most patients with advanced intraabdominal malignancies are moderately dehydrated, they are admitted the day before surgery and vigorously hydrated. Inadequate hydration results in a propensity for these patients to become hypotensive at the initiation of the hemofiltration. The patient's core temperature was maintained above 36°C (96.8°F) by preheating the substitution solutions and warming the operating room to 61°C (69.8°F).

Mitomycin C (20 to 30 mg/m^2) was infused intraarterially over 20 to 25 min. This was followed by 5-FU (500 to 750 mg/m^2) delivered over 10 min. In every case the hemofiltration was initiated before the drug administration and then continued for another 30 min following the completion of the arterial drug infusion. The total hemofiltration time was 60 to 70 min. The re-

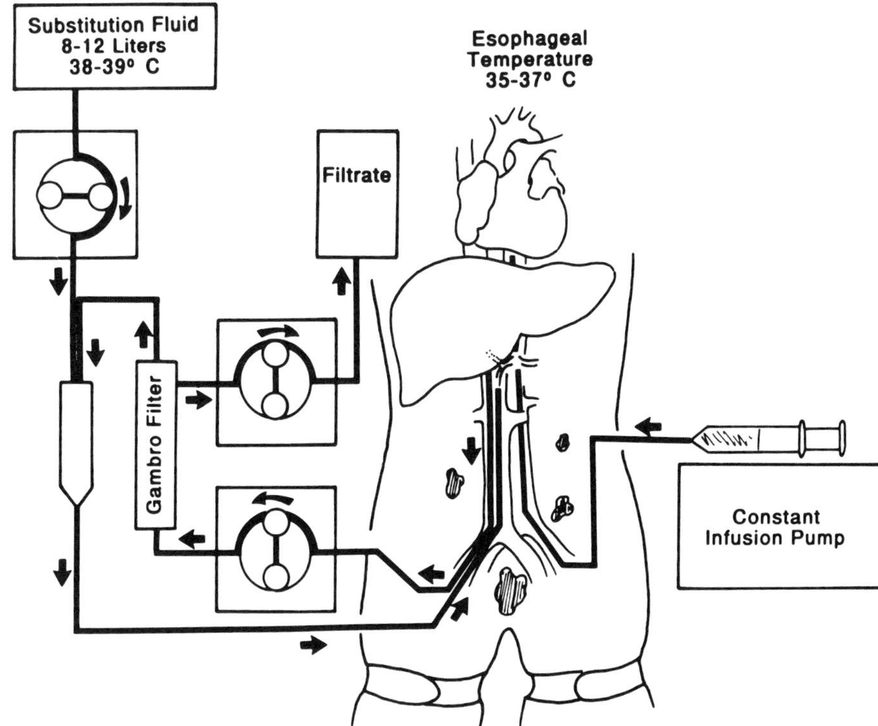

FIG. 89-3. Diagram for regional chemotherapy with extracorporeal hemofiltration. A balanced hemofiltration with a flow rate of 350 to 500 mL/min and an ultrafiltration rate of 150 mL/min is maintained for 1 h, while the chemotherapeutic agent(s) are infused over the first 30/35 min by a constant infusion pump.

gional chemotherapy plus hemofiltration was repeated every 4 to 5 weeks depending on the degree of myelosuppression. The patients in this series were treated with 1 to 4 hemofiltration procedures for an average of 2.1 procedures.

RESULTS

Every patient undergoing regional chemotherapy plus extracorporeal hemofiltration completed the treatments without major complications.

Of the 11 patients treated with regional chemotherapy plus hemofiltration, 2 (18 percent) with advanced pelvic disease and 1 (9 percent) with both liver and pelvic recurrences achieved a complete response as determined by computed tomography (CT), alkaline phosphatase, and CEA. Upon exploration, 1 patient was found to have a small area of residual tumor involving the bladder, which was treated by partial cystectomy. This patient then underwent a second hemofiltration and remained free of disease at over 30 months follow-up. The second patient also underwent exploratory surgery. This patient had residual disease involving the left ureter in the pelvis, which was resected, as well as a small area of residual carcinomatosis in the left upper quadrant. This patient lived more than 2 years and then succumbed to pulmonary metastases. The third patient's disease progressed in a new area of the liver after 4 months.

Two patients (18 percent) with peritoneal disease and liver metastases achieved a partial response. One of these patients, who had extensive peritoneal carcinomatosis, achieved a good partial response and then went 8 months without further therapy before developing symptomatic recurrent disease. Four patients (36 percent), essentially those with combined liver and peritoneal metastases, maintained a stable disease state for an average of 8 months. Two patients (18 percent) with extensive disease and multiple sites of recurrence had no response to therapy. Thus, their disease progressed after a single course of treatment.

The total body clearance of MMC is effectively increased by the use of regional chemotherapy in combination with extracorporeal hemofiltration. The pharmacokinetics of MMC shows that the peak serum drug level is rapidly lowered by 70 percent over 20 to 40 min following the completion of the drug infusion (Fig. 89-4). Similarly, it was found that 5-FU could be rapidly recaptured by the extracorporeal hemofiltration system. The reduction in plasma drug levels was a re-

Table 89-3
Hemofiltration Substitution Solutions[a]

3 L N/S	+ 30 meq $CaCl_2$
3 L N/S	+ 18 meq $MgCl_2$
3 L N/S	+ 12 meq KCl
3 L D5W	+ 450 meq $NaHCO_3$

[a]All four solutions infused simultaneously.

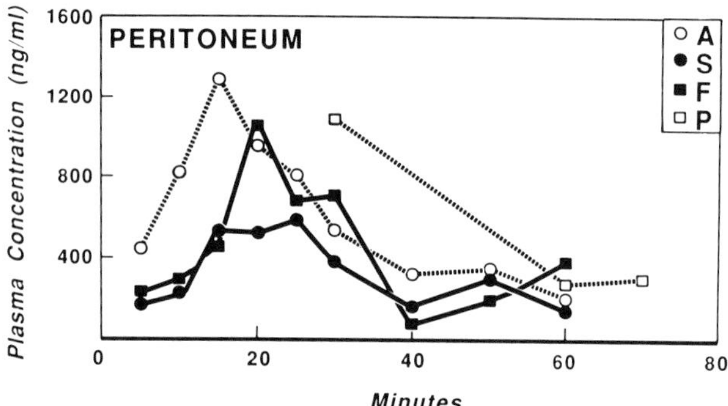

FIG. 89-4. Pharmacokinetics of mitomycin C within the regional chemotherapy with hemofiltration (RC-H) system. *A*. The effect of RC-H during an aortic abdominal infusion using 40 mg of MMC.

flection of a combination of drug recaptured, drug metabolized by the liver, and drug remaining attached to the microtubing within the hemofilter. The actual drug detectable in the ultrafiltrate following the completion of hemofiltration represented only 25 to 30 percent of the total drug dose. Peripheral plasma drug levels were also examined during hemofiltration, and the pharmacokinetics of MMC or 5-FU was similar to that found in the central vascular compartment. When the peripheral blood was studied 30 min after the end of hemofiltration, no rebound of MMC or 5-FU was demonstrable.

COMPLICATIONS

Only 4 patients have developed significant complications due to the regional chemotherapy plus hemofiltration. In three of these, the problem was related to the severe thrombocytopenia which developed. One patient had received 30 mg/M^2 of mitomycin-C and two developed severe thrombocytopenia following a third treatment of regional chemotherapy plus hemofiltration. Currently, the total dose of MMC has been limited 22 mg/m^2. One patient developed an infection and thrombosis of an implanted catheter and port system which required surgical replacement.

REFERENCES

1. Boring CC, Squires TS, Tong T: Cancer statistics 1993. *CA* 43:7–27, 1993.
2. Willett CG, Tepper JE, Cohen AM, et al: Failure patterns following curative resection of colonic carcinoma. *Ann Surg* 200:685–690, 1984.
3. Galandiuk S, Wieand HS, Moertel CG, et al: Patterns of recurrence after curative resection of carcinoma of the colon and rectum. *Surg Gynecol Obstet* 174:27–32, 1992.
4. August DA, Ottow RT, Sugarbaker PH: Clinical perspective of human colorectal cancer metastasis. *Cancer Metast* 3:303–324, 1984.
5. Martin EW Jr, Minton JP, Carey LC: CEA-directed second-look surgery in the asymptomatic patient after primary resection of colorectal cancer. *Ann Surg* 202:310–317, 1985.
6. Pearlman NW, Donohue RE, Stiegmann GV, et al: Pelvic and sacropelvic exenteration for locally advanced or recurrent anorectal cancer. *Arch Surg* 122:537–541, 1987.
7. Wanebo HJ, Gaker DL, Whitehill R, et al: Pelvic recurrence of rectal cancer. *Ann Surg* 205:482–495, 1987.
8. Wanebo HJ, Koness RJ, Turk PS, et al: Composite resection of posterior pelvic malignancy. *Ann Surg* 215:685–695, 1992.
9. Laurie JA, Moertel CG, Fleming TR, et al: Surgical adjuvant therapy of large-bowel carcinoma: An evaluation of levamisole and the combination of levamisole and fluorouracil. *J Clin Oncol* 7:1441–1456, 1989.
10. Moertel CG, Fleming TR, Macdonald JS, et al: Levamisole and fluorouracil for adjuvant therapy of resected colon carcinoma. *N Engl J Med* 322:352–358, 1990.
11. van de Velde CJH: The staging of hepatic metastases arising from colorectal cancer. *Recent Results Cancer Res* 100:85–90, 1986.
12. Schroy PC III, Cohen A, Winawer SJ, et al: New chemotherapeutic drug sensitivity assay for colon carcinomas in monolayer culture. *Cancer Res* 48:3236–3244, 1988.
13. Klopp CT, Alford TC, Bateman J, et al: Fractionated intraarterial cancer chemotherapy with bis-amine hydrochloride: A preliminary report. *Ann Surg* 132:811–832, 1950.
14. Beirman HR, Shimkin MB, Byron RL Jr, et al: The effects of intra-arterial administration of nitrogen mustard. *Fifth Int Cancer Cong Paris* 1950, p186.
15. Bierman HR, Byron RL, Kelly KH: Treatment of inoperable visceral and regional metastases by intra-arterial catheterization. *Cancer Res* 11:236, 1951.
16. Kokame GM, Krementz ET, Creech O Jr: Regional chemotherapy, in Ulin AW, Gollub SS (eds): *Surgical Bleeding: Handbook for Medicine, Surgery, and Specialties*. New York, McGraw-Hill, 1966, pp 475–486.
17. Buchwald H, Grage TB, Cassilopoulos PP, et al: Intra-arterial infusion chemotherapy for hepatic carcinoma using a totally implantable infusion pump. *Cancer* 45:866–869, 1980.
18. Niederhuber JE, Ensminger W, Gyves J, et al: Regional chemotherapy of colorectal cancer metastatic to the liver. *Cancer* 53:1336–1343, 1984.
19. Eckman WW, Patlak CS, Fenstermacher JD: A critical evaluation of the principles governing the advantages of intra-arterial infusions. *J Pharmacokinet Biopharm* 2:257–285, 1974.
20. Chen H-SG, Gross JR: Intra-arterial infusion of anticancer drugs: Theoretic aspects of drug delivery and review of responses. *Cancer Treat Rep* 64:31–40, 1980.
21. Ensminger WD, Gyves JW: Clinical pharmacology of hepatic arterial chemotherapy. *Semin Oncol* 10:176–182, 1983.
22. Ensminger WD, Gyves JW: Regional cancer chemotherapy. *Cancer Treat Rep* 68:101–115, 1984.
23. Collins JM: Pharmacokinetics and clinical monitoring, in Chabner BA, Collins JM (eds): *Cancer Chemotherapy: Principles and Practice*. Philadelphia, Lipincott, 1990, pp 16–31.
24. Chang AE, Collins JM, Speth PAJ, et al: Phase I study of intraarterial iododeoxyuridine in patients with colorectal liver metastases. *J Clin Oncol* 7:662–668, 1989.
25. Dedrick RL, Oldfield EH, Collins JM: Arterial drug infusion with extracorporeal removal: I. Theoretical basis with particular reference to the brain. *Cancer Treat Rep* 68:373–380, 1984.
26. Niederhuber JE, Grochow LB: Status of infusion chemotherapy for the treatment of liver metastases, in Principles and Practices of Oncology: Updates 3:1–9, 1989.
27. Patt YZ, Peters RE, Chuang VP, et al: Palliation of pelvic recurrence of colorectal cancer with intra-arterial 5-fluorouracil and mitomycin. *Cancer* 56:2175–2180, 1985.

28. Percivale P, Nobile MT, Vidili MG, et al: Treatment of colorectal cancer pelvic recurrences with hypogastric intra-arterial 5-fluorouracil by means of totally implantable port systems. *Reg Cancer Treat* 3:143–146, 1990.
29. Estes NC, Morphis JG, Hornback NB, et al: Intraarterial chemotherapy and hyperthermia for pain control in patients with recurrent rectal cancer. *Am J Surg* 152:597–601, 1986.
30. Goldstein LJ, Galski H, Fojo A, et al: Expression of a multidrug resistance gene in human cancers. *J Natl Cancer Inst* 81:116–124, 1989.
31. Link KH, Aigner KR, Kuehn W, et al: Prospective correlative chemosensitivity testing in high-dose intraarterial chemotherapy for liver metastases. *Cancer Res* 46:4837–4840, 1986.
32. Dedrick RL: Arterial drug infusion: Pharmacokinetic problems and pitfalls. *J Natl Cancer Inst* 80:84–89, 1988.
33. Kim DK, Watson RC, Pahnke LD, et al: Tumor vascularity as a prognostic factor for hepatic tumor. *Ann Surg* 185:31–34, 1977.
34. Daly JM, Kemeny N, Sigurdson ER, et al: Regional infusion for colorectal hepatic metastases. *Arch Surg* 122:1273–1277, 1987.
35. Tseng MH, Park HC: Pelvic intra-arterial mitomycin C infusion in previously treated patients with metastatic, unresectable, pelvic colorectal cancer and angiographic determination of tumor vascularity. *J Clin Oncol* 3:1093–1100, 1985.
36. Vaupal P: Hypoxia in neoplastic tissue. *Microvasc Res* 13:399–408, 1977.
37. Susuki K, Bruce WR, Baptista J: Characterization of cytotoxic steroids in human feces and their putative role in the etiology of human colon cancer. *Cancer Lett* 33:307–317, 1986.
38. Creech O Jr, Krementz ET, Ryan RF, et al: Chemotherapy of cancer: Regional perfusion utilizing an extracorporeal circuit. *Ann Surg* 148:616–632, 1958.
39. Ryan RF, Schramel RJ, Creech O Jr: Value of perfusion in pelvic surgery. *Dis Colon Rectum* 6:297–300, 1963.
40. Mitchell RB, Ratain MJ, Vogelzang NJ: Experimental rationale for continuous infusion chemotherapy, in Lokich JJ (ed): *Cancer Chemotherapy by Infusion*. Chicago, Precept Press, 1990, pp 3–34.
41. Wile A, Smolin M: Hyperthermic pelvic isolation-perfusion in the treatment of refractory pelvic cancer. *Arch Surg* 122:1321–1325, 1987.
42. Muller H, Aigner KR: Isolated pelvic perfusion for nonresectable pelvic tumors. *Reg Cancer Treat* 4:31, 1991.
43. Aigner KR: Methodische Ansatze zur optimierung des Konzentrations-Zeit-Faktors in der regionalen Chemotherapie, in Seeber S, Aigner KR, Enghofer E (eds): *Die lokoregionale Tumortherapie, Moglichkeiten und Grenzen*. Berlin, de Gruyter, 1988, pp. 81–93.
44. Muchmore JH, Krementz ET, Carter RD, et al: Treatment of abdominal malignant neoplasms using regional chemotherapy with hemofiltration. *Arch Surg* 126:1390–1396, 1991.
45. Aigner KR, Muller H, Walter H, et al: Drug filtration in high-dose regional chemotherapy. *Contrib Oncol* 29:261–280, 1988.
46. Muchmore JH, Krementz ET, Carter RD, et al: Concomitant high-dose intraarterial chemotherapy plus hemofiltration in treating advanced regional abdominal malignancies. *Reg Cancer Treat* 3:211–215, 1990.
47. Muchmore JH, Preslan J, Meyer M, et al: Pharmacokinetics of high-dose intra-arterial chemotherapy with concomitant hemofiltration (HICCF). *Proceedings of the Annual Meeting of the American Association for Cancer Research 30;* A1138, 1989.
48. Link KH, Staib L, Beger HG: Influence of exposure concentration and exposure time $C \times T$ on toxicity of cytostatic drugs to HT29 human colorectal carcinoma cells. *Reg Cancer Treat* 2:189–197, 1989.
49. Fjuii A: A new chemotherapy using combination hemodialysis and direct hemoperfusion. *J Jpn Soc Cancer Ther* 15:1121–1130, 1980.

PART 15

Systemic Therapy for Recurrent or Metastatic Disease

CHAPTER 90

Principles of Chemotherapy for Colorectal Cancer

Richard L. Schilsky

OVERVIEW

The development of chemotherapy for colorectal cancer has paralleled the development of 5-fluorouracil (5-FU) as an effective antineoplastic agent. Synthesized by Heidelberger et al.[1] in 1957 and introduced into clinical trials soon thereafter, 5-FU remains the single most effective chemotherapy drug for treatment of colorectal cancer. During the past 35 years, the biochemical pharmacology of the drug has been clearly elucidated and a variety of routes and schedules of administration have been explored in the clinic. Despite vast experience with the drug, the optimal manner in which 5-FU should be administered and its primary mechanism of action in human tumors have not yet been determined. Nevertheless, 5-FU remains widely used in treatment of a number of solid tumors not only because of its inherent antitumor activity but because of its synergistic interactions with other antitumor agents and with radiation. Knowledge of the biochemical pharmacology of the drug has led to the development of several rationally designed combination chemotherapy programs that appear to be superior to single-agent 5-FU in treatment of advanced colorectal cancer, although further clinical testing is necessary to define the optimal treatment regimen.

Other classes of chemotherapeutic agents have little utility in treatment of colorectal cancer. Response rates of 10 to 15 percent have been reported for the nitrosoureas such as carmustine and semustine.[2-4] These drugs produce delayed and cumulative bone marrow toxicity, late-onset renal failure, and pulmonary fibrosis; they are also potent leukemogens.[5] Their routine use in treatment of colorectal cancer cannot be recommended. Mitomycin C also produces responses of short duration in 10 to 15 percent of patients.[6-8] Its potential for hematologic and renal toxicity, particularly hemolytic-uremic syndrome, diminishes enthusiasm for its routine use.

Although dozens of new drugs have been screened, there is not convincing evidence of meaningful efficacy for any of them. Paclitaxel (Taxol), a recently introduced novel microtubule inhibitor, produced minor responses in some patients with advanced colorectal cancer during phase I testing.[9] Phase II studies performed to evaluate paclitaxel efficacy have not demonstrated significant activity in colorectal cancer.[10] Of greater interest is irinotecan (CPT-11), a novel topoisomerase I inhibitor recently introduced into clinical trial. In preliminary studies, a 46 percent response rate was observed in 17 patients with advanced colorectal cancer.[11] These observations are particularly encouraging in view of preclinical data suggesting that colonic tumors may be uniquely sensitive to inhibition of topoisomerase I.[12] Clinical trials combining CPT-11 with 5-FU and leucovorin have recently begun.

Despite the limited number of drugs available with activity against colorectal cancer, efforts have been made to combine agents empirically in an attempt to produce more effective treatment regimens. Considerable enthusiasm was generated for the addition of semustine to 5-FU following the report from the Mayo Clinic of a small randomized comparison of semustine, vincristine, and 5-FU (MOF) versus 5-FU alone in patients with metastatic colorectal cancer.[13] The objective response rate for MOF was more than twice that for 5-FU (43 versus 19 percent), but no significant survival advantage was observed. Subsequent attempts to confirm this superiority have produced variable results, and response rates for MOF or MF (semustine and 5-FU) regimens have ranged from 4 to 40 percent.[7,14–20] Other studies attempting to substitute mitomycin C for the nitrosourea or to employ multiple nitrosoureas such as MOF + streptozotocin have not produced greater objective tumor regression than expected from 5-FU alone.[21–24]

More recently, the addition of cisplatin to 5-FU has been evaluated based on preclinical studies demonstrating synergy between these agents. While initial phase II studies demonstrated response rates of 30 to 40 percent, several randomized trials (Table 90-1) failed to demonstrate any advantage of the combination over 5-FU alone in response rate or survival.[25–30] In view of the increased toxicity that results from addition of cisplatin, these regimens cannot be recommended for routine clinical use.

Because there are a limited number of effective agents for treatment of colorectal cancer, most recent studies have focused on biochemical modulation of 5-FU and on alterations of the route and schedule of 5-FU administration in an attempt to define the optimal way of utilizing this drug. Investigations of the mechanisms of drug resistance in colonic cancer are also ongoing and may provide important insights that will result in the design of more effective chemotherapy regimens. This chapter will focus on mechanisms of drug resistance in colonic cancer and on recent insights into the biochemical and clinical pharmacology of 5-FU, which provide the scientific foundation for most of the current treatment approaches in this disease.

DRUG RESISTANCE IN COLORECTAL CANCER

The resistance of colorectal cancers to virtually all classes of antineoplastic drugs is a major obstacle to the successful treatment of these tumors. The biochemical mechanisms of drug resistance in colorectal tumors have not yet been well characterized and are likely to vary considerably among individual tumors. Resistance mechanisms that appear to play a role in many tumors include enhanced efflux of drugs due to overexpression of P-glycoprotein; inactivation of drugs due to increased cellular levels of glutathione and glutathione transferases; enhanced cellular repair of drug-induced injury due to overexpression of DNA repair enzymes; and increased levels of thymidylate synthase (TS), the target enzyme for 5-FU.

Multidrug Resistance

The phenomenon of multidrug resistance (MDR) is manifest as the ability of malignant cells to develop cross-resistance to a variety of lipophilic drugs that share little functional or structural similarity.[31] Antitumor agents that are affected by the MDR phenotype

Table 90-1
Randomized Studies of Combination 5-FU + Cisplatin versus 5-FU Alone in Patients with Advanced Colorectal Cancer

Authors	*5-FU dose*	*Cisplatin dose*	*Response, percent*	*Survival, weeks*
Poon et al.[25]	a) 500 mg/m^2/day × 5 q 5 weeks	—	10	No difference
	b) 325 mg/m^2/day × 5 q 5 weeks	20 mg/m^2/day × 5	15	
Kemeny et al.[26]	a) 1000 mg/m^2/day × 5 q 4 weeks	—	3	52
	b) 1000 mg/m^2/day × 5 q 4 weeks	20 mg/m^2/day × 5	25	43
Lokich et al.[27]	a) 300 mg/m^2/day × 10 weeks	—	33	42
	b) 300 mg/m^2/day × 10 weeks	20 mg/m^2/week	31	48
Loehrer et al.[28]	a) 15 mg/kg/week	—	19	39
	b) 15 mg/kg/week	60 mg/m^2 q 3 weeks	22	40
LaBianca et al.[29]	a) 600 mg/m^3/week	—	15	56
	b) 600 mg/m^2/week	60 mg/m^2 q 3 weeks	20	43
Diaz-Rubio et al.[30]	a) 1000 mg/m^2/day × 5	—	23	39
	b) 1000 mg/m^2/day × 5	100 mg/m^2 q 4 weeks	21	51

Table 90-2
Anticancer Agents Associated with Multidrug Resistance

Antitumor antibiotics	Daunorubicin, doxorubicin, actinomycin D, mitoxantrone, mitomycin C
Tubulin-binding drugs	Vincristine, vinblastine, taxol
Topoisomerase inhibitors	Etoposide, teniposide
Antimetabolites	Trimetrexate

are shown in Table 90-2. The hallmark of MDR is the appearance in tumor cells of a 170-kDa membrane glycoprotein, called P-glycoprotein (P-gp), that functions as an energy-dependent active efflux pump.[32] P-glycoprotein is one of a family of membrane-associated transport proteins that are highly conserved in nature. In humans, the P-gp molecule is encoded by the MDR-1 gene and amplification or overexpression of this gene is sufficient to produce the MDR phenotype.[33–35] Although the normal function of P-gp is unknown, it can be detected in a variety of normal tissues, including the stomach, jejunum, colon, biliary canaliculi, and proximal renal tubules.[36,37] This distribution has led to speculation that MDR-1 gene expression plays an important role in transmembrane movement of environmental toxins. MDR-1 RNA levels are detectable in many intrinsically drug-resistant human tumors—including colonic, renal, and pancreatic carcinomas—and an increase in MDR-1 gene expression has been noted after an initial response to chemotherapy in tumors such as acute leukemia, breast cancer, and malignant lymphoma.[38–40] High levels of MDR-1 RNA are found in more than 80 percent of untreated colonic tumors, with the highest levels detectable in well- and moderately well differentiated tumors.[39] Immunohistochemical studies employing monoclonal antibodies directed against P-gp have recently demonstrated expression of P-gp in nearly 90 percent of stage B_2 colon carcinomas, with significantly increased immunoreactivity detected at the invasive front of the tumor.[41]

A variety of noncytotoxic drugs have now been found to interact with P-gp and compete with antitumor drugs for binding sites on the molecule.[42–46] Drugs such as calcium channel blockers, cyclosporine, and tamoxifen are able to reverse MDR in vitro and have now been brought to clinical trial in an attempt to overcome resistance to drugs such as vinblastine, etoposide, and doxorubicin (Table 90-3). Phase I clinical trials have demonstrated the feasibility of administering MDR-modulating agents with antineoplastic drugs and have suggested some efficacy for this approach, particularly in treatment of refractory hematologic malignancies.[47–50] Further studies are necessary to determine if MDR modulation will result in improved treatment for colorectal cancers.

Table 90-3
Agents Able to Reverse MDR in Vitro

Class of agent	*Example*
Calcium channel blockers	Verapamil
Calmodulin inhibitors	Phenothiazines
Immunosuppressive drugs	Cyclosporine A
Antiestrogens	Tamoxifen
Detergents	Cremophor EL
Steroid hormones	Progesterone

Glutathione and Glutathione Transferase

Glutathione (GSH) is a nonprotein thiol compound important in a number of intracellular processes, including binding and detoxification of reactive oxygen species, environmental toxins, and drugs. Increased levels of GSH have been detected in alkylating agent and cisplatin-resistant human ovarian cancer cell lines and have been implicated as the mechanism of drug resistance in these cells.[51–53] Increased activity of glutathione-S-transferases (GST), enzymes involved in conjugation of toxic molecules to GSH, also appears to contribute to drug resistance in some human tumor cell lines.[54–56] The GSTs are a family of isoenzymes with distinctive isoelectric properties encoded by separate gene families. The anionic GST π is the isoenzyme most commonly associated with drug resistance in human tumors.[57] In human colonic cancers, GST π RNA levels are increased an average of 3.7-fold over levels in normal colon surrounding the tumor. In one recent study of 23 untreated colon cancers, levels of GSH, GST, and GSH peroxidase were significantly higher in tumors than in surrounding normal tissue, ranging from 1.5 to fivefold higher than normal.[58]

Further evidence for the role of GSH in drug resistance comes from studies demonstrating that depletion of cellular GSH stores can restore sensitivity to alkylating agents and cisplatin. Buthionine sulfoximine (BSO) is a synthetic amino acid that binds to the enzyme gamma glutamyl cysteine synthetase, thereby inhibiting production of GSH. In human ovarian cancer cells resistant to melphalan and cisplatin, GSH depletion by BSO results in enhanced sensitivity to the cytotoxic effects of these drugs, a result also demonstrated in tumor-bearing animals.[59–61] Buthionine sulfoximine has recently entered clinical trial in combination with melphalan. Preliminary results suggest that BSO does deplete cellular GSH levels in peripheral blood cells without producing unacceptably severe toxicity.[62] Determination of the value of this approach in treatment of human tumors will require further study.

DNA Repair

Repair of drug-induced DNA injury is believed to be a fundamental mechanism of resistance to alkylating agents, cisplatin, nitrosoureas, and ionizing radiation. Although the biochemical mechanisms responsible for repair of mammalian DNA are incompletely characterized at present, it appears that nucleotide excision repair is the primary mechanism by which cells repair drug-induced DNA injury.[63,64] This process presumably requires the activity of a series of enzymes to recognize the damage, incise the DNA on either side of the damaged segment, generate new DNA to replace the excised portion, and ligate the new DNA segment to the existing DNA strand. A human excision repair gene designated ERCC-1 has recently been isolated and cloned and shares significant homology to yeast and bacterial excision-repair genes.[65]

The cellular response to DNA damage includes arrest of the cell cycle in G2 phase as well as induction of repair enzymes.[66] Cell cycle arrest presumably allows repair of potentially lethal DNA damage before mitosis occurs. Premature entry of alkylating agent–treated cells into mitosis following exposure to caffeine results in increased DNA damage and cell death.[67]

The net cytotoxic effects of drugs such as alkylating agents and cisplatin represent the balance between DNA injury and repair, and amplified repair mechanisms appear to play a role in tumor cell resistance to these drugs. Human ovarian cancer cells selected in vitro for resistance to cisplatin display a threefold increase in unscheduled DNA synthesis, representing increased repair.[67] Similar results have been found in ovarian cancer cells obtained from a patient who was clinically resistant to cisplatin therapy.[68] Recently, increased expression of the excision repair gene ERCC-1 has been reported in ovarian cancer cells selected in vitro for cisplatin resistance.[69]

In addition to excision repair of DNA, cells contain enzymes able to remove alkyl moieties from DNA, thereby repairing drug-induced injury without excision of the affected DNA segment. A specific example is the protein O^6-alkyl guanine transferase (AGT) that repairs DNA injury produced by chloroethyl nitrosoureas.[70] Cells containing large amounts of this protein are relatively resistant to this class of antitumor agents. Elevated levels of AGT have been detected in nearly 50 percent of newly diagnosed colonic carcinomas and may be responsible for nitrosourea resistance in such cases.[58]

A better understanding of the biochemical mechanisms of DNA repair may lead to effective new strategies to circumvent resistance in the clinic. Aphidocolin, an inhibitor of DNA polymerases alpha and gamma, inhibits the unscheduled DNA synthesis observed in cisplatin-resistant cell lines and produces a 3.5-fold enhancement of cisplatin cytotoxicity.[67] Similar results have been obtained with agents such as cytosine arabinoside and hydroxyurea.[71] DNA methylating agents such as dacarbazine or synthetic alkyl oligodeoxynucleotides such as O^6-benzylguanine have been used effectively in vitro and in tumor-bearing animals to reverse resistance to nitrosoureas.[72] These agents deplete cells of AGT, thereby increasing their vulnerability to alkylation of DNA at the O^6 position of guanine. Strategies such as these have recently been introduced into clinical trial to determine their feasibility and efficacy.[73]

CELLULAR PHARMACOLOGY OF 5-FLUOROURACIL

The predominant pathway of 5-FU activation and cytotoxicity has not been determined with certainty for any human tumor and may well vary considerably among tumor types. Intracellularly, 5-FU is metabolized to fluorouridine monophosphate (FUMP) and subsequently converted to the active nucleotide forms fluorouridine triphosphate (FUTP) and fluorodeoxyuridine monophosphate (FdUMP) (Fig. 90-1).[74–77] In many experimental tumors, FdUMP inhibition of thymidylate synthase (TS), and thereby of DNA synthesis, appears to be the primary mechanism of cytotoxicity.[78–81] In other systems, however, FUTP incorporation into RNA and interference with RNA processing and function appears to be the primary determinant of drug effect.[82–84] Recent data suggest that incorporation of 5-FdUTP into DNA may produce single-strand breaks that also contribute to the drug's cytotoxicity.[85–92] In human colonic cancer cells, the primary effect of 5-FU appears to be influenced by the duration of drug exposure, with short-term exposure favoring RNA-directed effects and prolonged exposure favoring DNA-directed cell killing.[93]

Thymidylate synthase is the only de novo source of thymidylate in the cell and, as such, is a key enzyme in mammalian DNA synthesis. This enzyme catalyzes the reductive methylation of deoxyuridylate by 5-10 methylene tetrahydrofolate to form thymidylate and dihydrofolate (Fig. 90-2). In the presence of sufficient reduced folate, 5-FdUMP forms a covalent ternary complex with the enzyme, which is slowly dissociable.[94–98] Binding of 5-FdUMP to TS is enhanced by

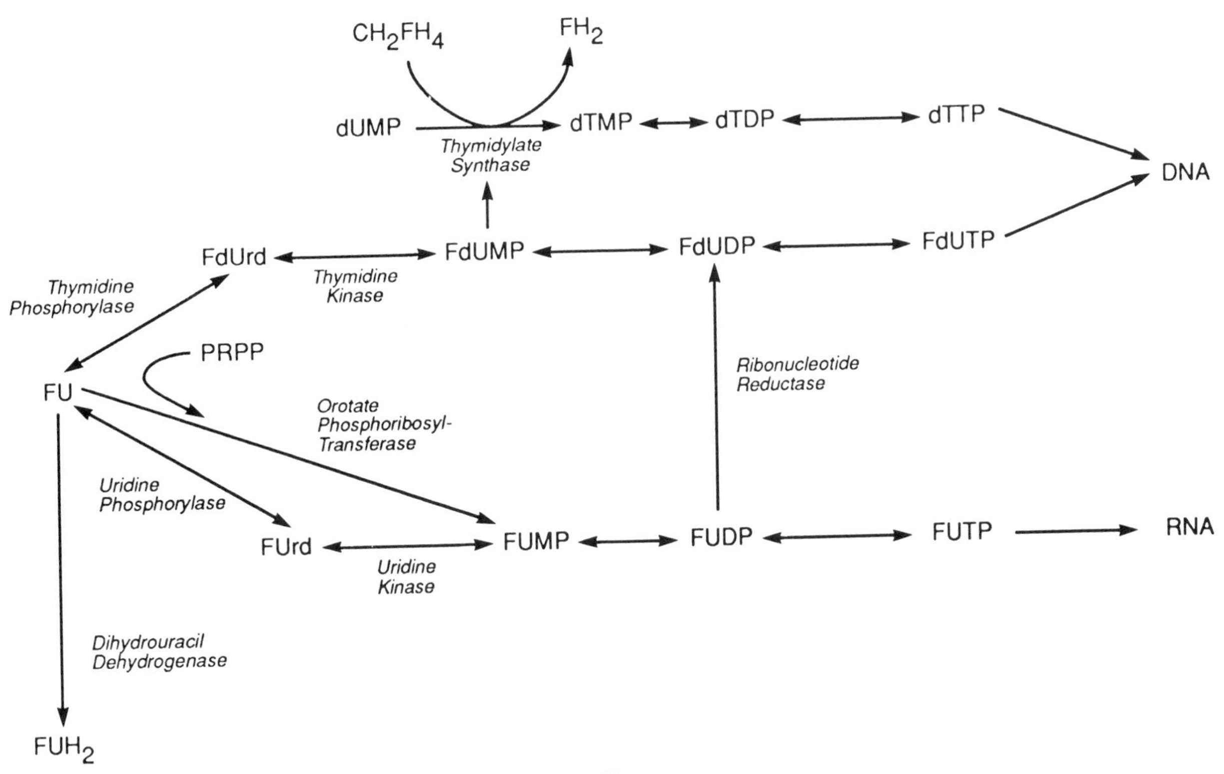

FIG. 90-1. Metabolic pathways and sites of action of 5-fluorouracil.

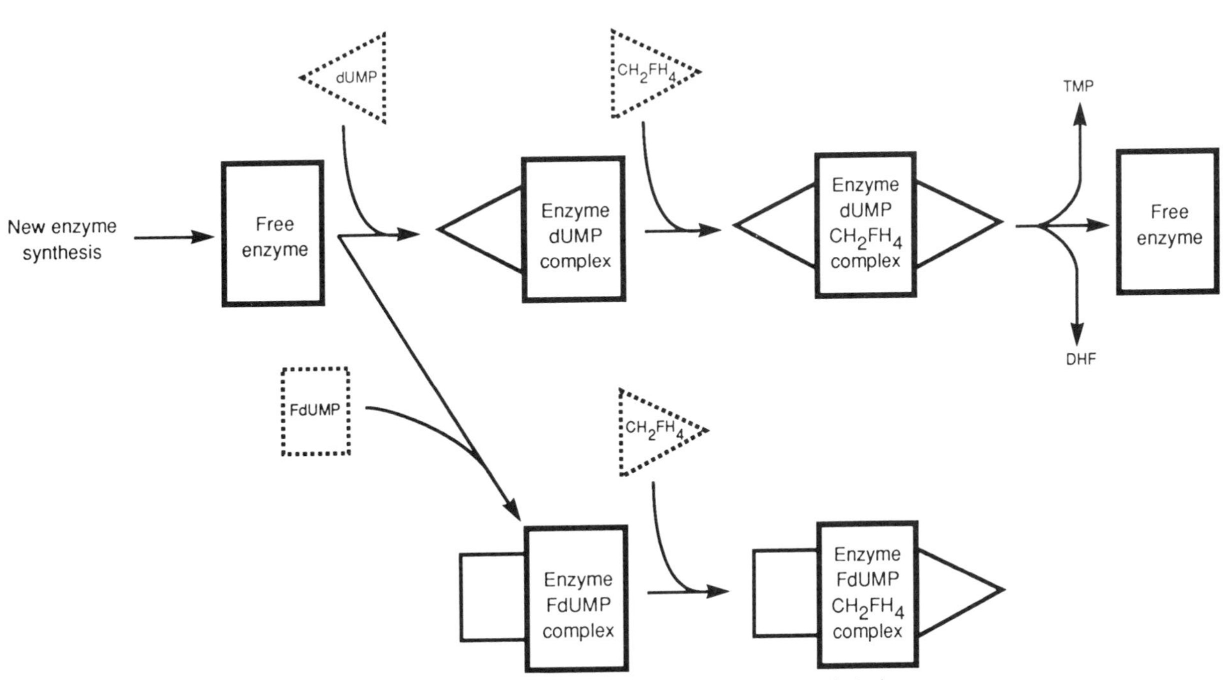

FIG. 90-2. Thymidylate synthase (TS) reaction. TS normally catalyzes the reductive methylation of dUMP by CH_2 FH_4 to form thymidylate (TMP) and dihydrofolate (DHF). In the presence of FdUMP, a covalent ternary complex is formed, resulting in TS inhibition.

Table 90-4
Determinants of Sensitivity to 5-Fluorouracil

Activity of enzymes required for 5-FU activation (e.g., uridine and thymidine phosphorylase and kinase)
Availability of cofactors required for 5-FU activation (e.g., phosphoribosyl pyrophosphate)
Amount of thymidylate synthase
Availability of reduced folates
Size of endogenous pools of UTP and dUMP
Activity of nucleoside transport processes
Activity of catabolic pathways

high concentrations of 5-10-CH_2-FH_4 and by polyglutamation of the folate.[99–101] The importance of cellular folate pools as biochemical determinants of FdUMP-TS binding has been underscored recently by the demonstration that the cytotoxic effects of 5-FU can be markedly enhanced by the provision of adequate amounts of reduced folate cofactor.[102–106] In both mouse leukemia cells and human colonic carcinoma cells, the cytotoxic effect of 5-FU can be enhanced at least threefold by the provision of 10 μM 5-formyl tetrahydrofolate (leucovorin) in the culture medium. This potentiation of 5-FU effect appears to be due primarily to stabilization of the FdUMP-enzyme-folate ternary complex and prolonged enzyme inhibition rather than to an increase in the extent of TS inhibition by the drug.

A number of factors are important in determining the sensitivity of tumor cells to 5-FU. These are summarized in Table 90-4 and include the activity of enzymes such as uridine and thymidine phosphorylase and kinase that are necessary for activation of the drug[107–109]; the availability of cofactors such as phosphoribosyl pyrophosphate that is necessary for 5-FU activation by orotic acid phosphoribosyl transferase[110]; the size of the endogenous pools of deoxyuridine monophosphate (dUMP) and uridine triphosphate (UTP) that compete with the drug for enzyme binding and incorporation into RNA,[111–113] and the amount of TS[114–116] and availability of reduced folates. The activity of nucleoside transport processes[117] and uptake of preformed thymidine from the extracellular fluid may also play a role in determining the outcome of treatment with 5-FU.

BIOCHEMICAL MODULATION OF 5-FLUOROURACIL

Biochemical modulation refers to the use of one or more agents to enhance the activation and/or cytotoxicity of another agent. The result may be either additive or synergistic cytotoxicity. Most often, biochemical modulation has been used to enhance the intracellular activation of antimetabolite drugs. For this purpose, modulating agents have been selected that enhance the activity of enzymes required for activation of cytotoxic drugs, increase the availability of cofactors required by cytotoxic drugs, or deplete cells of endogenous substrates that compete with drugs for binding to target enzymes. Each of these strategies has been employed in an attempt to enhance the antitumor activity of 5-FU.

Although biochemical modulation strategies often produce synergistic cytotoxicity to tumor cells in vitro, the successful application of these strategies in the clinic has been hampered by many factors. Foremost among these has been the problem of selectivity. Since modulation strategies rarely exploit biochemical pathways that are unique to tumor cells, increased toxicity to normal tissues may occur, resulting in little improvement in therapeutic index. Another problem that may be encountered is inability to achieve plasma concentrations of the modulating agent sufficient to produce the desired biochemical effect due to poor bioavailability, conversion in vivo to inactive metabolites, or the appearance of dose-limiting toxicity.

Since the role of the modulating agent is primarily adjunctive, it need not be administered at its maximally tolerated dose but only at a dose high enough to achieve the desired biochemical effect. Clinical trials of biochemical modulation strategies should therefore include biochemical as well as clinical end points to determine if the desired biochemical effect has, in fact, been achieved. Such studies are difficult to perform, particularly in solid tumors, due to the relative inaccessibility of metastatic solid tumors to biopsy, the small amounts of tissue obtained, and the frequent admixture of normal stromal elements that may confound interpretation of biochemical results.

5-FU/Leucovorin

The modulation of 5-FU by leucovorin is perhaps the most successful biochemical modulation strategy to be brought from the laboratory to the clinic. Following oral or parenteral administration, leucovorin (LV, 5-formyl FH_4) is readily converted to 5-methyl tetrahydrofolate, the primary circulating folate in humans (Fig. 90-3). Intracellularly, 5-methyl FH_4 donates its methyl group in the formation of homocysteine from methionine, thereby liberating tetrahydrofolate.[118] The entry of 5-formyl FH_4 into the reduced folate pool is mediated by the folate interconverting enzymes 5-10 methenyl FH_4 cyclohydrolase and 5-10 methylene FH_4 dehydrogenase as well as by several purine synthetic enzymes.[119,120] Once converted to 5-10 CH_2 FH_4, LV is able to serve as a one-carbon donor in the TS reaction and to interact with FdUMP in binding to the enzyme.

While it is clear from many preclinical experiments and randomized clinical trials that leucovorin can enhance the cytotoxicity and clinical effectiveness of 5-FU, a number of questions remain unanswered. In

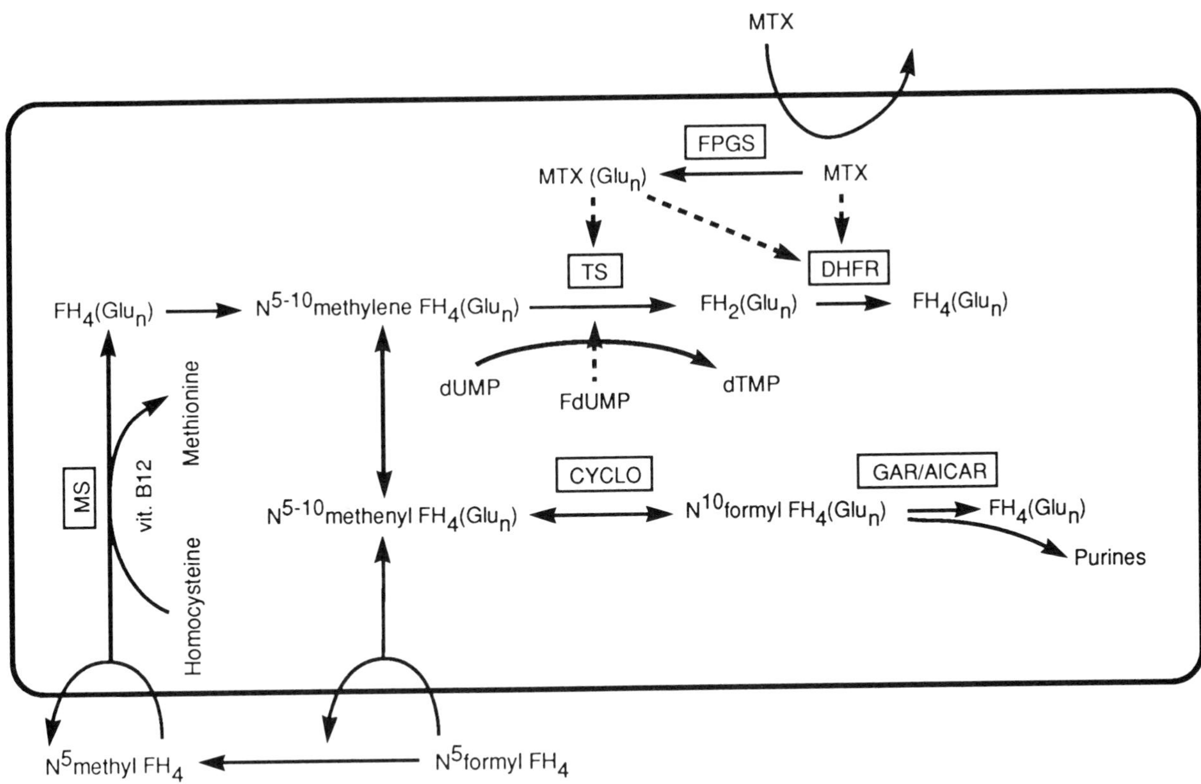

FIG. 90-3. Folate metabolic pathways. Glu, glutamyl; FPGS, folyl polyglutamate synthetase; DHFR, dihydrofolate reductase; TS, thymidylate synthase; dUMP, deoxyuridylate; dTMP, thymidylate; FdUMP, fluorodeoxyuridylate; MS, methionine synthetase; GAR, glycinamide ribotide transformylase; AICAR, amino imidazole carboxamide ribotide transformylase; Cyclo, 5, 10 methenyl FH_4 cyclohydrolase. Broken lines indicate enzyme inhibition.

preclinical model systems, exposure to leucovorin prior to 5-FU appears necessary for optimal cell kill, although the optimal duration of exposure to LV has not yet been determined. As in the case of other reduced folates, 5-10 CH_2 FH_4 is converted intracellularly to polyglutamate derivatives, formed from the sequential addition of glutamic acid residues to the terminal glutamate of the molecule. Polyglutamates of 5-10 CH_2 FH_4 bind with greater affinity to TS and are less readily dissociated and therefore provide enhanced stability to the FdUMP-TS-folate ternary complex.[99–101] The formation of folate polyglutamates in tumor cells is related primarily to the duration of exposure to exogenous folate, although great heterogeneity exists among tumor cell lines in the ability to form polyglutamates. Zhang and colleagues[121] have demonstrated that the IC_{50}s of fluorodeoxyuridine in HCT-8 human colonic cancer cells are similar, following 24-h or 5-day exposures to leucovorin. However the IC_{50} of fluorodeoxyuridine in a renal cell carcinoma line decreased significantly as the duration of exposure to LV was prolonged from 24 h to 5 days, suggesting that, in some cells, prolonged exposure to LV may enhance fluoropyrimidine's effects by permitting increased synthesis of folate polyglutamates.

Another unsettled question concerns the optimal concentration or dose of leucovorin necessary to potentiate 5-FU effects. Most in vitro studies suggest that concentrations of the biologically active L-isomer of LV of at least 1 μM are necessary. Considerable heterogeneity exists among tumor types, however; in some systems, LV concentrations as high as 10 μM are required for optimal effects. Grem and colleagues[122] have demonstrated that expansion of intracellular folate pools is proportional to the extracellular concentration of leucovorin but that a 50- to 100-fold increase in extracellular concentration is required to produce a twofold expansion of intracellular pools. This suggests that small changes in the administered dose of LV may have only minimal effects on intracellular folate levels.

The clinical formulation of leucovorin is a racemic mixture of stereoisomers around the C6 carbon of the pteridine ring. Virtually all of the biological activity of the compound resides in the L-isomer. Following intravenous injection of commercially available leucovorin, the L-isomer disappears from plasma with a half-life of approximately 30 min while clearance of the D-isomer is considerably slower and proceeds with a half-life of approximately 8 h.[123,124] These pharmacokinetic differences lead to the accumulation of high concentrations of D-LV relative to L-LV in plasma and have raised concern that the D-stereoisomer might interfere with the cellular uptake or biological activity of the L-isomer and thereby antagonize its effectiveness.

Several in vitro studies have evaluated interactions between the LV isomers at the level of membrane transport, expansion of cellular folate pools, and folate polyglutamation. No antagonistic effects of the D-LV isomer have been observed, leading to the conclusion that it is biologically inert.[122, 125] Nevertheless, a pure L-LV formulation has recently been introduced into clinical trial. Preliminary clinical studies demonstrate that it has pharmacokinetics and clinical effects virtually identical to those obtained with the racemic formulation.[126,127]

The observation that 5-FU/LV regimens are not effective in treatment of all patients with colorectal cancer reflects the great heterogeneity of 5-FU pharmacology in human tumors. Spears and colleagues[128] studied the formation of FdUMP and the inhibition of TS in human colonic carcinomas obtained by biopsy shortly after administration of an intravenous bolus dose of 5-FU. Significant heterogeneity in FdUMP levels and TS inhibition was observed among 37 colorectal adenocarcinomas, with the majority of tumors having less than 85 percent inhibition of TS at 20 to 400 min following the 5-FU dose. Also of note is that many tumors contained relatively low levels of FdUMP or had high levels of dUMP, the natural substrate for TS. In a similar study, Peters and colleagues[129] also demonstrated significant variability in TS levels in human colonic tumors and found that those tumors with the highest free enzyme levels following a dose of 5-FU were least likely to respond to therapy. In a follow-up study, these investigators compared the effects of 5-FU—administered with either high-dose (500 mg/m^2) or low-dose (25 mg/m^2) LV—on TS activity determined at the time of tumor resection 48 h later.[130] High-dose but not low-dose LV was found to potentiate 5-FU inhibition of TS significantly. Moreover, this effect was selective for colonic tumors and not observed in normal liver. In patients with breast cancer, Swain and colleagues[131] have demonstrated that the addition of LV to 5-FU significantly prolongs TS inhibition and that persistence of enzyme inhibition appears to correlate with response to therapy. These studies suggest that the utility of 5-FU/LV regimens in treatment of individual patients will depend on the TS level in the tumor, the extent of formation of FdUMP, and the duration of TS inhibition following administration of chemotherapy, which may be related to the dose of LV administered.

5-Fluorouracil/Methotrexate

The sequence-dependent synergism of methotrexate (MTX) and 5-FU has been extensively investigated, and it is clear that inhibition of de novo purine synthesis by MTX enhances 5-FU activation and cytotoxicity by increasing cellular pools of phosphoribosyl pyrophosphate (PRPP), a necessary cofactor for conversion of 5-FU to 5-FUTP by orotic acid phosphoribosyl transferase (Fig. 90-1).[131] In vitro, these events have been documented in a variety of murine and human tumor cell lines, with optimal synergy demonstrated in human tumor cells when the interval between exposure to the drugs is at least 24 h.[132–134] The reverse sequence of administration, 5-FU followed by MTX, is antagonistic in most experimental models.[135] In clinical studies, MTX administration 24 h prior to 5-FU has been demonstrated to increase tissue levels of PRPP and enhance the antitumor efficacy of 5-FU. Many MTX dosages (ranging from 40 to 800 mg/m^2), intervals (1 to 24 h before 5-FU), and schedules have been reported.[136–142] Although there is no regimen proven to be superior to 5-FU alone, a randomized clinical trial has confirmed the importance of a 24-h interval between administration of MTX and 5-FU to achieve maximal enhancement of 5-FU antitumor effects.[143]

N-(Phosponoacetyl)-L-Aspartate/5-Fluorouracil

N-(phosphonoacetyl)-L-aspartate (PALA) is a transition state inhibitor of aspartate transcarbamylase, the second step in the de novo pathway of pyrimidine biosynthesis (Fig. 90-4). Pretreatment with PALA leads to depletion of intracellular UTP and cytidine triphosphate (CTP) pools, thus increasing the ratio of 5-FUTP to UTP and the incorporation of FUTP into RNA.[82,144–146] Inhibition of pyrimidine biosynthesis also results in increased availability of PRPP and decreased formation of orotic acid, favoring the activation of 5-FU to FUMP. Depletion of uridine diphosphate (UDP) and cytidine diphosphate (CDP) potentially results in decreased dUMP formation and less competition with FdUMP for binding to TS. Early clinical studies of 5-FU/PALA were flawed by using the maximally tolerated dose of PALA rather than the minimally effective dose, which necessitated reducing the dose of 5-FU, thereby compromising the effectiveness of the regimen.[147] Preclinical studies in murine models and phase I clinical trials have demonstrated that a PALA dose of 250 mg/m^2 is sufficient to inhibit whole-body de novo pyrimidine production.[148] This observation has led to the design of a new series of PALA/5-FU studies that employ low-dose PALA and high-dose 5-FU in an attempt to achieve optimal modulation of 5-FU effects.[149,150]

5-Fluorouracil/Interferon

Preclinical data in a variety of solid tumor cell lines suggest a synergistic interaction between 5-FU and interferon.[151–154] The mechanism of this effect is as yet unknown, although interferon has been shown to en-

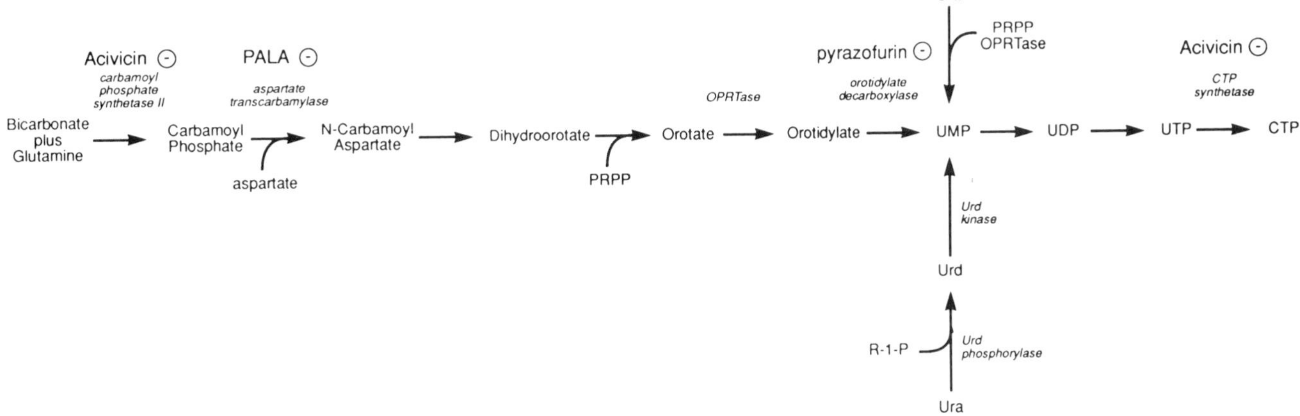

FIG. 90-4. Inhibitors of pyrimidine biosynthesis and their sites of action.

hance conversion of 5-FU to 5-FdUMP, reduce cellular levels of TS, and inhibit thymidine salvage pathways, all of which would tend to enhance 5-FU effects. In addition to these biochemical interactions, clinical trials have demonstrated reduced 5-FU clearance in the presence of interferon.[122,155,156] These observations have led to the introduction of 5-FU/interferon regimens into clinical trial.

5-Fluorouracil/Hydroxyurea

Inhibition of TS by FdUMP leads to accumulation of deoxyuridine monophosphate (dUMP), the natural substrate for the enzyme. High levels of dUMP impair binding of FdUMP to TS and may thereby diminish the effectiveness of 5-FU chemotherapy. In mammalian tissues, dUMP is formed by two enzymatic pathways, the reduction of CDP by ribonucleotide reductase and the deamination of deoxycytidine monophosphate (dCMP) by deoxycytidine deaminase. Studies in murine leukemia models have demonstrated therapeutic synergy when hydroxyurea (HU) or other inhibitors of ribonucleotide reductase are combined with fluoropyrimidines.[157] Thus far, clinical experience with HU modulation of 5-FU has been limited.

Dipyridamole/5-Fluorouracil

Dipyridamole is a nucleoside transport inhibitor that is able to block cellular uptake of nucleosides from extracellular fluid and thereby potentiate the cytotoxicity of a number of antimetabolites. In human colonic carcinoma cells, dipyridamole enhances the cytotoxicity of 5-FU in a dose-dependent manner.[158] This effect appears to be due to blockade of fluorodeoxyuridine efflux from cells by dipyridamole, resulting in enhanced intracellular retention of 5-FdUMP.[159] Increased DNA fragility and inhibition of uptake of preformed thymidine by dipyridamole may also contribute to enhanced cytotoxicity of 5-FU. Preliminary clinical trials of the combination of dipyridamole and 5-FU have revealed that concentrations of non-protein-bound dipyridamole necessary to enhance 5-FU cytotoxicity in vitro cannot be achieved clinically.[160,161] Furthermore, dipyridamole has been shown to enhance 5-FU clearance and decrease its steady-state concentration. These observations indicate that dipyridamole will not be clinically useful as a modulator of 5-FU effects but suggest that a more potent nucleoside transport inhibitor might potentially be beneficial.

5-Fluorouracil/Levamisole

In randomized clinical trials, the combination of 5-FU with the antihelminthic agent levamisole has been clearly shown to prolong the survival of patients with Dukes stage C colonic cancer treated in the adjuvant setting. The mechanism by which levamisole potentiates 5-FU effects is presently unknown. In vitro, levamisole has no direct cytotoxic effects, nor does it enhance 5-FU cytotoxicity at clinically achievable concentrations.[162] At high concentrations, however, both levamisole and its metabolite, *p*-hydroxy levamisole, potentiate the inhibitory effects of 5-FU against a variety of human tumor cell lines.[163] This effect does not appear to be mediated by inhibition of TS or by incorporation of 5-FU into RNA and does not require a direct interaction between the drugs; pretreatment of cells with levamisole is sufficient to enhance 5-FU toxicity. Inhibition of phosphatases by levamisole has been proposed as the mechanism responsible for its potentiation of 5-FU effects. Since levamisole is administered orally, it is possible that hepatic concentrations of the drug and its metabolite are substantially higher than concentrations observed in the peripheral blood and may be sufficient to potentiate the effects of 5-FU via this mechanism.

DRUG INTERACTIONS THAT REDUCE NORMAL TISSUE TOXICITY OF 5-FLUOROURACIL

Allopurinol

Normal tissues appear to preferentially activate 5-FU by orotic acid phosphoribosyl transferase (OPRT'ase) (Fig. 90-1). It therefore may be possible to exploit differences between 5-FU activation in normal tissues and tumors to minimize the toxic effects of the drug yet preserve its antitumor efficacy. Allopurinol nucleotides inhibit orotic acid decarboxylase, leading to expansion of intracellular orotic acid pools and inhibition of 5-FU activation by OPRT'ase.[164] In many normal tissues, this results in decreased toxicity, while tumor cells continue to activate 5-FU by alternative pathways.[165] Clinical studies employing allopurinol with 5-FU have produced variable results. Some have demonstrated amelioration of 5-FU toxicity by allopurinol, resulting in a significant increase in the maximally tolerated dose of 5-FU. Other studies, however, have shown the combination to be associated with enhanced neurotoxicity.[166–169] Allopurinol mouthwashes have been employed with variable success to ameliorate 5-FU–induced mucositis.[170]

Uridine

Uridine has been explored as an agent to ameliorate the toxicity of 5-FU based on the hypothesis that the toxic effects of 5-FU result from incorporation of 5-FU into RNA while the antitumor effects are derived primarily from inhibition of TS. In tumor-bearing mice, administration of pharmacologic doses of uridine following 5-FU reduced host toxicity without affecting the antitumor activity of the drug.[171] Uridine administration expanded UTP pools and increased the clearance of [^{3}H] 5-FU from RNA and DNA in both normal and tumor tissues.[172] Other studies in animals have confirmed that uridine rescue permits a substantial increase in the maximally tolerated dose of 5-FU, leading to enhanced antitumor effects.[173]

Clinical trials of 5-FU/uridine have recently begun.[174] Doses of uridine up to 12 g/m^2 administered as a 1-h infusion are well tolerated and produce plasma concentrations as high as 1 to 2 m*M*.[175] This schedule is not effective in ameliorating 5-FU-induced myelosuppression, however. Prolonged continuous intravenous infusion of uridine has also been explored but is complicated by dose-limiting fever.[176] An intermittent infusion schedule of 2 to 3 g/m^2 given as a 3-h infusion alternating with a 3-h rest period over 72 h is tolerable and effective in ameliorating 5-FU induced leukopenia.[174] Oral administration of uridine has also been explored, but its utility is limited by poor bioavailability.[177] Clearly, further studies are needed to determine whether uridine can be used effectively to selectively rescue normal tissues in humans and thereby improve the therapeutic index of 5-FU.

Thymidine

Although thymidine is able to reverse the cytotoxicity of 5-FU in many cell lines, it has not been effective as an agent to ameliorate 5-FU toxicity in the clinic. Indeed clinical trials of the thymidine/5-FU combination have produced severe toxicity due primarily to a pharmacokinetic interaction between the drugs that results in delayed 5-FU clearance.[178,179] In vivo, thymidine is rapidly converted to thymine, which competes with 5-FU for catabolism by dihydropyrimidine dehydrogenase. The result is a markedly prolonged half-life of 5-FU in plasma; enhanced renal excretion of unchanged drug, reflecting decreased metabolism; and markedly enhanced clinical toxicity.

RESISTANCE TO 5-FLUOROURACIL

Although 5-FU is the most widely used drug in treatment of colorectal cancer, it is clear that only a minority of patients respond to therapy and that complete responses are exceedingly rare. The mechanisms of resistance to 5-FU in human tumors are incompletely characterized at present. Given the multiple sites of action of 5-FU in cells, it is likely that multiple mechanisms of resistance exist and that more than one mechanism may be operative in any individual tumor.

In experimental tumors, a number of mechanisms of resistance to 5-FU have been elucidated. These are summarized in Table 90-5 and include decreased incorporation of 5-FU into RNA; altered binding of FdUMP by TS; increased cellular levels of TS due to gene amplification or overexpression[180,181]; decreased activity of enzymes necessary for 5-FU activation such as thymidine kinase[182,183]; increased activity of intracellular phosphatases, leading to decreased FdUMP levels; and relative deficiency of intracellular reduced folates. A human ovarian cancer cell line established from a patient who was clinically resistant to chemotherapy with 5-FU and cisplatin has been found to have decreased incorporation of 5-FU into DNA, compared to cells obtained prior to therapy, as the primary defect in 5-FU pharmacology.[184]

Table 90-5
Mechanisms of Resistance to 5-Fluorouracil

Decreased incorporation into RNA
Altered binding of FdUMP by thymidylate synthase
Increased thymidylate synthase levels
Decreased activity of thymidine kinase
Deficiency of intracellular reduced folates
Decreased incorporation of 5-FU into DNA

Cross-resistance to multiple chemotherapeutic agents is a common problem in clinical oncology. It is therefore interesting to note that human tumor cells selected in vitro for resistance to either doxorubicin or cisplatin display cross-resistance to 5-FU. Doxorubicin-resistant human breast cancer cells that express increased amounts of P-gp as well as glutathione-S-transferase also contain a 40- to 50-fold increase in TS levels compared to drug-sensitive cells due to overexpression but not amplification of the TS gene.[185] Similarly, cisplatin-resistant human ovarian cancer cells display marked cross-resistance to 5-FU associated with significantly increased TS activity.[186] A three- to fourfold increase in TS levels has also been noted in both cell lines and human tumors following exposure to 5-FU and appears to be due to increased translational efficiency following binding of FdUMP to the enzyme.[187] This upregulation of TS translation, which is abolished by exposure to gamma interferon, may be a clinically relevant mechanism of 5-FU resistance.

The recent development of a monoclonal antibody to human TS will facilitate the detection of increased TS levels in human tumors and normal tissues.[188] In an immunohistochemical study of TS levels in 177 patients with rectal cancer enrolled on NSABP protocol R01, TS expression was found to be an independent prognostic factor for both disease-free and overall survival.[189]

It is likely that multiple mechanisms of 5-FU resistance exist in human tumors. The application of modern immunologic and molecular genetic techniques to the study of 5-FU resistance may ultimately lead to the design of therapies to circumvent resistance and an improved clinical outcome following 5-FU treatment.

CLINICAL PHARMACOLOGY OF 5-FLUOROURACIL

Bioavailability of 5-FU after oral administration is highly variable due to erratic absorption and variable first-pass metabolism in the liver.[190,191] Therefore the drug is usually administered intravenously. Following intravenous bolus injection of conventional drug doses (400 to 600 mg/m^2), peak plasma levels of 0.1 to 1.0 mM are obtained. The drug is then rapidly metabolized at both hepatic and extrahepatic sites and disappears from plasma with a half-life of 6 to 20 min.[192–195] Continuous infusion of 5-FU at doses of 500 to 1000 mg/m^2 results in steady-state plasma concentrations of 1 to 5 μM. Regardless of the schedule of drug administration, there is considerable interindividual variation in 5-FU pharmacokinetics.

5-FU displays nonlinear pharmacokinetics.[193,196,197] With increasing drug dose, there is a decrease in total body clearance, a prolongation of elimination half-life, a disproportionate increase in area-under-the-concentration-versus-time curve (AUC) and a fall in hepatic extraction ratio. This nonlinear behavior is most likely due to saturation of the metabolic pathways responsible for 5-FU elimination. More than 80 percent of administered 5-FU is eliminated by conversion to dihydrofluorouracil, which is further metabolized to α-fluoro-β-ureido-propionic acid, α-fluoro-β-alanine, and carbon dioxide.[198–200] Approximately 15 percent of administered drug is excreted unchanged in the urine. The initial metabolic step in the degradation of 5-FU is mediated by the enzyme dihydropyrimidine dehydrogenase (DPD).[201] Kindred studies of patients experiencing severe 5-FU toxicity following administration of a standard dose of the drug have identified DPD deficiency as a rare pharmacogenetic syndrome with an autosomal recessive pattern of inheritance.[202] Affected individuals are unable to eliminate the drug normally and have sustained high plasma levels and severe toxicity. The prevalence of DPD deficiency in the general population is unknown and the impact, if any, of the heterozygous phenotype on 5-FU pharmacokinetics has not been determined. Large-scale population screening studies are presently under way in an attempt to estimate the frequency of DPD deficiency. This clinical syndrome should be considered in patients who experience unusually severe 5-FU toxicity at standard doses.

Better understanding of the clinical pharmacology of 5-FU may lead to more precision in dosing and a better therapeutic index. Recent studies by several investigators have begun to examine the pharmacodynamics of 5-FU. In patients receiving a 5-day continuous infusion of 5-FU at a dose of 15 mg/kg/day, Au et al.[203] showed that a steady-state concentration (C_{ss}) of greater than 1.5μM was predictive of myelosuppression. Bone marrow toxicity occurred in 10/12 cycles when the C_{ss} was greater than 1.5μM and in 0/13 cycles when the C_{ss} was less than 1.5μM. Van Groeningen and coworkers[204] studied patients receiving bolus 5-FU at doses of 500 to 720 mg/m^2. These workers found a correlation between the risk of toxicity and the AUC following 5-FU administration.

Thyss and colleagues[205] conducted a preliminary analysis of patients with head and neck cancer who received 5-FU 1000 mg/m^2/day × 5 and cisplatin.[205] In 29 patients receiving 63 cycles of therapy, 14 cycles were associated with gastrointestinal toxicity and 12 were associated with hematologic toxicity. Risk of toxicity was highly correlated with an AUC greater than 30,000 ng × h/mL. Santini and colleagues[206] updated this experience in describing 170 patients who received 477 cycles of this regimen. A retrospective analysis of 89 patients and 228 cycles of therapy disclosed a good relationship between AUC (days 1 to 5) as well as between the "half-cycle" AUC (days 0 to 3) and toxicity. A threshold day 0 to 3 AUC (AUC_{0-3}) of 15,000 ng × h/mL was determined which identified patients at greatest risk of toxicity. Then, 81 patients were studied prospectively through 249 cycles of therapy. AUC_{0-3} was measured, and if it exceeded 15,000 ng × h/mL, the dose of 5-FU was reduced for the remainder of the infusion. No attempt was made to escalate doses if the AUC_{0-3} was low. Dose adjustments were made only to avoid unacceptable toxicity. Using this approach, the incidence of severe toxicity was reduced from 20 percent in the first 89 patients studied to 12 percent in the prospectively studied patients. Despite the reduction in dose, response appeared to be improved using this approach: there was a 47 percent complete response rate for the prospective series compared to 31 percent for the retrospective series, suggesting that dose intensity improved because more patients received all of their scheduled cycles.

Yoshida and colleagues[207] have recently reported a relationship between C_{ss} days 1, 2, and 3 and toxicity during therapy of colonic cancer with continuous infusion 5-FU (190 to 600 mg/m^2/day). No clear relationship of C_{ss} to "effectiveness" of therapy was found. However, the variety of doses studied, lack of specified response criteria, lack of delineation as to reasons for dose and duration of infusion, and the small number of patients studied make this report difficult to interpret.

Hillcoat and colleagues[208] presented data suggesting that a higher AUC for infusion 5-FU was associated with a more favorable response to therapy in gastrintestinal cancer. This study, however, included only 27 patients and included stable disease as a category of response.

Relationships between 5-FU dose, systemic exposure, and toxicity were also explored during a phase I trial of continuous infusion 5-FU with or without dipyridamole.[209] A total of 42 patients were studied during 114 cycles of 5-FU at doses ranging from 185 to 3600 mg/m^2/day × 3 days. Mean 5-FU C_{ss} increased in a nonlinear fashion with increasing 5-FU dosage. Variability within dosage levels was approximately two- to threefold, with overlapping concentrations displayed between dosage levels. These observations have important implications, since some patients at the higher dosage levels had systemic exposures that were lower than those noted in some patients treated at lower dosage levels. Pharmacodynamic relationships could be established between 5-FU C_{ss} and frequency of stomatitis or extent of leukopenia.

These studies suggest that, even though 5-FU is a prodrug requiring intracellular activation, the application of sound pharmacologic principles to dosing of the drug can result in increased dose intensity, reduced toxicity and, perhaps, greater antitumor efficacy.

REFERENCES

1. Heidelberger C, Chaudhuari NK, Danenberg P, et al: Fluorinated pyrimidines: A new class of tumor inhibitory compounds. *Nature* 179:663–666, 1957.
2. Carter SK: Large bowel cancer: The current status of treatment. *J Natl Cancer Inst* 56:3–10, 1976.
3. Moertel CG: Therapy of advanced gastrointestinal cancer with the nitrosoureas. *Cancer Chemother* 3/4:27, 1973.
4. Macdonald JS, Neefe J: Chemotherapy in the management of gastrointestinal cancer. *Abdom Surg* 21:126–131, 1979.
5. Boice JD, Greene MH, Killen JY Jr, et al: Leukemia and preleukemia after adjuvant treatment of gastrointestinal cancer with semustine (methyl-CCNU). *N Engl J Med* 309:1079–1083, 1983.
6. Moertel CG: Clinical management of advanced gastrointestinal cancer. *Cancer* 36:675, 1975.
7. Moertel CG: Chemotherapy of gastrointestinal cancer. *N Engl J Med* 299:1049–1052, 1978.
8. Wasserman TH, Comis RL, Goldsmith M, et al: Tabular analysis of clinical chemotherapy of solid tumors. *Cancer Chemother Rep* 6:399, 1975.
9. Rowinsky EK, Cazenave LA, Donehower RC: Taxol: A novel investigational antimicrotubule agent. *J Natl Cancer Inst* 82:1247–1259, 1990.
10. Rowinsky EK, Onetto N, Canetta R, et al: Taxol: The first of the taxanes, an important new class of antitumor agents. *Semin Oncol* 19:646–662, 1992.
11. Shimada Y, Yoshino M, Wakui A, et al: Phase II study of CPT-11, a new camptothecin derivative, in patients with metastatic colorectal cancer. *Proc Am Soc Clin Oncol* 10:135, 1991.
12. Giovanella BC, Stehlin JS, Wall ME, et al: DNA topoisomerase I–targeted chemotherapy of human colon cancer in xenografts. *Science* 246:1046–1048, 1989.
13. Moertel CG, Schutt AJ, Hahn RG, et al: Therapy of advanced colorectal cancer with a combination of 5-fluorouracil, methyl 3-cis (2-chlorethyl)-1-nitrosourea and vincristine. *J Natl Cancer Inst* 54:69–71, 1975.
14. Posey L, Morgan LR: Methyl CCNU versus methyl CCNU and 5-fluorouracil in carcinoma of the large bowel. *Cancer Treat Rep* 61:1453–1458, 1977.
15. Baker LH, Talley RW, Matter R, et al: Phase III comparison of the treatment of advanced gastrointestinal cancer with bolus weekly 5-FU vs. methyl-CCNU plus bolus weekly 5-FU: A Southwest Oncology Group study. *Cancer* 38:1–7, 1976.
16. Falkson G, Falkson HC: Fluorouracil, methyl-CCNU, and vincristine in cancer of the colon. *Cancer* 38:1468–1470, 1976.
17. Macdonald JS, Kisner DF, Smythe T, et al: 5-Fluorouracil (5-FU), methyl-CCNU and vincristine in the treatment of advanced colorectal cancer: Phase II study utilizing weekly 5-FU. *Cancer Treat Rep* 60:1597, 1976.
18. Kemeny N, Yagoda A, Braun D Jr, et al: Randomized study of 2 different schedules of methyl CCNU, 5-FU, and vincristine for metastatic colorectal carcinoma. *Cancer* 43:78–82, 1979.
19. Engstrom P, MacIntyre J, Douglass H Jr, et al: Combination chemotherapy of advanced bowel cancer. *Proc AACR-ASCO* 19:384, 1978.
20. Kemeny N, Yagoda A, Braun J: Metastatic colorectal carcinoma: A prospective trial of methyl CCNU, 5-fluorouracil (5FU) and vincristine (MOF) versus MOF plus streptozotocin (MOF-strep). *Cancer* 51:20–25, 1983.
21. Buroker T, Kim PN, Groppe C, et al: 5-FU infusion with mitomycin C vs. 5FU infusion with methyl CCNU in the

treatment of advanced colon cancer. *Cancer* 42:1228–1233, 1978.
22. Gastrointestinal Tumor Study Group: Phase II study of methyl CCNU, vincristine, 5-fluorouracil and streptozotocin in advanced colorectal cancer. *J Clin Oncol* 2:770–773, 1984.
23. Richards FD, Case LD, White DR, et al: Combination chemotherapy (5-fluorouracil, methyl-CCNU, mitomycin C) versus 5-fluorouracil alone for advanced previously untreated colorectal carcinoma: A phase III study of the Piedmont Oncology Association. *J Clin Oncol* 4:565–570, 1986.
24. Buroker TR, Moertel CG, Fleming TR, et al: A controlled evaluation of recent approaches to biochemical modulation of enhancement of 5-fluorouracil therapy in colorectal carcinoma. *J Clin Oncol* 3:1624–1631, 1985.
25. Poon MA, O'Connell MJ, Moertel CG, et al: Biochemical modulation of fluorouracil: Evidence of significant improvement of survival and quality of life in patients with advanced colorectal carcinoma. *J Clin Oncol* 7:1407–1418, 1989.
26. Kemeny N, Israel K, Niedzwiecki D, et al: Randomized study of continuous infusion fluorouracil versus fluorouracil plus cis-platin in patients with metastatic colorectal cancer. *J Clin Oncol* 8:313–318, 1990.
27. Lokich J, Cantrell J, Ahlgren J, et al: A phase III trial of protracted infusional 5-FU vs. PIF plus weekly bolus cisplatin in advanced measurable colon cancer. *Proc Am Soc Clin Oncol* 8:104, 1989.
28. Loehrer PJ, Turner S, Kubilis P, et al: A prospective randomized trial of fluorouracil versus fluorouracil plus cis-platin in the treatment of metastatic colorectal cancer: A Hoosier Oncology Group trial. *J Clin Oncol* 6:642–648, 1988.
29. Labianca R, Pancera G, Cesana B, et al: Cis-platin + 5-fluorouracil versus 5-fluorouracil alone in advanced colorectal cancer: A randomized study. *Eur J Cancer Clin Oncol* 24:1579–1581, 1988.
30. Diaz-Rubio E, Milla A, Jimeno J, et al: Lack of clinical synergism between cis-platin and 5-fluorouracil in advanced colorectal cancer: Results of a randomized study. *Proc Am Soc Clin Oncol* 7:110, 1988.
31. Beck WT: The cell biology of multiple drug resistance. *Biochem Pharmacol* 36:2879–2887, 1987.
32. Juranka PF, Zastawny RL, Ling V: P-glycoprotein: Multidrug resistance and a superfamily of membrane-associated transport proteins. *FASEBJ* 3:2583–2592, 1989.
33. Gros P, Croop J, Roninson I, et al: Isolation and characterization of DNA sequences amplified in multi-drug resistant hamster cells. *Proc Natl Acad Sci USA* 83:337–341, 1986.
34. Roninson IB, Chin JE, Choi KG, et al: Isolation of human mdr DNA sequences amplified in multi-drug resistant KB carcinoma cells. *Proc Natl Acad Sci USA* 83:4538–4542, 1986.
35. Ueda K, Cardarelli C, Gottesman MM, et al: Expression of a full length cDNA for the human MDR 1 gene confers resistance to colchicine, doxorubicin and vinblastine. *Proc Natl Acad Sci USA* 84:3004–3008, 1987.
36. Thiebaut F, Tsuruo T, Hamada H, et al: Cellular localization of the multidrug resistance gene product P-glycoprotein in normal human tissues. *Proc Natl Acad Sci USA* 84:3004–7738, 1987.
37. Fojo A, Ueda K, Slamon DJ, et al: Expression of a multidrug resistance gene in human tumors and tissues. *Proc Natl Acad Sci USA* 84:265–269, 1987.
38. Goldstein LJ, Galski H, Fojo A, et al: Expression of a multidrug resistance gene in human cancers. *J Natl Cancer Inst* 81:116–124, 1989.
39. Mizoguchi T, Yamada K, Furukawa T, et al: Expression of the MDR 1 gene in human gastric and colorectal carcinomas. *J Natl Cancer Inst* 82:1679–1683, 1990.
40. Fojo AT, Shen D-W, Mickley LA, et al: Intrinsic drug resistance in human kidney cancer is associated with expression of a human multidrug resistance gene. *J Clin Oncol* 5:1922–1927, 1987.
41. Sinicrope FA, Hart J, Brasitus TA, et al: Localization of P-glycoprotein and carcinoembryonic antigen in human colon carcinoma. *Proc Am Assoc Cancer Res* 34:231, 1993.
42. Ford JM, Hait WN: Pharmacology of drugs that alter multidrug resistance in cancer. *Pharmacol Rev* 42:155–199, 1990.
43. Tsuruo T, Iida H, Tsukagoshi S, et al: Increased accumulation of vincristine and Adriamycin in drug-resistant P388 tumor cells following incubation with calcium antagonists and calmodulin inhibitors. *Cancer Res* 42:4730–4733, 1982.
44. Safa A, Glover CJ, Sewell JL, et al: Identification of the multidrug resistance–related membrane glycoprotein as an acceptor for calcium channel blockers. *J Biol Chem* 262: 7884–7888, 1987.
45. Gaveriaux C, Boesch D, Boelsterli JJ, et al: Overcoming multidrug resistance in Chinese hamster ovary cells in vitro by cyclosporin A and non-immunosuppressive derivatives. *Br J Cancer* 60:867–871, 1989.
46. Willingham M, Cornwell M, Cardarelli CS, et al: Single cell analysis of daunomycin uptake and efflux in multi-driug resistant and sensitive KB cells: Effects of verapamil and other drugs. *Cancer Res* 46:5941–5946, 1986.
47. Sonneveld P, Durie BGM, Lokhorst HM, et al: Modulation of multidrug resistant multiple myeloma by cyclosporin. *Lancet* 1:255–259, 1992.
48. Yahanda AM, Adler KM, Fisher GA, et al: Phase I trial of etoposide with cyclosporine as a modulator of multidrug resistance. *J Clin Oncol* 10:1624–1634, 1992.
49. Miller TP, Grogan TM, Dalton WS, et al: P-glycoprotein expression in malignant lymphoma and reversal of clinical drug resistance with chemotherapy plus high dose verapamil. *J Clin Oncol* 9:17–24, 1991.
50. Dalton WS, Grogan TM, Meltzer PS, et al: Drug resistance in multiple myeloma and non-Hodgkin's lymphoma: Detection of P-glycoprotein and potential circumvention by addition of verapamil to chemotherapy. *J Clin Oncol* 7:415–424, 1989.
51. Ahmad S, Okine L, Le B, et al: Elevation of glutathione in phenylalanine mustard-resistant murine L1210 leukemia cells. *J Biol Chem* 262:15048–15053, 1987.
52. Green JA, Vistica DT, Young RC, et al: Potentiation of melphalan cytotoxicity in human ovarian cancer cell lines by glutathione depletion. *Cancer Res* 44:5427–5431, 1984.
53. Perez RP, Hamilton TC, Ozols RF: Resistance to alkylating agents and cisplatin: Insights from ovarian carcinoma model systems. *Pharmacol Ther* 48:19–27, 1990.
54. Buller AL, Clapper ML, Tew KD: Glutathione-S-transferases in nitrogen mustard-resistant and sensitive cell lines. *Mol Pharmacol* 31:575–578, 1987.
55. Cole SPC, Downes HF, Mirski SEL, et al: Alterations in glutathione and glutathione-related enzymes in a multidrug resistant small cell lung cancer cell line. *Mol Pharmacol* 37:192–197, 1990.
56. Batist G, Tupule A, Sinha BK, et al: Overexpression of a novel anionic glutathione transferase in multidrug resistant human breast cancer cells. *J Biol Chem* 261:15544–15549, 1986.
57. Moscow JA, Fairchild CR, Madden MJ, et al: Expression of anionic glutathione-S-transferase and P-glycoprotein genes in human tissues and tumors. *Cancer Res* 49:1422–1428, 1989.
58. Redmond SMS, Joncourt F, Buser K, et al: Assessment of P-glycoprotein, glutathione based detoxifying enzymes and O6-alkyl guanine DNA alkyltransferase as potential indica-

tors of constitutive drug resistance in human colorectal tumors. *Cancer Res* 51:2092–2097, 1991.

59. Hamilton TC, Winker MA, Louie KG, et al: Augmentation of Adriamycin, melphalan and cisplatin cytotoxicity in drug resistant and sensitive human ovarian carcinoma cell lines by buthionine sulfoximine mediated glutathione depletion. *Biochem Pharmacol* 34:2583–2586, 1985.
60. Ozols R, Louie K, Plowman J, et al: Enhanced melphalan cytotoxicity in human ovarian cancer in vitro and in tumor-bearing nude mice by buthionine sulfoximine depletion of glutathione. *Biochem Pharmacol* 36:147–153, 1987.
61. Hansson J, Edgren M, Ehrsson H, et al: Effect of D, L-buthionine-S, R-sulfoximine on cytotoxicity and DNA cross-linking induced by bifunctional DNA-reactive cytostatic drugs in human melanoma cells. *Cancer Res* 48:19–26, 1988.
62. Bailey H, Mulcahy RT, Tutsch KD, et al: Glutathione levels and $\gamma-$glutamylcysteine synthase activity in patients undergoing phase I treatment with L-buthionine sulfoximine and melphalan. *Proc Am Assoc Cancer Res* 33:479, 1992.
63. Friedberg E: The molecular biology of nucleotide excision repair of DNA: Recent progress. *J Cell Sci Suppl* 6:1–23, 1987.
64. Sancor A, Sancor G: DNA repair enzymes. *Annu Rev Biochem* 57:29–67, 1988.
65. van Duin M, Wit J, Odijk H, et al: Molecular characterization of the human excision repair gene ERCC-1: cDNA cloning and amino acid homology with the yeast DNA repair gene. RAD 10. *Cell* 44:913–923, 1986.
66. Sorenson C, Eastman A: Mechanism of cis-diammine-dichloroplainum (II)-induced cytotoxicity: Role of G2 arrest and DNA double-strand breaks. *Cancer Res* 48:4484–4488, 1988.
67. Masuda H, Ozols R, Lai G, et al: Increased DNA repair as a mechanism of acquired resistance to cis-diammine dichloroplatinum (II) in human ovarian cancer cell lines. *Cancer Res* 48:5713–5716, 1988.
68. Lai G, Ozols R, Smyth J, et al: Enhanced DNA repair and resistance to cisplatin in human ovarian cancer. *Biochem Pharmacol* 37:4597–4600, 1993.
69. Reed E, Ormond P, Bohr V, et al: Expression of the human DNA repair gene ERCC-1 relates to cisplatin resistance in human ovarian cancer cells. *Proc Am Assoc Cancer Res* 30:448, 1989.
70. Robins P, Harris AL, Goldsmith I, et al: Cross-linking of DNA induced by chloroethylnitrosourea is prevented by O6-methylguanine-DNA-methyltransferase. *Nucleic Acids Res* 11:7743–7758, 1983.
71. Swinnen L, Barnes D, Fisher S, et al: 1-D-arabinofuranosylcytosine and hydroxyurea production of cytotoxic synergy with cis-diamminedichloroplatinum II and modification of platinum-induced DNA interstrand cross-linking. *Cancer Res* 49:1383–1389, 1989.
72. Mitchell RB, Moschel RC, Dolan ME: Effect of O6-benzyl guanine on the sensitivity of human tumor xenografts to 1,3-bis (2-chloroethyl)-1-nitrosourea and on DNA interstrand crosslink formation. *Cancer Res* 52:1171–1175, 1992.
73. Panella TJ, Smith DC, Schold SC, et al: Modulation of O6-alkylguanine-DNA alkyltransferase mediated carmustine resistance using streptozotocin: A phase I trial. *Cancer Res* 52:2456–2459, 1992.
74. Kessel D, Deacon J, Coffey B, et al: Some properties of a pyrimidine phospho-ribosyltransferase from murine leukemia cells. *Mol Pharmacol* 8:731–739, 1972.
75. Houghton JA, Houghton PJ: Elucidation of pathways of 5-fluorouracil metabolism in xenografts of human colorectal adenocarcinoma. *Eur J Clin Oncol* 19:807–815, 1983.
76. Finan PJ, Kiklitis PA, Chisholm EM, et al: Comparative levels of tissue enzymes concerned in the early metabolism of 5-fluorouracil in normal and malignant human colorectal tissue. *Br J Cancer* 50:711–715, 1984.
77. Schwartz PM, Moir RD, Hyde CM, et al: Role of uridine phosphorylase in the anabolism of 5-fluorouracil. *Biochem Pharmacol* 34:3585–3589, 1985.
78. Klubes P, Connelly K, Cerna I, et al: Effects of 5-fluorouracil on 5-fluorodeoxyuridine 5'-monophosphate and 2-deoxyuridine 5'-monophosphate pools, and DNA synthesis in solid mouse L1210 and rat Walker 256 tumors. *Cancer Res* 38:2325–2331, 1978.
79. Laskin JD, Evans MR, Slocum HK, et al: Basis for natural variation in sensitivity to 5-fluorouracil in mouse and human cells in culture. *Cancer Res* 39:383–390, 1979.
80. Evans RM, Laskin JD, Hakala MT: Assessment of growth limiting events caused by 5-fluorouracil in mouse cells and in human cells *Cancer Res* 40:4113–4122, 1980.
81. Maybaum J, Ullman B, Mandel HG, et al: Regulation of RNA- and DNA-directed actions of 5-fluoropyrimidines in mouse T-lymphoma (S-49) cells. *Cancer Res* 40:4209–4215, 1980.
82. Spiegelman S, Sawyer R, Nayak R, et al: Improving the antitumor activity of 5-fluorouracil by increasing its incorporation into RNA via metabolic modulation. *Proc Natl Acad Sci USA* 77:4966–4970, 1980.
83. Kufe DW, Egan EM: Enhancement of 5-fluorouracil incorporation into human lymphoblast ribonucleic acid. *Biochem Pharmacol* 30:129–133, 1981.
84. Kufe DW, Major PP: 5-Fluorouracil incorporation into human breast carcinoma RNA correlates with cytotoxicity. *J Biol Chem* 256:9802–9805, 1981.
85. Herrick D, Major PP, Kufe DW: Effect of methotrexate on incorporation and excision of 5-fluorouracil residues in human breast carcinoma DNA. *Cancer Res* 42:5015–5017, 1982.
86. Cheng Y-C, Nakayama K: Effects of 5-fluoro-2'deoxyuridine on DNA metabolism in HeLa cells. *Mol Pharmacol* 23:171–174, 1983.
87. Tanaka M, Kimura K, Yoshida S: Enhancement of the incorporation of 5-fluorodeoxyuridylate into DNA of HL-60 cells by metabolic modulations. *Cancer Res* 43:5145–5150, 1983.
88. Kufe DW, Scott P, Fram R, et al: Biologic effect of 5-fluoro-2'-deoxyuridine incorporation in L1210 deoxyribonucleic acid. *Biochem Pharmacol* 32:1337–1340, 1983.
89. Major PP, Egan E, Herrick D, et al: 5-Fluorouracil incorporation in DNA of human breast carcinoma cells. *Cancer Res* 42:3005–3009, 1982.
90. Schuetz JD, Wallace HJ, Diasio RB: 5-Fluorouracil incorporation into DNA of CF-1 mouse bone marrow cells as a possible mechanism of toxicity. *Cancer Res* 44:1358–1363, 1984.
91. Yoshioka A, Tanaka S, Hiraoka O, et al: Deoxyribonucleoside riphosphate imbalance—Fluorodeoxyuridine-induced DNA double strand breaks in mouse FM3A cells and the mechanism of cell death. *J Biol Chem* 262:8235–8241, 1987.
92. Lonn U, Lonn S: DNA lesions in human neoplastic cells and cytotoxicity of 5-fluoropyrimidines. *Cancer Res* 46:3866–3870, 1986.
93. Aschele C, Sobrero A, Faderan MA, et al: Novel mechanisms of resistance to 5-fluorouracil in human colon cancer (HCT-8) sublines following exposure to two different clinically relevant dose schedules. *Cancer Res* 52:1855–1864, 1992.
94. Galivan JH, Maley GF, Maley F: Factors affecting substrate

binding in *Lactobacillus casei* thymidylate synthetase as studied by equilibrium dialysis. *Biochemistry* 15:356–362, 1976.

95. Lockshin A, Danenberg PV, Murinson DS, et al: Thymidylate synthetase and 2' deoxyuridylate form a tight complex in the presence of pteroyltriglutamate. *J Biol Chem* 254:12285–12288, 1979.
96. Murinson DS, Anderson T, Schwartz HS, et al: Competitive binding radioassay for 5-fluorodeoxyuridine 5'-monophosphate in tissues. *Cancer Res* 39:2471–2475, 1979.
97. Lockshin A, Danenberg PV: Biochemical factors affecting the tightness of 5-fluorodeoxyuridylate binding to human thymidylate synthetase. *Biochem Pharmacol* 30:247–257, 1981.
98. Washtien WL, Santi DV: Assay of intracellular free and macromolecular-bound metabolites of 5'-fluorodeoxyuridine and 5-fluorouracil. *Cancer Res* 39:3397–3404, 1979.
99. Romanini A, Lin JT, Niedzwiecki D, et al: Role of folylpolyglutamates in biochemical modulation of fluoropyrimidines by leucovorin. *Cancer Res* 51:789–793, 1991.
100. Priest DG, Mangum M: Relative affinity of 5,10-methylene tetrahydrofolate polyglutamates for the *Lactobacillus casei* thymidylate synthase-5-fluorodeoxyuridylate binary complex. *Arch Biochem Biophys* 210:118–123, 1981.
101. Radparvar S, Houghton PJ, Houghton JA: Effect of polyglutamylation of 5,10-methylene tetrahydrofolate on the binding of 5-fluoro-2'-deoxyuridylate to thymidylate synthase purified from a human colon adenocarcinoma xenograft. *Biochem Pharmacol* 38:335–342, 1989.
102. Ullman B, Lee M, Martin DW, et al: Cytotoxicity of 5-fluoro-2'-deoxyuridine: requirement for reduced folate cofactors and antagonism by methotrexate. *Proc Natl Acad Sci USA* 75:980–983, 1978.
103. Houghton JA, Maroda SJ, Phillips JO, et al: Biochemical determinants of responsiveness to 5-fluorouracil and its derivatives in xenografts of human colorectal adenocarcinomas in mice. *Cancer Res* 41:144–149, 1981.
104. Evans RM, Laskin JD, Hakala MT: Effects of excess folates and deoxyinosine on the activity and site of action of 5-fluorouracil. *Cancer Res* 41:3288–3295, 1981.
105. Yin M-B, Zakrzewski SF, Hakala MT: Relationship of cellular folate cofactor pools to the activity of 5-fluorouracil. *Mol Pharmacol* 23:190–197, 1983.
106. Keyomarsi K, Moran RG: Folinic acid augmentation of the effects of fluoropyrimidines on murine and human leukemic cells. *Cancer Res* 46:5229–5235, 1986.
107. Reyes P, Hall TC: Synthesis of 5-fluorouridine 5'-phosphate by a pyrimidine phosphoribosyltransferase of mammalian origin: II. Correlation between the tumor levels of the enzyme and 5-fluorouracil-promoting increase in survival of tumor-bearing mice. *Biochem Pharmacol* 18:2587–2590, 1969.
108. Ardalan B, Cooney DA, Jayaram HN, et al: Mechanisms of sensitivity and resistance of murine tumors to 5-fluorouracil. *Cancer Res* 40:1431–1437, 1980.
109. Peters GJ, Laurensse E, Leyva A, et al: Sensitivity of human, murine and rat cells to 5-fluorouracil and 5'deoxy-5-fluorouridine in relation to drug-metabolizing enzymes. *Cancer Res* 46:20–28, 1986.
110. Ardalan B, Villacorte D, Heck D, et al: Phosphoribosyl pyrophosphate pool size and tissue levels as a determinant of 5-fluorouracil response in murine colonic adenocarcinomas. *Biochem Pharmacol* 31:1989–1992, 1982.
111. Myers CE, Young RC, Chabner BA: Biochemical determinants of 5-fluorouracil response in vivo: The role of deoxyuridylate pool expansion. *J Clin Invest* 56:1231–1238, 1975.
112. Berger SH, Hakala MT: Relationship of dUMP and free FdUMP pools to inhibition of thymidylate synthase by 5-fluorouracil. *Mol Pharmacol* 25:303–309, 1984.
113. Houghton JA, Weiss KD, Williams LG, et al: Relationship between 5-fluoro-2'deoxyuridylate, 2'deoxyuridylate, and thymidylate synthase activity subsequent to 5-fluorouracil administration in xenografts of human colon adenocarcinomas. *Biochem Pharmacol* 35:1351–1358, 1986.
114. Washtien WL: Thymidylate synthase levels as a factor in 5-fluorodeoxyuridine and methotrexate cytotoxicity in gastrointestinal tumor cell lines. *Mol Pharmacol* 21:723–728, 1982.
115. Priest DG, Ledford BE, Doig MT: Increased thymidylate synthetase in 5-fluorodeoxyuridine-resistant cultured hepatoma cells. *Biochem Pharmacol* 29:1549–1553, 1980.
116. Jenh C-H, Geyer PK, Baskin F, et al: Thymidylate synthase gene amplification in fluorodeoxyuridine-resistant mouse cell lines. *Mol Pharmacol* 28:80–85, 1985.
117. Sobrero AF, Moir RD, Bertino JR, et al: Defective facilitated diffusion of nucleosides, a primary mechanism of resistance to 5-fluoro-2'deoxyuridine in the HCT-8 human carcinoma. *Cancer Res* 45:3155–3160, 1985.
118. Nixon PF, Slutsky G, Nahas A, et al: The turnover of folate coenzymes in murine lymphoma cells. *J Biol Chem* 248:5932–5936, 1973.
119. Nahas A, Nixon PF, Bertino JR: Uptake and metabolism of N5 formyl tetrahydrofolate by L1210 leukemia cells. *Cancer Res* 32:1416–1421, 1972.
120. Matherly LH, Barlowe CR, Phillips VM, et al: The effects of 4-aminoantifolates on 5-formyltetrahydrofolate metabolism in L1210 cells: A biochemical basis for the selectivity of leucovorin rescue. *J Biol Chem* 262:710–717, 1987.
121. Zhang Z-G, Harstrick A, Rustum YM: Modulation of fluoropyrimidines: Role of dose and schedule of leucovorin administration. *Semin Oncol* 19(suppl 3):10–15, 1992.
122. Grem JL, Chu E, Boarman D, et al: Biochemical modulation of fluorouracil with leucovorin and interferon: Preclinical and clinical investigations. *Semin Oncol* 19(suppl 3):36–44, 1992.
123. Straw JA, Szapary D, Wynn WT: Pharmacokinetics of the diastereoisomers of leucovorin after intravenous and oral administration to normal subjects. *Cancer Res* 44:3114–3119, 1984.
124. Schilsky RL, Ratain MJ: Clinical pharmacokinetics of high dose leucovorin calcium after intravenous and oral administration. *J Natl Cancer Inst* 82:1411–1415, 1990.
125. Bertrand R, Jolivet J: Lack of interference by the unnatural isomer of 5-formyltetrahydrofolate with the effects of the natural isomer in leucovorin preparations. *J Natl Cancer Inst* 81:1175–1178, 1989.
126. Etienne M-C, Thyss A, Bertrand Y, et al: l-Folinic acid versus d, l-folinic acid in rescue of high dose methotrexate therapy in children. *J Natl Cancer Inst* 84:1190–1195, 1992.
127. Rustum YM, Zhang Z-G, Frank C, et al: Pharmacokinetics of the biologically active isomer, 6-S leucovorin in patients with advanced colorectal cancer. *Proc Am Assoc Cancer Res* 32:174, 1991.
128. Spears CP, Gustavsson BG, Berne M, et al: Mechanisms of innate resistance to thymidylate synthase inhibition after 5-fluorouracil. *Cancer Res* 48:5894–5900, 1988.
129. Peters GJ, van Groeningen CJ, van der Wilt CL, et al: Time course of inhibition of thymidylate synthase in patients treated with fluorouracil and leucovorin. *Semin Oncol* 19(suppl 3):26–35, 1992.
130. Peters GJ, Hoekman K, van Groeningen CJ, et al: High dose leucovorin but not low dose leucovorin potentiates 5-fluo-

rouracil induced inhibition of thymidylate synthase in human colon tumors. *Proc Am Soc Clin Oncol* 12:135, 1993.

131. Swain SM, Lippman ME, Egan EF, et al: Fluorouracil and high dose leucovorin in previously treated patients with metastic breast cancer. *J Clin Oncol* 7:890–899, 1989.
132. Benz C, Tillis T, Tattelman E, et al: Optimal scheduling of methotrexate and 5-fluorouracil in human breast cancer. *Cancer Res* 42:2081–2086, 1982.
133. Donehower RC, Allegra JC, Lippman ME, et al: Combined effects of methotrexate and 5-fluoropyrimidines on human breast cancer cells in serum-free tissue culture. *Eur J Cancer* 16:655–661, 1980.
134. Bertino JR, Sawicki WL, Linquist CA, et al: Schedule-dependent antitumor effects of methotrexate and 5-fluorouracil. *Cancer Res* 37:327–328, 1977.
135. Tattersall MHN, Jackson RC, Connors TA, et al: Combination chemotherapy: The interaction of methotrexate and 5-fluorouracil. *Eur J Cancer* 9:733–739, 1973.
136. Cantrell J, Hart R, Taylor R, et al: A phase II trial of continuous infusion (CI) 5-FU and weekly low dose cis-platin (DDP) in colorectal carcinoma. *Proc Am Soc Clin Oncol* 5:84, 1986.
137. Mehrotra S, Rosenthal CJ, Gardner B: Biochemical modulation of antineoplastic response in colorectal carcinoma: 5-Fluorouracil (F), high dose methotrexate (M) with calcium leukovorin (L) rescue (FML) in two sequences of administration. *Proc Am Soc Clin Oncol* 1:95, 1982.
138. Mahajan SL, Ajan JA, Kanoj A, et al: Comparison of two schedules of sequential high-dose methotrexate (MTX) and 5-fluorouracil (5-FU) for metastatic colorectal carcinoma. *Proc Am Soc Clin Oncol* 2:122, 1983.
139. Rangineni RR, Ajani JA, Bedikian AY, et al: Sequential conventional dose methotrexate (MTX) and 5-fluorouracil (5-FU) in the primary therapy of metastatic colorectal carcinoma. *Proc Am Soc Clin Oncol* 2:125, 1983.
140. Hansen R, Ritch P, Anderson T: Sequential methotrexate (MTX), 5-fluorouracil (5-FU), and leucovorin (LCV) in colorectal cancer. *Proc Am Soc Clin Oncol* 2:117, 1983.
141. Drapkin R, McAloon E, Lyman G: Sequential methotrexate (MTX) and 5-fluorouracil in advanced measurable colorectal cancer. *Proc Am Soc Clin Oncol* 2:118, 1983.
142. Kemeny NE, Ahmed T, Michaelson RA, et al: Activity of sequential low dose methotrexate and fluorouracil in advanced colorectal carcinoma: Attempt at correlation with tissue and blood levels of phosphoribosylpyrophosphate. *J Clin Oncol* 2:311–315, 1984.
143. Marsh JC, Bertino JR, Katz KH, et al: The influence of drug interval on the effect of methotrexate and fluorouracil in the treatment of advanced colorectal cancer. *J Clin Oncol* 9:371–380, 1991.
144. Ardalan B, Glazer RI, Kensler TW, et al: Synergistic effects of 5-fluorouracil and N-(phosphonacetyl)-L-aspartate on cell growth and ribonucleic acid synthesis in a human mammary carcinoma. *Biochem Pharmacol* 30:2045–2049, 1981.
145. Liang CM, Donehower RC, Chabner BA: Biochemical interactions between N-(phosphonacetyl)-L-aspartate and 5-fluorouracil. *Mol Pharmacol* 21:224–230, 1982.
146. Moore CE, Friedman J, Valdivieso M, et al: Aspartate carbamoyltransferase activity, drug concentrations and pyrimidine nucleotides in tissue from patients treated with N-(phosphonacetyl)-L-aspartate. *Biochem Pharmacol* 31:3317–3321, 1982.
147. Grem JL, King SA, O'Dwyer PJ, et al: Biochemistry and clinical activity of N-(phosphonacetyl)-L-aspartate: A review. *Cancer Res* 48:4441–4454, 1988.
148. Martin DS, Stolfi RL, Sawyer RC, et al: Therapeutic utility of utilizing low doses of N-(phosphonacetyl)-L-aspartic acid in combination with 5-fluorouracil: A murine study with clinical relevance. *Cancer Res* 43:2317–2321, 1998.
149. Ardalan B, Singh G, Silberman H: A randomized phase I and II study of short-term infusion of high dose fluorouracil with or without N-(phosphonacetyl)-L-aspartic acid in patients with advanced pancreatic and colorectal cancers. *J Clin Oncol* 6:1053–1058, 1988.
150. O'Dwyer PJ, Paul AR, Walczak J, et al: Phase II study of biochemical modulation of fluorouracil by low dose PALA in patients with colorectal cancer. *J Clin Oncol* 8:1497–1503, 1990.
151. Elias L, Crissman HA: Interferon effects upon the adenocarcinoma 38 and HL-60 cell lines: Antiproliferative responses and synergistic interactions with halogenated pyrimidine antimetabolites. *Cancer Res* 48:4868–4873, 1988.
152. Wadler S, Wersto R, Weinberg V, et al: Interaction of fluorouracil and interferon in human colon cancer cell lines: Cytotoxic and cytokinetic effects. *Cancer Res* 50:5735–5739, 1990.
153. Elias L, Sandoval JM: Interferon effects upon fluorouracil metabolism by HL-60 cells. *Biochem Biophys Res Commun* 163:867–874, 1989.
154. Chu E, Zinn S, Boarman D, et al: The interaction of gamma interferon and 5-fluorouracil in the H630 human colon carcinoma cell line. *Cancer Res* 50:5834–5840, 1990.
155. Grem JL, McAtee N, Murphy RF, et al: A pilot study of interferon alfa-2a in combination with fluorouracil plus high dose leucovorin in metastatic gastrointestinal carcinoma. *J Clin Oncol* 9:1811–1820, 1991.
156. Yee K, Allegra CJ, Steinberg SM, et al: Decreased catabolism of fluorouracil in peripheral blood mononuclear cells during combination therapy with fluorouracil, leucovorin and interferon α-2a. *J Natl Cancer Inst* 84:1820–1825, 1992.
157. Moran RG, Danenberg PV, Heidelberger C: Therapeutic response of leukemic mice treated with fluorinated pyrimidines and inhibitors of deoxyuridylate synthesis. *Biochem Pharmacol* 31:2929–2935, 1982.
158. Grem JL, Fischer PH: Augmentation of 5-fluorouracil cytotoxicity in human colon cancer cells by dipyridamole. *Cancer Res* 45:2967–2972, 1985.
159. Grem JL, Fischer PH: Alteration of fluorouracil metabolism in human colon cancer cells by dipyridamole with a selective increase in fluorodeoxyuridine monophosphate levels. *Cancer Res* 46:6191–6199, 1986.
160. Grem JL: Biochemical modulation of fluorouracil by dipyridamole: Preclinical and clinical experience. *Semin Oncol* 19(suppl 3):56–65, 1992.
161. Remick SC, Grem JL, Fischer PH, et al: A phase I trial of 5-fluorouracil and dipyridamole administered by 72 hour concurrent continuous infusion. *Cancer Res* 50:2667–2672, 1990.
162. Grem JL, Allegra CJ: Toxicity of levamisole and 5-fluorouracil in human colon carcinoma cells. *J Natl Cancer Inst* 81:1413–1417, 1989.
163. Kovach JS, Svingen PA, Schaid DJ: Levamisole potentiation of fluorouracil antiproliferative activity mimicked by orthovanadate, an inhibitor of tyrosine phosphatase. *J Natl Cancer Inst* 84:515–519, 1992.
164. Schwartz PM, Handschumacher RE: Selective antagonism of 5-fluorouracil cytotoxicity by 4-hydroxypyrazolo-pyrimidine (allopurinol) in vitro. *Cancer Res* 39:3095–3101, 1979.
165. Houghton JA, Houghton PJ: 5-Fluorouracil in combination with hypoxanthine and allopurinol: Toxicity and metabolism in xenografts of human colonic carcinomas in mice. *Biochem Pharmacol* 29:2077–2080, 1980.
166. Campbell TN, Howell SB, Pfeifle C, et al: High-dose allopurinol modulation of 5-FU toxicity: Phase I trial of an out-

patient dose schedule. *Cancer Treat Rep* 66:1723–1727, 1982.

167. Pfeifle CE, Wung WE: Effect of allopurinol on the toxicity of high-dose 5-fluorouracil administered by intermittent bolus injection. *Cancer* 51:220–225, 1983.
168. Fox RM, Woods RL, Tattersall MHN: Allopurinol modulation of high-dose fluorouracil toxicity. *Cancer Treat Rev* 6 (suppl):143–147, 1979.
169. Wooley PV, Ayoob MJ, Smith FP, et al: A controlled trial of the effect of 4-hydroxy-pyrazolopyrimidine (allopurinol) on the toxicity of a single bolus dose of 5-fluorouracil. *J Clin Oncol* 3:103–109, 1985.
170. Clark PI, Slevin ML: Allopurinol mouthwashes and 5-fluorouracil induced oral toxicity. *Eur J Surg Oncol* 11:267–268, 1985.
171. Martin DS, Stolfi RL, Sawyer RC, et al: High-dose 5-fluorouracil with delayed uridine "rescue" in mice. *Cancer Res* 42:3864–3870, 1982.
172. Sawyer RC, Stolfi RL, Spiegelman S, et al: Effect of uridine on the metabolism of 5-fluorouracil in the CD8F1 murine mammary carcinoma system. *Pharm Res* 2:69–75, 1984.
173. Klubes P, Cerna I: Use of uridine rescue to enhance the antitumor selectivity of 5-fluorouracil. *Cancer Res* 43:3182–3186, 1983.
174. van Groeningen CJ, Peters GJ, Pinedo HM: Modulation of fluorouracil toxicity with uridine. *Semin Oncol* 19(suppl 3):148–154, 1992.
175. Leyva A, van Groeningen CJ, KraaL I, et al: Phase I and pharmacokinetic studies of high-dose uridine intended for rescue from 5-fluorouracil toxicity. *Cancer Res* 44:5928–5933, 1984.
176. van Groeningen CJ, Leyva A, KraaL I, et al: Clinical and pharmacokinetic studies of prolonged administration of high-dose uridine intended for rescue from 5-FU toxicity. *Cancer Treat Rep* 70:745–750, 1986.
177. van Groeningen CJ, Peters GJ, Nadal JC, et al: Clinical and pharmacological study of orally administered uridine. *J Natl Cancer Inst* 83:437–441, 1991.
178. Woodcock TM, Martin DS, Damin LEM, et al: Clinical trials with thymidine and fluorouracil: A phase I and clinical pharmacologic evaluation. *Cancer* 45:1135–1143, 1980.
179. Au JL-S, Rustum YM, Ledesma EJ, et al: Clinical pharmacological studies of concurrent infusion of 5-fluorouracil and thymidine in treatment of colorectal carcinomas. *Cancer Res* 42:2930–2937, 1982.
180. Berger SH, Jenh C-H, Johnson LF, et al: Thymidylate synthase overproduction and gene amplification in fluorodeoxyuridine-resistant human cells. *Mol Pharmacol* 28:461–467, 1985.
181. Clark JL, Berger SH, Mittelman A, et al: Thymidylate synthase gene amplification in a colon tumor resistant to fluoropyrimidine chemotherapy. *Cancer Treat Rep* 71:261–265, 1987.
182. Mulkins MA, Heidelberger C: Biochemical characterization of fluoropyrimidine-resistant murine leukemic cell lines. *Cancer Res* 42:965–973, 1982.
183. Piper AA, Fox R: Biochemical basis for the differential sensitivity of human T- and B-lymphocyte lines to 5-fluorouracil. *Cancer Res* 42:3753–3760, 1982.
184. Chu E, Lai G-M, Zinn S, et al: Resistance of a human ovarian cancer line to 5-fluorouracil associated with decreased levels of 5-fluorouracil in DNA. *Mol Pharmacol* 38:410–417, 1990.
185. Chu E, Drake JC, Koeller DM, et al: Induction of thymidylate synthase associated with multidrug resistance in human breast and colon cancer cell lines. *Mol Pharmacol* 39:136–143, 1991.
186. Hill BT, Shellard SA, Hosking LK, et al: Characterization of a cisplatin-resistant human ovarian carcinoma cell line expressing cross resistance to 5-fluorouracil but collateral sensitivity to methotrexate. *Cancer Res* 52:3110–3118, 1992.
187. Allegra C, Chu E: Autoregulatory translational control of thymidylate synthase. Proceedings of the 7th NCI-EORTC Symposium on new drugs in cancer therapy, Amsterdam, 1992.
188. Johnston PG, Drake JC, Trepel J, et al: Immunological quantitation of thymidylate synthase using the monoclonal antibody TS 106 in fluorouracil sensitive and resistant human cancer cell lines. *Cancer Res* 52:4306–4312, 1992.
189. Johnston PG, Fisher E, Rockette HE, et al: Thymidylate synthase expression is an independent predictor of survival/disease-free survival in patients with rectal cancer. *Proc Am Soc Clin Oncol* 12:202, 1993.
190. Finch RE, Bending MR, Lant AF: Plasma levels of 5-fluorouracil after oral and intravenous administration in cancer patients. *Br J Clin Pharmacol* 7:613–617, 1979.
191. Christophidis N, Vajda FJE, Lucas I, et al: Fluorouracil therapy in patients with carcinoma of the large bowel: A pharmacokinetic comparison of various rates and routes of administration. *Clin Pharmacokinet* 3:330–336, 1978.
192. MacMillan WE, Wolberg WH, Welling PG: Pharmacokinetics of fluorouracil in humans. *Cancer Res* 38:3479–3482, 1978.
193. McDermott BJ, van der Berg HW, Murphy RF: Nonlinear pharmacokinetics for the elimination of 5-fluorouracil after intravenous administration in cancer patients. *Cancer Chemother Pharmacol* 9:173–178, 1982.
194. Heggie GD, Sommadossi J-P, Cross DS, et al: Clinical pharmacokinetics of 5-fluorouracil and its metabolites in plasma, urine, and bile. *Cancer Res* 47:2203–2206, 1987.
195. Erlichman C, Fine S, Elhakim T: Plasma pharmacokinetics of 5-FU given by continuous infusion with allopurinol. *Cancer Treat Rep* 70:903–904, 1986.
196. Collins JM, Dedrick RL, King FG, et al: Nonlinear pharmacokinetic models for 5-fluorouracil in man: Intravenous and intraperitoneal routes. *Clin Pharm Ther* 28:235–246, 1980.
197. Wagner JG, Gyves JW, Stetson PL, et al: Steady-state nonlinear pharmacokinetics of 5-fluorouracil during hepatic arterial and intravenous infusions in cancer patients. *Cancer Res* 46:1499–1506, 1986.
198. Mukherjee KL, Boohar J, Wentland D, et al: Studies on fluorinated pyrimidines: XVI. Metabolism of 5-fluorouracil-2-C14 and 5-fluoro-2′-deoxyuridine-2-C14 in cancer patients. *Cancer Res* 23:49–66, 1963.
199. Diasio RB, Schuetz JD, Wallace HJ, et al: Dihydrofluorouracil: A fluorouracil catabolite with antitumor activity in murine and human cells. *Cancer Res* 45:4900–4903, 1985.
200. Sweeny FJ, Barnes S, Diasio RB: Formation of conjugates of 2-fluoro-beta-alanine and bile acids during the metabolism of 5-fluorouracil and 5-fluoro-2-deoxyuridine in the isolated perfused rat liver. *Cancer Res* 48:2010–2014, 1988.
201. Harris BE, Song R, Soong S-J, et al: Relationship between dihydropyrimidine dehydrogenase activity and plasma 5-fluorouracil levels with evidence for circadian variation of enzyme activity and plasma drug levels in cancer patients receiving 5-fluorouracil by protracted continuous infusion. *Cancer Res* 50:197–201, 1990.
202. Harris BE, Carpenter JT, Diasio RB: Severe 5-fluorouracil toxicity secondary to dihydropyrimidine dehydrogenase deficiency. *Cancer* 68:499–501, 1991.
203. Au JLS, Rustum YM, Ledesma EJ, et al: Clinical pharmacological studies of concurrent infusion of 5-fluorouracil and

thymidine in treatment of colorectal cancer. *Cancer Res* 42:2930–2938, 1982.

204. van Groeningen CJ, Pinedo HM, Heddes J, et al: Pharmacokinetics of 5-fluorouracil assessed with a sensitive mass spectrometric method in patients on a dose escalation schedule. *Cancer Res* 48:6956–6961, 1988.
205. Thyss A, Milano G, Renee N, et al: Clinical and pharmacokinetic study of 5-FU in continuous 5-day infusions for head and neck cancer. *Cancer Chemother Pharmacol* 16:64–66, 1986.
206. Santini J, Milano G, Thyss A, et al: 5-FU therapeutic monitoring with dose adjustment leads to improved therapeutic index in head and neck cancer. *Br J Cancer* 59:287–290, 1989.
207. Yoshida T, Araki E, Ligo M, et al: Clinical significance of monitoring serum levels of 5-fluorouracil by continuous infusion in patients with advanced colonic cancer. *Cancer Chemother Pharmacol* 26:352–354, 1990.
208. Hillcoat B, McCullough PB, Figueredo AT, et al: Clinical response and plasma levels of 5-fluorouracil in patients with colonic cancer treated by drug infusion. *Br J Cancer* 38:719–724, 1978.
209. Trump DL, Egorin MJ, Forrest A, et al: Pharmacokinetic and pharmacodynamic analysis of fluorouracil during 72 hour continuous infusion with and without dipyridamole. *J Clin Oncol* 9:2027–2035, 1991.

CHAPTER 91

Trial Design in Phase I and Phase II Studies

David Kelsen

HIGHLIGHTS

Colorectal cancers are relatively resistant to most forms of currently available chemotherapy. Drug development is an urgent priority. The methodology for phase I and phase II trials involving chemotherapy alone has been well established. Carefully defined study objectives, patient eligibility criteria, dose escalation schema, and toxicity assessment are mandatory. Phase I trials are toxicity- and dose-establishment studies. Once a phase I trial has determined the maximum tolerated dose, phase II trials are begun. Phase II trials have as their major objective the assessment of response rates, particularly in patients who have not received prior chemotherapy. While phase I studies of single-agent chemotherapy alone are rather straightforward, the development of multimodality regimens for rectal and anal canal tumors have made this type of phase I trial significantly more complicated. The doses or approach of one modality should be held constant while the other modality is the variable. Regional therapy has both systemic and local toxicities which must be assessed separately in phase I and phase II trials.

CONTROVERSIES

As is the case with other solid tumors, a major question revolves around the entrance of patients who have not received prior chemotherapy into these trials. While this is important for patients with highly responsive tumors that are curable with chemotherapy (such as leukemias, lymphomas, or germ cell tumors), it is far less controversial for patients with colorectal cancer. Since overall response rates are low (20 to 35 percent with regimens such as 5-fluorouracil and leucovorin), with only rare complete remissions and almost never cures, most investigators feel that it is ethically justified to offer new, innovative therapies with either chemotherapy or biological response modifiers to patients with advanced metastatic colorectal cancer who have not received prior treatment. Carefully performed phase I trials for multimodality treatment in which either chemotherapy or radiation are varied while the other modalities are held constant have not been widely employed. Particularly controversal is the question of whether or not patients with potentially curable disease (although their risk of recurrence may be high) should be encouraged to participate in these trials.

FUTURE DIRECTIONS

The major goals of drug development, for use either alone or in combination with radiation and surgery, are the identification of active new single agents, the development of new regimens combining biologic response modifiers with conventional chemotherapy, and the employment of multimodality techniques.

Patients with adenocarcinomas of the colon and rectum frequently present with or eventually develop metastatic cancer. Chemotherapy has played a major role in the palliation of advanced disease, and most trials have focused on this patient population. More recently, chemotherapy has been accepted as a standard adjuvant treatment for patients with colonic cancer who have had the primary tumor resected but are at high risk for recurrence.[1] Similarly, in rectal cancer, combined-modality approaches involving chemotherapy and radiation following operation (or, more recently, before operation) have undergone widespread study, and postoperative radiation plus 5-fluorouracil (5-FU) chemotherapy is routinely employed.[2,3] Unfortunately, current available systemic chemotherapy for advanced colorectal cancer has been only modestly effective in inducing response and has had even less of an effect on survival. Even in the adjuvant setting, there is room for substantial progress. There is a pressing need for the development of new, more effective systemic therapies for these patients. In anal canal cancers, chemotherapy with concurrent radiation has been firmly established as primary treatment.[4,5] The majority of patients with this rare neoplasm are cured, usually without major surgical intervention. However, even here high-risk patients populations can be identified in whom currently available primary therapy is still unsatisfactory. Moreover, among those few patients with anal canal cancers who develop recurrent disease and systemic metastasis, chemotherapy (while useful for palliation) fails to cure the vast majority. Thus, newer chemotherapy regimens are important.

PHASE I, PHASE II, AND PHASE III TRIALS

The techniques whereby new drugs for single-modality systemic chemotherapy are developed have been well described.[6,7] Once preclinical studies have identified an active new agent or agents, animal toxicology studies are performed. These indicate the major expected side effects. Following completion of the animal toxicology studies, phase I studies are initiated.

The goal of phase I therapy is to determine the maximum tolerated dose (MTD) of a given agent, and the toxicities associated with it, using a specific dosing schedule. Phase II trials use the dose and treatment schedule from the phase I studies to identify those tumors for which the new treatment has efficacy. Phase III studies, which are beyond the scope of this chapter, use a random-assignment design to determine whether the new treatment is more effective than currently accepted therapy. This determination of effectiveness involves either an improvement in overall survival (which is the most desirable end point), disease-free and overall survival in adjuvant studies, or an improvement in quality of life and function. Toxicity is important in phase III trials, as an effective treatment may be too toxic for routine use. This would mandate further modifications of the therapy. It should be noted that phase II trials involving larger groups of patients should already, in theory, have identified such toxicities.

It is important to determine carefully, in advance, the objectives of a given treatment. This is especially crucial in combined-modality therapy, which is an important advance in the treatment of colorectal and anal canal cancers. The overlapping toxicities of the different modalities of radiation, chemotherapy, and surgery must be carefully considered in designing multimodality phase I and phase II trials. Studies involving, for example, concurrent chemotherapy and radiation have in the past been performed as phase II trials without first determining (using phase I techniques) the appropriate doses of the two different modalities. This may have a serious impact on either the effectiveness of treatment or on the development of unexpected side effects.

OBJECTIVES

Simply and clearly stated study objectives are vital to ensure that the question being asked in a given trial can be successfully answered in view of the number of patients being treated. It is highly desirable that one major, focused question be answered by any given trial. This is especially important in phase I studies. Important questions such as those involving pharmacokinetics and pharmacodynamics are subsidiary and are considered to be secondary objectives.

PATIENT ELIGIBILITY

While phase I studies of agents just beginning their clinical trials are usually performed in patients who have received prior treatment and who are by definition incurable, combined-modality studies with phase I aspects may include previously untreated patients. Another group of previously untreated patients who are frequently offered entrance into phase I studies are those who do not have measurable or evaluable disease (see below). For both phase I and phase II trials, minimally acceptable organ system function is needed in order to adequately assess toxicity. For example, a maximum allowable serum creatinine of 1.5 mg/100 mL and a maximum serum bilirubin of ≤ 1.5–2.0 mg/100 mL are usually protocol entrance requirements. For some agents, specific minimal acceptable pulmonary, cardiac, or neurologic function may also be protocol requirements.

Many phase I or II studies performed in the 1960s and early 1970s involved patients who were extremely ill or debilitated. It was found that the toxicity seen in this population did not reflect that seen in patients who were more fit. That is, the MTD of a new agent on a

Table 91-1
Karnofsky Performance Status (PS)

Able to carry on normal activity; no special care is needed	100%	Normal; no complaints; no evidence of disease
	90%	Able to carry on normal activity; minor signs or symptoms of disease
	80%	Normal activity with effort; some signs or symptoms of disease
Unable to work; able to live at home; cares for most personal needs; a varying amount of assistance is needed	70%	Cares for self; unable to carry on normal activity or to do active work
	60%	Requires occasional assistance but is able to care for most of his needs
	50%	Requires considerable assistance and frequent medical care
Unable to care for self; requires equivalent of institutional or hospital care; disease may be progressing rapidly	40%	Disabled; requires special medical care and assistance
	30%	Severely disabled; hospitalization is indicated, although death not imminent
	20%	Very sick; hospitalization necessary; active supportive treatment necessary
	10%	Moribund; fatal processes progressing rapidly
	0%	Dead

given schedule was significantly underestimated when compared to doses achievable in a population that was healthier. It is extremely important for both phase I and phase II trials that eligibility requirements include a patient's performance status (a general measure of "fitness"). There are many scales for measuring this factor. One widely used indicator is the Karnofsky Performance Scale (Table 91-1). In general, patients entering investigational phase I or phase II trials have a Karnofsky performance status (KPS) of 50 or greater. Many recent trials limit entrance of patients to those with a KPS of 60 or greater. These patients, while they may be symptomatic, are ambulatory and do not require hospitalization for reasons other than treatment.

While most phase I trials are performed in patients with a variety of malignancies, they are usually limited to patients with solid tumors. Phase I trials leading to phase II studies in leukemias are usually limited to patients with that disease. More recently, multimodality studies dealing with a single solid tumor (i.e., rectal cancer) have been performed. These studies include elements not usually assessed in traditional phase I studies, such as radiation toxicity enhancement.

Since in phase I trials the major question being asked does not involve tumor response, the presence of tumor masses that can be measured by physical examination or a radiographic study such as computed tomography (CT) or magnetic resonance imaging (MRI) is not usually required. It should be understood that *measurable disease* requires a mass in which (by standard convention) two perpendicular diameters can be followed. Most investigators consider *evaluable disease* to be that in which a single diameter can be obtained or that with indistinct borders. To declare response in this circumstance, more than the usual 50 percent decrease in size is needed.

The major end point of phase I trials is the determination of the MTD, leading to a recommended dose for phase II studies. In order to achieve this objective, phase I studies begin by treating small cohorts of patients, using a fixed dose and schedule of the new agent. The starting dose is based on preclinical toxicity obtained from animal models. This is usually one-tenth of the LD10 (the lowest dose causing fatal toxicity in 10 percent of the study animals, usually mice) expressed as milligrams per square millimeter of body surface area.

Phase I studies then follow a set plan of escalation. Usually, three patients are treated per level. If no toxicity is encountered, the next level is open to patient accrual. Dose escalation should be performed only after enough time has passed to observe acute side effects. Dose escalation commonly uses a modified Fibonacci schema. In this mathematical formula, the second level is usually 100 percent higher than the starting dose. Subsequent levels give smaller and smaller increments on a percentage basis. By the fourth step, dose escalation is usually 50 percent above the preceding level. At the highest levels, no more than a one-third increase above the preceding level should be used. Other dose escalation schedules have also been proposed.

When any toxicity is seen at a given level, a minimum of two to three additional patients should be treated at that level. Several different toxicity schemas have been designed to describe different grades of toxicity. Shown in Table 91-2 is an example of the widely

Table 91-2
Common Toxicity Criteria

Toxicity	*Grade*				
	0	*1*	*2*	*3*	*4*
			Blood/Bone Marrow		
WBC	≥4.0	3.0–3.9	2.0–2.9	1.0–1.9	<1.0
PLT	WNL	75.0—normal	50.0–74.9	25.0–49.9	<25.0
Hgb	WNL	10.0—normal	8.0–10.0	6.5–7.9	<6.5
Granulocytes/ bands	≥2.0	1.5–1.9	1.0–1.4	0.5–0.9	<0.5
Lymphocytes	≥2.0	1.5–1.9	1.0–1.4	0.5–0.9	<0.5
Hemorrhage (clinical)	None	Mild, no transfusion	Gross, 1–2 units transfusion per episode	Gross, 3–4 units transfusion per episode	Massive, >4 units transfusion per episode
Infection	None	Mild	Moderate	Severe	Life-threatening
			Gastrointestinal		
Nausea	None	Able to eat reasonable intake	Intake significantly decreased but can eat	No significant intake	—
Vomiting	None	1 episode in 24 h	2–5 episodes in 24 h	6–10 episodes in 24 h	>10 episodes in 24 h, or requiring parenteral support
Diarrhea	None	Increase of 2–3 stools/day over pre-Rx	Increase of 4–5 stools/day, or nocturnal stools, or moderate cramping	Increase of 7–9 stools/day, or incontinence, or severe cramping	Increase of ≥10 stools/day or grossly bloody diarrhea, or need for parenteral support
Stomatitis	None	Painless ulcers, erythema, or mild soreness	Painful erythema, edema, or ulcers, but can eat	Painful erythema, edema, or ulcers, and cannot eat	Requires parenteral or enteral support
			Liver		
Bilirubin	WNL	—	<1.5 × N	1.5–3.0 × N	>3.0 × N
Transaminase (SGOT, SGPT)	WNL	≤2.5 × N	2.6–5.0 × N	5.1–20.0 × N	>20.0 × N
Alk phos or 5′ nucleotidase	WNL	≤2.5 × N	2.6–5.0 × N	5.1–20.0 × N	>20.0 × N
Liver—clinical	No change from baseline	—	—	Precoma	Hepatic coma
			Kidney, Bladder		
Creatinine	WNL	<1.5 × N	1.5–3.0 × N	3.1–6.0 × N	>6.0 × N
Proteinuria	No change	1+ or <0.3 g% or <3 g/L	2–3+ or 0.3–1.0 g% or 3–10 g/L	4+ or >1.0 g% or >10 g/L	Nephrotic syndrome
Hematuria	Neg	Micro only	Gross, no clots	Gross + clots	Requires transfusion
Alopecia	No loss	Mild hair loss	Pronounced or total hair loss	—	—
Pulmonary	None or no change	Asymptomatic, with abnormality in PFT's	Dyspnea on significant exertion	Dyspnea at normal level of activity	Dyspnea at rest
			Heart		
Cardiac dysrhythmias	None	Asymptomatic, transient, requiring no therapy	Recurrent or persistent, no therapy required	Requires treatment	Requires monitoring; or hypotension, or ventricular tachycardia, or fibrillation

Table 91-2 (*Continued*)
Common Toxicity Criteria

Toxicity	*Grade* 0	1	2	3	4
Cardiac function	None	Asymptomatic, decline of resting ejection fraction by less than 20% of baseline value	Asymptomatic, decline of resting ejection fraction by more than 20% of baseline value	Mild CHF, responsive to therapy	Severe or refractory CHF
Cardiac—ischemia	None	Nonspecific T-wave flattening	Asymptomatic, ST and T wave changes suggesting ischemia	Angina without evidence for infarction	Acute myocardial infarction
Cardiac—pericardial	None	Asymptomatic effusion, no intervention required	Pericarditis (rub, chest pain, ECG changes)	Symptomatic effusion; drainage required	Tamponade; drainage urgently required
			Blood Pressure		
Hypertension	None or no change	Asymptomatic, transient increase by greater than 20 mmHg (D) or to >150/100 if previously WNL. No treatment required	Recurrent or persistent increase by greater than 20 mmHg (D) or to >150/100 if previously WNL. No treatment required	Requires therapy	Hypertensive crisis
Hypotension	None or no change	Changes requiring no therapy (including transient orthostatic hypotension)	Requires fluid replacement or other therapy but not hospitalization	Requires therapy and hospitalization; resolves within 48 h of stopping the agent	Requires therapy and hospitalization for >48 h after stopping the agent
			Neurologic		
Neurosensory	None or no change	Mild paresthesias, loss of deep tendon reflexes	Mild or moderate objective sensory loss; moderate paresthesias	Severe objective sensory loss or paresthesias that interfere with function	—
Neuromotor	None or no change	Subjective weakness; no objective findings	Mild objective weakness without significant impairment of function	Objective weakness with impairment of function	Paralysis
Neurocortical	None	Mild somnolence or agitation	Moderate somnolence or agitation	Severe somnolence, agitation, confusion, disorientation, or hallucinations	Coma, seizures, toxic psychosis
Neurocerebellar	None	Slight incoordination, dysdiadokinesis	Intention tremor, dysmetria, slurred speech, nystagmus	Locomotor ataxia	Cerebellar necros
Neuromood	No change	Mild anxiety or depression	Moderate anxiety or depression	Severe anxiety or depression	Suicidal ideation
Neuroheadache	None	Mild	Moderate or severe but transient	Unrelenting and severe	—
Neuroconstipation	None or no change	Mild	Moderate	Severe	Ileus >96 h

Table 91-2 (*Continued*)
Common Toxicity Criteria

Toxicity	*Grade* 0	1	2	3	4
Neurohearing	None or no change	Asymptomatic hearing loss on audiometry only	Tinnitus	Hearing loss interfering with function but correctable with hearing aid	Deafness not correctable
Neurovision	None or no change	—	—	Symptomatic subtotal loss of vision	Blindness
Skin	None or no change	Scattered macular or papular eruption or erythema that is asymptomatic	Scattered macular or papular eruption or erythema with pruritus or other associated symptoms	Generalized symptomatic macular, papular, or vesicular eruption	Exfoliative dermatitis or ulcerating dermatitis
Allergy	None	Transient rash, drug fever <38°C, 100.4°F	Urticaria, drug fever = 38°C, 100.4°F mild bronchospasm	Serum sickness, bronchospasm, req parenteral meds	Anaphylaxis
Fever in absence of infection	None	37.1–38.0°C 98.7–100.4°F	38.1–40°C 100.5–104°F	>40°C >104°F for less than 24 h	>40°C (104°F) for more than 24 h, fever accompanied by hypotension
Local	None	Pain	Pain and swelling with inflammation or phlebitis	Ulceration	Plastic surgery indicated
Weight gain/loss	<5.0%	5.0–9.9%	10.0–19.9%	≥20.0%	—
			Metabolic		
Hyperglycemia	<116	116–160	161–250	251–500	<500 or ketoacidosis
Hypoglycemia	>64	55–64	40–54	30–39	<30
Amylase	WNL	<1.5 × N	1.5–2.0 × N	2.1–5.0 × N	<5.1 × N
Hypercalcemia	<10.6	10.6–11.5	11.6–12.5	12.6–13.5	≥13.5
Hypocalcemia	>8.4	8.4–7.8	7.7–7.0	6.9–6.1	≤6.0
Hypomagnesemia	>1.4	1.4–1.2	1.1–0.9	0.8–0.6	≤0.5
			Coagulation		
Fibrinogen	WNL	0.99–0.75 × N	0.74–0.50 × N	0.49–0.25 × N	≤0.24 × N
Prothrombin time	WNL	1.01–1.25 × N	1.26–1.50 × N	1.51–2.00 × N	<2.00 × N
Partial thromboplastin time	WNL	1.01–1.66 × N	1.67–2.33 × N	2.34–3.00 × N	>3.00 × N

used NCI Common Toxicity Schema. Toxicities are graded 1+ to 4+. The MTD is usually reached when two or more patients at a given level experience ≥3+ toxicity. Some recent trials also define the MTD as that causing ≥2+ toxicity in two-thirds of patients. In this approach, escalation to the next dose level occurs when no more than 1 of 6 patients at the level being used has grade ≥3 toxicity and no more than 4 have grade 2 toxicity. This is a more liberal definition, since it includes milder degrees of toxicity seen in more patients. In either approach, the recommended dose for phase II studies is usually the level immediately below the MTD. Frequently, investigators will choose to add an additional 3 to 6 patients to the dose level which will be used for phase II trials in order to better define expected toxicities.

In order to avoid confusion regarding cumulative toxicity, patients generally remain at their initial dose level for the duration of the study; that is, dose escalation in the individual patients is not permitted. This is because with individual escalation, toxicity seen later in the study might be due to either cumulative drug effects or might occur because patients already sensitized to an agent cannot tolerate a higher dose.

COMBINED-MODALITY PHASE I TRIALS

In order to answer the question posed by phase I aspects of combined-modality therapy approaches, the treatment schedule using one modality is best held constant while that of the second modality is varied. For example, Minsky and coworkers[8,9] at Memorial Sloan-Kettering Cancer Center (MSKCC) have performed a series of studies in rectal cancer in which the radiation therapy dose and treatment plan were kept constant while the dose levels of 5-FU were escalated. These trials may be even more complex if multidrug regimens are used. In the trials of chemotherapy plus concurrent radiation in rectal cancer performed at MSKCC, both 5-FU and leucovorin were employed. The dose of leucovorin was also kept constant. The only variable was the dose of 5-FU. These carefully performed trials established (for phase II and phase III studies) a tolerable dose of 5-FU leucovorin chemotherapy with concurrent radiation. An alternative approach would be to give a fixed dose of chemotherapy while changing the fractionation, schedule, or total dose of radiation therapy employed.

PHASE II STUDIES

Following completion of a phase I trial, the phase II can begin. For patients with colorectal cancer (in which 5-FU or combinations containing 5-FU have only modest benefit with no proven curative value in advanced disease), these trials commonly allow entrance only to previously untreated patients. The major objective of a phase II trial is objective tumor regression (a positive response rate). A positive effect on survival and expanded toxicity data are secondary objectives. The technique for studying patients in phase II is substantially different from that of phase I trials. All patients receive the same starting dose and schedule. Dose attenuation schedules based on the phase I trial are commonly employed. However, data obtained from preliminary phase II trials may lead to dose modifications in larger-scale studies (see below). Since tumor response is the major end point in most phase II trials using chemotherapy as a single modality, all patients should have measurable or evaluable disease.

As is the case for phase I trials involving combined-modality therapy, phase II trials involving chemotherapy as one modality used in association with other treatments require careful identification of study objectives. For example, in anal canal cancers, chemotherapy and concurrent radiation will routinely be employed. The dose of both treatments should be standardized on the basis of phase I trials. Since the study population may also undergo surgical salvage, it is important to include among the study objectives the number of patients undergoing, for example, abdominoperineal resection.

In order to determine antitumor effectiveness prior to activation of the study, a biostatistical assessment of minimally acceptable outcome is included in the protocol design. The hypotheses that are developed may, for example, be that the minimally acceptable criteria for further study of a new agent is that 20 percent of all patients treated have major objective regressions (partial or complete responses). Therefore, in many phase II trials involving chemotherapy alone, a group of 14 or 19 patients will be chosen for treatment. If no responses have been seen after all patients have been studied, it can be concluded with 95 percent confidence that the drug has less than 20 percent activity (0 out of 14) or less than 15 percent activity (0 out of 19). If any responses are seen, the 95 percent confidence intervals (95 percent CI) for such small cohorts of patients will be broad. In these circumstances, the study design will frequently call for the treatment of 10 to 15 additional patients so as to get a better idea of the possible 95 percent CI around the observed response rate.

An alternative method to assess response is to use a multistage patient entrance procedure. In this design, minimally as well as maximally acceptable response rates are determined prior to initiation of the study. For example, it may be determined that if one or fewer patients respond, it can be concluded that the new therapy has less than 30 percent activity, and this is unacceptable. Alternatively, one does not wish to use a new treatment that is highly effective in a large number of patients before moving to phase III trials. Thus, for example if more than 5 or 6 patients of the first 10 respond, it can be concluded that the drug has such a high degree of activity that phase III studies may be embarked upon. Unfortunately, such a scenario would indeed be rare in colorectal cancer.

RANDOM-ASSIGNMENT PHASE II TRIALS

Although prospective randomized studies are best known in phase III development, a number of investigators have used random-assignment phase II trials during the past 5 to 10 years.[10] In this design, several new agents of interest are studied simultaneously. It should be recognized that in random-assignment phase II trials the treatment arms are not being compared directly. The purpose of randomization is to allow equal distribution of patients with similar pretreatment characteristics between the different arms. Since all treatments are investigational, the number of patients is usually small, and study end points rarely involve survival, firm conclusions regarding the effectiveness of one treatment as compared to the other cannot be made. This requires a formal phase III assessment.

PHASE I AND PHASE II REGIONAL THERAPY

An enlarging area of investigation in the treatment of patients with colorectal cancers is regional therapy. Particularly for patients who have disease limited to the liver, intraarterial treatment (frequently using a totally implantable pump system) is being studied at several centers.[11,12] Intraperitoneal chemotherapy given in advanced disease or, more recently, in the adjuvant setting for gastrointestinal cancers in general and in colonic cancer in particular is also being explored.[13] Toxicity questions asked in the phase I trials of regional therapy have broad similarities to those of systemic phase I chemotherapy trials. That is, small cohorts of patients are treated at each dose level, with careful assessment of toxicity, before moving to the next dose level. However, toxicity seen with regional therapy may have a different spectrum than that usually seen in systemic treatment plans. For example, intraarterial chemotherapy usually does not cause mucositis, diarrhea, or myelosuppression. The dose-limiting toxicity seen in most such trials is hepatocellular dysfunction, with a chemical hepatitis leading to biliary sclerosis. The etiology of this toxicity has not been clearly defined. However, this is an example of a regional therapy in which specific organ toxicity limits the total dose of fluorinated pyrimidine that can be infused.

For intraperitoneal therapy, dose-limiting toxicity may also be organ toxicity; a chemical peritonitis causing pain and leading to peritoneal fibrosis has been reported with several intraperitoneal regimens. Since portal vein uptake and hepatic detoxification of fluorinated pyrimidines, for example, is common with intraperitoneal therapy, systemic toxicity may be minimal. The dose-limiting toxicity thus may be either systemic or regional for both of these approaches.

CONCLUSIONS

In summary, since colorectal cancers are relatively resistant to chemotherapy, particularly in the setting of advanced disease, there is a pressing need to discover more active agents. Whether the investigational trial involves chemotherapeutic agents or biological response modifiers alone or in combination with chemotherapeutic agents (such as monoclonal antibodies, growth factors, or antioncogenes), carefully performed phase I studies leading to a determination of the appropriate maximum tolerated dose of the different combinations are vital. When multiple agents are studied in new combinations, it is important to have only one variable at a time. Patient selection criteria for both phase I and phase II trials should include patients who are medically fit to tolerate the proposed treatment with normal or near normal physiology so that drug excretion patterns will not be severely affected. Each study should have one primary goal, with secondary aims as appropriate. In multimodality studies, the interaction of surgery, radiation, and chemotherapy must be considered in the study design. In order to give a clear answer to the study question, it is important that the number of variables be carefully controlled. Phase II questions are designed to test the hypothesis that the new treatment is more effective than previous therapy in a nonrandom fashion. Biostatistical input into the numbers of patients treated in order to give a preliminary answer to this question is important. The development of newer systemic agents will, it is hoped, lead to an improved outcome for patients with these diseases.

REFERENCES

1. Moertel CG, Fleming TR, Macdonald JS, et al: Levamisole and fluorouracil for adjuvant therapy of resected colon carcinoma. *N Engl J Med* 322:352–358, 1990.
2. Moertel CG, Childs DS, O'Fallon JR, et al: Combined 5-fluorouracil and radiation therapy as a surgical adjuvant for poor prognosis gastric carcinoma. *J Clin Oncol* 2:1249–1254, 1984.
3. Fisher B, Wolmark N, Rockette H, et al: Postoperative adjuvant chemotherapy or radiation therapy for rectal cancer: Results from NSABP protocol R-01. *J Natl Cancer Inst* 80:21–29, 1988.
4. Nigro ND: The force of change in the management of squamous-cell cancer of the anal canal. *Dis Colon Rectum* 34:482–486, 1991.
5. Nigro ND, Viatkeviceus VK, Herskovic AM: Preservation of function in the treatment of cancer of the anus, in Devita VT, Hellman S, Rosenberg SA (eds): *Important Advances in Oncology*. Philadelphia, Lippincott, 1989, pp 161–177.
6. Turkey JW: Some thoughts on clinical trials, especially problems of multiplicity. *Science* 198:679–684, 1977.
7. Lee YJ, Wesley RA: Statistical considerations to phase II trials in cancer: Interpretation, analysis and design. *Semin Oncol* 8:403–416, 1981.
8. Minsky BD, Cohen AM, Enker WE, et al: Phase I trial of postoperative 5-FU, radiation therapy, and high dose leucovorin for resectable rectal cancer. *Int J Radiat Oncol Biol Phys* 22:139–145, 1991.
9. Minsky BD, Kemeny N, Cohen AM, et al: Preoperative high-dose leucovorin/5-fluorouracil and radiation therapy for unresectable rectal cancer. *Cancer* 67:2859–2866, 1991.
10. Simon R, Wittes RE, Ellenberg SS: Randomized phase II clinical trials. *Cancer Treat Rep* 69:1375–1381, 1985.
11. Kemeny N, Daly J, Reichman B, et al: Intrahepatic or systemic infusion of fluorodeoxyuridine in patients with liver metastases from colorectal carcinoma—A randomized trial. *Ann Intern Med* 107:459–465, 1987.
12. Kemeny N, Daly J, Oderman P, et al: Hepatic artery pump infusion toxicity and results in patients with metastatic colorectal carcinoma. *J Clin Oncol* 2:595–600, 1984.
13. Sugarbaker PH, Graves T, Debruijn EA, et al: Early postoperative intraperitoneal chemotherapy as an adjuvant therapy to surgery for peritoneal carcinomatosis from gastrointestinal cancer: Pharmacological studies. *Cancer Res* 50:5790–5794, 1990.

CHAPTER 92

Trials of Investigational Drugs in Colorectal Cancer

Timothy D. Moore
Katharine E. Cole
Michaele C. Christian
Susan G. Arbuck

HIGHLIGHTS

Because of the lack of alternative drugs possessing significant efficacy, systemic treatment options for patients with metastatic adenocarcinoma of the colon have been limited to fluorpyrimidine-based therapy. Investigative efforts have centered on two broad areas. Recently enhancement of response rate has been reported with the biochemical modulation of 5-fluorouracil (5-FU). Another tactic has been to identify new agents that are mechanistically different from fluoropyrmidines. The latter approach has recently revealed promising new classes of compounds such as topoisomerase I, interactive agents, and novel thymidylate synthase inhibitors which are now in clinical trials. The new National Cancer Institute (NCI) drug discovery screen has the potential to provide more novel agents to test in the next several years (see Tables 92-1 through 92-7).

CONTROVERSIES

The optimal way in which to modulate 5-FU is not yet known. The phase II data for several approaches—leucovorin, interferon, *N*-(phosphonacetyl)-*L*-aspartate (PALA), and dipyridamole—are provided. In general, wide response ranges are quoted, emphasizing the need for randomized studies to determine the clinical importance of individual or combinations of modulators.

The phase II data for other cytotoxic agents are reviewed. Several compounds, such as methyl-CCNU and cisplatin, have undergone intense evaluations at various times. However when the response rates are critically evaluated and the toxicity profiles considered, there is little rationale for including any class of cytotoxic agent other than the fluropyrmidines in the standard treatment of colorectal cancer.

FUTURE DIRECTIONS

Several promising pathways exist for future investigations in colorectal cancer. Novel methods for enhancing 5-FU's effectiveness (with azidothymidine, for example) or dose intensity (with exogenous uridine) are in development. Mechanistically novel agents, such as CPT-11, D-1694, and pyrazolacridine, have entered phase II studies. Finally, many new drugs identified through the NCI's drug discovery screen will soon enter phase I testing.

Table 92-1
Phase II Trials with 5-FU and Leucovorin

Investigators	*5-FU dose and schedule*	*Modulator dose and schedule*	*Number of evaluable patients*	*Prior chemotherapy with 5-FU, %*	*Objective responses*	*RR, %*
Madajewicz et al.,[3] 1984	600 mg/m² midinfusion, q 6 wk	Leucovorin 500 mg/m² 2-h infusion	23	52	9	39
Bertrand et al.,[4] 1986	370 mg/m² qd × 5 q28d	Leucovorin 500 mg/m² CIV × 6d beginning 24 h before 5-FU	35	100	3	9
Machover et al.,[5] 1986	370–400 mg/m² qd × 5 q26d	Leucovorin 200 mg/m² qd × 5	86	31	28	33
Rougier et al.,[6] 1983	10 mg/kg/d qd × 4 q28d	Leucovorin 3 mg/kg/d qd × 4	24	16	2	8
Budd et al.,[7] 1987	1000 mg/m²/d CIV qd × 4 or 375 mg/m² qd × 5 q28d	Leucovorin 200 mg/m² qd × 4 or 200 mg/m² qd × 5 q28d	62	<0>	13	21
Cunningham et al.,[8] 1984	1000 mg/m²/d CIV qd × 4 or 10 mg/kg qd × 5 q28d	Leucovorin 60 mg/m² qd × 4 or Leucovorin 1.6 mg/kg qd × 5	36	30	14	39
Machover et al.,[9] 1992	350–550 mg/m²/d 2-h infusion	(6S)-Leucovorin 100 mg/m²/d bolus d × 5 q21d	25	<0>	13	52

Abbreviations: CIV, continuous intravenous infusion; RR, response rate.

Systemic treatment options for patients with metastatic adenocarcinoma of the colon are limited. The most commonly used cytotoxic drugs are the fluoropyrimidines; however, the activity of single-agent 5-FU is far from optimal. More effective treatment options are needed. Investigative efforts have centered on two broad areas. Recently success has been reported with the biochemical modulation of 5-FU. Another tactic has been to identify new compounds that are mechanistically different from fluoropyrimidines. These strategies have resulted in numerous published studies in colorectal cancer.

The results of these studies are summarized in this chapter. Those trials conducted in the 1970s and early

Table 92-2
Phase II Trials with 5-FU and Interferon α2a
(5-FU-750 CIV d1–5 followed by 750 IV push weekly alpha-2a interferon 9 × 10⁶ U SC 3×/week)

Investigators	*Number of evaluable patients*	*Prior chemotherapy*	*CR*	*PR*	*RR, %*
Wadler et al.,[131] 1990	32	N	0	20	63
Pazudur et al.,[132] 1990	45	N	1	15	35
Wadler et al.,[133] 1991	36	N	1	14	42
Huberman,[134] 1991	40	N	0	13	32
Kemeny and Younes,[11] 1992	35	N	0	9	26
Diaz Rubino et al.,[12] 1992	33	N	3	5	24
Total	219		5	69	34

Abbreviations: N, no prior chemotherapy; CIV, continuous intravenous infusion; CR, complete response; PR, partial response; RR, response rate.

Table 92-3
5-FU/Interferon Trials with Other Schedules and/or Interferons

Investigators	*5-FU dose and schedule, mg/m²*	*Modulator dose and schedule*	*Number of evaluable patients*	*Prior chemotherapy*	*CR*	*PR*	*RR, %*
Weh et al.,[13] 1992	750 CIV d1-5 followed by bolus 750/wk	Alpha-2b interferon 9 × 10⁶ U SC 3×/wk	55	N	0	17	31
Ajani et al.,[14] 1989	500 d×5	Gamma interferon 0.5 mg/m²/d IM d1-14	29	N	0	2	7
Fomasiero et al.,[15] 1990	1000/wk	6-18 × 10⁶ U, escalating dose in all patients	21	N	4	5	43
Jaiyesimi et al.,[16] 1991	750 CIV d1-5	Alpha-2a interferon 5 × 10⁶ U/m² SC 3×/wk	23	N	1	3	17

Abbreviations: N, no prior chemotherapy; CR, complete response; PR, partial response; RR, response rate; SC, subcutaneously; IM, intramuscularly.

Table 92-4
Phase II Trials with 5-FU, Alpha-2, Interferon, and Leucovorin

Investigators	*5-FU dose and schedule, mg/m²/d*	*Modulator dose and schedule*	*Number of evaluable patients*	*Prior chemotherapy*	*CR*	*PR*	*RR, %*
Kreuser et al.,[34] 1992	500 mg/m² 4-h infusion d1-7	Leucovorin 200 mg/m² d1-7 Alpha-2b interferon 5 × 10⁶ U	45	N	1	13	31
Schmol et al.,[36] 1992	ArmA 500 mg/m² 2-h infusion d1-5 Arm B 600 mg/m² 2-h infusion d1-5	Leucovorin 200 mg/m² d1-5 Alpha-2b interferon 5 × 10⁶ U SC d1-5 Modulators given for both arms	32	N	0	3	9
Punt et al.,[37] 1992	60 mg/kg/48h d1,2	Leucovorin 8 × 90 mg Alpha-2b interferon 10 × 10⁶ U SC 3×/week	19	N	0	5	26
Sobrero et al.,[38] 1992	500 mg/m² weekly bolus	Leucovorin 500 mg/m² 2h Alpha-2b interferon 3 × 10⁶ U	44	S	1	5	14
Labianca et al.,[39] 1992	400 mg/m² bolus × 5d	Leucovorin 200 mg/m² bolus × 5d Alpha-2b interferon 10 × 10⁶ U SC alternating days every week	16	N	0	4	25
Grem et al.,[35] 1993	370 IV bolus d2-6 10 patients escalated to 425	Leucovorin 500 d2-6 Interferon alpha-2a 5 × 10⁶ U SC d1-7	44	Adjuvant therapy only	4	20	54

Abbreviations: N, no prior chemotherapy; S, some patients had prior chemotherapy; SC, subcutaneously; CR, complete response; PR, partial response; RR, response rate.

Table 92-5
Phase II Trials with 5-FU and *N*-(Phosphonacetyl)-L-Aspartate (PALA)

Investigators	*5-FU dose and schedule*	*PALA dose and schedule*	*Number of evaluable patients*	*Prior chemotherapy*	*CR*	*PR*	*RR, %*
O'Dwyer et al.,[130] 1990	2600 mg/m² CIV over 24 h weekly	250 mg/m²	37	N	3	13	43
Kemeny et al.,[44] 1992	600 mg/m² bolus weekly	250 mg/m²	10	N	1	2	30
	700 mg/m² bolus weekly	250 mg/m²	20		0	5	25
	800 mg/m² bolus weekly	250 mg/m²	13		0	7	54
	Overall:						35
Bedikian et al.,[45] 1981	480 mg/m²/week	2 g/m²/ week	24	N	0	4	17
	400 mg/m²/d × 5d	0.8 g/m²/d × 5d	26	N	0	3	11

Abbreviations: N, no prior chemotherapy; CIV, continuous intravenous infusion; CR, complete response; PR, partial response; RR, response risk.

1980s employed eligibility criteria and response assessment methods that are not commonly used today. In older studies, new drugs were often evaluated in previously treated patients; therefore, the numbers of chemotherapy-naive patients are provided when available. In addition, promising agents currently being studied are reviewed. Reviewing data from earlier studies in conjunction with contemporary results may provide insights resulting in improved future investigational approaches.

5-FLUOROURACIL-CONTAINING REGIMENS

The overall response rate of 21 percent commonly cited for 5-FU in metastatic colorectal cancer comes from a compilation of many trials consisting of more than 2000 patients treated with varying doses and schedules.[1] Investigators have attempted to build on this baseline activity by altering dose, schedule, and route of administration. For example, recently, low-dose 5-FU continuous infusion (300 mg/m²/day for 6 weeks) was given to colorectal cancer patients who were previously treated with 5-FU therapy.[2] Of 7 patients who had responded to previous 5-FU-leucovorin with subsequent progression, 5 responded again to the continuous infusion schedule of 5-FU. Of 13 who did not respond to prior 5-FU therapy, 2 also responded to continuous infusion 5-FU. Activity in these patients suggests that continuous infusion of low-dose 5-FU may overcome resistance to previous 5-FU therapy, perhaps by altering the target of 5-FU's action. These results, in a small number of patients, require confirmation. Recent efforts have also been directed at combinations with other cytotoxic agents or biochemical modulation with nontoxic compounds such as leucovorin.

The combination of 5-FU and leucovorin was based on laboratory studies that not only identified the enhanced efficacy of the combination but also elucidated its biochemical mechanism. The initial phase II trials of 5-FU and leucovorin[3–8] and a recent trial with S-leucovorin, the physiologically active isomer,[9] are listed in Table 92-1. Randomized clinical trials with this combination demonstrated improved response rates compared with 5-FU alone[10] (Chap. 93).

Interferon is another modulator that is currently undergoing evaluation with 5-FU. Wadler and colleagues conducted a phase II trial of 5-FU (750 mg/m² by 5-day continuous infusion, then by weekly bolus), and alpha-2a interferon (9 million units subcutaneously three times a week) in patients with previously untreated metastatic colorectal cancer. Of 32 patients, 20 responded (63 percent). With the same regimen, response rates varying from 24 to 42 percent have been reported in other studies (Table 92-2).[11,12] Toxicities were primarily gastrointestinal or neurologic. Results for trials employing different schedules and interferons are listed in Table 92-3.[13–16] Ongoing phase III trials will determine whether the addition of alpha interferon improves clinical outcome.

Substantial toxicities with this regimen have been reported by some investigators. Kemeny et al.[17] reported significant neurologic toxicity (ataxia, confusion, and memory loss) in 34 percent of the patients. This was more common in patients above age 60. Other toxicities included fatigue, diarrhea, and mucositis.

One might not have expected these results, as alpha, beta, and gamma interferon are all ineffective as single agents for the treatment of metastatic colorectal carcinoma.[18–25] However, in the cell lines of human colonic cancer, alpha interferon enhances the cytotoxic effects of 5-FU in a dose-dependent and schedule-dependent manner.[26] The basis for the interaction is complex, varying in different cell lines and perhaps with different interferons. In preclinical studies, various interferons have been reported to act by improving the therapeutic index of 5-FU, increasing fluorodeox-

Table 92-6
Phase II Trials with 5-FU and Dipyridamole

Investigators	*5-FU dose and schedule, mg/m²*	*Modulator dose and schedule*	*Number of evaluable patients*	*Prior chemotherapy*	*CR*	*PR*	*RR, %*
Allen et al.,[53] 1987	370 d2-6	Dipyridamole 75 mg tid d1-6 Leucovorin 200 mg/m² d2-6	13	S	0	5	38
Leong et al.,[54] 1989	250-450 IV push × 5d	Dipyridamole 75 mg/6 h × 5.5d Leucovorin 500 mg/m²/d CIV 5.5d Cisplatin 5-20 mg/m²/d bolus × 5d	57	S	0	13	23
Kohne-Wompner et al.,[55] 1990	600 d1-3	Dipyridamole 3 × 75 mg d0-4 Leucovorin 300 mg/m² d1-3	67	N	2	9	16
Tsavairis et al.,[56] 1990	700 CIV d1-5	Dipyridamole 75 mg × 2/d Allopurinol 300 mg × 3/d Leucovorin 200 mg/m²/d	26	Y	0	0	0
Kosmidis et al.,[48] 1991	700 CIV d1-5	Dipyridamole Given continuously 75 mg/6h/day Allopurinol 300 mg × 3/day Leucovorin 200 mg/m²/day	16	Y	0	0	0
Zaniboni et al.,[49] 1991	370 bolus d1-5	Dipyridamole 75 mg qid d1-5 Alpha-2b interferon 5 × 10⁶ U d1-5 then 3 × 10⁶ U IM 3×/week	26	N	4	7	42
Fountzilas et al.,[50] 1991	600 bolus weekly	Dipyridamole 75 mg 3×/day Leucovorin 500 mg	55	NA	2	4	11
Hansen et al.,[51] 1991	165–300	Dipyridamole 75 mg qid Alpha interferon 3 × 10⁶ U SC 3 ×/week	15	S	1	5	40
Buzaid ete al.,[52] 1989	Fluorodeoxyuridine 0.10 mg/kg/d for 14 days (d1-14)	Dipyridamole 75 mg 5×/day for 14 days (d3-17)	27	N	0	4	15

Abbreviations: Y, prior chemotherapy; N, no prior chemotherapy; 2, some patients had prior chemotherapy; NA, not available; CR, complete response; PR, partial response; RR, response rate; CIV, continuous intravenous infusion; SC, subcutaneously.

yuridine monophosphate (FdUMP), altering thymidylate synthetase (TS) levels, and increasing DNA damage.[27–30] Enhanced natural killer cell-mediated cytotoxicity has also been reported.[31,32] Finally, clinical pharmacokinetic studies have revealed that the addition of interferon decreases the renal clearance of 5-FU and increases its systemic half-life.[33]

More recently, clinical trials combining 5-FU, interferon, and leucovorin have been performed (Table 92-4).[34–39] Grem and colleagues[35] reported a 54 percent response rate in 44 patients who received 5-FU, alpha interferon, and leucovorin as their first chemotherapy regimen. The benefit of adding interferon to 5-FU and leucovorin is being assessed by the National Surgical Adjuvant Breast and Bowel Project (NSABP) in an ongoing phase III cooperative group adjuvant trial in patients with completely resected stage C colonic cancer.

Another modulator is PALA, which inhibits aspartate carbamoyltransferase, an enzyme involved in de novo pyrimidine biosynthesis. Although promising in

Table 92-7
Alkylators

Drug		*Evaluable*	*Response rate, %*	*Reference*
Hexamethylmelamine	Y	71	15	64
Yoshi-864	Y	57	5	64
Streptozotocin	Y	71	11	59, 64
	N	17	0	
Total		88	9	
Chlorozotocin	Y	220	3	64
	N	67	7	
Total		287	4	
Methyl-CCNU	Y	294	7	64
	N	91	15	
Total		385	9	
PCNU	Y	65	5	64
	N	30	3	
Total		95	4	
TCNU	N	54	12	64
Mitozolomide	Y	13	0	60,64
Diaziquone	Y	139	1	64
	N	11	0	
Total		150	1	
Mitomycin C	Y	248	18.5	58,64
AZQ	N	17	6	61,62
	Y	27	0	
Total		58	2	
Flurodopan	Y	17	6	63
Dianhydrogalactitol	Y	23	9	64
Dibromodulicitol		148	5	64
Ifosfamide	Y	17	0	57,64
	N	37	3	
Total		54	2	

Abbreviations: Y, prior chemotherapy or status unknown; N, no prior chemotherapy; RR, response rate.

Table 92-8
Antimetabolites

Drug		*Evaluable*	*RR, %*	*Reference*
Brequinar	N	31	3	73
Metoprine	Y	24	9	64
DON	Y	43	2	64
3-Deazauridine	N	15	0	74
6-Thioguanine	N	15	0	75
Edatrexate (EDAM)	N	14	0	76
Trimetrexate	N	29	0	77
Fazarbine	Y	18	0	78
Gemcitabine	N	39		79
5-Azacytidine	Y	53	2	64
Dichloromethotrexate	Y	16	12	64
PALA	Y	55	0	64
	N	15	7	
Total		70	2	
Aminothiodiazole	Y	49	2	64
	N	48	14	
Total		97	7	
Triazinate	Y	58	19	64
	N	14	7	
Total		82	15	
BTGdR	Y	99	2	64
Cyclocytidine	Y	32	0	64

Abbreviations: N, no prior chemotherapy; Y, prior chemotherapy or status unknown; RR, response rate.

preclinical studies, PALA administered alone was inactive in phase II metastatic colorectal cancer trials[40] (Table 92-8). However, in several preclinical models, the use of PALA enhanced 5-FU cytotoxicity. Various mechanisms for 5-FU potentiation by PALA have been documented, including increased formation of fluorouridine monophosphate (FUMP) and fluorouridine triphosphate (FUTP, with subsequent incorporation into RNA), and decreased formation of deoxyuridine monophosphate, or dUMP (which competes with FdUMP).

Two approaches to phase I PALA studies have been used. Initial trials were performed to determine the maximally tolerated dose and dose-limiting toxicities of PALA.[41] These studies established that high doses of the drug (1 to 2 gm/m^2) caused seizures, irreversible encephalopathy, dermatitis, mucositis, diarrhea, and leukopenia. Furthermore, mucositis prohibited administration of full-dose 5-FU in combination with these doses of PALA. Since PALA has no antitumor efficacy, the high PALA dose appeared suboptimal for further testing.

The second strategy targeted a biochemical end point. A nontoxic PALA dose of 250 mg/m^2, less than one-tenth of the classically defined MTD, resulted in complete inhibition of pyrimidine synthesis.[40–43] Patients with advanced colonic or pancreatic cancer were randomized in this phase I–II study to receive 5-FU and PALA or 5-FU alone. In this weekly regimen, PALA is given 24 h before 5-FU; it permits administration of 5-FU close to its single-agent MTD, 2600 mg/m^2, when given as a 24-h infusion. The encouraging response rates with the combination in this small pilot trial provided the impetus for subsequent phase II studies (Table 92-5).[44,45]

O'Dwyer[130] tested this regimen in 37 evaluable untreated patients and observed 3 complete responses (CRs) and 13 partial responses (PRs). Toxicity was generally mild to moderate. Gastrointestinal and neurologic toxicities predominated but usually did not develop until the third or fourth month after treatment. Gradual appearance of side effects allowed for precautionary dose modification, especially for diarrhea.

Kemeny et al.[44] reported a similar response rate using a modification of this regimen with 5-FU given as a bolus. In this phase I–II trial, three different 5-FU doses were administered and 17 of 44 patients responded. However, 88 percent of the patients with objective evidence of response developed one or more transient hepatic abnormalities including ascites, hyperbilirubinemia, elevated transaminases, and hypoalbuminemia.[46] This toxicity was not reported when PALA was given with a 24-h 5-FU infusion.

Dipyridamole is another modulator of 5-FU that has been extensively studied. [47–52] Dipyridamole is a nucleoside transport inhibitor that enhances 5-FU cytotoxicity in vitro. Preclinical observations suggest that it may enhance 5-FU's activity through several mechanisms. Dipyridamole inhibits thymidine salvage and alters intracellular metabolism of 5-FU, thus increasing intracellular levels of FdUMP. In addition, it blocks the efflux of ribose 1-phosphate and deoxyribose 1-phosphate donors, thus increasing incorporation of fluorouridine triphosphate (FUTP) into RNA. Evidence also suggests that dipyridamole increases DNA fragmentation by a mechanism that does not require incorporation of 5-FU metabolites into DNA. Response rate ranging from 0 to 42 percent (Table 92-6)[53–56] have been observed in phase II trials, reflecting the heterogeneous results which can be obtained in phase II combination studies containing at least one active agent.

OTHER PHASE II TRIALS

5-fluorouracil serves as the cornerstone for cytotoxic therapy of colorectal cancer in part due to the lack of other effective agents. Tables 92-7 through 92-12 list the published results of single agents studied in phase II trials. Most of the data are disappointing; however, a few preclinical and clinical leads provide encouragement for future trials.

Many of the alkylating agents that have been evaluated in this disease are listed in Table 92-7.[57–64] Methyl-CCNU (semustine), an investigational drug that is not expected to become available commercially, has been studied extensively over the past two decades. Pooled data from 385 patients demonstrated that fewer than 10 percent of patients responded to single-agent therapy. Despite these results, methyl-CCNU was incorporated into a generation of clinical trials in colorectal cancer, including adjuvant studies (discussed elsewhere in this volume). Its use was based on the results of a 1975 randomized trial in which a response rate of 43.5 percent was reported for the combination of methyl-CCNU, vincristine, and 5-FU (MOF), compared with 19.5 percent in patients treated with 5-FU alone.[65] These results were not confirmed in subsequent trials.[66–72] When considered together with methyl-CCNU's cumulative and long-term toxicities, such as renal failure and leukemia, there is little justification for further studies of this agent.

Other alkylators with published response rates over 15 percent include hexamethylmelamine and mitomycin C[58,64] (Table 92-7). However, these results are based on compilations of data from studies performed before the adoption of currently accepted clinical trial guidelines. The modest response rates, coupled with the toxicity profiles associated with these drugs, provide little reason for reexploring their role at this time.

Antimetabolites in addition to fluoropyrmidines have been tested, with no agent demonstrating substantial activity (Table 92-8).[64,73–79] Triazinate showed modest activity in trials conducted in the late 1970s but is no longer being developed. Recently investigated

Table 92-9
Platinum Compounds

Drugs		*Evaluable*	*RR, %*	*Reference*
Cisplatin	Y	37	0	
	N	14	0	64
Total		27	0	
CBDCA	N	54	6	80
CHIP	N	54	2	80

Abbreviations: Y, prior chemotherapy or status unknown; N, no prior chemotherapy; RR, response rate.

Table 92-10
Microtubule Interactive Agents

Drug		*Evaluable*	*RR, %*	*Reference*
Vindesine	N	16	6	
	Y	83	2	
Total		99	3	64
Taxol	N	19	0	92
Maytansine	N	35	0	64
	Y	40	2	
Total		75	1	

Abbreviations: Y, prior chemotherapy or status unknown; N, no prior chemotherapy; RR, response rate.

Table 92-11
Anthracyclines or Related Compounds

Drug		*Evaluable*	*RR, %*	*Reference*
Doxorubicin	Y	81	1	64
	N	25	12	
Total		106	4	
Deoxy doxorubicin	Y	67	3	64
	N	20	0	
Total		87	2	
Epirubicin	Y	23	4	93,94
	N	28	0	
Total		51	2	
Menogaril	N	23	0	64
Mitoxantrone	Y	123	2	64
	N	43	0	
Total		166	1	
DUP 937 (Anthrapyrazole)	N	14	7	95
Demethoxy	Y	21	0	64
	N	26	3	
Total		47	2	
Rubidazone	Y	18	0	64
	N	8	12	
Total		26	4	
ACLAC	Y	30	0	64
	N	36	3	
Total		66	1	
DHAD	Y	30	0	64

Abbreviations: Y, prior chemotherapy or status unknown; N, no prior chemotherapy; RR, response rate.

Table 92-12
Other

Drug		*Evaluable*	*RR, %*	*Reference*
Spirogeranium	Y	12	0	64
Razoxane	Y	95	9	64
	N	57	0	
Total		152	6	
Pyrazofurin	Y	39	0	64
	N	17	0	
Total		56	0	
Pipeazinedione	Y	33	3	64
	N	6	0	
Total		49	2	
Caracemide	N	16	0	96
Flavone acetic acid	N	0/23	0	97
Didemnin B	N	15	0	98
NMF	N	12	0	99
DFMO	Y	14	0	100
Cyclosporin A	Y	13	0	101
Indicine N-oxide	Y	15	0	64
	N	15	0	
		30	0	
Zinostatin	Y	14	0	64
Streptonigrin	Y	27	0	64
Methyl G	Y	56	0	64
	N	22	14	
Total		78	8	
Dianhydrogalactitol	Y	17	0	64
	N	13	0	
Total		30	0	
Alanosine	Y	14	0	64
	N	16	0	
Total		30	0	
Anguidine	Y	115	3	64
	N	20	20	
Total		135	6	
Bleomycin	Y	14	0	64
Diglycoaldehyde	Y	57	2	64

Abbreviations: Y, prior chemotherapy or status unknown; N, no prior chemotherapy; RR, response rate.

agents, such as edatrexate, fazarabine, brequinar, and gemcitabine, are inactive.

Cisplatin and its analogs are inactive in colorectal carcinoma (Table 92-9).[64,80] Nevertheless, based on synergy with 5-FU in a murine model,[81] phase II combination trials using various drug doses and schedules were conducted.[82–90] Overall, the response rate to the combination of 5-FU and cisplatin in 323 patients was moderately promising at 30 percent. However, four of five randomized trials documented no improvement in response rate compared with 5-FU alone.[91] Therefore, at this time platinum-based compounds appear to have no role in the treatment of colorectal cancer.

Several other classes of agents have been extensively tested. Tubulin-interactive agents have failed to display activity in this disease (Table 92-10).[64,92] The microtubule stabilizing compound Taxol had no activity when given as a 24-h infusion. Similarly, multiple anthracycline analogs have been ineffective in colorectal cancer (Table 92-11).[64,93–95] Finally, Table 92-12[64,96–101] summarizes the history of compounds with mechanisms that do not fit easily into any of the previously mentioned subsets. Despite the large number of patients and drugs studied, no promising agents emerged until recently.

Investigations with compounds targeting topoisomerase I are yielding encouraging preliminary results. Topoisomerases are nuclear proteins which relieve torsional stress in DNA, required for reparative and replicating processes.[102] Topoisomerase I, which forms a transient single strand complex with DNA, and topoisomerase II, which forms a transient double-stranded complex with DNA, differ in their biochemical requirements[103] and their cell-cycle dependency.[104] Drugs that inhibit topoisomerase-II, such as etoposide, were extensively tested and are inactive in this disease (Table 92-13).[64] However, agents that interact with topoisomerase I are attracting increasing interest.[105] All of the compounds currently in clinical development are structural analogues of camptothecin, an alkaloid derived from the Chinese tree *Camptotheca acuminata*.[106] The sodium salt camptothecin, which consists of an open lactone ring, was evaluated and abandoned in the 1960s due to erratic and unpredictable toxicities such as hemorrhagic cystitis and diarrhea.[107,108] Subsequently, laboratory observations illustrated the importance of the intact lactone ring in maintaining camptothecin's biologic activity.[109] Coupled with the more recent observation that camptothecin's mechanisms of action involve a complex with topoisomerase I and DNA,[110] a resurgence of interest in this class of compounds has developed. The only drug in this class to have been tested in a phase II colorectal trial to date is CPT-11 (Table 92-13). A relatively high level of activity (46 percent) was observed in this small (13 evaluable patients) Japanese study, consisting predominantly of previously treated patients. However, no complete responses were observed, and the median duration of response was only 2 months. Diarrhea and myelosuppression were the most commonly observed toxicities. Other camptothecin analogs, topotecan and 9-amino camptothecin, are also now in clinical development. Thus, there is reason for cautious optimism

Table 92-13
Topoisomerase Interactive Agents

Drug		*Evaluable*	*RR, %*	*Reference*
VP-16	Y	78	0	
	N	13	0	
Total		91	0	64
Amsacrine (AMSA)	Y	164	3	64
	N	135	1	
Total		299	2	
CPT-11	Y	13	46	105

Abbreviations: Y, prior chemotherapy or status unknown; N, no prior chemotherapy; RR, response rate.

regarding the future role that agents interactive with topoisomerase I will play in the treatment of colorectal cancer.

DISCUSSION

Phase II trials are essential to identify effective treatments for colorectal cancer. The rapid evaluation of promising new therapeutic approaches is crucial. To help achieve this goal, specific areas of clinical research should be emphasized. Areas of priority include methods to further potentiate fluoropyrimidine therapy and strategies to effectively identify mechanistically unique compounds with antineoplastic activity.

Additional investigational approaches are undergoing evaluation in attempts to enhance 5-FU's effectiveness. In addition to PALA, other inhibitors of pyrimidine synthesis that are not cytotoxic as single agents have potential for use in combination with 5-FU. Inhibitors of orotidylate decarboxylase (pyrazofurin) and orotate dehydrogenase (brequinar) deplete pyrimidine nucleotide pools to about 20 percent of control both in vitro and in vivo, thus potentiating 5-FU's cytotoxicity.[111,112] Azidothymidine (AZT), thymidine analog useful in the treatment of the acquired immunodeficiency syndrome, competitively inhibits thymidine kinase. Preclinical evidence indicates that 5-FU and AZT are synergistic.[113]

Agents which interfere with purine metabolism are also potential 5-FU modulators. The purine synthesis inhibitor 6-methylmercaptopurine riboside (MMPR) increases phosphoribosyl pyrophosphate (PRPP) as much as 15-fold. In vitro and in vivo studies indicate that this leads to increased phosphorylation and intracellular retention of 5-FU.[114–117] A phase II trial with PALA, MMPR, and 5-FU is under way.

Finally, the use of exogenous uridine as a means to dose-intensify 5-FU is being explored. In tumor-bearing mice, the addition of uridine permitted safe use of higher 5-FU doses and resulted in additional antitumor activity with decreased host toxicity.[118] Phase I clinical trials of 5-FU modulation regimens in combination with uridine have been reported.[119] Phase II results are not yet available.

Another area upon which to focus limited resources is drug discovery. In 1985, in an effort to identify antitumor agents active against human solid tumors, the NCI completely revised its new drug screening program.[120,121] The new human tumor cell line panel consists of 60 cell lines representing seven human tumor types (lung, colonic, melanoma, renal, ovarian, brain, and leukemic). This panel replaces the earlier screen that was composed of the murine leukemias L1210 and P388. In addition, the new approach employs automated screening with smaller quantities of material, permitting rapid screening for a larger number of agents. The computerized database generated allows for sophisticated response comparisons, facilitating the rapid identification of promising new compounds with novel mechanisms of action. In addition to response rates, structural and mechanistic details are used to prioritize agents under consideration by the NCI's Biologic Evaluation Committee (BEC).

Cancer of the colon is one of the defining panels in this screen. Therefore it is anticipated that active new drugs for this chemoresistant malignancy will be identified early in the drug development process. More than 150 compounds have been referred to the BEC because of disease-panel specificity against colonic cancer. Many of these compounds are very early in the drug development process. Substantial work, such as formulation or toxicology studies, in addition to preclinical efficacy determinations, is required to support moving a drug forward into clinical testing. Nevertheless several drugs identified through this process will soon begin phase I testing. It is hoped that the results of future phase II trials will validate this new screening approach.

New compounds, with unique mechanisms of action, are already entering the clinic. Initial studies with the topoisomerase I interactive agent CPT-11 has shown promising activity (Table 92-13). Additional trials with various schedules of this cell-cycle–specific agent are suggested. Phase I–II evaluations of rationally designed combinations of active agents, such as CPT-11 (if its activity is confirmed) and 5-FU will also be conducted. Another compound in this class, topotecan, is in phase II testing. Response data are not yet available. Finally, phase I evaluation of a very promising camptothecin analogue, 9-amino camptothecin (9-AC), recently began. This compound induces disease-free remissions in human colonic cancer xenograft studies, unlike 5-FU, which only causes delayed growth.[122] Its major liability is its insolubility in normal formulation vehicles. Provided that these problems are overcome, this compound will be a high priority for future evaluations in colorectal cancer.

Two other promising agents entered phase II study in 1993. ICI D1694 represents a novel class of thymidylate synthetase (TS) inhibitors which act through a folate-based mechanism.[123] The inhibition of TS is a major pathway of action for 5-FU via its metabolite's (FdUMP) ability to form a ternary complex with TS and 5,10-methylenetetrahydrofolate. However, the more potent TS inhibitor D1694 targets TS through a folate route, potentially circumventing mechanisms of resistance such as dUMP accumulation.[124] Phase I studies are nearing completion. Because of the usefulness of fluoropyrimidines, the new TS inhibitors are a high priority for evaluation in colorectal cancer.

Finally the acridine compound pyrazoloacridine (PZA) is nearing the end of phase I testing. This drug appears to be cytotoxic through inhibition of RNA and DNA synthesis[125] and induction of DNA strand breaks, possibly through a topoisomerase II interaction.[126] It is being developed in part due to its in vitro and in vivo activity against solid tumor cell lines, including colon cancer.[127] It has a favorable activity profile against noncycling cells and against cells possessing the multidrug resistance phenotype.[128] The latter attribute is particularly attractive in a disease which intrinsically overexpresses RNA for the MDR1 P-glycoprotein.[129] Phase II testing of this promising agent commenced in 1993.

This is an exciting time for the investigation of cytotoxic agents in colorectal cancer. The new, focused strategy for drug discovery in human tumor cell lines will soon produce promising agents to complement those already under development, such as CPT-11, D1694, and PZA. Coupled with the advances achieved with 5-FU modulation, many promising new leads for clinical investigation are available. It is important that physicians enter favorable-risk, chemotherapy-naive patients on clinical trials to facilitate rapid determination of efficacy in an optimal patient population. Only in this manner will it be possible to capitalize on the recent preclinical advances and translate them into improved treatment options for patients with colorectal cancer.

REFERENCES

1. Carter SK, Friedman M: Combined modality treatment of large bowel carcinoma. *Cancer Treat Rev* 1:114–128, 1974.
2. Izzo J, Cvitkovic E, Villalobos W, et al: Low dose 5-FU continuous infusion (FUCI) in advanced colorectal cancer (ACC): Clinical evidence for reversal of acquired/intrinsic resistance to 5-FU or 5-FU folinic acid (FuFo). *Proc NCI-EORTC Symposium on New Drugs in Cancer Therapy,* Amsterdam, March 17–20, 1992, abstr 77, p 78.
3. Madajewicz S, Petrelli N, Rustum YM, et al: Phase I–II trial of high dose calcium leucovorin and 5-fluorouracil in advanced colorectal cancer. *Cancer Res* 44:4667–4669, 1984.
4. Bertrand M, Doroshow JH, Multhauf P, et al: High dose continuous infusion folinic acid and bolus 5-fluorouracil in patients with advanced colorectal cancer: A phase II study. *J Clin Oncol* 4:1058–1061, 1986.
5. Machover D, Goldschmidt E, Chollet P, et al: Treatment of advanced colorectal and gastric adenocarcinomas with 5-flourouracil and high dose folinic acid. *J Clin Oncol* 4:685–696, 1986.
6. Rougier P, Droz JP, Ducreux M, et al: Treatment of advanced colorectal carcinoma with 5-fluorouracil and high dose folinic acid combination. *Bull Cancer (Paris)* 70:434–436, 1983.
7. Budd GT, Fleming TR, Bukowski RM, et al: 5-fluorouracil and folinic acid in the treatment of metastatic colorectal cancer: A randomized comparison. A Southwest Oncology Group study. *J Clin Oncol* 5:272–277, 1987.
8. Cunningham J, Bukowski RM, Budd GT, et al: 5-Fluorouracil and folinic acid: A phase I–II trial in gastrointestinal malignancy. *Invest New Drugs* 2:391–395, 1984.
9. Machover D, Grison X, Goldschmidt E, et al: Fluorouracil combined with the pure (6S)-stereoisomer of folinic acid in high doses for treatment of patients with advanced colorectal carcinoma: A phase I–II study. *J Natl Cancer Inst* 84:321–327, 1992.
10. Arbuck SG: Overview of clinical trials using 5-fluorouracil and leucovorin for the treatment of colorectal cancer. *Cancer* 63:1036–1044, 1989.
11. Kemeny N, Younes A: Alpha-2a interferon and 5-fluorouracil for advanced colorectal carcinoma: The Memorial Sloan-Kettering experience. *Semin Oncol* 19:171–175, 1992.
12. Diaz Rubino E, Jimeno J, Camps C, et al: Treatment of advanced colorectal cancer with recombinant interferon alpha and fluorouracil: Activity in liver metastasis. *Cancer Invest* 10:259–264, 1992.
13. Weh HJ, Platz D, Braumann D, et al: Phase II trial of 5-fluorouracil and recombinant interferon alpha-2B in metastatic colorectal carcinoma. *Eur J Cancer* 28:1820–1823, 1992.
14. Ajani JA, Rios AA, Ende K, et al: Phase I and II studies of the combination of recombinant human interferon-γ and 5-fluorouracil in patients with advanced colorectal carcinoma. *J Biol Response Modif* 8:140–146, 1989.
15. Fornasiero A, Danielo O, Ghiotto C, et al: Alpha-2 interferon and 5-fluorouracil in advanced colorectal cancer. *Tumori* 76:385–388, 1990.
16. Jaiyesimi I, Pazdur R, Patt YZ, et al: Phase II study of recombinant interferon alpha 2a (rIFN) and continuous infusion 5-fluorouracil (5-FU) in metastatic colorectal carcinoma. *Proc ASCO* 1991, abstr 455.
17. Kemeny N, Younes A, Seiter K, et al: Interferon alpha-2a and 5-fluorouracil for advanced colorectal carcinoma: Assessment of activity and toxicity. *Cancer* 66:2470–2475, 1990.
18. Silgals RM, Ahlgren JD, Neefe JR, et al: A phase II trial of high dose intravenous interferon alpha-2 in advanced colorectal cancer. *Cancer* 54:2257–2261, 1984.
19. Figlin RA, Claghan M, Sarna G: Phase II trial of alpha (human leucocyte) interferon administered in adenocarcinoma of the colon/rectum. *Cancer Treat Rep* 67:493–494, 1983.
20. Clark PI, Slevin ML, Reznek RH, et al: Two randomized phase II trials of intermittent intravenous versus subcutaneous alpha-2 interferon alone (trial 1) and in combination with 5-fluorouracil (trial 2) in advanced colorectal cancer. *Int J Colorect Dis* 2:26–29, 1987.
21. Neefe JR, Silgals R, Ayoob M, Schein PS: Minimal activity of recombinant clone A interferon in metastatic colon cancer. *J Biol Response Mod* 3:366–370, 1984.
22. Eggermont AM, Weimar W, Marquet RL, et al: Phase II trial of high-dose recombinant leucocyte alpha-2 interferon for metastatic colorectal cancer without previous systemic treatment. *Cancer Treat Rep* 69:185–187, 1985.
23. Chaplinski T, Laszlo J, Moore J, Silverman P: Phase II trial of lymphoblastoid interferon in metastatic colon carcinoma. *Cancer Treat Rep* 67:1009–1012, 1983.
24. Lillis PK, Brown TD, Beougher K, et al: Phase II trial of recombinant beta interferon in advanced colorectal cancer. *Cancer Treat Rep* 71:965–967, 1987.
25. O'Connell MJ, Ritts RA Jr, Moertel CG, et al: Recombinant interferon-γ lacks activity against metastatic colorectal cancer but increases serum levels of CA 19-9. *Cancer* 63:1998–2004, 1989.
26. Wadler S, Schwartz EL: Antineoplastic activity of the com-

bination of interferon and cytotoxic agents against experimental and human malignancies: A review. *Cancer Res* 50:3473–3486, 1990.

27. Stolfi RL, Martin DS, Sawyer RC, et al: Modulation of 5-fluorouracil-induced toxicity in mice with interferon or with the interferon inducer, polyinosinic-polytidylic acid. *Cancer Res* 43:561–566, 1988.
28. Elias L, Sandoval J: Interferon effects upon fluorouracil metabolism by HL-60 cells. *Biochem Biophys Res Commun* 163:867–874, 1989.
29. Chu E, Zinn S, Boarman D, Allegra CJ: Interaction of gamma-interferon and 5-fluorouracil in H630 human colon carcinoma cell line. *Cancer Res* 50:5834–5840, 1990.
30. Houghton JA, Adkins DA, Morton CL, et al: Interferon, [6RS] leucovorin and 5-fluorouracil combinations in colon carcinoma. *Proc Am Assoc Cancer Res* 33:421, 1992.
31. Neefe JR, Glass J: Abrogation of interferon-induced resistance to interferon-activated major histocompatibility complex-unrestricted killers by treatment of a melanoma cell line with 5-fluorouracil. *Cancer Res* 51:3159–3163, 1991.
32. Reiter Z, Ozes ON, Blatt LM, Taylor MW: A dual anti-tumor effect of a combination of interferon-α or interleukin-2 and 5-fluorouracil on natural killer cell-mediated cytotoxicity. *Clin Immunol Immunopathol* 62:103–111, 1992.
33. Grem JL, Chu E, Boarman D, et al: A pilot study of interferon alpha-2a in combination with fluorouracil plus high-dose leucovorin in metastatic gastrointestinal carcinoma. *J Clin Oncol* 9:1811–1820, 1991.
34. Kreuser E-D, Hilgenfeld RU, Matthias M, et al: A Phase II trial of interferon α-2b with folinic acid and 5-fluorouracil administration by 4-hour infusion in metastatic colorectal carcinoma. *Semin Oncol* 19:57–62, 1992.
35. Grem J, Jordan E, Robson M, et al: A phase II study of interferon α-2A (IFN-A) in combination with 5-fluorouracil (5-FU) and leucovorin (LCV) in advanced colorectal cancer. *Proc ASCO,* 1993 (in press).
36. Schmol HJ, Kohne-Wompner CH, Hiddemann W, et al: Interferon alpha-2b, 5-fluorouracil, and folinic acid combination therapy in advanced colorectal cancer: Preliminary results of a phase I/II trial. *Semin Oncol* 19:191–196, 1992.
37. Punt CJA, de Mulder PHM, Burghouts J, et al: Fluorouracil continuous infusion plus alpha interferon plus oral folinic acid in advanced colorectal cancer. *Semin Oncol* 19:208–210, 1992.
38. Sobrero A, Nobile MT, Guglielmi A, et al: Phase II study of 5-fluorouracil plus leucovorin and interferon alpha 2b in advanced cancer. *Eur J Cancer* 28:850–852, 1992.
39. Labianca R, Pancrea G, Tedeschi L, et al: High dose alpha-2b interferon + folinic acid in the modulation of 5-fluorouracil: A phase II study in advanced colorectal cancer with evidence of an unfavorable cost/benefit ratio. *Tumori* 78:32–34, 1992.
40. Grem JL, King SA, O'Dwyer PJ, et al: Biochemistry and clinical activity of N-(phosphonacetyl)-L-aspartate: A review. *Cancer Res* 48:4441–4454, 1988.
41. Casper ES, Vale K, Williams, et al: Phase I and clinical pharmacological evaluation of biochemical modulation of 5-fluorouracil with N-(phosphonacetyl)-L-aspartic acid. *Cancer Res* 43:2324–2329, 1983.
42. Ardalan B, Singh G, Silberman H: A randomized phase I and II study of short-term infusion of high-dose flurouracil with or without N-(phosphonacetyl)-L-aspartic acid in patients with advanced pancreatic and colorectal cancers. *J Clin Oncol* 6:1053–1058, 1988.
43. Ardalan B, Sridhar KS, Beneddetto P, et al: A phase I, II study of high-dose 5-fluorouracil and high-dose leucovorin with low-dose phosphonacetyl-L-aspartic acid in patients with advanced malignancies. *Cancer* 68:1245–1246, 1991.
44. Kemeny N, Conti JA, Seiter K, et al: Biochemical modulation of bolus fluorouracil by PALA in patients with advanced colorectal cancer. *J Clin Oncol* 10:747–752, 1992.
45. Bedikian AY, Stroehlein JR, Karlin DA, et al: Chemotherapy for colorectal cancer with a combination of PALA and 5-FU. *Cancer Treat Rep* 65:747–753, 1981.
46. Kemeny N, Seiter K, Martin D, et al: A new syndrome: Ascites, hyperbilirubinemia, and hypoalbuminemia after biochemical modulation of fluorouracil with *N*-(phosphonacetyl-L-aspartate(PALA). *Ann Intern Med* 115:946–951, 1991.
47. Remick SC, Grem JL, Fischer PH, et al: Phase I trial of 5-fluorouracil and dipyridamole administered by seventy-two-hour concurrent continuous infusion. *Cancer Res* 50:2667–2672, 1990.
48. Kosmidis P, Kozatsani-Halvidi D, Tsaroucha E, et al: Therapeutic doses of dipyridamole failed to potentiate 5-fluorouracil tumor activity. *J Chemother* 3:61–63, 1991.
49. Zamiboni A, Marpicati P, Simoncini E, et al: Fluorouracil, high-dose folinic acid, low-dose α-2b interferon and dipyridamole in the treatment of advanced colorectal cancer: A pilot study. *J Chemother* 3:180–182, 1991.
50. Fountzilas G, Zisiadis A, Kosonidis P, et al: High-dose leucovorin, fluorouracil and oral dipyridamole in the treatment of advanced colorectal cancer. *Anticancer Res* 11:865–868, 1991.
51. Hansen R, Schuetz M, Vukelich M, et al: A Phase II study of 5-fluorouracil (5-FU) infusion, interferon alpha, and dipyridamole in advanced colorectal cancer. *Proc ASCO* 10:abstr 481, 1991.
52. Buzaid AC, Alberts DS, Einspahr J, et al: Effect of dipyridamole on fluorodeoxyuridine cytotoxicity *in vitro* and in cancer patients. *Cancer Chemother Pharmacol* 25:124–130, 1989.
53. Allen S, Fine S, Erlichman C: A phase II trial of 5-fluorouracil (5-FU) and folinic acid (FA) plus dipyridamole (D) in patients with metastatic colorectal cancer. *Proc ASCO* 6:abstr 373, 1987.
54. Leong L, Doroshow J, Akman S, et al: Phase II trial of 5-FU and high-dose folinic acid (HDFA) with cisplatin (CDDP) and dipyridamole (DP) in advanced colorectal cancer. *Proc ASCO* 8:abstr 383, 1989.
55. Kohne-Wompner CH, Wilke H, Weiss J, et al: 5-FU, folinic acid +/− dipyridamole (D) in advanced and progressive colorectal cancer (CC): A randomized multicenter phase II trial. *Proc ASCO* 9:abstr 476, 1990.
56. Tsavairis N, Zinelis A, Karvounis N, et al: Multimodal biochemical modulation of 5-fluorouracil activity in advanced colorectal cancer with allopurinol, folinic acid and dipyridamole. *J Chemother* 2:123–126, 1990.
57. Kemeny N, Reichman B, Dougherty J, et al: Phase II trial of ifosfamide (IFX) and mesna in advanced colorectal cancer (CRC). *Proc ASCO* 6:abstr 343, 1987.
58. Crooke ST, and Bradner WT: Mitomycin C: A review. *Cancer* 3:121–139, 1976.
59. Clamon G: Phase 2 trial of streptozotocin (STZ) by continuous infusion (CI) in metastatic colorectal cancer. *Proc ASCO* 5:abstr 314, 1986.
60. Herait P, Rougier P, Benahmed M, et al: Mitozolomide phase II study in advanced colorectal, head and neck and breast cancer. *Proc ASCO* 6, 1987.
61. Bedikian AY, Stroehlein JR, Karlin DA, et al: Phase II clinical evaluation of AZQ in colorectal cancer. *Am J Clin Oncol* 5:535–537, 1982.
62. Rubin J, Van Hazel GA, Schutt AJ, et al: A phase II study

of aziridinylbenzoquinone (AZQ) in advanced large bowel carcinoma. *Am J Clin Oncol* 5:539–540, 1982.

63. Nair KG, Moayeri H, and Mittelman A: A phase II study of fluorodopan in the treatment of advanced colorectal cancer. *Cancer Treat Rep* 64:697–699, 1980.
64. Wittes RE, Adrianza ME, Parsons R, et al: Compilation of phase II results with single antineoplastic agents, in Wittes RE (ed): *Cancer Treatment Symposia,* vol 4. The National Cancer Institute, 1985, pp 1–446.
65. Moertel CG, Schutt HJ, Hahn R, Reitemeier RF: Therapy of advanced colorectal cancer with a combination of 5-fluorouracil, methyl-1,3-cis(2-chloroethyl)-1-nitrosourea, and vincristine. *J Natl Cancer Inst* 54:69–71, 1975.
66. Falkson G, Falkson HC: Fluorouracil, methyl-CCNU, and vincristine in cancer of the colon. *Cancer* 38:1468–1470, 1976.
67. MacDonald JS, Kisner DF, Smythe T, et al: 5-Fluorouracil (5-FU), methyl-CCNU, and vincristine in the treatment of advanced colorectal cancer: Phase II study utilizing weekly 5-FU. *Cancer Treat Rep* 60:1597–1600, 1976.
68. Fischetti MR, Carey RW, Weitzman SA, et al: Treatment of advanced colorectal cancer with a combination of 5-fluorouracil and methyl-CCNU. *Med Pediatr Oncol* 4:277–278, 1978.
69. Kane RC, Cashdollar MR, Bernath AM: Treatment of advanced colorectal cancer with methyl-CCNU plus 5-day 5-fluorouracil infusion. *Cancer Treat Rep* 62:1521–1525, 1978.
70. Lokich JJ, Skarin AT, Mayer RJ, Frei E III: Lack of effectiveness of combined 5-fluorouracil and methyl-CCNU therapy in advanced colorectal cancer. *Cancer* 40:2792–2796, 1977.
71. Baker LH, Talley RW, Matter R, et al: Phase III comparison of the treatment of advanced gastrointestinal cancer with bolus weekly 5-FU versus methyl-CCNU and weekly 5-FU: A Southwest Oncology Group study. *Cancer* 38:1–7, 1976.
72. Joss RA, Goldberg RS, Yates JW: Combination chemotherapy of colorectal cancer with 5-fluorouracil, methyl-1,3-cis(2-chorethyl)-1-nitrosourea, and vincristine. *Med Pediatr Oncol* 7:251–255, 1979.
73. Moore M, Robert F, Cripps M, et al: A Phase II study of brequinar sodium (DUP 785, NSC 368390) in gastrointestinal (GI) cancers (CA). *Proc ASCO* 10:abstr 478, 1991.
74. Bruno S, Creaven PJ, Iedesma E, et al: Phase II study of 3-deazauridine in advanced colorectal adenocarcinoma. *Am J Clin Oncol* 5:69–71, 1982.
75. Rubin J, Shutt AJ, Pitot HC: A Phase II study of intravenous 6-thioguanine (NSC-752) in advanced colorectal carcinoma. *Am J Clin Oncol* 15:236–238, 1992.
76. Kemeny N, Israel K, Hehir M: Phase II trial of 10-Edam in patients with advanced colorectal carcinoma. *Am J Clin Oncol* 13:42–44, 1990.
77. Ajani J, Abbruzzese J, Blackburn R, et al: Phase II evaluation of trimetrexate (TMTX) in patients with advanced colorectal carcinoma (CRC). *Proc ASCO* 7:abstr 442, 1988.
78. Ben-Baruch N, Denicoff A, Goldspiel B, et al: Phase II trial of fazarabine (F) in colon cancer (CC) and breast cancer (BC). *Proc ASCO* 10:abstr 147, 1991.
79. Fink U, Molle B, Daschner H, et al: Phase II study of gemcitabine in metastatic colorectal cancer. *Proc ASCO* 11:abstr 507, 1992.
80. Asbury RF, Kramer A, Green M, et al: A phase II study of carboplatin and CHIP in patients with metastatic colon carcinoma. *Am J Clin Oncol* 12:416–419, 1989.
81. Schabel FM Jr, Trader WM, Laster WR, et al: Cis-dichlorodiammine-platinum (II): Combination chemotherapy and cross-resistance studies with tumors of mice. *Cancer Treat Rep* 63:1459–1473, 1979.
82. Shephard KV, Faintuch J, Bitran JD, et al: Treatment of metastatic colorectal carcinoma with cisplatin and 5-FU. *Cancer Treat Rep* 69:123–124, 1985.
83. Loehrer PJ Sr, Einhorn LH, Williams SD, et al: Cisplatin plus 5-FU for the treatment of adenocarcinoma of the colon. *Cancer Treat Rep* 69:1359–1363, 1985.
84. Cantrell JE Jr., Hart RD, Taylor RF, Harvey JH, Jr: Pilot trial of prolonged continuous-infusions 5-fluorouracil a weekly cisplatin and advanced colorectal cancer. *Cancer Treat Rep* 71:615–618, 1987.
85. Dy C, Gil A, Algarra SM, et al: combination chemotherapy of cisplatin and 5-FU in advanced colorectal carcinoma. *Cancer Treat Rep* 70:465–468, 1986.
86. Galligioni E, Canobbio L, Figoli F, et al: Cisplatin and 5-fluorouracil combination chemotherapy in advanced and/or metastatic colorectal carcinoma: A phase II study. *Eur J Cancer Oncol* 23:657–661, 1987.
87. Posner MR, Belliveau JF, Weitberg AB, et al: Continuous-infusion cisplatin and bolus 5-fluorouracil in colorectal carcinoma. *Cancer Treat Rev* 71:975–977, 1987.
88. Kemeny N, Niedzwiecki D, Reichman B, et al: Cisplatin and 5-fluorouracil infusion for metastatic colorectal carcinoma: Differences in survival in two patient groups with similar response rates. *Cancer* 63:1065–1069, 1989.
89. LoRusso P, Pazdur R, Redman BG, et al: Low-dose continuous infusion of 5-fluorouracil and cisplatin: Phase II evaluation in advanced colorectal carcinoma. *Am J Clin Oncol* 12:486–490, 1989.
90. O'Connell MJ, Moertel CG, Kvols LK, et al: Clinical trial of cisplatin and intensive course 5-fluorouracil for the treatment of advanced colorectal cancer. *Am J Clin Oncol* 9:192–195, 1986.
91. Mayer RJ: Chemotherapy for metastatic colorectal cancer. *Cancer* 70:1414–1424, 1992.
92. Rowinsky EK, Onetto N, Canetta RM, et al: Taxol: The first of the taxanes, an important new class of antitumor agents. *Semin Oncol* 19:646–662, 1992.
93. Michaelson R, Kemeny N, Young C: Phase II evaluation of 4′-epi-doxorubicin in patients with advanced colorectal carcinoma. *Cancer Treat Rep* 66:1757–1758, 1992.
94. Maroun JA, Cripps C, Verma S, et al: Phase II study of high dose epirubicin (E) in advanced colorectal carcinoma. *Proc ASCO* 8:abstr 435, 1989.
95. Skillings J, Maroun J, Natale R, et al: A phase II study of DUP 937 in GI cancers. *Proc ASCO* 11:abstr 540, 1992.
96. Melink TJ, Van Echo DA, Tait N, et al: Phase II trial of caracemide administered by 5-day continuous infusion in advanced colorectal carcinoma. *Proc ASCO* 7:abstr 438, 1988.
97. Kaye SB, Clavel M, Dodion P, et al: Phase II trials with flavone acetic acid (NCS 347512, LM 975) in patients with advanced carcinoma of the breast, colon, head and neck and melanoma. *Invest New Drug* 8:595–599, 1990.
98. Rossof AH, Rowland J, Khandekar J, et al: Phase II trial of didemnin B in previously untreated patients with measurable metastatic colorectal carcinoma: An Illinois Cancer Council Study. *Proc ASCO* 8:abstr 439, 1989.
99. Tchekmedyian NS, Kaplan RS, Elias EG, et al: Phase II study of n-methylformamide (NMF) in colorectal cancer. *Proc ASCO* 5:abstr 92, 1986.
100. Abeloff MD, Rosen ST, Luk GD, et al: Phase II trial of α-difluoromethylornithine, an inhibitor of polyanine synthesis, in advanced small cell lung cancer and colon cancer. *Cancer Treat Rep* 70:843–845, 1986.
101. Marsh JC, Ganpule SR, Durivage H: Phase II study of cyclosporin A as a second-line therapy in metastatic colorectal cancer. *Proc Am Assoc Cancer Res* 30:abstr 1023, 1989.
102. Osheroff N: Biochemical basis for the interactions of type I

and type II topoisomerases with DNA. *Pharmacol Ther* 41:223–241, 1989.

103. Sutcliffe JA, Gootz TD, Barrett JF: Biochemical characteristics and physiological significance of major DNA topoisomerases. *Antimicrob Agents Chemother* 33:2027–2033, 1989.

104. Schneider E, Hsiang YH, Liu L: DNA topoisomerases as anticancer drug targets. *Adv Pharmacol* 21:149–183, 1990.

105. Shimada Y, Yoshino N, Wakui A, et al: Phase II study of CPT-11, new camptothecin derivative, in patients with metastatic colorectal cancer. *Proc ASCO* 10:abstr 408, 1991.

106. Wall ME, Wani MC, Cook CE, et al: Plant antitumor agents: 1. The isolation and structure of camptothecin, a novel alkaloidal leukemia and tumor inhibitor from *Camptotheca acuminata*. *J Am Chem Soc* 83:3888–3890, 1966.

107. Gottlieb JA, Guarino AM, Call JB, et al: Preliminary pharmacologic and clinical evaluation of camptothecin sodium. *Cancer Chemother Rep* 54:461–479, 1970.

108. Muggia FM, Creaven PJ, Hansen HH, et al: Phase I clinical trial of weekly and daily oral treatment with camptothecin sodium. *Cancer Chemother Rep* 56:515–521, 1972.

109. Damishefsky S, Quick J, Horwitz SB: Synthesis and biological activity in the camptothecin series. *Tetrahedron Lett* 27:2525–2528, 1973.

110. Hsiang YH, Hertzberg R, Hecht S, Liu LF: Camptothecin induced protein-linked DNA breaks via mammalian DNA topoisomerase I. *J Biol Chem* 260:14873–14878, 1985.

111. Moyer JD, Smith PA, Levy EJ, et al: Kinetics of N-(phosphonacetyl)-L-aspartate and pyrazofurin depletion of pyrimidine ribonucleotide and deoxyribonucleotide pools and their relationship to nucleic acid synthesis in intact and permeabilized cells. *Cancer Res* 42:4525–4531, 1982.

112. Pizzorno G, Wiegand R, Lentz KS, Handschumacher RE: Brequinar potentiates 5-fluorouracil antitumor activity in a murine model colon 38 tumor by tissue-specific modulation of uridine nucleotide pools. *Cancer Res* 52:1660–1665, 1992.

113. Weber G, Ichikawa S, Nagai M, Natsumeda Y: Azidothymidine inhibition of thymidine kinase and synergistic cytotoxicity with methotrexate and 5-fluorouracil in rat hepatoma and human colon cancer cells. *Cancer Commun* 2:129–133, 1990.

114. Martin DS, Stolfi RL, Sawyer RC, et al: An overview of thymidine. *Cancer* 45:1117–1128, 1980.

115. Kufe DW, Egan EM: Enhancement of 5-fluorouracil incorporation into human lymphoblast ribonucleic acid. *Biochem Pharmacol* 30:129–133, 1981.

116. O'Dwyer PJ, Hughes GR, Colofiore J, et al: Phase I trial of fluorouracil modulation by N-phosphonacetyl-L-aspartate and 6-methylmercaptopurine riboside: Optimization of 6-methylmercaptopurine riboside dose and schedule through biochemical analysis of sequential tumor biopsy specimens. *J Natl Cancer Inst* 83:1235–1240, 1991.

117. Bennett LL Jr, Brockman RW, Schnebli HP, et al: Activity and mechanism of action of 6-methyltiopurine ribonucleoside in cancer cells resistant to 6-mercaptopurine. *Nature* 2-5:1276–1279, 1965.

118. Martin DS, Stolfi RL, Sawyer RC, et al: High-dose 5-fluorouracil with delayed uridine "rescue" in mice. *Cancer Res* 42:3964–3970, 1982.

119. Kemeny N, Conti J, Martin D, et al: Oral uridine (UR) protects from 5-fluorouracil (FU) toxicity in metastatic colorectal carcinoma: Phase I/II trial of phosphonacetyl-L-aspartic acid (PALA) + FU with UR as a rescue agent. *Proc Am Soc Clin Oncol* 11:171, 1992.

120. Boyd MR: Status of the NCI Preclinical Antitumor Drug Discovery and Development Program. *Principles Practice Oncol Update* 3:1–12, 1989.

121. Grever MR, Schepartz SA, Chabner BA: The National Cancer Institute: Cancer Drug Discovery and Development Program. *Semin Oncol* 19:622–638, 1992.

122. Giovanella BC, Stehlin JS, Wall ME, et al: DNA topoisomerase I-targeted chemotherapy of human colon cancer in xenografts. *Science* 246:1046–1048, 1989.

123. Marsham PR, Hughes LR, Jackman AL, et al: Quinazoline antifolate thymidylate synthetase inhibitors: Heterocyclic-benzoyl ring modifications. *J Med Chem* 34:1594–1605, 1991.

124. Jackman AL, Taylor GA, Gibson W, et al: ICI D1694, a quinazoline antifolate thymidylate synthetase inhibitor that is a potent inhibitor of L1210 tumor cell growth *in vitro* and *in vivo:* A new agent for clinical study. *Cancer Res* 51:5579–5586, 1991.

125. Sebolt JS, Scavone SV, Pinter CD, et al: Pyrazoloacridine, a new class of anticancer agents with selectivity against solid tumors *in vitro*. *Cancer Res* 47:4299–4303, 1987.

126. Jackson RC, Sebolt JS, Shillis JL, et al: The pyrazolacridines: Approaches to the development of a carcinoma-selective cytotoxic agent. *Cancer Invest* 8:39–47, 1990.

127. LoRusso P, Wozniak AJ, Polin L, et al: Antitumor efficacy of PD115934 against solid tumors of mice. *Cancer Res* 50:4900–4905, 1990.

128. Sebolt J, Havlick M, Hamelehle K, et al: Activity of the pyrazolacridines against multidrug-resistant tumor cells. *Cancer Chemother Pharmacol* 24:219–224, 1989.

129. Goldstein LJ, Galski H, Fojo A, et al: Expression of a multidrug resistance gene in human cancers. *J Natl Cancer Inst* 81:116–124, 1989.

130. O'Dwyer PJ, Paul AR, Walczak J, et al: Phase II study of biochemical modulation of fluorouracil by low dose PALA in patients with colorectal cancer. *J Clin Oncol* 8:1497–1503, 1990.

131. Wadler S, Wiernik PH: Clinical update on the role of fluorouracil and recombinant interferon alfa-2a in the treatment of colorectal carcinoma. *Sem Oncol* 17 (suppl 1):16–21, 1990.

132. Pazdur R, Ajani JA, Patt YZ, et al: Phase II study of fluorouracil and recombinant interferon alfa-2a in previously untreated advanced colorectal carcinoma. *J Clin Oncol* 8:2027–2031, 1990.

133. Wadler S, Lembersky B, Atkins M, et al: Phase II trial of fluorouracil and recombinant interferon alfa-2a in patients with advanced colorectal carcinoma: An Eastern Cooperative Oncology Group study. *J Clin Oncol* 9:1806–1810, 1991.

134. Huberman M, McClay E, Atkins M, et al: Phase II trial of 5-fluorouracil and recombinant interferon alpha-2a in advanced colorectal cancer. *Proc Am Soc Clin Oncol* 10:153, 1991.

CHAPTER 93

Randomized Trials with 5-Fluorouracil in the Treatment of Advanced Colorectal Cancer

Peter J. O'Dwyer
Carl J. Minnitti

The progress of treatment in colorectal cancer provides one of the most compelling examples of the importance of the randomized clinical trial in establishing the role of therapeutic interventions. 5-Fluorouracil (5-FU) was the first agent with established activity in this disease.[1] The trial that defined this activity was a randomized trial of two schedules of 5-FU administration published in 1972.[2] In this trial, 5-day infusion produced higher responses than a daily bolus schedule. A later study showed that higher response rates and improved survival were associated with an aggressive daily and alternate-day regimen, followed by weekly treatment.[3] This trial defined how 5-FU would be given for the next 20 years. During this period, numerous investigations of empirically derived combination regimens failed to show an improvement over conventional single-agent 5-FU. More recently, when studies have been designed with a basis in the mechanism of cytotoxicity of 5-FU, some improvement in response rates and survival has emerged. This has provided the stimulus for a number of trials directed to maximizing the activity of 5-FU in colorectal cancer through the modulation of its intracellular metabolism.

Randomized Clinical Trials

As the definition of benefit from a novel treatment evolves to encompass qualitative endpoints, the design of the clinical trials that support its worth is subject to increasing scrutiny. The randomized clinical trial has become the standard by which advances are proved. Support by the National Cancer Institute (NCI) for large-scale studies with sufficient power to provide definitive answers to therapeutic questions has culminated in the highly successful Intergroup mechanism, by which adequate accrual to address therapeutically important questions is assured.[4] These studies have established many of the principles that currently govern the management of colorectal cancer.

The design of the randomized clinical trial is simple, and the random assignment of patients clearly helps to ensure that a comparable patient population is accrued to each treatment arm. However, randomization alone will not compensate for the entry of inadequate number of patients to distinguish important differences between the arms. Further, unless the population is stratified for important prognostic factors, a simple randomization is likely by chance alone to yield arms that have imbalance in major determinants of outcome unrelated to therapy. The early trials of adjuvant therapy of colorectal cancer suffered from some of these problems. The Veteran's Administration Surgical Oncology Group (VASOG) studies that provided an initial indication of the benefit of adjuvant 5-FU included substantial numbers of patients (496 to 1346 patients per arm) but no prospective stratification for disease stage.[5] These studies may be contrasted with current trial designs [such as those of the Intergroup or of National Surgical Adjuvant Breast and Bowel Project (NSABP)] in which prognostic factors are carefully controlled for and large numbers of patients entered.

More subtle sources of bias must be sought in evaluating randomized trial design. How is the randomization conducted? The use of codes that may be broken by the treatment team must be avoided. However, in trials of cancer treatments, it is not usually feasible for a study to be double-blind, because of the differing toxicity of treatment. A recent study by Laufman and colleagues[6] was an exception: by using the appropriate placebo on each arm, intravenous and oral leucovorin were shown to be equivalent in combination with 5-FU. Bias may also be generated in the analysis of these trials. Unplanned analyses of the data have to be figured into power calculations, and if acted upon, may lead to erroneous conclusions and premature termination of the study. Well-defined strategies for interim analysis of trials have been widely used and should be specified at the outset.[7]

These potential sources of error, coupled with the wish to obtain data on subsets of the overall accrual, have led to a reevaluation of the design of the randomized clinical trial. Rigorous prospective description of the treatment groups, with stratification for the clinical and biological determinants of outcome, will yield results that are likely to stand the test of a confirmatory study and to guide the management of an individual patient with a particular mix of risk factors.

Efficacy of Chemotherapy for Advanced Colorectal Cancer

Randomized clinical trials have generated the most definitive results in colorectal cancer. This observation prompts the inevitable question: Has 5-FU-based chemotherapy been demonstrated to afford benefit to patients with advanced colorectal cancer? Clearly, responses have been documented, and patients may survive longer with one treatment than with another. The initial reports of an investigation of 5-FU and leucovorin showed a quality-of-life benefit for the best arm.[8] Symptomatic improvement, weight gain, and a better performance status were more frequently associated with the superior arm. However, none of these findings establish definitively the value of chemotherapy in advanced disease.

Practically, it is not likely that a chemotherapy treatment versus a supportive care control trial could be mounted in the 1990s. However, a design that might complement such a trial was recently reported by the Nordic Gastrointestinal Cancer Group[9] (Table 93-1). A total of 183 patients were randomized to receive a 5-FU-containing regimen at the time of diagnosis of metastatic colorectal cancer or to receive the same regimen at the time of presentation with symptoms after a period of observation. The patient groups were comparable for prognostic factors. The group that received early therapy had better survival and quality of life than the group with delayed therapy. This important randomized trial defines the appropriate therapeutic approach to metastatic colorectal cancer: treat at time of diagnosis.

It also answers some of the concerns surrounding the efficacy of chemotherapy. One may argue that since the patients who got early treatment (and who had better survival) had *more* chemotherapy than those who received delayed treatment, a deleterious effect of chemotherapy would have produced the opposite result. Therefore, if chemotherapy does not compromise survival, the randomized studies currently available support its routine use in this disease.

Endpoints of Trials in Advanced Colorectal Cancer

The major criteria for evaluating the efficacy of a treatment in advanced colorectal cancer are response, survival, and quality of life. Hitherto response and survival have been deemed most important. These criteria define benefit in diseases in which chemotherapy produces high rates of tumor shrinkage and the potential for cure exists. In small cell lung and ovarian cancers, a favorable impact on response rates was followed by improvement in survival. However, in chemotherapy-resistant solid tumors, this concordance does not always exist.

A recent study of five chemotherapy regimens in non–small cell lung cancer provides a striking example.[10] The regimen with the highest response rate was a combination of mitomycin, vinblastine, and cisplatin (20 percent); that with the lowest response rate was single-agent carboplatin (9 percent). Despite this, the analysis of survival showed that patients treated with carboplatin survived longer than those on arms with higher response rates. In colorectal cancer, a number of examples are available (as will be detailed) where response rates are superior on one arm without a difference in survival.

If response rates do not necessarily imply an advantage in survival, one might ask if there are other con-

Table 93-1
Randomized Trial of Treatment with Methotrexate, 5-Fluorouracil, and Leucovorin Administered at Initial Diagnosis versus Chemotherapy at Onset of Symptoms

Arm	n	*Median symptom-free survival, months*	*Median survival, months*
Treat at diagnosis	92	10	14
Treat when symptomatic	91	2	9

SOURCE: Nordic Gastrointestinal Tumor Adjuvant Chemotherapy Group. (*J Clin Oncol* 10:904–911, 1992. With permission.)

sequences of a response that would indicate that a patient has received benefit from treatment. Performance status changes and weight gain are useful but not very sensitive indicators of quality of life. The need for the application of validated quality-of-life assessment instruments to the major randomized trials is increasingly apparent. The instruments chosen should be simple, easy to administer, reproducible, and appropriate for both the disease state and the treatment. The responses should be quantifiable as continuous variables, and the analysis should provide information about specific areas of benefit or lack of benefit. Several such scales have been devised and have been found to be reproducible in pilot studies.[11-13] The major cooperative groups are including quality-of-life analyses at all levels of clinical investigation, and familiarity with their use and potential role will be desirable to fully interpret the results of future phase III trials.

SCHEDULING OF 5-FU

Thirty years after the introduction of 5-FU to clinical use, there remains controversy concerning its optimal schedule of administration. That controversy has increased in recent years thanks to technological developments permitting long-term infusion to be administered in the outpatient setting. Early reports by Sullivan et al.[14] suggested that, by decreasing the administration rate of 5-FU, a larger total dose could be given with equal toxicity. This observation generated interest in the concept of more frequent dose schedules, and randomized trials in the 1970s evaluated both the toxicity and efficacy of various regimens. An apparent advantage for frequent administration culminated in trials of long-term infusions in recent years.

Pharmacologic Considerations

The principal justification for protracted dose schedules is that by providing a longer exposure to drugs with a short half-life, one exposes more cancer cells during a critical phase of the cell cycle. However, the effects of schedule in preclinical models have not to our knowledge been examined in vivo. The NCI preclinical database contains no studies of 5-FU schedules, the development of which preceded the implementation of such detailed analyses. As a result, evidence for possible schedule dependency must be sought in the in vitro setting.

In vitro studies on colon carcinoma cell lines, using 5-FU at varying concentrations and lengths of treatment, support the schedule-dependency of 5-FU. Drewinko and Yang[15] demonstrated that extending the length of exposure markedly increased the degree of cell kill for all concentrations of 5-FU. Calabro-Jones and colleagues[16] demonstrated that prolonged exposure to 5-FU resulted in pronounced cytotoxicity at concentrations that are clinically achievable in plasma. These results form the basis for the many infusional schedules used today. It is of interest that recent work with another human colon carcinoma cell line (WiDr) confirms these observations and demonstrates further that the interaction of leucovorin and 5-FU is schedule-dependent.[17]

More recently, the issue of schedule has been addressed by Aschele and colleagues.[18] Resistant subclones of HCT-8 human colon adenocarcinoma were selected after repeated brief exposures or after continuous long-term exposures. Mechanisms of resistance differed markedly among the lines. Those selected after a "bolus" type of drug exposure had decreased incorporation of 5-FU into RNA. The clones produced after protracted drug exposure ("infusional") manifested an inability to accumulate polyglutamylated reduced folates, and they recovered thymidylate synthase activity more rapidly than the sensitive line. These data support the relevance of scheduling to mechanisms of cytotoxicity and, by extension, to mechanisms of resistance in human tumors.

Additional evidence for schedule-dependency comes from the toxicity analyses of human studies. Infusional schedules are associated with mucositis and neurotoxicity, while a higher incidence of myelosuppression occurs with intermittent bolus regimens. These data suggest that certain cell types are more sensitive to one particular mechanism than to another. The pharmacologic determinants of drug action in different cell types were addressed by Houghton et al.[19] In colonic mucosa, toxicity was proportional to the incorporation of 5-FU into RNA, while antitumor activity was better correlated with thymidylate synthase (TS) inhibition.

Mechanisms of Cytotoxicity

Two major mechanisms of cytotoxicity are associated with 5-FU administration, one directed to DNA and the other to RNA. 5-FU enters cells by simple diffusion, and is retained following ribophosphorylation, which is chiefly accomplished by orotidine phosphoribosyl transferase. A necessary cofactor in that reaction is phosphoribosyl pyrophosphate (PRPP), the intracellular supply of which is required for both pyrimidine and purine synthesis. Inhibition of the latter (as by methotrexate or MMPR) makes available PRPP, which in turn results in greater intracellular retention of 5-FU and greater conversion to its active nucleotide derivatives.[20]

Conversion of 5-fluorouridine 5′-monophosphate (5-FUMP) along the ribonucleotide pathway to 5-fluorouridine 5′-triphosphate (5-FUTP) results in the incorporation of fluorinated uracil nucleotides into all forms of RNA. The resulting inhibition of normal RNA processing has been associated with cytotoxicity.[21] In some models, the extent of RNA incorporation correlates with cytotoxicity in vitro and antitumor efficacy in vivo.[22] As noted above, others have found that while RNA incorporation in colonic mucosal cells is correlated with toxicity, this relationship is not clearly maintained in the tumor cell, in which a DNA-directed mechanism is a better predictor of activity.[19]

Inhibition of DNA synthesis by 5-FU results from its incorporation to deoxyribonucleotide derivatives. 5-Fluorodeoxyuridine monophosphate (5-FdUMP) is an inhibitor of TS. Binding to the enzyme is enhanced several-fold by the sequential binding of reduced folate (in the form of 5,10-methylenetetrahydrofolate) to form a stable ternary complex.[23] The extent of TS inhibition in cultured tumor cells and of cytotoxicity achieved is dependent upon the availability of reduced folate.[24,25] In cells in which the TS-directed mechanism obtains, cytotoxicity is reversed by exogenous thymidine. In the studies of Calabro-Jones et al.[16] alluded to above, exogenous thymidine had no effect on the cytotoxicity of any of the schedules. This finding is unusual, and its further investigation may indicate how schedule manipulation may alter the balance between RNA- and DNA-directed cytotoxicity mechanisms.

An additional result of anabolism along the deoxyribonucleotide pathway is the incorporation of 5-fluoro-2′-deoxyuridine 5′-triphosphate (5-FdUTP) into DNA. Studies by Herrick et al.[26] have associated this effect with cytotoxicity, which may result from the excision of fluorinated uracil residues by DNA-associated glycosylases, resulting in single strand breaks. It is hypothesized that fragmentation of DNA, the repair of which is limited by the unavailability of thymidine, is the ultimate mechanism of cytotoxicity following TS inhibition. Similarly, TS inhibition results in depression of 2′-deoxyuridine 5′-triphosphate (dUTP) formation; a several-fold expansion of dUTP pools results in its incorporation into DNA also.[27] Persistence of unrepaired DNA double strand breaks is associated with cell death.

Randomized Clinical Studies of Short-Term Infusional 5-FU Administration

The standard administration of 5-FU has relied on short-term infusions. Several clinical trials have been conducted to investigate the role of various regimens (Table 93-2). As early as 1972, Moertel et al.[28] performed a double-blind randomized study of 149 patients with cancer of the large bowel. A rapid bolus injection of 5-FU 13.5 mg/kg/day for 5 consecutive days was compared to a 5-day 2-h infusion of an equitoxic dose. There were no differences in response or

Table 93-2
Randomized Trials of Short-Term Infusional versus Bolus 5-Fluorouracil Administration

Author	*Primary site*	*Schedule*	*5-FU schedule*	N	*CR, %*	*PR, %*	*(CR + PR) RR, %*	*Median survival*	*Comments*
Moertel et al.[28]	Colon	CI	25 kg/day × 5 (2 h)	75	NS	NS	12	NS	Similar toxicity
		B	13.5/kg/day × 5	74	NS	NS	12	NS	Double-blind study
Seifert et al.[2]	Colon	CI	30/kg/day × 5	34	NS	NS	44	8 months	Average survival, 6 months in both groups; groups not equally matched
		B	12 kg/day × 5	36	NS	NS	22	2 months	
Ansfield et al.[3]	Colon	B	12 mg/kg/day × 5, then 6 mg/kg/day every other day × 11, then 15 mg/kg weekly	35	NS	NS	33	55 weeks	More intensive treatment associated with improved response ratio and survival
		B	15 mg × 4 weekly	35	NS	NS	13		Infusional schedule not tested in study
		B	500 mg total × 4, then weekly	36	NS	NS	14	40 weeks	
		PO	15 mg/kg/day × 6, then weekly	35	NS	NS	13	NS	
								NS	
Kish et al.[34]	Head/Neck	CI	1000/m²/day × 4 + cisplatin 100/m² D1	18	22	50	72	27 weeks	Myelosuppression B > CI
		B	600/m² days 12 and 8 + cisplatin 100/m² D1	20	10	10	20	20 weeks	Stomatitis CI > B (RR = $p < .001$)
Rougier et al.[29]	Colon	CI	750/m²/day × 7 q 3 weeks	78	—	—	19	10 months	*Dose intensity* CI = 1369 mg/m²/week
		B	500/m²/day × 5 q 4 weeks (30 min)	77	—	—	8	9 months	B = 558 mg/m²/week (RR = $p = .02$)

Abbreviations: NS, not stated; CI, continuous infusion over 24 h; B, bolus; PO, oral; RR, response rate; CR, complete response; PR, partial response. Doses are in milligrams. Days of treatment are consecutive unless otherwise stated.

toxicity between these infusion durations, indicating that toxicity and response are unrelated to peak drug levels.

A more extreme difference in schedules was investigated by Seifert and colleagues,[2] who compared a 5-day continuous infusion to daily bolus treatment. This trial demonstrated a higher response rate with the continuous infusion but no difference in overall survival. Differences in pretreatment characteristics between the groups may have contributed to the observed response rates. More leukopenia followed bolus administration, while mucositis predominated with the infusional schedule.

Ansfield et al.[3] compared four different regimens of 5-FU at varying dose intensities. This landmark prospective, randomized study included 198 patients with colonic cancer and 163 patients with breast cancer. The first regimen consisted of 5-FU at 12 mg/kg/day for 5 days as a bolus injection, then 6 mg/kg every other day for 11 doses, then 15 mg/kg (about 550 mg/m^2) weekly. The second arm was 15 mg/kg weekly as a bolus injection. The third arm was 500-mg total dose given for 4 consecutive days, then weekly. The last arm was 15 mg/kg/day orally for 6 days, then weekly. The response rates in colorectal cancer were 33, 13, 14, and 13 percent respectively. The median survival was 15 weeks longer with the first, more intensive schedule. There were no significant differences in response rates or survival in the patients with breast cancer. This important trial demonstrated that a more intensive treatment regimen results in higher response rates and prolonged survival in patients with colorectal cancer. However, since toxicity was not equal on each arm, the influence of schedule as distinct from dose intensity cannot be gauged.

Rougier et al.[29] recently reported a randomized study comparing a short-term 7-day continuous infusion of 5-FU every 3 weeks (dose intensity of 1369 mg/m^2/week) with a 5-day bolus regimen (30 min) every 4 weeks (dose intensity of 558 mg/m^2/week). The response rate was higher for the infusional arm (19 versus 8 percent) but again no difference was detected in survival. With the exception of more hand-foot syndrome and stomatitis in the infusion arm, the toxicities were similar.

Intermittent infusions have also been investigated on weekly and 2-weekly schedules. Ardalan et al.[30] performed a phase I trial of 5-FU with and without aspartate carbamyltransferase (PALA) on a weekly 24-h infusion schedule. A dose of 2600 mg/m^2/week was recommended for further study. The addition of PALA did not appear to influence the toxicity of 5-FU in this regimen. We have recently confirmed the maximum tolerated dose (MTD) of 5-FU in a phase II trial of this schedule,[31] and a phase III trial to determine the role of PALA as a modulator of 5-FU in this regimen is under way in the Eastern Cooperative Oncology Group.

Schilsky et al.[32] found a maximum tolerated dose of 6 g/m^2 when 5-FU was administered as a 24-h infusion every 2 weeks. Others are investigating a 72-h infusion repeated every 3 weeks in combination with modulators (PALA, leucovorin, dipyridamole).[33] Of these schedules, only the 24-h weekly regimen is being tested prospectively.

Finally, some information concerning schedule may be adduced from studies of 5-FU in combination. Kish et al.[34] demonstrated substantially higher response rates (72 versus 20 percent) in patients with head and neck cancer with a 4-day infusional schedule of 5-FU compared to bolus therapy when both groups were given with cisplatin. Median survival was not significantly different, despite a threefold higher dose intensity on the infusional arm. These differences are unlikely to reflect solely the schedule-dependency of 5-FU cytotoxicity in this disease. The superiority of response rates to infusion in this setting may reflect potentiation by or of cisplatin, a somewhat different issue, but one which needs consideration in the development of combination regimens.

Overall, these trials of commonly used regimens do not easily lend themselves to conclusions regarding the merits of short-term infusional schedules. The more striking relationship is that of response to planned dose intensity. Hryniuk et al.[35] have presented an analysis that supports the role of dose intensity in response to 5-FU in colorectal cancer. Given equal dose intensity, it seems unlikely that a 5-day infusion would be markedly superior to a 5-day bolus regimen of single-agent 5-FU.

Randomized Clinical Studies of Long-Term Infusional 5-FU Administration

The availability of technology permitting the protracted and safe administration of cytotoxic drugs stimulated activity in this area in the 1980s. Infusional schedules of 5-FU have ranged from several hours to several months, and several randomized studies have been conducted (Table 93-3). A 14-day infusional regimen was compared to bolus treatment by Weinerman et al.[36] in a trial involving 184 patients with metastatic colonic cancer. Patients were treated with 350 mg/m^2/day as a continuous infusion for 14 days or 450 mg/m^2/day for five bolus doses. No difference in response rate or survival was detected.

In 1981, Lokich et al.[37] reported the results of a phase I study in which a dose of 300 mg/m^2/day for 60 days was well tolerated, with mucositis as the predominant toxicity. This result spawned numerous phase II trials using the protracted infusion of 5-FU[38–48]; among over 300 patients with colorectal cancer, the average response rate was 36 percent.[49] It was also demon-

Table 93-3
Randomized Trials of Long-Term Infusional versus Bolus 5-Fluorouracil Administration

Author	*Primary site*	*Schedule*	*5-FU schedule*	N	*CR, %*	*PR, %*	*(CR+PR) RR, %*	*Median survival*	*Comments*
Lokich et al.[50]	Colon	CI	300/m²/day × 10 weeks	87	5	25	30	10.3 months	32% of B group crossed over to CI
		B	500/m²/day × 5 q 5 weeks	87	0	7	7	11 months	(*RR* = $p < .001$)
Weinerman et al.[36]	Colon	CI	350 m²/day × 14 day	92	1	11	12	9.5 months	
		B	450/m²/day × 5	92	1	5	6	9.5 months	(*RR* = $p = .34$)
Hansen et al.[51,52]	Colon	CI	300/m²/day (indefinite)	162	3	22	27	13 months	only CI plus cisplatin better than B in RR
		CI+P	300/m²/day (indefinite) + cisplatin 20/m²/week	162	4	28	32	13.3 months	($p = .02$) CI no better than B
		B	500/m²/day × 5, then 600/m² weekly	161	4	15	19	10.6 months	No survival differences

Abbreviations: NS, not stated; CI, continuous infusion over 24 h; B, bolus; PO, oral; RR, response rate; CR, complete response; PR, partial response. Doses are in milligrams. Days of treatment are consecutive unless otherwise stated.

strated that in a small number of patients who were refractory to bolus 5-FU, a secondary response could be achieved with the long-term infusional schedule.[44]

The Mid-Atlantic Oncology Program (MAOP) compared this protracted infusional regimen to bolus therapy in 174 patients with untreated metastatic colorectal cancer.[50] A higher response rate (7 versus 30 percent) favored the infusional group, but the median survival was no different. A confounding issue in that study is that 32 percent of the bolus group crossed over to receive infusional therapy, and this may have affected the survival data. Leukopenia was more frequent with the bolus treatment, while the hand-foot syndrome (plantar-palmar erythrodysesthesia) developed in 24 percent of the infusional group.

Hansen et al.[51,52] have reported the preliminary results of a large Eastern Cooperative Oncology Group (ECOG) study involving 479 patients with colorectal cancer. Bolus 5-FU was compared to long-term infusional therapy with or without the addition of cisplatin. Both of the infusional arms produced higher response rates than the bolus arm, but only the one containing cisplatin reached statistical significance. The addition of cisplatin did not significantly improve response rates compared to 5-FU infusion alone. There was no significant survival difference among the three groups.[52]

An initial presentation of an ongoing Southwest Oncology Group randomized phase II trial is consistent with these findings: response rates to protracted infusion are among the highest of the seven experimental arms, but survival is not significantly different from the more standard regimens.

In summary, eight randomized trials have compared various infusional regimens of 5-FU to more standard bolus regimens. Of those with published results, four have shown a statistically significant improvement in response rates, but no substantial impact on survival has been demonstrated in any of these trials. The effect of greater tumor cell kill seems to be insufficient in patients with advanced disease to suppress the emergence and overgrowth of resistant disease that ultimately determines survival. Beyond a palliative role, however, the benefits of a greater cell kill from infusional therapy may have therapeutic relevance where fewer tumor cells are present. Further investigation of these infusional regimens by well-designed clinical trials in the adjuvant setting are warranted to test the hypothesis that responses to therapy in advanced disease promise clinical benefit. Such trials are under way in cooperative groups.

Schedule-dependence alone may not, however, account for differences in response rates with these regimens. Table 93-4 presents an analysis of the dose intensity achieved by various 5-FU regimens. The infusional schedules result in the highest dose intensities among the commonly used regimens. Hryniuk et al.[35] reported that dose intensity has a substantial influence on response rate in colorectal cancer. But can one legitimately compare the dose intensity of different schedules of a schedule-dependent drug? The in vitro data of Calabro-Jones et al.[16] indicate that exposures longer than 24 h require a higher area under the curve (AUC) to affect cytotoxicity. The principal message appears to be that extrapolation from imperfect models will not substitute for direct clinical testing.

Table 93-4
Dose Intensity of 5-Fluouracil on Various Schedules of Administration

Schedule	*Tolerable phase II dose, mg/m²*	*Dose intensity, g/m²/week*
Weekly IV bolus	600	0.6
5-Day bolus	450	0.56
5-Day infusion	1000	1.25
Continuous daily infusion	300	2.1
Weekly 24-h infusion	2600	2.6

EMPIRICAL COMBINATIONS WITH 5-FU

The success of empirical regimens of combination chemotherapy in "responsive" solid tumors led to attempts in the 1970s to derive empirical combinations with greater efficacy than that of 5-FU alone. It was hoped that the meager response rates associated with the use of other single agents might translate into superior activity in combination with 5-FU. This position was justified in part by the demonstration in murine models of synergistic interaction between 5-FU and alkylating agents, vinca alkaloids, and other drugs. A series of randomized trials was conducted by all of the active cooperative groups over a 10- to 15-year time frame.[54–66] No regimen emerged with activity any greater than that of the control arm. While many of the trials had numbers that would currently be viewed as equivalent to a randomized phase II study, none showed sufficient promise to warrant further testing in advanced disease. Interestingly, the vestiges of regimens that achieved popularity in this era remain in some current adjuvant regimens. The combination of methyl CCNU, vincristine, and 5-FU was tested in the initial study of adjuvant treatment for colonic cancer by the NSABP: subsequent studies have eliminated the nitrosourea because of its leukemogenic potential.

Clearly, empirical combinations cannot translate to the clinic the beneficial interactions between 5-FU and other agents observed in preclinical models. This experience is pertinent to the current state of development of new and promising agents in colorectal cancer. The negative results from previous empirical efforts suggest that future combination regimens be designed with a clear understanding of the pharmacologic interaction between the individual components.

BIOCHEMICAL MODULATION OF 5-FU

Principles of Biochemical Modulation

Appreciation of the cellular pharmacology of drug action has resulted in strategies to manipulate the pathways of activation and detoxication, particularly of antimetabolites. These efforts have been especially rewarding in the modulation of 5-FU and have resulted in improved treatment of colorectal cancer and possibly of other tumors. The success of the initial trials of 5-FU modulated by leucovorin has prompted the evaluation of additional modulation regimens aimed at the further potentiation of its activity.

Biochemical modulation may be defined as the use of one or more agents, which may themselves be devoid of anticancer activity, to influence the activity or the toxicity of an active antitumor drug.[67] By this definition, biochemical modulation clearly differs from combination chemotherapy, in which, as described by DeVita,[68] each of the drugs should have antitumor activity and should be used at maximum tolerated doses. A different approach to dose is required in biochemical modulation regimens. In this context, the dose of the modulator should be sufficient to maximize the desired biochemical effect but not more, since toxicity from the modulator may itself limit the dose of the active antitumor drug (the "effector agent").[67] In some cases, overlapping toxicity between the modulating and effector agents may require a compromise in the dose of each. Hence it is important to approach the development of these regimens through careful biochemical analysis. Establishing the dose of the modulator that results in the desired biochemical endpoint is a requirement of the design of an optimal regimen that will maximize the cytotoxicity of the effector agents. Failure to recognize this principle has resulted in the clinical testing of several unsuccessful regimens in the past.

Modulation of the Interaction of FdUMP with TS

The elucidation of the mechanism of inhibition of TS stimulated attempts to potentiate 5-FU activity by maximizing the intracellular reduced folate concentrations. The source of reduced folate for these studies is 5-formyl-tetrahydrofolate, leucovorin (LV). The sequence of developmental studies that culminated in randomized trials of 5-FU and LV is detailed extensively by Schilsky and Arbuck in this volume and will not be reiterated here. The initial clinical trials of 5-FU in combination with LV by Machover et al.[69] and Madajewicz et al.[70] resulted in partial responses in approximately 40 percent of previously untreated patients. These results stimulated a series of randomized clinical trials in which three schedules of 5-FU and LV in combination were tested: a weekly regimen, a daily x5 bolus regimen, and a daily x5 infusional regimen (Table 93-5). Inspection of the studies reveals that the majority of the trials showed a greater percentage of responding patients following treatment with 5-FU/LV than with 5-FU alone. Since most of the trials were

Table 93-5
Randomized Trials of 5-Fluorouracil/Leucovorin versus 5-Fluorouracil

Study	*Design*	N	*Response rate (5-FU versus 5-FU/LV), percent*	*Survival advantage*
GITSG[71]	5-FU_{500}/day × 5 vs 5-FU_{600}/LV_{500} vs 5-FU_{600}/LV_{25} weekly	382	12 vs 19 vs 28	No
NCOG[72]	5-FU weekly vs 5-FU_{400}/LV_{200} daily × 5	162	18 vs 16	No
GOIRC[73]	5-FU/day × 5 vs 5-FU_{400}/LV_{200} daily × 5	181	18 vs 16	No
GISCAD[74]	5-FU/day × 5 vs 5-FU_{400}/LV_{200} daily × 5	182	10 vs 21	No
GeNOVA[75]	5-FU weekly vs 5-FU_{600}/LV_{500} weekly	148	8 vs 23	No
PMH[76]	5-FU/day × 5 vs 5-FU_{370}/LV_{200} daily × 5	130	15 vs 30	Yes
City of Hope[77]	5-FU/day × 5 vs 5-FU_{370}/LV_{500} daily × 5	79	5 vs 45	No
Roswell Park[78]	5-FU/day × 11 vs 5-FU_{600}/LV_{500} weekly	53	11 vs 48	No
Bologna[79]	5-FU weekly vs 5-FU_{600}/LV_{200} weekly	64	3 vs 26	No
NCCTG[9,80]	5-FU/day × 5 vs 5-FU_{425}/LV_{20} versus 5-FU_{370}/LV_{200} daily × 5	212	10 vs 43 vs 26	Yes

SOURCE: Adapted in part from Ref. 81.

restricted to patients with measurable disease, this endpoint seems quite solid and has been confirmed in a recent metaanalysis.[81] The analysis of survival in this metaanalysis, however, suggests that, overall, no significant survival benefit exists for this strategy.

This conclusion may, however, illustrate one of the pitfalls of metaanalysis. Only two studies show a better survival for the 5-FU/LV treatment. Both administer the regimen on a 5-day schedule; if scheduling is indeed important, as discussed above, the more frequent administration regimen may optimize results. Further, the lower dose of LV (20 mg/m^2) used in the superior arm of the North-Central Cancer Treatment Group (NCCTG) trial may indeed impact on selectivity.[79] This was the only 5-day study with a low-dose LV arm.

Most of the randomized trials, in order to facilitate the assessment of both response and survival, required patients to have measurable disease. The positive trials were not so restricted, and some 42 percent of the patients in the NCCTG study had nonmeasurable disease. In addition to higher response rates in the measurable patients, a substantial survival advantage was observed in patients with both measurable and nonmeasurable disease.[80] An implication of this result is that optimal sensitization by LV may occur in patients with a small burden of tumor cells. The active investigation of this hypothesis is under way by virtue of the incorporation of 5-FU/LV regimens in adjuvant trials.

As a consequence of these results, 5-FU/LV has become the standard treatment for advanced colorectal cancer. Based on the NCCTG trial, the preferred schedule is that in which 5-FU (425 mg/m^2) is administered with low-dose (20 mg/m^2) LV on a regimen of 5 daily doses repeated every 4 or 5 weeks. Despite the increment in response rate afforded by the addition of LV to 5-FU, complete remissions in colorectal cancer are unusual; further clinical and preclinical work is needed to optimize the use of 5-FU in this disease. In the paragraphs that follow, we will examine alternative approaches to modulating 5-FU that have been or will soon be incorporated into randomized clinical trials.

Additional Targets for Modulation of 5-FU

Inhibition of Pyrimidine Synthesis

Biochemical Rationale. Natural uridine nucleosides and nucleotides compete for both the anabolic pathways of 5-FU metabolism and for binding of FdUMP to TS. Several inhibitors of pyrimidine synthesis have been shown to deplete uridine nucleotide pools and have been evaluated as anticancer drugs in clinical trials. None has emerged as a useful cytotoxic drug in its own right, but several have potential for use in combination with 5-FU. Inhibitors of orotidylate decarboxylase (pyrazofurin), aspartate carbamyltransferase (PALA), and orotate dehydrogenase (brequinar) have been shown to deplete cells of pyrimidine nucleotide pools to about 20 percent of control, a level which presumably results from the unimpeded action of salvage enzymes.[82–83] Each has been shown in vitro to potentiate the cytotoxicity of 5-FU, by only PALA has received extensive testing in vivo and in clinical trials.

Collins and Stark[84] synthesized PALA as an analog of the transition-state intermediate of the aspartate carbamyltransferase reaction. PALA is a potent inhibitor of aspartate transcarbamylase, with a Ki of 1.1×10^{-8} *M* for the enzyme derived from human spleen cells.[85] Inhibition of aspartate carbamyltranferase blocks de novo pyrimidine synthesis and is lethal to mammalian cells in culture.[86,87] PALA treatment markedly depletes pyrimidine nucleotide pools in vivo, in tumors and normal tissue, in a dose-dependent manner.[86,88,89] Studies in murine tumors in vivo showed that depletion of pyrimidine pools at low PALA doses correlated with sensitivity; resistant tumors required higher doses to achieve equivalent effects.[90]

Nucleotide pool changes in tumor cells in vivo were both dose and time-dependent. In sensitive tumors, low doses of PALA were as effective as higher doses in depleting uridine 5′-triphosphate (UTP) pools.[91] Martin et al.[91] showed that a dose of PALA, which would deplete UTP pools to 60 percent of control in tumor, enhanced the incorporation of 5-FU into tumor RNA but not into that of normal epithelium or bone marrow. The preclinical studies support the concept that PALA's depletion of uracil nucleotide pools reaches a plateau with increasing PALA dose, and that further increasing this dose provides no advantage in either antitumor efficacy or cell activity.

Clinical Trials with PALA. As noted above, the optimization of doses in a biochemical modulation regimen may be required to avoid reducing the dose of the active anticancer drug. Early studies of PALA and 5-FU showed that the use of maximally tolerated doses of PALA did not permit the administration of full doses of 5-FU because of severe mucositis.[92] These studies have been reviewed extensively.[93] Since PALA has no antitumor efficacy in colorectal cancer, the effect of reducing the 5-FU dose was to eliminate any response advantage for the combination. Casper and colleagues[94] conducted a phase I reevaluation of PALA with biochemical endpoints and showed that the biochemical effects of a dose of 250 mg/m^2 were indistinguishable from those of a dose of 2 g/m^2.[94] On the assumption that the effects in the whole body reflect those in the tumor, the dose of 250 mg/m^2 was recommended for further study of PALA as a modulator. In phase I reevaluations of PALA and 5-FU, the addition of PALA did not require reduction of the 5-FU dose.[94,95] In a group of patients with a variety of gastrointestinal malignancies, a high response rate was observed.[95] A full phase II trial in colorectal cancer was performed at Fox Chase Cancer Center: 16 of 37 (43 percent) patients responded and median survival was 17 months.[96]

Two multiarm randomized studies are currently under way to isolate the role of PALA in this regimen. Patients with previously untreated colorectal cancer are randomized to receive either 5-FU alone or 5-FU in combination with PALA. In both trials patients with measurable and nonmeasurable disease are being enrolled; the major endpoint of interest in survival. These trials will determine if this mechanism of modulation has therapeutic utility.

Modulation of Purine Metabolism

Biochemical Rationale. The ribophosphorylation of 5-FU (and thus its intracellular retention) depends on the availability of phosphoribosyl pyrophosphate (PRPP).[97] About two-thirds of available intracellular PRPP is used for purine synthesis. Inhibition of purine synthesis thus makes available PRPP, the levels of which can serve as a marker for the biochemical efficacy of this intervention. Treatment of cells in culture with inhibitors of purine synthesis is associated with a three- to sevenfold expansion of PRPP pools.[98] Two such inhibitors are currently being evaluated in combination with 5-FU. The antifolate methotrexate is polyglutamylated to a species that results in the inhibition of glycinamide ribotide (GAR) transformylase, either directly or through an accumulation of oxidized folate as a consequence of dihydrofolate reductase (DHFR) inhibition.[99] The synergistic action of methotrexate and 5-FU has been shown to depend on (1) the order of their administration, methotrexate preceding 5-FU; (2) the interval between them (18 to 24 h); and (3) the dose of MTX (not well established, but probably about 100 mg/m^2).[67]

Another inhibitor of purine synthesis is 6-methylmercaptopurine riboside (MMPR), which does not interact with folate pools. MMPR is phosphorylated intracellularly by adenosine kinase; the monophosphate inhibits phosphoribosyl aminotransferase, an early step in purine synthesis.[100] Both in vitro and in vivo studies demonstrate that MMPR may increase phosphoribosyl PRPP levels as much as 15-fold, which leads to increased phosphorylation and intracellular retention of 5-FU.[101] This effect, in turn, enhances 5-FU incorporation into RNA more than fivefold.[98] Kufe and Egan[98] and others showed that MMPR potentiated the cytotoxic effects of 5-FU in vitro and in vivo. Martin et al.[102] have shown that the addition of methotrexate (MTX) or MMPR to a PALA/5-FU regimen leads to enhanced therapeutic effect in the CD8F1 autochthonous breast model.

Clinical Trials. Clinical studies with the combination of methotrexate and 5-FU have yielded mixed results. An extensive listing of studies up to 1986 suggested that longer intervals between methotrexate and 5-FU yielded higher response rates in various diseases.[67] A recent randomized study by Marsh et al.[103] showed superior response rates with a 24-h versus a 1-h interval between methotrexate and 5-FU in colorectal cancer: the response rate with the superior regimen was equivalent to that of 5-FU/LV or PALA/5-FU.

Clinical studies of MMPR in combination with 5-FU have been performed on both weekly and 5-daily-dose schedules. However the optimal dose and timing of

MMPR administration in human studies had not been defined.[104,105] In a recent phase I trial, three dose levels of MMPR—75, 150, and 225 mg/m^2—were tested.[106] Biochemical effects were most pronounced at the two highest doses, at which over half of the patients showed a twofold or greater increase in tumor PRPP content. However, despite a low dose (1300 mg/m^2) of 5-FU, unacceptable mucositis was observed at the highest dose. This toxicity precluded further MMPR dose escalation; therefore, the 150 mg/m^2 dose level was selected for further development. Continued escalation of 5-FU was undertaken to identify a regimen for phase II testing. The maximum tolerated dose of 5-FU was 2300 mg/m^2. Phase II studies are under way with this regimen in colorectal cancer.

Thus it has been shown that inhibition of purine synthesis results in favorable biochemical changes in tumor tissue. The clinical results with MTX/5-FU suggest that potentiation of 5-FU by disruption of purine metabolism may be achieved. These studies establish a rational regimen for further testing of this approach to 5-FU modulation. Further, the lack of an effect of MMPR on folate metabolism will permit the addition of LV to the regimen without the risk of reversing the antipurine effect, as is the case with MTX. In a recent randomized clinical trial in colorectal cancer, the addition of MTX did not increase the activity of 5-FU/LV.[107]

Modulation by Interferons

The interferons have no activity in the treatment of either colonic cancer cells in vitro or colonic tumors in patients. However, Elias and Crissman[108] demonstrated a dose-related enhancement by alpha interferon of the cytotoxicity of 5-FU in vitro to a colonic cancer cell line.[108] They and others subsequently demonstrated that alpha interferon promoted enhanced formation of FdUMP, which was shown to result from an increase in the activity of the anabolizing enzyme pyrimidine nucleoside phosphorylase.[109]

Chu and colleagues[110] proposed an additional mechanism of interferon action. Treatment with 5-FU appears to result in an increase in the cellular content of TS protein in vitro and in vivo. This effect appears to be at the level of translation and may be a direct consequence of enzyme inhibition. The increase in thymidylate synthase activity induced by 5-FU is abolished by interferon (in this case, gamma interferon), and cells remain sensitive to subsequent doses of treatment.

Wadler and Wiernik[111] performed a pilot clinical study of a combination of 5-FU and interferon in patients with advanced colorectal cancer; 63 percent of the patients responded. This high response rate was confirmed in cooperative group studies (26 to 42 percent), and the regimen is currently undergoing testing in three large-scale randomized studies. Preliminary results of these studies have been presented.[112,113]

Other trials are addressing issues such as the optimal dose of interferon, while Grem and colleagues[114] have devised a combination of 5-FU, interferon, and LV that appears to have substantial activity in some gastrointestinal tumors. As an additional approach to the modulation TS, the use of interferon deserves further study.

Resistance Mechanisms and Clinical Results

The higher response rates achieved with regimens involving biochemical modulation of 5-FU suggests that greater tumor cell kill is obtained without added toxicity. This implies that the modulatory strategies are successful in overcoming one or more mechanisms of drug resistance. Such an inference must be made cautiously, however: comparisons with historical data are notoriously misleading, and many of the randomized studies had more toxicity on the modulation arm. This leaves open the possibility that intensifying the dose of single-agent 5-FU to yield equivalent toxicity might produce higher response rates. Such a conclusion is supported by the preclinical data of Martin et al.[91] and the clinical analyses of Hryniuk et al.[35] The most convincing evidence to support an effective modulation comes from the NCCTG study of 5-FU versus 5-FU/LV.[8] In each arm the dose of 5-FU was varied in an attempt to produce equivalent toxicity. A clear advantage in response rate and in survival was still observed. Thus the role of modulation LV seems established.

Unfortunately the precise mechanism of resistance overcome by this strategy has not been elucidated. Berger et al.[115] have described TS mutants resistant to 5-FU: the addition of LV in vitro markedly potentiates the cytotoxicity of 5-FU to such lines. The mutant enzyme has lower affinity for FdUMP and more rapid dissociation of the ternary complex.[116] A determination of the relationship between response to 5-FU/LV and presence of a TS mutation would be of interest. Similarly, amplification of the gene encoding TS is described as a resistance mechanism, but the relationship to clinical response is unknown.[117] An analysis of TS-related resistance mechanisms is needed in association with clinical trials, and the tools for such studies are available.

An inherent difficulty of correlative studies is the multiplicity of additional mechanisms that may lead to variability in the metabolism of 5-FU or of its necessary cofactors (namely, the activity of folylpolyglutamate synthetase, discussed above). The interpretation of clinical trials is further complicated by variability in the pharmacokinetics of 5-FU and of modulating agents and heterogeneity among the populations of cells in a given tumor. Nonetheless, the identification

Table 93-6
Current Phase III Trials of Therapies for Advanced Colorectal Cancer

Institution	*Protocol*	*Study Design*
SAKK	EU-92012 SAKK-4190	5-FU_{400} days 1–5 bolus vs 5-FU_{400} days 1–5 bolus LV_{20} days 1–5 bolus
MRC (UK)	MRC-CR04 EU-91020	5-FU_{1200} days 1,2; LV_{200} days 1,2 vs 5-FU_{1200} days 1,2; LV_{200} days 1,2; IFN-α 6 million U qod
Hoosier Oncology Group	HOG-GI89-1	5-FU_{450} days 1–5 bolus, then 5-FU 15 mg/kg weekly 5-FU_{450} days 1–5 bolus, then 15 mg/kg weekly; LV_{150} days 1–3
Intergroup CLB-9092	EST-2290	5-FU_{2600} 24-h infusion weekly vs $PALA_{25}0$; 5-FU $_{2600}$ 24-h infusion weekly vs 5-FU $_{600}$ bolus weekly; LV_{500} oral vs 5-FU_{600} bolus weekly; LV_{500} IV vs 5-FU_{750} days 1–5 infusion, then 5-FU_{250} weekly; IFN-α 9 million U thrice weekly
North Central	NCCTG-894652 MAYO-894652	5-FU_{370} days 1–5 bolus; 1-LV_{100} days 1–5 vs 5-FU_{370} days 1–5 bolus; days 1–LV_{500} oral days 1–5 vs 5-FU_{350} days 1–5 bolus; days 1–LV_{200} IV days 1–5
CRC (UK)	CRC-88003	5-FUdR 0.2 mg/kg/days × 14 vs symptomatic treament only
EORTC	EORTC-40909	5-FU 60 mg/kg by 48 h infusion hr × 4 then q2h; 1 h TX_{40} before each 5-FU vs 5-FU 60 mg/kg by 48 h infusion h × 4, then q2h MTX $_{40}$ before each 5-FU; $PALA_{250}$ 24 h before each 5-FU
MAOP	MAOP 5288	5-FU_{300} infusion/day × 70 vs $PALA_{250}$ weekly; 5-FU_{100} infusion/day × 70

of phenotypic or genotypic markers of resistance to fluoropyrimidines would assist in the identification of subsets of patients with a high or low likelihood of response and for whom alternative approaches must be designed.

In conclusion, there appears to have been a therapeutic advance through the use of biochemical modulation strategies in treating advanced colorectal cancer. The superiority of modulated regimens will, it is hoped, be established in the adjuvant setting, where they may contribute to the cure of this disease. Continued development of antipyrimidine and antipurine strategies should be undertaken, along with well-designed clinical studies. These approaches, coupled with exciting results in the development of new drugs, promise to improve the treatment of this resistant disease.

ONGOING RANDOMIZED STUDIES IN COLORECTAL CANCER

The perceived failure of an empirical approach to have an impact on advanced colorectal has led to a focus on the part of the major cooperative groups in the United States and in Europe upon biochemical modulation strategies (Table 93-6). The aggregate of these studies will help to indicate which modulatory strategies have promise and may be developed further and which may be abandoned. A focus on the optimal means of delivery of 5-FU is particularly pertinent at this time, when it may be anticipated that novel options for the treatment of advanced colorectal cancer will be available in the near future.

In conclusion, it may be suggested that the relatively large number of therapeutic trials in colorectal cancer have culminated in small gains in the setting of advanced disease. These gains have been defined through well-designed randomized clinical trials. In turn, the regimens emerging from such trials appear to afford even greater and perhaps curative benefit to patients in the adjuvant setting. Optimization of 5-FU administration seems unlikely to alter the ultimate fate of the patient with advanced disease. However, lessons learned in that environment may produce dramatic effects in early-stage disease.

REFERENCES

1. Heidelberger C: Fluorinated pyrimidines and their nucleosides; in Sartorelli AC, Johns DG (eds): *Handbook of Ex-*

perimental Pharmacology: Antineoplastic and Immunosuppressive Agents, vol 38, part 2. Berlin; Springer-Verlag, 1975, pp 193–231.

2. Seifert P, Baker LH, Reed M, et al: Comparison of continuously infused 5-fluorouracil with bolus treatment of patients with colorectal adenocarcinoma. *Cancer* 36:123–128, 1975.
3. Ansfield F, Klotz J, Nealon T: A phase III study comparing the clinical utility of four regimens of 5-fluorouracil. *Cancer* 39:34–40, 1977.
4. Wittes RE, Friedman MA, Simon R: Some thoughts on the future of clinical trials in cancer. *Cancer Treat Rep* 70:241–250, 1986.
5. Friedman MA, Hamilton JM: Progress in the adjuvant therapy of large bowel cancer, in DeVita VT, Hellman S, Rosenberg SA (eds): *Cancer: Principles and Practice of Oncology.* Philadelphia, Lippincott, 1993. pp 273–296.
6. Laufman LR, Bukowski RM, Collier MA, et al: A randomized, double-blind trial of fluorouracil plus placebo vs fluorouracil plus oral leucovorin in patients with metastatic colorectal cancer. *J Clin Oncol,* 1993 (in press).
7. O'Brien PC, Fleming TR: A multiple testing procedure for clinical trials. *Biometrics* 45:905–923, 1979.
8. Poon MA, O'Connell MJ, Moertel CG, et al: Biochemical modulation of fluorouracil: Evidence of significant improvement of survival and quality of life in patients with advanced colorectal carcinoma. *J Clin Oncol* 7:1407–1418, 1989.
9. Nordic Gastrointestinal Tumor Adjuvant Therapy Group: Expectancy or primary chemotherapy in patients with advanced asymptomatic colorectal cancer. A randomized trial. *J Clin Oncol* 10:904–911, 1992.
10. Bonomi PD, Finkelstein DM, Ruckdeschel JC, et al: Combination chemotherapy vs single agents followed by combination chemotherapy in stage IV non-small cell lung cancer: A study of the Eastern Cooperative Oncology Group. *J Clin Oncol* 7:1602–1613, 1989.
11. Finkelstein DM, Cassileth BR, Bonomi PD, et al: A pilot study of the functional living index-cancer (FLIC) scale for the assessment of quality of life for metastatic lung cancer patients. *Am J Clin Oncol* 11:630–633, 1988.
12. Nayfield SG, Hailey PJ: Quality of life assessment in cancer clinical trials. Bethesda, Maryland, U.S. Department of Health and Human Services, 1990.
13. Cella DF, Tulsky DS: Measuring quality of life today: methodologic aspects. *Oncology* 4:29–38, 1990.
14. Sullivan RD, Young CW, Miller E, et al: The clinical effects of continuous administration of fluorinated pyrimidines (5-fluorouracil and 5-fluoro-2'-deoxyuridine). *Cancer Chemother Rep* 8:77–83, 1960.
15. Drewinko B, Yang LY: Cellular basis for the inefficacy of 5-FU in human colon carcinoma. *Cancer Treat Rep* 69:1391–1398, 1985.
16. Calabro-Jones PM, Byfield JE, Ward JF, Sharp TR: Time-dose relationships for 5-fluorouracil cytotoxicity against human epithelial cancer cells *in vitro. Cancer Res* 42:4413–4420, 1982.
17. Moran RG, Scanlon KL: Schedule-dependent enhancement of the cytotoxicity of fluoropyrimidines to human carcinoma cells in the presence of folinic acid. *Cancer Res* 51:4618–4623, 1991.
18. Aschele C, Sobrero A, Faderan MA, Bertino JR: Novel mechanism(s) of resistance to 5-fluorouracil in human colon cancer (HCT 8) sublines following exposure to two different clinically relevant dose schedules. *Cancer Res* 52:1855–1864, 1992.
19. Houghton JA, Houghton PJ, Wooten RS: Mechanism of induction of the gastrointestinal toxicity in the mouse by 5-fluorouracil, 5-fluorouridine and 5-fluoro-2'-deoxyuridine. *Cancer Res* 39:2406–2413, 1979.
20. Kufe DW, Egan EM: Enhancement of 5-fluorouracil incorporation into human lymphoblast ribonucleic acid. *Biochem Pharmacol* 30:129–133, 1981.
21. Maybaum J, Ullmann B, Mandel HG, et al: Regulation of DNA- and RNA-directed actions of 5-fluoropyrimidines in mouse T-lymphoma (S-24) cells. *Cancer Res* 40:4209–4215, 1980.
22. Kufe D, Major P: 5-fluorouracil incorporation into human breast carcinoma RNA correlates with cytotoxicity. *J Biol Chem* 256:9802–9805, 1981.
23. Santi DV, McHenry CS: 5-fluoro-2'-deoxyuridylate: Covalent complex with thymidylate synthetase. *Proc Natl Acad Sci USA* 69:1855–1857, 1972.
24. Evans RM, Laskin JD, Hakala MT: Effect of excess folates and deoxyinosine on the activity and site of action of 5-fluorouracil. *Cancer Res* 41:3288–3295, 1981.
25. Berger SH, Hakala MT: Relationship of dUMP and free FdUMP pools to inhibition of thymidylate synthase by 5-fluorouracil. *Mol Pharmacol* 25:303–309, 1984.
26. Herrick DJ, Major PP, Kufe DW: Effect of methotrexate on incorporation and excision of 5-fluorouracil residues in human breast carcinoma DNA. *Cancer Res* 42:5015–5017, 1982.
27. Ingraham HA, Dickey L, Goulian M: DNA fragmentation and cytotoxicity from increased cellular deoxyuridylate. *Biochemistry* 25:3225–3230, 1986.
28. Moertel CG, Schutt AJ, Reitemeier RJ, et al: A comparison of 5-fluorouracil administered by slow infusion and rapid injection. *Cancer Res* 32:2717–2719, 1972.
29. Rougier Ph, Paillot B, Laplanche A, et al: End results of a multicentric randomized trial comparing 5-FU in continuous systemic infusion to bolus administration in measurable metastatic colorectal cancer. *Proc ASCO* 11:163, 1992.
30. Ardalan B, Singh G, Silberman H: A randomized phase I and II study of short-term infusion of high-dose fluorouracil with or without *N*-(phosphonacetyl)-L-aspartic acid in patients with advanced pancreatic and colorectal cancers. *J Clin Oncol* 6:1053–1058, 1988.
31. Haas NB, Hines JB, Hudes GR, et al: Phase I trial of 5-FU by 24 hour infusion weekly. *Investigational New Drugs,* 1993 (in press).
32. Schilsky RL, Perry MC, Citron ML: High dose 5-fluorouracil therapy for advanced gastrointestinal malignancy. *Proc ASCO* 7:102, 1988.
33. Remick SC, Grem JL, Fischer PH, et al: Phase I trial of 5-fluorouracil and dipyridamole administered by 72 hour concurrent continuous infusion. *Cancer Res* 50:2667–2672, 1990.
34. Kish JA, Ensley JF, Jacobs J, et al: A randomized trial of cisplatin + 5-fluorouracil infusion and cisplatin + 5-fluorouracil bolus for recurrent and advanced squamous cell carcinoma of the head and neck. *Cancer* 56:2740–2744, 1985.
35. Hryniuk WM, Eigueredo A, Goodyear M: Applications of dose intensity to problems in chemotherapy of breast and colorectal cancer. *Semin Oncol* 14:3–11, 1987.
36. Weinerman B, Shah A, Fields A, et al: A randomized trial of continuous systemic infusion vs bolus therapy with 5-fluorouracil in metastatic measurable colorectal cancer. *Proc ASCO* 9:103, 1990.
37. Lokich J, Bothe A, Fine N, et al: Phase I study of protracted venous infusion of 5-fluorouracil. *Cancer* 48:3565–3568, 1981.
38. Lokich J, Fine N, Perri J, et al: Protracted ambulatory venous infusion of 5-fluorouracil. *Am J Clin Oncol* 6:103–107, 1983.
39. Cabellero GA, Ausman RK, Quebbeman EJ: Long term, ambulatory, continuous intravenous infusion of 5-fluorouracil

for treatment of advanced adenocarcinomas. *Cancer Treat Rep* 69:13–15, 1985.

40. Benedetto P, Bogos M, Morillo G, et al: Chronic continuous infusion of 5-fluorouracil (CCI-FU) in previously untreated patients with measurable metastatic colorectal cancer. *Proc ASCO* 5:92, 1986.
41. Belt RJ, Davidner ML, Myron MC, et al: Continuous low-dose 5-fluorouracil (5-FU) for adenocarcinoma: Confirmation of activity. *Proc ASCO* 4:90, 1985.
42. Leichman L, Leichman CG, Kinzie J, et al: Long-term low dose 5-fluorouracil (5FU) in advanced measurable colon cancer: No correlation between toxicity and efficacy. *Proc ASCO* 4:86, 1985.
43. Quebbeman E, Ausman R, Hansen R, et al: Long term ambulatory treatment of metastatic colorectal adenocarcinoma by continuous intravenous infusion of 5-fluorouracil. *J Surg Oncol* 30:60–65, 1985.
44. Hansen R, Quebbeman E, Ausman R, et al: Continuous systemic 5-fluorouracil (5-FU) infusion in advanced colorectal cancer: Results in 91 patients. *J Surg Oncol* 40:177–181, 1989.
45. Wade JL, Herbst S, Greenburg A: Prolonged venous infusion (PVI) or 5-fluorouracil (5-FU) for metastatic colon cancer: A follow-up report. *Proc ASCO* 7:94, 1988.
46. Faintuch JS, Shepard KV, Gaynor E, et al: Continuous infusion 5-FU—A dose escalating schedule. *Proc ASCO* 5:93, 1986.
47. Kuo S, Finck S, Cho J, et al: Continuous ambulatory infusional 5-fluorouracil (5-FU) chemotherapy in advanced colorectal cancer: A single institutional retrospective study. *Proc ASCO* 8:126, 1989.
48. Reiter B, Schreibman S, Adler S, et al: Treatment of colorectal cancer with 5FU by infusion in a community oncology practice. *Proc ASCO* 6:74, 1987.
49. Hansen RM: 5-Fluorouracil by protracted venous infusion: A review of recent clinical studies. *Cancer Invest* 9:637–642, 1991.
50. Lokich JJ, Ahlgren JD, Gullo JJ, et al: A prospective randomized comparison of continuous infusion fluorouracil with a conventional bolus schedule in metastatic colorectal carcinoma: A Mid-Atlantic Oncology Program Study. *J Clin Oncol* 7:425–432, 1989.
51. Hansen R, Ryan L, Anderson T, et al: A phase III trial of bolus 5-FU vs protracted infusion 5-FU +/− cisplatin in metastatic colorectal cancer: An ECOG study. *Proc ASCO* 10:154, 1991.
52. Hansen R, Ryan L, Anderson T, et al: A Phase III trial of bolus 5-FU vs protracted infusion 5-FU +/− cisplatin in metastatic colorectal cancer: An ECOG study. *Proc ASCO* 11:171, 1992.
53. Leichman CG, Fleming TR, Muggia FM, et al: Fluorouracil schedules and modulation in advanced colorectal cancer: A Southwest Oncology Group Screening Trial. *Proc ASCO* 12:198, 1993.
54. Berman R, Giles GR, Malhotra A, et al: Randomized trial of melphalan plus 5-fluorouracil (5-FU) versus methyl-CCNU plus 5-FU in patients with advanced colorectal cancer. *Cancer Treat Rep* 62:457–459, 1978.
55. Buroker T, Wojtaszak B, Dindogru A, et al: Phase II trial of ftorafur with mitomycin C versus ftorafur with methyl-CCNU in untreated colorectal cancer. *Cancer Treat Rep* 62:689–692, 1978.
56. Bedikian AY, Valdivieso M, Mavligit GM, et al: Sequential chemoimmunotherapy of colorectal cancer: Evaluation of methotrexate, Baker's Antifol and levamisole. *Cancer* 42: 2169–2176, 1978.
57. Douglass HO Jr, Lavin PT, Woll J, et al: Chemotherapy of advanced measurable colon and rectal carcinoma with oral 5-fluorouracil, alone or in combination with cyclophosphamide or 6-thioguanine, with intravenous 5-fluorouracil or beta-2'-deoxythioguanosine or with oral 3(4-methyl-cyclohexyl)-1(2-chlorethyl)-1-nitrosourea: A phase II-III study of the Eastern Cooperative Oncology Group (EST 4273). *Cancer* 42:2538–2545, 1978.
58. Richards F 2d, Muss HB, Cooper R, et al: Chemotherapy versus chemoimmunotherapy in advanced adenocarcinoma of the colon and rectum: A prospective randomized study. *Cancer* 43:91–96, 1979.
59. White DR, Richards F 2d, Muss HB, et al: Therapy of advanced colorectal carcinoma with 5-fluorouracil and cyclophosphamide in combination with either CCNU or methotrexate. *Cancer* 45:662–665, 1980.
60. Engstrom PF, MacIntyre JM, Douglass HO Jr, et al: Combination chemotherapy of advanced colorectal cancer utilizing 5-fluorouracil, semustine, dacarbazine, vincristine, and hydroxyurea: A phase III trial by the Eastern Cooperative Oncology Group (EST:4275). *Cancer* 49:1555–1560, 1982.
61. Kemeny N, Yagoda A, Braun D Jr: Metastatic colorectal carcinoma: A prospective randomized trial of methyl-CCNU, 5-fluorouracil (5-FU) and vincristine (MOD) versus MOF plus streptozotocin (MOF-Strep). *Cancer* 51:20–24, 1983.
62. Presant CA, Denes AE, Liu C, Bartolucci AA: Prospective randomized reappraisal of 5-fluorouracil (5-FU) in metastatic colorectal carcinoma: A comparative trial with 6-thioguanine. *Cancer* 53:2610–2614, 1984.
63. Engstrom PF, MacIntyre M, Mittelman A, Klaassen DJ: Chemotherapy of advanced colorectal carcinoma: Fluorouracil alone vs two drug combinations using fluorouracil, hydroxyurea, semustine, dacarbazine, razoxane, and mitomycin: A phase III trial by the Eastern Cooperative Oncology Group (EST:1278). *Am J Clin Oncol* 7:313–318, 1984.
64. Richards F 2d, Case LD, White DR, et al: Combination chemotherapy (5-fluorouracil, methyl-CCNU, mitomycin C) versus 5-fluorouracil alone for advanced previously untreated colorectal carcinoma: A phase III study of the Piedmont Oncology Assocation. *J Clin Oncol* 4:565–570, 1986.
65. O'Connell MJ, Schutt AJ, Moertel CG, et al: A randomized clinical trial of combination chemotherapy in advanced colorectal cancer. *Am J Clin Oncol* 10:320–324, 1987.
66. Loehrer PJ Sr, Turner S, Kubilis P, et al: A prospective randomized trial of fluorouracil versus fluorouracil plus cisplatin in the treatment of metastatic colorectal cancer: A Hoosier Oncology Group trial. *J Clin Oncol* 6:642–648, 1988.
67. Leyland-Jones B, O'Dwyer PJ: Biochemical modulation: application of laboratory models to the clinic. *Cancer Treat Rep* 70:219–229, 1986.
68. DeVita VT: The relationship between tumor mass and resistance to chemotherapy. *Cancer* 51:1209–1220, 1983.
69. Machover D, Goldschmidt E, Chollet P, et al: Treatment of advanced colorectal and gastric adenocarcinomas with 5-fluorouracil and high-dose folinic acid. *J Clin Oncol* 4:685–696, 1986.
70. Madajewicz S, Petrelli N, Rustum YM, et al: Phase I-II trial of high-dose calcium leucovorin and 5-fluorouracil in advanced colorectal cancer. *Cancer Res* 44:4667–4669,1984.
71. Petrelli N, Douglass HO, Herrera L, et al: The modulation of fluorouracil with leucovorin in metastatic colorectal carcinoma: A prospective randomized phase III trial. *J Clin Oncol* 7:1419–1426, 1989.
72. Valone FH, Friedman MA, Wittlinger PS, et al: Treatment of patients with advanced colorectal carcinomas with fluorouracil alone, high-dose leucovorin plus fluorouracil, or sequential methotrexate, fluorouracil, and leucovorin: A randomized trial of the Northern California Oncology Group. *J Clin Oncol* 7:1427–1436, 1989.

73. Di Costanzo F, Bartolucci R, Calabresi F, et al: Fluorouracil-alone vs high-dose folinic acid and fluorouracil in advanced colorectal cancer: A randomized trial of the Italian Oncology Group for Clinical Research (COIRC). *Ann Oncol* 3:371–376, 1992.
74. Labianca R, Pancera G, Aitini E, et al: Folinic acid + 5-fluorouracil (5-FU) versus equidose 5-FU in advanced colorectal cancer: Phase III study of "GISCAD" (Italian Group for the Study of Digestive Tract Cancer). *Ann Oncol* 2:673–679, 1991.
75. Nobile MT, Rosso R, Sertoli MR, et al: Randomized comparison of weekly bolus 5-fluorouracil with or without leucovorin in metastatic colorectal carcinoma. *Eur J Cancer* 28A:1823–1827, 1992.
76. Erlichman C, Fine S, Wong A, et al: A randomized trial of fluorouracil and folinic acid in patients with metastatic colorectal carcinoma. *J Clin Oncol* 6:469–475, 1988.
77. Doroshow JH, Multhauf P, Leong L, et al: Prospective randomized comparison of fluorouracil versus fluorouracil and high-dose continuous infusion leucovorin calcium for the treatment of advanced measurable colorectal cancer in patients previously unexposed to chemotherapy. *J Clin Oncol* 8:491–501, 1990.
78. Petrelli N, Herrera L, Rustum Y, et al: A prospective randomized trial of 5-fluorouracil versus 5-fluorouracil and high-dose leucovorin versus 5-fluorouracil and methotrexate in previously untreated patients with advanced colorectal carcinoma. *J Clin Oncol* 5:1559–1565, 1987.
79. Martoni A, Cricca A, Guaraldi M, et al: Weekly regimen of 5-FU vs 5-FU plus intermediate dose folinic acid in the treatment of advanced colorectal cancer. *Anticancer Res* 12:607–612, 1992.
80. Poon MA, O'Connell MJ, Wieand HS, et al: Biochemical modulation of fluorouracil with leucovorin: Confirmatory evidence of improved therapeutic efficacy in advanced colorectal cancer. *J Clin Oncol* 9:1967–1972, 1991.
81. Advanced colorectal cancer metaanalysis project (ACCNAP): Modulation of fluorouracil by leucovorin in patients with advanced colorectal cancer: Evidence in terms of response rate. *J Clin Oncol* 10:896–903, 1992.
82. Moyer JD, Smith PA, Levy EJ, Handschumacher RE: Kinetics of *N*-(phosphonacetyl)-L-aspartate and pyrazofurin depletion of pyrimidine ribonucleotide and deoxyribonucleotide pools and their relationship to nucleic acid synthesis in intact and permeabilized cells. *Cancer Res* 42:4525–4531, 1982.
83. Pizzorno G, Wiegand R, Lentz SK, Handschumacher RE: Brequinar potentiates 5-fluruoracil antitumor activity in a murine model colon 38 tumor by tissue-specific modulation of uridine nucleotide pools. *Cancer Res* 52:1660–1665, 1992.
84. Collins KD, Stark GR: Aspartate transcarbamylase. Interaction with the transition-state analog *N*-(phosphonacetyl)-L-aspartate. *J Biol Chem* 246:6599–6605, 1971.
85. Moore EC, Friedman J, Valdivieso M, et al: Aspartate carbamoyl tranferase activity, drug concentrations, and pyrimidine nucleotides in tissue from patients treated with *N*-(phosphonacetyl)-L-aspartate. *Biochem Pharmacol* 31:3317–3321, 1982.
86. Swyryd A, Seaver SS, Stark GR: *N*-phosphonacetyl-L-aspartate, a potent transition state analog inhibitor of aspartate transcarbamylase, blocks proliferation of mammalian cells in culture. *J Biol Chem* 249:6945–6950, 1974.
87. Karle JM, Anderson LW, Cysyk RL: Effect of plasma concentrations of uridine on pyrimidine biosynthesis in cultured L1210 cells. *J Biol Chem* 259:67–72, 1984.
88. Kensler TW, Mutter G, Hankerson JG, et al: Mechanism of resistance of variants of the Louis lung cancer to *N*-(phosphonacetyl)-L-aspartic acid. *Cancer Res* 41:894–904, 1981.
89. Moyer JD, Handschumacher RE: Selective inhibition of pyrimidine synthesis and depletion of nucleotide pools by *N*-(phosphonacetyl)-L-aspartate. *Cancer Res* 39:3089–3094, 1979.
90. Moyer JD, Smith PA, Levy EJ, Handschumacher RE: Kinetics of *N*-(phosphonacetyl)-L-aspartate and pyrazofurin depletion of pyrimidine ribonucleotide and deoxyribonucleotide pools and their relationship to nucleic acid synthesis in intact and permeabilized cells. *Cancer Res* 42:4525–4531, 1982.
91. Martin DS, Stolfi RL, Sawyer RC, et al: Therapeutic utility of utilizing low doses of *N*-(phosphonacetyl)-L-aspartic acid in combination with 5-fluorouracil: A murine study with clinical relevance. *Cancer Res* 43:2317–2321, 1983.
92. Buroker TR, Moertel CG, Fleming TR, et al: A controlled evaluation of recent approaches to biochemical modulation or enhancement of 5-fluorouracil therapy in colorectal carcinoma. *J Clin Oncol* 3:1624–1631, 1985.
93. O'Dwyer PJ: The role of low-dose PALA in biochemical modulation. *Pharmacol Ther* 48:371–380, 1990.
94. Casper ES, Vale K, Williams LJ, et al: Phase I and clinical pharmacological evaluation of biochemical modulation of 5-fluorouracil with *N*-(phosphonacetyl)-L-aspartic acid. *Cancer Res* 43:2334–2329, 1983.
95. Ardalan B, Singh G, Silberman H: A randomized phase I and II study of short-term infusion of high-dose fluorouracil with or without *N*-(phosphonacetyl)-L-aspartic acid in patients with advanced pancreatic and colorectal cancers. *J Clin Oncol* 6:1053–1058, 1988.
96. O'Dwyer PJ, Paul AR, Walczak J, et al: Phase II study of biochemical modulation of 5-fluorouracil by low-dose PALA in patients with colorectal cancer. *J Clin Oncol* 8:1497–1503, 1990.
97. Houghton JA, Houghton PJ: Elucidation of pathways of 5-fluorouracil metabolism in xenografts of human colorectal adenocarcinoma. *Eur J Cancer Clin Oncol* 19:807–815, 1983.
98. Kufe DW, Egan EM: Enhancement of 5-fluorouracil incorporation into human lymphoblast ribonucleic acid. *Biochem Pharmacol* 30:129–133, 1981.
99. Allegra CA, Fine RL, Drake JC, Chabner BA: The effect of methotrexate on intracellular folate pools in human MCF-7 breast cancer cells: Evidence for direct inhibition of purine synthesis. *J Biol Chem* 261:6478–6485, 1986.
100. Bennett LL Jr, Brockman RW, Schnebli HP, et al: Activity and mechanism of action of 6-methylthiopurine ribonucleoside in cancer cells resistant to 6-mercaptopurine. *Nature* 205:1276–1279, 1965.
101. Martin DS, Stolfi RL, Sawyer RC, et al: An overview of thymidine. *Cancer* 45:1117–1128, 1980.
102. Martin DS, Stolfi RL, Sawyer RC, et al: Biochemical modulation of 5-fluorouracil and cytosine arabinoside with emphasis on thymidine, PALA and 6-methylmercaptopurine riboside, in Tattersall MHN, Fox RM (eds): *Nucleosides and Cancer Treatment*. Academic Press, Australia, 1981, pp 339–382.
103. Marsh JC, Bertino JR, Katz KH, et al: Influence of drug interval on the effect of methotrexate on fluorouracil in the treatment of advanced colorectal cancer. *J Clin Oncol* 9:371–380, 1991.
104. Crabtree GW, Wiemann MC, Spremulli EN, et al: Phase I clinical trial of the combination of 6-methylmercaptopurine riboside (MMPR) and 5-fluorouracil (5-FU). *Proc ASCO* 3:36, 1984.
105. Peters WP, Weiss G, Kufe DW: Phase I trial of combination

therapy with continuous infusion MMPR and continuous infusion 5-FU. *Cancer Chemother Pharmacol* 13:136–138, 1984.

106. O'Dwyer PJ, Hudes GR, Colofiore J, et al: Phase I trial of fluorouracil modulation by *N*-phosphonacetyl-L-aspartate and 6-methylmercaptopurine riboside: Optimization of 6-methylmercaptopurine riboside dose and schedule through biochemical analysis of sequential tumor biopsy specimens. *J Natl Cancer Inst* 83:1235–1240, 1991.
107. Glimelius B: Biochemical modulation of 5-fluorouracil: A randomized comparison of sequential methotrexate, 5-fluorouracil and leucovorin vs sequential 5-fluorouracil and leucovorin in patients with advanced symptomatic colorectal cancer: The Nordic Gastrointestinal Tumor Adjuvant Therapy Group. *Ann Oncol* 4:235–240, 1993.
108. Elias L, Crissman JA: Interferon effects upon the adenocarcinoma 38 and HL60 cell lines: Antiproliferative responses and synergistic interactions with halogenated pyrimidine anti-metabolites. *Cancer Res* 48:4868–4873, 1988.
109. Schwartz EL, Hoffman M, O'Connor CJ, Wadler S: Stimulation of 5-fluorouracil metabolite activation by interferon alpha in human colon carcinoma cells. *Biochem Biophys Res Commun* 182:1232–1239, 1992.
110. Chu E, Zinn S, Boarman D, Allegra CJ: Interaction of γ-interferon and 5-fluorouracil in the H630 human collon carcinoma cell line. *Cancer Res* 50:5834–5840, 1990.
111. Wadler S, Wiernik PH: Clinical update on the role of fluorouracil and recombinant interferon alfa-2a in the treatment of colorectal cancer. *Semin Oncol* 17 (suppl 1): 16–21, 1990.
112. York M, Greco FA, Figlin RA, et al.: A randomized phase III trial comparing 5-FU with or without interferon α2A for advanced colorectal cancer. *Proc ASCO* 12:200, 1993.
113. Kocha W: 5-fluorouracil plus interferon α2A (Roferon-A) vs 5-fluorouracil plus leucovorin in metastatic colorectal cancer: Results of a multicenter, multinational phase III study. *Proc ASCO* 12:193, 1993.
114. Grem JL, McAtee N, Murphy RF, et al: A pilot study of interferon-alfa-2a in combination with fluorouracil plus high-dose leucovorin in metastatic gastrointestinal carcinoma. *J Clin Oncol* 9:1811–1820, 1991.
115. Berger SH, Barbour KW, Berger FG: A naturally occurring variation in thymidylate synthase structure is associated with a reduced response to 5-fluoro-2'-deoxyuridine in a human colon tumor cell line. *Mol Pharmacol* 34:480–484, 1988.
116. Hughey CT, Barbour KW, Berger FG, Berger SH: Functional effects of a naturally occurring amino acid substitution in human thymidylate synthase. *Mol Pharmacol* 44:316–323, 1993.
117. Berger SH, Chung-Her J, Johnson LF, Berger FG: Thymidylate synthase overproduction and gene amplification in fluorodeoxyuridine-resistant human cells. *Mol Pharmacol* 28:461–467, 1987.

CHAPTER 94

Cellular Immunotherapy

Howard D. J. Edington
Michael T. Lotze

HIGHLIGHTS

Immunotherapy as a cancer treatment is not new; however, advances in molecular biology and mammalian gene transfer technology have ushered in a new era of understanding and therapeutic potential for patients with colorectal cancer and other malignancies. This chapter, based in part on a recent review, discusses treatment strategies involving cellular immunotherapy.[1] Approaches can be thought of as active or passive in nature, with administration of modified tumor constituting the former and transfer of immune cells, the latter.

CONTROVERSIES

The principal controversy involving immunotherapeutic approaches to cancer therapy is simply whether the tumor-bearing host (patient) can recognize his or her tumor as foreign and mount an immune response. Additional controversies include how to amplify and direct the antitumor immune response and how best to select patients who are likely to benefit from immune-based therapies.

FUTURE DIRECTIONS

The fairly recent fusion of cellular immunology and molecular biology, along with dramatic advances in both fields, will lead to an improved understanding of the pathogenesis of colorectal cancer as well as the process of malignant transformation at the genetic level. The role of oncogenes and suppressor genes will be further defined. Clarification of the role played by the p53 gene in the process of malignant transformation will have particular relevance to the management of colorectal malignancies. It is anticipated that exciting advances in gene transfer techniques will facilitate the development of novel "gene therapy" and "immunotherapy" approaches to established disease. The same knowledge will facilitate both early detection and the design of adjuvant therapy and disease prevention strategies.

Carcinoma of the colon and rectum accounts for 13 percent of malignancies in both males and females in the United States.[2] Survival rates have improved only slightly despite efforts targeted toward early detection and prevention through dietary manipulation. While surgical resection remains the single most effective therapy, the management of all patients with colorectal carcinoma remains a challenge. Patients with metastatic disease may expect a response rate of 15 to 20 percent to conventional drug therapy; the mean duration of the response is on the order of 12 to 18 months with 5-fluorouracil (5-FU) alone. Combinations with biologic agents including leucovorin and alpha interferon have increased the response rates to 50 percent; however, obtaining a durable response is still a problem.[3] Patients with advanced local regional disease have a dismal 5-year survival of approximately 15 to 25 percent.[4] Even when the tumor is detected at an early clinical stage and the patient treated with curative intent, the recurrence rates can be as high as 30 to

50 percent.[5–7] It is apparent, therefore, that further advances must be made in both adjuvant therapy and the treatment of established disease.

Immunotherapy is a reasonable treatment option for some cancer patients. The use of immunotherapy as front-line treatment for some malignancies—alpha interferon for hairy cell leukemia and interleukin-2 (IL-2) for metastatic renal cell carcinoma—is now clearly established.[8] Although thought to be new, immunotherapy as an approach to cancer treatment has been explored for some time. W. B. Coley, a surgeon at Memorial Sloan Kettering, noted in the 1800s that sarcoma patients who developed a wound infection seemed to have a more favorable prognosis. He then initiated some of the first clinical immunotherapy trials. Coley's toxins (bacterial products) were administered to patients with metastatic sarcoma.[9]

The potential use of immunotherapy for the treatment of malignancy depends upon several assumptions. The most important of these is that an antigenic difference exist between malignant and normal cells, that such an antigenic difference is expressed by all malignant cells, and that the host can recognize the difference and respond appropriately. The second set of assumptions implies that the tumor-bearing host is functionally immunodeficient in that an antitumor response is somehow blocked or inactivated. Goals of immunotherapy are to increase the host response to the tumor (active immunotherapy) and/or to provide agents such as monoclonal antibodies or immune effector cells (passive immunotherapy) that are themselves immunologically active and theoretically depend less upon a host response. (The use of monoclonal antibodies is discussed in Chap. 95) Cellular immunotherapy will be described in terms of both active and passive philosophies. It is clear, however, that the categories are mechanistically interrelated and are not mutually exclusive. Either tumor cells or lymphoid effector cells may be transferred to the tumor-bearing host. Tumor cell administration represents an active form of immunotherapy and is frequently described as a vaccination approach. The aim is to generate a host response to the administered tumor cells, which are usually altered ex vivo to increase their immunogenicity. Ideally a response to the transferred cells will be amplified and an antitumor response to the patient's established tumor will develop. Many feel that the term *vaccination* is inappropriate, since it suggests mechanistic analogies to viral vaccination approaches which may be inaccurate; *immunization* may be the preferred term. Adoptive cellular therapy using lymphoid effector cells is a passive form of immunotherapy in which cells with antitumor activity are grown ex vivo and transferred back to the tumor-bearing host. This approach has been suggested by the observation that lymphoid cells freshly isolated from tumor-bearing patients appear to be essentially anergic, at least with respect to the host tumor, and that a form of "tolerance" has developed. Both tumor-infiltrating lymphocytes (TILs) and natural killer (NK) cells immediately isolated from a patient's tumor demonstrate minimal antitumor lytic activity when tested against autologous and allogeneic tumor targets in vitro.[10,11] These same effector cells fail to bind to autologous tumor and do not produce IL-2 in response to tumor.[12] A similar lack of responsiveness has been noted for monocytes isolated from women with ovarian cancer.[13–15] Although the mechanism for this tolerance is ill defined and is obviously a central question for tumor immunologists, it is clear that the functional anergy can, in some cases, be reversed following ex vivo culture. Culture conditions are controlled to promote a preferential expansion of reactive lymphoid cell subsets that does not occur in the tumor-bearing host. The characterization of a number of cytokines, including the interleukins and interferons, that promote the growth and activation of lymphoid cell subsets has greatly facilitated the ex vivo culture of these cells. It is anticipated that a number of cytokines currently undergoing preclinical evaluation will be tested in clinical trials in the near future, and properties of some of these cytokines will be discussed (see below).

It is clear that immunotherapy is effective for some malignancies, including renal cell carcinoma, melanoma, and some hematologic malignancies. A central question remains—whether these particular tumors are somehow uniquely immunogenic and whether the same principles may apply to other tumor types, including colorectal carcinoma. A number of observations suggest that colorectal tumors may elicit an inflammatory response which, in turn, appears to have a favorable effect on prognosis. For patients with Dukes B and C colonic cancer, the presence of an inflammatory infiltrate in the resected specimen was associated with an 89 percent 5-year survival, compared with 46 percent for those whose tumor showed no such infiltrate.[16] These findings have been confirmed by others.[17–19]

ACTIVE SPECIFIC IMMUNOTHERAPY

Autologous Tumor Cell Vaccines

Hanna, Hoover, and associates[15,20–24] have developed a bacillus Calmette-Guérin (BCG) autologous tumor vaccination strategy for the treatment of patients with colorectal cancer. Human trials were based on data gathered from extensive preclinical investigations using a chemically induced hepatocarcinoma in a guinea pig model. Initial experiments involved the direct injection of BCG into intradermal tumor nodules. Regression of the treated nodule was observed. Interestingly, regional nodal metastases also regressed and systemic immunity developed. Treated animals rapidly rejected a second tumor challenge several weeks after BCG injection. Subsequent experiments proved that this approach was most effective for small tumor burdens and seemed to be dependent on macrophages and cytotoxic lymphocytes. Similar results could be attained using a vaccination of BCG and live irradiated tumor instead of intralesional injections. The investigators concluded that live cells were optimal for effective vaccination, that BCG promoted the recruitment of a host cellular infiltrate to the vaccination site, that antigen presentation occurred during the period of inflammation, and that sensitization and the development of tumor-specific immunity occurred in the regional nodal basin.

Animal data facilitated the design of a randomized prospective adjuvant trial of active specific immunotherapy (ASI) in patients undergoing resection of grades B_2, C_1, C_2, and C_3 colonic or rectal carcinoma. Tumor cell suspensions were prepared from resection specimens. Autologous tumor cells (10^7 cells) were radiated (200 Gy), mixed with BCG (10^7), and given twice as an intradermal injection (1 week apart). On the third week, irradiated tumor cells alone were injected. Most treated patients developed vaccination-site ulceration and regional adenopathy, while 67 percent developed delayed cutaneous hypersensitivity (DCH) responses to autologous tumor (compared to 9 percent of nonimmunized patients).[23] This response correlated positively with survival. Initial data analysis (mean follow-up = 28 months) showed a significant improvement in disease-free survival ($p = .035$) and overall survival ($p = .023$). Data concerning 80 patients were available for the most recent analysis. Patients were grouped into those with rectal cancer (33) and colonic cancer (47). In the colonic cancer group, 24 patients received ASI; there were 5 recurrences and 3 deaths compared to 12 recurrences and 7 deaths in the observation group ($n = 23$). These numbers reflect a significant decrease in recurrence rate ($p = .021$) for those patients undergoing ASI but no change in death rate. In the rectal cancer group, 16 patients were observed (10 recurrences and 7 deaths) and 17 patients received ASI (11 recurrences and 10 deaths). No difference in disease-free survival or overall survival was noted.[1,24]

A smaller trial also using a BCG–autologous tumor vaccine approach has been reported by Jessup and colleagues[25] from the M. D. Anderson Hospital. A total of 11 patients received immunotherapy; 8 of the 11 had rectal cancer. No complications were associated with the treatment and delayed-type hypersensitivity (DTH) responses were observed in most patients (10/11).[25] Although statistical inference is difficult, a difference in recurrence rate (18 percent treated versus 32 percent observation) was noted after 25 to 43 months of follow-up.

Patients treated with autologous tumor cells infected with modified Newcastle disease virus (to augment vaccine immunogenicity) demonstrated increased cellular responses to the inoculation, suggesting that a host immune response to autologous tumor can be stimulated via vaccination-type approaches.[26]

Synergism between vaccination-type immunotherapy and chemotherapy has been demonstrated in several animal models, including the guinea pig hepatocarcinoma model discussed above. Although the functional importance and even existence of suppressor cells has been debated, it has been proposed that cyclophosphamide may break tumor tolerance by depleting suppressor cells and thus facilitate immune manipulations. In turn, the inflammatory reaction incited by BCG or other immune modulators may, by altering vascular permeability, increase the delivery of cyclophosphamide to the tumor. A number of animal studies have confirmed synergy between cyclophosphamide and immunotherapy and suggest additional clinical trials.[27]

Clinical immunotherapy trials including cyclophosphamide are being initiated at the University of Pittsburgh as well as elsewhere.[1]

CYTOKINE GENE THERAPY VACCINATION

Eradication or regression of tumor following direct injection with cytokines, which themselves have no direct antitumor activity, suggested that an immune response could be generated by providing the cytokine in a paracrine fashion.[28] In this instance the cytokine might be viewed as an adjuvant analogous to BCG, *C. parvum*, or Freund's adjuvant used in conventional vaccination approaches. The use of genetically altered cells to serve as an adjuvant has been proposed. Both fibroblasts and lymphoid cells transfected with the IL-2 gene engineered to constitutively produce IL-2 have also been used as cellular delivery systems for IL-2.[29,30] A number of animal tumors have been transfected with the IL-2 gene including murine colorectal, sarcoma and melanoma lines.[31,32] Rejection of transfected tumor as well as nontransfected tumor injected concurrently occurred. Tumor rejection depended on the presence of CD8+ T cells but did not require CD4+ T cells. Rejection of tumor was associated with the development of immunity to later challenge with nontransfected tumor. In this model, minimal effect on established (nontransfected) tumor was seen. Numerous other cytokines have been transfected into various tumor systems including tumor necrosis factor (TNF), gamma-interferon (INF-γ), granulocyte colony stimulating factor (G-CSF), and IL-7. The observations are similar to those following IL-2 transfection.[33–36] The most disappointing observation from these studies is the general lack of therapeutic effect on established tumor. There are, however, several studies that do seem hopeful. Restifo et al.,[37] using an IFN-γ transfected tumor model, demonstrated an increased host response possibly related to improved antigen presentation by the transfected tumor. TILs were induced, which could then be expanded ex vivo and adoptively transferred back to the host with subsequent regression of nontransfected (established) tumor. Transfection of IL-4 into a murine renal cell carcinoma was associated with not only regression of transfected tumor and subsequent immunity but also a modest antitumor effect on nontransfected tumor.[38] Another report utilizing TNF-transfected tumor as a "vaccine" demonstrated reduction of established pulmonary metastases.[39]

PASSIVE IMMUNOTHERAPY

Adoptive Cellular Therapy

Adoptive cellular therapy depends on the use of cytokines to promote in vitro expansion and activation of the selected effector cell population. Lymphoid cells are harvested, purified, and cultured in media containing appropriate growth factors. Cells are expanded and then returned (adoptive transfer) back to the patient.

In vitro characterization of the LAK (lymphoid-activated killer) phenomenon was reported in 1980 by Yron and associates,[40] an observation that depended on the earlier description of IL-2 and its T-cell growth-promoting activities.[41] The phenomenon describes the in vitro lysis of labeled fresh tumor targets by lymphoid cells which have been preincubated in IL-2 or other lymphokines.[42] The effect is not major histocompatibility complex (MHC)-restricted and a variety of different fresh tumors are lysed by LAK cells. Cells with LAK activity appear to spare most normal cells. The LAK cell population is heterogenous, yet the lytic activity is ascribed primarily to the CD3$^-$/CD56$^+$ or NK-cell subpopulation.[43]

LAK Therapy

Murine studies conducted at the National Cancer Institute demonstrated that adoptive transfer of LAK cells combined with IL-2 administration mediated a dramatic regression of established tumor in a variety of models.[44,45] The data suggested that the transfer of LAK cells alone was not sufficient to effect significant antitumor activity and that concurrent administration of IL-2 was necessary, suggesting an in vivo dependence of transferred LAK for IL-2. Early trials of IL-2/LAK therapy in humans were guided by animal data. Patients with a variety of metastatic tumors were

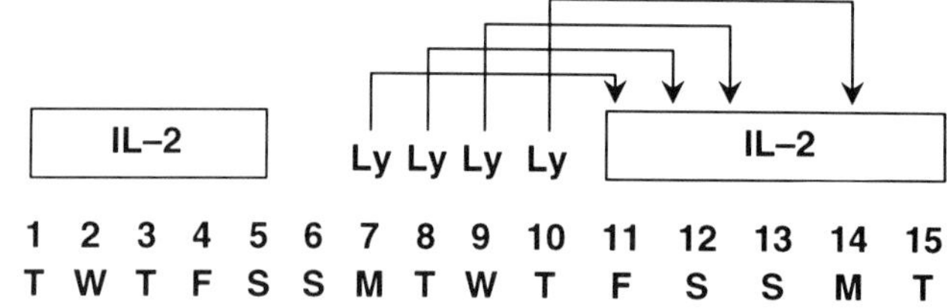

FIG. 94-1. Schedule of LAK-cell infusions accompanied by the administration of systemic IL-2 given intravenously.

treated with adoptive transfer of up to 15×10^{10} autologous LAK cells which had been cultured and expanded in IL-2 ex vivo. LAK-cell infusions were accompanied by the administration of systemic IL-2 given intravenously (720,000 IU/kg) according to the schedule in Fig. 94-1. Although most responses occurred in patients with melanoma or renal cell carcinoma, a 17 percent response rate was noted for patients with metastatic colorectal carcinoma. Similar response rates were documented by the IL-2/LAK working group (see Table 94-1).[46] Unfortunately the therapy is not without adverse side effects. The toxicity is caused by the IL-2, is dose-related, and effects usually reverse quickly when treatment is discontinued. The toxicity is most directly related to the induction of a profound capillary leak syndrome leading to the end-organ damage characteristic of a shock state, including severe peripheral and pulmonary edema as well as hepatic and cardiac insufficiency. Hematologic changes include thrombocytopenia and anemia. Nausea, vomiting, chills, and fever occur frequently and generally respond to symptomatic treatment.[47]

Our recently reported prospective study of IL-2 and LAK versus IL-2 alone in 181 patients suggested no overall benefit of the infusion of LAK; however, 2/8 patients with colorectal cancer treated with LAK plus IL-2 showed partial responses, compared with 0/10 colorectal cancer patients treated with IL-2 alone.[48] These initial results were viewed with cautious optimism; however, unsolved problems include the significant toxicity related to IL-2 and incomplete re-

Table 94-1
Results of the IL-2/LAK Working Group

Type of cancer	*Total*	*Complete regression*	*Partial regression*	*Objective regression rate, %*
Renal cell	32	2	3	16
Melanoma	32	1	5	19
Colorectal	19	1	2	16

SOURCE: From Rosenberg SA: Adoptive cellular therapy: Clinical applications, in Devita VT Jr, Hellman S, Rosenberg SA (eds): *Biologic Therapy of Cancer.* Philadelphia, Lippincott, 1991, p 217.

sponses. Currently, efforts to solve these problems involve testing additional cytokines which ideally have similar growth-promoting activities but less toxicity, exploring different delivery approaches (local versus systemic), and testing different effector-cell populations.

CYTOKINES

Other cytokines which show promise in preclinical evaluations for use in cellular therapy include IL-4, IL-7, IL-10, IL-12, and the interferons.

Interleukin-4

Interleukin-4 was first described as a B-cell growth factor and termed B-cell stimulating factor 1 (BCSF-1).[49] It was later found to have weak T-cell growth activity alone but synergized with IL-2 in promoting in vitro growth of TILs (see below) and inhibited the nonspecific LAK activity associated with IL-2. The side effects of IL-4 in humans, although similar to those of IL-2, do not seem to include the same degree of profound hypotension.[50] Trials utilizing the combination of IL-2 and IL-4 in conjunction with cellular therapy (gene-marked TILs; see below) have been initiated at the University of Pittsburgh.

Interleukin-7

Interleukin-7 shares a number of characteristics with IL-4. It was originally described as a B-cell growth factor and later shown to have T-cell growth activity.[51,52] Like IL-4, IL-7 may generate LAK activity (low in comparison to that of IL-2) and has synergistic effects when combined with IL-2.[53] Preclinical evaluation of IL-7 suggests a potential role for IL-7 for in vitro expansion of effector-cell populations.[53,54]

Interleukin-10

Interleukin-10 is produced by B cells and activated type 2 T-helper cells (Th_2). It inhibits the production of IL-2 and gamma interferon by Th_1 cells.[55,56] Interleukin-10 is considered by many to be an immunosuppressive cytokine in that it inhibits the stimulation of a cellular immune response.[57] Interesting in this regard is the striking homology of IL-10 cDNA with the BamH1 fragment (BCRF-1) of the Epstein-Barr virus genome, suggesting that IL-10 may facilitate host viral tolerance.[58] While it seems counterintuitive that an 'immunosuppressive" cytokine might have clinical utility in tumor immunotherapy, IL-10 has costimulatory activity with IL-2, IL-4, and IL-7 in promoting growth of murine T cells and also acts as a cytotoxic T-cell differentiation factor.[59]

Interleukin-12

Interleukin-12 is a recently described heterodimeric cytokine which appeared to be identical to a cytokine independently described as NK-cell stimulatory factor (NKSF).[60] Effects of IL-12 include LAK induction and T-cell growth activity. We and others have demonstrated significant antitumor activity of IL-12 alone and in conjunction with IL-2 in in vivo animal models utilizing a colorectal tumor. The antitumor effects of IL-12 appear, at least in part, to be mediated via the induction of high levels of gamma interferon.[61]

ADHERENT NATURAL KILLER CELL (A-NK) THERAPY

LAK cells represent a heterogenous population of cells that include both activated T cells and NK cells. It has been proposed that the interaction of the T and NK cells in this population may deleteriously affect the antitumor activity of the bulk preparation.[62,63] A simple, effective technique has been developed to select NK cells from peripheral blood mononuclear cells (PBMCs) based on the ability of activated NK cells to adhere to plastic.[64] These activated or adherent NK cells (A-NK cells) may be expanded to large numbers in culture. They represent a population rich in the CD3-Leu19+ phenotype and may be used for adoptive immunotherapy. In a rodent pulmonary metastases model, adoptive immunotherapy with A-NK cells and IL-2 was more effective than that with unfractionated LAK and IL-2.[65] These results were the basis for the initiation of an ongoing clinical protocol for the systemic therapy of patients with melanoma and renal cell carcinoma.[66] In addition, a protocol for the regional treatment of patients with unresectable hepatic metastatic disease from a colorectal primary has been initiated. Patients with isolated, unresectable hepatic colorectal metastases undergo leukapheresis. A-NK cells are purified and expanded in IL-2 in culture over 2 weeks. Cells are then reinfused via a hepatic artery catheter placed into either the right or left hepatic artery via percutaneous Seldinger technique. Concurrently the patients receive IL-2 according to a decreasing dose regimen (1 $mg/m^2/6$ h, 1 $mg/m^2/12$ h, 1 $mg/m^2/24$ h, then 0.25 $mg/m^2/24$ h $\times$ 3 days). The cycle is repeated 14 days later. This protocol will assess the concept of regional cellular immunotherapy, with each patient serving as his or her own control by contrasting the response in the left lobe with that in the right lobe of the liver as well as the efficacy of a decreasing IL-2 regimen. The first patient has just had treatment initiated on this trial.

TIL THERAPY

While clinical trials using the relatively nonspecific LAK cells were ongoing, several groups were investigating the potential for highly specific T-cell immunotherapy. Tumor-infiltrating lymphocytes (TILs) are T cells isolated from fresh tumor and grown in culture in the presence of IL-2 or other lymphokines with T-cell growth-promoting activity (IL-4, IL-7, and possibly others). These TILs are CD8+ and express the IL-2 receptor as well as HLA-DR.[67] Tumor lysis mediated by TILs is highly specific, MHC-restricted, and appears to be 50 to 100 times more effective on a per cell basis than LAK lysis.[68] T cells with antitumor specificity may be isolated from the draining nodal basin as well as from the primary tumor. Nodal cells—referred to as in vitro sensitized cells (IVS)—are similar to TILs and may be expanded in vitro and then used for adoptive transfer.[69]

One trial combining adoptive transfer of autologous TILs with systemic IL-2 and cyclophosphamide achieved a 29 percent response rate for patients with metastatic renal cell carcinoma and a 23 percent response rate for patients with melanoma. Cyclophosphamide augments the antitumor effects of TIL therapy in animal models.[70] We are aware of only two patients with colorectal cancer who have received TIL/IL-2 treatment. One patient had no response; however, another, who had peritoneal carcinomatosis at the time of laparotomy, had a minor response (25 percent) in a hepatic lesion and was later made disease free at reoperation. Interestingly, at the time of her reexploration, the peritoneal carcinomatosis had regressed completely and the hepatic lesion and a small implant in the illopsoas muscle were the only apparent foci of tumor; these were readily resected. The patient is currently without evidence of disease after 3 years of follow-up.

A number of conclusions were drawn from both clinical trials and the animal experiments evaluating TIL transfer: overall response rates were higher than for LAK/IL-2 and responses were seen in some patients who had previously failed IL-2/LAK therapy. The TILs appeared to traffic and localize preferentially in locations involved with tumor.[71,72] The latter observation has particular relevance to future efforts utilizing genetically engineered TIL cells (see below).

ACTIVATED MONOCYTES

The monocyte and the macrophage are involved in the regulation of the immune response. Their presence in regressing tumors has suggested a potential in vivo antitumor activity.[73] Monocytes isolated from animals immunized with tumor demonstrated lytic activity against the immunizing tumor in an in vitro assay.[74] Macrophages may generate antitumor responses via diverse mechanisms. They are involved in the regulation of cytolytic T-lymphocyte responses and other cellular activities by releasing various cytokines and growth factors. Tumor lysis by activated monocytes may be effected by direct spontaneous lytic activity and by antibody-dependent cell cytotoxicity.[75] Lysis of tumor by activated monocytes is relatively nonspecific, similar to lysis mediated by LAK cells. Activated monocytes demonstrate lytic activity toward both allogeneic and xenogeneic tumor targets while leaving normal cells intact.[76]

A variety of monocyte-activating substances have been identified, including BCG, endotoxin, interferon, and muramyl dipeptide.[77] Animal studies have confirmed in vivo antitumor activity of adoptively transferred monocytes. Regression of pulmonary metastases in a murine melanoma model was mediated by adoptive transfer of muramyl dipeptide–activated monocytes.[78] A reduction of pulmonary metastases in a murine fibrosarcoma model was effected by BCG-activated monocytes.[79]

In 1984, a phase I–II clinical trial for patients with peritoneal carcinomatosis was initiated at the National Cancer Institute. The regional (intraperitoneal) adoptive transfer of gamma interferon–activated monocytes was assessed. Preoperatively, patients underwent leukapheresis. Monocytes were purified by countercurrent elutriation and cells were incubated in polytetrafluoroethylene-coated flasks containing recombinant gamma interferon (1000 U/mL). Patients underwent a debulking laparotomy with removal of all gross disease, and a Tenckhoff catheter was placed. Autologous monocytes activated ex vivo were then adoptively transferred into the peritoneal cavity. Monocyte harvesting, activation, and transfer were repeated weekly for 16 weeks. At the end of the treatment period, a second laparotomy was performed and any residual disease resected. Patients with minimal resectable disease were treated with resection and six additional monocyte infusions. Treatments could be administered on an outpatient basis and were generally well tolerated. Six patients were treated on this pilot protocol (see Table 94-2). Results are difficult to interpret due to the small number of patients, disease heterogeneity, and multimodality therapy.[80]

A similar phase I study has been conducted by Faradji and associates[81] in France. Nine patients with peritoneal carcinomatosis were treated. Autologous monocytes were harvested by leukapheresis and purified by counterflow elutriation. Monocytes were activated ex vivo by incubating them with 1 μg liposomal muramyldipeptide derivative (MTP-PE)/10^6 monocytes for 18 h. The cells were infused into the peritoneal cavity via a peritoneal catheter inserted at laparotomy, and this peritoneal infusion was repeated

Table 94-2
Pilot Protocol

Sex/age	*Diagnosis*	*Treatment*	*Period of follow-up*	*Current status*
F/40	Pseudomyxoma peritonei	Debulking surgery and activated monocytes	20 months	NED[a]
F/33	Pseudomyxoma peritonei	Debulking surgery and activated monocytes	4 months	NED[a]
F/40	Peritoneal carcinomatosis 2⁰ to right colon primary with unresectable pelvic mass	Debulking surgery, activated monocytes, and radiation	30 months	NED[a]
M/52	Peritoneal carcinomatosis 2⁰ to right colon cancer	Debulking surgery and activated monocytes switched to IP 5-FU	10 months	AWD
F/39	Peritoneal carcinomatosis 2⁰ to left colon primary with unresectable pelvic mass	Debulking surgery and activated monocytes	8 months	Died of surgical complications; no disease on peritoneal surfaces at autopsy
M/45	Carcinomatosis following sigmoid resection	Debulking surgery and activated monocytes	12 months	NED following resection of pulmonary metastases

Abbreviations: NED, no evidence of disease; IP, intraperitoneal; AWD, alive with disease.

[a]Patient identified as responder to local regional surgery and immunotherapy treatment strategy.

weekly for 5 weeks. Elevated levels of IL-1, IL-6, TNF, and increased procoagulant activity detected in the postinfusion peritoneal fluid suggested that the infused monocytes remain activated in vivo. Indium-111 labeling studies demonstrated that the infused monocytes remain localized to the peritoneal cavity for up to 7 days. Data regarding therapeutic effects of the infused cells were not available from this study; however, the treatment was well tolerated, with fever, chills, and abdominal pain occurring in the minority of patients.[81] Clinical trials using muramyldipeptide liposomes for patients with sarcoma have just begun at the M. D. Anderson Hospital.

GENETICALLY ENGINEERED EFFECTOR CELLS

The observation that TILs appear to traffic and localize preferentially to sites of tumor involvement makes the concept of genetically engineering these cells to produce constitutive biologicals with antitumor activity very attractive. The goals are to localize potentially toxic therapy and amplify the immune response locally. Trials are currently in progress at the Surgery Branch of the National Cancer Institute, testing the efficacy of TILs engineered to constitutively produce TNF. Tumor necrosis factor has significant toxicity when given systemically in humans. Fever, chills, and a shocklike state are common, with systemic hypotension representing the dose-limiting toxicity. The MTD from multiple clinical trials appears to be about 200 g/m^2. The dose of TNF required to induce hemorrhagic tumor necrosis in mice on the basis of body surface area is 1000 g/m^2. There is obviously a significant gap between the dose of TNF required for in vivo tumor necrosis and the apparent MTD. It is possible that if higher doses could be administered safely to humans or if they could be delivered locally, more responses might be seen. It is hoped that the TILs will preferentially localize to tumor deposits and produce locally high levels of TNF that might not be systemically tolerated or to at least upregulate locally the immune response to the tumor.

In addition to cytokine genes, many other gene transfer strategies may be useful. For example, introduction of the herpes thymidine kinase gene into effector cells using retroviral vectors and their delivery to a tumor site or directly into tumors via adoptive transfer of viral producer lines may have a therapeutic role when the patient is treated with ganciclovir, which is converted to its toxic form in the presence of thymidine kinase.

ADJUVANT CELLULAR THERAPY

A number of conclusions may be drawn from animal data and early trials utilizing LAK and IL-2 for patients with metastatic disease:

1. Regression of metastatic tumor (melanoma, renal cell carcinoma, and colorectal carcinoma in humans) can be

mediated by the administration of IL-2 alone or in conjunction with LAK cells.
2. Therapeutic effect appeared to be proportional to the number of LAK cells transferred and the dose of IL-2 given.
3. In animal models, LAK/IL-2 therapy is most effective for small tumor burdens.

These conclusions served as the basis for the initiation in 1986 of an adjuvant trial using LAK and IL-2 for patients with resectable colorectal hepatic metastases. The trial was performed at the Surgery Branch of the National Cancer Institute. For patients undergoing hepatic resection for colorectal metastases, no effective adjuvant therapy exists and patients have a 5-year survival of 25 percent or less.[82]

Patients with resectable colorectal hepatic metastases and no other detectable evidence of disease underwent resection with curative intent and were randomized to receive no additional therapy or to receive three courses of high-dose IL-2 and LAK cells (four LAK cell infusions per course) over a 9-month period. Patients were stratified according to status of their resection margins (positive or negative for residual tumor) and number of nodules. Patients are followed and disease-free and overall survival recorded. Updated data regarding clinical outcome should be available soon. Preliminary analysis suggests that a small increase in disease-free survival will be noted for the group treated with adjuvant therapy.

CONCLUSIONS AND FUTURE DIRECTIONS

The role and nature of immunotherapeutic options for patients with colorectal carcinoma are evolving. Major obstacles include expense, toxicity, lack of specificity, and incomplete responses. Attempts to decrease IL-2–related toxicity include the evaluation of other cytokines with T-cell growth activity, including IL-7, IL-10, and IL-12. It is hoped that one or more of these may have clinical utility either alone or in conjunction with adoptive cellular therapy. Regional delivery approaches seek to minimize systemic toxicity and locally upregulate the immune response. Selective vascular perfusion and local regional delivery—for example, to the peritoneum—are two such strategies.

Advances in molecular biology and techniques of mammalian gene transfer are occurring rapidly. Effector cells are being engineered to increase their antitumor activity or to act as drug delivery vehicles. Additional understanding of the role played by the p53 gene in the malignant transformation process in colorectal cancers will facilitate the development of novel interventional strategies. For example, efforts to directly target the immune response to the mutant p53 protein or the overexpressed wild-type protein are under way in a number of laboratories.

REFERENCES

1. Edington HD, Lotze MT: Immunotherapy, in Wanebo HJ (ed): *Colorectal Cancer.* St Louis, Mosby, 1993, pp 540–562.
2. Boring CC, Squires TS, Tong T: Cancer statistics 1993. *CA* 43:7–27, 1993.
3. Mayer RJ: Chemotherapy for metastatic colorectal cancer. *Cancer* 70:1414–1424, 1992.
4. Goligher JC: *Surgery of the Anus, Rectum and Colon,* 3d ed. London, Baillere, Tindall, 1975.
5. Gilbert SG: Symptomatic local tumor failure following abdomino-perineal resection. *Int J Radiat Oncol Biol Phys* 4:801–807, 1978.
6. Gunderson LL, Tepper JE, Dosoretz DE, et al: Patterns of failure after treatment of gastrointestinal cancer. *Cancer Treat Symp* 2:181–197, 1983.
7. Pihl E, Hughes ESR, McDermott FT, et al: Disease free survival and recurrence after resection of colorectal carcinoma. *J Surg Oncol* 16:333–341, 1981.
8. Quesada JR, Reuben J, Manning JT, et al: Alpha interferon for induction of remission in hairy cell leukemia. *N Engl J Med* 310:15–18, 1984.
9. Coley WB: The treatment of inoperable sarcoma with the mixed toxins of erysipelas and bacillus prodigiosus. *JAMA* 31:389–395, 1898.
10. Balch CM, Riley LB, Bao Y-J, et al: Patterns of human tumor-infiltrating lymphocytes in 120 human cancers. *Arch Surg* 125:200–205, 1990.
11. Hersey P, MacDonald MJ, Schiberi SD, et al: Clonal analysis of cytotoxic T-lymphocytes against autologous melanoma. *Cancer Immunol Immunother* 22:15–23, 1986.
12. Itoh K, Tilden AB, Balch CM: Interleukin-2 activation of cytotoxic T-lymphocytes infiltrating into human metastatic melanomas. *Cancer Res* 46:3011–3017, 1986.
13. Kleinerman ES, Zwelling LA, Howser A, et al: Defective monocyte killing in patients with malignancies and restoration of function during chemotherapy. *Lancet* 2:1102—1105, 1980.
14. Peri G, Polentarutti N, Sessa C, et al: Tumoricidal activity of macrophages isolated from human ascitic and solid ovarian carcinomas: Augmentation by interferon, lymphokines and endotoxin. *Int J Cancer* 28:143–151, 1981.
15. Hanna MG Jr, Peters LC: Immunotherapy of established micrometastases with a bacillus Calmette-Guérin tumor cell vaccine. *Cancer Res* 38:204–209, 1978.
16. Murray D, Hreno A, Dutton J, et al: Prognosis in colon cancer: A pathologic reassessment. *Arch Surg* 110:908–913, 1975.
17. Jass JR, Atkin WS, Cuzick I, et al: The grading of rectal cancer: Histological perspectives and a multivariate analysis of 447 cases. *Histopathology* 10:437–459, 1986.
18. Carlon CA, Fabris G, Arslan-Pagnini C, et al: Prognostic correlations of operable carcinoma of the rectum. *Dis Colon Rectum* 28:47–50, 1985.
19. Svennevig JL, Lunde OC, Holter J, et al: Lymphoid infiltration and prognosis in colorectal carcinoma. *Br J Cancer* 49:375–377, 1984.
20. Hoover HC Jr, Peters LC, Brandhorst JS, et al: Therapy of spontaneous metastases with an autologous tumor vaccine in a guinea pig model. *J Surg Res* 30:409–415, 1981.
21. Hanna MG Jr, Peters LC: Specific immunotherapy of established visceral micrometastases by BCG–tumor cell vaccine alone or as an adjunct to surgery. *Cancer* 42:2613–2625, 1978.
22. Hanna MG, Brandhorst JS, Peters L: Active-specific immunotherapy of residual micrometastasis: An evaluation of sources, doses and ratios of BCG with tumor cells. *Cancer Immunol Immunother* 7:165–173, 1979.
23. Hoover HC Jr, Surdyke M, Dangel R, et al: Delayed cuta-

neous hypersensitivity to autologous tumor cells in colorectal cancer patients immunized with an autologous tumor cell: Bacillus Calmette-Guérin vaccine. *Cancer Res* 44:1671–1676, 1984.

24. Hoover HC, Surdyke MG, Brandhorst JS, et al: Five year follow-up of a controlled trial of active specific immunotherapy in colorectal cancer. *Proc ASCO* 9:106, 1990.
25. Jessup MJ, McBride CM, Ames FC, et al: Active specific immunotherapy of Dukes' B2 and C colorectal carcinoma comparison of two doses of the vaccine. *Cancer Immunol Immunother* 21:233–239, 1986.
26. Lehner B, Schlag P, Liebrich W, et al: Postoperative active specific immunization in curatively resected colorectal cancer patients with a virus modified autologous tumor cell vaccine. *Cancer Immunol Immunother* 32:173–178, 1990.
27. Dye ES, North RJ: T cell-mediated immunosuppression as an obstacle to adoptive immunotherapy of the P815 mastocytoma and its metastases. *J Exp Med* 154:1033–1042, 1981.
28. Bubenik J, Indorva M: Cancer immunotherapy using local interleukin-2 administration. *Immunol Lett* 16:305–310, 1987.
29. Bubenik J, Simova J, Jandlova T: Immunotherapy of cancer using local administration of lymphoid cells transformed by IL-2 cDNA and constitutively producing IL-2. *Immunol Lett* 23:287–292, 1990.
30. Bubenik J, Voitenok NN, Kieler J, et al: Local administration of cells containing an inserted IL-2 gene and producing IL-2 inhibits growth of human tumors in Nu/Nu mice. *Immunol Lett* 19:279–282, 1988.
31. Fearon ER, Pardol DM, Itaya T, et al: IL-2 production by tumor cells bypasses T helper function in the generation of an antitumor response. *Cell* 60:297–403, 1990.
32. Gansbacher B, Zier K, Daniels B: Interleukin 2 gene transfer into tumor cells abrogates tumorigenicity and induces protective immunity. *J Exp Med* 172:1217–1224, 1990.
33. Miyatake SI, Nishihara K, Kikuchi H, et al.: Efficient tumor suppression by glioma-specific murine cytotoxic T lymphocytes transfected with IFN-γ gene. *J Natl Cancer Inst* 82:217–220, 1990.
34. Asher AL, Mule JJ, Kasid A, et al: Murine tumor cells transduced with the gene for TNF-α: Evidence for paracrine immune effects of TNF against tumors. *J Immunol* 146:3227–3234, 1991.
35. Colombo MP, Ferrari G, Stoppacciaro S, et al: Granulocyte CSF gene transfer suppresses tumorigenicity of a murine adenocarcinoma in vivo. *J Exp Med* 173:889–897, 1991.
36. Blankenstein T, Qin Z, Uberla K, et al: Tumor suppression after tumor cell-targeted tumor necrosis factor-α gene transfer. *J Exp Med* 173:1047–1052, 1991.
37. Restifo NP, Spiess PJ, Karp SE, et al: A nonimmunogenic sarcoma transduced with the cDNA for IFN-• elicits CD8 + T cells against the wild-type tumor: Correlation with antigen presentation capability. *J Exp Med* 175(6):1423–1431, 1992.
38. Golumbek PT, Lazenby AJ, Levitsky HI, et al: Treatment of established renal cancer by tumor cells engineered to secrete interleukin-4. *Science* 254:713–716, 1991.
39. Marincola RM, Karp SE, Mule JJ, et al: Injection of murine sarcoma cells engineered to secrete human TNF-alpha causes regression of established pulmonary metastases. *Proc Am Assoc Cancer Res* 33:350, 1992.
40. Yron I, Wood TA, Spiess PJ, et al: In vitro growth of murine T cells: V. The isolation and growth of lymphoid cells infiltrating syngeneic solid tumors. *J Immunol* 125:238–245, 1980.
41. Morgan DA, Ruscetti FW, Gallo RG: Selective in vitro growth of T-lymphocytes from normal bone marrows. *Science* 193:1007–1008, 1976.
42. Rosenstein M, Yron I, Kaufmann Y, et al: Lymphokine-activated killer cells: Lysis of fresh syngeneic natural killer–resistant murine tumor cells by lymphocytes cultured in interleukin-2. *Cancer Res* 44:1946–1953, 1984.
43. Topalian SL, Rosenberg SA: Adoptive cellular therapy: Basic principles, in Devita VT, Hellman S, Rosenberg SA (eds): *Biologic Therapy of Cancer.* Philadelphia, Lippincott, 1991, pp 178–196.
44. LaFreniere R, Rosenberg SA: Successful immunotherapy of murine experimental hepatic metastases with lymphokine-activated killer cells and recombinant interleukin-2. *Cancer Res* 45:3735–3740, 1985.
45. Mule JJ, Shu S, Schwarz SL, et al: Adoptive immunotherapy of established pulmonary metastases with LAK cells and recombinant interleukin-2. *Science* 225:1487–1489, 1984.
46. Hawkin MJ: PPO updates IL-2/LAK. *Pract Oncol* 3(8):1–14, 1989.
47. Lotze MT, Matory YL, Rayner AA, et al: Clinical effects and toxicity of interleukin-2 in patients with cancer. *Cancer* 58:2764–2772, 1986.
48. Rosenberg SA, Lotze MT, Yang JC, et al: Prospective randomized trial of high-dose interleukin-2 alone or in conjunction with lymphokine-activated killer cells for the treatment of patients with advanced cancer. *J Natl Cancer Inst* 85:622–632, 1993.
49. Howard M, Farrar J, Hilfiker M, et al: Identification of a T cell derived B cell growth factor distinct form interleukin-2. *J Exp Med* 155:914, 1982.
50. Kawakami Y, Custer MC, Rosenberg SA, et al: IL-4 regulates IL-2 induction of lymphokine activated killer activity from human lymphocytes. *J Immunol* 142:3452–3461, 1989.
51. Lotze MT: Transplantation and adoptive cellular therapy of cancer: The role of T-cell growth factors. *Cell Transpl* 2:33–47, 1993.
52. Namen AE, Schmierer AE, March CJ, et al: B cell precursor growth promoting activity. *J Exp Med* 167:988–1002, 1988.
53. Edington HDJ, Lotze MT: Interleukin-7 induces weak LAK activity from murine splenocytes late after culture when compared to interleukin-2. *J Cell Biochem* 15F(suppl):145, 1991.
54. Jicha DL, Mule JJ, Rosenberg S: Interleukin-7 generates antitumor CTL against murine sarcomas with efficacy in cellular adoptive immunotherapy. *J Exp Med* 174:1511–1521, 1991.
55. Mosman TR, Cherwinski MW, Bond MA, et al: Two types of murine helper T cell clones: I. Definition according to profiles of lymphokine activities and secreted proteins. *J Immunol* 136:238, 1986.
56. O'Garra AG, Stapleton V, Pearce J, et al: Production of cytokines by mouse B cells: B lymphomas and normal B cells produce interleukin-10. *Int Immunol* 2:821, 1990.
57. Fiorentino DF, Bond MW, Mosman TR: Two types of mouse T-helper cell: IV. Th_2 clones secrete a factor that inhibits cytokine production by Th_1 clones. *J Exp Med* 170:2081–2088, 1989.
58. Moore KW, Vieira DF, Fiorentino ML, et al: Homology of cytokine synthesis inhibitory factor (IL-10) to the Epstein-Barr virus gene BCRF1. *Science* 248:1230–1234, 1990.
59. Chen WF, Zlotnik A: IL-10: A novel cytotoxic T cell differentiation factor. *J Immunol* 147:528–534, 1991.
60. Stern AS, Podlaski FJ, Hulmes JD, et al: Purification to homogeneity and partial characterization of cytotoxic lymphocyte maturation factor from B-lymphoblastoid cells. *Proc Natl Acad Sci USA* 87:6806–6812, 1990.
61. Nastala CL, Edington H, McKinney TG, et al: Interleukin-12 mediates potent anti-tumor effects in murine models in association with elevated serum nitric oxide and interferon-γ. (manuscript in preparation)
62. Ortlado JR, Mason A, Overton R: Lymphokine-activated killer cells: Analysis of progenitor and effectors. *J Exp Med* 164:1193–1205, 1986.

63. Herberman RB, Hiserodt JC, Vujanovic N, et al: Lymphokine-activated killer cell activity: Characteristics of effector cells and their progenitors in blood and spleen. *Immunol Today* 8:178–181, 1987.
64. Melder RJ, Whiteside TL, Vujanovic NL, et al: A new approach to generating antitumor effectors for adoptive immunotherapy using human adherent lymphokine-activated killer cells. *Cancer Res* 48:3461–3469, 1988.
65. Schwarz RE, Vujanovic NL, Hiserodt JC: Enhanced antimetastatic activity of lymphokine-activated killer cells purified and expanded by their adherence to plastic. *Cancer Res* 49:1441–1446, 1989.
66. Whiteside TL, Ernstoff MS, Nair S, et al: *In vitro* generation and *in vivo* effects of adherent-lymphokine activated killer (A-LAK) cells and IL-2 in patients with solid tumors, in RE Schmidt (ed): *Natural Killer Cells: Biology and Clinical Application: 6th International NK Cell Workshop*. Switzerland, Basel, Karger, 1990, pp 293–302.
67. Topalian SL, Rosenberg SA: Adoptive cellular therapy: Basic principles, in DeVita VT, Hellman S, Rosenberg SA (eds): *Biologic Therapy of Cancer.* Philadelphia, Lippincott, 1991, pp 178–196.
68. Spiess PJ, Yank JC, Rosenberg SA: In vivo antitumor activity of tumor infiltration lymphocytes expanded in recombinant interleukin-2. *J Natl Cancer Inst* 79:1067–1075, 1987.
69. Shu S, Chou T, Rosenberg SA: Generation from tumor-bearing mice of lymphocytes with in vivo therapeutic efficacy. *J Immunol* 139:295–304, 1987.
70. Topalian SL, Rosenberg SA: Tumor infiltrating lymphocytes: Evidence for specific immune reactions against growing cancers in mice and humans, in Devita VT, Hellman S, Rosenberg SA (eds): *Important Advances in Oncology*. Philadelphia, Lippincott, 1991, pp 19–41.
71. Griffith KD, Read EJ, Carasquillo CS, et al: In vivo distribution of adoptively transfered indium-111 labeled tumor infiltrating lymphocytes and peripheral blood lymphocytes in patients with metastatic melanoma. *J Natl Cancer Inst* 81:1709–1717, 1989.
72. Fisher B, Packard BS, Read EJ, et al: Tumor localization of adoptively transferred indium-111 labeled tumor infiltrating lymphocytes in patients with metastatic melanoma. *J Clin Oncol* 7:250–261, 1989.
73. Evans R: Macrophages and the tumor bearing host. *Br J Cancer* 28(suppl 1):19–25, 1973.
74. Bennet B: Specific suppression of tumor growth by isolated peritoneal macrophages from immunized mice. *J Immunol* 95:656–664, 1965.
75. Tagliabue AA, Mantovani A, Kilgallen M, et al: Natural cytotoxicity of mouse monocytes and macrophages. *J Immunol* 122:2363–2370, 1979.
76. Fidler IJ, Kleinerman ES: Lymphokine activated human blood monocytes destroy tumor cells but not normal cells under cocultivation conditions. *J Clin Oncol* 2:937–943, 1984.
77. Mantovani A, Dean JH, Jerrells TR, et al: Augmentation of tumoricidal activity of human monocytes and macrophages by lymphokines. *Int J Cancer* 25:691–699, 1980.
78. Fidler IJ, Barnes Z, Fogler WE, et al: Involvement of macrophages in the eradication of established metastases following intravenous injection of liposomes containing macrophage activations. *Cancer Res* 42:496–501, 1982.
79. Liotta L, Gattozzi C, Kleinerman J, et al: Reduction of tumor cell entry into vessels by BCG activated macrophages. *Br J Cancer* 36:639–641, 1977.
80. Edington HD, Stevenson HC, Sugarbaker PH: Local-regional approach to peritoneal carcinomatosis combining cytoreductive surgery with adoptive immunotherapy utilizing gamma interferon activated autologous monocytes, in Aigner J (ed): *Regional Cancer Treatment*. Basel, Karger, 1988.
81. Faradji A, Bohbot A, Frost H: Phase I study of liposomal MTP-PE-activated autologous monocytes administered intraperitoneally to patients with peritoneal carcinomatosis. *J Clin Oncol* 9:1251–1260, 1991.
82. Foster JH, Ensminger WF: Treatment of metastatic cancer to the liver, in Devita VT, Hellman S, Rosenberg SA (eds): *Principles and Practice of Oncology*. Philadelphia, Lippincott, 1985, pp 2117–2132.

CHAPTER 95

Monoclonal Antibodies in the Therapy of Colorectal Cancer

Chaitanya R. Divgi
Steven M. Larson

The first antibodies to be infused in humans were directed against carcinoembryonic antigen (CEA), which is expressed in increased amounts in colonic cancer. Subsequently, the largest number of clinical studies with monoclonal antibodies (mAbs) has been in the diagnosis and treatment of colorectal carcinoma. These studies have established "proof of principle," ie., that monoclonal antibodies can selectively target tumor. As a result, several ongoing trials are being carried out with a view to determining whether antibodies have any utility in the therapy of colorectal carcinoma.

As with chemotherapy, the early encouraging clinical results with therapeutic antibodies have been in the treatment of nonsolid tumors such as B-cell lymphoma and myelogenous leukemia, where significant cytoreduction without accompanying toxicity has been reported. Encouraging results have also been seen in immunotherapy of neuroblastoma, a pediatric solid tumor, where prolonged clinical remissions have been achieved. While there are important biological differences between nonsolid and solid tumors with respect to access of the therapeutic modality to the cytotoxic agent, these results have provided new impetus to the study of cancer immunotherapy using mAbs.

Most mAbs used in therapy trials have been conjugated with radionuclides. Radioimmunotherapy (RIT) with mAbs labeled with large doses of radioactivity [either iodine-131 (^{131}I) or yttrium-90 (^{90}Y)] has largely been limited to phase I trials. These have shown that there is little or no toxicity associated with the mAb; that toxicity with the radioimmunoconjugate may be predicted by the nature of the radionuclide and is largely hematopoietic; and that murine mAbs are limited to single use because of their immunogenicity. No major clinical responses have been reported. Immunotoxins, monoclonal antibodies to which toxins such as ricin or *Pseudomonas* exotoxin have been conjugated, have also been reported to cause prolonged major responses in patients with B-cell lymphoma. Trials with unconjugated mAbs have been fewer. Adjuvant administration of mAb 17-1A in patients with colorectal cancer has been shown to significantly increase both disease-free and overall survival, despite (or perhaps due to) an immune response by the host.

Current mAbs are murine in origin and provoke an immune response (human anti-mouse Ab, or HAMA) in the host that precludes effective utilization more than once. Biotechnological developments have made available potentially nonimmunogenic antigen-binding proteins, including humanized mAbs (where the antigen-binding portions of the murine mAb are grafted onto a human immunoglobulin backbone) and single-chain antigen-binding proteins (sFv), where the antigen-binding portions are produced in nonmammalian cells, with suitable linkers to allow conjugation of toxins, drugs, or radionuclides. These should permit repeated use of these "antigen-binding proteins," permitting multiple radioimmunodiagnostic and therapeutic studies.

The increasing use of murine mAbs in the clinical setting with associated HAMA formation means that in vitro assays that utilize murine mAbs (including most serum CEA assays) may give erroneous results in patients who have received murine mAbs. This fact should be borne in mind whenever a serum serologic assay gives results that do not fit the clinical situation.

There is little doubt that mAbs will be increasingly used in the treatment of colorectal cancer, as they offer specificity without significant toxicity. The development of "tailored" antigen-binding molecules will result in the emergence of various nonimmunogenic molecules for diagnosis (where smaller more rapidly clearing radiolabeled molecules will be used to screen for disease) and for therapy (where these molecules will be utilized by themselves, for their immunologic effector function, or conjugated with cytotoxic agents). While the overall field is still in its infancy, principles of mAb behavior in humans have emerged that will direct future development. These principles are elucidated and possible directions outlined in the following review.

OVERVIEW

Antibodies, especially mAbs, appear to be ideal for both the detection (when attached with appropriate radionuclides) and therapy (when attached with radionuclides, toxins, or chemotherapeutic agents) of cancer, as they offer unique characteristics of specificity and nontoxicity. Antibodies against colorectal cancer antigens have been studied for almost two decades. The largest number of clinical trials utilizing radiolabeled Abs have been carried out in colorectal carcinoma. Since the pioneering work of Goldenberg et al.[1] and of Mach et al.,[2] utilizing Abs against CEA, over 100 clinical trials have been carried out utilizing Abs against antigens expressed preferentially in colorectal carcinoma.[3,4]

Several broad statements regarding the overall development of the field may be made. Carcinoembryonic antigen has been the antigen system against which the vast majority of Abs, mostly murine, have been developed.[1–5] TAG-72 (a tumor associated glycoprotein found in most mucinous adenocarcinomas) is another secreted antigen against which mAbs have been studied.[6,7] In fact, the first mAb approved by the Food and Drug Administration (FDA), ONCOSCINT, for use in the detection of metastatic extrahepatic abdominal colorectal cancer, is ^{111}In-labeled B72.3, a murine anti-TAG-72 mAb. Another prominent secreted antigen studied has been 17-1A. Monoclonal Abs against nonsecreted antigens have been fewer, prominent among them being 19-9[8] and A33.[9]

Phase I therapeutic clinical trials with anticolonic cancer mAbs are in the process of completion.[10–16] These have utilized both unlabeled and radiolabeled murine mAbs. Therapeutic trials have shown little or no toxicity related to the mAb; dose-limiting toxicity with radiolabeled mAbs is hematopoietic. No major responses have been seen in established disease. Intriguing early work from Riethmüller et al.[16] suggests that adjuvant therapy of metastatic colorectal carcinoma with 17-1A, a murine IgG_{2a} against a secreted cell-surface antigen expressed in secretory endothelium, significantly improves disease-free survival.

A common problem with murine Abs has been the development, after initial injection, of a human anti-murine Ab (HAMA) response in the patient, precluding repeat administration.[17,18] Immunosuppressive agents have been and are continuing to be used to alleviate the response, with uncertain success. The issue has been approached in three ways: (1) by decreasing the size of the antigen-reactive molecule, either by fragmentation of the intact immunoglobulin to its reactive fragments (by enzyme digestion or genetic engineering), with the expectation that the smaller molecule will be cleared more rapidly and thus be less immunogenic; (2) by replacing non-antigen-binding portions of the murine immunoglobulin with human sequences, by genetic engineering, resulting in chimeric Abs with a murine Fv on a human framework, or humanized Abs where only the complementarity-determining regions (CDRs) are murine in origin; and (3) by developing human Abs by obtaining human Ab-producing lymphocytes capable of production in vitro. These approaches all appear promising and will all probably be of utility depending upon the specific clinical situation.

Indeed, there is little doubt that mAbs will play a major role in the therapy of colorectal cancer. Several general principles regarding major antigen systems, choice of radiolabel, selection of antigen-binding protein, and clinical role may be proposed:

1. Density and distribution of antigen expression in tumor tissue is critical to adequate Ab targeting. Homogeneously expressed nonsecreted antigens may be the ideal targets.
2. The degree of antigen expression in nontumor tissue, if any, will determine the amount of mAb necessary for adequate tumor targeting. Moreover, differential Ab uptake by tumor (tumor-nontumor ratio) needs to be considerable both for adequate tumor visualization [in radioimmunodetection (RID)] as well as for immunotherapy.

These above principles serve to underscore the central role of immunohistochemistry in the preclinical development of mAbs and the importance of dose-escalation studies in the clinical assessment of mAbs.

3. Immunogenicity of murine Ab limits, if not obviates, repeat infusions. This mandates development of less immunogenic molecules.

ANTIGENS/ANTIBODIES

Monoclonal Antibodies

Antibodies are part of a family of immunoglobulins produced in mammals by B lymphocytes. The development of hybridoma technology by Kohler and Milstein[19] in 1975 made it possible to produce large quantities of mAbs which recognized human tumor-associated antigens. Most currently used Abs belong to the IgG subclass. The IgG molecule, with a molecular weight between 150 and 180 kDa, consists of two heavy and two light polypeptide chains connected by disulfide bonds. Pepsin splits part of the constant region (F_C) to produce an $F(ab')_2$ fragment. The enzyme papain splits the Ab molecule into one Fc fragment and two Fab' fragments.

The first clinical trials using radiolabeled Abs were carried out using Abs against CEA. Goldenberg et al.,[1] in 1978, used radioiodinated polyclonal anti-CEA Abs from a variety of species in patients with metastatic colonic cancer and showed that in vivo localization of Ab in tumor could be ascertained by gamma camera imaging. Mach et al.,[2] in 1981, showed that ^{131}I-labeled mAb against CEA localized in gastrointestinal neoplasms and that detection rates could be improved by single photon emission computed tomography. There have been a large number of clinical trials subsequently in several distinct antigenic systems in colonic cancer.

A majority of clinical trials have been carried out using mAbs against *secreted antigens,* especially CEA. TAG-72 is a large (> 1000-kDa) glycoprotein expressed in most mucinous and differentiated adenocarcinomas, especially colonic. B72.3 is the first mAb to be developed against TAG-72,[6,20] and "second-generation" mAbs of higher affinity and comparable biodistribution (e.g., CC49) are currently being tested in radioimmunodetection and radiotherapy trials.[21,22] Of note is the fact that expression of CEA and TAG-72 antigens in tissue can be studied using paraffin-fixed tissue. 17-1A reacts against a secreted antigen (epithelial surface antigen, or ESA) found in most secretory epithelium.[23] Monoclonal Ab 17-1A has been used in clinical trials, both in the detection and therapy of colon cancer.

There have been fewer studies with antibodies against *nonsecreted cell surface antigens*. Prominent among them have been 19-9 and A33. The former is a nonsecreted blood-group-related antigen that has been studied in limited clinical trials,[8] while the latter has been extensively studied in our institution both in RID[9] and phase I RIT[11] trials. It reacts against a high-molecular-weight antigen found on more than 95 percent of colonic cancers as well as on the normal colonocyte. The antigen-Ab complex appears to be internalized by macropinocytosis into the cell, theoretically allowing efficient intracellular delivery of toxins and chemotherapeutic agents into the cell. In contrast to CEA, expression of the A33 antigen can only be studied in fresh frozen tissue.

Antibodies against *stromal antigens* offer exciting diagnostic and therapeutic possibilities, as there is a considerable stromal framework (consisting largely of activated fibroblasts) in most colonic carcinomas. F19 is an mAb developed by Rettig et al.[24] at this center that reacts against the stromal component of most epithelial carcinomas. A recently concluded trial with ^{131}I-F19 in presurgical metastatic colonic cancer patients showed excellent targeting to tumor in most cases, with no significant uptake by normal tissue.[25]

CEA

Jean-Pierre Mach and his group[2,26] were the first to study mAbs against CEA in patients with colorectal cancer; the group at the University of Lausanne is in the forefront of radioimmunotherapy with ^{131}I-labeled anti-CEA mAbs.[15] There have been no major responses in their therapy trials, and, as in other trials, dose-limiting toxicity has been hematopoietic. The group is continuing to work with less immunogenic chimeric and humanized mAbs to determine whether dose fractionation via multiple infusions of radiolabeled mAb can result in significant responses. Goldenberg et al.[27] in this country are continuing to look at the radioimmunotherapeutic potential of Ab fragments against the CEA antigen and have reported that with the Fab' molecule, there is little or no induction of an antimurine immune response.

TAG-72

We have completed a phase I radioimmunotherapy trial with ^{131}I-labeled CC49, a murine IgG_1 mAb that reacts against the TAG-72 antigen with higher affinity than B72.3.[28] There were no major responses. The maximum tolerated dose in heavily pretreated patients was 75 mCi/m^2. Dose-limiting toxicity has been hematopoietic. Prior chemotherapy influences the severity of marrow depression. We modified the trial to include patients minimally pretreated with chemotherapy; the maximum tolerated dose in this latter group was 90 mCi/m^2. Figure 95-1 shows a patient's whole-body scan a week after treatment with ^{131}I-CC49. Notice the excellent uptake in sites of known disease.

A33

A33 is a murine IgG_{2a} that reacts against a high-molecular-weight surface antigen found on over 95 percent of colorectal cancers studied as well as on normal colonocytes. We are currently evaluating its role in radioimmunotherapy. With ^{131}I-labeled A33, dose-limiting hematopoietic toxicity and maximum tolerated dose were similar to those seen with CC49 (i.e., 75 mCi/m^2).[29] Since A33 is internalized into the cell following interaction with antigen,[30] we evaluated the utility of ^{125}I-A33 in radioimmunotherapy: ^{125}I decays via electron capture, resulting in the emission of a burst of energy close (usually 3 to 4 cell diameters) to the site of decay.[31] At doses of up to 300 mCi/m^2, there

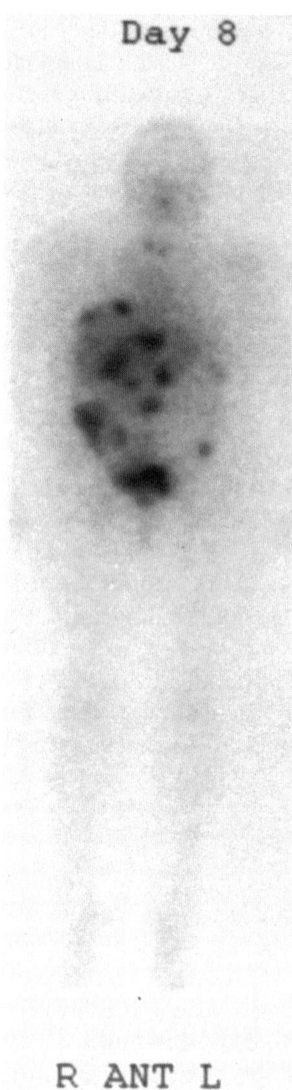

FIG. 95-1. Anterior whole-body planar gamma camera image taken 8 days after infusion of 130 mCi ^{131}I-CC49 in a patient with metastatic colonic carcinoma. Note the excellent uptake in sites of disease in the abdomen. Most of the peritoneal disease was not visualized on a companion CT scan.

has been no significant toxicity: dose escalation is ongoing.

17-1A

Monoclonal Ab 17-1A has been studied in several clinical trials, both its murine (IgG_{2a}) and chimeric (IgG_3) forms have been studied. It reacts against an antigen found on epithelial secretory surfaces (hence named *epithelial surface antigen* by some) that is shed into serum.

Riethmüller et al. (Ref. 16 and personal communication, 1993) found that disease-free survival was significantly increased in colonic cancer patients who received adjuvant immunotherapy with mAb 17-1A, both in its IgG_3 and IgG_{2a} forms. Their data hold promise for adjuvant immunotherapy; humanized mAbs may further improve the utility of adjuvant immunotherapy, although Riethmüller's data (personal communication, 1993) suggest that survival is longer in patients who develop high titers of antimurine antibodies (the trial involves multiple infusions of the murine mAbs).

Immunotherapy

Antibodies can be used in immunotherapy in several ways. By themselves, mAbs have been studied for possible activation of *immunologic effector function*. The most notable such trial has been that of Riethmüller et al. (personal communication, 1993), who have used mAb 17-1A, a murine IgG_{2a} with complement activation properties, in an adjuvant trial in patients with colonic cancer. They have reported increased disease-free survival, with toxicity being limited to allergic signs and symptoms following repeat infusions. While *immunotoxins* and *chemoimmunoconjugates* are being studied in the preclinical setting, no clinical trials have as yet been initiated in colorectal cancer. It is worth mentioning, however, that trials of various forms of ricin, a potent immunotoxin, conjugated with murine mAbs, are being conducted in patients with B-cell lymphoma, with encouraging initial clinical results.

Most immunotherapy trials have been conducted using *radioimmunoconjugates,* where radionuclides are attached to Abs, permitting selective delivery by Ab of cytotoxic radioactivity to tumor sites. The radionuclides used in clinical trials thus far are detailed below.

Radionuclides

Most therapeutic radionuclides in current clinical use emit cytotoxic beta-minus (β^-) radiation. Beta radiation results in the deposition of low energy over relatively long distances (2 to 4 mm) and is therefore described as low *linear energy transfer* (LET) radiation. Alpha or electron capture radiation, by contrast, are high LET types of radiation and deposit relatively large amounts of radiation over small (20- to 50-μm) distances. Iodine-131 (^{131}I) and yttrium-90 (^{90}Y) are two nuclides studied in β^- radioimmunotherapy trials. While ^{131}I has been used in numerous trials, ^{90}Y has been less extensively studied, presumably because of difficulties regarding stable conjugation of radiometal to antibody. At present, ^{125}I, which decays by electron capture with consequent high LET radiation, is being studied at Memorial Sloan-Kettering Cancer Center and at the University of Alabama in Birmingham in phase I radioimmunotherapy trials; it is conjugated with mAbs which internalize following antigen-antibody interaction. Work by Adelstein and colleagues[31] has demonstrated that for high-LET radionuclides to have cytotoxic potential, the site of decay should be at or near the nucleus; electron capture decay occurring at the cell surface is much less cytotoxic than comparable β^- radiation. As of now, there are no other therapeutic trials utilizing high-LET-decaying radionuclides, presumably because no other suitable internalizing mAbs have been identified. For the same reason, there are no immunotoxin trials in colonic cancer, as the toxin must be internalized to be cytotoxic.

Radioiodine

Perhaps the most commonly used iodine isotope is ^{131}I. It is easily available, relatively inexpensive, and easy to attach to antibodies. Its $T_{1/2}$ of 8 days makes it possible to study the kinetics of antibody uptake by target tissue over time by external imaging; its beta-minus emission makes it a useful agent for radioimmunotherapy. The radionuclide, however, has some disadvantages. The $T_{1/2}$ of 8 days results in significant radiation dose to normal organs, limiting total dose. The high gamma-ray energy of 364 keV necessitates special collimation for current gamma cameras. Finally, dehalogenation in vivo necessitates administration of blocking quantities of stable iodine (as Lugol's solution), despite which there is uptake of radioactivity in thyroid and stomach.

Iodine-125 has been extensively used to label antibodies. Its low photon energies preclude external gamma-camera imaging at diagnostically acceptable doses; however, these same low photon energies are ideal for autoradiography as well as for intraoperative detection using gamma-detector probes. Moreover, its high LET radiation (considerably cytotoxic over a few cell diameters) may make it the ideal radionuclide for radioimmunotherapy with internalizing mAbs. Iodine-124 has an energetic decay scheme and a $T_{1/2}$ of approximately 4 days; it emits positrons which can be detected by positron emission tomography (PET) and emits Auger electrons upon decay, raising interesting therapeutic possibilities. The nuclide, however, must be produced in specially configured cyclotrons. Attachment of this nuclide to antibodies is still experimental, though preliminary results are promising.

Radiometals

Yttrium-90 is a radiometal that can be attached to monoclonal antibodies by chelation, the same method used for the attachment of ^{111}In, although it is as yet unclear whether chelates suitable for ^{111}In conjugation to mAbs work as well for ^{90}Y (the reverse is believed to be true).[32] Other radiometals being considered for radioimmunotherapy include gallium-66 (^{66}Ga), a positron emitter, that, like ^{124}I, decays by electron capture. Lutetium-167, a lanthanide that can also be attached to mAbs by chelation, has also been used in a radioimmunotherapy trial in patients with colorectal cancer. Dose-limiting toxicity with these, as with radioiodine, has been myelosuppression. No major responses have been seen in colorectal cancer, though there have been encouraging results in patients with metastatic ovarian cancer treated intraperitoneally with ^{90}Y-labeled HMFG1, a murine antimucin antibody.

Rhenium

Rhenium-186 (^{186}Re) and rhenium-188 are nuclides that decay by β^- emission and can be conjugated to antibodies either directly or indirectly via a linker. Development of methodology permitting stable conjugation of technetium-99m (^{99m}Tc) to mAbs had kindled interest in the feasibility of using ^{186}Re for therapy, especially since this nuclide has not only more energetic β^- emission than ^{131}I but also a low-energy gamma emission permitting imaging and biodistribution studies. ^{186}Re HEDP is currently being used for palliation of bone pain in patients with metastatic skeletal disease. There are currently no clinical trials using ^{186}Re-labeled mAbs in colorectal cancer.

Labeling of Nuclides to Antibodies

Most current radioiodination methods involve iodination of tyrosyl residues found throughout the Ab molecule. This is accomplished either through liquid-phase interactions with agents such as chloramine T, or with solid-phase reagents such as iodogen. These methods are easy and reproducible and have been used extensively in clinical trials. They suffer from two important drawbacks: (1) dehalogenation in vivo can be considerable and (2) there may be significant loss in immunoreactivity (see below) as tyrosyl residues throughout the Ab molecule (i.e., including the antigen-binding region) are labeled. To overcome these drawbacks, several investigators have reported successful attachment of iodine to Abs via a conjugate, resulting in site-specific halogenation and decreased in vivo dehalogenation. These methods all involve initial iodination of a conjugate, which is then attached to the antibody, usually in a site-specific manner (i.e., to the Fc or hinge region of the molecule).

Yttrium-90 and other metal radionuclides are attached to antibodies via a chelating agent. Early chelation methods, usually with diethyleneamine tetraacetic acid, resulted in considerable hepatic uptake, presumably by transchelation of the radiometal in vivo. Subsequent progress in reducing hepatic uptake of radiolabel and decreasing the rate of radiometal detachment from the mAb in vivo has usually involved modifying the DTPA molecule or using macrocyclic chelates. It is still unclear whether a particular chelate will work as well with one radiometal (such as ^{111}In) as with another (such as ^{90}Y).[32]

CLINICAL TRIALS

Summary of Results in Other Tumors

Significant responses have been seen with immunotoxins against B-cell lymphoma, with a form of ricin (either the A chain or a blocked ricin molecule) being attached to internalizing Abs.[33] Phase I therapy trials carried out in B-cell lymphoma, neuroblastoma, and myelogenous leukemia have shown that there is significant cytoreduction of disease following treatment with radiolabeled Abs. Press et al.[34] at the University of Washington in Seattle have achieved complete clinical remissions in over 40 percent of patients with B-cell lymphoma,[34] as have Kaminski et al.[35] at the University of Michigan at Ann Arbor. The former group utilizes very high doses of ^{131}I labeled with antibodies against the CD21 and CD19 antigens, with resultant significant hematopoietic toxicity necessitating rescue with autologous bone marrow. The latter group has seen comparable results using nonhematotoxic doses of ^{131}I labeled with anti-CD20 antibody. It is as yet unclear whether using higher doses will result in longer-lasting remissions. One of the interesting features of B-cell lymphoma is that repeat administration of murine Abs frequently does not result in altered serum clearance; this is presumably because an antimouse response cannot be mounted by the (diseased) B-cells. An antimurine response is also not seen, for unclear reasons, in children with neuroblastoma treated with ^{131}I-labeled 3F8, an Ab developed by Nai-Kong Cheung. Immunotherapy with 3F8 has been shown to be effective in the treatment of stage IV neuroblastoma, and initial results with ^{131}I-3F8 suggest that radioimmunotherapy with subsequent autologous marrow rescue (the marrow being purged ex vivo by chemotherapy) results in a greater percentage of clinical remissions (Nai-Kong Cheung, personal communication, 1993).

Schwartz et al.[36] at Memorial Sloan-Kettering Cancer Center recently reported on radioimmunotherapy of myelogenous leukemia using ^{131}I-M195, an Ab against the CD33 receptor. Significant *selective* cytoreduction was noted in almost all patients administered doses of 105 mCi/m^2 of radioiodine, with no organ toxicity. However, in this series there was HAMA development, precluding repeat administration of radioimmunotherapy.

Radioimmunotherapy has been carried out with intraperitoneal ^{90}Y-labeled HMFG1 in adjuvant patients with ovarian carcinoma.[37] As with other trials, myelosuppression was dose-limiting; the study suggested that disease-free survival was prolonged in these patients.

Immunotherapy of Colorectal Carcinoma

Current phase I therapy trials with conjugated mAbs have shown that there is no major toxicity associated with the immunoglobulin. Toxicity has been limited to the conjugate and in the case of radioimmunoconjugates is primarily hematopoietic, consisting of thrombocytopenia followed by neutropenia. While toxicity seen thus far has been reversible, it seems likely that marrow insult following radioimmunotherapy may be long-lasting, thus putting the patient at increased risk for hematopoietic toxicity following subsequent hematotoxic chemotherapy. Nonhematopoietic toxicity has not been seen (in those trials where autologous marrow rescue has been used).

The lack of major responses in phase I therapy trials utilizing mAbs in metastatic colorectal cancer, even at maximum tolerated doses, suggests that alternative approaches need to be studied and make it unlikely that currently available mAbs will be useful in the therapy of bulky disease. However, the development of rapidly clearing, nonimmunogenic antigen-binding proteins may make it possible to treat established inoperable disease, as may the advent of nonimmunogenic immunoglobulins capable of activating immunologic effector function.

The development of single-chain antigen-binding proteins (sFvs)[38] makes it likely that these agents, conjugated with radionuclides or drugs, may find a place for regional (e.g., hepatic arterial) therapy. Their smaller size should result in greater extraction of the immunoconjugate from the vascular system and also allow greater penetration into tumor.[39,40] The lack of immunogenicity of the small molecules will enable repeated infusion.

As with all solid tumors, regardless of the form of therapy considered, bulkier disease is difficult if not impossible to treat successfully. Adjuvant therapy with mAbs appears promising; further study in this regard is warranted, especially with nonimmunogenic mAbs. Riethmüller et al. (Riethmüller G., personal communication, 1993) have shown that there is significant increase in disease-free as well as overall survival in patients with colonic cancer. Their program involves multiple infusions of considerable amounts of unlabeled mAb in an adjuvant setting. While there is an HAMA response, they speculate that the anti-idiotypic response may in fact be responsible for the improved disease-free survival, perhaps by stimulating an anti-anti-idiotypic response in patients after multiple infusions. This, of course, would not be as significant with relatively nonimmunogenic humanized mAbs, but the repeated administration of appropriate humanized mAb in an adjuvant setting should provoke immunologic effector function and be perhaps as useful as preliminary data have shown.

Anecdotally, patients who have received specific mAbs may show significant response to subsequent chemotherapy (Kemeny N, personal communication, 1993). Combination chemo- and immunotherapy may prove useful in the treatment of established metastatic colorectal cancer, and suitable trials are being planned at Memorial Sloan-Kettering Cancer Center and elsewhere.

FUTURE THERAPEUTIC STRATEGIES

Three major facets of anticancer antibodies need further elucidation: affinity, immunogenicity, and serum clearance. Higher-affinity, faster clearing mAbs will probably increase differential delivery to tumor and improve visualization and therapeutic potential. Nonimmunogenic molecules will allow repeated administration for radioimmunodetection as well as immunotherapy. Major developments in this regard are outlined.

Human Antibodies

Steis et al.[41] have conducted clinical trials with anti–colonic cancer mAbs (IgM) utilizing Epstein-Barr virus–transformed peripheral blood lymphocytes obtained from immunized patients. These mAbs are less than ideal because of their large size (increasing serum half-life and perhaps preventing sufficient penetration into tumor), their not very high affinity, and problems associated with maintenance of Ab-producing colonies in tissue culture. The same group is now studying human IgGs against colonic carcinoma, with encouraging initial clinical results. Heterohybridomas using sensitized human B lymphocytes and myeloma cells, capable of producing human IgG, have been developed; clinical trials with these and other nonimmunogenic Abs, however, are at least a few years away. Further exploration of these novel methods to produce all-human mAbs is important, as these molecules will almost certainly not be immunogenic; sequencing of the human complementarity determining regions (CDRs; see below) will permit development of antigen-binding proteins of human origin with suitable clearance and affinity characteristics.

Genetically Engineered Antigen-Binding Proteins

It is now possible to determine the gene sequence for murine mAbs and to isolate the gene(s) responsible for the *CDR* as well as the *variable region (Fv)* of the murine immunoglobulin. Transfection of a suitable mammalian immunoglobulin-producing cell with the gene sequence for the Fv along with that for human immunoglobulin (IgG)–constant regions results in production of *chimeric* Ab. Generally, chimeric Abs are less immunogenic than their murine counterparts. However, their immunogenicity (resulting in the development of *human antichimeric Ab,* or *HACA*) as well as their serum clearance has been extremely variable.[42] Attention has thus now become focused on *humanized* mAbs, with murine CDRs on a human IgG backbone. Clinical trials are being carried out with humanized mAbs in Hodgkin's disease, myelogenous leukemia, and lymphoma; these have shown that the Ab is not immunogenic. It appears likely, based on data available regarding endogenous human IgG, that slow serum clearance may be a problem, though the trials carried out thus far in nonsolid tumors have shown no difference between the serum clearance of humanized Ab and that of its murine counterpart (Waldmann TA and Scheinberg DA, personal communication, 1993). Genetic engineering should make possible the development of "designer" proteins that have suitable clearance characteristics (e.g., by deletion of one or more constant regions) with/without suitable immunologic characteristics (e.g., human IgG_1 molecules when effector function is desired; human IfG_3 molecules if relatively rapid clearance without effector function is warranted; deletion of the CH2 region of the immunoglobulin molecule if rapid serum clearance is desired without significant diminution of effector function). Although the (murine) CDRs constitute less than 10 percent of the entire IgG molecule, HAHA may be a problem, although initial data from clinical trials with humanized mAbs in patients with hematologic malignancies have shown no evidence of HAHA or altered clearance upon repeat administration. Finally, Fc-receptor-mediated binding may cause nonspecific accumulation of humanized IdG_1 mAb in normal lymph nodes.[43]

Availability of the gene sequence for the antigen-binding protein and its transfection into suitable mammalian or bacterial cells makes theoretically possible the production of a host of antigen-binding proteins, ranging from intact immunoglobulin to CDR constructs. None has been studied in clinical trials to date. *Single-chain antigen-binding proteins (sFvs)* are constructs of CDR, produced by transfection of *Escherichia coli* with the CDR-encoding gene along with suitable linker genes.[37] These sFvs have been shown to clear the blood rapidly and specifically localize in xenograft models; unlike Fab' fragments, they are not retained in renal parenchyma.[39] In addition, penetration into tumor appears greater with these smaller molecules.[40] Clinical trials with these interesting constructs are planned, and they may eventually prove useful not only for rapid RID but also for regional if not systemic immunotherapy.

CONCLUSIONS

Monoclonal Abs offer the promise, for perhaps the first time, of selective targeting of therapeutic agents to cancer. Initial trials have shown that Ab administration is nontoxic; toxicity is limited to the conjugate attached to the antibody, being myelosuppression with radionuclides and hepatotoxicity with toxins such as ricin. It appears unlikely that there will be significant reduction of bulky disease with Abs against solid tumors, such as colonic cancer. However, adjuvant therapy with Abs appears promising, with increased disease-free survival reported in solid tumors, including ovarian and colorectal cancer. Multiple infusions of therapeutic Abs are necessary before any significant responses can be expected; with the development of newer, nonimmunogenic molecules, multiple infusions appear to be feasible. Immunotherapy will undoubtedly be a part of the therapeutic armamentarium of colonic cancer in the not-too-distant future.

REFERENCES

1. Goldenberg DM, Deland F, Kim E, et al: Use of radiolabeled antibodies to CEA for the detection and localization of diverse cancers by external photoscanning. *N Engl J Med* 298:1384–1388, 1978.
2. Mach J-P, Buchegger F, Forni M, et al: Use of radiolabeled monoclonal anti-CEA antibodies for the detection of human carcinomas by external photoscanning and tomoscintigraphy. *Immunol Today* 2:239–249, 1981.
3. Kramer EL, Larson SM: Tumor targeting with radiolabeled antibody for diagnosis and therapy. *Immunol Allergy Clin North Am* 11:301–339, 1991.
4. Goldenberg DM: Monoclonal antibodies in cancer detection and therapy. *Am J Med* 94:297–312, 1993.
5. Divgi CR, McDermott K, Griffin TW, et al: Lesion-by-lesion comparison of computerized tomography and indium-111-labeled monoclonal antibody C110 radioimmunoscintigraphy in colorectal carcinoma: A multicenter trial. *J Nucl Med* 34:1656–1661, 1993.
6. Johnson VG, Schlom J, Paterson AJ, et al: Analysis of a human tumor-associated glycoprotein (TAG-72) using monoclonal antibody B72.3. *Cancer Res* 46:850–857, 1986.
7. Colcher D, Esteban JM, Carrasquillo JA, et al: Quantitative analyses of selected radiolabeled monoclonal antibody localization in metastatic lesions of colorectal cancer patients. *Cancer Res* 47:1185–1189, 1987.
8. Hnatowich DJ, Griffin TW, Kosciuczyk C, et al: Pharmacokinetics of an indium-111 labeled monoclonal antibody in cancer patients. *J Nucl Med* 26:849–858, 1985.
9. Welt S, Divgi CR, Real FX, et al: Quantitative analysis of antibody localization in human metastatic colon cancer: A phase I study of monoclonal antibody A33. *J Clin Oncol* 8:1894–1906, 1990.
10. Divgi CR, Kemeny N, Cordon-Cardo C, et al: Phase I radioimmunotherapy trial with iodine-131 labeled monoclonal antibody CC49 in patients with metastatic colorectal carcinoma. *Proc AMSCO* 10:A699, 1991.
11. Welt S, Divgi CR, Kemeny N, et al: Phase I/II study of iodine-131 monoclonal antibody A33 in patients with advanced colorectal carcinoma. *Proc AMSCO* 11:A489, 1992.
12. Meredith RF, Khazaeli MB, Plott WE, et al: Phase I trial of iodine-131-chimeric B72.3 (human IgG4) in metastatic colorectal cancer. *J Nucl Med* 33:23–29, 1992.
13. Meredith RF, Khazaeli MB, Liu T, et al: Dose fractionation of radiolabeled antibodies in patients with metastatic colon cancer. *J Nucl Med* 33:1648–1653, 1992.
14. Britton KE, Buraggi GL, Bares R, et al: A brief guide to the practice of radioimmunoscintigraphy and radioimmunotherapy in cancer: Report of the European Association of Nuclear Medicine Task Group on the clinical utility of labeled antibodies. *Int J Biol Markers* 4:106–118, 1989.
15. Bichof-Delaloye A, Delaloye B: Diagnostic applications and therapeutic approaches with different preparations of anti-CEA antibodies. *Int J Biol Markers* 7:193–197, 1992.
16. Riethmüller G, Johnson JP: Monoclonal antibodies in the detection and therapy of micrometastatic epithelial cancers. *Curr Opin Immunol* 4:647–655, 1992.
17. Shawler DL, Bartholomew RM, Smith LM, Dillman RO: Human immune response to multiple injections of murine monoclonal IgG. *J Immunol* 135:1530–1535, 1985.
18. Blottiere HM, Douillard JY, Koprowski H, Steplewski Z: Immunoglobulin class and immunoglobulin G subclass analysis of human anti-mouse antibody response during monoclonal antibody treatment of cancer patients. *Cancer Res* 50:1051s–1054s, 1990.
19. Kohler G, Milstein C: Continuous cultures of fused cell secreting antibody of predefined specificity. *Nature* 256:495–497, 1975.
20. Colcher D, Esteban J, Carrasquillo JA, et al: Complementation of intracavitary and intravenous administration of a monoclonal antibody (B72.3) in patients with carcinoma. *Cancer Res* 47:4218–4224, 1987.
21. Gallinger S, Reilly RM, Kirsh JC, et al: Comparative dual label study of first and second generation antitumor-associated glycoprotein-72 monoclonal antibodies in colorectal cancer patients. *Cancer Res* 53:271–278, 1993.
22. Divgi CR, Scott AM, McDermott K, et al: Clinical comparison of radiolocalization of two monoclonal antibodies (mabs) against the tag-72 antigen. *Int J Appl Rad Biol (B)* 21:9–15, 1994.
23. Moldofsky PJ, Powe J, Mulhern CB Jr, et al: Metastatic colon carcinoma detected with radiolabeled F(ab'2) monoclonal antibody fragments. *Radiology* 149:549–555, 1983.
24. Rettig WJ, Garin-Chesa P, Beresford HR, et al: Cell-surface glycoproteins of human sarcomas: Differential expression in normal and malignant tissues and cultured cells. *Proc Natl Acad Sci USA* 85:3110–3114, 1988.
25. Welt S, Rettig WG, Divgi CR, et al: Phase I localization study of iodine-131-monoclonal antibody F19 detecting an activation antigen of neoplastic stroma. *Proc Annu Meet Am Assoc Cancer Res* 33:A1900, 1992.
26. Mach JP, Buchegger F, Pelegrin A, et al: Progress in radiolabeled monoclonal antibodies for diagnosis and therapy, in Fortner JG, Rhoads JE, (eds): *Accomplishments in Cancer Research*. Philadelphia, Lippincott, 1989, pp 222–256.
27. Goldenberg DM, Wlodkowski TJ, Sharkey RM, et al: Colorectal cancer imaging with iodine-123 labeled CEA monoclonal antibody fragments. *J Nucl Med* 34:61–70, 1993.
28. Divgi CR, Scott AM, Dantis L, et al: Phase I radioimmunotherapy trial with iodine-131-monoclonal antibody CC49 in metastatic colon cancer. *J Nucl Med,* in press, 1994.
29. Welt S, Divgi CR, Kemeny N, et al: Phase I/II radioimmunotherapy study with iodine-131-monoclonal antibody A33 in metastatic colon cancer. *J Clin Oncol,* in press, 1994.
30. Barendswaard EC, Welt S, Scott AM, et al: Therapy of human colon cancer transplants in nu/nu mice with iodine-125 and iodine-131-monoclonal antibody A33. *Proc Annu Meet Am Assoc Cancer Res* 34:A2844, 1993.
31. Kassis AI, Sastry KSR, Adelstein SJ: Intracellular localization of auger electron emitters: Biophysical dosimetry. *Radiat Prot Dosim* 13:245–248, 1985.
32. Gansow, OA, Brechbiel MW, Mirzadeh S, et al: Chelates and antibodies: Current methods and new directions. *Cancer Treat Res* 51:153–171, 1990.
33. Grossbard ML, Press OW, Appelbaum FR, et al: Monoclonal antibody-based therapies of lymphoma and leukemia. *Blood* 80:863–878, 1992.
34. Press OW, Eary JF, Appelbaum FR, et al: Radiolabeled-antibody therapy of B-cell lymphoma with autologous bone marrow support. *N Engl J Med* 329:1219–1224, 1993.
35. Kaminski MS, Zasadny KR, Francis IR, et al: Radioimmu-

notherapy of B-cell lymphoma with ^{131}I-B1 (anti-CD20) antibody. *N Engl J Med* 329:459–465, 1993.
36. Schwartz MA, Lovett DR, Redner A, et al: Dose-escalation trial of M195 labeled with iodine-131 for cytoreduction and marrow ablation in relapsed or refractory myeloid leukemias. *J Clin Oncol* 11:294–303, 1993.
37. Hird V, Maraveyas A, Snook D, et al: Adjuvant therapy of ovarian cancer with radioactive monoclonal antibody. *Br J Cancer* 68:403–406, 1993.
38. Bird RE, Hardman KD, Jacobson JW, et al: Single-chain antigen-binding proteins. *Science* 242:423–426, 1988.
39. Milenic DE, Yokota T, Filpula DR, et al: Construction, binding properties, metabolism, and tumor targeting of a single-chain Fv derived from the pancarcinoma monoclonal antibody CC49. *Cancer Res* 51:6363–6371, 1991.
40. Yokota T, Milenic DE, Whitlow M, et al: Microautoradiographic analysis of the normal organ distribution of radioiodinated single-chain Fv and other immunoglobulin forms. *Cancer Res* 53:3776–3783, 1993.
41. Steis RG, Carrasquillo JA, McCabe R, et al: Toxicity, immunogenicity, and tumor radioimmunodetecting ability of two human monoclonal antibodies in patients with metastatic colorectal carcinoma. *J Clin Oncol* 8:476–490, 1990.
42. LoBuglio AF, Wheeler RH, Trang J, et al: Mouse/human chimeric monoclonal antibody in man: Kinetics and immune response. *Proc Natl Acad Sci USA* 86:4220–4224, 1989.
43. Lubeck MD, Steplewski Z, Baglia F, et al: The interaction of murine IgG subclass proteins with human monocyte Fc receptors. *J Immunol* 135:1299–1304, 1985.

CHAPTER 96

Development of Generic Vaccines for Colorectal Carcinoma

Philip O. Livingston

HIGHLIGHTS

Colorectal carcinomas (CRC) have a rich variety of differentiation antigens and oncogene products which appear to be ideal targets for active specific immunotherapy with tumor vaccines. Recent advances in our ability to extract or synthesize carbohydrate antigens and to sequence, clone, and express genes for protein antigens raises the possibility that a polyvalent generic vaccine against CRC can be produced. Its immunogenicity will be greatly improved by the availability of conjugate and recombinant vector vaccine technologies and potent new immunologic adjuvants. Results of recently completed preclinical and clinical trials confirm the potential of this approach. In addition, improved disease-free interval and survival have been demonstrated in a small randomized trial of autologous colonic carcinoma vaccine. Attempts to confirm these results and to identify the relevant antigens for inclusion in generic vaccines are under way.

CONTROVERSIES

The first major controversy, or unknown, in the field of tumor vaccinology in general and CRC vaccinology in particular is whether differentiation antigens and wild-type *ras* and p53 gene products are relevant antigens for active specific immunization against CRC or whether distinct antigens (which may be different on each carcinoma and are not expressed on any normal tissues, such as the gene products resulting from *ras* and p53 mutations or mutations at other loci) are more important. In either case, once the relevant antigens are identified, their immunogenicity will be greatly augmented by approaches described in this chapter, and it is expected that a significant immune response against them will result. While most of the antigens of colorectal carcinomas will be recognized by B cells and all of the protein antigens are likely to be recognized on antigen-presenting cells by CD4+ (helper) T cells, the second major unknown is whether any relevant CRC antigens are bound by tumor-cell class I MHC molecules at the cell surface, where they would be necessary targets for cytotoxic T-cell attack. Specific 1: CD8+ T-cell activation resulting in cell-mediated cytotoxicity; 2: CD4+ T-cell activation resulting in macrophage activation, inflammatory reactions, and help for antibody production and cell-mediated cytotoxicity; or 3: B-cell activation resulting in IgM and IgG antibody production and consequently improved antigen presentation are all mechanisms capable of initiating rejection reactions. A third major unknown is which of these mechanisms are important for CRC rejection.

FUTURE DIRECTIONS

Antigenic heterogeneity appears to be an inherent feature of malignancy, and genetically based heterogeneity in immune responsiveness is an inherent feature of the host immune response. Consequently, immunization against single tumor antigens will probably not be broadly applicable and polyvalent CRC vaccines are more likely to be effective. If efficacy of the autologous CRC vaccine recently described by Hoover and Hanna[55] is demonstrated in a second randomized trial, identification of the antigens recognized by these patients will be an excellent starting point for such a quest. Since the relevant tumor antigens will be differentiation antigens (autoantigens) or mutated autoantigens, which are poorly immunogenic, approaches such as conjugate and recombinant vector vaccines and the use of potent immunologic adjuvants will be required to augment their immunogenicity. Additional approaches will undoubtedly result from continuing advances in our understanding of antigen processing, presentation, and recognition. Application of these various immunization approaches in a stepwise manner—guided initially by serologic or cell-mediated immune responses induced in immunized patients and subsequently by results of randomized clinical trials—is quite likely to be productive. Active specific immunotherapy of CRC with generic polyvalent tumor vaccines will be added to the short list of modalities effective in the adjuvant setting and may have impact in patients with limited measurable CRC as well.

Physicians have dreamed of treating cancer with tumor vaccines ever since the first successful vaccines against infectious diseases were developed. While immunization prior to tumor challenge is generally most successful, the immune system has been shown to have the power to destroy a considerable burden of growing allogeneic tumor transplanted intentionally in mice or accidentally in humans.[1,2] Since metastatic tumors rarely regress spontaneously, emphasis must be placed on focusing this power on tumor antigens which are normally tolerated. Experimental animals can regularly be induced to mount strong immune reactions against poor immunogens such as differentiation antigens (antigens expressed on a subset of cells in tissues of common embryonic origin) following vaccination with appropriately constructed vaccines. Autoimmune attack on the corresponding normal organ results[3-6] unless tolerance is reinforced by injection of the normal antigen prior to immunization,[7] a finding which emphasizes the wisdom of immunizing patients who are free of detectable disease or have low tumor burdens. These findings form the basis for the assumption that, by appropriate active specific immunization with tumor vaccines, it should be feasible to harness the power and precision of the immune system to combat cancer. Immunization against a single tumor antigen is not likely to be as effective as immunization against multiple tumor antigens, partly because the resulting immune response against the cancer will be that much greater. More importantly, however, antigenic heterogeneity is an inherent feature of malignancy and genetically based heterogeneity of responsiveness to individual antigenic epitopes is an inherent feature of the host immune response. The goal is, therefore, to construct a generic polyvalent vaccine against CRC for use in the adjuvant setting after surgical ablation of all or most known disease.

Construction of optimally immunogenic tumor vaccines is a multistep process (see Fig. 96-1). There are a variety of differentiation antigens and mutated oncogene products which are particularly well suited for vaccines against CRC. These are discussed in the first

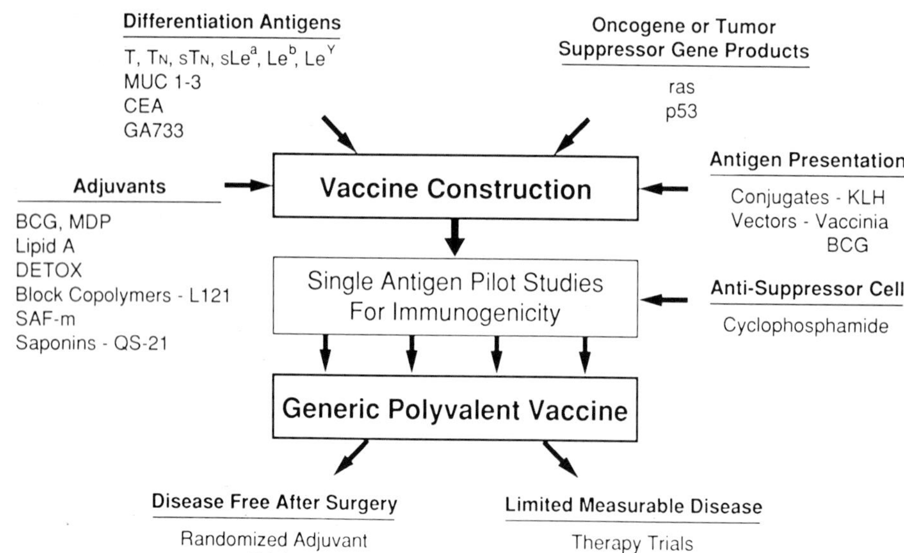

FIG. 96-1. Construction of generic tumor vaccines for colorectal cancer.

section of this review. In order to render these antigens sufficiently immunogenic, recent advances in tumor vaccinology must be applied. This is reviewed in the second section. In the final section, results of completed pilot and randomized tumor vaccine trials in patients with CRC are reviewed and ongoing trials and plans for future trials are discussed.

THE ANTIGENS OF COLORECTAL CARCINOMA

A great variety of antigens have been identified on CRC, many of which are discussed in other chapters of this text. Only those with low expression on normal tissues are discussed here. These can be subdivided into differentiation antigens and oncogene or tumor-suppressor-gene products.

The differentiation antigens of CRC that are particularly relevant for vaccine construction include blood group-related carbohydrate antigens, mucin antigens, and the glycoproteins carcinoembryonic antigen (CEA) and GA733-2. T, Tn, sialyl Tn (sTn), sialyl-Lewis^{a} (sLe^{a}), Le^{b}, and Le^{y}, are blood group-related carbohydrate antigens expressed on CRC (reviewed in Refs. 8 and 9). The structure of these antigenic epitopes is shown in Fig. 96-2. Each is abundantly expressed on 70 to 95 percent of colon cancers. Their availability as targets on CRC or other cancers for immune attack in humans has been confirmed with regard to T, sTn, and sLe^{a} antigens by sensitive imaging with murine monoclonal antibodies.[10–12] Each of these antigens is also expressed to a lesser extent on a variety of normal epithelial tissues predominantly at the luminal surface of secretory cells, a location which is relatively inaccessible to immune attack. While T, Tn, and sTn are exclusively expressed covalently attached to serine or threonine on mucin molecules, the Lewis epitopes are expressed as O- or N-linked moieties on glycoproteins and as glycolipids at the cell surface. The mucins are secreted into the bowel lumen by normal colonic epithelial cells but accumulate in the vicinity of colonic carcinoma cells, where they are available as targets for immune attack.

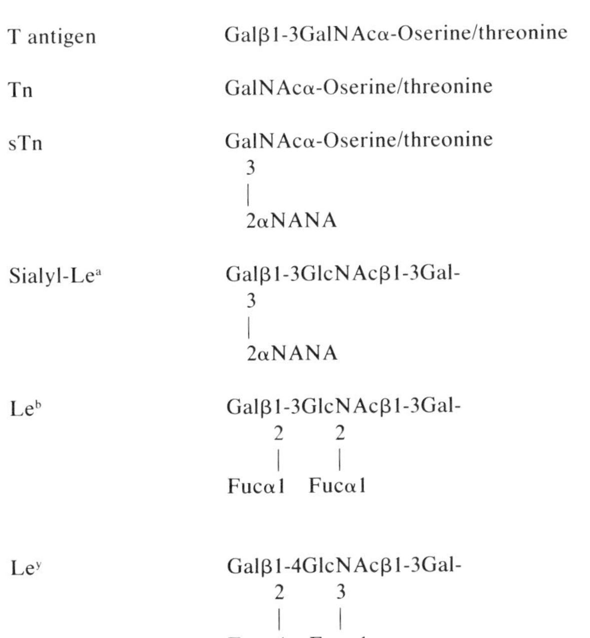

FIG. 96-2. Structure of blood group–related carbohydrate antigenic epitopes of colorectal carcinoma.

The peptide backbones of tumor mucins may also be targets for immune attack. They contain a large extracellular component made up of multiple copies of 20 to 27 amino acid tandem repeats and a cytoplasmic tail.[13,14] Three mucins have been identified on colorectal carcinomas—MUC1, MUC2, and MUC3—of which MUC2 and MUC3 appear to be predominant.[15–18] It has been suggested that the peptide backbones are not fully glycosylated by carcinomas, resulting in exposure to the immune system of peptide sequences which are not normally exposed. Consequently, a variety of peptide-specific monoclonal antibodies show specificity for the carcinoma-associated mucin, though the amino acid sequences in both normal and carcinoma mucins are probably the same. MUC1, expressed most widely on breast and pancreatic carcinomas, also contains epitopes recognized by cytotoxic T cells from patients with breast and pancreatic cancer.[19] Paradoxically, while these reactions are tumor-specific, they are major histocompatibility cluster (MHC) unrestricted, presumably due to the highly repetitive nature of mucins, which is hypothesized to allow cross-linking of T-cell receptors on mucin-specific T cells. The amino acid sequences of MUC2 and MUC3 have also been described (reviewed in Refs. 15 and 18), but less is known about the dominant B- and T-cell epitopes of these mucins or whether they can serve as tumor-associated antigens. Moreover, cytotoxic T cells reactive with them have not been described.

The CEA gene belongs to the immunoglobulin supergene family and consists of approximately 20 genes (reviewed in Ref. 20). Splice variants of the individual genes and posttranslational modifications (i.e., by glycosylation, as described for the mucins) greatly increase the number of CEA-related molecules. As with the other differentiation antigens described on human cancers, CEA is also present in normal colonic mucosa, but at lower concentrations than seen in CRC. Also, while some antigens in the CEA family are significantly expressed in a variety of normal tissues, others have a more restricted distribution (reviewed in Ref. 20). CEA is a 180-kDa oncofetal protein and a well-characterized tumor-associated antigen on many human cancers. Radiolabeled anti-CEA monoclonal antibodies have been used to identify metastases in

CRC patients with elevated CEA levels. Tumor sites were identified in 20 of 21 patients as confirmed at laparotomy or fine-needle biopsy. Significant uptake in normal tissues related to antibody specificity was not seen.[21] Kantor et al.[22] have described specific immunization against human CEA in mice by immunization with recombinant human CEA-vaccinia virus constructs which resulted in antibody, helper-T-cell, and cytotoxic-T-cell responses, as well as protection against challenge and regression of 7-day-old colonic adenocarcinomas expressing human CEA. It remains to be proven, however, whether human B cells or T cells can be induced to recognize CEA. As yet, despite the many murine antibodies that have been described against CEA, no human sera or T cells have been shown to react with CEA or CEA-expressing tumor cells.

GA733-2 antigen is a 40-kDa cell-surface glycoprotein which is assumed to be a differentiation antigen associated with a variety of epithelial carcinomas and their corresponding normal tissues. Murine monoclonal antibody C017-1A, which recognizes this antigen, has imaged the majority of colorectal carcinoma tumor sites in 52 patients; somewhat lower levels of uptake were detected in the normal colonic mucosa. Therapy trials with C017-1A and the additional murine monoclonal antibody GA733 have both resulted in occasional clinical responses in the absence of significant toxicity to normal epithelial tissues. The GA733-2 antigen is identical to another adenocarcinoma-associated antigen (KSA), and cDNAs coding for them have been sequenced.[23–25] The antigen is a 232 amino acid protein containing a single transmembrane domain of 23 amino acids and a 26–amino acid cytoplasmic domain. Low-level antibody titers against GA733 have been induced in CRC patients by anti-idiotype vaccines,[26,27] and T-cell activation in some of these same patients by the GA733-2 antigen has recently been detected (Herlyn, personal communication).

Oncogene products may be able to function as tumor-specific CRC antigens. The oncogene and tumor-suppressor-gene alterations associated with CRCs have been described in considerable detail in earlier chapters of this book. The familial adenomatous polyposis (FAP) and deleted in colonic carcinoma (DCC) genes are deleted or underexpressed in colonic carcinomas and the *myc* gene is not known to be mutated, though it does appear to be overexpressed in some tumors. These gene products, therefore, are not good candidates for vaccine construction. The *ras* and p53 gene alterations result in production of mutated gene products in 50 and 75 percent (respectively) of colonic cancers, and these are generally associated with prominent overexpression (reviewed in Refs. 28 and 29). Mutations offer the prospect of completely tumor-specific antigens, while the marked overexpression frequently seen in these carcinomas raises the possibility that even the wild-type (normal) portions of these gene products can serve as targets for immune attack. Murine monoclonal antibodies against wild-type p53 stain 75 percent of colorectal carcinomas[30] but do not stain normal tissues. Consideration of wild-type *ras* and p53 gene products as targets for immune attack and as immunogens for generic vaccine construction greatly facilitates vaccine construction, because several different *ras* mutations can occur at each of two locations (codons 12 and 61),[29,31] and p53 mutations at more than 50 locations have been described.[28] Antibodies against wild-type p53 have been identified in the sera of patients with breast or lung cancer,[31,32] confirming the potential immunogenicity of wild-type p53. However, *ras* and p53 are nuclear antigens which could only function as targets for immune attack against tumor cells if they were processed and presented as peptides by MHC class I or II molecules, as described below. Peace et al.[33] have described CD4+ helper T-cell recognition of transforming proteins encoded by mutated *ras* protooncogenes in mice immunized with the mutated peptides.[33] It remains to be determined, however, whether human T cells can recognize mutated or wild-type *ras* or p53 peptides naturally processed and presented by tumor cells.

AUGMENTING THE IMMUNOGENICITY OF COLORECTAL CARCINOMA ANTIGENS

Basis for the Poor Host Immune Response against Tumor Antigens

The tumor antigens described above are each appealing targets for vaccine construction; but since immune responses against them are seldom seen in patients with colonic cancer, it is clear that they are not normally very immunogenic. Additional approaches are needed to augment their immunogenicity—approaches which are not required for the standard vaccines against viral or bacterial diseases with which we are familiar. What is the basis for this difference? Tumors utilize a variety of mechanisms for eluding the host immune response. These include the shedding of tumor antigens, creating a "smokescreen effect"[34]; antigenic modulation (the temporary loss of tumor antigen in the presence of host immune response)[35]; antigenic heterogeneity (the genetic loss of antigens as a consequence of selection by the host immune response)[36]; and induction of suppression of the immune response by specific suppressor cells and other mechanisms.[37,38] More important than any of these, however, is the fact that tumor antigens are simply poor immunogens. The basis for this and for the approaches described below for overcoming their poor immunogenicity lies in the way antigens are processed by antigen-presenting cells (APCs) and recognized by T cells and B cells.

Protein antigens are broken down to peptides and presented at the cell surface[39] (1) as chains of 8 or 9 amino acids in the antigen-binding groove of MHC class I molecules (HLA-A, B, or C) to cytotoxic (CD8+) T cells or (2) as chains of 12 to 18 amino acids in the antigen-binding groove of MHC class II molecules (HLA-DP, DQ, or DR) to helper (CD4+) T cells. Antigens presented in the class I groove originate in the cell cytosol, where the processing begins. Processing is completed in the endoplasmic reticulum and Golgi compartments, and the peptides join with class I molecules in the post-Golgi compartment and are transported to the cell surface. These antigens are normally self antigens, mutated self antigens, or antigens of viruses or other intracellular parasites. Most cells in the body express class I MHC and so are potential APCs for cytotoxic T cells. Tumor cells have been known to evade this "responsibility" by global loss of HLA class I antigens or by focal loss of the particular HLA class I molecules responsible for presenting the relevant tumor antigens.[40] Escape from immune detection may result.

Antigens presented by class II MHC molecules are extrinsic antigens, such as those from most bacterial infections and standard vaccines. These antigens are endocytosed and processed in the endosomes. They encounter class II molecules following fusion of the endosomes with vesicles transporting class II molecules and are transported to the cell surface. Class II molecules are normally present on APCs such as B cells, macrophages, and dendritic cells; upon activation by various cytokines, however, class II molecules can be present on a variety of other cells as well. The relative importance of CD4+ T helper and CD8+ cytotoxic T cells in host immunity against cancer appears to vary with different tumor antigens (reviewed in Ref. 41). CD4+ T cells are vital for activating B cells for antibody production and improved antigen presentation, activating macrophages for inflammation and delayed-type hypersensitivity responses (DTH), and activating NK cells and CD8+ cytotoxic T cells for direct tumor lysis.

While T cells recognize exclusively processed peptides presented in linear fashion in the MHC antigen binding groove, B cells recognize predominantly unprocessed antigens in their normal tertiary configuration but require the help of T cells for full antibody production. For complex foreign antigens such as most bacteria or viruses, a variety of T cells recognize different antigenic epitopes, and sufficient T cell help for DTH and antibody production results. Similarly, complex intracellular pathogens activate a variety of cytotoxic T cells and—to the extent that these pathogens become extracellular—helper T cells as well. This process is less effective when single peptides are the immunogens because (1) some individuals may not be able to recognize that particular peptide and (2) at least initially, the quantity of helper-T-cell reactivity resulting from the small pool of T cells able to recognize this peptide is far less than that resulting from recognition of a more complex protein. This lack of T-cell responsiveness is compounded when the tumor antigen is a normal self antigen (such as differentiation antigens) to which the host is partially tolerant or a mutated normal self antigen with a single new or deleted amino acid. No detectable immune response may result.

Approaches for Overcoming the Poor Immunogenicity of Tumor Antigens

Irradiated Whole Tumor Cell Vaccines

Since CRC does not generally induce a detectable antitumor response in the host, it makes little sense to remove and then reinject these autologous cells unless significant steps are taken to augment their immunogenicity. Mixture with immunologic adjuvants such as bacillus Calmette-Guérin (BCG) is one approach toward this end. Another is transfection of these cells with cytokine genes such as IL2 or IL4, which greatly magnify the immune response against the transfected tumor cells. Both approaches result in protection from tumor challenge and cure of minimal disease in animal tumor models.[42–44] Approaches used with autologous tumor cells have the advantage that they can immunize against unknown antigens which may be uniquely present on that patient's tumor. However, making vaccines for each patient is a labor-intensive approach, and not all patients have sufficient tumor available. Also, this approach may not be the best method for immunization against well-defined antigens. While most tumors express the differentiation antigens and oncogene products described above, some express more than others, and high expressors may be far more immunogenic than average or low expressing cell lines, as has been shown for ganglioside GM2 in melanoma cells.[45] Vaccination with allogeneic CRC cell lines selected for optimal expression of one or more of these antigens is one solution. However, for cytotoxic T-cell activation, the tumor cells must share the pertinent MHC class I molecule, and this would need to be known for each antigen and each patient. This is a cumbersome approach to immunizing against known tumor antigens and may be required only if these antigens are not available in synthetic or purified form for the more effective approaches described below.

Anti-idiotype Antibody Vaccines

The region of an antibody which is unique to that antibody is termed the *idiotype*. It includes the antigen binding site and, since it is unique, if used for immunization it can induce activated B cells producing anti-idiotypic antibodies with variable regions mimicking the original antigen. These activated B cells can be used to prepare hybridomas resulting in anti-idiotypic monoclonal antibodies (mAbs). The use of "internal image" (resembling the original antigen) anti-idiotype antibodies for immunization may have advantages over the original antigen: (1) Compared to carbohydrate antigens such as T or sTn disaccharides, a protein simulation of the original antigen may more readily induce T-cell help because proteins are more readily processed and presented to T cells than carbohydrates. This might result in increased production of IgG antibodies and perhaps T-cell-mediated immunity. (2) For complex glycoprotein antigens, the anti-idiotypic antigen is available in amounts adequate for preclinical and clinical studies, while the original antigen may not be. Murine anti-idiotype mAbs presumed to bear an "internal image" mimicking the original antigen have been effectively used for immunization and protection against experimental infections and tumors (reviewed in Refs. 46 and 47).

Conjugate Vaccines for Induction of T-Cell Help

This approach derives from Landsteiner's classic experiments with hapten conjugation and has been used successfully to augment the immunogenicity of a variety of peptide and carbohydrate antigens. It is based on the concept of split tolerance. Studies of immunologic tolerance and ways to overcome it have shown in multiple experimental systems that T-cell unresponsiveness is more rapidly induced and more easily maintained than B-cell unresponsiveness. Levels of circulating antigens suitable for maintaining T-cell tolerance frequently fail to maintain B-cell tolerance. Consequently, if T-cell help is provided by covalent attachment of poorly immunogenic antigens to immunogenic proteins or use of the corresponding xenogeneic antigens (i.e., rat thyroglobulin in mice), antibodies can be produced to tolerated T-cell-dependent antigens. A variety of experimental autoimmune diseases have been induced by the use of this approach (reviewed in Refs. 3 through 6). Immunization of infants with diptheria toxoid conjugated to *Haemophilus influenzae* type B capsular polysaccharide but not the B polysaccharide alone results in IgG antibody production and protection from *Haemophilus influenzae* meningitis.[48] We and others have used this approach for the induction of high-titer IgM and IgG antibodies against GD3 ganglioside and sTn and T antigens, three antigens which normally result only in low-titer IgM antibodies.[49–51] B-cell activation by approaches such as these results in improved antigen-presenting capacity for the B cells and has been reported to facilitate T-cell activation against autoantigens.[52,53]

Viral and Mycobacterial Vectors for Induction of Cytotoxic T Cells

Vaccination with recombinant viruses or mycobacteria expressing the relevant tumor antigens as a consequence of transfer of the relevant gene is another approach being used for immunization against cancer. Following vaccination, infection by the vector results in intracellular production of antigen and its expression in the context of class I as well as class II MHC antigens. Induction of cytotoxic as well as helper T cells results. This approach is being used with a number of viruses and many different antigens (reviewed in Ref. 54). With regard to vaccines against CRC, transfected vaccinia viruses have been used for immunization against epithelial tumor mucin antigen[55] and CEA.[56] Recombinant BCG may also be particularly suitable for this approach because BCG has been safely used to immunize millions of people, is a strong immunopotentiating agent, persists in vivo for a long period of time, induces immune responses for many years, and recombinant BCG has recently successfully induced long-lived helper and cytotoxic T-lymphocyte responses against transfected antigens in mice.[57]

Immunologic Adjuvants

The term *immunologic adjuvant* designates an agent that increases the specific immune response to antigens. The relative importance of depot effect (sequestration of antigen for slow release and more efficient antigen processing), macrophage activation, and T-cell and B-cell activation in augmenting immune responses following adjuvant use remains an open question and is probably dependent on the antigen used. Primarily because of the need for adjuvants to augment the immunogenicity of recombinant peptide and purified carbohydrate vaccines against infectious diseases, a number of potent new adjuvants have been prepared and are in various phases of preclinical and clinical testing. These include (1) pluronic triblock copolymers such as L121,[58] which are known to activate complement and macrophages and facilitate attachment of antigen to lipid-aqueous interfaces; (2) SAF-m, which contains muramyl dipeptide (MDP) analogue threonyl MDP, L121, and squalane[59]; (3) DETOX, which contains an endotoxin lipid A analogue and mycobacterial cell-wall skeletons[60]; and (4) QS-21, which is a purified Quil A saponin fraction.[61] Of these adjuvants, QS-21 is unique in that it has been reported to induce cytotoxic T-cell activity against peptide antigens in addition to the usual helper T cell activity and antibody responses.[62] This may be due to a mild lytic activity of QS-21 (saponins are hemolysins), which may facilitate passage of antigen from the endosome into the cytosol. Based on studies comparing antibody titers and DTH responses against a variety of carbohydrate and protein antigens,[50,63] we have selected SAF-m and QS-21 as particularly potent adjuvants suitable for study in humans and are currently conducting phase I clinical trials with them.

VACCINATION TRIALS IN PATIENTS WITH COLORECTAL CARCINOMA

Immunization trials with an autologous CRC cell vaccine, anti-idiotype vaccines, and several blood group–related carbohydrate antigen vaccines have been conducted in CRC patients. These early efforts reveal both the promise of the approach and the difficulties in its implementation.

Autologous Colorectal Carcinoma Cell Vaccine

Hoover and Hanna[64] have described the results of a trial in which 98 patients with stages B_2, B_3, and C CRC, who were free of all evidence of disease after surgery, were randomized to receive either irradiated viable autologous tumor cells obtained from surgical specimens and mixed with BCG or no therapy. Three vaccinations were given at 1-week intervals beginning approximately a month after surgery, and the patients were then followed for evidence of disease progression. While these vaccines were not prepared with any particular antigens in mind and no screen for postimmunization reactivity against particular tumor antigens was conducted, the approach was based on a long series of studies with the guinea pig line-10 hepatic carcinoma model. The model identified viability of BCG and tumor cells, number of BCG organisms and tumor cells, their ratio, and the vaccination schedule as important variables, and these were all applied optimally in the clinical trial. The procedure was as follows: 10^7 viable tumor cells which had been irradiated with 20,000 rads plus 10^7 viable BCG organisms were mixed and injected intradermally into the skin of each thigh and one deltoid area sequentially at 1-week intervals. The third immunization contained tumor cells alone without BCG. Among the 80 evaluable patients, 18 were excluded for a variety of reasons. Among the 47 evaluable patients with cancer of the colon, the reported difference in recurrence rate between the 24 vaccinated patients and 23 controls at 40 and 60 months was approximately 20 and 40 percent, respectively (p = .021), while the difference in death rate was 10 and 20 percent at the same intervals (p = .099).[64] A recent update of these data shows that the survival difference has increased and that the p value has become significant (p = <.05) (Hanna, personal communication). Interestingly, among the 33 rectal carcinoma patients who were vaccinated, there was no improvement in disease-free interval and survival. Whether this relates to differences in tumor antigenicity and immunogenicity or the impact of postsurgical irradiation in the rectal carcinoma patients remains unknown. Skin tests for delayed hypersensitivity reactions to the autologous tumor cells were performed at intervals after immunization in 20 patients, and reactivity correlated with improved prognosis.[64] A similar correlation between DTH responses to autologous CRC cells and prognosis has been described by Liebrich et al.[65] for 23 patients vaccinated with autologous CRC cells infected with Newcastle disease virus. Expression of HLA class II molecules (HLA-DR and HLA-DP) on the colorectal carcinoma cells used by Hoover and Hanna for vaccine production also correlated with improved prognosis.[66] Addition of gamma interferon to the cell medium was shown to further increase expression of HLA class II molecules. Based on these studies, additional randomized trials have been initiated by the Eastern Cooperative Oncology Group (ECOG) to confirm the recurrence and survival benefit for vaccination with autologous colonic carcinoma cells and BCG. Patients with stage B_2 and stage B_3 colonic carcinoma were randomized to receive three vaccinations at 1-week intervals or no treatment, those with stage C CRC received vaccinations plus 5-FU and levamisole or 5-FU and levamisole alone.

Encouraging as these results are, this approach to vaccine construction has several drawbacks. Many patients with stage C colonic carcinoma do not have sufficient cells for vaccine construction, and tumor-cell processing and vaccine construction may not be readily applicable to the majority of regional medical centers. The major drawback, however, is that since the relevant antigens in this vaccine are not known, it is difficult to envision ways to improve the vaccine (with the possible exception of pretreatment of cells with gamma interferon to improve antigen presentation). Hoover and Hanna,[64] aware of these points and the need for a generic vaccine for CRC, are endeavoring to identify the relevant antigens through human monoclonal antibodies obtained by fusion of lymphocytes from immunized patients. If a second randomized trial confirms the benefit of this tumor-cell vaccine, considerable effort will be extended nationwide on identifying the relevant antigens.

Anti-idiotype Vaccines

Herlyn and coworkers[26,27] have immunized two groups of CRC patients with polyclonal goat anti-idiotype antibodies raised against murine monoclonal antibodies C017-1A and GA733. The two monoclonal antibodies recognize different epitopes on the same 37- to 40-kDa glycoprotein, which is associated with the cell surface of more than 85 percent of metastatic CRCs. Of 30 patients with advanced CRC who were immunized with purified goat antibodies (Ab2) against C017-1A,[26] 6 showed partial clinical responses. But since these patients also received chemotherapy, the clinical responses cannot be attributed solely to immunotherapy. Most patients developed increased titers of reactivity against CRC cells and inhibited binding of the goat anti-idiotype antibody (Ab2) to C017-1A, suggesting that the human serum Ab3 and mouse C017-1A recognize the same epitope. An additional group of 12 patients who were free of disease after surgery were immunized with goat Ab2 against GA733.[27] Of these patients, 5 developed increased reactivity against CRC cells as well as against the immunizing antibody. Sera from these patients specifically inhibited the binding of GA733 to tumor cells, suggesting once again that they recognize the same epitope as GA733. Recently the GA733 antigen has been purified and shown to induce a proliferative response in these immunized patients (Herlyn, personal communication). Trials with the polyclonal and new monoclonal anti-idiotype antibodies mimicking the GA733 and C017-1A epitopes of GA733 antigen are ongoing at Wistar Institute and Thomas Jefferson University Hospital. In addition, the GA733 antigen has recently been cloned and active specific immunotherapy trials are planned for 1994. Vaccines containing GA733 protein plus alum or BCG will be administered four times in phase I trials conducted at Thomas Jefferson University Hospital by Mastrangelo. All trials involve Dukes D patients with measurable disease. The immunogenicity of the anti-idiotype vaccines and GA733 antigen vaccines will be compared to determine the optimal approach for immunization against the C017-1A/GA733 antigen.

Blood Group–Related Carbohydrate Antigens

We have immunized small groups of high-risk Dukes B, C, and D CRC patients who were free of detectable disease after surgery with Tn, sTn, and T antigen vaccines. Our goal has been the development of a consistently immunogenic polyvalent vaccine—one that we could then test for clinical effect in patients with limited measurable disease and in a randomized trial in the adjuvant setting (see Fig. 96-1). Initially, mucin obtained from ovine sheep submaxillary glands (OSM) which expressed large amounts of Tn and sTn was used for vaccine construction.[67] It was anticipated that the xenogeneic mucin backbone would serve as an immunogenic carrier, magnifying the immunogenicity of the two carbohydrate epitopes. In all, 6 patients were treated with OSM alone, 8 patients were treated with OSM plus the immunologic adjuvant DETOX, and 6 additional patients were treated with OSM plus BCG. Pre- and postvaccination sera were tested by ELISA and dot-blot immune stains for antibodies reactive with OSM and related antigens. IgM antibody titers increased in 4 of 8 patients receiving the DETOX vaccine, 5 of 6 patients receiving the BCG vaccine, and 0 of 6 patients receiving no adjuvant. The specificity of the induced antibodies was confirmed by testing on synthetic sTn and Tn-HSA conjugates. Median IgM pre- and postvaccination titers were 1/20 and 1/80 for Tn-HSA and 1/10 and 1/320 for sTn-HSA. Low-level IgG antibody titers against sTn-HSA were detected in occasional patients. There was no significant toxicity except for that resulting from the immunologic adjuvants. These results demonstrated that Tn and especially sTn can be recognized by the human immune system but that the mucin protein backbone was an ineffective carrier and failed to induce sufficient T-cell help for IgG antibody production. Consequently, we have tested the immunogenicity of synthetic T and sTn-KLH conjugates prepared by Koganty and Longenecker (Biomira Inc., Edmonton, Alberta, Canada). A total of 6 patients each were vaccinated with T-KLH alone, T-KLH plus Detox, and sTn-KLH plus Detox (unpublished results). While no significant antibody induction occurred after immunization with T-KLH alone, high-titer IgM and IgG antibodies resulted against synthetic T or synthetic sTn in the other groups. Interestingly, while IgM antibodies induced in T-KLH and sTn-KLH vaccinated patients reacted as well with the natural T and sTn epitopes expressed on various mucins or tumor cells, the IgG antibodies reacted poorly or not at all with these natural sources of T and sTn antigens. Our results suggest that in the presence of T-cell help (as provided by KLH), the T and sTn disaccharide epitopes recognized by B cells are different than the natural T and sTn epitopes which are normally attached by serine or threonine to a tumor mucin backbone. These results are similar to those described by MacLean et al.[42,61] in patients with ovarian cancer vaccinated with T-KLH and sTn-KLH plus Detox except that the anti-T and sTn antigen IgG antibodies induced in ovarian cancer patients reacted (though with lower titers) with the natural antigens as well. The basis for this difference remains unexplained. Our data emphasize the importance of conjugation of weakly immunogenic differentiation antigens to highly immunogenic carrier molecules such as KLH and the requirement for using potent immunologic adjuvants. We plan to test sTn-serine-KLH and T-serine-KLH constructs with the more potent immunologic adjuvant QS-21 during 1994 in preparation for construction and testing of polyvalent vaccines containing several of these antigens.

Ongoing Trials

Clinical trials with tumor vaccines against CRC (as described above) by Hoover and Hanna (ECOG) and Herlyn and Mastrangelo (Wistar Institute and Thomas Jefferson University Hospital) are continuing. In addition, Schirrmacher (Heidelberg, Germany) is conducting a randomized trial comparing vaccination with Newcastle disease virus-infected autologous CRC cells to no treatment in patients with resected liver metastases.[68] Control patients will be eligible for vaccination after further recurrences. Schlom at the National Cancer Institute has initiated a trial for patients with measurable metastatic CRC using vaccinia virus transfected with the CEA gene.

REFERENCES

1. Wilson RE, Hager EB, Hampers CI, et al: Immunologic rejection of human cancer transplanted with a renal allograft. *N Engl J Med* 278:479, 1968.
2. Zukoski CF, Killen DA, Ginn E, et al: Transplanted carcinoma in immunosuppressed patients. *Transplantation* 9:71, 1970.
3. Weigle WO: *Autoimmunity: Genetic, Immunologic, Virologic and Clinical Aspects*. New York, Academic Press, 1977, p 141.
4. Stuart JM, Cremer MA, Townes AS, et al: Type II collagen-induced arthritis in rats. *J Exp Med* 155:1, 1982.
5. Paterson PY: LT/EAE and MS quest. *Cell Immunol* 82:55, 1983.
6. Allison AC: *Autoimmunity: Genetic, Immunologic, Virologic and Clinical Aspects*. New York, Academic Press, 1977, p 91.
7. Rose NR: Autoimmune diseases. *Sci Am* 244:80, 1981.
8. Lloyd KO: Blood group antigens as markers for normal differentiation and malignant change in human tissues. *Am J Clin Pathol* 87:129–139, 1987.
9. Blaszczyk M, Steplewski Z, Koprowski H: Carbohydrate antigens associated with gastrointestinal tumors, in Nasser, J (ed): *Tumor Markers*. New York, Praeger, 1987, pp 79–117.
10. MacLean GD, McEwan A, Noujaim AA, et al: A novel strategy for cancer immunoscintigraphy. *Antibody Immunoconj Radiopharm* 2:15, 1989.
11. Colcher D, Esteban JM, Carrasquillo JA, et al: Quantitation analyses of selective radiolabeled monoclonal antibody localization in metastatic lesions of colorectal cancer patients. *Cancer Res* 47:1185–1189, 1987.
12. Cohn KH, Welt S, Banner WP, et al: Localization of radioiodinated monoclonal antibody in colorectal cancer. *Arch Surg* 122:1425–1429, 1987.
13. Burchell J, Taylor-Papadimitriou J, Boshell M, et al: A short sequence, within the amino acid tandem repeat of a cancer-associated mucin, contains immunodominant epitopes. *Int J Cancer* 44:691–696, 1989.
14. Gendler S, Lancaster C, Taylor-Papadimitriou J, et al: Molecular cloning and expression of human tumor-associated polymorphic epithelial mucin. *J Biol Chem* 265:15286–15293, 1990.
15. Gum JR, Byrd JC, Hicks JW, et al: Molecular cloning of human intestinal mucin cDNAs. *J Biol Chem* 264:6480–6487, 1989.
16. Gum JR, Hicks JW, Swallow DM, et al: Molecular cloning of cDNAs derived from a novel human intestinal mucin gene. *Biochem Biophys Res Commun* 171:407–415, 1990.
17. Gendler SJ, Spicer AP, Lalani E-N, et al: Structure and biology of a carcinoma-associated mucin, MUC1. *Am Rev Respir Dis* 144:S42–S47, 1991.
18. Porchet N, Cong NV, Dufosse J, et al: Molecular cloning and chromosomal localization of a novel human tracheobronchial mucin cDNA containing tandemly repeated sequences of 48 base pairs. *Biochem Biophys Res Commun* 175:414–422, 1991.
19. Barnd D, Lan M, Metzgar R, Finn O: Specific, MHC-unrestricted recognition of tumour-associated mucins by human cytotoxic T cells. *Proc Natl Acad Sci USA* 86:7159–7163, 1989.
20. Thompson JA, Grunert F, Zimmerman W: Carcinoembryonic antigen gene family: Molecular biology and clinical perspectives. *J Clin Lab Anal* 5:344–366, 1991.
21. Griffin TW, Brill AB, Stevens S, et al: Initial clinical study of Indium-111-labeled clone 110 anticarcinoembryonic antigen antibody in patients with colorectal cancer. *J Clin Oncol* 9:631–640, 1991.
22. Kantor J, Irvine K, Abrams S, et al: Antitumor activity and immune responses induced by a recombinant carcinoembryonic antigen-vaccinia virus vaccine. *J Natl Cancer Inst* 84:1084–1091, 1992.
23. Szala S, Froehlich M, Scollon M, et al: Molecular cloning of cDNA for the carcinoma-associated antigen GA733-2. *Proc Natl Acad Sci USA* 87:3452–3546, 1990.
24. Perez MS, Walker LE: Isolation and characterization of a cDNA encoding the KS1/4 epithelial carcinoma marker. *J Immunol* 142:3662–3667, 1989.
25. Strand J, Hamilton AE, Beavers LS, et al: Molecular cloning and characterization of a human adenocarcinoma/epithelial cell surface antigen complementary DNA. *Cancer Res* 49: 314–317, 1989.
26. Herlyn D, Wettendorff M, Schmoll E, et al: Anti-idiotype immunization of cancer patients: Modulation of the immune response. *Proc Natl Acad Sci USA* 84:8055–8059, 1987.
27. Herlyn D, Benden A, Kane M, et al: Anti-idiotype cancer vaccine: Preclinical and clinical studies. *In Vivo* 5:615, 1991.
28. Levine AJ: The p53 tumor suppressor gene product. *Cancer Survey* 12:59–79, 1992.
29. Bos JL: Ras oncogenes in human cancer: A review. *Cancer Res* 49:4682, 1989.
30. Cunningham J, Lust JA, Schaid DJ, et al: Expression of p53 and 17p allelic loss in colorectal carcinoma. *Cancer Res* 52:1974–1980, 1992.
31. Winter SF, Minna JD, Johnson BE, et al: Development of antibodies against p53 in lung cancer patients appears to be dependent on the type of p53 mutation. *Cancer Res* 52:4168–4174, 1992.
32. Crawford LV, Pim DC, Bulbrook RD: Detection of antibodies against the cellular protein p53 in sera from patients with breast cancer. *Int J Cancer* 30:403–408, 1982.
33. Peace DJ, Chen W, Nelson H, Cheever MA: T cell recognition of transforming proteins encoded by mutated ras protooncogenes. *J Immunol* 146:2059–2065, 1991.
34. Hellstrom KE, Hellstrom I, Nepom JT: Specific blocking factors: Are they important? *Biophys Biochem Acta* 473:121–148, 1977.
35. Old LJ, Boyse EA, Stokert E: Antigenic properties of experimental leukemias: I. Serological studies in vitro with spontaneous and radiation-induced leukemias. *J Natl Cancer Inst* 31:977, 1963.
36. Pimm MV, Baldwin RW: Antigenic differences between primary methylcholanthrene-induced rat sarcomas and post surgical recurrences. *Intl J Cancer* 20:37, 1977.
37. Fujimoto S, Greene M, Sehon AH: Regulation of the immune response to tumor antigens: II. The nature of immunosuppressor cells in tumor-bearing hosts. *J Immunol* 116:800, 1976.
38. North RJ: Down-regulation of the antitumor immune response. *Adv Cancer Res* 45:1–43, 1985.
39. Yewdell JW, Bennink JR: Cell biology of antigen processing and presentation to MHC Class I molecule-restricted T lymphocytes. *Adv Immunol* 52:1–123, 1994.
40. Browning MJ, Bodmer W: MHC antigens and cancer: Implications for T cell surveillance, in Old L (ed): *Current Opinion in Immunology,* vol 4. Philadelphia, Current Biology Ltd., 1992, p 613.
41. Greenberg, P, Klarnet J, Sugarwara H, et al: Requirement for

antigen specific induction and expression of CD4+ and CD8+ T cell responses to tumors, in Finn O, Lotze M (eds): *Cellular Immunity in the Immunotherapy of Cancer.* New York, Wiley-Liss, 1990, pp 235–242.

42. Fearon ER, Pardoll DM, Itaya T, et al: Interleukin-2 production by tumor cells bypasses T helper function in the generation of antitumor response. *Cell* 60:397–403, 1990.
43. Gansbacher B, Bannerji R, Daniels B, et al: Retroviral vector-mediated γ-interferon gene transfer into tumor cells generates potent and long lasting antitumor immunity. *Cancer Res* 50:7820–7825, 1990.
44. Hanna MG, Brandhorst JS, Peters LC: Active specific immunotherapy of residual micrometastasis. *Cancer Immunol Immunother* 7:165–173, 1979.
45. Livingston PO, Natoli EJ Jr, Jones Calves M, et al: Vaccines containing purified GM2 antibodies in melanoma patients. *Proc Natl Acad Sci USA* 84:2911–2915, 1987.
46. Poskitt DC, Jean-Francois MJB, Turnbull S, et al: Internal image (Ab2β) anti-idiotype vaccines: Theoretical and practical aspects. *Vaccine* 9:792–796, 1991.
47. Köhler H, Raychaudhuri S, Chen J-J: Tumor idiotype vaccines: Correlation of the idiotype-recognizing T-cell repertoire with tumor growth. *Vaccine Res* 1:33–45, 1992.
48. Eskola J, Käyhty H, Takala AK, et al: A randomized prospective field trial of a conjugate vaccine in the protection of infants and young children against invasive *Haemophilus influenzae* type b disease. *N Engl J Med* 323:1381–1387, 1990.
49. Helling F, Lloyd KO, Oettgen HF, Livingston PO: Increased immunogenicity of GD3 ganglioside after covalent attachment to proteins. *Proc Am Assoc Cancer Res* 33:335, 1992.
50. Livingston PO, Koganty R, Longenecker BM, et al: Studies on the immunogenicity of synthetic and natural Thomsen-Friedenreich (TF) antigens in mice: Augmentation of the response by Quil A and SAF-m adjuvants and analysis of the specificity of the responses. *Vaccine Res* 1:99–109, 1992.
51. MacLean GD, Bowen-Yacyshyn MB, Samuel J, et al: Active immunization of human ovarian cancer patients against a common carcinoma (Thomsen-Friedenreich) determinant using a synthetic carbohydrate antigen. *J Immunother* 11:292–305, 1992.
52. Lin R-H, Mamula MJ, Hardin JA, Janeway CA Jr: Induction of autoreactive B cells allows priming of autoreactive T cells. *J Exp Med* 173:1433–1439, 1991.
53. Sopori ML, Donaldson LA, Savage SM: T lymphocyte heterogeneity in the rat. *Cell Immunol* 128:427–437, 1990.
54. Tartaglia J, Pincus S, Paoletti E: Poxvirus-based vectors as vaccine candidates. *Immunology* 10:13–30, 1990.
55. Hareuveni M, Gautier C, Kieny M-P, et al: Vaccination against tumor cells expressing breast cancer epithelial tumor antigen. *Proc Natl Acad Sci USA* 87:9498–9502, 1990.
56. Irvine K, Kantor J, Snoy P, Schlom J: Characterization of immunological responses using a CEA recombinant vaccinia virus in non-human primates. *Proc Am Assoc Cancer Res* 33:334, 1992.
57. Stover CK, de la Cruz VF, Fuerst TR, et al: New use of BCG for recombinant vaccines. *Nature* 351:456–460, 1991.
58. Hunter R, Olsen M, Buynitzky S: Adjuvant activity of non-ionic block copolymers: IV. Effect of molecular weight and formulation of titre and isotype of antibody. *Vaccine* 9:250–256, 1991.
59. Allison AC, Byars NE: An adjuvant formulation that selectively elicits the formation of antibodies of protective isotypes and of cell-mediated immunity. *J Immunol Meth* 95:157–168, 1986.
60. Mitchell MS, Kan-Mitchell J, Kempf RA, et al: Active specific immunotherapy for melanoma: Phase I trial of allogeneic lysates and a novel adjuvant. *Cancer Res* 48:5883–5893, 1988.
61. Kensil CR, Patel U, Lennick M, Marciani D: Separation and characterization of saponins with adjuvant activity from Quillaja saponaria molina cortex. *J Immunol* 146:431–437, 1991.
62. Newman MJ, Wu JY, Gardner BH, et al: Saponin adjuvant induction of ovalbumen-specific CD8 + cytotoxic T-lymphocyte responses. *J Immunol* 148:2357, 1992.
63. Livingston PO, Calves MJ, Helling F, et al: GD3/proteosome vaccines include consistent IgM antibodies against the ganglioside GD3. *Vaccine,* in press, 1994.
64. Hoover HC Jr, Hanna MG Jr: Immunotherapy by active specific immunization: Clinical applications, in Devita VT Jr, Hellman S, Rosenberg SA (eds): *Biologic Therapy of Cancer.* Philadelphia, Lippincott, 1991, pp 670–682.
65. Liebrich W, Schlag P, Manasterski M, et al: In vitro and clinical characterisation of a Newcastle disease virus-modified autologous tumour cell vaccine for treatment of colorectal cancer patients. *Eur J Cancer* 27:703–710, 1991.
66. Ransom JH, Pelle B, Hanna MG Jr: Expression of class II major histocompatibility complex molecules correlates with human colon tumor vaccine efficacy. *Cancer Res* 52:3460–3466, 1992.
67. O'Boyle KP, Zamore R, Adluri S, et al: Immunization of colorectal cancer patients with modified ovine submaxillary gland mucin and adjuvants induces IgM and IgG antibodies to sialylated Tn. *Cancer Res,* 52:5663, 1992.
68. MacLean GD, Reddish M, Koganty RR, et al: Immunization of breast cancer patients using a synthetic sialyl-Tn glycoconjugate plus Detox™ adjuvant. 36:215–222, 1993.

PART 16

Other Colorectal Tumors

CHAPTER 97

Carcinoid Tumors

Philip B. Paty
Elin R. Sigurdson

HIGHLIGHTS

Carcinoid tumors are neuroendocrine neoplasms whose clinical behavior ranges from benign to highly aggressive. Malignant behavior is generally confined to those tumors 2.0 cm or greater in diameter. Carcinoids of the appendix are usually found incidentally, and nearly all cases are cured by simple appendectomy. In the rectum, 80 to 90 percent of carcinoids are small, submucosal nodules found incidentally on proctoscopy; these early lesions are cured by local excision. The remaining rectal and colonic carcinoids are larger, symptomatic lesions, and the clinical presentation, diagnostic evaluation, and treatment are similar to colorectal adenocarcinoma. Overall survival following treatment of symptomatic lesions is poor due to frequent presentation with advanced-stage disease. Hepatic metastases are common, typically multifocal, and rarely amenable to surgical removal. The malignant carcinoid syndrome is rare.

CONTROVERSIES

The use of local excision versus radical resection for treatment of intermediate to large rectal carcinoids is controversial. Because the frequency of local invasion and metastases increases with the size of the primary tumor, traditional treatment for larger rectal lesions has been radical surgery. However, the benefit of resection has been questioned. For lesions 2.0 cm or greater in diameter and for those with involved regional lymph nodes, the long-term survival is poor, in some series less than 5 percent, regardless of treatment. Some believe the morbidity of radical resection is unwarranted and advocate local excision.

FUTURE DIRECTIONS

Metastatic disease to the liver and lungs is the major cause of death from carcinoid tumor. Currently no systemic therapy has proven efficacy. New biological approaches that target pathways of hormone production may be useful in control of symptoms and in development of tumor-specific chemotherapy. Aggressive treatment of symptomatic liver metastases with surgical debulking plus hepatic artery embolization warrants investigation. Additional biological studies are needed to define better prognostic markers and identify molecular targets for new therapies.

Adenocarcinoma, with its assorted histologic subtypes, accounts for nearly 98 percent of the malignant tumors arising in the colon and rectum. Clinical encounters with other cancers are uncommon and require special vigilance for proper diagnosis and management. In this chapter and the following two chapters, the three most common nonadenocarcinoma cancers—carcinoid tumor, lymphoma, and sarcoma—are reviewed. The relative frequency and clinical features of these colorectal cancers are summarized in Table 97-1.

Carcinoid tumors are neuroendocrine neoplasms whose clinical behavior may be benign or highly malignant. They are derived from enterochromaffin (EC)

Table 97-1
Malignant Neoplasms of the Colon and Rectum Other Than Adenocarcinoma

Histologic type	*Relative frequency*	*Clinical features*
Carcinoid		Clinical behavior indolent to highly aggressive. Malignant forms usually 2 cm or larger. Second neoplasms are common (15–40%).
	1.3% of rectal neoplasms	80% are benign submucosal nodules; 20% are symptomatic and grossly malignant.
	0.3% of colonic neoplasms	Usually symptomatic. Liver metastases in 30 to 40% at presentation.
	50% of appendiceal neoplasms	Incidental mass in appendectomy specimen. Malignant forms are rare.
Lymphoma	0.2% of colorectal cancers	Variable symptoms, obstruction common. Cecum and rectum are most frequent sites. Single, multiple, and diffuse lesions occur. Determine primary versus secondary GI involvement.
Sarcoma	0.1% of colorectal cancers	Variable symptoms, can masquerade as abscess. Some 50% require laparotomy for diagnosis. Regional lymph nodes involved in 12%; peritoneal or liver metastases in 40%.

cells, secretory cells within the intestinal or respiratory epithelium that take up (argyrophilic) and often reduce (argentaffinic) silver stains.[1-3] These EC cells produce a wide range of biogenic amines, neuropeptides, and peptide hormones—secretory products which are also found in carcinoid tumors. Such tumors have been characterized together with other amine precursor uptake (APU) and decarboxylation neoplasms (medullary carcinoma of the thyroid, pheochromocytoma, pancreatic islet cell tumors) as APUDomas.[4]

Gastrointestinal sites account for 85 to 95 percent of all clinically encountered carcinoids, the most common specific sites being the appendix (35 percent), small intestine (23 percent), and rectum/rectosigmoid (12 percent).[5] The colon is involved in approximately 6 percent of cases, with the cecum accounting for about half of these.[5,6] Because many carcinoids are asymptomatic and never detected, the true incidence of these tumors is unknown. Clinical management is highly dependent upon site of origin and is discussed below for appendiceal, colonic, and rectal tumors.

PATHOLOGY

Carcinoid tumors are commonly classified on the basis of embryologic origin from the foregut (bronchi, stomach, duodenum, pancreas), midgut (jejunum, ileum, cecum, appendix), and hindgut (left colon, rectum). This schema can be clinically useful because of the morphologic, biochemical, and clinical properties associated with each group.[7] Distinctive features of hindgut carcinoids include weak silver staining (argentaffin-negative, argyrophil-variable), low serotonin and 5-hydroxytryptophan content, increased frequency of bone metastases, and rare association with the malignant carcinoid syndrome.

Histologically, a typical carcinoid tumor is composed of small, uniform cells arranged in orderly bands or ribbons (Fig. 97-1). The cells have benign cytologic features, and mitotic figures are rare.[2] Dense neurosecretory granules are abundant in the cytoplasm. Immunohistochemical stains can demonstrate numerous peptides, including chromogranin, neuron-

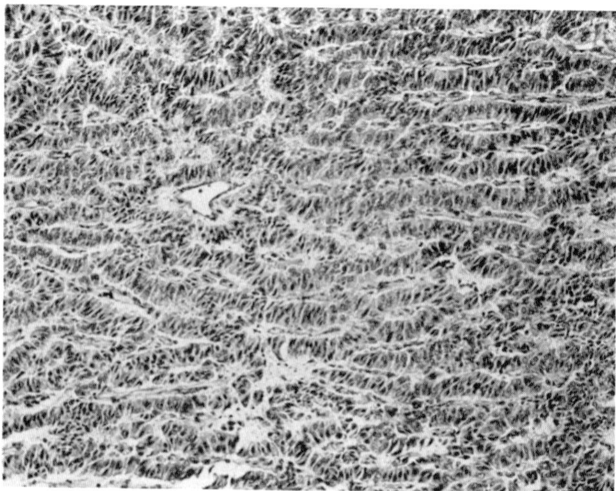

FIG. 97-1. Carcinoid tumor of colon, showing ribbonlike pattern (× 100). (Courtesy of S. Sternberg, M.D., New York.)

specific enolase, 5-hydroxytryptamine (serotonin), 5-hydroxytryptophan, neurotensin, calcitonin, insulin, gastrin, ACTH, and others.[8–10] Immunohistochemical staining patterns are helpful in diagnosis but have no prognostic value.[11]

Classification and nomenclature of tumors with atypical histology is not well standardized. Some authors regard only the most well-differentiated neuroendocrine tumors as carcinoids, whereas others include a wide range of anaplastic variants.[11–14] Loosely defined terms such as *atypical carcinoid* and *malignant carcinoid* have been used to describe neuroendocrine tumors showing various degrees of pleomorphism, mitoses, necrosis, or undifferentiated morphology. The confusion is magnified by the existence of "composite" tumors, which display both glandular and neuroendocrine features.[12,15,16] Inclusion of aggressive undifferentiated and small cell tumors may in part account for the poor survival statistics reported for large bowel carcinoids.[11,12] Five growth patterns—insular, trabecular, glandular, undifferentiated, and mixed—have been described and represent the most widely accepted diagnostic criteria for carcinoid tumors.[9,10,17]

The malignant potential of a carcinoid tumor cannot be predicted by its histologic appearance.[2,18] Demonstration of metastatic disease is the only unequivocal proof of malignancy. Tumor size is the most useful guide in predicting the likelihood of metastatic spread, as demonstrated for appendiceal, rectal, colonic, and small bowel carcinoids.[2,19–22] Lesions less than 1 cm in diameter are virtually never associated with metastatic spread and are treated by conservative surgery. Lesions of 2 cm or greater diameter are often symptomatic, frequently have regional metastases, and usually require bowel resection. Management of intermediate-size lesions is individualized on the basis of other prognostic factors and clinical judgment. Management of lesions at specific sites is discussed below.

APPENDICEAL CARCINOIDS

Incidence

Carcinoids are the most common neoplasm found in the appendix, accounting for about 50 percent of the total.[19,21] It has been estimated that a carcinoid tumor is found once in every 200 to 300 appendectomy specimens.[19] The tumor is rarely seen in young children or elderly adults and is most prevalent in young adults in the third and fourth decades of life.[19,21] Males and females are believed to be equally affected, although detection rates are higher in females because of a higher incidence of pelvic surgery.

Clinical Presentation

Appendiceal carcinoids are encountered in three clinical settings.[19] Approximately 90 percent are incidental findings and are removed en passant with the appendix during laparotomy for another condition. A large portion of these tumors are not suspected until the pathologist sections the appendix. Others are apparent at laparotomy, but the appearance is nonspecific: a round, oval, or fusiform enlargement of the appendix, either concentric or eccentric, usually near the tip. A second clinical presentation, involving approximately 10 percent of cases, is acute appendicitis. In only one-third of cases is the carcinoid tumor an obstructing factor that contributes to the appendicitis; in two-thirds, the tumor is located near the tip of the appendix, distal and unrelated to the inflammatory process. A third, extremely rare presentation is the malignant carcinoid syndrome. Workup and treatment are identical to carcinoid syndrome caused by carcinoids of small bowel origin.

Treatment and Results

Nearly all appendiceal carcinoids are small and grossly confined to the appendix. In the classic report of Moertel et al.[19] of 144 cases, metastases were found at operation in only two cases. In both instances, the diameter of the primary tumor was greater than 2.0 cm. Long-term follow-up of the 142 other tumors, all grossly localized to the appendix, showed no evidence of tumor recurrence following simple appendectomy.[19,23] Local invasion into the muscle wall, lymphatic channels, peritoneal surface, and mesentery was common but had no prognostic significance.[19,23] Subsequent collected series and case reports have confirmed that regional lymph node metastases from appendiceal carcinoids smaller than 2.0 cm are exceedingly rare.[24–27]

Treatment by simple appendectomy is widely agreed to be adequate for the vast majority of appendiceal carcinoids. The problem is identifying those rare cases that may benefit from more extensive surgery. Based on current knowledge, right hemicolectomy, primary or staged, should be performed in two situations: (1) tumors 2.0 cm or greater in diameter, and (2) tumors with proven metastases to regional lymph nodes. For tumors 1.0 to 1.9 cm in diameter, simple appendectomy remains standard treatment and will be curative in nearly all cases;[19,23] right hemicolectomy has been recommended for tumors within this group showing extensive mesenteric invasion but remains controversial because of sparse data.[27,28] For tumors at the base of the appendix, cecectomy may be required to ensure clear margins.

RECTAL CARCINOIDS

Incidence

Carcinoid tumors have been estimated to account for 1.3 percent of all neoplasms of the rectum and rectosigmoid.[5,29] The great majority are small, benign-appearing nodules found incidentally on proctoscopic examination. Their frequency of detection is approximately 1 in every 2500 proctoscopies.[30] These tumors are discovered most commonly in the fifth and sixth decades of life and are distributed equally between men and women.[18,22,30]

Clinical Presentation

Rectal carcinoids arise from the deep mucosa. The typical appearance is a small (<1.0 cm), solitary, firm, submucosal nodule on the anterior wall of the rectum. However, appearances vary and include small polypoid forms and larger, ulcerated, malignant forms.[31] Multicentricity is rare. Diagnosis requires biopsy and histologic evaluation. The microscopic appearance is identical to that of carcinoids at other sites, although only a minority of rectal carcinoids take up or reduce silver stains.[11]

Clinical presentation for 80 to 90 percent of cases is an asymptomatic nodule found on proctoscopy for screening or for evaluation of another condition. The vast majority prove to be unaggressive neoplasms that are cured by simple removal. In fact, management by biopsy alone or by incomplete removal is rarely associated with recurrence.[31] The remaining 10 to 20 percent of cases present with a range of symptoms indistinguishable from those of adenocarcinoma of the rectum: bleeding, change in defecation pattern, obstruction, tenesmus, and pain. Almost all symptomatic lesions are aggressive cancers that are ultimately fatal.[13,20,31] Such marked differences in presentation and outcome have caused some authors to distinguish "benign" and "malignant" forms; however, no histopathologic, biochemical, or genetic differences have been found to suggest the existence of two biological forms of this neoplasm.[31]

Metastatic involvement of the liver can be seen at initial presentation. This may be clinically silent or, in advanced cases, may present with cachexia, weakness, right-upper-quadrant pain, and fatigue. In most cases liver metastases are multifocal and not amenable to surgical treatment. Liver resection may rarely be offered for palliation of symptomatic tumors and for treatment of localized tumors that can be completely resected. Liver metastases from colorectal carcinoids rarely produce the malignant carcinoid syndrome. Additional sites of potential metastatic spread are the lungs, bone, spleen, pancreas, adrenals, broad ligament, and kidneys.[21]

Treatment and Results

Local excision is adequate treatment for early, asymptomatic lesions. Radical resection has generally been used for tumors at highest risk for metastatic spread to regional lymph nodes. Tumor size, ulceration, symptoms, invasion of the muscularis propria, and mitotic rate have been found to correlate with the presence of lymph node metastasis.[13,18,20,22,30–32] Tumor size is the most useful prognostic factor. Tumors less than 1.0 cm in diameter are only rarely (0 to 3 percent) associated with metastatic disease.[22,30] Tumors 1.0 to 1.9 cm in diameter are found to have metastases in about 10 percent of cases.[18,22,30,32] Tumors greater than 2.0 cm are associated with regional lymph node or liver metastases in 80 to 100 percent of cases.[13,22,30,31] Radical resection has traditionally been recommended for rectal carcinoids 2 cm or more in diameter.

Invasion of the muscularis propria has been proposed as an additional indication for radical resection.[18,20,32] Overall, about one-third of rectal carcinoids treated surgically are locally invasive into muscle, and 60 percent of these are associated with metastatic disease.[33] Some 80 percent of tumors greater than 2 cm in diameter invade muscle, but the presence or absence of muscle invasion does not add prognostic information.[32,33] Only 20 percent of tumors less than 2 cm in diameter invade muscle. In this group, the presence of muscle invasion increases the risk of metastatic disease from 2 percent to 40 to 48 percent.[32,33]

Despite widespread recognition of these prognostic factors, the proper use and benefit of radical resection is debatable.[13,29,31,32] Most patients with large, symptomatic, invasive tumors will die of distant metastatic disease regardless of treatment.[13,31] In one series, all patients with tumors larger than 2 cm in diameter or with regional lymph node metastases died of disease, with a median survival time of less than 1 year.[13] Five-year survival rates for large tumors are reported at 5 to 40 percent.[13,18,31] Ultimate cure rates are undoubtedly even lower, because relapse up to 10 years after surgical treatment can occur.[13,31] It is therefore reasonable to question whether patients with regional disease are curable. For many advanced tumors, local excision may provide equivalent local control and palliation of symptoms with less morbidity.[13]

Current treatment guidelines are controversial but can be summarized as follows. Tumors less than 1 cm in diameter may be endoscopically removed, fulgurated, or locally excised. Regardless of method, the goal of treatment should be complete ablation. Tumors 1.0 to 1.9 cm in diameter should be treated initially by full-thickness local excision. Tumors confined to the submucosa require no further treatment. Tumors invading into or through the muscularis propria are at higher risk of lymph node metastases and may be considered, on a selective basis, for radical resection. For tumors larger than 2 cm in diameter, there is no standard management, and treatment should be recommended on an individual basis. For older patients with accessible lesions, palliative local excision may be the best option. For younger patients and for lesions of the upper rectum, anterior resection may be preferable. Before radical surgery is undertaken, distant metastases should be excluded by abdominal computed tomography and chest x-rays.

COLONIC CARCINOIDS

Incidence

Colonic carcinoids represent approximately 0.3 percent of all cancers of the colon.[5,6] These tumors are most commonly found in patients in the sixth, seventh, and eighth decades of life and occur with equal frequency in men and women.[5,6] The age-adjusted incidence for the United States has been estimated at 0.31 cases/100,000 population/year.[6]

Clinical Presentation

The clinical presentation of carcinoids of the colon is indistinguishable from adenocarcinoma of the colon.[5,34] Most patients seek medical attention because of pain, partial obstruction, bleeding, anemia, diarrhea, weight loss, or malaise. Approximately 4 percent of patients present with the malignant carcinoid syndrome or elevated urinary 5-hydroxyindoleacetic acid (5-HIAA), and nearly all have lesions arising in the right colon, which is derived from the embryonic midgut.[34] Tumor detection is by barium enema or colonoscopy. The tumors are distributed throughout the colon, with several series noting a preponderance of cecal lesions.[5,6,12,34] Most are advanced lesions, with regional lymph node metastases found in 60 percent and liver metastases in 30 to 40 percent.[6,12,34]

Treatment and Results

Treatment is by standard hemicolectomy. Overall patient survival is estimated at 25 to 37 percent at 5 years.[6,34] Poor outcome is explained primarily by the large number of advanced tumors at presentation. The small subset (15 to 20 percent) of carcinoids that are found and resected at an early stage (<2 cm in diameter, confined to bowel wall) are associated with 5-year survival rates in excess of 80 percent.[6] In some series, inclusion of undifferentiated and anaplastic variants may contribute to the low cure rates.[11,12] Resection of hepatic metastases is usually not feasible due to multifocal disease but is recommended when complete removal can be accomplished safely. Over 70 percent of patients with hepatic metastases die within 1 year.[6]

ASSOCIATED NEOPLASMS

Approximately 15 to 40 percent of patients with gastrointestinal carcinoids will have a second neoplasm, either synchronous or metachronous.[5,6,13,27,35] Over two-thirds involve the gastrointestinal tract and include additional carcinoid tumors, colorectal cancers and polyps, and gastric cancers. A wide array of other cancers are also described, with breast, bladder, and lung being the most frequent sites.[27,36] The clinical significance of associated neoplasms is attested to by one report in which 19 percent of patients with colonic carcinoids died of metachronous gastrointestinal cancer.[6] Every patient with carcinoid tumor should be thoroughly screened for second neoplasms, including a complete evaluation of the gastrointestinal tract.

POSTOPERATIVE FOLLOW-UP

Patients undergoing potentially curative surgery are followed in a fashion similar to that for patients with gastrointestinal carcinomas. Physical examination, liver function tests, and abdominal computed tomography are the usual methods of evaluation. Some tumors progress slowly, and isolated local or liver recurrences should be considered for surgical resection. The malignant carcinoid syndrome is rarely seen but may occasionally develop in patients with right-sided colonic tumors.

CHEMOTHERAPY AND RADIATION THERAPY

There is no standard chemotherapy with proven efficacy for carcinoid tumor. Metastatic disease may remain stable for long periods and not require intervention. The largest experience with chemotherapy for carcinoid tumors is for treatment of liver metastases. Streptozotocin, 5-fluorouracil, methotrexate, doxorubicin, cyclophosphamide, carboplatinum, interferon, and octreotide have been tested in phase II trials.[2,37–39] The best response rates for combination therapy are between 20 and 40 percent with most responses lasting only a few months. Toxicity can be significant.

Because of these disappointing results, chemotherapy should be restricted to clinical trials for metastatic disease that is symptomatic or progressing. Palliation for symptomatic liver metastases may also be achieved with hepatic artery embolization or surgical debulking. Radiation therapy has been used for palliation of symptomatic bone and skin metastases.[40] At present there is no role for chemotherapy or radiation therapy in an adjuvant setting.

REFERENCES

1. Masson P: Carcinoids (argentaffin-cell tumors) and nerve hyperplasia of the appendicular mucosa. *Am J Pathol* 4:181–212, 1928.
2. Moertel CG: An odyssey in the land of small tumors. *J Clin Oncol* 5:1503–1522, 1987.
3. Kultschitzky N: Zur Frage uber den Bau des Darmkanals. *Arch Mikrosk Anat* 49:7, 1897.
4. Pearse AGE, Tabor TT: Embryology of the diffuse neuroendocrine system and its relationship to the common peptides. *Fed Proc* 38:2288, 1979.
5. Godwin JD II: Carcinoid tumors: An analysis of 2837 cases. *Cancer* 36:560–569, 1975.
6. Ballantyne GH, Savoca PE, Flannery JT, et al: Incidence and mortality of carcinoids of the colon: Data from the Connecticut Tumor Registry. *Cancer* 69:2400–2405, 1992.
7. Williams ED, Sanders M: The classification of carcinoid tumors. *Lancet* 1:238, 1963.
8. Dawson IMP: The endocrine cells of the gastrointestinal tract and the neoplasms which arise from them, in Morson BC (ed): *Pathology of the Gastrointestinal Tract: Current Topics in Pathology*. New York, Springer-Verlag, 1976, pp 222–258.
9. Soga J, Tazawa K: Pathologic analysis of carcinoids: Histologic re-evaluation of 62 cases. *Cancer* 28:990–998, 1971.
10. Martin ED, Potet F: Pathology of endocrine tumors of the GI tract. *Clin Gastroenterol* 3:511–532, 1974.
11. Federspiel BH, Burke AP, Sobin LH, et al: Rectal and colonic carcinoids: A clinicopathologic study of 84 cases. *Cancer* 65:135–140, 1990.
12. Staren ED, Gould VE, Warren WH, et al: Neuroendocrine carcinomas of the colon and rectum: A clinicopathologic evaluation. *Surgery* 104:1080–1089, 1988.
13. Sauven P, Ridge JA, Quan SH, et al: Anorectal carcinoid tumors: Is aggressive surgery warranted? *Ann Surg* 211:67–71, 1990.
14. Shirouzu K, Isomot H, Kakegawa T, et al: Treatment of rectal carcinoid tumors. *Am J Surg* 160:262–265, 1990.
15. Rutledge RH, Alexander JW: Primary appendiceal malignancies: Rare but important. *Surgery* 111:244–250, 1992.
16. Hamada Y, Oishi A, Shoji T, et al: Endocrine cells and prognosis in patients with colorectal carcinoma. *Cancer* 69:2641–2646, 1992.
17. Johnson LA, Lavin P, Moertel CG, et al: Carcinoids: The association of histologic growth pattern and survival. *Cancer* 51:882–889, 1983.
18. Orloff MJ: Carcinoid tumors of the rectum. *Cancer* 28:175–180, 1971.
19. Moertel CG, Dockerty MB, Jedd ES: Carcinoid tumors of the vermiform appendix. *Cancer* 21:270–278, 1968.
20. Peskin GW, Orlof MJ: A clinical study of 25 patients with carcinoid tumors of the Rectum. *Surg Gynecol Obstet* 109:673, 1959.
21. Wilson H, Cheek RC, Sherman RT, et al: Carcinoid tumors. *Curr Probl Surg* 7:1–51, 1971.
22. Bates H: Carcinoid tumors of the rectum: A statistical review. *Dis Colon rectum* 9:90, 1966.
23. Moertel CG, Weiland LH, Nagorney DM, et al: Carcinoid tumors of the small intestine and appendix. *N Engl J Med* 317:1699–1701, 1987.
24. Dent TL, Batsakis JG, Lindenauer SM: Carcinoid tumors of the appendix. *Surgery* 73:828–832, 1973.
25. Dunn JP: Carcinoid tumors of the appendix: Twenty-one cases, with a review of the literature. *NZ Med J* 95:73–76, 1982.
26. Syracuse DC, Perzin KH, Price JB, et al: Carcinoid tumors of the appendix: Mesoappendiceal extension and nodal metastases. *Ann Surg* 190:58–63, 1979.
27. Thompson GB, van Heerden JA, Martin JK, et al: Carcinoid tumors of the gastrointestinal tract: Presentation, management, and prognosis. *Surgery* 98:1054–1062, 1985.
28. Bowman GA, Rosenthal D: Carcinoid tumors of the appendix. *Am J Surg* 146:700–703, 1983.
29. Quan SHQ, Bader C, Berg JW: Carcinoid tumors of the rectum. *Dis Colon Rectum* 7:197–206, 1964.
30. Caldarola VT, Jackman RJ, Moertel CG, et al: Carcinoid tumors of the rectum. *Am J Surg* 107:844–849, 1964.
31. Burke M, Shepherd N, Mann CV: Carcinoid tumours of the rectum and anus. *Br J Surg* 74:358–361, 1987.
32. Naunheim KS, Zeitels J, Kaplan EL, et al: Rectal carcinoid tumors: Treatment and prognosis. *Surgery* 94:670–675, 1983.
33. Bates H: Carcinoid tumors of the rectum. *Dis Colon Rectum* 5:270–280, 1962.
34. Rosenberg JM, Welch JP: Carcinoid tumors of the colon: A study of 72 patients. *Am J Surg* 149:775–779, 1985.
35. Greenberg RS, Baumgarten DA, Clark WS, et al: Prognostic factors for gastrointestinal and bronchopulmonary carcinoid tumors. *Cancer* 60:2476–2483, 1987.
36. Moertel CG, Sauer WG, Dockerty MB, et al: Life history of the carcinoid tumor of the small intestine. *Cancer* 14:901–912, 1961.
37. Moertel CG: Treatment of carcinoid tumor and the malignant carcinoid syndrome. *J Clin Oncol* 1:727, 1983.
38. Saltz L, Trochanowski B, Buckley M, et al: Octreotide as an antineoplastic agent in the treatment of functional and nonfunctional neuroendocrine tumors. *Cancer* 72:244–248, 1993.
39. Saltz L, Lauwers G, Wisegerg J, et al: A phase II trial of carboplatin in patients with advanced APUD tumors. *Cancer* 72:619–622, 1993.
40. Maton PN, Hodgson HJF: Carcinoid tumors and the carcinoid syndrome, in Bouchier IAD, Allan RN, Hodgson HJF, et al (eds): *Textbook of Gastroenterology*. London, Bailliére-Tindall, 1984, 620.

CHAPTER 98

Sarcoma

Philip B. Paty
Elin R. Sigurdson

HIGHLIGHTS

Virtually all colorectal sarcomas are leiomyosarcomas that arise from smooth muscle cells of the intestinal wall. Presenting symptoms and endoscopic findings may be nonspecific, requiring surgical exploration for diagnosis. Complete resection is possible in 50 to 60 percent. Metastases to the peritoneal cavity and liver are common. Only 10 to 20 percent of completely resected patients are cured of disease. Patients with low-grade tumors live significantly longer than those with high-grade tumors. Despite disappointing cure rates, radical resection provides good palliation. Neither radiation therapy nor chemotherapy has any proven efficacy as adjuvant therapies.

CONTROVERSIES

The roles of sphincter-saving resections and local excision for rectal sarcoma are unclear. Traditional treatment has been abdominoperineal resection. Local excision has a rational basis given the low incidence of lymph node involvement by colorectal sarcomas, but most of the existing data suggest that recurrence rates after local excision of rectal sarcoma are unacceptably high.

FUTURE DIRECTIONS

Anecdotal case reports suggest that adjuvant radiation therapy may expand the role of sphincter-preserving surgery for rectal sarcoma. Randomized trials of adjuvant radiation for soft tissue sarcoma of the extremity indicate that adjuvant radiation improves local control; these trials provide a strong rationale for use of adjuvant radiation for anorectal sarcoma.

INCIDENCE

Sarcomas of the large intestine account for approximately 0.1 percent of all colorectal malignant tumors.[1–3] Their annual incidence has been estimated at 0.45 cases per million persons.[2] Adults of all ages can be affected; most cases occur in the fifth and sixth decades of life.[4,5] Males are affected more often than females (M:F ratio 1.8:1).[1,4–7]

PATHOLOGY

Sarcomas of the gastrointestinal (GI) tract arise from the stromal cells of the intestinal wall. Although intestinal fibrosarcoma,[8] angiosarcoma,[9] malignant fibrous histiocytoma,[6] hemangiopericytoma,[1] and other histologic types occur, in adults over 95 percent of GI sarcomas are leiomyosarcomas.[1,6] Leiomyosarcomas are derived from the smooth muscle cells of the muscularis propria and muscularis mucosa.[4] They can be found throughout the alimentary tract, with 5 percent occurring in the esophagus, 50 percent in the stomach, 30 percent in the small bowel, and 15 percent in the colon and rectum. Leiomyosarcoma of the anal canal is an extremely rare tumor that has been described in only a few case reports.[4,10–12] The morphology, clinical behavior, and treatment of leiomyosarcoma are similar regardless of the site of origin within the GI tract.[4,6]

Intestinal leiomyosarcomas are composed of elongated cells that grow in fascicles (Fig. 98-1). Masson trichrome stain demonstrates myofibrils that run longitudinally through the cytoplasm. An epithelial variant composed of round, clear cells has been called "leiomyoblastoma"; because its clinical behavior is no different, it has been recommended that this term be abandoned.[7] A variety of grading systems have been used.[1,4,7,13] All utilize mitotic activity, necrosis, and cellularity as the important criteria. Assignment of grade as either "high" or "low"[1,7] is the preferred system, since it is hard to demonstrate a difference in clinical behavior among three or four groups.[4,13]

Distinguishing benign (leiomyoma) and low-grade malignant forms on morphologic grounds is a well-recognized problem.[7,14,15] Neither small size nor lack of mitotic activity, the most important criteria for the diagnosis of leiomyoma, assures a benign clinical course.[7] In a retrospective study of 56 intestinal smooth muscle tumors followed for a minimum of 10 years, the designation *leiomyoma* could be given to only 2 tumors (3 percent).[7] The other 54 tumors recurred after surgical treatment, some at postoperative intervals greater than 15 years.[7] Because local or distant relapse will occur in at least 80 to 90 percent of cases, the pathologic designation of any smooth-muscle tumor of the intestine as "benign" must be viewed with skepticism.[7]

No single pathologic staging system is widely used. Presentation with metastatic disease and high-grade tumor are the most important prognostic variables.[1,4,6] Tumor size is important in univariate analysis but is highly correlated with and secondary in importance to grade.[1] In general, site within the GI tract has not been found to be of major prognostic importance.[4,6] However, for large intestinal sarcomas, patients with colonic tumors are more likely to present with advanced, metastatic tumors than patients with rectal sarcomas.[1]

The common sites of metastases are the peritoneal cavity and the liver. Lung metastases are less common and usually occur in combination with metastases to the peritoneum or liver.[1] Metastases to regional lymph nodes have been observed in about 12 percent of colorectal sarcomas.[1]

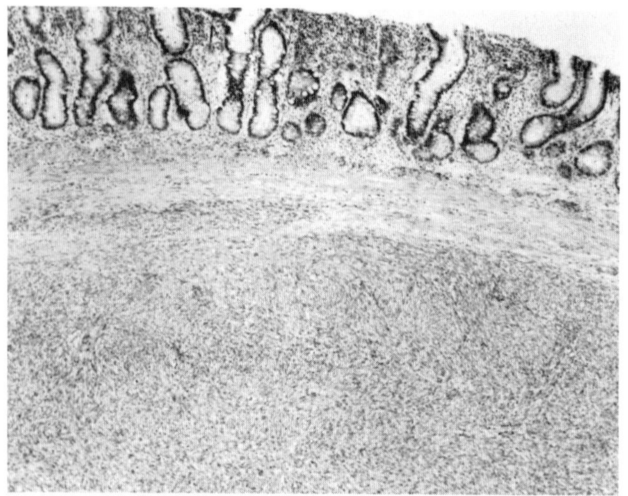

A

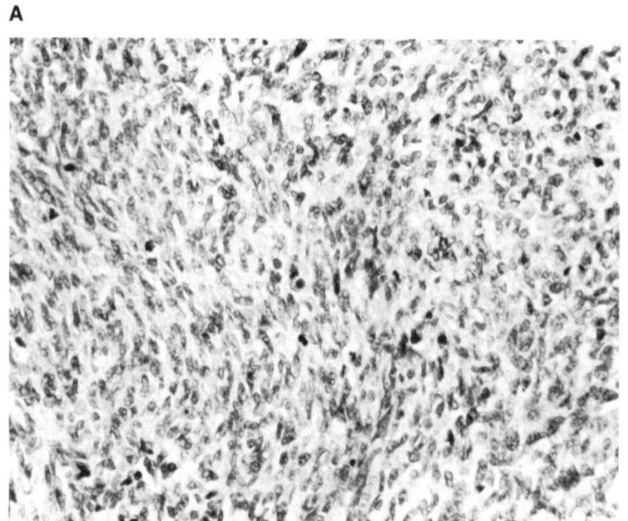

B

FIG. 98-1. *A*. Leiomyosarcoma of colon involving the submucosa (40×). *B*. High-grade leiomyosarcoma with numerous mitotic figures (250×). (Courtesy of S. Sternberg, M.D., New York.)

CLINICAL PRESENTATION

Pain (abdominal, pelvic, or rectal), bleeding, and changes in bowel habits are the most common presenting symptoms.[1,4,5] Rare presentations include hemoperitoneum, intussusception, volvulus, partial bowel obstruction, and abscess.[1,5] Recognition that approximately 8 percent of cases will masquerade as inflammatory disease—diverticulitis, appendiceal abscess, perirectal abscess—is important, because these presentations may lead to delays in diagnosis.[1]

The endoscopic and radiographic appearance of large bowel sarcomas is usually that of a submucosal mass, although polypoid forms do occur.[5] Focal ulceration is present in 40 to 50 percent.[5,14] Large tumor size, dumbbell shape, irregular mucosal pattern, and a barium-filled tumor cavity are signs suggestive of leiomyosarcoma on barium enema.[4] Endoscopic biopsy is often nondiagnostic. The correct histologic diagnosis is appreciated in fewer than half of the cases at the time of operation.[2]

TREATMENT AND RESULTS

Treatment is by radical resection whenever complete removal of tumor can be accomplished. Complete resection is possible in approximately 50 to 60 percent of cases.[1,4] Most unresectable tumors have metastasized to the liver or the peritoneal cavity at the time of exploration.[1] Because of the short life expectancy, attempts to resect metastatic disease are not recommended. Partial resections are, in general, not believed to benefit the patient.[1]

Local excision for low rectal lesions has been performed by experienced surgeons on a selective basis for small, low-grade tumors.[16] However, there are inadequate data to evaluate the optimal selection criteria and results of this approach. When data are accumulated from many small reports in the literature, the overall local recurrence rate following local excision is excessive (68 percent) and is significantly inferior to the local recurrence rate achieved by abdominoperineal resection (20 percent).[5] Local excision with adjuvant radiation for small anal sarcomas has given good short-term results in two case reports.[11,12]

Of patients resected for cure, approximately 20 to 30 percent will develop local failure and 60 to 90 percent will ultimately develop distant metastases.[1,4,5] The risk of local failure applies both to colonic and rectal tumors.[1] Patients remain at risk for relapse for up to 15 years. A credible assessment of treatment results therefore requires that survivors be followed for at least 10 years.[1,2,4,7]

The available data suggest that only 10 to 20 percent of all completely resected patients are cured of disease.[1,2,4,5] Patients with low-grade tumors live significantly longer (median survival, 5 to 10 years) than those with high-grade tumors (median survival, 2 to 3 years).[1,4,7] Despite the disappointing long-term cure rates, radical resection does provide good palliation for many years. For colonic tumors, hemicolectomy with radical mesenteric resection is recommended, given the 10 percent risk of lymph node metastases. Most patients with rectal tumors have been treated with abdominoperineal resection.[1,5] Sphincter-sparing resections have been reported and, with proper selection, do not appear to compromise treatment.[17]

CHEMOTHERAPY AND RADIATION THERAPY

Because of the rarity of gastrointestinal sarcomas, there is only anecdotal experience with chemotherapy and radiation therapy. In most instances, these modalities have been used in an attempt to palliate unresectable symptomatic tumors. Although the high relapse rates after surgical resection make adjuvant therapy appealing in theory, the efficacy of adjuvant chemotherapy and radiation therapy for these tumors is unknown. Trials designed solely for gastrointestinal sarcomas are not feasible. Trials of adjuvant chemotherapy for retroperitoneal sarcomas have shown no benefit.[18,19] On the other hand, adjuvant radiotherapy for soft tissue sarcoma of the extremity does reduce local recurrence.[20] Local excision plus high-dose radiation therapy for anorectal sarcomas has provided good short-term results in a few reported cases[11,12,17] and suggests that wider use of adjuvant radiation therapy for selected anorectal sarcomas might enhance local control.

REFERENCES

1. Meijer S, Peretz T, Gaynor JJ, et al: Primary colorectal sarcoma: A retrospective review and prognostic factor study of 50 consecutive patients. *Arch Surg* 125:1163–1168, 1993.
2. Friesen R, Moyana TN, Murray RB, et al: Colorectal leiomyosarcomas: A pathologic study with long-term follow-up. *Can J Surg* 35:505–508, 1992.
3. Dukes CE, Bussey HJ: Sarcoma and melanoma of the rectum. *Br J Cancer* 1:30–37, 1947.
4. Akwari OE, Dozois RR, Weiland LH, et al: Leiomyosarcoma of the small and large bowel. *Cancer* 42:1375–1384, 1978.
5. Khalifa AA, Bong WL, Rao VK, et al: Leiomyosarcoma of the rectum: Report of a case and review of the literature. *Dis Colon Rectum* 29:427–432, 1986.
6. McGrath PC, Neifeld JP, Lawrence W, et al: Gastrointestinal sarcomas: Analysis of prognostic factors. *Ann Surg* 206:706–710, 1987.
7. Evans HL: Smooth muscle tumors of the gastrointestinal tract: A study of 56 cases followed for a minimum of 10 years. *Cancer* 56:2242–2250, 1985.
8. Bonser RS, McMaster P, Acland PC, et al: Fibrosarcoma of the transverse colon. *J Surg Oncol* 31:34–35, 1986.
9. Taxy JB, Battifora H: Angiosarcoma of the gastrointestinal tract: A report of three cases. *Cancer* 62:210216, 1988.
10. Wolfson P, Oh C: Leiomyosarcoma of the rectum: Report of a case. *Dis Colon Rectum* 20:600–602, 1977.
11. Minsky BD, Mies C, Rich TA: Leiomyosarcoma of the anus treated with sphincter preserving surgery and radiation therapy. *J Surg Oncol* 32:89–91, 1986.
12. Minsky BD, Cohen AM, Hajdu SI: Conservative management of anal leiomyosarcoma. *Cancer* 68:1640–1643, 1991.
13. MacDougall PM: The cancer risk in ulcerative colitis. *Lancet* 2:655–658, 1966.
14. Ranchod J, Kempson RL: Smooth muscle tumors of the gastrointestinal tract and retroperitoneum: A pathologic analysis of 100 cases. *Cancer* 39:255–262, 1977.
15. He LJ, Wang BS, Chen CC: Smooth muscle tumours of the digestive tract: Report of 160 cases. *Br J Surg* 75:184–186, 1988.
16. Quan SH, Berg JW: Leiomyoma and leiomyosarcoma of the rectum. *Dis Colon Rectum* 5:415–425, 1962.

17. Minsky BD, Cohen AM, Hajdu SI, et al: Sphincter preservation in rectal sarcoma. *Dis Colon Rectum* 33:319322, 1990.
18. Glenn J, Sindelar WF, Kinsella T, et al: Results of multimodality therapy of resectable soft tissue sarcoma of the retroperitoneum. *Surgery* 97:316–325, 1985.
19. Bramwell V, Rouesse W, Steward A, et al: European experience of adjuvant chemotherapy for soft tissue sarcoma: Interim report of a randomized trial of CYVADIC versus control, in Ryan JR, Baker LO (eds): *Recent Concepts in Sarcoma Treatment*. Tarpon Springs, Fla, Kluwer, 1988.
20. Brennan MF, Hilaris B, Shiu MH, et al: Local recurrence in soft tissue sarcoma: A randomized trial of brachytherapy. *Arch Surg* 122:1289–1293, 1987.

CHAPTER 99

Lymphoma

Philip B. Paty
Elin R. Sigurdson

HIGHLIGHTS

Lymphomatous involvement of the large intestine may be primary or secondary. Primary colorectal lymphomas are non-Hodgkin's lymphomas (NHL), many of which have histologies not seen in NHL of nodal origin. Presenting symptoms are nonspecific, and endoscopic biopsy is often inadequate to establish a diagnosis. Staging should include computed tomography (CT) of the abdomen and pelvis, chest films, peripheral blood smear, and bone marrow biopsy/aspiration. Unlike treatment of nodal lymphomas, surgical resection of colorectal lymphomas has a major, sometimes curative role. Surgery, radiation therapy, and chemotherapy have been used individually and in combination, but optimal therapy is unknown. For localized tumors, surgical resection is recommended.

CONTROVERSIES

Surgical resection, radiation therapy, and combination chemotherapy each have curative potential in colorectal lymphoma. However, treatment guidelines are controversial. The use of adjuvant radiation after surgical resection of colonic lymphomas is particularly controversial, given the difficulty in defining radiation fields, the risk of toxicity to the small intestine, and the availability of active chemotherapy regimens as an alternative.

FUTURE DIRECTIONS

Modern multidrug chemotherapy regimens used successfully for nodal lymphomas have yet to be adequately tested for their efficacy in treating gastrointestinal (GI) lymphomas. Adjuvant combination chemotherapy given postoperatively has been reported to increase survival in small, nonrandomized series. As more experience is gained, the role of combination chemotherapy in adjuvant and primary therapy is likely to expand.

Lymphomas of the large intestine are rare but interesting neoplasms that share many features with lymphomas arising in other gastrointestinal sites. Varied clinical presentation, complex histology and staging, and nonstandardized treatment make clinical management of these tumors most challenging. Unlike treatment of lymphomas arising in nodal areas, surgical resection plays a major, sometimes curative role.

INCIDENCE

Lymphoma accounts for only 0.2 percent of all primary malignancies of the large intestine.[1,2] The disease can occur in children but is most commonly seen in adults in the fourth to seventh decades of life.[1,3–6] Several series report a slight preponderance of males.[2,7–11]

DIAGNOSIS AND STAGING

Lymphomatous involvement of the GI tract may be primary or secondary. This distinction, which is not always straightforward, is important because of significant differences in treatment and prognosis. Primary GI lymphomas are believed to arise in the small bowel from Peyer's patches and in the stomach and large intestine from lymphocytes associated with the mucosa.[1,9,12] Virtually all these tumors are NHL. Gastrointestinal involvement by Hodgkin's disease is extremely rare, occurring in only 0.25 percent of cases.[8] In contrast, GI tumors account for approximately 10 to 15 percent of all NHL at the time of diagnosis.[3] Secondary infiltration of the GI tract by lymphoma of nodal origin is infrequent at diagnosis but becomes more common in the late stages of disease; at autopsy, 50 to 70 percent of patients dying of NHL have demonstrable infiltration of the intestine.[13] Management of secondary lymphomas are considered separately at the end of this chapter.

The criteria for diagnosis of primary GI lymphoma were first stated in 1961 by Dawson et al.[14] and have been modified little. Tumors are considered primary when (1) a tumor mass in the intestine is confirmed histologically as lymphoma; (2) palpable peripheral adenopathy and hepatosplenomegaly are absent; (3) there is no evidence of lymphoma on standard chest films or chest CT scan; (4) peripheral blood smear and bone marrow aspiration/biopsy are normal. Nearly all primary intestinal lymphomas present with symptoms referable to the GI tract.

The most common site of origin is the stomach (60 percent), followed by the small intestine (25 percent) and the large intestine (15 percent).[10] Within the large bowel, the cecum and rectum are most frequently involved.[3] Many cecal lesions are large and also involve the ileum, making their precise site of origin uncertain.[3]

Two separate lesions will present synchronously in about 5 percent of patients.[1,3] Multiple lymphomatous nodules involving all or a portion of the large bowel, so-called multiple lymphomatous polyposis, account for 10 to 25 percent of colorectal lymphomas and are sometimes accompanied by lymphomatous lesions in the small bowel or stomach.[1,3,15]

The usual routes of spread for GI lymphomas are via lymphatics to regional and retroperitoneal nodes and by invasion into adjacent organs. Spread outside the abdomen is uncommon. Even among patients who do not respond to therapy, disease usually remains confined to the abdomen at the time of death.[10] The Ann Arbor system commonly used for nodal lymphomas is unsatisfactory for primary intestinal lymphomas because it does not adequately distinguish between patients with varying degrees of intraabdominal disease.[16] Several alternative staging systems have been proposed, including the Dukes system,[1] the TNM system,[7] the Manchester system,[17] and the modified systems of Rao[10] and of Musshoff.[18] For prognosis, it is important to distinguish between involvement of regional/mesenteric lymph nodes and retroperitoneal lymph nodes (Table 99-1).

HISTOLOGY

Lymphomas of the colon and rectum encompass a broad range of histologic types. Only a minority are recognizable as types found in nodal lymphomas.[9] Most are polymorphic (Fig. 99-1) and difficult to characterize by standard pathologic classifications such as those of Kiel, Luke-Collins, or Rappaport.[1,19,20] The vast majority of large bowel lymphomas express B-cell surface markers and exhibit a diffuse growth pattern.[1] Plasmacytoid differentiation is seen in 25 percent of cases (versus 5 percent of nodal lymphomas) and is important because it defines a low-grade, favorable

Table 99-1
Pathologic Staging Systems for Primary Gastrointestinal Lymphoma

Ann Arbor[1]	*Rao et al.*[10]	*Musshoff et al.*[16]	*Extent of disease*	*Relative frequency,*[10] *percent*	*5-year survival,*[10] *percent*
IE	IE	IE	Tumor confined to bowel wall	26	87
IIE	IIE	IIE_1	Tumor with spread to regional lymph nodes	26	67
IIE	IIIE	IIE_2	Tumor with nodal involvement beyond regional lymph nodes (i.e., iliac, paraaortic)	17	40
IIIE–IV	IVE	IIIE–IV	Tumor with spread to other organs within abdomen (i.e., liver, spleen) or beyond abdomen (i.e., chest, bone marrow)	31	13

SOURCE: From Ref. 29. (© W. B. Saunders Co. Reproduced by permission.)

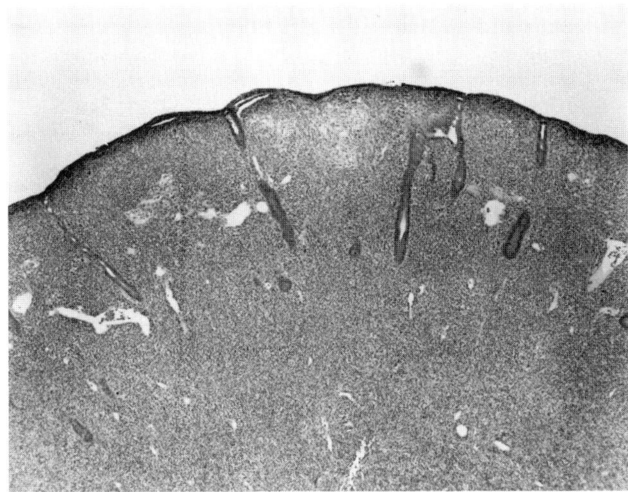

A

B

FIG. 99-1. *A*. Malignant lymphoma, colon, involving mucosa and submucosa (20 ×). *B*. Diffuse, mixed small- and large-cell type lymphoma (250 ×). (Courtesy of S. Sternberg, M.D., New York.)

group.[19] High-grade tumors containing large, blastlike, noncleaved cells account for 30 to 40 percent of cases and have a less favorable outcome.[1,19]

CLINICAL PRESENTATION

Nearly all tumors are symptomatic when diagnosed, and the clinical presentation is indistinguishable from that of colorectal adenocarcinoma. Rectal and rectosigmoid lymphomas most commonly present with rectal bleeding and/or diarrhea.[4,15] For cecal lesions, abdominal pain and weight loss are the predominant symptoms, and a mass is usually palpable.[3,12] Approximately 25 percent of colonic lesions present with bowel obstruction; intussusception is present in half of these cases.[3,21] Perforation is rare at presentation but can occur with radiation therapy or chemotherapy.[1]

Endoscopic and radiographic appearances are highly variable. Five patterns on barium enema have been described: (1) mucosal nodularity, (2) endo-exoenteric mass with mucosal destruction, (3) intraluminal mass, (4) mural infiltration producing anhaustral segments or strictures, and (5) extraluminal-mesenteric mass causing extrinsic compression.[22] The tumors have no distinctive features when visualized endoscopically, and endoscopic biopsy is often inadequate to establish the diagnosis of lymphoma.[3,4]

Whenever colorectal lymphoma is suspected preoperatively, a complete staging evaluation should be obtained: CT scan of the abdomen and pelvis, chest films, peripheral blood smear, and bone marrow biopsy/aspiration. Involvement of superficial lymph nodes or Waldeyer's ring should be excluded by physical examination. Extraintestinal involvement beyond the abdominal lymph nodes usually indicates lymphoma of nodal origin.

Several groups at risk for colorectal lymphoma have been identified. Long-standing ulcerative colitis can give rise to colonic lymphoma; the mean duration of colitic symptoms is 12 years (range, 5 to 30 years).[1,23] The diagnosis is often heralded by a flare in symptoms. Several reports of rectal lymphoma in homosexual men with acquired immunodeficiency syndrome (AIDS) suggest that they are at increased risk for this disease; most of the lymphomas were high in grade and followed an aggressive course.[24–27] Recipients of organ transplants who are taking immunosuppressive drugs are at high risk for colonic lymphoma and often present with perforation.[28]

TREATMENT AND RESULTS

Optimal therapy for GI lymphoma is unknown. The contributions of surgery, radiation therapy, and chemotherapy to outcome are difficult to assess from the available retrospective data. Most series are small, and comparisons between series are hampered by differences in inclusion criteria, staging, and histologic classification. Chemotherapy and radiotherapy have been utilized inconsistently and frequently with substandard regimens.

For colonic lymphoma, surgical resection is the primary treatment modality. Surgical exploration is the initial intervention in over 95 percent of cases, and complete resection is achieved in 50 to 80 percent of those explored.[2,3,11,12,27] For patients presenting with perforation, obstruction, or intussusception, surgery may be lifesaving. In others in whom the diagnosis is uncertain, surgical exploration provides definitive information regarding tumor histology and stage.

Radical colectomy alone can be curative, with 5-year survival rates of 16 to 58 percent.[1,2,17,26] For completely resected stage I tumors, survival has been reported between 67 to 87 percent.[10,17,26] It is more common for surgical resection to be performed in combination with postoperative radiation therapy or chemotherapy. Stage of disease and performance of complete resection are the most important determinants of survival. In addition, high tumor grade and T-cell lineage are consistent poor risk factors. Overall, 5- and 10-year survival rates for colonic lymphoma are about 50 percent.[3,10,12,17]

Abdominal radiation therapy has been used after colonic resection for tumors that are node-positive, bulky, transmural, or incompletely resected. Use of adjuvant radiation is, however, problematic because a wide field is needed and the small intestine has a low tolerance for radiation. Therefore, whole abdominal radiation is generally given at a dose of 2000 to 2500 cGy.[12,29] Several authors have reported improved survival in patients receiving postoperative radiation for GI lymphoma,[2,27,30] but in the absence of prospective data, these reports remain speculative. More recently, adjuvant combination chemotherapy has been reported by several groups to improve survival.[12,26,31]

For primary rectal lymphoma, both surgical resection and radiation therapy have been used successfully as primary therapy.[1,4,15,27] Survival rates for patients treated surgically are in the range of 50 to 60 percent.[1,4,32] For patients treated with primary radiation, complete responses can be achieved in the majority, but survival rates are 20 percent or less.[1,4,15,32] For tumors amenable to complete removal, most authors recommend surgical resection followed by adjuvant pelvic radiation. If complete removal is not feasible, treatment by radiation and chemotherapy is indicated.[1,4,32] As more experience is gained with multidrug regimens effective in nodal lymphomas, chemotherapy may assume an expanded role for many GI lymphomas.[29]

SECONDARY LYMPHOMA

Secondary involvement of the intestine by nodal lymphomas becomes increasingly common during the course of the disease. Most intestinal lesions are clinically silent but can be detected at autopsy.[33] Approximately 3 percent of lymphoma patients will develop symptomatic involvement of the large intestine.[33] The left colon and rectum are the most frequently involved sites, and involvement is often multicentric.[3,4,34]

Nearly all patients have advanced disease. Median survival is in the range of 9 to 18 months.[3,4,34] Primary therapy is directed at the systemic disease and usually consists of chemotherapy alone. Radiation may be effective in palliation of symptomatic rectal lesions. Surgical intervention is reserved for palliation of intestinal obstruction, bleeding, perforation, or other complications.[4]

REFERENCES

1. Shepherd NA, Hall PA, Coates PJ, et al: Primary malignant lymphoma of the colon and rectum: A histopathological and immunohistochemical analysis of 45 cases with clinicopathological correlations. *Histopathology* 12:235–252, 1988.
2. Contreary K, Nance FC, Becker WF: Primary lymphomas of the gastrointestinal tract. *Ann Surg* 191:593–598, 1980.
3. Wychulis AR, Beahrs OH, Woolner LB: Malignant lymphoma of the colon. *Arch Surg* 93:215–225, 1966.
4. Devine RM, Beart RW, Wolff BG: Malignant lymphoma of the rectum. *Dis Colon Rectum* 29:821–824, 1986.
5. Lewin KJ, Ranchod M, Dorfman RF: Lymphomas of the gastrointestinal tract: A study of 117 cases presenting with gastrointestinal disease. *Cancer* 42:693–707, 1978.
6. Fleming ID, Turk PS, Murphy SB, et al: Surgical implications of primary gastrointestinal lymphoma of childhood. *Arch Surg* 125:252–256, 1990.
7. Lim FE, Hartmen AS, Tan EGG, et al: Factors in the prognosis of gastric lymphoma. *Cancer* 39:1715–1720, 1977.
8. Wood NL, Coltman CA: Localized primary extranodal Hodgkin's disease. *Ann Intern Med* 78:113–118, 1973.
9. Isaacson PG, Spencer J, Wright DH: Classifying primary gut lymphomas. *Lancet* 2:1148–1149, 1988.
10. Rao AR, Kagan AR, Potyk D, et al: Management of gastrointestinal lymphoma. *Am J Clin Oncol* 7:213–219, 1984.
11. Hwang WS, Yao JCT, Cheng SS, et al: Primary colorectal lymphoma in Taiwan. *Cancer* 70:575–580, 1992.
12. Auger MJ, Allan NC: Primary ileocecal lymphoma: A study of 22 patients. *Cancer* 65:358–361, 1990.
13. Isaacson P, Wright DH, Judd MA, et al: Primary gastrointestinal lymphomas: A classification of 66 cases. *Cancer* 43: 1805–1819, 1979.
14. Dawson IMP, Conner JS, Morson BC: Primary malignant lymphoid tumors of the intestinal tract: Report of 37 cases with a study of factors influencing prognosis. *Br J Surg* 49:80–89, 1961.
15. Vanden Heule B, Taylor CR, Terry R, et al: Presentation of malignant lymphoma in the rectum. *Cancer* 49:2602–2607, 1982.
16. Carbone P, Kaplan H, Musshoff K, et al: Report of the committee on Hodgkin's disease staging. *Cancer Res* 31:1860–1861, 1971.
17. Blackledge G, Bush H, Dodge OG, et al: Study of gastrointestinal lymphoma. *Clin Oncol* 5:209–219, 1979.
18. Musshoff K: Kliniche Stadieneinteilung der Nicht-Hodgkin-Lymphome. *Strahlentherapie* 153:218–221, 1977.
19. Filippa DA, Lieberman PH, Weingrad DN, et al: Primary lymphomas of the gastrointestinal tract: Analysis of prognostic factors with emphasis on histological type. *Am J Surg Pathol* 7:363–372, 1983.
20. Hall PA, Jass JR, Levison PA, et al: Classification of primary gut lymphomas. *Lancet* 2:958–959, 1988.
21. Jalleh RP, Semeraro D, Vellacott KD: Cecocolic intussusception in multiple lymphomatous polyposis of the gastrointestinal tract: Report of a case. *Dis Colon Rectum* 33:424–426, 1990.
22. O'Connell DJ, Thompson AJ: Lymphoma of the colon: The spectrum of radiologic changes. *Gastrointest Radiol* 2:377–385, 1978.
23. Renton P, Balckshaw AJ: Colonic lymphoma complicating ulcerative colitis. *Br J Surg* 63:542–545, 1976.
24. Burkes RL, Meyer PR, Gill PS, et al: Rectal lymphoma in homosexual men. *Arch Intern Med* 146:913–915, 1986.
25. Lee MH, Waxman M, Gillooley J: Primary malignant lymphoma of the anorectum in homosexual men. *Dis Colon Rectum* 29:413–416, 1986.

26. Richards MA: Lymphoma of the colon and rectum. *Postgrad Med J* 62:615–620, 1986.
27. Naqvi MS, Burrows L, Kark AE: Lymphoma of the gastrointestinal tract: Prognostic guides based on 162 cases. *Ann Surg* 170:221–231, 1969.
28. Phillips DL, Keeffe EB, Benner KG, et al: Colonic lymphoma in the transplant patient. *Dig Dis Sci* 34:150–154, 1989.
29. Haber DA, Mayer RJ: Primary gastrointestinal lymphoma. *Semin Oncol* 15:154–169, 1988.
30. Gospodarowicz MK, Bush RS, Brown TC, et al: Curability of gastrointestinal lymphoma with combined surgery and radiation. *Int J Radiat Oncol Biol Phys* 9:3–9, 1983.
31. Bush RS, Ash CL: Primary lymphoma of the gastrointestinal tract. *Radiology* 92:1349–1354, 1969.
32. Perry PM, Cross RM, Morson BC: Primary malignant lymphoma of the rectum (22 cases). *Proc R Soc Med* 65:8, 1972.
33. Rosenberg SA, Diamond HO, Jaslowitz B, et al: Lymphosarcoma: A review of 1269 cases. *Medicine* 40:31, 1961.
34. Herrmann R, Panahon AM, Barcos MP, et al: Gastrointestinal involvement in non-Hodgkin's lymphoma. *Cancer* 46:215–222, 1980.

PART 17

Anal Cancer

CHAPTER 100

Overview, Epidemiology, and Etiology

Brenda Shank

HIGHLIGHTS

The epidemiology of anal carcinoma is presented with overall incidence rates in the United States and a further breakdown by gender, race, histology, and age.

Possible etiologic and contributory factors are discussed in detail. Etiologic factors considered are human papilloma virus (HPV), other infectious agents (HSV-2, HIV, *Chlamydia,* gonorrhea), oncogenes, and carcinogens (smoking and other chemicals). Contributing factors considered are homosexuality, immunosuppression, Crohn's disease, and chronic anorectal disease.

CONTROVERSIES

The predisposing role of condylomata and anal carcinoma may reflect a host state of enhanced susceptibility to multiple infections (e.g., immunosuppression, excessive exposure to viral agents from anal intercourse), since HPV-16 is highly correlated with anal cancer (but not condylomata) and HPV-6/11 are highly correlated with condylomata (but not anal cancer).

The contribution of other associations, such as chronic anorectal disease, is still unclear, as is the etiologic mechanism of current cigarette smoking, which is clearly contributory.

FUTURE DIRECTIONS

Further studies of the interactions of HPV and smoking with oncogene changes would be very important in the understanding of the mechanism of anal cancer induction.

Prospective studies with antiviral agents in high-risk patients would also be of great interest.

Cancer of the anal area may be divided into two very distinct regions: the anal canal and the anal margin. Tumors of the anal margin may be considered similar in histology, behavior, prognosis, and staging to epidermoid carcinoma of the skin. The treatment of carcinoma of the anal canal, which once required an abdominoperineal resection for cure, has become one of the triumphs of modern multimodality therapy. No longer is colostomy required even for large primary tumors, and overall survival has been increased.

Recent epidemiologic and laboratory studies have found interesting correlations of the human papilloma virus (HPV), as well as other etiologic agents, with the development of cancer of the anal canal.

EPIDEMIOLOGY

Incidence and Mortality

Cancer in the anal region is extremely rare; only 1 to 2 percent of large bowel cancers arise in this area.[1-3]

Table 100-1
Cases of Anal, Anal Canal, and Anorectal Malignancies in the United States by Histology

Histology	No. cases (% of total cases[a])			
	Both sexes	Females	Males	Ratio
Squamous cell carcinoma	296 (47)	102	194	1.9:1 } 2:1
Transitional cell	170 (27)	51	119	2.3:1 } 2:1
Adenocarcinoma	94 (15)	52	42	1:1.2
Carcinoma, NOS	18 (3)	5	13	
Papillary, villous (adeno) carcinoma	16 (3)	9	7	
Other:				
Mucinous adenocarcinoma	13 (2)			
Melanoma	7 (1)			
Mucoepidermoid carcinoma	3			
Adenosquamous carcinoma	2			
Carcinoid	1			
Rhabdomyosarcoma	1			
Leiomyosarcoma	1			
Paget's disease	1			

[a]With known histology.
Abbreviations: NOS = not otherwise specified.
SOURCE: Adapted from Young et al.[4]

In the United States, according to surveillance, epidemiology, and end results (SEER) data, the average annual age-adjusted incidence rate is only 0.6 cases per 100,000.[4] Nonwhite females have the highest incidence (0.9 per 100,000); the lowest incidence (0.5 per 100,000) is among white, Anglo, and Hispanic males. In the 5-year period from 1973–1977, there were only 626 reported cases nationwide. Of these, 125 were defined as being in the anal canal, 214 in the anus, and 287 in other parts of the rectum (anorectum). During the same period, only 19 deaths were reported. The majority of tumors were squamous cell carcinoma (47 percent) and transitional cell carcinoma (27 percent), with a few other histologies (Table 100-1). Melanoma was found only 1 percent of the time.

In a recent analysis, there was no trend of increasing incidence of melanoma with time, as there has been for skin melanoma.[5] There was an increased incidence in northern latitudes (north of 40° latitude).

Sex

In the United States, in contrast to rectal cancer, women have a higher incidence of anal canal carcinoma, with a ratio of about 2:1 for both squamous cell carcinoma and transitional cell carcinoma (Table 100-1). A similar female preponderance (2.3:1) was found for melanoma also.[6] A higher incidence of cancer of the anal canal in women has also been seen in the rest of the western world,[7–9] but a strong male preponderance was noted in New Delhi, India.[10] In one series of 195 patients in Paris, France,[11] the male/female ratio was as high as 6:1.

Recent studies have suggested a higher incidence in male homosexuals, presumably from anal intercourse.[12–18] In a case-control study by Daling et al.[18] (148 patients with anal cancer and 166 controls with colonic cancer), it was found that a history of anal-receptive intercourse in men (but not in women) was highly associated with anal cancer, with a relative risk (RR) of 33.1.

In a study by Peters and Mack[12] of 970 Los Angeles County residents, the incidence of squamous and transitional cell anal carcinomas was six times greater in single men than in married men ($p < .001$). Single women were not at increased risk. In the group below 35 years of age, anal carcinoma was more common in men; this was the reverse of the sex ratio for the group above 35 years of age, in whom there was a substantial female predominance. This was consistent with the authors' hypothesis that anal sexual activity is related to anal cancer. Mechanisms postulated were physical irritation of the anal canal, genital carcinogens (e.g., lubricants), or the transmission of oncogenic viruses by sexual contact. An increased risk for single men (RR = 2.2) was also found in Great Britain.[19] In contrast, unmarried women had a decreased risk of anal cancer (RR = 0.6).

Age

The incidence of anal carcinoma steadily increases after age 30 (Fig. 100-1),[4] reaching 4.7 per 100,000 after age 85. Published series of *treated* patients consist primarily of those between 50 and 80 years old. In one study, 80 percent of *canal* tumors occurred in people

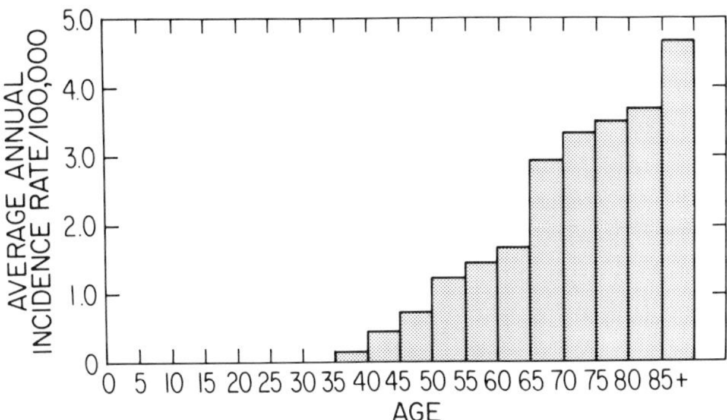

FIG. 100-1. Average annual age-specific incidence rate per 100,000 as a function of age. (From Young et al.,[4] SEER data.)

over age 60, whereas more than 50 percent of *margin* carcinomas developed in people under age 60.[8] In the Peters and Mack[12] series, an increased incidence in men below age 45 was seen in the prior decade; this increase was not found in men above age 45 years or in women of any age. An interesting case report[20] described the almost simultaneous development of squamous cell carcinoma of the anus at age 46 in dizygotic twins who had been separated since they were 20 years old; they had never married and were both heavy smokers and alcoholics, with several convictions and incarcerations.

An analysis of anorectal melanoma[5] demonstrated that the mean age at diagnosis was 70 years (range, 41 to 91 years), with a steadily increasing incidence with age.

ETIOLOGY

Human Papilloma Virus

In recent years, considerable evidence has accumulated implicating the human papilloma virus (HPV) in the pathogenesis of anal cancer. It has long been noted that a relationship exists between this virus and the development of anogenital warts (condyloma acuminata) in the general population[21–27] and in male homosexuals;[28] these may evolve into anal cancer after an interval of 5 to 40 years.[27]

In the case-control study reported by Daling et al.,[18] squamous cell carcinoma (but not transitional cell carcinoma) was strongly correlated with a history of genital warts (RR = 26.9 for heterosexual males, 32.5 for females). Of the 14 patients who had tumors that were positive for HPV, 64 percent had a history of warts. In a study spanning 28 years,[29] 41 of 500 women with condylomata developed anogenital malignancies, compared with only 1 of 246 men.

DNA, specifically from HPV type 16, has been found frequently in invasive squamous cell carcinoma (Table 100-2),[30–33] in contrast to condylomata, in which types 6 and 11, but not 16, are found frequently.[32,34,35]

In one Canadian study,[34] no HPV was found in 13 patients with invasive squamous cell carcinoma of the anal canal. In a study from six other geographic areas, HPV type 16 occurred at a high prevalence in patients with anal canal carcinoma, but there were distinct geographic differences (Table 100-2).[36] In a study using the polymerase chain reaction (PCR) for amplification of

Table 100-2
Frequency of HPV DNA Types in Anal Squamous Cell Carcinomas

		HPV DNA types						
Study (No. pts.)	*Geographic area*	*6*	*11*	*16*	*18*	*31*	*Unclassified, percent*	*Total, percent*
Beckman et al.[30] (70)	Seattle, Washington	12%	0%	14%	1%	—	6	33
Palmer et al.[31] (41)	London, England	0%	0%	56%	5%	—	—	61
Taxy et al.[32] (12)	Illinois	6/11 8%		17%	0%	0%	—	—
Duggan et al.[34] (13)	Alberta, Canada	6 / 0%	11 / 0%	0%	0%	—	—	0
Scholefield et al.[36] (173)	United Kingdom	—	—	43%	—	—	—	—
	Switzerland	—	—	43%	—	—	—	—
	Brazil	—	—	47%	—	—	—	—
	Poland	—	—	35%	—	—	—	—
	South Africa	—	—	11%	—	—	—	—
	India	—	—	3%	—	—	—	—
Kiyabu et al.[33] (4)	Los Angeles, California	—	—	100%	25%	—	—	100
Palefsky et al.[35] (24)	San Francisco, California	6/11 15%		77%	0%	23%	—	85

DNA sequences,[33] HPV type 16 was found in all four anal cancers studied, one of which also contained type 18. Other carcinomas in the genital area tested for HPV types 16 and 18 also were frequently positive for HPV-16, and, occasionally, HPV-18 (70 percent HPV-positivity in all sites); in oropharyngeal sites, HPV-16 was found 36 percent of the time and HPV-18 was not found.

A premalignant condition, anal intraepithelial neoplasia (AIN), was found in 28 percent (23/82) of patients who had HPV infection measured by DNA hybridization.[37] The incidence of AIN was significantly greater in homosexual men with HPV (17/28) than in heterosexual men with HPV (1/26); it was not observed in women with HPV unless cervical intraepithelial neoplasia was present. In a study from England,[38] 5 of 18 women with squamous cell carcinoma of the anus had a prior cervical malignancy (2 invasive and 3 in situ carcinomas); all 5 were positive for HPV DNA type 16 (and not types 6, 11, or 18) in anal and cervical archival tissue. In the study by Palefsky et al.,[35] (Table 100-2), HPV-16 was associated with high-grade AIN as well as invasive cancer, while HPV-6 and HPV-11 were primarily associated with condylomata and low-grade AIN. This is also supported by a study of 19 cases of high-grade AIN diagnosed in routinely excised hemorroidal tissue.[39] In 7/9 (78 percent) of these cases studied by in situ hybridization for HPV mRNA, HPV was found (5 type 16, 1 type 18, and 1 types 6 and 18).

In a 7-year cohort study of homosexual men, Goedert et al.[40] detected anal epithelial atypia in association with HPV detected by DNA hybridization but not by polymerase chain reaction, suggesting that atypia was related to a high level of replicative but not dormant HPV. There also appeared to be an increased reactivation of HPV in the presence of HIV-induced immunodeficiency.

Evidence for HPV in anal adenocarcinomas is scanty. In an Australian study,[41] HPV RNA transcripts were detected in 73 percent of 41 epidermoid carcinomas but in none of 6 anal and 11 rectal adenocarcinomas. Grade 3 AIN was not seen in the surrounding epithelium in any of the 9 HPV RNA-negative tumors but was seen in 14 of 25 RNA-positive tumors; one explanation may be the loss of dependence on RNA expression for maintenance of the neoplastic state as the tumor develops. In a study from New York[42] using PCR to detect HPV DNA, 2 of 6 anal adenocarcinomas had HPV-18, while no HPV was detected in 7 adenocarcinomas of the rectum or colon. In cloacogenic carcinoma, two published studies[43,44] disagree with each other. In a study from British Columbia,[43] none of 14 cases of anal cloacogenic carcinoma was positive for HPV DNA, while 12 of 21 cases of invasive squamous carcinoma were positive for types 16/18 HPV and 2 of 21 for types 6/11. In another study of cloacogenic carcinoma (4 cases from New York and 1 from Spain),[44] HPV DNA type 16/18 was present in 4 of 5, in the nuclei of tumor cells in 3 cases and only in the in situ component of the carcinoma in 1 case.

Other studies have shown linkages between homosexuality, immunosuppression, HPV infection, and/or abnormal cytologic smears.[45–50] In spite of all the evidence linking homosexuality, HPV, and anal cancer, Oriel[51] has suggested caution in assuming direct causality and stressed the need for more studies, including prospective cohort studies of men with anal HPV infection. Caussy et al.[49] proposed a viral interaction model in which HIV-related immunodeficiency allows reactivation of latent HPV, with subsequent development of epithelial abnormality. It is certainly possible but not proven that such abnormalities may progress further, with additional environmental insults, to frank malignancy. Other environmental influences are discussed further on in this chapter. At the genetic level, zur Hausen[52] has reviewed a possible mechanism of carcinogenesis with HPV. In cancer cells, there appears to be an interruption in host intracellular control of downregulation of specific HPV genes (E6, E7), which exists in normal replicating cells. He suggests that this may be due to structural modifications of the respective host-cell genes acquired during the interval of HPV DNA persistence.

Other Infections

When there was no history of genital warts in the analysis of Daling et al.,[18] anal cancer was associated with herpes simplex virus (HSV) type 2 (RR = 4.1) and *Chlamydia* (RR = 2.3) in women and with gonorrhea in men (RR = 17.2). In another study,[53] positive HSV-2 titer was associated with anal cancer in women in a univariate analysis ($p = .0017$), but it was not an independent predictor in a multivariate analysis. Finally, in a study from San Francisco,[35] HSV DNA was detected only in association with advanced disease, in 5 of 13 patients with cancer and 3 of 4 patients with high-grade AIN. Epstein-Barr virus and cytomegalovirus DNA were also sought, but were not detected in 40 specimens.

Although a relationship with HIV infection/AIDS has been suggested,[54,55] an Italian study[56] showed that among 435 HIV-associated tumors in abusers of intravenous drugs, anal tumors were extremely rare.

Oncogenes

A group from the United Kingdom[57] has explored the relationship of oncogenes to squamous cell carcinomas of the anus. Invasive cancer, AIN grade III, and hemorrhoids were assessed for HPV DNA and also for c-*myc*, p53, and retinoblastoma (*Rb-1*) gene abnormalities. HPV-16 was detected in 38 of 50 cancers (76 percent) and HPV-18 in 4 of 50 (8 percent). Amplification of c-*myc* was shown in 15 of 50 cancers (30 percent), of which 13 were positive for HPV-16 and one was positive for HPV-18 (not statistically significant correlation). Amplification of c-*myc* was not observed in any of the 5 AIN or 41 hemorrhoid DNAs analyzed, suggesting that c-*myc* amplification is likely to be a late event in anal malignancy. Gross rearrangement or loss of p53 or *Rb-1* loci was not observed in any of the tissues, but 3 tumors negative for HPV were heterozygous for p53 point mutations whereas 6 HPV-positive tumors and 2 hemorrhoids were wild-type sequence. This supports the idea that loss of p53 wild-type function is important in the etiology of anal cancers.

Although HPV-16 can be shown to cooperate in vitro with activated *ras* oncogenes in cellular transformation, it was suggested, in a series of screened anal tumors, that *ras* activation was not a common event in the genesis of these tumors and that when it did occur it did not appear to cooperate with HPV.[58]

OTHER ASSOCIATED CONDITIONS

Chronic Anorectal Disease

Anal cancer has been associated with anal fistulas, fissures, hemorrhoids, abscesses, leukoplakia, and lymphogranuloma venereum, but vigorous studies of relative risk have rarely been done. One recent study from California,[26] in which cases of anal and rectal squamous cell carcinoma were analyzed in comparison with randomly selected controls, showed that in addition to an increased risk with genital warts, there was an elevated risk for homosexual males who had a history of anal fissure or fistula (RR = 9.1). In heterosexual males and females, the risk was also increased (RR = 2.4) with a history of anal fissure or fistula as well as with a history of more than 12 episodes of hemorrhoids (RR = 2.6).

Crohn's Disease

A group from Australia[59] presented a case report of a patient with anal carcinoma complicating Crohn's disease and tabulated 6 other cases reported in the literature. There was no evidence that Crohn's disease increased the risk of developing anal cancer. Another study from St. Mark's Hospital, London, in the same year,[60] described 10 patients with local malignancy in the setting of anal and rectosigmoid Crohn's disease, 8 with adenocarcinoma of the anus, rectum, or sigmoid and 2 with squamous cell carcinoma of the anus. No HPV DNA was identified in any of the archival material. No firm evidence for an etiologic role of Crohn's disease in the development of anal squamous cell cancer was offered, but the authors speculate that immunosuppressive treatment for Crohn's disease and/or chronic inflammation could possibly contribute to the development of anorectal cancer.

Immunosuppression

Immunosuppression is a major factor increasing the risk of the development of anal cancer, perhaps through a viral oncogenic mechanism. Renal transplant patients, immunosuppressed with a variety of agents (especially prednisone and azathioprine), had a 100-fold increase in anogenital tumors compared with the rest of the population.[61] In several of the patients described in that study, there was a prior history of condylomata (29 percent) or herpes genitalis. A study in heart transplant patients[62] demonstrated a 4 percent incidence of malignant tumors (11 of 275 patients at risk $\geqslant$ 1 months after transplantation). Most (5) were squamous cell carcinomas, but only 1 was of the anus; the others were skin (2), esophagus (1), and larynx (1). Prior radiation therapy may also play a role,[9,63,64] perhaps through immunosuppression.

CHEMICAL CARCINOGENS

Smoking

Smoking has now been implicated in several studies as an important risk factor for the development of anal cancer, as it has been for cancer of the mouth, lung, bladder, and cervix. In the case-control study described by Daling et al.,[18] *current* cigarette smoking was a major risk factor in both sexes (RR = 7.7 in women, 9.4 in men). This supports the earlier report by Daniell,[65] who reported that 54 percent of 13 women with anal cancer were current smokers, while only 26 percent of 202 age-matched patients with colonic cancer were current smokers.

In a matched control study from Kansas,[53] cigarette smoking was implicatd in a univariate analysis along with other factors but was the only one of these factors shown to be an independent and significant factor upon multivariate analysis (p = .0126). Two other independent factors which had not been associated on univariate analysis were significant: previous use of hemorrhoid preparations and history of disturbed bowel habits for more than a month. Both of these latter associations could be the result of the anal cancer rather than a cause.

In the report by Holly et al.,[26] cigarette smoking was a significant independent risk factor for male homosexuals (RR = 1.9 for 20 pack-years and 5.2 for 50 pack-years), but not for females and heterosexual males, when multivariate analysis was done. In the latter groups, the risk was elevated with smoking but the associations were not statistically significant. Daling et al.[66] have presented more recent data in their case-control studies of patients with anogenital cancer in the Washington State and British Columbia area. Patients studied had cancers of the vulva, vagina, cervix, anus, and pelvis. With the exception of cervical cancer, the adjusted odds ratio (OR) was substantially elevated for current cigarette smoking, with the highest risks for anal cancer (OR = 5.2 for females and 14.6 for males) and for vulvar cancer (OR = 4.8). There was a somewhat increased risk among current smokers by number of years smoked for anal cancer only and an indication at all sites of an increased risk with the number of cigarettes smoked per day. The risk among former smokers was considerably less for most sites (for anal cancer, OR = 1.7 for females and 2.0 for males). There was no difference for women or men in the percentage of current smokers among HPV-negative and HPV-positive patients with anal cancer. These authors discuss the possibility that the influence of smoking could be mediated by immune suppression as well as by the direct effect of a carcinogen in cigarette smoke; they allude to their laboratory studies in which *N*-nitrosomethylurea (similar to compounds in tobacco) appears to have a direct role in inducing a malignant phenotype in HPV-18-immortalized keratinocytes.

Animal Studies

In mouse studies, anal squamous cell carcinomas have been induced by chemical carcinogens: 1,2-dimethylhydrazine (DMH)[67] and methylazoxymethanol acetate (MAM acetate).[68] Epidermal growth factor (EGF) was shown to promote the DMH-induced anal squamous cell carcinomas but not colorectal adenocarcinomas.[67]

In summary, HPV-16 is the strongest candidate for a direct role in the genesis of anal carcinoma, but other infectious agents, notably HSV-2 in women and gonorrhea in men, are also implicated. Other contributory factors are immunosuppression and current cigarette smoking. The association of condylomata, which appear to be related to HPV-6/11, may be more a reflection of host conditions, such as immunosuppression.

REFERENCES

1. Grinnell RS: An analysis of forty-nine cases of squamous cell carcinoma of the anus. *Surg Gynecol Obstet* 98:29–39, 1954.
2. Richards JC, Beahrs OH, Woolner LB: Squamous cell carcinoma of the anus, anal canal, and rectum in 109 patients. *Surg Gynecol Obstet* 114:475–481, 1962.
3. Sawyers JL, Herrington JL Jr, Main FB: Surgical considerations in the treatment of epidermoid carcinoma of the anus. *Ann Surg* 157:817–824, 1963.
4. Young JL, Percy CL, Asire AJ: *Surveillance, Epidemiology, and End Results: Incidence and Mortality Data, 1973–77*. National Cancer Institute Monograph 57. Bethesda MD, National Institutes of Health, Public Health Service, 1981.
5. Weinstock MA: Epidemiology and prognosis of ano-rectal malignant melanoma. *Proc ASCO* 11:350, 1992.
6. Nicholls RJ, Ritchie JK, Wadsworth J, et al: Total excision or restorative resection for carcinoma of the middle third of the rectum. *Br J Surg* 66:625–627, 1979.
7. Morson BC, Volkstadt H: Malignant melanoma of the anal canal. *J Clin Pathol* 16:126–132, 1963.
8. McConnell EM: Squamous cell carcinoma of the anus: A review of 96 cases. *Br J Surg* 57:89–92, 1970.
9. Wolfe HRI, Bussey HJR: Squamous cell carcinoma of the anus. *Br J Surg* 55:295–301, 1968.
10. Kapur BML, Dhawan IK, Singhal KK: Epidermoid carcinoma of the anorectum: Review of 31 cases. *Dis Colon Rectum* 20:252–254, 1977.
11. Salmon RJ, Zafrani B, Habib A, et al: Prognosis of cloacogenic and squamous cancers of the anal canal. *Dis Colon Rectum* 29:336–340, 1986.
12. Peters RK, Mack TM: Patterns of anal carcinoma by gender and marital status in Los Angeles County. *Br J Cancer* 48:629–636, 1983.
13. Cantril ST, Green JP, Schall GL, et al: Primary radiation therapy in the treatment of anal carcinoma. *Int J Radiat Oncol Biol Phys* 9:1271–1278, 1983.
14. Cooper HS, Patchefsky AS, Marks G: Cloacogenic carcinoma of the anorectum in homosexual men: An observation of four cases. *Dis Colon Rectum* 22:557–558, 1979.
15. Li FP, Osborn D, Cronin CM: Anorectal squamous carcinoma in two homosexual men. *Lancet* 2:391, 1982.
16. Austin DF: Etiologic clues from descriptive epidemiology: Squamous carcinoma of the rectum or anus. *Natl Cancer Inst Monogr* 62:89–90, 1982.
17. Daling JR, Weiss NS, Klopfenstein LL, et al: Correlates of homosexual behavior and the incidence of anal canal cancer. *JAMA* 247:1988–1990, 1982.
18. Daling JR, Weiss NS, Hislop G, et al: Sexual practices, sexually transmitted diseases, and the incidence of anal cancer. *N Engl J Med* 317:973–977, 1987.
19. Cohen AM: Purse-string placement for transanal intraluminal circular stapling. *Dis Colon Rectum* 29:532–533, 1986.
20. Jovanovic L, Babich M, Thomas K, et al: Simultaneous cloacogenic carcinoma in dizygotic twins. *Cancer* 59:1233–1235, 1987.
21. Siegel A: Malignant transformation of condyloma acuminatum: Review of the literature and case report. *Am J Surg* 103:613–617, 1962.
22. Friedberg MJ, Serlin O: Condyloma acuminatum: Its association with malignancy. *Dis Colon Rectum* 6:352–355, 1963.
23. Oriel JD, Whimster IW: Carcinoma in situ associated with virus-containing anal warts. *Br J Dermatol* 84:71–73, 1971.
24. Prasad ML, Abcarian H: Malignant potential of perianal condyloma acuminatum. *Dis Colon Rectum* 23:191–197, 1980.
25. Longo WE, Ballantyne GH, Gerald WL, et al: Squamous cell carcinoma in situ in condyloma acuminatum. *Dis Colon Rectum* 29:503–506, 1986.
26. Holly E, Whittemore AS, Aston DA, et al: Anal cancer incidence: Genital warts, anal fissure or fistula, hemorrhoids, and smoking. *J Natl Cancer Inst* 81:1726–1731, 1989.
27. zur Hausen H: Human papillomaviruses and their possible role in squamous cell carcinomas. *Curr Top Microbiol Immunol* 78:1–30, 1977.
28. Croxson T, Chabon AB, Rorat E, et al: Intraepithelial carcinoma of the anus in homosexual men. *Dis Colon Rectum* 27:325–330, 1984.
29. Chuang TY, Perry HO, Kurland LT, et al: Condyloma acuminatum in Rochester, Minnesota, 1950–1978. *Arch Dermatol* 257:337–340, 1987.
30. Beckmann AM, Daling JR, Sherman KJ, et al: Human papillomavirus infection and anal cancer. *Int J Cancer* 43:1042–1049, 1989.

31. Palmer JG, Scholefield JH, Coates PJ, et al: Anal cancer and human papillomaviruses. *Dis Colon Rectum* 32:1016–1022, 1989.
32. Taxy JB, Gupta PK, Gupta JW, et al: Anal cancer: Microscopic condyloma and tissue demonstration of human papillomavirus capsid antigen and viral DNA. *Arch Pathol Lab Med* 113:1127–1131, 1989.
33. Kiyabu MT, Shibata D, Arnheim N, et al: Detection of human papillomavirus in formalin-fixed, invasive squamous carcinomas using the polymerase chain reaction. *Am J Surg Pathol* 13:221–224, 1989.
34. Duggan MA, Borras VF, Inoue M, et al: Human papillomavirus DNA determination of anal condylomata, dysplasias, and squamous carcinomas with in situ hybridization. *Am J Clin Pathol* 92:16–21, 1989.
35. Palefsky JM, Holly EA, Gonazales J, et al: Detection of human papillomavirus DNA in anal intraepithelial neoplasia and anal cancer. *Cancer Res* 51:1014–1019, 1991.
36. Scholefield JH, Kerr IB, Shepherd NA, et al: Human papillomavirus type 16 DNA in anal cancer from six different countries. *Gut* 32:674–676, 1991.
37. Scholefield JH, Sonnex C, Talbot IC, et al: Anal and cervical intraepithelial neoplasia: Possible parallel. *Lancet* 2:765–769, 1989.
38. Dixon AR, Pringle JH, Holmes JT, et al: Cervical intraepithelial neoplasia and squamous cell carcinoma of the anus in sexually active women. *Postgrad Med J* 67:557–559, 1991.
39. Foust RL, Dean PJ, Stoler MH, et al: Intraepithelial neoplasia of the anal canal in hemorrhoidal tissue: A study of 19 cases. *Hum Pathol* 22:528–534, 1919.
40. Goedert JJ, Causey D, Palefsky J, et al: Anal pap smears and human papilloma viruses (HPV) in a 7-year cohort study of homosexual men. *Proc Am Soc Clin Oncol* 9:3, 1990.
41. Higgins GD, Uzelin DM, Phillips GE, et al: Differing characteristics of human papillomavirus RNA-positive and RNA-negative anal carcinomas. *Cancer* 68:561–567, 1991.
42. Koulos J, Symmans F, Chumas J, et al: Human papillomavirus detection in adenocarcinoma of the anus. *Mod Pathol* 4:58–61, 1991.
43. Wolber R, Dupuis B, Thiyagaratnam P, et al: Anal cloacogenic and squamous carcinomas: Comparative histologic analysis using in situ hybridization for human papillomavirus DNA. *Am J Surg Pathol* 14:176–182, 1990.
44. Aparicio-Duque R, Mittal KR, Chan W, et al: Cloacogenic carcinoma of the anal canal and associated viral lesions: An in situ hybridization study for human papilloma virus. *Cancer* 68:2422–2425, 1991.
45. Palefsky J, Gonzalez J, Greenblatt R, et al: Anal intraepithelial neoplasia and anal papillomavirus infection among homosexual males with group IV HIV disease. *JAMA* 263:1911–1916, 1990.
46. Kiviat N, Rompalo A, Bowden R, et al: Anal human papillomavirus infection among human immunodeficiency virus-seropositive and -seronegative men. *J Infect Dis* 162:358–361, 1990.
47. Law CL, Qassim M, Thompson CH, et al: Factors associated with clinical and sub-clinical anal human papillomavirus infection in homosexual men. *Genitourin Med* 67:92–98, 1991.
48. Melbye M, Palefsky J, Gonzalez J, et al: Immune status as a determinant of human papillomavirus detection and its association with anal epithelial abnormalities. *Int J Cancer* 46:203–206, 1990.
49. Caussy D, Goedert JJ, Palefsky J, et al: Interaction of human immunodeficiency and papilloma viruses: Association with anal epithelial abnormality in homosexual men. *Int J Cancer* 46:214–219, 1990.
50. Palefsky JM: Human papillomavirus-associated anogenital neoplasia and other solid tumors in human immunodeficiency virus-infected individuals. *Curr Opin Oncol* 3:881–885, 1991.
51. Oriel JD: Human papillomaviruses and anal cancer (editorial). *Genitourin Med* 65:213–215, 1989.
52. zur Hausen H: Papillomaviruses in anogenital cancer as a model to understand the role of viruses in human cancers. *Cancer Res* 49:4677–4681, 1989.
53. Holmes F, Borek D, Owen-Kummer M, et al: Anal cancer in women. *Gastroenterology* 95:107–111, 1988.
54. Lorenz HP, Wilson W, Leigh B, et al: Squamous cell carcinoma of the anus and HIV infection. *Dis Colon Rectum* 34:336–338, 1991.
55. Cone LA, Woodard DR, Potts BE, et al: An update on the acquired immunodeficiency syndrome (AIDS): Associated disorders of the alimentary tract. *Dis Colon Rectum* 29:60–64, 1986.
56. Monfardini S, Vaccher E, Lazzarin A, et al: Characterization of AIDS-associated tumors in Italy: Report of 435 cases of an IVDA-based series. *Cancer Detect Prev* 14:391–393, 1990.
57. Crook T, Wrede D, Tidy J, et al: Status of c-myc, p53 and retinoblastoma genes in human papillomavirus positive and negative squamous cell carcinomas of the anus. *Oncogene* 6:1251–1257, 1991.
58. Hiorns LR, Scholefield JH, Palmer JG, et al: Ki-ras oncogene mutations in non-HPV-associated anal carcinoma. *J Pathol* 161:99–103, 1990.
59. Lumley JW, Stitz RW: Crohn's disease and anal carcinoma: An association? A case report and review of the literature. *Aust NZ J Surg* 61:76–77, 1991.
60. Gilbert JM, Mann CV, Scholefield J, et al: The aetiology and surgery of carcinoma of the anus, rectum and sigmoid colon in Crohn's disease: Negative correlation with human papillomavirus type 16 (HPV16). *Eur J Surg Oncol* 17:507–513, 1991.
61. Penn I: Cancers of the anogenital region in renal transplant recipients. *Cancer* 58:611–616, 1986.
62. Couetil J-P, McGoldrick JP, Wallwork J, et al: Malignant tumors after heart transplantation. *J Heart Transpl* 9:622–626, 1990.
63. Cabrera A, Tsukada Y, Pickren JW, et al: Development of lower genital carcinomas in patients with anal carcinoma: A more than casual relationship. *Cancer* 19:470–480, 1966.
64. Goligher JC: *Surgery of the Anus, Rectum and Colon,* 3d ed. London, Baillere Tindall, 1975, p 815.
65. Daniell HW: Re: Causes of anal carcinoma. *JAMA* 254:358, 1985.
66. Daling JR, Sherman KJ, Hislop TG, et al: Cigarette smoking and the risk of anogenital cancer. *Am J Epidemiol* 135:180–189, 1992.
67. Kingsnorth AN, Abu-Khalaf M, Ross JS, et al: Relationship of chronic anorectal disease to carcinoma. *Arch Surg* 75:352–361, 1957.
68. Chaos A, Garrido H, Fernandez-Villoria JM: Carcinoma associated with fistula in ano. *Int Surg* 58:497–499, 1973.

CHAPTER 101

Perianal Disease

Joe J. Tjandra
Victor W. Fazio

HIGHLIGHTS

Perianal Paget's disease, Bowen's disease, and basal cell carcinoma are discussed in this chapter. Paget's disease is an intraepithelial *adenocarcinoma,* while Bowen's disease is an intraepithelial *squamous cell* carcinoma. They commonly present in elderly patients as a pruritic perianal rash refractory to standard dermatologic treatments. As a result, the diagnosis is often delayed. Perianal Paget's disease is associated with a higher incidence of underlying anorectal malignancy than Bowen's disease and has a higher risk of progression to invasive cancer. The best treatment of perianal Paget's disease and Bowen's disease is wide local excision provided that invasive cancer is not present. As microscopic disease often extends beyond clinically apparent disease, lesion mapping will be helpful in guiding the extent of surgical excision. By contrast, basal cell carcinoma has a low invasive potential and can be managed by conservative local excision, as for cutaneous basal cell carcinoma elsewhere.

CONTROVERSIES

The histogenesis of Paget's cells remains controversial. Perianal Paget's disease also appears to be biologically different from its mammary counterpart and seems to consist of more than one disease. Similarly, the association of Bowen's disease with underlying anorectal malignancy and other cutaneous malignancy is not clear.

FUTURE DIRECTIONS

Immunohistochemical studies have confirmed the glandular nature of Paget's cells and may be helpful in elucidating their histogenesis. As both Paget's disease and Bowen's disease are uncommon conditions, a central registry will be helpful in collecting data for prospective review.

PERIANAL PAGET'S DISEASE

Perianal Paget's disease is an uncommon entity. Thus far, about 100 cases have been reported. The true incidence is not known, as many cases are unreported or unrecognized. The first case of perianal Paget's disease was reported by Darier and Couillard[1] in 1893, 19 years after Sir James Paget[2] first described the characteristic breast lesion. The cytologic features of Paget's cells that are pathognomonic of Paget's disease, however, were first described by George Thin.[3]

Clinicopathologic Features

Perianal Paget's disease tends to occur in the elderly in the sixth to seventh decade (Table 101-1) as a slowly enlarging erythematous, eczematous, and often sharply demarcated perianal skin rash. This rash may be oozing or scaling (Fig. 101-1) and is often accompanied by intractable pruritus ani.

There is often a delay in the accurate diagnosis of Paget's disease because of its clinical similarity to Bowen's disease, malignant melanoma, anal basaloid

Table 101-1
Comparison of Perianal Paget's Disease with Bowen's Disease[4,6,15]

	Paget's disease	*Bowen's disease*
Age	60s–70s	50s
Gender	Males = Females	More Females
Underlying malignancy	~70%	? no relationship
Progression to invasive cancer	40%	6%
Paget's cells versus Bowenoid cells	PAS +ve[a]	PAS −ve

[a]PAS, periodic acid-Schiff.
Abbreviations: +ve, positive; −ve, negative.

carcinoma, dermatitis, hidradenitis suppurative, and Crohn's disease.[4]

The diagnosis must be confirmed by biopsy and by identification of the characteristic Paget's cells. These (Fig. 101-2) appear microscopically as large, rounded cells with abundant pale-staining cytoplasm and a large nucleus that is often displaced to the periphery

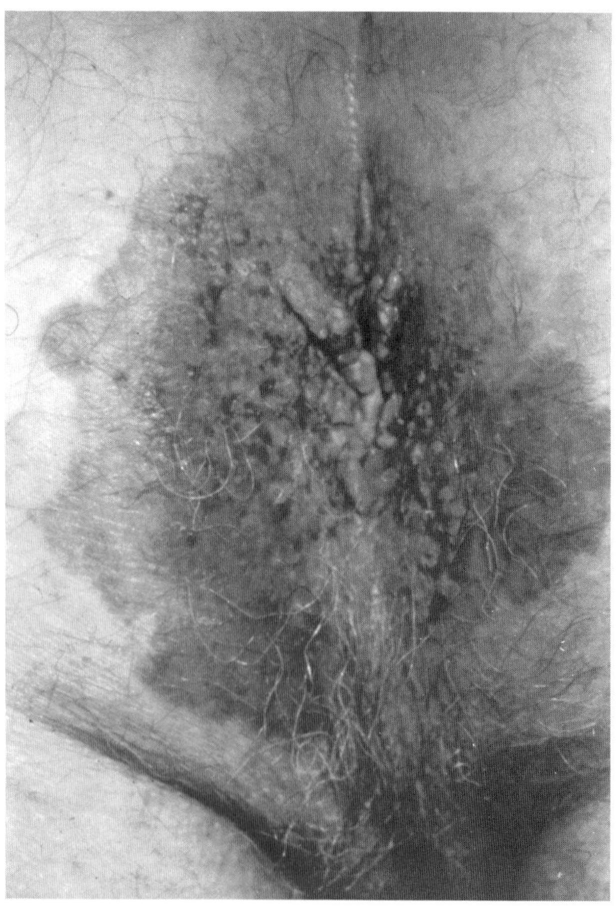

FIG. 101-1. Perianal Paget's disease presenting as a rash. (From Tjandra.[4] Reproduced by permission.)

of the cell, giving a signet-ring appearance.[4] Paget's cells also contain a mucoprotein (sialomucin) which stains positive with periodic acid-Schiff, mucicarmine, and alcian blue at pH 2.5.

Histogenesis of Paget's Cells

In a collective review of 55 cases of perianal Paget's disease,[4] 69 percent were associated with underlying malignancy. These included apocrine and eccrine carcinoma (36 percent), rectal adenocarcinoma (22 percent), and anal carcinoma (11 percent). The remaining 31 percent had no underlying malignancy. Such a wide spectrum of presentation indicates that perianal Paget's disease is probably more than one disease, with different pathologic processes. In this respect, Paget's disease in the perianal region is biologically different from its mammary counterpart, which is invariably associated with underlying breast carcinoma.

The histogenesis of Paget's cells is highly controversial. There are four main theories to explain the different patterns of presentation. First, Paget's cells may arise from underlying carcinoma of the apocrine or eccrine sweat glands with secondary epidermal involvement, as in mammary Paget's disease. Second, Paget's cells may be metastatic from underlying rectal adenocarcinoma,[5] exemplified by similarity of the mucin in Paget's cells and the underlying carcinoma cells in some cases. Third, there are simultaneous multicentric neoplastic changes in the epidermis, apocrine structures, and the glandular elements of the rectum. Finally, it is suggested that Paget's cells arise from the pleuripotential ectodermal basal cell as an adenocarcinoma in situ, with a long preinvasive phase. Thus, the last theory would explain those cases with no underlying malignancy.[6,7]

Whatever the theories, perianal Paget's disease is best regarded as an intraepithelial adenocarcinoma. The glandular origin of Paget's cells is supported by the presence of carcinoembryonic antigen and low-molecular-weight cytokeratins.[8,9] Some preliminary studies have suggested that patients with a higher risk of malignancy may have different immunohistochemical staining patterns.[10]

Management

Careful clinical assessment should include rectal and proctosigmoidoscopic examinations to evaluate the extent of involvement and the possible underlying malignancy. The role of endoluminal ultrasound is not clear, but it may be helpful in assessing the presence and depth of tumor invasion. Colonoscopy or barium enema is performed unless the patient is elderly and frail and there is a low index of suspicion that underlying colorectal neoplasm exists. Preliminary diagnostic biopsy from both the center and the edges of the

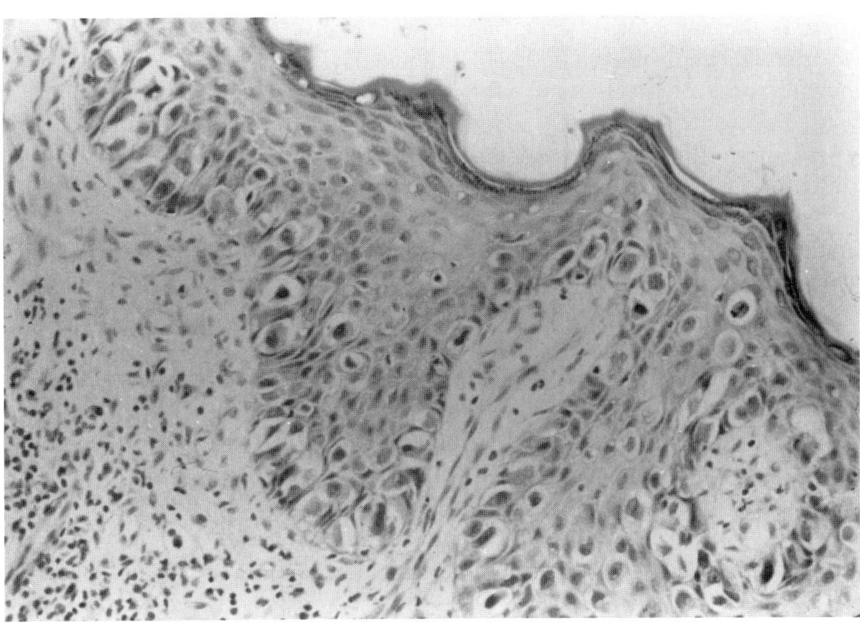

FIG. 101-2. Paget's cells in the anal mucosa (H&E, ×100). (From Tjandra.[4] Reproduced by permission.)

lesion should be performed to confirm the diagnosis and to detect any underlying carcinoma.

In the absence of invasive carcinoma, wide local excision is the treatment of choice. As microscopic evidence of Paget's disease may extend within the epidermis beyond clinically apparent disease, lesion mapping prior to surgery is helpful.[6] It has been the authors' practice to perform 2- to 3-mm biopsies 1 cm from the edge of the lesion and in all four quadrants of the perineum (Fig. 101-3). Biopsies are also taken at the dentate line and the anal verge. This precise lesion mapping will guide subsequent wide local excision. The margins of resection are examined by frozen section to assure complete excision. If the extent of excision is large, a split-thickness skin graft may be done.

If underlying invasive anorectal carcinoma is present, the treatment is that of the underlying malignancy—that is, abdominoperineal excision of the rectum with wide excision of the cutaneous lesion. Inguinal lymph node dissection may be necessary if the nodes are shown to be involved on fine-needle aspiration cytology.

Nonoperative treatments for perianal Paget's disease include topical bleomycin, topical 1% 5-fluorouracil, cryosurgery, chemotherapy, and radiotherapy. The results with these modalities are variable and experience has been limited. These treatments may have a role in elderly and frail patients with minimal symptoms.

Prognosis

The prognosis is good after adequate excision when there is no underlying carcinoma. The prognosis is

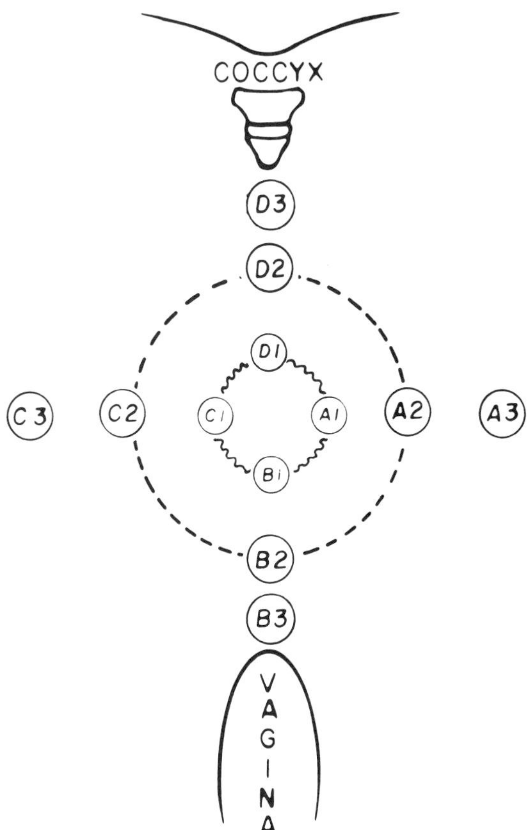

FIG. 101-3. Quadrant biopsy of the perineum. (1) dentate line; (2) anal verge; (3) perineum. (From Beck et al.[15] Reproduced by permission.)

worse in the presence of underlying carcinoma of the sweat glands and worst in patients with underlying adenocarcinoma of the rectum, with few 5-year survivors. Because of the delay in diagnosis (average 4 years), approximately 25 percent of patients with invasive perianal Paget's disease will already have metastasized.[11,12] Common sites of metastases include the inguinal and pelvic lymph nodes, liver, bone, lung, and brain.

Local recurrence is common. It arises because of inadequate excision, associated invasive carcinoma, or a general "field change." Recurrent disease may develop 10 years or more after initial surgery,[13] requiring repeat excisions. Thus lifelong surveillance for recurrences and for the development of metachronous invasive carcinoma of the rectum and anal canal is important. Appropriate follow-up includes an annual complete physical examination, proctosigmoidoscopy, punch biopsy of any new lesion, and random biopsies at the edges of the split-thickness skin graft as needed. Colonoscopy is also performed at 3-year intervals.

PERIANAL BOWEN'S DISEASE

Perianal Bowen's disease is uncommon; about 100 cases have been reported to date. This slow-growing intraepithelial squamous cell carcinoma (carcinoma in situ) was first described by John T. Bowen[14] in 1912 as a chronic atypical epithelial proliferation.

Clinicopathologic Features

Common presenting symptoms include nonspecific complaints of perianal pruritus, burning, or spotty bleeding. Bowen's disease occurs most commonly in the fifth decade (Table 101-1). Grossly, the lesions appear as raised, irregular, erythematous, occasionally pigmented, scaly or crusted plaques with eczematoid features (Fig. 101-4). The differential diagnosis of these lesions includes leukoplakia, Paget's disease, invasive squamous carcinoma, condyloma acuminatum,

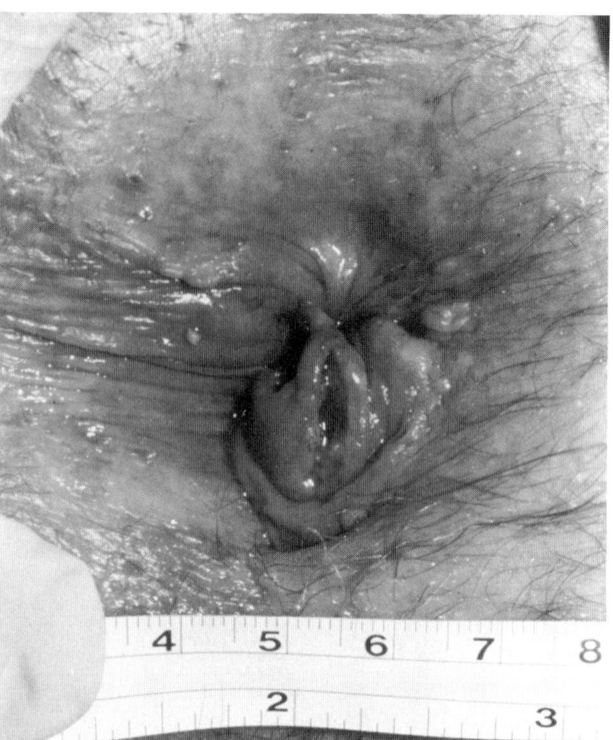

FIG. 101-4. Perianal Bowen's disease.

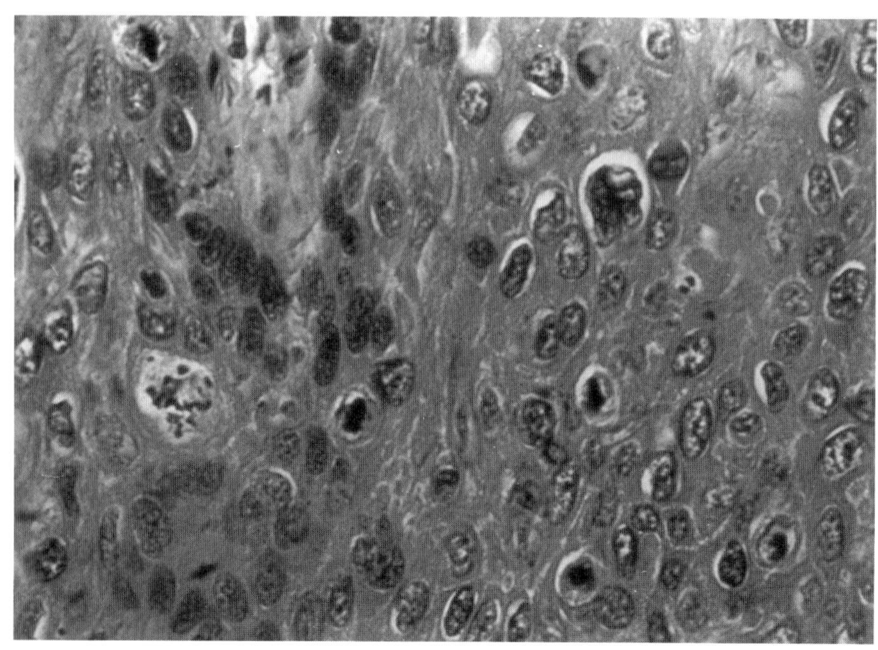

FIG. 101-5. Microscopic appearance of Bowen's disease (H&E, ×100).

dermatitis, eczema, and caudad spread of a rectal carcinoma.[15]

The typical microscopic appearance is that of in situ squamous cell carcinoma with Bowenoid cells,[16] which are multinucleated giant cells with large hyperchromatic nuclei, giving a halo effect (Fig. 101-5). In contrast to the Paget's cell, Bowenoid cells are negative on periodic acid-Schiff (PAS) stain. Invasive squamous carcinoma may develop in 6 percent of patients[15] and, when present, often manifests itself clinically as foci of ulceration. If early and adequate treatment is not given, many of these will develop metastases.

Association with Internal Malignancy

Graham and Helwig[17] reported that about 75 percent of patients with Bowen's disease develop synchronous or metachronous internal malignancies or primary carcinoma of the skin. In their experience, the commonest sites of internal malignancies were the respiratory tract, gastrointestinal tract, genitourinary organs, and reticuloendothelial system. Additionally, about 40 percent of patients developed other premalignant and malignant cutaneous lesions within 7 years of the onset of perianal Bowen's disease.[17]

However, a critical analysis[18] of published data failed to support any relationship between Bowen's disease and the subsequent development of internal malignancies. Additionally, a recent collective survey of experience with perianal Bowen's disease showed the incidence of subsequent nonsquamous malignancy to be low, at 4.7 percent.[19] This view is in keeping with the authors' own experience.[15]

Management

Any suspicious perianal lesion or one that fails to respond to conventional therapy within a month should be biopsied.[15] Full-thickness biopsies from both the center and the edges of the lesion are important to both confirm the diagnosis of Bowen's disease and exclude an invasive carcinoma. A colonoscopy is performed unless the patient is elderly and frail.

Wide local excision is the treatment of choice, as Bowen's cells may extend beyond the gross margins of the lesion.[20] It has been the authors' practice to perform lesion mapping, as for perianal Paget's disease.[15]

Residual wound defects can be closed primarily or left to heal by secondary intention if less than 30 percent of the circumference of the anal canal is involved. Defects larger than 50 percent of the circumference of the anal canal are covered by a split-thickness skin graft either at the initial operation or within 3 to 4 days of excision. For defects between 30 to 50 percent of the circumference, judgment between these alternatives depends on the elasticity of the local tissues and the presence of any preexisting anal stenosis (e.g., after previous hemorrhoidectomy).

Bowen's disease may extend into the anal canal, requiring wide excision of the anal mucosa and skin grafting. Compression of the split-thickness skin graft in the anal canal by a finger cot filled with cotton balls is helpful. Satisfactory anal continence after total excision of the anal canal followed by skin grafting has been reported.[21]

Perioperative preparation includes good mechanical bowel preparation, antibiotic prophylaxis, and—for 5 to 6 days after surgery—confinement of bowel function by codeine or diphenoxylate with atropine (Lomotil).

Prognosis

Using these techniques of lesion mapping and wide local excision, there has been no local recurrence in a report of 21 patients.[15] None of the patients developed anal stenosis or fecal incontinence.[15]

Long-term follow-up is necessary to detect recurrent perianal Bowen's disease. However, there has been no logical regimen for follow-up in view of the limited experience of most centers. We adopt a follow-up regimen similar to that used for perianal Paget's disease.

Basal Cell Carcinoma

This is a rare condition, comprising 0.2 percent of anorectal neoplasms.[22]

Clinical Features

Basal-cell carcinoma of the anal margin usually affect patients in the sixth decade and occurs more frequently in men than in women. Clinically, the lesions resemble cutaneous basal cell carcinomas found elsewhere, being characterized by a central ulceration with irregular and rolled edges. Less commonly, they may extend into the anal canal. The clinical course tends to be one of slow progression, with a low invasive potential.

The diagnosis is often delayed and common misdiagnoses include hemorrhoids, anal fissure, and perianal eczema. The histologic appearance is similar to that of cutaneous basal cell carcinoma elsewhere and must be distinguished from that of basaloid carcinomas (cloacogenic or transitional cell), which have a different biological behavior.

Management

Local excision with 5- to 10-mm margins is the treatment of choice. Local recurrence in 29 percent of patients was noted in a report[22]; most such recurrences are adequately dealt with by reexcision. Abdominoperineal resection is reserved for the uncommon circumstances of large lesions invading the anal sphincters. Mortality as a result of the basal cell carcinoma is highly uncommon.

REFERENCES

1. Darier J, Couillard P: Sur un cas de maladie de Paget de la region perineo-anale scrotale. *Soc Franc Dermatol Syph* 4:25–31, 1893.
2. Paget J: On disease of the mammary areola preceding cancer of the mammary gland. *St Bartholomew Hosp Res London* 10:87–89, 1874.
3. Thin G: Malignant papillary dermatitis of the nipple and the breast tumors with which it is found associated. *Br Med J* 1:760–763, 1881.
4. Tjandra J: Perianal Paget's disease: Report of three cases. *Dis Colon Rectum* 312:462–466, 1988.
5. Wood WS, Culling CF: Perianal Paget's disease: Histochemical differentiation utilizing the boohydride-KOH-PAS reaction. *Arch Pathol* 99:442–445, 1975.
6. Beck DE, Fazio VW: Perianal Paget's disease. *Dis Colon Rectum* 30:263–266, 1987.
7. Jones RE, Austin C, Ackerman AB: Extramammary Paget's disease: A critical reexamination. *Am J Dermatopathol* 1: 101–132, 1979.
8. Nagle RB, Lucas DO, McDaniel KM, et al: New evidence linking mammary and extramammary Paget cells to a common cell phenotype. *Am J Clin Pathol* 83:431–438, 1984.
9. Kariniemi AL, Ramaekers F, Lehto P, et al: Paget cells express cytokeratins typical of glandular epithelia. *Br J Dermatol* 112:179–183, 1985.
10. Armitage NC, Jass JR, Richman PI, et al: Paget's disease of the anus: A clinicopathological study. *Br J Surg* 76:60–63, 1989.
11. Grodsky L: Uncommon nonkeratinizing cancers of the anal canal and perianal region. *NY State J Med* 65:894–901, 1965.
12. Helwig EG, Graham JH: Anogenital (extramammary) Paget's disease: A clinicopathologic study. *Cancer* 16:387–403, 1963.
13. Williams SL, Rogers LW, Quan SHQ: Perianal Paget's disease: Report of seven cases. *Dis Colon Rectum* 19:30–40, 1976.
14. Bowen JT: Precancerous dermatoses: A study of two cases of chronic atypical epithelial proliferation. *J Cutan Dis* 30:241–255, 1912.
15. Beck DE, Fazio VW, Jagelman DG, et al: Perianal Bowen's disease. *Dis Colon Rectum* 31:419–422, 1988.
16. Strauss RJ, Fazio V: Bowen's disease of the anal and perianal area: A report and analysis of twelve cases. *Am J Surg* 137:231–234, 1979.
17. Graham JH, Helwig EB: Bowen's disease and its relationship to systemic cancer. *Arch Dermatol* 83:738, 1961.
18. Arbesman H, Ransohoff DE: Is Bowen's disease a predictor for the development of internal malignancy? A methodological critique of the literature. *JAMA* 257:516–518, 1987.
19. Marfing TE, Abel ME, Gallagher DM: Perianal Bowen's disease and associated malignancies: Results of a survey. *Dis Colon Rectum* 30:782–785, 1987.
20. Harrison EGJ, Beahrs OH, Hill JR: Anal and perianal malignant neoplasms: Pathology and treatment. *Dis Colon Rectum* 9:255–267, 1966.
21. Reynolds VH: Preservation of anal function after total excision of the anal mucosa for Bowen's disease. *Ann Surg* 199:563–568, 1984.
22. Nielsen OV, Jensen SL: Basal cell carcinoma of the anus—A clinical study of 34 cases. *Br J Surg* 68:856–857, 1981.

CHAPTER 102

Anal Carcinoma: Anatomy, Staging, and Prognostic Variables

Paul E. Savoca
W. Douglas Wong

HIGHLIGHTS

Anal cancers may be located outside the canal (perianal), at the lower end of the canal (anal margin or verge), or within the anal canal above or below the dentate line. The major prognostic factors for potentially curable lesions are size, depth of penetration, and regional nodal status.

CONTROVERSIES

Confusion over definitions of anal cancer based on location continues to make comparison of various treatments difficult.

FUTURE DIRECTIONS

Standardization of terminology and staging will allow improved comparison of treatment end results.

ANATOMY

The word *anus* is derived from the Greek meaning "end" and refers to the terminal 4 to 6 cm of the human gastrointestinal tract. This sophisticated muscular unit is responsible for maintaining continence, thereby conferring the ability to willfully defer defecation until a socially appropriate time. Although short, the anus is an area of the gastrointestinal tract which contains an abundant mix of cell types and may give rise to an equally abundant variety of neoplasms.

Much confusion persists among clinicians as to the precise anatomy of the anus and perianal region. These nuances are critical to the clinician and patient, as accurate classification of neoplasms in this area is important in determining treatment and predicting curability. Simple inspection of the perianal area with the buttocks separated serves to distinguish the skin of the buttock from the *perianal skin*. The latter appears darker and contains no hair. Histologically, the perianal skin is distinguished by its lack of epidermal appendages, such as hair follicles and sweat ands.

Anatomists define the *anal canal* as that region extending from the anal verge to the junction between squamous and columnar epithelium (the dentate or pectinate line). However, the surgeon defines the anal canal by topographic landmarks assessed with the examining finger. To the surgeon, the anal canal is the area between the anal verge and the anorectal ring. The anorectal ring is an easily palpable structure which corresponds to the junction of the puborectalis portion of the levator ani muscle with the external anal sphincter (Fig. 102-1). This definition includes the *anal transitional zone,* which extends roughly 1.5 to 2.0 cm proximal to the dentate line and includes the columns of Morgagni. Derived from the embryonic cloaca, the anal transitional zone is an area of unique histologic

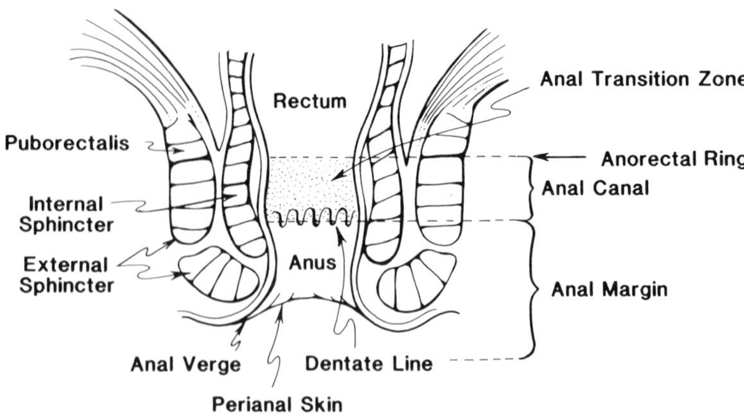

FIG. 102-1. Anatomy of the anus and perianal region. Note the anatomic boundaries of the anal canal and anal margin.

diversity where squamous, columnar, and transitional epithelia can be found.

In addition to a knowledge of the topographic anal canal anatomy, an exact understanding of the anatomy of the anal sphincter mechanism is important in order to assess depth of penetration of anal canal neoplasms and predict functional results after excisional therapy. The anal sphincter mechanism is made up of two concentric rings of muscle (Fig. 102-2). The inner bundle or internal sphincter is continuous with the inner circular muscle coat of the rectum and is primarily responsible for resting anal canal pressures, though the relative contribution of each of the components of the sphincter mechanism has recently been debated. The outer bundle, the external sphincter, is continuous with the puborectalis portion of the levator ani muscle. A conceptual model of the external sphincter mechanism was proposed by Shafik.[1] In this model, the external sphincter is composed of three muscular rings—designated subcutaneous, superficial, and deep portions—which act as a single functional unit (Fig. 102-3). The subcutaneous portion lies distal to the internal sphincter immediately beneath the perianal skin; its fibers mingle with those of the superficial transverse perinei and superficial external sphincter. The superficial external sphincter is oval-shaped and surrounds the internal sphincter. The fibers arise from the coccyx posteriorly and surround the anus. Anteriorly, the fibers attach to the perineal body. The deep portion of the external sphincter lies just below the pelvic floor, and it also surrounds the internal sphincter. Muscle fibers of the puborectalis muscle mingle with the proximal portion of this muscle, which is thought to act in conjunction with it.

The internal sphincter is autonomically innervated and therefore an involuntary muscle. The external sphincter has somatic innervation and is therefore a voluntary muscle primarily responsible for generating squeeze pressures. The internal sphincter is innervated by both sympathetic and parasympathetic fibers. Sympathetic nerves from the hypogastric plexus located at the aortic bifurcation descend as the hypogastric nerves and are responsible for anal sphincter contraction. Parasympathetic innervation from S_2, S_3, and S_4 travel lateral and anterior to the rectum and join with the hypogastric nerves to form the inferior hypogastric plexi. Mixed fibers from these plexi innervate the bladder, prostate, and penis as well as the internal sphincter. The external sphincter receives motor innervation from the inferior rectal nerve, a branch of the pudendal nerve. Derived from S_2, S_3, and S_4, the pudendal nerve exits the pelvis between the coccygeus and piriformis muscles and courses along the lateral walls of the ischiorectal fossa, accompanied by the internal pudendal artery and vein. The inferior rectal nerve traverses the ischiorectal fossa with the

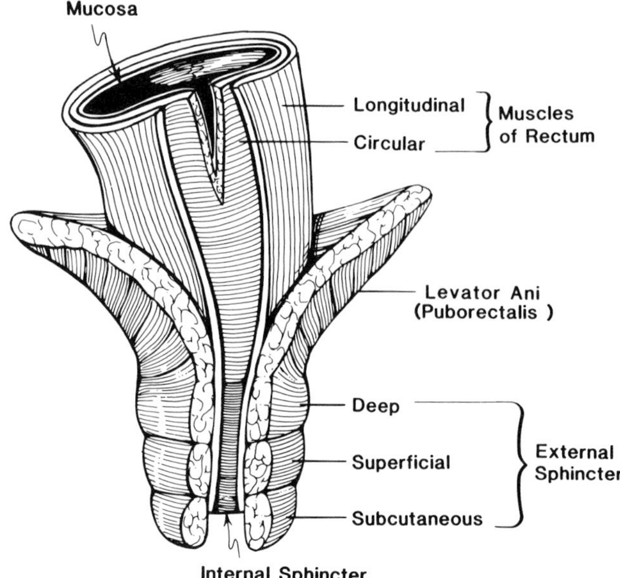

FIG. 102-2. Anatomy of the external anal sphincter. The three portions of the external sphincter—subcutaneous, superficial, and deep—are shown in relation to the rectal musculature.

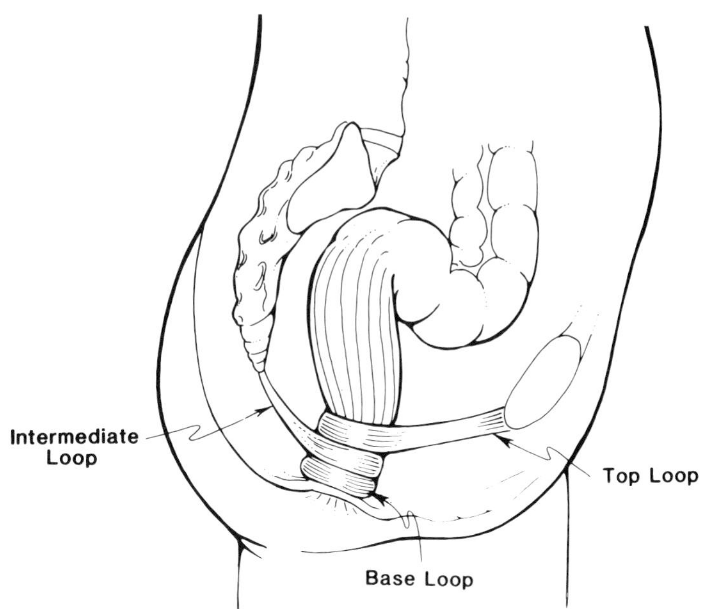

FIG. 102-3. The "triple loop" model of the external sphincter. The three components of the external sphincter with their respective attachments are shown. (*Adapted from Shafik.*[1])

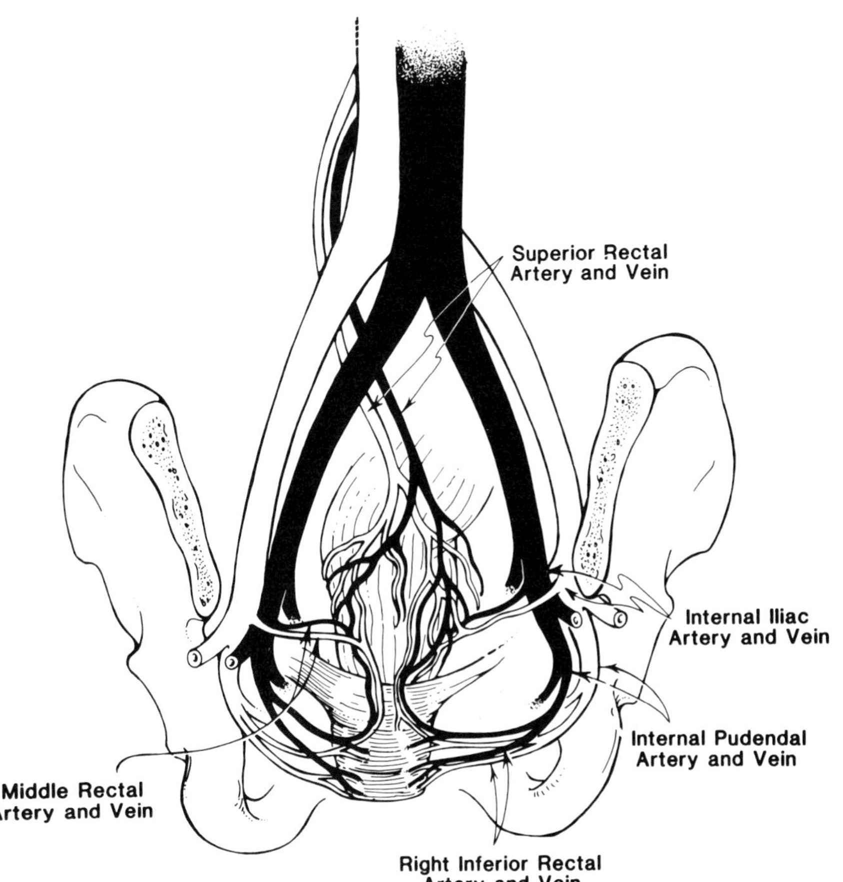

FIG. 102-4. Posterior view of the blood supply of the rectum and anus.

inferior rectal artery and vein to innervate the external sphincter. It also gives branches to the penis and vagina. Below the dentate line, cutaneous sensation is carried via the inferior rectal nerve.

Blood supply to the anus is via the inferior rectal artery, a branch of the internal pudendal artery (Fig. 102-4). Blood returns from the anus via two routes. Above the dentate line, venous blood returns via the superior rectal vein, a branch of the inferior mesenteric vein, and enters the portal circulation after joining usually with the splenic vein posterior to the body of the pancreas. Below the dentate line, blood returns via the middle and inferior rectal veins, which are branches of the internal iliac and internal pudendal veins respectively, to join the systemic circulation via the inferior vena cava. The anal region therefore represents an important area of portal-systemic connection.

Lymphatic drainage of the anal canal parallels arterial routes (Fig. 102-5). Lymphatics in the proximal anal canal drain along the superior and middle rectal vessels into the hypogastric and inferior mesenteric nodes proximally as well as laterally, traversing the ischiorectal fossa to the internal iliac nodes. Lymphatics from the lower anal canal distal to the dentate line drain to the superficial inguinal lymph nodes. The spread of anal and perianal neoplasms can be predicted based on a knowledge of this anatomy, as the tumor often spreads by direct extension through the lymphatic system and via the bloodstream. Tumors can also spread directly into adjacent tissues and occasionally upward in a submucosal plane for 5 to 6 cm before ulcerating into the rectum.[2]

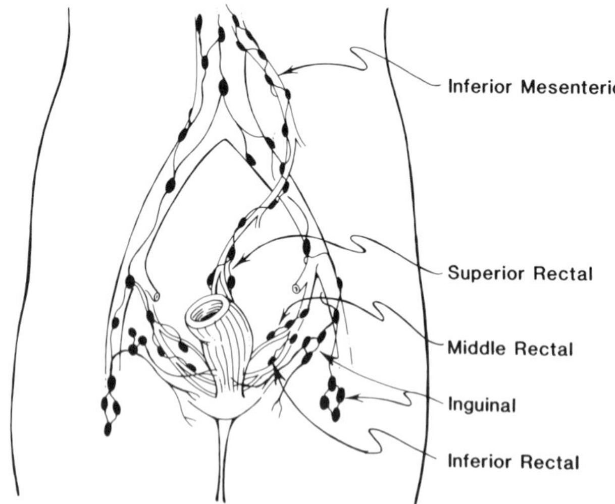

FIG. 102-5. Lymphatic drainage of the anus. Lesions distal to the dentate line drain laterally across the perineum to the superficial inguinal nodes; lesions astride the dentate line drain along the interior and middle rectal vessels to the hypogastric nodes (additionally or to the inguinal nodes). Proximal lesions may also drain along the rectum and superior hemorrhoidal vessels to the inferior mesenteric nodes.

CLASSIFICATION AND STAGING

Substantial confusion exists over the classification and staging of anal neoplasms. This stems from lack of a precise, universally accepted anatomic definition of the anal canal and anal margin as well as imprecise and subjective diagnostic tests. The divergent anatomic views mentioned earlier have led to considerable difficulty in the classification of these tumors. Several different classifications were used, depending on what center was reporting the data. Groups at St. Mark's and other centers considered all lesions distal to the dentate line to be anal margin lesions, while others, most notably the group at the Mayo Clinic, considered only lesions below the anal verge to be anal margin neoplasms. As Cummings[3] stated, the problem with classification is of more than academic interest because of the differences in patterns of spread and survival reported by most authors, which indicate that anal margin neoplasms have a considerably more favorable prognosis.[3] The World Health Organization has issued a standard: *Anal canal neoplasms are defined as lesions arising from the anorectal ring proximally (including the anal transitional zone) to the dentate line distally. Anal margin neoplasms are defined as those lesions arising distal to the dentate line to the junction of the perianal skin with the hair-bearing skin of the buttock.* This classification seems to have gained widespread acceptance in the literature in recent years.

The major histologic types of carcinoma of the anus are shown in Table 102-1. The vast majority of carcinomas of the anal canal are squamous cell carcinomas. However, many variants exist, including mucoepidermoid, transitional, cloacogenic, and basaloid. Early reports emphasized the differences between these tumors and suggested a more favorable prognosis for pure basaloid lesions.[4,5] While these terms are important for the precise pathologic description of these lesions, long-term survival has been found to be identi-

Table 102-1
Malignant Lesions of the Anal Canal and Anal Margin

Anal canal lesions	*Anal margin lesions*
Squamous cell carcinoma	Paget's disease
Malignant melanoma	Bowen's disease
Sarcoma	Basal cell carcinoma
Adenocarcinoma	Squamous cell carcinoma
Small cell carcinoma	

cal, thus rendering the nomenclature cumbersome and of little clinical significance. As such, these lesions should all be referred to simply as squamous carcinomas. Other uncommon but distinctly different tumors of this region include adenocarcinoma (arising in either an anal gland, duct, or fistula), melanoma, sarcoma, and small cell carcinoma.

In contrast, carcinomas of the anal margin lend themselves more easily to precise histologic definition. These lesions include Bowen's disease (intraepithelial squamous cell carcinoma), Paget's disease (intraepithelial adenocarcinoma), basal cell carcinoma, and squamous cell carcinoma. Like skin tumors, these lesions are characterized by a rather indolent course with a propensity for local invasion rather than distant metastasis (see Chap. 101).

A clinical staging system should serve several important purposes. First, it should provide a convenient and accurate method for categorizing lesions in such a way as to predict outcome; second, it should have some bearing on treatment decisions. Accurate staging of anal and perianal neoplasms has been difficult owing to the controversies regarding anatomy mentioned earlier and the lack of precise knowledge of prognostic variables. However, in 1978, the Union Internationale Contre le Cancer (UICC) established a staging system for both anal canal and anal margin lesions which incorporated a clinical staging system and a pathologic staging system after surgery.[6] After much criticism and revision, the American Joint Committee on Cancer (AJCC) adopted the same staging system. The unified AJCC/UICC staging system developed in 1987 is the system in current use and is shown in Table 102-2.

Development of a standardized staging system is usually based on knowledge of prognostic variables for a given lesion. For most tumors of the gastrointestinal tract, size, depth of penetration, histologic grade, and the presence or absence of nodal or distant metastatic disease have proved important. Unfortunately, much of this information has been difficult to obtain for anal carcinoma. The relative rarity of this lesion makes analysis difficult. In addition, it may be especially difficult or impossible to assess tumor size and depth of invasion accurately even if examination under anesthesia is performed. While evaluation of regional nodal spread and distant metastases has been possible, confusing nomenclature regarding histology has made it difficult to correlate tumor grade with survival. Thus, the current staging system is based on available data and parameters which can be fairly easily determined clinically.

Recently, transrectal ultrasonography (TRUS) has been increasingly utilized as a preoperative staging tool for patients with rectal and anal cancer (Fig. 102-6). Normal anatomy as seen on anal sonography is

Table 102-2
AJCC/UICC Staging System for Carcinoma of the Anal Canal and Anal Margin

Primary Tumor (T)
T_X Primary tumor cannot be assessed
T_0 No evidence of primary tumor
T_{is} Carcinoma in situ
T_1 ≤ 2 cm in greatest dimension
T_2 > 2 cm but ≤ 5 cm in greatest dimension
T_3 > 5 cm in greatest dimension
Anal canal
T_4 Invading adjacent structures: vagina, urethra, or bladder. Involvement of sphincter muscle alone is not classified as T_4
Anal margin
T_4 Invading deep extradermal structure: skeletal muscle or bone

Regional Lymph Node Involvement (N)
N_X Regional lymph nodes cannot be assessed
N_0 No regional lymph node involvement
Anal canal
N_1 Metastases to perirectal lymph nodes
N_2 Metastases to unilateral internal iliac and/or unilateral inguinal lymph nodes
N_3 Metastases to perirectal and inguinal lymph nodes and/or bilateral internal iliac and/or bilateral inguinal lymph nodes
Anal margin
N_1 Metastases to ipsilateral inguinal lymph nodes

Distant Metastases (M)
M_X Distant metastases cannot be assessed
M_0 No distant metastases
M_1 Distant metastases present

STAGING			
Stage 0	T_{is}	N_0	M_0
Stage I	T_1	N_0	M_0
Stage II	T_2	N_0	M_0
	T_3	N_0	M_0
Anal canal			
Stage IIIA	T_4	N_0	M_0
	T_{1-3}	N_1	M_0
Stage IIIB	T_4	N_1	M_0
	Any T	$N_{2,3}$	M_0
Anal margin			
Stage III	T_4	N_0	M_0
	Any T	N_1	M_0
Both			
Stage IV	Any T	Any N	M_1

shown in Fig. 102-7. With this modality, an inner distinct, highly echogenic layer can be identified which corresponds to mucosa and submucosa above the dentate line and to anal epithelium/subepithelial connective tissue and perirectal tissue below the dentate line. Surrounding this layer lies a low-echogenicity layer which corresponds to the internal sphincter. Distally, the external sphincter can be identified and, cranially, the puborectalis portion of the levator ani muscle can be seen as a U-shaped, mixed-echogenicity tissue continuous with the external sphincter.

Utilizing this technique, Goldman et al.[7] prospectively analyzed 50 patients with anal epidermoid car-

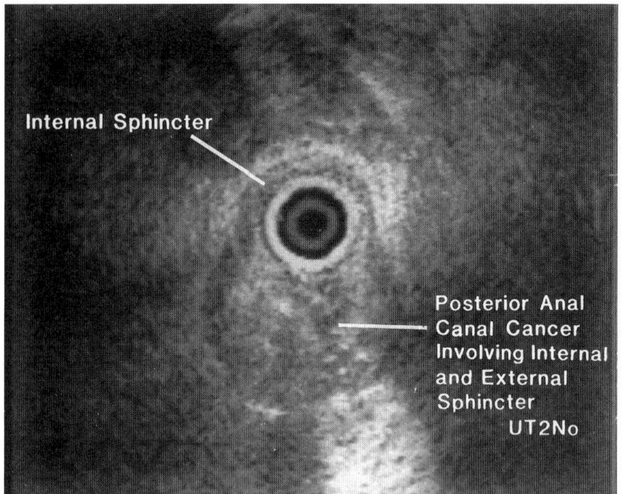

FIG. 102-6. Endoanal sonogram of a posterior anal canal carcinoma involving the internal and external anal sphincter.

cinoma and were able to classify depth of tumor invasion accurately into four levels:

UT_1: Tumor confined to anal epithelium and subendothelial connective tissue (mucosa and submucosa)
UT_2: Tumor limited to sphincter muscle/muscularis propria
UT_3: Tumor through sphincter muscle/muscularis propria
UT_4: Tumor penetrating into surrounding organs

In this study, tumor size, depth of invasion, and tumor volume were measured and TRUS staging was compared with clinical stage as assessed by digital exam. Clinical and ultrasound staging was correlated with the AJCC/UICC staging system. Two-thirds of clinical stage T_1 and T_2 lesions had ultrasonographic evidence of penetration of the anorectal muscular wall (UT_3 and UT_4). This was also the case in all clinical stage T_3 and T_4 lesions. In addition, TRUS staging accurately predicted response to radiation therapy. All lesions staged as clinical T_{1-2} and UT_{1-2} had complete response to radiation therapy, whereas only 64 percent of lesions at clinical stage T_{1-2}/UT_{3-4} responded and no lesions at clinical stage T_{3-4}/UT_{3-4} responded. The authors therefore concluded that TRUS could complement digital examination in the staging of anal carcinoma. The TRUS approach may prove to be a useful adjunct to the present TNM staging system, as these lesions are increasingly treated with chemoradiation; hence excision of the entire lesion for pathologic examination may never be performed.

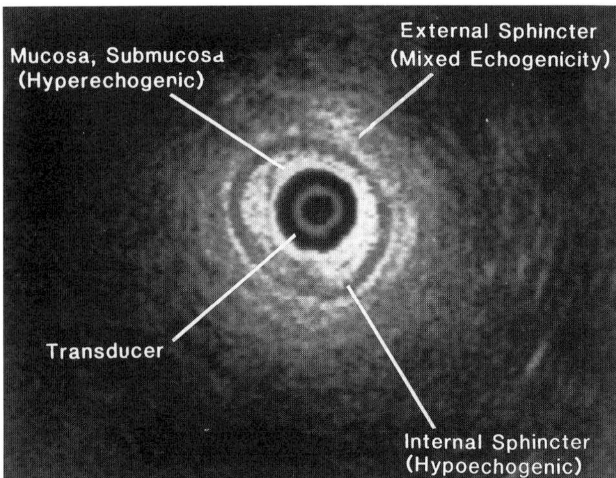

FIG. 102-7. Normal anal anatomy as seen by endoanal ultrasonography. First bright (hyperechogenic) layer represents mucosa and submucosa. Circular hypoechogenic structure (black) represents internal anal sphincter. External sphincter appears as mixed echogenicity structure.

PROGNOSTIC VARIABLES

Premalignant Lesions

For patients with intraepithelial neoplasia (Bowen's disease and Paget's disease), prognosis depends primarily on whether or not an invasive cancer has developed and whether adequate (not radical) surgical excision has been accomplished. These lesions are virtually 100 percent curable with wide local excision.[8,9]

Naturally, patients in whom diagnosis has been delayed and who develop invasive cancer have a worse prognosis. For Bowen's disease, there is progression to invasive carcinoma in 2 to 6 percent of cases.[10–12] In Paget's disease, progression to invasive carcinoma has been reported to be as high as 40 percent in untreated lesions, though experience with this lesion is quite limited.[13]

INVASIVE CANCERS

Location. The prognosis for carcinoma of the anal margin is quite favorable. Reported survival ranges between 68 and 100 percent, although local recurrence can be as high as 50 percent.[9,14] It may therefore be said that location—i.e., anal margin versus anal canal—is of prognostic importance. Only Paradise et al.[15] found no difference in survival between those with anal canal and anal margin lesions. Conversely, overall survival for anal canal lesions varies according to therapeutic regimen but has been reported in the range of 50 to 70 percent.[16,17]

Histologic Type. As mentioned earlier, no difference exists in survival for patients with the various histologic types of anal canal carcinoma. Several series suggested that cloacogenic carcinomas were somewhat more favorable; however, this has not been borne out in numerous subsequent studies.[4,5] Uncommonly, patients may develop a "small cell" variety of carcinoma of the anus which is similar histologically to small cell carcinoma of the lung. These patients seem to have a worse prognosis and a propensity for early metastatic disease.[18]

Aside from this rare tumor, Shepherd et al.[19] found that degree of differentiation had only marginal prognostic significance. He also found that other histologic features—such as degree of keratinization, nuclear pleomorphism, and lymphocytic infiltration—were not predictive of tumor behavior. The general consensus with regard to tumor grade has been that it may play some role in determining the biological behavior of these tumors but is probably not of major significance. It therefore has not been included in the AJCC/UICC staging system.

Tumor Size. In several early reports, tumor size was observed to correlate well with clinical outcome in patients with anal carcinoma. Goldman et al.[20] retrospectively studied 43 patients with anal canal cancers and found that T_1 and T_2 lesions had greater than an 80 percent 5-year survival, while T_3 and T_4 lesions were associated with survival of less than 20 percent. Smith et al.[16] found similar results in patients treated with the Nigro protocol. Boman et al.[18] reported that all 13 patients with tumors less than 2 cm in diameter were cured with local excision alone. Kuehn el al.,[21] Wanebo et al.,[22] and Salmon et al.[4] reported similar results regardless of treatment modality.

Shepherd et al.[19] performed a multivariate analysis of prognostic factors in patients with anal canal cancer and found tumor thickness to be a strongly statistically significant predictor of outcome in these patients. Patients with lesions up to 10 mm thick had an 85 percent 5-year survival, patients with tumors between 11 and 20 mm thick had a 55 percent 5-year survival, while patients with tumors 21 to 30 mm thick had a 25 percent 5-year survival.[19] Salmon et al.[4] expressed tumor size in terms of degree of involvement of the anal canal circumference and related this to survival. Overall actuarial survival in his 195 cases treated primarily with radiation therapy was 58 percent at 5 years. For tumors involving one-fourth of the anal canal, survival was 68 percent, and for those occupying one-half of the circumference, survival was 62 percent. Survival dropped to 33 and 18 percent for lesions occupying three-fourths and the entire circumference, respectively.[4] In summary, tumor size appears to be an important prognostic factor, though recent studies have suggested that depth of invasion may be more predictive of eventual outcome.

Depth of Invasion. This parameter is considered by many authors to be the single most important prognostic factor in patients with anal carcinoma. Numerous studies utilizing both clinical and radiologic evaluation, including transrectal ultrasound, have suggested this.[7,23] Corman et al.[24] studied 29 patients treated surgically at the Lahey Clinic over a 20-year period from 1950 to 1970. They found an 83 percent survival in patients with tumors extending into the submucosa, 88.9 percent survival in those invading muscle, and 33.6 percent survival in those with tumors invading the soft tissue. Schraut et al.[8] reviewed 47 patients treated at the University of Chicago and concluded that local excision could be performed for in situ or microinvasive lesions with 100 percent survival. Shepherd et al.,[19] in addition to incriminating tumor thickness as mentioned above, found that anatomic depth of invasion correlated extremely well with eventual outcome in their series of over 200 patients.

Thus prognosis seems related to tumor size, but it is unclear whether the independent variable in this situation is actual tumor size or depth of invasion. For clinical staging purposes, tumor size is clearly easier to assess. However, other modalities, such as TRUS, may impact upon this in the future. Other important prognostic factors include lymph node status and DNA ploidy.

Lymph Node Involvement. Metastases to inguinal lymph nodes have long been associated with a poor prognosis in patients with anal cancer. Corman et al.[24] noted a 28.6 percent survival in patients with positive inguinal nodes, while Schraut et al.[8] had no long-term survivors. Salmon et al.[4] found that lymph node involvement paralleled tumor size, which, in turn, was directly related to patient outcome. However, Greenall et al.[25] noted a 55 percent survival in patients undergoing groin dissection for clinically positive lymph nodes. More recently, Shepherd et al.[19] found that lymph node status was strongly predictive of outcome in patients undergoing local excision as well as those undergoing APR, and that this parameter along with depth of invasion and DNA ploidy were the only variables which accurately predicted outcome as predicted in a multivariate analysis. Overall, inguinal node metastases represent an ominous sign in patients with anal carcinoma and their prognosis remains poor despite aggressive therapy.

DNA Ploidy. This exciting and fairly recent technologic advance is rapidly gaining prominence as a predictor of the biological behavior of many types of tumors, including breast, pancreatic, colonic, and rectal as well as anal carcinomas. Scott et al.,[26] at the Mayo Clinic, retrospectively performed flow cytometric analysis of paraffin-embedded tissue and successfully obtained DNA histograms in 117 patients with anal carcinoma. In this study, 70 percent of lesions were diploid and 30 percent were nondiploid. The nondiploid lesions tended to be poorly differentiated, invasive into the anal sphincter mechanism, and associated with lymph node metastases. Despite this, survival differences were not statistically significant for either tetraploid or aneuploid tumors. However, Shepherd et al.[19] found 23 percent of 184 anal cancers to be nondiploid, and survival in these patients was significantly worse. Although data at this point are sparse, flow cytometry of fresh tissue specimens may prove to be a valuable indicator of prognosis in patients with anal carcinoma. Further study is clearly warranted to ascertain the exact nature of this relationship.

Although somewhat difficult to interpret due to radically changing treatment modalities employed during the last 15 years, the prognosis of patients with anal carcinoma seems related to three important factors: location, depth of invasion/tumor size, and lymph node status. While depth of invasion is difficult to assess clinically, this seems related to tumor size and advances may be forthcoming as more experience is gained with TRUS. This may prove quite useful, as surgery is now only rarely utilized as primary therapy for anal cancer and complete tissue specimens may not be available for pathologic staging in the majority of patients. Lymph node involvement continues to be a grave prognostic sign. Although lymphadenectomy had been suggested in the past to confer survival advantage, it carries significant morbidity and has not been shown to improve survival.[25] Recently, some encouraging results have been observed with nodal irradiation, which may limit morbidity and improve subsequent quality of life, albeit briefly. DNA ploidy is a promising new technology which may yield important insight into the biological behavior of these tumors but clearly requires further study.

REFERENCES

1. Shafik A: A concept of the anatomy of the anal sphincter mechanism and physiology of defecation. *Dis Colon Rectum* 30:970–975, 1981.
2. Wolfe HRI, Bussey HJR: Squamous cell carcinoma of the anus. *Br J Surg* 55:295–301, 1968.
3. Cummings BJ: The place of radiation therapy in the treatment of carcinoma of the anal canal. *Cancer Treat Rev* 9:125–147, 1982.
4. Salmon RJ, Zafrani B, Habib A, et al: Prognosis of cloacogenic and squamous cancers of the anal canal. *Dis Colon Rectum* 29:336–340, 1986.
5. Serota AI, Weil M, Williams RA, et al: Anal cloacogenic carcinoma. *Arch Surg* 116:454–459, 1981.
6. Harmer MH (ed): *TNM Classification of Malignant Tumors*, 3rd ed. Geneva, Switzerland, 1978, pp 77–81.
7. Goldman S, Glimelius B, Norming U, et al: Transanorectal ultrasonography in anal carcinoma: A prospective study of 21 patients. *Acta Radiol* 29:337–341, 1988.
8. Schraut WH, Wang CH, Dawson PJ, et al: Depth of invasion, location, and size of cancer of the anus dictate operative treatment. *Cancer* 51:1291–1296, 1983.
9. Beahrs OH, Wilson SM: Carcinoma of the anus. *Ann Surg* 184:422–428, 1976.
10. Marfing TE, Abel ME, Gallgher DM: Perianal Bowen's disease and anorectal malignancies: Results of a survey. *Dis Colon Rectum* 30:782–785, 1987.
11. Grodsky L: Intraepidermal cancer of the anus: Evolution to invasive growth. *Calif Med* 87:412–415, 1957.
12. Graham JH, Helwig EB: Bowen's disease and its relationship to systemic cancer. *Arch Dermatol* 83:738, 1961.
13. Stearns MW, Grodsky L, Harrison EG, et al: Malignant anal lesions. *Dis Colon Rectum* 9:315–327, 1966.
14. Greenall MJ, Quan SHQ, Stearns MW, et al: Epidermoid cancer of the anal margin. *Am J Surg* 149:95–101, 1985.
15. Paradis P, Douglass HO Jr, Holyoke ED: The clinical implications of a staging system for carcinoma of the anus. *Surg Gynecol Obstet* 141:411–416, 1975.
16. Smith DE, Muff NS, Shetali HS: Preoperative radiation and chemotherapy for anal and rectal cancer. *Am J Surg* 143:595–598, 1982.
17. Greenall MJ, Quan SHQ, Urmacher C, et al: Treatment of epidermoid carcinoma of the anal canal. *Surg Gynecol Obstet* 161:509–517, 1985.
18. Boman BM, Moertel CG, O'Connell MJ, et al: Carcinoma of the anal canal: A clinical and pathologic study of 188 cases. *Cancer* 54:114–125, 1984.
19. Shepherd NA, Scholefield JH, Love SB, et al: Prognostic factors in anal squamous carcinoma: A multivariate analysis of clinical, pathological, and flow cytometric parameters in 235 cases. *Histopathology* 16:545–555, 1990.
20. Goldman S, Auer G, Erhardt K, et al: Prognostic significance of clinical stage, histologic grade, and nuclear DNA content in squamous-cell carcinoma of the anus. *Dis Colon Rectum* 30:444–448, 1987.
21. Kuehn PG, Eisenberg H, Reed JF: Epidermoid carcinoma of the perianal skin and anal canal. *Cancer* 22:932–938, 1968.
22. Wanebo H, Furrell W, Constable W: Multimodality approach to surgical management of locally advanced epidermoid carcinoma of the anorectum. *Cancer* 47:2817–2826, 1981.
23. Goldman S, Glimelius B, Glas U, et al: Management of anal epidermoid carcinoma—An evaluation of treatment results in two population-based series. *Int J Colorect Dis* 4:234–243, 1989.
24. Corman ML, Haggitt RC: Carcinoma of the anal canal. *Surg Gynecol Obstet* 145:674–676, 1977.
25. Greenall M, Magill G, Quan S, et al: Recurrent epidermoid cancer of the anus. *Cancer* 57:1437–1441, 1986.
26. Scott NA, Beart RW Jr, Weiland LH, et al: Carcinoma of the anal canal and flow cytometric DNA analysis. *Br J Cancer* 60:56–58, 1989.

PART 18

Epidermoid Carcinoma

CHAPTER 103

Epidermoid Carcinoma of the Anus—Primary Surgical Therapy

Malcolm C. Veidenheimer

HIGHLIGHTS

The classic surgical treatment for epidermoid carcinoma of the anus by abdominoperineal resection and colostomy has largely been replaced by newer modalities of treatment.

CONTROVERSIES

Nonsurgical management is so successful that primary surgical treatment of patients with anal carcinoma may not be indicated. However, some authors believe that regardless of whether the lesion is in the anal canal or at the anal margin, local excision could be considered when the lesion measures less than 2 cm in diameter. Whether lymph node dissection improves survival when nodal involvement has occurred is debatable.

FUTURE DIRECTIONS

With increasing evidence of the effectiveness of nonsurgical therapy, primary surgical management may consist of procuring histologic proof of malignancy and assisting in the pathologic staging of the disease.

LOCAL EXCISION VERSUS RADICAL RESECTION

Most authors do not clearly differentiate between carcinoma of the anal canal and carcinoma at the anal margin. The tendency has been to consider local treatment for lesions less than 2.0 cm to 2.5 cm in diameter that have not invaded deeply into the underlying tissue. Five-year survival figures for local treatment of such lesions vary from 25 to 83 percent.[1] A series[2] from the Mayo Clinic reported a 93 percent 5-year survival rate for patients having local excision of a lesion less than 2 cm in diameter. Jensen and colleagues,[3] however, found that when the lesions were treated by local excision, a recurrent tumor developed in 63 percent of patients with a lesion at the anal margin and in 91 percent of those with a lesion of the anal canal.

Survival figures for patients who had abdominoperineal resection are similar to figures for patients who had local excision. Operative mortality associated with abdominoperineal resection in several reported series[2,4] ranged from 2 to 6 percent, with 5-year survival rates of 24 to 71 percent. Before the advent of combined-modality therapy, the 5-year survival rate after abdominoperineal resection from Memorial Sloan-Kettering Cancer Center in New York[5] was 33 percent. A further review of the literature by Adam and Efron,[6] up to 1987, showed that radical surgery produced 5-year survival rates of 46 to 64 percent.

Successive series[2,7,8] of patients treated by radical surgery at the Mayo Clinic reported 5-year survival rates of 61 to 68 percent. The concept held by many physicians that carcinoma of the anal canal is associated with a worse prognosis than carcinoma at the anal margin is not substantiated by the experiences of physicians at St. Mark's Hospital in London.[9] Only 6 percent of patients with anal carcinoma seen at that institution had local excision. The 5-year survival rate was 62 percent for patients having abdominoperineal resection for carcinoma of the anal canal, as compared with 36 percent for patients having abdominoperineal resection for carcinoma at the anal margin. Brown and colleagues[10] found no difference in outcome when they compared carcinoma of the anal canal and perianal squamous cell carcinoma treated by either local or radical operation. The poor results obtained by surgical treatment led these authors to state, "Despite the traditional role of surgery in the treatment of squamous cell carcinoma of the anus, operation alone no longer constitutes adequate therapy." Proponents of multimodality therapy, such as Leichman and Cummings,[11] also point out the poor results obtained by primary surgical treatment.

LYMPH NODES

Lymph nodes positive for metastatic carcinoma have been found in about 30 percent of patients who underwent retrieval of pelvic lymph nodes at the time of radical operation.[2,12] Inguinal lymph nodes were positive in 15 to 20 percent of patients sampled.[12,13] Work from Memorial Sloan-Kettering Cancer Center[5] suggests that extended resection does not improve survival. Inguinal lymph node dissection performed in concert with abdominoperineal resection resulted in a 10 to 20 percent 5-year survival for patients having positive nodes.[12,14]

Late recognition of involved inguinal lymph nodes subsequent to primary treatment of the tumor has occurred in as many as 25 percent of patients. When lymph nodes are the only area of metastatic disease, 5-year survival after lymph node dissection occurs in up to 60 percent of patients.[2,12]

SUMMARY

Patients with small lesions of the anal canal or at the anal margin may do well with local excision. Larger lesions have traditionally been treated by radical abdominoperineal resection with colostomy. Synchronous dissection of lymph nodes in the groin may result in unnecessary removal of inflammatory lymph nodes. Metachronous lymph node dissection is associated with a high survival rate when no other evidence of disease exists.

None of these modalities of therapy seems to offer results comparable to those after combined-modality treatment with radiation and chemotherapy.[15]

REFERENCES

1. Gordon PH: Squamous-cell carcinoma of the anal canal. *Surg Clin North Am* 68:1391–1399, 1988.
2. Boman BM, Moertel CG, O'Connell MJ, et al: Carcinoma of the anal canal: A clinical and pathologic study of 188 cases. *Cancer* 54:114–125, 1984.
3. Jensen SL, Hagen K, Harling H, et al: Long-term prognosis after radical treatment for squamous-cell carcinoma of the anal canal and anal margin. *Dis Colon Rectum* 31:273–278, 1988.
4. Gordon PH: Current status: Perianal and anal canal neoplasms. *Dis Colon Rectum* 33:799–808, 1990.
5. Quan SH: Anal and para-anal tumors. *Surg Clin North Am* 58:591–603, 1978.
6. Adam YG, Efron G: Current concepts and controversies concerning the etiology, pathogenesis, diagnosis and treatment of malignant tumors of the anus. *Surgery* 101:253–266, 1987.
7. Beahrs OH, Wilson SM: Carcinoma of the anus. *Ann Surg* 184:422–428, 1976.
8. Hohm W, Jackman RJ: Anorectal squamous-cell carcinoma: Conservative or radical treatment? *JAMA* 188:241–244, 1964.
9. Pinna-Pintor M, Northover JMA, Nicholls RJ: Squamous cell carcinoma of the anus at one hospital from 1948 to 1984. *Br J Surg* 76:806–810, 1989.
10. Brown DK, Oglesby AB, Scott DH, et al: Squamous cell carcinoma of the anus: A twenty-five-year retrospective. *Am Surg* 54:337–342, 1988.
11. Leichman LP, Cummings BJ: Anal carcinoma. *Curr Probl Cancer* 14:121–159, 1990.
12. Golden GT, Horsley JS III: Surgical management of epidermoid carcinoma of the anus. *Am J Surg* 131:275–280, 1976.
13. Stearns MW Jr, Urmacher C, Sternberg SS, et al: Cancer of the anal canal. *Curr Probl Cancer* 4:1–44, 1980.
14. Greenall MJ, Quan SHQ, Urmacher C, et al: Treatment of epidermoid carcinoma of the anal canal. *Surg Gynecol Obstet* 161:509–517, 1985.
15. Northover JMA: Place de la chirurgie dans le cancer épidermoïde de l'anus. *Lyon Chir* 87:82–84, 1991.

CHAPTER 104

Anal Cancer: Radiation, with and without Chemotherapy

Bernard J. Cummings

HIGHLIGHTS

The management of epidermoid cancer of the anal canal has changed dramatically over the past two decades, following the introduction of treatment with combined radiation and chemotherapy. This change has been brought about without any randomized trial comparison with radical surgery, which was the established treatment in most centers, or with radical radiation, which had been favored by some as an alternative to surgery. Cooperative group studies have subsequently shown that randomized trials can be done with this relatively uncommon cancer. However, the consistently high cure rates with preservation of anorectal function reported with combined radiation and chemotherapy and with radiation alone have now rendered formal randomized comparisons with radical surgery unnecessary. Currently about two-thirds of all patients who present with anal epidermoid cancers are cured, and anorectal function is preserved in about 90 percent of those cured by radiation with/without chemotherapy.

CONTROVERSIES

While there is little doubt that radiation with/without chemotherapy is generally to be preferred to radical surgery as initial treatment, there is still considerable debate over whether the addition of chemotherapy truly adds to what can be achieved with radiation alone. Two randomized trials in progress address this question for the combination of 5-fluorouracil (5-FU) and mitomycin C (MMC) with radiation. Comparison with historical controls suggests that there is improved local control when certain cytotoxic drugs are combined with radiation, at least for larger cancers. The most effective drugs and schedules are not yet established, but 5-FU plus MMC and 5-FU plus cisplatin given concurrently with radiation are the combinations currently in greatest favor. There is no consensus over the minimum effective radiation doses and over radiation techniques, particularly in relation to the regional lymph node groups which should be irradiated and in how to deliver homogeneous radiation to the anal area without producing excessive toxicity. The most effective way of determining whether the local anal cancer has been controlled and the timing of biopsies following radiation have also led to different recommendations.

FUTURE DIRECTIONS

Investigators have been steadily escalating the doses of radiation given together with chemotherapy, to the point where doses are now approaching those used when radiation is the sole treatment modality. It is becoming apparent that a single-dose protocol for tumors of all sizes is probably not appropriate and increases the risk of toxicity for patients with small cancers. Future randomized trials are likely to compare different chemotherapy combinations coupled with standardized radiation doses; however, they will require very large numbers of patients to demonstrate differences, since tumor control rates with several drug and radiation combinations are of the order of 85 percent and differences between the more effective combinations are likely to be no greater than about 10 percent. Future trials may well place greater emphasis on identifying differences in the risks of toxicity with various schedules which produce equivalent tumor control and cure rates. More detailed physiologic studies of anorectal function after treatment with radiation with/without chemotherapy may well reveal unanticipated differences in toxicity and in quality of life following treatment. There have so far been few biological studies to identify the characteristics of those anal tumors which are not eradicated by radiation or radiation plus chemotherapy. Similarly, the 10 to 20 percent of patients who will develop extrapelvic metastases and would benefit from studies of systemic adjuvant treatment cannot at present be readily identified. Although numerous laboratory studies have explored the interactions between radiation and cytotoxic drugs, the relevance of many of these experiments to clinical practice is uncertain, and development of a laboratory tumor system which truly mimics the clinical treatment of epidermoid anal cancers would greatly facilitate the design of future trials.

Radiation therapy, either alone or combined with cytotoxic chemotherapy, is now the preferred method of treatment for epidermoid cancers of the anal canal. Although there have been no randomized trials to compare the merits of radiation therapy with radical surgery, which was formerly the way by which such cancers were managed in most centers, the many reports of the successful use of radiation-based protocols to both cure epidermoid anal cancers and preserve anorectal function have led to general acceptance of initial treatment with either radiation or radiation plus chemotherapy. While the effectiveness of radiation combined with drugs has been the principal reason for this change in management, there are many questions still to be resolved, not the least being whether the addition of chemotherapy really leads to better results than treatment with radiation alone.

Several different conventions are used to define the boundaries of the anal canal.[1] In this chapter, the canal is defined as extending from a proximal limit at the palpable upper border of the anal sphincters and puborectalis muscle of the anorectal ring to a distal boundary at the anal verge, where the walls of the canal come into contact in their resting state and where the specialized mucosa of the anal canal merges with the perianal skin. Because several histologically distinct variants of cancers of the anal canal appear to have similar natural histories and respond similarly to radiation therapy, most reports group squamous cell carcinomas, both keratinizing and nonkeratinizing, and basaloid cancers together as epidermoid cancers, and this usage will also be followed here.

Control of a primary epidermoid cancer of the anal canal and its regional lymph node metastases carries a high likelihood of cure, since extrapelvic metastases are relatively infrequent in this disease. Because radiation therapy can eradicate epidermoid cancer within the pelvis while conserving the function of many of the local normal tissues, it offers potential advantages over radical surgery in the management of anal cancer. Although 75[2] to 90 percent[3] of anal cancers have invaded the sphincters or beyond by the time of diagnosis, it is very uncommon for the sphincters to have been damaged to such an extent that continence is irrevocably lost. In the Princess Margaret Hospital series, only 7 of 150 (5 percent) consecutive patients were incontinent for solid stool or had anovaginal fistulas when they were assessed for treatment.[4] While the specialized muscles of the sphincters are not reconstituted as the cancer regresses following radiation, the resulting fibrotic scar does not usually impair continence to a greater degree than did the original cancer. The major lymphatic groups at risk of metastases—the inguinal, internal iliac, and pararectal nodes—are located within a volume which can tolerate the radiation doses necessary to control metastases. At initial diagnosis, pelvic lymph node metastases are present in about 30 percent of patients[3,5] and inguinal metastases are found in up to 20 percent.[5,6]

RADIATION THERAPY

The risks of radionecrosis associated with some radiotherapy techniques, and concern over whether low-energy orthovoltage radiation or interstitial radiation could sterilize pelvic lymph node metastases, had led to a general preference for radical surgery as the treatment for anal cancer.[7] However, during the past four decades, the development of modern radiation equipment and improved treatment techniques, together with better understanding of the natural history of anal cancer, helped radiation therapy gain greater acceptance in many centers.

Interstitial Radiation

Tumor control and survival rates with interstitial therapy have varied widely, reflecting the criteria used by different investigators to select patients. The best results were obtained in relatively small cancers confined to the distal anal canal.[7] Localized interstitial treatment proved capable of curing many smaller primary anal cancers but allowed regional node metastases to grow unchecked. The likelihood of nodal metastases increases as the cancer invades the sphincters[8] and as the size of the tumor increases above about 2 cm.[3] Small, superficial, well-differentiated squamous cell cancers of the canal which are associated with a less than 10 percent risk of nodal metastases are relatively uncommon and were generally managed by local excision rather than radiation therapy.

To reduce the inhomogeneities of dose distribution which can occur when larger tumors are implanted and to decrease the risk of necrosis from large-volume high-dose implants, Papillon[9] recommended fractionated interstitial therapy, rather than the more traditional single-implant session designed to deliver 40 to 50 Gy over 3 to 4 days (Paris system) or 55 Gy over 7 days (Manchester system).[10] Papillon[9] suggested an initial single-plane implant of 40 Gy at the margin of the lesion followed 2 months later by a further 25 to 30 Gy over 2 to 3 days. Of the 88 patients treated by Papillon with interstitial radiation, 68 percent survived 5 years disease-free and 17 percent died within 5 years from anal cancer. The control rate with single-stage radiation was 76 percent (25/33) compared to 92 percent (50/55) after two-stage or split-course treatment. However, 14 of 88 (16 percent) cancers recurred in the pelvic nodes, and only 6 of these patients were salvaged.

While 80 percent of the patients in Papillon's series retained anorectal function, James et al.[10] found that function could be preserved in only 40 percent (27/68) of patients with anal or perianal cancers treated exclusively with interstitial radiation. In that series, local tumor control was obtained in 27 of 42 (62 percent) tumors less than 5 cm in size but in only 6 of 26 (23 percent) larger than 5 cm or associated with inguinal node metastases. Of the 33 patients apparently cured by radiation, 6 needed surgery for radionecrosis (9 percent of the overall group of 68, 18 percent of those cured by radiation). As a result of experiences such as these, interstitial radiation is now used infrequently as the sole method of treating anal cancer.

External Beam Radiation

With the development of modern megavoltage equipment, it became possible to include both the anal cancer and the regional lymph nodes, especially those in the perirectal and pelvic wall areas, in a volume which received a relatively homogeneous dose. Some centers also elected to include the inguinal and external iliac nodes in a single volume of irradiation, while others preferred to restrict treatment to the posterior pelvis. Radical radiation doses in the range of 50 Gy in 4 weeks to 65 Gy in 6 to 7 weeks were commonly prescribed. The dose-limiting tissues proved to be the perineal skin and anal and rectal mucosa. These doses are close to the limit of tolerance for these tissues for conventionally fractionated radiation delivered once daily and 4 to 5 times per week. Because the perineal skin is particularly sensitive and reacts briskly and uncomfortably to radiation, it was often necessary to interrupt treatment to allow acute dermatitis, diarrhea, and tenesmus to settle, and some centers adopted schedules with elective breaks in treatment, especially when using larger radiation volumes.[11,12] Those using these split-course schedules found that high-dose radiation was better tolerated. While there was no apparent reduction in control or cure rates with the more protracted split-course external beam schedules or with two-phase interstitial radiation, the interruption of radiation in this way may in theory allow some repopulation of the tumor during the break in treatment.

Selected results of the treatment of anal canal cancers with radiation therapy alone are shown in Table 104-1. It is very uncommon for epidermoid anal cancers to recur at the primary site later than about 2 years after radiation. Therefore, whenever possible in Table 104-1 and similar tables in this chapter, tumor control rates are cited at 2 years or longer after treatment. Control rates in all these tables exclude additional local tumor control achieved by surgical salvage.

As would be anticipated, control rates are better for smaller cancers. Survival rates at 5 years in those series which included both large and small tumors range from about 45 to 65 percent and are typical of those in the literature. They are also similar to those quoted for surgery.[5,13] It is more difficult to compare the complication rates in the different series because of the varying criteria used to define toxicity. Serious late complications generally included local tissue necrosis, particularly in the anal canal and adjacent skin, and severe proctitis which could not be controlled by treatment short of surgery. The average risk of serious complications in the series listed in Table 104-1 is about 10 percent, with a range of 2 to 14 percent based on a denominator which includes all patients treated. The complication rates in several series were higher when larger tumors were treated, possibly because more scarring occurred in the anal sphincters and adjacent tissues as the cancers regressed or because of a tendency to prescribe higher radiation doses for larger tumors.[11,12] Lesser degrees of radiation-associated toxicity—such as perianal and anorectal telangiectasia,

Table 104-1
Selected Results of Radiation Therapy

Reference	*Radiation, grays/fractions/time*	*Primary tumor control*		*Serious complications*	*5-Year survival, percent*
Newman et al.[70]	50 Gy/20/4 wk	42/52 (81%) (≤ 5 cm)	13/20 (65%) (> 5 cm or T_4)[a]	6/72 (8%)	66, actuarial
Otim-Oyet et al.[71]	60–65 Gy/30–33/6–7 wk	15/22 (68%) (≤ 4 cm)	8/17 (47%) (> 4 cm or T_4)	1/42 (2%)	52, cause specific
Doggett et al.[68]	Avg 63 Gy/5–7 wk	27/35 (77%) (≤ 4.5 cm)	—	2/35 (6%)	92, actuarial
Salmon et al.[14]	60–65 Gy/6–7 wk	—	106/150 (71%) (all sizes and T_4)	15/150 (10%)	55, actuarial
Eschwege et al.[11]	60–65 Gy/26–30/6–11 wk (some split course)	—	52/64 (81%) (all sizes and T_4)	9/64 (14%)	46, crude
Schlienger et al.[12]	40–45 Gy/16–18/5 wk plus 20–25 Gy/8–10 at 12 wk	73/101 (72%) (≤ 4 cm)	55/92 (60%) (> 4 cm or T_4)	21/193 (11%)	65, determinate
Papillon and Montbarbon[15]	42 Gy/10/2.5 wk plus 20 Gy implant at 11 wk (some plus 5-FU and MMC)	78/84 (93%) (≤ 4 cm)	117/138 (85%) (> 4 cm)	7/222 (3%)	65, crude

[a]T_4 = includes cases involving vaginal mucosa and in some series invasion of other pelvic organs.

occasional rectal bleeding, and urgency of defecation—are relatively common after high-dose pelvic radiation but are not usually a serious inconvenience to the patient.[12,14] Overall, anorectal function is retained by about 65 percent of all patients treated by external beam radiation treatment and by about 85 percent of those in whom the cancer is eradicated by radiation.

Combined External and Interstitial Radiation

A combination of external beam and interstitial radiation has been advocated as a means of delivering radiation to the primary tumor and regional lymph nodes, coupled with additional treatment to the primary cancer. Papillon and his colleagues[9,15] in Lyon have reported the largest series treated in this fashion. They designed a split-course approach in which, after initial external beam therapy, further interstitial treatment was delayed for 8 weeks to allow for recovery of the pelvic tissues and some regression of the primary tumor. They also elected to treat only a relatively small volume of the posterior pelvis with external beam radiation, further reducing the risk of serious damage to normal tissues. The initial cobalt-60 external beam treatment was relatively intense, combining perineal and presacral arc therapy to deliver about 35 Gy tumor dose in 10 fractions in 19 days (tissue maximum dose 42 Gy). This was followed 2 months later by a single-plane iridium-192 implant of 15 to 20 Gy over 15 to 28 (Paris system). Additional radiation was given to palpable pelvic or perirectal lymph node masses. The results Papillon and Montbarbon[15] achieved by this approach are included in Table 104-1. Comparable results have been achieved in smaller series by others[16–18] using similar selection criteria and treatment techniques, although they have sometimes encountered somewhat higher rates of late complications than the exemplary 3 percent reported by Papillon and Montbarbon.[15] Anorectal function was retained by about 90 percent of those whose cancer was controlled by combined external and interstitial radiation. It should be noted that Papillon and others who adopted his techniques reserved efforts at anorectal conservation for patients with mobile cancers which did not involve more than three-quarters of the anal circumference and which had not infiltrated the vaginal mucosa or other pelvic structures. Several of the other series treated by external radiation alone summarized in Table 104-1 included more advanced tumors.

Management of Residual Primary Cancer

The evaluation of tumor regression and control following radical radiation treatment has almost invariably been based on clinical assessment, with biopsies being reserved for patients suspected clinically of harboring residual or recurrent cancer. When radiation has been unsuccessful, appreciable numbers of patients with localized and resectable cancer have been salvaged by surgery, usually abdominoperineal resection. Following high-dose radiation treatment, surgery may be associated with delays in perineal healing, but the risk of other major complications has not been increased unduly.

Control of Regional Lymph Nodes

The presence of inguinal or pelvic lymph node metastases at the time of initial treatment is not a contraindication to the treatment of anal cancer with radiation therapy. The identification of nodal metastases is frequently associated with a poorer prognosis, but these nodes may be managed successfully by radiation alone or by a combination of radiation and limited surgery. Papillon and Montbarbon[15] reported long-term disease-free survival in 11 of 19 patients (60 percent) with inguinal node metastases managed by limited groin dissection followed by 45 Gy (fractionation not given). Schlienger et al.[12] controlled abnormal nodes in 17 of 24 patients (71 percent) with doses of about 60 to 65 Gy in 6 to 7 weeks. There is both direct and indirect evidence that radiation can control metastases to perirectal and pelvic wall nodes. Papillon and Montbarbon[15] noted that 9 of 31 patients with clinically abnormal perirectal or pelvic wall nodes died of cancer, implying that radiation controlled these metastases in at least 71 percent (22/31).[15] Also, in patients treated by abdominoperineal resection without prior radiation, the risk of pelvic nodal metastases is commonly about 30 percent.[3,5] However, in series in which a substantial component of the radiation dose is given by external beam techniques which encompass the nodes at greatest risk, the rate of tumor recurrence in the pelvis is much less than 30 percent, indicating that the expected pelvic node metastases are eradicated by radiation.

COMBINED RADIATION AND CHEMOTHERAPY

The impetus to manage most patients with anal cancer by radiation rather than by surgery came not from any widespread acceptance of radical radiation but from an innovative combination of low-dose radiation therapy combined with cytotoxic chemotherapy introduced as adjuvant treatment prior to abdominoperineal resection. The prototypical radiochemotherapy schedule for anal cancer was developed by Nigro et al.[19] and published in 1974.

A number of variations on the Nigro approach have been devised subsequently, based largely on the following principles. A drug has been selected for combination with radiation, either because it was expected to interact with radiation to increase cytotoxicity or because it was known to produce responses in metastatic anal cancer or in cancers of similar histologic type and it was hoped that the combination would improve control of primary anal cancers. Protocols which combine radiation and cytotoxic drugs for anal cancer have ostensibly sought mainly to exploit drug-radiation interactions which would improve the control of cancer within the volume irradiated rather than to have any effect on extrapelvic metastases. In some cases the desired improvement in therapeutic ratio has not been achieved because of excessive toxicity to normal tissue. Most protocols have been based on a strategy of concurrent radiation and chemotherapy, although more recently some have favored delivery of chemotherapy prior to radiation. Sequential multimodality therapy is less likely to lead to interaction between the drugs and radiation but may allow higher doses of each modality to be used without producing excessive damage to normal tissue.[20] There is a considerable amount of laboratory data available on the effects of combining drugs with radiation, some of which has been used to design clinical protocols, although conclusions from such experiments are often inconsistent and the relevance of such data to the clinical treatment of anal cancers is unclear. There is relatively little information on the response of primary anal cancers to cytotoxic drugs, and most protocols have been designed by analogy with the responses to cytotoxic drugs of squamous cell cancers in other sites, or with the more limited data obtained from the treatment of recurrent or metastatic anal cancers. The drugs most frequently combined with radiation to treat epidermoid anal cancers are 5-FU, used either alone or in combination with MMC or with platinum analogues (cisplatin and carboplatin), and bleomycin.

Radiation, 5-Fluorouracil, and Mitomycin C

In 1974 Nigro et al.[19] published their observations on 3 patients treated preoperatively with a combination of radiation therapy, 5-FU, and MMC or its analogue porfiromycin. This combination was intended to reduce the risk of pelvic recurrence after abdominoperineal resection. The anal tumor regressed in all 3 patients, and in two who underwent resection no residual cancer could be found; the patient who declined surgery had a complete response and the tumor did not recur. With experience, Nigro and his colleagues established a protocol which combined 30 Gy in 15 treatments in 3 weeks together with a bolus injection of MMC 15 mg/m^2 on the first day of radiation and a continuous intravenous infusion of 5-FU 1000 mg/m^2/24 h for 96 h on days 1 through 4 of radiation, the 5-FU infusion being repeated on days 29 through 32.[21] This protocol was designed to exploit additive effects with radiation of drugs to which the investigators had observed responses in advanced or metastatic anal cancer and to benefit from possible synergistic interaction between radiation and 5-FU.[22] The decision to give 5-FU concurrently with radiation was based on selected clinical[23] and laboratory[24] studies which had indicated increased cytotoxicity and possible synergistic interaction when 5-FU was administered in close conjunction with radiation. Continuous infusions of 5-FU had been shown to be less marrow-toxic than bolus injections, and it was anticipated that infusions of 5-FU could be combined safely with the more marrow-toxic MMC.[22] None of the major premises used in designing this protocol—namely, the preference for the drugs selected rather than for other cytotoxics, for infusional rather than bolus 5-FU, for bolus MMC, and for the administration of 5-FU and MMC concurrently with radiation rather than sequentially—has been evaluated systematically as the optimal management for epidermoid anal cancer. For this cancer, 5-FU is still generally given by short-term intensive infusion rather than by bolus injection or by other schedules, and both 5-FU and MMC are usually given concomitantly with the first few days of radiation. In their early reports, Nigro et al.[19] advised that abdominoperineal resection should be performed 4 to 6 weeks after radiation, irrespective of the extent of clinical regression of the anal cancer. However, when it became apparent that complete tumor regression occurred in the majority of patients and that later recurrence was uncommon, they recommended that the site of the primary tumor be biopsied electively and that radical surgery be performed only in those with histopathologically apparent residual cancer.[25]

As chemoradiation was adopted more widely, the original protocol was modified by other investigators, principally by increases in the dose of radiation, by omission of the second infusion of 5-FU except when given concurrently with radiation, and by limitation of biopsies to only those in whom cancer was suspected clinically. Table 104-2 shows selected protocols which indicate the range of radiation doses used and the comparative consistency of the doses of cytotoxic drugs. These protocols have been arranged in approximately ascending order of the intensity of radiation dose. There has been at least a twofold variation in the doses of radiation, which have ranged from 30 Gy in 3 weeks to 60 Gy in 6 weeks or more. The higher doses are still somewhat below those used when radiation is the sole treatment (see Table 104-1). The dose of 5-FU has usually been 1000 mg/m^2/24 h by continuous infusion over 96 h, with some centers delivering a second course of 5-FU concurrently with the latter part of the more protracted radiation schedules. A single bolus injection of MMC in doses of from 10 to 15 mg/m^2 is given at the start of radiation and is repeated in only a few protocols.

The overall primary tumor control rates at 2 years or longer after treatment for the series cited range from about 65 to 85 percent (Table 104-2). In most series, higher radiation doses, usually equivalent to 45 Gy in 5 weeks or more and often supplemented with local boost irradiation, have controlled about 75 percent of cancers larger than 4 or 5 cm in size, including circumferential tumors or cancers which have invaded other pelvic organs.[26] Radiation doses of about 30 Gy in 3 weeks to 41 Gy in 5 weeks have proven capable of eradicating up to about 90 percent of anal cancers 3 cm or less in diameter when combined with 5-FU and

Table 104-2
Selected Results of Concurrent Radiation, 5-Fluorouracil, and Mitomycin C

Reference	*Chemotherapy* 5-FU[a]	*Chemotherapy* Mitomycin C	*Radiation, grays/fractions/time*	*Primary tumor control*		*Regional node control*	*5-Year survival*
Leichman et al.[21]	1000 mg/m^2/24 h IVI d 1–4 and d 29–32	15 mg/m^2 IVB d 1	30 Gy/15/d 1–21	31/34 (91%) (≤ 5 cm)	7/10 (70%) (> 5 cm)	NS	80%, crude
Sischy et al.[49]	1000 mg/m^2/24 h IVI d 2–5 and d 28–31	10 mg/m^2 IVB d 1	40.8 Gy/24/d 1–35	22/26 (85%) (< 3 cm)	32/50 (64%) (≥ 3 cm)	NA	73%, 3 years actuarial
Cummings et al.[28]	1000 mg/m^2/24 h IVI d 1–4 and d 43–46	10 mg/m^2 IVB d 1 and d 43	48–50 Gy/24–20/d 1–58 (split course)	25/27 (93%) (≤ 5 cm)	16/20 (80%) (> 5 cm or T_4)	4/5	65%, actuarial
Schneider et al.[29]	1000 mg/m^2/24 h IVI d 1–4 and d 29–32	10 mg/m^2 IVB d 1 and d 29	50 Gy/25–28/d 1–35 ± boost	21/22 (95%) (≤ 5 cm)	14/19 (74%) (> 5 cm or T_4)	3/4	77%, actuarial
Papillon and Montbarbon[15]	600 mg/m^2/24 h IVI (120 h) d 1–5	12 mg/m^2 IVB d 1	42 Gy/10/d 1–19 plus interstitial boost 20 Gy d 78	—	57/70 (81%) (≥ 4 cm)	NS	NS
Tanum et al.[56]	1000 mg/m^2/24 h IVI d 1–4	10–15 mg/m^2 IVB d 1	50–54 Gy/25–27/d 1–35	28/30 (93%) (≤ 5 cm)	42/56 (75%) (> 5 cm or T_4)	NS	72%, actuarial
Cummings et al.[28]	1000 mg/m^2/24 h IVI d 1–4	10 mg/m^2 IVB d 1	50 Gy/20/d 1–28	3/3 (≤ 5 cm)	11/13 (85%) (> 5 cm or T_4)	3/3	75%, actuarial
Doci et al.[30]	750 mg/m^2/24 h IVI (120 h) d 1–5/d 43–47/ d 85–89	15 mg/m^2 IVB d 1/d 43/d 85	54–60 Gy/30–33/d 1–53 (split course)	28/38 (74%) (≤ 5 cm)	9/17 (53%) (> 5 cm)	8/8	81%, actuarial

[a]All infusions 96 h except where shown.

Abbreviations: IVI, continuous intravenous infusion; IVB, intravenous bolus injection; NS, not stated; NA, not applicable; T_4, invading adjacent organs.

MMC. The optimum radiation doses and techniques and chemotherapy doses are not known, and data relating the tumor control rates and the toxicity associated with the various protocols remain of considerable interest.

Regional lymph node metastases have also been controlled readily by the combination of radiation, 5-FU, and MMC, and the finding of nodal metastases on initial assessment does not contraindicate the use of combined-modality treatment or efforts to conserve anorectal function. In most series, the node groups affected have been treated by radiation doses similar to those delivered to the primary anal cancers, sometimes following local excision of enlarged inguinal nodes. Using this approach, lymph nodes have been controlled in 75 percent or more of those with abnormally enlarged nodes (many confirmed as metastases by biopsy prior to treatment).[27–30] And in those patients who underwent abdominoperineal resection following complete regression of the primary anal cancer with chemoradiation, the absence of metastatic lymph nodes in the tissues excised offers indirect evidence of the ability of the combination therapy to control regional node metastases as well as the primary tumor. As is the case with treatment by radiation alone, the finding of lymph node metastases at presentation has generally portended a relatively poorer prognosis even when the regional node metastases have themselves been controlled. Elective irradiation of clinically negative inguinal nodes with doses as low as 24 Gy in 2.5 wk combined with 5-FU and MMC has been sufficient to prevent late failure in these nodes.[28]

The survival rates shown in Table 104-2 are somewhat better than those usually ascribed to treatment with radical radiation alone. However, several of the early studies with concurrent radiation, 5-FU, and MMC excluded patients with locally advanced cancers or with regional node metastases; it will be necessary to await the outcome of randomized trials to determine whether tumor control and survival rates are truly improved by the combination.

The severity of acute normal tissue reactions within the volume irradiated has often been increased when 5-FU and MMC were given concomitantly with radiation. The tissues and organs principally affected are the skin of the perineum, the anorectum, and other bowel within the treatment volume. Some patients have had severe marrow depression, sometimes associated with secondary sepsis. Toxicity has occasionally led to death,[29,30] in contrast to treatment with radiation alone, where a fatal outcome from acute toxicity is extremely rare. Because the doses of drugs used have been fairly constant, the severity and frequency of the reactions are more readily correlated to changes in the radiation doses. However, even at doses as low as 30 Gy in 3 weeks, the addition of concurrent 5-FU and MMC resulted in severe acute toxicity in 5 to 10 percent (5 of 104 patients in Nigro's series[31] and 3 of 29 treated by Pipard).[18] At higher radiation doses, severe toxicity was more common. When a 96-h infusion of 5-FU (1000 mg/m^2/24 h) and a single bolus injection of MMC (10 mg/m^2) were given concurrently with the start of radical pelvic radiation (50 Gy in 20 fractions in 4 weeks) to a moderately large volume, grade 3 or greater toxicity (RTOG scale) occurred in 12 of 16 patients (75 percent). Similar radiation doses and techniques without concomitant chemotherapy resulted in severe toxicity in only 9 of 30 patients (30 percent).[32] The risk of acute toxicity from combined radiation and 5-FU and MMC was reduced to 36 percent (12 of 33) by decreasing the daily fractional dose from 2.5 to 2 Gy and by the adoption of planned split-course treatment.[32] In the series of Tanum et al.,[33] even at a daily fractional radiation dose of only 2 Gy, no more than 51 percent of patients who received a single 96-h infusion of 5-FU and one bolus injection of MMC at the start of radiation reached the planned total dose of 50 Gy without needing an interruption in treatment. The severity of acute toxicity has generally been modified mainly by altering the daily and total doses of radiation therapy—although the doses of second courses of 5-FU and MMC have also been adjusted, principally in response to the severity of oral mucositis and diarrhea and depression of hematologic indices with the initial course of drugs rather than to reactions within the irradiated tissues.

The risks of serious late normal tissue toxicity can also be correlated in part with the intensity of radiation treatment, although—because of the different conventions used to report toxicity—direct comparison of the results of the various series is difficult. In Table 104-3 the reported rates of serious late toxicity are compared according to the total radiation dose intended, the fractional daily dose, and the radiation treatment volume and field arrangement. In general, the lower the daily fractional dose, the lower the risk of late morbidity for similar total doses, and this is consistent with radiobiological theory. The high rate of late toxicity in the Toronto series[28] in patients who received uninterrupted radical radiation to 50 Gy in 4 weeks at 2.5 Gy per fraction concomitantly with 5-FU and MMC may be due in part to the difficulty in separating out damage consequential on the severe acute soft-tissue morbidity also seen with this schedule. An unexpected finding was the report from Papillon that the addition of 5-FU and MMC to his relatively intense radiation schedule (42 Gy given dose, approximately 35 Gy tumor dose, in 10 fractions in 19 days) was not associated with any increase in major early or late toxicity (Papillon, personal communication, June 1990). It seems most likely that this is due to the smaller volume of tissue irradiated by the Lyon technique and the use

Table 104-3
Late Toxicity after Radiation, 5-Fluorouracil, and Mitomycin C

Reference	*Serious morbidity, %*	*Total radiation, grays/fractions/time*	*Dose per fraction, Gy*	*Radiation, volume/fields*
Leichman et al.[21]	0/44 (0)	30 Gy/15/3 wk	2	AP:PA[a] pelvis to L5-S1
Sischy et al.[49]	2/79 (3)	40.8 Gy/24/5 wk	1.7	AP:PA pelvis to L5-S1
Cummings et al.[28]	1/33 (3)	48 Gy/24/8 wk (split)	2	AP:PA pelvis to S3 to 24 Gy, plus 4-field box or perineal
Doci et al.[30]	2/56 (4)	54–60 Gy/30–33/ 8 wk (split)	1.8	AP:PA pelvis to S3, plus perineal
Schneider et al.[29]	3/41 (7)	50 Gy/25–28/5 wk ± boost	1.8–2	AP:PA pelvis to S3 or 4-field
Tanum et al.[56]	14/89 (16)	50–54 Gy/25–27/ 5–8 wk	2	AP:PA pelvis to S1 to S3
Cummings et al.[28]	5/14 (36)	50 Gy/20/8 wk (split)	2.5	AP:PA pelvis to S3 to 25 Gy, plus 4-field box or perineal
Cummings et al.[28]	10/16 (63)	50 Gy/20/4 wk	2.5	AP:PA pelvis to S5 or S3 to 35 Gy, plus 4-field box or perineal
Papillon and Montbarbon[15]	— (< 5)	42 Gy/10/2.5 wk + boost	4.2	Perineal plus posterior pelvic arc

[a]AP:PA, anterior-posterior opposed fields.

of a direct perineal portal, rather than the larger volumes with beams tangential to the perineum favored in many other centers (see discussion of radiation technique, below). Despite the intensity of reactions reported in some series, anorectal function has been lost due to late toxicity in no more than 5 to 10 percent of patients and usually only in those who have received higher radiation doses. The most common causes of loss of function are anal ulceration or stricture, rectal bleeding, and incontinence due to fibrosis. Overall, anorectal function is reported to have been preserved in about two-thirds of all patients treated and in about 90 percent of those whose primary tumor was controlled by radiation, 5-FU, and MMC.

Although most investigators have administered 5-FU and MMC on the same days as radiation, there are some reports of the sequential use of the drugs in the week prior to radiation (Table 104-4). The results of sequential therapy appear to be inferior to those achieved with similar total doses of drugs and radiation delivered concurrently. However, differences in the stages of the cancers treated and different intervals between the completion of treatment and evaluation of tumor regression may account for the apparent advantages of concomitant treatment. Acute toxicity occurred with about equal frequency in these series, with 5 of 58 (9 percent) patients requiring hospitalization for toxicity in the sequential radiochemotherapy series[34,35]

Table 104-4
Concurrent versus Sequential 5-Fluorouracil, Mitomycin C, and Radiation

Reference	*5-FU*	*Mitomycin C*	*Radiation, grays/fractions/time*	*Biopsy or surgery*	*Complete regression, histologic negative*	*Survival*
Concurrent						
Nigro[31]	1000 mg/m²/24 h IVI (96 h) d 1–4 and d 29–32	15 mg/m² IVB d 1	30 Gy/15/d 1–21	Approx d 73	83/93 (89%)	80%, 5 years
Meeker et al.[36]	1000 mg/m²/24 h IVI (96 h) d 1–4 and d 29–32	15 mg/m² IVB d 1	30 Gy/15/d 1–21	Approx d 53–74	14/16 (88%)	87%, 40 months
Sequential						
Miller et al.[34]	750 mg/m²/24 h IVI (120 h) d 1–5	15 mg/m² IVB d 1	30 Gy/15/d 7–28	Approx d 56–72	19/42 (45%)	82%, 5 years
Secco et al.[35]	750 mg/m²/12 h IVI d 1–5	15 mg/m²/12 h IVI d 1	30 Gy/15/d 8–27	Approx d 55–69	3/14 (21%)	63%, 42 months

IVI = continuous intravenous infusion.
IVB = intravenous bolus injection.

compared with 10 of 123 (8 percent) when the drugs and radiation were given concurrently.[31,36] Two elderly patients in the series of Secco et al.[35] who were treated with sequential chemotherapy and radiation died of debility attributed to the chemotherapy. No serious late complications were reported in any of these series. While there have been no formal clinical studies to evaluate the effects of varying the sequencing of 5-FU and MMC with radiation, the differences in the results shown in Table 104-4 are consistent with those laboratory studies which suggest a time-dependent interaction between exposure to radiation and to 5-FU.[20,24,37]

The combination of radiation with concurrent 5-FU and MMC remains the most widely used form of chemoradiation for epidermoid anal cancer.

Radiation and 5-Fluorouracil

5-Fluorouracil alone has been combined with radiation in four protocols. Each was based on different premises resulting in marked differences in both drug and radiation schedules.

In 1983, Byfield et al.[38] described a clinical protocol based on their laboratory studies, which had suggested that 5-FU should be delivered in maximally tolerated doses and that it should be present for a prolonged period after each radiation treatment.[37] They concluded that a cyclical program of radiation (10 Gy in 4 fractions over days 1 to 4) with concurrent 5-FU (25 mg/kg/24 h by continuous intravenous infusion for 120 h over days 1 to 5) would most closely mimic the conditions of their laboratory experiments. They found that the cycles could be repeated after rest periods of about 9 days, during which oral mucositis and anorectal and perineal reactions settled. The primary tumor was controlled in 9 of 10 patients and regional node metastases were eradicated in 2 of 2 patients who received from 3 to 5 cycles. No serious late effects were observed up to 2 years after treatment. Schedules of this type have not been studied by others.

In contrast to these short, intensive cycles, Hughes et al.,[39] used conventional pelvic radiation of 45 Gy in 25 fractions in 5 weeks followed by local boost irradiation to the anal area; they gave concomitant 5-FU by continuous intravenous infusion at a dose of 300 mg/m^2/24 h throughout the initial 5 weeks of radiation. The intent was to deliver higher total doses of 5-FU. Also, if 5-FU at that daily dose level interacts with radiation, such prolonged infusions might be more effective than the more commonly used 4- or 5-day infusions. Acute gastrointestinal toxicity led to alteration of the chemotherapy schedule in 10 of 24 (42 percent) patients and to interruption of radiation therapy in 7 (29 percent). One patient died of acute toxicity. To reduce toxicity, the investigators recommended that the 5-FU be given on 5 days each week rather than 7, a change in dose which effectively rendered the total amount of 5-FU delivered over 25 days comparable to that in two more intensive 96-h infusions. In a later report, Rich et al.[40] noted that this combination controlled the primary tumor in 26 of 39 (67 percent) patients and that control rates for cancers over 2 cm in diameter were improved when the radiation dose was increased. The control rates for these larger tumors were 5 of 13 (38 percent) at <45 Gy, 9 of 13 (69 percent) at 50 to 55 Gy, and 7 of 8 (88 percent) at 60 to 66 Gy (external beam plus boost). There were apparently no serious late complications.

The third approach to combining radiation and 5-FU was developed by Cummings et al.,[28] who deleted MMC from split-course radiation protocols of 48 to 50 Gy over 8 weeks in which patients received two 96-h infusions of 5-FU 1000 mg/m^2/24 h. This was done to reduce acute morbidity and because of uncertainty concerning the role of MMC in treating anal cancer. Acute toxicity, particularly marrow depression, was reduced, but it was also found that the primary tumor control rate with radiation and 5-FU alone was only 58 percent (36/62) compared to 87 percent (41/47) when both 5-FU and MMC had been used. However, the likelihood of controlling regional lymph node metastases did not decrease with the omission of MMC, and regional control was achieved in all 15 patients with nodal metastases.

The Radiation Therapy Oncology Group (RTOG) has completed a randomized trial which addressed the merits of 5-FU with and without MMC in combination with radiation. The initial report of the RTOG study[41] did not describe as great an advantage from the inclusion of MMC in the protocol as that found in the nonrandomized study in Toronto.[28] In the RTOG trial, 310 patients received pelvic radiation, 45 Gy in 25 fractions in 5 weeks, with concomitant 5-FU 1000 mg/m^2/24 h by continuous infusion for 96 h starting on days 1 and 29 of radiation therapy. Patients were randomized to this schedule with/without MMC 10 mg/m^2 by bolus injection on days 1 and 29. At evaluation 6 weeks after the completion of treatment, histopathologically positive biopsies were obtained from 13 percent of those treated by radiation and 5-FU and from 8 percent of those who received both 5-FU and MMC. The 2-year overall survival rates were 79 percent with MMC and 81 percent without MMC. There was considerably greater toxicity in patients who received MMC. With additional follow-up, this study will clarify the role of MMC combined with short infusions of 5-FU. Further trials will be needed to address the issues raised by the models of repeated cycles or long-term continuous infusions of 5-FU.

Radiation, 5-Fluorouracil, and Platinum Analogues

The combination of 5-FU and cisplatin has produced high tumor response rates in squamous cell cancers of

Table 104-5
Selected Results of Radiation, 5-Fluorouracil, and Platinum

Reference	Chemotherapy: 5-FU	Chemotherapy: Platinum	Radiation, grays/fractions/time	Primary tumor complete response rates to chemotherapy and radiation	Survival
Concurrent					
Gerard et al.[72]	1000 mg/m²/24 h IVI (96 h) d 1–4	P 25 mg/m² IVB d 1–4	42 Gy/10/d 1–19 plus interstitial boost d 63–64	NS/19	94% 3 years actuarial (all tumors ≤ 5 cm)
Rich et al.[40]	300 mg/m²/24 h IVI 5 d (120 h)/wk d 1–42	P 4 mg/m²/24 h IVI 5 d/wk d 1–42	45–54 Gy/25–30/d 1–42	20/21 (95%)	91% 2 years actuarial
Induction Chemotherapy					
Brunet et al.[44]	1000 mg/m²/24 h IVI (120 h) d 2–6; Repeat cycles d 22, d 43	P 100 mg/m² IVB d 1, d 22, d 43	45 Gy/25/d 64–99 plus boost	17/19 (89%)	No cancer deaths, 10–40 months
Svensson et al.[45]	1000 mg/m²/24 h IVI (120 h) d 1–5; Repeat cycles d 29, d 57	CarboP 300–350 mg/m² IVB d 1, d 29, d 57	66 Gy/33/d 79–125	6/6 (100%)	No recurrence, 8–21 months
Alternating					
Roca et al.[73]	750 mg/m²/24 h IVI (120 h) d 2–7/d 23–28	P 50 mg/m² IVB d 1–2/d 22–23	20 Gy/10/d 8–21/d 29–42 plus boost	18/25 (72%)	87% 5 years actuarial

Abbreviations: NS, not stated; P, cisplatin; CarboP, carboplatin; IVI, continuous intravenous infusion; IVB, intravenous bolus injection.

the head, neck, and esophagus. Cisplatin has also been found to have radiosensitizing properties in some laboratory experiments.[42] Complete clinical regression of primary anal cancer has been reported after treatment with cisplatin alone.[43] On the basis of this background, cisplatin and 5-FU are now being combined both sequentially and concurrently with radiation to treat anal cancers.

Several of the studies summarized in Table 104-5 have been reported in abstract only, and follow-up is generally short so that there are few data on survival, long-term tumor control rates, or late toxicity. There have been high response rates with all schedules.

While most investigators use conventional bolus injections of platinum agents, Rich et al.[40] have extended their studies with long-term infusions of 5-FU by adding similar continuous infusions of cisplatin, again to exploit any radiosensitizing interaction with each daily radiation fraction.

The three studies with induction chemotherapy have provided some information on the response rates of primary anal cancers to the combination of 5-FU and platinum analogues. Brunet et al.[44] reported complete clinical regression in 7 of 17 patients (41 percent) after three cycles of 5-FU and cisplatin. Svensson et al.[45] observed complete or near complete responses in all 6 patients treated with three cycles of 5-FU and carboplatin. On the other hand, Rougier et al.[46] saw no complete responses, but they had 7 partial responses in 9 advanced tumors after two cycles of a combination of 5-FU, cisplatin, cyclophosphamide, and bleomycin.

The relative merits of MMC compared with platinum analogues in combination with 5-FU and radiation will probably be resolved only by a randomized trial.

Radiation and Bleomycin

Investigators in Sweden have combined bleomycin with radiation to treat squamous cell cancers of the anal canal.[47] They elected not to treat the basaloid variant of anal epidermoid cancer with this combination. Bleomycin was given by intramuscular injection in a dose of 5 mg, 1 h prior to each of the first 15 radiation treatments in an overall course of 60 Gy in 30 fractions in 8 weeks, split course after 40 Gy. There was no increase in late toxicity, but the severity of the acute perineal reaction led to interruption of treatment in 5 of 10 patients before the planned dose of 40 Gy in 4 weeks, whereas radiation did not have to be interrupted in any of the 13 patients managed by radiation alone. In this study, which was not randomized, the combination of radiation and bleomycin did not appear to improve the local tumor control rate.

Bleomycin was also included in two multidrug programs, one including cisplatin and described earlier,[46] and the other including methotrexate, vincristine, cyclophosphamide, and concomitant radiation to 60 Gy in 6 weeks.[48] The schedule used for the latter combination was described as tolerable. There was complete response in 11 of 13 patients, but 2 patients suffered later recurrences. No long-term follow-up was presented for this pilot study.

So far, bleomycin does not appear to play a major role in the treatment of primary anal cancer.

Identification of Residual Cancer

The evaluation of the site of the primary cancer following chemoradiation has provoked a variety of recommendations, based principally on clinical examination and tissue biopsy and to a lesser extent on serum markers. It is of interest to contrast these recommendations with the usual practice after the treatment of anal cancer with radiation alone, when only areas clinically suspected of residual or recurrent cancer are biopsied. Nigro[31] and others[34,36,49] have recommended elective biopsies from the site of the original cancer, following combined radiation and chemotherapy. The need for such biopsies and their timing and interpretation remain controversial.

In the large series from several centers collected by Nigro,[31] and in other series also,[34,36,50] there was very good correlation between the clinical and histologic assessment of complete tumor regression, so that little additional information would seem to have been gained from the biopsies. Also, a negative biopsy does not preclude tumor recurrence and the need for clinical examination at intervals after treatment. In Nigro's[31] series treated with radiation, 5-FU, and MMC, residual carcinoma was identified in the biopsy specimens of only 1 of 62 patients who had complete clinical tumor regression. Local recurrence was found within the next 12 months in 7 of 61 (11 percent) patients who had had negative biopsies initially. Tanum et al.[33] obtained multiple-core needle biopsies from the anal area following 5-FU, MMC, and radiation. At 1 month after treatment, 39 of 86 (45 percent) patients had a residual mass on clinical examination, but biopsies were positive in only 8 of the 39 (21 percent). At 3 months, 16 of 78 (20 percent) patients still had a palpable tumor, and 6 of these 16 masses (38 percent) yielded positive biopsies. Since it was the policy of Tanum's group to recommend abdominoperineal resection if a positive biopsy was obtained, it may be assumed that residual cancer in the 6 abnormal biopsies found at 3 months was missed at the 1-month examination. An additional 4 local recurrences were identified more than 3 months after treatment. This study provides striking evidence of the discordance between the presence of a palpable residual mass at the site of the original cancer and the ability to identify apparently intact and potentially viable cancer cells in biopsies from the mass. And since irradiated cells do not usually manifest loss of reproductive integrity until they undergo mitosis and cell viability cannot be readily established by histopathology, it is possible that some of the "positive" masses may well have resolved if biopsy had been deferred.

The sometimes slow regression of anal cancers also favors a conservative policy with respect to biopsy after treatment. Cummings et al.[28] plotted the temporal pattern of complete regression after radiation alone and after radiation combined with 5-FU and MMC or with 5-FU alone. Although in that study more cancers were eradicated completely by 5-FU, MMC, and radiation than by other treatments, there were no obvious differences in the regression patterns following the different regimens (Fig. 104-1). About 75 percent

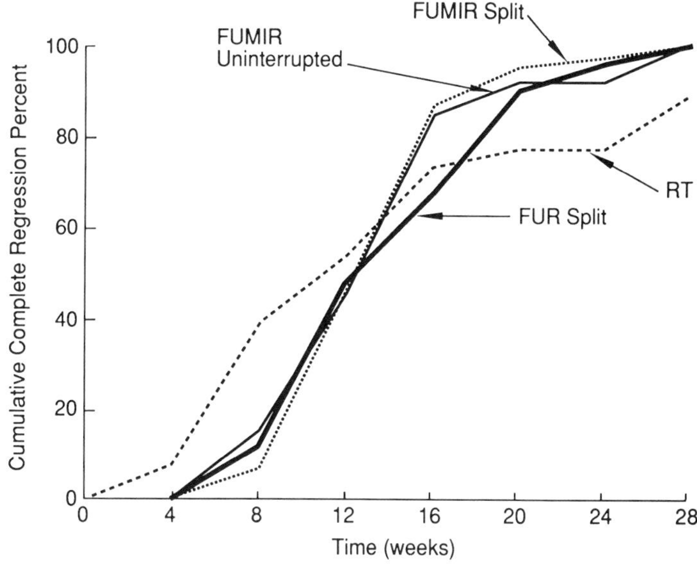

FIG. 104-1. Cumulative complete regression rates for epidermoid anal cancers treated by radiation alone (26 patients); 5-FU, MMC, and continuous radical radiation (FUMIR uninterrupted, 13 patients); 5-FU, MMC, and split-course radiation (FUMIR split, 38 patients); and 5-FU and split course radiation (FUR split, 38 patients). The cumulative clinical regression rates are shown for all patients who had a measurable tumor at the start of radiation treatment (time 0) and for whom the approximate date of complete tumor regression was available. The temporal rate of tumor regression is similar for all treatments. (From Cummings et al.[28] Reproduced by permission.)

of those tumors which were destined to regress completely were no longer detectable clinically by about 16 weeks from the start of treatment, but some tumors took up to 6 months or more to involute. Schlienger et al.[12] reported that after treatment with radical radiation alone, the mean time to complete clinical regression was 3 months, but occasionally the anal tumor mass took up to 12 months to disappear. Several authors have suggested elective biopsy as early as 6 weeks after the completion of radiation and chemotherapy.[31,34,41] Since this would be only about 10 to 14 weeks from the start of treatment, some patients may have had unnecessary additional treatment. There is no evidence to suggest that salvage rates are increased by elective biopsy shortly after the completion of chemoradiation compared to a policy of deferred selective biopsy based on clinical assessment. Multiple biopsies, or attempts to excise the whole scar at the site of an extensive primary tumor, may cause necrosis. Biopsies are better reserved for patients in whom treatment failure is suspected because of an enlarging tumor or anal symptoms.

Serum markers such as squamous cell carcinoma antigen[51,52] and carcinoembryonic antigen[53] have been evaluated. They do not appear to offer any advantage over clinical examination and selective biopsies in monitoring the status of anal cancer after treatment.

Management of Local/Regional Residual or Recurrent Cancer

When the presence of recurrent cancer is confirmed, further treatment must be individualized according to the extent of the recurrence and whether it is thought that the patient might tolerate further efforts to conserve anorectal function. Some centers have successfully given additional radiation alone[54] or radiation and chemotherapy.[22,27,41] Surgery, usually abdominoperineal resection, is recommended when further attempts to conserve anorectal function are not indicated. The risks of pelvic surgery after previous radiochemotherapy appear to be similar to those after comparable doses of radiation alone. Although some have suggested that surgical salvage rates are low after radiation or radiation and chemotherapy,[21,55] this is by no means a universal finding.[28,30,56] Local/regional control is frequently achieved by appropriate surgery, and although extrapelvic metastases are more frequent in some series in such patients, this probably reflects a more aggressive natural history of cancers which recur rather than any causal relationship between the biological behavior of the cancer and its initial treatment by radiation or radiation and cytotoxic drugs. In an effort to improve the outcome in patients undergoing surgery for residual cancer after preoperative 5-FU, MMC, and radiation, Michaelson et al.[50] gave several courses of MMC and 5-FU as postoperative adjuvant therapy. However, recurrence rates were similar whether or not patients received this additional chemotherapy and there was significant morbidity.

MECHANISMS OF INTERACTION BETWEEN CYTOTOXIC DRUGS AND RADIATION

There is considerable controversy as to whether the combinations of drugs and radiation used to treat anal cancer act by simple additive cytotoxicity or by synergistic interaction. Further clarification of these mechanisms would enable protocols to be refined more effectively and lessen the current dependence on empiricism. Steel and Peckham[57] have proposed broad concepts which facilitate discussion of combinations of radiation and chemotherapy. They suggested that interactions be considered under the headings of spatial cooperation, independence of drug and radiation action, protection of normal tissues from the effects of radiation by drugs, and enhancement of tumor response.

1. *Spatial cooperation*. There is no evidence to suggest that relapse outside the volume irradiated is less likely as a result of the cytotoxic drugs given concurrently or sequentially with radiation. Extrapelvic metastases have been reported after initial treatment in from about 10 to 20 percent of patients treated by surgery,[3,13] irradiation alone,[12,28] radiation with one or two courses of concurrent 5-FU and MMC,[28,31,56] and by two 96-h infusions of 5-FU with radiation.[28] There are no data for other combinations and schedules. The randomized trials in progress may provide further information, but it is probable that the relatively low doses of chemotherapy currently used in combined-modality protocols are insufficient to have any effect as systemic adjuvant treatment.

2. *Independence of drug and radiation action*. There is overlap rather than independence in the acute side effects in the pelvic tissues exposed to both radiation and 5-FU or bleomycin and, to a lesser extent, MMC and cisplatin. In most series which have employed concurrent treatment, the doses of either radiation or cytotoxic drugs or both have been reduced below those usually delivered when either modality is given alone. However, while acute toxicity has been exacerbated, most investigators have not found similar increases in late morbidity.

3. *Protection of normal tissues*. None of the cytotoxic drugs used so far to treat anal cancer appears to confer any protection from radiation effects on the pelvic tissues.

4. *Enhancement of tumor response*. Under the classification suggested by Steel and Peckham,[57] if an agent which is generally inactive on its own is combined with radiation and produces an increase in response over that seen with radiation alone, this en-

hancement is called *sensitization*. However, since all of the drugs used in multimodality programs for anal cancer do have some cytotoxic activity against that tumor, it is probably better to avoid the term *sensitization,* although this description is applied loosely in many papers which describe the treatment of anal cancer with radiation and concurrent chemotherapy. In the more complex situation in which both drug and radiation (or drug and drug, etc.) are cytotoxic, Steel and Peckham suggested the term *enhancement* to describe any situation in which the administration of one agent apparently increases the effect of the other or in which the effect of the combination appears to be greater than expected. This latter phenomenon is sometimes called *synergism* or *potentiation*. The evidence for enhancement in the treatment of anal cancers with radiation and cytotoxic drugs is inconclusive, and the merits of treating patients with either concurrent or sequential chemotherapy and radiation rather than radiation alone remain to be proved.

The improvement in pelvic control rates seen in some nonrandomized studies in which attempts have been made to match patients treated by radiation with those treated by similar doses and techniques together with cytotoxic drugs (Table 104-6) have not yet been confirmed by the randomized trials in progress. If there is any superiority from combined-modality treatment, it may be due to additive cytotoxicity rather than to enhancement. The possible improvement in outcome from delivering 5-FU and MMC concurrently with radiation rather than sequentially (see Table 104-4), does appear to favor enhancement rather than additivity, but the treatment schedules and other parameters in these nonrandomized series were not identical. Initial clinical response rates to sequential, concurrent, and alternating schedules of platinum analogues, 5-FU, and radiation do not point to any major differences in outcome for various schedules of treatment with this combination.

The many laboratory studies of the interaction of cytotoxic drugs and radiation give conflicting results and are of uncertain relevance to the clinical treatment of anal cancer. One frequently cited experiment with 5-FU and radiation is that reported by Byfield et al.,[37] who found synergistic interaction when HeLa and HT29 cell suspensions were subjected to prolonged exposure to cytotoxic levels of 5-FU after single doses of radiation. This experiment is considered to support the use of continuous infusions of 5-FU concurrently with radiation. On the other hand, Weinberg and Rauth[58] observed only additive and in some conditions subadditive effects when a squamous cell tumor SCC/ToVII implanted in mice was exposed to continuous infusions of 5-FU and concurrent multiple radiation fractions. Similarly, there is a lack of consistency regarding the nature of possible interactions between radiation and MMC,[59,60] cisplatin,[20,42] and bleomycin.[20,61] It is evident that results depend on the experimental system and the end points studied. It is not yet clear that the empirically derived protocols currently in clinical use are optimal and based on well-founded biological principles.

TECHNIQUES OF RADIATION THERAPY

The treatment of anal cancers presents special challenges because of the irregularities and curvatures of the perineum and lower pelvis, which make the achievement of homogeneous radiation distributions difficult. Also, the perineal skin is particularly sensitive to radiation, and the regional lymph nodes are not immediately adjacent to the anal canal or confined to the posterior pelvis. Major controversies in the design of radiation techniques include (1) selection of the lymph node groups to be treated, (2) the desirability of avoiding high dose radiation delivered tangentially to the perineum, and (3) the role of interstitial therapy.

1. Despite the relatively good control rates achieved when inguinal node metastases are clinically apparent, many investigators prefer to prevent the development of such metastases by electively irradiating clinically normal inguinal nodes rather than restricting treatment

Table 104-6
Radiation Alone Compared with Radiation, 5-Fluorouracil and Mitomycin C

		Primary tumor control	
Reference	*Primary tumor size*	*Radiation, historical*	*Radiation, 5-FU, and MMC*
Papillon and	≤ 4 cm	78/84 (93%)	—
Montbarbon[15]	> 4 cm	51/77 (66%)	57/70 (81%)
Pipard[18]	> 4 cm	16/23 (69%)	23/29 (79%)
Cummings et al.[28]	≤ 2 cm	6/6	8/8
	2.1–5 cm	13/23 (57%)	20/22 (91%)
	> 5 cm or T_4[a]	10/24 (42%)	27/33 (82%)

[a] T_4 = invading adjacent organs.

to only those patients with proven node metastases. The risk of late inguinal node failure in patients managed by surgery alone without elective groin dissection ranges from about 10 to 25 percent[3,62] and in patients treated by radiation therapy in whom the inguinal nodes were not treated electively from about 10 to 20 percent.[9,11,63] The inguinal nodes may be irradiated in continuity with the anal canal and posterior pelvic structures by anterior and posterior opposed pelvic fields or by separate inguinal portals combined with posterior pelvic fields. Elective nodal irradiation, alone or in combination with chemotherapy, has reduced the risk of late failure in the inguinal region to less than 5 percent.[9,63,64] It is not possible to demonstrate improved survival from such elective nodal irradiation because of the way in which the studies have been conducted and reported.

There is also some disagreement over which pelvic node groups should be irradiated. While there is little argument about the need to treat the perirectal and distal internal iliac nodes,[9,65] some investigators have advocated irradiating all the pelvic and pericolonic lymph nodes to at least the junction of the fifth lumbar and first sacral vertebrae.[18,27,49] Treatment of such large volumes increases the risk of acute and late morbidity, especially from damage to the small bowel. Many centers concentrate on the distal pelvis or reduce the volume after about 30 Gy in 3 weeks, so as to treat the internal and external iliac nodes and the perirectal nodes below the lower border of the sacroiliac joints.[22,63] Others have suggested that only the presacral internal iliac and perirectal nodes need be treated if other node groups are not clinically abnormal.[9] Figure 104-2 illustrates the comparative areas encompassed by different field arrangements.

2. Most of the techniques used to treat the anal canal and the regional nodes involve radiation beams tangential to the perineum. Papillon[9] has argued that the risk of perineal fibrosis and ulceration can be reduced by use of a direct perineal portal without the addition of tissue-equivalent bolus over the anus, so that some skin sparing is obtained. This technique is relatively awkward and requires a difficult match with the radiation field which encompasses the posterior pelvic lymph nodes. Nevertheless, Papillon[9] and others have demonstrated that such techniques are feasible and effective and are associated with low risks of serious morbidity. Figure 104-3 shows a transverse isodose distribution for a technique in which half the dose is delivered through anterior and posterior opposed pelvic fields and half through a four-field arrangement to the anal region;[63] this is compared to a sagittal distribution for a direct perineal portal combined with a posterior sacral arc field.[9] Inhomogeneities of dose in the distal pelvis around the anal canal can be reduced by devices such as transmission block

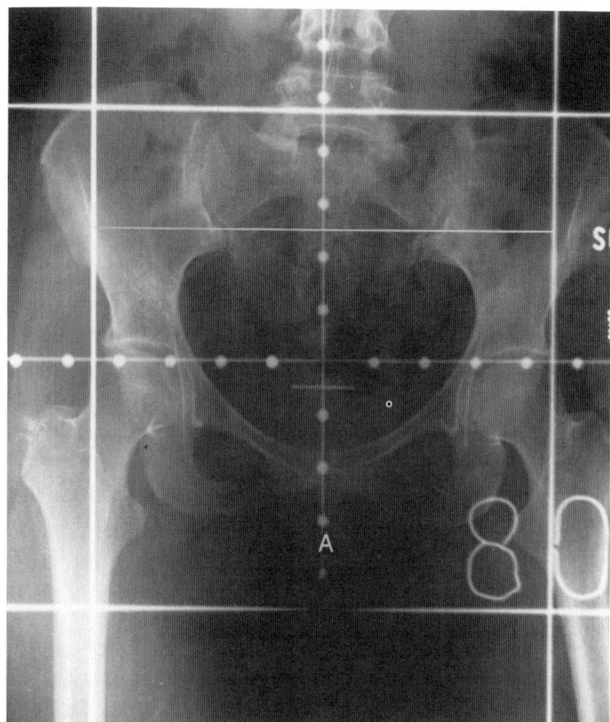

A

B

FIG. 104-2. *A*. Radiograph showing extent of pelvic tissues covered by fields which include the anal canal (anal orifice = A) and the inguinal and pelvic nodes in continuity. The upper border is placed at L5-S1 or at about S3 by different investigators. Corner shielding is not shown. *B*. Radiograph showing the volume covered in the technique developed by Papillon.[9] A direct perineal field 8 cm diameter (*arrow*) is matched to a posterior pelvic field 7 cm wide, with a lower border 7 cm above the anal orifice (A) and an upper border at L5-S1.

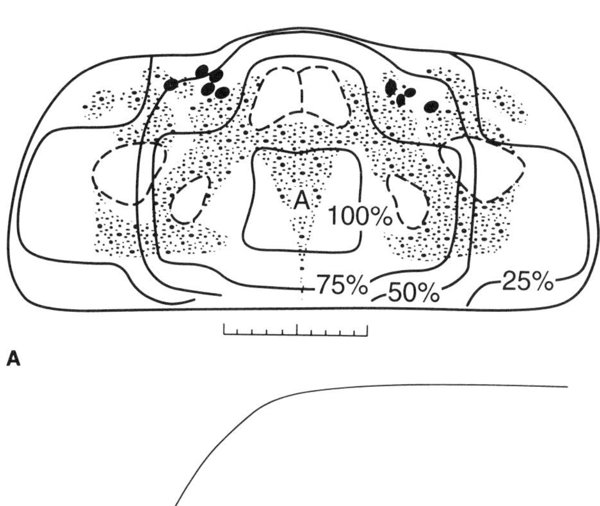

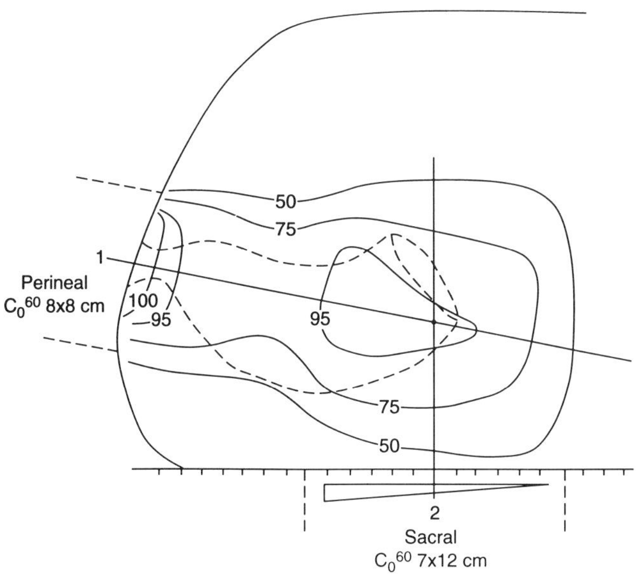

FIG. 104-3. *A*. Composite transverse isodose distribution through the anal canal (A) for technique in which half the tumor dose is given by large anterior-posterior opposed fields with cobalt-60 or 6-MV photons and half the tumor dose is given with 18-MV photons to a reduced volume by a four-field anterior-posteriorlateral arrangement. Isodoses normalized to 100 percent. (From Cummings.[63] Reproduced by permission.) *B*. Sagittal isodose distribution of cobalt-60 irradiation to posterior pelvis. Through a perineal field (1) 8 × 8 cm, and a sacral field (2) 7 cm wide × 12 cm long, a minimum tumor dose of 30 Gy in 10 fractions in 19 days is given to a target volume approximating the 75 percent isodose. Isodoses normalized to 100 percent. (From Papillon.[9] Reproduced by permission.)

filters,[66] although radiation beams remain tangential to the perineum with such techniques.

3. Many prescriptions incorporate boost irradiation to the primary anal tumor, and this may be delivered by either reduced-volume external beam therapy, which may be associated with some of the problems outlined above, or by interstitial implant therapy. Papillon[9] recommended that interstitial treatment should be given with a single plane of needles which should not encompass more than part of the anal circumference so as to lessen the risk of later stricture and that a template should be used to ensure the regular spacing of the radioactive needles. However, others have used more extensive implants without apparently encountering undue toxicity.[67]

CONCLUSION AND FUTURE DIRECTIONS

Although many centers prefer chemoradiation to radiation alone, there are as yet no completed randomized comparisons to support this preference. The United Kingdom Coordinating Committee for Cancer Research (UKCCCR) and the European Organization for the Research and Treatment of Cancer (EORTC) are each conducting trials in which radiation alone is compared with similar doses of radiation combined with 96-h infusions of 5-FU and bolus injections of MMC. Comparisons with historical controls in single centers (Table 104-6) and between centers (Tables 104-1 and 104-2) do suggest that the addition of 5-FU and MMC to radiation improves local tumor control rates relative to those obtained with similar doses of radiation, and similar trends may be claimed for 5-FU combined with platinum cytotoxics. The benefit is seen principally with larger tumors, for very good control and cure rates have been achieved with radical radiation alone for cancers up to 3 or 4 cm in size.[15,68,69] However, review of Table 104-2 also suggests that, in combination with 5-FU and MMC at least, radiation doses rather lower than those generally used for radical radiation alone can control smaller tumors up to about 3 cm or even 5 cm in size. The minimum dose of radiation, alone or combined with cytotoxic drugs, needed to eradicate anal cancers of different sizes and detailed dose-response data are not known. Combined-modality schedules for these smaller tumors based on less than radical doses of radiation may reduce the risk of toxicity from high-dose radiation but do expose the patient to the potential side effects of the cytotoxic drugs.

Although the several cooperative group studies in progress demonstrate that it is possible to carry out randomized trials with this uncommon cancer, it may be more productive in future studies to seek clinically significant differences in the risks of severe acute and late morbidity rather than differences in tumor control rates. Several combinations of drugs and radiation appear capable of producing local control in about 85 percent of patients, and demonstration of small differences in tumor control rates may require very large numbers of patients and not be particularly relevant in clinical practice. Functional studies may be particularly helpful in discriminating between protocols, because although about 90 percent of all patients in whom the primary cancer is controlled by radiation-based treatment now retain anorectal function, this function is not always normal, with some degree of fecal urgency and bleeding from postradiation telangiectatic vessels being common. Detailed physiologic studies of anorectal function may help to identify the least toxic schedules and techniques of radiation with/without chemotherapy.

Biological studies may eventually disclose the features which make from 10 to 15 percent of epidermoid anal cancers, sometimes including quite small tumors, resistant to radiation and to the several combinations of radiation and drugs currently in use; they may also indicate which patients might benefit from experimental protocols. Similarly, there has been little enthusiasm for studies of longer-term chemotherapy as systemic adjuvant treatment in view of the relatively low risk of extrapelvic metastases from epidermoid anal cancers. However, as control rates for pelvic tumors improve, extrapelvic metastases have become increasingly important in determining survival, and identification of biological markers of metastatic potential would help select patients for trials of systemic adjuvant therapy.

The treatment of anal cancer with drugs and radiation has been stimulated by and has prompted laboratory studies of the interaction of radiation and cytotoxic drugs. The relevance of some of the experimental systems, other than for the study of mechanisms, may be questioned, and it is to be hoped that a laboratory tumor system which truly mimics clinical epidermoid anal cancer will be developed.

The considerable variation in the results obtained in different centers and the well-known hazards of comparing groups of patients which have not been randomized appropriately make it difficult to reach firm conclusions on the benefits and disadvantages of the various treatment approaches for anal cancer. While the randomized trials in progress will undoubtedly add to our knowledge of the relative merits of certain types of combined-modality treatment and of radiation alone, rightly or wrongly the effectiveness of chemoradiation has led to a general awareness that epidermoid anal cancers can frequently be cured without the need to sacrifice anorectal function, and combinations of radiation and cytotoxic chemotherapy have become the preferred treatment in most centers.

REFERENCES

1. Cummings BJ: Current management of epidermoid carcinoma of the anal canal. *Gastroenterol Clin North Am* 16:125–142, 1987.
2. Paradis P, Douglass HO Jr, Holyoke ED: The clinical implications of a staging system for carcinoma of the anus. *Surg Gynecol Obstet* 141:411–416, 1975.
3. Boman BM, Moertel CG, O'Connell MJ, et al: Carcinoma of the anal canal: A clinical and pathologic study of 188 cases. *Cancer* 54:114–125, 1984.
4. Leichman LP, Cummings BJ: Anal carcinoma. *Curr Probl Cancer* 14:121–159, 1990.
5. Golden GT, Horsley JS III: Surgical management of epidermoid carcinoma of the anus. *Am J Surg* 131:275–280, 1976.
6. Greenall MJ, Quan SHQ, Urmacher C, et al: Treatment of epidermoid carcinoma of the anal canal. *Surg Gynecol Obstet* 161:509–517, 1985.
7. Cummings BJ: The place of radiation therapy in the treatment of carcinoma of the anal canal. *Cancer Treat Rev* 9:125–147, 1982.
8. Dougherty B, Evans H: Carcinomas of the anal canal: A study of 79 cases. *Am J Clin Pathol* 83:159–164,1985.
9. Papillon J: *Rectal and Anal Cancers.* New York, Springer-Verlag, 1982.
10. James RD, Pointon RS, Martin S: Local radiotherapy in the management of squamous carcinoma of the anus. *Br J Surg* 72:282–285, 1985.
11. Eschwege F, Lasser P, Chavy A, et al: Squamous cell carcinoma of the anal canal: Treatment by external beam irradiation. *Radiother Oncol* 3:145–150, 1985.
12. Schlienger M, Krzisch C, Pene F, et al: Epidermoid carcinoma of the anal canal: Treatment results and prognostic variables in a series of 242 cases. *Int J Radiat Oncol Biol Phys* 17:1141–1151, 1989.
13. Greenall MJ, Quan SHQ, DeCosse J: Epidermoid cancer of the anus. *Br J Surg* 72:S97–S103, 1985.
14. Salmon RJ, Fenton J, Asselain B, et al: Treatment of epidermoid anal canal cancer. *Am J Surg* 147:43–48, 1984.
15. Papillon J, Montbarbon JF: Epidermoid carcinoma of the anal canal: A series of 276 cases. *Dis Colon Rectum* 30:324–333, 1987.
16. Dubois JB, Garrigues JM, Pujol H: Cancer of the anal canal: Report on the experience of 61 patients. *Int J Radiat Oncol Biol Phys* 20:575–580, 1991.
17. Kin N, Pigneux J, Auvray H, et al: Our experience of conservative treatment of anal canal carcinoma combining external irradiation and interstitial implants: 32 cases treated between 1973 and 1982. *Int J Radiat Oncol Biol Phys* 14:253–259, 1988.
18. Pipard G: Combination therapy of anal canal cancer, a report on external irradiation with or without chemotherapy followed by interstitial iridium 192, in Sauer R (ed): *Interventional Radiation Therapy, Techniques, Brachytherapy.* Berlin, Springer-Verlag, 215–219, 1991.
19. Nigro ND, Vaitkevicius VK, Considine B Jr: Combined therapy for cancer of the anal canal: A preliminary report. *Dis Colon Rectum* 17:354–356, 1974.
20. Steel GG: The search for therapeutic gain in the combination of radiotherapy and chemotherapy. *Radiother Oncol* 11:31–35, 1988.
21. Leichman L, Nigro N, Vaitkevicius VK, et al: Cancer of the anal canal: Model for preoperative adjuvant combined modality therapy. *Am J Med* 211:216–278, 1985.
22. Nigro ND, Viatkevicius VK, Herskovic AM: Preservation of function in the treatment of cancer of the anus, in Devita VT, Hellman S, Rosenberg SA (eds): *Important Advances in Oncology.* Philadelphia, Lippincott, 1989, pp 161–177.
23. Moertel CG, Childs DS, Reitemeier RJ, et al: Combined 5-fluorouracil and supervoltage radiation therapy of locally unresectable gastrointestinal cancer. *Cancer* 2:865–867, 1969.
24. Vietti T, Eggerding F, Valeriote F: Combined effect of x-radiation and 5-fluorouracil on survival of transplanted leukemia cells. *J Natl Cancer Inst* 47:865–870, 1971.
25. Buroker TR, Nigro N, Bradley G, et al: Combined therapy for cancer of the anal canal: A follow-up report. *Dis Colon Rectum* 20:677–678, 1977.
26. Cummings BJ: Preservation of anorectal function in advanced epidermoid anal cancer (abstract). *Dis Colon Rectum* 34:P4, 1991.
27. Flam MS, John M, Mowry P, et al: Definitive combined modality therapy of carcinoma of the anus: A report of 30 cases

including results of salvage therapy in patients with residual disease. *Dis Colon Rectum* 30:495–502, 1987.

28. Cummings BJ, Keane TJ, O'Sullivan B, et al: Epidermoid anal cancer: Treatment by radiation alone or by radiation and 5-fluorouracil with and without mitomycin C. *Int J Radiat Oncol Biol Phys* 21:1115–1125, 1991.
29. Schneider IHF, Grabenbauer GG, Reck T, et al: Combined radiation and chemotherapy for epidermoid carcinoma of the anal canal. *Int J Colorect Dis* 7:192–196, 1992.
30. Doci R, Zucali R, Bombelli L, et al: Combined chemoradiation therapy for anal cancer. *Ann Surg* 215:150–156, 1992.
31. Nigro ND: An evaluation of combined therapy for squamous cell cancer of the anal canal. *Dis Colon Rectum* 27:763–766, 1984.
32. Cummings BJ: Anal canal carcinomas. *Front Radiat Ther Oncol* 26:131–141, 1992.
33. Tanum G, Tveit KM, Karlsen KO: Chemoradiotherapy of anal carcinoma: Tumor response and acute toxicity. *Oncology* 50:14–17, 1993
34. Miller EJ, Quan SHQ, Thaler HT: Treatment of squamous cell carcinoma of the anal canal. *Cancer* 67:2038–2041, 1991.
35. Secco GB, Sertoli MR, Scarpati D: Preoperative chemotherapy and radiotherapy in the management of epidermoid carcinoma of the anal canal. *Tumori* 73:151–153, 1987.
36. Meeker WR, Sickle-Santanello BJ, Philpott G, et al: Combined chemotherapy, radiation and surgery for epithelial cancer of the anal canal. *Cancer* 57:525–529, 1986.
37. Byfield JE, Calabro-Jones P, Klisak I, et al: Pharmacologic requirements for obtaining sensitization of human tumor cells in vitro to combined 5-fluorouracil or ftorafur and x-rays. *Int J Radiat Oncol Biol Phys* 8:1923–1933, 1982.
38. Byfield JE, Barone RM, Sharp TR, et al: Conservative management without alkylating agents of squamous cell anal cancer using cyclical 5-FU alone and x-ray therapy. *Cancer Treat Rep* 67:709–712, 1985.
39. Hughes LL, Rich TA, Delclos L, et al: Radiotherapy for anal cancer: Experience from 1979–1987. *Int J Radiat Oncol Biol Phys* 17:1153–1160, 1989.
40. Rich TA, Ajani JA, Morrison WH, et al: Chemoradiation for anal cancer: Continuous infusion 5-fluorouracil +/− cisplatin (abstract). *Radiother Oncol* 24(suppl):S104, 1992.
41. Flam MS, John MJ, Peters T, et al: Radiation and 5-fluorouracil (5-FU) vs radiation, 5-FU, mitomycin C (MMC) in the treatment of anal canal carcinoma: Preliminary results of a phase II randomized RTOG/ECOG intergroup trial (abstract). *Proc ASCO* 12:192, 1993.
42. Dewit L: Combined treatment of radiation and cis-diamminedichloroplatinum (II): A review of experimental and clinical data. *Int J Radiat Oncol Biol Phys* 13:403–426, 1987.
43. Salem P, Habboubi N, Nannasissie E, et al: Effectiveness of cisplatin in the treatment of anal squamous cell carcinoma. *Cancer Treat Rep* 69:891–893, 1985.
44. Brunet R, Becouarn Y, Pigneux J, et al: Cisplatine (P) et flurouracile (FU) en chimiotherapie neoadjuvante des carcinomes epidermoides du canal anal. *Lyon Chir* 87:77–78, 1991.
45. Svensson C, Kaigas M, Goldman S: Induction chemotherapy with carboplatin and 5-fluorouracil in combination with radiotherapy in loco-regionally advanced epidermoid carcinoma of the anus—Preliminary results. *Int J Colorectal Dis* 7:122–124, 1992.
46. Rougier P, Marin JL, Lasser P, et al: Chimiotherapie neo-adjuvante dans les carcinomes epidermoides evalues du canal anal: Etude pilote, in Jacquillat C, Weil M, Khayat D (eds): *Neo-Adjuvant Chemotherapy*. Cambridge, John Libbey Eurotext, 1988, pp 57–62.
47. Glimelius B, Pahlman L: Radiation therapy of anal epidermoid carcinoma. *Int J Radiat Oncol Biol Phys* 13:305–312, 1987.
48. Johnson Buarque E, Gomes Filho F, Guarischi A, et al: Outpatient radiochemotherapy for anal epidermoid carcinoma (abstract). *Proc ASCO* 11:190, 1992.
49. Sischy B, Doggett RLS, Krall JM, et al: Definitive irradiation and chemotherapy for radiosensitization in management of anal carcinoma: Interim report on Radiation Therapy Oncology Group study No. 8314. *J Natl Cancer Inst* 81:850–856, 1989.
50. Michaelson RA, Magill GB, Quan SHQ, et al: Pre-operative chemotherapy and radiation therapy in the management of anal epidermoid carcinoma. *Cancer* 51:390–395, 1983.
51. Fontana X, Lagrange JL, Francois E, et al: Assessment of "squamous cell carcinoma antigen" (SCC) as a marker of epidermoid carcinoma of the anal canal. *Dis Colon Rectum* 34:126–131, 1991.
52. Petrelli NJ, Shaw N, Bhargava A, et al: Squamous cell carcinoma antigen as a marker for squamous cell carcinoma of the anal canal. *J Clin Oncol* 6:782–785, 1988.
53. Tanum G, Stenwig AE, Bormer OP, et al: Carcinoembryonic antigen in anal carcinoma. *Acta Oncol* 31:333–335, 1992.
54. Haghbin M, Sischy B, Hinson J: A long-term follow-up of definitive conservative therapy for anal canal carcinoma (abstract). *Proc ASCO* 4:81, 1985.
55. Zelnick RS, Haas PA, Ajlouni M, et al: Results of abdominoperineal resections for failures after combination chemotherapy and radiation therapy for anal canal cancers. *Dis Colon Rectum* 35:574–578, 1992.
56. Tanum G, Tveit K, Karlsen KO, et al: Chemotherapy and radiation therapy for anal carcinoma. *Cancer* 67:2462–2466, 1991.
57. Steel GG, Peckham MJ: Exploitable mechanisms in combined radiotherapy-chemotherapy: The concept of additivity. *Int J Radiat Oncol Biol Phys* 5:85–91, 1979.
58. Weinberg MJ, Rauth AM: 5-Fluorouracil infusions and fractionated doses of radiation: Studies with a murine squamous cell carcinoma. *Int J Radiat Oncol Biol Phys* 13:1691–1699, 1987.
59. Rockwell S: Cytotoxicities of mitomycin C and x-rays to aerobic and hypoxic cells in vitro. *Int J Radiat Oncol Biol Phys* 8:1035–1039, 1982.
60. Siemann DW, Keng PC: Responses of tumor cell subpopulations to single modality and combined modality therapies. *NCI Monogr* 6:101–105, 1988.
61. Wu DZ, Zhang YQ, Keng P, et al: The interaction between bleomycin and radiation on cell survival and DNA damage in mammalian cell cultures. *Int J Radiat Oncol Biol Phys* 11:2125–2131, 1985.
62. Stearns MW Jr, Urmacher C, Sternberg SS, et al: Cancer of the anal canal. *Curr Probl Cancer* 4:1–44, 1980.
63. Cummings BJ: Carcinoma of the anal canal, in Perez CA, Brady LW (eds): *Principles and Practice of Radiation Oncology*, 2d ed. Philadelphia, Lippincott, 1992, pp 830–837.
64. Rousseau J, Mathieu G, Fenton J, et al: La telecobaltotherapie des cancers du canal anal. *J Radiol Electrol Med Nucl* 54:622–626, 1973.
65. Wade DS, Herrera L, Castillo NB, et al: Metastases to the lymph nodes in epidermoid carcinoma of the anal canal studied by a clearing technique. *Surg Gynecol Obstet* 169:238–242, 1989.
66. King GC, Sonnik DA, Kalend AM, et al: Transmission block technique for the treatment of the pelvis and perineum including the inguinal lymph nodes: Dosimetric considerations. *Med Dosim* 18:7–12, 1993.
67. Syed AM, Puthawala A, Neblett D, et al: Primary treatment of the lower rectum and anal canal by a combination of exter-

nal irradiation and interstitial implant. *Radiology* 128:199–203, 1978.

68. Doggett SW, Green JP, Cantril ST: Efficacy of radiation therapy alone for limited squamous cell carcinoma of the anal canal. *Int J Radiat Oncol Biol Phys* 15:1069–1072, 1988.
69. Martenson JA, Gunderson LL: Radiation therapy without chemotherapy in the management of cancer of the anal canal. *Cancer* 71:1736–1740, 1993.
70. Newman G, Calverley DC, Acker BD, et al: The management of carcinoma of the anal canal by external beam radiotherapy, experience in Vancouver 1971–1988. *Radiother Oncol* 25:196–202, 1992.
71. Otim-Oyet D, Ford H, Fisher C, et al: Radical radiotherapy for carcinoma of the anal canal. *Clin Oncol* 2:84–89, 1990.
72. Gerard JP, Romestaing P, Mahe M, et al: Cancer du canal anal: Role de l'association 5-FU-cisplatinum. *Lyon Chir* 87:74–76, 1991.
73. Roca E, Pennella E, Milano C, et al: Efficacy of cisplatin (DDP) with fluorouracil (5-FU) and alternating radiotherapy (RT) as first line treatment in anal cancer (ACC): Long term results (abstract). *Proc ASCO* 12:206, 1993.

CHAPTER 105

Surgical Therapy of Recurrent Epidermoid Carcinoma of the Anal Canal

Lemuel Herrera
Pedro Luna
Cesar Garcia

HIGHLIGHTS

Although the treatment of primary squamous cell carcinoma of the anal canal has changed dramatically during the last decade from abdominoperineal resection to a chemoradiation and sphincter-saving approach, the treatment of recurrent disease continues to present a formidable management challenge.

CONTROVERSIES

Disparity of opinions among clinicians is probably based on the paucity of cases seen, expectations from therapy, and observed results. It is not often recognized that for most individuals with recurrent disease, cure is generally an unrealistic end point. Palliation can be achieved, although at a significant price for short-lived relief and in selective cases.

FUTURE DIRECTIONS

Once the limitations of current therapy are recognized, the management goals will focus acutely on preserving and/or maximizing quality of life. The fact that there have been occasional cases in which chemotherapy has resulted in complete and long-lasting disappearance of systemic metastases indicates that there is a subset of patients whose tumors are exquisitely sensitive to this treatment. Thus, tumor characterization by a biochemical or molecular biological profile and drug-resistance mechanisms seem to be logical directions for further investigation. Defined identification of individual risk factors for recurrence may result in better follow-up. The early recognition of recurrent disease aided by a reliable tumor marker may result in more efficacious therapeutic interventions.

There has been a gradual but continuous and progressive adoption of a multidisciplinary chemoradiation-based approach as the primary treatment for epidermoid carcinoma of the anal canal (ECAC) following documentation by surgical biopsy and staging by the TNM classification system.[1] Because chemoradiation can attain long-lasting local control with preservation of sphincter function in a high percentage of these patients, this approach has relegated abdominoperineal resection (APR) to the role of a salvage procedure.

Despite this newly acquired knowledge, there are still a significant number of patients who continue to receive as primary treatment, single-modality therapies such as local excision, APR, and radiation therapy. These modalities, purportedly used with the intent to cure, are associated with significantly higher recurrence rates than those obtained with the multidisciplinary approach.[2] A number of these patients will present with either a persistence or a local recurrence of the tumor and may be considered candidates for surgery. For these individuals, however, although cure is generally an unrealistic goal, effective palliation may be an achievable end point. Thus, when palliation is recommended, the surgeon should state clearly and in advance the specific symptom he or she hopes to relieve. The chosen end point must aim for preservation or enhancement of quality of life. These palliative interventions should be chosen carefully and on an individual basis, with the expected benefits weighed against the potential risks. In these clinical settings, considerable clinical judgment is required.

Because primary ECAC and recurrences are uncommon, few institutions or investigators have had the opportunity to treat large numbers of patients in carefully stratified clinical settings. Thus, the majority of studies attempting to define the sequence of events of biological importance in these tumors have been retrospective and based on heterogeneous data collected over a long period of time. In addition, there are wide variations in the duration and type of follow-up, therapeutic approaches, methods of analysis, and end points, with therapies seldom matched to careful and uniform tumor stratifications. Because of the heterogeneity of the results, these studies cannot be subjected to an objective and meaningful analysis; therefore, at present, the clinician has to follow an empirical and pragmatic approach.

At the time of diagnosis of residual or recurrent local disease, there is often no evidence of systemic involvement (Fig. 105-1). Thus, at least on a theoretical basis, surgical ablative procedures may be considered as a possible mode of definitive therapy with a curative intent. Ablative interventions could include a variety of exenterative procedures of the pelvic organs and can be useful for central pelvic recurrences. These operations can be performed alone or in combination with removal of perineal, pararectal, or groin metastases or in conjunction with radiation therapy and/or chemotherapy, but their biological value as a positive intervention altering the natural history of the disease has yet to be established. Nonresectional approaches for patients not considered candidates for surgery consist mainly of electrocoagulation, cryotherapy, and laser therapy.

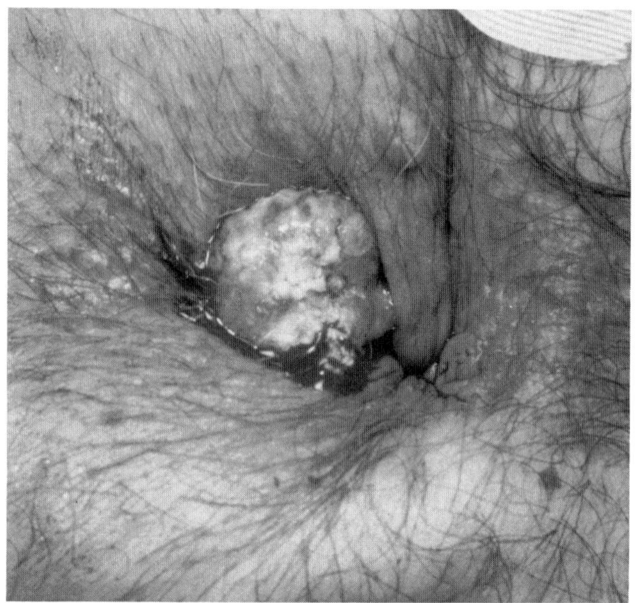

A

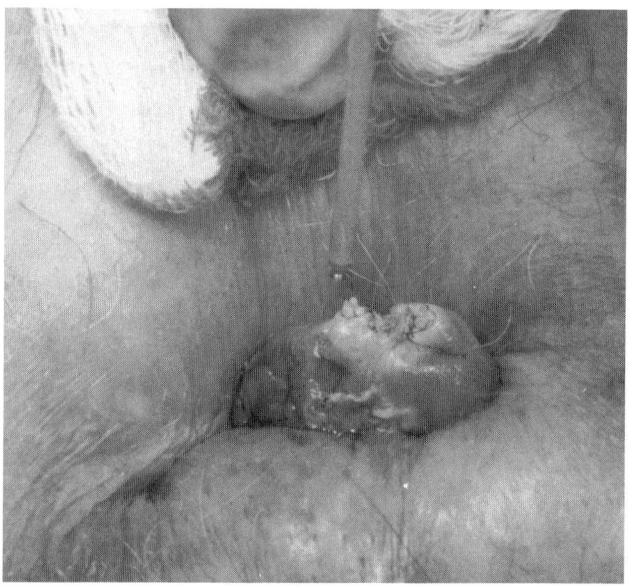

B

FIG. 105-1. *A*. Local recurrence initial chemoradiation therapy. *B*. Ablation/vaporization with an Nd:YAG laser.

PATTERNS OF RECURRENCE

Recurrence of ECAC can occur in one pattern or a combination of patterns. It can be (1) local; (2) local/regional, involving muscle, pelvic perirectal fat, and adjacent lymph nodes; (3) local/regional with discontinuous involvement of the pelvic lymph nodes; or (4) systemic involvement with visceral metastases. These patterns of recurrence may be helpful in stratifying patients for clinical management and study (Fig. 105-2).

SURGICAL THERAPY FOR RESIDUAL OR RECURRENT DISEASE

In deciding whether or not surgery may be helpful in this setting, several factors must be taken into account. These include an understanding of the patterns

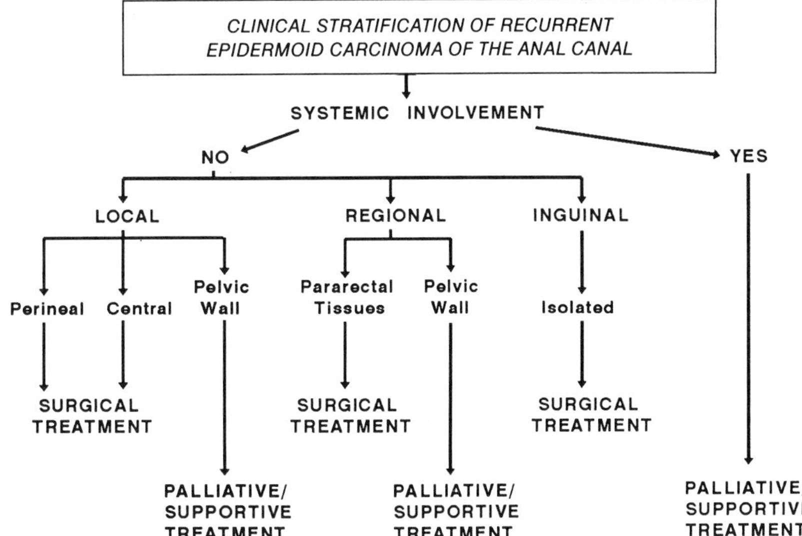

FIG. 105-2. Algorithm detailing the clinical stratification of recurrent epidermoid carcinoma of the anal canal.

of spread and their significance in terms of their outcome, the various clinical settings, and the overall health and performance status of the patient. It should be understood by all involved in the care of these patients that, in general, experience supports the contention that recurrent and possibly residual ECAC is incurable. Thus, the intent of the surgical procedure should not be ambiguous. Goals must be discussed clearly and in advance, with the aim to preserve, maintain, or enhance the quality of life of the patient, as the patient's life span is already limited and can usually be measured in months. Other relevant considerations may include the daily needs related to patient hygiene and the family's resources. Extensive local/regional disease often renders patients unable to care for themselves; thus, skilled and extensive medical assistance may be required. For these patients, a practical surgical aim is to facilitate local care and hygiene, even though the end points of enhanced survival and improved performance status are not applicable.

One must also be aware that many of these carcinomas share relevant etiologic factors. They often occur in immunosuppressed patients, for whom aggressive therapeutic interventions may represent a significantly increased risk for infectious complications, as in the HIV-positive patient.

Surgery for residual and/or recurrent ECAC can be classified as (1) resectional (i.e., wide local excision, APR, pelvic exenteration) or (2) nonresectional (i.e., electrocoagulation, cryosurgery, laser surgery).

Resectional Therapy

Resection may be necessary as part of a multidisciplinary approach, usually as a salvage attempt for residual or recurrent disease. Great care and judgment are necessary for recommendation for wide resections following chemoradiation treatment, because there is usually a "healing ridge" at the site of the primary tumor. This usually represents fibrosis and is not evidence of tumoral activity. When recurrence is suspected, we have elected to take a small incisional biopsy of the "ridge," using a True-Cut needle to take serial biopsies of the perirectal tissue at 1-cm intervals especially at the base of the lesion through the intact perianal skin. At this stage, we can stratify the tumor recurrence appropriately only after histologic examination of morphologic abnormalities detected by physical examination or imaging procedures, sometimes aided by the use of TA-4, an associated tumor antigen.[5] However, at times, this diagnosis can be exceedingly difficult or even impossible,[3,4] and resection will be necessary to establish it. The practical aim of resectional therapy for residual or recurrent ECAC is removal of all tumor with histologically healthy margins and careful outlining of the tumor bed with metallic markers for possible external radiotherapy or the installation of guides for brachytherapy at high doses to restricted fields if this has not been employed previously.

A "salvage" APR (Fig. 105-3) or exenteration may be particularly applicable to patients who have recurrence in the central portion of the pelvis without attachments to the pelvic wall. A median survival close to 2 years can be expected (Table 105-1). Unfortunately, this type of extensive surgery usually is not applicable to those who seem to need it most—that is, debilitated patients with locally advanced disease, those with end-stage systemic disease, and those with extrapelvic involvement. Furthermore, we have not observed a definitive improvement when such surgery is used in combination with either radiation therapy or chemotherapy; however, we have seen significant treatment-related toxicity, as observed by others.[6]

Surgical resection may be helpful to stop hemorrhage or to relieve intestinal or ureteral obstruction

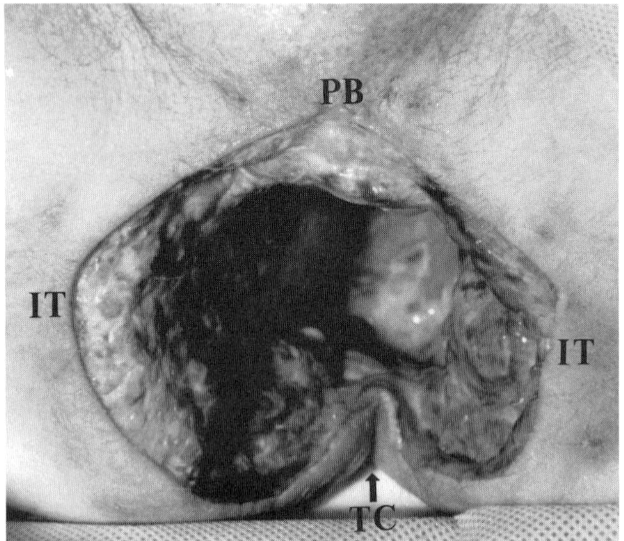

FIG. 105-3. Pelvic-perineal defect following resection. The limits of the resection are the perineal body (PB) ventrally, the tip of the coccyx (TC) dorsally, and the ischial tuberosities (IT) laterally.

produced by the pelvic tumor, or it may be useful in dealing with complications of radiation therapy. However, resection usually is not helpful in relieving pelvic pain, as pain is the result of invasion to the sacral plexus. For these painful local/regional recurrences, rhizotomy or a similar neurosurgical approach to analgesia must be considered.[7]

Lymph node metastases may have a preference for pararectal, internal iliac, external inguinal, preaortic, or mesenteric lymph nodes or a combination of these, but it is important to realize that these metastases do not occur in an orderly fashion.[8] Centrally located pararectal lymph nodes should be included in exenterative procedures if the dissection encompasses a wide lateral dissection of the pelvis and perineum.

Inguinal lymph node metastases may require a groin dissection.[9] Abdominoperineal resection and inguinal lymphadenectomy have been performed simultaneously for primary tumors and synchronous lymph node metastases, with a 5-year survival rate of 10 to 20 percent.[10] This is a very interesting observation,

Table 105-1
Results of Surgical Treatment of Recurrent Epidermoid Carcinoma of the Anal Canal[a]

Pt	Age, years	Sex	Pretreatment tumor stage	Initial treatment	Disease-free interval, months	Pattern of recurrence	Treatment	Follow-up, months	Current status	Comments
1	63	M	$T_2N_0M_0$	APR	32	Regional	Right inguinal lymphadenectomy	27	Alive; disease-free	
2	85	F	$T_2N_0M_0$	APR	8	Local/regional	Right inguinal lymphadenectomy; RT	23	Dead; progressive pelvic disease	
3	60	F	$T_1N_0M_0$	APR	71	Regional	Right inguinal lymphadenectomy; CT	1	Alive; disease-free	
4	57	M	$T_4N_0M_0$	RT		Local	Total pelvic exenteration		Dead; operative death	Residual disease[b]
5	41	M	$T_4N_0M_0$	RT		Local	Total pelvic exenteration		Dead; operative death	Residual disease[b]
6	43	M	$T_2N_0M_0$	RT	2	Local	APR for persistent disease	92	Alive; disease-free	
7	70	F	$T_3N_0M_0$	RT	4	Local	APR	44	Alive; disease-free	
8	65	F	$T_2N_0M_0$	RT	4	Local	APR	43	Alive; disease-free	
9	63	F	$T_4N_0M_0$	RT	6	Local	APR	13	Alive; disease-free	
10	68	F	$T_2N_0M_0$	RT	12	Local	APR	34	Dead; progressive pelvic disease	Regional recurrence 21 months after APR
11	65	F	$T_4N_0M_0$	RT	9	Regional	Right inguinal lymphadenectomy	16	Alive; disease-free	
12	62	F	$T_1N_0M_0$	Local excision	33	Local	APR	60	Alive; disease-free	
13	55	M	$T_4N_2M_0$	RT/CT	2	Local/distant	APR for persistent disease	6	Dead; pulmonary metastases	Persistent disease
14	69	F	$T_4N_0M_0$	RT/CT	8	Local/regional	APR; right inguinal lymphadenectomy	18	Alive; disease-free	
15	70	F	$T_1N_0M_0$	Local excision/CT	30	Local/regional	RT/APR	33	Dead; carcinomatosis	APR 25 months after RT

[a]Of 90 patients with epidermoid carcinoma of the anal canal, 40 had recurrence; 15 of these 40 patients were treated with surgery.
[b]Found at autopsy.
Abbreviations: APR, abdominoperineal resection; CT, chemotherapy; F, female; M, male; RT, radiation therapy.

since we regard lymph node metastases as a harbinger of systemic involvement.[11] Even more interesting is that when lymph nodes become clinically positive during follow-up (metachronous) and are the only site of failure, 5-year survival rates as high as 60 percent can still be obtained following radical lymphadenectomy[10] (Table 105-1). If performed meticulously, radical lymphadenectomy can be associated with low late morbidity in terms of lymphedema, but there is still significant early morbidity in terms of seromas and wound infections.

Metachronous inguinal lymph node metastases can be documented by needle aspiration biopsy and/or local lymph node excision. If lymph nodes are positive, nonsurgical options may include radiation or chemoradiation therapy provided that the area has not previously been included in the radiation field. Such a nonsurgical option may result in less morbidity and less lymphedema of the lower extremity compared with radical inguinal or ilioinguinal dissections, but these modalities are not yet accepted as standard treatment approaches.[9]

Anecdotally, exenteration in combination with other treatments has been reported to have beneficial longstanding results in other tumors provided that healthy margins have been obtained. It should be clear that the concept of cytoreduction (debulking), leaving residual tumor, is not applicable, because there is no chemotherapy available that may produce predictable beneficial results in this clinical setting.[12]

Some local recurrences following local excision of small ECAC can be managed, again, by reexcision with healthy margins. Other recurrences involve the soft tissues extensively, making it impossible to differentiate the tissue planes affected, and cannot be eliminated by anything less than a major resection. Recurrent tumors may produce tenesmus and symptoms related to their friability as well as marked and continued bleeding. They can also produce signs and symptoms related to progressive compression and invasion of the pelvic soft tissues, bone, and nerve roots. This type of pain is difficult to localize and control and may tax the pain-control team significantly.[7] These recurrent tumors are often extensive and bulky owing to their rapid growth. Bowel and ureteral obstruction and a persistent foul-smelling mucous discharge are common. Although most patients die within a few weeks as a consequence of the tumor burden and cachexia, the management of these clinical conditions remains extremely difficult.

When visceral and systemic patterns of spread occur, the lung and liver are the most common sites of involvement, followed by peritoneum and bone,[9] visceral and subcutaneous tissue, and the kidneys.[13] In this clinical setting, the role of surgery, if any, is extremely limited, as the patient's survival is usually short, measurable in weeks.

For associated complications produced by radiotherapy—such as incontinence, radiation enteritis, and small bowel obstruction—specific surgical interventions with a palliative intent may need to be individualized.[14]

Nonresectional Therapy

Fecal Diversion

A colostomy is helpful to relieve obstruction of the large bowel and to manage rectosigmoid bleeding. It should be noted that this type of fecal diversion has all of the disadvantages of a colostomy but is seldom associated with the possible benefits of resection of a localized process. It may not represent a gain in quality of life, and tenesmus usually cannot be relieved by this method. Moreover, survival is very short following this procedure (Table 105-1).

Electrocoagulation

A significant advantage of electrocoagulation is that it can be performed on an outpatient basis under regional or general anesthesia with a regular electrocoagulation unit. It may help to prevent a colostomy by relieving the obstruction through destruction of the luminal tumor. Fever is a common complication. Antibiotic coverage is usually recommended, as there is always the danger of bowel perforation and the introduction of bacteria to damaged perirectal tissues, with the subsequent development of an abscess.

Laser Vaporization

The use of various lasers, such as the Nd:YAG laser, and photodynamic therapy (PDT) have been found to be useful options in the treatment of these patients for control of local manifestations of the disease. These procedures can often be performed without anesthesia in an outpatient setting; only mild sedation is necessary. Although the complication rate is low and the procedure is well tolerated, treatments must be repeated frequently. Significant palliation of mucous discharge and cessation of hemorrhage can be obtained and obstruction can be alleviated successfully. However, the proper role of laser treatment in the management of these patients is still being defined.

Photodynamic Therapy

Photodynamic therapy (PDT) is an innovative approach to local ablation of tumors using a photosensitizer and an activating light.[15] Although, in theory, the activating light in PDT can be a laser or other light source, an argon-dye laser is commonly used. We have employed PDT in the clinical setting of unresectable pelvic recurrences and as an adjunct to salvage APR (Fig. 105-4). In the latter instance, it has been associ-

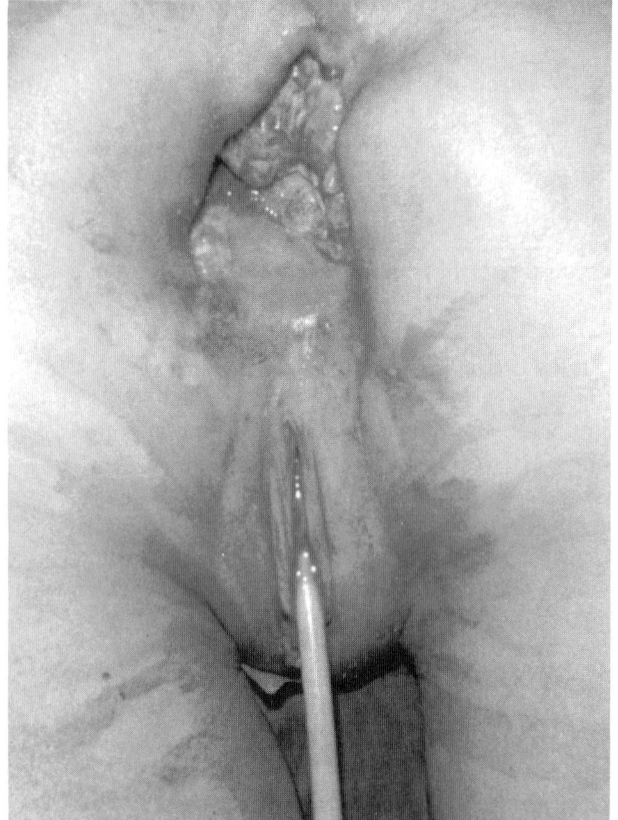

A

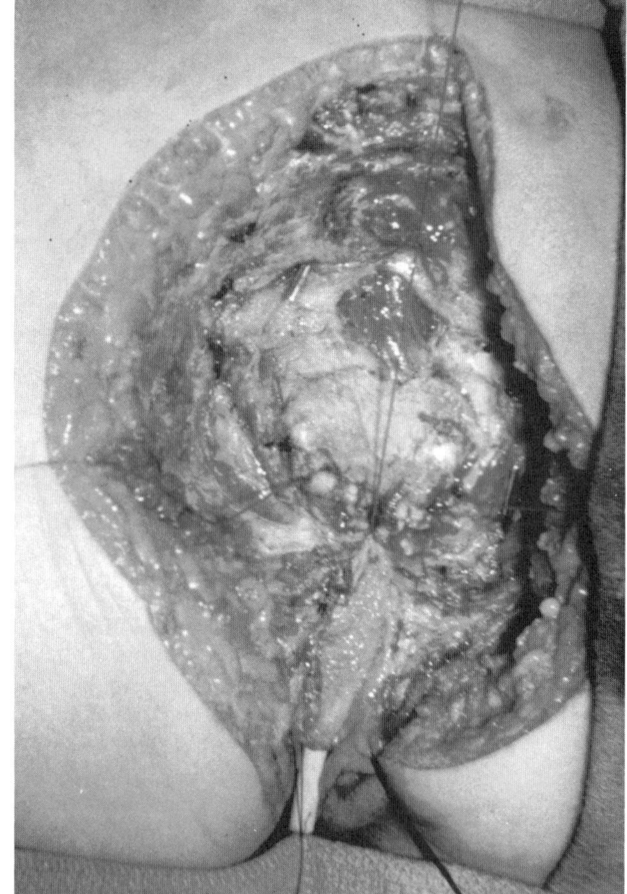

B

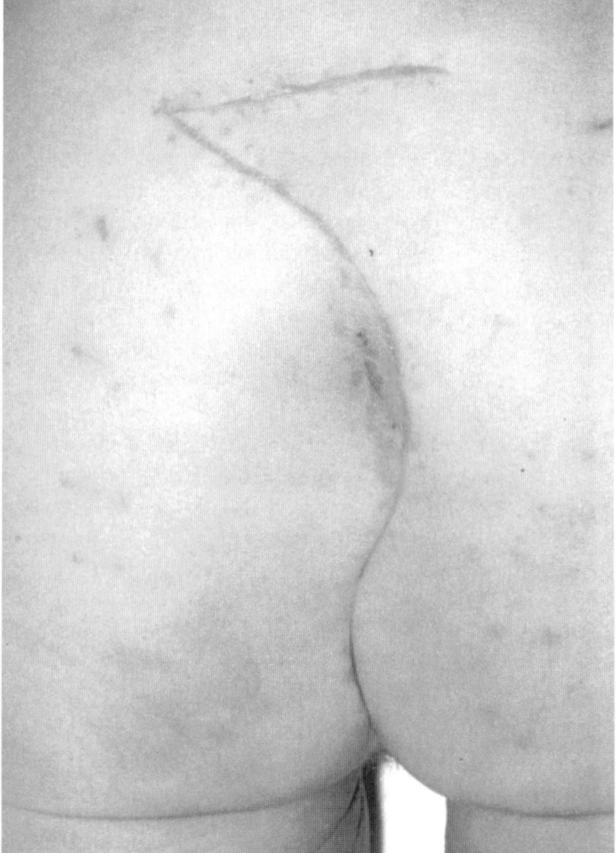

C

D

FIG. 105-4. *A*. Local recurrence in a 34-year-old woman following abdominoperineal resection. *B*. Wide local excision. *C*. Treatment with photodynamic therapy to the surface. *D*. Clinical photograph at 4 weeks' follow-up examination. The patient is alive without evidence of disease 7 years after the procedure.

ated in at least one case with a long disease-free survival (> 7 years).

Brachytherapy

The implantation of radioactive sources directly into tumors or tumoral beds may have the potential to be helpful, as high doses of localized radiation are delivered to the microscopic residual disease while sparing surrounding tissues. Surgery may be required for implantation of the plastic guides. We have used this modality in two patients with pelvic recurrences who had undergone previous radiation therapy, with some relief of pain but no objective, quantifiable tumor response.

Cryotherapy

Cryotherapy (Fig. 105-5) works by freezing tissues. It produces necrosis, which then is followed by sloughing and consequent lessening of the tumor bulk. Therapy is administered with a cryosurgical probe (a hollow, metal tubular device) cooled to −38°F with circulating liquid nitrogen. The probe can be applied to or embedded in the tumor, and freezing is induced rapidly, with the probe adhering quickly to the tissue. A significant advantage is that only the portion of tissue that whitens is destroyed, and the extent of destruction is easily monitored and controllable. Most patients tolerate the procedure well and recover rapidly. No anesthesia is usually required, only a mild sedative to ensure patient comfort. Cryotherapy significantly palliates symptoms of mucous discharge, bleeding, and possibly obstruction. Perianal and pelvic pain can be lessened temporarily. Disadvantages of this form of treatment include management of the large amount of discharged malodorous and necrotic tissue, which may persist for several days, and the need for repeated treatments.

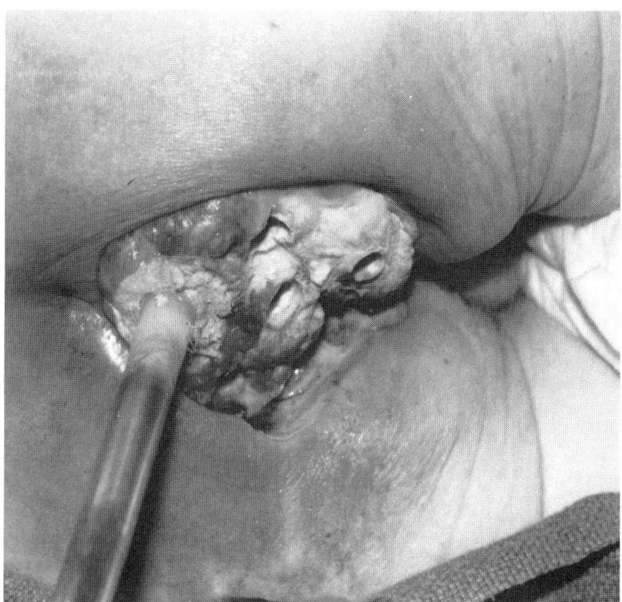

FIG. 105-5. Cryotherapy.

For patients who present with extensive distant metastases and/or symptomatic local disease and are found not to be candidates for resection, these nonresectional therapies may be options for palliation, making the ultimate course much more manageable. For this group of patients and their families, the concept of hospice care must be introduced early. Issues related to dying should be presented in a positive and dignified manner, using appropriate support personnel.

SUMMARY

There is a role for surgical interventions in the management of residual and/or recurrent epidermoid carcinoma of the anal canal. Prognostic factors present at the time of diagnosis of the primary tumor should be taken into account in defining the intended goal of the various therapeutic options. Often, local recurrences are associated with T1 or T2 tumors, whereas distant metastases are associated with T4 tumors. The clinician must be aware of the expected predicted success or failure of specific modalities of treatment and the methods of follow-up that may lead to early diagnosis of recurrence amenable to surgical treatment. One must attempt to classify the patient into an expected stratified pattern of recurrence. The extent of resection with "curative" intent must be determined only after a thorough evaluation that rules out extensive and advanced disease stages in which surgery may not be able to remove all tumor and produce healthy margins, as cytoreductive surgery is not applicable in this clinical setting. In addition, the choice of therapeutic procedure must take into consideration the fact that for many of these individuals, cure is an unrealistic goal. However, it remains true that there are the anecdotal accounts of patients with recurrent disease and distant metastases who have responded to regional and systemic chemotherapy consisting of 5-fluorouracil and cisplatin with radiation therapy; therefore, if the patient's general condition is fair, a closely monitored, vigorous surgical approach may be reasonable. Exceptions are represented by those patients with central pelvic-perineal recurrences and those with metachronous development of lymph node metastases in the groin, in whom resection has resulted in acceptable disease-free survival and gains in terms of quality of life.

Although resectional and nonresectional approaches can result in significant palliation of specific symptoms, these procedures must be chosen carefully and only after a comprehensive assessment indicates that the expected benefits clearly outweigh the potential risks and that the proposed end results will enhance the patient's quality of life.

REFERENCES

1. American Joint Committee on Cancer: Beahrs OH, Henson DE, Hutter RV, et al (eds): *Manual for the Staging of Cancer,* 3d ed. Philadelphia, Lippincott, 1988, pp 81–85, 113–138.
2. Dobrowsky W: Radiotherapy of epidermoid anal canal cancer. *Br J Radiol* 62:53–58, 1989.
3. Papillon J, Montbarbon JF, Gerard JP, et al: Interstitial curietherapy in the conservative treatment of anal and rectal cancers. *Int J Radiat Oncol Biol Phys* 17:1161–1169, 1989.
4. Leichman L, Nigro N, Vaitkevicius VK, et al: Cancer of the anal canal: Model for preoperative adjuvant combined modality therapy. *Am J Med* 78:211–215, 1985.
5. Petrelli NJ, Palmer M, Herrera L, Bhargava A: The utility of squamous cell carcinoma antigen for the follow-up of patients with squamous cell carcinoma of the anal canal. *Cancer* 70:35–39, 1992.
6. Tanum GL: Treatment of relapsing anal carcinoma. *Acta Oncol* 32:33–35, 1993.
7. Rodriguez-Bigas M, Petrelli NJ, Herrera L, West C: Intrathecal phenol rhizotomy for management of pain in recurrent unresectable carcinoma of the rectum. *Surg Gynecol Obstet* 173:41–44, 1991.
8. Wade DS, Herrera L, Castillo NB, Petrelli NJ: Metastases to lymph nodes in epidermoid carcinoma of the anal canal studied by a clearing technique. *Surg Gynecol Obstet* 169:238–242, 1989.
9. Greenall MJ, Magill GB, Quan SHQ, DeCosse JJ: Recurrent epidermoid cancer of the anus. *Cancer* 57:1437–1441, 1986.
10. Lopez MJ, Bliss DP Jr, Kraybill WG, Soybel DI: Carcinoma of the anal region. *Curr Probl Surg* 26:531–600, 1989.
11. Clark J, Petrelli N, Herrera L, Mittelman A: Epidermal carcinoma of the anal canal. *Cancer* 57:400–406, 1986.
12. Herrara L, Garcia C, Luna P, et al: The results of surgical treatment of epidermoid carcinoma of the anal canal. *Int J Surg Sci*, in press.
13. Jensen SL, Hagen K, Harling H, et al: Long-term prognosis after radical treatment for squamous cell carcinoma of the anal canal and anal margin. *Dis Colon Rectum* 31:273–278, 1988.
14. Schlienger M, Krzisch C, Pene F, et al: Epidermoid carcinoma of the anal canal: Treatment results and prognostic variables in a series of 242 cases. *Int J Radiat Oncol Biol Phys* 17:1141–1151, 1989.
15. Herrera L: Photodynamic therapy for colorectal neoplasia. *Semin Colon Rectal Surg* 3:57–61, 1992.

CHAPTER 106

Chemotherapy of Persistent, Recurrent, or Metastatic Cancer

Marshall S. Flam

HIGHLIGHTS

While the role of chemotherapy employed for radioenhancement with pelvic radiation in the definitive treatment of epidermoid malignancies of the anal region is now well defined, the role of postradiation systemic chemotherapy is not. Both the rarity of this malignancy and the impressive success of definitive chemoradiation in the complete eradication of this tumor in the majority of patients treated have resulted in a limited number of patients who require systemic therapy. Consequently, experience with systemic treatment without concomitant radiation is limited and controlled clinical trials nonexistent.

This chapter attempts to (1) categorize the types of patients with advanced disease; (2) identify the optimal treatment within each category of patients with advanced anal cancer based upon a comprehensive review of the literature; and (3) identify which systemic chemotherapeutic agents have the greatest activity against anal cancer, thereby paving the way for new approaches to all patients with this neoplasm.

CONTROVERSIES

With the acceptance of definitive chemoradiation in lieu of abdominoperineal resection in the primary treatment of carcinoma of the anal canal, the major areas of controversy are now in the management of the 10 to 20 percent of patients who fail to achieve complete tumor eradication (persistent disease) and in the 10 to 20 percent who relapse after achieving biopsy-proven complete tumor eradication with chemoradiation (recurrent disease). Should the salvage management of these two groups be surgical or nonsurgical? Are these two groups biologically the same or different and should their management be the same or different?

An additional issue revolves around the need to identify which chemotherapeutic agents are most active against this neoplasm. At this time we really do not know enough regarding the relative efficacy of chemotherapeutic agents against this tumor. The two agents now employed in the definitive chemoradiation of anal cancer, namely 5-fluorouracil (5-FU) and mitomycin C, appear to be capable of improving local control due to their radioenhancing capabilities; yet their activity either individually or in combination against this tumor without radiation appears to be limited.

FUTURE DIRECTIONS

The need to identify systemic agents with greater activity against anal cancer is obvious and pressing. The most efficacious drug combinations can be identified in clinical trials employing patients with advanced disease or by applying combination chemotherapy "up front" in a neoadjuvant fashion before definitive radiation or chemoradiation. Once the most effective combinations of systemic agents are identified, their employment with radiation in the primary treatment of anal cancer and in nonsurgical salvage regimens is likely to further improve the outcome for all patients with this neoplasm.

CLASSIFICATION

The following is a proposal for the classification of advanced-disease anal cancer patients who would potentially benefit from systemic treatment:

1. Primary chemoradiation failures
2. Recurrence after initially successful chemoradiation
    a. Local recurrence only
    b. Distant ± local recurrence
3. Recurrence after surgery
4. Metachronous nodal relapse
5. Presentation with distant metastases

SALVAGE THERAPY OF CHEMORADIATION FAILURES

In 1974, Nigro et al.[1] introduced a program of pelvic radiation, 5-FU infusion, and mitomycin C as a preoperative regimen for the treatment of epidermoid carcinoma of the anal canal. Subsequently, the high incidence of local tumor eradication and cure rates led this regimen as a definitive treatment in lieu of "traditional" abdominoperineal resection. With over 500 published patients treated with variations of this regimen over the past 18 years, the incidence of initial complete tumor eradication is 80 to 90 percent, in series in which both modalities are employed concomitantly,[4–15] but considerably lower in series employing the modalities sequentially.[16–18] Table 106-1 summarizes the initial local-treatment failure rates and salvage management (usually by abdominoperineal resection) of these failures in the major published series employing primary chemoradiation.

In 1987 the University of California San Francisco/Fresno group[8] reported the employment of a chemoradiation salvage regimen in four patients in whom local treatment had failed. All four achieved complete tumor eradication without additional late toxicity and without abdominoperineal resection. The chemoradiation salvage regimens employed by our group and the treatment outcome are demonstrated in Tables 106-2 and 106-3. Cho et al.[13] report 3 of 20 patients with residual disease following chemoradiation salvaged by

Table 106-1
Initial Local Treatment Failures of Combined Chemoradiation in Carcinoma of the Anus: Survey of Published Series

Institution	*No. of patients*	*No. of local failures, %*	*Salvage therapy of local failures*	*No. of deaths in local failures*	*No. alive with disease*	*No. salvaged*	*Percent NED, entire group*
Wayne State[4]	45	7 (15)	6 APR; 1 No Rx	7	0	0	84
U. Rochester[5,6]	29	[a]	9 interstitial implants	3	1	5	77
Memorial[16,17]	37	15 (40)	15 APR	4	1	10	78
Princess Margaret[7]	60	6 (10)	5 APR 1 Loc Exc	2	0	4	75[b]
U. Kentucky[9]	19	3 (16)	3 APR	0	0	3	100
U. Geneva[10]	29[c]	4[c] (14)	4 APR	1[d]	1	3	84
UCSF-Fresno[2]	30	4 (13)	4 CT-RT	1[d]	0	4	100
Grant-Ohio[13]	20	3 (15)	1 APR	0	0	1	95
			1 CT-RT	0	0	1	
			1 RT	0	0	1	
Henry Ford[14]	30	12 (40)	9 APR	12	0	0	53
Milan[18]	56	7 (12)	6 APR	3	1	3	77

[a]9/27 demonstrated "residual nodularity" and were implanted without biopsy. Thus, actual local failure rate before "implantation is unknown. Figures in table assume all patients with residual nodularity had residual tumor prior to implantation.

[b]10/60 failed with distant metastases; only 1 of 10 distant failures are in the local-failure group.

[c]Patients treated with an interstitial iridium implant in lieu of 2nd cycle of 5-FU plus external radiation.

[d]Dead of intercurrent disease but free of cancer following salvage treatment.

Abbreviations: NED, no evidence of disease; APR, abdominoperineal resection; Rx, therapy; CT-RT, chemoradiation; RT, radiation therapy; Loc Exc, local excision.

Table 106-2
Salvage Chemoradiation of Initial Chemoradiation Failures[a]

Case	*RT boost/RT total, cGy*	*5-FU, infusion*	*MMC*	*CDDP*	*MTX*	*5-FU, bolus*
A	1000/5320	1250/day × 4	—	100	—	—
B	1600/5720	—	—	—	200[b]	600[b]
C	900/5040	1000/day × 4	15	—	—	—
D	900/5040	1000/day × 4	—	100	—	—
E	1500/5280	1000/day × 4	—	75	—	—
F	900/5040	1000/day × 4	—	100	—	—

[a]All chemotherapy doses are in mg/m^2.

[b]5-FU (bolus) given 1 h after methotrexate infusion initiated; methotrexate infused over 30 min and followed by leucovorin 10 mg/m^2 PO q6h × five doses, starting 24 h after methotrexate infusion initiated.

Abbreviations: RT, radiation therapy; cGy, centigray; 5-FU, 5-fluorouracil; MMC, mitomycin C; CCDP, cisplatin; MTX, methotrexate.

chemoradiation with 5-FU and cisplatin (1 patient) or additional radiation (1 patient). Whether additional chemoradiation can salvage a significant proportion of patients with persistent local tumor following definitive chemoradiation is currently under evaluation by the Radiation Therapy Oncology Group (RTOG).[19] Under this protocol, 14 of 28 patients with residual tumor following definitive chemoradiation have been rendered disease-free on postsalvage biopsy employing a regimen of radiation, 5-FU, and cisplatin. As the vast majority of patients with anal cancer do not have distant metastases at presentation,[20] it would appear reasonable to manage patients with residual local tumor following primary chemoradiation with additional chemoradiation before resorting to abdominoperineal surgical salvage.

METACHRONOUS NODAL RELAPSE

The discussion of the management of patients who present with involved inguinal or pelvic lymph nodes is outside the scope of this chapter. In contrast to synchronous lymph node metastases, metachronous inguinal relapses can be successfully salvaged by radical groin dissection, with 5-year survival rates of 42 to 75 percent.[21–23] In this clinical setting, the use of postoperative adjuvant chemotherapy should be considered. However, the limited number of cases make a controlled clinical trial not feasible.

TREATMENT OF LOCAL RECURRENCE FOLLOWING SUCCESSFUL INITIAL CHEMORADIATION

The patterns of relapse in anal cancer differ depending upon the initial treatment modality (Table 106-4). In published series employing initial resective surgery and/or radiation, local recurrence at the primary site, pelvis, and/or regional nodes predominates.[22–24] In series employing the synchronous application of radiation and chemotherapy, relapse *outside* the pelvis is relatively more frequent than local relapse.[24,25] This would suggest that the improved rates of primary tumor eradication obtained with chemoradiation are due to the radioenhancing effect of chemotherapy, producing improved local control, rather than its effect upon micrometastatic disease.

Table 106-3
Analysis of Salvage Chemoradiation of Initial Treatment Failures—6 Cases

Case/Age/Sex/Stage	*Residual disease*	*Postsalvage BX*	*Relapse, months*	*Survival, months*
A 56/F/T_3N_0	Microscopic (BX+)	Not done	37[a]	78[b]
B 63/M/T_3N_0	Palpable mass (BX+)	Not done	—	4[c]
C 63/M/T_3N_0	Palpable mass	Neg	—	37[c]
D 55/F/T_3N_0	Palpable mass	Neg	—	75 (NED)
E 62/F/T_3N_1	Palpable mass (BX+)	Pos	NR	14[b]
F 65/F/T_3N_0	Microscopic (BX+)	Neg	—	62 (NED)

[a]Distant relapse without local relapse.

[b]Died of disease.

[c]Died of intercurrent disease, free of cancer.

Abbreviations: BX, biopsy; NED, no evidence of disease; NR, no response, never cleared primary tumor.

Table 106-4
Patterns of Relapse in Representative Series Employing Varied Primary Treatment Regimens

Authors	Treatment	No. of patients	Site of relapse					Total D/total F, percent	Total F/total T, percent
			P	P+N	N	P+D±N	D		
Frost et al.[22]	APR	109	29	NS	20	NS	11	11/60 (18)	60/109 (55)
Bowman et al.[23]	APR	114	12	7	8	5	6	11/46 (24)	46/114 (40)
Cummings et al.[24]	RT	57	12	5	1	9	1	10/28 (36)	28/57 (49)
	5-FU + RT	65	21	0	2	5	3	8/31 (26)	31/65 (48)
	5-FU + MMC + RT	69	7	1	0	5	7	12/20 (60)	20/69 (33)
Flam and John[25]	5-FU + MMC + RT + salvage CT-RT[a]	37	1	1	0	3	2	5/ 7 (71)	7/37 (19)

Abbreviations: P, primary site; N, regional nodes; D, distant metastases; F, failures; T, total treated; NS, not stated; APR, abdominoperineal resection; 5-FU, 5-fluorouracil infusion; RT, pelvic radiation; MMC, mitomycin C.

[a]Six patients with residual tumor were treated with salvage chemoradiation, including cisplatin.

Theoretically it is necessary to make a distinction between patients who fail to achieve complete primary tumor regression following initial combined modality therapy (persistent disease) and those who recur locally more than 6 months following completion of treatment (recurrent disease). Thus, patients who recur 6 months or more after complete response are more likely to have larger tumors than those with persistent disease, as the latter group undergoes more frequent observation at a time when their tumors are regressing. Additionally, malignancies that recur after complete regression are more likely to have been repopulated by cells that have been selected for resistance to both radiation and chemotherapy. Finally, the amount of radiation that can be employed after chemoradiation is limited and would be less likely to be effective, even with concomitant radioenhancers, if applied after a hiatus of more than a few weeks (prolonged split). These factors lead one to suspect that the effectiveness of salvage chemoradiation for local relapse (in contrast to local persistence) would probably not be adequate to avert the eventual need for radical surgery and, consequently, abdominoperineal resection should be considered the treatment of choice for any local recurrence developing 6 months or more from completion of chemoradiation. Nevertheless, the actual salvage rate of local relapse by abdominoperineal resection is difficult to quantitate from reported chemoradiation series. Doci et al.[15] treated 56 patients with a definitive chemoradiation regimen employing 5-FU, 2 to 3 doses of mitomycin C, and 5400 cGy radiation. Forty-nine patients achieved complete response. Twelve of these 49 patients (24 percent) developed a local recurrence after a median interval of 8 months (range 2 to 45 months). Eleven of the 12 patients underwent surgery (9APR, 1 local excision, 1 local excision plus chemoradiation), while one unresectable patient received additional chemoradiation. Eight of the 11 patients were successfully salvaged, while 3 patients died of distant metastases. This experience suggests that surgical salvage of patients initially treated with chemoradiation is effective for local relapse in contrast to local persistence.

The application of adjuvant chemotherapy with the most active regimens against metastatic disease should be considered for patients with local relapse following salvage surgery.

TREATMENT OF PATIENTS WITH DISTANT METASTATIC DISEASE

A majority of patients with cancer of the anal canal treated with chemotherapy within the last 15 years have been treated with concurrent chemoradiation. Accordingly, the activity of chemotherapy alone is difficult to assess. To discern what drugs are active against epidermoid carcinoma of the anal canal one must look to (1) studies employing chemotherapy prior to radiation, chemoradiation, or surgery; (2) patients who relapse following treatment of the primary with surgery or chemoradiation; and (3) rare patients who present with metastatic disease.

Intraarterial Infusion Chemotherapy in the Treatment of Recurrent and Metastatic Anal Carcinoma

Table 106-5 summarizes the individual case reports detailing the experience with intraarterial infusion of the liver and pelvis employing a variety of chemotherapeutic agents, including cisplatin, 5-FU, 5-floxuridine, (FUdR), nitrogen mustard, bleomycin, and combinations of these drugs. A complete remission has been reported in only one patient receiving FUdR and cisplatin infused into the hepatic artery.[26] Partial re-

Table 106-5
Intraarterial Chemotherapy in Recurrent and Metastatic Anal Carcinoma

Reference	*Drugs*	*Site*	*No. of patients and response*	*Comments*
27	CDDP, 5-FU	Pelvis Bone	1 PR	Hypogastric artery, 75% decrease mass + bone healing after four doses.
34	5-FU	Liver	1 NR	3-month hepatic artery infusion.
30	Bleomycin	Pelvis	3 PR 2 NR	Aortic bifurcation: 200 mg over 5 days + oral methyl-CCNU (4/5).
49	Nitrogen mustard	Pelvis	2 NR	Perineal recurrence after surgery.
29	5-FU	Pelvis	2 PR	Unresectable primary; APR after hypogastric artery infusion. NED after 2 and 4 years.
26	CDDP, FUdR	Liver	1 PR 1 CR	Bone progression after 2 cycles; NED after 17 months.
28	5-FU, bleomycin MMC	Pelvis	1 PR	Femoral artery infusion.
25	FUdR	Liver	2 NR	One patient also received 30 Gy hepatic radiation.

Abbreviations: 5-FU, 5-fluorouracil; CDDP, cisplatin; FUdR, 5-floxuridine; MMC, mitomycin C; PR, partial response; CR, complete response; NR, no response; NED, no evidence of disease; Gy, gray.

sponses have been reported with intraarterial infusion of combinations of cisplatin plus 5-FU,[27] 5-FU, bleomycin, and mitomycin C;[28] and with 5-FU[29] and bleomycin[30] into the pelvis. All of these reported partial responses were of short duration. Mackman and Johnson[29] report two patients with locally advanced anal primaries who were resectable following hypogastric artery infusion of 5-FU. Both patients survived more than 2 years. The limited number of reports make evaluation of the efficacy of intraarterial infusion difficult.

Single-Agent Chemotherapy in the Treatment of Recurrent and Metastatic Anal Carcinoma

The single-agent experience in the treatment of carcinoma of the anal canal is summarized in Table 106-6. Seven reports detailing the experience with only *12* patients are summarized. Three reports, including 6 patients, detail the results with cisplatin as a single agent. Among these, 4 partial remissions and 1 complete remission are reported. A discrepancy of response by disease site is noted in two patients.[31,32] Thus, Fischer et al.[31] report complete response in lymph node sites but partial response in the primary and in lung metastases. Ohzato et al.[32] report partial remissions in two patients in lung and liver metastases but no response in the primary. The only complete response reported employed cisplatin as a continuous 5-day infusion every 4 weeks.[33]

Three reports encompassing four patients detail the results of treatment with 5-FU administered as a single agent.[34–36] A variety of treatment schedules were implemented and no response was reported. Continuous infusion of 5-FU over 4 to 5 days was not administered in any of these case reports. Carey[35] reports a partial response of lung metastases to 5-FU and cisplatin after failure to respond to 5-FU alone. It would appear from this limited experience that low-dose or bolus 5-FU administered as a single agent against anal canal carcinoma is relatively inactive.

Three reports encompassing 5 patients treated with a variety of agents other than 5-FU and cisplatin are summarized in Table 106-6.[31,36,37] Partial remissions of pulmonary metastases were described for 1 patient with semustine (methyl-CCNU)[36] and 1 patient with doxorubicin (Adriamycin).[31] The use of ifosfamide in 2 patients[37] and bleomycin in 1 patient[31] resulted in no responses. Single-agent data in this miscellaneous group are too limited to make generalizations regarding activity of any of these drugs.

Combination Chemotherapy in the Treatment of Recurrent and Metastatic Anal Carcinoma Employing 5-FU and Cisplatin or Mitomycin

Table 106-7 summarizes the case reports and series of patients treated with 5-FU in combination with either mitomycin or cisplatin. Three reports encompassing 4 patients receiving a variety of schedules of 5-FU infusion with 15 mg/m^2 of mitomycin C indicate limited activity of this combination[31,38,39] despite the fact that it is the most commonly received combination used in conjunction with radiation for primary treatment. No complete responders and 3 partial responders are reported.

The combination of 5-FU infusion plus cisplatin in a variety of schedules is noted in Table 106-7. Three

Table 106-6
Single-Agent Chemotherapy in Recurrent and Metastatic Anal Carcinoma

Reference	*No. of patients*	*Drug*	*Dose*	*Schedule*	*Site*	*Response*	*Comments*
31	1	CDDP	2 mg/kg	IV q2wk × 8	Pelvis, node, lung	PR CR PR	Prior RX: BLEO, ADM, 5-FU + MMC.
33	3	CDDP	20 mg/m²/d + 50 mg/m²/d	5-d infusion q4wk 3 h infusion × 2d q28d	Primary + nodes	1 CR 2 PR	NED after 3 cycles, both lost to follow-up.
32	2	CDDP	NS	NS	Lung	?PR Liver	Primary did not respond.
34	2	5-FU	500 mg	IV q4wk	Liver	NR	
35	1	5-FU	500 mg/m²/d	IV bolus × 5d	Lung	NR	Subsequent PR to 5-FU + CDDP
36	1	5-FU	15 mg/kg	PO biweekly	Lung	NR	Subsequent PR to semustine; 75% decrease after 2 cycles. Response duration, 15 months. NR to STZ, VM-26, HMM.
31	1	ADM	55 mg/m²	IV q3wk	Lung	PR	8 months duration.
31	1	BLEO	10 mg	IV q1wk	Lung	NR	Pulmonary metastases developed during pelvic radiation + BLEO.
37	2	IFOS	1.5 g/m²/d	IV × 5 q21d	NS	NR	Broad phase II trial.

Abbreviations: CDDP, cisplatin; BLEO, bleomycin; ADM, Adriamycin; MMC, mitomycin C; HMM, hexamethylmelamine; 5-FU, fluorouracil; IFOS, ifosfamide; STZ, streptozotocin; VM-26, teniposide; PR, partial remission; CR, complete remission; NR, no response; NS, not stated in report; NED, no evidence of disease.

Table 106-7
Combination Chemotherapy with 5-Fluorouracil and Cisplatin or Mitomycin C in Recurrent and Metastatic Anal Carcinoma

Reference	*No. of patients*	*Drugs*	*Schedule*	*Sites*	*Response*	*Comments*
31	1	5-FU + MMC	350 mg/m²IV bolus 15 mg/m²IV q3 wk × 2	Lung	PD	Previous Rx: BLEO, ADM.
38	2	5-FU + MMC	750 mg/m²/d × 5 CI 15 mg/m² d 1	Pelvis	PR	
39	1	5-FU + MMC	1 g/m²/d × 4 CI 15 mg/m² d 1	Pelvis	PR	75% decrease after 2 cycles, then APR resulting in NED status.
27	1	5-FU + CDDP	1 g/m² d 2–5 CI CDDP 100 mg/m² d 1	Nodes	CR	After 3 cycles.
35	1	5-FU + CDDP	1 g/m²/d × 4 CI 50 mg/m² d 4	Lung	PR	Prior failure of 5-FU bolus.
26	1	5-FU + CDDP	1 gm/m²/d × 3 CI 30 mg/m²/d × 3 q4wk	Liver Pelvis	PR CR	Response >15 months.
40	22	5-FU + CDDP	1 g/m²/d CI × 5 in 16 pts × 4 in 6 pts 100 mg/m² d 1	Primary	6 CR (27%) 13 PR (59%) 3 NR (14%)	Neoadjuvant; Subsequent RT-CT or RT; 20 NED.
41	20	5-FU + CDDP	1 g/m²/d × 5 CI 100 mg/m² d 1 or 2 q3–4wk	7 pelvis 6 pelvis + distant 6 distant	2 CR (liver, liver + pelvis) 9 PR CR + PR = 55%	Duration of remission = 2–11 months (5.6 median). Sites: 10 liver, 2 skin, 4 lung, 2 node, 1 bone.

Abbreviations: 5-FU, 5-fluorouracil; MMC, Mitomycin C; BLEO, bleomycin; ADM, Adriamycin; CDDP, cisplatin; PR, partial response; PD, progressive disease; CR, complete remission; NR, no response; RT, radiation therapy; CT-RT, chemoradiation; CI, continuous infusion; NED, no evidence of disease.

individual case reports encompassing 3 patients are noted and all patients have experienced either a partial or complete remission.[26,27,35] Importantly, two major series[40,41] encompassing 42 patients employed 5-FU as a continuous infusion for 4 to 5 days and cisplatin at 100 mg/m^2 on day 1. Brunet et al.[40] employed this combination as primary treatment in a neoadjuvant fashion prior to subsequent treatment with radiation or chemoradiation. All patients had a measurable primary tumor without metastases. An impressive response rate of 86 percent is reported (27 percent complete response and 59 percent partial response). Of 22 patients, 20 were rendered disease-free without surgery. This is the only study reported in which neoadjuvant chemotherapy is employed; it clearly indicates the efficacy of the 5-FU and cisplatin combination without radiation against the primary tumor. Mahjoubi et al.[41] employed the same regimen of 5-FU plus cisplatin in 20 patients with recurrent disease. Primary treatment consisted of surgery in 4, radiation in 7, surgery plus radiation in 4, and radiation plus chemotherapy in 4, while 1 patient presented with liver metastases at diagnosis. Two complete responses (liver and liver plus pelvis) plus 9 partial responses were noted, with a duration of 2 to 11 months (median 5.6 months). The response rate was 55 percent. There is no breakdown of sites of metastatic disease demonstrating partial responses. This study clearly demonstrates the activity of cisplatin and 5-FU to be significant but less effective in recurrent disease after radiation than when used in a neoadjuvant fashion prior to radiation.

Combination Chemotherapy without Fluoropyrimidines in the Treatment of Recurrent and Metastatic Anal Carcinoma

Table 106-8 summarizes a variety of case reports and series in which chemotherapy combinations *without* 5-FU are employed against metastatic or recurrent disease. No complete responders are reported with any of these combinations, although a number of partial responses are noted. Wilking et al.[42] report on the combination of bleomycin, vincristine, methotrexate, and leucovorin in 15 patients. Three partial responses of short duration were noted in inguinal lymph nodes; however, toxicity with this treatment was severe and there were 4 deaths. Magill and Quan[43] report on two cisplatin-based regimens employed in 27 patients who had previously been treated with 5-FU, mitomycin, and radiation. A total of 19 patients treated with the CVB regimen (cisplatin, vinblastine, and bleomycin)

Table 106-8
Combination Chemotherapy without Fluoropyrimidines in Recurrent and Metastatic Anal Carcinoma

Reference	*No. of patients*	*Drugs*	*Schedule*	*Sites*	*Response*	*Comments*
48	1	VCR	0.75 mg IV	Pelvis	CR	VCR 6 h prior to
		BLEO	30 mg IV BIW × 12	Lung	PR	BLEO.
33	1	CDDP	20 mg/m^2/d × 5 CI	Primary	NR	25% decrease tumor,
		MTX	50 mg/m^2 d1 + 15 IV			neutropenic sepsis.
		VCR	1.4 mg/m^2 d 1 IV			
		BLEO	15 mg IM d 1,5,15			
42	15	BLEO	10 mg/m^2/d × 5 CI	8 node	3 PR	3 PR in inguinal nodes,
		VCR	1.2 mg/m^2 IV d 6	2 liver		duration 1–5 months,
		MTX	75 mg/m^2 IV bolus 175 mg/m^2 over 12 h d 6	1 lung 3 nonmeasurable		severe toxicity, 4 deaths.
		LEUCO	15 mg IV q6h × 6 q4wk			
43	19	CDDP	120 mg/m^2 d 1	NA	5/17 MR	Major response; no
		VLB	4 mg/m^2 d 1			details of site +
		BLEO	10 mg/m^2 IV d 3 10 mg/m^2/d CI d 3–6			response.
43	8	MTX	30 mg/m^2 d 1	NA	2/17 MR	Major response; no
		VLB	3 mg/m^2 d 1			details of site +
		ADM	30 mg/m^2 d 2			response.
		CDDP	70 mg/m^2 d 2			
44	25	MMC	10 mg/m^{2}IV q4wk × 2 then q10wk	NA	11/19 PR	ECOG—EST 72-82 Phase II. All failed
		ADM	30 mg/m^{2}IV q4wk × 2 then q5wk			chemoradiation. CR = 0%, PR = 58%
		CDDP	60 mg/m^{2}IV q4wk × 2 then q5wk			of evaluable patients.

Abbreviations: VCR, vincristine; BLEO, bleomycin; CDDP, cisplatin; MTX, methotrexate; ADM, Adriamycin; LEUCO, leucovorin; VLB, vinblastine; CR, complete remission; NA, not available; PR, partial remission; NR, no response; MR, major response; CI, continuous infusion; BIW, twice per week.

demonstrated 5 of 17 major responses, but further details are not supplied. Eight patients treated with the M-VAC regimen (methotrexate, vinblastine, Adriamycin, and cisplatin) demonstrated 2 of 7 major responses. Hahn[44] employed the combination of mitomycin C, Adriamycin, and cisplatin in 25 patients who had failed chemoradiation. A 58 percent partial response rate but no complete responses were observed in this phase II Eastern Cooperative Oncology Group (ECOG) study. It appears that none of the nonfluorouracil combinations reported and summarized in Table 106-8 are as active against recurrent or metastatic anal carcinoma as the combination of 5-FU infusion and cisplatin.

Other Chemotherapy Regimens

From 1979 to 1990, 37 patients were enrolled in a pilot study employing pelvic radiation, 5-FU infusion, and two doses of mitomycin as a definitive nonoperative regimen.[2] Patients with residual disease on posttreatment biopsy were then treated with a chemoradiation salvage regimen employing boost perineal radiation, 5-FU infusion, and cisplatin.[8] In all, 6 patients relapsed after achieving complete remission and 4 ultimately died of cancer while 5 additional patients presented with metastatic disease, 3 after failing chemoradiation administered at other institutions.

A group of 12 patients (5 with metastatic disease at presentation, 6 relapsing after achieving complete remission, and 1 failing to achieve complete remission) studied at the University of California San Francisco/San Joaquin Valley represent a database for the assessment of the responsiveness of this tumor to chemotherapy.[25] Table 106-9 summarizes the response rates of 13 chemotherapy regimens by site of metastatic disease. Responses were observed in pelvis/perineum (5/10), lymph node (4/13), lung (3/10), liver (3/13), and bone (0/2). The most active regimens were sequential methotrexate, 5-FU, and leucovorin (8/9);[45] 5-FU infusion plus cisplatin (3/5); weekly low-dose doxorubicin (3/8); and 5-FU infusion plus mitomycin (1/2). No responses were observed for infusion doxorubicin with or without vincristine (0/5), etoposide (0/6) and vinblastine plus dacarbazine infusion (0/2), or alpha interferon (0/2).

In summary, our experience would indicate that metastatic and recurrent carcinoma of the anal canal is most responsive to the combination of methotrexate–5-FU–leucovorin, 5-FU infusion plus cisplatin, and weekly low-dose doxorubicin.

CONCLUSIONS

In reviewing all published experience in conjunction with our own experience, a number of conclusions can be drawn:

1. The most active chemotherapy regimen against anal canal cancer is 5-fluorouracil infusion and cisplatin.
2. This combination is considerably more active when employed in a neoadjuvant fashion initially with or without radiation compared with its employment against recurrent disease developing after radiation or chemoradiation.

Table 106-9
Response to Chemotherapy by Site of Metastases: 12 Patients with Advanced Anal Carcinoma

	Site of metastatic disease					
Chemotherapy regimen	*Pelvis/Perineum*	*Lymph node*	*Liver*	*Lung*	*Bone*	*Response rates, CR + PR/total*
5-FU infusion + MMC			1 NR	1 PR		1 / 2
5-FU infusion + CDDP		1 CR	1 PR; 2 NR	1 CR		3 / 5
MTX-5-FU-leucovorin	4 CR	2 PR	2 PR	1 NR		8 / 9
Adriamycin infusion		1 NR	1 NR	1 NR		0 / 3
Adriamycin weekly	1 PR	1 PR; 1 NR	1 NR	1 PR; 1 NR	2 NR	3 / 8
Adriamycin + VCR infusion	1 NR	1 NR				0 / 2
Etoposide	1 NR	1 NR	1 NR	3 NR		0 / 6
5-FU-VCR-DTIC	1 NR	1 NR				0 / 2
Vinblastine-DTIC	1 NR	1 NR				0 / 2
Mitoxanthrone		1 NR	1 NR			0 / 2
Methotrexate				1 NR		0 / 1
FUdR—hepatic artery			2 NR[a]			0 / 2
Interferon	1 NR	2 NR	1 NR			0 / 4
TOTALS	4 CR; 1 PR; 5 NR	1 CR; 3 PR; 9 NR	3 PR; 10 NR	1 CR; 2 PR; 7 NR	2 NR	
CR + PR/Total	5 / 10	4 / 13	3 / 13	3 / 10	0 / 2	

Abbreviations: CR, complete remission (complete disappearance of all measureable disease); PR, partial response (> 50% reduction in measureable disease); NR, no response or progression of disease; 5-FU, 5-fluorouracil; MMC, mitomycin C; CDDP, cisplatin, VCR, vincristine; DTIC = dacarbazine; FUdR, 5-floxuridine; MTX–5-FU, leucovorin: sequential methotrexate, 5-FU, leucovorin (Ref. 45).

[a]One patient treated with IA-FUdR + radiation to liver.

3. The active combination of sequential methotrexate-5-FU-leucovorin has not been adequately tested and should be evaluated in a neoadjuvant fashion prior to definitive chemoradiation to assess its efficacy.
4. The combination of 5-FU infusion and mitomycin against recurrent or metastatic disease is inadequate treatment as is 5-FU alone.
5. There appears to be no advantage to direct intraarterial infusion chemotherapy with or without radiation for recurrent disease.
6. Combinations of chemotherapy and radiation for recurrent or metastatic disease are of low efficacy with the possible exception of treatment of pelvic recurrence in patients who have been initially treated by abdominoperineal resection.
7. Some activity is reported for adriamycin, methyl-CCNU, and bleomycin preceded by vincristine. Responses with these agents are usually partial and of short duration.
8. The data base for most available chemotherapeutic agents is limited and many newer drugs such as carboplatin, taxol, iphosphamide, and etoposide have never been adequately evaluated.
9. There are no data regarding the efficacy of biotherapeutic modalities such as interferon, interleukin, and monoclonal antibody therapy in this disease.
10. Future use of chemotherapeutic agents against this malignancy will not significantly impact survival when used in the setting of recurrent or metastatic disease. Consequently greater efforts should be made to organize studies employing neoadjuvant chemotherapy prior to definitive chemoradiation to assess the efficacy of chemotherapeutic agents and their impact on complete remission rates and survival.

REFERENCES

1. Nigro ND, Vaitkeviceus VK, Considine B Jr: Combined therapy for cancer of the anal canal: A preliminary report. *Dis Colon Rectum* 17:354–356, 1974.
2. Flam MS, John M, Lovalvo L, et al: Definitive nonsurgical therapy for epithelial malignancies of the anal canal: A report of 12 cases. *Cancer* 51:1378–1387, 1983.
3. Cummings BJ: The place of radiation therapy in the treatment of carcinoma of the anal canal. *Cancer Treat Rev* 9:125–147, 1982.
4. Leichman L, Nigro N, Vaitkeviceus VK, et al: Cancer of the anal canal: Model for preoperative adjuvant combined modality therapy. *Am J Med* 211:216–278, 1985.
5. Sischy B: The use of radiation therapy combined with chemotherapy in the management of squamous cell carcinoma of the anus and marginally resectable adenocarcinoma of the rectum. *Int J Radiat Oncol Biol Phys* 11:1587–1593, 1985.
6. Hagbin M, Sischy B, Hinson J: A long term follow up of definitive conservative therapy for anal canal carcinoma. *Proc ASCO* 4:81, 1985.
7. Cummings B, Keane T, Thomas G, et al: Results and toxicity of the treatment of anal canal carcinoma by radiation therapy or radiation therapy and chemotherapy. *Cancer* 54:2062–2068, 1984.
8. Flam MS, John M, Mowry P, et al: Definitive combined modality therapy of carcinoma of the anus: A report of 30 cases including results of salvage therapy in patients with residual disease. *Dis Colon Rectum* 30:495–502, 1987.
9. Meeker WR Jr, Sickie-Santanello BJ, Philpott G, et al: Combined chemotherapy, radiation and surgery for epithelial cancer of the anal canal. *Cancer* 57:525–529, 1986.
10. Pipard G, Peytremann R, Marti MC: Conservative multidisciplinary treatment of locally advanced epidermoid and cloacogenic cancer of the anal canal (abstract). *Proc ASCO* 5:268, 1986.
11. Sischy B, Doggett RLS, Krall JM, et al: Definitive irradiation and chemotherapy for radiosensitization in management of anal carcinoma: Interim report on radiation therapy, oncology group study No. 8314. *J Natl Cancer Inst* 81:850–856, 1989.
12. Habr-Gama A, da Silva e Sous AH Jr, Nadalin W, et al: Epidermoid carcinoma of the anal canal: Results of treatment by combined chemotherapy and radiation therapy. *Dis Colon Rectum* 32:773–777, 1989.
13. Cho CC, Taylor CW, Padmanabhan A, et al: Squamous cell carcinoma of the anal canal: Management with combined chemo-radiation therapy. *Dis Colon Rectum* 34:675–678, 1991.
14. Zelnick RS, Haas PA, Ajlouni M, et al: Results of abdominoperineal resections for failures after combination chemotherapy and radiation therapy for anal canal cancers. *Dis Colon Rectum* 35:574–578, 1992.
15. Doci R, Zucali R, Bombelli L, et al: Combined chemoradiation therapy for anal cancer: A report of 56 cases. *Ann Surg* 215:150–156, 1992.
16. Michaelson RA, Magill GB, Quan SHQ, et al: Pre-operative chemotherapy and radiation therapy in the management of anal epidermoid carcinoma. *Cancer* 51:390–395, 1983.
17. Enker WE, Heilweil M, Janov AJ, et al: Improved survival in epidermoid carcinoma of the anus in association with pre-operative multi-disciplinary therapy. *Arch Surg* 121:1386–1390, 1986.
18. Secco GB, Sertoli MR, Scarpati D, et al: Preoperative chemotherapy and radiotherapy in the management of epidermoid carcinoma of the anal canal. *Tumori* 73:151–155, 1987.
19. Flam MS, John MJ, Peters T, et al: Radiation and 5-fluorouracil (5-FU) vs. radiation, 5-FU, mitomycin-C (MMC) in the treatment of anal canal carcinoma: Preliminary results of a phase III randomized RTOG/ECOG intergroup trial (abstract). *Proc Asco* 12:192, 1993.
20. Cummings BJ: Radiation therapy and chemoradiation in the treatment of primary anal canal carcinoma. *Compr Ther* 9:59–65, 1983.
21. Greenall M, Magill G, Quan S, et al: Recurrent epidermoid cancer of the anus. *Cancer* 57:1437–1441, 1986.
22. Frost DB, Richards PC, Montague ED, et al: Epidermoid cancer of the anorectum. *Cancer* 53:1285–1293, 1984.
23. Boman BM, Moertel CG, O'Connell MJ, et al: Carcinoma of the anal canal: A clinical and pathologic study of 188 cases. *Cancer* 54:114–125, 1984.
24. Cummings BJ, Keane TJ, O'Sullivan B, et al: Epidermoid anal cancer: Treatment by radiation alone or by radiation and 5-fluorouracil with and without mitomycin C. *Int J Radiat Oncol Biol Phys* 21:1115–1125, 1991.
25. Flam MS, John MJ: The management of advanced epidermoid anal carcinoma (abstract). *J Cancer Res Clin Oncol (Suppl)* 116:852, 1990.
26. Ajani J, Carrasco H, Jackson D, et al: Combination of cisplatin plus fluoropyrimidine chemotherapy effective against liver metastases from carcinoma of the anal canal. *Am J Med* 87:221–224, 1989.
27. Khater R, Frenay M, Bourry J, et al: Cisplatin plus 5-fluorouracil in the treatment of metastatic anal squamous cell car-

cinoma: A report of two cases. *Cancer Treat Rep* 70:1345–1346, 1986.
28. Mieno K, Takeda Y, Satoi Y, et al: Effects of intra-arterial infusion chemotherapy in local recurrence of anal cancer. *Gan To Kagako Ryoho* 16:3007–3010, 1989.
29. Mackman S, Johnson RO: Infusion of 5-fluorouracil into the hypogastric artery for massive anal carcinoma. *Am J Surg* 113:699–701, 1967.
30. Lindell TD, Moseley S, Fletcher WS: Combination CCNU and bleomycin therapy for squamous cell carcinoma. *Am Surg* 40:281–289, 1974.
31. Fisher W, Herbst K, Sims J, et al: Metastatic cloacogenic carcinoma of the anus: Sequential responses to Adriamycin and cis-dicholorodiamineplatinum (II). *Cancer Treat Rep* 62:91–97, 1978.
32. Ohzato H, Satomi T, Sakita I: Two cases of cloacogenic carcinoma of the anal canal: Chemotherapeutic effect of cis-platinum. *Nippon Geka Gakkai Zasshi* 89:291–295, 1988.
33. Salem P, Habboubi N, Nannasissie E, et al: Effectiveness of cisplatin in the treatment of anal squamous cell carcinoma. *Cancer Treat Rep* 69:891–893, 1985.
34. Kheir S, Hickey RC, Martin RG, et al: Cloacogenic carcinoma of the anal canal. *Arch Surg* 104:407–415, 1972.
35. Carey RW: Regression of pulmonary metastases from cloacogenic carcinoma after cisplatin and 5-fluorouracil treatment. *J Clin Gastroenterol* 6:257–259, 1984.
36. Zimm S, Wampler GL: Response of metastatic cloacogenic carcinoma to treatment with semustine. *Cancer* 48:2575–2576, 1981.
37. Coleman RE, Clarke J, Harper PG: A phase two study of ifosfamide for squamous carcinomas (abstract). *Fourth European Conference on Clinical Oncology and Cancer Nursing* 4:255, 1987.
38. Quan SHQ, Magill GB, Leaming RH, et al: Multidisciplinary preoperative approach to the management of epidermoid carcinoma of the anus and anorectum. *Dis Colon Rectum* 21:89–91, 1978.
39. Barni S, Frigerio F, Lissoni P, et al: Anal squamous cell carcinoma arising on radio-dermatitis cured with chemotherapy alone: Case report. *Tumori* 73:423–424, 1987.
40. Brunet R, Sadek H, Vignoud J, et al: Cisplatin (P) and 5 fluorouracil (5FU) for the neoadjuvant treatment (Tt) of epidermoid anal carcinoma (EACC). *Proc ASCO* 9:104, 1990.
41. Mahjoubi M, Sadek H, Francois E, et al: Epidermoid anal canal carcinoma (EACC): Activity of cisplatin (P) and continuous 5-fluorouracil (5FU) in metastatic (M) and/or local recurrent (LR) disease. *Proc ASCO* 9:114, 1990.
42. Wilking N, Petrelli N, Herrera L, et al: Phase II study of combination of bleomycin, vincristine and high-dose methotrexate (BOM) with leucovorin rescue in advanced squamous cell carcinoma of the anal canal. *Cancer Chemother Pharmacol* 15:300–302, 1985.
43. Magill GB, Quan S: Salvage chemotherapy of anal epidermoid carcinoma with cisplatin based protocols. *Proc ASCO* 8:117, 1989.
44. Hahn G: ECOG Phase II study—EST 72-82, personal communication, November 1992.
45. Gerwirtz AM, Cadman E: Preliminary report on the efficacy of sequential methotrexate and 5-fluorouracil in advanced breast cancer. *Cancer* 47:2552–2555, 1981.
46. Blot WJ, Fraumeni FJ, Stone BJ: Geographic patterns of large bowel cancer in the US. *J Natl Cancer Inst* 57:1225–1231, 1976.
47. Cady B, Persson AV, Monson DO: Changing patterns of colorectal cancer. *Cancer* 33:433–436, 1974.
48. Livingston R, Bodey G, Gottlieb J, et al: Kinetic scheduling of vincristine and bleomycin in patients with lung cancer and other malignant tumors. *Cancer Chemother Rep* 57:219–224, 1973.
49. Sawyers JL: Epidermoid cancer of the perianus and the anal canal. *Surg Clin North Am* 45:1173–1178, 1965.

PART 19

Other Anal Cancers

CHAPTER 107

Adenocarcinoma of the Anal Canal

Richard L. Nelson

HIGHLIGHTS

Adenocarcinoma of the anal canal is a rare form of a rare tumor. Both basaloid and keratinizing tumors of the anal canal are more prevalent. There is no histologic, biological, or etiologic uniformity within the category of anal adenocarcinomas, so that this rare entity must be further subdivided by several parameters before it can be characterized. One generalization that can be relied upon is that these tumors tend to secrete more mucus than typical rectal adenocarcinomas, and it is the copious secretion of mucus that often characterizes their clinical presentation.

CONTROVERSIES

Several questions have been asked in previous reports of anal adenocarcinoma. The first relates to etiology, specifically whether a single etiologic mechanism could be responsible for all tumors. Proposed mechanisms or associations have included:

Cancers arising in anal glands
Cancers arising in preexisting fistulas in ano
Anal sexual intercourse, with and without venereal infection
Congenital anorectal duplications
Crohn's disease
Metastasis from a proximal colorectal adenocarcinoma to a chronic fistula in ano
Apocrine gland cancers
Paget's disease of the anus
Radiation for nonintestinal cancer

Several of these etiologic associations raise the issue of cancer prevention. Specifically, would definitive treatment of the benign precursor eliminate the risk of cancer—in for instance, treatment of tumors found arising in a chronic fistula in ano? Because of the rarity and apparent heterogeneity of adenocarcinoma of the anal canal, no comparative or analytic epidemiologic studies have been done that might resolve this question. Anal cancers of all histologies have been associated with certain sexual practices. There are also no reports that deal with prevention measures (once abstinence is no longer possible) in this instance.

A third area of some controversy is whether histology differentiates anal adenocarcinoma from anal squamous or cloacogenic tumors in the determination of natural history and allocation to optimal therapy. It may be that the gross anatomic location of the tumor alone determines the above and that histology is superfluous.

FUTURE DIRECTIONS

No comparative studies related to therapy have been reported because of the rarity of the tumor, so issues of radical surgery versus combined chemotherapy and radiation therapy versus radiation therapy alone have not been assessed. The natural history and modes of spread of anal adenocarcinoma have also not been well described. Both the biological and therapeutic issues are resolvable through a combination of careful review of existing data and prospective cooperative treatment studies.

INCIDENCE AND TYPES OF ANAL ADENOCARCINOMA

Adenocarcinoma of the anal canal and perianal region is a very rare tumor. One author has estimated that 10 percent of anal cancers are adenocarcinomas, almost certainly an overestimate.[1] It has further been estimated that anal cancers in general represent only 1 percent of all colorectal tumors, so that it can be estimated that about 100 cases of anal adenocarcinoma occur within the United States each year. Unlike the relative uniformity with which colonic adenocarcinoma presents itself, the clinical history, presentation, and etiologic associations of anal adenocarcinoma are so varied that that group of 100 patients would have to be further divided into five or six subgroups in order to describe the classic features of the illness systematically.

Adenocarcinoma of the Rectum Extending into the Anal Canal

In this rather common situation, an intraluminal rectal tumor exists, extending into the anal canal and often out of the anal orifice.[2] Biopsy will confirm the histology, though the biopsy will often have to be performed in the operating room under anesthesia because of the associated pain. Extension of the tumor into the sphincters will usually cause intense pain, limiting the ability to perform endoscopy and biopsy without anesthesia (Fig. 107-1*A*). Treatment is no different than for a rectal adenocarcinoma, though extension will limit mobility and resectability unless preoperative adjuvant therapy is given.[2,3]

Colloid Carcinoma

It is this tumor that is found underlying the eczematoid perianal skin eruption known as Paget's disease. If this is a tumor arising from anal glands, with the Paget's disease being a superficial manifestation of the deeper tumor, it differs markedly from other tumors of supposed anal gland etiology in several parameters. There is no palpable tumor mass; the Paget's disease is all that is clinically apparent (Fig. 107-2). The tumor diffusely infiltrates the perianal dermis and ischiorectal fossae; the Paget's disease does not encompass its anatomic limits. The nature of mucous secretion and gland formation is quite different from that in other tumors.[1] One significant area of similarity with other anal gland cancers is the absence, on anoscopy, of any visible intraluminal tumor. Pain is often not a prominent feature of the tumor. Treatment will be discussed below.

Anal Gland Cancer

Anal gland cancers are often of mixed histology, with basaloid or squamous elements coexisting with glandular elements.[4] There is usually no intraanal tumor to be seen and the presentation is often as a perianal abscess or fistula in ano. The tumor itself, in a fistula tract, may be very subtle. This is one reason why chronic fistulas must always be biopsied (Fig. 107-3). Radical surgery alone has been associated with poor prognosis even in apparently limited disease.

Cancer Arising in a Chronic Fistula in Ano

Some patients with long-standing fistulas in ano develop cancers that may be due to chronic inflammation within the fistula tract (Figs. 107-3 and 107-4). This is analogous to Marjolin's ulcer cancers in chronic burn scars or perhaps intestinal cancer in patients with chronic inflammatory bowel disease. It is the chronicity of the preexisting fistula, which is often present for 20 years or more, that separates this type of cancer from the anal gland cancers described above.[2,4]

Proximal Colorectal Adenocarcinoma Metastasizing to an Anal Canal Wound, Such as a Chronic Fistula

Intraluminal metastasis of proximal colorectal cancer to normal mucosa has never been documented, though the possibility is often casually discussed. It was proposed many years ago that suture-line recurrence after resection of colonic cancer is due to intraluminal implantation of tumor cells in more "fertile ground"—that is, the cut surface of the bowel. In surgical specimens, viable tumor cells were easily found floating freely within the lumen of the intestine. Luminal ligation prior to tumor mobilization was proposed to limit this possibility, and clinical studies seemed to support this practice.[5] Though suture-line recurrences are now felt to be predominantly nodal persistence of tumor that grows into the intestinal lumen, the idea of "fertile ground" for tumor cell implantation may be relevant in the context of granulation tissue, particularly lining the tract of a chronic fistula in ano. The coexistence of a chronic fistula, a proximal cancer, and cancer within the fistula has been reported, and one case has been seen by the author. Though two primary tumors, one of the colorectum and one of the fistula, also explain this phenomenon, the possibility of intraluminal spread is great enough to mandate that colonoscopy be

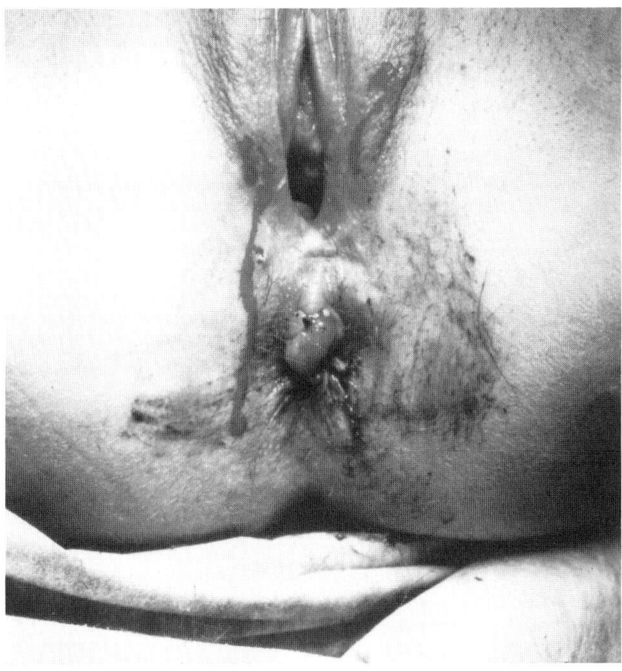

A

B

FIG. 107-1. *A*. Anal mass thought to be a hemorrhoid by a referring physician. *B*. This was found to be a large rectal cancer in a young woman with familial polyposis.

performed on all individuals with cancers in anal fistulas or wounds.[4]

Polypoid Adenocarcinomas, Similar to Colorectal Cancers

Polyps of the anal canal are, unlike proximal colonic polyps, often inflammatory or hypertrophic lesions related to chronic fissures or hemorrhoids. In addition, prolapsing hemorrhoids themselves may often be polypoid in appearance. Yet true adenomas and polypoid adenocarcinomas of the anal canal that are otherwise identical to proximal colorectal tumors do exist. They often have considerable stalks, because of the shearing that occurs in the anal canal. Biopsy should be excisional and attempted only in the operating room with regional anesthetic, sphincter relaxation, and the instruments necessary to control the loss of blood, which is often substantial. Careful excisional biopsy can be curative if margins are free of tumor and the histology is favorable (see Chap. 47, on cancer in polyps). Piecemeal or inadequate excision, as might occur during "U bends" during colonoscopy, creates real therapeutic dilemmas that risk loss of the patient's anorectum.

Adenocarcinomas Causing Atypical Fissures in Ano

Benign fissures, appropropriately recognized and expeditiously treated, can be cured almost instantly. The greatest danger in the evaluation and treatment of fissures is the failure to recognize atypical fissures. Atypical fissures are common manifestations of systemic diseases such as Crohn's disease, tuberculosis of the gastrointestinal tract, venereal infections, acute leukemia, and malignant lymphoma.[6] In addition, local tumors, most commonly basaloid or cloacogenic cancers but also adenocarcinoma of the anal canal (Fig. 107-5), may present as atypical fissures. Delay in diagnosis or inappropriate therapy (such as sphincterotomy) would be catastrophic for patients with all the above conditions. Pain and bleeding are the presenting symptoms. The fissure is characteristically not limited to the anoderm, as benign fissures are, but is contiguous with the anal mucosa. Benign fissure is usually a young person's disease. When an elderly person presents with any fissure, particularly one atypical in appearance, a diagnosis must be obtained expeditiously. Though operative biopsy is needed to establish the diagnosis of adenocarcinoma of the anal canal, other diagnoses must be ruled out, especially leukemia, before the patient is subjected to the risks of anesthesia and biopsy.

ETIOLOGIC RELATIONSHIPS

Several etiologic relationships to adenocarcinoma of the anal canal exist that have not already been dis-

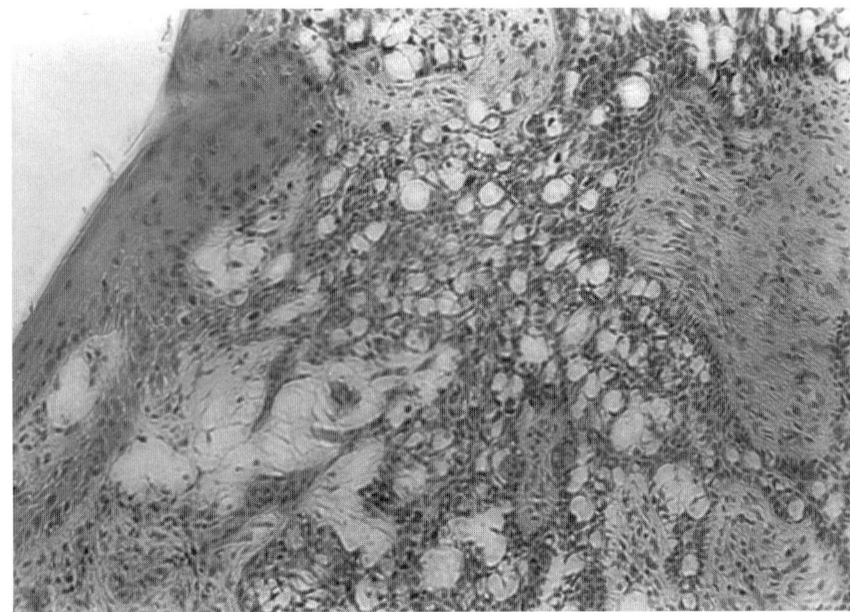

FIG. 107-2. Paget's cells in the dermis with underlying colloid carcinoma in what appeared grossly to be only excoriated or eczematoid anoderm.

cussed. The first is Crohn's disease, a chronic idiopathic inflammatory disease of the gastrointestinal tract in which perianal manifestations are common. Malignant degeneration of involved tissues, including those of the anal canal, is also reported in Crohn's disease patients.[4,7,8] The risk of cancer in these patients is particularly troublesome because the symptoms of Crohn's disease relapse—bleeding and weight loss—are indistinguishable from those of cancer. Aggressive intervention, either diagnostic or resectional, every time symptoms arise would be excessive for the majority of patients and would result in many becoming intestinal cripples. There is a fine line to tread in Crohn's disease patients between conservatism and negligence.

Anal sexual intercourse is regularly practiced by roughly 5 percent of American males and 10 percent of American females.[9] In some segments of our society, it is the most common form of birth control. The public health consequences of this once arcane practice are now well known, relating to a number of venereally spread infections including AIDS, the most

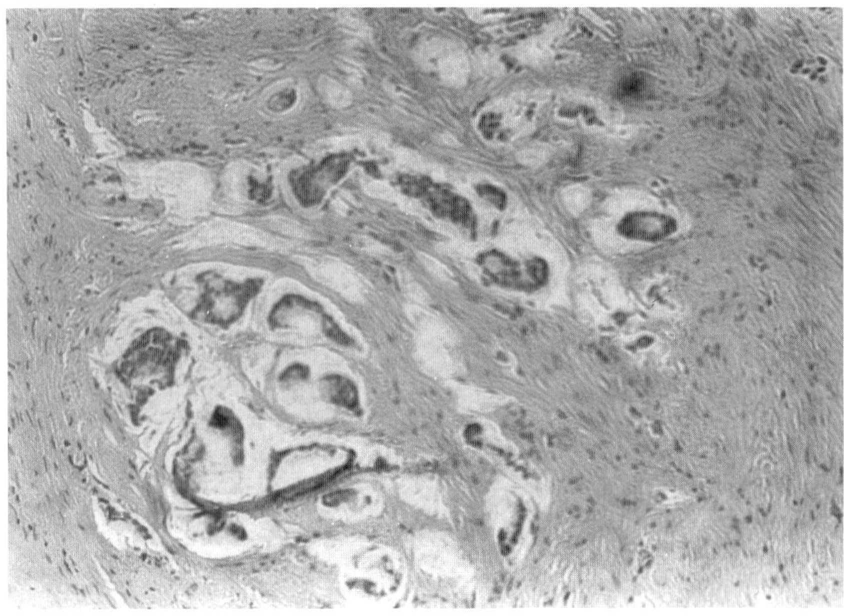

FIG. 107-3. Unsuspected carcinoma in an operative biopsy of the wall of a chronic anal fistula.

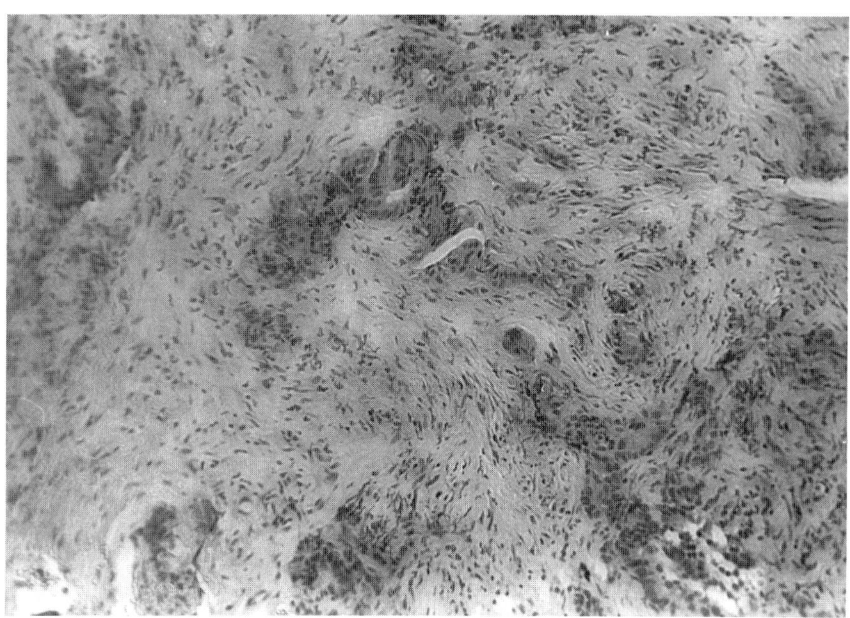

FIG. 107-4. Carcinoma in a chronic fistula in ano.

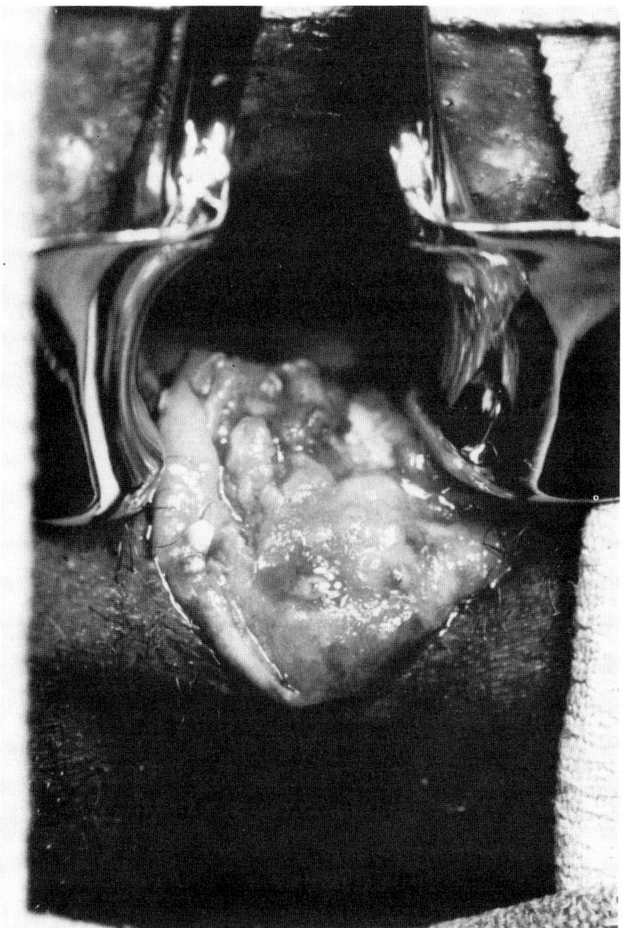

FIG. 107-5. Atypical fissure with the irregular borders and contiguous extension into the anal mucosa typical of anal cancer.

catastrophic of these. Anal cancer of all histologic types has been reported to be far more common among individuals who practice anal intercourse than those who do not.[10] Obvious markers of risk include other venereally spread diseases such as condylomata acuminatum. Anoscopic examination must be performed frequently in all individuals with histories of anal venereal infection or who are known to practice anal intercourse. The specific cause of the tumor risk is unknown.

Several other relationships have been hypothesized for tumors of the anal canal in general and adenocarcinoma in particular. The first is apocrine gland cancers, though apocrine glands do not exist in the anal canal. Rectal duplications are often written about and almost never seen. Radiation therapy for pelvic malignancies has been rarely reported to be associated with subsequent anorectal tumors, though the risk in these individuals is probably no greater than in nonradiated persons.

NATURAL HISTORY

There is no large data set from which to draw patterns of spread and recurrence for this rare disease. The experience is therefore anecdotal and limited in its generalizability. As stated above, the category of adenocarcinoma of the anal canal comprises very heterogeneous subcategories. With that disclaimer, it can be said that in the author's experience, adenocarcinoma of the anal canal is an aggressive disease, somewhat more so than the more prevalent cloacogenic cancers. It must be aggressively treated. In an earlier report from the author's institution, three of four individuals treated by surgery alone died of cancer.[4] The pattern of recurrence was pelvic only in one and diffuse carcinomatosis in the other two, even though the disease was apparently only local at the time of surgery.

THERAPY

Therapeutic options include local excision, abdominoperineal excision of the rectum and anus with permanent colostomy, radiotherapy with or without combined chemotherapy and with or without either of the above operative procedures. There are no comparative studies that would permit rigorous analysis of the risks and benefits of each option. The choice is therefore once again based upon anecdotal experience.

Alternatively, it may be possible to draw upon experience from more prevalent tumors in which adequate therapeutic analyses have been performed if those tumors are biologically analogous to the rarer tumor. In this instance it seems reasonable to use such an analogy.

The treatment of cloacogenic cancer of the anal canal has been revolutionized in the past two decades by the application of combined chemotherapy and radiotherapy before surgery.[11] The method is known as the "Nigro" or "Wayne State" protocol, in which 5-fluorouracil and mitomycin C are given concomitant with pelvic radiotherapy (see Chap. 70). This author has treated 5 patients with adenocarcinoma of the anal canal with this protocol in recent years. Of these, 1 has died of unrelated causes and the other 4 are free of disease, with at least 2 years of follow-up for each. One cancer was a fistula cancer, two were polypoid lesions, one was ulcerating with pelvic nodal metastases, and one was a colloid carcinoma associated with Paget's disease. Radical surgery was performed in only two of the patients, in one case after local recurrence following a local excision. No excision was done in the patient with colloid cancer; indeed, none was possible because of the diffuse nature of the disease.

SUMMARY

It has long been the practice of the author's colorectal surgery service to explore patients with anal pain in the operating room under anesthesia, with sphincter relaxation, lights, and instruments that will allow adequate and safe examination, biopsy, and therapeutic procedures, such as drainage of abscesses, polypectomy, or fistulotomy. This is the most compassionate and efficacious way to evaluate a patient with anal pain and/or suspected anal canal cancer.[4,6] Whether aggressive intervention in benign disease of the anal canal, such as fistulotomy, might prevent some anal cancers is only speculation, but it seems a reasonable speculation. Certainly unsuspected cancers of the anal canal will be diagnosed earlier by early surgical evaluation of anal pain.

On the basis of very limited data, it would seem best to assume that all anal canal adenocarcinomas are biologically analogous to other tumors of the anal canal and are best treated as such.

REFERENCES

1. Spjut HJ: Pathology of neoplasms, in Spratt JS (ed): *Neoplasms of the Colon, Rectum, and Anus: Mucosal and Epithelial*. Philadelphia, Saunders, 1984.
2. Goligher JC: *Surgery of the Anus, Rectum and Colon,* 3d ed. London, Balliére, Tindall, 1975, p 826.
3. Sischy B: The use of radiation therapy combined with chemotherapy in the management of squamous cell carcinoma of the anus and marginally resectable cancer of the rectum. *Int J Radiat Oncol Biol Phys* 11:1587–1593, 1985.
4. Nelson RL, Prasad ML, Abcarian H: Anal carcinoma presenting as a perirectal abscess or fistula. *Arch Surg* 120:632–635, 1985.
5. McGrew EA, Laws JF, Cole WH: Free malignant cells in relation to recurrence of carcinoma of the colon. *JAMA* 154:1251–1254, 1954.
6. Nelson RL, Abcarian H: Complications of rectal surgery. *Surg Rounds* 9:37–48, 1986.
7. Greenstein AJ, Gennuso R, Sachar DB, et al: Extraintestinal cancers in inflammatory bowel disease. *Cancer* 56:2914–2921, 1985.
8. Slater G, Greenstein A, Aufses AH: Anal carcinoma in patients with Crohn's disease. *Ann Surg* 199:348–350, 1984.
9. Bolling DR, Voeller B: AIDS and heterosexual anal intercourse. *JAMA* 258:474, 1987.
10. Daling JR, Weiss NS, Hislop G, et al: Sexual practices, sexually transmitted diseases, and the incidence of anal cancer. *N Engl J Med* 317:973–977, 1987.
11. Nigro ND: The force of change in the management of squamous-cell cancer of the anal canal. *Dis Colon Rectum* 34:482–486, 1991.

CHAPTER 108

Anorectal Melanoma

Stuart H. Q. Quan

Anorectal melanoma is extremely rare and virulent; the appropriate surgical treatment remains unclear.

INCIDENCE

Since the first reported case in 1854,[1] approximately 600 patients with anorectal melanoma have been described in the world's literature, mostly in isolated case reports and a few in larger single-institutional series of 10 or more patients. Indeed, the entire population of Sweden from 1970 to 1984 and that of Israel from 1960 to 1981 yielded only 49 and 30 patients, respectively, with this tumor.[2,3] The Memorial Sloan–Kettering Cancer Center (MSKCC) reports 85 patients collected over a period of over 60 years,[4–7] which represents only 0.6 percent of approximately 12,000 malignant tumors seen in the distal 15 cm of the lower intestinal tract over the same time span.

RACE, AGE, SEX

With the exception of an occasional report of this rare tumor in black or Asian patients, an overwhelming majority of these patients are Caucasian. In our own series, only three were black and one was half Asian and half black. The remainder of the MSKCC patients were all Caucasian. The youngest patient was 27 years old and the oldest was 85. The average and median ages were 58 and 59, respectively. There were 39 males and 46 females.

SIGNS AND SYMPTOMS

The overwhelming initial symptom in over two-thirds of patients is bleeding. Pain, change in bowel habits, and the feeling that there may be hemorrhoids or polyps present are the next most common complaints. Two of the patients in the MSKCC series had diagnoses of anorectal melanoma established on tissues removed at hemorrhoidectomy, and one other patient's diagnosis was made from an office polypectomy. Less common symptoms are tenesmus, induration, or a sense of an abnormal mass. Systemic signs of weight loss and abdominal distension are indicative of advanced disease.

The primary tumor varies in appearance from that of a small, benign-looking, grapelike growth, not unlike a hemorrhoid occurring at the mucocutaneous junction (see Fig. 108-1), to that of a large, ulcerating, deeply pigmented tumor occluding the anal canal. Obvious melanotic discoloration was visible in only half of our patients. A smaller number had melanin deposits demonstrable only under the microscope, and a few patients were diagnosed as having amelanotic melanoma. Most of the tumors arose from the anoderm, but three occurred in the rectum several centimeters above the dentate line. No other primary sites were found in these patients. We assume that these tumors arose from either heterotopic epithelium or some mucosal spread, although, at the time, no microscopic stepped serial sections of the anus and rectum were taken to prove or disprove these hypotheses.

PATHOLOGIC FEATURES AND PROGNOSIS

An indication of the advanced stage of the disease (and therefore the poor prognosis) was reflected in the size of the primary tumor in the MSKCC series. Only 25 percent of the patients had tumors less than 1 cm in diameter. The rest had tumors up to 6 cm in diameter (average, 4 cm).

There may or may not be a correlation between tumor thickness and survival after treatment. By optical micrometric measurement (Breslow technique), the thickness of the tumor as it extended from the mucosal surface to the point of deepest penetration into the anal wall was found to be less than 2 mm in only three patients. All three were alive and well 13 or more years after diagnosis and abdominoperineal resection. The other seven who survived 5-year-plus s disease had

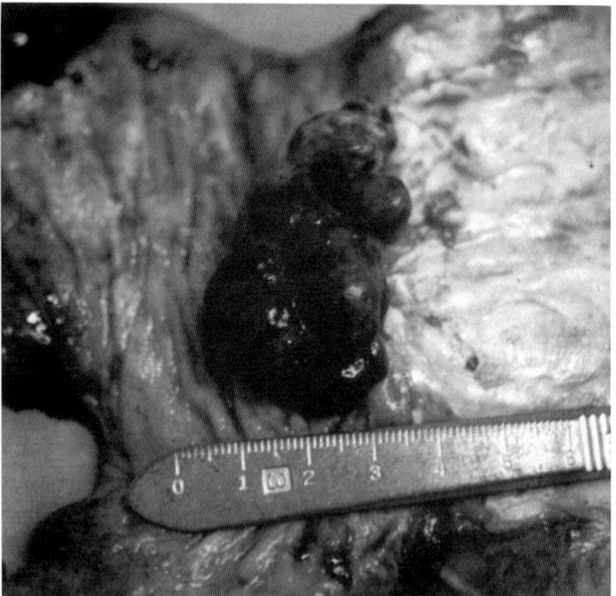

FIG. 108-1. Gross appearance of a typical polypoid anal melanoma in an abdominoperineal resection specimen.

thicker tumors, but their exact depth was not recorded.

Microscopically, melanoma in the anorectum differs little from the cutaneous form of this tumor. The melanocytes would take a spindle, epithelioid, nevoid, or other shape to invade the underlying lamina propria and rectal mucosa in the areolar or haphazard pattern. The mitotic rate varies markedly from tumor to tumor.

TREATMENT RESULTS

Historically, the collected surgical experience with malignant melanoma of the anorectum has varied between being ultra-conservative[2,3,8–12] to being ultra-radical,[13–17] with no clear choice of either being definitive or ideal. Two obvious reasons come readily to mind to explain this wide range of therapeutic approach: First, the tumor is so rare that no expertise and experience can be accumulated from one source; second, the prognosis is so poor that some surgeons, adopting a pessimistic view, choose local surgical control of the lesion only.

In our own institutional experience, only 1 of the 10 patients who has survived 5 years or more disease-free had undergone only a local excision and subsequent groin dissections. This was a 44-year-old woman who was first correctly diagnosed upon the discovery of a positive groin metastasis. The diagnosis of a primary melanoma of the anal canal had been missed in a hemorrhoidectomy done elsewhere 1 year previously. She underwent local reexcision of the primary site and is alive and well without evidence of the disease 6 years after the hemorrhoidectomy and 5 years after subsequent bilateral metachronous groin dissections.

Of the patients who survived 5 years or more disease-free, 9 had undergone abdominoperineal resection; 1 was found to have metastatic mesenteric lymph nodes (Table 108-1). Although 9 out of 85 represents only a 10 percent 5-year survival rate, these patients nevertheless represent the largest single series thus far reported that showed successful treatment by abdominoperineal resection. If, however, one considers only the subset of the 43 patients in our series who received abdominoperineal resection as primary treatment, the 9 patients then represent a more encouraging 27 percent 5-year survival rate. Of interest is the fact that all 5-year survivors have been women.

We have also used conservative therapeutic approaches, including local excision alone or combined with groin dissection, local excision followed by de-

Table 108-1
Patients Who Survived Five Years

No.	*Sex*	*Age*	*Site*	*Size, cm*	*Treatment*	*Status follow-up, months*
1	F	47	Rectum	5	APR, RT	DOC, 96
2	F	45	Anus	3	APR	DOD, 60
3	F	64	Anus	NA	APR	DOC, 314
4	F	64	Anus	3	APR	NED, 70
5	F	68	Anus	2	APR, Bil. ELND	DOC, 270
6	F	67	Rectum	2.5	APR	NED, 171
7	F	53	Rectum	3	APR, Post. vaginectomy	NED, 150
8	F	52	Anus	1	WLE, TLND, ELND resect. pelvic nodal metastasis	NED, 126
9	F	61	Anus	0.5	APR	NED, 92
10	F	48	Anus	1.5	APR	DOD, 87

Abbreviations: APR, abdominal perineal resection; DOC, died of complications; DOD, dead of disease 5 years after treatment; ELND, elective inguinal lymphadenectomy; RT, radiotherapy; TLND, therapeutic inguinal lymphadenectomy; WLE, wide local excision.

layed rectal resection, and local tumor destruction by cryosurgery or fulguration. With the exception of the unique 5-year-plus survivor previously described, the mean survival for these patients was only 22 months. Besides local or radical surgery, various combinations and additions of chemotherapy, chemoimmunotherapy, local radiation therapy, immunotherapy, and/or autoclonal antibody therapy have also been tried, but with little expectation of prolonging survival.

We conclude then that, despite the rarity of cure for anorectal melanoma as reported in the medical literature, our recommended treatment for stage I to stage III anal melanoma in acceptable-risk surgical patients continues to be abdominoperineal resection of the rectum with adequate mesenteric lymphatic dissection plus extramesenteric lymph node dissection if indicated. As adjuvant strategies prove effective for cutaneous melanoma, such approaches can also be applied to patients with this rare disease.

REFERENCES

1. Moore W: Recurrent melanoma of the rectum after previous removal from the verge of the anus in a man age sixty-five. *Lancet* 1:290, 1857.
2. Goldman S, Glimelius B, Pahlman L: Anorectal malignant melanoma in Sweden: Report of 49 cases. *Dis Colon Rectum* 33:874–877, 1990.
3. Siegal B, Cohen D, Jacob ET: Surgical treatment of anorectal melanomas. *Am J Surg* 146:336–338, 1983.
4. Quan SHQ, White JE, Deddish MR: Malignant melanoma of the anorectum. *Dis Colon Rectum* 2:275–283, 1959.
5. Quan SHQ, Deddish MR: Noncutaneous melanoma. *Cancer* 16:111–114, 1966.
6. Wanebo HJ, Woodruff JM, Quan SHQ, et al: Anorectal melanoma. *Cancer* 47:1891–1900, 1981.
7. Brady MS, Karelius JP, Quan SHQ: Anorectal melanoma. A 64-year experience at MEKCC. To be published.
8. Cooper PH, Mills SE, Allen MS Jr: Malignant melanoma of the anus: Report of 12 patients and analysis of 255 additional cases. *Dis Colon Rectum* 25:693–703, 1982.
9. Pyper PC, Parks TG: Melanoma of the anal canal. *Br J Surg* 71:671–672, 1984.
10. Ward MWN, Romano G, Nicholls RJ: The surgical treatment of anorectal malignant melanoma. *Br J Surg* 73:68–69, 1986.
11. Slingluff CL, Vollmer RT, Seigler HF: Anorectal melanoma: Clinical characteristics and results of surgical management in 24 patients. *Surgery* 107:1–9, 1990.
12. Ross M, Pezzi C, Pezzi T, et al: Patterns of failure in anorectal melanoma. *Arch Surg* 125:313–316, 1990.
13. Pack GT, Oropeza R: A comparative study of melanoma and epidermoid carcinoma of the anal canal: A review of 20 melanomas and 29 epidermoid carcinomas. *Dis Colon Rectum* 10:161–176, 1967.
14. Chiu YS, Unni KK, Beart RW Jr: Malignant melanoma of the anorectum. *Dis Colon Rectum* 23:122–124, 1980.
15. Bolivar JC, Harris JW, Branch W, et al: Melanoma of the anorectal region. *Surg Gynecol Obstet* 154:337–341, 1982.
16. Baskies AM, Sugarbaker EV, Chretien PB, et al: Anorectal melanoma: The role of posterior exenteration. *Dis Colon Rectum* 25:772–777, 1982.
17. Freedman LS: Malignant melanoma of the anorectal region: Two cases of prolonged survival. *Br J Surg* 71:164–165, 1984.

PART 20

Pain Management

CHAPTER 109

Colorectal and Anal Cancer Pain: Pathophysiology, Assessment, Syndromes, and Management

Nathan I. Cherny
Kathleen M. Foley

HIGHLIGHTS

The success of cancer pain therapy is dependent upon the ability of the clinician to assess the presenting problems, recognize and evaluate pain syndromes, and formulate a comprehensive care plan. Management of cancer pain problems requires familiarity with a range of therapeutic options including antineoplastic therapies and analgesic pharmacotherapy as well as anesthetic, neurosurgical, psychological, and physiatric techniques. Currently available techniques can provide adequate relief to a vast majority of patients. Pharmacologic therapy is the mainstay of cancer pain management, but other concurrent interventions may be required to manage difficult pain problems. Successful pain management is characterized by the implementation of the techniques with the most favorable therapeutic index for the prevailing circumstances, along with provision for repeated evaluations to ensure that an optimal balance between pain relief and adverse effects is maintained. In all cases, these analgesic treatments must be skillfully integrated with the management of other symptoms.

CONTROVERSIES

Continuing controversies pertaining to opioid selection, optimal schedule and route of administration, risks of tolerance and addiction, and concern for side effects all affect patient care. There is a paucity of controlled trials addressing these issues as well those regarding the relative roles of primary therapies, adjuvant drugs, and anesthetic and neurosurgical techniques. The palliative index of surgery, chemotherapy, and radiotherapy in the management of advanced symptomatic disease is largely unknown.

FUTURE DIRECTIONS

Basic research clarifying understanding of pain pathophysiology will, it is hoped, yield more specific analgesic tools. Analgesic pharmacotherapy will be further enhanced by ongoing studies involving novel routes of opioid administration, prevention of opioid side effects, and new adjuvant analgesic agents. Integration of quality-of-life and pain measurement methodologies into clinical studies of primary therapies will provide secondary endpoint data vital to optimal therapeutic decision making.

Patients with colorectal cancer are heterogeneous in their experience of pain and symptom distress. Clinicians who care for these patients must be prepared to manage a diverse spectrum of problems, ranging from the treatment of acute procedure-related pain to the management of chronic unremitting pain in patients with advanced disease.[1] Although established analgesic strategies can benefit most patients,[2] undertreatment is common.[3,4]

In general, approximately one-third of cancer patients undergoing active therapy and as many as 70 to 90 percent of those with advanced disease experience pain.[4] In a survey of ambulatory patients with colonic cancer, "persistent or frequent" pain during the prior 2 weeks was reported by 52 of 181 patients (28.7 percent), the median duration of pain was 4 weeks (range <1 to 468 weeks), approximately 90 percent of these patients experienced pain more than 25 percent of the time, and the average pain severity was "moderate." More than half of the patients interviewed reported that pain interfered moderately or greater with their enjoyment of life, general activity, sleep, and mood.[5] In a study of patients admitted for hospice care, 49 percent of patients with colorectal cancer had severe pain at presentation.[6]

The prevalence of acute and chronic cancer pain and the burden of distress and suffering engendered by this symptom oblige the treating clinician to be skilled in the assessment and treatment of this problem. Relief of pain in cancer patients is an ethical imperative, and it is incumbent upon clinicians to maximize the knowledge, skill, and diligence needed to attend to this task.[7–9] The success of cancer pain therapy is dependent upon the ability of the clinician to assess the presenting problems, identify and evaluate pain syndromes, and formulate a comprehensive care plan with provision for reevaluation and follow-up. Cancer pain is a dynamic problem, and successful management requires a continuity of care that provides an appropriate level of vigilance and responds quickly, flexibly, and expertly to the changing needs of the patient.[10–12] This approach recognizes the need to incorporate pain treatment within a broader therapeutic agenda, in which needs for tumor control, symptom palliation (physical and psychological), and functional rehabilitation are concurrently addressed.[10,13]

PAIN—GENERAL PRINCIPLES

The Nature of Pain

Pain and Nociception

Nociception. Nociception is defined as the activity produced in the nervous system by potentially tissue-damaging stimuli. Although nociception cannot be directly observed, in the clinical setting it is inferred to occur whenever a tissue-damaging stimulus impinges upon a pain-sensitive structure.

Pain. The complex relationship between tissue injury and pain is emphasized in the definition of pain promulgated by the International Association for the Study of Pain: "an unpleasant sensory and emotional experience associated with actual or potential tissue damage or described in terms of such damage."[14]

Pain is the perception of nociception, and like other perceptions is determined by an interaction between activity in sensorineural pathways and a variety of behavioral and psychologic factors. In addition to nociceptive stimuli, two other mechanisms contributing to pain perception can be inferred: neuropathic and psychological processes (Fig. 109-1). Although psychologic processes can strongly influence the expression and impact of pain,[15,16] nociceptive and neuropathic factors predominate in the cancer population.[17]

Cancer Pain Pathophysiology

Pain Pathways

Nociceptors. Nociceptors are widely distributed in skin, muscle, connective tissues, and viscera.[18–22] A variety of subtypes have been identified. The best-characterized somatic nociceptors have thinly myelinated fibers sensitive to noxious mechanical stimuli (high-threshold mechanoreceptors) or unmyelinated fibers that respond to mechanical, thermal, and chemical stimuli. Visceral nociceptors are similar morphologically and likewise respond to discrete sets of noxious stimuli.[19] All nociceptors may become sensitized by noxious stimuli and thereafter demonstrate spontaneous activity, a lower threshold, and a more intense response.[20] These primary sensory afferents have their cell bodies in the dorsal root ganglion; their axons enter the spinal cord by way of the dorsal root and, generally, ascend for one or two segments in Lissauer's tracts and synapse in the laminae of the dorsal horn.

The Dorsal Horn. The neuroanatomy and neurochemistry of the dorsal horn are extraordinarily complex.[21–23] A large number of putative neurotransmitters or neuromodulators, including peptides, amino acids, monoamines and other compounds, have been implicated in the processing of nociceptive input at the first central synapse.[24]

Ascending Pathways. Several ascending pathways arise from second-order neurons and decussate in the central gray spinal cord to become the neospinothalamic and paleospinothalamic tracts.[21,22] The neospinothalamic tract, which projects monosynaptically to the ventrobasal complex of the thalamus, subserves pain intensity and localization. Multiple polysynaptic pathways (together termed the *paleospinothalamic*

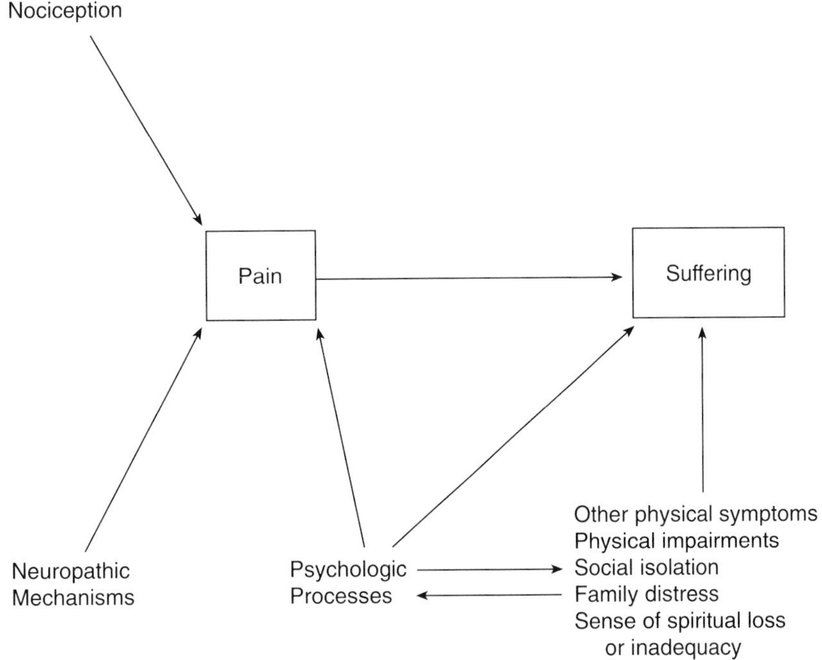

FIG. 109-1. Factors contributing to pain and the relationship between pain and suffering (see text). (From Portenoy RK: Cancer pain: Pathophysiology and syndromes. Lancet 339:1026–1031, 1992. Reproduced by permission.)

tracts), which connect with various brainstem and subcortical sites, contribute to autonomic and affective responses and to the activation of pain modulating systems.

Segmental and Supraspinal Pain Modulation. Nociception is modulated by both segmental and suprasegmental systems, a concept originally modeled in the gate-control theory.[25] Neurotransmitters such as dopamine, serotonin, norepinephrine, and the endogenous opioid peptides (i.e., enkephalin, beta-endorphin, and dynorphin) play a significant role in this modulatory system. Segmental processes may involve the activation of inhibitory interneurons by myelinated nonnociceptive afferent fibers. The most important of the descending inhibitory pathways arises in the periaqueductal gray nuclei of the midbrain, synapses in the raphae magnus nucleus of the medulla, and projects to the dorsal horn via the dorsal longitudinal fasciculus.[23,26]

Endogenous opioids are involved in this modulatory system at multiple sites through a large number of distinct compounds and receptor subtypes.[27,28] Subpopulations of opioid receptors are localized in the ascending and descending pain pathways. These receptors mediate the multiple pharmacologic effects of the opioid analgesics. The periaqueductal gray (PAG) region in the midbrain and the dorsal horn in the spinal cord are rich in opioid receptors and represent the supraspinal and spinal sites that mediate opioid analgesia. Direct administration of opioids into the PAG region or spinal cord[29] inhibits pain transmission.

Visceral Pain Pathways. Pain impulses arising from the viscera are transmitted by unmyelinated afferent fibers in the sympathetic nerves that have their cell bodies in the thoracolumbar dorsal root ganglia (T2–L3). Specifically, the innervation of pelvic viscera arises from T10–L1. At the dorsal horn, sympathetic afferent nerves account for approximately 10 percent of afferent fibers (the other 90 percent arise from somatic structures). The visceral afferent fibers terminate in the dorsal horn where they synapse with ascending viscerosomatic neurons in the spinothalamic tracts.

Pain Mechanisms

Inferences about the pathophysiologic mechanisms that may be responsible for the pain are valuable in the assessment and management of cancer pain. As suggested previously, three broad categories of pain mechanisms may be posited: ongoing nociception, neuropathic processes, and psychological influences. From information acquired through the assessment process, these mechanisms can be used to label pain according to the predominant pathophysiology that is inferred to exist. The clinical lexicon now commonly refers to *nociceptive pain* and *neuropathic pain*.[30,31] A third category, which is sometimes termed *idiopathic pain*,[31] includes both those pains that are presumed to have an organic etiology that has not yet been identified and those that are perceived to have a psychological cause.[32]

Nociceptive Pain. *Nociceptive pain* is the term applied to pain that is perceived to be commensurate with tissue damage associated with an identifiable somatic or visceral lesion. The persistence of pain is related to ongoing activation of nociceptors. Nociceptive pain that originates from somatic structures (also known as somatic pain) is typically well localized and described as sharp, aching, throbbing, or pressure-like. Pain originating from viscera (visceral pain) is often more diffuse and is usually described as gnawing or cramping when due to obstruction of a hollow viscus and as aching, sharp, or throbbing when due to involvement of organ capsules or other mesentery. From the clinical perspective, nociceptive pains (particularly somatic pains) often respond to opioid drugs[31,33] or to interventions that ameliorate or denervate the peripheral lesion.

Neuropathic Pain. The term *neuropathic pain* is applied to pain associated with injury to peripheral or central neural structures.[34] This term implies that the pain is believed to be sustained by aberrant somatosensory processing at sites in the peripheral or central nervous system[34,35] and is most strongly suggested when a dysesthesia occurs in a region of motor, sensory, or autonomic dysfunction that is attributable to a discrete neurologic lesion.[35] The diagnosis can be challenging. In many cases, the diagnosis is inferred from the distribution of the pain and identification of a lesion in neural structures that innervate this region.

Although neuropathic pain can be described in terms of pain characteristics or site of injury, it is useful to distinguish these syndromes according to the presumed site or "generator" of the aberrant neural activity that sustains the pain (Table 109-1).[35] Peripheral neuropathic pain is caused by injury to a peripheral nerve or nerve root and is presumably sustained by aberrant processes originating in the nerve root, plexus, or nerve. Neuropathic pains believed to be sustained by a central generator include sympathetically maintained pain and a group of syndromes traditionally known as the *deafferentation pains*. Sympathetically maintained pain (also known as *reflex sympathetic dystrophy* or *causalgia*) may occur following injury to soft tissue, peripheral nerve, viscera, or central nervous system and is characterized by focal autonomic dysregulation in a painful region (e.g., vasomotor or pilomotor changes, swelling, or sweating abnormalities) or by trophic changes.[36]

The diagnosis of neuropathic pain has important clinical implications. Neuropathic pains are widely believed to respond relatively less well to opioid drugs than nociceptive pains.[31,37,38] Optimal treatment may

Table 109-1
Taxonomy of Neuropathic Pain by Putative Predominating Mechanism

1. Predominantly "central" pain generator
   a. Deafferentation pain[a]
   b. Sympathetically maintained pain[b]
2. Predominantly "peripheral" pain generator
   a. Painful mononeuropathy
   b. Painful polyneuropathy

[a]Can follow injury to peripheral or central neural structures.

[b]Can follow injury to peripheral neural or somatic structures; rarely caused by damage to central structures.

depend on the use of so-called adjuvant analgesics[35,39] or other specific approaches, such as sympathetic nerve block.

Idiopathic Pain. Pain that is perceived to be excessive for the extent of identifiable organic pathology can be termed *idiopathic*. Some patients with idiopathic pain present with affective and behavioral disturbances sufficient to infer a predominating psychologic pathogenesis, in which case a specific psychiatric diagnosis can be applied.[32] When this inference cannot be made, however, the label *idiopathic* should be retained, and assessments should be repeated at appropriate intervals. Idiopathic pain in general and pain related to a psychiatric disorder specifically are uncommon in the cancer population, notwithstanding the importance of psychologic factors in the quality of life.

Pain, Psychologic Distress, and Suffering

Pain and Psychologic Distress

The relationship between pain and psychologic well-being is complex and reciprocal. Mood disturbance and beliefs about the meaning of pain in relation to illness have been shown to be significant predictors of perceived pain intensity,[40,41] and the perceived meaning of the pain is a major determinant of function and mood.[42] In one large prospective study,[15] the prevalence of cancer-related pain was 39 percent in those who had a psychiatric diagnosis and only 19 percent in those without such a diagnosis. In the group with pain, the most important psychiatric diagnoses included adjustment disorders with depressed mood, mixed depression and anxiety, and major depression.[15] The relationship between pain and psychologic distress is further demonstrated by the observation that uncontrolled pain is a major factor in cancer-related suicide[43–45] and that psychiatric symptoms have commonly been observed to disappear with adequate pain relief.[46]

The presence of cancer pain can disturb normal processes of coping and adjustment, which are fundamental reactions to the stresses imposed by the cancer and its treatment.[47,48] Pain may augment a sense of vulnerability, contributing to a preoccupation with the potential for catastrophic outcomes.[47] In some cases, unrealistic or distorted attitudes toward the pain problem (e.g., assumptions, beliefs, expectations) can undermine the ability to cope, so that the patient becomes utterly helpless and desperate.[47] This situation can be reflected in the development of pain behaviors characterized by increasing passivity and dependency or the uncontrolled expression of negative attitudes and feelings. These behaviors can, in turn, exacerbate social isolation.[47]

Suffering. Suffering is the perception of distress engendered by all the adverse factors that together undermine quality of life.[49] Pain may contribute profoundly to suffering, but numerous other factors—such as the experience of other symptoms, progressive physical impairment, or psychosocial disturbances—may be equally or more important[50] (Fig. 109-1). Suffering and pain are therefore best regarded as related but discrete experiences which have distinct clinical implications. Analgesia alone may not lessen suffering; consequently, pain therapy is not the sole objective in the supportive care of the cancer patient. Rather, pain therapy must be a critical component of a more comprehensive therapeutic plan designed to address the diverse factors that impair quality of life.[10,13]

Pain Features and Syndrome Identification

A syndrome is a temporal and qualitative convergence of symptoms and signs, which conforms to a recognized pattern. Specific syndromes may be associated with distinct etiologies, pathophysiologies, and prognostic and therapeutic implications. In the context of cancer pain, syndromes are defined by the association of particular pain characteristics and physical signs with specific complications of the underlying disease or its treatment.

Pain Characteristics

Evaluation of pain characteristics provides some of the raw data essential for syndrome identification. The most important of the characteristics are as follows:

Pain Intensity. In the cancer population, evaluation of pain intensity is pivotal to therapeutic decision making. The selection of an analgesic drug, route and dose of administration, and rate of dose titration may all be influenced by reported pain intensity. Furthermore, intensity may also help characterize the pain mechanisms and underlying syndrome. For example, clinical observation strongly suggests that the pain associated with radiation-induced nerve injury is rarely severe; the occurrence of severe pain in a previously irradiated region, therefore, suggests the existence of recurrent neoplasm or a radiation-induced second primary.[51]

Pain Quality. The quality of the pain often suggests its pathophysiology. As noted previously, somatic nociceptive pains are usually well localized and described as sharp, aching, throbbing, or pressurelike. Visceral nociceptive pains are generally diffuse and may be gnawing or crampy when due to obstruction of a hollow viscus or aching, sharp, or throbbing when due to involvement of organ capsules or mesentery. Neuropathic pains may be described as burning, tingling, or shocklike.[52]

Pain Distribution. Patients with cancer pain commonly experience pain at more than one site.[5,53–55] The number of pain sites has been identified as a salient determinant of the impact of pain on mood and function.[5] The distinction between focal, multifocal, and generalized pain may be important in the selection of therapy, such as nerve blocks, radiotherapy, or surgical approaches.

The distribution of the pain often clarifies its relationship to the underlying organic lesion. The term *focal pain,* which is used to denote one site of pain, also denotes pain that is experienced in the region of the underlying lesion. The term *referred pain* is applied when pain is experienced in a distribution remote to the lesion. Pain referral patterns, which have been characterized for both nociceptive (somatic and visceral) pain and neuropathic pain,[19,56,57] must be recognized to evaluate the underlying organic etiology. For example, neuropathic pain is associated with several characteristic patterns including (1) pain referred anywhere in the distribution of peripheral nerves from a lesion involving the nerve itself or the plexus from which it arises, (2) pain referred to the dermatome innervated by a damaged nerve root (radicular pain), (3) pain referred anywhere in the region of the body innervated by a damaged central pathway, and (4) symmetrical extremity pain from a peripheral neuropathy. Somatic and visceral nociceptive stimuli may similarly be associated with characteristic pain referral patterns. Familiarity with pain referral patterns is essential to target appropriate diagnostic and therapeutic maneuvers. For example, a patient with a past history of colonic cancer who develops progressive shoulder pain and has no evidence of focal pathology must undergo evaluation of the region above and below the diaphragm to exclude the possibility of referred pain from diaphragmatic irritation.

Temporal Relationships. Cancer-related pain may be acute or chronic. *Acute pain* is defined by a recent onset and a natural history characterized by transience. Most frequently, acute pain is associated with a well-defined onset and a readily identifiable cause, such as chemotherapy-induced stomatitis or a post–lumbar puncture headache. The pain is often associated with overt pain behaviors (such as moaning, grimacing, and splinting), anxiety, or signs of generalized sympathetic hyperactivity, including diaphoresis, hypertension, and tachycardia.

Chronic pain has been identified by persistence for 3 months or more beyond the usual course of an acute illness or injury, a pattern of recurrence at intervals over months or years, or by association with a chronic pathologic process.[58] Chronic tumor-related pain is usually insidious in onset and has a course which is characterized by fluctuations in intensity. Pain often increases progressively with tumor growth and may regress with tumor shrinkage (in response to anticancer therapy). Chronic pain due to cancer may be associated with affective disturbances (anxiety and/or depression) and vegetative symptoms, such as asthenia, anorexia, and sleep disturbance; overt pain behaviors and sympathetic hyperactivity are often absent.[59]

Transitory exacerbations of severe pain over a baseline of moderate pain or less may be described as *breakthrough pain*.[60] Breakthrough pains can occur in either acute or chronic pain states. In a survey of patients with chronic cancer pain, almost two-thirds experienced severe or excruciating breakthrough pains.[60] These exacerbations may be precipitated by volitional actions of the patient—such as movement, micturition, cough or defecation (incident pains)—or by nonvolitional events such as bowel distention. Spontaneous fluctuations in pain intensity can also occur without an identifiable precipitant.

Whereas acute pains experienced by cancer patients are usually related to diagnostic and therapeutic interventions, chronic pains are most commonly caused by direct tumor infiltration. Adverse consequences of cancer therapy—including surgery, chemotherapy, and radiation therapy—account for 15 to 25 percent of chronic cancer pain problems; a small proportion of the chronic pains experienced by cancer patients are caused by pathology unrelated to either the cancer or the cancer therapy.[53,55,61–63]

ASSESSMENT OF CANCER PAIN PROBLEMS

General Considerations

Cancer pain assessment has two major objectives: (1) the accurate characterization of pain, including the pain syndrome and inferred pathophysiology, and (2) the evaluation of the impact of the pain and the role it plays in the overall suffering of the patient. This assessment is predicated on the establishment of a trusting relationship with the patient. Even with such a relationship, however, the clinician should not be cavalier about the potential for underreporting of symptoms. Symptoms are frequently described as complaints, and there is a common perception that the "good patient" refrains from complaining.[64] The clinicians must maintain a clinical posture that affirms relief of pain and suffering as central goals of therapy and encourages open and effective communication about symptoms. If the patient is either unable or unwilling to describe the pain, a family member may have to be questioned to assess the distress or disability of the patient. The prevalence of pain is so great that an open-ended question about the presence of pain should be included at each patient visit in routine oncologic practice.

A practical approach to the assessment of cancer pain incorporates a stepwise approach that begins with data collection and ends with a clinically relevant formulation (Table 109-2).

Data Collection

The History in Cancer Pain Assessment

A careful review of the past medical history and chronology of the cancer is important to place the pain problem in context. The pain-related history must elucidate the relevant pain characteristics as well as the responses of the patient to previous disease-modifying and analgesic therapies. The presence of multiple pain problems is common, and if more than one is reported, each must be assessed independently. The use of validated pain assessment instruments can provide a format for communication between the patient and health care professionals and can also be used to monitor the adequacy of therapy.[42,65–67]

The consequences of the pain must also be assessed. These may include impairment in activities of daily living; psychological, familial, and professional dysfunction; disturbed sleep, appetite, and vitality; and financial concerns. The psychiatric history, current level of anxiety or depression, suicidal ideation, and the perceived meaning of the pain are all very relevant to therapy. Pervasive dysfunctional attitudes such as pessimism, idiosyncratic interpretation of pain, self-blame, catastrophizing, and perceived loss of personal control can be detected through careful questioning. It is important to assess the patient-family interaction and to note both the kind and frequency of pain behaviors and the nature of the family response.

Most patients with cancer pain have multiple other symptoms.[54,68,69] It is incumbent upon the clinician to evaluate the severity and distress caused by symptoms other than pain. Symptom checklists and quality-of-life measures may contribute to this comprehensive evaluation.[70,71]

Table 109-2
Stepwise Assessment of the Patient with Cancer Pain

Step 1: Data collection

Pain-related history	*Other relevant history*	*Available laboratory and imaging data*	*Physical examination*
Chronology Characteristics Impact on function Prior treatment Other pain history	Disease-related Other symptoms Psychiatric history Social resources		

Step 2: Provisional assessment

Provisional pain diagnosis	*Global assessment*	*Concurrent concerns*
1. Syndrome identification	1. Extent of disease	1. Other symptoms
2. Inferred pathophysiology	2. Relative priority of goals of care Prolongation of survival Augmentation of function Provision of comfort	2. Untreated concurrent diseases 3. Psychosocial needs 4. Rehabilitative needs 5. Financial needs

Step 3: Diagnostic investigations and other assessments

Diagnostic investigations	*Other assessments*
1. Symptom specific 2. Extent of disease	1. Psychological 2. Social 3. Financial 4. Functional

Step 4: Initial formulation and problem list

1. Pain syndromes and pathophysiology
2. Extent of diseases
3. Concurrent concerns
4. Anticipated contingencies

Step 5: Patient review and formulation of prioritized problem list

Current problems	*Anticipated contingencies*
1.	1. ....
2.	2. ....
3.	3. ....
4.	4. ....

Step 6: Multimodality therapeutic plan

1. Primary treatment:
   - Chemotherapy
   - Radiotherapy
   - Surgery
   - Immunotherapy
   - Other
2. Symptom-directed pharmacotherapy
3. Treatment of concurrent disease processes
4. Rehabilitative approaches
5. Psychologic approaches
6. Anesthetic approaches
7. Neurosurgical approaches

SOURCE: Adapted from Cherny NI, Portenoy RK: Cancer pain pathophysiology, assessment and syndromes, in Wall PD and Melzack R (eds): *Textbook of Pain*, 3rd ed. New York: Churchill Livingstone, 1994, pp 787–823. Reproduced by permission.

Examination

A physical examination, including a neurologic evaluation, is a necessary part of the initial pain assessment. The need for a thorough neurologic assessment is justified by the high prevalence of painful neurologic conditions in patients with cancer pain.[17,72] The physical examination should attempt to identify the underlying etiology of the pain problem, clarify the extent of the underlying disease, and discern the relationship of the pain complaint to the disease.

Review of Previous Investigations

Careful review of previous laboratory and imaging studies can provide important information about the cause of the pain as well as the extent of the underlying disease.

Provisional Assessment

The information derived from the initial data collection provides the basis for a provisional pain diagnosis, assessment of global disease status, and identification of other concurrent concerns. The provisional pain diagnosis includes an assessment of the likely pathophysiology and pain syndrome. An understanding of disease status requires an evaluation of the extent of the disease, the prognosis, and the anticipated goals of therapy.[73] Evaluation of concurrent concerns includes other symptoms and related psychosocial problems.

Diagnostic Investigations and Additional Assessment

Additional investigations are often required to clarify areas of uncertainty in the provisional assessment.[17] The extent and type of diagnostic investigation must be appropriate to the patient's general status and the overall goals of care.

The lack of a definitive finding on an investigation should not be used to override a compelling clinical diagnosis. To minimize the risk of error, the physician ordering the diagnostic procedures should personally review them with the radiologist to correlate pathologic changes with the clinical findings. Pain should be managed during the diagnostic evaluation. Comfort will improve compliance and reduce the distress associated with procedures. No patient should be inadequately evaluated because of poorly controlled pain.

Formulation and Therapeutic Planning

The evaluation should enable the clinician to appreciate the nature of the pain, its impact, and concurrent concerns that further undermine quality of life. The findings of this evaluation should be reviewed with the patient and appropriate others. Through candid discussion, current problems can be prioritized to reflect their importance to the patient.

This evaluation may also identify potential outcomes that would benefit from contingency planning. Examples include advance medical directives, evaluation of resources for home care, prebereavement interventions with the family, and the provision of assistive devices in anticipation of compromised ambulation.

ACUTE PAIN SYNDROMES

Cancer-related acute pain syndromes are most commonly due to diagnostic and therapeutic interventions (Table 109-3). Although some tumor-related pains have an acute onset (such as pain from a pathologic fracture), most of these will tend to be chronic or recurrent unless effective treatment for the underlying lesion is provided. Of the acute pain syndromes, only herpetic neuralgia will be addressed in this chapter.

Table 109-3
Acute Pain Syndromes in Colorectal and Anal Cancer

Acute pain associated with diagnostic and therapeutic interventions
Acute pain associated with diagnostic interventions
Arterial or venous blood sampling
Lumbar puncture
Colonoscopy
Myelography
Percutaneous biopsy
Acute postoperative pain
Acute pain caused by other therapeutic interventions
Pleurodesis
Tumor embolization
Suprapubic catheterization
Intercostal catheter
Nephrostomy insertion
Acute pain associated with analgesic techniques
Injection pain
Opioid headache
Spinal opioid hyperalgesia syndrome
Epidural injection pain
Acute pain associated with anticancer therapies
Acute pain associated with chemotherapy infusion techniques
Intravenous infusion pain
Hepatic artery infusion pain
Intraperitoneal chemotherapy abdominal pain
Acute pain associated with chemotherapy toxicity
Mucositis
Corticosteroid-induced perineal discomfort
Steroid pseudorheumatism
Colony stimulating factor–induced bone pain
5-fluorouracil–induced anginal chest pain
Acute pain associated with immunotherapy
Interferon (IFN)–induced acute pain
Acute pain associated with radiotherapy
Incident pains
Acute radiation enteritis and proctocolitis
Subacute radiation myelopathy
Acute pain associated with infection
Acute herpetic neuralgia
Abdominal or pelvic abscess

Acute Herpetic Neuralgia

Cancer patients have a fivefold increased incidence of acute herpetic neuralgia over the general population.[74] Pain or itch usually precedes the development of the rash by several days and may occasionally occur without the development of skin eruption.[75] The pain, which may be continuous or lancinating, may persist for several weeks after the resolution of the rash and usually resolves within 2 months.[75] Pain persisting beyond this interval is referred to as *postherpetic neuralgia*. Postherpetic neuralgia is two to three times more frequent in the cancer population than the general population.[74] Patients with postherpetic neuralgia and cancer who describe changes in the pattern of pain or the development of new neurologic deficits may have tumor-related pain that exacerbates the existing neuropathic pain. The dermatomal location of the varicella zoster infection shows a significant correlation with the site of the malignancy, and exacerbations occur twice as frequently in previously irradiated dermatomes as in nonirradiated areas.[74] Dissemination of the infection is twice as frequent in patients with active tumor compared with those who are in remission.[76] In patients receiving chemotherapy, the infection usually develops at a median time of less than 1 month after the completion of chemotherapy.

Table 109-4
Chronic Pain Syndromes in Colorectal and Anal Cancer

Tumor-related pain syndromes
Visceral pain syndromes
Hepatic distention syndrome
Midline retroperitoneal syndrome
Chronic intestinal obstruction
Peritoneal carcinomatosis
Malignant perineal pain
Malignant pelvic floor myalgia
Ureteric obstruction
Pain syndromes due to tumor involvement of the peripheral nervous system
Malignant lumbosacral plexopathy and radiculopathy
Bone pain syndromes
Vertebral syndromes
Back pain and epidural (spinal cord and cauda equina) compression
Pain syndromes of the bony pelvis and hip
Headache and facial pain syndromes
Intracerebral tumor
Leptomeningeal metastases
Base-of-skull metastases
Painful cranial neuralgias
Chronic pain syndromes associated with cancer therapy
Postchemotherapy pain syndromes
Avascular necrosis of femoral or humeral head
Plexopathy associated with intraarterial infusion
Chronic postsurgical pain syndromes
Phantom anus pain
Postsurgical pelvic floor myalgia
Chronic postradiation pain syndromes
Radiation-induced lumbosacral plexopathy
Chronic radiation enteritis and proctitis
Burning perineum syndrome
Chronic radiation myelopathy
Osteoradionecrosis

CHRONIC PAIN SYNDROMES (TABLE 109-4)

Pain Syndromes Due to Tumor Involvement of Viscera and Adjacent Structures

Pain may be caused by pathology involving the luminal organs of the gastrointestinal or genitourinary tracts, the parenchymal organs, the peritoneum, or the retroperitoneal soft tissues. Obstructions of hollow viscus—including intestine, biliary tract, and ureter—produce visceral nociceptive syndromes that are well described in the surgical literature.[77] Pain arising from retroperitoneal and pelvic lesions may involve mixed nociceptive and neuropathic mechanisms if both somatic structures and nerve plexuses are involved.

Hepatic Distension Syndrome

The liver is the most common visceral site of metastases arising from colonic and rectal neoplasms. Pain-sensitive hepatic structures include the liver capsule, vascular structures, and biliary tract.[78,79] Nociceptive afferents that innervate these structures travel via the celiac plexus, phrenic nerve, and lower right intercostal nerves. Extensive intrahepatic metastases or gross hepatomegaly associated with cholestasis may produce discomfort in the right subcostal region of the abdomen and, less commonly, in the right midback or flank.[78,79] Referred pain may be experienced in the right neck or shoulder or in the region of the right scapula.[78] The pain, which is usually described as a dull aching, may be exacerbated by movement, pressure in the abdomen, and deep inspiration. It is commonly accompanied by symptoms of anorexia and nausea. Physical examination may reveal a hard, irregular subcostal mass that descends with respiration and is dull to percussion. Other features of hepatic failure may be present. Imaging of the hepatic parenchyma by either ultrasound or computed tomography (CT) will usually identify the presence of space-occupying lesions.

Occasional patients develop an acute subcostal pain exacerbated by respiration. Physical examination may demonstrate a palpable or audible rub. These findings suggest the development of an overlying peritonitis, which may occur in response to some acute event such as a hemorrhage into a metastasis.

Midline Retroperitoneal Syndrome

Retroperitoneal lymphadenopathy involving the upper abdomen may produce pain by invasion into deep somatic structures of the posterior abdominal wall,

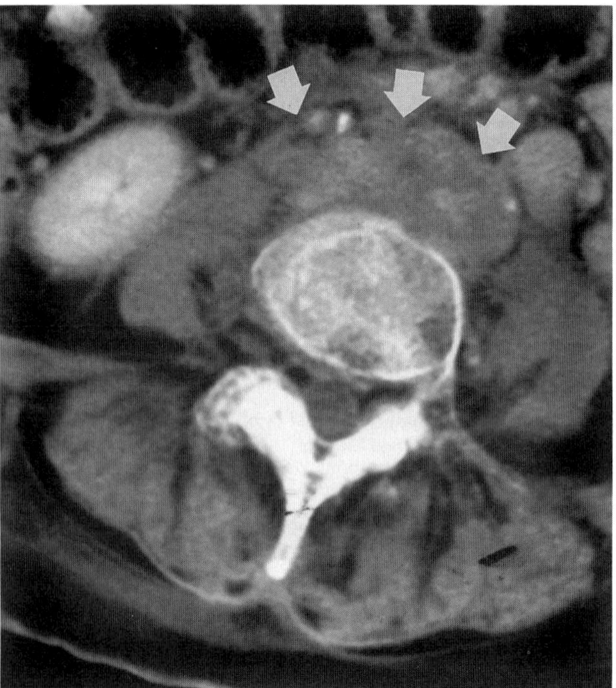

FIG. 109-2. Abdominal CT scan of a 52-year-old woman with metastatic carcinoma of the colon who presented with upper abdominal and mid-back pain. There is lymphadenopathy in the retroperitoneal space immediately anterior to the vertebral body (arrows). (Adapted from Cherny NI, Portenoy RK: Cancer pain pathophysiology, assessment and syndromes, in Wall PD, Melzack R (eds): *Textbook of Pain, 3rd ed.* New York, Churchill Livingstone, 1994, in press. Reproduced by permission.)

distortion of pain-sensitive connective tissue and vascular structures, local inflammation, and direct infiltration of the celiac plexus. The pain is experienced in the epigastrium, in the low thoracic region of the back, or in both locations. It is usually dull and boring in character, exacerbated with recumbency, and improved by sitting. The diagnosis is confirmed by CT or magnetic resonance imaging (MRI) of the upper abdomen (Fig. 109-2). If tumor is identified in the paravertebral space or a vertebral body metastasis is identified, consideration should be given to careful evaluation of the epidural space.

Chronic Intestinal Obstruction

Abdominal pain is an almost invariable manifestation of chronic intestinal obstruction, which may occur in patients with colonic, rectal, or anal cancers.[80,81] The factors that contribute to this pain include contractions of smooth muscle; mesenteric tension, and mural ischemia. Obstructive symptoms may be due primarily to the tumor or, more likely, to a combination of mechanical obstruction and other processes such as autonomic neuropathy and ileus from metabolic derangements and drugs. Both continuous and colicky pain occur.[80,81] The pain is referred to the dermatomes corresponding to the spinal segments supplying the affected viscera. Vomiting, anorexia, and constipation are important associated symptoms. Abdominal radiographs taken in both the supine and erect positions may demonstrate the presence of air-fluid levels and intestinal distention. Scanning of the abdomen by CT or MRI can assess the extent and distribution of intraabdominal neoplasm, which has implications for subsequent treatment options.

Peritoneal Carcinomatosis

Colorectal cancer is among the most common causes of peritoneal carcinomatosis.[82] This condition can cause peritoneal inflammation, mesenteric tethering, malignant adhesions, and ascites,[83] all of which can cause pain. Mesenteric tethering and tension can cause a diffuse abdominal or low back pain. Tense, malignant ascites may produce a diffuse abdominal discomfort as well as a distinct stretching pain in the anterior abdominal wall. Adhesions can also cause obstruction of hollow viscus, with intermittent colicky pain.[84] Computed tomography may demonstrate evidence of ascites, omental infiltration, and peritoneal nodules.

Perineal Pain

Colorectal and anal cancers are the neoplastic diseases most commonly responsible for perineal pain.[85] The pain, which is typically described as constant and aching, is often aggravated by sitting or standing and may be associated with tenesmus or bladder spasms.[85] Perineal pain is most commonly caused by either local extension or local recurrence of tumor,[85] and postoperative recurrence of perineal pain is highly suggestive of local recurrence.[85] The pathologic finding of perineural invasion in resected tumor is highly predictive of the likelihood of local recurrence (80 percent); the vast majority of such recurrences (90 percent) are associated with pain as the predominant symptom.[86]

Tumor invasion of the musculature of the deep pelvis can also result in a syndrome that appears similar to the so-called tension myalgia of the pelvic floor.[87] The pain is typically described as a constant ache or heaviness that is exacerbated by upright posture. When due to tumor, the pain may be concurrent with other types of perineal pain. Digital examination of the pelvic floor may reveal local tenderness or palpable tumor.

Ureteric Obstruction

Carcinoma of the rectum is one of the most common tumors associated with this complication.[88,89] Pain may or may not accompany ureteric obstruction. When present, it is typically a dull, chronic discomfort in the flank. Colicky pain and pain radiating into the groin or genitalia can also occur. More frequently, unilateral

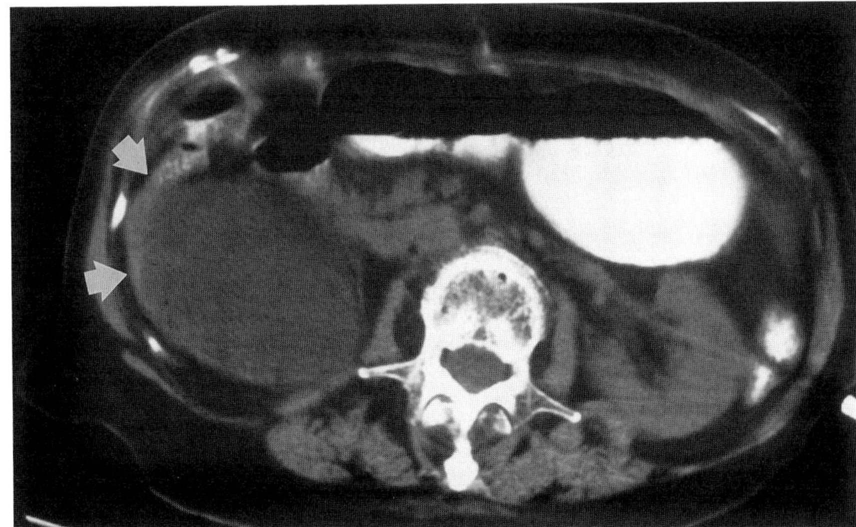

FIG. 109-3. Abdominal CT scan demonstrating massive right-sided hydronephrosis with marked cortical thinning (arrows) from a patient with a pelvic recurrence of rectal carcinoma who developed right-sided loin pain. (Adapted from Cherny NI, Portenoy RK: Cancer pain pathophysiology, assessment and syndromes, in Wall PD, Melzack R (eds): *Textbook of Pain, 3rd ed.* New York, Churchill Livingstone, 1994, in press. Reproduced by permission.)

obstruction is discovered following an incidental finding of unilateral hydronephrosis. Bilateral obstruction typically presents with symptoms of nausea, anorexia, lethargy, delirium, or anuria. Ureteric obstruction can be complicated by pyelonephritis or pyelonephrosis, which often present with features of sepsis, flank pain, and dysuria. Diagnosis of ureteric obstruction can be confirmed by the demonstration of hydronephrosis on renal sonography.[90,91] The level of obstruction can be demonstrated by pyelography, and CT scanning techniques will usually demonstrate the cause (Fig. 109-3).[88,91]

Pain Syndromes Involving the Peripheral Nervous System

Lumbosacral Plexopathy

In the cancer population, lumbosacral plexopathy is usually caused by neoplastic infiltration or compression. Polyradiculopathy from leptomeningeal metastases or epidural metastases can mimic lumbosacral plexopathy, and the evaluation of the patient must consider these lesions as well (see below). Occasional patients develop lumbosacral plexopathy as a result of surgical trauma, radiation therapy, infarction, cytotoxic damage, infection in the pelvis or psoas muscle, abdominal aneurysm, or idiopathic lumbosacral neuritis.[92–96]

Malignant Lumbosacral Plexopathy. Colorectal cancer is among the most common causes of malignant lumbosacral plexopathy.[51,97] In general, tumors involve the plexus by direct extension from intrapelvic neoplasm; metastases account for only one-fourth of the cases.[97] In one study, two-thirds of patients developed plexopathy within 3 years of their primary diagnosis and one-third presented within 1 year.[97]

Pain is the first symptom reported by most patients with malignant lumbosacral plexopathy and is experienced by almost all patients during the course of the disease. The pain may be experienced in the lower abdomen, inguinal region, buttock, or leg.[97] The quality is usually aching, pressurelike, or stabbing. Most patients also experience numbness, paresthesias, and weakness weeks to months after the pain begins. Common signs include leg weakness that involves multiple myotomes, sensory loss that crosses dermatomes, reflex asymmetry, focal tenderness, leg edema, and positive direct or reverse straight-leg-raising signs.

Upper plexus involvement occurs in almost one-third of patients[97] and is most commonly due to direct extension from a colorectal tumor. Pain may be experienced in the lower abdomen, flank, iliac crest, or anterolateral thigh. Examination findings include sensory, motor and reflex changes in a L1-4 distribution. A subgroup of these patients presents with a syndrome characterized by pain and paresthesias limited to the lower abdomen or inguinal region, with occasional sensory loss and no motor findings. Computed tomography in the latter patients may show tumor adjacent to the L1 vertebra (the L1 syndrome)[97] or along the pelvic side wall, where it presumably damages the ilioinguinal, iliohypogastric, or genitofemoral nerve. Another subgroup of patients have neoplastic involvement of the psoas muscle and present with a syndrome characterized by upper lumbosacral plexopathy and painful flexion of the ipsilateral hip, with positive psoas muscle stretch test. This has been termed the *malignant psoas syndrome*.[98]

A lower plexopathy occurs in just over 50 percent of patients[97] and in this population is usually due to direct extension from a rectal cancer. Pain may be localized in the buttocks and perineum or referred to the

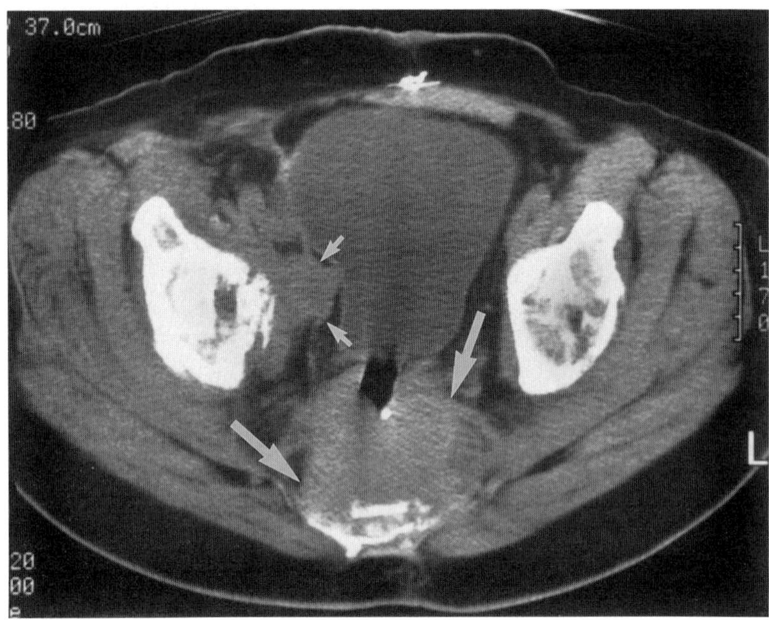

FIG. 109-4. Pelvic CT scan demonstrating a presacral mass that erodes the sacrum (large arrows) and involves the plexus in the right pelvic sidewall (small arrows). (Adapted from Cherny NI, Portenoy RK: Cancer pain pathophysiology, assessment and syndromes, in Wall PD, Melzack R (eds): *Textbook of Pain, 3rd ed.* New York, Churchill Livingstone, 1994, in press. Reproduced by permission.)

posterolateral thigh and leg. Associated symptoms and signs conform to an L4-S1 segmental distribution. Examination may reveal weakness or sensory changes in the L5 and S1 dermatomes and depressed ankle jerks. Other findings include leg edema, bladder or bowel dysfunction, sacral or sciatic notch tenderness, and a positive straight-leg-raising test. A pelvic mass may be palpable.

Sacral plexopathy may occur from direct extension of a sacral lesion or a presacral mass. This may present with predominant involvement of the lumbosacral trunk, characterized by pain over the dorsal media foot and sole and weakness of knee flexion, ankle dorsiflexion, and inversion. Other patients demonstrate particular involvement of the coccygeal plexus, with prominent sphincter dysfunction and perineal pain.

A panplexopathy with involvement in a L1-S3 distribution occurs in almost one-fifth of patients with lumbosacral plexopathy.[97] Local pain may occur in the lower abdomen, buttocks, or perineum. Referred pain can be experienced anywhere in distribution of the plexus. Leg edema is extremely common. Neurologic deficits may be confluent or patchy over the L1-S3 distribution, and the straight-leg-raising test is usually positive.

Autonomic dysfunction, particularly anhydrosis and vasodilatation, has been associated with plexus and peripheral nerve injuries[99] and has been reported as the presenting symptom of metastatic lumbosacral plexopathy.[100,101] These findings may help in determining the anatomic location of the lesion.[102]

Cross-sectional imaging, with either CT or MRI, is the usual diagnostic procedure to evaluate lumbosacral plexopathy (Fig. 109-4). Scanning should be done from the level of the L1 vertebral body, through the sciatic notch. When CT scanning techniques are being used, images should include bone and soft tissue windows. Definitive imaging of the epidural space adjacent to the plexus should be considered in the patient who has features indicative of a relatively high risk of epidural extension, including bilateral symptoms or signs, unexplained incontinence, or a prominent paraspinal mass.[97,103]

Bone Pain

Bone metastases arising from carcinomas of the colon or rectum have a low incidence, but by virtue of the high prevalence of these conditions, they accounted for over 20 percent of bone metastases observed on autopsy study.[104] Bone metastases potentially cause pain by multiple mechanisms, including endosteal or periosteal nociceptor activation by mechanical distortion or release of chemical mediators (such as prostaglandins, bradykinin, substance P, and histamine) and by tumor growth into adjacent soft tissues and nerves.[105]

Bone pain due to metastatic tumor must be differentiated from less common types of chronic bone pain in cancer patients. Nonneoplastic causes in this population include osteoporotic pathologic fractures and focal osteonecrosis, which may be idiopathic or related to the use of corticosteroids or previous radiotherapy.

In general, the vertebrae are the most common sites of bony metastases.[106,107] Vertebral metastases of colorectal tumors most commonly arise in the lumbosacral spine.[106,108] The early recognition of pain syndromes due to neoplastic invasion of vertebral bodies is essential, since pain usually precedes compression of adjacent neural structures and prompt primary therapy directed at the lesion may prevent the subsequent development of neurologic deficits. This recognition often requires substantial clinical acumen; referral of pain is common, and the associated symptoms and signs can mimic a variety of other disorders, both malignant (e.g., paraspinal masses) and nonmalignant.

Vertebral Syndromes

Atlantoaxial Destruction and Odontoid Fractures. Destruction of the atlas or fracture of the odontoid process typically presents with nuchal or occipital pain. Pain often radiates over the posterior aspect of the skull to the vertex and is exacerbated by movement of the neck, particularly flexion.[109] Pathologic fracture may result in secondary subluxation, with ensuing compression of the spinal cord at the cervicomedullary junction.

C7-T1 Syndrome. Invasion of C7 or T1 vertebrae can result in pain referred to the interscapular region. These lesions may be missed if radiographic evaluation is mistakenly targeted to the painful area caudal to the site of damage. Additionally, visualization of the appropriate region on routine radiographs may be inadequate due to obscuration by overlying bone and mediastinal shadows. Bone scintigraphy may assist in targeting additional diagnostic imaging procedures, particularly CT or MRI.

T12-L1 Syndrome. T12 or L1 vertebral lesions can refer pain to the ipsilateral iliac crest or the sacroiliac joint. Imaging procedures directed at pelvic bones will therefore miss the source of the pain.

Sacral Syndrome. Severe focal pain radiating to buttocks, perineum, or posterior thighs may accompany destruction of the sacrum. The pain is often exacerbated by sitting or lying and is relieved by standing or walking. Lateral spread to involve muscles that rotate the hip (e.g., the pyriformis muscle) may produce a malignant "pyriformis syndrome," characterized by buttock or posterior leg pain that is exacerbated by internal rotation of the hip. Local extension of the tumor mass may also involve the sacral plexus, resulting in neurologic deficits, most importantly sphincter dysfunction (see below).

Back Pain and Epidural Spinal Cord Compression

In general, epidural compression (EC) of the spinal cord or cauda equina is a common neurologic complication of cancer, occurring in up to 10 percent of patients;[110] tumors of the distal gastrointestinal tract account for less than 5 percent of these episodes.[106,108,111] Most EC is caused by posterior extension of vertebral body metastasis to the epidural space, others are caused by tumor extension from the posterior arch of the vertebra or infiltration of a paravertebral tumor through the intervertebral foramen.

Untreated EC leads inevitably to neurologic compromise, ultimately including paraplegia or quadriplegia. Effective treatment can potentially prevent these complications. The efficacy of treatment is determined by numerous factors, the most salient of which is the degree of neurologic impairment at the time therapy is initiated. Of patients who begin treatment while ambulatory, 75 percent remain so; the efficacy of treatment declines to 30 to 50 percent for those who begin treatment while markedly paretic, and it is less than 10 percent for those who are plegic.[103,106,110,112,113] Treatment generally involves the administration of corticosteroids (see below) and radiotherapy (RT). Surgical decompression is considered for some patients with radioresistant tumors, those who have previously received maximal RT to the involved field, those with spinal instability, and those for whom no other tissue is available for histologic diagnosis.[110,111] Decompressive laminectomy for posteriorly located lesions and anterior vertebrectomy with spinal stabilization for lesions arising from the vertebral body are the currently recommended procedures.[114–116] Decompressive laminectomy in the setting of vertebral body collapse is not recommended because of the risk of neurologic deterioration or spinal instability (22 to 25 percent) induced by the procedure.[117,118]

Back pain, however, is a nonspecific symptom, which can result from bony or paraspinal metastases without epidural encroachment, from retroperitoneal or leptomeningeal tumor, or from a large variety of other benign conditions including musculoskeletal disorders.[110] Since it is impracticable to pursue an extensive evaluation in every patient who develops back pain, the assessment of this symptom must include a systematic evaluation that determines the likelihood of EC and thereby selects patients appropriate for further investigation of the epidural space. The selection process is based on symptoms and signs and the results of simple and inexpensive imaging techniques. The clinical features suggestive of epidural extension are listed in Table 109-5.

Imaging Modalities. Definitive imaging of the epidural space confirms the existence of EC (and thereby indicates the necessity and urgency of treatment), determines the extent of epidural encroachment (which influences prognosis and may alter the therapeutic approach), and defines the appropriate radiation portals.[119] The options for definitive imaging include MRI, myelography, and CT myelography (Figs. 109-5 and 109-6). MRI, which is noninvasive and offers accurate soft tissue imaging and multiplanar views, is generally preferred. Myelography remains the investigative mo-

Table 109-5
Clinical Features Suggestive of Epidural Spinal Cord and Cauda Equina Compression

Clinical features	*Notes*
Rapid progression of back pain	Ominous occurrence
Radicular pain	Can be intermittent, constant or lancinating Usually unilateral in cervical and lumbosacral regions Usually bilateral in the thorax Exacerbated by recumbency, cough, sneeze, or Valsalva
Weakness	Segmental: suggestive of radiculopathy Lumbosacral multisegmental: suggestive of cauda equina compression Pyramidal distribution: suggestive of spinal cord compression Variable rate of progression After development of weakness, 30 percent develop paraplegia within 7 days
Sensory abnormalities	May also begin segmentally May ultimately evolve to a sensory level Upper level of sensory findings may correspond to the location of the epidural tumor
Bladder and bowel dysfunction	Generally occurs late Early symptoms of conus medullaris or cauda equina lesion
Musculoskeletal features	Scoliosis Asymmetrical wasting of paravertebral musculature Gibbus (palpable step) in the dorsal spine Spinal tenderness to percussion

dality of choice for patients who lack access to MRI and those unable to undergo the procedure. MRI is relatively contraindicated in patients with severe claustrophobia and absolutely contraindicated for patients with metallic implants, cardiac pacemakers, or aneurysm clips.

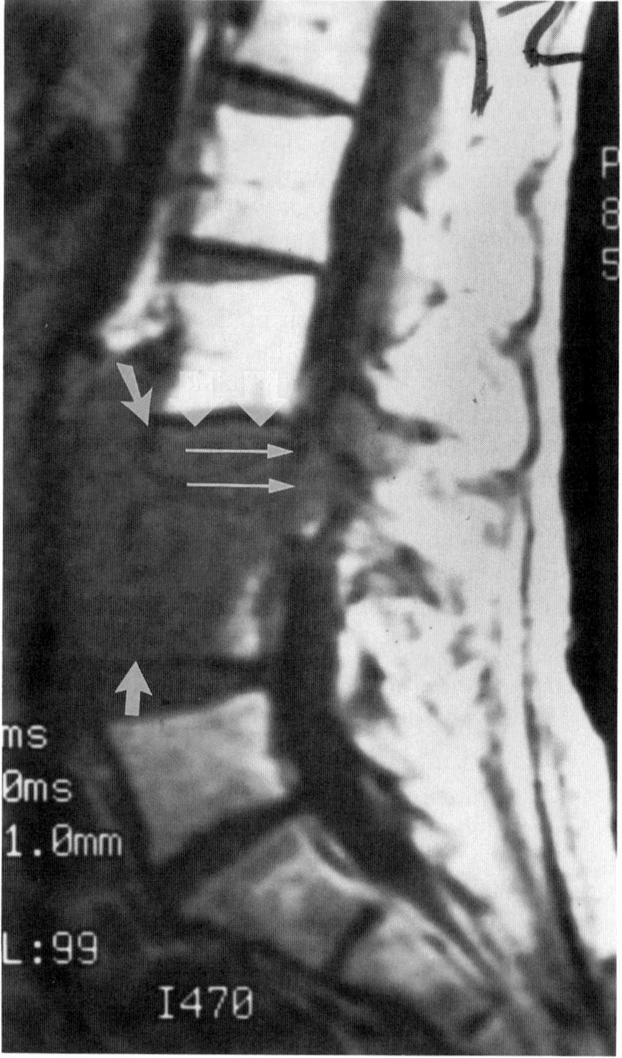

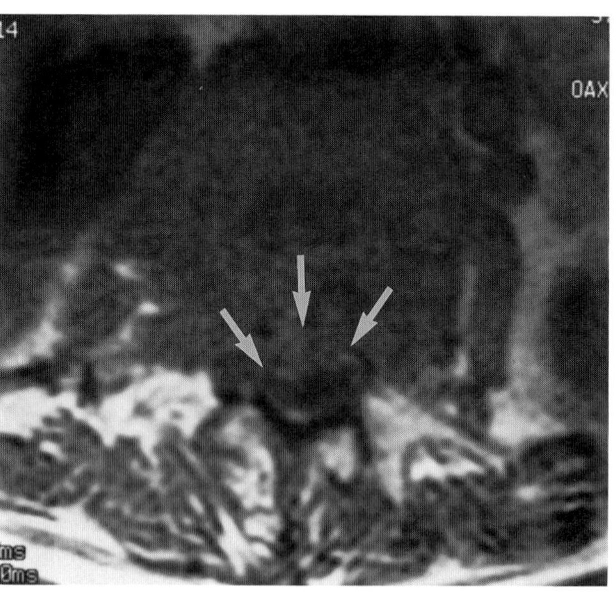

FIG. 109-5. Sagittal and axial MRI scans of the lumbar spine in a 56-year-old woman with carcinoma of the colon who presented with back pain and L3 radicular pain in the right leg. The sagittal scan demonstrates extensive destruction of both L3 and L4 vertebral bodies (vertical arrows). There is posterior extension of the tumor into the epidural space which compresses the spinal cord (horizontal arrows). The axial scan performed through L3 demonstrates complete obliteration of the epidural space (arrows) and severe compression of the thecal sac. (Adapted from Cherny NI, Portenoy RK: Cancer pain pathophysiology, assessment and syndromes, in Wall PD, Melzack R (eds): *Textbook of Pain, 3rd ed.* New York, Churchill Livingstone, 1994, in press. Reproduced by permission.)

Algorithm for the Investigation of Cancer Patients with Back Pain. Given the prevalence and the potentially dire consequences of EC and the recognition that back pain is a marker of early (and therefore treatable) EC, algorithms have been developed to guide the evaluation of back pain in the cancer patient. The objective of these algorithms is to select a subgroup who should undergo definitive imaging of the epidural space from among the large number of patients who develop back pain.[119] Effective treatment of EC before irreversible neurologic compromise occurs is the overriding goal of these approaches. One such algorithm defines both the urgency and course of the evaluation (Fig. 109-7).

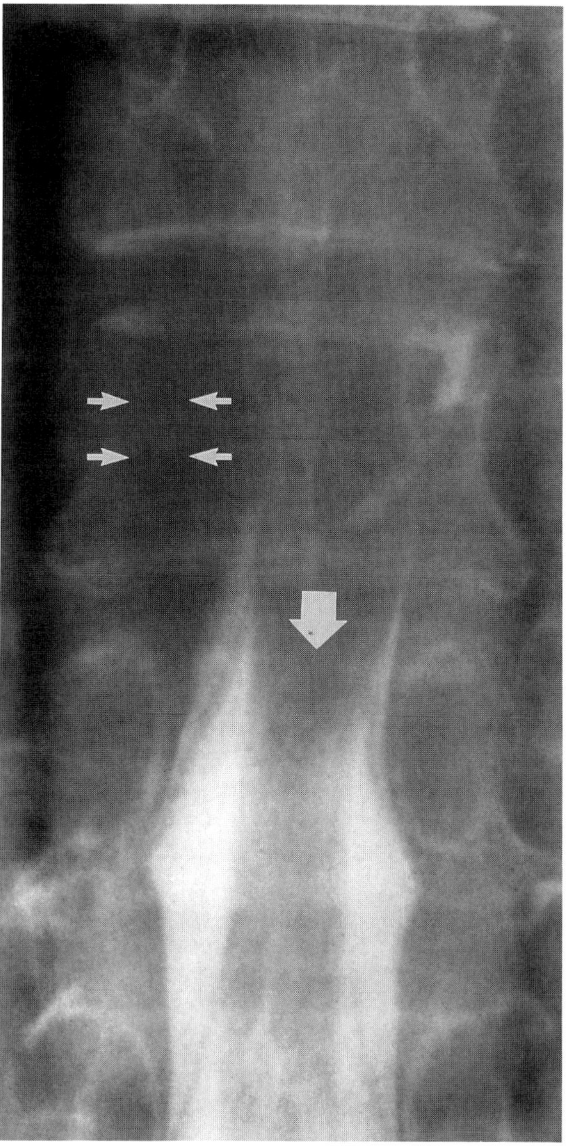

FIG. 109-6. Segment of a thoracic myelogram (T8, 9, 10, and 11) performed on a 54-year-old woman with severe mid-back pain. There is a complete block to the flow of contrast at the T9 level (large arrow). The left pedicle of the T9 vertebra is absent due to metastatic erosion (small arrows). (Adapted from Cherny NI, Portenoy RK: Cancer pain pathophysiology, assessment and syndromes, in Wall PD, Melzack R (eds): *Textbook of Pain, 3rd ed.* New York, Churchill Livingstone, 1994, in press. Reproduced by permission.)

Patients with emerging symptoms and signs indicative of spinal cord or cauda equina dysfunction are designated group 1. The evaluation (and, if appropriate, treatment) of these patients should proceed on an emergency basis. Unless contraindicated, these patients should receive an intravenous dose of corticosteroid before epidural imaging is performed. High-dose dexamethasone is customarily used. One regimen advocates an initial intravenous bolus of 100 mg followed by 96 mg/day in divided doses, which is tapered over 3 to 4 weeks.

Patients with symptoms and signs of radiculopathy or stable or mild signs of spinal cord or cauda equina dysfunction are designated group 2. These patients are also usually treated presumptively with a corticosteroid (typically with a more moderate dose) and are scheduled for definitive imaging of the epidural space as soon as possible.

Group 3 patients have back pain and no symptoms or signs suggesting EC. These patients should be evaluated in routine fashion beginning with plain spine radiographs. The presence at the appropriate level of any abnormality consistent with neoplasm indicates a high probability (60 percent) of EC.[120] Definitive imaging of the epidural space is strongly indicated in patients who have >50 percent vertebral body collapse, and it is generally recommended for patients with pedicle erosion. In patients with back pain and normal bone radiography, a positive scintigram at the site of pain is associated with a 12 to 17 percent likelihood of epidural disease.[103,121] If both radiographs and scintigraphy are normal but the patient has severe or progressive pain, evaluation with CT or preferably MRI may still be warranted.

Pain Syndromes of the Bony Pelvis and Hip

The pelvis and hip are common sites of metastatic involvement. The weight-bearing function of these structures, essential for normal ambulation, contributes to the propensity of disease at these sites to cause incident pain with ambulation.

Hip Joint Syndrome. Tumor involvement of the acetabulum or head of the femur typically produces localized hip pain, which is aggravated by weight bearing and movement of the hip. The pain may radiate to the knee or medial thigh, and occasionally this is the only site of pain.[122] Medial extension of acetabular tumor can involve the lumbosacral plexus as it traverses the pelvic side wall. Plain radiographs and bone scintigraphy usually demonstrate bony involvement; however, CT and MRI tomographic techniques are more

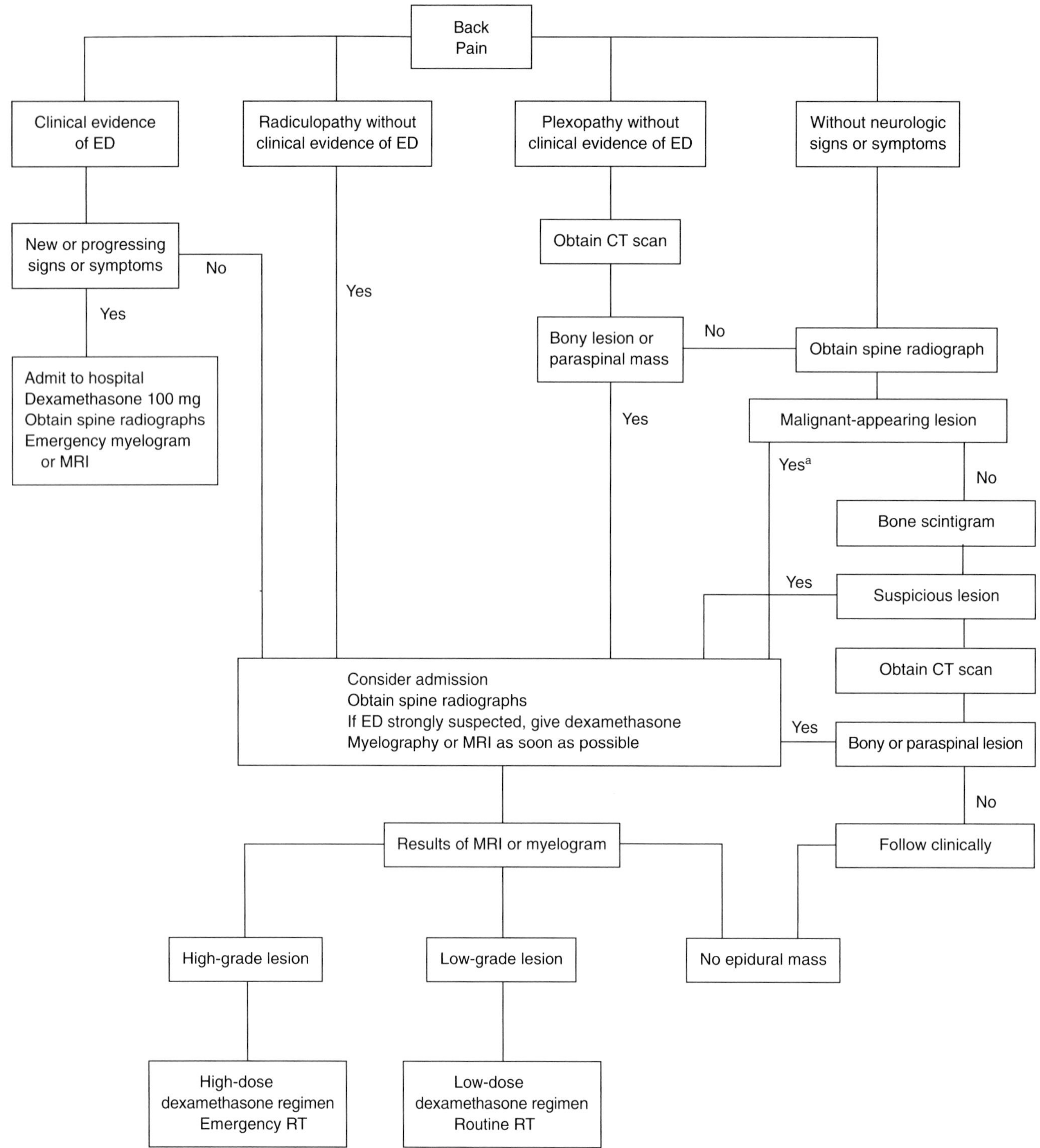

[a] Definitive imaging is strongly recommended if vertebral collapse is present. The clinician may consider foregoing definitive imaging if lesion is limited to the body of the vertebra. A CT scan may be needed to define the limits of the lesion; definitive imaging should be done if the bony cortex adjacent to the spinal canal is compromised.

FIG. 109-7. Algorithm for the management of back pain in the cancer patient. Abbreviations: ED, epidural disease; CT, computed tomography; MRI, magnetic resonance imaging; RT, radiation therapy. Abbreviations: ED, epidural disease; CT, computed tomography; MRI, magnetic resonance imaging; RT, radiation therapy. (From Portenoy RK; Evaluation of back pain in the patient with cancer. J Back Pain Musculoskel Rehab, 3:44–52, 1992. Reproduced by permission.)

sensitive, and they also demonstrate the extent of adjacent soft tissue involvement.[123]

Headache and Facial Pain

Tumor-related headache is a relatively uncommon cancer pain problem in the colorectal and anal cancer population. Cancer-related headache results from traction, inflammation, or infiltration of pain-sensitive structures in the head and neck.[124]

Brain Metastases

The incidence of cerebral metastases in patients with colorectal cancer is approximately 5 percent.[125,126] Headache is a common presenting symptom in patients with brain metastases, occurring in 60 to 90 percent; patients with multiple metastases and those with posterior fossa metastases are most likely to report this symptom.[126–128] The quality of the headache may be throbbing or steady, and the intensity is usually mild to moderate. The location may be local or generalized; when lateralized, it usually overlies the site of the lesion, but posterior fossa lesions often cause a bifrontal headache.[124] The headache is often worse in the morning and is exacerbated by stooping, sudden head movement, or Valsalva maneuvers (cough, sneeze, or strain).

Leptomeningeal Metastases

Leptomeningeal metastases, characterized by diffuse or multifocal involvement of the subarachnoid space by metastatic tumor, are rare in colorectal carcinoma. Generalized headache and radicular pain in the low back and buttocks are the most common pains associated with leptomeningeal metastases.[129,130] The headache may be associated with changes in mental status, nausea, vomiting, tinnitus, and nuchal rigidity. Focal or multifocal neurologic symptoms or signs may involve any level of the neuraxis.[131,132] The diagnosis is confirmed through analysis of the cerebrospinal fluid (CSF) which may reveal elevated pressure, elevated protein, depressed glucose, lymphocytic pleocytosis, and positive cytology. Ninety percent of patients ultimately show positive cytology, but multiple analyses may be required.[129,130,133]

Base-of-Skull Metastases

Bony metastases to the base of skull are associated with well-described clinical syndromes,[134] named according to the site of metastatic involvement: orbital, parasellar, middle fossa, jugular foramen, occipital condyle, clivus, and sphenoid sinus (Table 109-6). When base-of-skull metastases are suspected, CT scan with bone window settings is the diagnostic procedure of choice to evaluate bony disease;[134] MRI is most sensitive for assessing soft tissue extension; and CSF analysis may be needed to exclude leptomeningeal metastases.[135]

Table 109-6
Pain Syndromes Associated with Base-of-Skull Metastases

Syndrome	*Usual presentation*
Orbital	Progressive ipsilateral retroorbital and supraorbital pain
Parasellar	Unilateral supraorbital and frontal headache may be associated with diplopia, may be opthalmoparesis or papilledema, or may demonstrate hemianopsia or quadrantinopsia
Middle cranial fossa	Facial numbness in the distribution of second or third divisions of the trigeminal nerve, paresthesias or pain referred to the cheek or jaw
Jugular foramen	Hoarseness of dysphagia, pain referred to the ipsilateral ear or mastoid, occasionally glossopharyngeal neuralgia with or without syncope
Occipital condyle	Unilateral occipital pain worsened with neck flexion and associated with stiffness of the neck
Clivus	Vertex headache, which is often exacerbated by neck flexion; lower cranial nerve (VI–XII) dysfunction (may become bilateral)
Sphenoid sinus	Bifrontal headache radiating to the temporal region and intermittent retroorbital pain

Painful Cranial Neuralgias

Glossopharyngeal and trigeminal neuralgias can occur from metastases in the base of the skull or leptomeninges. Each of these syndromes has a characteristic presentation.[135] Early diagnosis is critical to prevent progressive neurologic injury.

Chronic Pain Syndromes Associated with Cancer Therapy

Most treatment-related pains caused by tissue-damaging procedures are acute and are remarkable for their predictability and self-limited natural history. Chronic treatment-related pain syndromes are associated with either a persistent nociceptive complication of an invasive treatment, such as a postsurgical abscess, or, more commonly, to neural injury.[135] In some cases, these syndromes occur long after the therapy is completed, resulting in a difficult differential diagnosis between recurrent disease and a complication of therapy.

Chronic Postsurgical Pain Syndromes

Phantom Anus Syndrome. Phantom pain is perceived to arise from a resected body structure, as if the structure were still contiguous with the body. A phantom anus pain syndrome occurs in approximately 15 percent of patients who undergo abdominoperineal resection of the rectum.[136,137] Phantom anus pain may develop either in the early postoperative period or after a latency of months to years.[136,138] Late-onset pain is almost always associated with tumor recurrence.[138]

Postsurgical Pelvic Floor Myalgia. Surgical trauma to the pelvic floor can cause a residual pelvic floor myalgia, which—like the neoplastic syndrome described previously—mimics so-called tension myalgia.[87] The risk of disease recurrence associated with this condition is not known, and its natural history has not been defined. In patients who have undergone anorectal resection, this condition must be differentiated from the phantom anus syndrome (see above).

Postsurgical Lumbosacral Plexopathy. Surgical trauma to the lumbosacral plexus during deep pelvic resection can result in persistent neurologic dysfunction and pain.

Chronic Postradiation Pain Syndromes

Chronic pain occurring as a complication of radiation therapy tends to occur late in the course of a patient's illness. These syndromes must always be differentiated from recurrent tumor.

Radiation-Induced Lumbosacral Plexopathy. Radiation fibrosis of the lumbosacral plexus is rare and may occur from 1 to over 30 years following radiation treatment. Radiation-induced plexopathy typically presents with progressive weakness and leg swelling; pain is not usually a prominent feature.[139] Weakness begins distally in the L5-S1 segments and is slowly progressive. The symptoms and signs are often bilateral.[139] If CT scanning demonstrates a lesion, it is usually a nonspecific diffuse infiltration of the tissues. Electromyography may show myokymic discharges.[139]

Chronic Radiation Enteritis and Proctitis. Chronic enteritis and proctocolitis occur as a delayed complication in 2 to 10 percent of patients who undergo abdominal or pelvic radiation therapy.[140,141] The rectum and rectosigmoid are more commonly involved than the small bowel,[141] a pattern that may relate to the retroperitoneal fixation of the former structures. The latency is variable (3 months to 30 years).[140,141] Chronic radiation injury to the rectum can present as proctitis (with bloody diarrhea, tenesmus, and cramping pain), obstruction due to stricture formation, or fistulas to the bladder or vagina.[140,141] Radiation damage to the small bowel typically causes colicky abdominal pain, which can be associated with chronic nausea or malabsorption.[140,141] Barium studies may demonstrate a narrow tubular bowel segment resembling that of Crohn's disease or ischemic colitis. Endoscopic imaging and biopsy may be necessary to distinguish suspicious lesions from recurrent cancer.[141]

Burning Perineum Syndrome. Persistent perineal discomfort is an uncommon delayed complication of pelvic radiotherapy. After a latency of 6 to 18 months, persistent burning pain develops in the perianal region; the pain may extend anteriorly to involve the vagina or scrotum.[142] In patients who have had abdominoperineal resection, phantom anus pain and recurrent tumor are major elements in the differential diagnosis. Appropriate studies must be done to exclude recurrent neoplasm.

Chronic Radiation Myelopathy. Chronic radiation myelopathy is a late complication of spinal cord irradiation that is rarely seen in this population. The latency interval is highly variable but is most commonly 12 to 14 months. Common presentations include a progressive Brown-Sequard syndrome[143] or partial transverse myelopathy. Sensory symptoms, including pain, typically precede the development of progressive motor and autonomic dysfunction.[144] Imaging studies, particularly MRI, are important to exclude an epidural lesion and to demonstrate the nature and extent of intrinsic cord pathology, which may include atrophy, swelling, or syrinx.[144] The course of chronic radiation myelopathy is usually characterized by steady progression over months, followed by a subsequent phase of slow progression or stabilization.

Osteoradionecrosis. Osteoradionecrosis is a late complication of radiotherapy which, though usually painless, may be characterized by the development of a painful focus of necrotic bone. Overlying tissue breakdown can occur spontaneously or as a result of trauma.[145,146] Delayed development of a painful ulcer must be differentiated from tumor recurrence.

MANAGEMENT OF CHRONIC CANCER PAIN

General Considerations

Optimal management of pain problems in this population requires familiarity with a range of therapeutic options including antineoplastic therapies, analgesic pharmacotherapy, and anesthetic, neurosurgical, psychological, and physiatric techniques (Table 109-7). Successful pain management is characterized by the implementation of the techniques with the most favorable therapeutic index for the prevailing circumstances along with provision for repeated evaluations, so that a favorable balance between pain relief and adverse effects is maintained.[147–149] Currently available techniques can provide adequate relief to a vast majority of patients.

Table 109-7
Analgesic Therapies for Cancer Pain

Therapy	*Examples*
Primary therapy	Chemotherapy Radiotherapy Hormone therapy Immunotherapy Surgery Antibiotics
Systemic analgesic pharmacotherapy	Nonopioid analgesics Opioids Adjuvant analgesics
Anesthetic techniques	Intraspinal opioids Neural blockade
Neurosurgical techniques	Rhizotomy Cordotomy
Physiatric techniques	Orthoses Physical therapy
Psychologic techniques	Relaxation training Distraction techniques
Neurostimulatory techniques	Transcutaneous electrical nerve stimulation (TENS) Dorsal column stimulation Deep brain stimulation Acupuncture

Primary Therapy

The assessment process may reveal a cause for the pain that is amenable to etiologically directed primary therapy. For pain produced by tumor infiltration or compression, antineoplastic treatment with surgery, radiotherapy, chemotherapy, or other novel approaches may be considered. Pain caused by infections may be amenable to antibiotic therapy or drainage procedures. If successful, such primary therapy can have profound analgesic consequences.

Radiotherapy

Although it is generally true that RT has a pivotal role in the palliative treatment of bone metastases,[150,151] epidural spinal cord compression,[150] and cerebral metastases,[152] data specific to metastases arising from the colon, rectum, and anus are not available. Guidelines for the evaluation of the role of palliative RT have been described: a high likelihood of efficacy should be anticipated, the treatment should not entail significant risk of adverse effects, the duration of treatment should be short, and it should offer a greater palliative index than other available therapeutic modalities.[153] There is a paucity of data regarding the efficacy of RT in the management of pelvic plexopathic pain. There is a stated impression that palliative RT for malignant lumbosacral plexopathy often yields partial relief of short duration.[153] The results with the perineal pain of low sacral plexopathy and the phantom anus syndrome are more encouraging.[153,154] Hepatic RT, with 2000 to 3000 rad, is generally well tolerated and can relieve the pain of hepatic capsular distention in 50 to 90 percent of patients.[155–158]

Chemotherapy

The therapeutic index of chemotherapy in the management of cancer pain is related to the balance between its antineoplastic efficacy and cost factors of toxicity and out-of-hospital opportunity cost. There is little information on the specific analgesic or quality-of-life benefit of chemotherapy.[159] Chemotherapy has been reported to be of analgesic value in patients with and without significant tumor shrinkage.[160] Patients with advanced colonic or rectal cancer have a relatively low likelihood of objective tumor response (10 to 40 percent) to chemotherapy.[161] Palliative chemotherapy for colorectal cancer should be administered as a trial of therapy in addition to specific analgesic treatment. Squamous cell cancer of the anus, in contrast, can be highly responsive to combined-modality treatment, and an impressive cure rate is reported even with advanced disease.[162,163] The response to salvage chemotherapy for recurrent anal cancer is variable, and long duration of initial response is predictive of a higher likelihood of second response.

Surgery

Surgery may have a role in the relief of symptoms caused by specific mechanical problems such as obstruction of a hollow viscus, unstable bony structures, and compression of neural structures.[159,164–167] Against the potential benefits must be weighed the considerations of the likelihood and duration of benefit, the direct risks of surgery, and the anticipated length of hospitalization and convalescence.[164] Clinical experience suggests that the surgical interventions of high palliative index include the stabilization of pathologic fractures, the relief of remediable bowel obstructions, and the drainage of symptomatic ascites. Paracentesis may provide prompt relief from the pain and discomfort of tense ascites. The duration of relief is generally short unless large volumes are drained. Large-volume paracentesis, up to 5 to 10 L, can provide more durable palliation[164,168] and can be drained with small risk of hypotension[168,169] or diminution of serum protein levels.[170] Radical surgery to excise locally advanced disease in patients with no evidence of metastatic spread may be of both palliative and survival value to some patients.[171–173] Successful management of pain associated with uncontrollable recurrent pelvic tumors ulcerating through the perineum after radical surgical debridement with perineal reconstruction has been reported.[174]

Antibiotic Therapy

Antibiotics may be analgesic when the source of the pain involves infection. Illustrative examples include chronic sinus infections, pelvic abscess, pyelonephrosis, and osteitis pubis.[175,176] In some cases, infections may be occult and confirmed only by the symptomatic relief provided by empiric treatment with these drugs.[177,178]

Analgesic Therapy—An Overview

For the large majority of patients, pain management involves specific analgesic approaches. Systemic pharmacologic therapy is the mainstay[13,61,179] and should be integrated with psychological and physiatric techniques. Anesthetic and neurosurgical techniques should be considered for the patient who has not obtained satisfactory pain relief. In all cases, these analgesic treatments must be skillfully integrated with the management of other symptoms.

The "Analgesic Ladder" Approach to Systemic Pharmacotherapy

An expert committee convened by the Cancer Unit of the World Health Organization (WHO) has proposed a useful approach to drug selection for cancer pain, which has become known as the "analgesic ladder."[179]

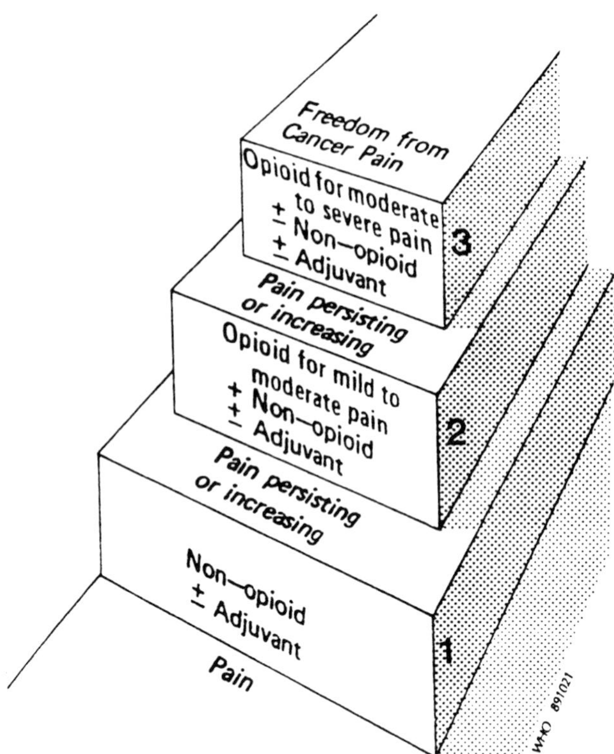

FIG. 109-8. WHO Three-step analgesic ladder. [From Cancer Pain Relief and Palliative Care: Report of a WHO Expert Committee. Geneva, World Health Organization, 1990 (WHO Technical Report Series, No. 804), Fig. 1. Reproduced by permission.]

Combined with appropriate dosing guidelines, this approach is capable of providing adequate relief to 70 to 90 percent of patients.[180–184] Emphasizing that pain intensity should be the prime consideration in the selection of analgesia, the approach advocates three basic steps, as outlined in Fig. 109-8:

1. Patients with mild to moderate cancer-related pain should be treated with a nonopioid analgesic, which should be combined with an adjuvant analgesic if a specific indication for one exists. For example, a patient with continual leg pain of mild to moderate intensity caused by postradiation lumbosacral plexopathy may benefit from a tricyclic antidepressant agent in addition to acetaminophen.
2. Patients who are relatively intolerant of drugs and present with moderate to severe pain or who fail to achieve adequate relief after a trial of a nonopioid analgesic should be treated with a "weak" opioid (e.g., codeine, oxycodone, or propoxyphene); this drug is typically combined with a nonopioid and may be coadministered with an adjuvant analgesic.
3. Patients who present with severe pain or fail to achieve adequate relief following appropriate administration of drugs on the second rung of the analgesic ladder should receive a "strong" opioid, which may also be combined with a nonopioid analgesic or an adjuvant drug.

Systemic Analgesic Pharmacotherapy

Nonopioid Analgesics

General Considerations. The nonopioid analgesics are useful alone for mild to moderate pain (step 1 of the analgesic ladder) and provide additive analgesia when combined with opioid drugs in the treatment of more severe pain. Unlike opioid analgesics, these drugs have a "ceiling" effect for analgesia and produce neither tolerance nor physical dependence. The nonopioid analgesics comprise numerous subclasses (Table 109-8). Some of these agents, like aspirin and the NSAIDs, inhibit the enzyme cyclooxygenase and consequently block the biosynthesis of prostaglandins, inflammatory mediators known to sensitize peripheral nociceptors.[185] A central mechanism is also likely[186] and appears to predominate in acetaminophen analgesia.[187]

Dosing. The optimal administration of nonopioid analgesics requires an understanding of their clinical pharmacology,[188] including potential adverse effects and dosing guidelines appropriate in the management of cancer pain. The concept of dose titration is particularly important in this population. Since the minimal effective analgesic dose is unknown for any individual patient and both analgesic and side effects of these drugs are, at least in part, dose-dependent, it is reasonable to initiate therapy at a relatively low dose and then explore the dose-response relationship through gradual dose escalation until the ceiling dose is reached.

Adverse Effects. Safe administration of these agents requires familiarity with their potential adverse effects.[188] Aspirin and the other NSAIDs have a broad spectrum of potential toxicity: bleeding diathesis due to inhibition of platelet aggregation, peptic ulcer disease, and renal impairment are the most common. Infrequent adverse effects include confusion, precipitation of cardiac failure, and exacerbation of hypertension. Particular caution is required in the administration of these agents to patients at increased risk of adverse effects, including those with blood clotting disorders, a predilection to peptic ulceration, or impaired renal function as well as those receiving concurrent corticosteroid therapy and the elderly.

Table 109-8
Commonly Used Nonopioid Analgesics

Chemical class	*Generic name*	*Half life, hours*	*Starting dose, mg*	*Maximum recommended dose, mg/day*	*Comments*
Nonacidic	Acetaminophen	3–4	750 q4h	6000	Available over the counter
Salicylates	Aspirin	3–12	650 q4–6h	6000	Available over the counter
	Diflunisal	8–12	500 q12h	1500	Less GI toxicity than aspirin
	Choline magnesium trisalicylate	8–12	1000 q12h	4000	Minimal GI toxicity. No effect on platelet function at usual doses
	Salsalate	8–12	1000 q12h	4000	Minimal GI toxicity. No effect on platelet function at usual doses
Proprionic acids	Ibuprofen	3–4	400 q6h	4200	Available over the counter
	Naproxen	1–3	250 q12h	1000	
	Fenoprofen	2–3	200 q6h	3200	
Acetic acids	Indomethacin	4–5	25 q12h	200	Sustained-release and rectal preparations
	Sulindac	14	150 q12h	400	
	Diclofenac	2	25 q8h	200	
	Ketorolac tromethamine	4–7	30 q6h	240	Oral or parenteral preparation
Oxicams	Piroxicam	45	20 q24h	40	

Acetaminophen has fewer adverse effects than the acidic nonopioid analgesics; gastrointestinal toxicity is rare and there are no adverse effects on platelet function. Hepatic toxicity is possible, however, and patients with chronic alcoholism and liver disease can develop severe hepatotoxicity even when the drug is taken in usual therapeutic doses.[189] Acute overdose of acetaminophen can produce hepatic necrosis, and death can occur after a single dose of 10 g or more.[190]

Opioid Analgesics—Basic Pharmacology

Opioid Receptor Interactions. Based on their interactions with the various receptor subtypes, opioid compounds can be divided into agonist, agonist-antagonist, and antagonist classes (Table 109-9).[191] The pure agonist drugs (Table 109-10) are most commonly used in clinical pain management.

The mixed agonist-antagonist opioids (pentazocine, nalbuphine, and butorphanol) and the partial agonist opioids (buprenorphine and probably dezocine) play a minor role in the management of cancer pain.[61,147] The factors limiting their utility in this setting include the existence of a ceiling effect for analgesia, the precipitation of withdrawal in patients physically dependent to opioid agonists, and the problem of dose-dependent psychotomimetic side effects that exceed those of pure agonist drugs.

Dose-Response Relationship. The pure agonist opioid drugs appear to have no ceiling effect to analgesia. As the dose is raised, analgesic effects increase until either analgesia is achieved or the patient loses consciousness. Furthermore, this increase in effect occurs as a log-linear function: dose increments on a logarithmic scale yield linear increases in analgesia.[37] In practice, the appearance of adverse effects—including confusion, sedation, nausea, vomiting, or respiratory depression—imposes a limit on the useful dose. The efficacy of any particular drug in a specific patient will be determined by the degree of analgesia produced following dose escalation prior to the development of unmanageable side effects.

Table 109-9
Classification of Opioid Analgesics

Agonists	*Partial agonists*	*Agonist/antagonists*
Morphine	Buprenorphine	Pentazocine
Codeine	Dezocine	Butorphanol
Oxycodone		Nalbuphine
Heroin		
Oxymorphone		
Meperidine		
Levorphanol		
Hydromorphone		
Methadone		
Fentanyl		
Sufentanil		
Alfentanil		
Propoxyphene		

Relative Potency and Equianalgesic Doses. Relative analgesic potency is the ratio of the dose of two analgesics required to produce the same analgesic effect. By convention, the relative potency of each of the commonly used opioids is based upon a comparison to 10 mg of parenteral morphine.[192] Equianalgesic dose information (Table 109-10) provides guidelines for dose selection when drug or route of administration are changed. Equianalgesic doses provide a useful reference point but should not be considered as standard starting doses or as providing a firm guideline in switching between opioids. Numerous variables may influence the appropriate dose for the individual patient, including pain severity, prior opioid exposure (and the degree of cross-tolerance this confers), age, route of administration, level of consciousness, and metabolic abnormalities.

"Weak" versus "Strong" Opioids. The division of opioid agonists into "weak" versus "strong" opioids was incorporated into the original analgesic ladder proposed by the World Health Organization.[179] This distinction is not based on a fundamental difference in the pharmacology of the pure agonist opioids but rather reflects the customary manner in which these drugs are used.

Opioid Agonists (Table 109-10)

Codeine. Codeine is the most commonly used opioid analgesic for the management of mild to moderate pain. It is the standard drug against which all drugs for mild or moderate pain are compared. Codeine is a prodrug and is metabolized in the liver to morphine and norcodeine. It is most commonly used in combination with aspirin or acetaminophen.

Oxycodone. Oral oxycodone is used in both step 2 and step 3 of the analgesic ladder. Combined with aspirin or acetaminophen in products that provide 5 mg of oxycodone per tablet, it is a useful drug for moderate pain. It is also available as a single entity, however, and doses can be escalated to manage severe pain effectively.[193,194]

Propoxyphene (Dextropropoxyphene). Propoxyphene is a congener of methadone. It is metabolized to norpropoxyphene, which has a long half-life and is associated with excitatory effects, including tremulousness and seizures.[195] These effects are dose-related and do not appear to pose a clinical problem at the doses of propoxyphene typically administered for moderate pain in the nontolerant patient.[194]

Morphine. Based on its availability and clinician familiarity with its use, morphine has been designated as

Table 109-10
Opioid Agonist Drugs

Drug	*Dose, mg, equianalgesic to 10 mg IM morphine*		*Half life, h*	*Duration of action, h*	*Comments*
	IM	*PO*			
"Weak" opioids					
Codeine	130	200	2–3	2–4	Usually combined with a nonopioid
Oxycodone	15	30	2–3	2–4	Usually combined with a nonopioid
Propoxyphene	100	50	2–3	2–4	Usually combined with nonopioid. Norpropoxyphene toxicity may cause seizures
"Strong" opioids					
Morphine	10	30 (repeated dose) 60 (single dose)	2–3	3–4	Multiple routes of administration available. Controlled release available. M6G accumulation in renal failure
Hydromorphone	1.5	7.5	2–3	2–4	No known active metabolites. Multiple routes available.
Methadone	10	20	15–190	4–8	Plasma accumulation may lead to delayed toxicity. Dosing should be initiated on an "as needed" basis
Meperidine	75	300	2–3	2–4	Low oral bioavailability. Normeperidine toxicity limits utility. Contraindicated in renal failure and patients taking MAO inhibitors
Oxymorphone	1	10 (P.R.)	2–3	3–4	No oral formulation available. Less histamine release
Heroin	5	60	0.5	3–4	High-solubility morphine prodrug, not available in the United States
Levorphanol	2	4	12–15	4–8	Plasma accumulation may lead to delayed toxicity
Fentanyl[a] transdermal system				48–72	Patches available to deliver 25, 50, 75, and 100 μg/h 12 h to peak effect

[a]Transdermal fentanyl 100 μg/h is approximately equianalgesic to parenterally infused morphine sulphate 4 mg/h.

the prototypical agent for step 3 of the analgesic ladder.[179] The World Health Organization has placed oral morphine on the essential drug list, and preparations are available for oral, rectal, parenteral, and intraspinal administration.

Morphine undergoes glucuronidation at the 3 and 6 positions. Although morphine-3-glucuronide (M3G), the major metabolite,[196] has negligible affinity for opioid receptors, morphine-6-glucuronide (M6G) binds to opioid receptors[197] and produces potent opioid effects in animals[197–199] and in humans.[197,200,201] In patients with impaired renal function, high concentrations of M6G have been associated with toxicity.[200,202] Although further studies are needed to clarify the clinical importance of this and other metabolites, the data available are adequate to recommend caution when administering morphine to patients with renal disease.

Single-dose studies of morphine in postoperative cancer patients demonstrated in IM to PO potency ratio of 1 : 6.[203] However, both bioavailability data[204] and surveys of patients receiving the drug chronically suggest that a ratio of 1 : 3 or 1 : 2 is more appropriate.[55] The reason for the discrepancy between relative potency estimates derived from single-dose versus chronic dosing studies probably relates to both methodology[205] and to the pharmacokinetics and pharmacodynamics of M6G. Relative to morphine, M6G concentration is higher with oral than with parenteral administration; this may lead to an increase in the relative potency of the orally administerea drug.

The development of controlled-release morphine preparations, which can be administered on an 8- or 12-h schedule, has had a major impact on clinical practice. These preparations provide improved convenience of dosing and can be particularly useful in eliminating the need for frequent dosing during the nighttime hours.[206] Controlled-release morphine should not be used to titrate the dose rapidly in patients with severe pain. At least 24 h is required to approach steady-state plasma concentration after dosing is initiated or changed, and these kinetics may complicate efforts to identify the appropriate dose rapidly. Dose finding in these situations is performed more efficiently with an immediate-release morphine preparation.[207] When the effective dose is identified, the patient may be converted to a controlled-release preparation using a milligram-to-milligram conversion.[207]

Heroin. Heroin is a highly soluble semisynthetic opioid analgesic prepared by diacetylating morphine. Heroin is a prodrug which is rapidly biotransformed to 6-acetylmorphine and morphine to produce its analgesic effect.[208] Following oral administration of heroin, only morphine can be measured in the blood.[209] Although it is available in Canada and England, heroin is not licensed in the United States.

Hydromorphone. Hydromorphone is another morphine congener with a short half-life that is a very useful alternative to morphine. Hydromorphone is a versatile drug that can be administered by the oral, rectal, parenteral, and intraspinal routes. Because of its significant solubility and the availability of a high-concentration preparation (10 mg/mL), it has been widely used by subcutaneous infusion. A recent study has demonstrated that the bioavailability of this drug by continuous subcutaneous infusion is approximately 80 percent of that by the intravenous route.[210]

Meperidine (Pethidine). Meperidine is a short-half-life synthetic opioid agonist with a profile of potential adverse effects that limits its utility as an analgesic for chronic cancer pain. Meperidine is *N*-demethylated to normeperidine, which is an active metabolite that is twice as potent as a convulsant and half as potent as an analgesic than its parent compound. Accumulation of normeperidine after repetitive dosing of meperidine can result in central nervous system excitability characterized by subtle mood effects, tremors, multifocal myoclonus, and occasionally seizures.[211,212] Although accumulation of normeperidine is most likely to affect patients with overt renal disease, toxicity is sometimes observed in patients with normal renal function.[211,213] These potential adverse effects relatively contraindicate meperidine for the management of chronic cancer pain. Given the availability of alternative drugs that lack these toxicities, the use of normeperidine in acute pain management can also be questioned.[214]

Methadone. Methadone is a synthetic opioid with a very long plasma half-life, which averages approximately 24 h (range from 13 to over 100 h). This long half-life notwithstanding, most patients require dosing at a 4- to 8-h interval to maintain analgesic effects.[215] After treatment is initiated or the dose is increased, plasma concentration rises for a prolonged period, and this may be associated with delayed onset of side effects.[216,217] Serious adverse effects can be avoided if the initial period of dosing is accomplished with "as needed" administration and patients are carefully monitored. When steady state has been achieved, scheduled dose frequency should be determined by the duration of analgesia following each dose. Oral and parenteral preparations of methadone are available. Subcutaneous infusion of methadone can be associated with the development of skin toxicity.[218]

Oxymorphone. Oxymorphone is another short-half-life congener of morphine. Injectable and rectal formulations are available in the United States. Oxymorphone is less likely to produce histamine release than morphine[219,220] and may have particular utility for patients who develop itch in response to other opioids.[221]

Levorphanol. Levorphanol is a morphine congener with a long half-life (12 to 16 h). Like methadone, this drug may accumulate following the initiation of therapy or dose escalation. Levorphanol is commonly used as a second-line agent in patients with chronic pain who cannot tolerate morphine. The possibility that this drug may be particularly useful in morphine-tolerant patients has been proposed on the basis of its affinity for receptors (kappa-3 and delta) that are presumably not involved in morphine analgesia.[222]

Fentanyl. Fentanyl is a semisynthetic opioid characterized by high potency and lipophilicity. Fentanyl has been used parenterally and intraspinally to manage postoperative and obstetric pain. The recent development of a transdermal system (see below) has broadened its clinical utility to the management of patients with chronic cancer pain.[223–225] A transmucosal preparation is under development and may be useful in the management of acute pain, including "breakthrough" pain in the cancer population.[226]

Opioid Selection

The most important factors in the selection of an opioid are the intensity and other characteristics of the pain, patient age, influence of underlying illness, and characteristics of the opioid and concurrent medications.

Pain Intensity. In the United States, the most common products used in the management of mild to moderate pain contain acetaminophen or aspirin plus codeine or oxycodone. In the absence of limiting side effects, the dose of this drug can be increased until the maximum dose of the nonopioid co-analgesic is attained (e.g., 4000 to 6000 mg acetaminophen). If a patient has tolerated a combination product extremely well but no longer obtains satisfactory analgesia from a quantity that increases the risk of toxicity from the nonopioid component, the opioid contained in the combination product can be increased as a single entity. More commonly, however, patients who fail to obtain adequate analgesia at these maximal doses are switched to a "strong" opioid, the dose of which is then titrated upward. Patients who present with severe pain should be treated with a strong opioid from the start.

Although somatic and visceral pain are generally more responsive to opioid analgesics than neuropathic pain,[33] it should be recognized that opioid responsiveness is a continuum and appropriate dose escalation will identify many patients with neuropathic pain who will achieve adequate relief.[37] Thus a trial of opioid therapy should be administered to all patients with pain of sufficient severity, regardless of inferred pathophysiology.

Patient Age. For the younger patient without major organ failure, any of the available agonist opioids can be selected. Convenience of administration should be a major determinant; morphone sulfate may be preferred, since it is available as a controlled-release preparation that allows an 8- to 12-h dosing interval. For the elderly and those with major organ failure, short-half-life drugs are preferred. These drugs, which include morphine, hydromorphone and oxycodone, require a relatively short period to achieve stable plasma concentrations and are therefore simpler to titrate and monitor.

Coexisting Disease. Pharmacokinetic studies of meperidine, pentazocine, and propoxyphene have revealed that severe liver disease may decrease the clearance and increase the bioavailability and half-lives of these drugs. In contrast, the metabolism of morphine and methadone are not altered in patients with liver disease.[227] Patients with renal impairment may accumulate the active metabolites of propoxyphene (norpropoxyphene), meperidine (normeperidine) and morphine (M6G).[200,202,228,229]

Drug Interactions. The potential for additive side effects and serious toxicity from drug combinations must be recognized. The sedative effect of an opioid may add to that produced by numerous other centrally acting drugs, such as anxiolytics, neuroleptics, and antidepressants. Likewise, the constipatory effects of opioids are worsened by drugs with anticholinergic effects. Severe adverse reactions—including excitation, hyperpyrexia, convulsions and death—have been reported after the administration of meperidine to patients treated with a monoamine oxidase inhibitor.[230]

Response to Previous Trials of Opioid Therapy. For the patient who is opioid-naive, the above considerations predominate. For some patients, sequential trials of different opioid drugs may be necessary to find the optimal balance between analgesia and side effects. Interindividual variability in opioid responses, the existence of incomplete cross-tolerance to opioid analgesia, and incomplete cross-sensitivity to adverse effects explain the potential utility of switching to an alternative opioid.[231]

Routes of Systemic Opioid Administration

Opioid should be administered by the least invasive and safest route capable of providing adequate analgesia. In a survey of patients with advanced cancer, more than half required two or more routes of administration prior to death, and almost a quarter required three or more.[54]

Oral. The oral route of opioid administration remains the most important and appropriate in routine practice. Most patients can use the oral route throughout most of their illness. Orally administered drugs have a slower onset of action, delayed peak time, and a longer duration of effect than parenterally administered drugs. The time to peak effect depends on the drug and the nature of the formulation; however, for most immediate-release oral formulations, peak effect is typically achieved after 60 min. The oral route of drug administration is not appropriate in patients who have impaired swallowing or gastrointestinal obstruction, and some patients who require a rapid onset of analgesia after each dose may not benefit significantly from this route. For highly tolerant patients, the inability to prescribe a manageable oral opioid program—due to the excessive number of tablets or volume of oral solution to be ingested—may be an indication for the use of a nonoral route.

The switch between oral and parenteral routes requires careful attention to relative potency to avoid subsequent overdosing or underdosing. Equianalgesic doses (Tables 109-10) should be consulted to guide dose selection. The potencies of the subcutaneous, intramuscular, and intravenous routes are conventionally considered equivalent for the purpose of these calculations. If possible, the problems associated with switching the route of administration can be minimized by accomplishing the change in steps (e.g., slowly reducing the parenteral dose and increasing the oral dose over a 2- to 3-day period).

Rectal. The rectal route is a noninvasive alternative to the parenteral route for patients unable to take oral opioids.[232] Rectal suppositories containing hydromorphone, oxymorphone, and morphine are available in the United States (oxycodone suppositories are available elsewhere). The potency of opioids administered rectally is believed to approximate that of oral dosing.[233]

Transdermal. The transdermal route of administration is another noninvasive alternative for the patient unable to tolerate oral medication.[225] The first opioid available by the transdermal route is fentanyl. The transdermal system consists of a drug reservoir that is separated from the skin by a copolymer membrane that controls the rate of drug delivery to the skin surface. Drug is released into the skin at a nearly constant amount per unit of time. The dosing interval for each system is usually 72 h, but it may be as short as 48 h. Empirically, the indications for the transdermal route include intolerance of oral medication, poor compliance with oral medication, and, occasionally, the desire to provide a trial of fentanyl to patients who have reacted unfavorably to other opioids.[225] The 12-h delay until steady state is achieved limits the utility of this mode of delivery for patients with unstable pain problems.

Sublingual. The sublingual approach has limited utility due to the lack of true sublingual formulations in the United States, poor absorption of most drugs, and the inability to deliver high doses or prevent swallowing of the dose.[232,234] Sublingual administration of an injectable formulation is occasionally used in the relatively nontolerant patient who transiently loses the option of oral dosing. On the basis of bioavailability data, sublingual absorption appears to be best with lipophilic opioids such as fentanyl or methadone.[234]

Parenteral. Repeated bolus injections can be administered by the intravenous, intramuscular, or subcutaneous routes. Repetitive parenteral injections are usually effective but may be associated with prominent "bolus" effects (toxicity at peak concentration and/or pain breakthrough at the trough). Repetitive IM injections are a common practice, but they are painful and offer no pharmacokinetic advantage; their use is not recommended.

Continuous parenteral infusions may be administered intravenously or subcutaneously. The major indication for continuous infusion is inability to swallow or absorb opioids; continuous infusion is also used in some patients whose high opioid requirement renders oral treatment impractical.[235–239]

Continuous subcutaneous infusion can easily be used by ambulatory patients. A range of pumps is available, which vary in complexity and cost and in the ability to provide patient-controlled "rescue doses" as an adjunct to a continuous basal infusion (see below).[238] Clinical experience suggests that dosing may proceed in a manner identical to that of continuous IV infusion. Continuous subcutaneous delivery of drug combinations may be indicated when pain is accompanied by nausea, anxiety, or agitation. Antiemetics, neuroleptics, or anxiolytics may be combined with the opioid provided they are nonirritant, miscible, and stable in combined solution. Experience has been reported with metoclopramide, haloperidol, scopolamine, cyclizine, methotrimeprazine, chlorpromazine, and midazolam.[240]

Opioid Dosing Guidelines

Schedule of Administration. Patients with continuous or frequent pain generally benefit from scheduled "around-the-clock" dosing, which can provide the patient with continuous relief by preventing the pain from recurring. Around-the-clock scheduled dosing must be used cautiously in patients with no previous opioid exposure, who may develop opioid toxicity as plasma concentration rises toward steady-state levels; in the cancer population, this is most likely to become a problem when drugs with long half-lives, such as methadone or levorphanol, are used.

All patients who receive an around-the-clock opioid regimen should also be offered "rescue doses." The rescue dose is a supplemental dose of the opioid that is offered on an as-needed basis. It provides an important means to treat pain that breaks through the regular schedule. The rescue drug is typically identical to that administered on a continuous basis with the exception of transdermal fentanyl (since none is available); the use of an alternative short-half-life opioid for the rescue dose is recommended in this situation. The frequency with which the rescue dose can be offered depends on the time to peak effect for the drug and the route of administration. Oral rescue doses are offered up to every 1 to 2 h and parenteral doses are offered up to every 15 to 30 min. Clinical experience suggests that the size of the rescue dose should be equivalent to approximately 5 to 15 percent of the 24-h baseline dose. The integration of scheduled dosing with rescue doses provides a method for safe and rational stepwise dose escalation which is applicable to all routes of opioid administration.

In some settings, an as-needed dosing regimen without an around-the-clock regimen should be considered. Dosing on an as-needed basis provides additional safety during the initiation of opioid therapy in the opioid-naive patient, particularly when rapid dose escalation is needed. This technique is strongly recommended at the start of methadone therapy. As-needed dosing may also be appropriate for patients who have rapidly decreasing analgesic requirements or intermittent pain separated by pain-free intervals. Some patients who require as-needed dosing should be considered for formal patient-controlled analgesia.

Patient-controlled analgesia (PCA) is a technique of parenteral drug administration (see above) in which the patient controls a pump that delivers an analgesic according to parameters set by the physician. Use of a PCA device allows patients to overcome variations in both pharmacokinetic and pharmacodynamic factors by carefully titrating the rate of opioid administration to meet their individual analgesic needs.[241–246] Long-term PCA in cancer patients is most commonly accomplished via the subcutaneous route, using an ambulatory infusion device.[238,247,248] It is indicated for patients who are unable to tolerate oral medications and have fluctuations in pain intensity, patients with intense breakthrough pain requiring rapid relief, or patients requiring systemic opioid therapy at doses that cannot otherwise be conveniently administered.

Starting Dose. A patient who is relatively nontolerant, having had only some exposure to a weak opioid, should generally begin one of the strong opioids at a dose equivalent to 5 to 10 mg IM morphine every 3 to 4 h. If morphine is used, an IM : oral relative potency ratio for morphine of 1 : 3 is conventional. When patients on higher doses of opioids are switched to an alternative opioid drug, the starting dose of the new drug should be reduced to 50 to 75 percent of the equianalgesic dose (and to less when the switch is to methadone) to account for incomplete cross-tolerance.

Dose Titration. At all times, inadequate relief should be addressed through gradual escalation of dose until adequate analgesia is reported or unmanageable side effects supervene. Because opioid response increases linearly with the log of the dose, dose escalations less than 30 to 50 percent are not likely to improve analgesia significantly. Doses can become extremely large during this process of titration. The absolute dose is immaterial as long as the balance between analgesia and side effects remains favorable. In one retrospective study of patients with advanced cancer, the average daily opioid requirement was equivalent to 400 to 600 mg of IM morphine, but approximately 10 percent of patients required more than 2000 mg and one patient required over 35,000 mg/24 h.[54]

The rate of dose titration depends on the severity of the pain. Patients who present with very severe pain are sometimes best managed by repeated parenteral administration of a dose every 15 to 30 min until the pain is partially relieved. Patients with moderate pain, who are treated with short-half-life opioids, can undergo dose increments as often as twice daily. The dose of controlled-release preparations of oral morphine or transdermal fentanyl can be increased every 24 to 48 h.

The Problem of Tolerance. Tolerance is a pharmacologic effect characterized by the need for increasing doses to maintain the same effects. Tolerance to the various opioid effects develops at different rates. For example, tolerance to respiratory depression, somnolence, and nausea generally develop rapidly, whereas tolerance to opioid-induced constipation develops very slowly if at all.[249] From the clinical perspective, the concern is that tolerance will develop to the analgesic effect of the drug and that this will necessitate rapid dose escalation, which may continue until the drug is no longer useful. Indeed, tolerance to opioid side effects is clinically desirable and allows effective dose titration to proceed. It is important to recognize that analgesic tolerance is seldom the dominant factor in the need for opioid dose escalation. Rather, most patients who require an escalation in dose to manage increasing pain have demonstrable progression of disease.[67,249–251] There are two important implications of this observation: (1) concern about chemical tolerance should not impede the use of opioids early in the course of the disease and (2) worsening pain in a patient receiving a stable dose of opioids should not be attributed to tolerance but should be assessed as presumptive evidence of disease progression or recurrence.

Adverse Effects and Their Management

Successful opioid therapy requires that the benefits of analgesia and other desirable effects clearly outweigh treatment-related adverse effects. This implies that a detailed understanding of adverse opioid effects and strategies to prevent and manage them are essential skills for all involved in cancer pain management.

Respiratory Depression. Respiratory depression is potentially the most serious adverse effect of opioid therapy. Respiratory depression occurs as a consequence of activation of specific receptors (mu2) in the lower brainstem,[252] which may result in impairment of all phases of respiratory activity (rate, minute volume, and tidal exchange). With repeated administration, tolerance to this effect develops rapidly, and it is a very rare event in the cancer patient whose opioid dose is titrated carefully against pain. Clinically significant respiratory depression is always accompanied by other signs of central nervous system (CNS) depression, including sedation and mental clouding. Respiratory compromise accompanied by tachypnea and anxiety is never a primary opioid event. When respiratory depression occurs in such patients, alternative explanations (e.g., pneumonia or pulmonary embolism) should be sought. Opioid-induced respiratory depression can also occur if the stimulus of the pain is removed suddenly (as may occur following neurolytic procedures) and the opioid dose is not reduced.

If clinically significant respiratory depression occurs, naloxone should be used to improve ventilation. The goal of this therapy is to improve respiration without causing systemic withdrawal. Small bolus injection of dilute naloxone (0.4 mg in 10 mL saline) should be titrated against respiratory rate. In the comatose patient, an endotracheal tube should be placed to assist ventilation and prevent aspiration. Specific caution is required for patients who have received chronic meperidine therapy, since naloxone may precipitate seizures by blocking the depressant action of meperidine and allowing the convulsant activity of normeperidine to be manifest.[253] If the patient is arousable, and the peak plasma levels of the opioid have already been reached, the opioid dose should be withheld, and the patient should be monitored until improved.

Sedation. Initiation of opioid therapy or significant dose escalation commonly induces sedation that usually persists for days to weeks until tolerance to this effect develops. Some patients have a persistent problem with sedation, particularly if other confounding factors exist. These factors include the use of other sedating drugs or coexistent diseases, such as dementia, metabolic encephalopathy, or brain metastases. Management of persistent sedation is best accomplished with a stepwise approach (Table 109-11). First, nonessential CNS-depressant medications such as neuroleptics, antidepressants, anxiolytics, or antihistamines should be discontinued. Second, those patients who are experiencing adequate analgesia should undergo a modest dose reduction of their opioid (e.g., 25 percent). Third, the use of a psychostimulant, such as dextroamphetamine[254] or methylphenidate,[255,256] should be considered.

Cognitive Impairment and Delirium. For patients and their families, confusion is a greatly feared effect of the opioid drugs.[64] Mild cognitive impairment is common following the initiation of opioid therapy or dose escalation.[257] Like sedation, however, pure opioid-induced encephalopathy appears to be transient in most patients, persisting from days to a week or two. Although persistent confusion attributable to opioid alone occurs, the etiology of persistent delirium is usually multifactorial, and opioids are one of several contributing factors, including electrolyte disorders, neoplastic involvement of the CNS, sepsis, vital organ failure, and hypoxemia.[258] A stepwise approach to the management of delirium in this setting is presented in Table 109-12. Treatment of the delirium with a neuroleptic drug may be helpful while its cause is being sought and treated. Haloperidol in low doses (0.5 to 1.0 mg PO or 0.25 to 0.5 mg IV or IM) is most commonly recommended because of its efficacy and low incidence of cardiovascular and anticholinergic effects.

Table 109-11
Management of Opioid-Induced Sedation

1. Discontinue nonessential CNS-depressant medications
2. If analgesia is satisfactory, reduce opioid dose by 25%
3. If analgesia is unsatisfactory, try addition of a psychostimulant
4. If somnolence persists, consider:
   - Addition of a coanalgesic that will allow reduction in opioid dose
   - Change to an alternative opioid drug
   - A change in opioid route to the intraspinal route
   - A trial of other anesthetic, neurolytic or neurosurgical options

Table 109-12
Management of Opioid-Induced Delirium

1. Discontinue nonessential centrally acting medications
2. If analgesia is satisfactory, reduce opioid dose by 25%
3. Exclude sepsis or metabolic derangement
4. If delirium persists, consider:
   - Trial of neurolytic (e.g., haloperidol)
   - Change to an alternative opioid drug
   - A change in opioid route to the intraspinal route
   - A trial of other anesthetic, neurolytic, or neurosurgical options

Constipation. Constipation is the most common adverse effect encountered during chronic opioid therapy.[55,61,147,259,260] Opioids bind to peripheral receptors in the gut, prolonging colonic transit time by increasing segmental contractions, decreasing propulsive peristalsis, and reducing intraluminal fluid content by increasing salt and water absorption across the intestinal mucosa. Central opioid receptors are also presumably involved in colonic transit and the urge to defecate.[261,262] The likelihood of opioid-induced constipation is so great that laxative medications should be prescribed prophylactically to most patients.[55,61,147,259,263–265] The differential diagnosis of constipation includes ileus and mechanical obstruction (due to tumor or adhesions). Rectal impaction by fecal matter and the finding of extensive fecal shadowing on abdominal radiographs suggest a diagnosis of constipation.

Combination therapy is frequently used. A softening agent (docusate) can be coadministered with a cathartic (e.g., senna, bisocodyl, or phenolphthalein). The doses of these drugs should be increased as necessary and an osmotic laxative (e.g., milk of magnesia) should be added if needed. Chronic lactulose therapy is an alternative that some patients prefer, and occasional patients are managed with intermittent colonic lavage using an oral bowel preparation such as GoLYTELY. Rare patients with refractory constipation can undergo a trial of oral naloxone, which has a bioavailability of less than 3 percent. A small series of patients has been reported in whom an oral dose of 3 to 12 mg reversed constipation without compromising analgesia or precipitating systemic withdrawal.[259] If oral naloxone is used, the initial dose should be small (0.8 to 1.2 mg once or twice daily), and the dose should be escalated by small steps until either favorable effects occur or the patient develops abdominal cramps, diarrhea, or any other adverse effect.

Nausea and Vomiting. In ambulatory patients, the incidence of nausea and vomiting has been estimated to be 10 to 40 percent and 15 to 40 percent, respectively.[266] Opioids may produce these effects through stimulation of the medullary chemoreceptor trigger zone, enhanced vestibular sensitivity, and increased gastric antral tone. Tolerance to these effects usually develops within weeks, and routine prophylactic administration of an antiemetic is not necessary except in patients with a history of severe opioid-induced nausea and vomiting.[260] Patients should have access to an antiemetic at the start of therapy in case the need for one should arise. Anecdotally, the use of prochlorperazine and metoclopramide has usually been sufficient to manage opioid-induced nausea. Metoclopramide is preferred if nausea is associated with early satiety, bloating, or postprandial vomiting. Patients with vertigo or prominent movement-induced nausea should also be considered for a trial of scopolamine or meclizine. In patients with more severe or persistent symptoms, a switch to an alternative opioid should be considered.

Myoclonus. Myoclonus is a dose-related adverse effect of all opioids. Mild and infrequent myoclonus is common and may resolve spontaneously with the development of tolerance to this effect. Myoclonus can be symptomatic and distressing. Benzodiazepines (particularly clonazepam),[267] barbiturates, or valproate may be of value in the management of this symptom. If symptomatic myoclonus is refractory to treatment, the opioid should be switched and consideration should be given to alternative strategies for pain management.

Urinary Retention. Opioid analgesics increase smooth muscle tone and can occasionally cause bladder spasm or an increase in sphincter tone. The latter effect can lead to urinary retention.[191] This is an infrequent problem that is usually observed in elderly male patients. Tolerance can develop rapidly, but catheterization may be necessary to manage transient problems.

Understanding the Problems of Physical and Psychological Dependence or Addiction

Concern about physical dependence, psychological dependence, and abusive drug-related behaviors augments the fear of opioid drugs and contributes substantially to the undertreatment of pain.[64,265,268–271]

Physical Dependence. Physical dependence is a pharmacologic property of opioid drugs defined by the development of an abstinence (withdrawal) syndrome following either abrupt dose reduction or administration of an antagonist. Despite the observation that physical dependence is most commonly observed in patients taking large doses over a prolonged period of time, withdrawal has also been observed in patients after low doses or short duration of treatment. If repeated doses are administered for several days, it is prudent to use a tapering schedule to stop the drug and to avoid agonist-antagonist drugs, such as pentazocine. If these simple precautions are taken, physical dependence will not become a problem clinically.

True physical dependence should be clearly differentiated from the situation of "therapeutic dependence," whereby the patient requires a specific pharmacotherapy to control a symptom or disease process. This relationship is well illustrated by the requirement of patients with congestive heart failure for cardiotonic and diuretic medications or the reliance of insulin-dependent diabetics on insulin therapy. In these situations, undermedication or withdrawal of treatment results in serious untoward consequences for the patient. Patients with chronic cancer pain have an analogous relationship to their analgesic therapy. This relationship may or may not be associated with the development of physical dependence, but it is virtually never associated with addiction.

Psychologic Dependence or Addiction. Psychologic dependence, commonly called addiction, is a psychologic and behavioral syndrome characterized by a continued craving for an opioid drug to achieve a psychic effect which is associated with aberrant drug-related behavior, including compulsive drug seeking and continued (or escalating) use despite harm to the user or others.

The medical use of opioids for cancer pain is very rarely associated with the development of addiction.[268] In the only prospective study that attempted to address the risk of addiction, 11,882 patients with no history of abuse who received at least one opioid preparation in the hospital setting were monitored; there were only 4 cases of reasonably well-documented psychologic dependence with abuse behaviors.[272] Although there are no prospective studies in patients with chronic cancer pain, there is a broad anecdotal experience that affirms the extremely low risk of iatrogenic psychologic dependence in this population.[13,55,61,67,179,260,264,265,269,273–275] Health care providers, patients, and families often require vigorous and repeated reassurance that the risk of addiction is extremely small.

The distress engendered in patients who have a therapeutic requirement for analgesic drugs but who continue to experience unrelieved pain is occasionally expressed in behaviors that are reminiscent of those stemming from psychologic dependence, such as intense concern about opioid availability. The absence of use-despite-harm and the elimination of these behaviors by sustained pain relief, usually produced by dose escalation, distinguishes the patient from the true addict. Misunderstanding of these phenomena may lead the clinician to inappropriately stigmatize the patient with the label *addict,* which may compromise care and erode the doctor-patient relationship.[276] In the setting of unrelieved pain, abnormal drug-related behaviors require careful assessment, renewed efforts to manage the pain, and the avoidance of stigmatizing labels.

Table 109-13
Painful Conditions Commonly Responding to Corticosteroid Therapy

Raised intracranial pressure
Acute spinal cord compression
Superior vena cava syndrome
Metastatic bone pain
Neuropathic pain due to infiltration or compression by tumor
Symptomatic lymphedema
Hepatic capsular distention

Adjuvant Analgesics—General Considerations

The term *adjuvant analgesic* describes a drug that has a primary indication other than pain but which is analgesic in some painful conditions. These drugs may be combined with primary analgesics in any of the three steps of the analgesic ladder to improve analgesic outcome in patients who cannot otherwise attain an acceptable balance between relief and side effects from opioid drugs.

Whenever an adjuvant analgesic is selected, differences between the use of the drug for its primary indication and its use as an analgesic must be appreciated. Since the nature of dose-dependent analgesic effects has not been characterized for most of these drugs, dose titration is reasonable with virtually all. Low initial doses are appropriate, given the desire to avoid early side effects. There is great interpatient and intrapatient variability in the response to all adjuvant analgesics, including those within the same class. These observations suggest the potential utility of sequential trials of adjuvant analgesics. The process of sequential drug trials, like the use of low initial doses and dose titration, should be explained to the patient at the start of therapy, so as to enhance compliance and reduce the distress that may occur if treatments fail.

Multipurpose Adjuvant Medications

Corticosteroids. Corticosteroids are among the most widely used adjuvant analgesics.[277,278] They have been demonstrated to have analgesic effects,[279] to significantly improve quality of life,[280–282] and to have beneficial effects on appetite, nausea, mood, and malaise in this population.[279,283,284] Painful conditions that commonly respond to corticosteroids are listed in Table 109-13. Patients with advanced cancer who experience pain and other symptoms that may respond to steroids are usually given a small dose (e.g., dexamethasone 1 to 2 mg twice daily). An acute episode of very severe pain related to epidural spinal cord compression, bony metastases, or lumbosacral plexopathy that cannot be promptly reduced with opioids may respond dramatically to a short course of relatively high doses[285] (e.g., dexamethasone 100 mg followed initially by 96 mg/day in divided doses). In all cases, following pain reduction, the dose should gradually be lowered to the minimum needed to sustain relief.

Neuroleptic Drugs. Neuroleptic drugs have a limited role in the management of cancer pain. Methotrimeprazine has been very useful in bedridden patients with advanced cancer who experience pain associated with anxiety, restlessness, nausea, or a propensity to bowel obstruction. In the United States, methotrimeprazine is approved only for repetitive intramuscular administration, but extensive experience has affirmed that it may also be given by continuous subcutaneous administration,[239] subcutaneous bolus injection, or brief intravenous infusion (administration over 20 to 30 min).

Adjuvants Used for Neuropathic Pain

Neuropathic pain is generally less responsive to opioid therapy than nociceptive pain and therapeutic outcome may be improved by the addition of an adjuvant medication. For purposes of adjuvant drug selection, distinction is drawn between continuous, lancinating, and sympathetically mediated neuropathic pain (Table 109-14).

Antidepressant Medications. There is evidence that antidepressant drugs have analgesic effects in diverse types of chronic pain.[39,286,287] In the cancer population, these drugs are commonly used to manage continuous neuropathic pains that have not responded adequately to an opioid and lancinating neuropathic pains that are refractory to other specific adjuvant agents. These compounds are also useful in patients with pain complicated by depression and insomnia. The evidence for analgesic efficacy is greatest for the tertiary amine tricyclic drugs, such as amitriptyline, doxepin, and imipramine, and for secondary amine drugs, such as desipramine and nortryptyline.[287–291] The secondary amine drugs have fewer side effects and are preferred when concern about sedation, anticholinergic effects, or cardiovascular toxicity is high. There is very limited evidence that trazodone and maprotiline are analgesic and virtually no data in support of fluoxetine.[39]

Table 109-14
A Guide to the Selection of Adjuvant Analgesics for Neuropathic Pain Based on Clinical Characteristics

Continuous pain	*Lancinating pain*	*Sympathetically maintained pain*
Tricyclic antidepressants	Anticonvulsant drugs	Phenoxybenzamine
Amitriptyline	Carbamazepine	Prazosin
Doxepin	Phenytoin	Corticosteroid
Imipramine	Clonazepam	Nifedipine
Desipramine	Valproate	
Nortriptyline	Baclofen	
Oral local anesthetics	Oral local anesthetics	
Mexiletine		
Clonidine		
Capsaicin		

Anticonvulsant Drugs. Selected anticonvulsant drugs appear to be analgesic for the lancinating dysesthesias that characterize diverse types of neuropathic pain.[39,292] Clinical experience also supports the use of these agents in patients with episodic neuropathic pains that are nonlancinating but which have a paroxysmal onset and, to a far lesser extent, in those with neuropathic pains characterized solely by continuous dysesthesias. Most practitioners begin with carbamazepine because of the extraordinarily good response rate observed in trigeminal neuralgia, but this drug must be used cautiously in patients with thrombocytopenia, those at risk for bone marrow failure (e.g., following chemotherapy), and those whose blood counts must be monitored to determine disease status.

Baclofen. Baclofen, a gamma-aminobutyric acid (GABA) agonist, is a proven analgesic for trigeminal neuralgia[293,294] and is often employed in the management of lancinating pains due to neural injury of any type.

Oral Local Anesthetics. Oral local anesthetic drugs are important to consider in the management of neuropathic pains characterized by continuous and lancinating dysesthesias.[39] Since the supporting evidence for this use is far less abundant than that available for other drug classes, it is reasonable to undertake a trial with an oral local anesthetic in patients with continuous dysesthesias who fail to respond adequately to or who cannot tolerate the tricyclic antidepressants and in patients with lancinating pains refractory to trials of anticonvulsant drugs and baclofen (see below). Mexiletine is the safest of these drugs.[39,295,296]

Clonidine. Clonidine is an alpha$_2$ adrenergic agonist that has established antinociceptive effects.[39] A trial of oral or transdermal clonidine can be considered in neuropathic pain refractory to opioids and other adjuvants.

Capsaicin. Capsaicin depletes peptides in small primary afferent neurons, including those that are putative mediators of nociceptive transmission (e.g., substance P). Anecdotal data suggest that topical administration of capsaicin 0.025% cream may relieve some forms of neuropathic pain.[297–299] A higher concentration (0.075%) is also available, and it is reasonable to try this product in patients who do not benefit from the lower-concentration product.

Pimozide. Pimozide, a phenothiazine neuroleptic with activity against lancinating neuropathic pain, is occasionally used, but it is associated with a high incidence of adverse effects, including physical and mental slowing, tremor, and slight parkinsonian symptoms.[300] It should be considered following failed trials with other drugs.

Adjuvant Drugs for Sympathetically Maintained Pain. Anecdotal reports suggest that trials of phenoxybenzamine,[301] prazosin,[302] propranolol,[303] and nifedipine[304] can be considered in this setting.

Adjuvant Analgesics Used for Bone Pain

Anti-Inflamatory Drugs. Anecdotally, nonsteroidal anti-inflammatory drugs appear to be particularly efficacious in pain of this type, and corticosteroids are often advocated in difficult cases.[39,105]

Bisphosphonates and Calcitonin. Bisphosphonates, analogs of inorganic pyrophosphate that inhibit osteoclast activity, have been demonstrated to relive malignant bone pain in several surveys and controlled trials.[39,305] Two recent placebo-controlled trials of pamidronate in patients with advanced cancer demonstrated significant reduction of bone pain.[306,307] Although a similar trial of sodium etidronate demonstrated no beneficial effects,[308] treatment of refractory bone pain with one of these agents is appropriate. Similarly, the evidence that repeated doses of subcutaneous calcitonin significantly reduce bone pain is equivocal,[309,310] but it is reasonable to consider a trial with this drug (e.g., salmon calcitonin 100 to 200 IU twice daily subcutaneously for several weeks) in refractory cases.

Radiolabeled Isotopes. Early trials also suggest that radiolabeled agents that are absorbed at areas of high bone turnover may be useful in the treatment of metastatic bone pain.[311–315] Further studies are needed to identify the risks and benefits of each agent and the durability of the effects produced.

Other Noninvasive Analgesic Techniques

Psychologic Therapies in Cancer Pain

Psychologic approaches are an integral part of the care of the cancer patient with pain. Cognitive-behavioral interventions can help patients decrease the perception of distress engendered by the pain experience through the development of new coping skills and the modification of thoughts, feelings, and behaviors.[47] Essential to these methods is the development of the skill of self-monitoring; the ability to observe one's emotional and behavioral responses in a relatively objective, semidetached manner so as to notice dysfunctional reactions and interactions and to learn to control them.

Behavioral Techniques. Behavioral techniques seek to enhance coping skills. Relaxation methods reduce muscular tension, emotional arousal, and mental confusion and can enhance pain tolerance.[316] Systematic desensitization reduces the anticipatory anxiety that leads to avoidant behaviors in situations of anticipated hurt. For example, when patients are immobilized by the fear of incident pain, they are encouraged to perform the avoided activity in very small steps, so that they gradually become used to performing the activity without experiencing the anticipated pain. Contingency management is a technique whereby dysfunctional pain behaviors, such as excessive complaining, are targeted to be replaced by an alternative "well" behavior by selective positive reinforcement of the well behavior only.[317]

Cognitive Techniques. Cognitive techniques are applied to thoughts, images, and attitudes rather than behaviors. In situations where the pain cannot be immediately or totally relieved, obsessive focusing of attention on pain (hypervigilance) may contribute to a counterproductive increase in anxiety and distress. Cognitive coping techniques, including distraction and focusing, are mental skills aimed to reduce the distress of the pain experience.[318] Successful implementation requires that the patient believe that the presence of the pain does not carry the implication of immediate danger[47] and depends upon the patient's ability to focus attention on neutral or positive objects in the imagination or the environment. Various techniques have been described and the therapist must determine which is most consistent with the patient's habitual coping strategies.[318]

Physiatric Techniques

Physiatric techniques are important to optimize function in the patient with chronic cancer pain,[319] and physiatric modalities such as electrical stimulation, medical heat treatments, and cryotherapy are all useful adjuncts in the treatment of musculoskeletal pain in the cancer patient. Treatment of lymphedema of the lower limb by use of wraps, pressure stockings, and intermittent sequential pneumatic pump devices can improve function and relieve pain and heaviness.[320] Utilization of orthotic devices, to immobilize and support painful or weakened structures, and assistive devices can be of great value to patients with pain precipitated by weight bearing or ambulation. Particular examples include the use of orthotic devices for patients with low back pain related to vertebral metastases or ankle splinting for the patient with foot drop caused by lumbosacral plexopathy.

Transcutaneous Electrical Nerve Stimulation

Transcutaneous electrical nerve stimulation (TENS) is associated with reduction in the threshold and perception of pain. The mechanism by which pain is attenuated is not well defined; local neural blockade, branch block in the dorsal horn, and activation of a central inhibitory system have all been proposed.[321,322] Clinical experience suggests that this modality is a useful adjunct in the management of mild to moderate musculoskeletal pain.

Anesthetic and Neurosurgical Analgesic Techniques for Pain Refractory to Systemic Pharmacotherapy

Anesthetic and neurosurgical techniques are important for the patient who has not obtained satisfactory pain relief using systemically administered opioids and adjuvant analgesics. In the Italian validation study of the WHO analgesic ladder, anesthetic and neurosurgical techniques were required in less than 30 percent of patients. Even when these methods are implemented, concurrent systemic pharmacotherapy will be required.[181] The major indications for these techniques are presented in Table 109-15.

Regional Analgesia

Epidural and Intrathecal Opioids. The delivery of low opioid doses near the sites of activity in the spinal cord may decrease supraspinally mediated adverse effects. Compared to neuroablative therapies, spinal opioids have the advantage of preserving normal sensitivity and sympathetic function. In the absence of

Table 109-15
Anesthetic and Neurosurgical Analgesic Techniques for Pain Refractory to Systemic Pharmacotherapy and Their Indications

Technique	*Clinical situation in which it should be considered*
Spinal opioids	Systemic opioid analgesia complicated by unmanageable supraspinally mediated adverse effects
Celiac plexus block	Refractory malignant pain involving the upper abdominal viscera including the upper retroperitoneum, liver, small bowel, and proximal colon
Lumbar sympathetic blockage	Sympathetically maintained pain involving the legs
Chemical rhizotomy	Refractory bilateral pelvic or lumbosacral plexus pain in a patient confined to bed and with urinary diversion
Transacral neurolysis	Refractory pain limited to the perineum
Cordotomy	Refractory unilateral pain arising below midthoracic level
Myelotomy	Not generally recommended (see text)
Dorsal root entry zone (DREZ) lesion	Refractory lumbosacral plexopathy in a patient with a prolonged life expectancy

Table 109-16
Adverse Effects of Chronic Intraspinal Opioids (Median %)

	Epidural	*Intrathecal*
Investigators	27	16
No. patients	4530	975
Duration (days)	100 (1–700)	91 (3–579)
Pain on injection	21 (0–27)	0 (0)
Severe respiratory depression	1 (0–18)	0.6 (0–4)
Pruritus	16 (1–68)	21 (0–30)
Urinary retention	12 (0–24)	22 (0–53)
Nausea, vomiting	18 (7–22)	27 (0–68)
Headache		15 (0–22)
Dysphoria or euphoria	8 (0–30)	8 (0–14)
Infection, superficial	4 (0–9)	8 (0–10)
Infection, severe	1 (0–7)	1.5 (0–10)

SOURCE: Adapted from De Castro et al.[331]

contraindications (such as the presence of epidural tumor, bleeding diathesis, or sepsis), a temporary trial of spinal opioid therapy should be performed to assess the potential benefits of this approach before implantation of a permanent catheter. Opioid selection for intraspinal delivery is influenced by several factors. Hydrophilic drugs, such as morphine and hydromorphone, have a prolonged half-life in cerebrospinal fluid and significant rostral redistribution.[323–325] Lipophilic opioids such as fentanyl and sufentanil, which have less rostral redistribution[326] may be preferable for segmental analgesia at the level of spinal infusion. In some patients, the addition of a low concentration of a local anesthetic, such as 0.25% bupivacaine, to an intraspinal opioid has been demonstrated to increase analgesic effect without increasing toxicity.[327–330] Several types of intraspinal delivery systems involving portable and implanted infusion pumps have been described. The adverse effects of pooled prospective data from 24 investigators and over 5000 patients have recently been presented (Table 109-16).[331] The potential morbidity from these procedures indicates the need for a well-trained clinician and long-term monitoring in the care of patients who undergo this approach.

Anesthetic Neuroablative Techniques for Sympathetically Mediated Pain and Visceral Pain

Celiac Plexus Block. Neurolytic celiac plexus blockade (NCPB) can be considered in the management of pain caused by malignancy of the upper abdominal viscera, including the upper retroperitoneum, liver, small bowel, and proximal colon.[332–334] Analgesic response rates in the region of 50 to 90 percent are reported, with a duration of effect of from 1 to 12 months.[332–334] Common transient complications include postural hypotension and diarrhea.[332–334] Posterior spread of neurolytic solution may lead to the involvement of lower thoracic and lumbar somatic nerves and can result in severe neuralgias in the region of the lower rib cage or upper thigh. Uncommon complications include pneumothorax, retroperitoneal hematoma, and paraparesis.

Lumbar Sympathetic Blockade. Lumbar sympathetic blockade should be considered for sympathetically maintained pain involving the legs. The risk of sphincter dysfunction with this technique is small.[333]

Anesthetic and Neurosurgical Neuroablative Techniques for Somatic and Neuropathic Pain

Chemical Rhizotomy. Chemical rhizotomy is an effective method of pain control for patients with advanced malignancy and otherwise refractory pelvic, perineal, or plexopathic pain.[335,336] The aim of subarachnoid and epidural neurolysis is to produce a chemical rhizotomy, thus interrupting the afferent pathways from the affected area. Because of the significant risk of increasing the patient's disability through motor weakness, sphincter incompetence, and loss of positional sense, chemical rhizotomy is best reserved for patients already confined to bed and with urinary diversion.

Subarachnoid techniques involving the use of absolute alcohol and phenol are well described.[333] Alcohol is hypobaric and is administered with the patient placed in the lateral oblique position, with the painful side uppermost. Phenol solutions are hyperbaric and viscous, and the technique requires that the patient lie on the painful side in a semilateral/supine position so that the posterior nerve roots are dependent. In addition to its neurolytic effect, phenol has an initial local anesthetic action, producing warmth, tingling, or a prickling sensation over the distribution the affected nerve. The hyperbaricity of phenol is of particular advantage in the production of saddle-block anesthesia in patients with midline pain owing to pelvic cancer.

Epidural rhizotomy is an alternative technique that involves epidural catheter placement with the tip close to the center of the segmental area to be blocked. After a local anesthetic test dose is injected to confirm placement, small doses of phenol or alcohol are injected at 1-day intervals until the desired analgesic result is obtained. Approximately 1 to 3 mL is injected on each occasion. With phenol-in-saline solutions, onset of pain relief is rapid (1 to 2 min).

Satsifactory analgesia is achieved in about 50 percent of patients.[333] Adverse effects can be related to the injection technique (spinal headache, mechanical neural damage, infection, and arachnoiditis) or to the neurolysis of nerve fibers not concerned in the mediation of pain. Complications include motor paresis (5 to 20 percent), sphincter dysfunction (5 to 60 percent), impairment of touch and proprioception, and dysesthesias.[333] Fortunately, neurologic deficits are usually transient, although fatal meningitis, paraplegia, and permanent impairment of sphincteric function have been recorded.[333] Patient counseling regarding the risks involved in these techniques is essential.

Transacral Neurolysis. Refractory pain limited to the perineum may be amenable to neurolysis of the S4 nerve root via the ipsilateral posterior sacral foramen.[337] This technique is associated with minimal risk of motor impairment.

Cordotomy. Cordotomy is a procedure whereby the anterolateral spinothalamic tract is ablated to produce contralateral hypesthesia to pain and temperature.[338,339] The patient with severe unilateral pain arising in the torso or lower extremity, such as that due to tumor involving the pelvic side wall, is most likely to benefit from this procedure.[336] The percutaneous cervical cordotomy is performed under local anesthesia, with biplanar fluoroscopic monitoring. A miniature electrode is inserted into the anterolateral quadrant of the cervical spine through a C1-C2 puncture. With the patient awake, it is possible to test placement of the electrode to ensure adequate somatotopic localization before an ablative thermal lesion is made with a radiofrequency generator[338] The open cordotomy is performed either through posterior laminectomy or by an anterior low cervical approach. Open cordotomy is now generally reserved for patients who are unable to lie in the supine position or who are not cooperative enough to undergo a percutaneous procedure.[338]

Significant pain relief is achieved in more than 90 percent of patients during the period immediately following the procedure.[336,338–340] Fifty percent of surviving patients have recurrent pain after 1 year and repeat cordotomy may be necessary. The neurologic complications of cordotomy include paresis, ataxia, and bladder dysfunction.[340] The complications are usually transient but are protracted and disabling in approximately 5 percent of cases. Rarely, patients with a long duration of survival (>12 months) develop a delayed-onset dysesthetic pain. The most serious potential complication is respiratory dysfunction, which may occur in the form of phrenic nerve paralysis or as sleep-induced apnea.[341] The latter is a result of the interruption of ascending reticular pathways. Because of these concerns, bilateral high cervical cordotomies or a unilateral cervical cordotomy ipsilateral to the site of a solely functioning lung are not recommended.

Myelotomy. Surgical myelotomy aims to interrupt the decussating spinothalamic fibers subserving both sides of the body so as to produce symmetrical loss of pain and temperature sensation in the subserved dermatomes.[342] The analgesia produced by this technique is often suboptimal and of short duration.[342] It has been suggested that refractory midline perineal pain, the most specific indication of commissural myelotomy, is more easily and effectively controlled with chemical rhizotomy.[343]

Lesions of the Dorsal Root Entry Zone. The dorsal root entry zone (DREZ) lesion results from an ablative procedure of the substantia gelatinosa Rolandi and the surrounding tracts designed to destroy dorsal horn neurons in those spinal segments that correspond to the patient's pain. The procedure is performed under general anesthesia and requires a multilevel laminectomy. Pain relief from lesions not associated with nerve root avulsion is observed in only 30 to 50 percent of cases,[344] and there is very little experience in the application of this technique to cancer pain. The patient with refractory lumbosacral plexopathy resulting from treatment (radiation, chemotherapy, or surgery), or one who has tumor-related deafferentation pain and a reasonable life expectancy could be considered for this procedure. Complications of DREZ procedures include increasing neurologic dysfunction with loss of proprioception and dysesthesias.

CONCLUSION

Among patients with colorectal and anal cancer, the experience of acute pain is virtually universal, and a large proportion develop chronic pain in the setting of incurable disease. The illness experience of the patient with locally extensive or metastatic disease can be long, and adequate symptom control is a major clinical challenge that can extend over many months or years. The individual practitioner can effectively treat the majority of pain problems by attending to careful pain assessment and implementing analgesic therapy.[1] Currently available analgesic techniques can provide adequate relief to the vast majority of patients, most of whom will respond to systemic pharmacotherapy alone. Comprehensive continuing care requires the integration of this expertise with management of other symptoms and the psychosocial needs of the patient. Cancer is a dynamic problem, and successful ongoing management requires a continuity of care that provides an appropriate level of monitoring and responds quickly, flexibly, and expertly to the changing needs of the patient. Patients with refractory pain or unremitting suffering related to other losses or distressing symptoms should have access to specialists in pain management or palliative medicine who can provide an approach capable of addressing these complex problems.

REFERENCES

1. Balch CM: The surgeon's expanded role in cancer care. *Cancer* 3:604–609, 1990.
2. Jorgensen L, Mortensen MB, Jensen NH, et al: Treatment of cancer pain patients in a multidisciplinary pain clinic. *Pain Clinic* 3:83–89, 1990.
3. Stjernsward J, Teoh N: The scope of the cancer pain problem, in Foley KM, Bonica JJ, Ventafridda V (eds): *Second International Congress on Cancer Pain,* vol 16. New York, Raven Press, 1990, pp 7–12.
4. Bonica JJ: Treatment of cancer pain: Current status and future needs, in Fields HL, Dubner R, Cervero F (eds): *Advances in Pain Research and Therapy,* vol 9. New York, Raven Press, 1989, pp 589–616.
5. Portenoy RK, Miransky J, Thaler HT, et al: Pain in ambulatory patients with lung or colon cancer: Prevalence, characteristics and impact. *Cancer* 70:1616–1624, 1992.
6. Brescia FJ, Portenoy RK, Ryan M, et al: Pain, opioid use, and survival in hospitalized patients with advanced cancer. *J Clin Oncol* 10:149–155, 1992.
7. Edwards RB: Pain management and the values of health care providers, in Hill CS, Fields WS (eds): *Drug Treatment of Cancer Pain in a Drug Oriented Society: Advances in Pain Research and Therapy,* vol 11. New York, Raven Press, 1989, pp 101–112.
8. Wanzer SH, Federman DD, Adelstein SJ, et al: The physician's responsibility toward hopelessly ill patients—A second look. *N Engl J Med* 120:844–849, 1989.
9. Martin RS: Mortal values: Healing, pain and suffering, in Hill CS, Fields WS (eds): *Drug Treatment of Cancer Pain in a Drug Oriented Society: Advances in Pain Research and Therapy,* vol 11. New York, Raven Press, 1989, pp 19–26.
10. Ventafridda V: Continuing care; A major issue in cancer pain management. *Pain* 36:137–143, 1989.
11. Shegda LM, McCorkle R: Continuing care in the community. *J Pain Symptom Management* 5:279–286, 1990.
12. Coyle N: A model of continuity of care for cancer patients with chronic pain. *Med Clin North Am* 71:259–270, 1987.
13. World Health Organization: *Cancer Pain Relief and Palliative Care.* Geneva, World Health Organization, 1990, p 75.
14. International Association for the Study of Pain, Subcommittee on Taxonomy: Pain terms: A list with definitions and notes on usage. *Pain* 8:249–252, 1980.
15. Derogatis LR, Morrow GR, Fetting J, et al: The prevalence of psychiatric disorders among cancer patients. *JAMA* 249:751–757, 1983.
16. Breitbart W: Psychiatric management of cancer pain. *Cancer* 63:2336–2342, 1989.
17. Gonzales GR, Elliot KJ, Portenoy RK, et al: The impact of a comprehensive evaluation in the management of cancer pain. *Pain* 47:141–144, 1991.
18. Mense S, Stahnke M: Responses in muscle afferent fibers of slow conduction velocity to contractions and ischaemia in the cat. *J Physiol (London)* 342:343–348, 1983.
19. Ness TJ, Gebhart GE: Visceral pain: A review of experimental studies. *Pain* 41:167–234, 1990.
20. Perl ER: Characterization of nociceptors and their activation of neurons in the superficial dorsal horn: First step for the sensation pain, in Kruger L, Liebeskind JC (eds): *Advances in Pain Research and Therapy,* vol 6. New York, Raven Press, 1984, pp 23–52.
21. Besson JM, Chaouch A: Peripheral and spinal mechanisms of nociception. *Physiol Rev* 67:67–186, 1987.
22. Willis WD: *The Pain System: The Neural Basis of Nociceptive Transmission in the Mammalian Nervous System.* Basel, Karger, 1985.
23. Duggan AW, Weihe E: Central transmission of impulses in the nociceptor events in the superficial dorsal horn, in Basbaum AI, Besson J-M (eds): *Towards a New Pharmacotherapy of Pain.* New York, Wiley, 1991, pp 35–67.
24. Kocher L, Anton F, Reeh PW, et al: The effect of carrageenan-induced inflammation on the excitability of unmyelinated skin nociceptors in the rat. *Pain* 29:363–373, 1987.
25. Melzack R, Wall PD: Pain mechanisms: A new theory. *Science* 150:971–978, 1965.
26. Basbaum AI, Fields HL: Endogenous pain control systems: Brainstem spinal pathways and endorphin circuitry. *Annu Rev Neurosci* 7:309–338, 1984.
27. Evans CJ, Hammond DL, Fredrickson RCA: The opioid peptides, in Pasternak GW (ed): *The Opiate Receptors.* Clifton, New Jersey, Humana Press, 1988, pp 23–74.
28. Dickenson AH: Mechanisms of the analgesic actions of opiates and opioids. *Br Med J* 47:690–702, 1991.
29. Yaksh TL: Direct evidence that spinal serotonin and noradrenaline terminals mediate the spinal antinociceptive effects of morphine in the periaqueductal gray. *Brain Res* 160:180–185, 1979.
30. Ventafridda V, Caraceni A: Cancer pain classification: a controversial issue. *Pain* 46:1–2, 1991.
31. Arner S, Meyerson BA: Lack of analgesic effect of opioids on neuropathic and idiopathic forms of pain. *Pain* 33:11–23, 1988.
32. American Psychiatric Association: Somatoform disorders, in *Diagnostic and Statistical Manual of Mental Disorders,* 3rd ed. Washington DC, American Psychiatric Association, 1987, pp 255–267.
33. Cherny NI, Thaler HT, Friedlander-Klar H, et al: Opioid responsiveness of neuropathic cancer pain: Combined analysis of single-dose analgesic trials (abstract). *Proc Am Soc Clin Oncol* 11:abst 1330, 1992.
34. Devor M, Basbaum AI, Bennett GJ, et al: Group report: Mechanisms of neuropathic pain following peripheral injury, in Basbaum A, Besson J-M (eds): *Towards a New Pharmacotherapy of Pain.* New York: Wiley, 417–440, 1991.

35. Portenoy RK: Issues in the management of neuropathic pain, in Basbaum A, Besson J-M (eds): *Towards a New Pharmacotherapy of Pain*. New York, Wiley, 1991, pp 393–416.
36. Janig W, Blumberg H, Boas RA, et al: The reflex sympathetic dystrophy syndrome: Consensus statement and general recommendations for diagnosis and clinical research, in Bond MR, Charlton JE, Woolf CJ (eds): *Proceedings of the VIth World Congress on Pain. Pain Research and Clinical Management,* vol 4. Amsterdam, Elsevier, 1991, pp 373–382.
37. Portenoy RK, Foley KM, Inturrisi CE: The nature of opioid responsiveness and its implications for neuropathic pain: New hypotheses derived from studies of opioid infusions. *Pain* 43:273–286, 1990.
38. Dubner R: A call for more science, not more rhetoric, regarding opioids and neuropathic pain. *Pain* 47:1–2, 1991.
39. Portenoy RK: Adjuvant analgesics in pain management, in Doyle D, Hanks GW, MacDonald N (eds): *Oxford Textbook of Palliative Medicine*. Oxford England, Oxford University Press, 1993, pp 187–203.
40. Bond MR, Pearson IB: Psychosocial aspects of pain in women with advanced cancer of the cervix. *J Psychosom Res* 13:13–21, 1969.
41. Barkwell DP: Ascribed meaning: A critical factor in coping and pain attenuation in patients with cancer-related pain. *J Palliat Care* 7(3):5–14, 1991.
42. Daut RL, Cleeland CS: The prevalence and severity of pain in cancer. *Cancer* 50:1913–1918, 1982.
43. Bolund C: Medical and care factors in suicides by cancer patients in Sweden. *J Psychosoc Oncol* 3:31–52, 1985.
44. Breitbart W: Suicide in the cancer patient. *Oncology* 1:49–54, 1987.
45. Cleeland CS: The impact of pain on the patient with cancer. *Cancer* 54:2635–2641, 1984.
46. Breitbart W: Cancer pain and suicide, in Foley KM, Bonica JJ, Ventafridda V (eds): *Second International Congress on Cancer Pain*. (*Advances in Pain Research and Therapy,* vol 16.) New York, Raven Press; 1990, pp 399–412.
47. Fishman B: The treatment of suffering in patients with cancer pain: Cognitive behavioral approaches, in Foley KM, Bonica JJ, Ventafridda V (eds): *Second International Congress on Cancer Pain*. (*Advances in Pain Research and Therapy,* vol 16.) New York, Raven Press, 1990, pp 301–316.
48. Lazarus RS, Folkman C: *Stress, Appraisal and Coping*. New York, Springer Verlag, 1984.
49. Cassel EJ: The nature of suffering and the goals of medicine. *N Engl J Med* 306:639–645, 1982.
50. Ventafridda V, DeConno F, Ripamonti C, et al: Quality of life assessment during a palliative care program. *Ann Oncol* 1:415–420, 1990.
51. Jaeckle KA: Nerve plexus metastases. *Neurol Clin* 9:857–866, 1991.
52. Boureau F, Doubrere JF, Luu M: Study of verbal description in neuropathic pain. *Pain* 42:145–152, 1990.
53. Banning A, Sjogren P, Henriksen H: Pain causes in 200 patients referred to a multidisciplinary cancer pain clinic. *Pain* 45:45–48, 1991.
54. Coyle N, Adelhardt J, Foley KM, et al: Character of terminal illness in the advanced cancer patient: Pain and other symptoms during last four weeks of life. *J Pain Symptom Mgt* 5:83–89, 1990.
55. Twycross RG, Lack SA. Symptom control in far-advanced cancer: Pain relief. London, Pitman, 1984.
56. Kellgren JG: On distribution of pain arising from deep somatic structures with charts of segmental pain areas. *Clin Sci* 4:35–46, 1939.
57. Torebjork HE, Ochoa JL, Schady W: Referred pain from intraneural stimulation of muscle fascicles in the median nerve. *Pain* 18:145–156, 1984.
58. Bonica JJ, Ventafridda V, Twycross RG: Cancer pain, in Bonica JJ (ed): *The Management of Pain,* 2nd ed. Philadelphia, Lea & Febiger, 1990, pp 400–460.
59. McCaffery M, Thorpe DM: Differences in perception of pain and the development of adversarial relationships among health care providers, in Hill CS, Fields WS (eds): *Drug Treatment of Cancer Pain in a Drug Oriented Society*. (*Advances in Pain Research and Therapy,* vol 11.) New York, Raven Press, 1989, pp 19–26.
60. Portenoy RK, Hagen NA: Breakthrough pain: Definition, prevalence, and characteristics. *Pain* 41:273–281, 1990.
61. Foley KM: The treatment of cancer pain. *N Engl J Med* 313:84–95, 1985.
62. Foley KM: Clinical assessment of pain. *Acta Anaesth Scand* 74(suppl):91–96, 1982.
63. Twycross RG, Fairfield S: Pain in far-advanced cancer. *Pain* 14:303–310, 1982.
64. Cleeland CS: Pain control: public and physician's attitudes, in Hill CS, Fields WS (eds): *Drug Treatment of Cancer Pain in a Drug-Oriented Society,* vol 11. New York, Raven Press, 1989, pp 81–89.
65. Melzack R: The McGill pain questionnaire: Major properties and scoring methods. *Pain* 1:277–299, 1975.
66. Fishman B, Pasternak S, Wallenstein SL, et al: The Memorial Pain Assessment Card: A valid instrument for the evaluation of cancer pain. *Cancer* 60:1151–1158, 1987.
67. Foley KM: Controversies in cancer pain: Medical perspective. *Cancer* 63:2257–2265, 1989.
68. Ventafridda V, Ripamonti C, De Conno F, et al: Symptom prevalence and control during cancer patients' last days of life. *J Palliat Care* 6:7–11, 1990.
69. Reuben DB, Mor V, Hiris J: Clinical symptoms and length of survival in patients with terminal cancer. *Arch Intern Med* 148:1586–1591, 1988.
70. Moinpour CM, Feigl P, Metch B, et al: Quality of life endpoints in cancer clinical trials. *J Natl Cancer Inst* 81:485–495, 1989.
71. Moinpour CM, Hayden KA, Thomson IM, et al: Quality of life assessment in Southwest Oncology Group trials. *Oncology* 4(5):79–84, 1990.
72. Clouston P, De Angelis L, Posner JB: The spectrum of neurologic disease in patients with systemic cancer. *Ann Neurol* 31:268–273, 1992.
73. Haines IE, Zalcberg J, Buchanan JD: Not-for-resuscitation orders in cancer patients: Principles of decision making. *Med J Aust* 153:225–229, 1990.
74. Rusthoven JJ, Ahlgren P, Elhakim T, et al: Risk factors for varicella zoster disseminated infection among adult cancer patients with localized zoster. *Cancer* 62:1641–1646, 1988.
75. Portenoy RK, Duma C, Foley KM: Acute herpetic and postherpetic neuralgia: Clinical review and current management. *Ann Neurol* 20:651–664, 1986.
76. Rusthoven JJ, Ahlgren P, Elhakim T, et al: Varicella-zoster infection in adult cancer patients: A population study. *Arch Inter Med* 148:1561–1566, 1988.
77. Silen W: Cope's *Early Diagnosis of the Acute Abdomen,* 16th ed. New York, Oxford, 1983.
78. Mulholland MW, Debas H, Bonica JJ: Diseases of the liver, biliary system and pancreas, in Bonica JJ (ed): *The Management of Pain* vol 2. Philadelphia, Lea & Febiger, 1990, pp 1214–1231.
79. Coombs DW: Pain due to liver capsular distention, in Ferrer-Brechner T (ed): *Common Problems in Pain Management.*

(*Common Problems in Anesthesia.*) Chicago, Year Book, 1990, pp 247–253.

80. Ventafridda V, Ripamonti C, Caraceni A, et al: The management of inoperable gastrointestinal obstruction in terminal cancer patients. *Tumori* 76:389–393, 1990.
81. Baines MJ: Management of malignant intestinal obstruction in patients with advanced cancer, in Foley KM, Bonica JJ, Ventafridda V (eds): *Second International Congress on Cancer Pain.* (*Advances in Pain Research and Therapy,* vol 16.) New York, Raven Press, 1990, pp 327–336.
82. Walsch D, Williams G: Surgical biopsy studies of omental and peritoneal nodules. *Br J Surg* 58:428–432, 1971.
83. Bender MD: Diseases of the peritoneum, mesentery and diaphragm, in Sleisenger MH, Fordtran JS (eds): *Gastrointestinal Disease: Pathophysiology, Diagnosis, Management,* 4th ed. Philadelphia, Saunders, 1989, pp 1932–1967.
84. Lynch MA, Cho KC, Jeffrey RJ, et al: CT of peritoneal lymphomatosis. *Am J Roentgenol* 151:713–715, 1988.
85. Stillman M: Perineal pain: Diagnosis and management, with particular attention to perineal pain of cancer, in Foley KM, Bonica JJ, Ventafrida V (eds): *Second International Congress on Cancer Pain.* (*Advances in Pain Research and Therapy,* vol 16.) New York, Raven Press, 1990, pp 359–377.
86. Seefeld PH, Bargen JA: The spread of carcinoma of the rectum: Invasion of lymphatics, veins and nerves. *Ann Surg* 118:76–90, 1943.
87. Sinaki M, Merritt JL, Stilwell GK: Tension myalgia of the pelvic floor. *Mayo Clin Proc* 52:717–722, 1977.
88. Greenfield A, Resnick MI: Genitourinary emergencies. *Semin Oncol* 16:516–520, 1989.
89. Talner LB: Specific causes of obstruction, in Pollack HM (ed): *Clinical Urography,* vol 2. Philadelphia, Saunders, 1990, pp 1629–1751.
90. Frohlich EP, Bex P, Nissenbaum MM, et al: Comparison between renal ultrasonography and excretory urography in cervical cancer. *Int J Gynaecol Obstet* 34:49–54, 1991.
91. Fair WR: Urologic emergencies, in DeVita VT, Hellman S, Rosenberg SA (eds): *Cancer Principles and Practice of Oncology,* 3rd ed. Philadelphia, Lippincott, 1989, pp 2016–2028.
92. Chad DA, Bradley WG: Lumbosacral plexopathy. *Semin Neurol* 7:97–104, 1987.
93. Garcia-Diaz J, Balseiro J, Calandre L, et al: Aortic dissection presenting with neurologic signs. *N Engl J Med* 318:1070, 1988.
94. Brown MJ, Asbury AK: Diabetic neuropathy. *Ann Neurol* 15:2–12, 1984.
95. Evans BA: Lumbosacral plexus neuropathy. *Neurology* 31:1327–1330, 1981.
96. Bradley WG, Chad D, Verghese JP, et al: Painful lumbosacral plexopathy with elevated erythrocyte sedimentation rate: A treatable inflammatory syndrome. *Ann Neurol* 15:457–464, 1984.
97. Jaeckle KA, Young DF, Foley KM: The natural history of lumbosacral plexopathy in cancer. *Neurology* 35:8–15, 1985.
98. Stevens MJ, Gonet YM: Malignant psoas syndrome: Recognition of an oncologic entity. *Australas Radiol* 34:150–154, 1990.
99. Brodal A: *Neurological Anatomy.* Oxford, England, Oxford University Press, 1981, pp 527–530, 756–758.
100. Dalmau J, Graus F, Marco M: "Hot and dry foot" as initial manifestation of neoplastic lumbosacral plexopathy. *Neurology* 39:871–872, 1989.
101. Gilchrist JM, Moore M: Lumbosacral plexopathy in cancer patients. *Neurology* 35:1392, 1985.
102. Evans RJ, Watson CPN: Lumbosacral plexopathy in cancer patients. *Neurology* 35:1392–1393, 1985.
103. Portenoy RK, Galer BS, Salamon O, et al: Identification of epidural neoplasm: Radiography and bone scintigraphy in the symptomatic and asymptomatic spine. *Cancer* 64:2207–2213, 1989.
104. Abrams HL, Spiro R, Goldstein N: Metastases in carcinoma: Analysis of 1000 autopsied cases. *Cancer* 23:74–85, 1950.
105. Nielsen OS, Munro AJ, Tannock IF: Bone metastases: Pathophysiology and management policy. *J Clinical Oncol* 9:509–524, 1991.
106. Gilbert RW, Kim JH, Posner JB: Epidural spinal cord compression from metastatic tumor: Diagnosis and treatment. *Ann Neurol* 3:40–51, 1978.
107. Sorensen S, Borgesen SE, Rohde K, et al: Metastatic epidural spinal cord compression: Results of treatment and survival. *Cancer* 65:1502–1508, 1990.
108. Stark RJ, Henson RA, Evans SJW: Spinal metastases: A retrospective survey from a general hospital. *Brain* 105:189–197, 1982.
109. Phillips E, Levine AM: Metastatic lesions of the upper cervical spine. *Spine* 14:1071–1077, 1989.
110. Posner JB: Back pain and epidural spinal cord compression. *Med Clin North Am* 71:185–206, 1987.
111. Grant R, Papadopoulos SM, Greenberg HS: Metastatic epidural spinal cord compression. *Neurol Clin* 9:825–841, 1991.
112. Ruff RL, Lanska DJ: Epidural metastases in prospectively evaluated in veterans with cancer and back pain. *Cancer* 63:2234–2241, 1989.
113. Barcena A, Lobato RD, Rivas JJ, et al: Spinal metastatic disease: Analysis of factors determining functional prognosis and choice of treatment. *Neurosurgery* 15:820–827, 1984.
114. Sundaresan N, Galicich JH, Lane JM, et al: Treatment of neoplastic epidural cord compression by vertebral resection and stabilization. *J Neurosurg* 63:676–684, 1985.
115. Sundaresan N, Galicich JH, Bains MS, et al: Vertebral body resection in the treatment of cancer involving the spine. *Cancer* 53:1393–1396, 1984.
116. Harrington KD: Anterior cord decompression and spinal stabilization for patients with metastatic lesions of the spine. *J Neurosurg* 61:107–117, 1984.
117. Brice J, McKissock W: Surgical treatment of malignant extradural tumors. *Br J Med* 1:1341–1346, 1965.
118. Findlay GF: The role of vertebral body collapse in the management of malignant spinal cord compression. *J Neurol Neurosurg Psychiatry* 50:151–154, 1987.
119. Portenoy RK, Lipton RB, Foley KM: Back pain in the cancer patient: An algorithm for evaluation and management. *Neurology* 37:134–138, 1987.
120. Rodichok LD, Harper GR, Ruckdeschel JC, et al: Early diagnosis of spinal epidural metastases. *Am J Med* 70:1181–1188, 1981.
121. O'Rourke T, George CB, Redmond J: Spinal computed tomography and computer tomographic metrimazide myelography in the early diagnosis of spinal metastatic disease. *J Clin Oncol* 4:576–581, 1986.
122. Sim FH: Metastatic bone disease: Lesions of the pelvis and hip, in: Sim FH (ed): *Diagnosis and Management of Metastatic Bone Disease: A Multidisciplinary Approach.* New York, Raven Press, 1988, pp 183–198.
123. Beatrous TE, Choyke PL, Frank JA: Diagnostic evaluation of cancer patients with pelvic pain: Comparison of scintigraphy, CT, and MR imaging. *Am J Roentgenol* 155:85–88, 1990.
124. Posner JB: Headache and other head pain, in Wyngaaden JB, Smith LH, Claude Bennett J (ed): *Cecil's Textbook of*

Medicine, 19th ed. Philadelphia, Saunders, 1992, pp 2117–2123.

125. Wright DC, Delaney TF: Treatment of metastatic cancer to the brain, in DeVita VT, Hellman S, Rosenberg SA (eds): *Cancer: Principles and Practice of Oncology*, 3rd ed. Philadelphia, Lippincott, 1989, pp 2245–2261.
126. Forsyth PA, Posner JB: Headache associated with intracranial neoplasms, in Olesen J, Tfelt-Hansen P, Welch KMA (eds): *The Headaches*. New York, Raven Press, 1993, pp 705–714.
127. Fadul C, Misulis KE, Wiley RG: Cerebellar metastases: Diagnostic and management considerations. *J Clin Oncol* 5:1110–1115, 1987.
128. Posner JB, Chernik NL: Intracranial metastases from systemic cancer. *Adv Neurol* 19:575–587, 1978.
129. Wasserstrom WR, Glass JP, Posner JB: Diagnosis and treatment of leptomeningeal metastasis from solid tumors: Experience with 90 patients. *Cancer* 49:759–772, 1982.
130. Kaplan JG, DeSouza TG, Farkash A, et al: Leptomeningeal metastases: Comparison of clinical features and laboratory data of solid tumors, lymphomas and leukemias. *J Neurooncol* 9:225–229, 1990.
131. Glass PJ, Foley KM: Carcinomatous meningitis, in Harris JR, Hellman S, Henderson IC, et al (eds): *Breast Diseases*. Philadelphia, Lippincott, 1991, pp 700–710.
132. Henson RA, Urich H: *Cancer and the Nervous System*. Boston, Blackwell, 1982, pp 100–119, 368–405.
133. Olsen ME, Chernik NL, Posner JB: Infiltration of the leptomeninges by systemic cancer. *Arch Neurol* 30:122–137, 1974.
134. Greenberg HS, Deck MDF, Vikram B, et al: Metastasis to the base of the skull: Clinical findings in 43 patients. *Neurology* 31:530–537, 1981.
135. Elliott K, Foley KM: Neurologic pain syndromes in patients with cancer. *Neurol Clin* 7:333–360, 1989.
136. Boas RA: Phantom anus syndrome, in Bonica JJ, Lindblom U, Iggo A (eds): *Proceedings of the Third World Congress on Pain*. (*Advances in Pain Research and Therapy*, vol 5.) New York, Raven Press, 1983, pp 947–951.
137. Ovesen P, Kroner K, Ornsholt J, et al: Phantom-related phenomena after rectal amputation: Prevalence and characteristics. *Pain* 44:289–291, 1991.
138. Boas RA: Post-surgical perineal pain in cancer: A 5 year follow-up. *Pain* (suppl 5):376, 1990.
139. Thomas JE, Cascino TL, Earl JD: Differential diagnosis between radiation and tumor plexopathy of the pelvis. *Neurology* 35:1–7, 1985.
140. Buchi K: Radiation proctitis: Therapy and prognosis. *JAMA* 265:1180, 1991.
141. Earnest DL, Trier JS: Radiation enteritis and colitis, in Sleisenger MH, Fordtran JS (eds): *Gastrointestinal Disease: Pathophysiology, Diagnosis, Management*, vol 2. Philadelphia, Saunders, 1989, pp 1369–1382.
142. Minsky B, Cohen A: Minimizing the toxicity of radiation therapy in rectal cancer. *Oncology* 2:21–25, 1988.
143. Jellinger K, Strum KW: Delayed radiation in myelopathy in man. *J Neurol Sci* 14:389–408, 1971.
144. Cascino TL: Radiation myelopathy, in Rottenberg DA (ed): *Neurological Complications of Cancer Treatment*. Boston, Butterworth-Heinemann, pp 1991, 69–78.
145. Epstein JB, Wong FLW, Stephenson-Moore P: Osteoradionecrosis: Clinical experience and a proposal for classification. *J Oral Maxillofacial Surg* 45:104–110, 1987.
146. Epstein JB, Schubert MM, Scully C: Evaluation and treatment of pain in patients with orofacial cancer. *Pain Clin* 4:3–20, 1991.
147. Foley KM, Inturrisi CE: Analgesic drug therapy in cancer pain: Principles and practice. *Med Clin North Am* 71:207–232, 1987.
148. Belgrade MJ: Control of pain in cancer patients. *Postgrad Med* 85:319–323, 1989.
149. Ferrell BR, Wisdom C, Wenzl C: Quality of life as an outcome variable in the management of cancer pain. *Cancer* 11:2321–2327, 1989.
150. Bates T: A review of local radiotherapy in the treatment of bone metastases and cord compression. *Int J Radiat Oncol Biol Phys* 23:217–222, 1992.
151. Bates T, Yarnold JR, Blitzer P, et al: Bone metastasis consensus statement. *Int J Radiat Oncol Biol Phys* 23:215–216, 1992.
152. Coia LR: The role of radiotherapy in the treatment of brain metastases. *Int J Radiat Oncol Biol Phys* 23:239–244, 1992.
153. Bosch A: Radiotherapy. *Clin Oncol* 3:47–53, 1984.
154. Dobrowsky W, Schmidt AP: Radiotherapy for presacral recurrence following radical surgery for rectal carcinoma. *Dis Colon Rectum* 28:917–919, 1985.
155. Borgelt BB, Gelber R, Brady LW, et al: The palliation of hepatic metastases: Results of a Radiation Therapy Oncology Group pilot study. *Int J Radiat Oncol Biol Phys* 7:587–591, 1981.
156. Prassad B, Lee M, Hendrickson FR: Irradiation of hepatic metastases. *Int J Radiat Oncol Biol Phys* 2:129–132, 1977.
157. Sherman DM, Weichselbaum R, Order SE, et al: Palliation of hepatic metastatases. *Cancer* 41:2013–2017, 1978.
158. Minsky BD, Leibel S: The treatment of hepatic metastases from colorectal cancer with radiation therapy alone or combined with chemotherapy or misonidazole. *Cancer Treat Rev* 16:213–219, 1989.
159. MacDonald N: The role of medical and surgical oncology in the management of cancer pain, in Foley KM, Bonica JJ, Ventafrida V (eds): *Second International Congress on Cancer Pain*. (*Advances in Pain Research and Therapy*, vol 16.) New York, Raven Press, 1990, pp 27–39.
160. Patt YZ, Peters RE, Chuang VP, et al: Palliation of pelvic recurrence of colorectal cancer with intra-arterial 5-fluorouracil and mitomycin. *Cancer* 56:2175–2180, 1985.
161. Bruckner HW, Motwani BT: Chemotherapy of advanced cancer of the colon and rectum. *Semin Oncol* 18:443–461, 1991.
162. Cummings BJ: Anal cancer. *Int J Radiat Oncol Biol Phys* 19:1309–1315, 1990.
163. Tanum G, Tveit K, Karlsen KO, et al: Chemotherapy and radiation therapy for anal carcinoma: Survival and late morbidity. *Cancer* 67:2462–2466, 1991.
164. Boraas M: Palliative surgery. *Semin Oncol* 12:368–374, 1985.
165. Sundaresan N, DiGiacinto GV: Antitumor and anti nociceptive approaches to control cancer pain. *Med Clin North Am* 71:329–348, 1987.
166. Williams MR: The place of surgery in terminal care, in Saunders C (ed): *The Management of Terminal Disease*. London, Edward Arnold, 1984.
167. Petrelli NJ, Velez A, Herrera L, et al: Ileal conduits for recurrent unresectable colorectal adenocarcinoma. *Am J Surg* 150:239–242, 1985.
168. Ross GJ, Kessler HB, Clair MR, et al: Sonographically guided paracentesis for palliation of symptomatic malignant ascites. *Am J Roentgenol* 153:1309–1311, 1989.
169. Cruikshank DP, Buchsbaum HJ: Effects of rapid paracentesis: Cardiovascular dynamics and body fluid composition. *JAMA* 225:1361, 1973.
170. Lifshitz S, Buchsbaum HJ: The effect of paracentesis on serum proteins. *Gynecol Oncol* 4:347, 1976.

171. Montesani C, Ribotta G, De MR, et al: Extended resection in the treatment of colorectal cancer. *Int J Colorect Dis* 6:161–164, 1991.
172. Williams LJ, Huddleston CB, Sawyers JL, et al: Is total pelvic exenteration reasonable primary treatment for rectal carcinoma? *Ann Surg* 207:670–678, 1988.
173. Takagi H, Morimoto T, Yasue M, et al: Total pelvic exenteration for advanced carcinoma of the lower colon. *J Surg Oncol* 28:59–62, 1985.
174. Temple WJ, Ketcham AS: Surgical palliation for recurrent rectal cancers ulcerating in the perineum. *Cancer* 65:1111–1114, 1990.
175. Burney RE, Faulkner DJ: Recurrent abdominal abscess caused by retained colorectum after proctocolectomy. *Surgery* 104:580–582, 1988.
176. Butch RJ, Wittenberg J, Mueller PR, et al: Presacral masses after abdominoperineal resection for colorectal carcinoma: The need for needle biopsy. *Am J Roentgenol* 144:309–312, 1985.
177. Bruera E, McDonald N: Intractable pain in patients with advanced head and neck tumors: A possible role of local infection. *Cancer Treat Rep* 70:691–692, 1986.
178. Coyle N, Portenoy RK: Infection as a cause of rapidly increasing pain in cancer patients. *J Pain Symptom Mgt* 6:266–269, 1991.
179. World Health Organization: *Cancer Pain Relief.* Geneva: World Health Organization, 1986, p 74.
180. Walker VA, Hoskin PJ, Hanks GW, et al: Evaluation of WHO analgesic guidelines for cancer pain in a hospital-based palliative care unit. *J Pain Symptom Mgt* 3:145–150, 1988.
181. Ventafridda V, Tamburini M, Caraceni A, et al: A validation study of the WHO method for cancer pain relief. *Cancer* 59:851–856, 1987.
182. Takeda F: Results of field-testing in Japan of WHO Draft Interim Guidelines on Relief of Cancer Pain. *Pain Clin* 1:83–89, 1986.
183. Schug SA, Zech D, Dorr U: Cancer pain management according to WHO analgesic guidelines. *J Pain Symptom Mgt* 5:27–32, 1990.
184. Grond S, Zech D, Schug SA, et al: Validation of the World Health Organisation guidelines for cancer pain relief during the last days and hours of life. *J Pain Symptom Mgt* 6:411–422, 1991.
185. Vane JR: Inhibition of prostaglandin synthesis as a mechanism of action for aspirin-like drugs. *Nature New Biol* 234:231–238, 1971.
186. Willer JC, DeBrouckert T, Bussel B, et al: Central analgesic effect of ketoprofen in humans: Electrophysiologic evidence for a supraspinal mechanism in a double-blind and crossover study. *Pain* 38:1–8, 1989.
187. Piletta P, Porchett HC, Dayer P: Central analgesic effect of acetaminophen but not of aspirin. *Clin Pharmacol Ther* 49:350–354, 1991.
188. Brooks PM, Wood AJJ: Nonsteroidal antiinflammatory drugs—Differences and similarities. *N Engl J Med* 324:1716–1725, 1991.
189. Seeff LB, Cuccherini BA, Zimmerman HI, et al: Acetaminophen hepatotoxicity in alcoholics. *Ann Intern Med* 104:399–404, 1986.
190. Insel PA: Analgesic-antipyretics and antiinflammatory agents: Drugs employed in the treatment of rheumatoid arthritis and gout, in Gilman AG, Rall TW, Nies AS, et al (eds): *The Pharmacological Basis of Therapeutics,* 8th ed. New York, Pergamon Press, 1990, pp 638–681.
191. Jaffe JH, Martin WR: Opioid analgesics and antagonists, in Gilman AG, Rall TW, Nies AS, et al (eds): *The Pharmacological Basis of Therapeutics,* 8th ed. New York: Pergamon Press, 1990, pp 485–521.
192. Houde RW, Wallenstein SL, Beaver WT: Evaluation of analgesics in patients with cancer pain, in Lasagna L (ed): *International Encyclopedia of Pharmacology and Therapeutics,* vol 1. New York, Pergamon Press, 1966, pp 59–67.
193. Kalso E, Vainio A: Morphine and oxycodone hydrochloride in the management of cancer pain. *Clin Pharmacol Ther* 47:639–646, 1990.
194. De Conno F, Ripamonti C, Sbannotto A, et al: A clinical study on the use of codeine, oxycodone, dextropropoxyphene, buprenorphine and pentazocine in cancer pain. *J Pain Symptom Mgt* 6:423–427, 1991.
195. Inturrisi CE, Colburn WN, Verebey K, et al: Propoxyphene and norpropoxyphene kinetics after single and repeated doses of propoxyphene. *Clin Pharmacol Ther* 31:157–167, 1982.
196. Sawe J, Svensson JO, Rane A: Morphine metabolism in cancer patients on increasing oral doses—No evidence for autoinduction or dose dependence. *J Clin Pharmacol* 16:85–93, 1983.
197. Paul D, Standifer KM, Inturrisi CE, et al: Pharmacological characterization of morphine-6 beta-glucuronide, a very potent morphine metabolite. *J Pharmacol Exp Ther* 251:477–483, 1989.
198. Pasternak GW, Bodnar RJ, Clarke JA, et al: Morphine-6-glucuronide, a potent Mu agonist. *Life Science* 41:2845–2849, 1987.
199. Shimomura K, Kamata O, Ueki S, et al: Analgesic effects of morphine glucuronides. *Tohoku J Exp Med* 105:45–51, 1971.
200. Osborne RJ, Joel SP, Slevin ML: Morphine intoxication in renal failure: The role of morphine-6-glucuronide. *Br J Med* 292:1548–1549, 1986.
201. Hanna MH, Peat SJ, Woodham M, et al: Analgesic efficacy and CSF pharmacokinetics of intrathecal morphine-6-glucuronide: Comparison with morphine. *Br J Anaesth* 64:547–550, 1990.
202. Hagen N, Foley KM, Cerbones DJ, et al: Chronic nausea and morphine-6-glucuronide. *J Pain Symptom Mgt* 6:125–128, 1991.
203. Houde RW, Wallenstein SL, Beaver WT: Clinical measurement of pain, in de Stevens G (ed): *Analgesics.* New York, Academic Press, 1965, pp 75–122.
204. Sawe J, Dahlstrom B, Paazlow L, et al: Morphine kinetics in cancer patients. *Clin Pharmacol Ther* 30:629–634, 1981.
205. Kaiko RF: Commentary: Equianalgesic dose ratio of intramuscular/oral morphine, 1 : 6 versus 1 : 3, in Foley KM, Inturrisi CE (eds): *Opioid Analgesics in the Management of Clinical Pain.* (*Advances Pain Research and Therapy,* vol 8.) New York, Raven Press, 1986, pp 87–94.
206. Arkinstall WW, Goughnour BR, White JA, et al: Control of severe pain with sustained-release morphine tablets v. oral morphine solution. *Can Med Assoc J* 140:653–657, 1989.
207. Warfield CA: Guidelines for the use of MS Contin tablets in the management of cancer pain. *Postgrad Med J* 67:12–16, 1991.
208. Inturrisi CE, Max MB, Foley KM, et al: The pharmacokinetics of heroin in patients with chronic pain. *N Engl J Med* 310:1213–1217, 1984.
209. Saltzburg D, Inturrisi CE, Greenslade R, et al: Blood profiles of heroin (H) and metabolites during repeated oral administration in cancer pain patients. *Proc Am Soc Clin Oncol,* 1988.
210. Moulin DE, Kreeft JH, Murray PN, et al: Comparison of continuous subcutaneous and intravenous hydromorphone

infusions for management of cancer pain. *Lancet* 465–468, 1991.

211. Szeto HH, Inturrisi CE, Houde R, et al: Accumulation of normeperidine, an active metabolite of meperidine, in patients with renal failure or cancer. *Ann Intern Med* 85:738–741, 1977.
212. Eisendrath SJ, Goldman B, Douglas J, et al: Meperidine-induced delirium. *Am J Psychiatry* 144:1062–1065, 1987.
213. Kaiko RF, Foley KM, Grabinski PV, et al: Central nervous system excitatory effects of meperidine in cancer patients. *Ann Neurol* 13:180–185, 1983.
214. Agency for Health Care Policy and Research, Acute Pain Management Panel: Acute pain management: Operative or medical procedures and trauma, *Clinical Practice Guideline*. Washington, DC, US Department of Health and Human Services, 1992.
215. Grochow L, Sheidler V, Grossman S, et al: Does intravenous methadone provide longer lasting analgesia than intravenous morphine? A randomized double-blind study. *Pain* 38:151–157, 1989.
216. Inturrisi CE, Portenoy RK, Max MB, et al: Pharmacokinetic-pharmacodynamic (PK-PD) relationships of methadone infusions in patients with cancer pain. *Clin Pharmacol Ther* 47:565–570, 1990.
217. Inturrisi CE, Colburn WA, Kaiko RF, et al: Pharmacokinetics and pharmacodynamics of methadone in patients with chronic pain. *Clin Pharmacol Ther* 41:392–401, 1987.
218. Bruera E, Fainsinger R, Moore M, et al: Local toxicity with subcutaneous methadone: Experience of two centers. *Pain* 45:141–145, 1991.
219. Sinatra RS, Hyde NH, Harrison DM: Oxymorphone revisited. *Semin Anesth* 8:208–215, 1988.
220. Hermens JM, Harifin JM, Hirshman CA: Comparison of histamine release in human skin mast cells by morphine, fentanyl and oxymorphone. *Anesthesiology* 62:124–129, 1985.
221. Rogers A: Considering histamine release in prescribing opioid analgesics. *J Pain Symptom Mgt* 6:44–45, 1991.
222. Moulin DE, Ling GS, Pasternak GW: Unidirectional cross tolerance between morphine and levorphanol in the rat. *Pain* 33:233–239, 1988.
223. Varvel JR, Shafter SL, Hwang SS, et al: Absorption characteristics of transdermally administered fentanyl. *Anesthesiology* 70:928–934, 1989.
224. Gourlay GK, Kowalski SR, Plummer JL, et al: The efficacy of transdermal fentanyl in the treatment of postoperative pain: A double blind comparison of fentanyl and placebo systems. *Pain* 40:21–28, 1990.
225. Calis KA, Kohler DR, Corso DM: Transdermally administered fentanyl for pain management. *Clin Pharmacol* 11:22–36, 1992.
226. Fine PG, Marcus M, DeBoer AJ, et al: An open label study of oral transmucosal fentanyl citrate (OTFC) for the treatment of breakthrough cancer pain. *Pain* 45:149–155, 1991.
227. Hasselstrom J, Eriksson LS, Persson A, et al: The metabolism and bioavailability of morphine in patients with severe liver cirrhosis. *Br J Clin Pharmacol* 29:289–297, 1990.
228. Chan GL, Matzke GR: Effects of renal insufficiency on the pharmacokinetics and pharmacodynamics of opioid analgesics. *Drug Intell Clin Pharm* 21:773–783, 1987.
229. Sawe J, Svensson JO, Odar-Cederlof I: Kinetics of morphine in patients with renal failure (letter). *Lancet* 2:211, 1985.
230. Inturrisi CE, Umans JG: Meperidine biotransformation and central nervous system toxicity in animals and humans, in Foley KM, Inturrisi CE (ed): *Opioid Analgesics in the Management of Clinical Pain*. (*Advances in Pain Research and Therapy*, vol 8.) New York, Raven Press, 1986, pp 143–154.
231. Galer BS, Coyle N, Pasternak GW, et al: Individual variability in the response to different opioids: Report of five cases. *Pain* 49:87–91, 1992.
232. Ripamonti C, Bruera E: Rectal, buccal, and sublingual narcotics for the management of cancer pain. *J Palliat Care* 7:30–35, 1991.
233. Hanning CD: The rectal absorption of opioids, in Benedetti C, Chapman CR, Giron G (eds): *Opioid Analgesia*. (*Advances in Pain Research and Therapy*, vol 14.) New York, Raven Press, 1990, pp 259–269.
234. Weinberg DS, Inturrisi CE, Reidenberg B, et al: Sublingual absorption of selected opioid analgesics. *Clin Pharmacol Ther* 44:335–342, 1988.
235. Portenoy RK: Continuous intravenous infusions of opioid drugs. *Med Clin North Am* 71:233–241, 1987.
236. Bruera E, Brenneis C, Michaud M, et al: Use of the subcutaneous route for the administration of narcotics in patients with cancer pain. *Cancer* 62:407–411, 1988.
237. Davenport HT: Subcutaneous narcotics. *Anaesthesia* 45: 413, 1990.
238. Swanson G, Smith J, Bulich R, et al: Patient-controlled analgesia for chronic cancer pain in the ambulatory setting: A report of 117 patients. *J Clin Oncol* 7:1903–1908, 1989.
239. Storey P, Hill HH, St Louis R, et al: Subcutaneous infusions for control of cancer symptoms. *J Pain Symptom Mgt* 5:33–41, 1990.
240. Oliver DJ: Syringe drivers in palliative care: A review. *Palliat Med* 2:21–26, 1988.
241. Chapman CR: Giving the patient control of opoioid analgesic administration, in Hill CS, Fields WS (eds): *Drug Treatment of Cancer Pain in a Drug Oriented Society,* (*Advances in Pain Research and Therapy,* vol 11.) New York, Raven Press, 1989, pp 339–351.
242. Kerr IG, Sone M, Deangelis C, et al: Continuous narcotic infusion with patient-controlled analgesia for chronic cancer pain in outpatients. *Ann Intern Med* 108:554–557, 1988.
243. Hill HF, Mackie AM, Coda BA, et al: Patient-controlled analgesic administration: A comparison of steady-state morphine infusions with bolus doses. *Cancer* 67:873–882, 1991.
244. Egbert AM, Parks LH, Short LM, et al: Randomized trial of postoperative patient-controlled analgesia vs intramuscular narcotics in frail elderly men. *Arch Intern Med* 150:1897–1903, 1990.
245. Lange MP, Dahn MS, Jacobs LA: Patient-controlled analgesia versus intermittent analgesia dosing. *Heart Lung* 17:495–498, 1988.
246. Hill HF, Mackie AM, Coda BA: Patient-controlled analgesic infusion, in Max MB, Portenoy RK, Laska E (eds): *The Design of Analgesic Clinical Trials*. (*Advances in Pain Research and Therapy,* vol 18.) New York, Raven Press, 1991, pp 507–524.
247. Coyle N, Mauskop A, Maggard J: Continuous subcutaneous infusions of opiates in cancer patients with pain. *Oncol Nurs Forum* 13:53–57, 1986.
248. Bruera E, Brenneis C, Michaud M, et al: Patient-controlled subcutaneous hydromorphone versus continuous subcutaneous infusion for the treatment of cancer pain. *J Natl Cancer Inst* 80:1152–1154, 1988.
249. Foley KM: Clinical tolerance to opioids, in Basbaum AI, Bessom JM (eds): *Towards a New Pharmacology of Pain,* Dahlem Konfrenzen. Chichester, England, Wiley, 1991, pp 181–204.
250. Kanner RM, Foley KM: Patterns of narcotic drug use in a cancer pain clinic. *Ann NY Acad Sci* 362:161–172, 1981.
251. Coyle N, Adelhardt J, Foley KM, et al: Character of terminal illness in the advanced cancer patient: Pain and other

symptoms during the last four weeks of life. *J Pain Sympt Mgmt* 5:83–89, 1990.

252. Ling GSFF, Spiegel K, Lockhart SH, et al: Separation of opioid analgesia from respiratory depression: Evidence for different receptor mechanisms. *J Pharmacol Exp Ther* 232:149–155, 1985.
253. Umans JG, Inturrisi CE: Antinociceptive activity and toxicity of meperidine and normeperidine in mice. *J Pharmacol Exp Ther* 223:203–206, 1982.
254. Forrest WH, Brown BW, Brown CR, et al: Dextroamphetamine with morphine for the treatment of postoperative pain. *N Engl J Med* 296:712–715, 1977.
255. Bruera E, Brenneis C, Patterson AH, et al: Use of methylphenedate as an adjuvant to narcotic analgesics in patients with advanced cancer. *J Pain Symptom Mgt* 4:3–6, 1989.
256. Bruera E, Chadwich S, Brenneis C, et al: Methylphenidate associated with narcotics for the treatment of cancer pain. *Cancer Treat Rep* 71:67–70, 1987.
257. Bruera E, Macmillan K, Hanson J, et al: The cognitive effects of the administration of narcotic analgesics in patients with cancer pain. *Pain* 39:13–16, 1989.
258. Breitbart W, Holland JC: Psychiatric complications of cancer. *Curr Ther Hematol Oncol* 3:268–275, 1988.
259. Sykes NP: Oral naloxone in opioid associated constipation. *Lancet* 337:1475, 1991.
260. Walsh TD: Prevention of opioid side effects. *J Pain Symptom Mgt* 5:363–367, 1990.
261. Kaufman PN, Krevsky B, Malmud LS, et al: Role of opiate receptors in the regulation of colonic transit. *Gastroenterology* 94:1351–1356, 1988.
262. Rogers M, Cerda JJ: The narcotic bowel syndrome. *J Clin Gastroenterol* 11:132–135, 1989.
263. McQuay HJ, Carroll D, Faura CC, et al: Oral morphine in cancer pain: Influences on morphine and metabolite concentration. *Clin Pharmacol Ther* 48:236–244, 1990.
264. Inturrisi CE: Management of cancer pain. *Cancer* 63:2308–2320, 1989.
265. Hill CS, Fields WS: Drug *Treatment of Cancer Pain in a Drug Oriented Society. (Advances in Pain Research and Therapy,* vol 11.) New York, Raven Press, 1989.
266. Campora E, Merlini L, Pace M, et al: The incidence of narcotic induced emesis. *J Pain Symptom Mgt* 6:428–430, 1991.
267. Eisele JH, Grigsby EJ, Dea G: Clonazepam treatment of myoclonic contractions associated with high dose opioids: A case report. *Pain* 49:231–232, 1992.
268. Schuster CR: Does treatment of cancer pain with narcotics produce junkies? in Hill CS, Fields WS (eds): *Drug Treatment of Cancer Pain in a Drug Oriented Society. (Advances in Pain Research and Therapy,* vol 11.) New York, Raven Press, 1989, pp 1–3.
269. Foley KM: The decriminalization of cancer pain, in Hill CS, Field H (eds): *Drug Treatment of Cancer Pain in a Drug Oriented Society. (Advances in Pain Research and Therapy,* vol 11.) New York, Raven Press, 1989, pp 5–18.
270. Jaffe JH: Misinformation: Euphoria and addiction, in Hill CS, Fields WS (eds): *Drug Treatment of Cancer Pain in a Drug Oriented Society. (Advances in Pain Research and Therapy,* vol 11.) New York, Raven Press, 1989, pp 163–174.
271. Morgan JP: American opiophobia: Customary underutilization of opioid analgesics, in Hill CS, Fields WS (eds): *Drug Treatment of Cancer Pain in a Drug Oriented Society. (Advances in Pain Research and Therapy,* vol 11.) New York, Raven Press, 1989, pp 181–189.
272. Porter J, Jick H: Addiction rare in patients treated with narcotics (letter). *N Engl J Med* 302:123, 1980.
273. American College of Physicians Health and Public Policy Committee: Drug therapy for severe chronic pain in terminal illness. *Ann Intern Med* 99:870–880, 1983.
274. American Pain Society: *Principles of Analgesic Use in the Treatment Acute Pain and Chronic Cancer Pain: A Concise Guide to Medical Practice,* 2nd ed. Skokie, Illinois, American Pain Society, 1989.
275. Chapman CR, Hill HF: Prolonged morphine self-administration and addiction liability. *Cancer* 63:1636–1644, 1989.
276. Weissman DE, Haddox JD: Opioid pseudoaddiction—An iatrogenic syndrome. *Pain* 36:363–366, 1989.
277. Ettinger AB, Portenoy RK: The use of corticosteroids in the treatment of symptoms associated with cancer. *J Pain Symptom Mgt* 3:99–103, 1988.
278. Walsh TD: Adjuvant analgesic therapy in cancer pain, in Foley KM, Bonica JJ, Ventafrida V (eds): *The Second International Conference on Cancer Pain. (Advances in Pain Research and Therapy,* vol 16.) New York, Raven Press, 1990, pp 155–168.
279. Bruera E, Roca E, Cedaro L, et al: Action of oral methylprednisolonoe in terminal cancer patients: A prospective randomized double-blind study. *Cancer Treat Rep* 69:751–754, 1985.
280. Della Cuna GR, Pellegrini A, Piazzi M: Effect of methylprednisolone sodium succinate on quality of life in preterminal cancer patients: A placebo-control multicenter study. *Eur J Clin Oncol* 29:1817–1821, 1989.
281. Tannock I, Gospodarowicz M, Meakin W, et al: Treatment of metastatic prostatic cancer with low-dose prednisone: Evaluation of pain and quality of life as pragmatic indices of response. *J Clin Oncol* 7:590–597, 1989.
282. Popiela T, Lucchi R, Giongo F: Methylprednisolone as palliative therapy for female terminal cancer patients: The Methylprednisolone Female Preterminal Cancer Study Group. *Eur J Cancer Clin Oncol* 25:1823–1829, 1989.
283. Moertel CG, Shuttle A, Reitemeier R, et al: Corticosteroid therapy of preterminal gastrointestinal cancer. *Cancer* 33:1607–1609, 1974.
284. Wilcox JC, Corr J, Shaw J, et al: Prednisolone as appetite stimulant in patients with cancer. *Br Med J* 288:27, 1984.
285. Greenberg HS, Kim J, Posner JB: Epidural spinal cord compression from metastatic tumor: Results with a new treatment protocol. *Ann Neurol* 8:361–366, 1980.
286. Walsh TD: Antidepressants in chronic pain. *Clin Neuropharmacol* 6:271–295, 1983.
287. Panerai AE, Bianchi M, Sacerdote P, et al: Antidepressants in cancer pain. *J Palliat Care* 7:42–44, 1991.
288. Breivik H, Rennemo F: Clinical evaluation of combined treatment with methadone and psychotropic drugs in cancer patients. *Acta Anaesth Scand* 74:135–140, 1982.
289. Magni G, Arsie D, DeLeo D: Antidepressants in the treatment of cancer pain: A survey in Italy. *Pain* 29:347–353, 1987.
290. Hugues A, Chauvergne J, Lissilour T, et al: L'imipramine utilisee comme antalgique majeur en carcinologie: Etude de 118 cas. *Presse Med* 71:1073–1074, 1963.
291. Walsh TD: Controlled study of imipramine and morphine in chronic pain due to cancer (abstract), in *Proc 5th Annu Meet Am Soc Clin Oncol* 1986, p. 237.
292. Swerdlow M: Anticonvulsant drugs and chronic pain. *Clin Neuropharmacol* 7:51–82, 1984.
293. Fromm GH, Terrence CF, Chattha AS: Baclofen in the treatment of trigeminal neuralgia: Double-blind study and long-term follow-up. *Ann Neurol* 15:240–244, 1984.
294. Fromm GH: Trigeminal neuralgia and related disorders, in Portenoy RK (ed): *Pain: Mechanisms and Syndromes.*

(*Neurology Clinics*, vol 7.) Philadelphia, Saunders, 1989, pp 305–319.

295. CAST (Cardiac Arrhythmia Suppression Trial) Investigators: Preliminary report: Effect of encainide and flecainide on mortality in a randomized trial of arrhythmia suppression after acute myocardial infarction. *N Engl J Med* 321:406–412, 1989.
296. Horn HR, Hadidian Z, Johnson JL, et al: Safety evaluation of tocainide in an American emergency use program. *Am Heart J* 100:1037–1040, 1980.
297. Bernstein JE, Bideevs DR, Dahl MV, et al: Treatment of chronic postherpetic neuralgia with topical capsaicin. *J Am Acad Dermatol* 17:93–96, 1987.
298. Watson CPN, Evans RJ, Watt VR: Postherpetic neuralgia and topical capsaicin. *Pain* 33:333–340, 1988.
299. Watson CPN, Evans RJ, Watt VR: The post-mastectomy pain syndrome and the effect of topical capsaicin. *Pain* 38:177–186, 1989.
300. Lechin F, van der Dijs B, Lechin ME, et al: Pimozide therapy for trigeminal neuralgia. *Arch Neurol* 9:960–962, 1989.
301. Ghostine SY, Comair YG, Turner DM, et al: Phenoxybenzamine in the treatment of causalgia. *J Neurosurg* 60:1263–1268, 1984.
302. Abram SE, Lightfoot RW: Treatment of longstanding causalgia with prazosin. *Reg Anaesth* 6:79–81, 1981.
303. Simson G: Propranolol for causalgia and Sudek's atrophy. *JAMA* 227:327, 1974.
304. Prough DS, McLeskey CH, Poehling GG, et al: Efficacy of oral nifedipine in the treatment of reflex sympathetic dystrophy. *Anesthesiology* 62:796–799, 1985.
305. Kanis JA, McCloskey EV, Taube T, et al: Rationale for the use of bisphosphonates in bone metastases. *Bone* 12:8–13, 1991.
306. Van Holten-Verzantvoort ATM, Zwinderman AH, Aaronson NK, et al: The effect of supportive pamidronate treatment on aspects of quality of life of patients with advanced breast cancer. *Eur J Cancer* 27:544–549, 1991.
307. Clarke NW, Holbrook IB, McClure J, et al: Osteoclast inhibition by pamidronate in metastatic prostate cancer: A preliminary study. *Br J Cancer* 63:420–423, 1991.
308. Smith JA: Palliation of painful bone metastases from prostate cancer using sodium etidronate: Results of a randomized, prospective, double-blind, placebo-controlled study. *J Urol* 141:85–87, 1989.
309. Hindley AC, Hill AB, Leyland MJ, et al: A double-blind controlled trial of salmon calcitonin in pain due to malignancy. *Cancer Chemother Pharmacol* 9:71–74, 1982.
310. Blomquist C, Elomaa I, Porkka L, et al: Evaluation of salmon calcitonin treatment in bone metastases from breast cancer—A controlled trial. *Bone* 9:45–51, 1988.
311. Eisenhut M, Berberich R, Kimmig B, et al: Iodine-131-labeled diphosphonates for palliative treatment of bone metastases: II. Preliminary clinical results with Iodine-131 BDP3. *J Nuclear Med* 27:1255–1261, 1986.
312. Maxon HR, Deutsch EA, Thomas SR, et al: Initial experience with 186-Re(Sn)-HEDP in the treatment of painful skeletal metastases. *J Nucl Med* 29:776, 1988.
313. Silberstein EB, Williams C: Strontium-89 therapy for the pain of osseous metastases. *J Nucl Med* 26:345–348, 1985.
314. Turner JH, Claringbold BG, Heatherington EL, et al: A phase 1 study of samarium-153 ethylenedi-amenetetramethylene phosphonate therapy for disseminated skeletal metastases. *J Clin Oncol* 7:1926–1931, 1989.
315. Lewington VJ, McEwan AJ, Ackery DM, et al: A prospective, randomised double-blind crossover study to examine the efficacy of strontium-89 in pain palliation in patients with advanced prostate cancer metastatic too bone. *Eur J Cancer* 27:954–958, 1991.
316. Linton SL, Melin L: Applied relaxation in the management of cancer pain. *Behav Psychother* 11:337–350, 1983.
317. Fordyce WE: *Behavioral Methods for Chronic Pain and Illness*. St. Louis, Mosby, 1976.
318. Turk D, Meichenbaum D, Genest M: *Pain and Behavioral Medicine*. New York, Guilford Press, 1983.
319. Gamble GL, Kinney CL, Brown PS, et al: Cardiovascular, pulmonary, and cancer rehabilitation: 5. Cancer rehabilitation: management of pain, neurologic and other clinical problems. *Arch Phys Med Rehabil* 71(Suppl 4):247–251, 1990.
320. Brennan MJ: Management of lymphedema: Review of pathophysiology and treatment. *J Pain Symptom Mgt* 7:110–116, 1992.
321. Long DM: Fifteen years of transcutaneous electrical stimulation for pain control. *Stereotact Funct Neurosurg* 56:2–19, 1991.
322. Bushnell MC, Marchand S, Tremblay N, et al: Electrical stimulation of peripheral and central pathways for the relief of musculoskeletal pain. *Can J Physiol Pharmacol* 69:697–703, 1991.
323. Moulin DE, Inturrisi CE, Foley KM: Epidural and intrathecal opioids: Cerebrospinal fluid and plasma pharmacokinetics in cancer pain patients, in Foley KM, Inturrisi CE (eds): *Opioid Analgesics in the Management of Clinical Pain.* (*Advances in Pain Research and Therapy,* vol 8.) New York, Raven Press, 1986, pp 369–384.
324. Max MB, Inturrisi CE, Kaiko RF, et al: Epidural and intrathecal opiates: Cerebrospinal fluid and plasma profiles in patients with chronic cancer pain. *Clin Pharmacol Ther* 38:631–641, 1985.
325. Brose WG, Tanalian DL, Brodsky JB, et al: CSF and blood pharmacokinetics of hydromorphone and morphine following lumbar epidural administration. *Pain* 45:11–17, 1991.
326. Chrubasik J, Wust H, Schulte MJ, et al: Relative analgesic potency of epidural fentanyl, alfentanil, and morphine in treatment of postoperative pain. *Anesthesiology* 68:929–933, 1988.
327. Du Pen SL, Ramsey DH: Compounding local anesthetics and narcotics for epidural analgesia in cancer out patients. *Anasthesiology* 69:A404, 1988.
328. Nitescu P, Appelgren L, Linder LE, et al: Epidural versus intrathecal morphine-bupivicaine: Assessment of consecutive treatment in advanced cancer pain. *J Pain Symptom Mgt* 5:18–26, 1990.
329. Hogan Q, Haddox JD, Abram S, et al: Epidural opiates and local anesthetics for the management of cancer pain. *Pain* 46:271–279, 1991.
330. Sjoberg M, Appelgren L, Einarsson S, et al: Long-term intrathecal morphine and bupivacaine in "refractory" cancer pain: Results from the first series of 52 patients. *Acta Anaesth Scand* 35:30–43, 1991.
331. De Castro MD, Meynadier MD, Zenz MD: *Regional Opioid Analgesia.* (*Developments in Critical Care Medicine and Anesthesiology,* vol 20.) Dordrecht, Netherlands, Kluwer, 1991, p 633.
332. Brown DL, Bulley CK, Quiel EC: Neurolytic celiac plexus blockade for pancreatic cancer pain. *Anesth Anals* 66:869–873, 1987.
333. Cousins MJ: Dwyer B, Gibb D: Chronic pain and neurolytic blockade, in Cousins MJ, Bridenbaugh PO (eds): *Neural Blockade in Clinical Anesthesia and Management of Pain,* 2nd ed. Philadelphia, Lippincott, 1988, pp 1053–1084.
334. Bonica JJ, Buckley FP, Moricca G, et al: Neurolytic block-

ade and hypophysectomy, in Bonica JJ (ed): *The Management of Pain,* vol 2, 2nd ed. Philadelphia, Lea & Febiger, 1990, pp 1980–2039.

335. Hellendoorn SM, Overweg VKJ: Perineal pain: A case report. *Eur J Surg Oncol* 14:197–198, 1988.
336. Ischia S, Luzzani A, Ischia A, et al: Subarachnoid neurolytic block (L5-S1) and unilateral percutaneous cervical cordotomy in the treatment of pain secondary to pelvic malignant disease. *Pain* 20:139–149, 1984.
337. Robertson DH: Transsacral neurolytic nerve block: An alternative approach to intractable perineal pain. *Br J Anaesth* 55:873–875, 1983.
338. Arbit E: Neurosurgical management of cancer pain, in Foley KM, Bonica JJ, Ventafrida V (eds): *Second International Congress on Cancer Pain.* (*Advances in Pain Research and Therapy,* vol 16.) New York, Raven Press, 1990, pp 289–300.
339. Rosomoff HL, Carroll F, Brown J: Percutaneous radiofrequency cervical cordotomy: Technique. *J Neurosurg* 23: 639–644, 1965.
340. Tasker RR, Tsuda T, Howrylyshn P: Percutaneous cordotomy—The lateral high cervical technique, in Schmidek HH, Sweet WH (eds): *Operative Neurosurgical Technique: Indications, Methods and Results.* New York, Grune & Stratton, 1988, pp 1191–1205.
341. Polatty RC, Cooper KR: Respiratory failure after percutaneous cordotomy. *South Med J* 79:367–379, 1986.
342. Rosomoff HL, Papo I, Loeser JD, et al: Neurosurgical operations on the spinal cord, in Bonica JJ (ed): *The Management of Pain,* 2nd ed. Philadelphia, Lea & Febiger, 1990, pp 2067–2081.
343. Papo I: Spinal posterior rhizotomy and commisural myelotomy in the treatment of cancer pain, in Bonicca JJ, Ventafridda V (ed): (*Advances in Pain Research and Therapy,* vol 2.) New York, Raven Press, 1979, pp 325–337.
344. Ishijima B, Shimoji K, Shimizu H, et al: Lesions of spinal and trigeminal dorsal root entry zone for deafferentation pain: Experience of 35 cases. *Appl Neurophysiol* 51:175–187, 1988.

Cancer of the Colon, Rectum, and Anus

Index

Page numbers followed by "f" indicate figures; page numbers followed by "t" indicate tables.